19th International Conference on Principles of Knowledge Representation and Reasoning (KR2022)

Haifa, Israel
31 July – 5 August 2022

Editors:

Gabriele Kern-Isberner
Gerhard Lakemeyer
Thomas Meyer

ISBN: 978-1-7138-6108-9

Printed from e-media with permission by:

Curran Associates, Inc.
57 Morehouse Lane
Red Hook, NY 12571

Some format issues inherent in the e-media version may also appear in this print version.

International Joint Conference on Artificial Intelligence (IJCAI)
Information Sciences Institute/USC 4676
Admiralty Way, Marina del Rey
CA 90292
USA

Phone: +49 (761) 203-8221
Fax: +49 (761) 203-8222

nebel@ijcai.org

Additional copies of this publication are available from:

Curran Associates, Inc.
57 Morehouse Lane
Red Hook, NY 12571 USA
Phone: 845-758-0400
Fax: 845-758-2633
Email: curran@proceedings.com
Web: www.proceedings.com

TABLE OF CONTENTS

MAIN TRACK

SPECIAL SESSION ON KR AND MACHINE LEARNING

1 CONFERENCE COMMITTEE

General Chair

Gerhard Lakemeyer (RWTH Aachen University, Germany)

Program Chairs

Gabriele Kern-Isberner (TU Dortmund, Germany)
Thomas Meyer (University of Cape Town and CAIR, South Africa)

Applications and Systems Track

Alessandro Antonucci (IDSIA, Switzerland)
Matthias Thimm (University of Hagen, Germany)

Recently Published Research Track

Sebastian Rudolph (TU Dresden, Germany)
Ivan Varzinczak (Université d'Artois and CRIL, France)

Special Session: KR and Machine Learning

Fabio Cozman (University of Sao Paulo, Brazil)
Steven Schockaert (Cardiff University, UK)

Special Session: KR and Robotics

Gabriella Cortellessa (National Research Council, Italy)
Enrico Motta (The Open University, UK)

Workshops and Tutorials

Stefan Borgwardt (TU Dresden, Germany)
Maria Vanina Martinez (CONICET and Universidad de Buenos Aires, Argentina)

Doctoral Consortium

Giovanni Casini (ISTI - CNR, Italy)
Jandson Santos Ribeiro Santos (University of Hagen, Germany)

Local Organization

Ofer Arieli (Academic College of Tel Aviv-Yaffo, Israel)

Sponsorship

Martin Homola (Comenius University of Bratislava, Slovakia)
Vladislav Ryzhikov (Birkbeck, University of London, UK)

Publicity

Elena Botoeva (University of Kent, UK)
Jesse Heyninck (Open Universiteit, the Netherlands)
Marco Wilhelm (TU Dortmund, Germany)

Diversity and Inclusion

Yazmin Ibanez-Garcia (Cardiff University, UK)
Abhaya Nayak (Macquarie University, Sydney, Australia)
Renata Wassermann (University of Sao Paulo, Brazil)

2 AREA CHAIRS AND PROGRAM COMMITTEE

Area Chairs

Alessandro Antonucci (IDSIA, Switzerland)
Franz Baader (TU Dresden, Germany)
Pietro Baroni (University of Brescia, Italy)
Christoph Beierle (University of Hagen, Germany)
Vaishak Belle (University of Edinburgh, UK)
Salem Benferhat (CRIL, University of Artois, France)
Richard Booth (Cardiff University, UK)
Gerhard Brewka (Leipzig University, Germany)
Pedro Cabalar (University of Corunna, Spain)
Diego Calvanese (Free University of Bozen-Bolzano, Italy)
Fabio Cozman (University of Sao Paulo, Brazil)
James Delgrande (Simon Fraser University, Canada)
Thomas Eiter (TU Wien, Austria)
Esra Erdem (Sabanci University, Turkey)
Anthony Hunter (University College London, UK)
Joao Leite (Universidade NOVA de Lisboa, Portugal)
Domenico Lembo (Sapienza University of Rome, Italy)
Leonid Libkin (University of Edinburgh, UK)
Sheila McIlraith (University of Toronto, Canada)
Rafael Peñaloza (University of Milano-Bicocca, Italy)
Marco Ragni (TU Chemnitz, Germany)
Sebastian Rudolph (TU Dresden, Germany)
Sebastian Sardina (RMIT University, Australia)
Torsten Schaub (University of Potsdam, Germany)
Steven Schockaert (Cardiff University, UK)
Guillermo R. Simari (Universidad Nacional del Sur, Argentina)
Tran Cao Son (New Mexico State University, Mexico)
Christian Strasser (Ruhr-University Bochum, Germany)
Matthias Thimm (University of Hagen, Germany)
Francesca Toni (Imperial College London, UK)
Ivan Varzinczak (Université d'Artois and CRIL, France)
Stefan Woltran (TU Wien, Austria)

Program Committee (Main Technical Program)

Mehwish Alam (FIZ Karlsruhe and AIFB Institute, KIT, Germany)
Leila Amgoud (IRIT, CNRS, France)
Daan Apeldoorn (University Medical Center of the Johannes Gutenberg University Mainz, Germany)
Carlos Areces (FaMAF, Universidad Nacional de Córdoba, Argentina)
Ofer Arieli (Academic College of Tel Aviv-Yaffo, Israel)
Marcello Balduccini (Saint Joseph's University, USA)
Chitta Baral (Arizona State University, USA)
Ringo Baumann (Leipzig University, Germany)
Dorothea Baumeister (Heinrich-Heine-Universität Düsseldorf, Germany)
Bartosz Bednarczyk (TU Dresden, Germany and University of Wrocław, Poland)
Michael Beetz (Technical University of Munich, Germany)
Elena Bellodi (University of Ferrara, Italy)
Leopoldo Bertossi (Skema Business School, Montreal, Canada)
Meghyn Bienvenu (CNRS, University of Bordeaux, France)

Stefano Bistarelli (University of Perugia, Italy)
Alexander Bochman (Holon Institute of Technology, Israel)
Bart Bogaerts (Vrije Universiteit Brussel, Belgium)
Thomas Bolander (Technical University of Denmark, Denmark)
Annemarie Borg (Utrecht University, Netherlands)
Elena Botoeva (University of Kent, UK)
Zied Bouraoui (CRIL, Université d'Artois, France)
Pierre Bourhis (CNRS CRIStAL, France)
Camille Bourgaux (DI ENS, CNRS, France)
Loris Bozzato (Fondazione Bruno Kessler, Italy)
Tanya Braun (University of Münster, Germany)
Krysia Broda (Imperial College London, UK)
Maximiliano Budan (CONICET and Universidad Nacional del Sur, Argentina)
David Carral (LIRMM, Inria, University of Montpellier, CNRS, France)
Giovanni Casini (ISTI - CNR, Italy)
Federico Cerutti (University of Brescia, Italy)
Ismail Ilkan Ceylan (University of Oxford, UK)
Jake Chandler (Ludwig Maximilian University of Munich, Germany)
Agnese Chiatti (The Open University, UK)
Gianluca Cima (CNRS, University of Bordeaux, France)
Oana Cocarascu (King's College London, UK)
Andrea Cohen (ICIC, CONICET-UNS, Argentina)
Marco Console (Sapienza University of Rome, Italy)
Carl Corea (University of Koblenz-Landau, Germany)
Fabio Aurelio D'Asaro (University of Verona, Italy)
Artur D'Avila Garcez (City University London, UK)
Giuseppe De Giacomo (Sapienza University of Rome, Italy)
Ronald de Haan (University of Amsterdam, Netherlands)
Thomas Demeester (Ghent University, Belgium)
Marc Denecker (KU Leuven, Belgium)
Martín Diéguez (University of Pau, France)
Clare Dixon (University of Manchester, UK)
Didier Dubois (ADRIA Team, IRIT-CNRS, France)
Wolfgang Faber (Alpen-Adria-Universität Klagenfurt, Austria)
Marcelo A. Falappa (Universidad Nacional del Sur, Argentina)
Jorge Fandinno (University of Nebraska at Omaha, USA)
Eduardo Fermé (Universidade da Madeira, Portugal)
Tommaso Flaminio (IIIA - CSIC, Spain)
Sergio Flesca (University of Calabria, Italy)
Giorgos Flouris (ICS, FORTH, Greece)
Sarah Alice Gaggl (TU Dresden, Germany)
Alejandro Garcia (Universidad Nacional del Sur, Argentina)
Martin Gebser (Alpen-Adria-Universität Klagenfurt, Austria)
Hector Geffner (ICREA and Universitat Pompeu Fabra, Spain)
Malik Ghallab (LAAS-CNRS, France)
Massimiliano Giacomin (University of Brescia, Italy)
Laura Giordano (DISIT, Università del Piemonte Orientale, Italy)
Valentina Gliozzi (Universita di Torino, Italy)
Lluis Godo (IIIA - CSIC, Spain)
Lucía Gómez Álvarez (TU Dresden, Germany)
Ricardo Gonçalves (Universidade NOVA de Lisboa, Portugal)
Martin Grohe (RWTH Aachen University, Germany)
Paulo T. Guerra (Federal University of Ceara, Brazil)
Ricardo Guimarães (University of Bergen, Norway)
Victor Gutierrez-Basulto (Cardiff University, UK)
Joseph Halpern (Cornell University, USA)
Markus Hecher (TU Wien, Austria)
Fredrik Heintz (Linköping University, Sweden)
Joachim Hertzberg (University of Osnabrueck, Germany)
Andreas Herzig (CNRS, IRIT, Univ. Toulouse, France)
Jesse Heyninck (Open Universiteit, the Netherlands)
Matthias Hofer (Universität Bayreuth, Germany)
Steffen Hölldobler (TU Dresden, Germany)
Martin Homola (Comenius University of Bratislava, Slovakia)
Aaron Hunter (British Columbia Institute of Technology, Canada)
Giovambattista Ianni (University of Calabria, Italy)
Yazmin A. Ibanez-Garcia (Cardiff University, UK)
Katsumi Inoue (NII, Japan)
Tomi Janhunen (Tampere University, Finland)
Matti Järvisalo (University of Helsinki, Finland)
Patric Jensfelt (KTH Royal Institute of Technology, Sweden)
Jianmin Ji (University of Science and Technology of China, China)
Jean Christoph Jung (Universität Hildesheim, Germany)
Antonis Kakas (University of Cyprus, Cyprus)
Yevgeny Kazakov (University of Ulm, Germany)
Kristian Kersting (TU Darmstadt, Germany)
Toryn Q. Klassen (University of Toronto, Canada)
Matthias Knorr (Universidade NOVA de Lisboa, Portugal)
Boris Konev (University of Liverpool, UK)
Sébastien Konieczny (CRIL - CNRS, France)
Roman Kontchakov (Birkbeck, University of London, UK)
Patrick Koopmann (TU Dresden, Germany)
Frederic Koriche (CRIL, Université d'Artois, France)
Egor V. Kostylev (University of Oslo, Norway)
Alisa Kovtunova (TU Dresden, Germany)
Markus Krötzsch (TU Dresden, Germany)
Oliver Kutz (Free University of Bozen-Bolzano, Italy)
Ondřej Kuželka (Czech Technical University in Prague, Czech Republic)
Evelina Lamma (ENDIF, University of Ferrara, Italy)
Gianfranco Lamperti (University of Brescia, Italy)
Jérôme Lang (CNRS, LAMSADE, Université Paris-Dauphine, France)
Davide Lanti (Free University of Bozen-Bolzano, Italy)
Tiep Le (New Mexico State University, USA)
Francesco Leofante (Imperial College London, UK)
Nicola Leone (University of Calabria, Italy)
Yves Lespérance (York University, Canada)
Sebastian Link (University of Auckland, New Zealand)
Francesca Alessandra Lisi (Università degli Studi di Bari Aldo Moro, Italy)
Emiliano Lorini (IRIT, France)
Thomas Lukasiewicz (University of Oxford, UK)
Tim Lyon (TU Dresden, Germany)

Marco Manna (University of Calabria, Italy)
Marco Maratea (DIBRIS, University of Genova, Italy)
Pierre Marquis (Univ. Artois, CNRS, CRIL / Institut Universitaire de France, France)
Maria Vanina Martinez (CONICET and Universidad de Buenos Aires, Argentina)
Nicolas Maudet (LIP6, Sorbonne Université, France)
Kuldeep S. Meel (National University of Singapore, Singapore)
John-Jules Meyer (Utrecht University, Netherlands)
Ralf Möller (University of Luebeck, Germany)
Marco Montali (Free University of Bozen-Bolzano, Italy)
Leora Morgenstern (Palo Alto Research Center, USA)
Sriraam Natarajan (University of Texas at Dallas, USA)
Abhaya Nayak (Macquarie University, Sydney, Australia)
Andreas Niskanen (University of Helsinki, Finland)
Zoran Ognjanović (Mathematical Institute of the Serbian Academy of Sciences and Arts, Serbia)
Andrea Orlandini (National Research Council, Italy)
Magdalena Ortiz (TU Wien, Austria)
Ana Ozaki (University of Bergen, Norway)
Aline Paes (Universidade Federal Fluminense, Brazil)
Maurice Pagnucco (University of New South Wales, Australia)
Francesco Parisi (University of Calabria, Italy)
Andrea Passerini (University of Trento, Italy)
Fabio Patrizi (Sapienza University of Rome, Italy)
Heiko Paulheim (University of Mannheim, Germany)
Pavlos Peppas (University of Patras, Greece)
Ron Petrick (Heriot-Watt University, UK)
Andreas Pieris (University of Edinburgh, UK, and University of Cyprus, Cyprus)
Ramon Pino Perez (Université d'Artois, France)
Antonella Poggi (Sapienza University of Rome, Italy)
Enrico Pontelli (New Mexico State University, USA)
Nico Potyka (Imperial College London, UK)
Henri Prade (IRIT, CNRS, France)
Carlo Proietti (National Research Council, Italy)
Antonio Rago (Imperial College London, UK)
Anna Rapberger (TU Wien, Austria)
Jandson Santos Ribeiro Santos (University of Hagen, Germany)
Francesco Ricca (University of Calabria, Italy)
Tjitze Rienstra (Maastricht University, Netherlands)
Fabrizio Riguzzi (University of Ferrara, Italy)
Andrey Rivkin (Free University of Bozen-Bolzano, Italy)
Odinaldo Rodrigues (King's College London, UK)
Ricardo Oscar Rodriguez (Universidad de Buenos Aires, Argentina)
Francesca Rossi (IBM)
Jörg Rothe (Heinrich-Heine-Universität Düsseldorf, Germany)
Hans Rott (University of Regensburg, Germany)
Marie-Christine Rousset (University of Grenoble Alpes, France)
Alessandra Russo (Imperial College London, UK)
Vladislav Ryzhikov (Birkbeck, University of London, UK)
Orkunt Sabuncu (TED University, Turkey)
Joshua Sack (California State University, Long Beach, USA)
Chiaki Sakama (Wakayama University, Japan)
Zeynep G. Saribatur (TU Wien, Austria)
Ken Satoh (NII and Sokendai, Japan)
Uli Sattler (University of Manchester, UK)
Kai Sauerwald (University of Hagen, Germany)
Domenico Fabio Savo (University of Bergamo, Italy)
Federico Scafoglieri (Sapienza University of Rome, Italy)
Konstantin Schekotihin (Alpen-Adria Universität Klagenfurt, Austria)
Klaus-Dieter Schewe (Zhejiang University, China)
Ute Schmid (University of Bamberg, Germany)
Renate A. Schmidt (University of Manchester, UK)
Christoph Schwering (University of New South Wales, Australia)
Nicolas Schwind (AIST, Japan)
Dietmar Seipel (Julius-Maximilians-Universität Würzburg, Germany)
Luciano Serafini (Fondazione Bruno Kessler, Italy)
Gerardo Simari (Universidad Nacional del Sur and CONICET, Argentina)
Mantas Simkus (TU Wien, Austria)
Marlo Souza (Federal University of Bahia, Brazil)
Mohan Sridharan (University of Birmingham, UK)
Frieder Stolzenburg (Harz University of Applied Sciences, Germany)
Hannes Strass (TU Dresden, Germany)
Karim Tabia (CRIL CNRS UMR 8188, Université d'Artois, France)
Prasad Tadepalli (Oregon State University, USA)
Balder ten Cate (University of Amsterdam, Netherlands)
Eugenia Ternovska (Simon Fraser University, Canada)
Michael Thielscher (University of New South Wales, Australia)
Nicolas Troquard (Free University of Bozen-Bolzano, Italy)
Mirek Truszczynski (University of Kentucky, USA)
Efthymia Tsamoura (Samsung AI Research)
Anni-Yasmin Turhan (TU Dresden, Germany)
Markus Ulbricht (University of Leipzig, Germany)
Alessandro Umbrico (National Research Council, Italy)
Mauro Vallati (University of Huddersfield, UK)
Leon van der Torre (University of Luxembourg, Luxembourg)
Frank Van Harmelen (Vrije Universiteit Amsterdam, Netherlands)
Joost Vennekens (KU Leuven, Belgium)
Srdjan Vesic (CRIL, CNRS, Université d'Artois, France)
Carlos Viegas Damásio (Universidade NOVA de Lisboa, Portugal)
Serena Villata (CNRS, Laboratoire d'Informatique, Signaux et Systèmes de Sophia-Antipolis, France)
Jirka Vomlel (Academy of Sciences, Czech Republic)
Johannes P. Wallner (TU Graz, Austria)
Kewen Wang (Griffith University, Australia)
Renata Wassermann (University of Sao Paulo, Brazil)
Marco Wilhelm (TU Dortmund, Germany)
Diedrich Wolter (University of Bamberg, Germany)
Frank Wolter (University of Liverpool, UK)
Jiajun Wu (Stanford University, USA)

Guohui Xiao (University of Bergen, Norway)
Michael Zakharyaschev (Birkbeck, University of London, UK)
Marina Zanella (University of Brescia, Italy)
Jessica Zangari (University of Calabria, Italy)
Gerson Zaverucha (Federal University of Rio de Janeiro, Brazil)
Riccardo Zese (University of Ferrara, Italy)

Program Committee (Recent Published Research Track)

Pedro Cabalar (University of Corunna, Spain)
Federico Cerutti (University of Brescia, Italy)
James Delgrande (Simon Fraser University, Canada)
Thomas Eiter (TU Wien, Austria)
Hector Geffner (ICREA and Universitat Pompeu Fabra, Spain)
Andreas Herzig (CNRS, IRIT, Univ. Toulouse, France)
Jesse Heyninck (Open Universiteit, the Netherlands)
C. Maria Keet (University of Cape Town, South Africa)
Emanuel Kieroński (University of Wrocław, Poland)
Jérôme Lang (CNRS, LAMSADE, Université Paris-Dauphine, France)
Michel Leclère (LIRMM, Inria, University of Montpellier, France)
Vladimir Lifschitz (University of Texas at Austin, USA)
Pierre Marquis (Univ. Artois, CNRS, CRIL / Institut Universitaire de France)
Marie-Laure Mugnier (University of Montpellier, France)
Guillermo R. Simari (Universidad Nacional del Sur, Argentina)
Marija Slavkovik (University of Bergen, Norway)
Mohan Sridharan (University of Birmingham, UK)
Michael Thomazo (Inria, DIENS, ENS, CNRS, PSL University, France)
Francesca Toni (Imperial College London, UK)
Mirek Truszczynski (University of Kentucky, USA)

Additional Reviewers

Marco Alberti
Tahar Allouche
Damiano Azzolini
Pedro Barahona
Linus Boes
Benedikt Bollig
Paola Daniela Budán
Elisa Böhl
Francesco Calimeri
Pierre Carbonnelle
Valentin Cassano
Burkhard Englert
Francesco Faloci
Krisztina Fruzsa
Marco Gavanelli
Gregory Gelfond
Maximilian Heinrich
Anna Maria Kerkmann
Christian Laußmann
Oscar Lima Carrion
Xinghan Liu
Djordje Markovic
Ivan Mercanti
Katsumi Nitta
Magdalena Ortiz
Volkan Patoglu
Francesco Percassi
Simona Perri
Cosimo Persia
Johannes Rabold
Mostafa Sakr
Francesco Santini
Stephan Scheele
Kenneth Skiba
Mate Soos
Kazuko Takahashi
Pierre Tassel
Carlo Taticchi
Satyadharma Tirtarasa
Kees van Berkel
Linde Vanbesien
Toshiko Wakaki
Marcel Waleska
Zhe Wang
Hiroaki Yamada
Honghua Zhang
Zhiqiang Zhuang

3 PREFACE

Knowledge Representation and Reasoning (KR) is a well-established and lively field of research within Artificial Intelligence. KR builds on the fundamental thesis that knowledge can be represented in an explicit declarative form, suitable for processing by dedicated symbolic reasoning engines. This enables the exploitation of knowledge that would otherwise be implicit through semantically grounded inference mechanisms. Consequently, KR has contributed to the theory and practice of various areas in AI, including agents, automated planning and natural language processing, and to fields beyond AI, including data management, semantic web, verification, software engineering, robotics, computational biology, and cyber security.

The KR conference series is the leading forum for timely in-depth presentation of progress in the theory and principles underlying the representation and computational management of knowledge and beliefs. Since 1989, it has been fostering not only communication and a cross-fertilization of ideas within the area but also collaboration across research boundaries. Its topics are diverse and cover a broad spectrum of research topics. To showcase the role of KR in key areas and in support of topic diversity, KR 2022 included for the third time the following tracks and special sessions in addition to the main conference track:

- *Applications and Systems Track:* This track invited submissions of papers on emerging and deployed applications of KR, describing all aspects of the development, deployment, and evaluation of KR systems to solve real-world problems, including interesting case studies and benchmarks, and discussing research experience and lessons learned.
- *Recent Published Research Track:* This track provided a forum to discuss important results related to KR that appeared recently in selective journals and conferences, but have not been previously presented at KR conferences.
- *Special Session on KR and Machine Learning:* This special session invited submissions of papers on synergistic integration of KR and machine learning methods. This topic has witnessed a growing interest over the past few years, partly due to increased activities in the field of explainable AI.
- *Special Session on KR and Robotics:* This special session invited submissions of papers on synergistic integration of KR and Robotics methods.

We received 218 submissions (180 full papers, 38 short papers) to the main technical program (including the Applications and Systems track, and the Special Sessions on KR and Machine Learning, and KR and Robotics), of which 58 (26.6%) were accepted (51 full papers and 7 short papers). In addition, we received 21 submissions to the Recently Published Research Track, of which 17 were accepted for presentation at the conference.

The following papers received the best paper awards of KR 2022:

- *Ray Reiter Best Paper Award:* "The Topology of Surprise" by Alexandru Baltag, Nick Bezhanishvili and David Fernández-Duque.
- *Ray Reiter Best Paper Award Runner-Up:* "Conservative Extensions for Existential Rules" by Jean Christoph Jung, Carsten Lutz, and Jerzy Marcinkowski.
- *Marco Cadoli Best Student Paper Award:* "Finite Entailment of UCRPQs over ALC Ontologies" by Victor Gutierrez-Basulto, Albert Gutowski, Yazmin Ibanez-Garcia, and Filip Murlak.
- *Marco Cadoli Best Student Paper Award Runner-Up:* "On Syntactic Forgetting with Strong Persistence" by Matti Berthold.

The award winners were selected from nominations made by area chairs and PC members by this year's award committee, consisting of Birte Glimm, Pierre Marquis, and Francesca Toni; we thank them all for contributing their time and expertise to this special task.

The program of KR 2022 included four invited talks by prominent researchers that focused on traditional KR fields, as well as established connections to applications and other research communities:

- Yejin Choi (University of Washington, USA): *Neuro-Symbolic Adventures on Commonsense Knowledge and Reasoning*
- Ulrike Hahn (Birkbeck University of London, UK): *Probabilities, Reasoning, and Argumentation*
- Anthony Hunter (University College London, UK): *From Non-monotonic Reasoning to Argumentation and Commonsense* (Great Moments in KR Talk)
- Leonid Libkin (University of Edinburgh, UK): *Graph Queries: Do We Study What Matters?*

Since KR 2022 took place as one of 12 conferences at FLoC 2022, the Federated Logic Conference, its attendants could also enjoy the topical diversity of invited talks from other FLoC 2022 conferences.

Continuing the good tradition of previous KR conferences, KR 2022 also hosted sessions that aimed at integrating young scientists into the KR family and connecting members of our research community in general:

- *Doctoral Consortium (DC):* The Doctorial Consortium students delivered lightning talks during a session of the main conference, followed by a poster session where they could discuss their work with other conference participants. They also enjoyed a joint lunch with the DC organizers and mentors.
- *Diversity & Inclusion (D&I):* For the second time, this year's conference included a session devoted to fostering diversity and inclusion in our research community, as well as further D&I-related activities.

Continuing the *Future of KR* session at KR 2021, we had a plenary session on *Current and Future Challenges in Knowledge Representation and Reasoning*, presenting results from a very recent Dagstuhl Perspectives Workshop.

In addition, KR 2020 initiated the tradition of *Test of Time* awards, which were continued at KR 2022. The Test of Time award is for a paper published at least 15 years ago (counting from 2022) which has stood the test of time. This year the award went to "Combining Answer Set Programming with Description Logics for the Semantic Web", published in KR 2004 and Artificial intelligence 172 (12-13) (2008) by Thomas Eiter, Giovambattista Ianni, Thomas Lukasiewicz, Roman Schindlauer, and Hans Tompits.

For the very first time KR 2022 also awarded the *KR Early Career Award*. Researchers eligible for this award need to have completed their doctoral degree in 2020 or 2021. This year the award went to Markus Hecher from TU Vienna for his analysis of the paramaterized complexity of fundamental problems in artificial intelligence.

We are very grateful to our award committee—Meghyn Bienvenu, Frank Wolter, and Diego Calvanese—for contributing their time, expertise, and effort in selecting the winners.

As in recent years, KR 2022 solicited workshop and tutorial proposals via an open call. The following workshops and tutorials with a variety of interesting and timely topics could be offered to KR 2022 and FLoC 2022 attendants:

- WS: *Third Workshop on Explainable Logic-Based Knowledge Representation* (XLoKR 2022)
- WS: *Third Workshop on Parameterized Complexity of Computational Reasoning* (PCCR 2022)
- Tutorial: *Assumption-Based Nonmonotonic Reasoning*, Alexander Bochmann
- Tutorial: *Belief Change, Ontology Repair and Evolution*, Renata Wassermann
- Tutorial: *DatalogMTL: Theory and Practice of Temporal Reasoning*, Bernardo Cuenca, Przemysław Andrzej Wałega, Dingmin Wang, Michael Zakharyaschev, Guohui Xiao, Vladislav Ryzhikov
- Tutorial: *Hybrid Temporal Situation Calculus Planning with Continuous Processes: Semantics*, Mikhail Soutchanski
- Tutorial: *Referring Expressions in Artificial Intelligence and Knowledge Representation Systems*, David Toman, Grant Weddell
- Tutorial: *Logic meets Learning + Explainable Machine Learning*, Vaishak Belle

After two years of virtual KR conferences due to the Corona pandemic (KR 2020 and KR 2021), KR 2022 could be organized as a physical conference at the Technion in Haifa, Israel. This decision was confirmed on May 1, 2022, because the overall health situation was improving, and most countries returned to (almost) normal life over the summer of 2022. Nevertheless, for those authors who still could not travel for some reason, FLoC 2022 made it possible to present video talks. Two of our invited talks (those by Yejin Choi and Ulrike Hahn) were given as remote talks. In this way, we were happy to see large parts of the KR community meeting in person again after three years while also allowing for integrating the scientific contributions of those who could not come.

We wish to thank everyone who contributed to making KR 2022 a success. We start with our Special Sessions and Track Chairs who significantly supported us in ensuring diversity of topics and establishing connections to other communities: Alessandro Antonucci and Matthias Thimm (Applications & Systems Track), Fabio Cozman and Steven Schockaert (Special Session on KR & Machine Learning), Gabriella Cortellessa and Enrico Motta (Special Session on KR & Robotics), and Sebastian Rudolph and Ivan Varzinczak (Recently Published Research Track). We also thank this year's Area Chairs for the crucial role they played in the review and selection process, as well as our Program Committee members and additional reviewers for their thorough and timely reviews of the submissions. Next, let us acknowledge the important activities that enriched the technical program of KR 2022. We are grateful to Stefan Borgwardt and Maria Vanina Martinez for selecting and coordinating the Workshop and Tutorial program, to Giovanni Casini and Jandson Santos Ribeiro Santos for organizing this year's Doctoral Consortium, and to Yazmin Ibanez-Garcia, Abhaya Nayak, and Renata Wassermann for organizing the Diversity & Inclusion session and activities. We also would like to thank François Schwarzentruber for enriching the program of KR 2022 with a piano concert. A big thank you goes to our local chair Ofer Arieli for helping us to arrange KR 2022, and to the FLoC 2022 Organizing Committee for providing a beautiful environment to the conference. We also thank Martin Homola and Vladislav Ryzhikov who so successfully recruited funding and sponsors, and our Publicity Chairs Elena Botoeva, Jesse Heyninck, and Marco Wilhelm for taking care of the KR 2022 website and for spreading information on the conference via mailing lists and on social platforms.

Finally, we would like to thank all of our colleagues who contributed to the continued success of the KR conference series through their active participation in KR 2022.

Gabriele Kern-Isberner and Thomas Meyer
Program Chairs

Gerhard Lakemeyer
General Chair

4 INVITED TALKS

Neuro-Symbolic Adventures on Commonsense Knowledge and Reasoning

Yejin Choi, University of Washington, USA

Neural language models, as they grow in scale, continue to surprise us with utterly nonsensical and counterintuitive errors despite their otherwise remarkable performances on numerous leaderboards. In this talk, I will argue that it is time to challenge the currently dominant paradigm of task-specific supervision built on top of large-scale self-supervised neural networks. First, I will highlight the importance of unsupervised, inference-time algorithms that can make significantly better lemonades out of off-the-shelf neural language models via flexible differentiable reasoning and discrete inference with predicate logic. Next, I will highlight the importance of melding explicit and declarative knowledge encoded in symbolic knowledge graphs with implicit and observed knowledge encoded in neural language models, with newest updates on ATOMIC 10x and distilled COMET, demonstrating a machine-authored KB that wins, for the first time, over a human-authored KB in all criteria: scale, accuracy, and diversity.

Yejin Choi is Brett Helsel Professor at the Paul G. Allen School of Computer Science & Engineering at the University of Washington and a senior research manager at AI2 overseeing the project Mosaic. Her research investigates a wide range of problems including commonsense knowledge and reasoning, neuro-symbolic integration, multimodal representation learning, and AI for social good. She is a co-recipient of the NAACL Best Paper Award in 2022, the ACL Test of Time award in 2021, the CVPR Longuet-Higgins Prize in 2021, a NeurIPS Outstanding Paper Award in 2021, the AAAI Outstanding Paper Award in 2020, the Borg Early Career Award in 2018, the inaugural Alexa Prize Challenge in 2017, IEEE AI's 10 to Watch in 2016, and the ICCV Marr Prize in 2013.

Probabilities, Reasoning, and Argumentation

Ulrike Hahn, Birkbeck University of London, UK

The talk will review different ways in which the study of human cognition has invoked probabilities, and examine the extent to which laypeople match up to probabilistic norms. This provides both evidence on the breadth of challenge faced by computational systems seeking to tackle real-world reasoning problem and indicates where computational systems could most usefully provide support.

Ulrike Hahn is a professor at the Department of Psychological Sciences at Birkbeck College, University of London, where she also serves as director of the Centre for Cognition, Computation and Modelling. Ulrike Hahn's research interests are, first and foremost, questions of human rationality. Her research examines human judgment, decision-making, and the rationality of everyday argument. She is presently particularly interested in the role of perceived source reliability for our beliefs, including our beliefs as parts of larger communicative social networks. Ulrike Hahn has served as a member of the Senior Editorial Board of Topics in Cognitive Science, as an Action Editor for Cognitive Psychology, as an Action Editor for Psychonomic Bulletin and a consulting editor for Psychological Review. She was awarded the Cognitive Section Prize by the British Psychological Society, the Kerstin Hesselgren Professorship by the Swedish Research Council, and the Anneliese Maier Research Award by the Alexander von Humboldt Foundation. She is a fellow of the German National Academy of Science (Leopoldina), a fellow of the Association for Psychological Science, a corresponding member of the Bayerische Akademie der Wissenschaften, and she holds an honorary doctorate from Lund University, Sweden.

From Non-monotonic Reasoning to Argumentation and Commonsense (Great Moments in KR Talk)

Anthony Hunter, University College London, UK

Interest in non-monotonic reasoning arose from the need to model how people in everyday life use defeasible knowledge (i.e., knowledge that is normally correct but can have exceptions). One path of research that has evolved from this is computational models of argument. This is concerned with modelling the human ability to handle incomplete and conflicting situations through the identification and analysis of arguments and counterarguments. A key problem in computational models of argument is the need to handle enthymemes. These are arguments that have some premises, and possibly the claim, being implicit. To understand enthymemes, for example exchanged during a dialogue, we often require commonsense reasoning. Whilst the need to formalise commonsense reasoning was a driver for research in non-monotonic reasoning, the questions of how to formalise commonsense reasoning, and how to acquire the knowledge necessary for commonsene reasoning, remain largely unanswered. In this talk, we will review the fields of non-monotonic reasoning, computational models of argument, and commonsense reasoning, and focus on the handling of enthymemes.

Anthony Hunter is Professor of Artificial Intelligence, and Head of the Intelligent Systems Group, in the UCL Department of Computer Science. He is a graduate of the University of Bristol and Imperial College London. He did his PhD in the Department of Computing at Imperial College on the topic of defeasible reasoning (supervised by Professor Dov Gabbay). After a couple of post-doctoral positions at Imperial (on the role of non-monotonic reasoning in machine learning, and on the analysis of inconsistency in specifications), he moved to University College London (UCL). He has published over 200 papers on knowledge representation and reasoning. His primary interest has been on computational models of argument (including deductive argumentation, probabilistic argumentation, persuasion, and enthymemes), and related topics including commonsense reasoning, paraconsistent reasoning, knowledge aggregation, and measures of inconsistency. His research has been funded by EPSRC, the Royal Society, the Leverhulme Trust, the Alan Turing Institute, and Innovate UK.

Graph Queries: Do We Study What Matters?

Leonid Libkin, University of Edinburgh, UK

Graph queries are studied extensively by many communities: data management, AI, Semantic Web. The development of the theoretical models of such queries happened in between the two eras of prominence of graphs: the early network data model (later overridden by relational) and more recent models of RDF and especially property graphs, gaining prominence in the last decade. Classical theory gives us the fundamental notion of Regular Path Queries (RPQ) and its many derivatives: CRPQs, UCRPQs, 2UCRPQs, ECRPQs, RDPQs, GXPath etc. This is still the model that dominates in research literature. Applications follow a different path however. A number of successful graph query languages including Cypher, PGQL, and GSQL led to the development of a new international standard called GQL (Graph Query Language). The core of GQL is inspired by RPQs in the same way the Hoover dam is inspired by a beaver blocking a local creek: the essence is similar, but the end result is not. However, GQL is still work in progress and even when finished it will come in the shape of hundreds of pages of specs, rather than a simple mathematical definition. The goal of this talk is to give such a definition to the community, and issue a call to change the main language of study to reflect graph languages that will dominate the practical landscape for decades to come.

Leonid Libkin is a professor of computer science at the University of Edinburgh and query language researcher at RelationalAI; he is also affiliated with École Normale Supérieure in Paris. He was previously scientific advisor to Neo4j, professor at the University of Toronto, and member of research staff at Bell Laboratories in Murray Hill. He received his PhD from the University of Pennsylvania in 1994. His main research interests are in the areas of data management and logic in computer science. He has written five books and over 250 technical papers. His awards include a Marie Curie Chair Award, a Royal Society Wolfson Research Merit Award, and six Best Paper Awards. He has chaired program committees of major database and logic conferences (PODS, LICS, ICDT), and served as chair of the 2010 Federated Logic Conference and general chair of PODS. He is an ACM fellow, a fellow of the Royal Society of Edinburgh, and a member of Academia Europaea.

5 SPONSORS

The KR 2022 conference was partially supported by the following organizations.

Platinum Sponsor

The Artificial Intelligence Journal

Artificial Intelligence
www.elsevier.com/locate/artint

Silver Sponsor

KR Inc. (Principles of Knowledge Representation & Reasoning)

Bronze Sponsors

The National Science Foundation

NSF

The Academic College of Tel Aviv-Yaffo

THE ACADEMIC of TEL AVIV-YAFFO

The European Association for Artificial Intelligence

EurAi

MAIN TRACK

A Gödel Calculus for Linear Temporal Logic

Juan Pablo Aguilera[1,2] , **Martín Diéguez**[3] , **David Fernández-Duque**[1,4] , **Brett McLean**[1]
[1]Department of Mathematics WE16, Ghent University
[2]Institute of Discrete Mathematics and Geometry, Vienna University of Technology
[3]University of Angers
[4]ICS of the Czech Academy of Sciences
{Juan.Aguilera, Brett.McLean, David.FernandezDuque}@UGent.be
Martin.DieguezLodeiro@univ-angers.fr

Abstract

We consider Gödel temporal logic (GTL), a variant of linear temporal logic based on Gödel–Dummett propositional logic. In recent work, we have shown this logic to enjoy natural semantics both as a fuzzy logic and as a superintuitionistic logic. Using semantical methods, the logic was shown to be PSPACE-complete. In this paper we provide a deductive calculus for GTL, and show this calculus to be sound and complete for the above-mentioned semantics.

1 Introduction

Despite their potential usefulness in areas such as spatio-temporal reasoning (Artemov, Davoren, and Nerode 1997) or vague temporal reasoning (Davies 1996), the combination of linear temporal logic with a modal or non-classical base tends to lead to high computational complexity (Balbiani et al. 2018) or even undecidability (Konev et al. 2006; Vidal 2021). Nevertheless, our recent work (Aguilera et al. 2022) provides a promising avenue for fuzzy temporal reasoning. There, we show that linear temporal logic (LTL) over a Gödel–Dummett base is PSPACE-complete, which is optimal for a logic interpreting classical LTL.

The methods used in (Aguilera et al. 2022) are model-theoretic and leave open the question of whether a proof-theoretic approach is possible. Here, we aim to close this gap by employing techniques used to establish completeness of an intuitionistic LTL in (Boudou, Diéguez, and Fernández-Duque 2017) with 'eventually' but without 'henceforth.' As we will see, the complications that led to omitting 'henceforth' in that work can be solved by incorporating the *dual implication* into our language, a connective that is to implication what disjunction is to conjunction. Aside from the technical advantages it afford us, it has been argued by Rauszer (1980) that dual implication is useful for reasoning with incomplete or inconsistent information.

Previously, LTL based on the intermediate logic of here-and-there (Heyting 1930) was axiomatized by Balbiani and Diéguez (2016). This logic allows for three truth values and is the basis for temporal answer set programming (Aguado et al. 2021; Aguado et al. 2013). Another combination of here-and-there, modal logic and Rauszer's co-implication has been studied in (Balbiani and Diéguez 2018).

Gödel logics and their extensions with possibility theory (Dubois, Lang, and Prade 1987) have been extensively studied in (Dellunde, Godo, and Marchioni 2011). These extensions have applications in the field of logic programming (Alsinet and Godo 2013; Blandi, Godo, and Rodríguez 2005). Aside from this, a version of the 'next' fragment of intuitionistic LTL was axiomatized by (Kojima and Igarashi 2011) and a logic with 'next' and 'eventually' (but not henceforth) by (Boudou, Diéguez, and Fernández-Duque 2017). Intuitionistic LTL with 'henceforth' has not been axiomatized, but (Boudou et al. 2021) showed that logics with the latter tense are more sensitive to choice of semantics than those without it and (Chopoghloo and Moniri 2021) provided a strongly complete infinitary calculus.

We recently showed that GTL possesses two natural semantics, corresponding to whether it is viewed as a fuzzy logic or as a superintuitionistic logic (Aguilera et al. 2022). As a fuzzy logic, propositions take values in $[0, 1]$, and truth values of compound propositions are defined using standard operations on the reals. As a superintuitionistic logic, models consist of bi-relational structures equipped with a partial order to interpret implication intuitionistically and a function to interpret the LTL tenses. We showed that the set of validities for either of these semantics coincides, and in fact coincides with the set of validities for a third class of structures we call *non-deterministic quasimodels*. Similar structures were used to prove upper complexity bounds for dynamic topological logic (Fernández-Duque 2009) and intuitionistic temporal logic (Fernández-Duque 2018). In the setting of GTL, they can be used to prove that the validity problem is decidable: while the logic does not enjoy the finite model property for either the fuzzy or the superintuitionistic semantics, it *does* enjoy the finite quasimodel property.

(Diéguez and Fernández-Duque 2018; Fernández-Duque 2012) have shown that quasimodels also come in handy in completeness proofs. There are two main reasons for this. First, as quasimodels are somewhat more flexible than proper models, it is easier to construct them. Thus our task is to construct a quasimodel falsifying a given non-derivable formula. Once constructed, we can use unwinding techniques to produce a proper bi-relational model from our quasimodel. The second advantage is that it allows us to use techniques normally available only for logics enjoying the finite model property, such as fully characterizing a given structure using a finite formula. In fact, contrary to the classical case, we will assign two characteristic formulas to each state w of our quasimodels, $\chi^+(w)$ and $\chi^-(w)$, characterizing the 'positive' and 'negative' information available in w.

Aside from these points, our completeness proof involves several stages that should be standard to those familiar with temporal logic: a *canonical model* $\mathfrak{C}$ is built, which correctly interprets $\bigcirc$ but not $\Diamond$ and $\Box$. In order to remedy this, a modified filtration $\mathfrak{C}/_\Sigma$ is built, which *does* interpret all tenses correctly when restricted to the set of formulas Σ, but fails to have a deterministic successor relation. Finally, an unwinding procedure is applied to $\mathfrak{C}/_\Sigma$ to obtain a bi-relational model. This unwinding is somewhat more complex than in the classical case, but fortunately we may appeal to results of (Aguilera et al. 2022) to conclude that any formula falsified in $\mathfrak{C}/_\Sigma$ is also falsified in a suitable unwinding of $\mathfrak{C}/_\Sigma$.

2 Syntax and Semantics

In this section we first introduce the temporal language we work with and then two possible semantics for this language: real semantics and bi-relational semantics.

Fix a countably infinite set $\mathbb{P}$ of propositional variables. Then the **Gödel temporal language** $\mathcal{L}$ is defined by the grammar (in Backus–Naur form):

$$\varphi,\psi := p \mid \varphi\wedge\psi \mid \varphi\vee\psi \mid \varphi\Rightarrow\psi \mid \varphi\Leftarrow\psi \mid \bigcirc\varphi \mid \Diamond\varphi \mid \Box\varphi,$$

where $p \in \mathbb{P}$. Here, $\bigcirc$ is read as 'next', $\Diamond$ as 'eventually', and $\Box$ as 'henceforth'. The connective $\Leftarrow$ is dual (or co-) implication and represents the operator dual to implication (Wolter 1998). We also use $\bot$ (respectively $\top$) as a shorthand for $p\Leftarrow p$ (respectively $p\Rightarrow p$) for some fixed variable p, and we use $\neg\varphi$ (respectively $\sim\varphi$) as a shorthand for $\varphi\Rightarrow\bot$ (respectively $\top\Leftarrow\varphi$), and $\varphi\Leftrightarrow\psi$ (not related to dual implication) as a shorthand for $(\varphi\Rightarrow\psi)\wedge(\psi\Rightarrow\varphi)$.

We now introduce the first of our semantics for the Gödel temporal language: *real semantics*, which views $\mathcal{L}$ as a fuzzy logic (enriched with temporal modalities). In the definition, $[0,1]$ denotes the real unit interval.

Definition 1 (real semantics)**.** A **flow** is a pair $\mathcal{T} = (T, S)$, where T is a set and $S\colon T \to T$ is a function. A **real valuation** on $\mathcal{T}$ is a function $V\colon \mathcal{L}\times T \to [0,1]$ such that, for all $t \in T$, the following equalities hold.

$$\begin{array}{rcl}
V(\bot,t) &=& 0\\
V(\varphi\wedge\psi,t) &=& \min\{V(\varphi,t),V(\psi,t)\}\\
V(\varphi\vee\psi,t) &=& \max\{V(\varphi,t),V(\psi,t)\}\\
V(\varphi\Rightarrow\psi,t) &=& \begin{cases} V(\psi,t) & \text{if } V(\varphi,t) > V(\psi,t)\\ 1 & \text{if } V(\varphi,t)\le V(\psi,t)\end{cases}\\
V(\varphi\Leftarrow\psi,t) &=& \begin{cases} V(\varphi,t) & \text{if } V(\varphi,t) > V(\psi,t)\\ 0 & \text{if } V(\varphi,t)\le V(\psi,t)\end{cases}\\
V(\bigcirc\varphi,t) &=& V(\varphi,S(t))\\
V(\Diamond\varphi,t) &=& \sup_{n<\omega} V(\varphi,S^n(t))\\
V(\Box\varphi,t) &=& \inf_{n<\omega} V(\varphi,S^n(t))
\end{array}$$

A flow $\mathcal{T}$ equipped with a valuation V is a **real (Gödel temporal) model**.

The second semantics, *bi-relational semantics*, views $\mathcal{L}$ as an intuitionistic logic (temporally enriched).

Definition 2 (bi-relational semantics)**.** A **(Gödel temporal) bi-relational frame** is a quadruple $\mathcal{F} = (W, T, \le, S)$ where $(W,\le)$ is a linearly ordered set and (T,S) is a flow. A **bi-relational valuation** on $\mathcal{F}$ is a function $[\![\cdot]\!] : \mathcal{L} \to 2^{W\times T}$ such that, for each $p\in\mathbb{P}$, the set $[\![p]\!]$ is *downward closed* in its first coordinate, and the following equalities hold.

$$\begin{array}{rcl}
[\![\bot]\!] &=& \varnothing\\
[\![\varphi\wedge\psi]\!] &=& [\![\varphi]\!]\cap[\![\psi]\!]\\
[\![\varphi\vee\psi]\!] &=& [\![\varphi]\!]\cup[\![\psi]\!]\\
[\![\varphi\Rightarrow\psi]\!] &=& \{(w,t)\in W\times T \mid \forall v\le w((v,t)\in[\![\varphi]\!] \\
&& \qquad\text{implies } (v,t)\in[\![\psi]\!])\}\\
[\![\varphi\Leftarrow\psi]\!] &=& \{(w,t)\in W\times T \mid \exists v\ge w((v,t)\in[\![\varphi]\!] \\
&& \qquad\text{and } (v,t)\notin[\![\psi]\!])\}\\
[\![\bigcirc\varphi]\!] &=& (\mathrm{id}_W\times S)^{-1}[\![\varphi]\!]\\
[\![\Diamond\varphi]\!] &=& \bigcup_{n<\omega}(\mathrm{id}_W\times S)^{-n}[\![\varphi]\!]\\
[\![\Box\varphi]\!] &=& \bigcap_{n<\omega}(\mathrm{id}_W\times S)^{-n}[\![\varphi]\!]
\end{array}$$

where $(\mathrm{id}_W\times S)$ is the function such that $(\mathrm{id}_W\times S)(w,t) = (w,S(t))$. Given $(w,t)\in W\times T$, we say that $S((w,t)) \stackrel{\text{def}}{=} (w,S(t))$. A bi-relational frame $\mathcal{F}$ equipped with a valuation $[\![\cdot]\!]$ is a **(Gödel temporal) bi-relational model**.

This semantics combines standard semantics for the implications based on $\le$ (read downward) and for the tenses based on S: for example, $(w,t)\in[\![\Diamond\varphi]\!]$ if and only if there exists $n\ge 0$ such that $(w,S^n(t))\in[\![\varphi]\!]$. Note that, by structural induction, the valuation of *any* $\varphi\in\mathcal{L}$ is downward closed in its first coordinate, in the sense that if $(w,t)\in[\![\varphi]\!]$ and $v\le w$, then $(v,t)\in[\![\varphi]\!]$.

Validity of $\mathcal{L}$-formulas is defined in the usual way.

Definition 3 (validity)**.** Given a real model $\mathcal{X} = (T,S,V)$ and a formula $\varphi\in\mathcal{L}$, we say that φ is **globally true** on $\mathcal{X}$, written $\mathcal{X}\models\varphi$, if for all $t\in T$ we have $V(\varphi,t)=1$. Given a bi-relational model $\mathcal{X} = (\mathcal{F},[\![\cdot]\!])$ and a formula $\varphi\in\mathcal{L}$, we say that φ is **globally true** on $\mathcal{X}$, written $\mathcal{X}\models\varphi$, if $[\![\varphi]\!] = W\times T$.

If $\mathcal{X}$ is a flow or a bi-relational frame, we write $\mathcal{X}\models\varphi$ and say φ is **valid** on $\mathcal{X}$, if φ is globally true for every valuation on $\mathcal{X}$. If Ω is a class of flows, frames, or models, we say that $\varphi\in\mathcal{L}$ is **valid** on Ω if, for every $\mathcal{X}\in\Omega$, we have $\mathcal{X}\models\varphi$. If φ is not valid on Ω, it is **falsifiable** on Ω.

We define the logic $\mathsf{GTL}_{\mathbb{R}}$ to be the set of $\mathcal{L}$-formulas that are valid over the class of all flows and the logic $\mathsf{GTL}_{\mathrm{Rel}}$ to be the set of $\mathcal{L}$-formulas that are valid over the class of all bi-relational frames. The main theorem of (Aguilera et al. 2022) is that these logics coincide:

Theorem 4. $\mathsf{GTL}_{\mathbb{R}} = \mathsf{GTL}_{\mathrm{Rel}}$. *That is, for each $\varphi\in\mathcal{L}$, φ is valid over the class of real Gödel temporal models if and only if it is valid over the class of all Gödel temporal bi-relational models.*

3 The Calculus

We begin by establishing our basic calculus for logics over $\mathcal{L}$. It is obtained by adapting the standard axioms and inference rules of LTL (Lichtenstein and Pnueli 2000), as well as their dual versions.

Definition 5. The logic GTL is the least set of $\mathcal{L}$-formulas closed under the following axioms and rules.

I **All (substitution instances of) intuitionistic tautologies (see e.g. (Mints 2000))**

II **Axioms and rules of H-B logic:**

A $\varphi \Rightarrow (\psi \vee (\varphi \Leftarrow \psi))$

B $\dfrac{\varphi \Rightarrow \psi}{(\varphi \Leftarrow \theta) \Rightarrow (\psi \Leftarrow \theta)}$

C $\dfrac{\varphi \Rightarrow \psi \vee \gamma}{(\varphi \Leftarrow \psi) \Rightarrow \gamma}$

III **Linearity axioms:**

A $(\varphi \Rightarrow \psi) \vee (\psi \Rightarrow \varphi)$

B $\neg((\varphi \Leftarrow \psi) \wedge (\psi \Leftarrow \varphi))$

IV **Temporal axioms:**

A $\neg \bigcirc \bot$

B $\bigcirc(\varphi \vee \psi) \Rightarrow (\bigcirc\varphi \vee \bigcirc\psi)$

C $(\bigcirc\varphi \wedge \bigcirc\psi) \Rightarrow \bigcirc(\varphi \wedge \psi)$

D $\bigcirc(\varphi \Rightarrow \psi) \Leftrightarrow (\bigcirc\varphi \Rightarrow \bigcirc\psi)$

E $\Box(\varphi \Rightarrow \psi) \Rightarrow (\Box\varphi \Rightarrow \Box\psi)$

F $\Box(\varphi \Rightarrow \psi) \Rightarrow (\Diamond\varphi \Rightarrow \Diamond\psi)$

G $\Box\varphi \Rightarrow \varphi \wedge \bigcirc\Box\varphi$

H $\varphi \vee \bigcirc\Diamond\varphi \Rightarrow \Diamond\varphi$

I $\Box(\varphi \Rightarrow \bigcirc\varphi) \Rightarrow (\varphi \Rightarrow \Box\varphi)$

J $\Box(\bigcirc\varphi \Rightarrow \varphi) \Rightarrow (\Diamond\varphi \Rightarrow \varphi)$

V **Back–up confluence axiom:**

$\bigcirc(\varphi \Leftarrow \psi) \Rightarrow (\bigcirc\varphi \Leftarrow \bigcirc\psi)$

VI **Standard modal rules:**

A $\dfrac{\varphi,\ \varphi \Rightarrow \psi}{\psi}$ B $\dfrac{\varphi}{\bigcirc\varphi}$ C $\dfrac{\varphi}{\Box\varphi}$

Axiom group II concerns the relationship between $\Rightarrow$ and $\Leftarrow$. In particular, Axiom II.A is used in C. Rauszer's axiomatization of intuitionistic logic with co-implication (called H-B logic) (Rauszer 1974). The Gödel–Dummett axiom III.A and its order dual III.B are used to force the connectives $\Rightarrow$ and $\Leftarrow$ to be implemented on locally linear posets (i.e. posets that are a disjoint union of linear orders).

Axioms IV.C, IV.D, and IV.E are standard modal axioms (viewing $\bigcirc$ as a box-type modality). In particular they hold in any normal modal logic, although of course GTL is not itself normal by virtue of being strictly sub-classical. Axiom IV.F is a dual version of IV.E; such dual axioms are often needed in intuitionistic modal logic, since $\Diamond$ and $\Box$ are not typically interdefinable. The axioms IV.A and IV.B have to do with the passage of time being deterministic in linear temporal logic: IV.A characterises seriality and IV.B characterises (partial) functionality, thus together they constrain temporal accessibility to be a total function.

The co-inductive axiom IV.G states that if something will henceforth be the case, then it is true now and, moreover, in the next moment, it will still henceforth be the case, and IV.I is successor induction, as time is interpreted over the natural numbers. Axioms IV.H and IV.J are their duals. Note that 'henceforth' is interpreted reflexively. All rules of group VI.A are standard modal logic deduction rules, and in particular any normal modal logic is closed under these rules.

Most of the axioms are either included in the axiomatization of intuitionistic LTL (Boudou, Diéguez, and Fernández-Duque 2017) or a variant of one of them (e.g. a contrapositive). From this, we easily derive the following.

Proposition 6. *The above calculus is sound for the class of real models, as well as for the class of bi-relational models.*

Proof. The rules II.B and II.C are readily seen to preserve validity. We check Axioms V and III.B; all other rules or axioms have been shown to be sound for intuitionistic or bi-relational models in the literature (see e.g. (Balbiani et al. 2018; Rauszer 1974)).

For Axiom V, it suffices to check its validity on the class of bi-relational models. Let $\mathcal{M} = (W, T, \leq, S, [\![\cdot]\!])$ be a bi-relational model and suppose that $(w,t) \in [\![\bigcirc(\varphi \Leftarrow \psi)]\!]$; we must show that $(w,t) \in [\![\bigcirc\varphi \Leftarrow \bigcirc\psi]\!]$. From $(w,t) \in [\![\bigcirc(\varphi \Leftarrow \psi)]\!]$ we see that $(w, S(t)) \in [\![\varphi \Leftarrow \psi]\!]$; hence there is $(v, S(t)) \geq (w, S(t))$ with $(v, S(t)) \in [\![\varphi]\!] \setminus [\![\psi]\!]$. But then $(v, S(t)) \in [\![\bigcirc\varphi]\!] \setminus [\![\bigcirc\psi]\!]$, witnessing that $(w,t) \in [\![\bigcirc\varphi \Leftarrow \bigcirc\psi]\!]$.
For Axiom III.B, let us assume towards a contradiction that $\neg((\varphi \Leftarrow \psi) \wedge (\psi \Leftarrow \varphi))$ is not valid with respect to bi-relational models, so we can find $\mathcal{M}$ as above and $(w,t) \in \mathcal{M}$ such that $(w,t) \notin [\![\neg((\varphi \Leftarrow \psi) \wedge (\psi \Leftarrow \varphi))]\!]$. Therefore, there exists $(v,t) \leq (w,t)$ such that $(v,t) \in [\![(\varphi \Leftarrow \psi) \wedge (\psi \Leftarrow \varphi)]\!]$. Therefore, $(v,t) \in [\![\varphi \Leftarrow \psi]\!]$ and $(v,t) \in [\![\varphi \Leftarrow \psi]\!]$. Therefore, there exists $(v',t) \geq (v,t)$ and $(v'',t) \geq (v,t)$ such that $(v',t) \in [\![\varphi]\!] \setminus [\![\psi]\!]$ and $(v'',t) \in [\![\psi]\!] \setminus [\![\varphi]\!]$. Since $(W, \leq)$ is a linear order, either $(v',t) \leq (v'',t)$ or $(v',t) \geq (v'',t)$. In the former case we get that $(v',t) \in [\![\psi]\!]$ and in the latter case we get that $(v'',t) \in [\![\varphi]\!]$; in any case we reach a contradiction. ☐

Our main objective is to show that our calculus is indeed complete; proving this will take up the remainder of this paper.

As we show next, we can also derive the converses of some of these axioms. Below, for a set of formulas Γ we define $\bigcirc\Gamma = \{\bigcirc\varphi : \varphi \in \Gamma\}$, and empty conjunctions and disjunctions are defined by $\bigwedge \varnothing = \top$ and $\bigvee \varnothing = \bot$.

Lemma 7. *Let $\varphi \in \mathcal{L}$ and $\Gamma \subseteq \mathcal{L}$ be finite. Then the following formulas belong to* GTL.

1. $\bigcirc\bigvee\Gamma \Leftrightarrow \bigvee\bigcirc\Gamma$

2. $\bigcirc\bigwedge\Gamma \Leftrightarrow \bigwedge\bigcirc\Gamma$

3. $\Diamond\varphi \Rightarrow \varphi \vee \bigcirc\Diamond\varphi$

4. $\varphi \wedge \bigcirc\Box\varphi \Rightarrow \Box\varphi$

5. $(\varphi \Leftarrow \varphi) \Rightarrow \psi$

6. $(\varphi \Leftarrow \psi) \Rightarrow \varphi$

4 Labelled Systems and Quasimodels

Quasimodels will be a central tool in our completeness proof. These were originally introduced in (Fernández-Duque 2009) for *dynamic topological logic*, a classical predecessor of *intuitionistic temporal logic*, for which quasimodels were also used in (Fernández-Duque 2018). In this section we will introduce labelled spaces, labelled systems, and finally, quasimodels. Quasimodels can be viewed as a sort of nondeterministic generalisation of bi-relational models. Quasimodels are a great advantage to us since GTL has the finite quasimodel property (any falsifiable formula is falsifiable in a finite quasimodel), despite not having the finite model property for either the real or the bi-relational semantics (Aguilera et al. 2022).

Definition 8. Let $\Sigma \subseteq \mathcal{L}$ be closed under subformulas and $\Phi^+, \Phi^- \subseteq \Sigma$. We say that the pair $\Phi = (\Phi^+, \Phi^-)$ is a **two-sided Σ-type** if:

1. $\Phi^- \cap \Phi^+ = \varnothing$,
2. if $\varphi \wedge \psi \in \Phi^+$, then $\varphi, \psi \in \Phi^+$,
3. if $\varphi \wedge \psi \in \Phi^-$, then $\varphi \in \Phi^-$ or $\psi \in \Phi^-$,
4. if $\varphi \vee \psi \in \Phi^+$, then $\varphi \in \Phi^+$ or $\psi \in \Phi^+$,
5. if $\varphi \vee \psi \in \Phi^-$, then $\varphi, \psi \in \Phi^-$,
6. if $\varphi \Rightarrow \psi \in \Phi^+$, then $\varphi \in \Phi^-$ or $\psi \in \Phi^+$,
7. if $\varphi \Rightarrow \psi \in \Phi^-$, then $\psi \in \Phi^-$,
8. if $\varphi \Leftarrow \psi \in \Phi^-$, then $\varphi \in \Phi^-$ or $\psi \in \Phi^+$,
9. if $\varphi \Leftarrow \psi \in \Phi^+$, then $\varphi \in \Phi^+$,
10. if $\Diamond\varphi \in \Phi^-$, then $\varphi \in \Phi^-$,
11. if $\Box\varphi \in \Phi^+$, then $\varphi \in \Phi^+$.

If moreover $\Sigma = \Phi^- \cup \Phi^+$, we may say that Φ is **saturated**. The set of saturated two-sided Σ-types will be denoted $\mathbb{T}_\Sigma$. Given $\Phi, \Psi \in \mathbb{T}_\Sigma$, we write

$$\Phi \leq_\Sigma \Psi \text{ if and only if } \Phi^- \subseteq \Psi^- \text{ and } \Phi^+ \supseteq \Psi^+.$$

Often we want Σ to be finite, in which case we write $\Sigma \Subset \mathcal{L}$ to indicate that $\Sigma \subseteq \mathcal{L}$ and Σ is finite and closed under subformulas. We remark that if $\Phi \in \mathbb{T}_\Sigma$, then $\Phi^- = \Sigma \setminus \Phi^+$ (and vice-versa), but it is convenient to view Φ as a pair, since both the 'positive' and 'negative' information will play an important role.

A partially ordered set $(A, \leq)$ is **locally linear** if it is a disjoint union of linear posets. If $a, b \in A$, we write $a \lesseqgtr b$ if $a \leq b$ or $b \leq a$. We call the set $\{b \in A : b \lesseqgtr a\}$ the **linear component** of a; by assumption, linear components partition A.

Definition 9. Let $\Sigma \subseteq \mathcal{L}$ be closed under subformulas. A **Σ-labelled space** is a triple $\mathcal{W} = (|\mathcal{W}|, \leq_\mathcal{W}, \ell_\mathcal{W})$, where $(|\mathcal{W}|, \leq_\mathcal{W})$ is a locally linear poset and $\ell \colon |\mathcal{W}| \to \mathbb{T}_\Sigma$ a monotone function, in the sense that

$$w \leq_\mathcal{W} v \text{ implies } \ell_\mathcal{W}(w) \leq_\Sigma \ell_\mathcal{W}(v),$$

and such that for all $w \in |\mathcal{W}|$:

- whenever $\varphi \Rightarrow \psi \in \ell^-_\mathcal{W}(w)$, there is $v \leq_\mathcal{W} w$ such that $\varphi \in \ell^+_\mathcal{W}(v)$ and $\psi \in \ell^-_\mathcal{W}(v)$;
- whenever $\varphi \Leftarrow \psi \in \ell^+_\mathcal{W}(w)$, there is $v \geq_\mathcal{W} w$ such that $\varphi \in \ell^+_\mathcal{W}(v)$ and $\psi \in \ell^-_\mathcal{W}(v)$.

The Σ-labelled space $\mathcal{W}$ **falsifies** $\varphi \in \mathcal{L}$ if $\varphi \in \ell_\mathcal{W}(w)^-$ for some $w \in W$. The **height** of $\mathcal{W}$ is the supremum of all n such that there is a chain $w_1 <_\mathcal{W} w_2 <_\mathcal{W} \ldots <_\mathcal{W} w_n$.

If $\mathcal{W}$ is a labelled space, elements of $|\mathcal{W}|$ will sometimes be called **worlds**. When clear from context we will omit subscripts and write, for example, $\leq$ instead of $\leq_\mathcal{W}$.

Recall that a subset S of a poset $(P, \leq)$ is **convex** if $s \in S$ whenever $a, b \in S$ and $a \leq s \leq b$. A **convex relation** between posets $(A, \leq_A)$ and $(B, \leq_B)$ is a binary relation $R \subseteq A \times B$ such that for each $x \in A$ the image set $\{y \in B \mid x \ R \ y\}$ is convex with respect to $\leq_B$, and for each $y \in B$ the preimage set $\{x \in A \mid x \ R \ y\}$ is convex with respect to $\leq_A$. The relation R is **fully confluent** if it validates the four following conditions:

Forth–down
if $x \leq_A x' \ R \ y'$ there is y such that $x \ R \ y \leq_B y'$,

Forth–up
if $x' \geq_A x \ R \ y$ there is y' such that $x' \ R \ y' \geq_B y$,

Back–down
if $x' \ R \ y' \geq_B y$ there is x such that $x' \geq_A x \ R \ y$,

Back–up
if $x \ R \ y \leq_B y'$ there is x' such that $x \leq_A x' \ R \ y'$.

In other words, R is fully confluent if $\leq_A \circ R = R \circ \leq_B$ and $\geq_A \circ R = R \circ \geq_B$.

Definition 10. Let $\Sigma \subseteq \mathcal{L}$ be closed under subformulas. Suppose that $\Phi, \Psi \in \mathbb{T}_\Sigma$. The ordered pair (Φ, Ψ) is **sensible** if it satisfies the following conditions:

1. If $\bigcirc\varphi \in \Phi^+$, then $\varphi \in \Psi^+$.
2. If $\bigcirc\varphi \in \Phi^-$, then $\varphi \in \Psi^-$.
3. If $\Diamond\varphi \in \Phi^+$, then $\varphi \in \Phi^+$ or $\Diamond\varphi \in \Psi^+$.
4. If $\Diamond\varphi \in \Phi^-$, then $\varphi \in \Phi^-$ and $\Diamond\varphi \in \Psi^-$.
5. If $\Box\varphi \in \Phi^+$, then $\varphi \in \Phi^+$ and $\Box\varphi \in \Psi^+$.
6. If $\Box\varphi \in \Phi^-$, then $\varphi \in \Phi^-$ or $\Box\varphi \in \Psi^-$.

A pair (w, v) of worlds in a labelled space $\mathcal{W}$ is **sensible** if $(\ell(w), \ell(v))$ is sensible. A relation $S \subseteq |\mathcal{W}| \times |\mathcal{W}|$ is **sensible** if every pair in S is sensible. Further, S is **ω-sensible** if

- whenever $\Diamond\varphi \in \ell^+_\mathcal{W}(w)$, there are $n \geq 0$ and v such that $w \ S^n \ v$ and $\varphi \in \ell^+_\mathcal{W}(v)$;
- whenever $\Box\varphi \in \ell^-_\mathcal{W}(w)$, there are $n \geq 0$ and v such that $w \ S^n \ v$ and $\varphi \in \ell^-_\mathcal{W}(v)$.

Recall that a binary relation is said to be **serial** if every element of the domain is related to some element of the codomain.

A **labelled system** is a labelled space $\mathcal{W}$ equipped with a serial, fully confluent, convex sensible relation $R_\mathcal{W} \subseteq |\mathcal{W}| \times |\mathcal{W}|$. If moreover $R_\mathcal{W}$ is ω-sensible, we say that $\mathcal{W}$ is a **Σ-quasimodel.**

Any bi-relational model can be regarded as a Σ-quasimodel: If $\mathcal{X} = (W, T, \leq, S, [\![\cdot]\!])$ is a bi-relational model and $x \in W \times T$, we can assign a Σ-type $\ell_\mathcal{X}(x)$ to x given by

$$\ell_\mathcal{X}(x)^+ = \{\psi \in \Sigma \mid x \in [\![\psi]\!]\}$$
$$\ell_\mathcal{X}(x)^- = \{\psi \in \Sigma \mid x \notin [\![\psi]\!]\}.$$

Note that this assignment of types is $\leq_\Sigma$-monotone. We also set $R_\mathcal{X} = \{((w,t),(w,S(t))) \mid w \in W, t \in T\}$; it is obvious that $R_\mathcal{X}$ is ω-sensible. Henceforth we will tacitly identify $\mathcal{X}$ with its associated Σ-quasimodel.

The following is proved in (Aguilera et al. 2022).

Theorem 11. *Given $\varphi \in \mathcal{L}$, the following are equivalent:*

1. *φ is falsifiable.*
2. *φ is falsifiable in a quasimodel.*
3. *φ is falsifiable in a finite quasimodel.*

5 The Canonical Model

In this section we construct a standard canonical model for GTL. In the presence of $\Diamond$ and $\Box$, the standard canonical model is only a labelled system, rather than a proper bi-relational model. Nevertheless, it will be a useful ingredient in our completeness proof. Since we are working over an intermediate logic, the role of maximal consistent sets will be played by complete types, as defined below. The notation $\vdash$ always refers to derivability in the calculus defined in Section 3. Below, recall that by convention, $\bigwedge \varnothing = \top$ and $\bigvee \varnothing = \bot$.

Definition 12. Given two sets of formulas $\Gamma, \Delta \subseteq \mathcal{L}$, we say that Δ is a consequence of Γ, denoted by $\Gamma \vdash \Delta$, if there exist finite (possibly empty) $\Gamma' \subseteq \Gamma$ and $\Delta' \subseteq \Delta$ such that $\vdash \bigwedge \Gamma' \Rightarrow \bigvee \Delta'$ (i.e. $\bigwedge \Gamma' \Rightarrow \bigvee \Delta' \in \mathsf{GTL}$).

We say that a pair of sets $\Phi = (\Phi^+, \Phi^-) \in \mathcal{L} \times \mathcal{L}$ is **consistent** if $\Phi^+ \not\vdash \Phi^-$. A saturated, consistent pair is a **complete type**. The set of complete types will be denoted $\mathbb{T}_\infty$.

Note that we are using the standard interpretation of $\Gamma \vdash \Delta$ in Gentzen-style calculi. When working within a turnstile, we will follow the usual proof-theoretic conventions of writing Γ, Δ instead of $\Gamma \cup \Delta$, and writing φ instead of $\{\varphi\}$. Observe that there is no clash in terminology regarding the use of the word *type*.

Lemma 13. *If Φ is a complete type then Φ is a saturated two-sided $\mathcal{L}$-type.*

Proof. Let Φ be a complete type. Observe that Φ is already saturated by definition, so it remains to check that it satisfies all conditions of Definition 8. Condition 1 follows from the consistency of Φ. For condition 10 we use Axiom IV.H: if $\Diamond\varphi \in \Phi^-$ and $\varphi \in \Phi^+$ we would have that Φ is inconsistent; hence $\varphi \in \Phi^-$. Condition 11 is proved using Axiom IV.G. The remaining conditions are left to the reader. □

As with maximal consistent sets, complete types satisfy a Lindenbaum property. Below, if (Γ, Δ) and (Γ', Δ') are pairs of sets of formulas, we say that (Γ', Δ') **extends** (Γ, Δ) if $\Gamma \subseteq \Gamma'$ and $\Delta \subseteq \Delta'$.

Lemma 14 (Lindenbaum lemma). *Let $\Gamma, \Delta \subseteq \mathcal{L}$. If $\Gamma \not\vdash \Delta$, then there exists a complete type Φ extending (Γ, Δ).*

Proof. The proof is standard, but we provide a sketch. Let $\varphi \in \mathcal{L}$. Note that either $\Gamma, \varphi \not\vdash \Delta$ or $\Gamma \not\vdash \Delta, \varphi$, for otherwise by a cut rule (which is intuitionistically derivable) we would have $\Gamma \vdash \Delta$. Thus we can add φ to Γ or to Δ, and by repeating this process for each element of $\mathcal{L}$ (or using Zorn's lemma) we can find a suitable Φ. □

Before defining the canonical model, recall that for a set of formulas Γ, we have $\circ\Gamma \stackrel{\text{def}}{=} \{\circ\varphi \mid \varphi \in \Gamma\}$. We also define

$$\ominus\Gamma \stackrel{\text{def}}{=} \{\varphi \mid \circ\varphi \in \Gamma\}.$$

Given a set A, let $\mathbb{I}_A$ denote the identity function on A. The canonical model $\mathfrak{C}$ is defined as the labelled structure

$$\mathfrak{C} = (|\mathfrak{C}|, \leq_{\mathfrak{C}}, S_{\mathfrak{C}}, \ell_{\mathfrak{C}}),$$

where $|\mathfrak{C}| = \mathbb{T}_\infty$ is the set of complete types, $\Phi \leq_{\mathfrak{C}} \Psi$ if $\Phi \leq_{\mathcal{L}} \Psi$ (i.e., if $\Phi^- \subseteq \Psi^-$ and $\Phi^+ \supseteq \Psi^+$), $S_{\mathfrak{C}}(\Phi) = (\ominus\Phi^+, \ominus\Phi^-)$, and $\ell_{\mathfrak{C}}(\Phi) = \Phi$. We will usually omit writing $\ell_{\mathfrak{C}}$, as it has no effect on its argument.

Next we show that $\mathfrak{C}$ is an $\mathcal{L}$-labelled system. We begin by showing that it is based on a labelled space.

Lemma 15. *$(|\mathfrak{C}|, \leq_{\mathfrak{C}}, \ell_{\mathfrak{C}})$ is a $\mathcal{L}$-labelled space.*

Proof. We know that $\leq_{\mathcal{L}}$ is a partial order and restrictions of partial orders are partial orders, so $\leq_{\mathfrak{C}}$ is a partial order. Moreover, $\ell_{\mathfrak{C}}$ is the identity, so $\Phi \leq_{\mathfrak{C}} \Psi$ implies that $\ell_{\mathfrak{C}}(\Phi) \leq_{\mathcal{L}} \ell_{\mathfrak{C}}(\Psi)$.

To prove that $(|\mathfrak{C}|, \leq_{\mathfrak{C}})$ is locally linear, assume towards a contradiction that it is not. We consider two cases:

1. There exist Φ, Ψ and Θ such that $\Phi \leq_{\mathcal{L}} \Psi$ and $\Phi \leq_{\mathcal{L}} \Theta$, but $\Psi \not\leq_{\mathcal{L}} \Theta$ and $\Theta \not\leq_{\mathcal{L}} \Psi$. By definition, there exist two formulas $\varphi \in \Theta^+ \setminus \Psi^+$ and $\psi \in \Psi^+ \setminus \Theta^+$. It is easy to see that $\varphi \Rightarrow \psi \notin \Theta^+$ and $\psi \Rightarrow \varphi \notin \Psi^+$. This would imply that Axiom III.A does not belong to Φ^+—a contradiction.
2. There exist Φ, Ψ and Θ such that $\Phi \geq_{\mathcal{L}} \Psi$ and $\Phi \geq_{\mathcal{L}} \Theta$, but $\Psi \not\geq_{\mathcal{L}} \Theta$ and $\Theta \not\geq_{\mathcal{L}} \Psi$. Then it is easy to see that there exist two formulas $\varphi \in \Psi^+ \setminus \Theta^+$ and $\psi \in \Theta^+ \setminus \Psi^+$ such that $\varphi \Leftarrow \psi \in \Psi^+$ and $\psi \Leftarrow \varphi \in \Theta^+$. From $\Phi \geq_{\mathcal{L}} \Psi$, $\Phi \geq_{\mathcal{L}} \Theta$, and some intuitionistic reasoning we conclude that $(\varphi \Leftarrow \psi) \wedge (\psi \Leftarrow \varphi) \in \Phi^+$, which contradicts Axiom III.B.

We finish by considering the conditions on $\Rightarrow$ and $\Leftarrow$. Let us consider $\Phi \in |\mathfrak{C}|$:

- If $\varphi \Rightarrow \psi \in \Phi^-$ then, by Condition 7 of Definition 8, $\psi \in \Phi^-$. Let us define $u = (\Phi^+ \cup \{\varphi\}, \{\psi\})$, and let us assume by contradiction that u is not consistent. This means that there exists $\gamma \in \Phi^+$ such that $\gamma \wedge \varphi \Rightarrow \psi \in \mathsf{GTL}$. By propositional reasoning, $\gamma \Rightarrow (\varphi \Rightarrow \psi) \in \mathsf{GTL}$. Since $\gamma \in \Phi^+$ and Φ is consistent, $\varphi \Rightarrow \psi \notin \Phi^-$—a contradiction. Therefore, u is consistent and, by Lemma 14, it can be extended to a complete type Ψ. From the definition of u we can conclude that $\Psi \leq_{\mathcal{L}} \Phi$, $\varphi \in \Psi^+$, and $\psi \in \Psi^-$ as required.
- If $\varphi \Leftarrow \psi \in \Phi^+$ then, by Condition 9, $\varphi \in \Phi^+$. Let us define $u = (\{\varphi\}, \Phi^- \cup \{\psi\})$, and let us assume by contradiction that u is not consistent. This means that there exists $\gamma \in \Phi^-$ such that $\varphi \Rightarrow \psi \vee \gamma \in \mathsf{GTL}$. By Rule II.C, we get $(\varphi \Leftarrow \psi) \Rightarrow \gamma \in \mathsf{GTL}$. Since $\gamma \in \Phi^-$, we deduce that $\varphi \Leftarrow \psi \notin \Phi^+$—a contradiction. By Lemma 14, u can be extended to a complete type Ψ. It is easy to check that $\Phi \leq_{\mathcal{L}} \Psi$, $\varphi \in \Psi^+$, and $\psi \in \Psi^-$ as required. □

Lemma 16. *$S_{\mathfrak{C}} \colon |\mathfrak{C}| \to |\mathfrak{C}|$ is well defined.*

Proof. Let $\Phi \in |\mathfrak{C}|$ and $\Psi = S_{\mathfrak{C}}(\Phi)$; we must check that $\Psi \in |\mathfrak{C}| = \mathbb{T}_\infty$. Recall that $\Psi^+ = \ominus\Phi^+$ and $\Psi^- = \ominus\Phi^-$. To see that Ψ is saturated, let $\varphi \in \mathcal{L}$ be so that $\varphi \notin \Psi^-$. It follows that $\circ\varphi \notin \Phi^-$, but Φ is saturated, so $\circ\varphi \in \Phi^+$ and thus $\varphi \in \Psi^+$. Since φ was arbitrary, $\Psi^- \cup \Psi^+ = \mathcal{L}$. Next we check that Ψ is consistent. If not, let $\Gamma \subseteq \Psi^+$ and $\Delta \subseteq \Psi^-$ be finite and such that $\bigwedge \Gamma \Rightarrow \bigvee \Delta \in \mathsf{GTL}$. Using VI.B and IV.D we see that $\circ \bigwedge \Gamma \Rightarrow \circ \bigvee \Delta \in \mathsf{GTL}$, which in view of Lemma 7 implies that $\bigwedge \circ\Gamma \Rightarrow \bigvee \circ\Delta \in \mathsf{GTL}$ as well. But $\bigcirc\Gamma \subseteq \Phi^+$ and $\bigcirc\Delta \subseteq \Phi^-$, contradicting the fact that Φ is consistent. We conclude that $\Psi \in |\mathfrak{C}|$. □

Lemma 17. *$S_\mathfrak{C}$ is fully confluent.*

Proof. We check the four conditions:

Forth–down, forth–up: Let Φ, Ψ be such that $\Phi \leq_\mathcal{L} \Psi$. Since $S_\mathfrak{C}$ is a function, these properties amount to showing that $S_\mathfrak{C}(\Phi) \leq_\mathcal{L} S_\mathfrak{C}(\Psi)$. If $\varphi \in \left(S_\mathfrak{C}(\Psi)\right)^+$ then $\bigcirc\varphi \in \Psi^+$, which since $\Phi \leq_\mathcal{L} \Psi$ implies that $\bigcirc\varphi \in \Phi^+$ and hence $\varphi \in \left(S_\mathfrak{C}(\Phi)\right)^+$. Similarly we can check that if $\varphi \in \left(S_\mathfrak{C}(\Phi)\right)^-$ then $\varphi \in \left(S_\mathfrak{C}(\Psi)\right)^-$, so that $S_\mathfrak{C}(\Phi) \leq_\mathcal{L} S_\mathfrak{C}(\Psi)$, as needed.

Back–up: Let Φ, Ψ, and Θ be such that $\Psi = S_\mathfrak{C}(\Phi)$ and $\Psi \leq_\mathcal{L} \Theta$, and let us define $u = (\ominus\Theta^+, \Phi^- \cup \ominus\Theta^-)$. Assume toward a contradiction that u is not consistent. Therefore, there exist $\gamma \in \Phi^-$, $\varphi \in \Theta^+$, and $\psi \in \Theta^-$ such that $\bigcirc\varphi \Rightarrow (\gamma \vee \bigcirc\psi) \in \mathsf{GTL}$. By Lemma 7(6, we get that $(\bigcirc\varphi \Leftarrow \bigcirc\psi) \Rightarrow \gamma \in \mathsf{GTL}$. Since $\gamma \in \Phi^-$ and Φ is consistent and saturated, we have $\bigcirc\varphi \Leftarrow \bigcirc\psi \in \Phi^-$. By Axiom V, $\bigcirc(\varphi \Leftarrow \psi) \Rightarrow (\bigcirc\varphi \Leftarrow \bigcirc\psi) \in \Phi^+$. Since $\bigcirc\varphi \Leftarrow \bigcirc\psi \in \Phi^-$ and Φ is consistent and saturated, we have $\bigcirc(\varphi \Leftarrow \psi) \in \Phi^-$. Since $\Psi = S_\mathfrak{C}(\Phi)$, we have $\varphi \Leftarrow \psi \in \Psi^- \subseteq \Theta^-$. Thus either $\varphi \in \Theta^-$ or $\psi \in \Theta^+$—a contradiction. By Lemma 14, u can be extended to a complete type Υ, which satisfies $\Phi \leq_\mathcal{L} \Upsilon$ and $\Theta = S_\mathfrak{C}(\Upsilon)$, as required.

Back–down: Let Φ, Ψ, and Θ be such that $\Psi = S_\mathfrak{C}(\Phi)$ and $\Theta \leq_\mathcal{L} \Psi$ and define $u = (\Phi^+ \cup \ominus\Theta^+, \ominus\Theta^-)$ and assume that u is not consistent. This means that there exists $\gamma \in \Phi^+$, $\varphi \in \Theta^+$, and $\psi \in \Theta^-$ such that $\gamma \wedge \bigcirc\varphi \Rightarrow \bigcirc\psi \in \mathsf{GTL}$. By propositional reasoning, $\gamma \Rightarrow (\bigcirc\varphi \Rightarrow \bigcirc\psi) \in \mathsf{GTL}$, so $\bigcirc\varphi \Rightarrow \bigcirc\psi \in \Phi^+$. By Axiom IV.D, $\bigcirc(\varphi \Rightarrow \psi) \in \Phi^+$. Since $\Psi = S_\mathfrak{C}(\Phi)$, we have $\varphi \Rightarrow \psi \in \Psi^+ \subseteq \Theta^+$. Therefore $\psi \in \Theta^+$—a contradiction. By Lemma 14, u can be extended to a complete type Υ. It can be checked that $\Upsilon \leq_\mathcal{L} \Phi$ and $\Theta = S_\mathfrak{C}(\Upsilon)$, as required. □

Lemma 18. *$S_\mathfrak{C}$ is a convex relation.*

Proof. Since $S_\mathfrak{C}$ is a function, images of points are singletons, hence automatically convex. Thus we need only prove that preimages are convex. We proceed by contradiction. Let us take $\Upsilon \in |\mathfrak{C}|$ and let us define $\mathcal{A} = S_\mathfrak{C}^{-1}(\Upsilon)$ and let us assume that $\mathcal{A}$ is not convex. This means that there exist $\Phi, \Psi, \Theta \in |\mathfrak{C}|$ such that $\Phi, \Psi \in \mathcal{A}$ and $\Phi \leq_\mathcal{L} \Theta \leq_\mathcal{L} \Psi$, but $\Theta \notin \mathcal{A}$. Since $\Phi, \Psi \in \mathcal{A}$ and $\Theta \notin \mathcal{A}$, it follows that $S_\mathfrak{C}(\Phi) = S_\mathfrak{C}(\Psi) = \Upsilon \neq S_\mathfrak{C}(\Theta)$. We consider two cases:

- there exists $\bigcirc\varphi \in \Theta^+$ such that $\varphi \notin \Upsilon^+$. Then $\bigcirc\varphi \in \Phi^+$, so $\varphi \in \Upsilon^+$—a contradiction.
- there exists $\bigcirc\varphi \in \Theta^-$ such that $\varphi \notin \Upsilon^-$. Then $\bigcirc\varphi \in \Psi^-$ so $\varphi \in \Upsilon^-$—a contradiction. □

Lemma 19. *$S_\mathfrak{C}$ is sensible.*

Proof. Let us consider Φ, Ψ such that $\Psi = S_\mathfrak{C}(\Phi)$. We consider the conditions for (Φ, Ψ) to be sensible.

If $\bigcirc\varphi \in \Phi^+$ then $\varphi \in \Psi^+$ by the definition of $S_\mathfrak{C}$. If $\bigcirc\varphi \notin \Phi^+$ then $\bigcirc\varphi \in \Phi^-$ and, by definition, $\varphi \in \Psi^-$.

If $\Diamond\varphi \in \Phi^+$ and $\varphi \notin \Phi^+$, it follows that $\varphi \in \Phi^-$. By Lemma 7, $\Diamond\varphi \Rightarrow \varphi \vee \bigcirc\Diamond\varphi \in \mathsf{GTL}$, so we cannot have that $\bigcirc\Diamond\varphi \in \Phi^-$, and hence $\bigcirc\Diamond\varphi \in \Phi^+$, so that $\Diamond\varphi \in \Psi^+$. Similarly, if $\Diamond\varphi \in \Phi^-$ we have that $\bigcirc\Diamond\varphi \in \Phi^-$, for otherwise we obtain a contradiction from IV.H. Therefore, $\Diamond\varphi \in \Psi^-$ as well.

If $\Box\varphi \in \Phi^+$ then, by Axiom IV.G we get $\varphi, \bigcirc\Box\varphi \in \Phi^+$. Since $\Psi = S_\mathfrak{C}(\Phi)$, we get $\Box\varphi \in \Psi^+$. Conversely, assume that $\Box\varphi \in \Phi^-$. By Lemma 7, $\varphi \wedge \bigcirc\Box\varphi \in \Phi^-$, so either $\varphi \in \Phi^-$ or $\bigcirc\Box\varphi \in \Phi^-$ (giving in the second case $\Box\varphi \in \Psi^-$). In either case we reach the desired conclusion. □

We remark the general fact that given a Σ_1-labelled system and a subformula-closed $\Sigma_2 \subseteq \Sigma_1$, one can restrict the labelling to Σ_2 in the natural way (by replacing its output at any point by its intersection with Σ_2). Doing so yields a Σ_2-labelled system. This is easily verifiable from the definitions.

Proposition 20. *The canonical model $\mathfrak{C}$ is an $\mathcal{L}$-labelled system. Restricting the labelling to any subformula-closed $\Sigma \subseteq \mathcal{L}$ yields a Σ-labelled system.*

Proof. For the first claim, we need for the following three properties to hold: 1. $(|\mathfrak{C}|, \leq_\mathfrak{C}, \ell_\mathfrak{C})$ is a labelled space; 2. $S_\mathfrak{C}$ is a serial, fully confluent, convex sensible relation; and 3. $\ell_\mathfrak{C}$ has $\mathbb{T}_\mathcal{L}$ as its codomain. The first item is Lemma 15. $S_\mathfrak{C}$ is serial since it is a well defined function by Lemma 16, and it is a fully confluent, convex, sensible relation by Lemmas 17, 18, and 19. Finally, if $\Phi \in |\mathfrak{C}|$ then $\ell_\mathfrak{C}(\Phi) = \Phi$, which is an element of $\mathbb{T}_\mathcal{L}$ by Lemma 13.

The second claim follows from the observation preceding the proposition. □

6 The Canonical Quasimodel

In this section we describe a finite quotient $\mathfrak{C}/_\Sigma$ of the canonical labelled system $\mathfrak{C}$ constructed in Section 5, and we show that $\mathfrak{C}/_\Sigma$ is a Σ-labelled system. Later, in Section 8, we will show that $\mathfrak{C}/_\Sigma$ is also ω-sensible and thus a quasimodel.

We obtain $\mathfrak{C}/_\Sigma$ from $\mathfrak{C}$ in two steps. First, we will take a bisimulation quotient to obtain a finite Σ-labelled space equipped with a fully confluent sensible relation. The second step will be to extend the sensible relation to be convex, yielding a finite Σ-labelled system.

We describe the quotient explicitly, noting afterwards that it is a particular type of bisimulation quotient. The assumption that Σ is finite is only needed at the end: if Σ is finite then $\mathfrak{C}/_\Sigma$ will be finite. So for now let Σ be any subformula-closed subset of $\mathcal{L}$, and let $\mathfrak{C} = (|\mathfrak{C}|, \leq_\mathfrak{C}, S_\mathfrak{C}, \ell_\mathfrak{C})$ be the canonical labelled system, which by Proposition 20 is a Σ-labelled system when $\ell_\mathfrak{C}$ is restricted to a Σ-labelling, which we assume (and henceforth denote by ℓ).

For $\Phi \in |\mathfrak{C}|$, define $L(\Phi) = \{\ell(\Psi) \mid \Psi \lesseqgtr \Phi\}$. We define the binary relation $\sim$ on $|\mathfrak{C}|$ by

$$\Phi \sim \Psi \iff (\ell(\Phi), L(\Phi)) = (\ell(\Psi), L(\Psi)).$$

If Σ is finite, then clearly $|\mathfrak{C}|/{\sim}$ is finite.

Note that $\sim$ is the largest relation that is simultaneously a bisimulation with respect to the relations $\leq$ and $\geq$, with Σ

treated as the set of atomic propositions that bisimilar worlds must agree on.

Now define a partial order $\leq_Q$ on the equivalence classes $|\mathfrak{C}|/{\sim}$ of $\sim$ by

$$[\Phi] \leq_Q [\Psi] \iff L(\Phi) = L(\Psi) \text{ and } \ell(\Phi) \geq \ell(\Psi),$$

noting that this is well-defined and is indeed a partial order.

Since each set $L(\Phi)$ can be linearly ordered by inclusion and $\ell(\Phi) \in L(\Phi)$, the poset $(|\mathfrak{C}|/{\sim}, \leq_Q)$ is a disjoint union of linear orders. By defining ℓ_Q by

$$\ell_Q([\Phi]) = \ell(\Phi)$$

we obtain a Σ-labelled space $(|\mathfrak{C}|/{\sim}, \leq_Q, \ell_Q)$; it is not hard to check that this labelling is inversely monotone and that the clauses for $\Rightarrow$ and $\Leftarrow$ hold with this labelling.

Now define the binary relation R_Q on $|\mathfrak{C}|/{\sim}$ to be the smallest relation such that $[\Phi] \; R_Q \; [S(\Phi)]$, for all $\Phi \in |\mathfrak{C}|$.

Lemma 21. *The relation R_Q is fully confluent and sensible.*

Proof. It is clear that R_Q is sensible. For confluence, suppose $[\Phi] \; R_Q \; [S(\Phi)]$. To see that the forth–up condition holds, suppose further that $[\Phi] \leq_Q [\Psi]$. Then as $\ell(\Phi) \in L(\Phi) = L(\Psi)$ there is some $\Theta \geq \Phi$ with $[\Psi] = [\Theta]$. Then we have $[\Theta] \; R_Q \; [S(\Theta)]$ and $[S(\Phi)] \leq_Q [S(\Theta)]$, as required for the forth–up condition. The proofs of the remaining three confluence conditions are entirely analogous. □

As promised, we now have a Σ-labelled space equipped with a fully confluent sensible relation. We now transform this labelled space into a Σ-labelled system by making the additional relation convex by fiat.

Define R_Q^+ by $X \; R_Q^+ \; Y$ if and only if there exist $X_1 \leq_Q X \leq_Q X_2$ and $Y_1 \leq_Q Y \leq_Q Y_2$ such that $X_2 \; R_Q \; Y_1$ and $X_1 \; R_Q \; Y_2$. Now define $\mathfrak{C}/\Sigma = (|\mathfrak{C}|/{\sim}, \leq_Q, R_Q^+, \ell_Q)$.

Lemma 22. *The structure $\mathfrak{C}/\Sigma$ is a Σ-labelled system.*

Proof. We already know that $(|\mathfrak{C}|/{\sim}, \leq_Q, \ell_Q)$ is a Σ-labelled space. First we must check R_Q^+ is still fully confluent and sensible.

For the forth–down condition, suppose $X \leq_Q X' \; R_Q^+ \; Y'$. Then by the definition of R_Q^+, there are some $X_2 \geq_Q X'$ and $Y_1 \leq_Q Y'$ such that $X_2 \; R_Q \; Y_1$. Since $X \leq_Q X' \leq_Q X_2$, by the forth–down condition for R_Q there is some $Y \leq_Q Y_1$ with $X \; R_Q \; Y$ and therefore $X \; R_Q^+ \; Y$. Since $Y \leq_Q Y_1 \leq_Q Y'$, we are done. The proof that the forth–up condition holds is just the order dual of that for forth–down. The proofs of the back–down and back–up conditions are similar.

To see that R_Q^+ is sensible, suppose $X \; R_Q^+ \; Y$ and that $\bigcirc\varphi \in \Sigma$. Take $X_1 \leq_Q X \leq_Q X_2$ and $Y_1 \leq_Q Y \leq_Q Y_2$ such that $X \; R_Q \; Y_1$. Then

$$\begin{aligned} \bigcirc\varphi \in \ell_Q(X) &\Longrightarrow \bigcirc\varphi \in \ell_Q(X_1) \\ &\Longrightarrow \varphi \in \ell_Q(Y_2) \\ &\Longrightarrow \varphi \in \ell_Q(Y) \\ &\Longrightarrow \varphi \in \ell_Q(Y_1) \\ &\Longrightarrow \bigcirc\varphi \in \ell_Q(X_2) \quad \Longrightarrow \bigcirc\varphi \in \ell_Q(X), \end{aligned}$$

so $\bigcirc\varphi \in \ell_Q(X) \iff \varphi \in \ell_Q(Y)$. The $\Diamond$ and $\Box$ cases are similar.

Finally, we show that R_Q^+ is convex. Firstly, for the image condition, if $X \; R_Q^+ \; Y_1$ and $X \; R_Q^+ \; Y_2$ with $Y_1 \leq_Q Y \leq Y_2$, then by the definition of R_Q^+ we can find $X_2 \geq_Q X$ and $Y_1' \leq_Q Y_1$ with $X_2 \; R_Q \; Y_1'$, and similarly $X_1 \leq_Q X$ and $Y_2' \geq_Q Y_2$ with $X_1 \; R_Q \; Y_2'$. Since then $X_1 \leq_Q X \leq_Q X_2$ and $Y_1' \leq_Q Y \leq_Q Y_2'$, by the definition of R_Q^+ we conclude that $X \; R_Q^+ \; Y$. The preimage condition is completely analogous. This completes the proof that $\mathfrak{C}/\Sigma$ is a Σ-labelled system. □

Lemma 23. *Suppose Σ is finite, and write $\|\Sigma\|$ for its cardinality. Then the height of $\mathfrak{C}/\Sigma$ is bounded by $\|\Sigma\| + 1$, and the cardinality of the domain $|\mathfrak{C}|/{\sim}$ of $\mathfrak{C}/\Sigma$ is bounded by $(\|\Sigma\| + 1) \cdot 2^{\|\Sigma\|(\|\Sigma\|+1)+1}$*

Proof. Each element of the domain of $\mathfrak{C}/\Sigma$ is a pair (ℓ, L) where L is a (nonempty) subset of $\wp\Sigma$ and $\ell \in L$. Since L is linearly ordered by inclusion, it has height at most $\|\Sigma\| + 1$. There are $(2^{\|\Sigma\|})^i$ subsets of $\wp\Sigma$ of size i, so there are at most $\sum_{i=1}^{\|\Sigma\|+1} (2^{\|\Sigma\|})^i$ distinct L. The sum is bounded by $2^{\|\Sigma\|(\|\Sigma\|+1)+1}$. The factor of $\|\Sigma\| + 1$ corresponds to choice of an $\ell \in L$, for each L. □

Thus we have an exponential bound on the size of $\mathfrak{C}/\Sigma$. Later, once we prove $\mathfrak{C}/\Sigma$ is a quasimodel, the decidability of GTL can be inferred from this bound. See (Aguilera et al. 2022) for a more direct proof of decidability using the same quotient construction. However, for our purposes, it suffices to observe that $\mathfrak{C}/\Sigma$ is finite.

7 Characteristic Formulas

Next we show that there exist formulas defining points in the canonical quotient, i.e. to each $w \in |\mathfrak{C}/\Sigma|$ we assign formulas 'distinguishing' w. In fact, we need two versions of such formulas, as we can define them to be either true or false outside of the linear component of w. First, we define a formula $\chi_\Sigma^+(w)$ (or $\chi^+(w)$ when Σ is clear from context) such that for all $\Gamma \in |\mathfrak{C}|$, $\chi^+(w) \in \Gamma$ if and only if $w = [\Gamma']$ for some $\Gamma' \geq \Gamma$. Dually, we define $\chi^-(w) = \chi_\Sigma^-(w)$ so that for all $\Gamma \in |\mathfrak{C}|$, $\chi^-(w) \notin \Gamma$ if and only if $w = [\Gamma']$ for some $\Gamma' \leq \Gamma$. Compared to (Diéguez and Fernández-Duque 2018), these formulas require dual implication, as they must look 'up' and 'down' the model. In this section, we write $\mathfrak{C}/\Sigma = (|\mathfrak{C}/\Sigma|, \leq, R, \ell)$. We will omit subindices on the ℓ and L functions.

Definition 24. Fix $\Sigma \Subset \mathcal{L}$. Given $\Delta \in \mathbb{T}_\Sigma$, define $\overrightarrow{\Delta} = \bigwedge \Delta^+ \Rightarrow \bigvee \Delta^-$ and $\overleftarrow{\Delta} = \bigwedge \Delta^+ \Leftarrow \bigvee \Delta^-$. Given $w \in |\mathfrak{C}/\Sigma|$, we define a formula $\chi^0(w) = \chi_\Sigma^0(w)$ by

$$\chi^0(w) := \bigwedge_{\Delta \in L(w)} {\sim}\overrightarrow{\Delta} \wedge \bigwedge_{\Delta \notin L(w)} \neg\overleftarrow{\Delta}.$$

Then define $\chi^+(w) = \chi_\Sigma^+(w)$ by

$$\chi^+(w) = \overleftarrow{\ell(w)} \wedge \chi^0(w)$$

and $\chi^-(w) = \chi^-_\Sigma(w)$ by

$$\chi^-(w) = \chi^0(w) \Rightarrow \overrightarrow{\ell(w)}.$$

Proposition 25. *Given $w \in |\mathfrak{C}/\Sigma|$ and $\Gamma \in |\mathfrak{C}|$,*

1) $\chi^0(w) \in \Gamma^+$ if and only if $L(\Gamma) = L(w)$,
2) $\chi^+(w) \in \Gamma^+$ if and only if $[\Gamma] \leq w$, and
3) $\chi^-(w) \in \Gamma^-$ if and only if $[\Gamma] \geq w$.

Proof. Let $w \in |\mathfrak{C}/\Sigma|$ and $\Gamma \in |\mathfrak{C}|$.

1) First assume that $\chi^0(w) \in \Gamma^+$, so that $\bigwedge_{\Delta \in L(w)} \sim\overrightarrow{\Delta} \in \Gamma^+$ and $\bigwedge_{\Delta \notin L(w)} \neg\overleftarrow{\Delta} \in \Gamma^+$. Let $\Delta \in L(w)$. From $\sim\overrightarrow{\Delta} \in \Gamma^+$, we obtain $\Phi \geq \Gamma$ such that $\overrightarrow{\Delta} \notin \Phi^+$. Hence there is $\Phi_\Delta \leq \Phi$ with $\bigwedge \Delta^+ \in \Phi^+_\Delta$ and $\bigvee \Delta^- \in \Phi^-_\Delta$, i.e. $\ell(\Phi_\Delta) = \Delta$. From local linearity we see that $\Phi_\Delta \lesseqgtr \Gamma$; hence $\Delta = \ell(\Phi_\Delta) \in L(\Gamma)$.

Similarly, if $\Delta \in \mathbb{T}_\Sigma \setminus L(w)$, for any $\Psi \leq \Gamma$ we have that $\overleftarrow{\Delta} \notin \Psi^+$, so that there is no $\Psi_\Delta \geq \Psi$ with $\bigwedge \Delta^+ \in \Psi^+_\Delta$ and $\bigvee \Delta^- \in \Psi^-_\Delta$. Thus there is no $\Psi_\Delta \lesseqgtr \Gamma$ with $\bigwedge \Delta^+ \in \Psi^+_\Delta$ and $\bigvee \Delta^- \in \Psi^-_\Delta$, i.e. $\Delta \notin L(\Gamma)$ (for the $\Psi_\Delta \geq \Gamma$ case, set $\Psi = \Gamma$; for $\Psi_\Delta \leq \Gamma$ set $\Psi = \Psi_\Delta$).

The converse follows by similar reasoning. Assume that $L(\Gamma) = L(w)$. Then from $\Delta \in L(\Gamma)$ we readily obtain $\sim\overrightarrow{\Delta} \in \Gamma^+$, and similarly from $\Delta \notin L(\Gamma)$ we obtain $\neg\overleftarrow{\Delta} \in \Gamma^+$, from which we obtain by propositional reasoning $\chi^0(w) \in \Gamma^+$.

2) If $\chi^+(w) \in \Gamma^+$ then $\chi^0(w) \in \Gamma^+$, hence $L(\Gamma) = L(w)$, while $\overleftarrow{\ell(w)} \in \Gamma^+$ implies that there is some $\Gamma' \geq \Gamma$ with $\ell(\Gamma') = \ell(w)$. This shows that $w = [\Gamma'] \geq [\Gamma]$, as claimed.

3) This item is similar to the previous, except that we observe that if $L(\Gamma) \neq L(w)$, then $\chi^-(w) \notin \Gamma^-$. □

Remark 26. Note that the formula $\chi^+_\Sigma(w)$ makes essential use of dual implication, as properties of $w \geq [\Gamma]$ do not affect truth values in Γ in the language with $\Rightarrow$ alone. In contrast, the formulas χ^-_Σ are similar to the formulas $\mathrm{Sim}(w)$ of (Diéguez and Fernández-Duque 2018), although we remark that dual implication is still needed to describe the full linear component of w.

Next we establish some provable properties of each of χ^+_Σ and χ^-_Σ. We begin with the former.

Proposition 27. *Given $w \in |\mathfrak{C}/\Sigma|$ and $\psi \in \Sigma$:*

1) If $\psi \in \ell^-(w)$, then $\vdash \chi^+(w) \Rightarrow (\chi^+(w) \Leftarrow \psi)$.
2) If $\psi \in \ell^+(w)$, then $\vdash \chi^+(w) \Rightarrow \psi$.
3) For any $w \in |\mathfrak{C}/\Sigma|$, $\vdash \chi^+(w) \Rightarrow \circ \bigvee_{wRv} \chi^+(v)$.

Proof. 1) Let $\Gamma \in |\mathfrak{C}|$ and assume that $\psi \in \ell^-(w)$ and $\chi^+(w) \in \Gamma^+$; by properties of the canonical model, it suffices to show that $(\chi^+(w) \Leftarrow \psi) \in \Gamma^+$. From $\chi^+(w) \in \Gamma$ and Proposition 25 we obtain $\Delta \leq \Gamma$ such that $[\Delta] = w$, hence $\chi^+(w) \in \Delta^+$ and $\psi \in \Delta^-$, yielding $(\chi^+(w) \Leftarrow \psi) \in \Gamma$.

2) If $\psi \in \ell^+(w)$, as above, let $\Gamma \in |\mathfrak{C}|$ be such that $\chi^+(w) \in \Gamma^+$, and $\Delta \leq \Gamma$ with $[\Delta] = w$. Then $\psi \in \Delta^+$, yielding $\psi \in \Gamma^+$.

3) Let Γ be such that $\chi^+(w) \in \Gamma$, so that there is $\Delta \leq \Gamma$ with $[\Delta] = w$. Then $w\ R\ [S_\mathfrak{C}(\Delta)]$ by definition, and moreover $\chi^+([S_\mathfrak{C}(\Delta)]) \in S_\mathfrak{C}(\Delta^+)$ implies that $\circ\chi^+([S_\mathfrak{C}(\Delta)]) \in \Delta^+$. Thus $\circ\chi^+([S_\mathfrak{C}(\Delta)]) \in \Gamma^+$ by downward persistence, so that $\bigvee_{wRv} \chi^+(v) \in \Gamma^+$. □

The formula χ^-_Σ behaves 'dually', as established below.

Proposition 28. *Given $w \in |\mathfrak{C}/\Sigma|$ and $\psi \in \Sigma$:*

1) If $\psi \in \ell^-(w)$, then $\vdash \psi \Rightarrow \chi^-(w)$.
2) If $\psi \in \ell^+(w)$, then $\vdash (\psi \Rightarrow \chi^-(w)) \Rightarrow \chi^-(w)$.
3) For any $w \in |\mathfrak{C}/\Sigma|$, $\vdash \circ \bigwedge_{wRv} \chi^-(v) \Rightarrow \chi^-(w)$.

Proof. 1) Assume that $\psi \in \ell^-(w) \cap \Gamma^+$ and write $w = [\Delta]$. Then $\psi \in \Delta^-$, which means we cannot have $\Gamma \geq \Delta$. Hence Proposition 25 implies that $\chi^-(w) \notin \Gamma^-$, i.e. $\chi^-(w) \in \Gamma^+$.

2) Suppose that $\psi \in \ell^+(w)$ and proceed to prove the claim by contrapositive. If $\chi^-(w) \in \Gamma^-$ for some $\Gamma \in |\mathfrak{C}|$, then there is $\Delta \leq \Gamma$ such that $w = [\Delta]$. But then $\chi^-(w) \in \Delta^-$ and $\psi \in \Delta^+$, which implies that $(\psi \Rightarrow \chi^-(w)) \in \Delta^-$, hence also $(\psi \Rightarrow \chi^-(w)) \in \Gamma^-$, as required.

3) Proceed by contrapositive. If $\chi^-(w) \in \Gamma^-$ for some $\Gamma \in |\mathfrak{C}|$, then there is $\Delta \leq \Gamma$ such that $w = [\Delta]$. We have that $w\ R\ [S_\mathfrak{C}(\Delta)]$ by definition. Letting $v = [S_\mathfrak{C}(\Delta)]$, we have that $\chi^-(v) \in S^-_\mathfrak{C}(\Delta)$, hence $\circ\chi^-(v) \in \Delta^-$, and by downward persistence, $\circ\chi^-(v) \in \Gamma^-$. Hence $\circ \bigwedge_{wRv} \chi^-(v) \in \Gamma^-$. □

8 Completeness

The formulas $\chi^\pm_\Sigma$ are fundamental in our completeness proof; specifically, we will use them to show that $\mathfrak{C}/\Sigma$ is ω-sensible, hence a quasimodel. Since validity over the class of quasimodels is equivalent to real validity by Theorem 11, completeness will follow. The following lemma is the first step towards establishing ω-sensibility. Once again, we write $\mathfrak{C}/\Sigma = (|\mathfrak{C}/\Sigma|, \leq, R, \ell)$, and as usual R^* is the transitive, reflexive closure of R.

Lemma 29. *If $\Sigma \Subset \mathcal{L}$ and $w \in |\mathfrak{C}/\Sigma|$, then*

1. $\vdash \bigvee_{wR^*v} \chi^+(v) \Rightarrow \circ \bigvee_{wR^*v} \chi^+(v)$, and
2. $\vdash \circ \bigwedge_{wR^*v} \chi^-(v) \Rightarrow \bigwedge_{wR^*v} \chi^-(v)$.

Proof. The first item follows from Proposition 27(3), as for any $v \in R^*(w)$ we have that

$$\vdash \chi^+(v) \Rightarrow \circ \bigvee_{vRu} \chi^+(u).$$

Since $v\ R\ u$ implies that $w\ R^*\ u$ by transitivity,

$$\vdash \chi^+(v) \Rightarrow \circ \bigvee_{wR^*u} \chi^+(u).$$

Since v was arbitrary, we obtain

$$\vdash \bigvee_{wR^*v} \chi^+(v) \Rightarrow \bigcirc \bigvee_{wR^*u} \chi^+(u),$$

which by a change of variables yields the original claim.
Item 2 is similar, but uses Proposition 28(3). □

In order to complete our proof that $\mathfrak{C}/_\Sigma$ is ω-sensible, it suffices to apply induction to the formulas of Lemma 29.

Proposition 30.

1. *If $w \in |\mathfrak{C}/_\Sigma|$ and $\Diamond\psi \in \ell^+(w)$, then there is $v \in R^*(w)$ such that $\psi \in \ell^+(v)$.*
2. *If $w \in |\mathfrak{C}/_\Sigma|$ and $\Box\psi \in \ell^-(w)$, then there is $v \in R^*(w)$ such that $\psi \in \ell^-(v)$.*

Proof. **1.** Towards a contradiction, assume that $w \in |\mathfrak{C}/_\Sigma|$ and $\Diamond\psi \in \ell^+(w)$ but, for all $v \in R^*(w)$, $\psi \in \ell^-(w)$. By Lemma 29, $\vdash \bigcirc \bigwedge_{wR^*v} \chi^-(v) \Rightarrow \bigwedge_{wR^*v} \chi^-(v)$. By the $\Diamond$-induction axiom IV.J and standard modal reasoning, $\vdash \Diamond \bigwedge_{wR^*v} \chi^-(v) \Rightarrow \bigwedge_{wR^*v} \chi^-(v)$; in particular,

$$\vdash \Diamond \bigwedge_{wR*v} \chi^-(v) \Rightarrow \chi^-(w). \tag{1}$$

Now let $v \in R^*(w)$. By Proposition 28(1) and the assumption that $\psi \in \ell^-(v)$ we have that $\vdash \psi \Rightarrow \chi^-(v)$, and since v was arbitrary, $\vdash \psi \Rightarrow \bigwedge_{wR^*v} \chi^-(v)$. Using distributivity IV.F we further have that $\vdash \Diamond\psi \Rightarrow \Diamond \bigwedge_{wR^*v} \chi^-(v)$. This, along with (1), shows that $\vdash \Diamond\psi \Rightarrow \chi^-(w)$. However, by Proposition 27(2) and our assumption that $\Diamond\psi \in \ell^+(w)$ we have that $\vdash \big(\Diamond\psi \Rightarrow \chi^-(w)\big) \Rightarrow \chi^-(w)$. Hence by modus ponens we obtain $\vdash \chi^-(w)$. Writing $w = [\Gamma]$, Proposition 25 yields $\chi^-(w) \notin \Gamma^+$, but this contradicts $\vdash \chi^-(w)$. We conclude that there is $v \in R^*(w)$ with $\psi \in \ell^+(v)$, as needed.

2. This is similar to the first item, but dualised. Towards a contradiction, assume that $w \in |\mathfrak{C}/_\Sigma|$ and $\Box\psi \in \ell^-(w)$ but, for all $v \in R^*(w)$, $\psi \in \ell^+(w)$. By Lemma 29, $\vdash \bigvee_{wR^*v} \chi^+(v) \Rightarrow \bigcirc \bigvee_{wR^*v} \chi^+(v)$. By the $\Box$-induction axiom IV.I, $\vdash \bigvee_{wR^*v} \chi^+(v) \Rightarrow \Box \bigvee_{wR^*v} \chi^+(v)$; in particular,

$$\vdash \chi^+(w) \Rightarrow \Box \bigvee_{wR^*v} \chi^+(v). \tag{2}$$

Now let $v \in R^*(w)$. By Proposition 27(2) and the assumption that $\psi \in \ell^+(v)$, we have that $\vdash \chi^+(v) \Rightarrow \psi$, and since v was arbitrary, $\vdash \bigvee_{wR^*v} \chi^+(v) \Rightarrow \psi$. Using distributivity IV.E we further have that $\vdash \Box \bigvee_{wR^*v} \chi^+(v) \Rightarrow \Box\psi$. This, along with (2), shows that

$$\vdash \chi^+(w) \Rightarrow \Box\psi. \tag{3}$$

By Proposition 27(1) and our assumption that $\Box\psi \in \ell^-(w)$ we have that $\vdash \chi^+(w) \Rightarrow \big(\chi^+(w) \Leftarrow \Box\psi\big)$, hence by (3) and Rule II.B we obtain $\vdash \chi^+(w) \Rightarrow (\Box\psi \Leftarrow \Box\psi)$. In view of Lemma 7.5, this implies that $\chi^+(w)$ is contradictory. Writing $w = [\Gamma]$, Proposition 25 yields $\chi^+(w) \in \Gamma$, which once again is impossible. We conclude that there is $v \in R^*(w)$ with $\psi \in \ell^-(v)$. □

Corollary 31. *If $\Sigma \Subset \mathcal{L}$, then $\mathfrak{C}/_\Sigma$ is a quasimodel.*

Proof. By Lemma 22, $\mathfrak{C}/_\Sigma$ is based on a labelled system, while by Proposition 30, R is ω-sensible. By definition, $\mathfrak{C}/_\Sigma$ is a quasimodel. □

We are now ready to prove that our calculus is complete.

Theorem 32. *If $\varphi \in \mathcal{L}$ is valid, then $\vdash \varphi$.*

Proof. We prove the contrapositive. Suppose φ is an unprovable formula and let Σ be the set of subformulas of φ. Since φ is unprovable, there is $\Gamma \in |\mathfrak{C}|$ with $\varphi \in \Gamma^-$. Hence $[\Gamma] \in |\mathfrak{C}/_\Sigma|$ is a point in a quasimodel falsifying φ, so that by Theorem 11, φ is not valid. □

9 Concluding Remarks

We have provided a sound and complete calculus for the Gödel temporal logic GTL. These results further cement GTL as a privileged logic for fuzzy temporal reasoning and pave the way for a proof-theoretic treatment of these logics. Among the challenges in this direction is the design of cut-free or cyclic calculi.

In proving our main results, we have developed tools for the treatment of superintuitionistic temporal logics, specifically identifying the usefulness of combining 'henceforth' with co-implication. We believe that this insight will lead to completeness proofs for related logics, including intuitionistic LTL, where complete calculi for 'eventually' are available, but not so for 'henceforth'. Along these lines, it should be remarked that the techniques of (Diéguez and Fernández-Duque 2018) should lead to a sound and complete calculus for the logic with $\Rightarrow$, $\bigcirc$ and $\Diamond$ (but no co-implication or henceforth), although such a result does not follow immediately from the present work.

Another subject that would be worth studying in the near future is bisimulation in Gödel temporal logic. This tool has been used to determine that temporal operators are not interdefinable in the intuitionistic temporal setting (Balbiani et al. 2018; Balbiani et al. 2020). For the class of temporal here-and-there models, 'henceforth' is a basic operator that cannot be defined, while 'eventually' becomes definable in terms of 'henceforth', 'next', and implication (Balbiani et al. 2018; Balbiani et al. 2020). When introducing co-implication, results on definability exist in the literature: for a combination of the logic of here-and-there, co-implication and the basic modal logic K, it has been proven by (Balbiani and Diéguez 2018) that modal operators become interdefinable. We do not know if co-implication has the same effect to our Gödel temporal logic; a negative answer would require a suitable notion of bisimulation preserving both implications, as well as the temporal operators.

In a different direction, logics such as PDL or CTL may also enjoy naturally axiomatizable Gödel counterparts. The techniques developed here and by (Aguilera et al. 2022) could very well be applicable in these settings.

Acknowledgements

This work has been partially supported by FWO-FWF grant G030620N/I4513N (J.P.A. and D.F.D.), FWO grant 3E017319 (J.P.A.), the projects EL4HC and étoiles montantes CTASP at Région Pays de la Loire, France (M.D.), the COST action CA-17124 (M.D. and D.F.D.), and SNSF–FWO Lead Agency Grant 200021L_196176/G0E2121N (B.M. and D.F.D.).

References

Aguado, F.; Cabalar, P.; Diéguez, M.; Pérez, G.; and Vidal, C. 2013. Temporal equilibrium logic: a survey. *Journal of Applied Non-Classical Logics* 23(1-2):2–24.

Aguado, F.; Cabalar, P.; Diéguez, M.; Pérez, G.; Schaub, T.; Schuhmann, A.; and Vidal, C. 2021. Linear-time temporal answer set programming. *Theory and Practice of Logic Programming* 1–55.

Aguilera, J. P.; Diéguez, M.; Fernández-Duque, D.; and McLean, B. 2022. Time and gödel: Fuzzy temporal reasoning in PSPACE. *CoRR* abs/2205.00574.

Alsinet, T., and Godo, L. 2013. A complete calculus for possibilistic logic programming with fuzzy propositional variables. *CoRR* abs/1301.3832.

Artemov, S.; Davoren, J.; and Nerode, A. 1997. Modal logics and topological semantics for hybrid systems. *Technical Report MSI 97-05.*

Balbiani, P., and Diéguez, M. 2016. Temporal here and there. In Loizos, M., and Kakas, A., eds., *Logics in Artificial Intelligence*, 81–96. Springer.

Balbiani, P., and Diéguez, M. 2018. Here and there modal logic with dual implication. In Bezhanishvili, G.; D'Agostino, G.; Metcalfe, G.; and Studer, T., eds., *Advances in Modal Logic 12, proceedings of the 12th conference on Advances in Modal Logic, held in Bern, Switzerland, August 27–31, 2018*, 63–82. College Publications.

Balbiani, P.; Boudou, J.; Diéguez, M.; and Fernández-Duque, D. 2018. Bisimulations for intuitionistic temporal logics. *arXiv* 1803.05078.

Balbiani, P.; Boudou, J.; Diéguez, M.; and Fernández-Duque, D. 2020. Intuitionistic linear temporal logics. *ACM Trans. Comput. Log.* 21(2):14:1–14:32.

Blandi, L.; Godo, L.; and Rodríguez, R. O. 2005. A connection between similarity logic programming and Gödel modal logic. In Montseny, E., and Sobrevilla, P., eds., *Proceedings of the Joint 4th Conference of the European Society for Fuzzy Logic and Technology and the 11th Rencontres Francophones sur la Logique Floue et ses Applications, Barcelona, Spain, September 7–9, 2005*, 775–780. Universidad Polytecnica de Catalunya.

Boudou, J.; Diéguez, M.; Fernández-Duque, D.; and Kremer, P. 2021. Exploring the jungle of intuitionistic temporal logics. *Theory Pract. Log. Program.* 21(4):459–492.

Boudou, J.; Diéguez, M.; and Fernández-Duque, D. 2017. A decidable intuitionistic temporal logic. In *26th EACSL Annual Conference on Computer Science Logic, CSL 2017, August 20–24, 2017, Stockholm, Sweden*, 14:1–14:17.

Chopoghloo, S., and Moniri, M. 2021. A strongly complete axiomatization of intuitionistic temporal logic. *J. Log. Comput.* 31(7):1640–1659.

Davies, R. 1996. A temporal-logic approach to binding-time analysis. In *Proceedings, 11th Annual IEEE Symposium on Logic in Computer Science, New Brunswick, New Jersey, USA, July 27–30, 1996*, 184–195.

Dellunde, P.; Godo, L.; and Marchioni, E. 2011. Extending possibilistic logic over Gödel logic. *International Journal of Approximate Reasoning* 52(1):63–75. Tenth European Conference on Symbolic and Quantitative Approaches to Reasoning with Uncertainty (ECSQARU 2009).

Diéguez, M., and Fernández-Duque, D. 2018. An intuitionistic axiomatization of 'Eventually'. In Bezhanishvili, G.; D'Agostino, G.; Metcalfe, G.; and Studer, T., eds., *Advances in Modal Logic 12, proceedings of the 12th conference on Advances in Modal Logic, held in Bern, Switzerland, August 27–31, 2018*, 199–218. College Publications.

Dubois, D.; Lang, J.; and Prade, H. 1987. Theorem proving under uncertainty - A possibility theory-based approach. In McDermott, J. P., ed., *Proceedings of the 10th International Joint Conference on Artificial Intelligence. Milan, Italy, August 23–28, 1987*, 984–986. Morgan Kaufmann.

Fernández-Duque, D. 2009. Non-deterministic semantics for dynamic topological logic. *Ann. Pure Appl. Log.* 157(2-3):110–121.

Fernández-Duque, D. 2012. A sound and complete axiomatization for dynamic topological logic. *Journal of Symbolic Logic* 77(3):947–969.

Fernández-Duque, D. 2018. The intuitionistic temporal logic of dynamical systems. *Log. Methods Comput. Sci.* 14(3).

Heyting, A. 1930. Die formalen Regeln der intuitionistischen Logik. In *Sitzungsberichte der Preussischen Akademie der Wissenschaften*. Deutsche Akademie der Wissenschaften zu Berlin. 42–56.

Kojima, K., and Igarashi, A. 2011. Constructive linear-time temporal logic: Proof systems and Kripke semantics. *Information and Computation* 209(12):1491 – 1503.

Konev, B.; Kontchakov, R.; Wolter, F.; and Zakharyaschev, M. 2006. Dynamic topological logics over spaces with continuous functions. In Governatori, G.; Hodkinson, I.; and Venema, Y., eds., *Advances in Modal Logic*, volume 6, 299–318. London: College Publications.

Lichtenstein, O., and Pnueli, A. 2000. Propositional temporal logics: Decidability and completeness. *Logic Journal of the IGPL* 8(1):55–85.

Mints, G. 2000. *A Short Introduction to Intuitionistic Logic*. University Series in Mathematics. Springer.

Rauszer, C. 1974. A formalization of the propositional calculus of H-B logic. *Studia Logica* 33(1):23–34.

Rauszer, C. 1980. *An algebraic and Kripke-style approach to a certain extension of intuitionistic logic*. Warszawa: Instytut Matematyczny Polskiej Akademi Nauk.

Vidal, A. 2021. On transitive modal many-valued logics. *Fuzzy Sets Syst.* 407:97–114.

Wolter, F. 1998. On logics with coimplication. *Journal of Philosophical Logic* 27(4):353–387.

Proceedings of the 19th International Conference on Principles of Knowledge Representation and Reasoning
Main Track

Automatic Synthesis of Dynamic Norms for Multi-Agent Systems

Natasha Alechina[1] , **Giuseppe De Giacomo**[2] , **Brian Logan**[1,3] , **Giuseppe Perelli**[2]
[1]Utrecht University
[2]Sapienza University of Rome
[3]University of Aberdeen
{n.a.alechina, b.s.logan}@uu.nl, perelli@di.uniroma1.it, degiacomo@diag.uniroma1.it

Abstract

Norms have been widely proposed to coordinate and regulate behaviour in multi-agent systems (MAS). We consider the problem of synthesising and revising the set of norms in a normative MAS to satisfy a design objective expressed in Alternating Time Temporal Logic (ATL*). ATL* is a well-established language for strategic reasoning, which allows the specification of norms that constrain the strategic behaviour of agents. We focus on dynamic norms, that is, norms corresponding to Mealy machines, that allow us to place different constraints on the agents' behaviour depending on the state of the norm and the state of the underlying MAS. We show that synthesising dynamic norms is $(k+1)$-EXPTIME where k is the alternation depth of quantifiers in the ATL* specification. Note that for typical cases of interest, k is either 1 or 2. We also study the problem of removing existing norms to satisfy a new objective, which we show to be 2EXPTIME-complete.

1 Introduction

Norms have been widely proposed as a way of coordinating and regulating behaviour in multi-agent systems (MAS) (Chopra et al. 2018). Intuitively, a *norm* expresses a pattern of desired or undesired behaviour. Examples of norms include traffic laws stating how an agent should drive, hygiene rules introduced during a pandemic, and social conventions, such as greeting someone the first time you see them each day. Norms may be generated by the designer or administrator of a MAS (prescriptive norms), e.g., traffic laws, or emerge spontaneously from interactions between agents (emergent norms) (Haynes et al. 2017). In what follows, we focus on prescriptive norms designed by the developer or administrator of a normative MAS, rather than norms that emerge spontaneously.

Norms may be implemented in a MAS through regimentation or enforcement (Grossi, Aldewereld, and Dignum 2006). A *regimented* norm is impossible to violate due to the design of the MAS. For example, only authorised users can login to the system. *Enforcement* imposes a sanction on an agent when a norm is violated, e.g., a fine or social disapproval. In the interests of brevity, we focus on regimented norms, however our approach can be easily modified to produce norms where sanctions are imposed when the norm is violated.

Rather than modelling norms as forbidding some actions in a given state of the environment (static norms), we model them as automata (Mealy machines), as this allows us to take into account the relevant history of the system. In general, it is not reasonable to assume that the entire history of a MAS is recorded in the state of the environment. For example, we may consider a norm that forbids greeting someone the agent already met on the same day, or making more than n support requests in a fixed period of time, or performing an experiment before ethical approval has been obtained, etc. We refer to such automata-based norms as *dynamic norms*. Such dynamic norms were introduced in (Huang et al. 2016; Perelli 2019).

We focus on the problem of the *automated synthesis of dynamic norms*: given a multi-agent system and an objective (a formula in ATL*), is there a dynamic norm that, when implemented in the MAS, ensures the objective is satisfied? We also consider a problem of removing dynamic norms in order to satisfy ATL* objectives. There has been considerable work on norm synthesis for static norms, e.g., (Morales et al. 2015; Morales et al. 2018; Bulling and Dastani 2016). For example, Bulling and Dastani (2016) consider norm synthesis for LTL objectives. In their approach, agents are assumed to have LTL-defined preferences with numerical values and the aim of the synthesis is to produce a norm that enforces the objective for some Nash equilibrium. There has been less work on the synthesis of dynamic norms. In (Huang et al. 2016) the synthesis of dynamic norms to satisfy Computation Tree Logic (CTL) objectives is considered, and in (Perelli 2019), the synthesis of dynamic norms for LTL objectives and Nash equilibria.

In this paper, we present a new approach to the automated synthesis of dynamic norms to satisfy objectives expressed in ATL*. In contrast to objectives expressed in LTL, ATL* allows us to place constraints on the strategies of particular groups of agents. We consider a very general setting of norm synthesis in multi-agent systems, in which only the actions the agents may perform, the norms already in force, and the system objective to be achieved are specified. In particular, we make no assumptions about the goals, preferences or states of agents, as in designing open multi-agent systems where agents are developed by different organisations or developers, such information is often unavailable. The system objectives and norms we consider are also very general. We show that synthesising dynamic norms in this setting is $(k + 1)$-EXPTIME where k is the alternation of quantifiers in the ATL* specification. Note that for typical cases of interest, k is either 1 or 2. We also study the problem of removing existing norms to satisfy a new objective, which we show to be 2EXPTIME-complete.

2 Framework

In this section we introduce our framework for reasoning about dynamic norms in multi-agent systems, and briefly recall some necessary preliminaries.

2.1 System Models

We model a normative multi-agent system as a particular kind of game, similar to concurrent game structures, but extended with norms. For example, if the MAS is a city, then norms are things like traffic laws, hygiene rules, social conventions, etc. that apply there. Norms do not have to apply to all agents in the same way. For example, some traffic gets priority; small children are exempt from wearing face masks; children are not allowed to drive a car. These considerations are reflected in the definition below.

A *k-normed Multi-Agent System* (k-MAS), sometimes also called *game*, $\mathcal{G}$ is a tuple:

$$\langle \mathrm{Ag}, \mathrm{Ac}, \mathrm{AP}, \mathsf{Cap}, (\mathrm{Nrm}_i)_{i\leq k}, \vec{\mathsf{q}}_0, \mathsf{tr}, (\mathsf{illegal}_i)_{i\leq k}, (\eta_i)_{i\leq k}\rangle$$

where:

- $\mathrm{Ag} = \{1, \ldots, N\}$ is a finite set of N *agents*, denoted by natural numbers;
- Ac is a finite set of *actions* that agents can perform (in some state of the environment);
- AP is a finite set of *atomic propositions*; an assignment of truth values to AP determines environment states of the system;
- $\mathsf{Cap} : \mathrm{Ag} \times 2^{\mathrm{AP}} \to 2^{\mathrm{Ac}}$ is a *capability function* that assigns to each agent in each environment state the set of actions it is capable of performing in that state;
- Nrm_i is a finite set of *normative states*, one for each $i \leq k$, with $\vec{\mathrm{Nrm}} = \mathrm{Nrm}_1 \times \ldots \times \mathrm{Nrm}_k$, being the *normative vector state space*;
- $\vec{\mathsf{q}}_0 \in \vec{\mathrm{Nrm}}$ is a designated *initial normative state*;
- $\mathsf{tr} : 2^{\mathrm{AP}} \times \mathrm{Ac}^{\mathrm{Ag}} \to 2^{\mathrm{AP}}$ is a *transition function* that determines the next state of the environment given the current state of the environment and the actions performed by the agents;
- $\mathsf{illegal}_i : \mathrm{Nrm}_i \times 2^{\mathrm{AP}} \to 2^{\mathrm{Ac}\times\mathrm{Ag}}$ is the *illegality function* that returns a set pairs of actions and agents that are illegal given the current state of a norm and the environment;
- $\eta_i : \mathrm{Nrm}_i \times 2^{\mathrm{AP}} \to \mathrm{Nrm}_i$ is a *normative function* that determines the next state of a norm given the current state of the norm and the environment.

Intuitively, starting from the empty set of atomic propositions[1] and from the initial vector of normative states $\vec{\mathsf{q}}_0$, a game moves forward according to the transition function, triggered by an action tuple $\vec{a} \in \mathrm{Ac}^{\mathrm{Ag}}$, changing the underlying evaluation of the propositions in AP. Simultaneously, each normative component is updated by the corresponding normative function.

A *configuration* of $\mathcal{G}$ is a tuple $c = (\pi, \vec{\mathsf{q}}) \in 2^{\mathrm{AP}} \times \vec{\mathrm{Nrm}}$. Sometimes, with an abuse of notation, we denote by $\mathsf{illegal}_i(\mathsf{q}_i, \pi, j) \doteq \{a \in Ac : (a, j) \in \mathsf{illegal}_i(\mathsf{q}_i, \pi)\}$ the set of actions that are made illegal for agent j by the i-th normative component. Analogously, for a configuration $c = (\pi, \vec{\mathsf{q}})$, by $\mathsf{Avl}_{\mathcal{G}}(c, j) \doteq \mathsf{Cap}(j, \pi) \setminus (\cup_{i\leq k}\mathsf{illegal}_i(\mathsf{q}_i, \pi, j))$, we denote the set of actions available to agent j in configuration c, where $\vec{\mathsf{q}}^i$ is the i-th component of $\vec{\mathsf{q}}$.

The set $\mathsf{Avl}_{\mathcal{G}}(c) \doteq \mathsf{Avl}_{\mathcal{G}}(c, 1) \times \ldots \times \mathsf{Avl}_{\mathcal{G}}(c, N)$ denotes the action vectors that are available in a configuration c.

Note that agents can select only actions that are in their capability and that are allowed by each normative component. More precisely, at each configuration $c = (\pi, \vec{\mathsf{q}})$, each agent j can select only an action $a^j \in \mathsf{Avl}_{\mathcal{G}}(c, j)$. Once each agent j has chosen an available action a^j and the corresponding action vector $\vec{a} = (a^1, \ldots, a^k)$ is formed, the system moves its components forward to the configuration $(\pi', \vec{\mathsf{q}}')$, with $\pi' = \mathsf{tr}(\pi, \vec{a})$ and $\vec{\mathsf{q}}' = (\eta_1(\mathsf{q}^1, \pi), \ldots, \eta_k(\mathsf{q}^k, \pi))$.

A *legal run*, or simply *run* is an infinite sequence $r \in (2^{\mathrm{AP}} \times \vec{\mathrm{Nrm}})^\omega$ such that, for each $n \in \mathbb{N}$, there exists an action vector $\vec{a}_n \in \mathsf{Avl}_{\mathcal{G}}(r_n)$, such that

$$r_{n+1} = (\mathsf{tr}(\pi_n, \vec{a}_n), \eta_1(\mathsf{q}_n^1, \pi_n), \ldots, \eta_k(\mathsf{q}_n^k, \pi_n))$$

with $r_n = (\pi_n, \vec{\mathsf{q}}_n)$. We use the notation $r_{\leq n}$ to denote the prefix of r up to and including r_n. Similarly, $r_{\geq n}$ is the suffix of r starting from r_n. Moreover, we write $c \xrightarrow{\vec{a}} c'$ to denote that the action vector $\vec{a}$ determines a transition from configuration c to configuration c'.

Intuitively, a run is an infinite sequence that, starting from a given configuration, evolves according to the action vectors as the agents select them. A run is *initial* if it starts from the initial configuration, that is, $r_0 = (\emptyset, \vec{\mathsf{q}}_0)$.

A *strategy* for agent j in the game $\mathcal{G}$ is a Mealy machine of the form

$$\sigma_j = (S_j, s_j^0, \vec{\mathrm{Nrm}} \times 2^{\mathrm{AP}}, \mathrm{Ac}, \delta_j, \tau_j).$$

Intuitively, a strategy is a machinery that, for each internal state $s \in S_j$ and a configuration $c = (\pi, \vec{\mathsf{q}})$ of $\mathcal{G}$, selects an action in Ac determined by $\tau_j(s, (\pi, \vec{\mathsf{q}}))$ and updates its internal state $\delta_j(s, (\pi, \vec{\mathsf{q}}))$ accordingly. Clearly, not every strategy is available in the game, only those that comply with the *normative requirements* specified by the game itself. We say that a strategy σ_j is *legal* with respect to $\mathcal{G}$ if, and only if, $\tau_j(s, (\pi, \vec{\mathsf{q}})) \in \mathsf{Avl}(\vec{\mathsf{q}}, \pi, j)$. From now on, we restrict our attention to legal strategies, and, unless otherwise stated, we refer to them simply as strategies. Moreover, for simplicity, for a given strategy σ_j and a finite sequence $\hat{r} \in (2^{\mathrm{AP}} \times \vec{\mathrm{Nrm}})^*$, by $\sigma_j(\hat{r}) \in \mathrm{Ac}$ we denote the action determined by the action function τ_j in σ_j after the sequence $\hat{r}$ has been fed to the internal transition function δ_j.[2]

[1]The assumption that the initial state is empty is made for convenience; the developments below would go through for an arbitrary initial state.

[2]Note that any conventional strategy $\sigma : (2^{\mathrm{AP}})^* \to \mathrm{Ac}$ has a

Consider a subset $A \subseteq \mathrm{Ag}$ of agents and a set of strategies σ_A, one for each agent $j \in A$. We say that a run r is *compatible* with σ_A if, for every $n \in \mathbb{N}$, it holds that there exists an action vector $\vec{a}_n$, with $a_n^j = \sigma_j(r_{\leq n})$ for each $j \in A$ and $\sigma_j \in \sigma_A$, such that r_{n+1} is obtained from r_n by applying $\vec{a}_n$. Essentially, a run r is compatible with σ_A if it can be generated when the agents in A play according to their respective strategies. The set of runs starting from a given configuration c and compatible with σ_A is denoted by $\mathsf{out}_{\mathcal{G}}(c, \sigma_A)$. Observe that the set of runs of a given k-MAS $\mathcal{G}$ starting from a configuration c, sometimes denoted $\mathsf{Paths}_{\mathcal{G}}(c)$, can also be written as $\mathsf{out}_{\mathcal{G}}(c, \emptyset)$. Moreover, when it is clear from the context, we omit the subscript and simply write $\mathsf{Paths}(c)$ or $\mathsf{out}(c, \sigma_A)$.

2.2 ATL*– Alternating-Time Temporal Logic

We use Alternating-Time Temporal Logic (ATL*) to express system objectives. For example, we may want a particular group of agents to be able to achieve a temporal goal, such as provide timely assistance to sick people or respond to other emergencies. Or, we may want to preclude a group of agents from achieving a goal, such as having a road race on a residential street. Norms are synthesised and added to the system in order to satisfy new objectives. Note that this means that new norms may make previous objectives unachievable (e.g. if speeds over 20 mph are made uniformly illegal, then ambulances also cannot drive at more than 20 mph). However, we can always add old objectives conjunctively to the new one when synthesising norms.

We now recall the syntax of ATL* and provide a definition of its semantics over a k-MAS. We start with the definition of the syntax.

ATL* formulas are built inductively from the set of atomic propositions AP and agents Ag, by using the following grammar, where $p \in \mathrm{AP}$ and $A \subseteq \mathrm{Ag}$:

$$\varphi := p \mid \neg\varphi \mid \varphi \wedge \varphi \mid \mathtt{X}\varphi \mid \varphi \mathtt{U} \varphi \mid \langle\langle A \rangle\rangle \varphi.$$

As syntactic sugar we also use $\varphi_1 \vee \varphi_2 \doteq \neg(\neg\varphi_1 \wedge \neg\varphi_2)$, $\varphi_1 \rightarrow \varphi_2 \doteq \neg\varphi_1 \vee \varphi_2$, $\varphi_1 \leftrightarrow \varphi_2 \doteq (\varphi_1 \rightarrow \varphi_2) \wedge (\varphi_2 \rightarrow \varphi_1)$, $[\![A]\!]\varphi \doteq \neg\langle\langle A \rangle\rangle\neg\varphi$, $\mathtt{F}\varphi \doteq \mathsf{true}\mathtt{U}\varphi$, and $\mathtt{G}\varphi \doteq \neg\mathtt{F}\neg\varphi$.

Intuitively, $\langle\langle A \rangle\rangle\psi$ means that each agent in A has a strategy such that, whatever the agents $\mathrm{Ag} \setminus A$ do, the resulting outcome satisfies ψ. This translates into the semantics as follows. For a given k-MAS $\mathcal{G}$ and a run r over it, the semantics of an ATL* formula φ, denoted $\mathcal{G}, r \models \varphi$, is given recursively as follows:

- $\mathcal{G}, r \models p$ iff $p \in \pi_0$, with $r_0 = (\pi_0, \vec{\mathsf{q}}_0)$ for some $\vec{\mathsf{q}}_0 \in \vec{\mathrm{Nrm}}$;
- $\mathcal{G}, r \models \neg\varphi$ iff $\mathcal{G}, r \not\models \varphi$;
- $\mathcal{G}, r \models \varphi_1 \wedge \varphi_2$ iff both $\mathcal{G}, r \models \varphi_1$ and $\mathcal{G}, r \models \varphi_2$.
- $\mathcal{G}, r \models \langle\langle A \rangle\rangle\varphi$ iff there is a strategy σ_A such that $\mathcal{G}, r' \models \varphi$, for all $r' \in \mathsf{out}(r_0, \sigma_A)$;
- $\mathcal{G}, r \models \mathtt{X}\varphi$ iff $\mathcal{G}, r_{\geq 1} \models \varphi$;
- $\mathcal{G}, r \models \varphi_1 \mathtt{U} \varphi_2$ iff there exists $j \in \mathbb{N}$ such that $\mathcal{G}, r_{\geq i} \models \varphi_1$, for all $i < j$, and $\mathcal{G}, r_{\geq j} \models \varphi_2$.

The *model-checking problem* for ATL* is: given a structure $\mathcal{G}$, a run r and an ATL* formula φ, does it hold that $\mathcal{G}, r \models \varphi$? Although the result below was established for concurrent game structures (essentially, 0-MAS without normative components), it also holds for k-MAS.

Theorem 1. *(Alur, Henzinger, and Kupferman 2002, Theorem 5.6) The model-checking problem for ATL* is 2EXPTIME-complete.*

2.3 ATL* for Strategic Permission and Prohibition

In this section, we introduce two important classes of normative specifications, *strategic permissions* and *strategic prohibitions*, which can be expressed in ATL* in a simple way.

Definition 1 (Strategic Permission)**.** *A strategic permission is a positive Boolean combination of formulas of the form $\langle\langle A \rangle\rangle\varphi$, where φ is a purely temporal formula (not containing any strategy quantification $\langle\langle A' \rangle\rangle$).*

Intuitively, a strategic permission objective $\langle\langle A \rangle\rangle\varphi$ ensures that the agent(s) A have the strategic ability to bring about φ. Strategic permissions are a form of reachability property that specify that agents should have the freedom to do something if they wish. Note that a norm satisfying a strategic permission may restrict the actions of agents not in A, that is, that the agents $\mathrm{Ag} \setminus A$ may be constrained so that they not have a strategy to prevent A achieving ϕ. For example,

Example 1 (Strategic Permission)**.** *The property that ambulances should be able to park in their designated places at a hospital can be expressed in ATL* as $\bigwedge_{i \in A} \langle\langle i \rangle\rangle \mathtt{G}(\mathtt{ready}_i \rightarrow \mathtt{X}\ \mathtt{park}_i)$, where A is the set of ambulances, $\mathtt{ready}_i$ stands for 'ambulance i is ready to park' and $\mathtt{park}_i$ stands for 'ambulance i is parked in its designated place'.*

This property can be enforced by making it illegal for all agents different from i to park in i's place.

Definition 2 (Strategic Prohibition)**.** *A strategic prohibition is a positive Boolean combination of formulas of the form $\neg\langle\langle A \rangle\rangle\varphi$, where φ is a purely temporal formula.*

A strategic prohibition objective $\neg\langle\langle A \rangle\rangle\varphi$ ensures that the agent(s) A do *not* have the strategic ability to bring about φ. Strategic prohibitions are a form of safety property that specify that agents should not have the freedom to bring something about even if they wish to. In general, a norm satisfying a strategic prohibition restricts the actions of agents in A. For example,

Example 2 (Strategic Prohibition)**.** *The property that a set of juvenile delinquents D should not be able to organise a road race can be expressed in ATL* as $\neg\langle\langle D \rangle\rangle \mathtt{F}\ \mathtt{road\_race}$.*

corresponding strategy of the form $\sigma : (2^{\mathrm{AP}} \times \vec{\mathrm{Nrm}})^* \rightarrow \mathrm{Ac}$, because the system is deterministic and the next normative state can be computed from the previous normative and environment state. Here we consider regular strategies, that is, those that can be represented as a Mealy machines. This is not a limitation, as, when the specification language is ω-regular, if a strategy satisfying the specification exists, then a regular strategy also exists. Moreover, this representation means strategies have a compact form, and is similar to the form of dynamic norms introduced later.

This property can be enforced by making it illegal for all agents to drive fast, but such a blanket prohibition may conflict with a strategic permission allowing ambulances to drive fast: $\bigwedge_{i\in A}\langle\langle i\rangle\rangle \mathtt{G\,X\,speed}_i^{\geq 20}$. A norm that makes driving fast illegal only for agents in D will not violate the latter property.

2.4 ATL* with Strategy Context

For technical purposes, we also make use of an extension of ATL*, namely ATL* with strategy context (Laroussinie and Markey 2015), denoted ATL^*_{sc}, in which another form of quantification $\langle\langle\cdot A\cdot\rangle\rangle\varphi$ is used, together with its dual $[\![\cdot A\cdot]\!]\varphi$, defined as $\neg\langle\langle\cdot A\cdot\rangle\rangle\neg\varphi$. Formulas of ATL^*_{sc} are interpreted over the same structures as ATL* together with a strategy context. More formally, for a given k-MAS $\mathcal{G}$ and a set of strategies σ_B for the subset $B \subseteq \text{Ag}$ of agents, we write:

- $\mathcal{G}, r \models_{\sigma_B} \langle\langle\cdot A\cdot\rangle\rangle\varphi$ if there is a strategy σ_A such that $\mathcal{G}, r' \models_{\sigma_B\circ\sigma_A} \varphi$, for all $r' \in \mathsf{out}(r_0, \sigma_B \circ \sigma_A)$;

where $\sigma_B \circ \sigma_A \doteq \sigma_B \cup \sigma_{A\setminus B}$ denotes the set of strategies obtained from σ_B by adding strategies of σ_A that are for agents in A but not in B.

The *quantifier alternation*, or simply *alternation* of a ATL^*_{sc} formula φ is the number of times an existential quantification $\langle\langle\cdots\rangle\rangle$ is followed by a universal one $[\![\cdots]\!]$, and vice-versa. The model checking problem for ATL^*_{sc} was shown to have a TOWER-complete complexity in (Laroussinie and Markey 2015), whose height depends on the number of alternations in the formula. More precisely, they show that model checking an ATL^*_{sc} formula with h alternations is $(h+1)$-EXPTIME-complete.

Theorem 2. *(Laroussinie and Markey 2015, Corollary 14) The model-checking problem for an ATL^*_{sc} formula with h nested strategy quantifiers is $(h+1)$-EXPTIME-complete.*

2.5 Norms

A *Norm* over a k-MAS $\mathcal{G}$ is a Mealy machine of the form

$$\mathcal{N} = \langle \text{Nrm}, \mathsf{q}_0, 2^{\text{AP}}, 2^{\text{Ac}\times\text{Ag}}, \eta, \mathsf{illegal}\rangle$$

A norm takes a state of the world as input and returns a set pairs of actions and agents that are illegal given the current state of a norm and the environment. $\mathcal{N}$ is well-defined on every k-MAS $\mathcal{G}$ having the same set Ag of agents, Ac of actions and AP of propositions.

Example 3. *A trivial norm (that does not impose any restrictions) can be defined as follows:* $\text{Nrm} = \{\mathsf{q}_0\}$, $\eta(\mathsf{q}_0, \pi) = \mathsf{q}_0$ *for all* $\pi \in 2^{\text{AP}}$, *and* $\mathsf{illegal}(\mathsf{q}_0, \pi) = \emptyset$ *for all* π.

Example 4. *A norm that forbids agent j executing action a after encountering proposition p twice can be defined as* $\text{Nrm} = \{\mathsf{q}_0, \mathsf{q}_1, \mathsf{q}_2\}$, *where for* $i \in \{0, 1\}$, $\eta(\mathsf{q}_i, \pi) = \mathsf{q}_i$ *if* $p \notin \pi$, $\eta(\mathsf{q}_i, \pi) = \mathsf{q}_{i+1}$ *if* $p \in \pi$, $\mathsf{illegal}(\mathsf{q}_i, \pi) = \emptyset$ *for all* π*; and* $\eta(\mathsf{q}_2, \pi) = \mathsf{q}_2$ *for all* π, $\mathsf{illegal}(\mathsf{q}_2, \pi) = \{(a, j)\}$.

The following example is adapted from (Huang et al. 2016) (slightly simplified for brevity).

Example 5. *In a system consisting of n producers and m consumers, the norm prevents producers failing to supply consumers whose 'turn' it is to be served. Actions of each producer j are of the form $B \subseteq \{1, \ldots, m\}$, corresponding to serving the set of consumers B. If it is the turn of consumer i, then illegal actions are B such that $i \notin B$. This norm can be defined as follows:* $\text{Nrm} = \{\mathsf{q}_1, \ldots, \mathsf{q}_m\}$, *(the states of the norm correspond to which consumer's turn it is),* $\eta(\mathsf{q}_i, \pi) = \mathsf{q}_{i+1(mod\ m)}$ *for all* π, $\mathsf{illegal}(\mathsf{q}_i, \pi) = \{(B, j) \mid i \notin B\}$.

Conditional prohibition norms introduced in (Tinnemeier et al. 2009) are tuples of the form (condition, prohibited property, deadline, sanction). Condition is a propositional formula that describes states after which the prohibition comes into effect (until a state satisfying the deadline is reached). Sanction is either a negative utility or an indication that violating the norm is impossible (the norm is regimented). A regimented conditional prohibition norm can also be defined in our formalism.

Example 6. *A norm which prohibits agent j moving between the start and the end of some procedure can be defined as follows.* $\text{Nrm} = \{\mathsf{q}_1, \mathsf{q}_2\}$, $\eta(\mathsf{q}_1, \pi) = \mathsf{q}_1$ *if start* $\notin \pi$ *and* $\eta(\mathsf{q}_1, \pi) = \mathsf{q}_2$ *otherwise.* $\mathsf{illegal}(\mathsf{q}_1, \pi) = \emptyset$ *and* $\mathsf{illegal}(\mathsf{q}_2, \pi) = \{move\}$.

Consider a norm $\mathcal{N}_{k+1}$ whose components are all indexed with $k+1$. We can implement $\mathcal{N}_{k+1}$ on a k-MAS $\mathcal{G}$ to obtain a $(k+1)$-MAS defined as the tuple $\mathcal{G} \oplus \mathcal{N}_{k+1} = \langle \text{Ag}, \text{Ac}, \text{AP}, \mathsf{Cap}, (\text{Nrm}_i)_{i\leq k+1}, \vec{\mathsf{q}}_0, \mathsf{tr}, (\mathsf{illegal}_i)_{i\leq k+1}, (\eta_i)_{i\leq k+1}\rangle$, containing an extra normative state component, which are the states of $\mathcal{N}_{k+1}$, and whose evolution is determined by its normative function η_{k+1}.

Intuitively, $\mathcal{N}_{k+1}$ introduces more restrictions on the actions for the agents when implemented in a given k-MAS $\mathcal{G}$. Indeed, for every configuration c in the original game and its extension with the state of $\mathcal{N}_{k+1}$, c', it holds that $\mathsf{Avl}_{\mathcal{G}\oplus\mathcal{N}_{k+1}}(c', j) \subseteq \mathsf{Avl}_{\mathcal{G}}(c, j)$ for every agent $j \in \text{Ag}$.

Observe also that every normative state component i of a k-MAS $\mathcal{G}$ can be regarded as a norm $\mathcal{N}_i = \langle \text{Nrm}_i, e_0^i, 2^{\text{AP}}, 2^{\text{Ac}\times\text{Ag}}, \eta_i, \mathsf{illegal}_i\rangle$ and so $\mathcal{G}$ can be obtained from a 0-MAS where the norms $\mathcal{N}_1 \ldots, \mathcal{N}_k$ have been applied one by one. A norm $\mathcal{N}_i$ can also be removed from $\mathcal{G}$, denoted $\mathcal{G} \ominus \mathcal{N}_i$, resulting in a $(k-1)$ MAS.

2.6 Norm Synthesis and Revision

We can now define the two problems addressed in this paper. The first is *Norm Synthesis*, which is the problem of finding a norm $\mathcal{N}$ for a k-MAS $\mathcal{G}$ that, if implemented, makes a given ATL* formula φ true over $\mathcal{G} \oplus \mathcal{N}$.

Definition 3 (Norm Synthesis)**.** *For a given k-MAS $\mathcal{G}$ and an ATL* formula φ, determine whether there exists a norm $\mathcal{N}_{k+1}$ such that $\mathcal{G} \oplus \mathcal{N}_{k+1} \models \varphi$.*

On the other hand, *Norm Removal* is the opposite problem. That is, given a k-MAS $\mathcal{G}$, to identify a subset $\{\mathcal{N}_{\iota_1}, \ldots \mathcal{N}_{\iota_h}\}$ of the already implemented norms that, if removed, make a given ATL^*_{sc} formula true.

Definition 4 (Norm Removal)**.** *For a given k-MAS $\mathcal{G}$ and an ATL* formula φ, determine whether there exists a subset $\{\mathcal{N}_{\iota_1}, \ldots \mathcal{N}_{\iota_h}\}$ of norms such that $\mathcal{G} \ominus \mathcal{N}_{\iota_1} \ominus \ldots \ominus \mathcal{N}_{\iota_h} \models \varphi$.*

3 Automated Norm Synthesis

We start by solving Norm Synthesis. We do this by reinterpreting norms of a given k-MAS $\mathcal{G}$ as strategies of an accessory k-MAS $\mathcal{G}'$, reducing the norm synthesis to strategy synthesis in this accessory game.

In order to simplify our reasoning, first observe that a k-MAS $\mathcal{G}$ can always be regarded as a 1-MAS where the only applied norm is the product of the k norms given in $\mathcal{G}$. For this reason, from now on, we assume without loss of generality that $\mathcal{G}$ is a 1-MAS.

To illustrate Norm Synthesis, we use the following running example.

Example 7. *$\mathcal{G}_{ex}$ has two agents, 1 and 2, two actions $wait$ and ask, two propositions $rest$ and $work$. Agent 1 can only do $wait$. Agent 2 can always do $wait$ and ask. The transition function is: if both agents perform $wait$, then $rest$ becomes true. If agent 2 performs ask, then $work$ becomes true. The initial norm is trivial (it has one state and no illegal actions). The task is to synthesise a norm that will enable agent 1 to have two consecutive moments of rest after $work$ becomes true: $\varphi_{rest} = \langle\langle 1 \rangle\rangle \mathtt{G}(work \rightarrow \mathtt{X}(rest \wedge \mathtt{X} rest))$.*

Consider, for instance, a strategy for Agent 2 defined as $\sigma_2 = \langle S_2, s_2^0, 2^{\mathrm{AP}}, \mathrm{Ac}, \delta_2, \tau_2 \rangle$,[3] with $S_2 = \{s_2^0\}$, $\delta_2(s_2^0, \pi) = s_2^0$ and $\tau_2(s_2^0, \pi) = ask$, for each $\pi \in 2^{\mathrm{AP}}$. Note that this strategy prevents φ_{rest} from becoming true, as there is no strategy for Agent 1 that, combined with σ_2, makes the temporal part satisfied. To prevent Agent 2 from repeatedly executing ask, we can implement a norm that works as a counter: once the proposition $work$ becomes true, Agent 2 is not allowed to execute action ask twice in a row.

In the following, we show how to solve Norm Synthesis automatically, by employing the construction of an accessory game. The definitions are inspired by the *encoding game* defined in (Perelli 2019).

Construction 1 (Accessory game)**.** *Consider a 1-MAS $\mathcal{G} = \langle \mathrm{Ag}, \mathrm{Ac}, \mathrm{AP}, \mathsf{Cap}, \mathrm{Nrm}_1, \mathsf{q}_0^1, \mathsf{tr}, \mathsf{illegal}_1, \eta_1 \rangle$ and define the accessory 1-MAS as:*

$$\mathcal{G}' = \langle \mathrm{Ag}', \mathrm{Ac}', \mathrm{AP}', \mathsf{Cap}', \mathrm{Nrm}_1, \mathsf{q}_0^1, \mathsf{tr}', \mathsf{illegal}_1', \eta_1' \rangle,$$

where

- $\mathrm{Ag}' = \{0\} \cup \mathrm{Ag}$ *includes a 0-agent, sometimes called the* normative agent*;*
- $\mathrm{Ac}' = \mathrm{Ac} \cup (2^{\mathrm{Ac} \times \mathrm{Ag}})$ *includes all possible sets of pairs of actions and agents as possible actions;*
- $\mathrm{AP}' = \mathrm{AP} \cup (\mathrm{Ac} \times \mathrm{Ag})$ *includes the set of pairs of actions and agents in the atomic propositions;*
- $\mathsf{Cap}'(j, \pi') = \begin{cases} 2^{\mathrm{Ac} \times \mathrm{Ag}}, & \text{if } j = 0 \\ \mathsf{Cap}(j, \pi'_{\restriction \mathrm{AP}}) \setminus (\{j\} \cap \pi'), & \text{o/w} \end{cases}$
- $\mathsf{tr}'(\pi', \vec{a}) = \mathsf{tr}(\pi'_{\restriction \mathrm{AP}}, \vec{a}_{-0}) \cup \vec{a}_0$*;*
- $\mathsf{illegal}'(\mathsf{q}_1, \pi') = \mathsf{illegal}(\mathsf{q}_1, \pi'_{\restriction \mathrm{AP}})$*;*
- $\eta'(\mathsf{q}_1, \pi') = \eta(\mathsf{q}_1, \pi'_{\restriction \mathrm{AP}})$.

[3]Note that we consider only 2^{AP} as input alphabet, since only the trivial norm is currently implemented in the game.

The idea of this construction is to embed the reasoning about the existence of norms in terms of a strategy in the accessory game. To do so, we add to $\mathcal{G}$ an extra agent, the normative agent, whose capability is precisely that of *preventing* actions of other agents. To suitably encode this capability, we also expand the state and action spaces of the game with all possible subsets of pairs of agents and actions. The transition function τ' mimics τ with regards to the evaluation of AP and copies the action taken by the normative agent into the next state. The capability function Cap' is also extended accordingly. It prescribes agent 0 to take actions that correspond to the output of the norm for $\mathcal{G}$ (the set of pairs of actions and agents that are illegal according to the norm). Regarding the other agents, it assigns the subset of actions originally available in $\mathcal{G}$ which are not prevented by the action taken by the normative agent in the previous step.

Example 8. *The accessory game corresponding to $\mathcal{G}_{ex}$ is $\mathcal{G}'$ where:*

- $\mathrm{Ag}' = \{0, 1, 2\}$*;*
- $\mathrm{Ac}' = \{wait, ask\} \cup 2^{\{wait, ask\} \times \{1,2\}}$*;*
- $\mathrm{AP}' = \{work, rest\} \cup \{(wait, 1), (wait, 2), (ask, 1), (ask, 2)\}$*;*
- $\mathsf{Cap}'(0, \pi') = 2^{\{wait, ask\} \times \{1,2\}}$*, and* $\mathsf{Cap}'(j, \pi') = \mathsf{Cap}(j, \pi'_{\restriction \mathrm{AP}}) \setminus (\{j\} \cap \pi')$*, for* $j = 1, 2$*. For instance, it holds that* $\mathsf{Cap}'(2, \{work, (2, ask)\}) = \{wait\}$.
- $\mathsf{tr}'(\pi', \vec{a}) = \mathsf{tr}(\pi'_{\restriction \mathrm{AP}}, \vec{a}_{-0}) \cup \vec{a}_0$. *For instance, it holds that* $\mathsf{tr}'(\{work\}, (wait, wait, \{(2, ask)\})) = \{rest, (2, ask)\}$*;*
- $\mathsf{illegal}'(\mathsf{q}_1, \pi')$ *and* $\eta'(\mathsf{q}_1, \pi')$ *defined as in Construction 1.*

We can now make a connection between norms for $\mathcal{G}$ and strategies of agent 0 in $\mathcal{G}'$. Indeed, a strategy for the normative agent is of the form $\sigma_0 = \langle S_0, s_0^0, \mathrm{Nrm}_1 \times 2^{\mathrm{AP}'}, \mathrm{Ac}', \delta_0, \tau_0 \rangle$. Observe that $\mathsf{Cap}'(0, \pi') = 2^{\mathrm{Ac} \times \mathrm{Ag}}$, and the set $2^{\mathrm{AP}'} = 2^{\mathrm{AP} \cup (\mathrm{Ac} \times \mathrm{Ag})}$ is isomorphic to $2^{\mathrm{AP}} \times 2^{\mathrm{Ac} \times \mathrm{Ag}}$. This allows us to rewrite the strategy as $\sigma_0 = \langle S_0, s_0^0, \mathrm{Nrm}_1 \times 2^{\mathrm{AP}} \times 2^{\mathrm{Ac} \times \mathrm{Ag}}, 2^{\mathrm{Ac} \times \mathrm{Ag}}, \delta_0, \tau_0 \rangle$, from which a corresponding norm can be constructed.

Construction 2 (Norm construction)**.** *For a given strategy $\sigma_0 = \langle S_0, s_0^0, \mathrm{Nrm}_1 \times 2^{\mathrm{AP}} \times 2^{\mathrm{Ac} \times \mathrm{Ag}}, 2^{\mathrm{Ac} \times \mathrm{Ag}}, \delta_0, \tau_0 \rangle$ of agent 0 in $\mathcal{G}'$, the norm $\mathcal{N}_{\sigma_0}$ for $\mathcal{G}$ is defined as:*

$$\langle S_0 \times \mathrm{Nrm}_1 \times 2^{\mathrm{Ac} \times \mathrm{Ag}}, (s_0, \mathsf{q}_0, \emptyset), 2^{\mathrm{AP}}, 2^{\mathrm{Ac} \times \mathrm{Ag}}, \eta, \mathsf{illegal} \rangle,$$

where $\eta((s, \mathsf{q}_1, A), \pi) = (s', \mathsf{q}_1', A')$, with

- $s' = \delta_0(s, (\mathsf{q}_1, \pi \cup A))$,
- $\mathsf{q}_1' = \eta_1(\mathsf{q}_1, \pi)$*, and*
- $A' = \tau_0(s, (\mathsf{q}_1, \pi \cup A), \pi)$,

and $\mathsf{illegal}((s, \mathsf{q}_1, A), \pi) = \tau_0(s, (\mathsf{q}_1, \pi \cup A), \pi)$*, for every* $s \in S_0$*,* $\mathsf{q}_1 \in \mathrm{Nrm}_1$*, and* $A \in 2^{\mathrm{Ac} \times \mathrm{Ag}}$.

On the other hand, we can generate a strategy for the normative agent.

Construction 3 (Strategy construction). *For a given norm* $\mathcal{N}_2 = \langle \text{Nrm}_2, \mathsf{q}_0^2, 2^{\text{AP}}, 2^{\text{Ac}\times\text{Ag}}, \eta_2, \mathsf{illegal}_2 \rangle$ *in* $\mathcal{G}$, *the strategy* $\sigma_{\mathcal{N}_2}$ *for agent* 0 *in* $\mathcal{G}'$ *is defined as:*

$$\langle S, s_0, \text{Nrm}_1 \times 2^{\text{AP}'}, \text{Ac}', \delta, \tau \rangle,$$

where $S = \text{Nrm}_2$, $s_0 = \mathsf{q}_0^2$, *and the internal and output functions are defined as:*

- $\delta(\mathsf{q}_2, (\mathsf{q}_1, \pi')) = \eta_2(\mathsf{q}_2, \pi'_{\restriction \text{AP}})$,
- $\tau(\mathsf{q}_2, (\mathsf{q}_1, \pi')) = \mathsf{illegal}_2(\mathsf{q}_2, \pi'_{\restriction \text{AP}})$,

for every $\mathsf{q}_2 \in \text{Nrm}_2$ *and* $\pi' \in 2^{\text{AP}'}$.

Note that a run r in $\mathcal{G}'$ belongs to the set $(2^{\text{AP}'} \times \text{Nrm}_1)^\omega$. By $r_{\restriction \text{AP}}$ we denote the sequence in $(2^{\text{AP}})^\omega$ obtained from r by projecting out everything but the sequence of evaluations in AP. Analogously, such projection can be extended to sets of runs. In particular, we consider $\mathsf{Paths}_{\mathcal{G}'}(c)_{\restriction \text{AP}}$ to be the set of projections over all possible paths in $\mathcal{G}'$ starting from configuration c, and $\mathsf{out}_{\mathcal{G}'}(\sigma_A, c)_{\restriction \text{AP}}$ as the projections of outcomes in $\mathcal{G}'$ with initial configuration c, with σ_A be the strategy profile for the set A of agents.

There is a connection between σ_0 and the corresponding norm. Precisely, they produce runs in games that relate to the same projections over AP, as stated by the lemma below.

Lemma 1. *For a given* 1*-MAS* $\mathcal{G}$, *its accessory game* $\mathcal{G}'$, *and a state* $\pi \in 2^{\text{AP}}$, *the following two statements hold:*

1. *For every strategy* σ_0 *of agent* 0 *in* $\mathcal{G}'$, *it holds that* $\mathsf{out}_{\mathcal{G}'}(\sigma_0, (\pi, \mathsf{q}_0^1))_{\restriction \text{AP}} = \mathsf{Paths}_{\mathcal{G}\oplus\mathcal{N}_{\sigma_0}}(\pi, \vec{\mathsf{q}}_0)_{\restriction \text{AP}}$;
2. *For every norm* $\mathcal{N}$ *on* $\mathcal{G}$, *it holds that* $\mathsf{Paths}_{\mathcal{G}\oplus\mathcal{N}}(\pi, \vec{\mathsf{q}}_0)_{\restriction \text{AP}} = \mathsf{out}_{\mathcal{G}'}(\sigma_{\mathcal{N}}, (\pi, \mathsf{q}_0^1))_{\restriction \text{AP}}$.

Proof. We prove the two statements separately.

1. The proof proceeds by double inclusion. For the left to right direction, consider a sequence $r'_{\restriction \text{AP}} \in \mathsf{out}_{\mathcal{G}'}(\sigma_0, (\pi, \mathsf{q}_0^1))_{\restriction \text{AP}}$ and let r' be a run in $\mathcal{G}'$ from which $r'_{\restriction \text{AP}}$ is obtained by projection. By contradiction, let us assume that r'_{AP} does not belong to $\mathsf{Paths}_{\mathcal{G}\oplus\mathcal{N}_{\sigma_0}}(\pi, \vec{\mathsf{q}}_0)_{\restriction \text{AP}}$ and let $h \in \mathbb{N}$ be the greatest natural number for which $(r'_{\leq h})_{\restriction \text{AP}} \cdot r'' \in \mathsf{Paths}_{\mathcal{G}\oplus\mathcal{N}_{\sigma_0}}(\pi, \vec{\mathsf{q}}_0)_{\restriction \text{AP}}$, for some sequence r''. More specifically, there does not exist any sequence $\hat{r}$ such that $(r'_{\leq h+1})_{\restriction \text{AP}} \cdot \hat{r} \in \mathsf{Paths}_{\mathcal{G}\oplus\mathcal{N}_{\sigma_0}}(\pi, \vec{\mathsf{q}}_0)_{\restriction \text{AP}}$. Now, consider a sequence of action vectors $\vec{a}^0, \ldots, \vec{a}^h$ in $\mathcal{G}'$ such that, for every $h' \leq h$, it holds that $r'_{h'} \xrightarrow{\vec{a}^{h'}} r'_{h'+1}$ and $\vec{a}_0^{h'}$ is always the action selected by σ_0 as the execution evolves. Note that such a sequence exists, as the run r' belongs to $\mathsf{out}_{\mathcal{G}'}(\sigma_0, (\pi, \mathsf{q}_0^1))_{\restriction \text{AP}}$. By the construction of $\mathcal{N}_\sigma$, we obtain that the sequence $(\vec{a}^0)_{-0}, \ldots, (\vec{a}^h)_{-0}$ generates a partial run in $\mathcal{G} \oplus \mathcal{N}_{\sigma_0}$, denoted $r_0, \ldots, r_{h+1}$ that can be extended to a run $r \in \mathsf{Paths}_{\mathcal{G}\oplus\mathcal{N}_{\sigma_0}}(\pi, \vec{\mathsf{q}}_0)_{\restriction \text{AP}}$ in a way that $(r_{h\leq h+1})_{\restriction \text{AP}} = (r'_{h\leq h+1})_{\restriction \text{AP}}$, resulting in a contradiction with h being the greatest number for which such property holds, and subsequently that $r'_{\text{AP}} \notin \mathsf{Paths}_{\mathcal{G}\oplus\mathcal{N}_{\sigma_0}}(\pi, \vec{\mathsf{q}}_0)_{\restriction \text{AP}}$.

For the right to left direction, consider a sequence $r'_{\restriction \text{AP}} \in \mathsf{Paths}_{\mathcal{G}\oplus\mathcal{N}_{\sigma_0}}(\pi, \vec{\mathsf{q}}_0)_{\restriction \text{AP}}$ and let r' be a run in $\mathcal{G} \oplus \mathcal{N}_{\sigma_0}$ from which $r'_{\restriction \text{AP}}$ is obtained by projection. By contradiction, let us assume that r'_{AP} does not belong to $\mathsf{out}_{\mathcal{G}'}(\sigma_0, (\pi, \mathsf{q}_0^1))_{\restriction \text{AP}}$ and let $h \in \mathbb{N}$ be the greatest natural number for which $(r'_{\leq h})_{\restriction \text{AP}} \cdot r'' \in \mathsf{out}_{\mathcal{G}'}(\sigma_0, (\pi, \mathsf{q}_0^1))_{\restriction \text{AP}}$, for some sequence r''. More specifically, there does not exist any sequence $\hat{r}$ such that $(r'_{\leq h+1})_{\restriction \text{AP}} \cdot \hat{r} \in \mathsf{out}_{\mathcal{G}'}(\sigma_0, (\pi, \mathsf{q}_0^1))_{\restriction \text{AP}}$. Now, consider a sequence of action vectors $\vec{a}^0, \ldots, \vec{a}^h$ in $\mathcal{G} \oplus \mathcal{N}$ such that, for every $h' \leq h$, it holds that $r'_{h'} \xrightarrow{\vec{a}^{h'}} r'_{h'+1}$ Note that such sequence exists as the run r' belongs to $\mathsf{Paths}_{\mathcal{G}\oplus\mathcal{N}_{\sigma_0}}(\pi, \vec{\mathsf{q}}_0)_{\restriction \text{AP}}$. By the construction of $\mathcal{N}_\sigma$, we obtain that the sequence $(\vec{a}^0, a_0^0), \ldots, (\vec{a}^h, a_0^h)$, with $a_0^0, \ldots a_0^h$ being the sequence of actions generated by σ_0 generates a partial run in $\mathcal{G}'$, denoted $r_0, \ldots, r_{h+1}$ that can be extended to a run $r \in \mathsf{out}_{\mathcal{G}'}(\sigma_0, (\pi, \mathsf{q}_0^1))_{\restriction \text{AP}}$ in a way that $(r_{h\leq h+1})_{\restriction \text{AP}} = (r'_{h\leq h+1})_{\restriction \text{AP}}$, resulting in a contradiction with h being the greatest number for which such property holds, and subsequently that $r'_{\text{AP}} \notin \mathsf{out}_{\mathcal{G}'}(\sigma_0, (\pi, \mathsf{q}_0^1))_{\restriction \text{AP}}$.

2. The proof proceeds by double inclusion. For the left to right direction, consider a sequence $r'_{\restriction \text{AP}} \in \mathsf{Paths}_{\mathcal{G}\oplus\mathcal{N}}(\pi, \vec{\mathsf{q}}_0)_{\restriction \text{AP}}$ and let r' be a run in $\mathcal{G} \oplus \mathcal{N}$ from which $r'_{\restriction \text{AP}}$ is obtained by projection. By contradiction, let us assume that r'_{AP} does not belong to $\mathsf{out}_{\mathcal{G}'}(\sigma_{\mathcal{N}}, (\pi, \mathsf{q}_0^1))_{\restriction \text{AP}}$ and let $h \in \mathbb{N}$ be the greatest natural number for which $(r'_{\leq h})_{\restriction \text{AP}} \cdot r'' \in \mathsf{out}_{\mathcal{G}'}(\sigma_{\mathcal{N}}, (\pi, \mathsf{q}_0^1))_{\restriction \text{AP}}$, for some sequence r''. More specifically, there does not exist any sequence $\hat{r}$ such that $(r'_{\leq h+1})_{\restriction \text{AP}} \cdot \hat{r} \in \mathsf{out}_{\mathcal{G}'}(\sigma_{\mathcal{N}}, (\pi, \mathsf{q}_0^1))_{\restriction \text{AP}}$. Now, consider a sequence of action vectors $\vec{a}^0, \ldots, \vec{a}^h$ in $\mathcal{G} \oplus \mathcal{N}$ such that, for every $h' \leq h$, it holds that $r'_{h'} \xrightarrow{\vec{a}^{h'}} r'_{h'+1}$ Note that such a sequence exists, as the run r' belongs to $\mathsf{Paths}_{\mathcal{G}\oplus\mathcal{N}}(\pi, \vec{\mathsf{q}}_0)_{\restriction \text{AP}}$. By the construction of $\sigma_{\mathcal{N}}$, we obtain that the sequence $(\vec{a}^0, a_0^0), \ldots, (\vec{a}^h, a_0^h)$, with $a_0^0, \ldots a_0^h$ being the sequence of actions generated by $\sigma_{\mathcal{N}}$ generates a partial run in $\mathcal{G}'$, denoted $r_0, \ldots, r_{h+1}$ that can be extended to a run $r \in \mathsf{out}_{\mathcal{G}'}(\sigma_{\mathcal{N}}, (\pi, \mathsf{q}_0^1))_{\restriction \text{AP}}$ in a way that $(r_{h\leq h+1})_{\restriction \text{AP}} = (r'_{h\leq h+1})_{\restriction \text{AP}}$, resulting in a contradiction with h being the greatest number for which the property holds, and subsequently that $r'_{\text{AP}} \notin \mathsf{out}_{\mathcal{G}'}(\sigma_{\mathcal{N}}, (\pi, \mathsf{q}_0^1))_{\restriction \text{AP}}$.

For the right to left direction, consider a sequence $r'_{\restriction \text{AP}} \in \mathsf{out}_{\mathcal{G}'}(\sigma_{\mathcal{N}}, (\pi, \mathsf{q}_0^1))_{\restriction \text{AP}}$ and let r' be a run in $\mathcal{G}'$ from which $r'_{\restriction \text{AP}}$ is obtained by projection. By contradiction, let us assume that r'_{AP} does not belong to $\mathsf{Paths}_{\mathcal{G}\oplus\mathcal{N}}(\pi, \vec{\mathsf{q}}_0)_{\restriction \text{AP}}$ and let $h \in \mathbb{N}$ be the greatest natural number for which $(r'_{\leq h})_{\restriction \text{AP}} \cdot r'' \in \mathsf{Paths}_{\mathcal{G}\oplus\mathcal{N}}(\pi, \vec{\mathsf{q}}_0)_{\restriction \text{AP}}$, for some sequence r''. More specifically, there does not exist any sequence $\hat{r}$ such that $(r'_{\leq h+1})_{\restriction \text{AP}} \cdot \hat{r} \in \mathsf{Paths}_{\mathcal{G}\oplus\mathcal{N}}(\pi, \vec{\mathsf{q}}_0)_{\restriction \text{AP}}$. Now, consider a sequence of action vectors $\vec{a}^0, \ldots, \vec{a}^h$ in $\mathcal{G}'$ such that, for every $h' \leq h$, it holds that $r'_{h'} \xrightarrow{\vec{a}^{h'}} r'_{h'+1}$ and $\vec{a}_0^{h'}$ is always the action selected by $\sigma_{\mathcal{N}}$ as the execution evolves. Note that such a sequence exists, as the run r' belongs to $\mathsf{out}_{\mathcal{G}'}(\sigma_{\mathcal{N}}, (\pi, \mathsf{q}_0^1))_{\restriction \text{AP}}$. By the construction of $\sigma_{\mathcal{N}}$, we obtain that the sequence $(\vec{a}^0)_{-0}, \ldots, (\vec{a}^h)_{-0}$ generates a partial run in $\mathcal{G} \oplus \mathcal{N}$, denoted $r_0, \ldots, r_{h+1}$ that can be extended to a run $r \in \mathsf{Paths}_{\mathcal{G}\oplus\mathcal{N}}(\pi, \vec{\mathsf{q}}_0)_{\restriction \text{AP}}$ in such a way that $(r_{h\leq h+1})_{\restriction \text{AP}} = (r'_{h\leq h+1})_{\restriction \text{AP}}$, resulting in a contradiction with h being the greatest number for which such property holds, and subsequently that $r'_{\mathrm{AP}} \notin \mathsf{Paths}_{\mathcal{G}\oplus\mathcal{N}}(\pi, \vec{\mathsf{q}}_0)_{\restriction\mathrm{AP}}$. □

Lemma 1 establishes the equivalence between norms in $\mathcal{G}$ and their corresponding strategies in $\mathcal{G}'$, in the sense that they allow/disallow the same set of possible outcomes.

We now show that, once a norm $\mathcal{N}$ is implemented, it is also possible to establish a correspondence between agents' strategies in $\mathcal{G} \oplus \mathcal{N}$ and $\mathcal{G}'$, when agent 0 is employing the corresponding strategy $\sigma_{\mathcal{N}}$. Indeed, consider again a 1-MAS $\mathcal{G}$ and the accessory $\mathcal{G}'$ as defined above. We have the following:

Construction 4 (Outgoing strategy mapping). *Consider a norm $\mathcal{N}_2$ over $\mathcal{G}$ with $\sigma_{\mathcal{N}}$ being the corresponding strategy in $\mathcal{G}'$ for the normative agent. Moreover, consider an agent $j \in \mathrm{Ag}$ and a strategy σ_j for j in $\mathcal{G} \oplus \mathcal{N}_2$ of the form $\sigma_j = \langle S_j, s_k^0, \mathrm{Nrm}_1 \times \mathrm{Nrm}_2 \times 2^{\mathrm{AP}}, \mathrm{Ac}, \delta_j, \tau_j \rangle$. The* outgoing strategy *σ'_j for agent $j \in \mathrm{Ag}$ in $\mathcal{G}'$ is defined as*

$$\langle S'_j, s_k^{0\prime}, \mathrm{Nrm}_1 \times 2^{\mathrm{AP}'}, \mathrm{Ac}', \delta'_j, \tau'_j \rangle,$$

where $S'_j = S_j \times \mathrm{Nrm}_2$, $s_k^{0\prime} = (s_k^0, \mathsf{q}_2^0)$, and the internal and output functions are defined as:

- $\delta'_j((s, \mathsf{q}_2), (\mathsf{q}_1, \pi')) = (\delta_j(s, (\mathsf{q}_1, \mathsf{q}_2, \pi'_{\restriction\mathrm{AP}})), \eta_2(\mathsf{q}_2, \pi'_{\restriction\mathrm{AP}}))$;
- $\tau'_j((s, \mathsf{q}_2), (\mathsf{q}_1, \pi')) = \tau_j(s, (\mathsf{q}_1, \mathsf{q}_2, \pi'_{\restriction\mathrm{AP}}))$.

On the other hand, we can map a strategy in $\mathcal{G}'$ back to a strategy in $\mathcal{G} \oplus \mathcal{N}$.

Construction 5 (Incoming strategy mapping). *Consider a strategy σ'_j in $\mathcal{G}'$ for agent j, given as $\sigma'_j = \langle S'_j, s_k^{0\prime}, \mathrm{Nrm}_1 \times 2^{\mathrm{AP}'}, \mathrm{Ac}', \delta'_j, \tau'_j \rangle$.*
The incoming strategy *for agent j in $\mathcal{G} \oplus \mathcal{N}_2$ is defined as*

$$\sigma_j = \langle S_j, s_k^0, \mathrm{Nrm}_1 \times \mathrm{Nrm}_2 \times 2^{\mathrm{AP}}, \mathrm{Ac}, \delta_j, \tau_j \rangle,$$

where $S_j = S'_j$, $s_k^0 = s_k^{0\prime}$, and the internal and output functions are defined as:

- $\delta_j(s, (\mathsf{q}_1, \mathsf{q}_2, \pi)) = \delta'_j(s, (\mathsf{q}_1, \pi \cup \mathsf{illegal}_2(\mathsf{q}_2, \pi)))$;
- $\tau_j(s, (\mathsf{q}_1, \mathsf{q}_2, \pi)) = \tau'_j(s, (\mathsf{q}_1, \pi \cup \mathsf{illegal}_2(\mathsf{q}_2, \pi)))$.

As for norms and strategies for agent 0, the same kind of correspondence holds between strategies for the agents in the two structures, as the following lemma states.

Lemma 2. *For a given 1-MAS $\mathcal{G}$, its accessory game $\mathcal{G}'$, a pair $(\mathcal{N}, \sigma_0)$ of the corresponding norm and normative agent strategy, a set $A \subseteq \mathrm{Ag}$ of agents, and a state $\pi \in 2^{\mathrm{AP}}$, the following two statements hold:*

1. *For every strategy σ_A in $\mathcal{G} \oplus \mathcal{N}$ it holds that $\mathsf{out}_{\mathcal{G}\oplus\mathcal{N}}(\pi, \vec{\mathsf{q}}_0, \sigma_A)_{\restriction\mathrm{AP}} = \mathsf{out}_{\mathcal{G}'}((\pi, \mathsf{q}_0^1), \sigma_0 \cup \sigma'_A)_{\restriction\mathrm{AP}}$;*
2. *For every strategy σ'_A in $\mathcal{G}'$ it holds that $\mathsf{out}_{\mathcal{G}'}((\pi, \mathsf{q}_0^1), \sigma_0 \cup \sigma'_A)_{\restriction\mathrm{AP}} = \mathsf{out}_{\mathcal{G}\oplus\mathcal{N}}(\pi, \vec{\mathsf{q}}_0, \sigma_A)_{\restriction\mathrm{AP}}$.*

Proof. We prove the two statements separately.

1. The proof proceed by double inclusion. For the left to right direction, consider a sequence $r'_{\restriction\mathrm{AP}} \in \mathsf{out}_{\mathcal{G}\oplus\mathcal{N}}(\pi, \vec{\mathsf{q}}_0, \sigma_A)_{\restriction\mathrm{AP}}$ with r' being a run in $\mathcal{G} \oplus \mathcal{N}$ from which $r'_{\restriction\mathrm{AP}}$ is obtained by projection. By contradiction, let us assume that r'_{AP} does not belong to $\mathsf{out}_{\mathcal{G}'}((\pi, \mathsf{q}_0^1), \sigma_0 \cup \sigma'_A)_{\restriction\mathrm{AP}}$ and let $h \in \mathbb{N}$ be the greatest natural number for which $(r'_{\leq h})_{\restriction\mathrm{AP}} \cdot r'' \in \mathsf{out}_{\mathcal{G}'}((\pi, \mathsf{q}_0^1), \sigma_0 \cup \sigma'_A)_{\restriction\mathrm{AP}}$, for some sequence r''. More specifically, there does not exist any sequence $\hat{r}$ such that $(r'_{\leq h+1})_{\restriction\mathrm{AP}} \cdot \hat{r} \in \mathsf{out}_{\mathcal{G}'}((\pi, \mathsf{q}_0^1), \sigma_0 \cup \sigma'_A)_{\restriction\mathrm{AP}}$. Now, consider a sequence of action vectors $\vec{a}^0, \ldots, \vec{a}^h$ in $\mathcal{G} \oplus \mathcal{N}$ such that, for every $h' \leq h$, it holds that $r'_{h'} \xrightarrow{\vec{a}^{h'}} r'_{h'+1}$ and $\vec{a}_j^{h'}$ is always the action selected by σ_j, for each $j \in A$, as the execution evolves. Note that such a sequence exists, as the run r' belongs to $\mathsf{out}_{\mathcal{G}\oplus\mathcal{N}}(\pi, \vec{\mathsf{q}}_0, \sigma_A)_{\restriction\mathrm{AP}}$. By the construction of $\sigma_{\mathcal{N}}$ and σ'_A, we obtain that the sequence $(\vec{a}^0, a_0^0), \ldots, (\vec{a}^h, a_0^h)$ with $a_0^0, \ldots, a_0^h$ being he sequence of actions generated by $\sigma_{\mathcal{N}}$, generates a partial run in $\mathcal{G}'$, denoted $r_0, \ldots, r_{h+1}$ that can be extended to a run $r \in \mathsf{out}_{\mathcal{G}'}((\pi, \mathsf{q}_0^1), \sigma_0 \cup \sigma'_A)_{\restriction\mathrm{AP}}$ in such a way that $(r_{h\leq h+1})_{\restriction\mathrm{AP}} = (r'_{h\leq h+1})_{\restriction\mathrm{AP}}$, resulting in a contradiction with h being the greatest number for which such property holds, and subsequently that $r'_{\mathrm{AP}} \notin \mathsf{out}_{\mathcal{G}'}((\pi, \mathsf{q}_0^1), \sigma_0 \cup \sigma'_A)_{\restriction\mathrm{AP}}$.

For the right to left direction, consider a sequence $r'_{\restriction\mathrm{AP}} \in \mathsf{out}_{\mathcal{G}'}((\pi, \mathsf{q}_0^1), \sigma_0 \cup \sigma'_A)_{\restriction\mathrm{AP}}$ with r' being a run in $\mathcal{G}'$ from which $r'_{\restriction\mathrm{AP}}$ is obtained by projection. By contradiction, let us assume that r'_{AP} does not belong to $\mathsf{out}_{\mathcal{G}\oplus\mathcal{N}}(\pi, \vec{\mathsf{q}}_0, \sigma_A)_{\restriction\mathrm{AP}}$ and let $h \in \mathbb{N}$ be the greatest natural number for which $(r'_{\leq h})_{\restriction\mathrm{AP}} \cdot r'' \in \mathsf{out}_{\mathcal{G}\oplus\mathcal{N}}(\pi, \vec{\mathsf{q}}_0, \sigma_A)_{\restriction\mathrm{AP}}$, for some sequence r''. More specifically, there does not exist any sequence $\hat{r}$ such that $(r'_{\leq h+1})_{\restriction\mathrm{AP}} \cdot \hat{r} \in \mathsf{out}_{\mathcal{G}\oplus\mathcal{N}}(\pi, \vec{\mathsf{q}}_0, \sigma_A)_{\restriction\mathrm{AP}}$. Now, consider a sequence of action vectors $\vec{a}^0, \ldots, \vec{a}^h$ in $\mathcal{G}'$ such that, for every $h' \leq h$, it holds that $r'_{h'} \xrightarrow{\vec{a}^{h'}} r'_{h'+1}$ and $\vec{a}_j^{h'}$ is always the action selected by σ_j, for each $j \in A \cup \{0\}$, as the execution evolves. Note that such a sequence exists, as the run r' belongs to $\mathsf{out}_{\mathcal{G}'}((\pi, \mathsf{q}_0^1), \sigma_0 \cup \sigma'_A)_{\restriction\mathrm{AP}}$.

By the construction of $\sigma_{\mathcal{N}}$ and σ'_A of Construction 3 and Construction 4, respectively, we obtain that the sequence $(\vec{a}^0)_{-0}, \ldots, (\vec{a}^h)_{-0}$ generates a partial run in $\mathcal{G} \oplus \mathcal{N}$, denoted $r_0, \ldots, r_{h+1}$ that can be extended to a run $r \in \mathsf{out}_{\mathcal{G}\oplus\mathcal{N}}(\pi, \vec{\mathsf{q}}_0, \sigma_A)_{\restriction\mathrm{AP}}$ in such a way that $(r_{h\leq h+1})_{\restriction\mathrm{AP}} = (r'_{h\leq h+1})_{\restriction\mathrm{AP}}$, resulting in a contradiction with h being the greatest number for which such property holds, and subsequently that $r'_{\mathrm{AP}} \notin \mathsf{out}_{\mathcal{G}\oplus\mathcal{N}}(\pi, \vec{\mathsf{q}}_0, \sigma_A)_{\restriction\mathrm{AP}}$.

2. Note that the proof of this statement is identical to the previous one, except for the fact that this time we use Construction 2 and Construction 5 for $\mathcal{N}_{\sigma_0}$ and σ_A, respectively. □

An immediate consequence of Lemma 1 and Lemma 2 is that the existence of a norm in $\mathcal{G}$ can be restated as the existence of the corresponding strategy for agent 0 in $\mathcal{G}'$.

Lemma 3. *For a given 1-MAS $\mathcal{G}$ and an ATL* formula φ, the following two statements are equivalent:*

1. *There exists a norm $\mathcal{N}$ over $\mathcal{G}$ such that $\mathcal{G} \oplus \mathcal{N} \models \varphi$*
2. *$\mathcal{G}' \models \langle\langle \cdot 0 \cdot \rangle\rangle \varphi'$, where φ' is obtained from φ by replacing all strategy quantifiers $\langle\langle A \rangle\rangle$ with $\langle\langle \cdot A \cdot \rangle\rangle$.*

Proof. We prove the equivalence by double implication. Both directions proceed by structural induction on the formula φ. Here, for simplicity, we show only the base case of $\varphi = \langle\!\langle A \rangle\!\rangle \psi$, with $\psi \in LTL$, as all the others are a simple variant of this.

To prove that Statement 1 implies Statement 2, assume that $\mathcal{G} \oplus \mathcal{N} \models \varphi$. Therefore, there exists σ_A such that $r \models \psi$ for every $r \in (\mathsf{out}_{\mathcal{G}\oplus\mathcal{N}}(\sigma_A, \emptyset))_{\restriction \mathrm{AP}}$.[4] Then, consider the strategy σ'_A in $\mathcal{G}'$ obtained from σ_A by applying Construction 4. By Lemma 2, we obtain that $(\mathsf{out}_{\mathcal{G}\oplus\mathcal{N}}(\sigma_A, \emptyset))_{\restriction \mathrm{AP}} = (\mathsf{out}_{\mathcal{G}'}(\sigma'_A \cup \sigma_{\mathcal{N}}, \emptyset))_{\restriction \mathrm{AP}}$ with $\sigma_{\mathcal{N}}$ obtained from $\mathcal{N}$ by applying Construction 3, which in turns implies that $\mathcal{G}' \models \langle\!\langle \cdot 0 \cdot \rangle\!\rangle \varphi'$.

The other direction proceeds as follows. Assume that $\mathcal{G}' \models \langle\!\langle \cdot 0 \cdot \rangle\!\rangle \langle\!\langle A \rangle\!\rangle \psi$. Therefore, there exists a strategy σ_0 for agent 0 and a strategy profile σ'_A, such that $r \models \psi$ for every $r \in (\mathsf{out}_{\mathcal{G}'}(\sigma'_A \cup \sigma_{\mathcal{N}}, \emptyset))_{\restriction \mathrm{AP}}$. Now consider the norm $\mathcal{N}_{\sigma_0}$ obtained from Construction 2 and the strategy profile σ_A obtained from Construction 5. By Lemma 2, we obtain that $(\mathsf{out}_{\mathcal{G}'}(\sigma'_A \cup \sigma_{\mathcal{N}}, \emptyset))_{\restriction \mathrm{AP}} = (\mathsf{out}_{\mathcal{G}\oplus\mathcal{N}_{\sigma_0}}(\sigma_A, \emptyset))_{\restriction \mathrm{AP}}$ and so that $\mathcal{G} \oplus \mathcal{N}_{\sigma_0} \models \langle\!\langle A \rangle\!\rangle \psi$. □

Example 9. *The formula from Example 7 is translated into* ATL^*_{sc} *as* $\langle\!\langle \cdot 0 \cdot \rangle\!\rangle \langle\!\langle \cdot 1 \cdot \rangle\!\rangle \mathtt{G}(work \to \mathtt{X}(rest \wedge \mathtt{X} rest))$. *A possible norm (corresponding to a strategy for 0) is:* $\mathrm{Nrm} = \{\mathsf{q}_0, \mathsf{q}_1, \mathsf{q}_2\}$, *where* $\eta(\mathsf{q}_0, \pi) = \mathsf{q}_0$ *if* $work \notin \pi$, *else* $\eta(\mathsf{q}_0, \pi) = \mathsf{q}_1$; $\eta(\mathsf{q}_1, \pi) = \mathsf{q}_2$ *and* $\eta(\mathsf{q}_2, \pi) = \mathsf{q}_0$ *if* $rest \in \pi$, *else* $\eta(\mathsf{q}_1, \pi) = \mathsf{q}_1$ *and* $\eta(\mathsf{q}_2, \pi) = \mathsf{q}_2$. $\mathsf{illegal}(\mathsf{q}_0, \pi) = \emptyset$ *and* $\mathsf{illegal}(\mathsf{q}_1, \pi) = \mathsf{illegal}(\mathsf{q}_2, \pi) = \{(2, ask)\}$.

As a consequence of the lemma, the norm synthesis problem for a MAS $\mathcal{G}$ and an ATL* objective φ can be reduced to the model-checking of an $\mathrm{ATL}^*_{\mathrm{sc}}$ formula over the accessory game $\mathcal{G}'$. The complexity of such a procedure depends on the number h of alternation quantifiers in the formula and the first quantifier modality. More precisely, it is $(h+1)$-EXPTIME for existential ATL*, that is, the fragment of ATL* with formulas starting with an existential quantification, and $(h+2)$-EXPTIME for universal ATL*. The reason for this is that the resulting $\mathrm{ATL}^*_{\mathrm{sc}}$ formula comes with an extra alternation, if the original ATL* formula φ begins with a universal quantification.

Theorem 3. *The following two statements hold:*

1. *Norm Synthesis for a k-MAS for an existential ATL* formula with alternation quantifier h can be solved in $(h+1)$-EXPTIME.*
2. *Norm Synthesis for a k-MAS for a universal ATL* formula with alternation quantifier h can be solved in $(h+2)$-EXPTIME.*

Notice that the two fragments introduced in Section 2.3 are both of alternation 1. In particular, formulas for strategic permission (Cf. Definition 1) are in the existential ATL* fragment, whereas formulas for strategic prohibition (Cf. Definition 2) are in the universal ATL* fragment. Therefore, combining this with the complexity results of Theorem 3, we obtain the following corollary.

[4] Note that we can consider the projection over AP as the formula ψ ranges over the same set of atomic propositions.

Corollary 1. *The following two hold:*

1. *Norm Synthesis for a k-MAS for a strategic permission specification can be solved in 2-EXPTIME.*
2. *Norm Synthesis for a k-MAS for a strategic prohibition specification can be solved in 3-EXPTIME.*

It is worth mentioning a further special case that arises with strategic prohibition specifications, when every agent is mentioned in the universal quantification. In this case, the alternation of the formula is 0, as there is no implicit existential quantification, as in Example 2. For this case, the complexity is 2EXPTIME.

Observe that we can obtain a Norm Synthesis algorithm by the following steps. First, we use Construction 1 to reduce from Norm Synthesis to model checking $\mathrm{ATL}^*_{\mathrm{sc}}$. Note that such translation is both effective and polynomial in the size of the original k-MAS $\mathcal{G}$. Then, we solve the corresponding model checking instance by employing any applicable procedure, returning a normative strategy σ_0, if available. Finally, by employing Construction 2 on σ_0, we obtain a norm for $\mathcal{G}$. Again, the construction is both effective and polynomial in the size of σ_0. Moreover, Lemma 3 and Theorem 3 combined guarantee the procedure to solve the original Norm Synthesis problem correctly.

4 Norm Removal

Regarding Norm Removal, note that the solution space is finite, as it is given by the 2^k possible subsets of norms that are implemented in a k-MAS. Therefore, it suffices to model-check the ATL* formula φ against all possible 2^k removals of norms.

Theorem 4. *The norm removal problem is 2EXPTIME-complete w.r.t. the size of the ATL* formula and EXPTIME w.r.t. the number of norms implemented.*

5 Related Work

There is an extensive literature on using norms of differing types for the formal analysis and design of single- and multi-agent systems. In some approaches, norms correspond to labelling some states in a state transition system as 'violating', e.g., (Meyer and Wieringa 1993). For example, in (Astefanoaei et al. 2009; Dennis, Tinnemeier, and Meyer 2010; Dastani, Grossi, and Meyer 2013), norms are represented by "counts-as" rules characterising violation states (e.g., a state where an agent exceeds the speed limit "counts as" a violation). Other kinds of norms label some transitions as violating, e.g., (Ågotnes, van der Hoek, and Wooldridge 2010), or label particular paths through the system as violating, e.g., (Bulling, Dastani, and Knobbout 2013). For example, conditional prohibitions with deadlines and sanctions (Dignum et al. 2004; Boella and van der Torre 2004; Boella, Broersen, and van der Torre 2008; Tinnemeier et al. 2009) are of the form $P(c, \varphi, d, s)$ where c is the detachment condition (when a state satisfying c is encountered the prohibition becomes active), φ is the state property which is prohibited to bring about, and d is the deadline (after a state satisfying d is encountered, the prohibition is no longer active), and s is a sanction (explained below). Modulo a translation between state-based and action-based prohibitions (Alechina, Dastani, and Logan 2018), regimented conditional prohibitions are clearly a special case of the norms considered in this paper.

What happens as a result of implementing a norm also varies. For example, in some approaches the violating states or transitions are removed (norm regimentation). We can then check whether some desirable properties (objectives) are satisfied in the resulting smaller system, see, e.g., (Ågotnes et al. 2007). In other approaches, violating states or paths are labelled with sanctions (norm enforcement). Sanctions are 'fines' applied to violating traces (in the special case of regimented norms, like the ones we consider in this paper, the trace is terminated). Again, we can check whether it is possible to execute a 'good' behaviour without incurring a sanction, or it is impossible to execute a 'bad' behaviour without incurring a sanction, see, e.g., (Alechina, Dastani, and Logan 2013). However, the aim in such approaches is to *verify* whether some property is true after implementing a norm, rather than to *synthesise* a norm, that, if implemented, will satisfy the property as in our approach.

The first formal treatment of norm synthesis (social laws to coordinate agents' behaviour) was proposed in (Shoham and Tennenholtz 1995), see also (Fitoussi and Tennenholtz 2000). There, norms are constraints on agent behaviours of the form (a, φ), which are interpreted as: in a state satisfying φ action a is prohibited. The objectives are essentially strategy existence properties (or strategic permissions in our terminology). The decision form of the synthesis problem of 'useful social laws' (enabling the objectives) is shown to be NP-complete. In (Christelis and Rovatsos 2009), an EXPTIME algorithm for synthesising state-based prohibitions was proposed. In a somewhat different approach to norm synthesis, (Corapi et al. 2011) use ILP to synthesise norms from use cases. In (Morales et al. 2015; Morales et al. 2018) on-line norm synthesis is proposed as a more feasible way of synthesising norms when the state space is not known in advance. In (van der Hoek, Roberts, and Wooldridge 2007), the problem of synthesising norms is reduced to model-checking in ATL (a fragment of ATL*). In (Bulling and Dastani 2016), norm synthesis is studied in a setting similar to ours, but where agent preferences are known and it is possible to consider Nash equilibria. The system is represented as a CGS. Agents' preferences are represented by a list of pairs (φ_j, u_j), where φ_j is an LTL formula and u_j is a natural number (utility). Nash equilibrium is defined in terms of the utilities obtained by the agents when adopting a given strategy. The system objective is represented by a normative choice function, which is also an LTL formula. Their 'regimenting norms' are closest to norms considered in this paper, and are of the form $(\varphi, \mathcal{A}, \bot)$ where φ is a propositional formula and $\mathcal{A} \subseteq Act^n$ is a set of joint actions. The norm makes $\mathcal{A}$ illegal in states satisfying φ. Rather than removing illegal actions, they are redirected to loop in the same state (have no effect).[5] Clearly, such norms are less expressive than the dynamic norms in our approach. The problems considered in (Bulling and Dastani 2016) are weak and strong implementation, and norm-based mechanism design. A norm weakly implements a normative behaviour function if there exists a Nash equilibrium that satisfies the LTL formula. A norm strongly implements iff all Nash equilibria satisfy the formula. Weak implementation is Σ_2^P-complete in the size of the CGS, preferences, objective and norm. The strong implementation problem can be solved by a deterministic polynomial-time oracle Turing machine that can make two non-adaptive queries to an oracle in Σ_2^P and is both Σ_2^P-hard and Π_2^P-hard. Weak implementation existence is Σ_2^P-complete. Strong implementation existence is Σ_3^P-complete.

Dynamic norms were introduced in (Huang et al. 2016; Perelli 2019). In (Huang et al. 2016), dynamic absolute or regimented prohibitions similar to the ones in this paper are considered. The illegality function returns a joint action rather than a set of pairs of an action and agent, as in (Bulling and Dastani 2016). The language for specifying objectives is Computation Tree Temporal Logic (CTL). The main result is that the norm synthesis problem is EXPTIME-complete. Other problems considered are two versions of norm recognition problem. In (Perelli 2019), the synthesis of dynamic norms for LTL objectives and Nash equilibria is shown to be 2EXPTIME-complete when considering the existence of a Nash equilibrium satisfying the objective, and in 3EXPTIME for enforcing all Nash equilibria to satisfy the objective. Since our language for objectives is more expressive, it is not surprising that the complexity of synthesis for our setting is higher.

6 Conclusion

We proposed a framework for modelling dynamic norms that enforce constraints on agent strategies in multi-agent systems in order to satisfy system objectives stated in ATL*. These norms are more general than regimented state-based prohibitions and conditional prohibitions, and are *dynamic*, so can constrain strategies in a more flexible way. We prove that the norm synthesis problem is decidable in $(k+1)$-EXPTIME; however for two important classes of objectives, strategic permissions and strategic prohibitions, it is in 2EXPTIME and 3EXPTIME, respectively. We conjecture that the $(k+1)$-EXPTIME bound is tight, but leave the proof of hardness for future work. Another possible direction of future research is synthesis of minimally constraining norms.

Acknowledgments

This work is partially supported by the ERC Advanced Grant WhiteMech (No. 834228), by the EU ICT-48 2020 project TAILOR (No. 952215), by the PRIN project RIPER (No. 20203FFYLK), and by the JPMorgan AI Faculty Research Award "Resilience-based Generalized Planning and Strategic Reasoning".

[5]The authors mention that in previous work they removed illegal joint actions entirely. However this caused problems with actions still being available to individual agents, while a joint action was impossible. In our approach, we avoid this problem by making individual rather than joint actions illegal.

References

Ågotnes, T.; van der Hoek, W.; Rodríguez-Aguilar, J. A.; Sierra, C.; and Wooldridge, M. J. 2007. On the logic of normative systems. In Veloso, M. M., ed., *IJCAI 2007, Proceedings of the 20th International Joint Conference on Artificial Intelligence*, 1175–1180.

Ågotnes, T.; van der Hoek, W.; and Wooldridge, M. 2010. Robust normative systems and a logic of norm compliance. *Logic Journal of the IGPL* 18(1):4–30.

Alechina, N.; Dastani, M.; and Logan, B. 2013. Reasoning about normative update. In *Proceedings of the Twenty Third International Joint Conference on Artificial Intelligence (IJCAI 2013)*, 20–26. AAAI Press.

Alechina, N.; Dastani, M.; and Logan, B. 2018. Norm specification and verification in multiagent systems. In Chopra, A.; van der Torre, L.; Verhagen, H.; and Villata, S., eds., *Handbook of Normative Multiagent Systems*, 29–55. College Publications.

Alur, R.; Henzinger, T. A.; and Kupferman, O. 2002. Alternating-time temporal logic. *J. ACM* 49(5):672–713.

Astefanoaei, L.; Dastani, M.; Meyer, J.; and de Boer, F. 2009. On the semantics and verification of normative multiagent systems. *International Journal of Universal Computer Science* 15(13):2629–2652.

Boella, G., and van der Torre, L. 2004. Regulative and constitutive norms in normative multiagent systems. In *Proceedings of the Ninth International Conference on Principles of Knowledge Representation and Reasoning (KR'04)*, 255–266.

Boella, G.; Broersen, J.; and van der Torre, L. 2008. Reasoning about constitutive norms, counts-as conditionals, institutions, deadlines and violations. In *Proceedings of the International Conference on Principles and Practice of Multi-Agent Systems (PRIMA)*, 86–97.

Bulling, N., and Dastani, M. 2016. Norm-based mechanism design. *Artif. Intell.* 239:97–142.

Bulling, N.; Dastani, M.; and Knobbout, M. 2013. Monitoring norm violations in multi-agent systems. In *Twelfth International conference on Autonomous Agents and Multi-Agent Systems (AAMAS'13)*, 491–498.

Chopra, A.; van der Torre, L.; Verhagen, H.; and Villata, S., eds. 2018. *Handbook of Normative Multiagent Systems*. College Publications.

Christelis, G., and Rovatsos, M. 2009. Automated norm synthesis in an agent-based planning environment. In *Proceedings of The 8th International Conference on Autonomous Agents and Multiagent Systems*, 161–168.

Corapi, D.; Russo, A.; Vos, M. D.; Padget, J. A.; and Satoh, K. 2011. Normative design using inductive learning. *Theory Pract. Log. Program.* 11(4-5):783–799.

Dastani, M.; Grossi, D.; and Meyer, J.-J. 2013. A logic for normative multi-agent programs. *Journal of Logic and Computation, special issue on Normative Multiagent Systems* 23(2):335–354.

Dennis, L. A.; Tinnemeier, N. A. M.; and Meyer, J.-J. C. 2010. Model checking normative agent organisations. In Dix, J.; Fisher, M.; and Novák, P., eds., *Computational Logic in Multi-Agent Systems - 10th International Workshop, CLIMA X, Revised Selected and Invited Papers*, volume 6214 of *Lecture Notes in Computer Science*, 64–82. Springer.

Dignum, F.; Broersen, J.; Dignum, V.; and Meyer, J.-J. C. 2004. Meeting the deadline: Why, when and how. In *Proceedings of the International Workshop on Formal Approaches to Agent-Based Systems (FAABS)*, 30–40.

Fitoussi, D., and Tennenholtz, M. 2000. Choosing social laws for multi-agent systems: Minimality and simplicity. *Artificial Intelligence* 119(1):61–101.

Grossi, D.; Aldewereld, H.; and Dignum, F. 2006. *Ubi Lex, Ibi Poena* : Designing norm enforcement in e-institutions. In Noriega, P.; Vázquez-Salceda, J.; Boella, G.; Boissier, O.; Dignum, V.; Fornara, N.; and Matson, E., eds., *Coordination, Organizations, Institutions, and Norms in Agent Systems II - AAMAS 2006 and ECAI 2006 International Workshops, COIN 2006, Revised Selected Papers*, volume 4386 of *Lecture Notes in Computer Science*, 101–114. Springer.

Haynes, C.; Luck, M.; McBurney, P.; Mahmoud, S.; Vitek, T.; and Miles, S. 2017. Engineering the emergence of norms: a review. *The Knowledge Engineering Review* 32.

Huang, X.; Ruan, J.; Chen, Q.; and Su, K. 2016. Normative Multiagent Systems: The Dynamic Generalization. 1123–1129.

Laroussinie, F., and Markey, N. 2015. Augmenting ATL with strategy contexts. *Inf. Comput.* 245:98–123.

Meyer, J.-J. C., and Wieringa, R. J. 1993. Deontic logic: A concise overview. In Meyer, J.-J. C., and Wieringa, R., eds., *Deontic Logic in Computer Science: Normative System Specification*. John Wiley & Sons. 3–16.

Morales, J.; López-Sánchez, M.; Rodríguez-Aguilar, J. A.; Vasconcelos, W. W.; and Wooldridge, M. J. 2015. Online automated synthesis of compact normative systems. *ACM Trans. Auton. Adapt. Syst.* 10(1):2:1–2:33.

Morales, J.; Wooldridge, M. J.; Rodríguez-Aguilar, J. A.; and López-Sánchez, M. 2018. Off-line synthesis of evolutionarily stable normative systems. *Auton. Agents Multi Agent Syst.* 32(5):635–671.

Perelli, G. 2019. Enforcing Equilibria in Multi-Agent Systems. 188–196.

Shoham, Y., and Tennenholtz, M. 1995. On social laws for artificial agent societies: off-line design. *Artificial Intelligence* 73(1-2):231–252.

Tinnemeier, N.; Dastani, M.; Meyer, J.-J. C.; and van der Torre, L. 2009. Programming normative artifacts with declarative obligations and prohibitions. In *Proceedings of the IEEE/WIC/ACM International Joint Conferences on Web Intelligence and Intelligent Agent Technologies, WI-IAT'09*, volume 2, 145 –152.

van der Hoek, W.; Roberts, M.; and Wooldridge, M. J. 2007. Social laws in alternating time: effectiveness, feasibility, and synthesis. *Synthese* 156(1):1–19.

Pushing Optimal ABox Repair from $\mathcal{EL}$ Towards More Expressive Horn-DLs

Franz Baader, Francesco Kriegel
Theoretical Computer Science, Technische Universität Dresden, Dresden, Germany
{franz.baader,francesco.kriegel}@tu-dresden.de

Abstract

Ontologies based on Description Logic (DL) represent general background knowledge in a terminology (TBox) and the actual data in an ABox. DL systems can then be used to compute consequences (such as answers to certain queries) from an ontology consisting of a TBox and an ABox. Since both human-made and machine-learned data sets may contain errors, which manifest themselves as unintuitive or obviously incorrect consequences, repairing DL-based ontologies in the sense of removing such unwanted consequences is an important topic in DL research. Most of the repair approaches described in the literature produce repairs that are not optimal, in the sense that they do not guarantee that only a minimal set of consequences is removed. In a series of papers, we have developed an approach for computing optimal repairs, starting with the restricted setting of an $\mathcal{EL}$ instance store, extending this to the more general setting of a quantified ABox (where some individuals may be anonymous), and then adding a static $\mathcal{EL}$ TBox.

Here, we extend the expressivity of the underlying DL considerably, by adding nominals, inverse roles, regular role inclusions and the bottom concept to $\mathcal{EL}$, which yields a fragment of the well-known DL Horn-$\mathcal{SROIQ}$. The ideas underlying our repair approach still apply to this DL, though several non-trivial extensions are needed to deal with the new constructors and axioms. The developed repair approach can also be used to treat unwanted consequences expressed by certain conjunctive queries or regular path queries, and to handle Horn-$\mathcal{ALCOI}$ TBoxes with regular role inclusions.

1 Introduction

Description Logics (DLs) (Baader et al. 2017) are a prominent family of logic-based knowledge representation formalisms, which offer a good compromise between expressiveness and the complexity of reasoning and are the formal basis for the Web ontology language OWL.[1] The palette of well-investigated DLs with optimized reasoning support goes from the inexpressive and tractable DLs of the $\mathcal{EL}$ and DL-Lite families (Baader, Brandt, and Lutz 2005; Calvanese et al. 2007), on which the OWL 2 profiles OWL 2 EL and OWL 2 QL are based, all the way up to the N2ExpTime-complete DL $\mathcal{SROIQ}$ (Horrocks, Kutz, and Sattler 2006; Kazakov 2008), which is the DL underlying OWL 2. The consequence-based reasoning approach developed for the $\mathcal{EL}$ family (Baader, Brandt, and Lutz 2005) can be extended to Horn fragments of more expressive DLs, which yields practical "pay as you go" reasoning procedures for these fragments, though they are no longer tractable (Kazakov 2009; Ortiz, Rudolph, and Šimkus 2010).

Like all large human-made digital artefacts, the ontologies employed in applications often contain errors, and this problem is only exacerbated if parts of the ontology (e.g., the data) are automatically generated using inexact methods based on information retrieval or machine learning. Errors are usually detected when reasoning finds an inconsistency or generates consequences that are unintuitive or obviously wrong in the application domain. For the developers of a DL-based ontology it is often quite hard to see how the ontology needs to be modified such that the unwanted consequences no longer follow from the repaired ontology, but as few as possible other consequences are lost.

Classical DL repair approaches based on axiom pinpointing compute maximal subsets of the ontology that do not have the unwanted consequences (Parsia, Sirin, and Kalyanpur 2005; Schlobach et al. 2007; Baader and Suntisrivaraporn 2008). Such repairs depend on the syntactic form of the ontology: if a certain fact is expressed by a single strong axiom rather than an equivalent set of weaker ones, then too many consequences may be lost when removing this strong axiom. To overcome this problem, more fine-grained approaches for repairing DL-based ontologies have been developed (Horridge, Parsia, and Sattler 2008; Lam et al. 2008; Du, Qi, and Fu 2014; Troquard et al. 2018; Baader et al. 2018). These approaches are, however, still not optimal since they apply some restrictions on how the ontology can be changed, based on its syntactic form. In particular, they usually do not add new objects to the ABox.

To see why new objects may be needed to achieve optimality, assume that the ABox contains the information that Kim, who is rich and famous, is Ann's child, expressed by the assertions $\mathit{Famous}(\mathit{KIM})$, $\mathit{Rich}(\mathit{KIM})$, and $\mathit{child}(\mathit{ANN}, \mathit{KIM})$, and that we want to remove the consequence $\exists\, \mathit{child}.(\mathit{Rich} \sqcap \mathit{Famous})(\mathit{ANN})$. If we decide to keep the assertion that Kim is Ann's child, then we need to remove either $\mathit{Rich}(\mathit{KIM})$ or $\mathit{Famous}(\mathit{KIM})$. However, if we decide that this Kim is not Ann's child after all, simply removing the role assertion $\mathit{child}(\mathit{ANN}, \mathit{KIM})$ would

[1] https://www.w3.org/TR/owl2-overview/

also remove implied consequences for Ann. This can be avoided by adding the assertions $child(ANN, x)$, *Rich*(x), $child(ANN, y)$, and *Famous*(y), where x and y are anonymous individuals, which are formally represented in a quantified ABox (qABox) by existentially quantified variables. This example illustrates the main idea underlying the optimal repair approach introduced in (Baader et al. 2020): the use of quantified ABoxes and the construction of appropriate anonymous copies of individuals. The main technical problem to solve in (Baader et al. 2020) was to find out which copies with what properties are needed to achieve optimality. This work dealt with an input ontology consisting only of a qABox, and assumed that the unwanted consequences are instance relationships $C(a)$ for $\mathcal{EL}$ concepts C.

In (Baader et al. 2021), we extended this approach to a setting where, in addition to the qABox, the ontology contains an $\mathcal{EL}$ TBox, which is assumed to be correct, and thus cannot be changed during repair. To add consequences implied by the TBox, we saturate the qABox by using the concept inclusions as rewrite rules before repairing the qABox. If, in our example, the TBox contained the concept inclusion *Celebrity* $\sqsubseteq$ $Rich \sqcap Famous$ and the ABox contained *Celebrity*(KIM) rather than *Rich*(KIM) and *Famous*(KIM), then saturation would add the latter two assertions. If then *Celebrity*(KIM) is removed in the repair, these two consequences can still be preserved. However, when repairing the saturated qABox, care must be taken that the TBox cannot re-introduce assertions that have been removed by the repair. For example, in the case where the unwanted consequence is *Rich*(KIM), it is not enough to remove this assertion from the saturated qABox: one also needs to remove *Celebrity*(KIM) since together with the TBox it implies *Rich*(KIM). The problem with saturation is that, in the presence of cyclic concept inclusions, such as $Rich \sqsubseteq \exists child.Rich$, it may not terminate. This is not just a problem of our repair *approach*, but may prevent the existence of optimal repairs (see Example 9 below). In (Baader et al. 2021), two approaches are considered to overcome this problem. On the one hand, one can restrict the attention to TBoxes that are cycle-restricted as introduced in (Baader, Borgwardt, and Morawska 2012). On the other hand, if one is only interested in answers to instance queries, one can apply a weaker saturation operation, called IQ-saturation, which always terminates for $\mathcal{EL}$.

In this paper, we extend the expressivity of the DL used to formulate the TBox and the unwanted consequences considerably, by adding nominals, inverse roles, role inclusion axioms, and the bottom concept to $\mathcal{EL}$. To obtain a decidable DL and guarantee the existence of optimal repairs, we restrict the set of role inclusion axioms to being regular, as in the DL $\mathcal{SROIQ}$. In addition, we first consider the case without the bottom concept, and only later deal with the additional problems caused by the fact that bottom may cause the ontology to become inconsistent. Computability of the set of optimal repairs and the fact that this set *covers* all repairs (in the sense that every repair is entailed by an optimal one) follows from a "small repair" property, which can be shown using an adaptation of the well-known filtration technique (Baader et al. 2017). However, even disregarding the impracticality of an algorithm that computes the optimal repairs by looking at all qABoxes up to a certain size bound, this does not lead to a viable methods for choosing an appropriate optimal repair since it would require the knowledge engineer to choose among exponentially many repairs of exponential size. In contrast, the *canonical repairs* (which cover all optimal repairs) constructed by our extension of the repair approach in (Baader et al. 2021) are characterized by so-called *repair seeds*, which are of polynomial size. The knowledge engineer can choose among these by answering a polynomial number of instance queries (i.e., queries about which instance relationships hold in the application domain).

The added expressivity generates new challenges, which require non-trivial adaptations of our approach for constructing canonical repairs. Since nominals in the TBox can imply equality between individuals, we extend qABoxes by equality assertions, to be able to represent such consequences in the saturated qABox, and we also must repair unwanted equalities. We deal with role inclusion axioms and inverse roles by using finite automata, which can represent the infinitely many implied role inclusions in a finite way. Technically, this is where we make use of the restriction to regular sets of role inclusion axioms. To handle inconsistency caused by bottom, we consider not only "local" unwanted consequences of the form $C(a)$, but also "global" ones of the form $\exists\{x\}.\{C(x)\}$. If, in our example, the TBox additionally says that rich and poor are disjoint, using the concept inclusion $Poor \sqcap Rich \sqsubseteq \bot$, and the qABox states that Ann has an (anonymous) child that is a poor celebrity, then the entailed inconsistency can be repaired by preventing the consequence $\exists\{x\}.\{(Poor \sqcap Rich)(x)\}$.

The added expressivity also allows us to specify interesting kinds of unwanted consequences other than instance relationships. On the one hand, we can deal with regular reachability queries, which are similar to regular path queries (Calvanese, Eiter, and Ortiz 2009). On the other hand, we can also treat certain kinds of conjunctive queries. The problem of repairing w.r.t. conjunctive queries to qABoxes has already been considered, in the guise of achieving compliance for relational datasets with labelled nulls, in (Grau and Kostylev 2019). However, this work does not allow for background TBoxes, and the notion of optimality used there is different from ours since it restricts the possible changes to the qABox to a sequence of certain anonymization operations. Finally, our repair approach can also deal with Horn-$\mathcal{ALCOI}$-TBoxes together with sets of regular role inclusion axioms.

Due to space restrictions, full proofs of our results are given in (Baader and Kriegel 2022).

2 Preliminaries

First, we introduce the DL $\mathcal{ELROI}$ employed to formulate terminological background knowledge, and the quantified ABoxes with equalities used to represent the data. Then we describe how such an ABox can be saturated w.r.t. the terminological knowledge, and finally define regular sets of role inclusions and show how to represent them using finite automata.

2.1 The Description Logic $\mathcal{ELROI}$

The DL $\mathcal{ELROI}$ extends $\mathcal{EL}$ with (complex) role inclusions ($\mathcal{R}$), nominals ($\mathcal{O}$), and inverse roles ($\mathcal{I}$). Let Σ be a *signature*, i.e., a disjoint union of finite, non-empty sets Σ_I, Σ_C, and Σ_R of *individual names*, *concept names*, and *role names*, respectively. A *role* is either a role name or an *inverse role* r^- for some role name $r \in \Sigma_\mathsf{R}$. For a role R we write R^- to denote r^- if $R = r$ is a role name and r if $R = r^-$ is an inverse role. Concept descriptions C of $\mathcal{ELROI}$ are constructed using the grammar rule

$$C ::= \top \mid A \mid \{a\} \mid C \sqcap C \mid \exists R.C,$$

where A ranges over concept names, a over individual names, and R over roles. An *atom* is a concept name A, a *nominal* $\{a\}$, or an *existential restriction* $\exists R.C$. Each concept description C is a conjunction of atoms, with $\top$ corresponding to the empty conjunction. We denote the set of these atoms as $\mathsf{Conj}(C)$.

A *concept inclusion (CI)* is of the form $C \sqsubseteq D$ for concept descriptions C, D, and a *role inclusion (RI)* is of the form $\varepsilon \sqsubseteq S$ or $R_1 \circ \cdots \circ R_n \sqsubseteq S$ for roles $R_1, \dots, R_n, S$ and $n \geq 1$. In the following, when we write $R_1 \circ \cdots \circ R_n \sqsubseteq S$, we assume that $n \geq 0$, where $R_1 \circ \cdots \circ R_n$ for $n = 0$ stands for ε. A *TBox* is a finite set of CIs, an *RBox* is a finite set of RIs, and a pair $(\mathcal{T}, \mathcal{R})$ consisting of a TBox $\mathcal{T}$ and an RBox $\mathcal{R}$ is called a *terminology*. A *concept assertion* $C(a)$ is a shorthand for the CI $\{a\} \sqsubseteq C$, and a *role assertion* $r(a, b)$ abbreviates $\{a\} \sqsubseteq \exists r.\{b\}$. Furthermore, $r^-(a, b)$ means $r(b, a)$.

The semantics of $\mathcal{ELROI}$ is defined as usual (Baader et al. 2017; Horrocks, Kutz, and Sattler 2006) using the notion of an *interpretation* $\mathcal{I} = (\mathsf{Dom}(\mathcal{I}), \cdot^\mathcal{I})$, which assigns subsets $C^\mathcal{I}$ of $\mathsf{Dom}(\mathcal{I})$ to concepts C and binary relations $R^\mathcal{I}$ on $\mathsf{Dom}(\mathcal{I})$ to roles R according to the semantics of the constructors. Individual names a are mapped to elements $a^\mathcal{I}$ of $\mathsf{Dom}(\mathcal{I})$, without requiring the *unique name assumption*, i.e., $a^\mathcal{I} = b^\mathcal{I}$ is allowed for distinct individual names a, b. Models of TBoxes and RBoxes are also defined in the usual way. We say that the terminology $(\mathcal{T}, \mathcal{R})$ *entails* a CI or RI α (written $(\mathcal{T}, \mathcal{R}) \models \alpha$) if α holds in every model of $\mathcal{T}$ and $\mathcal{R}$. In case $(\mathcal{T}, \mathcal{R}) \models C \sqsubseteq D$ we say that C *is subsumed by* D w.r.t. $(\mathcal{T}, \mathcal{R})$, and may write $C \sqsubseteq^{\mathcal{T},\mathcal{R}} D$ to express this.

Note that other interesting axioms concerning roles can be expressed using RIs and inverse roles. Reflexivity, transitivity, and symmetry of r can respectively be enforced by the RIs $\varepsilon \sqsubseteq r$, $r \circ r \sqsubseteq r$, and $r \sqsubseteq r^-$, and *range restrictions* $\mathsf{Ran}(r) \sqsubseteq C$ can be expressed by CIs $\exists r^-.\top \sqsubseteq C$.

This last observation shows that subsumption in $\mathcal{ELROI}$ is actually undecidable since it was shown in (Baader, Lutz, and Brandt 2008) that subsumption in $\mathcal{EL}$ w.r.t. RIs and range restrictions is undecidable. We will avoid this problem by imposing a restriction on RBoxes (see Section 2.4).

2.2 Quantified ABoxes with Equalities

Quantified ABoxes were first introduced in (Baader et al. 2020), but they were also considered, as relational datasets with labelled nulls, in (Grau and Kostylev 2019), and their existentially quantified variables correspond to the "anonymous individuals" in the OWL 2 standard. Also, as explained in (Baader et al. 2020), quantified ABoxes are basically the same as Boolean conjunctive queries. Here, we extend this notion by allowing for equality assertions, but for simplicity still use the name "quantified ABoxes" for the extended formalism. Equality assertions are used to represent implied equality between individuals; e.g., the CI $\{a\} \sqsubseteq \{b\}$ implies that a and b must always be interpreted by the same element of the domain.

Let Σ be a signature. A *quantified ABox (qABox)* $\exists X.\mathcal{A}$ over Σ consists of a finite set X of *variables*, which is disjoint with Σ, and a *matrix* $\mathcal{A}$, which is a finite set of *concept assertions* $A(u)$, *role assertions* $r(u, v)$, and *equality assertions* $a \equiv b$, where $A \in \Sigma_\mathsf{C}$, $r \in \Sigma_\mathsf{R}$, $u, v \in \Sigma_\mathsf{I} \cup X$, and $a, b \in \Sigma_\mathsf{I}$. An *object name* of $\exists X.\mathcal{A}$ is either an element of Σ_I or a variable in X. We denote the set of these objects as $\mathsf{Obj}(\exists X.\mathcal{A})$. If X is empty, then we sometimes drop the quantifier $\exists\emptyset$.

The interpretation $\mathcal{I}$ is a *model* of $\exists X.\mathcal{A}$ (written $\mathcal{I} \models \exists X.\mathcal{A}$) if there is a *variable assignment* $\mathcal{Z}\colon X \to \mathsf{Dom}(\mathcal{I})$ such that the augmented interpretation $\mathcal{I}[\mathcal{Z}]$ that additionally maps each variable x to $\mathcal{Z}(x)$ is a model of the matrix $\mathcal{A}$, i.e., $u^{\mathcal{I}[\mathcal{Z}]} \in A^\mathcal{I}$ for each $A(u) \in \mathcal{A}$, $(u^{\mathcal{I}[\mathcal{Z}]}, v^{\mathcal{I}[\mathcal{Z}]}) \in r^\mathcal{I}$ for each $r(u, v) \in \mathcal{A}$, and $a^\mathcal{I} = b^\mathcal{I}$ for each $a \equiv b \in \mathcal{A}$. Given a terminology $(\mathcal{T}, \mathcal{R})$ and qABoxes $\exists X.\mathcal{A}$ and $\exists Y.\mathcal{B}$, we say that $\exists X.\mathcal{A}$ *entails* $\exists Y.\mathcal{B}$ w.r.t. $(\mathcal{T}, \mathcal{R})$ (written $\exists X.\mathcal{A} \models^{\mathcal{T},\mathcal{R}} \exists Y.\mathcal{B}$) if every model of $\exists X.\mathcal{A}$ and $(\mathcal{T}, \mathcal{R})$ is also a model of $\exists Y.\mathcal{B}$. If both the TBox $\mathcal{T}$ and the RBox $\mathcal{R}$ are empty, then we omit the suffix "w.r.t. $(\mathcal{T}, \mathcal{R})$" and write $\models$ instead of $\models^{\mathcal{T},\mathcal{R}}$. Similar simplifications are made if one of them is empty.

For qABoxes without equality assertions, it was shown in (Baader et al. 2020) that entailment can be characterized using homomorphisms. In our extended setting, we need to adapt the definition of a homomorphism between qABoxes. To this purpose, we consider the equivalence relation $\approx_{\exists X.\mathcal{A}}$ on $\mathsf{Obj}(\exists X.\mathcal{A})$ induced by the equality assertions in $\exists X.\mathcal{A}$, which is defined as the reflexive, symmetric, transitive closure of the relation $\{\, (a, b) \mid a \equiv b \in \mathcal{A} \,\}$. We sometimes write $\approx$ for $\approx_{\exists X.\mathcal{A}}$ if the qABox is clear from the context, and denote the equivalence classes by $[u]_{\exists X.\mathcal{A}}$. Since there are no equality assertions involving variables, each equivalence class of a variable is a singleton set.

Definition 1. A *homomorphism* h from a qABox $\exists X.\mathcal{A}$ to a qABox $\exists Y.\mathcal{B}$ is a mapping $h\colon \mathsf{Obj}(\exists X.\mathcal{A}) \to \mathsf{Obj}(\exists Y.\mathcal{B})$ that satisfies the following conditions:

(Hom1) $a \approx_{\exists X.\mathcal{A}} b$ implies $h(a) \approx_{\exists Y.\mathcal{B}} h(b)$ for all individual names a, b.

(Hom2) $h(a) = a$ for each individual name a.

(Hom3) For each concept assertion $A(t) \in \mathcal{A}$, there is an object name v such that $v \approx_{\exists Y.\mathcal{B}} h(t)$ and $A(v) \in \mathcal{B}$.

(Hom4) For each role assertion $r(t, u) \in \mathcal{A}$, there are object names v, w such that $v \approx_{\exists Y.\mathcal{B}} h(t)$, $w \approx_{\exists Y.\mathcal{B}} h(u)$, and $r(v, w) \in \mathcal{B}$.

Based on this notion of homomorphism, entailment between qABoxes with equality assertions can now be characterized as follows.

Conjunction Rule. If $\mathcal{B}$ contains the assertion $(C_1 \sqcap \cdots \sqcap C_n)(t)$ for $n \neq 1$, then remove it from $\mathcal{B}$ and add the assertions $C_1(t), \ldots, C_n(t)$ to $\mathcal{B}$.

Existential Restriction Rule. If $\mathcal{B}$ contains the assertion $\exists R.C(t)$, then remove it from $\mathcal{B}$, add a fresh variable y to Y, and add the assertions $R(t, y)$ and $C(y)$ to $\mathcal{B}$.

Nominal Rule. If $\mathcal{B}$ contains the assertion $\{a\}(t)$, then remove it from $\mathcal{B}$ and, if t is an individual name, then add the equality $t \equiv a$ to $\mathcal{B}$; otherwise replace every occurrence of t in $\mathcal{B}$ by a and remove t from Y.

Concept Inclusion Rule. If $\mathcal{T}$ contains the CI $C \sqsubseteq D$ and $\mathcal{B}$ entails the concept assertion $C(t)$, but not $D(t)$, then add the concept assertion $D(t)$ to $\mathcal{B}$.

Role Inclusion Rule. If $\mathcal{R}$ contains the RI $R_1 \circ \cdots \circ R_n \sqsubseteq S$ and $\mathcal{B}$ entails the role assertions $R_1(t_0, t_1), \ldots, R_n(t_{n-1}, t_n)$, but not $S(t_0, t_n)$, then add the role assertion $S(t_0, t_n)$ to $\mathcal{B}$.

Figure 1: The saturation rules are exhaustively applied to a qABox $\exists Y.\mathcal{B}$ w.r.t. a terminology $(\mathcal{T}, \mathcal{R})$, starting with $\exists Y.\mathcal{B} := \exists X.\mathcal{A}$ for an input qABox $\exists X.\mathcal{A}$.

Proposition 2. *The qABox $\exists X.\mathcal{A}$ is entailed by the qABox $\exists Y.\mathcal{B}$ iff there exists a homomorphism from $\exists X.\mathcal{A}$ to $\exists Y.\mathcal{B}$.*

As in the case of qABoxes without equality assertions, this provides us with an NP decision procedure for entailment. NP-hardness already holds without equality assertions (Baader et al. 2020).

We often need to consider the matrix $\mathcal{A}$ of a quantified ABox $\exists X.\mathcal{A}$ alone, without the quantifier prefix. We can view $\mathcal{A}$ to be an "ordinary" ABox without quantifiers (or equivalently as a qABox with empty quantifier prefix) by extending the signature to $\Sigma \cup X$, where variables are treated as individuals. This allows us to evaluate entailment expressions like $\mathcal{A} \models C(x)$, where C is a concept description and $x \in X$, using interpretations and models for the extended signature.

2.3 Saturation

The purpose of saturation is to extend a given qABox $\exists X.\mathcal{A}$ with enough consequences derived using the terminology $(\mathcal{T}, \mathcal{R})$ such that entailment from $\exists X.\mathcal{A}$ w.r.t. $(\mathcal{T}, \mathcal{R})$ is the same as entailment from its saturation $\mathsf{sat}^{\mathcal{T},\mathcal{R}}(\exists X.\mathcal{A}) = \exists Y.\mathcal{B}$ w.r.t. the empty terminology. The rules in Figure 1 extend the CQ-saturation rules in (Baader et al. 2021) such that nominals, inverse roles, and RIs are taken into account. Note that, during saturation, the matrix $\mathcal{B}$ may contain complex concept assertions, but after termination all concept assertions are again restricted to concept names. The semantics of qABoxes with complex concept assertions is defined in the obvious way.

In general, application of the saturation rules need not terminate, already in the $\mathcal{EL}$ setting considered in (Baader et al. 2021). But there the restriction to cycle-restricted TBoxes guarantees termination, where an $\mathcal{EL}$ TBox $\mathcal{T}$ is cycle-restricted if there is no concept C and roles $r_1, \ldots, r_n$ $(n \geq 1)$ such that $C \sqsubseteq_{\mathcal{T}} \exists r_1. \cdots \exists r_n.C$. For $\mathcal{ELROI}$ terminologies, the RBox may cause non-termination even if the TBox is cycle-restricted.

Example 3. Consider the $\mathcal{ELROI}$ TBox $\mathcal{T} := \{A \sqsubseteq \exists r.\top, \exists s.\top \sqsubseteq \exists s.A\}$, the RBox $\mathcal{R} := \{r \sqsubseteq s\}$, and the qABox $\exists\emptyset.\mathcal{A}$ with $\mathcal{A} := \{A(a)\}$. The TBox $\mathcal{T}$ is cycle-restricted and saturation of $\exists\emptyset.\mathcal{A}$ with $(\mathcal{T}, \emptyset)$ terminates after a has received an r-successor x_1. However, w.r.t. $(\mathcal{T}, \mathcal{R})$, the role inclusion rule makes x_1 also an s-successor of a. The concept inclusion rule then adds an s-successor y_1 of a and the assertion $A(y_1)$. But now y_1 receives an r-successor x_2, which becomes an s-successor of y_1, etc.

Since our repair approach works on saturated qABoxes, it can only be applied in the presence of terminologies $(\mathcal{T}, \mathcal{R})$ that are terminating in the following sense.

Definition 4. The terminology $(\mathcal{T}, \mathcal{R})$ is *terminating* if, for each qABox $\exists X.\mathcal{A}$, there is a finite sequence of applications of the saturation rules in Figure 1 to $\exists X.\mathcal{A}$ resulting in a qABox to which no more rule applies. We then denote this qABox as $\mathsf{sat}^{\mathcal{T},\mathcal{R}}(\exists X.\mathcal{A})$ and call it the *saturation* of $\exists X.\mathcal{A}$ w.r.t. $(\mathcal{T}, \mathcal{R})$.

We refrain here from giving our own decidable sufficient condition for termination of a terminology $(\mathcal{T}, \mathcal{R})$. Instead, we point out that one can translate the concept inclusions in $\mathcal{T}$ and the role inclusions in $\mathcal{R}$ into a set of existential rules, and that saturation then corresponds to applying the so-called chase. One can thus try to use one of the numerous acyclicity conditions guaranteeing chase termination proposed in the database and rules communities (see, e.g., (Grau et al. 2013)) to show termination of $(\mathcal{T}, \mathcal{R})$. The saturation obtained in case of termination has the following important property.

Theorem 5. *Let $(\mathcal{T}, \mathcal{R})$ be a terminating terminology and $\exists X.\mathcal{A}$ a quantified ABox. Then, for every qABox $\exists Z.\mathcal{C}$, the following statements are equivalent:*

1. $\exists X.\mathcal{A} \models^{\mathcal{T},\mathcal{R}} \exists Z.\mathcal{C}$.
2. $\mathsf{sat}^{\mathcal{T},\mathcal{R}}(\exists X.\mathcal{A}) \models \exists Z.\mathcal{C}$.
3. *There is a homomorphism from $\exists Z.\mathcal{C}$ to $\mathsf{sat}^{\mathcal{T},\mathcal{R}}(\exists X.\mathcal{A})$.*

In (Baader et al. 2021), a different kind of saturation, called IQ-saturation, was introduced, which always terminates. Using IQ-saturation in the repair process was shown to be sufficient if one is only interested in instance queries. However, due to the presence of inverse roles in $\mathcal{ELROI}$, it is easy to see that finite IQ-saturations cannot always work (see (Baader and Kriegel 2022) for an example).

2.4 Regular RBoxes

As pointed out at the end of Section 2.1, subsumption is undecidable in $\mathcal{ELROI}$ if arbitrary RBoxes are allowed. In (Baader, Lutz, and Brandt 2008), tractability of $\mathcal{EL}^{++}$ is ensured by restricting the interaction between range restrictions and RIs. Since, in our setting, range restrictions are expressed using inverse roles and CIs, it is not clear how to adapt this solution. Instead, we use the regularity restriction imposed in (Horrocks, Kutz, and Sattler 2006; Kazakov 2008) to make $\mathcal{SROIQ}$ decidable, which is required by our repair approach anyway.

Definition 6. An RBox $\mathcal{R}$ is *regular* if, for each role R, the language $L_{\mathcal{R}}(R) := \{ S_1 \cdots S_n \mid S_1 \circ \cdots \circ S_n \sqsubseteq^{\mathcal{R}} R \}$ is regular. The sublogic of $\mathcal{ELROI}$ that only supports regular RBoxes is denoted by $\mathcal{ELR}_{\mathsf{reg}}\mathcal{OI}$.

Since $\mathcal{ELR}_{\mathsf{reg}}\mathcal{OI}$ is a fragment of Horn-$\mathcal{SROIQ}$, it inherits the complexity upper-bound of 2ExpTime (Ortiz, Rudolph, and Šimkus 2010). The exact complexity of subsumption in $\mathcal{ELR}_{\mathsf{reg}}\mathcal{OI}$ is open, with the best lower-bound of ExpTime inherited from $\mathcal{ELI}$ (Baader, Lutz, and Brandt 2008).

To the best of our knowledge, it is not known whether RBox regularity is decidable. Decidability of the closely related regularity problem for pure context-free grammars has been open for a long time (Maurer, Salomaa, and Wood 1980). However, there exist syntactic restrictions that guarantee regularity (Horrocks, Kutz, and Sattler 2006; Kazakov 2010), and if these restrictions apply then one can effectively construct (exponentially large) finite automata accepting the regular languages $L_{\mathcal{R}}(R)$.

Let $\mathcal{R}$ be a regular RBox, and for each role R, let $\mathfrak{A}_R = (Q_R, \Sigma_{\mathsf{R}}^{\pm}, i_R, \Delta_R, F_R)$ be a finite automaton (with set of states Q_R, the alphabet $\Sigma_{\mathsf{R}}^{\pm}$ of all roles, initial state i_R, transition relation Δ_R, and set of final states F_R) accepting $L_{\mathcal{R}}(R)$, i.e., such that $L(\mathfrak{A}_R) = L_{\mathcal{R}}(R)$. We assume without loss of generality (but in the worst-case paid for by another exponential blowup) that each automaton $\mathfrak{A}_R$ is deterministic. In addition, we assume that $\mathfrak{A}_R$ does not contain states that are unreachable from the initial state or from which no final state can be reached, and further that the sets Q_R for different R are pairwise disjoint and are all disjoint with the signature Σ. For each state $q \in Q_R$, the automaton $\mathfrak{A}_{\mathcal{R}}(q) := (Q_R, \Sigma_{\mathsf{R}}^{\pm}, q, \Delta_R, F_R)$ is obtained from $\mathfrak{A}_R$ by replacing the initial state i_R with q. We will use existential restrictions of the form $\exists q.C$ for $q \in Q_R$ as abbreviations for the (possibly infinite) disjunction $\bigsqcup\{ \exists S_1.\cdots\exists S_n.C \mid S_1 \cdots S_n \in L(\mathfrak{A}_{\mathcal{R}}(q)) \}$, i.e., in each interpretation $\mathcal{I}$, $(\exists q.C)^{\mathcal{I}}$ is defined to be

$$\bigcup\{ (\exists S_1.\cdots\exists S_n.C)^{\mathcal{I}} \mid S_1 \cdots S_n \in L(\mathfrak{A}_{\mathcal{R}}(q)) \}.$$

Entailment for such existential restrictions can be characterized as follows.

Lemma 7. *Given a qABox $\exists X.\mathcal{A}$, an object t of it, a terminology $(\mathcal{T}, \mathcal{R})$ with regular $\mathcal{R}$, $\mathcal{ELROI}$ concept descriptions C, D, and a state q. Then the following holds:*

1. $\mathcal{A} \models^{\mathcal{T},\mathcal{R}} \exists q.C(t)$ *iff there is a word* $S_1 \cdots S_n \in L(\mathfrak{A}_{\mathcal{R}}(q))$ *such that* $\mathcal{A} \models^{\mathcal{T},\mathcal{R}} \exists S_1.\cdots\exists S_n.C(t)$,
2. $D \sqsubseteq^{\mathcal{T},\mathcal{R}} \exists q.C$ *iff there is a word* $S_1 \cdots S_n \in L(\mathfrak{A}_{\mathcal{R}}(q))$ *such that* $D \sqsubseteq^{\mathcal{T},\mathcal{R}} \exists S_1.\cdots\exists S_n.C$.

If the terminology is terminating, we can decide whether the conditions for entailment stated in Lemma 7 hold. Basically, to check whether $\mathcal{A} \models^{\mathcal{T},\mathcal{R}} \exists q.C(t)$ holds, we simply need to find an accepting run of the automaton $\mathfrak{A}_{\mathcal{R}}(q)$ such that the accepted word corresponds to a path in the saturation $\mathsf{sat}^{\mathcal{T},\mathcal{R}}(\exists X.\mathcal{A})$ that starts with t and ends with an instance of C. This boils down to a reachability test in the product of the automaton with the saturation. The second condition in Lemma 7 can be reduced to the first one.

3 Optimal and Canonical Repairs

In this section, we first extend the notion of an (optimal) repair, as introduced in (Baader et al. 2021), to the more expressive DL $\mathcal{ELROI}$ and a setting where the repair request, which describes which consequences are to be removed, also contains global unwanted consequences. For regular sets of role inclusions, we show that every repair is entailed by a repair containing a bounded number of individuals. From this, we derive that the set of optimal repairs can effectively be computed and covers all repairs. Then, we extend the construction of canonical repairs of (Baader et al. 2021) from $\mathcal{EL}$ to $\mathcal{ELR}_{\mathsf{reg}}\mathcal{OI}$. The set of canonical repairs can effectively be computed, covers all repairs and thus contains all optimal repairs, and a repair seed determining such a canonical repair can be chosen by answering a polynomial number of instance queries. Throughout the section, we assume (unless specified otherwise) that $\exists X.\mathcal{A}$ is a quantified ABox, $\mathcal{T}$ an $\mathcal{ELROI}$ TBox, $\mathcal{R}$ a regular RBox, all defined over the same signature Σ, and that $(\mathcal{T}, \mathcal{R})$ is terminating.

Definition 8. A *repair request* $\mathcal{P}$ is a union of a finite set $\mathcal{P}_{\mathsf{loc}}$ of $\mathcal{ELROI}$ concept assertions, the *local* request, and of a finite set $\mathcal{P}_{\mathsf{glo}}$ of $\mathcal{ELROI}$ concept descriptions, the *global* request. A *repair* of $\exists X.\mathcal{A}$ for $\mathcal{P}$ w.r.t. $(\mathcal{T}, \mathcal{R})$ is a quantified ABox $\exists Y.\mathcal{B}$ that fulfills the following properties:

(Rep1) $\exists X.\mathcal{A} \models^{\mathcal{T},\mathcal{R}} \exists Y.\mathcal{B}$,

(Rep2) $\exists Y.\mathcal{B} \not\models^{\mathcal{T},\mathcal{R}} C(a)$ for each $C(a) \in \mathcal{P}_{\mathsf{loc}}$,

(Rep3) $\exists Y.\mathcal{B} \not\models^{\mathcal{T},\mathcal{R}} \exists\{x\}.\{D(x)\}$ for each $D \in \mathcal{P}_{\mathsf{glo}}$.

This repair is *optimal* if there is no repair $\exists Z.\mathcal{C}$ such that $\exists Z.\mathcal{C} \models^{\mathcal{T},\mathcal{R}} \exists Y.\mathcal{B}$, but $\exists Y.\mathcal{B} \not\models^{\mathcal{T},\mathcal{R}} \exists Z.\mathcal{C}$. We say that a set of repairs $\mathfrak{S}$ *covers* all repairs if every repair is entailed w.r.t. $(\mathcal{T}, \mathcal{R})$ by a repair in $\mathfrak{S}$.

Obviously, $\exists X.\mathcal{A}$ has a repair for $\mathcal{P}$ w.r.t. $(\mathcal{T}, \mathcal{R})$ iff the terminology alone does not imply any of the unwanted consequences in $\mathcal{P}$, since then the empty ABox is a repair. The restriction to terminating terminologies and regular RBoxes is needed to ensure that any repair problem has a finite set of optimal repairs covering all repairs. The proof of Proposition 2 in (Baader et al. 2018) contains an example with non-terminating terminology where there is no optimal repair, though there is a repair. However, in this proof it is only shown that there cannot be an optimal repair that is an ABox. While this proof can be adapted to deal also with qABoxes, we present here a modified example with exactly one optimal repair, which however does not cover all repairs.

Example 9. Assume that $\mathcal{T} := \{A \sqsubseteq \exists r.A,\ \exists r.A \sqsubseteq A\}$, $\mathcal{R} := \emptyset$, $\mathcal{A} := \{A(a), B(a)\}$, and $\mathcal{P} := \{(A \sqcap B)(a)\}$. Then $\exists\{x\}.\{A(a), A(x), B(x)\}$ is an optimal repair of $\exists\emptyset.\mathcal{A}$ for $\mathcal{P}$ w.r.t. $(\mathcal{T}, \mathcal{R})$. However, there are also repairs in which the concept assertion $B(a)$ is retained, and $A(a)$ is removed. To see that there cannot be an optimal repair containing $B(a)$, first note that $\mathcal{A}$ together with $\mathcal{T}$ does not imply the existence of any role cycle, and thus no repair can contain such a cycle. Consequently, for an optimal repair $\exists Y.\mathcal{B}$ containing $B(a)$, there is an upper bound n on the length of role chains starting from a. Adding $r(a, y_1), r(y_2, y_3), \ldots, r(y_n, y_{n+1})$ for fresh existentially quantified variables $y_1, \ldots, y_{n+1}$ to

$\exists Y.\mathcal{B}$ then yields a new repair that strictly implies $\exists Y.\mathcal{B}$, which contradicts the assumed optimality of this repair.

The following example shows that non-regularity of the RBox may prevent all repairs from being covered by a finite set of repairs.

Example 10. The RBox $\mathcal{R} := \{r^- \circ s \circ r \sqsubseteq s\}$ is not regular since $L_\mathcal{R}(s) = \{(r^-)^i s r^i \mid i \geq 0\}$ is a context-free language over the alphabet $\{r^-, s, r\}$ known to be non-regular. Together with the TBox $\mathcal{T} := \{\exists s.A \sqsubseteq A,\ \exists s.B \sqsubseteq B\}$, this RBox yields a terminating terminology. Consider the ABox $\mathcal{A} := \{r(a,a), s(a,a), A(a), B(a)\}$ and the repair request $\mathcal{P} = \mathcal{P}_{\mathsf{glo}} := \{A \sqcap B\}$. It is not hard to see that, for each $n \geq 1$, the qABox $\exists X_n.\mathcal{A}_n$ is a repair of $\exists\emptyset.\mathcal{A}$ for $\mathcal{P}$ w.r.t. $(\mathcal{T},\mathcal{R})$, where $X_n := \{x_1,\ldots,x_n\}$ and

$$\begin{aligned}\mathcal{A}_n := \{\, & r(a,x_1), r(x_1,x_2),\ldots, r(x_{n-1},x_n),\\ & s(a,a), s(x_1,x_1),\ldots, s(x_n,x_n),\\ & A(a), A(x_1), A(x_2),\ldots, A(x_{n-1}), B(x_n)\,\}.\end{aligned}$$

Assume that $\mathfrak{S}$ is a finite set of repairs of $\exists\emptyset.\mathcal{A}$ for $\mathcal{P}$ w.r.t. $(\mathcal{T},\mathcal{R})$ that covers all repairs, and let n be larger than the maximal number of objects occurring in the elements of $\mathfrak{S}$. Without loss of generality we assume that the elements of $\mathfrak{S}$ are saturated w.r.t. $(\mathcal{T},\mathcal{R})$. Then there must exist a repair $\exists Y.\mathcal{B}$ in $\mathfrak{S}$ such that there is a homomorphism h from $\exists X_n.\mathcal{A}_n$ to $\exists Y.\mathcal{B}$. Since $\mathcal{B}$ contains less than n objects, there must be i,j with $1 \leq i < j \leq n$ such that $h(x_i) = h(x_j)$. Consequently, $h(x_n)$ is reachable from $h(a)$ with the role r both in n steps and in $m < n$ steps, where $m = n-(j-i)$. Since $h(x_m)$ is also reachable in m steps from $h(a)$ and $s(h(a),h(a))$ must be in $\mathcal{B}$, the fact that $\exists Y.\mathcal{B}$ is saturated implies that $s(h(x_n),h(x_m))$ must belong to $\mathcal{B}$. Since $A(x_m) \in \mathcal{A}_n$ yields $A(h(x_m)) \in \mathcal{B}$, this implies that $A(h(x_n)) \in \mathcal{B}$. However, since $B(x_n) \in \mathcal{A}_n$ also yields $B(h(x_n) \in \mathcal{B}$, this contradicts our assumption that $\exists Y.\mathcal{B}$ is a repair for $\mathcal{P}$.

The Small Repair Property If we restrict the attention to terminating terminologies with regular RBoxes $\mathcal{R}$, then we can show that the repairs of a certain bounded size cover all repairs. For an $\mathcal{ELROI}$ TBox $\mathcal{T}$ and a repair request $\mathcal{P}$, let $\mathsf{Sub}(\mathcal{T},\mathcal{P})$ denote the set of concept descriptions occurring in $\mathcal{T}$ and $\mathcal{P}$ and $\mathsf{Atoms}(\mathcal{T},\mathcal{P})$ the set of atoms in this set. To take the RBox into account, we introduce the set of *$\mathcal{R}$-extended atoms* $\mathsf{Atoms}_\mathcal{R}(\mathcal{T},\mathcal{P})$, which is obtained from $\mathsf{Atoms}(\mathcal{T},\mathcal{P})$ by replacing each $\exists R.C \in \mathsf{Atoms}(\mathcal{T},\mathcal{P})$ with the existential restrictions $\exists q.C$, where q ranges over Q_R (i.e., the set of states of the automaton for $L_\mathcal{R}(R)$).

Proposition 11. *Let $(\mathcal{T},\mathcal{R})$ be a terminating $\mathcal{ELROI}$ terminology with regular RBox, $\mathcal{P}$ an $\mathcal{ELROI}$ repair request, $\exists X.\mathcal{A}$ a (w.l.o.g) saturated qABox with m objects, and $n := |\mathsf{Atoms}(\mathcal{T},\mathcal{P}) \cup \mathsf{Atoms}_\mathcal{R}(\mathcal{T},\mathcal{P})|$. Then every repair of $\exists X.\mathcal{A}$ for $\mathcal{P}$ w.r.t. $(\mathcal{T},\mathcal{R})$ is entailed w.r.t. $(\mathcal{T},\mathcal{R})$ by a repair that contains at most $m\cdot 2^n$ objects.*

This proposition can be shown by adapting the well-known filtration technique, e.g., used in (Baader et al. 2017) to prove the finite model property for $\mathcal{ALC}$. Let $\exists Y.\mathcal{B}$ be a repair of $\exists X.\mathcal{A}$ for $\mathcal{P}$ w.r.t. $(\mathcal{T},\mathcal{R})$, and assume without loss of generality that it is saturated. Since $\exists X.\mathcal{A}$ entails every repair and is also assumed to be saturated, there is a homomorphism h from $\exists Y.\mathcal{B}$ to $\exists X.\mathcal{A}$. For objects u of $\exists Y.\mathcal{B}$, we set $t(u) := \{\, C \mid C \in \mathsf{Atoms}(\mathcal{T},\mathcal{P}) \cup \mathsf{Atoms}_\mathcal{R}(\mathcal{T},\mathcal{P})$ and $\mathcal{B} \models C(u)\,\}$, and define the equivalence relation $\sim$ on these objects as

$$u \sim v \text{ iff } t(u) = t(v) \text{ and } h(u) = h(v).$$

Obviously, $\sim$ has at most $m\cdot 2^n$ equivalence classes $[u]_\sim$. The filtration $\exists Z.\mathcal{C}$ has these equivalence classes as objects, with the class $[a]_\sim$ standing for the individual a. The classes inherit their concept and role assertions from the ones of their elements in $\mathcal{B}$ (see (Baader and Kriegel 2022) for details). We can then show, for all $C \in \mathsf{Atoms}(\mathcal{T},\mathcal{P}) \cup \mathsf{Atoms}_\mathcal{R}(\mathcal{T},\mathcal{P})$ and for all $u \in \mathsf{Obj}(\exists Y.\mathcal{B})$, that

$$\mathcal{C} \models C([u]_\sim) \text{ iff } \mathcal{B} \models C(u).$$

Since $\exists Y.\mathcal{B}$ is a saturated repair, this implies that $\exists Z.\mathcal{C}$ is saturated w.r.t. $\mathcal{T}$ and does not entail (w.r.t. $\mathcal{T}$) any of the unwanted consequences specified by $\mathcal{P}$. The filtration $\exists Z.\mathcal{C}$ need not be saturated w.r.t. $\mathcal{R}$, but we can show that its saturation w.r.t. $\mathcal{R}$ does not entail additional instance relationships for atoms in $\mathsf{Atoms}(\mathcal{T},\mathcal{P}) \cup \mathsf{Atoms}_\mathcal{R}(\mathcal{T},\mathcal{P})$. This implies that, also w.r.t. $(\mathcal{T},\mathcal{R})$, the filtration does not entail any of the unwanted consequences in $\mathcal{P}$. Finally, it is easy to check that $u \mapsto [u]_\sim$ is a homomorphism from the repair $\exists Y.\mathcal{B}$ to the filtration $\exists Z.\mathcal{C}$, and that $[u]_\sim \mapsto h(u)$ is a homomorphism from $\exists Z.\mathcal{C}$ to the input qABox $\exists X.\mathcal{A}$. Thus, the filtration $\exists Z.\mathcal{C}$ is a repair with at most $m\cdot 2^n$ objects that entails $\exists Y.\mathcal{B}$.

Since, for a fixed signature and up to renaming of variables, there are only finitely many qABoxes containing at most $m\cdot 2^n$ objects, we can effectively construct the set of optimal repairs of $\exists X.\mathcal{A}$ for $\mathcal{P}$ w.r.t. $(\mathcal{T},\mathcal{R})$ by enumerating these qABoxes, then removing the ones that are not repairs, and finally removing from the remaining set the elements that are strictly entailed by an other element.

Theorem 12. *Let $\exists X.\mathcal{A}$ be a qABox, $(\mathcal{T},\mathcal{R})$ a terminating $\mathcal{ELROI}$ terminology with regular RBox whose associated automata can effectively be computed, and $\mathcal{P}$ an $\mathcal{ELROI}$ repair request. Then the set of all optimal repairs of $\exists X.\mathcal{A}$ for $\mathcal{P}$ w.r.t. $(\mathcal{T},\mathcal{R})$ can, up to equivalence, effectively be computed, and every repair is entailed by an optimal repair.*

The following example shows that the "automata atoms" in $\mathsf{Atoms}_\mathcal{R}(\mathcal{T},\mathcal{P})$ are needed for the filtration.

Example 13. Assume that $\mathcal{T} := \emptyset$, $\mathcal{R} := \{r \circ r \sqsubseteq s\}$, $\mathcal{A} := \{r(a,b), r(b,c), s(a,c)\}$, and $\mathcal{P} := \{\exists s.\top(a)\}$. The qABox $\exists\{x\}.\{r(a,b), r(x,c)\}$ is a (saturated) repair of $\exists\emptyset.\mathcal{A}$ for $\mathcal{P}$ w.r.t. $(\mathcal{T},\mathcal{R})$. If we used only $\mathsf{Atoms}(\mathcal{T},\mathcal{P}) = \{\exists s.\top\}$ for the filtration, then the objects b and x would be identified since they behave the same w.r.t. this concept in the repair. Thus, $[a]_\sim$ would have $[x]_\sim = [b]_\sim$ as r-successor in the filtration, which in turn would have $[c]_\sim$ as r-successor. This shows that the filtration would have $\exists s.\top(a)$ as a consequence, and thus would not be a repair. The regular language $L_\mathcal{R}(s) = \{rr, s\}$ is accepted by a deterministic automaton with three states, q_0, q_1, q_2, where q_0 is initial and q_2 is final, r-transitions from q_0 to q_1 and from q_1 to q_2, and an s-transition from q_0 to q_2. Since the object x belongs to $\exists q_1.\top$, but b does not, they are not identified in the filtration that takes the concepts in $\mathsf{Atoms}_{\mathcal{R}}(\mathcal{T},\mathcal{P}) = \{\exists q_i.\top \mid 0 \leq i \leq 2\}$ into account.

Canonical Repairs Instead of blindly searching for optimal repairs among the very large set of "small" repairs, we now show how the considerably smaller set of canonical repairs, which contains all optimal repairs, can be constructed from repair seeds. Such a repair seed is of polynomial size, and it basically specifies which atoms in $\mathsf{Atoms}(\mathcal{T},\mathcal{P}) \cup \mathsf{Atoms}_{\mathcal{R}}(\mathcal{T},\mathcal{P})$ need to be removed for each individual.

From now on, we assume that $\exists Y.\mathcal{B}$ is the saturation of $\exists X.\mathcal{A}$ w.r.t. $(\mathcal{T},\mathcal{R})$. Our canonical repairs will actually be computed from $\exists Y.\mathcal{B}$. As mentioned in the introduction, to achieve optimality, it is not sufficient to remove assertions from this qABox. We must also generate anonymous copies of its objects. Basically, these copies are induced by pairs $(u,\mathcal{K})$ where u is an object in $\mathcal{B}$ and $\mathcal{K} \subseteq \mathsf{Atoms}_{\mathcal{R}}(\mathcal{T},\mathcal{P})$ is a set of atoms C such that u is an instance of C in $\exists Y.\mathcal{B}$. Putting an atom into $\mathcal{K}$ means that the copy of u induced by $(u,\mathcal{K})$ should not be an instance of C.

Recall that $\mathsf{Conj}(C)$ is the set of all top-level conjuncts of a concept description C. The set $\mathsf{Conj}_{\mathcal{R}}(C)$ is obtained from $\mathsf{Conj}(C)$ by replacing each existential restriction $\exists R.D \in \mathsf{Conj}(C)$ with $\exists i_R.D$. The sets $\mathcal{K}$ used to construct copies of u must be repair types for u.

Definition 14. Let u be an object name of $\exists Y.\mathcal{B}$. A *repair type* for u is a set $\mathcal{K} \subseteq \mathsf{Atoms}_{\mathcal{R}}(\mathcal{T},\mathcal{P})$ satisfying:

(RT1) If $C \in \mathcal{K}$, then $\mathcal{B} \models C(u)$.

(RT2) If $D \in \mathsf{Sub}(\mathcal{T},\mathcal{P}) \cup \mathsf{Atoms}_{\mathcal{R}}(\mathcal{T},\mathcal{P})$ with $\mathcal{B} \models D(u)$ and $C \in \mathcal{K}$ with $D \sqsubseteq^{\mathcal{T},\mathcal{R}} C$, then $\mathsf{Conj}_{\mathcal{R}}(D) \cap \mathcal{K} \neq \emptyset$.

(RT3) If $E \in \mathcal{P}_{\mathsf{glo}}$ and $\mathcal{B} \models E(u)$, then $\mathsf{Conj}_{\mathcal{R}}(E) \cap \mathcal{K} \neq \emptyset$.

The first condition says that only concept assertions that really hold for u need to be removed. The second condition ensures that concept assertions that are removed for u cannot be reintroduced by the terminology. The third condition has the effect that no copy can be an instance of a concept description that occurs in the global request.

In the canonical repairs, one of the copies of each individual will stand for this individual, whereas the other copies are variables. In addition, some individuals that are equal w.r.t. $\exists Y.\mathcal{B}$ may no longer be equal in the repair. The repair seed makes these decisions explicit.

Definition 15. A *repair seed* $\mathcal{S}$ consists of an equivalence relation $\approx_{\mathcal{S}}$ on $\mathsf{Obj}(\exists Y.\mathcal{B})$ that is a refinement of $\approx_{\exists Y.\mathcal{B}}$ (i.e., $\approx_{\mathcal{S}} \subseteq \approx_{\exists Y.\mathcal{B}}$) and of a function that maps each equivalence class $[a]_{\mathcal{S}}$ of an individual a w.r.t. $\approx_{\mathcal{S}}$ to a repair type $\mathcal{S}_{[a]_{\mathcal{S}}}$ for a, such that the following conditions are fulfilled:

(RS1) If $C(a) \in \mathcal{P}_{\mathsf{loc}}$ and $\mathcal{B} \models C(a)$, then $\mathsf{Conj}_{\mathcal{R}}(C) \cap \mathcal{S}_{[a]_{\mathcal{S}}} \neq \emptyset$.

(RS2) If a, b are individuals and $\{a\} \in \mathsf{Atoms}(\mathcal{T},\mathcal{P})$, then $\{a\} \in \mathcal{S}_{[b]_{\mathcal{S}}}$ iff $a \approx_{\exists Y.\mathcal{B}} b$ and $a \not\approx_{\mathcal{S}} b$.

The first condition guarantees that the repair induced by the seed satisfies the local request. The second condition ensures that the decision made by the seed that two individuals should no longer be equal is respected in the repair.

In contrast to the case of $\mathcal{EL}$ (Baader et al. 2021), not every repair seed induces a canonical repair. The seed must satisfy an additional admissibility conditions. Due to space constraints, we can neither provide the definition of admissibility nor the one of canonical repairs here. They can be found in (Baader and Kriegel 2022), as can the proof of the next theorem.

Theorem 16. *For every admissible repair seed $\mathcal{S}$, the induced canonical repair can effectively be computed, is saturated w.r.t. $(\mathcal{T},\mathcal{R})$, and is a repair of $\exists X.\mathcal{A}$ for $\mathcal{P}$ w.r.t. $(\mathcal{T},\mathcal{R})$. Conversely, every repair of $\exists X.\mathcal{A}$ for $\mathcal{P}$ w.r.t. $(\mathcal{T},\mathcal{R})$ is entailed by such a canonical repair.*

Since all admissible repair seeds can effectively be generated, Theorem 12 can also be obtained as a corollary to this theorem. Even in the case without a terminology, not all canonical repairs need to be optimal (Baader et al. 2020), but we expect even the non-optimal ones to be quite good w.r.t. preserving consequences. One advantage of canonical repairs is that each one can be characterized by a polynomial-size repair seed, which can be generated by the knowledge engineers by making a polynomial number of decisions based on their domain knowledge. Another advantage is that the optimized approach for generating a canonical repair from a repair seed introduced in (Baader et al. 2021) for $\mathcal{EL}$ can be extended to $\mathcal{ELROI}$. More details on these advantages can be found in (Baader and Kriegel 2022).

4 Extensions and Applications

In this section we present several extensions to the repair framework. Section 4.1 shows how inconsistencies can be repaired that come into play when the bottom concept $\bot$ is added. Section 4.2 deals with repair requests formulated as conjunctive queries. Finally, Section 4.3 briefly mentions additional extensions that cannot be presented in detail here.

4.1 Adding the Bottom Concept and Repairing Inconsistencies

The DL $\mathcal{ELROI}(\bot)$ ($\mathcal{ELR}_{\mathsf{reg}}\mathcal{OI}(\bot)$) extends $\mathcal{ELROI}$ ($\mathcal{ELR}_{\mathsf{reg}}\mathcal{OI}$) with the bottom concept $\bot$, which is always interpreted as the empty set. If $\bot$ is available in the TBox, then qABoxes may become inconsistent w.r.t. terminologies. We call the quantified ABox $\exists X.\mathcal{A}$ *consistent* w.r.t. a terminology $(\mathcal{T},\mathcal{R})$ if there is a model of $\exists X.\mathcal{A}$ and $(\mathcal{T},\mathcal{R})$, and *inconsistent* otherwise. For instance, the qABox $\{A(a)\}$ is inconsistent w.r.t. the TBox $\{A \sqsubseteq \bot\}$

Since any concept assertion (qABox) is entailed w.r.t. $(\mathcal{T},\mathcal{R})$ by a qABox that is inconsistent w.r.t. $(\mathcal{T},\mathcal{R})$, any non-empty repair request to an inconsistent qABox requires us also to get rid of the inconsistency. In addition, the definition of what is a repair needs to be revised since (Rep1) is trivially satisfied in case $\exists X.\mathcal{A}$ is inconsistent w.r.t. $(\mathcal{T},\mathcal{R})$. Any qABox $\exists Y.\mathcal{B}$ satisfying (Rep2) and (Rep3) is thus a repair, even if $\exists Y.\mathcal{B}$ is completely unrelated to $\exists X.\mathcal{A}$. Hence, there cannot be an optimal repair since we can always extend a given repair by adding completely unrelated assertions.

Fortunately, in $\mathcal{ELROI}(\bot)$ we can divide the TBox into a positive and an "unsatisfiable" part, where the unsatisfiable part plays a rôle when an inconsistency is derived, but has no effect otherwise. To be more precise, consider an $\mathcal{ELROI}(\bot)$ TBox $\mathcal{T}$. Since each concept containing $\bot$ is equivalent to $\bot$, we can assume without loss of generality that each concept description occurring in $\mathcal{T}$ is either $\bot$ or does not contain $\bot$ as a subconcept. After removing tautological CIs $\bot \sqsubseteq C$, it follows that $\mathcal{T}$ is a disjoint union of a TBox $\mathcal{T}_+$ in which $\bot$ does not occur (the *positive part*) and of a TBox $\mathcal{T}_\bot$ containing only CIs of the form $C \sqsubseteq \bot$ where C does not contain $\bot$ (the *unsatisfiable part*). We can characterize inconsistency by means of this partitioning of $\mathcal{T}$, and show that $\mathcal{T}_\bot$ is only relevant for causing an inconsistency.

Proposition 17. *The following holds for every $\mathcal{ELROI}(\bot)$ terminology $(\mathcal{T}, \mathcal{R})$:*

1. *The quantified ABox $\exists X.\mathcal{A}$ is inconsistent w.r.t. $(\mathcal{T}, \mathcal{R})$ iff there is a CI $C \sqsubseteq \bot$ in $\mathcal{T}_\bot$ such that $\exists X.\mathcal{A} \models^{\mathcal{T}_+,\mathcal{R}} \exists\{x\}.\{C(x)\}$.*
2. *If $\exists X.\mathcal{A}$ is consistent w.r.t. $(\mathcal{T}, \mathcal{R})$, then $\exists X.\mathcal{A} \models^{\mathcal{T},\mathcal{R}} \exists Y.\mathcal{B}$ iff $\exists X.\mathcal{A} \models^{\mathcal{T}_+,\mathcal{R}} \exists Y.\mathcal{B}$.*

Motivated by the second statement of this proposition, we now use $\mathcal{T}_+$ rather than $\mathcal{T}$ in (Rep1), and of course additionally require the repair to be consistent. Also note that it does not make sense to use $\bot$ in the repair request.

Definition 18. Consider a qABox $\exists X.\mathcal{A}$, an $\mathcal{ELROI}$ repair request $\mathcal{P}$, and an $\mathcal{ELROI}(\bot)$ terminology $(\mathcal{T}, \mathcal{R})$. An *inconsistency repair* of $\exists X.\mathcal{A}$ for $\mathcal{P}$ w.r.t. $(\mathcal{T}, \mathcal{R})$ is a qABox $\exists Y.\mathcal{B}$ such that

(IRep1) $\exists X.\mathcal{A} \models^{\mathcal{T}_+,\mathcal{R}} \exists Y.\mathcal{B}$

(IRep2) $\exists Y.\mathcal{B}$ is consistent w.r.t. $(\mathcal{T}, \mathcal{R})$,

(IRep3) $\exists Y.\mathcal{B} \not\models^{\mathcal{T},\mathcal{R}} C(a)$ for each $C(a) \in \mathcal{P}_{\mathsf{loc}}$, and

(IRep4) $\exists Y.\mathcal{B} \not\models^{\mathcal{T},\mathcal{R}} \exists\{x\}.\{D(x)\}$ for each $D \in \mathcal{P}_{\mathsf{glo}}$.

This inconsistency repair is *optimal* if it is not strictly entailed by another inconsistency repair w.r.t. $(\mathcal{T}, \mathcal{R})$.

Due to the second statement in Proposition 17, the notion of an inconsistency repair coincides with that of a repair as introduced in Definition 8 if $\exists X.\mathcal{A}$ is consistent w.r.t. $(\mathcal{T}, \mathcal{R})$. If $\exists X.\mathcal{A}$ is inconsistent w.r.t. $(\mathcal{T}, \mathcal{R})$, then the first statement in Proposition 17 shows that (IRep2) can be enforced by extending the global request with the concepts C for which $C \sqsubseteq \bot \in \mathcal{T}_\bot$. Given a repair request $\mathcal{P}$, we denote the extended request obtained this way as $\mathcal{P}^{\mathcal{T}_\bot}$.

Theorem 19. *Consider a qABox $\exists X.\mathcal{A}$, an $\mathcal{ELROI}$ repair request $\mathcal{P}$, and an $\mathcal{ELROI}(\bot)$ terminology $(\mathcal{T}, \mathcal{R})$. If $(\mathcal{T}, \mathcal{R})$ is inconsistent, then there are no inconsistency repairs of $\exists X.\mathcal{A}$ w.r.t. $(\mathcal{T}, \mathcal{R})$. Otherwise, the (optimal) inconsistency repairs of $\exists X.\mathcal{A}$ for $\mathcal{P}$ w.r.t. $(\mathcal{T}, \mathcal{R})$ coincide with the (optimal) repairs of $\exists X.\mathcal{A}$ for $\mathcal{P}^{\mathcal{T}_\bot}$ w.r.t. $(\mathcal{T}_+, \mathcal{R})$.*

If $\mathcal{R}$ is regular and $(\mathcal{T}_+, \mathcal{R})$ is terminating, then we can apply the approach described in the previous section to compute all optimal inconsistency repairs.

4.2 Repairs for Conjunctive Queries

Until now, we have only allowed the use of $\mathcal{ELROI}$ concept queries in the repair request. We now extend this to conjunctive queries (CQs). More precisely, we employ Boolean conjunctive queries (BCQs), i.e., CQs without answer variables. This is in line with the fact that we only considered concept queries where the answer variable was either instantiated with an individual or existentially quantified. In (Grau and Kostylev 2019), CQs with answer variables are employed in the policy (which corresponds to our repair request), with the meaning that such a CQ should not have any answer tuple in the repair. This can clearly be expressed using the finitely many BCQs obtained by instantiating the answer variables with all answer tuples. As already mentioned above, BCQs and qABoxes are merely syntactic variants of each other (Baader et al. 2020). For this reason, we avoid introducing BCQs formally and use qABoxes instead.

Definition 20. A *qABox repair request* $\mathcal{P}$ is a finite set of qABoxes. Given a qABox $\exists X.\mathcal{A}$, a terminology $(\mathcal{T}, \mathcal{R})$, and a qABox repair request $\mathcal{P}$, a *repair* of $\exists X.\mathcal{A}$ for $\mathcal{P}$ w.r.t. $(\mathcal{T}, \mathcal{R})$ is a qABox $\exists Y.\mathcal{B}$ that satisfies

(CQRep1) $\exists X.\mathcal{A} \models^{\mathcal{T},\mathcal{R}} \exists Y.\mathcal{B}$, and

(CQRep2) $\exists Y.\mathcal{B} \not\models^{\mathcal{T},\mathcal{R}} \exists Z.\mathcal{C}$ for each $\exists Z.\mathcal{C} \in \mathcal{P}$.

It is *optimal* if it is not strictly entailed by another repair.

Since both concept assertions $C(a)$ and global repair requests $\exists\{x\}.\{C(x)\}$ for $\mathcal{ELROI}$ concept descriptions C can be rewritten into equivalent qABoxes, using the first three rules in Figure 1, the repair requests and repairs introduced in Definition 8 are a special case of the qABox repair requests and repairs introduced here. We will now investigated under what conditions a rewriting in the other direction is possible.

Definition 21. An *$\mathcal{ELROI}$ rewriting* of the qABox $\exists Z.\mathcal{C}$ is an $\mathcal{ELROI}$ concept description C such that $\exists Z.\mathcal{C}$ and $\exists\{x\}.\{C(x)\}$ are equivalent.

By adapting the notion of c-acyclicity introduced in (Alexe et al. 2011), we can give (effectively checkable) conditions characterizing the existence of such a rewriting. Basically, the qABox is translated into an appropriate undirected graph, and the condition for c-acyclicity says that every cycle must contain an individual (see (Baader and Kriegel 2022) and (Alexe et al. 2011) for more details). Furthermore, we need the notion of a *core*, which is a qABox such that each endomorphism on it is bijective. Each qABox $\exists X.\mathcal{A}$ has a computable and (up to renaming) unique core to which it is equivalent (Hell and Nešetřil 1992). It will be denoted in the following as $\mathsf{core}(\exists X.\mathcal{A})$.

Proposition 22. *A qABox has an $\mathcal{ELROI}$ rewriting iff its core is connected and c-acyclic.*

A detailed proof of this proposition can be found in (Baader and Kriegel 2022). The proof of the if-direction is constructive in the sense that it shows how the rewriting can be computed. Thus, if all qABoxes in a given qABox repair request are $\mathcal{ELROI}$ rewritable, then we can reduce qABox repair to $\mathcal{ELROI}$ repair.

Example 23. As an example of a qABox that is not c-acyclic we consider $\exists\{x, y\}.\{r(a, x), s(x, y), s(y, x)\}$. It has a cycle from x to y and then back that does not involve an individual. It is not $\mathcal{ELROI}$ rewritable since an $\mathcal{ELROI}$ concept could only enforce going back from y to the predecessor x if one of them were an individual whose name can be used in the concept. In contrast, the qABox $\exists\{y\}.\{s(a,y), s(y,a)\}$, which is c-acyclic, has the $\mathcal{ELROI}$ rewriting $\{a\} \sqcap \exists s.\exists s.\{a\}$. Note that the qABox $\exists\{x,y\}.\{s(x,y), r(x,y)\}$ is also not c-acyclic. Again, an $\mathcal{ELROI}$ concept cannot enforce that there is a joint s- and r-successor of x. The qABox $\exists\{y\}.\{s(a,y), r(a,y)\}$ has the $\mathcal{ELROI}$ rewriting $\exists r^-.\{a\} \sqcap \exists s^-.\{a\}$.

Considering Proposition 22, one might think that non-connectedness of $\mathsf{core}(\exists Z.\mathcal{C})$ for $\exists Z.\mathcal{C} \in \mathcal{P}$ could be an impediment to reducing qABox repair to $\mathcal{ELROI}$ repair. However, this is not the case: it is sufficient that all connected components of $\mathsf{core}(\exists Z.\mathcal{C})$ are $\mathcal{ELROI}$ rewritable. To be more precise, let $\mathfrak{H}(\mathcal{P})$ be the set of all hitting sets of $\{\, \mathsf{CoCo}(\mathsf{core}(\exists Z.\mathcal{C})) \mid \exists Z.\mathcal{C} \in \mathcal{P} \text{ and } \exists X.\mathcal{A} \models^{\mathcal{T},\mathcal{R}} \exists Z.\mathcal{C} \,\}$, where the operator CoCo yields the set of connected components of an input qABox.

Lemma 24. *$\exists Y.\mathcal{B}$ is a repair of $\exists X.\mathcal{A}$ for $\mathcal{P}$ w.r.t. $(\mathcal{T},\mathcal{R})$ iff there is a hitting set $\mathcal{H}$ in $\mathfrak{H}(\mathcal{P})$ such that $\exists Y.\mathcal{B}$ is a repair of $\exists X.\mathcal{A}$ for $\mathcal{H}$ w.r.t. $(\mathcal{T},\mathcal{R})$.*

According to our previous considerations, we can compute the optimal repairs for such a hitting set $\mathcal{H}$ if each component in $\mathcal{H}$ has an $\mathcal{ELROI}$ rewriting. The elements of $\mathcal{H}$ are connected components of the cores of the elements of $\mathcal{P}$. Since such a core is c-acyclic iff all its connected components are so, it is thus sufficient to require that the cores of the elements of $\mathcal{P}$ are c-acyclic. Under this assumption, the set of all optimal repairs of $\exists X.\mathcal{A}$ for $\mathcal{P}$ w.r.t. $(\mathcal{T},\mathcal{R})$ is then obtained by collecting the optimal repairs of $\exists X.\mathcal{A}$ for $\mathcal{H}$ w.r.t. $(\mathcal{T},\mathcal{R})$ for all hitting set $\mathcal{H}$ in $\mathfrak{H}(\mathcal{P})$, and then removing elements from this set that are strictly entailed by other elements.

Theorem 25. *Let $\exists X.\mathcal{A}$ be a qABox, $(\mathcal{T},\mathcal{R})$ a terminating terminology with a regular RBox whose associated automata can effectively be computed, and $\mathcal{P}$ be a qABox repair request. Then the set of all optimal repairs of $\exists X.\mathcal{A}$ for $\mathcal{P}$ w.r.t. $(\mathcal{T},\mathcal{R})$ can be effectively computed if $\mathsf{core}(\exists Z.\mathcal{C})$ is c-acyclic for all qABoxes $\exists Z.\mathcal{C}$ in $\mathcal{P}$. In addition, each repair is then entailed by an optimal repair.*

Without restrictions on the qABoxes in the repair request, the set of optimal repairs need not cover all repairs in the sense stated in the theorem, even if the qABox to be repaired is an ABox and the terminology is empty. In fact, it follows from (Nešetřil and Tardif 2000, Corollary 3.5) that the ABox $\{r(a,a)\}$ has no optimal repair for the repair request consisting of the qABox $\exists\{x\}.\{r(x,x)\}$. But the empty ABox is a repair, which is thus not entailed by an optimal one.

4.3 Further Extensions

The repair framework developed in this paper can also be used to deal with regular path expressions in the repair request, Horn-$\mathcal{ALCOI}$ TBoxes, and qABoxes that have a static part that must not be changed. The basic idea is to create an $\mathcal{ELROI}$ terminology over an extended signature that is a conservative extension of the input terminology, and in which such extensions can be expressed. Our repair approach is then applied w.r.t. this terminology. However, the repairs obtained this way may still contain names not occurring in the original signature, and thus these additional symbols need to be removed from these repairs appropriately.

We illustrate this for the case of *regular path expressions*, which are regular expressions over the alphabet of all roles. In repair requests, the concepts may now contain such expressions in place of roles. The semantics is defined by interpreting union, concatenation, and Kleene-star in the regular expressions as union, composition, and reflexive-transitive closure of binary relations, and the empty word as the identity relation. For example, the concept assertion $(\exists r^*.\{b\})(a) \in \mathcal{P}$ then says that, in the repair, there should not be an (empty or non-empty) r-path from a to b. To express the regular expression r^*, we introduce a new role name $\lceil r^* \rceil$ and extend the RBox with the RIs $\varepsilon \sqsubseteq \lceil r^* \rceil$, $r \sqsubseteq \lceil r^* \rceil$, and $\lceil r^* \rceil \circ \lceil r^* \rceil \sqsubseteq \lceil r^* \rceil$. In the repair request, we now use $\lceil r^* \rceil$ in place of r^*. A repair computed for this modified request may still contain the new name $\lceil r^* \rceil$, but we can simply remove all assertions containing it to obtain a repair in the original signature.

If a part of the given qABox is known to be correct, one may want to keep this part static when repairing (i.e., the repair should still imply this static part). Since our TBoxes are static and concept and role assertions can be expressed using nominals, the idea is now to move the static part of the qABox to the TBox. However, to express assertions involving variables, the signature needs to be extended by adding these variables as individual names.

More details on how to deal with these two extensions and on how Horn-$\mathcal{ALCOI}$ TBoxes can be expressed can be found in (Baader and Kriegel 2022).

5 Conclusion

We have shown that the approaches for computing optimal repairs developed in our previous work can be extended to a considerably more expressive DL, which covers most of the DL $\mathcal{EL}^{++}$ underlying the OWL 2 EL profile, but also has inverse roles. Our main result is that, in this setting, optimal repairs can effectively be computed and cover all repairs in the sense that every repair is entailed by an optimal one. In addition, we have demonstrated that this repair approach can deal with several other interesting repair problems.

The paper actually provides two proofs of the main result, one based on showing a small repair property by filtration, and another one based on the construction of canonical repairs. We believe the second approach to be more useful in practice. In fact, when repairing a given quantified ABox w.r.t. an $\mathcal{ELROI}$ terminology, first computing all optimal repairs and then expecting the knowledge engineer to choose an appropriate one among (potentially) exponentially many exponentially large optimal repairs does not appear to be a practically viable repair approach. Since our canonical repairs are determined by polynomially large repair seeds, such a repair can be chosen by making polynomially many decisions regarding certain instance relationships. Once a repair seed is chosen, the induced canonical repair is always exponentially large. However, by adapting the optimized repair approach of (Baader et al. 2021) to our more expressive language, we can obtain considerably smaller optimized repairs.

Acknowledgements

This work was partially supported by the AI competence center ScaDS.AI Dresden/Leipzig and the German Research Foundation (DFG) in Project 430150274 ("Repairing Description Logic Ontologies") and SFB/TRR 248 ("Foundations of Perspicuous Software Systems"). We thank the anonymous reviewers for their helpful comments. In particular, one of the reviewers provided us with Example 10 and the idea that filtration can be used to show the small repair property.

References

Alexe, B.; ten Cate, B.; Kolaitis, P. G.; and Tan, W. C. 2011. Characterizing schema mappings via data examples. *ACM Trans. Database Syst.* 36(4):23:1–23:48.

Baader, F., and Kriegel, F. 2022. Pushing optimal ABox repair from $\mathcal{EL}$ towards more expressive Horn-DLs (extended version). LTCS-Report 22-02, Chair of Automata Theory, Institute of Theoretical Computer Science, Technische Universität Dresden, Dresden, Germany. https://doi.org/10.25368/2022.131.

Baader, F., and Suntisrivaraporn, B. 2008. Debugging SNOMED CT using axiom pinpointing in the description logic $\mathcal{EL}^+$. In *Proceedings of the International Conference on Representing and Sharing Knowledge Using SNOMED (KR-MED'08)*.

Baader, F.; Horrocks, I.; Lutz, C.; and Sattler, U. 2017. *An Introduction to Description Logic*. Cambridge University Press.

Baader, F.; Kriegel, F.; Nuradiansyah, A.; and Peñaloza, R. 2018. Making repairs in description logics more gentle. In Thielscher, M.; Toni, F.; and Wolter, F., eds., *Principles of Knowledge Representation and Reasoning: Proceedings of the Sixteenth International Conference, KR 2018*, 319–328. AAAI Press.

Baader, F.; Kriegel, F.; Nuradiansyah, A.; and Peñaloza, R. 2020. Computing compliant anonymisations of quantified ABoxes w.r.t. $\mathcal{EL}$ policies. In Pan, J. Z.; Tamma, V. A. M.; d'Amato, C.; Janowicz, K.; Fu, B.; Polleres, A.; Seneviratne, O.; and Kagal, L., eds., *The Semantic Web – ISWC 2020 – 19th International Semantic Web Conference, Proceedings, Part I*, volume 12506 of *Lecture Notes in Computer Science*, 3–20. Springer.

Baader, F.; Koopmann, P.; Kriegel, F.; and Nuradiansyah, A. 2021. Computing optimal repairs of quantified ABoxes w.r.t. static $\mathcal{EL}$ TBoxes. In Platzer, A., and Sutcliffe, G., eds., *Automated Deduction - CADE 28 - 28th International Conference on Automated Deduction, Proceedings*, volume 12699 of *Lecture Notes in Computer Science*, 309–326. Springer.

Baader, F.; Borgwardt, S.; and Morawska, B. 2012. Extending unification in $\mathcal{EL}$ towards general TBoxes. In Brewka, G.; Eiter, T.; and McIlraith, S. A., eds., *Principles of Knowledge Representation and Reasoning: Proceedings of the Thirteenth International Conference, KR 2012*. AAAI Press.

Baader, F.; Brandt, S.; and Lutz, C. 2005. Pushing the $\mathcal{EL}$ envelope. In Kaelbling, L. P., and Saffiotti, A., eds., *IJCAI-05, Proceedings of the Nineteenth International Joint Conference on Artificial Intelligence*, 364–369. Professional Book Center.

Baader, F.; Lutz, C.; and Brandt, S. 2008. Pushing the $\mathcal{EL}$ envelope further. In Clark, K., and Patel-Schneider, P. F., eds., *Proceedings of the Fourth OWLED Workshop on OWL: Experiences and Directions*, volume 496 of *CEUR Workshop Proceedings*. CEUR-WS.org.

Calvanese, D.; Giacomo, G. D.; Lembo, D.; Lenzerini, M.; and Rosati, R. 2007. Tractable reasoning and efficient query answering in description logics: The *DL-Lite* family. *J. Autom. Reason.* 39(3):385–429.

Calvanese, D.; Eiter, T.; and Ortiz, M. 2009. Regular path queries in expressive description logics with nominals. In Boutilier, C., ed., *IJCAI 2009, Proceedings of the 21st International Joint Conference on Artificial Intelligence*, 714–720.

Du, J.; Qi, G.; and Fu, X. 2014. A practical fine-grained approach to resolving incoherent OWL 2 DL terminologies. In *Proc. of the 23rd ACM Int. Conf. on Information and Knowledge Management, (CIKM'14)*, 919–928.

Grau, B. C., and Kostylev, E. V. 2019. Logical foundations of linked data anonymisation. *J. Artif. Intell. Res.* 64:253–314.

Grau, B. C.; Horrocks, I.; Krötzsch, M.; Kupke, C.; Magka, D.; Motik, B.; and Wang, Z. 2013. Acyclicity notions for existential rules and their application to query answering in ontologies. *J. Artif. Intell. Res.* 47:741–808.

Hell, P., and Nešetřil, J. 1992. The core of a graph. *Discret. Math.* 109(1-3):117–126.

Horridge, M.; Parsia, B.; and Sattler, U. 2008. Laconic and precise justifications in OWL. In Sheth, A. P.; Staab, S.; Dean, M.; Paolucci, M.; Maynard, D.; Finin, T. W.; and Thirunarayan, K., eds., *The Semantic Web - ISWC 2008, 7th International Semantic Web Conference, Proceedings*, volume 5318 of *Lecture Notes in Computer Science*, 323–338. Springer.

Horrocks, I.; Kutz, O.; and Sattler, U. 2006. The even more irresistible $\mathcal{SROIQ}$. In Doherty, P.; Mylopoulos, J.; and Welty, C. A., eds., *Proceedings, Tenth International Conference on Principles of Knowledge Representation and Reasoning*, 57–67. AAAI Press.

Kazakov, Y. 2008. $\mathcal{RIQ}$ and $\mathcal{SROIQ}$ are harder than $\mathcal{SHOIQ}$. In Brewka, G., and Lang, J., eds., *Principles of Knowledge Representation and Reasoning: Proceedings of the Eleventh International Conference, KR 2008*, 274–284. AAAI Press.

Kazakov, Y. 2009. Consequence-driven reasoning for Horn $\mathcal{SHIQ}$ ontologies. In Boutilier, C., ed., *IJCAI 2009, Proceedings of the 21st International Joint Conference on Artificial Intelligence*, 2040–2045.

Kazakov, Y. 2010. An extension of complex role inclusion axioms in the description logic $\mathcal{SROIQ}$. In Giesl, J., and Hähnle, R., eds., *Automated Reasoning, 5th International Joint Conference, IJCAR 2010, Proceedings*, volume 6173 of *Lecture Notes in Computer Science*, 472–486. Springer.

Lam, J. S. C.; Sleeman, D. H.; Pan, J. Z.; and Vasconcelos, W. W. 2008. A fine-grained approach to resolving unsatisfiable ontologies. *J. Data Semant.* 10:62–95.

Maurer, H. A.; Salomaa, A.; and Wood, D. 1980. Pure grammars. *Inf. Control.* 44(1):47–72.

Nešetřil, J., and Tardif, C. 2000. Duality theorems for finite structures (characterising gaps and good characterisations). *J. Comb. Theory, Ser. B* 80(1):80–97.

Ortiz, M.; Rudolph, S.; and Šimkus, M. 2010. Worst-case optimal reasoning for the Horn-DL fragments of OWL 1 and 2. In Lin, F.; Sattler, U.; and Truszczynski, M., eds., *Principles of Knowledge Representation and Reasoning: Proceedings of the Twelfth International Conference, KR 2010.*

Parsia, B.; Sirin, E.; and Kalyanpur, A. 2005. Debugging OWL ontologies. In Ellis, A., and Hagino, T., eds., *Proc. of the 14th International Conference on World Wide Web (WWW'05)*, 633–640. ACM.

Schlobach, S.; Huang, Z.; Cornet, R.; and Harmelen, F. 2007. Debugging incoherent terminologies. *J. Automated Reasoning* 39(3):317–349.

Troquard, N.; Confalonieri, R.; Galliani, P.; Peñaloza, R.; Porello, D.; and Kutz, O. 2018. Repairing ontologies via axiom weakening. In McIlraith, S. A., and Weinberger, K. Q., eds., *Proceedings of the Thirty-Second AAAI Conference on Artificial Intelligence, (AAAI-18)*, 1981–1988. AAAI Press.

The Topology of Surprise

Alexandru Baltag[1] , **Nick Bezhanishivili**[1] , **David Fernández-Duque**[2,3]
[1]ILLC, University of Amsterdam
[2]ICS of the Czech Academy of Sciences
[3]Department of Mathematics WE16, Ghent University
{A.Baltag,N.Bezhanishvili}@uva.nl, fernandez@cs.cas.cz

Abstract

In this paper we present a topological epistemic logic, with modalities for knowledge (modeled as the universal modality), knowability (represented by the topological interior operator), and unknowability of the actual world. The last notion has a non-self-referential reading (modeled by Cantor derivative: the set of limit points of a given set) and a self-referential one (modeled by Cantor's perfect core of a given set: its largest subset without isolated points). We completely axiomatize this logic, showing that it is decidable and PSPACE-complete, and we apply it to the analysis of a famous epistemic puzzle: the Surprise Exam Paradox.

1 Introduction

Epistemic logic has been formalized by Hintikka within the framework of possible-world semantics in relational (Kripke) models, and later rediscovered by game theorists (Aumann 1995) in the setting of partitional models (corresponding to the special case of S5 Kripke models, based on equivalence relations). In these forms, it has been used in Computer Science to reason about distributed systems, in AI to reason about agent-based knowledge representation, and in Philosophy to explore issues in formal epistemology.

An alternative interpretation of modal logic is based not on Kripke frames, but on topological spaces. This semantics can be traced back to McKinsey and Tarski (McKinsey and Tarski 1944). When the modal $\Diamond$ is interpreted as topological closure Cl and the modal $\Box$ as topological interior Int, one obtains a semantics for the modal logic S4. McKinsey and Tarski also suggested a second topological semantics, obtained by interpreting the modal $\Diamond$ as Cantor derivative (where recall that the derivative $d(A)$ of a set A consists of all limit points of A). The modal logic of Cantor derivative is semantically more expressive than the modal logic of the interior/closure operators: the latter can be defined in terms of derivative, but not vice-versa.

Since then, the usefulness of topological structures in Computer Science and Knowledge Representation has been well established. As noticed by Vickers (Vickers 1989) and Abramsky (Abramsky 1991), the notion of observability and its logic require a topological setting. Abstract notions of computability also involve topological structures, with a famous example being the Scott topology. Research on spatial reasoning, in both topological and metric incarnations, is also of significant interest for AI. More recently, developments in Formal Learning Theory (Kelly 1996; Brecht and Yamamoto 2010; Baltag, Gierasimczuk, and Smets 2015) and Distributed Computing (Goubault, Ledent, and Rajsbaum 2020) have taken a topological turn. Moreover, recent work in epistemic logic (Baltag et al. 2016; Özgün 2017; Baltag et al. 2019b) on modelling and reasoning about evidence and knowability uses topological structures.

These applications are based mostly on the notion of topological interior. Our paper builds on this existing work, but is the first to show the usefulness for Knowledge Representation of other topological notions, such as Cantor derivative. From a technical point of view, our formalism is obtained by adding to the logic of Cantor derivative a global modality (quantifying over all points), an operator capturing the perfect core $d^{\infty}(A)$ of a set A (defined as the largest subset of A that is equal to its own derivative) and a dynamic update modality (that goes from the original space to some definable subspace). Building on our previous work on topological μ-calculus (Baltag, Bezhanishvili, and Fernández-Duque 2021), we give a complete axiomatization, as well as decidability and complexity results. Our proof is natural and not difficult to grasp, due in large part to subtle technical innovations which allow for a much more direct approach than that of related results in the literature (see e.g. (Fernández-Duque 2011; Goldblatt and Hodkinson 2017)).

From a conceptual point of view, the key contribution of our paper is that we develop a logic of evidence-based knowledge, knowability, and (un)knowability of the actual world; and moreover, we apply it to the analysis of a famous epistemic paradox: the Surprise Examination paradox.

We start by adopting the learning-theoretic reading of topology (Kelly 1996; Baltag, Gierasimczuk, and Smets 2015; Baltag et al. 2019b), in which a topological space is a way to represent the actual and potential evidence that some (anonymous) agent may observe. The points of the space represent possible worlds (or possible states of the world): all the possibilities that are consistent with the agent's current knowledge. A proposition is known if it is true in all possible worlds. The potential evidence (that might be observed in the future) forms a topological basis $\mathcal{B}$: if a world x belongs to a basic open set $x \in U \in \mathcal{B}$, then the agent may observe proposition U in world x. The topological interior operator $\mathrm{Int}(A)$ captures the *knowability* of proposition A through observations $U \in \mathcal{B}$. When the agent gains more knowledge, some possibilities are eliminated (being ruled out by the new information), and thus the space shrinks to a subspace: this corresponds to performing a knowledge update (described in our logic by dynamic update modalities).

While each of the above epistemic readings of standard topological notions are already known from the literature, the epistemic meaning of Cantor's derivative and the perfect core is not so obvious. In this paper, we propose a novel and very natural learning-theoretic interpretation of derivative. Essentially, the derivative $d(A)$ is the proposition asserting that *the actual world is unknowable (through observations), even if given (the additional information)* A.[1] Finally, the epistemic meaning of the perfect core $d^\infty(A)$ can be reconstructed from its fixed-point definition: essentially, $d^\infty(A)$ is the *self-referential version of Cantor's derivative*, i.e. the proposition asserting that "A is true, but the actual world is unknowable even given *this* information" (where 'this' refers to the very proposition that we are defining).

The main motivation for the introduction of the perfect core modality comes from our analysis of the Surprise Exam Paradox. The story says that a Student knows for sure that the date of the exam has been fixed in one of the five (working) days of next week. But he doesn't know in which day. The Teacher (who is known to be always truthful) announces that the *exam's date will be a surprise*: even in the evening before the exam, the Student will still not know for sure that the exam is tomorrow. Intuitively, the Student can then prove (by backward induction, starting with Friday) that *the exam cannot take place in any day of the week*: first, if the exam would be on Friday, then it wouldn't be a surprise (-since Friday is the last possible day, by Thursday evening the Student would know it); since the Teacher (truthfully) announced that the exam will be a surprise, it follows that the exam will not take place on Friday. But once Friday is eliminated, the Student can repeat the same argument, until all days are eliminated. But this is a contradiction (since we assumed the Student *knows* there will be an exam).

In some versions of the puzzle, there is an even more "paradoxical" follow-up: the assumption that the Teacher never lies is weakened, to allow the Student some way out. After deriving the above contradiction, he concludes that the Teacher lied: the exam will *not* be a surprise. Confident that, whenever the exams comes, he will somehow get to know it an evening in advance (and thus be able to study in that last evening), the Student parties every day. Then, when the exam comes (say, on Wednesday), it *will* indeed be a complete surprise! So the Teacher told the truth after all?!

[1]Indeed, prior to this paper, the dominant interpretation of derivative in the epistemological literature was Steinsvold's reading in terms of "belief" (Steinsvold 2007). That interpretation has been criticized as not correctly reflecting the intuitive properties of belief and its relations to knowledge (Baltag et al. 2019a). Though new, our interpretation is closer to an older work (Parikh 1992), based on a different framework: multi-agent $S5$ Kripke frames. In that setting, derivative is connected to ignorance (rather than to unknowability): the agent does not know the actual world.

In this paper, we give a full analysis of the paradox using our topological epistemic logic. We distinguish between non-self-referential interpretations of Teacher's announcement (which can be formalized using Cantor derivative) and self-referential interpretations (which are captured using the perfect core modality). The first interpretation was pursued (in a non-topological, and less transparent, setting) in (Gerbrandy 2007), and shown to be paradox-free: the only conclusion is that the exam cannot be on Friday, but the elimination process cannot be iterated. However, most logicians consider that the most natural (and intended) interpretation is the second, self-referential one. As in the above intuitive argumentation, this does lead to a contradiction. The correct conclusion is that a Teacher who is known to be always truthful *cannot make* such an announcement (since if she did, it would be a lie). In this, we agree with the verdict given in (Quine 1953). However, we also show that the above contradiction is only produced by the special evidential topology underlying the Surprise Exam Story. By changing the topology, we obtain "non-paradoxical" versions, in which the Teacher *can* truthfully make similar future-oriented self-referential "surprise" announcements. Our conclusion (against the opinions of many philosophical logicians) is that epistemic self-referentiality is *not* the cause of the apparent 'paradoxicality' of the Surprise Exam Paradox.

2 The Evidential Topology

As preliminaries, we recall here some notions from General Topology. In the view of our epistemic applications, we strengthen somewhat the standard notion of topological base, obtaining a concept that we call "strong base".

2.1 Topological Preliminaries

Definition 2.1 (Topology, strong base, open and closed sets, neighborhoods)**.** *A* ***strong (topological) base*** *on a set X (called a* space, *and whose elements $x \in X$ are called* points*) is a family $\mathcal{B} \subseteq \mathcal{P}(X)$ of subsets of X (called* basic open *sets), with the property that it is* closed under finite intersections*: if $\mathcal{U} \subseteq \mathcal{B}$ is any finite subfamily, then $\bigcap \mathcal{U} \in \mathcal{T}$. This is in fact equivalent to requiring that a base is closed only under binary intersections (if $U, V \in \mathcal{B}$, then $U \cap V \in \mathcal{B}$) and contains the whole space (i.e. $X \in \mathcal{B}$).*[2] *A* basic neighborhood *of a point $x \in X$ is a basic open set $U \in \mathcal{B}$ with $x \in U$.*

A ***topology*** *on a set X is a strong base $\mathcal{T} \subseteq \mathcal{P}(X)$, that satisfies the additional requirement that: it is* closed under arbitrary (possibly infinite) unions*: if $\mathcal{U} \subseteq \mathcal{T}$ is any subfamily, then $\bigcup \mathcal{U} \in \mathcal{T}$. The pair $(X, \mathcal{T})$ is a* ***topological space*** *and the sets $U \in \mathcal{T}$ are called* open *sets.*[3] *Their complements $X - U$ (with $U \in \mathcal{T}$) are called* closed, *and have dual closure properties to the opens. A* neighborhood *of a point $x \in X$ is an open set $U \in \mathcal{T}$ with $x \in U$.*

[2]This last condition follows from applying closure under finite intersections to the empty family $\mathcal{U} = \emptyset \subseteq \mathcal{B}$, since $\bigcap \emptyset = X$.

[3]By applying closure under unions to the empty family $\mathcal{U} = \emptyset$, it is easy to see that $\emptyset$ is open (as well as closed, being the complement $X - X$ of the open set X).

Operators in a Topological Space [Interior, closure, derivative] An *interior point* of a set $A \subseteq X$ is a point $x \in X$ s.t. there exists a neighborhood $U \in \mathcal{T}$ (of x) with $x \in U \subseteq A$. Given a strong basis $\mathcal{B}$ for the topology $\mathcal{T}$, it is easy to see that x is an interior point of A iff there exists a *basic* neighborhood $U \in \mathcal{B}$ (of x) s.t. $x \in U \subseteq A$. The ***interior*** $\text{Int}(A)$ of a set $A \subseteq X$ is the set of all its interior points. A point $x \in X$ is *close* to a set $A \subseteq X$ if all its (basic) neighborhoods intersect A: for all $U \in \mathcal{T}$ (or equivalently, for all $U \in \mathcal{B}$) s.t. $x \in U$ we have $U \cap A \neq \emptyset$. The ***closure*** $\text{Cl}(A)$ of the set A is the set of all points that are close to A. A *limit point* of a set $A \subseteq X$ is a point $x \in X$ s.t. every (basic) neighborhood U of x contains a point $y \in A$ with $y \neq x$; equivalently, x is a limit point of A iff $x \in \text{Cl}(A - \{x\})$. The ***(Cantor) derivative*** $d(A)$ of a set A is the set of all the limit points of A. It is easy to see that $\text{Cl}(A) = A \cup d(A)$. A non-limit point $x \in A - d(A)$ is called *isolated* in A.

It is important to note that operators Int, Cl and d are *monotonic* operators, e.g. in particular $A \subseteq B$ implies $d(A) \subseteq d(B)$.

Generated Topology The *topology generated by* a strong base $\mathcal{B} \subseteq \mathcal{P}(X)$ is the smallest topology $\mathcal{T} \subseteq \mathcal{P}(X)$ s.t. $\mathcal{B} \subseteq \mathcal{T}$. We then say that $\mathcal{B}$ is a *base for* $\mathcal{T}$. The generated topology can be explicitly characterized as consisting of all possible unions of basic opens: $\mathcal{T} = \{\bigcup \mathcal{U} : \mathcal{U} \subseteq \mathcal{B}\}$.

Subspace Topology Every subset $A \subseteq X$ of a topological space $(X, \mathcal{T})$ is a ***subspace*** of the original space, when endowed with the subspace topology $\mathcal{T}_A = \{A \cap U : U \in \mathcal{T}\}$. Every strong base $\mathcal{B}$ for $\mathcal{T}$ induces a corresponding strong base for $\mathcal{T}_A$, obtained by taking $\mathcal{B}_A = \{A \cap U : U \in \mathcal{B}\}$. All the above topological notions can be relativized to a subspace: e.g. for any subset $P \subseteq A$, we can define its relative interior $\text{Int}_A(P)$ in A, closure $\text{Cl}_A(P)$ in A and derivative $d_A(P)$ in A, by applying the above definitions in the subspace A. It is easy to see that $\text{Int}_A(P) = A \cap \text{Int}(P \cup (X - A))$, $\text{Cl}_A(P) = A \cap \text{Cl}(P)$, and $d_P(A) = A \cap d(P)$.

Perfect Sets and Perfect Core A set $A \subseteq X$ is said to be ***perfect*** if $A = d(A)$. The ***perfect core*** of a set A is a subset of A denoted by $d^\infty(A)$, and defined as the largest perfect subset of A.[4] The perfect core $d^\infty(A)$ is the largest fixed point of the relative derivative operator $d_A : \mathcal{P}(A) \to \mathcal{P}(A)$, that takes subsets $P \subseteq A$ into their relative derivative $d_A(P) = A \cap d(P)$ in A.[5] This fixed point exists (by the Knaster-Tarski fixed point theorem) because of the *monotonicity* of the relative derivative operator d_A (itself a consequence of the monotonicity of derivative and intersection). Using standard μ-calculus notation for this largest fixed point, we can thus write

$$d^\infty(A) = \nu P. A \cap d(P).$$

[4]Here, "largest" is used in the sense of inclusion: so the perfect core $d^\infty(A)$ is the unique set B satisfying the following three conditions: (1) $B \subseteq A$; (2) $B = d(B)$; (3) every set B' satisfying conditions (1) and (2) is included in B.

[5]Once again, "largest" is taken here in the sense of inclusion.

Cantor-Bendixson Rank For any set $A \subseteq X$, we define a transfinite sequence of subsets of A, by putting:

$$d^0(A) = A, \qquad d^{\alpha+1}(A) = d_A(d^\alpha(A)) = A \cap d^\alpha(A),$$

$$d^\lambda(A) = \bigcap_{\alpha<\lambda} d^\alpha(A) \text{ for limit ordinals } \lambda.$$

It is easy to check that this is a descending sequence

$$A = d^0(A) \supseteq d(A) = d^1(A) \supseteq \ldots \supseteq d^\alpha(A) \supseteq \ldots,$$

which thus must reach a *fixed point*; i.e. there must exist an ordinal α s.t. $d^{\alpha+1}(A) = d^\alpha(A)$. The smallest such ordinal is called the ***(Cantor-Bendixson) rank*** of A, denoted by $\text{rank}(A)$. Moreover, *the fixed point of the above iterative process $d^\alpha(A)$ is the perfect core*:

$$d^{\text{rank}(A)}(A) = d^\infty(A).$$

2.2 The Epistemic Interpretation of Topology

We proceed now to explain the intended epistemic interpretation of the above topological notions, in terms of observable evidence and information updates.

Possible Worlds, Knowledge, Observable Evidence, Evidential Topology We think of the points $x \in X$ as representing *possible worlds* (or possible states of the world): all the possibilities that are consistent with some (anonymous) agent's information. Only one of these points represents the *actual world* (the true state of affairs), but the agent may not know which one: all she knows for certain is that it belongs to the set X. Every subset $P \subseteq X$ represents a "proposition", which may be "true" (i.e., hold) in a given world or not. A proposition P is "known" for certain only if it is true in all possible worlds that are consistent with the agent's information, i.e. if $P = X$. A strong basis $\mathcal{B} \subseteq \mathcal{P}(X)$ represents our agent's *potential evidence*: the properties of the world that can in principle be *directly observed* by the agent. When $x \in U \in \mathcal{B}$, the agent may observe the truth of proposition U in world x. Note that only the observable properties that are *true* in a world x will be observed in x (i.e. we assume observations to be sound or "correct"). So in world x the observable evidence corresponds to basic neighborhoods of the point x. Note also that this is *not* yet "evidence in hand" (that the agent already possesses), but "evidence out there" (that might observed in the future). The two conditions that underlie our definition of strong basis have a clear epistemic meaning: closure under binary intersections says that our agent is *able to accumulate observations*: after observing propositions U and V, the agent will in effect have observed the truth of the conjunction $U \cap V$ (coming to know that $x \in U \cap V$); while the condition $X \in \mathcal{B}$ says that the agent can directly *observe the truth of a tautology*.

Knowability and Conditional Knowability Interior points $x \in \text{Int}(P)$ represent worlds in which proposition P is *knowable* (or " verifiable") based on direct observations: P is true at x, and this fact can be known after some more evidence about x is observed. This interpretation follows directly from the definition: $x \in \text{Int}(P)$ holds iff there exists some observable evidence that entails P (i.e. $U \in \mathcal{B}$ with

$x \in U \subseteq P$). So, as an epistemic proposition, $\mathrm{Int}(P)$ says that *proposition P can be known from observations.* More generally, the proposition $\mathrm{Int}(A \Rightarrow P) = \mathrm{Int}((X - A) \cup P)$ captures *conditional knowability*: it says that *P can be known (from observations) given A.*

Unknowability and Falsifiability The complement $X - \mathrm{Int}(P)$ thus corresponds to "unknowability" of P, while the closure $\mathrm{Cl}(P) = X - \mathrm{Int}(X - P)$ corresponds to unfalsifiability of P: $x \in \mathrm{Cl}(P)$ means that, no matter what more evidence about x will be observed, P will never be known to be false. Note though that *our notion of unknowability is not an absolute barrier to knowledge*: it only expresses the fact that P cannot be known by direct observations (of evidence observable by the agent). Such an 'unknowable' P may still become known based on information received from another source (e.g. another agent).

Verifiable and Falsifiable Propositions The open sets $U \in \mathcal{T}$ represent *(inherently) verifiable propositions*: the ones having the property that they are knowable/verifiable whenever they are true (cf. (Vickers 1989; Kelly 1996)). This interpretation is backed by the following equivalence:

$$P \in \mathcal{T} \text{ iff } P \subseteq \mathrm{Int}(P).$$

Similarly, the closed sets represent *(inherently) falsifiable propositions*: whenever they are false, they can become known to be false after some more evidence is observed.

Knowledge Updates The move from the original topology on X to the subspace topology on some subset $A \subseteq X$ corresponds to performing an *update* of the agent's knowledge base with the proposition A: the possible worlds not satisfying A are eliminated, so the agent comes to know A after that. The update can be the result of a direct observation $A \in \mathcal{B}$; but it can also be the result of some communication from some outside source of information (e.g. an announcement from some other agent), in which case it is quite possible that $A \notin \mathcal{B}$ (i.e. A is *not* observable by our agent). However, for this update-by-elimination to be justified, it is essential that our agent *knows for certain that the source of the new information is absolutely reliable* (e.g. the other, informing agent is telling the truth).[6] The relativized interior $\mathrm{Int}_A(P) = A \cap \mathrm{Int}(P \cup (X - A))$ in the subspace topology will then capture a notion of *updated knowability* (after updating with P, the agent can come to know A based on further observations).

Examples of Evidential Topologies

- *Complete ignorance*: the **trivial topology** $\mathcal{T} = \{\emptyset, X\}$ on a set X;
- *Omniscience (God's topology)*: the **discrete topology** $\mathcal{T} = \mathcal{P}(X) = \{Y | Y \subseteq X\}$ on X;
- Knowledge based on *measurements of a point on a line*: the **standard topology of real numbers** $X = \mathbb{R}$, with the topology $\mathcal{T}$ generated by the strong basis $\mathcal{B} = \{(a, b) : a, b \in \mathbb{Q}, a < b\}$ (open intervals with rational endpoints);
- Knowledge based on *measurements in space*: the **standard topology on** $\mathbb{R}^n$, with state space $X = \mathbb{R}^n$ and topology $\mathcal{T} = \{$ countable unions of rational open balls$\}$, i.e. $A \subseteq \mathbb{R}^n$ is open iff it is of the form $A = \bigcup_{i=1}^{\infty} \{x \in \mathbb{Q}^n | d(x, a_i) < b_i\}$, where $a_i, b_i \in \mathbb{Q}^n$ and d is the Euclidean distance in n-dimensional space $\mathbb{R}^n$. A strong basis for this topology consists of all finite intersections of rational open balls.

Concrete Example: The Policeman and the Speeding Car A policeman may use radars with varying accuracy to determine whether a car is speeding in a 50 mph speed-limit zone. Then the *the set of possible worlds* is $X = (0, \infty)$ (since we assume the car is known to be *moving*). The strong base

$$\mathcal{B} = \{(a, b) : a, b \in \mathbb{Q}, 0 < a < b < \infty\}$$

consists of *all possible measurement results by arbitrarily accurate radars*. The topology $\mathcal{T}$ generated by $\mathcal{B}$ is the *standard topology on real numbers* (restricted to X). "*Speeding*" is the proposition $S = (50, \infty)$.

Suppose now that a radar with accuracy shows mph 51 ± 2 mph. This induces an *update*: the original space X shrinks to the subspace $A = (49, 53)$. In this updated space, "*Speeding*" becomes $S_A = (50, 53)$. Still, even now (in the subspace A, i.e. after the radar reading), the policeman does *not know* that the car is speeding (since $S_A \neq A$). However, the property "the car is speeding" *is in principle verifiable* (by the policeman): *if* the car is indeed speeding, then its velocity must be some $x \in S_A = (50, 53)$. Given a more accurate radar, the policeman can obtain a better measurement (a, b) with $x \in (a, b) \subseteq S_A$. This is reflected in the fact that $S_A = (50, 53)$ is *open* in the standard topology.

In contrast, *Not-Speeding* $NS = (0, 50]$ is *in general not verifiable* (not open). This means that *whether NS is knowable or not depends on the actual speed*! For instance, NS is knowable in the world in which the speed is $x = 49$. But it is *not* knowable in the world $x = 50$. On the other hand, not-speeding NS is in general falsifiable (closed in X): whenever it is false, it can be disproved by a sufficiently accurate measurement of the speed.

The Epistemic Interpretation of Cantor Derivative To understand the derivative, recall the equivalence:

$$x \in d(A) \text{ iff } x \in \mathrm{Cl}(A - \{x\}).$$

But note that $\mathrm{Cl}(A - \{x\}) = X - \mathrm{Int}(X - (A - \{x\})) = X - \mathrm{Int}((X - A) \cup \{x\}) = X - Int(A \Rightarrow \{x\})$. Using our interpretation of $X - P$ as negation of the proposition P, and of $\mathrm{Int}(A \Rightarrow P)$ as conditional knowability (of P given A), we conclude that

$$x \in d(A) \quad \text{iff} \quad x \text{ is not knowable given } A.$$

So, as an epistemic proposition, Cantor's derivative $d(A)$ says that "*the actual world is unknowable given A*".

The Epistemic Meaning of the Perfect Core Looking now at the perfect core $d^{\infty}(A)$, we can infer its epistemic meaning from the above fixed-point identity:

$$d^{\infty}(A) = \nu P. A \cap d(P).$$

[6] When this is not the case, other forms of updating are to be considered (in which the non-A worlds are *not* eliminated, but only considered in some sense less plausible, or less probable, than the A-worlds).

The perfect core can thus be understood as the *self-referential version of Cantor's derivative*: $d^{\infty}(A)$ captures the epistemic proposition "A is true, but the actual world is unknowable given *this* information" (where 'this' refers to the very proposition that we are defining). As we'll see, this is precisely the kind of self-referential statement that plays a key role in the Surprise Examination Paradox.

3 The Logic of Derivative and Perfect Core

In this section we introduce the formal syntax and semantics of our logic. We begin by defining the formal languages $\mathcal{L}_{\langle\cdot\rangle}$ and $\mathcal{L}$ we will work with:

Syntax. The language $\mathcal{L}_{\langle\cdot\rangle}$ of dynamic-epistemic logic of derivative and perfect core consists of formulas recursively defined by the following BNF:

$$\varphi ::= p \mid \neg\varphi \mid \varphi\wedge\varphi \mid \Diamond\varphi \mid \odot\varphi \mid \widehat{K}\varphi \mid \langle\varphi\rangle\varphi$$

The language $\mathcal{L}$ of (static) epistemic logic of derivative and perfect core is the fragment of $\mathcal{L}_{\langle\cdot\rangle}$ obtained by eliminating all dynamic modalities $\langle\varphi\rangle$.

Semantics. We interpret this language on **epistemic topo-models** $\mathbf{M} = (X, \mathcal{T}, \|\cdot\|)$: topological spaces $(X, \mathcal{T})$ with a valuation function (mapping every atomic sentence p into a subset $\|p\| \subseteq X$). The semantics is given by extending this valuation recursively to all of $\mathcal{L}_{\langle\cdot\rangle}$, defining $\|\varphi\|_{\mathbf{M}}$ using the usual clauses for Booleans, while

$$\|\Diamond\varphi\|_{\mathbf{M}} = d(\|\varphi\|_{\mathbf{M}})$$

is the Cantor derivative of $\|\varphi\|_{\mathbf{M}}$ wrt the topology $\mathcal{T}$, and

$$\|\odot\varphi\|_{\mathbf{M}} = d^{\infty}\|\varphi\|_{\mathbf{M}} = \nu P.\big(\|\varphi\|_{\mathbf{M}} \cap d(P)\big)$$

is the perfect core of $\|\varphi\|_{\mathbf{M}}$. The operator $\widehat{K}$ is just the global existential modality, quantifying existentially over all possible worlds: $\|\widehat{K}\varphi\|_{\mathbf{M}} = X$ if $\|\varphi\|_{\mathbf{M}} \neq \emptyset$, otherwise $\|\widehat{K}\varphi\|_{\mathbf{M}} = \varnothing$. Finally, $\langle\varphi\rangle\psi$ is the dynamic modality for epistemic updates, whose semantics is given by evaluating ψ in the updated model: if, for any subset $A \subseteq X$, we put $\mathbf{M} = (A, \mathcal{T}_A, \|\cdot\|_A)$ for the updated model, with the subspace topology $\mathcal{T}_A = \{U \cap A : U \in \mathcal{T}\}$ and relativized valuation $\|p\|_A = \|p\| \cap A$, then we set

$$\|\langle\varphi\rangle\psi\|_{\mathbf{M}} = \|\psi\|_{\|\varphi\|},$$

where $\|\varphi\| = \|\varphi\|_{\mathbf{M}}$ is the valuation of φ in the original model. As usual, we may write $(\mathbf{M}, x) \models \varphi$ iff $x \in \|\varphi\|_{\mathbf{M}}$. When the model $\mathbf{M}$ is clear from the context, we may skip it, writing e.g. $\|\varphi\|$ and $x \models \varphi$.

In an epistemic context, we read $\widehat{K}$ as *epistemic possibility*: $\widehat{K}\varphi$ says that "as far our agent knows, φ *may* be true", in the sense that φ is consistent with the agent's information. We read $\Diamond\varphi$ as saying that "the actual world is unknowable (through observations) given φ"; we read $\odot\varphi$ as a self-referential statement, saying that "φ is true, but the actual world is unknowable (through observation) given *this* information" (where 'this information' refers to the very proposition we are defining); finally, we read $\langle\varphi\rangle\psi$ as saying that "φ holds, and ψ will also hold after updating with φ".

Abbreviations: We will use the standard abbreviations for propositional connectives $\varphi\vee\psi$, $\varphi\Rightarrow\psi$, $\varphi\Leftrightarrow\psi$, $\top$ and $\bot$, as well as the following additional ones: $\Box\varphi := \neg\Diamond\neg\varphi$, $K\varphi := \neg\widehat{K}\neg\varphi$, $\widehat{\mathcal{K}}\varphi := \varphi\vee\Diamond\varphi$, and $\mathcal{K}\varphi := \neg\widehat{\mathcal{K}}\neg\varphi$. To justify these notations, note that K is just the universal modality (quantifying universally over all worlds that are possible according to our agent), $\Diamond$ is just the closure modality and $\mathcal{K}$ is just the interior modality: $\|K\varphi\| = X$ iff $\|\varphi\| = X$, and $\|K\varphi\| = \emptyset$ otherwise; $\|\widehat{\mathcal{K}}\varphi\| = \mathrm{Cl}(\|\varphi\|)$; and $\|\mathcal{K}\varphi\| = \|\varphi\wedge\Box\varphi\| = \mathrm{Int}(\|\varphi\|)$. So, given our interpretation of possible worlds, closure and interior, we can read $K\varphi$ as "φ is known" (to our agent), $\mathcal{K}\varphi$ as "φ is knowable" (through observations by our agent), and read $\widehat{\mathcal{K}}\varphi$ as "φ cannot be falsified" (by any observations by the agent).

Theorem 3.1. ***[Completeness for $\mathcal{L}_{\langle\cdot\rangle}$]*** *The following system is a sound and complete axiomatization of the dynamic-epistemic logic of Cantor derivative and perfect core $\mathcal{L}_{\langle\cdot\rangle}$:*

- *Axioms and Rules of Propositional Logic.*
- *Necessitation Rule, and Distribution (=Kripke's Axiom), for the modalities K, $\Box$ and $[\varphi]$.*[7]
- *Positive and negative introspection for knowledge:*
$$K\varphi \Rightarrow KK\varphi \qquad \neg K\varphi \Rightarrow K\neg K\varphi$$
- *Positive Introspection of Knowability* (if φ is knowable, then it is knowable to be knowable)*:* $\mathcal{K}\varphi \Rightarrow \mathcal{K}\mathcal{K}\varphi$
- *Knowledge implies knowability:* $K\varphi \Rightarrow \mathcal{K}\varphi$
- *Monotonicity rule for the perfect core:* $\dfrac{\varphi\rightarrow\psi}{\odot\varphi\rightarrow\odot\psi}$
- *Fixed Point Axiom:* $\odot\varphi \Rightarrow (\varphi\wedge\Diamond\odot\varphi)$
- *Induction Axiom:* $\mathcal{K}(\varphi\Rightarrow\Diamond\varphi) \Rightarrow (\varphi\Rightarrow\odot\varphi)$
- *Reduction axioms for update modalities:*
$$\langle\varphi\rangle p \Leftrightarrow (\varphi\wedge p)$$
$$\langle\varphi\rangle\neg\theta \Leftrightarrow (\varphi\wedge\neg\langle\varphi\rangle\theta)$$
$$\langle\varphi\rangle\widehat{K}\theta \Leftrightarrow (\varphi\wedge\widehat{K}\langle\varphi\rangle\theta)$$
$$\langle\varphi\rangle\Diamond\theta \Leftrightarrow (\varphi\wedge\Diamond\langle\varphi\rangle\theta)$$
$$\langle\varphi\rangle\odot\theta \Leftrightarrow \odot\langle\varphi\rangle\theta$$

Proving soundness is an easy verification. Completeness follows immediately from putting together the following two results:

Theorem 3.2. ***[Provable Co-expressivity of $\mathcal{L}_{\langle\cdot\rangle}$ and $\mathcal{L}$]*** *Every formula in the language $\mathcal{L}_{\langle\cdot\rangle}$ is provably equivalent*[8] *to some formula in the static fragment $\mathcal{L}$. Hence, the two logics $\mathcal{L}_{\langle\cdot\rangle}$ and $\mathcal{L}$ have the same expressivity.*[9]

[7] In fact, Necessitation for $\Box$ follows from Necessitation for K and the axiom "Knowledge implies knowability".

[8] This means that the equivalence is provable in the above axiomatic system for $\mathcal{L}_{\langle\cdot\rangle}$.

[9] But they differ in succinctness: formulas in $\mathcal{L}_{\langle\cdot\rangle}$ can be in general exponentially more succinct than their translations in $\mathcal{L}$. In addition, they can capture the desired dynamic-epistemic scenarios in a much more transparent and direct way than their translations. This makes dynamic modalities very useful for applications, and justifies our choice of the larger language $\mathcal{L}_{\langle\cdot\rangle}$.

Theorem 3.3. *[Completeness for $\mathcal{L}$] The system obtained from the above axiomatic system for $\mathcal{L}_{\langle\cdot\rangle}$ by eliminating all axioms and rules that refer to dynamic modalities (specifically: eliminating Necessitation and Distribution for $[\varphi]$, as well as all the reduction axioms) is a sound and complete axiomatization of the static epistemic logic of Cantor derivative and perfect core $\mathcal{L}$.*

Proof Summary While the proof of Theorem 3.2 is an easy induction (using the reduction axioms to gradually push the dynamic modalities past other operators and then eliminate them), the proof of Theorem 3.3 is highly non-trivial, and uses methods that we developed in our recent work on topological μ-calculus (Baltag, Bezhanishvili, and Fernández-Duque 2021). Hence, we only give here a bird's eye overview of this proof. Essentially, we start from the canonical model Ω (comprising all maximally consistent theories accessible from some fixed theory), a standard construction in modal logic. But we should stress that Ω is *not* our intended model.[10] Indeed, the usual Truth Lemma fails for our logic $\mathcal{L}$ in the canonical model: formulas are not necessarily satisfied in Ω by the theories that contain them. Next, for any given finite set of formulas Σ, we select a special submodel of the canonical model Ω^{Σ} (called the Σ-final model), consists of "Σ-final theories": essentially, these are the ones whose cluster is locally definable by some formula in Σ. Our goal will be to show that the Truth Lemma does hold in Ω^{Σ} for Σ-formulas. It is easy to show that Ω^{Σ} satisfies the usual Existential Witness Lemma for modalities $\Diamond$ and $\widehat{K}$ (and formulas in Σ), but extending this to the perfect core modality $\odot$ requires some work. Another key ingredient in our proof is the fact that Ω^{Σ} is "essentially" a finite object: though possibly infinite in size, it has finite 'depth', and moreover it contains only finitely many bisimilarity classes. As a consequence, the largest fixed points of the operators $P \mapsto d_{\|\varphi\|}(P)$ (that define $\|\odot\varphi\|$) are all attained in Ω^{Σ} below some fixed *finite* stage of the Cantor-Bendixson process. We then use these ingredients to prove our Truth Lemma for the final model Ω^{Σ}.

The full details are in the Appendix to the extended version (see Supplementary Material), where we also use the selection method to obtain a finite submodel of Ω^{Σ} that satisfies the same relevant formulas, and then analyzing the complexity of the selection algorithm, thus proving:

Theorem 3.4. *[FMP, Decidability and Complexity] The (static and dynamic) logics of Cantor derivative and perfect core have the strong finite model property (and hence they are decidable). Moreover, the satisfiability problem for the static logic $\mathcal{L}$ is* PSPACE*-complete.*

Some Technical-Historical Connections. As mentioned in the Introduction, McKinsey and Tarski (McKinsey and Tarski 1944) were the first to look at the modal logic of topological closure and topological interior. In our notations, these are captured by the knowability modalities $\widehat{\mathcal{K}}$ and $\mathcal{K}$. They showed that this is the same as the modal logic of reflexive-transitive frames, more precisely the modal logic S4. In our formalism, the axiom 4 corresponds to our axiom of Positive Introspection for knowability: $\mathcal{K}\varphi \Rightarrow \mathcal{K}\mathcal{K}\varphi$. We refer to (van Benthem and Bezhanishvili 2007) for an overview of results on topological completeness of modal logics above S4.

As also mentioned in the Introduction, McKinsey and Tarski also considered the modal logic of Cantor derivative. Esakia (Esakia 2001; Esakia 2004) showed that the derivative logic of all topological spaces is the same as the logic of weakly-transitive frames, namely the modal logic wK4 $=$ K $+$ w4, where w4 is the weak transitivity axiom: $\Diamond\Diamond p \rightarrow \Diamond p \vee p$. In our formalism, this is easily seen to be *equivalent* to the above-mentioned axiom of Positive Introspection for knowability. Indeed, given our definition of knowability, the axiom $\mathcal{K}\varphi \Rightarrow \mathcal{K}\mathcal{K}\varphi$ can be unfolded into

$$(\varphi \wedge \Box\varphi) \Rightarrow \Box\Box\varphi.$$

This is a Sahlqvist formula (see e.g. (Chagrov and Zakharyaschev 1997)) corresponding to the weak-transitivity condition on relational models, whose equivalent dual form is Esakia's weak transitivity axiom w4.

4 Surprise: Non-Self-Referential Version

There are many 'solutions' to the Surprise Exam Paradox in the literature (Quine 1953; McLelland and Chihara 1975; Wright and Sudbury 1977; Sorensen 1984; Chow 1998; Hall 1999; Gerbrandy 2007; Levi 2009). Some of them concern different versions of the puzzle, in which some of the assumptions are suspended , e.g. the Student may *not know for sure* (but only believe) that there will be an exam next week, or that the Teacher always tells the truth. Though interesting, these provide "easy" ways to avoid the contradiction, so we will ignore these weakened versions, focusing on the version in which these assumptions are granted. Even so, most of the solutions proposed in the literature are unfortunately informal, or only half formalized. Gerbrandy's approach (Gerbrandy 2007) is one of the few exceptions. We hereby briefly summarize his approach.

Gerbrandy's Solution The setting uses the older, non-topological version of our dynamic-epistemic logic, more precisely the so-called Public Announcement Logic: an epistemic model $\mathbf{M} = (X, \|\cdot\|)$ is simply given by a set of possible worlds X together with a valuation map; the logic is restricted to the fragment generated by atomic sentences, Boolean connectives, the knowledge operator $K\varphi$ (modeled as universal modality) and the dynamic update operators $[\varphi]\theta$ (also called 'public announcement', and modeled by relativization to the *subset* $\|\varphi\|$, with no subspace topological structure). Like our logic, this logic is single-agent: the Teacher is only treated as an infallible *source* of truthful information, not as an agent. So the knowledge operator K refers to the Student's knowledge. Knowability $\mathcal{K}\varphi$, derivative modality $\Diamond\varphi$ and perfect core $\odot\varphi$ do not belong to this language. But the update modalities are still eliminable, via the reduction laws for Booleans and knowledge.

More specifically, the set $X = \{x_1, x_2, x_3, x_4, x_5\}$ consists of five possible worlds, with the obvious meaning: for

[10]In fact, the notion of truth in the canonical model will play no role in this paper: we never evaluate our formulas in it. Instead, we only use a few basic syntactic properties of this model.

each $1 \leq i \leq 5$, x_i is the world in which the exam will come in the corresponding i^{th} day of the week. The language has 5 atomic sentences $\{p_i : 1 \leq i \leq 5\}$, where p_i means "the exam will be in the ith day". The valuation is again obvious: $\|p_i\| = \{x_i\}$. Clearly, this model satisfies $K(\bigvee_{i=1}^{5} p_i)$, which captures one of the main assumptions of the puzzle: the Student knows for sure there will be an exam in the next week. Furthermore, for each $1 \leq i \leq 5$, the passage of the previous days without any exam can be 'simulated' in this logic by an update with the sentence $\bigwedge_{j=1}^{i-1} \neg p_j$: indeed, this is the information gained by the Student by the evening of day $i-1$. Hence, Gerbrandy formalizes Teacher's announcement as the sentence

$$\text{SURPRISE} := \bigwedge_{i=1}^{5} [\bigwedge_{j=1}^{i-1} \neg p_j] \neg K p_i.$$

This sentence says that, no matter in which day i will the exam come, by the evening of day $i-1$ the Student will not know for sure that the exam will be the next day. Using the reduction axioms, this formula can be simplified to

$$\text{SURPRISE} \Leftrightarrow \bigwedge_{i=1}^{5} \neg K(\bigvee_{j=1}^{i} p_j).$$

Finally, the assumption that the Student knows for sure that the Teacher never lies is implemented by performing an update with the sentence SURPRISE: all worlds in which the sentence is false are eliminated, and the model shrinks to $\|\text{SURPRISE}\|$. But, using the above static equivalent, it is easy to see that, in the model X the sentence SURPRISE is false only in world w_5 (in which the exam is on Friday) and true in all the others. Hence, the model shrinks to $\|\text{SURPRISE}\| = \{x_1, x_2, x_3, x_4\}$.

Thus, according to Gerbrandy, *the only valid conclusion is that the exam cannot be on Friday*: the first elimination step in the informal reasoning underlying the 'paradox' is the only correct one. All further elimination steps are *not* justified: e.g., the second step (eliminating Thursday) would require performing *a second update* with the sentence SURPRISE. But the Teacher only announced the sentence once! The sentence SURPRISE was true before being announced (assuming the exam won't be on Friday), but *nothing guarantees that the sentence will still be true after this announcement*: the Teacher did not claim *that*! If say, the exam will be on Thursday, then the sentence SURPRISE changes its truth value (from true to false) after the Teacher's announcement: this does not in any way contradict the truthfulness of Teacher's announcement (since it *was true* at the moment when it was announced). So the apparent 'paradox' only points to the existence of sentences that change their truth value after being announced.[11]

A first objection to the above approach is that it gives a very "low level" formalization of the sentence SURPRISE, that is highly dependent on irrelevant details (such as the number of days in the week, the linear temporal order of the observable evidence in the form of day-passing, etc). If we change the story to cover 2 weeks, the sentence SURPRISE changes. Even worse: we can build similar stories, to which the above approach simply cannot be applied, since e.g. the number of worlds is infinite, the potential observations are also infinitely many, and they cannot be arranged in any salient linear order. Let us look now at such an example.

Infinite Surprise Let us denote the set of positive integers by $\mathbb{N}$. It is known that the Teacher chose a point x belonging to the set

$$A = \{0\} \cup \{1/n : n \in \mathbb{N}\} \cup \{1/n(n+1) : n \in \mathbb{N}\}$$

and marked it on the real line drawn on a board. The Student can perform observations, measuring the position of the point, with any arbitrary precision $\epsilon > 0$ (by building better and better measurement devices); but obviously, he can never measure the position with infinite precision ($\epsilon = 0$)! But the Teacher (who is known to be always truthful) tells the Student: "*No matter how good your measurement is, you will never know the exact position of the point!*"

Intuitively, the Student can reproduce the Surprise Exam argument to conclude that $x \notin A$, obtaining a contradiction (since he *knows* that $x \in A$). First, if the point is of the form $x = \frac{1}{n(n+1)}$ for some $n \in \mathbb{N}$, then he eventually be able to know its location exactly, if he continues increasing the precision of his measurements: indeed, whenever he will reach a precision $\epsilon < |\frac{1}{n(n+1)} - \frac{1}{(n+1)(n+2)}| = \frac{1}{n(n+1)(n+2)}$, then his measurement will yield an open interval of the form $(a-\epsilon, a+\epsilon) \ni x$, whose only intersection with A is the singleton $\{x\} = \{\frac{1}{n(n+1)}\}$ consisting of the exact position. But this contradicts the Teacher's announcement (that he will never know the exact position); this contradiction rules out all points of the form $\frac{1}{n(n+1)}$, so x must belong to the set $\{0\} \cup \{1/n : n \in \mathbb{N}\}$. By repeating the argument, the Student can rule out next all points of the form $x = \frac{1}{n}$ (with $n \in \mathbb{N}$), since in any such case he will eventually be able to know its location exactly (whenever he reaches a precision $\epsilon < |\frac{1}{n} - \frac{1}{(n)(n+1)}| = \frac{1}{n(n+1)}$), concluding that x *must belong to the singleton set* $\{0\}$. So now the Student *knows* the exact location $x = 0$ (without even having had to do any measurement), again contradicting Teacher's announcement!

Though the argument is essentially identical to the Surprise Exam, it cannot be treated using the above approach, due to the fact that both the possible worlds and the possible observations (measurement intervals) are infinite.

This is where the topological approach comes to the rescue. By abstracting away from day-passing or measurements, and considering them to be just special cases of families of observable evidence, given in the form of strong topological bases, we can see the sentence SURPRISE simply says that "*the actual world is not knowable through observations*". Using our semantics, this is captured by the formula

$$\text{SURPRISE} := \Diamond\top,$$

where $\Diamond$ is the derivative modality wrt the evidential topology (generated by the basis $\mathcal{B}$). In the case of our Infinite

[11]Such examples are called 'Moore sentences' and are by now well-understood as non-paradoxical utterings, easily dealt with in the framework of Dynamic Epistemic Logic.

Surprise, it is clear what the evidential topology is: the *standard* topology on the set A, generated by the family $\mathcal{B} = \{(a, b) \cap A : a, b \in \mathbb{Q}, a < b\}$ of (relativized) open intervals with rational endpoints. Applying Gerbrandy's analysis to this topological version, we see that $\|\text{SURPRISE}\|_A = \|\Diamond\top\|_A = d_A(A) = d(A) = \{0\} \cup \{\frac{1}{n} : n \in \mathbb{N}\}$ (since all other points are isolated in A), and we can thus conclude that *only this first elimination step is correct*: the only information that can be extracted from Teacher's announcement is that $x \in \{\frac{1}{n} : n \in \mathbb{N}\}$. Further elimination steps are not justified: though true when it was announced, the sentence $\Diamond\top$ may have changed its truth value after the announcement.

Going back to the original Surprise Exam story, what is the evidential topology in that case? Since "observations" correspond there to the passing of days without exams, the relevant strong base is

$$\mathcal{B} = \{O_1, O_2, O_3, O_4, O_5\},$$

where $O_i = X - \{x_j : j < i\} = \{x_j : i \leq j\}$. Here, $O_1 = X$ corresponds to the trivial tautological observation (before Monday) that the exam will be in one of the 5 days of next week; O_2 corresponds to the negative observation after Monday morning: that the exam was not on Monday (hence it will be in one of the remaining four days); etc. The generated evidential topology is $\mathcal{T} = \{\emptyset\} \cup \mathcal{B}$. Once again, as in Gerbrandy's analysis, $\|\Diamond\top\| = X - \{x_5\} = \{x_1, x_2, x_3, x_4\}$ (since x_5 is the only isolated point in this topology).

We have thus obtained a uniform treatment of the puzzle, that simplifies and generalizes Gerbrandy's solution.

5 Surprise: Self-Referential Version

While the above formalization of the sentence SURPRISE seems natural at first sight, there is something profoundly odd about it. The teacher announced that the *exam's date **will** be a surprise*: this seemed to point to the *actual future*, as it will unfold *after* this announcement is made. However, the above formalization allows for the possibility that the announcement was meant to be true only before the announcement (or counterfactually: if no such announcement was made), but to possibly change its truth value to false after the announcement is made. In that case, in what sense can one still claim that the Teacher was truthful in her announcement about "will" happen?

Looking at the sentence $\Diamond\top$ (or at Gerbrandy's more complicated non-topological counterpart), we can see that the best way to describe it in natural language is a counterfactual statement of the type: "*the exam's date **would** have been a surprise, if I didn't make this very announcement*". Moreover, this interpretation in terms of a counterfactual (instead of the actual) future seems to be crucial for Gerbrandy's 'solution' of the paradox.

However, this is *not* what the Teacher said, and it does *not* sound like the most natural interpretation of her statement. When referring to the future in an announcement, it is typically implicitly assumed that the speaker factors in her own announcement action: thus, she is expected to use the word "will" to refer to what will happen after she makes the announcement. "It will be a surprise" means that it *will* be so, not that it would have been so in some other possible future.

Thus, to understand the Teacher's statement we need to make explicit its implicit self-referentiality, reading it as "*You will not know in advance the exam day (i.e. after hearing **this** very announcement)*". Most authors who wrote about the paradox agree that *this self-referential interpretation is the intended one*.

Gerbrandy was aware of this interpretation (without formalizing it), but like many other logicians he thought that it leads to a genuine, Liar-like paradox, because of its circularity. In contrast, other logicians, such as Quine, argued in older work (Quine 1953) that there is no real paradox, but only an impossible assumption: the conclusion should only be that a *source who is known to always tell the truth cannot make such a (future-oriented, implicitly self-referential) announcement* (since that would be a lie).

Using our derivative and dynamic modalities, we can formalize the self-referential announcement as a 'circular' proposition P satisfying the equation

$$P = \langle P \rangle \Diamond\top.$$

Moreover, this is *all* that is claimed in the Teacher's announcement: there is no other implicit information in it. This means that we are looking at the *most general statement* satisfying the equation, i.e. the *largest fixed point* of the operator $P \mapsto \langle P \rangle \Diamond\top$. Using standard μ-calculus notation, we can write the statement as

$$\text{SURPRISE}^{\infty} := \nu P.\langle P \rangle \Diamond\top,$$

and call it the *self-referential surprise announcement*. Although the above formalization is not in our language $\mathcal{L}_{\langle\cdot\rangle}$ (but only in its fixed-point extension), it can be given an equivalent formulation. Using our reduction laws, we can see that $\langle P \rangle \Diamond\top$ is equivalent to $P \wedge \Diamond\langle P \rangle\top$, which in turn is equivalent to $P \wedge \Diamond P$. So the sentence SURPRISE^{∞} is equivalent to any of the following formulas:

$$\nu P.P \wedge \Diamond P = \nu P.\Diamond P = \nu P.(\top \wedge \Diamond P) = \odot\top.$$

Thus, the formula $\odot\top$, denoting the perfect core of our space $\|\odot\top\|_X = d^{\infty}(X)$, captures the full self-referential meaning of the surprise announcement SURPRISE^{∞}. There is nothing paradoxical with this type of self-referentiality: the monotonicity of the derivative operator ensures the existence of the fixed point. If a Teacher who is known never to lie made this announcement, that would induce an update that shrinks the original space X to its perfect core X^{∞}.

We can now recognize the successive eliminative steps in the Student's reasoning as corresponding to the Cantor-Bendisxon process of calculating the perfect core: the first step eliminates the isolated point x_5, calculating the Cantor derivative $d^1(X) = X - \{x_5\}$; the next step calculates $d^2(X) = X - \{x_4, x_5\}$; etc. After five steps, we reach a fixed point $d^5(X) = d^{\infty}(X) = \emptyset$. A similar remark applies to our above Infinite Surprise example: the first step yields $d^1(A) = \{0\} \cup \{\frac{1}{n} : n \in \mathbb{N}\}$; the next step yields $d^2(A) = \{0\}$; finally, the third step reaches the fixed point

$d^3(A) = d^\infty(A) = \emptyset$. And since in both cases the perfect core is empty, a contradiction is actually reached!

But, in this interpretation, *all the elimination steps are justified* (unlike in Gerbrandy's counterfactual interpretation). The conclusion is that, in the self-referential version of the story, *the Student's entire inductive eliminative reasoning is entirely correct*! The contradiction obtained in the end ($\|\text{SURPRISE}^\infty\| = d^\infty(X) = \emptyset$) only shows that *the update with* SURPRISE$^\infty$ *cannot be truthfully performed in this case*: if it is known that the Teacher never lies, then *the statement* SURPRISE$^\infty$ *is false, and in fact known to be false*, regardless of the day of the exam.

Liar-like paradox? Not really. The sentence SURPRISE$^\infty$ has in any case some definite truth value, unlike the Liar sentences. As already mentioned, one of the assumptions of the story must simply be false: either it is *not known for sure that the Teacher always tells the truth*, or else the Teacher *never makes this self-referential announcement* in these particular situations (since it would be a lie). The *appearance* of paradox is due to the fact in this specific example the only fixed point is the empty set. However, a proposition with empty extension is by definition *not* paradoxical, but just false (in all possible worlds).

But this doesn't validate the Students' ultimate conclusion (in the follow-up story): partying every day is *not* justified. *That last follow-up step is the Student's only mistake.* If the Student gives up the first assumption (that he knew that the Teacher never lies), then the whole iterative elimination reasoning is *blocked*: even the first step is no longer justified! So, in that case, the Student can no longer be sure that the Teacher lies: she may be lying, or she may be telling the truth. All bets are off, the exam might come any day. Studying every day, instead of partying, is now the only safe option.

Our diagnosis agrees with Quine's: a Teacher who is known not to lie cannot truthfully make the announcement SURPRISE$^\infty$ in our two examples. But, contrary to Quine, Gerbrandy and other philosophical logicians, we claim that this impossibility result is *not* due to the self-referential character of the announcement. Self-referentiality is only dangerous when applied to non-monotonic operators (such as negation, e.g. the Liar). But derivative is monotonic, so *the type of self-referentiality involved in the Surprise story is innocuous.*[12] In fact, the sentence SURPRISE$^\infty$ can even be *true* in some situations! To see this, let us consider a modified version of the above Infinite Surprise example.

Infinite Surprise with a Twist Everything goes as in the Infinite Surprise story, except that this time the Teacher choses a point x belonging to the set $B = A \cup [1,2]$, where $A = \{0\} \cup \{\frac{1}{n} : n \in \mathbb{N}\} \cup \{\frac{1}{n(n+1)} : n \in \mathbb{N}\}$ is the set in the previous (untwisted) version of Infinite Surprise. The same Cantor-Bendixson inductive process of elimination can be now used to show that the perfect core is $d^4(B) = d^\infty(B) = [1,2]$. In this situation, an update with the same self-referential sentence SURPRISE$^\infty$ shrinks the set of possible points to the subspace $[1,2]$. In other words, an announcement of this sentence by a Teacher known to lie simply conveys the information that the actual points satisfies $x \in [1,2]$. A smart Student should be able to correctly infer this information, by applying the same type of "paradoxical" reasoning as in the above examples. But no contradiction is reached now: this scenario *can* happen, and if the point really is in $[1,2]$ then the Teacher told the truth!

The conclusion of our analysis is that, in any Surprise-like paradox, *the appearance of "paradoxicality" is not due to self-referentiality, but only to the fact that the perfect core happens to be empty*. The existence of non-empty perfect sets is a topological fact, that has important epistemic consequences: the self-referential sentence involved in Surprise-like scenarios *can* in fact be *true* (even if in the standard story it turns out to be false). The Surprise Exam 'Paradox' is not a paradox at all, and the Students' inductive process of elimination is a correct logical argument[13]: just a special case of the inductive Cantor-Bendixson process of calculating the perfect core! Thus, our analysis reveals deep connections between the apparent paradox and classical work in Analysis and Topology.

6 Concluding Remarks

In this paper, we developed a unified topological interpretation of knowledge, observable evidence, knowability and knowledge updates, and studied a notion of "epistemic surprise" (expressing the unknowability of the actual world), that comes in two flavors: a non-self-referential version (described by Cantor derivative) and a self-referential one (described by the perfect core). We applied these notions to the analysis of the Surprise Exam Paradox, gave a complete axiomatization of the associated logic, and proved that it is decidable and that its static fragment is PSPACE-complete.

Some outstanding open questions still remain. First, what is the *complexity of our dynamic logic* $\mathcal{L}_{\langle\cdot\rangle}$? Although the reduction to $\mathcal{L}$ is exponential, we conjecture that $\mathcal{L}_{\langle\cdot\rangle}$ is still PSPACE-complete. Second: developing a *multi-agent version* of our logic would be of great value for studying epistemic dialogues, security protocols and other multi-agent epistemic scenarios and puzzles. In future work, we plan to tackle these open problems and their applications.

[12] In contrast, the Liar sentence requires a fixed point for negation/complementation, which doesn't exist in a Boolean algebra. Another possible source of the feeling of paradox given by the Surprise Exam story might be the *negative* form of the Surprise sentence, as expressed in natural language, which makes it superficially similar to the Liar sentence. Thus, its self-referentiality may *look* dangerous at first sight. But looks are deceiving: in the expression "the actual world can be known, given P", the proposition P appears conditionally, and thus in a negative position; hence, when we negate this expression (saying "the world cannot be known, given P"), P reverts to a positive position. This explains the monotonicity of Cantor's derivative (and relative derivative), and thus the non-paradoxical nature of SURPRISE$^\infty$.

[13] With the obvious exception of the follow-up story: as we explained above, going to party every day (after giving up on the initial assumption that it was known that the Teacher never lies) is the Student's only mistake.

Acknowledgments

The third author was supported by the FWO-FWF Lead Agency grant G030620N (FWO)/I4513N (FWF).

References

Abramsky, S. 1991. Domain theory in logical form. *Ann. Pure Appl. Logic* 51(1-2):1–77.

Aumann, R. 1995. Backward induction and common knowledge of rationality. *Games and Economic Behavior* 8:6–19.

Baltag, A.; Bezhanishvili, N.; and Fernández-Duque, D. 2021. The topological mu-calculus: completeness and decidability. In *Proc. of LICS 36*, 1–13. IEEE Press.

Baltag, A.; Bezhanishvili, N.; Özgün, A.; and Smets, S. 2016. Justified belief and the topology of evidence. In *Proc. of WoLLIC 2016*, volume 9803 of *LNCS*, 83–103. Springer.

Baltag, A.; Bezhanishvili, N.; Ozgun, A.; and Smets, S. 2019a. A topological approach to full belief. *JPL* 48:205–244.

Baltag, A.; Gierasimczuk, N.; Özgün, A.; Sandoval, A. L. V.; and Smets, S. 2019b. A dynamic logic for learning theory. *Journal of Logical and Algebraic Methods in Programming* 109:100485.

Baltag, A.; Gierasimczuk, N.; and Smets, S. 2015. On the solvability of inductive problems: A study in epistemic topology. In *Proc. of TARK 2015*, 81–98. ENTCS.

Brecht, M., and Yamamoto, A. 2010. Topological properties of concept spaces. *Information & Computation* 208(4):327–340.

Chagrov, A., and Zakharyaschev, M. 1997. *Modal Logic*. New York: The Clarendon Press.

Chow, T. Y. 1998. The surprise examination or unexpected hanging paradox. *American Mathematical Monthly* 105:41—-51.

Esakia, L. 2001. Weak transitivity—a restitution. In *Logical investigations, No. 8 (Russian) (Moscow, 2001)*. Moscow: "Nauka". 244–255.

Esakia, L. 2004. Intuitionistic logic and modality via topology. *Annals of Pure and Applied Logic* 127(1-3):155–170. Provinces of logic determined.

Fernández-Duque, D. 2011. Tangled modal logic for spatial reasoning. In Walsh, T., ed., *IJCAI 2011, Proceedings of the 22nd International Joint Conference on Artificial Intelligence, Barcelona, Catalonia, Spain, July 16-22, 2011*, 857–862. IJCAI/AAAI.

Gerbrandy, J. 2007. The surprise examination in dynamic epistemic logic. *Synthese* 155:21–33.

Goldblatt, R., and Hodkinson, I. 2017. Spatial logic of tangled closure operators and modal mu-calculus. *Ann. Pure Appl. Log.* 168(5):1032–1090.

Goubault, E.; Ledent, J.; and Rajsbaum, S. 2020. A simplicial complex model for dynamic epistemic logic to study distributed task computability. *Information & Computation*.

Hall, N. 1999. How to set a surprise exam. *Mind* 108(432):647–703.

Kelly, K. T. 1996. *The Logic of Reliable Inquiry*. Oxford University Press.

Levi, K. 2009. The solution to the surprise exam paradox. *Southern Journal of Philosophy* 47(2):131–158.

McKinsey, J. C. C., and Tarski, A. 1944. The algebra of topology. *Ann. of Math.* 45:141–191.

McLelland, J., and Chihara, C. 1975. The surprise examination paradox. *JPL* 4(1):71–89.

Özgün, A. 2017. *Evidence in Epistemic Logic : A Topological Perspective*. Ph.D. Dissertation, ILLC, Univ. of Amsterdam and Univ. of Lorraine.

Parikh, R. 1992. Finite and infinite dialogues. In *Logic from Computer Science*, 481–497. Springer.

Quine, M. V. 1953. On a so-called paradox. *Mind* 62(245):65–67.

Sorensen, R. 1984. Recalcitrant variations of the prediction paradox. *Australasian Journal of Philosophy* 69(4):355–362.

Steinsvold, C. 2007. *Topological models of belief logics*. Ph.D. Dissertation, City University of New York.

van Benthem, J., and Bezhanishvili, G. 2007. Modal logics of space. In *Handbook of spatial logics*. Dordrecht: Springer. 217–298.

Vickers, S. 1989. *Topology via Logic*. Cambridge: Cambridge University Press.

Wright, C., and Sudbury, A. 1977. The paradox of the unexpected examination. *Australasian Journal of Philosophy* 55(1):41—58.

Proceedings of the 19th International Conference on Principles of Knowledge Representation and Reasoning
Main Track

On Syntactic Forgetting with Strong Persistence

Matti Berthold
Universität Leipzig
berthold@informatik.uni-leipzig.de

Abstract

It is generally agreed upon that so-called *strong persistence* $(\mathbf{SP})$ captures best the essence of *forgetting* in logic programming. While classes of operators, such as F_{R} and F_{SP}, that satisfy immediate relaxations of $(\mathbf{SP})$, and in the case of F_{SP}, even $(\mathbf{SP})$ whenever possible, have been characterized semantically, many practical questions have yet to be addressed. This technical paper aims to answer one of them: How can atoms be forgotten from a program without having to calculate its exponential number of models? To this end, we introduce two concrete representatives of F_{R} and F_{SP} that forget sets of atoms by syntactical manipulation of a program's rules. This may in many cases prevent exponential blowups and produce a forgetting result that is close to the original program.

1 Introduction

The research area of *forgetting* has recently seen ample amounts of progress in the context of logic programming. Intuitively, forgetting means that bits of a program are removed in such a way that the logical connections between the remaining bits are left intact. Forgetting might be necessary, for example, to tend to legal requests to remove information of a user from a knowledge base, or, to simplify it by removing unnecessary data.

Recent studies investigated several forgetting properties and identified *Strong Persistence* $(\mathbf{SP})$ to most accurately describe the essence of forgetting (Gonçalves, Knorr, and Leite 2016a). $(\mathbf{SP})$, however, is not always obtainable (Gonçalves, Knorr, and Leite 2016b). Therefore forgetting operators have been defined semantically, satisfying different relaxations of $(\mathbf{SP})$, among them F_{R} and F_{SP}, where notably F_{SP} does satisfy $(\mathbf{SP})$, whenever possible (Gonçalves et al. 2017).

While it is possible to obtain specific forgetting results from the desired semantics by counter-models construction (Cabalar and Ferraris 2007), this process necessarily involves calculating an exponential number of interpretations. In many cases, such blowups can be avoided by constructing a forgetting result purely by syntactically manipulating the input program.

In the literature there exists a number of such syntactic forgetting operators (Zhang and Foo 2006; Eiter and Wang 2008; Knorr and Alferes 2014; Gonçalves et al. 2021), however, most of them do not satisfy the most basic properties, much less $(\mathbf{SP})$ (cf. (Berthold et al. 2019) for an overview).

The only syntactic operator to satisfy $(\mathbf{SP})$, whenever possible, f_{SP}, only forgets one atom. To this end, it was proven to conform to the semantics of class F_{SP}. But can f_{SP} be iterated to correctly forget arbitrary sets of atoms?

Example 1. *Consider forgetting p and q from program P_1:*

$$a \leftarrow p, q. \qquad q \leftarrow not\, p. \qquad p \leftarrow not\, not\, p.$$

The only remaining atom, a, is implied by p and q, who are mutually exclusive. Since a can therefore not be deduced, one would expect the result of forgetting to be the empty program.[1] *And indeed, if we first forget q and then p via f_{SP}, we arrive at our desired result. Forgetting q first yields $\mathsf{f}_{SP}(P_1, q)$:*

$$\cancel{a \leftarrow p, not\, p.} \qquad p \leftarrow not\, not\, p.$$

where the appearance of q in the rule $a \leftarrow p, q.$ is simply replaced by $not\, p$, which implied q before. The resulting rule can then be disregarded, as p and $not\, p$ are unsatisfiable together. Forgetting p subsequently naturally yields the empty program, i.e. $\mathsf{f}_{SP}(\mathsf{f}_{SP}(P_1, q), p) = \emptyset$.

Observe what happens if the order of forgetting p and q is reversed: Forgetting p first yields $\mathsf{f}_{SP}(P_1, p)$:

$$a \leftarrow q, not\, not\, a. \qquad q \leftarrow not\, not\, q.$$

where the cyclic dependency on p is transferred to a and q, but the information that a was only implied by a contradiction is lost. Forgetting q thereafter yields $\mathsf{f}_{SP}(\mathsf{f}_{SP}(P_1, p), q)$:

$$a \leftarrow not\, not\, a.$$

which is not our desired forgetting result.

Apparently, f_{SP} is sensitive to the order in which atoms are forgotten. We will show that, worse yet, for both classes, F_{R} and F_{SP}, there are instances such that forgetting atoms iteratively in *any* order will create a result deviating from forgetting all atoms at once. This proves the existing forgetting operator f_{SP} insufficient for forgetting arbitrary sets of atoms from programs by F_{SP} semantics, and illustrates that concrete forgetting procedures for both F_{R} and F_{SP} necessarily are quite complex.

This paper introduces the syntactic operators f_R and f^*_{SP} to overcome these issues, that forget any set of atoms correctly by the semantics of F_{R} and F_{SP}.

[1] This intuition coincides with F_{SP}.

The paper is structured as follows: Sec. 2 recalls the basics of logic programming and the semantics of forgetting. Sec. 3 collects a number of auxiliary syntactic operators that are used when forgetting. We put a particular emphasis on their connection to HT-semantics and provide some insights that are essential to our main results.

The operators f_R and f^*_{SP} are defined and proven to be correct in Sec. 4 and 5 respectively. Finally Sec. 6 contains the intuitions behind the operators, as well as some positive results demonstrating their performance. We close the paper with a discussion in Sec. 7.

2 Background

Logic Programs We assume a *propositional signature* Σ. A *logic program* P over Σ is a finite set of *rules* of the form

$$a_1 \vee \ldots \vee a_k \leftarrow b_1, ..., b_l, not\, c_1, ..., not\, c_m, \\ not\, not\, d_1, ..., not\, not\, d_n,$$

where all $a_1, \ldots, a_k, b_1, \ldots, b_l, c_1, \ldots, c_m$, and $d_1, \ldots, d_n$ are atoms of Σ (Lifschitz, Tang, and Turner 1999). Such rules r are also written more succinctly as

$$H(r) \leftarrow B^+(r), not\, B^-(r), not\, not\, B^{--}(r),$$

where $H(r) = \{a_1, \ldots, a_k\}$, $B^+(r) = \{b_1, \ldots, b_l\}$, $B^-(r) = \{c_1, \ldots, c_m\}$, and $B^{--}(r) = \{d_1, \ldots, d_n\}$, and we will use both forms interchangeably. Given a rule r, $H(r)$ is called the *head* of r, and $B(r) = B^+(r) \cup not\, B^-(r) \cup not\, not\, B^{--}(r)$ is called the *body* of r, where, for a set A of atoms, $not\, A = \{not\, q \mid q \in A\}$ and $not\, not\, A = \{not\, not\, q \mid q \in A\}$.

$\Sigma(P)$ and $\Sigma(r)$ denote the set of atoms appearing in P and r, respectively.

Given a program P and an *interpretation*, i.e., a set $I \subseteq \Sigma$ of atoms, the *reduct* of P given I, is defined as $P^I = \{H(r) \leftarrow B^+(r) \mid r \in P$ such that $B^-(r) \cap I = \varnothing$ and $B^{--}(r) \subseteq I\}$. An *HT-interpretation* is a pair $\langle X, Y \rangle$ s.t. $X \subseteq Y \subseteq \Sigma$. Given a program P, an HT-interpretation $\langle X, Y \rangle$ is an *HT-model of* P, $\langle X, Y \rangle \models P$, iff $Y \models P$ and $X \models P^Y$, where $\models$ both denotes the standard satisfaction relation for classical logic and for HT-logic.[2] An HT-interpretation $\langle X, Y \rangle$ is *total* iff $X = Y$. Given a rule r, $\langle X, Y \rangle \models r$, iff $\langle X, Y \rangle \models \{r\}$. We admit that the set of HT-models of a program P is restricted to $\Sigma(P)$ even if $\Sigma(P) \subset \Sigma$. We denote by $\mathcal{HT}(P)$ the set of *all HT-models of* P. A set of atoms Y is an *answer set* of P iff $\langle Y, Y \rangle \in \mathcal{HT}(P)$, and there is no $X \subset Y$ such that $\langle X, Y \rangle \in \mathcal{HT}(P)$. We term HT-models $\langle X, Y \rangle$ s.t. $X \subset Y$ *witnesses*. The set of all answer sets of P is denoted by $\mathcal{AS}(P)$. Two programs P_1, P_2 are *equivalent* iff $\mathcal{AS}(P_1) = \mathcal{AS}(P_2)$ and *strongly equivalent*, $P_1 \equiv P_2$, iff $\mathcal{AS}(P_1 \cup R) = \mathcal{AS}(P_2 \cup R)$ for any program R. It is well-known that $P_1 \equiv P_2$ exactly when $\mathcal{HT}(P_1) = \mathcal{HT}(P_2)$ (Lifschitz, Pearce, and Valverde 2001). Given a set $V \subseteq \Sigma$, the *V-exclusion* of a set of answer sets (a set of HT-interpretations) $\mathcal{M}$, denoted $\mathcal{M}_{\parallel V}$, is $\{X \backslash V \mid X \in \mathcal{M}\}$ ($\{\langle X \backslash V, Y \backslash V \rangle \mid \langle X, Y \rangle \in \mathcal{M}\}$).

[2]For brevity, parentheses, commas and union signs within HT-interpretations may be omitted, such that, for example, $\langle \varnothing, Ypq \rangle$ means $\langle \varnothing, Y \cup \{p, q\} \rangle$.

Forgetting: Properties and Operators Let $\mathcal{P}$ be the set of all logic programs. A *forgetting operator* is a (partial) function $\mathsf{f} : \mathcal{P} \times 2^\Sigma \to \mathcal{P}$. The program $\mathsf{f}(P, V)$ is interpreted as the *result of forgetting about V from P*. Moreover, $\Sigma(\mathsf{f}(P, V)) \subseteq \Sigma(P) \backslash V$ is usually required. In the following we introduce some well-known properties for forgetting operators (Gonçalves, Knorr, and Leite 2016a).

Strong persistence is presumably the best known one (Knorr and Alferes 2014). It requires that the result of forgetting $\mathsf{f}(P, V)$ is strongly equivalent to the original program P, modulo the forgotten atoms.

(SP) f satisfies *strong persistence* iff, for each program P and each set of atoms V, we have: $\mathcal{AS}(P \cup R)_{\parallel V} = \mathcal{AS}(\mathsf{f}(P, V) \cup R)$ for all programs R with $\Sigma(R) \subseteq \Sigma \backslash V$.

Notably, **(SP)** can be decomposed into the following three properties, i.e. an operator f satisfies **(SP)** iff f satisfies all **(wC)**, **(sC)** and **(SI)**, where

(wC) f satisfies *weakened consequence* iff, for each P and each set of atoms V: $\mathcal{AS}(\mathsf{f}(P, V)) \supseteq \mathcal{AS}(P)_{\parallel V}$.

(sC) f satisfies *strengthened consequence* iff, for each P and each set of atoms V: $\mathcal{AS}(\mathsf{f}(P, V)) \subseteq \mathcal{AS}(P)_{\parallel V}$.

Strong invariance requires that rules not mentioning atoms to be forgotten can be added before or after forgetting.

(SI) f satisfies *strong invariance* iff, for each program P and each set of atoms V, we have: $\mathsf{f}(P, V) \cup R \equiv \mathsf{f}(P \cup R, V)$ for all programs R with $\Sigma(R) \subseteq \Sigma \backslash V$.

Note that the presented properties are often considered for certain subclasses such as *disjunctive*, *normal* or *Horn programs*. Moreover, they naturally extend over classes of forgetting operators, where a class satisfies a property, iff all its members do.

In the light of the impossibility for a forgetting operator to satisfy **(SP)** for all pairs $\langle P, V \rangle$, called *forgetting instances*, where P is a program and V is a set of atoms to be forgotten from P (Gonçalves, Knorr, and Leite 2016b), **(SP)** was defined for concrete forgetting instances. A forgetting operator f satisfies $\mathbf{(SP)}_{\langle P, V \rangle}$, if $\mathcal{AS}(\mathsf{f}(P, V) \cup R) = \mathcal{AS}(P \cup R)_{\parallel V}$, for all programs R with $\Sigma(R) \subseteq \Sigma \backslash V$. A sound and complete criterion Ω characterizes when it is not possible to forget while satisfying $\mathbf{(SP)}_{\langle P, V \rangle}$.

The definition of Ω is rather technical. To decide Ω for a given $\langle P, V \rangle$, all total models $\langle YA, YA \rangle$ with $Y \subseteq \Sigma(P) \backslash V$ and $A \subseteq V$ are *considered* for which there are no witnesses $\langle YA', YA \rangle \in \mathcal{HT}(P)$ with $A' \subset A$. For each $Y \subseteq \Sigma(P) \backslash V$ all such *relevant* $A \subseteq V$ are collected:

$$Rel^Y_{\langle P, V \rangle} := \{A \subseteq V \mid \langle Y \cup A, Y \cup A \rangle \in \mathcal{HT}(P) \text{ and } \\ \nexists A' \subset A \text{ s.t. } \langle Y \cup A', Y \cup A \rangle \in \mathcal{HT}(P)\}.$$

Then, an instance $\langle P, V \rangle$ *satisfies criterion* Ω iff between the considered total models with matching unforgotten part Y, there is no least element, with respect to their witnesses modulo V, more formally, iff there is $Y \subseteq \Sigma \backslash V$ such that the set of sets $\mathcal{R}^Y_{\langle P, V \rangle} := \{R^{Y,A}_{\langle P, V \rangle} \mid A \in Rel^Y_{\langle P, V \rangle}\}$ is non-empty and has no least element, where

$$R^{Y,A}_{\langle P, V \rangle} := \{X \backslash V \mid \langle X, Y \cup A \rangle \in \mathcal{HT}(P)\}.$$

Example 2. *Consider the forgetting instance $\langle P_2, \{p\}\rangle$, where P_2 has the following HT-models*[3]*:*

$$\langle apq, apq\rangle \quad \langle aq, aq\rangle \quad \langle ap, ap\rangle$$
$$\langle \varnothing, apq\rangle \quad \langle a, aq\rangle \quad \langle a, ap\rangle$$

Both $\langle apq, apq\rangle$ and $\langle aq, aq\rangle$ are considered, whereas $\langle ap, ap\rangle$ is not, because of $\langle a, ap\rangle$. $\langle apq, apq\rangle$ and $\langle aq, aq\rangle$ match w.r.t. $Y = \{a, q\}$, but none of them is least w.r.t. their witnesses modulo p. Hence $\langle P_2, \{p\}\rangle$ satisfies Ω.

Corresponding to the Ω criterion the classes $\mathsf{F_R}$ and $\mathsf{F_{SP}}$ specify the HT-models of the forgetting result. It was shown that $\mathsf{F_{SP}}$ satisfies $(\mathbf{SP})_{\langle P,V\rangle}$ for all instances $\langle P, V\rangle$ that do not satisfy Ω. Moreover, in the case where Ω is satisfied, $\mathsf{F_{SP}}$ still exhibits desirable behavior, such as satisfying $(\mathbf{SI})$ and $(\mathbf{wC})$, two of three characterizing criterions of $(\mathbf{SP})$. $\mathsf{F_R}$ on the other hand always satisfies $(\mathbf{sC})$ and $(\mathbf{SI})$, which makes it an ideal choice, if no new answer sets should be created (Gonçalves et al. 2017).

The classes $\mathsf{F_R}$ and $\mathsf{F_{SP}}$ are are defined as follows:

$$\mathsf{F_R} := \{\mathsf{f} \mid \mathcal{HT}(\mathsf{f}(P,V)) = \{\langle X,Y\rangle \mid Y \subseteq \Sigma(P)\backslash V \wedge X \in \bigcup \mathcal{R}^{Y}_{\langle P,V\rangle}\}, \text{ for all programs } P \text{ and } V \subseteq \Sigma\},$$

$$\mathsf{F_{SP}} := \{\mathsf{f} \mid \mathcal{HT}(\mathsf{f}(P,V)) = \{\langle X,Y\rangle \mid Y \subseteq \Sigma(P)\backslash V \wedge X \in \bigcap \mathcal{R}^{Y}_{\langle P,V\rangle}\}, \text{ for all programs } P \text{ and } V \subseteq \Sigma\}.$$

where $\mathsf{F_R}$ collects the union of all witnesses modulo V of the considered models, and $\mathsf{F_{SP}}$ collects their intersection.

Example 3. *We assume $\mathsf{f} \in \mathsf{F_R}$. The following graph contains programs as nodes, represented by their respective set of HT-models. Two nodes P_i and P_j are connected by an edge labeled V, iff $\mathsf{f}(P_i, V) = P_j$. An edge from P_i to P_j is additionally labeled with Ω, iff $\langle P_i, V\rangle$ satisfies Ω. The program P_2 from Exm. 2 is in the topmost box.*

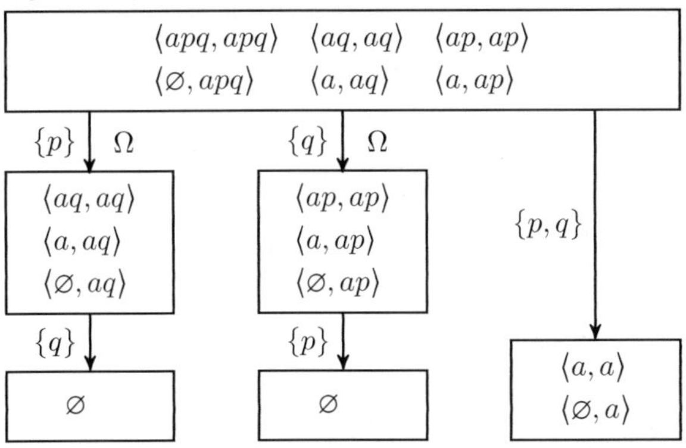

If p is forgotten from P_2, then $Rel^{\{a,q\}}_{\langle P_2,\{p\}\rangle} = \{\varnothing, \{p\}\}$. Hence $\langle aq, aq\rangle \models \mathsf{f}(P_2, \{p\})$. Since $\langle a, aq\rangle \models P_2$, and $\langle \varnothing, apq\rangle \models P_2$, we get $\langle a, aq\rangle \models \mathsf{f}(P_2, \{p\})$ and $\langle \varnothing, aq\rangle \models \mathsf{f}(P_2, \{p\})$. For all $Y \subseteq \Sigma(P_2)\backslash V$, s.t. $Y \neq \{a, q\}$, we have $Rel^{Y}_{\langle P_2,\{p\}\rangle} = \varnothing$, which entails $\langle Y, Y\rangle \not\models \mathsf{f}(P_2, \{p\})$

[3]Given a set of HT-interpretations M, satisfying $\langle X, Y\rangle \in M \Rightarrow \langle Y, Y\rangle \in M$, there exists a program P with $\mathcal{HT}(P) = M$ (Cabalar and Ferraris 2007). In the following examples each set of models represents the program that can be derived by the counter-models construction.

Example 4. *Now assume $\mathsf{f} \in \mathsf{F_{SP}}$ instead, and the same graphical representation of forgetting as in Exm. 3. When p is forgotten from P_2, then $\langle aq, aq\rangle \models \mathsf{f}(P_2, \{p\})$, for the same reason as in Exm. 3, since $Rel^{\{a,q\}}_{\langle P_2,\{p\}\rangle} \neq \varnothing$, but, since $\langle ap, apq\rangle \not\models P_2$, and $\langle a, apq\rangle \not\models P_2$, we get $\langle a, aq\rangle \not\models \mathsf{f}(P_2, \{p\})$. In addition, $\langle q, aq\rangle \not\models P_2$, and $\langle \varnothing, aq\rangle \not\models P_2$ entail $\langle \varnothing, aq\rangle \not\models \mathsf{f}(P_2, \{p\})$. As before, for all $Y \subseteq \Sigma(P_2)\backslash V$, s.t. $Y \neq \{a, q\}$, we have $Rel^{Y}_{\langle P_2,\{p\}\rangle} = \varnothing$, which entails $\langle Y, Y\rangle \not\models \mathsf{f}(P_2, \{p\})$*

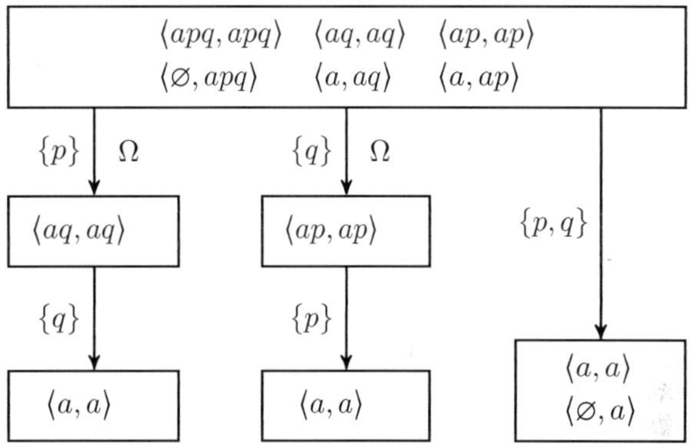

Whereas arbitrary sets of atoms can be forgotten, based on the HT-models defined by $\mathsf{F_R}$ and $\mathsf{F_{SP}}$ via the counter-models construction (Cabalar and Ferraris 2007) – a procedure not unlike determining a formula in CNF based on classical models – purely syntactical manipulations following $\mathsf{F_{SP}}$ semantics have only been defined to forget single atoms, and for $\mathsf{F_R}$ up until now there are none whatsoever.

Examples 3 and 4 witness that in general atoms cannot be forgotten iteratively by the semantics of $\mathsf{F_R}$ and $\mathsf{F_{SP}}$, which, for one, proves f_{SP} unfit to correctly forget multiple atoms.

3 Syntactic Tools

Defining syntactic forgetting operators obeying the semantics of $\mathsf{F_R}$ and $\mathsf{F_{SP}}$ comes down to two points: i) identifying which rules an interpretation is contradicted by, and ii) constructing rules that contradict interpretations as semantically defined. In this chapter we collect and introduce essential tools needed to do these two things.

Firstly, to avoid complications and unnecessary calculations caused by redundant (parts of) rules, we bring programs into a normal formal as has been done in previous related work (Inoue and Sakama 1998; 2004; Cabalar, Pearce, and Valverde 2007; Slota and Leite 2011; Knorr and Alferes 2014). The construction used by Berthold et al. in 2019 applies to programs with disjunctive heads and double negation, and eliminates non-minimal rules (Brass and Dix 1999).

First off, there is a number of redundancies that can be removed easily, by considering each rule individually.

Example 5. *Consider the following rules:*

$$a \vee b \leftarrow a. \qquad a \vee b \leftarrow not\, a.$$
$$b \leftarrow a, not\, a. \qquad b \leftarrow a, not\, not\, a.$$
$$b \leftarrow not\, a, not\, not\, a.$$

The three rules in the left column are tautological, they are satisfied by any interpretation, and can thus be disregarded.

The two rules in the right column contain redundant literals. An interpretation satisfying the body of the top rule, i.e. not a cannot at the time satisfy a in the rule's head. Therefore a can be omitted. For the bottom rule it holds that any interpretation satisfying a in the rule's body also satisfies not not a, hence not not a can be omitted.

Further, some rules are weaker (have more models) than other rules. Such *non-minimal* rules can also be disregarded. We broaden the notion of non-minimality, that has been used by Berthold et al., by adapting subsumption of rules (Cabalar, Pearce, and Valverde 2007).

Definition 1. *Given two rules r and s, s subsumes r, in symbols $s \leq r$, iff:*

1. $H(s) \subseteq H(r) \cup B^-(r)$,
2. $B^+(s) \subseteq B^+(r) \cup B^{--}(r)$,
3. $B^-(s) \subseteq B^-(r)$,
4. $B^{--}(s) \subseteq B^{--}(r) \cup B^+(r)$, *and*
5. $B^+(s) \cap B^{--}(r) = \emptyset$ *or* $H(s) \cap H(r) = \emptyset$.

Subsumption is such that, if a rule s subsumes a rule r, then s has no more HT-models than r. In other words it contains at least as much information, and r is redundant.

A rule r is *minimal in P*, iff it is not (strictly) subsumed by another rule s in P, i.e. iff $\neg\exists s \in P : s \leq r \wedge r \nleq s$.

Example 6. *Consider the following program P_6:*

$$a \leftarrow not\,not\,b. \qquad a \leftarrow c, not\,not\,b. \qquad \leftarrow b, not\,a.$$

In (Berthold et al. 2019), only the middle rule is non-minimal in P_6, since it contains more literals than the rule on the left. In this paper, we additionally deem the right hand rule non-minimal, since it is subsumed by the left hand rule.

Programs in normal form do not contain redundant parts of rules, non-minimal rules, nor tautologies, where a rule r is *tautological* iff $H(r) \cap B^+(r) \neq \emptyset$, or $B^+(r) \cap B^-(r) \neq \emptyset$, or $B^-(r) \cap B^{--}(r) \neq \emptyset$.

Definition 2. *Let P be a program. We say that P is in* normal form *iff the following conditions hold:*

- *P does not contain tautological rules;*
- *if $a \in H(r)$, then not $a \notin B(r)$;*
- *if $a \in B(r)$, then not not $a \notin B(r)$;*
- *all rules in P are minimal.*

Any program can be transformed into a strongly equivalent program in normal form.

Definition 3. *Let P be a program. The normal form $NF(P)$ is obtained from P by:*

1. *removing all tautological rules;*
2. *removing all atoms a from $B^{--}(r)$ in the remaining rules r, whenever $a \in B^+(r)$;*
3. *removing all atoms a from $H(r)$ in the remaining rules r, whenever $a \in B^-(r)$;*
4. *removing from the resulting program all rules that are not minimal.*

Proposition 1. *Let P be a program. Then, $NF(P)$ is in normal form and is strongly equivalent to P.*

The first three steps of the normal form construction only require checking each rule by itself. Checking whether a rule in a program P is non-minimal requires a comparison to each other rule in P. Hence the normal form construction has polynomial complexity.

Proposition 2. *Let P be a program. Then, the normal form $NF(P)$ can be computed in* PTIME.

The q-exclusion notation is short hand to remove an atom.

Definition 4 (q-exclusion)**.** *Given an atom $q \in \Sigma$, and a set of literals L, a rule r and a program P over Σ, the q-exclusions are $L^{\setminus q} := L \setminus \{q, not\,q, not\,not\,q\}$, $r^{\setminus q} := H^{\setminus q}(r) \leftarrow B^{\setminus q}(r)$ and $P^{\setminus q} := \{r^{\setminus q} \mid r \in P\}$.*

A rule in a program in normal form can only contain a given atom q in six different ways. We define a partition of a program along these occurrences.

Definition 5. *Given a program P in normal form over Σ and an atom $q \in \Sigma$, P is partitioned according to the occurrence of q, i.e. $\mathsf{occ}(P, q) := \langle R, R_0, R_1, R_2, R_3, R_4 \rangle$, where*

$$\begin{aligned} R &:= \{r \in P \mid q \notin \Sigma(r)\} \\ R_0 &:= \{r \in P \mid q \in B(r)\} \\ R_1 &:= \{r \in P \mid not\,q \in B(r)\} \\ R_2 &:= \{r \in P \mid not\,not\,q \in B(r), q \notin H(r)\} \\ R_3 &:= \{r \in P \mid not\,not\,q \in B(r), q \in H(r)\} \\ R_4 &:= \{r \in P \mid not\,not\,q \notin B(r), q \in H(r)\} \end{aligned}$$

By partitioning a program along the occurrences of an atom, we are able to identify some first correspondences between rules and models – if an interpretation is not a model of a program, it is contradicted by a rule with a certain occurrence of q.

Proposition 3. *Given a program P in normal form over Σ, $X \subseteq Y \subseteq \Sigma$, and an atom $q \in \Sigma$, with $q \notin Y$, and $\mathsf{occ}(P, q) = \langle R, R_0, R_1, R_2, R_3, R_4 \rangle$. Then the following equivalencies hold:*

$$\begin{aligned} \langle X, Y \rangle \not\models P &\Leftrightarrow \exists r \in R \cup R_1 \cup R_4 : \langle X, Y \rangle \not\models r \\ \langle Xq, Yq \rangle \not\models P &\Leftrightarrow \exists r \in R \cup R_0 \cup R_2 : \langle Xq, Yq \rangle \not\models r \\ \langle X, Yq \rangle \not\models P &\Leftrightarrow \exists r \in R \cup R_2 \cup R_3 \cup R_4 : \langle X, Yq \rangle \not\models r \end{aligned}$$

The next construction conversely identifies, which interpretations *are* models of a program.

The *as-dual* construction (Berthold et al. 2019) generalizes constructions that collect sets of conjunctions of literals aiming to replace negated occurrences of a literal (Eiter and Wang 2008; Knorr and Alferes 2014). It takes into account disjunctions and double negations, and can be used more generally to collect literals describing possible ways to satisfy rules independently of a given atom. Applying the construction to the rules containing q in the head, the as-dual describe exactly how q can be falsified.

Example 7. *Consider the following program P_7:*

$$a \vee q \leftarrow b. \qquad\qquad q \leftarrow c.$$

If b does not hold, q cannot be derived from the first rule. Likewise, q cannot be derived from the first rule, if a is not false. Further, q cannot be derived from the second rule, if c does not hold. Hence q is falsified by the following two sets of literals: $\{not\, b, not\, c\}$ and $\{not\, not\, a, not\, c\}$.

Definition 6. *Given a program $P = \{r_1, \dots, r_n\}$ over Σ and an atom $q \in \Sigma$, then:*

$$\mathcal{D}^q_{as}(P) := \{\{l_1, \dots, l_n\} \mid l_i \in not\, B^{\setminus q}(r_i) \cup not\, not\, H^{\setminus q}(r_i), 1 \leq i \leq n\},$$

where, for a set S of literals, $not\, S = \{not\, s \mid s \in S\}$ and $not\, not\, S = \{not\, not\, s \mid s \in S\}$, where, for $p \in \Sigma$, we assume the simplification $not\, not\, not\, p = not\, p$ and $not\, not\, not\, not\, p = not\, not\, p$.

The as-dual can also be applied more generally, to any program P to gain sets of literals proving P to be satisfied independently of an atom q.

Example 8. *Let P_8 consist of the following two rules:*

$$a \leftarrow q, b. \qquad c \leftarrow d, not\, not\, q.$$

Then each set in $\mathcal{D}^q_{as}(P_8)$ =

$$\{ \quad \{not\, not\, a, not\, not\, c\}, \quad \{not\, b, not\, not\, c\}, \quad \{not\, not\, a, not\, d\}, \quad \{not\, b, not\, d\} \quad \}$$

describes how P_8 can be satisfied independently of q.

By applying the as-dual to certain subsets of a program, we are able to construct rules that contradict some models of a program.

Proposition 4. *Given a program P in normal form over Σ, $Y \subseteq \Sigma$, and an atom $q \in \Sigma$, with $q \notin Y$, and $\mathsf{occ}(P,q) = \langle R, R_0, R_1, R_2, R_3, R_4 \rangle$. Then the following implications hold:*

$$\langle Y, Y \rangle \models P \Rightarrow \exists D \in \mathcal{D}^q_{as}(R_1 \cup R_4) : \langle Y, Y \rangle \not\models\ \leftarrow D$$
$$\langle Yq, Yq \rangle \models P \Rightarrow \exists D \in \mathcal{D}^q_{as}(R_0 \cup R_2) : \langle Yq, Yq \rangle \not\models\ \leftarrow D$$
$$\langle Y, Yq \rangle \models P \Rightarrow \exists D \in \mathcal{D}^q_{as}(R_3 \cup R_4) : \langle Y, Yq \rangle \not\models\ \leftarrow D$$

In the case that $R = \varnothing$ the first and second implication hold in both directions.

We define the product of rules (resp. of programs) and double negation of rules to be able to construct rules (resp. programs) that unite the models of two given rules (resp. of programs).

Definition 7 (Product of Rules). *Let r_1 and r_2 be rules. Their* product *$r_1 \times r_2$, is defined as:*

$$H(r_1) \cup H(r_2) \leftarrow B(r_1) \cup B(r_2)$$

Proposition 5. *Let r_1, r_2 be rules over Σ, and $X \subseteq Y \subseteq \Sigma$,*

$$Y \models r_1 \times r_2 \Leftrightarrow Y \models r_1 \vee Y \models r_2$$
$$X \models \{r_1 \times r_2\}^Y \Leftrightarrow X \models \{r_1\}^Y \vee X \models \{r_2\}^Y$$

Definition 8 (Product of Programs). *Let P_1 and P_2 be programs. Their* product *$P_1 \times P_2$, is defined as:*

$$\{r_1 \times r_2 \mid r_1 \in P_1 \wedge r_2 \in P_2\}$$

Proposition 6. *Let P_1, P_2 be programs over Σ, and $X \subseteq Y \subseteq \Sigma$,*

$$Y \models P_1 \times P_2 \Leftrightarrow Y \models P_1 \vee Y \models P_2$$
$$X \models (P_1 \times P_2)^Y \Leftrightarrow X \models P_1^Y \vee X \models P_2^Y$$

In general, $\mathcal{HT}(P_1) \cup \mathcal{HT}(P_2) = \mathcal{HT}(P_1 \times P_2)$ does not hold, e.g. $\langle \varnothing, ab \rangle \not\models \{a \leftarrow\}$ and $\langle \varnothing, ab \rangle \not\models \{\leftarrow b\}$, but $\langle \varnothing, ab \rangle \models \{a \leftarrow b\}$. To get around this, we define the double negation of a rule to be able to reason about, whether the second item Y of an HT-model $\langle X, Y \rangle$ is a classical model, and therefore whether the corresponding total model $\langle Y, Y \rangle$ is a potential answer set.

Definition 9. *Given a rule r, we define the* double negation *of r, i.e. $not\, not\, r$, as:*

$$not\, not\, r := \leftarrow not\, H(r) \cup not\, not\, B(r)$$

Proposition 7. *Given a rule r over Σ, and $X \subseteq Y \subseteq \Sigma$, the following statement holds:*

$$Y \models r \Leftrightarrow \langle X, Y \rangle \models not\, not\, r$$

Using the double negation, for example, we can construct $P = \{a \leftarrow\} \times \{not\, not\ \leftarrow b\} = \{a \leftarrow not\, not\, b\}$, such that $\langle \varnothing, ab \rangle \not\models P$, and $\mathcal{HT}(P) = \mathcal{HT}(\{a \leftarrow\}) \cup \mathcal{HT}(\{\leftarrow b\})$.

Any rule r subsumes $not\, not\, r$. In order not to lose double negated rules, we therefore restrict the normal form construction NF to its first three steps, denoted nf, when necessary (in Def. 10 and Def. 11).

All the aforementioned correspondences between models and rules remain, when an atom q is removed from a rule as well as from an interpretation.

Proposition 8. *Given a program P in normal form over Σ, $X \subset Y \subseteq \Sigma$, and an atom $q \in \Sigma$, with $q \notin Y$, and $\mathsf{occ}(P,q) = \langle R, R_0, R_1, R_2, R_3, R_4 \rangle$. Then the following equivalences hold:*

$$\langle Y, Y \rangle \not\models P \Leftrightarrow \exists r \in R_1 \cup R_4 : \langle Y, Y \rangle \not\models not\, not\, r^{\setminus q} \vee \exists r \in R : \langle Y, Y \rangle \not\models r$$
$$\langle X, Y \rangle \not\models P \Leftrightarrow \exists r \in R \cup R_1 \cup R_4 : \langle X, Y \rangle \not\models r^{\setminus q}$$
$$\langle Yq, Yq \rangle \not\models P \Leftrightarrow \exists r \in R_0 \cup R_2 : \langle Y, Y \rangle \not\models not\, not\, r^{\setminus q} \vee \exists r \in R : \langle Y, Y \rangle \not\models r$$
$$\langle Y, Yq \rangle \not\models P \Leftrightarrow \langle Yq, Yq \rangle \not\models P \vee \exists r \in R_3 \cup R_4 : \langle Y, Y \rangle \not\models not\, not\, r^{\setminus q}$$
$$\langle Y, Yq \rangle \models P \Leftrightarrow \langle Yq, Yq \rangle \models P \wedge \exists D \in \mathcal{D}^q_{as}(R_3 \cup R_4) : \langle Y, Y \rangle \not\models\ \leftarrow D$$
$$\langle Xq, Yq \rangle \not\models P \Leftrightarrow \exists r \in R \cup R_0 \cup R_2 : \langle X, Y \rangle \not\models r^{\setminus q}$$
$$\langle X, Yq \rangle \not\models P \Leftrightarrow \langle Yq, Yq \rangle \not\models P \vee \exists r \in R \cup R_2 \cup R_3 \cup R_4 : \langle X, Y \rangle \not\models r^{\setminus q}$$

If additionally $R = \varnothing$, then

$$\langle Y, Y \rangle \models P \Leftrightarrow \exists D \in \mathcal{D}^q_{as}(R_1 \cup R_4) : \langle Y, Y \rangle \not\models\ \leftarrow D$$
$$\langle Yq, Yq \rangle \models P \Leftrightarrow \exists D \in \mathcal{D}^q_{as}(R_0 \cup R_2) : \langle Y, Y \rangle \not\models\ \leftarrow D$$

For all $r_2 \in R_2$:

$$\langle Yq, Yq \rangle \not\models r_2 \Leftrightarrow \langle Y, Yq \rangle \not\models r_2, \text{ and}$$
$$\langle Xq, Yq \rangle \not\models r_2 \Leftrightarrow \langle X, Yq \rangle \not\models r_2.$$

The rules identified in Prop. 8 constitute the essential building blocks, used to define f_R and f^*_{SP}.

4 Relativized Forgetting

Now, we define f_R, such that $\mathsf{f}_R \in \mathsf{F}_\mathsf{R}$. To that end, for each $A \subseteq V$, we define an auxiliary operator f_R^A that determines, whether A is relevant for a given $Y \subseteq \Sigma(P)\backslash V$ ($A \in Rel^Y_{\langle P,V\rangle}$), and whether for this A there exists a witness $\langle XA'', YA\rangle$, with $A'' \subseteq A$. We construct these $\mathsf{f}_R^A(P,V)$, such that they contradict $\langle Y,Y\rangle$, iff A is not relevant w.r.t. Y, i.e. $\langle Y,Y\rangle \nvDash \mathsf{f}_R^A(P,V) \Leftrightarrow A \notin Rel^Y_{\langle P,V\rangle}$, and such that, if A is relevant, $\mathsf{f}_R^A(P,V)$ satisfies all the witnesses modulo V that belong to $\langle YA, YA\rangle$, i.e. $\langle X,Y\rangle \vDash \mathsf{f}_R^A(P,V) \Leftrightarrow A \in Rel^Y_{\langle P,V\rangle} \land \exists A'' \subseteq A : \langle XA'', YA\rangle \vDash P$.

F_R is such that $\mathcal{HT}(\mathsf{f}_R(P,V)) = \bigcup_{A\subseteq V} \mathcal{HT}(\mathsf{f}_R^A(P,V))$, so we define f_R as the conjunction all f_R^A by $\times$, to construct a program that unites all of their the models.

The operators f_R^A are defined inductively. We therefore first define them for one atom. If one atom q is forgotten from a program P, there are two subsets of $\{q\}$. In other words, for any $Y \subseteq \Sigma$, we have $Rel^Y_{\langle P,\{q\}\rangle} \subseteq \{\varnothing, \{q\}\}$.

For forgetting one atom q it holds that $\{q\} \in Rel^Y_{\langle P,\{q\}\rangle}$, iff $\langle Yq, Yq\rangle \vDash P$ and $\langle Y, Yq\rangle \nvDash P$. Using Prop. 8, we are able to construct rules, contradicting $\langle Y,Y\rangle$, iff $\{q\} \notin Rel^Y_{\langle P,\{q\}\rangle}$, and otherwise, if $\{q\}$ is relevant, satisfying $\langle X,Y\rangle$ iff $\langle Xq, Yq\rangle \vDash P$ or $\langle X, Yq\rangle \vDash P$.

Definition 10 (f_R^+). *Given a program P in normal form over Σ and $q \in \Sigma$ s.t. $\mathsf{occ}(P,q) = \langle R, R_0, R_1, R_2, R_3, R_4\rangle$. Then:*

$$\mathsf{f}_R^+(P,q) := nf(A \cup B \cup C \cup D)$$

where:

$$A := \{\leftarrow D \mid D \in \mathcal{D}^q_{as}(R_3 \cup R_4)\}$$
$$B := \{not\, not\, r^{\backslash q} \mid r_0 \in R_0 \cup R_2\}$$
$$C := \{r^{\backslash q} \mid r \in R \cup R_2\}$$
$$D := \{(r_0 \times r')^{\backslash q} \mid r_0 \in R_0, r' \in R_3 \cup R_4\}$$

The four sets A, B, C and D making up $\mathsf{f}_R^+(P,q)$ directly correspond to the conclusions in Prop. 8. If $\langle Yq, Yq\rangle \nvDash P$, a rule $r \in B \cup C$ contradicts $\langle Y,Y\rangle$. If $\langle Y, Yq\rangle \vDash P$, then a rule $r \in A$ contradicts $\langle Y,Y\rangle$. Otherwise, if both $\langle Xq, Yq\rangle \nvDash P$ and $\langle X, Yq\rangle \nvDash P$, then a rule in $C \cup D$ contradicts $\langle X,Y\rangle$.

Proposition 9. *Given a program P over Σ, an atom $q \in \Sigma$, and sets X and Y, s.t. $X \subset Y \subseteq \Sigma\backslash\{q\}$, then:*

$$\langle Y,Y\rangle \vDash \mathsf{f}_R^+(P,q) \Leftrightarrow \{q\} \in Rel^Y_{\langle P,\{q\}\rangle}$$

If $\{q\} \in Rel^Y_{\langle P,\{q\}\rangle}$, then:

$$\langle X,Y\rangle \vDash \mathsf{f}_R^+(P,q) \Leftrightarrow \langle Xq, Yq\rangle \vDash P \lor \langle X, Yq\rangle \vDash P$$

It holds that $\varnothing \in Rel^Y_{\langle P,\{q\}\rangle} \Leftrightarrow \langle Y,Y\rangle \vDash P$. Once again, we utilize Prop. 8 to construct an auxiliary program.

Definition 11 (f_R^-). *Given a program P in normal form over Σ and $q \in \Sigma$ s.t. $\mathsf{occ}(P,q) = \langle R, R_0, R_1, R_2, R_3, R_4\rangle$. Then:*

$$\mathsf{f}_R^-(P,q) := nf(A \cup B)$$

where:

$$A := \{r'^{\backslash q} \mid r' \in R \cup R_1 \cup R_4\}$$
$$B := \{not\, not\, r'^{\backslash q} \mid r' \in R_1 \cup R_4\}$$

Proposition 10. *Given a program P over Σ, an atom $q \in \Sigma$, and sets X and Y, s.t. $X \subset Y \subseteq \Sigma\backslash\{q\}$, then:*

$$\langle Y,Y\rangle \vDash \mathsf{f}_R^-(P,q) \Leftrightarrow \varnothing \in Rel^Y_{\langle P,\{q\}\rangle}$$

If $\varnothing \in Rel^Y_{\langle P,\{q\}\rangle}$, then:

$$\langle X,Y\rangle \vDash \mathsf{f}_R^-(P,q) \Leftrightarrow \langle X,Y\rangle \vDash P$$

Now, using f_R^+ and f_R^- as building blocks, we inductively construct f_R^A for V of arbitrary sizes. We assume an arbitrary ordering on the signature Σ to be able to fix a concrete forgetting result. However, the subsequent propositions are independent of this ordering and hence there is no loss of generality. We leave the question about whether the given ordering has a meaningful impact on the forgetting result for future studies – the resulting program $\mathsf{f}_R(P,V)$ is correct anyhow.

Definition 12 (f_R^A). *Let P be a program over Σ, and $A \subseteq \{q_1, q_2, \dots, q_n\} = V \subseteq \Sigma$, s.t. $0 < n$, then:*

$$\mathsf{f}_R^A(P,\varnothing) := P$$
$$\mathsf{f}_R^A(P,V) := \mathsf{f}_R^{\otimes_n}(\mathsf{f}_R^{A\backslash q_n}(P, V\backslash\{q_n\}), q_n)$$

where:

$$\mathsf{f}_R^{\otimes_n} := \begin{cases} \mathsf{f}_R^+, & \text{if } q_n \in A \\ \mathsf{f}_R^-, & \text{otherwise} \end{cases}$$

For $|V| = n$ the auxiliary functions f_R^A consist of n nested functions calls f_R^+ or f_R^-. For example, given a program P, $V = \{p,q\}$ and $A = \{p\}$, $\mathsf{f}_R^A(P,V) = \mathsf{f}_R^-(\mathsf{f}_R^+(P,p),q)$. Prop. 11 generalizes Prop. 9 and Prop. 10, and can be proven by induction.

Proposition 11. *Given a program P over Σ, and sets X, Y, A and V, s.t. $A \subseteq V \subseteq \Sigma$, and $X \subseteq Y \subseteq \Sigma\backslash V$, then*

$$\langle Y,Y\rangle \vDash \mathsf{f}_R^A(P,V) \Leftrightarrow A \in Rel^Y_{\langle P,V\rangle}$$

If $A \in Rel^Y_{\langle P,V\rangle}$, then:

$$\langle X,Y\rangle \vDash \mathsf{f}_R^A(P,V) \Leftrightarrow \exists A'' \subseteq A : \langle XA'', YA\rangle \vDash P$$

F_R is such that all considered total models and their witnesses (modulo V) are collected. In other words, for any $\mathsf{f} \in \mathsf{F}_\mathsf{R}$ we have

$$\mathcal{HT}(\mathsf{f}(P,V)) = \bigcup_{A\subseteq V} \mathcal{HT}(\mathsf{f}_R^A(P,V))$$

Therefore, we define the result of forgetting f_R, by using the $\times$ operator.

Definition 13 (f_R). *Let P be a program over Σ in normal form and $V \subseteq \Sigma$.*

$$\mathsf{f}_R(P,V) := NF(\bigtimes_{A\subseteq V} \mathsf{f}_R^A(P,V))$$

Using Prop. 6, Prop. 11 and the fact that any $\langle Y,Y\rangle$ is contradicted by a double negated rule, we arrive at:

Theorem 1. $\mathsf{f}_R \in \mathsf{F}_\mathsf{R}$

5 Forgetting with Strong Persistence

Next, we define f^*_{SP}, such that $\mathsf{f}^*_{SP} \in \mathsf{F}_{\mathsf{SP}}$. For any program P and set V, the forgetting result $\mathsf{f}^*_{SP}(P,V)$ has a subset of the models of $\mathsf{f}_R(P,V)$, but the same total models, i.e.:

$$\langle Y,Y\rangle \models \mathsf{f}^*_{SP}(P,V) \Leftrightarrow \langle Y,Y\rangle \models \mathsf{f}_R(P,V).$$

In other words, $\mathsf{f}^*_{SP}(P,V)$ and $\mathsf{f}_R(P,V)$ only differ in their witnesses. We hence construct $\mathsf{f}^*_{SP}(P,V)$ by adding rules to $\mathsf{f}_R(P,V)$ that contradict the remaining witnesses. We call these additional rules $\mathsf{f}_W(P,V)$.

Example 9. *Consider P_2 from earlier, where*

$$\mathcal{HT}(\mathsf{f}_R(P_2,\{p\})) = \{\langle aq,aq\rangle, \langle a,aq\rangle, \langle\varnothing,aq\rangle\}.$$

$\mathsf{f}_W(P_2,\{p\})$ specifically contradicts $\langle a,aq\rangle$ and $\langle\varnothing,aq\rangle$, s.t.

$$\mathcal{HT}(\mathsf{f}_R(P_2,\{p\}) \cup \mathsf{f}_W(P_2,\{p\})) = \{\langle aq,aq\rangle\}.$$

As for f_R, we define f_W by the help of auxiliary operators for every $A \subseteq V$. Each $\mathsf{f}^A_W(P,V)$ contradicts $\langle X,Y\rangle$, i.e. $\langle X,Y\rangle \not\models \mathsf{f}^A_W(P,V)$, iff $A \in Rel^Y_{\langle P,V\rangle}$ and $\forall A'' \subseteq A : \langle XA'',YA\rangle \not\models P$, where $X \subseteq Y \subseteq \Sigma$.

Also as before, the auxiliary operators f^A_W are defined inductively by nested calls of f^+_W and f^-_W.

Definition 14 (f^+_W)**.** *Given a program P in normal form over Σ and $q \in \Sigma$ s.t. $\mathsf{occ}(P,q) = \langle R,R_0,R_1,R_2,R_3,R_4\rangle$, then:*

$$\mathsf{f}^+_W(P,V) := NF(A \cup B)$$

where:

$$A := \{(r_0 \times r' \times not\,not\,r)^{\backslash q} \times \leftarrow D \mid r_0 \in R_0,\ r,r' \in R_3 \cup R_4, D \in \mathcal{D}^q_{as}(R_0 \cup R_2)\}$$

$$B := \{(r \times not\,not\,r')^{\backslash q} \times \leftarrow D \mid r \in R \cup R_2, r' \in R_3 \cup R_4, D \in \mathcal{D}^q_{as}(R_0 \cup R_2)\}$$

The operator f^+_W creates a rule contradicting $\langle X,Y\rangle$ iff $\{q\} \in Rel^Y_{\langle P,V\rangle}$ and $\langle Xq,Yq\rangle, \langle X,Yq\rangle \notin \mathcal{HT}(P)$. According to Prop. 8, $\{q\} \in Rel^Y_{\langle P,V\rangle}$ entails the existence of $D \in \mathcal{D}^q_{as}(P)$ and $r \in R_3 \cup R_4$, s.t. $\langle X,Y\rangle \not\models \leftarrow D$ and $\langle X,Y\rangle \not\models not\,not\,r^{\backslash q}$. Also, $\langle Xq,Yq\rangle \not\models P \wedge \langle X,Yq\rangle \not\models P$ implies the existence of an $r \in R \cup R_2$, s.t. $\langle X,Y\rangle \not\models r^{\backslash q}$, or $r_0 \in R_0$, and $r' \in R_3 \cup R_4$, s.t. $\langle X,Y\rangle \not\models r_0^{\backslash q} \times r'^{\backslash q}$. Hence the sets A and B.

Proposition 12. *Given a program P over Σ, an atom $q \in \Sigma$, and sets X and Y, s.t. $X \subseteq Y \subseteq \Sigma\backslash\{q\}$, then:*

$$\{q\} \in Rel^Y_{\langle P,\{q\}\rangle} \wedge \langle Xq,Yq\rangle \not\models P \wedge \langle X,Yq\rangle \not\models P \Leftrightarrow \langle X,Y\rangle \not\models \mathsf{f}^+_W(P,q)$$

Definition 15 (f^-_W)**.** *Given a program P in normal form over Σ and $q \in \Sigma$ s.t. $\mathsf{occ}(P,q) = \langle R,R_0,R_1,R_2,R_3,R_4\rangle$, then:*

$$\mathsf{f}^-_W(P,V) := NF(A)$$

where:

$$A := \{r'^{\backslash q} \times \leftarrow D \mid r' \in R \cup R_1 \cup R_4, D \in \mathcal{D}^q_{as}(R_1 \cup R_4)\}$$

Again, using Prop. 8, $\varnothing \in Rel^Y_{\langle P,V\rangle}$ implies the existence of $D \in \mathcal{D}^q_{as}(P)$ s.t. $\langle X,Y\rangle \not\models \leftarrow D$, and if $\langle X,Y\rangle \not\models P$ then there is a rule $r \in R \cup R_1 \cup R_4$ s.t. $\langle X,Y\rangle \not\models r^{\backslash q}$.

Proposition 13. *Given a program P over Σ, an atom $q \in \Sigma$, and sets X and Y, s.t. $X \subseteq Y \subseteq \Sigma\backslash\{q\}$, then:*

$$\varnothing \in Rel^Y_{\langle P,\{q\}\rangle} \wedge \langle X,Y\rangle \not\models P \Leftrightarrow \langle X,Y\rangle \not\models \mathsf{f}^-_W(P,q)$$

Example 10. *Recall P_1 from the beginning,*

$$\mathsf{f}^+_W(P_1,\{p\}) = \{a \leftarrow q, not\,not\,a\} \cup \varnothing$$
$$\mathsf{f}^-_W(P_1,\{p\}) = \{q \leftarrow not\,not\,q\}$$

Now, the operators f^A_W are defined inductively.

Definition 16 (f^A_W)**.** *Let P be a program over Σ, and $A \subseteq \{q_1,q_2,\dots,q_n\} = V \subseteq \Sigma$, s.t. $0 < n$, then:*

$$\mathsf{f}^A_W(P,\varnothing) := P$$
$$\mathsf{f}^A_W(P,V) := \mathsf{f}^{\otimes_n}_W(\mathsf{f}^{A\backslash q_n}_W(P\backslash R, V\backslash\{q_n\}), q_n) \cup R$$

where:

$$\mathsf{f}^{\otimes_n}_W := \begin{cases} \mathsf{f}^+_W, & \text{if } q_n \in A \\ \mathsf{f}^-_W, & \text{otherwise} \end{cases}$$
$$R := \{r \in P \mid V \cap \Sigma(r) = \varnothing\}$$

Prop. 14 generalizes Prop. 12 and Prop. 13, and can be proven by induction. For technical reasons we assume R to be empty. This assumption can be made without loss of generality, since F_{SP} satisfies (**SI**).

Proposition 14. *Given a program P over Σ, and sets X, Y, A and V, s.t. $A \subseteq V \subseteq \Sigma$, $X \subseteq Y \subseteq \Sigma\backslash V$, and $R = \{r \in P \mid V \cap \Sigma(r) = \varnothing\} = \varnothing$, then:*

$$A \in Rel^Y_{\langle P,V\rangle} \wedge \forall A'' \subseteq A : \langle XA'',YA\rangle \not\models P \Leftrightarrow \langle X,Y\rangle \not\models \mathsf{f}^A_W(P,V)$$

Now, $\mathsf{f}_W(P,V)$ is the union of all $\mathsf{f}^A_W(P,V)$.

Definition 17 (f_W)**.** *Given a program P in normal form over Σ and $V \subseteq \Sigma$. Then:*

$$\mathsf{f}_W(P,V) := NF(\bigcup_{A\subseteq V} \mathsf{f}^A_W(P,V))$$

The union of programs satisfies the intersections of their models. Hence the next proposition.

Proposition 15. *Given a program P over Σ in normal form, three sets of atoms X, Y and V, s.t. $X \subseteq Y \subseteq \Sigma$, $V \subseteq \Sigma$, and $R = \{r \in P \mid V \cap \Sigma(r) = \varnothing\} = \varnothing$, then:*

$$\exists A \in Rel^Y_{\langle P,V\rangle} \text{ s.t. } \forall A'' \subseteq A. \langle XA'',YA\rangle \not\models P \Leftrightarrow \langle X,Y\rangle \not\models \mathsf{f}_W(P,V)$$

We arrive at the end. f^*_{SP} is (the normal form of) the union of f_R and f_W, and a member of F_{SP}.

Definition 18 (f^*_{SP})**.** *Let P be a program over Σ in normal form and $V \subseteq \Sigma$.*

$$\mathsf{f}^*_{SP}(P,V) := NF(\mathsf{f}_W(P,V) \cup \mathsf{f}_R(P,V))$$

Theorem 2. $\mathsf{f}^*_{SP} \in \mathsf{F}_{\mathsf{SP}}$

6 Intuitions and Results

The operators f_R and f^*_{SP} and their components are defined methodologically, to match the semantics F_R and F_SP. Nonetheless, their results can be observed to bear some intuitive sense. In fact, they implement adjusted versions of all the derivation rules of f_{SP}. In other words, all the intuitions about f_{SP} apply to f_R and f^*_{SP}.

To make a comparison, we recall the definition of f_{SP}, rephrased to be more compact, and to match our notation using '×'. Notably, derivation rules **3a** and **7** have been merged into **3a**. This simplification is possible, due to the application of the normal form construction.

Definition 19 (f_{SP}). *Let P be a program in normal form over Σ, $q \in \Sigma$, and $\mathsf{occ}(P,q) = \langle R, R_0, R_1, R_2, R_3, R_4\rangle$, then $\mathsf{f}_{SP}(P,q) := NF(\mathbf{0} \cup \mathbf{1a} \cup \mathbf{2a} \cup \mathbf{3a} \cup \mathbf{1b} \cup \mathbf{2b} \cup \mathbf{3b} \cup \mathbf{4} \cup \mathbf{5} \cup \mathbf{6})$, where:*

$$\mathbf{0} = R$$
$$\mathbf{1a} = \{(r_0 \times r_4)^{\setminus q} \mid r_0 \in R_0, r_4 \in R_4\}$$
$$\mathbf{2a} = \{(r_0 \times r_3)^{\setminus q} \times not\,not\,r'^{\setminus q} \mid r_0 \in R_0, r_3 \in R_3, r' \in R_1 \cup R_4\}$$
$$\mathbf{3a} = \{(r_0 \times r_3 \times not\,not\,r'_3)^{\setminus q} \times \leftarrow D \mid r_0 \in R_0, r_3, r'_3 \in R_3,\ D \in \mathcal{D}^q_{as}(R_0 \cup R_2)\}$$
$$\mathbf{1b} = \{r_2^{\setminus q} \times r'^{\setminus q} \mid r_2 \in R_2, r' \in R_1 \cup R_4\}$$
$$\mathbf{2b} = \{r_2^{\setminus q} \times not\,not\,r'^{\setminus q} \mid r_2 \in R_2,\ r' \in R_1 \cup R_4\}$$
$$\mathbf{3b} = \{(r_2 \times not\,not\,r_3)^{\setminus q} \times \leftarrow D \mid r_2 \in R_2, r_3 \in R_3,\ D \in \mathcal{D}^q_{as}(R_0 \cup R_2)\}$$
$$\mathbf{4} = \{r'^{\setminus q} \times \leftarrow D \mid r' \in R_1 \cup R_4, D \in \mathcal{D}^q_{as}(R_3 \cup R_4)\}$$
$$\mathbf{5} = \{r'^{\setminus q} \times not\,not\,r^{\setminus q} \mid r' \in R_1 \cup R_4,\ r \in R_0 \cup R_2\}$$
$$\mathbf{6} = \{r'^{\setminus q} \times \leftarrow D \mid r' \in R_1 \cup R_4, D \in \mathcal{D}^q_{as}(R_1 \cup R_4)\}$$

In the case of forgetting one atom, f_R implements the derivation rules **0**, **1a**, **2a**, **1b**, **2b**, **4** and **5**. The operators f^+_R and f^-_R respectively gather half of each derivation rule. These halves are then conjoined by ×. The outputs of f^+_R (resp. f^-_R) are indicated in the definition above in blue (resp. red) text colors. For example, given that $r_0 \in R_0$ and $r_4 \in R_4$, f^+_R produces $(r_0 \times r_4)^{\setminus q}$, while f^-_R produces $r_4^{\setminus q}$. Also $(r_0 \times r_4)^{\setminus q} \times r_4^{\setminus q} = (r_0 \times r_4)^{\setminus q}$ – hence the purple text in **1a**.

Example 11. *Consider forgetting q from the program P_{11}:*

$$a \leftarrow q. \qquad b \leftarrow not\,q. \qquad q \leftarrow c.$$

*Then $\mathsf{f}_{SP}(P_{11},q)$ is derived by **1a**, **4** and **5**; $\mathsf{f}^+_R(P_{11},q)$ and $\mathsf{f}^-_R(P_{11},q)$ each include half of these derived rules.*

$$\mathsf{f}_R(P_{11},q) = \mathsf{f}_{SP}(P_{11},q) = \{a \leftarrow c\,; b \leftarrow not\,c\,; b \leftarrow not\,a\}$$
$$\mathsf{f}^+_R(P_{11},q) \supseteq \{a \leftarrow c\,;\ \leftarrow not\,c\,;\ \leftarrow not\,a\}$$
$$\mathsf{f}^-_R(P_{11},q) \supseteq \{\ \leftarrow c\,;\ b \leftarrow\ \}$$

After conjoining the results f^+_R and f^-_R by ×, all halves that have been put together 'incorrectly' are eliminated by the normal form construction. For the scope of this paper, we rely on the normal form construction to eliminate these redundancies – An efficient implementation might not produce them in the first place.

When multiple atoms are forgotten via f_R the pattern as indicated in Def. 19 repeats recursively. Consider, for example, forgetting $V = \{q_1, q_2\}$ from P. Then, first, $\mathsf{f}^+_R(P,q_1)$ and $\mathsf{f}^-_R(P,q_1)$ are calculated – the rules that are indicated in blue (resp. red), but they are not immediately conjoined by ×. Before, f^+_R and f^-_R are applied to them.

Now, the operator f_W implements the remaining derivation rules **3a**, **3b** and **6** in a way that circumvents the issue we alluded to in the introduction.

Example 12. *Consider again the first example, where forgetting p and q from program P_1 via f_{SP} in one order produces an incorrect result. Why is that? $P_1 = \{r_1, r_2, r_3\}$, where:*

$$r_1 = a \leftarrow p, q. \quad r_2 = q \leftarrow not\,p. \quad r_3 = p \leftarrow not\,not\,p.$$

Forgetting p yields $\mathsf{f}_{SP}(P_1,p) = \{r_4, r_5\}$, where:

$$r_4 = a \leftarrow q, not\,not\,a. \qquad r_5 = q \leftarrow not\,not\,q.$$

*The initial program contains a self-cycle r_3, which amounts to a choice of whether p is true or not. Rules r_4 and r_5 which are derived by **3a** and **6** in $\mathsf{f}_{SP}(P_1,p)$ mimic this choice by giving self-cycles to rules r_1 and r_2 that depend on p. However, the information that they were derived from mutually exclusive rules is lost. Therefore, when q is forgotten from $\mathsf{f}_{SP}(P_1,p)$, r_6 is derived by **3a**, as if r_4 and r_5 (and hence r_1 and r_2) are independent of each other. $\mathsf{f}_{SP}(\mathsf{f}_{SP}(P_1,p),q) = \{r_6\}$, where:*

$$r_6 = a \leftarrow not\,not\,a.$$

The operator f_W circumvents the creation of r_6 by compartmentalizing r_4 and r_5:

$$\mathsf{f}^+_W(P_1,p) = \{r_4\} \qquad \mathsf{f}^-_W(P_1,p) = \{r_5\}$$

and

$$\mathsf{f}^+_W(\{r_4\},q) = \mathsf{f}^-_W(\{r_4\},q) = \mathsf{f}^+_W(\{r_5\},q) = \mathsf{f}^-_W(\{r_5\},q) = \varnothing$$

Hence $\mathsf{f}_W(P_1,\{p,q\}) = \varnothing$, and thus $\mathsf{f}^*_{SP}(P_1,\{p,q\}) = \varnothing$.

6.1 Computational Advantage

While for some forgetting instances exponential blowups are inevitable (Eiter and Kern-Isberner 2018), forgetting via the semantics of a program will always be exponential with respect to the number of its atoms. In many scenarios forgetting by syntactic manipulations is much simpler.

Example 13 (Inevitable Blowup). *Consider forgetting q from the following program P_{13}:*

$$a \leftarrow not\,q. \qquad q \leftarrow b_1, c_1. \qquad \ldots \qquad q \leftarrow b_n, c_n.$$

The programs $\mathsf{f}_R(P_{13},q)$ and $\mathsf{f}^*_{SP}(P_{13},q)$ are exponentially large with respect to n.

We present some scenarios where forgetting via f_R and f^*_{SP} clearly outperforms forgetting via the semantics, and provide formal results proving that the result of forgetting by f_R and f^*_{SP} are more similar to the initial program than the result of forgetting by the semantics.

We denote the results of the counter-models method variation in (Wang, Wang, and Zhang 2013), (Wang et al. 2014) from the expected HT models f^{sem}_R and f^{sem}_{SP} respectively.

Example 14 (Computational Blowup). *Consider forgetting q from P_{14}:*

$$a \leftarrow q. \qquad q \leftarrow b_1, \ldots, b_n.$$

where

$$\mathsf{f}_R(P_{14}, \{q\}) = \mathsf{f}^*_{SP}(P_{14}, \{q\}) = \{a \leftarrow b_1, \ldots, b_n\}$$

are derived rather quickly through

$$\begin{aligned}\mathsf{f}_R(P_{14}, \{q\}) &= NF(\mathsf{f}^+_R(P_{14}, q) \times \mathsf{f}^-_R(P_{14}, q)) \\ &= \{a \leftarrow b_1, \ldots, b_n\},\end{aligned}$$

where

$$\begin{aligned}\mathsf{f}^+_R(P_{14}, q) = \{&a \leftarrow b_1, \ldots, b_n; \\ &\leftarrow not\, a, not\, not\, b_1, \ldots, not\, not\, b_n\}\end{aligned}$$

$$\mathsf{f}^-_R(P_{14}, q) = \{\leftarrow b_1, \ldots, b_n; \leftarrow not\, not\, b_1, \ldots, not\, not\, b_n\}$$

and

$$\begin{aligned}\mathsf{f}^*_{SP}(P_{14}, \{q\}) &= \mathsf{f}_R(P_{14}, \{q\}) \cup \mathsf{f}^+_W(P_{14}, q) \cup \mathsf{f}^-_W(P_{14}, q) \\ &= \mathsf{f}_R(P_{14}, \{q\}) \cup \emptyset \cup \emptyset \\ &= \{a \leftarrow b_1, \ldots, b_n\},\end{aligned}$$

but deriving

$$\begin{aligned}\mathsf{f}^{sem}_R(P_{14}, \{q\}) = \mathsf{f}^{sem}_{SP}(P_{14}, \{q\}) = \\ \{ \leftarrow b_1, \ldots, b_n, not\, a; \\ a \leftarrow b_1, \ldots, b_n, not\, not\, a \}\end{aligned}$$

involves checking 3^{n+2} interpretations.

Example 15 (Blowup of the Forgetting Result). *Consider forgetting q from P_{15}:*

$$a \leftarrow b, not\, q. \qquad c \leftarrow d, not\, q. \qquad e \leftarrow f, not\, q.$$

then $\mathsf{f}_R(P_{15}, \{q\}) = \mathsf{f}^*_{SP}(P_{15}, \{q\}) =$

$$a \leftarrow b. \qquad c \leftarrow d. \qquad e \leftarrow f.$$

while $\mathsf{f}^{sem}_R(P_{15}, \{q\})$ and $\mathsf{f}^{sem}_{SP}(P_{15}, \{q\})$ both contain 127 rules, which, no doubt, in no way resemble P_{15}.

The attentive reader might notice that the number of auxiliary operators f^A_R and f^A_W is exponential with respect to the size of V, which seems to counteract the savings of not having to calculate an exponential number of interpretations.

Proposition 16. *Let P_1, P_2 and R be programs over Σ,*

$$(P_1 \cup R) \times (P_2 \cup R) \equiv (P_1 \times P_2) \cup R.$$

Since f^+_R and f^-_R both simply pass on rules R not mentioning q_i, the proposition above can be utilized to factor out any rule not mentioning q_i of its respective recursive step, thus limiting potential exponential blowups. If an intermediate result does not mention q_i at all, the recursive step can be skipped, halving the size of the recursive sub-tree. For f_W the hope is that some intermediate results are empty, to be able to prune the recursive tree as well.

Furthermore, most of the time V is much smaller than $\Sigma(P)$, which is why in practice the complexity is expected to be significantly smaller compared to the semantic approach.

The operator f_{SP} has been proven to produce more favorable results compared to f^{sem}_{SP}. To that end, Berthold et al. defined a distance measure between logic programs, and proved that the result of f_{SP} is closer to the initial program than f^{sem}_{SP}. These results directly translate to f_R and f^*_{SP}.

7 Conclusion and Discussion

Strong persistence $(\mathbf{SP})$ most accurately describes that the relations of remaining atoms are left intact after forgetting. Due to its general impossibility, a number of relaxations of $(\mathbf{SP})$ have been proposed and investigated. Notably, $(\mathbf{SP})$ decomposes into the three properties $(\mathbf{sC})$, $(\mathbf{wC})$ and $(\mathbf{SI})$, where an operator f satisfies $(\mathbf{SP})$ iff f satisfies all $(\mathbf{wC})$, $(\mathbf{sC})$ and $(\mathbf{SI})$.

The classes of operators $\mathsf{F_R}$ and $\mathsf{F_{SP}}$ each guarantee two of those three properties, and in the case of $\mathsf{F_{SP}}$, even all three, and thus $(\mathbf{SP})$, whenever possible.

$\mathsf{F_R}$ and $\mathsf{F_{SP}}$ are defined by the semantics of their forgetting result, i.e. they do not define concrete functions, and up until now the only way to forget via their definitions, was to calculate the exponential number of models of a given input, to apply them, and then to construct a new program from the resulting models. This process is necessarily computationally hard, and its result may in no way resemble the input.

This paper introduced two novel operators f_R and f^*_{SP}, to circumvent these two issues. They forget atoms from a program purely by syntactically manipulating its rules, avoiding having to calculate the exponential number of its models, and creating a result that in some way resembles its origin.

We proved their membership in $\mathsf{F_R}$ resp. $\mathsf{F_{SP}}$, and therefore that f_R and f^*_{SP} inherit several (desirable) properties (Gonçalves et al. 2017).

Corollary 3. f_R *satisfies* $(\mathbf{sC})$, $(\mathbf{SI})$, $(\mathbf{PP})$ *and* $(\mathbf{SE})$, *but not* $(\mathbf{wE})$, $(\mathbf{W})$, $(\mathbf{wC})$, *nor* $(\mathbf{CP})$.

Corollary 4. f^*_{SP} *satisfies* $(\mathbf{wC})$, $(\mathbf{SI})$, $(\mathbf{PP})$ *and* $(\mathbf{SE})$, *but not* $(\mathbf{wE})$, $(\mathbf{W})$, $(\mathbf{sC})$, *nor* $(\mathbf{CP})$.
Further, if $\langle P, V\rangle$ satisfies $\neg\Omega$, then f^*_{SP} satisfies $(\mathbf{SP})_{\langle P,V\rangle}$.

Further, we provided examples that illustrate that members of $\mathsf{F_R}$ and $\mathsf{F_{SP}}$ cannot always forget atoms iteratively. Constructing forgetting results according to their semantics is therefore necessarily involved. The operator f_{SP}, for example, that has previously been shown to adhere to $\mathsf{F_{SP}}$ semantics, has thus been proven to be unfit to correctly forget arbitrary sets of atoms by $\mathsf{F_{SP}}$ semantics.

In the context of modular logic programming, $(\mathbf{SP})$ can be relaxed to $(\mathbf{UP})$, where the result of forgetting is only required to have the same answer set (modulo V) under the addition of facts (Gonçalves et al. 2019).

There exists a semantic class $\mathsf{F_{UP}}$, that guarantees $(\mathbf{UP})$, and interestingly for us, also guarantees $(\mathbf{sC})$ and $(\mathbf{wC})$, with a representative $\mathsf{f}_u \in \mathsf{F_{UP}}$ (Gonçalves et al. 2021), that too, if applicable, forgets atoms through syntactic manipulation. In other words, with f_R, f^*_{SP} and f_u at our disposal, we can now syntactically forget satisfying any two properties of $(\mathbf{wC})$, $(\mathbf{sC})$ and $(\mathbf{SI})$.

One future line of research is to explore how forgetting translates to other formalisms, as has been done for abstract argumentation (Baumann and Berthold 2022). Another one is to investigate forgetting from logic programs with variables. In this larger context, forgetting can mean a number of things: the removal of all occurrences of a predicate, the removal of all occurrences of an individual, or perhaps, the removal of all occurrences of certain individuals within some predicates, to, for example, just forget certain information about an entity.

Acknowledgements

Quite obviously, this work is a continuation of my master's thesis, which was mainly supervised by Ricardo Gonçalves. I want, therefore, to take the opportunity to express my gratitude for his support and efforts throughout the process.
Back then, he was the one to tell me that there might be a wrong forgetting order, when iterating f_{SP}, using a notation that I adapted in Exm. 3 and 4. I hope you like my fix!
Further, I thank the anonymous reviewers for all of their useful hints.
This work was supported by the German Federal Ministry of Education and Research (BMBF, 01IS18026B-F) by funding the competence center for Big Data and AI "ScaDS.AI" Dresden/Leipzig.

References

Baumann, R., and Berthold, M. 2022. Limits and possibilities of forgetting in abstract argumentation. In *Proceedings of (IJCAI-22)*. To appear.

Berthold, M.; Gonçalves, R.; Knorr, M.; and Leite, J. 2019. A syntactic operator for forgetting that satisfies strong persistence. *Theory and Practice of Logic Programming* 19(5-6):1038–1055.

Brass, S., and Dix, J. 1999. Semantics of (disjunctive) logic programs based on partial evaluation. *Journal of Logic Programming* 40(1):1–46.

Cabalar, P., and Ferraris, P. 2007. Propositional theories are strongly equivalent to logic programs. *Theory and Practice of Logic Programming* 7(6):745–759.

Cabalar, P.; Pearce, D.; and Valverde, A. 2007. Minimal logic programs. In *Proceedings of (ICLP-07)*. Springer.

Eiter, T., and Kern-Isberner, G. 2018. A brief survey on forgetting from a knowledge representation and reasoning perspective. *KI - Künstliche Intelligenz*.

Eiter, T., and Wang, K. 2008. Semantic forgetting in answer set programming. *Artificial Intelligence* 172(14):1644–1672.

Gonçalves, R.; Knorr, M.; Leite, J.; and Woltran, S. 2017. When you must forget: Beyond strong persistence when forgetting in answer set programming. *Theory and Practice of Logic Programming* 17(5-6):837–854.

Gonçalves, R.; Janhunen, T.; Knorr, M.; Leite, J.; and Woltran, S. 2019. Forgetting in modular answer set programming. In *Proceedings of (AAAI-19)*, 2843–2850. AAAI Press.

Gonçalves, R.; Janhunen, T.; Knorr, M.; and Leite, J. 2021. On syntactic forgetting under uniform equivalence. In *Proceedings of (JELIA-21)*, volume 12678 of *Lecture Notes in Computer Science*, 297–312. Springer.

Gonçalves, R.; Knorr, M.; and Leite, J. 2016a. The ultimate guide to forgetting in answer set programming. In *Proceedings of (KR-16)*, 135–144.

Gonçalves, R.; Knorr, M.; and Leite, J. 2016b. You can't always forget what you want: On the limits of forgetting in answer set programming. In *Proceedings of (ECAI-16)*, 957–965.

Inoue, K., and Sakama, C. 1998. Negation as failure in the head. *Journal of Logic Programming* 35(1):39–78.

Inoue, K., and Sakama, C. 2004. Equivalence of logic programs under updates. In *Proceedings of (JELIA-04)*. Springer.

Knorr, M., and Alferes, J. J. 2014. Preserving strong equivalence while forgetting. In *Proceedings of (JELIA-14)*, volume 8761 of *LNCS*, 412–425. Springer.

Lifschitz, V.; Pearce, D.; and Valverde, A. 2001. Strongly equivalent logic programs. *ACM Transactions on Computational Logic* 2(4):526–541.

Lifschitz, V.; Tang, L. R.; and Turner, H. 1999. Nested expressions in logic programs. *Annals of Mathematics and Artificial Intelligence* 25(3-4):369–389.

Slota, M., and Leite, J. 2011. Back and forth between rules and SE-models. In *Proceedings of (LPNMR-11)*. Springer.

Wang, Y.; Zhang, Y.; Zhou, Y.; and Zhang, M. 2014. Knowledge forgetting in answer set programming. *Journal of Artificial Intelligence Research* 50:31–70.

Wang, Y.; Wang, K.; and Zhang, M. 2013. Forgetting for answer set programs revisited. In *Proceedings of (IJCAI-13)*, 1162–1168. IJCAI/AAAI.

Zhang, Y., and Foo, N. Y. 2006. Solving logic program conflict through strong and weak forgettings. *Artificial Intelligence* 170(8-9):739–778.

Counting Queries over $\mathcal{ELHI}_\bot$ Ontologies

Meghyn Bienvenu[1] , **Quentin Manière**[1] , **Michaël Thomazo**[2]
[1]CNRS, University of Bordeaux, Bordeaux INP, LaBRI, Talence, France
[2]Inria, DI ENS, ENS, CNRS, University PSL, Paris, France
{meghyn.bienvenu, quentin.maniere}@u-bordeaux.fr, michael.thomazo@inria.fr

Abstract

While ontology-mediated query answering most often adopts (unions of) conjunctive queries as the query language, some recent works have explored the use of counting queries coupled with DL-Lite ontologies. The aim of the present paper is to extend the study of counting queries to Horn description logics outside the DL-Lite family. Through a combination of novel techniques, adaptations of existing constructions, and new connections to closed predicates, we achieve a complete picture of the data and combined complexity of answering counting conjunctive queries (CCQs) and cardinality queries (a restricted class of CCQs) in $\mathcal{ELHI}_\bot$ and its various sublogics. Notably, we show that CCQ answering is 2EXP-complete in combined complexity for $\mathcal{ELHI}_\bot$ and every sublogic that extends $\mathcal{EL}$ or DL-Lite$^{\mathcal{H}}_{\text{pos}}$. Our study not only provides the first results for counting queries beyond DL-Lite, but it also closes some open questions about the combined complexity of CCQ answering in DL-Lite.

1 Introduction

Ontology-mediated query answering (OMQA) facilitates access to data through the use of ontologies, which provide a convenient vocabulary for query formulation and capture domain knowledge that can be exploited to obtain more complete query results. The OMQA approach has been extensively studied over the past fifteen years (Poggi et al. 2008; Bienvenu and Ortiz 2015; Xiao et al. 2018), leading to the identification of ontology languages that are well suited to OMQA due to their attractive computational properties. Particular attention has been paid to Horn description logics of the DL-Lite and $\mathcal{EL}$ families (Calvanese et al. 2007; Baader, Brandt, and Lutz 2005).

While most work on OMQA considers that the user query is a conjunctive query (CQ), there has been significant interest in exploring the possibility of adopting more expressive query languages for OMQA. In particular, several works have investigated ways of equipping CQs with some form of counting (Calvanese et al. 2008; Kostylev and Reutter 2015; Feier, Lutz, and Przybylko 2021). A recent approach, proposed in (Bienvenu, Manière, and Thomazo 2020) as a generalization of (Kostylev and Reutter 2015), considers *counting conjunctive queries (CCQs)* that are syntactically defined like standard CQs except that some variables may be designated as *counting variables*. In each model of the knowledge base, we can count the number of possible assignments to the counting variables that make the query answer hold. As the count value may differ between models, the goal is to identify intervals that provide upper and lower bounds on the count values across all models.

The problem of answering CCQs is intractable, in both data and combined complexity, for common DL-Lite dialects such as DL-Lite$_{\text{core}}$ and DL-Lite$^{\mathcal{H}}_{\text{core}}$(Kostylev and Reutter 2015). Recent works have shown that intractability arises even for simple forms of CCQs (Calvanese et al. 2020a; Bienvenu, Manière, and Thomazo 2021). However, some interesting tractable cases have also been identified, notably, rooted CCQs (Bienvenu, Manière, and Thomazo 2020; Calvanese et al. 2020a; Nikolaou et al. 2019) and cardinality queries (Bienvenu, Manière, and Thomazo 2021) coupled with DL-Lite$_{\text{core}}$ ontologies. Query rewriting techniques have also begun to be explored (Calvanese et al. 2020b). However, despite these advances, we still have only a partial understanding of CCQ answering in common DL-Lite dialects, and the precise combined complexity has remained elusive: the current bounds for DL-Lite$^{\mathcal{H}}_{\text{core}}$ are between coNEXP and coN2EXP (Kostylev and Reutter 2015). Moreover, to the best of our knowledge, CCQ answering has not yet been studied for DLs outside the DL-Lite family.

In this paper, we extend the study of CCQ answering to other well-known Horn description logics, such as $\mathcal{EL}$ and the more expressive $\mathcal{ELHI}_\bot$. The techniques used in the DL-Lite context do not readily transfer to $\mathcal{EL}$ due to the presence of conjunction, and in any case, our results show that they do not achieve the optimal combined complexity even for DL-Lite. We therefore develop a new approach based upon the observation that there exists a model minimizing the count value that consists of an arbitrary structure $\mathcal{I}^*$ containing all assignments for the counting variables, augmented with structures that are tree-shaped, provided we ignore edges to and from $\mathcal{I}^*$. Importantly, we can bound the size of the central component $\mathcal{I}^*$, which enables us to explore all possible options for $\mathcal{I}^*$. Checking whether a given $\mathcal{I}^*$ can be extended to a model preserving the minimum count value can be done by specifying a set of *patterns* (intuitively representing a pair of adjacent elements), and testing via local consistency conditions whether they can be coherently assembled. This latter step takes inspiration from a CQ answering technique for existential rules

	Combined complexity						*Data complexity*
	DL-Lite$_{pos}$	DL-Lite$_{core}$	DL-Lite$^{\mathcal{H}}_{pos}$	DL-Lite$^{\mathcal{H}}_{core}$	$\mathcal{EL}(\mathcal{H}_\bot), \mathcal{EL}(\mathcal{HI})$	$\mathcal{EL}(\mathcal{H})\mathcal{I}_\bot$	$\mathcal{EL}(\mathcal{HI}_\bot)$
Concept	NL	coNP	NL	coNP‡	EXP	coNEXP	coNP
Role	NL	coNP	coNP‡	coNP‡	EXP	coNEXP	coNP
CCQ	coNEXP†	coNEXP†	2EXP	2EXP	2EXP	2EXP	coNP

Figure 1: Complexity results for CCQs and cardinality queries, all bounds are tight. †/ ‡: previously known upper / lower bound.

(Thomazo et al. 2012), and is also similar in spirit to type-elimination style procedures, which have been employed for reasoning with expressive DLs, see e.g. (Rudolph, Krötzsch, and Hitzler 2012; Eiter et al. 2009).

Using this new approach, we are able to establish a 2EXP upper bound in combined complexity for $\mathcal{ELHI}_\bot$. A matching lower bound, which applies to both $\mathcal{EL}$ and DL-Lite$^{\mathcal{H}}_{pos}$, is obtained by establishing a novel connection between CCQ answering and OMQA with closed predicates. This yields 2EXP-completeness for a wide range of Horn DLs and closes the combined complexity gap for CCQ answering in DL-Lite$^{\mathcal{H}}_{core}$. We further prove a coNEXP lower bound for DL-Lite$_{pos}$, which matches an existing coNEXP upper bound, yielding the precise combined complexity for DL-Lite$_{core}$ as well. We also explore how to shrink the size of the models implicitly generated by our procedure, producing models with bounded size which we use to show that CCQ answering is coNP-complete in data complexity for all logics between $\mathcal{EL}$ and $\mathcal{ELHI}_\bot$.

In addition to CCQs, we also investigate the special case of cardinality queries, which correspond to Boolean atomic CCQs and allow us to ask for (bounds on) the number of members of a given concept or role. We obtain a complete picture of data and combined complexity of answering cardinality queries in $\mathcal{ELHI}_\bot$ and its various sublogics. While the data complexity is coNP-complete for all considered logics, the combined complexity ranges from NL or coNP in DL-Lite logics to EXP or coNEXP for $\mathcal{EL}$ and its extensions. We achieve these results using a variety of the techniques: refinements of our approach for general CCQs, adaptations of existing constructions, and further reductions involving closed predicates. Figure 1 summarizes the complexity results for both CCQs and cardinality queries.

Paper Organization Section 2 introduces the necessary preliminaries, in particular, the syntax and semantics of the considered DLs and the definition of CCQs. Sections 3 and 4 present our complexity results for CCQs and cardinality queries, respectively, and sketch the underlying techniques (an appendix with full proofs can be found in the long version of this paper, available on arXiv). Section 5 concludes with a discussion of future work.

2 Preliminaries

Knowledge Bases We assume mutually disjoint sets $\mathsf{N_C}$, $\mathsf{N_R}$, and $\mathsf{N_I}$ of *concept, role, and individual names*. A *knowledge base (KB)* $\mathcal{K} = (\mathcal{T}, \mathcal{A})$ consists of an ABox $\mathcal{A}$ and a TBox $\mathcal{T}$. An *ABox* is a finite set of *concept assertions* $\mathrm{A}(\mathsf{b})$ (with $\mathrm{A} \in \mathsf{N_C}$, $\mathsf{b} \in \mathsf{N_I}$) and *role assertions* $\mathrm{P}(\mathsf{a}, \mathsf{b})$ (with $\mathrm{P} \in \mathsf{N_R}$, $\mathsf{a}, \mathsf{b} \in \mathsf{N_I}$). We denote by $\mathsf{Ind}(\mathcal{A})$ the set of individuals occurring in an ABox $\mathcal{A}$.

A *TBox* is a finite set of axioms. In $\mathcal{ELHI}_\bot$, TBoxes consist of *concept inclusions* $\mathrm{B}_1 \sqsubseteq \mathrm{B}_2$, *positive role inclusions* $\mathrm{R}_1 \sqsubseteq \mathrm{R}_2$, and *negative role inclusions*[1] $\mathrm{R}_1 \sqcap \mathrm{R}_2 \sqsubseteq \bot$, where the R_i are *roles* drawn from $\mathsf{N}_\mathsf{R}^\pm = \{\mathrm{P}, \mathrm{P}^- \mid \mathrm{P} \in \mathsf{N_R}\}$ and the B_i are *(complex) concepts* constructed as follows:

$$\mathrm{B} := \bot \mid \top \mid \mathrm{A} \mid \mathrm{B}_1 \sqcap \mathrm{B}_2 \mid \exists \mathrm{R}.\mathrm{B} \quad \text{with } \mathrm{A} \in \mathsf{N_C}, \mathrm{R} \in \mathsf{N}_\mathsf{R}^\pm$$

Various sublogics of $\mathcal{ELHI}_\bot$ can be obtained by disallowing role inclusions, inverse roles, and/or the bottom construct. For example, $\mathcal{EL}$ is obtained by removing all three features, while $\mathcal{ELI}_\bot$ corresponds to disallowing role inclusions (retaining inverse roles and $\bot$). We shall also consider some DL-Lite dialects that are fragments of $\mathcal{ELHI}_\bot$. The most expressive, DL-Lite$^{\mathcal{H}}_{core}$, allows positive and negative role inclusions, and restricted forms of concept inclusions:

$$\mathrm{D}_1 \sqsubseteq \mathrm{D}_2 \quad \mathrm{D}_1 \sqcap \mathrm{D}_2 \sqsubseteq \bot \quad \mathrm{D}_i := \mathrm{A} \mid \exists \mathrm{R}.\top$$

with $\mathrm{A} \in \mathsf{N_C}, \mathrm{R} \in \mathsf{N}_\mathsf{R}^\pm$. The logics DL-Lite$^{\mathcal{H}}_{pos}$, DL-Lite$_{core}$, and DL-Lite$_{pos}$ are obtained respectively by dropping negative inclusions, role inclusions, or both features.

We shall use $\mathsf{sig}(\mathcal{T})$ (resp. $\mathsf{sig}(\mathcal{K})$) to denote the *signature* of a TBox $\mathcal{T}$ (resp. KB $\mathcal{K}$), i.e. the set of concept and role names appearing in $\mathcal{T}$ (resp. $\mathcal{K}$).

Semantics of KBs An interpretation takes the form $\mathcal{I} = (\Delta^\mathcal{I}, \cdot^\mathcal{I})$, where $\Delta^\mathcal{I}$ is a non-empty set (called the domain) and $\cdot^\mathcal{I}$ is the interpretation function that maps each $\mathrm{A} \in \mathsf{N_C}$ to $\mathrm{A}^\mathcal{I} \subseteq \Delta^\mathcal{I}$, each $\mathrm{P} \in \mathsf{N_R}$ to $\mathrm{P}^\mathcal{I} \subseteq \Delta^\mathcal{I} \times \Delta^\mathcal{I}$, and each $\mathsf{a} \in \mathsf{N_I}$ to $\mathsf{a}^\mathcal{I}$. In this paper, we will make the *Standard Names Assumption* by setting $\mathsf{a}^\mathcal{I} = \mathsf{a}$. Note however that our results only rely upon the weaker *Unique Names Assumption* (UNA), which stipulates that $\mathsf{a}^\mathcal{I} \neq \mathsf{b}^\mathcal{I}$ whenever $\mathsf{a} \neq \mathsf{b}$.

The function $\cdot^\mathcal{I}$ naturally extends to roles and complex concepts: $(\mathrm{P}^-)^\mathcal{I} = \{(y, x) \mid (x, y) \in \mathrm{P}^\mathcal{I}\}$, $\bot^\mathcal{I} = \emptyset$, $\top^\mathcal{I} = \Delta^\mathcal{I}$, $(\mathrm{B}_1 \sqcap \mathrm{B}_2)^\mathcal{I} = \mathrm{B}_1^\mathcal{I} \cap \mathrm{B}_2^\mathcal{I}$ and $(\exists \mathrm{P}.\mathrm{B})^\mathcal{I} = \{d \mid (d, e) \in \mathrm{P}^\mathcal{I}, e \in \mathrm{B}^\mathcal{I}\}$. An inclusion $\mathrm{G} \sqsubseteq \mathrm{H}$ is satisfied in $\mathcal{I}$ if $\mathrm{G}^\mathcal{I} \subseteq \mathrm{H}^\mathcal{I}$; an assertion $\mathrm{A}(\mathsf{b})$ (resp. $\mathrm{P}(\mathsf{a}, \mathsf{b})$) is satisfied in $\mathcal{I}$ if $\mathsf{b} \in \mathrm{A}^\mathcal{I}$ (resp. $(\mathsf{a}, \mathsf{b}) \in \mathrm{P}^\mathcal{I}$). An interpretation is a *model* of a TBox $\mathcal{T}$ (resp. KB $\mathcal{K}$) if it satisfies all axioms in $\mathcal{T}$ (resp. axioms and assertions in $\mathcal{K}$). A KB is *satisfiable* if it has at least one model. An inclusion (resp. assertion) Φ is *entailed* from $\mathcal{T}$ (resp. $\mathcal{K}$), written $\mathcal{T} \models \Phi$ (resp. $\mathcal{K} \models \Phi$), if Φ is satisfied in every model of $\mathcal{T}$ (resp. $\mathcal{K}$).

[1]We follow e.g. (Bienvenu et al. 2014) by including negative role inclusions in $\mathcal{ELHI}_\bot$, so that it has DL-Lite$^{\mathcal{H}}_{core}$ as a sublogic.

Example 1. *Consider the ABox $\mathcal{A}_e := \{\mathrm{A}_1(\mathsf{a}), \mathrm{B}(\mathsf{b})\}$ and the $\mathcal{ELHI}_\bot$ TBox $\mathcal{T}_e$:*

$$\mathrm{A}_1 \sqsubseteq \exists \mathrm{R}.\mathrm{A}_2 \quad \mathrm{A}_2 \sqsubseteq \exists \mathrm{R}.\mathrm{A}_1 \quad \mathrm{B} \sqsubseteq \exists \mathrm{R}.\mathrm{B} \quad \mathrm{R} \sqcap \mathrm{R}^- \sqsubseteq \bot$$
$$\mathrm{A}_2 \sqsubseteq \exists \mathrm{R}.\overline{\mathrm{B}} \quad \overline{\mathrm{B}} \sqsubseteq \exists \mathrm{R}.\mathrm{C} \quad \mathrm{B} \sqsubseteq \mathrm{C} \quad \mathrm{B} \sqcap \overline{\mathrm{B}} \sqsubseteq \bot$$

Our example KB is $\mathcal{K}_e := (\mathcal{T}_e, \mathcal{A}_e)$. Figures 2a and 2c depict models of $\mathcal{K}_e$.

We can view an interpretation $\mathcal{I}$ as a (possibly infinite) set of assertions $\mathcal{A}_\mathcal{I} = \{\mathrm{A}(e) \mid e \in \mathrm{A}^\mathcal{I}, \mathrm{A} \in \mathsf{N_C}\} \cup \{\mathrm{P}(e, e') \mid (e, e') \in \mathrm{P}^\mathcal{I}, \mathrm{P} \in \mathsf{N_R}\}$. We say that $\mathcal{I}$ is *$\mathcal{T}$-satisfiable* if $\mathcal{T} \cup \mathcal{A}_\mathcal{I}$ has a model, and it is *$\mathcal{T}$-saturated* if $\mathcal{A}_\mathcal{I}$ contains every assertion entailed by $(\mathcal{T}, \mathcal{A}_\mathcal{I})$.

Counting Queries We consider counting queries as defined in (Bienvenu, Manière, and Thomazo 2020) (which generalizes the queries considered in (Kostylev and Reutter 2015; Calvanese et al. 2020a)). A *counting conjunctive query (CCQ)* takes the form $q(\mathbf{x}) = \exists \mathbf{y} \exists \mathbf{z}\, \psi(\mathbf{x}, \mathbf{y}, \mathbf{z})$, where $\mathbf{x}, \mathbf{y}, \mathbf{z}$ are tuples of *answer, existential, and counting variables*, respectively, and ψ is a conjunction of concept and role atoms with terms from $\mathsf{N_I} \cup \mathbf{x} \cup \mathbf{y} \cup \mathbf{z}$. We use $\mathsf{terms}(q)$ for the set of all terms occurring in q, and we treat queries as sets of atoms when convenient. The usual notion of *conjunctive query (CQ)* is captured by CCQs without counting variables (i.e. $\mathbf{z} = \emptyset$). A CCQ q is *Boolean* if $\mathbf{x} = \emptyset$. *Concept cardinality queries* are Boolean CCQs of the form $\exists z\, \mathrm{A}(z)$ ($\mathrm{A} \in \mathsf{N_C}$), while *role cardinality queries* have the form $\exists z_1, z_2\, \mathrm{R}(z_1, z_2)$ ($\mathrm{R} \in \mathsf{N_R}$).

A *match* for a CCQ q in an interpretation $\mathcal{I}$ is a homomorphism from q into $\mathcal{I}$, i.e. a function π that maps each term in q to an element of $\Delta^\mathcal{I}$ such that $\pi(t) = t$ when $t \in \mathsf{N_I}$, $\pi(t) \in \mathrm{A}^\mathcal{I}$ for every $\mathrm{A}(t) \in q$, and $(\pi(t), \pi(t')) \in \mathrm{P}^\mathcal{I}$ for every $\mathrm{P}(t, t') \in q$. If a match π maps $\mathbf{x}$ to $\mathbf{a}$, then the restriction of π to $\mathbf{z}$ is called a *counting match (c-match)* of $q(\mathbf{a})$ in $\mathcal{I}$. The set of *answers* to q in $\mathcal{I}$, denoted $q^\mathcal{I}$, contains all pairs $(\mathbf{a}, [m, M])$, with $m, M \in \mathbb{N} \cup \{+\infty\}$, such that the number of distinct c-matches of $q(\mathbf{a})$ in $\mathcal{I}$ belongs to the interval $[m, M]$. A *certain answer* to q w.r.t. $\mathcal{K}$ is an answer in every model of $\mathcal{K}$, that is a pair from $\bigcap_{\mathcal{I} \models \mathcal{K}} q^\mathcal{I}$.

As usual, it is sufficient to consider the Boolean case: $(\mathbf{a}, [m, M])$ is a certain answer to a CCQ $q(\mathbf{x})$ iff $(\emptyset, [m, M])$ is a certain answer to the Boolean CCQ $q(\mathbf{a})$ obtained by replacing $\mathbf{x}$ with $\mathbf{a}$. Thus, from now on, *we focus on Boolean CCQs*, and work with candidate answers $[m, M]$ in place of $(\emptyset, [m, M])$.

We further observe that since $\mathcal{ELHI}_\bot$ cannot restrict the size of models, the least upper bound M in a certain answer $[m, M]$ is: 0 if the underlying CQ is unsatisfiable w.r.t. $\mathcal{T}$, 1 if q has a match in every model but $\mathbf{z} = \emptyset$; and $+\infty$ otherwise. As the first two cases can be readily handled using existing techniques, *we focus on identifying certain answers of the form $[m, +\infty]$*.

Example 2. *Let $q_e := \exists y\, \exists z\, \mathrm{R}(y, z) \wedge \mathrm{C}(z)$ be a Boolean CCQ. Intervals $[0, +\infty]$ and $[1, +\infty]$ are certain answers to q_e over $\mathcal{K}_e$. Interval $[4, +\infty]$ is not as the models depicted on Figures 2a and 2c contain only 3 matches for q_e.*

To clarify how our notion of certain answer relates to standard OMQA semantics, we note that a Boolean CQ q is entailed from $\mathcal{K}$ iff $[1, +\infty]$ is a certain answer to q over $\mathcal{K}$.

Complexity Given a $\mathcal{ELHI}_\bot$ knowledge base $\mathcal{K} = (\mathcal{T}, \mathcal{A})$, a Boolean CCQ q, and an integer $m \geq 0$ (in binary), we are interested in the complexity of deciding whether $[m, +\infty]$ is a certain answer to q w.r.t. $\mathcal{K}$. We will consider the two usual complexity measures: *combined complexity* which is in terms of the size of the whole input, and *data complexity* which is only in terms of the size of $\mathcal{A}$ and m ($\mathcal{T}$ and q are treated as fixed). If O is a TBox, ABox, KB, or CCQ, then the *size* of O, denoted $|O|$, is the number of occurrences of concept and role names in O.

Normal form As is standard (see e.g. (Bienvenu et al. 2014)), we work with $\mathcal{ELHI}_\bot$ TBoxes in a convenient *normal form*, where every concept inclusion has one of the following restricted shapes:

$$\mathrm{A} \sqsubseteq \bot \qquad \top \sqsubseteq \mathrm{A} \qquad \mathrm{A}_1 \sqcap \mathrm{A}_2 \sqsubseteq \mathrm{A}$$
$$\mathrm{A}_1 \sqsubseteq \exists \mathrm{R}.\mathrm{A}_2 \qquad \exists \mathrm{R}.\mathrm{A}_1 \sqsubseteq \mathrm{A}_2$$

with $\mathrm{A}, \mathrm{A}_1, \mathrm{A}_2 \in \mathsf{N_C}, \mathrm{R} \in \mathsf{N_R^\pm}$. Through the introduction of fresh concept names, we can transform in polynomial time any TBox $\mathcal{T}$ into a normal-form TBox $\mathcal{T}'$ that is a model-conservative extension of $\mathcal{T}$ (hence, indistinguishable from $\mathcal{T}$ from the point of view of queries). We therefore *assume w.l.o.g. that all considered TBoxes are in normal form.*

Closed Predicates A *KB with closed predicates* consists of a KB $(\mathcal{T}, \mathcal{A})$ and a set $\Sigma \subseteq \mathsf{N_C} \cup \mathsf{N_R}$ of *closed predicates*. An interpretation $\mathcal{I}$ is a *model of* $(\mathcal{T}, \mathcal{A}, \Sigma)$ if it is a model of $(\mathcal{T}, \mathcal{A})$ which interprets the closed predicates according to $\mathcal{A}$, i.e. $\mathrm{A}^\mathcal{I} = \{\mathsf{a} \mid \mathrm{A}(\mathsf{a}) \in \mathcal{A}\}$ for every $\mathrm{A} \in \Sigma \cap \mathsf{N_C}$ and $\mathrm{P}^\mathcal{I} = \{(\mathsf{a}, \mathsf{b}) \mid \mathrm{P}(a, b) \in \mathcal{A}\}$ for every $\mathrm{P} \in \Sigma \cap \mathsf{N_R}$. Query entailment is then defined as for classical KBs, but using this modified notion of model.

3 General Case of CCQs

This section presents our main contributions: a decision procedure and associated tight complexity bounds for CCQ answering in $\mathcal{ELHI}_\bot$ and its sublogics.

To improve readability, we have split the section into several parts. Section 3.1 presents a double-exponential-time decision procedure, whose correctness proof is detailed in Section 3.2. We explain, in Section 3.3, how to shrink the size of the models implicitly generated by our procedure, which we use to show coNP data complexity. Finally, in Section 3.4, we prove the required lower bounds.

3.1 Decision Procedure

In this subsection, we devise a procedure that computes in double-exponential time the minimum amount of c-matches, which immediately yields the following upper bound:

Theorem 1. *CCQ answering in $\mathcal{ELHI}_\bot$ is in* 2EXP *w.r.t. combined complexity.*

Let us fix a satisfiable KB $\mathcal{K} = (\mathcal{T}, \mathcal{A})$ and a (Boolean) CCQ q. The next lemma provides an upper bound on the minimal number of c-matches.

Lemma 1. *There exists a model of $\mathcal{K}$ with less than $M := (|\mathsf{Ind}(\mathcal{A})| + 3\,|\mathcal{T}|\,2^{|\mathcal{T}|})^{|q|}$ c-matches for q.*

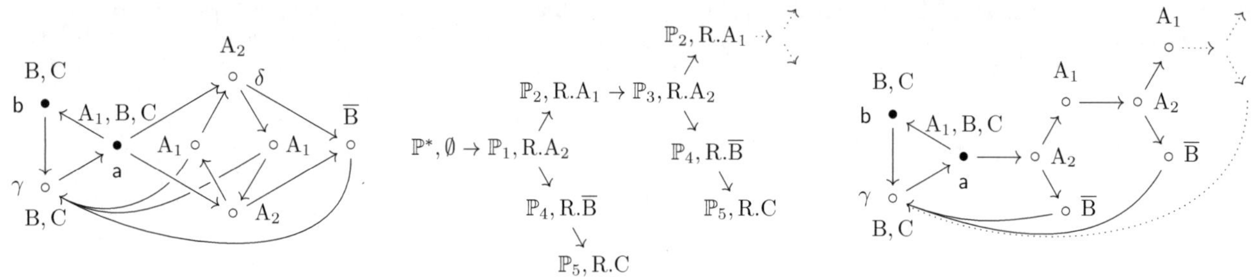

(a) A model $\mathcal{I}_e$ of $\mathcal{K}_e$.

(b) Pattern tree $\mathcal{P}_e$.

(c) Model $\mathcal{I}_e^{\diamond}$ built from $\mathbb{P}_e^*$.

Figure 2: Interpretations and pattern tree used along our examples, labels for the only role R have been omitted for readability.

Proof sketch. We can exhibit a model having at most $|\mathsf{Ind}(\mathcal{A})| + 3\,|\mathcal{T}|\,2^{|\mathcal{T}|}$ elements. □

It follows that in any model $\mathcal{I}$ having a minimum number of c-matches, the set $\Delta^* \subseteq \Delta^{\mathcal{I}}$ of elements appearing in the image of a c-match has size at most $M \cdot |q|$. We can thus iterate over all such Δ^*, and even over all induced interpretations $\mathcal{I}^* = \mathcal{I}_{|\Delta^*}$, in double-exponential time w.r.t. combined complexity. The core task will then be to determine, given such a candidate $\mathcal{I}^*$, whether we can extend $\mathcal{I}^*$ into a model of $\mathcal{K}$ *without introducing new c-matches*.

Let us fix our candidate $\mathcal{I}^*$ and see how to check for a suitable extension. The challenging axioms to handle are those of the form $\mathrm{A} \sqsubseteq \exists \mathrm{R.B}$, as they might require us to introduce new elements. We define the set $\Omega := \{\mathrm{R.B} \mid \mathrm{A} \sqsubseteq \exists \mathrm{R.B} \in \mathcal{T}\}$ and call its members *(existential) heads*. Importantly, as our correctness proof will establish, it is sufficient to consider extensions of $\mathcal{I}^*$ which are obtained by adding tree-shaped structures of new elements, plus some edges between the new elements and $\Delta^{\mathcal{I}^*}$ (we may need to use elements from $\Delta^{\mathcal{I}^*}$ as witnesses for existential heads to avoid new query matches). This property enables us to build such an extension by piecing together local interpretations corresponding to the addition of a single edge, using two distinguished symbols ⊚ and ⊛ as placeholders for fresh elements. We shall call these building blocks *patterns*, as they are inspired by a notion of the same name introduced for CQ answering with existential rules (Thomazo et al. 2012).

Patterns not only consist of a local interpretation, but also other information needed to ensure that assembled patterns do not violate any TBox axioms or introduce any new matches. In particular, we shall keep track of (partial) query matches involving the local elements using the notion of a coherent specification. Intuitively, such a specification tells us which matches should be realized in the constructed extension, and naturally contains at least the matches of subqueries of q already realized in the local interpretation.

Definition 1. *Let $\mathcal{I}$ be an interpretation.*

- *The* specification $\mathfrak{M}^{\mathcal{I}}$ induced by $\mathcal{I}$ *is the set of pairs (r, π) such that $r \subseteq q$ and $\pi : r \to \mathcal{I}$ is a (full) match.*
- *A* coherent specification $\mathfrak{M}$ *over $\mathcal{I}$ is a set of pairs (r, π) where $r \subseteq q$ and π is a partial mapping from* $\mathsf{terms}(r)$ *to $\Delta^{\mathcal{I}}$ such that $\mathfrak{M}$ contains $\mathfrak{M}^{\mathcal{I}}$ and if $(r_1, \pi_1), (r_2, \pi_2) \in \mathfrak{M}$ with π_1 and π_2 defined and equal on* $\mathsf{var}(r_1) \cap \mathsf{var}(r_2)$, *then $(r_1 \cup r_2, \pi_1 \cup \pi_2) \in \mathfrak{M}$.*

To check the compatibility of different specifications, we will need to be able to restrict them to a subdomain:

Definition 2. *The* restriction of a specification $\mathfrak{M}$ *over an interpretation $\mathcal{I}$ to a domain $\Delta \subseteq \Delta^{\mathcal{I}}$, denoted $\mathfrak{M}_{|\Delta}$, is the set of pairs (r, π') such that π' is the restriction of some π to $\pi^{-1}(\Delta)$ for some $(r, \pi) \in \mathfrak{M}$.*

Remark 1. *Induced specifications and restrictions of coherent specifications are both coherent specifications.*

Patterns will contain a further kind of information called a prediction, defined next. The purpose will be explained in more detail once we introduce links between patterns, but roughly it serves to coordinate the successor patterns of a pattern to avoid violating negative role inclusions.

Definition 3. *A* prediction *is a function* $\mathsf{next} : \Omega \to \Delta^{\mathcal{I}^*} \cup \Omega$ *verifying that: for all $\mathrm{R_1.B_1}, \mathrm{R_2.B_2} \in \Omega$, if $\mathcal{T} \models \mathrm{R_1} \sqcap \mathrm{R_2} \sqsubseteq \bot$, then* $\mathsf{next}(\mathrm{R_1.B_1}) \neq \mathsf{next}(\mathrm{R_2.B_2})$.

We now formally define the central notion of pattern, relative to $\mathcal{I}^*$ and a candidate specification $\mathfrak{M}^*$ over $\mathcal{I}^*$.

Definition 4. *A* pattern $\mathbb{P}$ *(w.r.t. $\mathcal{I}^*$ and $\mathfrak{M}^*$) is a tuple* $(\mathfrak{fr}^{\mathbb{P}}, \mathfrak{gen}^{\mathbb{P}}, \mathfrak{I}^{\mathbb{P}}, \mathfrak{M}^{\mathbb{P}}, \mathsf{next}_{\mathbb{P}})$ *where:*

- *The frontier and generated domains $\mathfrak{fr}^{\mathbb{P}}$ and $\mathfrak{gen}^{\mathbb{P}}$ are* disjoints *sets of elements from $\Delta^{\mathcal{I}^*} \cup \{⊚, ⊛\}$;*
- *$\mathfrak{I}^{\mathbb{P}}$ is a $\mathcal{T}$-saturated and $\mathcal{T}$-satisfiable interpretation with $\Delta^{\mathfrak{I}^{\mathbb{P}}} = \Delta^{\mathcal{I}^*} \cup \mathfrak{fr}^{\mathbb{P}} \cup \mathfrak{gen}^{\mathbb{P}}$ and such that $\mathfrak{I}^{\mathbb{P}}_{|\Delta^{\mathcal{I}^*}} = \mathcal{I}^*$;*
- *$\mathfrak{M}^{\mathbb{P}}$ is a coherent specification of q over $\mathfrak{I}^{\mathbb{P}}$ that preserves $\mathfrak{M}^*$, that is $(\mathfrak{M}^{\mathbb{P}})_{|\Delta^{\mathcal{I}^*}} = \mathfrak{M}^*$;*
- $\mathsf{next}_{\mathbb{P}}$ *is a prediction.*

We shall be interested in two types of patterns. The (unique) *initial pattern* $\mathbb{P}^* := (\emptyset, \Delta^{\mathcal{I}^*}, \mathcal{I}^*, \mathfrak{M}^*, \mathsf{Id})$ simply represents $\mathcal{I}^*$ and $\mathfrak{M}^*$. All other patterns of interest represent additions of a pair of adjacent elements, and $\mathfrak{fr}^{\mathbb{P}}$ and $\mathfrak{gen}^{\mathbb{P}}$ will be singletons (representing these two elements).

Example 3. *In our running example, $\Delta^*_{\mathrm{e}} := \{\mathsf{a}, \mathsf{b}, \gamma\}$ (z maps to only these elements). The initial pattern $\mathbb{P}^*_{\mathrm{e}}$ has frontier $\emptyset$, generated terms Δ^*_{e}, interpretation $\mathcal{I}^*_{\mathrm{e}} := (\mathcal{I}_{\mathrm{e}})_{|\Delta^*_{\mathrm{e}}}$ depicted in Figure 3a, and specification $\mathfrak{M}^*_{\mathrm{e}} := (\mathfrak{M}^{\mathcal{I}_{\mathrm{e}}})_{|\Delta^*_{\mathrm{e}}}$. Non-initial patterns will be illustrated later.*

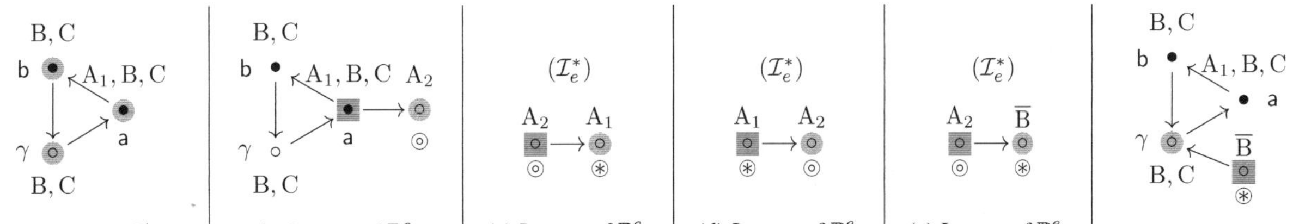

(a) Interp. $\mathcal{I}^*_e$. (b) Interp. of $\mathbb{P}^e_1$. (c) Interp. of $\mathbb{P}^e_2$. (d) Interp. of $\mathbb{P}^e_3$. (e) Interp. of $\mathbb{P}^e_4$. (f) Interp. of $\mathbb{P}^e_5$.

Figure 3: Interpretations of patterns from Example 4.

We now define how to combine patterns together, and first, *when* it is necessary to combine them.

Definition 5. *We say that* $\mathrm{R.B} \in \Omega$ *is* applicable *to* e *in a pattern* $\mathbb{P}$ *if* $e \in \mathfrak{gen}^{\mathbb{P}}$ *and there exists* $\mathrm{A} \sqsubseteq \exists\mathrm{R.B} \in \mathcal{T}$ *with* $e \in \mathrm{A}^{\mathfrak{I}^{\mathbb{P}}}$ *but* $e \notin (\exists\mathrm{R.B})^{\mathfrak{I}^{\mathbb{P}}}$.

When a head is applicable to a pattern, we need to find another pattern that can realize the head. This is formalized by the following notion of link between patterns, which requires that the two patterns are compatible (Conditions 1, 2, 3), the second pattern realizes the head (Condition 4), and certain consistency conditions hold (Conditions 5, 6).

Definition 6. *Let* $\mathrm{R.B}$ *be an applicable head on* e_1 *in a pattern* $\mathbb{P}_1$. *There is a* $(\mathrm{R.B}, e_1)$*-link from* $\mathbb{P}_1$ *to* $\mathbb{P}_2$ *if:*

1. $\mathfrak{fr}^{\mathbb{P}_2} = \{e_1\}$ *and* $\mathfrak{gen}^{\mathbb{P}_2}$ *is a singleton, say* $\{e_2\}$*;*
2. *For all concept name* A, *we have* $e_1 \in \mathrm{A}^{\mathfrak{I}^{\mathbb{P}_1}}$ *iff* $e_1 \in \mathrm{A}^{\mathfrak{I}^{\mathbb{P}_2}}$*;*
3. $\mathfrak{M}^{\mathbb{P}_1}_{|\Delta^{\mathcal{I}^*} \cup \{e_1\}} = \mathfrak{M}^{\mathbb{P}_2}_{|\Delta^{\mathcal{I}^*} \cup \{e_1\}}$*;*
4. $e_2 \in \mathrm{B}^{\mathfrak{I}^{\mathbb{P}_2}}$ *and for all* $\mathrm{P} \in \mathsf{N_R}$: $\mathrm{P}^{\mathfrak{I}^{\mathbb{P}_2}} = \mathrm{P}^{\mathcal{I}^*} \cup \{(e_1, e_2) \mid \mathcal{T} \models \mathrm{R} \sqsubseteq \mathrm{P}\} \cup \{(e_2, e_1) \mid \mathcal{T} \models \mathrm{R}^- \sqsubseteq \mathrm{P}\}$
5. *If ever* $e_2 \in \Delta^{\mathcal{I}^*} \cap \mathfrak{fr}^{\mathbb{P}_1}$, *then* $\mathfrak{I}^{\mathbb{P}_1} \cup \mathfrak{I}^{\mathbb{P}_2}$ *is* $\mathcal{T}$*-satisfiable.*
6. *If* $e_2 \in \Delta^{\mathcal{I}^*}$, *then* $e_2 = \mathsf{next}_{\mathbb{P}_1}(\mathrm{R.B})$.

We denote $\mathbb{L}^{\mathrm{R.B}}_{\mathbb{P}_1, e_1}$ *the set of patterns* $\mathbb{P}_2$ *such that there is a* $(\mathrm{R.B}, e_1)$*-link from* $\mathbb{P}_1$ *to* $\mathbb{P}_2$.

Remark 2. *Predictions are used in Condition 6 to avoid problematic situations where two successor patterns merge back to the same element of* $\Delta^{\mathcal{I}^*}$. *Specifically, if we have a* $\mathrm{R}_1.\mathrm{B}_1$*-link from* $\mathbb{P}_0$ *to* $\mathbb{P}_1$ *and a* $\mathrm{R}_2.\mathrm{B}_2$*-link from* $\mathbb{P}_0$ *to* $\mathbb{P}_2$, *with* $\mathcal{T} \models \mathrm{R}_1 \sqcap \mathrm{R}_2 \sqsubseteq \bot$, *then* $\mathsf{next}_{\mathbb{P}_0}(\mathrm{R}_1.\mathrm{B}_1) \neq \mathsf{next}_{\mathbb{P}_0}(\mathrm{R}_2.\mathrm{B}_2)$, *preventing* $\mathbb{P}_1$ *and* $\mathbb{P}_2$ *from using the same element of* $\Delta^{\mathcal{I}^*}$ *as generated term (which would violate* $\mathcal{T}$*). Condition 5 is similar in spirit, handling the case of the pattern* $\mathbb{P}_1$ *using the frontier element of* $\mathbb{P}_0$ *as a generated term.*

Example 4. *We consider patterns* $\mathbb{P}^e_1, \ldots, \mathbb{P}^e_5$ *whose interpretations are depicted in Figure 3. Frontier terms are indicated by square-purple and generated terms by circle-green. Predictions are* Id *except for* $\mathsf{next}_{\mathbb{P}^e_4}$, *which maps* R.C *to* γ. *Specifications* $\mathfrak{M}_i$ *are given by:* $\mathfrak{M}_1 = \mathfrak{M}^*_e \cup \{(\alpha_\mathrm{R}, (y, z) \mapsto (\mathsf{a}, \circledcirc)), (\alpha_\mathrm{R}, z \mapsto \circledcirc), (\alpha_\mathrm{R}, y \mapsto \circledcirc)\}$*;* $\mathfrak{M}_5 = \mathfrak{M}^*_e \cup \{(q_e, (y, z) \mapsto (\circledast, \gamma)), (\alpha_\mathrm{R}, (y, z) \mapsto (\circledast, \gamma)), (\alpha_\mathrm{R}, z \mapsto \circledast)\}$*;* $\mathfrak{M}_4 = \mathfrak{M}_1 \cup \mathfrak{M}_5 \cup \{(\alpha_\mathrm{R}, (y, z) \mapsto (\circledcirc, \circledast))\}$*;* $\mathfrak{M}_2 = \mathfrak{M}_4 \setminus \{(\alpha_\mathrm{R}, z \mapsto \circledast)\}$*;* $\mathfrak{M}_3 = \mathfrak{M}_5 \cup \{(\alpha_\mathrm{R}, (y, z) \mapsto (\mathsf{a}, \circledcirc)), (\alpha_\mathrm{R}, (y, z) \mapsto (\circledast, \circledcirc)), (\alpha_\mathrm{R}, y \mapsto \circledcirc)\}$, *where* α_R *denotes* $\mathrm{R}(y, z)$. *Observe that* $\mathfrak{M}_i$ *may include (partial) matches which are not present in* $\mathbb{P}^e_i$*'s interpretation but are useful for linking patterns, e.g.* $(q_e, (y, z) \mapsto (\circledast, \gamma))$ *in* $\mathfrak{M}_4$ *enables a* $(\mathrm{R.C}, \circledast)$*-link from* $\mathbb{P}^e_4$ *to* $\mathbb{P}^e_5$ *(see Example 5).*

We now characterize patterns that cannot be used to satisfy a head without introducing a new c-match.

Definition 7. *A pattern* $\mathbb{P}$ *is* rejecting *if one of the two following conditions holds:*

- *There exists* $(q, \pi) \in \mathfrak{M}^{\mathbb{P}}$ *with* $\pi(\mathbf{z}) \cap \{\circledcirc, \circledast\} \neq \emptyset$*;*
- *There exists an existential head* R.B *that applies on* e *in* $\mathbb{P}$ *such that all patterns* $\mathbb{P}' \in \mathbb{L}^{\mathrm{R.B}}_{\mathbb{P}, e}$ *are rejecting.*

A pattern is accepting if it is not rejecting.

The acceptance of the initial pattern $\mathbb{P}^*$ is a sufficient condition ensuring $\mathcal{I}^*$ extends to a model having no more c-matches than encoded in $\mathfrak{M}^*$, i.e. the pairs $(q, \pi) \in \mathfrak{M}^*$ such that π is defined for all counting variables.

Lemma 2. *If* $\mathbb{P}^* := (\emptyset, \Delta^*, \mathcal{I}^*, \mathfrak{M}^*, \mathsf{Id})$ *is accepting, then there exists a model* $\mathcal{I}^\diamondsuit$ *such that* $\mathcal{I}^* \subseteq \mathcal{I}^\diamondsuit$ *and if* $\pi : q \to \mathcal{I}^\diamondsuit$ *is a c-match, then* $(q, \pi) \in \mathfrak{M}^*$. *In particular,* $\mathcal{I}^\diamondsuit$ *has at most as many c-matches as those encoded in* $\mathfrak{M}^*$.

Furthermore, the minimum amount of c-matches is reached among initial patterns due to the following result:

Lemma 3. *If* $\mathcal{I}$ *is a model of* $\mathcal{K}$ *with* m *c-matches, then there exists an accepting initial pattern whose specification encodes* exactly m *c-matches.*

Before proving Lemmas 2 and 3, let us recap the overall double-exponential procedure underlying Theorem 1:

Proof of Theorem 1. We consider all possible initial patterns $\mathbb{P}^*$ with an interpretation domain Δ^* such that $\mathsf{Ind}(\mathcal{A}) \subseteq \Delta^*$ and $|\Delta^*| \leq M|q|$ (recall Lemma 1). Every such $\mathbb{P}^*$ is of single-exponential size w.r.t. combined complexity (observe that its specification $\mathfrak{M}^*$ corresponds to a subset of $2^q \times (\Delta^* \cup \{\uparrow\})^q$, where $\uparrow$ is a fresh symbol witnessing the use of *partial* mappings), and thus are double-exponential in number (up to isomorphism) and can be enumerated in double-exponential time. For each such $\mathbb{P}^*$, we construct in double-exponential time the set of all possible descendant patterns of $\mathbb{P}^*$ (which are of single-exponential size, having at most $|\Delta^*| + 2$ elements). We then check whether each possible pattern ($\mathbb{P}^*$ or candidate descendant) is in fact a well-defined pattern, in particular, its interpretation is $\mathcal{T}$-satisfiable and $\mathcal{T}$-saturated. These verifications can be done in double-exponential time, recalling that KB satisfiability and instance checking are in EXP for $\mathcal{ELHI}_\bot$ (even the variant with negative role inclusions, see e.g. (Bienvenu et al. 2014)). Acceptance of $\mathbb{P}^*$ is tested (again in deterministic exponential time) by repeatedly iterating over the set of patterns and removing those that are rejecting either due to their specification, or due to the removal of all patterns that could provide a link for an applicable head. If $\mathbb{P}^*$ is found to be accepting and $\mathfrak{M}^*$ encodes m c-matches, then Lemma 2 ensures the existence of a model with at most m c-matches. Conversely, Lemma 3 ensures that we can find the smallest such m among the accepting initial patterns. □

3.2 Proofs of Lemmas 2 and 3

We now prove the central lemmas of the correctness proof.

From Accepting Patterns to Models To prove Lemma 2, let us suppose we are given an initial pattern $\mathbb{P}^* := (\emptyset, \Delta^*, \mathcal{I}^*, \mathfrak{M}^*, \mathsf{Id})$ that is accepting. Our aim is to construct a model $\mathcal{I}^\diamond$ that extends $\mathcal{I}^*$ and is such that $(q, \pi) \in \mathfrak{M}^*$ for every c-match $\pi : q \to \mathcal{I}^\diamond$.

We proceed as follows. For each accepting descendant pattern $\mathbb{P}$ (w.r.t. $\mathcal{I}^*$ and $\mathfrak{M}^*$) and each head R.B applicable to e in $\mathbb{P}$, we choose an accepting pattern $\mathsf{ch}^{\mathrm{R.B}}_{\mathbb{P},e}$ from $\mathbb{L}^{\mathrm{R.B}}_{\mathbb{P},e}$. Then, starting from $\mathbb{P}^*$, we build a tree-shaped set of words, whose letters consist of an accepting pattern and existential head, and which witnesses the acceptance of $\mathbb{P}^*$.

Definition 8. *The* pattern tree $\mathcal{P}$ *is defined as the smallest set of words such that:*

- $(\mathbb{P}^*, \emptyset) \in \mathcal{P}$;
- *If* $w \cdot (\mathbb{P}, h) \in \mathcal{P}$ *and* R.B *is applicable to* e *in* $\mathbb{P}$, *then* $w \cdot (\mathbb{P}, h) \cdot (\mathsf{ch}^{\mathrm{R.B}}_{\mathbb{P},e}, \mathrm{R.B}) \in \mathcal{P}$.

It remains to 'glue' together the interpretations $\mathfrak{J}^{\mathbb{P}}$ according to the structure of $\mathcal{P}$. Since a pattern $\mathbb{P}$ may occur more than once, we create a copy of $\mathfrak{J}^{\mathbb{P}}$ for each node in $\mathcal{P}$ of the form $w \cdot (\mathbb{P}, h)$. We do not duplicate however elements from $\mathcal{I}^*$ as they precisely are those we want to reuse. Hence only the frontier term and the generated term may be duplicated (provided they do not belong to Δ^*). When a node $w \cdot (\mathbb{P}_1, h_1) \cdot (\mathbb{P}_2, h_2)$ is encountered, we merge the frontier term of $\mathbb{P}_2$ with the already-introduced copy of the generated element from $\mathbb{P}_1$ on which h_2 is applied (which is the only element in $\mathfrak{fr}^{\mathbb{P}_2}$). Therefore, when considering such a node $w \cdot (\mathbb{P}_1, h_1) \cdot (\mathbb{P}_2, h_2)$, the only element we might have to introduce is a copy of the generated term e of $\mathbb{P}_2$ (unless $e \in \Delta^*$), which we shall simply name $w \cdot (\mathbb{P}_1, h_1) \cdot (\mathbb{P}_2, h_2)$. Formally, the copying and merging of elements is achieved by the following family of duplicating functions, defined inductively for each $w \cdot (\mathbb{P}, h) \in \mathcal{P}$.

$$\lambda_{w\cdot(\mathbb{P},h)} : \Delta^{\mathfrak{J}^{\mathbb{P}}} \to \Delta^{\mathcal{I}^*} \cup \{w, w\cdot(\mathbb{P},h)\}$$
$$e \mapsto \begin{cases} e & \text{if } e \in \Delta^{\mathcal{I}^*} \\ w & \text{if } e \in \mathfrak{fr}^{\mathbb{P}} \setminus \Delta^{\mathcal{I}^*} \\ w\cdot(\mathbb{P},h) & \text{if } e \in \mathfrak{gen}^{\mathbb{P}} \setminus \Delta^{\mathcal{I}^*} \end{cases}$$

Note that if $e \in \mathfrak{fr}^{\mathbb{P}_2} \setminus \Delta^{\mathcal{I}^*}$, then $e \in \mathfrak{gen}^{\mathbb{P}_1} \setminus \Delta^{\mathcal{I}^*}$, hence

$$\lambda_{w\cdot(\mathbb{P}_1,h_1)\cdot(\mathbb{P}_2,h_2)}(e) = \lambda_{w\cdot(\mathbb{P}_1,h_1)}(e) = w\cdot(\mathbb{P}_1,h_1).$$

The desired model $\mathcal{I}^\diamond$ can then be defined as follows:

$$\mathcal{I}^\diamond := \bigcup_{w\cdot(\mathbb{P},h)\in\mathcal{P}} \lambda_{w\cdot(\mathbb{P},h)}(\mathfrak{J}^{\mathbb{P}}).$$

Example 5. *The patterns introduced in Example 4 are sufficient to witness that* $\mathbb{P}^*_e$ *is accepting. The initial part of* $\mathcal{P}_e$ *is depicted in Figure 2b. The resulting* $\mathcal{I}^\diamond_e$ *is depicted in Figure 2c. Notice how it inherits the tree-shaped structure of* $\mathcal{P}_e$ *up to roles collapsing back in* $\mathcal{I}^*_e$.

By definition, each $\lambda_{w\cdot(\mathbb{P},h)}$ is a homomorphism from $\mathfrak{J}^{\mathbb{P}}$ to $\mathcal{I}^\diamond$. Due to Condition 2, the shared element of linked patterns must belong to the same concepts, so concept membership in $\mathcal{I}^\diamond$ transfers back to $\mathfrak{J}^{\mathbb{P}}$:

Lemma 4. *For all* $w \cdot (\mathbb{P}, h) \in \mathcal{P}$, *for all* $e \in \Delta^{\mathfrak{J}^{\mathbb{P}}}$ *and for all* $\mathrm{A} \in \mathsf{N_C}$, *if* $\lambda_{w\cdot(\mathbb{P},h)}(e) \in \mathrm{A}^{\mathcal{I}^\diamond}$, *then* $e \in \mathrm{A}^{\mathfrak{J}^{\mathbb{P}}}$.

An analogous property fails however for roles, as two patterns $\mathbb{P}_1 = \mathsf{ch}^{h_1}_{\mathbb{P},e}$ and $\mathbb{P}_2 = \mathsf{ch}^{h_2}_{\mathbb{P},e}$ may reuse the same element from Δ^*, that is, $\mathfrak{gen}^{\mathbb{P}_1} = \mathfrak{gen}^{\mathbb{P}_2} \in \Delta^*$. In that case, satisfied roles in $\mathcal{I}^\diamond_{|\Delta}$ where $\Delta := \lambda_{w\cdot(\mathbb{P},h)\cdot(\mathbb{P}_1,h_1)}(\mathfrak{J}^{\mathbb{P}_1})$ may not be satisfied in $\mathfrak{J}^{\mathbb{P}_1}$. Conditions 5 and 6 allow us to show the following weaker property, sufficient for our purposes:

Lemma 5. *For all* $w \cdot (\mathbb{P}, h) \in \mathcal{P}$, $d, e \in \Delta^{\mathfrak{J}^{\mathbb{P}}}$, *and* $\mathrm{P} \in \mathsf{N_R}$: *if* $(\lambda_{w\cdot(\mathbb{P},h)}(d), \lambda_{w\cdot(\mathbb{P},h)}(e)) \in \mathrm{P}^{\mathcal{I}^\diamond}$, *then* $\mathfrak{J}^{\mathbb{P}}$ *remains* $\mathcal{T}$*-satisfiable if we add* (d, e) *to* $\mathrm{P}^{\mathfrak{J}^{\mathbb{P}}}$.

A similar lemma (given in the appendix) allows us to lift query matches from $\mathcal{I}^\diamond$ to patterns, yielding the following:

Proposition 1. $\mathcal{I}^\diamond$ *is a model of* $\mathcal{K}$ *whose c-matches are included in those encoded in* $\mathfrak{M}^*$.

From a Model to an Accepting Initial Pattern We now turn to the proof of Lemma 3. We fix a model $\mathcal{I}$ of $\mathcal{K}$, and our task is to construct an accepting initial pattern having the same number of c-matches as $\mathcal{I}$.

Let Δ^* be the subset of $\Delta^{\mathcal{I}}$ consisting of all individuals in $\mathcal{A}$ and all elements e such that $e = \pi(z)$ for some $\pi : q \to \mathcal{I}$ and counting variable z. Set $\mathcal{I}^* := \mathcal{I}_{|\Delta^*}$ and $\mathfrak{M}^* := (\mathfrak{M}^{\mathcal{I}})_{|\Delta^*}$. Notice in particular that the number of c-matches for q encoded in $\mathfrak{M}^*$ is exactly the number of c-matches for q in $\mathcal{I}$. We claim that $\mathbb{P}^* := (\emptyset, \Delta^*, \mathcal{I}^*, \mathfrak{M}^*, \mathsf{Id})$ is accepting.

To prove this, we shall build a set of patterns, whose every pattern $\mathbb{P}$ is *not trivially rejecting*, i.e. $\mathbb{P}$ does not satisfy the base-case condition of a rejecting pattern, and which is *realized in* $\mathcal{I}$, meaning that $\mathfrak{J}^{\mathbb{P}}$ homomorphically embeds into $\mathcal{I}$. Observe that the initial pattern $\mathbb{P}^*$ satisfies both conditions. To pursue the construction, given any pattern $\mathbb{P}$ satisfying the two conditions and a head h applicable to $\mathbb{P}$, we show how to extract from $\mathcal{I}$ another $\mathbb{Q}$ which satisfies the conditions and which makes h hold for $\mathbb{P}$. Since the number of patterns is finite, every sequence of patterns constructed in such a manner either leads to a trivially accepting pattern (i.e. one with no applicable heads) or loops back to an already explored pattern satisfying the conditions. It follows that all patterns in the set are accepting (in particular, $\mathbb{P}^*$).

To formalize the construction, we shall introduce a function τ associating to each pattern $\mathbb{P}$ a homomorphism $\mathfrak{J}^{\mathbb{P}} \to \mathcal{I}$. Furthermore, we shall assume that, for every $\mathrm{R.A} \in \Omega$, we have chosen a function $\mathsf{succ}^{\mathcal{I}}_{\mathrm{R.A}}$ that maps every element $e \in (\exists \mathrm{R.A})^{\mathcal{I}}$ to an element $e' \in \Delta^{\mathcal{I}}$ such that $(e, e') \in \mathrm{R}^{\mathcal{I}}$ and $e' \in \mathrm{A}^{\mathcal{I}}$. The construction begins with $\mathbb{P}^*$, for which we set $\tau(\mathbb{P}^*) := \mathsf{Id}_{\mathcal{I}^* \to \mathcal{I}}$. Next we take some already constructed pattern $\mathbb{P}_1$ with its associated function $\tau(\mathbb{P}_1)$, and consider a head R.B that is applicable to e_1 in $\mathbb{P}_1$. Since R.B applies to e, there must exist $\mathrm{A} \in \mathsf{N_C}$ such that $e \in \mathrm{A}^{\mathfrak{I}^{\mathbb{P}_1}}$ and $\mathcal{T} \models \mathrm{A} \sqsubseteq \exists\mathrm{R.B}$. Set $e_1' := \tau(\mathbb{P}_1)(e_1)$. Since $\tau(\mathbb{P}_1)$ is a homomorphism and $\mathcal{I}$ is a model of $\mathcal{T}$, we obtain $e_1' \in (\exists\mathrm{R.B})^{\mathcal{I}}$ and can set $e_2' := \mathsf{succ}^{\mathcal{I}}_{\mathrm{R.B}}(e_1')$. If $e_2' \in \Delta^*$, then we set $e_2 := e_2'$, otherwise we set e_2 to either ⊚ or ⊛ such that $e_1 \neq e_2$.

We can now define the new pattern $\mathbb{P}_2$. Its frontier is e_1 and its generated term is e_2. Its interpretation is given by:

$$\begin{array}{rcl} \mathrm{C}^{\mathfrak{I}^{\mathbb{P}_2}} & := & \mathrm{C}^{\mathcal{I}^*} \cup \{e_k \mid e_k' \in \mathrm{C}^{\mathcal{I}}, k = 1, 2\} \\ \mathrm{P}^{\mathfrak{I}^{\mathbb{P}_2}} & := & \mathrm{P}^{\mathcal{I}^*} \cup \{(e_1, e_2) \mid \mathcal{T} \models \mathrm{R} \sqsubseteq \mathrm{P}\} \\ & & \cup \{(e_2, e_1) \mid \mathcal{T} \models \mathrm{R}^- \sqsubseteq \mathrm{P}\} \end{array}$$

Its specification is $(\mathfrak{M}^{\mathcal{I}})_{|\Delta^* \cup \{e_1', e_2'\}}$ in which e_1' (resp. e_2') has been replaced by e_1 (resp. e_2). Its prediction maps a head h to the value of $\mathsf{succ}^{\mathcal{I}}_h(e_2')$ if it is defined, else to h. Finally, we let $\tau(\mathbb{P}_2)$ be the function that maps elements of Δ^* to themselves, e_1 to e_1' and e_2 to e_2'. Recalling that $\mathcal{I}$ is a model, of $\mathcal{K}$ it is then straightforward to verify that $\mathbb{P}_2$ is a well-defined not-trivially-rejecting pattern, satisfying $\mathbb{P}_2 \in \mathbb{L}^{\mathrm{R.B}}_{\mathbb{P}_1, e_1}$, and such that $\tau(\mathbb{P}_2)$ is indeed a homomorphism.

Example 6. *In the model $\mathcal{I}_e$, depicted in Figure 2a, we can set $\mathsf{succ}^{\mathcal{I}_e}_{\mathrm{R.A}_2}(\mathsf{a}) := \delta$ (other choices of successors are unique), and then apply the preceding construction to obtain the accepting patterns from Example 4.*

3.3 Obtaining Bounded-Size Optimal Models

To obtain optimal models of bounded size, we start from the pattern tree $\mathcal{P}$ and model $\mathcal{I}^\diamond$ we constructed from an accepting initial pattern. It remains to merge elements of $\mathcal{I}^\diamond$ to obtain a model of the required size. To identify similar elements, we consider their neighbourhoods.

Definition 9. *Consider an interpretation $\mathcal{I}$ and an element $c \in \Delta^{\mathcal{I}}$. Its n-neighbourhood $\mathcal{N}^{\mathcal{I},\Delta}_n(c)$ w.r.t. a subdomain $\Delta \subseteq \Delta^{\mathcal{I}}$ is defined inductively as:*

$$\mathcal{N}^{\mathcal{I},\Delta}_0(c) := \{c\}$$
$$\mathcal{N}^{\mathcal{I},\Delta}_{n+1}(c) := \mathcal{N}^{\mathcal{I},\Delta}_n(c) \cup \left\{ e \;\middle|\; \begin{array}{l} \exists d \in \mathcal{N}^{\mathcal{I},\Delta}_n(c) \setminus \Delta, \\ \exists \mathrm{R} \in \mathsf{N}^{\pm}_{\mathsf{R}},\ (d, e) \in \mathrm{R}^{\mathcal{I}} \end{array} \right\}$$

Observe that we stop adding successors when we reach Δ.

To characterize neighbourhoods in $\mathcal{I}^\diamond$ (w.r.t. domain Δ^*), we focus on the tree-like structure inherited from $\mathcal{P}$. Recall that we kept a *single* pattern for each head R.B applicable to an element e of a pattern $\mathbb{P}$, namely $\mathsf{ch}^{\mathrm{R.B}}_{\mathbb{P},e}$. We can thus consider the bijection σ mapping $(\mathbb{P}^*, \emptyset) \cdot (\mathbb{P}_1, h_1) \cdots (\mathbb{P}_n, h_n)$ (with $n \geq 1$) to $ah_1 \ldots h_n$, where a is such that $\mathfrak{fr}^{\mathbb{P}_1} = \{a\}$; we extend σ to Δ^* by letting $\sigma(e) = e$ for $e \in \Delta^*$. Inspired by the notion of interleaving used in the DL-Lite setting (Kostylev and Reutter 2015), we define the *interlacing* $\mathcal{I}' := \sigma(\mathcal{I}^\diamond)$, obtained by renaming elements of $\mathcal{I}^\diamond$ using σ. Denote by $\Delta^\circ := \Delta^* \cup \sigma(\mathcal{P} \setminus \mathbb{P}^*)$ the forest-shaped domain that is to $\mathcal{I}'$ what $\mathcal{P}$ is to $\mathcal{I}^\diamond$. We define an associated mapping $f' : \Delta^\circ \to \mathcal{I}'$ by setting $f' := \sigma \circ f \circ \sigma^{-1}$ where f maps each element of Δ^* to itself and each $w \cdot (\mathbb{P}, h) \in \mathcal{P}$ to $\lambda_{w \cdot (\mathbb{P}, h)}(e)$ where $\mathfrak{gen}^{\mathbb{P}} = \{e\}$.

The definition of $\mathcal{I}'$ ensures that every $c \in \Delta^{\mathcal{I}'} \setminus \Delta^*$ belongs to $\sigma(\mathcal{P} \setminus \mathbb{P}^*)$ and thus $c = aw$ for some $a \in \Delta^*$ and word $w \in \Omega^*$. The tree-shaped structure of Δ° ensures that for all n, there exists a unique prefix $r_{n,c}$ of aw such that *(i)* $f'(r_{n,c}) \in \mathcal{N}^{\mathcal{I}',\Delta^*}_n(c)$ and *(ii)* for any $d \in \mathcal{N}^{\mathcal{I}',\Delta^*}_n(c)$, there exists a unique word $w^d_{n,c}$ such that $d = f'(r_{n,c} \cdot w^d_{n,c})$.

This leads us to characterize the n-neighbourhood of an element $c \in \mathcal{I}'$ via the following function $\chi_{n,c}$, whose domain Ω_n is the set of words over Ω with length $\leq 2n$. Notice that, departing from (Kostylev and Reutter 2015), we keep track of *sets* of satisfied concepts, in order to handle conjunctions of concepts in the left-hand sides of axioms.

$$\chi_{n,c} : \Omega_n \to \Delta^* \cup 2^{\mathsf{sig}(\mathcal{T})} \cup \{\emptyset\}$$
$$w \mapsto \begin{cases} \emptyset & \text{if } f'(r_{n,c}w) \text{ undefined} \\ f'(r_{n,c}w) & \text{if } f'(r_{n,c}w) \in \Delta^* \\ \{\mathrm{A} \in \mathsf{sig}(\mathcal{T}) \mid f'(r_{n,c}w) \in \mathrm{A}^{\mathcal{I}'}\} & \text{otherwise} \end{cases}$$

We can now introduce the equivalence relation we use to merge elements:

Definition 10. *The equivalence relation $\sim_n$ on $\Delta^{\mathcal{I}'}$ is defined as follows: an element $e \in \Delta^*$ is $\sim_n$-equivalent only to itself; elements c_1, c_2 from $\Delta^{\mathcal{I}'} \setminus \Delta^*$ are $\sim_n$-equivalent iff $w^{c_1}_{n,c_1} = w^{c_2}_{n,c_2}$, $\chi_{n,c_1} = \chi_{n,c_2}$, and $|c_1| = |c_2| \mod 2|q|+3$.*

We obtain a finite model of the required size by merging elements with respect to $\sim_{|q|+1}$.

Theorem 2. *The interpretation $\mathcal{J} := \mathcal{I}'/\!\sim_{|q|+1}$ is a model of $\mathcal{K}$ that has at most as many c-matches for q as $\mathcal{I}^\diamond$. Its size is polynomial w.r.t. data complexity, double-exponential w.r.t. combined complexity, and single-exponential if the size of the CCQ q is fixed.*

Proof sketch. The key to proving that the amount of c-matches does not increase through the quotient operation is to exhibit suitable local homomorphisms. Indeed, a match of q in $\mathcal{J}$ maps each connected component C of q into a $|q|$-neighbourhood $\mathcal{N}^{\mathcal{J},\overline{\Delta^*}}_{|q|}(\overline{c})$, where $\overline{c}$ denotes the equivalence class of c w.r.t. $\sim_{|q|+1}$ and $\overline{\Delta^*}$ stands for the set $\{\overline{e} \mid e \in \Delta^*\}$. By exhibiting a homomorphism $\rho_c : \mathcal{N}^{\mathcal{J},\overline{\Delta^*}}_{|q|}(\overline{c}) \to \mathcal{N}^{\mathcal{I}',\Delta^*}_{|q|}(c)$ such that $\rho^{-1}_{n,c}(\overline{\Delta^*}) \subseteq \overline{\Delta^*}$, we can find a match of C in $\mathcal{I}'$. Such matches for q's connected components together form a match of the full q in $\mathcal{I}'$. It is mostly straightforward to show that $\mathcal{J}$ is a model, except for negative role inclusions, where the homomorphisms ρ_c are needed to move violations of $\mathrm{R}_1 \sqcap \mathrm{R}_2 \sqsubseteq \bot$ in $\mathcal{J}$ back into $\mathcal{I}'$. The claimed upper bounds are obtained by analyzing the size of $\mathcal{J}$ (i.e. counting the equivalence classes in $\Delta^{\mathcal{J}}$), keeping in mind that due to Lemma 1, we may assume that $|\Delta^*| \leq |\mathsf{Ind}(\mathcal{A})| + |q|\,(|\mathsf{Ind}(\mathcal{A})| + 3\,|\mathcal{T}|\,2^{|\mathcal{T}|})^{|q|}$. □

From Theorem 2, it follows that there exists a model minimizing the amount of c-matches with polynomial size w.r.t. data complexity. One can therefore non-deterministically guess this interpretation before verifying it is indeed a model and comparing its amount of c-matches with the input integer. The two latter steps can be done in (deterministic) polynomial time w.r.t. data complexity, yielding an upper bound in data complexity for CCQ answering, matching the corresponding results in the DL-Lite setting (Kostylev and Reutter 2015; Bienvenu, Manière, and Thomazo 2020).

Theorem 3. *CCQ answering in $\mathcal{ELHI}_\bot$ is in* coNP *w.r.t. data complexity.*

3.4 Matching Lower Bounds

We now provide 2EXP lower bounds for $\mathcal{EL}$ and DL-Lite$^{\mathcal{H}}_{\text{pos}}$, which together with Theorem 1, establish the 2EXP-completeness of CCQ answering for $\mathcal{ELHI}$ and every sublogic that extends $\mathcal{EL}$ or DL-Lite$^{\mathcal{H}}_{\text{pos}}$. The proofs are by reduction from the problem of answering Boolean union of conjunctive queries (BUCQs) over KBs with closed predicates, proven 2EXP-hard in (Ngo, Ortiz, and Šimkus 2016).

Theorem 4. *CCQ answering in $\mathcal{EL}$ is* 2EXP*-hard w.r.t. combined complexity.*

Proof sketch. Consider an $\mathcal{EL}$ KB $\mathcal{K} = (\mathcal{T}, \mathcal{A}, \Sigma)$ with closed predicates and a BUCQ $q = \bigvee_{k=1}^{l} q_k$. Examining the 2EXP-hardness proof from (Ngo, Ortiz, and Šimkus 2016), we may assume that Σ consists only of concept names and each q_k is connected and has only variables as terms.

Pick a fresh individual aux not used in $\mathcal{A}$, and let $\mathcal{A}'$ be obtained from $\mathcal{A}$ by adding $\mathrm{A}(\mathsf{aux})$ for every concept name A in $\mathcal{K}$ and $\mathrm{P}(\mathsf{aux}, \mathsf{aux})$ for every role name P in $\mathcal{K}$. Consider the KB $\mathcal{K}' = (\mathcal{T}, \mathcal{A}')$ and the CCQ q' built as the conjunction of (i) all of the CQs q_k in q (with all variables treated as counting variables), (ii) the query $q_{\mathrm{A}} = \exists z_{\mathrm{A}}\ \mathrm{A}(z_{\mathrm{A}})$ for each $A \in \Sigma$, and (iii) the queries $q_{\mathrm{P}}^{+} = \exists z_{\mathrm{P}}^{+}\ \mathrm{P}(z_{\mathrm{P}}^{+}, \mathsf{aux})$ and $q_{\mathrm{P}}^{-} = \exists z_{\mathrm{P}}^{-}\ \mathrm{P}(\mathsf{aux}, z_{\mathrm{P}}^{-})$ for each role name P from $\mathcal{K}$. For each $\mathrm{A} \in \Sigma$, let n_{A} be the number of individuals a such that $\mathrm{A}(\mathsf{a}) \in \mathcal{A}$, and set $N := \prod_{\mathrm{A} \in \Sigma}(n_{\mathrm{A}} + 1)$. To complete the proof, one can show that $N + 1$ is a certain answer to q' over $\mathcal{K}'$ iff $\mathcal{K}$ entails q. □

Theorem 5. *CCQ answering in DL-Lite$^{\mathcal{H}}_{\text{pos}}$ is* 2EXP*-hard w.r.t. combined complexity.*

Proof. As the 2EXP-hardness proof for DL-Lite$^{\mathcal{H}}_{\text{core}}$ from (Ngo, Ortiz, and Šimkus 2016) does not involve negative inclusions, we can employ the same approach as for $\mathcal{EL}$ (the added aux assertions cannot lead to inconsistency). □

We thus close the open question of the combined complexity of CCQ answering in DL-Lite$^{\mathcal{H}}_{\text{core}}$. Note that our lower bound applies even to the subclass of CCQs whose every variable is a counting variable, as considered in (Kostylev and Reutter 2015; Calvanese et al. 2020a).

The preceding lower bound does not apply to DL-Lite$_{\text{pos}}$, for which coNEXP membership has been shown (Kostylev and Reutter 2015; Bienvenu, Manière, and Thomazo 2020). We pinpoint the exact complexity by giving a matching lower bound, via a reduction from the exponential grid tiling problem. Here again the lower bound holds even when restricted to CCQs with only counting variables.

Theorem 6. *CCQ answering in DL-Lite$_{\text{pos}}$ is* coNEXP*-hard w.r.t. combined complexity.*

4 Cardinality Queries

In this section, we focus on the restricted class of cardinality queries, which allow one to count the number of elements belonging to a given concept or role name.

To reduce the number of cases to be studied, we first notice that role cardinality queries are always harder than concept cardinality queries for the logics we consider.

Theorem 7. *Let $\mathcal{L}$ be a sublogic of $\mathcal{ELHI}_\bot$ that can express $\mathrm{A} \sqsubseteq \exists \mathrm{P}.\top$ ($\mathrm{A} \in \mathsf{N_C}$, $\mathrm{P} \in \mathsf{N_R}$). Then concept cardinality query answering over $\mathcal{L}$ KBs can be polynomially reduced to role cardinality query answering over $\mathcal{L}$ KBs.*

Proof. Take a concept cardinality query $q_{\mathrm{A}} = \exists z \mathrm{A}(z)$ and a KB $\mathcal{K} = (\mathcal{T}, \mathcal{A})$. We pick a fresh role name $\mathrm{P} \notin \mathsf{sig}(\mathcal{K})$, and consider the role cardinality query $q_{\mathrm{P}} = \exists z_1, z_2\ \mathrm{P}(z_1, z_2)$ and modified TBox $\mathcal{T}' := \mathcal{T} \cup \{\mathrm{A} \sqsubseteq \exists \mathrm{P}.\top\}$.

Any model $\mathcal{I}$ of $\mathcal{K}$ can be extended to a model $\mathcal{I}'$ of $\mathcal{K}' = (\mathcal{T}', \mathcal{A})$ by setting $\mathrm{P}^{\mathcal{I}'} := \{(e, e) \mid e \in \mathrm{A}^{\mathcal{I}}\}$. Indeed, this ensures satisfaction of the additional axiom $\mathrm{A} \sqsubseteq \exists \mathrm{P}.\top$. Moreover, as no new domain elements were introduced, axioms $\top \sqsubseteq \mathrm{B}$ from $\mathcal{T}$ remain satisfied, and all other axioms are not affected since $\mathrm{P} \notin \mathsf{sig}(\mathcal{T})$.

Notice that q_{A} has *exactly* as many matches in $\mathcal{I}$ as q_{P} has in $\mathcal{I}'$, hence an interval $[m, +\infty]$ is a certain answer to q_{A} over $\mathcal{K}$ iff it is a certain answer to q_{P} over $\mathcal{K}'$. □

4.1 Results for $\mathcal{EL}$ and its Extensions

The next two results, together with Theorem 7, establish that cardinality query answering is coNEXP-complete w.r.t. combined complexity in $\mathcal{ELHI}_\bot$ and $\mathcal{ELI}_\bot$.

Theorem 8. *Role cardinality query answering in $\mathcal{ELHI}_\bot$ is in* coNEXP *w.r.t. combined complexity.*

Proof. Theorem 2 proves that the minimal number of matches is reached with a model of exponential size. □

Theorem 9. *Concept cardinality query answering in $\mathcal{ELI}_\bot$ is* coNEXP*-hard w.r.t. combined complexity.*

Proof sketch. The proof proceeds by reduction from the complement of the Succinct-3COL problem, known to be NEXP-complete (Papadimitriou and Yannakakis 1986). □

The coNEXP lower bound relies on KBs that only admit exponentially large models. For logics admitting polynomial-sized models, the complexity slightly decreases.

Theorem 10. *Let $\mathcal{L}$ be a sublogic of $\mathcal{ELHI}_\bot$ for which every satisfiable KB admits a polynomial-sized model. Then role cardinality query answering over $\mathcal{L}$ KBs is in* EXP.

Proof sketch. The key observation is that, for logics with polysize models and single-atom queries, the optimal number of matches is bounded polynomially in the size of the KB. We can thus iterate over all polynomial-sized ABoxes that could represent the restriction of an optimal model to the ABox and elements in matches. We test whether such an ABox extends to a model without new matches by performing a satisfiability check, taking the query role as closed predicate. This gives a deterministic single-exponential time procedure, since satisfiability of $\mathcal{ELHI}_\bot$ KBs with closed predicates is in EXP (Ngo, Ortiz, and Šimkus 2016). □

Corollary 1. *Role cardinality query answering in $\mathcal{ELH}_\bot$ is in* EXP *w.r.t. combined complexity.*

Proof sketch. We observe that a variant of the compact canonical model used in the combined approach (Lutz, Toman, and Wolter 2009), provides a model also for $\mathcal{ELH}_\bot$ KBs with negative role inclusions. □

Corollary 2. *Role cardinality query answering in $\mathcal{ELHI}$ is in* EXP *w.r.t. combined complexity.*

Proof. Existence of polynomial-sized models is trivial due to the absence of negative inclusions. For example, extending $\mathcal{A}$ with every possible fact constructed from $\mathsf{Ind}(\mathcal{A})$ and $\mathsf{sig}(\mathcal{K})$ yields a model of $\mathcal{K} = (\mathcal{T}, \mathcal{A})$. □

We conclude this subsection by providing matching lower bounds for concept cardinality queries in $\mathcal{EL}$.

Theorem 11. *Concept cardinality query answering in $\mathcal{EL}$ is* EXP*-hard w.r.t. combined complexity.*

Proof sketch. The proof is by reduction from the problem of deciding if an $\mathcal{EL}$ KB with closed predicates is satisfiable, proven EXP-hard in (Ngo, Ortiz, and Šimkus 2016). □

Theorem 12. *Concept cardinality query answering in $\mathcal{EL}$ is* coNP*-hard w.r.t. data complexity.*

Proof sketch. We reduce the complement of the graph 3-colorability problem to answering the cardinality query $\exists z\ \mathrm{B}(z)$ w.r.t. the TBox $\mathcal{T}$ containing $\mathrm{A} \sqsubseteq \exists \mathrm{R.B}$ and $\exists \mathrm{R.C_k} \sqcap \exists \mathrm{E}.(\exists \mathrm{R.C_k}) \sqsubseteq \mathrm{B}$ for $k \in \{1, 2, 3\}$. □

4.2 Results for DL-Lite

The data complexity picture being already known from the literature (Bienvenu, Manière, and Thomazo 2021), we focus on combined complexity.

We start by establishing tractabililty for DL-Lite$^{(\mathcal{H})}_{\mathsf{pos}}$ KBs.

Theorem 13. *Concept cardinality query answering in DL-Lite$_{\mathsf{pos}}$ is* NL*-hard w.r.t. combined complexity.*

Proof sketch. We proceed by reduction from the st-connectivity problem, known to be NL-complete (Immerman 1999). □

Theorem 14. *Concept cardinality query answering in DL-Lite$^{\mathcal{H}}_{\mathsf{pos}}$ is in* NL *w.r.t. combined complexity.*

Proof. Let $q_{\mathrm{C}} = \exists z\, \mathrm{C}(z)$ be a concept cardinality query. Starting from the canonical model $\mathcal{C}_\mathcal{K}$ of a KB $\mathcal{K} = (\mathcal{T}, \mathcal{A})$, the minimal number of matches can easily be computed.

- If there exists an individual $\mathsf{a} \in \mathsf{Ind}(\mathcal{A})$ such that $\mathcal{K} \models \mathrm{C}(\mathsf{a})$, then we can collapse all anonymous elements onto one such individual (the choice doesn't matter), obtaining a model in which matches are exactly such individuals a, which is clearly minimal (recall we make the UNA). We can check whether $\mathcal{K} \models \mathrm{C}(\mathsf{a})$ in NL (Artale et al. 2009)
- Otherwise, if there exists an anonymous match in $\mathcal{C}_\mathcal{K}$, then we collapse all anonymous elements onto a chosen ABox individual, obtaining a model with a single match for q_{C}, which is clearly optimal. Existence of an anonymous match can be checked in NL (Artale et al. 2009).
- Otherwise, there are no matches in $\mathcal{C}_\mathcal{K}$, hence 0 is the minimal number of matches.

Notice that we do not need to actually compute the model corresponding to the optimal number of matches, and we only need to compare that number to the input integer. □

Theorem 15. *Role cardinality query answering in DL-Lite$_{\mathsf{pos}}$ is in* NL *w.r.t. combined complexity.*

Proof sketch. The proof relies on the same principle as Theorem 14, with a more sophisticated case analysis. □

Note that the preceding theorem concerns DL-Lite$_{\mathsf{pos}}$ rather than DL-Lite$^{\mathcal{H}}_{\mathsf{pos}}$, as role cardinality query answering in DL-Lite$^{\mathcal{H}}_{\mathsf{pos}}$ is coNP-hard even w.r.t. data complexity.

The introduction of disjointness axioms also leads to intractability, even for concept cardinality queries.

Theorem 16. *Concept cardinality query answering in DL-Lite$_{\mathsf{core}}$ is* coNP*-hard w.r.t. combined complexity.*

Proof. Let $\mathcal{G} = (\mathcal{V}, \mathcal{E})$ be an undirected graph, and consider

$$\mathcal{T}_\mathcal{G} = \bigcup_{v \in \mathcal{V}} \{\mathrm{A} \sqsubseteq \exists \mathrm{V}, \exists \mathrm{V}^- \sqsubseteq \mathrm{C}\} \cup \bigcup_{\{v_1, v_2\} \in \mathcal{E}} \{\exists \mathrm{V}_1^- \sqsubseteq \neg \exists \mathrm{V}_2^-\}.$$

It is easily verified that $\mathcal{G} \in \mathsf{3COL}$ iff $[4, +\infty] \notin q^{\mathcal{K}_\mathcal{G}}$ for the KB $\mathcal{K}_\mathcal{G} := (\mathcal{T}_\mathcal{G}, \{\mathrm{A}(\mathsf{a})\})$ and query $q = \exists z\, \mathrm{C}(z)$. □

Theorem 17. *Role cardinality query answering in DL-Lite$^{\mathcal{H}}_{\mathsf{core}}$ is in* coNP *w.r.t. combined complexity.*

Proof sketch. One guesses a small counterexample to $[m, +\infty]$ being a certain answer, relying on the existence of small models, atomicity of the query, and Theorem 3 of (Ngo, Ortiz, and Šimkus 2016). □

5 Outlook

In this paper, we have extended the study of CCQ answering to Horn DLs outside the DL-Lite family, establishing a complete picture of the combined and data complexity of the problems of answering CCQs and cardinality queries in $\mathcal{ELHI}_\bot$ and its various sublogics. Interestingly, the new techniques we devised also allowed us to close some open questions concerning the combined complexity of CCQ answering in DL-Lite. Going forward, the main challenge is to develop practical algorithms. A first direction is to look for restrictions on the query or ontology that ensure polynomial data complexity for logics of the $\mathcal{EL}$ family. Second, it would be desirable, for $\mathcal{EL}$ but also for DL-Lite, to develop more refined coNP procedures that are amenable to implementation using SAT solvers. We believe that our improved understanding of the structure of optimal models will prove helpful for both of these research directions.

Acknowledgments

Partially supported by ANR project CQFD (ANR-18-CE23-0003).

References

Artale, A.; Calvanese, D.; Kontchakov, R.; and Zakharyaschev, M. 2009. The DL-Lite family and relations. *Journal of Artificial Intelligence Research (JAIR)* 36:1–69.

Baader, F.; Brandt, S.; and Lutz, C. 2005. Pushing the $\mathcal{EL}$ envelope. In *Proceedings of the 19th international joint conference on Artificial intelligence (IJCAI)*, 364–369.

Bienvenu, M., and Ortiz, M. 2015. Ontology-mediated query answering with data-tractable description logics. In *Tutorial Lectures of the 11th Reasoning Web International Summer School (RW)*, 218–307.

Bienvenu, M.; Calvanese, D.; Ortiz, M.; and Simkus, M. 2014. Nested regular path queries in description logics. In *Proceedings of the 14th International Conference on Principles of Knowledge Representation and Reasoning (KR)*, 218–227.

Bienvenu, M.; Manière, Q.; and Thomazo, M. 2020. Answering counting queries over DL-Lite ontologies. In *Proceedings of the 29th International Joint Conference on Artificial Intelligence (IJCAI)*, 1608–1614.

Bienvenu, M.; Manière, Q.; and Thomazo, M. 2021. Cardinality queries over DL-Lite ontologies. In *Proceedings of the 30th International Joint Conference on Artificial Intelligence (IJCAI)*, 1801–1807.

Calvanese, D.; Giacomo, G. D.; Lembo, D.; Lenzerini, M.; and Rosati, R. 2007. Tractable reasoning and efficient query answering in description logics: The DL-Lite family. *Journal of Automated Reasoning (JAR)* 39(3):385–429.

Calvanese, D.; Kharlamov, E.; Nutt, W.; and Thorne, C. 2008. Aggregate queries over ontologies. In *Proceedings of the 2nd International Workshop on Ontologies and Information Systems for the Semantic Web (ONISW)*, 97–104.

Calvanese, D.; Corman, J.; Lanti, D.; and Razniewski, S. 2020a. Counting query answers over a DL-Lite knowledge base. In *Proceedings of the 29th International Joint Conference on Artificial Intelligence (IJCAI)*, 1658–1666.

Calvanese, D.; Corman, J.; Lanti, D.; and Razniewski, S. 2020b. Rewriting count queries over DL-Lite TBoxes with number restrictions. In *Proceedings of the 33rd International Workshop on Description Logics (DL)*.

Eiter, T.; Lutz, C.; Ortiz, M.; and Simkus, M. 2009. Query answering in description logics: the knots approach. In *Proceedings of the 16th International Workshop on Logic, Language, Information and Computation (WoLLIC)*, 26–36.

Feier, C.; Lutz, C.; and Przybylko, M. 2021. Answer counting under guarded TGDs. In *Proceedings of the 24th International Conference on Database Theory (ICDT)*.

Immerman, N. 1999. Descriptive complexity.

Kostylev, E. V., and Reutter, J. L. 2015. Complexity of answering counting aggregate queries over DL-Lite. *Journal of Web Semantics (JWS)* 94–111.

Lutz, C.; Toman, D.; and Wolter, F. 2009. Conjunctive query answering in the description logic $\mathcal{EL}$ using a relational database system. In *Proceedings of the 21st International Joint Conference on Artificial Intelligence (IJCAI)*, 2070–2075.

Ngo, N.; Ortiz, M.; and Šimkus, M. 2016. Closed predicates in description logics: results on combined complexity. In *Proceedings of the 15th International Conference on Principles of Knowledge Representation and Reasoning (KR)*, 237–246.

Nikolaou, C.; Kostylev, E. V.; Konstantinidis, G.; Kaminski, M.; Grau, B. C.; and Horrocks, I. 2019. Foundations of ontology-based data access under bag semantics. *Journal of Artificial Intelligence (AIJ)* 91 – 132.

Papadimitriou, C. H., and Yannakakis, M. 1986. A note on succinct representations of graphs. *Information and Control* 71(3):181–185.

Poggi, A.; Lembo, D.; Calvanese, D.; De Giacomo, G.; Lenzerini, M.; and Rosati, R. 2008. Linking data to ontologies. *Journal of Data Semantics (JoDS)* 10:133–173.

Rudolph, S.; Krötzsch, M.; and Hitzler, P. 2012. Type-elimination-based reasoning for the description logic $\mathcal{SHIQ}b_s$ using decision diagrams and disjunctive datalog. *Logical Methods in Computer Science (LMCS)* 8(1).

Thomazo, M.; Baget, J.; Mugnier, M.; and Rudolph, S. 2012. A generic querying algorithm for greedy sets of existential rules. In *Proceedings of the 13th International Conference on Principles of Knowledge Representation and Reasoning (KR)*.

Xiao, G.; Calvanese, D.; Kontchakov, R.; Lembo, D.; Poggi, A.; Rosati, R.; and Zakharyaschev, M. 2018. Ontology-based data access: a survey. In *Proceedings of the 27th International Joint Conference on Artificial Intelligence (IJCAI)*, 5511–5519.

Defining Defense and Defeat in Abstract Argumentation From Scratch – A Generalizing Approach

Lydia Blümel and **Markus Ulbricht**
Department of Computer Science, Leipzig University
mulbricht@informatik.uni-leipzig.de

Abstract

We propose a general framework to investigate semantics of Dung-style argumentation frameworks (AFs) by means of a generic defeat notion formalized by refute operators. After establishing the technical foundations, we propose natural generic versions of Dung's classical semantics. We demonstrate how classical as well as recent proposals can be captured by our approach when utilizing suitable notions of refutal. We perform an investigation of basic properties which semantics inherit from the underlying refute operator. In particular, we show under which conditions a counterpart to Dung's fundamental lemma can be inferred and how it ensures the existence of the generalized version of complete extensions. We contribute to a principle-based study of AF semantics by discussing properties tailored to compare different refute operators. Finally, we report computational complexity results for basic reasoning tasks which hold in our general framework.

1 Introduction

Since Dung's seminal 1995 paper (Dung 1995) introducing abstract argumentation frameworks (AFs), the field of formal argumentation has become a vibrant research area in Artificial Intelligence. Research in AFs is driven by investigating the behavior of semantics formalizing jointly acceptable sets of arguments (cf. (Baroni, Caminada, and Giacomin 2018) for an overview). Over the years, many fundamental properties typically considered for non-monotonic formalisms have been studied for abstract argumentation semantics. Among others, central issues like existence and uniqueness (Weydert 2011; Baumann and Spanring 2015), replaceability (Oikarinen and Woltran 2011; Baumann 2016), expressibility (Dunne et al. 2015), as well as general modularity and locality properties were studied (Baroni and Giacomin 2007; Baumann 2011; Baroni, Giacomin, and Liao 2018).

Due to the considerable amount of semantics that have been proposed in the literature, researchers have developed proposals in order to objectively assess their quality for different scenarios. This resulted in a comprehensive collection of so-called *principles* (Baroni and Giacomin 2007; van der Torre and Vesic 2018), i.e. properties that formalize (un-)desirable characteristics of semantics. The principles range from basic concepts which hold by definition for most semantics to rather technical requirements which formalize different concepts of step-wise computability of extensions.

The principle-based analysis reveals that most commonly accepted semantics are either based on the notion of admissibility or naivity. In a nutshell, admissibility requires that a set of arguments is capable of defending itself (that is, counter-attacking any argument challenging it) in the given AF, whereas naivity is not concerned with defense at all.

However, these two concepts do not always yield intuitive results. Let us illustrate the sometimes undesired behavior by considering the following example AFs. The formal theoretical background for AFs can be found in Section 2.

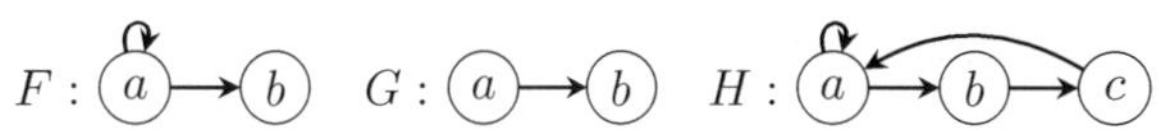

Suppose we are in a setting where we wish to neglect the self-attacker a in F. Then b should be acceptable which is however not the case for any admissible-based semantics. As a possible solution we could consider naivity-based semantics. But since they completely disregard the notion of defense we then would also accept b in G. This is clearly undesired though since in G, b is attacked by the undisputed argument a. Naivity-based semantics which also make use of the SCC-recursive scheme (Baroni, Giacomin, and Guida 2005) would handle F and G quite well, but due to their reliance on the structure of the given graph, the AF H would be treated unsatisfactory: It consists of a single SCC only and therefore this approach collapses to the underlying base function (we refer the reader to (Baroni, Giacomin, and Guida 2005) for more details on SCC-recursive semantics).

These observations motivated the proposal of some recent approaches which are tailored to find "good" ways to disregard some of the attacking arguments in certain situations (Bodanza and Tohmé 2009; Dondio and Longo 2021; Baumann, Brewka, and Ulbricht 2020b; Dauphin, Rienstra, and van der Torre 2021). Comparing the characteristics of such non-classical semantics in a formal way is a challenging endeavor, since all of them make (more or less implicit) use of different defense notions by disregarding certain attackers of the given extension. Thus, a comprehensive understanding of these semantics requires delving into and comparing the varying underlying concepts. Moreover, the usual principles considered in the literature (Baroni and Giacomin 2007; van der Torre and Vesic 2018) are not concerned with different versions of defense making it hard to use them when assessing what a "good" weak version of admissibility is.

In this paper, we contribute to this line of research and propose a unifying approach for investigating defense notions, their implications for the induced semantics, and their suitability for certain scenarios. The key observation in our proposal is that Dung's defense is based on the conception that each attacker of a given argument shall be *refuted* by the defending set. Therefore, by altering the definition of "refute" we obtain versions of Dung's theory, which are familiar in their spirit, but suitable for our purpose.

Our main contributions can be summarized as follows:

- After recalling the necessary AF background in Section 2 we introduce our general framework in Section 3. Based on a generic refute operator δ we develop a defense notion and a generalization of the characteristic function, yielding counterparts to Dung's semantics.
- We demonstrate how recent proposals from the literature can be captured by our approach and the underlying defense notion of the semantics is revealed (Section 4).
- We discuss formal properties of our general semantics based on the characteristics of the specified refute operator. Most notably, we obtain a natural generalization of Dung's fundamental lemma (Section 5).
- We propose abstract principles, tailored to investigate refute operators and evaluate the ones we introduced throughout the paper (Section 6).
- We investigate the computational complexity of basic reasoning tasks for semantics based on polynomial-time computable refute operators (Section 7).

2 Background

We fix a non-finite background set $\mathcal{U}$. An *argumentation framework* (AF) (Dung 1995) is a directed graph $F = (A, R)$ with a set of arguments $A \subseteq \mathcal{U}$ and the attack relation $R \subseteq A \times A$. If not stated otherwise we assume any AF to be finite and we use $\mathcal{F}$ for the set of all these graphs. If $(a, b) \in R$ we say that a *attacks* b as well as a *attacks* (the set) E given that $b \in E \subseteq A$. This situation is denoted as $a \rightarrow b$ or $a \rightarrow E$, respectively; we define $E \rightarrow a$ analogously.

We frequently use the so-called *range* of a set E defined as $E^{\oplus} = E \cup E^{+}$ where $E^{+} = \{a \in A \mid E \text{ attacks } a\}$. We also let $E^{-} = \{a \in A \mid a \text{ attacks } E\}$. If $E = \{a\}$ is a singleton, we write a^{+} and a^{-} instead of $\{a\}^{+}$ and $\{a\}^{-}$. By $F{\downarrow_E}$ we denote F projected to the arguments in E, i.e. $F{\downarrow_E} = (E, R \cap (E \times E))$. The E-*reduct of* F is the AF $F^{E} = (E^{*}, R \cap (E^{*} \times E^{*}))$ where $E^{*} = A \setminus E^{\oplus}$. This means, F^{E} is the subframework of F obtained by removing the range of E, i.e. $F^{E} = F{\downarrow_{A \setminus E^{\oplus}}}$. For an AF $F = (B, S)$ we let $A(F) = B$ and $R(F) = S$.

A *semantics* is a function $\sigma : \mathcal{F} \rightarrow 2^{2^{\mathcal{U}}}$ with $F = (A, R) \mapsto \sigma(F) \subseteq 2^{A}$. This means, a semantics returns a set of subsets of A, so-called σ-*extensions*. We say that an argument $a \in A$ is *credulously accepted* if $a \in \bigcup \sigma(F)$. Similarly, a is considered as *skeptically accepted* if $|\sigma(F)| \geq 1$ and $a \in \bigcap \sigma(F)$. In case of uniquely defined semantics, i.e. $|\sigma(F)| = 1$ for any F we may simply speak of *accepted* arguments as both notions coincide.

In this paper we consider several semantics which are in spirit based on Dung's classical *admissible*, *complete*, *preferred*, *grounded* and *stable* semantics (abbr. ad, co, pr, gr, stb). All mentioned semantics satisfy conflict-freeness. A set $E \subseteq A$ is conflict-free in F (for short, $E \in cf(F)$) iff for no $a, b \in E$, $a \rightarrow b$. For the present paper it will be convenient to utilize the so-called *characteristic function* Γ_F to define the semantics. For $E \subseteq A$ we have $\Gamma_F(E) = \{a \in A \mid E \text{ defends } a\}$. A set E *defends* a if $b \rightarrow a$ implies $E \rightarrow b$.

Definition 2.1. *Let $F = (A, R)$ be an AF and $E \in cf(F)$.*

1. $E \in ad(F)$ *iff* $E \subseteq \Gamma_F(E)$,
2. $E \in co(F)$ *iff* $E = \Gamma_F(E)$,
3. $E \in pr(F)$ *iff E is $\subseteq$-maximal in* $co(F)$,
4. $E \in gr(F)$ *iff E is $\subseteq$-minimal in* $co(F)$,
5. $E \in stb(F)$ *iff E attacks any* $a \in A \setminus E$.

3 Defeat and Defense

Defense and defeat are fundamental cornerstones in abstract argumentation and before generalizing these notions, we shall reflect about which basic principles we want to modify, and which we want to preserve.

The first observation we are going to make is that the notion of "defense" is actually based on the attack relation, i.e. a set E of arguments defends some $a \in A$ if $E \rightarrow b$ for each b s.t. $b \rightarrow a$. Since Dung AFs represent attacks between arguments, it is natural to stipulate that an argument a is acceptable by default, and for each attacker b there needs to be some reason to reject b, i.e. arguments attacking a represent threats for the acceptance of it and hence need to be taken care of. We therefore want to preserve the basic idea that an argument is *defended* if each attacker is countered.

So we observe that if "defense" means each attacking argument is defeated, it suffices to adjust the notion of defeat. For Dung's classical semantics, the notion of "E defeats a" is defined as $\exists b \in E : b \rightarrow a$. So defeat is merely syntactical (and existential quantified); a choice which is natural from an intuitive point of view, but technically speaking rather arbitrary. The aforementioned choice also ties together the notion of "conflict" (there is an attack between two arguments) and "defeat" (an extension defeats an argument).

Let us separate these notions by introducing a general concept of refutal. Given an AF $F = (A, R)$, we expect a refute operator to assign to a set E of arguments the subset of A which is refuted by E. We do not impose any further restriction and therefore end up with the following.

Definition 3.1. *Let $F = (A, R)$ be an AF. A* refute operator *is a mapping $\delta : 2^{A} \rightarrow 2^{A}$; E δ-refutes a if $a \in \delta(E)$.*

If the underlying AF is not clear from context, we denote the refute operator by $\delta(F, E)$ to emphasize F. If δ and δ' are two refute operators we write $\delta \subseteq \delta'$ if $\delta(E) \subseteq \delta'(E)$ holds for each set E of arguments in each AF $F = (A, R)$.

Definition 3.2 (Classical Refutal)**.** *Let $F = (A, R)$ be an AF. The classical refute operator is $\delta_c(E) = E^{+}$.*

Let us introduce a novel refute operator as well. For this, suppose we want it to behave as close as possible to the classical δ_c, but disregard self-attacking arguments.

Definition 3.3. *Let $F = (A, R)$ be an AF. For $E \subseteq A$ we define δ_{self} as $\delta_{self}(E) = E^+ \cup \{a \in A \mid a \to a\}$.*

Example 3.4. *Consider the following AF F and $E = \{b\}$.*

$F:$ 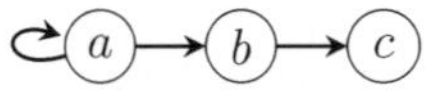

Then $\delta_c(E) = \{c\}$, whereas $\delta_{self}(E) = \{a, c\}$. For $E' = \{a, b\}$ we get $\delta_c(E') = \delta_{self}(E') = \{a, b, c\}$.

Having established a general notion of refutal, let us now define conflict-freeness. As mentioned before, the intuitive idea of our proposal is to separate the notions of "conflict' and "defeat". We interpret $a \to E$ resp. $E \to a$ as "conflict between E and a" and $a \in \delta(E)$ as "E refutes a". For a set E to be conflict-free, we insist both notions are respected.

Definition 3.5. *Let $F = (A, R)$ be an AF and δ a refute operator. A set E of arguments is δ-conflict free ($E \in cf_\delta(F)$) iff i) $E \in cf(F)$ and ii) $E \cap \delta(E) = \emptyset$.*

Example 3.6. *Consider again our AF from Example 3.4. The only δ_c-conflict free sets are $cf_{\delta_c}(F) = \{\emptyset, \{b\}, \{c\}\}$. Since δ_c and δ_{self} only disagree regarding self-attacking arguments, we infer $cf_{\delta_{self}}(F) = cf_{\delta_c}(F)$.*

Let us collect some basic properties of cf_δ.

Proposition 3.7. *For any AF F and refute operator δ, i) $\emptyset \in cf_\delta(F)$, ii) $cf_{\delta_c}(F) = cf(F)$, and iii) if δ is monotonic, then $E' \notin cf_\delta(F)$ if there is $E \subseteq E'$ with $E \notin cf_\delta(F)$.*

For our definition of δ-defense we view each argument a with $a \to E$ as a potential threat to our extension. In order to take care of this threat, E must refute a, i.e. $a \in \delta(E)$. As for usual defense, this condition must hold for each threat.

Definition 3.8. *For an AF $F = (A, R)$ and refute operator δ, $E \subseteq A$ δ-defends $a \in A$ iff $b \in \delta(E)$ for each $b \in a^-$.*

Example 3.9. *Returning to our Example 3.4, the set $E = \{b\}$ δ_{self}-defends itself because $a \in \delta_{self}(E)$, while it does not δ_c-defend itself since $a \notin \delta_c(E) = E^+$. Again, both notions agree that $E' = \{a, b\}$ defends itself.*

Based on our generalized version of defense, let us define the natural induced characteristic function as well.

Definition 3.10. *Let $F = (A, R)$ be an AF and δ a refute operator. The δ-characteristic function Γ_δ is the mapping $\Gamma_\delta : 2^A \to 2^A$ with $\Gamma_\delta(E) = \{a \in A \mid E\ \delta\text{-defends}\ a\}$.*

Note $\Gamma(E) = \Gamma_{\delta_c}(E)$ for the classical refute operator δ_c. The characteristic function is a fundamental concept in AFs and therefore requires a suitable generalization for our setting. However, as the following example illustrates we need to carefully assess the behavior we expect.

Example 3.11. *Recall our AF F from Example 3.4. The set $E = \{b\}$ δ_{self}-defends the self-attacker a: We already saw $\delta_{self}(E) = \{a, c\}$. Since $a^- = \{a\}$ we get $a^- \subseteq \delta_{self}(E)$ and thus $a \in \Gamma_{\delta_{self}}(E)$. In contrast, $a \notin \Gamma(E)$.*

We therefore anticipate that a generalized version of complete semantics would insist that E cannot be an extension without a if δ_{self} is the considered refute operator. That is, we would be forced to include a self-attacking argument in our extension. The problematic behavior stems from the fact that a conflict-free set E δ_{self}-defends an argument which is also refuted by E. For Dung-semantics this cannot happen.

Proposition 3.12. *Let $F = (A, R)$ be an AF. If $E \in cf(F)$, then $\Gamma(E) = \Gamma(E) \setminus E^+$. That is, for the classical refute operator δ_c we have $\Gamma_{\delta_c}(E) = \Gamma_{\delta_c}(E) \setminus \delta_c(E)$.*

This property is a cornerstone in Dung's theory as it is the main ingredient for the proof of his fundamental lemma. However, as we already saw for the quite simple refute operator δ_{self}, we cannot guarantee this behavior in general. We will thus refine our δ-characteristic function before defining the semantics. Later in Section 5.3 we will revisit this requirement and investigate in which cases it is necessary and under which conditions we can drop it.

Definition 3.13. *Let $F = (A, R)$ be an AF and δ a refute operator. The polished δ-characteristic function χ_δ is the mapping $\chi_\delta : 2^A \to 2^A$ with $\chi_\delta(E) = \Gamma_\delta(E) \setminus \delta(E)$.*

Example 3.14. *In Example 3.4 we have $\chi_{\delta_{self}}(\{b\}) = \{b\}$.*

We are ready to define the generalized versions of Dung's semantics from the paper (Dung 1995).

Definition 3.15. *Let F be an AF and δ a refute operator.*

1. *$E \in ad_\delta(F)$ iff $E \subseteq \chi_\delta(E)$,*
2. *$E \in co_\delta(F)$ iff $E = \chi_\delta(E)$,*
3. *$E \in pr_\delta(F)$ iff E is $\subseteq$-maximal in $co_\delta(F)$,*
4. *$E \in gr_\delta(F)$ iff E is $\subseteq$-minimal in $co_\delta(F)$,*
5. *$E \in stb_\delta(F)$ iff $E \in cf_\delta(F)$ and $E \cup \delta(E) = A(F)$.*

The attentive reader may have observed that we did not impose $E \in cf_\delta(F)$ as a precondition. Indeed, using the polished characteristic function this property is implicit.

Proposition 3.16. *For any AF F and refute operator E we have that $E \in ad_\delta(F)$ implies $E \in cf_\delta(F)$.*

Example 3.17. *For the AF F from before we already found $cf_{\delta_{self}}(F) = \{\emptyset, \{b\}, \{c\}\}$. The three sets and their refuted arguments are as follows.*

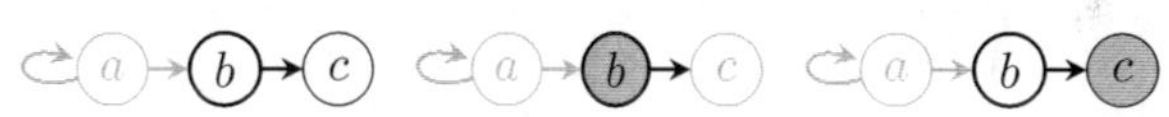

$\chi_{\delta_{self}}(\emptyset) = \{b\}$ $\quad \chi_{\delta_{self}}(\{b\}) = \{b\}$ $\quad \chi_{\delta_{self}}(\{c\}) = \{b\}$

We have $b \notin \delta_{self}(\{c\})$ and hence $\{c\} \notin ad_{\delta_{self}}(F)$. Moreover, $\emptyset \in ad_{\delta_{self}}(F)$ is easy to see, but $\chi_{\delta_{self}}(\emptyset) = \{b\}$ yields $\emptyset \notin co_{\delta_{self}}(F)$. From the previous example we recall $\chi_{\delta_{self}}(\{b\}) = \{b\}$ and hence $\{b\} \in co_{\delta_{self}}(F)$. This also implies $\{b\} \in pr_{\delta_{self}}(F) = gr_{\delta_{self}}(F) = co_{\delta_{self}}(F)$. From $\delta_{self}(\{b\}) = \{a, c\} = A \setminus \{b\}$ we also infer that $\{b\} \in stb_{\delta_{self}}(F)$; there is no other δ-stable extension.

Using χ_δ is not necessary to define ad_δ as we show next. For the general version of admissibility, we can always use Γ_δ instead. The issue described in Example 3.18 which gave rise to define the polished version χ_δ only applies to complete-based semantics.

Proposition 3.18. *Given an AF F and a refute operator δ, we have that $E \in ad_\delta(F)$ iff $E \in cf_\delta(F)$ and $E \subseteq \Gamma_\delta(E)$.*

Let us finish this section by formalizing that the semantics from Definition 3.15 faithfully generalize Dung's semantics.

Proposition 3.19. *For $\delta = \delta_c$ we have $\sigma_\delta(F) = \sigma(F)$ for each AF F and $\sigma \in \{ad, co, gr, pr, stb\}$.*

4 Defense Notions of Non-classical Semantics

Before delving into various formal properties of our new notions, let us demonstrate how our approach captures several non-classical semantics in a quite natural way. In this section, we consider three different families of semantics based on proposals from the literature. Since we do not intend to discriminate based on any specific order, we will simply proceed chronologically.

The aim of this section is to provide the reader with a selection of examples of possible refute operators capturing recently proposed non-classical semantics from the literature. The subsequent sections are designed in a way that a full understanding of these examples is not necessary in order to follow the remainder of the paper.

4.1 Cogent Semantics

Bodanza and Tohmé presented alternative semantics with the goal to limit the effect of self-defeating arguments (Bodanza and Tohmé 2009). In a nutshell, the idea is that defense is not required against each argument in the given AF, but only against ones which are serious enough in a certain sense. The latter concept is implemented as follows.

Definition 4.1. *Let $F = (A, R)$ be an AF. A set $E \subseteq A$ is called cogent ($E \in cog(F)$) iff for any X the following holds: If $X \in ad(F{\downarrow}_{X \cup E})$, then $E \in ad(F{\downarrow}_{X \cup E})$.*

Then *sustainable* extensions are defined as maximal cogent, i.e. $E \in sus(F)$ iff E is maximal in $cog(F)$.

Example 4.2. *Consider the following AFs F and G*

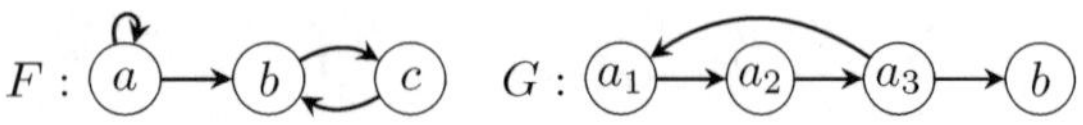

We verify that $E = \{b\} \in cog(F)$. Observe that $X \in ad(F{\downarrow}_{X \cup E})$ can never be the case for some set X containing the self-attacker a. Thus, the only conflict-free candidates for X are $\emptyset$, $\{b\}$, and $\{c\}$; in all cases, $E \in ad(F{\downarrow}_{X \cup E})$ holds. Similarly, we find $\{c\} \in cog(F)$. Since the emptyset is also cogent, $cog(F) = \{\emptyset, \{b\}, \{c\}\}$. Consider now G. In this case, $E = \{b\} \notin cog(G)$. The reason is that we can set $X = \{a_3\}$ and in the subframework $F{\downarrow}_{X \cup E}$ the argument b cannot counterattack a_3. A similar reasoning can be applied to any argument in G and in summary we obtain $cog(G) = \{\emptyset\}$.

It turns out that cogency is closely related to classical admissibility. Formally, the only difference is that self-attacking arguments are disregarded since they can never be in any cogent set. Consequently, cogent semantics can be captured by the refute operator δ_{self} we already introduced.

Definition 4.3. *Let $F = (A, R)$ be an AF. The* cogency *refute operator δ_{cog} is given as $\delta_{cog} = \delta_{self}$.*

The following theorem formalizes that δ_{self} is the suitable refute operator to capture the cogent semantics family.

Theorem 4.4. *For any AF F we have $E \in cog(F)$ iff $E \in ad_{\delta_{self}}(F)$, $E \in sus(F)$ iff $E \in pr_{\delta_{self}}(F)$.*

Thus, we have successfully extracted the underlying defense notion of cogent semantics. As a by-product, we obtain natural notions of "complete" and "grounded" semantics by considering $co_{\delta_{self}}$ and $gr_{\delta_{self}}$, respectively.

4.2 Undecidedness Blocking

The paper (Dondio and Longo 2021) proposes a weakened version of admissibility which is based on the following idea of "undecidedness blocking": Suppose we are given an argument a which is undecided w.r.t. some admissible extension E in the sense that $a \notin E^{\oplus}$. Then, each argument a' attacked by a cannot be accepted, i.e. $a' \notin E$. If even $a' \notin E^{+}$ holds, then a' is also undecided. This may lead to chains of undecided arguments of an arbitrary length. Dondio and Longo therefore propose an approach where the effect of undecided arguments is limited. The original definition is given in terms of labelings. However, we can find a convenient equivalent characterization via extensions.

Definition 4.5. *A set $E \subseteq A$ is called weakly ub-complete ($E \in co^{wu}(F)$) if $E \in cf(F)$ and $\Gamma(E) \subseteq E$.*

Example 4.6. *Recall our two AFs form Example 4.2. We find $co^{wu}(F) = \{\emptyset, \{b\}, \{c\}\}$ so one might wonder whether the definition of co^{wu} yields some kind of "defense" notion. The answer is affirmative, but the underlying notion is quite subtle which is nicely illustrated in G: Here, $\{b\} \in co^{wu}(G)$ as well since b clearly does not defend either of the a_i. However, consider the situation when choosing e.g. a_1:*

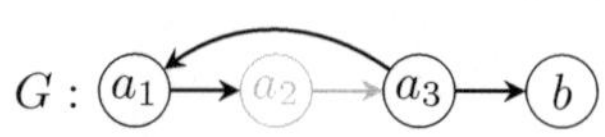

We have $\Gamma(\{a_1\}) = \{a_3\}$ so it does not hold that $\Gamma(\{a_1\}) \subseteq \{a_1\}$. However, simply iterating Γ does not help to fix this issue since $\{a_1, a_3, b\}$ is not conflict-free in G. Indeed, $co^{wu}(G) = \{\emptyset, \{b\}\}$, i.e. the arguments in the odd cycle cannot be chosen. We want to mention though that the acceptability of b does not depend on a_1, a_2, a_3 forming an odd cycle. Consider H given as follows.

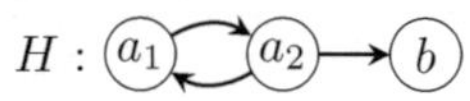

Here $\{b\} \in co^{wu}(H)$ as well since $\{b\}$ does neither defend a_1 nor a_2. In summary, $co^{wu}(H) = \{\emptyset, \{b\}, \{a_1\}, \{a_2\}\}$.

The behavior of the previous example generalizes to the following idea: Whenever E defends some set E' which in turn attacks E, then $E \notin co^{wu}(F)$. The same is true if E' defends some E'' attacking E and so on. A concise way to formalize this observation is the reduct $F^E = F{\downarrow}_{A \setminus E^{\oplus}}$.

Proposition 4.7. *Let $F = (A, R)$ be an AF and $E \in cf(F)$. There is some $E' \in co^{wu}(F)$ with $E \subseteq E'$ iff $G \in gr(F^E)$ does not attack E in F.*

We can consequently think of a "defense" notion which is based on the grounded extension of F^E. Indeed, we can capture the semantics co^{ub} as follows.

Definition 4.8. *For an $F = (A, R)$ and $E \subseteq A$ define the* wu *operator as $\delta_{wu}(E) = \{a \in A \mid a \notin (gr(F^E) \cup E)\}$.*

Theorem 4.9. *Let $F = (A, R)$ be an AF and $E \subseteq A$. Then $E \in co^{wu}(F)$ iff $E \in co_{\delta_{wu}}(F)$.*

We hence extracted the underlying defense notion of the undecidedness blocking principle. Versions of "admissible", "grounded", and "preferred" semantics can be obtained by considering $ad_{\delta_{wu}}$, $gr_{\delta_{wu}}$, and $pr_{\delta_{wu}}$, respectively.

4.3 Recursive "Weak Admissibility"

Weak admissibility as proposed in (Baumann, Brewka, and Ulbricht 2020b) is based on a recursive definition utilizing the reduct F^E. The intuition is that arguments in E are accepted, those in E^+ are rejected and out of those in $A \setminus E^\oplus$, attackers y of E are of concern. In order to assess such a y as "serious" enough to be a threat, it has to be weakly admissible in the reduct F^E, leading to the following definition.

Definition 4.10. *Let $F = (A, R)$ be an AF. $E \subseteq A$ is called* weakly admissible *in F ($E \in ad^w(F)$) iff*

1. $E \in cf(F)$, and

2. for any attacker y of E we have $y \notin \bigcup ad^w(F^E)$.

Example 4.11. *Let us discuss our examples from the previous subsections. Regarding F, for both $E = \{b\}$ and $E' = \{c\}$ it holds that the corresponding reduct F^E and $F^{E'}$ contains only the self-attacker a. Since self-attacking arguments can never be weakly admissible, $ad^w(F) = \{\emptyset, \{b\}, \{c\}\}$ follows. Observe that in an AF consisting of an odd cycle a_1, a_2, a_3, no argument occurs in a weakly admissible extension. It follows that $ad^w(G) = \{\emptyset, \{b\}\}$. Since $\{a_1\}, \{a_2\} \in ad^w(H)$, b cannot survive without a_1, so we conclude $ad^w(H) = \{\emptyset, \{a_1\}, \{a_2\}, \{a_1, b\}\}$.*

The decisive feature of weak admissibility is that arguments which are not acceptable in the reduct F^E are disregarded. The natural refute operator hence is the following.

Definition 4.12. *Let $F = (A, R)$ be an AF. The* weak refute operator *δ_w is for each set E of arguments given as $\delta_w(E) = E^+ \cup \{a \in F^E \mid a \notin \bigcup ad^w(F^E)\}$.*

Intuitively, an argument a is δ_w-refuted by E iff it is either attacked by E or occurring in the reduct without being credulously accepted there. We formalize that δ_w is suitable for our purpose as it captures weakly admissible semantics.

Theorem 4.13. *Let $F = (A, R)$ be an AF and $E \subseteq A$. Then $E \in ad^w(F)$ iff $E \in ad_{\delta_w}(F)$.*

The paper also presents a notion of defense and the induced weak complete, preferred, and grounded semantics.

Definition 4.14. *Let $F = (A, R)$ be an AF. Given two sets $E, X \subseteq A$. We say E weakly defends (or simply, w-defends) X iff for any attacker y of X we have,*

1. E attacks y, or

2. $y \notin E$, $y \notin \bigcup ad^w(F^E)$ and $X \subseteq X' \in ad^w(F)$.

Definition 4.15. *Let $F = (A, R)$ be an AF. A set $E \subseteq A$ is called* weakly complete *in F ($E \in co^w(F)$) iff $E \in ad^w(F)$ and if E w-defends $X \supseteq E$, then $X = E$.*

Weakly grounded (gr^w) and preferred (pr^w) are defined as minimal resp. maximal weakly complete sets. In the paper (Dauphin, Rienstra, and van der Torre 2021) the notion of weak defense has been further investigated and interesting alternatives are proposed, but within the scope of this contribution we stick with Definition 4.15. The following result establishes a natural fixed-point characterization for co^w.

Theorem 4.16. *Let $F = (A, R)$ be an AF and $E \subseteq A$. Then $E \in co^w(F)$ iff $E \in co_{\delta_w}(F)$.*

Corollary 4.17. *Let F be an AF. Then i) $E \in pr^w(F)$ iff $E \in pr_{\delta_w}(F)$ and ii) $E \in gr^w(F)$ iff $E \in gr_{\delta_w}(F)$.*

5 Basic Properties

In this section we examine basic properties of semantics based on general refute operators. This investigation is inspired by the behavior of the classical semantics, i.e. we particularly focus on the following questions.

- Is there a suitable version of the Fundamental Lemma?
- Under which conditions do complete extensions exist?
- Can we infer that the grounded extension is unique?

Our investigation requires caution since the classical refute operator $\delta_c(E) = E^+$ is a simple syntactical one with intuitive properties. Moving to a general mapping δ is thus a challenging endeavour at first glance. However, it turns out that under some mild conditions we can answer the above questions affirmatively for a general refute operator δ. First, let us mention that $\emptyset$ is admissible for any operator.

Lemma 5.1. *Let $F = (A, R)$ be an AF and δ a refute operator. Then $\emptyset \in ad_\delta(F)$. In particular, $ad_\delta(F) \neq \emptyset$.*

5.1 The Fundamental Lemma

The above Lemma 5.1 is simple, yet our first major building block in finding conditions ensuring $co_\delta(F)$ exists. Dung's classical proof for the existence of complete extensions starts with some admissible set and then applies:

Lemma 5.2 (Fundamental lemma)**.** *Let $F = (A, R)$ be an AF and $E \in ad(F)$. If E defends a, then $E \cup \{a\} \in ad(F)$.*

Unfortunately, we cannot expect this property to hold for any conceivable refute operator. Our goal is thus to find conditions ensuring this property. However, before doing so let us establish that a natural counterpart to the fundamental lemma indeed yields the existence of complete extensions.

Definition 5.3. *A refute operator* induces the fundamental lemma *if for any AF $F = (A, R)$ and $E \in ad_\delta(F)$ the following holds: If $a \in \chi_\delta(E)$, then $E \cup \{a\} \in ad_\delta(F)$.*

Theorem 5.4. *Let $F = (A, R)$ be an AF. If δ induces the fundamental lemma, then $co_\delta(F) \neq \emptyset$.*

Proof. We have $\emptyset \subseteq \chi_\delta(\emptyset)$. If even "=" holds, we are done. So let $E_1 = \{a_1\}$ for some $a \in \chi_\delta(\emptyset)$ and for each $i \geq 2$ we set $E_i = E_i \cup \{a_i\}$ for some $a_i \in \chi_\delta(E_{i-1}) \setminus E_{i-1}$. Since δ induces the fundamental lemma, a simple induction shows that $E_i \cup \{a_i\} \in ad_\delta(F)$ for each i and $a_i \notin E_{i-1}$, i.e. $E_{i-1} \subsetneq E_i$. By finiteness of A, this procedure stops after at most $|A|$ steps with some E_i satisfying $E_i = \chi_\delta(E_i)$. □

Our goal is thus to find natural conditions ensuring that our given refute operator δ induces the fundamental lemma. We show that this can be ensured by the following two conditions (which are both satisfied by δ_c):

Definition 5.5. *We say χ_δ satisfies*

- cf-monotonicity *if for any AF $F = (A, R)$ and $E, E' \in cf_\delta(F)$ we have that $E \subseteq E'$ implies $\chi_\delta(E) \subseteq \chi_\delta(E')$;*
- conflict-free transfer *if for any AF $F = (A, R)$ and $E \in ad_\delta(F)$ we have $E \cup \{a\} \in cf_\delta(F)$ for each $a \in \chi_\delta(E)$.*

We can show that in general, this two properties indeed suffice in order to infer the fundamental lemma.

Proposition 5.6. *Let F be an AF and δ a refute operator. If χ_δ satisfies both cf-monotonicity and conflict-free transfer, then δ induces the fundamental lemma.*

Proof. Let $E \in ad_\delta(F)$ and $a \in \chi_\delta(E)$. By conflict-free transfer, $E \cup \{a\} \in cf_\delta(F)$. Since $E \in ad_\delta(F)$ we can apply cf-monotonicity and find $\chi_\delta(E) \subseteq \chi_\delta(E \cup \{a\})$. By definition of $E \in ad_\delta(F)$, we have $E \subseteq \chi_\delta(E)$. From $a \in \chi_\delta(E)$ we can therefore also infer $E \cup \{a\} \subseteq \chi_\delta(E)$. □

As we show next, Proposition 5.6 is applicable to δ_{cog}. Although this is not the case for δ_{wu}, this refute operator induces the fundamental lemma nonetheless.

Proposition 5.7. *The refute operator δ_{self} satisfies both cf-monotonicity and conflict-free transfer, δ_{wu} induces the fundamental lemma but does not satisfy cf-monotonicity.*

In contrast, the following shows that δ_w does not induce the fundamental lemma and thus by Proposition 5.6 cannot satisfy both cf-monotonicity and conflict-free transfer.

Example 5.8. *In the AF F below $\{d\}$ is δ_w-defended by $\emptyset$ but $\{d\} \notin ad_{\delta_w}(F)$.*

I :
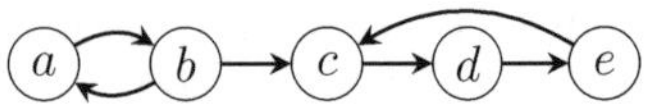

Nonetheless $co_{\delta_w}(F) \neq \emptyset$ for any AF F, so the fundamental lemma is no necessary condition.

5.2 Grounded and Preferred Extensions

Next we want to give a criterion ensuring that gr_δ is always unique. As before our inspiration comes from the behavior of the classical semantics. Notably, the following property is a natural counterpart to conflict-free transfer.

Definition 5.9. *Let δ a refute operator. The polished characteristic function χ_δ satisfies* admissibility transfer *if for any AF F and $E \in ad_\delta(F)$ we have $\chi_\delta(E) \in ad_\delta(F)$.*

Theorem 5.10. *Let $F = (A, R)$ be an AF and δ a refute operator. If χ_δ satisfies cf-monotonicity and admissibility transfer, then $|gr_\delta(F)| = 1$ and the unique δ-grounded extension $G \in gr_\delta(F)$ satisfies $G = \bigcup_{i \in \mathbb{N}} \chi^i_\delta(\emptyset)$.*

Proof. Let $E \in co_\delta(F)$. By cf-monotonicity we have $\chi_\delta(\emptyset) \subseteq \chi_\delta(E)$. Now by induction and due to admissibility transfer we infer $\chi^i_\delta(\emptyset) \subseteq \chi^i_\delta(E)$ for each integer i. For some i, $\chi^i_\delta(\emptyset) = \chi^{i+1}_\delta(\emptyset)$, i.e. G is complete Since $E \in co_\delta(F)$ we have $E = \chi^i_\delta(E)$ and thus, $G \subseteq E$. □

Theorem 5.10 is applicable to both δ_{cog} and δ_{wu}.

Proposition 5.11. *The refute operators δ_{self} and δ_{wu} satisfy admissibility transfer.*

Since gr_{δ_w} is not unique in general (Baumann, Brewka, and Ulbricht 2020b) we can be certain that δ_w does not satisfy both cf-monotonicity and admissibility transfer. The final property of classical semantics we inspect more closely here is regarding preferred semantics: They are defined as maximal complete extensions, but this is equivalent to maximal admissible sets. Remarkably, the same properties ensuring uniqueness of gr also yield this equivalence. First consider an auxiliary lemma which establishes the technical property we require. Then we infer the desired property.

Lemma 5.12. *Let $F = (A, R)$ be an AF and δ a refute operator. Let $E \in ad_\delta(F)$. If the polished characteristic function χ_δ satisfies both cf-monotonicity and admissibility transfer, then there is some $E' \in co_\delta(F)$ with $E \subseteq E'$.*

Proposition 5.13. *Let $F = (A, R)$ be an AF and δ a refute operator. If the polished characteristic function χ_δ satisfies both cf-monotonicity and admissibility transfer, then $pr_\delta(F) = \{E \subseteq A \mid E$ is maximal in $ad_\delta(F)\}$.*

Proof. For ($\subseteq$) let $E \in co_\delta(F)$. If E is not maximal in $ad_\delta(F)$, then there is some $E' \in ad_\delta(F)$ with $E \subsetneq E'$. By Lemma 5.12, there is $E'' \in co_\delta(F)$ with $E \subsetneq E' \subseteq E''$, contradiction. The other direction ($\supseteq$) is analogous. □

Observe that we can thus infer the following result which, to the best of our knowledge, has not been stated explicitly in the original papers where the semantics have been proposed.

Corollary 5.14. *For any AF F we have $pr_\delta(F) = \{E \subseteq A \mid E$ is maximal in $ad_\delta(F)\}$ for $\delta \in \{\delta_{self}, \delta_{wu}\}$.*

Proposition 5.13 is not applicable to δ_w, but due to (Baumann, Brewka, and Ulbricht 2020b), $pr^w(F) = \{E \subseteq A \mid E$ is maximal in $ad^w(F)\}$ holds nonetheless.

5.3 Polished Refute Operators

We recall that our semantics based on a refute operator δ were defined in terms of the polished characteristic function $\chi_\delta(E) = \Gamma_\delta(E) \setminus \delta(E)$. Since $\chi_\delta(E)$ and $\Gamma_\delta(E)$ coincide for Dung's semantics whenever E is conflict-free (see Proposition 3.12), one could argue that χ_δ is a faithful generalization of the classical characteristic function on its own. Nonetheless, let us investigate situations where $\Gamma_\delta = \chi_\delta$.

Definition 5.15. *We call δ* polished *if for each AF $F = (A, R)$ we have $\chi_\delta(E) = \Gamma_\delta(E)$ for each $E \in cf_\delta(F)$.*

We can give the following general negative result. Let us stipulate the notation $A^\circ = \{a \in A \mid a \to a\}$.

Proposition 5.16. *Let $F = (A, R)$ be an AF. A refute operator δ s.t. $A^\circ \subseteq \delta(E)$ for each $E \subseteq A$ is not polished.*

Proof. Let $F = (\{a\}, \{(a, a)\})$. By assumption $\delta(\emptyset) = \{a\}$. However, this means $\emptyset$ refutes each attacker of a which implies $a \in \Gamma_\delta(\emptyset)$ as well. Thus, $\chi_\delta(\emptyset) = \emptyset \subsetneq \{a\} = \Gamma_\delta(\emptyset)$. Since $\emptyset \in cf_\delta(F)$, δ is not polished. □

As we will later see when considering the *self attack refute* principle, δ_{self} and δ_w satisfy $A^\circ \subseteq \delta(E)$ for each $E \subseteq A$ in any AF F (see Table 1). We hence infer:

Corollary 5.17. *Both δ_{self} and δ_w are not polished.*

Recall that the semantics based on δ_{self}, δ_{wu}, and δ_w are tailored to limit the impact self-defeating arguments have on the reasoning in F. We thus assume a setting where it is desired to disregard self-attackers. Hence, we want to emphasize that the above corollary is not a flaw of the refute operators. Rather, Proposition 5.16 suggests that refute operators serving this purpose will in general not tend to be polished. As the last observation we make in this section we will show that, in contrast, a refute operator which is stricter than Dung's classical refute will always be polished.

Proposition 5.18. *Let $F = (A, R)$ be an AF and δ a refute operator. If $\delta(E) \subseteq E^+$ for each $E \subseteq A$, then δ is polished.*

	δ_c	δ_{self}	δ_{wu}	δ_w
Induces fundamental lemma	✓	✓	✓	✗
cf-monotonicity	✓	✓	✗	✗
Conflict-free transfer	✓	✓	✓	✓
Admissibility transfer	✓	✓	✓	✗
Polished	✓	✗	✗	✗
Requiring attacks	✓	✓	✓	✓
Refute possible	✓	✓	✓	✓
Monotonicity	✓	✓	✗	✗
Self-attack refutal	✗	✓	✗	✓
Self-attack neglection	✗	✓	✗	✓
Additivity	✓	✓	✗	✗
Context-free	✓	✗	✗	✗
Generalize classical defense	✓	✓	✓	✓
Tractable	✓	✓	✓	✗

Table 1: Refute Operator Principles

6 Principles and Their Relationships

Within the last decade, AF semantics have been extensively studied w.r.t. certain *principles*, i.e. properties which are satisfied (or not) by certain semantics. This line of research helps establishing a comprehensive understanding of their behavior. In view of this, the present paper gives rise to approaching this endeavor in terms of the underlying refute operator, i.e. this section is driven by the following research questions.

- Can we investigate principles which are satisfied by semantics by considering the underlying refute operator?
- What are the principles a refute operator should satisfy?

As we already mentioned, the non-classical semantics considered in this paper all serve the purpose of minimizing the damage caused by self-defeating arguments. Inspired by this, we also want to consider some specific principles devised to compare semantics of this kind, i.e. we study:

- What is a "good" weak version of admissibility?

Throughout this section we assume an arbitrary but fixed AF $F = (A, R)$. The attentive reader will observe that we only discuss a small selection of the usual principles mentioned in the literature. This choice is made due to space restrictions; a comprehensive study of this matter is left for future work. A summary of all principles and which refute operators satisfy them is reported in Table 1.

6.1 Defense and Defeat

We start by some basic properties of refute and defense operators. Our first principles establish some basic ideas of refute operators we intuitively expect. For classical refute $\delta_c(E) = E^+$ these are all clear, but since in our general setting δ is an arbitrary mapping, we want to mention them here in our general investigation.

Principle 6.1 (Requiring Attacks). *A refute operator δ re-*quires attacks *if $a^- = \emptyset$ implies $a \notin \delta(E)$ for each $E \subseteq A$.*

Principle 6.2 (Refute Possible). *A refute operator δ satisfies the* refute possible *principle if for each argument $a \in \mathcal{U}$ there is some AF $F = (A, R)$ and $E \subseteq A$ s.t. $a \in \delta(E)$.*

So these principles simply formalize that refutal of an argument should in general be possible, but not without presence of another argument questioning it. We want to emphasize that requiring attacks does not distinguish whether some attack stems from E, i.e. it is possible for a refute operator to satisfy it, but we still have $a^- \cap E = \emptyset$ for an argument $a \in \delta(E)$. Full absence of any attack within the given AF however renders δ trivial.

Fact 6.3. *If $R = \emptyset$, i.e. $F = (A, \emptyset)$, and δ requires attacks, then $\delta(E) = \emptyset$ for each $E \subseteq A$. Moreover, $gr_\delta(F) = \{A\}$.*

Next we consider monotonicity of δ. It is clear that this is an important property, but as we saw already in the last sections, not every reasonable operator satisfies it.

Principle 6.4 (Monotonicity). *A refute operator δ satisfies* monotonicity *if $E \subseteq E' \subseteq A$ implies $\delta(E) \subseteq \delta(E')$.*

The next principles are concerned with self-attackers and how they influence the refuted sets of arguments. This aspect is interesting for applications where the presence of such arguments shall not influence the outcome of a discussion, as is the case for our examples from Section 4.

Principle 6.5 (Self-Attack Refute). *A refute operator δ satisfies* self-attack refutal *if $A^\circ \subseteq \delta(E)$ for each E.*

Let us also consider an even stronger version of this principles formalizing that self-attackers do not have any influence on the attacked arguments whatsoever (at least if E itself does not contain a self-attacker). For this, we let F° be the AF after removing self-attackers, i.e. $F^\circ = F\downarrow_{A\setminus A^\circ}$.

Principle 6.6 (Self-Attack Neglection). *A refute operator δ satisfies* self-attack neglection *if for each $E \subseteq A(F^\circ)$, $a \in A$ it holds that $a \in \delta(F, E)$ iff $(a, a) \in R$ or $a \in \delta(F^\circ, E)$.*

Observe that for refute operators which behave in a certain sense intuitively, we would expect that self-attack refutal implies self-attack neglection. For this, suppose E does not contain any self-attacker. Then any self-attacker a is refuted due to self-attack refutal. For arguments which are no self-attackers, the condition $a \in \delta(F, E)$ iff $a \in \delta(F^\circ, E)$ simply implies that the present self-attackers do not influence whether or not E refutes a. Since E does not contain any self-attacker, we would expect this behavior.

More broadly, the following principles consider the interaction of arguments with each other in E as well as the sensitivity to the remaining AF.

Principle 6.7 (Additivity). *A refute operator δ satisfies* additivity *if $\delta(E) = \bigcup_{e \in E} \delta(\{e\})$ for each $\emptyset \neq E \subseteq A$.*

Principle 6.8 (Context-free). *A refute operator δ is* context-free *if $\delta(F, E) = \delta(F', E)$ where $F' = (A, R')$ is an AF satisfying $(a, b) \in R$ iff $(a, b) \in R'$ for each $a \in E$.*

The latter condition formalizes that E has the same outgoing attacks in F'. For example, classical refute based on out-going attacks satisfies both additivity and context-free since $E^+ = \bigcup_{e \in E}\{e\}^+$ and E^+ depends solely on E and its out-going attacks. On the other hand, we can formalize that under mild conditions a refute operator which disregards self-attacking arguments cannot be context-free.

Proposition 6.9. *There is no refute operator satisfying requiring attacks, self-attack refutal, and context-free.*

With the addition of the additivity principle one might now expect that there should be some quite natural characterization of the classical refute operator $\delta_c(E) = E^+$. However, it is still surprisingly difficult to capture δ_c in terms of our abstract properties. At least for semantics which are more liberal than ad – i.e. we have that $\bigcup ad(F) \subseteq \bigcup ad_\delta(F)$ – we can achieve this as follows.

Proposition 6.10. *Let δ be a refute operator satisfying requiring attacks, context-free, and additivity. If $\bigcup ad(F) \subseteq \bigcup ad_\delta(F)$, then $\delta(E) = E^+$ for each set E of arguments satisfying $E \cap A^\circ = \emptyset$.*

For our final principle regarding refute operators, let us have a closer look at the notion of defense. The following relates χ_δ to the classical operator Γ, formalizing that χ_δ contains at least the classically defended arguments.

Principle 6.11. *A refute operator δ* generalizes classical defense *if for each AF $F = (A, R)$ and $E \in cf(F)$ it holds that $\Gamma(E) \subseteq \chi_\delta(E)$.*

In particular refute operators designed to yield more liberal versions of ad –like the ones we consider in the present paper– should adhere to this property since it would not make sense for these to credulously accept fewer arguments than Γ. To conclude our discussion on principles for refute operators we turn our attention to Table 1 summarizing which operators satisfy which of our novel principles.

Theorem 6.12. *Satisfaction of principles by the refute operators considered in this paper is as depicted in Table 1.*

6.2 Weak Admissibility Notions

In this section we discuss a selection of principles which are tailored to compare semantics devised to yield more liberal notions of defense. As is the case for our running example semantics, we will assume that the underlying motivation is to limit the effect of contradictory or self-attacking arguments whose status is undecided. We start with a simple property, stating that the given semantics is more liberal than ad which formalizes that we indeed accept more arguments.

Principle 6.13. *A semantics σ satisfies* ad-liberalization *if for each AF F, $\bigcup ad(F) \subseteq \bigcup \sigma(F)$ and there is some AF F_0 s.t. $\bigcup ad(F_0) \subsetneq \bigcup \sigma(F_0)$.*

This is a basic requirement for the semantics sharing our underlying motivation, with the exception of the "grounded" version. Next we recall a property from (Baumann, Brewka, and Ulbricht 2020a) formalizing that a semantics disregards self-attackers.

Principle 6.14. *A semantics σ satisfies* neglection of self-attackers *if for any AF F, $\sigma(F) = \sigma(F^\circ)$.*

Interestingly, the way semantics are defined based on a general refute operator allows us to infer satisfaction in an intuitive way by means of the behavior of δ.

Proposition 6.15. *If δ satisfies self-attack neglection, then σ satisfies neglection of self-attackers for each $\sigma \in \{ad_\delta, co_\delta, gr_\delta, pr_\delta, stb_\delta\}$.*

As a corollary, we obtain that the considered semantics based on δ_{self} and δ_w satisfy neglection of self-attackers.

Next we introduce a property which can be viewed as a generalization of neglection of self-attackers where we make use of unattacked arguments, i.e. a set U of arguments s.t. $(a, b) \in R$ with $b \in U$ implies $a \in U$. The underlying idea is as follows. Given some unattacked set U of arguments where $\sigma(F{\downarrow_U}) = \{\emptyset\}$. Then, as in the case of self-attackers, no argument in U is acceptable. A semantics following the intuition that arguments which can never be accepted shall not be able to cause any harm can now be expected to behave as if U was not part of the AF at all. We call this property the *separation property*.

Principle 6.16. *A semantics σ satisfies the* separation property *if for any AF F and any unattacked $U \subseteq A$ the following holds: If $\sigma(F{\downarrow_U}) = \{\emptyset\}$, then $\sigma(F) = \sigma(F{\downarrow_{A \setminus U}})$.*

The separation property can grasp, among others, the idea that an unresolved odd cycle can be removed from the AF.

Example 6.17. *Consider F, G, and H from Example 4.11. Semantics which require extensions to be conflict-free as well as satisfying the separation property treat F like the even cycle consisting of b and c. If in addition no argument in an isolated odd cycle is accepted, G is equivalent to the isolated argument b. In case of H, however, the separation property will most likely not make any difference since the even cycle a_1 and a_2 yields two accepted arguments for most semantics.*

6.3 On the Relation to Classical Principles

We conclude our discussion on principles by recalling some of the most basic ones from the literature and investigating them by means of our general framework.

Definition 6.18. *A semantics σ satisfies*

- defense *if $E \subseteq \Gamma(E)$ for each $F \in \mathcal{F}$, $E \in \sigma(F)$;*
- reinstatement *if $\Gamma(E) \subseteq E$ for each $F \in \mathcal{F}$, $E \in \sigma(F)$;*
- I-maximality *if $\sigma(F)$ forms an antichain for each $F \in \mathcal{F}$.*

We can ensure satisfaction of defense whenever δ is more cautious than δ_c.

Proposition 6.19. *Let δ be a refute operator s.t. $\delta \subseteq \delta_c$. Then for each $\sigma \in \{ad_\delta, co_\delta, pr_\delta, gr_\delta, stb_\delta\}$, the semantics σ satisfies defense.*

The reinstatement property holds for complete-based semantics whenever δ generalizes classical defense. Clearly, this cannot be ensured for δ-admissible extensions in general ad is exclusively concerned with defense of the set E.

Proposition 6.20. *Let δ be a refute operator generalizing classical defense. Then for each $\sigma \in \{co_\delta, pr_\delta, gr_\delta, stb_\delta\}$, the semantics σ satisfies reinstatement.*

Moreover, I-maximality holds by definition for any version of grounded and preferred semantics. Observe that, at least if δ is defined in a somewhat counter-intuitive way, we cannot be certain that stb_δ adheres to I-maximality.

Proposition 6.21. *Let δ be a refute operator. Then for each $\sigma \in \{pr_\delta, gr_\delta\}$, the semantics σ satisfies I-maximality.*

To concludes this section, let us consider Table 2 reporting satisfaction of principles formulated for semantics.

Theorem 6.22. *Satisfaction of principles by the semantics considered in this paper is as depicted in Table 2.*

	δ_c	δ_{self}	δ_{wu}	δ_w
Ad-liberal.	✗	ad	ad	ad
Self-attack neg	✗	✓	✗	✓
Sep prop.	✗	✗	✗	✓
Defense	✓	✗	gr	✗
Reinstatement	$\sigma \neq ad_\delta$	$\sigma \neq ad_\delta$	$\sigma \neq ad_\delta$	$\sigma \neq ad_\delta$
I-maximality	gr, pr, stb	gr, pr, stb	gr, pr	gr, pr, stb

Table 2: Semantics Principles. Here a checkmark means the property holds for each induced σ. Similarly, $\sigma \neq ad_\delta$ indicates that the property holds for all except $_\delta$. A crossmark indicates satisfaction for none of them. Gray entries are known from the literature

7 Computational Complexity

The computational complexity of reasoning in AFs is well-studied for the usual semantics (Dvorák and Dunne 2018). In this section we discuss generic membership results we can infer from the properties of the refute operator. We assume the reader to be familiar with the polynomial hierarchy.

Definition 7.1. *A refute operator is* tractable *if for each AF $F = (A, R)$ and $E \subseteq A$, the set $\delta(E)$ can be computed in polynomial time.*

If we are given a tractable refute operator, we can infer the following upper bounds for the standard reasoning tasks.

Proposition 7.2. *Let δ be a tractable refute operator. Deciding whether a set $E \subseteq A$ of arguments in an AF $F = (A, R)$ satisfies $E \in \sigma_\delta(F)$ is tractable for each $\sigma \in \{ad, co, stb\}$ and in* coNP *for $\sigma \in \{gr, pr\}$.*

Proposition 7.3. *Let δ be a tractable refute operator. Deciding whether an argument $a \in A$ is credulously accepted w.r.t. σ_δ in an AF $F = (A, R)$ is in* NP *for $\sigma \in \{ad, co, pr, stb\}$ and in Σ_2^P for $\sigma = gr$.*

Regarding skeptical reasoning, we need to check $\sigma(F) \neq \emptyset$ in addition to the actual reasoning task. So we reduce our attention to cases where this is unnecessary. From our results from Section 5 we know that refute operators inducing the fundamental lemma ensure $co_\delta(F) \neq \emptyset$.

Proposition 7.4. *For δ tractable and inducing the fundamental lemma, deciding whether $a \in A$ is skeptically accepted w.r.t. σ_δ in an AF $F = (A, R)$ is trivial for $\sigma = ad$, in* coNP *for $\sigma \in \{co, gr\}$ and in Π_2^P for $\sigma = pr$.*

The computational complexity of the grounded extension is surprisingly high in general considering that reasoning with Dung's classical variant is tractable. The latter cannot be attributed to the fact that reasoning with the minimal complete extension(s) is an easy task in general. Rather, this stems from the fact that gr can be computed by iterating the characteristic function Γ. This observation yields:

Theorem 7.5. *Let δ be a tractable refute operator s.t. χ_δ satisfies cf-monotonicity and admissibility transfer. Then the following reasoning tasks are tractable. Deciding $a \in A$ is i) credulously accepted w.r.t. gr_δ, ii) skeptically accepted w.r.t. gr_δ, iii) skeptically accepted w.r.t. co_δ.*

Let us now come to the operators considered in this paper. Clearly, the classical refute operator $\delta_c(E) = E^+$ is tractable. The same is true for δ_{cog} and δ_{wu}.

Proposition 7.6. *The operators δ_{cog} and δ_{wu} are tractable.*

The same is not true for δ_w as the complexity analysis provided in (Dvorák, Ulbricht, and Woltran 2021) shows. By applying the reduction given in this paper, we can infer that the underlying decision problem is PSPACE-complete.

Proposition 7.7. *Deciding whether two input $E, X \subseteq A$ of arguments in an input AF $F = (A, R)$ satisfy $E = \delta_w(X)$ is* PSPACE*-complete.*

8 Discussion

Generalizing the underlying defense or refute notion in AFs is conceptually not novel. A recent example is the paper (Vassiliades et al. 2021) where the authors use different kinds of attacks, some of which are capable of inducing conflicts, whereas others can contribute to defense. The paper (Yu et al. 2021) uses an adjusted notion of defense for a multi-agent setting. In (Fan and Toni 2015) so-called related admissibility is the theoretical foundation for computing dialectical explanations for acceptance of arguments.

As mentioned in the introduction, several recent proposals attempt to find a middle ground between naivity-based and admissibility-based semantics (Bodanza and Tohmé 2009; Dondio 2018; Dondio and Longo 2021; Baumann, Brewka, and Ulbricht 2020b; Dauphin, Rienstra, and van der Torre 2021), but also semantics defined by the SCC-recursive scheme (Baroni, Giacomin, and Guida 2005), in particular $cf2$ and $stage2$ (Dvořák and Gaggl 2014), can be seen as semantics of this kind. The recently introduced weak admissibility (Baumann, Brewka, and Ulbricht 2020b) is already well-studied (Baumann, Brewka, and Ulbricht 2020a; Dauphin, Rienstra, and van der Torre 2020; Dvorák, Ulbricht, and Woltran 2021) and interestingly, the approach discussed in (Dondio and Longo 2021) also contributes a principle-based comparison. The paper (Dauphin, Rienstra, and van der Torre 2020) also proposes novel SCCs-based semantics.

Our research induces several interesting future work directions. First, our Theorem 4.16 does not hold for the alternatives proposed in (Dauphin, Rienstra, and van der Torre 2021), thus finding suitable refute operators would broaden the results. The same is true for SCC-based semantics like the ones introduced in (Dauphin, Rienstra, and van der Torre 2020). As a general observation, it is probably not straightforward how our approach could capture the SCC-recursive scheme. The present paper generalizes Dung's classical semantics, but one could also consider generalized versions of e.g. ideal (Dung, Mancarella, and Toni 2007), eager (Caminada 2007), or semi-stable (Caminada 2006) semantics. Our analysis in Section 5 was focused on the existence of complete extensions, so it would be interesting to find conditions ensuring the existence of δ-stable extensions, as done in (Dung 1995) for the classical semantics. One could also propose and investigate further refute operators, in particular notions which are more cautious than admissibility, similar in spirit to strong admissibility (Caminada 2014). Finally the investigation of further principles would be conceivable, in particular generalized versions of those discussed in Section 6.3, by phrasing them in terms of χ_δ.

Acknowledgements

This work was supported by the German Research Foundation (DFG, BA 6170/2-1) and the German Federal Ministry of Education and Research (BMBF, 01/S18026A-F) by funding the competence center for Big Data and AI "ScaDS.AI" Dresden/Leipzig.

References

Baroni, P., and Giacomin, M. 2007. On principle-based evaluation of extension-based argumentation semantics. *Artificial Intelligence* 171:675–700.

Baroni, P.; Caminada, M.; and Giacomin, M. 2018. Abstract argumentation frameworks and their semantics. In *Handbook of Formal Argumentation*. College Publications.

Baroni, P.; Giacomin, M.; and Guida, G. 2005. SCC-recursiveness: a general schema for argumentation semantics. *Artif. Intell.* 168(1-2):162–210.

Baroni, P.; Giacomin, M.; and Liao, B. 2018. Locality and modularity in abstract argumentation. In *Handbook of Formal Argumentation*. College Publications. chapter 19.

Baumann, R., and Spanring, C. 2015. Infinite argumentation frameworks - on the existence and uniqueness of extensions. In *Essays Dedicated to Gerhard Brewka on the Occasion of His 60th Birthday*, volume 9060, 281–295. Springer.

Baumann, R.; Brewka, G.; and Ulbricht, M. 2020a. Comparing weak admissibility semantics to their dung-style counterparts - reduct, modularization, and strong equivalence in abstract argumentation. In *Proc. KR 2020, September 12-18, 2020*, 79–88.

Baumann, R.; Brewka, G.; and Ulbricht, M. 2020b. Revisiting the foundations of abstract argumentation: Semantics based on weak admissibility and weak defense. In *Proc. AAAI 2020*, 2742–2749. AAAI Press.

Baumann, R. 2011. Splitting an argumentation framework. In *Proc. LPNMR 2011*, 40–53. Springer.

Baumann, R. 2016. Characterizing equivalence notions for labelling-based semantics. In *Proc KR 2016*, 22–32.

Bodanza, G. A., and Tohmé, F. A. 2009. Two approaches to the problems of self-attacking arguments and general odd-length cycles of attack. *Journal of Applied Logic* 7(4):403–420. Special Issue: Formal Models of Belief Change in Rational Agents.

Caminada, M. 2006. Semi-stable semantics. *COMMA* 144:121–130.

Caminada, M. 2007. Comparing two unique extension semantics for formal argumentation: ideal and eager. In *Proc. BNAIC 2007*, 81–87. Utrecht University Press.

Caminada, M. 2014. Strong admissibility revisited. In *Computational Models of Argument - Proceedings of COMMA 2014*, 197–208.

Dauphin, J.; Rienstra, T.; and van der Torre, L. 2020. A principle-based analysis of weakly admissible semantics. In *Proc. COMMA 2020*, volume 326 of *Frontiers in Artificial Intelligence and Applications*, 167–178. IOS Press.

Dauphin, J.; Rienstra, T.; and van der Torre, L. 2021. New weak admissibility semantics for abstract argumentation. In *Proc. CLAR 2021*, volume 13040 of *Lecture Notes in Computer Science*, 112–126. Springer.

Dondio, P., and Longo, L. 2021. Weakly complete semantics based on undecidedness blocking. *arXiv preprint arXiv:2103.10701*.

Dondio, P. 2018. A proposal to embed the in dubio pro reo principle into abstract argumentation semantics based on topological ordering and undecidedness propagation. In *Proceedings of the 2nd Workshop on Advances In Argumentation In Artificial Intelligence, 2018*, volume 2296 of *CEUR Workshop Proceedings*, 42–56. CEUR-WS.org.

Dung, P. M.; Mancarella, P.; and Toni, F. 2007. Computing ideal sceptical argumentation. *Artificial Intelligence* 171(10):642–674.

Dung, P. M. 1995. On the acceptability of arguments and its fundamental role in nonmonotonic reasoning, logic programming and n-person games. *Artificial Intelligence* 77(2):321–357.

Dunne, P. E.; Dvořák, W.; Linsbichler, T.; and Woltran, S. 2015. Characteristics of multiple viewpoints in abstract argumentation. *Artificial Intelligence* 228:153–178.

Dvorák, W., and Dunne, P. E. 2018. Computational problems in formal argumentation and their complexity. In *Handbook of Formal Argumentation*. College Publications.

Dvořák, W., and Gaggl, S. A. 2014. Stage semantics and the scc-recursive schema for argumentation semantics. *Journal of Logic and Computation* 26(4):1149–1202.

Dvorák, W.; Ulbricht, M.; and Woltran, S. 2021. Recursion in abstract argumentation is hard - on the complexity of semantics based on weak admissibility. In *Proc AAAI 2021*, 6288–6295. AAAI Press.

Fan, X., and Toni, F. 2015. On computing explanations in argumentation. In *Proceedings of the Twenty-Ninth AAAI Conference on Artificial Intelligence, January 25-30, 2015, Austin, Texas, USA*, 1496–1502. AAAI Press.

Oikarinen, E., and Woltran, S. 2011. Characterizing strong equivalence for argumentation frameworks. *Artificial Intelligence* 175:1985–2009.

van der Torre, L., and Vesic, S. 2018. The principle-based approach to abstract argumentation semantics. In *Handbook of Formal Argumentation*. College Publications.

Vassiliades, A.; Flouris, G.; Patkos, T.; Bikakis, A.; Bassiliades, N.; and Plexousakis, D. 2021. A multi attack argumentation framework. In *International Conference on Logic and Argumentation*, 417–436. Springer.

Weydert, E. 2011. Semi-stable extensions for infinite frameworks. In *Benelux Conference on Artificial Intelligence*, 336–343.

Yu, L.; Chen, D.; Qiao, L.; Shen, Y.; and van der Torre, L. 2021. A principle-based analysis of abstract agent argumentation semantics. In *Proc. KR 2021, Online event, November 3-12, 2021*, 629–640.

Sticky Policies in OWL2: Extending $\mathcal{PL}$ with Fixpoints and Transitive Closure

Piero A. Bonatti, **Luigi Sauro**,
Università di Napoli Federico II
{pab, luigi.sauro}@unina.it

Abstract

$\mathcal{PL}$ is a low-complexity profile of OWL2, expressly designed to encode data usage policies and personal data protection regulations - such as the GDPR - in a machine understandable way. With $\mathcal{PL}$, the compliance of privacy policies with the GDPR and with the data subjects' consent to processing can be checked automatically and in real time. In this paper, we extend $\mathcal{PL}$ to support "sticky policies". They are a sort of license that applies to data transfers, and specifies how the recipient can use the data. Sticky policies may be "recursive", i.e. they may apply not only to the first data transfer, but also to all subsequent transfer operations that the (direct or indirect) recipients may execute in the future. Recursive sticky policies can be encoded with fixpoints or transitive role closure. In this paper we prove that such extensions make compliance checking intractable. Since the scalability of compliance checking is a major requirement in this area, these results justify a specialized, polynomial-time approach to encoding sticky policies.

1 Introduction

The European General Data Protection Regulation (GDPR) has changed the landscape of personal data processing. Due to the heavy sanctions and reputation loss incurred in case of violations, the legal entities that process personal data (*controllers* in GDPR's terminology), are calling for automated support to compliance. The European H2020 projects SPECIAL[1] and TRAPEZE[2] tackle this need by means of semantic technnologies, that effectively yield reliability, interoperability, extensibility, flexibility, usability and scalability (Bonatti, Sauro, and Langens 2021). In particular, usability and scalability have been addressed in SPECIAL by identifying a profile of OWL2, called OWL2-PL (policy language), that is simpler to grasp for users with no background in logic, and can be processed very efficently using specialized reasoners (Bonatti et al. 2020). The description logic correponding to OWL2-PL is called $\mathcal{PL}$. One of the goals of TRAPEZE is extending $\mathcal{PL}$ with additional constructs, so as to support more general use cases. In this paper we focus on extending $\mathcal{PL}$ to support *sticky policies*. They are a sort of license that applies to data transfers, and specifies how direct and indirect recipients can use the data. Before delving into technical details, let us summarize the basic features of the semantic policy framework of SPECIAL and TRAPEZE that we are going to enrich.

The privacy policies of controllers, the consent to processing of data subjects, and the personal data protection regulations themselves are all policies. A policy can be identified with the set of operations authorized by the policy; such operations can be abstracted as tuples of attributes (Bonatti, De Capitani di Vimercati, and Samarati 2002). Accordingly, the semantic policy framework encodes policies in OWL2 as classes of reified tuples. In the personal data protection domain, the characteristic attributes of operations include (not exclusively) the data category being processed, the purpose and the nature of the processing, the third parties with which data are shared, the legal basis of the processing, and other information related to the regulation (Bonatti et al. 2020). For example, a privacy policy stating that email addresses are transferred to third parties for advertising purposes, based on the data subject's consent, is encoded in description logics as follows:

$$\begin{aligned}&\exists \mathsf{has\_data}.\mathsf{Email} \sqcap \\ &\quad \exists \mathsf{has\_processing}.\mathsf{Transfer} \sqcap \\ &\quad \exists \mathsf{has\_purpose}.\mathsf{Advertising} \sqcap \\ &\quad \exists \mathsf{has\_legal\_basis}.\mathsf{Consent}\,.\end{aligned}$$

A (privacy) policy P *complies* with a policy P' (a consent statement or regulation) if, and only if, all the operations authorized by P are also authorized by P', that is, P is a subclass of P'. Thus, compliance checking is naturally reduced to *subsumption checking* in description logic. For example, if Email is a subclass of Contact (contact data) and Advertising a subclass of Marketing, then the above policy complies with the consent to transferring contact data to third parties for marketing purposes, which is formalized as:

$$\begin{aligned}&\exists \mathsf{has\_data}.\mathsf{Contact} \sqcap \\ &\quad \exists \mathsf{has\_processing}.\mathsf{Transfer} \sqcap \\ &\quad \exists \mathsf{has\_purpose}.\mathsf{Marketing}\,.\end{aligned}$$

Note that the classical semantics of subsumption checking (based on entailment) treats policies as *closed* policies, that is, only what is explicitly allowed is permitted. For example, a privacy policy whose purpose is not subsumed by Marketing would not comply with the above consent statement.

[1] https://specialprivacy.ercim.eu/
[2] https://trapeze-project.eu/

Data transfers can be constrained with sticky policies. For instance, the above consent statement can be refined to state that third parties are allowed (only) to directly use the data subject's contact information for marketing purposes (which implicitly forbids further transfers to third parties, if we assume that Transfer is *not* subsumed by DirectUse):

$$\begin{array}{l}\exists\mathsf{has\_data.Contact}\sqcap\\ \quad\exists\mathsf{has\_processing.Transfer}\sqcap\\ \quad\exists\mathsf{has\_purpose.Marketing}\sqcap\\ \quad\exists\mathsf{sticky.}(\\ \qquad\exists\mathsf{has\_data.Contact}\sqcap\\ \qquad\exists\mathsf{has\_processing.DirectUse}\sqcap\\ \qquad\exists\mathsf{has\_purpose.Marketing})\,.\end{array}$$

Property "sticky" should be functional in order to avoid the ambiguities that may arise from the application of different, overlapping policies.

By nesting sticky policies, one may allow further transfers to third parties, as in the following expression:

$$P_0 \sqcap \exists\mathsf{sticky}.(P_1 \sqcap \exists\mathsf{sticky}.(P_2 \sqcap \ldots \exists\mathsf{sticky}.P_n \ldots))\,.$$

Here the controller should satisfy P_0, while its direct recipients have to satisfy P_1; in turn, their recipients should satisfy P_2, and so on. Clearly, the above concept regulates only finite disclosure chains of length n. In general, however, disclosure chains can be unbounded. Then sticky policies should be *recursive*, that is, they should identically apply to all (direct and indirect) recipients, and allow each of them to further transfer data to other third parties. Formally, one would like to express something like the infinitary concept

$$P_0 \sqcap \exists\mathsf{sticky}.(P_1 \sqcap \exists\mathsf{sticky}.(P_1 \sqcap \exists\mathsf{sticky}.(P_1 \sqcap \ldots)))\,.$$

Logic provides at least two ways of expressing the above class with a finite expression: greatest fixpoint operators (ν) and transitive role closure (R^+). Since sticky is a functional property, the following are equivalent to the above concept:

$$P_0 \sqcap \nu X.(\exists\mathsf{sticky}.(P_1 \sqcap X))\,,$$
$$P_0 \sqcap (\exists\mathsf{sticky}.P_1) \sqcap \forall\mathsf{sticky}^+.(\exists\mathsf{sticky}.P_1)\,.$$

Accordingly, in this paper, we are going to investigate the extensions of $\mathcal{PL}$ with greatest fixpoints, universal quantifiers, and transitive role closure. The ultimate goal is supporting sticky policies in a very efficient manner, as some of the use cases of interest to the industrial partners of SPECIAL and TRAPEZE require to complete thousands of compliance checks per second.

Example 1 (Streaming Scenario)**.** Telecom providers, that today are also Internet providers, receive from their base stations about 15000 call records per second, and almost 10000 probing records per second from their wi-fi network. The data contained in the aforementioned records are of great interest for strategic applications and services, such as location-based services and taylored recommendations; however, call and probing records contain personal data, and the European regulation on data protection prohibits the above usage without the consent of the data subjects. Without consent, even storing the data temporarily, waiting for a batch process to discard the records that cannot be processed, is illegal. Then the description of how and why each application processes the data must be checked in real-time for compliance with the consent statements that apply to the records being processed. This scenario is further complicated by the fact that each data subject can withdraw or modify her consent anytime, and that she may selectively decide to opt in or out each processing option (e.g. a customer might accept only location tracking, and not internet tracking). □

More generally, subsumption checks are going to be as frequent as access control checks in our target applications. Therefore, the semantic policy framework must satisfy extreme scalability requirements, that are not common in the knowledge representation area. Thus, an implied necessary requirement is that *subsumption checking must be possible in deterministic polynomial time*, and the degree of the polynomial should be low.

In (Bonatti et al. 2020), it has been proved – both theoretically and experimentally – that $\mathcal{PL}$ satisfies the scalability requirement, and that real policies can be checked for compliance in a few hundreds of μ-seconds using a sequential Java implementation (i.e. a technology that is not intrinsically performant). The challenge now is supporting sticky policies while preserving the performance of $\mathcal{PL}$.

In sections 3 and 4 we prove that the extensions of $\mathcal{PL}$ with ν, and with the combination of $\forall$ and transitive role closure – respectively – are intractable. We prove lower complexity bounds at the first level of the polynomial hierarchy; they suffice to conclude that the above extensions of $\mathcal{PL}$ are not suitable for our purposes. Concerning upper complexity bounds, the complexity of the logics supporting ν and transitive role closure is typically much higher, namely, EXPTIME or harder, if a full set of boolean operators is supported. In our setting, getting a tighter complexity estimate is difficult, due to the limited expressiveness of $\mathcal{PL}$; this aspect is further detailed in section 6.

The intractability results justify a tractable approach tailored to the use cases, based on a restricted language $\mathcal{PL}_0^{\mathsf{sticky}}$ that will be illustrated in section 5. This language preserves the asymptotic complexity of reasoning of $\mathcal{PL}$, so it is a promising approach to sticky policy representation.

The basic notions about description logics and $\mathcal{PL}$ are recalled in the next section. Related and future works are discussed in section 6.

2 Preliminary Definitions

We assume the reader to be familiar with the basic notions of Description Logics (DL) (Baader et al. 2003). Here we recall only the aspects needed for this work. The DL languages of our interest are built from countably infinite sets of concept names ($\mathsf{N_C}$), role names ($\mathsf{N_R}$), and concrete property names ($\mathsf{N_F}$). An *interpretation* $\mathcal{I}$ is a structure $\mathcal{I} = (\Delta^{\mathcal{I}}, \cdot^{\mathcal{I}})$ where $\Delta^{\mathcal{I}}$ is a nonempty set, and the *interpretation function* $\cdot^{\mathcal{I}}$ is such that (i) $A^{\mathcal{I}} \subseteq \Delta^{\mathcal{I}}$ if $A \in \mathsf{N_C}$; (ii) $R^{\mathcal{I}} \subseteq \Delta^{\mathcal{I}} \times \Delta^{\mathcal{I}}$ if $R \in \mathsf{N_R}$; (iii)$f^{\mathcal{I}} \subseteq \Delta^{\mathcal{I}} \times \mathbb{N}$ if $f \in \mathsf{N_F}$, where $\mathbb{N}$ denotes the set of natural numbers.

Compound concepts and roles are built from concept names, role names, and the logical constructors listed in Ta-

Name	Syntax	Semantics
transitive closure	R^+	$\bigcup_{i\geq 1}(R^i)^{\mathcal{I}} \quad (R \in \mathsf{N_R})$
top	$\top$	$\top^{\mathcal{I}} = \Delta^{\mathcal{I}}$
bottom	$\bot$	$\bot^{\mathcal{I}} = \emptyset$
complement	$\neg C$	$\neg C^{\mathcal{I}} = \Delta^{\mathcal{I}} \setminus C^{\mathcal{I}}$
intersection	$C \sqcap D$	$(C \sqcap D)^{\mathcal{I}} = C^{\mathcal{I}} \cap D^{\mathcal{I}}$
union	$C \sqcup D$	$(C \sqcup D)^{\mathcal{I}} = C^{\mathcal{I}} \cup D^{\mathcal{I}}$
existential restriction	$\exists R.C$	$\{d \in \Delta^{\mathcal{I}} \mid \exists (d,e) \in R^{\mathcal{I}} : e \in C^{\mathcal{I}}\}$
universal restriction	$\forall R.C$	$\{d \in \Delta^{\mathcal{I}} \mid \forall (d,e) \in R^{\mathcal{I}} : e \in C^{\mathcal{I}}\}$
interval restrictions	$\exists f.[\ell, u]$	$\{d \in \Delta^{\mathcal{I}} \mid \exists i \in [\ell, u] : (d,i) \in f^{\mathcal{I}}\}$

Table 1: Syntax and semantics of some DL constructs.

$\mathcal{PL}$ axiom α	$\mathcal{I} \models \alpha$ iff:
$A \sqsubseteq B$	$A^{\mathcal{I}} \subseteq B^{\mathcal{I}}$
$A_1 \sqcap \cdots \sqcap A_n \sqsubseteq B$	$A_1^{\mathcal{I}} \cap \cdots \cap A_n^{\mathcal{I}} \subseteq B^{\mathcal{I}}$
$\mathsf{disj}(A, B)$	$A^{\mathcal{I}} \cap B^{\mathcal{I}} = \emptyset$
$\mathsf{range}(R, A)$	$(x,y) \in R^{\mathcal{I}} \rightarrow y \in A^{\mathcal{I}}$
$\mathsf{func}(R)$	$(x,y) \in R^{\mathcal{I}} \wedge (x,z) \in R^{\mathcal{I}} \rightarrow y = z$

Table 2: Axioms for $\mathcal{PL}$ knowledge bases. Here A, with possible subscripts, and B range over concept names while R is a role name.

ble 1. We use metavariables A, B for concept names, C, D for (possibly compound) concepts, R, S for role names, and f, g for concrete property names. The third column shows how to extend the valuation $\cdot^{\mathcal{I}}$ of an interpretation $\mathcal{I}$ to compound expressions; in the first row, let $(R^1)^{\mathcal{I}} = R^{\mathcal{I}}$ and $(R^i)^{\mathcal{I}} = R^{\mathcal{I}} \circ (R^{i-1})^{\mathcal{I}}$, for all $i > 1$.

In (Bonatti et al. 2020) several extensions of $\mathcal{PL}$ are considered, where knowledge bases can be expressed with fragments of Horn-$\mathcal{SRIQ}$, under suitable restriction related to import-by-query and knowledge compilation techniques, cf. (Bonatti et al. 2020). Here, we consider only the axioms that suffice to prove our lower bounds. These axioms and the corresponding semantics are shown in Table 2.[3] As usual, an interpretation $\mathcal{I}$ is a model of a $\mathcal{PL}$ knowledge base $\mathcal{KB}$ (in symbols, $\mathcal{I} \models \mathcal{KB}$) if and only if $\mathcal{I} \models \alpha$, for all axioms α occurring in $\mathcal{KB}$.

In $\mathcal{PL}$, the query language differs from the knowledge base language, and is equipped with the constructs needed to express policies. Specifically, a *simple $\mathcal{PL}$ concept* is defined by the following grammar, where $A \in \mathsf{N_C}$, $R \in \mathsf{N_R}$, and $f \in \mathsf{N_F}$:

$$C ::= A \mid \bot \mid \exists f.[l,u] \mid \exists R.C \mid C \sqcap C\,.$$

A *full $\mathcal{PL}$ concept* is a union $D_1 \sqcup \ldots \sqcup D_n$ of simple $\mathcal{PL}$ concepts ($n \geq 1$). $\mathcal{PL}$'s *subsumption queries* are inclusions $C \sqsubseteq D$ where C, D are full $\mathcal{PL}$ concepts. A $\mathcal{PL}$ subsumption query $C \sqsubseteq D$ is *simple* if both C and D are simple.

If $\mathcal{KB}$ entails a subsumption query $C \sqsubseteq D$ (in symbols, $\mathcal{KB} \models C \sqsubseteq D$), then we say that C *complies with* D (under $\mathcal{KB}$). Compliance checking is in general coNP-complete, however it downgrades to P whenever the query $C \sqsubseteq D$ is *interval safe*, that is: for all interval constraints $\exists f.[l,u]$ and $\exists f'.[l',u']$ occurring in C and D, respectively, either $[l,u] \subseteq [l',u']$ or $[l,u] \cap [l',u'] = \emptyset$ (Bonatti et al. 2020).

Notably, coming back to the general case where C and D may contain partially overlapping intervals, and $C = C_1 \sqcup \cdots \sqcup C_n$, it is always possible to turn $C \sqsubseteq D$ into an equivalent, interval safe query by splitting the intervals of C in a suitable way. The resulting concept C' has size $O(|C| \cdot |D|^c)$, where $c = \max_{1 \leq i \leq n} c_i$ and each c_i is the number of interval constraints occurring in C_i, for $i = 1, \ldots, n$. Fortunately, the exponent c is a fixed constant in our use cases, therefore, C' can be computed in polynomial time and compliance checking is tractable. In particular, policy encoding requires at most one interval constraint per simple concept (such interval is used to specify how long data are kept by the controller). In the following, no more details about these complexity issues will be needed; the interested reader is referred to (Bonatti et al. 2020) for a complete discussion.

Hereafter, in order to keep different sources of complexity cleanly separated in the complexity analysis, we consider (and extend) the restricted logic $\mathcal{PL}_0$ obtained from $\mathcal{PL}$ by disallowing interval constraints – therefore, in $\mathcal{PL}_0$, subsumptions are vacuously interval safe, and subsumption checking is tractable. $\mathcal{PL}$ will be considered again in section 6.

Next, let us define the greatest fixpoint operator ν that will be used in section 3 to augment the query language. To this aim, we consider a supplementary countably infinite set $\mathsf{N_V}$ of *variables*; similarly to an atomic concept, a variable X is interpreted as a set of individuals, $X^{\mathcal{I}} \subseteq \Delta^{\mathcal{I}}$. Let $\mathcal{E}$ be a subset of $\Delta^{\mathcal{I}}$; by $\mathcal{I}[X \rightarrow \mathcal{E}]$ we mean the interpretation such that X is interpreted as $\mathcal{E}$, and all the other symbols are interpreted as in $\mathcal{I}$. Then, the semantics of a fixpoint concept $\nu X.C$ is the following:

$$(\nu X.C)^{\mathcal{I}} = \bigcup \{\mathcal{E} \subseteq \Delta^{\mathcal{I}} \mid \mathcal{E} \subseteq C^{\mathcal{I}[X \rightarrow \mathcal{E}]}\}\,.$$

Finally, a pointed interpretation is a pair $(\mathcal{I}, d)$, where $d \in \Delta^{\mathcal{I}}$. We say that $(\mathcal{I}, d)$ satisfies a concept C (in symbols, $\mathcal{I}, d \models C$) iff $d \in C^{\mathcal{I}}$. We also say that $(\mathcal{I}, d)$ is a model of a knowledge base $\mathcal{KB}$ if $\mathcal{I} \models \mathcal{KB}$.

3 $\mathcal{PL}$ with Fixpoints

Let $\mathcal{PL}_0^{\nu}$ be the extension of $\mathcal{PL}_0$ where greatest fixpoints may occur in subsumption queries. At a first glance, $\mathcal{PL}_0^{\nu}$ constitutes a promising way of encoding sticky policies, due to its similarity with $\mathcal{EL}$ with greatest fixpoints, that has been proved to be tractable in (Lutz, Piro, and Wolter 2010).

However, the interplay of greatest fixpoints with functional roles (that are supported only in $\mathcal{PL}$) makes subsumption checking at least coNP-hard. This holds not only for

[3]Interestingly, the axioms listed in Table 2 also suffice to axiomatize the vocabularies that are actually employed in the use cases of SPECIAL and TRAPEZE. Such vocabularies are being developed by the DPVCG,[4] a community group of the W3C devoted to the development of standardized data privacy vocabularies.

$\mathcal{PL}$, but also for all the description logics that support $\sqcap$, $\sqsubseteq$, and func in knowledge base axioms, and $\sqcap$, $\exists$, and ν in subsumption queries.

Theorem 2. *Let $\mathcal{DL}$ be any description logics that supports $\sqcap$, $\sqsubseteq$, and* func *in knowledge base axioms, and $\sqcap$, $\exists$, and ν in subsumption queries. Subsumption checking in $\mathcal{DL}$ is coNP-hard.*

Proof. The proof is by reduction of the validity problem to subsumption checking. Let $\phi = \bigvee_{i=1}^{m} \ell_{i,1} \wedge \ell_{i,2} \wedge \ell_{i,3}$ be any propositional formula in 3-DNF, and let $x_1, \ldots, x_k$ be the propositional variables occurring in ϕ. Introduce a fresh concept name A_i for each x_i and a fresh concept name $\bar{A}_i$ for each negative literal $\neg x_i$. For each propositional literal ℓ, let $\tilde{\ell}$ denote the corresponding concept name. Informally speaking, the knowledge base $\mathcal{KB}$ encodes ϕ in such a way that if an individual d satisfies ϕ (up to the correspondence between literals and concepts), then d satisfies also a distinguished atomic concept F that represents the truth of ϕ. More formally, let $\mathcal{KB}$ consist of the following axioms, where each concept B_i represents the truth of the i-th disjunct of ϕ:

$$\tilde{\ell}_{i,1} \sqcap \tilde{\ell}_{i,2} \sqcap \tilde{\ell}_{i,3} \sqsubseteq B_i$$
$$B_i \sqsubseteq F$$
$$\mathsf{func}(R)$$

(where $i = 1, \ldots, m$). The use of role R will be explained later.

Greatest fixpoints are used to create periodic chains of instance types. To make this more precise, we need some auxiliary definitions. First, for all $i = 1, \ldots, k$ (where k is the number of propositional variables in ϕ), define

$$\begin{aligned} C_i^1 &= A_i \sqcap \exists R.X \\ C_i^{j+1} &= \bar{A}_i \sqcap \exists R.C_i^j \end{aligned}$$

(where X is a concept variable). For example,

$$\begin{aligned} C_i^2 &= \bar{A}_i \sqcap \exists R.(A_i \sqcap \exists R.X) \\ C_i^3 &= \bar{A}_i \sqcap \exists R.(\bar{A}_i \sqcap \exists R.(A_i \sqcap \exists R.X)) \\ C_i^4 &= \bar{A}_i \sqcap \exists R.(\bar{A}_i \sqcap \exists R.(\bar{A}_i \sqcap \exists R.(A_i \sqcap \exists R.X))) \\ &\vdots \end{aligned}$$

Note that the instances of any concept $\nu X.C_i^j$ are the first elements of infinite R-chains where A_i is satisfied (at least) every j steps, while the other elements satisfy (at least) $\bar{A}_i$.

Let $p_1 = 2, p_2 = 3, p_3 = 5, \ldots, p_k$ be the first k prime numbers, and define:

$$C = \prod_{i=1}^{k} \nu X.C_i^{p_i} \,. \tag{1}$$

Claim: ϕ is valid iff $\mathcal{KB} \models C \sqsubseteq \nu X.(F \sqcap \exists R.X)$.

First we prove the "only if" part of the claim. If ϕ is valid, then for all models $\mathcal{I}$ of $\mathcal{KB}$ and all individuals $d \in \Delta^{\mathcal{I}}$, the following clearly holds: If d belongs to $A_i^{\mathcal{I}}$ or $\bar{A}_i^{\mathcal{I}}$ for all $i = 1, \ldots, k$, then $d \in F^{\mathcal{I}}$. Note that C forces all the direct and indirect R-successors of its instances to be in $A_i^{\mathcal{I}}$ or $\bar{A}_i^{\mathcal{I}}$, for all $i = 1, \ldots, k$, so all such successors are in $F^{\mathcal{I}}$. It follows, by definition of ν, that all the instances of C belong to $\nu X.(F \sqcap \exists R.X)$, which proves the "only if" part of the claim.

To prove the "if" part of the claim, suppose that ϕ is not valid, and construct a counterexample $\mathcal{I}$ to the subsumption as follows. Let $\Delta^{\mathcal{I}}$ be an infinite set $\{d_i \mid i \in \mathbb{N}\}$. Let $R^{\mathcal{I}} = \{(d_i, d_{i+1}) \mid i \in \mathbb{N}\}$. For all $i \in \mathbb{N}$ and $j = 1, \ldots, k$, let $d_i \in A_j^{\mathcal{I}}$ iff $i \bmod p_j = 0$, and let $\bar{A}_j^{\mathcal{I}} = \Delta^{\mathcal{I}} \setminus A_j^{\mathcal{I}}$. Finally, for all $i = 1, \ldots, m$, let $B_i^{\mathcal{I}} = (\tilde{\ell}_{i,1} \sqcap \tilde{\ell}_{i,2} \sqcap \tilde{\ell}_{i,3})^{\mathcal{I}}$ and $F^{\mathcal{I}} = \bigcup_{i=1}^{m} B_i^{\mathcal{I}}$. By construction, we have both that $\mathcal{I}$ satisfies $\mathcal{KB}$, and $d_1 \in C^{\mathcal{I}}$. Moreover, since the numbers $p_1, \ldots, p_k$ that determine the periodic behavior of C's fixpoints are distinct prime numbers, the individuals $d_1, d_2, \ldots, d_i, \ldots$ collectively satisfy all possible combinations of literal encodings that contain no pair of complementary concepts A_j and $\bar{A}_j$ ($j = 1, \ldots, k$). So the concepts satisfied by $\mathcal{I}$'s elements represent all possible truth assignments to $x_1, \ldots, x_k$.[5] One of this truth assignments falsifies ϕ, by assumption, so – by construction – there exists $d_j \in \Delta^{\mathcal{I}}$ such that $d_j \notin F^{\mathcal{I}}$. As a consequence, $d_1 \notin \nu X.(F \sqcap \exists R.X)$. This proves that $C^{\mathcal{I}} \not\subseteq \nu X.(F \sqcap \exists R.X)^{\mathcal{I}}$, which completes the proof of the claim.

The reduction is correct by the claim; we are only left to show that it can be computed in polynomial time. The size of the knowledge base and the size of the concept $\nu X.(F \sqcap \exists R.X)$ are obviously polynomial in the size of ϕ, so we only have to provide a polynomial bound on the size of C. In order to see this, we use a results by Rosser (Rosser 1941). The kth prime number p_k is bounded by

$$p_k < k(\log k + \log\log k + 2)$$

so, for sufficiently large k, $p_k < 2k^2$. It follows that the length of each concept $\nu X.C_i^{p_i}$ in (1) is $O(k^2)$ and the entire concept C is $O(k^3)$, so the reduction can be computed in polynomial time.[6] □

As a corollary, subsumption checking in $\mathcal{PL}_0^{\nu}$ is coNP-hard, even if neither disjointness axioms nor range axioms are used, and only one functional role is used.

4 $\mathcal{PL}$ with Universal Restrictions and Transitive Role Closure

Transitive role closure provides an alternative way of expressing sticky policies. Transitive closure can be regarded as a restricted form of fixpoint: every concept of the form $\forall R^+.C$ can be expressed with ν as $\nu X.\forall R.(C \sqcap X)$. So, reasoning in $\mathcal{PL}_0$ with transitive role closure might turn out to be less complex than reasoning in $\mathcal{PL}_0$ with greatest fixpoints. Unfortunately, tractability is not preserved, due to the interplay of $\forall$ and $\exists$. We are going to prove that the NP-complete EXACT COVER (XC) problem can be reduced

[5] In particular, each propositional interpretation $\{x_{i_1}, \ldots, x_{i_n}\}$ corresponds to the element d_h with $h = \prod_{l=1}^{n} p_{i_l}$.

[6] It is not hard to see that it can even be computed in logarithmic space.

to subsumption in two extensions of $\mathcal{PL}_0$ that employ the operators $\forall$ and $\cdot^+$ needed to encode sticky policies.

We prove these results by adapting a reduction of XC to concept (un)satisfiability in $\mathcal{ALE}$, extensively illustrated in (Donini 2003, Sec. 3.3.1). Let us first recall the definition of the problem:

Definition 3 (EXACT COVER, XC). *Given a finite set* $U = \{u_1, \dots, u_n\}$ *and a family* $\mathcal{M} = \{M_1, \dots, M_m\}$ *of subsets of* U*, decide whether there exist an* exact cover *of* U*, that is, a family of mutually disjoint sets* $M_{i_1}, \dots, M_{i_q}$ *whose union equals* U*.*

The following lemma introduces the reduction and states its correctness :

Lemma 4. (Donini 2003) *An instance of* XC *has an exact cover if, and only if, the concept* $C_\mathcal{M}$ *defined below is unsatisfiable:*

$$C_\mathcal{M} = C_1^1 \sqcap \ldots \sqcap C_1^m \sqcap D$$

where each C_l^j *is inductively defined as*

$$C_{2n+1}^j = \top \quad \textit{(base case)}$$

$$C_l^j = \begin{cases} \exists R.C_{l+1}^j & \textit{either } l \le n \wedge u_l \in M_j \textit{ or} \\ & n < l \le 2n \wedge u_{l-n} \in M_j \\ \forall R.C_{l+1}^j & \textit{either } l \le n \wedge u_l \notin M_j \textit{ or} \\ & n < l \le 2n \wedge u_{l-n} \notin M_j \end{cases}$$

and $D = \underbrace{\forall R.\forall R.\ldots\forall R}_{2n}.\bot$.

Example 5. Let $U = \{u_1, u_2\}$ and $\mathcal{M} = \{M_1, M_2\}$, where $M_1 = \{u_1\}$ and $M_2 = \{u_2\}$. Concept $C_\mathcal{M}$ is

$$\begin{array}{ll} \exists R.\forall R.\exists R.\forall R.\top \sqcap & (C_1^1) \\ \forall R.\exists R.\forall R.\exists R.\top \sqcap & (C_1^2) \\ \forall R.\forall R.\forall R.\forall R.\bot & (D) \end{array}$$

Note that this instance of XC has an exact cover ($\mathcal{M}$ itself) and $C_\mathcal{M}$ is indeed inconsistent. □

Lemma 4 was proved by showing that an exact cover exists iff the tableaux for $C_\mathcal{M}$ has a clash, caused by a node labelled with both $\top$ and $\bot$, where $\top$ has been introduced by some of the concepts C_1^j and $\bot$ has been introduced by D. Clearly, the same result can be obtained by replacing $\top$ (that is not supported in $\mathcal{PL}$) with a concept name A. So, from Lemma 4, we get:

Corollary 6. *Let* $C_\mathcal{M}^A$ *be the concept resulting from* $C_\mathcal{M}$ *by replacing each occurrence of* $\top$ *with concept name* A*. An instance of* XC *has an exact cover if, and only if, the concept* $C_\mathcal{M}^A$ *is unsatisfiable.*

It follows that subsumption is intractable in the extension of $\mathcal{PL}_0$ with $\forall$, that will be denoted by $\mathcal{PL}_0^\forall$.

Corollary 7. *Subsumption checking in* $\mathcal{PL}_0^\forall$ *is NP-hard, even if the knowledge base is empty.*

Proof. The exact cover problem is reduced to subsumption as follows: let A and B two distinct concept names. For a given instance of XC, the corresponding concept $C_\mathcal{M}^A$ and B have no symbols in common, therefore $C_\mathcal{M}^A \sqsubseteq B$ is valid iff $C_\mathcal{M}^A$ is unsatisfiable. Then this corollary immediately follows from Corollary 6. □

As a last attempt to restore tractability, one may consider another extension of $\mathcal{PL}_0$ where the problematic quantifier $\forall$ can be used only in conjunction with transitive role closure (as required by sticky policy modeling), and viceversa. In other words, expressions like $\forall R^+.C$ and $\exists R.C$ are permitted, while $\forall R.C$ and $\exists R^+.C$ are disallowed. This logic will be denoted with $\mathcal{PL}_0^{\forall+}$. This attempt is motivated by the observation that if $\forall R$ were replaced with $\forall R^+$ in $C_\mathcal{M}^A$, then the resulting concept would not capture exact covers anymore.

Example 8. Let $U = \{u_1, u_2, u_3\}$ and $\mathcal{M} = \{M_1, M_2\}$, where $M_1 = \{u_1\}$ and $M_2 = \{u_2\}$. The replacement of $\forall R$ with $\forall R^+$ in $C_\mathcal{M}^A$ yields:

$$\begin{array}{l} \exists R.\forall R^+.\forall R^+.\exists R.\forall R^+.\forall R^+.A \sqcap \\ \forall R^+.\exists R.\forall R^+.\forall R^+.\exists R.\forall R^+.A \sqcap \\ \forall R^+.\forall R^+.\forall R^+.\forall R^+.\forall R^+.\forall R^+.\bot \end{array}$$

The concepts in the first two lines create an infinite sequence of R-successors that clashes with the concept in the third line. So the above concept is inconsistent although this instance of XC has no exact covers. □

Unfortunately, the restriction on $\forall$ and $\cdot^+$ does not yield a tractable logic, either. First note that the reduction reported in Lemma 4 works equally well if different roles are used at each level, as in the following example.

Example 9. The concept $C_\mathcal{M}$ illustrated in Example 5 could be equivalently replaced with

$$\begin{array}{l} \exists R_1.\forall R_2.\exists R_3.\forall R_4.\top \sqcap \\ \forall R_1.\exists R_2.\forall R_3.\exists R_4.\top \sqcap \\ \forall R_1.\forall R_2.\forall R_3.\forall R_4.\bot\,. \end{array}$$

□

This version preserves the correspondence with XC stated in Lemma 4, because the tableaux produced by the two reductions have the same structure and differ only in the role names. Now each $\forall R_i$ can be equivalently replaced with $\forall R_i^+$; more precisely, it is easy to verify that also this second change preserves the structure of the tableaux for $C_\mathcal{M}$, and that the only difference is that $\forall R_i$ is replaced by $\forall R_i^+$ in node labels.

As a consequence of the above discussion, subsumption checking in $\mathcal{PL}_0^{\forall+}$ is intractable due to the following reduction from XC:

Lemma 10. *An instance of* XC *has an exact cover if, and only if, the concept* $C'^A_\mathcal{M}$ *defined below is unsatisfiable:*

$$C'^A_\mathcal{M} = C'^1_1 \sqcap \ldots \sqcap C'^m_1 \sqcap D'$$

where each C'^j_l *is inductively defined as*

$$C'^j_{2n+1} = A \quad \textit{(base case)}$$

$$C'^j_l = \begin{cases} \exists R_l.C'^j_{l+1} & \textit{either } l \le n \wedge u_l \in M_j \textit{ or} \\ & n < l \le 2n \wedge u_{l-n} \in M_j \\ \forall R_l^+.C'^j_{l+1} & \textit{either } l \le n \wedge u_l \notin M_j \textit{ or} \\ & n < l \le 2n \wedge u_{l-n} \notin M_j \end{cases}$$

and $D' = \forall R_1^+.\forall R_2^+.\ldots.\forall R_{2n}^+.\bot$.

The lower complexity bound (next theorem) can be proved by analogy with the proof of Corollary 7, using $C'^{A}_{\mathcal{M}}$ and Lemma 10 in place of $C^{A}_{\mathcal{M}}$ and Corollary 6.

Theorem 11. *Subsumption checking in* $\mathcal{PL}_0^{\forall+}$ *is NP-hard.*

5 Towards A Tractable Approach

Here we introduce a language tailored to the encoding of sticky policies. Such a specialized approach is motivated by the intractability results proved in the previous sections. The complexity caused by the interactions between ν and $\exists$ identified in section 3 will be avoided by restricting the language so as to allow only simple, linear recursions whose cyclic behavior has period 1.

Definition 12 (Pol,$\mathcal{PL}_0^{\mathsf{sticky}}$). *Let* Pol *be the least language containing:*

- *all the simple concepts of* $\mathcal{PL}_0$ *with no occurrence of* sticky *(called* sticky-free *concepts);*
- *all the concepts* $C \sqcap \exists\mathsf{sticky}.D$ *such that* C *is a* sticky-free $\mathcal{PL}_0$ *concept and* D *a* ν*-free concept in* Pol*;*
- *all the concepts* $C \sqcap \nu X.\exists(\mathsf{sticky}.D \sqcap X)$ *such that* C *and* D *are* sticky-free $\mathcal{PL}_0$ *concepts.*

$\mathcal{PL}_0^{\mathsf{sticky}}$ *knowledge bases are* $\mathcal{PL}$ *knowledge bases containing only axioms from Table 2, and at least the axiom* func(sticky)*, that must also be the unique axiom where* sticky *occurs.* $\mathcal{PL}_0^{\mathsf{sticky}}$ *subsumption queries are expressions* $C \sqsubseteq D$ *where* C *and* D *are in* Pol.

Example 13. The following policies are in Pol and can be used in $\mathcal{PL}_0^{\mathsf{sticky}}$ subsumption queries:

∃has_data.Contact ⊓
∃has_processing.Transfer ⊓
∃has_purpose.Marketing ⊓
∃sticky.(
  ∃has_data.Contact ⊓
  ∃has_processing.Transfer ⊓
  ∃has_purpose.Marketing ⊓
  ∃sticky.(
    ∃has_data.Contact ⊓
    ∃has_processing.DirectUse ⊓
    ∃has_purpose.Marketing)) .

∃has_data.Contact ⊓
∃has_processing.Transfer ⊓
∃has_purpose.Marketing ⊓
νX.∃sticky.(
  ∃has_data.Contact ⊓
  ∃has_processing.SomeProcessing ⊓
  ∃has_purpose.Marketing ⊓ X) . □

$\mathcal{PL}_0^{\mathsf{sticky}}$ subsumption checking can be reduced to the same problem in $\mathcal{PL}_0$. To see this, we first prove a lemma that considers the four possible cases in which the given $\mathcal{PL}_0^{\mathsf{sticky}}$ subsumption contains the fixpoint operator ν (the other $\mathcal{PL}_0^{\mathsf{sticky}}$ subsumptions are just classic $\mathcal{PL}_0$ subsumptions). Each case is reduced to a small number of $\mathcal{PL}_0$ subsumptions.

Lemma 14. *Let* $\mathcal{KB}$ *be a* $\mathcal{PL}_0^{\mathsf{sticky}}$ *knowledge base, and let* C*,* D*,* E*, and* F *be* sticky-free Pol *concepts.*

1. $\mathcal{KB} \models C \sqcap \nu X.\exists\mathsf{sticky}.(D \sqcap X) \sqsubseteq E \sqcap \nu X.\exists\mathsf{sticky}.(F \sqcap X)$ *iff some of the following conditions hold:*
   - $\mathcal{KB} \models C \sqsubseteq \bot$,
   - $\mathcal{KB} \models D \sqsubseteq \bot$,
   - *both* $\mathcal{KB} \models C \sqsubseteq E$ *and* $\mathcal{KB} \models D \sqsubseteq F$ *hold;*
2. *if* G *is* ν*-free, then* $\mathcal{KB} \models G \sqsubseteq C \sqcap \nu X.\exists\mathsf{sticky}.(D \sqcap X)$ *iff* $\mathcal{KB} \models G \sqsubseteq \bot$*;*
3. *if* E *is both* ν*-free and* sticky-free*, then* $\mathcal{KB} \models C \sqcap \nu X.\exists\mathsf{sticky}.(D \sqcap X) \sqsubseteq E$ *iff either* $\mathcal{KB} \models C \sqsubseteq E$ *or* $\mathcal{KB} \models D \sqsubseteq \bot$*;*
4. *if* G *is* ν*-free but not* sticky-free*, that is,*

$$G = G_0 \sqcap \exists\mathsf{sticky}.(G_1 \sqcap \exists\mathsf{sticky}.(...\exists\mathsf{sticky}.G_n...)) \quad (2)$$

   (where $G_0, \ldots, G_n$ *are* sticky-free $\mathcal{PL}_0$ *concepts), then* $\mathcal{KB} \models C \sqcap \nu X.\exists\mathsf{sticky}.(D \sqcap X) \sqsubseteq G$ *iff some of the following conditions hold:*
   - $\mathcal{KB} \models C \sqsubseteq \bot$,
   - $\mathcal{KB} \models D \sqsubseteq \bot$,
   - *both* $\mathcal{KB} \models C \sqsubseteq G_0$ *and* $\mathcal{KB} \models D \sqsubseteq G_1 \sqcap \ldots \sqcap G_n$ *hold;*

Proof. We start by proving statement 2. Since G is ν-free, it belongs to $\mathcal{PL}_0$, therefore – if consistent w.r.t. $\mathcal{KB}$– it has a finite tree-shaped model that satisfies $\mathcal{KB}$ (Bonatti et al. 2020). In such models, the concept on the right-hand side (that has only infinite models) is empty, so the subsumption is false. It follows easily that the subsumption holds iff $\mathcal{KB} \models G \sqsubseteq \bot$. This proves 2.

Proof of 3, "if". If $\mathcal{KB} \models C \sqsubseteq E$, then the subsumption holds because its left-hand side is subsumed by C and $\sqsubseteq$ is transitive. If $\mathcal{KB} \models D \sqsubseteq \bot$, then also $\mathcal{KB} \models \nu X.\exists\mathsf{sticky}.(D \sqcap X) \sqsubseteq \bot$, so the subsumption holds because its left-hand side is subsumed by $\bot$.

Proof of 3, "only if". By contraposition, assume that $\mathcal{KB} \not\models C \sqsubseteq E$ and $\mathcal{KB} \not\models D \sqsubseteq \bot$. Then there exist two pointed interpretations $(\mathcal{I}_1, d_1)$ and $(\mathcal{I}_2, d_2)$, that are models of $\mathcal{KB}$, and satisfy the sticky-free concepts $C \sqcap \neg E$ and D, respectively. We may assume w.l.o.g. that $\mathcal{I}_1$ and $\mathcal{I}_2$ are disjoint. Define an interpretation $\mathcal{J}$ as the union of $\mathcal{I}_1$ and $\mathcal{I}_2$ extended with the following definition of sticky: $\mathsf{sticky}^{\mathcal{J}} = \{(d_1, d_2), (d_2, d_2)\}$. By construction, $\mathcal{J}$ satisfies $\mathcal{KB}$: indeed, the union of $\mathcal{I}_1$ and $\mathcal{I}_2$ satisfies $\mathcal{KB}$ by the disjoint model union property (Bonatti et al. 2020), and the definition of sticky satisfies func(sticky), that is the unique axiom involving sticky in $\mathcal{KB}$. Moreover, by construction, $(\mathcal{J}, d_1)$ satisfies the left-hand side of the subsumption but not E. Then $\mathcal{J}$ witnesses that the subsumption does not hold.

Proof of 1. The "if" part is straightforward and left to the reader. The "only if" part is proved similarly to the previous case. More precisely, by contraposition, assume that $\mathcal{KB} \not\models C \sqsubseteq \bot$, $\mathcal{KB} \not\models D \sqsubseteq \bot$, and either $\mathcal{KB} \not\models C \sqsubseteq E$ or $\mathcal{KB} \not\models D \sqsubseteq F$ holds. In the former case, construct a counterexample $(\mathcal{J}, d_1)$ to the subsumption by composing two models of $C \sqcap \neg E$ and D, respectively, as shown in the proof of statement 3. Similarly, in the latter case, construct a counterexample $(\mathcal{J}, d_1)$ to the subsumption by composing two models of C and $D \sqcap \neg F$, respectively.

Proof of 4, "if". Let FP denote the fixpoint expression in the left-hand side of the subsumption, and note that the left-hand side is equivalent to:

$$C \sqcap \underbrace{\exists \mathsf{sticky}.(D \sqcap \exists \mathsf{sticky}.(\ldots \exists \mathsf{sticky}.(D}_{n \text{times}} \sqcap FP)\ldots))$$

This makes the left-hand side directly comparable with (2). Now the "if" part is straightforward and left to the reader.

Proof of 4, "only if". By contraposition, assume that $\mathcal{KB} \not\models C \sqsubseteq \bot$, $\mathcal{KB} \not\models D \sqsubseteq \bot$, and either $\mathcal{KB} \not\models C \sqsubseteq G_0$ or $\mathcal{KB} \not\models D \sqsubseteq G_1 \sqcap \ldots \sqcap G_n$ holds. In the former case, obtain a counterexample to the subsumption by composing two models of $C \sqcap \neg G_0$ and D, respectively, as shown in the proof of 3. In the latter case, there exists i $(1 \leq i \leq n)$ such that $\mathcal{KB} \not\models D \sqsubseteq D_i$. Then obtain a counterexample to the subsumption by composing two models of C and $D \sqcap \neg G_i$, respectively, using the same approach as in 3. □

As a consequence of the above lemma, we get:

Theorem 15. *Subsumption checking in $\mathcal{PL}_0^{\mathsf{sticky}}$ can be done in polynomial time.*

Proof. $\mathcal{PL}_0^{\mathsf{sticky}}$ subsumption checking can always be reduced to subsumption checking in $\mathcal{PL}_0$. In particular, for all given $\mathcal{PL}_0^{\mathsf{sticky}}$ subsumptions $C \sqsubseteq D$, either C and D are ν-free (so $C \sqsubseteq D$ is a $\mathcal{PL}_0$ subsumption), or $C \sqsubseteq D$ falls in one of the four cases covered by Theorem 14. For each of these cases, Theorem 14 provides an equivalent set of subsumption checks that involve $\mathcal{PL}_0$ concepts only (as ν-free $\mathcal{PL}_0^{\mathsf{sticky}}$ concepts are $\mathcal{PL}_0$ concepts). Since subsumption checking in $\mathcal{PL}_0$ is in PTIME, the same holds for $\mathcal{PL}_0^{\mathsf{sticky}}$. □

Note that, in the worst case, a subsumption check in $\mathcal{PL}_0^{\mathsf{sticky}}$ is reduced to four subsumption checks in $\mathcal{PL}_0$, therefore $\mathcal{PL}_0^{\mathsf{sticky}}$ preserves the asymptotic complexity of compliance checking in $\mathcal{PL}_0$.

6 Discussion and Related Work

The approach to sticky policies outlined in the previous section is only a first step towards a complete tractable solution. The language $\mathcal{PL}_0^{\mathsf{sticky}}$ does not yet support some of the features of $\mathcal{PL}$, such as intervals and unions. These two features are related, because the normalization of intervals that makes $\mathcal{PL}$ subsumption queries interval-safe (hence tractable) introduces unions. Some of these unions may occur within the range of ν, and it is not possible – in general – to move them to the top level to reduce general policies to mere unions of Pol concepts. Therefore, it is necessary to investigate the interplay of fixpoints and unions, and its potential impact on complexity. We conjecture that – with a careful definition of $\mathcal{PL}^{\mathsf{sticky}}$ – interval safety can still be obtained efficiently (given the natural restrictions satified by policies), and that the proof of Theorem 14 can be generalized to prove that tractability is preserved also in the presence of intervals and unions. Of course, the theoretical complexity analysis shall be complemented by an experimental performance evaluation to see if the ad hoc framework meets the scalability requirements of use cases.

Another limitation of the current version of $\mathcal{PL}_0^{\mathsf{sticky}}$ is that a single consent policy cannot permit both finite and infinite data transfer chains at the same time (cf. Theorem 14, point 2), while in some cases it may be useful to state that any number of transfers is permitted. Thus, $\mathcal{PL}_0^{\mathsf{sticky}}$ should be extended to support classes that may contain both finite and infinite chains, such as:

$$\nu X.\big((\exists \mathsf{sticky}.(C \sqcap X)) \sqcup D\big) ,$$

where C is a policy that admits transfers and D a policy that does not admit transfers. This provides an independent motivation for introducing unions within the scope of ν.

It is not easy to turn the lower complexity bounds presented in this paper into exact characterizations. On the one hand, the extensions of $\mathcal{PL}$ that we considered make it possible to axiomatize complex, exponentially large structures, like those used in some proofs of PSPACE-hardness; on the other hand, the limited expressiveness of $\mathcal{PL}$ (and in particular the restrictions on union and negation) makes it difficult to use those structures to reconstruct the complexity results that have been proved for DLs that (unlike $\mathcal{PL}$) support a full set of boolean concept operators. An additional difficulty stems from the fact that, in $\mathcal{PL}$'s extensions, fixpoints and transitive role closures may occur only in the queries and cannot be used inside axioms.

The logic $\mathcal{PL}_0^{\forall}$ investigated in Section 4 is similar to $\mathcal{FL}_0$, in some respects. It has been proved in (Nebel 1990) that subsumption checking in $\mathcal{FL}_0$ is coNP-complete for acyclic TBoxes.

Fixpoints have been extensively investigated in the context of description logics, see for example (Calvanese, Giacomo, and Lenzerini 1999; Bonatti and Peron 2004; Bonatti et al. 2008; Lutz, Piro, and Wolter 2010; Franconi and Toman 2011). Most of these papers deal with expressive logics whose reasoning tasks are at least EXPTIME-hard (sometimes even undecidable). The only exception is (Lutz, Piro, and Wolter 2010), that proves the tractability of $\mathcal{EL}$ with greatest fixpoints. This logic and $\mathcal{PL}_0^{\nu}$ have several traits in common. The intractability of $\mathcal{PL}_0^{\nu}$ is due to the interplay of functionality axioms (not supported by $\mathcal{EL}$) with the fixpoints occurring in the queries.

The seminal work that started the investigation of transitive role closures is (Sattler 1996). One of its results is the proof that extending $\mathcal{ALC}$ with transitive role closure makes concept satisfiability EXPTIME-complete. Subsumption checking has the same complexity because, in $\mathcal{ALC}$ and its extensions, concept satisfiability and subsumption checking are mutually reducible to each other. The complexity of transitive role closure in $\mathcal{EL}$ has been studied in (Haase and Lutz 2008). It is proved that subsumption checking is complete for coNP, PSPACE, and EXPTIME if TBoxes are empty, acyclic, and cyclic, respectively.

It may be interesting to investigate whether regular path queries can be used to model sticky policies. A rich set of results on nested regular path queries and low-complexity DLs can be found in (Bienvenu et al. 2014). However, this paper deals with query evaluation, while the counterpart of compliance checking (i.e. subsumption checking) is query containment.

We conclude by pointing out that the same approach adopted for data usage policies works out of the box for *licenses in financial data markets*, an area that has similar requirements (i.e. support to data transfers, and need for massive and reliable compliance checking, in order to reduce the risks of sanctions due to license violations). Moreover, the "Share Alike" Creative Commons licence has a transitive nature, much like sticky policies. These observations open up a brand new range of applications for $\mathcal{PL}$ and its extensions.

Acknowledgments

This work is funded by the European Union with grant n. 883464. The autors are grateful to the anonymous reviewers for their insightful and constructive comments.

References

Baader, F.; Calvanese, D.; McGuinness, D. L.; Nardi, D.; and Patel-Schneider, P. F., eds. 2003. *The Description Logic Handbook: Theory, Implementation, and Applications*. Cambridge University Press.

Bienvenu, M.; Calvanese, D.; Ortiz, M.; and Simkus, M. 2014. Nested regular path queries in description logics. In Baral, C.; Giacomo, G. D.; and Eiter, T., eds., *Principles of Knowledge Representation and Reasoning: Proceedings of the Fourteenth International Conference, KR 2014, Vienna, Austria, July 20-24, 2014*. AAAI Press.

Bonatti, P. A., and Peron, A. 2004. On the undecidability of logics with converse, nominals, recursion and counting. *Artif. Intell.* 158(1):75–96.

Bonatti, P. A.; Lutz, C.; Murano, A.; and Vardi, M. Y. 2008. The complexity of enriched mu-calculi. *Log. Methods Comput. Sci.* 4(3).

Bonatti, P. A.; Ioffredo, L.; Petrova, I. M.; Sauro, L.; and Siahaan, I. S. R. 2020. Real-time reasoning in OWL2 for GDPR compliance. *Artif. Intell.* 289:103389.

Bonatti, P. A.; De Capitani di Vimercati, S.; and Samarati, P. 2002. An algebra for composing access control policies. *ACM Trans. Inf. Syst. Secur.* 5(1):1–35.

Bonatti, P. A.; Sauro, L.; and Langens, J. 2021. Representing consent and policies for compliance. In *IEEE European Symposium on Security and Privacy Workshops, EuroS&P 2021, Vienna, Austria, September 6-10, 2021*, 283–291. IEEE.

Calvanese, D.; Giacomo, G. D.; and Lenzerini, M. 1999. Reasoning in expressive description logics with fixpoints based on automata on infinite trees. In Dean, T., ed., *Proceedings of the Sixteenth International Joint Conference on Artificial Intelligence, IJCAI 99, Stockholm, Sweden, July 31 - August 6, 1999. 2 Volumes, 1450 pages*, 84–89. Morgan Kaufmann.

Donini, F. M. 2003. Complexity of reasoning. In Baader et al. (2003). 96–136.

Franconi, E., and Toman, D. 2011. Fixpoints in temporal description logics. In Walsh, T., ed., *IJCAI 2011, Proceedings of the 22nd International Joint Conference on Artificial Intelligence, Barcelona, Catalonia, Spain, July 16-22, 2011*, 875–880. IJCAI/AAAI.

Haase, C., and Lutz, C. 2008. Complexity of subsumption in the family of description logics: Acyclic and cyclic tboxes. In Ghallab, M.; Spyropoulos, C. D.; Fakotakis, N.; and Avouris, N. M., eds., *ECAI 2008 - 18th European Conference on Artificial Intelligence, Patras, Greece, July 21-25, 2008, Proceedings*, volume 178 of *Frontiers in Artificial Intelligence and Applications*, 25–29. IOS Press.

Lutz, C.; Piro, R.; and Wolter, F. 2010. Enriching $\mathcal{EL}$-concepts with greatest fixpoints. In Coelho, H.; Studer, R.; and Wooldridge, M. J., eds., *ECAI 2010 - 19th European Conference on Artificial Intelligence, Lisbon, Portugal, August 16-20, 2010, Proceedings*, volume 215 of *Frontiers in Artificial Intelligence and Applications*, 41–46. IOS Press.

Nebel, B. 1990. Terminological reasoning is inherently intractable. *Artif. Intell.* 43(2):235–249.

Rosser, B. 1941. Explicit bounds for some functions of prime numbers. *American Journal of Mathematics* 63(1):211–232.

Sattler, U. 1996. A concept language extended with different kinds of transitive roles. In Görz, G., and Hölldobler, S., eds., *KI-96: Advances in Artificial Intelligence, 20th Annual German Conference on Artificial Intelligence, Dresden, Germany, September 17-19, 1996, Proceedings*, volume 1137 of *Lecture Notes in Computer Science*, 333–345. Springer.

Region-Based Merging of Open-Domain Terminological Knowledge

Zied Bouraoui[1], **Sébastien Konieczny**[1], **Thanh Ma**[1], **Nicolas Schwind**[2], **Ivan Varzinczak**[1]
[1]CRIL, Univ. Artois & CNRS, France
[2]National Institute of Advanced Industrial Science and Technology, Tokyo, Japan
nicolas-schwind@aist.go.jp, {bouraoui,konieczny,ma,varzinczak}@cril.fr

Abstract

This paper introduces a novel method for merging open-domain terminological knowledge. It takes advantage of the Region Connection Calculus (RCC5), a formalism used to represent regions in a topological space and to reason about their set-theoretic relationships. To this end, we first propose a faithful translation of terminological knowledge provided by several and potentially conflicting sources into region spaces. The merging is then performed on these spaces, and the result is translated back into the underlying language of the input sources. Our approach allows us to benefit from the expressivity and the flexibility of RCC5 while dealing with conflicting knowledge in a principled way.

1 Introduction

Commonsense knowledge is playing an increasingly important role in the development of AI systems. Such knowledge is available, for example, in large open-domain terminological knowledge bases Cyc or SUMO as ontological knowledge, in knowledge graphs (KGs) such as DBpedia and WikiData, and as semantic markup (e.g., RDFa). Ontologies, as frameworks for expressing terminological knowledge, encode structured relations about the concepts and properties of a given domain. In this paper, we focus on terminological knowledge about concepts that can be expressed using ontologies as these latter are playing an important role in areas such as semantic web (Homburg, Staab, and Janke 2020), information retrieval (Chen et al. 2019), natural language processing (Rospocher and Corcoglioniti 2018), and machine learning (Hohenecker and Lukasiewicz 2020), among others. For instance, Bouraoui and Schockaert (2018) have shown that knowledge encoded in ontologies, as prior conceptual knowledge, is useful for learning concept representations from few examples.

However, the available ontologies (and KGs, as simple ontologies) are inevitably incomplete, where several rules and facts are missing. Several methods have been proposed for automated ontology (KG) completion (Beltagy et al. 2013; Rocktäschel and Riedel 2017; Li, Bouraoui, and Schockaert 2019) that exploit statistical regularities in a given ontology to predict plausible missing rules or facts. Unfortunately, meaningful knowledge is difficult to predict, especially when only a few examples of facts or rules are available. Moreover, as most of the existing approaches are mainly based on statistical regularities, the resulting predictions might be conflicting with each other. A repair-based mechanism is then required to maintain the consistency of the set of terminological statements, i.e., ensure that there are no conflicting (or contradictory) statements. In the same perspective, to widen the coverage of terminological knowledge to several domains and to deal with incompleteness and conflicting statements, one may combine knowledge from several sources. However, it turns out that merging open-domain knowledge bases is a particularly challenging task as pointed out, for example, in (Tanon et al. 2016) reporting the different problems and difficulties encountered when merging Freebase with WikiData. Conflicting information may occur when the statements of several sources are simply gathered together. Ontology merging and alignment / matching has also attracted much attention in the literature (Thiéblin, Haemmerlé, and Trojahn 2018; Chang, wei Chen, and Zhang 2019; Benferhat et al. 2019; Zhao and Zhang 2016; Laadhar et al. 2017; Thiéblin, Haemmerlé, and Trojahn 2018). The approach generally consists in studying an equivalence matching between a source and target taxonomy. In this work, we assume that all knowledge encoded by the different sources are already aligned and mapped to each other. Namely, we suppose that they share the same terminology. Hence, while ontology alignment (or matching) is the process of determining correspondences between terminologies of ontologies, ontology *merging* aims to combine two (or more) ontologies having the same terminology while handling conflicting statements.

Let us consider an example to illustrate the merging problem. Assume that a first source says that the concept $Paper$ is disjoint with the concept $Document$, while another source says that every $Paper$ is a $Document$. Obviously enough, these two statements are conflicting. To be faithful to both sources while resolving conflicts, a sensible choice would be to assume that $Paper$ and $Document$ are not disjoint concepts, but every $Paper$ is not necessarily a $Document$, that is, the two concepts *partially overlap*. This kind of result is clearly consistent and can be seen as a good compromise between both sources. Finding a meaningful and relevant compromise between sources during the merging process is difficult to obtain. This is mainly due the fact that ontology languages (Description Logics for example) are not expressive enough to capture salient knowledge that might emerge during the merging process. The simple example pointed out above clearly shows some pieces of knowledge that should be taken into account during the merging process, but that cannot be captured in the ontology language. The problem of ontology (or DL) merging is close to the problem of belief merging in a propositional setting (Benferhat et al. 2019; Benferhat et al. 2014; Kumar and Harding 2016; Wang et al. 2012; Patricia, Konieczny, and Marquis 2008). For instance, Benferhat *et al.* (2019) studied merging assertional bases in the *DL-Lite* fragment. They have determined the minimal subsets of assertions to resolve conflicts based on the inconsistency minimization principle. Bouraoui et al. (2020a) proposed a model-based merging operator for merging $\mathcal{EL}$ ontologies which solves semantic conflicts that arise during the merging process.

In this paper, to handle the merging problem, we take inspiration from conceptual spaces, which are geometric representation frameworks, in which the objects are represented as points in a topological space, and concepts are modelled as regions (Haarslev and Möller 1997; Gärdenfors 2000; Douven et al. 2022). Motivated by the fact that conceptual knowledge in an ontology can be to some extent modelled as geometric objects and constraints on metric spaces (Bouraoui et al. 2020b), this paper proposes a method for ontology merging that takes advantage of *qualitative spatial reasoning* to find out a relevant compromise between sources while resolving conflicts. Qualitative spatial reasoning is a suitable paradigm for efficiently reasoning about spatial entities and their relationships, where knowledge is represented as a so-called *qualitative constraint network (QCN)*. Spatial information is usually represented in terms of basic or non-basic relations in a qualitative calculus, where reasoning tasks are then formulated as solving a set of qualitative constraints (Randell, Cui, and Cohn 1992; Cohn et al. 1997; Bhatt et al. 2011; Sioutis, Long, and Janhunen 2020). In particular, the Region Connection Calculus (RCC) is a well-studied formalism for qualitative topological representation and reasoning, including its subsets *RCC-5* (Schockaert and Li 2013) and *RCC-8* (Randell, Cui, and Cohn 1992). Two significant advantages of the RCC framework are its ability to reason efficiently about the relationships between spatial entities, and its ability to deal with conflicts in qualitative constraint merging as shown in (Condotta et al. 2010; Thau, Bowers, and Ludäscher 2009). In short, the representation of region constraints into QCNs allows for more expressivity than when using DL rules (or constraints). In particular, QCNs are expressive enough to allows for disjunctions in the constraints.

Several QCN merging operators have been introduced in the literature (e.g., (Condotta et al. 2009; Condotta et al. 2010; Thau, Bowers, and Ludäscher 2009; Julien and Westphal 2012). Roughly speaking, these operators compute a distance between QCN scenarios and the input QCNs. Then the scenarios with a minimal distance are selected as the best candidates for the merged result. Taking inspiration from these works, in this paper we take advantage of the RCC-5 formalism and propose a method for merging open-domain terminological knowledge (simply called ontologies) using QCNs. We first show how to translate such knowledge into qualitative spaces while preserving its semantics and properties. Second, we propose a merging operator that produces a single and consistent region space representing a compromise between sources. Lastly, we show how to express the region space in the input ontology language while maintaining all relevant information.

The proofs of propositions are available online[1].

2 Background

Our method is based on two complementary frameworks for merging open-domain terminological knowledge: we rely on a lightweight Description Logic (DL) framework to encode knowledge and use RCC-5 and qualitative constraints for performing the merging. This section briefly recalls the technical background required on these two topics.

Description Logics. $\mathcal{EL}$ is a family of lightweight DLs, which underlies the Ontology Web Language profile OWL2-EL, that is considered as one of the main representation formalisms to express terminological knowledge (Baader, Brandt, and Lutz 2005). The main ingredients of DLs are individuals, concepts, and roles, which correspond at the semantic level to objects, sets of objects, and binary relations between objects. More formally, let N_C, N_R, N_I be three pairwise disjoint sets where N_C denotes a set of atomic concepts, N_R denotes a set of atomic relations (roles), and N_I denotes a set of individuals. In this paper, we consider $\mathcal{EL}_\perp$ concept expressions (Kriegel 2020) which are built according to the following grammar:

$$C ::= \top \mid \perp \mid N_C \mid C \sqcap C \mid \exists r.C \text{ where } r \in N_R.$$

Let $C, D \in N_C$, $a, b \in N_I$, and $r \in N_R$. An $\mathcal{EL}$ ontology $O = \langle \mathcal{T}, \mathcal{A} \rangle$ (a.k.a. knowledge base) comprises two components, the TBox (Terminological Box denoted by $\mathcal{T}$) and ABox (denoted by $\mathcal{A}$). The TBox consists of a set of General Concept Inclusion (GCI) axioms of the form $C \sqsubseteq D$, meaning that C is more specific than D or simply C is subsumed by D, and axioms of the form $C \sqcap D \sqsubseteq \perp$, meaning that C and D are disjoint concepts. The ABox is a finite set of assertions on individual objects of the form $C(a)$ or $r(a, b)$.

The semantics is given in terms of interpretations $\mathcal{I} = (\Delta^\mathcal{I}, \cdot^\mathcal{I})$, which consist of a non-empty interpretation domain $\Delta^\mathcal{I}$ and an interpretation function $\cdot^\mathcal{I}$ that maps each individual $a \in N_I$ into an element $a^\mathcal{I} \in \Delta^\mathcal{I}$, each concept $A \in N_C$ into a subset $A^\mathcal{I} \subseteq \Delta^\mathcal{I}$, and each role $r \in N_R$ into a subset $r^\mathcal{I} \subseteq \Delta^\mathcal{I} \times \Delta^\mathcal{I}$.

A summary of the syntax and semantics of $\mathcal{EL}_\perp$ is shown in Table 1. An interpretation $\mathcal{I}$ is said to be a model of (or satisfies) an axiom Φ in the form of the left column in the table, denoted by $\mathcal{I} \models \Phi$, when the corresponding condition in the right column is satisfied. For instance, $\mathcal{I} \models C \sqsubseteq D$ if and only if $C^\mathcal{I} \subseteq D^\mathcal{I}$. Similarly, $\mathcal{I}$ satisfies a concept (resp. role) assertion, denoted by $\mathcal{I} \models C(a)$ (resp. $\mathcal{I} \models r(a, b)$), if $a^\mathcal{I} \in C^\mathcal{I}$ (resp. $(a^\mathcal{I}, b^\mathcal{I}) \in r^\mathcal{I}$). An interpretation $\mathcal{I}$ is a model of an ontology O if it satisfies all the axioms and assertions in O. An ontology is said to be consistent if it has

[1] https://arxiv.org/abs/2205.02660

Syntax	Semantics
$C \sqsubseteq D$	$C^{\mathcal{I}} \subseteq D^{\mathcal{I}}$
r	$r^{\mathcal{I}} \subseteq \Delta^{\mathcal{I}} \times \Delta^{\mathcal{I}}$
a	$a^{\mathcal{I}} \in \Delta^{\mathcal{I}}$
$C \sqcap D$	$C^{\mathcal{I}} \cap D^{\mathcal{I}}$
$\top$	$\Delta^{\mathcal{I}}$
$\bot$	$\emptyset$
$\exists r.C$	$\{x \in \Delta^{\mathcal{I}} \mid \exists y \in \Delta^{\mathcal{I}} s.t.(x, y) \in r^{\mathcal{I}}, y \in C^{\mathcal{I}}\}$

Table 1: Syntax and semantics of $\mathcal{EL}_{\bot}$

Name (Symbol)	Syntax	Semantics
Proper Part of (PP)	$v_C\{PP\}v_D$	$v_C^{\mathcal{S}} \subset v_D^{\mathcal{S}}$
Inverse PP of (PPi)	$v_C\{PPi\}v_D$	$v_D^{\mathcal{S}} \subset v_C^{\mathcal{S}}$
Equals (EQ)	$v_C\{EQ\}v_D$	$v_C^{\mathcal{S}} = v_D^{\mathcal{S}}$
Disjoint From (DR)	$v_C\{DR\}v_D$	$v_C^{\mathcal{S}} \cap v_D^{\mathcal{S}} = \emptyset$
Partially Overlaps (PO)	$v_C\{PO\}v_D$	$v_C^{\mathcal{S}} \cap v_D^{\mathcal{S}} \neq \emptyset$ $v_C^{\mathcal{S}} \not\subseteq v_D^{\mathcal{S}}, v_D^{\mathcal{S}} \not\subseteq v_C^{\mathcal{S}}$

Table 2: Syntax and semantics of *RCC-5*, $v_C, v_D \in V$.

a model. Otherwise, it is inconsistent. An axiom Φ is entailed by an ontology, denoted by $\mathcal{O} \models \Phi$, if Φ is satisfied by every model of $\mathcal{O}$. We say that C is subsumed by D w.r.t. an ontology $\mathcal{O}$ iff $\mathcal{O} \models C \sqsubseteq D$. Similarly, we say that a is an instance of C w.r.t. $\mathcal{O}$ iff $\mathcal{O} \models C(a)$. An interpretation $\mathcal{I} = (\Delta^{\mathcal{I}}, \cdot^{\mathcal{I}})$ is said to be *fulfilling* when each concept name in the ontology is non-empty in $\mathcal{I}$, i.e., for each concept $C_i \in N_C$, $\cdot^{\mathcal{I}}(C_i) \neq \emptyset$.

The main reasoning task that is considered in terminological ontologies is classification. It consists in computing all the entailed subsumptions ($C \sqsubseteq D$) (and equivalences ($C \equiv D$)) that hold between atomic concepts of an ontology, or the concepts $\top$ or $\bot$. Such a procedure is described in (Baader, Brandt, and Lutz 2005), which first consists in transforming the ontology into a normal form using a set of rules, and then performing a classification reasoning process using the set of inference (completion) rules (see (Baader, Brandt, and Lutz 2005) for more details). In this paper, we assume that the input ontologies are provided in a specific normal form, to which we apply completion rules for classification. This classification step is to normalize the input ontologies. The reason of conducting normalization is to handle and transform the complex axioms into the axioms of all atomic concepts to be simpler for the translation process. That is, before translating the input ontologies into a region-based representation, we assume that each of them is in the *strict normal form*, i.e., if its TBox $\mathcal{T}$ only consists of inclusions of the fundamental form: $A \sqsubseteq B$, $A \sqcap B \sqsubseteq \bot$, $A \sqsubseteq \exists r.B$ and $\exists r.A \sqsubseteq B$ where $A, B \in N_C$. Such an assumption is made without loss of generality, since for each ontology $\mathcal{O}$, one can compute an ontology $\mathcal{O}'$ in the strict normal form in polynomial time (Baader, Brandt, and Lutz 2005).

Region Connection and Qualitative Constraints. The RCC (Region Connection Calculus) formalism allows one to represent and reason about the relationships between spatial entities (Randell, Cui, and Cohn 1992). Among the fragments of the RCC theory, RCC-5 fragment is expressive enough to reason about set-theoretic relations between regions (Bennett 1994; Peter and Thomas 1997). In RCC-5, regions can simply be interpreted as non-empty subsets of a given set and the focus is given on a set $\mathcal{B} = \{DR, PO, EQ, PP, PPi\}$ of five binary relations between regions called *basic relations*. The set $\mathcal{B}$ forms a jointly exhaustive and pairwise disjoint set of relations, that is, each pair of regions satisfies exactly one relation from $\mathcal{B}$: the relation DR (resp. PO, EQ, PP) holds between two regions whenever the two regions are disjoint (resp. when they partially overlap, are equal, when the first is a strict subset of the second), and PPi is the converse of PP. Based on $\mathcal{B}$, more complex pieces of information about the relative positions of a set of regions can be represented by means of qualitative constraint networks (QCNs). Formally, a QCN is a pair $\mathcal{N} = \langle V, \Psi \rangle$, where $V = \{v_C, v_D, \ldots\}$ is a set of region variables representing the spatial entities and Ψ is a set of binary constraints between these entities. Each constraint $\Psi_{CD} \in \Psi$ is a mapping from $V \times V$ to $2^{\mathcal{B}}$, and is simply denoted by $\Psi_{CD} = v_C\ \varphi\ v_D$, where $\varphi \subseteq 2^{\mathcal{B}}$; and Ψ_{CD} is said to be a singleton constraint whenever φ is a singleton.

An interpretation of a QCN $\mathcal{N}$ is defined as $\mathcal{S} = (\mathcal{D}^{\mathcal{S}}, \cdot^{\mathcal{S}})$, where $\mathcal{D}^{\mathcal{S}}$ is a non-empty set (the domain of the regions), and $\cdot^{\mathcal{S}}$ is an interpretation function which maps each variable v_C to a non-empty subset $v_C^{\mathcal{S}}$ of $\mathcal{D}^{\mathcal{S}}$. Table 2 precises how singleton constraints from Ψ are interpreted in RCC-5, i.e., an interpretation $\mathcal{S}$ of $\mathcal{N}$ satisfies a singleton constraint Ψ_{CD}, denoted by $\mathcal{S} \models \mathcal{N}$, if the relation between $v_C^{\mathcal{S}}$ and $v_D^{\mathcal{S}}$ according to the table is satisfied (e.g., $\mathcal{S} \models v_C\{PP\}v_D\}$ whenever $v_C^{\mathcal{S}} \subset v_D^{\mathcal{S}}$). The satisfaction relation is extended to any (non-singleton) constraint from $2^{\mathcal{B}}$ as follows: for each $\varphi \in 2^{\mathcal{B}}$, $\mathcal{S} \models v_C\ \varphi\ v_D$ iff $\mathcal{S} \models v_C\ \{\varphi_i\}\ v_D$ for some $\varphi_i \in \varphi$ (e.g., $\mathcal{S} \models v_C\{PP, EQ\}v_D$ iff $\mathcal{S} \models v_C\{PP\}v_D$ or $v_C\{EQ\}v_D\}$). An interpretation $\mathcal{S}$ of a QCN $\mathcal{N} = \langle V, \Psi \rangle$ is said to be a solution of $\mathcal{N}$, denoted by $\mathcal{S} \models \mathcal{N}$, iff $\mathcal{S} \models \Psi_{CD}$ for each $\Psi_{CD} \in \Psi$. A QCN is consistent iff it admits a solution. A sub-network of $\mathcal{N}$ is a QCN $\mathcal{N}' = \langle V, \Psi' \rangle$ such that $\Psi' \subseteq \Psi$. A quasi-atomic QCN $\langle V, \Psi \rangle$ is a QCN where for each $v_C, v_D \in V$, there is a unique constraint $\Psi_{CD} \in \Psi$, and where Ψ_{CD} is either a singleton or $\Psi_{CD} \in \{\{PP, EQ\}, \{PPi, EQ\}\}$. A scenario of a QCN is a quasi-atomic sub-network of $\mathcal{N}$. Noteworthy, a QCN is consistent if it admits a consistent scenario.

3 Merging Framework Description

This short section summarizes our method for merging open-domain terminological knowledge (i.e., ontologies) using qualitative constraint networks (QCNs). As highlighted in the introduction, QCNs are expressive enough to capture some relevant information that might emerge during the merging process, which in turn allows one to select a consistent compromise between sources when expressing the merging result.

The first task is to find a "faithful translation" from an ontology to a QCN that preserves the semantics and maintains the initial knowledge encoded in the ontology. Then, it is assumed that every input ontology is translated into a QCN, so we are given a multiset of QCNs, also called *profile*. The second task is then to define a merging operator that associates the QCN profile into a single QCN, representing the QCN profile in a global and consistent way. As constraints of the merged QCN are *sets* of basic relations, this QCN cannot be translated back into the target ontology language in the general case. So we select one of its "best" consistent scenarios which, in contrast, can be expressed as an ontology.

More precisely, our approach involves the following main steps:

1. The translation of terminological knowledge sources (i.e., the input ontologies given in the strict normal form) into QCNs (Section 4). In this step, we present a translation function that ensures the faithfulness of the translation from an ontology into a QCN.
2. The definition of a QCN merging operator (Section 5). Exploiting the notion of "distance" between basic relations and constraints, this step associates the input QCN profile (the translated ontologies) with a single merged, consistent QCN.
3. The selection of a "best" consistent scenario of the merged QCN as a candidate of the merged result (Section 6). This selection process takes advantage of the notion of distance between scenarios and some plausible instantiation of the input ontologies (i.e., some interpretations).
4. The translation of the selected consistent scenario back into an ontology, i.e., the underlying language of the input sources (Section 7).

4 Translating Terminological Knowledge into QCNs

In this section, we present a translation function from any ontology to a QCN. More precisely, we (1) map atomic concepts names into QCN variables and axioms into constraints, and (2) show that the translation is faithful to the TBox of the initial ontology.

Definition 1 (Forward translation $\tau_{\triangleright}$). *A **forward translation** is a function $\tau_{\triangleright} : N_C \longrightarrow V$ s.t. $\tau_{\triangleright}(C) \stackrel{\text{def}}{=} v_C$. $\tau_{\triangleright}$ is extended to map axioms in the (strict) normal form into constraints as follows:*

- $\tau_{\triangleright}(C \sqsubseteq D) \stackrel{\text{def}}{=} \tau_{\triangleright}(C)\{PP, EQ\}\tau_{\triangleright}(D)$, *and*
- $\tau_{\triangleright}(C \sqcap D \sqsubseteq \bot) \stackrel{\text{def}}{=} \tau_{\triangleright}(C)\{DR\}\tau_{\triangleright}(D)$.

Moreover, $\tau_{\triangleright}$ is extended to translate ontologies in the (strict) normal form into a set of constraints in the expected way: $\tau_{\triangleright}(O) \stackrel{\text{def}}{=} \{\tau_{\triangleright}(\Phi) \mid \Phi \in O\}$.

To show that the translation is faithful, we provide a "semantic" mapping from O to $\tau_{\triangleright}(O)$, and conversely. Let us first show how models of O correspond to solutions of $\tau_{\triangleright}(O)$:

Definition 2 (Flattening of an interpretation). *Let $\mathcal{I} = (\Delta^{\mathcal{I}}, \cdot^{\mathcal{I}})$ be a fulfilling interpretation. With $\mathcal{S}_{\mathcal{I}} \stackrel{\text{def}}{=} (\Delta^{\mathcal{I}}, \cdot^{\mathcal{S}_{\mathcal{I}}})$ we denote the **flattening of** $\mathcal{I}$, where $\cdot^{\mathcal{S}_{\mathcal{I}}} : V \longrightarrow 2^{\Delta^{\mathcal{I}}}$ is such that $(v_C)^{\mathcal{S}_{\mathcal{I}}} = C^{\mathcal{I}}$.*

Notably, non-fulfilling interpretations are not considered (are irrelevant) in the paper because the corresponding translation regions cannot be empty (are non-empty subsets) in RCC-5.

Theorem 1. *Let O be an ontology, and let $\mathcal{I}$ be a fulfilling interpretation of O such that $\mathcal{I} \models O$. Then $\mathcal{S}_{\mathcal{I}} \models \tau_{\triangleright}(O)$.*

The other way around, let us show how solutions of $\tau_{\triangleright}(O)$ correspond to interpretations satisfying all axioms from O.

Definition 3 (Inflation of a solution). *Let $\mathcal{S} = (\mathcal{D}^{\mathcal{S}}, \cdot^{\mathcal{S}})$ be a semantic solution to a QCN $\mathcal{N}$ over V. With $\mathcal{I}_{\mathcal{S}} \stackrel{\text{def}}{=} (\Delta^{\mathcal{I}_{\mathcal{S}}}, \cdot^{\mathcal{I}_{\mathcal{S}}})$, where $\Delta^{\mathcal{I}_{\mathcal{S}}} = \mathcal{D}^{\mathcal{S}}$ and, for every $A \in N_C$, $A^{\mathcal{I}_{\mathcal{S}}} = (v_A)^{\mathcal{S}}$, we call $\mathcal{I}_{\mathcal{S}}$ an **inflation of** $\mathcal{S}$.*

Intuitively, the inflation of $\mathcal{S}$ corresponds to an interpretation blown up from $\mathcal{S}$ by interpreting atomic concept names in the same way their corresponding variable names are "populated" by the solution. Notice that there are as many possible inflations of $\mathcal{S}$ as there are ways of interpreting N_R and N_I over $\Delta^{\mathcal{I}_{\mathcal{S}}}$. An immediate consequence of Definition 3 is that every inflation of a solution $\mathcal{S}$ is fulfilling.

Theorem 2. *Let O be an ontology and let $\mathcal{S}$ be a solution of $\tau_{\triangleright}(O)$. Then there is an inflation $\mathcal{I}_{\mathcal{S}}$ of $\mathcal{S}$ s.t. $\mathcal{I}_{\mathcal{S}} \models \Phi$ for each axiom Φ of O.*

Theorems 1 and 2 establish that our translation is faithful, i.e., that the set of all fulfilling models of an ontology O are captured precisely in its translated QCN $\tau_{\triangleright}(O)$.

5 QCN Merging

We reduce the merging of a profile of ontologies $\mathcal{P} = \langle O^1, \ldots, O^n \rangle$ to the merging of a profile of QCNs $\mathcal{N} = \langle \mathcal{N}^1, \ldots, \mathcal{N}^n \rangle$, where for each $i \in \{1, \ldots, n\}$, $\mathcal{N}^i = (V, \Psi^i) = \tau_{\triangleright}(O^i)$, based on the faithful translation given the previous section. Inspired by works on syntactical QCN merging (Condotta et al. 2010), this QCN merging process is summarized as follows. We associate with the profile $\mathcal{N}$ a single merged and consistent QCN $\mathcal{N} = (V, \Psi)$ representing $\mathcal{N}$ in a "global" way. This is performed in a constraint-wise fashion: for each pair of variables $v_C, v_D \in V$, we associate each basic relation $b \in \mathcal{B}$ with a value representing its *distance* to the profile of constraints $\mathscr{C}_{CD} = \langle \Psi^1_{CD}, \ldots, \Psi^n_{CD} \rangle$. This distance is the key tool to form the constraint Ψ_{CD} of the merged QCN $\mathcal{N}$. Intuitively, each constraint Ψ_{CD} corresponds to the set of basic relations with the lowest distances to the profile $\mathscr{C}_{CD}$, while ensuring that the resulting QCN is consistent.

Example 1. *Consider the profile of ontologies $\mathcal{P} = \langle O^1, O^2, O^3, O^4 \rangle$ that encodes the following knowledge about the four concepts of Paper, Text, Document and Book, respectively denoted by P, T, D and B*[2].

[2]An implementation to illustrate our method is also made available at the following link: https://github.com/ontologymerging/MergingOntologyWithQCN.

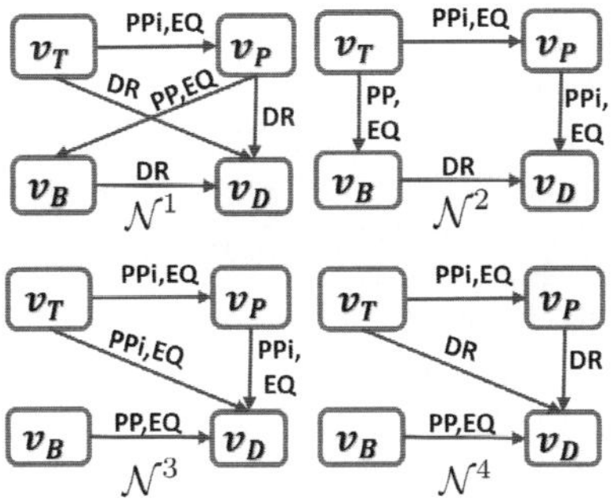

Figure 1: QCN profile of Example 1

- $O^1 = \langle \mathcal{T}^1 = \{P \sqsubseteq T, T \sqcap D \sqsubseteq \bot, P \sqsubseteq B, P \sqcap D \sqsubseteq \bot, B \sqcap D \sqsubseteq \bot\}, \mathcal{A}^1 = \{P(p_1), T(p_1), T(t_1), D(d_1), B(p_1), B(b_1)\}\rangle$,
- $O^2 = \langle \mathcal{T}^2 = \{P \sqsubseteq T, T \sqsubseteq B, D \sqsubseteq B, D \sqsubseteq P\}, \mathcal{A}^2 = \{P(p_2), P(d_2), T(p_2), T(t_2), D(d_2), B(p_2), B(b_2)\}\rangle$,
- $O^3 = \langle \mathcal{T}^3 = \{B \sqsubseteq D, D \sqsubseteq P, P \sqsubseteq T, D \sqsubseteq T\}, \mathcal{A}^3 = \{P(p_3), T(t_3), T(p_3), D(d_3), B(b_3)\}\rangle$,
- $O^4 = \langle \mathcal{T}^4 = \{D \sqcap P \sqsubseteq \bot, P \sqsubseteq T, B \sqsubseteq D, T \sqcap B \sqsubseteq \bot, T \sqcap D \sqsubseteq \bot\}, \mathcal{A}^4 = \{P(p_4), T(t_4), T(p_4), D(b_4), D(d_4), B(b_4)\}\rangle$.

Using the forward translation $\tau_\triangleright$ presented in the previous section, one associates with $\mathcal{P}$ a profile of QCNs $\langle \tau_\triangleright(O^i)\rangle = \langle \mathcal{N}^i\rangle$ ($i \in \{1, \ldots, 4\}$). The four QCNs are depicted in Figure 1 (to alleviate the figures, we do not represent the Ψ_{CD} when $\Psi_{CD} = \mathcal{B}$, i.e., when the QCN does not provide any information between the relationship between v_C and v_D).

Although we do not require it in the general case, note that in this example each ontology O^i is consistent, i.e., the TBox of each input ontology does not contain conflicting information. As a direct consequence of Theorem 1, each QCN is consistent. However, simply combining these QCNs can easily lead to conflicts. For instance, there is no basic relation shared in the constraints Ψ^1_{BD} and Ψ^3_{BD}, since in $\mathcal{N}^1$ we have that *Book* $\{DR\}$ *Document* whereas in $\mathcal{N}^3$ we have that *Book* $\{PP, EQ\}$ *Document*. This calls for our QCN merging procedure.

5.1 Computing a Distance between a Basic Relation and a Profile of Constraints

We start by considering a distance between basic relations. Firstly introduced in (Freksa 1992) in the context of temporal reasoning, the notion of *conceptual neighborhood* (CN) between relations was later adapted to QCN merging in (Condotta, Kaci, and Schwind 2008) to define such a distance. Intuitively, two basic relations $b, b' \in \mathcal{B}$ are CNs if a continuous transformation of two regions which satisfy the basic relation $b \in B$ leads them to directly satisfy the basic relation b' without satisfying any other basic relation from $\mathcal{B}$. For instance, PP and EQ are CNs since "shrinking" a first region C initially equal to another region D directly makes it a proper part of D. This results in the neighborhood relation $\{(DR, PO), (PO, DR), (PO, PP), (PP, PO), (PO, PPi), (PPi, PO), (PP, EQ), (EQ, PP), (PPi, EQ), (EQ, PPi)\}$. This neighborhood relation induces a *neighborhood graph* $\mathcal{G}$ whose vertices are the elements of $\mathcal{B}$, and where there is an edge between two basic relations $b, b' \in \mathcal{B}$ whenever b and b' are CNs according the neighborhood relation. The distance $d(b, b')$ between two basic relations b and b' is defined as the length of the shortest path between b and b' in the neighborhood graph. For instance, $d(DR, PO) = 1$ since DR and PO are CNs, and $d(DR, EQ) = 3$ since DR and PO (resp. (PO, PP) and (PP, EQ)) are CNs, but DR and EQ are not. This distance is extended to a distance between a basic relation $b \in \mathcal{B}$ and a constraint $\varphi \in 2^{\mathcal{B}}$, defined as $d(b, \varphi) = \min_{b' \in \varphi} d(b, b')$. Lastly, given two variables $v_C, v_D \in V$, the distance between each $b \in \mathcal{B}$ and the profile of constraints $\mathscr{E}_{CD} = \langle \Psi^1_{CD}, \ldots, \Psi^n_{CD}\rangle$ is defined by $d(b, \mathscr{E}_{CD}) = \sum_{i \in \{1,\ldots,n\}} d(b, \Psi^i_{CD})$.

Example 1 (continued). *Let us focus on Text (T) and Document (D). We have $\mathscr{E}_{TD} = \langle \Psi^1_{TD}, \Psi^2_{TD}, \Psi^3_{TD}, \Psi^4_{TD}\rangle = \langle \{DR\}, \mathcal{B}, \{PPi, EQ\}, \{DR\}\rangle$. For the distance between the basic relation PP and $\mathscr{E}_{TD}$, we have that $d(PP, \mathscr{E}_{TD}) = d(b, \Psi^1_{TD}) + d(b, \Psi^2_{TD}) + d(b, \Psi^3_{TD}) + d(b, \Psi^4_{TD})$, where:*

$$d(PP, \Psi^1_{TD}) = d(PP, \{DR\}) = d(PP, DR) = 2,$$
$$d(PP, \Psi^2_{TD}) = d(PP, \mathcal{B}) = d(PP, PP) = 0,$$
$$d(PP, \Psi^3_{TD}) = d(PP, \{PPi, EQ\}) = d(PP, EQ) = 1,$$
$$d(PP, \Psi^4_{TD}) = d(PP, \{DR\}) = d(PP, DR) = 2.$$

We get that $d(PP, \mathscr{E}_{TD}) = 5$. The distances between each basic relation from $\mathcal{B}$ and the profile of constraints $\mathscr{E}_{CD}$ for each pair of variables $v_C, v_D \in V$ is summarized in Table 3.

$\mathscr{E}$ / $\mathcal{B}$	$\mathscr{E}_{TP}$	$\mathscr{E}_{TB}$	$\mathscr{E}_{TD}$	$\mathscr{E}_{PB}$	$\mathscr{E}_{PD}$	$\mathscr{E}_{BD}$
DR	8	2	2	2	4	6
PO	4	2	3	1	4	4
PP	4	2	5	0	6	3
PPi	0	3	4	1	4	4
EQ	0	3	6	0	6	3

Table 3: Distances between relations from $\mathcal{B}$ and the profile of constraints $\mathscr{E}_{CD}$, for each pair of variables $v_C, v_D \in V$.

5.2 Using the Distance to Build a Merged Consistent QCN

We now describe our procedure which associates a profile of QCNs with a merged, consistent QCN. This takes advantage of the distance between basic relations and a profile of constraints $\mathscr{E}_{CD}$. Let us first formally define two intermediate functions $relax_{CD}$ and val_{CD} which are used in our procedure. Given a total preorder[3] $\preceq$ over a finite set E, let us denote by $\min(E, \preceq)$ the set of minimal elements of E w.r.t. $\preceq$,

[3] A total preorder over a set E is a total, symmetric and transitive relation.

i.e., $\min(E, \preceq) = \{e \in E \mid \forall e' \in E, e \preceq e'\}$. Each pair of variables v_C, v_D is associated with a total preorder $\preceq_{CD}$ over the basic relations from $\mathcal{B}$ defined for all $b, b' \in \mathcal{B}$ as $b \preceq_{CD} b'$ iff $d(b, \mathscr{E}_{CD}) \leq d(b', \mathscr{E}_{CD})$. Then the function $relax_{CD}$ is a mapping $relax_{CD} : 2^{\mathcal{B}} \mapsto 2^{\mathcal{B}}$ defined for each $\varphi \in 2^{\mathcal{B}}$ as $relax_{CD}(\varphi) = \varphi \cup \min(\mathcal{B} \setminus \varphi, \preceq_{CD})$. It corresponds to the *relaxation* of a constraint φ w.r.t.. the total preordering $\preceq_{CD}$. Noteworthy, $relax_{CD}(\emptyset)$ corresponds to the set of basic relations with a minimal distance to the profile of constraints $\mathscr{E}_{CD}$. The function val_{CD} is a mapping $val_{CD} : 2^{\mathcal{B}} \mapsto \mathbb{N}$ defined for each $\varphi \in 2^{\mathcal{B}}$ as $val_{CD}(\varphi) = \max_{b \in \varphi} d(b, \mathscr{E}_{CD})$. For instance, according to Table 3 and focusing on *Book* and *Document* (cf. $\mathscr{E}_{BD}$), we get that $PP, EQ \preceq_{BD} PO, PPi \preceq_{BD} DR$, that $relax_{BD}(\emptyset) = \{PP, EQ\}$, that $relax_{BD}(\{PP, EQ\}) = \{PP, EQ, PO, PPi\}$, and that $val_{BD}(\{PP, EQ\}) = 3$.

We are ready to introduce our main procedure, whose outline is given in Algorithm 1 that defines an initial QCN $\mathcal{N}$ by setting each one of its constraints Ψ_{CD} to the set of basic relations from $\mathcal{B}$ having a distance to the profile of constraints $\mathscr{E}_{CD}$ that is minimal (lines 2 to 5). If this QCN is consistent, then it is returned as the merged QCN (line 12). If not, some of the constraints of $\mathcal{N}$ are relaxed in line 7, in the sense that some basic relations are added to these constraints. Such a set of constraints S is selected as follows. In line 7, S is first restricted to those constraints from $\mathcal{N}$ which *can* be relaxed, i.e., those constraints not equal to $\mathcal{B}$. Among those candidate constraints, one selects in line 8 the constraints Ψ_{CD} having a highest value $val_{CD}(\Psi_{CD})$. Indeed, we do not want to relax first the constraints consisting of basic relations which are "close" to the input profile, but rather would one prioritize the relaxation of more "controversial" constraints, i.e., those with a high value according to val_{CD}. For instance, let us look back at Table 3. It can be seen that $d(PPi, \mathscr{E}_{TP}) = d(EQ, \mathscr{E}_{TP}) = 0$, and thus $val_{TP}(\{PPi, EQ\}) = 0$; this low value reflects the consensus between sources on the fact that one of the basic relations PPi, EQ holds between *Text* and *Paper*, and indeed it can be verified that the axiom $P \sqsubseteq T$ is consistent with each input TBox. On the contrary, one has that $val_{PD}(\{DR, PO, PPi\}) = 4$; this higher value reflects a disagreement between the input sources about the relationship between the concepts of *Paper* and *Document*. And in the general case, whenever possible and in order to restore the consistency of the merged QCN, it is a sensible choice to keep unchanged those constraints unanimely accepted by the input sources, and rather weaken first the most disputed constraints. This "relaxation" process is repeated iteratively until the resulting QCN is consistent which, obviously enough, is guaranteed after a finite number of iterations.

Example 1 (continued). *Initially, the merged QCN* $\mathcal{N} = \langle V, \Psi \rangle$ *is defined by the following set of constraints, which correspond the basic relations highlighted in Table 3 (this QCN is also depicted in Figure 2(a)):*

$$\Psi_{TP} = \{PPi, EQ\} \qquad \Psi_{TB} = \{DR, PO, PP\}$$
$$\Psi_{TD} = \{DR\} \qquad \Psi_{PB} = \{PP, EQ\}$$
$$\Psi_{PD} = \{DR, PO, PPi\} \quad \Psi_{BD} = \{PP, EQ\}$$

This QCN is inconsistent. One can see that the constraints Ψ_{PB} *and* Ψ_{BD} *imply by transitivity that the relation between* P *and* D *must be* PP *or* EQ, *yet* $\Psi_{PD} \cap \{PP, EQ\} = \emptyset$. *Then the constraint* Ψ_{PD} *is selected (cf. line 8 in the algorithm) as the only candidate for relaxation at this point, since* $val_{PD}(\Psi_{PD}) = 4$, *which is the highest value among all constraints. And since* $relax_{PD}(\Psi_{PD}) = \mathcal{B}$, *one updates* Ψ_{PD} *to* $\mathcal{B}$ *which results in the QCN depicted in Figure 2(b). This QCN is, again, inconsistent (in this case, explaining its inconsistency is more complex as it involves dependencies between all four variables. We omit the details for space reasons). Then the constraint* Ψ_{BD} *is selected for relaxation* ($val_{BD}(\Psi_{BD}) = 3$) *and one updates* Ψ_{BD} *to* $\{PP, EQ, PO, PPi\}$. *The resulting QCN (cf. Figure 2(c)) is consistent and returned by the procedure.*

Algorithm 1: Computing a merged QCN

input: A profile of QCNs $\mathcal{N} = \langle \mathcal{N}_1, \ldots, \mathcal{N}_n \rangle$
output: A merged, consistent QCN $\mathcal{N}$

```
1  begin
       // Initialization of the output QCN N
2      Ψ ⟵ {Ψ_CD | v_C, v_D ∈ V}
3      foreach (v_C, v_D) ∈ V × V do
4          Ψ_CD ⟵ relax_CD(∅)
5      N ⟵ (V, Ψ)
6      while N is not consistent do
           // One relaxes some constraints of N
7          S ⟵ {Ψ_CD | Ψ_CD ∈ Ψ, Ψ_CD ≠ B}
8          S ⟵ arg max{val_CD(Ψ_CD) | Ψ_CD ∈ S)}
9          foreach Ψ_CD ∈ S do
10             Ψ_CD ⟵ relax_CD(Ψ_CD)
11         N ⟵ (V, Ψ)
12     return N
```

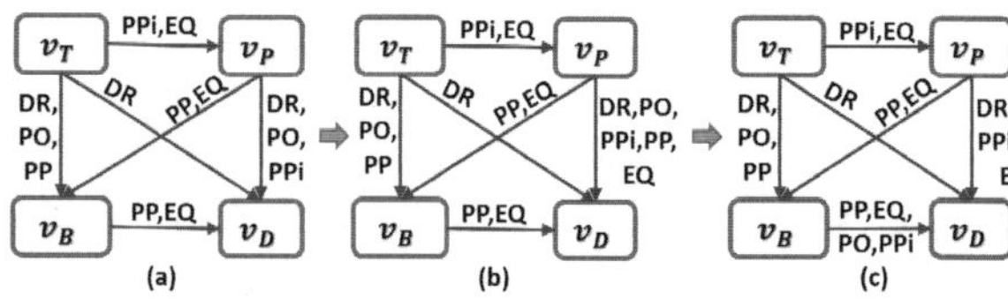

Figure 2: The QCNs iteratively generated by our algorithm. Fig. 2(c) corresponds to the final consistent merged QCN.

Algorithm 1 runs in a time that is polynomial on the size of the input QCN profile, given access to an NP oracle in one step (line 6). Indeed, (i) checking the consistency of an RCC-5 QCN can be performed by taking advantage of a standard SAT solver (Condotta, Nouaouri, and Sioutis 2016), (ii) the number of possible relaxations of a given constraint is bounded by a constant (the number of RCC-5 basic relations), and as a consequence, the number of iterations performed in the loop starting from line 6 is in $O(|V \times V|)$; and (iii) the functions $relax_{CD}$ and val_{CD} are computed in $O(1)$ since the distance d is computed in $O(1)$, again because the number of RCC-5 basic relations is bounded by a constant. This makes the complexity of Algorithm 1 in FP^{NP}, that is reminiscent of the complexity of the inference problem for propositional belief merging, i.e., P^{NP},

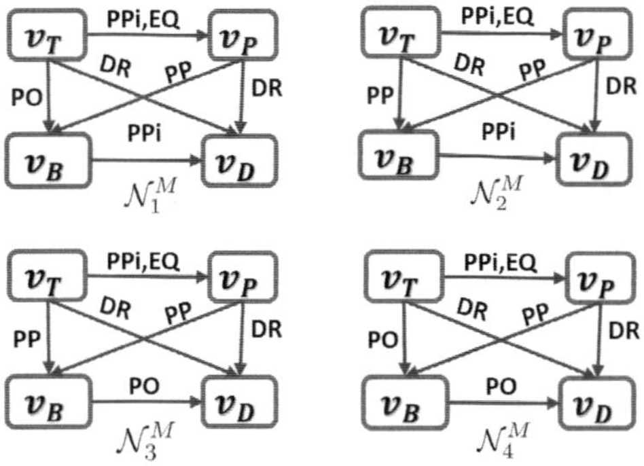

Figure 3: The consistent scenarios of the merged QCN.

for a vast majority of the existing operators (Konieczny and Marquis 2004).

Notably, the QCN merging step we propose in our framework can be seen as an adaptation of (Condotta et al. 2010) that allows one to work with a single QCN as a merged result (the output of Algorithm 1). Nevertheless, the work of Condotta et al. (Condotta et al. 2010) does not provide such a procedure.

6 Selecting a Representative Scenario of the Merged QCN

Once we have obtained a merged, consistent QCN, our goal is to express it in our initial (target) ontology language. However, not every constraint Ψ_{CD} from the QCN (i.e., a subset of $\mathcal{B}$) can easily be translated as a set of axioms, since non-singleton constraints express some disjunctive information between two concepts/regions. Moreover, since the merged QCN is consistent, one can remark it necessarily admits at least one consistent scenario, and since a scenario involves singleton constraints (as well as the two constraints $\{PP, EQ\}$, $\{PPi, EQ\}$), it can easily be translated into a single ontology, as will be shown in the next section. Then our aim is to (i) focus on all consistent scenarios of the merged QCN, and (ii) select one representative scenario. This can be done by exploiting information provided by the input ABoxes as we intend to show in the rest of this section.

In our running example, the merged QCN admits four consistent scenarios which are depicted in Figure 3. Let us first discuss why these four scenarios seem to be reasonable candidates to the input ontologies / QCNs provided by the sources. First, note that all input ontologies state that $Paper \sqsubseteq Text$ ($v_T\{PPi, EQ\}v_P$ in the QCN profile). And it can be seen that this consensus is reflected in the four candidate scenarios, which entail that information. Second, while the two sources O_1 and O_4 state that $Text$ and $Document$ are disjoint concepts ($v_T\{DR\}v_D$ in the corresponding input QCNs), only one source says that $Document \sqsubseteq Text$ ($v_T\{PP, EQ\}v_D$). In this case, it make sense to follow the point of view of the majority of the sources. And accordingly, in all four scenarios we have that $v_T\{DR\}v_D$, thus $Text$ and $Document$ are disjoint concepts. Third, the source O_1 states that $Paper \sqsubseteq Book$ and all other sources have no information on these concepts. It is sensible to keep this information in the merged result, and accordingly all four scenarios entail that information. More, one sees that $v_P\{PP\}v_B$ holds in all scenarios, i.e., that $Paper$ is a *strict* part of $Book$, or stated otherwise, that both concepts cannot be equal while keeping the relationships between the remaining concepts consistent. This emergent property is also an interesting feature of the merging process. Last, the reason why there are four, equally reasonable, candidate scenarios is that some strong disagreements hold on the relationships between the concepts $Text$ and $Book$ on the one hand, and the concepts $Book$ and $Document$ on the other hand. Accordingly, the only differences between the four scenarios hold on the constraints between these two pairs of concepts ($v_T\{PO\}v_B$ / $v_T\{PP\}v_B$, and $v_B\{PPi\}v_D$ / $v_B\{PO\}v_D$).

What remains to be done is to select one of these four scenarios. For this purpose, one takes advantage of the ABoxes from the input ontologies and see how these ABoxes relate to each scenario. To be as faithful as possible to what each input source says, instead of simply considering each input ABox as such, one considers the "closure" of it according to its corresponding TBox. For instance, if a given source states that $Paper \sqsubseteq Text$ in its TBox and that $Paper(p)$ in its ABox, then it makes sense to also consider that $Text(p)$ also holds in that source's implicit knowledge. Formally, let $O = \langle \mathcal{T}, \mathcal{A} \rangle$ be an ontology. The *deductive closure of* $\mathcal{A}$ w.r.t. $\mathcal{T}$, denoted by $Cl_{\mathcal{T}}(\mathcal{A})$, is defined as $Cl_{\mathcal{T}}(\mathcal{A}) \stackrel{\text{def}}{=} \{B(a) \mid B \in N_C,\ a \in N_I,\ O \models B(a)\}$ (Baader et al. 2007; Benferhat, Bouraoui, and Tabia 2015). Accordingly, $\langle \mathcal{T}, \mathcal{A} \rangle$ is logically equivalent to $\langle \mathcal{T}, Cl_{\mathcal{T}}(\mathcal{A}) \rangle$.

To select the representative scenario, we define a distance between a scenario and the set of all input (closed) ABoxes, and then use this distance to choose the scenario. The representative scenario is the one having a minimal distance. So given a scenario, the idea is to count the number of individuals in each input ABox which raise a conflict w.r.t. the constraints of that scenario. This can naturally be done for any scenario constraint $v_C\ \varphi\ v_D$ where $\varphi \neq \{PO\}$. For instance, if $Paper(p)$ and $Document(p)$ hold in the ABox of a given source, and $v_P\{DR\}v_D$ holds in the scenario under consideration, then according to that ABox p is an individual that raises a conflict with that scenario. Another example is if $Paper(p)$ holds but not $Text(p)$, then p is not a member of the concept $Text$ in the ABox (recall that ABoxes are closed w.r.t. their TBox); in that case p raises a conflict with the constraints $v_P\ \varphi\ v_T$ when $\varphi \in \{\{PP\}, \{EQ\}, \{PP, EQ\}\}$. More formally, given an ABox $\mathcal{A}$, a scenario constraint $v_C\ \varphi\ v_D$ where $\varphi \neq \{PO\}$, and an individual p, we say that *p raises a conflict with* φ *w.r.t* $\mathcal{A}$ when:

$$\begin{array}{ll} C(p) \in \mathcal{A}, D(p) \notin \mathcal{A} & \text{when } \varphi \subseteq \{PP, EQ\}, \\ D(p) \in \mathcal{A}, C(p) \notin \mathcal{A} & \text{when } \varphi \subseteq \{PPi, EQ\}, \\ C(p), D(p) \in \mathcal{A} & \text{when } \varphi = \{DR\}. \end{array}$$

And the number of conflicts raised by an ontology $O = \langle \mathcal{T}, \mathcal{A} \rangle$ w.r.t. a a scenario constraint $v_C\ \varphi\ v_D$ where $\varphi \neq \{PO\}$, is defined as $nbConf(O, \varphi) = |\{p \in N_I \mid p \text{ raises a conflict with } \varphi \text{ w.r.t. } Cl_{\mathcal{T}}(\mathcal{A})\}|$.

The case of PO is more complex. Indeed, it can be easily seen that no individual can raise a conflict with

$v_C\{PO\}v_D$. This is because all basic relations $\mathcal{B} \setminus \{PO\}$ express explicit dependencies between concepts / regions, whereas PO is a complementary relation that (explicitly) expresses a notion of *independency* between concepts. For instance, the concepts $Smoker$ and $Researcher$ can naturally be thought of as independent concepts, in the sense that one can easily find in a real-world context individuals that are members of either both concepts, only one of them, and none of them (note that this should not be confused with the case of DR, which expresses an explicit dependency between concepts, e.g., the concepts Dog and Cat.) So to evaluate the number of "conflicts" raised by an ABox w.r.t. a constraint $v_C\{PO\}v_D$, we propose to count how "unbalanced" the number of conflicts are w.r.t. the remaining forms of constraints. Formally, focusing on the scenario constraint between two variables v_C and v_D, $nbConf(O, \varphi) = \max_{\varphi' \neq \{PO\}} nbConf(O, \varphi')) - \min_{\varphi' \neq \{PO\}} nbConf(O, \varphi'))$. For instance, when $nbConf(O, \{PP, EQ\}) = nbConf(O, \{PPi, EQ\}) = nbConf(O, \{DR\})$, then $nbConf(O, \{PO\}) = 0$: since individuals can be found equally (i) in both underlying concepts, and (ii) in one concept but not the other, O raises no conflict w.r.t. $\{PO\}$.

We have now a way to select the representative scenario from a given set of candidates. The distance between a scenario $\mathcal{N}^M$ and the input profile of ontologies $\mathcal{P} = \langle O^1, \ldots, O^n \rangle$ is simply defined as the overall number of conflicts raised by all input ABoxes w.r.t. all constraints of $\mathcal{N}^M$, i.e., $d(\mathcal{N}^M, \mathcal{P}) = \sum_{i \in \{1,\ldots,n\}, \varphi \in \mathcal{N}^M} nbConf(O^i, \varphi)$. Given a set of candidate scenarios, the representative scenario is then the one having a minimal distance.

Example 1 (continued). *Let us go back to our running example. We have that* $Cl_{\mathcal{T}^3}(\mathcal{A}^3) = \{P(p_3), P(b_3), P(d_3), T(t_3), T(d_3), T(b_3), T(p_3), D(d_3), D(b_3), B(b_3)\}$. *So focusing on* $Text$ *and* $Book$ *(i.e., on the scenario constraints between the variables* v_T *and* v_B*), we have that* $nbConf(O^3, \{PP\}) = |\{t_3, d_3, p_3\}| = 3$, *and one can easily verify that* $nbConf(O^3, \{PO\}) = |\{t_3, d_3, p_3\}| = 3 - 0 = 3$. *Summing up all conflicts, we get that* $d(\mathcal{N}_1^M, \mathcal{P}) = 20$, $d(\mathcal{N}_2^M, \mathcal{P}) = 18$, $d(\mathcal{N}_3^M, \mathcal{P}) = 22$, *and* $d(\mathcal{N}_4^M, \mathcal{P}) = 24$. *Hence, the scenario* $\mathcal{N}_2^M$ *is selected as a representative scenario of the merged QCN.*

7 Translating the Representative Scenario into a Terminological Knowledge

The last step of our framework is to translate back the resulting selected representative scenario into an ontology. The translation is defined as follows.

Definition 4 (Backward translation $\tau_\triangleleft$)**.** *A* ***backward translation*** *is a function* $\tau_\triangleleft : V \longrightarrow C$ *s.t.* $\tau_\triangleleft(v_C) \stackrel{\text{def}}{=} C$. $\tau_\triangleleft$ *is extended to map constraints into an ontology as follows, where* A', C', *and* D' *are new concept names and* a, b, *and* c *new individual names:*[4]

- $\tau_\triangleleft(v_C\{EQ\}v_D) \stackrel{\text{def}}{=} \langle\{C \equiv D\}, \emptyset\rangle$;
- $\tau_\triangleleft(v_C\{DR\}v_D) \stackrel{\text{def}}{=} \langle\{C \sqcap D \sqsubseteq \bot\}, \emptyset\rangle$;
- $\tau_\triangleleft(v_C\{PO\}v_D) \stackrel{\text{def}}{=} \langle\{A' \sqsubseteq C \sqcap D, C' \sqsubseteq C, C' \sqcap D \sqsubseteq \bot, D' \sqsubseteq D, D' \sqcap C \sqsubseteq \bot\}, \{A'(a), C(c), C(a), D(d), D(a), C'(c), D'(d)\}\rangle$;
- $\tau_\triangleleft(v_C\{PP, EQ\}v_D) \stackrel{\text{def}}{=} \langle\{C \sqsubseteq D\}, \emptyset\rangle$;
- $\tau_\triangleleft(v_C\{PPi, EQ\}v_D) \stackrel{\text{def}}{=} \langle\{D \sqsubseteq C\}, \emptyset\rangle$;
- $\tau_\triangleleft(v_C\{PP\}v_D) \stackrel{\text{def}}{=} \langle\{C \sqsubseteq D, D' \sqsubseteq D, C \sqcap D' \sqsubseteq \bot\}, \{D'(d), C(c), D(d), D(c)\}\rangle$, *and*
- $\tau_\triangleleft(v_C\{PPi\}v_D)) \stackrel{\text{def}}{=} \langle\{D \sqsubseteq C, C' \sqsubseteq C, D \sqcap C' \sqsubseteq \bot\}, \{C'(c), D(d), C(d), D(c)\}\rangle$.

Moreover, $\tau_\triangleleft$ *is extended to translate a set of constraints into an ontology in the (strict) normal form in the expected way:* $\tau_\triangleleft(\mathcal{N}) \stackrel{\text{def}}{=} \langle\mathcal{T}, \mathcal{A}\rangle$, *where* $\mathcal{T} \stackrel{\text{def}}{=} \bigcup_{\tau_\triangleleft(\Psi)=\langle\mathcal{T}',\mathcal{A}'\rangle, \Psi\in\mathcal{N}} \mathcal{T}'$ *and* $\mathcal{A} \stackrel{\text{def}}{=} \bigcup_{\tau_\triangleleft(\Psi)=\langle\mathcal{T}',\mathcal{A}'\rangle, \Psi\in\mathcal{N}} \mathcal{A}'$.

Accordingly, our back translation is faithful. Using again the notions of inflation and flattening (cf. Definitions 2 and 3), we show that the set of solutions of a scenario $\mathcal{N}$ are captured precisely in its translated ontology $\tau_\triangleleft(\mathcal{N})$.

Theorem 3. *Let* $\mathcal{N}$ *be a scenario and* $\mathcal{S}$ *be solution of* $\mathcal{N}$. *Then there is an inflation* $\mathcal{I}_\mathcal{S}$ *of* $\mathcal{S}$ *s.t.* $\mathcal{I}_\mathcal{S}$ *is a model of* $\tau_\triangleleft(\mathcal{N})$.

Theorem 4. *Let* $\mathcal{N}$ *be a scenario and let* $\mathcal{I}$ *be a fulfilling interpretation of* $\tau_\triangleleft(\mathcal{N})$ *such that* $\mathcal{I}$ *is a model of* $\tau_\triangleleft(\mathcal{N})$. *Then* $\mathcal{S}_\mathcal{I} \models \mathcal{N}$.

Example 1 (continued)**.** *Let us translate the selected scenario* $\mathcal{N}_2^M$ *into an ontology. From Definition 4, we get that:* $\tau_\triangleleft(\mathcal{N}_2^M) = \langle\{(\Psi_{TP})\ P \sqsubseteq T,\ (\Psi_{TD})\ T \sqcap D \sqsubseteq \bot,\ (\Psi_{PD})\ P \sqcap D \sqsubseteq \bot,\ (\Psi_{TB})\ T \sqsubseteq B,\ SubBo1 \sqsubseteq B,\ SubBo1 \sqcap T \sqsubseteq \bot,\ (\Psi_{PB})\ P \sqsubseteq B,\ SubBo2 \sqsubseteq B,\ SubBo2 \sqcap P \sqsubseteq \bot,\ (\Psi_{BD})\ D \sqsubseteq B,\ SubBo3 \sqsubseteq B,\ SubBo3 \sqcap D \sqsubseteq \bot\}, \{T(t_1), SubBo1(s_1), B(t_1), B(s_1), P(p_1), SubBo2(s_2), B(p_1), B(s_2), D(d_1), SubBo3(s_3), B(d_1), B(s_3)\}\rangle$.

8 Conclusion

In this paper, we introduced a terminological knowledge merging procedure based on qualitative reasoning over region spaces, by providing a two-way translation between terminological knowledge and RCC-5 based qualitative constraint networks. Accordingly, even if the input sources are inconsistent when simply combined together, our approach returns a consistent result. It also remains as close as possible to the input sources, i.e., by preserving as much information as possible.

We have assumed that all input ontologies were provided in a strict normal form. Notably, the process of translating an ontology into another equivalent ontology in strict normal form can be done in polynomial time, but this process also allows one to obtain a full classification of all initial atomic concepts, for instance by taking advantage of axioms involving constraints between complex concepts of the type $\exists r.C$ (Baader, Brandt, and Lutz 2005). For the scope of our paper, we have focused on the merging of all atomic concepts from the input ontologies, since considering more complex concepts may lead to consider constraints of higher arity in the translated qualitative constraint networks (e.g., for each role

[4]Notice that the constraint $\{PO\}$ cannot be translated into a set of GCIs only, whence the use of ABox assertions in the translation.

r in the signature, the assertion $\exists r.A \sqsubseteq \exists r.B$ holds when $A \sqsubseteq B$ holds, which would correspond to a constraint of arity four in the translation), and our merging procedure does not allow for these types of constraints. These kind of considerations will be investigated in a future work. Further work will also include the empirical evaluation of our method. Moreover, an approach for representing regions and points in vector spaces (combining natural language processing) is another next interesting direction for merging ontologies.

Acknowledgments

This work has benefited from the support of the AI Chair BE4musIA of the French National Research Agency (ANR-20-CHIA-0028) and FEI INS2I 2022-EMILIE.

References

Baader, F.; Calvanese, D.; Mcguinness, D.; Nardi, D.; and Patel-Schneider, P. 2007. *The Description Logic Handbook: Theory, Implementation, and Applications*. Cambridge University Press.

Baader, F.; Brandt, S.; and Lutz, C. 2005. Pushing the $\mathcal{EL}$ Envelope. In *Proceedings of the 19th International Joint Conferences on Artificial Intelligence (IJCAI'05)*, 364–369.

Beltagy, I.; Chau, C.; Boleda, G.; Garrette, D.; Erk, K.; and Mooney, R. 2013. Montague meets Markov: Deep semantics with probabilistic logical form. In *Second Joint Conference on Lexical and Computational Semantics (*SEM)*, 11–21.

Benferhat, S.; Bouraoui, Z.; Lagrue, S.; and Rossit, J. 2014. Min-based Assertional Merging Approach for Prioritized DL-Lite Knowledge Bases. In *Proceedings of the 8th International Conference on Scalable Uncertainty Management (SUM'14)*, 8–21.

Benferhat, S.; Bouraoui, Z.; Papini, O.; and Würbel, E. 2019. Assertional removed sets merging of dl-lite knowledge bases. In *Proceedings of the 13th International Conference of Scalable Uncertainty Management (SUM'19)*, 207–220.

Benferhat, S.; Bouraoui, Z.; and Tabia, K. 2015. How to select one preferred assertional-based repair from inconsistent and prioritized dl-lite knowledge bases? In *Proceedings of the 24th International Conference on Artificial Intelligence (IJCAI'15)*, 1450–1456.

Bennett, B. 1994. Spatial Reasoning with Propositional Logics. In *Proceedings of the 4th International Conference on Principles of Knowledge Representation and Reasoning (KR'94)*, 51–62.

Bhatt, M.; Guesgen, H.; Wölfl, S.; and Hazarika, S. 2011. Qualitative Spatial and Temporal Reasoning: Emerging Applications, Trends, and Directions. *Spatial Cognition & Computation* 11:1–14.

Bouraoui, Z., and Schockaert, S. 2018. Learning Conceptual Space Representations of Interrelated Concepts. In *Proceedings of the 27th International Joint Conference on Artificial Intelligence (IJCAI'18)*, 1760–1766.

Bouraoui, Z.; Konieczny, S.; Ma, T. T.; and Varzinczak, I. 2020a. Model-based Merging of Open-Domain Ontologies. In *Proceedings of the 33rd IEEE International Conference on Tools with Artificial Intelligence (ICTAI'20)*, 29–34.

Bouraoui, Z.; Camacho-Collados, J.; Anke, L. E.; and Schockaert, S. 2020b. Modelling Semantic Categories using Conceptual Neighborhood. In *Proceedings of the 34th AAAI Conference on Artificial Intelligence (AAAI'20)*, 7448–7455.

Chang, F.; wei Chen, G.; and Zhang, S. 2019. FCAMap-KG Results for OAEI 2019. In *Proceedings of the 18th International Semantic Web Conference (OM@ISWC'19)*, 138–145.

Chen, Z.; Yu, S.; Shengxian, W.; and Dianhai, Y. 2019. RLTM: An Efficient Neural IR Framework for Long Documents. In *Proceedings of the 28th International Joint Conference on Artificial Intelligence (IJCAI'19)*, 5457–5463.

Cohn, A.; Bennett, B.; Gooday, J.; and Gotts, M. 1997. Qualitative Spatial Representation and Reasoning with the Region Connection Calculus. *GeoInformatica* 275–316.

Condotta, J.-F.; Kaci, S.; Marquis, P.; and Schwind, N. 2009. Merging Qualitative Constraint Networks in a Piecewise Fashion. In *Proceedings of the 21st IEEE International Conference on Tools with Artificial Intelligence (ICTAI'09)*, 605–608.

Condotta, J.-F.; Kaci, S.; Marquis, P.; and Schwind, N. 2010. A Syntactical Approach to Qualitative Constraint Networks Merging. In *Proceedings of the 17th International Conference on Logic Programming and Automated Reasoning (LPAR'10)*, 233–247.

Condotta, J.-F.; Kaci, S.; and Schwind, N. 2008. A Framework for Merging Qualitative Constraints Networks. In *Proceedings of the 21st International Florida Artificial Intelligence Research Society Conference (FLAIRS'08)*, 586–591.

Condotta, J.-F.; Nouaouri, I.; and Sioutis, M. 2016. A SAT Approach for Maximizing Satisfiability in Qualitative Spatial and Temporal Constraint Networks. In *Proceedings of the 15th International Conference on Principles of Knowledge Representation and Reasoning (KR'16)*, 342–442.

Douven, I.; Elqayam, S.; Gärdenfors, P.; and Mirabile, P. 2022. Conceptual spaces and the strength of similarity-based arguments. *Cognition* 218:104951.

Freksa, C. 1992. Temporal reasoning based on semi-intervals. *Artificial Intelligence* 54(1):199–227.

Gärdenfors, P. 2000. *Conceptual Spaces: The Geometry of Thought*. US: MIT Press.

Haarslev, V., and Möller, R. 1997. SBox: A Qualitative Spatial Reasoner. In *Proceedings of the 11th International Workshop on Qualitative Reasoning (QR'97)*, 105–113.

Hohenecker, P., and Lukasiewicz, T. 2020. Ontology Reasoning with Deep Neural Networks. In *Proceedings of the 29th International Joint Conference on Artificial Intelligence (IJCAI'20)*, 5060–5064.

Homburg, T.; Staab, S.; and Janke, D. 2020. Geosparql+: Syntax, semantics and system for integrated querying of graph, raster and vector data. In *Proceedings of the 19th International Semantic Web Conference (ISWC'20)*, 258–275.

Julien, H., and Westphal, M. 2012. Revising Qualitative Constraint Networks: Definition and Implementation. In *Proceedings of the 24th IEEE International Conference on Tools with Artificial Intelligence (ICTAI'12)*, 548–555.

Konieczny, S., and Marquis, P. 2004. DA2 merging operators. *Artificial Intelligence* 157:49–79.

Kriegel, F. 2020. Most specific consequences in the description logic $\mathcal{EL}$. *Discrete Applied Mathematics* 172–204.

Kumar, S. K., and Harding, J. A. 2016. Description logic–based knowledge merging for concrete- and fuzzy-domain ontologies. *Journal of Engineering Manufacture* 954–971.

Laadhar, A.; Ghozzi, F.; Megdiche, I.; Ravat, F.; Teste, O.; and Gargouri, F. 2017. POMap results for OAEI 2017. In *Proceedings of the 16th International Semantic Web Conference (ISWC'17)*, 1–7.

Li, N.; Bouraoui, Z.; and Schockaert, S. 2019. Ontology Completion Using Graph Convolutional Networks. In *Proceedings of the 18th International Semantic Web Conference (ISWC'19)*, 435–452.

Patricia, E.; Konieczny, S.; and Marquis, P. 2008. Conflict-based merging operators. In *Proceedings of the 11st International Conference on Principles of Knowledge Representation and Reasoning (KR'08)*, 348–357.

Peter, J., and Thomas, D. 1997. A Complete Classification of Tractability in RCC-5. *Journal of Artificial Intelligence Research* 211–221.

Randell, D. A.; Cui, Z.; and Cohn, A. G. 1992. A spatial logic based on regions and connection. In *Proceedings of the 3rd International Conference on Principles of Knowledge Representation and Reasoning (KR'92)*, 165–176.

Rocktäschel, T., and Riedel, S. 2017. End-to-end differentiable proving. In *Proceedings of the 31st International Conference on Neural Information Processing Systems (NIPS'17)*, 3791–3803.

Rospocher, M., and Corcoglioniti, F. 2018. Joint Posterior Revision of NLP Annotations via Ontological Knowledge. In *Proceedings of the 27th International Joint Conference on Artificial Intelligence (IJCAI'18)*, 4316–4322.

Schockaert, S., and Li, S. 2013. Combining RCC5 relations with betweenness information. In *Proceedings of the 23rd International Joint Conference on Artificial Intelligence (IJCAI'13)*, 1083–1089.

Sioutis, M.; Long, Z.; and Janhunen, T. 2020. On Robustness in Qualitative Constraint Networks. In *Proceedings of the 29th International Joint Conference on Artificial Intelligence (IJCAI'20)*, 1813–1819.

Tanon, T. P.; Vrandecic, D.; Schaffert, S.; Steiner, T.; and Pintscher, L. 2016. From Freebase to Wikidata: The Great Migration. In *Proceedings of the 25th International World Wide Web Conference (WWW'16)*, 1419–1428.

Thau, D.; Bowers, S.; and Ludäscher, B. 2009. Merging Taxonomies under RCC-5 Algebraic Articulations. *Journal of Computing Science and Engineering* 109–126.

Thiéblin, É.; Haemmerlé, O.; and Trojahn, C. 2018. CANARD complex matching system. In *Proceedings of the 17th International Semantic Web Conference (OM@ISWC'18)*, 138–143.

Wang, Z.; Wang, K.; Jin, Y.; and Qi, G. 2012. Ontomerge: A system for merging DL-Lite ontologies. *CEUR Workshop Proceedings* 969:16–27.

Zhao, M., and Zhang, S. 2016. FCA-Map results for OAEI 2016. In *Proceedings of the 15th International Semantic Web Conference (OM@ISWC'16)*, 1–7.

Proceedings of the 19th International Conference on Principles of Knowledge Representation and Reasoning
Main Track

Revisiting Semiring Provenance for Datalog

Camille Bourgaux[1], Pierre Bourhis[2], Liat Peterfreund[3], Michaël Thomazo[1]
[1]DI ENS, ENS, CNRS, PSL University & Inria, Paris, France
[2]CRIStAL, CNRS, University of Lille, Inria, Lille, France
[3]LIGM, CNRS, Université Gustave Eiffel, ENPC, Paris, France
camille.bourgaux@ens.fr, pierre.bourhis@inria.fr,
liat.peterfreund@univ-eiffel.fr, michael.thomazo@inria.fr

Abstract

Data provenance consists in bookkeeping meta information during query evaluation, in order to enrich query results with their trust level, likelihood, evaluation cost, and more. The framework of semiring provenance abstracts from the specific kind of meta information that annotates the data. While the definition of semiring provenance is uncontroversial for unions of conjunctive queries, the picture is less clear for Datalog. Indeed, the original definition might include infinite computations, and is not consistent with other proposals for Datalog semantics over annotated data. In this work, we propose and investigate several provenance semantics, based on different approaches for defining classical Datalog semantics. We study the relationship between these semantics, and introduce properties that allow us to analyze and compare them.

1 Introduction

Datalog is a rule language widely studied both in the database community, where it is seen as a query language, and in the KR community, as an ontology language.

In relational databases, the framework of *semiring provenance* was introduced to generalize computations over annotated databases, e.g., the semantics of probabilistic databases (Senellart 2017), the bag semantics, lineage or why-provenance (Cheney, Chiticariu, and Tan 2009). In this framework, the semantics of positive relational algebra queries over databases annotated with elements of any commutative semiring is inductively defined on the structure of the query (Green, Karvounarakis, and Tannen 2007; Green and Tannen 2017). *Provenance semirings* are expressions (such as polynomials) built from variables associated to each tuple of the database (Green 2009). A provenance expression provides a general representation of how tuples have been used to derive a query result, and can be faithfully evaluated in any semiring in which the considered provenance semiring can be homomorphically embedded.

Semiring provenance has also been studied for Datalog queries, for which it was defined based on the set of all *derivation trees* for the query (Green, Karvounarakis, and Tannen 2007; Deutch et al. 2014; Deutch, Gilad, and Moskovitch 2018). However, this definition seems less axiomatic than in the case of relational databases. Indeed, there may be infinitely many derivation trees, leading to infinite provenance expressions, while Datalog programs have finite models that can be computed efficiently (Abiteboul, Hull, and Vianu 1995). A consequence is that this definition is valid only for a restricted class of semirings, namely ω-continuous. Recently, Dannert et al. (2021) restrict the semiring even further by considering fully-chain complete semirings in order to extend provenance definition to logical languages featuring negation and fixed-point. Even if numerous useful semirings are ω-continuous, or can be extended to a such semiring, infinite provenance expressions may be considered unintuitive in some cases. Consider, for example, the counting semiring (i.e., natural numbers with standard operations) for which provenance of positive relational algebra queries corresponds to their bag semantics. This semiring can be extended to an ω-continuous one by adding ∞ to the natural numbers, hence providing a way to capture the bag semantics for Datalog queries (Mumick, Pirahesh, and Ramakrishnan 1990; Green, Karvounarakis, and Tannen 2007). However, query answers having infinite multiplicities may not seem very natural or informative. Moreover, alternative bag semantics for languages close to Datalog have been defined, and would not lead to such infinite multiplicities when applied to Datalog. This is in particular the case of the bag semantics for ontology-based data access (Nikolaou et al. 2017; Nikolaou et al. 2019), which corresponds to one of the two semantics proposed for source-to-target tuple generating dependencies in the context of data exchange (Hernich and Kolaitis 2017). Interestingly, these bag semantics are not based on derivation trees but are *model-theoretic* semantics: they define annotated interpretations, and conditions for rules satisfaction over such interpretations. Such model-theoretic semantics have also been used in other contexts to evaluate Datalog and variants over annotated databases, such as fuzzy Datalog (Achs and Kiss 1995) or description logic knowledge bases annotated with provenance tokens (Calvanese et al. 2019; Bourgaux et al. 2020). Finally, yet other semantics definitions have been proposed for some use cases. For instance, Zhao, Subotic, and Scholz (2020) consider *minimal depth proof trees*, which correspond to a Datalog *evaluation algorithm*, with the intended use of understanding the computation of the result, and guiding debugging.

The fact that the above semantics are not encompassed by the definition of semiring provenance for Datalog, along with the need of handling infinite computations which are entailed by this definition, motivate us to investigate alternative natural semantics that might be a better fit in different contexts.

In this paper we introduce several natural provenance semantics for Datalog over annotated data. Our definitions are based on different classical approaches: model-theoretic, execution-based and proof tree-based. They capture the semantics mentioned previously, and are inspired by practical needs. For instance, our semantics definition based on minimal depth derivation trees capture the behavior of Datalog engines, such as Soufflé (Soufflé 2020), that store only minimal depth derivation trees instead of storing them all (which might be impossible in case there are infinitely many); Our semantics based on non-recursive derivation trees (in which a fact is not derived from itself) resembles the approach taken by some graph query languages, e.g., SPARQL and Cypher, to handle queries with possibly infinite outputs by allowing to explicitly restrict the output to include only simple paths. In addition, some of the semantics suggested in the paper are closely related to paradigms for weighted reasoning in the context of words and trees (Esparza and Luttenberger 2011; Stüber and Vogler 2008).

After defining these different semantics, we study under which conditions they coincide and investigate their connections. We then provide a general framework for defining such provenance semantics, and present several properties relevant for provenance semantics that allow us to compare them. We briefly discuss some complexity issues in conclusion. Proofs and additional discussion are available in the appendix of (Bourgaux et al. 2022).

2 Preliminaries

2.1 Datalog

We use the standard Datalog settings (cf. (Abiteboul, Hull, and Vianu 1995) part D).

Syntax Let **P**, **C**, and **V** be mutually disjoint, possibly infinite sets of *predicates*, *constants*, and *variables* respectively. Elements of $\mathbf{C} \cup \mathbf{V}$ are called *terms*. An *atom* has the form $p(t_1, \ldots, t_n)$ where $p \in \mathbf{P}$ is an n-ary predicate, and t_i's are terms. A *fact* (or *ground atom*) is a variable-free atom. A *(Datalog) rule* is an expression: $\forall \vec{x} \forall \vec{y} (\phi(\vec{x}, \vec{y}) \to \psi(\vec{x}))$ where $\vec{x}$ and $\vec{y}$ are tuples of variables and $\phi(\vec{x}, \vec{y})$ and $\psi(\vec{x})$ are conjunctions of atoms whose variables are $\vec{x} \cup \vec{y}$ and $\vec{x}$ respectively. We call $\phi(\vec{x}, \vec{y})$ and $\psi(\vec{x})$ the *body* and *head* of the rule, respectively. From now on, we assume that rules are in *normalized form*, i.e., the head consists of a single atom $H(\vec{x})$, and quantifiers are implicit. The *domain* $\mathcal{D}(\mathcal{A})$ of a set $\mathcal{A}$ of atoms is the set of terms that appear in its atoms.

A *database* D is a finite set of facts, and a *Datalog program (or ontology)* Σ is a finite set of Datalog rules. The *schema* of D (resp. Σ) denoted $\mathcal{S}(D)$ (resp. $\mathcal{S}(\Sigma)$) is the set of predicates that appear in its atoms.[1]

Semantics The semantics of Datalog can classically be defined in three ways: through models, fixpoints or derivation trees. All three definitions rely on the notion of homomorphism: a *homomorphism* from a set $\mathcal{A}$ of atoms to a set $\mathcal{B}$ of atoms is a function $h : \mathcal{D}(\mathcal{A}) \to \mathcal{D}(\mathcal{B})$ such that $h(t) = t$ for all $t \in \mathbf{C}$, and $p(t_1, \ldots, t_n) \in \mathcal{A}$ implies $h(p(t_1, \cdots, t_n)) := p(h(t_1), \ldots, h(t_n)) \in \mathcal{B}$. We denote by $h(\mathcal{A})$ the set $\{h(p(t_1, \ldots, t_n)) \mid p(t_1, \ldots, t_n) \in \mathcal{A}\}$. The homomorphism definition is extended to conjunctions of atoms by viewing them as the sets of atoms they contain.

A set I of facts is a *model* of a rule $r := \phi(\vec{x}, \vec{y}) \to \psi(\vec{x})$, denoted by $I \models r$, if every homomorphism h from $\phi(\vec{x}, \vec{y})$ to I is also a homomorphism from $\psi(\vec{x})$ to I; it is a *model* of a Datalog program Σ if $I \models r$ for every $r \in \Sigma$; it is a *model* of a database D if $D \subseteq I$. A fact α is *entailed* by D and Σ, denoted $\Sigma, D \models \alpha$, if $\alpha \in I$ for every model I of Σ and D.

Example 1. *Let Σ contain the rules $B(x) \to A(x)$, $R(x,y) \wedge A(y) \to B(x)$, and $R(x,y) \to R(y,x)$, and $D := \{B(a), B(b), R(a,b), R(b,a)\}$. Each model of D and Σ contains all facts in D as well as $A(a)$ and $A(b)$, which are thus entailed by Σ, D.*

An equivalent way to define the entailment of a fact α by D and Σ is to check if there is a homomorphism from α to a specific model, defined as the *least fixpoint* containing D of the immediate consequence operator: An immediate consequence for D and Σ is either $\alpha \in D$, or α such that there exists a rule $r := \phi(\vec{x}, \vec{y}) \to \psi(\vec{x})$ and a homomorphism h from $\phi(\vec{x}, \vec{y})$ to D such that $h(\psi(\vec{x})) = \alpha$.

Finally, a third definition relies on derivation trees.

Definition 1 (Derivation Tree). *A derivation tree t of a fact α w.r.t. a database D and a program Σ is a finite tree whose leaves are labeled by facts from D and non-leaf nodes are labeled by triples $(p(t_1, \ldots, t_m), r, h)$ where*

- *$p(t_1, \ldots, t_m)$ is a fact over the schema $\mathcal{S}(\Sigma)$;*
- *r is a rule from Σ of the form $\phi(\vec{x}, \vec{y}) \to p(\vec{x})$;*
- *h is a homomorphism from $\phi(\vec{x}, \vec{y})$ to the facts of the labels of the node children, such that $h(p(\vec{x})) = p(t_1, \ldots, t_m)$;*
- *there is a bijection f between the node children and the atoms of $\phi(\vec{x}, \vec{y})$, such that for every $q(\vec{z}) \in \phi(\vec{x}, \vec{y})$, $f(q(\vec{z}))$ is of the form $(h(q(\vec{z})), r', h')$ or is a leaf labeled by $h(q(\vec{z}))$.*

Moreover, if $(p(t_1, \cdots, t_m), r, h)$ or $p(t_1, \cdots, t_m)$ is the root of t, then $p(t_1, \cdots, t_m) = \alpha$.

Example 2. *Let Σ contain $r_1 := R(x,y) \to H(x,x)$, $r_2 := R(x,y) \to H(x,y)$ and $r_3 := S(x,y,z) \wedge S(x,z,y) \to H(x,x)$. If $D = \{R(a,a), S(a,b,c), S(a,c,b)\}$, then the fact $\alpha := H(a,a)$ has the following derivation trees*

(α, r_1, h)	(α, r_2, h)	(α, r_3, h_3)	(α, r_3, h'_3)
$R(a,a)$	$R(a,a)$	$S(a,b,c)$ $S(a,c,b)$	$S(a,c,b)$ $S(a,b,c)$

where $h(x) = h(y) = a$, $h_3(x) = a$, $h_3(y) = b$, $h_3(z) = c$ and $h'_3(x) = a$, $h'_3(y) = c$, $h'_3(z) = b$.

Note that when the program at hand is recursive (i.e., the dependency graph of its predicates contains cycles) a fact may have infinitely many derivation trees. Figure 1 depicts some of the infinitely many derivation trees of $A(a)$ from Example 1. In this example, and from this point on, we omit rules and homomorphisms from trees when there is no ambiguity.

[1] Note that we do not require the set of predicates of atoms appearing in heads of rules to be disjoint from $\mathcal{S}(D)$; naturally, all of our results are valid under this assumption as well.

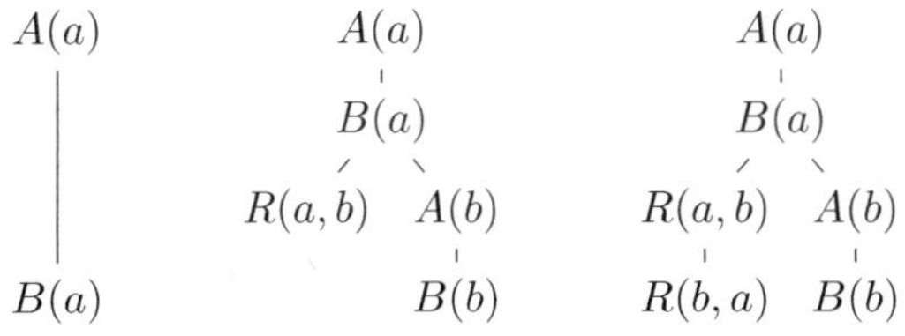

Figure 1: Some derivation trees of $A(a)$ in Example 1.

Queries A *conjunctive query* (CQ) is an existentially quantified formula $\exists\vec{y}\,\phi(\vec{x},\vec{y})$ where $\phi(\vec{x},\vec{y})$ is a conjunction of atoms with variables in $\vec{x}\cup\vec{y}$; a *union of conjunctive queries* (UCQ) is a disjunction of CQs (over the same free variables). A query is *Boolean* if it has no free-variables. A set of facts I satisfies a Boolean CQ (BCQ) $q := \exists\vec{y}\,\phi(\vec{y})$, written $I \models q$, if and only if there is a homomorphism from $\phi(\vec{y})$ to I. A BCQ q is *entailed* by a Datalog program Σ and database D, written $\Sigma, D \models q$, if and only if $I \models q$ for every model I of Σ and D. Note that $\Sigma, D \models q$ if and only if $\Sigma \cup \{\phi(\vec{y}) \rightarrow \mathsf{goal}\}, D \models \mathsf{goal}$, where goal is a nullary predicate such that $\mathsf{goal} \notin \mathcal{S}(\Sigma)\cup\mathcal{S}(D)$. A tuple of constants $\vec{a}$ is an *answer* to a CQ $q(\vec{x}) := \exists\vec{y}\,\phi(\vec{x},\vec{y})$ over Σ and D if $\vec{a}$ and $\vec{x}$ have the same arity and $\Sigma, D \models q(\vec{a})$ where $q(\vec{a})$ is the BCQ obtained by replacing the variables from $\vec{x}$ with the corresponding constants from $\vec{a}$. When $\Sigma = \emptyset$, it amounts to the existence of a homomorphism from $q(\vec{a})$ to D, which corresponds to the semantics of CQs over relational databases.

2.2 Annotated Databases

To equip databases with extra information, their facts might be annotated with, e.g., trust levels, clearance degree required to access them, or identifiers to track how they are used.

In the framework of semiring provenance, annotations are elements of algebraic structures known as commutative semirings. A *semiring* $\mathbb{K} = (K, +_{\mathbb{K}}, \times_{\mathbb{K}}, 0_{\mathbb{K}}, 1_{\mathbb{K}})$ is a set K with distinguished elements $0_{\mathbb{K}}$ and $1_{\mathbb{K}}$, equipped with two binary operators: $+_{\mathbb{K}}$, called the *addition*, which is an associative and commutative operator with identity $0_{\mathbb{K}}$, and $\times_{\mathbb{K}}$, called the *multiplication*, which is an associative operator with identity $1_{\mathbb{K}}$. It also holds that $\times_{\mathbb{K}}$ distributes over $+_{\mathbb{K}}$, and $0_{\mathbb{K}}$ is annihilating for $\times_{\mathbb{K}}$. When multiplication is commutative, the semiring is said to be *commutative*. We use the convention according to which multiplication is applied before addition to omit parentheses. We omit the subscript of operators and distinguished elements when there is no ambiguity.

Definition 2. *An* annotated database *is a triple $(D, \mathbb{K}, \lambda)$ where D is a database, $\mathbb{K} = (K, +_{\mathbb{K}}, \times_{\mathbb{K}}, 0_{\mathbb{K}}, 1_{\mathbb{K}})$ is a semiring, and $\lambda : D \mapsto K \setminus \{0_{\mathbb{K}}\}$ maps facts into semiring elements different from $0_{\mathbb{K}}$.*

Example 3 (Ex. 1 cont'd)**.** *The semiring $\mathbb{N} = (\mathbb{N}, +, \times, 0, 1)$ of the natural numbers equipped with the usual operations is used for bag semantics. The tropical semiring $\mathbb{T} = (\mathbb{R}_{+}^{\infty}, \mathsf{min}, +, \infty, 0)$ is used to compute minimal-cost paths. We define $\lambda_{\mathbb{N}} : D \mapsto \mathbb{N}\setminus\{0\}$ by $\lambda_{\mathbb{N}}(B(a)) = 3$, $\lambda_{\mathbb{N}}(B(b)) = 1$, $\lambda_{\mathbb{N}}(R(a,b)) = 2$, $\lambda_{\mathbb{N}}(R(b,a)) = 1$; And $\lambda_{\mathbb{T}} : D \mapsto \mathbb{R}_{+}$ by $\lambda_{\mathbb{T}}(B(a)) = 10$, $\lambda_{\mathbb{T}}(B(b)) = 1$, $\lambda_{\mathbb{T}}(R(a,b)) = 5$, $\lambda_{\mathbb{T}}(R(b,a)) = 2$.*

We next list some possible properties of semirings. A semiring is *$+$-idempotent* (resp. *$\times$-idempotent*) if for every $a \in K$, $a + a = a$ (resp. $a \times a = a$). It is *absorptive* if for every $a, b \in K$, $a \times b + a = a$. It is *positive* if for every $a, b \in K$, $a \times b = 0$ if and only if ($a = 0$ or $b = 0$), and $a + b = 0$ if and only if $a = b = 0$. Finally, an important class is that of ω-continuous commutative semirings in which infinite sums are well-defined. Given a semiring, we define the binary relation $\sqsubseteq$ such that $a \sqsubseteq b$ if and only if there exists $c \in K$ such that $a + c = b$. A commutative semiring is *ω-continuous* if $\sqsubseteq$ is a partial order, every (infinite) ω-chain $a_0 \sqsubseteq a_1 \sqsubseteq a_2 \ldots$ has a least upper bound $\sup((a_i)_{i\in\mathbb{N}})$, and for every a, $a + \sup((a_i)_{i\in\mathbb{N}}) = \sup((a + a_i)_{i\in\mathbb{N}})$ and $a \times \sup((a_i)_{i\in\mathbb{N}}) = \sup((a \times a_i)_{i\in\mathbb{N}})$.

The semantics of queries from the positive relational algebra, and in particular of UCQs, over annotated databases is defined inductively on the structure of the query (Green, Karvounarakis, and Tannen 2007). Intuitively, joint use of data (conjunction) corresponds to multiplication, and alternative use of data (union or projection) corresponds to addition.

Example 4 (Ex. 3 cont'd)**.** *The BCQ $\exists xy\,(R(x,y) \wedge B(y))$ is entailed from $(D, \mathbb{N}, \lambda_{\mathbb{N}})$ with multiplicity $\lambda_{\mathbb{N}}(R(a,b)) \times \lambda_{\mathbb{N}}(B(b)) + \lambda_{\mathbb{N}}(R(b,a)) \times \lambda_{\mathbb{N}}(B(a)) = 5$, and from $(D, \mathbb{T}, \lambda_{\mathbb{T}})$ with minimal cost $\mathsf{min}(\lambda_{\mathbb{T}}(R(a,b)) + \lambda_{\mathbb{T}}(B(b)), \lambda_{\mathbb{T}}(R(b,a)) + \lambda_{\mathbb{T}}(B(a))) = 6$.*

A semantics of Datalog over annotated databases has been defined by Green, Karvounarakis, and Tannen (2007) using derivation trees, that we shall name the *all-tree semantics*. It associates to each fact α entailed by Σ and D the following sum, where $T_D^{\Sigma}(\alpha)$ is the set of all derivation trees for α w.r.t. Σ and D and $\Lambda(t) := \prod_{v \text{ is a leaf of } t} \lambda(v)$ is the $\mathbb{K}$-annotation of the derivation tree t (since $\mathbb{K}$ is commutative, the result of the product is well-defined).

$$\mathcal{P}^{\mathrm{AT}}(\Sigma, D, \mathbb{K}, \lambda, \alpha) := \sum_{t \in T_D^{\Sigma}(\alpha)} \Lambda(t).$$

Since $T_D^{\Sigma}(\alpha)$ may be infinite, $\mathcal{P}^{\mathrm{AT}}$ is well-defined for all Σ, $(D, \mathbb{K}, \lambda)$ and α only in the case where $\mathbb{K}$ is ω-continuous.

Example 5 (Ex. 3 cont'd)**.** *The fact $\alpha := A(a)$ is entailed with minimal cost: $\mathcal{P}^{AT}(\Sigma, D, \mathbb{T}, \lambda_{\mathbb{T}}, \alpha) = \mathsf{min}_{t\in T_D^{\Sigma}(\alpha)} \Sigma_{v \text{ is a leaf of } t} \lambda_{\mathbb{T}}(v) = 3$. Since $\mathbb{N}$ is not ω-continuous, $\mathcal{P}^{AT}(\Sigma, D, \mathbb{N}, \lambda_{\mathbb{N}}, \alpha)$ is not defined.*

2.3 Provenance Semirings

Provenance semirings have been introduced to abstract from a particular semiring by associating a unique provenance token to each fact of the database, and building expressions that trace their use. Given a set X of *variables* that annotate the database, a *provenance semiring* $Prov(X)$ is a semiring over a space of provenance expressions with variables from X.

Various such semirings were introduced in the context of relational databases (Green 2009): The most expressive annotations are provided by the *provenance polynomials* semiring $\mathbb{N}[X] := (\mathbb{N}[X], +, \times, 0, 1)$ of polynomials with coefficients from $\mathbb{N}$ and variables from X, and the usual operations. Less general provenance semirings include, for example, the semiring $\mathbb{B}[X] := (\mathbb{B}[X], +, \times, 0, 1)$ of polynomials with Boolean coefficients, and the semiring $PosBool(X) := (PosBool(X), \vee, \wedge, \mathsf{false}, \mathsf{true})$ of positive Boolean expressions.

In the Datalog context, it is important to allow for infinite provenance expressions, as there can be infinitely many derivation trees. A *formal power series* with variables from X and coefficients from K is a mapping that associates to each monomial over X a coefficient in K. A formal power series S can be written as a possibly infinite sum $S = \Sigma_{m \in \mathsf{mon}(X)} S(m)m$ where $\mathsf{mon}(X)$ is the set of monomials over X and $S(m)$ is the coefficient of the monomial m. The set of formal power series with variables from X and coefficients from K is denoted $K[\![X]\!]$. Green, Karvounarakis, and Tannen (2007) define the *Datalog provenance semiring* as the semiring $\mathbb{N}^\infty[\![X]\!]$ of formal power series with coefficients from $\mathbb{N}^\infty = \mathbb{N} \cup \{\infty\}$.

A *semiring homomorphism* from $\mathbb{K} = (K, +_\mathbb{K}, \times_\mathbb{K}, 0_\mathbb{K}, 1_\mathbb{K})$ to $\mathbb{K}' = (K', +_{\mathbb{K}'}, \times_{\mathbb{K}'}, 0_{\mathbb{K}'}, 1_{\mathbb{K}'})$ is a mapping $h : K \to K'$ such that $h(0_\mathbb{K}) = 0_{\mathbb{K}'}$, $h(1_\mathbb{K}) = 1_{\mathbb{K}'}$, and for all $a, b \in K$, $h(a +_\mathbb{K} b) = h(a) +_{\mathbb{K}'} h(b)$ and $h(a \times_\mathbb{K} b) = h(a) \times_{\mathbb{K}'} h(b)$. A semiring homomorphism between ω-continuous semirings is *ω-continuous* if it preserves least upper bounds: $h(\sup((a_i)_{i \in \mathbb{N}})) = \sup((h(a_i))_{i \in \mathbb{N}})$.

Following Deutch et al. (2014), we say that a provenance semiring $Prov(X)$ *specializes* correctly to a semiring $\mathbb{K}$, if any valuation $\nu : X \to K$ extends uniquely to a (ω-continuous if $Prov(X)$ and $\mathbb{K}$ are ω-continuous) semiring homomorphism $h : Prov(X) \to K$, allowing the computations for $\mathbb{K}$ to factor through the computations for $Prov(X)$. A provenance semiring $Prov(X)$ is *universal for a set of semirings* if it specializes correctly to each semiring of this set. Green, Karvounarakis, and Tannen (2007) showed that $\mathbb{N}[X]$ is universal for commutative semirings, and $\mathbb{N}^\infty[\![X]\!]$ is universal for commutative ω-continuous semirings.

3 Alternative Semantics

In this section we propose several natural ways of defining the semantics of Datalog over annotated databases, and investigate their connections. We have seen that the semantics of Datalog can equivalently be defined through models, fixpoints or derivation trees. The semantics we propose also fall into these three approaches. For presentation purposes, we see each semantics as a partial function $\mathcal{P}$ that associates to a Datalog program Σ, annotated database $(D, \mathbb{K}, \lambda)$, and fact α, a semiring element $\mathcal{P}(\Sigma, D, \mathbb{K}, \lambda, \alpha)$.

3.1 Model-Based Semantics

We first investigate two provenance semantics based on Datalog's model-theoretic semantics. In both cases, we will define interpretations (I, μ^I) where I is a set of facts and μ^I is a function that annotates facts of I, and formulate requirements for them to be models of Σ and $(D, \mathbb{K}, \lambda)$, extending standard models of Σ and D with fact annotations.

Annotated Model-based Hernich and Kolaitis (2017) define two bag semantics in the context of data exchange: the *incognizant* and *cognizant* semantics. The difference between them arise from the two different semantics of bag union: the incognizant semantics uses the maximum-based union, while the cognizant semantics uses the sum-based union.

In more details, both semantics are based on the following semantics for source-to-target tuple generating dependencies (s-t tgds): a pair (I, J) of source and target instances satisfies an s-t tgd $q_1(\vec{x}) \to q_2(\vec{x})$ if for every answer $\vec{a}$ to q_1 over I, $\vec{a}$ is an answer to q_2 over J with at least the same multiplicity. Given a set of s-t tgds Σ and a source I, a target J is an *incognizant solution* for I w.r.t. Σ if (I, J) satisfies every s-t tgd in Σ. It is a *cognizant solution* if for every $r \in \Sigma$, there is a target instance J_r such that (I, J_r) satisfies r and $\uplus J_r \subseteq J$, where $\uplus$ denotes the sum-union of bags (i.e., the multiplicity of each element of the sum-union is equal to the sum of its multiplicities). The incognizant (resp. cognizant) *certain answers* to a query q w.r.t. Σ on I are defined using bag intersection of the answers over the incognizant (resp. cognizant) solutions for I w.r.t. Σ, i.e., the multiplicity of an answer is the minimum of its multiplicities over the solutions. Note that for BCQs, the only possible certain answer is the empty tuple.

For example, consider $\Sigma = \{B(x) \to A(x), C(x) \to A(x)\}$ and $D = \{(B(a), 1), (C(a), 1)\}$. Under the incognizant semantics, the multiplicity of the certain answer of the Boolean query $A(a)$ w.r.t. Σ and D is 1 while under the cognizant semantics it is 2. Indeed, $J = \{(A(a), 1)\}$ is an incognizant solution for D w.r.t. Σ as it satisfies both s-t tgds, but is not a cognizant solution as the sum of multiplicities that arise from the two rules is 2.

It is easy to show that the cognizant semantics is equivalent to $\mathcal{P}^{\mathrm{AT}}$ on the counting semiring $\mathbb{N} = (\mathbb{N}, +, \times, 0, 1)$, and thus coincides with the classical bag semantics for Datalog. However, we have seen that the incognizant and cognizant semantics differ. Moreover, note that in the field of ontology-based data access, the bag semantics defined by Nikolaou et al. for DL-Lite$_R$ (2017; 2019) coincides with the *incognizant* semantics, thus disagrees with the classical Datalog bag semantics (Mumick, Pirahesh, and Ramakrishnan 1990; Green, Karvounarakis, and Tannen 2007).

We hence define a provenance semantics that coincides with these semantics when used with the counting semiring. Since it is based on greatest lower bounds, it is defined on a restricted class of semirings.

Let $\mathbb{K} = (K, +, \times, 0, 1)$ be a commutative ω-continuous semiring such that for every $K' \subseteq K$, the greatest lower bound $\inf(K')$ of K' is well defined (i.e., there exists a unique $z \in K$ such that $z \sqsubseteq x$ for every $x \in K'$ and every z' such that $z' \sqsubseteq x$ for every $x \in K'$ is such that $z' \sqsubseteq z$), Σ be a Datalog program, and $(D, \mathbb{K}, \lambda)$ be an annotated database. We define $\mathbb{K}$*-annotated interpretations* as pairs (I, μ^I) where I is a set of facts, and μ^I is a function from I to K. We say that a $\mathbb{K}$-annotated interpretation (I, μ^I) is a *model* of Σ and $(D, \mathbb{K}, \lambda)$, denoted by $(I, \mu^I) \models (\Sigma, D, \mathbb{K}, \lambda)$, if

1. $D \subseteq I$, and for every $\alpha \in D$, $\lambda(\alpha) \sqsubseteq \mu^I(\alpha)$;
2. for every $\phi(\vec{x}, \vec{y}) \to H(\vec{x})$ in Σ, whenever there is a homomorphism $h : \phi(\vec{x}, \vec{y}) \mapsto I$, then $h(H(\vec{x})) \in I$ and
$$\sum_{h' : \phi(\vec{x}, \vec{y}) \mapsto I, h'(\vec{x}) = h(\vec{x})} \; \prod_{\beta \in h'(\phi(\vec{x}, \vec{y}))} \mu^I(\beta) \sqsubseteq \mu^I(h(H(\vec{x}))).$$

The *annotated model-based provenance semantics* $\mathcal{P}^{\mathrm{AM}}$ is defined by

$$\mathcal{P}^{\text{AM}}(\Sigma, D, \mathbb{K}, \lambda, \alpha) := \inf(\{\mu^I(\alpha) | (I, \mu^I) \models (\Sigma, D, \mathbb{K}, \lambda)\}).$$

Proposition 1. *If the Datalog rules in Σ are (1) s-t tgds, or (2) formulated in DL-Lite$_R$, then for every BCQ q, $\mathcal{P}^{AM}(\Sigma \cup \{q \rightarrow \text{goal}\}, D, \mathbb{N}, \lambda_{\mathbb{N}}, \text{goal})$ is equal to the multiplicity of the empty tuple in (1) the incognizant certain answers or (2) the bag certain answers to q w.r.t. Σ and $(D, \mathbb{N}, \lambda_{\mathbb{N}})$.*

Set-Annotated Model-based We adapt the work on provenance for the description logics DL-Lite$_R$ and $\mathcal{ELH}^r$ (Calvanese et al. 2019; Bourgaux et al. 2020), where the semiring is assumed to be a $\times$-idempotent provenance semiring $Prov(X)$ and rules are also annotated. Annotated models of annotated knowledge bases are defined as set of facts annotated with sets of monomials from $Prov(X)$. Given a fact α and a monomial m over X, $(\Sigma, D, Prov(X), \lambda_X) \models (\alpha, m)$ holds when m belongs to the annotation set of α in every models of Σ and $(D, Prov(X), \lambda_X)$.

To obtain an analog provenance semantics for Datalog, we define interpretations which associate facts with (possibly infinite) *sets of annotations*, and formulate the requirements for them to be models of Σ and $(D, \mathbb{K}, \lambda)$.

Let $\mathbb{K} = (K, +, \times, 0, 1)$ be a commutative ω-continuous semiring, Σ be a Datalog program, and $(D, \mathbb{K}, \lambda)$ be an annotated database. We define $\mathbb{K}$*-set-annotated interpretations* as pairs (I, μ^I) where I is a set of facts, and μ^I is a function from I to the *power-set of* K. We say that a $\mathbb{K}$-set-annotated interpretation (I, μ^I) is a model of Σ and $(D, \mathbb{K}, \lambda)$, denoted by $(I, \mu^I) \models (\Sigma, D, \mathbb{K}, \lambda)$, if

1. $D \subseteq I$, and for every $\alpha \in D$, $\lambda(\alpha) \in \mu^I(\alpha)$;
2. for every $\phi(\vec{x}, \vec{y}) \rightarrow H(\vec{x})$ in Σ, whenever there is a homomorphism $h : \phi(\vec{x}, \vec{y}) \mapsto I$, then $h(H(\vec{x})) \in I$ and if $h(\phi(\vec{x}, \vec{y})) = \beta_1 \wedge \dots \wedge \beta_n$, $\{\Pi_{i=1}^n k_i \mid (k_1, \dots, k_n) \in \mu^I(\beta_1) \times \dots \times \mu^I(\beta_n)\} \subseteq \mu^I(h(H(\vec{x})))$.

The *set-annotated model-based provenance semantics* $\mathcal{P}^{\text{SAM}}$ is defined by

$$\mathcal{P}^{\text{SAM}}(\Sigma, D, \mathbb{K}, \lambda, \alpha) := \sum_{k \in \bigcap_{(I, \mu^I) \models (\Sigma, D, \mathbb{K}, \lambda)} \mu^I(\alpha)} k.$$

Connections between semantics Let $\sqsubseteq$ be the binary relation between provenance semantics such that $\mathcal{P} \sqsubseteq \mathcal{P}'$ if and only if $\mathcal{P}(\Sigma, D, \mathbb{K}, \lambda, \alpha) \sqsubseteq \mathcal{P}'(\Sigma, D, \mathbb{K}, \lambda, \alpha)$ for every Σ, $(D, \mathbb{K}, \lambda)$ and α on which $\mathcal{P}$ and $\mathcal{P}'$ are well-defined.

Proposition 2. *The following holds:*

$$\mathcal{P}^{AM} \sqsubseteq \mathcal{P}^{AT} \text{ and } \mathcal{P}^{SAM} \sqsubseteq \mathcal{P}^{AT}.$$

Next examples show that $\mathcal{P}^{\text{AM}}$ and $\mathcal{P}^{\text{SAM}}$ are incomparable.

Example 6. *Let $\Sigma = \{A(x) \rightarrow \text{goal}, B(x) \rightarrow \text{goal}\}$, $D = \{A(a), B(a)\}$, $\lambda_{\mathbb{N}}(A(a)) = 2$ and $\lambda_{\mathbb{N}}(B(a)) = 3$.*

Annotated models of Σ and $(D, \mathbb{N}, \lambda_{\mathbb{N}})$ are such that $\mu^I(\text{goal}) \geq 3$, so $\mathcal{P}^{AM}(\Sigma, D, \mathbb{N}, \lambda_{\mathbb{N}}, \text{goal}) = 3$.

Set-annotated models of Σ and $(D, \mathbb{N}, \lambda_{\mathbb{N}})$ are such that $\{2, 3\} \subseteq \mu^I(\text{goal})$, so $\mathcal{P}^{SAM}(\Sigma, D, \mathbb{N}, \lambda_{\mathbb{N}}, \text{goal}) = 5$.

Hence $\mathcal{P}^{AM}(\Sigma, D, \mathbb{N}, \lambda_{\mathbb{N}}, \text{goal}) < \mathcal{P}^{SAM}(\Sigma, D, \mathbb{N}, \lambda_{\mathbb{N}}, \text{goal})$.

Example 7. *Let $\Sigma = \{R(x, y) \rightarrow \text{goal}\}$, $D = \{R(a, b), R(a, c)\}$, $\lambda_{\mathbb{N}}(R(a, b)) = 2$ and $\lambda_{\mathbb{N}}(R(a, c)) = 2$.*

Annotated models of Σ and $(D, \mathbb{N}, \lambda_{\mathbb{N}})$ are such that $\mu^I(\text{goal}) \geq 4$, so $\mathcal{P}^{AM}(\Sigma, D, \mathbb{N}, \lambda_{\mathbb{N}}, \text{goal}) = 4$.

Set-annotated models of Σ and $(D, \mathbb{N}, \lambda_{\mathbb{N}})$ are such that $\{2\} \subseteq \mu^I(\text{goal})$, so $\mathcal{P}^{SAM}(\Sigma, D, \mathbb{N}, \lambda_{\mathbb{N}}, \text{goal}) = 2$.

Hence $\mathcal{P}^{AM}(\Sigma, D, \mathbb{N}, \lambda_{\mathbb{N}}, \text{goal}) > \mathcal{P}^{SAM}(\Sigma, D, \mathbb{N}, \lambda_{\mathbb{N}}, \text{goal})$.

Despite of their inherently different approaches, $\mathcal{P}^{\text{AM}}$, $\mathcal{P}^{\text{SAM}}$ and $\mathcal{P}^{\text{AT}}$ coincide on a large class of semirings.

Proposition 3. *If $\mathbb{K}$ is a commutative $+$-idempotent ω-continuous semiring, then for every Σ, $(D, \mathbb{K}, \lambda)$, and α, $\mathcal{P}^{AM}(\Sigma, D, \mathbb{K}, \lambda, \alpha) = \mathcal{P}^{SAM}(\Sigma, D, \mathbb{K}, \lambda, \alpha) = \mathcal{P}^{AT}(\Sigma, D, \mathbb{K}, \lambda, \alpha)$.*

Additional insights on the connection between definitions can be gained by considering the provenance semiring $\mathbb{N}^\infty[\![X]\!]$: the monomials with non-zero coefficients are the same with all semantics but their coefficients may differ ($\mathcal{P}^{\text{AT}}$ leading to the highest coefficients by Proposition 2).

Proposition 4. *Let λ_X be an injective function from D to X.*

- *A monomial occurs in $\mathcal{P}^{AT}(\Sigma, D, \mathbb{N}^\infty[\![X]\!], \lambda_X, \alpha)$ if and only if it occurs in $\mathcal{P}^{AM}(\Sigma, D, \mathbb{N}^\infty[\![X]\!], \lambda_X, \alpha)$.*
- *$\mathcal{P}^{SAM}(\Sigma, D, \mathbb{N}^\infty[\![X]\!], \lambda_X, \alpha)$ is obtained by setting all non-zero coefficients to 1 in $\mathcal{P}^{AT}(\Sigma, D, \mathbb{N}^\infty[\![X]\!], \lambda_X, \alpha)$.*

An example where $\mathcal{P}^{\text{AT}}$ and $\mathcal{P}^{\text{AM}}$ or $\mathcal{P}^{\text{SAM}}$ differ on $\mathbb{N}^\infty[\![X]\!]$ is the following: Let Σ contain $A(x) \rightarrow B(x)$, $B(x) \rightarrow A(x)$, $D = \{A(a)\}$ and $\lambda_X(A(a)) = x$. Since there are infinitely many derivation trees for $A(a)$, $\mathcal{P}^{\text{AT}}(\Sigma, D, \mathbb{K}, \lambda_X, A(a)) = \infty x$ while for $\mathcal{P} \in \{\mathcal{P}^{\text{AM}}, \mathcal{P}^{\text{SAM}}\}$, $\mathcal{P}(\Sigma, D, \mathbb{N}^\infty[\![X]\!], \lambda_X, A(a)) = x$, as $\{A(a), B(a)\}$ with both facts annotated with x (resp. $\{x\}$) is a (resp. set-)annotated model for Σ and $(D, \mathbb{N}^\infty[\![X]\!], \lambda_X)$.

Note that $\mathcal{P}^{\text{AM}}$ and $\mathcal{P}^{\text{SAM}}$ can still lead to infinite provenance expressions: Let $\Sigma = \{A(x) \wedge B(x) \rightarrow A(x)\}$, $D = \{A(a), B(a)\}$, $\lambda_X(A(a)) = x$ and $\lambda_X(B(a)) = y$. For $\mathcal{P} \in \{\mathcal{P}^{\text{AM}}, \mathcal{P}^{\text{SAM}}\}$, $\mathcal{P}(\Sigma, D, \mathbb{N}^\infty[\![X]\!], \lambda_X, A(a)) = x + xy + xy^2 + xy^3 + \dots$.

3.2 Execution- and Tree-Based Semantics

We saw that when annotations are present there is more than one way to define a model-based semantics for Datalog and that it differs from the all-tree semantics. We now investigate definitions based on classical Datalog evaluation algorithms.

We extend the notion of *immediate consequence operator* describing the application of rules onto facts, with the computation of annotation. To this end, we introduce the *annotation aware immediate consequence operator* T_Σ. Applying T_Σ on a set of annotated facts $(I, \mathbb{K}, \lambda)$ results in $(I_{T_\Sigma}, \mathbb{K}, \lambda_{T_\Sigma})$ where I_{T_Σ} is the result of applying the immediate consequence operator to Σ and I, and λ_{T_Σ} annotates facts in I_{T_Σ} with the relational provenance (over $(I, \mathbb{K}, \lambda)$) of the UCQ formed by the bodies of the rules that create them. Formally,

$$I_{T_\Sigma} := \{H(\vec{a}) \mid I \models \exists \vec{y}\, \phi(\vec{a}, \vec{y}),\ \phi(\vec{x}, \vec{y}) \rightarrow H(\vec{x}) \in \Sigma\}$$

$$\lambda_{T_\Sigma}(H(\vec{a})) := \sum_{\substack{h(\vec{x}) = \vec{a},\ I \models h(\phi(\vec{x}, \vec{y})) \\ \phi(\vec{x}, \vec{y}) \rightarrow H(\vec{x}) \in \Sigma}} \ \prod_{\beta \in h(\phi(\vec{x}, \vec{y}))} \lambda(\beta)$$

We define a union operator for annotated databases (over the same semiring): $(I, \mathbb{K}, \lambda) \cup (I', \mathbb{K}, \lambda') := (I \cup I', \mathbb{K}, \lambda'')$ where $\lambda''(\alpha) := \lambda(\alpha) + \lambda'(\alpha)$ where we slightly abuse notation by setting $\lambda(\alpha) = 0$ if $\alpha \notin I$, and $\lambda'(\alpha) = 0$ if $\alpha \notin I'$.

Naive Evaluation / All Trees In the naive evaluation algorithm, all rules are applied in parallel until a fixpoint is reached. The 'annotation aware' version of it is as follows: We set $I^0_{\mathsf{n}}(\Sigma, D, \mathbb{K}, \lambda) := (D, \mathbb{K}, \lambda)$, and define inductively $I^{i+1}_{\mathsf{n}}(\Sigma, D, \mathbb{K}, \lambda) := T_\Sigma(I^i_{\mathsf{n}}(\Sigma, D, \mathbb{K}, \lambda)) \cup (D, \mathbb{K}, \lambda)$. Note that the subscript n of I_{n} is an abbreviation for 'naive', and the superscript i indicates how many times T_Σ was applied.

Let $(I^i_{\mathsf{n}}, \mathbb{K}, \lambda^i_{\mathsf{n}})$ denote $I^i_{\mathsf{n}}(\Sigma, D, \mathbb{K}, \lambda)$. We say that $I^i_{\mathsf{n}}(\Sigma, D, \mathbb{K}, \lambda)$ *converges* if there is some k such that $I^\ell_{\mathsf{n}} = I^k_{\mathsf{n}}$ for every $\ell \geq k$, and $\sup(\lambda^i_{\mathsf{n}}(\alpha))$ exists for every $\alpha \in I^k_{\mathsf{n}}$.

Proposition 5. *For every $\Sigma, D, \mathbb{K}, \lambda$, if $\mathbb{K}$ is ω-continuous then $I^i_{\mathsf{n}}(\Sigma, D, \mathbb{K}, \lambda)$ converges.*

In this case, we define $I^\infty_{\mathsf{n}} := I^k_{\mathsf{n}}$ and $\lambda^\infty_{\mathsf{n}} := \sup_{i\to\infty} \lambda^i_{\mathsf{n}}$. The *naive execution provenance semantics* $\mathcal{P}^{\mathrm{NE}}$ is defined by

$$\mathcal{P}^{\mathrm{NE}}(\Sigma, D, \mathbb{K}, \lambda, \alpha) := \begin{cases} \lambda^\infty_{\mathsf{n}}(\alpha) & \alpha \in I^\infty_{\mathsf{n}} \\ 0 & \text{otherwise} \end{cases}$$

and is equivalent to the all-tree semantics.

Proposition 6. *It holds that $\mathcal{P}^{NE} = \mathcal{P}^{AT}$.*

Optimized Naive Evaluation / Minimal Depth Trees We consider an optimized version of the naive algorithm that stops as soon as the desired fact is derived. We define the 'annotation aware' version of this algorithm by $I^0_{\mathsf{o},\alpha}(\Sigma, D, \mathbb{K}, \lambda) := (D, \mathbb{K}, \lambda)$, and

$$I^{i+1}_{\mathsf{o},\alpha}(\Sigma, D, \mathbb{K}, \lambda) := \begin{cases} T_\Sigma(I^i_{\mathsf{o},\alpha}(\Sigma, D, \mathbb{K}, \lambda)) \cup (D, \mathbb{K}, \lambda) & \alpha \notin I^i_{\mathsf{o},\alpha} \\ I^i_{\mathsf{o},\alpha}(\Sigma, D, \mathbb{K}, \lambda) & \text{otherwise} \end{cases}$$

where $I^i_{\mathsf{o},\alpha}$ is such that $I^i_{\mathsf{o},\alpha}(\Sigma, D, \mathbb{K}, \lambda) := (I^i_{\mathsf{o},\alpha}, \mathbb{K}, \lambda^i_{\mathsf{o},\alpha})$.

Proposition 7. *For every $\Sigma, D, \mathbb{K}, \lambda$, and α such that $\Sigma, D \models \alpha$, there exists $k \geq 0$ such that $I^k_{\mathsf{o},\alpha}(\Sigma, D, \mathbb{K}, \lambda) = I^\ell_{\mathsf{o},\alpha}(\Sigma, D, \mathbb{K}, \lambda)$ for every $\ell \geq k$.*

With k as provided by Proposition 7, we define the *optimized execution provenance semantics* $\mathcal{P}^{\mathrm{OE}}$ by:

$$\mathcal{P}^{\mathrm{OE}}(\Sigma, D, \mathbb{K}, \lambda, \alpha) := \begin{cases} \lambda^k_{\mathsf{o},\alpha}(\alpha) & \alpha \in I^k_{\mathsf{o},\alpha} \\ 0 & \text{otherwise} \end{cases}$$

We show that an equivalent tree-based semantics can be obtained by considering only minimal depth trees for the desired fact. This approach has been considered useful, for example to present a 'small proof' for debugging (Zhao, Subotic, and Scholz 2020). Formally, let $\texttt{depth}(t)$ denote the depth of tree t. We say that $t \in T^\Sigma_D(\alpha)$ is *of minimal depth* if for every $t' \in T^\Sigma_D(\alpha)$ it holds that $\texttt{depth}(t) \leq \texttt{depth}(t')$. The *minimal depth tree provenance semantics* $\mathcal{P}^{\mathrm{MDT}}$ is defined by

$$\mathcal{P}^{\mathrm{MDT}}(\Sigma, D, \mathbb{K}, \lambda, \alpha) := \sum_{\substack{t \in T^\Sigma_D(\alpha) \\ \text{is of minimal depth}}} \Lambda(t)$$

and is equivalent to the optimized naive execution.

Proposition 8. *It holds that $\mathcal{P}^{OE} = \mathcal{P}^{MDT}$.*

Seminaive Evaluation / Hereditary Minimal Depth Trees In the seminaive evaluation algorithm, facts are derived only once. We introduce a new consequence operator Δ_Σ that derives only new facts and is defined as follows: $\Delta_\Sigma(I, \mathbb{K}, \lambda) := (I_{\Delta_\Sigma}, \mathbb{K}, \lambda_{\Delta_\Sigma})$ where $T_\Sigma(I, \mathbb{K}, \lambda) := (I_{T_\Sigma}, \mathbb{K}, \lambda_{T_\Sigma})$, $I_{\Delta_\Sigma} := I_{T_\Sigma} \setminus I$, and λ_{Δ_Σ} is the restriction of λ_{T_Σ} to I_{Δ_Σ}. We can now define the annotation aware version of the seminaive evaluation: $I^0_{\mathsf{sn}}(\Sigma, D, \mathbb{K}, \lambda) := (D, \mathbb{K}, \lambda)$ and $I^{i+1}_{\mathsf{sn}}(\Sigma, D, \mathbb{K}, \lambda) := I^i_{\mathsf{sn}}(\Sigma, D, \mathbb{K}, \lambda) \cup \Delta_\Sigma(I^i_{\mathsf{sn}}(\Sigma, D, \mathbb{K}, \lambda))$.

Proposition 9. *For every $\Sigma, D, \mathbb{K}, \lambda$, there exists $k \geq 0$ such that $I^k_{\mathsf{sn}}(\Sigma, D, \mathbb{K}, \lambda) = I^\ell_{\mathsf{sn}}(\Sigma, D, \mathbb{K}, \lambda)$ for every $\ell \geq k$.*

Note that, unlike in Proposition 5, we do not require $\mathbb{K}$ to be ω-continuous. With k provided by Proposition 9, the *seminaive execution provenance semantics* $\mathcal{P}^{\mathrm{SNE}}$ is defined by

$$\mathcal{P}^{\mathrm{SNE}}(\Sigma, D, \mathbb{K}, \lambda, \alpha) := \begin{cases} \lambda^k_{\mathsf{sn}} & \alpha \in I^k_{\mathsf{sn}} \\ 0 & \text{otherwise} \end{cases}$$

To capture this with the tree-based approach we need to further restrict all subtrees to be of minimal depth. Formally, a derivation tree $t \in T^\Sigma_D(\alpha)$ is a *hereditary minimal-depth (derivation) tree* if for every node n of t labeled by (β, r, h), the subtree t_β with root n is a minimal-depth derivation tree for β. The *hereditary minimal depth tree provenance semantics* $\mathcal{P}^{\mathrm{HMDT}}$ is defined by

$$\mathcal{P}^{\mathrm{HMDT}}(\Sigma, D, \mathbb{K}, \lambda, \alpha) := \sum_{\substack{t \in T^\Sigma_D(\alpha) \\ \text{is hereditary minimal-depth}}} \Lambda(t)$$

and is equivalent to the seminaive execution.

Proposition 10. *It holds that $\mathcal{P}^{SNE} = \mathcal{P}^{HMDT}$.*

3.3 Non-Recursive Tree-Based Semantics

Both execution-based semantics $\mathcal{P}^{\mathrm{OE}}$ and $\mathcal{P}^{\mathrm{SNE}}$ take into account finite subsets of derivation trees (and hence converge). Is there a more informative tree-based semantics (i.e., one that takes into account a bigger subset of derivation trees) that still converges? We present such a semantics based on the intuition that deriving a fact from itself is redundant.

Formally, a *non-recursive (derivation) tree* is a derivation tree that does not contain two nodes labeled with the same fact and such that one is the descendant of the other. The *non-recursive tree provenance semantics* $\mathcal{P}^{\mathrm{NRT}}$ is defined by

$$\mathcal{P}^{\mathrm{NRT}}(\Sigma, D, \mathbb{K}, \lambda, \alpha) := \sum_{\substack{t \in T^\Sigma_D(\alpha) \\ \text{is non-recursive}}} \Lambda(t).$$

Connections between semantics Next proposition follows from the fact that hereditary minimal-depth trees are of minimal-depth and non recursive. The sets of minimal depth trees and non-recursive trees are incomparable, so that $\mathcal{P}^{\mathrm{NRT}} \not\sqsubseteq \mathcal{P}^{\mathrm{MDT}}$ and $\mathcal{P}^{\mathrm{MDT}} \not\sqsubseteq \mathcal{P}^{\mathrm{NRT}}$.

Proposition 11. *The following hold:*

$$\mathcal{P}^{HMDT} \sqsubseteq \mathcal{P}^{NRT} \sqsubseteq \mathcal{P}^{AT} \quad \textit{and} \quad \mathcal{P}^{HMDT} \sqsubseteq \mathcal{P}^{MDT} \sqsubseteq \mathcal{P}^{AT}$$

Moreover $\mathcal{P}^{\mathrm{NRT}}$ and $\mathcal{P}^{\mathrm{AT}}$ coincide on specific semirings.

Proposition 12. *For every $\Sigma, D, \mathbb{K}, \lambda$ and α, if $\mathbb{K}$ is a commutative absorptive ω-continuous semiring, then $\mathcal{P}^{NRT}(\Sigma, D, \mathbb{K}, \lambda, \alpha) = \mathcal{P}^{AT}(\Sigma, D, \mathbb{K}, \lambda, \alpha)$.*

If $\mathbb{K}$ is not absorptive, there exists Σ, $(D, \mathbb{K}, \lambda)$ and α such that $\mathcal{P}^{\text{NRT}}(\Sigma, D, \mathbb{K}, \lambda, \alpha) \neq \mathcal{P}^{\text{AT}}(\Sigma, D, \mathbb{K}, \lambda, \alpha)$, even in the case where $\mathbb{K}$ is $+$-idempotent and $\times$-idempotent: Let Σ consist of the rule $A(x) \wedge B(x) \to A(x)$ and $D = \{A(a), B(a)\}$. Then $\mathcal{P}^{\text{NRT}}(\Sigma, D, \mathbb{K}, \lambda, A(a)) = \lambda(A(a))$ while $\mathcal{P}^{\text{AT}}(\Sigma, D, \mathbb{K}, \lambda, A(a)) = \lambda(A(a)) + \lambda(A(a)) \times \lambda(B(a))$.

The other semantics differ even under strong restrictions.

Example 8. *This example shows that $\mathcal{P}^{NRT}$, $\mathcal{P}^{MDT}$ and $\mathcal{P}^{HMDT}$ differ even if $\mathbb{K}$ is $+$ and $\times$-idempotent and absorptive.*

$$\begin{aligned}\textit{Let } \Sigma =& \{B(x) \wedge C(x) \to A(x),\ D(x) \to B(x),\\ & E(x) \to C(x),\ F(x) \to E(x)\}\\ D =& \{C(a),\ D(a),\ E(a),\ F(a)\}\end{aligned}$$

The three derivation trees of $A(a)$ w.r.t. Σ and D are non-recursive, but only the first two are of minimal depth and only the first one is a hereditary minimal-depth tree.

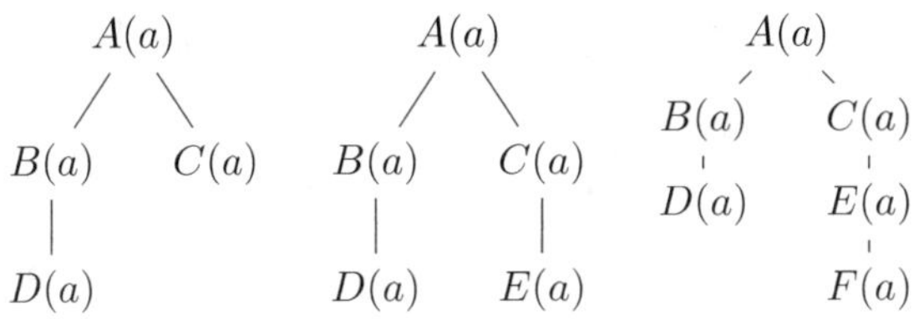

Thus, if $(D, \mathbb{K}, \lambda)$ is such that $\lambda(C(a)) = c$, $\lambda(D(a)) = d$, $\lambda(E(a)) = e$, and $\lambda(F(a)) = f$ then

$$\begin{aligned}\mathcal{P}^{NRT}(\Sigma, D, \mathbb{K}, \lambda, A(a)) =& c \times d + d \times e + d \times f\\ \mathcal{P}^{MDT}(\Sigma, D, \mathbb{K}, \lambda, A(a)) =& c \times d + d \times e\\ \mathcal{P}^{HMDT}(\Sigma, D, \mathbb{K}, \lambda, A(a)) =& c \times d\end{aligned}$$

4 Basics Properties

In this section, we provide a framework allowing to compare the provenance semantics presented in the previous section. It is clear that they all fulfill the following definition.

Definition 3 (Provenance semantics). *A* provenance semantics *is a partial function that assigns to a Datalog program Σ, annotated database $(D, \mathbb{K}, \lambda)$ and fact α, an element $\mathcal{P}(\Sigma, D, \mathbb{K}, \lambda, \alpha)$ in K such that:*

1. *$\Sigma, D \not\models \alpha$ implies $\mathcal{P}(\Sigma, D, \mathbb{K}, \lambda, \alpha) = 0_{\mathbb{K}}$.*
2. *If $\mathbb{K}$ is positive, $\mathcal{P}(\Sigma, D, \mathbb{K}, \lambda, \alpha) = 0_{\mathbb{K}}$ implies $\Sigma, D \not\models \alpha$.*

We call the semiring domain *of $\mathcal{P}$ the maximal set S of semirings such that $\mathcal{P}(\Sigma, D, \mathbb{K}, \lambda, \alpha)$ is defined for every $\mathbb{K} \in S$, and every Σ, $(D, \mathbb{K}, \lambda)$ and α.*

Intuitively, Definition 3 means that the semantics reflects fact (non)-entailment. It is extremely permissive: We could define such a semantics that associates to each entailed fact a random semiring element different from zero, and does not bring any information beyond facts entailment. In the sequel, we state and discuss a number of properties that may be expected to be satisfied by a provenance semantics.

Throughout this section, when not stated otherwise, $\mathcal{P}$, Σ, D, $\mathbb{K}$, λ and α denote respectively an arbitrary provenance semantics, Datalog program, database, commutative semiring $(K, +, \times, 0, 1)$, function from D to $K \setminus \{0\}$, and fact. We phrase properties as conditions, and say that $\mathcal{P}$ *satisfies* a property if it satisfies the condition. We also denote by λ_X an injective function $\lambda_X : D \mapsto X$.

4.1 Compatibility with Classical Notions

Property 1 is a sanity check: if a Datalog program amounts to a UCQ, the provenance should be the same as the one defined for relational databases (Green, Karvounarakis, and Tannen 2007). A Datalog program Σ is *UCQ-defined* if its rules are of the form $\phi(\vec{x}, \vec{y}) \to H(\vec{x})$ where H is a predicate that does not occur in the body of any rule. In this case, the equivalent UCQ Q^{Σ} of Σ is $\bigcup_{\phi(\vec{x},\vec{y}) \to H(\vec{x}) \in \Sigma} \exists \vec{y} \phi(\vec{x}, \vec{y})$.

Property 1 (Algebra Consistency). *If Σ is UCQ-defined with rule head $H(\vec{x})$ and $H \notin \mathcal{S}(D)$, then for every tuple $\vec{a}$ of same arity as $\vec{x}$, the relational provenance of $Q^{\Sigma}(\vec{a})$ is equal to $\mathcal{P}(\Sigma, D, \mathbb{K}, \lambda, H(\vec{a}))$.*

While Property 1 considers the behavior of a provenance semantics on a restricted class of queries, we can alternatively consider its behavior on a specific semiring. Boolean provenance has a very natural definition, based on the database subsets that entail the query, and is widely used, notably for probabilistic databases (Senellart 2017), but also for ontology-mediated query explanation (e.g., in Datalog$^{+/-}$ or description logics (Ceylan et al. 2019; Ceylan et al. 2020)). It is formalized with the semiring $PosBool(X)$.

Property 2 (Boolean Compatibility).

$$\mathcal{P}(\Sigma, D, PosBool(X), \lambda_X, \alpha) = \bigvee_{\substack{D' \subseteq D\\ \Sigma, D' \models \alpha}} \bigwedge_{\beta \in D'} \lambda_X(\beta)$$

Property 2 expresses 'insensibility' to syntax, that is, every provenance semantics that satisfies Property 2 agrees on equivalent programs (i.e., those that have the same models) for the semiring $PosBool(X)$. This is related to ideas from (Green 2009) on the provenance of equivalent UCQs.

4.2 Compatibility with Specialization

Semiring provenance has been introduced to abstract from the particular semiring at hand, and factor the computations in some provenance semiring which specializes correctly to any semiring of interest. The next property allows one to do so, and is thus highly desirable (Bourgaux et al. 2022).

Property 3 (Commutation with Homomorphisms). *If there is a semiring homomorphism h from $\mathbb{K}_1$ to $\mathbb{K}_2$, then $h(\mathcal{P}(\Sigma, D, \mathbb{K}_1, \lambda, \alpha)) = \mathcal{P}(\Sigma, D, \mathbb{K}_2, h \circ \lambda, \alpha)$.*

We call Property 3 restricted to ω-continuous homomorphisms *Commutation with ω-Continuous Homomorphisms*.

Specializing correctly is all the more useful when $\mathcal{P}$ is well-defined for a lot of semirings, in particular on all commutative or at least all commutative ω-continuous semirings.

Property 4 (Any (ω-Continuous) Semiring). *$\mathcal{P}$ satisfies the* Any Semiring Property *(resp.* Any ω-Continuous Semiring Property*) if the semiring domain of $\mathcal{P}$ contains the set of all commutative (resp. commutative ω-continuous) semirings.*

4.3 Joint and Alternative Use of the Data

How is the actual usage of the data reflected in the provenance semantics? The next property formalizes that multiplication reflects joint use of the data, and addition alternative use. For the rest of this section, we set goal to be a nullary predicate not in $\mathcal{S}(\Sigma) \cup \mathcal{S}(D)$.

Property 5 (Joint and Alternative Use). *For all tuples of facts* $(\alpha_1^1, \cdots, \alpha_{n_1}^1), \ldots, (\alpha_1^m, \cdots, \alpha_{n_m}^m)$, *it holds that*

$$\mathcal{P}(\Sigma', D, \mathbb{K}, \lambda, \mathsf{goal}) = \Sigma_{i=1}^m \Pi_{j=1}^{n_i} \mathcal{P}(\Sigma, D, \mathbb{K}, \lambda, \alpha_j^i)$$

where $\Sigma' = \Sigma \cup \{\bigwedge_{j=1}^{n_i} \alpha_j^i \rightarrow \mathsf{goal} \mid 1 \leq i \leq m\}$.

We weaken the above by referring to each mode separately:

Property 6 (Joint Use). *For all facts* $\alpha_1, \cdots, \alpha_n$,

$$\mathcal{P}(\Sigma', D, \mathbb{K}, \lambda, \mathsf{goal}) = \Pi_{j=1}^n \mathcal{P}(\Sigma, D, \mathbb{K}, \lambda, \alpha_j)$$

where $\Sigma' = \Sigma \cup \{\bigwedge_{j=1}^n \alpha_j \rightarrow \mathsf{goal}\}$.

Property 7 (Alternative Use). *For all facts* $\alpha_1, \cdots, \alpha_m$,

$$\mathcal{P}(\Sigma', D, \mathbb{K}, \lambda, \mathsf{goal}) = \Sigma_{i=1}^m \mathcal{P}(\Sigma, D, \mathbb{K}, \lambda, \alpha_i)$$

where $\Sigma' = \Sigma \cup \{\alpha_i \rightarrow \mathsf{goal} \mid 1 \leq i \leq m\}$.

4.4 Fact Roles in Entailment

After considering how facts can be combined or used alternatively to entail a result, we ponder their possible roles w.r.t. the entailment. Property 8 asserts that the original annotation of a fact takes part in the provenance of its entailment.

Property 8 (Self). *If* $\alpha \in D$, *then* $\lambda(\alpha) \sqsubseteq \mathcal{P}(\Sigma, D, \mathbb{K}, \lambda, \alpha)$.

Moreover, if a database fact cannot be alternatively derived using the rules, then its provenance should be exactly its original annotation. To phrase this property we use the *grounding* Σ_D of Σ w.r.t. D, defined by $\Sigma_D = \{h(\phi(\vec{x}, \vec{y})) \rightarrow h(H(\vec{x})) \mid \phi(\vec{x}, \vec{y}) \rightarrow H(\vec{x}) \in \Sigma, h : \vec{x} \cup \vec{y} \mapsto \mathcal{D}(D)\}$. It holds that $\Sigma, D \models \alpha$ if and only if $\Sigma_D, D \models \alpha$.

Property 9 (Parsimony). *If* $\alpha \in D$ *does not occur in any rule head in* Σ_D *then* $\mathcal{P}(\Sigma, D, \mathbb{K}, \lambda, \alpha) = \lambda(\alpha)$.

Parsimony Property together with other constraints guarantee Algebra Consistency Property.

Proposition 13. *If* $\mathcal{P}$ *satisfies Properties 5 (Joint and Alternative Use) and 9 (Parsimony), and is such that for every* $\Sigma, D, \mathbb{K}, \lambda, \alpha$, $\mathcal{P}(\Sigma, D, \mathbb{K}, \lambda, \alpha) = \mathcal{P}(\Sigma_D, D, \mathbb{K}, \lambda, \alpha)$, *then it satisfies Property 1 (Algebra Consistency).*

Property 10 states that $\mathcal{P}$ reflects the necessity of a fact for the entailment. We say that $\beta \in D$ is *necessary* to $\Sigma, D \models \alpha$ if $\Sigma, D \setminus \{\beta\} \not\models \alpha$, and denote by *Nec* the set of such facts.

Property 10 (Necessary Facts). *There exists* $e \in K$ *such that* $\mathcal{P}(\Sigma, D, \mathbb{K}, \lambda, \alpha) = \Pi_{\beta \in Nec} \lambda(\beta) \times e$.

A fact is *usable* to $\Sigma, D \models \alpha$ if it occurs in some derivation tree in $T_D^\Sigma(\alpha)$. Usable facts are related to the notion of *lineage* (Cui, Widom, and Wiener 2000) and can be defined without resorting to derivation trees (Bourgaux et al. 2022). Intuitively, if a fact is not usable to derive another fact, it should not have any influence on its provenance.

Property 11 (Non-Usable Facts). *For every* λ' *that differs from* λ *only on facts that are not usable to* $\Sigma, D \models \alpha$, *it holds that* $\mathcal{P}(\Sigma, D, \mathbb{K}, \lambda, \alpha) = \mathcal{P}(\Sigma, D, \mathbb{K}, \lambda', \alpha)$.

4.5 Data Modification

The last two properties indicate how provenance is impacted when facts are inserted or deleted.

Property 12 (Insertion). *For every* $(D', \mathbb{K}, \lambda')$ *such that* $D \cap D' = \emptyset$,

$$\mathcal{P}(\Sigma, D, \mathbb{K}, \lambda, \alpha) + \mathcal{P}(\Sigma, D', \mathbb{K}, \lambda', \alpha) \sqsubseteq \mathcal{P}(\Sigma, D \cup D', \mathbb{K}, \lambda \cup \lambda', \alpha).$$

Maintaining provenance upon fact deletion is very useful in practice. We formalize this using a provenance semiring, which allows us to keep track of the facts. A partial evaluation of a provenance expression $p(X)$ over variables X is an expression obtained from $p(X)$ by replacing some of the variables by a given value.

Property 13 (Deletion). *For every provenance semiring* $Prov(X)$ *and* $D' \subseteq D$, *if* λ' *is the restriction of* λ_X *to* D' *and* $\Delta = D \setminus D'$, *then* $\mathcal{P}(\Sigma, D', Prov(X), \lambda', \alpha)$ *is equal to the partial evaluation of* $\mathcal{P}(\Sigma, D, Prov(X), \lambda_X, \alpha)$ *obtained by setting the annotations of facts in* Δ *to* 0*:* $\mathcal{P}(\Sigma, D, Prov(X), \lambda_X, \alpha)[\{\lambda_X(x) = 0\}_{x \in \Delta}]$.

5 Semantics Analysis w.r.t. Properties

In this section, we analyze the semantics proposed in Section 3 w.r.t. the properties introduced in Section 4. The properties each semantics satisfies are summarized in Table 1. Proofs of the positive cases are given in the appendix of (Bourgaux et al. 2022) and we discuss the negative cases, which may be more characteristic, in the sequel.

	$\mathcal{P}^{\mathtt{AT}}$	$\mathcal{P}^{\mathtt{NRT}}$	$\mathcal{P}^{\mathtt{MDT}}$	$\mathcal{P}^{\mathtt{HMDT}}$	$\mathcal{P}^{\mathtt{AM}}$	$\mathcal{P}^{\mathtt{SAM}}$
Algebra Consistency	✓	✓	✓	✓		
Boolean Compat.	✓	✓			✓	✓
Com. with Hom.		✓	✓	✓		
Com. with ω-Cont.	✓	✓	✓	✓		
Any Semiring		✓	✓	✓		
Any ω-Cont. Sem.	✓	✓	✓	✓		✓
Joint and Alt. Use	✓	✓				
Joint Use	✓	✓		✓	✓	
Alternative Use	✓	✓				
Self	✓	✓	✓	✓	✓	✓
Parsimony	✓	✓	✓	✓	✓	✓
Necessary Facts	✓	✓	✓	✓		✓
Non-Usable Facts	✓	✓	✓	✓	✓	✓
Insertion	✓	✓				
Deletion	✓	✓			✓	✓

Table 1: Does a property hold for a provenance semantics?

5.1 Tree- and Execution-Based Semantics Cases

We first discuss $\mathcal{P}^{\mathtt{MDT}}$ and $\mathcal{P}^{\mathtt{HMDT}}$, which have not been much investigated and stand out compared to $\mathcal{P}^{\mathtt{AT}}$ and $\mathcal{P}^{\mathtt{NRT}}$. The next example shows that they do not satisfy the Boolean Compatibility, Joint and Alternative Use, Alternative Use, Insertion and Deletion Properties.

Example 9. *Consider* Σ *and* $(D, Prov(X), \lambda_X)$ *as follows.*

$$\Sigma = \{A(x) \rightarrow \mathsf{goal},\ B(x) \rightarrow \mathsf{goal},\ C(x) \rightarrow B(x)\}$$
$$D = \{A(a),\ C(a)\} \text{ with } \lambda_X(A(a)) = a,\ \lambda_X(C(a)) = c$$

It holds that both $\mathcal{P}^{MDT}(\Sigma, D, Prov(X), \lambda_X, \mathsf{goal})$ *and* $\mathcal{P}^{HMDT}(\Sigma, D, Prov(X), \lambda_X, \mathsf{goal})$ *are equal to* a. *For* $\mathcal{P} \in \{\mathcal{P}^{MDT}, \mathcal{P}^{HMDT}\}$ *we then have the following:*
(i) *The Boolean provenance of* goal *is* $a \vee c$, *hence* $\mathcal{P}$ *does not satisfy the Boolean Compatibility Property.*
(ii) *Since* $\mathcal{P}(\emptyset, D, Prov(X), \lambda_X, A(a)) = a$ *and* $\mathcal{P}(\emptyset, D, Prov(X), \lambda_X, C(a)) = c$, $\mathcal{P}$ *does not satisfy the Alternative Use, nor the Joint and Alternative Use Property.*
(iii) *Let* $D' = \{\mathsf{goal}\}$ *and* $\lambda'(\mathsf{goal}) = g$. *It holds that* $\mathcal{P}(\Sigma, D \cup D', Prov(X), \lambda_X \cup \lambda'_X, \mathsf{goal}) = g$, *which is different from* $\mathcal{P}(\Sigma, D, Prov(X), \lambda_X, \mathsf{goal}) + \mathcal{P}(\Sigma, D', Prov(X), \lambda'_X, \mathsf{goal}) + e$ *for every* $e \in Prov(X)$. *Hence* $\mathcal{P}$ *does not satisfy the Insertion Property.*
(iv) *Let* $D' = D \setminus \{A(a)\} = \{C(a)\}$. *The partial evaluation of* $\mathcal{P}(\Sigma, D, Prov(X), \lambda_X, \mathsf{goal})$ *where* a *is set to* 0 *is equal to* 0 *while* $\mathcal{P}(\Sigma, D', Prov(X), \lambda_X, \mathsf{goal}) = c$. *Hence* $\mathcal{P}$ *does not satisfy the Deletion Property.*

We now illustrate the difference between $\mathcal{P}^{\text{HMDT}}$ and $\mathcal{P}^{\text{MDT}}$: $\mathcal{P}^{\text{HMDT}}$ satisfies the Joint Use Property while $\mathcal{P}^{\text{MDT}}$ does not.

Example 10. *Let* $\Sigma = \{C(x) \rightarrow B(x),\ D(x) \rightarrow A(x)\}$, $D = \{B(a), C(a), D(a)\}$ *and* $\lambda(B(a)) = b$, $\lambda(C(a)) = c$, $\lambda(D(a)) = d$, *and consider* $\Sigma' = \Sigma \cup \{A(a) \wedge B(a) \rightarrow \mathsf{goal}\}$. $\mathcal{P}^{MDT}(\Sigma', D, \mathbb{K}, \lambda, \mathsf{goal}) = b \times d + c \times d$ *while* $\mathcal{P}^{MDT}(\Sigma, D, \mathbb{K}, \lambda, A(a)) = d$ *and* $\mathcal{P}^{MDT}(\Sigma, D, \mathbb{K}, \lambda, B(a)) = b$. *Hence* $\mathcal{P}^{MDT}$ *does not satisfy the Joint Use Property.*

We conclude this discussion with the remark that $\mathcal{P}^{\text{AT}}$ satisfies the Commutation with ω-Continuous Homomorphisms but not the Commutation with Homomorphisms Property.

Example 11. *Consider the semiring* $\mathbb{N}^\infty$ *with the classical operations, and define* $\mathbb{N}^{\infty,\infty'}$ *as its extension by an element* ∞' *such that for every* $n \in \mathbb{N} \cup \{\infty\}$, $n + \infty' = \infty'$, *and* $n \times \infty' = \infty'$ *if* $n \neq 0$, *and* 0 *otherwise. Both semirings are* ω*-continuous and* $h : \mathbb{N}^\infty \mapsto \mathbb{N}^{\infty,\infty'}$ *defined by* $h(n) = n$ *for every* $n \in \mathbb{N}$, $h(\infty) = \infty'$ *is a semiring homomorphism (which is not* ω*-continuous). Assume that* $\mathcal{P}^{AT}(\Sigma, D, \mathbb{N}^\infty, \lambda, \mathsf{goal}) = \Sigma_{i \in \mathbb{N}} 1 = \infty$. *Then* $h(\mathcal{P}^{AT}(\Sigma, D, \mathbb{N}^\infty, \lambda, \mathsf{goal})) = \infty'$ *is different from* $\mathcal{P}^{AT}(\Sigma, D, \mathbb{N}^{\infty,\infty'}, h \circ \lambda, \mathsf{goal}) = \Sigma_{i \in \mathbb{N}} h(1) = \infty$.

5.2 Model-Based Semantics Cases

On $+$-idempotent semirings, $\mathcal{P}^{\text{AM}}$ and $\mathcal{P}^{\text{SAM}}$ coincide with $\mathcal{P}^{\text{AT}}$ so verify the same properties, and the semiring $\mathbb{B}[\![X]\!]$ of formal power series with Boolean coefficients can be used to compute them in any $+$-idempotent semiring (Bourgaux et al. 2022). However, on non-idempotent semirings, they do not satisfy several properties, and in particular the Commutation with (ω-Continuous) Homomorphisms Properties.

Example 12. *Let* $\Sigma = \{A(x) \rightarrow \mathsf{goal}, B(x) \rightarrow \mathsf{goal}\}$ *and* $D = \{A(a), B(a)\}$ *and consider the provenance semiring* $\mathbb{N}^\infty[\![X]\!]$ *with* $\lambda_X(A(a)) = x$ *and* $\lambda_X(B(a)) = y$.

It holds that both $\mathcal{P}^{AM}(\Sigma, D, \mathbb{N}^\infty[\![X]\!], \lambda_X, \mathsf{goal})$ *and* $\mathcal{P}^{SAM}(\Sigma, D, \mathbb{N}^\infty[\![X]\!], \lambda_X, \mathsf{goal})$ *are equal to* $x + y$.

Consider now the semiring $\mathbb{N}^\infty$, $\lambda_{\mathbb{N}}(A(a)) = 2$ *and* $\lambda_{\mathbb{N}}(B(a)) = 2$. *Both* $\mathcal{P}^{AM}(\Sigma, D, \mathbb{N}^\infty, \lambda_{\mathbb{N}}, \mathsf{goal})$ *and* $\mathcal{P}^{SAM}(\Sigma, D, \mathbb{N}^\infty, \lambda_{\mathbb{N}}, \mathsf{goal})$ *are equal to* 2.

For $\mathcal{P} \in \{\mathcal{P}^{AM}, \mathcal{P}^{SAM}\}$ *we then have the following:*
(i) *Let* h *be a* ω*-continuous homomorphism from* $\mathbb{N}^\infty[\![X]\!]$ *to* $\mathbb{N}^\infty$ *such that* $h(x) = 2$ *and* $h(y) = 2$. *Since* $h(x + y) = h(x) + h(y) = 4$, $\mathcal{P}$ *does not satisfy the Commutation with* ω*-Continuous Homomorphisms Property.*
(ii) *The relational provenance of* $Q^\Sigma()$ *w.r.t.* $\mathbb{N}^\infty$ *and* $\lambda_{\mathbb{N}}$ *is* 4 *so* $\mathcal{P}$ *does not satisfy the Algebra Consistency Property.*
(iii) $\mathcal{P}(\emptyset, D, \mathbb{N}^\infty, \lambda_{\mathbb{N}}, A(a)) + \mathcal{P}(\emptyset, D, \mathbb{N}^\infty, \lambda_{\mathbb{N}}, B(a)) = 4$ *so* $\mathcal{P}$ *does not satisfy the Alternative Use nor the Joint and Alternative Use Property.*
(iv) *Since* $\mathcal{P}(\Sigma, \{A(a)\}, \mathbb{N}^\infty, \lambda_{\mathbb{N}}, \mathsf{goal}) + \mathcal{P}(\Sigma, \{B(a)\}, \mathbb{N}^\infty, \lambda_{\mathbb{N}}, \mathsf{goal}) = 4$ *is strictly greater than* $\mathcal{P}(\Sigma, D, \mathbb{N}^\infty, \lambda_{\mathbb{N}}, \mathsf{goal})$, $\mathcal{P}$ *does not satisfy the Insertion Property.*

Moreover, $\mathcal{P}^{\text{SAM}}$ does not satisfy the Joint Use Property.

Example 13. *Let*

$$\Sigma = \{A(x) \rightarrow \mathsf{g}_1, A(x) \rightarrow \mathsf{g}_2, B(x) \rightarrow \mathsf{g}_1, B(x) \rightarrow \mathsf{g}_2\}$$
$$D = \{A(a), B(a)\} \text{ with } \lambda_X(A(a)) = x, \lambda_X(B(a)) = y.$$

Both $\mathcal{P}^{SAM}(\Sigma, D, \mathbb{N}^\infty[\![X]\!], \lambda_X, \mathsf{g}_1)$ *and* $\mathcal{P}^{SAM}(\Sigma, D, \mathbb{N}^\infty[\![X]\!], \lambda_X, \mathsf{g}_2)$ *are equal to* $x + y$ *but* $\mathcal{P}^{SAM}(\Sigma \cup \{\mathsf{g}_1 \wedge \mathsf{g}_2 \rightarrow \mathsf{goal}\}, D, \mathbb{N}^\infty[\![X]\!], \lambda_X, \mathsf{goal}) = x^2 + y^2 + xy \neq (x + y)^2$.

We show that $\mathcal{P}^{\text{AM}}$ does not satisfy the Necessary Facts Property in the appendix of (Bourgaux et al. 2022) because we needed to craft a specific semiring to get a counter-example.

6 Complexity Considerations and Conclusion

In this paper, we present alternative provenance semantics for Datalog based on models, execution algorithms and derivation trees, and compare them through the lens of different properties. $\mathcal{P}^{\text{NRT}}$ is the only one that satisfies all the studied properties but does not coincide with an execution based semantics contrary to the other tree-based semantics $\mathcal{P}^{\text{AT}}$, $\mathcal{P}^{\text{MDT}}$, and $\mathcal{P}^{\text{HMDT}}$. The equivalence between the tree-based $\mathcal{P}^{\text{AT}}$, $\mathcal{P}^{\text{NRT}}$ and model-based $\mathcal{P}^{\text{AM}}$ and $\mathcal{P}^{\text{SAM}}$ definitions on absorptive semirings may also indicates a robust provenance on this restricted setting.

One of the main complexity sources of Datalog provenance stems from its infinite representation. Deutch et al. (2014) studied semirings for which the provenance expressions given by $\mathcal{P}^{\text{AT}}$ are finite, and showed that they can be represented by polynomial size circuits. We show that the annotations produced at each iteration of our execution algorithms can be represented by arithmetic circuits of polynomial size in the data (Bourgaux et al. 2022). Consequently, both $\mathcal{P}^{\text{MDT}}$ and $\mathcal{P}^{\text{HMDT}}$ can be represented by polynomial size circuits regardless of the semiring. On the contrary, we show that (assuming $\mathsf{P} \neq \mathsf{NP}$) there is no polynomially computable circuit that computes $\mathcal{P}^{\text{NRT}}$ on $\mathbb{N}^\infty[\![X]\!]$, by a reduction from a result by Arenas, Conca, and Pérez (2012). Whether it is possible to polynomially compute circuits for $\mathcal{P}^{\text{NRT}}$ on provenance semirings less expressive than $\mathbb{N}^\infty[\![X]\!]$ but non-absorptive remains open.

Acknowledgements

This work is supported by the ANR project CQFD (ANR-18-CE23-0003).

References

Abiteboul, S.; Hull, R.; and Vianu, V. 1995. *Foundations of Databases*. Addison-Wesley.

Achs, Á., and Kiss, A. 1995. Fuzzy extension of datalog. *Acta Cybern.* 12(2):153–166.

Arenas, M.; Conca, S.; and Pérez, J. 2012. Counting beyond a yottabyte, or how SPARQL 1.1 property paths will prevent adoption of the standard. In Mille, A.; Gandon, F.; Misselis, J.; Rabinovich, M.; and Staab, S., eds., *Proceedings of the 21st World Wide Web Conference 2012, WWW 2012, Lyon, France, April 16-20, 2012*, 629–638. ACM.

Bourgaux, C.; Ozaki, A.; Peñaloza, R.; and Predoiu, L. 2020. Provenance for the description logic elhr. In Bessiere, C., ed., *Proceedings of the Twenty-Ninth International Joint Conference on Artificial Intelligence, IJCAI 2020*, 1862–1869. ijcai.org.

Bourgaux, C.; Bourhis, P.; Peterfreund, L.; and Thomazo, M. 2022. Revisiting semiring provenance for Datalog. arxiv.org/abs/2202.10766.

Calvanese, D.; Lanti, D.; Ozaki, A.; Peñaloza, R.; and Xiao, G. 2019. Enriching ontology-based data access with provenance. In Kraus, S., ed., *Proceedings of the Twenty-Eighth International Joint Conference on Artificial Intelligence, IJCAI 2019, Macao, China, August 10-16, 2019*, 1616–1623. ijcai.org.

Ceylan, İ. İ.; Lukasiewicz, T.; Malizia, E.; and Vaicenavicius, A. 2019. Explanations for query answers under existential rules. In Kraus, S., ed., *Proceedings of the Twenty-Eighth International Joint Conference on Artificial Intelligence, IJCAI 2019, Macao, China, August 10-16, 2019*, 1639–1646. ijcai.org.

Ceylan, İ. İ.; Lukasiewicz, T.; Malizia, E.; and Vaicenavicius, A. 2020. Explanations for ontology-mediated query answering in description logics. In Giacomo, G. D.; Catalá, A.; Dilkina, B.; Milano, M.; Barro, S.; Bugarín, A.; and Lang, J., eds., *ECAI 2020 - 24th European Conference on Artificial Intelligence, 29 August-8 September 2020, Santiago de Compostela, Spain*, volume 325 of *Frontiers in Artificial Intelligence and Applications*, 672–679. IOS Press.

Cheney, J.; Chiticariu, L.; and Tan, W. C. 2009. Provenance in databases: Why, how, and where. *Found. Trends Databases* 1(4):379–474.

Cui, Y.; Widom, J.; and Wiener, J. L. 2000. Tracing the lineage of view data in a warehousing environment. *ACM Trans. Database Syst.* 25(2):179–227.

Dannert, K. M.; Grädel, E.; Naaf, M.; and Tannen, V. 2021. Semiring provenance for fixed-point logic. In Baier, C., and Goubault-Larrecq, J., eds., *29th EACSL Annual Conference on Computer Science Logic, CSL 2021, January 25-28, 2021, Ljubljana, Slovenia (Virtual Conference)*, volume 183 of *LIPIcs*, 17:1–17:22. Schloss Dagstuhl - Leibniz-Zentrum für Informatik.

Deutch, D.; Milo, T.; Roy, S.; and Tannen, V. 2014. Circuits for datalog provenance. In Schweikardt, N.; Christophides, V.; and Leroy, V., eds., *Proc. 17th International Conference on Database Theory (ICDT), Athens, Greece, March 24-28, 2014*, 201–212. OpenProceedings.org.

Deutch, D.; Gilad, A.; and Moskovitch, Y. 2018. Efficient provenance tracking for datalog using top-k queries. *VLDB J.* 27(2):245–269.

Esparza, J., and Luttenberger, M. 2011. Solving fixed-point equations by derivation tree analysis. In Corradini, A.; Klin, B.; and Cîrstea, C., eds., *Algebra and Coalgebra in Computer Science*, 19–35. Berlin, Heidelberg: Springer Berlin Heidelberg.

Green, T. J., and Tannen, V. 2017. The semiring framework for database provenance. In Sallinger, E.; den Bussche, J. V.; and Geerts, F., eds., *Proceedings of the 36th ACM SIGMOD-SIGACT-SIGAI Symposium on Principles of Database Systems, PODS 2017, Chicago, IL, USA, May 14-19, 2017*, 93–99. ACM.

Green, T. J.; Karvounarakis, G.; and Tannen, V. 2007. Provenance semirings. In Libkin, L., ed., *Proceedings of the Twenty-Sixth ACM SIGACT-SIGMOD-SIGART Symposium on Principles of Database Systems, June 11-13, 2007, Beijing, China*, 31–40. ACM.

Green, T. J. 2009. Containment of conjunctive queries on annotated relations. In Fagin, R., ed., *Database Theory - ICDT 2009, 12th International Conference, St. Petersburg, Russia, March 23-25, 2009, Proceedings*, volume 361 of *ACM International Conference Proceeding Series*, 296–309. ACM.

Hernich, A., and Kolaitis, P. G. 2017. Foundations of information integration under bag semantics. In *32nd Annual ACM/IEEE Symposium on Logic in Computer Science, LICS 2017, Reykjavik, Iceland, June 20-23, 2017*, 1–12. IEEE Computer Society.

Mumick, I. S.; Pirahesh, H.; and Ramakrishnan, R. 1990. The magic of duplicates and aggregates. In McLeod, D.; Sacks-Davis, R.; and Schek, H., eds., *16th International Conference on Very Large Data Bases, August 13-16, 1990, Brisbane, Queensland, Australia, Proceedings*, 264–277. Morgan Kaufmann.

Nikolaou, C.; Kostylev, E. V.; Konstantinidis, G.; Kaminski, M.; Grau, B. C.; and Horrocks, I. 2017. The bag semantics of ontology-based data access. In Sierra, C., ed., *Proceedings of the Twenty-Sixth International Joint Conference on Artificial Intelligence, IJCAI 2017, Melbourne, Australia, August 19-25, 2017*, 1224–1230. ijcai.org.

Nikolaou, C.; Kostylev, E. V.; Konstantinidis, G.; Kaminski, M.; Grau, B. C.; and Horrocks, I. 2019. Foundations of ontology-based data access under bag semantics. *Artif. Intell.* 274:91–132.

Senellart, P. 2017. Provenance and probabilities in relational databases. *SIGMOD Rec.* 46(4):5–15.

Soufflé. 2020. https://souffle-lang.github.io/index.html.

Stüber, T., and Vogler, H. 2008. Weighted monadic datalog. *Theoretical Computer Science* 403(2):221–238.

Zhao, D.; Subotic, P.; and Scholz, B. 2020. Debugging large-scale datalog: A scalable provenance evaluation strategy. *ACM Trans. Program. Lang. Syst.* 42(2):7:1–7:35.

Normalisations of Existential Rules: Not so Innocuous!

David Carral[1], **Lucas Larroque**[2*], **Marie-Laure Mugnier**[1], **Michaël Thomazo**[3]
[1]LIRMM, Inria, University of Montpellier, CNRS, Montpellier, France
[2]DI ENS, ENS, CNRS, PSL University, Paris, France
[3]Inria, DI ENS, ENS, CNRS, PSL University, Paris, France
{david.carral, michael.thomazo}@inria.fr, lucas.larroque@ens.psl.eu, mugnier@lirmm.fr

Abstract

Existential rules are an expressive knowledge representation language mainly developed to query data. In the literature, they are often supposed to be in some normal form that simplifies technical developments. For instance, a common assumption is that rule heads are atomic, i.e., restricted to a single atom. Such assumptions are considered to be made without loss of generality as long as all sets of rules can be normalised while preserving entailment. However, an important question is whether the properties that ensure the decidability of reasoning are preserved as well. We provide a systematic study of the impact of these procedures on the different chase variants with respect to chase (non-)termination and FO-rewritability. This also leads us to study open problems related to chase termination of independent interest.

1 Introduction

Existential rules are an expressive knowledge representation language mainly developed to query data (Baget et al. 2009; Calì, Gottlob, and Lukasiewicz 2009). Such rules are an extension of first-order function-free Horn rules (like those of Datalog) with existentially quantified variables in the rule heads, which allows to infer the existence of unknown individuals.

Querying a knowledge base (KB) $\mathcal{K} = \langle \mathcal{R}, F \rangle$, where $\mathcal{R}$ is a set of existential rules and F a set of facts, consists in computing all the answers to queries that are logically entailed from $\mathcal{K}$. Two main techniques have been developed, particularly in the context of the fundamental (Boolean) conjunctive queries. The *chase* is a bottom-up process that expands F by rule applications from $\mathcal{R}$ towards a fixpoint. It produces a *universal* model of $\mathcal{K}$, i.e., a model of $\mathcal{K}$ that homomorphically maps to all models of $\mathcal{K}$, which is therefore sufficient to decide query entailment. *Query rewriting* is a dual technique, which consists in rewriting a query q with the rules in $\mathcal{R}$ into a query q' such that q is entailed by $\mathcal{K}$ if and only if q' is entailed by F solely.

Conjunctive query answering being undecidable for existential rules (Beeri and Vardi 1981), both the chase and query rewriting may not terminate. There is however a wide range of rule subclasses defined by syntactic restrictions that ensure *chase termination* on any set of facts (see, e.g., various acyclicity notions in (Grau et al. 2013)) or the existence, for any conjunctive query, of a (finite) rewriting into a first-order query, a property referred to as *FO-rewritability* (Calvanese et al. 2007).

In the literature, existential rules are often supposed to be in some normal form that simplifies technical developments. For instance, a common assumption is that rule heads are atomic, i.e., restricted to a single atom. On the one hand, the use of single-head rules greatly simplifies the presentation of theoretical arguments (e.g., (Calì, Gottlob, and Pieris 2012)). On the other hand, this restriction may also simplify implementations; e.g., the optimisation procedure presented in (Tsamoura et al. 2021) exploits single-head rules to clearly establish the provenance of each fact computed during the chase. Moreover, after normalisation, we can apply existing methods to effectively determine if the chase terminates for an input single-head existential rule set if this set is linear (Leclère et al. 2019) or guarded (Gogacz, Marcinkowski, and Pieris 2020). Normal form assumptions are often made without loss of generality as long as all sets of rules can be normalised while preserving all interesting entailments. However, an important question is whether the properties that ensure the decidability of reasoning are preserved as well. In particular, what is the impact of common normalisation procedures on fundamental properties like chase termination or FO-rewritability?

In fact, the chase is a family of algorithms, which differ from each other in their termination properties. Here, we consider the four main chase variants, namely: the *oblivious* chase (Calì, Gottlob, and Kifer 2008a), the *semi-oblivious* (aka skolem) chase (Marnette 2009), the *restricted* (aka standard) chase (Fagin et al. 2003) and the *core* chase (Deutsch, Nash, and Remmel 2008). As the core chase has the inconvenience of being non-monotonic (i.e., the produced set of facts does not grow monotonically), we actually study a monotonic variant that behaves similarly regarding termination, namely the *equivalent* chase (Rocher 2016). The ability of a chase variant to halt on a given KB is directly related to its power of reducing logical redundancies introduced by rules. The oblivious chase blindly performs all possible rule applications, while the equivalent chase terminates exactly when the KB admits a finite universal model. The other variants lie between these two extremes. For practical efficiency reasons, the most implemented variant is the restricted chase. However, it is the only variant sensitive to

*Our work started when Lucas was intern at LIRMM-Inria.

	$\mathbb{O}$	$\mathbb{SO}$	$\exists$-$\mathbb{R}$	$\forall$-$\mathbb{R}$	$\exists$-$\mathbb{DF}$-$\mathbb{R}$	$\forall$-$\mathbb{DF}$-$\mathbb{R}$	$\mathbb{E}$
Single-Piece	=	+	$\neq$	$\neq$	$\neq$	$\neq$	=
One-Way	=	=	−	−	−	−	−
Two-Way	=	=	+	−	=	=	=

Table 1: Impact on chase termination. Chase variants are denoted as follows: $\mathbb{O}$: Oblivious; $\mathbb{SO}$: semi-oblivious; ($\mathbb{DF}$-)$\mathbb{R}$: (Datalog-first) restricted; $\mathbb{E}$: equivalent.

the order of rule applications: for a given KB, there may be sequences of rule applications that terminate, while others do not. We study a natural strategy, called *Datalog-first restricted chase*, which prioritises Datalog rules (whose head does not include existential quantifiers) thus achieving termination in many real-world cases (Carral, Dragoste, and Krötzsch 2017). Moreover, experiments have shown that it is indeed a very efficient strategy (Urbani et al. 2018).

On the other hand, we consider two well-known normalisation procedures of a set of rules: *single-piece*-decomposition, which breaks rule heads into subsets called pieces and outputs a logically equivalent rule set (Baget et al. 2011; König et al. 2013); and *atomic*-decomposition, which requires to introduce fresh predicates and outputs a set of atomic-head rules that form a conservative extension of the original set, hence preserve entailment (Calì, Gottlob, and Kifer 2008b; Calì, Gottlob, and Pieris 2012).

Contributions. We provide a systematic study of the impact of these procedures on the different chase variants with respect to chase (non-)termination and FO-rewritability. This also leads us to solve some open problems related to chase termination, which are of independent interest.

Although the relationships between most chase variants with respect to chase termination are well understood (Grahne and Onet 2018), the question remained open regarding the restricted chase and its Datalog-first version. Unexpectedly, we found that Datalog-first strategies are not always optimal: we exhibit a rule set $\mathcal{R}$ such that the restricted chase has a terminating sequence on any KB $\langle\mathcal{R}, F\rangle$ but there is a KB $\langle\mathcal{R}, F\rangle$ on which no Datalog-first strategy terminates (Section 3).

While it appears that none of the considered decompositions influences FO-rewritability, the situation is very different concerning chase termination, as summarized in Table 1. Note that we distinguish between two behaviors for restricted chases: $\exists$ means that at least one chase sequence terminates on any KB ("sometimes-termination") and $\forall$ that all sequences terminate on any KB ("termination"). Single-piece-decomposition (Section 4) has no impact on the oblivious and equivalent chases (noted =), a positive impact on the semi-oblivious chase (noted +), and an erratic impact on (Datalog-first-)restricted chase (noted $\neq$). The standard atomic-decomposition (Section 5), called *one-way* in the table, has a negative impact on all chase variants, except for the (semi-)oblivious ones. Looking for a well-behaved atomic-decomposition procedure, we study a new one, named *two-way* (Section 6). A salient property of this decomposition is that it preserves the existence of a finite universal model. As shown in the table, two-way behaves better than one-way: it preserves (sometimes-)termination of the Datalog-first restricted chase and may even improve the sometimes-termination of the restricted chase. However, the negative impact on the termination of the restricted chase remains. These findings led us to an intriguing question: does a computable normalisation procedure exist that produces atomic-head rules and exactly preserves the termination of the restricted chase? We show that the answer is negative by a complexity argument (Section 7). More specifically, we study the decidability status of the following problem: Given a KB $\mathcal{K} = \langle\mathcal{R}, F\rangle$, does the restricted chase terminate on $\mathcal{K}$? We show that the associated membership problem is at least at the second level of the arithmetical hierarchy (precisely Π_2^0-hard) when there is no restriction on $\mathcal{R}$, while it is recursively enumerable (in Σ_1^0) when $\mathcal{R}$ is a set of atomic-head rules. Since $\Sigma_1^0 \subsetneq \Pi_2^0$, we obtain the negative answer to our question.

The complete proofs for all of the results in this paper can be found on an arXiv submission with the same name.

2 Preliminaries

First-Order Logic (FOL) We define $\texttt{Preds}$, $\texttt{Cons}$, and $\texttt{Vars}$ to be mutually disjoint, countably infinite sets of *predicates*, *constants*, and *variables*, respectively. Every $P \in \texttt{Preds}$ has an *arity* $\mathsf{ar}(P) \geq 0$. Let $\texttt{Terms} = \texttt{Cons} \cup \texttt{Vars}$ be the set of *terms*. We write lists $t_1, \ldots, t_n$ of terms as $\vec{t}$ and often treat them as sets. For a formula or set thereof U, let $\texttt{Preds}(U)$, $\texttt{Cons}(U)$, $\texttt{Vars}(U)$, and $\texttt{Terms}(U)$ be the sets of all predicates, constants, variables, and terms that occur in U, respectively.

An *atom* is a FOL formula $P(\vec{t})$ with P a $|\vec{t}|$-ary predicate and $\vec{t} \in \texttt{Terms}$. For a formula U, we write $U[\vec{x}]$ to indicate that $\vec{x}$ is the set of all free variables that occur in U.

Definition 1. An *(existential) rule* R is a FOL formula

$$\forall\vec{x}\forall\vec{y}.\big(B[\vec{x},\vec{y}] \to \exists\vec{z}.H[\vec{x},\vec{z}]\big) \qquad (1)$$

where $\vec{x}$, $\vec{y}$, and $\vec{z}$ are pairwise disjoint lists of variables; and B and H are (finite) non-empty conjunctions of atoms, called the *body* and the *head* of R, respectively. The set $\vec{x}$ is the *frontier* of R. If $\vec{z}$ is empty, then R is a *Datalog* rule.

Next, we often denote a rule such as R above by $B \to H$ or $B \to \exists\vec{z}.H$, omitting all or some quantifiers.

A *factbase* F is an existentially closed (finite) conjunction of atoms. A *Boolean conjunctive query* (BCQ) has the same form as a factbase, and we often identify both notions.A *knowledge base* (KB) $\mathcal{K}$ is a tuple $\langle\mathcal{R}, F\rangle$ with $\mathcal{R}$ a rule set and F a factbase. We often identify rule bodies, rule heads, and factbases with (finite) sets of atoms.

Given atom sets F and F', a *homomorphism* π from F to F' is a function with domain $\texttt{Vars}(F)$ such that $\pi(F) \subseteq F'$; π is an *isomorphism* from F to F' if additionally, π is injective and π^{-1} is a homomorphism from F to F'. A homomorphism π from F to F' is a *retraction* if π is the identity over $\texttt{Vars}(F) \cap \texttt{Vars}(F')$ (next, we often use this notion with $F' \subseteq F$).

We identify logical interpretations with atom sets. An atom set F *satisfies* a rule $R = B \rightarrow H$ if, for every homomorphism π from B to F, there is an extension $\hat{\pi}$ of π with $\hat{\pi}(H) \subseteq F$; equivalently, F is a *model* of R. An atom set $\mathcal{M}$ is a *model of a factbase* F if there is a homomorphism from F to $\mathcal{M}$, and it is a *model of a KB* $\langle \mathcal{R}, F \rangle$ if it is a model of F and satisfies all rules in $\mathcal{R}$. Given KBs or atom sets A and B, A *entails* B, written $A \models B$, if every model of A is a model of B; A and B are *equivalent* if $A \models B$ and $B \models A$. Given atom sets F and F', it is known that $F \models F'$ iff there is a homomorphism from F' to F.

Definition 2. A model $\mathcal{M}$ of a KB $\mathcal{K}$ is *universal* if there is a homomorphism from $\mathcal{M}$ to every model of $\mathcal{K}$.

Every KB $\mathcal{K}$ admits some (possibly infinite) universal model. Hence, $\mathcal{K} \models Q$ for any BCQ Q iff there is a homomorphism from a universal model of $\mathcal{K}$ to Q. The *BCQ entailment* problem takes as input a KB $\mathcal{K}$ and a BCQ Q and asks if $\mathcal{K} \models Q$; it is undecidable (Beeri and Vardi 1981).

Next, we will consider transformations of rule sets that introduce fresh predicates. To specify the relationships between a rule set and its decomposition, we will rely on the notion of conservative extension:

Definition 3 (Conservative extension)**.** Let $\mathcal{R}$ and $\mathcal{R}'$ be two rule sets such that $\texttt{Preds}(\mathcal{R}) \subseteq \texttt{Preds}(\mathcal{R}')$. The set $\mathcal{R}'$ is a *conservative extension* of the set $\mathcal{R}$ if (1) the restriction of any model of $\mathcal{R}'$ to the predicates in $\texttt{Preds}(\mathcal{R})$ is a model of $\mathcal{R}$, and (2) any model $\mathcal{M}$ of $\mathcal{R}$ can be extended to a model $\mathcal{M}'$ of $\mathcal{R}'$ that has the same domain (i.e., $\texttt{Terms}(\mathcal{M}) = \texttt{Terms}(\mathcal{M}')$) and agrees with $\mathcal{M}$ on the interpretation of the predicates in $\texttt{Preds}(\mathcal{R})$ (i.e., they have the same atoms with predicates in $\texttt{Preds}(\mathcal{R})$).

When $\mathcal{R}'$ is a conservative extension of $\mathcal{R}$, for any factbase F the KBs $\langle \mathcal{R}, F \rangle$ and $\langle \mathcal{R}', F \rangle$ entail the same (closed) formulas on $\texttt{Preds}(\mathcal{R})$, in particular BCQs.

The chase The chase is a family of procedures that repeatedly apply rules to a factbase until a fixpoint is reached. We formally define such procedures before stating their correctness with respect to factbase entailment in Proposition 7.

Definition 4 (Triggers and derivations)**.** Given a fact set F, a *trigger* t on F is a tuple $\langle R, \pi \rangle$ with $R = B \rightarrow \exists \vec{z}.H$ a rule and π a homomorphism from B to F. Let $\mathsf{support}(t) = \pi(B)$ and $\mathsf{output}(t) = \pi^R(H)$, where π^R is the extension of π that maps every variable $z \in \vec{z}$ to the fresh variable z_t that is unique for z and t. A *derivation* from a KB $\mathcal{K} = \langle \mathcal{R}, F \rangle$ is a sequence $\mathcal{D} = (\emptyset, F_0), (t_1, F_1), \ldots$ such that:

1. Every F_i in $\mathcal{D}$ is a factbase; moreover, $F_0 = F$.
2. Every t_i in $\mathcal{D}$ is a trigger $\langle R, \pi \rangle$ on F_{i-1} such that $R \in \mathcal{R}$, $\mathsf{output}(t_i) \not\subseteq F_{i-1}$, and $F_i = F_{i-1} \cup \mathsf{output}(t_i)$.

The *result* of $\mathcal{D}$, written $\mathsf{res}(\mathcal{D})$, is the union of all the factbases in $\mathcal{D}$. Let $\mathsf{triggers}(\mathcal{D})$ be the set of all triggers in $\mathcal{D}$ and $\mathsf{length}(\mathcal{D}) = |\mathsf{triggers}(\mathcal{D})|$ be the length of $\mathcal{D}$.

Different chase variants build specific derivations according to different criteria of trigger applicability. Below, the letters $\mathbb{O}$, $\mathbb{SO}$, $\mathbb{R}$, and $\mathbb{E}$ respectively refer to so-called oblivious, semi-oblivious, restricted, and equivalent[1] variants.

Definition 5 (Applicability)**.** A trigger $t = \langle R, \pi \rangle$ on a factbase F is (i) $\mathbb{O}$*-applicable* on F if $\mathsf{output}(t) \not\subseteq F$, (ii) $\mathbb{SO}$*-applicable* on F if $\mathsf{output}(t') \not\subseteq F$ for every trigger $t' = (R, \pi')$ with $\pi(x) = \pi'(x)$ for all $x \in \mathsf{fr}(R)$, (iii) $\mathbb{R}$*-applicable* on F if there is no retraction from $F \cup \mathsf{output}(t)$ to F, and (iv) $\mathbb{E}$*-applicable* on F if there is no homomorphism from $F \cup \mathsf{output}(t)$ to F.

Example 1. *Consider the KB $\mathcal{K} = \langle \mathcal{R}, F \rangle$ with $\mathcal{R} = \{R = P(x, y) \rightarrow \exists z.P(y, z) \wedge P(z, y)\}$ and $F = \{P(a, b)\}$ with a and b some constants. The trigger $t_1 = (R, \pi_1)$ with $\pi_1 = \{x \mapsto a, y \mapsto b\}$ is $\mathbb{X}$-applicable on $F_0 = F$ (for any $\mathbb{X}$), and $\mathsf{output}(t_1) = \{P(b, z_{t_1}), P(z_{t_1}, b)\}$. There are two new triggers on $F_1 = F \cup \mathsf{output}(t_1)$, both $\mathbb{O}$- and $\mathbb{SO}$-applicable, but neither $\mathbb{R}$- nor $\mathbb{E}$-applicable. For instance, consider $t_2 = (R, \pi_2)$ with $\pi_2 = \{x \mapsto b, y \mapsto z_{t_1}\}$ and $\mathsf{output}(t_2) = \{P(z_{t_1}, z_{t_2}), P(z_{t_2}, z_{t_1})\}$: there is a retraction from $F_1 \cup \mathsf{output}(t_2)$ to F_1, which maps z_{t_2} to b.*

Definition 6 (($\mathbb{DF}$-)$\mathbb{X}$-Chase)**.** For an $\mathbb{X} \in \{\mathbb{O}, \mathbb{SO}, \mathbb{R}, \mathbb{E}\}$, an $\mathbb{X}$*-derivation from a KB* $\mathcal{K} = \langle \mathcal{R}, F \rangle$ is a derivation $\mathcal{D}$ such that every trigger $t_i \in \mathsf{triggers}(\mathcal{D})$ is $\mathbb{X}$-applicable on F_i; $\mathcal{D}$ is a $\mathbb{DF}$-$\mathbb{X}$*-derivation* if it gives priority to Datalog rules: for any $t_i = \langle R, \pi \rangle \in \mathsf{triggers}(\mathcal{D})$, if R is a non-Datalog rule, then F_{i-1} satisfies every Datalog rule in $\mathcal{R}$. A ($\mathbb{DF}$-)$\mathbb{X}$-derivation $\mathcal{D}$ is *fair* if for every F_i occurring in $\mathcal{D}$ and trigger t $\mathbb{X}$-applicable on F_i, there is some $j > i$ such that t is not $\mathbb{X}$-applicable on F_j. A ($\mathbb{DF}$-)$\mathbb{X}$-derivation is *terminating* if it is fair and finite.

The result of any fair $\mathbb{X}$-derivation is a universal model of the KB, for $\mathbb{X} \in \{\mathbb{O}, \mathbb{SO}, \mathbb{R}\}$, and has a retraction to a universal model for $\mathbb{X} = \mathbb{E}$. Therefore, we obtain:

Proposition 7. *Consider a BCQ Q, a KB $\mathcal{K}$, and some fair $\mathbb{X}$-derivation $\mathcal{D}$ from $\mathcal{K}$ where $\mathbb{X} \in \{\mathbb{Y}, \mathbb{DF}\text{-}\mathbb{Y}\}$ and $\mathbb{Y} \in \{\mathbb{O}, \mathbb{SO}, \mathbb{R}, \mathbb{E}\}$. Then, $\mathcal{K} \models Q$ iff $\mathsf{res}(\mathcal{D}) \models Q$.*

Decidable Classes of Rule Sets We now define classes of rule sets that ensure the decidability of BCQ entailment, based either on chase termination or on query rewritability.

Definition 8 (Chase-Terminating Sets)**.** For a $\mathbb{Y} \in \{\mathbb{O}, \mathbb{SO}, \mathbb{R}, \mathbb{E}\}$ and an $\mathbb{X} \in \{\mathbb{Y}, \mathbb{DF}\text{-}\mathbb{Y}\}$, let $CT^{\mathbb{X}}_{\forall\forall}$ (resp. $CT^{\mathbb{X}}_{\forall\exists}$) be the set of all rule sets $\mathcal{R}$ such that every (resp. some) fair $\mathbb{X}$-derivation from every KB $\langle \mathcal{R}, F \rangle$ is finite.

When $\mathcal{R} \in CT^{\mathbb{X}}_{\forall\forall}$ (resp. $CT^{\mathbb{X}}_{\forall\exists}$), $\mathcal{R}$ ensures the *termination* (resp. *sometimes termination*) of the $\mathbb{X}$-chase.

Example 2. *Consider the KB $\mathcal{K} = \langle \mathcal{R}, F \rangle$ from Example 1. All fair $\mathbb{O}$- or $\mathbb{SO}$-derivations from $\mathcal{K}$ are infinite. The only one fair $\mathbb{R}$-derivation (resp. $\mathbb{E}$-derivation) from $\mathcal{K}$ is $\mathcal{D} = (\emptyset, F_0), (t_1, F_1)$. Any fair $\mathbb{R}$-derivation from a KB with $\mathcal{R}$ is finite and hence, $\mathcal{R} \in CT^{\mathbb{R}}_{\forall\forall}$ (and $\mathcal{R} \in CT^{\mathbb{E}}_{\forall\forall}$).*

[1]The equivalent chase behaves as the better-known core chase regarding termination: it halts exactly when the KB has a finite universal model. The difference lies in the fact that the core chase computes a minimal universal model (i.e., a core). The equivalent chase has the advantage of being monotonic ($\forall i, F_i \subseteq F_{i+1}$).

Definition 9 (FO-rewritability)**.** A rule set $\mathcal{R}$ is *FO-rewritable* if for any BCQ Q, there is a (finite) BCQ set $\{Q_1, \ldots, Q_n\}$ such that, for every factbase F, $\langle \mathcal{R}, F\rangle \models Q$ iff $F \models Q_i$ for some $1 \le i \le n$.

In our proofs, we rely on a property equivalent to FO-rewritability: the bounded derivation depth property, which has the advantage of being based on (a breadth-first version of) the chase (Calì, Gottlob, and Lukasiewicz 2009). See (Gottlob et al. 2014) about the equivalence between both properties.

Definition 10 (BDDP). For a rule R and a factbase F, let $R(F) \supseteq F$ be the minimal factbase that includes $\mathsf{output}(t)$ for every trigger t with R. For a rule set $\mathcal{R}$, let $\mathcal{R}(F) = \bigcup_{R \in \mathcal{R}} R(F)$. For a KB $\mathcal{K} = \langle \mathcal{R}, F\rangle$, let $\mathsf{Ch}_0(\mathcal{K}) = F$ and $\mathsf{Ch}_i(\mathcal{K}) = \mathcal{R}(\mathsf{Ch}_{i-1}(\mathcal{K}))$ for every $i \ge 1$.

A rule set $\mathcal{R}$ has the *bounded derivation depth property (BDDP)* if, for any BCQ Q, there is some $k \ge 0$ such that, for every factbase F, $\langle \mathcal{R}, F\rangle \models Q$ iff $\mathsf{Ch}_k(\langle \mathcal{R}, F\rangle) \models Q$.

Normalisation Procedures Finally, we formally define normalisation procedures and their impact on the above properties. A *normalisation procedure* is a function f that maps rule sets to rule sets (complying with a certain shape) such that for any rule set $\mathcal{R}$, $\langle \mathcal{R}, F\rangle \models Q$ iff $\langle f(\mathcal{R}), F\rangle \models Q$ for any factbase F and BCQ Q on $\mathtt{Preds}(\mathcal{R})$.

Definition 11. Consider some $\mathbb{X} \in \{\mathbb{O}, \mathbb{SO}, \mathbb{R}, \mathbb{DF}\text{-}\mathbb{R}, \mathbb{E}\}$. Then, a normalisation procedure f:

- *Preserves termination* of the $\mathbb{X}$-chase if $f(CT^{\mathbb{X}}_{\forall\forall}) \subseteq CT^{\mathbb{X}}_{\forall\forall}$; it preserves *sometimes-termination* of the $\mathbb{X}$-chase if $f(CT^{\mathbb{X}}_{\forall\exists}) \subseteq CT^{\mathbb{X}}_{\forall\exists}$.
- *Preserves non-termination* of the $\mathbb{X}$-chase if $f(\overline{CT^{\mathbb{X}}_{\forall\forall}}) \subseteq \overline{CT^{\mathbb{X}}_{\forall\forall}}$. Otherwise, f *may gain termination.*
- *Preserves rewritability* if it maps FO-rewritable rule sets to FO-rewritable rule sets.

3 Generality of Chase-Terminating Rule Sets

One of our goals is to study normalisation procedures that preserve membership over the sets of chase-terminating rule sets from Definition 8. To be systematic, we clarify the equality and strict-subset relations between these sets in Theorems 12 and 13, respectively. Grahne and Onet already proved most of the claims in these theorems (see Theorem 4.5, Propositions 4.6 and 4.7, and Corollary 4.8 in (Grahne and Onet 2018)); we reprove some of them again to be self-contained. However, note that all results regarding Datalog-first chase variants are our own contribution.

Theorem 12. *For every* $\mathbb{X} \in \{\mathbb{O}, \mathbb{SO}, \mathbb{E}\}$, *we have that*

$$CT^{\mathbb{X}}_{\forall\forall} = CT^{\mathbb{X}}_{\forall\exists} = CT^{\mathbb{DF}\text{-}\mathbb{X}}_{\forall\forall} = CT^{\mathbb{DF}\text{-}\mathbb{X}}_{\forall\exists}$$

Sketch. To show that the theorem holds if $\mathbb{X} = \mathbb{O}$ (resp. $\mathbb{X} = \mathbb{SO}$), it suffices to prove that all fair $\mathbb{X}$-derivations from an input KB $\mathcal{K}$ produce the same result (resp. same result up to isomorphism); see forthcoming Lemma 16.

All fair $\mathbb{E}$-derivations from an input KB $\mathcal{K}$ are finite iff $\mathcal{K}$ admits a finite universal model (Rocher 2016). Hence, the theorem holds if $\mathbb{X} = \mathbb{E}$. □

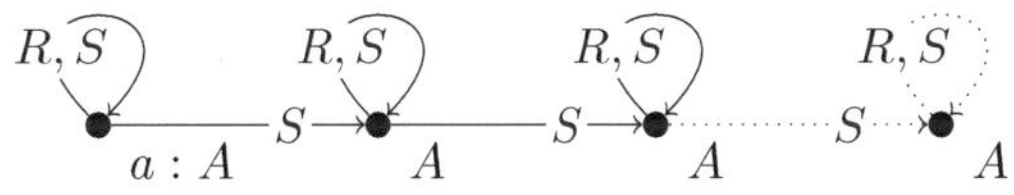

Figure 1: The only result of the $\mathbb{DF}$-$\mathbb{R}$-chase from the KB $\mathcal{K} = \langle \mathcal{R}, \{A(a)\}\rangle$ introduced in the proof of Theorem 13

The equalities in Theorem 12 simplify our work: for instance, if a function preserves termination of the oblivious chase, then we know that it also preserves sometimes-termination of this variant. Alas, the remaining sets of chase-terminating rule sets are not equal:

Theorem 13. *The following hold:*

$$\begin{aligned} CT^{\mathbb{O}}_{\forall\forall} \subset CT^{\mathbb{SO}}_{\forall\forall} \subset CT^{\mathbb{R}}_{\forall\forall} \subset CT^{\mathbb{DF}\text{-}\mathbb{R}}_{\forall\forall} \\ \subset CT^{\mathbb{DF}\text{-}\mathbb{R}}_{\forall\exists} \subset CT^{\mathbb{R}}_{\forall\exists} \subset CT^{\mathbb{E}}_{\forall\forall} \end{aligned}$$

Sketch. The subset inclusions follow by definition; we present some rule sets to show that these are strict:

$$\{P(x,y) \to \exists z.P(x,z)\} \in CT^{\mathbb{SO}}_{\forall\forall} \setminus CT^{\mathbb{O}}_{\forall\forall}$$

$$\{P(x,y) \to \exists z.P(y,z) \wedge P(z,y)\} \in CT^{\mathbb{R}}_{\forall\forall} \setminus CT^{\mathbb{SO}}_{\forall\forall}$$

$$\begin{aligned} &\{P(x,y) \to \exists z.P(y,z), \\ &\quad P(x,y) \to P(y,x)\} \in CT^{\mathbb{DF}\text{-}\mathbb{R}}_{\forall\forall} \setminus CT^{\mathbb{R}}_{\forall\forall} \end{aligned}$$

$$\begin{aligned} &\{P(x,y) \to \exists z.P(y,z) \wedge P(z,y), \\ &\quad P(x,y) \to \exists z.P(y,z)\} \in CT^{\mathbb{DF}\text{-}\mathbb{R}}_{\forall\exists} \setminus CT^{\mathbb{DF}\text{-}\mathbb{R}}_{\forall\forall} \end{aligned}$$

$$\begin{aligned} &\{P(x,y) \to \exists z.P(y,z), \\ &\quad P(x,y) \wedge P(y,z) \to P(y,x)\} \in CT^{\mathbb{E}}_{\forall\forall} \setminus CT^{\mathbb{R}}_{\forall\exists} \end{aligned}$$

Moreover, the rule set $\mathcal{R} = \{(2\text{–}6)\}$ is in $CT^{\mathbb{R}}_{\forall\exists} \setminus CT^{\mathbb{DF}\text{-}\mathbb{R}}_{\forall\exists}$:

$$A(x) \to R(x,x) \tag{2}$$

$$R(x,y) \wedge S(y,z) \to S(x,x) \tag{3}$$

$$A(x) \wedge S(x,y) \to A(y) \tag{4}$$

$$A(x) \to \exists z.R(x,z) \tag{5}$$

$$R(x,y) \to \exists z.S(y,z) \tag{6}$$

To show that $\mathcal{R} \notin CT^{\mathbb{DF}\text{-}\mathbb{R}}_{\forall\exists}$ we prove that the KB $\mathcal{K} = \langle \mathcal{R}, \{A(a)\}\rangle$ does not admit terminating $\mathbb{DF}$-$\mathbb{R}$-derivations. Specifically, all fair $\mathbb{DF}$-$\mathbb{R}$-derivations from $\mathcal{K}$ yield the same result, which is depicted in Figure 1. Rule (2) is applied first, then the following pattern is repeated: apply rule (6) followed by Datalog rules (3), (4) and (2). Rule (5) is never applicable since priority is given to rule (2). To show that $\mathcal{R} \in CT^{\mathbb{R}}_{\forall\exists}$ we verify that every KB of the form $\langle \mathcal{R}, F\rangle$ admits a terminating $\mathbb{R}$-derivation. We can produce such a derivation by exhaustively applying the rules in $\mathcal{R}$ in the following order:[2] first, apply rules (4), (5) and (6); then, apply (3); finally, apply (2). □

Our main achievement is showing that $CT^{\mathbb{R}}_{\forall\exists} \setminus CT^{\mathbb{DF}\text{-}\mathbb{R}}_{\forall\exists}$ is non-empty; thus proving that Datalog-first strategies are not necessarily the most terminating for the restricted chase.

[2]To understand why this strategy results in a terminating $\mathbb{R}$-derivation, we suggest to first try it on $F = \{A(a)\}$, which yields $\{A(a), R(a, z_1), S(z_1, z_2), S(a, a), R(a, a)\}$.

4 Single-Piece Decomposition

The single-piece decomposition (piece-decomposition in short) is a procedure that splits a rule $R = B \to \exists z.H$ into several rules $R_1, \ldots, R_n$ that have the same body as R, and whose head is a subset of H that (directly or indirectly) shares some existential variable in H.

Definition 14. The *piece graph* of a rule $R = B \to \exists \vec{z}.H$ is the graph whose vertices are the atoms in H, and with an edge between a and a' if $\vec{z} \cap \mathtt{Vars}(a) \cap \mathtt{Vars}(a')$ is non-empty. A *(rule) piece* of R is the conjunction of atoms corresponding to a (connected) component of its piece graph.

The *piece-decomposition* of a rule $R = B \to \exists \vec{z}.H$ is the rule set $\mathsf{sp}(R) = \{B \to \exists \vec{v}.H' \mid H' \text{ is a piece of } R\}$. For a rule set $\mathcal{R}$, let $\mathsf{sp}(\mathcal{R}) = \bigcup_{R \in \mathcal{R}} \mathsf{sp}(R)$.

Example 3. *Consider the rule* (7) *and its single-piece decomposition* $\mathsf{sp}((7)) = \{(8\text{–}10)\}$*:*

$$R(x,y) \to \exists z,u.P(x,z) \land A(z) \land A(u) \land P(x,y) \quad (7)$$
$$R(x,y) \to \exists z.P(x,z) \land A(z) \quad (8)$$
$$R(x,y) \to \exists u.A(u) \quad (9)$$
$$R(x,y) \to P(x,y) \quad (10)$$

Piece-decomposition is indeed a normalisation procedure, since it preserves logical equivalence:

Proposition 15. *A rule set* $\mathcal{R}$ *is equivalent to the set* $\mathsf{sp}(\mathcal{R})$*.*

The following lemma is later applied to show that the piece-decomposition preserves termination of the oblivious and semi-oblivious chase in Theorem 18:

Lemma 16. *Consider some fair* $\mathbb{X}$*-derivations* $\mathcal{D}$ *and* $\mathcal{D}'$ *from a KB* $\mathcal{K}$*. If* $\mathbb{X} = \mathbb{O}$*, then* $\mathsf{res}(\mathcal{D}) = \mathsf{res}(\mathcal{D}')$*. If* $\mathbb{X} = \mathbb{SO}$*, then* $\mathsf{res}(\mathcal{D})$ *is isomorphic to* $\mathsf{res}(\mathcal{D}')$*.*

Definition 17. Given some $\mathbb{X} \in \{\mathbb{O}, \mathbb{SO}\}$ and a KB $\mathcal{K}$, let $\mathsf{Ch}_{\mathbb{X}}(\mathcal{K})$ be some (arbitrarily chosen) atom set that is isomorphic to the result of all fair $\mathbb{X}$-derivations from $\mathcal{K}$.

Theorem 18. *The piece-decomposition preserves the termination of the* $\mathbb{O}$*-chase and* $\mathbb{SO}$*-chase.*

Sketch. Consider some $\mathbb{X} \in \{\mathbb{O}, \mathbb{SO}\}$ and some $\mathbb{X}$-derivation $\mathcal{D}$ from a KB $\mathcal{K} = \langle \mathcal{R}, F \rangle$. We can show via induction on $\mathcal{D}$ that there is an injective homomorphism from $\mathsf{Ch}_{\mathbb{X}}(\langle \mathsf{sp}(\mathcal{R}), F \rangle)$ to $\mathsf{Ch}_{\mathbb{X}}(\mathcal{K})$. Therefore, finiteness of $\mathsf{Ch}_{\mathbb{X}}(\mathcal{K})$ implies finiteness of $\mathsf{Ch}_{\mathbb{X}}(\langle \mathsf{sp}(\mathcal{R}), F \rangle)$. □

The piece-decomposition does not preserve the termination of any restricted chase variant. The reason is that it allows for intertwining the application of split rules that come from different original rules, resulting in new application strategies that may lead to non-termination.

Theorem 19. *The piece-decomposition does not preserve termination of the* $\mathbb{R}$*- or the* $\mathbb{DF}$*-*$\mathbb{R}$*-chase.*

Sketch. Consider the rule set $\mathcal{R} = \{(11), (12)\}$ and its piece-decomposition $\mathsf{sp}(\mathcal{R}) = \{(12\text{–}14)\}$:

$$P(x,y) \to P(y,y) \land A(y) \quad (11) \qquad P(x,y) \to P(y,y) \quad (13)$$
$$A(x) \to \exists z.P(x,z) \quad (12) \qquad P(x,y) \to A(y) \quad (14)$$

The set $\mathcal{R}$ is in $CT^{\mathbb{R}}_{\forall\forall}$ because triggers with (12) are not $\mathbb{R}$-applicable to the output of triggers with (11). The set $\mathsf{sp}(\mathcal{R})$ is not in $CT^{\mathbb{R}}_{\forall\forall}$ because the KB $\langle \mathsf{sp}(\mathcal{R}), \{A(a)\} \rangle$ admits the following non-terminating $\mathbb{R}$-derivation $(\emptyset, F_0), (t_1, F_1), \ldots$:

$$F_0 = \{A(a)\}, \qquad F_4 = \{P(z_1, z_1)\} \cup F_3,$$
$$F_1 = \{P(a, z_1)\} \cup F_0, \qquad F_5 = \{A(z_2)\} \cup F_4,$$
$$F_2 = \{A(z_1)\} \cup F_1, \qquad F_6 = \{P(z_2, z_3)\} \cup F_5,$$
$$F_3 = \{P(z_1, z_2)\} \cup F_2, \qquad \ldots$$

This derivation is built by first applying rule (12) (leading to F_1), then indefinitely repeating the sequence of rule applications (14), (12), and (13). In contrast, the only fair $\mathbb{R}$-derivation with $\mathcal{R}$ would apply (12) then (11), leading to $\{A(a), P(a, z_1), P(z_1, z_1), A(z_1)\}$.

To get a similar behavior with the $\mathbb{DF}$-$\mathbb{R}$ chase, we introduce "dummy" existential variables in rules (11) and (12), so that their piece-decomposition has no Datalog rules:

$$P(x,y,v) \to \exists u,w.P(y,y,u) \land A(y,w) \quad (15)$$
$$A(x,v) \to \exists z,u.P(x,z,u) \quad (16)$$

Applying analogous arguments we can show that $\mathcal{R}' = \{(15), (16)\}$ is in $CT^{\mathbb{DF}\text{-}\mathbb{R}}_{\forall\forall}$ and that $\mathsf{sp}(\mathcal{R}')$ is not. □

Initially, we believed that the piece-decomposition would preserve sometimes-termination of the $\mathbb{R}$-chase. Our intuition was that, given a terminating $\mathbb{R}$-derivation from a KB $\mathcal{K} = \langle \mathcal{R}, F \rangle$, we could replicate this derivation from $\langle \mathsf{sp}(\mathcal{R}), F \rangle$ by applying the split rules in $\mathsf{sp}(\mathcal{R})$ piece by piece. Surprisingly, this is not always possible:

Theorem 20. *The piece-decomposition does not preserve the sometimes-termination of the* $\mathbb{R}$*-chase.*

Sketch. The following set $\mathcal{R} = \{(17\text{–}22)\}$ is in $CT^{\mathbb{R}}_{\forall\exists}$ and its piece-decomposition $\mathsf{sp}(\mathcal{R}) = \{(18\text{–}24)\}$ is not. The set $\mathcal{R}$ is adapted from $\{(2\text{–}6)\}$ (proof of Th. 13). Note that (17) is split into two equivalent rules (23) and (24). To show that $\mathsf{sp}(\mathcal{R}) \notin CT^{\mathbb{R}}_{\forall\exists}$, we start again from $\{A(a)\}$. Again, some R-atom is created and leads to apply other rules. With $\mathcal{R}$, applying (17) then (18) creates an atom of form $R(y_1, z_1)$, while with $\mathsf{sp}(\mathcal{R})$, applying (23) then (18) creates an atom $R(y_1, y_1)$. This loop leads to non-termination.

$$A(x) \to \exists y,z.U(x,y) \land H(y,x) \land U(x,z) \land H(z,x) \quad (17)$$
$$U(x,y) \land U(x,z) \to R(y,z) \quad (18)$$
$$U(x,z) \land R(y,z) \to \exists v.R(z,v) \quad (19)$$
$$R(x,y) \land R(y,z) \to \exists v.S(z,v) \quad (20)$$
$$R(x,y) \land S(y,z) \to S(x,x) \quad (21)$$
$$A(x) \land U(x,y) \land S(y,z) \to \exists v.H(z,v) \land A(v) \quad (22)$$
$$A(x) \to \exists y.U(x,y) \land H(y,x) \quad (23)$$
$$A(x) \to \exists z.U(x,z) \land H(z,x) \quad (24)$$

□

Theorem 21. *The piece-decomposition does not preserve the sometimes-termination of the* $\mathbb{DF}$*-*$\mathbb{R}$*-chase.*

Sketch. The set $\mathcal{R} = \{(25\text{–}29)\}$ is in $CT^{\mathbb{DF}\text{-}\mathbb{R}}_{\forall\exists}$ while $\mathsf{sp}(\mathcal{R}) = \{(26\text{–}31)\}$ is not. Note that the only difference with $\{(2\text{–}6)\}$ is the atom $H(x, y)$ in the first rule, making it non-Datalog, which prevents its early application.

$$A(x) \to \exists y.R(x, x) \wedge H(x, y) \qquad (25)$$
$$R(x, y) \wedge S(y, z) \to S(x, x) \qquad (26)$$
$$A(x) \wedge S(x, y) \to A(y) \qquad (27)$$
$$A(x) \to \exists y.R(x, y) \quad (28) \qquad A(x) \to R(x, x) \quad (30)$$
$$R(x, y) \to \exists z.S(y, z) \quad (29) \qquad A(x) \to \exists y.H(x, y) \quad (31)$$

□

Since piece-decomposition preserves logical equivalence (Proposition 15), one directly obtains that it preserves termination of the equivalent chase. Indeed, $\langle \mathcal{R}, F\rangle$ admits a finite universal model iff $\langle \mathsf{sp}(\mathcal{R}), F\rangle$ admits one:

Theorem 22. *The piece-decomposition preserves the termination of the* $\mathbb{E}$*-chase.*

The piece-decomposition may gain termination:

Theorem 23. *The piece-decomposition may gain termination (and sometimes-termination) of the* $\mathbb{SO}$*-, the* $\mathbb{R}$*-, and the* $\mathbb{DF}$*-*$\mathbb{R}$*-chase but not of the* $\mathbb{O}$*- and* $\mathbb{E}$*-chase.*

Sketch. Consider the set $\mathcal{R} = \{P(x, y) \to \exists z.P(x, z) \wedge R(x, y)\}$, which is not in $CT^{\mathbb{SO}}_{\forall\forall}$, $CT^{\mathbb{R}}_{\forall\exists}$, $CT^{\mathbb{R}}_{\forall\forall}$, $CT^{\mathbb{DF}\text{-}\mathbb{R}}_{\forall\exists}$, or $CT^{\mathbb{DF}\text{-}\mathbb{R}}_{\forall\forall}$. However, $\mathsf{sp}(\mathcal{R})$ is in all of these sets.

Concerning the $\mathbb{O}$-chase, we show via induction that $\mathsf{Ch}_{\mathbb{O}}(\langle \mathcal{R}, F\rangle)$ and $\mathsf{Ch}_{\mathbb{O}}(\langle \mathsf{sp}(\mathcal{R}), F\rangle)$ are isomorphic for any rule set $\mathcal{R}$ and factbase F (where $\mathsf{Ch}_{\mathbb{O}}(\cdot)$ is the function from Definition 17, which maps a KB to its only $\mathbb{O}$-chase result). Hence, all $\mathbb{O}$-derivations from $\langle \mathcal{R}, F\rangle$ are terminating iff all $\mathbb{O}$-derivations from $\langle \mathsf{sp}(\mathcal{R}), F\rangle$ are terminating. Concerning the $\mathbb{E}$-chase, we rely again on Proposition 15. □

To show that the piece-decomposition preserves FO-rewritability we show that it preserves the BDDP property.

Theorem 24. *A rule set* $\mathcal{R}$ *is BDDP iff* $\mathsf{sp}(\mathcal{R})$ *is BDDP.*

Sketch. We can prove by induction that, for any KBs $\langle \mathcal{R}, F\rangle$ and any $i \geq 1$, the factbases $\mathsf{Ch}_i(\langle \mathcal{R}, F\rangle)$ and $\mathsf{Ch}_i(\langle \mathsf{sp}(\mathcal{R}), F\rangle)$ are isomorphic. □

5 One-Way Atomic Decomposition

Piece-decomposition may not produce atomic-head rules; a useful restriction considered in many contexts. The following procedure is classically used to produce such rules:

Definition 25. The *one-way atomic decomposition* of a rule $R = B[\vec{x}, \vec{y}] \to \exists \vec{z}.H[\vec{x}, \vec{z}]$ is the rule set $\mathit{1ad}(R)$ that contains the rule $B \to \exists \vec{z}.X_R(\vec{x}, \vec{z})$ and, for each atom $P(\vec{t}) \in H$, the rule $X_R(\vec{x}, \vec{z}) \to P(\vec{t})$, where X_R is a fresh predicate unique for R, of arity $|\vec{x}| + |\vec{z}|$. Given a rule set $\mathcal{R}$, let $\mathit{1ad}(\mathcal{R}) = \bigcup_{R \in \mathcal{R}} \mathit{1ad}(R)$.

Example 4. *Consider the rule* (32) *and its one-way atomic decomposition* $\mathit{1ad}((32)) = \{(33\text{–}35)\}$*:*

$$R(x, y) \to \exists z.P(x, z) \wedge S(x, y, z) \qquad (32)$$
$$R(x, y) \to \exists z.X_{(32)}(x, y, z) \qquad (33)$$
$$X_{(32)}(x, y, z) \to P(x, z) \qquad (34)$$
$$X_{(32)}(x, y, z) \to S(x, y, z) \qquad (35)$$

Note that piece-decomposition would not decompose rule (32)*, i.e.,* $\mathsf{sp}((32)) = \{(32)\}$

Strictly speaking, $\mathcal{R}$ and $\mathit{1ad}(\mathcal{R})$ cannot be logically equivalent because they are built on different sets of predicates; however, it is straighforward to check that $\mathit{1ad}(\mathcal{R})$ is a conservative extension of $\mathcal{R}$. Therefore, one-way atomic decomposition is indeed a normalisation procedure.

The following is a corollary of forthcoming Theorem 34:

Theorem 26. *The one-way atomic decomposition preserves termination of the* $\mathbb{O}$*- and* $\mathbb{SO}$*-chase.*

An interesting phenomenon occurs with the one-way atomic decomposition: the notions of $\mathbb{SO}$-applicability on $\mathcal{R}$ and $\mathbb{R}$-applicability on $\mathit{1ad}(\mathcal{R})$ coincide:

Lemma 27. *Consider a KB* $\langle \mathcal{R}, F\rangle$ *and a finite derivation* $\mathcal{D} = (\emptyset, F_0), (t_1, F_1), \ldots, (t_n, F_n)$ *from* $\langle \mathit{1ad}(\mathcal{R}), F\rangle$*. Then, a trigger* t *with a rule in* $\mathit{1ad}(\mathcal{R})$ *is* $\mathbb{R}$*-applicable on* F_n *iff it is* $\mathbb{SO}$*-applicable on* F_n*.*

Proof. ($\Rightarrow$): from Definition 5. ($\Leftarrow$): Let $t = (R, \pi)$ with $R \in \mathit{1ad}(\mathcal{R})$. If R is Datalog, the notions of $\mathbb{SO}$- and $\mathbb{R}$-applicability coincide for every factbase. Otherwise, R is of the form $B[\vec{x}, \vec{y}] \to \exists \vec{z}.X_{R'}(\vec{x}, \vec{z})$ where $X_{R'} \notin \mathtt{Preds}(\mathcal{R})$ and $R' \in \mathcal{R}$ is of the form $B[\vec{x}, \vec{y}] \to \exists \vec{z}.H[\vec{x}, \vec{z}]$. If t is $\mathbb{SO}$-applicable on F_n, then, for every trigger $t' = (R, \pi')$ with $\pi(\vec{x}) = \pi'(\vec{x})$, it holds that $\mathsf{output}(t') \not\subseteq F_n$. By Definition 25, R is the only rule in $\mathit{1ad}(\mathcal{R})$ with $X_{R'}$ in its head, hence $\pi''(X_{R'}(\vec{x}, \vec{z})) \notin F_n$ for every extension π'' of π. Hence, t is $\mathbb{R}$-applicable on F_n. □

Intuitively, Lemma 27 implies that, after applying the one-way atomic decomposition, $\mathbb{R}$-applicability becomes as loose and unrestrictive as $\mathbb{SO}$-applicability. Therefore:

Theorem 28. *The one-way atomic decomposition does not preserve termination nor sometimes-termination of the* $\mathbb{R}$*- or the* $\mathbb{DF}$*-*$\mathbb{R}$*-chase.*

Proof. By Theorem 13, there is a rule set $\mathcal{R} \notin CT^{\mathbb{SO}}_{\forall\forall}$ that is in $CT^{\mathbb{R}}_{\forall\forall}$, $CT^{\mathbb{DF}\text{-}\mathbb{R}}_{\forall\forall}$, $CT^{\mathbb{DF}\text{-}\mathbb{R}}_{\forall\exists}$, and $CT^{\mathbb{R}}_{\forall\exists}$.[3] By Theorem 26, $\mathit{1ad}(\mathcal{R})$ is not in $CT^{\mathbb{SO}}_{\forall\forall}$; that is, there is some KB $\mathcal{K}$ of the form $\langle \mathit{1ad}(\mathcal{R}), F\rangle$ that does not admit any terminating $\mathbb{SO}$-derivation. By Lemma 27, every terminating $\mathbb{R}$-derivation from $\mathcal{K}$ is also a terminating $\mathbb{SO}$-derivation from $\mathcal{K}$. Therefore, $\mathcal{K}$ does not admit any terminating $\mathbb{R}$-derivation, hence $\mathit{1ad}(\mathcal{R})$ is not in $CT^{\mathbb{R}}_{\forall\forall}$, $CT^{\mathbb{DF}\text{-}\mathbb{R}}_{\forall\forall}$, $CT^{\mathbb{DF}\text{-}\mathbb{R}}_{\forall\exists}$, or $CT^{\mathbb{R}}_{\forall\exists}$. □

Theorem 29. *The one-way atomic decomposition does not preserve the termination of the* $\mathbb{E}$*-chase.*

[3] Such rule set in given in the proof of Theorem 13; see also $\{(36)\}$ in the proof of Theorem 29.

Proof. Consider the rule set $\mathcal{R} = \{(36)\}$ (see also Example 1) and its decomposition $1ad(\mathcal{R}) = \{(37\text{–}39)\}$:

$$P(x,y) \rightarrow \exists z.\ P(y,z) \wedge P(z,y) \quad (36)$$

$$P(x,y) \rightarrow \exists z.X_{(36)}(y,z) \quad (37)$$

$$X_{(36)}(y,z) \rightarrow P(y,z) \quad (38)$$

$$X_{(36)}(y,z) \rightarrow P(z,y) \quad (39)$$

The rule set $\mathcal{R}$ is in $CT^{\mathbb{E}}_{\forall\forall}$ since every $\mathbb{E}$-derivation from a KB $\langle \mathcal{R}, F\rangle$ yields a finite result, which is a subset of $F \cup \{P(a,z_a), P(z_a,a) \mid a \in \texttt{Terms}(F), z_a \notin \texttt{Terms}(F)\}$.

The rule set $1ad(\mathcal{R})$ is not in $CT^{\mathbb{E}}_{\forall\forall}$ since the KB $\mathcal{K} = \langle 1ad(\mathcal{R}), \{P(a,b)\}\rangle$ has no terminating $\mathbb{E}$-derivation. In fact, all fair $\mathbb{E}$-derivations from $\mathcal{K}$ yield the same result:

$$\{P(a,b), X_{(36)}(b,z_1), P(b,z_1), P(z_1,b)\} \cup$$
$$\{X_{(36)}(z_i,z_{i+1}), P(z_i,z_{i+1}), P(z_{i+1},z_i) \mid i \geq 1\}$$

□

Again, to show that the one-way decomposition preserves FO-rewritability, we show that it preserves BDDP.

Theorem 30. *A rule set $\mathcal{R}$ is BDDP iff $1ad(\mathcal{R})$ is BDDP.*

Sketch. ($\Rightarrow$): For factbases F restricted to the original vocabulary Σ, we prove that $\mathsf{Ch}_i(F,\mathcal{R}) = \mathsf{Ch}_{2i}(F, 1ad(\mathcal{R}))_{|\Sigma}$. Dealing with arbitrary factbases is tackled by a weakening of this correspondence. ($\Leftarrow$): If $\mathcal{R}$ is not BDDP, there are Q and $\{F_i\}_{i\in\mathbb{N}}$ such that for all i, $F_i, \mathcal{R} \models Q$ and $\mathsf{Ch}_i(F_i,\mathcal{R}) \not\models Q$. Since for all F_i on Σ, $\mathsf{Ch}_i(F_i,\mathcal{R}) = \mathsf{Ch}_{2i}(F_i, 1ad(\mathcal{R}))_{|\Sigma}$, it holds that $\mathsf{Ch}_{2i}(F_i, 1ad(\mathcal{R})) \not\models Q$, hence $1ad(\mathcal{R})$ is not BDDP. □

6 Two-Way Atomic Decomposition

Despite the fact that it produces a conservative extension of the original rule set, the one-way atomic decomposition does not preserve the existence of a finite universal model; hence, it does not preserve equivalent chase termination.

Example 5. *As in the proof of Theorem 29, consider $\mathcal{R} = \{(36)\}$, its decomposition $1ad(\mathcal{R}) = \{(37\text{–}39)\}$, and the factbase $F = \{P(a,b)\}$. Then, $\mathcal{U} = \{P(a,b), P(b,z_1), P(z_1,b)\}$ is a finite universal model for $\langle\mathcal{R},F\rangle$ that cannot be extended (keeping the same domain) into is a universal model of $\langle 1ad(\mathcal{R}), F\rangle$. Indeed, the set*

$$\{P(a,b), P(b,z_1), P(z_1,b), X_{(36)}(b,z_1), X_{(36)}(z_1,b)\}$$

is the smallest extension of $\mathcal{U}$ that is a model for $\langle 1ad(\mathcal{R}), F\rangle$, but it is not universal.

Hence, we define a notion similar to that of conservative extension, but whose purpose is to guarantee the preservation of the equivalent chase termination.

Definition 31. Let $\mathcal{R}$ and $\mathcal{R}'$ be two rule sets such that $\texttt{Preds}(\mathcal{R}) \subseteq \texttt{Preds}(\mathcal{R}')$. The set $\mathcal{R}'$ is a *universal-conservative extension* of the set $\mathcal{R}$ if, for any factbase F with $\texttt{Preds}(F) \subseteq \texttt{Preds}(\mathcal{R})$,

1. The restriction of any universal model of $\langle\mathcal{R}', F\rangle$ to the predicates in $\texttt{Preds}(\mathcal{R})$ is a universal model of $\langle\mathcal{R}, F\rangle$.
2. Any universal model $\mathcal{M}$ of $\langle\mathcal{R}, F\rangle$ can be extended to a universal model of $\langle\mathcal{R}', F\rangle$ that has the same domain and agrees with $\mathcal{M}$ on the interpretation of $\texttt{Preds}(\mathcal{R})$.

We now introduce a normalisation procedure that produces universal-conservative extensions:

Definition 32. The *two-way atomic decomposition* of a rule $R = B[\vec{x},\vec{y}] \rightarrow \exists\vec{z}.H[\vec{x},\vec{z}]$ is the rule set $2ad(R) = 1ad(R) \cup \{H[\vec{x},\vec{z}] \rightarrow X_R(\vec{x},\vec{z})\}$, with X_R the fresh predicate in $1ad(R)$. For a rule set $\mathcal{R}$, we let $2ad(\mathcal{R}) = \bigcup_{R\in\mathcal{R}} 2ad(R)$.

Example 6. *Consider again the rule* (32) *from Example 4. Then its two-way atomic decomposition is $2ad((32)) = 1ad((32)) \cup \{(40)\}$:*

$$P(x,z) \wedge S(x,y,z) \rightarrow X_{(32)}(x,y,z) \quad (40)$$

We establish that this new decomposition is indeed a normalisation procedure that has the desired property.

Proposition 33. *The rule set $2ad(\mathcal{R})$ is a conservative extension and a universal-conservative extension of $\mathcal{R}$.*

We can now focus our interest again on chase termination. Both atomic decompositions behave like the single-piece decomposition (Theorem 18) regarding the oblivious and the semi-oblivious chase:

Theorem 34. *Both atomic decompositions preserve the termination of the $\mathbb{O}$-chase and the $\mathbb{SO}$-chase.*

Sketch. Consider $\mathbb{X} \in \{\mathbb{O}, \mathbb{SO}\}$ and $\mathcal{K} = \langle\mathcal{R},F\rangle$ a KB. First note that for these $\mathbb{X}$-chases, applying a rule cannot prevent the application of another rule. Hence, since $1ad(\mathcal{R}) \subseteq 2ad(\mathcal{R})$, it is sufficient to prove the result for $2ad(\mathcal{R})$. The proof is similar to that of Theorem 18: we show by induction on an arbitrary derivation $\mathcal{D}$ from $\mathcal{K}$ that there is an injective homomorphism from $\mathsf{Ch}_{\mathbb{X}}(\langle 2ad(\mathcal{R}), F\rangle)$ restricted to the predicates in $\texttt{Preds}(\mathcal{R})$ to $\mathsf{Ch}_{\mathbb{X}}(\mathcal{K})$, which leads to a similar conclusion. □

The behavior of the restricted chase is again less easily characterized, as we will see in the next results.

Theorem 35. *The two-way atomic decomposition preserves sometimes-termination of the $\mathbb{R}$-chase; it may also gain termination of this chase variant.*

Sketch. To prove preservation, consider a KB $\mathcal{K} = \langle\mathcal{R},F\rangle$ such that $\mathcal{R} \in CT^{\mathbb{R}}_{\forall\exists}$. Then, there is a terminating $\mathbb{R}$-derivation $\mathcal{D}$ from $\mathcal{K}$. We can then show by induction that if a trigger $t = (R,\pi)$ with $R = B \rightarrow H$ is applied at some step, the trigger $t' = (B \rightarrow X_R, \pi)$ is applicable at the same step, then the triggers $t_i = (X_R \rightarrow H_i, \pi^R)$ also are, and that applying t' and all the t_i successively yields the same result (when restricted to the predicates in $\mathcal{R}$) as applying t. This shows that we can replicate a terminating derivation, and thus that the sometimes-termination is preserved.

We now present an example where we gain termination. Consider the rule set $\mathcal{R} = \{(41\text{–}45)\}$:

$$A(x) \rightarrow \exists y,z\ R(x,x,x) \wedge R(x,y,z) \quad (41)$$

$$R(x,y,z) \rightarrow \exists t.R(x,x,t) \quad (42)$$

$$R(x,x,y) \rightarrow \exists z.S(x,y,z) \quad (43)$$
$$R(x,x,y) \wedge S(x,y,z) \rightarrow S(x,x,x) \quad (44)$$
$$A(x) \wedge S(x,x,y) \rightarrow A(y) \quad (45)$$

There is no terminating $\mathbb{R}$-derivation on the KB $\langle \mathcal{R}, \{A(a)\}\rangle$ but there is one on $\langle 2ad(\mathcal{R}), F\rangle$ for any F. □

Theorem 36. *The two-way atomic decomposition does not preserve the termination of the* $\mathbb{R}$*-chase.*

Proof. Consider the rule set $\mathcal{R} = \{(36)\}$ introduced in the proof of Theorem 29 and $2ad(\mathcal{R}) = \{(37\text{–}39), (46)\}$:

$$P(x,y) \rightarrow \exists z.\ P(y,z) \wedge P(z,y) \quad (36)$$
$$P(x,y) \rightarrow \exists z.X_{(36)}(y,z) \quad (37)$$
$$X_{(36)}(y,z) \rightarrow P(y,z) \quad (38)$$
$$X_{(36)}(y,z) \rightarrow P(z,y) \quad (39)$$
$$P(y,z) \wedge P(z,y) \rightarrow X_{(36)}(y,z) \quad (46)$$

The $\mathbb{R}$-chase yields the same result as the $\mathbb{E}$-chase on $\mathcal{R}$, so $\mathcal{R} \in CT^{\mathbb{R}}_{\forall\forall}$. We then construct an infinite derivation from $\langle 2ad, P(a,b)\rangle$. First, apply (37), and (38). Then, repeat the following pattern: (37), (38) (on the new variable), then (39) and (46) (on the variables of the previous loop). Applying (37) again before applying (46) yields an infinite chain. □

Again, the $\mathbb{R}$-chase is not well-behaved with respect to atomic decomposition. However, the $\mathbb{DF}$-$\mathbb{R}$-chase behaves exactly as desired regarding the two-way atomic decomposition. In fact, we can show an even stronger result: any $\mathbb{DF}$-$\mathbb{R}$-derivation from a KB $\langle \mathcal{R}, F\rangle$ can be replicated by a $\mathbb{DF}$-$\mathbb{R}$-derivation from $\langle 2ad(\mathcal{R}), F\rangle$, and conversely.

Theorem 37. *The 2-way atomic decomposition has no impact on the (sometimes-)termination of the* $\mathbb{DF}$-$\mathbb{R}$*-chase; i.e.,* $CT^{\mathbb{DF}\text{-}\mathbb{R}}_{\forall\forall} = 2ad(CT^{\mathbb{DF}\text{-}\mathbb{R}}_{\forall\forall})$ *and* $CT^{\mathbb{DF}\text{-}\mathbb{R}}_{\forall\exists} = 2ad(CT^{\mathbb{DF}\text{-}\mathbb{R}}_{\forall\exists})$.

Sketch. One can prove that any fair $\mathbb{DF}$-$\mathbb{R}$-derivation $\mathcal{D}$ from $\langle \mathcal{R}, F\rangle$ with $\mathcal{R} \in CT^{\mathbb{DF}\text{-}\mathbb{R}}_{\forall\forall}$ can be replicated to yield a fair $\mathbb{DF}$-$\mathbb{R}$-derivation $\mathcal{D}'$ from $\langle 2ad(\mathcal{R}), F\rangle$ such that $\mathcal{D}'$ is finite if and only if $\mathcal{D}$ is. The reciprocal is also true. □

The following result follows from Proposition 33

Theorem 38. *: The two-way atomic decomposition preserves the termination of the* $\mathbb{E}$*-chase.*

The single-piece decomposition may gain termination for some chase variants (Theorem 23); we are interested to know if the same can happen with atomic decompositions. Unfortunately, there is no way for a non-terminating rule set to gain termination, as stated next:

Proposition 39. *If a chase variant does not terminate on a rule set* $\mathcal{R}$*, it does not terminate on* $1ad(\mathcal{R})$ *and* $2ad(\mathcal{R})$.

Sketch. For each trigger with a rule R in the original infinite fair derivation, one can consider the corresponding triggers with $1ad(R)$ or $2ad(R)$, and thus produce an infinite fair derivation. □

Regarding FO-rewritability, the two-way atomic decomposition behaves similarily to the one-way atomic decomposition (which can be proven similarly, see Theorem 30).

Theorem 40. *A rule set* $\mathcal{R}$ *is BDDP iff* $2ad(\mathcal{R})$ *is BDDP.*

7 No Normalisation for the Restricted Chase

Normalisation procedures studied so far do not maintain the status of the termination of the $\mathbb{R}$-chase. This raises the question of the existence of such a procedure. We show here that no computable function can map rule sets to sets of rules having atomic head while preserving termination and non-termination of the $\mathbb{R}$-chase. To do that, we show that with atomic-head rules, the class of rule sets $CT^{\mathbb{R}}_{F\forall}$ for which every fair $\mathbb{R}$-derivation from $\langle \mathcal{R}, F\rangle$ is finite is a recursively enumerable set. With arbitrary rules, we show it is hard for Π^0_2, the second level of the arithmetic hierarchy (Rogers 1987). A complete problem for Π^0_2 is to decide whether a given Turing machine halts on every input word; it remains complete when inputs are restricted to words on a unary alphabet.

Proposition 41. *For any factbase* F*, the subset of* $CT^{\mathbb{R}}_{F\forall}$ *composed of sets of atomic-head rules is recognizable.*

Sketch. With atomic-head rules, it is known that the existence of an infinite fair restricted derivation is equivalent to the existence of an infinite restricted derivation (Gogacz, Marcinkowski, and Pieris 2020). Using König's lemma, one can show that the chase terminates iff there exists a k such that any fair $\mathbb{R}$-derivation is of length at most k. □

Proposition 42. *There exists a factbase* F *such that* $CT^{\mathbb{R}}_{F\forall}$ *is* Π^0_2*-hard.*[4]

Sketch. Given a Turing machine (TM) M whose input alphabet is unary, we build a KB $\mathcal{K} = \langle \mathcal{R}_w \cup \mathcal{R}_M, F\rangle$ s.t. every fair $\mathbb{R}$-derivation from $\mathcal{K}$ is finite iff M halts on every input. Regardless the chase variant, simulating a TM with a rule set such that the chase terminates whenever the TM halts is classical; we reuse the rule set $\mathcal{R}_M$ provided in (Bourgaux et al. 2021), which we recall in Figure 4 for self-containment. We show that we can assume wlog that all the rules of $\mathcal{R}_M$ are applied after all the rules of $\mathcal{R}_w$ (listed in Figure 3). The set $\mathcal{R}_w$ is used to generate from F arbitrarily large input tape representations in a terminating way. To ensure that any fair $\mathbb{R}$-derivation from $\langle \mathcal{R}_w, F\rangle$ terminates, we reuse the emergency brake technique from (Krötzsch, Marx, and Rudolph 2019), which allows one to stop the derivation at any desired length. The representation of an input word of length j is a set of atoms of the shape $\{\mathtt{Nxt}(c^j_i, c^j_{i+1}), \mathtt{S}_1(c^j_i) \mid 0 \leq i < j\} \cup \{\mathtt{S}\_(c^j_j), \mathtt{Frst}(c^j_0), \mathtt{End}(c^j_j)\}$. As detailed below, the factbase F contains the representation of the input words of length 0 and 1 (Item 1), atoms used as seeds to build larger words (Item 2) and atoms that initialize the emergency brake (Items 3 and 4):

1. $\mathtt{Frst}(c^1_0), \mathtt{S}_1(c^1_0), \mathtt{Nxt}(c^1_0, c^1_1), \mathtt{End}(c^1_1), \mathtt{S}\_(c^1_1),$ $\mathtt{Frst}(c^0_0), \mathtt{End}(c^0_0), \mathtt{S}\_(c^0_0)$
2. $\mathtt{Int}(a), \mathtt{NF}(a, nf_1), \mathtt{R}(nf_1), \mathtt{NF}(nf_1, b), \mathtt{D}(nf_1, b)$

[4]Note that this contradicts the first item of Theorem 5.1 in (Grahne and Onet 2018). However, no proof is given for that statement, which is uncorrectly attributed to (Deutsch, Nash, and Remmel 2008).

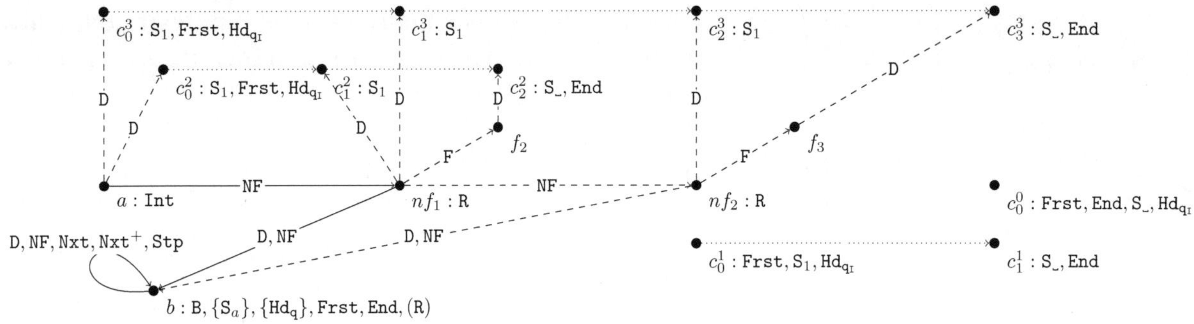

Figure 2: The effect of $\mathcal{R}_w$ on F: Dashed atoms are $\mathtt{D}, \mathtt{F}$ or $\mathtt{NF}$ atoms generated by the chase; $\mathtt{Nxt}$ atoms used by $\mathcal{R}_M$ are dotted.

$$\mathtt{B}(b) \wedge \mathtt{NF}(z,x) \wedge \mathtt{R}(x) \rightarrow \exists y.\mathtt{NF}(x,y) \wedge \mathtt{R}(y) \wedge \mathtt{D}(y,b) \wedge \mathtt{NF}(y,b) \quad (47)$$

$$\mathtt{B}(b) \rightarrow \mathtt{R}(b) \quad (48)$$

$$\mathtt{NF}(x,y) \rightarrow \exists z.\mathtt{F}(y,z) \quad (49)$$

$$\mathtt{F}(x,y) \rightarrow \exists z.\mathtt{D}(y,z) \wedge \mathtt{End}(z) \wedge \mathtt{S}_\_(z) \quad (50)$$

$$\mathtt{NF}(t,x) \wedge \mathtt{NF}(x,y) \wedge \mathtt{D}(y,z) \rightarrow \exists u.\mathtt{Nxt}(u,z) \wedge \mathtt{D}(x,u) \wedge \mathtt{S}_1(u) \quad (51)$$

$$\mathtt{NF}(t,x) \wedge \mathtt{F}(x,y) \wedge \mathtt{D}(y,z) \rightarrow \exists u.\mathtt{Nxt}(u,z) \wedge \mathtt{D}(x,u) \wedge \mathtt{S}_1(u) \quad (52)$$

$$\mathtt{Int}(x) \wedge \mathtt{NF}(x,y) \wedge \mathtt{D}(y,z) \rightarrow \exists u.\mathtt{Nxt}(u,z) \wedge \mathtt{D}(x,u) \wedge \mathtt{S}_1(u) \wedge \mathtt{Frst}(u) \quad (53)$$

$$\mathtt{Frst}(x) \rightarrow \mathtt{Hd}_{\mathtt{q_I}}(x) \quad (54)$$

Figure 3: Rules $\mathcal{R}_w$ to create the initial tapes

3. $\mathtt{B}(b), \mathtt{F}(b,b), \mathtt{NF}(b,b), \mathtt{D}(b,b), \mathtt{Nxt}(b,b), \mathtt{Lst}(b), \mathtt{Frst}(b)$
4. $\mathtt{Hd_s}(b), \mathtt{S}_l(b), \mathtt{End}(b), \mathtt{Stp}(b,b), \mathtt{Nxt}^+(b,b)$

The chase works as follows: after generating a *non-final* (NF) chain with Rule (47), the *brake* (B) is made *real* (R) by Rule (48), which prevents any extension of the non-final chain through restricted rule applications. A *final* (F) element is added after each non-final element by Rule (49), and from each final element a tape is created, by traversing the chain, marking as *done* (D) processed elements, thanks to Rules (50)-(53). Figure 2 depicts the result of any $\mathbb{R}$-chase derivation from $\langle \mathcal{R}_w, F\rangle$ in which $\mathtt{R}(b)$ has been derived after exactly one application of Rule (47). Rule (54) sets the initial state on the first cell. □

As it is known recursively enumerable sets are a strict subsets of Π_2^0 (Rogers 1987), the following theorem follows.

Theorem 43. *No computable function f exists that maps rule sets to rule sets having atomic-head rules such that $\mathcal{R} \in CT_{\forall\forall}^{\mathbb{R}}$ if and only if $f(\mathcal{R}) \in CT_{\forall\forall}^{\mathbb{R}}$.*

$$\mathtt{Nxt}(x,y) \rightarrow \mathtt{Nxt}^+(x,y)$$
$$\mathtt{Nxt}^+(x,y) \wedge \mathtt{Nxt}^+(y,z) \rightarrow \mathtt{Nxt}^+(x,z)$$
$$\mathtt{Nxt}(x,y) \wedge \mathtt{Stp}(x,z) \wedge \mathtt{Stp}(y,w) \rightarrow \mathtt{Nxt}(z,w)$$
$$\mathtt{End}(x) \wedge \mathtt{Stp}(x,z) \rightarrow \exists v.\mathtt{Nxt}(z,v) \wedge \mathtt{S}_\_(v) \wedge \mathtt{End}(v)$$
$$\mathtt{Hd_q}(x) \wedge \mathtt{Nxt}^+(x,y) \wedge \mathtt{S}_c(y) \rightarrow \exists z.\mathtt{Stp}(y,z) \wedge \mathtt{S}_c(z)$$
$$\mathtt{Hd_q}(x) \wedge \mathtt{Nxt}^+(y,x) \wedge \mathtt{S}_c(y) \rightarrow \exists z.\mathtt{Stp}(y,z) \wedge \mathtt{S}_c(z)$$
$$\mathtt{Hd_q}(x) \wedge \mathtt{S}_a(x) \rightarrow \exists z.\mathtt{Stp}(x,z) \wedge \mathtt{S}_b(z)$$
$$\mathtt{Hd_q}(x) \wedge \mathtt{S}_a(x) \wedge \mathtt{Stp}(x,z) \wedge \mathtt{Nxt}(z,w) \rightarrow \mathtt{Hd_r}(w)$$
$$\mathtt{Hd_q}(x) \wedge \mathtt{S}_a(x) \wedge \mathtt{Stp}(x,z) \wedge \mathtt{Nxt}(w,z) \rightarrow \mathtt{Hd_r}(w)$$

Figure 4: Rules $\mathcal{R}_M$ for the Turing Machine simulation: the last three rules are instantiated w.r.t.the transition function of M.

This applies in particular to normalisation procedures producing rule sets with atomic-head rules.

8 Conclusion

As shown in this paper, normalisation procedures do have an impact, sometimes unexpected, on chase termination. This is particularly true regarding the restricted chase, which is the most relevant in practice but also the most difficult to control. We extend the understanding of its behavior by three results. We show that the Datatog-first strategy is in fact not always the most terminating, which goes against a common belief. We introduce a new atomic-decomposition (two-way), which behaves nicely, in particular regarding the Datalog-first restricted chase, but still has a negative impact on the restricted chase termination. This leads to us to show a more fundamental decidability result, which implies that no computable atomic-decomposition exists that exactly preserves the termination of the restricted chase (i.e., termination and non-termination). Note however that our result does not rule out the existence of a computable normalisation procedure into atomic-head rules that would improve the termination of the restricted chase, although this seems unlikely. Future work includes investigating normalisation procedures for first-order logical formulas, to translate these into the existential rule framework.

Acknowledgements

This work was partly supported by the ANR project CQFD (ANR-18-CE23-0003).

References

Baget, J.; Leclère, M.; Mugnier, M.; and Salvat, E. 2009. Extending decidable cases for rules with existential variables. In *IJCAI*, 677–682.

Baget, J.; Leclère, M.; Mugnier, M.; and Salvat, E. 2011. On rules with existential variables: Walking the decidability line. *Artif. Intell.* 175(9-10):1620–1654.

Beeri, C., and Vardi, M. Y. 1981. The implication problem for data dependencies. In *International Colloquium on Automata, Languages, and Programming*, 73–85. Springer.

Bourgaux, C.; Carral, D.; Krötzsch, M.; Rudolph, S.; and Thomazo, M. 2021. Capturing homomorphism-closed decidable queries with existential rules. In Bienvenu, M.; Lakemeyer, G.; and Erdem, E., eds., *Proceedings of the 18th International Conference on Principles of Knowledge Representation and Reasoning, KR 2021, Online event, November 3-12, 2021*, 141–150.

Calì, A.; Gottlob, G.; and Kifer, M. 2008a. Taming the infinite chase: Query answering under expressive relational constraints. In *Proceedings of the Eleventh International Conference on Principles of Knowledge Representation and Reasoning*, KR'08, 70–80. AAAI Press.

Calì, A.; Gottlob, G.; and Kifer, M. 2008b. Taming the infinite chase: Query answering under expressive relational constraints. In Brewka, G., and Lang, J., eds., *Principles of Knowledge Representation and Reasoning: Proc. of the Eleventh International Conference, KR 2008, Sydney, Australia, September 16-19, 2008*, 70–80. AAAI Press.

Calì, A.; Gottlob, G.; and Lukasiewicz, T. 2009. A general datalog-based framework for tractable query answering over ontologies. In *PODS*, 77–86. ACM.

Calì, A.; Gottlob, G.; and Pieris, A. 2012. Towards more expressive ontology languages: The query answering problem. *Artif. Intell.* 193:87–128.

Calvanese, D.; De Giacomo, G.; Lembo, D.; Lenzerini, M.; and Rosati, R. 2007. Tractable reasoning and efficient query answering in description logics: The DL-Lite family. *Journal of Automated Reasoning (JAR)* 39(3):385–429.

Carral, D.; Dragoste, I.; and Krötzsch, M. 2017. Restricted chase (non)termination for existential rules with disjunctions. In Sierra, C., ed., *Proceedings of the Twenty-Sixth International Joint Conference on Artificial Intelligence, IJCAI 2017, Melbourne, Australia, August 19-25, 2017*, 922–928. ijcai.org.

Deutsch, A.; Nash, A.; and Remmel, J. B. 2008. The chase revisited. In Lenzerini, M., and Lembo, D., eds., *Proc. of the 27th ACM SIGMOD-SIGACT-SIGART Symp. on Principles of Database Systems, PODS 2008*, 149–158. ACM.

Fagin, R.; Kolaitis, P. G.; Miller, R. J.; and Popa, L. 2003. Data exchange: Semantics and query answering. In Calvanese, D.; Lenzerini, M.; and Motwani, R., eds., *Database Theory - ICDT 2003, 9th International Conference, Siena, Italy, January 8-10, 2003, Proc.*, volume 2572 of *Lecture Notes in Computer Science*, 207–224. Springer.

Gogacz, T.; Marcinkowski, J.; and Pieris, A. 2020. All-instances restricted chase termination. In Suciu, D.; Tao, Y.; and Wei, Z., eds., *Proceedings of the 39th ACM SIGMOD-SIGACT-SIGAI Symposium on Principles of Database Systems, PODS 2020, Portland, OR, USA, June 14-19, 2020*, 245–258. ACM.

Gottlob, G.; Kikot, S.; Kontchakov, R.; Podolskii, V. V.; Schwentick, T.; and Zakharyaschev, M. 2014. The price of query rewriting in ontology-based data access. *Artif. Intell.* 213:42–59.

Grahne, G., and Onet, A. 2018. Anatomy of the chase. *Fundam. Informaticae* 157(3):221–270.

Grau, B. C.; Horrocks, I.; Krötzsch, M.; Kupke, C.; Magka, D.; Motik, B.; and Wang, Z. 2013. Acyclicity notions for existential rules and their application to query answering in ontologies. *J. Artif. Intell. Res.* 47:741–808.

König, M.; Leclère, M.; Mugnier, M.; and Thomazo, M. 2013. Sound, complete and minimal ucq-rewriting for existential rules. *CoRR* abs/1311.3198.

Krötzsch, M.; Marx, M.; and Rudolph, S. 2019. The power of the terminating chase (invited talk). In Barceló, P., and Calautti, M., eds., *22nd International Conference on Database Theory, ICDT 2019, March 26-28, 2019, Lisbon, Portugal*, volume 127 of *LIPIcs*, 3:1–3:17. Schloss Dagstuhl - Leibniz-Zentrum für Informatik.

Leclère, M.; Mugnier, M.; Thomazo, M.; and Ulliana, F. 2019. A single approach to decide chase termination on linear existential rules. In Barceló, P., and Calautti, M., eds., *Proceedings of the 22nd International Conference on Database Theory, ICDT 2019, Lisbon, Portugal*, volume 127 of *LIPIcs*, 18:1–18:19. Schloss Dagstuhl - Leibniz-Zentrum für Informatik.

Marnette, B. 2009. Generalized schema-mappings: from termination to tractability. In Paredaens, J., and Su, J., eds., *Proc. of the Twenty-Eigth ACM SIGMOD-SIGACT-SIGART Symp. on Principles of Database Systems, PODS 2009, June 19 - July 1, 2009, Providence, Rhode Island, USA*, 13–22. ACM.

Rocher, S. 2016. *Querying Existential Rule Knowledge Bases: Decidability and Complexity.* Ph.D. Dissertation, University of Montpellier, France.

Rogers, H. 1987. *Theory of Recursive Functions and Effective Computability.* Cambridge, MA, USA: MIT Press.

Tsamoura, E.; Carral, D.; Malizia, E.; and Urbani, J. 2021. Materializing knowledge bases via trigger graphs. *Proc. VLDB Endow.* 14(6):943–956.

Urbani, J.; Krötzsch, M.; Jacobs, C. J. H.; Dragoste, I.; and Carral, D. 2018. Efficient model construction for horn logic with vlog - system description. In *IJCAR*, volume 10900 of *Lecture Notes in Computer Science*, 680–688. Springer.

A General Framework for Modelling Conditional Reasoning - Preliminary Report

Giovanni Casini[1,2] **, Umberto Straccia**[1]
[1]ISTI-CNR, Pisa, Italy
[2]CAIR, University of Cape Town, Cape town, South Africa
{giovanni.casini, umberto.straccia}@isti.cnr.it

Abstract

We introduce and investigate here a formalisation for conditionals that allows the definition of a broad class of reasoning systems. This framework covers the most popular kinds of conditional reasoning in logic-based KR: the semantics we propose is appropriate for a structural analysis of those conditionals that do not satisfy closure properties associated to classical logics.

1 Introduction

Conditionals are generally considered the backbone of human (and AI) reasoning: the "if-then" connection between two propositions is the stepping stone of arguments and a lot of the research effort in formal logic has focused on this kind of connection. A conditional connection satisfies different properties according to the kind of arguments it is used for. The classical material implication is appropriate for modelling the "if-then" connection as it is used in Mathematics, but the equivalence between the material implication $A \rightarrow B$ and $\neg A \vee B$ is not appropriate for many other contexts. Different kinds of reasoning use different kinds of conditionals, modelling, among others, *presumptive reasoning* (e.g. "Birds typically fly"), *normative reasoning* (e.g. "if you have had alcohol, you should not drive"), *casual reasoning* (e.g. "if you throw a stone against that window, then you will break it"), *probabilistic reasoning* (e.g. "if you go out in this weather, you will probably get a cold"), *fuzzy reasoning* (e.g. "if the temperature is hot, then the fan speed is high"), or *counterfactual reasoning* (e.g. "if I were you, I wouldn't do that").

In different contexts we associate to the "if-then" expressions distinct modalities, each of them validating different argumentation patterns. A common way of formalising different reasoning patterns that are or are not endorsed in a specific reasoning context is through *structural properties*. That is, formal constraints specifying that a set of conditionals is closed under certain reasoning patterns. This kind of analysis was used already in classical logic, as the class of Tarskian logical consequence relations have been characterised in terms of three main properties:

Reflexivity: $A \models A$ (Ref)

Monotonicity: $\frac{A \models C,\ \models B \rightarrow A}{B \models C}$ (Mon)

Cut: $\frac{A \wedge B \models C,\ A \models B}{A \models C}$ (Cut) .

Referring to structural properties in analysing conditional logics has become a standard in some areas (Gabbay 1995; Makinson 1994; Makinson and van der Torre 2000). However, let us note that while some properties may appear obvious in everyday reasoning, these may become in fact undesirable depending on the reasoning context in which we apply them. For example, a property like

Right Conjunction: $\frac{A \Rightarrow B,\ A \Rightarrow C}{A \Rightarrow (B \wedge C)}$ (And)

dictates that if an agent believes "if A then B" and "if A then C", then it should also believe that "if A then B and C" ($\Rightarrow$ stands for conditional implication). For instance, if an agent believes that typically birds fly and that typically birds nest on trees, it is reasonable to require for a rational agent to abide to the (And) property, and, thus, to believe the conjunction of the two, i.e. typically birds fly *and* nest on trees.

While the (And) property is required in presumptive reasoning, it is not considered appropriate for other kinds of reasoning, as, for example, in a probabilistic context (Hawthorne and Makinson 2007) or in deontic reasoning. In the latter case, in some kind of normative reasoning involving incompatible preferences, (And) is not a desirable reasoning pattern: an agent could believe $\texttt{saturday} \Rightarrow \texttt{party}$ ("On Saturday night I would like to go to a party") and $\texttt{saturday} \Rightarrow \texttt{tv}$ ("On Saturday night I would like to stay home watching TV"), but not $\texttt{saturday} \Rightarrow \texttt{party} \wedge \texttt{tv}$ ("On Saturday night I would like to go to a party and to stay home watching TV").

Another property that is usually satisfied in most of the reasoning contexts is

Right Weakening: $\frac{A \Rightarrow B,\ \models B \rightarrow C}{A \Rightarrow C}$ (RW) .

(RW) simply states that if an agent believes "if A then B", then it believes also "if A then C" for any (classical) consequence C of B. For example, it is reasonable to impose that believing that presumably birds fly implies also believing that presumably birds move, since flying implies moving.

However, there are contexts in which (RW) gives back counter-intuitive results, as in some forms of deontic and causal reasoning (Casini, Meyer, and Varzinczak 2019a), as illustrated by the following examples:

- "if you are involved in a car accident, you should remain on the spot" is an acceptable norm, but "if you are involved in a car accident, you should remain on the spot or paint yourself in blue" is not as acceptable;
- "if you turn the wheel of a moving car, the car will move in a circle" is meaningful, while "If you turn the wheel of a moving car, the car will move" is not really that meaningful;
- "if you throw a stone against the window, it will break" is meaningful, but "If you throw a stone against the window, it will break or Ann will drink tea" is not.

(RW) is a property that is strongly connected to the traditional semantics that is used to formalise conditional reasoning, i.e. possible-worlds semantics. In fact, most formalisations of conditional reasoning have been built using a possible-worlds semantics by referring more or less directly to classical modal operators. Using such an approach it has been possible to define logical systems modelling various kinds of non-classical reasoning.

On the other hand, relying on possible worlds means relying on closed logical theories, and such an approach enforces some properties (e.g. logical omniscience) that may be in conflict with some modelling goals. Some works have already considered ways of combining a possible world approach with some constrained forms of (RW) (Casini, Meyer, and Varzinczak 2019a; Rott 1989). Let us anticipate that, in contrast to those approaches, we will consider here a kind of intentional semantics instead.

One limit of the possible-worlds approach to the formalisation of conditionals "if *condition* C holds, then *effect* D holds with a given *modality*" is that it accounts for the modality that is associated with the truth of D given the truth of C. However, it does not account for whether the truth of D given the truth of C has any relevance for the kind of reasoning we are considering. The centrality of the notion of *relevance* in conditional reasoning has already been pointed out in (Delgrande 2011). However what 'relevance' means in the context of conditional reasoning remains still vague nowadays.

As we are going to show in the next section, our formalisation focuses on choice functions that model what the *agent considers as relevant effects and relevant conditions*. Our work is somewhat inspired by (Rott 2001) that also suggested the use of choice functions in modelling the semantics of conditionals.

The paper is organised as follows. In the next section we introduce some background concepts we will rely on in our formalisation of conditionals. In Section 3 we illustrate our formalisation of conditionals, while Section 4 describes how we may accommodate various structural properties within our approach. Section 5 discusses how to formalise entailment relations in our framework and shows possible future developments. Eventually, Section 6 summarises our contribution.

2 Preliminaries

We use a conditional language containing conditionals of the form $C \Rightarrow D$. We do not consider here the possibility of nesting the conditionals or combining them via propositional operators.

Let $\mathcal{L}$ be a finitely generated propositional language, with logical connectives $\neg, \vee, \wedge, \rightarrow$ and $\leftrightarrow$ and propositional symbol $\bot$ having usual meaning. Capital letters $A, B, \ldots$ will be used to refer to propositions, while $\mathcal{A}, \mathcal{B}, \ldots$ will refer to sets of propositions. With $\models$ we denote the classical propositional consequence relation.

Our language will be $\mathcal{L}_{\Rightarrow}$, the conditional language built on top of $\mathcal{L}$: namely,

$$\mathcal{L}_{\Rightarrow} \equiv_{\text{def}} \{C \Rightarrow D \mid C, D \in \mathcal{L}\} .$$

On the semantics side we will use a relation $\leq \subseteq \mathcal{L} \times \mathcal{L}$ among propositional formulae, where $A \leq B$ iff $\models A \rightarrow B$, so that $\leq$ generates the classical lattice semantics over propositional formulas, with $\vee$ and $\wedge$ represented by the *join* and *meet* operations, respectively. The relations $<$ and $\equiv$ are defined as usual from $\leq$. Note that, using $\leq$ as a representation of $\rightarrow$, $A < B$ represents $A \rightarrow B$ and $\neg(B \rightarrow A)$, while $A \equiv B$ is a representative of $A \leftrightarrow B$. Of course, $\leq$ is reflexive and transitive.

With $\min_{\leq}(\mathcal{A})$ we denote the *minimal* elements in $\mathcal{A}$ w.r.t. $\leq$, i.e. $\min_{\leq}(\mathcal{A}) \equiv_{\text{def}} \{B \in \mathcal{A} \mid \nexists C \in \mathcal{A} \text{ s.t. } C < B\}$, while $\mathcal{A}^{\uparrow} \equiv_{\text{def}} \{B \mid A \leq B \text{ for some } A \in \mathcal{A}\}$ and $\mathcal{A}^{\downarrow} \equiv_{\text{def}} \{B \mid B \leq A \text{ for some } A \in \mathcal{A}\}$ (we will write $A^{\uparrow}, A^{\downarrow}$ for $\{A\}^{\uparrow}, \{A\}^{\downarrow}$).
We are going to use a well-known order among sets of formulae, based on $\leq$: the *Smyth* order $\preceq$ over power sets (see, e.g. (Straccia, Ojeda-Aciego, and Damásio 2009, Section 3) for a short introduction).[1] Specifically,

$$\mathcal{A} \preceq \mathcal{B} \text{ iff } \forall B \in \mathcal{B}\, \exists A \in \mathcal{A} \text{ s.t. } A \leq B .$$

We also write $\mathcal{A} \cong \mathcal{B}$ iff $\mathcal{A} \preceq \mathcal{B}$ and $\mathcal{B} \preceq \mathcal{A}$.

A *choice* function is a set-valued function $h \colon \mathcal{L} \rightarrow 2^{\mathcal{L}}$, mapping a formula to a set of formulae. We say that h is *Smyth-monotone*, or simply *S-monotone*, iff for every $A, B \in \mathcal{L}$, if $A \leq B$ then $h(A) \preceq h(B)$. Furthermore, $A \in \mathcal{L}$ is a *fixed-point* of h iff $A \in h(A)$ (see, e.g. (Straccia, Ojeda-Aciego, and Damásio 2009)).

Eventually, we say that h is $\star$*-closed*, where $\star \in \{\leq, \equiv\}$, iff for all $A, B, C \in \mathcal{L}$, if $A \in h(C)$ and $B \star A$ then $B \in h(C)$.[2] On the other hand, we will say that h is $\star$*-closed*, where $\star \in \{\wedge, \vee\}$, iff for all $A, B, C \in \mathcal{L}$, if $A \in h(C)$ and $B \in h(C)$ then $A \star B \in h(C)$.

3 Semantics

We build our semantics on top of two choice functions, f and g, representing what an agent considers as relevant connections. Specifically, a *conditional interpretation* $\mathcal{I}$ is a pair

$$\mathcal{I} = (f, g)$$

[1] Orders of this type are often used in the context of so-called *power domains* (Knijnenburg 1993; Knijnenburg 1996; Plotkin 1976; Smyth 1978; Winskel 1985).

[2] Note that for $\leq$ order matters as $\leq$ is not symmetric.

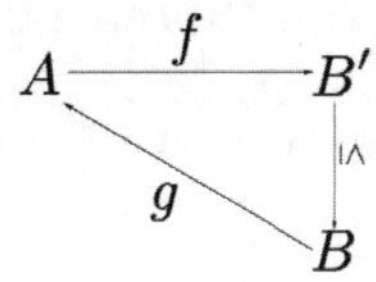

Figure 1: Graphical representation of $\mathcal{I} \Vdash A \Rightarrow B$.

s.t. $f : \mathcal{L} \to 2^{\mathcal{L}}$ and $g : \mathcal{L} \to 2^{\mathcal{L}}$. f represents the *relevant effects* of a proposition, and g the *possible conditions* for a proposition to hold.

Definition 1 (Satisfaction). *Let $\mathcal{I} = (f, g)$ be a conditional interpretation. $\mathcal{I}$* satisfies *a conditional $A \Rightarrow B$, denoted $\mathcal{I} \Vdash A \Rightarrow B$, iff the following conditions hold:*

1. *there is $B' \in \mathcal{L}$ s.t. $B' \in f(A)$ and $B' \leq B$; and*
2. *$A \in g(B)$.*

$A \Rightarrow B$ is satisfiable *(has a* model*) if there is a conditional interpretation $\mathcal{I}$ such that $\mathcal{I} \Vdash A \Rightarrow B$. A set of conditionals is* satisfiable *(has a* model*) iff each conditional in it is so.*

Fig. 1 gives a graphical representation of the satisfaction relation: $\mathcal{I} \Vdash A \Rightarrow B$ iff there is a "triangle" $A \xrightarrow{f} B' \leq B \xrightarrow{g} A$. We indicate with $A \triangle B$ that there is a triangle $A \xrightarrow{f} B' \leq B \xrightarrow{g} A$ passing through some $B' \leq B$.

The meaning of the above definition has an epistemic flavour: an agent accepts a conditional connection between A and B if B is a logical consequence of some *relevant effect* B' of A ($B' \in f(A)$), and A is recognised as a *relevant condition* for B ($A \in g(B)$).

Given an interpretation $\mathcal{I}$, with $S_{\mathcal{I}}$ we indicate the set of conditionals satisfied by $\mathcal{I}$, i.e. $S_{\mathcal{I}} \equiv_{\text{def}} \{A \Rightarrow B \mid \mathcal{I} \Vdash A \Rightarrow B\}$.

Let us note that our class of interpretations is quite generic and, in particular, can represent any set of conditionals. In fact, given a set of conditionals S, we may define a model $\mathcal{I}$ characterising it, that is, satisfying exactly the conditionals in S (i.e., $S_{\mathcal{I}} = S$). To do so, given S, we construct a conditional interpretation w.r.t. S

$$\mathcal{I}_S = (f_S, g_S)$$

in the following way:

1. define the following sets: $\mathcal{A}_B \equiv_{\text{def}} \{A \mid A \Rightarrow B \in S\}$ and $\mathcal{C}_A \equiv_{\text{def}} \{B \mid A \Rightarrow B \in S\}$.
2. for every $D \in \mathcal{L}$, we set

$$f_S(D) = \min_{\leq}(\mathcal{C}_D) \text{ and } g_S(D) = \mathcal{A}_D .$$

$\mathcal{I}_S$ characterises S, as the following proposition proves.

Proposition 1. *Given a set of conditionals S, $\mathcal{I}_S$ is its* characteristic model, *that is, a conditional $A \Rightarrow B$ is in S iff $\mathcal{I}_S \Vdash A \Rightarrow B$.*

Proof. From left to right. Assume $A \Rightarrow B$ is in S. Then, by definition of $\mathcal{I}_S$, we have that $A \in g_S(B)$ and there is a $B' \in f_S(A)$ s.t. $B' \leq B$ (it could be B itself). Hence $\mathcal{I}_S \Vdash A \Rightarrow B$.

From right to left. Assume $\mathcal{I}_S \Vdash A \Rightarrow B$. Then $A \in g_S(B)$, and that, by construction of $\mathcal{I}_S$, can be only if $A \Rightarrow B \in S$. □

Please note that, as we have proved Proposition 1 for any arbitrary set of conditionals S, the following immediate corollary tells us that the class of conditional interpretations $\mathcal{I} = (f, g)$ do not impose any form of closure under any structural property.

Corollary 1. *The class of conditional interpretations can represent any set of conditionals.*

Corollary 2. *Any set of conditionals S is satisfiable.*

4 Structural Properties

In the following, we are going to show that by constraining the functions f and g, it is possible to enforce the closure of the set of conditionals under structural properties that are considered as appropriate for modelling various kinds of reasoning. We start by analysing some classical reasoning patterns.

At first, as f and g range over formulae and not over possible worlds, i.e. logically closed theories, *Definition 1 does not imply any form of closure under logical equivalence.* Such a behaviour may be desirable in some epistemic contexts in which we would like to avoid some form of a priori *logical omniscience* (Fagin et al. 1995). That is, the well known reasoning patterns of *Left Logical Equivalence* (LLE) and *Right Logical Equivalence* (RLE) do not hold in general in our framework. However, if these are desired, it is quite straightforward to enforce (LLE) and (RLE) in our setting. Specifically, for

Left Logical Equivalence:

$$\frac{A \Rightarrow C, \quad A \equiv B}{B \Rightarrow C} \quad \text{(LLE)}$$

it suffices to impose the following semantic constraints on a conditional interpretation $\mathcal{I} = (f, g)$:

(LLE$_{\mathcal{I}}$) for all A, B:

1. if $A \equiv B$, then $f(A) = f(B)$;
2. g is $\equiv$-closed.

Similarly, for

Right Logical Equivalence:

$$\frac{A \Rightarrow B, \quad B \equiv C}{A \Rightarrow C} \quad \text{(RLE)}$$

the semantic constraint to be imposed on a conditional interpretation $\mathcal{I} = (f, g)$ is:

(RLE$_{\mathcal{I}}$) for all A, B:

1. if $A \equiv B$, then $g(A) = g(B)$.

The conditions (LLE$_{\mathcal{I}}$) and (RLE$_{\mathcal{I}}$) characterise the classes of the conditional interpretations satisfying, respectively, (LLE) and (RLE). In fact, it can be shown that[3]

[3]Since the proof is straightforward we omit it.

Proposition 2. *A set of conditionals S is closed under (LLE) (resp. (RLE)) iff it can be characterised by a conditional model $\mathcal{I} = (f, g)$ that satisfies (LLE$_\mathcal{I}$) (resp. (RLE$_\mathcal{I}$)).*

Another basic property is *Reflexivity*, that simply states that for every proposition A it holds 'If A, then A'. Despite appearing as an obviously valid conditional, there are some contexts in which it is not a desirable property. Consider for example a deontic system expressing recommendations, in which $A \Rightarrow B$ is read as "if A holds, then B would be preferrable". This kind of conditionals can result quite counterintuitive if it embeds reflexivity (see e.g. (Makinson and van der Torre 2000)): while "if there is an act of violence, then you should call the police" appears to be a reasonable conditional, to be forced to conclude "if there is an act of violence, then there should be an act of violence" is counter-intuitive. Reflexivity does not hold in our framework, though if we would like to have this pattern, it suffices to impose a simple constraint on conditional interpretations. For

Reflexivity:

$$A \Rightarrow A \quad \text{(Ref)}$$

the semantic constraint to be imposed on a conditional interpretation $\mathcal{I} = (f, g)$ is:

(Ref$_\mathcal{I}$) for all A:

1. A is a fixed-point of both f and g.

Proposition 3. *A set of conditionals S is closed under (Ref) iff it can be characterised by a conditional model $\mathcal{I} = (f, g)$ that satisfies (Ref$_\mathcal{I}$).*

Proof. From right to left. Assume that S is characterised by some conditional model $\mathcal{I} = (f, g)$ that satisfies (Ref$_\mathcal{I}$), that is, $S = S_\mathcal{I}$. We have to show that $S_\mathcal{I}$ is closed under (Ref), and it is immediate to see that (Ref$_\mathcal{I}$) implies $\mathcal{I} \Vdash A \Rightarrow A$ for every A.

From left to right. Let S be a set of conditionals closed under (Ref). We need to prove that there is a conditional interpretation $\mathcal{I} = (f, g)$ characterising it and satisfying (Ref$_\mathcal{I}$). We can define such an $\mathcal{I}$ by slightly modifying the characteristic model $\mathcal{I}_S = (f_S, g_S)$. Specifically, it suffices to consider $\mathcal{I} = (f, g)$, where $g(A) = g_S(A)$ and $f(A) = f_S(A) \cup \{A\}$, for every A. Clearly, $\mathcal{I}$ satisfies (Ref$_\mathcal{I}$). The proof that $A \Rightarrow B \in S$ iff $\mathcal{I} \Vdash A \Rightarrow B$ is analogous to the proof of Proposition 1, considering also that S is closed under (Ref). □

As next, we consider more elaborate structural properties. We start with considering the *Cut* reasoning pattern, one of the main structural properties in classical logic (cf. Section 1). So, for

Cut:

$$\frac{A \wedge B \Rightarrow C, \quad A \Rightarrow B}{A \Rightarrow C} \quad \text{(Cut)}$$

the semantic constraints to be imposed on a conditional interpretation $\mathcal{I} = (f, g)$ are:

(Cut$_\mathcal{I}$) for all A, B, C:

1. If $A \triangle B$, then $f(A) \preceq f(A \wedge B)$;
2. If $A \in g(B)$ and $A \wedge B \in g(C)$, then $A \in g(C)$.

Then, we can show that

Proposition 4. *A set of conditionals S is closed under (Cut) iff it can be characterised by a conditional model $\mathcal{I} = (f, g)$ that satisfies (Cut$_\mathcal{I}$).*

Proof. From right to left. Assume that S is characterised by some conditional model $\mathcal{I} = (f, g)$ that satisfies (Cut$_\mathcal{I}$), that is $S = S_\mathcal{I}$. We need to prove that $S_\mathcal{I}$ is closed under (Cut). Suppose $\mathcal{I} \Vdash A \Rightarrow B$ and $\mathcal{I} \Vdash A \wedge B \Rightarrow C$. Then there is some $C' \in f(A \wedge B)$ s.t. $C' \leq C$. Since $f(A) \preceq f(A \wedge B)$ there is some $C'' \in f(A)$ s.t. $C'' \leq C'$, that is, $C'' \leq C$. Regarding g, we have $A \in g(B)$ and $A \wedge B \in g(C)$, hence $A \in g(C)$. $C'' \in f(A)$ and $A \in g(C)$ imply $\mathcal{I} \Vdash A \Rightarrow C$. Therefore, $S_\mathcal{I}$ is closed under (Cut).

From left to right. Let S be a set of conditionals closed under (Cut). We need to prove that there is a conditional interpretation $\mathcal{I} = (f, g)$ characterising it and satisfying (Cut$_\mathcal{I}$). Let us consider the characteristic model $\mathcal{I}_S$.We need to prove that it satisfies the two conditions of (Cut$_\mathcal{I}$). So, assume $A \triangle B$ and $C \in f_S(A \wedge B)$. $A \triangle B$ implies $\mathcal{I}_S \Vdash A \Rightarrow B$, that by Proposition 1 implies $A \Rightarrow B \in S$. By construction of $\mathcal{I}_S$, $C \in f_S(A \wedge B)$ implies that $A \wedge B \Rightarrow C \in S$. From $\{A \Rightarrow B, A \wedge B \Rightarrow C\} \subseteq S$ and (Cut) we have that $A \Rightarrow C \in S$, and, by Proposition 1, $\mathcal{I}_S \Vdash A \Rightarrow C$. Therefore, there is a C' s.t. $C' \in f_S(A)$ and $C' \leq C$. That is, $f_S(A) \leq_S f_S(A \wedge B)$ holds. Regarding the second condition on g_S, let $A \in g_S(B)$ and $A \wedge B \in g_S(C)$. By construction of $\mathcal{I}_S$, $A \Rightarrow B$ and $A \wedge B \Rightarrow C$ are in S, and by (Cut) $A \Rightarrow C \in S$. Therefore, by construction of $\mathcal{I}_S$, $A \in g_S(C)$, which concludes the proof. □

As next, we address *monotonicity* (cf. Section 1), also a main property of classical logic. It states that strengthening the antecedent of a conditional from a logical point of view, we still preserve the effects. For example, the conditional `horse` $\Rightarrow$ `mammal` in a monotonic system imposes to conclude that any kind of horse is a mammal, e.g. `horse` $\wedge$ `mustang` $\Rightarrow$ `mammal`. That is, (Mon) makes our conditionals *strict*, in the sense that they do not admit exceptions. So, for

Monotonicity:

$$\frac{A \Rightarrow C, \quad \models B \rightarrow A}{B \Rightarrow C} \quad \text{(Mon)}$$

the semantic constraints to be imposed on a conditional interpretation $\mathcal{I} = (f, g)$ are:

(Mon$_\mathcal{I}$)

1. f is S-Monotone;
2. g is $\leq$-closed.

Proposition 5. *A set of conditionals S is closed under (Mon) iff it can be characterised by a conditional model $\mathcal{I} = (f, g)$ that satisfies (Mon$_\mathcal{I}$).*

Proof. From right to left. Assume that S is characterised by some conditional model $\mathcal{I} = (f, g)$ that satisfies (Mon$_\mathcal{I}$), that is, $S = S_\mathcal{I}$. We need to prove that $S_\mathcal{I}$ is closed under

(Mon). Assume $\mathcal{I} \Vdash A \Rightarrow C$ and $\models B \rightarrow A$, i.e. $B \leq A$. $\mathcal{I} \Vdash A \Rightarrow C$ implies that there is some $B' \in f(A)$ s.t. $B' \leq C$. By S-Monotonicity $f(B) \preceq f(A)$ and, thus, there is some $B'' \in f(B)$ s.t. $B'' \leq B'$, that implies $B'' \leq C$. As g is $\leq$-closed and $B \leq A$, $A \in g(C)$ implies $B \in g(C)$. Hence $\mathcal{I} \Vdash B \Rightarrow C$. Therefore, $S_\mathcal{I}$ is closed under (Mon).

From left to right. Let S be a set of conditionals closed under (Mon). We need to prove that there is a conditional interpretation $\mathcal{I} = (f, g)$ characterising it and satisfying (Mon$_\mathcal{I}$). Let us consider the characteristic model $\mathcal{I}_S$ of S as by Proposition 1. We need to prove that it satisfies the two conditions of (Mon$_\mathcal{I}$). So, let $B \leq A$, and let $C \in f_S(A)$. By construction of $\mathcal{I}_S$, $C \in f_S(A)$ implies that $A \Rightarrow C \in S$, and by (Mon) $B \Rightarrow C \in S$. By construction of $\mathcal{I}_S$, either $C \in f_S(B)$, or there is a $C' \in f_S(B)$ s.t. $C' \leq C$. Hence f_S is S-Monotone. Also the $\leq$-closure of g_S is an immediate consequence of the closure under (Mon) of S and the definition of g_S in $\mathcal{I}_S$, , which concludes the proof. □

As by Section 1, (And) is a property that appears desirable in many contexts, but may have some exceptions. For

Right Conjunction:

$$\frac{A \Rightarrow B, \quad A \Rightarrow C}{A \Rightarrow (B \wedge C)} \qquad \text{(And)}$$

the semantic constraints to be imposed on a conditional interpretation $\mathcal{I} = (f, g)$ that characterise (And) are:

(And$_\mathcal{I}$) for all A, B:

1. if $B, C \in \min_{\leq}(f(A))$, then $B \equiv C$;
2. $g(A) \cap g(B) \subseteq g(B \wedge C)$.

Proposition 6. *A set of conditionals S is closed under (And) iff it can be characterised by a conditional model $\mathcal{I} = (f, g)$ that satisfies (And$_\mathcal{I}$).*

Proof. From right to left. Assume that S is characterised by some conditional model $\mathcal{I} = (f, g)$ that satisfies (And$_\mathcal{I}$), that is, $S = S_\mathcal{I}$. We need to prove that $S_\mathcal{I}$ is closed under (And). Assume $\mathcal{I} \Vdash A \Rightarrow B$ and $\mathcal{I} \Vdash A \Rightarrow C$. Then there is some $B' \in f(A)$ s.t. $B' \leq B$ and some $C' \in f(A)$ s.t. $C' \leq C$. $\min_{\leq}(f(A))$ contains some B^* s.t. $B^* \leq B$ and some C^* s.t. $C^* \leq C$. By the first condition of (And$_\mathcal{I}$) we have $B^* \equiv C^*$, and as a consequence we have $B^* \leq C$ and eventually $B^* \leq B \wedge C$. Regarding g, we have $A \in g(B)$ and $A \in g(C)$, hence $A \in g(B \wedge C)$. $B^* \in f(A)$, $B^* \leq B \wedge C$ and $A \in g(B \wedge C)$ together imply $\mathcal{I} \Vdash A \Rightarrow (B \wedge C)$. Therefore, $S_\mathcal{I}$ is closed under (And).

From left to right. Let S be a set of conditionals closed under (And). We need to prove that there is a conditional interpretation $\mathcal{I} = (f, g)$ characterising it and satisfying (And$_\mathcal{I}$). Let us consider the characteristic model $\mathcal{I}_S$ of S as by Proposition 1. We need to prove that it satisfies the two conditions of (And$_\mathcal{I}$). So, assume there are three propositions A, B, C s.t. $B, C \in \min_{\leq}(f_S(A))$ and $B \not\equiv C$. From the construction of $\mathcal{I}_S$ we have that $B, C \in \min_{\leq}(f_S(A))$ implies that $B \wedge C \notin f_S(A)$, and that for any A, B, if $B \in f_S(A)$, then $\mathcal{I}_S \Vdash A \Rightarrow B$. Hence we have $\mathcal{I}_S \Vdash A \Rightarrow B$ and $\mathcal{I}_S \Vdash A \Rightarrow C$, but not $\mathcal{I}_S \Vdash A \Rightarrow B \wedge C$, against the closure of S under (And). Regarding the second condition, for all A, B, $A \in g_S(B)$ iff $\mathcal{I}_S \Vdash A \Rightarrow B$. Let $A \in g_S(B) \cap g_S(C)$. Then $\mathcal{I}_S \Vdash A \Rightarrow B$, $\mathcal{I}_S \Vdash A \Rightarrow C$, and, by (And), $\mathcal{I}_S \Vdash A \Rightarrow B \wedge C$, that implies $A \in g_S(B \wedge C)$, which concludes the proof. □

Reasoning by cases is another well-known characteristics of classical reasoning, which is formalised by the *Left Disjunction* reasoning pattern. To deal with it, for

Left Disjunction: $\frac{A \Rightarrow C,\ B \Rightarrow C}{A \vee B \Rightarrow C}$ (Or)

the semantic constraints to be imposed on a conditional interpretation $\mathcal{I} = (f, g)$ that characterise (Or) are:

(Or$_\mathcal{I}$) for all A, B:

1. $\min_{\leq}(f(A)^{\uparrow} \cap f^{\uparrow}(B)) \subseteq f(A \vee B)$;
2. g is $\vee$-closed.

Proposition 7. *A set of conditionals S is closed under (Or) iff it can be characterised by a conditional model $\mathcal{I} = (f, g)$ that satisfies (Or$_\mathcal{I}$).*

Proof. From right to left. Assume that S is characterised by a conditional model $\mathcal{I} = (f, g)$ that satisfies (Or$_\mathcal{I}$), that is, $S = S_\mathcal{I}$. We need to prove that $S_\mathcal{I}$ is closed under (Or). Assume $\mathcal{I} \Vdash A \Rightarrow C$ and $\mathcal{I} \Vdash B \Rightarrow C$. Then there are $C' \in f(A)$ s.t. $C' \leq C$, and $C'' \in f(B)$ s.t. $C'' \leq C$. Then there must be some C^* s.t. $C' \leq C^*$, $C'' \leq C^*$, and $C^* \leq C$ (C itself satisfies the constraint), and the minimal among them w.r.t. $\leq$ are in $f(A \vee B)$ by condition 1. of (Or$_\mathcal{I}$). Hence in $f(A \vee B)$ there is some C^* s.t. $C^* \leq C$. But, $\mathcal{I} \Vdash A \Rightarrow C$ and $\mathcal{I} \Vdash B \Rightarrow C$ imply also that $A, B \in g(C)$ and, thus, as g is $\vee$-closed, $A \vee B \in g(C)$. Therefore, we can conclude $\mathcal{I} \Vdash A \vee B \Rightarrow C$. Therefore, $S_\mathcal{I}$ is closed under (Or).

From left to right. Let S be a set of conditionals closed under (Or). We need to prove that there is a conditional interpretation $\mathcal{I} = (f, g)$ characterising it and satisfying (Or$_\mathcal{I}$). So, let us consider the characteristic model $\mathcal{I}_S$ as by Proposition 1. At first, we show that $\mathcal{I}_S$ satisfies the second condition of (Or$_\mathcal{I}$). In fact, by construction of $\mathcal{I}_S$, for all C, D, if $C \in g_S(D)$ then $C \Rightarrow D \in S$. Therefore, as S is closed under (Or), g_S must be $\vee$-closed. On the other hand, if $\mathcal{I}_S$ does not satisfy the first condition of (Or$_\mathcal{I}$), we transform $\mathcal{I}_S$ into a model $\mathcal{I}'$ by extending f_S only. Specifically, it is sufficient that for every disjunction $A \vee B$ we add the set $\min_{\leq}(f_S)^{\uparrow}(A) \cap f_S^{\uparrow}(B))$ to $f_S(A \vee B)$. Now, it is easily verified that indeed $\mathcal{I}'$ satisfies exactly the same set of conditionals as $\mathcal{I}_S$, i.e. S. In fact, in $\mathcal{I}'$ we have an extension of f_S, while g_S stays the same. Therefore, as by construction of $\mathcal{I}_S$, $C \in g(D)$ iff $C \Rightarrow D \in S$, the same holds for $\mathcal{I}'$ and, thus, the set of satisfied conditionals by $\mathcal{I}'$ remains the same as for $\mathcal{I}_S$, i.e. S, which concludes the proof. □

As mentioned in Section 1, *Right Weakening* is a property that is generally desirable in many context with some exceptions. To support the reasoning pattern of

Right Weakening:

$$\frac{A \Rightarrow B, \quad \models B \rightarrow C}{A \Rightarrow C} \qquad \text{(RW)}$$

the semantic constraint to be imposed on a conditional interpretation $\mathcal{I} = (f, g)$ that characterise (RW) is:

($RW_{\mathcal{I}}$) for all A, B:

1. if $A \leq B$ then $g(A) \subseteq g(B)$.

Proposition 8. *A set of conditionals S is closed under (RW) iff it can be characterised by a conditional model $\mathcal{I} = (f, g)$ that satisfies ($RW_{\mathcal{I}}$).*

Proof. From right to left. Assume that S is characterised by a conditional model $\mathcal{I} = (f, g)$ that satisfies ($RW_{\mathcal{I}}$), that is, $S = S_{\mathcal{I}}$. We need to prove that $S_{\mathcal{I}}$ is closed under (RW). So, assume $\mathcal{I} \Vdash A \Rightarrow B$ and $\models B \to C$, i.e. $B \leq C$. Then there is some $B' \in f(A)$ s.t. $B' \leq B$, and consequently $B' \leq C$. Since $B \leq C$, $A \in g(B)$, by condition 1. we have $A \in g(C)$. Hence $\mathcal{I} \Vdash A \Rightarrow C$. $S_{\mathcal{I}}$ is closed under (RW).

From left to right. Let S be a set of conditionals closed under (RW). We need to prove that there is a conditional interpretation $\mathcal{I} = (f, g)$ characterising it and satisfying ($RW_{\mathcal{I}}$). So, consider the characteristic model $\mathcal{I}_S$, assume $B \leq C$, i.e. $\models B \to C$, and let $A \in g_S(B)$. By construction of $\mathcal{I}_S$, $A \in g_S(B)$ implies $\mathcal{I} \Vdash A \Rightarrow B$, that, by (RW), implies $\mathcal{I} \Vdash A \Rightarrow C$. By construction of $\mathcal{I}_S$, $A \in g_S(C)$, as desired. □

So far, we have taken under consideration most of the properties characterising classical entailment. However, we still miss two important consistency properties: namely, *ex falso quodlibet* and *consistency preservation*. The former is a classical property strongly connected with classical implication and entailment, and stating that we can conclude anything from a false premise. This property, for example, is not fully desirable in counterfactual reasoning, where we would like to be able to reason coherently about false situation, but that are at least conceivable. Nevertheless, to support the reasoning pattern of

Ex Falso Quodlibet:

$$\frac{\models \neg A}{A \Rightarrow B} \qquad \text{(EFQ)}$$

the semantic constraints to be imposed on a conditional interpretation $\mathcal{I} = (f, g)$ that characterise (EFQ) are:

($EFQ_{\mathcal{I}}$) for all A: if $A \equiv \bot$, then

1. $\bot \in f(A)$;
2. $A \in g(B)$, for all B.

Proposition 9. *A set of conditionals S is closed under (EFQ) iff it can be characterised by a conditional model $\mathcal{I} = (f, g)$ that satisfies ($EFQ_{\mathcal{I}}$).*

Proof. From right to left. Assume that S is characterised by a conditional model $\mathcal{I} = (f, g)$ that satisfies ($EFQ_{\mathcal{I}}$), that is, $S = S_{\mathcal{I}}$. We need to prove that $S_{\mathcal{I}}$ is closed under (EFQ). Assume $\models \neg A$. We need to prove that $\mathcal{I} \Vdash A \Rightarrow B$ holds for all B. $\models \neg A$ implies $A \equiv \bot$, hence, by ($EFQ_{\mathcal{I}}$), we have $\bot \in f(A)$, $\bot \leq B$ and, thus, $A \in g(B)$. Therefore, $\mathcal{I} \Vdash A \Rightarrow B$ and, thus, $S_{\mathcal{I}}$ is closed under (EFQ).

From left to right. Let S be a set of conditionals closed under (EFQ). We need to prove that there is a conditional interpretation $\mathcal{I} = (f, g)$ characterising it and satisfying ($EFQ_{\mathcal{I}}$). So, consider the characteristic model $\mathcal{I}_S$ and let $\models \neg A$. By (EFQ), $A \Rightarrow \bot \in S$ follows, and, since $\bot \in \min_{\leq}(\mathcal{C}_D)$, $\bot \in f_S(A)$ holds. Furthermore, by (EFQ), $A \Rightarrow B \in S$ holds, for all $B \in \mathcal{L}$. Therefore, by construction of $\mathcal{I}_S$, $A \in g_S(B)$ holds, for any $B \in \mathcal{L}$ and, thus, $\mathcal{I}_S$ satisfies ($EFQ_{\mathcal{I}}$), which concludes the proof. □

Please note that (EFQ) is an immediate consequence of (RLE), (And) and (RW). However, we may have contexts that do not satisfy some of these three properties, but still satisfies (EFQ). If this is the case, the semantic constraint ($EFQ_{\mathcal{I}}$) has to be considered.

Consistency preservation tells us that we cannot conclude absurdity from a classically consistent premise. To support the reasoning pattern of

Consistency Preservation:

$$\frac{A \Rightarrow B, \quad \models \neg B}{\models \neg A} \qquad \text{(Con)}$$

the semantic constraint to be imposed on a conditional interpretation $\mathcal{I} = (f, g)$ that characterise (Con) is:

($Con_{\mathcal{I}}$) for all A,

1. if $B \in f(A)$, for some $B \leq \bot$, then $A \leq \bot$.

Please note that only if we assume (RLE) we can express (Con) in the classical (equivalent) forms

$$\frac{A \Rightarrow \bot}{\models \neg A} \qquad \frac{\not\models \neg A}{A \not\Rightarrow \bot}$$

where the reading of the latter is: "if $\neg A$ is not a tautology then the conditional $A \Rightarrow \bot$ cannot be concluded".

Proposition 10. *A set of conditionals S is closed under (Con) iff it can be characterised by a conditional model $\mathcal{I} = (f, g)$ that satisfies ($Con_{\mathcal{I}}$).*

Proof. From right to left. Assume that S is characterised by a conditional model $\mathcal{I} = (f, g)$ that satisfies ($Con_{\mathcal{I}}$), that is $S = S_{\mathcal{I}}$. We need to prove that S is closed under (Con). So, assume $\mathcal{I} \Vdash A \Rightarrow B$ and $\models \neg B$, i.e. $B \leq \bot$. We need to prove that $\models \neg A$ holds. $\mathcal{I} \Vdash A \Rightarrow B$ implies that there is $B' \in f(A)$ s.t. $B' \leq B$, hence $B' \leq \bot$. Therefore, by ($Con_{\mathcal{I}}$) we have $A \leq \bot$, that is, $\models \neg A$.

From left to right. Let S be a set of conditionals satisfying (Con). We need to prove that there is a conditional interpretation $\mathcal{I} = (f, g)$ characterising it and satisfying ($Con_{\mathcal{I}}$). We prove that the characteristic model $\mathcal{I}_S$ is such an interpretation, by proving that for any A, if $\bot < A$ then there is no $B \leq \bot$ s.t. $B \in f_S(A)$. Let $\bot < A$ and $B \leq \bot$; hence $\not\models \neg A$ and $\models \neg B$. By (Con), $A \Rightarrow B \notin S$. By construction of $\mathcal{I}_S$, $A \Rightarrow B \notin S$ implies that B is not in $f_S(A)$, since otherwise we would have $A \Rightarrow B \in S$. □

A stronger property that connects conditional reasoning to classical entailment is *supraclassicality*, that is, the conditional systems extends classical reasoning. To support the reasoning pattern of

Supraclassicality: $\frac{\models A \to B}{A \Rightarrow B}$ (Sup)

the semantic constraints to be imposed on a conditional interpretation $\mathcal{I} = (f, g)$ that characterise (Sup) are:

(Con$_\mathcal{I}$) for all A,

1. A is a fixed-point of f;
2. $A^{\downarrow} \subseteq g(A)$.

Proposition 11. *A set of conditionals S is closed under (Sup) iff it can be characterised by a conditional model $\mathcal{I} = (f, g)$ that satisfies (Sup$_\mathcal{I}$).*

Proof. From right to left. Assume that S is characterised by a conditional model $\mathcal{I} = (f, g)$ and, thus, $S = S_\mathcal{I}$, that satisfies (Sup$_\mathcal{I}$). We need to prove that $S_\mathcal{I}$ is closed under (Sup). So, assume $\models A \rightarrow B$, i.e. $A \leq B$. Then $A \in B^{\downarrow}$, hence $A \in g(B)$, $A \in f(A)$, and $A \leq B$, hence $\mathcal{I} \Vdash A \Rightarrow B$.

From left to right. Let S be a set of conditionals satisfying (Sup). We need to prove that there is a conditional interpretation $\mathcal{I} = (f, g)$ characterising it and satisfying (Sup$_\mathcal{I}$). Consider the characteristic model $\mathcal{I}_S$: it clearly satisfies the second condition, the one over g. It is possible it does not satisfy the condition over f, in case S contains some conditional $A \Rightarrow B$ with $B < A$. To cover such a case it is sufficient to modify $\mathcal{I}_S$ into a model $\mathcal{I}$ in the same way as done in the proof of Proposition 3. $\mathcal{I}$ is a characteristic model of S satisfying both the conditions in (Sup$_\mathcal{I}$). □

Please note that (i) (Sup) is a consequence of (Ref) and (RW) together, but it is not equivalent to the combination of those two properties; and (ii) if we change the second condition in (Sup$_\mathcal{I}$) into $A^{\downarrow} = g(A)$, we model the classical propositional entailment (proof omitted).

A main portion of the research in conditional reasoning has focused on forms of defeasible reasoning. Defeasible reasoning is characterised by a degree of uncertainty connected some of the drawn conclusions that may be revised when faced with more complete and specific information. Presumptive reasoning, that is, reasoning based on expectations, represents the most popular context in which it is necessary to constraint (Mon). The basic form of constrainted monotonicity is *Cautious Monotonicity*. To support the reasoning pattern of

Cautious Monotonicity:

$$\frac{A \Rightarrow B, \quad A \Rightarrow C}{A \wedge B \Rightarrow C} \qquad \text{(CM)}$$

the semantic constraints to be imposed on a conditional interpretation $\mathcal{I} = (f, g)$ that characterise (CM) are:

(CM$_\mathcal{I}$) for all A, B,

1. if $A \triangle B$, then $f(A \wedge B) \preceq f(A)$;
2. if $A \in g(B) \cap g(C)$ then $A \wedge B \in g(C)$.

Proposition 12. *A set of conditionals S is closed under (CM) iff it can be characterised by a conditional model $\mathcal{I} = (f, g)$ that satisfies (CM$_\mathcal{I}$).*

Proof. From right to left. Assume that S can be characterised by a conditional model $\mathcal{I} = (f, g)$ and, thus, $S = S_\mathcal{I}$, that satisfies (CM$_\mathcal{I}$). We need to prove that $S_\mathcal{I}$ is closed under (CM). So, assume $\mathcal{I} \Vdash A \Rightarrow B$ and $\mathcal{I} \Vdash A \Rightarrow C$. Therefore, there is some $C' \in f(A)$ s.t. $C' \leq C$, and $f(A \wedge B) \leq_S f(A)$. As a consequence, there is some $C'' \in f(A \wedge B)$ s.t. $C'' \leq C'$, that is, $C'' \leq C$. Regarding g, we have $A \in g(B)$ and $A \in g(C)$, hence $A \wedge B \in g(C)$. Therefore, $\mathcal{I} \Vdash A \wedge B \Rightarrow C$ holds.

From left to right. Let S be a set of conditionals closed under (CM). We need to prove that there is a conditional interpretation $\mathcal{I} = (f, g)$ characterising it and satisfying (CM$_\mathcal{I}$). Consider the characteristic model $\mathcal{I}_S$ as by Proposition 1. We need to prove that it satisfies the two conditions of (CM$_\mathcal{I}$). Let $A \triangle B$ and $C \in f_S(A)$. $A \triangle B$ implies $\mathcal{I}_S \Vdash A \Rightarrow B$, which by Proposition 1 implies $A \Rightarrow B \in S$. By construction of $\mathcal{I}_S$, $C \in f_S(A)$ implies that $A \Rightarrow C \in S$. From $\{A \Rightarrow B, A \Rightarrow C\} \subseteq S$ and (CM) we have that $A \wedge B \Rightarrow C \in S$, and, by Proposition 1, $\mathcal{I}_S \Vdash A \wedge B \Rightarrow C$. That is, there is a C' s.t. $C' \in f_S(A \wedge B)$ and $C' \leq C$. Therefore, $f_S(A \wedge B) \preceq f_S(A)$ holds. Regarding the second condition on g_S, let $A \in g_S(B) \cap g_S(C)$. By construction of $\mathcal{I}_S$, $A \Rightarrow B$ and $A \Rightarrow C$ are in S, and by (CM) $A \wedge B \Rightarrow C \in S$, that is, by construction of $\mathcal{I}_S$, $A \wedge B \in g_s(C)$, which concludes the prove. □

Beyond being a desirable property from the point of view of many reasoning contexts, such as presumptive and prototypical reasoning (Kraus, Lehmann, and Magidor 1990), (CM) if formally important because combining it with (Cut) we obtain *Cumulativity*:

Cumulativity:

$$\text{If } A \Rightarrow B \text{ then } (A \Rightarrow C \text{ iff } A \wedge B \Rightarrow C) \qquad \text{(Cumul)}$$

(Cumul) is formally important because entailment relations satisfying (Cumul) satisfy also *Idempotence*, a classical closure property.

The semantic constraints to be imposed on a conditional interpretation $\mathcal{I} = (f, g)$ that characterise (Cumul) are obtained by combining (Cut$_\mathcal{I}$) and (CM$_\mathcal{I}$): that is,

(Cumul$_\mathcal{I}$) for all A, B, C,

1. If $A \triangle B$ then $f(A) \cong f(A \wedge B)$;
2. If $A \in g(B)$ then ($A \in g(C)$ iff $A \wedge B \in g(C)$).

Proceeding in this way we can introduce many other structural properties / reasoning patterns as formal constraints specified over the the functions f and g. For example, consider (AntiRW), a form of constrained (RW) (Casini, Meyer, and Varzinczak 2019a):

Anti Right Weakening:

$$\frac{A \Rightarrow B, \models B \rightarrow C, \models C \rightarrow D, A \not\Rightarrow C}{A \not\Rightarrow D} \qquad \text{(AntiRW)}$$

Or, equivalently,

$$\frac{A \Rightarrow B, \models B \rightarrow C, \models C \rightarrow D, A \Rightarrow D}{A \Rightarrow C} \qquad \text{(AntiRW*)}$$

(AntiRW), that is implied by (RW), states that we can weaken the conclusions, but, once we *block* the right weakening process, we cannot recover it anymore. It is a property that, for example, appears appropriate for some causal or deontic forms of reasoning (see (Casini, Meyer, and Varzinczak 2019a) for details).

We can enforce (AntiRW) in our framework via the following semantic constraints:

(AntiRW$_\mathcal{I}$) for all A, B, C, D,

1. if $A \in g(B)$, $A \in g(D)$ and $B \leq D$ then $B \leq C \leq D$ implies $A \in g(C)$.

Proposition 13. *A set of conditionals S is closed under (AntiRW) iff it can be characterised by a conditional model $\mathcal{I} = (f, g)$ that satisfies (AntiRW$_\mathcal{I}$).*

Proof. From right to left. Assume that S can be characterised by a conditional model $\mathcal{I} = (f, g)$ and, thus, $S = S_\mathcal{I}$, that satisfies (AntiRW$_\mathcal{I}$). We prove that $S_\mathcal{I}$ is closed under (AntiRW*) (that is equivalent to (AntiRW)). So, assume $\mathcal{I} \Vdash A \Rightarrow B$ and $\mathcal{I} \Vdash A \Rightarrow D$, with $B \leq C \leq D$. Then there is some $B' \in f(A)$ s.t. $B' \leq B \leq C \leq D$. Also, $A \in g(B)$ and $A \in g(D)$, that, by condition 1. of (AntiRW$_\mathcal{I}$), imply $A \in g(C)$. The latter and $B' \leq C$ imply $\mathcal{I} \Vdash A \Rightarrow C$, as desired.

From left to right. Let S be a set of conditionals closed under (AntiRW*). We need to prove that there is a conditional interpretation $\mathcal{I} = (f, g)$ characterising it and satisfying (AntiRW$_\mathcal{I}$). Let us consider the characteristic model $\mathcal{I}_S$, and we prove that it satisfies the condition (AntiRW$_\mathcal{I}$). So, let $A \in g_S(B)$, $A \in g_S(D)$, and $B \leq C \leq D$. By the construction of $\mathcal{I}_S$ we have $\mathcal{I}_S \Vdash A \Rightarrow B$ and $\mathcal{I}_S \Vdash A \Rightarrow D$. Since $B \leq C \leq D$ and S is closed under (AntiRW*), $\mathcal{I}_S \Vdash A \Rightarrow C$, that implies $A \in g_S(C)$. Hence condition 1. is satisfied, which completes the prove. □

Finally, let $\mathcal{P}$ be the set of structural properties presented in this section. We have taken under consideration each of them, and we have given a semantic counterpart in our framework. Each semantic property is a sufficient condition for obtaining a characterising model, but not a necessary condition. Specifically, given any set of conditionals S closed under some structural property (X), we have proved that there must be a characterising model satisfying (X$_\mathcal{I}$), not that every model characterising S must satisfy (X$_\mathcal{I}$).

In the following, we clarify whether all these semantic properties are compatible among them. That is, given a set of conditionals closed under some of the structural properties in $\mathcal{P}$, we are going to answer to the problem whether there is a characterising model closed under all the correspondent semantic properties.

Proposition 14. *Let $\mathcal{X} \subseteq \mathcal{P}$ be a set of structural properties in $\mathcal{P}$, and $\mathcal{X}_\mathcal{I}$ be the set of the correspondent semantic properties. If a set S of conditionals is closed under the properties in $\mathcal{X}$, then there is a conditional interpretation characterising S and satisfying all the properties in $\mathcal{X}_\mathcal{I}$.*

Proof. (Sketch) Let $\mathcal{P}' = \mathcal{P} \setminus \{$(Ref),(Sup),(Or)$\}$. If $\mathcal{X} \subseteq \mathcal{P}'$ the proof is straightforward: as seen in the proof of the propositions in this section, given a set S satisfying any property in $\mathcal{P}'$, the characteristic model $\mathcal{I}_S$ satisfies the correspondent semantic property. So, if we are dealing only with properties in $\mathcal{P}'$, the characteristic model of S is the model we are looking for. It remains to take under consideration the combinations between properties in $\mathcal{P}'$ and $\{$(Ref),(Sup),(Or)$\}$.

For (Ref) in Proposition 3 we have extended f_S in the model $\mathcal{I}_S$ into a function f s.t. $f(A) = f_S(A) \cup \{A\}$ for every proposition A, and that the new model satisfies the same set of conditionals S. It is easy to check that the satisfaction of any property in $\mathcal{P}$ and of their semantic counterparts is preserved in this extension of f, with the only exception of (LLE), that requires a further extension of f: namely, for every A, $f(A) = f_S(A) \cup \{B \mid B \equiv A\}$. It is easy to check that, given any set of conditionals closed under (LLE) and (Ref), this further extension of f w.r.t. f_S does not affect neither the set of conditionals satisfied by the model (that is, it is still the characteristic model of the initial set S), nor the satisfaction of the other semantic properties.

For (Sup) we introduce the same extension to f_S, and the same argument applies.

For (Or) in Proposition 7, we define a model $\mathcal{I}$ that extends $\mathcal{I}_S$ by adding $\min_\leq(f_S(A)^\uparrow \cap f_S(B)^\uparrow$ to $f_S(A \vee B)$, for every disjunction $A \vee B$. Again, this change of $\mathcal{I}_S$ does not affect any of the other semantic properties, apart from (LLE), that requires an extra change as for (Ref) and (Sup): we need to extend f_S imposing $f(C) = f_S(C) \cup \min_\leq(f_S(A)^\uparrow \cap f_S(B)^\uparrow)$ to any C s.t. $C \equiv (A \vee B)$ for some disjunction $A \vee B$. As for (Ref) and (Sup), this extra change does not affect the set of the satisfied conditionals and the satisfaction of the other semantic properties, which completes the prove. □

5 Entailment and Future Work

Most of the results in this paper are *representational* ones showing how conditional interpretations are appropriate for modelling different forms of closure. The next step is the definition of an actual reasoning systems in this framework: we start from a finite set of conditionals $\mathcal{K} = \{A_1 \Rightarrow B_1, \ldots, A_n \Rightarrow B_n\}$, and we would like to derive new conditionals according to reasoning patterns satisfied, or, more generally, according to some predefined functions f and g. In this preliminary report, we present only intuition behind our approach that aims at modelling conditionals entailed by predefined functions f and g.

To do so, we consider the following example for illustrative purposes, showing how one may derive new conditionals, for instance, under (Ref) and (Cut).

Example 1. *Let $\mathcal{K} = \{\texttt{feline} \Rightarrow \texttt{carnivore}, \texttt{feline} \wedge \texttt{carnivore} \Rightarrow \texttt{mammal}\}$ (we use only the initials of the propositional letters in what follows). The conditionals in $\mathcal{K}$ represent the information an agent is aware of. That is, if $A \Rightarrow B \in \mathcal{K}$ then the agent is aware that B is a relevant effect of A and A is a relevant condition for B. Formally, this translates into a model $\mathcal{I} = (f, g)$ where, for every A,*

$$f(A) \equiv_{def} \{B \mid A \Rightarrow B \in \mathcal{K}\}$$
$$g(A) \equiv_{def} \{B \mid B \Rightarrow A \in \mathcal{K}\} .$$

Hence in the present case we have $f(\texttt{f}) = \{\texttt{c}\}$, $f(\texttt{f} \wedge \texttt{c}) = \{\texttt{m}\}$ and $f(A) = \emptyset$ for any other formula A; $g(\texttt{c}) = \{\texttt{f}\}$,

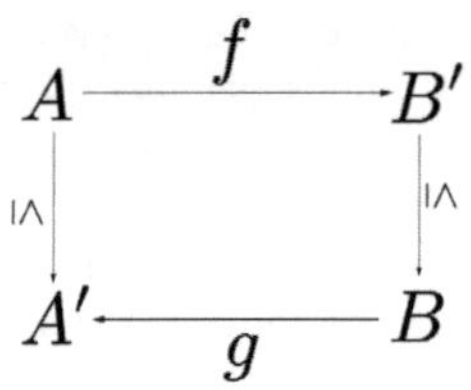

Figure 2: Alternative configuration for $\mathcal{I} \Vdash A \Rightarrow B$.

$g(\mathtt{m}) = \{\mathtt{f} \wedge \mathtt{c}\}$ and $g(A) = \emptyset$ for any other formula A. This model satisfies only the conditionals in $\mathcal{K}$, and in order to impose the closure under (Ref) and (Cut), we impose the satisfaction of (Ref$_\mathcal{I}$) and (Cut$_\mathcal{I}$) by extending f and g into, respectively, f' and g': in order to satisfy (Ref$_\mathcal{I}$) we add A to $f(A)$ and $g(A)$ for every formula A, while to satisfy (Cut$_\mathcal{I}$) we need to add $\mathtt{m}$ to $f(\mathtt{f})$ (for condition 1.) and $\mathtt{f}$ to $g(\mathtt{m})$ (for condition 2.). Hence, we end up with the model $\mathcal{I}' = (f', g')$ with $f'(\mathtt{f}) = \{\mathtt{c}, \mathtt{m}, \mathtt{f}\}$, $f(\mathtt{f} \wedge \mathtt{c}) = \{\mathtt{m}, \mathtt{f} \wedge \mathtt{c}\}$ and $f(A) = \{A\}$ for any other formula A; $g(\mathtt{c}) = \{\mathtt{f}, \mathtt{c}\}$, $g(\mathtt{m}) = \{\mathtt{f}, \mathtt{f} \wedge \mathtt{c}, \mathtt{m}\}$ and $g(A) = \{A\}$ for any other formula A. To determine which conditionals are satisfied by $\mathcal{I}'$, we have to look for 'triangles' (see Fig. 1) that occur under f', g' and $\leq$. In this case, one may verify that indeed $\mathcal{I}'$ satisfies also $\mathtt{f} \Rightarrow \mathtt{m}$, i.e., $\mathcal{I}' \Vdash \mathtt{f} \Rightarrow \mathtt{m}$ ("a feline is a mammal") and all the reflexive conditionals.

Therefore, the main idea to formalise reasoning is, given a knowledge base $\mathcal{K}$, to build a model characterising $\mathcal{K}$ and then to modify its f and g according to the reasoning patterns we would like to implement. The first step is to define closure operations over f and g that result into the smallest extension of $\mathcal{K}$ satisfying the desired properties, in line with classical Tarskian approach to entailment. This is the approach taken in Example 1, that is compatible with the structural proprieties we have considered here: all of them can be used also as derivation rules, and are compatible with the existence of a single smallest closure.

The following step would be the definition of forms of reasoning that are stronger from the inferential point of view, looking at more complex structural properties that allow for multiple smallest closed extensions. This would be in line with some popular approaches for modelling defeasible reasoning using possible-worlds semantics: they take under consideration more complex structural properties like *Rational Monotonicity*, and define the entailment relations referring to specific semantic constructions (Lehmann and Magidor 1992; Lehmann 1995; Pearl 1990; Casini, Meyer, and Varzinczak 2019b).

Beyond the development of decision procedures built on top of this semantics, we would also like to point out the flexibility of our approach. In particular working on the variation of two aspects: (i) the configuration of the satisfaction relation; and (ii) the interpretation of the relation $\leq$.

For example, we have also considered the satisfaction relation of a conditional $A \Rightarrow B$ based on the rectangle in Fig. 2, which extends the one based on triangle illustrated in Fig. 1: namely, $\mathcal{I} \Vdash A \Rightarrow B$ iff there is a "rectangle" $A \xrightarrow{f} B' \leq B \xrightarrow{g} A' \geq A$. Now, in case $\leq$ is transitive, as it is if $A \leq B$ is interpreted as $\models A \rightarrow B$, such a configuration imposes the closure under the following property (proof omitted):

$$\frac{A \Rightarrow B,\ \ C \Rightarrow D,\ \ A \leq C,\ \ B \leq D}{A \Rightarrow D}$$

Such a property may be counter-intuitive as it imposes implicitly a form of restricted (Mon) and (RW) that is not always desired. However such a reasoning pattern may become interesting if, for example, we interpret $A \leq C$ as stating that C is *similar* to A instead: from $A \Rightarrow B, C \Rightarrow D$, C similar to A, and D similar to B we derive $A \Rightarrow D$. This kind of reinterpretation of $\leq$ would allow the analysis of totally different kinds of reasoning, depending on the meaning of $\leq$ and its properties, such as e.g. reflexivity, constrained forms of transitivity or symmetry.

We are looking forward to investigate entailment procedures and interpretation variants of $\leq$ in more detail.

6 Conclusions

There have been a few attempts to formalise non-classical forms of conditional reasoning that do not satisfy properties, like (RW), that are endemic in the possible-worlds semantics, e.g. (Casini, Meyer, and Varzinczak 2019a; Rott 2019). The approach we consider here is quite different from that usually found in the literature, as our semantics renounces the use of possible worlds: reasoning is modelled through the manipulation of the choice functions f and g, which we believe, is more flexible than the possible-worlds approach. Clearly, if we consider forms of reasoning that satisfy at least (LLE), (RLE), and (Anti-RW), we may revert also to the possible-worlds framework as presented in (Casini, Meyer, and Varzinczak 2019a). The relationship between that semantics and the present one still needs to be investigated, however. Beside, let us note that another system, a deontic one, that satisfies implicitly (only) (RLE) has been presented by Parent and van der Torre (2014), and is based on the semantics of I/O logics (Makinson and van der Torre 2000).

In summary, in this preliminary work, we have only started to investigate conditionals $A \Rightarrow B$ via the manipulation of the set-valued functions f (the relevant effects of A) and g (relevant conditions for B). Moreover, as mentioned in Section 5, we think that by modifying the interpretation and the properties of $\leq$ the present semantics also paves the way to accommodate and analyse various other different kinds of non-classical reasoning.

Acknowledgments

This research was partially supported by TAILOR (Foundations of Trustworthy AI – Integrating Reasoning, Learning and Optimization), a project funded by EU Horizon 2020 research and innovation programme under GA No 952215.

References

Casini, G.; Meyer, T.; and Varzinczak, I. 2019a. Simple conditionals with constrained right weakening. In *Proceedings of the Twenty-Eighth International Joint Conference on*

Artificial Intelligence, IJCAI-19, 1632–1638. International Joint Conferences on Artificial Intelligence Organization.

Casini, G.; Meyer, T.; and Varzinczak, I. 2019b. Taking defeasible entailment beyond rational closure. In Calimeri, F.; Leone, N.; and Manna, M., eds., *Logics in Artificial Intelligence - 16th European Conference, JELIA 2019, Rende, Italy, May 7-11, 2019, Proceedings*, volume 11468 of *Lecture Notes in Computer Science*, 182–197. Springer.

Delgrande, J. P. 2011. What's in a default? thoughts on the nature and role of defaults in nonmonotonic reasoning. In Brewka, G.; Marek, V.; and Truszczynski, M., eds., *Nonmonotonic Reasoning. Essays Celebrating Its 30th Anniversary*. College Publications.

Fagin, R.; Halpern, J.; Moses, Y.; and Vardi, M. 1995. *Reasoning about Knowledge*. MIT Press.

Gabbay, D. M. 1995. A general theory of structured consequence relations. *Theoria* 10(2):49–78.

Hawthorne, J., and Makinson, D. 2007. The quantitative/qualitative watershed for rules of uncertain inference. *Studia Logica* 86(2):247–297.

Knijnenburg, P. 1993. Algebraic domains, chain completion and the plotkin powerdomain construction. Technical Report RUU-CS-93-03, Department of Information and Computing Sciences, Utrecht University.

Knijnenburg, P. M. W. 1996. A note on the smyth powerdomain construction. *Fundamenta Informaticae* 26(2):133–139.

Kraus, S.; Lehmann, D.; and Magidor, M. 1990. Nonmonotonic reasoning, preferential models and cumulative logics. *Artif. Intell.* 44:167–207.

Lehmann, D., and Magidor, M. 1992. What does a conditional knowledge base entail? *Artif. Intell.* 55:1–60.

Lehmann, D. 1995. Another perspective on default reasoning. *Annals of Mathematics and Artificial Intelligence* 15(1):61–82.

Makinson, D., and van der Torre, L. 2000. Input/output logics. *Journal of Philosophical Logic* 29(4):383–408.

Makinson, D. 1994. General patterns in nonmonotonic reasoning. In *Handbook of Logic in Artificial Intelligence Nad Logic Programming, Vol. Iii*. Oxford: Clarendon Press. 35–110.

Parent, X., and van der Torre, L. 2014. "Sing and Dance!". In Cariani, F.; Grossi, D.; Meheus, J.; and Parent, X., eds., *Deontic Logic and Normative Systems*, 149–165. Cham: Springer International Publishing.

Pearl, J. 1990. System Z: a natural ordering of defaults with tractable applications to nonmonotonic reasoning. In *Proceedings of the 3rd Conference on Theoretical Aspects of Rationality and Knowledge (TARK)*.

Plotkin, G. D. 1976. A powerdomain construction. *SIAM Journal on Computing* 5(3):452–487.

Rott, H. 1989. A nonmonotonic conditional logic for belief revision. part 1: Semantics and logic of simple conditionals. In Fuhrmann, A., and Morreau, M., eds., *The Logic of Theory Change, Workshop, Konstanz, FRG, October 13-15, 1989, Proceedings*, volume 465 of *Lecture Notes in Computer Science*, 135–181. Springer.

Rott, H. 2001. *Change, Choice and Inference: A Study of Belief Revision and Nonmonotonic Reasoning*. Oxford University Press.

Rott, H. 2019. Difference-making conditionals and the relevant ramsey test. *The Review of Symbolic Logic* 1–32.

Smyth, M. B. 1978. Power domains. *J. Comput. Syst. Sci.* 16(1):23–36.

Straccia, U.; Ojeda-Aciego, M.; and Damásio, C. V. 2009. On fixed-points of multi-valued functions on complete lattices and their application to generalized logic programs. *SIAM Journal on Computing* 8(5):1881–1911.

Winskel, G. 1985. On powerdomains and modality. *Theor. Comput. Sci.* 36:127–137.

Proceedings of the 19th International Conference on Principles of Knowledge Representation and Reasoning
Main Track

Rediscovering Argumentation Principles Utilizing Collective Attacks

Wolfgang Dvořák[1] , **Matthias König**[1] , **Markus Ulbricht**[2] , **Stefan Woltran**[1]
[1]TU Wien, Institute of Logic and Computation
[2]Leipzig University, Department of Computer Science
{dvorak, mkoenig, woltran}@dbai.tuwien.ac.at, mulbricht@informatik.uni-leipzig.de

Abstract

Argumentation Frameworks (AFs) are a key formalism in AI research. Their semantics have been investigated in terms of *principles*, which define characteristic properties in order to deliver guidance for analysing established and developing new semantics. Because of the simple structure of AFs, many desired properties hold almost trivially, at the same time hiding interesting concepts behind syntactic notions. We extend the principle-based approach to Argumentation Frameworks with Collective Attacks (SETAFs) and provide a comprehensive overview of common principles for their semantics. Our analysis shows that investigating principles based on decomposing the given SETAF (e.g. directionality or SCC-recursiveness) poses additional challenges in comparison to usual AFs. We introduce the notion of the reduct as well as the modularization principle for SETAFs which will prove beneficial for this kind of investigation. We then demonstrate how our findings can be utilized for incremental computation of extensions and give a novel parameterized tractability result for verifying preferred extensions.

1 Introduction

Abstract argumentation frameworks (AFs) as proposed by Dung (1995) in his seminal paper are nowadays a classical research area in knowledge representation and reasoning. In AFs, arguments are interpreted as abstract entities and thus the focus is solely on the relationship between them, i.e. which arguments are in conflict with each other. Consequently, an AF is simply a directed graph, where the vertices are interpreted as arguments and edges as attacks between them. Within the last years, several semantics for AFs have been proposed in order to formalize jointly acceptable sets of arguments, see, e.g., (Baroni, Caminada, and Giacomin 2018). Different semantics have different features, yielding more or less beneficial behavior in varying contexts. In order to assess and compare the characteristics of semantics in a formal and objective way, researchers pay increasing attention to perform principles-based analyses of AF semantics, i.e. formalizing properties semantics should satisfy in different situations. We refer the reader to (van der Torre and Vesic 2017) for a recent overview.

In the present paper we consider Argumentation Frameworks with collective attacks (SETAFs), introduced by Nielsen and Parsons (2006). SETAFs generalize Dung-style AFs in the sense that some arguments can only be effectively defeated by a collection of attackers, yielding a natural representation as a directed hypergraph. Many key semantic properties of AFs have been shown to carry over to SETAFs, see e.g. (Nielsen and Parsons 2006; Flouris and Bikakis 2019). Moreover, work has been done on expressiveness (Dvořák, Fandinno, and Woltran 2019), and translations from SETAFs to AFs (Polberg 2017; Flouris and Bikakis 2019). Also the hypergraph structure of SETAFs has recently been subject of investigation (Dvořák, König, and Woltran 2021a; Dvořák, König, and Woltran 2021b). However, a thorough principle-based analysis of SETAF semantics is still unavailable. In this paper, we will close this gap by investigating the common SETAF semantics w.r.t. to a comprehensive selection of principles, inspired from similar proposals that have been studied for Dung-AFs.

Although we will see that in many cases the behavior generalizes from AFs to the setting with collective attacks, our study also reveals situations where caution is required and thus emphasizes properties we deem natural for AFs. In fact, many AF principles like SCC-recursiveness (Baroni, Giacomin, and Guida 2005) or the recently introduced modularization property (Baumann, Brewka, and Ulbricht 2020a) are concerned with partial evaluation of the given graph and step-wise computation of extensions. We will pay special attention to these kind of principles since (a) they require to establish novel technical foundations when generalizing the underlying structure from simple graphs to hypergraphs and (b) have immediate implications for the design of solvers. Along the way, we will also introduce a SETAF version for the reduct (Baumann, Brewka, and Ulbricht 2020b) of an AF which has proven to be a handy tool when investigating argumentation semantics.

The main contribution of this paper is to show that our natural extensions of the AF principles are well-behaving for SETAFs. We show that basic properties are preserved, as well as their implications in terms of the structure of extensions. More specifically our contributions are as follows.

- After giving necessary preliminaries in Section 2 we introduce for SETAFs the counterparts to the most important basic principles from the literature in Section 3.
- We propose the E-reduct SF^E for a SETAF SF and a set E of arguments and investigate its core properties, includ-

ing the modularization property for SETAFs (Section 4). Moreover, we use the reduct to provide alternative characterizations of SETAFs semantics.

- We introduce uninfluenced sets of arguments in SETAFs as the counterpart of unattacked sets in AFs. We then propose and investigate a SETAF version of the directionality and non-interference principles (Section 5) and the SCC-recursiveness (Section 6).
- We discuss the computational implications of modularization, directionality and SCC-recursiveness in Section 7. In particular we illustrate the potential for incremental algorithms.

Technical proofs that are omitted due to space constraints are provided at https://arxiv.org/abs/2205.03151. Some of the results reported in this article evolved from the paper (Dvořák et al. 2021) presented at the NMR 2021 workshop.

2 Background

We briefly recall the definitions of SETAFs and its semantics (see, e.g., (Bikakis et al. 2021)). Throughout the paper, we assume a countably infinite domain $\mathfrak{A}$ of possible arguments.

A SETAF is a pair $SF = (A, R)$ where $A \subseteq \mathfrak{A}$ is a finite set of *arguments*, and $R \subseteq (2^A \setminus \{\emptyset\}) \times A$ is the *attack relation*. For an attack $(T, h) \in R$ we call T the *tail* and h the *head* of the attack. SETAFs (A, R), where for all $(T, h) \in R$ it holds that $|T| = 1$, amount to (standard Dung) AFs. In that case, we usually write (t, h) to denote the set-attack $(\{t\}, h)$. Moreover, for a SETAF $SF = (A, R)$, we use $A(SF)$ and $R(SF)$ to identify its arguments A and its attack relation R, respectively.

Given a SETAF (A, R), we write $S \mapsto_R a$ if there is a set $T \subseteq S$ with $(T, a) \in R$. Moreover, we write $S' \mapsto_R S$ if $S' \mapsto_R a$ for some $a \in S$. For $S \subseteq A$, we use S_R^+ to denote the set $\{a \mid S \mapsto_R a\}$ and define the *range* of S (w.r.t. R), denoted $S_R^\oplus$, as the set $S \cup S_R^+$.

Example 2.1. Consider the SETAF $SF = (A, R)$ with arguments $A = \{a, b, c, d, e, f, g, h\}$ and attack relation

$$R = \{(a, b), (\{b, d\}, c), (b, d), (d, b), (d, e), (e, d), (\{d, f\}, h), (f, g), (g, f), (g, h), (h, g)\};$$

the collective attacks $(\{b, d\}, c), (\{d, f\}, h)$ are highlighted.

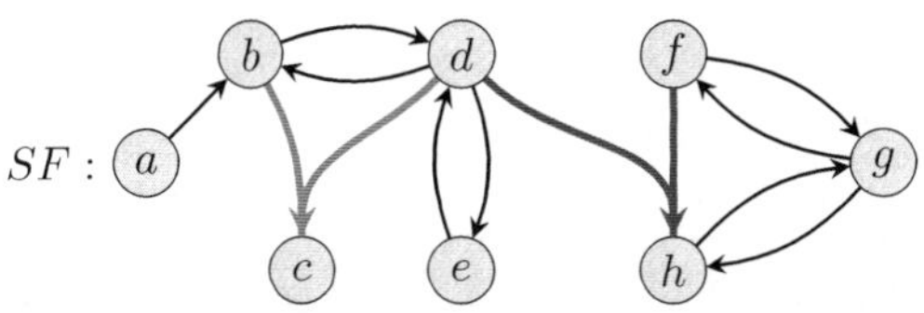

The well-known notions of conflict and defense from classical Dung-style AFs naturally generalize to SETAFs.

Definition 2.2. Given a SETAF $SF = (A, R)$, a set $S \subseteq A$ is *conflicting* in SF if $S \mapsto_R a$ for some $a \in S$. A set $S \subseteq A$ is *conflict-free* in SF, if S is not conflicting in SF, i.e. if $T \cup \{h\} \not\subseteq S$ for each $(T, h) \in R$. $cf(SF)$ denotes the set of all conflict-free sets in SF.

Definition 2.3. Given a SETAF $SF = (A, R)$, an argument $a \in A$ is *defended* (in SF) by a set $S \subseteq A$ if for each $B \subseteq A$, such that $B \mapsto_R a$, also $S \mapsto_R B$. A set $T \subseteq A$ is defended (in SF) by S if each $a \in T$ is defended by S (in SF).

Moreover, we make use of the *characteristic function* Γ_{SF} of a SETAF $SF = (A, R)$, defined as $\Gamma_{SF}(S) = \{a \in A \mid S \text{ defends } a \text{ in } SF\}$ for $S \subseteq A$.

The semantics we study in this work are the grounded, admissible, complete, preferred, stable, naive, stage and semi-stable semantics, which we will abbreviate by *grd*, *adm*, *com*, *pref*, *stb*, *naive*, *stage* and *sem*, respectively (Bikakis et al. 2021).

Definition 2.4. Given a SETAF $SF = (A, R)$ and a conflict-free set $S \in cf(SF)$. Then,

- $S \in adm(SF)$, if S defends itself in SF,
- $S \in com(SF)$, if $S \in adm(SF)$ and $a \in S$ for all $a \in A$ defended by S,
- $S \in grd(SF)$, if $S = \bigcap_{T \in com(SF)} T$,
- $S \in pref(SF)$, if $S \in adm(SF)$ and $\nexists T \in adm(SF)$ s.t. $T \supset S$,
- $S \in stb(SF)$, if $S \mapsto_R a$ for all $a \in A \setminus S$,
- $S \in naive(SF)$, if $\nexists T \in cf(SF)$ with $T \supset S$,
- $S \in stage(SF)$, if $\nexists T \in cf(SF)$ with $T_R^\oplus \supset S_R^\oplus$, and
- $S \in sem(SF)$, if $S \in adm(SF)$ and $\nexists T \in adm(SF)$ s.t. $T_R^\oplus \supset S_R^\oplus$.

The relationship between the semantics has been clarified in (Dvořák, Greßler, and Woltran 2018; Flouris and Bikakis 2019; Nielsen and Parsons 2006) and matches with the relations between the semantics for Dung AFs, i.e. for any SETAF SF:

$$stb(SF) \subseteq sem(SF) \subseteq pref(SF) \subseteq com(SF) \subseteq adm(SF)$$
$$stb(SF) \subseteq stage(SF) \subseteq naive(SF) \subseteq cf(SF)$$

To extend the graph-related terminology to the directed hypergraph structure of SETAFs, we often take the *primal graph* (Dvořák, König, and Woltran 2021a) as a starting point. Intuitively, collective attacks are "split up" in order to obtain a directed graph with a similar structure as the original SETAF.

Definition 2.5 (Primal Graph). Let $SF = (A, R)$ be a SETAF. Its *primal graph* is defined as $primal(SF) = (A, R')$ with $R' = \{(t, h) \mid (T, h) \in R, t \in T\}$.

Example 2.6. Recall the SETAF SF from Example 2.1. Its primal graph $primal(SF)$ looks as follows.

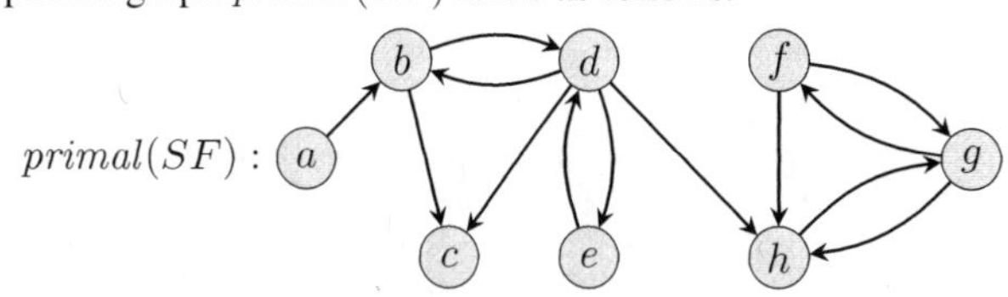

Finally, we introduce the notion of the *projection*, which we will revisit and redefine in Sections 5 and 6.

Definition 2.7 (Projection). Let $SF = (A, R)$ be a SETAF and $S \subseteq A$. We define the *projection* $SF\downarrow_S$ of SF w.r.t. S as $(S, \{(T', h) \mid (T, h) \in R, h \in S, T' = T \cap S, T' \neq \emptyset\})$.

	grd	*adm*	*com*	*stb*	*pref*	*naive*	*sem*	*stage*
Conflict-freeness	✓	✓	✓	✓	✓	✓	✓	✓
Defense	✓	✓	✓	✓	✓	✗	✓	✗
Admissibility	✓	✓	✓	✓	✓	✗	✓	✗
Reinstatement	✓	✗	✓	✓	✓	✗	✓	✗
CF-reinstatement	✓	✗	✓	✓	✓	✓	✓	✓
Naivety	✗	✗	✗	✓	✗	✓	✗	✓
I-maximality	✓	✗	✗	✓	✓	✓	✓	✓
Allowing abstention	✓	✓	✓	✗	✗	✗	✗	✗
Crash resistance	✓	✓	✓	✗	✓	✓	✓	✓
Modularization	✓	✓	✓	✓	✓	✗	✓	✗
Directionality	✓	✓	✓	✗	✓	✗	✗	✗
Non-interference	✓	✓	✓	✗	✓	✓	✓	✓
SCC-recursiveness	✓	✓	✓	✓	✓	✗	✗	✗

Table 1: An overview of our results regarding SETAF principles.

3 Basic Principles

We start our principles-based analysis of SETAF semantics by generalizing basic principles from AFs. Satisfaction (or non-satisfaction) of principles allows us to distinguish semantics with respect to fundamental properties that are crucial in certain applications. The principles we consider have natural counterparts for Dung-style AFs, simply by applying them to SETAFs where $|T| = 1$ for each tail. We therefore formalize the following observation:

Observation 3.1. *Let P be a SETAF-principle that properly generalizes an AF-principle P^{AF} in the sense that for SETAFs SF with $|T| = 1$ for each $(T, h) \in R(SF)$, every semantics σ satisfies P iff it satisfies P^{AF}. Then if a semantics σ does not satisfy P^{AF}, then σ does not satisfy P.*

As all of our principles properly generalize the respective AF-principles, whenever a principle is not satisfied for AFs, this translates to the corresponding SETAF principle as well.

Next, we follow (van der Torre and Vesic 2017) and introduce analogous principles for SETAFs. Our first set of principles is concerned with basic properties of semantics.

Definition 3.2. The following properties are said to hold for a semantics σ if the listed condition holds for each SETAF $SF = (A, R)$ and each set $E \in \sigma(SF)$.

- *conflict-freeness*: $E \in cf(SF)$
- *defense*: each $a \in E$ is defended
- *admissibility*: $E \in adm(SF)$
- *reinstatement*: $a \in E$ for each a defended by E
- *CF-reinstatement*: $a \in E$ for each a defended by E s.t. $E \cup \{a\} \in cf(SF)$

These principles formalize requirements which oftentimes do or do not hold immediately by definition of the given semantics. We do not discuss these in detail here; the respective (non-)satisfaction results are reported in Table 1.

The next principles make statements about the structure of the extensions of a given semantics σ. Here, I-maximality is due to Baroni and Giacomin (2007).

Definition 3.3. The following properties are said to hold for a semantics σ if the listed condition holds for each SETAF $SF = (A, R)$ and each $E, E' \in \sigma(SF)$.

- *naivety* iff there is no $E' \in cf(SF)$ s.t. $E' \supset E$
- *I-maximality* iff $E \subseteq E'$ implies $E = E'$

Whether the naivety principle is satisfied can be seen by closely inspecting the definition of the semantics. I-maximality results for SETAFs have been shown in (Dvořák, Fandinno, and Woltran 2019).

The principle of allowing abstention can be attributed to Baroni, Caminada, and Giacomin (2011).

Definition 3.4. A semantics σ satisfies *allowing abstention* if for all SETAFs $SF = (A, R)$, for all $a \in A(SF)$, if there exist $E, E' \in \sigma(SF)$ with $a \in E$ and $a \in E'^{+}_{R}$ then there exists a $D \in \sigma(SF)$ such that $a \notin D^{\oplus}_{R}$.

Allowing abstention is satisfied by complete semantics, since—as in AFs—if there exist $E, E' \in com(SF)$ with $a \in E$ and $a \in E'^{+}$, this means $a \notin G^{\oplus}$ where $G \in grd(SF)$.

For the last principle we discuss within this section, which is due to Caminada, Carnielli, and Dunne (2012), we require another notion. We call a SETAF $SF' = (A', R')$ *contaminating* for a semantics σ if for every SETAF $SF = (A, R)$ with $A \cap A' = \emptyset$, it holds that $\sigma(SF \cup SF') = \sigma(SF')$, where $SF \cup SF'$ is the SETAF $(A \cup A', R \cup R')$.

Definition 3.5 (Crash resistance)**.** A semantics σ satisfies *crash resistance* if there is no contaminating SETAF for σ.

As in the case for AFs, *stb* is the only semantics considered in this paper which is not crash-resistant. The reason is that one can choose SF' to be an isolated odd cycle, yielding $stb(SF \cup SF') = \emptyset$ for any SETAF SF. The other semantics are more robust in this regard and yield $\sigma(SF \cup SF') = \{E \cup E' \mid E \in \sigma(SF), E' \in \sigma(SF')\}$ whenever $A \cap A' = \emptyset$.

In the following sections we will introduce and investigate further principles regarding computational properties.

4 Reduct and Modularization

In this section, we will generalize the modularization property (Baumann, Brewka, and Ulbricht 2020a), which yields concise alternative characterizations for the classical semantics in AFs, to SETAFs. As a first step, we require the so-called reduct of a SETAF.

4.1 The SETAF Reduct

In the remainder of this paper, the *reduct* of a SETAF w.r.t. a given set E will play a central role. Intuitively, the reduct w.r.t. E represents the SETAF that result from "accepting" E and rejecting what is defeated now, while not deciding on the remaining arguments. To illustrate the idea, consider the following example:

Example 4.1. Recall the SETAF SF from Example 2.1. Consider the singleton $\{a\}$. If we view a as accepted, then b is rejected. This means that the attack from b to d can be disregarded. However, we also observe that c cannot be attacked anymore since attacking it requires both b and d. Now consider $\{f\}$. Interpreting f as accepted renders g rejected. In addition, in order to attack h only one additional argument (namely d) is required. Thus, if we let $E = \{a, f\}$, then we expect the SETAF SF^{E} –with the intuitive meaning that a and f are set to true– to look as follows.

SF^E :

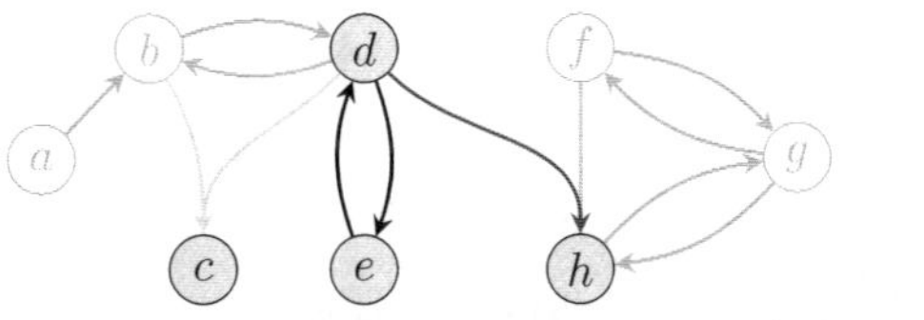

As we can see, the above depicted SETAF reflects the situation after E is set to true: e.g. c is defended and in order to defeat h, only d is required.

That is, in the reduct SF^E, we only need to consider arguments that are still undecided, i.e. all arguments neither in E nor attacked by E. As illustrated in the example, some attacks that involve deleted arguments are preserved which is in contrast to the AF-reduct (Baumann, Brewka, and Ulbricht 2020a). In particular, if the arguments in the tail of an attack are "accepted" (i.e. in E), the attack can still play a role in attacking or defending. If the tail of an attack (T, h) is already attacked by E, we can disregard (T, h).

Definition 4.2. Given a SETAF $SF = (A, R)$ and $E \subseteq A$, the *E-reduct of SF* is the SETAF $SF^E = (A', R')$, with

$$\begin{aligned} A' &= A \setminus E^{\oplus}_R \\ R' &= \{(T \setminus E, h) \mid (T, h) \in R,\, T \cap E^{+}_R = \emptyset, \\ &\qquad T \not\subseteq E,\, h \in A'\} \end{aligned}$$

Thereby, the condition $T \cap E^{+}_R = \emptyset$ captures cases like the attack $(\{b, d\}, c)$ from our example: b is attacked by E, and thus, the whole attack gets removed. The reason why we take $(T \setminus E, h)$ as our attacks is the partial evaluation as in the attack $(\{d, f\}, h)$ after setting f to true: only d is now left required in order to "activate" the attack against h.

Example 4.3. Given the SETAF SF from Example 4.1 as well as $E = \{a, f\}$ as before, the reduct SF^E is the SETAF depicted above, i.e. $SF^E = \{A', R'\}$ with $A' = \{c, d, e, h\}$ and $R' = \{(d, e), (e, d), (d, h)\}$.

We start our formal investigation of the reduct with a technical lemma to settle some basic properties.

Lemma 4.4. *Given a SETAF $SF = (A, R)$ and two disjoint sets $E, E' \subseteq A$. Let $SF^E = (A', R')$.*

1. *If there is no $S \subseteq A$ s.t. $S \mapsto_R E'$, then the same is true in SF^E.*
2. *Assume E does not attack $E' \in cf(SF)$. Then, E defends E' iff there is no $S' \subseteq A'$ s.t. $S' \mapsto_{R'} E'$.*
3. *Let $E \in cf(SF)$. If $E \cup E'$ does not attack E in SF and $E' \subseteq A'$, with $E' \in cf(SF^E)$ then $E \cup E' \in cf(SF)$.*
4. *Let $E \cup E' \in cf(SF)$. If $E' \mapsto_{R'} a$, then $E \cup E' \mapsto_R a$.*
5. *If $E \cup E' \in cf(SF)$, then $SF^{E \cup E'} = \left(SF^E\right)^{E'}$.*

4.2 The Modularization Property

Having established the basic properties of the SETAF reduct, we are now ready to introduce the modularization property (Baumann, Brewka, and Ulbricht 2020a).

Definition 4.5 (Modularization)**.** A semantics σ satisfies *modularization* if for all SETAFs SF, for every $E \in \sigma(SF)$ and $E' \in \sigma(SF^E)$, we have $E \cup E' \in \sigma(SF)$.

Modularization allows us to build extensions iteratively. After finding such a set $E \subseteq A$ we can efficiently compute its reduct SF^E and pause before computing an extension E' for the reduct in order to obtain a larger extension $E \cup E'$ for SF. Hence, this first step can be seen as an intermediate result that enables us to reduce the computational effort of finding extensions in SF, as the arguments whose status is already determined by accepting E do not have to be considered again. Instead, we can reason on the reduct SF^E (see Section 7). In the following, we establish the modularization property for admissible and complete semantics.

Theorem 4.6 (Modularization Property)**.** *Let SF be a SETAF, $\sigma \in \{adm, com\}$ and $E \in \sigma(SF)$.*

1. *If $E' \in \sigma(SF^E)$, then $E \cup E' \in \sigma(SF)$.*
2. *If $E \cap E' = \emptyset$ and $E \cup E' \in \sigma(SF)$, then $E' \in \sigma(SF^E)$.*

Proof. (for $\sigma = adm$) Let $SF^E = (A', R')$.

1) Since E is admissible and $E' \subseteq A'$, E' does not attack E. By Lemma 4.4, item 3, $E \cup E' \in cf(SF)$. Now assume $S \mapsto_R E \cup E'$. If $S \mapsto_R E$, then $E \mapsto_R S$ by admissibility of E. If $S \mapsto_R E'$, there is $T \subseteq S$ s.t. $(T, e') \in R$ for some $e' \in E'$. In case $E \mapsto_R T$, we are done. Otherwise, $(T \setminus E, e') \in R'$ and by admissibility of E' in SF^E, $E' \mapsto_{R'} T \setminus E$. By Lemma 4.4, item 4, $E \cup E' \mapsto_R T \setminus E$.

2) Now assume $E \cup E' \in adm(SF)$. We see $E' \in cf(SF^E)$ as follows: If $(T', e') \in R'$ for $T' \subseteq E'$ and $e' \in E'$, then there is some $(T, e') \in R$ with $T' = T \setminus E$. Hence $E \cup E' \mapsto_R E'$, contradiction. Now assume E' is not admissible in SF^E, i.e. there is $(T', e') \in R'$ with $e' \in E'$ and E' does not counterattack T' in SF^E. Then there is some $(T, e') \in R$ with $T' = T \setminus E$ and $T \cap E^{+}_R = \emptyset$. By admissibility of $E \cup E'$, $E \cup E' \mapsto_R T$, say $(T^*, t) \in R$, $T^* \subseteq E \cup E'$ and $t \in T$. Since $E \cup E'$ is conflict-free, $T^* \cap E^{+}_R = \emptyset$ and thus we either have a) $T^* \subseteq E$, contradicting $T \cap E^{+}_R = \emptyset$, or b) $(T^* \setminus E, t) \in R'$ and $t \in T'$, i.e. E' counterattacks T' in SF^E contradicting the above assumption. □

The result for complete semantics can be obtained by using Lemma 4.4, items 2 and 5. Note that the modularization property also holds for *stb*, *pref*, and *sem* semantics. However, the only admissible set in the reduct w.r.t. a stable/preferred/semi-stable extension is the empty set, rendering the property trivial. The exact relation is captured by the following alternative characterizations of the semantics under our consideration.

Proposition 4.7. *Let $SF = (A, R)$ be a SETAF, $E \in cf(SF)$ and $SF^E = (A', R')$.*

1. *$E \in stb(SF)$ iff $SF^E = (\emptyset, \emptyset)$,*
2. *$E \in adm(SF)$ iff $S \mapsto_R E$ implies $S \setminus E \not\subseteq A'$,*
3. *$E \in pref(SF)$ iff $E \in adm(SF)$ and $\bigcup adm\left(SF^E\right) = \emptyset$,*
4. *$E \in com(SF)$ iff $E \in adm(SF)$ and no argument in SF^E is unattacked,*
5. *$E \in sem(SF)$ iff $E \in pref(SF)$ and there is no $E' \in pref(SF)$ s.t. $A(SF^{E'}) \subset A(SF^E)$.*

Proof. The characterizations for *stb* and *adm* are straightforward and *pref* is due to the modularization property of *adm*. For $com(SF)$ we apply Lemma 4.4, item 2, to each singleton E' occurring in SF^E. For *sem* recall that range-maximal preferred extensions are semi-stable. □

From the characterization of complete semantics provided in Proposition 4.7 we infer that for any SETAF SF the complete extensions $E \in com(SF)$ satisfy $grd(SF^E) = \{\emptyset\}$ implying modularization for *grd*. Moreover, as the grounded extension G is the least complete, we can utilize modularization of *adm* and obtain G by the following procedure: (1) add the set of unattacked arguments U into G, (2) repeat step (1) on SF^U until there are no unattacked arguments.

5 Directionality and Non-Interference

In this section we discuss the principles directionality and non-interference. Intuitively, these principles give information about the behavior of "separate" parts of a framework. In order to formalize this separation-property, we start of with the notion of unattacked sets of arguments[1]. For directionality (Baroni and Giacomin 2007) we have to carefully consider this notion in order to obtain a natural generalization of the AF case preserving the intended meaning. A naive definition of unattacked sets will lead to nonsensical results: assume a set S is unattacked in a SETAF $SF = (A, R)$ whenever it is not attacked from "outside", i.e. if the condition $A \setminus S \not\mapsto_R S$ holds.

Example 5.1. Consider now the following SETAF (a) and its projections (b), (c) w.r.t. the "unattacked" set $S = \{a, c\}$.

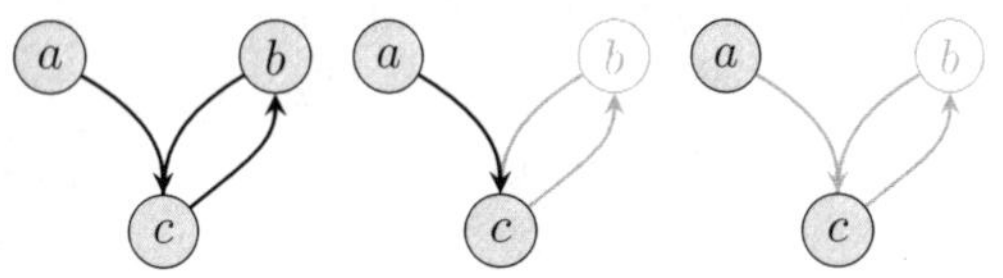

(a) (b) (c)

Note that $\{a, c\}$ is stable in (a). If we now consider the projection $SF{\downarrow_S}$—see (b)—we find that $\{a, c\}$ is not stable, falsifying directionality. However, one might argue that this is due to the credulous nature of our projection-notion. We could easily consider a different proper generalization of the projection, namely $SF{\downarrow^*_S} = (S, \{(T, h) \mid (T, h) \in R, T \cup \{h\} \subseteq S\})$. In this more skeptical version we delete attacks if any of the arguments in the tail are not in the projected set—see (c). However, we still cannot obtain the desired results: in (a) we find $\{a\}$ to be the unique grounded extension, while in (c) $\{a, c\}$ is grounded, again falsifying directionality. As for the directionality principle we do not want to add additional arguments or attacks and we exhausted all possible reasonable projection notions for this small example, we conclude that the underlying definition of *unattacked* sets was improper. We therefore suggest a different definition—and at the same time suggest to think of these sets rather as "uninfluenced" than "unattacked". In AFs, clearly both notions coincide. However, we still argue that the concept of "influence" captures the true nature of directionality in a more intuitive and precise manner. Moreover, note that in the case of uninfluenced sets both notions of projection coincide, as well as the notion of *restriction* (see Definition 6.5) for arbitrary sets $D \subseteq A \setminus S$.

[1] While in the previous section we used "unattacked arguments", i.e. arguments that are not the head of any attack, unattacked *sets of arguments* allow for attacks within the set.

Definition 5.2 (Influence). Let $SF = (A, R)$ be a SETAF. An argument $a \in A$ *influences* $b \in A$ if there is a directed path from a to b in $primal(SF)$. A set $S \subseteq A$ is *uninfluenced* in SF if no $a \in A \setminus S$ influences any $b \in S$. We denote the set of uninfluenced sets by $US(SF)$.

Utilizing this notion, we can properly generalize directionality (Baroni and Giacomin 2007).

Definition 5.3 (Directionality). A semantics σ satisfies *directionality* if for all SETAFs SF and every $S \in US(SF)$ it holds $\sigma(SF{\downarrow_S}) = \{E \cap S \mid E \in \sigma(SF)\}$.

We will revisit directionality at the end of the next section, as we can utilize SCC-recursiveness to show that *grd*, *com*, and *pref* satisfy directionality. Similarly, we generalize *non-interference* (Caminada, Carnielli, and Dunne 2012), which has an even stronger requirement. $S \subseteq A$ is *isolated* in $SF = (A, R)$, if S is uninfluenced and $A \setminus S$ is uninfluenced, i.e. there are no edges in $primal(SF)$ between S and $A \setminus S$.

Definition 5.4 (Non-interference). A semantics σ satisfies *non-interference* iff for all SETAFs SF and all isolated $S \subseteq A(SF)$, it holds $\sigma(SF{\downarrow_S}) = \{E \cap S \mid E \in \sigma(SF)\}$.

Clearly, directionality implies non-interference. It is easy to see from the respective definitions that also naive, semi-stable, and stage semantics satisfy non-interference.

6 SCC-Recursiveness

SCC-recursiveness (Baroni, Giacomin, and Guida 2005) can be seen as a tool to iteratively compute extensions, or an alternative characterization of many semantics. SCC-recursiveness formalizes the intuition that the acceptance status of an argument depends only on its ancestors—i.e., the arguments that feature a directed path to the argument in question. In Section 5 we captured this concept with the notion of *influence*. In a nutshell, an argument a "influences" an argument b in a SETAF SF if there is a directed path from a to b in $primal(SF)$. It is therefore reasonable to investigate SCCs (strongly connected components) with this idea in mind. In particular, our definition of SCCs captures the equivalence classes w.r.t. the influence relation.

Definition 6.1 (SCCs). Let SF be a SETAF. By $SCCs(SF)$ we denote the set of strongly connected components of SF, which we define as the sets of arguments contained in the strongly connected components of $primal(SF)$.

Example 6.2. Recall our SETAF from before.

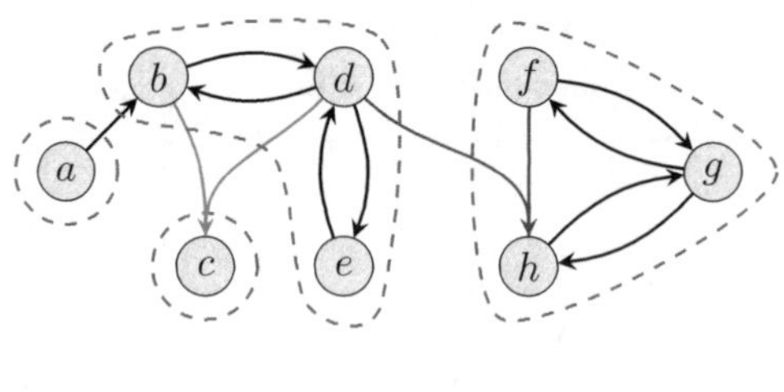

In this SETAF, we have the four SCCs $\{a\}, \{b, d, e\}, \{c\}$, and $\{f, g, h\}$, as depicted in dashed lines.

Analogously to (Baroni, Giacomin, and Guida 2005), we partition the arguments in defeated, provisionally defeated and undefeated ones. Intuitively, accepting a defeated argument would lead to a conflict, the provisionally defeated cannot be defended and will therefore be rejected (while not being irrelevant for defense of other arguments), and the undefeated form the candidates for extensions. We obtain the following formal definition of the sets we just described.

Definition 6.3. Let $SF = (A, R)$ be a SETAF. Moreover, let $E \subseteq A$ be a set of arguments and $S \in SCCs(SF)$ be an SCC. We define the set of defeated arguments $D_{SF}(S, E)$, provisionally defeated arguments $P_{SF}(S, E)$, and undefeated arguments $U_{SF}(S, E)$ w.r.t. S, E as

$$D_{SF}(S, E) = \{a \in S \mid E \setminus S \mapsto_R a\},$$
$$P_{SF}(S, E) = \{a \in S \mid A \setminus (S \cup E^+) \mapsto_R a\} \setminus D_{SF}(S, E),$$
$$U_{SF}(S, E) = S \setminus (D_{SF}(S, E) \cup P_{SF}(S, E)).$$

Moreover, we set $UP_{SF}(S, E) = U_{SF}(S, E) \cup P_{SF}(S, E)$.

In order to properly investigate SCC-recursiveness, we need the notion of the *restriction*. The restriction coincides with the *projection* on AFs (cf. Definition 2.7). However, in the following we will argue that the projection does not capture the intricacies of this process. Ultimately, we will see that for a reasonable restriction we need semantic tools that are similar to the reduct. For that, we revisit Example 5.1.

Example 6.4. Consider the following SETAFs (a) and (b).

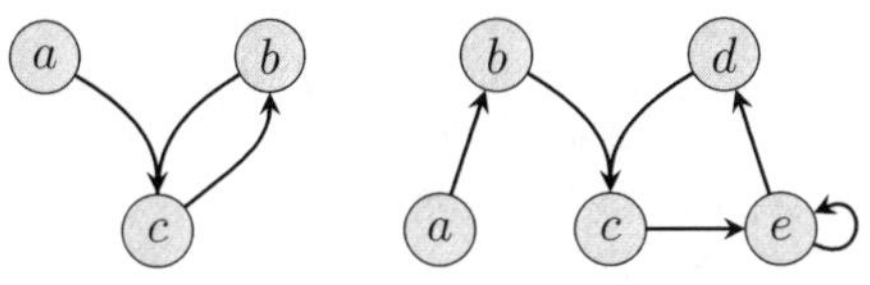

(a) (b)

In (a), assume we accept the argument a. Now for the remaining SCC $\{b, c\}$ the projection $SF\downarrow_{\{b,c\}}$ yields the attacks (b, c) and (c, b), as one might expect. In (b), assume we accept a and therefore reject b. The projection $SF\downarrow_{\{c,d,e\}}$ yields a cycle of length 3, and none of the remaining arguments can be accepted. However, as c is defended this is not the expected behavior. One might argue that this notion of projection is too credulous, i.e., attacks remain that have to be discarded. Recall Example 5.1 where we defined an alternative projection, namely $SF\downarrow_S^* = (S, \{(T, h) \mid (T, h) \in R, T \cup \{h\} \subseteq S\})$. Now, one can check that we get the expected results in (b). However, in (a) $SF\downarrow_{\{b,c\}}^*$ only features the attack (c, b), and it incorrectly seems like we cannot accept b. We solve this problem by adapting the notion of *restriction* such that both cases are handled individually. We keep track of a set of rejected arguments and discard attacks once an argument in its tail is discarded—these attacks are irrelevant to the further evaluation of the SETAF.

Definition 6.5 (Restriction). Let $SF = (A, R)$ be a SETAF and let $S, D \subseteq A$. We define the *restriction* of SF w.r.t. S and D as the SETAF $SF\Downarrow_S^D = (S', R')$ where

$$S' = (A \cap S) \setminus D$$
$$R' = \{(T \cap S', h) \mid (T, h) \in R, h \in S', T \cap D = \emptyset, T \cap S' \neq \emptyset\}.$$

The restriction handles both cases of Example 6.4 according to our intuition. In (a) the SETAF $SF\Downarrow_{\{b,c\}}^{\emptyset}$ contains b and c, and as we accepted the part tail of $(\{a, b\}, c)$ outside $\{b, c\}$ (namely a), the attack (b, c) is kept. In (b) $SF\Downarrow_{\{c,d,e\}}^{\{b\}}$ contains the "attack-chain" $(c, e), (e, d)$, and as the tail of $(\{b, d\}, c)$ is already defeated, we disregard (d, c). We want to emphasize that this example illustrates how the notion of projection is akin to the SETAF-reduct: indeed, constructing $SF\Downarrow_S^D$ consists in projecting to a certain set of arguments and then i) removing attacks where defeated arguments are involved as well as ii) partially evaluating the remaining tails. Formally, the connection is as follows.

Lemma 6.6. *Let $SF = (A, R)$ be a SETAF and let $E, S \subseteq A$. Then $SF\Downarrow_S^{(E\setminus S)^+} = SF^{(E\setminus S)}\downarrow_S$.*

Let us now formally introduce SCC-recursiveness (Baroni, Giacomin, and Guida 2005) as a SETAF principle. Extensions are recursively characterized as follows: if the SETAF SF consists of a single SCC, the *base function* $\mathcal{BF}$ of the semantics yields the extensions. For SETAFs that consist of more SCCs we apply the *generic selection function* $\mathcal{GF}$, where SF is evaluated separately on each SCC, taking into account arguments that are defeated by previous SCCs

Definition 6.7 (SCC-recursiveness). A semantics σ satisfies *SCC-recursiveness* if for all SETAFs $SF = (A, R)$, it holds that $\sigma(SF) = \mathcal{GF}(SF)$, where $\mathcal{GF}(SF) \subseteq 2^A$ is defined as: $E \subseteq A \in \mathcal{GF}(SF)$ if and only if

- if $|SCCs(SF)| = 1$, $E \in \mathcal{BF}(SF)$,
- otherwise, $\forall S \in SCCs(SF)$ it holds $E \cap S \in \mathcal{GF}(SF\Downarrow_{UP_{SF}(S,E)}^{(E\setminus S)^+})$,

where $\mathcal{BF}$ is a function that maps a SETAF $SF = (A, R)$ with $|SCCs(SF)| = 1$ to a subset of 2^A.

In the following subsections we will investigate and refine SCC-recursiveness for the different semantics under our consideration. For the proofs we loosely follow the structure of (Baroni, Giacomin, and Guida 2005), incorporating our SETAF-specific notions.

6.1 Stable Semantics

We start with stable semantics, as this is the easiest case.

Example 6.8. Recall Example 6.2 and consider the stable extension $E = \{a, c, d, f\}$ of SF. Let $S = \{b, d, e\}$. Indeed, $E \cap S = \{d\}$ is a stable extension of the projected SETAF $SF\Downarrow_S^{(E\setminus S)^+} = (\{d, e\}, \{(d, e), (e, d)\})$.

In this section we will show that this is no coincidence, i.e. *stb* satisfies SCC-recursiveness. For the investigation of SCC-recursiveness in stable semantics we use the fact that there are no undecided arguments. Thus, in each step we do not have to keep track of as much information from previous SCCs. Formally, we obtain the following auxiliary lemma.

Lemma 6.9. *Let SF be a SETAF and $E \in stb(SF)$, then for all $S \in SCCs(SF)$ it holds $P_{SF}(S, E) = \emptyset$.*

Proof. For an argument a to be provisionally defeated, there has to be an attack (T, a) with $T \not\subseteq (E \cup E^+)$, a contradiction to the requirement of stable extensions. □

We continue with the main technical underpinning for the SCC-recursive characterization of stable semantics. Intuitively, Proposition 6.10 states that an extension E is "globally" stable in SF if and only if for each of its SCCs S it is "locally" stable in $SF\Downarrow^{(E\setminus S)^+}_{UP_{SF}(S,E)}$.

Proposition 6.10. *Let $SF = (A, R)$ be a SETAF and let $E \subseteq A$, then $E \in stb(SF)$ if and only if $\forall S \in SCCs(SF)$ it holds $(E \cap S) \in stb(SF\Downarrow^{(E\setminus S)^+}_{UP_{SF}(S,E)})$.*

Proof. Let $SF' = SF\Downarrow^{(E\setminus S)^+}_{UP_{SF}(S,E)}$ be the "local" SETAF w.r.t. an arbitrary SCC $S \in SCCs(SF)$. If we assume E is globally stable, we need to show that (1) $(E \cap S)$ is contained in the local SETAF, i.e. $E \cap S \subseteq UP_{SF}(S, E)$, (2) $(E \cap S)$ is locally conflict-free, (3) $(E \cap S)$ (locally) attacks all arguments not in it. For 1. note that by global conflict-freeness there cannot be an $a \in D_{SF}(S, E) \cap E$. Also 2. follows from global conflict-freeness, as any violation of local conflict-freeness by an attack $(T, h) \in R(SF')$ would imply the existence of an attack $(T', h) \in R$ with $T \subseteq T' \subseteq E$. For 3. consider an arbitrary argument $a \in A(SF') \setminus E$. As E is globally stable, we know $E \mapsto_R a$. Moreover, as we assume $a \in A(SF')$ we know a is not defeated, i.e. (parts of) an attack towards a appears in $R(SF')$, establishing that $(E \cap S)$ is locally stable. For the other direction, assume E is locally stable for every SCC. Global conflict-freeness follows from local conflict-freeness, as any attack (T, h) with $T \cup \{h\} \subseteq E$ would imply a conflict in the SCC of h. It remains to show that $E \mapsto_R a$ for all $a \in A \setminus E$. For a's SCC S, either $a \in D_{SF}(S, E)$ (and we are done) or $a \in UP_{SF}(S, E)$, in which case it is locally attacked, and by construction of the restriction globally attacked. □

This leads us the the characterization of stable extensions. The base function is $stb(SF)$, the base case follows immediately. The composite case follows from Proposition 6.10.

Theorem 6.11. *Stable semantics is SCC-recursive.*

6.2 Admissible Sets

As already mentioned, when investigating stable semantics we can use the observation that each argument is either in E or defeated by E. For admissibility-based semantics, undecidedness of arguments is also possible which we need to handle in our SCCs as well. This is reflected in the definition due to an added second component of $\mathcal{GF}$ which intuitively collects all arguments that can still be defended within the current SCC. We account for this in Definition 6.16 by maintaining a set of candidate arguments C. Moreover, the particular case of SETAFs gives rise to a novel scenario, where certain attacks are present in an SCC, but not applicable.

Example 6.12. Recall our SETAF from before.

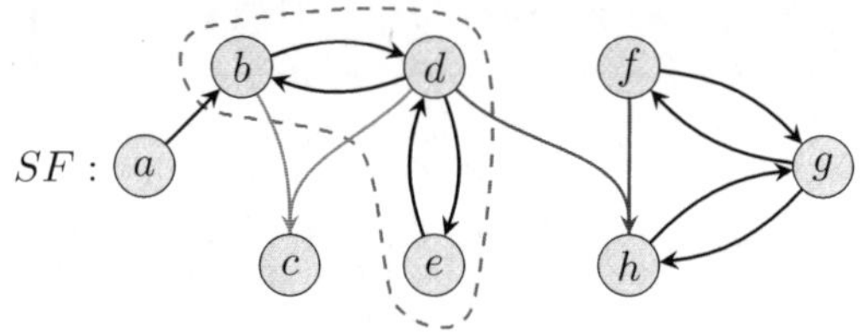

Let $E = \emptyset$. First consider $S = \{b, d, e\}$. Then

$$D_{SF}(S, E) = \emptyset \qquad SF\Downarrow^{(E\setminus S)^+}_{UP_{SF}(S,E)} = (S', R')$$
$$P_{SF}(S, E) = \{b\} \qquad S' = \{b, d, e\}$$
$$U_{SF}(S, E) = \{d, e\} \quad R' = \{(b, d), (d, b), (d, e), (e, d)\}$$

In contrast to the situation we saw for stable semantics we now also need to bear in mind that b cannot be defended by arguments in S (due to a). Hence the additional information in $\mathcal{GF}$ is required. Now let $T = \{f, g, h\}$. Then

$$D_{SF}(T, E) = \emptyset \qquad SF\Downarrow^{(E\setminus T)^+}_{UP_{SF}(T,E)} = (T', R'')$$
$$P_{SF}(T, E) = \emptyset \qquad T' = \{f, g, h\}$$
$$U_{SF}(T, E) = \{f, g, h\} \quad R'' = \{(f, h), (g, h), (h, g), (f, g), (g, f)\}$$

We now observe that although there is an attack from f to h in $SF\Downarrow^{\emptyset}_{T}$, the argument h can actually not be defeated by f, because this would require d to be present in our extension. Note however that we cannot delete the attack (f, h), as this would mean we could accept h—without defending h against the attack from $\{d, f\}$. Consequently, we will keep track of these attacks that have to be considered for defense, but cannot themselves be used to defend an argument. We will call attacks of this kind *mitigated*.

Definition 6.13 (Mitigated Attacks)**.** Let $SF = (A, R)$ be a SETAF. Moreover, let $E \subseteq A$ and $S \in SCCs(SF)$. We define the set of *mitigated attacks* as follows: $M_{SF}(S, E) = \{(T, h) \in R(SF\Downarrow^{(E\setminus S)^+}_{UP_{SF}(S,E)}) \mid \forall (T', h) \in R : T' \supseteq T \Rightarrow (T' \setminus T) \not\subseteq E\}$.

For the computation of mitigated attacks only the ancestor SCCs are relevant. In particular, the set $(T' \setminus T)$ is contained in ancestor SCCs of S for each attack $(T', h) \in R$. To account for these novel scenarios we adapt the notion of acceptance. We have to assure that the "counter-attacks" used for defense are not mitigated.

Definition 6.14 (Semantics Considering C, M)**.** Let $SF = (A, R)$ be a SETAF, and let $E, C \subseteq A$ and $M \subseteq R$. An argument $a \in A$ is *acceptable considering M w.r.t. E* if for all $(T, a) \in R$ there is $(X, t) \in R \setminus M$ s.t. $X \subseteq E$ and $t \in T$.

- E is *admissible in C considering M*, denoted by $E \in adm(SF, C, M)$, if $E \subseteq C$, $E \in cf(SF)$, and each $a \in E$ is acceptable considering M w.r.t. E.
- E is *complete in C considering M*, denoted by $E \in com(SF, C, M)$, if $E \in adm(SF, C, M)$ and E contains all $a \in C$ acceptable considering M w.r.t. E.
- E is *preferred in C considering M*, denoted by $E \in pref(SF, C, M)$, if $E \in adm(SF, C, M)$ and there is no $E' \in adm(SF, C, M)$ with $E' \supset E$.

The *characteristic function* $F^M_{SF,C}$ *of* SF *in* C *considering* M is the mapping $F^M_{SF,C} : 2^C \to 2^C$ where $F^M_{SF,C}(E) = \{a \in C \mid a \text{ is acceptable considering } M \text{ w.r.t. } E\}$.

- E is *grounded in* C *considering* M, denoted by $E \in grd(SF, C, M)$, if E is the least fixed point of $F^M_{SF,C}$.

Setting $C = A$ and $M = \emptyset$ recovers the original semantics, in these cases we will omit writing the respective parameter. The standard relationships hold for this generalization of the semantics, as the following result illustrates.

Theorem 6.15. *Let* SF *be a SETAF, and let* $C \subseteq A$ *and* $M \subseteq R$. *Then, (1)* $F^M_{SF,C}$ *is monotonic, (2)* $E \in grd(SF, C, M)$ *is the least set in* $com(SF, C, M)$ *w.r.t.* $\subseteq$, *and (3)* $E \in pref(SF, C, M)$ *are the maximal sets in* $com(SF, C, M)$ *w.r.t.* $\subseteq$.

We now redefine Definition 6.7 in order to capture the admissibility-based semantics.

Definition 6.16 (SCC-recursiveness)**.** A semantics σ satisfies *SCC-recursiveness* if and only if for all SETAFs $SF = (A, R)$ it holds $\sigma(SF) = \mathcal{GF}(SF, A, \emptyset)$, where $\mathcal{GF}(SF, C, M) \subseteq 2^A$ is defined as:

$E \subseteq A \in \mathcal{GF}(SF, C, M)$ if and only if

- if $|SCCs(SF)| = 1$, $E \in \mathcal{BF}(SF, C, M)$,
- otherwise, $\forall S \in SCCs(SF)$ it holds $E \cap S \in \mathcal{GF}(SF{\Downarrow}^{(E\setminus S)^+}_{UP_{SF}(S,E)}, U_{SF}(S, E) \cap C, M_{SF}(S, E))$,

where $\mathcal{BF}$ maps $SF = (A, R)$ with $|SCCs(SF)| = 1$ and sets $C \subseteq A$, $M \subseteq R$ to a subset of 2^A.

Towards an SCC-recursive characterization of admissible sets we discuss the following auxiliary results. Lemma 6.17 shows that global acceptability implies local acceptability, Lemma 6.18 shows the converse direction.

Lemma 6.17. *Let* $SF = (A, R)$ *be a SETAF, let* $E \in adm(SF)$ *be an admissible set of arguments, and let* a *be acceptable w.r.t.* E *in* SF, *where* a *is in the SCC* S.

Then it holds $a \in U_{SF}(S, E)$ *and* a *is acceptable w.r.t.* $(E \cap S)$ *in* $SF{\Downarrow}^{(E\setminus S)^+}_{UP_{SF}(S,E)}$ *considering* $M_{SF}(S, E)$. *Moreover,* $(E \cap S)$ *is conflict-free in* $SF{\Downarrow}^{(E\setminus S)^+}_{UP_{SF}(S,E)}$.

Proof. By the fundamental lemma (Nielsen and Parsons 2006) we get $E \cup \{a\} \in adm(SF)$, and in particular $a \in U_{SF}(S, E)$ and $(E \cap S) \subseteq U_{SF}(S, E)$ for all $S \in SCCs(SF)$. The key idea is that if (parts of) attacks towards an argument $x \in E$ appear on the local level, (parts of) a global counter-attack also appear in x's SCC. This applies both to $(E \cap S)$ and a. Regarding local conflict-freeness, this follows from the global admissibility of E: there would be a defending attack $(T, h) \in R$ against any attack violating local conflict-freeness with $T \cup \{h\} \subseteq E$, a contradiction. □

Lemma 6.18. *Let* $SF = (A, R)$ *be a SETAF, let* $E \subseteq A$ *such that* $(E \cap S) \in adm(SF{\Downarrow}^{(E\setminus S)^+}_{UP_{SF}(S,E)}, U_{SF}(S, E), M_{SF}(S, E))$ *for all* $S \in SCCs(SF)$. *Moreover, let* $S' \in SCCs(SF)$ *and let* $a \in U_{SF}(S', E)$ *be acceptable w.r.t.* $(E \cap S')$ *in* $SF{\Downarrow}^{(E\setminus S')^+}_{UP_{SF}(S',E)}$ *considering* $M_{SF}(S', E)$. *Then* a *is acceptable w.r.t.* E *in* SF.

Proof. We distinguish in 3 cases the relationship of an attack $(T, a) \in R$ to S': (1) $T \subseteq S'$. Either $T \cap D_{SF}(S', E) \neq \emptyset$ or there is a non-mitigated local counter-attack that corresponds to a global counter-attack. (2) $T \subseteq A \setminus S'$. But then $T \cap E^+_R \neq \emptyset$. (3) $T \cap S' \neq \emptyset$ and $T \cap (A \setminus S') \neq \emptyset$. Here we proceed as in (1). In all cases a is defended. □

Combining these two results we obtain the SCC-recursive characterization of admissible sets.

Proposition 6.19. *Let* $SF = (A, R)$ *be a SETAF and let* $E \subseteq A$ *be a set of arguments. Then* $\forall C \subseteq A$ *it holds* $E \in adm(SF, C)$ *if and only if* $\forall S \in SCCs(SF)$ *it holds* $(E \cap S) \in adm(SF{\Downarrow}^{(E\setminus S)^+}_{UP_{SF}(S,E)}, U_{SF}(S, E) \cap C, M_{SF}(S, E))$.

Proof. From Lemma 6.17 we get the "$\Rightarrow$" direction. For the "$\Leftarrow$" direction we first establish global conflict-freeness. Assume towards contradiction there is an attack $(T, h) \in R$ with $T \cup \{h\} \subseteq E$. We distinguish in 3 cases the relationship of T to h's SCC S: (1) $T \subseteq S$ contradicts local conflict-freeness. (2) $T \subseteq A \setminus S$ contradicts our assumption $h \in U_{SF}(S, E)$. It has to be $E \mapsto_R T$, as otherwise part of the attack appears locally, violating local conflict-freeness. This attack $(X, t) \in E$ with $X \subseteq E$, where again we can handle the relationship of X to t's SCC S. Again, case (1) and (2) lead to contradictions, and due to finiteness we can only apply (3) until we encounter an initial SCC. Inductively, we get back to the initial case, a contradiction. Hence, global conflict-freeness holds. Global defense follows from Lemma 6.18. □

The base function for admissible sets is $adm(SF, C, M)$. We will utilize this result to obtain the characterizations of the other (admissibility-based) semantics.

Theorem 6.20. *Admissible semantics is SCC-recursive.*

6.3 Further Semantics

Utilizing the characterization of admissible sets, we can formalize the SCC-recursive scheme grounded, complete, and preferred extensions in a similar manner. The key idea is that local admissibility implies global admissibility and vice versa. The respective minimality/maximality restrictions also carry over in both directions.

Proposition 6.21. *Let* $SF = (A, R)$ *be a SETAF, let* $E \subseteq A$, *and let* $\sigma \in \{grd, com, pref\}$. *Then* $\forall C \subseteq A$ *it holds* $E \in \sigma(SF, C)$ *if and only if* $\forall S \in SCCs(SF)$ *it holds* $(E \cap S) \in \sigma(SF{\Downarrow}^{(E\setminus S)^+}_{UP_{SF}(S,E)}, U_{SF}(S, E) \cap C, M_{SF}(S, E))$.

As it is the case with AFs, the respective base functions $grd(SF, C, M)$, $com(SF, C, M)$, and $pref(SF, C, M)$ can be obtained in the same way as for admissible semantics.

Theorem 6.22. *Grounded, complete, and preferred semantics are SCC-recursive.*

Concerning the base function for *grd* we can use that each SCC is either cyclic or contains exactly one argument and no attack. We can thus alternatively characterize the base function as $\mathcal{BF}(SF, C) = \{\{a\}\}$ if $A(SF) = C = \{a\}, R(SF) = \emptyset$ and $\mathcal{BF}(SF, C) = \{\emptyset\}$ otherwise.

6.4 Connection to Directionality

As it is the case in AFs, we can obtain results regarding directionality using SCC-recursiveness if the base function always admits at least one extension (Baroni and Giacomin 2007). First note that for an uninfluenced set U any SCC S with $S \cap U \neq \emptyset$ has to be contained in U, as well as all ancestor SCCs of S. Then, by the SCC-recursive characterization we get the following general result, subsuming the semantics under our consideration.

Proposition 6.23. *Let σ be a semantics such that for all SETAFs SF and all $C \subseteq A(SF)$, $M \subseteq R(SF)$ it holds $\mathcal{BF}(SF, C, M) \neq \emptyset$. If σ satisfies SCC-recursiveness then it satisfies directionality.*

7 Incremental Computation

In this section we briefly discuss the computational implications of a semantics satisfying directionality, modularization, or SCC-recursiveness. First, for a semantics σ satisfying directionality an argument a is in some extension (in all extensions) if and only if it is in some extension (in all extensions) of the framework that is restricted to the arguments that influence a. That is, when deciding credulous or skeptical acceptance of an argument, in a preprocessing step, we can shrink the framework to the relevant part. The property of modularization is closely related to CEGAR style algorithms for preferred semantics that can be implemented via iterative SAT-solving (Dvořák et al. 2014). In order to compute a preferred extension we can iteratively compute a non-empty admissible set of the current framework, build the reduct w.r.t. this admissible set, and repeat this procedure on the reduct until the empty set is the only admissible set. The preferred extension is then given by the union of the admissible sets.

Finally, for SCC-recursive semantics we can iteratively compute extensions along the SCCs of a given framework (see (Baumann 2011; Liao, Jin, and Koons 2011; Baroni, Giacomin, and Liao 2014; Cerutti et al. 2014) for such approaches for AFs). That is, in the initial SCCs we simply compute the extensions and then for each of them proceed on the remaining SCCs. We then iteratively proceed on SCCs in their order. To evaluate an SCC that is attacked by other ones we have to take the attacks from earlier SCCs into account and, as we have already fixed our extension there, we can simply follow the SCC-recursive schema. We next illustrate this for stable semantics.

Example 7.1. Consider the following SETAF SF.

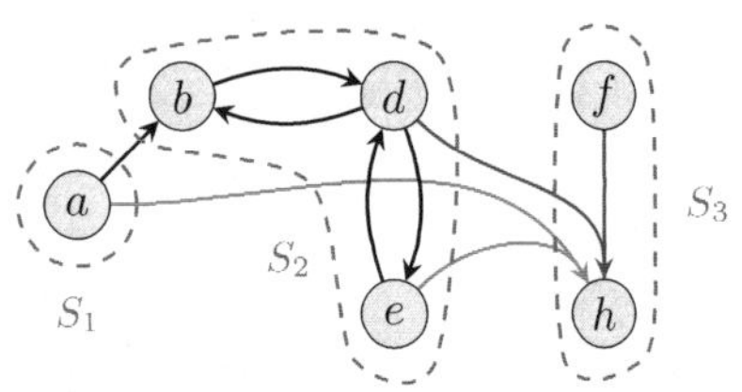

We can iteratively compute the stable extensions of SF as follows: in the first SCC $S_1 = \{a\}$ we simple compute all the stable extensions, i.e., $stb(SF\Downarrow^{\emptyset}_{S_1}) = \{\{a\}\}$. We then proceed with $\{a\}$ as extension E for the part of the SETAF considered so far. Next we consider S_2 and adapt it to take E into account. As $(E \setminus S_2)^+ = \{b\}$ we only have to delete the argument b from S_2 before evaluating the SCC and thus we obtain $SF\Downarrow^{\{b\}}_{S_2} = (\{d, e\}, \{(d, e), (e, d)\})$. Combining these with E we obtain two stable extensions $E_1 = \{a, d\}$, $E_2 = \{a, e\}$ for $SF\Downarrow^{\emptyset}_{S_1 \cup S_2}$. We proceed with S_3 and first consider E_1. As $(E_1 \setminus S_3)^+ = \{b, e\}$ we do not remove arguments from S_3. However, as $d \in E_1$ we cannot delete the attack $(\{d, f\}, h)$ but have to replace it by the attack (f, h). We then have $stb(SF\Downarrow^{\{b,e\}}_{S_3}) = \{\{f\}\}$ and thus obtain the first stable extensions of SF $\{a, d, f\}$. Now consider E_2. We have that E_2 attacks h, i.e., $(E_2 \setminus S_3)^+ = \{b, d, h\}$, and thus we have to remove h before evaluating S_3 and thus obtain $SF\Downarrow^{\{b,d,h\}}_{S_3} = (\{f\}, \emptyset)$. We end up with $\{a, e, f\}$ as the second stable extension of SF.

The computational advantage of the incremental computation is that certain computations are performed over single SCCs instead of the whole framework. This is in particular significant for preferred semantics where the $\subseteq$-maximality check can be done within the SCCs. Notice that verifying a preferred extension is in general coNP-complete (Dvořák and Dunne 2018; Dvořák, Greßler, and Woltran 2018). However, given our results regarding the SCC-recursive scheme, the following parameterized tractability result is easy to obtain.

Theorem 7.2. *Let SF be a SETAF where $|S| \leq k$ for all $S \in SCCs(SF)$. Then we can verify a given preferred extensions in $O(2^k \cdot poly(|SF|))$ for some polynomial poly.*

8 Conclusion

In this work, we systematically analyzed semantics for SETAFs using a principles-based approach (see Table 1 for an overview of the investigated properties). We pointed out interesting concepts that help us to understand the principles more deeply: edge cases that for AFs are hidden behind simple syntactic notions have to be considered explicitly for SETAFs, revealing semantic peculiarities that are already there in the special case. To this end, we highlight the usefulness of the *reduct* in this context—many seemingly unrelated notions from various concepts boil down to formalizations closely related to the reduct. We particularly focused on computational properties like modularization and SCC-recursiveness. The latter concept has recently been investigated for Abstract Dialectical Frameworks in a different context by Gaggl, Rudolph, and Straß (2021). However, it is not immediately clear how their results apply in the context of SETAFs. Future work hence includes the investigation of this connection. Moreover, the reduct for SETAFs and the generalization of the recursive scheme for SETAFs allow for the definition of new semantics that have not yet been studied in the context of collective attacks. An interesting direction for future works is investigating semantics *cf2* (Baroni, Giacomin, and Guida 2005) and *stage2* (Dvořák and Gaggl 2016), as well as the family of semantics based on weak admissibility (Baumann, Brewka, and Ulbricht 2020b).

Acknowledgments

This research has been supported by the Vienna Science and Technology Fund (WWTF) through project ICT19-065, the Austrian Science Fund (FWF) through project P32830, and by the German Federal Ministry of Education and Research (BMBF, 01/S18026A-F) by funding the competence center for Big Data and AI "ScaDS.AI" Dresden/Leipzig.

References

Baroni, P., and Giacomin, M. 2007. On principle-based evaluation of extension-based argumentation semantics. *Artif. Intell.* 171(10-15):675–700.

Baroni, P.; Caminada, M.; and Giacomin, M. 2011. An introduction to argumentation semantics. *Knowledge Eng. Review* 26(4):365–410.

Baroni, P.; Caminada, M.; and Giacomin, M. 2018. Abstract argumentation frameworks and their semantics. In Baroni, P.; Gabbay, D.; Giacomin, M.; and van der Torre, L., eds., *Handbook of Formal Argumentation*. College Publications. chapter 4, 159–236.

Baroni, P.; Giacomin, M.; and Guida, G. 2005. SCC-recursiveness: a general schema for argumentation semantics. *Artif. Intell.* 168(1-2):162–210.

Baroni, P.; Giacomin, M.; and Liao, B. 2014. On topology-related properties of abstract argumentation semantics. A correction and extension to dynamics of argumentation systems: A division-based method. *Artif. Intell.* 212:104–115.

Baumann, R.; Brewka, G.; and Ulbricht, M. 2020a. Comparing weak admissibility semantics to their dung-style counterparts - reduct, modularization, and strong equivalence in abstract argumentation. In *Proceedings of the 17th International Conference on Principles of Knowledge Representation and Reasoning, KR 2020*, 79–88.

Baumann, R.; Brewka, G.; and Ulbricht, M. 2020b. Revisiting the foundations of abstract argumentation - semantics based on weak admissibility and weak defense. In *Proceedings of the Thirty-Fourth AAAI Conference on Artificial Intelligence, AAAI 2020*, 2742–2749. AAAI Press.

Baumann, R. 2011. Splitting an argumentation framework. In *Proceedings of the 11th International Conference on Logic Programming and Nonmonotonic Reasoning, LPNMR 2011*, volume 6645 of *Lecture Notes in Computer Science*, 40–53. Springer.

Bikakis, A.; Cohen, A.; Dvořák, W.; Flouris, G.; and Parsons, S. 2021. Joint attacks and accrual in argumentation frameworks. *FLAP* 8(6):1437–1501.

Caminada, M.; Carnielli, W. A.; and Dunne, P. E. 2012. Semi-stable semantics. *J. Log. Comput.* 22:1207–1254.

Cerutti, F.; Giacomin, M.; Vallati, M.; and Zanella, M. 2014. An SCC recursive meta-algorithm for computing preferred labellings in abstract argumentation. In *Proceedings of the 14th International Conference on Principles of Knowledge Representation and Reasoning, KR 2014*. AAAI Press.

Dung, P. M. 1995. On the acceptability of arguments and its fundamental role in nonmonotonic reasoning, logic programming and n-person games. *Artif. Intell.* 77(2):321–358.

Dvořák, W., and Dunne, P. E. 2018. Computational problems in formal argumentation and their complexity. In *Handbook of Formal Argumentation*. College Publications. chapter 14, 631–687. Also appears in IfCoLog Journal of Logics and their Applications 4(8):2557–2622.

Dvořák, W., and Gaggl, S. A. 2016. Stage semantics and the scc-recursive schema for argumentation semantics. *J. Log. Comput.* 26(4):1149–1202.

Dvořák, W.; Järvisalo, M.; Wallner, J. P.; and Woltran, S. 2014. Complexity-sensitive decision procedures for abstract argumentation. *Artif. Intell.* 206(0):53 – 78.

Dvořák, W.; König, M.; Ulbricht, M.; and Woltran, S. 2021. A reduct-driven study of argumentation frameworks with collective attacks. In *Proceedings of the 19th International Workshop on Non-Monotonic Reasoning (NMR) 2021, colocated with KR 2021*.

Dvořák, W.; Fandinno, J.; and Woltran, S. 2019. On the expressive power of collective attacks. *Argument Comput.* 10(2):191–230.

Dvořák, W.; Greßler, A.; and Woltran, S. 2018. Evaluating SETAFs via answer-set programming. In *Proceedings of the Second International Workshop on Systems and Algorithms for Formal Argumentation (SAFA 2018)*, volume 2171 of *CEUR Workshop Proceedings*, 10–21. CEUR-WS.org.

Dvořák, W.; König, M.; and Woltran, S. 2021a. Graph-classes of argumentation frameworks with collective attacks. In *Proceedings of the 17th European Conference on Logics in Artificial Intelligence JELIA 2021*, volume 12678 of *Lecture Notes in Computer Science*, 3–17. Springer.

Dvořák, W.; König, M.; and Woltran, S. 2021b. On the complexity of preferred semantics in argumentation frameworks with bounded cycle length. In *Proceedings of the 17th International Conference on Principles of Knowledge Representation and Reasoning, KR 2021*, 671–675.

Flouris, G., and Bikakis, A. 2019. A comprehensive study of argumentation frameworks with sets of attacking arguments. *Int. J. Approx. Reason.* 109:55–86.

Gaggl, S. A.; Rudolph, S.; and Straß, H. 2021. On the decomposition of abstract dialectical frameworks and the complexity of naive-based semantics. *J. Artif. Intell. Res.* 70:1–64.

Liao, B. S.; Jin, L.; and Koons, R. C. 2011. Dynamics of argumentation systems: A division-based method. *Artif. Intell.* 175(11):1790–1814.

Nielsen, S. H., and Parsons, S. 2006. A generalization of Dung's abstract framework for argumentation: Arguing with sets of attacking arguments. In *Proceedings of the 3rd International Workshop on Argumentation in Multi-Agent Systems, ArgMAS 2006*, volume 4766 of *Lecture Notes in Computer Science*, 54–73. Springer.

Polberg, S. 2017. *Developing the Abstract Dialectical Framework*. Ph.D. Dissertation, Vienna University of Technology, Institute of Information Systems.

van der Torre, L., and Vesic, S. 2017. The principle-based approach to abstract argumentation semantics. *FLAP* 4(8):2735–2778.

Public and Private Affairs in Strategic Reasoning

Nathanaël Fijalkow[1] , **Bastien Maubert**[2] , **Aniello Murano**[2] , **Sasha Rubin**[3] and **Moshe Vardi**[4]
[1]CNRS & LaBRI, France
[2]Università degli Studi di Napoli "Federico II", Italy
[3]University of Sydney, Australia
[4]Rice University, U.S.A.

Abstract

Do agents know each others' strategies? In multi-process software construction, each process has access to the processes already constructed; but in typical human-robot interactions, a human may not announce their strategy to the robot (indeed, the human may not even know their own strategy). This question has often been overlooked when modeling and reasoning about multi-agent systems. In this work we study how it impacts strategic reasoning.

To do so we consider Strategy Logic (SL), a well-established and highly expressive logic for strategic reasoning. Its usual semantics, which we call "white-box semantics", models systems in which agents "broadcast" their strategies. By adding imperfect information to the evaluation games for the usual semantics, we obtain a new semantics called "black-box semantics", in which agents keep their strategies private. We consider the model-checking problem and show that the black-box semantics has much lower complexity than white-box semantics for an important fragment of Strategy Logic.

1 Introduction

In multi-agent systems, strategies tell agents what actions to take in order to try and achieve their goals. The strategy that an agent decides or chooses to use at a point in time may or may not depend on the strategies chosen by the other agents. For example, in typical agent applications such as human-robot interaction, a human may not announce its strategy to the robot (indeed, the human may not even be aware of their own strategy); on the other hand, in multi-process software construction projects one might assume that each process knows the strategy of the other processes already constructed. The purpose of this paper is to encapsulate this distinction in Strategy Logic (SL), a powerful logical formalism able to express a wide range of game-theoretic strategic concepts, such as winning strategies and Nash equilibria (Mogavero et al. 2014).

There are a number of strategic logics of varying expressiveness and complexities, among which the influential ATL/ATL* (Alur, Henzinger, and Kupferman 2002), which extend the branching-time logics CTL/CTL* with strategic modalities, ATL with strategy contexts (Laroussinie and Markey 2015), which remembers past strategies when evaluating new strategic modalities, and Strategy Logic and its fragments (Chatterjee, Henzinger, and Piterman 2010; Mogavero et al. 2014; Mogavero et al. 2017; Belardinelli et al. 2019; Aminof et al. 2019; Cermák, Lomuscio, and Murano 2015), which treat strategies as first-order variables. These logics are typically interpreted over multi-agent transition systems (known as "concurrent game structures") in which agents take simultaneous actions resulting in the next state. The usual semantics of these logics is what we call "white-box", which means, intuitively, that agents announce their strategies. We illustrate this with a simple example.

Consider the game of matching pennies in which two players, Alice and Bob, simultaneously choose Heads or Tails, and the objective of Bob is to match Alice's choice. Consider the property "for every strategy of Alice there exists a strategy of Bob such that the pennies match", which we could write in SL as

$$\forall s_A \, \exists s_B \, (\text{Alice}, s_A)(\text{Bob}, s_B)\text{Match},$$

where (a, s) indicates that agent a is assigned strategy s. Under the usual interpretation of quantifiers, this property is true: for a strategy s_A of Alice, the same strategy for Bob provides a witness to the satisfaction of the formula. And indeed this formula holds true in the usual semantics of SL, which reflects the usual mathematical interpretation.

This interpretation, however, is not always the desired one. In the example, a strategy s_B for Bob exists for each strategy s_A of Alice, but s_B depends on Alice's strategy s_A, and Bob is not able to know which strategy to pick unless Alice first announces her strategy. In most agent-based scenarios, however, agents are assumed to choose their strategies in secret and not announce them to their opponents. In such settings, if one wants $\exists s_B$ to express not only the existence of a strategy, but the ability for the agent to choose it, then a different type of semantics for such strategic properties is required, in which Bob's strategy is not allowed to depend at all on Alice's strategy. We call this interpretation "black-box" semantics, in contrast to the usual "white-box" semantics where strategies are publicly announced.

In this work, we define Strategy Logic with black-box semantics, and study its expressiveness and complexity.

1.1 Related Work

One thread in the history of strategic logics for multi-agent systems is the search for an expressive logic with elementary complexity. ATL* can express the existence or absence of winning strategies for a coalition, and has elementary complexity: its model-checking problem is 2-EXPTIME-complete, i.e., no harder than solving games with LTL winning conditions (which can be expressed in ATL*). Richer logics can naturally express game-theoretic concepts such as the existence of Nash equilibria, including ATL* with strategy contexts and Strategy Logic. However, model checking these logics is nonelementary decidable, with one exponential per alternation between existential and universal strategy quantifiers (Laroussinie and Markey 2013; Mogavero et al. 2017).

Then started a line of work that aims at taming the complexity of Strategy Logic, both by studying fragments or considering variations on the semantics. One approach is to restrict to positional strategies, i.e., strategies that only look at the current state rather than current history, which leads to a PSPACE-complete model-checking problem (Čermák et al. 2018). However, positional strategies are not adequate for general LTL objectives – the memory required may be double-exponential in the size of the formula already for very simply formulas encoding the synthesis problem (Pnueli and Rosner 1989).

Concerning fragments, the One-Goal fragment of SL is computationally no harder than ATL*, but it cannot express the existence of Nash equilibria. Other fragments have been introduced that can express it. One important fragment is Nested-Goals (Mogavero et al. 2014), whose formulas consist of a prefix of strategy quantifiers followed by a Boolean combination of *goals*, i.e., formulas of the form $\flat\psi$ where $\flat$ is a sequence of strategy assignments for all agents, and ψ is an LTL formula which can have nested goals as atomic propositions. New strategy quantifications inside goals are also allowed if they start independent subsentences. Nested-Goals SL under the white-box semantics is very expressive and can express most properties of interest (it subsumes ATL*, it can express existence of Nash and subgame perfect equilibria), but its model-checking problem is nonelementary, as for the full logic (Mogavero et al. 2014).

One proposal to explain the source of complexity in such logics is that in the usual semantics of these logics, strategies quantified later on in the formula can depend on the entirety of strategies quantified before. Typically, in a formula of the form $\forall s\, \exists t\, \varphi$, the action chosen by strategy t in any history h can depend on the action chosen by s on h and its prefixes, but also *future* histories of the form hh', and even on *counterfactual* histories that are neither prefixes of h nor continuations thereof. The case was made that such dependencies are unnatural in many cases of interest, and that avoiding them may also reduce drastically the complexity. These dependencies were studied in depth in (Mogavero et al. 2014) and later in (Gardy, Bouyer, and Markey 2020). A semantics in which future and counterfactual dependencies can be forbidden was proposed for the Nested-Goals fragment, called behavioural semantics (Mogavero et al. 2017). This involves a heavy mathematical machinery called dependence maps, related to Skolem functions for first-order logic, and the complexity of which explains why it was only defined for the Nested-Goals fragment and not the full logic. We observe that although the behavioural semantics forbids future and counterfactual dependencies, it allows for concurrent ones, which is not natural in many settings (see the matching penny example for instance).

The concept of dependence between quantifiers has also been much studied in classical logic. Among the most influential formalisms one can cite branching quantifiers (Henkin and Karp 1965), independence-friendly logic (Hintikka 1998) and Dependence Logic (Väänänen 2007).

Our work can be seen as a novel approach to the problem of dependencies in Strategy Logic.

1.2 Contributions

We consider Branching-time Strategy Logic (BSL), which adds to SL a quantifier on possible outcomes of the strategies currently bound to agents. This quantifier can be simulated in classic SL with white-box semantics by quantifying on strategies for agents that are not bound to any strategy, but this no longer works with the black-box semantics of strategy quantification, hence our choice to consider BSL.

After recalling the usual Tarski-style white-box semantics of BSL, we propose an equivalent definition via evaluation games; see (Hintikka and Sandu 1997) for an overview of game-theoretic semantics. These are two-player games played between Eloise and Abelard, where Eloise tries to prove that the given formula is true in the given model, while Abelard tries to prove the opposite. A formula is defined to be true in a model if Eloise has a winning strategy in the corresponding evaluation game. Our new black-box semantics for BSL is then obtained by hiding the universally quantified strategies so that Eloise's strategies cannot depend on them when she chooses existentially quantified ones, thus obtaining an imperfect-information evaluation game, reminiscent of Dependence Logic's evaluation games with imperfect information (Väänänen 2007).

We then focus on the "Nested-Goals" fragment of BSL, which we call BSL[NG]. We show that BSL[NG] with black-box semantics is strictly more expressive than ATL*, can express existence of Nash or subgame perfect equilibria, but still enjoys an elementary model-checking problem, which we prove to be 3-EXPTIME-complete. To obtain the upper-bounds we observe that under black-box semantics, existential and universal strategy quantifiers commute, and thus black-box BSL[NG] translates into white-box BSL[NG] with only one alternation in strategy quantifiers.

Finally we introduce and discuss an extension of BSL that combines the two semantics, white-box and black-box, in a single logic with two kinds of strategy quantifiers: public quantifiers from the white-box semantics, and private quantifiers from the black-box one.

Outline In Section 2 we recall the classic white-box semantics of BSL. In Section 3 we present an alternative, equivalent definition of this semantics via evaluation games, we define the new black-box semantics by adding imperfect information to those evaluation games, and we discuss this new semantics. We study the model-checking problem for BSL[NG] with black-box semantics in Section 4. In Section 5 we discuss a logic merging both semantics. We conclude in Section 6.

2 Classic Strategy Logic

2.1 Games

For the rest of the paper we fix a number of parameters: AP is a finite set of *atomic propositions* (denoted $p, q, r, \ldots$), Ag is a finite set of *agents* or *players* (denoted $a, b, c, \ldots$), Act is a finite set of *actions* (usually denoted α), and Var is a finite set of *strategy variables* (usually denoted s).

Definition 1 (Game). *A concurrent game structure $\mathcal{G}$ (or game for short) is a tuple (V, v_0, Δ, ℓ) where:*

- *V is the set of* positions,
- *$v_0 \in V$ is the* initial position,
- *$\Delta : V \times Act^{Ag} \to V$ is the* transition function,
- *$\ell : V \to 2^{AP}$ is the* labeling function.

Joint actions. In a position $v \in V$, each player $a \in \text{Ag}$ chooses an action $\alpha_a \in \text{Act}$, and the game proceeds to the position $\Delta(v, \boldsymbol{\alpha})$, where $\boldsymbol{\alpha} \in \text{Act}^{\text{Ag}}$ stands for the *joint action* $(\alpha_a)_{a\in\text{Ag}}$. Given a joint action $\boldsymbol{\alpha} = (\alpha_a)_{a\in\text{Ag}}$ and $a \in \text{Ag}$, we let $\boldsymbol{\alpha}_a$ denote α_a.

Plays and strategies. A *play* π is an infinite word over V, and a *history* h is a finite prefix of a play. For a play $\pi = v_1v_2\ldots$ and an index $i \in \mathbb{N}$, history $\pi_{\leq i} = v_1 \ldots v_i$ is the prefix of π up until position i. Plays is the set of plays, and Hist the set of histories. A *strategy* is a function $\sigma : \text{Hist} \to \text{Act}$, and Str is the set of all strategies. The length of a history h is written $|h|$ and its last position $\text{last}(h)$.

Assignments and bindings. An *assignment* is a partial function $\chi : \text{Var} \to \text{Str}$ that interprets strategy variables, and a *binding* is a partial function $\beta : \text{Ag} \to \text{Str}$ that binds some agents to strategies. We write $\chi[s \mapsto \sigma]$ for the assignment that maps s to σ and is equal to χ on the rest of its domain, and similarly for bindings. For a binding β we also let $\beta[a \mapsto \emptyset]$ be the binding that is undefined on a and otherwise equal to β. We say that an agent is *bound* by β if it is in its domain $\text{dom}(\beta)$.

Outcomes. Given a binding β and a history $h = h' \cdot v_0$ we let $\text{Out}(h, \beta)$ be the set of plays that can be obtained starting from h when each agent a bound by β plays according to $\beta(a)$, i.e., the set of plays of the form $h' \cdot v_0v_1v_2\ldots$ where for each $i \geq 0$ there exists a joint action $\boldsymbol{\alpha}$ where $\boldsymbol{\alpha}_a = \beta(a)(h' \cdot v_0 \ldots v_{i-1})$ for each agent a bound by β, such that $v_{i+1} \in \Delta(v_i, \boldsymbol{\alpha})$.

Turn-based games. While concurrent game structures provide the models of Strategy Logic, we will also use *turn-based games* to define the semantics of the logics. These games, where players play in turns, can be seen as a particular case of the games defined above, but it is convenient to use specialized notations. In such cases the set of positions $V = \uplus_{a\in\text{Ag}}V_a$ is partitioned between the players, and when in position $v \in V_a$ player a directly chooses the next position. Transitions are thus described by a relation $\Delta \subseteq V \times V$. Histories and plays are as before, a strategy for a player a is a function $V^*V_a \to V$ that respects the transitions, and outcomes are plays that follows the fixed strategies.

2.2 Syntax of Strategy Logic

We first present the full Strategy Logic. We consider Branching-time Strategy Logic (BSL), the branching-time variant of SL (Knight and Maubert 2015; Fijalkow et al. 2018; Berthon et al. 2021), which contains an *outcome quantifier* that quantifies on possible outcomes given the current history and binding, as well as an *unbinding operator* that releases an agent from its current strategy. The main reason to consider BSL is that it is expressively equivalent to SL (Knight and Maubert 2015) but allows explicit quantification on outcomes, while in usual SL this has to be simulated by strategy quantifications and bindings. Such artificial strategy quantifications may increase the computational complexity of evaluating the formula. But using strategy quantifiers instead of outcomes quantifiers is also a problem when considering unorthodox semantics for strategy quantification as we do here.

Definition 2. *The syntax of* BSL *is given by the following grammar:*

$$\varphi ::= p \mid \neg\varphi \mid \varphi \vee \varphi \mid \exists s\, \varphi \mid (a, s)\varphi \mid (a, \emptyset)\varphi \mid \mathbf{E}\psi$$
$$\psi ::= \varphi \mid \neg\psi \mid \psi \vee \psi \mid \mathbf{X}\psi \mid \psi\mathbf{U}\psi$$

where $p \in AP$, $a \in Ag$ and $s \in Var$.

As usual we define $\top = p \vee \neg p$, $\varphi \wedge \varphi' = \neg(\neg\varphi \vee \neg\varphi')$, $\forall s\, \varphi = \neg\exists s\, \neg\varphi$, $\mathbf{A}\psi = \neg\mathbf{E}\neg\psi$, $\mathbf{F}\psi = \top\mathbf{U}\psi$ and $\mathbf{G}\psi = \neg\mathbf{F}\neg\psi$. Without loss of generality we will assume that each strategy variable s is quantified at most once in each formula, which allows us to talk about *existentially quantified* and *universally quantified* variables.

Formulas of type φ are called *history formulas*, those of type ψ are called *outcome formulas*. We define $\text{HistSub}(\varphi)$ and $\text{OutSub}(\varphi)$ as the sets of history and outcome subformulas of φ, respectively. We say that a strategy variable appears *free* in a formula if it appears (in a binding operator) out of the scope of a strategy quantifier. A *sentence* is a history formula without free variables.

Remark 1. *Note that when all agents are bound to a strategy, i.e., when β is defined for all agents, this determines a unique outcome: $Out(h, \beta)$ is a singleton for any history h. As a result $\mathbf{E}\psi$ and $\mathbf{A}\psi$ are equivalent when evaluated in such a complete binding (see Definition 4), and we may thus omit the outcome quantifier. For instance if we have $Ag = \{a, b\}$, we may write $\exists s\, \forall t\, (a, s)(b, t)\mathbf{X}p$ instead of $\exists s\, \forall t\, (a, s)(b, t)\mathbf{A}\mathbf{X}p$.*

We also introduce the Nested-Goals fragment of BSL. The idea of Nested-Goals is that strategy quantifiers come in blocks, each followed by a Boolean combination of *goals* (written $\flat$), which consist of a sequence of strategy bindings or unbindings, followed by an outcome quantifier and outcome formula, in such a way that each block of quantifiers starts a closed formula whose semantics is independent of previous quantifiers and bindings. Goals can also be nested, allowing the rebinding of agents to previously quantified strategies along an outcome formula. This very expressive fragment subsumes ATL* and can in addition express complex game-theoretic notions such as existence of Nash Equilibria or Subgame Perfect Equilibria.

Definition 3. BSL[NG] *consists of formulas generated by the following grammar:*

$$\Phi ::= \exists s\,\Phi \mid \phi$$
$$\phi ::= \phi \vee \phi \mid \neg\phi \mid \flat$$
$$\flat ::= (a, s)\flat \mid (a, \emptyset)\flat \mid \mathbf{E}\psi$$
$$\psi ::= p \mid \flat \mid \Phi \mid \neg\psi \mid \psi \vee \psi \mid \mathbf{X}\psi \mid \psi\mathbf{U}\psi$$

where $p \in AP$, $a \in Ag$ and $s \in Var$, with the following syntactic constraint: each subformula Φ of an outcome formula ψ must be a closed sentence, meaning that it either unbinds or rebinds to newly quantified strategies all agents that were bound above Φ, before each outcome quantifier $\mathbf{E}$. Such a formula is called an independent subsentence.

Since independent subsentences can be evaluated independently, we will sometimes treat them as atomic propositions. For instance when considering the model-checking problem, a bottom-up model-checking procedure can start by evaluating innermost independent subsentences and decorate the model with atomic propositions indicating where they hold. Seeing independent subsentences as atomic formulas leads to the *flat fragment* of BSL[NG], denoted by BSL[NG,f] and defined by the same grammar as above, except that Φ is removed from the production rule for outcome formulas, which becomes:

$$\psi ::= p \mid \flat \mid \neg\psi \mid \psi \vee \psi \mid \mathbf{X}\psi \mid \psi\mathbf{U}\psi$$

Example 1. *Write $Ag = \{a_1, \ldots, a_n\}$, and consider that each agent a_i aims at making true some property expressed by an* LTL *formula ψ_i. Define the following formula*

$$\Phi_{NE} = \exists s_1 \ldots \exists s_n \forall t$$
$$\bigwedge_{i=1}^{n} (Ag_{-i}, \boldsymbol{s}_{-i})(a_i, t)\psi_i \to (Ag, \boldsymbol{s})\psi_i,$$

where $(Ag, \boldsymbol{s})$ is a shorthand for $(a_1, s_1) \ldots (a_n, s_n)$ and, similarly, notation $(Ag_{-i}, \boldsymbol{s}_{-i})$ is a shorthand for $(a_1, s_1) \ldots (a_{i-1}, s_{i-1})(a_{i+1}, s_{i+1}) \ldots (a_n, s_n)$. Φ_{NE} expresses that there exists a Nash Equilibrium for objectives ψ_i. This formula is in BSL[NG], *and even in its flat fragment as it does not contain any strategy quantifier under an outcome quantifier (each ψ_i is a pure* LTL *formula).*

Consider now formula

$$\Phi_{SPE} = \exists s_1 \ldots \exists s_n\, (Ag, \boldsymbol{s})\mathbf{AG}\, \forall t$$
$$\bigwedge_{i=1}^{n} (a_i, t)\psi_i \to \psi_i,$$

which expresses that there exists a Subgame Perfect equilibrium. It is not in the Nested Goals fragment: indeed the subformula on the second line is of type Φ, but each conjunct only rebinds one agent (a_i) before the outcome quantifier[1]*, leaving other agents bound to strategies from the previous block of strategy quantifiers.*

One could consider rewriting into the equivalent formula

$$\Phi'_{SPE} = \exists s_1 \ldots \exists s_n\, (Ag, \boldsymbol{s})\mathbf{AG}\, \forall t$$
$$\bigwedge_{i=1}^{n} (Ag_{-i}, \boldsymbol{s}_{-i})(a_i, t)\psi_i \to (Ag, \boldsymbol{s})\psi_i,$$

[1]which is implicit here, see Remark 1

but the latter is still not part of the Nested Goals fragment. Indeed here in the subformula of the second line each agent is bound again, but only one is bound to a newly quantified strategy. All the remaining agents are bound to strategies quantified in the first part of the formula.

However, since the universal quantification $\forall t$ commutes with the universal quantification on points of outcomes $\mathbf{AG}$ and with the binding $(Ag, \boldsymbol{s})$ (which does not involve t), one can instead rewrite Φ_{SPE} as follows:

$$\Phi''_{SPE} = \exists s_1 \ldots \exists s_n \forall t\, (Ag, \boldsymbol{s})\mathbf{AG}$$
$$\bigwedge_{i=1}^{n} (a_i, t)\psi_i \to (Ag, \boldsymbol{s})\psi_i,$$

This formula is in BSL[NG], *and even in its flat fragment.*

We conclude this section by recalling the usual semantics of BSL.

2.3 White-box Semantics of Strategy Logic

We recall the classical Tarski-style semantics of BSL formulas, which we call *white-box* and denote $\models_\square$. In the next section we will provide a new equivalent definition via evaluation games.

Definition 4 (White-box semantics)**.** *Let $\mathcal{G}$ be a game. A history formula φ (resp. outcome formula ψ) is evaluated in an assignment χ for free variables of φ (resp. ψ), a binding β and a history h (resp. a play π and an index $i \in \mathbb{N}$). We define $\mathcal{G}, \chi, \beta, h \models_\square \varphi$ and $\mathcal{G}, \chi, \beta, \pi, i \models_\square \psi$ inductively as follows (we omit $\mathcal{G}$):*

$\chi, \beta, h \models_\square p$	if	$p \in \ell(last(h))$
$\chi, \beta, h \models_\square \neg\varphi$	if	$\chi, \beta, h \not\models_\square \neg\varphi$
$\chi, \beta, h \models_\square \varphi \vee \varphi'$	if	$\chi, \beta, h \models_\square \varphi$ or $\chi, \beta, h \models_\square \varphi'$
$\chi, \beta, h \models_\square \exists s\, \varphi$	if	$\exists \sigma \in Str$ s.t. $\chi[s \mapsto \sigma], \beta, h \models_\square \varphi$
$\chi, \beta, h \models_\square (a, s)\varphi$	if	$\chi, \beta[a \mapsto \chi(s)], h \models_\square \varphi$
$\chi, \beta, h \models_\square (a, \emptyset)\varphi$	if	$\chi, \beta[a \mapsto \emptyset], h \models_\square \varphi$
$\chi, \beta, h \models_\square \mathbf{E}\psi$	if	$\exists \pi \in Out(h, \beta)$ s.t. $\chi, \beta, \pi, \lvert h\rvert \models_\square \psi$
$\chi, \beta, \pi, i \models_\square \varphi$	if	$\chi, \beta, \pi_{\leq i} \models_\square \varphi$
$\chi, \beta, \pi, i \models_\square \neg\psi$	if	$\chi, \beta, \pi, i \not\models_\square \psi$
$\chi, \beta, \pi, i \models_\square \psi \vee \psi'$	if	$\chi, \beta, \pi, i \models_\square \psi$ or $\chi, \beta, \pi, i \models \psi'$
$\chi, \beta, \pi, i \models_\square \mathbf{X}\psi$	if	$\chi, \beta, \pi, i+1 \models_\square \psi$
$\chi, \beta, \pi, i \models_\square \psi\mathbf{U}\psi'$	if	$\exists j \geq i$ s.t. $\chi, \beta, \pi, j \models_\square \psi'$, and $\forall k \in [i, j)$, $\chi, \beta, \pi, k \models_\square \psi$

For a sentence φ we write $\mathcal{G} \models_\square \varphi$ if $\mathcal{G}, \emptyset, \emptyset, v_0 \models_\square \varphi$.

In this paper we focus on strategy quantification, and in particular alternation of existential and universal quantifiers. In the white-box semantics of a formula $\forall s.\exists s'.\varphi$ the strategy σ chosen for s is publicly announced, in the sense that s' can depend on σ. Technically this is due to the fact that the evaluation of $\exists s'.\varphi$ is carried out with σ in the assignment $\chi[s \mapsto \sigma]$. Let us illustrate this on a very simple example.

Example 2. *"Cop and robber" is a one-step concurrent two-player game. Both the cop and the robber pick either* LEFT *or* RIGHT *at the same time, and the cop catches the robber if their choices match (see Figure 1).*

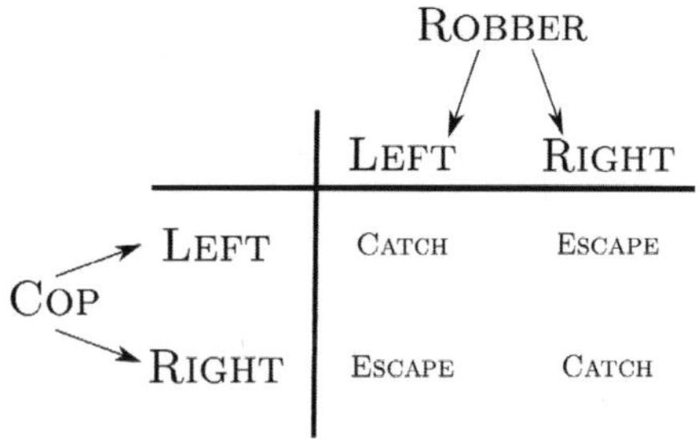

Figure 1: Cop and robber

Consider the BSL *formula*

$$\varphi = \forall s\, \exists t\, (\text{COP}, s)(\text{ROBBER}, t)\text{ESCAPE}$$

*It expresses that for every strategy of the cop there is a strategy of the robber which ensures that she escapes (*ESCAPE *is a formula which expresses that the outcome of the one-shot game is* ESCAPE*).*

In the white-box semantics, we have $\mathcal{G} \models_\square \varphi$. Indeed, when the robber picks a strategy, the cop's strategy s has already been publicly announced, hence choosing $t \neq s$ ensures an escape. We will get back to this example with the black-box semantics.

3 Black-box Semantics

In this section we introduce and discuss the new black-box semantics, which we define via evaluation games. We first introduce an alternative definition of the usual white-box semantics via evaluation games with perfect information, and then describe how to obtain the black-box semantics by hiding the chosen strategies in the games for the white-box semantics, thus obtaining games with imperfect information. We refer to, e.g., (Hodges and Väänänen 2019) for an introduction to game semantics for classical logic.

3.1 White-box Evaluation Games

Given a game $\mathcal{G}$ and a BSL sentence Φ, we define the evaluation game $\mathbb{G}_\square(\mathcal{G}, \Phi)$. It is a turn-based game played between two players: Eloise (also written E), who aims at proving that $\mathcal{G} \models_\square \Phi$, and Abelard (A), who challenges this claim.

The set $V_{\mathcal{G},\Phi}$ of positions in $\mathbb{G}_\square(\mathcal{G}, \Phi)$ is the union of

$$\{(\chi, \beta, h, \varphi, \mathrm{P}) \mid \varphi \in \text{HistSub}(\Phi), \mathrm{P} \in \{\mathrm{E}, \mathrm{A}\}\}$$

and

$$\{(\chi, \beta, \pi, i, \psi, \mathrm{P}) \mid \psi \in \text{OutSub}(\Phi), \mathrm{P} \in \{\mathrm{E}, \mathrm{A}\}\}$$

and the initial position is $(\emptyset, \emptyset, v_0, \Phi, V)$. Negation is dealt with by switching the roles of the players in trying to prove or disprove the current subformula, the idea being that Eloise succeeds in proving that $\neg\varphi$ holds if Abelard fails to prove that φ holds. Component $\mathrm{P} \in \{\mathrm{E}, \mathrm{A}\}$ in a position $(\chi, \beta, h, \varphi, \mathrm{P})$ indicates who of Eloise or Abelard is trying to prove subformula φ true in the current context; this is determined by whether the number of negations above subformula φ is even or odd[2]. We call P the *player in charge* and let $\overline{\mathrm{P}}$ denote its opponent.

Positions of the form $(\chi, \beta, h, p, \mathrm{P})$ are terminal, meaning that the game ends. Such a position with $\mathrm{P} = \mathrm{E}$ is *winning* for Eloise if $p \in \ell(\text{last}(h))$, otherwise it is winning for Abelard, and vice versa when $\mathrm{P} = \mathrm{A}$. Moves in other types of positions are as follows.

- $\neg$-positions: from $(\chi, \beta, h, \neg\varphi, \mathrm{P})$ the game goes to $(\chi, \beta, h, \varphi, \overline{\mathrm{P}})$, and similarly from $(\chi, \beta, \pi, i, \neg\psi, \mathrm{P})$ the game goes to $(\chi, \beta, \pi, i, \psi, \overline{\mathrm{P}})$.
- $\vee$-positions: from $(\chi, \beta, h, \varphi \vee \varphi', \mathrm{P})$, P moves either to $(\chi, \beta, h, \varphi, \mathrm{P})$ or to $(\chi, \beta, h, \varphi', \mathrm{P})$. Similarly for positions of the form $(\chi, \beta, \pi, i, \psi \vee \psi', \mathrm{P})$.
- $\exists s$-positions: from $(\chi, \beta, h, \exists s\, \varphi, \mathrm{P})$, P chooses some $\sigma \in \text{Str}$ and moves to $(\chi[s \mapsto \sigma], \beta, h, \varphi, \mathrm{P})$.
- (a, s)-positions: from $(\chi, \beta, h, (a, s)\varphi, \mathrm{P})$, the game moves to $(\chi, \beta[a \mapsto \chi(s)], h, \varphi, \mathrm{P})$.
- $(a, \emptyset)$-positions: from $(\chi, \beta, h, (a, s)\varphi, \mathrm{P})$, the game moves to $(\chi, \beta[a \mapsto \emptyset], h, \varphi, \mathrm{P})$.
- **E**-positions: from $(\chi, \beta, h, \mathbf{E}\psi, \mathrm{P})$, P chooses some outcome $\pi \in \text{Out}(\chi, h)$ and moves to $(\chi, \beta, \pi, |h|, \varphi, 0)$.
- φ-positions: from $(\chi, \beta, \pi, i, \varphi, \mathrm{P})$ the game goes to $(\chi, \beta, \pi_{\leq i}, \varphi, \mathrm{P})$
- **X**-positions: from $(\chi, \beta, \pi, i, \mathbf{X}\psi, \mathrm{P})$, the game moves to $(\chi, \beta, \pi, i + 1, \psi, \mathrm{P})$.
- **U**-positions: from $(\chi, \beta, \pi, i, \psi\mathbf{U}\psi', \mathrm{P})$, P chooses between $(\chi, \beta, \pi, i, \psi', \mathrm{P})$ and $(\chi, \beta, \pi, i, \psi \wedge \mathbf{X}\psi\mathbf{U}\psi', \mathrm{P})$.

A play is *winning* if either it reaches a winning terminal position, or it remains from some point onwards in **U**-positions with $\mathrm{P} = \mathrm{A}$ (meaning that Abelard is trying to prove true some formula $\psi\mathbf{U}\psi'$ but keeps postponing forever the realization of ψ').

A *strategy* for Eloise defines a move for every history in $\mathbb{G}_\square(\mathcal{G}, \Phi)$ ending in a situation where Eloise has a choice to make. A strategy for Eloise is *winning* if all plays consistent with this strategy are winning.

Lemma 1 (Correctness of the evaluation game). *$\mathcal{G} \models_\square \Phi$ if, and only if, Eloise has a winning strategy in $\mathbb{G}_\square(\mathcal{G}, \Phi)$ from the initial position.*

3.2 Black-box Evaluation Games

The intuition behind the black-box semantics is that when a strategy is universally quantified, it is fixed but not publicly announced, so that later existentially quantified strategies cannot depend on them. This is mathematically formalised by constraining the information available to Eloise in the evaluation game, making it an imperfect-information game in the classical sense for games played on graphs, where an

[2]Note that all along Eloise tries to prove that the initial formula holds in the game. Roles change only for subformulas: Eloise proves that $\neg\varphi$ is true if Abelard cannot prove that φ is true.

equivalence relation models indistinguishable positions, and strategies are required to be consistent with observations, i.e., they should assign the same actions to equivalent histories (Doyen and Raskin 2011).

We define the fact that a sentence Φ of BSL is satisfied in a game $\mathcal{G}$ with the black-box semantics, written $\mathcal{G} \models_\blacksquare \Phi$, via an evaluation game $\mathbb{G}_\blacksquare(\mathcal{G}, \Phi)$.

The game $\mathbb{G}_\blacksquare(\mathcal{G}, \Phi)$ is similar to $\mathbb{G}_\square(\mathcal{G}, \Phi)$ (it has the same set of positions $V_{\mathcal{G},\varphi}$, same moves and same winning condition), except that it has imperfect information: we define an equivalence relation $\sim$ over $V_{\mathcal{G},\Phi}$ by letting two positions be equivalent if they are identical except possibly for the interpretation of universally quantified variables. We then require that Eloise play similarly in equivalent situations, thus forcing her to choose existentially quantified strategies independently from the universally quantified strategies chosen by Abelard.

Formally, define $(\chi, \beta, h, \varphi, \mathrm{P}) \sim (\chi', \beta', h', \varphi', \mathrm{P}')$ if $\beta = \beta'$, $h = h'$, $\varphi = \varphi'$, $\mathrm{P} = \mathrm{P}'$ and for all $s \in \mathrm{Var}$ existentially quantified in Φ, we have $\chi(s) = \chi'(s)$. Similarly, define $(\chi, \beta, \pi, i, \psi, \mathrm{P}) \sim (\chi', \beta', \pi', i', \psi', \mathrm{P}')$ if $\beta = \beta'$, $\pi = \pi'$, $i = i'$, $\psi = \psi'$, $\mathrm{P} = \mathrm{P}'$ and for all $s \in \mathrm{Var}$ existentially quantified in Φ, we have $\chi(s) = \chi'(s)$. We then let $[V_{\mathcal{G},\Phi}]_\sim$ denote the quotient of $V_{\mathcal{G},\Phi}$ by $\sim$, and require that Eloise's strategies be defined on $[V_{\mathcal{G},\Phi}]^*_\sim$ instead of $V^*_{\mathcal{G},\Phi}$ as in $\mathbb{G}_\square(\mathcal{G}, \Phi)$.

Definition 5 (Black-box semantics). *Let $\mathcal{G}$ be a game, Φ a* BSL *sentence and φ a history subformula of Φ. Then $\mathcal{G}, \chi, \beta, h \models_\blacksquare \varphi$ if Eloise has a winning strategy in $\mathbb{G}_\blacksquare(\mathcal{G}, \Phi)$ from position $(\chi, \beta, h, \varphi, \mathrm{E})$.*

We start by proving the following central property, which is that under black-box semantics existential and universal strategy quantifiers commute. The proof also serves to illustrate how the game semantics works.

Lemma 2. *For every formula of the form $\forall s\, \exists t\, \Phi$, for every game $\mathcal{G}$, assignment χ, binding β and history h, it holds that*

$$\mathcal{G}, \chi, \beta, h \models_\blacksquare \forall s\, \exists t\, \Phi \quad \textit{iff} \quad \mathcal{G}, \chi, \beta, h \models_\blacksquare \exists t\, \forall s\, \Phi$$

Proof. The right-to-left direction is clear. The other one follows directly from the definition of the black-box semantics: assume that $\mathcal{G}, \chi, \beta, h \models_\blacksquare \forall s\, \exists t\, \Phi$, i.e., Eloise has a winning strategy in the corresponding evaluation game from position $(\chi, \beta, h, \neg\exists s\, \neg\exists t\, \Phi, \mathrm{E})$. The game moves to $(\chi, \beta, h, \exists s\, \neg\exists t\, \Phi, \mathrm{A})$, where Abelard chooses a strategy σ, then to $(\chi[s \mapsto \sigma], \beta, h, \neg\exists t\, \Phi, \mathrm{A})$, and then to $(\chi[s \mapsto \sigma], \beta, h, \exists t\, \Phi, \mathrm{E})$. Let σ' be the strategy chosen by Eloise's winning strategy in this position. By definition of the imperfect-information evaluation game, the strategy σ' picked by Eloise's winning strategy is the same for any choice made by Abelard for t, and the position $(\chi[s \mapsto \sigma, t \mapsto \sigma'], \beta, h, \Phi, \mathrm{E})$ is winning for Eloise for any σ. As a result Eloise has a winning strategy from $(\chi, \beta, h, \exists t\, \neg\exists s\, \neg\Phi, \mathrm{E})$, which is to pick σ', and this concludes the proof. □

Example 3. *Let us get back to Example 2. Intuitively, if the cop keeps its strategy private, then there is no way for the robber to pick a strategy that ensures she escapes. This is the kind of situation that the black-box semantics is designed to capture, and we claim that indeed $\mathcal{G} \not\models_\blacksquare \varphi$. This is because a strategy for Eloise for the subformula $\psi = \exists t\, (\textsc{Cop}, s)(\textsc{Robber}, t)$* Escape *does not see what strategy Abelard has chosen for s. In other words, it must make the same choice for all s, but there is no strategy t for the* Robber *that ensures she will escape for any s.*

Example 4. *The point of this example is to illustrate a subtelty of the black-box semantics for existential quantifiers. We consider a variant of the cop and robber game from Example 2: now there are two cops,* $\textsc{Cop}_1$ *and* $\textsc{Cop}_2$*, and one robber. All three agents choose* Left *or* Right *at the same time, and the cops catch the robber if at least one of the two cops chooses the same direction as the robber.*

Consider the SL *formula*

$$\exists s_1\, \exists s_2\, \forall t\, (\textsc{Cop}_1, s_1)(\textsc{Cop}_2, s_2)(\textsc{Robber}, t)\ \textsc{Catch}$$

It expresses that there exist strategies for the two cops ensuring to catch the robber, and intuitively it should hold: two strategies s_1 and s_2 that pick different directions are witnesses for the satisfaction of this formula. And indeed we have that $\mathcal{G} \models_\blacksquare \Phi$.

There are two aspects of the evaluation game that account for this. First, only the valuation of universally *quantified strategies is hidden, while existential ones are visible to Eloise. Second, all existentially quantified strategies are chosen by Eloise, and that a formula is said to hold if there exists a winning strategy for Eloise. This meta existential quantification on Eloise's strategies effectively quantifies on all existentially quantified strategies of the formula at once, making it possible for s_2 to depend on s_1. A consequence of this is that the semantics would remain unchanged if all strategies (both existentially and universally quantified) were hidden in the evaluation game $\mathbb{G}_\blacksquare(\mathcal{G}, \Phi)$.*

Example 5. *Consider again formulas Φ_{NE} and Φ''_{SPE} from Example 1. In both formulas, all existential quantifications on strategies are made* before *universal ones, so that black-box and white-box semantics coincide for these formulas.*

From the last example we get:

Proposition 1. *The existence of Nash Equilibria and Subgame Perfect Equilibria can be expressed in* BSL[NG] *with black-box semantics.*

3.3 Comparison with ATL*

We briefly recall the syntax and semantics of ATL*.

Formulas are given by the following grammar:

$$\varphi ::= p \mid \neg\varphi \mid \varphi \vee \varphi \mid \langle A \rangle \psi$$
$$\psi ::= \varphi \mid \neg\psi \mid \psi \vee \psi \mid \mathbf{X}\psi \mid \psi \mathbf{U} \psi$$

where $p \in \mathrm{AP}$ and $A \subseteq \mathrm{Ag}$.

A formula of type φ is evaluated in a position of a game, and a formula of type ψ is evaluated in a play. We only recall the semantics for the coalition operator $\langle A \rangle \psi$, whose intuitive meaning is that coalition A has a strategy to ensure that ψ holds: $\mathcal{G}, v \models \langle A \rangle \psi$ holds if there exists a strategy profile $\{\sigma_a\}_{a \in A}$ such that for all outcomes $\pi \in \mathrm{Out}(v, (a, \sigma_a)_{a \in A})$ formula ψ holds in π. The dual operator $[A]\psi$ is defined as $\neg\langle A\rangle\neg\psi$, and means that for any strategy of coalition A there exists an outcome that satisfies ψ.

ATL* formulas can be translated to BSL with black-box semantics. Such a translation can be defined by induction, where all cases are trivial but the coalition quantifier which is as follows: assuming that $\text{Ag} = \{a_1, \ldots, a_n\}$ and $A = \{a_{i_1}, \ldots, a_{i_k}\}$, $\langle A\rangle\psi$ is translated as

$$\exists s_1 \ldots \exists s_k (\text{Ag}, \emptyset)(a_1, s_1) \ldots (a_k, s_k)\mathbf{A}\psi',$$

where ψ' is the translation of ψ.

Observe that each block of strategy quantifiers is followed by a unique goal which starts by unbinding all agents, and all new bindings are made with newly quantified strategies. As a result, this translation produces only formulas in the Nested Goals fragment. In addition, each block of strategy quantifiers consists in only existential operators (when translating $\langle A\rangle$) or only universal ones (when translating $[A]$), so that the white-box and black-box semantics coincide for the obtained formulas.

It follows that BSL[NG] with black-box semantics subsumes ATL*. We show that it is actually strictly more expressive.

Proposition 2. *BSL[NG] with black-box semantics is strictly more expressive than ATL*.*

Proof. We adapt the proof from (Mogavero et al. 2014) that One-Goal SL with white-box semantics is strictly more expressive than ATL*. Consider the two concurrent game structures in Figure 2. We have three agents a, b and c, and two actions 0 and 1 in $\mathcal{G}_1$, three actions 0, 1 and 2 in $\mathcal{G}_2$. In both games the initial position is v_0. The transitions are defined by the sets of joint moves $J_1 = \{00*, 11*\}$ and $J_2 = \{00*, 11*, 12*, 200, 202, 211\}$ ($\overline{J_i}$ denotes the complement of J_i). It is proved in (Mogavero et al. 2014, Theorem 4.4) that both games satisfy the same ATL* formulas.

Consider now the BSL[NG] formula

$$\Phi = \exists s_a \forall s_b\, (a, s_a)(b, s_b)\mathbf{EX}\neg p$$

It is quite easy to see that $\mathcal{G}_1 \not\models_{\blacksquare} \Phi$, while $\mathcal{G}_2 \models_{\blacksquare} \Phi$. Indeed in $\mathcal{G}_1$ no matter which action is chosen by a, if b plays the same action then the game goes to v_1, where p holds. In $\mathcal{G}_2$ instead, if agent a plays 2, then no matter what strategy is played by b, c has a way to reach v_2 where p does not hold. Observe that in Φ there is no universal quantifier under an existential one, so that white-box and black-box semantics coincide for this formula. □

4 Model Checking

In this section we show that model checking BSL[NG] with black-box semantics is 3-EXPTIME-complete.

4.1 Upper Bound

We establish the result for the flat fragment. It can then be lifted to BSL[NG] via a marking algorithm that evaluates independent subsentences in a bottom-up fashion. But first we recall the notion of alternation depth of a formula.

Definition 6. *The alternation depth of a formula in BSL[NG,f] is the maximum number of alternations between existential and universal strategy quantifiers.*

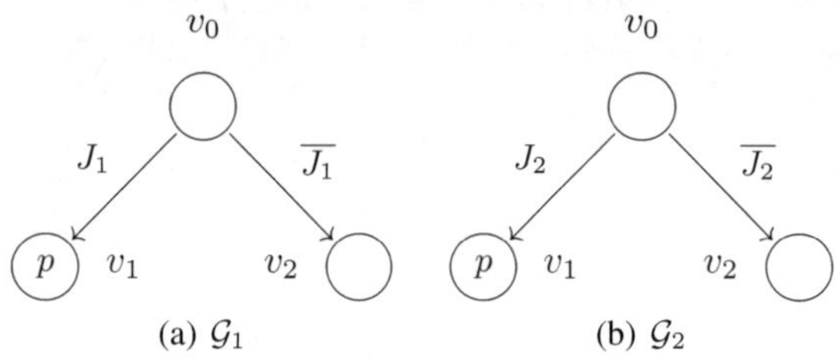

Figure 2: Games $\mathcal{G}_1$ and $\mathcal{G}_2$

We now establish the following about the flat fragment:

Proposition 3. *Model checking BSL[NG,f] with black-box semantics is in 3-EXPTIME.*

Proof. Let Φ be a formula in the flat fragment of BSL[NG]. It is of the form $\Phi = Q\phi$, where Q is a block of strategy quantifiers and ϕ contains no strategy quantifier. By Lemma 2, existential quantifiers in Q can be permuted with universal ones, thus obtaining an equivalent formula $\Phi' = Q'\phi$ where Q' consists of a block of existential strategy quantifiers followed by a block of universal ones. Φ' has alternation depth 1 and model checking BSL formulas with alternation depth k can be done in time at most $(k+2)$-exponential in the size of the formula (Berthon et al. 2021, Proposition 5.4).[3] □

Note that formulas obtained by the translation from ATL* to BSL[NG,f] presented in Section 3.3 have zero alternation of strategy quantifiers, so that they fall in a fragment of BSL[NG,f] whose model checking is actually in 2-EXPTIME, as for ATL*.

4.2 Lower Bound

We prove the following:

Proposition 4. *Model checking BSL[NG,f] with black-box semantics is 3-EXPTIME-hard.*

Proof. It is shown in (Laroussinie and Markey 2014, Theorem 4.11) that model checking EQ^kCTL^* is $(k+1)$-EXPTIME hard for $k > 0$, where EQ^kCTL^* is the fragment of Quantified CTL* with all second-order quantifiers at the beginning of the formula, starting with an existential quantification and with $k-1$ alternations. The reduction from model checking for Quantified CTL* to that of BSL with white-box semantics presented in (Laroussinie and Markey 2015; Berthon et al. 2021), when applied to formulas of EQ^kCTL^*, produces formulas in BSL[NG,f] with alternation $k-1$. Taking $k = 2$, we obtain formulas in which the

[3] More precisely (Berthon et al. 2021) considers a notion of *simulation depth* which allows for a finer analysis, and they prove that formulas with simulation depth k can be model checked in $(k+1)$-exponential time. Formulas of alternation depth k as defined here have simulation depth at most $k+1$, hence the result. Some formulas of alternation k have simulation depth only k, but defining simulation depth would be cumbersome and unnecessary to obtain our 3-EXPTIME upper bound.

only strategy quantifiers consist of an initial block of existential quantifiers followed by a block of universal ones. For such formulas, the black-box semantics coincides with the white-box one. We thus obtain the desired lower bound. □

Propositions 3 and 4 entail that:

Theorem 1. *Model checking* BSL[NG] *with black-box semantics is 3-EXPTIME-complete.*

Up to our knowledge, BSL[NG] is the first logic that strictly subsumes ATL*, can express Nash equilibria and subgame perfect Equilibria, and yet enjoys a model-checking problem with elementary complexity.

5 Strategy Logic with Mixed Announcements

We now introduce a logic that combines the white-box and black-box semantics, by allowing two kinds of strategy quantification: public (white-box) and private (black-box). This logic subsumes both BSL with white-box semantics and BSL with black-box semantics, and is written $\mathsf{BSL}_{\square\blacksquare}$.

Definition 7 (Syntax). *The set of* $\mathsf{BSL}_{\square\blacksquare}$ *formulas is given by the following grammar:*

$$\varphi ::= p \mid \neg\varphi \mid \varphi \vee \varphi \mid \exists^{\square} s\, \varphi \mid \exists^{\blacksquare} s\, \varphi \mid (a, s)\varphi \mid (a, \emptyset)\varphi \mid \mathbf{E}\psi$$
$$\psi ::= \varphi \mid \neg\psi \mid \psi \vee \psi \mid \mathbf{X}\psi \mid \psi\mathbf{U}\psi$$

where $p \in AP$, $a \in Ag$ *and* $s \in Var$.

Define $\forall^{\square} s\, \varphi = \neg\exists^{\square}\neg\varphi$ and $\forall^{\blacksquare} s\, \varphi = \neg\exists^{\blacksquare}\neg\varphi$. Strategy variables introduced by white-box quantifiers $\exists^{\square} s$ are called *publicly quantified*, while those introduced by black-box quantifiers $\exists^{\blacksquare} s$ are called *privately quantified*.

We now define the semantics $\models_{\square\blacksquare}$ of $\mathsf{BSL}_{\square\blacksquare}$ via yet another evaluation game, obtained by refining the information accessible to Eloise in the black-box evaluation games. More precisely, for a game $\mathcal{G}$ and a sentence Φ we define the evaluation game $\mathbb{G}_{\square\blacksquare}(\mathcal{G}, \Phi)$ as follows: the set of positions $V^{\square\blacksquare}_{\mathcal{G},\Phi}$ is again the union of

$$\{(\chi, \beta, h, \varphi, \mathrm{P}) \mid \varphi \in \mathrm{HistSub}(\Phi), \mathrm{P} \in \{\mathrm{E}, \mathrm{A}\}\} \text{ and}$$
$$\{(\chi, \beta, \pi, i, \psi, \mathrm{P}) \mid \psi \in \mathrm{OutSub}(\Phi), \mathrm{P} \in \{\mathrm{E}, \mathrm{A}\}\},$$

the initial position is $(\emptyset, \emptyset, v_0, \Phi, V)$, and moves are defined similarly to the games for white-box and black-box semantics. In particular, for the two types of strategy quantifiers, moves are as follows:

- $\exists^{\square} s$-positions: from $(\chi, \beta, h, \exists^{\square} s\, \varphi, \mathrm{P})$, P chooses some $\sigma \in \mathrm{Str}$ and moves to $(\chi[s \mapsto \sigma], \beta, h, \varphi, \mathrm{P})$.
- $\exists^{\blacksquare} s$-positions: from $(\chi, \beta, h, \exists^{\blacksquare} s\, \varphi, \mathrm{P})$, P chooses some $\sigma \in \mathrm{Str}$ and moves to $(\chi[s \mapsto \sigma], \beta, h, \varphi, \mathrm{P})$.

The only difference is in the definition of the equivalence relation on positions. Formally, we define $(\chi, \beta, h, \varphi, \mathrm{P}) \sim_{\square\blacksquare} (\chi', \beta', h', \varphi', \mathrm{P}')$ if $\beta = \beta'$, $h = h'$, $\varphi = \varphi'$, $\mathrm{P} = \mathrm{P}'$ and for all variables $s \in$ Var that are either existentially quantified or universally *publicly* quantified in Φ, we have $\chi(s) = \chi'(s)$; similarly for $(\chi, \beta, \pi, i, \psi, \mathrm{P}) \sim_{\square\blacksquare} (\chi', \beta', \pi', i', \psi', \mathrm{P}')$. Strategies of Eloise are defined on $[V^{\square\blacksquare}_{\mathcal{G},\Phi}]^*_{\sim_{\square\blacksquare}}$. The interpretation is that Eloise cannot observe which strategies are chosen by Abelard for universal black-box quantifiers.

Definition 8 (Mixed announcements semantics). *Let* $\mathcal{G}$ *be a game,* Φ *a* $\mathsf{BSL}_{\square\blacksquare}$ *sentence and* φ *a history subformula of* Φ. *Then* $\mathcal{G}, \chi, \beta, h \models_{\square\blacksquare} \varphi$ *if Eloise has a winning strategy in* $\mathbb{G}_{\square\blacksquare}(\mathcal{G}, \Phi)$ *from position* $(\chi, \beta, h, \varphi, \mathrm{E})$.

First, note that by definition of the semantics, and in particular by definition of $\sim_{\square\blacksquare}$, public or private quantification makes a difference only for *universal* quantification, so that we may write $\exists s$ instead of $\exists^{\square} s$ or $\exists^{\blacksquare} s$.

We now illustrate with two examples how BSL with mixed announcements can be used to model subtle scenarios in which agents in a system may or may not be informed of other agents' strategies.

Example 6. *Let us discuss another variant of the cop and robber game from Example 2 with two cops and one robber. Consider the* $\mathsf{BSL}_{\square\blacksquare}$ *formula:*

$$\Phi = \forall^{\blacksquare} s_1 \forall^{\blacksquare} t\, \exists s_2 (\textsc{Cop}_1, s_1)(\textsc{Cop}_2, s_2)(\textsc{Robber}, t)\textsc{Catch}$$

It expresses that the second cop can choose a strategy s_2 *ensuring a catch irrespective of both the strategies of the first cop* (s_1) *and of the robber* (t). *Note that here it is quite natural to require that* s_2 *does not depend on* t, *which is why* t *is quantified privately. Whether* s_2 *should be allowed to depend on* s_1 *or not depends on whether the two cops can communicate along a private channel, and the point of this example is to show that this can be formalised in* BSL *with mixed announcements.*

The formula above does not hold: $\mathcal{G} \not\models_{\square\blacksquare} \Phi$. *Indeed, to ensure a catch,* s_2 *should choose the direction not chosen by* s_2. *But since* s_1 *is kept private,* s_2 *cannot depend on it. However, by replacing* $\forall^{\blacksquare} s_1$ *with* $\forall^{\square} s_1$, *the formula becomes true on this game, because* s_2 *can make the opposite choice of* s_1 *to ensure a catch.*

Example 7. *All examples so far were one-step concurrent games. To illustrate the expressive power of strategy logic with mixed announcements, let us consider a multiagent system involving temporal reasoning. The game is called "cop and smuggler": at each time step, the smuggler chooses either* LEFT, RIGHT, *or* WAIT, *and the cop chooses either* LEFT *or* RIGHT. *If at some point the two choices coincide, the cop catches the robber. The outcome is illustrated in Figure 3. The objective of the smuggler is to smuggle as much as possible.*

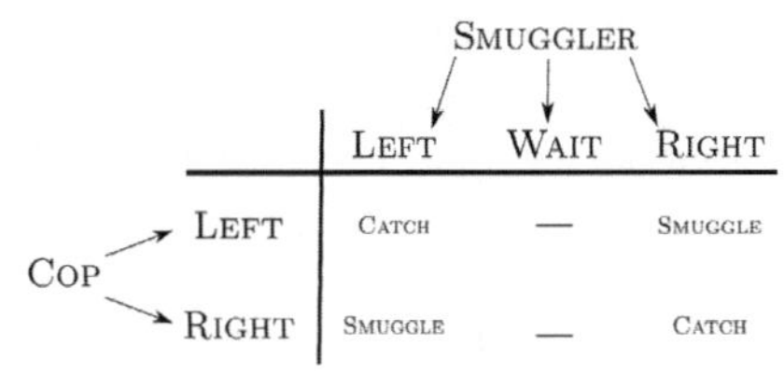

Figure 3: Cop and smuggler

Consider the $\mathsf{BSL}_{\square\blacksquare}$ *formula:*

$$\forall^{\square} t\, (\textsc{Smuggler}, t) \Big(\mathbf{AGF}\, (\textsc{Left} \vee \textsc{Right}) \rightarrow \exists s\, (\textsc{Cop}, s)\, \mathbf{F}\, \textsc{Catch}\Big)$$

It expresses that for all strategies of the robber that attempts to smuggle infinitely often, i.e., does not wait forever, there exists a catching strategy for the cop. The formula holds if t is publicly announced (as in the formula above), and it does not otherwise.

6 Conclusion

Strategy logic with black-box semantics is a natural logic for reasoning about agent-based scenarios in which agents do not announce their strategies. Its Nested-Goals fragment is situated in a middle ground between the expressiveness of SL with white-box semantics and the elementary complexity of ATL^*. Indeed, similarly to SL with white-box semantics, it can express certain complex solution concepts such as Nash equilibria. On the other hand, similarly to ATL^*, it has an elementary complexity, i.e., a 3-EXPTIME-complete model-checking problem, which is much closer to ATL^* (2-EXPTIME-complete) than SL with white-box semantics (non-elementary).

The behavioural semantics discussed in the related works, which also aims at obtaining a natural and expressive semantics for SL with good computational complexity, is defined only for the Nested-Goals fragment and relies on complex dependency maps. In contrast our black-box semantics is defined for the whole logic BSL via intuitive evaluation games with imperfect information.

One direction for future work is to establish the complexity of model checking the full BSL with black-box semantics, as well as that of the logic with mixed announcements $\mathsf{BSL}_{\square\blacksquare}$. Another would be to draw inspiration from independence-friendly logic (Mann, Sandu, and Sevenster 2011) and dependence logic (Väänänen 2007) to define a *team semantics* for Strategy Logic with private announcements. Indeed these logics study mechanisms of dependence among variables in classical logic, which is closely related to what we study here. Dependence logic considers semantics based on imperfect-information games, as we do, but also has a Tarski-style semantics based on *teams*: intuitively a formula is not evaluated with respect to a single assignment for free variables, but a set of assignments, which allows formalizing dependencies between variables.

References

Alur, R.; Henzinger, T. A.; and Kupferman, O. 2002. Alternating-time temporal logic. *J. ACM* 49(5):672–713.

Aminof, B.; Kwiatkowska, M.; Maubert, B.; Murano, A.; and Rubin, S. 2019. Probabilistic strategy logic. In Kraus, S., ed., *IJCAI'19*, 32–38. ijcai.org.

Belardinelli, F.; Jamroga, W.; Kurpiewski, D.; Malvone, V.; and Murano, A. 2019. Strategy logic with simple goals: Tractable reasoning about strategies. In Kraus, S., ed., *Proceedings of the Twenty-Eighth International Joint Conference on Artificial Intelligence, IJCAI 2019, Macao, China, August 10-16, 2019*, 88–94. ijcai.org.

Berthon, R.; Maubert, B.; Murano, A.; Rubin, S.; and Vardi, M. Y. 2021. Strategy logic with imperfect information. *ACM Trans. Comput. Log.* 22(1):5:1–5:51.

Čermák, P.; Lomuscio, A.; Mogavero, F.; and Murano, A. 2018. Practical verification of multi-agent systems against slk specifications. *Inf. Comput.* 261:588–614.

Cermák, P.; Lomuscio, A.; and Murano, A. 2015. Verifying and synthesising multi-agent systems against one-goal strategy logic specifications. In Bonet, B., and Koenig, S., eds., *Proceedings of the Twenty-Ninth AAAI Conference on Artificial Intelligence, January 25-30, 2015, Austin, Texas, USA*, 2038–2044. AAAI Press.

Chatterjee, K.; Henzinger, T. A.; and Piterman, N. 2010. Strategy Logic. *Inf. Comput.* 208(6):677–693.

Doyen, L., and Raskin, J.-F. 2011. Games with imperfect information: Theory and algorithms. In *Lectures in Game Theory for Computer Scientists*. 185–212.

Fijalkow, N.; Maubert, B.; Murano, A.; and Rubin, S. 2018. Quantifying bounds in strategy logic. In *CSL'18*, volume 23.

Gardy, P.; Bouyer, P.; and Markey, N. 2020. Dependences in strategy logic. *Theory Comput. Syst.* 64(3):467–507.

Henkin, L., and Karp, C. R. 1965. Some remarks on infinitely long formulas. *Journal of Symbolic Logic* 30(1).

Hintikka, J., and Sandu, G. 1997. Game-theoretical semantics. In van Benthem, J., and ter Meulen, A., eds., *Handbook of Logic and Language*. North Holland / Elsevier. 361–410.

Hintikka, J. 1998. Informational independence as a semantical phenomenon. In *Paradigms for Language Theory and Other Essays*. Springer. 52–70.

Hodges, W., and Väänänen, J. 2019. Logic and Games. In Zalta, E. N., ed., *The Stanford Encyclopedia of Philosophy*. Metaphysics Research Lab, Stanford University, Fall 2019 edition.

Knight, S., and Maubert, B. 2015. Dealing with imperfect information in strategy logic. In *SR'15*.

Laroussinie, F., and Markey, N. 2013. Satisfiability of ATL with strategy contexts. In *GandALF'13*, 208–223.

Laroussinie, F., and Markey, N. 2014. Quantified CTL: expressiveness and complexity. *Log. Methods Comput. Sci.* 10(4).

Laroussinie, F., and Markey, N. 2015. Augmenting ATL with strategy contexts. *Inf. Comput.* 245:98–123.

Mann, A. L.; Sandu, G.; and Sevenster, M. 2011. *Independence-friendly logic: A game-theoretic approach*, volume 386. Cambridge University Press.

Mogavero, F.; Murano, A.; Perelli, G.; and Vardi, M. Y. 2014. Reasoning about strategies: On the model-checking problem. *ACM Trans. Comput. Log.* 15(4):34:1–34:47.

Mogavero, F.; Murano, A.; Perelli, G.; and Vardi, M. 2017. Reasoning about strategies: on the satisfiability problem. *Logical Methods in Computer Science* 13(1).

Pnueli, A., and Rosner, R. 1989. On the synthesis of a reactive module. In *POPL'89*, 179–190.

Väänänen, J. 2007. *Dependence logic: A new approach to independence friendly logic*, volume 70. Cambridge University Press.

Compound Conditionals as Random Quantities and Boolean Algebras

Tommaso Flaminio[1] , **Angelo Gilio**[2,*] , **Lluis Godo**[1] , **Giuseppe Sanfilippo**[3]
[1]IIIA - CSIC, Campus de la UAB, Barcelona, Spain
[2]Department SBAI, University of Rome "La Sapienza", Rome, Italy (*retired)
[3] Department of Mathematics and Computer Science, University of Palermo, Palermo, Italy
{tommaso, godo}@iiia.csic.es, angelo.gilio@sbai.uniroma1.it, giuseppe.sanfilippo@unipa.it

Abstract

Conditionals play a key role in different areas of logic and probabilistic reasoning, and they have been studied and formalised from different angles. In this paper we focus on the de Finetti's notion of conditional as a three-valued object, with betting-based semantics, and its related approach as random quantity as mainly developed by two of the authors. Compound conditionals have been studied in the literature, but not in full generality. In this paper we provide a natural procedure to explicitly attach conditional random quantities to arbitrary compound conditionals that also allows us to compute their previsions. By studying the properties of these random quantities, we show that, in fact, the set of compound conditionals can be endowed with a Boolean algebraic structure. In doing so, we pave the way to build a bridge between the long standing tradition of three-valued conditionals and a more recent proposal of looking at conditionals as elements from suitable Boolean algebras.

1 Introduction

Conditional expressions are pivotal in representing knowledge and reasoning abilities of intelligent agents. Conditional reasoning features in a wide range of areas spanning non-monotonic reasoning (Adams 1975; Dubois and Prade 1994; Benferhat, Dubois, and Prade 1997; Kern-Isberner 2001; Gilio 2002; Gilio and Sanfilippo 2013b; Beierle et al. 2018), causal inference (Halpern 2016; van Rooij and Schulz 2019), and more generally reasoning under uncertainty (Halpern 2003; Coletti and Scozzafava 2002; Pfeifer and Sanfilippo 2017; Sanfilippo et al. 2018) or conditional preferences (Ghirardato 2002; Vantaggi 2010; Coletti, Petturiti, and Vantaggi 2019). Bruno de Finetti was one of the first who put forward an analysis of conditionals beyond the realm of conditional probability theory arguing that they cannot be described within the bounds of classical logic (de Finetti 1936; de Finetti 1937). He expressed this by referring to them as *trievents*: a conditional, denoted as $(a|b)$, is a basic object to be read "a given b" that turns out to be true if both a and b are true, false if a is false and b is true, and *void* if b is false.

The vast literature on conditionals also includes the study of *compound* conditionals, that is to say, those expressions obtained by combining basic conditionals like $(a|b)$ by usual logical operations of "and", "or", "negation" and so forth, see, e.g., (Schay 1968; Calabrese 1987; McGee 1989; Goodman, Nguyen, and Walker 1991; Jeffrey 1991; Edgington 1995; Milne 1997; Nguyen and Walker 1994; Stalnaker and Jeffrey 1994; Kaufmann 2009; Ciucci and Dubois 2013).

In this line, and based on de Finetti's original conception, (Gilio and Sanfilippo 2013a; Gilio and Sanfilippo 2014; Gilio and Sanfilippo 2019; Gilio and Sanfilippo 2020; Gilio and Sanfilippo 2021a; Gilio and Sanfilippo 2021b) propose and develop an approach to interpret both basic and compound conditionals as random quantities. This approach has been proved to allow for a suitable *numerical representation* of conditionals and some families of compound conditional expressions. Indeed, as we will recall in Section 2, starting from trivents $(a|b)$ regarded as random quantities taking values in a three-element set $\{0, 1, x\}$, where x is a real value in $[0, 1]$ representing a conditional probability, one can extend such representation also to cover more complex conditional formulas.

An alternative, more logically-oriented approach to conditionals has been put forward in e.g. (van Fraassen 1976) or (Goodman and Nguyen 1994)'s Conditional Event algebras, and more recently in (Flaminio, Godo, and Hosni 2020) in a finitary context. These papers formalise conditional expressions in an algebraic setting, and therefore provide a *symbolic representation* of them. In this approach, as it is common in logico-algebraic representations, neither basic expressions $(a|b)$ nor compound conditional formulas necessarily have a numerical counterpart, as their interpretation remains at the symbolic level. However, this does not forbid, as shown in (Flaminio, Godo, and Hosni 2020), to consider e.g. a fully compatible probabilistic layer on top of it.

In the present paper we will put forward an analysis that takes inspiration from both of the above settings and proposes a numerical representation of conditionals that, in addition, also allows for a logico-symbolic representation. In particular, we will:

- present a natural and uniform procedure to interpret compound conditionals as random quantities;
- investigate the numerical and logical properties of such a representation for compound conditionals via their associated random quantities; and
- prove that, at the logical level, the present approach, leads

to the same results of (Flaminio, Godo, and Hosni 2020), where the authors showed that compound symbolic conditionals can be endowed with a Boolean algebra structure.

Let us further remark that the apparent contradiction between the perspective that looks at three-valued conditionals as numerical random quantities as done, e.g., in (Gilio and Sanfilippo 2014; Gilio and Sanfilippo 2021a), and the Boolean algebraic perspective on conditionals used in (Flaminio, Godo, and Hosni 2020) to reason about them, actually dissolves once we precisely set at which level the numerical and the symbolic representation intervene. Proofs of main results can be found in the Arxiv version (Flaminio et al. 2022).

The present paper is organized as follows. In the next Section 2 we will recall in some more details the original approach of (de Finetti 1936) (Subsection 2.1) and the one that followed of (Gilio and Sanfilippo 2014) (Subsection 2.2). The interpretation of compound conditionals in terms of conditional random quantities will be the subject of Section 3. There we will also provide examples in order for our basic construction to be clear. In Section 4 we will then prove numerical and also logical properties of the random quantities that represent compound conditionals, and in Section 5 we will examine some probabilistic aspects. The comparison between the algebras arising from the random quantities studied here and the Boolean algebras of conditionals of (Flaminio, Godo, and Hosni 2020) will be the topic of Section 6, where we prove that they are indeed isomorphic. In the last Section 7 we will gather some conclusions and remarks about future work on this subject.

2 Some Preliminary Comments on Conjoined Conditionals

In this section, in order to better understand the formalism and results of this paper, we recall some notions given in the approach by Gilio-Sanfilippo, and their relation with the notions and results given here.

We will denote here events by capital letters, such as $A, B, H, K, \ldots$. Moreover, we denote random quantities by capital letters, such as $X, Y, Z \ldots$. In particular, X_A will denote the indicator function of an event A.

2.1 The Conditional Prevision in the Approach of de Finetti

Given a random quantity Z and an event $H \neq \bot$, in the approach of de Finetti (1935) the conditional prevision $\mathbb{P}(Z|H)$ can be assessed by applying the following conditional bet:

1) you are asked to assess the value $z = \mathbb{P}(Z|H)$, by knowing that if H is true then the bet is in effect;

2) if the bet has effect, then you pay z and you receive the random amount Z; otherwise, if H is false, the bet is null;

3) the checking of coherence for the assessment $z = \mathbb{P}(Z|H)$ is made by only considering the cases where the bet has effect.

We observe that for the random quantity $Z{\cdot}X_H + zX_{\overline{H}}$, by linearity of the prevision, it holds that

$$\mathbb{P}(Z{\cdot}X_H + zX_{\overline{H}}|H) = \mathbb{P}(Z{\cdot}X_H|H) + zP(\bar{H}|H) = \\ = \mathbb{P}(Z|H) + z\cdot 0 = \mathbb{P}(Z|H).$$

On the other hand,

$$\mathbb{P}(Z{\cdot}X_H + zX_{\overline{H}}) = \mathbb{P}(Z{\cdot}X_H) + zP(\bar{H}) = \\ = \mathbb{P}(Z|H)P(H) + zP(\bar{H}) = zP(H) + zP(\bar{H}) = z.$$

In other words, if $\mathbb{P}(Z|H) = z$, we have the following equalities:

$$\mathbb{P}(Z{\cdot}X_H + zX_{\overline{H}}) = \mathbb{P}(Z{\cdot}X_H + zX_{\overline{H}}|H) = \mathbb{P}(Z|H) = z. \tag{1}$$

Now, consider the random quantity $Z{\cdot}X_H + yX_{\overline{H}}$, under the assumptions that:

(i) $y = \mathbb{P}(Z{\cdot}X_H + yX_{\overline{H}})$;

(ii) in order to check the coherence of the assessment y, we discard the cases where you receive back the paid amount y (whatever y be), that is we discard the case where H is false (bet called off).

Of course, $y = z$ satisfies both (i) and (ii).

Question: is it coherent to assess $y \neq z$?

We show below that the answer is NO.
Indeed, if we make a bet on the random quantity

$$(Z{\cdot}X_H + zX_{\overline{H}}) - (Z{\cdot}X_H + yX_{\overline{H}}) = (z - y)X_{\overline{H}},$$

we should agree to pay $z - y$ by receiving $(z - y)X_{\overline{H}} \in \{0, z - y\}$. As when H is false we receive back the paid amount $z-y$ (whatever $z-y$ be), this case must be discarded for checking the coherence of the assessment $z - y$. Then, we should pay $z - y$ by knowing that (when the bet is not called off) we receive 0. Therefore, by coherence, $z-y = 0$, that is $y = z = \mathbb{P}(Z|H)$.

In other words, to assess the conditional prevision $\mathbb{P}(Z|H)$ is equivalent to assess the prevision $\mathbb{P}(Z{\cdot}X_H + zX_{\overline{H}})$. Thus, the conditional random quantity $Z|H$ can be defined as

$$Z|H = ZX_H + zX_{\overline{H}}, \text{ where } z = \mathbb{P}(ZX_H + zX_{\overline{H}}). \tag{2}$$

In this way we can look at z both as the conditional prevision $\mathbb{P}(Z|H)$ *à la de Finetti*, and as the prevision of the conditional random quantity $Z|H = ZX_H + zX_{\overline{H}}$. In particular, given two events A and $H \neq \emptyset$, if $x = \mathbb{P}(X_{AH} + xX_{\overline{H}})$, then $x = P(A|H)$ and hence

$$X_{A|H} = X_{AH} + P(A|H)X_{\overline{H}}. \tag{3}$$

Note that, as $ZX_H|H = Z|H$ and $X_{\overline{H}}|H = 0$, one has

$$(Z|H)|H = (ZX_H + zX_{\overline{H}})|H = \\ = ZX_H|H + zX_{\overline{H}}|H = Z|H.$$

Moreover, as $ZX_H|\bar{H} = 0$ and $X_{\overline{H}}|\bar{H} = 1$, it holds that

$$(Z|H)|\bar{H} = (ZX_H + zX_{\overline{H}})|\bar{H} = ZX_H|\bar{H} + zX_{\overline{H}}|\bar{H} = z.$$

2.2 The Conjunction in the Approach by Gilio & Sanfilippo

We recall that in the approach by Gilio and Sanfilippo the compound conditionals, like conjunctions and disjunctions, are defined as conditional random quantities, in the setting of coherence, see e.g. (Gilio and Sanfilippo 2014; Gilio and Sanfilippo 2019; Gilio and Sanfilippo 2021b). In this section, in order to make explicit the numerical aspects, we recall these notions by using the notations of the current paper. Then, the indicator of an event A, or a conditional event $A|H$ is denoted (not by the same symbol, but) by X_A, or $X_{(A|H)}$, respectively. Likewise, the conjunction $(A|H) \wedge (B|K)$ is denoted by $X_{(A|H)\wedge(B|K)}$, and so on.

In the setting of coherence, given a probability assessment $P(A|H) = x, P(B|K) = y$, the conjunction of $A|H$ and $B|K$ is defined as

$$X_{(A|H)\wedge(B|K)} = \begin{cases} 1, & \text{if } AHBK \text{ is true,} \\ 0, & \text{if } \bar{A}H \vee \bar{B}K \text{ is true,} \\ x, & \text{if } \bar{H}BK \text{ is true,} \\ y, & \text{if } AH\bar{K} \text{ is true,} \\ z, & \text{if } \bar{H}\bar{K} \text{ is true,} \end{cases} \quad (4)$$

where z is the prevision of $X_{(A|H)\wedge(B|K)}$, which (in the framework of the betting scheme) is the amount to be paid in order to receive the random amount $X_{(A|H)\wedge(B|K)}$. We observe that

$$X_{(A|H)\wedge(B|K)} = X_{AHBK} + xX_{\overline{H}BK} + yX_{AH\overline{K}} + zX_{\overline{H}\overline{K}}, \quad (5)$$

where $z = \mathbb{P}(X_{AHBK} + xX_{\overline{H}BK} + yX_{AH\overline{K}} + zX_{\overline{H}\overline{K}})$. Then, by applying (2), where H is replaced by $H \vee K$ and Z is replaced by $X_{AHBK} + xX_{\overline{H}BK} + yX_{AH\overline{K}}$, we have

$$Z \cdot X_{H\vee K} = (X_{AHBK} + xX_{\overline{H}BK} + yX_{AH\overline{K}})X_{H\vee K} = \\ = X_{AHBK} + xX_{\overline{H}BK} + yX_{AH\overline{K}},$$

and it follows that

$$X_{AHBK} + xX_{\overline{H}BK} + yX_{AH\overline{K}} + zX_{\overline{H}\overline{K}} = \\ = (X_{AHBK} + xX_{\overline{H}BK} + yX_{AH\overline{K}})|(H \vee K).$$

Hence, from (5) we obtain

$$X_{(A|H)\wedge(B|K)} = (X_{AHBK} + xX_{\overline{H}BK} + yX_{AH\overline{K}})|(H \vee K),$$

with

$$z = \mathbb{P}(X_{AHBK} + xX_{\overline{H}BK} + yX_{AH\overline{K}})|H \vee K) = \\ = P(AHBK|H \vee K) + xP(\bar{H}BK|H \vee K) + \quad (6) \\ + yP(AH\bar{K}|H \vee K).$$

We observe that, if $P(H \vee K) > 0$,

$$z = \frac{P(AHBK) + xP(\bar{H}BK) + yP(AH\bar{K})}{P(H \vee K)},$$

which is the well known formula given in (Kaufmann 2009) and in (McGee 1989).
In addition, by observing that

$$X_{(AHBK|H\vee K)} = X_{AHBK} + P(AHBK|H \vee K)X_{\overline{H}\overline{K}}, \\ xX_{(\overline{H}BK|H\vee K)} = xX_{\overline{H}BK} + xP(\bar{H}BK|H \vee K)X_{\overline{H}\overline{K}}, \\ yX_{(AH\overline{K}|H\vee K)} = yX_{AH\overline{K}} + yP(AH\bar{K}|H \vee K)X_{\overline{H}\overline{K}},$$

from (6) we obtain

$$X_{(AHBK|H\vee K)} + xX_{(\overline{H}BK|H\vee K)} + yX_{(AH\overline{K}|H\vee K)} \\ = X_{AHBK} + xX_{\overline{H}BK} + yX_{AH\overline{K}} + zX_{\overline{H}\overline{K}}.$$

Finally, $X_{(A|H)\wedge(B|K)}$ coincides with the random quantity $X_{(AHBK|H\vee K)} + xX_{(\overline{H}BK|H\vee K)} + yX_{(AH\overline{K}|H\vee K)}$.

In the next example we illustrate an application related to compound conditionals obtained when we consider a *double-bet* in soccer betting.

Example 2.1. Consider two soccer matches: (1) Barcelona–Real Madrid; (2) Juventus–Napoli. For each (uncancelled) match the possible outcomes are: *Home win*, *Draw*, and *Away win*. Let us consider two single bets on the events "Barcelona wins" and "Juventus draws". In a single bet, if a match is cancelled your stake will be refunded (the bet is called off). Then, actually, we have to consider two conditional bets: "Barcelona wins, given that match 1 is not cancelled" and "Juventus draws, given that match 2 is not cancelled". Define the events A ="Barcelona wins", B ="Juventus draws", H = "the match 1 is not cancelled", and K = "the match 2 is not cancelled". In the bet on $A|H$, with $P(A|H) = x$, you pay r and you receive $rQ_1X_{AH} + rX_{\overline{H}}$, where $Q_1 = \frac{1}{x}$. Similarly, in the bet on $B|K$, with $P(B|K) = y$, you pay r and you receive $rQ_2X_{BK} + rX_{\overline{K}}$, where $Q_2 = \frac{1}{y}$. A *double-bet* on "Barcelona wins and Juventus draws" is a linked series of the two single bets, where the return from one bet is automatically staked on the other bet. More precisely, you pay r by receiving the return on one bet, for instance $r(Q_1X_{AH} + X_{\overline{H}})$, which then is staked on the other bet, by receiving the global return $r(Q_1X_{AH} + X_{\overline{H}})(Q_2X_{BK} + X_{\overline{K}}) = rQ_1Q_2X_{AHBK} + rQ_2X_{\overline{H}BK} + rQ_1X_{AH\overline{K}} + rX_{\overline{H}\overline{K}}$. Notice that, if a match is cancelled, the bet will revert to a single bet on the remaining match, and if both matches are cancelled the double-bet is void and your stake will be refunded. In the particular case where $r = \frac{1}{Q_1Q_2} = xy$, it holds that $rQ_1Q_2 = 1$, $rQ_2 = x$, and $rQ_1 = y$; then, the random amount you receive becomes

$$X_{AHBK} + xX_{\overline{H}BK} + yX_{AH\overline{K}} + xyX_{\overline{H}\overline{K}},$$

which, from (5), coincides with $X_{(A|H)\wedge(B|K)}$, where $z = xy$. Then, the double-bet is a bet on the conjoined conditional $(A|H) \wedge (B|K)$ = "(Barcelona wins, given that match 1 is not cancelled) and (Juventus draws, given that match 2 is not cancelled)", where the prevision of the conjunction coincides with $P(A|H)P(B|K)$.

Notice that, under logical independence of the events A, H, B, K, the assessment $P(A|H) = x$, $P(B|K) = y$ and $\mathbb{P}[X_{(A|H)\wedge(B|K)}] = xy$ is coherent. Indeed, $xy \in [z', z'']$, where $z' = \max\{x + y - 1, 0\}$ and $z'' = \min\{x, y\}$ are the tightest lower and upper bounds for the coherent extensions $z = \mathbb{P}[X_{(A|H)\wedge(B|K)}]$ of the assessment (x, y) (Gilio and Sanfilippo 2014, Theorem 7). Likewise double-bets, multiple-bets can be formalized by exploiting the notion of conjunction of n conditional events.

2.3 Relation with the Present Approach

For notational convenience, in the rest of the paper we will use lower case letters for events involved in (compound) conditionals; hence, for instance, we will denote by $(a|b)$ a conditional event and by $(a|b) \wedge (c|d)$ the conjunction of $(a|b)$ and $(c|d)$. Moreover, in order to distinguish the logical aspects from the numerical ones, with each compound conditional t we will associate a suitable random quantity X_t, whose numerical values are the conditional previsions of some intermediate objects, called reducts. In particular, with the conjunction $(a|b) \wedge (c|d)$ we will associate a random quantity $X_{(a|b)\wedge(c|d)}$, whose numerical values are conditional previsions associated with the reducts determined by the following partition which corresponds to the one in (4): $\{abcd,\ \bar{a}b \vee \bar{c}d,\ \bar{b}cd,\ ab\bar{d},\ \bar{c}\bar{d}\}$. As we will see more in general later, the reducts associated with the elements of the partition above are denoted by $1,\ 0,\ (a|b),\ (c|d),\ (a|b) \wedge (c|d)$, respectively. From them we obtain the respective numerical values $1, 0, x, y, z$ of $X_{(a|b)\wedge(c|d)}$, which are interpreted by the following conditional previsions:

$$1 = \mathbb{P}(1|\Omega),\ 0 = \mathbb{P}(0|\Omega),\ x = \mathbb{P}(X_{(a|b)}|b),\\ y = \mathbb{P}(X_{(c|d)}|d),\ z = \mathbb{P}[X_{(a|b)\wedge(c|d)}|(c \vee d)].$$

We observe that, based on (2), it could be verified that

$$x = \mathbb{P}(X_{(a|b)}|b) = P(a|b),\ y = \mathbb{P}(X_{(c|d)}|d) = P(c|d),\\ z = \mathbb{P}[X_{(a|b)\wedge(c|d)}|(c \vee d)] = \mathbb{P}[X_{(a|b)\wedge(c|d)}].$$

Thus, $X_{(a|b)\wedge(c|d)}$ is nothing else than the conjunction between the conditional events $(a|b)$ and $(c|d)$ defined in (4). We remark that, by this approach, each compound conditional t is not explicitly defined, but we operate on it by means of the associated random quantity X_t.
Notice that, given a probability assessment $(x_1, \ldots, x_n)$ on a family $\{(a_1|b_1), \ldots, (a_n|b_n)\}$, where $x_i = P(a_i|b_i)$, the possible values of the random vector $(X_{(a_1|b_1)}, \ldots, X_{(a_n|b_n)})$ coincide with the so-called points Q_h's. By these points a geometrical approach for checking coherence and for propagation can be developed (Gilio and Sanfilippo 2020; Gilio and Sanfilippo 2021b).

3 General Compound Conditionals as Conditional Random Quantities

From now on we will be considering a fix *finite* Boolean algebra of ordinary events $\mathbf{A} = (A, \wedge, \vee, \neg, \bot, \top)$. For the sake of a lighter notation, we will also use ab for the conjunction $a \wedge b$ of events a and b, $\bar{a}$ for $\neg a$ of the event a, while we will keep denoting the disjunction of a and b by $a \vee b$.

In this setting, the set of the atoms $\mathrm{at}(\mathbf{A})$ of the algebra of events $\mathbf{A}$, can be identified with the set Ω of interpretations for $\mathbf{A}$, i.e. the set of Boolean algebra homomorphisms $w : \mathbf{A} \to \{0, 1\}$. Indeed, we will say that an event $a \in \mathbf{A}$ is *true* (resp. *false*) under an interpretation (or possible world) $w \in \Omega$ when $w(a) = 1$ (resp. $w(a) = 0$), also denoted as $w \models a$ (resp. $w \not\models a$).

As we anticipated in the previous section, conditional events of the form "if a then b", or "a given b", where a and b are events from $\mathbf{A}$ with b different from $\bot$, will be denoted by pairs $(a|b)$. We will also let $A|A' = \{(a|b) : a \in A, b \in A'\}$, where $A' = A\backslash\{\bot\}$, be the set of all conditionals that can be built from $\mathbf{A}$, that will be also called *basic conditionals. Compound conditionals*, then, are combinations of basic ones by operations of negation, conjunction and disjunction, that we will keep denoting them as $\neg, \wedge$ and $\vee$ without danger of confusion. Denote by $\mathbb{T}(A)$ the term algebra of type $(\wedge, \vee, \neg, \bot, \top)$ over the set $A|A'$, so that its support $\mathbb{T}(A)$ is the set of arbitrary terms generated from $A|A'$ (taken as variables) over the signature $(\neg, \wedge, \vee, \bot, \top)$. For instance, if $a, c, e \in A$ and $b, d, f \in A'$, then $(a|b) \wedge (c|d)$ or $(a|b) \vee ((c|d) \wedge \neg(e|f))$ are examples of compound conditionals from $\mathbb{T}(A)$. One of our ultimate aims will be to present a Boolean algebra obtained from $\mathbb{T}(A)$ that extends $\mathbf{A}$.

In the rest of the section we will further extend the random quantity-based approach to conditionals and propose an unambiguous procedure to interpret any compound conditional as a suitable random quantity.

For every $t \in \mathbb{T}(A)$, let us denote by $Cond(t) = \{(a_1|b_1), \ldots, (a_n|b_n)\}$ the set of basic conditionals appearing in t, and by $\mathbf{b}(t) = b_1 \vee \ldots \vee b_n$ the disjunction of the antecedents in $Cond(t)$.

Definition 3.1. Let $w \in \Omega$ be a classical interpretation and let $t \in \mathbb{T}(A)$ be a term. The *w-reduct* of t, denoted t^w, is the term in $\mathbb{T}(A)$, called the *w-reduct of* t, obtained from t by the following procedure:

(1) replace each $(a_i|b_i) \in Cond(t)$ by 1 if $w \models a_ib_i$, and by 0 if $w \models \bar{a}_ib_i$,
(2) apply the following reduction rules to subterms of t until no further reduction is possible:
$$\neg 1 := 0, \qquad \neg 0 := 1,$$
$$r \wedge 1 = 1 \wedge r := r, \quad r \wedge 0 = 0 \wedge r := 0, \quad \text{where the } r$$
$$r \vee 1 = 1 \vee r := 1, \quad r \vee 0 = 0 \vee r := r,$$
denotes a subterm of t.

This symbolic reduction procedure has some interesting properties. First of all, $w \models \neg\mathbf{b}(t)$, then no reduction is possible and hence $t^w = t$. Second, the reduction commutes with the operation symbols, in the following sense:

Lemma 3.2. *For every terms $t \in \mathbb{T}(A)$ and for every $w \in \Omega$, the following hold: (i) $(\neg t)^w = \neg t^w$; (ii) $(t \wedge s)^w = t^w \wedge s^w$; (iii) $(t \vee s)^w = t^w \vee s^w$.*

We will denote by $Red(t) = \{t^w | w \in \Omega$ the set of w-reducts of t, and by $Red^0(t) = Red(t)\backslash\{t\}$, the set of its *proper w-reducts*.

Example 3.3. Let $t = (a|b) \wedge ((c|d) \vee \neg(e|f))$ and let w such that $w(a) = 1, w(b) = 0, w(c) = 0, w(d) = 0, w(e) = 1, w(f) = 1$, i.e. $w \models a\bar{b}\bar{c}\bar{d}ef$. Then

$$t^w = (a|b) \wedge ((c|d) \vee \neg 1) = (a|b) \wedge ((c|d) \vee 0) = (a|b) \wedge (c|d).$$

Let w' such that $w' \models abc\bar{d}ef$. Then

$$t^{w'} = 1 \wedge ((c|d) \vee \neg 1) = (c|d) \vee 0 = (c|d).$$

Further, if w'' is such that $w'' \models abcdef$, then $t^{w''} = 1 \wedge (1 \vee \neg 1) = 1 \wedge (1 \vee 0) = 1$. In fact, one can check that $Red^0(t) = \{1, 0, (a|b), (c|d), \neg(e|f), (a|b) \wedge (c|d), (a|b) \wedge \neg(e|f), (c|d) \vee \neg(e|f)\}$.

Now, we recall the notion of conditional prevision of a random quantity.

Definition 3.4. Let $X : \Omega \to [0,1]$ be a random quantity, and let $b \in A$ be an event. Then, given a conditional probability $P : A \times A' \to [0,1]$, the *conditional prevision of* X *given* b is defined as:

$$\mathbb{P}(X|b) = \sum_{w \in \Omega} X(w) \cdot P(w|b) = \sum_{w \in \Omega : w \models b} X(w) \cdot P(w|b).$$

The next definition presents a suitable way to associate a random quantity to every compound conditional $t \in \mathbb{T}(A)$.

Definition 3.5. Let $\mathbf{A}$ be a finite Boolean algebra and $P : A \times A' \to [0,1]$ a conditional probability on $\mathbf{A}$. For every term t in $\mathbb{T}(A)$, we define the random quantity $X_t : \Omega \to [0,1]$ as follows: for every $w \in \Omega$,

$$X_t(w) := \mathbb{P}(X_{t^w}|\mathbf{b}(t^w)).$$

If $t^w = 1$ or $t^w = 0$, we take $\mathbf{b}(t^w) = \top$, and hence $X_1 = 1$ or $X_0 = 0$ respectively. Thus, $X_1(w) = 1$ or $X_0(w) = 0$.

Regarding this definition, some observations are in order here:
(i) As we have observed before, if $w \models \bar{\mathbf{b}}(t)$ then $t^w = t$, and thus $X_t(w) = \mathbb{P}(X_t|\mathbf{b}(t))$, and hence $\mathbb{P}(X_t|\bar{\mathbf{b}}(t)) = \mathbb{P}(X_t|\mathbf{b}(t))$.
(ii) The above definition of X_t strongly depends on the assumed conditional probability P of $A \times A'$. Actually, once we fix the initial conditional probability P on $A \times A'$, all random quantities X_t are fully determined. Indeed, the above Definition 3.5 is in fact a recursive definition, since

$$\mathbb{P}(X_{t^w}|\mathbf{b}(t^w)) = \sum_{w'} X_{t^w}(w') \cdot P(w'|\mathbf{b}(t^w)),$$

and in turn, $X_{t^w}(w') = \mathbb{P}(X_{(t^w)^{w'}}|\mathbf{b}((t^w)^{w'}))$, and so on, until reaching basic conditionals.
(iii) As a consequence, in general different conditional probabilities P and P' on $\mathbf{A}$ will define different random quantities X_t for the same term t.
(iv) In the case t is of the form $t = (a|\top)$, the associated random quantity X_t coincides with the indicator function of a, that is, $X_t(w) = 1$ whenever $w \models a$, and $X_t(w) = 0$ otherwise. This shows that $(a|\top)$ can indeed be indentified with the plain event a. In this case, for the sake of a lighter notation, we will write X_a instead of $X_{(a|\top)}$.

Notation 1. From now on, for simplicity, for any $t \in \mathbb{T}(A)$, we will write $\mathbb{P}^c(X_t)$ for $\mathbb{P}(X_t|\mathbf{b}(t))$.

Displayed in another way, the random quantity X_t can be specified as follows: let $Red^0(t) = \{t^w | w \in \Omega\} = \{t_1, t_2, ..., t_k\}$ and let $\{E_1, E_2, ..., E_k\}$ be the corresponding subsets of interpretations leading to a same element of $Red^0(t)$, then

$$X_t(w) = \mathbb{P}(X_{t^w}|\mathbf{b}(t^w)) = \\ = \begin{cases} \mathbb{P}^c(X_{t_1}), & \text{if } w \models E_1 \\ \dots, & \dots \\ \mathbb{P}^c(X_{t_k}), & \text{if } w \models E_k \\ \hdashline \mathbb{P}^c(X_t), & \text{if } w \models \neg(E_1 \vee \dots \vee E_k) \end{cases}$$

where the dashed line separates those cases where the interpretation w belongs to $\mathbf{b}(t)$ from those which do not.

In this setting, it is clear that X_t is in fact the following linear combination of the indicator functions of the events defining an associated partition:

$$X_t = \mathbb{P}^c(X_{t_1})X_{E_1} + \dots + \mathbb{P}^c(X_{t_k})X_{E_k} + \mathbb{P}^c(X_t)X_{E_{k+1}}$$

where $E_{k+1} = \bar{E}_1 \wedge \dots \wedge \bar{E}_k = \bar{\mathbf{b}}(t)$, and hence

$$\mathbb{P}^c(X_t) = \mathbb{P}^c(X_{t_1}) \cdot P(E_1|\mathbf{b}(t)) + \dots + \mathbb{P}^c(X_{t_k}) \cdot P(E_k|\mathbf{b}(t)).$$

We remark that, from (i) above and from (1), it holds that

$$\begin{aligned} &\mathbb{P}(X_t) = \mathbb{P}(X_t \cdot X_{\mathbf{b}(t)}) + \mathbb{P}(X_t \cdot X_{\bar{\mathbf{b}}(t)}) = \\ &= \mathbb{P}(X_t|\mathbf{b}(t))P(\mathbf{b}(t)) + \mathbb{P}(X_t|\bar{\mathbf{b}}(t))P(\bar{\mathbf{b}}(t)) = \\ &= \mathbb{P}^c(X_t)P(\mathbf{b}(t)) + \mathbb{P}^c(X_t)P(\bar{\mathbf{b}}(t)) = \mathbb{P}^c(X_t). \end{aligned} \tag{7}$$

In other words, formula (7) shows that the prevision of X_t coincides with the conditional prevision $\mathbb{P}^c(X_t)$.

We end this section by exemplifying the above definition of X_t for selected known cases of compound conditionals t that will be helpful in next sections.

Example 3.6. Let $t = (a|b)$. Then, by applying the above definition, we get

$$t^w = \begin{cases} 1, & \text{if } w \models ab \\ 0, & \text{if } w \models \bar{a}b \\ (a|b), & \text{if } w \models \bar{b} \end{cases} \qquad \mathbf{b}(t^w) = \begin{cases} \top, & \text{if } w \models ab \\ \top, & \text{if } w \models \bar{a}b \\ b, & \text{if } w \models \bar{b} \end{cases}$$

and thus we have:

$$X_{(a|b)}(w) = \mathbb{P}(X_{t^w}|\mathbf{b}(t^w)) = \\ = \begin{cases} \mathbb{P}(X_1|\top) = 1, & \text{if } w \models ab \\ \mathbb{P}(X_0|\top) = 0, & \text{if } w \models \bar{a}b \\ \mathbb{P}(X_{(a|b)}|b), & \text{if } w \models \bar{b} \end{cases} .$$

Now, since $P(w|b) = 0$ whenever $w \models \bar{b}$, we have

$$\begin{aligned} &\mathbb{P}(X_{(a|b)}|b) = \\ &= 1 \cdot P(ab|b) + 0 \cdot P(\bar{a}b|b) + \mathbb{P}(X_{(a|b)}|b) \cdot 0 = \\ &= P(ab|b) = P(a|b). \end{aligned}$$

Therefore we get the following well-known three-valued representation of a conditional $(a|b)$:

$$X_{(a|b)}(w) = \begin{cases} 1, & \text{if } w \models ab \\ 0, & \text{if } w \models \bar{a}b \\ P(a|b), & \text{if } w \models \bar{b} \end{cases} .$$

Equivalently, in agreement with (3), $X_{(a|b)}$ can be expressed as the following linear combination of the indicator functions of the events ab and $\bar{b}$:

$$X_{(a|b)} = 1X_{ab} + 0X_{\bar{a}b} + P(a|b)X_{\bar{b}} = X_{ab} + P(a|b)X_{\bar{b}}.$$

Example 3.7. Now let $t = \neg(a|b)$, the negation of $(a|b)$. Then, by applying the above definition, we get:

$$t^w = \begin{cases} \neg 1 := 0, & \text{if } w \models ab \\ \neg 0 := 1, & \text{if } w \models \bar{a}b \\ \neg(a|b), & \text{if } w \models \bar{b} \end{cases} ,$$

$$\mathbf{b}(t^w) = \begin{cases} \top, & \text{if } w \models ab \\ \top, & \text{if } w \models \bar{a}b \\ b, & \text{if } w \models \bar{b} \end{cases},$$

and thus we have: $X_{\neg(a|b)}(w) =$

$$= \mathbb{P}(X_{t^w}|\mathbf{b}(t^w)) = \begin{cases} 0, & \text{if } w \models ab \\ 1, & \text{if } w \models \bar{a}b \\ \mathbb{P}(X_{\neg(a|b)}|b), & \text{if } w \models \bar{b} \end{cases}.$$

Now, since $P(w|b) = 0$ whenever $w \models \neg b$, we have

$$\begin{aligned} &\mathbb{P}(X_{\neg(a|b)}|b) = \\ &= 0 \cdot P(ab|b) + 1 \cdot P(\bar{a}b|b) + \mathbb{P}(X_{\neg(a|b)}|b) \cdot 0 \\ &= P(\bar{a}b|b) = P(\bar{a}|b) = 1 - P(a|b). \end{aligned}$$

Therefore the final expression for $X_{\neg(a|b)}$ is

$$X_{\neg(a|b)}(w) = \begin{cases} 0, & \text{if } w \models ab \\ 1, & \text{if } w \models \bar{a}b \\ 1 - P(a|b), & \text{if } w \models \bar{b} \end{cases}.$$

That is to say, $X_{\neg(a|b)} = 1 - X_{(a|b)} = X_{(\bar{a}|b)}$.

Example 3.8. Let us examine again the case of a conjunction of two conditionals $t = (a|b) \wedge (c|d)$ from the current perspective. Here we have $\mathbf{b}(t) = b \vee d$, and

$$X_t(w) = \begin{cases} 1, & \text{if } w \models abcd \\ 0, & \text{if } w \models (\bar{a}b) \vee (\bar{c}d) \\ \mathbb{P}^c(a|b), & \text{if } w \models b\bar{c}d \\ \mathbb{P}^c(c|d), & \text{if } w \models ab\bar{d} \\ \hdashline \mathbb{P}^c((a|b) \wedge (c|d)), & \text{if } w \models \bar{b}\bar{d} \end{cases}$$

Now, we know that $\mathbb{P}^c(a|b) = P(a|b)$ and $\mathbb{P}^c(c|d) = P(c|d)$. Then, using the above definition we get:

$$\begin{aligned} \mathbb{P}^c((a|b) \wedge (c|d)) &= \mathbb{P}(X_{(a|b) \wedge (c|d)}|b \vee d) \\ &= P(abcd|b \vee d) + P(a|b) \cdot P(\bar{b}cd|b \vee d) + \\ &+ P(c|d) \cdot P(ab\bar{d}|b \vee d), \end{aligned}$$

that coincides, when $P(b \vee d) > 0$, with the formula given in (McGee 1989; Kaufmann 2009).

Let us now consider two particular cases:

- First, consider the case $a \leqslant b = c \leqslant d$. Then $t = (a|b) \wedge (b|d)$, $\mathbf{b}(t) = b \vee d = d$, and moreover:
  - $abcd = abd = ad = a$
  - $(\bar{a}b) \vee (\bar{c}d) = (\bar{a}b) \vee (\bar{b}d) = (\bar{a}bd) \vee (\bar{a}\bar{b}d) = \bar{a}d$
  - $\bar{b}cd = \bar{b}b = \bot$
  - $ab\bar{d} = a\bar{d} = \bot$

  Hence, the above general definition reduces to:

$$X_{(a|b) \wedge (b|d)}(w) = \begin{cases} 1, & \text{if } w \models a \\ 0, & \text{if } w \models \bar{a}d \\ \mathbb{P}^c((a|b) \wedge (b|d)), & \text{if } w \models \bar{d} \end{cases}$$

  where $\mathbb{P}^c((a|b) \wedge (b|d)) = 1 \cdot P(a|d) = P(a|d) = \mathbb{P}^c((a|d))$ and thus $X_{(a|b) \wedge (b|d)}(w) = X_{(a|d)}(w)$ for all w. Thus, from the numerical point of view, the compound conditional $(a|b) \wedge (b|d)$ behaves as the basic conditional $(a|d)$. See also (Gilio and Sanfilippo 2020, formulas (55) and (56)) where it is also observed that $P(a|d) = P(a|b)P(b|d)$ (*compound probability theorem*).

- Consider now the case $b = d$. Then $t = (a|b) \wedge (c|b)$ and $\mathbf{b}(t) = b$. In this case the above general expression reduces to the following one:

$$X_t(w) = \begin{cases} 1, & \text{if } w \models abc \\ 0, & \text{if } w \models (\bar{a} \vee \bar{c})b = \overline{ac}b \\ \mathbb{P}^c((a|b) \wedge (c|b)), & \text{if } w \models \bar{b}, \end{cases}$$

  where $\mathbb{P}^c((a|b) \wedge (c|b)) = 1 \cdot P(abc|b) = P(ac|b) = \mathbb{P}^c((ac|b))$, and therefore it is clear that $X_{(a|b) \wedge (c|b)}(w) = X_{(a \wedge c|b)}(w)$ for all w. Thus, in this case, we see that the compound conditional $(a|b) \wedge (c|b)$ actually behaves like the basic conditional $(a \wedge c|b)$.

Example 3.9. Finally, let us consider a more complex compound conditional $t = (a|b) \wedge ((c|d) \vee \neg(e|f))$. Again, by the above definition, we get its associated random quantity:

$$X_t(w) = \begin{cases} 1, & \text{if } w \models ab(cd \vee \bar{e}b) \\ 0, & \text{if } w \models \bar{a}b \vee \bar{c}def \\ \mathbb{P}^c((a|b)), & \text{if } w \models b(cd \vee \bar{e}f) \\ \mathbb{P}^c((a|b) \wedge (c|d)), & \text{if } w \models \bar{b}def \\ \mathbb{P}^c((a|b) \wedge \neg(e|f)), & \text{if } w \models \bar{b}\bar{c}d\bar{f} \\ \mathbb{P}^c((c|d)), & \text{if } w \models ab\bar{d}ef \\ \mathbb{P}^c(\neg(e|f)), & \text{if } w \models ab\bar{c}d \\ \mathbb{P}^c((c|d) \vee \neg(e|f)), & \text{if } w \models ab\bar{d}\bar{f} \\ \hdashline y, & \text{if } w \models \bar{b}\bar{d}\bar{f} \end{cases}$$

where $y = \mathbb{P}^c((a|b) \wedge ((c|d) \vee \neg(e|f)))$, and for simplicity, we have written $\mathbb{P}^c(s)$ for $\mathbb{P}^c(X_s)$, i.e. for $\mathbb{P}(X_s|\mathbf{b}(s))$.

We end this section with the following remark on a betting interpretation for compound conditionals $t \in \mathbb{T}(A)$. A bet between a gambler and a bookmaker on X_t is specified as follows:

- The gambler pays to the bookmaker: $\mathbb{P}^c(X_t)$
- In a situation $w \in \Omega$, the gambler receives from the bookmaker: $X_t(w) = \mathbb{P}^c(X_{t^w})$

Note that if $w \models \neg\mathbf{b}$ then $t^w = t$, and thus $\mathbb{P}^c(X_{t^w}) = \mathbb{P}^c(X_t)$, i.e. what the gambler receives is what he has payed, i.e. it represents the situation in which the bet is called off. We observe that coherence requires that the prevision of the random gain must be equal to zero. Indeed, given t, X_t is specified as:

$$X_t(w) = \begin{cases} \mathbb{P}^c(X_{E_1}), & \text{if } w \models E_1 \\ \dots & \dots \\ \mathbb{P}^c(X_{E_k}), & \text{if } w \models E_k \\ \hdashline \mathbb{P}^c(X_t), & \text{if } w \models \neg(E_1 \vee \dots \vee E_k) \end{cases}.$$

In this setting, the balance of the betting for the bookmaker in a given situation w such that $w \models E_i$ is what he receives, $\mathbb{P}(X_t)$, minus what he pays to the gambler, X_t, that is:

$$G(w) = \mathbb{P}(X_t) - X_t(w) = \mathbb{P}^c(X_t) - \mathbb{P}^c(X_{E_i}).$$

Moreover, when $w \models \mathbf{b}(t)$, it holds that $G(w) = \mathbb{P}^c(X_t) - \mathbb{P}^c(X_t) = 0$. Then, the prevision of the random quantity G of the balance will be:

$$\begin{aligned} &\mathbb{P}(G) = \textstyle\sum_{w \in \Omega} G(w)P(w|\mathbf{b}(t)) = \\ &= \textstyle\sum_{i=1}^k (\mathbb{P}^c(X_t) - \mathbb{P}^c(X_{E_i}))P(E_i|\mathbf{b}(t)) = \\ &= \mathbb{P}^c(X_t) \textstyle\sum_{i=1}^k P(E_i|\mathbf{b}(t)) - \sum_{i=1}^k \mathbb{P}^c(X_{E_i})P(E_i|\mathbf{b}(t)) = \\ &= \mathbb{P}^c(X_t) - \mathbb{P}^c(X_t) = 0. \end{aligned}$$

Remark 3.10. Example 2.1 can be generalized to compound conditionals. For instance, we can construct a bet on the disjunction $t = (a|b) \vee (c|d)$, or on the compound $t = (a|b) \vee (c|d) \wedge (e|f)$, and so on.

4 Properties of Compound Conditionals

In this section we show some key properties of the random quantities associated to certain forms of compound quantities that will allow us to show they can be endowed somehow with a Boolean algebraic structure

We start by showing that if two compound conditional terms t and t' are such that $\mathbf{b}(t) \equiv \mathbf{b}(t')$, to check whether they have the same associated random quantity, it is enough to check whether the random quantities take the same value over those worlds satisfying the disjunction $\mathbf{b}(t)$. A related result is given in (Gilio and Sanfilippo 2014, Theorem 4).

Lemma 4.1. *Let $t, t' \in \mathbb{T}(A)$ such that $\mathbf{b}(t) \equiv \mathbf{b}(t')$ and $X_t(w) = X_{t'}(w)$ for each $w \in \Omega$ such that $w \models \mathbf{b}(t)$. Then $X_t = X_{t'}$.*

Proof. It is enough to show that $X_t(w) = X_{t'}(w)$ when $w \models \neg\mathbf{b}(t)$. Due to the fact that if $w \models \neg\mathbf{b}(t)$ then $X_t(w) = \mathbb{P}(X_t|\mathbf{b}(t))$, this is equivalent to show that $\mathbb{P}(X_t|\mathbf{b}(t)) = \mathbb{P}(X_{t'}|\mathbf{b}(t))$. But these previsions only depend on the values of X_t and $X_{t'}$ on w's such that $w \models \mathbf{b}(t)$, and by hypothesis they coincide. □

Clearly, if $\mathbf{b}(t) \equiv \mathbf{b}(t')$ and $t^w = t'^w$ then $X_t(w) = \mathbb{P}(X_{t^w}|\mathbf{b}(t)) = \mathbb{P}(X_{t'^w}|\mathbf{b}(t)) = X_{t'}(w)$. Hence we have the following corollary.

Corollary 4.2. *If $\mathbf{b}(t) = \mathbf{b}(t')$ and $t^w = t'^w$ for each $w \in \Omega$ such that $w \models \mathbf{b}(t)$, then $X_t = X_{t'}$.*

Proposition 4.3. *Let $t \in \mathbb{T}(A)$ and let s be a subterm of t. Further let $s' \in \mathbb{T}(A)$ such that $\mathbf{b}(s) = \mathbf{b}(s')$ and $X_{s^w} = X_{s'^w}$ for all $w \models \mathbf{b}(s)$, and let t' be the term obtained by uniformly replacing s by s' in t. Then $X_t = X_{t'}$.*

Proof. It follows from the recursive definition of X_t and that, for any $w \in \Omega$, t^w can be computed from the w-reducts of its subterms (Lemma 3.2). □

Next we show that the random quantities for compound conditionals satisfy properties very familiar from a Boolean algebraic perspective.

Proposition 4.4. *For every $t, s, r \in \mathbb{T}(A)$ the following conditions hold:*

1. $X_t = X_{t\wedge t}$;
2. $X_{t\wedge s} = X_{s\wedge t}$;
3. $X_{t\wedge(s\wedge r)} = X_{(t\wedge s)\wedge r}$;
4. $X_{t\wedge\neg t} = 0$;
5. $X_{\neg(t\wedge s)} = X_{\neg t\vee\neg s}$;
6. $X_{t\wedge(s\vee r)} = X_{(t\wedge s)\vee(t\wedge r)}$;
7. $X_{t\vee s} = X_t + X_s - X_{t\wedge s}$;
8. $X_{\neg t} = 1 - X_t$ *and hence* $X_{\neg\neg t} = X_t$;
9. *If* $a \leqslant b$, *then* $X_{(a|b)\wedge(a|b\vee c)} = X_{a|b\vee c}$

The proof of Proposition 4.4 is not included due to lack of space, but we notice that items (1)-(8) are proved in a similar way by induction on the complexity of the terms involved, and where the base cases are those only involving basic conditionals. Many of these base cases are proved in previous examples.

Now we show that compound conditionals actually form a Boolean algebra. In order to do it we first properly arrange the compound conditionals in equivalence classes each of which contains terms from $\mathbb{T}(A)$ that provides the same random quantity under *any* given conditional probability.

More precisely, recalling observation (ii) after Def. 3.5, let us define the binary relation $\equiv$ on $\mathbb{T}(A)$ as follows: for all $t, s \in \mathbb{T}(A)$, $t \equiv s$ iff $X_t = X_s$ under any conditional probability P on $A \times A'$.

It is immediate to check that $\equiv$ is an equivalence relation. Thus, let $\mathbb{T}(A)$ to be the quotient $\mathbb{T}(A)/\equiv$. If we denote by $[t]$ the equivalence class of a generic term $t \in \mathbb{T}(A)$ under $\equiv$, define operations on $\mathbb{T}(A)$ as follows: for all $[t], [s] \in \mathbb{T}(A)$, $[t]\wedge^*[s] = [s\wedge t]$, $[t]\vee^*[s] = [s\vee t]$, $\neg^*[t] = [\neg t]$, $0 = [(\bot|\top)]$, $1 = [(\top|\top)]$.

By Proposition 4.3, the above operations are well defined. Moreover, the following holds:

Theorem 4.5. *For every finite Boolean algebra $\mathbf{A}$, the structure $\mathcal{T}(\mathbf{A}) = (\mathbb{T}(A)/\equiv, \wedge^*, \vee^*, \neg^*, 0, 1)$ is a Boolean algebra.*

Proof. By Proposition 4.4, the operations $\wedge^*, \vee^*, \neg^*$ and constants $0, 1$ satisfy all the required equations for $\mathcal{T}(\mathbf{A})$ being a Boolean algebra. □

Remark 4.6. Notice that, given $[t]$ and $[s]$ in $\mathcal{T}(\mathbf{A})$, $[t] \leqslant [s]$ in the lattice order of $\mathcal{T}(\mathbf{A})$ iff $[t] \wedge^* [s] = [t]$ iff $[t \wedge s] = [t]$ iff $X_{t\wedge s} = X_t$.

Next proposition shows that well-known properties of conditionals also hold in the setting of the present paper.

Proposition 4.7. *The following properties hold in $\mathcal{T}(\mathbf{A})$:*

(i) $[(a|a)] = 1$
(ii) $[(a|b) \wedge (c|b)] = [(a \wedge c|b)]$
(iii) $[\neg(a|b)] = [(\bar{a}|b)]$
(iv) $[(a \wedge b|b)] = [(a|b)]$
(v) $[(a|b) \wedge (b|c)] = [(a|c)]$, *if* $a \leqslant b \leqslant c$
(vi) *if* $a \leqslant b$, *then* $[(a|b \vee c)] \leqslant [(a|b)]$ *for all* c.

Proof. For each one of the equalities above, of the form $[t] = [s]$, we proved in previous examples, that $X_t = X_s$. As for the last claim, apply Proposition 4.4 (9). Then the claim follows by the definition of $\mathcal{T}(\mathbf{A})$. □

5 Probability of Compound Conditionals

Since $\mathcal{T}(\mathbf{A})$ is a Boolean algebra, we are allowed to define probabilities on it. In this section we will show that the previsions $\mathbb{P}(X_t)$'s of the random quantities X_t's determine in fact a probability on $\mathcal{T}(\mathbf{A})$.

Definition 5.1. Given a conditional probability $P : A \times A' \to [0, 1]$, we define the mapping $P^* : \mathbb{T}(A) \to [0, 1]$ as follows: for every $t \in \mathbb{T}(A)$, $P^*(t) =_{def} \mathbb{P}(X_t)$. In other words, based on (7)

$$P^*(t) = \mathbb{P}(X_t) = \mathbb{P}^c(X_t) = \mathbb{P}(X_t|\mathbf{b}(t)) = \\ = \sum_w X_t(w) \cdot P(w|\mathbf{b}(t)) = \sum_w \mathbb{P}^c(X_{t^w}) \cdot P(w|\mathbf{b}(t)).$$

From the above definition, it is cleat that if t and t' are terms such $t \equiv t'$, then $P^*(t) = P^*(t')$.

Proposition 5.2. *Any given conditional probability $P : A \times A' \to [0,1]$ fully determines the probabilities $P^*(t)$ for all compound conditional $t \in \mathbb{T}(A)$.*

Proof. Let $t \in \mathbb{T}(A)$ such that $Cond(t) = \{(a_1|b_1), \ldots, (a_n|b_n)\}$. We have seen that $P^*((a_i|b_i)) = P(a_i|b_i)$. Suppose that for every $s \in Red^0(t)$, there is a family of conditionals $C_s \subseteq A \times A'$ such that $P^*(s)$ is of the form $P^*(s) = f_s(\{P(c_i|d_i) : (c_i|d_i) \in C_s\})$ for some function f_s. Then, by definition, we have

$$P^*(t) = \mathbb{P}(X_t) = \sum_{w \in W} \mathbb{P}^c(X_{t^w}) \cdot P(w|\mathbf{b}(t)) = \\ = \sum_{w \in W} P^*(t^w) \cdot P(w|\mathbf{b}(t)) = \\ = \sum_{w \in W} f_{t^w}(\{P(c|d) : (c|d) \in C_{t^w}\}) \cdot P(w|\mathbf{b}(t)),$$

the latter expression clearly only depending on P. □

Moreover, the following is a direct consequence of Proposition 4.4.

Corollary 5.3. *For every $t, s, r \in \mathbb{T}(A)$ the following conditions hold:*

1. $P^*(t) = P^*(t \wedge t)$
2. $P^*(t \wedge s) = P^*(s \wedge t)$
3. $P^*(t \wedge (s \wedge r)) = P^*((t \wedge s) \wedge r)$
4. $P^*(t \wedge \neg t) = 0.$
5. $P^*(\neg(t \wedge s)) = P^*(\neg t \vee \neg s)$
6. $P^*(t \wedge (s \vee r)) = P^*((t \wedge s) \vee (t \wedge r))$
7. $P^*(t) = 1$ *if* $X_t = 1$
8. $P^*(t) = 0$ *if* $X_t = 0$
9. $P^*(t \vee s) = P^*(t) + P^*(s) - P^*(t \wedge s)$
10. $P^*(\neg t) = 1 - P^*(t).$

Notice that the items 6,7,8, and 9 of the above corollary together with the above remarked fact that $t \equiv t'$ implies $P^*(t) = P^*(t')$, show that P^* naturally induces a probability on the algebra $\mathcal{T}(\mathbf{A})$ that we will still denote by the same symbol.

Corollary 5.4. *For every conditional probability P on $A \times A'$ the map P^* is a probability measure on $\mathcal{T}(\mathbf{A})$.*

Furthermore, as we have checked in Example 3.6, for every basic conditional $(a|b)$ we have $P^*((a|b)) = P(a|b)$, thus complying with *the Equation* (Edgington 1995), or *Stalnaker's hypothesis*, see, e.g., (Douven and Dietz 2011; Sanfilippo et al. 2020). The next example shows how to compute the probability P^* of a (more complex) compound conditional.

Example 5.5. Continuing the above Example 3.9 for $t = (a|b) \wedge ((c|d) \vee \neg(e|f))$, we have $\mathbf{b}(t) = b \vee d \vee f$ and using the above Definition 5.1 we get:

$$P^*(t) = \mathbb{P}(X_t) = \mathbb{P}(X_t|\mathbf{b}(t)) = P(abcd \vee \bar{e}f)|b \vee d \vee f) + \\ + P(a|b)P(\bar{b}(cd \vee \bar{e}f)|b \vee d \vee f) + \\ + P^*((a|b) \wedge (c|d))P(\bar{b}\bar{d}ef|b \vee d \vee f) + \\ + P^*((a|b) \wedge \neg(e|f))P(\bar{b}\bar{c}d\bar{f}|b \vee d \vee f) + \\ + P(c|d)P(ab\bar{d}ef|b \vee d \vee f) + \\ + (1 - P(e|f))P(ab\bar{c}d|b \vee d \vee f) + \\ + P^*((c|d) \vee \neg(e|f))P(ab\bar{d}\bar{f}|b \vee d \vee f).$$

6 Boolean Algebras of Random Variables and Boolean Algebras of Conditionals

The above Theorem 4.5, tells us that the random quantities that represent conditionals form a Boolean algebra. Actually, in (Flaminio, Godo, and Hosni 2020), the authors presented a way to construct Boolean algebras of conditionals that also represent conditional statements, although following a different line of thoughts.

For the sake of clarity, let us briefly recall how a Boolean algebras of conditional $\mathcal{C}(\mathbf{A})$ is defined for every Boolean algebra $\mathbf{A}$. Consider the free Boolean algebra Free$(A|A)$ generated by the set $A|A$ of all pairs $(a, b) \in A \times A$ such that $b \neq \bot$, in the language $\wedge, \vee, \neg, \top^*$. Every pair $(a, b) \in A|A$ will be henceforth denoted by $(a|b)$. Then, one considers the following set of basic requirements the algebra $\mathcal{C}(\mathbf{A})$ should satisfy:

(R1) For all $b \in A'$, the conditional $(b|b)$ will be the top element of $\mathcal{C}(\mathbf{A})$ and $(\neg b|b)$ will be the bottom;

(R2) Given $b \in A'$, the set of conditionals $A|b = \{(a|b) : a \in A\}$ will be the domain of a Boolean subalgebra of $\mathcal{C}(\mathbf{A})$, and in particular when $b = \top$, this subalgebra will be isomorphic to $\mathbf{A}$;

(R3) In a conditional $(a|b)$ we can replace the consequent a by $a \wedge b$, that is, the conditionals $(a|b)$ and $(a \wedge b|b)$ represent the same element of $\mathcal{C}(\mathbf{A})$;

(R4) For all $a \in A$ and all $b, c \in A'$, if $a \leqslant b \leqslant c$, then the result of conjunctively combining the conditionals $(a|b)$ and $(b|c)$ must yield the conditional $(a|c)$.

Notice that (R4) encodes a sort of restricted chaining of conditionals and it is inspired by the chain rule of conditional probabilities: $P(a|b) \cdot P(b|c) = P(a|c)$ whenever $a \leqslant b \leqslant c$.

One then proceeds by considering the smallest congruence relation $\equiv_{\mathfrak{C}}$ on Free$(A|A)$ satisfying:

(C1) $(b|b) \equiv_{\mathfrak{C}} \top^*$, for all $b \in A'$;

(C2) $(a_1|b) \wedge (a_2|b) \equiv_{\mathfrak{C}} (a_1 \wedge a_2|b)$, for all $a_1, a_2 \in A$, $b \in A'$;

(C3) $\neg(a|b) \equiv_{\mathfrak{C}} (\bar{a}|b)$, for all $a \in A$, $b \in A'$;

(C4) $(a \wedge b|b) \equiv_{\mathfrak{C}} (a|b)$, for all $a \in A$, $b \in A'$;

(C5) $(a|b) \wedge (b|c) \equiv_{\mathfrak{C}} (a|c)$, for all $a \in A$, $b, c \in A'$ such that $a \leqslant b \leqslant c$.

Note that (C1)-(C5) faithfully account for the requirements R1-R4 where, in particular, (C2) and (C3) account for R2. Finally, the algebra $\mathcal{C}(\mathbf{A})$ is formally defined as follows.

Definition 6.1. For every Boolean algebra $\mathbf{A}$, the *Boolean algebra of conditionals* of $\mathbf{A}$ is the quotient structure $\mathcal{C}(\mathbf{A}) = \text{Free}(A|A)/_{\equiv_{\mathfrak{C}}}$.

By definition, the algebra $\mathcal{C}(\mathbf{A})$ is finite whenever so is $\mathbf{A}$. In particular, if $\mathbf{A}$ is atomic with atoms $\alpha_1, \ldots, \alpha_n$, in (Flaminio, Godo, and Hosni 2020) it is shown that the atoms of $\mathcal{C}(\mathbf{A})$ are all in the following form: let $\langle \beta_1, \ldots, \beta_{n-1} \rangle$ be a sequence of pairwise different atoms of $\mathbf{A}$. Then, $(\beta_1|\top) \wedge (\beta_2|\overline{\beta_1}) \wedge (\beta_{n-1}|\overline{\beta_1} \wedge \ldots \wedge \overline{\beta_{n-2}})$ is an atom of $\mathcal{C}(\mathbf{A})$ and indeed all atoms of $\mathcal{C}(\mathbf{A})$ have that form for some sequence of atoms of $\mathbf{A}$ of length $n-1$. For any such sequence $\langle\alpha\rangle$, we will write $\omega_{\langle\alpha\rangle}$ to denote its associated atom of $\mathcal{C}(\mathbf{A})$.

For every sequence $\langle\alpha\rangle$, $\omega_{\langle\alpha\rangle}$ clearly belongs to $\mathbb{T}(\mathbf{A})$. Thus it makes sense to look at these terms inside $\mathcal{T}(\mathbf{A})$.

Theorem 6.2. *For every finite Boolean algebra* $\mathbf{A}$ *with atoms* $\alpha_1, \ldots, \alpha_n$, *the set* $\mathrm{at}(\mathcal{T}(\mathbf{A}))$ *of atoms of* $\mathcal{T}(\mathbf{A})$ *coincides with the set* $\{[\omega_{\langle\alpha\rangle}] \in \mathcal{T}(\mathbf{A}) : \omega_{\langle\alpha\rangle}$ *is an atom of* $\mathcal{C}(\mathbf{A})\}$.

Proof. Direct inspection on the proofs of Proposition 4.3 and Theorem 4.4 from (Flaminio, Godo, and Hosni 2020) where the authors proved that $\mathrm{at}(\mathcal{C}(\mathbf{A}))$ is the set of atoms of $\mathcal{C}(\mathbf{A})$, shows that the unique properties of $\mathcal{C}(\mathbf{A})$ needed in their proofs are the basic properties of Boolean algebras (in particular commutativity and associativity of $\wedge$ and distributivity), plus the following:

- If $a \leqslant b$, then for all c, $[(a|b \vee c)] \leqslant [(a|b)]$ (see part (ii) in the proof of (Flaminio, Godo, and Hosni 2020, Theorem 4.4));
- for all $a \neq \bot$, $[(a|a)] = 1$ and $[(\bot|a)] = 0$ (see part (b) in the proof of (Flaminio, Godo, and Hosni 2020, Proposition 4.3));
- $[(a|b)] = \bigvee_{\alpha \in \mathrm{at}(\mathbf{A}):\alpha \leqslant a}[(\alpha|b)]$; (see (a) in the proof of (Flaminio, Godo, and Hosni 2020, Proposition 4.3)).

All these properties hold in $\mathcal{T}(\mathbf{A})$, whence the same proofs apply to this case. □

Corollary 6.3. *For every finite Boolean algebra* $\mathbf{A}$, $\mathcal{T}(\mathbf{A})$ *is isomorphic to* $\mathcal{C}(\mathbf{A})$.

Proof. Two Boolean algebras with the same cardinality are isomorphic. □

In (Flaminio, Godo, and Hosni 2020) it is proved that any (unconditional) positive probability P on $\mathbf{A}$ canonically extends to a positive probability μ_P on $\mathcal{C}(\mathbf{A})$ such that for every basic conditional $(a|b)$, $\mu_P(a|b) = P(a \wedge b)/P(b)$.

We can finally apply the latter result and the above Theorem 6.2 to show our final outcome, for which we still need a previous lemma on the factorization of the probability P^* on the atoms of $\mathcal{T}(\mathbf{A})$, that is in fact a particular case of (Gilio and Sanfilippo 2020, Thm 18).

Lemma 6.4. *Let* $\mathbf{A}$ *be a finite Boolean algebra with* $\mathrm{at}(\mathbf{A}) = \{\alpha_1, \ldots, \alpha_n\}$ *and let* P *be a conditional probability on* $A \times A'$. *Then,*

$$P^*((\alpha_1|\top) \wedge (\alpha_2|\overline{\alpha_1}) \wedge \ldots \wedge (\alpha_{n-1}|\alpha_{n-1} \vee \alpha_n)) = \\ = P(\alpha_1) \cdot P(\alpha_2|\overline{\alpha_1}) \cdot \ldots \cdot P(\alpha_{n-1}|\alpha_{n-1} \vee \alpha_n).$$

We observe that, if P is a positive probability on $\mathbf{A}$, for each basic conditional $(a|b)$, $P^*(a|b) = P(a \wedge b)/P(b) = \mu_P(a|b)$. Our last result shows that P^* and μ_P coincide on every compound conditional as well.

Theorem 6.5. *Given a positive probability* P *on* $\mathbf{A}$ *and any* $t \in \mathbb{T}(A)$, $P^*(t) = \mu_P(t)$, *once we identify the elements of* $\mathcal{T}(\mathbf{A})$ *with those of* $\mathcal{C}(\mathbf{A})$.

Proof. By Lemma 6.4, P^* coincides with μ_P on the atoms of $\mathcal{T}(\mathbf{A})$, and hence on the whole algebra. □

7 Conclusions

In the present paper we have put forward an investigation on compound conditionals that, starting from the original setting proposed by de Finetti, aims at representing them in terms of conditional random quantities. Technically speaking, we start by a finite Boolean algebra $\mathbf{A}$ of events and a (coherent) conditional probability P on $A \times A'$, where $A' = A \backslash \{\bot\}$. Then, to each term t written in the language having as variables basic conditionals of the form $(a|b)$ (for $a \in A$ and $b \in A'$), we first consider, for each interpretation $w \in \Omega$ the reduct t^w of t, and then we associate to t a conditional random quantity $X_t : \Omega \to [0, 1]$, that assigns to each $w \in \Omega$ the value $X_t(w)$ given by the conditional prevision $\mathbb{P}(X_{t^w}|\mathbf{b}(t^w))$.

By doing this, we have presented a natural and uniform procedure to interpret compound conditionals as random quantities and we have investigated the numerical and logical properties of such representation for compound conditionals via their associated random quantities. Our main contribution concerns the possibility of defining operations among conditionals by an iterative procedure. Furthermore, we have proved that these operations allow us to regard the set of those numerical representations as a Boolean algebra $\mathcal{T}(\mathbf{A})$. This latter result provides in turn a numerical counterpart of the construction explored in (Flaminio, Godo, and Hosni 2020), where the authors showed that compound symbolic conditionals, satisfying certain identities, can be endowed with a suitable Boolean algebra structure $\mathcal{C}(\mathbf{A})$. In particular, we have shown that the two algebraic structures that arise from these numerical and the symbolic representations of conditionals turn out to be isomorphic. Moreover, any conditional probability P on $A \times A'$ extends in the same way to both algebras $\mathcal{T}(\mathbf{A})$ and $\mathcal{C}(\mathbf{A})$.

As for future work we plan to generalize Theorem 6.5 to the case in which P is a conditional probability on $A \times A'$. Moreover, we aim at studying the extension of the random quantity-based approach to compound conditionals developed in this paper to deal with general forms of iterated conditionals, see e.g. (Sanfilippo et al. 2020; Gilio and Sanfilippo 2021c). Finally, we plan to study possible applications of compound conditionals to non-monotonic reasoning from conditional bases and to conditional logics more in general, in the line of possible interrelationships with different areas as discussed in (Aucher et al. 2019). Another interesting area of application of compound conditionals to be further explored is the area of psychology of uncertain reasoning (Elqayam et al. 2020).

Acknowledgments

The authors thank the anonymous referees for their comments. Flaminio and Godo acknowledge partial support by the MOSAIC project (EU H2020-MSCA-RISE-2020 Project 101007627) and also by the Spanish project PID2019-111544GB-C21 funded by MCIN/AEI/10.13039/501100011033. Sanfilippo acknowledges support by the FFR2020-FFR2021 projects of University of Palermo, Italy.

References

Adams, E. W. 1975. *The logic of conditionals*. Dordrecht: Reidel.

Aucher, G.; Égré, P.; Kern-Isberner, G.; and Poggiolesi, F. 2019. Conditional logics and conditional reasoning: New joint perspectives (Dagstuhl seminar 19032). *Dagstuhl Reports* 9(1):47–66.

Beierle, C.; Eichhorn, C.; Kern-Isberner, G.; and Kutsch, S. 2018. Properties of skeptical c-inference for conditional knowledge bases and its realization as a constraint satisfaction problem. *Ann. Math. Artif. Intell.* 83(3-4):247–275.

Benferhat, S.; Dubois, D.; and Prade, H. 1997. Nonmonotonic reasoning, conditional objects and possibility theory. *Artificial Intelligence* 92:259–276.

Calabrese, P. 1987. An algebraic synthesis of the foundations of logic and probability. *Information Sciences* 42(3):187 – 237.

Ciucci, D., and Dubois, D. 2013. A map of dependencies among three-valued logics. *Information Sciences* 250:162 – 177.

Coletti, G., and Scozzafava, R. 2002. *Probabilistic logic in a coherent setting*. Dordrecht: Kluwer.

Coletti, G.; Petturiti, D.; and Vantaggi, B. 2019. Dutch book rationality conditions for conditional preferences under ambiguity. *Ann. Oper. Res.* 279(1-2):115–150.

de Finetti, B. 1936. La Logique de la Probabilité. In *Actes du Congrès International de Philosophie Scientifique, Paris, 1935*. Hermann et Cie Éditeurs, Paris. IV 1 – IV 9.

de Finetti, B. 1937. La prévision: ses lois logiques, ses sources subjectives. *Annales de l'Institut Henri Poincaré* 7(1):1–68.

Douven, I., and Dietz, R. 2011. A puzzle about Stalnaker's hypothesis. *Topoi* 31–37.

Dubois, D., and Prade, H. 1994. Conditional objects as nonmonotonic consequence relationships. *IEEE Trans. on Syst. Man and Cybernetics,* 24(12):1724 –1740.

Edgington, D. 1995. On conditionals. *Mind* 104:235–329.

Elqayam, S.; Douven, I.; Evans, J. S. B. T.; and Cruz, N. 2020. *Logic and Uncertainty in the Human Mind: A Tribute to David E. Over*. Oxon: Routledge.

Flaminio, T.; Gilio, A.; Godo, L.; and Sanfilippo, G. 2022. Compound conditionals as random quantities and Boolean algebras (version with proofs). arxiv.org/abs/2204.14131.

Flaminio, T.; Godo, L.; and Hosni, H. 2020. Boolean algebras of conditionals, probability and logic. *Artificial Intelligence* 286:103347.

Ghirardato, P. 2002. Revisiting savage in a conditional world. *Economic Theory* 20(1):83–92.

Gilio, A., and Sanfilippo, G. 2013a. Conjunction, disjunction and iterated conditioning of conditional events. In *Synergies of Soft Computing and Statistics for Intelligent Data Analysis*, volume 190 of *AISC*. Berlin: Springer. 399–407.

Gilio, A., and Sanfilippo, G. 2013b. Quasi conjunction, quasi disjunction, t-norms and t-conorms: Probabilistic aspects. *Information Sciences* 245:146–167.

Gilio, A., and Sanfilippo, G. 2014. Conditional random quantities and compounds of conditionals. *Studia Logica* 102(4):709–729.

Gilio, A., and Sanfilippo, G. 2019. Generalized logical operations among conditional events. *Applied Intelligence* 49(1):79–102.

Gilio, A., and Sanfilippo, G. 2020. Algebraic aspects and coherence conditions for conjoined and disjoined conditionals. *International Journal of Approximate Reasoning* 126:98 – 123.

Gilio, A., and Sanfilippo, G. 2021a. On compound and iterated conditionals. *Argumenta* 6(2):241–266.

Gilio, A., and Sanfilippo, G. 2021b. Compound conditionals, Frchet-Hoeffding bounds, and Frank t-norms. *International Journal of Approximate Reasoning* 136:168–200.

Gilio, A., and Sanfilippo, G. 2021c. Iterated conditionals and characterization of p-entailment. In Vejnarová, J., and Wilson, N., eds., *Symbolic and Quantitative Approaches to Reasoning with Uncertainty, ECSQARU 2021*, volume 12897 of *LNCS*. Springer International Publishing. 629–643.

Gilio, A. 2002. Probabilistic reasoning under coherence in System P. *Annals of Mathematics and Artificial Intelligence* 34:5–34.

Goodman, I. R., and Nguyen, H. T. 1994. A theory of conditional information for probabilistic inference in intelligent systems: II. product space approach. *Inf. Sci.* 76(1-2):13–42.

Goodman, I. R.; Nguyen, H. T.; and Walker, E. A. 1991. *Conditional Inference and Logic for Intelligent Systems: A Theory of Measure-Free Conditioning*. North-Holland.

Halpern, J. Y. 2003. *Reasoning about Uncertainty*. Cambridge, MA, USA: MIT Press.

Halpern, J. Y. 2016. *Actual Causality*. The MIT Press.

Jeffrey, R. 1991. Matter-of-Fact Conditionals. *Proceedings of the Aristotelian Society, Supplementary Volume* 65:161–183.

Kaufmann, S. 2009. Conditionals right and left: Probabilities for the whole family. *Journal of Philosophical Logic* 38:1–53.

Kern-Isberner, G. 2001. *Conditionals in Nonmonotonic Reasoning and Belief Revision – Considering Conditionals as Agents*. Lecture Notes in Artificial Intelligence, Springer.

McGee, V. 1989. Conditional probabilities and compounds of conditionals. *Philosophical Review* 98(4):485–541.

Milne, P. 1997. Bruno de Finetti and the Logic of Conditional Events. *British Journal for the Philosophy of Science* 48(2):195–232.

Nguyen, H. T., and Walker, E. A. 1994. A history and introduction to the algebra of conditional events and probability logic. *IEEE Transactions on Systems, Man, and Cybernetics* 24(12):1671–1675.

Pfeifer, N., and Sanfilippo, G. 2017. Probabilistic squares and hexagons of opposition under coherence. *International Journal of Approximate Reasoning* 88:282–294.

Sanfilippo, G.; Pfeifer, N.; Over, D.; and Gilio, A. 2018. Probabilistic inferences from conjoined to iterated conditionals. *International Journal of Approximate Reasoning* 93(Supplement C):103 – 118.

Sanfilippo, G.; Gilio, A.; Over, D.; and Pfeifer, N. 2020. Probabilities of conditionals and previsions of iterated conditionals. *International Journal of Approximate Reasoning* 121:150 – 173.

Schay, G. 1968. An algebra of conditional events. *Journal of Mathematical Analysis and Applications* 24:334–344.

Stalnaker, R., and Jeffrey, R. 1994. Conditionals as random variables. In Eells, E., and Skyrms, B., eds., *Probability and Conditionals: Belief Revision and Rational Decision*. New York, NY, USA: Cambridge University Press. 31–46.

van Fraassen, B. 1976. Probabilities of conditionals. *Foundations of Probability Theory, Statistical Inference, and Statistical Theories of Science* 1:261–308. cited By 89.

van Rooij, R., and Schulz, K. 2019. Conditionals, causality and conditional probability. *Journal of Logic, Language and Information* 28(1):55–71.

Vantaggi, B. 2010. Incomplete preferences on conditional random quantities: Representability by conditional previsions. *Math. Soc. Sci.* 60(2):104–112.

Proceedings of the 19th International Conference on Principles of Knowledge Representation and Reasoning
Main Track

Interpolants and Explicit Definitions in Extensions of the Description Logic $\mathcal{EL}$

Marie Fortin , Boris Konev , Frank Wolter
University of Liverpool
{mfortin, konev, wolter}@liverpool.ac.uk

Abstract

We show that the vast majority of extensions of the description logic $\mathcal{EL}$ do not enjoy the Craig interpolation nor the projective Beth definability property. This is the case, for example, for $\mathcal{EL}$ with nominals, $\mathcal{EL}$ with the universal role, $\mathcal{EL}$ with a role inclusion of the form $r \circ s \sqsubseteq s$, and for $\mathcal{ELI}$. It follows in particular that the existence of an explicit definition of a concept or individual name cannot be reduced to subsumption checking via implicit definability. We show that nevertheless the existence of interpolants and explicit definitions can be decided in polynomial time for standard tractable extensions of $\mathcal{EL}$ (such as $\mathcal{EL}^{++}$) and in ExpTime for $\mathcal{ELI}$ and various extensions. It follows that these existence problems are not harder than subsumption which is in sharp contrast to the situation for expressive DLs. We also obtain tight bounds for the size of interpolants and explicit definitions and the complexity of computing them: single exponential for tractable standard extensions of $\mathcal{EL}$ and double exponential for $\mathcal{ELI}$ and extensions. We close with a discussion of Horn-DLs such as Horn-$\mathcal{ALCI}$.

1 Introduction

The *projective Beth definability property* (PBDP) of a description logic (DL) $\mathcal{L}$ states that a concept or individual name is explicitly definable under an $\mathcal{L}$-ontology $\mathcal{O}$ by an $\mathcal{L}$-concept using symbols from a signature Σ of concept, role, and individual names if, and only if, it is implicitly definable using Σ under $\mathcal{O}$. The importance of the PBDP for DL research stems from the fact that it provides a polynomial time reduction of the problem to decide the existence of an explicit definition to the well understood problem of subsumption checking. The existence of explicit definitions is important for numerous knowledge engineering tasks and applications of description logic ontologies, for example, the extraction of equivalent acyclic TBoxes from ontologies (ten Cate et al. 2006; ten Cate, Franconi, and Seylan 2013), the computation of referring expressions (or definite descriptions) for individuals (Artale et al. 2021b), the equivalent rewriting of ontology-mediated queries into concepts (Seylan, Franconi, and de Bruijn 2009; Lutz, Seylan, and Wolter 2019; Toman and Weddell 2021), the construction of alignments between ontologies (Geleta, Payne, and Tamma 2016), and the decomposition of ontologies (Konev et al. 2010).

The PBDP is often investigated in tandem with the *Craig interpolation property* (CIP) which states that if an $\mathcal{L}$-concept is subsumed by another $\mathcal{L}$-concept under some $\mathcal{L}$-ontology then one finds an interpolating $\mathcal{L}$-concept using the shared symbols of the two input concepts only. In fact, the CIP implies the PBDP and the interpolants obtained using the CIP can serve as explicit definitions.

Many standard Boolean DLs such as $\mathcal{ALC}$, $\mathcal{ALCI}$, and $\mathcal{ALCQI}$ enjoy the CIP and PBDP and sophisticated algorithms for computing interpolants and explicit definitions have been developed (ten Cate, Franconi, and Seylan 2013). Important exceptions are the extensions of any of the above DLs with nominals and/or role hierarchies. In fact, it has recently been shown that the problem of deciding the existence of an interpolant/explicit definition becomes 2ExpTime-complete for $\mathcal{ALCO}$ ($\mathcal{ALC}$ with nominals) and for $\mathcal{ALCH}$ ($\mathcal{ALC}$ with role hierarchies). This result is in sharp contrast to the ExpTime-completeness of the same problem for $\mathcal{ALC}$ itself inherited from the ExpTime-completeness of subsumption under $\mathcal{ALC}$-ontologies (Artale et al. 2021a).

Our aim in this article is threefold: (1) determine which members of the $\mathcal{EL}$-family of DLs enjoy the CIP/PBDP; (2) investigate the complexity of deciding the existence of interpolants/explicit definitions for those that do not enjoy it; and (3) establish tight bounds on the size of interpolants/explicit definitions and the complexity of computing them.

In what follows we discuss our main results. It has been shown in (Konev et al. 2010; Lutz, Seylan, and Wolter 2019) already that $\mathcal{EL}$ and $\mathcal{EL}$ with role hierarchies enjoy the CIP and PBDP. Rather surprisingly, it turns out that none of the remaining standard DLs in the $\mathcal{EL}$-family enjoy the CIP nor the PBDP.

Theorem 1. *The following DLs do not enjoy the CIP nor PBDP:*

1. *$\mathcal{EL}$ with the universal role,*
2. *$\mathcal{EL}$ with nominals,*
3. *$\mathcal{EL}$ with a single role inclusion $r \circ s \sqsubseteq s$,*
4. *$\mathcal{EL}$ with role hierarchies and a transitive role,*
5. *the extension $\mathcal{ELI}$ of $\mathcal{EL}$ with inverse roles.*

In Points 2 to 5, the CIP/PBDP also fails if the universal role can occur in interpolants/explicit definitions.

Theorem 1 also has interesting consequences that are not explicitly stated. For instance, it follows that neither the DL $\mathcal{EL}^{++}$ introduced in (Baader, Brandt, and Lutz 2005) nor the extension of $\mathcal{ELI}$ with any combination of nominals, role hierarchies, or transitive roles enjoy the CIP/PBDP. With the exception of the failure of the CIP/PBDP for $\mathcal{EL}$ with nominals (without the universal role in interpolants/explicit definitions) (Artale et al. 2021b), our results are new.

It follows from Theorem 1 that the behaviour of extensions of $\mathcal{EL}$ is fundamentally different from extensions of $\mathcal{ALC}$: adding role hierarchies to $\mathcal{ALC}$ does not preserve the CIP/PBDP (Konev et al. 2009) but it does for $\mathcal{EL}$; on the other hand, adding the universal role or inverse roles to $\mathcal{ALC}$ preserves the CIP/PBDP (ten Cate, Franconi, and Seylan 2013) but it does not for $\mathcal{EL}$.

Theorem 1 leaves open the behaviour of a few natural DLs between $\mathcal{EL}$ and its extension with arbitrary role inclusions. For instance, what happens if one only adds transitive roles or, more generally, role inclusions using a single role name only? To cover these cases we show a general result that implies that these DLs enjoy the CIP and PBDP. In particular, it follows that in Point 4 of Theorem 1 the combination of role hierarchies with a transitive role is necessary for failure of the CIP/PBDP.

We next discuss our main result about tractable extensions of $\mathcal{EL}$.

Theorem 2. *For $\mathcal{EL}$ and any extension with any combination of nominals, role inclusions, the universal role, or $\bot$, the existence of interpolants and explicit definitions is in* PTIME. *If an interpolant/explicit definition exists, then there exists one of at most exponential size that can be computed in exponential time. This bound is optimal.*

It follows that for tractable extensions of $\mathcal{EL}$ the complexity of deciding the existence of interpolants and explicit definitions does not depend on the CIP/PBDP, in sharp contrast to the behaviour of $\mathcal{ALCO}$ and $\mathcal{ALCH}$. Moreover, the proof shows how interpolants and explicit definitions can be computed from the canonical models introduced in (Baader, Brandt, and Lutz 2005), if they exist. It applies derivation trees (first introduced in (Bienvenu, Lutz, and Wolter 2013) for DLs without nominals and role hierarchies) to estimate the size of interpolants and provide an exponential time algorithm for computing them.

Theorem 3. *For $\mathcal{ELI}$ and any extension with any combination of nominals, the universal role, or $\bot$, the existence of interpolants and explicit definitions is* EXPTIME*-complete. If an interpolant/explicit definition exists, then there exists one of at most double exponential size that can be computed in double exponential time. This bound is optimal.*

The proof of Theorem 3 shows how an interpolant or explicit definition can be extracted from a (potentially infinite) tree-shaped canonical model. The EXPTIME complexity bound is proved using an encoding as an emptiness problem for tree automata that also uses derivation trees. It does not seem possible to obtain tight bounds on the size of interpolants using derivation trees; instead we generalize transfer sequences for this purpose (also first introduced in (Bienvenu, Lutz, and Wolter 2013)).

In the final section, we consider expressive Horn-DLs such as Horn-$\mathcal{ALCI}$. We first observe that Theorem 3 also holds for Horn-$\mathcal{ALCI}$ and extensions with nominals and the universal role, provided one asks for interpolants and explicit definitions in $\mathcal{ELI}$ (and extensions with nominals and the universal role, respectively). If one admits expressive Horn-concepts as interpolants or explicit definitions, then sometimes interpolants and explicit definitions exist that previously did not exist. We show that nevertheless the CIP/PBDP also fail in this case for DLs including Horn-$\mathcal{ALC}$, $\mathcal{ELI}$, and Horn-$\mathcal{ALCI}$.

Detailed proofs are given in the arxiv version of this article: https://arxiv.org/abs/2202.07186.

2 Related Work

The CIP and PBDP have been investigated extensively in databases, with applications to query rewriting under views and query compilation (Toman and Weddell 2011; Benedikt et al. 2016). The computation of explicit definitions under Horn ontologies can be seen as an instance of query reformulation under constraints (Deutsch, Popa, and Tannen 2006) which has been a major research topic for many years. The Chase and Backchase approach that is central to this research closely resembles our use of canonical models. We do not assume, however, that the chase terminates. In (Benedikt et al. 2016; 2017), it is shown that the reformulation of CQs into CQs under tgds can be reduced to entailment using Lyndon interpolation of first-order logic. By linking reformulation into CQs and definability using concepts, this approach can potentially be used to obtain alternative proofs of complexity upper bounds for the existence of interpolants and explicit definitions in our languages. Also relevant is the investigation of interpolation in basic modal logic (Maksimova and Gabbay 2005) and hybrid modal logic (Areces, Blackburn, and Marx 2001; ten Cate 2005).

The main aim of this article is to investigate explicit definability of concept and individual names under ontologies. We have therefore chosen a definition of the CIP and interpolants that generalizes the projective Beth definability property and explicit definability in a natural and useful way, following (ten Cate, Franconi, and Seylan 2013). There are, however, other notions of Craig interpolation that are of interest. Of particular importance for modularity and various other purposes is the following version: if $\mathcal{O}$ is an ontology and $C \sqsubseteq D$ an inclusion such that $\mathcal{O} \models C \sqsubseteq D$, then there exists an ontology $\mathcal{O}'$ in the shared signature of $\mathcal{O}$ and $C \sqsubseteq D$ such that $\mathcal{O} \models \mathcal{O}' \models C \sqsubseteq D$. This property has been considered for $\mathcal{EL}$ and various extensions in (Sofronie-Stokkermans 2008; Konev et al. 2010). Currently, it is unknown whether there exists any interesting relationship between this version of the CIP and the version we investigate in this article.

Craig interpolants should not be confused with uniform interpolants (or forgetting) (Lutz, Seylan, and Wolter 2012; Lutz and Wolter 2011; Nikitina and Rudolph 2014; Koopmann and Schmidt 2015). Uniform interpolants generalize Craig interpolants in the sense that a uniform interpolant is an interpolant for a fixed antecedent and any formula implied by the antecedent and sharing with it a fixed set of symbols.

Interpolant and explicit definition existence have only recently been investigated for logics that do not enjoy the CIP or PBDP. Extending work on Boolean DLs we discussed already, it is shown that they become harder than validity also in the guarded and two-variable fragment (Jung and Wolter 2021). The interpolant existence problem for linear temporal logic LTL is considered in (Place and Zeitoun 2016). In the context of referring expressions, explicit definition existence is investigated in (Artale et al. 2021b), see also (Borgida, Toman, and Weddell 2016).

3 Preliminaries

Let $\mathsf{N_C}$, $\mathsf{N_R}$, and $\mathsf{N_I}$ be disjoint and countably infinite sets of *concept*, *role*, and *individual names*. A *role* is a role name r or an *inverse role* r^-, with r a role name. *Nominals* take the form $\{a\}$, where a is an individual name. The *universal role* is denoted by u. $\mathcal{ELIO}_u$*-concepts* C are defined by the following syntax rule:

$$C, C' \quad ::= \quad \top \mid A \mid \{a\} \mid C \sqcap C' \mid \exists r.C$$

where A ranges over concept names, a over individual names, and r over roles (including the universal role). Fragments of $\mathcal{ELIO}_u$ are defined as usual. For example, $\mathcal{ELI}$*-concepts* are $\mathcal{ELIO}_u$-concepts without nominals and the universal role, and $\mathcal{EL}$*-concepts* are $\mathcal{ELI}$-concepts without inverse roles. Given any of the DLs $\mathcal{L}$ introduced above, an $\mathcal{L}$*-concept inclusion* ($\mathcal{L}$*-CI*) takes the form $C \sqsubseteq D$ with C, D $\mathcal{L}$-concepts. An $\mathcal{L}$*-ontology* $\mathcal{O}$ is a finite set of $\mathcal{L}$-CIs.

We also consider ontologies with *role inclusions (RIs)*, expressions of the form $r_1 \circ \cdots \circ r_n \sqsubseteq r$ with $r_1, \ldots, r_n, r$ role names. An $\mathcal{ELO}_u$-ontology with RIs is called an $\mathcal{ELRO}_u$*-ontology*. A set of RIs is a *role hierarchy* if all its RIs are of the form $r \sqsubseteq s$ with r, s role names.

A *signature* Σ is a set of concept, role, and individual names, uniformly referred to as *(non-logical) symbols*. We follow common practice and do not regard the universal role u as a non-logical symbol as its interpretation is fixed. We use $\mathsf{sig}(X)$ to denote the set of symbols used in any syntactic object X such as a concept or an ontology. If $\mathcal{L}$ is a DL and Σ a signature, then an $\mathcal{L}(\Sigma)$*-concept* C is an $\mathcal{L}$-concept with $\mathsf{sig}(C) \subseteq \Sigma$. The *size* $||X||$ of a syntactic object X is the number of symbols needed to write it down.

The semantics of DLs is given in terms of *interpretations* $\mathcal{I} = (\Delta^\mathcal{I}, \cdot^\mathcal{I})$, where $\Delta^\mathcal{I}$ is a non-empty set (the *domain*) and $\cdot^\mathcal{I}$ is the *interpretation function*, assigning to each $A \in \mathsf{N_C}$ a set $A^\mathcal{I} \subseteq \Delta^\mathcal{I}$, to each $r \in \mathsf{N_R}$ a relation $r^\mathcal{I} \subseteq \Delta^\mathcal{I} \times \Delta^\mathcal{I}$, and to each $a \in \mathsf{N_I}$ an element $a^\mathcal{I} \in \Delta^\mathcal{I}$. The interpretation $C^\mathcal{I} \subseteq \Delta^\mathcal{I}$ of a concept C in $\mathcal{I}$ is defined as usual, see (Baader et al. 2017). An interpretation $\mathcal{I}$ *satisfies* a CI $C \sqsubseteq D$ if $C^\mathcal{I} \subseteq D^\mathcal{I}$ and an RI $r_1 \circ \cdots \circ r_n \sqsubseteq r$ if $r_1^\mathcal{I} \circ \cdots \circ r_n^\mathcal{I} \subseteq r^\mathcal{I}$. We say that $\mathcal{I}$ is a *model of* an ontology $\mathcal{O}$ if it satisfies all inclusions in it. If α is a CI or RI, we write $\mathcal{O} \models \alpha$ if all models of $\mathcal{O}$ satisfy α. We write $\mathcal{O} \models C \equiv D$ if $\mathcal{O} \models C \sqsubseteq D$ and $\mathcal{O} \models D \sqsubseteq C$.

An ontology is in *normal form* if its CIs are of the form

$$\top \sqsubseteq A, \quad A_1 \sqcap A_2 \sqsubseteq B, \quad A \sqsubseteq \{a\}, \quad \{a\} \sqsubseteq A,$$

and

$$A \sqsubseteq \exists r.B, \quad \exists r.B \sqsubseteq A$$

where A, A_1, A_2, B are concept names, r is a role or the universal role, and a is an individual name. It is well known that for any $\mathcal{ELIO}_u$-ontology $\mathcal{O}$ with or without RIs one can construct in polynomial time a conservative extension $\mathcal{O}'$ using the same constructors as $\mathcal{O}$ that is in normal form.

$\mathcal{L}(\Sigma)$-concepts can be characterized using $\mathcal{L}(\Sigma)$-*simulations* which we define next. Let $\mathcal{I}$ and $\mathcal{J}$ be interpretations. A relation $S \subseteq \Delta^\mathcal{I} \times \Delta^\mathcal{J}$ is called an $\mathcal{ELO}(\Sigma)$*-simulation* between $\mathcal{I}$ and $\mathcal{J}$ if the following conditions hold:

1. if $d \in A^\mathcal{I}$ and $(d, e) \in S$, then $e \in A^\mathcal{J}$, for all $A \in \mathsf{N_C} \cap \Sigma$;
2. if $d = a^\mathcal{I}$ and $(d, e) \in S$, then $e = a^\mathcal{J}$, for all $a \in \mathsf{N_I} \cap \Sigma$;
3. if $(d, d') \in r^\mathcal{I}$ and $(d, e) \in S$, then there exists e' with $(e, e') \in r^\mathcal{J}$ and $(d', e') \in S$, for all $r \in \mathsf{N_R} \cap \Sigma$.

S is called an $\mathcal{ELO}_u(\Sigma)$*-simulation* if $\Delta^\mathcal{I}$ is the domain of S and an $\mathcal{ELIO}(\Sigma)$*-simulation* if Condition 3 also holds for inverse roles from Σ. Condition 2 is dropped if $\mathcal{L}$ does not use nominals. We write $(\mathcal{I}, d) \preceq_{\mathcal{L},\Sigma} (\mathcal{J}, e)$ if there exists an $\mathcal{L}(\Sigma)$-simulation S between $\mathcal{I}$ and $\mathcal{J}$ with $(d, e) \in S$. We write $(\mathcal{I}, d) \leq_{\mathcal{L},\Sigma} (\mathcal{J}, e)$ if $d \in C^\mathcal{I}$ implies $e \in C^\mathcal{J}$ for all $\mathcal{L}(\Sigma)$-concepts C. The following characterization is well known (Lutz and Wolter 2010; Lutz, Piro, and Wolter 2011).

Lemma 1. *Let* $\mathcal{L} \in \{\mathcal{EL}, \mathcal{EL}_u, \mathcal{ELO}, \mathcal{ELO}_u, \mathcal{ELI}, \mathcal{ELI}_u\}$. *Then* $(\mathcal{I}, d) \preceq_{\mathcal{L},\Sigma} (\mathcal{J}, e)$ *implies* $(\mathcal{I}, d) \leq_{\mathcal{L},\Sigma} (\mathcal{J}, e)$. *The converse direction holds if* $\mathcal{J}$ *is finite.*

4 Craig Interpolation Property and Projective Beth Definability Property

We introduce the Craig interpolation property (CIP) as defined in (ten Cate, Franconi, and Seylan 2013) and the projective Beth definability property (PBDP) and prove Theorem 1 from the introduction to this article. We observe that the CIP implies the PBDP, but lack a proof of the converse direction. Nevertheless, all DLs considered in this paper enjoying the PBDP also enjoy the CIP.

Set $\mathsf{sig}(\mathcal{O}, C) = \mathsf{sig}(\mathcal{O}) \cup \mathsf{sig}(C)$, for any ontology $\mathcal{O}$ and concept C. Let $\mathcal{O}_1, \mathcal{O}_2$ be $\mathcal{L}$-ontologies and let C_1, C_2 be $\mathcal{L}$-concepts. Then an $\mathcal{L}$-concept D is called an $\mathcal{L}$*-interpolant*[1] for $C_1 \sqsubseteq C_2$ under $\mathcal{O}_1, \mathcal{O}_2$ if

- $\mathsf{sig}(D) \subseteq \mathsf{sig}(\mathcal{O}_1, C_1) \cap \mathsf{sig}(\mathcal{O}_2, C_2)$;
- $\mathcal{O}_1 \cup \mathcal{O}_2 \models C_1 \sqsubseteq D$;
- $\mathcal{O}_1 \cup \mathcal{O}_2 \models D \sqsubseteq C_2$.

Definition 1. *A DL* $\mathcal{L}$ *has the Craig interpolation property (CIP) if for any* $\mathcal{L}$*-ontologies* $\mathcal{O}_1, \mathcal{O}_2$ *and* $\mathcal{L}$*-concepts* C_1, C_2 *such that* $\mathcal{O}_1 \cup \mathcal{O}_2 \models C_1 \sqsubseteq C_2$ *there exists an* $\mathcal{L}$*-interpolant for* $C_1 \sqsubseteq C_2$ *under* $\mathcal{O}_1, \mathcal{O}_2$.

[1] Important variations of this definition are to drop $\mathcal{O}_2$ in Point 2 and $\mathcal{O}_1$ in Point 3, respectively, or to consider only one ontology $\mathcal{O} = \mathcal{O}_1 = \mathcal{O}_2$ and regard the signature Σ of the interpolant as an input given independently from $\mathcal{O}, C_1, C_2$. This has an effect on the CIP, but our results on interpolant computation and existence are not affected.

We next define the relevant definability notions. Let $\mathcal{O}$ be an ontology and A a concept name. Let $\Sigma \subseteq \text{sig}(\mathcal{O})$ be a signature. An $\mathcal{L}(\Sigma)$-concept C is an *explicit $\mathcal{L}(\Sigma)$-definition of A under $\mathcal{O}$* if $\mathcal{O} \models A \equiv C$. We call A *explicitly definable in $\mathcal{L}(\Sigma)$ under $\mathcal{O}$* if there is an explicit $\mathcal{L}(\Sigma)$-definition of A under $\mathcal{O}$. The Σ-reduct $\mathcal{I}_{|\Sigma}$ of an interpretation $\mathcal{I}$ coincides with $\mathcal{I}$ except that no symbol that is not in Σ is interpreted in $\mathcal{I}_{|\Sigma}$. A concept A is called *implicitly definable using Σ under $\mathcal{O}$* if the Σ-reduct of any model $\mathcal{I}$ of $\mathcal{O}$ determines the set $A^{\mathcal{I}}$; in other words, if $\mathcal{I}$ and $\mathcal{J}$ are both models of $\mathcal{O}$ such that $\mathcal{I}_{|\Sigma} = \mathcal{J}_{|\Sigma}$, then $A^{\mathcal{I}} = A^{\mathcal{J}}$. It is easy to see that implicit definability can be reformulated as a standard reasoning problem as follows: a concept name $A \notin \Sigma$ is implicitly definable using Σ under $\mathcal{O}$ iff $\mathcal{O} \cup \mathcal{O}_\Sigma \models A \equiv A'$, where $\mathcal{O}_\Sigma$ is obtained from $\mathcal{O}$ by replacing every symbol X not in Σ (including A) uniformly by a fresh symbol X'.

Definition 2. *A DL $\mathcal{L}$ has the projective Beth definable property (PBDP) if for any $\mathcal{L}$-ontology $\mathcal{O}$, concept name A, and signature $\Sigma \subseteq$ sig($\mathcal{O}$) the following holds: if A is implicitly definable using Σ under $\mathcal{O}$, then A is explicitly $\mathcal{L}(\Sigma)$-definable under $\mathcal{O}$.*

Remark 1. The CIP implies the PBDP. To see this, assume that an $\mathcal{L}$-ontology $\mathcal{O}$, concept name A and a signature Σ are given, and that A is implicitly definable from Σ under $\mathcal{O}$. Then $\mathcal{O} \cup \mathcal{O}_\Sigma \models A \equiv A'$, with $\mathcal{O}_\Sigma$ defined above. Take an $\mathcal{L}$-interpolant C for $A \sqsubseteq A'$ under $\mathcal{O}, \mathcal{O}_\Sigma$. Then C is an explicit $\mathcal{L}(\Sigma)$-definition of A under $\mathcal{O}$.

Remark 2. The PBDP implies that implicitly definable nominals are explicitly definable and that, more generally, every implicitly definable concept C is explicitly definable. This can be shown by adding $A \equiv C$ to the ontology for a fresh concept name A and asking for an explicit definition of A in the extended ontology.

Remark 3. The CIP and PBDP are invariant under adding $\bot$ (interpreted as the empty set) to the languages introduced above. The straightforward proof is given in the appendix of the full version.

We next prove that the majority of tractable extensions of $\mathcal{EL}$ does not enjoy the CIP nor PBDP.

Theorem 1. *The following DLs do not enjoy the CIP nor PBDP:*

1. *$\mathcal{EL}$ with the universal role,*
2. *$\mathcal{EL}$ with nominals,*
3. *$\mathcal{EL}$ with a single role inclusion $r \circ s \sqsubseteq s$,*
4. *$\mathcal{EL}$ with role hierarchies and a transitive role,*
5. *$\mathcal{EL}$ with inverse roles.*

In Points 2 to 5, the CIP/PBDP also fails if the universal role can occur in interpolants/explicit definitions.

Proof. We first show that $\mathcal{EL}_u$ does not enjoy the PBDP. Point 1 then follows using Remark 1. We define an $\mathcal{EL}_u$-ontology $\mathcal{O}_u$, signature Σ, and concept name A such that A is implicitly definable using Σ under $\mathcal{O}_u$ but not $\mathcal{EL}_u(\Sigma)$-explicitly definable under $\mathcal{O}_u$. Define $\mathcal{O}_u$ as the following set of CIs:

$$A \sqsubseteq B, \quad D \sqcap \exists u.A \sqsubseteq E, \quad B \sqsubseteq \exists r.C$$

$$C \sqsubseteq D, \quad B \sqcap \exists r.(C \sqcap E) \sqsubseteq A,$$

and let $\Sigma = \{B, D, E, r\}$. We have $\mathcal{O}_u \models A \equiv B \sqcap \forall r.(D \rightarrow E)$,[2] so A is implicitly definable using Σ under $\mathcal{O}_u$. The interpretations $\mathcal{I}$ and $\mathcal{I}'$ given in Figure 1 show that A is not explicitly $\mathcal{EL}_u(\Sigma)$-definable under $\mathcal{O}_u$. Indeed, $\mathcal{I}$

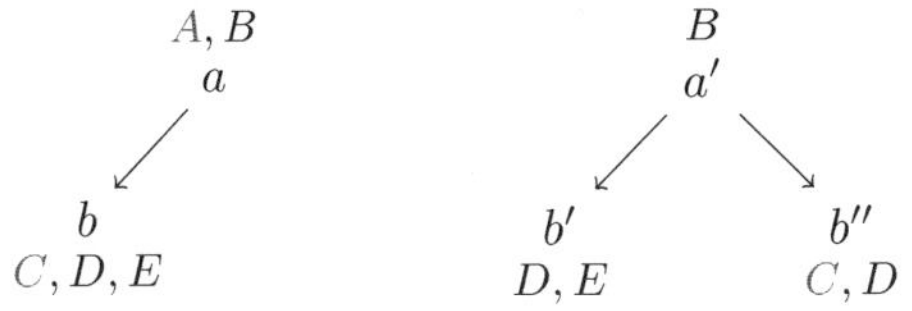

Figure 1: Interpretations $\mathcal{I}$ (left) and $\mathcal{I}'$ (right) used for $\mathcal{O}_u$.

and $\mathcal{I}'$ are both models of $\mathcal{O}_u$, $a \in A^{\mathcal{I}}$, $a' \notin A^{\mathcal{I}'}$, and the relation $\{(a, a'), (b, b')\}$ is a $\mathcal{EL}_u(\Sigma)$-simulation between $\mathcal{I}$ and $\mathcal{I}'$. As $\mathcal{EL}_u(\Sigma)$-concepts are preserved under $\mathcal{EL}_u(\Sigma)$-simulations (Lemma 1), if $\mathcal{O}_u \models A \equiv F$ for some $\mathcal{EL}_u(\Sigma)$-concept F, then from $a \in A^{\mathcal{I}}$ we obtain $a \in F^{\mathcal{I}}$. This implies $a' \in F^{\mathcal{I}'}$, and so $a' \in A^{\mathcal{I}'}$. As $a' \notin A^{\mathcal{I}'}$, we obtain a contradiction.

We next prove Point 2. An example from (Artale et al. 2021b) shows that $\mathcal{ELO}$ does not enjoy the CIP/PBDP. Here we show that $\mathcal{ELO}$ does not enjoy the CIP/PBDP, even if interpolants/explicit defintions are from $\mathcal{ELO}_u$. Let $\mathcal{O}_n$ contain the following CIs:

$$A \sqsubseteq \exists r.(E \sqcap \{c\}), \quad \top \sqsubseteq \exists s.(Q_2 \sqcap \exists s.\{c\})$$

$$\exists s.(Q_1 \sqcap Q_2 \sqcap \exists s.\{c\}) \sqsubseteq A, \quad \exists s.E \sqsubseteq Q_1$$

and let $\Sigma = \{c, s, Q_1\}$. Observe that A is implicitly definable using Σ under $\mathcal{O}_n$ as $\mathcal{O}_n \models A \equiv \forall s.(\exists s.\{c\} \rightarrow Q_1)$. The relation $\{(a, a'), (b, b'), (c, c')\}$ is an $\mathcal{ELO}_u(\Sigma)$-simulation between the interpretations $\mathcal{I}$ and $\mathcal{I}'$ defined in Figure 2. Now we can apply the same argument as in Point 1 to show that A is not explicitly $\mathcal{ELO}_u(\Sigma)$-definable under $\mathcal{O}_n$.

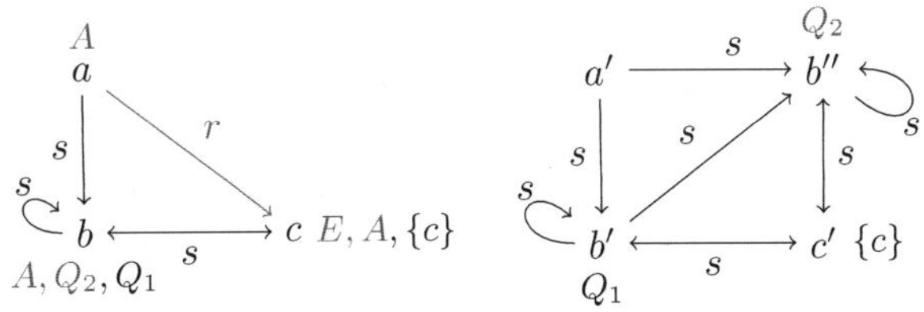

Figure 2: Interpretations $\mathcal{I}$ (left) and $\mathcal{I}'$ (right) used for $\mathcal{O}_n$.

For Point 3, let $\mathcal{O}_r$ contain

$$A \sqsubseteq \exists r.E, \quad E \sqsubseteq \exists s.B, \quad \exists s.B \sqsubseteq A, \quad r \circ s \sqsubseteq s,$$

and let $\Sigma = \{s, E\}$. Then A is implicitly definable using Σ under $\mathcal{O}_r$ since

$$\mathcal{O}_r \models \forall x(A(x) \leftrightarrow \exists y(E(y) \wedge \forall z(s(y,z) \rightarrow s(x,z)))).$$

We show that there does not exist any $\mathcal{EL}_u(\Sigma)$-explicit definition of A under $\mathcal{O}_r$. The interpretations $\mathcal{I}$ and $\mathcal{I}'$ given

[2]Here and in what follows we use standard $\mathcal{ALC}$ syntax and semantics and set $C \rightarrow D := \neg C \sqcup D$ (Baader et al. 2017).

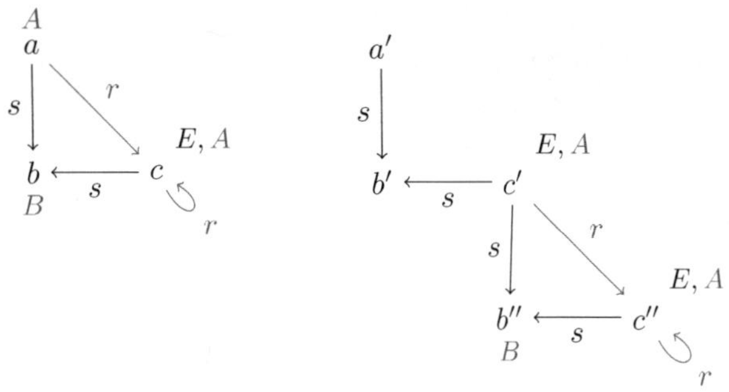

Figure 3: Interpretations $\mathcal{I}$ (left) and $\mathcal{I}'$ (right) used for $\mathcal{O}_r$.

in Figure 3 are both models of $\mathcal{O}_r$, $a \in A^{\mathcal{I}}$, $a' \notin A^{\mathcal{I}'}$, and the relation $\{(a, a'), (b, b'), (c, c')\}$ is an $\mathcal{EL}_u(\Sigma)$-simulation between $\mathcal{I}$ and $\mathcal{I}'$. One can now show in the same way as in Point 1 that no $\mathcal{EL}_u(\Sigma)$-definition of A under $\mathcal{O}_r$ exists.

Point 4 is shown in the appendix of the full version using a modification of the ontology used for Point 3.

To prove Point 5, obtain an $\mathcal{ELI}$-ontology $\mathcal{O}_i$ from $\mathcal{O}_u$ defined above by replacing the second CI of $\mathcal{O}_u$ by $D \sqcap \exists r^-.A \sqsubseteq E$. Let, as before, $\Sigma = \{B, D, E, r\}$. Then A is implicitly definable from Σ under $\mathcal{O}_i$ (the same explicit definition works), but A is not explicitly $\mathcal{ELI}_u(\Sigma)$-definable under $\mathcal{O}_i$ (the same interpretations $\mathcal{I}$ and $\mathcal{I}'$ work). □

We next discuss a general positive result on interpolation and explicit definition existence that shows that Theorem 1 is essentially optimal. A set $\mathcal{R}$ of RIs is *safe* for a signature Σ if for each RI $r_1 \circ \cdots \circ r_n \sqsubseteq r \in \mathcal{R}, n \geq 1$, if $\{r_1, \ldots, r_n, r\} \cap \Sigma \neq \emptyset$ then $\{r_1, \ldots, r_n, r\} \subseteq \Sigma$.

Theorem 4. *Let $\mathcal{O}_1, \mathcal{O}_2$ be $\mathcal{EL}$-ontologies with RIs, C_1, C_2 be $\mathcal{EL}$-concepts, and set $\Sigma = sig(\mathcal{O}_1, C_1) \cap sig(\mathcal{O}_2, C_2)$. Assume that the set of RIs in $\mathcal{O}_1 \cup \mathcal{O}_2$ is safe for Σ and $\mathcal{O}_1 \cup \mathcal{O}_2 \models C_1 \sqsubseteq C_2$. Then an $\mathcal{EL}$-interpolant for $C_1 \sqsubseteq C_2$ under $\mathcal{O}_1$, $\mathcal{O}_2$ exists.*

The proof technique is based on simulations and similar to (Konev et al. 2010; Lutz, Seylan, and Wolter 2019). Theorem 4 has a few interesting consequences. For instance, $\mathcal{EL}$ with transitive roles enjoys both the CIP and PBDP since transitivity is expressed by the role inclusion $r \circ r \sqsubseteq r$ which is safe for any signature (as it only uses a single role name).

5 Interpolant and Explicit Definition Existence

We introduce interpolant and explicit definition existence as decision problems and establish a polynomial time reduction of the latter to the former. We then show that it suffices to consider ontologies in normal form and that the addition of $\bot$ does not affect the complexity of the decision problems.

Definition 3. *Let $\mathcal{L}$ be a DL. Then* $\mathcal{L}$-interpolant existence *is the problem to decide for any $\mathcal{L}$-ontologies $\mathcal{O}_1, \mathcal{O}_2$ and $\mathcal{L}$-concepts C_1, C_2 whether there exists an $\mathcal{L}$-interpolant for $C_1 \sqsubseteq C_2$ under $\mathcal{O}_1, \mathcal{O}_2$.*

Observe that interpolant existence reduces to checking $\mathcal{O}_1 \cup \mathcal{O}_2 \models C_1 \sqsubseteq C_2$ for logics with the CIP but that this is not the case for logics without the CIP.

Definition 4. *Let $\mathcal{L}$ be a DL. Then* $\mathcal{L}$-explicit definition existence *is the problem to decide for any $\mathcal{L}$-ontology $\mathcal{O}$, signature Σ, and concept name A whether A is explicitly definable in $\mathcal{L}(\Sigma)$ under $\mathcal{O}$.*

Remark 4. There is a polynomial time reduction of $\mathcal{L}$-explicit definition existence to $\mathcal{L}$-interpolant existence. Moreover, any algorithm computing $\mathcal{L}$-interpolants also computes $\mathcal{L}$-explicit definitions and any bound on the size of $\mathcal{L}$-interpolants provides a bound on the size of $\mathcal{L}$-explicit definitions. The proof is similar to the proof of Remark 1.

We next observe that replacing the original ontologies by a conservative extension preserves interpolants and explicit definitions. Thus, it suffices to consider ontologies in normal form and interpolants for inclusions between concept names.

Lemma 2. *Let $\mathcal{O}_1, \mathcal{O}_2$ be ontologies and C_1, C_2 concepts in any DL $\mathcal{L}$ considered in this paper. Then one can compute in polynomial time $\mathcal{L}$-ontologies $\mathcal{O}_1', \mathcal{O}_2'$ in normal form and with fresh concept names A, B such that an $\mathcal{L}$-concept C is an interpolant for $C_1 \sqsubseteq C_2$ under $\mathcal{O}_1, \mathcal{O}_2$ iff it is an interpolant for $A \sqsubseteq B$ under $\mathcal{O}_1', \mathcal{O}_2'$.*

Proof. Let $\mathcal{O}_1'$ and $\mathcal{O}_2'$ be normal form conservative extensions of $\mathcal{O}_1 \cup \{A \equiv C\}$ and, respectively, $\mathcal{O}_2 \cup \{B \equiv D\}$, computed in polynomial time. One can show that $\mathcal{O}_1'$ and $\mathcal{O}_2'$ are as required. □

Remark 5. Assume that $\mathcal{L}$ is any of the DLs introduced above and let $\mathcal{L}_\bot$ denote its extension with $\bot$. Then $\mathcal{L}$-interpolant existence and $\mathcal{L}$-explicit definition existence can be reduced in polynomial time to $\mathcal{L}_\bot$-interpolant existence and $\mathcal{L}_\bot$-explicit definition existence, respectively. The converse direction also holds modulo an oracle deciding whether $\mathcal{O} \models C \sqsubseteq \bot$.

6 Interpolant and Explicit Definition Existence in Tractable $\mathcal{EL}$ Extensions

The aim of this section is to analyse interpolants and explicit definitions for extensions of $\mathcal{EL}$ with any combination of nominals, role inclusions, or the universal role. We show the following result from the introduction.

Theorem 2. *For $\mathcal{EL}$ and any extension with any combination of nominals, role inclusions, the universal role, or $\bot$, the existence of interpolants and explicit definitions is in* PTIME. *If an interpolant/explicit definition exists, then there exists one of at most exponential size that can be computed in exponential time. This bound is optimal.*

Before we start with a sketch of the proof we give instructive examples showing that the exponential bound on the size of explicit definitions is optimal.

Example 1. Variants of the following example have already been used for various succinctness arguments in DL. Let

$$\begin{aligned} \mathcal{O}_b \;=\; & \{A \sqsubseteq M \sqcap \exists r_1.B_1 \sqcap \exists r_2.B_1\} \cup \\ & \{B_i \sqsubseteq \exists r_1.B_{i+1} \sqcap \exists r_2.B_{i+1} \mid 1 \leq i < n\} \cup \\ & \{B_n \sqsubseteq B, \exists r_1.B \sqcap \exists r_2.B \sqsubseteq B, B \sqcap M \sqsubseteq A\} \end{aligned}$$

and $\Sigma_0 = \{r_1, r_2, B_n, M\}$. A triggers a marker M and a binary tree of depth n whose leafs are decorated with B_n. Conversely, if B_n is true at all leafs of a binary tree of depth n, then B is true at all nodes of the tree and B together with M entail A at its root. Let, inductively, $C_0 := B_n$ and $C_{i+1} = \exists r_1.C_i \sqcap \exists r_2.C_i$, for $0 < i < n$, and $C = M \sqcap C_n$. Then C is the smallest explicit $\mathcal{EL}(\Sigma_0)$-definition of A under $\mathcal{O}_b$. Next let

$$\begin{aligned}\mathcal{O}_p &= \{r_i \circ r_i \sqsubseteq r_{i+1} \mid 0 \leq i < n\} \cup \\ &\quad \{A \sqsubseteq \exists r_0.B, B \sqsubseteq \exists r_0.B, \exists r_n.B \sqsubseteq A\}\end{aligned}$$

and $\Sigma_1 = \{r_0, B\}$. Then $\exists r_0^{2^n}.B$ is the smallest explicit $\mathcal{EL}(\Sigma_1)$-definition of A under $\mathcal{O}_p$.

Observe that using $\mathcal{O}_b$ one enforces explicit definitions of exponential size by generating a binary tree of linear depth whereas using $\mathcal{O}_p$ this is achieved by generating a path of exponential length. The latter can only happen if role inclusions are used in the ontology. One insight provided by the exponential upper bound on the size of explicit definitions in Theorem 2 is that the two examples cannot be combined to enforce a binary tree of exponential depth.

To continue with the proof we introduce ABoxes as a technical tool that allows us to move from interpretations to (potentially incomplete) sets of facts and concepts. An *ABox* $\mathcal{A}$ is a (possibly infinite) set of assertions of the form $A(x)$, $r(x,y)$, $\{a\}(x)$, and $\top(x)$ with $A \in \mathsf{N_C}$, $r \in \mathsf{N_R}$, $a \in \mathsf{N_I}$, and x, y individual variables (we call individuals used in ABoxes variables to distinguish them from individual names used in nominals). We denote by $\text{ind}(\mathcal{A})$ the set of individual variables in $\mathcal{A}$. A Σ-*ABox* is an ABox using symbols from Σ only. Models of ABoxes are defined as usual. We do not make the unique name assumption.

Every interpretation $\mathcal{I}$ defines an ABox $\mathcal{A}_\mathcal{I}$ by identifying every $d \in \Delta^\mathcal{I}$ with a variable x_d and taking $A(x_d)$ if $d \in A^\mathcal{I}$, $r(x_c, x_d)$ if $(c,d) \in r^\mathcal{I}$, $\{a\}(x_d)$ if $a^\mathcal{I} = d$. Conversely, ABoxes $\mathcal{A}$ define interpretations in the obvious way (by identifying variables x, y if $\{a\}(x), \{a\}(y) \in \mathcal{A}$). We associate with every ABox $\mathcal{A}$ a directed graph $G_\mathcal{A} = (\text{ind}(\mathcal{A}), \bigcup_{r \in \mathsf{N_R}} \{(x,y) \mid r(x,y) \in \mathcal{A}\})$. Let Γ be a set of individual names. Then $\mathcal{A}$ is *ditree-shaped modulo* Γ if after dropping some facts of the form $r(x,y)$ with $\{a\}(y) \in \mathcal{A}$ for some $a \in \Gamma$, it is *ditree-shaped* in the sense that $G_\mathcal{A}$ is acyclic and $r(x,y) \in \mathcal{A}$ and $s(x,y) \in \mathcal{A}$ imply $r = s$. A *pointed ABox* is a pair $\mathcal{A}, x$ with $x \in \text{ind}(\mathcal{A})$. Then $\mathcal{ELO}_u(\Sigma)$-concepts correspond to pointed Σ-ABoxes $\mathcal{A}, x$ such that $\mathcal{A}$ is ditree-shaped modulo $\mathsf{N_I} \cap \Sigma$ and $\mathcal{ELO}(\Sigma)$-concepts correspond to *rooted* pointed Σ-ABoxes $\mathcal{A}, x$ such that $\mathcal{A}$ is ditree-shaped modulo $\mathsf{N_I} \cap \Sigma$, where $\mathcal{A}, x$ is called rooted if for every $y \in \text{ind}(\mathcal{A})$ there is a path from x to y in $G_\mathcal{A}$. We write $\mathcal{O}, \mathcal{A} \models C(x)$ if $x^\mathcal{I} \in C^\mathcal{I}$ for every model $\mathcal{I}$ of $\mathcal{O}$ and $\mathcal{A}$.

Given an $\mathcal{ELRO}_u$-ontology $\mathcal{O}$ in normal form and a concept name A, one can construct in polynomial time the *canonical model* $\mathcal{I}_{\mathcal{O},A}$ *of* $\mathcal{O}$ *and* A using the approach introduced in (Baader, Brandt, and Lutz 2005). More generally, the canonical model $\mathcal{I}_{\mathcal{O},\mathcal{A}}$ for an ABox $\mathcal{A}$ and ontology $\mathcal{O}$ can be constructed in polynomial time and is a model of both $\mathcal{O}$ and $\mathcal{A}$ such that for any $\mathcal{ELO}_u$-concept C using symbols from $\mathcal{O}$ only and any $x \in \text{ind}(\mathcal{A})$,

(†) $\mathcal{O}, \mathcal{A} \models C(x)$ iff $x \in C^{\mathcal{I}_{\mathcal{O},\mathcal{A}}}$,

details are given in the appendix of the full version. We let $\mathcal{I}_{\mathcal{O},A} = \mathcal{I}_{\mathcal{O},\mathcal{A}}$ with $\mathcal{A} = \{A(\rho_A)\}$. Note that in (Baader, Brandt, and Lutz 2005) the condition (†) is only stated for subconcepts C of the ontology $\mathcal{O}$, thus (†) requires a proof.

Example 2. The interpretations $\mathcal{I}$ defined in the proof of Theorem 1 define canonical models $\mathcal{I}_{\mathcal{O},A}$ with $\rho_A = a$ for the ontologies $\mathcal{O} \in \{\mathcal{O}_u, \mathcal{O}_n, \mathcal{O}_r, \mathcal{O}_i\}$. The interpretations $\mathcal{I}'$ define canonical models $\mathcal{I}_{\mathcal{O},\mathcal{A}_\mathcal{O}^\Sigma}$ with $\mathcal{A}_\mathcal{O}^\Sigma$ the Σ-reduct of $\mathcal{I}_{\mathcal{O},A}$ regarded as an ABox and $\rho_A = a'$.

The *directed unfolding* of a pointed Σ-ABox $\mathcal{A}, x$ into a pointed Σ-ABox $\mathcal{A}^u, x$ that is ditree-shaped modulo $\Sigma \cap \mathsf{N_I}$ is defined in the standard way. In the *rooted directed unfolding*, nodes that cannot be reached from x via role names are dropped.

Assume now that $\mathcal{O}$ is in normal form and A a concept name. Let $\mathcal{A}_{\mathcal{O},A}^\Sigma$ be the Σ-reduct of the canonical model $\mathcal{I}_{\mathcal{O},A}$, regarded as an ABox. Denote by $\mathcal{A}_{\mathcal{O},A}^{\Sigma,u}, \rho_A$ the directed unfolding of $\mathcal{A}_{\mathcal{O},A}^\Sigma, \rho_A$, by $\mathcal{A}_{\mathcal{O},A}^{\downarrow\Sigma}, \rho_A$ the sub-ABox of $\mathcal{A}_{\mathcal{O},A}^\Sigma$ rooted in ρ_A, and by $\mathcal{A}_{\mathcal{O},A}^{\downarrow\Sigma,u}, \rho_A$ its rooted directed unfolding. Theorem 2 is a direct consequence of the following characterization of interpolants.

Theorem 5. *There exists a polynomial p such that the following conditions are equivalent for all $\mathcal{ELRO}_u$-ontologies $\mathcal{O}_1, \mathcal{O}_2$ in normal form, concept names A, B, and $\Sigma = sig(\mathcal{O}_1, A) \cap sig(\mathcal{O}_2, B)$:*

1. *An $\mathcal{ELO}_u$-interpolant for $A \sqsubseteq B$ under $\mathcal{O}_1, \mathcal{O}_2$ exists;*
2. $\mathcal{O}_1 \cup \mathcal{O}_2, \mathcal{A}_{\mathcal{O}_1 \cup \mathcal{O}_2, A}^\Sigma \models B(\rho_A)$;
3. *there exists a finite subset $\mathcal{A}$ of $\mathcal{A}_{\mathcal{O}_1 \cup \mathcal{O}_2, A}^{\Sigma,u}$ with $|ind(\mathcal{A})| \leq 2^{p(||\mathcal{O}_1 \cup \mathcal{O}_2||)}$ such that the $\mathcal{ELO}_u$-concept corresponding to $\mathcal{A}, \rho_A$ is an $\mathcal{ELO}_u$-interpolant for $A \sqsubseteq B$ under $\mathcal{O}_1, \mathcal{O}_2$.*

The same equivalences hold if in Points 1 to 3, $\mathcal{ELO}_u$ is replaced by $\mathcal{ELO}$, $\mathcal{A}_{\mathcal{O}_1 \cup \mathcal{O}_2, A}^\Sigma$ by $\mathcal{A}_{\mathcal{O}_1 \cup \mathcal{O}_2, A}^{\downarrow\Sigma}$, and $\mathcal{A}_{\mathcal{O}_1 \cup \mathcal{O}_2, A}^{\Sigma,u}$ by $\mathcal{A}_{\mathcal{O}_1 \cup \mathcal{O}_2, A}^{\downarrow\Sigma,u}$.

In Point 3, $\mathcal{A}$ can be computed in exponential time, if it exists.

Note that the polynomial time decidability of interpolant existence follows from Point 2 of Theorem 5 (and the tractability of $\mathcal{ELRO}_u$ (Baader, Brandt, and Lutz 2005)).

Example 3. Our proof of Theorem 2 can be regarded as an application of Theorem 5: by Example 2, the interpretations $\mathcal{I}$ and $\mathcal{I}'$ coincide with the canonical models $\mathcal{I}_{\mathcal{O},A}$ and $\mathcal{I}_{\mathcal{O},\mathcal{A}_{\mathcal{O},A}^\Sigma}$ and so $\rho_A = a' \notin A^{\mathcal{I}_{\mathcal{O},\mathcal{A}_{\mathcal{O},A}^\Sigma}}$ is equivalent to $\mathcal{O}, \mathcal{A}_{\mathcal{O},A}^\Sigma \not\models A(\rho_A)$ (Point 2 in Theorem 5).

The following example illustrates the difference between the existence of explicit definitions in $\mathcal{ELO}$ and $\mathcal{ELO}_u$ and thus the need for moving to the ABoxes $\mathcal{A}_{\mathcal{O},A}^{\downarrow\Sigma}$, and $\mathcal{A}_{\mathcal{O},A}^{\downarrow\Sigma,u}$ if one does not admit the universal role in explicit definitions.

Example 4. Let $\mathcal{O} = \{A \sqsubseteq \{b\}, A \sqsubseteq \exists r.B, B \sqsubseteq \exists s.A\}$ and let $\Sigma = \{b, B\}$. Then A is explicitly $\mathcal{ELO}_u(\Sigma)$-definable under $\mathcal{O}$ since $\mathcal{O} \models A \equiv \{b\} \sqcap \exists u.B$ but A

is not explicitly $\mathcal{ELO}(\Sigma)$-definable. Note that in this case $\mathcal{A}^{\Sigma}_{\mathcal{O},A} = \{\{b\}(\rho_A), B(y)\}$ but $\mathcal{A}^{\downarrow\Sigma}_{\mathcal{O},A} = \{\{b\}(\rho_A)\}$.

We next sketch the proof idea for Theorem 5 for the case with universal role in interpolants. We show "1. $\Rightarrow$ 2.", observe that "3. $\Rightarrow$ 1." is trivial, and then sketch the proof of "2. $\Rightarrow$ 3." and the exponential time algorithm computing interpolants, details are provided in the appendix of the full version. For "1. $\Rightarrow$ 2." assume that C is an $\mathcal{ELO}_u(\Sigma)$-concept with (i) $\mathcal{O}_1 \cup \mathcal{O}_2 \models A \sqsubseteq C$ and (ii) $\mathcal{O}_1 \cup \mathcal{O}_2 \models C \sqsubseteq B$. By (†) and (i), $\mathcal{A}^{\Sigma}_{\mathcal{O}_1\cup\mathcal{O}_2,A} \models C(\rho_A)$. But then by (ii) $\mathcal{O}_1 \cup \mathcal{O}_2, \mathcal{A}^{\Sigma}_{\mathcal{O}_1\cup\mathcal{O}_2,A} \models B(\rho_A)$, as required.

If one does not impose a bound on the size of $\mathcal{A}$ in Point 3, then one can prove "2. $\Rightarrow$ 3." using compactness and a generalization of *unraveling tolerance* according to which $\mathcal{O}_1 \cup \mathcal{O}_2, \mathcal{A}^{\Sigma}_{\mathcal{O}_1\cup\mathcal{O}_2,A}$ and $\mathcal{O}_1 \cup \mathcal{O}_2, \mathcal{A}^{\Sigma,u}_{\mathcal{O}_1\cup\mathcal{O}_2,A}$ entail the same $C(\rho_A)$ (Lutz and Wolter 2017; Hernich et al. 2020). As we are interested in an exponential bound on the size of $\mathcal{A}$ (and a deterministic exponential time algorithm computing it) we require a more syntactic approach. Our proof of "2. $\Rightarrow$ 3." is based on *derivation trees* which represent a derivation of a fact $C(a)$ from an ontology $\mathcal{O}$ and ABox $\mathcal{A}$ using a labeled tree. Our derivation trees generalize those introduced in (Bienvenu, Lutz, and Wolter 2013; Baader et al. 2016) to languages with nominals and role inclusions. Reflecting the use of individual names and concept names in the construction of the domain of the canonical model (Baader, Brandt, and Lutz 2005), we assume $a \in \Delta := \mathsf{ind}(\mathcal{A}) \cup ((\mathsf{N_C} \cup \mathsf{N_I}) \cap \mathsf{sig}(\mathcal{O}))$ and $C \in \Theta := \{\top\} \cup (\mathsf{N_C} \cap \mathsf{sig}(\mathcal{O})) \cup \{\{a\} \mid a \in \mathsf{N_I} \cap \mathsf{sig}(\mathcal{O})\}$. Then a derivation tree (T, V) for $(a, C) \in \Delta \times \Theta$ is a tree T with a labeling function $V : T \to \Delta \times \Theta$ such that $V(\varepsilon) = (a, C)$ and (V, T) satisfies rules stating under which conditions the label of n is derived in one step from the labels of the successors of n. To illustrate, the existence of successors n_1, n_2 of n with $V(n_1) = (a, C_1)$ and $V(n_2) = (a, C_2)$ justifies $V(n) = (a, C)$ if $\mathcal{O} \models C_1 \sqcap C_2 \sqsubseteq C$. The rules are given in the appendix of the full version, we only discuss the rule used to capture derivations using RIs: $V(n) = (a_1, C)$ is justified if there are role names $r_2, \dots, r_{2k-2}, r$ such that (a_{2k}, C') is a label of a successor of n, $\mathcal{O} \models \exists r.C' \sqsubseteq C$, $\mathcal{O} \models r_2 \circ \cdots \circ r_{2k-2} \sqsubseteq r$, and the situation depicted in Figure 4 holds, where the "dotted lines" stand for 'either $a_i = a_{i+1}$ or some $(a_i, \{c\}), (a_{i+1}, \{c\})$ with $c \in \mathsf{N_I}$ are labels of successors of n', and $\hat{r}_i$ stands for 'either $r(a_i, a_{i+1}) \in \mathcal{A}$ or some (a_i, C_i) is a label of a successor of n and $\mathcal{O} \models C_i \sqsubseteq \exists r_i.\{a_{i+1}\}$ if $a_{i+1} \in \mathsf{N_I}$ and $\mathcal{O} \models C_i \sqsubseteq \exists r_i.a_{i+1}$ if $a_{i+1} \in \mathsf{N_C}$'. Moreover, for all $a_i \neq a_1$, $1 \leq i \leq 2k$, there exists a successor of n with label (a_i, D) for some D. The soundness of this rule should be clear, completeness can be shown similarly to the analysis of canonical models.

The length of the sequence $a_1, \dots, a_{2k}$ can be exponential (for instance, in Example 1 for the fact (ρ_A, A) in $\mathcal{O}_p, \mathcal{A}^{\Sigma_1}_{\mathcal{O}_p,A}$). One can show, however, that its length can be bounded without affecting completeness by $2^{q(||\mathcal{O}||+||\mathcal{A}||)}$ with q a polynomial. The following lemma summarizes the main properties of derivation trees.

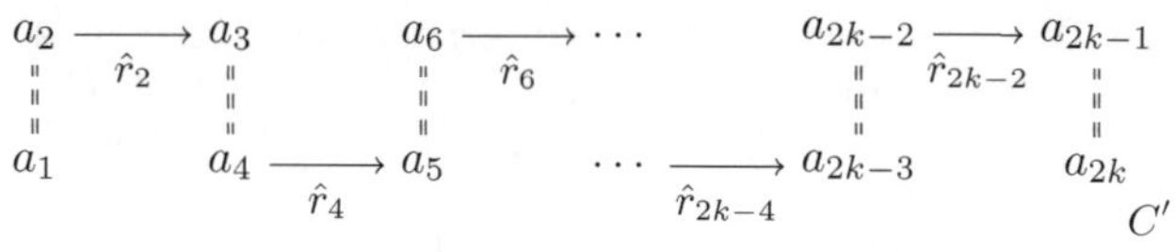

Figure 4: Rule for Role Inclusions.

Lemma 3. *Let $\mathcal{O}$ be an $\mathcal{ELRO}_u$-ontology in normal form and $\mathcal{A}$ a finite sig($\mathcal{O}$)-ABox. Then*

1. *$\mathcal{O}, \mathcal{A} \models A(x)$ if and only if there is a derivation tree for $A(x)$ in $\mathcal{O}, \mathcal{A}$. Moreover, if a derivation tree exists, then there exists one of depth and outdegree bounded by $(||\mathcal{A}|| + ||\mathcal{O}||) \times ||\mathcal{O}||$ which can be constructed in exponential time in $||\mathcal{O}|| + ||\mathcal{A}||$.*
2. *If (T, V) is a derivation tree for $A(x)$ in $\mathcal{O}, \mathcal{A}$ of at most exponential size, then one can construct in exponential time (in $||\mathcal{A}|| + ||\mathcal{O}||$) a derivation tree (T', V') for $A(x)$ in $\mathcal{O}, \mathcal{A}^u$ with $\mathcal{A}^u$ the directed unfolding of $\mathcal{A}$ modulo $\Sigma = sig(\mathcal{A}) \cap \mathsf{N_I}$ and T' of the same depth as T and such that the outdegree of T' does not exceed $\max\{3, 3n\}$ with n the length of the longest chain $a_1 \cdots a_n$ used in the rule for RIs in the derivation tree (T, V).*

Proof. We sketch the idea. For Point 1, the bound on the depth of derivation trees can be proved by observing that one can assume (using a standard pumping argument) that the labels of distinct nodes on a single path are distinct and the bound on the outdegree can be proved by observing that one can trivially assume that all successor nodes of a node have distinct labels. For the construction of derivation trees, let F_n denote the set of facts in $\Delta \times \Theta$ for which there is a derivation tree of depth at most n. Then one can construct in exponential time derivation trees for all facts in any F_n, $n \leq (||\mathcal{A}||+||\mathcal{O}||)\times||\mathcal{O}||$ by starting with derivation trees of depth 0 for members of F_0, and then constructing derivation trees of depth $i+1$ for members of F_{i+1} using the trees for members of $F_0, \dots, F_i$. For Point 2, the transformation of (T, V) into (T', V') is by induction over rule application, the only interesting step being the rule for RIs. Using the ontology $\mathcal{O}_p$ of Example 1 one can see that the exponential blow-up of the outdegree is unavoidable. □

We are now in the position to complete the sketch of the proof of "2. $\Rightarrow$ 3." Assume that Point 2 holds. Then $\mathcal{O}_1 \cup \mathcal{O}_2, \mathcal{A}^{\Sigma}_{\mathcal{O}_1\cup\mathcal{O}_2,A} \models B(\rho_A)$. By Point 1 of Lemma 3 we can construct a derivation tree (T, V) for (ρ_A, B) in $\mathcal{O}_1 \cup \mathcal{O}_2, \mathcal{A}^{\Sigma}_{\mathcal{O}_1\cup\mathcal{O}_2,A}$ of polynomial depth and outdegree in exponential time. By Point 2 of Lemma 3 we can transform (T, V) into a derivation tree (T', V') for (ρ_A, B) in $\mathcal{O}_1 \cup \mathcal{O}_2, \mathcal{A}^{\Sigma,u}_{\mathcal{O}_1\cup\mathcal{O}_2,A}$ in exponential time. Now let $\mathcal{A}$ be the restriction of $\mathcal{A}^{\Sigma,u}_{\mathcal{O}_1\cup\mathcal{O}_2,A}$ to all $x \in \mathsf{ind}(\mathcal{A}^{\Sigma,u}_{\mathcal{O}_1\cup\mathcal{O}_2,A})$ which occur in a label of V'. Then (T', V') is also a derivation tree for (ρ_A, B) in $\mathcal{O}_1 \cup \mathcal{O}_2, \mathcal{A}$ and so $\mathcal{O}_1 \cup \mathcal{O}_2, \mathcal{A} \models B(\rho_A)$. It follows that the $\mathcal{ELO}_u(\Sigma)$-concept corresponding to $\mathcal{A}$ is an interpolant for $A \sqsubseteq B$ under $\mathcal{O}_1 \cup \mathcal{O}_2$. Its size is at most exponential in $||\mathcal{O}_1 \cup \mathcal{O}_2||$ since (T', V') is at most exponential in $||\mathcal{O}_1 \cup \mathcal{O}_2|| + ||\mathcal{A}^{\Sigma}_{\mathcal{O}_1\cup\mathcal{O}_2,A}||$, and so also in $||\mathcal{O}_1 \cup \mathcal{O}_2||$.

7 Interpolant and Explicit Definition Existence in $\mathcal{ELI}$ and Extensions

We analyze interpolants and explicit definitions for $\mathcal{ELI}$ and its extensions with nominals and universal roles, and show the following result from the introduction.

Theorem 3. *For $\mathcal{ELI}$ and any extension with any combination of nominals, the universal role, or $\bot$, the existence of interpolants and explicit definitions is* ExpTime*-complete. If an interpolant/explicit definition exists, then there exists one of at most double exponential size that can be computed in double exponential time. This bound is optimal.*

The double exponential lower bound on the size of explicit definitions and interpolants is shown in the appendix of the full version. The proof is inspired by similar lower bounds for the size of FO-rewritings and uniform interpolants (Lutz and Wolter 2010; Nikitina and Rudolph 2014). To prove the remaining claims of Theorem 3, we lift Theorem 5 to $\mathcal{ELI}$. The main differences are that (1) we now associate undirected graphs with ABoxes and also unfold along inverse roles; (2) that canonical models become potentially infinite but tree-shaped; (3) that therefore deciding the new variant of Point 2 of Theorem 5 is not an instance of standard entailment checking in $\mathcal{ELI}$, instead we give a reduction to emptiness checking for tree automata; and (4) that to bound the size of $\mathcal{A}$ in Point 3, we employ transfer sequences (and not derivation trees) to represent how facts are derived.

In more detail, associate with every ABox $\mathcal{A}$ the undirected graph $G^u_{\mathcal{A}} = (\text{ind}(\mathcal{A}), \bigcup_{r\in\mathsf{N_R}}\{\{x,y\} \mid r(x,y) \in \mathcal{A}\})$. We say that $\mathcal{A}$ is *tree-shaped* if $G^u_{\mathcal{A}}$ is acyclic, $r(x,y) \in \mathcal{A}$ and $s(x,y) \in \mathcal{A}$ imply $r = s$, and $r(x,y) \in \mathcal{A}$ implies $s(y,x) \notin \mathcal{A}$ for any s. $\mathcal{A}$ is *tree-shaped modulo a set Γ of individual names* if after dropping some facts $r(x,y)$ with $\{a\}(x)$ or $\{a\}(y) \in \mathcal{A}$ for some $a \in \Gamma$ it is tree-shaped. We observe that $\mathcal{ELIO}_u(\Sigma)$-concepts correspond to pointed Σ-ABoxes $\mathcal{A}, x$ such that $\mathcal{A}$ is tree-shaped modulo $\mathsf{N_I} \cap \Sigma$. $\mathcal{ELIO}(\Sigma)$-concepts correspond to *weakly rooted* pointed Σ-ABoxes $\mathcal{A}, x$ such that $\mathcal{A}$ is tree-shaped modulo $\mathsf{N_I} \cap \Sigma$, where $\mathcal{A}, x$ is called weakly rooted if for every $y \in \text{ind}(\mathcal{A})$ there is a path from x to y in $G^u_{\mathcal{A}}$.

For every $\mathcal{ELIO}_u$-ontology $\mathcal{O}$ and concept A there exists a (potentially infinite) pointed canonical model $\mathcal{I}_{\mathcal{O},A}, \rho_A$ such that the ABox $\mathcal{A}_{\mathcal{O},A}$ corresponding to $\mathcal{I}_{\mathcal{O},A}$ is tree-shaped modulo $\mathsf{N_I} \cap \text{sig}(\mathcal{O})$. The property (†) used in the context of canonical models for tractable extensions of $\mathcal{EL}$ holds here as well. We also require the *undirected unfolding* of a pointed Σ-ABox $\mathcal{A}, x$ into a pointed Σ-ABox $\mathcal{A}^*, x$ which is tree-shaped modulo $\Sigma \cap \mathsf{N_I}$. In the *rooted undirected unfolding*, nodes that cannot be reached from x via roles are dropped.

Assume now that $\mathcal{O}$ is in normal form and A a concept name. Let $\mathcal{A}^{\Sigma}_{\mathcal{O},A}$ be the Σ-reduct of the canonical model $\mathcal{I}_{\mathcal{O},A}$, regarded as an ABox. Denote by $\mathcal{A}^{\Sigma,*}_{\mathcal{O},A}, \rho_A$ the undirected unfolding of $\mathcal{A}^{\Sigma}_{\mathcal{O},A}, \rho_A$, by $\mathcal{A}^{\downarrow_w\Sigma}_{\mathcal{O},A}, \rho_A$ the sub-ABox of $\mathcal{A}^{\Sigma}_{\mathcal{O},A}$ weakly rooted in ρ_A, and by $\mathcal{A}^{\downarrow_w\Sigma,*}_{\mathcal{O},A}, \rho_A$ its rooted undirected unfolding. Then we lift Theorem 5 as follows.

Theorem 6. *There exists a polynomial p such that the following conditions are equivalent for all $\mathcal{ELIO}_u$-ontologies $\mathcal{O}_1, \mathcal{O}_2$ in normal form, concept names A, B, and $\Sigma = \mathit{sig}(\mathcal{O}_1, A) \cap \mathit{sig}(\mathcal{O}_2, B)$:*

1. *An $\mathcal{ELIO}_u$-interpolant for $A \sqsubseteq B$ under $\mathcal{O}_1, \mathcal{O}_2$ exists;*
2. *$\mathcal{O}_1 \cup \mathcal{O}_2, \mathcal{A}^{\Sigma}_{\mathcal{O}_1\cup\mathcal{O}_2,A} \models B(\rho_A)$;*
3. *there exists a finite subset $\mathcal{A}$ of $\mathcal{A}^{\Sigma,*}_{\mathcal{O}_1\cup\mathcal{O}_2,A}$ with $|\mathit{ind}(\mathcal{A})| \leq 2^{2^{p(||\mathcal{O}_1\cup\mathcal{O}_2||)}}$ such that the $\mathcal{ELIO}_u$-concept corresponding to $\mathcal{A}, \rho_A$ is an $\mathcal{ELIO}_u$-interpolant for $A \sqsubseteq B$ under $\mathcal{O}_1, \mathcal{O}_2$.*

The same equivalences hold if in Points 1 to 3, $\mathcal{ELIO}_u$ is replaced by $\mathcal{ELIO}$, $\mathcal{A}^{\Sigma}_{\mathcal{O}_1\cup\mathcal{O}_2,A}$ by $\mathcal{A}^{\downarrow_w\Sigma}_{\mathcal{O}_1\cup\mathcal{O}_2,A}$, and $\mathcal{A}^{\Sigma,*}_{\mathcal{O}_1\cup\mathcal{O}_2,A}$ by $\mathcal{A}^{\downarrow_w\Sigma,*}_{\mathcal{O}_1\cup\mathcal{O}_2,A}$.

In Point 3, $\mathcal{A}$ can be computed in double exponential time, if it exists.

We first sketch how tree automata are used to show that Point 2 entails an exponential time upper bound for deciding the existence of an interpolant. To this end we represent finite prefix-closed subsets $\mathcal{A}$ of $\mathcal{A}^{\Sigma}_{\mathcal{O}_1\cup\mathcal{O}_2,A}$ as trees and design

- a non-determistic tree automaton over finite trees (NTA), $\mathfrak{A}_1$, that accepts exactly those trees that represent prefix-closed finite subsets of $\mathcal{A}^{\Sigma}_{\mathcal{O}_1\cup\mathcal{O}_2,A}$;
- a two-way alternating tree automaton over finite trees (2ATA), $\mathfrak{A}_2$, that accepts exactly those trees that represent a pointed ABox $\mathcal{A}, \rho$ with $\mathcal{O}_1 \cup \mathcal{O}_2, \mathcal{A} \models B(\rho)$.

Similar tree automata techniques have been used e.g. in (Jung et al. 2020). $\mathfrak{A}_1$ is constructed using the definition of canonical models; its states are essentially types occuring in the canonical model and it can be constructed in exponential time. The 2ATA $\mathfrak{A}_2$ tries to construct a derivation tree for $B(\rho)$ in $\mathcal{O}_1 \cup \mathcal{O}_2, \mathcal{A}$, given as input a tree representing $\mathcal{A}, \rho$. It has polynomially many states, and can thus be turned into an equivalent NTA with exponentially many states (Vardi 1998). By taking the intersection with $\mathfrak{A}_1$, one can then check in exponential time whether $L(\mathfrak{A}_1) \cap L(\mathfrak{A}_2) \neq \emptyset$, that is, whether $\mathcal{O}_1 \cup \mathcal{O}_2, \mathcal{A}^{\Sigma}_{\mathcal{O}_1\cup\mathcal{O}_2,A} \models B(\rho_A)$.

We return to the proof of Theorem 6. The interesting implication is "2. $\Rightarrow$ 3." and the double exponential computation of interpolants. In this case we use transfer sequences to obtain a bound on the size of the subset $\mathcal{A}$ of $\mathcal{A}^{\Sigma,*}_{\mathcal{O}_1\cup\mathcal{O}_2,A}$ needed to derive $B(\rho_A)$ (we note that for $\mathcal{ELI}$ without nominals one can also use the automata encoding above). Transfer sequences describe how facts are derived in a tree-shaped ABox and allow to determine when individuals a and b behave sufficiently similar so that the subtree rooted at a can be replaced by the subtree rooted at b (Bienvenu, Lutz, and Wolter 2013) without affecting a derivation. This technique can be used to show that one can always choose a prefix closed subset $\mathcal{A}$ of $\mathcal{A}^{\Sigma,*}_{\mathcal{O}_1\cup\mathcal{O}_2,A}$ of at most exponential depth. This also implies that $\mathcal{A}$ can be obtained in double exponential time by constructing the canonical model up to depth $2^{q(||\mathcal{O}_1\cup\mathcal{O}_2||)}$ with q a polynomial.

8 Expressive Horn Description Logics

We address two questions regarding expressive Horn-DLs. (1) Can our results for $\mathcal{ELI}$ and extensions be lifted to more expressive Horn-DLs? (2) In the examples provided in the proof of Theorem 1 we sometimes (for example, for $\mathcal{EL}_u$ and $\mathcal{ELI}$) construct explicit Horn-DL definitions to show implicit definability of concept names. Are Horn-DL concepts always sufficient to obtain an explicit definition if an implicit definition exists? We provide a positive answer to (1) if one only admits $\mathcal{ELIO}_u$-concepts (or fragments) as interpolants/explicit definitions and a negative answer to (2) in the sense that $\mathcal{ELI}$ and various other Horn-DLs do not enjoy the CIP/PBDP even if one admits Horn-DL concepts as interpolants/explicit definitions.

We introduce expressive Horn DLs (Hustadt, Motik, and Sattler 2005), presented here in the form proposed in (Lutz and Wolter 2012). *Horn-$\mathcal{ALCIO}_u$-concepts* R and *Horn-$\mathcal{ALCIO}_u$-CIs* $L \sqsubseteq R$ are defined by the syntax rules

$$R, R' ::= \top \mid \bot \mid A \mid \neg A \mid \{a\} \mid \neg\{a\} \mid R \sqcap R' \mid L \rightarrow R \mid \exists r.R \mid \forall r.R$$

$$L, L' ::= \top \mid \bot \mid A \mid L \sqcap L' \mid L \sqcup L' \mid \exists r.L$$

with A ranging over concept names, a over individual names, and r over roles (including the universal role). As usual, the fragment of Horn-$\mathcal{ALCIO}_u$ without nominals and the universal role is denoted by Horn-$\mathcal{ALCI}$ and Horn-$\mathcal{ALC}$ denotes the fragment of Horn-$\mathcal{ALCI}$ without inverse roles.

Theorem 7. *Let $(\mathcal{L}, \mathcal{L}')$ be the pair (Horn-$\mathcal{ALCI}$, $\mathcal{ELI}$) or the pair (Horn-$\mathcal{ALCIO}_u$, $\mathcal{ELIO}_u$). Then*

- *deciding the existence of an $\mathcal{L}'$-interpolant for an $\mathcal{L}'$-CI $C \sqsubseteq D$ under $\mathcal{L}$-ontologies $\mathcal{O}_1, \mathcal{O}_2$ is* EXPTIME*-complete;*
- *deciding the existence of an explicit $\mathcal{L}'(\Sigma)$-definition of a concept name A under an $\mathcal{L}$-ontology $\mathcal{O}$ is* EXPTIME*-complete.*

Moreover, if an $\mathcal{L}$-interpolant/explicit definition exists, then there exists one of at most double exponential size that can be computed in double exponential time.

Theorem 7 follows from Theorem 3 and the fact that for any $\mathcal{L}$-ontology one can construct in polynomial time an $\mathcal{L}'$-ontology in normal form that is a conservative extension of $\mathcal{L}$ (see (Bienvenu et al. 2016) for a similar result). We next show that despite the fact that Horn-$\mathcal{ALCI}$-concepts sometimes provide explicit definitions if none exist in $\mathcal{ELI}$ (proof of Theorem 1), they are not sufficient to prove the CIP/PBDP.

Theorem 8. *There exists an ontology $\mathcal{O}$ in Horn-$\mathcal{ALC}$ (and in $\mathcal{ELI}$), a signature Σ, and a concept name A such that A is implicitly definable using Σ under $\mathcal{O}$ but does not have an explicit Horn-$\mathcal{ALCI}_u(\Sigma)$-definition.*

Proof. We modify the ontology used in the proof of Point 1 of Theorem 1. Let $\Sigma = \{B, D_1, E, r, r_1\}$ and let $\mathcal{O}$ contain $B \sqcap \exists r.(C \sqcap E) \sqsubseteq A$ and the following CIs:

$$A \sqsubseteq B, \quad B \sqsubseteq \forall r.F, \quad B \sqsubseteq \exists r.C, \quad C \sqsubseteq F \sqcap \forall r_1.D_1,$$

$$F \sqsubseteq \exists r_1.D_1 \sqcap \exists r_1.M,$$
$$A \sqsubseteq \forall r.((F \sqcap \exists r_1.(D_1 \sqcap M)) \rightarrow E).$$

Intuitively, the final two CIs should be read as

$$F \sqsubseteq \exists r_1.D_1$$
$$A \sqsubseteq \forall r.((F \sqcap \forall r_1.D_1) \rightarrow E)$$

and the concept name M is introduced to achieve this in a projective way as the latter CI is not in Horn-$\mathcal{ALCI}$.

A is implicitly definable using Σ under $\mathcal{O}$ since

$$\mathcal{O} \models A \equiv B \sqcap \forall r.(\forall r_1.D_1 \rightarrow E).$$

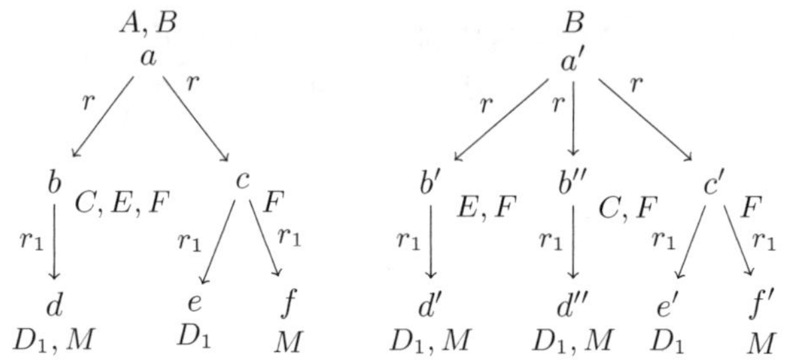

Figure 5: Interpretations $\mathcal{I}$ (left) and $\mathcal{I}'$ (right).

To show that A is not explicitly Horn-$\mathcal{ALCI}_u(\Sigma)$-definable under $\mathcal{O}$ consider the interpretations $\mathcal{I}$ and $\mathcal{I}'$ in Figure 5. The claim follows from the facts that $\mathcal{I}$ and $\mathcal{I}'$ are models of $\mathcal{O}$, $a \in A^{\mathcal{I}}$, $a' \notin A^{\mathcal{I}'}$, but $a \in F^{\mathcal{I}}$ implies $a' \in F^{\mathcal{I}'}$ holds for every Horn-$\mathcal{ALCI}_u(\Sigma)$-concept F. The latter can be proved by observing that there exists a Horn-$\mathcal{ALCI}_u(\Sigma)$-simulation between $\mathcal{I}$ and $\mathcal{I}'$ (Jung et al. 2019) containing $(\{a\}, a)$, we refer the reader to the appendix of the full version. To obtain an example in $\mathcal{ELI}$, it suffices to take a conservative extension of $\mathcal{O}$ in $\mathcal{ELI}$. □

9 Discussion

For a few important extensions of $\mathcal{EL}/\mathcal{ELI}$ the complexity of interpolant and explicit definition existence remains to be investigated. Examples include extensions of $\mathcal{ELI}$ with role inclusions, and extensions of $\mathcal{EL}$ or $\mathcal{ELI}$ with functional roles or more general number restrictions. It would also be of interest to investigate interpolant existence if Horn-concepts are admitted as interpolants (using, for example, the games introduced in (Jung et al. 2019)). Finally, the question arises whether there exists at all a decidable Horn language extending, say, Horn-$\mathcal{ALCI}$, with the CIP/PBDP. We note that Horn-FO enjoys the CIP (Exercise 6.2.6 in (Chang and Keisler 1998)) but is undecidable and that we show in the appendix of the full version that the Horn fragment of the guarded fragment does not enjoy the CIP/PBDP.

Acknowledgments

This research was supported by the EPSRC UK grant EP/S032207/1.

References

Areces, C.; Blackburn, P.; and Marx, M. 2001. Hybrid logics: Characterization, interpolation and complexity. *J. Symb. Log.* 66(3):977–1010.

Artale, A.; Jung, J. C.; Mazzullo, A.; Ozaki, A.; and Wolter, F. 2021a. Living without Beth and Craig: Explicit definitions and interpolants in description logics with nominals and role hierarchies. In *Proc. of AAAI*.

Artale, A.; Mazzullo, A.; Ozaki, A.; and Wolter, F. 2021b. On free description logics with definite descriptions. In *Proc. of KR*.

Baader, F.; Bienvenu, M.; Lutz, C.; and Wolter, F. 2016. Query and predicate emptiness in ontology-based data access. *J. Artif. Intell. Res.* 56:1–59.

Baader, F.; Horrocks, I.; Lutz, C.; and Sattler, U. 2017. *An Introduction to Description Logic*. Cambridge University Press.

Baader, F.; Brandt, S.; and Lutz, C. 2005. Pushing the $\mathcal{EL}$ envelope. In *Proc. of IJCAI*, 364–369.

Benedikt, M.; Leblay, J.; ten Cate, B.; and Tsamoura, E. 2016. *Generating Plans from Proofs: The Interpolation-based Approach to Query Reformulation*. Synthesis Lectures on Data Management. Morgan & Claypool Publishers.

Benedikt, M.; Kostylev, E. V.; Mogavero, F.; and Tsamoura, E. 2017. Reformulating queries: Theory and practice. In *IJCAI*, 837–843.

Bienvenu, M.; Hansen, P.; Lutz, C.; and Wolter, F. 2016. First order-rewritability and containment of conjunctive queries in horn description logics. In *IJCAI*, 965–971.

Bienvenu, M.; Lutz, C.; and Wolter, F. 2013. First-order rewritability of atomic queries in Horn description logics. In *Proc. of IJCAI*.

Borgida, A.; Toman, D.; and Weddell, G. E. 2016. On referring expressions in query answering over first order knowledge bases. In *Proc. of KR*, 319–328.

Chang, C., and Keisler, H. J. 1998. *Model Theory*. Elsevier.

Deutsch, A.; Popa, L.; and Tannen, V. 2006. Query reformulation with constraints. *SIGMOD Rec.* 35(1):65–73.

Geleta, D.; Payne, T. R.; and Tamma, V. A. M. 2016. An investigation of definability in ontology alignment. In Blomqvist, E.; Ciancarini, P.; Poggi, F.; and Vitali, F., eds., *Proc. of EKAW*, 255–271.

Hernich, A.; Lutz, C.; Papacchini, F.; and Wolter, F. 2020. Dichotomies in ontology-mediated querying with the guarded fragment. *ACM Trans. Comput. Log.* 21(3):20:1–20:47.

Hustadt, U.; Motik, B.; and Sattler, U. 2005. Data complexity of reasoning in very expressive description logics. In *IJCAI*, 466–471.

Jung, J. C., and Wolter, F. 2021. Living without Beth and Craig: Definitions and interpolants in the guarded and two-variable fragments. In *Proc. of LICS*.

Jung, J. C.; Papacchini, F.; Wolter, F.; and Zakharyaschev, M. 2019. Model comparison games for horn description logics. In *Proc. of LICS*, 1–14. IEEE.

Jung, J. C.; Lutz, C.; Martel, M.; and Schneider, T. 2020. Conservative extensions in horn description logics with inverse roles. *J. Artif. Intell. Res.* 68:365–411.

Konev, B.; Lutz, C.; Walther, D.; and Wolter, F. 2009. Formal properties of modularisation. In *Modular Ontologies*, volume 5445 of *Lecture Notes in Computer Science*. Springer. 25–66.

Konev, B.; Lutz, C.; Ponomaryov, D. K.; and Wolter, F. 2010. Decomposing description logic ontologies. In *Proc. of KR*. AAAI Press.

Koopmann, P., and Schmidt, R. A. 2015. Uniform interpolation and forgetting for ALC ontologies with aboxes. In *Proc. of AAAI*, 175–181. AAAI Press.

Lutz, C., and Wolter, F. 2010. Deciding inseparability and conservative extensions in the description logic EL. *J. Symb. Comput.* 45(2):194–228.

Lutz, C., and Wolter, F. 2011. Foundations for uniform interpolation and forgetting in expressive description logics. In *Proc. of IJCAI*, 989–995. IJCAI/AAAI.

Lutz, C., and Wolter, F. 2012. Non-uniform data complexity of query answering in description logics. In Brewka, G.; Eiter, T.; and McIlraith, S. A., eds., *Proc. of KR*.

Lutz, C., and Wolter, F. 2017. The data complexity of description logic ontologies. *Logical Methods in Computer Science* 13(4).

Lutz, C.; Piro, R.; and Wolter, F. 2011. Description logic tboxes: Model-theoretic characterizations and rewritability. In Walsh, T., ed., *Proc. of IJCAI*, 983–988. IJCAI/AAAI.

Lutz, C.; Seylan, I.; and Wolter, F. 2012. An automata-theoretic approach to uniform interpolation and approximation in the description logic EL. In *Proc. of KR*. AAAI Press.

Lutz, C.; Seylan, I.; and Wolter, F. 2019. The data complexity of ontology-mediated queries with closed predicates. *Logical Methods in Computer Science* 15(3).

Maksimova, L., and Gabbay, D. 2005. *Interpolation and Definability in Modal and Intuitionistic Logics*. Clarendon Press.

Nikitina, N., and Rudolph, S. 2014. (Non-)succinctness of uniform interpolants of general terminologies in the description logic EL. *Artif. Intell.* 215:120–140.

Place, T., and Zeitoun, M. 2016. Separating regular languages with first-order logic. *Log. Methods Comput. Sci.* 12(1).

Seylan, I.; Franconi, E.; and de Bruijn, J. 2009. Effective query rewriting with ontologies over dboxes. In *Proc. of IJCAI*, 923–925.

Sofronie-Stokkermans, V. 2008. Interpolation in local theory extensions. *Log. Methods Comput. Sci.* 4(4).

ten Cate, B.; Conradie, W.; Marx, M.; and Venema, Y. 2006. Definitorially complete description logics. In *Proc. of KR*, 79–89. AAAI Press.

ten Cate, B.; Franconi, E.; and Seylan, İ. 2013. Beth definability in expressive description logics. *J. Artif. Intell. Res.* 48:347–414.

ten Cate, B. 2005. Interpolation for extended modal languages. *J. Symb. Log.* 70(1):223–234.

Toman, D., and Weddell, G. E. 2011. *Fundamentals of Physical Design and Query Compilation.* Synthesis Lectures on Data Management. Morgan & Claypool Publishers.

Toman, D., and Weddell, G. E. 2021. FO rewritability for OMQ using beth definability and interpolation. In Homola, M.; Ryzhikov, V.; and Schmidt, R. A., eds., *Proc. of DL.* CEUR-WS.org.

Vardi, M. Y. 1998. Reasoning about the past with two-way automata. In *Proc. of ICALP'98*, 628–641.

Proceedings of the 19th International Conference on Principles of Knowledge Representation and Reasoning
Main Track

Unique Characterisability and Learnability of Temporal Instance Queries

Marie Fortin[1] , **Boris Konev**[1] , **Vladislav Ryzhikov**[2] ,
Yury Savateev[2] , **Frank Wolter**[1] , **Michael Zakharyaschev**[2]
[1]Department of Computer Science, University of Liverpool, UK
[2]Department of Computer Science, Birkbeck, University of London, UK
{marie.fortin,boris.konev,wolter@liverpool.ac.uk}, {vlad,yury,michael}@dcs.bbk.ac.uk

Abstract

We aim to determine which temporal instance queries can be uniquely characterised by a (polynomial-size) set of positive and negative temporal data examples. We start by considering queries formulated in fragments of propositional linear temporal logic *LTL* that correspond to conjunctive queries (CQs) or extensions thereof induced by the until operator. Not all of these queries admit polynomial characterisations but by restricting them further to path-shaped queries we identify natural classes that do. We then investigate how far the obtained characterisations can be lifted to temporal knowledge graphs queried by 2D languages combining *LTL* with concepts in description logics $\mathcal{EL}$ or $\mathcal{ELI}$ (i.e., tree-shaped CQs). While temporal operators in the scope of description logic constructors can destroy polynomial characterisability, we obtain general transfer results for the case when description logic constructors are within the scope of temporal operators. Finally, we apply our characterisations to establish (polynomial) learnability of temporal instance queries using membership queries in the active learning framework.

1 Introduction

Constructing queries or, more generally, logical concepts describing individuals of interest, can be difficult. Providing support to a user to cope with this problem has been a major research topic in databases, logic, and knowledge representation. For instance, in reverse engineering of database queries and concept descriptions (Martins 2019; Lehmann and Hitzler 2010; Jung et al. 2020), one aims to identify a query using a set of positively and negatively labelled examples of answers and non-answers, respectively; and in active learning approaches, one aims to identify a query by asking an oracle (e.g., domain specialist) whether an example is an answer or a non-answer to the query (Angluin, Frazier, and Pitt 1992; Funk, Jung, and Lutz 2021; ten Cate and Dalmau 2021).

Recently, the *unique characterisation* of a query by a finite (ideally, polynomial-size) set of positive and negative example answers has been identified as a fundamental link between queries and data (ten Cate and Dalmau 2021). Namely, we say that a query $\boldsymbol{q}$ *fits* a pair $E = (E^+, E^-)$ of sets E^+ and E^- of pointed databases $(\mathcal{D}, a)$ if $\mathcal{D} \models \boldsymbol{q}(a)$ for $(\mathcal{D}, a) \in E^+$, and $\mathcal{D} \not\models \boldsymbol{q}(a)$ for $(\mathcal{D}, a) \in E^-$. Then E *uniquely characterises* $\boldsymbol{q}$ within a class $\mathcal{Q}$ of queries if $\boldsymbol{q}$ is the only (up to equivalence) query in $\mathcal{Q}$ that fits E.

Unique (polynomial) characterisations can be used to illustrate, explain, and construct queries. They are also a 'non-procedural' necessary condition for (polynomial) learnability using membership queries in Angluin's (1987b) framework of active learning, where membership queries to the oracle take the form 'does $\mathcal{D} \models \boldsymbol{q}(a)$ hold?'. It is shown by ten Cate and Dalmau (2021) that, for classes of conjunctive queries (CQs), it is often a sufficient condition as well.

In many applications, queries are required to capture the temporal evolution of individuals, making their formulation even harder. The aim of this paper is to start an investigation of the (polynomial) characterisability of temporal instance queries. We first consider one-dimensional data instances of the form $(\delta_0, \dots, \delta_n)$, where δ_i is the set of atomic propositions that are true at timestamp i, describing the temporal behaviour of a single individual, and queries formulated in fragments of propositional linear temporal logic *LTL*. Although rather basic as a temporal data model, this restriction allows us to focus on the purely temporal aspect of unique characterisability. We then generalise our results, where possible, to standard two-dimensional temporal data instances, in which the δ_i are replaced by non-temporal data instances and queries are obtained by combining fragments of *LTL* with $\mathcal{ELI}$-concept queries (or tree-shaped CQs), thereby combining a well established formalism for accessing temporal data (Chomicki and Toman 2018) with the basic concept descriptions for tractable data access from description logic (Baader et al. 2017).

Our initial observation is that already very primitive temporal queries are not uniquely characterisable. For example[1], consider the query $\boldsymbol{q} = \Diamond_r(A \wedge B)$ with the operator $\Diamond_r$ 'now or later' (interpreted by $\leq$ over linearly ordered timestamps). By the pigeonhole principle, no finite example set E can distinguish $\boldsymbol{q}$ from a query $\boldsymbol{q}' = \Diamond_r(A \wedge (\Diamond_r B \wedge \Diamond_r(A \wedge \dots)))$ with sufficiently many alternating A and B. Similarly, the query $\boldsymbol{q} = \bigcirc A$ with the 'next time' operator $\bigcirc$ is not distinguishable by a finite example set from $\boldsymbol{q}' = (\bigcirc \dots \bigcirc A) \mathsf{U} A$ with the strict 'until' operator U and sufficiently many $\bigcirc$ on its left-hand side.

Aiming to identify natural and useful classes of temporal queries enjoying (polynomial) characterisability, in this

[1]For detailed explanations and omitted proofs, the reader is referred to the full Arxiv version (Fortin et al. 2022b) of this paper.

paper we consider the conjunctive fragment of *LTL*. To begin with, we focus on two classes of path CQs: the class $\mathcal{Q}_p[\bigcirc, \Diamond_r]$ of queries of the form

$$\boldsymbol{q} = \rho_0 \wedge \boldsymbol{o}_1(\rho_1 \wedge \boldsymbol{o}_2(\rho_2 \wedge \cdots \wedge \boldsymbol{o}_n\rho_n)), \quad (1)$$

where $\boldsymbol{o}_i \in \{\bigcirc, \Diamond_r\}$ and ρ_i is a conjunction of atomic propositions, and also the class $\mathcal{Q}_p^\sigma[\mathsf{U}]$ of U-queries of the form

$$\boldsymbol{q} = \rho_0 \wedge (\lambda_1 \mathsf{U} (\rho_1 \wedge (\lambda_2 \mathsf{U} (\dots (\lambda_n \mathsf{U} \rho_n) \dots)))), \quad (2)$$

where λ_i is a conjunction of atoms or $\bot$. The superscript σ in $\mathcal{Q}_p^\sigma[\mathsf{U}]$ indicates that queries are formulated in a finite signature σ, a condition required because of the universal quantification implicit in U. Our first main result is a syntactic criterion of (polynomial) characterisability of $\mathcal{Q}_p[\bigcirc, \Diamond_r]$-queries. In fact, it turns out that the query $\Diamond_r(A \wedge B)$ mentioned above epitomises the cause of non-characterisability in $\mathcal{Q}_p[\bigcirc, \Diamond_r]$. It follows, in particular, that the restriction $\mathcal{Q}_p[\bigcirc, \Diamond]$ of $\mathcal{Q}_p[\bigcirc, \Diamond_r]$ to queries with $\bigcirc$ and strict eventuality $\Diamond = \bigcirc\Diamond_r$ is polynomially characterisable. Our second main result is that all $\mathcal{Q}_p^\sigma[\mathsf{U}]$-queries with $\subseteq$-incomparable λ_i and ρ_i, for each i, are polynomially characterisable within $\mathcal{Q}_p^\sigma[\mathsf{U}]$. Although we show that all $\mathcal{Q}_p^\sigma[\mathsf{U}]$-queries are exponentially characterisable, it remains open whether they are polynomially characterisable in $\mathcal{Q}_p^\sigma[\mathsf{U}]$.

The essential property that distinguishes $\mathcal{Q}_p[\bigcirc, \Diamond_r]$ and $\mathcal{Q}_p^\sigma[\mathsf{U}]$ from other queries is that they do not admit temporal branching as, for instance, in $\Diamond A \wedge \Diamond B$. In fact, we show that even within the class of queries using only $\wedge$ and $\Diamond$ and with a bound on the number of branches, not all queries are polynomially characterisable. A first step towards positive results covering non-path queries is made for the case of queries in which all branches are of equal length.

Our next aim is to generalise the obtained results to 2D temporal queries combining *LTL* with the description logic constructor $\exists P$ of $\mathcal{ELI}$. Our first main result is negative: even queries of the form $\exists P.\boldsymbol{q}_1 \wedge \cdots \wedge \exists P.\boldsymbol{q}_n$, in which $\boldsymbol{q}_i \in \mathcal{Q}_p[\bigcirc, \Diamond]$, are not polynomially characterisable. The situation changes drastically, however, if we consider queries of the form (1) or (2), in which ρ_i and λ_i are $\mathcal{ELI}$-queries. Indeed, we generalise our polynomial characterisability results for $\mathcal{Q}_p[\bigcirc, \Diamond_r]$ and $\mathcal{Q}_p^\sigma[\mathsf{U}]$ to such queries using recent results on the computation of frontiers in the lattice of $\mathcal{ELI}$-queries (ten Cate and Dalmau 2021) and proving a new result on split partners in the lattice of $\mathcal{EL}$-queries (where $\mathcal{EL}$ denotes $\mathcal{ELI}$ without inverse roles).

Finally, we discuss applications of our results to learning temporal instance queries using membership queries of the form 'does $\mathcal{D} \models \boldsymbol{q}$ hold?'. As we always construct example sets effectively, our unique (exponential) characterisability results imply (exponential-time) learnability with membership queries. Obtaining polynomial-time learnability from polynomial characterisations is more challenging. A main result here is that $\mathcal{Q}_p[\bigcirc, \Diamond_r]$ with $\mathcal{ELI}$-queries is polynomial-time learnable with membership queries, assuming the learner is given the target query size in advance.

2 Related Work

Our contribution is closely related to work on active learnability of formal languages and on learning temporal logic formulas interpreted over finite and infinite traces. It is also related to learning database queries and other formal expressions for accessing data. In the former area, the seminal paper by Angluin (1987a) has given rise to a large body of work on active learning of regular languages or variations, for example, (Shahbaz and Groz 2009; Aarts and Vaandrager 2010; Cassel et al. 2016; Howar and Steffen 2018). This work has mainly focused on learning various types of finite state machines or automata using a combination of membership queries with other powerful types of queries such as equivalence queries. The use of two or more types of queries is motivated by the fact that otherwise one cannot efficiently learn a wide variety of important languages, including regular languages. In fact, the main difference between this work and our contribution is that we focus on queries for which the corresponding formal languages form only a small subset of the regular languages and it is this restriction that enables us to focus on characterisability and learnability with membership queries.

Rather surprisingly, there has hardly been any work on active learning of temporal formulas over finite or infinite traces; we refer the reader to (Camacho and McIlraith 2019), also for a discussion of the relationship between learning automata and *LTL*-formulas. In contrast, passive learning of *LTL*-formulas has recently received significant attention; see (Lemieux, Park, and Beschastnikh 2015; Neider and Gavran 2018; Fijalkow and Lagarde 2021; Fortin et al. 2022a) and, in the context of explainable AI, also (Camacho and McIlraith 2019) for an overview.

In the database and KR communities, there has been extensive work on identifying queries and concept descriptions from data examples. For instance, in reverse engineering of queries, the goal is typically to decide whether there is a query that fits (or separates) a set of positive and negative examples. Relevant work under the closed world assumption include (Arenas and Diaz 2016; Barceló and Romero 2017) and under the open world assumption (Gutiérrez-Basulto, Jung, and Sabellek 2018; Funk et al. 2019). Related work on active learning not yet discussed include the identification of $\mathcal{EL}$-queries (Funk, Jung, and Lutz 2021) and ontologies (Konev, Ozaki, and Wolter 2016; Konev et al. 2017), and of schema-mappings (ten Cate, Dalmau, and Kolaitis 2013; ten Cate et al. 2018). Again this work differs from our contribution as it focuses on learning using membership and equivalence queries rather than only the former. The use of unique characterisations to explain and construct schema mappings has been promoted and investigated by Kolaitis (2011) and Alexe et al. (2011).

Combining *LTL* and description logics for temporal conceptual modelling and data access has a long tradition (Lutz, Wolter, and Zakharyaschev 2008; Artale et al. 2017). For querying purposes, sometimes description logic concepts have been replaced by general CQs. Our restriction to $\mathcal{ELI}$-concepts instead of general CQs is motivated by results of (ten Cate and Dalmau 2021) showing that only CQs that are acyclic modulo cycles through the answer variables are polynomially characterisable within the class of CQs. Hence very strong acyclicity conditions are needed to ensure polynomial characterisability. We conjecture that our results can be extended to this class.

The class of queries in which no $\exists P$ is within the scope of temporal operators was first introduced by (Baader, Borgwardt, and Lippmann 2015; Borgwardt and Thost 2015) in the context of monitoring applications. The lcs and msc in temporal DLs are considered by Tirtarasa and Turhan 2022.

3 Preliminaries

By a *signature* we mean any finite set $\sigma \neq \emptyset$ of *atomic concepts* $A, B, C, \dots$ representing observations, measurements, events, etc. A *σ-data instance* is any finite sequence $\mathcal{D} = (\delta_0, \dots, \delta_n)$ with $\delta_i \subseteq \sigma$, saying that $A \in \delta_i$ happened at moment i. The *length* of $\mathcal{D}$ is $\max(\mathcal{D}) = n$ and the *size* of $\mathcal{D}$ is $|\mathcal{D}| = \Sigma_{i \leq n}|\delta_i|$. We do not distinguish between $\mathcal{D}$ and its variants of the form $(\delta_0, \dots, \delta_n, \emptyset, \dots, \emptyset)$.

We access data by means of *queries*, $\boldsymbol{q}$, constructed from atoms, $\bot$ and $\top$ using $\wedge$ and the temporal operators $\bigcirc$, $\Diamond$, $\Diamond_r$ and U. The set of atomic concepts occurring in $\boldsymbol{q}$ is denoted by $sig(\boldsymbol{q})$. The set of queries that only use the operators from $\Phi \subseteq \{\bigcirc, \Diamond, \Diamond_r, \mathsf{U}\}$ is denoted by $\mathcal{Q}[\Phi]$; $\mathcal{Q}^\sigma[\Phi]$ is the restriction of $\mathcal{Q}[\Phi]$ to a signature σ. The *size* $|\boldsymbol{q}|$ of $\boldsymbol{q}$ is the number of symbols in $\boldsymbol{q}$, and the *temporal depth* $tdp(\boldsymbol{q})$ of $\boldsymbol{q}$ is the maximum number of nested temporal operators in $\boldsymbol{q}$.

$\mathcal{Q}[\bigcirc, \Diamond, \Diamond_r]$-queries can be equivalently defined as *tree-shaped* conjunctive queries (CQs) with the binary predicates *suc*, $<$, $\leq$ over $\mathbb{N}$, and atomic concepts as unary predicates. Each such CQ is a set $Q(t_0)$ of assertions of the form $A(t)$, $suc(t, t')$, $t < t'$, and $t \leq t'$, with a distinguished variable t_0, such that, for every variable t in $Q(t_0)$, there exists exactly one path from t_0 to t along the binary predicates *suc*, $<$, $\leq$.

The set of $\mathcal{Q}[\bigcirc, \Diamond, \Diamond_r]$-queries with *path-shaped* CQ counterparts is denoted by $\mathcal{Q}_p[\bigcirc, \Diamond, \Diamond_r]$. Such queries $\boldsymbol{q}$ take the form (1), where $\boldsymbol{o}_i \in \{\bigcirc, \Diamond, \Diamond_r\}$ and ρ_i is a conjunction of atoms (the empty conjunction is $\top$). Similarly, $\mathcal{Q}_p[\mathsf{U}]$-queries take the form (2).

Given a data instance $\mathcal{D} = (\delta_0, \dots, \delta_n)$, the *truth-relation* $\mathcal{D}, \ell \models \boldsymbol{q}$, for $\ell < \omega$, is defined as follows:

$$\mathcal{D}, \ell \models A \text{ iff } A \in \delta_\ell, \qquad \mathcal{D}, \ell \models \top, \qquad \mathcal{D}, \ell \not\models \bot,$$
$$\mathcal{D}, \ell \models \boldsymbol{q}_1 \wedge \boldsymbol{q}_2 \text{ iff } \mathcal{D}, \ell \models \boldsymbol{q}_1 \text{ and } \mathcal{D}, \ell \models \boldsymbol{q}_2,$$
$$\mathcal{D}, \ell \models \bigcirc \boldsymbol{q} \text{ iff } \mathcal{D}, \ell + 1 \models \boldsymbol{q},$$
$$\mathcal{D}, \ell \models \Diamond \boldsymbol{q} \text{ iff } \mathcal{D}, m \models \boldsymbol{q}, \text{ for some } m > \ell,$$
$$\mathcal{D}, \ell \models \Diamond_r \boldsymbol{q} \text{ iff } \mathcal{D}, m \models \boldsymbol{q}, \text{ for some } m \geq \ell,$$
$$\mathcal{D}, \ell \models \boldsymbol{q}_1 \mathsf{U} \boldsymbol{q}_2 \text{ iff there is } m > \ell \text{ such that } \mathcal{D}, m \models \boldsymbol{q}_2 \text{ and } \mathcal{D}, k \models \boldsymbol{q}_1, \text{ for all } k \text{ with } \ell < k < m.$$

Note that $\mathcal{D}, n \models \Diamond\top \wedge \bigcirc\top \wedge (\boldsymbol{q} \mathsf{U} \top)$ as $(\delta_0, \dots, \delta_n, \emptyset)$ is a variant of $\mathcal{D}$. We write $\boldsymbol{q} \models \boldsymbol{q}'$ if $\mathcal{D}, \ell \models \boldsymbol{q}$ implies $\mathcal{D}, \ell \models \boldsymbol{q}'$ for any $\mathcal{D}$ and ℓ. If $\boldsymbol{q} \models \boldsymbol{q}'$ and $\boldsymbol{q}' \models \boldsymbol{q}$, we call $\boldsymbol{q}$ and $\boldsymbol{q}'$ *equivalent* and write $\boldsymbol{q} \equiv \boldsymbol{q}'$. Since $\bigcirc\boldsymbol{q} \equiv \bot\mathsf{U}\boldsymbol{q}$, $\Diamond\boldsymbol{q} \equiv \top\mathsf{U}\boldsymbol{q}$ and $\Diamond\boldsymbol{q} \equiv \bigcirc\Diamond_r\boldsymbol{q}$, one can assume that $\mathcal{Q}[\bigcirc, \Diamond] \subseteq \mathcal{Q}[\mathsf{U}]$, $\mathcal{Q}[\Diamond] \subseteq \mathcal{Q}[\bigcirc, \Diamond_r]$ and $\mathcal{Q}[\bigcirc, \Diamond_r] = \mathcal{Q}[\bigcirc, \Diamond_r, \Diamond]$.

4 Unique Characterisability

An *example set* is a pair $E = (E^+, E^-)$ with finite sets E^+ and E^- of data instances that are called *positive* and *negative examples*, respectively. A query $\boldsymbol{q}$ *fits* E if $\mathcal{D}^+, 0 \models \boldsymbol{q}$ and $\mathcal{D}^-, 0 \not\models \boldsymbol{q}$, for all $\mathcal{D}^+ \in E^+$ and $\mathcal{D}^- \in E^-$. We say that E *uniquely characterises* $\boldsymbol{q}$ within a class $\mathcal{Q}$ of queries if $\boldsymbol{q}$ fits E and $\boldsymbol{q} \equiv \boldsymbol{q}'$ for any $\boldsymbol{q}' \in \mathcal{Q}$ that fits E. If all $\boldsymbol{q} \in \mathcal{Q}$ are characterised by some E within $\mathcal{Q}' \supseteq \mathcal{Q}$, we call $\mathcal{Q}$ *uniquely characterisable* within $\mathcal{Q}'$. Further, $\mathcal{Q}$ is *polynomially characterisable* within $\mathcal{Q}' \supseteq \mathcal{Q}$ if there is a polynomial f such that every $\boldsymbol{q} \in \mathcal{Q}$ is characterised within $\mathcal{Q}'$ by some E of size $|E| \leq f(|\boldsymbol{q}|)$, where $|E| = \Sigma_{\mathcal{D} \in (E^+ \cup E^-)}|\mathcal{D}|$. Let $\mathcal{Q}^n$ be the set of queries in $\mathcal{Q}$ of size at most n. We say that $\mathcal{Q}$ is *polynomially characterisable for bounded query size* if there is a polynomial f such that every $\boldsymbol{q} \in \mathcal{Q}^n$ is characterised by some E of size $\leq f(n)$ within $\mathcal{Q}^n$.

Observe that (polynomial) characterisability is anti-monotone: if a query $\boldsymbol{q}$ is (polynomially) characterisable within $\mathcal{Q}$ and $\mathcal{Q}' \subseteq \mathcal{Q}$, then $\boldsymbol{q}$ is (polynomially) characterisable within $\mathcal{Q}'$. In counterexamples to characterisability, we therefore only provide the smallest natural class of queries within which non-characterisability holds. The following examples illustrate (non-)characterisability within the classes $\mathcal{Q}_p[\Diamond_r]$ and $\mathcal{Q}_p[\bigcirc, \Diamond_r]$.

Example 1. (i) Recall from Section 1 that $\Diamond_r(A \wedge B)$ is not uniquely characterisable within $\mathcal{Q}_p[\Diamond_r]$. The same argument shows non-characterisability of $\Diamond(A \wedge B)$ within $\mathcal{Q}_p[\Diamond_r, \Diamond]$. On the other hand, the query $\Diamond(A \wedge B)$ is characterised within $\mathcal{Q}_p[\Diamond, \bigcirc]$ by the example set with positive examples $(\emptyset, \{A, B\})$ and $(\emptyset, \emptyset, \{A, B\})$ and negative examples $(\emptyset, \{A\})$ and $(\emptyset, \{B\})$.

(ii) The conjunction of atoms does not always lead to non-characterisability within classes of queries with $\Diamond_r$. For example, $\boldsymbol{q} = \Diamond_r(A \wedge \bigcirc(A \wedge B))$ is characterised within $\mathcal{Q}_p[\bigcirc, \Diamond_r]$ by $E = (E^+, E^-)$ in which E^+ contains two data instances $(\{A\}, \{A, B\})$ and $(\emptyset, \{A\}, \{A, B\})$ and E^- also two instances:

$$(\emptyset, \emptyset, \{A, B\}), \quad (\emptyset, \{A\}, \{A\}, \{B\}, \{A, B\}).$$

The intuition here is that some instances from E^- have to satisfy the query $\Diamond_r(A \wedge \bigcirc(B \wedge \Diamond_r(A \wedge B)))$ as well as the query $\Diamond_r(A \wedge \bigcirc(A \wedge \Diamond_r(A \wedge B)))$.

(iii) While the query $\Diamond_r(A \wedge B)$ from (i) is not characterisable, there is a polynomial f such that, for all $n \in \mathbb{N}$, it is characterisable within $\mathcal{Q}_p^n[\bigcirc, \Diamond_r]$ by some E_n of size $\leq f(n)$. Namely, we take $E^+ = \{(\{A, B\}), (\emptyset, \{A, B\})\}$ and $E^- = \{(\underbrace{\{A\}, \{B\}, \dots, \{A\}, \{B\}}_{n \text{ times}})\}$.

Observe that one can always separate $\boldsymbol{q} \in \mathcal{Q}[\bigcirc, \Diamond_r]$ from any other $\boldsymbol{q}' \in \mathcal{Q}[\bigcirc, \Diamond_r]$ with $sig(\boldsymbol{q}') \supsetneq \text{sig}(\boldsymbol{q}) = \sigma$ using the positive example $(\sigma, \dots, \sigma)$ with $tdp(\boldsymbol{q})+1$-many copies of σ. One can therefore focus on characterisability within the relevant class of queries over the same signature as the input query. However, this is not the case for $\mathcal{Q}[\mathsf{U}]$:

Example 2. The query $\boldsymbol{q} = \bot \,\mathsf{U}\, A \equiv \bigcirc A$ is not uniquely characterisable within $\mathcal{Q}_p[\mathsf{U}]$. Indeed, suppose $\boldsymbol{q}$ fits E and σ comprises all atoms occurring in E. Then $\mathcal{D}, 0 \models C \,\mathsf{U}\, A$ iff $\mathcal{D}, 0 \models \bigcirc A$, for all $\mathcal{D}$ in E and $C \notin \sigma$, and so E does not characterise $\boldsymbol{q}$. On the other hand, for the signature $\sigma = \{A, B\}$, the query $\boldsymbol{q}$ is characterised within $\mathcal{Q}_p^\sigma[\mathsf{U}]$ by the example set (E^+, E^-) in which $E^+ = \{(\emptyset, \{A\})\}$ and $E^- = \{(\sigma, \{B\}, \{A\})\}$ as $A \,\mathsf{U}\, A \equiv (A \wedge B) \,\mathsf{U}\, A \equiv \bigcirc A$.

As noted in Section 1, $\bot$ U A is not uniquely characterisable within $\mathcal{Q}^{\{A\}}[\mathsf{U}]$ because of nested U-operators on the left-hand side of U. This observation prompts us to consider the subclass $\mathcal{Q}^{\sigma}_{-}[\mathsf{U}]$ of $\mathcal{Q}^{\sigma}[\mathsf{U}]$-queries $\boldsymbol{q}$ in which any subquery $\boldsymbol{q}' \,\mathsf{U}\, \boldsymbol{q}''$ does not contain occurrences of U in $\boldsymbol{q}'$. Note that $\mathcal{Q}^{\sigma}_{p}[\mathsf{U}] \subseteq \mathcal{Q}^{\sigma}_{-}[\mathsf{U}]$. We show that $\mathcal{Q}^{\sigma}_{-}[\mathsf{U}]$ is uniquely characterisable. To simplify notation, we give σ-data instances as *words* over the alphabet 2^{σ} using the standard notation of regular languages. Instead of $\mathcal{D}, 0 \models \boldsymbol{q}$ we simply write $\mathcal{D} \models \boldsymbol{q}$. By the semantics of U, for any $\boldsymbol{q} \in \mathcal{Q}^{\sigma}_{-}[\mathsf{U}]$, we have

$$\sigma^d \not\models \boldsymbol{q} \text{ for } d \leq \mathit{tdp}(\boldsymbol{q}), \quad \sigma^d \models \boldsymbol{q} \text{ for } d > \mathit{tdp}(\boldsymbol{q}) \quad (3)$$

where σ^d is a word with d-many σ. Note also that there are finitely-many, say $N_d < \omega$, pairwise non-equivalent queries of any depth $d < \omega$ in $\mathcal{Q}^{\sigma}_{-}(\mathsf{U})$.

Lemma 3. *If $\boldsymbol{q}, \boldsymbol{q}' \in \mathcal{Q}^{\sigma}_{-}[\mathsf{U}]$ are of depth d and $\boldsymbol{q} \not\models \boldsymbol{q}'$, then there is $\mathcal{D}$ such that $\max(\mathcal{D}) \leq N_d$, $\mathcal{D} \models \boldsymbol{q}$ and $\mathcal{D} \not\models \boldsymbol{q}'$.*

Proof. Consider $\mathcal{D}$ of minimal length such that $\mathcal{D} \models \boldsymbol{q}$ and $\mathcal{D} \not\models \boldsymbol{q}'$. Let $\mathit{tp}(i)$ comprise all of the subqueries $\boldsymbol{s}$ of $\boldsymbol{q}$ and $\boldsymbol{q}'$ with $\mathcal{D}, i \models \boldsymbol{s}$. By the choice of $\mathcal{D}$, we have $\mathit{tp}(i) \neq \mathit{tp}(j)$ for any distinct $i, j \in [0, \max(\mathcal{D})]$ (otherwise we could cut the interval $[i, j)$ out of $\mathcal{D}$ to obtain a shorter instance separating $\boldsymbol{q}$ from $\boldsymbol{q}'$). It follows that $\max(\mathcal{D}) \leq N_d$. ❑

Theorem 4. *For any σ, $\mathcal{Q}^{\sigma}_{-}[\mathsf{U}]$ is uniquely characterisable.*

Proof. Any $\boldsymbol{q} \in \mathcal{Q}^{\sigma}_{-}(\mathsf{U})$ is uniquely characterised by E with

$$E^+ = \{\mathcal{D} \models \boldsymbol{q} \mid \max(\mathcal{D}) \leq N_{\mathit{tdp}(\boldsymbol{q})}\},$$
$$E^- = \{\mathcal{D} \not\models \boldsymbol{q} \mid \max(\mathcal{D}) \leq N_{\mathit{tdp}(\boldsymbol{q})}\}.$$

Indeed, let $\boldsymbol{q}' \in \mathcal{Q}^{\sigma}_{-}(\mathsf{U})$ fit E. Then $\mathit{tdp}(\boldsymbol{q}') = \mathit{tdp}(\boldsymbol{q})$ by (3), and so $\boldsymbol{q} \equiv \boldsymbol{q}'$ by Lemma 3. ❑

It follows from the proof that $\mathcal{Q}[\bigcirc, \Diamond]$ is uniquely characterisable as well.

5 Characterisability in $\mathcal{Q}_p[\bigcirc, \Diamond_r]$

In this section, we prove a criterion of (polynomial) unique characterisability of queries within $\mathcal{Q}_p[\bigcirc, \Diamond_r]$. The criterion is applicable to $\mathcal{Q}_p[\bigcirc, \Diamond, \Diamond_r]$-queries in a normal form, which is defined and illustrated below.

Example 5. It is readily checked that the $\mathcal{Q}_p[\bigcirc, \Diamond_r]$-query $\boldsymbol{q} = \bigcirc\Diamond_r\bigcirc\Diamond_r(A \wedge B \wedge C \wedge \Diamond_r(B \wedge \Diamond_r(B \wedge C)))$ is equivalent to the $\mathcal{Q}_p[\bigcirc, \Diamond, \Diamond_r]$-query $\boldsymbol{q}^{nf} = \Diamond\Diamond(A \wedge B \wedge C)$.

We define the normal form for $\mathcal{Q}_p[\bigcirc, \Diamond, \Diamond_r]$-queries represented as a first-order CQ by a list of atoms. For example, the query $\boldsymbol{q}^{nf}$ above is given by the CQ

$$\boldsymbol{q}^{nf}(t_0) = t_0 < t_1, t_1 < t_2, A(t_2), B(t_2), C(t_2)$$

with one free (answer) variable t_0 and existentially quantified t_1 and t_2. In general, any $\boldsymbol{q} \in \mathcal{Q}_p[\bigcirc, \Diamond, \Diamond_r]$ is represented as a CQ

$$\rho_0(t_0), R_1(t_0, t_1), \dots, \rho_{n-1}(t_{n-1}), R_n(t_{n-1}, t_n), \rho_n(t_n),$$

where ρ_i is a set of atoms, $\rho_i(t_i) = \{A(t_i) \mid A \in \rho_i\}$ and $R_i \in \{\mathit{suc}, <, \leq\}$. We divide $\boldsymbol{q}$ into *blocks* $\boldsymbol{q}_i$ such that

$$\boldsymbol{q} = \boldsymbol{q}_0 \mathcal{R}_1 \boldsymbol{q}_1 \dots \mathcal{R}_n \boldsymbol{q}_n \quad (4)$$

with $\mathcal{R}_i = R^i_1(t^i_0, t^i_1) \dots R^i_{n_i}(t^i_{n_i-1}, t^i_{n_i})$, for $R^i_j \in \{<, \leq\}$,

$$\boldsymbol{q}_i = \rho^i_0(s^i_0)\mathit{suc}(s^i_0, s^i_1)\rho^i_1(s^i_1) \dots \mathit{suc}(s^i_{k_i-1}, s^i_{k_i})\rho^i_{k_i}(s^i_{k_i})$$

and $s^i_{k_i} = t^{i+1}_0$, $t^i_{n_i} = s^i_0$. If $k_i = 0$, the block $\boldsymbol{q}_i$ is *primitive*. A primitive block $\boldsymbol{q}_i = \rho^i_0(s^i_0)$ with $i > 0$ and $|\rho^i_0| \geq 2$ is called a *lone conjunct* of $\boldsymbol{q}$.

Example 6. The query $\Diamond_r(A \wedge B)$ in Example 1(i), whose CQ representation is $t_0 \leq t_1, \rho_1(t_1)$, for $\rho_1 = \{A, B\}$, has a lone conjunct $\rho_1(t_1)$. In $\Diamond_r(A \wedge \bigcirc(A \wedge B))$ from Example 1(ii), represented as $t_0 \leq t_1$, $A(t_1), \mathit{suc}(t_1, t_2), \rho_1(t_2)$, the conjunct $\rho_1(t_2)$ is not lone.

Now, we say that $\boldsymbol{q}$ given by (4) is in *normal form* if the following conditions are satisfied:

(n1) $\rho^i_0 \neq \emptyset$ if $i > 0$, and $\rho^i_{k_i} \neq \emptyset$ if $i > 0$ or $k_i > 0$ (thus, of all the first/last ρ in a block, only ρ^0_0 can be empty);

(n2) each $\mathcal{R}_i$ is either a single $t^i_0 \leq t^i_1$ or a sequence of $<$;

(n3) $\rho^i_{k_i} \not\supseteq \rho^{i+1}_0$ if $\boldsymbol{q}_{i+1}$ is primitive and R_{i+1} is $\leq$;

(n4) $\rho^i_{k_i} \not\subseteq \rho^{i+1}_0$ if $i > 0$, $\boldsymbol{q}_i$ is primitive and R_{i+1} is $\leq$.

The queries in Example 6 are in normal form with two blocks each; the query $\boldsymbol{q}^{nf}$ above is in normal form with two blocks $\boldsymbol{q}_0 = \top(t_0)$ and $\boldsymbol{q}_1 = A(t_2) \wedge B(t_2) \wedge C(t_2)$.

Lemma 7. *Every query in $\mathcal{Q}_p[\bigcirc, \Diamond_r]$ is equivalent to a query in normal form that can be computed in linear time.*

A query $\boldsymbol{q} \in \mathcal{Q}_p[\bigcirc, \Diamond]$ is *safe* if it is equivalent to a query $\boldsymbol{q}' \in \mathcal{Q}_p[\bigcirc, \Diamond]$ in normal form not containing lone conjuncts. We are now in the position to formulate the criterion.

Theorem 8. (i) *A query $\boldsymbol{q} \in \mathcal{Q}_p[\bigcirc, \Diamond_r]$ is uniquely characterisable within $\mathcal{Q}_p[\bigcirc, \Diamond_r]$ iff $\boldsymbol{q}$ is safe.*

(ii) *Those queries that are uniquely characterisable within $\mathcal{Q}_p[\bigcirc, \Diamond_r]$ are actually polynomially characterisable within $\mathcal{Q}_p[\bigcirc, \Diamond_r]$.*

(iii) *The class $\mathcal{Q}_p[\bigcirc, \Diamond_r]$ is polynomially characterisable for bounded query size.*

(iv) *The class $\mathcal{Q}_p[\bigcirc, \Diamond]$ is polynomially characterisable.*

Proof sketch. A detailed proof is given in the full version. Here, we define a polysize example set $E = (E^+, E^-)$ characterising a query $\boldsymbol{q}$ in normal form (4), which does not contain lone conjuncts. Let b be the number of $\bigcirc$ and $\Diamond$ in $\boldsymbol{q}$ plus 1. For each block $\boldsymbol{q}_i$ in (4), we take two words

$$\bar{\boldsymbol{q}}_i = \rho^i_0 \dots \rho^i_{k_i}, \quad \bar{\boldsymbol{q}}_i \bowtie \bar{\boldsymbol{q}}_{i+1} = \rho^i_0 \dots (\rho^i_{k_i} \cup \rho^{i+1}_0) \dots \rho^{i+1}_{k_{i+1}}.$$

The set E^+ contains the data instances given by the words

- $\mathcal{D}_b = \bar{\boldsymbol{q}}_0 \emptyset^b \dots \bar{\boldsymbol{q}}_i \emptyset^b \bar{\boldsymbol{q}}_{i+1} \dots \emptyset^b \bar{\boldsymbol{q}}_n$,
- $\mathcal{D}_i = \bar{\boldsymbol{q}}_0 \emptyset^b \dots \bar{\boldsymbol{q}}_i \bowtie \bar{\boldsymbol{q}}_{i+1} \dots \emptyset^b \bar{\boldsymbol{q}}_n$ if $\mathcal{R}_{i+1}$ is $\leq$,
- $\mathcal{D}_i = \bar{\boldsymbol{q}}_0 \emptyset^b \dots \bar{\boldsymbol{q}}_i \emptyset^{n_{i+1}} \bar{\boldsymbol{q}}_{i+1} \dots \emptyset^b \bar{\boldsymbol{q}}_n$ otherwise.

Here, $\emptyset^b$ is a sequence of b-many $\emptyset$ and similarly for $\emptyset^{n_{i+1}}$. The set E^- contains all data instances of the form

- $\mathcal{D}^-_i = \bar{\boldsymbol{q}}_0 \emptyset^b \dots \bar{\boldsymbol{q}}_i \emptyset^{n_{i+1}-1} \bar{\boldsymbol{q}}_{i+1} \dots \emptyset^b \bar{\boldsymbol{q}}_n$ if $n_{i+1} > 1$;
- $\mathcal{D}^-_i = \bar{\boldsymbol{q}}_0 \emptyset^b \dots \bar{\boldsymbol{q}}_i \bowtie \bar{\boldsymbol{q}}_{i+1} \dots \emptyset^b \bar{\boldsymbol{q}}_n$ if $\mathcal{R}_{i+1}$ is a single $<$,

and also the data instances obtained from $\mathcal{D}_b$ by

(a) removing a single atom from some $\rho^i_j \neq \emptyset$ or removing the whole $\rho^i_j = \emptyset$, for $i \neq 0$ and $j \neq 0$, from some $\bar{\boldsymbol{q}}_i$;
(b) replacing $\bar{\boldsymbol{q}}_i = \rho^i_0 \dots \rho^i_l \rho^i_{l+1} \dots \rho^i_{k_i}$ ($k_i > 0$) by $\bar{\boldsymbol{q}}'_i \emptyset^b \bar{\boldsymbol{q}}''_i$, where $\bar{\boldsymbol{q}}'_i = \rho^i_0 \dots \rho^i_l$, $\bar{\boldsymbol{q}}''_i = \rho^i_{l+1} \dots \rho^i_{k_i}$ and $l \geq 0$;
(c) replacing some $\rho^i_l \neq \emptyset$, $0 < l < k_i$, by $\rho^i_l \emptyset^b \rho^i_l$;
(d) replacing $\rho^i_{k_i}$ ($k_i > 0$, $|\rho^i_{k_i}| \geq 2$) with $\rho^i_{k_i} \setminus \{A\} \emptyset^b \rho^i_{k_i}$, for some $A \in \rho^i_{k_i}$, or replacing ρ^i_0 ($k_i > 0$, $|\rho^i_0| \geq 2$) with $\rho^i_0 \emptyset^b \rho^i_0 \setminus \{A\}$, for some $A \in \rho^i_0$;
(e) replacing $\rho^0_0 \neq \emptyset$ with $\rho^0_0 \setminus \{A\} \emptyset^b \rho^0_0$, for some $A \in \rho^0_0$, if $k_0 = 0$, and with $\rho^0_0 \emptyset^b \rho^0_0$ if $k_0 > 0$.

The size of E is clearly polynomial in $|\boldsymbol{q}|$. It is readily seen that $\mathcal{D} \models \boldsymbol{q}$ for all $\mathcal{D} \in E^+$. To continue the proof sketch, note that $\mathcal{D} \models \boldsymbol{q}$ iff there is a *homomorphism* h from the set $var(\boldsymbol{q})$ of variables in $\boldsymbol{q}$ to $[0, \max(\mathcal{D})]$, i.e., $h(t_0) = 0$, $A(h(t)) \in \mathcal{D}$ if $A(t) \in \boldsymbol{q}$, $h(t') = h(t) + 1$ if $suc(t, t') \in \boldsymbol{q}$, and $h(t)\, R\, h(t')$ if $R(t, t') \in \boldsymbol{q}$ for $R \in \{<, \leq\}$. Using the assumption that $\boldsymbol{q}$ is in normal form, one can show that there is no homomorphism witnessing $\mathcal{D} \models \boldsymbol{q}$, for any $\mathcal{D} \in E^-$.

Suppose now that $\boldsymbol{q}' \in \mathcal{Q}_p[\bigcirc, \Diamond_r]$ in normal form is given and $\boldsymbol{q}' \not\equiv \boldsymbol{q}$. If $\mathcal{D}_b \not\models \boldsymbol{q}'$, we are done as $\mathcal{D}_b \in E^+$. Otherwise, let h be a homomorphism witnessing $\mathcal{D}_b \models \boldsymbol{q}'$. Then one can show that either the restriction of h to the blocks of $\boldsymbol{q}'$ is an isomorphism onto the blocks of $\boldsymbol{q}$ or there exists a data instance $\mathcal{D}$ obtained using one of the rules (a)–(e) such that a suitably modified h is a homomorphism from $\boldsymbol{q}'$ to $\mathcal{D}$. In the latter case, we are done as $\mathcal{D} \in E^-$ and $\mathcal{D} \models \boldsymbol{q}'$. In the former case, $\boldsymbol{q}$ and $\boldsymbol{q}'$ coincide with the exception of the sequences of $\Diamond$ and $\Diamond_r$ between blocks. Then $\boldsymbol{q}$ can be separated from $\boldsymbol{q}'$ using the examples $\mathcal{D}_i$ and $\mathcal{D}^-_i$. ❑

6 Polynomial Characterisability in $\mathcal{Q}^\sigma_p[\mathsf{U}]$

LTL-queries with U do not correspond to CQs (because of the universal quantification in its semantics), and so require a different approach. We view them as defining regular languages. With each $\mathcal{Q}^\sigma_p[\mathsf{U}]$-query of the form (2) we associate the following regular expression over the alphabet 2^σ:

$$\boldsymbol{q} = \rho_0 \lambda^*_1 \rho_1 \lambda^*_2 \dots \lambda^*_n \rho_n \lambda^*_{n+1} \tag{5}$$

where $\lambda_{n+1} = \emptyset$ and $\bot^* = \varepsilon$. We regard the words of the language $\boldsymbol{L}(\boldsymbol{q})$ over 2^σ as data instances. Clearly, $\mathcal{D}' \models \boldsymbol{q}$ iff there is $\mathcal{D} \in \boldsymbol{L}(\boldsymbol{q})$ such that $\mathcal{D} \Subset \mathcal{D}'$, i.e., $\mathcal{D} = (\delta_0, \dots, \delta_k)$ and $\mathcal{D}' = (\delta'_0, \dots, \delta'_k)$, for some $k < \omega$, and $\delta_i \subseteq \delta'_i$, for all $i \leq k$. The language $\boldsymbol{L}_{\boldsymbol{q}}$ of all σ-data instances $\mathcal{D} \models \boldsymbol{q}$ (regarded as words over 2^σ) can be given by the NFA $\mathfrak{A}_{\boldsymbol{q}}$ below, where each $\to_\alpha$, for $\alpha \neq \bot$, stands for all transitions $\to_\beta$ with $\alpha \subseteq \beta \subseteq \sigma$ (note that $\bot \notin \sigma$):

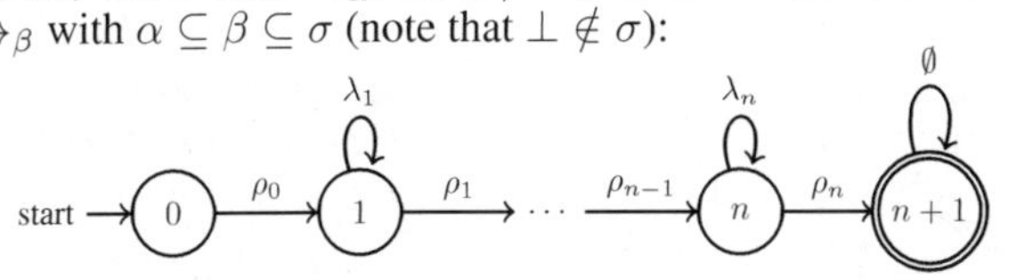

Without loss of generality we assume that all our $\boldsymbol{q}$ are *minimal* in the sense that by replacing any $\lambda_i \neq \bot$ with $\bot$ in $\boldsymbol{q}$ we obtain a query that is *not equivalent* to $\boldsymbol{q}$. For example, in minimal $\boldsymbol{q}$, $\rho_j \supseteq \dots \supseteq \rho_i \supseteq \lambda_i$ and $\lambda_l = \bot$ for all $l \in (j, i)$ imply $\rho_j \not\subseteq \lambda_j$ as otherwise $\lambda_j \mathsf{U} (\rho_j \wedge (\bot \mathsf{U} \dots (\lambda_i \mathsf{U} \varphi) \dots))$ is equivalent to $\bot \mathsf{U} (\rho_j \wedge (\bot \mathsf{U} \dots (\lambda_i \mathsf{U} \varphi) \dots))$. Using standard automata-theoretic techniques, one can show:

Theorem 9. *Any $\mathcal{Q}^\sigma_p[\mathsf{U}]$-queries $\boldsymbol{q} \not\equiv \boldsymbol{q}'$ can be separated by some $\mathcal{D}$ with* $\max(\mathcal{D}) \leq O((\min\{tdp(\boldsymbol{q}), tdp(\boldsymbol{q}')\})^2)$.

Using Theorem 9 in the proof of Theorem 4 we obtain:

Corollary 10. *The class $\mathcal{Q}^\sigma_p[\mathsf{U}]$ is exponentially characterisable within $\mathcal{Q}^\sigma_p[\mathsf{U}]$.*

The following examples illustrate difficulties in finding short unique characterisations of $\mathcal{Q}^\sigma_p[\mathsf{U}]$-queries, namely, that in general, data instances of different shapes and forms are needed to separate $\mathcal{Q}^\sigma_p[\mathsf{U}]$-queries. To unclutter notation we omit $\{\}$ in singletons like $\{A\}$.

Example 11. (a) The shortest data instance separating

$$\boldsymbol{q} = X\emptyset^* A\bot^* B\bot^* AB^* AA^* B\emptyset^*,$$
$$\boldsymbol{q}' = X\emptyset^* A\bot^* BA^* AB^* A\bot^* B\emptyset^*$$

is $\mathcal{D} = XABABBAAB$ with $\mathcal{D} \models \boldsymbol{q}$ and $\mathcal{D} \not\models \boldsymbol{q}'$ (e.g., $XABABAAB$ satisfies both $\boldsymbol{q}$ and $\boldsymbol{q}'$).

(b) For $l > 0$, let $\boldsymbol{q}_l = (AB^*)^{l-1} AA^* BB^*$. Then

$$XA^* \boldsymbol{q}_{l_1} \boldsymbol{q}_{l_2} \dots \boldsymbol{q}_{l_k} X\emptyset^* \ \not\equiv\ X\bot^* \boldsymbol{q}_{l_1} \boldsymbol{q}_{l_2} \dots \boldsymbol{q}_{l_k} X\emptyset^*,$$
$$XA^* \boldsymbol{q}_{l_1} \boldsymbol{q}_{l_2} \dots \boldsymbol{q}_{l_k} A\emptyset^* \ \equiv\ X\bot^* \boldsymbol{q}_{l_1} \boldsymbol{q}_{l_2} \dots \boldsymbol{q}_{l_k} A\emptyset^*.$$

If $1 < l_1 \leq \dots \leq l_k$, the former inequivalence is witnessed by the instance $XA^{l_1} BA^{l_2} B \dots A^{l_k} BA^{l_k} BX$. Less generally, $XA^* \boldsymbol{q}_2 \boldsymbol{q}_3 X\emptyset^* \not\equiv X\bot^* \boldsymbol{q}_2 \boldsymbol{q}_3 X\emptyset^*$ can be shown by $XAABAAABAAABX$ or by $XAABABAABABX$ (spot the difference and see ($\mathfrak{n}_2$) below).

Here, we consider the class $\mathcal{P}^\sigma[\mathsf{U}]$ of *peerless* queries given by (5), in which, for any i, either $\lambda_i = \bot$ or the sets λ_i and ρ_i are *incomparable* with respect to $\subseteq$. Our main result is that $\mathcal{P}^\sigma[\mathsf{U}]$ is polynomially characterisable within $\mathcal{Q}^\sigma_p[\mathsf{U}]$.

We start with a general observation. Consider two queries $\boldsymbol{q} = \rho_0 \lambda^*_1 \dots \lambda^*_n \rho_n \emptyset^*$ and $\boldsymbol{q}' = \rho_0 \mu^*_1 \dots \mu^*_n \rho_n \emptyset^*$. We say that $\lambda_i \neq \bot$ *subsumes* $\mu_j \neq \bot$ if either $i = j$ and $\mu_j \subseteq \lambda_i$, or $j < i$ and $\mu_j \rho_j \dots \rho_{i-1} \Subset \rho_j \dots \rho_{i-1} \lambda_i$, or $j > i$ and $\rho_i \dots \rho_{j-1} \mu_j \Subset \lambda_i \rho_i \dots \rho_{j-1}$. In the last two cases,

$$\mu_j \subseteq \rho_j \subseteq \dots \subseteq \rho_{i-1} \subseteq \lambda_i, \quad \mu_j \subseteq \rho_{j-1} \subseteq \dots \subseteq \rho_i \subseteq \lambda_i,$$

respectively. Note that, for peerless $\boldsymbol{q}$, the last inclusion is impossible. If λ_i and μ_j subsume each other, in which case $\lambda_i = \mu_j$, we call (λ_i, μ_j) a *matching pair*. Observe also that, for $\mathcal{D}^i_{\boldsymbol{q}} = \rho_0 \dots \rho_{i-1} \lambda_i \rho_i \dots \rho_n$, if $\mathcal{D}^i_{\boldsymbol{q}} \models \boldsymbol{q}'$, then λ_i subsumes some μ_j: $\rho_0 \dots \rho_n \emptyset \Subset \mathcal{D}^i_{\boldsymbol{q}}$ means that λ_i subsumes $\mu_{n+1} = \emptyset$, and $\rho_0 \dots \mu_j \dots \rho_n \Subset \mathcal{D}^i_{\boldsymbol{q}}$ that λ_i subsumes μ_j. The proof of the next lemma is given in the full version:

Lemma 12. *For any queries $\boldsymbol{q}$ and $\boldsymbol{q}'$ as above, either (i) each $\lambda_i \neq \bot$ subsumes μ_j occurring in some matching pair (λ_k, μ_j) or (ii) $\boldsymbol{q}$ and $\boldsymbol{q}'$ are separated by a data instance of the form $\mathcal{D}^i_{\boldsymbol{q}}$ or $\mathcal{D}^j_{\boldsymbol{q}'}$. Also, if $\boldsymbol{q}$ is peerless, λ_i can only subsume μ_j in the matching pair (λ_i, μ_j) with $i \geq j$, in which case $\mu_j = \rho_j = \dots = \rho_{i-1} = \lambda_i$.*

Note that the number of data instances of the form $\mathcal{D}^i_{\boldsymbol{q}'}$ for all possible $\mathcal{Q}^\sigma_p[\mathsf{U}]$-queries $\boldsymbol{q}'$ can be exponential in $|\sigma|$. The following example indicates how to overcome this issue.

Example 13. Let $\sigma = \{A, B, C, D, X\}$. To separate the query $X\{C, D\}^* A\emptyset^*$ from any $X\lambda^* A\emptyset^*$ with $A, D \notin \lambda$, we can use $\mathcal{D} = X\sigma \setminus \{A, D\}A$.

Theorem 14. *The class $\mathcal{P}^\sigma[\mathsf{U}]$ is polynomially characterisable within $\mathcal{Q}_p^\sigma[\mathsf{U}]$.*

Proof sketch. We show that any $\boldsymbol{q} = \rho_0\lambda_1^*\rho_1\lambda_2^* \dots \lambda_n^*\rho_n\emptyset^*$ in $\mathcal{P}^\sigma[\mathsf{U}]$ is characterised by the example set $E = (E^+, E^-)$ where E^+ contains all data instances of the following forms:

($\mathfrak{p}_0$) $\rho_0 \dots \rho_n$,

($\mathfrak{p}_1$) $\rho_0 \dots \rho_{i-1}\lambda_i\rho_i \dots \rho_n = \mathcal{D}^i_{\boldsymbol{q}}$,

($\mathfrak{p}_2$) $\rho_0 \dots \rho_{i-1}\lambda_i^k\rho_i \dots \rho_{j-1}\lambda_j\rho_j \dots \rho_n = \mathcal{D}^j_{i,k}$, for $i < j$ and $k = 1, 2$;

and E^- has all instances that are *not* in $\boldsymbol{L}(\boldsymbol{q})$ of the forms:

($\mathfrak{n}_0$) σ^n and $\sigma^{n-i}\sigma \setminus \{A\}\sigma^i$, for $A \in \rho_i$,

($\mathfrak{n}_1$) $\rho_0 \dots \rho_{i-1}\sigma \setminus \{A, B\}\rho_i \dots \rho_n$, for $A \in \lambda_i \cup \{\bot\}$ and $B \in \rho_i \cup \{\bot\}$,

($\mathfrak{n}_2$) for all i and $A \in \lambda_i \cup \{\bot\}$, *some* data instance

$$\mathcal{D}^i_A = \rho_0 \dots \rho_{i-1}(\sigma \setminus \{A\})\rho_i\lambda_{i+1}^{k_{i+1}} \dots \lambda_n^{k_n}\rho_n, \qquad (6)$$

if any, such that $\max(\mathcal{D}^i_A) \le (n+1)^2$ and $\mathcal{D}^i_A \not\models \boldsymbol{q}^\dagger$ for $\boldsymbol{q}^\dagger$ obtained from $\boldsymbol{q}$ by replacing λ_j, for all $j \le i$, with $\bot$. Note that $\mathcal{D}^i_A \not\models \boldsymbol{q}$ for peerless $\boldsymbol{q}$.

By definition, $\boldsymbol{q}$ fits E and $|E|$ is polynomial in $|\boldsymbol{q}|$. We prove in the full version that E uniquely characterises $\boldsymbol{q}$. ❑

One reason why this construction does not generalise to the whole $\mathcal{Q}_p^\sigma[\mathsf{U}]$ is that $\mathcal{D}^i_A \not\models \boldsymbol{q}^\dagger$ does not imply $\mathcal{D}^i_A \not\models \boldsymbol{q}$ for non-peerless $\boldsymbol{q}$, as shown by the following example:

Example 15. Let $\boldsymbol{q} = XA^*AB^*A\bot^*AB^*AA^*BB^*X\emptyset^*$. For any data instance $\mathcal{D}^3_\bot$ satisfying (6)—for example, $\mathcal{D}^3_\bot = XAA\sigma ABABX$—we have $\mathcal{D}^3_\bot \models \boldsymbol{q}$.

7 Characterisability in $\mathcal{Q}[\Diamond]$

In the previous two sections, we have investigated characterisability of path-shaped queries. Here, we first justify that restriction by exhibiting two examples that show how temporal branching can destroy polynomial characterisability in $\mathcal{Q}[\Diamond]$. Both examples make use of *unbalanced* queries, in which different branches have different length. We then show that this is no accident: one can at least partially restore polynomial characterisability for classes without unbalanced queries.

We start by observing that, without loss of generality, it is enough to consider conjunctions of path queries only:

Lemma 16. *For every $\boldsymbol{q} \in \mathcal{Q}[\Diamond]$, one can compute in polynomial time an equivalent query of the form $\boldsymbol{q}_1 \wedge \dots \wedge \boldsymbol{q}_n$ with $\boldsymbol{q}_i \in \mathcal{Q}_p[\Diamond]$, for $1 \le i \le n$.*

The first example showing non-polynomial characterisability is rather straightforward but requires unbounded branching and an unbounded number of atoms. We write queries $\boldsymbol{q} \in \mathcal{Q}_p^\sigma[\Diamond]$ of the form

$$\boldsymbol{q} = \rho_0 \wedge \Diamond(\rho_1 \wedge \Diamond(\rho_2 \wedge \dots \wedge \Diamond\rho_n)) \qquad (7)$$

as words $\rho_0\rho_1 \dots \rho_n$ over 2^σ (omitting but not forgetting $\lambda_i^* = \emptyset^*$ from (5)) and also use $\rho_0\rho_1 \dots \rho_n$ to denote the data instance defined by $\boldsymbol{q}$.

Example 17. Consider $\boldsymbol{q}_n = \boldsymbol{s}_1 \wedge \dots \wedge \boldsymbol{s}_n$, where $n \ge 2$ and each $\boldsymbol{s}_i$ is a word repeating n times the sequence $A_1 \dots A_n$ (of singletons) with omitted A_i. Now, consider the queries $\boldsymbol{q}_n^{\boldsymbol{p}} = \boldsymbol{q}_n \wedge \boldsymbol{p}$, where $\boldsymbol{p} = \Diamond(A_{i_1} \wedge \Diamond(A_{i_2} \wedge \dots \wedge \Diamond A_{i_n}))$ and $A_{i_1} \dots A_{i_n}$ is a permutation of $A_1 \dots A_n$. Then $\boldsymbol{q}_n^{\boldsymbol{p}} \models \boldsymbol{q}_n$ and $\boldsymbol{q}_n \not\models \boldsymbol{q}_n^{\boldsymbol{p}}$ as shown by the data instance $\boldsymbol{s}_{i_1}\boldsymbol{s}_{i_2} \dots \boldsymbol{s}_{i_n}$. Moreover, if $\mathcal{D} \models \boldsymbol{q}_n$, $\mathcal{D} \not\models \boldsymbol{p}$ and $\boldsymbol{p}' \neq \boldsymbol{p}$, then $\mathcal{D} \models \boldsymbol{p}'$. It follows that, in any $E = (E^+, E^-)$ uniquely characterising $\boldsymbol{q}_n$, the set E^+ contains at least $n!$ data instances.

The class $\mathcal{Q}_{\le n}[\Diamond]$ of queries of *branching factor* at most n contains all queries in $\mathcal{Q}[\Diamond]$ that are equivalent to a query of the form $\boldsymbol{q}_1 \wedge \dots \wedge \boldsymbol{q}_m$ with $m \le n$ and $\boldsymbol{q}_i \in \mathcal{Q}_p[\Diamond]$. We next provide an example of non-polynomial characterisability that requires four atoms and bounded branching only.

Example 18. Let $\sigma = \{A_1, A_2, B_1, B_2\}$, $\boldsymbol{q}_1 = \emptyset(\boldsymbol{s}\sigma)^n\boldsymbol{s}$, and $\boldsymbol{q}_2 = \emptyset\sigma^{2n+1}$, where $\boldsymbol{s} = \{A_1, A_2\}\{B_1, B_2\}$. Consider the set P of 2^{n+1}-many queries of the form $\emptyset\boldsymbol{s}_1 \dots \boldsymbol{s}_{n+1}$ with $\boldsymbol{s}_i$ either $\{A_1\}\{A_2\}$ or $\{B_1\}\{B_2\}$. Then $\boldsymbol{q}_1 \wedge \boldsymbol{q}_2 \not\models \boldsymbol{q}$ for any $\boldsymbol{q} \in P$ and, for any $\mathcal{D}$ with $\mathcal{D} \models \boldsymbol{q}_1 \wedge \boldsymbol{q}_2$, there is at most one $\boldsymbol{q} \in P$ with $\mathcal{D} \not\models \boldsymbol{q}$ (the proof is rather involved). It follows that $\boldsymbol{q}_1 \wedge \boldsymbol{q}_2 \not\models \boldsymbol{q}_1 \wedge \boldsymbol{q}_2 \wedge \boldsymbol{q}$ for all $\boldsymbol{q} \in P$, but 2^{n+1} positive examples are needed to separate $\boldsymbol{q}_1 \wedge \boldsymbol{q}_2$ from all $\boldsymbol{q}_1 \wedge \boldsymbol{q}_2 \wedge \boldsymbol{q}$ with $\boldsymbol{q} \in P$.

We next identify polynomially characterisable classes of $\mathcal{Q}[\Diamond]$-queries, assuming as before that $\rho_n \neq \emptyset$ in any $\boldsymbol{q}$ of the form (1). We call a query $\boldsymbol{q}_1 \wedge \dots \wedge \boldsymbol{q}_n \in \mathcal{Q}[\Diamond]$ with $\boldsymbol{q}_1, \dots, \boldsymbol{q}_n \in \mathcal{Q}_p[\Diamond]$ *balanced* if all $\boldsymbol{q}_i$ have the same depth; further, we call it *simple* if, in each $\boldsymbol{q}_i$ given by (1), $|\rho_j| = 1$ for all j. Let $\mathcal{Q}_b[\Diamond]$ denote the class of queries in $\mathcal{Q}[\Diamond]$ that are equivalent to a balanced query.

Theorem 19. (i) *The class of simple queries in $\mathcal{Q}_b[\Diamond]$ is polynomially characterisable within $\mathcal{Q}_b[\Diamond]$.*

(ii) *For any n, the class $\mathcal{Q}_b[\Diamond] \cap \mathcal{Q}_{\le n}[\Diamond]$ is polynomially characterisable.*

Proof sketch. Let $\boldsymbol{q} \in \mathcal{Q}_p^\sigma[\Diamond]$. We start with a lemma on the existence of polynomial-size σ-data instances $\mathcal{D}_{\boldsymbol{q},k}$ such that $\mathcal{D}_{\boldsymbol{q},k} \not\models \boldsymbol{q}$ and $\mathcal{D}_{\boldsymbol{q},k} \models \boldsymbol{q}'$ for all $\boldsymbol{q}' \in \mathcal{Q}_p^\sigma[\Diamond]$ with $\boldsymbol{q}' \not\models \boldsymbol{q}$ and $tdp(\boldsymbol{q}') \le k$. Note that such $\mathcal{D}_{\boldsymbol{q},k}$ do not exist in general.

Example 20. Let $\boldsymbol{q} = A \wedge B$. Then $A \not\models \boldsymbol{q}$ and $B \not\models \boldsymbol{q}$ but there does not exist any $\mathcal{D}_{\boldsymbol{q},0}$ such that $\mathcal{D}_{\boldsymbol{q},0} \not\models \boldsymbol{q}$, $\mathcal{D}_{\boldsymbol{q},0} \models A$ and $\mathcal{D}_{\boldsymbol{q},0} \models B$.

In the following lemma, we therefore assume that $\boldsymbol{q}$ does not speak about the initial timepoint.

Lemma 21. *Let $\boldsymbol{q} \in \mathcal{Q}_p^\sigma[\Diamond]$ be of the form $\Diamond\boldsymbol{q}'$ and let $k > 0$. Then one can construct in polynomial time a σ-data instance $\mathcal{D}_{\boldsymbol{q},k}$ such that $\mathcal{D}_{\boldsymbol{q},k} \not\models \boldsymbol{q}$ and $\mathcal{D}_{\boldsymbol{q},k} \models \boldsymbol{q}'$ for all $\boldsymbol{q}' \in \mathcal{Q}_p^\sigma[\Diamond]$ with $\boldsymbol{q}' \not\models \boldsymbol{q}$ and $tdp(\boldsymbol{q}') \le k$.*

Proof. Assuming that $\boldsymbol{q} = \Diamond(\rho_1 \wedge \Diamond(\rho_2 \wedge \dots \wedge \Diamond\rho_n))$ with $\rho_i = \{A_1^i, \dots, A_{n_i}^i\}$ for $i \ge 1$, we set

$$\mathcal{D}_{\boldsymbol{q},k} = \sigma\boldsymbol{s}_1^k\sigma \cdots \boldsymbol{s}_{n-1}^k\sigma\boldsymbol{s}_n^k,$$

where $s_i = \sigma \setminus \{A_1^i\} \dots \sigma \setminus \{A_{n_i}^i\}$. One can show by induction that $\mathcal{D}_{q,k}$ is as required. ❑

Using Lemma 21, for any $q \in \mathcal{Q}^\sigma[\Diamond]$, one can construct a polynomial-size set of negative examples as follows. Suppose $q = q_1 \wedge \dots \wedge q_n \in \mathcal{Q}^\sigma[\Diamond]$ with

$$q_i = \rho_0^i \wedge \Diamond(\rho_1^i \wedge \Diamond(\rho_2^i \wedge \dots \wedge \Diamond\rho_{n_i^i})).$$

Let $\rho = \bigwedge_{i=1}^n \rho_0^i$ and let q_i^- be q_i without the conjunct ρ_0^i, so Lemma 21 is applicable to q_i^-. Now let $E_{q,m}^-$ contain the σ-data instances $\mathcal{D}_{q_i^-,m}$ and $\sigma \setminus \{A\}\sigma^m$ for all $A \in \rho$.

Lemma 22. (i) *For any $\mathcal{D} \in E_{q,m}^-$, we have $\mathcal{D} \not\models q$.*

(ii) *For any $q' \in \mathcal{Q}^\sigma[\Diamond]$ with $q' \not\models q$ and $tdp(q') \le m$, there exists $\mathcal{D} \in E_{q,m}^-$ with $\mathcal{D} \models q'$.*

It follows from Lemma 22 that non-polynomial characterisability of $\mathcal{Q}[\Diamond]$-queries can only be caused by the need for super-polynomially-many positive examples. We now discuss the construction of positive examples in the proof of Theorem 19 (ii); part (i) is dealt with in the full version. Let $q = q_1 \wedge \dots \wedge q_m \in \mathcal{Q}_b^\sigma[\Diamond] \cap \mathcal{Q}_{\le n}^\sigma[\Diamond]$ with $m \le n$ and

$$q_i = \rho_0^i \wedge \Diamond(\rho_1^i \wedge \Diamond(\rho_2^i \wedge \dots \wedge \Diamond\rho_N^i)).$$

For any map $f\colon \{1, \dots, m\} \to \{1, \dots, N\}$, construct a σ-data instance $\mathcal{D}_f$ by inserting $\rho_{f(i)}^i$ into the data instance σ^N in position $f(i)$. Let E^+ contain the data instance $\rho\sigma^N$ for $\rho = \bigcup_{i=1}^m \rho_0^i$ and all the data instances $\mathcal{D}_f$. One can show that (E^+, E^-) characterises q in $\mathcal{Q}_b[\Diamond] \cap \mathcal{Q}_{\le n}[\Diamond]$. ❑

8 2D Temporal Instance Queries

Now we consider 'two-dimensional' query languages that combine instance queries (over the object domain) in the standard description logics $\mathcal{EL}$ and $\mathcal{ELI}$ (Baader et al. 2017) with the *LTL*-queries (over the temporal domain) considered above. Our aim is to understand how far the characterisability results of the previous sections can be generalised to the 2D case. A *relational signature* is a finite set $\Sigma \neq \emptyset$ of unary and binary predicate symbols. A *Σ-data instance* $\mathcal{A}$ is a finite set of *atoms* $A(a)$ and $P(a, b)$ with $A, P \in \Sigma$ and *individual names* a, b. Let $ind(\mathcal{A})$ be the set of individual names in $\mathcal{A}$. We assume that $P^-(a, b) \in \mathcal{A}$ iff $P(b, a) \in \mathcal{A}$, calling P^- the *inverse* of P (with $P^{--} = P$). Let $S := P \mid P^-$. *Temporal instance queries* are defined by the grammar

$$q := \top \mid \bot \mid A \mid \exists S.q \mid q_1 \wedge q_2 \mid op\, q \mid q_1 \mathbin{\mathsf{U}} q_2,$$

where $op \in \{\bigcirc, \Diamond, \Diamond_r\}$. Such queries without temporal operators are called *$\mathcal{ELI}$-queries*; those of them without inverses P^- are *$\mathcal{EL}$-queries*. A *temporal Σ-data instance $\mathcal{D}$* is a finite sequence $\mathcal{A}_0, \dots, \mathcal{A}_n$ of Σ-data instances. We set $ind(\mathcal{D}) = \bigcup_{i=1}^n ind(\mathcal{A}_i)$. For any $\ell \in \mathbb{N}$ and $a \in ind(\mathcal{D})$, the *truth-relation* $\mathcal{D}, a, \ell \models q$ is defined by induction:

$\mathcal{D}, a, \ell \models A$ iff $A(a) \in \mathcal{A}_\ell$,

$\mathcal{D}, a, \ell \models \exists S.q$ iff there is $b \in ind(\mathcal{A}_\ell)$ such that $S(a, b) \in \mathcal{A}_\ell$ and $\mathcal{D}, b, \ell \models q$,

with the remaining clauses being obvious generalisations of the *LTL* ones. An *example set* is a pair $E = (E^+, E^-)$ with finite sets E^+ and E^- of *pointed temporal data instances* $(\mathcal{D}, a)$ such that $a \in ind(\mathcal{D})$. We say that *q fits E* if $\mathcal{D}^+, a^+, 0 \models q$ and $\mathcal{D}^-, a^-, 0 \not\models q$, for all $(\mathcal{D}^+, a^+) \in E^+$ and $(\mathcal{D}^-, a^-) \in E^-$. As before, *$E$ uniquely characterises q* if q fits it and every q' fitting E is logically equivalent to q.

We need the following result on the unique characterisability of $\mathcal{ELI}$-queries.

Theorem 23 (ten Cate and Dalmau 2021)**.** *The class of $\mathcal{ELI}$-queries is polynomially characterisable.*

Theorem 24 is proved by constructing frontiers in the set of $\mathcal{ELI}$-queries partially ordered by entailment, where a set $\mathcal{F}$ of $\mathcal{ELI}$-queries is called a *frontier* of an $\mathcal{ELI}$-query q if the following hold:

- $q \models q'$ and $q' \not\models q$, for all $q' \in \mathcal{F}$;
- if $q \models q''$ for some $\mathcal{ELI}$-query q'', then $q'' \models q$ or there exists $q' \in \mathcal{F}$ with $q' \models q''$.

Theorem 24 (ten Cate and Dalmau 2021)**.** *A frontier $\mathcal{F}(q)$ of any $\mathcal{ELI}$-query q can be computed in polynomial time.*

Theorem 23 follows from Theorem 24. For any $\mathcal{ELI}$-query q, we denote by $\hat{q}$ the tree-shaped data instance defined by q with designated root a. Then q is characterised by E with $E^+ = \{\hat{q}\}$ and $E^- = \{\hat{r} \mid r \in \mathcal{F}(q)\}$.

For any unrestricted temporal query language $\mathcal{Q}[\Phi]$ and $\mathcal{L} \in \{\mathcal{EL}, \mathcal{ELI}\}$, we denote by $\mathcal{Q}[\Phi] \otimes \mathcal{L}$ the set of all temporal instance queries with operators in Φ with (for $\mathcal{ELI}$) or without (for $\mathcal{EL}$) inverse predicates. We generalise the path-shaped queries $\mathcal{Q}_p[\Phi]$ as follows: $\mathcal{Q}_p[\Phi] \otimes \mathcal{L}$ denotes the class of queries q in $\mathcal{Q}[\Phi] \otimes \mathcal{L}$ such that, for any subquery $q_1 \wedge q_2$ of q, either q_1 or q_2 do not have an occurrence of any operator in Φ that is not in the scope of $\exists S$. To illustrate, $\exists S.\Diamond A \wedge \Diamond\exists S.A$ is in $\mathcal{Q}_p[\Phi] \otimes \mathcal{L}$, but $\Diamond A \wedge \Diamond\exists S.A$ is not. We make two observations about unique characterisability in these 'full' combinations.

Theorem 25. (i) *$\mathcal{Q}[\bigcirc, \Diamond] \otimes \mathcal{EL}$ is uniquely characterisable.*

(ii) *$\mathcal{Q}_p[\bigcirc] \otimes \mathcal{ELI}$ and $\mathcal{Q}_p[\Diamond] \otimes \mathcal{ELI}$ are polynomially characterisable.*

Here, (i) is shown similarly to Theorem 4 (it remains open whether it can be extended to $\mathcal{Q}[\bigcirc, \Diamond] \otimes \mathcal{ELI}$); (ii) is proved by generalising Theorem 24 to temporal data instances.

We now show that the application of the DL constructor $\exists P$ to temporal queries with both $\bigcirc$ and $\Diamond$ destroys polynomial characterisability. Denote by $\mathcal{EL}(\mathcal{Q}_p[\bigcirc, \Diamond])$ the class of queries in $\mathcal{Q}_p[\bigcirc, \Diamond] \otimes \mathcal{EL}$ that contain no $\exists P$ in the scope of a temporal operator.

Theorem 26. *$\mathcal{EL}(\mathcal{Q}_p[\bigcirc, \Diamond])$ is not polynomially characterisable.*

Proof sketch. Consider queries $q_n = \exists P.q_1^n \wedge \dots \wedge \exists P.q_n^n$, in which each q_i^n corresponds to the regular expression

$$\underbrace{BB\emptyset^*A}_{1}\dots\underbrace{BB\emptyset^*A}_{i-1}\underbrace{\emptyset^*B\emptyset^*A}_{i}\underbrace{BB\emptyset^*A}_{i+1}\dots\underbrace{BB\emptyset^*A}_{n}\emptyset^*$$

(with omitted $\bot^* = \varepsilon$ in BB). One can show that any unique characterisation of q_n contains at least 2^n positive examples to separate it from all queries $q_n \wedge \exists P.s$ with

$$s = o_1(B \wedge \Diamond(A \wedge o_2(B \wedge \Diamond(A \wedge \dots \wedge o_n(B \wedge \Diamond A) \dots)))),$$

where o_i is $\bigcirc$ or $\Diamond\bigcirc$ if $i > 1$, and blank or $\Diamond$ if $i = 1$. ❑

The situation changes drastically if we do not admit temporal operators in the scope of $\exists P$. We start by investigating the class $\mathcal{Q}_p[\bigcirc, \Diamond_r](\mathcal{ELI})$ of queries of the form

$$\boldsymbol{q} = \boldsymbol{r}_0 \wedge \boldsymbol{o}_1(\boldsymbol{r}_1 \wedge \boldsymbol{o}_2(\boldsymbol{r}_2 \wedge \cdots \wedge \boldsymbol{o}_n \boldsymbol{r}_n)),$$

where the $\boldsymbol{r}_i$ are $\mathcal{ELI}$-queries and $\boldsymbol{o}_i \in \{\bigcirc, \Diamond_r\}$. We can generalise the CQ-representation, the normal form, and the notion of lone conjunct from $\mathcal{Q}_p[\bigcirc, \Diamond_r]$ to $\mathcal{Q}_p[\bigcirc, \Diamond_r](\mathcal{ELI})$ in a straightforward way. To formulate conditions (**n1**)–(**n4**), we replace the set inclusions '$\rho_i \subseteq \rho_j$' by entailment '$\boldsymbol{r}_i \models \boldsymbol{r}_j$'. For example, (**n4**) becomes

(**n4′**) $\boldsymbol{r}_0^{i+1} \not\models \boldsymbol{r}_{k_i}^i$ if $i > 0$, $\boldsymbol{q}_i$ is primitive and R_{i+1} is $\leq$.

The condition for lone conjuncts now requires that $\boldsymbol{r}$ is not equivalent to any $\boldsymbol{q}_1 \wedge \boldsymbol{q}_2$ with $\mathcal{ELI}$-queries $\boldsymbol{q}_1, \boldsymbol{q}_2$ such that $\boldsymbol{q}_i \not\models \boldsymbol{r}$ for $i = 1, 2$. Then one can show again that every $\mathcal{Q}_p[\bigcirc, \Diamond_r](\mathcal{ELI})$-query is equivalent to a query in normal form, which can be computed in polynomial time.

Theorem 27. *The statements of Theorem 8 (i)–(iv) also hold if one replaces $\mathcal{Q}_p[\bigcirc, \Diamond_r]$ by $\mathcal{Q}_p[\bigcirc, \Diamond_r](\mathcal{ELI})$.*

The proof generalises the example set defined in Theorem 8 using the frontiers provided by Theorem 24 as a *black box*. Indeed, in the definition of examples, replace ρ_i by $\hat{\boldsymbol{r}}_i$, the data instance corresponding to the $\mathcal{ELI}$-query $\boldsymbol{r}_i$, and replace '$\rho \setminus \{A\}$ for $A \in \rho$' by 'the data instance corresponding to a query in $\mathcal{F}(\boldsymbol{r})$'. We choose a single individual, a, as the root of these data instances. For example, item (a) becomes:

(a′) replacing some $\boldsymbol{r}_j^i$ by the data instance corresponding to a query in $\mathcal{F}(\boldsymbol{r}_j^i)$ or removing the whole $\boldsymbol{r}_j^i = \emptyset$ for $i \neq 0$ and $j \neq 0$ from some $\boldsymbol{q}_i$.

Next, consider the class $\mathcal{Q}_p[\mathsf{U}](\mathcal{L})$ of queries of the form

$$\boldsymbol{q} = \boldsymbol{r}_0 \wedge (\boldsymbol{l}_1 \,\mathsf{U}\, (\boldsymbol{r}_1 \wedge (\boldsymbol{l}_2 \,\mathsf{U}\, (\dots (\boldsymbol{l}_n \,\mathsf{U}\, \boldsymbol{r}_n) \dots)))), \quad (8)$$

where $\boldsymbol{r}_i$ is an $\mathcal{L}$-query and $\boldsymbol{l}_i$ is either an $\mathcal{L}$-query or $\bot$, for $\mathcal{L} \in \{\mathcal{EL}, \mathcal{ELI}\}$. For the same reason as in the 1D case, we fix a finite signature Σ of predicate symbols. Denote by $\mathcal{L}(\Sigma)$ and $\mathcal{Q}_p[\mathsf{U}](\mathcal{L})$ the set of queries in $\mathcal{L}$ and $\mathcal{Q}_p^\Sigma[\mathsf{U}](\mathcal{L})$, respectively, with predicate symbols in Σ. Aiming to generalise Theorem 14, we again translate set-inclusion to entailment, so the *peerless queries* $\mathcal{P}^\Sigma[\mathsf{U}](\mathcal{L})$ take the form (8) such that either $\boldsymbol{l}_i = \bot$ or $\boldsymbol{l}_i \not\models \boldsymbol{r}_i$ and $\boldsymbol{r}_i \not\models \boldsymbol{l}_i$.

Theorem 28. *Let Σ be a finite relational signature. Then $\mathcal{P}^\Sigma[\mathsf{U}](\mathcal{EL})$ is polynomially characterisable within $\mathcal{Q}_p^\Sigma[\mathsf{U}](\mathcal{EL})$, while $\mathcal{P}^\Sigma[\mathsf{U}](\mathcal{ELI})$ is exponentially, but not polynomially, characterisable within $\mathcal{Q}_p^\Sigma[\mathsf{U}](\mathcal{ELI})$.*

To prove Theorem 28, we generalise the example set from the proof of Theorem 14. The positive examples are straightforward: simply replace ρ_i and λ_i by the data instances corresponding to $\boldsymbol{r}_i$ and $\boldsymbol{l}_i$ (and choose a single root individual). For the negative examples, we have to generalise the construction of σ, $\sigma \setminus \{A\}$, and $\sigma \setminus \{A, B\}$. For σ, this is straightforward as its role can now be played by the Σ-data instance $\mathcal{A}_\Sigma = \{A(a), R(a,a) \mid A, R \in \Sigma\}$ for which $\mathcal{A}_\Sigma \models \boldsymbol{q}(a)$ for all $\boldsymbol{q} \in \mathcal{ELI}(\Sigma)$. For $\sigma \setminus \{A\}$ and $\sigma \setminus \{A, B\}$, we require *split partners* defined as follows. Let Q be a finite set of $\mathcal{L}(\Sigma)$-queries. A set $\mathcal{S}(Q)$ of pointed Σ-data instances $(\mathcal{A}, a)$ is called a *split partner* of Q in $\mathcal{L}(\Sigma)$ if the following conditions are equivalent for all $\mathcal{L}(\Sigma)$-queries $\boldsymbol{q}'$:

- $\mathcal{A} \models \boldsymbol{q}'(a)$ for some $(\mathcal{A}, a) \in \mathcal{S}(Q)$;
- $\boldsymbol{q}' \not\models \boldsymbol{q}$ for all $\boldsymbol{q} \in Q$.

Example 29. The split partner of $\{\boldsymbol{q} = A\}$ in $\mathcal{EL}(\Sigma)$ is the singleton set containing $(\mathcal{A}_\Sigma^{-A}, a)$ with $\mathcal{A}_\Sigma^{-A}$ defined as $\{B(a), R(a,b), R(b,b), B'(b) \mid B \in \Sigma \setminus \{A\}, R, B' \in \Sigma\}$.

Theorem 30. *Fix $n > 0$. For any set Q of $\mathcal{EL}(\Sigma)$-queries with $|Q| \leq n$, one can compute in polynomial time a split partner $\mathcal{S}(Q)$ of Q in $\mathcal{EL}(\Sigma)$. For $\mathcal{ELI}$, one can compute a split partner in exponential time, which is optimal as even for singleton sets Q of $\mathcal{ELI}(\Sigma)$-queries, no polynomial-size split partner of Q in $\mathcal{ELI}(\Sigma)$ exists in general.*

The proof, given in the full version, requires (as does $\mathcal{A}_\Sigma$) the construction of non-tree-shaped data instances. Our results for $\mathcal{ELI}$ are closely related to the study of generalised dualities for homomorphisms between relational structures (Foniok, Nesetril, and Tardif 2008; Nesetril and Tardif 2005) but use pointed relational structures. The construction of $\mathcal{S}(Q)$ for $\mathcal{ELI}$ is based on a construction first introduced in (Bienvenu et al. 2014).

We obtain the negative examples for $\boldsymbol{q}$ of the form (8) by taking the following pointed data instances $(\mathcal{D}, a)$ (assuming that split partners take the form $(\mathcal{A}, a)$ for a fixed a):

($\mathfrak{n}_0'$) $(\mathcal{A}_\Sigma^n, a)$ and $(\mathcal{A}_\Sigma^{n-i} \mathcal{A} \mathcal{A}_\Sigma^i, a)$, for $(\mathcal{A}, a) \in \mathcal{S}(\{\boldsymbol{r}_i\})$;

($\mathfrak{n}_1'$) $(\mathcal{D}, a) = (\hat{\boldsymbol{r}}_0 \dots \hat{\boldsymbol{r}}_{i-1} \mathcal{A} \hat{\boldsymbol{r}}_i \dots \hat{\boldsymbol{r}}_n, a)$ with $\mathcal{D}, a, 0 \not\models \boldsymbol{q}$ and $(\mathcal{A}, a) \in \mathcal{S}(\{\boldsymbol{l}_i, \boldsymbol{r}_i\}) \cup \mathcal{S}(\{\boldsymbol{l}_i\}) \cup \mathcal{S}(\{\boldsymbol{r}_i\}) \cup \{(\mathcal{A}_\Sigma, a)\}$;

($\mathfrak{n}_2'$) for all i and $(\mathcal{A}, a) \in \mathcal{S}(\{\boldsymbol{l}_i\}) \cup \{(\mathcal{A}_\Sigma, a)\}$, *some* data instance

$$(\mathcal{D}_\mathcal{A}^i, a) = (\hat{\boldsymbol{r}}_0 \dots \hat{\boldsymbol{r}}_{i-1} \mathcal{A} \hat{\boldsymbol{r}}_i \hat{\boldsymbol{l}}_{i+1}^{k_{i+1}} \hat{\boldsymbol{r}}_{i+1} \dots \hat{\boldsymbol{l}}_n^{k_n} \boldsymbol{r}_n, a),$$

if any, such that $\max(\mathcal{D}_\mathcal{A}^i) \leq (n+1)^2$ and $\mathcal{D}_\mathcal{A}^i, a, 0 \not\models \boldsymbol{q}^\dagger$ for $\boldsymbol{q}^\dagger$ obtained from $\boldsymbol{q}$ by replacing all $\boldsymbol{l}_j$, $j \leq i$, with $\bot$.

We illustrate the construction by generalising Example 2.

Example 31. For $\boldsymbol{q} = \bigcirc A$ and any relational signature $\Sigma \ni A$, we obtain, after removing redundant instances, that $E^+ = \{(\emptyset\{A(a)\}, a)\}$ and $E^- = \{(\mathcal{A}_\Sigma \mathcal{A}_\Sigma^{-A}\{A(a)\}, a)\}$ characterise $\boldsymbol{q}$ within $\mathcal{Q}_p^\Sigma[\mathsf{U}](\mathcal{EL})$.

We finally generalise Theorem 19 (ii) (part (i) is not interesting since simple queries do not generalise to any new class of $\mathcal{ELI}$-queries). Query classes such as $\mathcal{Q}[\Diamond](\mathcal{EL})$ are defined in the obvious way by replacing in $\mathcal{Q}[\Diamond]$-queries conjunctions of atoms by $\mathcal{EL}$-queries.

Theorem 32. *The class $\mathcal{Q}_b[\Diamond](\mathcal{EL}) \cap \mathcal{Q}_{\leq n}[\Diamond](\mathcal{EL})$ is polynomially characterisable for any $n < \omega$.*

Again the positive and negative examples are obtained from the 1D case by replacing σ by $\mathcal{A}_\Sigma$ and $\sigma \setminus \{A\}$ by appropriate split partners.

9 Applications to Learning

We apply our results on unique characterisability to exact learnability of temporal instance queries. Given a class $\mathcal{Q}$ of such queries, we aim to identify a *target query* $\boldsymbol{q} \in \mathcal{Q}$ using queries to an oracle. The learner knows $\mathcal{Q}$ and the signature σ (Σ in the 2D case) of $\boldsymbol{q}$. We allow only one type of queries, called *membership queries*, in which the learner picks a σ-data instance $\mathcal{D}$ and asks the oracle whether $\mathcal{D} \models \boldsymbol{q}$ holds. (In the 2D case, the learner picks a pointed Σ-data instance $(\mathcal{D}, a)$ and asks whether $\mathcal{D}, a, 0 \models \boldsymbol{q}$ holds.) The oracle answers 'yes' or 'no' truthfully. The class $\mathcal{Q}$ is *(polynomial time) learnable with membership queries* if there exists an algorithm that halts for any $\boldsymbol{q} \in \mathcal{Q}$ and computes (in polynomial time in the size of $\boldsymbol{q}$ and σ/Σ), using membership queries, a query $\boldsymbol{q}' \in \mathcal{Q}$ that is equivalent to $\boldsymbol{q}$. By default, the learner does not know $|\boldsymbol{q}|$ in advance but reflecting Theorem 8 (iii), we also consider the case when $|\boldsymbol{q}|$ is known (which is common in active learning).

Obviously, unique characterisability is a necessary condition for learnability with membership queries. Conversely, if there is an algorithm that computes, for every $\boldsymbol{q} \in \mathcal{Q}$, an example set that uniquely characterises $\boldsymbol{q}$ within $\mathcal{Q}^{sig(\boldsymbol{q})}$, then $\mathcal{Q}$ is learnable with membership queries: enumerate $\mathcal{Q}^{sig(\boldsymbol{q})}$ starting with the smallest query $\boldsymbol{q}$, compute a characterising set E for $\boldsymbol{q}$ and check using membership queries whether $\boldsymbol{q}$ is equivalent to the target query. Eventually the algorithm will terminate with a query that is equivalent to the target query. As all of our positive results on unique characterisability provide algorithms computing example sets, we directly obtain learnability with membership queries. Moreover, if the example sets are computed in exponential time, then we obtain an exponential-time learning algorithm: in the enumeration above only $|sig(\boldsymbol{q})|^{|\boldsymbol{q}|}$ queries are checked before the target query is found. Unfortunately, we cannot infer polynomial-time learnability from polynomial characterisability in this way.

A detailed analysis of polynomial-time learnability using membership queries is beyond the scope of this paper. Instead, we focus on one main result, the polynomial-time learnability of $\mathcal{Q}_p[\bigcirc, \Diamond](\mathcal{ELI})$.

Theorem 33. (i) *The class of safe queries in* $\mathcal{Q}_p[\bigcirc, \Diamond_r](\mathcal{ELI})$ *is polynomial-time learnable with membership queries.*

(ii) *The class* $\mathcal{Q}_p[\bigcirc, \Diamond_r](\mathcal{ELI})$ *is polynomial-time learnable with membership queries if the learner knows the size of the target query in advance.*

(iii) *The class* $\mathcal{Q}_p[\bigcirc, \Diamond](\mathcal{ELI})$ *is polynomially-time learnable with membership queries.*

Proof sketch. We consider the 1D case without $\mathcal{ELI}$-queries first. (i) Our proof strategy is to construct a query $\boldsymbol{q}'$ that agrees with $\boldsymbol{q}$ on the positive and negative examples for $\boldsymbol{q}'$ from Theorem 8. The algorithm proceeds by computing a data instance $\mathcal{D}$. Our aim is to arrive at $\mathcal{D}_b$ through iterations of steps, from which the required query can be 'read off'.

Step 1. First, identify the number of $\bigcirc$ and $\Diamond$ in $\boldsymbol{q}$ by asking membership queries of the form σ^k incrementally, starting from $k = 1$, and then set $b = \min\{k \mid \sigma^k \models \boldsymbol{q}\} + 1$ and $\mathcal{D}_0 = \sigma^b$. Initialise $\mathcal{D} = \mathcal{D}_0$.

Step 2. Suppose that a data instance $\mathcal{D}'$ is obtained from $\mathcal{D}$ by applying one of the rules (a)–(e) of Theorem 8. If $\mathcal{D}' \models \boldsymbol{q}$ then replace $\mathcal{D}$ with $\mathcal{D}'$. Repeat as long as possible. One can show that the number of applications of each rule is bounded by a polynomial in $|\sigma|$ and the size of $\boldsymbol{q}$, and so **Step 2** finishes in polynomial time.

Step 3. Suppose $\mathcal{D}$ contains $\emptyset^b \rho_0^i \emptyset^b$ and $|\rho_0^i| \geq 2$. Since rule (a) does not apply, every homomorphism $h\colon \boldsymbol{q} \to \mathcal{D}$ sends some $t_1, \dots, t_l$ to ρ_0^i, for $l \geq 1$. As $\boldsymbol{q}$ does not contain lone conjuncts, $\boldsymbol{q}$ contains singleton primitive blocks at positions $t_1, \dots, t_l$. Suppose $\rho_0^i = \{A_1, \dots, A_{|\rho_0^i|}\}$ and let $w = \{A_1\}\emptyset^b\{A_2\}\emptyset^b \dots \{A_{|\rho_0^i|}\}\emptyset^b$ (the order in which $A_1, \dots, A_{|\rho_0^i|}$, the elements of ρ_0^i, are enumerated does not matter, we fix any one). Let $\mathcal{D}_k^i$ be obtained from $\mathcal{D}$ by replacing $\emptyset^b \rho_0^i \emptyset^b$ with $\emptyset^b (w)^k$. Notice that, for $k = |\boldsymbol{q}|$, we have $\mathcal{D}_k^i \models \boldsymbol{q}$; however, the algorithm is not given this k. Instead, the algorithm incrementally iterates starting from $k = 1$ until $\mathcal{D}_k^i \models \boldsymbol{q}$. Since $k \leq |\boldsymbol{q}|$, this takes polynomially-many iterations. Let $\mathcal{D}'$ be obtained from $\mathcal{D}_k^i$ by removing primitive blocks as long as $\mathcal{D}' \models \boldsymbol{q}$. Notice that rules (a)–(e) do not apply to $\mathcal{D}'$. Replace $\mathcal{D}$ with $\mathcal{D}'$. Repeat **Step 3** as long as possible. Since no new lone conjuncts are introduced, the process finishes after polynomially-many steps.

Step 4. At this point of computation, the algorithm has identified all blocks of $\boldsymbol{q}$ but not the sequences of $\Diamond$ and $\Diamond_r$ between them. They can be easily determined based on the positive and negative examples $\mathcal{D}_i$ and $\mathcal{D}_i^-$.

The proof of (ii) is similar, with a modified **Step 3**. Finally, (iii) is a consequence of (ii) as the size of the query $\boldsymbol{q}$ does not exceed $n = |\sigma|b$.

We obtain a learning algorithm for $\mathcal{Q}_p[\bigcirc, \Diamond_r](\mathcal{ELI})$ by combining the learning algorithm above with the learning algorithm for $\mathcal{ELI}$-queries by ten Cate and Dalmau (2021) using the positive and negative examples given in Theorem 27. Note that the data instance $\mathcal{A}_\Sigma$ is now used instead of σ and that one has to 'unfold' such non tree-shaped data instances into tree-shaped ones. ❑

10 Conclusions

In this paper, we have considered temporal instance queries with *LTL* operators and started investigating their unique (polynomial) characterisability and exact learnability using membership queries. We have obtained both positive and negative results, depending on the available temporal operators and the allowed interaction between the temporal and object dimensions in queries. The results indicate that finding complete classifications of 1D and 2D temporal queries according to (polynomial) characterisability and learnability could be a very difficult task. In particular, interesting open problems include the polynomial characterisability of full $\mathcal{Q}_p^\sigma[\mathsf{U}]$, more general criteria of polynomial characterisability for temporal branching queries and other temporal operators, and the polynomial-time learnability of $\mathcal{Q}_p^\sigma[\mathsf{U}]$ and 2D extensions. From a conceptual viewpoint, it would be of interest to develop a framework that spells out explicitly the conditions that non-temporal queries should satisfy so that their combination with *LTL*-queries preserves polynomial characterisability and polynomial-time learnability.

Acknowledgments

This research was supported by the EPSRC UK grants EP/S032207 and EP/S032282 for the joint project 'quant^{MD}: Ontology-Based Management for Many-Dimensional Quantitative Data'.

References

Aarts, F., and Vaandrager, F. 2010. Learning i/o automata. In *International Conference on Concurrency Theory*, 71–85. Springer.

Alexe, B.; ten Cate, B.; Kolaitis, P. G.; and Tan, W. C. 2011. Characterizing schema mappings via data examples. *ACM Trans. Database Syst.* 36(4):23.

Angluin, D.; Frazier, M.; and Pitt, L. 1992. Learning conjunctions of Horn clauses. *Mach. Learn.* 9:147–164.

Angluin, D. 1987a. Learning regular sets from queries and counterexamples. *Inf. Comput.* 75(2):87–106.

Angluin, D. 1987b. Queries and concept learning. *Mach. Learn.* 2(4):319–342.

Arenas, M., and Diaz, G. I. 2016. The exact complexity of the first-order logic definability problem. *ACM Trans. Database Syst.* 41(2):13:1–13:14.

Artale, A.; Kontchakov, R.; Kovtunova, A.; Ryzhikov, V.; Wolter, F.; and Zakharyaschev, M. 2017. Ontology-mediated query answering over temporal data: A survey. In *Proc. of TIME 2017*, volume 90 of *LIPIcs*, 1:1–1:37. Schloss Dagstuhl, Leibniz-Zentrum für Informatik.

Baader, F.; Horrocks, I.; Lutz, C.; and Sattler, U. 2017. *An Introduction to Description Logics*. Cambride University Press.

Baader, F.; Borgwardt, S.; and Lippmann, M. 2015. Temporal query entailment in the description logic SHQ. *J. Web Semant.* 33:71–93.

Barceló, P., and Romero, M. 2017. The complexity of reverse engineering problems for conjunctive queries. In *Proc. of ICDT*, 7:1–7:17.

Bienvenu, M.; ten Cate, B.; Lutz, C.; and Wolter, F. 2014. Ontology-based data access: A study through disjunctive datalog, CSP, and MMSNP. *ACM Trans. Database Syst.* 39(4):33:1–33:44.

Borgwardt, S., and Thost, V. 2015. Temporal query answering in the description logic EL. In *Proc. of IJCAI 2015*, 2819–2825. AAAI Press.

Camacho, A., and McIlraith, S. A. 2019. Learning interpretable models expressed in linear temporal logic. In *Proc. of ICAPS 2018*, 621–630. AAAI Press.

Cassel, S.; Howar, F.; Jonsson, B.; and Steffen, B. 2016. Active learning for extended finite state machines. *Formal Aspects Comput.* 28(2):233–263.

Chomicki, J., and Toman, D. 2018. *Temporal Logic in Database Query Languages*. Springer. 3992–3998.

Fijalkow, N., and Lagarde, G. 2021. The complexity of learning linear temporal formulas from examples. *CoRR* abs/2102.00876.

Foniok, J.; Nesetril, J.; and Tardif, C. 2008. Generalised dualities and maximal finite antichains in the homomorphism order of relational structures. *Eur. J. Comb.* 29(4):881–899.

Fortin, M.; Konev, B.; Ryzhikov, V.; Savateev, Y.; Wolter, F.; and Zakharyaschev, M. 2022a. Reverse engineering of temporal queries with and without LTL ontologies: First steps (extended abstract). In *Proc. of DL'22*.

Fortin, M.; Konev, B.; Ryzhikov, V.; Savateev, Y.; Wolter, F.; and Zakharyaschev, M. 2022b. Unique Characterisability and Learnability of Temporal Instance Queries. *CoRR abs/2205.01651*.

Funk, M.; Jung, J. C.; Lutz, C.; Pulcini, H.; and Wolter, F. 2019. Learning description logic concepts: When can positive and negative examples be separated? In *Proc. of IJCAI*, 1682–1688.

Funk, M.; Jung, J. C.; and Lutz, C. 2021. Actively learning concepts and conjunctive queries under ELr-ontologies. In *Proc. of IJCAI 2021*, 1887–1893. ijcai.org.

Gutiérrez-Basulto, V.; Jung, J. C.; and Sabellek, L. 2018. Reverse engineering queries in ontology-enriched systems: The case of expressive Horn description logic ontologies. In *Proc. of IJCAI-ECAI*.

Hodkinson, I. M.; Wolter, F.; and Zakharyaschev, M. 2000. Decidable fragment of first-order temporal logics. *Ann. Pure Appl. Log.* 106(1-3):85–134.

Howar, F., and Steffen, B. 2018. Active automata learning in practice - an annotated bibliography of the years 2011 to 2016. In *Machine Learning for Dynamic Software Analysis: Potentials and Limits, International Dagstuhl Seminar 16172*, volume 11026 of *LNCS*, 123–148. Springer.

Jung, J. C.; Lutz, C.; Pulcini, H.; and Wolter, F. 2020. Logical separability of incomplete data under ontologies. In *Proc. of KR 2020*, 517–528.

Kolaitis, P. G. 2011. Schema Mappings and Data Examples: Deriving Syntax from Semantics (Invited Talk). In *Proc. of FSTTCS 2011*, volume 13 of *Leibniz International Proceedings in Informatics (LIPIcs)*, 25–25. Dagstuhl, Germany: Schloss Dagstuhl–Leibniz-Zentrum fuer Informatik.

Konev, B.; Lutz, C.; Ozaki, A.; and Wolter, F. 2017. Exact learning of lightweight description logic ontologies. *J. Mach. Learn. Res.* 18:201:1–201:63.

Konev, B.; Ozaki, A.; and Wolter, F. 2016. A model for learning description logic ontologies based on exact learning. In *Proc. of AAAI*, 1008–1015. AAAI Press.

Lehmann, J., and Hitzler, P. 2010. Concept learning in description logics using refinement operators. *Machine Learning* 78:203–250.

Lemieux, C.; Park, D.; and Beschastnikh, I. 2015. General LTL specification mining (t). In *Proc. of ASE*, 81–92. IEEE.

Lutz, C.; Wolter, F.; and Zakharyaschev, M. 2008. Temporal description logics: A survey. In *Proc. of TIME 2008*, 3–14. IEEE Computer Society.

Martins, D. M. L. 2019. Reverse engineering database queries from examples: State-of-the-art, challenges, and research opportunities. *Inf. Syst.* 83:89–100.

Neider, D., and Gavran, I. 2018. Learning linear temporal properties. In *Proc. of FMCAD 2018*, 1–10. IEEE.

Nesetril, J., and Tardif, C. 2005. Short answers to exponentially long questions: Extremal aspects of homomorphism duality. *SIAM J. Discret. Math.* 19(4):914–920.

Schild, K. 1993. Combining terminological logics with tense logic. In *Proc. of EPIA'93*, volume 727 of *LNCS*, 105–120. Springer.

Shahbaz, M., and Groz, R. 2009. Inferring mealy machines. In *International Symposium on Formal Methods*, 207–222. Springer.

ten Cate, B., and Dalmau, V. 2021. Conjunctive queries: Unique characterizations and exact learnability. In *Proc. of ICDT 2021*, volume 186 of *LIPIcs*, 9:1–9:24. Schloss Dagstuhl - Leibniz-Zentrum für Informatik.

ten Cate, B.; Kolaitis, P. G.; Qian, K.; and Tan, W. 2018. Active learning of GAV schema mappings. In *Proc. of PODS 2018*, 355–368. ACM.

ten Cate, B.; Dalmau, V.; and Kolaitis, P. G. 2013. Learning schema mappings. *ACM Trans. Database Syst.* 38(4):28:1–28:31.

Tirtarasa, S., and Turhan, A.-Y. 2022. Computing Generalizations of Temporal $\mathcal{EL}$ Concepts with Next and Global. In *Proc. of SAC'22*. Association for Computing Machinery.

Proceedings of the 19th International Conference on Principles of Knowledge Representation and Reasoning
Main Track

On the Expressive Power of Intermediate and Conditional Effects in Temporal Planning

Nicola Gigante[1] , **Andrea Micheli**[2] , **Enrico Scala**[3]
[1]Free University of Bozen-Bolzano, Italy
[2]Fondazione Bruno Kessler, Trento, Italy
[3]University of Brescia, Italy
nicola.gigante@unibz.it, amicheli@fbk.eu, enrico.scala@unibs.it

Abstract

Automated planning is the task of finding a sequence of *actions* that reach a desired goal, given a description of their applicability and their effects on the world. In *temporal* planning, actions have a duration and can overlap in time. In modern temporal planning formalisms, two features have been introduced which are very useful from a modeling perspective, but are not yet thoroughly understood: *intermediate conditions and effects* (ICE) and *conditional effects*. The expressive power of such constructs is yet not well comprehended, especially when time is dense, and no minimum separation is required between mutex events. This paper reveals that both ICE and conditional effects do *not* add expressive power with regards to common temporal planning formalisms. In particular, we show how they can be compiled away using a polynomial-size encoding that makes no assumptions on the time domain. This encoding advances our understanding of these features, and allow for their use with simple temporal planners that lack their support. Moreover, it provides a constructive proof showing that temporal planning with ICE and conditional effects remains PSPACE-complete.

1 Introduction

Automated planning is the task of finding a course of *actions* that, when executed starting from a known initial state, reaches a state satisfying a given goal condition. In *temporal planning*, actions have a non-zero duration, and can overlap in time. When multiple instances of the same action are allowed to overlap with themselves, temporal planning has been proved to be EXPSPACE-complete (Rintanen 2007) and *undecidable* (Gigante et al. 2020; Gigante et al. 2022), respectively on discrete and dense time domains, while it becomes PSPACE-complete, in both cases, without self-overlap of actions.

Different temporal planning formalisms have been introduced. PDDL 2.1 (Fox and Long 2003) extends the de-facto standard PDDL language with durative actions. The ANML language (Smith, Frank, and Cushing 2008), introduced in the context of space exploration, mixes features from action-based STRIPS-like formalisms such as PDDL with concepts taken from timeline-based planning languages (Frank and Jónsson 2003; Cesta et al. 2009; Gigante et al. 2017).

A few features of these formalisms exist that are very useful in practice but not yet well understood: *intermediate conditions and effects* (ICE), and *conditional effects*.

With ICE, an action can affect or be conditioned in time points different than the start and the end of its execution time interval. For example, an action might specify an effect to happen 5 time steps after its execution started, and at the same time require a given condition to hold in between 2 time steps after its starting and 5 time steps before its ending. This distinctive feature of the ANML language is not syntactically supported by PDDL 2.1 and, depending on some semantic assumptions about the underlying time domain, it is not clear if such a feature makes ANML more expressive.

With *conditional effects*, the effects of actions can be specified to apply or not depending on some state-dependent condition. For example, an action might be specified to set the truth of a proposition p at its end, only if a certain condition holds at its start. This feature, as formalized in PDDL 2.1, poses some challenges. Neither the polynomial nor the exponential encoding of classical conditional effects (Nebel 2000) work in the temporal case. In temporal planning the conditions under which a given effect is applied depend on the entire execution of the action (*e.g.*, an effect at the *start* of an action that depends on a condition evaluated *over all* the execution of the action), and this poses a significant challenge for the support of this feature. Conditional effects are available in PDDL 2.1, but are not supported by ANML; again, it is unclear whether PDDL 2.1 without such a feature is less expressive.

In this paper, we settle these questions, showing that both ICE and conditional effects *do not* add expressive power. We do so by providing a polynomial-size construction that encodes ICE and conditional effects into simple durative actions. This construction, which can be applied to both PDDL 2.1 and ANML problems, only assumes that self-overlap of actions is forbidden, and is independent from any assumption about the discrete or dense nature of the underlying time model, and from any assumption on the separation between mutex events (*ϵ-separation* or *non-zero separation* semantics). We are not aware of any compilations for conditional effects in temporal planning, and the only known compilation schemata for ICE only applies under ϵ-separation semantics (Fox, Long, and Halsey 2004; Smith 2003), which corresponds to assuming discrete time (Rintanen 2007).

Our construction employs *simultaneity constraints*, a

novel modeling technique that allows the endpoints of some actions, or whole actions, to always happen simultaneously. How to encode such constraints without particular assumptions on the time domain was not generally known before. Thanks to the terse encoding of these constraints, our compilation of ICE and conditional effects is quite lightweight, requiring only a handful of additional actions and fluents in the worst case.

Our results have a number of implications:

1. ICE and conditional effects do not increase the expressive power of temporal planning formalisms;
2. such features can be used with simple temporal planners that do not support them;
3. the homogeneous treatment of both features in terms of simultaneity constraints highlights a relationship between the two that was never noted before;
4. the temporal planning problem with both features, without self-overlap of actions, is still PSPACE-complete both on discrete and dense time.

The paper is structured as follows. After giving the necessary background information in Section 2, we introduce ICE and conditional effects in Section 3. Then, we introduce simultaneity constraints in Section 4, showing how to encode such constraints into temporal planning problems. Then, Section 5 uses simultaneity constraints to show how to encode ICE, while Section 6 turns its attention to conditional effects. Section 7 discusses related work, and Section 8 concludes with final remarks and mentions future work.

2 Background

Following Fox and Long (2003), this section introduces the temporal planning problem we are interested in. Given a set P of *propositions*, let $\mathbb{B}_P$ be the set of *Boolean formulas* over P.

Definition 1 (Temporal Planning Problem). *A temporal planning problem is a tuple $\mathcal{P} = \langle P, A, I, G\rangle$, where P is a set of propositions, A is a set of durative actions, $I \subseteq P$ is the initial state, and $G \in \mathbb{B}_P$ is the goal condition. A snap (instantaneous) action is a tuple $h = \langle \mathrm{pre}(h), \mathrm{eff}^+(h), \mathrm{eff}^-(h)\rangle$, where $\mathrm{pre}(h) \in \mathbb{B}_P$ is the precondition and $\mathrm{eff}^+(h), \mathrm{eff}^-(h) \subseteq P$ are two disjoint sets of propositions, called the* positive *and* negative *effects of h, respectively. We write $\mathrm{eff}(h)$ for $\mathrm{eff}^+(h) \cup \mathrm{eff}^-(h)$. A durative action $a \in A$ is a tuple $\langle a_\vdash, a_\dashv, \mathrm{pre}^\leftrightarrow(a), [L_a, U_a]\rangle$, where $a_\vdash$ and $a_\dashv$ are the* start *and* end *snap actions, respectively, $\mathrm{pre}^\leftrightarrow(a) \in \mathbb{B}_P$ is the* over-all condition, *and $L_a \in \mathbb{Q}_{>0}$ and $U_a \in \mathbb{Q}_{\geq 0} \cup \{\infty\}$ are the bounds on the action duration.*

The above definition corresponds to temporal planning as defined by PDDL 2.1 (without numeric variables). The problem is defined using a set-theoretic representation, where states are subsets of P, which is the universe of facts over which one can determine the status of things, and the possible transitions that may take place in the system. When interpreted as a state, a subset s of P lists those atoms which hold true in it and implicitly asserts false those which are not part of it (closed-world assumption). Conditions are Boolean formulas over P. The initial state I specifies what holds at the beginning, before execution, while action tuples in A specify the dynamics of the system, that is, how a state can change, and under which propositional and temporal conditions such changes may happen. An action tuple delegates the specification of the state transition to two *snap actions*: one is relative to when the durative action starts, and one to when the durative action ends. As classical planning actions, these instantaneous transitions are represented by a pair, which encodes the applicability of the transition ($\mathrm{pre}(h)$), and the effects that the transition has on the state when applied ($\mathrm{eff}^+(h)$ and $\mathrm{eff}^-(h)$). Unlike in classical planning problems, however, in temporal planning actions last for a certain time (they are *durative*), and their duration has to satisfy the given lower and upper time limits, that is, $[L_a, U_a]$. Moreover, since the state can change while the action is under execution, we can further require that all intermediate states satisfy a given invariant condition ($\mathrm{pre}^\leftrightarrow(a)$). Note that PDDL 2.1 allows for instantaneous classical actions to be defined alongside durative actions. Here, for simplicity we do not allow for this feature, but it would be straightforward to do so. Finally, the Boolean formula G determines what needs to be achieved in order for the problem to be solved.

A collection of action tuples from A, together with a starting time and a duration, is called a plan.

Definition 2 (Plan). *Let $\mathcal{P} = \langle P, A, I, G\rangle$ be a planning problem. A plan for $\mathcal{P}$ is a set of tuples $\pi = \{\langle a_1, t_1, d_1\rangle, \cdots, \langle a_n, t_n, d_n\rangle\}$, where, for each $1 \leq i \leq n$, $a_i \in A$ is a durative action, $t_i \in \mathbb{Q}_{\geq 0}$ is its start time, and $d_i \in \mathbb{Q}_{>0}$ is its duration.*

A plan can be understood as a set of timed decisions the agent can take over time. Indeed, each tuple of a plan defines what action needs to start (a_n), when it must be initiated (t_n), and how long it has to last (d_n). Note that this semantics assumes a *dense* time model, but all the constructions in this paper apply to a *discrete* time model as well.

In order to precisely state whether a given plan is valid with respect to the temporal planning problem it represents a candidate solution for, in the following we recall and summarize the state-transition model interpretation of a temporal plan given by Fox and Long (2003).

Definition 3 (Set of timed snap actions). *A timed snap action (TSA) is a pair $\langle t, h\rangle$, where $t \in \mathbb{Q}_{\geq 0}$ and h is a snap action. Given a plan $\pi = \{\langle a_1, t_1, d_1\rangle, \cdots, \langle a_n, t_n, d_n\rangle\}$, the set of TSAs of π is defined as:*

$$H(\pi) = \{\langle t, a_\vdash\rangle, \langle t + d, a_\dashv\rangle \mid \langle a, t, d\rangle \in \pi\}$$

Given a set of timed snap actions, we define the induced parallel plan as the sequence of sets of timed snap actions sharing the same time index. As we will see, the validity of plans can be stated by defining constraints over the induced parallel plan that can be extracted from the timed snap actions of a plan.

Definition 4 (Induced parallel plan). *Let π be a plan and let $H(\pi) = \{\langle t'_1, h_1\rangle, \cdots, \langle t'_m, h_m\rangle\}$ be the set of TSAs of π. The induced parallel plan for π is the sequence*

$\pi^{ind} = \langle\langle t''_1, \{h \mid \langle t''_1, h\rangle \in H(\pi)\}\rangle, \cdots, \langle t''_k, \{h \mid \langle t''_k, h\rangle \in H(\pi)\}\rangle\rangle$, *which is ordered and grouped with respect to the time index, that is,* $\forall i, j \in \{1, \cdots, k\}$, $i < j$ *if and only if* $t''_i < t''_j$, *and if* $t''_i = t''_j$, *then* $i = j$. *Given* $c_i = \langle a_i, t_i, d_i\rangle \in \pi$, *we denote by* $\pi^{ind}_{\vdash}(c_i) = x$, *with* $t''_x = t_i$, *and* $\pi^{ind}_{\dashv}(c_i) = y$, *with* $t''_y = t_i + d_i$, *the indexes of the pairs in* π^{ind} *containing, in the right hand side, the snap actions* $a_{i\vdash}$ *and* $a_{i\dashv}$ *relative to* c_i, *respectively.*

In order to define the validity of plans, we need to decide what happens to events that affect the same variables. We say that two snap actions are *mutex* whenever one interferes with at least one effect or precondition of the other. The concept is formally defined as follows.

Definition 5 (Mutex snap actions). *Given a set of propositions* P *and a Boolean formula* $\phi \in \mathbb{B}_P$, *let* $P(\phi)$ *be the set of propositions mentioned by* ϕ. *Two snap actions* h *and* z *are* mutually exclusive *(mutex), denoted by* $\text{mutex}(h, z)$, *if either* $P(\text{pre}(h)) \cap \text{eff}(z) \neq \varnothing$, *or* $P(\text{pre}(z)) \cap \text{eff}(h) \neq \varnothing$, *or* $\text{eff}^+(h) \cap \text{eff}^-(z) \neq \varnothing$, *or* $\text{eff}^+(z) \cap \text{eff}^-(h) \neq \varnothing$.

We are now ready to define the notion of plan validity. Intuitively, a plan is said to be valid if (i) the induced plan is a classical goal-reaching execution where all overall and duration constraints are satisfied, and (ii) mutex snap actions do not appear at the same time in a plan.

Given a set of propositions $s \subseteq P$, called *state*, and a condition $\phi \in \mathbb{B}_P$, we write $s \models \phi$ if s satisfies ϕ under the classical semantics of Boolean formulas.

Definition 6 (Plan validity). *Given a temporal planning problem* $\mathcal{P} = \langle P, A, I, G\rangle$ *and a plan* $\pi = \{\langle a_1, t_1, d_1\rangle, \cdots, \langle a_n, t_n, d_n\rangle\}$ *for* $\mathcal{P}$, *and* $\pi^{ind} = \langle\langle t'_1, B_1\rangle, \cdots, \langle t'_m, B_m\rangle\rangle$ *be its induced plan. Then,* π *is valid if the following statements hold:*

1. $\forall i \in \{1, \cdots, n\}$ $L_{a_i} \leq d_i \leq U_{a_i}$,
2. *there are no* $h, z \in B_i$, *with* $h \neq z$, *for some* $i \in \{1, \cdots, m\}$, *such that* $\text{mutex}(h, z)$,
3. *given* $s_0 = I$, *for all* $i \in \{1, \ldots, m\}$, *it holds that:*
   (a) $s_i = (s_{i-1} \setminus \bigcup_{h \in B_i} \text{eff}^-(h)) \cup \bigcup_{h \in B_i} \text{eff}^+(h)$;
   (b) $s_i \models \bigwedge_{h \in B_i} \text{pre}(h)$;
   (c) $s_m \models G$,
4. *for all* $c = \langle a, t, d\rangle \in \pi$ *and all* $\pi^{ind}_{\vdash}(c) \leq k < \pi^{ind}_{\dashv}(c)$, *we have* $s_k \models \text{pre}^{\leftrightarrow}(a)$.
5. *actions do not self-overlap*, i.e., *there are no* $1 \leq i, j \leq n$, *with* $i \neq j$, *such that* $a = a_i = a_j$ *and* $t_i \leq t_j \leq t_i + d_i$

Note that Item 2 of Definition 6 only assumes a non-zero time separation between mutex events (*non-zero separation* semantics), without assuming a concrete minimum amount of time (ϵ-*separation* semantics). The constructions in this paper do not depend on this assumption though, and work with ϵ-separation semantics as well. Note also that Item 5 explicitly excludes self-overlap of actions. This assumption is quite natural given that self-overlap leads to *undecidability* in dense time domains (Gigante et al. 2022).

3 ICE and Conditional Effects

In this section, we introduce the features that are the subject of this paper, that is, *intermediate conditions and effects* (ICE), and *conditional effects*.

ICE allow the modeler to state that something happens or has to happen in time points different from the start or the end of the action execution interval. An effect, for example, can be placed at k time steps after the start of the action, and a condition can be required to hold from k steps after the start to l steps before the end, and so on. Formally, planning problems with ICE can be defined as follows.

Definition 7 (Intermediate conditions and effects). *Given a positive rational number* $k \in \mathbb{Q}_{\geq 0}$, *an* ICE term *is either a term* $\mathsf{START} + k$ *or* $\mathsf{END} - k$.

An ICE effect *is a tuple* $e = \langle \tau, \text{eff}^+, \text{eff}^-\rangle$ *where* τ *is an ICE term and* eff^+ *and* eff^- *are sets of propositions.*

An ICE condition *is a pair* $c = \langle \tau_1, \tau_2, \phi\rangle$ *where* τ_1 *and* τ_2 *are ICE terms and* ϕ *is a Boolean formula, such that:*

1. *if* $\tau_1 \equiv \mathsf{START} + k$ *and* $\tau_2 \equiv \mathsf{START} + l$, *then* $k < l$;
2. *if* $\tau_1 \equiv \mathsf{END} - k$ *and* $\tau_2 \equiv \mathsf{END} - l$, *then* $k > l$;

Definition 8 (Planning problem with ICE). *A* durative action with ICE *is a tuple* $a = \langle a_\vdash, a_\dashv, \text{pre}^{\leftrightarrow}(a), [L_a, U_a], E_a, C_a\rangle$ *where* $a_\vdash$, $a_\dashv$, $\text{pre}^{\leftrightarrow}(a)$, L_a, *and* U_a *are defined as in Definition 1,* E_a *is a set of ICE effects, and* C_a *is a set of ICE conditions. A* planning problem with ICE *is a planning problem as in Definition 1 but made of durative actions with ICE.*

A thorough formal description of the semantics of ICE conditions and effects is beyond the scope of this paper, but can be found in the literature (Valentini, Micheli, and Cimatti 2020). Intuitively, an ICE effect $e = \langle \tau, \text{eff}^+, \text{eff}^-\rangle$ applies the positive effects eff^+ and the negative effects eff^- to the state at the time specified by τ: if $\tau = \mathsf{START} + k$, the effects are applied k time steps after the start of the action. Similarly, if $\tau = \mathsf{END} - k$, the effects are applied k time steps before the end of the action. An ICE condition $c = \langle \tau_1, \tau_2, \phi\rangle$ requires that ϕ holds during all the time points between τ_1 and τ_2 (extrema included).

Figure 1 shows an example usage of ICE. The setting is the operation of a production plant. A production machine makes some treatment over a part of the final product, which is done in 50 seconds. However, to avoid the part to oxidize and become useless, it has to be picked and stored within other 50 seconds. This can be modeled by making the action make-treatment 100 seconds long, with an intermediate effect at $t = 50$ that sets the *done* fluent, signaling the end of the treatment. Then, the pick action has to be executed within the next 50 seconds, because the end of make-treatment requires the *picked* fluent to be true.

We now turn our attention to conditional effects. In the context of temporal planning, they are defined by Fox and Long (2003) in their definition of PDDL 2.1. Intuitively, with conditional effects on durative actions, one can make the application of an effect depend on a combination of conditions evaluated at the start of, at the end of, and over all the interval of execution of the action. For example, one may say that at the start of an action the effect p is applied only if the formula θ holds at the end, and ψ holds true over

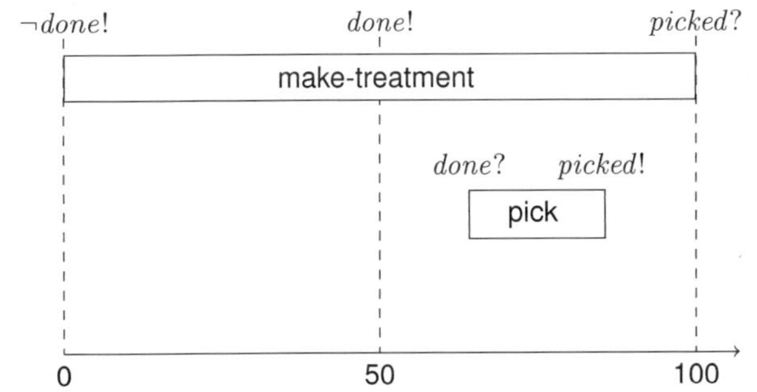

Figure 1: Example use case of ICE. Question marks denote conditions, exclamation marks denote effects.

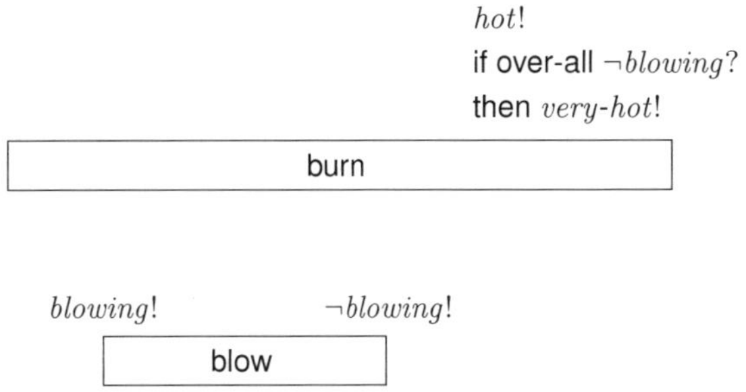

Figure 2: Example use case of conditional effects. Question marks denote conditions, exclamation marks denote effects.

the entire execution. Formally, we can define conditional effects as follows.

Definition 9 (Conditional effects). *Let P be a set of propositions. A* conditional effect *is a tuple $e = \langle \phi, \psi, \theta, \text{eff}_{\vdash}^{+}, \text{eff}_{\vdash}^{-}, \text{eff}_{\dashv}^{+}, \text{eff}_{\dashv}^{-} \rangle$, where $\phi \in \mathbb{B}_P$ is the* at-start *condition, $\psi \in \mathbb{B}_P$ is the* over-all *condition, $\theta \in \mathbb{B}_P$ is the* at-end *condition, $\text{eff}_{\vdash}^{+} \subseteq P$ and $\text{eff}_{\vdash}^{-} \subseteq P$ are the positive and negative* at-start *effects, and $\text{eff}_{\dashv}^{+} \subseteq P$ and $\text{eff}_{\dashv}^{-} \subseteq P$ are the positive and negative* at-end *effects.*

Definition 10 (Problem with conditional effects). *A durative action with conditional effects is a tuple $a = \langle a_{\vdash}, a_{\dashv}, \text{pre}^{\leftrightarrow}(a), [L_a, U_a], E_a \rangle$, where $a_{\vdash}$, $a_{\dashv}$, $\text{pre}^{\leftrightarrow}(a)$, L_a, and U_a are defined as in Definition 1, and E_a is a set of* conditional effects. *A* planning problem with conditional effects *is a problem $\mathcal{P} = \langle P, A, I, G \rangle$ where P, I and G are defined as in Definition 1, and A is a set of durative actions with conditional effects.*

Intuitively, if an action a is equipped with a conditional effect $e = \langle \phi, \psi, \theta, \text{eff}_{\vdash}^{+}, \text{eff}_{\vdash}^{-}, \text{eff}_{\dashv}^{+}, \text{eff}_{\dashv}^{-} \rangle$, and the action is executed, the positive and negative *at-start* and *at-end* effects $\text{eff}_{\vdash}^{+}$, $\text{eff}_{\vdash}^{-}$, $\text{eff}_{\dashv}^{+}$, $\text{eff}_{\dashv}^{-}$ are applied if and only if the *at-start* condition ϕ holds at the start of the execution, the *over-all* condition ψ holds during all the execution of the action (extrema excluded), and the *at-end* condition θ holds at the end of the execution. As in the case of ICE in the previous section, we do not delve into all the formal details of the semantics of planning problems with conditional effects, redirecting the reader to Fox and Long (2003).

The kind of situations that can be expressed with conditional effects in temporal planning is qualitatively different than what can be done in classical planning, because a condition can involve events that are very distant in the plan. For example, one may say that the effect of setting a fluent at the end of an action is applied only if some condition has held over all the execution of the action. This is what we use to express the use case depicted in Figure 2. An action burn is used to switch on a burner that has the purpose of increasing the temperature. The burner has only a single mode of operation and can be switched on only for a fixed amount of time, but the problem requires different temperature levels. For this reason, some air can be blown to balance the temperature (the blow action). Hence, if the burn action is executed alone, both the *hot* and *very-hot* fluents are set. If the blow action is executed in the middle, only the *hot* fluent is set.

Conditional effects emerge in various compilations from planning with state trajectory constraints (*e.g.*, (Torres and Baier 2015; Bonassi et al. 2021)) and conformant planning (*e.g.*, (Palacios and Geffner 2007; Grastien and Scala 2020; Scala and Grastien 2021) to classical planning. In the case of state-trajectory constraints, conditional effects are used to keep track of the side effect of each agent's decision on a monitoring automaton that represents the satisfiability status of the constraints. For example, Torres and Baier (2015) use a NFA automaton that accepts all plans that satisfy the provided trajectory constraints. In conformant planning problems, for example, Grastien and Scala (2020) use conditional effects to link the action effects with some assumption over the possible worlds in the agent's initial belief. In the resulting classical planning problem, the agent is required to find a plan that works for each such assumption. The support of conditional effects that can be conditioned throughout the entire execution of an action has the potential to extend such approaches to temporal planning problems as well.

4 Simultaneity Constraints

In order to show how to encode ICE and conditional effects into a temporal planning problem, we use the concept of *simultaneity constraint*.

We need some terminology first.

Definition 11 (Plan projection). *Let $\mathcal{P} = \langle P, A, I, G \rangle$ be a temporal planning problem and let A' be a set of actions such that $A' \cap A \neq \varnothing$. Given a plan π for $\mathcal{P}$, the* projection *of π over A', denoted $\pi|_{A'}$, is the plan obtained from π by removing any action $a \in A \setminus A'$.*

Intuitively, simultaneity constraints impose some snap actions to always happen at the same time. They are formally defined as follows.

Definition 12 (Simultaneity constraint). *Let $\mathcal{P} = \langle P, A, I, G \rangle$ be a temporal planning problem, and let a_{*_a} and b_{*_b} be two snap actions, where $*_a, *_b \in \{\vdash, \dashv\}$. A problem $\mathcal{P}' = \langle P', A', I', G' \rangle$* augments *$\mathcal{P}$ with the* simultaneity constraint *$a_{*_a} \mathbin{/\!/} b_{*_b}$ if any plan π is a valid plan for $\mathcal{P}'$ if and only if $\pi|_A$ is a valid plan for $\mathcal{P}$ and, for each $t \in \mathbb{Q}_{\geq 0}$*

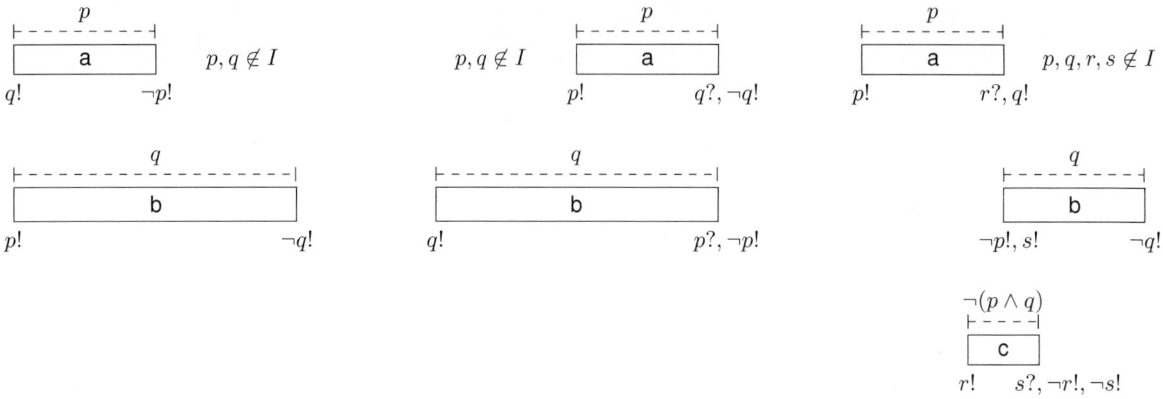

Figure 3: Schematics for the construction of $a_\vdash \mathbin{/\!/} b_\vdash$ (left), $a_\dashv \mathbin{/\!/} b_\dashv$ (center), and $a_\dashv \mathbin{/\!/} b_\vdash$ (right). Question marks denote conditions, exclamation marks denote effects, dashed lines denote overall conditions.

such that $(t, a_{*_a}) \in H(\pi)$, *we have* $(t, b_{*_b}) \in H(\pi)$, *and* vice versa, *for each* $t \in \mathbb{Q}_{\geq 0}$ *such that* $(t, b_{*_b}) \in H(\pi)$, *we have* $(t, a_{*_a}) \in H(\pi)$.

As an example, given two durative actions a and b, if we augment $\mathcal{P}$ with the simultaneity constraint $a_\dashv \mathbin{/\!/} b_\vdash$ we restrict valid plans for π to those where for each instance of a there is an instance of b where the end of a and the start of b are simultaneous, and *vice versa*.

We show now how to add a simultaneity constraint to a temporal planning problem. The encoding is different for the three cases of $a_\vdash \mathbin{/\!/} b_\vdash$ (both starting snap actions), $a_\dashv \mathbin{/\!/} b_\dashv$ (both ending snap actions), and $a_\dashv \mathbin{/\!/} b_\vdash$ (an ending and a starting snap action). The key ideas of how to encode simultaneity constraints in the three cases are shown in Figure 3. Let us understand how the encoding works intuitively before delving into the formal details. In the case of $a_\vdash \mathbin{/\!/} b_\vdash$, two fresh propositions p and q are introduced, which are initially set to false. The overall conditions of a and b are enriched by asking respectively p and q, while the starting effect of a sets q and the starting effect of b sets p. Now, a cannot start before the start of b because it needs p to hold, and b cannot start before the start of a because it needs q to hold. The result is that the two actions have to start together. The end effects of a and b then reset p and q to *false* to recover the initial state, allowing the construction to repeat if needed. A similar reasoning holds for $a_\dashv \mathbin{/\!/} b_\dashv$.

The case for $a_\dashv \mathbin{/\!/} b_\vdash$ is different, as it involves a *clip construction*. A third fresh action c is introduced, which is used to hold together a and b, alongside fresh propositions p, q, r, and s. The propositions r and s are used to force c to start before the end of a and end after the start of b, enclosing the two snap actions that we want to glue together. Then, a has overall condition p, while b has overall condition q, but C has overall condition $\neg(p \wedge q)$, thus a and b cannot overlap. Moreover, the end of a sets q, so the overall condition of C risks to be invalidated as soon as a ends. However, the start of b sets $\neg p$, hence the only way for the overall condition of C to stay satisfied is for $a_\dashv$ and $b_\vdash$ to happen at the same time. We can now formally define what we described above. Let us start from the case of $a_\vdash \mathbin{/\!/} b_\vdash$.

Definition 13 (Encoding of $a_\vdash \mathbin{/\!/} b_\vdash$). *Given a temporal planning problem* $\mathcal{P} = \langle P, A, I, G \rangle$, *two actions* $a, b \in A$, *and two propositions* p *and* q *(not necessarily in* P*), we denote as* $\text{enc}(a_\vdash \mathbin{/\!/} b_\vdash, \mathcal{P}, p, q)$ *the temporal planning problem* $\mathcal{P}' = \langle P', A', I', G' \rangle$ *defined as follows:*

1. $P' = P \cup \{p, q\}$;
2. $I' = I$ (i.e., *p and q start false) and* $G' = G$;
3. $A' = A \setminus \{a, b\} \cup \{a', b'\}$ *where* a' *and* b' *are like* a *and* b *excepting for what follows:*
   (a) $\text{eff}^+(a'_\vdash) = \text{eff}^+(a_\vdash) \cup \{q\}$;
   (b) $\text{eff}^-(a'_\dashv) = \text{eff}^-(a_\dashv) \cup \{p\}$;
   (c) $\text{pre}^\leftrightarrow(a') = \text{pre}^\leftrightarrow(a) \wedge p$;
   (d) $\text{eff}^+(b'_\vdash) = \text{eff}^+(b_\vdash) \cup \{p\}$;
   (e) $\text{eff}^-(b'_\dashv) = \text{eff}^-(b_\dashv) \cup \{q\}$;
   (f) $\text{pre}^\leftrightarrow(b') = \text{pre}^\leftrightarrow(b) \wedge q$;

For the case of $a_\dashv \mathbin{/\!/} b_\dashv$ the construction is as follows.

Definition 14 (Encoding of $a_\dashv \mathbin{/\!/} b_\dashv$). *Given a temporal planning problem* $\mathcal{P} = \langle P, A, I, G \rangle$, *two actions* $a, b \in A$, *and two propositions* p *and* q *(not necessarily in* P*), we denote as* $\text{enc}(a_\dashv \mathbin{/\!/} b_\dashv, \mathcal{P}, p, q)$ *the temporal planning problem* $\mathcal{P}' = \langle P', A', I', G' \rangle$ *defined as follows:*

1. $P' = P \cup \{p, q\}$;
2. $I' = I$ (i.e., *p and q start false) and* $G' = G$;
3. $A' = A \setminus \{a, b\} \cup \{a', b'\}$ *where* a' *and* b' *are like* a *and* b *excepting for what follows:*
   (a) $\text{eff}^+(a'_\vdash) = \text{eff}^+(a_\vdash) \cup \{p\}$;
   (b) $\text{eff}^-(a'_\dashv) = \text{eff}^-(a_\dashv) \cup \{q\}$;
   (c) $\text{pre}(a'_\dashv) = \text{pre}(a_\dashv) \wedge q$;
   (d) $\text{pre}^\leftrightarrow(a') = \text{pre}^\leftrightarrow(a) \wedge p$;
   (e) $\text{eff}^+(b'_\vdash) = \text{eff}^+(b_\vdash) \cup \{q\}$;
   (f) $\text{eff}^-(b'_\dashv) = \text{eff}^-(b_\dashv) \cup \{p\}$;
   (g) $\text{pre}(b'_\dashv) = \text{pre}(b_\dashv) \wedge p$;
   (h) $\text{pre}^\leftrightarrow(b') = \text{pre}^\leftrightarrow(b) \wedge q$;

The case of $a_\dashv \mathbin{/\!/} b_\vdash$ is encoded as follows.

Definition 15 (Encoding of $a_\dashv$ // $b_\vdash$). *Given a temporal planning problem $\mathcal{P} = \langle P, A, I, G\rangle$, two actions $a, b \in A$, and three propositions p, q, and r (not necessarily in P), we denote as* $\text{enc}(a_\dashv \;//\; b_\vdash, \mathcal{P}, p, q, r)$ *the temporal planning problem $\mathcal{P}' = \langle P', A', I', G'\rangle$ defined as follows:*

1. $P' = P \cup \{p, q\}$;
2. $I' = I$ (i.e., *p, q, r, and s start false) and* $G' = G$;
3. $A' = A \setminus \{a, b\} \cup \{a', b', c\}$, *where a' and b' are like a and b excepting for what follows:*
   (a) $\text{eff}^+(a'_\vdash) = \text{eff}^+ a_\vdash \cup \{p\}$;
   (b) $\text{eff}^+(a'_\dashv) = \text{eff}^+ a_\dashv \cup \{q\}$;
   (c) $\text{pre}(a'_\dashv) = \text{pre}(a_\dashv) \wedge r$;
   (d) $\text{pre}^\leftrightarrow(a') = \text{pre}^\leftrightarrow(a) \wedge p$;
   (e) $\text{eff}^-(b'_\vdash) = \text{eff}^-(b_\vdash) \cup \{p\}$;
   (f) $\text{eff}^+(b'_\vdash) = \text{eff}^+(b_\vdash) \cup \{s\}$;
   (g) $\text{eff}^-(b'_\dashv) = \text{eff}^-(b_\dashv) \cup \{q\}$;
   (h) $\text{pre}^\leftrightarrow(b') = \text{pre}^\leftrightarrow(b) \wedge q$;
   and $c = \langle c_\vdash, c_\dashv, \text{pre}^\leftrightarrow(c), [L_c, U_c]\rangle$ *is defined as follows:*
   (a) $\text{eff}^+(c_\vdash) = \{r\}$, $\text{eff}^-(c_\vdash) = \varnothing$;
   (b) $\text{eff}^+(c_\dashv) = \varnothing$, $\text{eff}^-(c_\dashv) = \{r, s\}$;
   (c) $\text{pre}(c_\vdash) = \top$, $\text{pre}(c_\dashv) = s$;
   (d) $\text{pre}^\leftrightarrow(c) = \neg(p \wedge q)$;
   (e) $L_a = U_a = \min\{L_a, L_b\}$.

One can check that the constructions in Definitions 13, 14 and 15 work as intended.

Lemma 1 (Soundness of simultaneity constraints encoding). *Given a temporal planning problem $\mathcal{P} = \langle P, A, I, G\rangle$, two actions $a, b \in A$, and three propositions $p, q, r \notin P$, then:*

1. *the planning problem* $\text{enc}(a_\vdash \;//\; b_\vdash, \mathcal{P}, p, q)$ *augments $\mathcal{P}$ with the simultaneity constraint $a_\vdash$ // $b_\vdash$;*
2. *the planning problem* $\text{enc}(a_\dashv \;//\; b_\dashv, \mathcal{P}, p, q)$ *augments $\mathcal{P}$ with the simultaneity constraint $a_\dashv$ // $b_\dashv$;*
3. *the planning problem* $\text{enc}(a_\dashv \;//\; b_\vdash, \mathcal{P}, p, q, r)$ *augments $\mathcal{P}$ with the simultaneity constraint $a_\dashv$ // $b_\vdash$.*

Another kind of simultaneity constraint will come useful later: a constraint that imposes a durative action to be simultaneous with one of a set of other actions.

Definition 16 (Simultaneity constraint between actions). *Let $\mathcal{P} = \langle P, A, I, G\rangle$ be a temporal planning problem, and let $a \in A$ and $b_0, \ldots, b_n \in A$ be durative actions. A problem $\mathcal{P}' = \langle P', A', I', G'\rangle$* augments *$\mathcal{P}$ with the simultaneity constraint a // $\{b_0, \ldots, b_n\}$ if any plan π is valid for $\mathcal{P}'$ if and only if $\pi|_A$ is valid for $\mathcal{P}$ and, for each instance of a executing in $\pi|_A$, there is an instance of one of $b_0, \ldots, b_n$ executing in $\pi|_A$ starting and ending exactly at the same time.*

Intuitively, if a is an action and $b_0, \ldots, b_n$ are actions, when we augment a problem $\mathcal{P}$ with a constraint a // $\{b_0, \ldots, b_n\}$, we impose that for each instance of a, at least one of $b_0, \ldots, b_n$ is executed exactly at the same time of a. To encode this constraint, we can at first observe that augmenting a problem with a // $\{b\}$ is equivalent to augmenting it with the two simultaneity constraints $a_\vdash$ // $b_\vdash$ and $a_\dashv$ // $b_\dashv$. Then, by reusing some auxiliary propositions, we can encode the disjunction between $b_0, \ldots, b_n$.

Definition 17 (Encoding of a // $\{b_0, \ldots, b_n\}$). *Given a temporal planning problem $\mathcal{P} = \langle P, A, I, G\rangle$ and actions $a, b_0, \ldots, b_n \in A$,* $\text{enc}(a \;//\; \{b_0, \ldots, b_n\}, \mathcal{P})$ *denotes the problem recursively defined as follows:*

$$\text{enc}(a \;//\; \varnothing, \mathcal{P}) = \mathcal{P}$$
$$\text{enc}(a \;//\; \{b_0, \ldots, b_n\}, \mathcal{P}) = \text{enc}(a_\vdash \;//\; b_{0\vdash}, \mathcal{P}'', p_1, q_1)$$
$$\text{where } \mathcal{P}'' = \text{enc}(a_\dashv \;//\; b_{0\dashv}, \mathcal{P}', p_2, q_2)$$
$$\mathcal{P}' = \text{enc}(a \;//\; \{b_0, \ldots, b_{n-1}\})$$

where $p_1, p_2, q_1, q_2 \notin P$ are four fresh propositions.

The recursive definition of $\text{enc}(a \;//\; \{b_0, \ldots, b_n\}, \mathcal{P})$ in Definition 17 augments the original problem $\mathcal{P}$, once for each action $\{b_0, \ldots, b_n\}$, with two simultaneity constraints that bind together $a_\vdash$ with $b_{i\vdash}$ and $a_\dashv$ with $b_{i\dashv}$. However, this construction does more than the simple combination of $a_\vdash$ // $b_{i\vdash}$ and $a_\dashv$ // $b_{i\dashv}$: by reusing the same propositions p_1, p_2, q_1, q_2 to encode the simultaneity constraints between the snap actions of a and $b_0, \ldots, b_n$, we make sure that the constructions shown in Figure 3 are satisfied by any one of the actions $b_0, \ldots, b_n$. One can check the following result.

Lemma 2 (Soundness of Definition 17). *Given a temporal planning problem $\mathcal{P} = \langle P, A, I, G\rangle$, and durative actions $a, b_0, \ldots, b_n \in A$, the temporal planning problem* $\text{enc}(a \;//\; \{b_0, \ldots, b_n\}, \mathcal{P})$ *augments $\mathcal{P}$ with the constraint a // $\{b_0, \ldots, b_n\}$.*

5 Intermediate Conditions and Effects

Thanks to the simultaneity constraints developed in Section 4, we can easily encode planning problem with ICE into a plain planning problem.

Theorem 1 (ICE encoding). *Given a planning problem with ICE $\mathcal{P} = \langle P, A, I, G\rangle$, there exists a planning problem $\mathcal{P}' = \langle P', A', I', G'\rangle$ such that any plan π is valid for $\mathcal{P}'$ if and only if $\pi|_A$ is valid for $\mathcal{P}$.*

Proof. Let $a = \langle a_\vdash, a_\dashv, \text{pre}^\leftrightarrow(a), [L_a, U_a], E_a, C_a\rangle$ be a durative action with ICE from $\mathcal{P}$. Then, a can be simply replaced by the corresponding plain durative action, after augmenting the problem with some auxiliary actions and suitable simultaneity constraints. How exactly this is done depends on the kind of ICE involved (see Figure 4):

1. For an ICE effect $\langle \mathsf{START} + k, \text{eff}^+, \text{eff}^-\rangle$, we add an auxiliary action e with $\text{eff}^+(e_\dashv) = \text{eff}^+$ and $\text{eff}^-(e_\dashv) = \text{eff}^-$, $L_e = U_e = k$, and we augment the problem with the simultaneity constraint $a_\vdash$ // $e_\vdash$.
2. Similarly, for an ICE effect $\langle \mathsf{END} - k, \text{eff}^+, \text{eff}^-\rangle$, we add an auxiliary action e with $\text{eff}^+(e_\vdash) = \text{eff}^+$ and $\text{eff}^-(e_\vdash) = \text{eff}^-$, $L_e = U_e = k$, and we augment the problem with the simultaneity constraint $a_\dashv$ // $e_\dashv$.
3. For an ICE condition $\langle \mathsf{START} + k, \mathsf{START} + l, \phi\rangle$ we add two auxiliary actions e_1 and e_2. We set $\text{pre}(e_{2\vdash}) = \text{pre}(e_{2\dashv}) = \text{pre}^\leftrightarrow(e_2) = \phi$, $L_{e_1} = U_{e_1} = k$, $L_{e_2} = U_{e_2} = l - k$, and we augment the problem with the constraints $a_\vdash$ // $e_{1\vdash}$ and $e_{1\dashv}$ // $e_{2\vdash}$.

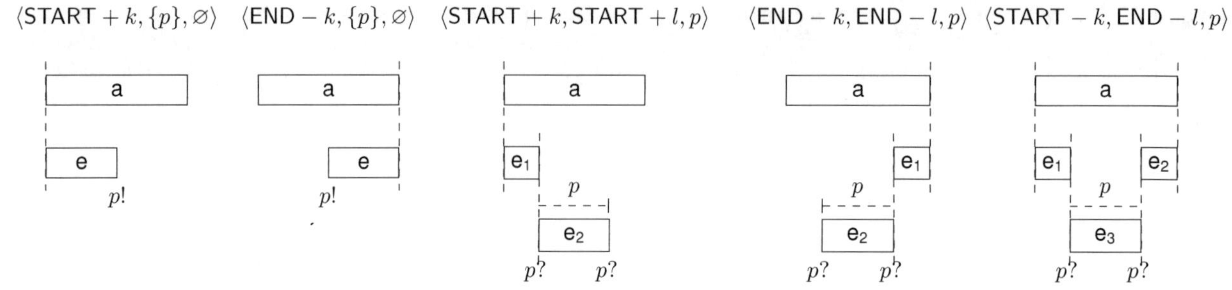

Figure 4: Constructions to encode ICE using simultaneity constraints. Question marks denote conditions, exclamation marks denote effects, horizontal dashed lines denote overall conditions, vertical dashed lines denote simultaneity constraints.

4. Similarly, for an ICE condition $\langle \mathsf{END} - k, \mathsf{END} - l, \phi \rangle$ we add two auxiliary actions e_1 and e_2. We set $\text{pre}(e_{2\vdash}) = \text{pre}(e_{2\dashv}) = \text{pre}^{\leftrightarrow}(e_2) = \phi$, $L_{e_1} = U_{e_1} = l$, $L_{e_2} = U_{e_2} = k - l$, and we augment the problem with the constraints $a_{\dashv} \mathbin{/\!/} e_{1\dashv}$ and $e_{1\vdash} \mathbin{/\!/} e_{2\dashv}$.
5. For an ICE condition $\langle \mathsf{START} + k, \mathsf{END} - k, \phi \rangle$, we add three auxiliary actions e_1, e_2, and e_3. We set $\text{pre}(e_{3\vdash}) = \text{pre}(e_{3\dashv}) = \text{pre}^{\leftrightarrow}(e_3) = \phi$, $L_{e_1} = U_{e_1} = k$, $L_{e_2} = U_{e_2} = l$, and we augment the problem with the constraints $a_{\vdash} \mathbin{/\!/} e_{1\vdash}$, $e_{1\dashv} \mathbin{/\!/} e_{3\vdash}$, $e_{3\dashv} \mathbin{/\!/} e_{2\vdash}$, and $e_{2\dashv} \mathbin{/\!/} a_{\dashv}$.

It can be checked that any plan π is valid for $\mathcal{P}'$ if and only if $\pi|_A$ is valid for $\mathcal{P}$. □

By applying this compilation of ICE to the example problem of Figure 1, we replace make-treatment with a corresponding plain durative action that has no intermediate effect. Then, we add action e with duration 50 that sets *done* true at its end, and is forced to start together with make-treatment by means of the simultaneity constraint $a_{\vdash} \mathbin{/\!/} e_{\vdash}$ with a = make-treatment. The rest of the problem is left untouched; it is easy to see that any plan starting the make-treatment action at time t needs to start e at the same time, causing the positive effect on *done* to happen at time $t + 50$, hence capturing the ICE semantics. Moreover, the plan where e is projected away is a valid plan for the original problem with ICE.

Note that the constructions employed in Theorem 1 produce only a few additional actions. In particular, one additional action is required for ICE effects, while five additional actions (including the actions needed for the encoding of simultaneity constraints) are needed to encode the most complex kind of ICE condition (*i.e.*, $\langle \mathsf{START} + k, \mathsf{END} - l, \phi \rangle$). In any case, the growth in size of the resulting problem is only polynomial. This fact, together with the complexity results by Gigante et al. (2022), implies the following.

Corollary 1 (Complexity of planning with ICE). *Finding whether a valid plan exists for a planning problem with ICE is PSPACE-complete.*

6 Conditional Effects

We focus now on how problems with conditional effects can be polynomially encoded into plain planning problems.

Theorem 2 (Conditional effects encoding). *Given a planning problem with conditional effects $\mathcal{P} = \langle P, A, I, G \rangle$, there exists a planning problem $\mathcal{P}' = \langle P', A', I', G' \rangle$ such that any plan π is valid for $\mathcal{P}'$ iff $\pi|_A$ is valid for $\mathcal{P}$.*

Proof. Figure 5 shows the construction for an example conditional effect. For a durative action a with conditional effect $e = \langle \phi, \psi, \theta, \text{eff}^+_{\vdash}, \text{eff}^-_{\vdash}, \text{eff}^+_{\dashv}, \text{eff}^-_{\dashv} \rangle$, we introduce five auxiliary actions b_0, b_1, b_2, b_3, and b'_3, and we augment the problem with the simultaneity constraint $a \mathbin{/\!/} \{b_0, b_1, b_2, b_3\}$ and $b_{3\vdash} \mathbin{/\!/} b'_{3\vdash}$. In this way, we create the situation depicted in the figure, with one of b_0, b_1, b_2, b_3 forced to happen simultaneous to a, and b'_3 forced to start at the start of b_3. Now, we set conditions and effects of b_0 to mimic the conditional effect, that is:

$$\text{pre}(b_{0\vdash}) = \phi \qquad \text{pre}^{\leftrightarrow}(b_0) = \psi \qquad \text{pre}(b_{0\dashv}) = \theta$$
$$\text{eff}^+(b_{0\vdash}) = \text{eff}^+_{\vdash} \quad \text{eff}^-(b_{0\vdash}) = \text{eff}^-_{\vdash} \quad \text{eff}^+(b_{0\dashv}) = \text{eff}^+_{\dashv}$$
$$\text{eff}^-(b_{0\dashv}) = \text{eff}^-_{\dashv}$$

Hence, b_0 is executed (simultaneously to a), only if all the conditions of the conditional effect are satisfied, applying the corresponding effects. We then handle the case where the conditions of the conditional effect are *not* satisfied. To this end, we set the conditions of b_1, b_2, and b'_3 accordingly:

$$\text{pre}(b_{1\vdash}) = \neg\phi \quad \text{pre}(b_{2\dashv}) = \neg\theta \quad \text{pre}(b'_{3\dashv}) = \neg\psi$$

In this way, b_1 is executed (simultaneously to a) when the *at-start* condition of the conditional effect is not satisfied, b_2 is executed when the *at-end* condition of the conditional effect is not satisfied, and b_3 is executed when the *over-all* condition of the conditional effect is not satisfied, *i.e.*, when there exists at least one time point (the end of b'_3) during the execution of the action where $\neg\psi$ holds. As the last detail, an auxiliary proposition x is introduced to force b'_3 to end before b_3, by setting $\text{eff}^+(b'_{3\vdash})$, $\text{eff}^-(b'_{3\dashv}) = \{x\}$ and $\text{pre}(b_{3\vdash}) = \neg x$. Note that, as noted in the figure, b_1, b_2, and b_3 are mutually exclusive with b_0 due to their conditions. However, b_1, b_2 and b_3 may potentially execute together with no harm.

One can check that the construction described above indeed encodes the given conditional effect. □

Consider the example problem of Figure 2: to compile away the conditional effect at the end of action burn we

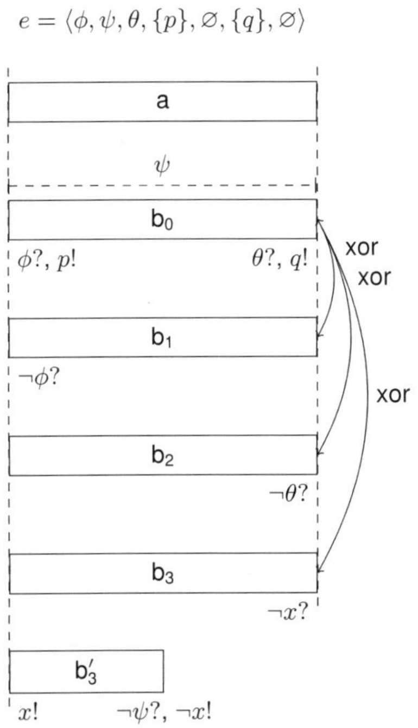

Figure 5: Constructions to encode conditional effects of a durative action using simultaneity constraints. Question marks denote conditions, exclamation marks denote effects, horizontal dashed lines denote overall conditions, vertical dashed lines denote simultaneity constraints, arrows denote mutual exclusion between actions.

only need the actions b_0, b_3 and b_3' of the above construction as the condition only involves an over-all constraint. The action burn in the resulting problem will only have the unconditional, end effect setting hot true, and either action b_0 or b_3 is required to be in parallel with burn. The action b_0 has an over-all condition $\neg blowing$ and an end effect setting $very\text{-}hot$ true, encoding the execution of the conditional effect. Instead, the action b_3 requires action b_3' to start at the same time of b_3 and by means of the end condition of b_3' checks if there exists a point within the duration of burn where $blowing$ is true, hence encoding the non-execution of the conditional effect.

Note that the cost of the encoding employed in Theorem 2 is only five actions for each conditional effect.

Corollary 2 (Complexity of planning with conditional effects)**.** *Finding whether a valid plan exists for a planning problem with conditional effects is PSPACE-complete.*

7 Related Work

Intermediate Conditions and Effects (ICE) as defined in this paper follow the abstract syntax of the Action Notation Modeling Language (ANML) (Smith, Frank, and Cushing 2008). The NDL planning language (Rintanen 2015) supports delayed effects with timing relative to the starting of the action. ICE is useful in several contexts, for example for modeling schedules and events (Valentini, Micheli, and Cimatti 2020) and to compile away duration uncertainty in temporal planning (Cimatti et al. 2018). Some planners natively support ICE (Bit-Monnot et al. 2020; Micheli and Scala 2019; Valentini, Micheli, and Cimatti 2020), but the majority of temporal planners do not.

Under the assumption of ϵ-separation semantics, two compilations for ICE have been presented in (Cimatti et al. 2018). These compilations build on the clip-action construction by Fox, Long, and Halsey (2004), and on the container-action construction by Smith (2003), respectively. The former construction introduces an additional action with duration $2 \times \epsilon$, forcing two snap-actions to happen at the same time by means of additional propositions. This effectively encodes a simultaneity constraint that can be used to encode ICE. The latter, instead, uses an envelope action that forces a fixed time distance between two or more actions that are constrained to happen one after the other. Note that the container-action compilation is less general than the clip, because it assumes that the actions have fixed durations.

Our compilation significantly extends the scope achievable by either of these existing compilations. First of all, we do not assume the ϵ-separation semantics: our compilation works both when the minimum time quantum must be specified by the user and when it is computed automatically by the planner. Moreover, our encoding uses less additional actions with respect to the previous compilations in general. In fact, to force the simultaneous execution of two starting or two ending snap-actions we do not use any additional durative action while both previous approaches require one additional action regardless of the type of snap actions involved.

Considering the example shown in Figure 1, the make-treatment action needs to be transformed into two actions aimed at capturing the effect at time 50. With the clip-action construction, we can create two actions each with duration 50, and can enforce the end of the first action to happen simultaneously (by means of an additional action) to the starting of the second. The first action sets $done$ true at its ending. With the container construction, instead, we can create two additional actions that are forced to happen in sequence and both during the make-treatment. The first lasts $50-\epsilon$ and sets $done$ at its end, while the second has duration $50 - 2 \times \epsilon$. In this way, these two actions are forced to happen at specific times within the duration of make-treatment and the ending of the first action lays exactly at time 50 after the start of make-treatment. Our compilation, instead, only uses one (not two!) additional action that lasts 50 units of time with an ending effect that sets $done$, and forces it to start together with make-treatment.

Conditional effects are an interesting modeling feature of temporal planning that has been largely ignored in the literature. We observe that neither the naïve exponential compilation of conditional effects nor the polynomial one presented in the seminal paper by Nebel (2000) for classical planning can be easily adapted to the context of temporal planning. In fact, neither compilation supports conditions specified at times different than the timing of the effect.

The naïve exponential compilation for classical planning works by creating one action for every possible combination of the conditional effects. For example, two conditional effects having preconditions ϕ and ψ respectively are compiled away by creating four copies of the action they belong to. Such actions have additional preconditions $\phi \wedge \psi$, $\phi \wedge \neg\psi$, $\neg\phi \wedge \psi$, and $\neg\phi \wedge \neg\psi$ respectively and each action has the appropriate effect given the precondition. This compilation is simple but is in general exponential and is not applicable in temporal planning for effects conditioned on the over-all constraint. For example, consider the situation depicted in Figure 2: the over-all constraint $\neg blowing$ cannot be easily negated to construct the copy of the action without the very-hot effect. In fact, the over-all constraint is falsified by the existence of a point where $blowing$ is true, and this is not easily expressible in a condition[1].

The polynomial compilation for classical planning works by encoding a set of conditional effects for a certain action a into a sequence of pairs of artificial actions that must be executed after a. Each pair encodes a single conditional effect and the two alternative actions are used to make the choice between applying the effect or skipping it.

For example, the pair of actions associated with a conditional effect having precondition ϕ is composed of one action having precondition ϕ and the (unconditional) effect, and another action with precondition $\neg\phi$ and no effect. Additional propositions are used to enforce the execution of exactly one action from each pair corresponding to each conditional effect after the execution of a.

In the context of temporal planning, this compilation suffers from the same limitation of the naïve exponential one. Moreover, in the case of ϵ-separation semantics, the sequence of actions introduced by the compilation would require a non-zero amount of time (in particular $\epsilon \times N$ where N is the number of contemporary conditional effects in case of ϵ-separation semantics). This timing is in general non-negligible and breaks the semantics of the compilation.

Our compilation of conditional effects takes inspiration from the polynomial compilation for classical planning: we also create a number of actions for each conditional effect. However, we overcome the over-all complication mentioned above by fully actively monitor each over-all condition appearing in conditional effects. Moreover, the simultaneity construction we use works regardless of the ϵ-separation semantics, thus maintaining the compilation polynomial without introducing artificial delays in the plan.

Both our techniques build on and generalize a construction to force the simultaneity of the start of two durative actions that to the best of our knowledge was first identified in the (unpublished) PhD thesis of William Cushing (Cushing 2012). The simultaneity construction for two starting points was used as an argument to reject the semantics of PDDL 2.1 and develop the message of the thesis. In this paper, we instead use and generalize this construction to force the simultaneity of any pair of clip actions and we show how it can be used to encode in the semantics of PDDL 2.1 (with or without ϵ-separation) both conditional effects and ICE.

Our construction is also related to a compilation of quantitative Allen relations presented in (Coles et al. 2019); in fact, our simultaneity operators can be seen as *starts-with*, *ends-with* or *meets* Allen constraints depending on the kind of clip actions involved. We remark that all previous compilations are limited to the ϵ-separation semantics, while our approach works with or without this assumption.

ICE and conditional effects, together with *over-all* conditions, also allows one to state that if during the interval execution of an action some condition ϕ holds, then there are two sub-intervals where two conditions ϕ' and ϕ'' hold. In the field of *interval temporal logics* (Della Monica et al. 2011), this effect is obtained by the *chop operator*. The interval temporal logic CDT, that results from considering this temporal operator, is *undecidable*, but here we can express the operator thanks to an implicit restriction to *existential* modal operators: we cannot state that *for all* the ways of splitting the interval in two subintervals, the two satisfies ϕ' and ϕ'', but only that one such splitting exists.

Finally, our computational complexity results build on the work by Gigante et al. (2022): we adopt their abstract language for temporal planning and we consider conditional effects and ICE, showing that the addition of such features does not impact the computational complexity of the planning problems regardless of the ϵ-separation semantics.

8 Conclusions

In this paper, we analyzed the expressive power of Intermediate Conditions and Effects (ICE) and conditional effects in action-based temporal planning languages. We showed that both these constructs do not add expressive power and that both features can be compiled away in an equivalent formulation irrespective of the assumptions on the semantics of time and the presence of ϵ-separation. Our encodings exploit a construction that forces the simultaneous execution of either two action endpoints or two entire durative actions. A secondary yet important consequence of our compilations is that they generalize recent results by Gigante et al. (2022). That is, the addition of ICE and conditional effects do not have any impact on the computational complexity of temporal planning, which remains PSPACE-complete when self-overlapping is prohibited. Last, but not least, we highlight that our results are constructive: our compilations can be used to approach problems featuring ICE or conditional effects even with planners that do not natively support them.

Following on from this last observation, in the future, we plan to empirically experiment with our compilations to evaluate the practical applicability on existing planners: this could open new venues for further research as the simultaneity constraints we used as a basis for our compilation could be in principle natively supported, hence providing a more efficient implementation of the ideas behind our encodings. Other directions of research include the analysis of other planning features such as the quantitative Allen-algebra constraints identified in (Coles et al. 2019). Speaking of Allen relations, it comes natural to see whether our constructions can be used to support a kind of *temporally extended goals* where, instead of LTL conditions, more expressive *interval* conditions can be expressed, for example in terms of (some fragment of) the Halpern and Shoham interval temporal logic (Della Monica et al. 2011).

[1]Note that this is *not* equivalent to an over-all $\neg blowing$ constraint, that would require $blowing$ to be false during the action.

Acknowledgements

Andrea Micheli and Enrico Scala have been partially supported by AIPlan4EU, a project funded by EU Horizon 2020 research and innovation programme under GA n. 101016442. Nicola Gigante has been partially supported by the TOTA project (*"Temporal Ontologies and Tableaux Algorithms"*) and by the STAGE project (*"Synthesis for Timeline-based Planning Games"*) by the Faculty of Computer Science, Free University of Bozen-Bolzano.

References

Bit-Monnot, A.; Ghallab, M.; Ingrand, F.; and Smith, D. E. 2020. FAPE: a constraint-based planner for generative and hierarchical temporal planning. *CoRR* abs/2010.13121.

Bonassi, L.; Gerevini, A. E.; Percassi, F.; and Scala, E. 2021. On planning with qualitative state-trajectory constraints in PDDL3 by compiling them away. In *Proceedings of the 31st International Conference on Automated Planning and Scheduling*, 46–50. AAAI Press.

Cesta, A.; Cortellessa, G.; Fratini, S.; Oddi, A.; and Rasconi, R. 2009. The APSI Framework: a Planning and Scheduling Software Development Environment. In *Proceedings of the 19th International Conference on Automated Planning and Scheduling*.

Cimatti, A.; Do, M.; Micheli, A.; Roveri, M.; and Smith, D. E. 2018. Strong temporal planning with uncontrollable durations. *Artif. Intell.* 256:1–34.

Coles, A. J.; Coles, A.; Martínez, M.; Savas, E.; Delfa, J. M.; de la Rosa, T.; E-Martín, Y.; and Olaya, A. G. 2019. Efficiently reasoning with interval constraints in forward search planning. In *Proceedings of the The Thirty-Third AAAI Conference on Artificial Intelligence*, 7562–7569. AAAI Press.

Cushing, W. A. 2012. *When is Temporal Planning Really Temporal?* Ph.D. Dissertation, Arizona State University. https://rakaposhi.eas.asu.edu/cushing-dissertation.pdf.

Della Monica, D.; Goranko, V.; Montanari, A.; and Sciavicco, G. 2011. Interval temporal logics: a journey. *Bull. EATCS* 105:73–99.

Fox, M., and Long, D. 2003. PDDL2.1: An Extension to PDDL for Expressing Temporal Planning Domains. *Journal of Artificial Intelligence Research* 20:61–124.

Fox, M.; Long, D.; and Halsey, K. 2004. An investigation into the expressive power of PDDL2.1. In de Mántaras, R. L., and Saitta, L., eds., *Proceedings of the 16th Eureopean Conference on Artificial Intelligence*, 328–342. IOS Press.

Frank, J., and Jónsson, A. 2003. Constraint-based Attribute and Interval Planning. *Constraints* 8(4):339–364.

Gigante, N.; Montanari, A.; Cialdea Mayer, M.; and Orlandini, A. 2017. Complexity of timeline-based planning. In *Proc. of the 27th International Conference on Automated Planning and Scheduling*, 116–124. AAAI Press.

Gigante, N.; Micheli, A.; Montanari, A.; and Scala, E. 2020. Decidability and complexity of action-based temporal planning over dense time. In *Proc. of the Thirty-Fourth AAAI Conference on Artificial Intelligence*, 9859–9866. AAAI Press.

Gigante, N.; Micheli, A.; Montanari, A.; and Scala, E. 2022. Decidability and complexity of action-based temporal planning over dense time. *Artif. Intell.* 307:103686.

Grastien, A., and Scala, E. 2020. CPCES: A planning framework to solve conformant planning problems through a counterexample guided refinement. *Artif. Intell.* 284:103271.

Micheli, A., and Scala, E. 2019. Temporal planning with temporal metric trajectory constraints. In *Proceedings of The Thirty-Third AAAI Conference on Artificial Intelligence*, 7675–7682. AAAI Press.

Nebel, B. 2000. On the compilability and expressive power of propositional planning formalisms. *J. Artif. Intell. Res.* 12:271–315.

Palacios, H., and Geffner, H. 2007. From conformant into classical planning: Efficient translations that may be complete too. In *Proceedings of the Seventeenth International Conference on Automated Planning and Scheduling*, 264–271. AAAI.

Rintanen, J. 2007. Complexity of concurrent temporal planning. In *Proc. of the 17th International Conference on Automated Planning and Scheduling*, 280–287.

Rintanen, J. 2015. Models of action concurrency in temporal planning. In Yang, Q., and Wooldridge, M. J., eds., *Proceedings of the Twenty-Fourth International Joint Conference on Artificial Intelligence*, 1659–1665. AAAI Press.

Scala, E., and Grastien, A. 2021. Non-deterministic conformant planning using a counterexample-guided incremental compilation to classical planning. In *Proceedings of the Thirty-First International Conference on Automated Planning and Scheduling*, 299–307. AAAI Press.

Smith, D.; Frank, J.; and Cushing, W. 2008. The anml language. In *KEPS 2008*.

Smith, D. E. 2003. The case for durative actions: A commentary on PDDL2.1. *J. Artif. Intell. Res.* 20:149–154.

Torres, J., and Baier, J. A. 2015. Polynomial-time reformulations of LTL temporally extended goals into final-state goals. In *Proceedings of the Twenty-Fourth International Joint Conference on Artificial Intelligence*, 1696–1703. AAAI Press.

Valentini, A.; Micheli, A.; and Cimatti, A. 2020. Temporal planning with intermediate conditions and effects. In *Proceedings of the Thirty-Fourth AAAI Conference on Artificial Intelligence*, 9975–9982. AAAI Press.

Finite Entailment of UCRPQs over $\mathcal{ALC}$ Ontologies

Víctor Gutiérrez-Basulto[1] , **Albert Gutowski**[2] , **Yazmín Ibáñez-García**[1] , **Filip Murlak**[2]
[1]Cardiff University, UK
[2]University of Warsaw, Poland
{a.gutowski, f.murlak}@mimuw.edu.pl, {gutierrezbasultov, ibanezgarciay}@cardiff.ac.uk

Abstract

We investigate the problem of *finite* entailment of ontology-mediated queries. We consider the expressive query language, unions of conjunctive regular path queries (UCRPQs), extending the well-known class of union of conjunctive queries, with regular expressions over roles. We look at ontologies formulated using the description logic $\mathcal{ALC}$, and show a tight 2ExpTime upper bound for entailment of UCRPQs. At the core of our decision procedure, there is a novel automata-based technique introducing a stratification of interpretations induced by the deterministic finite automaton underlying the input UCRPQ.

1 Introduction

At the intersection of knowledge representation and database theory lies the fundamental problem of *ontology-mediated query entailment (OMQE)*, where the background knowledge provided by an ontology is used to enrich the answers to queries posed to databases. In this context, description logics (DLs) are a widely accepted family of logics used to formulate ontologies. By now, the OMQE problem under the unrestricted semantics (reasoning over arbitrary models) is well understood for various query languages and DLs (Schneider and Simkus 2020). In contrast, for the *finite* OMQE problem, where one is interested in reasoning over finite models only, the overall landscape is rather incomplete. However, in recent years, the study of finite OMQE has been gaining traction, considering both lightweight and expressive DLs and (mostly) unions of conjunctive queries (Rosati 2008; Ibáñez-García, Lutz, and Schneider 2014; Rudolph 2016; Gogacz, Ibáñez-García, and Murlak 2018; Gogacz et al. 2019; Danielski and Kieronski 2019; Gogacz et al. 2020; Bednarczyk and Kieroński 2022).

In this paper we consider the problem of finite OMQE with unions of conjunctive regular path queries (UCRPQs) as the query language. UCRPQs (Florescu, Levy, and Suciu 1998; Calvanese et al. 2000) are a powerful navigational query language for graph databases in which one can express that two entities are related by a path of edges that can be specified by a regular language over binary relations. So, UCRPQs extend unions of conjunctive queries (UCQs) with atoms that might contain regular expressions that traverse the edges of the database. Indeed, path navigation is included in the query language XPath 2.0 for XML data, and it is also present in the SPARQL 1.1 query language for RDF data through the property path feature. Given the resemblance of instance data stored in ABoxes in DLs to graph-like data, several investigations on unrestricted entailment of various types of navigational query languages mediated by DL ontologies have been carried out (Stefanoni et al. 2014; Calvanese, Eiter, and Ortiz 2014; Bienvenu, Ortiz, and Simkus 2015; Gutiérrez-Basulto, Ibáñez-García, and Jung 2018; Gogacz et al. 2019; Bednarczyk and Rudolph 2019), yielding algorithmic approaches and optimal complexity bounds. For finite entailment of regular path queries mediated by DL ontologies, there are only undecidability results available (Rudolph 2016). The most relevant positive news are the decidability and computational complexity results by Danielski and Kieronski (2019) and Gogacz et al. (2020) on finite entailment of conjuctive queries with transitive closure over roles mediated by expressive DL ontologies.

We focus on ontologies formulated using the description logic $\mathcal{ALC}$. Note that entailment of UCRPQs over $\mathcal{ALC}$ ontologies is not *finitely controllable*, i.e. finite and unrestricted entailment do not coincide as it is *not* the case that for any $\mathcal{ALC}$ knowledge base $\mathcal{K}$ and any UCRPQ φ, it holds that $\mathcal{K}$ entails φ over all (unrestricted) models iff $\mathcal{K}$ entails φ over all finite models. By assuming that the represented world is finite, we can therefore not reuse existing complexity bounds or algorithmic approaches to UCRPQ entailment. From a usability perspective, the suitability of this assumption depends on the potential applications. A particular interest for navigational queries comes from bioinformatics and cheminformatics (Lysenko et al. 2016; Cook et al. 2016; Galgonek et al. 2016; Hu, Qiu, and Dumontier 2015; Rajabi and Sanchez-Alonso 2021; Chen et al. 2020). For instance, experts often need to find associations between entities in protein, cellular, drug, and disease networks (represented as graph databases), so that e.g. gene-disease-drug associations (corresponding to paths in the database) can be discovered for developing new treatment methods. In this type of applications, databases and the models they represent are clearly meant to be finite. Importantly, biochemical networks contain complex motifs involving e.g. *cycles* or cliques. This type of patterns can be described using UCRPQs, however, without the finiteness assumption these patterns could be disregarded as the associated query might not be entailed when reasoning over all models (including infinite ones).

1.1 Contribution

The main technical contribution of our investigation is the development of a dedicated automata-based method for entailment of UCRPQs over $\mathcal{ALC}$ ontologies, providing an optimal upper bound. More precisely, we obtain the following result, where the matching lower bound is inherited from (Ortiz and Simkus 2014).

Theorem 1. *Finite entailment of UCRPQs over $\mathcal{ALC}$ ontologies is* 2EXPTIME*-complete.*

In prior work, Rudolph (2016) showed that finite entailment of 2RPQs in $\mathcal{ALCIOF}$ is undecidable. Theorem 1 thus provides a key step towards delimiting the decidability boundary of finite OMQE with navigational queries.

At the heart of our approach to finite entailment of UCRPQs in $\mathcal{ALC}$ there is a stratification of interpretations induced by the deterministic finite automaton underlying the UCRPQ. This stratification builds upon the so-called *tape construction*, previously used to efficiently evaluate queries in the extension of XPath 1.0 where arbitrary regular expressions may appear as path expressions (Bojańczyk and Parys 2011). To realize the tape construction, our method represents UCRPQs by means of a semiautomaton $\mathcal{B}$ (Ginzburg 1968) and defines an expansion of $\mathcal{B}$, allowing to trace runs of $\mathcal{B}$ that begin in all possible states, on all infixes of the input word. We make interpretations $\mathcal{I}$ knowledgeable of the expansion by enriching paths of $\mathcal{I}$ with its possible runs and by associating edges of $\mathcal{I}$ with levels ℓ induced by the transitions of the expansion. In a similar fashion we also make CRPQs sensible of levels. With this at hand, we tackle finite entailment by eliminating the lowest level from a query and from an interpretation, and then recursively solving the simpler problem. At each step of this process, we should be able to arrange solutions to simpler problems in a hierarchical way so that we can reason over them. To this aim, we consider a variant of entailment that includes an *environment*, which will provide the necessary information to position the arranged solutions to simpler problems in the context of larger interpretations. To better keep track of the complexity of our recursive method, we introduce a modification of the entailment problem modulo environment in which we look at a particular type of finite models: (ℓ, ℓ')-*models*, which are models with edges of levels ℓ or higher that are 'consistent' w.r.t. queries referring to edges of level ℓ' or higher. We solve the problem of finding (ℓ, ℓ')-models recursively by increasing ℓ and ℓ' in an alternating way, until both reach the maximum level $n + 1$, with n the number of states of $\mathcal{B}$. This will mean solving finite entailment modulo environment, and thus standard finite entailment as well.

Missing proofs can be found in the technical report available at https://arxiv.org/pdf/2204.14261.pdf.

1.2 Related Work

We next discuss some existing work relevant to our study.

OMQE of Navigational Queries. As previously discussed, there exist various works on unrestricted entailment of navigational query languages mediated by DL ontologies. Most of them concentrate on extensions of regular path queries (RPQs), such as UCRPQs, and consider both Horn (Bienvenu, Ortiz, and Simkus 2015) and expressive DLs (Calvanese, Eiter, and Ortiz 2014; Gutiérrez-Basulto, Ibáñez-García, and Jung 2018; Gogacz et al. 2019; Bednarczyk and Rudolph 2019). There have been also some studies on entailment of graph XPath queries (Stefanoni et al. 2014; Bienvenu et al. 2014; Kostylev, Reutter, and Vrgoc 2014).

Finite OMQE. There exist various decidability results and optimal complexity bounds for finite entailment of union of conjunctive queries in Horn DLs (Rosati 2008; Ibáñez-García, Lutz, and Schneider 2014) and in expressive DLs from the $\mathcal{S}$ family (Gogacz, Ibáñez-García, and Murlak 2018; Gogacz et al. 2019; Danielski and Kieronski 2019). In most cases, the computational complexity coincides with that of the unrestricted case, but the algorithmic approaches are completely different. On the negative side, undecidability of finite entailment of UCQs in the more expressive DL $\mathcal{SHOIF}$ was shown by (Rudolph 2016), as well as the undecidability result for finite entailment of 2RPQs in $\mathcal{ALCIOF}$. Closer to our work are the positive results on finite entailment of UCQs with transitive closure over roles in expressive DLs allowing for transitivity or transitive closure over roles (Danielski and Kieronski 2019; Gogacz et al. 2020). These results close the distance to the undecidability frontier for finite entailment from a different angle by considering ontology languages more expressive than $\mathcal{ALC}$, but a subclass of UCRPQs as query language. In the context of database theory research, finite OMQE (also called open-world query entailment) has also been investigated; for instance, Amarilli and Benedikt (2020) study finite OMQE for inclusion dependencies and functional dependencies over relations of arbitrary arity, and Pratt-Hartmann (2009) looks at finite OMQE in the two-variable fragment of FOL with counting quantifiers.

Finite Controllability. There have been also a few works on finite controllability in the context of DLs. For instance, Bednarczyk and Kieroński (2022) recently showed that the $\mathcal{ZOI}$ and $\mathcal{ZOQ}$ members of the $\mathcal{Z}$ family are finitely controllable for UCQs. Beyond DLs, there have been several works on UCQ-finite controllability: for the guarded fragment of FOL (Bárány, Gottlob, and Otto 2014) or for various fragments of existential rules (Civili and Rosati 2012; Gogacz and Marcinkowski 2013; Baget et al. 2011; Amendola, Leone, and Manna 2018; Gottlob, Manna, and Pieris 2018). Closer to our study, is the work by Figueira, Figueira, and Baque (2020) on the classification of finitely and non-finitely controllable subclasses of CRPQs over ontologies formulated in the guarded-negation fragment of FOL or in the frontier fragment of existential rules. However, no complexity results or algorithms for finite entailment are provided for the non-finitely controllable cases.

2 Preliminaries

2.1 Description Logics

We consider a vocabulary consisting of countably infinite disjoint sets of *concept names* $\mathsf{N_C}$, *role names* $\mathsf{N_R}$, and *individual names* $\mathsf{N_I}$. $\mathcal{ALC}$-*concepts* C, D are defined by the grammar

$$C, D ::= A \mid \neg C \mid C \sqcap D \mid \exists r.C$$

where $A \in \mathsf{N_C}$ and $r \in \mathsf{N_R}$. We use standard abbreviations $\bot, \top, C \sqcup D$ and $\forall r.C$.

An $\mathcal{ALC}$*-TBox* $\mathcal{T}$ is a finite set of *concept inclusions (CIs)* $C \sqsubseteq D$, where C, D are $\mathcal{ALC}$-concepts. An *ABox* $\mathcal{A}$ is a finite non-empty set of *concept* and *role assertions* of the form $A(a), r(a, b)$, where $A \in \mathsf{N_C}$, $r \in \mathsf{N_R}$ and $\{a, b\} \subseteq \mathsf{N_I}$. We write $\mathsf{ind}(\mathcal{A})$ for the *set of individual names* occurring in $\mathcal{A}$. A *knowledge base (KB)* is a pair $\mathcal{K} = (\mathcal{T}, \mathcal{A})$. We write $\mathsf{CN}(\mathcal{K})$ and $\mathsf{rol}(\mathcal{K})$ for the *sets of all concept and role names* occurring in $\mathcal{K}$. We let $\|\mathcal{K}\|$ be the total size of the representation of $\mathcal{K}$.

Without loss of generality, we assume throughout the paper that all CIs are in one of the following *normal forms*:

$$\bigsqcap_i A_i \sqsubseteq \bigsqcup_j B_j, \quad A \sqsubseteq \exists r.B, \quad A \sqsubseteq \forall r.B,$$

where $A, A_i, B, B_j \in \mathsf{N_C}$, $r \in \mathsf{N_R}$, and empty disjunction and conjunction are equivalent to $\bot$ and $\top$, respectively. Additionally, for each $A \in \mathsf{CN}(\mathcal{K})$ there is a complementary $\bar{A} \in \mathsf{CN}(\mathcal{K})$ axiomatized with $\top \sqsubseteq A \sqcup \bar{A}$ and $A \sqcap \bar{A} \sqsubseteq \bot$.

2.2 Interpretations

The semantics is given as usual via *interpretations* $\mathcal{I} = (\Delta^\mathcal{I}, \cdot^\mathcal{I})$ consisting of a non-empty *domain* $\Delta^\mathcal{I}$ and an *interpretation function* $\cdot^\mathcal{I}$ mapping concept names to subsets of the domain and role names to binary relations over the domain, and individual names to elements of the domain. The interpretation of complex concepts C is defined in the usual way (Baader et al. 2017). An interpretation $\mathcal{I}$ is a *model of a TBox* $\mathcal{T}$, written $\mathcal{I} \models \mathcal{T}$ if $C^\mathcal{I} \subseteq D^\mathcal{I}$ for all CIs $C \sqsubseteq D \in \mathcal{T}$. It is a *model of an ABox* $\mathcal{A}$, written $\mathcal{I} \models \mathcal{A}$, if $\mathsf{ind}(\mathcal{A}) \subseteq \Delta^\mathcal{I}$, $a^\mathcal{I} = a$ for each $a \in \mathsf{ind}(\mathcal{A})$, $(a, b) \in r^\mathcal{I}$ for all $r(a, b) \in \mathcal{A}$, and $a \in A^\mathcal{I}$ for all $A(a) \in \mathcal{A}$. The first two conditions constitute the so-called *standard name assumption*. Finally, $\mathcal{I}$ is a *model of a KB* $\mathcal{K} = (\mathcal{T}, \mathcal{A})$, written $\mathcal{I} \models \mathcal{K}$, if $\mathcal{I} \models \mathcal{T}$ and $\mathcal{I} \models \mathcal{A}$.

An interpretation $\mathcal{I}$ is *finite* if $\Delta^\mathcal{I}$ is finite. An interpretation $\mathcal{I}'$ is a *sub-interpretation* of $\mathcal{I}$, written as $\mathcal{I}' \subseteq \mathcal{I}$, if $\Delta^{\mathcal{I}'} \subseteq \Delta^\mathcal{I}$, $A^{\mathcal{I}'} \subseteq A^\mathcal{I}$, and $r^{\mathcal{I}'} \subseteq r^\mathcal{I}$ for all $A \in \mathsf{N_C}$ and $r \in \mathsf{N_R}$. For $\Sigma \subseteq \mathsf{N_C} \cup \mathsf{N_R}$, $\mathcal{I}$ is an interpretation *over signature* Σ if $A^\mathcal{I} = \emptyset$ and $r^\mathcal{I} = \emptyset$ for all $A \in \mathsf{N_C} \setminus \Sigma$ and $r \in \mathsf{N_R} \setminus \Sigma$. The union $\mathcal{I} \cup \mathcal{J}$ of $\mathcal{I}$ and $\mathcal{J}$ is an interpretation such that $\Delta^{\mathcal{I} \cup \mathcal{J}} = \Delta^\mathcal{I} \cup \Delta^\mathcal{J}$, $A^{\mathcal{I} \cup \mathcal{J}} = A^\mathcal{I} \cup A^\mathcal{J}$, and $r^{\mathcal{I} \cup \mathcal{J}} = r^\mathcal{I} \cup r^\mathcal{J}$ for all $A \in \mathsf{N_C}$ and $r \in \mathsf{N_R}$.

A *unary* $\mathcal{K}$*-type* is a subset of $\mathsf{CN}(\mathcal{K})$ including either A or $\bar{A}$ for each $A \in \mathsf{CN}(\mathcal{K})$. For an interpretation $\mathcal{I}$ and an element $d \in \Delta^\mathcal{I}$, the *unary* $\mathcal{K}$*-type of* d *in* $\mathcal{I}$ is $\mathsf{tp}^\mathcal{I}(d) = \{A \in \mathsf{CN}(\mathcal{K}) \mid d \in A^\mathcal{I}\}$. We say that $\mathcal{I}$ *realizes* a unary $\mathcal{K}$-type τ if $\tau = \mathsf{tp}^\mathcal{I}(d)$ for some $d \in \Delta^\mathcal{I}$.

2.3 Queries and Finite Entailment

We next introduce the query language. We concentrate on Boolean queries, that is, queries without answer variables. The extension to queries with answer variables is standard; see, for example, (Glimm et al. 2008). A *conjunctive regular path query (CRPQ)* is a first-order formula

$$\varphi = \exists \mathbf{x}\, \psi(\mathbf{x})$$

such that $\psi(\mathbf{x})$ is constructed using $\wedge$ over atoms of the form $A(t)$ or $\mathcal{E}(t, t')$ where $A \in \mathsf{N_C}$, t, t' are variables from $\mathbf{x}$ or individual names from $\mathsf{N_I}$, and $\mathcal{E}$ is a *path expression* defined by the grammar

$$\mathcal{E}, \mathcal{E}' ::= r \mid \mathcal{E}^* \mid \mathcal{E} \cup \mathcal{E}' \mid \mathcal{E} \circ \mathcal{E}'$$

where $r \in \mathsf{N_R}$. Thus, $\mathcal{E}$ is essentially a regular expression over the (infinite) alphabet $\{r \mid r \in \mathsf{N_R}\}$. The set of individual names in φ is denoted with $\mathsf{ind}(\varphi)$. A *conjunctive query (CQ)* is a CRPQ that does not use the operators $*, \cup$ and $\circ$ in path expressions, and a *regular path query (RPQ)* consists of a single atom of the form $\mathcal{E}(t, t')$.

The semantics of CRPQs is defined via matches. Let us fix a CRPQ $\varphi = \exists \mathbf{x}\, \psi(\mathbf{x})$ and an interpretation $\mathcal{I}$. A *match for* φ *in* $\mathcal{I}$ is a function

$$\pi : \mathbf{x} \cup \mathsf{ind}(\varphi) \to \Delta^\mathcal{I}$$

such that $\pi(a) = a$, for all $a \in \mathsf{ind}(\varphi)$, and $\mathcal{I}, \pi \models \psi(\mathbf{x})$ under the standard semantics of first-order logic extended with a rule for atoms of the form $\mathcal{E}(t, t')$. More formally, we define:

- $\mathcal{I}, \pi \models \psi_1 \wedge \psi_2$ iff $\mathcal{I}, \pi \models \psi_1$ and $\mathcal{I}, \pi \models \psi_2$;
- $\mathcal{I}, \pi \models A(t)$ iff $\pi(t) \in A^\mathcal{I}$;
- $\mathcal{I}, \pi \models \mathcal{E}(t, t')$ iff $(\pi(t), \pi(t')) \in \mathcal{E}^\mathcal{I}$, where $\mathcal{E}^\mathcal{I}$ is defined inductively as $(\mathcal{E}^*)^\mathcal{I} = (\mathcal{E}^\mathcal{I})^*$, $(\mathcal{E}_1 \cup \mathcal{E}_2)^\mathcal{I} = \mathcal{E}_1^\mathcal{I} \cup \mathcal{E}_2^\mathcal{I}$, $(\mathcal{E}_1 \circ \mathcal{E}_2)^\mathcal{I} = \mathcal{E}_1^\mathcal{I} \circ \mathcal{E}_2^\mathcal{I}$.

An interpretation $\mathcal{I}$ *satisfies* φ, written $\mathcal{I} \models \varphi$, if there exists a match for φ in $\mathcal{I}$. A *union of CRPQs (UCRPQ)* is a finite set of CRPQs and a *union of CQs (UCQ)* is a finite set of CQs. An interpretation $\mathcal{I}$ satisfies an UCRPQ Φ, written as $\mathcal{I} \models \Phi$, if $\mathcal{I} \models \varphi$ for some $\varphi \in \Phi$. We say that $\mathcal{K}$ *finitely entails* Φ, written $\mathcal{K} \models_{\mathsf{fin}} \Phi$, if each finite model of $\mathcal{K}$ satisfies Φ. A model of $\mathcal{K}$ that does not satisfy Φ is a *counter-model*. The *finite entailment problem* asks if a given KB $\mathcal{K}$ finitely entails a given query Φ.

2.4 UCRPQs via Semiautomata

We work with UCRPQs represented by means of a *semiautomaton* (Ginzburg 1968) $\mathcal{B} = (Q, \Gamma, \delta)$ where Q is a finite set of states, $\Gamma \subseteq \{r \mid r \in \mathsf{N_R}\}$ is a finite alphabet—throughout the paper we assume $\Gamma = \mathsf{rol}(\mathcal{K})$, and $\delta : Q \times \Gamma \to Q$ is the transition function. A semiautomaton is essentially a deterministic finite automaton without initial and final states; a run of a semiautomaton $\mathcal{B}$ over a word w is defined just like for a finite automaton, except that it can begin in any state and there is no notion of accepting runs. Under this representation, an RPQ is an atom over a binary predicate of the form $\mathcal{B}_{q,q'}$ where $q, q' \in Q$ are states of $\mathcal{B}$. We let $\mathcal{I}, \pi \models \mathcal{B}_{q,q'}(t, t')$ iff $(\pi(t), \pi(t')) \in \mathcal{B}^\mathcal{I}_{q,q'}$ where $\mathcal{B}^\mathcal{I}_{q,q'}$ is the set of pairs (e, e') such that for some $n \in \mathbb{N}$ there exist $r_1, \dots, r_n \in \Gamma$ and $e_0, \dots, e_n \in \Delta^\mathcal{I}$ such that

- $e_0 = e$ and $e_n = e'$;

- $(e_{i-1}, e_i) \in (r_i)^{\mathcal{I}}$ for all $i \in \{1, \ldots, n\}$;
- there exists a run of $\mathcal{B}$ on the word $r_1 \ldots r_n$ that begins in state q and ends in state q'.

We also allow *edge atoms* of the form $r(x, x')$ for $r \in \Gamma$.

Each UCRPQ Φ can be effectively rewritten into a UCRPQ Φ' expressed by means of a semiautomaton $\mathcal{B}$ of size $k \cdot 2^{O(m)}$ where k is the number of path expressions in Φ and m is their maximal size. The size of CRPQs in Φ' is bounded by the size of CRPQs in Φ and $|\Phi'| = 2^{\text{poly}\|\Phi\|}$, where $\|\Phi\|$ is the total size of Φ.

For simplicity we work with KBs $\mathcal{K} = (\mathcal{T}, \mathcal{A})$ where the ABox $\mathcal{A}$ is *trivial*; that is, $\mathsf{ind}(\mathcal{A}) = \{a\}$ for some $a \in \mathsf{N_I}$ and $\mathcal{A}$ contains only concept assertions. The general finite entailment problem can be reduced to this special case using the following lemma.

Lemma 1. *Given an oracle for finite entailment for trivial ABoxes, the general finite entailment* $(\mathcal{T}, \mathcal{A}) \models_{\mathsf{fin}} \Phi$ *can be decided in time* $2^{\text{poly}(\|(\mathcal{T},\mathcal{A})\|)\cdot 2^{\text{poly}(\|\Phi\|)}}$ *using calls to the oracle for* $\mathcal{K}' = (\mathcal{T}, \mathcal{A}')$ *and* Φ' *consisting of* $2^{\text{poly}(\|\Phi\|)}$ *CRPQs of linear size over the same semiautomaton as* Φ.

2.5 Entailment Modulo Environment

We solve the entailment problem using a divide-and-conquer approach in which counter-models are decomposed into simpler ones, whose existence is easier to decide. Each level of this recursive procedure will involve certain modifications to the TBox. For complexity reasons we need to pay close attention to these changes, making sure that no blow-up is involved. To make it easier, we generalize the entailment problem by turning the modifications into a separate part of the input, which allows fixing the TBox for the duration of the whole procedure. At every level of the recursion, we will need to reason 'externally' about the way simpler pieces are put together to form the larger counter-model, and 'internally' about how to specify the required properties of a piece depending on what is happening outside. We will think of the models as induced subinterpretations of a larger interpretation. Dually, the remaining part of the larger interpretation can be seen as an external context, in which our models live. The relevant features of this context will be represented by environments, which we now define.

An *environment* $\mathcal{E} = (\Theta, \varepsilon)$ consists of a set Θ of unary types and a function $\varepsilon : \Theta \to 2^{\mathsf{rol}(\mathcal{K})\times\mathsf{CN}(\mathcal{K})}$. The intended meaning is that only types from Θ are allowed and each element of an allowed unary type τ has an r-edge to an element in the extension of B in the external context for each $(r, B) \in \varepsilon(\tau)$. Accordingly, we say that $\mathcal{I}$ is a *model of* $\mathcal{K}$ *modulo* $\mathcal{E}$ and write $\mathcal{I} \models^{\mathcal{E}} \mathcal{K}$ if $\mathcal{I}$ realizes only unary types from Θ and it is a model of $\mathcal{K}$ under the following *relaxed semantics of existential restrictions*:

- for every existential restriction $\exists r.B$ in $\mathcal{K}$ and every element $d \in \Delta^{\mathcal{I}}$, $d \in (\exists r.B)^{\mathcal{I}}$ iff either there is an r-edge in $\mathcal{I}$ from d to an element $e \in B^{\mathcal{I}}$ or $(r, B) \in \varepsilon\big(\mathsf{tp}^{\mathcal{I}}(d)\big)$.

(The semantics of universal restrictions is not altered and it is the environment's reponsibility to account for them.) Correspondingly, a query Φ is *finitely entailed by* $\mathcal{K}$ *modulo* $\mathcal{E}$, written $\mathcal{K} \models^{\mathcal{E}}_{\mathsf{fin}} \Phi$, if for each finite interpretation $\mathcal{I}$, if $\mathcal{I} \models^{\mathcal{E}} \mathcal{K}$ then $\mathcal{I} \models \Phi$. The problem of *finite entailment modulo environment* is to decide for a given KB $\mathcal{K}$, environment $\mathcal{E}$, and query Φ if $\mathcal{K} \models^{\mathcal{E}}_{\mathsf{fin}} \Phi$.

Note that finite entailment modulo environment and ordinary finite entailment are interreducible. In one direction, it is enough to take the set of all unary $\mathcal{K}$-types for Θ and set $\varepsilon(\tau) = \emptyset$ for all $\tau \in \Theta$. In the other direction, the conditions imposed on unary types and the relaxed semantics of existential restrictions can be expressed easily in the TBox. The latter reduction, however, might significantly increase the size of the TBox. It is easier to control the size of the input at different levels of the recursion when these conditions are explicitly represented in the environment.

3 Expansion and Decorations

In order to handle UCRPQs expressed by means of a semiautomaton $\mathcal{B}$ we need to be able to trace runs of $\mathcal{B}$ that begin in all possible states, on all infixes of the input word. We achieve this using the following construction.

Let us fix an arbitrary linear order on the set Q of the states of $\mathcal{B}$. The *expansion* of $\mathcal{B}$ is a semiautomaton $\widehat{\mathcal{B}}$ whose set of states is the set $\widehat{Q}$ of all permutations of Q. Thus, an element of $\widehat{Q}$ can be seen as a tuple $\mathbf{p} = (p_1, p_2, \ldots, p_n)$ such that p_i is the image of the ith state of $\mathcal{B}$ under the respective permutation. We refer to positions in this tuple as *levels*. In particular, the *level of* $q \in Q$ *in* $\mathbf{p}$ is the unique i such that $q = p_i$. Assuming $\delta : Q \times \mathsf{rol}(\mathcal{K}) \to Q$ is the transition function of $\mathcal{B}$, we define the transition function

$$\hat{\delta} : \widehat{Q} \times \mathsf{rol}(\mathcal{K}) \to \widehat{Q}$$

of $\widehat{\mathcal{B}}$ by letting $\hat{\delta}(\mathbf{p}, r)$ be the permutation $\mathbf{p}'$ obtained by listing all states appearing in the sequence

$$\delta(\mathbf{p}, r) = \big(\delta(p_1, r), \delta(p_2, r), \ldots, \delta(p_n, r)\big)$$

in the order of their first appearances, followed by all remaining states of $\mathcal{B}$ ordered as in Q. Note that the level of $\delta(p_i, r)$ in $\mathbf{p}'$ is at most i. Consider the set $P \subseteq \{1, 2, \ldots, n\}$ of levels i such that the level of $\delta(p_i, r)$ in $\mathbf{p}'$ is equal to i. It follows from the definition of $\mathbf{p}'$ that $P = \{1, 2, \ldots, \ell\}$ for some $\ell \in \{1, 2, \ldots, n\}$. We call this number ℓ the *level of transition* $\mathbf{p} \xrightarrow{r} \mathbf{p}'$.

From each run of $\widehat{\mathcal{B}}$ on a word w we can reconstruct all runs of $\mathcal{B}$ on w. Let $\mathbf{p}_0, \mathbf{p}_1, \ldots, \mathbf{p}_m$ be a run of $\widehat{\mathcal{B}}$ on w. Consider a run $q_0, q_1, \ldots, q_m$ of $\mathcal{B}$ on w. For $i = 0, 1, \ldots, m$, let ℓ_i be the level of q_i in $\mathbf{p}_i$. Any sequence $\ell_0, \ell_1, \ldots, \ell_m$ associated like this with a run of $\mathcal{B}$ will be called a *thread* in the run of $\widehat{\mathcal{B}}$ (see Fig. 1). Notice that two threads that begin at different levels can meet at the same level somewhere along the run; if this happens they remain equal until the end of the run. Also, threads can be born in the middle of a run of $\widehat{\mathcal{B}}$, but they never disappear. A crucial property of threads is that they are non-increasing sequences: the level of q_{i+1} in $\mathbf{p}_{i+1}$ is bounded by the level of q_i in $\mathbf{p}_i$.

Lemma 2. *Let* $\mathbf{p}_0, \mathbf{p}_1, \ldots, \mathbf{p}_m$ *be a run of* $\widehat{\mathcal{B}}$ *on* w, *and let* q, q' *be states of* $\mathcal{B}$. *There is a run of* $\mathcal{B}$ *on* w *from* q *to* q' *iff there exist positions* $0 \leq j_1 < j_2 < \cdots < j_k = m$, *levels* $n \geq \ell_1 > \ell_2 > \cdots > \ell_k \geq 1$, *and states* $q_0, q_1, \ldots, q_k$ *with* $1 \leq k \leq n$ *such that* $q_0 = q$, $q_k = q'$, *and*

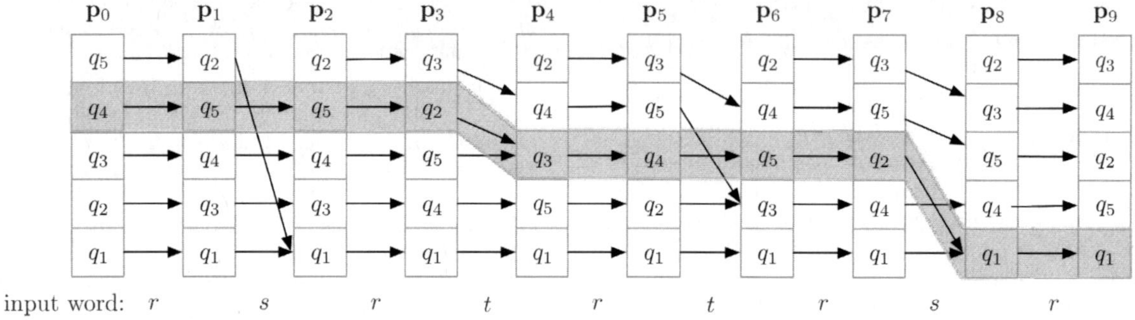

Figure 1: A thread in a run of the expansion of a semiautomaton.

- *the level of q_0 in $\mathbf{p}_0$ is ℓ_1 and the level of q_k in $\mathbf{p}_m$ is ℓ_k;*
- *for all $i \in \{1, 2, \ldots, k-1\}$, the level of q_i in $\mathbf{p}_{j_i}$ is ℓ_i and the level of $\delta(q_i, w[j_i+1])$ in $\mathbf{p}_{j_i+1}$ is ℓ_{i+1};*
- *for all $i \in \{1, 2, \ldots, k\}$, each transition taken in the segment of the run from $\mathbf{p}_{j_{i-1}+1}$ (or $\mathbf{p}_0$ for $i = 1$) to $\mathbf{p}_{j_i}$ has level at least ℓ_i.*

As an illustration of Lemma 2, consider the run of the expanded semiautomaton shown in Fig. 1. Tracing the run of the original semiautomaton on the same word, starting in state q_4, we discover the positions $j_1 = 3$ and $j_2 = 7$ where the corresponding thread drops to a lower level. Between these positions, the thread stays at the same level, beginning with $\ell_1 = 4$ (taking transitions of levels $5, 4, 5 \geq \ell_1$), followed by $\ell_2 = 3$ (taking transitions of levels $5, 3, 5 \geq \ell_2$), and $\ell_3 = 1$ (taking a transition of level $5 \geq \ell_3$).

The next step is to account for the possible runs of $\widehat{\mathcal{B}}$ over paths in the interpretation. Towards this goal, we decorate elements of the interpretation with states of $\widehat{\mathcal{B}}$. To avoid additional blow-up, we represent states of $\widehat{\mathcal{B}}$ using combinations of fresh concept names $C_{q,\ell}$ where q is a state of $\mathcal{B}$ and $\ell \in \{1, 2, \ldots, n\}$ is a level; we write $\mathsf{CN}(\widehat{\mathcal{B}})$ for the set of all $C_{q,\ell}$. For a state $\mathbf{p} = (p_1, p_2, \ldots, p_n)$ of $\widehat{\mathcal{B}}$, by $C_\mathbf{p}$ we mean the concept $C_{p_1,1} \sqcap C_{p_2,2} \sqcap \cdots \sqcap C_{p_n,n}$. We say that an element $e \in \Delta^\mathcal{I}$ is *decorated* with state $\mathbf{p}$ if $e \in C^\mathcal{I}_\mathbf{p}$. An interpretation $\mathcal{I}$ is *$\widehat{\mathcal{B}}$-decorated* if no element has incoming edges over different roles from $\mathsf{rol}(\mathcal{K})$ and $\mathcal{I}$ satisfies the CIs

$$C_\mathbf{p} \sqsubseteq \forall r.C_{\hat{\delta}(\mathbf{p},r)}, \quad C_\mathbf{p} \sqcap C_{\mathbf{p}'} \sqsubseteq \bot, \quad \top \sqsubseteq \bigsqcup_{\mathbf{p} \in \widehat{Q}} C_\mathbf{p}$$

for all states $\mathbf{p}, \mathbf{p}'$ of $\widehat{\mathcal{B}}$ such that $\mathbf{p} \neq \mathbf{p}'$. The axiomatization above is exponential in the size of $\mathcal{B}$, but we can do better.

Lemma 3. *Given $\mathcal{B}$ one can compute in polynomial time a TBox $\widehat{\mathcal{T}}_\mathcal{B}$ such that $\mathcal{I} \models \widehat{\mathcal{T}}_\mathcal{B}$ iff $\mathcal{I}$ is $\widehat{\mathcal{B}}$-decorated.*

To every edge in a $\widehat{\mathcal{B}}$-decorated interpretation $\mathcal{I}$ we can assign a level as follows. Consider elements $e, e' \in \Delta^\mathcal{I}$ such that $(e, e') \in r^\mathcal{I}$ for some $r \in \mathsf{rol}(\mathcal{K})$. Note that $(e, e') \notin s^\mathcal{I}$ for every $s \in \mathsf{rol}(\mathcal{K}) \setminus \{r\}$. Let $\mathbf{p}$ and $\mathbf{p}'$ be the states decorating e and e', respectively. It holds that $\mathbf{p} \xrightarrow{r} \mathbf{p}'$. By *the level of the edge* (e, e') we shall understand the level of this transition. A *level-ℓ interpretation* is a $\widehat{\mathcal{B}}$-decorated interpretation that does not contain edges of level strictly below ℓ; if $\ell > n$, this means that there are no edges at all. The following lemma is the key to our algorithm.

Lemma 4. *Consider a level-ℓ interpretation $\mathcal{I}$ and elements $e \in C^\mathcal{I}_{q,\ell}$ and $e' \in C^\mathcal{I}_{q',\ell}$. Then, $(e, e') \in \mathcal{B}^\mathcal{I}_{q,q'}$ iff there is a path from e to e' in $\mathcal{I}$.*

We make use of Lemma 4 by decomposing RPQs into segments corresponding to different levels, as was done for the runs of $\widehat{\mathcal{B}}$ in Lemma 2. To facilitate this, we make our queries aware of levels. A *$\widehat{\mathcal{B}}$-decorated CRPQ* is a CRPQ φ represented by means of semiautomaton $\mathcal{B}$ that contains exactly one atom of the form $C_{q,\ell}(x)$ and exactly one atom of the form $C_{q',\ell'}(x')$ for each atom $\mathcal{B}_{q,q'}(x, x')$ in φ. We call ℓ and ℓ' the *begin level* and the *end level* of atom $\mathcal{B}_{q,q'}(x, x')$ in φ, respectively. Because levels never increase in a thread of a run of $\widehat{\mathcal{B}}$, we can assume without loss of generality that $\ell \geq \ell'$ always holds. A *level-ℓ CRPQ* is a $\widehat{\mathcal{B}}$-decorated CRPQ that contains no RPQ atoms of end level strictly below ℓ. As all end levels are at most n, a level-ℓ CRPQ for $\ell > n$ contains no RPQ atoms; that is, it is a CQ. To *complete* a CRPQ φ means to turn it into a $\widehat{\mathcal{B}}$-decorated CRPQ φ' by adding unary atoms over concepts $C_{q,\ell}$ in an arbitrary minimal way. Each resulting φ' is called a *completion* of φ. Over $\widehat{\mathcal{B}}$-decorated interpretations, φ is equivalent to the union of its completions. The *completion of a UCRPQ* Φ is the union of all completions of all CRPQs in Φ.

We conclude this section by showing how to turn any counterexample to $\mathcal{K} \models^\mathcal{E}_{\mathsf{fin}} \Phi$ into a $\widehat{\mathcal{B}}$-decorated one. Let $\mathcal{I}$ be an interpretation over $\mathsf{CN}(\mathcal{K}) \cup \mathsf{rol}(\mathcal{K})$. The *product* of $\mathcal{I}$ and $\widehat{\mathcal{B}}$ is the interpretation $\mathcal{I} \times \widehat{\mathcal{B}}$ over $\mathsf{CN}(\widehat{\mathcal{B}}) \cup \mathsf{CN}(\mathcal{K}) \cup \mathsf{rol}(\mathcal{K})$ such that

- $\Delta^{\mathcal{I} \times \widehat{\mathcal{B}}} = \Delta^\mathcal{I} \times \mathsf{rol}(\mathcal{K}) \times \widehat{Q}$,
- $C^{\mathcal{I} \times \widehat{\mathcal{B}}} = C^\mathcal{I} \times \mathsf{rol}(\mathcal{K}) \times \widehat{Q}$ for all $C \in \mathsf{CN}(\mathcal{K})$,
- $C^{\mathcal{I} \times \widehat{\mathcal{B}}}_{q,\ell} = \Delta^\mathcal{I} \times \mathsf{rol}(\mathcal{K}) \times \{(p_1, p_2, \ldots, p_n) \in \widehat{Q} : p_\ell = q\}$ for all $q \in Q$ and $\ell \in \{1, 2, \ldots, n\}$,
- $r^{\mathcal{I} \times \widehat{\mathcal{B}}} = \big\{\big((e, s, \mathbf{p}), (e', r, \mathbf{p}')\big) : (e, e') \in r^\mathcal{I}, \mathbf{p} \xrightarrow{r} \mathbf{p}', s \in \mathsf{rol}(\mathcal{K})\big\}$ for $r \in \mathsf{rol}(\mathcal{K})$.

Note that if $\mathcal{I}$ is finite, so is $\mathcal{I} \times \widehat{\mathcal{B}}$.

Lemma 5. *Let Φ be a UCRPQ, $\mathcal{K}$ an $\mathcal{ALC}$ KB with a trivial ABox, and $\mathcal{E}$ an environment.*

- *$\mathcal{I} \times \widehat{\mathcal{B}}$ is a $\widehat{\mathcal{B}}$-decorated interpretation.*
- *If $\mathcal{I} \not\models \Phi$ then $\mathcal{I} \times \widehat{\mathcal{B}} \not\models \Phi$.*
- *If $\mathcal{I} \models^{\mathcal{E}} \mathcal{K}$ then $\mathcal{I} \times \widehat{\mathcal{B}} \models^{\mathcal{E}} \mathcal{K}$ up to identifying the unique individual a in $\mathcal{K}$ with some $(a, r, \mathbf{p}) \in \Delta^{\mathcal{I} \times \widehat{\mathcal{B}}}$.*

4 Core Computational Problem

To solve the entailment problem we eliminate the lowest level from the query and from the interpretation, and solve the problem with fewer levels recursively. Eliminating each level will involve interpretations built from pieces that are solutions for the simplified problem. Evaluating CRPQs over such interpretations requires breaking them down into fragments and it must accommodate single RPQs witnessed across multiple pieces.

For a UCRPQ Φ let $\tilde{\Phi}$ be the completion of an equivalent UCRPQ represented by means of a semiautomaton $\mathcal{B}$. A *fragment* of $\varphi \in \tilde{\Phi}$ is either of the following:

- a $\widehat{\mathcal{B}}$-decorated CRPQ of the form $C_{q_1,\ell_1}(y_1) \wedge \mathcal{B}_{q_1,q_2}(y_1, y_2) \wedge C_{q_2,\ell_2}(y_2)$ or $C_{q_1,\ell_1}(y_1) \wedge \mathcal{B}_{q_1,q_2}(y_1, y_2) \wedge C_{q_2,\ell_2}(y_2) \wedge r(y_2, y_3) \wedge C_{q_3,\ell_3}(y_3)$ where y_1, y_2, y_3 are fresh variables and $r \in \mathsf{rol}(\mathcal{K})$,
- a connected $\widehat{\mathcal{B}}$-decorated CRPQ that can be obtained from φ by dropping selected atoms, replacing selected RPQ atoms $\mathcal{B}_{q,q'}(x, x')$ by a subset of $\mathcal{B}_{q,q_1}(x, y_1)$, $r(y_1, y_2)$, $\mathcal{B}_{q_3,q'}(y_3, x')$ for some fresh variables y_1, y_2, y_3 and $r \in \mathsf{rol}(\mathcal{K})$, and completing the resulting CRPQ.

A fragment of Φ is a fragment of any of the CRPQs in $\tilde{\Phi}$. Importantly, a fragment of a fragment of Φ is also a fragment of Φ, and each $\varphi \in \tilde{\Phi}$ is a fragment of Φ. Up to renaming fresh variables, Φ has $2^{\mathrm{poly}(\|\Phi\|)}$ different fragments, despite $\mathcal{B}$ being exponential in $\|\Phi\|$.

We now enrich interpretations again by including information about matched fragments of Φ. For each fragment φ of Φ and each $\emptyset \neq V \subseteq \mathit{var}(\varphi)$ we choose a fresh concept name $A_{\varphi,V}$. We call an interpretation $\mathcal{I}$ *correct (wrt. Φ)* if $e \in A^{\mathcal{I}}_{\varphi,V}$ iff $\pi(V) = \{e\}$ for some match π for φ in $\mathcal{I}$. Assuming $\mathcal{I}$ is correct, $\mathcal{I} \models \Phi$ iff $A^{\mathcal{I}}_{\varphi,V} \neq \emptyset$ for some $\varphi \in \tilde{\Phi}$ and $\emptyset \neq V \subseteq \mathit{var}(\varphi)$. Correctness is not compositional: the union of two correct interpretations sharing a single element need not be correct. As our method of eliminating levels relies on such decompositions of interpretations, we replace correctness with a notion that is weaker, but compositional.

We first abstract the decomposition of a $\widehat{\mathcal{B}}$-decorated CRPQ induced by a match in a union of disjoint 'peripheric' interpretations, each sharing a single element with a single 'core' interpretation (Fig. 2 shows three 'peripheric' interpretations connected to the 'core' by single edges, included in the 'peripheric' interpretations). A *partition* of a $\widehat{\mathcal{B}}$-decorated CRPQ φ into $\varphi', \varphi_1, \ldots, \varphi_k$ is obtained as follows. Choose $X', X_1, \ldots X_k \subseteq \mathit{var}(\varphi)$ such that

- $X_i \cap X_j = \emptyset$ for all $i \neq j$;

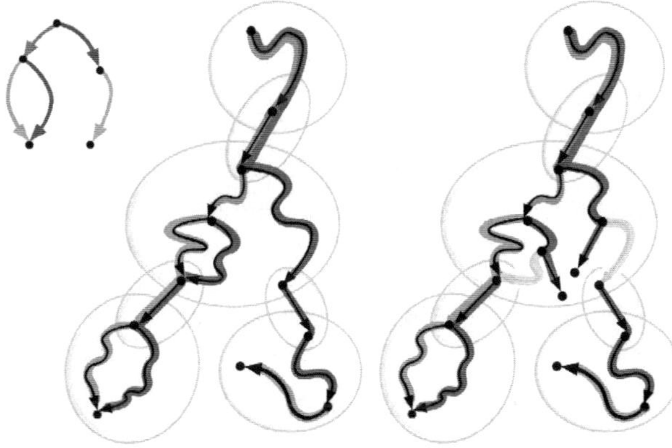

Figure 2: CRPQ φ is distributed over the bags constituting $\mathcal{I}$.

- for each atom of the form $r(x, x')$ in φ there exists i such that either $\{x, x'\} \subseteq X_i$ or $\{x, x'\} \subseteq X'$.

Based on $X', X_1, \ldots X_k$ define $\varphi', \varphi_1, \ldots, \varphi_k$ as follows. For each atom of the form $r(x, x')$ in φ choose i such that $\{x, x'\} \subseteq X_i$ and add $r(x, x')$ to φ_i or add $r(x, x')$ to φ' provided that $\{x, x'\} \subseteq X'$. For each RPQ atom $\mathcal{B}_{q,q'}(x, x')$ of begin level ℓ and end level ℓ' in φ do one of the following:

- provided that $\{x, x'\} \subseteq X'$, add $\mathcal{B}_{q,q'}(x, x')$ to φ';
- choose i such that $\{x, x'\} \subseteq X_i$ but $\{x, x'\} \not\subseteq X'$, and add $\mathcal{B}_{q,q'}(x, x')$ to φ_i (light green RPQ in Fig. 2);
- choose i such that $x \in X' \setminus X_i$ and $x' \in X_i \setminus X'$, a level m such that $\ell \geq m \geq \ell'$, a state p of $\mathcal{B}$, and a fresh variable y, and add $\mathcal{B}_{q,p}(x, y) \wedge C_{p,m}(y)$ to φ' and $C_{p,m}(y) \wedge \mathcal{B}_{p,q'}(y, x')$ to φ_i (blue and orange in Fig. 2);
- choose i such that $x \in X_i \setminus X'$ and $x' \in X' \setminus X_i$, a level m such that $\ell \geq m \geq \ell'$, a state p of $\mathcal{B}$, and a fresh variable y, and add $\mathcal{B}_{q,p}(x, y) \wedge C_{p,m}(y)$ to φ_i and $C_{p,m}(y) \wedge \mathcal{B}_{p,q'}(y, x')$ to φ' (dark green in Fig. 2);
- choose $i \neq j$ such that $x \in X_i \setminus X'$ and $x' \in X_j \setminus X'$, levels m, m' such that $\ell \geq m \geq m' \geq \ell'$, states p, p' of $\mathcal{B}$, and fresh variables y, y', add $\mathcal{B}_{q,p}(x, y) \wedge C_{p,m}(y)$ to φ_i, $C_{p,m}(y) \wedge \mathcal{B}_{p,p'}(y, y') \wedge C_{p',m'}(y')$ to φ', and $C_{p',m'}(y') \wedge \mathcal{B}_{p',q'}(y', x')$ to φ_j (purple in Fig. 2).

Note that for each $\mathcal{B}_{q,q'}(x, x')$ exactly one of the above actions can be performed and the choice of i and j is unique. To complete the construction, add to φ' all unary atoms of φ over variables already used in φ', and similarly for each φ_i. Observe that for each $X' \subseteq \mathit{var}(\varphi)$ there is exactly one choice of $X_1, X_2, \ldots, X_k$ (up to a permutation) such that the resulting $\varphi_1, \varphi_2, \ldots, \varphi_k$ are connected (regardless of the choice of p, p' and m, m'). Assuming that φ is a fragment of Φ, it then holds that so are $\varphi_1, \varphi_2, \ldots, \varphi_k$.

We call $\mathcal{I}$ *consistent (wrt. Φ)* if for each partition of a fragment φ of Φ into a CRPQ φ' and fragments $\varphi_1, \varphi_2, \ldots, \varphi_k$ with $\mathit{var}(\varphi_i) \cap \mathit{var}(\varphi_j) = \emptyset$ for $i \neq j$, $V_i = \mathit{var}(\varphi_i) \cap \mathit{var}(\varphi')$, and $\emptyset \neq V \subseteq \mathit{var}(\varphi) \cap \mathit{var}(\varphi')$, there is no match π for φ' in $\mathcal{I}$ such that $\pi(V_i) = \{e_i\} \subseteq \left(A_{\varphi_i,V_i}\right)^{\mathcal{I}}$ for all i but $\pi(V) = \{e\} \not\subseteq \left(A_{\varphi,V}\right)^{\mathcal{I}}$. Clearly, all correct interpretations are consistent. The converse is not true in general, but the following key property is preserved.

Lemma 6. *For every UCRPQ Φ and every consistent $\widehat{\mathcal{B}}$-decorated interpretation $\mathcal{I}$, if $A^{\mathcal{I}}_{\varphi,V} = \emptyset$ for each $\varphi \in \tilde{\Phi}$ and $\emptyset \neq V \subseteq var(\varphi)$, then $\mathcal{I} \not\models \Phi$.*

Consistency is sufficient to express entailment, but it does not yield well to the recursive elimination of levels. We generalize it by refining the information about matched fragments of Φ. We introduce fresh concepts $A^{\kappa}_{\varphi,V}$ where φ is a fragment of Φ, $\emptyset \neq V \subseteq var(\varphi)$,

$$\kappa : var(\varphi) \to \{1, 2, \dots, \ell\},$$

and $\kappa(V) = \{\ell\}$ for some $\ell \in \{1, 2, \dots, n+1\}$. We write $\mathsf{CN}^{\Phi}_{\ell}$ for the set of $A^{\kappa}_{\psi,V}$ such that $\kappa(V) = \{\ell\}$. Intuitively, κ is a synopsis of when specific fragments of ψ were matched during the recursive search for the model. Specifically, $\kappa(x) = \ell$ indicates that x was matched after all levels strictly below ℓ had been eliminated from the query, but while level ℓ was still present. Accordingly, ℓ-consistency, defined below, ensures that the synopses built so far are consistently updated while level ℓ is being handled.

We call $\mathcal{I}$ *ℓ-consistent (wrt. Φ)* if for each partition of a fragment φ of Φ into a CRPQ φ' of level ℓ and fragments $\varphi_1, \varphi_2, \dots, \varphi_k$ with $var(\varphi_i) \cap var(\varphi_j) = \emptyset$ for $i \neq j$, $V_i = var(\varphi_i) \cap var(\varphi')$, and $\emptyset \neq V \subseteq var(\varphi) \cap var(\varphi')$, there is no match π for φ' in $\mathcal{I}$ such that $\pi(V_i) = \{e_i\} \subseteq \left(A^{\kappa_i}_{\varphi_i,V_i}\right)^{\mathcal{I}}$ for all i but $\pi(V) = \{e\} \nsubseteq (A^{\kappa}_{\varphi,V})^{\mathcal{I}}$ where

- $\kappa_i(x) \leq \ell$ for all $x \in var(\varphi_i)$,
- $\kappa(x) = \kappa_i(x)$ for all $x \in var(\varphi_i) \setminus V_i$,
- $\kappa(x) = \ell$ for all $x \in var(\varphi) \cap var(\varphi')$.

We stress that while φ' has level ℓ, fragments $\varphi, \varphi_1, \dots, \varphi_k$ can have any level. Note also that ℓ-consistency speaks only of concept names in $\mathsf{CN}^{\Phi}_1 \cup \mathsf{CN}^{\Phi}_2 \cup \dots \cup \mathsf{CN}^{\Phi}_{\ell}$. Identifying $A_{\varphi,V}$ with $A^{\kappa}_{\varphi,V}$ for κ constantly equal to 1, we get that consistency and 1-consistency are equivalent.

In what follows, by an *(ℓ, ℓ')-interpretation* we mean an ℓ'-consistent level-ℓ interpretation. By an *(ℓ, ℓ')-model* of $\mathcal{K}$ modulo $\mathcal{E}$ we mean an (ℓ, ℓ')-interpretation that is model of $\mathcal{K}$ modulo $\mathcal{E}$. The actual problem we will be solving is the following *(ℓ, ℓ')-model problem* for $\ell \leq \ell'$: Given a KB $\mathcal{K}$ with a trivial ABox, an environment $\mathcal{E}$, and a UCRPQ Φ decide if there exists a finite (ℓ, ℓ')-model of $\mathcal{K}$ modulo $\mathcal{E}$.

By Lemma 5, entailment modulo environment (with trivial ABox) can be reduced to the $(1,1)$-model problem by modifying the environment to forbid all unary types containing $A^{\kappa}_{\varphi,V}$ for any $\varphi \in \tilde{\Phi}$, $\emptyset \neq V \subseteq var(\varphi)$, and κ constantly equal 1. Note that the reduction does not affect the query Φ, nor the KB $\mathcal{K}$. However, it introduces up to $2^{\mathrm{poly}(\|\Phi\|)}$ new concept names $A_{\varphi,V}$ and $C_{q,\ell}$. Consequently, the number of unary types is at most $2^{|\mathsf{CN}(\mathcal{K})|+2^{\mathrm{poly}(\|\Phi\|)}}$. It follows that the size of the environment is bounded by $2^{\|\mathcal{K}\|+2^{\mathrm{poly}(\|\Phi\|)}}$.

To solve the $(1,1)$-model problem we will proceed recursively, incrementing ℓ and ℓ' in an alternating fashion, until $\ell = \ell' = n+1$. At each level of the recursion we will be making multiple recursive calls. During the recursion the UCRPQ Φ and the TBox $\mathcal{T}$ will remain unchanged, but the ABox and the environment will evolve. Importantly, we will not introduce any new concepts, so the size of the environment will always be bounded by $2^{\|\mathcal{K}\|+2^{\mathrm{poly}(\|\Phi\|)}}$. The size of the ABox will be bounded by $\|\mathcal{K}\| + 2^{\mathrm{poly}(\|\Phi\|)}$ and the number of individuals will never grow. In consequence, the total cost of the algorithm can be computed as the cost of a single recursion step times the number of steps. In the following sections we will show that each recursion step can be carried out in time $2^{O(\|\mathcal{K}\|)+2^{\mathrm{poly}(\|\Phi\|)}}$, excluding the cost of the recursive calls. The depth of the recursion is $O(n) = 2^{\mathrm{poly}(\|\Phi\|)}$. The number of recursive calls within a single recursion step is also bounded by $2^{O(\|\mathcal{K}\|)+2^{\mathrm{poly}(\|\Phi\|)}}$. This means that the total number of recursion steps is $2^{\|\mathcal{K}\| \cdot 2^{\mathrm{poly}(\|\Phi\|)}}$ and so is the overall complexity of the recursive algorithm for the $(1,1)$-model problem.

5 Incrementing the Level of Queries

The main goal of this section is to solve the (ℓ, ℓ)-model problem by reduction to multiple instances of the $(\ell, \ell+1)$-model problem for $\ell \leq n$. The $(n+1, n+1)$-model problem is discussed briefly at the end of the section.

As a first step, we observe that it is enough to consider interpretations whose DAG of strongly connected components is a tree. For this purpose we define *tree-like* interpretations as those that can be decomposed into multiple finite subinterpretations, called *bags*, arranged into a (possibly infinite) tree such that: (1) all bags are pairwise disjoint; (2) between each parent and child bag there is a single edge, pointing from an element of the parent bag to an element of the child bag; (3) all other edges are between elements of the same bag. We think of edges between bags as 2-element interpretations, called *edge-bags*, sharing the origin with the parent bag and the target with the child bag. A tree-like interpretation is then a union of all its bags and edge-bags. Fig. 2 shows a tree-like interpretation with 4 bags and 3 edge-bags. In tree-like interpretations ℓ-consistency is a local property.

Lemma 7. *A tree-like interpretation is ℓ-consistent iff each of its bags and edge-bags is ℓ-consistent.*

Lemma 8. *There is a finite (ℓ, ℓ')-model of $\mathcal{K}$ modulo $\mathcal{E}$ iff there is a finite tree-like (ℓ, ℓ')-model of $\mathcal{K}$ modulo $\mathcal{E}$ whose bags are strongly connected.*

The next step is to eliminate the lowest level from the queries. An *$(\ell+1)$-reduct* of a level-ℓ CRPQ φ is any CRPQ that can be obtained from φ by first splitting each RPQ atom $\mathcal{B}_{q_1,q_2}(x_1, x_2)$ of begin level $\ell_1 > \ell$ and end level ℓ into $\mathcal{B}_{q_1,q_1'}(x_1, x_1') \wedge C_{q_1',\ell_1'}(x_1') \wedge r(x_1', x_2') \wedge C_{q_2',\ell}(x_2') \wedge \mathcal{B}_{q_2',q_2}(x_2', x_2)$ where $\ell_1 \geq \ell_1' \geq \ell+1$, and then dropping from the resulting CRPQ all atoms whose begin and end level is ℓ (all unary atoms are kept). Note that each $(\ell+1)$-reduct φ' of φ is a conjunction of at most $|\varphi|$ disjoint fragments of φ and that $var(\varphi) \subseteq var(\varphi')$.

Lemma 9. *Over $\widehat{\mathcal{B}}$-decorated interpretations, each level-ℓ CRPQ implies the union of its $(\ell+1)$-reducts. Over strongly-connected level-ℓ interpretations, each level-ℓ CRPQ is equivalent to the union of its $(\ell+1)$-reducts.*

Because Lemma 8 guarantees tree-like solutions with strongly connected bags, we can replace ℓ-consistency with *strong ℓ-consistency*: the only difference is that π ranges over matches of all possible $(\ell+1)$-reducts of φ', rather than over matches of φ' itself. We restate Lemma 8 as follows.

Lemma 10. *There is a finite (ℓ, ℓ)-model of $\mathcal{K}$ modulo $\mathcal{E}$ iff there is a finite tree-like level-ℓ model of $\mathcal{K}$ modulo $\mathcal{E}$ whose edge bags are ℓ-consistent and bags strongly ℓ-consistent.*

It remains to show how to find models of the latter form. Let us first see how to find one consisting of a single bag; that is, how to find a finite strongly ℓ-consistent level-ℓ model of $\mathcal{K}$ modulo $\mathcal{E}$. We will show that this amounts to finding a finite $(\ell, \ell+1)$-model of $\mathcal{K}$ modulo $\mathcal{E}'$ for one of the $(\ell+1)$-reducts $\mathcal{E}'$ of $\mathcal{E}$ described below.

Consider a fragment φ, a non-empty set $V \subseteq \mathit{var}(\varphi)$, a partition of φ into a CRPQ φ' of level ℓ, and fragments $\varphi_1, \varphi_2, \ldots, \varphi_k$, as in the definition of (strong) ℓ-consistency. Let $\kappa : \mathit{var}(\varphi) \to \{1, 2, \ldots, \ell\}$ be such that $\kappa\big(\mathit{var}(\varphi) \cap \mathit{var}(\varphi')\big) = \{\ell\}$. Let ψ' be an $(\ell+1)$-reduct of φ'. Consider CRPQs ψ with $\mathit{var}(\varphi) \subseteq \mathit{var}(\psi)$ that can be partitioned into ψ' and $\varphi_1, \varphi_2, \ldots, \varphi_k$. Choose the one with minimal $\mathit{var}(\psi)$. This amounts to merging back all RPQ atoms split during the partition of φ, provided that their segments were not affected by replacing φ' with ψ'. The CRPQ ψ is not a fragment, because it need not be connected: Figure 2 right illustrates passing from φ to ψ consisting of two disconnected fragments. Let $\psi_1, \psi_2, \ldots, \psi_m$ be the fragments constituting ψ and let $U_i = V \cap \mathit{var}(\psi_i)$. An *$(\ell+1)$-reduct* $\mathcal{E}'$ of $\mathcal{E}$ is constructed by iterating over all possible choices of φ, V, φ', $\varphi_1, \varphi_2, \ldots, \varphi_k$, ψ', κ, as above, and pruning $\mathcal{E}$ for each choice in one of the following ways:

- either pick i such that $U_i = \emptyset$ and remove all unary types that contain any $A^{\kappa_i}_{\psi_i, W_i}$ with $W_i \subseteq \mathit{var}(\psi_i) \cap \mathit{var}(\psi')$, $\kappa_i\big(\mathit{var}(\psi_i) \cap \mathit{var}(\psi')\big) = \{\ell+1\}$, and $\kappa_i(x) = \kappa(x)$ for all $x \in \mathit{var}(\psi_i) \setminus \mathit{var}(\psi')$;
- or remove all unary types that contain some $A^{\kappa_i}_{\psi_i, U_i}$ with $\kappa_i\big(\mathit{var}(\psi_i) \cap \mathit{var}(\psi')\big) = \{\ell+1\}$ and $\kappa(x) = \kappa_i(x)$ for all $x \in \mathit{var}(\psi_i) \setminus \mathit{var}(\psi')$, for each i such that $U_i \neq \emptyset$, but do not contain $A^{\kappa}_{\varphi, V}$.

Lemma 11. *$\mathcal{I}$ is a strongly ℓ-consistent level-ℓ model of $\mathcal{K}$ modulo $\mathcal{E}$ iff some interpretation that agrees with $\mathcal{I}$ over all role names and all concept names except $\mathsf{CN}^{\Phi}_{\ell+1}$ is an $(\ell+1)$-consistent level-ℓ model of $\mathcal{K}$ modulo $\mathcal{E}'$ for some $(\ell+1)$-reduct $\mathcal{E}'$ of $\mathcal{E}$.*

Finite models consisting of multiple bags can be constructed bottom-up by a least fixed point procedure, using Lemma 11 to find each bag.

Lemma 12. *The (ℓ, ℓ)-model problem for an $\mathcal{ALC}$ KB $\mathcal{K}$, a UCRPQ Φ, and an environment $\mathcal{E}$ can be solved in time*

$$2^{O(\|\mathcal{K}\|)+2^{\mathrm{poly}(\|\Phi\|)}}$$

given an oracle for the $(\ell, \ell+1)$-model problem (with the same UCRPQ and TBox).

At the bottom of the recursion we need to check if there exists a $(n+1, n+1)$-model for $\mathcal{K}$ modulo $\mathcal{E}$. Now, a $\widehat{\mathcal{B}}$-decorated interpretation is level-$(n+1)$ iff it is *discrete*; that is, it has no edges at all. This allows solving the problem by a direct inspection. Because the ABox is trivial and ℓ-consistency is preserved under restrictions of the domain, it is enough to go through all singleton interpretations.

Lemma 13. *The $(n+1, n+1)$-model problem for an $\mathcal{ALC}$ KB $\mathcal{K}$, a UCRPQ Φ, and an environment $\mathcal{E}$ can be solved in time $2^{O(\|\mathcal{K}\|)+2^{\mathrm{poly}(\|\Phi\|)}}$.*

6 Incrementing the Level of Models

In this section we solve the (ℓ, ℓ')-model problem by reduction to multiple instances of the (ℓ', ℓ')-model problem for $\ell < \ell'$; that is, we eliminate level-ℓ edges from the interpretations. Like in Section 5, we rely on tree-like models of a special form; this time, however, they may be infinite and an additional step is needed to turn them into finite ones.

A $\widehat{\mathcal{B}}$-decorated interpretation is *ℓ'-flat* if it is a tree-like interpretation where all edges between bags have level strictly below ℓ', whereas all edges inside bags have level at least ℓ'.

Lemma 14. *If there exists a finite (ℓ, ℓ')-model of $\mathcal{K}$ modulo $\mathcal{E}$ then there exists an ℓ'-flat (ℓ, ℓ')-model of $\mathcal{K}$ modulo $\mathcal{E}$ with bounded degree and bag size.*

In contrast to Lemma 8, the above only shows that the reformulated condition is necessary. We show that it is sufficient, by turning an arbitrary ℓ'-flat (ℓ, ℓ')-model of $\mathcal{K}$ modulo $\mathcal{E}$ with bounded degree and bag size into a finite (ℓ, ℓ')-model of $\mathcal{K}$ modulo $\mathcal{E}$. For this we use *coloured blocking*. For $d \in \Delta^{\mathcal{I}}$, the *$m$-neighbourhood $N^{\mathcal{I}}_m(d)$ of d* is the interpretation obtained by restricting $\mathcal{I}$ to elements $e \in \Delta^{\mathcal{I}}$ within distance m from d in $\mathcal{I}$, enriched with a fresh concept interpreted as $\{d\}$. A *colouring of $\mathcal{I}$ with k colours* is an extension $\mathcal{I}'$ of $\mathcal{I}$ to k fresh concept names $B_1, \ldots, B_k$ such that $B^{\mathcal{I}'}_1, \ldots, B^{\mathcal{I}'}_k$ is a partition of $\Delta^{\mathcal{I}'} = \Delta^{\mathcal{I}}$. We say that $d \in B^{\mathcal{I}'}_i$ has colour B_i. We call $\mathcal{I}'$ *m-proper* if for each $d \in \Delta^{\mathcal{I}'}$ all elements of $N^{\mathcal{I}'}_m(d)$ have different colours.

Fact 1 (Gogacz, Ibáñez-García, and Murlak 2018). *If $\mathcal{I}$ has bounded degree, then for all $m \geq 0$ there exists an m-proper colouring $\mathcal{I}'$ of $\mathcal{I}$ with finitely many colours. Consider interpretation $\mathcal{J}$ obtained from $\mathcal{I}'$ by redirecting some edges such that the old target and the new target have isomorphic m-neighbourhoods in $\mathcal{I}'$. Then, for each conjunctive query φ with at most $\sqrt{m}$ binary atoms, if $\mathcal{I} \not\models \varphi$, then $\mathcal{J} \not\models \varphi$.*

Let $\mathcal{I}$ be an ℓ'-flat (ℓ, ℓ')-model of $\mathcal{K}$ modulo $\mathcal{E}$ of bounded degree with bags of size at most M. In order to make Fact 1 applicable, we need to express the ℓ'-consistency condition over $\mathcal{I}$ by means of a finite set of conjunctive queries, rather than CRPQs. Towards this end, we show that over $\mathcal{I}$ each level-ℓ' CRPQ is equivalent to a UCQ. We rely on the following observation.

Lemma 15. *In a match of a $\widehat{\mathcal{B}}$-decorated CRPQ in a $\widehat{\mathcal{B}}$-decorated interpretation, each path witnessing an RPQ atom of end level at least ℓ' uses at most $n - \ell'$ edges of level strictly below ℓ'.*

We say that a CRPQ φ is *bounded by* K over an interpretation $\mathcal{J}$ if for each match of φ in $\mathcal{J}$ each RPQ atom of φ can be witnessed by a path of length at most K.

Lemma 16. *Let $\mathcal{J}$ be $\widehat{\mathcal{B}}$-decorated interpretation made up of disjoint level-ℓ' interpretations of size at most M connected by edges of level strictly below ℓ'. Assuming $\ell' \leq n$, each level-ℓ' CRPQ is bounded by $M(n-\ell'+1)^2$ over $\mathcal{J}$.*

For a $\widehat{\mathcal{B}}$-decorated CRPQ φ, let $\varphi^{(K)}$ be the UCQ obtained by taking the union of all CQs that can be obtained from φ by eliminating each RPQ atom $\mathcal{B}_{q,q'}(x,x')$ in one of the following ways: either remove the atom and equate variables x and x', or replace the atom with a CQ of the form

$$r_1(x,y_1) \wedge r_2(y_1,y_2) \wedge \cdots \wedge r_N(y_{N-1},x')$$

where $N \leq K$, $y_1,\ldots,y_{N-1}$ are fresh variables, and there is a run of $\mathcal{B}$ on $r_1 \ldots r_N$ that begins in q and ends in q'.

Fact 2. *If a $\widehat{\mathcal{B}}$-decorated CRPQ φ is bounded by K on an interpretation $\mathcal{J}$, then $\mathcal{J} \models \varphi$ iff $\mathcal{J} \models \varphi^{(K)}$.*

The final step before we can apply Fact 1 is to express ℓ'-consistency as query evaluation. Consider a partition of a fragment φ of Φ into a CRPQ φ' of level ℓ' and fragments $\varphi_1,\varphi_2,\ldots,\varphi_k$ with $var(\varphi_i)\cap var(\varphi_j)=\emptyset$ for $i\neq j$, $V_i = var(\varphi_i)\cap var(\varphi')$, and $\emptyset \neq V \subseteq var(\varphi)\cap var(\varphi')$. Let ψ be the CRPQ obtained from φ' as follows. Begin from a copy of φ'. For each $i \in \{1,\ldots,k\}$, add to ψ an atom $A^{\kappa_i}_{\varphi_i,V_i}(u)$ for some κ_i satisfying $\kappa_i(x) \leq \ell$ for all $x \in var(\varphi_i)$ and $\kappa_i(x)=\ell$ for all $x\in V_i$, and some variable u in V_i (V_i is nonempty, because φ is connected), and equate all variables in V_i. Similarly, add to ψ the atom $\bar{A}_{\varphi',V}(u)$ for some κ satisfying $\kappa(x)=\ell$ for all $x\in var(\varphi)\cap var(\varphi')$ and $\kappa(x)=\kappa_i(x)$ for all $x \in var(\varphi)\cap var(\varphi_i)$, and some $u\in V$, and equate all variables in V. Let $\Phi_{\ell'}$ be the union of all CRPQs ψ obtained as above for different choices of φ, φ', $\varphi_1,\varphi_2,\ldots,\varphi_k$, V, and $\kappa_1,\kappa_2,\ldots,\kappa_k$. Note that $\Phi_{\ell'}$ is a union of level-ℓ' CRPQs. If $\ell' > n$, $\Phi_{\ell'}$ is a UCQ.

Lemma 17. *If $\mathcal{J}$ is a $\widehat{\mathcal{B}}$-decorated interpretation, then $\mathcal{J}$ is ℓ'-consistent iff $\mathcal{J} \not\models \Phi_{\ell'}$.*

Let $K = M(n-\ell'+1)^2$. Let t be the maximal number of binary atoms in one CQ in $\Phi^{(K)}_{\ell'}$. (Note that if $\ell' > n$, the query $\Phi_{\ell'}$ is a UCQ and $\Phi^{(K)}_{\ell'}$ coincides with $\Phi_{\ell'}$.) Fix $m = t^2$ and let $\mathcal{I}'$ be an m-proper colouring of $\mathcal{I}$. On each infinite branch, select the first bag $\mathcal{M}$ such that for some bag $\mathcal{M}'$ higher on this branch, the m-neighbourhood of the target element e of the edge from the parent of $\mathcal{M}$ to $\mathcal{M}$ is isomorphic to the m-neighbourhood of the target e' of the edge from the parent of $\mathcal{M}'$ to $\mathcal{M}'$. Because the number of non-isomorphic m-neighbourhoods in a structure of bounded degree is bounded, the depth of the selected bags in the tree of bags is also bounded. The set of selected bags is finite and forms a maximal antichain. Let $\mathcal{F}$ be the interpretation obtained by taking the union of all strict ancestors of the selected bags, and for each element e as above, redirect the edge coming from the parent of $\mathcal{M}$ to e'.

Clearly, $\mathcal{F}$ is a finite level-ℓ interpretation. It is routine to check that $\mathcal{F} \models^{\mathcal{E}} \mathcal{K}$. It remains to prove that $\mathcal{F}$ is ℓ'-consistent. We know that $\mathcal{I}$ is ℓ'-consistent. By Lemma 17, $\mathcal{I} \not\models \Phi_{\ell'}$. By Lemma 16 and Fact 2, $\mathcal{I} \not\models \Phi^{(K)}_{\ell'}$. By Fact 1, $\mathcal{F} \not\models \Phi^{(K)}_{\ell'}$. By construction, $\mathcal{F}$ satisfies the assumptions of Lemma 16. Hence, by Lemma 16 and Fact 2, $\mathcal{F} \not\models \Phi_{\ell'}$. We conclude that $\mathcal{F}$ is ℓ'-consistent using Lemma 17.

Thus we have proved the converse of Lemma 14.

Lemma 18. *If there exists an ℓ'-flat (ℓ,ℓ')-model of $\mathcal{K}$ modulo $\mathcal{E}$ with bounded degree and bag size then there exists a finite (ℓ,ℓ')-model of $\mathcal{K}$ modulo $\mathcal{E}$.*

Combining Lemmas 6, 14, and 18, we get that there is a finite (ℓ,ℓ')-model of $\mathcal{K}$ modulo $\mathcal{E}$ iff there is a bounded-degree ℓ'-flat model of $\mathcal{K}$ modulo $\mathcal{E}$ whose bags are ℓ'-consistent and have bounded size. As in an ℓ'-flat model each bag is a level-ℓ' interpretation, when we restrict our search to one-bag models the problem is an instance of the (ℓ',ℓ')-model problem. Models consisting of multiple bags can be built coinductively top-down by means of a greatest fixed point algorithm (similar to type elimination), using the (ℓ',ℓ')-model problem to check if each bag exists.

Lemma 19. *The (ℓ,ℓ')-model problem for an $\mathcal{ALC}$ KB $\mathcal{K}$, a UCRPQ Φ, and an environment $\mathcal{E}$ can be solved in time*

$$2^{O(\|\mathcal{K}\|)+2^{\mathrm{poly}(\|\Phi\|)}}$$

given an oracle for the (ℓ',ℓ')-model problem (with the same UCRPQ and TBox).

7 Looking Forward (and Back)

This paper provides first positive results on finite entailment of navigational queries over DLs ontologies. The main technical contribution is an optimal automata-based 2EXPTIME upper bound for finite entailment of UCRPQs in $\mathcal{ALC}$.

Let us take a look back at our journey. We devised an expansion of the semiautomaton used to represent UCRPQs to keep track of its runs that begin in all possible states, on all infixes of the input word. By making interpretations and CRPQs knowledgeable of the runs of this expansion, we are able to associate levels to them as dictated by the transitions of the expansion. To solve the entailment problem, we use a recursive method eliminating the lowest level from the query and from the interpretation, and solving then the simpler problem. In particular, we look at problem of finding (ℓ,ℓ') models, and solve it by recursively increasing ℓ and ℓ' in an alternating way, until both reach a maximum level: Section 5 and 6 respectively address the increment of the query level and of the model. We finally showed what to do when $\ell=\ell'=n+1$, which as argued, is enough to solve the original finite entailment problem.

As for future work, the first immediate step is to extend our method to deal with test atoms of the form $A?$, which are usually available in UCRPQs. For the ontology language, we believe our method can be adapted to allow inverses, nominals or counting. Regarding more expressive query languages, the natural next step is to consider *two-way* CRPQs. Our current approach relies on the fact that information only flows forward, and it is not clear whether it can be adapted to deal with queries that can go back.

Acknowledgments

This work was supported by Poland's National Science Centre grant 2018/30/E/ST6/00042. It also benefited from inspiring discussions with Charles Paperman.

References

Amarilli, A., and Benedikt, M. 2020. Finite open-world query answering with number restrictions. *ACM Trans. Comput. Log.* 21(4):27:1–27:73.

Amendola, G.; Leone, N.; and Manna, M. 2018. Finite controllability of conjunctive query answering with existential rules: Two steps forward. In *IJCAI*, 5189–5193. ijcai.org.

Baader, F.; Horrocks, I.; Lutz, C.; and Sattler, U. 2017. *An Introduction to Description Logic*. Cambridge University Press.

Baget, J.-F.; Leclère, M.; Mugnier, M.-L.; and Salvat, E. 2011. On rules with existential variables: Walking the decidability line. *Artificial Intelligence* 175(9):1620–1654.

Bárány, V.; Gottlob, G.; and Otto, M. 2014. Querying the guarded fragment. *Log. Methods Comput. Sci.* 10(2).

Bednarczyk, B., and Kieroński, E. 2022. Finite entailment of local queries in the $\mathcal{Z}$ family of description logics. In *Proc. of AAAI-2022*.

Bednarczyk, B., and Rudolph, S. 2019. Worst-case optimal querying of very expressive description logics with path expressions and succinct counting. In *IJCAI*, 1530–1536. ijcai.org.

Bienvenu, M.; Calvanese, D.; Ortiz, M.; and Simkus, M. 2014. Nested regular path queries in description logics. In *KR*.

Bienvenu, M.; Ortiz, M.; and Simkus, M. 2015. Regular path queries in lightweight description logics: Complexity and algorithms. *J. Artif. Intell. Res.* 53:315–374.

Bojańczyk, M., and Parys, P. 2011. XPath evaluation in linear time. *J. ACM* 58(4):17:1–17:33.

Calvanese, D.; Giacomo, G. D.; Lenzerini, M.; and Vardi, M. Y. 2000. Containment of conjunctive regular path queries with inverse. In *KR*, 176–185. Morgan Kaufmann.

Calvanese, D.; Eiter, T.; and Ortiz, M. 2014. Answering regular path queries in expressive description logics via alternating tree-automata. *Inf. Comput.* 237:12–55.

Chen, C.; Huang, H.; Ross, K. E.; Cowart, J. E.; Arighi, C. N.; Wu, C. H.; and Natale, D. A. 2020. Protein ontology on the semantic web for knowledge discovery. *Scientific Data* 7(1):337.

Civili, C., and Rosati, R. 2012. A broad class of first-order rewritable tuple-generating dependencies. In *Datalog*, volume 7494 of *Lecture Notes in Computer Science*, 68–80. Springer.

Cook, C. E.; Bergman, M. T.; Finn, R. D.; Cochrane, G.; Birney, E.; and Apweiler, R. 2016. The European Bioinformatics Institute in 2016: Data growth and integration. *Nucleic acids research* 44:D20–D26.

Danielski, D., and Kieronski, E. 2019. Finite satisfiability of unary negation fragment with transitivity. In *MFCS*, volume 138 of *LIPIcs*, 17:1–17:15.

Figueira, D.; Figueira, S.; and Baque, E. P. 2020. Finite controllability for ontology-mediated query answering of CRPQ. In *KR*, 381–391.

Florescu, D.; Levy, A. Y.; and Suciu, D. 1998. Query containment for conjunctive queries with regular expressions. In *PODS*, 139–148. ACM Press.

Galgonek, J.; Hurt, T.; Michlíková, V.; Onderka, P.; Schwarz, J.; and Vondrášek, J. 2016. Advanced SPARQL querying in small molecule databases. *Journal of Cheminformatics* 8(1):31.

Ginzburg, A. 1968. *Algebraic Theory of Automata*. ACM Monograph Series. Academic Press.

Glimm, B.; Lutz, C.; Horrocks, I.; and Sattler, U. 2008. Conjunctive query answering for the description logic SHIQ. *J. Artif. Intell. Res.* 31:157–204.

Gogacz, T., and Marcinkowski, J. 2013. Converging to the chase - A tool for finite controllability. In *LICS*, 540–549. IEEE Computer Society.

Gogacz, T.; Gutiérrez-Basulto, V.; Ibáñez-García, Y.; Jung, J. C.; and Murlak, F. 2019. On finite and unrestricted query entailment beyond SQ with number restrictions on transitive roles. In *IJCAI*, 1719–1725. ijcai.org.

Gogacz, T.; Gutiérrez-Basulto, V.; Gutowski, A.; Ibáñez-García, Y.; and Murlak, F. 2020. On finite entailment of non-local queries in description logics. In *KR*, 424–433.

Gogacz, T.; Ibáñez-García, Y.; and Murlak, F. 2018. Finite query answering in expressive description logics with transitive roles. In *Proc. of KR-18*.

Gottlob, G.; Manna, M.; and Pieris, A. 2018. Finite model reasoning in hybrid classes of existential rules. In *IJCAI*, 1831–1837. ijcai.org.

Gutiérrez-Basulto, V.; Ibáñez-García, Y. A.; and Jung, J. C. 2018. Answering regular path queries over SQ ontologies. In *AAAI*, 1845–1852. AAAI Press.

Hu, W.; Qiu, H.; and Dumontier, M. 2015. Link analysis of life science linked data. In *ISWC (2)*.

Ibáñez-García, Y. A.; Lutz, C.; and Schneider, T. 2014. Finite model reasoning in Horn description logics. In *KR*.

Kostylev, E. V.; Reutter, J. L.; and Vrgoc, D. 2014. XPath for DL-Lite ontologies. In *Description Logics*.

Lysenko, A.; Roznovăţ, I. A.; Saqi, M.; Mazein, A.; Rawlings, C. J.; and Auffray, C. 2016. Representing and querying disease networks using graph databases. *BioData Mining* 9(1):23.

Ortiz, M., and Simkus, M. 2014. Revisiting the hardness of query answering in expressive description logics. In *RR*, volume 8741 of *Lecture Notes in Computer Science*, 216–223. Springer.

Pratt-Hartmann, I. 2009. Data-complexity of the two-variable fragment with counting quantifiers. *Inf. Comput.* 207(8):867–888.

Rajabi, E., and Sanchez-Alonso, S. 2021. Knowledge discovery using SPARQL property path: The case of disease data set. *Journal of Information Science* 47(5):677–687.

Rosati, R. 2008. Finite model reasoning in DL-Lite. In *ESWC*.

Rudolph, S. 2016. Undecidability results for database-inspired reasoning problems in very expressive description logics. In *KR*, 247–257. AAAI Press.

Schneider, T., and Simkus, M. 2020. Ontologies and data management: A brief survey. *Künstliche Intell.* 34(3):329–353.

Stefanoni, G.; Motik, B.; Krötzsch, M.; and Rudolph, S. 2014. The complexity of answering conjunctive and navigational queries over OWL 2 EL knowledge bases. *J. Artif. Intell. Res.* 51:645–705.

Proceedings of the 19th International Conference on Principles of Knowledge Representation and Reasoning
Main Track

Conservative Extensions for Existential Rules

Jean Christoph Jung[1], Carsten Lutz[2], Jerzy Marcinkowski[3]
[1]Institute of Computer Science, University of Hildesheim, Germany
[2]Institute of Computer Science, Leipzig University, Germany
[3]Institute of Computer Science, University of Wrocław, Poland
jungj@uni-hildesheim.de, clu@informatik.uni-leipzig.de, jma@cs.uni.wroc.pl

Abstract

We study the problem to decide, given sets T_1, T_2 of tuple-generating dependencies (TGDs), also called existential rules, whether T_2 is a conservative extension of T_1. We consider two natural notions of conservative extension, one pertaining to answers to conjunctive queries over databases and one to homomorphisms between chased databases. Our main results are that these problems are undecidable for linear TGDs, undecidable for guarded TGDs even when T_1 is empty, and decidable for frontier-one TGDs.

1 Introduction

Tuple-generating dependencies (TGDs) are an expressive constraint language that emerged in database theory, where it has various important applications (Abiteboul, Hull, and Vianu 1995). In knowledge representation, TGDs are used as an ontology language under the names of existential rules and Datalog$^\pm$ (Baget et al. 2011; Calì et al. 2010). For the purposes of this paper, however, we stick with the name of 'TGDs'. A major application of TGDs in KR is ontology-mediated querying where a database query is enriched with an ontology, aiming to deliver more complete answers and to extend the vocabulary available for query formulation (Bienvenu et al. 2014; Bienvenu and Ortiz 2015; Calvanese et al. 2009). The semantics of ontology-mediated querying can be given in terms of homomorphisms and the widely known chase procedure that makes explicit the logical consequences of a set of TGDs and a database.

As the use of unrestricted TGDs makes the evaluation of ontology-mediated queries undecidable, various computationally more well-behaved fragments have been identified. We consider linear TGDs, guarded TGDs, and frontier-one TGDs (Calì, Gottlob, and Lukasiewicz 2012; Baget et al. 2011; Calì, Gottlob, and Kifer 2013). For all of these, ontology-mediated query evaluation is decidable. Deferring a formal definition to Section 2 of this paper, we remark that guarded generalizes linear, and that frontier-one is orthogonal to both linear and guarded. Moreover, linear TGDs generalize description logics (DLs) of the DL-Lite family (Artale et al. 2009), while both guarded and frontier-one TGDs generalize DLs of the $\mathcal{ELI}$ family (Baader et al. 2017).

On top of bare-bones query evaluation, there are other natural problems that are suggested by the framework of ontology-mediated querying. Consider the following: given sets of TGDs T_1 and T_2 (formulated in any, potentially different schemas), a database schema Σ_D, and a query schema Σ_Q, decide whether T_2 is a Σ_D, Σ_Q-*CQ-conservative extension* of T_1, that is, whether for all Σ_D-databases D and conjunctive queries (CQ) $q(\bar{x})$ in schema Σ_Q, every tuple $\bar{c}$ that is an answer to q on D given T_1 is also an answer to q on D given T_2 (Botoeva et al. 2016). Note that this is a very relevant problem. If, for instance, T_2 is a Σ_D, Σ_Q-CQ-conservative extension of T_1 and vice versa, then we can safely replace T_1 with T_2 in any application where databases are formulated in schema Σ_D and queries in schema Σ_Q. CQ-conservative extensions have been studied for various DLs and are decidable for many members of the DL-Lite and $\mathcal{ELI}$ families (Konev et al. 2011; Jung et al. 2020). In this paper, we address the naturally emerging question whether decidability extends to the more general settings of linear, guarded, and frontier-one TGDs.

A natural problem related to CQ-conservative extensions is Σ_D, Σ_Q-*hom-conservative extension* which asks whether for every Σ_D-database, there is a Σ_Q-homomorphism[1] from the chase $\mathsf{chase}_{T_2}(D)$ of D with T_2 to $\mathsf{chase}_{T_1}(D)$ that is the identity on all constants in D. In fact, this problem corresponds to CQ-conservative extensions when CQs may be infinitary, and it is known that these two problems do not coincide even in the case of DLs (Botoeva et al. 2016). We study hom-conservative extensions along with CQ-conservative extensions. In addition, we consider the variant of CQ/hom-conservative extensions where the set of TGDs T_1 is required to be empty. We refer to this as Σ_D, Σ_Q-*CQ/hom-triviality*. Note that triviality is also a very natural problem as it asks whether the given set of TGDs T_2 says *anything at all* about Σ_D-databases as far as conjunctive queries and homomorphisms over schema Σ_Q are concerned. We observe that Σ_D, Σ_Q-CQ-triviality and Σ_D, Σ_Q-hom-triviality coincide even for unrestricted TGDs, and thus we only speak of Σ_D, Σ_Q-*triviality*. Our main results are as follows.

1. For linear TGDs, CQ- and hom-conservative extensions are undecidable, but triviality is decidable.
2. For guarded TGDs, triviality is undecidable.
3. For frontier-one TGDs, CQ- and hom-conservative extensions are decidable.

[1]A homomorphism that disregards symbols outside of Σ_Q.

We consider it remarkable that undecidability already appears for a class as restricted as linear TGDs. Regarding Point 1, we also determine the exact complexity of triviality for linear TGDs as being PSPACE-complete, and CONP-complete when the arity of relation symbols is bounded by a constant. Regarding Point 3, our algorithms yield 3EXPTIME upper bounds, while 2EXPTIME lower bounds can be imported from the DL $\mathcal{ELI}$, a fragment of frontier-one TGDs (Gutiérrez-Basulto, Jung, and Sabellek 2018; Jung et al. 2020). The exact complexity remains open.

Our undecidability results are proved by reductions from a convergence problem that concerns Conway functions (Conway 1972). In a database theory context, such a technique has been used in (Gogacz and Marcinkowski 2014). As the reader shall see, the reductions take place in the setting of Pyramus and Thisbe (Ovid 2008), a mythological couple that could only communicate through a crack in the wall and whose fate it was to never meet again in person. Bring some popcorn. The decidability result for hom-conservative extensions for frontier-one TGDs rests on the observation that whenever there is a database that witnesses non-conservativity, then there is such a database of bounded treewidth. This enables a decision procedure based on alternating tree automata. The case of CQ-conservative extensions is more intricate as it requires the use of *homomorphism limits*, that is, families of homomorphisms that can only look n steps 'into the model', for any n. It is not clear how the existence of homomorphism limits can be verified by tree automata. Our solution generalizes the approach to CQ-conservative extensions in $\mathcal{ELI}$ pursued in (Jung et al. 2020). In short, the idea is to push the use of homomorphism limits to parts of the chase that are Σ_Q-disconnected from the database and regular in shape, and to then characterize homomorphism limits from/into such regular (infinite) databases in terms of unbounded homomorphisms.

Related Work. We already mentioned the work on DLs from the DL-Lite and $\mathcal{ELI}$ families (Konev et al. 2011; Jung et al. 2020). For description logics such as $\mathcal{ALC}$ that support negation and disjunction, CQ- and hom-conservative extensions are undecidable (Botoeva et al. 2019). A different kind of conservative extension is obtained by replacing databases and query answers with logical consequences formulated in the ontology language (Ghilardi, Lutz, and Wolter 2006). While such conservative extensions are decidable in $\mathcal{ALC}$ (Ghilardi, Lutz, and Wolter 2006; Lutz, Walther, and Wolter 2007), they are undecidable in the guarded fragment and in the two-variable fragment of first-order logic (Jung et al. 2017). For existential rule languages, the difference between this version of conservative extensions and CQ-conservative extensions tends to be small (depending on the class of rules considered).

2 Preliminaries

Relational Databases. Fix countably infinite and pairwise disjoint sets of *constants* $\mathbf{C}$ and $\mathbf{N}$ and variables $\mathbf{V}$. We refer to the constants in $\mathbf{N}$ as *nulls*. A *schema* Σ is a set of relation symbols R with associated arity $\mathsf{ar}(R) \geq 1$. A Σ-*fact* is an expression of the form $R(\bar{c})$ with $R \in \Sigma$ and $\bar{c}$ is an $\mathsf{ar}(R)$-tuple of constants from $\mathbf{C} \cup \mathbf{N}$. A Σ-*instance* is a possibly infinite set of Σ-facts, and a Σ-*database* is a finite Σ-instance that uses only constants from $\mathbf{C}$. We write $\mathsf{adom}(I)$ for the set of constants from $\mathbf{C} \cup \mathbf{N}$ used in instance I. For an instance I and a schema Σ, $I|_\Sigma$ denotes the restriction of I to Σ, that is, the set of all facts in I that use a relation symbol from Σ. We say that I is *connected* (resp., Σ-*connected*) if the Gaifman graph of I (resp., $I|_\Sigma$) is connected and that I is of *finite degree* if the Gaifman graph of I has finite degree.

For a schema Σ, a Σ-*homomorphism* from instance I to instance J is a function $h : \mathsf{adom}(I) \to \mathsf{adom}(J)$ such that $R(h(\bar{c})) \in J$ for every $R(\bar{c}) \in I$ with $R \in \Sigma$. We say that h is *database-preserving* if it is the identity on all constants from $\mathbf{C}$ (but not necessarily from $\mathbf{N}$) and write $I \to_\Sigma J$ if there is a database-preserving Σ-homomorphism from I to J.

Conjunctive Queries. A *conjunctive query* (CQ) over a schema Σ takes the form $\exists \bar{y}\, \phi(\bar{x}, \bar{y})$ where $\bar{x}$ and $\bar{y}$ are tuples of variables from $\mathbf{V}$, ϕ is a set of *atoms* $R(\bar{z})$ with $R \in \Sigma$ and $\bar{z}$ a tuple of variables of length $\mathsf{ar}(R)$. We refer to the variables in $\bar{x}$ as the *answer variables* of q and denote a CQ with $q(\bar{x})$ to emphasize that it has answer variables $\bar{x}$. The *arity* of q is the length $|\bar{x}|$ of $\bar{x}$, and q is *Boolean* if it is of arity 0.

Every CQ $q(\bar{x})$ gives rise to a database D_q, known as the *canonical database* of q, by viewing variables as constants and atoms as facts. A Σ-*homomorphism* h from q to an instance I is a Σ-homomorphism from D_q to I. A tuple $\bar{c} \in \mathsf{adom}(I)^{|\bar{x}|}$ is an *answer* to q on I if there is a homomorphism h from q to I with $h(\bar{x}) = \bar{c}$. The *evaluation of* $q(\bar{x})$ *on* I, denoted $q(I)$, is the set of all answers to q on I.

For a CQ q, but also for any other syntactic object q, we use $||q||$ to denote the number of symbols needed to write q encoded as a word over a suitable alphabet.

TGDs. A *tuple-generating dependency* (TGD) ϑ is a first-order sentence $\forall \bar{x} \forall \bar{y}\, (\phi(\bar{x}, \bar{y}) \to \exists \bar{z}\, \psi(\bar{x}, \bar{z}))$ such that $q_\varphi = \exists \bar{y}\, \phi(\bar{x}, \bar{y})$ and $q_\psi = \exists \bar{z}\, \psi(\bar{x}, \bar{z})$ are CQs. We call ϕ and ψ the *body* and *head* of ϑ. The body may be the empty conjunction, that is, logical truth. The variables in $\bar{x}$ are the *frontier variables*. We may write ϑ as $\phi(\bar{x}, \bar{y}) \to \exists \bar{z}\, \psi(\bar{x}, \bar{z})$. An instance I *satisfies* ϑ, denoted $I \models \vartheta$, if $q_\phi(I) \subseteq q_\psi(I)$. It *satisfies* a set of TGDs T if $I \models \vartheta$ for each $\vartheta \in T$. We then also say that I is a *model* of T.

A TGD ϑ is *frontier-one* if it has exactly one frontier variable (Baget et al. 2011). It is *guarded* if its body is empty or contains a *guard atom* α that contains all variables in the body (Calì, Gottlob, and Kifer 2013). A TGD is *linear* if its body contains at most one atom. Clearly, every linear TGD is guarded. The *body width* of a set T of TGDs is the maximum number of variables in a rule body of a TGD in T, and the *head width* is defined accordingly.

Throughout this paper, we are going to make use of the well-known chase procedure for making explicit the consequences of a set of TGDs (Johnson and Klug 1984; Fagin et al. 2005; Calì, Gottlob, and Kifer 2013). Let I be an instance and T a set of TGDs. A TGD $\phi(\bar{x}, \bar{y}) \to \exists \bar{z}\, \psi(\bar{x}, \bar{z}) \in T$ is *applicable* at a tuple $\bar{c}$ of constants in I if $\phi(\bar{c}, \bar{c}') \subseteq I$ for some $\bar{c}'$ and there is no homomorphism h from $\psi(\bar{x}, \bar{z})$ to I such that $h(\bar{x}) = \bar{c}$. In this case, the *result* *of applying the TGD in I at $\bar{c}$* is the instance $I \cup \{\psi(\bar{c}, \bar{c}'')\}$ where $\bar{c}''$ is the tuple obtained from $\bar{z}$ by replacing each variable z with a fresh null, that is, a null that does not occur in I. We also refer to such an application as a *chase step*.

A *chase sequence for I with T* is a sequence of instances $I_0, I_1, \dots$ such that $I_0 = I$ and each I_{i+1} is the result of a chase step from I_i. The *result* of the chase sequence is the instance $J = \bigcup_{i \geq 0} I_i$. The chase sequence is *fair* if whenever a TGD from T is applicable to a tuple $\bar{c}$ in some I_i, then this application is a chase step in the sequence. Every fair chase sequence for I with T has the same result, up to homomorphic equivalence. Since for our purposes all results are equally useful, we use $\mathsf{chase}_T(I)$ to denote the result of an arbitrary, but fixed chase sequence for I with T and call $\mathsf{chase}_T(I)$ the *result of chasing I with T*. This version of the chase is often called the *restricted chase* and it ensures that $\mathsf{chase}_T(D)$ has finite degree, which shall be important for our proofs.

Lemma 1. *Let T be a set of TGDs and I an instance. Then for every model J of T with $I \subseteq J$, there is a homomorphism h from $\mathsf{chase}_T(I)$ to J that is the identity on $\mathsf{adom}(I)$.*

Note that if T is a set of frontier-one TGDs, then for any database D the instance $\mathsf{chase}_T(D)$ can be obtained from D by 'glueing' a (potentially infinite) instance onto each constant $c \in \mathsf{adom}(D)$. We denote this instance with $\mathsf{chase}_T(D)|_c^{\downarrow}$. A precise definition is given in the appendix.

Let T be a set of TGDs, $q(\bar{x})$ a CQ and D a database. A tuple $\bar{c} \in \mathsf{adom}(D)^{|\bar{x}|}$ is an *answer* to q on D w.r.t. T, written $D, T \models q(\bar{c})$, if $q(\bar{c})$ is logically follows from $D \cup T$ or, equivalently, if there is a homomorphism h from q to $\mathsf{chase}_T(D)$ with $h(\bar{x}) = \bar{c}$. The *evaluation of q on D w.r.t. T*, denoted $q_T(D)$, is the set of all answers to q on D w.r.t. T.

3 Conservative Extensions

We introduce the notions of conservative extension that are studied in this paper and the associated decision problems.

Definition 1. *Let T_1, T_2 be sets of TGDs and let Σ_D, Σ_Q be schemas called the* data schema *and* query schema*. Then*

- *T_2 is* Σ_D, Σ_Q-hom-conservative *over T_1, written $T_1 \models^{hom}_{\Sigma_D,\Sigma_Q} T_2$, if there is a database-preserving Σ_Q-homomorphism from $\mathsf{chase}_{T_2}(D)$ to $\mathsf{chase}_{T_1}(D)$ for all Σ_D-databases D;*
- *T_2 is* Σ_D, Σ_Q-CQ-conservative *over T_1, written $T_1 \models^{CQ}_{\Sigma_D,\Sigma_Q} T_2$, if $q_{T_2}(D) \subseteq q_{T_1}(D)$ for all Σ_D-databases D and all CQs q over schema Σ_Q.*
- *T_1 is Σ_D, Σ_Q-hom-trivial if T_1 is Σ_D, Σ_Q-hom-conservative over the empty set of TGDs, and likewise for* Σ_D, Σ_Q-CQ-triviality.

It is easy to see that logical entailment $T_1 \models T_2$ implies $T_1 \models^{\text{hom}}_{\Sigma_D,\Sigma_Q} T_2$ for all schemas Σ_D and Σ_Q, and that Σ_D, Σ_Q-hom-conservativity implies Σ_D, Σ_Q-CQ-conservativity. The following example from (Botoeva et al. 2016) shows that the converse fails.

Example 1. *Consider the following sets of TGDs that are both linear and frontier-one:*

$$T_1 = \{\, A(x) \to \exists y\, S(x,y), B(y), \quad B(x) \to \exists y\, R(x,y), B(y) \,\}$$

$$T_2 = \{\, A(x) \to \exists y\, S(x,y), B(y), \quad B(x) \to \exists y\, R(y,x), B(y) \,\}.$$

Let $\Sigma_D = \{A\}$ and $\Sigma_Q = \{R\}$. We recommend to the reader to verify that T_2 is not Σ_D, Σ_Q-hom-conservative over T_1 by trying to find a database-preserving homomorphism from $\mathsf{chase}_{T_2}(D)$ to $\mathsf{chase}_{T_1}(D)$, and that it is Σ_D, Σ_Q-CQ-conservative.

However, Σ_D, Σ_Q-hom-conservativity is equivalent to Σ_D, Σ_Q-CQ-conservativity with infinitary CQs. We refrain from making this precise and instead consider the converse, that is, Σ_D, Σ_Q-CQ-conservativity is equivalent to Σ_D, Σ_Q-hom-conservativity when the latter is defined in terms of a finitary version of homomorphisms that we introduce next.

Let I_1, I_2 be instances and $n \geq 0$, and let Σ be a schema. We write $I_1 \to^n_\Sigma I_2$ if for every induced subinstance I of I_1 with $|\mathsf{adom}(I)| \leq n$, there is a database-preserving Σ-homomorphism from I to I_2. We further write $I_1 \to^{\mathsf{lim}}_\Sigma I_2$ if $I_1 \to^n_\Sigma I_2$ for all $n \geq 1$.

Theorem 1. *Let T_1 and T_2 be sets of TGDs and Σ_D, Σ_Q schemas. Then $T_1 \models^{CQ}_{\Sigma_D,\Sigma_Q} T_2$ iff $\mathsf{chase}_{T_2}(D) \to^{\mathsf{lim}}_{\Sigma_Q} \mathsf{chase}_{T_1}(D)$.*

For triviality, the hom- and CQ-version coincide.

Lemma 2. *Let T_1, T_2 be sets of TGDs and Σ_D, Σ_Q schemas. Then T_1 and T_2 are Σ_D, Σ_Q-hom-trivial if and only if they are Σ_D, Σ_Q-CQ-trivial.*

Because of Lemma 2, we from now on disregard Σ_D, Σ_Q-CQ-triviality and refer to Σ_D, Σ_Q-hom-triviality simply as Σ_D, Σ_Q-*triviality*. We thus obtain the three decision problems *hom-conservativity*, *CQ-conservativity*, and *triviality*, defined in the obvious way. For instance, hom-conservativity means to decide, given finite sets of TGDs T_1, T_2 and finite schemas Σ_D, Σ_Q, whether T_2 is Σ_D, Σ_Q-hom-conservative over T_1.

We note that Lemma 2 is an immediate consequence of Theorem 1 and the following observation.

Lemma 3. *Let I_1, I_2 be instances such that I_1 is countable and I_2 is finite, and let Σ be a schema. If $I_1 \to^{\mathsf{lim}}_\Sigma I_2$, then $I_1 \to_\Sigma I_2$.*

We sketch the proof of Lemma 3, details are in the appendix. If $I_1 \to^{\mathsf{lim}}_\Sigma I_2$, then we find database-preserving Σ-homomorphisms $h_1, h_2, \dots$ from finite subinstances $J_1 \subseteq J_2 \subseteq \dots$ of I_1 to I_2 such that $I_1 = \bigcup_{i \geq 1} J_i$. If $h_1, h_2, \dots$ are compatible in the sense that $h_i(c) = h_j(c)$ whenever $h_i(c), h_j(c)$ are both defined, then $\bigcup_{i \geq 1} h_i$ is a Σ-homomorphism that witnesses $I_1 \to_\Sigma I_2$. If this is not the case, however, we can still manipulate $h_1, h_2, \dots$ into a compatible sequence $g_1, g_2, \dots$ by 'skipping homomorphisms', which is used in several proofs in this paper. We start with h_1 and observe that since J_1 and I_2 are finite, there are only

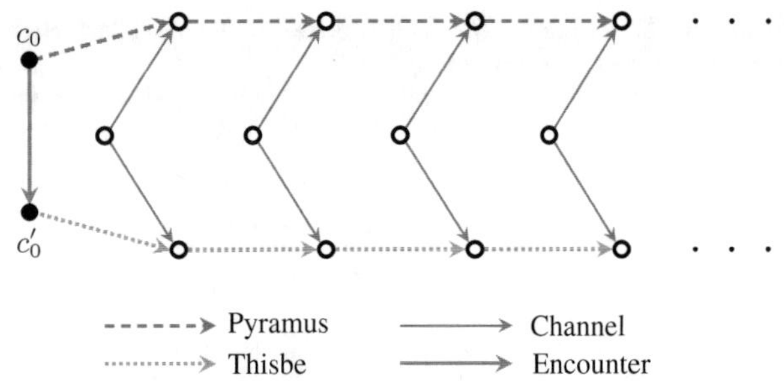

Figure 1: Chase generated by T_{myth}.

finitely many homomorphisms h from J_1 to I_2. Some such homomorphism must occur infinitely often in the restrictions of $h_1, h_2, \ldots$ to $\mathsf{adom}(J_1)$ and thus we find a subsequence $h_1', h_2', \ldots$ of $h_1, h_2, \ldots$ in which h_1' is compatible with all of $h_2', h_3', \ldots$. We proceed in the same way for h_2', then for h_3', ad infinitum, finding the desired sequence $g_1, g_2, \ldots$.

4 Undecidability

The aim of this section is to prove the following results.

Theorem 2. *The following problems are undecidable:*

1. *hom-conservativity for linear TGDs;*
2. *CQ-conservativity for linear TGDs;*
3. *triviality for guarded TGDs.*

We give a single proof that establishes Points 1 and 2. Attaining Point 3 requires a non-trivial modification of the proof. We start with the former, first highlighting the main mechanism that we use in our reduction.

4.1 The Main Mechanism

Consider the set of rules T_{myth}. It comprises three TGDs:

$$\begin{array}{rcl} \mathsf{Encounter}(p,t) & \rightarrow & \exists p',c,t'\ M(p,p',c,t',t) \\ M(p,p',c,t',t) & \rightarrow & \exists p'',c',t''\ M(p',p'',c',t'',t') \\ M(p,p',c,t',t) & \rightarrow & \mathsf{Pyramus}(p,p'),\mathsf{Thisbe}(t,t'), \\ & & \mathsf{Channel}(c,p'),\mathsf{Channel}(c,t'). \end{array}$$

Now consider the database $D = \{\mathsf{Encounter}(c_0, c_0')\}$. The instance $\mathsf{chase}_{T_{\mathsf{myth}}}(D)$, shown in Figure 1, will play an important role. Its intuitive meaning is that '*after an initial brief encounter, Pyramus and Thisbe have never met again, but forever remained able to connect via an (indirect) channel.*' Notice that we do not explicitly show relation M in Figure 1 as M is only a construction aid, needed to ensure that the TGDs in T_{myth} are linear. As Σ_Q, we will use the set of relation symbols in T_{myth} except M, plus a unary relation symbol Mouth. We advise the reader to not worry about the schema Σ_D at this point (it will actually be empty).

Let $\kappa = \langle [p_1, \ldots, p_n], [t_1, \ldots, t_n] \rangle$ be a pair of sequences of positive integers of the same length n. By River_κ, we mean the database that contains the following facts, an example being displayed in Figure 2:

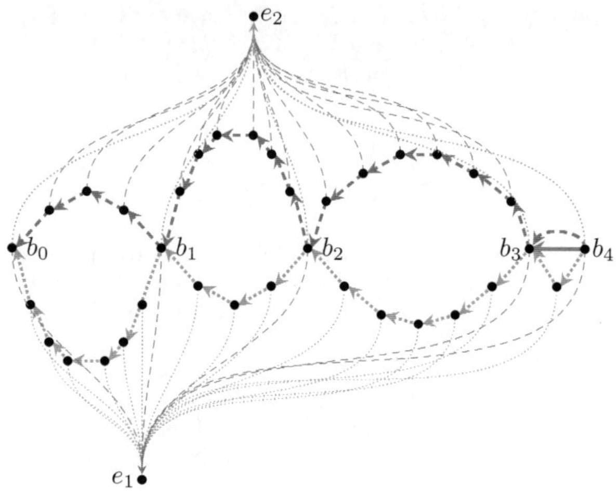

Figure 2: The database River_κ for $\kappa = \langle [4,7,7,1], [7,4,6,2] \rangle$.

- There are 3 kinds of constants. The *eternities* are e_1 and e_2. The *channel* is c, not shown in the picture. All remaining constants are called *worldly*.
- For $1 \leq i \leq n$ there is a Pyramus path of length p_i from b_i to b_{i-1} as well as a Thisbe path of length t_i from b_i to b_{i-1}. Constants b_i are called *bridges*.
- There is $\mathsf{Thisbe}(a, e_1)$ for each non-bridge constant a on each of the Thisbe-paths and there is $\mathsf{Pyramus}(a, e_2)$ for each non-bridge constant a on each of the Pyramus-paths. There are also $\mathsf{Thisbe}(a, e_2)$ and $\mathsf{Pyramus}(a, e_1)$ for each bridge constant a. In addition (and not in Figure 2), there are $\mathsf{Pyramus}(e_i, e_i)$ and $\mathsf{Thisbe}(e_i, e_i)$ for $i \in \{1, 2\}$.
- For each *worldly* constant a, there is $\mathsf{Channel}(c, a)$. Moreover, there are facts $\mathsf{Channel}(e_i, e_i)$, for $i \in \{1, 2\}$. These facts are not shown in Figure 2.
- There are $\mathsf{Encounter}(b_n, b_{n-1})$ and $\mathsf{Mouth}(b_0)$.

It is easy to see that $\mathsf{chase}_{T_{\mathsf{myth}}}(\mathsf{River}_\kappa)$ is obtained from River_κ by adding a copy of the instance shown in Figure 1, glueing the Encounter fact to the Encounter fact in River_κ (and adding some M-facts that are not important here). Now, let us leave to our readers the pleasure to notice that:

Observation 1. *There is a database-preserving Σ_Q-homomorphism from $\mathsf{chase}_{T_{\mathsf{myth}}}(\mathsf{River}_\kappa)$ to River_κ if and only if there exists $m \in \{1, \ldots, n-1\}$ such that $t_m \neq p_{m+1}$.*

Hint: As long as Pyramus and Thisbe walk down their respective river banks they are connected via the constant c. But for their union to last forever they need, at some point, to enter one of the eternities. Since eternity has no channel with the worldly constants (and the two eternities are not connected by a channel either), Pyramus and Thisbe both need to enter the same eternity, and they need to do it simultaneously. But this can only happen when one of them is in a bridge constant and the other in a non-bridge. □

That's nice, isn't it? But where could undecidability be lurking here?

4.2 Conway Functions

Let $\gamma, \alpha_0, \beta_0, \ldots, \alpha_{\gamma-1}, \beta_{\gamma-1}$ be positive integers such that $\beta_k | \gamma$ and $\beta_k | k\alpha_k$ for $0 \leq k < \gamma$ where as usual '|' denotes divisibility without remainder. For a positive integer n, define $F(n)$ by setting $F(n) = n\alpha_k/\beta_k$ for $k = n \bmod \gamma$. Thus, the remainder of n when dividing by γ determines the pair (α_k, β_k) used to compute the value $F(n)$. Note that due to the two divisibility conditions, the range of F contains only positive integers.

The function F is called the *Conway function defined by* $\gamma, \alpha_0, \beta_0, \ldots, \alpha_{\gamma-1}, \beta_{\gamma-1}$. We say that F *stops* if there exists an $n \in \mathbb{N}$ such that $F^n(2) = 1$, where F^n is F composed with itself, n times. There is no special meaning to the numbers 1 and 2 used here, we could choose otherwise. The following is well-known, see also (Gogacz and Marcinkowski 2014).

Theorem 3. *It is undecidable whether the Conway function defined by a given sequence* $\gamma, \alpha_0, \beta_0, \ldots, \alpha_{\gamma-1}, \beta_{\gamma-1}$ *stops.*

Take a sequence $\gamma, \alpha_0, \beta_0, \ldots, \alpha_{\gamma-1}, \beta_{\gamma-1}$ defining a Conway function F. We prove Points 1 and 2 of Theorem 2 by showing how to compute, given the sequence, sets T_1 and T_2 of linear TGDs along with schemas Σ_D, Σ_Q such that F does not stop if and only if T_2 is Σ_D, Σ_Q-hom-conservative over T_1 if and only if T_2 is Σ_D, Σ_Q-CQ-conservative over T_1. We assume without loss of generality that $F(1) = 1$ and $F(2) = 3$.

4.3 The Reduction

We say that $\kappa = \langle [p_1, \ldots, p_n], [t_1, \ldots, t_n] \rangle$ (or River_κ) is

- *locally correct* if the following conditions hold:
  1. $p_1 = 2$ and $p_n = 1$;
  2. $F(p_i) = t_i$ for $1 \leq i < n$;
- *correct* if it is locally correct and $t_i = p_{i+1}$ for $1 \leq i < n$.

The database River_κ shown in Figure 2 is not locally correct because $p_1 \neq 2$ and $t_n \neq 1$ (which must be the case as we assume $F(1) = 1$).

Clearly, F does not stop if and only if every locally correct River_κ is incorrect, and by Observation 1 this is the case if and only if for each locally correct sequence κ there exists a database-preserving Σ_Q-homomorphism from $\mathsf{chase}_{T_{\mathsf{myth}}}(\mathsf{River}_\kappa)$ to River_κ.

Now the plan is as follows. Take $\Sigma_D = \emptyset$. We define T_1 such that $\mathsf{chase}_{T_1}(\emptyset)$ is the 'disjoint union' of all locally correct databases River_κ. Our T_2 will be the union of T_1 and T_{myth}. A careful reader can notice that if this plan succeeds, then the proof of Point 1 of Theorem 2 will be completed. And it will indeed succeed, but not without one little nuance. This is the reason why we used quotations mark around the term 'disjoint union' above.

The set of TGDs T_1 is the union of two sets of linear TGDs T_{rec} and T_{proj}. As intended, T_1 generates the union of all locally correct databases River_κ. The mentioned nuance is that the union is not disjoint, but massively overlapping. However, this does not compromise correctness of the reduction.

The rules of T_{rec} will not mention symbols from Σ_Q. They instead use a schema Σ_F that consists of high arity relation symbols used as construction aids. We later use T_{proj} to relate these symbols to those in Σ_Q. More precisely, Σ_F contains relation symbols Start of arity 8, End of arity 5, Bridge of arity 4, WH^i_k (for WorkHorse) of arity $\alpha_k + \beta_k + 5$ for $0 \leq k, i < \gamma$, and BH_k (for BridgeHead) of arity $\alpha_k + \beta_k + 5$ for $0 \leq k < \gamma$. In what follows, we use $\dagger$ to denote the list of variables 'c, e_1, e_2'. With $+_\gamma$ and $-_\gamma$, we denote addition and subtraction in the ring $\mathbb{Z}_\gamma$.

Since $\Sigma_D = \emptyset$, first of all we need a rule that will create something out of nothing:

$$\rightarrow \ \exists \dagger, b_0, x_1, y_1, y_2, b_1 \ \mathsf{Start}(\dagger, b_0, x_1, y_1, y_2, b_1).$$

Later, T_{proj} will generate a Pyramus-path from b_1 via x_1 to b_0 and a Thisbe-path from b_1 via y_2 and y_1 to b_0, determining the lengths $p_1 = 2$ and $t_1 = 3$ of the river. Recall that local correctness prescribes $p_1 = 2$ and we assume $F(2) = 3$. We need to know that b_1 is a bridge:

$$\mathsf{Start}(\dagger, b_0, x_1, y_1, y_2, b_1) \ \rightarrow \ \mathsf{Bridge}(\dagger, b_1).$$

We now put our horses to work by adding, for $0 \leq k < \gamma$:

$$\mathsf{Bridge}(\dagger, b) \rightarrow \exists x_1, \ldots, x_{\beta_i}, y_1, \ldots, y_{\alpha_i} \quad \mathsf{WH}^{\beta_k}_k(\dagger, b, x_1, \ldots, x_{\beta_k}, b, y_1, \ldots, y_{\alpha_k})$$

and for $0 \leq k, i < \gamma$:

$$\mathsf{WH}^i_k(\dagger, x_0, x_1, \ldots, x_{\beta_k}, y_0, y_1, \ldots, y_{\alpha_k}) \rightarrow \exists z_1, \ldots, z_{\beta_k}, u_1, \ldots, u_{\alpha_k} \quad \mathsf{WH}^{i+_\gamma \beta_k}_k(\dagger, x_{\beta_k}, z_1, \ldots, z_{\beta_k}, y_{\alpha_k}, u_1, \ldots, u_{\alpha_k}).$$

$\mathsf{WH}^i_k(\dagger, c_0, c_1, \ldots, x_{\beta_k}, y_0, y_1, \ldots, y_{\alpha_k})$ promises to generate, via T_{proj}, a Pyramus-path of length β_k from x_{β_k} to x_0 and a Thisbe-path of length α_k from y_{α_k} to y_0. The above two rules thus patiently produce Pyramus- and Thisbe-paths that lead to b. The superscript $\cdot^i$ remembers how many Pyramus-edges have been produced since the last bridge, modulo γ, and the subscript $\cdot_k$ chooses a remainder class, that is, it expresses the promise that the Pyramus-path between the two bridges is of length n, for some number n with $n \bmod \gamma = k$.

Then, at some point, the next bridge can be reached:

$$\mathsf{WH}^{k-_\gamma \beta_k}_k(\dagger, x_0, x_1, \ldots, x_{\beta_k}, y_0, y_1, \ldots, y_{\alpha_k}) \rightarrow \exists z_1, \ldots, z_{\beta_k - 1}, u_1, \ldots, u_{\alpha_k - 1}, b \quad \mathsf{BH}_k(\dagger, x_{\beta_k}, z_1, \ldots, z_{\beta_k - 1}, b, y_{\alpha_k}, u_1, \ldots, u_{\alpha_k - 1}, b)$$

$$\mathsf{BH}_k(\dagger, x_{\beta_k}, z_1, \ldots, z_{\beta_k - 1}, b, y_{\alpha_k}, u_1, \ldots, u_{\alpha_k - 1}, b) \rightarrow \mathsf{Bridge}(\dagger, b).$$

In the first rule above, relation $\mathsf{WH}^{k-_\gamma \beta_k}_k$ indicates that we have seen m Pyramus-edges, for some m with $m \bmod \gamma = k -_\gamma \beta_k$, and that BH_k will generate β_k more Pyramus-edges, thus arriving at the promised remainder of k. It is also easy to see that if the chosen remainder class was k and the length of the Pyramus-path between two bridges produced by the above rules is n, then the length of the Thisbe-path is $F(n) = n\alpha_k/\beta_k$. Thus, Point 2 of local correctness is satisfied.

Finally, we want to produce the last[2] segment of the river:

$$\mathsf{Bridge}(\dagger, b) \rightarrow \exists b' \ \mathsf{End}(\dagger, b, b')$$

[2]Orographically the first, as we generate the river from the mouth to the source.

This will generate direct Pyramus- and Thisbe-edges from b' to b (recall that $F(1) = 1$).

The TGDs in T_{rec} generate the actual rivers as projections of the template produced by T_{rec}. We start at the mouth:

$$\begin{aligned}&\mathsf{Start}(\dagger, b_0, x_1, y_1, y_2, b_1) \rightarrow\\ &\quad \mathsf{Mouth}(b_0),\\ &\quad \mathsf{Pyramus}(x_1, b_0), \mathsf{Pyramus}(b_1, x_1), \mathsf{Pyramus}(x_1, e_2),\\ &\quad \mathsf{Thisbe}(y_1, b_0), \mathsf{Thisbe}(y_2, y_1), \mathsf{Thisbe}(b_1, y_2),\\ &\quad \mathsf{Thisbe}(y_1, e_1), \mathsf{Thisbe}(y_2, e_1),\\ &\quad \mathsf{Channel}(c, x_1), \mathsf{Channel}(c, y_1), \mathsf{Channel}(c, y_2),\\ &\quad \mathsf{Channel}(e_1, e_1), \mathsf{Pyramus}(e_1, e_1), \mathsf{Thisbe}(e_1, e_1)\\ &\quad \mathsf{Channel}(e_2, e_2), \mathsf{Pyramus}(e_2, e_2), \mathsf{Thisbe}(e_2, e_2).\end{aligned}$$

The rules for WH^i_k are then as expected:

$$\begin{aligned}&\mathsf{WH}^i_k(\dagger, x_0, x_1, \ldots, x_{\beta_k}, y_0, y_1, \ldots, y_{\alpha_k}) \rightarrow\\ &\quad \mathsf{Pyramus}(x_1, x_0), \ldots, \mathsf{Pyramus}(x_{\beta_k}, x_{\beta_k - 1}),\\ &\quad \mathsf{Pyramus}(x_1, e_2), \ldots, \mathsf{Pyramus}(x_{\beta_k}, e_2),\\ &\quad \mathsf{Thisbe}(y_1, y_0), \ldots, \mathsf{Thisbe}(y_{\alpha_k}, y_{\alpha_k - 1}),\\ &\quad \mathsf{Thisbe}(y_1, e_1), \ldots, \mathsf{Thisbe}(y_{\alpha_k}, e_1),\\ &\quad \mathsf{Channel}(c, x_1), \ldots, \mathsf{Channel}(c, x_{\beta_k}),\\ &\quad \mathsf{Channel}(c, y_1), \ldots, \mathsf{Channel}(c, y_{\alpha_k}).\end{aligned}$$

Rules for the relations BH_i are analogous, so we skip them. There are also rules for projecting relations Bridge and End:

$$\begin{aligned}&\mathsf{Bridge}(\dagger, b) \rightarrow \mathsf{Channel}(c, b), \mathsf{Pyramus}(b, e_1), \mathsf{Thisbe}(b, e_2)\\ &\mathsf{End}(\dagger, b, b') \rightarrow \mathsf{Pyramus}(b', b), \mathsf{Thisbe}(b', b),\\ &\qquad\qquad \mathsf{Encounter}(b, b').\end{aligned}$$

In the appendix, we show that:

Lemma 4. *F does not stop iff $T_2 = T_1 \cup T_{\text{myth}}$ is Σ_Q, Σ_D-hom-conservative over $T_1 = T_{\text{rec}} \cup T_{\text{proj}}$.*

This establishes Point 1 of Theorem 2. For the "if" direction, one shows that if $\mathsf{chase}_{T_2}(\emptyset) \rightarrow_{\Sigma_Q} \mathsf{chase}_{T_1}(\emptyset)$, then every locally correct river is incorrect, and thus F stops. Since rivers may be long, but are finite, it actually suffices that $\mathsf{chase}_{T_2}(\emptyset) \rightarrow^{\lim}_{\Sigma_Q} \mathsf{chase}_{T_1}(\emptyset)$ for F to stop, which by Theorem 1 gives Point 2 of Theorem 2.

For Point 3 of Theorem 2, we again want to use the toolkit above, in particular T_{myth} and Observation 1. But the situation is a bit different now. In the above reduction, we had at our disposal T_1 which was able to produce, from nothing, all the rivers we needed. So we could afford to have $\Sigma_D = \emptyset$. Now, however, we no longer have T_1, but only T_2, and our strategy is as follows. Recall that F stops if and only if there is a locally correct River_κ that is correct, and that River_κ is correct if there is no database-preserving Σ_Q-homomorphism from $\mathsf{chase}_{T_{\text{myth}}}(\mathsf{River}_\kappa)$ to River_κ. We use the database D to guess a River_κ that admits no such homomorphism. More precisely, we design T_2 so that it verifies the existence of a (single) locally correct river in D and only if successful generates a chase with T_{myth} at the Encounter fact of that river. Details are in the appendix.

5 Triviality for Linear TGDs

We show that for linear TGDs, Σ_D, Σ_Q-triviality is decidable and PSPACE-complete, while it is only coNP-complete when the arity of relation symbols is bounded by a constant. The upper bounds crucially rely on the observation that non-triviality is always witnessed by a *singleton database*, that is, a database that contains at most one fact. This was first noted (for CQ-conservative extensions) in the context of the decription logic DL-Lite (Konev et al. 2011).

Lemma 5. *Let T be a set of linear TGDs and Σ_D, Σ_Q schemas. Then T is Σ_D, Σ_Q-trivial iff $\mathsf{chase}_T(D) \rightarrow_{\Sigma_Q} D$ for all singleton Σ_D-databases D.*

So an important part of deciding triviality is to decide, given a set of TGDs T and a singleton database D, whether $\mathsf{chase}_T(D) \not\rightarrow_{\Sigma_Q} D$. The basis for this is the subsequent lemma.

Lemma 6. *Let T be a set of linear TGDs and D a singleton database. Then $\mathsf{chase}_T(D) \not\rightarrow_{\Sigma_Q} D$ implies that there is a connected database $C \subseteq \mathsf{chase}_T(D)$ that contains at most two facts and such that $C \not\rightarrow_{\Sigma_Q} D$.*

Lemmas 5 and 6 provide us with a decision procedure for triviality for linear TGDs. Given a finite set of linear TGDs T and finite schemas Σ_D and Σ_Q, all we have to do is iterate over all singleton Σ_D-databases D and over all $C \subseteq \mathsf{chase}_T(D)$ that contain at most two facts and check (in polynomial time) whether $C \rightarrow_{\Sigma_Q} D$. To identify the sets C, we can iterate over all exponentially many candidates and check for each of them whether $D, T \models q_C$, where q_C is C viewed as a Boolean CQ. This entailment check is possible in PSPACE (Gottlob, Manna, and Pieris 2015). This yields the PSPACE upper bound in the following result.

Theorem 4. *For linear TGDs, triviality is PSPACE-complete. It is coNP-complete if the arity of relation symbols is bounded by a constant.*

To obtain the coNP upper bound, we recall that when the arity of relation symbols is bounded by a constant, then the entailment check '$D, T \models q_C$' is in NP (Gottlob et al. 2014). To decide non-triviality, we may thus guess D and C and verify in polynomial time that $C \not\rightarrow_{\Sigma_Q} D$ and in NP that $D, T \models q_C$. For the lower bounds, we reduce entailments of the form $D, T \models \exists x\, A(x)$, with T a set of linear TGDs, to non-triviality for linear TGDs. This problem is PSPACE-hard in general (Casanova, Fagin, and Papadimitriou 1984) and it is common knowledge that it is NP-hard when the arity of relation symbols is bounded by a constant. The reduction goes as follows. Let D, T, and $\exists x\, A(x)$ be given. Introduce a fresh binary relation symbol R, set $\Sigma_D = \Sigma_Q = \{R\}$, and let T' be the extension of T with the TGDs

$$\begin{aligned} &\rightarrow \; q_D\\ A(u) \; &\rightarrow \; \exists x \exists y \exists z\, R(x, y), R(y, z)\end{aligned}$$

where q_D is D viewed as a Boolean CQ. Note that there is no homomorphism from $R(x, y), R(y, z)$ into the singleton Σ_D-database $\{R(c, c')\}$. Based on this, it is easy to verify that T' is Σ_D, Σ_Q-trivial iff $D, T \not\models \exists x\, A(x)$.

6 Frontier-One TGDs

The purpose of this section is to show the following.

Theorem 5. *For frontier-one TGDs, CQ-conservativity and hom-conservativity are decidable in* 3EXPTIME *(and* 2EXPTIME*-hard).*

2EXPTIME lower bounds carry over from the description logic $\mathcal{ELI}$, see (Gutiérrez-Basulto, Jung, and Sabellek 2018) for hom-conservativity and (Jung et al. 2020) for CQ-conservativity. They already apply when only unary and binary relation symbols are admitted. In the remainder of the section, we thus concentrate on the upper bounds.

Both in the case of hom-conservativity and CQ-conservativity, we first provide a suitable model-theoretic characterization and then use it to find a decision procedure based on tree automata. The case of CQ-conservativity is significantly more challenging because of the appearance of homomorphism limits.

6.1 Deciding Hom-Conservativity

We show that to decide hom-conservativity, it suffices to consider databases of bounded treewidth. Instead of using the standard notion of a tree decomposition, however, it is more convenient for us to work with so-called tree-like databases. Variations of these have been used for instance in (Benedikt, Bourhis, and Senellart 2012; Jung et al. 2018).

A *Σ-instance tree* is a triple $\mathcal{T} = (V, E, B)$ with (V, E) a directed tree and B a function that assigns a Σ-database $B(v)$ to every $v \in V$ such that the following conditions hold:

1. for every $a \in \bigcup_{v \in V} \mathsf{adom}(B(v))$, the restriction of (V, E) to the nodes $v \in V$ such that $a \in \mathsf{adom}(B(v))$ is a tree of depth at most one;
2. for every $(u, v) \in E$, $|\mathsf{adom}(B(u)) \cap \mathsf{adom}(B(v))| \leq 1$.

The *width* of the instance tree is the supremum of the cardinalities of $\mathsf{adom}(B(v))$, $v \in V$. A Σ-instance tree $\mathcal{T}$ defines an associated instance $I_\mathcal{T} = \bigcup_{v \in V} B(v)$. A Σ-instance I is *tree-like of width* k if there is a Σ-instance tree $\mathcal{T}$ of width k with $I = I_\mathcal{T}$.

Instance trees of width k are closely related to tree decompositions of width k in which the bags overlap in at most one constant. Condition 1, however, strengthens the usual connectedness condition to trees of depth 1. This strengthening is crucial for our constructions and not possible for other classes of TGDs such as guarded TGDs.

Theorem 6. *Let T_1 and T_2 be sets of frontier-one TGDs, and Σ_D and Σ_Q schemas. Let k be the body width of T_1. Then the following are equivalent:*

1. $T_1 \models^{hom}_{\Sigma_D, \Sigma_Q} T_2$;
2. $\mathsf{chase}_{T_2}(D) \rightarrow_{\Sigma_Q} \mathsf{chase}_{T_1}(D)$, *for all tree-like Σ_D-databases D of width at most k.*

The "1 $\Rightarrow$ 2"-direction is a direct consequence of the definition of hom-conservativity. For the "2 $\Rightarrow$ 1"-direction, let D be a Σ_D-database witnessing $T_1 \not\models^{\text{hom}}_{\Sigma_D, \Sigma_Q} T_2$, that is, $\mathsf{chase}_{T_2}(D) \not\rightarrow_{\Sigma_Q} \mathsf{chase}_{T_1}(D)$. We show in the appendix that the unraveling U of D into a (potentially infinite) tree-like Σ_D-instance of width k also satisfies $\mathsf{chase}_{T_2}(U) \not\rightarrow_{\Sigma_Q} \mathsf{chase}_{T_1}(U)$. Compactness then yields a finite subset U' of U that still satisfies $\mathsf{chase}_{T_2}(U') \not\rightarrow_{\Sigma_Q} \mathsf{chase}_{T_1}(U')$.

We show in the appendix how Theorem 6 can be used to reduce Σ_D, Σ_Q-hom-conservativity to the EXPTIME-complete emptiness problem of two-way alternating tree automata (2ATAs) and in this way obtain a 3EXPTIME upper bound. Here, we only give a sketch. Let T_1 and T_2 be sets of frontier-one TGDs, Σ_D and Σ_Q schemas, k the body width of T_1, and ℓ the head width of T_1.

The 2ATA works on input trees that encode a tree-like database D of width at most k along with a tree-like model I_0 of D and T_1 of width at most $\max\{k, \ell\}$. It verifies that $\mathsf{chase}_{T_2}(D) \not\rightarrow_{\Sigma_Q} I_0$. If such an I_0 is found, then $\mathsf{chase}_{T_2}(D) \not\rightarrow_{\Sigma_Q} \mathsf{chase}_{T_1}(D)$ because $\mathsf{chase}_{T_1}(D) \rightarrow I_0$. The converse is also true since $\mathsf{chase}_{T_1}(D)$ is tree-like of width $\max\{k, \ell\}$. In fact, the instance $\mathsf{chase}_{T_1}(D)|^{\downarrow}_{c}$ that the chase generates below each $c \in \mathsf{adom}(D)$ (see Section 2) is tree-like of width ℓ.

Since our homomorphisms are database-preserving and T_2 is a set of frontier-one TGDs, $\mathsf{chase}_{T_2}(D) \not\rightarrow_{\Sigma_Q} I_0$ if and only if there is a $c \in \mathsf{adom}(D)$ such that $\mathsf{chase}_{T_2}(D)|^{\downarrow}_{c} \not\rightarrow_{\Sigma_Q} I_0$. The 2ATA may thus check this latter condition, which it does by relying on the notion of a type. Since types also play a role in the subsequent sections, we make this precise.

Let T be a set of frontier-one TGDs. We use $\mathsf{bodyCQ}(T)$ to denote the set of unary or Boolean CQs that can be obtained by starting with the Boolean CQ $\exists y \exists \bar{z}\, \phi(y, \bar{z})$ with $\phi(y, \bar{z})$ the body of some TGD in T, then dropping any number of atoms, and then identifying variables. Finally, we may choose a variable as the answer variable and rename it to the fixed variable x (or stick with a Boolean CQ). A *T-type* is a subset $t \subseteq \mathsf{bodyCQ}(T)$ such that for some instance I that is a model of T and some $c \in \mathsf{adom}(I)$,

1. $q(x) \in t$ iff $c \in q(I)$ for all unary $q(x) \in \mathsf{bodyCQ}(T)$ and
2. $q \in t$ iff $I \models q$ for all Boolean $q \in \mathsf{bodyCQ}(T)$.

We then also use $\mathsf{tp}_T(I, c)$ to denote t. We assume that every type contains the additional formula $\mathsf{true}(x)$ (so that x is guaranteed to occur free in t). We may then view t as a unary CQ with free variable x and thus as a (canonical) database. For brevity, we use t also to denote both of these. $\mathsf{TP}(T)$ is the set of all T-types. Note that the number of types is double exponential in $||T||$. The type $\mathsf{tp}_T(\mathsf{chase}_T(D), c)$ tells us everything we need to know about c in the chase of a database D with T, as follows.

Lemma 7. *Let T be a set of frontier-one TGDs, I an instance, and $c \in \mathsf{adom}(I)$. Then $\mathsf{chase}_T(I)|^{\downarrow}_{c}$ and $\mathsf{chase}_T(J)|^{\downarrow}_{c}$ are homomorphically equivalent, where J is obtained from $\mathsf{tp}_T(\mathsf{chase}_T(I), c)$ by replacing the free variable x with c.*

The proof of Lemma 7 is straightforward by reproducing chase steps from the construction of $\mathsf{chase}_T(I)$ in $\mathsf{chase}_T(J)$ and vice versa. Details are omitted.

So to verify that $\mathsf{chase}_{T_2}(D) \not\rightarrow_{\Sigma_Q} I_0$, a 2ATA may guess a constant c in the database D represented by the input tree, and it may also guess the type $\mathsf{tp}_{T_2}(\mathsf{chase}_{T_2}(D), c)$. It then goes on to verify that $\mathsf{tp}_{T_2}(\mathsf{chase}_{T_2}(D), c)$ was guessed correctly (which is not entirely trivial as $\mathsf{chase}_{T_2}(D)$ is *not* encoded in the input). Exploiting Lemma 7, it then starts from type $\mathsf{tp}_{T_2}(\mathsf{chase}_{T_2}(D), c)$ to construct 'in its states' the instance $\mathsf{chase}_{T_2}(D)|_c^{\downarrow}$, simultaneously walking through the instance I_0 encoded by the input tree to verify that, as desired, $\mathsf{chase}_{T_2}(D)|_c^{\downarrow} \not\to_{\Sigma_Q} I_0$ (we actually build a 2ATA for verifying $\mathsf{chase}_{T_2}(D)|_c^{\downarrow} \to_{\Sigma_Q} I_0$ and then complement).

6.2 Deciding CQ-Conservativity

We start with showing that, also for deciding CQ-conservativity, it suffices to consider tree-like databases. In addition, it suffices to consider CQs q of arity 0 or 1.

Theorem 7. *Let T_1 and T_2 be sets of frontier-one TGDs, and Σ_D and Σ_Q schemas. Let k be the body width of T_1. Then the following are equivalent:*

1. $T_1 \models^{CQ}_{\Sigma_D,\Sigma_Q} T_2$;
2. $q_{T_2}(D) \subseteq q_{T_1}(D)$, *for all tree-like Σ_D-databases D of width at most k and connected Σ_Q-CQs q of arity 0 or 1.*

The proof of Theorem 7 first concentrates on restricting the shape of the database, using unraveling and compactness as in the proof of Theorem 6. In a second step, it is then not difficult to restrict also the shape of the CQ.

The following refinement of Theorem 1 is a straightforward consequence of Theorem 7.

Theorem 8. *Let T_1 and T_2 be sets of frontier-one TGDs, Σ_D and Σ_Q schemas, and k the body width of T_1. Then the following are equivalent:*

1. $T_1 \models^{CQ}_{\Sigma_D,\Sigma_Q} T_2$;
2. $\mathsf{chase}_{T_2}(D) \to^{\mathsf{lim}}_{\Sigma_Q} \mathsf{chase}_{T_1}(D)$, *for all tree-like Σ_D-databases D of width at most k.*

Although Theorem 8 looks very similar to Theorem 6, it does not directly suggest a decision procedure. In particular, it is not clear how tree automata can deal with homomorphism limits. We next work towards a more operative characterization that pushes the use of homomorphism limits to parts of the chase that are Σ_Q-disconnected from the database and regular in shape. As we shall see, this allows us to get to grips with homomorphism limits.

For a database D, with $\mathsf{chase}_T(D)|^{\mathsf{con}}_{\Sigma}$ we denote the union of all maximally Σ-connected components of $\mathsf{chase}_T(D)$ that contain at least one constant from $\mathsf{adom}(D)$.

Theorem 9. *Let T_1 and T_2 be sets of frontier-one TGDs, Σ_D and Σ_Q schemas, and k the body width of T_1. Then $T_1 \models^{CQ}_{\Sigma_D,\Sigma_Q} T_2$ iff for all tree-like Σ_D-databases D of width at most k, the following holds:*

1. $\mathsf{chase}_{T_2}(D)|^{\mathsf{con}}_{\Sigma_Q} \to_{\Sigma_Q} \mathsf{chase}_{T_1}(D)$;
2. *for all maximally Σ_Q-connected components I of $\mathsf{chase}_{T_2}(D) \setminus \mathsf{chase}_{T_2}(D)|^{\mathsf{con}}_{\Sigma_Q}$, one of the following holds:*
   (a) $I \to_{\Sigma_Q} \mathsf{chase}_{T_1}(D)$;
   (b) $I \to^{\mathsf{lim}}_{\Sigma_Q} \mathsf{chase}_{T_1}(D)|_c^{\downarrow}$ *for some $c \in \mathsf{adom}(D)$.*

The subsequent example illustrates the theorem.

Example 2. *Consider the sets of TGDs T_1, T_2 and the schemas Σ_D, Σ_Q from Example 1. Recall that T_2 is Σ_D, Σ_Q-CQ-conservative over T_1. Since Σ_D contains only the unary relation A, we may w.l.o.g. concentrate on the Σ_D-database $D = \{A(c)\}$. Clearly, Point 1 of Theorem 9 is satisfied.*

For Point 2, observe that $\mathsf{chase}_{T_2}(D) \setminus \mathsf{chase}_{T_2}(D)|^{\mathsf{con}}_{\Sigma_Q}$ contains only one maximally Σ_Q-connected component, which is of the form

$$I = \{R(c_1, c_0), R(c_2, c_1), \dots\}.$$

Moreover, $I \to^{\mathsf{lim}}_{\Sigma_Q} \mathsf{chase}_{T_1}(D)|_c^{\downarrow}$ and thus Point 2(b) is satisfied. Point 2(a) is not satisfied since $I \not\to_{\Sigma_Q} \mathsf{chase}_{T_1}(D)$.

The easier 'if' direction of the proof of Theorem 9 relies on the fact that, as per Theorem 7, we can concentrate on connected CQs of arity 0 or 1. The interesting direction is 'only if', distinguishing several cases and using several 'skipping homomorphism' arguments (see Lemma 3).

Points 1 and 2(a) of Theorem 9 are amenable to the same tree automata techniques that we have used for hom-conservativity. Point 2(b) achieves the desired expulsion of homomorphism limits, away from the database D to instances of regular shape. In fact, the number of possible T_1-types is independent of D and thus by Lemma 7 the number of distinct instances $\mathsf{chase}_{T_1}(D)|_c^{\downarrow}$ in Point 2(b) that have to be considered is also independent of D. Moreover, these instances are purely chase-generated and thus regular in shape. The same is true for the instances I in Point 2. We next take a closer look at the latter.

Let T be a set of frontier-one TGDs. A *T-labeled database* is a pair $A = (D, \mu)$ with D a database and $\mu : \mathsf{adom}(D) \to \mathsf{TP}(T)$. We associate A with a database D_A that is obtained by starting with D and then adding, for each $c \in \mathsf{adom}(D)$, a disjoint copy D' of the type $\mu(c)$ viewed as a database and glueing the copy of x in D' to c in D_A. We use T-labeled databases to describe fragments of chase-generated instances, and thus assume that D_A contains only null constants. We also associate A with a Boolean CQ q_A, obtained by viewing D_A as such a CQ.

A *labeled Σ-head fragment of T_2* is a T_2-labeled database (F, μ) such that F can be obtained by choosing a TGD $\phi(x, \bar{y}) \to \exists \bar{z}\, \psi(x, \bar{z}) \in T_2$ and taking a maximally Σ-connected component of ψ that does not contain the frontier variable. The following lemma follows from an easy analysis of the chase procedure. Proof details are omitted.

Lemma 8. *Let I be a maximally Σ_Q-connected component of $\mathsf{chase}_{T_2}(D) \setminus \mathsf{chase}_{T_2}(D)|^{\mathsf{con}}_{\Sigma_Q}$, as in Point 2 of Theorem 9. Then for some labeled Σ_Q-head fragment $A = (F, \mu)$ of T_2,*

1. $\mathsf{chase}_{T_2}(D) \models q_A$, *and*
2. *I is homomorphically equivalent to $\mathsf{chase}_T(D_A)|^{\mathsf{con}}_{\Sigma_Q}$.*

Clearly, the number of labeled Σ-head fragments of T_2 is independent of D, just like the number of T_1-types. It thus follows from Lemma 8 and what was said before it that the number of checks '$I \to^{\mathsf{lim}}_{\Sigma_Q} \mathsf{chase}_{T_1}(D)|_c^{\downarrow}$' in Point 2(b) of Theorem 9 does not depend on D: there is at most one such check for every labeled Σ-head fragment of T_2 and every T_1-type. We can do all these checks in a preprocessing step, before starting to build 2ATAs for CQ-conservativity that implement the characterization provided by Theorem 9. Whenever the 2ATA needs to carry out a check '$I \to^{\mathsf{lim}}_{\Sigma_Q}$

$\mathsf{chase}_{T_1}(D)|^{\downarrow}_{c}$' to verify Point 2(b), we can simply look up the precomputed result and let the 2ATA reject immediately if it is negative. Thus, the automata are completely freed from dealing with homomorphism limits.

6.3 Precomputing Homomorphism Limits

It remains to show how to actually achieve the precomputation of the tests '$I \rightarrow^{\lim}_{\Sigma_Q} \mathsf{chase}_{T_1}(D)|^{\downarrow}_{c}$' in Point 2(b) of Theorem 9. This is where we finally deal with homomorphism limits. The following theorem makes precise the problem that we actually have to decide.

Theorem 10. *Given two sets of frontier-one TGDs T_1 and T_2, a schema Σ, a labeled Σ-head fragment $A = (D, \mu)$ for T_2, and a T_1-type $\widehat{t}$, it can be decided in time triple exponential in $||T_1|| + ||T_2||$ whether $\mathsf{chase}_{T_2}(D_A)|^{\mathsf{con}}_{\Sigma} \rightarrow^{\lim}_{\Sigma} \mathsf{chase}_{T_1}(\widehat{t})$.*

We invite the reader to compare the decision problem formulated in Theorem 10 with Point 2(b) of Theorem 9 in the light of Lemmas 7 and 8. The decision procedure used to prove Theorem 10 is again based on tree automata. To enable their use, however, we first rephrase the decision problem in Theorem 10 in a way that replaces homomorphism limits with unbounded homomorphisms.

Let T_1, T_2, Σ, $A = (D, \mu)$, and $\widehat{t}$ be as in Theorem 10. Recall that A is associated with a database D_A and a Boolean CQ q_A. Here, we additionally use unary CQs q^c_A, for every $c \in \mathsf{adom}(D)$, which are defined exactly like q_A except that c is now the answer variable.

The main idea for proving Theorem 10 is to replace homomorphism limits into $\mathsf{chase}_{T_1}(\widehat{t})$ with homomorphisms into a class of instances $\mathcal{R}(T_1, \widehat{t})$ whose disjoint union should be viewed as a relaxation of $\mathsf{chase}_{T_1}(\widehat{t})$. In particular, this relaxation admits a homomorphism limit to $\mathsf{chase}_{T_1}(\widehat{t})$, but not a homomorphism. Let us make this precise.

We again use instance trees. This time, however, they are not based on directed trees, but on *directed pseudo-trees*, that is, finite or infinite directed graphs $G = (V, E)$ such that every node $v \in V$ has at most one incoming edge and G is connected and contains no cycle.[3] Note that infinite directed pseudo-trees need not have a root. For example, a two-way infinite path qualifies as a directed pseudo-tree.

A *T_1-labeled instance tree* has the form $\mathcal{T} = (V, E, B, \mu)$ with $\mathcal{T}' = (V, E, B)$ an instance tree (based on a directed pseudo-tree) and $\mu : \mathsf{adom}(I_{\mathcal{T}'}) \rightarrow \mathsf{TP}(T_1)$ a function that assigns a T_1-type to every element in $I_{\mathcal{T}'}$. For $v \in V$, we use μ_v to denote the restriction of μ to $\mathsf{adom}(B(v))$. Moreover, we set $I_{\mathcal{T}} = I_{\mathcal{T}'}$. We say that $\mathcal{T}$ is *$\widehat{t}$-proper* if the following conditions are satisfied:

1. for every $v \in V$, one of the following holds:
   (a) v is the root of (V, E), $B(v)$ has the form $\{\mathsf{true}(c_0)\}$, and $\mu(c_0) = \widehat{t}$;
   (b) there is a TGD ϑ in T_1 such that $B(v)$ is isomorphic to the head of ϑ and $\widehat{t}, T_1 \models q_{(B(v),\mu_v)}$;
2. for every $(u, v) \in E$ such that $B(u) \cap B(v)$ contains a (single) constant c, we have $\mu_u(c), T_1 \models q^c_{(B(v),\mu_v)}(x)$. That is: the constant x from the type $\mu_u(c)$ viewed as a database is an answer to the unary CQ $q^c_{(B(v),\mu_v)}$ w.r.t. T_1.

[3]Neither in the directed nor in the undirected sense, which is equivalent if every node has at most one incoming edge.

The announced class $\mathcal{R}(T_1, \widehat{t})$ consists of all instances I such that $I = I_{\mathcal{T}}$ for some $\widehat{t}$-proper T_1-labeled instance tree $\mathcal{T}$. It is easy to see that $\mathsf{chase}_{T_1}(\widehat{t}) \in \mathcal{R}(T_1, \widehat{t})$ as there is a $\widehat{t}$-proper T_1-labeled instance tree $\mathcal{T}$ such that $I_{\mathcal{T}} = \mathsf{chase}_{T_1}(\widehat{t})$. However, there are also instances $I \in \mathcal{R}(T_1, \widehat{t})$ that do not admit a homomorphism to $\mathsf{chase}(\widehat{t}, T_1)$. The following example illustrates their importance.

Example 3. *Consider $T_1, T_2, \Sigma_D, \Sigma_Q$ from Example 1 and I, D, c from Example 2. Let $\widehat{t} = \mathsf{tp}_{T_1}(\mathsf{chase}_{T_1}(D), c)$, that is, $\widehat{t} = \{A(x), \exists x\, A(x), \exists x\, B(x)\}$. Then $I \not\rightarrow \mathsf{chase}_{T_2}(\widehat{t})$. However, we find a $\widehat{t}$-proper T_1-labeled instance tree $\mathcal{T} = (V, E, B, \mu)$ such that $I \rightarrow I_{\mathcal{T}}$.*

We may construct $\mathcal{T}$ by starting with a single node v_0, $B(v_0) = \{R(c_1, c_0)\}$, and

$$\mu(c_0) = \mu(c_1) = \{B(x), \exists x\, A(x), \exists x\, B(x)\}.$$

Then repeatedly add a predecessor v_{i+1} of v_i, with $B(v_{i+1}) = \{R(c_{i+1}, c_i)\}$ and $\mu(c_{i+1}) = \mu(c_0)$, ad infinitum. The resulting tree $\mathcal{T}$ is $\widehat{t}$-proper and satisfies $I_{\mathcal{T}} = I$. Note that it does not have a root.

The next lemma is the core ingredient to the proof of Theorem 10. Informally, it states that when replacing $\mathsf{chase}_{T_1}(\widehat{t})$ with instances from $\mathcal{R}(T_1, \widehat{t})$, we may also replace homomorphism limits with homomorphisms.

Lemma 9. *Let I be a countable Σ-connected instance such that $\mathsf{adom}(I)$ contains only nulls. Then $I \rightarrow^{\lim}_{\Sigma} \mathsf{chase}_{T_1}(\widehat{t})$ iff there is an $\widehat{I} \in \mathcal{R}(T_1, \widehat{t})$ with $I \rightarrow \widehat{I}$.*

In the proof of Lemma 9, the laborious direction is 'only if', where one assumes that $I \rightarrow^{\lim}_{\Sigma} \mathsf{chase}_{T_1}(\widehat{t})$ and then uses finite subinstances $J_1 \subseteq J_2 \subseteq \cdots$ of I with $I = \bigcup_{i \geq 1} J_i$ and homomorphisms h_i from J_i to $\mathsf{chase}_{T_1}(\widehat{t})$, $i \geq 1$, to identify the desired instance $\widehat{I} \in \mathcal{R}(T_1, \widehat{t})$. This again involves several 'skipping homomorphisms' type of arguments.

Using Lemma 9, we give a decision procedure based on 2ATAs that establishes Theorem 10. The 2ATA accepts input trees encoding an instance $I \in \mathcal{R}(T_1, \widehat{t})$ that admits a Σ-homomorphism from $\mathsf{chase}_{T_2}(D_A)|^{\mathsf{con}}_{\Sigma}$.

7 Future Work

It would be interesting to determine the exact complexity of hom- and CQ-conservativity for frontier-one TGDs. We tend to think that these problems are 3EXPTIME-complete. Note that in the description logic $\mathcal{ELI}$, they are 2EXPTIME-complete (Jung et al. 2020).

It would also be interesting to study conservative extensions and triviality for other classes of TGDs that have been proposed in the literature. Of course, it would be of particular interest to identify decidable cases. Classes for which undecidability does not follow from the results in this paper include acyclic and sticky TGDs, which exist in several forms, see for instance (Calì, Gottlob, and Pieris 2010).

Acknowledgements

Carsten Lutz was supported by the DFG project LU 1417/3-1 QTEC and Jery Marcinkowski by the Polish National Science Centre (NCN) grant 2016/23/B/ST6/01438.

References

Abiteboul, S.; Hull, R.; and Vianu, V. 1995. *Foundations of Databases*. Addison-Wesley.

Artale, A.; Calvanese, D.; Kontchakov, R.; and Zakharyaschev, M. 2009. The DL-Lite family and relations. *J. Artif. Intell. Res.* 36:1–69.

Baader, F.; Horrocks, I.; Lutz, C.; and Sattler, U. 2017. *An Introduction to Description Logic*. Cambridge University Press.

Baget, J.; Mugnier, M.; Rudolph, S.; and Thomazo, M. 2011. Walking the complexity lines for generalized guarded existential rules. In *Proc. of IJCAI*, 712–717.

Benedikt, M.; Bourhis, P.; and Senellart, P. 2012. Monadic datalog containment. In *Proc. of ICALP*, volume 7392 of *LNCS*, 79–91. Springer.

Bienvenu, M., and Ortiz, M. 2015. Ontology-mediated query answering with data-tractable description logics. In *Reasoning Web*, 218–307.

Bienvenu, M.; ten Cate, B.; Lutz, C.; and Wolter, F. 2014. Ontology-based data access: A study through disjunctive Datalog, CSP, and MMSNP. *ACM Transactions on Database Systems* 39(4):33:1–33:44.

Botoeva, E.; Konev, B.; Lutz, C.; Ryzhikov, V.; Wolter, F.; and Zakharyaschev, M. 2016. Inseparability and conservative extensions of description logic ontologies: A survey. In *Proc. of Reasoning Web*, volume 9885 of *LNCS*, 27–89. Springer.

Botoeva, E.; Lutz, C.; Ryzhikov, V.; Wolter, F.; and Zakharyaschev, M. 2019. Query inseparability for $\mathcal{ALC}$ ontologies. *Artif. Intell.* 272:1–51.

Calì, A.; Gottlob, G.; Lukasiewicz, T.; Marnette, B.; and Pieris, A. 2010. Datalog+/-: A family of logical knowledge representation and query languages for new applications. In *Proc. of LICS*, 228–242. IEEE Computer Society.

Calì, A.; Gottlob, G.; and Kifer, M. 2013. Taming the infinite chase: Query answering under expressive relational constraints. *J. Artif. Intell. Res.* 48:115–174.

Calì, A.; Gottlob, G.; and Lukasiewicz, T. 2012. A general datalog-based framework for tractable query answering over ontologies. *J. Web Semant.* 14:57–83.

Calì, A.; Gottlob, G.; and Pieris, A. 2010. Advanced processing for ontological queries. *Proc. VLDB Endow.* 3(1):554–565.

Calvanese, D.; Giacomo, G. D.; Lembo, D.; Lenzerini, M.; Poggi, A.; Rodriguez-Muro, M.; and Rosati, R. 2009. Ontologies and databases: The DL-Lite approach. In *Reasoning Web*, volume 5689 of *LNCS*, 255–356.

Casanova, M. A.; Fagin, R.; and Papadimitriou, C. H. 1984. Inclusion dependencies and their interaction with functional dependencies. *J. Comput. Syst. Sci.* 28(1):29–59.

Conway, J. 1972. Unpredictable iterations. In *Proc. of 1972 Number Theory Conference*, 49–52.

Fagin, R.; Kolaitis, P. G.; Miller, R. J.; and Popa, L. 2005. Data exchange: semantics and query answering. *Theor. Comput. Sci.* 336(1):89–124.

Ghilardi, S.; Lutz, C.; and Wolter, F. 2006. Did I damage my ontology? A case for conservative extensions in description logics. In *Proc. of KR*, 187–197. AAAI Press.

Gogacz, T., and Marcinkowski, J. 2014. All-instances termination of chase is undecidable. In *Proc. of ICALP*, volume 8573 of *LNCS*, 293–304. Springer.

Gottlob, G.; Kikot, S.; Kontchakov, R.; Podolskii, V. V.; Schwentick, T.; and Zakharyaschev, M. 2014. The price of query rewriting in ontology-based data access. *Artif. Intell.* 213:42–59.

Gottlob, G.; Manna, M.; and Pieris, A. 2015. Polynomial rewritings for linear existential rules. In *Proc. of IJCAI*, 2992–2998. AAAI Press.

Gutiérrez-Basulto, V.; Jung, J. C.; and Sabellek, L. 2018. Reverse engineering queries in ontology-enriched systems: The case of expressive horn description logic ontologies. In *Proc. of IJCAI*, 1847–1853. ijcai.org.

Johnson, D. S., and Klug, A. C. 1984. Testing containment of conjunctive queries under functional and inclusion dependencies. *J. Comput. Syst. Sci.* 28(1):167–189.

Jung, J. C.; Lutz, C.; Martel, M.; Schneider, T.; and Wolter, F. 2017. Conservative extensions in guarded and two-variable fragments. In *Proc. of ICALP*, LIPIcs, 108:1–108:14.

Jung, J. C.; Lutz, C.; Martel, M.; and Schneider, T. 2018. Querying the unary negation fragment with regular path expressions. In *Proc. of ICDT*, volume 98 of *LIPIcs*, 15:1–15:18. Schloss Dagstuhl - Leibniz-Zentrum für Informatik.

Jung, J. C.; Lutz, C.; Martel, M.; and Schneider, T. 2020. Conservative extensions in horn description logics with inverse roles. *J. Artif. Intell. Res.* 68:365–411.

Konev, B.; Kontchakov, R.; Ludwig, M.; Schneider, T.; Wolter, F.; and Zakharyaschev, M. 2011. Conjunctive query inseparability of OWL 2 QL TBoxes. In *Proc. of AAAI*. AAAI Press.

Lutz, C.; Walther, D.; and Wolter, F. 2007. Conservative extensions in expressive description logics. In *Proc. of IJCAI*, 453–458.

Ovid. 2008. *Metamorphoses, first edition 8 AD, Translated by A. D. Melville. Introduction and notes by Edward John Kenney.* Oxford University Press.

The More the Worst-Case-Merrier: A Generalized Condorcet Jury Theorem for Belief Fusion

Jonas Karge and **Sebastian Rudolph**
Computational Logic Group, TU Dresden
{jonas.karge, sebastian.rudolph}@tu-dresden.de

Abstract

In multi-agent belief fusion, there is increasing interest in results and methods from social choice theory. As a theoretical cornerstone, the *Condorcet Jury Theorem* (CJT) states that given a number of equally competent, independent agents where each is more likely to guess the true out of two alternatives, the chances of determining this objective truth by majority voting increase with the number of participating agents, approaching certainty. Past generalizations of the CJT have shown that some of its underlying assumptions can be weakened. Motivated by requirements from practical belief fusion scenarios, we provide a significant further generalization that subsumes several of the previous ones. Our considered setting simultaneously allows for heterogeneous competence levels across the agents (even tolerating entirely incompetent or even malicious voters), and voting for any number of alternatives from a finite set. We derive practical lower bounds for the numbers of agents needed to give probabilistic guarantees for determining the true state through approval voting. We also demonstrate that the non-asymptotic part of the CJT fails in our setting for arbitrarily high numbers of voters.

1 Introduction

When aggregating pieces of information or judgments from several sources, one can have one of two goals in mind: One goal is to ensure a *fair* aggregation procedure that outputs a collective judgment which best reconciles the preferences held by each individual source – in such a case, "truth" emerges from the process itself in form of the aggregated judgment. Another goal presumes the existence of a *true* state of the world, independent from the consulted sources' inclinations, and strives for a procedure that has a high probability to determine this *objective truth*, even at the risk of "unfairly" discarding the information given by some sources. In this work, it is the second, *truth tracking* goal we have in mind.

The Condorcet Jury Theorem (CJT) is a venerable and prominent result from voting theory (Marquis de Condorcet 1785). In its simplest version, it states that a group of independent, equally competent, and reliable agents voting on two alternatives where one represents the true state of the world (but the agents do not directly know which), then majority voting best tracks this true state. The CJT's original purpose was to provide a strong justification for majority voting as method of societal decision making, as its outcome in a democratic procedure binds the rest of society (Young 1988). The CJT provides this justification by asserting that a large group of voters performs better at reaching the objectively correct decision – should one exist – than single individuals.

Lately, with waning focus on the human nature of voters, the CJT and its extensions have been the subject of great interest and found applications in various disciplines where a voter now is seen more generally as some "abstract agent" that could be instantiated by humans, but also by automated decision-making procedures drawing information, e.g., from sensors, pre-specified knowledge, and/or inferencing methods. Notable application fields include *information science*, e.g., for relating voting to link-based ranking of webpages (Masterton and Olsson 2016), and *machine learning*, where CJT-like results can be harnessed for evaluating the importance of diversity for the quality of consensus-clustering algorithms (Jain 2018) or for guaranteeing that sets of classifiers (typically referred to as an *ensembles*), whose individual decisions are aggregated by some sort of voting mechanism, outperform individual classifiers (Dietterich 2000; Lam 2000).

But also the *knowledge representation* area has seen significant recent influence from social choice theory. In particular, voting methods have been applied to multi-agent systems and information fusion, where pieces of information coming from potentially conflicting agents have to be merged into a collective knowledge base. In this setting, the aggregation process is realized by defining belief fusion operators that apply voting rules to propositional knowledge bases with the aim of tracking the correct piece of information (Pigozzi and Hartmann 2007). Subsequently, the CJT was formalized and generalized for the belief fusion framework, demonstrating how to best track the true state of the world when knowledge bases in an incomplete information setting are merged (Everaere, Konieczny, and Marquis 2010).

In the following, we will provide a high-level overview of the CJT and its generalizations.[1] In all settings, some number of agents votes on a finite set of alternatives. Thereby, it is always assumed that the true state of the world is among the alternatives that can be voted on.

Condorcet's Theorem. Condorcet's original setting is *dichotomic*, that is, the set of alternatives is restricted to two and each agent has to vote for exactly one of the two. Moreover,

[1] For a rigid formalization of these results, see Section 4.

a particular agent is said to be *reliable* if the probability that she votes for the true state of the world is strictly greater than one half. In a *homogenous* setting, the probability of voting for a particular alternative is the same across all agents. Additionally, the agents choices are assumed to be *independent*. That is, intuitively, knowing the choices of some of the agents does not provide any information on the choices of the other agents. Upon voting, the *majority* rule stipulates that the alternative that receives more than half of the votes wins. Note that in a dichotomic setting with an odd number of voters, the majority always produces a unique winner. From the above assumptions, Condorcet derived the following result:

Theorem 1 (Marquis de Condorcet 1785). *For odd-numbered homogenous groups of independent and reliable agents in a dichotomic voting setting, the probability that majority voting identifies the correct alternative*

(1) increases monotonically with the number of agents and

(2) converges to 1 *as the number of agents goes to infinity.*

Note that only (2), commonly referred to as the *asymptotic part* of the theorem or *Crowd Infallibility* is featured in most generalizations of the CJT (Ben-Yashar and Paroush 2000), while (1), the *non-asymptotic part*, also called *Growing Reliability*, has been demonstrated to be violated for a small number of agents when the homogeneity assumption is weakened (Owen, Grofman, and Feld 1989).

Naturally, the underlying assumptions seem quite strong: Voters are typically not equally competent. Moreover, agents often times will be presented more than two alternatives. Also, an agent might wish to abstain or to vote for more than one particular alternative at a time. Guided by these observations, various generalizations of the CJT have been established, relaxing some of the underlying assumptions. In the following, we briefly discuss some existing generalizations of the CJT that are central to our contribution.

Choosing from More Options. The first generalization we discuss is due to List and Goodin (2001), who generalized the CJT to any finite number of alternatives. As before, their setting still presumes homogeneous groups of independent agents, and each agent is supposed to pick exactly one of the alternatives. However, each agent is now seen as *reliable* if the probability that she votes for the correct alternative is strictly greater than the probability that she votes for any other alternative. Moreover, instead of majority voting, *plurality voting* is applied. That is, an alternative wins if it receives strictly more votes than any other alternative.

Theorem 2 (List and Goodin 2001). *For a homogenous group of independent and reliable agents where each agent votes for exactly one alternative from a finite set of alternatives, the probability that plurality voting identifies the correct alternative*

(1) is higher than that for any other alternative winning and

(2) converges to 1 *as the number of agents goes to infinity.*

Still, for this result it is assumed that all voters are equally reliable and that agents can vote for one alternative only.

Choosing Several Options or None. More recently, Everaere et al. (2010) generalized the CJT to settings where agents vote by choosing any subset from a finite set of alternatives. Again, they presume a homogeneous group of independent agents, but adjust the *reliability* criterion: It requires that the probability of the correct alternative being contained in the chosen set is strictly greater than that of any other.

The appropriate voting method is then *approval voting*, where an alternative wins if it is contained in more of the agent-picked-sets than any other.

Theorem 3 (Everaere, Konieczny, and Marquis 2010). *For a homogeneous group of independent and reliable agents, the probability that approval voting on finitely many alternatives identifies the correct alternative converges to* 1 *as the number of agents goes to infinity.*

While Everaere et al.'s result allows a more liberal voting scheme, it still relies on the – rather artificial – assumption that all agents are equally competent.

Heterogenous Competence. One has to acknowledge that, in most natural cases, there are agents more competent than others. Likewise, it would be practical if one could give (probabilistic) correctness guarantees even for cases where the group of agents contains a certain share of incompetent (or even malicious) agents. To this end, Owen et al. (1989) have shown a generalized CJT wherein, in a dichotomic setting, the homogeneity requirement is dropped and the reliability assumption is significantly weakened. They define *reliability* on a group-level rather than individually and merely require that the probability to vote for the correct alternative, *averaged across all agents*, is strictly greater than one half.

Theorem 4 (Owen, Grofman, and Feld 1989). *For a reliable group of independent agents in a dichotomic voting setting, the probability that majority voting identifies the correct alternative converges to* 1 *as the number of agents goes to infinity.*

Then again, while allowing for voter heterogeneity, this result is restricted to two alternatives where agents can vote for one alternative at a time only.

Our Contribution. As central contribution of this paper, we state (Section 4) and prove (Section 5) a generalization of the CJT that subsumes all the results discussed before. It establishes that the probability of approval voting identifying the correct alternative converges to 1 as the number of agents goes to infinity, in any setting where

(i) the set of choices to pick from is finite and fixed, but of arbitrary size,

(ii) upon voting, the agents can choose any number of alternatives from that set, and

(iii) we require group reliability, i.e., the average probability to vote for the true alternative is (by a fixed margin $\Delta p > 0$) greater than the average probability to vote for any other alternative.

We note that the existence of a fixed positive probability margin Δp is an implicit requirement in all mentioned versions of the CJT. All these results fail if the difference between the probabilities is allowed to approach zero as the number of voters grows (see Berend and Paroush 1998).

Further contributions of this paper are the following:

- We establish a formally rigorous unifying probabilistic framework that allows for comparing the discussed results and makes all underlying assumptions explicit (Section 4).
- We derive bounds for the minimal number of agents required to guarantee that the approval voting is successful with a probability higher than a given value $P_{\min}$, depending on the number m of choices and the probability margin Δp. It turns out that for different values of these parameters, different formulae provide better estimates.
- We discuss why an analogon to part (1) of the CJT cannot be established in our setting and provide corresponding counterexamples for arbitrarily large numbers of agents.

2 Motivational Scenario

To further motivate the use of the CJT for information fusion, we briefly discuss a hypothetical scenario based on an emerging technology called *Smart Dust*.

Smart Dust is a micro-electro-mechanical system (MEMS) with wireless, dust-sized components, called motes, that can carry sensors in order to provide information on their domain of application (Sharma and Sultana 2020). Possible applications range from general engineering and health to environmental monitoring (e.g., to support forecasting of natural disasters) (Haenggi 2016).

For instance, when applied to monitoring geological activity, a Smart Dust system consisting of possibly thousands of motes (Nerkar and Kumar 2016), spread across a region of interest, can be used to detect patterns known to precede major geological events such as earthquakes or landslides. The goal then is to assemble the individual motes' findings to derive predictions of such events occurring in the near future (Sharma and Sultana 2020). Key issues in collecting the data from the Smart Dust system include the aggregation of heterogeneous information and the management of uncertainty at various levels (Agogino, Granderson, and Qiu 2002).

In the CJT setting, we can see each sensor-carrying mote as an individual agent. In a hypothetical scenario, we can imagine a manufacturer of a Smart Dust system to give certain guarantees regarding the reliability of the provided motes. This may include a certain percentage of motes malfunctioning (through production errors or as a consequence of their deployment) as well as the probabilities of a functional mote to correctly identify patterns that precede earthquakes or landslides, and to distinguish these patterns from each other and from harmless geological activity in the area where it is applied. In this scenario, the probability of a mote correctly identifying such a pattern also depends on, for instance, its location in that area. The collection of motes/agents then has heterogeneously distributed levels of competence about which only statistical guarantees can be given.

Then, the data delivered by the plethora of motes has to be aggregated. To this end, it is conceivable to apply voting methods, where each potential prediction associated with a detected pattern constitutes a particular alternative to vote on. The generalization of the CJT proven in this paper justifies this strategy in principle and ensures that – given basic reliability guarantees – the probability of making the right prediction goes against 1 with a growing number of motes. Even more, our results providing lower bounds on this success probability depending on the number of agents, the number of alternatives, and certain quantified statistical reliability guarantees, allow us to give practical concrete estimates for the number of motes (or "kilograms of smart dust") that need to be deployed in order to successfully track the correct geodynamic situation.

3 Preliminaries

Probability Theory. While we assume the reader to be familiar with the foundations of probability, we briefly recall some basic notions and fix notations used. Following common practice we use X (usually with annotations) to denote random variables. For *Bernoulli random variables*, where X can only take values from $\{0, 1\}$, we let $p = \mathbb{P}(X = 1)$ denote the probability for X taking the value and obtain $\mathbb{P}(X = 0) = 1 - p$, where, as usual, $\mathbb{P}(.)$ is used to denote the *probability* of X taking the indicated values. Given a random variable X, we let $\mathbb{E}(X)$ denote the *expected value* of X, defined as $\sum_x X\mathbb{P}(X = x)$ whenever X ranges over finitely many values. Likewise, we define the *variance* $\mathbb{Var}(X)$ of X as $\mathbb{E}((X - \mathbb{E}(X))^2)$. For Bernoulli distributions with parameter p, we obtain $\mathbb{E}(X) = p$ and $\mathbb{Var}(X) = p(1 - p)$.

Voting. We assume a finite set $\mathcal{W} = \{\omega_1, \ldots, \omega_m\}$ of m items referred to as *choices*. We further assume a finite set $\mathcal{A} = \{a_1, \ldots, a_n\}$ of n *agents*.

Given $\mathcal{A}$ and $\mathcal{W}$, one *approval voting (instance)* is represented by the relation $V \subseteq \mathcal{A} \times \mathcal{W}$ where $(a_i, \omega_j) \in V$ means that agent a_i approves choice ω_j (meaning that she considers it more favourable or likely than any of the non-approved choices). Given an approval vote V, the *score* $\#_V\, \omega$ of some choice $\omega \in \mathcal{W}$ is defined as the overall number of votes that ω receives, i.e.,

$$\#_V\, \omega = |\{a_i \in \mathcal{A}_n \mid (a_i, \omega) \in V\}|.$$

We then say some choice $\omega \in \mathcal{W}$ *wins the approval vote* V if it receives strictly higher scores (that is: strictly more votes) than any other choice, that is,

$$\#_V\, \omega > \max_{\omega' \in \mathcal{W} \setminus \{\omega\}} \#_V\, \omega'.$$

Let us remark that other types of voting schemes can be obtained from approval voting. Whenever every agent is required to vote for exactly one choice (i.e., V is required to be a function), approval voting is identical to *plurality voting*. If one additionally requires $m = 2$, one obtains *majority voting*, since in the functional setting with two choices, a choice winning the approval vote means that it must obtain strictly more than half of all votes.

4 Truth Tracking through Voting

In the truth tracking setting, the choices represent possible *world states*, with the basic assumption that in each instantiation of the voting procedure, exactly one of these states $\omega_* \in \mathcal{W}$ is the true, actual world state. The agents are assumed not to have direct access to the information about the actual world state, but they might be able to obtain indications through some epistemic process (such as sensor readings).

Formal Probabilistic Model. As usual, the described scenario is modeled as a random process. This process generates ω_* as well as V and is governed by a joint probability distribution $\mathbb{P}$ over the Bernoulli (i.e., $\{0,1\}$-valued) random variables

$$\begin{matrix} X_*^{\omega_1}, & \ldots, & X_*^{\omega_m}, \\ X_1^{\omega_1}, & \ldots, & X_1^{\omega_m}, \\ \vdots & \vdots\vdots\vdots & \vdots \\ X_n^{\omega_1}, & \ldots, & X_n^{\omega_m}. \end{matrix}$$

The values taken by these random variables represent the outcome of a voting event as follows: $X_*^{\omega_j}$ is 1 if ω_j is the actual world state (i.e., $\omega_j = \omega_*$), and 0 otherwise, whereas $X_i^{\omega_j}$ is 1 if the ith agent voted for the jth world state (i.e., $(a_i, \omega_j) \in V$) and 0 otherwise. For brevity, we let $[\omega_* = \omega_j]$ denote the expression $X_*^{\omega_j}{=}1 \wedge \bigwedge_{\omega \in \mathcal{W} \setminus \{\omega_j\}} X_*^{\omega}{=}0$.

We next specify basic assumptions we make about the above joint distribution. Obviously, considering the described meaning of the joint distribution, we always require that $[\omega_j = \omega_*]$ holds for exactly one $\omega_j \in \mathcal{W}$.

One central and crucial assumption that we impose is that the agents do not influence each other in their decision whether or not to approve some choice.

Definition 1. *A joint distribution satisfies* agent approval independence *if, conditioned on the actual world state, the decision to approve any given ω_j is made independently across all agents, i.e., for any $\omega, \omega_j \in \mathcal{W}$ and any sequence $v_1, \ldots, v_n$ of values from $\{0,1\}$ the following holds:*

$$\mathbb{P}\Big(\bigwedge_{i=1}^{n} X_i^{\omega_j} = v_i \mid [\omega_*{=}\omega]\Big) = \prod_{i=1}^{n} \mathbb{P}\Big(X_i^{\omega_j} = v_i \mid [\omega_*{=}\omega]\Big).$$

In other words, in a setting satisfying agent approval independence, the joint probability of any given approval voting outcome referring to a given world state can be obtained as the product of the corresponding marginal probabilities, when controlling for the actual world state.

Next, we introduce a formal notion that will allow us to quantify how well the group of agents as a whole is able to estimate the actual true world state.

Definition 2. *A joint probability distribution satisfies Δp-* group reliability *for some $\Delta p > 0$, if the probability to approve the true world state, averaged across all agents, is at least by Δp higher than the averaged probability for approving any other state, i.e., for every $\omega, \omega' \in \mathcal{W}$ with $\omega \neq \omega'$ the following holds:*

$$\tfrac{1}{n}\sum_{i=1}^{n} \mathbb{P}\Big(X_i^{\omega}{=}1 \,|\, [\omega_*{=}\omega]\Big) \geq \Delta p + \tfrac{1}{n}\sum_{i=1}^{n} \mathbb{P}\Big(X_i^{\omega'}{=}1 \,|\, [\omega_*{=}\omega]\Big).$$

The previous two assumptions are required to obtain our result (and any of the prior results discussed in this paper), so we refer to this setting as *I&R* (for independent and reliable).

The assumptions introduced next are optional; they allow to constrain the setting further in order to formalize existing results in a uniform framework. The first such constraint requires the conditional approval probabilities to be uniform across all agents.

Definition 3. *A joint distribution satisfies* homogeneity *if, upon fixing the actual world state, the marginal probability to approve any given ω_j is the same for every agent, i.e., for any $\omega, \omega' \in \mathcal{W}$ and all $i, k \in \{1, \ldots, n\}$ the following holds:*

$$\mathbb{P}(X_i^{\omega} = 1 \mid [\omega_*{=}\omega']) = \mathbb{P}(X_k^{\omega} = 1 \mid [\omega_*{=}\omega']).$$

Another constraint realizes the plurality voting scheme by imposing that every agent must approve exactly one of the choices.

Definition 4. *A joint distribution satisfies* (vote) completeness *if for every $i \in \{1, \ldots, n\}$ the following holds:*

$$\textstyle\sum_{j=1}^{m} X_i^{\omega_j} = 1.$$

We conclude our framework by formally defining an appropriate notion characterizing the chance that the true world state is identified via an approval vote.

Definition 5. *Given a family $\mathcal{P}$ of joint probability distributions for n agents and a set $\mathcal{W}$ of m choices, the* approval vote worst-case success probability *$P_{m,n}^{\text{wcs}}$ is defined by*

$$\min_{\substack{\mathbb{P} \in \mathcal{P} \\ \omega \in \mathcal{W}}} \mathbb{P}\Big(\bigwedge_{\omega_\dagger \in \mathcal{W} \setminus \{\omega\}} \textstyle\sum_{k=1}^{n} X_k^{\omega} > \sum_{k=1}^{n} X_k^{\omega_\dagger} \mid [\omega_* = \omega]\Big).$$

In words, for m choices and n agents, given a family $\mathcal{P}$ of distributions adhering to a specific set of assumptions about the voting setting, $P_{m,n}^{\text{wcs}}$ expresses the guaranteed minimal probability that approval voting identifies the true world state.

Formulating CJT Versions. With the above notions in place, we can represent the previously shown versions of the CJT in a uniform way as follows, where the number $m \geq 2$ of choices and the group reliability parameter $\Delta p > 0$ are arbitrary but fixed throughout the limit process:

- Marquis de Condorcet: In any complete, homogeneous I&R setting holds $P_{2,n}^{\text{wcs}} \xrightarrow[n\to\infty]{} 1$.
- List and Goodin: In any complete, homogeneous I&R setting holds $P_{m,n}^{\text{wcs}} \xrightarrow[n\to\infty]{} 1$.
- Everaere, Konieczny, and Marquis: In any homogeneous I&R setting holds $P_{m,n}^{\text{wcs}} \xrightarrow[n\to\infty]{} 1$.
- Owen, Grofman, and Feld: In any complete I&R setting holds $P_{2,n}^{\text{wcs}} \xrightarrow[n\to\infty]{} 1$.

In the same vein, we can express our main theorem, which generalizes all of the above:

Theorem 5 (Generalized CJT). *In any I&R setting with fixed $m \geq 2$ and $\Delta p > 0$ holds $P_{m,n}^{\text{wcs}} \xrightarrow[n\to\infty]{} 1$.*

5 Proof of the Asymptotic Result

For the proof of our generalization of the (asymptotic part of) CJT, it is convenient to consider ω_* fixed (yet still unknown to the agents) and the remaining elements of $\mathcal{W}$ appropriately renamed, i.e., we let $\mathcal{W} = \{\omega_*, \omega_1, \ldots, \omega_{m-1}\}$. This is without loss of generality and allows for a more succinct formulation without conditional probabilities.

For every $\omega \in \mathcal{W}$, we let $p_1^{\omega}, \ldots, p_n^{\omega}$ denote the Bernoulli parameters of the random variables $X_1^{\omega}, \ldots, X_n^{\omega}$, respectively, which are independently distributed by assumption.

Then $\mathbb{E}(X_k^\omega) = p_k^\omega$ for all $k \in \{1, \dots, n\}$. We will make use of the average of the p_k^ω given by

$$\bar{p}^\omega = \frac{1}{n} \sum_{k=1}^n p_k^\omega.$$

We define for all ω, n, and k

$$\widetilde{X}_k^\omega = X_k^\omega - \mathbb{E}(X_k^\omega) = X_k^\omega - p_k^\omega$$

the centralized versions of all considered distributions. Observe that $\mathbb{E}(\widetilde{X}_k^\omega) = 0$ and

$$\mathbb{Var}(\widetilde{X}_k^\omega) = \mathbb{Var}(X_k^\omega) = p_k^\omega(1 - p_k^\omega) \leq \tfrac{1}{4}. \quad (1)$$

Moreover, for every $\omega \in \mathcal{W}$, we define the (original and centralized) distribution for the score received by ω by

$$X^\omega = \sum_{k=1}^n X_k^\omega \quad \text{and} \quad \widetilde{X}^\omega = \sum_{k=1}^n \widetilde{X}_k^\omega,$$

respectively, and note that

$$\begin{aligned} X^\omega &= \sum_{k=1}^n X_k^\omega = \sum_{k=1}^n \mathbb{E}(X_k^\omega) + \sum_{k=1}^n (X_k^\omega - \mathbb{E}(X_k^\omega)) \\ &= \sum_{k=1}^n p_k^\omega + \sum_{k=1}^n (X_k^\omega - \mathbb{E}(X_k^\omega)) \\ &= n\bar{p}^\omega + \sum_{k=1}^n \widetilde{X}_k^\omega = n\bar{p}^\omega + \widetilde{X}^\omega. \end{aligned} \quad (2)$$

Furthermore, note that (due to the independence of all $X_1^\omega, \dots, X_n^\omega$)

$$\mathbb{Var}(\widetilde{X}^\omega) = \mathbb{Var}(X^\omega) = \sum_{k=1}^n \mathbb{Var}(X_k^\omega) \leq \tfrac{n}{4}. \quad (3)$$

According to the group reliability assumption, there exists some (uniform) $\Delta p > 0$ such that for every n and $\omega_\dagger \in \mathcal{W} \setminus \{\omega_*\}$ holds

$$\bar{p}^{\omega_*} \geq \Delta p + \bar{p}^{\omega_\dagger}.$$

In the following, let $\omega_\dagger \in \mathcal{W} \setminus \{\omega_*\}$ denote an arbitrary but fixed "competitor" of ω_* in the approval vote. The strategy used toward showing the desired result starts by establishing a lower bound for the probability of ω_* winning against $\omega_\dagger$. Intuitively, this probability increases with growing n, since the distributions for $\frac{X^{\omega_*}}{n}$ and $\frac{X^{\omega_\dagger}}{n}$ will get concentrated more and more narrowly around $\bar{p}^{\omega_*}$ and $\bar{p}^{\omega_\dagger}$, respectively.[2]

To separate the scores of ω_* and $\omega_\dagger$, we make use of the threshold values

$$\theta^* = n(\bar{p}^{\omega_*} - \tfrac{\Delta p}{2}) \quad \text{as well as} \quad \theta^\dagger = n(\bar{p}^{\omega_\dagger} + \tfrac{\Delta p}{2})$$

and observe that $\theta^* \geq \theta^\dagger$ holds by construction, as the difference between $\bar{p}^{\omega_*}$ and $\bar{p}^{\omega_\dagger}$ is at least Δp. For the following, we will employ a popular inequality by Chebyshev.

Lemma 1 (Chebyshev 1867). *For any distribution X with finite $\mathbb{E}(X)$ and $\mathbb{Var}(X)$ and any real number r holds*

$$\mathbb{P}(|X - \mathbb{E}(X)| > r) \leq \tfrac{\mathbb{Var}(X)}{r^2}.$$

[2]This general observation regarding growing sums of independently distributed random variables also shows up in the popular Central Limit Theorem, but, as we will argue in Section 7, that theorem itself is not applicable in our case.

Then we can obtain a lower bound for the probability that in the course of an approval vote the correct choice ω_* receives more votes than some fixed competitor $\omega_\dagger$ as follows:

$$\begin{aligned} &\mathbb{P}(X^{\omega_*} > X^{\omega_\dagger}) \\ &\quad \text{introduce fixed separating thresholds} \\ &> \mathbb{P}(X^{\omega_*} > \theta^* \geq \theta^\dagger > X^{\omega_\dagger}) \\ &\quad \text{worst case, even if } X^{\omega_*}, X^{\omega_\dagger} \text{ maximally dependent} \\ &\geq 1 - \mathbb{P}(X^{\omega_*} \leq \theta^*) - \mathbb{P}(\theta^{\omega_\dagger} \leq X^{\omega_\dagger}) \\ &\quad \text{Equation (2) and Definitions of } \theta^* \text{ and } \theta^\dagger \\ &= 1 - \mathbb{P}(n\bar{p}^{\omega_*} + \widetilde{X}^{\omega_*} \leq n(\bar{p}^{\omega_*} - \tfrac{\Delta p}{2})) \\ &\qquad - \mathbb{P}(n(\bar{p}^{\omega_\dagger} + \tfrac{\Delta p}{2}) \leq n\bar{p}^{\omega_\dagger} + \widetilde{X}^{\omega_\dagger}) \\ &= 1 - \mathbb{P}(\widetilde{X}^{\omega_*} \leq -n\tfrac{\Delta p}{2}) - \mathbb{P}(n\tfrac{\Delta p}{2} \leq \widetilde{X}^{\omega_\dagger}) \qquad (4) \\ &\geq 1 - \mathbb{P}(|\widetilde{X}^{\omega_*}| \geq n\tfrac{\Delta p}{2}) - \mathbb{P}(n\tfrac{\Delta p}{2} \leq |\widetilde{X}^{\omega_\dagger}|) \\ &\quad \text{Chebyshev's inequality } (2\times) \\ &\geq 1 - \tfrac{\mathbb{Var}(\widetilde{X}^{\omega_*})}{(n\frac{\Delta p}{2})^2} - \tfrac{\mathbb{Var}(\widetilde{X}^{\omega_\dagger})}{(n\frac{\Delta p}{2})^2} \\ &\quad \text{Equation (3) } (2\times) \\ &\geq 1 - \tfrac{\frac{n}{4}}{(n\frac{\Delta p}{2})^2} - \tfrac{\frac{n}{4}}{(n\frac{\Delta p}{2})^2} = 1 - \tfrac{2}{n\Delta p^2} \qquad (5) \end{aligned}$$

Now, in order to obtain the probability for ω_* winning the approval vote against *all* competing $\omega_\dagger \in \mathcal{W} \setminus \{\omega_*\}$ simultaneously, we state

$$\begin{aligned} &\mathbb{P}(\textstyle\bigwedge_{\omega_\dagger \in \mathcal{W} \setminus \{\omega_*\}} X^{\omega_*} > X^{\omega_\dagger}) \\ &\quad \text{worst case, even if } X^{\omega_1}, X^{\omega_2}, \dots \text{ maximally dependent} \\ &\geq 1 - \textstyle\sum_{i=1}^{m-1} \mathbb{P}(X^{\omega_*} \leq X^{\omega_i}) \\ &= 1 - \textstyle\sum_{i=1}^{m-1} (1 - \mathbb{P}(X^{\omega_*} > X^{\omega_i})) \qquad (6) \\ &\quad \text{Equation (5)} \\ &> 1 - \textstyle\sum_{i=1}^{m-1} (1 - (1 - \tfrac{2}{n\Delta p^2})) = 1 - \tfrac{2(m-1)}{n\Delta p^2} \qquad (7) \end{aligned}$$

As this argument holds for every choice of ω_* and is valid for every I&R joint probability distribution, this allows us to conclude our desired result

$$P_{m,n}^{\text{wcs}} \xrightarrow[n \to \infty]{} 1, \quad (8)$$

which finishes the proof of the main theorem.

6 Estimates for Required Number of Agents

For the given proof, not much care was given to arrive at particularly tight bounds. Still, beyond the convergence behavior in the infinite, the obtained result allows to derive concrete guarantees in the finite: Provided the average probability of the true state being approved is known to be by Δp better than that of any competitor, the number n of agents needed to guarantee a success probability of at least $P_{\min}$ when choosing among m options is

$$n \geq \frac{2(m-1)}{\Delta p^2(1 - P_{\min})}. \quad (9)$$

That is, the number of agents needed grows linearly with the number of wrong alternatives offered, is inversely proportional to the admissible failure probability $1 - P_{\min}$, and depends inversely quadratically on the guaranteed margin between the average probabilities of right and wrong choice.

Better Bounds for High Values of $P_{\min}$ and/or m. The guarantees established via Equation (9) are still unsatisfactory, in particular when the required success probability and/or the number of choices are high. Assuming a generous margin of $\Delta p = 0.5$, the number of required voters for $m = 11$ and $P_{\min} = 0.9$ is 800 and grows to $80,000$ when requiring $P_{\min} = 0.99$ and letting $m = 101$. This raises the question of whether lower, more practical bounds can be obtained. Fortunately this is the case.

To this end, a crucial observation is that for Bernoulli random variables, their potential values are confined to the interval $[0, 1]$, so the probability of a value outside that interval being taken is 0. For the sum of (not necessarily identically distributed) independent random variables with this property, Hoeffding's inequality provides a tail estimate.

Lemma 2 (Hoeffding 1963). *Let $X_1, \ldots, X_n$ be independent random variables satisfying $\mathbb{P}(l_i \leq X_i \leq u_i) = 1$ for reals l_i, u_i. Consider the sum of these random variables, $X = \sum_{i=1}^n X_i$. Then for every real number $t > 0$ holds*

$$\mathbb{P}(X - \mathbb{E}(X) \geq t) \leq e^{-\frac{2}{\sum_{i=1}^n (u_i - l_i)^2} t^2}.$$

This allows for improving the established lower success probability bound for winning against one competitor:

$$\begin{aligned}
&\mathbb{P}(X^{\omega_*} > X^{\omega_\dagger}) \\
&\text{Equation (4)} \\
&\geq 1 - \mathbb{P}(\widetilde{X}^{\omega_*} \leq -n\tfrac{\Delta p}{2}) - \mathbb{P}(n\tfrac{\Delta p}{2} \leq \widetilde{X}^{\omega_\dagger}) \\
&\text{Hoeffding's theorem } (2\times) \text{ noting that } u_i - l_i = 1 \text{ for all } i \\
&\geq 1 - e^{-\frac{2}{n}(n\frac{\Delta p}{2})^2} - e^{-\frac{2}{n}(n\frac{\Delta p}{2})^2} = 1 - 2e^{-\frac{1}{2}n\Delta p^2} \qquad (10)
\end{aligned}$$

Then we obtain for the winning against all competitors:

$$\begin{aligned}
&\mathbb{P}(\textstyle\bigwedge_{\omega_\dagger \in \mathcal{W}\setminus\{\omega_*\}} X^{\omega_*} > X^{\omega_\dagger}) \\
&\text{Equation (6)} \\
&\geq 1 - \textstyle\sum_{i=1}^{m-1} (1 - \mathbb{P}(X^{\omega_*} > X^{\omega_i})) \\
&\text{Equation (10)} \\
&= 1 - \textstyle\sum_{i=1}^{m-1} (1 - (1 - 2e^{-\frac{1}{2}n\Delta p^2})) \\
&= 1 - (m-1)2e^{-\frac{1}{2}n\Delta p^2} \qquad (11)
\end{aligned}$$

And as estimate for the number of independent agents needed to surpass a success probability of $P_{\min}$:

$$n \geq \frac{2}{\Delta p^2} \ln \frac{2(m-1)}{1 - P_{\min}} \qquad (12)$$

Note that this significantly lowers the bounds in the cases considered above: for $\Delta p = 0.5$, $m = 11$ and $P_{\min} = 0.9$ the number of required voters is 42. For $P_{\min} = 0.99$ and $m = 101$, it grows only very moderately to 80. It is also easy to see that Equation (12) yields better estimates than Equation (9) for all possible values of Δp, m, and $P_{\min}$ due to the fact that $\ln(x) < x$ always holds.

Better Bounds for Large Δp. The improved bound still yields unintuitively high values under certain conditions. As an informative cornercase, consider $\Delta p = 1$. This means that the average probability to approve the true world state is by 1 higher than approving any other state. This condition can only be satisfied if every voter behaves perfectly, i.e., she always approves ω_* and never approves any competing $\omega_\dagger$. Under such fortunate circumstances, it is obvious that consulting just one agent (i.e., $n = 1$) must be sufficient, no matter how high $P_{\min}$ and m. However, upon inspection of Equation (12), even when fixing $\Delta p = 1$, we can obtain arbitrarily large values for n upon choosing high $P_{\min}$ and/or m. Note that very large values of Δp are not just of academic interest since there might be belief fusion scenarios wherein close-to-perfect sensors are deployed.

To appropriately handle such situations, we resort to a more careful analysis and refined estimates of tail probabilities. We state Jensen's inequality, recalling that a function $f : [l, h] \to \mathbb{R}$ from some real interval $[l, h]$ to the real numbers is *concave* if for any $x_1, x_2 \in [l, h]$ and every $t \in [0, 1]$ holds

$$f(tx_1 + (1-t)x_2) \geq tf(x_1) + (1-t)f(x_2).$$

Lemma 3 (Jensen 1906). *For any concave function $f : [l, u] \to \mathbb{R}$, real values $x_1, \ldots, x_n \in [l, u]$ and positive weights $w_1, \ldots, w_n > 0$ holds*

$$\frac{\sum_{i=1}^n w_i f(x_i)}{\sum w_i} \leq f\left(\frac{\sum_{i=1}^n w_i x_i}{\sum w_i}\right).$$

In particular, choosing $w_i = \frac{1}{n}$ for every $i \in \{1, \ldots, n\}$ yields

$$\tfrac{1}{n}\textstyle\sum_{i=1}^n f(x_i) \leq f\left(\tfrac{1}{n}\sum_{i=1}^n x_i\right).$$

That is, for concave functions, applying the function to the average of a collection of numbers yields a larger value than taking the average over the corresponding collection of function values. In particular, given values $p_1, \ldots, p_n$ and letting $\bar{p} = \frac{1}{n}\sum_{i=1}^n p_i$, we can use the observation that the function $f : x \mapsto x(1-x)$ is concave to obtain

$$\begin{aligned}
\tfrac{1}{n}\textstyle\sum_{i=1}^n p_i(1-p_i) &= \tfrac{1}{n}\textstyle\sum_{i=1}^n f(p_i) \leq f\left(\tfrac{1}{n}\sum_{i=1}^n p_i\right) \\
&= f(\bar{p}) = \bar{p}(1-\bar{p}). \qquad (13)
\end{aligned}$$

This insight allows us to obtain a better bound on the variance of the sum of the approvals for a given $\omega \in \mathcal{W}$:

$$\begin{aligned}
\mathbb{Var}(\widetilde{X}^{\omega}) &= \mathbb{Var}(X^{\omega}) \\
&= \textstyle\sum_{k=1}^n \mathbb{Var}(X_k^{\omega}) = \sum_{k=1}^n p_k^{\omega}(1 - p_k^{\omega}) \\
&\text{Equation (13)} \\
&\leq np^{\omega}(1 - p^{\omega}). \qquad (14)
\end{aligned}$$

As another ingredient, we make use of the *Chebyshev-Cantelli inequality*, a less commonly known variant of Chebyshev's inequality, which allows to infer good estimates for one-sided tail bounds of probability distributions.

Lemma 4 (Chebyshev 1867, Cantelli 1928). *For any distribution X with finite $\mathbb{E}(X)$ and $\mathbb{Var}(X)$ and any real number $\lambda > 0$ holds*

$$\mathbb{P}(X - \mathbb{E}(X) \geq \lambda) \leq \tfrac{\mathbb{Var}(X)}{\mathbb{Var}(X) + \lambda^2}.$$

Applying the above to $-X$ yields

$$\mathbb{P}(X - \mathbb{E}(X) \leq -\lambda) \leq \tfrac{\mathbb{Var}(X)}{\mathbb{Var}(X) + \lambda^2}.$$

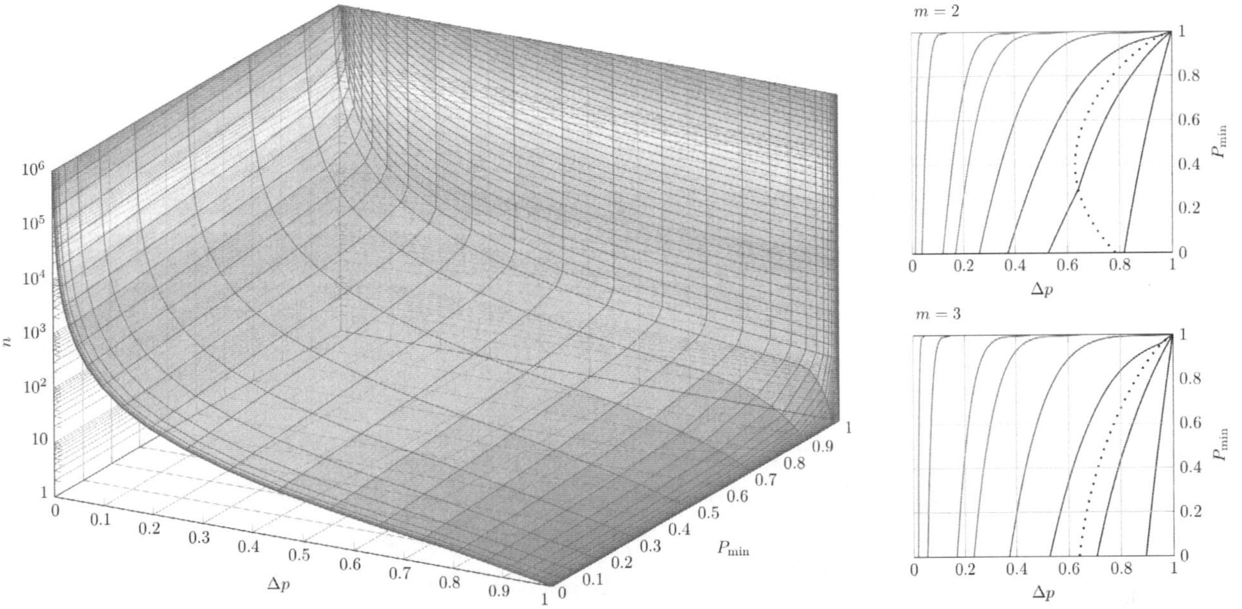

Figure 1: Left: Lower bound for n, given Δp and $P_{\min}$ for fixed $m = 2$. Plot cut off at $n = 10^6$, note that $n \xrightarrow[\Delta p \to 0]{} \infty$ and $n \xrightarrow[P_{\min} \to 1]{} \infty$.
Right: Contour lines for $n = 10^4$, 10^3, 100, 50, 20, 10, 5, and 2 (left to right), given $m = 2$ (top) and $m = 3$ (bottom). The dotted lines separate the area for large Δp, where Equation (12) provides the better estimate.

These tools allow us to arrive at an improved lower bound for the probability of ω_* winning against one competitor:

$$\begin{aligned}
&\mathbb{P}(X^{\omega_*} > X^{\omega_\dagger}) \\
&\text{Equation (4)} \\
&= 1 - \mathbb{P}(\widetilde{X}^{\omega_*} \le -n\tfrac{\Delta p}{2}) - \mathbb{P}(n\tfrac{\Delta p}{2} \le \widetilde{X}^{\omega_\dagger}) \\
&\text{Chebyshev-Cantelli inequality } (2\times) \\
&\ge 1 - \tfrac{\mathrm{Var}(\widetilde{X}^{\omega_*})}{\mathrm{Var}(\widetilde{X}^{\omega_*}) + (n\frac{\Delta p}{2})^2} - \tfrac{\mathrm{Var}(\widetilde{X}^{\omega_\dagger})}{\mathrm{Var}(\widetilde{X}^{\omega_\dagger}) + (n\frac{\Delta p}{2})^2} \\
&= \tfrac{n^2\Delta p^2}{4\mathrm{Var}(\widetilde{X}^{\omega_*}) + n^2\Delta p^2} + \tfrac{n^2\Delta p^2}{4\mathrm{Var}(\widetilde{X}^{\omega_\dagger}) + n^2\Delta p^2} - 1 \\
&\text{Equation (14)} \\
&\ge \tfrac{n^2\Delta p^2}{4np^{\omega_*}(1-p^{\omega_*}) + n^2\Delta p^2} + \tfrac{n^2\Delta p^2}{4np^{\omega_\dagger}(1-p^{\omega_\dagger}) + n^2\Delta p^2} - 1 \\
&\text{value minimal for } p^{\omega_*} = \tfrac{1+\Delta p}{2} \text{ and } p^{\omega_\dagger} = \tfrac{1-\Delta p}{2}\text{, cf. appendix} \\
&\ge \tfrac{n\Delta p^2}{(1-\Delta p^2) + n\Delta p^2} + \tfrac{n\Delta p^2}{(1-\Delta p^2) + n\Delta p^2} - 1 \\
&= \tfrac{2n\Delta p^2}{1+(n-1)\Delta p^2} - 1 = \tfrac{(n+1)\Delta p^2 - 1}{1+(n-1)\Delta p^2} \\
&= 1 - 2\tfrac{1-\Delta p^2}{1+(n-1)\Delta p^2}
\end{aligned} \tag{15}$$

This allows us to obtain a lower bound for the probability of ω_* winning the approval vote:

$$\begin{aligned}
&\mathbb{P}(\textstyle\bigwedge_{\omega_\dagger \in \mathcal{W} \setminus \{\omega_*\}} X^{\omega_*} > X^{\omega_\dagger}) \\
&\text{Equation (6)} \\
&\ge 1 - \textstyle\sum_{i=1}^{m-1} (1 - \mathbb{P}(X^{\omega_*} > X^{\omega_i})) \\
&\text{Equation (15)} \\
&\ge 1 - \textstyle\sum_{i=1}^{m-1} (1 - (1 - 2\tfrac{1-\Delta p^2}{1+(n-1)\Delta p^2})) \\
&= 1 - \tfrac{2(m-1)(1-\Delta p^2)}{1+(n-1)\Delta p^2}
\end{aligned} \tag{16}$$

Consequently, we obtain the following estimate for the number of independent agents needed to surpass a given success probability of $P_{\min}$:

$$n \ge 1 + 2\Big(\frac{1}{\Delta p^2} - 1\Big)\Big(\frac{m-1}{1-P_{\min}}\Big). \tag{17}$$

Note that now we obtain $n \ge 1$ whenever $\Delta p = 1$ as desired. It can also be checked that this estimate is superior to Equation (9) for all values of Δp, m, and $P_{\min}$. However, between the estimates Equation (12) and Equation (17) none dominates the other for all values; therefore it is advisable to determine the minimum of the two in every case. Thus we arrive at our final bound:

Theorem 6. *In a Δp-group reliable setting with m choices, the worst case approval vote success probability is at least $P_{\min}$ whenever the number of agents is equal or higher than*

$$\min\Big(\tfrac{2}{\Delta p^2}\ln Q, 1 + (\tfrac{1}{\Delta p^2} - 1)Q\Big), \tag{18}$$

where $Q = 2\frac{m-1}{1-P_{\min}}$ is the twofold ratio between the number of incorrect alternatives and the admissible error probability.

Figure 1 visualizes the thus established lower bounds of n depending on the parameters. While, in conformance with intuition, n goes against infinity as m grows, as $P_{\min}$ approaches 1, or as Δp approaches 0, the asymptotic behaviour is qualitatively different: ensuring very high success probabilities or managing large numbers of choices has a much more moderate influence on the number of agents to be employed than coping with small group reliability margins.

7 Failure of the Non-Asymptotic Statement

We recall the non-asymptotic part of the original CJT stating that for any two odd natural numbers $i, j \in \mathbb{N}$ with $i < j$, the probability that ω_* wins the majority vote in a setting with i agents is strictly smaller than the probability for a setting with j agents.

It has been observed before that this proposition fails when the homogeneity assumption is dropped, even when upholding completeness and confining the choices to two (Owen, Grofman, and Feld 1989). We will now formally show that this failure is not just an artifact for small agent numbers, but that it occurs for arbitrarily large n.

Theorem 7. *Let $k \in \mathbb{N}$. Given $\mathcal{W} = \{\omega_*, \omega_\dagger\}$ as well as average approval probabilities $\bar{p}^{\omega_*}$ and $\bar{p}^{\omega_\dagger} = 1 - \bar{p}^{\omega_*}$ with $\bar{p}^{\omega_*} - \bar{p}^{\omega_\dagger} = \Delta p$ satisfying $1 > \Delta p > 0$, then there exist $i, j \in \mathbb{N}$ with $j > i > k$ and corresponding joint distributions $\mathbb{P}$ and $\mathbb{P}'$ for complete approval voting settings over $\mathcal{W}$ with j and i agents, respectively, such that*

$$\mathbb{P}\Big(X^{\omega_*} > X^{\omega_\dagger}\Big) < \mathbb{P}'\Big(X^{\omega_*} > X^{\omega_\dagger}\Big).$$

In words, no matter how large the number of agents, if the concrete success probability is unknown, one can never be sure it will improve upon picking a setting with more agents.

We will show this by providing, for any given k and Δp concrete joint distributions where the success probability decreases despite an increasing number of agents. These distributions will be obtained, on the one hand, from the homogeneous setting underlying the original CJT and, on the other hand, from a scenario that we call the *experts & deniers setting*. In the following, let $\bar{p}^{\omega_*}$ and $\bar{p}^{\omega_\dagger}$ be fixed with $\bar{p}^{\omega_*} - \bar{p}^{\omega_\dagger} = \Delta p$ satisfying $1 > \Delta p > 0$. Due to the complete setting, we also know that $\bar{p}^{\omega_\dagger} = 1 - \bar{p}^{\omega_*}$ and thus $\bar{p}^{\omega_*} = \frac{1+\Delta p}{2}$ and $\bar{p}^{\omega_\dagger} = \frac{1-\Delta p}{2}$.

Definition 6. *For any $j \in \mathbb{N}$, let $\mathbb{P}_j^-$ denote the unique joint probability distribution for the j-agent homogeneous complete setting with choices $\mathcal{W} = \{\omega_*, \omega_\dagger\}$.*

This is the probability distribution underlying Condorcet's original theorem. We obtain the following coarse estimate of an upper bound for the probability of the approval vote leading to a correct outcome:

$$\begin{aligned}\mathbb{P}_j^-\left(X^{\omega_*} > X^{\omega_\dagger}\right) &< 1 - \mathbb{P}_j^-\left(X^{\omega_\dagger}{=}j\right)\\ &= 1 - (\bar{p}^{\omega_\dagger})^j\\ &= 1 - (\tfrac{1-\Delta p}{2})^j.\end{aligned}$$

Hence, given $\Delta p < 1$, we note that $\mathbb{P}_j^-\left(X^{\omega_*} > X^{\omega_\dagger}\right)$ is strictly smaller than 1 for every j.

This homogeneous setting will now be contrasted with the *experts & deniers setting*, which in a way represents the "most inhomogeneous" way of realizing a joint probability distribution with the given average probabilities. In such a setting, every but possibly one agent falls into one of two categories: she can be an *expert*, who always infallibly picks the right choice, or a *denier*, who persistently chooses the incorrect option. Notably, in such a setting, the outcome of the majority vote is almost deterministic: it can take at most two different values, namely the floor and the ceiling of the expected value.

Definition 7. *For any $i \in \mathbb{N}$, we let $\mathbb{P}_i^+$ denote the i-agent joint probability distribution with agent-wise Bernoulli parameters $p_1^{\omega_*}, p_1^{\omega_\dagger}, \ldots, p_i^{\omega_*}, p_i^{\omega_\dagger}$ defined by:*

$$p_\ell^{\omega_*} = \begin{cases} 1 & \ell \leq \lfloor i\bar{p}^{\omega_*} \rfloor \\ i\bar{p}^{\omega_*} - \lfloor i\bar{p}^{\omega_*} \rfloor & \lfloor i\bar{p}^{\omega_*} \rfloor < \ell \leq \lceil i\bar{p}^{\omega_*} \rceil \\ 0 & \lceil i\bar{p}^{\omega_*} \rceil < \ell \end{cases}$$

while $p_\ell^{\omega_\dagger} = 1 - p_\ell^{\omega_*}$. We refer to this type of distribution as the experts & deniers setting.

Inspecting $\mathbb{P}_i^+$, we see that $\bar{p}^{\omega_*}$ and $\bar{p}^{\omega_\dagger}$ are indeed the average approval probabilities of ω_* and $\omega_\dagger$, respectively. Also note that by construction, due to the near-deterministic nature of this setting, we have

$$\mathbb{P}_i^+(\lfloor i\bar{p}^{\omega_*} \rfloor \leq X^{\omega_*} \leq \lceil i\bar{p}^{\omega_*} \rceil) = 1 \text{ as well as}$$
$$\mathbb{P}_i^+(\lfloor i\bar{p}^{\omega_\dagger} \rfloor \leq X^{\omega_\dagger} \leq \lceil i\bar{p}^{\omega_\dagger} \rceil) = 1.$$

Then, whenever we pick $i \geq \frac{2}{\Delta p}$, we obtain

$$\lceil i\bar{p}^{\omega_\dagger} \rceil < i\bar{p}^{\omega_\dagger} + 1 \leq i\bar{p}^{\omega_\dagger} + i\Delta p - 1 = i\bar{p}^{\omega_*} - 1 < \lfloor i\bar{p}^{\omega_*} \rfloor,$$

and therefore with the above

$$\mathbb{P}_i^+(X^{\omega_*} > X^{\omega_\dagger}) = 1.$$

In words, whenever the number of agents is large enough, the experts & deniers setting ensures that the true world state will be identified with a probability of 1. From these observations, the proof of Theorem 7 follows immediately by picking $j > i > \max(k, \frac{2}{\Delta p})$ and letting $\mathbb{P}' = \mathbb{P}_i^+$ as well as $\mathbb{P} = \mathbb{P}_j^-$.

As an aside, the experts & deniers setting discussed here also serves as a good case in point to demonstrate that in the non-homogeneous setting, the Central Limit Theorem (CLT, which, in fact, comes handy to show homogeneous versions of the CJT) is not applicable. This holds even when resorting to the CLT formulations of Lyapunov (1900; 1902) or Lindeberg (1922) which can cope with sums of not identically distributed random variables. Both versions rely on the sum of the variances to grow indefinitely for $n \to \infty$. This is not the case for sequences of experts & deniers settings where most of the underlying Bernoulli parameters p_i^{ω} are 0 or 1, leading to a variance of 0. Indeed, such sequence do not converge against the normal distribution. This is the reason why we employed tail estimates in our proofs which are more robust against extremal variances.

8 Conclusion and Future Work

Motivated by multi-agent belief fusion scenarios, this paper established a generalized Condorcet Jury Theorem that holds under remarkably weak assumptions. That is, in the generalization presented here, agents are allowed to have heterogeneously distributed competence levels as long as the group of agents is on average more likely to vote for the correct alternative than any other alternative. It was shown that this holds for any finite number of alternatives under approval voting, where every agent is allowed to vote for any number of alternatives.

Beyond establishing this result, we were able to derive estimates for the number of independent agents necessary to guarantee a prescribed minimal probability, $P_{\min}$, of the aggregation process being successful, given the number m of alternatives, and the minimum distance Δp between the average approval probabilities for correct and wrong alternative.

Finally, we proved an impossibility result: When weakening the homogeneity assumption by allowing for average competence levels, part (1) of Condorcet's original jury theorem fails for any arbitrarily large number of agents. That is, the probability that the voting procedure yields the correct alternative cannot be guaranteed to increase when choosing a larger team of agents.

In future work, we intend to perform experiments to estimate whether there still is a significant margin between the theoretically established guarantees we provide and the statistical behavior observed when belief fusion through voting aggregation is simulated. If a significant difference were found, this would clearly motivate the search for even better, tighter theoretical bounds.

We also aim to integrate our generalized Condorcet Jury Theorem into the formal belief fusion framework: following the argument by Everaere, Konieczny, and Marquis (2010), our generalization gives rise to a new postulate for belief merging operators, based on group-reliability. Consequently, it is worthwhile to investigate which of the well-known operators used in the belief fusion literature satisfy this new postulate. The operators found to satisfy this new postulate are capable of tracking the true state of the world under the weak assumptions underlying our generalization of the CJT.

Moreover, it would be important to investigate to what extent our results can be maintained when allowing for a certain degree of mutual influence among the voters, thereby weakening the assumption of *independence*. Indeed, there exist results that extend the CJT in that direction. Ladha (1992) generalized the CJT in the dichotomic setting with majority voting by only restricting the average coefficients of correlations. On another note, Pivato (2017) generalized the CJT to a class of voting rules for more than two alternatives such as plurality voting and approval voting allowing for significant correlations among voters. Note that both these works weaken the requirement toward agent independence but impose that all participating agents are individually reliable, i.e., they cannot handle scenarios where unreliable or even malicious agents are involved. For future work, it is thus interesting to see to what extent the result shown here can be generalized to accommodate a moderate amount of correlation among voters, along the lines of the approaches mentioned above.

As a further generalization, it seems promising to look into scenarios where agents are allowed to give more fine-grained feedback than the simple approval or non-approval of alternatives. For example, Morreau (2021) recently proved a variant of the CJT that considers the aggregation of grades into the median grade assigned to some object in order to track the correct grade: In a peer review scenario, the reviewers assign scores to a given proposal, each of which represents a grade, i.e. a gradual evaluation of the object in question. This approach being restricted to finitely many grades, a natural generalization to consider would be to allow for real-valued evaluations of objects such as fuzzy values or probabilities. If such a generalization can be shown, one could, for instance, aggregate probabilistic statements with the aim of tracking the correct probability assessment of an event directly. Clearly, approaches along those lines will need to be compared to well-established methods of quantitative belief fusion for heterogeneous sources such as Bayesian frameworks, Dempster-Shafer theory as well as fuzzy and possibilistic approaches (Bloch et al. 2001).

Appendix

We briefly present the determination of the extremal value determination used in Equation (12). Our goal is to determine the minimal value of the following expression over all $p = \bar{p}^{\omega_*}$:

$$\begin{aligned}
&\tfrac{n^2\Delta p^2}{4np^{\omega_*}(1-p^{\omega_*})+n^2\Delta p^2} + \tfrac{n^2\Delta p^2}{4np^{\omega_\dagger}(1-p^{\omega_\dagger})+n^2\Delta p^2} - 1 \\
&= \frac{1}{\frac{4np^{\omega_*}(1-p^{\omega_*})}{n^2\Delta p^2}+1} + \frac{1}{\frac{4np^{\omega_*}(1-p^{\omega_\dagger})}{n^2\Delta p^2}+1} - 1 \\
&\text{substitute } u = \tfrac{4np^{\omega_*}(1-p^{\omega_*})}{n^2\Delta p^2} \text{ and } v = \tfrac{4np^{\omega_\dagger}(1-p^{\omega_\dagger})}{n^2\Delta p^2} \\
&= \tfrac{1}{u+1} + \tfrac{1}{v+1} - 1
\end{aligned}$$

We obtain the value of the $p = \bar{p}^{\omega_*}$ producing the minimum of this expression as the zeros of its first derivative. Consequently, letting $(.)'$ denote $\frac{\mathrm{d}}{\mathrm{d}p}(.)$, we find

$$\begin{aligned}
0 &= \left(\tfrac{1}{u+1} + \tfrac{1}{v+1} - 1\right)' = \left(\tfrac{1}{u+1}\right)' + \left(\tfrac{1}{v+1}\right)' \\
&= \tfrac{-u'}{(u+1)^2} + \tfrac{-v'}{(v+1)^2}.
\end{aligned}$$

Multiplying with $(u+1)^2(v+1)^2$, we obtain:

$$0 = -v'(u+1)^2 - u'(v+1)^2,$$

and further

$$\begin{aligned}
0 &= (2p - 1 - 2\Delta p)(p - p^2 + (n\tfrac{\Delta p}{2})^2)^2 \\
&\quad + (2p-1)((n\tfrac{\Delta p}{2})^2 + p - p^2 - \Delta p + 2p\Delta p - \Delta p^2)^2 \\
&= (2p - \Delta p - 1)\cdot \\
&\quad (2p^4 - 4p^3\Delta p - 4p^3 + 4p^2\Delta p^2 + 6p^2\Delta p \\
&\quad - 4p^2(n\tfrac{\Delta p}{2})^2 + 2p^2 - 2p\Delta p^3 - 4p\Delta p^2 \\
&\quad + 4p\Delta p(n\tfrac{\Delta p}{2})^2 - 2p\Delta p + 4p(n\tfrac{\Delta p}{2})^2 \\
&\quad + \Delta p^3 + \Delta p^2 - 2\Delta p(n\tfrac{\Delta p}{2})^2 + 2(n\tfrac{\Delta p}{2})^4).
\end{aligned}$$

As the second factor does not produce zeros under the given assumptions, we proceed with

$$\begin{aligned}
0 &= 2p - \Delta p - 1 \\
p &= \tfrac{1+\Delta p}{2},
\end{aligned}$$

which yields

$$\begin{aligned}
p^{\omega_*} &= p = \tfrac{1+\Delta p}{2} \text{ as well as} \\
p^{\omega_\dagger} &= p^{\omega_*} - \Delta p = \tfrac{1-\Delta p}{2}.
\end{aligned}$$

Acknowledgments

Sebastian Rudolph has received funding from the European Research Council (Grant Agreement no. 771779, DeciGUT). Jonas Karge was supported by by the Bundesministerium fur Bildung und Forschung (BMBF, Federal Ministry of Education and Research) in the Center for Scalable Data Analytics and Artificial Intelligence (ScaDS.AI). We are grateful for comments by Lucía Gómez Álvarez as well as the three anonymous reviewers.

References

Agogino, A. M.; Granderson, J.; and Qiu, S. 2002. Sensor validation and fusion with distributed 'smart dust' motes for monitoring and enabling efficient energy use. In *Proceedings of the AAAI 2002 Spring Symposium, 2002*, 51–57.

Ben-Yashar, R., and Paroush, J. 2000. A nonasymptotic condorcet jury theorem. *Social Choice and Welfare* 17:189–199.

Berend, D., and Paroush, J. 1998. When is Condorcet's Jury Theorem valid? *Social Choice and Welfare* 15:481–488.

Bloch, I.; Hunter, A.; Appriou, A.; Ayoun, A.; Benferhat, S.; Besnard, P.; Cholvy, L.; Cooke, R.; Cuppens, F.; Dubois, D.; Fargier, H.; Grabisch, M.; Kruse, R.; Lang, J.; Moral, S.; Prade, H.; Saffiotti, A.; Smets, P.; and Sossai, C. 2001. Fusion: General concepts and characteristics. *International Journal of Intelligent Systems* 16(10):1107–1134.

Cantelli, F. P. 1928. Sui confini della probabilita. *Atti del Congresso Internazional del Matematici* 6:47 – 59.

Chebyshev, P. L. 1867. Des valeurs moyennes. *Liouville's Journal de Mathématiques Pures et Appliquées* 12:177–184.

Marquis de Condorcet, M. J. A. N. C. 1785. *Essai sur l'application de l'analyse à la probabilité des décisions rendues à la pluralité des voix.* Imprimerie Royale, Paris.

Dietterich, T. G. 2000. Ensemble methods in machine learning. In *Multiple Classifier Systems*, 1–15. Berlin, Heidelberg: Springer Berlin Heidelberg.

Everaere, P.; Konieczny, S.; and Marquis, P. 2010. The epistemic view of belief merging: Can we track the truth? In Coelho, H.; Studer, R.; and Wooldridge, M. J., eds., *Proceedings of the 19th European Conference on Artificial Intelligence (ECAI 2010)*, volume 215 of *FAIA*, 621–626. IOS Press.

Haenggi, M. 2016. *Smart Dust: Sensor Network Applications, Architecture, and Design.* Boca Raton: Taylor & Francis. Chapter 1.

Hoeffding, W. 1963. Probability inequalities for sums of bounded random variables. *Journal of the American Statistical Association* 58(301):13–30.

Jain, B. J. 2018. Condorcet's jury theorem for consensus clustering. In Trollmann, F., and Turhan, A., eds., *Proceedings of the 41st German Conference on AI (KI 2018)*, volume 11117 of *LNCS*, 155–168. Springer.

Jensen, J. L. W. V. 1906. Sur les fonctions convexes et les inégalités entre les valeurs moyennes. *Acta Mathematica* 30:175 – 193.

Ladha, K. K. 1992. The Condorcet jury theorem, free speech, and correlated votes. *American Journal of Political Science* 36(3):617–634.

Lam, L. 2000. Classifier combinations: Implementations and theoretical issues. In Kittler, J., and Roli, F., eds., *Proceedings of the First International Workshop on Multiple Classifier Systems (MCS 2000)*, volume 1857 of *LNCS*, 77–86. Springer.

Lindeberg, J. W. 1922. Eine neue Herleitung des Exponentialgesetzes in der Wahrscheinlichkeitsrechnung. *Mathematische Zeitschrift* 15:211–225.

List, C., and Goodin, R. E. 2001. Epistemic democracy: Generalizing the Condorcet jury theorem. *Journal of Political Philosophy* 9(3):277–306.

Lyapunov, A. 1900. Sur une proposition de la théorie des probabilités. *Bulletin de l'Académie impériale des sciences de St. Pétersbourg* 13:359–386.

Lyapunov, A. 1902. Nouvelle forme du théorème sur la limite de probabilité. *Mémoires de l'Académie impériale des sciences de St. Pétersbourg* 12:1–24.

Masterton, G., and Olsson, E. J. 2016. Linking as voting: how the Condorcet jury theorem in political science is relevant to webometrics. *Scientometrics* 106:945–966.

Morreau, M. 2021. Democracy without enlightenment: A jury theorem for evaluative voting. *Journal of Political Philosophy* 29(2):188–210.

Nerkar, M. H., and Kumar, N. 2016. Smart Dust. *International Journal of Advanced Research in Computer and Communication Engineering* 5:685–691.

Owen, G.; Grofman, B.; and Feld, S. L. 1989. Proving a distribution-free generalization of the Condorcet Jury Theorem. *Mathematical Social Sciences* 17(1):1–16.

Pigozzi, G., and Hartmann, S. 2007. Aggregation in multiagent systems and the problem of truth-tracking. In Durfee, E. H.; Yokoo, M.; Huhns, M. N.; and Shehory, O., eds., *Proceedings of the 6th International Joint Conference on Autonomous Agents and Multiagent Systems (AAMAS 2007)*, 219–221. IFAAMAS.

Pivato, M. 2017. Epistemic democracy with correlated voters. *Journal of Mathematical Economics* 72(C):51–69.

Sharma, N., and Sultana, P. 2020. Earthquake monitoring and prediction system using smart dust – a novel approach. *International Journal of Scientific and Technology Research* 9(4):3103 – 3109.

Young, H. P. 1988. Condorcet's theory of voting. *The American Political Science Review* 82(4):1231–1244.

Computing Stable Conclusions under the Weakest-Link Principle in the ASPIC+ Argumentation Formalism

Tuomo Lehtonen[1] , **Johannes P. Wallner**[2] , **Matti Järvisalo**[1]
[1]University of Helsinki, Helsinki, Finland
[2]Graz University of Technology, Graz, Austria
{tuomo.lehtonen, matti.jarvisalo}@helsinki.fi, wallner@ist.tugraz.at

Abstract

Rephrasing argumentation semantics in terms of subsets of defeasible elements allows for gaining new insights for reasoning about acceptance in established fragments of the central structured argumentation formalism of ASPIC$^+$. We provide a non-trivial generalization of these recent results, capturing preferences in ASPIC$^+$. In particular, considering preferences under the weakest-link principle, we show that the stable semantics can be phrased in terms of subsets of defeasible elements. We employ the rephrasing for establishing both complexity results and practical algorithms for reasoning about acceptance in this variant of ASPIC$^+$. Justified by completeness for the second level of the polynomial hierarchy, we develop an iterative answer set solving based approach to reasoning about acceptance under the so-called elitist lifting in ASPIC$^+$ frameworks. Our implementation of the approach scales well in practice.

1 Introduction

Argumentation is an established area of knowledge representation and reasoning research, with the fundamental aim of drawing conclusions from internally inconsistent or incomplete knowledge bases (Baroni et al. 2018; Gabbay et al. 2021; Atkinson et al. 2017). Arguments most often have an intrinsic structure made explicit through derivations from more basic structures. Computational models for structured argumentation (Bondarenko et al. 1997; Cyras et al. 2018; García and Simari 2014; García and Simari 2018; Besnard and Hunter 2008; Besnard and Hunter 2018)—ASPIC$^+$ (Modgil and Prakken 2018; Modgil and Prakken 2013) among the most prominent formalisms—enable making the internal structure of arguments explicit. In its general form, ASPIC$^+$ allows for arguments that combine strict inference rules—capturing deductively valid inferences—and defeasible inference rules—capturing presumptive inference—as well as accounting for preferential information. On one hand, this generality enables application in various settings, including legal reasoning (Prakken et al. 2015; Prakken 2012), ontology-based data access (Yun and Croitoru 2016), intelligence analysis (Toniolo et al. 2015), and information extraction for online crime reports (Schraagen et al. 2018). On the other hand, developing insights on the complexity and algorithmic aspects of reasoning in ASPIC$^+$ is still called for and remains a challenge.

Recently, an answer set programming (ASP) (Niemelä 1999; Brewka et al. 2015) approach to reasoning in ASPIC$^+$ without preferences was proposed (Lehtonen, Wallner, and Järvisalo 2020). Based on phrasing argumentation semantics in terms of subsets of defeasible elements in ASPIC$^+$, the approach avoids a potentially exponential translation to Dung's abstract argumentation frameworks (Dung 1995) employed earlier for realizing reasoning in ASPIC$^+$ (Snaith and Reed 2012; Thimm 2017) altogether, and instead employs an ASP solver on a direct ASP encoding on the level of ASPIC$^+$ for the reasoning task at hand.

In this work we study possibilities of generalizing these recent insights to preferential reasoning in ASPIC$^+$. In particular, we consider an instantiation of ASPIC$^+$ composed of atomic sentences, including axioms and ordinary premises, and allowing asymmetric negation. Towards a computational approach supporting preferences, we formally extend the foundations of rephrasing semantics developed earlier (Lehtonen, Wallner, and Järvisalo 2020) to cover preferences under the central weakest-link principle and elitist lifting (Modgil and Prakken 2018), focusing on the stable semantics as the first goal.

We provide both new complexity results as well as algorithms for credulous and skeptical reasoning, together with an experimental evaluation of an implementation of the algorithms. The non-trivial extension we develop of the earlier rephrasing to incorporate preferential reasoning is central for these contributions. In terms of complexity results, we show Σ_2^P and Π_2^P completeness for credulous and skeptical reasoning, respectively, for ASPIC$^+$ frameworks satisfying prominent rationality criteria (Modgil and Prakken 2018). Furthermore, we establish that reasoning has milder complexity (NP- and coNP-complete) for the case without defeasible rules, thereby being of the same complexity as the case without preferences (Lehtonen, Wallner, and Järvisalo 2020). Our rephrasing is vital here, since an explicated abstract framework yields structures not bounded polynomially, and these complexity classes restrict algorithms (among other aspects) to polynomial space consumption. The complexity results clearly indicate that inclusion of preferences increase complexity of reasoning in ASPIC$^+$. Moreover, our rephrasing highlights that the jump in complexity is due to a particular type of attack ("contradictory rebut") when combined with preferential reasoning.

In addition to the complexity results, in light of completeness of acceptance for the second level of the polynomial hierarchy, we employ the rephrasing in developing ASP-based counterexample-guided abstraction refinement algorithms for credulous and skeptical reasoning in ASPIC$^+$ with preferences, making use of incremental ASP solving techniques, and show that an implementation of the approach shows promising scalability up to hundreds of sentences.

After recalling necessary preliminaries of ASPIC$^+$ in Section 2, we overview our complexity results in Section 3. The extended rephrasing with preferences is presented in two parts: in Section 4 defeats on assumption are presented and Section 5 shows the rephrasing of stable semantics. In Section 6 the novel algorithms are presented, and experiments are presented in Section 7. We conclude after discussing related works in Section 8. An extended version of the paper with formal proofs is available via the authors' webpages.

2 ASPIC$^+$ Framework

We recall background on ASPIC$^+$ (Modgil and Prakken 2018; Modgil and Prakken 2013; Prakken 2010). We assume a set (language) $\mathcal{L}$ composed of atoms x. We start with contrariness.

Definition 1. *Let a contrary function be* $^{-}: \mathcal{L} \rightarrow 2^{\mathcal{L}}$. *We say that* $a \in \mathcal{L}$ *is a contrary of* $b \in \mathcal{L}$ *if* $a \in \overline{b}$ *and* $b \notin \overline{a}$. *We say that* a *is a contradictory of* b *if* $a \in \overline{b}$ *and* $b \in \overline{a}$.

That is, contraries represent an asymmetric relation, while contradictories are symmetric. When a and b are contradictory to each other we sometimes write $-a = b$ (or $a = -b$). An atom may be a contradictory to several atoms.

A central part of an ASPIC$^+$ framework is a knowledge base $\mathcal{K} \subseteq \mathcal{L}$ comprised of a defeasible part (ordinary premises $\mathcal{K}_p$) and a non-defeasible part (axioms $\mathcal{K}_n$).

Definition 2. *A knowledge base is a set* $\mathcal{K}_n \cup \mathcal{K}_p = \mathcal{K} \subseteq \mathcal{L}$, *with disjoint sets* $\mathcal{K}_n$ *(axioms) and* $\mathcal{K}_p$ *(ordinary premises).*

Another part of ASPIC$^+$ is a set of rules over $\mathcal{L}$, denoted by $\mathcal{R}$. This set is composed of defeasible rules $a_1, \ldots, a_n \Rightarrow b$ and strict rules $a_1, \ldots, a_n \rightarrow b$. We denote the set of defeasible rules by $\mathcal{R}_d$ and the set of strict rules by $\mathcal{R}_s$. When we do not distinguish between strict or defeasible rules, we write $a_1, \ldots, a_n \rightsquigarrow b$. A partial function $n : \mathcal{R}_d \rightarrow \mathcal{L}$ gives names to defeasible rules. For a rule $r = a_1, \ldots, a_n \rightsquigarrow b$, we denote its head by $head(r) = b$ and its body by $body(r) = \{a_1, \ldots, a_n\}$.

For preferences, we consider preorders (i.e., reflexive and transitive binary relations) $\leq = \leq_p \cup \leq_d$, composed of a preorder on ordinary premises $\leq_p$ and a preorder on defeasible rules $\leq_d$.

Definition 3. *An argumentation theory (AT) is a tuple* $(\mathcal{L}, \mathcal{R}, n, ^{-}, \mathcal{K}, \leq)$, *with a knowledge base* $\mathcal{K} \subseteq \mathcal{L}$, *rules* $\mathcal{R} = \mathcal{R}_d \cup \mathcal{R}_s$ *over* $\mathcal{L}$, *a contrary function* $^{-}: \mathcal{L} \rightarrow 2^{\mathcal{L}}$, *a partial function* $n : \mathcal{R}_d \rightarrow \mathcal{L}$, *and a preorder* $\leq = \leq_p \cup \leq_d$.

Each part of an AT is assumed to be finite. Arguments are constructed from parts of an AT. An argument represents a "derivation tree" starting from elements in the knowledge base and uses rules to derive a conclusion.

Definition 4. *Given an AT* $T = (\mathcal{L}, \mathcal{R}, n, ^{-}, \mathcal{K}, \leq)$, *the set of arguments in* T *is inductively defined as follows.*

- *If* $x \in \mathcal{K}$, *then* $A = x$ *is an argument with* $\texttt{Conc}(A) = x$.
- *If* $A_1, \ldots, A_n$ *are arguments,* $x_i = \texttt{Conc}(A_i)$ *for* $1 \leq i \leq n$, *and* $(x_1, \ldots, x_n \rightsquigarrow x) \in \mathcal{R}$, *then* $A = A_1, \ldots, A_n \rightsquigarrow x$ *is an argument with* $\texttt{Conc}(A) = x$.

There are no other arguments.

We make use of the following shorthands.

Definition 5. *Let* $T = (\mathcal{L}, \mathcal{R}, n, ^{-}, \mathcal{K}, \leq)$ *be an AT, and* A *an argument in* T.

- *If* $A = x \in \mathcal{K}$ *then* $\texttt{Sub}(A) = \{A\}$ *and* $\texttt{Rules}(A) = \emptyset$.
- *If* $A = A_1, \ldots, A_n \rightsquigarrow x$, *then*
  $\texttt{Sub}(A) = \{A\} \cup \bigcup_{i=1}^{n} \texttt{Sub}(A_i)$,
  $\texttt{TopRule}(A) = (\texttt{Conc}(A_1), \ldots, \texttt{Conc}(A_n) \rightsquigarrow x)$, *and*
  $\texttt{Rules}(A) = \{\texttt{TopRule}(A)\} \cup \bigcup_{i=1}^{n} \texttt{Rules}(A_i)$.

Further, $\texttt{Prem}(A) = \texttt{Sub}(A) \cap \mathcal{K}$, $\texttt{Prem}_\texttt{d}(A) = \texttt{Prem}(A) \cap \mathcal{K}_p$, *and* $\texttt{DefRules}(A) = \texttt{Rules}(A) \cap \mathcal{R}_d$.

That is, we define shorthands for the subarguments (Sub) of an argument, the rules and defeasible rules in the argument (Rules and DefRules), the topmost rule (TopRule), the premises of the argument within the knowledge base (Prem), and the ordinary premises ($\texttt{Prem}_\texttt{d}$). Further, $\texttt{defPart}(A) = \texttt{Prem}_\texttt{d}(A) \cup \texttt{DefRules}(A)$. If $A \in \mathcal{K}$, then $\texttt{TopRule}(A)$ is undefined. We extend the shorthands for a set of arguments $\mathcal{A}$ as $\texttt{Conc}(\mathcal{A}) = \{\texttt{Conc}(A) \mid A \in \mathcal{A}\}$ and $\texttt{TopRule}(\mathcal{A}) = \{\texttt{TopRule}(A) \mid A \in \mathcal{A}\}$. For each shorthand $f \in \{\texttt{Sub}, \texttt{Rules}, \texttt{DefRules}, \texttt{Prem}, \texttt{Prem}_\texttt{d}\}$ returning a set, we define $f(\mathcal{A}) = \bigcup_{A \in \mathcal{A}} f(A)$. An argument A is an immediate subargument of $B = A_1, \ldots, A_n \rightsquigarrow x$ if $A \in \{A_1, \ldots, A_n\}$. We allow only finite structures as arguments (i.e., arguments which are "trees" of finite size), and consider as arguments those arguments A for which $\texttt{Sub}(A)$ is finite (disallowing infinite chaining of rules, e.g., via $x \rightsquigarrow x$), as also defined by Modgil and Prakken (2018).

Conflicts among arguments are defined via attacks between arguments.

Definition 6. *Given an AT* $T = (\mathcal{L}, \mathcal{R}, n, ^{-}, \mathcal{K}, \leq)$ *and two arguments* A *and* B *in* T, *argument* A *attacks argument* B *iff* A *undercuts, rebuts, or undermines* B, *where*

- A *undercuts* B *(on* B'*) iff* $\texttt{Conc}(A) \in \overline{n(r)}$ *for some* $B' \in \texttt{Sub}(B)$ *such that* $\texttt{TopRule}(B') = r$ *is defeasible;*
- A *rebuts* B *(on* B'*) iff* $\texttt{Conc}(A) \in \overline{x}$ *for some* $B' = B_1, \ldots, B_n \Rightarrow x \in \texttt{Sub}(B)$*; and*
- A *undermines* B *(on* x*) iff* $\texttt{Conc}(A) \in \overline{x}$ *and* $x \in \texttt{Prem}_\texttt{d}(B)$.

That is, an argument attacks another argument on the defeasible parts of the latter. Ordinary premises can be attacked by undermining, and defeasible rules can be attacked by rebutting the conclusion or undercutting the rule itself. For rebuts and undermining one distinguishes further if $\texttt{Conc}(A)$ and x are contraries or contradictories: in the former case we say that A contrary undermines (rebuts) B and in the latter that A contradictory undermines (rebuts) B.

The preorders $\leq_p$ and $\leq_d$ on the defeasible parts are lifted to strict partial orders (i.e., to irreflexive, asymmetric, and transitive binary relations) $\triangleleft_p$ and $\triangleleft_d$, via lifting operators. We focus on the elitist lifting (Modgil and Prakken 2018). As usual, the strict part of $\leq_p$ ($\leq_d$) is defined by $x <_p y$ iff $x \leq_p y$ and $y \not\leq_p x$ (same for $\leq_d$).

Definition 7. *Let $\leq$ be a preorder on a set X. Define $\triangleleft^{Eli}$ for two non-empty $Y, Z \subseteq X$ by $Y \triangleleft^{Eli} Z$ iff $\exists a \in Y$ s.t. $\forall b \in Z$ we have $a < b$. Moreover, $\emptyset \not\triangleleft^{Eli} Y$ and $Z \triangleleft^{Eli} \emptyset$ for each non-empty Z.*

That is, Z is preferred to Y if there is at least one element in Y that is strictly less preferred to each element in Z. The empty set is a special case, being strictly preferred to each non-empty set, and cannot be less preferred than any set.

For two preorders $\leq_p$ and $\leq_d$ and their liftings $\triangleleft^{Eli} = \triangleleft_p^{Eli} \cup \triangleleft_d^{Eli}$, one defines a strict partial order $\prec$ on arguments, denoting the preference (ranking) on arguments using certain principles. We omit the superscript *Eli* in the remainder of the paper. We focus here on the weakest-link principle, by which one considers all defeasible elements of arguments in the comparison. An argument B is strictly preferred to A ($A \prec B$) whenever

- if $\texttt{DefRules}(A) = \texttt{DefRules}(B) = \emptyset$, then $\texttt{Prem}_\texttt{d}(A) \triangleleft \texttt{Prem}_\texttt{d}(B)$;
- if $\texttt{Prem}_\texttt{d}(A) = \texttt{Prem}_\texttt{d}(B) = \emptyset$, then $\texttt{DefRules}(A) \triangleleft \texttt{DefRules}(B)$;
- else $\texttt{Prem}_\texttt{d}(A) \triangleleft \texttt{Prem}_\texttt{d}(B)$ and $\texttt{DefRules}(A) \triangleleft \texttt{DefRules}(B)$.

Defeats between arguments, i.e., successful attacks, are defined based on argument preferences as follows.

Definition 8. *Given an AT $T = (\mathcal{L}, \mathcal{R}, n, \overline{}, \mathcal{K}, \leq)$ and two arguments A and B in T, argument A defeats argument B iff A successfully undercuts, rebuts, or undermines B, where*

- *A successfully undercuts B if A undercuts B;*
- *A successfully rebuts B (on B') iff A contrary rebuts B, or A rebuts B on B' and $A \not\prec B'$; and*
- *A successfully undermines B (on x) iff A contrary undermines B, or A undermines B on x and $A \not\prec x$.*

In other words, an undercut always succeeds, as do contrary rebuts and undermining attacks. For intuition, an undercut attacks the very applicability of a rule, and such an attack takes precedence over preferences between arguments. Similarly, as contraries signal an asymmetric incompatibility of two atoms, the presence of a contrary of an atom x results in x being attacked regardless of preferences. Modgil and Prakken (2013; 2018) provide a discussion on this. For the contradictory variants of rebut and undermining (i.e., when conclusion of A and the ordinary premise or conclusion of a defeasible rule in B are contradictories of each other), the preference order $\prec$ on arguments decides whether the attack succeeds: if A is strictly less preferred to the attacked subargument, the attack fails, otherwise it is a defeat.

Example 1. *Let $T = (\mathcal{L}, \mathcal{R}, n, \overline{}, \mathcal{K}, \leq)$ be an AT with $\mathcal{L} = \{a, b, c, w, x, y, z\}$, $\mathcal{K}_p = \{a, b, c\}$, $\mathcal{K}_n = \emptyset$, $\overline{x} = \{z\}$, $\overline{z} = \{x\}$, $\overline{c} = \{y\}$, $\overline{n(r_1)} = \{w\}$, $\mathcal{R}_d = \{(r_1 : a \Rightarrow y), (r_2 : b \Rightarrow x)\}$, and $\mathcal{R}_s = \{(y \rightarrow z), (c \rightarrow w)\}$. We write names of defeasible rules by r_i before the rule. Moreover, let $a \leq_p b$ and $r_1 \leq_d r_2$. The AT is shown in Figure 1(left) with the arguments it gives rise to. Defeasible premises or inference is marked with dashed lines. The arguments and their defeat relation are shown on the right side of this figure. It holds that A_4 undercuts both A_5 and A_7 (on A_5), A_5 contrary undermines both A_1 and A_4 (on A_1), and A_7 contradictory rebuts A_6. Since x and z are contradictory to each other, but A_7 concludes z via a strict rule, it is the case that A_6 does not contradictory rebut A_7. Except for the last attack, all are successful and thus defeats, since $A_7 \prec A_6$ ($\texttt{Prem}_\texttt{d}(A_7) = \{a\} \triangleleft_p \{b\} = \texttt{Prem}_\texttt{d}(A_6)$ due to $a <_p b$ and $\texttt{DefRules}(A_7) = \{r_1\} \triangleleft_d \{r_2\} = \texttt{DefRules}(A_6)$ due to $r_1 <_d r_2$). The unsuccessful contradictory rebut is denoted as a dotted arrow.*

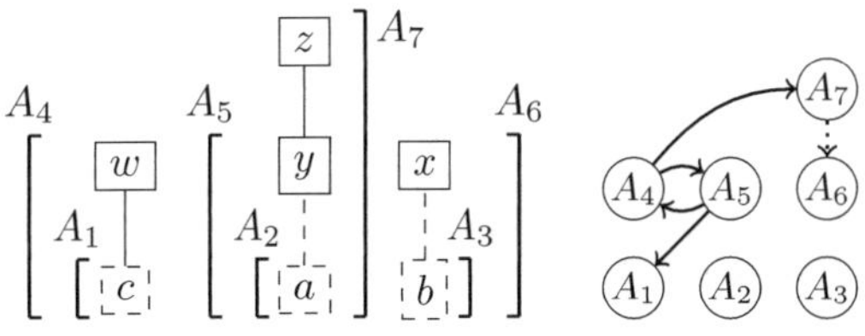

Figure 1: Example AT and corresponding AF

In ASPIC$^+$, there are important conditions which ensure satisfaction of rationality postulates, which might fail in the very general case (Modgil and Prakken 2018; Caminada 2018). It turns out that these conditions are useful for our computational approach, as well. These conditions constrain the set of strict rules in an AT, and we make use of three such conditions here, borrowing from Modgil and Prakken (2018).

A set of strict rules $\mathcal{R}_s$ is said to be closed under transposition if for each $a_1, \ldots, a_n \rightarrow b \in \mathcal{R}_s$ it holds that for each i, $1 \leq i \leq n$, we have $a_1, \ldots, a_{i-1}, b', a_{i+1}, \ldots, a_n \rightarrow a'_i \in \mathcal{R}_s$ for all contradictories $-b' = b$ and $-a'_i = a_i$, and at least one contradictory of each must exist. An AT T is strict-consistent if there are no arguments A, B with $\texttt{defPart}(A) = \texttt{defPart}(B) = \emptyset$ s.t. $\texttt{Conc}(A)$ is a contrary of $\texttt{Conc}(B)$, or $\texttt{Conc}(A)$ and $\texttt{Conc}(B)$ are contradictory to each other.

Definition 9. *We say an AT T is well-formed if*

- *$\mathcal{R}_s$ is closed under transposition,*
- *T is strict-consistent, and*
- *if x is a contrary of y then $y \notin \mathcal{K}_n$ and $y \neq head(r)$ for all $r \in \mathcal{R}_s$.*

For intuition, these conditions aim to avoid certain inconsistencies that may arise, with strict-consistency likely the most immediate: if an AT is not strict-consistent then there are a arguments composed only of axioms and strict rules concluding contrary or contradictory atoms. For details we refer the reader to the work of Modgil and Prakken (2018). We remark that we are using a subset of the conditions of "well-defined" ATs as defined by Modgil and Prakken (2018).

Semantics of ATs are defined via a translation to (abstract) argumentation frameworks (AFs) (Dung 1995). An AF is a pair $F = (\mathcal{A}, \mathcal{D})$ of a set of (abstract) arguments $\mathcal{A}$ and defeats $\mathcal{D} \subseteq \mathcal{A} \times \mathcal{A}$ between arguments. If $(A, B) \in \mathcal{D}$ we say that A defeats B. Similarly, $\mathcal{S} \subseteq \mathcal{A}$ defeats $B \in \mathcal{A}$ if there is an $A \in \mathcal{S}$ with $(A, B) \in \mathcal{D}$. We say that $\mathcal{S}$ defends an argument A if for each $B \in \mathcal{A}$ such that $(B, A) \in \mathcal{D}$, there is a $C \in \mathcal{S}$ such that $(C, B) \in \mathcal{D}$. We consider the AF semantics of conflict-free and admissible sets, and complete and stable extensions, with the corresponding functions $\sigma \in \{cf, adm, com, stb\}$. A semantics $\sigma(F) \subseteq 2^{\mathcal{A}}$ returns a set of extensions. An extension under a semantics σ is a σ-extension for short.

Definition 10. *Given an AF $F = (\mathcal{A}, \mathcal{D})$, a set $\mathcal{E} \subseteq \mathcal{A}$ is conflict-free (in F) if there are no A, B in $\mathcal{E}$ such that $(A, B) \in \mathcal{D}$. The set of all conflict-free sets of F is denoted by $cf(F)$. For an $\mathcal{E} \in cf(F)$, we have*

- *$\mathcal{E} \in adm(F)$ iff each $A \in \mathcal{E}$ is defended by $\mathcal{E}$;*
- *$\mathcal{E} \in com(F)$ iff $\mathcal{E} \in adm(F)$ and each A defended by $\mathcal{E}$ is in $\mathcal{E}$;*
- *$\mathcal{E} \in stb(F)$ iff $\mathcal{E}$ defeats each argument in $\mathcal{A} \setminus \mathcal{E}$.*

ATs can be translated to AFs as follows.

Definition 11. *Let $T = (\mathcal{L}, \mathcal{R}, n, ^-, \mathcal{K}, \leq)$ be an AT. An AF $F = (\mathcal{A}, \mathcal{D})$ corresponds to T if $\mathcal{A}$ is the set of all arguments in T and $\mathcal{D}$ the defeat relation based on T.*

Reasoning on ATs consists of checking whether a queried atom is warranted, by asking (credulously) whether there is a σ-extension having an argument concluding the atom, or (skeptically) whether all σ-extensions have such an argument.

Definition 12. *Given an AT $T = (\mathcal{L}, \mathcal{R}, n, ^-, \mathcal{K}, \leq)$ and an AF F corresponding to T, we say that $x \in \mathcal{L}$ is*

- *skeptically justified in T under semantics σ if in each $\mathcal{E} \in \sigma(F)$ there is an $A \in \mathcal{E}$ with $\texttt{Conc}(A) = x$;*
- *credulously justified in T under semantics σ if there is an $\mathcal{E} \in \sigma(F)$ with an $A \in \mathcal{E}$ s.t. $\texttt{Conc}(A) = x$.*

Example 2. *Continuing Example 1, the AF corresponding to the AT is shown in Figure 1 (right). There are two stable extensions: $\mathcal{E}_1 = \{A_1, A_2, A_3, A_4, A_6\}$ and $\mathcal{E}_2 = \{A_2, A_3, A_5, A_6, A_7\}$. Since $\texttt{Conc}(A_4) = w$, $A_4 \in \mathcal{E}_1$, and there is no argument in $\mathcal{E}_2$ with conclusion w, it holds that w is credulously but not skeptically justified under stable semantics.*

A useful property is that each complete extension of an AF corresponding to an AT is closed under subarguments, i.e., if $\mathcal{E}$ is complete and $A \in \mathcal{E}$, then all $\texttt{Sub}(A)$ are in $\mathcal{E}$, as well. Note that stable extensions are also complete extensions.

Proposition 1 (Modgil and Prakken 2013). *Let $T = (\mathcal{L}, \mathcal{R}, n, ^-, \mathcal{K}, \leq)$ be an AT, $F = (\mathcal{A}, \mathcal{D})$ the AF corresponding to T, and $\mathcal{E} \in com(F)$. It holds that $\mathcal{E}$ is closed under subarguments.*

Building on earlier work (Lehtonen, Wallner, and Järvisalo 2020), we utilize the concept of so-called assumptions (P, D) for a given AT $T = (\mathcal{L}, \mathcal{R}, n, ^-, \mathcal{K}, \leq)$, which represent parts of the defeasible elements: $P \subseteq \mathcal{K}_p$ and $D \subseteq \mathcal{R}_d$. We define $(P, D) \sqsubseteq (P', D')$ if $P \subseteq P'$ and $D \subseteq D'$.

Given a set of rules $\mathcal{R}$ and a set of atoms $L \subseteq \mathcal{L}$, we say that $x \in \mathcal{L}$ is derivable from L via $\mathcal{R}$, denoted by $L \vdash_{\mathcal{R}} x$, if (i) $x \in L$ or (ii) there is a sequence of rules $(r_1, \ldots, r_n)$ from $\mathcal{R}$ s.t. $head(r_n) = x$ and for each rule r_i it holds that each atom in the body of r_i is derived from rules earlier in the sequence or is in L, i.e., $body(r_i) \subseteq L \cup \bigcup_{j<i} head(r_j)$.

We extend the derivability notion to assumptions in a straightforward way: given an AT $T = (\mathcal{L}, \mathcal{R}, n, ^-, \mathcal{K}, \leq)$ and an assumption (P, D) in T, we say that from (P, D) one can derive (in T) an atom $x \in \mathcal{L}$, denoted by $(P, D) \vdash_T x$, if $P \cup \mathcal{K}_n \vdash_{D \cup \mathcal{R}_s} x$, i.e., x is derivable from the defeasible elements in the assumption and all non-defeasible parts in the AT. The deductive closure of an assumption in T is then defined as $Th_T(P, D) = \{x \in \mathcal{L} \mid (P, D) \vdash_T x\}$. We say that a rule r is applicable by an assumption (P, D) if $body(r) \subseteq Th_T(P, D)$, i.e., all elements of the body of r can be derived using the assumption. For an assumption (P, D) in T and an argument A in T we say that A is based on (P, D) if A uses only defeasible elements from this assumption, i.e., A is based on (P, D) in T if $\texttt{DefRules}(A) \subseteq D$ and $\texttt{Prem}_{\texttt{d}}(A) \subseteq P$.

Assumptions and arguments have a direct connection.

Proposition 2 (Lehtonen, Wallner, and Järvisalo 2020). *Let $T = (\mathcal{L}, \mathcal{R}, n, ^-, \mathcal{K}, \leq)$ be an AT and (P, D) an assumption in T. There is an argument A based on (P, D) in T with $\texttt{Conc}(A) = x$ iff $(P, D) \vdash_T x$.*

3 Complexity of Reasoning

In this section, we provide an overview of our complexity results for preferential reasoning under stable semantics in ASPIC$^+$. The rephrasing of stable semantics essential for the formal proofs of the complexity results (as well as for the algorithms presented in Section 6) is postponed until Sections 4–5.

While an AF corresponding to a given AT is, in general, not bounded polynomially in size w.r.t. the given AT, we showed (Lehtonen, Wallner, and Järvisalo 2020) that one can define criteria on assumptions (P, D) so that there is a direct correspondence between assumptions and extensions of arguments, without explicating the extension (and without constructing the corresponding AF), with assumptions being bounded polynomially regarding the input AT. Such an approach is essential to show complexity results for classes in the polynomial hierarchy (which are restricted to polynomial space). Concretely, assumptions, and criteria on assumptions, allow for a design of algorithms that operate in polynomial space, and fall into a class of the polynomial hierarchy, in the form of a non-deterministic construction of a (P, D) assumption and subsequent verification of the conditions imposed by the semantics.

Preferential reasoning is important to ASPIC$^+$, but obtaining criteria on assumptions reflecting preferences is, as we will show, non-immediate, and, moreover, increases computational complexity. Recall that preferences in ASPIC$^+$ lead to a modified attack structure (the defeat relation), which means that preferences change conflicts in the corresponding AF, an object we have to avoid explicitly constructing in order to obtain tight complexity results.

We show that preferential reasoning, under stable semantics, the weakest-link principle, and elitist lifting in ASPIC$^+$, remains on the same level of complexity in case no defeasible rules are present as in the case no preferences are present. This result, in fact, aligns reasoning under stable semantics in ASPIC$^+$ and assumption-based argumentation (ABA) with certain kinds of preferences (called ABA$^+$) (Čyras and Toni 2016) from the view of complexity (Lehtonen, Wallner, and Järvisalo 2021).

Theorem 3. *For ATs without defeasible rules and stable semantics, credulous justification is NP-complete and skeptical justification is coNP-complete.*

While hardness for these cases follows in a rather direct fashion from existing results (e.g., see hardness on AFs (Dvořák and Dunne 2018) or ASPIC$^+$ without preferences (Lehtonen, Wallner, and Järvisalo 2020)), membership results are based on our rephrasing that characterizes stable semantics in terms of conditions on assumption sets, formally presented in the next subsections.

However, in contrast, when including defeasible rules we show that reasoning jumps to the second level of the polynomial hierarchy, under prominent instantiations of ASPIC$^+$ satisfying rationality postulates, concretely what we refer to as well-formed ATs. These results clearly set ASPIC$^+$ and ABA$^+$ apart, in terms of computational complexity of reasoning. Hardness holds even in the case of no strict rules.

Theorem 4. *For well-formed ATs and stable semantics, credulous justification is Σ_2^P-complete and skeptical justification is Π_2^P-complete. Hardness holds even when there are no strict rules.*

For intuition on why well-formedness, i.e., conditions usually used for showing rationality postulates, are useful for showing complexity results, these conditions also lead to properties that allow to align stable extensions and stable assumptions in a more direct way. In the following section we present a rephrasing of defeats to the viewpoint of assumptions, where we clearly distinguish between two types of defeats with one being the underlying reason for the complexity jump, and subsequently highlight useful properties following from assuming well-formed ATs.

4 Defeats on Assumptions

In this section we investigate defeats defined on assumptions (P, D), and their relation to defeats on arguments, as a precursor to rephrasing semantics on assumptions.

It will be useful to classify defeats into two categories: one contains successful contradictory rebuts and the other category, which we call individual defeats, contains all other types of defeats.

Definition 13. *Let $T = (\mathcal{L}, \mathcal{R}, n, ^-, \mathcal{K}, \leq)$ be an AT, and A and B two arguments in T. We say that A individually defeats B if A*

- *successfully undercuts B,*
- *contrary rebuts B, or*
- *successfully undermines B.*

The reason for considering these two classes will become clear when considering their corresponding definitions on assumptions and their respective complexity. We define individual defeats on assumptions as follows.

Definition 14. *Let $T = (\mathcal{L}, \mathcal{R}, n, ^-, \mathcal{K}, \leq)$ be an AT, and (P, D) be an assumption in T. We say that (P, D) individually defeats an $x \in \mathcal{K}_p \cup \mathcal{R}_d$ if*

- *$x = p \in \mathcal{K}_p$ and*
  - *there is a contrary of p in $Th_T(P, D)$ (contrary undermine) or*
  - *there is a contradictory of p in $Th_T(P', D)$ with $P' = \{p' \in P \mid p' \not< p\}$ (contradictory undermine),*
- *$x = r \in \mathcal{R}_d$ and*
  - *$\overline{n(r)} \cap Th_T(P, D) \neq \emptyset$ (undercut),*
  - *there is a contrary of $head(r)$ in $Th_T(P, D)$ (contrary rebut).*

These conditions reflect individual defeats on arguments. Assumption (P, D) undermines an ordinary premise if one can derive a contrary of the premise or a contradictory using not less preferred premises. Undercuts and contrary rebuts on assumptions directly reflect undercuts and contrary rebuts on arguments (which do not require preference handling).

Next we show that an assumption (P, D) individually defeating x represents a set of arguments $\mathcal{S}$ for which the following holds: for each argument B containing x (as an ordinary premise or a defeasible rule) there is an argument $A \in \mathcal{S}$ individually defeating B. This motivates the name: the defeat targets a single defeasible element and does not require (more) context information on the defeated argument.

Proposition 5. *Let $T = (\mathcal{L}, \mathcal{R}, n, ^-, \mathcal{K}, \leq)$ be an AT, (P, D) be an assumption in T, and $x \in \mathcal{K}_p \cup \mathcal{R}_d$. There is an argument A based on (P, D) s.t. A individually defeats an argument B in T whenever $x \in \texttt{Prem}_\texttt{d}(B) \cup \texttt{DefRules}(B)$ iff (P, D) individually defeats x.*

What remains is the case of contradictory rebut. It turns out that phrasing contradictory rebuts on assumptions leads to a more complex condition.

Definition 15. *Let $T = (\mathcal{L}, \mathcal{R}, n, ^-, \mathcal{K}, \leq)$ be an AT, and (P, D) and (P', D') be assumptions in T. Further, let $W = Th_T(P'', D) \cup Th_T(P, D'')$ with*

- *$P'' = \{p \in P \mid \exists p' \in P', p \not< p'\}$ and*
- *$D'' = \{r \in D \mid \exists r' \in D', r \not< r'\}$.*

We say (P, D) contradictory rebuts (P', D') on $r' \in D'$ if

- *P' is non-empty and there is a contradictory of $head(r')$ in W, or*
- *P' is empty and there is a contradictory of $head(r')$ in $Th_T(P, D'')$.*

Sets P'' and D'' are chosen in a way to accommodate the preference induced by the elitist lifting (for each element there is one not more preferred). The case distinction reflects the weakest-link principle (if P' is empty only defeasible rules are taken into account; D' is non-empty).

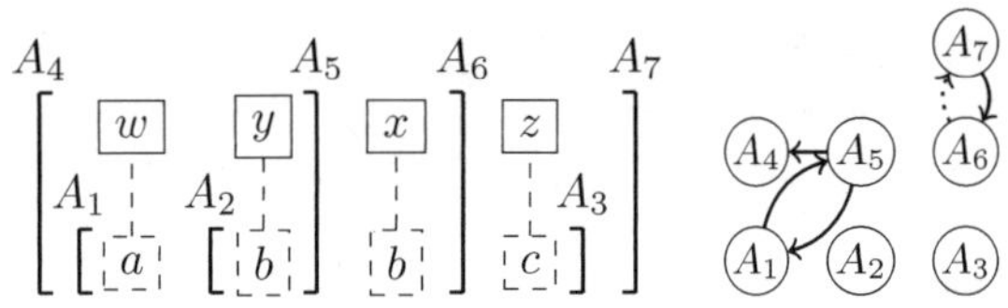

Figure 2: AT with $\mathcal{R}_s = \emptyset$ and corresponding AF

For individual defeats it holds that if an assumption individually defeats a defeasible element x, then this assumption (and its corresponding arguments) defeats all assumptions (arguments) individually containing the defeasible element x. In contrast, contradictory defeats are defined on assumptions contradictory rebutting a *specific* assumption (and as we will see, making no claim on sub-assumptions, for instance), which is why checking contradictory rebuts is computationally harder than checking individual attacks.

Example 3. *Let* $T = (\mathcal{L}, \mathcal{R}, n, ^-, \mathcal{K}, \leq)$ *be an AT with* $\mathcal{L} = \{a, b, c, w, x, y, z\}$, $\mathcal{K}_p = \{a, b, c\}$, $\mathcal{K}_n = \emptyset$, $\overline{x} = \{z\}$, $\overline{z} = \{x\}$, $\overline{a} = \{y\}$, $\overline{y} = \{a\}$, $\mathcal{R}_s = \emptyset$, *and* $\mathcal{R}_d = \{(r_1 : b \Rightarrow x), (r_2 : b \Rightarrow y), (r_3 : c \Rightarrow z), (r_4 : a \Rightarrow w)\}$. *Further, let* $a \leq_p b$, $b \leq_p c$, *and* $r_1 \leq_d r_3$. *The AT and corresponding AF are shown in Figure 2. Argument* A_5 *successfully contradictory undermines* A_1 *(and* A_4 *on* A_1*) and* A_1 *successfully contradictory rebuts* A_5. *The latter holds because* $\texttt{Prem}_\texttt{d}(A_1) = \{a\} \lhd \{b\} = \texttt{Prem}_\texttt{d}(A_5)$ *due to* $a <_p b$, *but* $\texttt{DefRules}(A_1) = \emptyset$ *and* $\emptyset \not\lhd \{r_2\} = \texttt{DefRules}(A_5)$. *Argument* A_7 *successfully contradictory rebuts* A_6, *but* A_6 *does not successfully contradictory rebut* A_7, *due to* $A_6 \prec A_7$ *(*$b <_p c$ *and* $r_1 <_d r_3$*). Consider* $P = \{b, c\}$ *and* $D = \{r_1, r_2\}$. *It holds that* (P, D) *individually defeats* a *(because we can derive the contradictory of* a *from* (P, D) *and neither* b *nor* c *is less preferred to* a*). For* $P' = \{a, c\}$ *and* $D' = \{r_3, r_4\}$ *it holds that* (P, D) *contradictory rebuts* (P', D') *on* r_3, *since with* $P'' = \{b, c\} = P$ *and* $D'' = \{r_1, r_2\} = D$ *we can derive a contradictory of* $head(r_3) = z$ *(namely* x*) by Definition 15. However,* (P, D) *does not contradictory rebut* $(P^*, D^*) = (\{c\}, \{r_3\})$ *on* r_3 *(the ingredients for* A_7*) since, again by Definition 15, neither from* $(\{c\}, D)$ *nor from* $(P, \{r_2\})$ *one can derive* x *(one requires* b *and defeasible rule* r_1*).*

That is, an assumption might contradictory rebut an assumption (P, D), but not $(P', D') \sqsubseteq (P, D)$. Next we state that if (P, D) contrary rebuts (P', D'), then there is an argument based on (P, D) successfully contradictory rebutting arguments containing exactly (P', D') as their defeasible part.

Proposition 6. *Let* $T = (\mathcal{L}, \mathcal{R}, n, ^-, \mathcal{K}, \leq)$ *be an AT, and* (P, D) *and* (P', D') *be assumptions in* T. *If* (P, D) *contradictory rebuts* (P', D') *on* r *then all arguments* B *in* T *with*

- $\texttt{Prem}_\texttt{d}(B) = P'$,
- $\texttt{DefRules}(B) = D'$, *and*
- $\texttt{TopRule}(B) = r$.

are successfully contradictory rebutted on B *by an argument* A *based on* (P, D).

5 Rephrasing Stability on Assumptions

In this section we make use of assumptions and defeats to define stable semantics on assumptions such that "stable assumptions" have a useful correspondence to stable extensions. In contrast to the case without preferences (Lehtonen, Wallner, and Järvisalo 2020), where a direct correspondence was possible, it turns out that defeasible rules, and even more, the *combination* of strict and defeasible rules, together with preferential reasoning, is a particular challenge for computation. General translation results (Modgil and Prakken 2018) that reduce an ASPIC$^+$ AT to an AT without strict rules or without defeasible rules are not directly usable in our case.[1]

We first show auxiliary results. First, a useful property is that if an argument attacks (but not necessarily defeats) another argument, this attack is present as a defeat, in a certain well-behaved manner, in case the underlying AT is well-formed (in particular closed under transposition). In case no strict rules exist at all, a rather strong condition holds: there is a defeat among subarguments of the two arguments involved in an attack. In case there are strict rules, which are closed under transposition, it can be the case that the defeat is "propagated" to a superargument of one of the two arguments (more precisely a superargument of a subargument of one of the two), but nevertheless in a controlled manner, as stated in the following lemma.

Lemma 7. *Let* T *be an AT with* $\mathcal{R}_s$ *closed under transposition, and* A *and* B *two arguments in* T *with* $\texttt{TopRule}(A) \in \mathcal{R}_s$. *If* A *unsuccessfully contradictory rebuts or unsuccessfully contradictory undermines* B, *then there is an argument* C *in* T *which defeats* A *and for every* $C' \in \texttt{Sub}(C)$ *with* $\texttt{TopRule}(C')$ *being defeasible or* $C' \in \mathcal{K}_p$ *it holds that* $C' \in \texttt{Sub}(A) \cup \texttt{Sub}(B)$.

Based on the lemma, the next proposition formalizes that attacks in well-formed ATs, do not, in a sense, disappear.

Proposition 8. *Let* $T = (\mathcal{L}, \mathcal{R}, n, ^-, \mathcal{K}, \leq)$ *be an AT, and argument* A *in* T *attacks argument* B *in* T.

- *If* $\mathcal{R}_s = \emptyset$, *then* A *defeats* B *or some* $B' \in \texttt{Sub}(B)$ *defeats* A.
- *If* $\mathcal{R}_s$ *is closed under transposition, then there is an argument* C *based on* $(\texttt{Prem}_\texttt{d}(A) \cup \texttt{Prem}_\texttt{d}(B), \texttt{DefRules}(A) \cup \texttt{DefRules}(B))$ *s.t.* C *defeats* A *or* B.

Example 4. *In the AT from Example 1,* A_7 *contradictory rebuts* A_6, *but* A_7 *does not defeat* A_6. *No subargument of* A_6 *defeats* A_7. *This exemplifies the fact that in presence of both strict and defeasible rules the first item of Proposition 8 does not hold. A simple example with only strict rules is obtained by considering two ordinary premises* a *and* b, *with* $a <_p b$ *and a strict rule* $a \rightarrow x$ *with* x *and* b *being contradictory. Then there are no defeats (the argument concluding* x *is strictly weaker than argument* b*); however, there is an attack based on contradictory undermining. Crucially the sets of strict rules are not closed under transposition.*

[1]While a translation of strict rules to defeasible ones has been proposed (Li and Parsons 2015), it turned out not to be valid (Li 2019) and hence not applicable for our case.

Another useful ingredient is a property related to subargument closure (see Proposition 1): if $\mathcal{E}$ is complete in an AT, then for each argument A whose defeasible elements are in $\mathcal{E}$ (i.e., $\texttt{defPart}(A) \subseteq \texttt{defPart}(\mathcal{E})$) it holds that $A \in \mathcal{E}$. In contrast to closure under subarguments, this kind of closure property does not hold in general (see extended version for an example); however, it does hold in case there are either no strict or no defeasible rules for complete semantics, and for well-formed ATs for stable semantics. Motivation for this property is that a correspondence of a (P, D) and an extension can be defined in a way that the extension contains all arguments that can be constructed using defeasible elements in (P, D) and strict components (strict rules, axioms) in an AT. Formally, for a semantics σ a set of ATs is closed under defeasible elements if for each $\mathcal{E} \in \sigma(F)$, for the AF F corresponding to T, it holds that all arguments A with $\texttt{defPart}(A) \subseteq \texttt{defPart}(\mathcal{E})$ are in $\mathcal{E}$.

Proposition 9. *The set of ATs with $\mathcal{R}_s = \emptyset$ or $\mathcal{R}_d = \emptyset$ is closed under defeasible elements for complete semantics and the set of ATs with $\mathcal{R}_s$ closed under transposition is closed under defeasible elements for stable semantics.*

We are now in a position to define stability on assumptions. We define w-stable assumptions for the case of well-formed ATs, and s-stable assumption for when there are only strict rules.

Definition 16. *Let $T = (\mathcal{L}, \mathcal{R}, n, ^-, \mathcal{K}, \leq)$ be a well-formed AT. Assumption (P, D) of T is w-stable if all D are applicable by (P, D) and*

1. *$\nexists x, y \in Th_T(P, D)$ such that x is a contrary of y, x and y are contradictory, or $x \in \overline{\{n(r) \mid r \in D\}}$,*
2. *(P, D) individually defeats all $p \in \mathcal{K}_p \setminus P$, and*
3. *(P, D) contradictory rebuts all (P', D') on some r' where*
   - *each rule in D' is applicable by (P', D'),*
   - *$D' \nsubseteq D$, and*
   - *$P' \subseteq P$ and $D' \subseteq D_U$, where D_U are the rules in $\mathcal{R}_d$ that are not individually defeated by (P, D).*

The first condition states that one cannot derive from this assumption x and y that are contrary or contradictory to each other, and that one cannot derive contraries/contradictories of names of rules in D. This ensures conflict-freeness. Individual defeats and contradictory rebuts among arguments based on a w-stable (P, D) are prevented (otherwise contrary or contradictory x and y are derivable, or contrary/contradictory of a rule name is derivable). The second condition is direct: if violated there is an argument (an ordinary premise) not defeated. The last condition takes care of undercuts and rebuts "outside" the set to be stable: D_U "removes" all possible arguments that are undercut or contrary rebutted (by individual defeat), and if there is an argument still possible, then this argument has P' and D' (exactly) as its defeasible elements, and it has to be the case that (P, D) contradictory rebuts (P', D').

Example 5. *Considering the AT from Example 3, it holds that (P, D) from the example is not a w-stable assumption (a corresponding stable extension containing all arguments based on (P, D) also does not exist): condition 1 is satisfied directly, and condition 2, as well. However, condition 3 is not satisfied: while (P, D) does contradictory rebut (P', D') from the example, it holds that (P, D) does not contradictory rebut (P^*, D^*). A w-stable assumption is $(\{a, b, c\}, \{r_3, r_4\})$.*

We show the correspondence between w-stable assumptions and stable extensions.

Theorem 10. *Let $T = (\mathcal{L}, \mathcal{R}, n, ^-, \mathcal{K}, \leq)$ be a well-formed AT, and $F = (\mathcal{A}, \mathcal{D})$ the corresponding AF to T.*

- *If (P, D) is a w-stable assumption in T, then $\mathcal{E} = \{A \mid$ A based on (P, D) in $T\}$ is a stable extension of F.*
- *If $\mathcal{E}$ is a stable extension of F, then (P, D) is a w-stable assumption of T with $P = \texttt{Prem}_\texttt{d}(\mathcal{E})$ and $D = \texttt{DefRules}(\mathcal{E})$.*

In the theorem, we see that closure under defeasible elements is utilized directly (e.g., via the construction of extensions from an assumption). Well-formedness is most visible in proving the correspondence. For an intuition, the proof of Proposition 8 (and Lemma 7) makes use of transposition: otherwise there might be a conflict derived on an assumption, but not present in a corresponding AF, since, e.g., if A attacks B, $A \prec B$, and the top rule of A is strict. Without transposition such a conflict might not materialize as a defeat in the AT (with transposition one may "chain" transposed rules to obtain a defeat).

We move on to the case of no defeasible rules. Here only individual defeats are present since rebuts require defeasible rules.

Definition 17. *Let $T = (\mathcal{L}, \mathcal{R}, n, ^-, \mathcal{K}, \leq)$ be an AT with $\mathcal{R}_d = \emptyset$. We say that $(P, \emptyset)$, $P \subseteq \mathcal{K}_p$, is s-stable in T if*

- *$(P, \emptyset)$ does not individually defeat any $p \in P$, and*
- *$(P, \emptyset)$ individually defeats all $p \in \mathcal{K}_p \setminus P$.*

If clear from the context, we write (P) instead of $(P, \emptyset)$.

Proposition 11. *Let $T = (\mathcal{L}, \mathcal{R}, n, ^-, \mathcal{K}, \leq)$ be an AT with $\mathcal{R}_d = \emptyset$, and $F = (\mathcal{A}, \mathcal{D})$ the corresponding AF to T.*

- *If (P) is an s-stable assumption in T, then $\mathcal{E} = \{A \mid$ A based on $(P, \emptyset)$ in $T\}$ is a stable extension of F.*
- *If $\mathcal{E}$ is a stable extension of F, then (P) is an s-stable assumption of T with $P = \texttt{Prem}_\texttt{d}(\mathcal{E})$.*

The preceding results directly lead to the result that checking credulous or skeptical justification is possible via inspecting stable assumptions instead of extensions.

Proposition 12. *Given an AT T which is well-formed (or which has empty $\mathcal{R}_d$), and an $x \in \mathcal{L}$, it holds that*

- *x is credulously justified in T under stable semantics iff there is a w-stable (s-stable) assumption (P, D) in T with $x \in Th_T(P, D)$, and*
- *x is skeptically justified in T under stable semantics iff in all w-stable (s-stable) assumptions (P, D) in T we have $x \in Th_T(P, D)$.*

We end this section with complexity results for verifying whether an assumption is s- or w-stable, which form the basis for the membership results of Theorem 3 and Theorem 4.

Algorithm 1 Credulous justification

Require: Well-formed AT T and queried atom $s \in \mathcal{L}$
Ensure: return YES if s is credulously justified in T under stable semantics, NO otherwise

1: $\pi \leftarrow \pi_{1,2}(T) \cup \{\leftarrow \texttt{not derived}(s)\}$
2: **while** π has an answer set M **do**
3:     **if** $\pi \cup \pi_{\neg 3}(M)$ has no answer sets **then return** YES
4:     **else** $\pi \leftarrow \pi \cup \pi_r(M)$
5: **return** NO

Algorithm 2 Skeptical justification

Require: Well-formed AT T and queried atom $s \in \mathcal{L}$
Ensure: return YES if s is skeptically justified in T under stable semantics, NO otherwise

1: $\pi \leftarrow \pi_{1,2}(T) \cup \{\leftarrow \texttt{derived(s)}\}$
2: **while** π has an answer set M **do**
3:     **if** $\pi \cup \pi_{\neg 3}(M)$ has no answer sets **then return** NO
4:     **else** $\pi \leftarrow \pi \cup \pi_r(M)$
5: **return** YES

Theorem 13. *Verifying whether an assumption is s-stable is in P, and verifying whether an assumption is w-stable is coNP-complete.*

6 Algorithm for Stable Semantics

Our approach to credulous acceptance under stable semantics is outlined as Algorithm 1. (The ASP encodings used are detailed in the extended version available online.) One ASP solver provides candidate solutions corresponding to assumptions (P, D) that derive the queried atom, satisfy Items 1–2 of Definition 16 and the applicability of every $r \in D$ (Lines 1–2). Another ASP solver checks for counterexamples to the solution candidate (Line 3). A counterexample is an assumption (P', D') such that (P, D) does not contradictory rebut it while the other conditions of Item 3 of Definition 16 hold. If there is no counterexample, the candidate is w-stable and thus the query is credulously justified (Line 3).

We employ two encodings, $\pi_{1,2}(T)$ for candidate generation and $\pi_{\neg 3}$ for counterexample finding, with the following properties: (P, D) derives s and satisfies the first two conditions in T iff there is an answer set M of $\pi_{1,2}(T) \cup \{\leftarrow \texttt{not derived(s)}\}$ with $P \cup D = \{p \in (\mathcal{K}_p \cup \mathcal{R}_d) \mid \textbf{in}(p) \in M\}$. The $\{\leftarrow \texttt{not derived(s)}\}$ is a constraint ruling out answers where s is not derivable from the guessed assumption set. The answer set M also indicates the premises and rules that (P, D) does not defeat individually. For verifying if the answer set corresponds to a w-stable assumption, it holds that (P', D') is a counterexample in T iff there is an answer set M' of $\pi_{\neg 3}(M)$ with $P' \cup D' = \{p \in (\mathcal{K}_p \cup \mathcal{R}_d) \mid \textbf{in}(p) \in M'\}$. If a counterexample is found, the current π is refined, via π_r, to exclude each $(P'', D'') \sqsubseteq (P, D)$ (Line 5); the encoding $\pi_r(M)$ enforces that some defeasible element that is not in the candidate in M needs to be in any future candidate. Excluding all subassumptions is valid, since if (P, D) does not contradictory rebut a counterexample (P', D'), then no subassumption of (P, D) can contradictory rebut (P', D') either (follows from Definition 15).

The algorithm for skeptical reasoning (Algorithm 2) follows with relatively minor changes from Algorithm 1. In short, it searches for a counterexample, namely, for a stable extension that does not contain the query s. For this, the constraint in Line 1 is changed to rule out answers where s is derivable from the guessed assumption set. Then the algorithm returns NO if it finds a suitable counterexample and YES otherwise.

7 Experiments

We implemented (available at https://bitbucket.org/coreo-group/aspforaspic/) the ASP-based CEGAR algorithms using the incremental Python interface of Clingo v5.5.1 (Gebser et al. 2019) under default parameters. The experiments were run on 2.60-GHz Intel Xeon E5-2670 8-core 64-GB machines with CentOS 7 under a per-instance 600-second time and 16-GB memory limit.

We generated ATs with $N = 100, 200, ...800$ atoms (i.e., members of $\mathcal{L}$ excluding the names for defeasible rules) as follows, selecting one queried non-premise atom per framework: all atoms aside from axioms and 10% of defeasible rules were assigned a contradictory or asymmetric contrary (each with equal probability); 5% of all atoms are axioms and 20% of atoms are premises. We varied the number of rules deriving each atom (rpa) and the sizes of rule bodies (rs): for each non-premise atom, the number of rules deriving the atom was chosen at random from $[1, 5]$ or $[1, 10]$, as was the number of atoms in the body of each rule body. When the head has a contradictory, a rule deriving it was chosen to be strict with a 10% probability and the atoms in the rule body were selected from the sentences that have a contradictory (closure under transposition requires each atom present in a strict rule to have a contradictory). Closure under transposition was enforced by creating the required additional strict rules. We generated preference relations over premises and defeasible rules for each framework by choosing for both a random permutation $(x_i)_{0<i\leq n}$ of the elements and for each $j < i$ setting x_i to be preferred to x_j with probability 30%. For each N and different combinations of rpa and rs we generated 10 frameworks.

Tables 1 and 2 give the number of timeouts and mean runtimes (in parentheses, with timeouts included as 600 s) of our approach for each N and choice of rs, rpa for credulous and skeptical reasoning, respectively. The empirical hardness of the instances depend on the parameters and reasoning tasks. Skeptical justification is empirically harder than credulous on all of the parameter families tested. The instances with many smaller rules seems the hardest for both reasoning tasks while the instances with fewer and smaller rules are comparatively easier.

In terms of systems for direct runtime comparison, there are few options currently. The Tweety library (Thimm 2017) offers one possible point of comparison. However, Tweety employs a translation to Dung AFs, and as its first step explicitly generates the arguments from a given AT. We observed that already the argument construction step fails (due

	#timeouts (mean runtime (s))					
N	rs=5, rpa=5		rs=5, rpa=10		rs=10, rpa=10	
100	0	(1)	0	(16)	0	(6)
200	0	(8)	4	(321)	0	(49)
300	1	(85)	6	(428)	0	(182)
400	0	(64)	4	(491)	3	(474)
500	4	(316)	10	(600)	10	(600)
600	0	(222)	10	(600)	10	(600)
700	1	(405)	10	(600)	10	(600)
800	3	(556)	10	(600)	10	(600)

Table 1: Timeouts and runtimes on credulous reasoning.

	#timeouts (mean runtime (s))					
N	rs=5, rpa=5		rs=5, rpa=10		rs=10, rpa=10	
100	0	(2)	0	(74)	0	(7)
200	0	(51)	8	(509)	0	(114)
300	1	(190)	10	(600)	1	(279)
400	7	(445)	9	(582)	5	(531)
500	9	(567)	10	(600)	10	(600)
600	8	(524)	10	(600)	10	(600)
700	9	(580)	10	(600)	10	(600)
800	10	(600)	10	(600)	10	(600)

Table 2: Timeouts and runtimes on skeptical reasoning.

to time or memory out) for all but seven of the benchmark instances (five of the succeeding instances had $N = 100$ and two $N = 200$). This further emphasizes the benefits of our AT-level ASP-based approach compared to approaches resorting to AF translation.

8 Related Work

For overviews on computational approaches to structured argumentation see, e.g., surveys by Dvořák and Dunne (2018) and Cerutti et al. (2018). Regarding rephrasing (sets of) arguments—or argument structures—in different forms, in assumption-based argumentation (Bondarenko et al. 1997; Cyras et al. 2018) semantics have been defined in terms of extensions of arguments and on subsets of assumptions, and recently extended with preferences, e.g., in ABA$^+$ (Čyras and Toni 2016). In ASPIC$^+$, preferred subtheories (Brewka 1989) and specific instantiations of ASPIC$^+$ have a semantic correspondence (Modgil and Prakken 2013). There are also connections between repairs of ontological knowledge bases and extensions of AFs instantiated from knowledge bases (Croitoru and Vesic 2013). By studying outcomes of rule-based systems and their instantiated arguments and attacks, certain subparts of the rule-base are connected to semantics of the resulting AF (Amgoud and Besnard 2019). Structured argumentation frameworks, including a fragment of ASPIC$^+$ (Heyninck and Straßer 2021) by making use of properties implying satisfaction of rationality postulates, have been connected to maximal consistent subset reasoning (see, e.g., the recent survey by Arieli, Borg, and Heyninck (2019)). In contrast, we consider ASPIC$^+$ with atomic strict and defeasible rules, contraries and contradictories, weakest-link principle, elitist lifting, and all forms of attacks and defeats defined on these based on (Modgil and Prakken 2018) (undermining, undercut, and rebut, with their contrary and contradictory versions), and present a rephrasing of stability in terms of defeasible elements of the given AT which is designed for computational purposes. We show correspondences for the fragments of (i) AT without defeasible rules and (ii) well-formed ATs. Conditions underlying well-formed ATs have been used earlier for showing satisfaction of properties regarding rationality. We show that these are also viable for computational purposes.

Computational complexity for structured argumentation includes several results, e.g., for assumption-based argumentation (Dimopoulos, Nebel, and Toni 2002; Cyras, Heinrich, and Toni 2021; Karamlou, Cyras, and Toni 2019; Lehtonen, Wallner, and Järvisalo 2021), for deductive argumentation, e.g., (Wooldridge, Dunne, and Parsons 2006; Hirsch and Gorogiannis 2010), and for DeLP, e.g., (Alfano et al. 2021). For ASPIC$^+$, complexity results were obtained for the case without preferences, upon which we build (Lehtonen, Wallner, and Järvisalo 2020). We present novel complexity results for ASPIC$^+$ with preferences.

Cerutti et al. (2018) provide a survey on systems for structured argumentation. Specific to ASPIC$^+$, the systems Tweety (Thimm 2017) and TOAST (Snaith and Reed 2012) implement reasoning for specific tasks. We were unable to obtain the source code for TOAST (Snaith and Reed 2012) from the authors for a further potential direct comparison. Further systems implementing reasoning in contexts drawing inspiration from ASPIC$^+$ (as considered here) include EPR (Visser 2008) and Arg2P (Calegari et al. 2022).

9 Conclusions

As a non-trivial extension of a recently proposed approach to reasoning in ASPIC$^+$, we established both complexity results and formal foundations for an incremental ASP approach to stable conclusions under the weakest-link principle. In terms of complexity, as the main contributions we established completeness for the second level of the polynomial hierarchy for both credulous and skeptical acceptance, thereby witnessing a jump in complexity due to inclusion of preferences. Pertaining to this complexity class, we proposed a counterexample-guided abstraction refinement style approach using incremental ASP solving for the task, scaling up to hundreds of atoms in practice. The approach circumvents a potential exponential blow-up intrinsic to approaches translating ASPIC$^+$ reasoning to abstract argumentation via formally rephrasing the semantics in terms of subsets of defeasible elements.

Our work opens up directions for further work, including extending the approach to further variants of preferential reasoning in ASPIC$^+$ and structured argumentation (Beirlaen et al. 2018; Young, Modgil, and Rodrigues 2016; Dyrkolbotn, Pedersen, and Broersen 2018; Heyninck and Straßer 2019), in terms of both complexity analysis and algorithms, as well as investigating computational properties of further fragments of ASPIC$^+$.

Acknowledgements

This work has been financially supported in part by Academy of Finland (grant 322869), University of Helsinki Doctoral Programme in Computer Science DoCS, and by the Austrian Science Fund (FWF) P35632. The authors wish to thank the Finnish Computing Competence Infrastructure (FCCI) for supporting this project with computational and data storage resources.

References

Alfano, G.; Greco, S.; Parisi, F.; Simari, G. I.; and Simari, G. R. 2021. Incremental computation for structured argumentation over dynamic DeLP knowledge bases. *Artif. Intell.* 300:103553.

Amgoud, L., and Besnard, P. 2019. A formal characterization of the outcomes of rule-based argumentation systems. *Knowledge and Information Systems* 61(1):543–588.

Arieli, O.; Borg, A.; and Heyninck, J. 2019. A review of the relations between logical argumentation and reasoning with maximal consistency. *Ann. Math. Artif. Intell.* 87(3):187–226.

Atkinson, K.; Baroni, P.; Giacomin, M.; Hunter, A.; Prakken, H.; Reed, C.; Simari, G. R.; Thimm, M.; and Villata, S. 2017. Towards artificial argumentation. *AI Magazine* 38(3):25–36.

Baroni, P.; Gabbay, D.; Giacomin, M.; and van der Torre, L., eds. 2018. *Handbook of Formal Argumentation*. College Publications.

Beirlaen, M.; Heyninck, J.; Pardo, P.; and Straßer, C. 2018. Argument strength in formal argumentation. *IfCoLog Journal of Logics and their Applications* 5(3):629–676.

Besnard, P., and Hunter, A. 2008. *Elements of Argumentation*. MIT Press.

Besnard, P., and Hunter, A. 2018. A review of argumentation based on deductive arguments. In Baroni et al. (2018). chapter 9, 437–484.

Bondarenko, A.; Dung, P. M.; Kowalski, R. A.; and Toni, F. 1997. An abstract, argumentation-theoretic approach to default reasoning. *Artif. Intell.* 93:63–101.

Brewka, G.; Delgrande, J. P.; Romero, J.; and Schaub, T. 2015. asprin: Customizing answer set preferences without a headache. In *AAAI*, 1467–1474. AAAI Press.

Brewka, G. 1989. Preferred subtheories: An extended logical framework for default reasoning. In *IJCAI*, 1043–1048. Morgan Kaufmann.

Calegari, R.; Omicini, A.; Pisano, G.; and Sartor, G. 2022. Arg2P: An argumentation framework for explainable intelligent systems. *J. Log. Comput.* 32(2):369–401.

Caminada, M. 2018. Rationality postulates: Applying argumentation theory for non-monotonic reasoning. In Baroni et al. (2018). chapter 15, 771–795.

Cerutti, F.; Gaggl, S. A.; Thimm, M.; and Wallner, J. P. 2018. Foundations of implementations for formal argumentation. In Baroni et al. (2018). chapter 15, 688–767.

Croitoru, M., and Vesic, S. 2013. What can argumentation do for inconsistent ontology query answering? In *SUM*, volume 8078 of *LNCS*, 15–29. Springer.

Čyras, K., and Toni, F. 2016. ABA+: Assumption-based argumentation with preferences. In *KR*, 553–556. AAAI Press.

Cyras, K.; Fan, X.; Schulz, C.; and Toni, F. 2018. Assumption-based argumentation: Disputes, explanations, preferences. In Baroni et al. (2018). chapter 7, 365–408.

Cyras, K.; Heinrich, Q.; and Toni, F. 2021. Computational complexity of flat and generic assumption-based argumentation, with and without probabilities. *Artif. Intell.* 293:103449.

Dimopoulos, Y.; Nebel, B.; and Toni, F. 2002. On the computational complexity of assumption-based argumentation for default reasoning. *Artif. Intell.* 141(1/2):57–78.

Dung, P. M. 1995. On the acceptability of arguments and its fundamental role in nonmonotonic reasoning, logic programming and n-person games. *Artif. Intell.* 77(2):321–358.

Dvořák, W., and Dunne, P. E. 2018. Computational problems in formal argumentation and their complexity. In Baroni et al. (2018). chapter 13, 631–688.

Dyrkolbotn, S. K.; Pedersen, T.; and Broersen, J. M. 2018. On elitist lifting and consistency in structured argumentation. *IfCoLog Journal of Logics and their Applications* 5(3):709–746.

Gabbay, D.; Giacomin, M.; Simari, G. R.; and Thimm, M., eds. 2021. *Handbook of Formal Argumentation*, volume 2. College Publications.

García, A. J., and Simari, G. R. 2014. Defeasible logic programming: Delp-servers, contextual queries, and explanations for answers. *Argument Comput.* 5(1):63–88.

García, A. J., and Simari, G. R. 2018. Argumentation based on logic programming. In Baroni et al. (2018). chapter 8, 409–435.

Gebser, M.; Kaminski, R.; Kaufmann, B.; and Schaub, T. 2019. Multi-shot ASP solving with clingo. *Theory Pract. Log. Program.* 19(1):27–82.

Heyninck, J., and Straßer, C. 2019. A fully rational argumentation system for preordered defeasible rules. In *AAMAS*, 1704–1712. IFAAMAS.

Heyninck, J., and Straßer, C. 2021. Rationality and maximal consistent sets for a fragment of ASPIC+ without undercut. *Argument & Compututation* 12(1):3–47.

Hirsch, R., and Gorogiannis, N. 2010. The complexity of the warranted formula problem in propositional argumentation. *J. Log. Comput.* 20(2):481–499.

Karamlou, A.; Cyras, K.; and Toni, F. 2019. Complexity results and algorithms for bipolar argumentation. In *AAMAS*, 1713–1721. IFAAMAS.

Lehtonen, T.; Wallner, J. P.; and Järvisalo, M. 2020. An answer set programming approach to argumentative reasoning in the ASPIC+ framework. In *KR*, 636–646. IJCAI.org.

Lehtonen, T.; Wallner, J. P.; and Järvisalo, M. 2021. Declarative algorithms and complexity results for assumption-based argumentation. *J. Artif. Intell. Res.* 71:265–318.

Li, Z., and Parsons, S. 2015. On argumentation with purely defeasible rules. In *SUM*, volume 9310 of *LNCS*, 330–343. Springer.

Li, Z. 2019. *A Purely Defeasible Argumentation Framework*. Ph.D. Dissertation, City University of New York.

Modgil, S., and Prakken, H. 2013. A general account of argumentation with preferences. *Artif. Intell.* 195:361–397.

Modgil, S., and Prakken, H. 2018. Abstract rule-based argumentation. In Baroni et al. (2018). chapter 6, 287–364.

Niemelä, I. 1999. Logic programs with stable model semantics as a constraint programming paradigm. *Ann. Math. Artif. Intell.* 25(3-4):241–273.

Prakken, H.; Wyner, A. Z.; Bench-Capon, T. J. M.; and Atkinson, K. 2015. A formalization of argumentation schemes for legal case-based reasoning in ASPIC+. *J. Log. Comput.* 25(5):1141–1166.

Prakken, H. 2010. An abstract framework for argumentation with structured arguments. *Argument & Computation* 1(2):93–124.

Prakken, H. 2012. Reconstructing Popov v. Hayashi in a framework for argumentation with structured arguments and Dungean semantics. *Artif. Intell. Law.* 20(1):57–82.

Schraagen, M.; Odekerken, D.; Testerink, B.; and Bex, F. 2018. Argumentation-driven information extraction for online crime reports. In *CIKM*, volume 2482 of *CEUR Workshop Proceedings*. CEUR-WS.org.

Snaith, M., and Reed, C. 2012. TOAST: online ASPIC$^+$ implementation. In *COMMA*, volume 245 of *FAIA*, 509–510. IOS Press.

Thimm, M. 2017. The Tweety library collection for logical aspects of artificial intelligence and knowledge representation. *Künstliche Intelligenz* 31(1):93–97.

Toniolo, A.; Norman, T. J.; Etuk, A.; Cerutti, F.; Ouyang, W. R.; Srivastava, M. B.; Oren, N.; Dropps, T.; Allen, J. A.; and Sullivan, P. 2015. Supporting reasoning with different types of evidence in intelligence analysis. In *AAMAS*, 781–789. ACM.

Visser, W. 2008. Implementation of argument-based practical reasoning. Master's thesis, Utrecht University.

Wooldridge, M. J.; Dunne, P. E.; and Parsons, S. 2006. On the complexity of linking deductive and abstract argument systems. In *AAAI*, 299–304. AAAI Press.

Young, A. P.; Modgil, S.; and Rodrigues, O. 2016. Prioritised default logic as rational argumentation. In *AAMAS*, 626–634. ACM.

Yun, B., and Croitoru, M. 2016. An argumentation workflow for reasoning in ontology based data access. In *COMMA*, volume 287 of *FAIA*, 61–68. IOS Press.

Proceedings of the 19th International Conference on Principles of Knowledge Representation and Reasoning
Main Track

Dynamic Deontic Logic for Permitted Announcements

Xu Li[1], Dov Gabbay[2,1], Réka Markovich[1]
[1]University of Luxembourg
[2]King's College London
{xu.li, reka.markovich}@uni.lu, dov.gabbay@kcl.ac.uk

Abstract

In this paper, we introduce and study a dynamic deontic logic for permitted announcements. In our logic framework, it is permitted to announce something if announcing it would not lead to forbidden knowledge. It is shown that the logic is not compact, and we propose a sound and weakly complete Hilbert-style axiomatisation. We also study the computational complexity of the model checking problem and the decidability of the satisfiability problem. Finally, we introduce a neighbourhood semantics with a strongly complete axiomatisation.

1 Introduction

Deontic logic is an area of logic that investigates normative concepts like obligation, permission and prohibition (Gabbay et al. 2013). It has applications in many areas of computer science, including legal knowledge representation. Recently, there has been increasing interest in studying deontic logic about knowledge or belief (Başkent, Loohuis, and Parikh 2012; Markovich and Roy 2021a). But little attention has been paid to deontic logic about epistemic actions like public announcements. Balbiani and Seban (2011) proposed a logic framework to reason about "permission to say something". In our view, however, their semantics does not reflect the intuition behind permitted announcements (see Section 6). Inspired by Aucher et al. (2011), we have developed an alternative logic of permitted announcements, called LPA, by interpreting "permitted announcements" as "announcements that would not lead to forbidden knowledge". As we will see later, it follows the well known Andersonian tradition in deontic logic. Since "knowledge" and "permission" are both well established concepts in epistemic logic and deontic logic respectively, the crucial question is how to capture all the logical principles of permitted announcements defined in this style as well as other metalogical properties of the resulting logic. Specifically, we address the following research questions in this paper:

1. What is a suitable language for talking about permitted announcements? What is a suitable semantics for characterising permitted announcements?
2. How to capture all logical principles about permitted announcements? We need to define a proof system and show that all and only the validities are provable.
3. Is the proposed axiomatisation strongly complete with respect to the formal semantics? If not, can we find an alternative semantics with which our axiomatisation is strongly complete?
4. What is the computational complexity of the model checking problem in the resulting logic framework? We propose a model checking algorithm and analyse its complexity.
5. Is the satisfiability problem decidable or not?

The resulting logic, LPA, enables us to reason about privacy policies. Aucher, Boella and van der Torre (2011) proposed a dynamic modal logic to reason about which information is permitted to be sent by a security monitor to comply with a privacy policy. A privacy policy there is just a finite and consistent set of formulas. By replacing the purely syntactical privacy policy by the general notions of permitted and forbidden knowledge characterised by relational models, we can reason about privacy policies. We explain the details of this point in Section 7.

This paper is structured as follows. We provide the definitions, explanations and semantic results of LPA in the next section. We address the model checking problem of LPA in Section 3. A sound and weakly complete axiomatisation for LPA is introduced in Section 4, and we also show the decidability there. We provide an alternative neighbourhood-like semantics in Section 5. We compare our paper with related literature in Sections 6 and 7. Section 8 concludes the paper and indicates some future work.

2 Language and Semantics

Let PROP be a countable infinite set of propositional variables and let vio be a propositional constant such that $vio \notin$ PROP.

Definition 1 (Language). *The* language $\mathcal{L}$ *is defined inductively by the following BNF grammar:*

$$\varphi ::= p \mid vio \mid \neg\varphi \mid (\varphi \wedge \varphi) \mid K\varphi \mid [\varphi]\varphi$$

where $p \in$ PROP. *Let* $\mathcal{L}_{el}$ *be the language without inductive constructs* vio *and* $[\varphi]\varphi$. *We define* $\mathbb{P}\varphi$ *as an abbreviation for* $\neg[\varphi]vio$. *Other propositional connectives are defined in the usual way.*

For every formula $\varphi \in \mathcal{L}$, let $sub(\varphi)$ be the set of all the subformulas of φ. For any set of formulas $\Gamma \subseteq \mathcal{L}$, we use $\textsc{prop}(\Gamma)$ to denote the set of propositional variables occurring in at least one formula in Γ. Given some $A \subseteq \textsc{prop}$, $\mathcal{L}_x(A)$ is the logical language $\mathcal{L}_x$ ($\mathcal{L}$, $\mathcal{L}_{el}$) restricted to propositional variables in A.

The intuitive reading of $K\varphi$ is "φ is known" and that of vio is "a violation has occurred". The formula $[\varphi]\psi$ is read as "after the announcement of φ, it holds that ψ". The formula $\mathbb{P}\varphi$ is an abbreviation for $\neg[\varphi]vio$, which states that "it is not the case that after the announcement of φ, a violation has occurred". Thus, $\mathbb{P}\varphi$ is intended to express that "it is permitted to announce φ".

Here are some brief remarks about our language. The use of the propositional constant vio dates back to Anderson (1958). But a more relevant reference is (Meyer 1987), where deontic logic about actions is reduced to a variant of dynamic logic by setting that $F\alpha = [\alpha]V$ and $P\alpha = \neg F\alpha$, where α is an action and $[\alpha]V$ means that "after the execution of α, one gets into trouble". Thus, an action α is forbidden (that is, $F\alpha$) if, after the execution of α, one gets into trouble; an action α is permitted (that is, $P\alpha$) if α is not forbidden. Concerning our paper, since public announcements are a type of action, we define $\mathbb{P}\varphi$ as $\neg[\varphi]vio$. [1]

We do not introduce operator O for obligation in our language. This is due to two considerations. First, we want to focus on our aim of developing a logic of permitted announcements. The current language is already sufficient for talking about permitted announcements. Second, adding obligation operator O to our language would allow us to express Åqvist's paradox, i.e. $OKp \to Op$ (Åqvist 1967).

In the following definition, we define the complexity of a formula, and it will be used in several proofs in our paper, including the completeness proof.

Definition 2 (Complexity). *For every formula $\alpha \in \mathcal{L}$, the* complexity *of α, with the notation $c(\alpha)$, is a positive integer inductively defined as follows: (1) $c(p) = c(vio) = 1$; (2) $c(\neg\varphi) = c(K\varphi) = 1 + c(\varphi)$; (3) $c(\varphi \wedge \psi) = 1 + \max(c(\varphi), c(\psi))$; (4) $c([\varphi]\psi) = (4 + c(\varphi)) \cdot c(\psi)$.*

The next lemma will be used in the completeness proof.

Lemma 3. *The following hold for every $\varphi, \psi, \chi \in \mathcal{L}$ (van Ditmarsch, van der Hoek, and Kooi 2008, page 187):*

1. $c(\psi) > c(\varphi)$ *if* $\varphi \in sub(\psi) \setminus \{\psi\}$
2. $c([\varphi]p) > c(\varphi \to p)$
3. $c([\varphi]\neg\psi) > c(\varphi \to \neg[\varphi]\psi)$
4. $c([\varphi](\psi \wedge \chi)) > c([\varphi]\psi \wedge [\varphi]\chi)$
5. $c([\varphi]K\psi) > c(\varphi \to K[\varphi]\psi)$
6. $c([\varphi][\psi]\chi) > c([\varphi \wedge [\varphi]\psi]\chi)$

Now we introduce the formal models for LPA.

Definition 4 (Models). *A* model *is a tuple $M = (W_0, W, \sim_0, R_0, V_0)$ such that:*

- *W_0 is a non-empty set called* the initial domain*;*
- *$W \subseteq W_0$ is a non-empty set called* the current domain*;*
- *$\sim_0 \subseteq W_0 \times W_0$ is an equivalence relation on W_0;*
- *$R_0 \subseteq W_0 \times W_0$ is a serial relation on W_0, i.e. for any $w \in W_0$, there is a $v \in W_0$ such that wR_0v;*
- *$V_0 : \textsc{prop} \to \wp(W_0)$ is a valuation.*

Given a model $M = (W_0, W, \sim_0, R_0, V_0)$, we define the initial model *of M as $M_0 = (W_0, W_0, \sim_0, R_0, V_0)$. For every state $w \in W_0$, we define $\sim_0(w) = \{v \in W_0 \mid w \sim_0 v\}$, $R_0(w) = \{v \in W_0 \mid wR_0v\}$ and $V_0(w) = \{p \in \textsc{prop} \mid w \in V_0(p)\}$. Finally, a* pointed model *is a pair M, w where M is a model and w is a state of M.*

Intuitively, if the equivalence relation $\sim_0$ holds between two states w, u, we mean that the two states are indistinguishable (to the agent we are modelling), whereas if the serial relation R_0 holds between w, u (i.e. wR_0u), it means that u is an ideal world for w. The states in W_0 are used to model the situation before any public announcement occurred. In contrast, the states in W are intended to represent the current situation where some public announcements may have occurred. Now we are ready to introduce the formal semantics for LPA.

Definition 5 (Semantics). *Given a model $M = (W_0, W, \sim_0, R_0, V_0)$, for every state $w \in W$ and formula $\alpha \in \mathcal{L}$, we inductively define that α is* satisfied *at w, with the notation $M, w \models \alpha$, as follows:*

$M, w \models p$	*iff*	$w \in V_0(p)$
$M, w \models \neg\varphi$	*iff*	*not* $M, w \models \varphi$
$M, w \models \varphi \wedge \psi$	*iff*	$M, w \models \varphi$ *and* $M, w \models \psi$
$M, w \models K\varphi$	*iff*	$M, u \models \varphi$ *for all* $u \in W$ *with* $w \sim_0 u$
$M, w \models vio$	*iff*	*there is* $\varphi \in \mathcal{L}_{el}$ *such that* $M, w \models \varphi$ *and* $M_0, u \not\models \varphi$ *for all* $u \in W_0$ *with* wR_0u [2]
$M, w \models [\varphi]\psi$	*iff*	$M, w \models \varphi$ *implies* $M\vert_\varphi, w \models \psi$

where $M|_\varphi = (W_0, [\![\varphi]\!]_M, \sim_0, R_0, V_0)$ and $[\![\varphi]\!]_M = \{w \in W \mid M, w \models \varphi\}$. The notion of validity is defined as usual.

The semantics for all our operators are standard (Plaza 1989; Gerbrandy and Groeneveld 1997), except for the constant vio. The semantics for vio reflects the intuition that a violation occurred if there is a true statement which is also forbidden to be the case (i.e. false in all ideal worlds). Recall that we define $\mathbb{P}\varphi$ as an abbreviation for $\neg[\varphi]vio$. Thus, to decide whether it is permitted to announce φ, we need to check the normative status of all epistemic formulas (instead of φ itself) after the announcement. The reason is that the announcement of φ may lead the agent to infer some other fact ψ which itself is forbidden to be known by him/her. In the general case, we cannot decide which propositions are epistemically related for which agents, so a proper solution

[1] Here we define permitted announcements as weak permission (Dignum, Meyer, and Wieringa 1994a). One can also consider the version of strong permission, i.e., $\mathbb{P}^+\varphi := [\varphi]\neg vio$.

[2] One may argue that the notion of "violation" defined here is too general since the normative status of propositional formulas are also taken into account. Alternatively, one can let φ range over $\mathcal{L}_{el} \backslash \mathcal{L}_{prop}$. However, we will not consider the alternative definition in this paper. One reason is that all of our results in this paper also hold for the alternative definition.

is the introduction of existential quantification over formulas in the definition of vio.

In our semantics, we assume that the permission of statements like $p \to Kq$ does not change with public announcements, which is reflected in the fact that we always go back to the initial model M_0 to decide whether a statement is permitted or not. This assumption is plausible in many cases. For example, we are not permitted to know the medical data of others even if we have been told about them. We also recognise that there may be cases where permission to know does change with communications. We leave that for future work.

The following example illustrates our semantics.

Example 6. *Consider a company where each branch has its own website. The headquarters create a privacy policy according to which the branches are allowed to publish their employees' names n on their websites under the 'Colleagues' menu point but they are not allowed to indicate their email addresses e as the company doesn't want the public to know them. However, if someone knows how the company generates the email addresses, they can infer them by knowing the names. In this case, even if the public could know the names, the branch shouldn't publish them to be in compliance with the privacy policy.*

This scenario can be represented by the models M and $M|_n$ in Figure 1. Model M characterises the public's initial knowledge and permission to know where the current state is w. We have $M, w \models K(n \to e)$ and $M, w \models \neg vio$ (since wR_0w). To characterise the situation after the announcement of n, we replace the current domain of M by $[\![n]\!]_M = \{w, v, x\}$, and the resulting model is $M|_n$. Since $M|_n, w \models vio$ (because $M|_n, w \models Ke$ and $M_0, s \not\models Ke$ for all $s \in W_0$ with wR_0s), we have $M, w \models [n]vio$, i.e. $M, w \not\models \mathbb{P}n$.

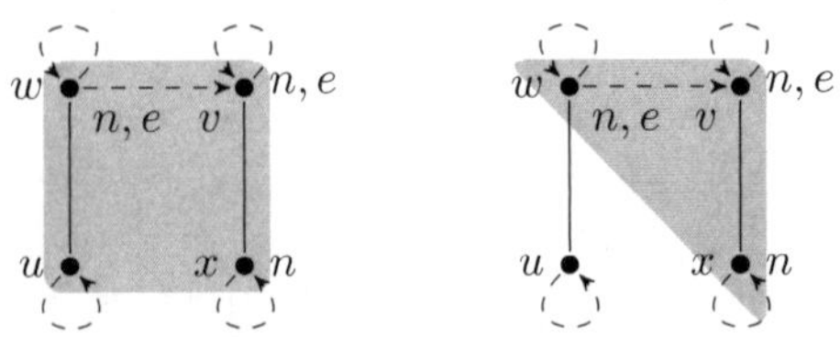

Figure 1: Two models $M = (W_0, W, \sim_0, R_0, V_0)$ (on the left) and $M|_n = (W_0, [\![n]\!]_M, R_0, V_0)$ (on the right). Worlds are nodes in the graph, and valuations are given by labelling the nodes with the true atoms. The current domains of each model consist of all the nodes in shaded areas. The epistemic relation $\sim_0$ and the deontic relation R_0 are represented by straight lines and dotted arrows respectively.

We list some semantic results in the next two propositions.

Proposition 7. *The following hold for every $\varphi, \psi, \chi \in \mathcal{L}$:*

1. $\models [\varphi]p \leftrightarrow (\varphi \to p)$
2. $\models [\varphi]\neg\psi \leftrightarrow (\varphi \to \neg[\varphi]\psi)$
3. $\models [\varphi](\psi \wedge \chi) \leftrightarrow ([\varphi]\psi \wedge [\varphi]\chi)$
4. $\models [\varphi]K\psi \leftrightarrow (\varphi \to K[\varphi]\psi)$
5. $\models [\varphi][\psi]\chi \leftrightarrow [\varphi \wedge [\varphi]\psi]\chi$
6. $\models vio \leftrightarrow [\top]vio$
7. $\models K(\varphi \leftrightarrow \psi) \to ([\varphi]vio \leftrightarrow [\psi]vio)$

Proof. We show the validity of only the last two items. Let $M = (W_0, W, \sim_0, R_0, V_0)$ be an arbitrary model and let $w \in W$.

6. Since $M, w \models \top$ and $M|_\top$ is identical to M, it is straightforward that $M, w \models vio \leftrightarrow [\top]vio$.
7. Suppose that $M, w \models K(\varphi \leftrightarrow \psi)$, we are supposed to show that $M, w \models [\varphi]vio \leftrightarrow [\psi]vio$. Without loss of generality, we only show $M, w \models [\varphi]vio \to [\psi]vio$. If $M, w \not\models \varphi$, then $M, w \not\models \psi$. By the semantics of operator $[\cdot]$, it is easy to see that $M, w \models [\varphi]vio$ and $M, w \models [\psi]vio$, thus $M, w \models [\varphi]vio \to [\psi]vio$. If $M, w \models \varphi$ (thus $M, w \models \psi$), we have $\sim_0(w) \cap [\![\varphi]\!]_M = \sim_0(w) \cap [\![\psi]\!]_M$. We can show the following claim by induction on the structure of χ:

   For every $\chi \in \mathcal{L}_{el}$ and $v \in \sim_0(w) \cap [\![\varphi]\!]_M$, $M|_\varphi, v \models \chi$ iff $M|_\psi, v \models \chi$.

   In particular, $M|_\varphi, w \models \chi$ iff $M|_\psi, w \models \chi$ for all $\chi \in \mathcal{L}_{el}$. If $M, w \models [\varphi]vio$, since $M, w \models \varphi$, then $M|_\varphi, w \models vio$. By the semantics, there must be a $\chi \in \mathcal{L}_{el}$ such that $M|_\varphi, w \models \chi$ and $M_0, v \not\models \chi$ for all $v \in R_0(w)$. Note that $M|_\psi, w \models \chi$ too, thus $M|_\psi, w \models vio$. Therefore $M, w \models [\psi]vio$ since $M, w \models \psi$. We have shown that $M, w \models [\varphi]vio \to [\psi]vio$. □

Proposition 8 (Properties of $\mathbb{P}$). *The following properties hold:*

1. $\models \mathbb{P}\varphi \to \varphi$;
2. $\models [\varphi]\mathbb{P}\psi \leftrightarrow (\varphi \to \mathbb{P}(\varphi \wedge [\varphi]\psi))$;
3. *If* $\models \varphi \leftrightarrow \psi$, *then* $\models \mathbb{P}\varphi \leftrightarrow \mathbb{P}\psi$;
4. $\models \neg vio \to (K\varphi \to \mathbb{P}\varphi)$;
5. $\models vio \to \neg\mathbb{P}\top$;
6. $\models vio \to (K\varphi \to \neg\mathbb{P}\varphi)$;
7. *Even if* $\models \varphi$, *it is not necessarily the case that* $\models \mathbb{P}\varphi$;
8. $\not\models \mathbb{P}\varphi \wedge \mathbb{P}\psi \to \mathbb{P}(\varphi \wedge \psi)$;
9. $\not\models \mathbb{P}(\varphi \wedge \psi) \to \mathbb{P}\varphi$;
10. $\not\models \mathbb{P}\varphi \to \mathbb{P}\mathbb{P}\varphi$.

Remark 1. Item 5 and 6 are about the behaviour of our permitted announcement operator in a violation state. Item 5 states that we are not permitted to announce tautologies in a violation state and item 6 states that we are also not permitted to announce facts that have already been known by the agent. One may argue that these are counter-intuitive since announcing them would not change the epistemic situation of the agent. Thus they are harmless and should be permitted. We answer the question by considering two cases: (1) The violation occurred because the agent must know some facts but he/she does not know it currently. In this case, we should tell them the facts, rather than hiding them by saying some tautologies or other known facts. (2) The agent knows some facts that are forbidden to be known by him/her. In this case, we can not remedy the situation by saying something more. Thus we should keep silence to prevent him/her from inferring new information from our announcements. It can be seen as that we are modelling a careful sender.

Remark 2. Questions may also arise on the relevance between announcements and the violation. For example, in item 5, announcing the tautology has nothing to do with the actual violation, so why should it be prohibited? We only mention here that the similar problem has been identified in dynamic deontic logic, i.e., whether an executed action *causes* the actual violation? So we could solve our problem using a method similar to that in (Dignum, Meyer, and Wieringa 1994a).

The next proposition shows that LPA has no compactness, so there would not be a strongly complete axiomatisation for LPA (Blackburn, de Rijke, and Venema 2001).

Proposition 9. *LPA is not compact.*

Proof. Consider a set of formulas $\Gamma = \{[\neg vio]\chi \to \chi \mid \chi \in \mathcal{L}_{el}\} \cup \{\neg vio \wedge [\neg vio]vio\}$. It is clear that Γ is unsatisfiable. Next, we show that any finite subset Γ' of Γ is satisfiable. Without loss of generality, we assume that $\neg vio \wedge [\neg vio]vio \in \Gamma'$. Let p^* be a propositional variable not in $\text{PROP}(\Gamma')$. Let $M = (W_0, W, \sim_0, R_0, V_0)$ be a model where:

- $W_0 = \{w, u, w', u'\}$;
- $W = \{w, u\}$;
- $\sim_0 = \{(w, w), (u, u), (w', w'), (u', u'), (w, u), (u, w), (w', u'), (u', w')\}$;
- $R_0 = \{(w, w'), (u, w'), (w', w'), (u', u')\}$;
- $V(p) = \varnothing$ for every $p \neq p^*$, $V(p^*) = \{u, u'\}$.

We illustrate M in Figure 2. We are going to show that $M, w \models \varphi$ for every $\varphi \in \Gamma'$. It is clear that (1) $M, w \models \neg vio$. Since $M, u \models p^*$ and $M_0, w' \not\models p^*$, then $M, u \models vio$. So $[\![\neg vio]\!]_M = \{w\}$, thus $M|_{\neg vio} = (W_0, \{w\}, \sim_0, R_0, V_0)$, as illustrated in Figure 2. Since $M|_{\neg vio}, w \models K\neg p^*$ and $M_0, w' \not\models K\neg p^*$, then $M|_{\neg vio}, w \models vio$, thus (2) $M, w \models [\neg vio]vio$. By induction on the structure of χ, we can prove the following claim:

> For every $\chi \in \mathcal{L}_{el}(\text{PROP}(\Gamma'))$ and $x \in \{w, u\}$, it is the case that $M, x \models \chi$ iff $M|_{\neg vio}, w \models \chi$. (†)

In particular, we have $M, w \models \chi$ iff $M|_{\neg vio}, w \models \chi$ for every $\chi \in \mathcal{L}_{el}(\text{PROP}(\Gamma'))$. It follows that (3) $M, w \models [\neg vio]\chi \to \chi$ for every $[\neg vio]\chi \to \chi \in \Gamma'$. From (1) – (3), it follows that $M, w \models \varphi$ for every $\varphi \in \Gamma'$. □

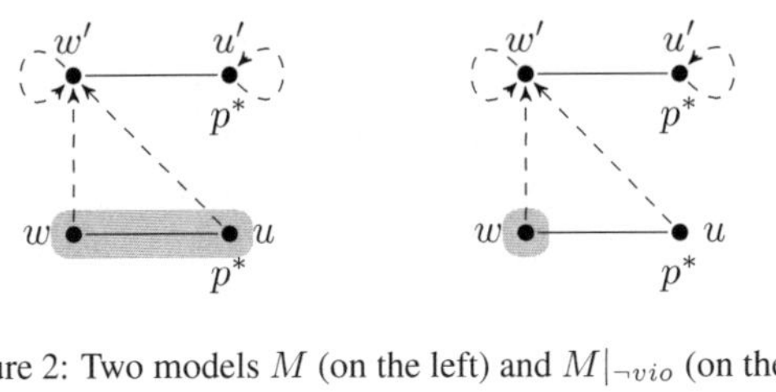

Figure 2: Two models M (on the left) and $M|_{\neg vio}$ (on the right).

3 Model Checking

Given a formula φ and a pointed model M, w, we want to check whether φ holds at M, w. This is the so-called model checking problem. It is not clear, at first sight, whether the problem is decidable in LPA, because the semantics of vio contains a quantification over all the formulas in $\mathcal{L}_{el}$. Thus, if we want to decide whether it is permitted to announce φ, it seems that we need to check all the epistemic formulas one by one. In this section, we show that if the number of propositional variables is restricted to a finite number, then we effectively resolve the "model checking" problem. More precisely, let $A \subset \text{PROP}$ be a finite set, and we will show that the following decision problem, denoted as $\text{MC}(\mathcal{L}(A))$, is decidable.

Input: a finite model $M = (W_0, W, \sim_0, R_0, V_0)$ for $\mathcal{L}(A)$ (i.e. the domain of the valuation V_0 is A), a state $w \in W$, and a formula $\varphi \in \mathcal{L}(A)$,[3]
Output: determination of whether φ is satisfied at w in M.[4]

Below, we focus on the model checking of vio since the satisfaction of other operators can be checked as in standard public announcement logic (Kooi and van Benthem 2004). The key point here is that, when the number of states in the model and that of propositional variables in the language are both restricted to be finite, the constant vio is satisfied in the current state if and only if there is no ideal state that is bisimilar to the current state (as shown in Proposition 13).

Definition 10 (Largest bisimulation). *Given two models $M = (W_0, W, \sim_0, R_0, V_0)$ and $M' = (W_0', W', \sim_0', R_0', V_0')$, we define the* largest bisimulation *between M and M' as a binary relation $\underline{\leftrightarrow} \subseteq W \times W'$ such that $w \underline{\leftrightarrow} v$ if:*

atoms $V_0(w) = V_0'(v)$.

forth *for all $x \in W$, if $w \sim_0 x$, then there is a $y \in W'$ such that $v \sim_0' y$ and $V_0(x) = V_0'(y)$.*

back *for all $y \in W'$, if $v \sim_0' y$, then there is a $x \in W$ such that $w \sim_0 x$ and $V_0'(y) = V_0(x)$.*

Definition 11 (Identity formula). *Given a model $M = (W_0, W, \sim_0, R_0, V_0)$, for every $w \in W$, let $\text{VAL}(w)$ be the formula $(\bigwedge_{p \in V_0(w)} p) \wedge (\bigwedge_{p \notin V_0(w)} \neg p)$. The* identity formula *of w, denoted as $\text{IDFORM}(w)$, is defined as follows:*

$$\text{VAL}(w) \wedge K(\bigvee_{v \in W \cap \sim_0(w)} \text{VAL}(v)) \wedge \bigwedge_{v \in W \cap \sim_0(w)} \neg K \neg \text{VAL}(v)$$

Lemma 12. *Let two models $M = (W_0, W, \sim_0, R_0, V_0)$ and $M' = (W_0', W', \sim_0', R_0', V_0')$ be given and let the largest bisimulation between M and M' be $\underline{\leftrightarrow}$. For every $w \in W$ and $v \in W'$, we have*

[3]Without specifying explicitly, the "models" mentioned in this section would be finite models for $\mathcal{L}(A)$.

[4]Here, strictly speaking, the notion of satisfaction should be distinguished from that in Definition 5. That is, the truth definition of vio should be replaced by the following:

> $M, w \models vio$ iff there is $\varphi \in \mathcal{L}_{el}(A)$ such that $M, w \models \varphi$ and $M_0, u \not\models \varphi$ for all $u \in W_0$ with wR_0u

1. *$w \leftrightarrows v$ iff for every $\varphi \in \mathcal{L}_{el}(A)$, it is the case that $M, w \models \varphi$ iff $M', v \models \varphi$;*
2. *If $(w, v) \notin \leftrightarrows$, then $M, w \models$ IDFORM(w) and $M', v \not\models$ IDFORM(w).*

Proof. We show only the first item. *From left to right*: Suppose that $w \leftrightarrows v$. Note that, in S5, every formula $\varphi \in \mathcal{L}_{el}$ is equivalent to a formula of the modal degree ≤ 1 (Cresswell and Hughes 1996). Thus, we can prove the lemma by considering four cases: p, $K\alpha$ (α is a propositional formula), $\neg\varphi$ and $\varphi \wedge \psi$, all of which are straightforward. *From right to left*: Suppose that $(w, v) \notin \leftrightarrows$. It is not hard to see that $M, w \models$ IDFORM(w) but $M', v \not\models$ IDFORM(w). □

Proposition 13. *Let $M = (W_0, W, \sim_0, R_0, V_0)$ be a model and let the largest bisimulation between M and M_0 be $\leftrightarrows$. For every state $w \in W$, it holds that $M, w \models vio$ iff for all $u \in W_0$ with wR_0u, $(w, u) \notin \leftrightarrows$.*

Proof. From left to right: Suppose $M, w \models vio$. Let $u \in W_0$ be an arbitrary state such that wR_0u. By the semantics of vio, there must be a formula $\varphi \in \mathcal{L}_{el}(A)$ such that $M, w \models \varphi$ and $M_0, u \not\models \varphi$. Therefore $(w, u) \notin \leftrightarrows$ by item 1 of Lemma 12. *From right to left*: Since $(w, u) \notin \leftrightarrows$, it follows from item 2 of Lemma 12 that $M, w \models$ IDFORM(w) and $M_0, u \not\models$ IDFORM(w). It is obvious that $M, w \models vio$. □

Now we can present a sound algorithm like that of Algorithm 1 to decide the truth of vio at some pointed model. A close look at Algorithm 1 delivers us the following theorem:

Theorem 14. MC$(\mathcal{L}$ (A)) *is in* $O(|W_0|^4 \times |A| \times |sub(\varphi)|)$.

Algorithm 1 Model checking for vio

Input: A model $M = (W_0, W, \sim_0, R_0, V_0)$ for $\mathcal{L}(A)$
Input: a state $w \in W$
Output "Yes" or "No"
  for each $u \in R_0(w)$ **do**
    Check if ISBISIMILAR((M,w),(M_0,v)). If yes:
    return "No"
  end for
  return "Yes"

  procedure ISBISIMILAR((M,w),(M_0,v))
    if $V_0(w) \neq V_0(v)$ **then**
      return False
    else
      for each $w' \in W \cap \sim_0(w)$ **do**
        Check if there is a $v' \in \sim_0(v)$ such that $V_0(w') = V_0(v')$. If not:
        return False
      end for
      for each $v' \in \sim_0(v)$ **do**
        Check if there is a $w' \in W \cap \sim_0(w)$ such that $V_0(w') = V_0(v')$. If not:
        return False
      end for
    end if
    return True
  end procedure

4 Axiomatisation

In this section, we first define a Hilbert-style axiomatisation **LPA** for the language $\mathcal{L}$ and prove that it is sound and complete with respect to the class of all models. The general idea behind the completeness proof is to prove weak completeness by constructing a finite canonical model. This can be achieved by taking maximal consistent sets in the finite closure of one formula instead of the whole language $\mathcal{L}$. However, we do not have a modal operator to describe the relation R_0 in models, so the crucial step is how to construct the relation R_0 in the finite canonical model.

Definition 15 (Axiomatisation). *The axiomatisation **LPA** for the language $\mathcal{L}$ is provided in Figure 3. A formula in $\mathcal{L}$ is a theorem of **LPA** if there is a proof for it. If φ is a theorem of **LPA**, we write $\vdash \varphi$.*

Axioms:	
(PL)	All propositional tautologies
(K)	$K(\varphi \to \psi) \to (K\varphi \to K\psi)$
(T)	$K\varphi \to \varphi$
(4)	$K\varphi \to KK\varphi$
(5)	$\neg K\varphi \to K\neg K\varphi$
(!Atom)	$[\varphi]p \leftrightarrow (\varphi \to p)$
(!Neg)	$[\varphi]\neg\psi \leftrightarrow (\varphi \to \neg[\varphi]\psi)$
(!Conj)	$[\varphi](\psi \wedge \chi) \leftrightarrow ([\varphi]\psi \wedge [\varphi]\chi)$
(!K)	$[\varphi]K\psi \leftrightarrow (\varphi \to K[\varphi]\psi)$
(!Comp)	$[\varphi][\psi]\chi \leftrightarrow [\varphi \wedge [\varphi]\psi]\chi$
(vio)	$vio \leftrightarrow [\top]vio$
($\mathbb{P}$)	$K(\varphi \leftrightarrow \psi) \to ([\varphi]vio \leftrightarrow [\psi]vio)$
Rules:	
(MP)	from φ and $\varphi \to \psi$, infer ψ
(Nec)	from φ, infer $K\varphi$

Figure 3: The axiomatization **LPA**

Definition 16 (Closure). *Given a formula $\varphi \in \mathcal{L}$, the* closure *of φ, with the notation $cl(\varphi)$, is the smallest set of formulas such that:*

- *$\varphi \in cl(\varphi)$;*
- *if $\psi \in cl(\varphi)$, then $sub(\psi) \subseteq cl(\varphi)$;*
- *if $\psi \in cl(\varphi)$ and ψ is not of the form $\neg\chi$, then $\neg\psi \in cl(\varphi)$;*
- *if $[\psi]p \in cl(\varphi)$, then $(\psi \to p) \in cl(\varphi)$;*
- *if $[\psi]\neg\chi \in cl(\varphi)$, then $(\psi \to \neg[\psi]\chi) \in cl(\varphi)$;*
- *if $[\psi](\chi \wedge \xi) \in cl(\varphi)$, then $[\psi]\chi \wedge [\psi]\xi \in cl(\varphi)$;*
- *if $[\psi]K\chi \in cl(\varphi)$, then $(\psi \to K[\psi]\chi) \in cl(\varphi)$;*
- *if $[\psi][\chi]\xi \in cl(\varphi)$, then $[\psi \wedge [\psi]\chi]\xi \in cl(\varphi)$;*
- *if $vio \in cl(\varphi)$, then $[\top]vio \in cl(\varphi)$;*
- *if $[\psi]vio$, $[\chi]vio \in cl(\varphi)$, then $K(\psi \leftrightarrow \chi) \in cl(\varphi)$.*

It is clear that $cl(\varphi)$ is finite for every formula φ. For any finite set of formulas Γ, let $\bigwedge\Gamma$ be the conjunction of all the formulas in Γ. The notion of "maximal consistent set" in a closure is defined as usual (van Ditmarsch, van der Hoek, and Kooi 2008). It is obvious that the set of all maximal consistent sets in $cl(\varphi)$ is finite for any formula φ.

Lemma 17. *Let φ be a formula. For any maximal consistent set of formulas Γ in $cl(\varphi)$, the following hold:*

1. *if $\vdash \bigwedge \Gamma \to \psi$ and $\psi \in cl(\varphi)$, then $\psi \in \Gamma$;*
2. *if $\psi \in cl(\varphi)$, then $\psi \in \Gamma$ iff $\neg\psi \notin \Gamma$;*
3. *if $\psi \wedge \chi \in cl(\varphi)$, then $\psi \wedge \chi \in \Gamma$ iff $\psi \in \Gamma$ and $\chi \in \Gamma$.*

In the remainder of this section, for convenience, we fix the formula $\varphi \in \mathcal{L}$. For every $\psi \in cl(\varphi)$, let $\|\psi\|$ be the set of all maximal consistent sets in $cl(\varphi)$ containing ψ. The Lindenbaum lemma can be proved in the standard way.

Lemma 18 (Lindenbaum)**.** *For every consistent set of formulas $\Sigma \subseteq cl(\varphi)$, there is a maximal consistent set Γ in $cl(\varphi)$ such that $\Sigma \subseteq \Gamma$.*

Now we define the notion of canonical pseudo-model, which is the main ingredient for constructing the canonical model in Definition 23.

Definition 19 (Canonical pseudo-model for $cl(\varphi)$)**.** *The* canonical pseudo-model *for $cl(\varphi)$ is a tuple $\mathsf{M} = (W, \sim, V)$ such that:*

- *W is the set of all maximal consistent sets in $cl(\varphi)$;*
- *$\sim \subseteq W \times W$ is such that $w \sim u$ iff $\{K\psi \mid K\psi \in w\} = \{K\psi \mid K\psi \in u\}$;*
- *V : PROP $\to \wp(W)$ is such that:*
  - *for all $p \in cl(\varphi)$, $w \in V(p)$ iff $p \in w$;*
  - *for all $w \in W$, there is a unique propositional variable $p_w \notin cl(\varphi)$ such that $V(p_w) = \{w\}$;*
  - *$V(p) = \varnothing$ for any other propositional variable.*

It is clear from the definition that $\sim$ is an equivalence relation. Note that V is well defined since W is finite. The following lemma can be shown in the standard way.

Lemma 20 (Existence)**.** *For every $w \in W$ and $K\psi \in cl(\varphi)$, if $K\psi \notin w$, then there must be a $u \in W$ such that $w \sim u$ and $\psi \notin u$.*

Lemma 21. *For every $w \in W$ and formulas $[\psi]vio, [\xi]vio \in cl(\varphi)$, if $[\psi]vio \notin w$ and $[\xi]vio \in w$, then $\sim(w) \cap \|\psi\| \neq \sim(w) \cap \|\xi\|$.*

Proof. Suppose $[\psi]vio \notin w$ and $[\xi]vio \in w$, then $K(\psi \leftrightarrow \xi) \notin w$. Otherwise, we would have $\vdash \bigwedge w \to ([\psi]vio \leftrightarrow [\xi]vio)$ by the axiom ($\mathbb{P}$) and we would have $\vdash \bigwedge w \to (\neg[\psi]vio \wedge [\xi]vio)$ by item 2 of Lemma 17, thereby contradicting the consistency of w.

Since $K(\psi \leftrightarrow \xi) \notin w$ and $K(\psi \leftrightarrow \xi) \in cl(\varphi)$, then by Lemma 20, it follows that there must be an $u \in W$ such that $w \sim u$ and $\psi \leftrightarrow \xi \notin u$.

Note that $\psi \in cl(\varphi)$. Then, by item 2 of Lemma 17, it follows that either $\psi \in u$ or $\neg\psi \in u$ (but not both). If $\psi \in u$, then $\xi \notin u$, thus $\sim(w) \cap \|\psi\| \neq \sim(w) \cap \|\xi\|$. If $\neg\psi \in u$, then $\psi \notin u$ and $\xi \in u$ (otherwise $\neg\xi \in u$ by item 2 of Lemma 17, thus $\psi \leftrightarrow \chi \in u$. Contradiction!). It also follows that $\sim(w) \cap \|\psi\| \neq \sim(w) \cap \|\xi\|$. □

Let $\psi_1, \psi_2, \ldots, \psi_n$ be an enumeration of all formulas ψ such that $[\psi]vio \in cl(\varphi)$ and there is a $w \in W$ with $[\psi]vio \notin w$. Next, we define the notion of "updates to the canonical pseudo-model", which also provides the ingredients for constructing the canonical model.

Definition 22 (Updates to the canonical pseudo-model)**.** *For each $1 \leq i \leq n$, we define the* update *to the canonical pseudo-model by ψ_i as a tuple $\mathsf{M}^i = (W^i, \sim^i, V^i)$ such that:*

- *$W^i = \|\psi_i\| \times \{i\}$;*
- *$\sim^i \subseteq W^i \times W^i$ is such that $(w, i) \sim^i (u, i)$ iff $w \sim u$;*
- *$V^i(p) = (V(p) \times \{i\}) \cap W^i$.*

Note that $\sim^i$ is an equivalence relation over W^i. Now, we are ready to define the canonical model for $cl(\varphi)$.

Definition 23 (Canonical model for $cl(\varphi)$)**.** *The* canonical model *$\mathcal{M}^c = (W_0^c, W^c, \sim_0^c, R_0^c, V_0^c)$ for $cl(\varphi)$ is defined as follows:*

- *$W_0^c = W \cup \bigcup_{1 \leq i \leq n} W^i \cup \{0\}$;*
- *$W^c = W$;*
- *$\sim_0^c = \sim \cup (\bigcup_{1 \leq i \leq n} \sim^i) \cup \{(0, 0)\}$;*
- *$R_0^c(w) = \{(w, i) \mid 1 \leq i \leq n$ and $[\psi_i]vio \notin w\} \cup \{0\}$ if $w \in W$,*
  $R_0^c(w) = \{w\}$ otherwise;
- *$V_0^c(p) = V(p) \cup \bigcup_{1 \leq i \leq n} V^i(p)$.*

We can verify that $\mathcal{M}^c$ is indeed a model. In the remainder of the section, let $[\![\varphi]\!] = [\![\varphi]\!]_{\mathcal{M}^c}$.

Lemma 24. *Let $1 \leq i \leq n$ and suppose that $\|\psi_i\| = [\![\psi_i]\!]$. Then for every $w \in W^c$ with $\mathcal{M}^c, w \models \psi_i$, it is the case that $\mathcal{M}^c|_{\psi_i}, w \models \chi$ iff $\mathcal{M}_0^c, (w, i) \models \chi$ for every $\chi \in \mathcal{L}_{el}$.*

Proof. Induction on the structure of χ. In the inductive case $K\xi$, note that $\sim^i((w, i)) = (\sim(w) \cap [\![\psi_i]\!]) \times \{i\}$ since we assume that $\|\psi_i\| = [\![\psi_i]\!]$. □

Lemma 25. *For every $\xi \in cl(\varphi)$ and $w \in [\![\xi]\!]$, if $\sim(w) \cap [\![\xi]\!] \neq \sim(w) \cap \|\psi_i\|$ for every $1 \leq i \leq n$ with $[\psi_i]vio \notin w$, then $\mathcal{M}^c|_\xi, w \models vio$.*

Proof. Let

$$\gamma = K(\bigvee_{u \in \sim(w) \cap [\![\xi]\!]} p_u) \wedge \bigwedge_{u \in \sim(w) \cap [\![\xi]\!]} \neg K \neg p_u.$$

It is clear that $\mathcal{M}^c|_\xi, w \models \gamma$. To show that $\mathcal{M}^c|_\xi, w \models vio$, it suffices to show that $\mathcal{M}_0^c, u \not\models \gamma$ for all $u \in R_0^c(w)$. If $u = 0$, it is clear that $\mathcal{M}_0^c, 0 \not\models \gamma$. If $u \neq 0$, then by the definition of R_0^c, there must be a $1 \leq i \leq n$ such that $[\psi_i]vio \notin w$ and $u = (w, i)$. By our assumption, we have $\sim(w) \cap \|\psi_i\| \neq \sim(w) \cap [\![\xi]\!]$.

If $\sim(w) \cap \|\psi_i\| \not\subseteq \sim(w) \cap [\![\xi]\!]$, there must be a $v \in \sim(w)$ such that $v \in \|\psi_i\|$ and $v \notin [\![\xi]\!]$. Note that, by the definitions of $\sim_0^c$ and $\sim^i$, we have that $\sim_0^c((w, i)) = \sim^i((w, i)) = (\sim(w) \cap \|\psi_i\|) \times \{i\}$. Thus $(v, i) \in \sim_0^c((w, i))$. Since $v \notin [\![\xi]\!]$, we have that $\mathcal{M}_0^c, (w, i) \models \neg K \neg (\bigwedge_{u \in \sim(w) \cap [\![\xi]\!]} \neg p_u)$ by the definition of V_0^c. Thus, $\mathcal{M}_0^c, (w, i) \not\models \gamma$.

If $\sim(w) \cap \|\psi_i\| \not\supseteq \sim(w) \cap [\![\xi]\!]$, it follows that there is a $v \in \sim(w)$ such that $v \in [\![\xi]\!]$ and $v \notin \|\psi_i\|$. Note that, by the definitions of $\sim_0^c$ and $\sim^i$, we have that $\sim_0^c((w, i)) = \sim^i((w, i)) = (\sim(w) \cap \|\psi_i\|) \times \{i\}$. Thus $(v, i) \notin \sim_0^c((w, i))$. Therefore $\mathcal{M}_0^c, (w, i) \not\models \neg K \neg p_v$ by the definition of V_0^c. Thus $\mathcal{M}_0^c, (w, i) \not\models \gamma$. □

Lemma 26 (Truth). *For every formula $\psi \in cl(\varphi)$, $\|\psi\| = [\![\psi]\!]$.*

Proof. Induction on $c(\psi)$:

Case p. For every $p \in cl(\varphi)$ and $w \in W^c$, we have that $p \in w$ iff $w \in V(p)$ iff $w \in V_0^c(p)$.

Case vio. *From left to right*: Suppose $vio \in w$. Since $[\top]vio \in cl(\varphi)$, then $[\top]vio \in w$ by the axiom (vio) and item 1 of Lemma 17. For every $1 \leq i \leq n$ such that $[\psi_i]vio \notin w$, since $[\psi_i]vio, [\top]vio \in cl(\varphi)$, $[\psi_i]vio \notin w$ and $[\top]vio \in w$, it follows from Lemma 21 that $\sim(w) \cap \|\psi_i\| \neq \sim(w) \cap \|\top\|$. Since $[\![\top]\!] = \|\top\| = W$, then $\sim(w) \cap \|\psi_i\| \neq \sim(w) \cap [\![\top]\!]$. Therefore $\mathcal{M}^c|_\top, w \models vio$ by Lemma 25. That is $\mathcal{M}^c, w \models vio$. *From right to left*: Suppose $vio \notin w$ and $\mathcal{M}^c, w \models vio$. Then $[\top]vio \notin w$ by the axiom (vio). Thus, there must be a $1 \leq i \leq n$ such that $\psi_i = \top$. By the definition of R_0^c, it must be the case that $wR_0^c(w,i)$. Note that $\|\top\| = [\![\top]\!] = W$, thus, by Lemma 24, we have

$$\mathcal{M}^c|_\top, w \models \chi \text{ iff } \mathcal{M}_0^c, (w,i) \models \chi \text{ for every } \chi \in \mathcal{L}_{el}.$$

But since we assume that $\mathcal{M}^c, w \models vio$ (thus $\mathcal{M}^c, w \models [\top]vio$ by item 6 of Proposition 7), then $\mathcal{M}^c|_\top, w \models vio$. By semantics, there must be a $\chi \in \mathcal{L}_{el}$ such that $\mathcal{M}^c|_\top, w \models \chi$ and $\mathcal{M}_0^c, (w,i) \not\models \chi$. Contradiction!

The cases for $\neg$, $\wedge$ and K are all straightforward and the cases for $[\xi]p$, $[\xi]\neg\xi'$, $[\xi](\xi_1 \wedge \xi_2)$, $[\xi]K\xi'$, and $[\xi][\xi_1]\xi_2$ follow directly from the induction hypothesis, Proposition 7, and the axioms (!Atom) – (!Comp). The case for $[\xi]vio$ remains to be considered.

From left to right: Suppose $[\xi]vio \in w$. If $\xi \notin w$, by the induction hypothesis, $\mathcal{M}^c, w \not\models \xi$. Thus $\mathcal{M}^c, w \models [\xi]vio$ by semantics. Therefore, we assume that $\xi \in w$. By the induction hypothesis, this implies that $\mathcal{M}^c, w \models \xi$. To prove that $\mathcal{M}^c, w \models [\xi]vio$, it suffices to show that $\mathcal{M}^c|_\xi, w \models vio$. For every $1 \leq i \leq n$ with $[\psi_i]vio \notin w$, since $[\psi_i]vio, [\xi]vio \in cl(\varphi)$, $[\psi_i]vio \notin w$ and $[\xi]vio \in w$, it follows from Lemma 21 that $\sim(w) \cap \|\psi_i\| \neq \sim(w) \cap \|\xi\|$. By the induction hypothesis that $\|\xi\| = [\![\xi]\!]$, we have that $\sim(w) \cap \|\psi_i\| \neq \sim(w) \cap [\![\xi]\!]$. Now we can apply Lemma 25 and obtain $\mathcal{M}^c|_\xi, w \models vio$. Therefore, $\mathcal{M}^c, w \models [\xi]vio$. *From right to left*: Suppose $[\xi]vio \notin w$ (thus $\xi \in w$) and $\mathcal{M}^c, w \models [\xi]vio$. It follows that there must be a $1 \leq i \leq n$ such that $\psi_i = \xi$. By the definition of R_0^c, it must be the case that $wR_0^c(w,i)$. Note that, by the induction hypothesis, we have $\|\xi\| = [\![\xi]\!]$ and $\mathcal{M}^c, w \models \xi$. Thus, by Lemma 24, we have

$$\mathcal{M}^c|_\xi, w \models \chi \text{ iff } \mathcal{M}_0^c, (w,i) \models \chi \text{ for every } \chi \in \mathcal{L}_{el}.$$

But since we assume $\mathcal{M}^c, w \models [\xi]vio$, then $\mathcal{M}^c|_\xi, w \models vio$. By semantics, there must be a $\chi \in \mathcal{L}_{el}$ such that $\mathcal{M}^c|_\xi, w \models \chi$ and $\mathcal{M}_0^c, (w,i) \not\models \chi$. Contradiction! □

Theorem 27 (Soundness and completeness). *For every $\varphi \in \mathcal{L}$, $\models \varphi$ iff $\vdash \varphi$.*

Proof. It is not hard to see that all the axioms and rules of standard epistemic logic S5 are valid. This, together with Proposition 7, implies that **LPA** is sound. For the completeness, suppose $\nvdash \varphi$. Then $\neg\varphi$ is consistent. Thus, by Lemma 18, there must be a maximal consistent set Γ in $cl(\varphi)$ such that $\neg\varphi \in \Gamma$. By Lemma 26, it follows that $\mathcal{M}^c, \Gamma \models \neg\varphi$. Thus, $\not\models \varphi$. □

Since the canonical model we constructed is finite, the next lemma follows immediately.

Lemma 28 (Finite model). *For any formula $\varphi \in \mathcal{L}$, if φ is satisfiable, then φ must be satisfied in a finite model.*

Theorem 29 (Decidability). *The satisfiability problem for LPA is decidable.*

5 A Neighbourhood-like Semantics

We have proven that **LPA** is weakly complete with respect to the semantics in Definition 5. However, by Proposition 9, **LPA** is not strongly complete, and we can never find such an axiomatisation. From a logical point of view, it would be interesting to find an alternative semantics with which **LPA** is strongly complete. In this section, we propose such a semantics for LPA in which the permitted announcements $\mathbb{P}\varphi$ undergoes a neighbourhood characterisation.

Definition 30 (Neighbourhood epistemic models). *A* neighbourhood epistemic model, *or simply* n-model, *is a tuple* $\mathsf{M} = (W, \sim, N, V)$ *such that:*

- *W is a non-empty set;*
- *$\sim \subseteq W \times W$ is an equivalence relation on W;*
- *$N : W \to \wp(\wp(W))$ is a neighbourhood function;*[5]
- *V : PROP $\to \wp(W)$ is a valuation.*

Definition 31 (n-model semantics). *Given an n-model $\mathsf{M} = (W, \sim, N, V)$, for every state $w \in W$ and formula $\alpha \in \mathcal{L}$, we inductively define that $\mathsf{M}, w \models^n \alpha$ as follows:*

$\mathsf{M}, w \models^n p$	*iff*	$w \in V(p)$
$\mathsf{M}, w \models^n vio$	*iff*	$\{v \in W \mid w \sim v\} \notin N(w)$
$\mathsf{M}, w \models^n \neg\varphi$	*iff*	*not* $\mathsf{M}, w \models^n \varphi$
$\mathsf{M}, w \models^n (\varphi \wedge \psi)$	*iff*	$\mathsf{M}, w \models^n \varphi$ *and* $\mathsf{M}, w \models^n \psi$
$\mathsf{M}, w \models^n K\varphi$	*iff*	*for all* $u \in W$ *with* $w \sim u$, $\mathsf{M}, u \models^n \varphi$
$\mathsf{M}, w \models^n [\varphi]\psi$	*iff*	$\mathsf{M}, w \models^n \varphi$ *implies* $\mathsf{M}|_\varphi, w \models^n \psi$

where $\mathsf{M}|_\varphi = (W_\varphi, \sim_\varphi, N_\varphi, V_\varphi)$ is defined as follows:

- $W_\varphi = [\![\varphi]\!]_\mathsf{M}$;
- $\sim_\varphi = \sim \cap ([\![\varphi]\!]_\mathsf{M} \times [\![\varphi]\!]_\mathsf{M})$;
- $N_\varphi(w) = \{U \mid U \in N(w) \,\&\, U \subseteq [\![\varphi]\!]_\mathsf{M}\}$;
- $V_\varphi(p) = V(p) \cap [\![\varphi]\!]_\mathsf{M}$.

Thus, in the n-model semantics, we have $\mathsf{M}, w \models^n \mathbb{P}\varphi$ iff

$$\mathsf{M}, w \models^n \varphi \text{ and } [\![\varphi]\!]_\mathsf{M} \cap \{v \in W \mid w \sim v\} \in N(w)$$

However, the relationship between the n-model semantics and the semantics in Definition 5 is not so straightforward.

Proposition 32. *For any model $M = (W_0, W, \sim_0, R_0, V_0)$ and $w \in W$, there is an n-model M and state w' in M such that $M, w \models \varphi$ iff $\mathsf{M}, w' \models \varphi$ for all formulas $\varphi \in \mathcal{L}$.*

[5]For every $w \in W$, each set in the neighbourhood $N(w)$ induces an equivalence relation over W. Thus, intuitively, the function N can be understood as specifying which epistemic situations are "good" at each state.

Sketch of Proof. We can construct the model $\mathsf{M} = (W', \sim', N', V')$ such that:

- $W' = W$, $\sim' = \sim_0 \cap (W \times W)$, $V'(p) = V_0(p) \cap W$;
- $N'(w) = \{[\![\psi]\!]_M \cap \sim_0(w) \mid \psi \in \mathcal{L} \,\&\, M, w \models \mathbb{P}\psi\}$;
- $w' = w$.

It is not hard to prove the proposition by induction on the structure of φ.

But the converse of the above proposition does not hold. That is, there is an n-model for which we can not find an equivalent model. Since it is not hard to find an n-model satisfying the set Γ introduced in the proof of Proposition 9, but Γ is unsatisfiable in our original semantics. The exact relationship between the n-model semantics and the original semantics is given by the following proposition.

Proposition 33. *For every $\varphi \in \mathcal{L}$, φ is satisfiable (under the semantics in Definition 5) iff φ is satisfied by an n-model.*

We can also show the following completeness theorem by the canonical model method.

Theorem 34. *The axiomatisation **LPA** is sound and strongly complete with respect to the n-model semantics.*

6 The Principles of Permitted Announcements

The work of Balbiani and Seban (2011) is the first attempt to study the notion of "permission to say something". Since our work is devoted to the same topic, we compare our paper with their work in a separate section.

In Balbiani and Seban's (2011) article, the operators $P(\psi, \varphi)$ and $O(\psi, \varphi)$ are introduced to express the notions that "after announcing ψ, it is permitted/obligatory to announce φ". It is clear that our operator $\mathbb{P}\varphi$ can be expressed in their framework as $P(\top, \varphi)$. Conversely, one can also interpret their operator $P(\psi, \varphi)$ as $[\psi]\mathbb{P}\varphi$ in LPA. We do not have an operator $\mathbb{O}\varphi$ to express that "it is obligatory to announce φ", which is clearly a direction for future work. However, the semantics for their logic is quite different from ours. In their framework, a ternary relation $\mathcal{P} \subseteq S \times \wp(S) \times \wp(S)$ is used to provide the semantics for $P(\psi, \varphi)$ in such a way that $\mathcal{M}, s \models P(\psi, \varphi)$ iff for some $(s, [\![\psi]\!], S'') \in \mathcal{P}, S'' \subseteq [\![\varphi]\!]$, where S is the domain of the model and $[\![\varphi]\!]$ is the truth set of φ. We observe that those permitted announcements are directly encoded in the ternary relation $\mathcal{P}$. This encoding is purely technical and serves only to distinguish between what is permitted and what is not permitted. It does not reflect the semantic intuition behind the permitted announcements. In contrast, our work gives an intuitively appealing interpretation of "permitted announcements". We also find different logical principles pertaining to permitted announcements.

The prominent principle of permitted announcements that is absent from the work of Balbiani and Seban (2011) but present in ours is the axiom ($\mathbb{P}$): $K(\varphi \leftrightarrow \psi) \rightarrow (\mathbb{P}\varphi \leftrightarrow \mathbb{P}\psi)$. It states that if two statements are known by the agent to be equivalent, then it is impossible that we are permitted to announce one statement to the agent while being forbidden to announce the other statement, because the actions of announcing φ and announcing ψ would bring the same set of knowledge in this case. From ($\mathbb{P}$), we can infer that $\mathbb{P}\top \rightarrow (K\varphi \rightarrow \mathbb{P}\varphi)$. It states that we are permitted to announce things that have already been known if the current situation is good. This is a trivial principle, but it is not valid in the work of Balbiani and Seban (2011).

Another missing principle is $[\varphi]\mathbb{P}\psi \leftrightarrow (\varphi \rightarrow \mathbb{P}(\varphi \wedge [\varphi]\psi))$, which is equivalent to $\langle\varphi\rangle\mathbb{P}\psi \leftrightarrow \mathbb{P}\langle\varphi\rangle\psi$, where $\langle\varphi\rangle\psi = \neg[\varphi]\neg\psi$. It can be understood as saying that "it is permitted to make an announcement that 'φ is true and after the announcement of φ, ψ is true' if and only if φ is true and it is permitted to announce ψ after φ has been announced". One may notice that it is a variant of a well-known property pertaining to sequel actions in dynamic deontic logic: $P(\alpha_1; \alpha_2) \leftrightarrow \langle\alpha_1\rangle P\alpha_2$ (Meyer 1987).

LPA also invalidates some principles pertaining to permitted announcements in the work of Balbiani and Seban (2011). One is the weakening of a permitted announcement: $\mathbb{P}(\varphi \wedge \psi) \rightarrow \mathbb{P}\varphi$.[6] This is because the announcement of φ may provide less information than the announcement of $\varphi \wedge \psi$. However, sometimes ignorance about some facts may be forbidden or, in other words, knowledge of these facts is obligatory. For example, in many countries, it is not permitted for a pharmacist to only advertise over-the-counter medicines to customers while not telling them the possible side-effects.

7 Related Work

Deontic logic about knowledge and belief. The notions of permission and prohibition to know have been studied by Cuppens and Demolombe (1996) in the context of security of databases. In their framework, the modalities $PK\varphi$ and $FK\varphi$ are introduced to express that "some users are permitted/forbidden to know that the database believes φ".[7] There are two binary relations in their models, one for knowledge and one for obligation. Thus $PK\varphi$ is true at some state w if there is some ideal world of w in which $K\varphi$ holds. LPA implicitly employs the same characterisation of permission to know in its truth definition for vio.

An important paradox of deontic logic about knowledge is Åqvist's paradox (Åqvist 1967). Our work is not aimed at solving that paradox. Our concern is how the change of knowledge brought by public announcements affects the normative status of the agent concerned. Various work are devoted to the study of how knowledge affects obligation, e.g. (Horty 2001; Pacuit, Parikh, and Cogan 2006; Grossi et al. 2021). In our work, we assume that knowledge does not affect permission to know. It would be interesting to extend our work such that permission to know interacts with knowledge. Recently, there have also been some work studying other deontic concepts of knowledge, like "the right to know" (Markovich and Roy 2021a; Markovich and Roy 2021b). Our work concerns the permission to say something. We plan to extend our work to

[6]We point out that this principle does not hold in the earlier work of Balbiani et al. (2009).

[7]We reformulate their notations for a clear presentation.

studying the notion of "having the right to say" and its role in the formalisation of freedom of speech.

Deontic logic about epistemic actions. We are heavily influenced by the work of Aucher et al. (2011) which proposes a dynamic modal logic for reasoning about which information is permitted to be sent by a security monitor in order to comply with a privacy policy. We improve their logic in the following respects: 1. A privacy policy in their logic is just a finite and consistent set of formulas (like OKq or $Kp \to PKq$) specifying the permitted and obligatory knowledge of the receiver. By encoding the privacy policy into relational models, we can reason about the privacy policy, rather than just check the permitted and forbidden knowledge according to a purely syntactic list. 2. We simplify the semantics. In their logic, they use the machinery of action models in dynamic epistemic logic (Baltag and Moss 2004). Though dynamic epistemic logic is powerful enough, we show that we do not need it if we are only dealing with permitted announcements. Our semantics is much simpler and the number of states will not grow exponentially with announcements. The latter is important for model checking. The idea of distinguishing between the initial and current domains in relational models can be found in the work of Baltag et al. (2018). 3. We also enhance their formal language so that we can talk about high-order expressions about permitted announcements like $\mathbb{P}\mathbb{P}\varphi$. But a problem follows from our approach. Aucher et al. (2011) can express the notion of compliance as a single compound formula. Thus, they easily get a complete axiomatisation for their logic. However, the constant vio in LPA can not be reduced. Thus, it is not so easy to propose a complete axiomatisation. Meanwhile, we also think that our axiomatisation is more revealing.

Van Benthem et al. (2009) propose a logic for protocols in dynamic epistmemic logic. We can interpret it as a logic for permitted epistemic actions. Due to the space limitation, we only mention here that the permitted epistemic actions (represented by the event models of dynamic epistemic logic) are listed in the protocols, and there is no the notion of "permitted knowledge" in their framework. Besides, our work can easily be extended to other epistemic actions by adding the vio constant to the language of dynamic epistemic logic (Baltag and Moss 2004). Van Ditmarsch and Seban (2012) extend their prior work (Balbiani and Seban 2011) to the multi-agent case. We can also study how to extend our work to the multi-agent case.

Dynamic deontic logic. Our work has a close relationship to dynamic deontic logic (Meyer 1987). In dynamic deontic logic, an action is permitted if performing it would not lead to getting into trouble. Thus, permissions about actions are reduced to the normative status after executing the actions. Our work can be seen as instantiating actions by public announcements. Compared to (Meyer 1987), our work has three differences: 1. The truth of vio depends on the structure of the model rather than the propositional truth values of a state. 2. Our language allows high-order expressions like $\mathbb{P}\mathbb{P}\varphi$. 3. There are no compositions of public announcements like the negation of a public announcement.

In the later developments of dynamic deontic logic, different definitions of permission have been proposed (Dignum, Meyer, and Wieringa 1994a). For example, the strong permission $P_{Strong}(\alpha)$ is defined as $[\alpha]\neg V$. Similarly, we can also study different variants of permitted announcements.

Van der Meyden et al. (1996) criticise Meyer's dynamic deontic logic because it contains a problematic validity: $\langle\alpha\rangle P\beta \to P(\alpha;\beta)$. The idea is that the action α may be a forbidden action. Thus, as per their example, even if we are permitted to remain silent after shooting the president, we are not permitted to shoot the president and remain silent. In LPA, we have an analogy: $\langle\varphi\rangle\mathbb{P}\psi \to \mathbb{P}\langle\varphi\rangle\psi$. However, what falls into the scope of $\mathbb{P}$ in the consequent of the implication is not a *sequel announcement* but a *single announcement* of formula $\langle\varphi\rangle\psi$. The free choice paradox (Ross 1941; Dignum, Meyer, and Wieringa 1994b) is another paradox concerning dynamic deontic logic. But, again, there is no notion of choice between two announcements in LPA.

The notion of "the negation of an action" in dynamic deontic logic has also been doubted by several authors (Broersen 2004; Wansing 2004; Sun and Huimin 2014; Ju and van Eijck 2016). Our work suggests the importance of a proper definition for the negation of public announcements.

8 Conclusions and Future Work

In this paper, we introduced a logic of permitted announcements by interpreting "permitted announcements" as "announcements that would not lead to forbidden knowledge". The language of LPA is obtained by augmenting public announcement logic with a constant vio, and the semantics for permitted announcements contains a quantification over all epistemic formulas. We captured all the logical principles of permitted announcements by the axiomatisation **LPA** and provided an alternative neighbourhood-like semantics with which **LPA** is strongly complete. It should be pointed out that the axiom ($\mathbb{P}$) would not be valid if assume a weaker logic for the knowledge operator K, e.g., the modal logic **K**. We conjecture that our technique can be adapted to show the completeness results when the base epistemic logic is stronger than **K4**. We also studied the computational complexity of the model checking problem and showed the decidability of the satisfiability problem. The computational complexity of the satisfiability problem for LPA is still unknown.

Our work gives new insights into the notion of "permitted announcements" and enables us to reason about privacy policies and other forms of regulated communication. Many issues are left for future research. The vital issue is how to incorporate the notion of "obligatory announcements". When we provided our semantics in this work, we assumed that permission to know does not change with public announcements, but it is natural to consider how to enable our framework to reason about the dynamics of permission to know. We can also consider, for instance, how to extend our framework to the multi-agent case, and how to incorporate epistemic actions other than public announcements.

Acknowledgments

We thank Leendert van der Torre for valuable discussions and comments on earlier drafts of this paper. We also thank three anonymous reviewers of KR 2022 for insightful remarks and Llio Humphreys for proofreading the paper. This work was supported by the Fonds National de la Recherche Luxembourg through the project Deontic Logic for Epistemic Rights (OPEN O20/14776480).

References

Anderson, A. R. 1958. A reduction of deontic logic to alethic modal logic. *Mind* 67(265):100–103.

Aucher, G.; Boella, G.; and van der Torre, L. 2011. A dynamic logic for privacy compliance. *Artificial Intelligence and Law* 19(2):187.

Balbiani, P., and Seban, P. 2011. Reasoning about permitted announcements. *Journal of Philosophical Logic* 40(4):445–472.

Balbiani, P.; van Ditmarsch, H.; and Seban, P. 2009. Reasoning about permitted announcements. In Herzig, A., and Lorini, E., eds., *(Electronic) proceedings of: ESSLLI 2009 workshop logical methods for social concepts, Bordeaux, France*.

Baltag, A., and Moss, L. S. 2004. Logics for epistemic programs. *Synthese* 139(2):165–224.

Baltag, A.; Özgün, A.; and Vargas Sandoval, A. L. 2018. APAL with memory is better. In Moss, L. S.; de Queiroz, R.; and Martinez, M., eds., *Logic, Language, Information, and Computation*, 106–129. Berlin, Heidelberg: Springer Berlin Heidelberg.

Başkent, C.; Loohuis, L. O.; and Parikh, R. 2012. On knowledge and obligation. *Episteme* 9(2):171–188.

Blackburn, P.; de Rijke, M.; and Venema, Y. 2001. *Modal Logic*, volume 53 of *Cambridge Tracts in Theoretical Computer Science*. Cambridge University Press.

Broersen, J. 2004. Action negation and alternative reductions for dynamic deontic logics. *Journal of Applied Logic* 2(1):153–168. The Sixth International Workshop on Deontic Logic in Computer Science.

Cresswell, M. J., and Hughes, G. E. 1996. *A new introduction to modal logic*. Routledge.

Cuppens, F., and Demolombe, R. 1996. A deontic logic for reasoning about confidentiality. In Brown, M. A., and Carmo, J., eds., *Deontic Logic, Agency and Normative Systems*, 66–79. London: Springer London.

Dignum, F.; Meyer, J.-J. C.; and Wieringa, R. 1994a. A dynamic logic for reasoning about sub-ideal states. In *ECAI'94 Workshop "Artificial Normative Reasoning"*.

Dignum, F.; Meyer, J.-J. Ch..; and Wieringa, R. J. 1994b. Contextual permission: A solution to the free choice paradox. In *Proceedings of the 2nd International Workshop on Deontic Logic in Computer Science (DEON 1994), Oslo, Norway, January 6-8, 1994*, 107–135.

Gabbay, D.; Horty, J.; Parent, X.; van der Meyden, R.; and van der Torre, L., eds. 2013. *Handbook of Deontic Logic and Normative Systems*. College Publications.

Gerbrandy, J., and Groeneveld, W. 1997. Reasoning about information change. *Journal of Logic, Language, and Information* 6(2):147–169.

Grossi, D.; Kooi, B.; Su, X.; and Verbrugge, R. 2021. How knowledge triggers obligation. In Ghosh, S., and Icard, T., eds., *Logic, Rationality, and Interaction*, 201–215. Cham: Springer International Publishing.

Horty, J. F. 2001. *Agency and Deontic Logic*. Oxford University Press.

Ju, F., and van Eijck, J. 2016. To do something else. In *Deontic Logic and Normative Systems. 13th International Conference, DEON 2016, Bayreuth, Germany, July 18-21, 2018*, 109–122.

Kooi, B., and van Benthem, J. 2004. Reduction axioms for epistemic actions. In Schmidt, R. A.; Pratt-Hartmann, I.; Reynolds, M.; and Wansing, H., eds., *AiML-2004: Advances in Modal Logic (Preliminary Proceedings)*, 197–211.

Markovich, R., and Roy, O. 2021a. Formalizing the right to know: Epistemic rights as normative positions. In *The First International Workshop on Logics for New-Generation Artificial Intelligence (LNGAI 2021)*.

Markovich, R., and Roy, O. 2021b. A logical analysis of freedom of thought. In *Deontic Logic and Normative Systems. 14th International Conference, DEON 2018, The Netherlands, 3-6 July, 2018*, 323–338.

Meyer, J.-J. C. 1987. A different approach to deontic logic: deontic logic viewed as a variant of dynamic logic. *Notre Dame Journal of Formal Logic* 29(1):109 – 136.

Pacuit, E.; Parikh, R.; and Cogan, E. 2006. The logic of knowledge based obligation. *Synthese* 149(2):311–341.

Plaza, J. 1989. Logics of public communications. In Emrich, M.; Pfeifer, M.; Hadzikadic, M.; and Ras, Z., eds., *Proceedings of the 4th International Symposium on Methodologies for Intelligent Systems*, 201–216.

Ross, A. 1941. Imperatives and logic. *Theoria* 7:53–71.

Sun, X., and Huimin, D. 2014. Stratified action negation for dynamic logic. In *26th BENELUX Conference on Artificial Intelligence (BNAIC)*.

van Benthem, J.; Gerbrandy, J.; Hoshi, T.; and Pacuit, E. 2009. Merging frameworks for interaction. *Journal of Philosophical Logic* 38(5):491–526.

van der Meyden, R. 1996. The Dynamic Logic of Permission. *Journal of Logic and Computation* 6(3):465–479.

van Ditmarsch, H., and Seban, P. 2012. A logical framework for individual permissions on public announcements. https://personal.us.es/hvd/newerpubs/hanspablo070212.pdf. Accessed: 2022-05-15.

van Ditmarsch, H.; van der Hoek, W.; and Kooi, B. 2008. *Dynamic Epistemic Logic*. Springer, Dordrecht.

Wansing, H. 2004. *On the Negation of Action Types: Constructive Concurrent PDL*. Dresden Preprints in theoretical philosophy and philosophical logic. Techn. Univ.

Åqvist, L. 1967. Good samaritans, contrary-to-duty imperatives, and epistemic obligations. *Noûs* 1(4):361–379.

Proceedings of the 19th International Conference on Principles of Knowledge Representation and Reasoning
Main Track

Epistemic Actions: Comparing Multi-agent Belief Bases with Action Models

Emiliano Lorini[1] , **Elise Perrotin**[2] , **François Schwarzentruber**[3]
[1]IRIT, CNRS and University of Toulouse, France
[2]CRIL, CNRS, France
[3]Univ Rennes, IRISA, France
emiliano.lorini@irit.fr, elise.perrotin@cril.fr, francois.schwarzentruber@ens-rennes.fr

Abstract

We compare the syntactic multi-agent belief base approach, and the dynamic epistemic logic possible world semantic approach. In the belief base approach, the language provides an implicit and an explicit belief operators, plus a dynamic modality for actions consisting in adding formulae to bases. For the semantic approach, we rely on action models of Dynamic Epistemic Logic (DEL). We first show how to translate a formula of the belief base approach into DEL: in particular, we provide a specific action model scheme corresponding to the addition of a formula in a belief base. Conversely, we identify a fragment of DEL that can be translated in the multi-agent belief base language.

1 Introduction

The formalization of epistemic states and their dynamics is one of the key topics in the area of knowledge representation and reasoning. There are two traditions in this area. On the one hand, there is epistemic logic which started with the seminal work of Hintikka (Hintikka 1962) on the logics of knowledge and belief. It was extended to the multi-agent setting at a later stage (Fagin et al. 1995; Meyer and van der Hoek 1995) and, more recently, to modeling knowledge and belief change with growing research on dynamic epistemic logic (DEL) (Baltag, Moss, and Solecki 1998; Baltag and Moss 2004; van Ditmarsch, van der Hoek, and Kooi 2007a). The standard approach to epistemic logic is extensional. Its formal semantics exploits the so-called multi-agent *Kripke models*, namely, multi-relational structures equipped with valuation functions for the interpretation of atomic formulas. Binary relations in a multi-agent Kripke model are called *epistemic (or doxastic) accessibility relations* and are used to describe the agents' epistemic states and uncertainty.

On the other hand, we have the so-called syntactic approach. It includes, for instance, work on belief base and knowledge base revision (Hansson 1993; 1999; Benferhat et al. 2002), belief base merging (Konieczny and Pérez 2002) and input-output logic (Makinson and van der Torre 2000). The syntactic approach typically leverages belief bases, or more generally knowledge bases, for representing what an agent knows or believes. A natural distinction in this approach is between explicit and implicit belief. An agent's explicit belief is seen as a piece of information in the agent's belief base, while an implicit belief corresponds to a piece of information that is derivable from the agent's belief base (i.e., included in the deductive closure of the agent's belief base). The syntactic approach was put forward among other things as a solution to the logical omniscience problem in virtue of the fact that an agent's beliefs are described either by a set of formulas which is not necessarily closed under deduction (Eberle 1974; Moore and Hendrix 1982) or by a set of formulas obtained by the application of an incomplete set of deduction rules (Konolige 1986; Jago 2009).

The two approaches have been recently reconciled in (Lorini 2018; 2020) in which a semantics for multi-agent epistemic logic using belief bases was proposed. The central idea of this semantics is that an agent's epistemic indistinguishability relation should be computed from the agent's belief base by stipulating that *a state is considered possible by the agent if and only if it satisfies all information in the agent's belief base*. Moreover, at a dynamic level, the dynamics of the agents' explicit and implicit beliefs are supposed to depend on how their belief bases change over time. For instance, by privately expanding its belief base with a new information α, an agent will start to explicitly believe α and, consequently, it will be able to deduce new facts from its expanded belief base.

In this paper we push forward the comparison between the two approaches by investigating the connection between the update semantics for DEL using so-called action models (Baltag, Moss, and Solecki 1998) and the update semantics for epistemic logic using belief bases introduced in (Lorini 2020). We believe comparing the two approaches is useful since each of them has its own advantages and disadvantages and it is important to have a clear understanding of their relationship. For instance, the extensional approach using multi-relational Kripke models and action models is general, as it allows us to model a large variety of multi-agent information dynamics, but it is not compact: even simple situations require big models. On the contrary, the syntactic approach is less general, but it represents information in a more compact way with the help of belief bases. We will answer the following questions: what is the extensional counterpart in terms of action model of the notion of belief base expansion? Which class of multi-agent information dynamics can be represented through update operations on belief bases? Both directions will be explored: from multi-agent belief bases to action models and back from action models to multi-agent belief bases. On the one hand, we will show how to translate the notion of private belief base expansion into a specific class of action models representing private information change. On the other hand, we will identify a specific class of "ruby" actions models that can be translated into the belief base semantics. In a "ruby" action model each agent privately learns a new fact and updates its beliefs accordingly assuming that the others do not learn anything. The non-trivial aspect of the construction from the DEL semantics to the belief base semantics lies in syntactically representing action models with belief bases.

The paper is organized as follows.[1] In Section 2 we present the background material on the language and the semantics for epistemic logic exploiting belief bases introduced in (Lorini 2020). Section 3 presents the background material on DEL: the notions of action model and product update between an epistemic model and an action model. In Section 4, we study the connection between the update semantics for epistemic logic using multi-agent belief bases and the DEL semantics using action models. We provide a polynomial embedding of the former into the latter and then we show how to represent "ruby" action models through the notion of private belief base expansion. In Section 5, we discuss the two semantics under the assumption of epistemic introspection. In Section 6, we discuss some related work.

2 Background on Multi-agent Belief Bases

This section presents the dynamic epistemic language for beliefs of both explicit and implicit types (Lorini 2020).

2.1 Language

Assume a countably infinite set of atomic propositions $Ap = \{p, q, \ldots\}$ and a finite set of agents $Ag = \{1, \ldots, n\}$. Let $2^{Ag*} = 2^{Ag} \setminus \{\emptyset\}$ be the set of non-empty coalitions.

We define the language in two steps. First define the language $\mathcal{L}_0$ by:

$$\mathcal{L}_0 \stackrel{\text{def}}{=} \quad \alpha \quad ::= \quad p \mid \neg\alpha \mid \alpha \wedge \alpha \mid \triangle_i \alpha,$$

where p ranges over Ap and i ranges over Ag. $\mathcal{L}_0$ is the language used to represent *explicit* beliefs. The formula $\triangle_i \alpha$ reads "agent i has the explicit belief that α". The language $\mathcal{L}_B$ extends $\mathcal{L}_0$ and is defined by:

$$\mathcal{L}_B \stackrel{\text{def}}{=} \quad \varphi \quad ::= \quad \alpha \mid \neg\varphi \mid \varphi \wedge \varphi \mid \Box_i \varphi \mid [+_J \alpha]\varphi,$$

where α ranges over $\mathcal{L}_0$, i over Ag and J over 2^{Ag*}.

The other Boolean constructions $\top$, $\bot$, $\vee$, $\rightarrow$ and $\leftrightarrow$ are defined from p, $\neg$ and $\wedge$ in the standard way. The formula $\Box_i \varphi$ reads "agent i implicitly believes that φ". The abbreviation $\Diamond_i \varphi \stackrel{\text{def}}{=} \neg\Box_i\neg\varphi$ defines the concept of belief compatibility. The formula $\Diamond_i \varphi$ reads "φ is compatible with agent i's explicit beliefs". The operator $[+_J \alpha]$ is used to model private belief expansion. Specifically, the formula $[+_J \alpha]\varphi$ reads "φ holds after every agent in the coalition J has expanded its belief base with α".

[1]The supplementary material contains the long version of this submission.

2.2 Belief Base Semantics

The formal semantics for the language $\mathcal{L}_B$ exploits belief bases. Unlike the standard Kripke semantics in which possible worlds and epistemic alternatives are primitive, they are here defined from the primitive concept of belief base.

Definition 1 (State) *A state is a tuple* $B = \big((B_i)_{i \in Ag}, V\big)$ *where* $B_i \subseteq \mathcal{L}_0$ *is agent i's belief base, and* $V \subseteq Ap$ *is the actual environment. The set of all states is noted* $\mathbf{S}$.

The following definition specifies truth conditions for formulas in the sublanguage $\mathcal{L}_0$.

Definition 2 (Satisfaction relation) *For any state* $B = \big((B_i)_{i \in Ag}, V\big) \in \mathbf{S}$:

$$\begin{aligned} B \models p &\iff p \in V, \\ B \models \neg\alpha &\iff B \not\models \alpha, \\ B \models \alpha_1 \wedge \alpha_2 &\iff B \models \alpha_1 \text{ and } B \models \alpha_2, \\ B \models \triangle_i \alpha &\iff \alpha \in B_i. \end{aligned}$$

Observe the set-theoretic interpretation of the explicit belief operators in the previous definition: agent i has the explicit belief that α if and only if α is included in its belief base. The following definition introduces the notion of epistemic alternative.

Definition 3 (Epistemic alternatives) *Let* $i \in Ag$. *Then,* $\mathcal{R}_i$ *is the binary relation on the set* $\mathbf{S}$ *such that, for all* $B = \big((B_i)_{i \in Ag}, V\big), B' = \big((B'_i)_{i \in Ag}, V'\big) \in \mathbf{S}$:

$$B\mathcal{R}_i B' \text{ if and only if } \forall \alpha \in B_i : B' \models \alpha.$$

$B\mathcal{R}_i B'$ means that B' is an epistemic alternative for agent i at B, that is to say, B' is a state that agent i considers possible at B. The idea of the previous definition is that B' is an epistemic alternative for agent i at B if and only if, B' satisfies all facts that agent i explicitly believes at B.

A multi-agent belief model (MAB), or simply model, is defined to be a state supplemented with a set of states, called *context*. The context Cxt is not necessarily equal to the set of all states $\mathbf{S}$, since there could be states in $\mathbf{S}$ incompatible with the general "laws of the domain" and, consequently, with the agents' epistemic states. For example, we might want to exclude from the context Cxt all states in which the propositions "1+1=2" and "1+1=3" are true concomitantly.

Definition 4 (Multi-agent belief model) *A multi-agent belief model (MAB) is a pair* (B, Cxt), *where* $B \in \mathbf{S}$ *and* $Cxt \subseteq \mathbf{S}$. *The class of MABs is noted* $\mathbf{M}$.

Note that in Definition 4 we do not require $B \in Cxt$. The following definition extends Definition 2 to the full language $\mathcal{L}_B$. Its formulas are interpreted with respect to MABs. (We omit Boolean cases, as they are defined in the usual way.)

Definition 5 (Satisfaction relation (cont.)) *Let* $(B, Cxt) \in \mathbf{M}$. *Then:*

$$\begin{aligned} (B, Cxt) \models \alpha &\iff B \models \alpha, \\ (B, Cxt) \models \Box_i \varphi &\iff \forall B' \in Cxt, \text{if } B\mathcal{R}_i B' \text{ then } \\ &\qquad (B', Cxt) \models \varphi, \\ (B, Cxt) \models [+_J \alpha]\varphi &\iff (B^{+_J \alpha}, Cxt) \models \varphi, \end{aligned}$$

with $V^{+_J \alpha} = V$, $B_i^{+_J \alpha} = B_i \cup \{\alpha\}$ *for all* $i \in J$, *and* $B_j^{+_J \alpha} = B_j$ *for all* $j \notin J$.

According to the previous definition, agent i implicitly believes that φ if and only if φ is true at all states in the context that i considers possible. Moreover, every agent in coalition J privately expands its belief base with α if every agent in J adds the information α to its belief base, while all agents outside of J keep their beliefs unchanged.

Let $\varphi \in \mathcal{L}_B$. Formula φ is said to be valid relative to the class $\mathbf{M}$, noted $\models_{\mathbf{M}} \varphi$, if and only if, for every $(B, Cxt) \in \mathbf{M}$, we have $(B, Cxt) \models \varphi$. Formula φ is said to be satisfiable for the class $\mathbf{M}$ if and only if $\neg\varphi$ is not valid for the class $\mathbf{M}$.

3 Background on DEL

An epistemic model is a Kripke structure (i.e. a graph) in which nodes are possible worlds and edges are labelled by agents.

Definition 6 *An* epistemic model $\mathcal{M} = (W, (R_i)_{i \in Ag}, V)$ *is a tuple where:*

- W *is a non-empty finite set of possible* worlds,
- $R_i \subseteq W \times W$ *is an* accessibility relation *for agent* i,
- $V : W \longrightarrow 2^{Ap}$ *is a* valuation function.

A static epistemic situation is then classically represented by a so-called pointed epistemic model, which is a pair $\mathcal{M}, w$ where w is the current world.

Example 1 *In Figure 1 (on the left), the epistemic model $\mathcal{M}$ contains two worlds w and u that are indistinguishable for both agents i and j. Moreover, the current world is w.*

To model epistemic actions (public/private announcements, etc.), DEL provides the notion of action model (Baltag, Moss, and Solecki 1998). An action model is also a Kripke structure. Nodes are atomic actions, also called events, labelled by a pair of pre- and post-conditions. The precondition $pre(a)$ of an atomic action a is the epistemic formula that should be true before the execution of a, and the postcondition function $post(a)$ assigns to each proposition p a new truth value obtained by the evaluation of the formula $post(a)(p)$.

Definition 7 *An* action model *is a tuple* $\mathcal{A} = (\mathsf{A}, (R_i^{\mathcal{A}})_{i \in Ag}, pre, post)$ *where:*

- A *is a non-empty finite set of possible* atomic actions,
- $R_i^{\mathcal{A}} \subseteq \mathsf{A} \times \mathsf{A}$ *is the* accessibility relation *on* A *for* i,
- $pre : \mathsf{A} \longrightarrow \mathcal{L}_{\mathbf{EL}}$ *is a* precondition function,
- $post : \mathsf{A} \times Ap \longrightarrow \mathcal{L}_{\mathbf{EL}}$ *is a* postcondition function.

Example 2 *In Figure 1 (top), the action model $\mathcal{A}$ contains two atomic actions a and a'. For a to be executed, its precondition p should be true. Then, action a assigns p to false. Action a' is always executable since its precondition is $\top$, and it does not change the value of any proposition. Action a is the current event and the sole possible action for agent i, while agent j considers that the trivial action a' happens. The pointed action model $\mathcal{A}, a$ corresponds to the private announcement of p to agent i and the private assignment of p to false for agent i (that is, only i sees that p has been assigned to false).*

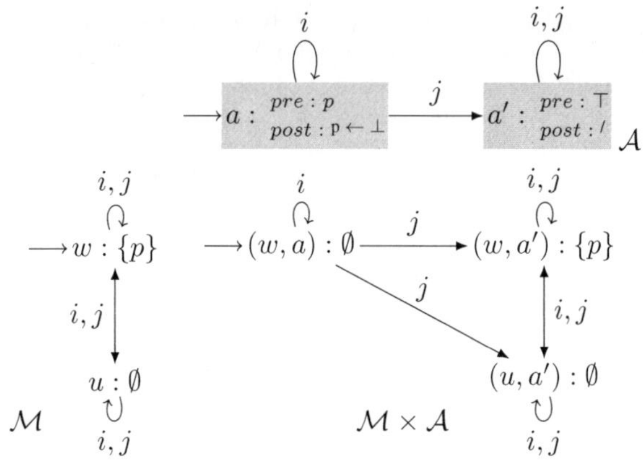

Figure 1: Example of product $\mathcal{M} \times \mathcal{A}$.

Now we recall the definition of the product $\mathcal{M} \times \mathcal{A}$ which corresponds to the epistemic model obtained by executing the action model $\mathcal{A}$ in the initial epistemic model $\mathcal{M}$.

Definition 8 *Let* $\mathcal{M} = (W, (R_i)_{i \in Ag}, V)$ *be a Kripke model. Let* $\mathcal{A} = (\mathsf{A}, (R_i^{\mathcal{A}})_{i \in Ag}, pre, post)$ *be an action model. The* product *of* $\mathcal{M}$ *and* $\mathcal{A}$ *is* $\mathcal{M} \times \mathcal{A} = (W', (R'_i)_{i \in Ag}, V')$ *where:*

1. $W' = \{(w, a) \in W \times \mathsf{A} \mid \mathcal{M}, w \models pre(a)\}$;
2. $(w, a) R'_i (w', a')$ *iff* $w R_i w'$ *and* $a R_i^{\mathcal{A}} a'$;
3. $V'((w, a)) = \{p \in Ap \mid \mathcal{M}, w \models post(a, p)\}$.

Worlds in $\mathcal{M} \times \mathcal{A}$ are pairs (w, a) in which the precondition of a holds in $\mathcal{M}, w$.

Example 3 *Figure 1 shows the resulting product $\mathcal{M} \times \mathcal{A}$ by executing $\mathcal{A}$ from $\mathcal{M}$. Note that the pair (u, a') is not present because the precondition p is not true in u. Note also that p is false in (w, a), due to the postcondition of a.*

The product of a pointed epistemic model $(\mathcal{M}, w)$ with a pointed event model $(\mathcal{A}, a)$ is defined as $(\mathcal{M}, w) \times (\mathcal{A}, a) := (\mathcal{M} \times \mathcal{A}, (w, a))$. It is defined only if $\mathcal{M}, w \models pre(a)$.We recall the language of DEL, noted $\mathcal{L}_{DEL}$, by extending standard epistemic logic with dynamic modalities $\langle \mathcal{A}, a \rangle$:

$$\varphi \ ::= \ \top \mid p \mid \neg\varphi \mid \varphi \wedge \varphi \mid \mathsf{K}_i\varphi \mid \langle \mathcal{A}, a \rangle \varphi$$

Formula $\mathsf{K}_i\varphi$ is read "agent i knows that φ". Formula $\langle \mathcal{A}, a \rangle \varphi$ is read "action $\mathcal{A}, a$ is executable, and after having executed it, φ holds".

Definition 9 *The truth conditions $\mathcal{M}, w \models \varphi$ are defined as follows (Boolean cases are omitted):*

- $\mathcal{M}, w \models p$ *if* $p \in V(w)$;
- $\mathcal{M}, w \models \mathsf{K}_i\varphi$ *if for all u such that* $w R_i u$, $\mathcal{M}, u \models \varphi$.
- $\mathcal{M}, w \models \langle \mathcal{A}, a \rangle \varphi$ *if* $\mathcal{M}, w \models pre(a)$ *and* $\mathcal{M} \times \mathcal{A}, (w, a) \models \varphi$.

We finish this section by recalling the notion of modal depth $md(\varphi)$ of a formula φ which is the maximum of the number of nested knowledge operators. It is defined by induction: $md(p) := 0$; $md(\neg\varphi) := md(\varphi)$; $md(\varphi \vee \psi) := \max(md(\varphi), md(\psi))$; $md(\mathsf{K}_i\varphi) = 1 + md(\varphi)$ and finally

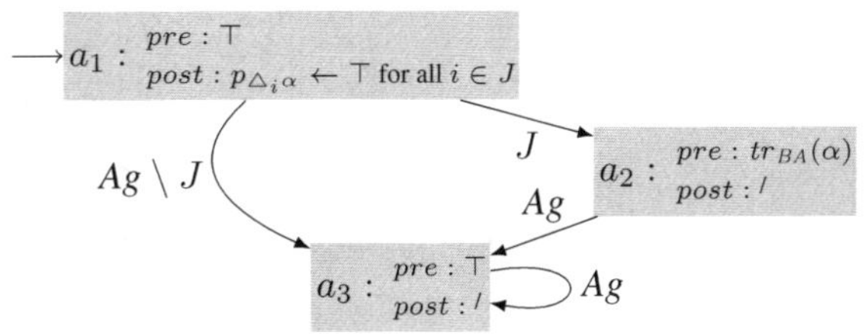

Figure 2: Action model $\mathcal{A}_{+_J\alpha}$ that simulates adding α in bases of agents in J.

$md(\langle \mathcal{A}, a \rangle)\varphi$ is the maximum of the modal depths of φ and the formulas written in $\mathcal{A}$.

The notion of bisimulation in modal logic has been refined to take the modal depth of formulas into account: the notion of n-bimilation noted $\leftrightarrows_n$. We have that $\mathcal{M}, w \leftrightarrows_n \mathcal{M}', w'$ iff $\mathcal{M}, w$ and $\mathcal{M}', w'$ agree on formulas of modal depth at most n (see Prop. 2.31 in (Blackburn, de Rijke, and Venema 2001) and Section 6.5 in (Van Ditmarsch, van Der Hoek, and Kooi 2007b)).

4 The Two Translations

In this section, we explore the connection between the DEL semantics using action models and the semantics using belief bases. We first investigate the direction from multi-agent belief bases to action models. Then, we investigate the other direction, from action models to multi-agent belief bases.

4.1 From Belief Base Operations to Action Models

We show how to embed the belief base semantics into the DEL action model semantics. In particular, we provide a polynomial satisfiability preserving translation tr_{BA} of the language $\mathcal{L}_B$ into $\mathcal{L}_{DEL}$. It is defined as follows:

$$\begin{aligned}
&tr_{BA}(p) = p,\\
&tr_{BA}(\neg\varphi) = \neg tr_{BA}(\varphi),\\
&tr_{BA}(\varphi_1 \wedge \varphi_2) = tr_{BA}(\varphi_1) \wedge tr_{BA}(\varphi_2),\\
&tr_{BA}(\triangle_i \alpha) = p_{\triangle_i \alpha} \wedge \mathsf{K}_i tr_{BA}(\alpha),\\
&tr_{BA}(\Box_i \varphi) = \mathsf{K}_i tr_{BA}(\varphi),\\
&tr_{BA}([+_J\alpha]\varphi) = [\mathcal{A}_{+_J\alpha}, a_1] tr_{BA}(\varphi),
\end{aligned}$$

where $\mathcal{A}_{+_J\alpha} = (\mathsf{A}, (R_i^{\mathcal{A}})_{i \in Ag}, pre, post)$ is the action model (see Figure 2) such that:

- $\mathsf{A} = \{a_1, a_2, a_3\}$;
- $\forall i \in J, R_i^{\mathcal{A}} = \{(a_1, a_2), (a_2, a_3), (a_3, a_3)\}$;
- $\forall i \in Ag \setminus J, R_i^{\mathcal{A}} = \{(a_1, a_3), (a_2, a_3), (a_3, a_3)\}$;
- $pre(a_1) = \top, pre(a_2) = tr_{BA}(\alpha), pre(a_3) = \top$;
- $post(a_2, p) = post(a_3, p) = p$ for all $p \in Ap$, $post(a_1, p) = p$ for all $p \notin \bigcup_{i \in J}\{p_{\triangle_i \alpha}\}$, and $post(a_1, p_{\triangle_i \alpha}) = \top$ if $i \in J$.

The following is the core result of this section highlighting the correctness of our polynomial embedding.

Theorem 1 *Let $\varphi \in \mathcal{L}_B$. Then, φ is satisfiable for the class* $\mathbf{M}$ *if and only if $tr_{BA}(\varphi)$ is DEL-satisfiable.*

PROOF.

The proof relies on the fact the language $\mathcal{L}_B$ can be equivalently interpreted relative to models of the form $\Omega = (S, \mathcal{B}, (\Rightarrow_i)_{i \in Ag}, \tau)$ where S is a non-empty set of states, $\mathcal{B} : Ag \times S \longrightarrow 2^{\mathcal{L}_0}$ is a belief base function, $\tau : Ap \longrightarrow 2^S$ is valuation function, $\Rightarrow_i \subseteq S \times S$ is agent i's epistemic accessibility relation. $\mathcal{L}_B$-formulas are interpreted with respect to pointed models (Ω, s) with $s \in S$ as follows (boolean cases are omitted for simplicity): (i) $(\Omega, s) \models p$ iff $s \in \tau(p)$, (ii) $(\Omega, s) \models \triangle_i \alpha$ iff $\alpha \in \mathcal{B}(i, s)$, (iii) $(\Omega, s) \models \Box_i \varphi$ iff $\forall s' \in S$, if $s \Rightarrow_i s'$ then $(\Omega, s') \models \varphi$, (iv) $(\Omega, s) \models [+_J\alpha]\varphi$ iff $(\Omega^{+_J\alpha}, s^*) \models \varphi$, where $\Omega^{+_J\alpha} = (S^{+_J\alpha}, \mathcal{B}^{+_J\alpha}, (\Rightarrow_i^{+_J\alpha})_{i \in Ag}, \tau^{+_J\alpha})$ with $s^* \notin S$ and:

- $S^{+_J\alpha} = S \cup \{s^*\}$,
- $\mathcal{B}^{+_J\alpha}(i, s') = \mathcal{B}(i, s)$ if $s' \neq s^*$,
- $\mathcal{B}^{+_J\alpha}(i, s^*) = \mathcal{B}(i, s)$ if $i \notin J$,
- $\mathcal{B}^{+_J\alpha}(i, s^*) = \mathcal{B}(i, s) \cup \{\alpha\}$ if $i \in J$,
- $\Rightarrow_i^{+_J\alpha} = \Rightarrow_i \cup \{(s^*, s') \mid s \Rightarrow_i s'\}$ if $i \notin J$,
- $\Rightarrow_i^{+_J\alpha} = \Rightarrow_i \cup \{(s^*, s') \mid s \Rightarrow_i s'$ and $(\Omega, s') \models \alpha\}$ if $i \in J$,
- $\tau^{+_J\alpha}(p) = \tau(p) \cup \{s^*\}$ if $s \in \tau(p)$,
- $\tau^{+_J\alpha}(p) = \tau(p)$ if $s \notin \tau(p)$.

In particular, for every $\varphi \in \mathcal{L}_B$, it is shown in (Lorini 2020) that φ is satisfiable for the class of multi-agent belief models $\mathbf{M}$ iff φ is satisfiable for the subclass of the previous models such that, for every $i \in Ag$ and for every $s \in S$, $\Rightarrow_i(s) \subseteq \bigcap_{\alpha \in \mathcal{B}(i,s)} ||\alpha||_{(\Omega,s)}$ with $||\alpha||_{(\Omega,s)} = \{s' \in S \mid (\Omega, s') \models \alpha\}$. Such a subclass is called the class of "notional" models and is noted $\mathbf{N}$. Given the previous semantic equivalence between the two classes $\mathbf{M}$ and $\mathbf{N}$ wrt language $\mathcal{L}_B$, in the rest of the proof we simply need work with the latter class.

We just need to show that φ is satisfiable for the class $\mathbf{N}$ if and only if $tr_{BA}(\varphi)$ is DEL-satisfiable. The left-to-right direction of the proof is by induction on the structure of φ and relies on a two-step transformation. The non-trivial case is $\psi = [+_J\alpha]\varphi$. Given a pointed notional model (Ω, s) satisfying φ we transform it into an isomorphic pointed epistemic model $\mathcal{M}, w$. Then, we compute the pointed notional model $(\Omega^{+_J\alpha}, s^*)$ on the one hand, and the epistemic model $\mathcal{M} \times \mathcal{A}_{+_J\alpha}, (w, a_1)$ on the other hand. We transform $(\Omega^{+_J\alpha}, s^*)$ into an isomorphic pointed epistemic model $(\mathcal{M}', w')$. We show that $\mathcal{M}', w'$ and $\mathcal{M} \times \mathcal{A}_{+_J\alpha}, (w, a_1)$ are bisimilar. The right-to-left direction is proved in an analogous way. ■

4.2 From Action Models to Belief Base Operations

In this section, we show how to polynomially translate a DEL fragment into $\mathcal{L}_B$. We focus on the DEL fragment, based on so-called *ruby action models*, that encompasses[2]

[2]if we ignore postconditions

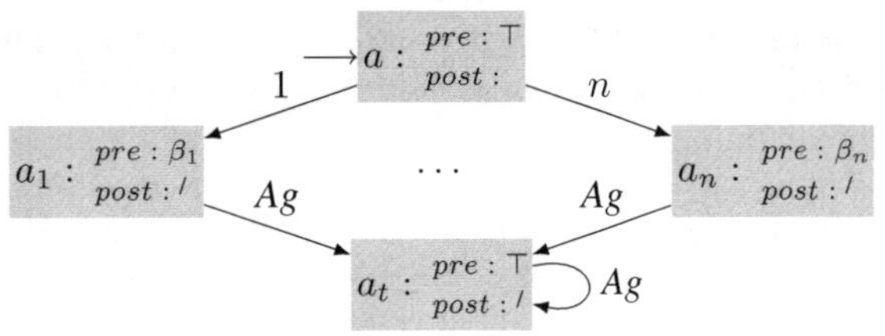

Figure 3: Pointed ruby action model $(\mathcal{A}, a)$.

the action models $\mathcal{A}_{+_J\alpha}$ used in the translation tr_{BA} (see Figure 2).

Ruby Action Models

Definition 10 *A ruby action model $\mathcal{A}, a$ is a pointed action model of the form given in Figure 3 where $\beta_1, \ldots, \beta_n$ are propositional formulas (that is, boolean combinations of propositional variables).*

A ruby action model corresponds to the concurrent private announcement of β_1 to agent $1, \ldots,$ of β_n to agent n. Interestingly, the action model $\mathcal{A}_{+_J\alpha}$ of Figure 2 in which we ignore the postcondition is equivalent to the ruby action model with $\beta_i = tr_{BA}(\alpha)$ for all $i \in J$ and $\beta_i = \top$ for all $i \notin J$.

In the definition of ruby action models, we suppose that the root a_0 is linked to a unique action a_i for agent i. This definition can be leveraged also if this uniqueness is not assumed: several i-successors can be replaced by a single i-successor whose precondition is the disjunction of the preconditions. While, the absence of i-successors can be replaced by a single i-successor whose precondition is $\bot$. The obtained ruby action model is equivalent to the original action model[3].

Note that ruby action models commute ($\mathcal{M} \times \mathcal{A} \times \mathcal{A}' = \mathcal{M} \times \mathcal{A}' \times \mathcal{A}$ when $\mathcal{A}$ and $\mathcal{A}'$ are ruby action models).

Translation We define a translation tr_{AB} from the DEL language with only ruby action models into the language $\mathcal{L}_B$ as follows:

$$
\begin{aligned}
tr_{AB}(p) &:= p \\
tr_{AB}(\neg\varphi) &:= \neg tr_{AB}(\varphi) \\
tr_{AB}(\varphi \wedge \psi) &:= tr_{AB}(\varphi) \wedge tr_{AB}(\psi) \\
tr_{AB}(\mathsf{K}_i\varphi) &:= \Box_i\varphi \\
tr_{AB}([\mathcal{A}, a]\varphi) &:= [tr_{Act}(\mathcal{A}, a)]tr_{AB}(\varphi)
\end{aligned}
$$

where $tr_{Act}(\mathcal{A}, a)$ is the sequence of operations that $[+_1\beta_1; \ldots; +_n\beta_n]$; when $\mathcal{A}, a$ is the action model depicted in Figure 3. Note that tr_{AB} is computable in polynomial time.

Theorem 2 *Let φ be a DEL formula only containing ruby action models. Then: φ is DEL satisfiable iff $tr_{AB}(\varphi)$ is satisfiable for the class* M.

[3]This is true because there is an emulation (see (van Eijck, Ruan, and Sadzik 2012)) between the original action model and the obtained ruby action model.

Before proving Theoreom 2, we need to make a detour and explain how to encode tree-like epistemic models. For the rest of the section, we suppose that Ap is finite and contains the atomic propositions in φ.

Tree-like Epistemic Models When a DEL formula is satisfiable, it is in a tree. This comes from the fact that epistemic logic has the tree-like model property (see Th. 5.2 in (Vardi 1996), or Proposition 2.15 in (Blackburn, de Rijke, and Venema 2001)), and that any DEL formula is equivalent to a formula in standard epistemic logic (van Ditmarsch, van der Hoek, and Kooi 2007a). We consider here tree-like epistemic models, in which the actual world is the root of the tree. Given a tree-like epistemic model τ with root w and a ruby action model $(\mathcal{A}, a)$, we call $\tau \times (\mathcal{A}, a)$ the connected component of $\tau \times \mathcal{A}$ containing the world (w, a). This component is still tree-like, and $(\tau \times (\mathcal{A}, a), (w, a))$ is bisimilar to $(\tau \times \mathcal{A}, (w, a))$.

We first give a function describing any tree-like epistemic model. We define $desc(\tau)$ by induction on τ:

$$desc(\textcircled{w}) = \mathsf{Prop}(w) \wedge \bigwedge_{i \in Ag} \Box_i \bot$$

desc(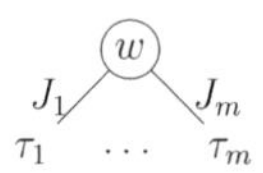) $= \mathsf{Prop}(w) \wedge \bigwedge_{i \in Ag} \Box_i \bigvee_{k \mid i \in J_k} desc(\tau_k) \wedge \bigwedge_{i,k \mid i \in J_k} \Diamond_i desc(\tau_k)$

where $\mathsf{Prop}(w)$ is $\bigwedge_{p \in Ap \mid p \text{ is true in } w} p \wedge \bigwedge_{p \in Ap \mid p \text{ is false in } w} \neg p$ (we restrict to relevant atomic propositions, so Ap is finite here). The formula $desc(\textcircled{w})$ intuitively describes the valuation in w and that there are no successors in w. The formula desc(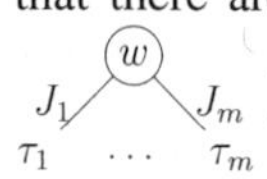) intuitively describes the valuation w, says that successors are among trees $\tau_1, \ldots, \tau_k$ and finally says that each tree $\tau_1, \ldots, \tau_k$ is present as a successor.

It is known that the DEL version of this function, which for any τ gives the formula $tr_{BA}(desc(\tau))$, describes epistemic models up to $depth(\tau)$-bisimulation (Moss 2007). We first show that this description function similarly describes belief bases up to bisimulation.

Proposition 1 *For any DEL formula φ in which there are no dynamic operators, for any state B, context Cxt and tree-like epistemic model τ with root w, if $B, Cxt \models desc(\tau)$ then $B, Cxt \models tr_{AB}(\varphi)$ iff $\tau, w \models \varphi$.*

PROOF.

This is shown by induction on φ. Suppose τ is of the form 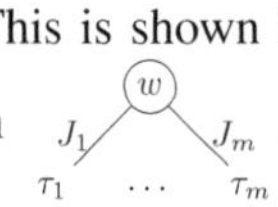.

The case of propositional variables is straightforward as $B, Cxt \models \mathsf{Prop}(w)$. The cases of boolean operators are standard.

If $B, Cxt \models \Box_i tr_{AB}(\varphi)$, consider w' such that wR_iw'. Then w' is the root of τ_k for some k such that $i \in J_k$.

As $B, Cxt \models desc(\tau)$, we have in particular $B, Cxt \models \Diamond_i desc(\tau_k)$. Hence there exists B' such that $B\mathcal{R}_iB'$ and $B', Cxt \models desc(\tau_k)$. But then by the induction hypothesis, $B', Cxt \models tr_{AB}(\varphi)$ iff $\tau_k, w' \models \varphi$, and $B', Cxt \models tr_{AB}(\varphi)$ as $B\mathcal{R}_iB'$. Hence $\tau, w' \models \varphi$ and $\tau, w \models \mathsf{K}_i\varphi$.

If $\tau, w \models \mathsf{K}_i\varphi$, consider B' such that $B\mathcal{R}_iB'$. Then there exists k such that $i \in J_k$ and $B', Cxt \models desc(\tau_k)$. Call w' the root of τ_k in τ. Then wR_iw' so $\tau, w' \models \varphi$, and by the induction hypothesis $B', Cxt \models tr_{AB}(\varphi)$ iff $\tau_k, w' \models \varphi$, the latter being equivalent to $\tau, w' \models \varphi$. Hence $B', Cxt \models tr_{AB}(\varphi)$ and $B, Cxt \models \Box_i tr_{AB}(\varphi)$. ■

In order to generalize this correspondence to formulas which *do* include dynamic operators, we must first establish that the translation of ruby action models effectively simulates the effects of these actions in belief bases. More precisely, the formula $tr_{BA}(desc(\tau)) \to [(\mathcal{A}, a)]tr_{BA}(desc(\tau \times (\mathcal{A}, a)))$ is valid in DEL for any tree-like epistemic model τ and pointed ruby action model $(\mathcal{A}, a)$; we show a corresponding property for belief bases.

Proposition 2 *For any tree-like epistemic model τ, for any ruby action model $(\mathcal{A}, a)$, state B and context Cxt, if $B \models desc(\tau)$ then $B^{tr(\mathcal{A},a)}, Cxt \models desc(\tau \times (\mathcal{A}, a))$.*

PROOF.

We show this by induction on the height on τ. Consider a ruby-like action model such as the one in Figure 3.

If $\tau = (w)$, then $\tau \times (\mathcal{A}, a)$ is equal to τ and $desc(\tau) = desc(\tau \times (\mathcal{A}, a)) = \mathsf{Prop}(w) \wedge \bigwedge_{i \in Ag} \Box_i \bot$. Consider then B and Cxt such that $B, Cxt \models desc(\tau)$. As $B^{tr_{Act}(\mathcal{A},a)}$ and B agree on all propositional variables, we have $B^{tr_{Act}(\mathcal{A},a)}, Cxt \models \mathsf{Prop}(w)$. Moreover, suppose that $B^{tr_{Act}(\mathcal{A},a)}\mathcal{R}_iB'$ for some agent i and some B' in Cxt: then $B\mathcal{R}_iB'$ as $B_i \subseteq B_i^{tr_{Act}(\mathcal{A},a)}$. But $B, Cxt \models \Box_i\bot$, so there can be no such state B', and therefore $B^{tr_{Act}(\mathcal{A},a)}, Cxt \models \Box_i\bot$ for all i. Hence $B^{tr_{Act}(\mathcal{A},a)}, Cxt \models desc(\tau)$.

Suppose now that τ is of the form 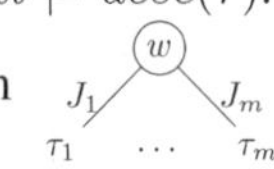

, and call w_k the root of τ_k for $1 \leqslant k \leqslant m$. Then $\tau \times (\mathcal{A}, a)$ is bisimilar to 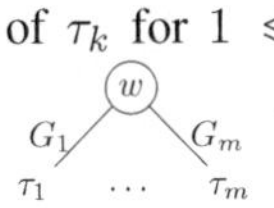

where for every $k \leqslant m$, $G_k = \{i \in J_k \mid \tau, w_k \models \beta_i\}$; and

$$desc(\tau \times (\mathcal{A}, a)) = \mathsf{Prop}(w) \wedge \bigwedge_{i \in Ag} \Box_i \bigvee_{k | i \in G_k} desc(\tau_k) \wedge \bigwedge_{i,k | i \in G_k} \Diamond_i desc(\tau_k).$$

Consider B and Cxt such that $B, Cxt \models desc(\tau)$. Once again, it is clear that $B^{tr_{Act}(\mathcal{A},a)}, Cxt \models \mathsf{Prop}(w)$. Consider now a state $B' \in Cxt$ such that $B^{tr_{Act}(\mathcal{A},a)}\mathcal{R}_iB'$. Then as before, $B\mathcal{R}_iB'$,and therefore $B', Cxt \models \bigvee_{k|i \in J_k} desc(\tau_k)$, that is, there exists a $k \leqslant m$ such that $i \in J_k$ and $B', Cxt \models desc(\tau_k)$. Moreover, as $\beta_i \in B^{tr_{Act}(\mathcal{A},a)}$, it must be the case that $B', Cxt \models \beta_i$. Then by Proposition 1, we have $\tau_k, w_k \models \beta_i$, hence $\tau, w_k \models \beta_i$ and $i \in G_k$. Therefore $B^{tr_{Act}(\mathcal{A},a)}, Cxt \models \Box_i \bigvee_{k|i \in G_k} desc(\tau_k)$ for all i in Ag.

It remains to show that $B^{tr_{Act}(\mathcal{A},a)}, Cxt \models \Diamond_i desc(\tau_k)$ for all i and k such that $i \in G_k$. Consider such a i and k: then $i \in J_k$ and $\tau, w_k \models \beta_i$. As $i \in J_k$ and $B, Cxt \models desc(\tau)$, we know that $B, Cxt \models \Diamond_i desc(\tau_k)$, that is, there exists some B' such that $B\mathcal{R}_iB'$ and $B', Cxt \models desc(\tau_k)$. But then by Proposition 1, $B', Cxt \models \beta_i$ as $\tau, w_k \models \beta_i$. Hence $B^{tr_{Act}(\mathcal{A},a)}\mathcal{R}_iB'$, and $B^{tr_{Act}(\mathcal{A},a)}, Cxt \models \Diamond_i desc(\tau_k)$. We conclude that $B^{tr_{Act}(\mathcal{A},a)}, Cxt \models desc(\tau \times (\mathcal{A}, a))$. ■

We can now extend the result of Proposition 1 to any formulas of the DEL language in which all actions are ruby action models.

Proposition 3 *For any formula φ of the DEL language in which all action models are ruby action models, for any state B, context Cxt and tree-like epistemic model τ with root w, if $B, Cxt \models desc(\tau)$ then $B, Cxt \models tr_{AB}(\varphi)$ iff $\tau, w \models \varphi$.*

PROOF.

We show this by induction on φ. We have shown all cases in the proof of Proposition 1 except for that of dynamic operators.

If $B, Cxt \models desc(\tau)$, then:

$$\begin{aligned}
&B, Cxt \models [tr_{Act}(\mathcal{A}, a)]tr_{AB}(\varphi)\\
&\text{iff } B^{tr_{Act}(\mathcal{A},a)}, Cxt \models tr_{AB}(\varphi)\\
&\text{iff } \tau \times \mathcal{A}, (w, a) \models \varphi \text{ (by IH with Proposition 2)}\\
&\text{iff } \tau, w \models [\mathcal{A}, a]\varphi.
\end{aligned}$$

This ends the proof. ■

Correctness of the Translation We are now ready to prove Theorem 2. We show both directions of the equivalence separately.

Proposition 4 *For any formula φ containing only ruby action models, if φ is DEL-satisfiable then $tr_{AB}(\varphi)$ is B-satisfiable.*

PROOF.

Suppose that φ is DEL-satisfiable. Then by the tree-like model property, φ is satisfied in a tree-like epistemic model $\tau = (W, (R_i)_{i \in Ag}, V)$ with root w: $\tau, w \models \varphi$. For each $v \in W$, consider a fresh variable p_v (appearing neither in φ not in $V(w)$ for $w \in W$) and define the model $\tau' = (W, (R_i)_{i \in Ag}, V')$ such that for all $v \in W$, $V'(v) = V(v) \cup \{p_v\}$. Then we also have $\tau', w \models \varphi$. Now define the state $B^v = \big((B_i^v)_{i \in Ag}, V^v\big)$ as follows:

$$B_i^v = \{\bigvee_{u | vR_iu} p_u\}$$

$$V^v = V'(v)$$

Consider the context $Cxt^W = \{B^v \mid v \in W\}$. Then $B^w, Cxt^W \models desc(\tau')$. Hence $B^w, Cxt^W \models tr_{AB}(\varphi)$? by Proposition 3. ■

Proposition 5 *For any formula φ containing only ruby action models, if $tr_{AB}(\varphi)$ is B-satisfiable then φ is DEL satisfiable.*

PROOF.
For any state B and context Cxt, define the epistemic model $\mathcal{M}^{B,Cxt} = (W^{B,Cxt}, (R_i^{B,Cxt})_{i\in Ag}, V^{B,Cxt})$, where:

$$W^{B,Cxt} = \{B\} \cup Cxt;$$
$$R_i^{B,Cxt} = \{(B,B') \mid B' \in Cxt \text{ and } B\mathcal{R}_i B'\} \cup \{(B',B'') \mid B',B'' \in Cxt \text{ and } B'\mathcal{R}_i B''\} \text{ for all } i \in Ag;$$
$$V^{B,Cxt}(B') = \{p \mid B' \models p\} \text{ for all } B' \in W.$$

An induction on φ proves that for any formula φ of the DEL language containing no dynamic operators, for any B and Cxt, $B, Cxt \models tr_{AB}(\varphi)$ iff $\mathcal{M}^{B,Cxt}, B \models \varphi$. (For the proof, remark that given B, Cxt, and any $B' \in Cxt$, $(M^{B,Cxt}, B')$ and $(M^{B',Cxt}, B')$ are equal when $B \in Cxt$ and bisimilar when $B \notin Cxt$.)

Consider now a formula φ of the DEL language only containing ruby action models, and suppose that $B, Cxt \models \varphi$ for some B and Cxt. We know that $M^{B,Cxt}, B$ is $md(\varphi)$-bisimilar to some tree-like epistemic model (τ, w) (consider the unravelling of $M^{B,Cxt}, B$ up to depth $md(\varphi)$), where w is the root of τ. In particular, $M^{B,Cxt}, B \models tr_{BA}(desc(\tau))$, hence $B, Cxt \models desc(\tau)$ as $tr_{BA}(desc(\tau))$ contains no dynamic operators. By Proposition 3, this implies that for any formula ψ of the DEL language only containing ruby action models, $B, Cxt \models tr_{AB}(\psi)$ iff $\tau, w \models \psi$. In particular, $\tau, w \models \varphi$, hence φ is DEL satisfiable. ■

5 Introspective Variant

In this section, we explain the changes to make to keep translations from $\mathcal{L}_B$ into $\mathcal{L}_{DEL}$, and from $\mathcal{L}_{DEL}$ into $\mathcal{L}_B$ wrt. to the introspective variant. The latter translation will however require some technical restrictions. The underlying epistemic logic is K45: the epistemic relations are transitive and Euclidean (see Def. 2.13 of (Van Ditmarsch, van Der Hoek, and Kooi 2007b)).

5.1 Definition

In (Lorini 2020) an alternative definition of the epistemic indistinguishability relation is given. It works for introspective agents that have perfect knowledge of their belief bases. Specifically, for a state to be considered possible by an introspective agent, (i) it must satisfy all information in the agent's actual belief base, and (ii) the agent should have the same belief base in the actual state and in the epistemically accessible state.

Definition 11 (Epistemic alternatives) *The introspective variant of the epistemic indistinguishability relation is the binary relation $\mathcal{R}_i \subseteq \mathbf{S} \times \mathbf{S}$ such that, for all $B = ((B_i)_{i\in Ag}, V), B' = ((B'_i)_{i\in Ag}, V') \in \mathbf{S}$:*

$$B\mathcal{R}_i^{Int} B' \text{ if and only if } (i) \forall\alpha \in B_i : B' \models \alpha, \quad (ii) B_i = B'_i.$$

In other words, the previous definition adds to Definition 3 the introspection condition (ii). It is easy to verify that the relation $\mathcal{R}_i^{Int}$ so defined is transitive and Euclidean.

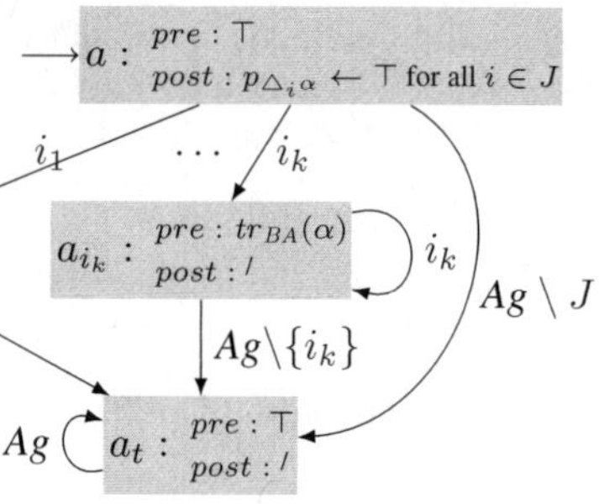

Figure 4: Action model $\mathcal{A}^{intr}_{+_J\alpha}$ that simulates adding α in bases of agents in $J = \{i_1, \ldots, i_k\}$ in the introspective variant.

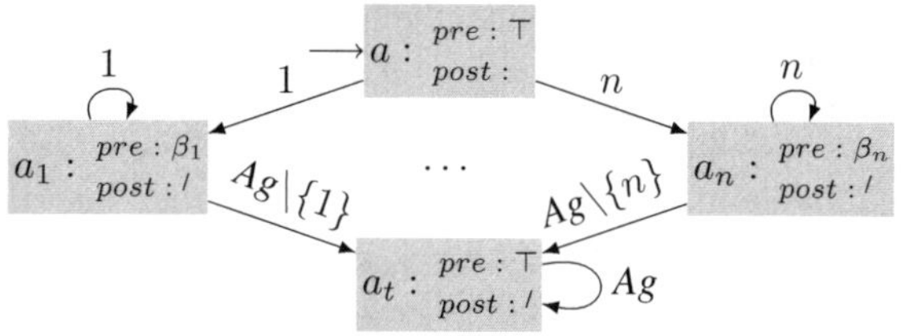

Figure 5: Introspective ruby action model.

5.2 From Belief Base Operations to Action Models

When considering introspective agents (i.e., when the epistemic indistinguishability relations are defined according to Definition 11), we need to slightly redefine the translation from the language $\mathcal{L}_B$ to the language $\mathcal{L}_{DEL}$ given in Section 4.1. In particular, we need to define a new translation tr^{intr}_{BA} whose lines 1-5 are identical to lines 1-5 of translation tr_{BA} and whose line 6 is:

$$tr^{intr}_{BA}([+_J\alpha]\varphi) = [\mathcal{A}^{intr}_{+_J\alpha}, a]tr^{intr}_{BA}(\varphi),$$

where $\mathcal{A}^{intr}_{+_J\alpha}$ is the action model for introspective agents depicted in Figure 4. The following theorem is the analog of Theorem 1 for introspective agents. We omit its proof since it is similar to that of Theorem 1.

Theorem 3 *Let the epistemic indistinguishability relation $\mathcal{R}_i$ be defined according to Definition 11 and let $\varphi \in \mathcal{L}_B$. Then, φ is satisfiable for the class $\mathbf{M}$ if and only if $tr^{intr}_{BA}(\varphi)$ is DEL-satisfiable.*

5.3 From Action Models to Belief Base Operations

In this section, we discuss the natural generalisation of tr_{AB} to the introspective case.

Introspective Ruby Action Models

Definition 12 *An introspective ruby action model $\mathcal{A}, a$ is a pointed action model of the form given in Figure 5 where $\beta_1, \ldots, \beta_n$ are propositional formulas.*

The translation tr^{intr}_{AB} differs from tr_{AB} given in Subsection 4.2 in two aspects. First the language is the DEL one with *introspective* ruby action models. Second, we need to add a special variable for each action model $\mathcal{A}$. We define:

$$tr^{intr}_{AB}([\mathcal{A}, a]\varphi) := [tr_{Act}(\mathcal{A}, a)]tr^{intr}_{AB}(\varphi)$$

where $tr_{Act}(\mathcal{A}, a)$ is the sequence of operations that $[+_1\beta_1; \ldots; +_n\beta_n; +_1p_{\mathcal{A}}; \ldots; +_np_{\mathcal{A}}; +_1p^1_{\mathcal{A}}; \ldots; +_np^n_{\mathcal{A}}]$; when $\mathcal{A}, a$ is the action model depicted in Figure 5, and where $p_{\mathcal{A}}$ and all $p^i_{\mathcal{A}}$ are fresh atomic propositions. Note that tr^{intr}_{AB} is still computable in polynomial time.

Just like the ruby action models of Definition 10, introspective ruby action models commute. Thus, the sole information of action model $\mathcal{A}$ being executed is sufficient; the order of the executions is not important. In other words, the propositions $p_{\mathcal{A}}$ are sufficient to represent the list of already executed actions. Also, as the variables $p_{\mathcal{A}}$ are fresh, they are supposed to be initially false.

Theorem 4 *Let φ be a DEL formula only containing introspective ruby action models. Then: φ is DEL K45-satisfiable implies $tr^{intr}_{AB}(\varphi)$ is satisfiable for the class $\mathbf{M}$ with the introspective relations.*

The proof of Theorem 4 is involved. We start by giving some definitions and notations surrounding introspective ruby action models. For any formula φ containing only introspective ruby action models, we call $\mathbf{Seq}(\varphi)$ the set of sequences of pointed action models corresponding to sequences of actions found in φ, defined inductively as:

$$\begin{aligned}\mathbf{Seq}(p) &= \{\epsilon\} \quad (\epsilon \text{ is the empty sequence})\\ \mathbf{Seq}(\varphi \wedge \psi) &= \mathbf{Seq}(\varphi) \cup \mathbf{Seq}(\varphi)\\ \mathbf{Seq}(\neg\varphi) &= \mathbf{Seq}(\varphi)\\ \mathbf{Seq}([\mathcal{A}, a]\varphi) &= \{(\mathcal{A}, e)\sigma \mid \sigma \in \mathbf{Seq}(\varphi)\\ &\qquad \text{and } e \text{ is an event in } \mathcal{A}\}\end{aligned}$$

Example 4 *For example, given two pointed action models $(\mathcal{A}, a)$ and $(\mathcal{A}', a')$, we have $\mathbf{Seq}([\mathcal{A}, a]p \wedge [\mathcal{A}', a'](q \wedge \neg[\mathcal{A}, a]p)) = \{(\mathcal{A}, e), (\mathcal{A}', e'), (\mathcal{A}', e')(\mathcal{A}, e) \mid e$ is an event of $\mathcal{A}$ and e' is an event of $\mathcal{A}'\}$.*

If w is a world in an epistemic model $\mathcal{M}$ and σ is a sequence $(\mathcal{A}_1, e_1) \ldots (\mathcal{A}_m, e_m)$ of pointed action models, we abbreviate the model $(\mathcal{M} \times \mathcal{A}_1) \times \cdots \times \mathcal{A}_m$ to $\mathcal{M} \times \sigma$ and the world $((w, e_1), \ldots, e_m)$ in $\mathcal{M} \times \sigma$ to (w, σ), when that world is defined in $\mathcal{M} \times \sigma$.

As ruby action models commute, the order of the ruby action models of a sequence σ does not matter when constructing $\mathcal{M} \times \sigma$; we will therefore be identifying any sequence σ of actions with the set of actions found in σ. In particular, two sequences σ and σ' are considered equal when they consist of the same actions.

Finally, given a sequence σ of introspective ruby action models, we call $Add_i(\sigma)$ the set of formulas β such that $+_i\beta$ appears in $tr_{Act}(\mathcal{A}, a)$ for some action $(\mathcal{A}, a)$ or $(\mathcal{A}, a_i)$ in σ. Formally:

$$\begin{aligned}Add_i(\sigma) = \{\beta \mid \exists (\mathcal{A}, e) \in \sigma, e \in \{a, a_i\}\\ \text{and } pre_{\mathcal{A}}(a_i) = \beta\}\end{aligned}$$

From Epistemic Models to Contexts Remark that introspective ruby action models preserve the K45 properties: the product of a K45 epistemic model with an introspective ruby action model is again a K45 epistemic model.

We now define contexts simulating the effects of actions in an epistemic model. Given a formula φ containing only introspective ruby action models and a K45 epistemic model $(\mathcal{M}, r)$ with $\mathcal{M} = (W, (R_i)_{i \in Ag}, V)$, we take for every action model $\mathcal{A}$ in φ three fresh variable $p_{\mathcal{A}}$, $p^i_{\mathcal{A}}$ and $p^t_{\mathcal{A}}$ appearing neither in φ nor in $V(w)$ for any $w \in W$, and we similarly take for every $w \in W$ a fresh variable p_w. We define the following context:

$$\begin{aligned}Cxt^{\varphi, \mathcal{M}} = \{B^{w,\sigma} \mid \sigma \in \mathbf{Seq}(\varphi) \text{ and}\\ (w, \sigma) \text{ is a world of } \mathcal{M} \times \sigma\}\end{aligned}$$

where for all $w \in W$ and $\sigma \in \mathbf{Seq}(\varphi)$, $B^{w,\sigma} = ((B^{w,\sigma}_i)_{i \in Ag,}, V^{w,\sigma})$ with:

$$\begin{aligned}B^{w,\sigma}_i =& \{ \bigvee_{v | w R_i v} p_v\} \cup \{p_{\mathcal{A}} \mid (\mathcal{A}, e) \in \sigma\} \cup Add_i(\sigma)\\ &\cup \{p^i_{\mathcal{A}} \mid (\mathcal{A}, e) \in \sigma, e \in \{a, a_i\}\}\\ &\cup \{p^t_{\mathcal{A}} \mid (\mathcal{A}, e) \in \sigma, e \notin \{a, a_i\}\}\\ V^{w,\sigma} =& V(w) \cup \{p_w\} \cup \{p_{\mathcal{A}} \mid (\mathcal{A}, e) \in \sigma\}\\ &\cup \{p^i_{\mathcal{A}} \mid i \in Ag, (\mathcal{A}, a_i) \in \sigma\} \cup \{p^t_{\mathcal{A}} \mid (\mathcal{A}, a_t) \in \sigma\}.\end{aligned}$$

Intuitively, we want every state $B^{w,\sigma}$ to correspond to the world (w, σ). The fresh variables identify the worlds of w, the actions models in σ, as well as instances of events a_i and a_t. The constraints in $B^{w,\sigma}_i$ correspond to the following properties:

- from the definition of product updates, it follows that is $(w, \sigma) R_i (w', \sigma')$ then $w R_i w'$;
- the inclusion of $p_{\mathcal{A}}$ for all $(\mathcal{A}, e) \in \sigma$ identify the world as being part of the model $\mathcal{M} \times \sigma$;
- $Add_i(\sigma)$ corresponds to the new beliefs introduced for i by σ in (w, σ);
- when $e \in \{a, a_i\}$ for some $(\mathcal{A}, e) \in \sigma$ then $e R_i e'$ iff $e' = a_i$;
- when $e \notin \{a, a_i\}$ for some $(\mathcal{A}, e) \in \sigma$ then $e R_i e'$ iff $e' = a_t$.

We are now going to show that this context corresponds to the collection of all models $\mathcal{M} \times \sigma$ for $\sigma \in \mathbf{Seq}(\varphi)$, which will then allow us to simulate model checking of φ in $\mathcal{M}$.

Proposition 6 *Let φ be a DEL formula containing only introspective ruby action models. Let $(\mathcal{M}, r)$ be a K45 epistemic model , and $Cxt^{\varphi, \mathcal{M}}$ be the corresponding context. Then $\mathcal{M}, r \models \varphi$ iff $B^r, Cxt^{\varphi, \mathcal{M}} \models tr^{intr}_{AB}(\varphi)$.*

Proof of Theorem 4 Suppose that φ is K45-satisfiable. Then φ is satisfiable in a K45 epistemic model. Consider a K45 epistemic model $(\mathcal{M}, r)$ satisfying φ. By Proposition 6, we have $B^{r,\epsilon}$, $Cxt^{\varphi, \mathcal{M}} \models tr^{intr}_{AB}(\varphi)$.

Other Direction Suppose that $tr^{intr}_{AB}(\varphi)$ is satisfiable. To adapt the proof of Proposition 5, we need to construct a K45 epistemic model for φ from the unravelling of the belief base inferred epistemic model for $tr^{intr}_{AB}(\varphi)$. The issue will be that the application of a_i *must* exactly correspond to the addition of the β_i in the belief bases. And the obtained state *must* be in the context. To cope with that, we simply suppose that the context is the set $\mathbf{S}$ of *all* states.

Theorem 5 *$tr^{intr}_{AB}(\varphi)$ is satisfiable for the class of states whose context is $\mathbf{S}$ implies φ is DEL K45-satisfiable.*

6 Related Work

Let us mention syntactic approaches for describing epistemic actions. Action models of DEL are captured up to n-bisimilarity by a language of programs introduced in (French, Hales, and Tay 2014). A logical language for capturing specific kinds of private/public announcements in which propositions expressing which agents are listening to the source is introduced in (Bolander et al. 2016). However in all of these approaches only actions are syntactic, while the underlying models remain Kripke structures.

As emphasized in the introduction, the multi-agent semantics for epistemic logic using belief bases was first introduced in (Lorini 2018; 2020). It allows us to represent both agents' beliefs about propositional facts and their higher-order beliefs (i.e., an agent i's belief about an agent j's belief).[4] It was applied to the formalization of a large variety of epistemic concepts and of aspects of both individual and collective epistemic reasoning including graded belief (Lorini and Schwarzentruber 2021a), distributed belief (Herzig et al. 2020), common belief (Lorini and Rapion 2022), multi-agent belief revision and planning (Lorini and Schwarzentruber 2021b; Davila et al. 2021). A preliminary comparison of this semantics and the DEL update semantics was given in (Lorini 2020) in which it was shown that private belief base expansion corresponds to a specific kind of DEL private announcement represented through arrow models (Kooi and Renne 2011). In particular, it was shown that the epistemic model obtained via private belief expansion is bisimilar to the epistemic model obtained via private announcement relative to the language of standard of epistemic logic.

The semantics for epistemic logic using belief bases can be seen as a way of defining a single 'canonical' model from the description of a state. This point was explored in (Lorini 2019) in the static setting of epistemic logic. In this paper, we extend the analysis to the dynamic setting (Theorem 2).

In the belief base approach, as seen in Definition 1, the state contains a set of formulas for each agent, and then a 'canonical' model is inferred by the relations of Definition 3. There are other approaches that define a 'canonical' model based on what agents see. The description of what agents see is either given by positions of agents in a geometrical environment (Balbiani, Gasquet, and Schwarzentruber 2013; Gasquet, Goranko, and Schwarzentruber 2016), or given by an abstract specification (Cooper et al. 2021). A similar idea is at the center of symbolic model checking for epistemic logic (van Benthem et al. 2015). Techniques described in Section 4 and 5 may also be applied to the comparison of these frameworks with action models.

[4]Related work on the connection between the syntactic representation of preferences based on priority graphs and Kripke models for preference representation can be found in (de Jongh and Liu 2009; Liu 2011; Souza and Moreira 2021). It was extended to deontic logic in (van Benthem, Grossi, and Liu 2014). This work is focused on the single-agent case and does not consider reasoning about higher-order beliefs or preferences.

7 Conclusion

This paper is about a seminal bridge between two opposite approaches for dynamic knowledge change: the syntactic one with belief base operations, and the semantic one with DEL action models (see Theorems 1 and 2). We also discussed the introspective case (see Theorems 3, 4, 5).

For going from belief bases to action models, we proposed action models for simulating the operation of privately expanding belief bases of some agents by an input α (see Figures 2 and 4). For the other direction, we restricted to so-called *ruby* action models (see Figures 3 and 5). For going from (ruby) action models to belief base operations, we adopted two different proof techniques. For the non-introspective case, we simply add each formula β_j to the base of agent j for simulating a ruby action model. We were also able to fully describe (tree-like) epistemic models obtained by product as a formula of $\mathcal{L}_B$. For the introspective case, the simulation of a ruby action model is more involved and requires the use of fresh atomic propositions.

Our work leaves many open questions for future work.

Modal Formulas. Currently, formulas in ruby action models are Boolean. We plan to generalize to any modal formulas. This is challenging because formulas in action models can only be about implicit beliefs, and the translation from implicit to explicit beliefs is not straightforward.

Belief Revision. Belief bases form an elegant formalism for bringing belief revision in a multi-agent context (Lorini and Schwarzentruber 2021b). We aim at studying the link with the plausibility models for multi-agent belief revision (Baltag and Smets 2006).

Epistemic Planning. On the one hand, multi-agent epistemic planning with belief bases is decidable, even with belief revision (Lorini and Schwarzentruber 2021b). On the other hand, epistemic planning in DEL when models are trees and propositional is also decidable (Bolander, Holm Jensen, and Schwarzentruber 2015). Future work will be devoted to investigate the connection between the two approaches to epistemic planning.

Public Announcement. Recently, the belief base approach was extended to capture a notion of public announcement (Lorini and Rapion 2022). This paper paves the way for investigating the connection between DEL-notions of public and semi-private announcement and corresponding notions expressed the belief base semantics.

Acknowledgements

This work is supported by the ANR projects CoPains ("Cognitive Planning in Persuasive Multimodal Communication") and BE4musIA ("Belief Change for better Multi-Source Information Analysis").

References

Balbiani, P.; Gasquet, O.; and Schwarzentruber, F. 2013. Agents that look at one another. *Log. J. IGPL* 21(3):438–467.

Baltag, A., and Moss, L. S. 2004. Logics for epistemic programs. *Synthese* 139 (2):165–224.

Baltag, A., and Smets, S. 2006. Dynamic belief revision over multi-agent plausibility models. In *Proceedings of LOFT*, volume 6, 11–24. University of Liverpool Liverpool.

Baltag, A.; Moss, L.; and Solecki, S. 1998. The logic of public announcements, common knowledge and private suspicions. In *Proceedings of the Seventh Conference on Theoretical Aspects of Rationality and Knowledge (TARK'98)*, 43–56. Morgan Kaufmann.

Benferhat, S.; Dubois, D.; Prade, H.; and Williams, M.-A. 2002. A practical approach to revising prioritized knowledge bases. *Studia Logica* 70(1):105–130.

Blackburn, P.; de Rijke, M.; and Venema, Y. 2001. *Modal Logic*. Cambridge: Cambridge University Press.

Bolander, T.; van Ditmarsch, H.; Herzig, A.; Lorini, E.; Pardo, P.; and Schwarzentruber, F. 2016. Announcements to attentive agents. *J. Log. Lang. Inf.* 25(1):1–35.

Bolander, T.; Holm Jensen, M.; and Schwarzentruber, F. 2015. Complexity results in epistemic planning. In *IJCAI 2015*, 2791–2797. AAAI Press.

Cooper, M. C.; Herzig, A.; Maffre, F.; Maris, F.; Perrotin, E.; and Régnier, P. 2021. A lightweight epistemic logic and its application to planning. *Artif. Intell.* 298:103437.

Davila, J. L. F.; Longin, D.; Lorini, E.; and Maris, F. 2021. A simple framework for cognitive planning. In *Proceedings of the Thirty-Fifth AAAI Conference on Artificial Intelligence (AAAI 2021)*, 6331–6339. AAAI Press.

de Jongh, D., and Liu, F. 2009. Preference, priorities and belief. In Gruene-Yanoff, T., and Hansson, S. O., eds., *Preference Change*. Springer. 85–108.

Eberle, R. A. 1974. A logic of believing, knowing and inferring. *Synthese* 26:356–382.

Fagin, R.; Halpern, J.; Moses, Y.; and Vardi, M. 1995. *Reasoning about Knowledge*. Cambridge: MIT Press.

French, T.; Hales, J.; and Tay, E. 2014. A composable language for action models. In Goré, R.; Kooi, B. P.; and Kurucz, A., eds., *Advances in Modal Logic 10, invited and contributed papers from the tenth conference on "Advances in Modal Logic," held in Groningen, The Netherlands, August 5-8, 2014*, 197–216. College Publications.

Gasquet, O.; Goranko, V.; and Schwarzentruber, F. 2016. Big brother logic: visual-epistemic reasoning in stationary multi-agent systems. *Auton. Agents Multi Agent Syst.* 30(5):793–825.

Hansson, S. O. 1993. Theory contraction and base contraction unified. *Journal of Symbolic Logic* 58(2):602–625.

Hansson, S. O. 1999. *A Textbook of Belief Dynamics: Theory Change and Database Updating*. Dordrecht, Netherland: Kluwer.

Herzig, A.; Lorini, E.; Perrotin, E.; Romero, F.; and Schwarzentruber, F. 2020. A logic of explicit and implicit distributed belief. In *Proceedings of the 24th European Conference on Artificial Intelligence (ECAI 2020)*, volume 325 of *Frontiers in Artificial Intelligence and Applications*, 753–760. IOS Press.

Hintikka, J. 1962. *Knowledge and Belief*. New York: Cornell University Press.

Jago, M. 2009. Epistemic logic for rule-based agents. *Journal of Logic, Language and Information* 18(1):131–158.

Konieczny, S., and Pérez, R. P. 2002. Merging information under constraints: a logical framework. *Journal of Logic and Computation* 12(5):773–808.

Konolige, K. 1986. *A deduction model of belief*. Los Altos: Morgan Kaufmann Publishers.

Kooi, B., and Renne, B. 2011. Arrow update logic. *Review of Symbolic Logic* 4(4):536–559.

Liu, F. 2011. *Reasoning about preference dynamics*, volume 354. Springer.

Lorini, E., and Rapion, E. 2022. Logical theories of collective attitudes and the belief base perspective. In *Proceedings of the 21st International Conference on Autonomous Agents and Multiagent Systems (AAMAS 2022)*. ACM.

Lorini, E., and Schwarzentruber, F. 2021a. A computationally grounded logic of graded belief. In *Proceedings of the 17th European Conference on Logics in Artificial Intelligence (JELIA 2021)*, volume 12678 of *Lecture Notes in Computer Science*, 245–261. Springer.

Lorini, E., and Schwarzentruber, F. 2021b. Multi-agent belief base revision. In Zhou, Z., ed., *Proceedings of the Thirtieth International Joint Conference on Artificial Intelligence, IJCAI 2021, Virtual Event / Montreal, Canada, 19-27 August 2021*, 1959–1965. ijcai.org.

Lorini, E. 2018. In praise of belief bases: Doing epistemic logic without possible worlds. In *Proceedings of the Thirty-Second AAAI Conference on Artificial Intelligence (AAAI-18)*, 1915–1922. AAAI Press.

Lorini, E. 2019. Exploiting belief bases for building rich epistemic structures. In Moss, L. S., ed., *Proceedings of the Seventeenth Conference on Theoretical Aspects of Rationality and Knowledge (TARK 2019)*, volume 297 of *EPTCS*, 332–353.

Lorini, E. 2020. Rethinking epistemic logic with belief bases. *Artificial Intelligence* 282.

Makinson, D., and van der Torre, L. 2000. Input/output logics. *Journal of Philosophical Logic* 29:383–408.

Meyer, J.-J. C., and van der Hoek, W. 1995. *Epistemic Logic for AI and Theoretical Computer Science*. Oxford: Cambridge University Press.

Moore, R. C., and Hendrix, G. G. 1982. Computational models of belief and the semantics of belief sentences. In Peters, S., and Saarinen, E., eds., *Processes, Beliefs, and Questions*, Synthese Language Library. Springer. 107–127.

Moss, L. S. 2007. Finite models constructed from canonical formulas. *Journal of Philosophical Logic* 36(6):605–640.

Souza, M., and Moreira, A. 2021. Belief base change as priority change: A study based on dynamic epistemic logic. *Journal of Logical and Algebraic Methods in Programming* 122.

van Benthem, J.; van Eijck, J.; Gattinger, M.; and Su, K. 2015. Symbolic model checking for dynamic epistemic logic. In *Proceedings of the 5th International Workshop on Logic, Rationality and Interaction (LORI 2015)*, volume 9394 of *LNCS*, 366–378. Springer-Verlag.

van Benthem, J.; Grossi, D.; and Liu, F. 2014. Priority structures in deontic logic. *Theoria* 80(2):116–152.

van Ditmarsch, H. P.; van der Hoek, W.; and Kooi, B. 2007a. *Dynamic Epistemic Logic*. Kluwer Academic Publishers.

Van Ditmarsch, H.; van Der Hoek, W.; and Kooi, B. 2007b. *Dynamic epistemic logic*, volume 337. Springer Science & Business Media.

van Eijck, J.; Ruan, J.; and Sadzik, T. 2012. Action emulation. *Synth.* 185(Supplement-1):131–151.

Vardi, M. Y. 1996. Why is modal logic so robustly decidable? In Immerman, N., and Kolaitis, P. G., eds., *Descriptive Complexity and Finite Models, Proceedings of a DIMACS Workshop 1996, Princeton, New Jersey, USA, January 14-17, 1996*, volume 31 of *DIMACS Series in Discrete Mathematics and Theoretical Computer Science*, 149–183. DIMACS/AMS.

Proceedings of the 19th International Conference on Principles of Knowledge Representation and Reasoning
Main Track

Ontology-Mediated Querying on Databases of Bounded Cliquewidth

Carsten Lutz[1], **Leif Sabellek**[2], **Lukas Schulze**[1]
[1]Department of Computer Science, Leipzig University, Germany
[2]Department of Computer Science, University of Bremen, Germany
{clu, lschulze}@informatik.uni-leipzig.de, sabellek@uni-bremen.de

Abstract

We study the evaluation of ontology-mediated queries (OMQs) on databases of bounded cliquewidth from the viewpoint of parameterized complexity theory. As the ontology language, we consider the description logics $\mathcal{ALC}$ and $\mathcal{ALCI}$ as well as the guarded two-variable fragment GF_2 of first-order logic. Queries are atomic queries (AQs), conjunctive queries (CQs), and unions of CQs. All studied OMQ problems are fixed-parameter linear (FPL) when the parameter is the size of the OMQ plus the cliquewidth. Our main contribution is a detailed analysis of the dependence of the running time on the parameter, exhibiting several interesting effects.

1 Introduction

Ontology-mediated querying is an established subfield of knowledge representation. The general aim is to enrich a database with an ontology to add domain knowledge and to extend the vocabulary available for query formulation (Bienvenu et al. 2014; Bienvenu and Ortiz 2015; Calvanese et al. 2009). Expressive description logics (DLs) such as $\mathcal{ALC}$ and $\mathcal{ALCI}$ are a popular choice for the ontology language as they underpin the widely used OWL DL profile of the OWL 2 ontology language. However, ontology-mediated querying with these languages is coNP-complete in data complexity even for simple atomic queries (AQs) of the form $A(x)$ and thus scales poorly to larger amounts of data. One reaction to this problem is to resort to approximate query answers, as done for example in (Zhou et al. 2015; Haga et al. 2021). A potential alternative is to only admit databases from a class that is sufficiently restricted so that non-approximate answers can be computed in PTime, or to decompose the input database into component databases from such a class.

The aim of this paper is to study ontology-mediated querying on classes of databases of bounded cliquewidth. This is relevant because such classes are maximal known ones on which ontology-mediated querying with DLs such as $\mathcal{ALC}$ and $\mathcal{ALCI}$ is in PTime in data complexity, even when unions of conjunctive queries (UCQs) are admitted as queries. This follows from a folklore translation of ontology-mediated querying into MSO_1 and the known result that MSO_1 has PTime data complexity on structures of bounded cliquewidth (Courcelle, Makowsky, and Rotics 2000). In fact, it even has linear time data complexity (when a k-expression for constructing the database is provided). We recall that bounded treewidth implies bounded cliquewidth since every database of treewidth k has cliquewidth at most $3 \cdot 2^{k-1}$ (Corneil and Rotics 2005). The converse is false because databases of bounded treewidth are sparse in the sense of graph theory, whereas databases of bounded cliquewidth may be dense.

We do not claim that databases encountered in practical applications typically have small cliquewidth. In fact, an empirical study of real-world databases has found that their treewidth tends to be high (Maniu, Senellart, and Jog 2019), and one may expect similar results for cliquewidth. The same study, however, also points out the opportunities that lie in the decomposition of a database into a part of high treewidth and parts of low treewidth, and this has in fact been used successfully to implement efficient querying (Wei 2010; Akiba, Sommer, and Kawarabayashi 2012; Maniu, Cheng, and Senellart 2017). While we are not aware that similar approaches based on cliquewidth have yet been studied, it seems entirely reasonable to pursue them. The work presented here may provide a foundation for such an endeavour.

In this paper, we focus on the framework of parameterized complexity theory. Linear time data complexity with a uniform algorithm trivially implies *fixed-parameter linearity (FPL)* when the parameter is the size of the ontology-mediated query (OMQ). Recall that FPL is defined like the more familiar *fixed-parameter tractability (FPT)* except that the running time may depend only linearly on the size of the database, that is, it must be $f(|Q|) \cdot |\mathcal{D}|$ where f is a computable function, Q the OMQ, and $\mathcal{D}$ the database. Our main goal is to determine the optimal running time of FPL algorithms for ontology-mediated querying on databases of bounded cliquewidth and to provide algorithms that achieve this running time.

As the ontology language, we consider the DLs $\mathcal{ALC}$ and $\mathcal{ALCI}$ and the more expressive guarded two-variable fragment GF_2 of first-order logic. As queries, we admit AQs, conjunctive queries (CQs), and UCQs. An *ontology-mediated query (OMQ)* combines an ontology and a query, and an *OMQ language* is determined by the choice of an ontology language and a query language. For instance, $(\mathcal{ALC}, \text{AQ})$ is the OMQ language that combines $\mathcal{ALC}$ ontologies with AQs. We find that the running time may be single or double exponential in $|Q|$, depending on the choice of the OMQ language. There are several surprising effects, which we highlight in the following. An overview is provided in Table 1.

We show that in $(\mathcal{ALCI}, \text{AQ})$, evaluating an OMQ Q on a database $\mathcal{D}$ is possible in time $2^{O(|Q| \cdot k)} \cdot |\mathcal{D}|$ where k is the cliquewidth of $\mathcal{D}$.[1] We assume here that a k-expression for constructing $\mathcal{D}$ is given (otherwise, the running time is cubic in $|\mathcal{D}|$ and thus FPT, but not FPL). Note that this implies FPL even when the parameter is the size of the OMQ plus the cliquewidth of the database (and so the cliquewidth of the database needs not be bounded by a constant). In (GF_2, AQ), in contrast, we achieve a running time of $2^{2^{O(|Q|)} \cdot k^2} \cdot |\mathcal{D}|$ and show that attaining $2^{2^{o(|Q|)}} \cdot \texttt{poly}(|\mathcal{D}|)$ is impossible even on databases of cliquewidth 2 unless the exponential time hypothesis (ETH) fails. This is interesting for several reasons. First, it is folklore that OMQ evaluation in (GF_2, AQ) is ExpTime-complete in combined complexity on unrestricted databases, and thus one has to 'pay' for the running time to be polynomial in $|\mathcal{D}|$ on databases of bounded cliquewidth by an exponential increase in the running time in $|Q|$. Second, the higher running time for (GF_2, AQ) compared to $(\mathcal{ALCI}, \text{AQ})$ is *not* due to the fact that GF_2 is more expressive than $\mathcal{ALCI}$. In fact, the GF_2 ontology used in the lower bound proof can be expressed in $\mathcal{ALC}$ and the increase in complexity is due to the higher succinctness of GF_2. And third, we also show that in (GF_2, AQ), OMQs can be evaluated in time $2^{O(|Q| \cdot k^2)} \cdot |\mathcal{D}|$ where k is the *treewidth* of $\mathcal{D}$. Thus, the exponential difference in complexity between $(\mathcal{ALCI}, \text{AQ})$ and (GF_2, AQ) that we observe for cliquewidth does not exist for treewidth.

The above results concern AQs, and transitioning to (U)CQs brings about some interesting differences. We show that in $(\mathcal{ALCI}, \text{UCQ})$, evaluation of an OMQ Q is possible in time $2^{|\mathcal{O}| \cdot k^{O(|q| \log(|q|))}} \cdot |\mathcal{D}|$ where $\mathcal{O}$ is the ontology in Q and q is the query in Q. This is complemented by the result that already in $(\mathcal{ALC}, \text{CQ})$, a running time of $2^{2^{o(|Q|)}} \cdot \texttt{poly}(|\mathcal{D}|)$ cannot be achieved even on databases of cliquewidth 3 unless ETH fails. This should be contrasted with the fact that OMQ evaluation in $(\mathcal{ALC}, \text{CQ})$ and $(\mathcal{ALC}, \text{UCQ})$ is ExpTime-complete in combined complexity on unrestricted databases (Lutz 2008) and thus also in these OMQ languages one has to pay for polynomial running time in $|\mathcal{D}|$ by an exponential increase in overall running time. Note however, that the increase is only in $|q|$, but not in $|\mathcal{O}|$. This is in contrast to the case of AQs where the size of queries is actually constant, and it is good news as queries tend to be much smaller than ontologies.

Finally we observe that, in $(\mathcal{ALCF}, \text{AQ})$, where $\mathcal{ALCF}$ is the extension of $\mathcal{ALC}$ with functional roles, OMQ evaluation on databases of treewidth 2 is coNP-hard in data complexity when the unique name assumption is not made.

Proof details are delegated to the appendix, see (Lutz, Sabellek, and Schulze 2022).

Related Work. Monadic second-order logic (MSO) comes in two versions: MSO_1 admits quantification only over sets of nodes while MSO_2 can additionally quantify over sets of edges. Courcelle's theorem states that MSO_2 model checking is FPL on graphs of bounded treewidth and (Courcelle, Makowsky, and Rotics 2000) shows the same for MSO_1 and graphs of bounded cliquewidth (when a k-expression is provided). The problem studied in the current paper can be translated into MSO_1, but this does not yield the tight complexities presented here. It was shown in (Kreutzer and Tazari 2010) that MSO_2 is not FPT for graph classes that have unbounded treewidth and are closed under substructures (under certain assumptions), see also (Ganian et al. 2014); results in this style do not appear to be known for MSO_1 and cliquewidth.

[1] We explain our use of the O-notation in the appendix.

	Bnd. CW	Bnd. TW	Unrestr.
$(\mathcal{ALC}(\mathcal{I}), \text{AQ})$	sngl exp	sngl exp	ExpTime
(GF_2, AQ)	dbl exp	sngl exp	ExpTime
$(\mathcal{ALC}, \text{(U)CQ})$	dbl exp	sngl exp	ExpTime
$(\mathcal{ALCI}, \text{(U)CQ})$	dbl exp	dbl exp	2ExpTime
$(\text{GF}_2, \text{(U)CQ})$	open	dbl exp	2ExpTime

Table 1: Overview of results

2 Preliminaries

Description Logics. Let $\mathsf{N_C}$, $\mathsf{N_R}$, and C be countably infinite sets of *concept names*, *role names*, and *constants*. A *role* is a role name r or an *inverse role* r^-, where r is a role name. Set $(r^-)^- = r$. $\mathcal{ALCI}$*-concepts* are generated by the rule

$$C, D ::= A \mid \neg C \mid C \sqcap D \mid C \sqcup D \mid \exists r.C \mid \forall r.C$$

where A ranges over concept names and r over roles. An $\mathcal{ALC}$*-concept* is an $\mathcal{ALCI}$-concept that does not use inverse roles. We use $\top$ to denote $A \sqcup \neg A$ for some fixed concept name A and $\bot$ for $\neg\top$. For $\mathcal{L} \in \{\mathcal{ALC}, \mathcal{ALCI}\}$, an $\mathcal{L}$-*ontology* is a finite set of *concept inclusions (CIs)* $C \sqsubseteq D$ with C and D $\mathcal{L}$-concepts. A *database* is a finite set of *facts* of the form $A(c)$ or $r(c, c')$ where $A \in \mathsf{N_C} \cup \{\top\}$, $r \in \mathsf{N_R}$, and $c, c' \in \mathsf{C}$. We use $\texttt{adom}(\mathcal{D})$ to denote the set of constants used in a database $\mathcal{D}$, also called its *active domain*. The *size* of a syntactic object X, denoted $|X|$, is the number of symbols needed to write X as a word over a finite alphabet using a suitable encoding.

The semantics is given in terms of *interpretations* $\mathcal{I} = (\Delta^\mathcal{I}, \cdot^\mathcal{I})$, we refer to (Baader et al. 2017) for details. An interpretation $\mathcal{I}$ *satisfies* a CI $C \sqsubseteq D$ if $C^\mathcal{I} \subseteq D^\mathcal{I}$, a fact $A(c)$ if $c \in A^\mathcal{I}$, and a fact $r(c, c')$ if $(c, c') \in r^\mathcal{I}$. We thus make the standard names assumption, that is, we interpret constants as themselves. This implies the unique name assumption. For $S \subseteq \Delta^\mathcal{I}$, we use $\mathcal{I}|_S$ to denote the restriction of $\mathcal{I}$ to domain S. An interpretation $\mathcal{I}$ is a *model* of an ontology or database if it satisfies all inclusions or facts in it. A database $\mathcal{D}$ is *satisfiable* w.r.t. an ontology $\mathcal{O}$ if there is a model $\mathcal{I}$ of $\mathcal{O}$ and $\mathcal{D}$.

We also consider the *guarded two-variable fragment* (GF_2) of first-order logic. In GF_2, only two fixed variables x and y are available and quantification is restricted to the pattern

$$\forall \bar{y}(\alpha(\bar{x}, \bar{y}) \rightarrow \varphi(\bar{x}, \bar{y})) \quad \exists \bar{y}(\alpha(\bar{x}, \bar{y}) \wedge \varphi(\bar{x}, \bar{y}))$$

where $\varphi(\bar{x}, \bar{y})$ is a GF_2 formula with free variables among $\bar{x} \cup \bar{y}$ and $\alpha(\bar{x}, \bar{y})$ is an atomic formula (possibly an equality) called the *guard* that uses all variables in $\bar{x} \cup \bar{y}$. Function symbols and constants are not admitted, and neither is equality in non-guard positions. We only admit relation symbols of arity one and two, identifying the former with concept names and the latter with role names. We may thus interpret GF_2 formulas in DL interpretations. A *GF_2-ontology* is a finite set of GF_2-sentences.

Queries. A *conjunctive query (CQ)* is of the form $q(\bar{x}) = \exists \bar{y}\, \varphi(\bar{x}, \bar{y})$, where $\bar{x}$ and $\bar{y}$ are tuples of variables and $\varphi(\bar{x}, \bar{y})$ is a conjunction of *concept atoms* $A(x)$ and *role atoms* $r(x, y)$, $A \in \mathsf{N_C}$, $r \in \mathsf{N_R}$, and x, y variables from $\bar{x} \cup \bar{y}$. We call the variables in $\bar{x}$ the *answer variables* of q, and use $\mathtt{var}(q)$ to denote $\bar{x} \cup \bar{y}$. We may write $\alpha \in q$ to indicate that α is an atom in q. For $V \subseteq \mathtt{var}(q)$, we use $q|_V$ to denote the restriction of q to the atoms that use only variables in V. A tuple $\bar{d} \in (\Delta^{\mathcal{I}})^{|\bar{x}|}$ is an *answer* to q on an interpretation $\mathcal{I}$ if there is a homomorphism h from q to $\mathcal{I}$ with $h(\bar{x}) = \bar{d}$. More details are in the appendix.

A *union of conjunctive queries (UCQ)* $q(\bar{x})$ is a disjunction of CQs with the same answer variables $\bar{x}$. A tuple $\bar{d} \in (\Delta^{\mathcal{I}})^{|\bar{x}|}$ is an *answer* to q on interpretation $\mathcal{I}$, written $\mathcal{I} \models q(\bar{d})$, if $\bar{d}$ is an answer to some CQ in q on $\mathcal{I}$. We use $q(\mathcal{I})$ to denote set of all answers to q on $\mathcal{I}$. The *arity* of q is the length of $\bar{x}$ and q is *Boolean* if it is of arity zero. An *atomic query (AQ)* is a CQ of the form $A(x)$ with A a concept name.

Ontology-Mediated Querying. An *ontology-mediated query (OMQ)* is a pair $Q = (\mathcal{O}, q)$ with $\mathcal{O}$ an ontology and q a query such as a UCQ. While OMQs are often defined to include an additional third component, the data signature, the problem of query evaluation studied in this paper is insensitive to that component, and so we omit it. We write $Q(\bar{x})$ to indicate that the answer variables of q are $\bar{x}$. A tuple $\bar{a} \in \mathtt{adom}(\mathcal{D})^{|\bar{x}|}$ is an *answer* to $Q(\bar{x})$ on a database $\mathcal{D}$, written $\mathcal{D} \models Q(\bar{a})$, if $\mathcal{I} \models q(\bar{a})$ for all models $\mathcal{I}$ of $\mathcal{O}$ and $\mathcal{D}$. When more convenient, we might alternatively write $\mathcal{D}, \mathcal{O} \models q(\bar{a})$. We write $Q(\mathcal{D})$ to denote the set of all answers to Q on $\mathcal{D}$. We use $(\mathcal{L}, \mathcal{Q})$ to denote the *OMQ language* that contains all OMQs Q in which $\mathcal{O}$ is formulated in the DL $\mathcal{L}$ and q in the query language $\mathcal{Q}$, such as in $(\mathcal{ALCI}, \text{UCQ})$ and (GF_2, AQ).

Let $(\mathcal{L}, \mathcal{Q})$ be an OMQ language. We write *OMQ evaluation in* $(\mathcal{L}, \mathcal{Q})$ to denote the problem to decide, given an OMQ $Q(\bar{x}) \in (\mathcal{L}, \mathcal{Q})$, a database $\mathcal{D}$, and a tuple $\bar{c} \in \mathtt{adom}(\mathcal{D})^{|\bar{x}|}$, whether $\bar{c} \in Q(\mathcal{D})$. A *parameterization* is a function κ that assigns to every input $Q, \mathcal{D}, \bar{c}$ a parameter $\kappa(Q, \mathcal{D}, \bar{c}) \in \mathbb{N}$. We will use $\kappa = |Q|$ in lower bounds and $\kappa = |Q| + k$ in upper bounds where k is the cliquewidth of $\mathcal{D}$ as defined below. OMQ evaluation is *fixed-parameter tractable (FPT) for* κ if it can be decided by an algorithm that runs in time $f(\kappa(Q, \mathcal{D}, \bar{c})) \cdot \mathtt{poly}(n)$ where f is a computable function, here and throughout the paper, $\mathtt{poly}$ denotes an unspecified polynomial, and n is the size of the input. *Fixed-parameter linearity (FPL) for* κ is defined analogously, with running time $f(\kappa(Q, \mathcal{D}, \bar{c})) \cdot O(n)$.

Treewidth and Cliquewidth. Treewidth describes how similar a graph (in our case: a database) is to a tree, and cliquewidth does the same for cliques (Courcelle and Engelfriet 2012). Due to space restrictions and since this article focuses on cliquewidth, we provide the definition of treewidth only in the appendix. Databases of cliquewidth k can be constructed by a k-expression as defined below, where k refers to the number of *labels* in the expression. For convenience, we use a reservoir of fresh concept names $L_1, L_2, \ldots$ as labels that may occur in databases, but not in ontologies and queries. We say that a constant $c \in \mathtt{adom}(\mathcal{D})$ is *labeled* i if $L_i(c) \in \mathcal{D}$. An *expression* s defines a database $\mathcal{D}_s$ built from four operations, as follows:

$\boldsymbol{s = \iota(\mathcal{D})}$ is the nullary operator for *constant introduction* where $i \geq 1$ and $\mathcal{D}$ is a database with $|\mathtt{adom}(\mathcal{D})| = 1$ that contains exactly one fact of the form $L_i(c)$, and $\mathcal{D}_s = \mathcal{D}$.

$\boldsymbol{s = s_1 \oplus s_2}$ is the binary operator for *disjoint union* where s_1 and s_2 are expressions such that $\mathtt{adom}(\mathcal{D}_{s_1}) \cap \mathtt{adom}(\mathcal{D}_{s_2}) = \emptyset$ and $\mathcal{D}_s = \mathcal{D}_{s_1} \cup \mathcal{D}_{s_2}$.

$\boldsymbol{s = \alpha^r_{i,j}(s')}$ is the unary operator for *role insertion* where r is a role name, $i, j \geq 1$ are distinct, and s' is an expression. It links all constants labeled i to all constants labeled j using role r, that is,

$$\mathcal{D}_s = \mathcal{D}_{s'} \cup \{r(a, b) \mid L_i(a) \in \mathcal{D}_{s'} \text{ and } L_j(b) \in \mathcal{D}_{s'}\}.$$

$\boldsymbol{s = \rho_{i \to j}(s')}$ is the unary operator for *relabeling* where $i, j \geq 1$ are distinct and s' is an expression. It changes all i-labels to j, that is,

$$\mathcal{D}_s = \mathcal{D}_{s'} \setminus \{L_i(c) \mid c \in \mathtt{adom}(\mathcal{D}_{s'})\} \cup \{L_j(c) \mid L_i(c) \in \mathcal{D}_{s'}\}.$$

An expression s is a *k-expression* if all labels in s are from $\{L_1, \ldots, L_k\}$. A database $\mathcal{D}$ has *cliquewidth* $k > 0$ if there is a k-expression s with $\mathcal{D}_s = \mathcal{D}$, but no k'-expression s' such that $k' < k$ and $\mathcal{D}_{s'} = \mathcal{D}$, up to facts of the form $L_i(c)$.

Example 1. *Consider the class of databases about schools that use the concept names* $\mathtt{Pupil}$, $\mathtt{Teacher}$ *and* $\mathtt{School}$ *as well as role names* $\mathtt{teaches}$, $\mathtt{worksAt}$ *and* $\mathtt{isClassmateOf}$, *and where each teacher works at exactly one school and can teach any number of pupils. The set of all pupils is partitioned into groups of pupils that are classmates of one another, and each teacher teaches exactly one such group. A basic database from that class is*

$$\begin{aligned}\mathcal{D} = \{&\mathtt{Pupil}(a_1), \mathtt{Pupil}(a_2), \mathtt{Teacher}(b), \mathtt{School}(c),\\ &\mathtt{worksAt}(b, c), \mathtt{teaches}(b, a_1), \mathtt{teaches}(b, a_2),\\ &\mathtt{isClassmateOf}(a_1, a_2), \mathtt{isClassmateOf}(a_2, a_1)\}.\end{aligned}$$

This database has cliquewidth 3, and in fact so does any database from the described class, independently of the number of pupils, teachers, and schools. When constructing k-expressions, it suffices to use up to two labels for pupils, one for teachers, and one for schools. With proper relabeling, no more than three labels are needed at the same time.

3 Upper Bounds and Algorithms

We prove that OMQ evaluation on databases of bounded cliquewidth is FPL when the parameter is the size of the OMQ plus the cliquewidth of the database and establish upper bounds on the overall running time.

3.1 $\mathcal{ALCI}$ with AQs

Theorem 1. *In $(\mathcal{ALCI}, AQ)$, an OMQ $Q = (\mathcal{O}, q)$ can be evaluated on a database $\mathcal{D}$ of cliquewidth k in time $2^{O(|\mathcal{O}| \cdot k)} \cdot |\mathcal{D}|$.*

Theorem 1 implies that OMQ evaluation in $(\mathcal{ALCI}, \text{AQ})$ is in FPL, and also that it is in linear time in data complexity when the cliquewidth of databases is bounded by a constant. As announced before, we assume here and in all subsequent upper complexity bounds that a k-expression s_0 for $\mathcal{D}$ is given as part of the input. In fact, the number of subexpressions of s_0 must be $O(|\mathcal{D}|)$, a condition that is satisfied by any reasonable k-expression for $\mathcal{D}$. These assumptions could clearly be dropped if, given a database $\mathcal{D}$ of cliquewidth k, we could compute a k-expression that generates $\mathcal{D}$ (or a sufficient approximation thereof) in time $2^{O(k)} \cdot |\mathcal{D}|$. It is an open problem whether this is possible, see e.g. (Downey and Fellows 2013). There is, however, an algorithm that computes, given a database $\mathcal{D}$ of cliquewidth k, in time $|\mathtt{adom}(\mathcal{D})|^3$ a k'-expression with $k' \leq 2^{3k-1}$ (Oum 2008). As a consequence, we obtain an analogue of Theorem 1 that does not require a k-expression for $\mathcal{D}$ to be given and where the time bound is replaced with $2^{|Q| \cdot 2^{O(k)}} \cdot |\mathcal{D}|^3$. While this no longer yields FPL, it still yields FPT.

To prove Theorem 1, it suffices to give an algorithm for database satisfiability w.r.t. an $\mathcal{ALCI}$ ontology that runs within the stated time bounds. To decide whether $\mathcal{D}, \mathcal{O} \models A(c)$, we may then simply check whether $\mathcal{D} \cup \{\overline{A}(c)\}$ is unsatisfiable w.r.t. the ontology $\mathcal{O} \cup \{\overline{A} \equiv \neg A\}$.

Assume that we are given as input a database $\mathcal{D}_0$, an ontology $\mathcal{O}$, and a k-expression s_0 that generates $\mathcal{D}_0$. We may assume w.l.o.g. that $\mathcal{O}$ takes the form $\{\top \sqsubseteq C_\mathcal{O}\}$ where $C_\mathcal{O}$ is an $\mathcal{ALCI}$-concept in negation normal form (NNF), that is, negation is only applied to concept names, but not to compound concepts. Every $\mathcal{ALCI}$-ontology $\mathcal{O}$ can be converted into this form in linear time (Baader et al. 2017).

Our algorithm traverses the k-expression s_0 bottom-up, computing for each subexpression s a succinct representation of the models of the database $\mathcal{D}_s$ and ontology $\mathcal{O}$. Before giving details, we introduce some relevant notions. We use $\mathtt{sub}(\mathcal{O})$ to denote the set of all concepts in $\mathcal{O}$, closed under subconcepts and $\mathtt{cl}(\mathcal{O})$ for the extension of $\mathtt{sub}(\mathcal{O})$ with the NNF of all concepts $\neg C$, $C \in \mathtt{sub}(\mathcal{O})$. Moreover, $\mathtt{cl}^\forall(\mathcal{O})$ denotes the restriction of $\mathtt{cl}(\mathcal{O})$ to concepts of the form $\forall r.C$ and $\mathtt{cl}^*(\mathcal{O})$ is $\{C \mid \forall r.C \in \mathtt{cl}(\mathcal{O})\}$. A *type for* $\mathcal{O}$ is a set $t \subseteq \mathtt{cl}(\mathcal{O})$ such that for some model $\mathcal{I}$ of $\mathcal{O}$ and some $d \in \Delta^\mathcal{I}$, $t = \{C \in \mathtt{cl}(\mathcal{O}) \mid d \in C^\mathcal{I}\}$. We then also denote t with $\mathtt{tp}_\mathcal{I}(d)$.

An *input output assignment (IOA)* for $\mathcal{O}$ is a pair $\gamma = (\mathtt{in}, \mathtt{out})$ with $\mathtt{in} : \{1, \dots, k\} \rightarrow 2^{\mathtt{cl}^*(\mathcal{O})}$ and $\mathtt{out} : \{1, \dots, k\} \rightarrow 2^{\mathtt{cl}^\forall(\mathcal{O})}$ total functions. For easier reference, we use $\gamma^\mathtt{in}$ to denote $\mathtt{in}$ and $\gamma^\mathtt{out}$ to denote $\mathtt{out}$. Every database $\mathcal{D}$ and model $\mathcal{I}$ of $\mathcal{D}$ and $\mathcal{O}$ give rise to an IOA $\gamma_{\mathcal{I},\mathcal{D}}$ for $\mathcal{O}$ defined by setting, for $1 \leq i \leq k$,

$$\gamma^\mathtt{in}_{\mathcal{I},\mathcal{D}}(i) = \mathtt{cl}^*(\mathcal{O}) \cap \bigcap_{L_i(c) \in \mathcal{D}} \mathtt{tp}_\mathcal{I}(c) \text{ and}$$

$$\gamma^\mathtt{out}_{\mathcal{I},\mathcal{D}}(i) = \mathtt{cl}^\forall(\mathcal{O}) \cap \bigcup_{L_i(c) \in \mathcal{D}} \mathtt{tp}_\mathcal{I}(c).$$

Intuitively, $\gamma^\mathtt{out}(i)$ lists outputs generated by label i in the sense that every concept $\forall r.C \in \gamma^\mathtt{out}(i)$ 'outputs' C to all constants labeled j when we use the $\alpha^r_{i,j}$ operation to introduce new role edges. It is then important that $C \in \gamma^\mathtt{in}(j)$, and in this sense $\gamma^\mathtt{in}(j)$ lists inputs accepted by label j.

The central idea of our algorithm is to compute, for each subexpression s of s_0, the set of IOAs

$$\Theta(s) = \{\gamma_{\mathcal{I},\mathcal{D}_s} \mid \mathcal{I} \text{ model of } \mathcal{D}_s \text{ and } \mathcal{O}\}.$$

It then remains to check whether $\Theta(s_0)$ is non-empty. The sets $\Theta(s)$ are computed as follows:

$\boldsymbol{s = \iota(\mathcal{D})}$: Set $\Theta(s) = \{\gamma_{\mathcal{I},\mathcal{D}} \mid \mathcal{I} \text{ model of } \mathcal{D} \text{ and } \mathcal{O}\}$.

$\boldsymbol{s = s_1 \oplus s_2}$: $\Theta(s)$ contains an IOA γ for each pair of IOAs $(\gamma_1, \gamma_2) \in \Theta(s_1) \times \Theta(s_2)$ defined by setting, for $1 \leq i \leq k$:

$$\gamma^\mathtt{in}(i) = \gamma_1^\mathtt{in}(i) \cap \gamma_2^\mathtt{in}(i) \quad \gamma^\mathtt{out}(i) = \gamma_1^\mathtt{out}(i) \cup \gamma_2^\mathtt{out}(i).$$

$\boldsymbol{s = \alpha^r_{i,j}(s')}$: $\Theta(s)$ is obtained from $\Theta(s')$ by removing IOAs that are ruled out by the additional role links. Formally, we keep in $\Theta(s)$ only those IOAs γ such that

a) if $\forall r.C \in \gamma^\mathtt{out}(i)$ then $C \in \gamma^\mathtt{in}(j)$ and

b) if $\forall r^-.C \in \gamma^\mathtt{out}(j)$ then $C \in \gamma^\mathtt{in}(i)$.

$\boldsymbol{s = \rho_{i \to j}(s')}$: for each $\widehat{\gamma} \in \Theta(s')$, $\Theta(s)$ contains the IOA γ defined as follows:

c) $\gamma^\mathtt{in}(i) = \mathtt{cl}^*(\mathcal{O})$ and $\gamma^\mathtt{out}(i) = \emptyset$

d) $\gamma^\mathtt{in}(j) = \widehat{\gamma}^\mathtt{in}(i) \cap \widehat{\gamma}^\mathtt{in}(j)$ and $\gamma^\mathtt{out}(j) = \widehat{\gamma}^\mathtt{out}(i) \cup \widehat{\gamma}^\mathtt{out}(j)$

e) $\gamma^\mathtt{in}(\ell) = \widehat{\gamma}^\mathtt{in}(\ell)$ and $\gamma^\mathtt{out}(\ell) = \widehat{\gamma}^\mathtt{out}(\ell)$ for all $\ell \in \{1, \dots, k\} \setminus \{i, j\}$.

We prove in the appendix that the algorithm is correct.

Lemma 1. *For all subexpressions s of s_0, $\Theta(s) = \{\gamma_{\mathcal{I},\mathcal{D}_s} \mid \mathcal{I}$ model of $\mathcal{D}_s$ and $\mathcal{O}\}$.*

The presented algorithm achieves the intended running time. We do a single bottom-up pass over s_0, considering each subexpression s, of which there are at most $O(|\mathcal{D}|)$ many. The size of each IOA in $\Theta(s)$ is $O(|\mathcal{O}| \cdot k)$ and there are at most $2^{O(|\mathcal{O}| \cdot k)}$ IOAs. It can be verified that each set $\Theta(s)$ can be constructed in time $2^{O(|\mathcal{O}| \cdot k)}$. For the case $s = \iota(\mathcal{D})$, this essentially amounts to enumerating all types for $\mathcal{O}$, more details are in the appendix.

3.2 $\mathcal{ALCI}$ with UCQs

Theorem 2. *In $(\mathcal{ALCI}, \text{UCQ})$, an OMQ $Q = (\mathcal{O}, q)$ can be evaluated on a database $\mathcal{D}$ of cliquewidth k in time $2^{|\mathcal{O}| \cdot k^{O(|q| \log(|q|))}} \cdot |\mathcal{D}|$.*

The algorithm used to prove Theorem 2 is a generalization of the one used for Theorem 1. It also traverses the k-expression s_0 bottom-up, computing for each subexpression s a set of IOAs that additionally are annotated with information about partial homomorphisms from CQs in the UCQ q into models of $\mathcal{D}_s$ and $\mathcal{O}$. The generalization is not entirely straightforward. First, the homomorphism may map some variables to elements of the model that are 'outside' of the database $\mathcal{D}_s$ while IOAs only store information about constants from $\mathcal{D}_s$. And second, we cannot even memorize all homomorphisms that map all variables into $\mathcal{D}_s$ as there may be $|\mathcal{D}_s|^{|q|}$ many of them, too many for FPL. Our solution to the first issue is to modify the ontology and UCQ so that variables need never be mapped outside of $\mathcal{D}$. We resolve the second issue by the observation that it suffices to memorize the *labels* of the constants in $\mathcal{D}_s$ to which variables are mapped, but not their precise identity. The generalized algorithm establishes Theorem 1 as a special case; we singled out the algorithm in the previous section for didactic reasons.

Assume that we are given as input an OMQ $Q(\bar{x}) = (\mathcal{O}, q) \in (\mathcal{ALCI}, \text{UCQ})$, a database $\mathcal{D}_0$, and a k-expression s_0 that generates $\mathcal{D}_0$. It is easy to see that we may assume w.l.o.g. that Q is Boolean, details are in the appendix. We may also assume the ontology $\mathcal{O}$ to contain a CI $\top \sqsubseteq A_\top$, with $A_\top$ not used anywhere else in $\mathcal{O}$, and that every CQ p in q contains the concept atom $A_\top(x)$ for every $x \in \mathtt{var}(p)$. This will prove useful for the constructions below.

An interpretation $\mathcal{I}$ is a *tree* if the undirected graph $G_\mathcal{I} = (V, E)$ with $V = \Delta^\mathcal{I}$ and $E = \{\{x, y\} \mid (x, y) \in r^\mathcal{I}$ for some $r\}$ is a tree and there are no self loops and multi-edges, the latter meaning that $(d, e) \in r_1^\mathcal{I}$ implies $(d, e) \notin r_2^\mathcal{I}$ for all distinct roles r_1, r_2. We call a model $\mathcal{I}$ of $\mathcal{D}_0$ *tree-extended* if it satisfies the following conditions:

- $r^\mathcal{I} \cap (\mathtt{adom}(\mathcal{D}_0) \times \mathtt{adom}(\mathcal{D}_0)) = \{(d, e) \mid r(d, e) \in \mathcal{D}_0\}$ for all role names r and
- if $\mathcal{I}$ is modified by setting $r^\mathcal{I} = r^\mathcal{I} \setminus (\mathtt{adom}(\mathcal{D}_0) \times \mathtt{adom}(\mathcal{D}_0))$ for all role names r, then the result is a disjoint union of trees and each of these trees contains exactly one constant from $\mathtt{adom}(\mathcal{D}_0)$.

The following is well-known, see for example (Lutz 2008).

Lemma 2. *If there is a model $\mathcal{I}$ of $\mathcal{D}_0$ and $\mathcal{O}$ such that $\mathcal{I} \not\models q$, then there is such a model $\mathcal{I}$ that is tree-extended.*

Lemma 2 provides the basis for the announced modification of $\mathcal{O}$ and the CQs in q: we extend $\mathcal{O}$ to an ontology $\mathcal{O}_q$ and q into a UCQ $\widehat{q}$ such that for every tree-extended model $\mathcal{I}$ of $\mathcal{D}_0$ and $\mathcal{O}_q$, $\mathcal{I} \models q$ iff $\mathcal{I}|_{\mathtt{adom}(\mathcal{D}_0)} \models \widehat{q}$. We then proceed to work with $\mathcal{O}_q$ and $\widehat{q}$ in place of $\mathcal{O}$ and q, which allows us to concentrate on homomorphisms from CQs in $\widehat{q}$ to models $\mathcal{I}$ of $\mathcal{D}$ and $\mathcal{O}_q$ that map all variables to $\mathtt{adom}(\mathcal{D}_0)$.

We next present the extension of $\mathcal{O}$. A Boolean or unary CQ p being a *tree* (without self-loops and multi-edges) is defined in the expected way. Note that a unary tree CQ p can be viewed as an $\mathcal{ALCI}$-concept C_p in an obvious way. For example, if $p(x) = \{A(x), r(y, x), s(y, z), B(z), r(y, z'), A(z')\}$, then $C_p = A \sqcap \exists r^-.(\exists s.B \sqcap \exists r.A)$. We use $\mathtt{trees}(q)$ to denote the set of all (Boolean) tree CQs that can be obtained from a CQ in q by first dropping atoms and then taking a contraction. When writing $p(x)$ with $p \in \mathtt{trees}(q)$ and $x \in \mathtt{var}(p)$, we mean p with x made answer variable. The ontology $\mathcal{O}_q$ is obtained from $\mathcal{O}$ by adding the following, and then converting to NNF:

- for every $p \in \mathtt{trees}(q)$ and $x \in \mathtt{var}(p)$, the CIs $A_{p(x)} \sqsubseteq C_{p(x)}$ and $C_{p(x)} \sqsubseteq A_{p(x)}$ where $A_{p(x)}$ is a fresh concept name;
- for every $p \in \mathtt{trees}(q)$, the CIs $A_p \sqsubseteq \exists r_p.C_p$, $C_p \sqsubseteq A_p$, and $\exists r.A_p \sqsubseteq A_p$ for every role r used in $\mathcal{O}$, where A_p is a fresh concept name and r_p a fresh role name.

Note that $|\mathcal{O}_q| \in |\mathcal{O}| \cdot 2^{O(|q| \cdot \log |q|)}$.

Towards defining the UCQ $\widehat{q}$, consider all CQs that can be obtained as follows. Start with a contraction p of a CQ from q, then choose a set of variables $S \subseteq \mathtt{var}(p)$ such that

$$p^- = p \setminus \{r(x, y) \in p \mid x, y \in S\}$$

is a disjoint union of tree CQs each of which contains at most one variable from S and at least one variable that is not from S. Include in $\widehat{q}$ all CQs that can be obtained by extending $p|_S$ as follows:

1. for every maximal connected component p' of p^- that contains a (unique) variable $x_0 \in S$, add the atom $A_{p'(x_0)}(x_0)$;
2. for every maximal connected component p' of p^- that contains no variable from S, add the atom $A_{p'}(z)$ with z a fresh variable.

It is easy to verify that in Points 1 and 2 above, the CQ p' is in $\mathtt{trees}(q)$ and thus CIs for p' have been introduced in the construction of $\mathcal{O}_q$. The number of CQs in $\widehat{q}$ is single exponential in $|q|$ and each CQ is of size at most $|q|$.

Lemma 3. *For every tree-extended model $\mathcal{I}$ of $\mathcal{D}_0$ and $\mathcal{O}_q$, $\mathcal{I} \models q$ iff $\mathcal{I}|_{\mathtt{adom}(\mathcal{D}_0)} \models \widehat{q}$.*

Let $\mathcal{Q}$ denote the set of all subqueries p of CQs in $\widehat{q}$, that is, p can be obtained from a CQ in $\widehat{q}$ by dropping atoms. A *decorated IOA* for $\mathcal{O}_q$ is a triple $\gamma = (\mathtt{in}, \mathtt{out}, S)$ where $(\mathtt{in}, \mathtt{out})$ is an IOA and S is a set of pairs (p, f) with $p \in \mathcal{Q}$ and $f : \mathtt{var}(p) \to \{1, \ldots, k\}$ a total function. We use $\gamma^{\mathtt{in}}$ to denote $\mathtt{in}$ and likewise for $\gamma^{\mathtt{out}}$ and γ^S. We argue in the appendix that the number of decorated IOAs is $2^{|\mathcal{O}| \cdot k^{O(|q| \log |q|)}}$.

Every database $\mathcal{D}$ and model $\mathcal{I}$ of $\mathcal{D}$ and $\mathcal{O}_q$ give rise to a decorated IOA $\gamma_{\mathcal{I},\mathcal{D}}$ for $\mathcal{O}_q$ where

- $\gamma^{\mathtt{in}}_{\mathcal{I},\mathcal{D}}$ and $\gamma^{\mathtt{out}}_{\mathcal{I},\mathcal{D}}$ are defined as in the previous section and
- γ^S contains all pairs (p, f) with $p \in \mathcal{Q}$ and f a function from $\mathtt{var}(p)$ to $\{1, \ldots, k\}$ such that there is a homomorphism h from p to $\mathcal{I}$ with $f(x) = i$ iff $L_i(h(x)) \in \mathcal{D}$ for all variables $x \in \mathtt{var}(p)$.

For all subexpressions s of s_0, our algorithm computes

$$\Theta(s) = \{\gamma_{\mathcal{I},\mathcal{D}_s} \mid \mathcal{I} \text{ is a tree-extended model of } \mathcal{D}_s \text{ and } \mathcal{O}_q\}.$$

By Lemma 3 and since every tree-extended model of $\mathcal{D}_0$ and $\mathcal{O}$ can be extended to a tree-extended model of $\mathcal{D}_0$ and $\mathcal{O}_q$, this implies that, as desired, $\mathcal{D}_0, \mathcal{O} \not\models q$ iff there is a decorated IOA $\gamma \in \Theta(s_0)$ such that γ^S contains no pair (p, f) with p a CQ in $\widehat{q}$. The sets $\Theta(s)$ are computed as follows:

$\boldsymbol{s = \iota(\mathcal{D})}$: $\Theta(s) = \{\gamma_{\mathcal{I},\mathcal{D}} \mid \mathcal{I}$ is a tree-extended model of $\mathcal{D}$ and $\mathcal{O}_q\}$.

$\boldsymbol{s = s_1 \oplus s_2}$: $\Theta(s)$ contains a decorated IOA γ for each pair $(\gamma_1, \gamma_2) \in \Theta(s_1) \times \Theta(s_2)$ where, for $1 \leq i \leq k$:

$$\gamma^{\mathtt{in}}(i) = \gamma_1^{\mathtt{in}}(i) \cap \gamma_2^{\mathtt{in}}(i) \quad \gamma^{\mathtt{in}}(i) = \gamma_1^{\mathtt{out}}(i) \cup \gamma_2^{\mathtt{out}}(i)).$$

and $\gamma^S = \gamma_1^S \cup \gamma_2^S \cup \{(p_1 \cup p_2, f_1 \cup f_2) \mid (p_i, f_i) \in \gamma_i^S$ for $i \in \{1, 2\}$, $p_1 \cup p_2 \in \mathcal{Q}$ and $\mathtt{var}(p_1) \cap \mathtt{var}(p_2) = \emptyset\}$.

$\boldsymbol{s = \alpha^r_{i,j}(s')}$: $\Theta(s)$ contains the decorated IOAs γ that can be obtained by choosing a $\widehat{\gamma} \in \Theta(s')$ that satisfies Conditions a) and b) from Section 3.1 and then defining

- $\gamma^{\mathtt{in}} = \widehat{\gamma}^{\mathtt{in}}$ and $\gamma^{\mathtt{out}} = \widehat{\gamma}^{\mathtt{out}}$;

- γ^S to be $\widehat{\gamma}^S$ extended with all pairs (p', f) such that $p' \in \mathcal{Q}$ and for some $(p, f) \in \widehat{S}$, p' can be obtained from p by adding zero or more atoms $r(x, y)$, subject to the condition that $f(x) = i$ and $f(y) = j$.

$s = \rho_{i \to j}(s')$: for each $\widehat{\gamma} \in \Theta(s')$, $\Theta(s)$ contains the decorated IOA γ obtained by defining

- $\gamma^{\mathtt{in}}$ and $\gamma^{\mathtt{out}}$ according to Conditions c) to e) in Section 3.1;
- γ^S to contain all pairs (p, f') such that for some $(p, f) \in \widehat{S}$, f' can be obtained by starting with f and then setting $f'(x) = j$ whenever $f(x) = i$.

Note that $\mathcal{Q}$ contains $A_\top(x)$ for every variable x in q and thus we can start with mapping subqueries that contain only a single variable x (and a dummy atom) in the $s = \iota(\mathcal{D})$ case. The algorithm achieves the intended goal.

Lemma 4. *For all subexpressions s of s_0, $\Theta(s) = \{\gamma_{\mathcal{I},\mathcal{D}_s} \mid \mathcal{I}$ is a tree-extended model of $\mathcal{D}_s$ and $\mathcal{O}_q\}$.*

The running time is analyzed in the appendix.

3.3 GF$_2$ with AQs

Theorem 3. *In (GF$_2$,AQ), an OMQ $Q = (\mathcal{O}, q)$ can be evaluated on a database $\mathcal{D}$ of cliquewidth k in time $2^{2^{O(|\mathcal{O}|)} \cdot k^2} \cdot |\mathcal{D}|$.*

As in Section 3.1, we may concentrate on the satisfiability of databases w.r.t. ontologies. To decide whether $\mathcal{D}, \mathcal{O} \models A(\bar{c})$, we then simply check whether $\mathcal{D} \cup \{\overline{A}(\bar{c})\}$ is unsatisfiable w.r.t. the ontology $\mathcal{O} \cup \{\forall \bar{x}\, (\overline{A}(\bar{x}) \to \neg A(\bar{x}))\}$. Note that this also captures 'binary AQs' $A(\bar{c})$.

Assume that we are given as input a GF$_2$-ontology $\mathcal{O}$, a database $\mathcal{D}_0$, and a k-expression s_0 that generates $\mathcal{D}_0$. For $i \in \{1, 2\}$, we use $\mathtt{cl}_i(\mathcal{O})$ to denote the set of all subformulas of $\mathcal{O}$ with at most i free variables, closed under single negation. For $i = 2$, we additionally assume that $\mathtt{cl}_i(\mathcal{O})$ contains all formulas $r(x, y)$ and $r(y, x)$ with r a role name that occurs in $\mathcal{D}_0$.[2] An *i-type for $\mathcal{O}$* is a set $t \subseteq \mathtt{cl}_i(\mathcal{O})$ such that for some model $\mathcal{I}$ of $\mathcal{O}$ and some $\bar{d} \in (\Delta^\mathcal{I})^i$,

$$t = \{\varphi(\bar{x}) \in \mathtt{cl}_i(\mathcal{O}) \mid \mathcal{I} \models \varphi(\bar{e}),$$
$$\bar{e} \text{ a subtuple of } \bar{d} \text{ of length } |\bar{x}| \in \{0, \ldots, i\}\}.$$

We then also denote t with $\mathtt{tp}^i_\mathcal{I}(\bar{d})$ and use $\mathtt{TP}_i$ to denote the set of all i-types for $\mathcal{O}$. For $t_1, t_2 \in \mathtt{TP}_1$ and $t \in \mathtt{TP}_2$, we say that t_1 and t_2 *are compatible with* t and write $t_1 \rightsquigarrow_t t_2$ if there is a model $\mathcal{I}$ of $\mathcal{O}$ and $d_1, d_2 \in \Delta^\mathcal{I}$ such that $\mathtt{tp}^1_\mathcal{I}(d_i) = t_i$ for $i \in \{1, 2\}$ and $\mathtt{tp}^2_\mathcal{I}(d_1, d_2) = t$. Note that every 1-type contains a 0-type and every 2-type contans a 0-type and two 1-types, identified by the subformulas that use free variable x and y, respectively.

We again traverse the k-expression s_0 bottom-up, computing for each subexpression s a representation of the models of the database $\mathcal{D}_s$ and ontology $\mathcal{O}$. This representation, however, is different from the ones in the previous sections and does not use IOAs. The reason is as follows. A concrete model $\mathcal{I}$ of $\mathcal{D}_s$ and $\mathcal{O}$ assigns a 1-type to every constant in $\mathcal{D}_s$ and thus a set T_i of 1-types to every label i. In $\mathcal{ALCI}$, we may represent each set T_i by the sets $\{\forall r.C \mid \exists t \in T_i : \forall r.C \in t\}$ and $\{C \in \mathtt{cl}^*(\mathcal{O}) \mid \forall t \in T_i : C \in t\}$ of an IOA because they contain all information that we need when using the $\alpha^r_{i,j}$ operator to introduce new edges. The virtue is that there are only single exponentially many IOAs. Now consider the GF$_2$-ontology $\mathcal{O}$ that contains the sentence

$$\forall x \forall y\, r(x, y) \to \bigwedge_{1 \le i \le n} (A_i(x) \leftrightarrow A_i(y)).$$

The 1-types in T_i may contain any combination of the formulas $A_1(x), \ldots, A_n(x)$ and for dealing with the $\alpha^r_{i,j}$ operator we clearly have to know all of them. However, there are double exponentially many sets of such combinations, and this results in a double exponential upper bound.

We now give details of how we represent models. A *multi-edge* is a set of atoms $r(x, y)$ and $r(y, x)$. Let $\mathcal{M}$ denote the set of all multi-edges that only use role names that occur in $\mathcal{D}_0$. For a database $\mathcal{D}$ and distinct $a, b \in \mathtt{adom}(\mathcal{D})$, we use $M_\mathcal{D}(a, b)$ to denote the multi-edge that consists of all atoms $r(x, y)$ such that $\mathcal{D}$ contains the fact $r(a, b)$, and $r(y, x)$ such that $\mathcal{D}$ contains the fact $r(b, a)$.

A *model abstraction* is a pair $\gamma = (T, E)$ where

- $T : \{1, \ldots, k\} \to 2^{\mathtt{TP}_1}$ is a partial function that associates each label with a set of 1-types;
- $E : \{1, \ldots, k\}^2 \to 2^{\mathtt{TP}_1 \times \mathcal{M} \times \mathtt{TP}_1}$ is a partial function that associates each pair of labels (i, j), where $i \neq j$, with a set of triples (t_1, M, t_2) from $\mathtt{TP}_1 \times \mathcal{M} \times \mathtt{TP}_1$

such that all 1-types in the ranges of T and E contain exactly the same subformulas of $\mathcal{O}$ that are sentences, that is, they contain the same 0-type. We use γ^0 to denote this 0-type, γ^T to denote T, and likewise for γ^E. We use multi-edges in model abstractions rather than 2-types as the former allow us to add edges later when the operator $\alpha^r_{i,j}$ is applied whereas the latter fix all edges from the beginning.

Every database $\mathcal{D}$ and model $\mathcal{I}$ of $\mathcal{D}$ give rise to a model abstraction $\gamma_{\mathcal{I},\mathcal{D}}$ defined by setting, for $1 \le i, j \le k$,

$$\gamma^T_{\mathcal{I},\mathcal{D}}(i) = \{\mathtt{tp}^1_\mathcal{I}(c) \mid L_i(c) \in \mathcal{D}\}$$
$$\gamma^E_{\mathcal{I},\mathcal{D}}(i, j) = \{(\mathtt{tp}^1_\mathcal{I}(c), M_\mathcal{D}(c, c'), \mathtt{tp}^1_\mathcal{I}(c')) \mid L_i(c) \in \mathcal{D} \text{ and } L_j(c') \in \mathcal{D}\}.$$

Our algorithm computes, for each subexpression s of s_0,

$$\Theta(s) = \{\gamma_{\mathcal{I},\mathcal{D}_s} \mid \mathcal{I} \text{ model of } \mathcal{D}_s \text{ and } \mathcal{O}\}.$$

It then remains to check whether $\Theta(s_0)$ is non-empty. The sets $\Theta(s)$ are computed as follows:

$s = \iota(\mathcal{D})$: Set $\Theta(s) = \{\gamma_{\mathcal{I},\mathcal{D}} \mid \mathcal{I} \text{ model of } \mathcal{D} \text{ and } \mathcal{O}\}$.

$s = s_1 \oplus s_2$: $\Theta(s)$ contains a model abstraction $\gamma = (T, F)$ for each pair of model abstractions $(\gamma_1, \gamma_2) \in \Theta(s_1) \times \Theta(s_2)$ with $\gamma^0_1 = \gamma^0_2$ defined by setting, for $1 \le i, j \le k$,

$$\gamma^T(i) = \gamma^T_1(i) \cup \gamma^T_2(i)$$
$$\gamma^E(i, j) = \gamma^E_1(i, j) \cup \gamma^E_2(i, j) \cup \{(t_1, \emptyset, t_2) \mid t_1 \in \gamma^T_1(i) \text{ and } t_2 \in \gamma^T_2(j)\} \cup \{(t_1, \emptyset, t_2) \mid t_1 \in \gamma^T_2(i) \text{ and } t_2 \in \gamma^T_1(j)\}.$$

[2]Recall that x and y are the two fixed (and distinct) variables admitted in GF$_2$.

$s = \alpha^r_{i,j}(s')$: $\Theta(s)$ contains a model abstraction γ for every model abstraction $\widehat{\gamma} \in \Theta(s')$ such that

(∗) for all $(t_1, M, t_2) \in \widehat{\gamma}^E(i,j)$, there is a $t \in \mathtt{TP}_2$ such that $M \cup \{r(x,y)\} \subseteq t$ and $t_1 \rightsquigarrow_t t_2$.

The model abstraction γ is defined like $\widehat{\gamma}$ except that

for all $(t_1, M, t_2) \in \widehat{\gamma}^E(i,j)$, add $r(x,y)$ to M, and
for all $(t_1, M, t_2) \in \widehat{\gamma}^E(j,i)$, add $r(y,x)$ to M.

$s = \rho_{i \to j}(s')$: for each $\widehat{\gamma} \in \Theta(s')$, $\Theta(s)$ contains the model abstraction γ defined like $\widehat{\gamma}$ except that, for $1 \le \ell \le k$,

$$\gamma^T(i) = \emptyset \qquad \gamma^E(i,\ell) = \emptyset$$
$$\gamma^T(j) = \widehat{\gamma}^T(j) \cup \widehat{\gamma}^T(i) \qquad \gamma^E(\ell,i) = \emptyset$$
$$\gamma^E(j,\ell) = \widehat{\gamma}^E(j,\ell) \cup \widehat{\gamma}^E(i,\ell)$$
$$\gamma^E(\ell,j) = \widehat{\gamma}^E(\ell,j) \cup \widehat{\gamma}^E(\ell,i).$$

The algorithm achieves the intended goal and runs within the stated time bounds.

Lemma 5. *For all subexpressions s of s_0, $\Theta(s) = \{\gamma_{\mathcal{I},\mathcal{D}_s} \mid \mathcal{I}$ model of $\mathcal{D}_s$ and $\mathcal{O}\}$.*

4 Lower Bounds

We prove that for (GF$_2$, AQ) and ($\mathcal{ALC}$, CQ), the double exponential running time in $|\mathcal{O}|$ cannot be improved unless the exponential time hypothesis (ETH) is false. The ETH states that if δ is the infimum of real numbers such that 3SAT can be solved in time $O(2^{\delta n})$, where n is the number of variables in the input formula, then $\delta > 0$. The following are the two main results of this section.

Theorem 4. *If the ETH is true, then there is no algorithm with running time $2^{2^{o(|Q|)}} \cdot \mathtt{poly}(|\mathcal{D}|)$ for OMQ evaluation in*

1. *(GF$_2$, AQ) on databases of cliquewidth 2;*
2. *($\mathcal{ALC}$, CQ) on databases of cliquewidth 3.*

Note that OMQ evaluation in (GF$_2$, AQ) and ($\mathcal{ALC}$, CQ) are only EXPTIME-complete in combined complexity on unrestricted databases. The former is folklore and the latter is proved in (Lutz 2008). Thus, Theorem 4 implies that, in these two OMQ languages, one has to pay for the running time to be polynomial in $|\mathcal{D}|$ on databases of bounded cliquewidth by an exponential increase in the running time in $|Q|$.

We now prove Theorem 4. A major contribution of the original paper bringing forward the ETH is the sparsification lemma, which implies the following useful consequence of the ETH (Impagliazzo, Paturi, and Zane 2001):

(∗) If the ETH is true, then 3SAT cannot be solved in time $2^{o(m)}$, with m the number of clauses of the input formula.

Both results in Theorem 4 are proved by contradiction against (∗), i.e. we show that an algorithm for these OMQ evaluation problems with running time $2^{2^{o(|Q|)}} \cdot \mathtt{poly}(|\mathcal{D}|)$ can be used to design an algorithm for 3SAT with running time $2^{o(m)}$, contradicting (∗). To achieve this, it suffices to give a polynomial time reduction from 3SAT to OMQ evaluation that produces an ontology of size $O(\log m)$ where m is the number of clauses in the input formula. For both points of Theorem 4, we first use a known reduction from 3SAT to LIST COLORING (Theorem 5) and then reduce LIST COLORING to OMQ evaluation. In LIST COLORING, the input is a graph in which every vertex is associated with a list of colors, and the question is whether it is possible to assign to each vertex a color from its list and obtain a valid coloring of the graph. Formally: Given an undirected graph $G = (V, E)$ and a set $C_v \subseteq \mathbb{N}$ of colors for each node $v \in V$, decide whether there is a map $f : V \to \mathbb{N}$ such that $f(v) \in C_v$ for every $v \in V$ and $f(u) \neq f(v)$ for every $\{u, v\} \in E$.

The following is proved in (Jansen 1996), Theorem 11. The graphs of cliquewidth 2 that are used in the proof are (non-disjoint) unions of two cliques.

Theorem 5. *There is a polynomial time reduction from 3SAT to LIST COLORING that turns a formula with m clauses into an instance of LIST COLORING with a connected graph of cliquewidth 2 and $O(m)$ colors.*

To prove Point 1 of Theorem 4, we reduce LIST COLORING to OMQ evaluation in (GF$_2$, AQ). To highlight the idea of the reduction, we first sketch the proof of a slightly weaker version of Point 1 of Theorem 4, namely that there is no algorithm with the stated running time on databases of cliquewidth 3 (instead of 2). Moreover, we use queries of the form $\exists x\, B(x)$ rather than AQs. As an intermediate, we consider the problem PRECOLORING EXTENSION, where the input is a number of colors k and a graph in which some nodes are already colored, and the question is whether the coloring can be extended to a k-coloring of the whole graph. Consider the following standard reduction from LIST COLORING to PRECOLORING EXTENSION (Fellows et al. 2011). For every vertex v and every color $c \notin C_v$, add a new vertex that is precolored with c and is only adjacent to v. This reduction increases the cliquewidth by at most 1, so when starting from Theorem 5, the resulting graphs have cliquewidth at most 3. It remains to reduce PRECOLORING EXTENSION to OMQ evaluation.

Without the precoloring, we may view the input graph to PRECOLORING EXTENSION as a database $\mathcal{D}$ by replacing every vertex by a constant and every edge $\{u, v\}$ by two facts $r(u, v)$ and $r(v, u)$. Let us assume that the number of colors is a power of 2, say 2^ℓ. Each of the 2^ℓ colors is assigned a unique bit string of length ℓ. Introduce concept names $A^j_1, \dots, A^j_\ell$ for $j \in \{0, 1\}$ and add the sentence $\forall x(A^0_i(x) \leftrightarrow \neg A^1_i(x))$ to the ontology $\mathcal{O}$, which says that every constant in $\mathcal{D}$ should be assigned a unique sequence of ℓ bits, representing a color. To express that adjacent vertices should be colored differently, we just have to say that their bit strings should differ in at least one place: $\forall x \forall y\, (r(x, y) \to \bigvee_{i=1}^{\ell} A^0_i(x) \leftrightarrow A^1_i(y))$. For every vertex v that is precolored by a color c, we add facts $A^j_i(v)$ that represent this color. As the query, choose $\exists x\, B(x)$ with B a fresh concept name. This query is implied if and only if $\mathcal{D}$ is not satisfiable w.r.t. $\mathcal{O}$, which is the case if and only if we started with a no-instance of PRECOLORING EXTENSION.

The following lemma improves the reduction to use only databases of cliquewidth 2 and AQs.

Lemma 6. *There is a polynomial time reduction from* LIST COLORING *on connected graphs of cliquewidth 2 to OMQ*

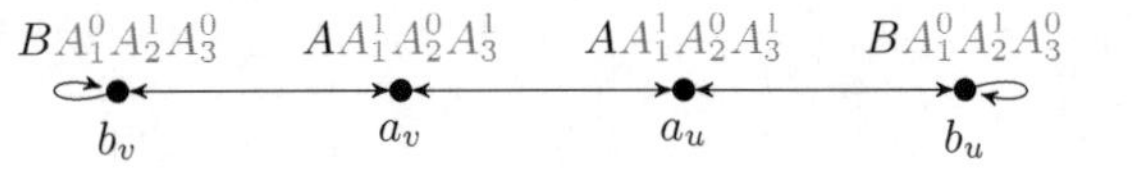

Figure 1: Black: Fragment of $\mathcal{D}$ that represents edge $\{u, v\} \in E$. Gray: Concept names that could appear in an interpretation where the coloring has a defect, for $\ell = 3$.

evaluation in $(\mathrm{GF}_2, \mathrm{AQ})$ *on databases of cliquewidth 2, where the constructed ontology is of size* $O(\log(k))$ *with* k *the number of distinct colors of the input graph.*

We are now ready to prove Point 1 of Theorem 4.

Proof. Assume for a contradiction that there is an algorithm with running time $2^{2^{o(|\mathcal{O}|)}} \cdot \texttt{poly}(|\mathcal{D}|)$ for OMQ evaluation in $(\mathrm{GF}_2, \mathrm{AQ})$ on databases of cliquewidth at most 2. Then the following is an algorithm for 3SAT. Given a formula in 3CNF with m clauses, apply the reduction from Theorem 5 followed by the one from Lemma 6. This yields an OMQ $Q \in (\mathrm{GF}_2, \mathrm{AQ})$ where the ontology $\mathcal{O}$ is of size $O(\log(m))$, a database $\mathcal{D}$ of cliquewidth 2 and an answer candidate $a \in \texttt{adom}(\mathcal{D})$. Use the algorithm for OMQ evaluation in $(\mathrm{GF}_2, \mathrm{AQ})$ whose existence we assumed on input $Q, \mathcal{D}$ and a. The running time of the first step is polynomial. The running time of the second step is $2^{2^{o(\log m)}} \cdot \texttt{poly}(|\mathcal{D}|)$, which is $2^{o(m)}$, contradicting the ETH. ❑

Interestingly, the reduction does not rely on the additional expressive power of GF_2 compared to $\mathcal{ALC}$, but rather on the ability of GF_2 to express certain statements more succinctly. To demonstrate this, we introduce the extension $\mathcal{ALC}^{=}$ of $\mathcal{ALC}$ with the following constructor:

If $A_1, \dots, A_n$ are concept names, then $\exists r.[A_1, \dots, A_n]_=$ is a concept. The semantics is defined as follows:

$$\exists r.[A_1, \dots, A_n]_=^{\mathcal{I}} = \{d \in \Delta^{\mathcal{I}} \mid \exists e \in \Delta^{\mathcal{I}} : (d, e) \in r^{\mathcal{I}} \text{ and } d \in A_i^{\mathcal{I}} \Leftrightarrow e \in A_i^{\mathcal{I}} \text{ for all } i \in \{1, \dots, n\}\}.$$

It is easy to see that the expressive power of $\mathcal{ALC}$ and of $\mathcal{ALC}^{=}$ are identical, as the additional constructor $\exists r.[A_1, \dots, A_n]_=$ can be expressed as

$$\bigsqcup_{C_1 \in \{A_1, \neg A_1\}} \cdots \bigsqcup_{C_n \in \{A_n, \neg A_n\}} (C_1 \sqcap \cdots \sqcap C_n \sqcap \exists r.(C_1 \sqcap \cdots \sqcap C_n)).$$

Note that the above concept is exponentially larger than the original one. In GF_2, in contrast, the new constructor can easily be expressed using only a linear size formula.

In the reduction used to prove Lemma 6, we may replace the GF_2 ontology by the following $\mathcal{ALC}^{=}$-ontology:

$$\begin{aligned}\mathcal{O} = &\{\exists s.[A_1, \dots, A_n]_= \sqsubseteq D\} \cup \\ &\{B \sqcap \exists r.[A_1, \dots, A_n, B]_= \sqsubseteq D\} \cup \\ &\{\exists r.D \sqsubseteq D, D \sqsubseteq \forall r.D, \exists s.D \sqsubseteq D, D \sqsubseteq \forall s.D\} \cup \\ &\{\top \sqsubseteq A_i^0 \sqcup A_i^1, A_i^0 \sqcap A_i^1 \sqsubseteq \bot \mid i \in \{1, \dots, \ell\}\}.\end{aligned}$$

Thus, Point 1 of Theorem 4 still holds if $(\mathrm{GF}_2, \mathrm{AQ})$ is replaced with $(\mathcal{ALC}^{=}, \mathrm{AQ})$.

To prove Point 2 of Theorem 4, we use a reduction that is similar to the one presented before Lemma 6. This time we are only allowed to use an $\mathcal{ALC}$ ontology, but also CQs in place of AQs, which again allows us to express succinctly that adjacent nodes have to be colored differently.

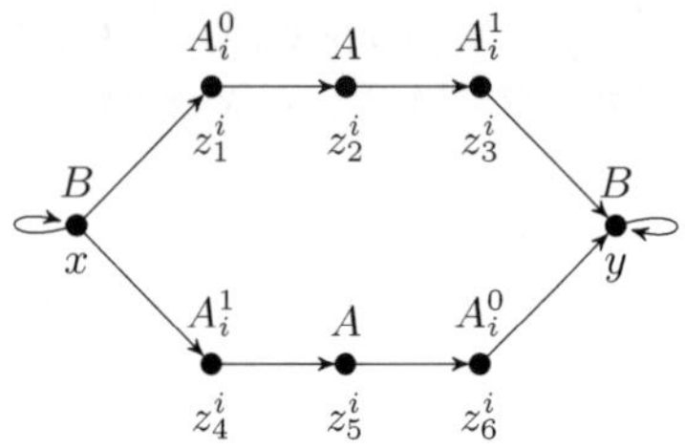

Figure 2: Gadget i of CQ q. Every edge represents an r-fact. The variables x and y are shared among gadgets.

Lemma 7. *There is a polynomial time reduction from* LIST COLORING *on connected graphs of cliquewidth 2 to OMQ evaluation in* $(\mathcal{ALC}, \mathrm{CQ})$ *on databases of cliquewidth 3, where the constructed OMQ is of size* $O(\log k)$*,* k *the number of distinct colors of the input graph.*

Proof. Let $G = (V, E)$ be an undirected graph of cliquewidth 2 and $C_v \subseteq \mathbb{N}$ a list of possible colors for every $v \in V$. We construct a database $\mathcal{D}$ of cliquewidth 3 and a Boolean OMQ $Q = (\mathcal{O}, q)$ from $(\mathcal{ALC}, \mathrm{CQ})$ such that G and C_v are a yes-instance for LIST COLORING if and only if $\mathcal{D} \not\models Q$. In contrast to what was described above, we do not carry out a reduction from LIST COLORING to PRE-COLORING EXTENSION as a separate first step, but build it directly into the main reduction. Let k be the number of distinct colors that occur, w.l.o.g. let $\bigcup_{v \in V} C_v = \{1, \dots, k\}$. Define $\ell = \lceil \log k \rceil$ and $L = \{1, \dots, 2^\ell\}$.

We use concept names A_i^j, $i \in \{1, \dots, \ell\}$ and $j \in \{0, 1\}$, another concept name B, one role name r, and constants a_v, b_v, a_v^c, and b_v^c for every $v \in V$ and $c \in L \setminus C_v$. The database is defined as

$$\begin{aligned}\mathcal{D} = &\{r(a_v, a_u), r(a_u, a_v) \mid \{u, v\} \in E\} \cup \\ &\{r(a_v, a_v^c), r(a_v^c, a_v) \mid v \in V, c \in L \setminus C_v\} \cup \\ &\{A_i^j(a_v^c) \mid v \in V, c \in L \setminus C_v \text{ and the } i\text{-th bit of } c \text{ is } j\} \cup \\ &\{r(a_v, b_v), r(b_v, a_v), r(b_v, b_v) \mid v \in V\} \cup \\ &\{r(a_v^c, b_v^c), r(b_v^c, a_v^c), r(b_v^c, b_v^c) \mid v \in V, c \in L \setminus C_v\} \cup \\ &\{A(a_v), A(a_v^c) \mid v \in V, c \in L \setminus C_v\} \cup \\ &\{B(b_v), B(b_v^c) \mid v \in V, c \in L \setminus C_v\}.\end{aligned}$$

Here, every constant a_v represents a vertex of G, and every constant a_v^c is a constant adjacent to a_v that is precolored with the color c. Furthermore, for every constant a_v (resp. a_v^c) there is a constant b_v (resp. b_v^c) such that b_v (resp. b_v^c) is adjacent only to a_v (resp. a_v^c). We refer to the b_v and b_v^c as the *copies* of a_v and a_v^c. Every copy has an r-selfloop and a unary marker B, and every non-copy has a unary marker A. Figure 1 depicts a part of the database. We argue in the appendix that $\mathcal{D}$ has cliquewidth 3.

Next, we construct the ontology, which has two purposes. First, we assign a unique color to every constant of the database. For every $i \in \{1, \dots, \ell\}$, we include the CIs $\top \sqsubseteq A_i^0 \sqcup A_i^1$ and $A_i^0 \sqcap A_i^1 \sqsubseteq \bot$. The second purpose is to assure that every copy b_v (resp. b_v^c) is colored using the anti-color of the color of a_v (resp. a_v^c). Here, the *anti-color* of a color c is the color obtained from c by flipping every bit, e.g. the anti-color of 10010 is 01101. Since the copies b_v and b_v^c carry the concept name B, this can be achieved using the following CIs for every $i \in \{1, \dots, \ell\}$ and $j \in \{0, 1\}$:

$$A \sqcap B \sqsubseteq \bot \qquad B \sqcap A_i^j \sqsubseteq \forall r.(B \sqcup A_i^{1-j}).$$

Now we construct the (Boolean) CQ q, whose purpose it is to detect a defect in the coloring. It is a union of ℓ gadgets, with gadget number i checking that the colors of two adjacent vertices agree on bit number i. We use two variables x and y, as well as variables $z_1^i, z_2^i, \dots, z_6^i$ for every $i \in \{1, \dots, \ell\}$. The variables x and y are shared between all the gadgets, whereas the variables $z_1^i, z_2^i, \dots, z_6^i$ belong to gadget number i. The i-th gadget is displayed in Figure 2. It is clear that the OMQ $(\mathcal{O}, q)$ is of size $O(\log k)$.

Claim. G and C_v are a yes-instance for LIST COLORING if and only if $\mathcal{D} \not\models Q$.

We only show the 'if' direction here as it demonstrates how the constructed CQ q can identify defects in the coloring. Let $\mathcal{I}$ be a model of $\mathcal{O}$ and $\mathcal{D}$ such that $\mathcal{I} \not\models q$. We show that G and the C_v are a yes-instance of LIST COLORING. Since $\mathcal{I}$ is a model of $\mathcal{O}$, every a_v is assigned a unique color c_v, encoded using the A_i^j. We define $f(v) = c_v$ for every $v \in V$. If any two adjacent constants a_u and a_v were colored with the same color $c = j_1 j_2 \dots j_\ell \in \{0, 1\}^\ell$, then we can construct a homomorphism h from q to $\mathcal{I}$ by $h(x) = b_v, h(y) = b_u$ and, if $j_i = 0$, then

$$h(z_1^i) = a_v, h(z_2^i) = a_u, h(z_3^i) = b_u$$
$$h(z_4^i) = b_v, h(z_5^i) = a_v, h(z_6^i) = a_u$$

and if $j_i = 1$, then

$$h(z_1^i) = b_v, h(z_2^i) = a_v, h(z_3^i) = a_u$$
$$h(z_4^i) = a_v, h(z_5^i) = a_u, h(z_6^i) = b_u .$$

Figure 1 depicts the case where $c = 101$. But we assumed that $\mathcal{I} \not\models q$, so every two adjacent a_v and a_u have different colors. Thus, f witnesses that G and the C_v are a yes-instance for LIST COLORING. ❑

With Lemma 7 at hand, the proof for Point 2 of Theorem 4 continues exactly as the proof of Point 1.

5 Bounded Treewidth

We prove two results that concern OMQ evaluation on databases of bounded treewidth, mainly to contrast with the results obtained for databases of bounded cliquewidth.

Theorem 6. *In (GF_2, AQ), an OMQ $Q = (\mathcal{O}, q)$ can be evaluated on a database $\mathcal{D}$ of treewidth k in time $2^{O(|\mathcal{O}| \cdot k^2)} \cdot |\mathcal{D}|$.*

Note that we obtain single exponential running time while Theorem 4 states that when treewidth is replaced by cliquewidth, we cannot be better than double exponential.

Theorem 7. *In (GF_2, UCQ), evaluating an OMQ $Q = (\mathcal{O}, q)$ on a database $\mathcal{D}$ of treewidth k is possible in time $2^{|\mathcal{O}| \cdot k^{O(|q| \log(|q|))}} \cdot |\mathcal{D}|$.*

Theorem 7 is relevant because we leave open the corresponding case for cliquewidth, that is, we do not even know whether OMQ evaluation in $(\mathrm{GF}_2, \mathrm{UCQ})$ on databases of bounded cliquewidth is in PTIME in data complexity. We remark that the overall running time in Theorem 7 cannot be improved to single exponential because OMQ evaluation in $(\mathcal{ALCI}, \mathrm{CQ})$ is 2EXPTIME-complete in combined complexity on databases of the form $\{A(c)\}$ (Lutz 2007).

We give a single algorithm that yields both Theorem 6 and 7. Assume that we are given as input an OMQ $Q = (\mathcal{O}, q) \in (\mathrm{GF}_2, \mathrm{UCQ})$, and a database $\mathcal{D}_0$ of treewidth k. As in the proof of Theorem 2, we may assume w.l.o.g. that Q is Boolean. In contrast to the case of cliquewidth, we do not need to assume that a tree decomposition is given as part of the input. In fact, a tree decomposition $T = (V, E, (B_v)_{v \in V})$ of $\mathcal{D}_0$ of width at most $2k + 1$ can be computed in time $2^{O(k)} \cdot |\mathtt{adom}(\mathcal{D}_0)|$ (Korhonen 2021).

Our algorithm traverses the tree decomposition T bottom-up. For every node v, we compute a representation of the models of $\mathcal{D}_v$ and $\mathcal{O}$, where $\mathcal{D}_v$ is the restriction of $\mathcal{D}_0$ to the constants that occur in the bags of the subtree of T rooted at v. Along with the representations of models, we keep track of partial homomorphisms from CQs in q to these models (we actually rewrite the query beforehand, in the style of Section 3.2). Details are in the appendix.

6 Conclusion

We leave open the interesting question whether OMQ evaluation in $(\mathrm{GF}_2, \mathrm{(U)CQ})$ on databases of bounded cliquewidth is in PTIME in data complexity. While all other OMQ languages studied in this paper are easily translated into MSO_1, this is not the case for $(\mathrm{GF}_2, \mathrm{(U)CQ})$. In fact, it is straightforward to express the problem MONOCHROMATIC TRIANGLE[3] in $(\mathrm{GF}_2, \mathrm{CQ})$ and to our knowledge it is open whether this problem can be expressed in MSO_1.

It would also be interesting to consider natural extensions of $\mathcal{ALCI}$. We believe that adding role inclusions has no impact on the obtained results. It is less clear what happens for transitive roles, number restrictions, and nominals. In the appendix, we make the following observation for the extension $\mathcal{ALCF}$ of $\mathcal{ALC}$ with (globally) functional roles.

Theorem 8. *OMQ evaluation in $(\mathcal{ALCF}, CQ)$ on databases of treewidth 2 is* CONP*-hard in data complexity if the unique name assumption is not made.*

The proof relies on an observation from (Figueira 2016). We conjecture that when the unique name assumption is made, fixed-parameter linearity is regained and can be proved using the methods in this paper.

It would also be very interesting to pursue the idea of decomposing databases into a (hopefully small) part of high cliquewidth and parts of low cliquewidth, with the aim of achieving efficiency in practical applications.

Acknowledgements

Supported by the DFG CRC 1320 EASE - Everyday Activity Science and Engineering.

[3]Can the edges of a given graph be colored with two colors without generating a monochromatic triangle?

References

Akiba, T.; Sommer, C.; and Kawarabayashi, K. 2012. Shortest-path queries for complex networks: exploiting low tree-width outside the core. In *Proc. of EDBT*, 144–155. ACM.

Baader, F.; Horrocks, I.; Lutz, C.; and Sattler, U. 2017. *An Introduction to Description Logic*. Cambridge University Press.

Bienvenu, M., and Ortiz, M. 2015. Ontology-mediated query answering with data-tractable description logics. In *Reasoning Web*, 218–307.

Bienvenu, M.; ten Cate, B.; Lutz, C.; and Wolter, F. 2014. Ontology-based data access: A study through disjunctive Datalog, CSP, and MMSNP. *ACM Transactions on Database Systems* 39(4):33:1–33:44.

Calvanese, D.; Giacomo, G. D.; Lembo, D.; Lenzerini, M.; Poggi, A.; Rodriguez-Muro, M.; and Rosati, R. 2009. Ontologies and databases: The DL-Lite approach. In *Reasoning Web*, volume 5689 of *LNCS*, 255–356.

Cormen, T. H.; Leiserson, C. E.; Rivest, R. L.; and Stein, C. 2022. *Introduction to algorithms*. MIT press.

Corneil, D. G., and Rotics, U. 2005. On the relationship between clique-width and treewidth. *SIAM Journal on Computing* 34(4):825–847.

Courcelle, B., and Engelfriet, J. 2012. *Graph Structure and Monadic Second-Order Logic - A Language-Theoretic Approach*, volume 138 of *Encyclopedia of mathematics and its applications*. Cambridge University Press.

Courcelle, B.; Makowsky, J. A.; and Rotics, U. 2000. Linear time solvable optimization problems on graphs of bounded clique-width. *Theory Comput. Syst.* 33(2):125–150.

Downey, R. G., and Fellows, M. R. 2013. *Fundamentals of parameterized complexity*, volume 4. Springer.

Fellows, M. R.; Fomin, F. V.; Lokshtanov, D.; Rosamond, F. A.; Saurabh, S.; Szeider, S.; and Thomassen, C. 2011. On the complexity of some colorful problems parameterized by treewidth. *Inf. Comput.* 209(2):143–153.

Figueira, D. 2016. Semantically acyclic conjunctive queries under functional dependencies. In *Proceedings of the 31st Annual ACM/IEEE Symposium on Logic in Computer Science*, 847–856.

Ganian, R.; Hlinený, P.; Langer, A.; Obdrzálek, J.; Rossmanith, P.; and Sikdar, S. 2014. Lower bounds on the complexity of mso_1 model-checking. *J. Comput. Syst. Sci.* 80(1):180–194.

Grädel, E. 1999. On the restraining power of guards. *J. Symb. Log.* 64(4):1719–1742.

Haga, A.; Lutz, C.; Sabellek, L.; and Wolter, F. 2021. How to approximate ontology-mediated queries. In *Proc. of KR*, 323–333.

Impagliazzo, R.; Paturi, R.; and Zane, F. 2001. Which problems have strongly exponential complexity? *J. Comput. Syst. Sci.* 63(4):512–530.

Jansen, K. 1996. Complexity results for the optimum cost chromatic partition problem. *Universität Trier, Mathematik/Informatik, Forschungsbericht* 96-41.

Korhonen, T. 2021. A single-exponential time 2-approximation algorithm for treewidth. *arXiv preprint arXiv:2104.07463*.

Kreutzer, S., and Tazari, S. 2010. Lower bounds for the complexity of monadic second-order logic. In *Proc. of LICS*, 189–198. IEEE Computer Society.

Lutz, C.; Sabellek, L.; and Schulze, L. 2022. Ontology-mediated querying on databases of bounded cliquewidth. *CoRR* abs/2205.02190.

Lutz, C. 2007. Inverse roles make conjunctive queries hard. In *Proc. of DL2007*, volume 250 of *CEUR Workshop Proceedings*. CEUR-WS.org.

Lutz, C. 2008. Two upper bounds for conjunctive query answering in SHIQ. In *Proc. of DL2008*, volume 353 of *CEUR Workshop Proceedings*. CEUR-WS.org.

Maniu, S.; Cheng, R.; and Senellart, P. 2017. An indexing framework for queries on probabilistic graphs. *ACM Trans. Database Syst.* 42(2):13:1–13:34.

Maniu, S.; Senellart, P.; and Jog, S. 2019. An experimental study of the treewidth of real-world graph data. In *Proc. of ICDT*, volume 127 of *LIPIcs*, 12:1–12:18. Schloss Dagstuhl - Leibniz-Zentrum für Informatik.

Oum, S.-I. 2008. Approximating rank-width and clique-width quickly. *ACM Transactions on Algorithms (TALG)* 5(1):1–20.

Wei, F. 2010. TEDI: efficient shortest path query answering on graphs. In *Proc. ofSIGMOD*, 99–110. ACM.

Zhou, Y.; Cuenca Grau, B.; Nenov, Y.; Kaminski, M.; and Horrocks, I. 2015. PAGOdA: Pay-as-you-go ontology query answering using a datalog reasoner. *J. Artif. Intell. Res.* 54:309–367.

Automating Reasoning with Standpoint Logic via Nested Sequents

Tim S. Lyon , Lucía Gómez Álvarez
Computational Logic Group, Faculty of Computer Science, TU Dresden
{timothy_stephen.lyon, lucia.gomez_alvarez}@tu-dresden.de

Abstract

Standpoint logic is a recently proposed formalism in the context of knowledge integration, which advocates a multi-perspective approach permitting reasoning with a selection of diverse and possibly conflicting standpoints rather than forcing their unification. In this paper, we introduce nested sequent calculi for propositional standpoint logics—proof systems that manipulate trees whose nodes are multisets of formulae—and show how to automate standpoint reasoning by means of non-deterministic proof-search algorithms. To obtain worst-case complexity-optimal proof-search, we introduce a novel technique in the context of nested sequents, referred to as *coloring*, which consists of taking a formula as input, guessing a certain coloring of its subformulae, and then running proof-search in a nested sequent calculus on the colored input. Our technique lets us decide the validity of standpoint formulae in CoNP since proof-search only produces a *partial* proof relative to each permitted coloring of the input. We show how all partial proofs can be fused together to construct a complete proof when the input is valid, and how certain partial proofs can be transformed into a counter-model when the input is invalid. These "certificates" (i.e. proofs and counter-models) serve as explanations of the (in)validity of the input.

1 Introduction

Standpoint Logic. The fact that knowledge bases (KBs) encode the standpoints of their creators (e.g. in the form of viewpoints, contextual factors or semantic commitments) is the source of well-known challenges in the area of knowledge integration. Since semantic heterogeneity between the sources is to be expected, inconsistencies may arise if we attempt to combine them into a single conflict-free conceptual model. To illustrate this, consider three KBs: C, a 'commonsense' representation of colours; H, a KB by a *house painting* business that reuses and extends C; and R, a KB that formalizes the *RYB color model*, from the fine arts tradition.

Example 1. *According to* C, *basic colours such as* `Blue` *and* `Green` *are disjoint.* H *complies with* C *and further specifies that* `Teal` *is* `Green`. *In contrast, according to* R *it is unequivocal that* `Teal` *is both* `Green` *and* `Blue`. *Generally, it is conceivable that* `Blue` *holds.*

These sources cannot be merged without the undesired effect of inconsistency, and circumventing it requires either

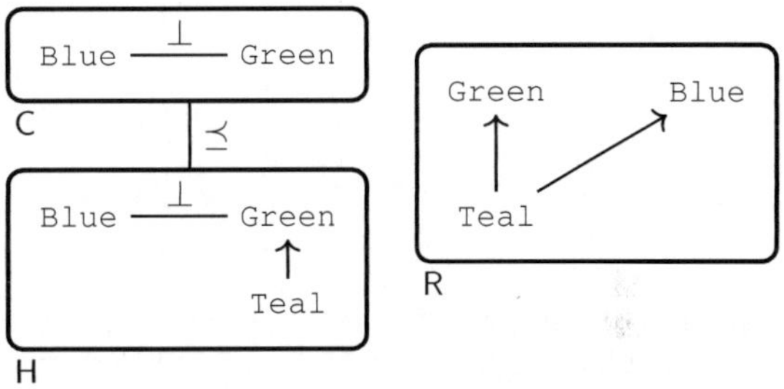

Figure 1: Diagrams of C, H and R. $\preceq$ indicates that H extends C.

knowledge weakening or duplication (Pesquita et al. 2013). Instead, one may wish to jointly reason with the KBs, treating them as alternative standpoints on a domain.

Standpoint logic (Gómez Álvarez and Rudolph 2021) is a simple multi-modal logic intended for the representation of knowledge relative to different, possibly conflicting, perspectives. The framework introduces the labeled modalities $\Box_s$ and $\Diamond_s$ for each standpoint s, where $\Box_s \varphi$ is read as "according to s, it is *unequivocal* that φ" and $\Diamond_s \varphi$ as "according to s, it is *conceivable* that φ". In addition, $s \preceq s'$ indicates that the standpoint s is *sharper* than s', that is, s complies with s' and further specifies it.

(F1) $\Box_{\mathsf{C}} \neg(\texttt{Blue} \land \texttt{Green}) \land \Box_{\mathsf{R}}(\texttt{Teal} \rightarrow (\texttt{Blue} \land \texttt{Green}))$

(F2) $(\mathsf{H} \preceq \mathsf{C})$ (F3) $\Box_{\mathsf{H}}(\texttt{Teal} \rightarrow \texttt{Green})$ (F4) $\Diamond_{*}(\texttt{Blue})$

The formulae (F1)-(F4) formalize Example 1, (illustrated in Figure 1) in propositional standpoint logic. (F1) encodes that `Blue` and `Green` are unequivocally disjoint according to standpoint C, while according to standpoint R it is unequivocal that `Teal` implies both `Blue` and `Green`. (F2) encodes that H includes the knowledge of C, and (F3) that `Teal` is `Green` according to H. Last, (F4) encodes that `Blue` holds under some interpretations by using the universal standpoint $*$, which sits atop any hierarchy of standpoints and is used to reference knowledge that is unequivocally true or conceivable among all perspectives.

In addition to representing unequivocal and conceivable facts (e.g. (F3) and (F4)), which may be relative to standpoints (e.g. (F1)), hold universally (e.g. (F4)), or establish a hierarchy of standpoints (e.g. (F2)), one may also express (in)determinate knowledge by means of the (definable) dual operators $\mathcal{I}_s$ and $\mathcal{D}_s$. The indeterminacy operator

$\mathcal{I}_s\varphi := \Diamond_s\varphi \wedge \Diamond_s\neg\varphi$ makes explicit that both φ and $\neg\varphi$ are conceivable in the context of s, thus making φ inherently indeterminate. Finally, the framework can be used to establish correspondences or bridges between the standpoints themselves. For instance, (F5) encodes that if something is `Teal` according to R, then it is `Green` for C and R.

(F5) $\Box_{\mathsf{R}}(\texttt{Teal}) \rightarrow (\Box_{\mathsf{C}}\,\texttt{Green} \wedge \Box_{\mathsf{R}}\,\texttt{Green})$

Natural reasoning tasks over multi-standpoint specifications include gathering unequivocal or undisputed knowledge, determining knowledge that is relative to a standpoint or a set of them, and contrasting the knowledge that can be inferred from different standpoints. To illustrate, let us assume $\Box_*\,\texttt{Teal}$ and examine some inferences that we can draw from this in the setting of Example 1. On the one hand, from (F5), (F3), and $\Box_*\,\texttt{Teal}$ we obtain that green is unequivocal for the three standpoints: $\Box_{\mathsf{C}}\,\texttt{Green}$, $\Box_{\mathsf{H}}\,\texttt{Green}$ and $\Box_{\mathsf{R}}\,\texttt{Green}$. On the other hand, we can infer the global indeterminacy of blue $\mathcal{I}_*\texttt{Blue}$, because (i) `Teal` holds universally, (ii) it is unequivocal for R that `Teal` implies `Blue` (F1), hence $\Diamond_*\,\texttt{Blue}$, and (iii) we know $\Box_{\mathsf{C}}\,\texttt{Green}$, which together with (F1) implies $\Box_{\mathsf{C}}\,\neg\texttt{Blue}$ and thus $\Diamond_*\,\neg\texttt{Blue}$.

Conveniently, the satisfiability problem in propositional standpoint logic is known to be NP-complete (Gómez Álvarez and Rudolph 2021), in pleasant contrast to the PSPACE-completeness normally exhibited by multi-modal epistemic logics, such as the closely related $\mathsf{KD45}_n$.[1] This result, obtained via a translation to one-variable first-order logic, makes the framework attractive in applied scenarios, and prompts our work to provide a suitable proof-theory for standpoint logic. Not only can our proof systems be leveraged to provide a proof-search procedure deciding the validity of standpoint formulae, but our proof-theoretic approach yields *witnesses*, that is, proofs of valid formulae and counter-models of invalid formulae. Such "certificates" (i.e. proofs and counter-models) possess explanatory value, and may be used, for instance, to trace the standpoints involved in a certain inference; e.g. when a global indeterminacy such as $\mathcal{I}_*\texttt{Blue}$ is inferred from a large collection of standpoints, we may want to gather the standpoints that hold contrasting views (in this case R and $\{\mathsf{H}, \mathsf{C}\}$, which can be easily extracted from a proof). Thus, our reliance on proof theory provides essential information that may be used to answer "why" a certain piece of information holds while still allowing "low" complexity reasoning.

Nested Sequents and Proof Theory. Since their inception, sequent systems—which consist of inference rules that syntactically manipulate pairs of multisets of formulae—have proven themselves fruitful in writing decision algorithms for logics (Dyckhoff 1992; Gentzen 1935a; Gentzen 1935b; Slaney 1997). A crucial feature of such systems, and their use in decidability, is the so-called *subformula property*, which a sequent system has *iff* the premise(s) of each inference rule only contain subformulae of the conclusion of the rule. (NB. Systems with the subformula property are also referred to as *analytic*.) With the goal of securing this property for proof systems for theories *beyond classical propositional logic* (e.g. the modal logics Kt and $\mathsf{S5}$), more sophisticated sequent systems extending Gentzen's original formalism were eventually proposed; e.g., see (Belnap 1982; Simpson 1994; Wansing 2002). In this paper, we employ one such extended formalism, viz. the *nested sequent formalism* (Brünnler 2009; Bull 1992; Kashima 1994; Poggiolesi 2009), which utilizes trees of multisets of formulae in deriving theorems. Such systems have proven well-suited for automated reasoning with modal and related logics, being used (for instance) in the writing of decision/proof-search algorithms (Brünnler 2009; Tiu, Ianovski, and Goré 2012) and the extraction of interpolants (Fitting and Kuznets 2015; Lyon et al. 2020).

Drawing on ideas from the *structural refinement* methodology, detailed in (Lyon 2021a) and used to provide nested sequent systems for diverse classes of modal and constructive logics (see (Lyon and van Berkel 2019; Lyon 2020; Lyon 2021b)), our first contribution in this paper is the introduction of analytic nested sequent systems (each dubbed $\mathsf{NS}(\mathcal{V})$ with $\mathcal{V}$ a certain parameter) for propositional standpoint logics (Gómez Álvarez and Rudolph 2021). For our second contribution, we exploit our nested systems to write concrete, *worst-case complexity-optimal* proof-search algorithms (deciding the validity of propositional standpoint formulae in CoNP), which apply inference rules from $\mathsf{NS}(\mathcal{V})$ *in reverse* on an input formula with the goal of building a proof thereof. Whereas typical proof-search algorithms operate deterministically and attempt to build a *complete* proof of the input, we introduce a novel technique (our third contribution) referred to as *coloring*, which performs proof-search *non-deterministically* and which only constructs a *partial* proof of the input relative to each non-deterministic choice. The technique of coloring involves first guessing a particular labeling of the subformulae of an input formula with *active* $\circ$ and *inactive* $\bullet$ labels, with the proof-search algorithm subsequently only processing data deemed active. An interesting consequence of this technique is the attainment of a CoNP proof-search algorithm as the partial proofs constructed during proof-search are at most polynomially larger than the input and only require polynomial time to compute. Moreover, in the instance where the input formula is invalid, we show how to construct a counter-model from failed proof-search, and in the instance where our input formula is valid, we provide a procedure that generates a *complete* proof witnessing the validity of the input formula by patching together all *partial* proofs (our fourth contribution).

Organization of Paper. Our paper is organized as follows: Sect. 2 presents the syntax and semantics of propositional standpoint logic. In Sect. 3, we introduce our nested sequent systems for propositional standpoint logics, proving such systems sound and concluding their completeness. In the penultimate section (Sect. 4), we introduce the method of coloring and show how to automate reasoning with standpoint logics, that is, we provide a (worst-case complexity-optimal) proof-search algorithm deciding the validity of propositional standpoint formulae in CoNP. The final section (Sect. 5) concludes the paper and discusses future work.

[1] Standpoint logic introduces sharpenings and stronger interaction axioms than $\mathsf{KD45}_n$, as discussed in (Gómez Álvarez 2020).

2 Standpoint Logic

Let us now specify the syntax of propositional standpoint logic (SL), denoted by $\mathbb{S}$.

Definition 1 (Syntax of Standpoint Logic). *Let $\mathcal{V} = \langle \mathcal{P}, \mathcal{S} \rangle$ be a* vocabulary *where $\mathcal{P}$ is a non-empty set of propositional variables and $\mathcal{S}$ is a set of standpoint symbols containing the distinguished symbol $*$, i.e. the* universal standpoint. *We define the language $\mathcal{L}_{\preceq} := \{s \preceq s' \mid s, s' \in \mathcal{S}\}$, and refer to formulae in $\mathcal{L}_{\preceq}$ as* sharpening statements. *The language $\mathcal{L}_{\mathcal{V}}$ is defined via the following grammar in BNF:*

$$\varphi ::= p \mid \neg p \mid (\varphi \vee \varphi) \mid (\varphi \wedge \varphi) \mid \Box_s \varphi \mid \Diamond_s \varphi$$

where $p \in \mathcal{P}$ and $s \in \mathcal{S}$. We also use $\top$ and $\bot$ as shorthands with the usual definitions.

Last, for $\Gamma \subseteq \mathcal{L}_{\preceq}$ and $\varphi \in \mathcal{L}_{\mathcal{V}}$, we define a standpoint implication *to be a formula of the form $\bigwedge \Gamma \rightarrow \varphi$, where $\bigwedge \Gamma$ is a conjunction of all elements of Γ, which equals $\top$ when Γ is empty.*

We make use of formulae in negation normal form as this will simplify the structures present in our nested systems and enhance the readability of our proof theory. To further simplify, we also assume w.l.o.g. that sets of sharpening statements are (1) free of cycles $s_1 \preceq s_2, \ldots, s_n \preceq s_1$ and (2) omit occurrences of $*$. Assumption (1) is permitted since any standpoint implication containing a cycle $s_1 \preceq s_2, \ldots, s_n \preceq s_1$ of standpoints is equivalent to one where the cycle is deleted and all occurrences of $s_1, \ldots, s_{n-1}$ are replaced by s_n in the formula. Regarding assumption (2), any sharpening statement with $*$ is either of the form $s \preceq *$, and is thus trivial (see Def. 4 below), or is of the form $* \preceq s$, in which case s can be systematically replaced by $*$ in a standpoint implication to obtain an equivalent one.

Definition 2 (Subformula and Size). *We define the set of* subformulae *of φ, denoted* $\text{sufo}(\varphi)$, *recursively as follows:*

- $\text{sufo}(p) := \{p\}$ *and* $\text{sufo}(\neg p) := \{\neg p\}$*;*
- $\text{sufo}(\heartsuit\psi) := \{\heartsuit\psi\} \cup \text{sufo}(\psi)$*;*
- $\text{sufo}(\psi \otimes \chi) := \{\psi \otimes \chi\} \cup \text{sufo}(\psi) \cup \text{sufo}(\chi)$.

with $\heartsuit \in \{\Diamond_s, \Box_s \mid s \in \mathcal{S}\}$ and $\otimes \in \{\vee, \wedge\}$. We say that ψ is a subformula *of φ iff $\psi \in \text{sufo}(\varphi)$, and define the* size *of a formula φ in $\mathcal{L}_{\mathcal{V}}$, denoted $|\varphi|$, to be equal to $|\text{sufo}(\varphi)|$, i.e. to the number of its subformulae.*

In what follows, we introduce the semantics of SL, defined over a structure of precisifications, which is akin to the usual structure of possible worlds. A *precisification* is a complete and consistent way in which the state of affairs can be described with a given vocabulary, and standpoints are modeled as sets of precisifications considered admissible. This strategy of modelling the variability of natural language as hyper-ambiguity is based on the theory supervaluationism (Fine 1975; Keefe and Smith 1997), which standpoint logic draws from (Gómez Álvarez and Bennett 2018; Gómez Álvarez, Bennett, and Richard-Bollans 2017).

Definition 3 (Standpoint Model). *Given a vocabulary $\mathcal{V}$, a model $\mathcal{M}$ (over $\mathcal{V}$) is a triple $\langle \Pi, \sigma, \delta \rangle$, where Π is a non-empty set of precisifications, $\sigma : \mathcal{S} \rightarrow 2^{\Pi}$, and $\delta : \mathcal{P} \rightarrow 2^{\Pi}$ with $\sigma(s) \neq \emptyset$ for all $s \in \mathcal{S}$ and $\sigma(*) = \Pi$. The set of all such models is denoted by $\mathfrak{M}_{\mathbb{S}}$.*

Definition 4 (Semantic Clauses). *Let $\Gamma \subseteq \mathcal{L}_{\preceq}$ and $\varphi, \psi \in \mathcal{L}_{\mathcal{V}}$. Moreover, let $\mathcal{M} = \langle \Pi, \sigma, \delta \rangle$ be a standpoint model with $\pi \in \Pi$. We recursively define the satisfaction of a formula on $\mathcal{M}$ at π accordingly:*

- $\mathcal{M}, \pi \models p$ *iff* $\pi \in \delta(p)$*;*
- $\mathcal{M}, \pi \models \neg p$ *iff* $\pi \notin \delta(p)$*;*
- $\mathcal{M}, \pi \models \varphi \wedge \psi$ *iff* $\mathcal{M}, \pi \models \varphi$ *and* $\mathcal{M}, \pi \models \psi$*;*
- $\mathcal{M}, \pi \models \varphi \vee \psi$ *iff* $\mathcal{M}, \pi \models \varphi$ *or* $\mathcal{M}, \pi \models \psi$*;*
- $\mathcal{M}, \pi \models \Diamond_s \varphi$ *iff for some* $\pi' \in \sigma(s)$, $\mathcal{M}, \pi' \models \varphi$*;*
- $\mathcal{M}, \pi \models \Box_s \varphi$ *iff for all* $\pi' \in \sigma(s)$, $\mathcal{M}, \pi' \models \varphi$*;*
- $\mathcal{M}, \pi \models s \preceq s'$ *iff* $\sigma(s) \subseteq \sigma(s')$*;*
- $\mathcal{M}, \pi \models \bigwedge \Gamma$ *iff* $\mathcal{M}, \pi \models s \preceq s'$ *for all* $s \preceq s' \in \Gamma$*;*
- $\mathcal{M}, \pi \models \bigwedge \Gamma \rightarrow \varphi$ *iff* $\mathcal{M}, \pi \models \bigwedge \Gamma$ *implies* $\mathcal{M}, \pi \models \varphi$*;*
- $\mathcal{M} \models \bigwedge \Gamma \rightarrow \varphi$ *iff* $\mathcal{M}, \pi \models \bigwedge \Gamma \rightarrow \varphi$ *for all* $\pi \in \Pi$.

A standpoint implication $\bigwedge \Gamma \rightarrow \varphi$ is defined to be valid *(relative to a vocabulary $\mathcal{V}$) iff it is true on each model $\mathcal{M} \in \mathfrak{M}_{\mathbb{S}}$; it is defined to be* invalid *(relative to $\mathcal{V}$) otherwise.*

For a vocabulary $\mathcal{V}$, the standpoint logic $\mathbb{S}(\mathcal{V})$ *is the set of all valid standpoint implications $\bigwedge \Gamma \rightarrow \varphi$ over $\mathfrak{M}_{\mathbb{S}}$.*

It is worth remarking that the specification of sharpening statements in a separate language (viz. $\mathcal{L}_{\preceq}$) and the above definition of satisfiability and validity contrast with the original presentation in (Gómez Álvarez and Rudolph 2021). However, this specification simplifies our treatment of sharpening statements, which previously served as atomic propositions in the language $\mathcal{L}_{\mathcal{V}}$. In fact, these statements are obsolete in extensions of the language allowing set theoretical combinations of standpoints in modalities (which is the object of current research). Moreover, in these extensions, the natural requirement of inner consistency (i.e. the non-emptiness of $\sigma(s)$, for each $s \in \mathcal{S}$) of standpoints is relaxed, which can be easily reflected in our nested sequent systems by dropping the (n_s) rule (see Fig. 2 in Section 3).

3 Nested Sequent Systems

We define a *nested sequent* (which we will also refer to as a *sequent*) to be a formula of the form $\Gamma \vdash \Delta$ with Γ and Δ defined via the following grammars in BNF:

$$\Gamma ::= s \preceq s' \mid \emptyset \mid \Gamma, \Gamma \quad \Delta ::= \Sigma \mid \Delta, (s)[\Sigma]_{\pi}$$

$$\Sigma ::= \varphi \mid \emptyset \mid \Sigma, \Sigma$$

where $s, s' \in \mathcal{S} \setminus \{*\}$, $\varphi \in \mathcal{L}_{\mathcal{V}}$, and π is among a countably infinite set of labels $\{\pi_i \mid i \in \mathbb{N} \setminus \{0\}\}$. We use Φ and Ψ (occasionally annotated) to denote nested sequents and note that we employ the use of labels as this proves useful in extracting a counter-model from failed proof-search (see Thm. 3). Moreover, each nested sequent $\Gamma \vdash \Delta$ with $\Delta = \Sigma_0, (s_1)[\Sigma_1]_{\pi_1}, \ldots, (s_n)[\Sigma_n]_{\pi_n}$ possesses a special structure; namely, the *antecedent* Γ is a set of sharpening statements of the form $s \preceq s'$, and the *consequent* Δ is a multiset encoding a tree of depth 1 whose nodes are multisets of formulae from $\mathcal{L}_{\mathcal{V}}$. The consequent Δ can be expressed graphically as follows:

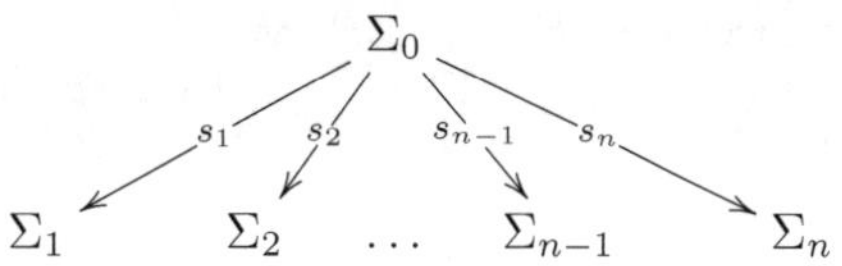

We refer to a multiset Σ_i occurring in the consequent of a nested sequent as a *component*, and note that components (along with the antecedent and consequent) are permitted to be empty $\emptyset$. Intuitively, components correspond to precisifications in a standpoint model. It is also worthwhile to define the relation $\preceq^*_\Gamma$ on standpoints as this will be used as a side condition dictating applications of certain inference rules:

Definition 5. *For a nested sequent $\Gamma \vdash \Delta$, let $\preceq^*_\Gamma \subseteq \mathcal{S} \times \mathcal{S}$ be the minimal reflexive and transitive relation such that*

- $s \preceq^*_\Gamma s'$ *for every* $s \preceq s' \in \Gamma$, *and*
- $s \preceq^*_\Gamma *$ *for every* $s \in \mathcal{S}$.

A nice feature of nested sequents is that such objects typically permit a formula translation, e.g. (Brünnler 2009; Bull 1992; Kashima 1994; Poggiolesi 2009), meaning that our logical semantics can be lifted to the language of our proof systems without introducing an extended semantics for nested sequents.

Definition 6 (Formula Interpretation)**.** *We define the* formula interpretation *of a nested sequent $\Gamma \vdash \Delta$ with $\Delta = \Sigma_0, (s_1)[\Sigma_1]_{\pi_1}, \dots, (s_n)[\Sigma_n]_{\pi_n}$ as follows:*

$$\iota(\Gamma \vdash \Delta) := \bigwedge \Gamma \rightarrow \bigvee \Sigma_0 \vee \bigvee_{1 \leq i \leq n} \Box_{s_i}(\bigvee \Sigma_i)$$

We define $\Gamma \vdash \Delta$ to be valid iff $\iota(\Gamma \vdash \Delta)$ is valid. Also, we note that $\bigwedge \emptyset = \top$ and $\bigvee \emptyset = \bot$, as usual.

A uniform presentation of our nested calculi is given in Fig. 2. We let $\mathsf{NS}(\mathcal{V})$ denote the corresponding nested sequent calculus over a vocabulary $\mathcal{V}$. Our inference rules make use of the brackets '{' and '}' in the consequent of a nested sequent to indicate that the displayed formula(e) occur in some component. In particular, given a nested sequent $\Gamma \vdash \Delta$, where Δ is of the form $\Sigma_0, (s_1)[\Sigma_1]_{\pi_1}, \dots, (s_i)[\Sigma_i]_{\pi_i}, \dots, (s_n)[\Sigma_n]_{\pi_n}$, the notation $\Gamma \vdash \Delta\{\varphi\}_{\pi_i}$ indicates that φ occurs in Σ_i; additionally, we use $\Gamma \vdash \Delta\{\varphi\}_{\pi_0}$ to indicate that φ occurs in Σ_0, i.e. the label π_0 is used to reference the multiset Σ_0 serving as the root of the tree encoded by the consequent.

To make the functionality of each rule in $\mathsf{NS}(\mathcal{V})$ precise, we explicitly state the operation performed by each rule. With the exception of the premise-free (id) rule, we explain for each rule how the *premise(s)* (the nested sequent(s) occurring above the horizontal inference line) are obtained from the *conclusion* (the nested sequent occurring below the horizontal inference line). This explanation is consistent with how the rules are applied (bottom-up) during proof-search as described in the following section. Also, in accordance with standard proof-theoretic terminology (Buss 1998; Takeuti 2013), we refer to the formula that is explicitly displayed in the conclusion of a rule as *principal*, and indicate the principal formulae in our explanation of the rules below to make this precise for the reader.

(id) A nested sequent is *initial*, and may be used to begin a derivation, so long as some component contains both p and $\neg p$ (the principal formulae);

$(\vee)$ If a component Σ_i of the conclusion contains $\varphi \vee \psi$ (the principal formula), then adding φ and ψ to Σ_i yields the premise;

$(\wedge)$ If a component Σ_i of the conclusion contains $\varphi \wedge \psi$ (the principal formula), then adding φ to Σ_i yields the left premise and adding ψ to Σ_i yields the right premise;

$(\Box_s)$ For any $s \in \mathcal{S}$, if a component Σ_i of the conclusion contains $\Box_s \varphi$ (the principal formula), then appending the consequent Δ with $(s)[\varphi]_{\pi'}$, where π' is fresh (i.e. it does not occur in the conclusion), yields the premise;

(n_s) For any $s \in \mathcal{S}$, we may append the consequent of the conclusion with $(s)[\emptyset]_{\pi'}$ to obtain the premise so long as π' is fresh;

$(\Diamond^1_s)$ For any $s \in \mathcal{S}$, if a component Σ_i of the conclusion contains $\Diamond_s \varphi$ (the principal formula), the consequent contains a nesting $(s')[\Sigma]_{\pi'}$, and $s' \preceq^*_\Gamma s$, then adding φ to the nesting $(s')[\Sigma]_{\pi'}$ yields the premise;

$(\Diamond^2_s)$ For any $s \in \mathcal{S}$, if the consequent contains a nesting of the form $(s')[\Diamond_s \varphi, \Sigma]_{\pi'}$ with $\Diamond_s \varphi$ the principal formula, and $s' \preceq^*_\Gamma s$, then adding φ to the nesting $(s')[\Diamond_s \varphi, \Sigma]_{\pi'}$ yields the premise;

$(\Diamond_*)$ If a component Σ_i of the conclusion contains $\Diamond_* \varphi$ (the principal formula), then prepending the consequent Δ with φ (i.e. adding φ to Σ_0) yields the premise.

Example 2. *Below, we provide an example of a nested sequent derivation. To minimize the width of the proof, we let φ denote $\Diamond_s \Diamond_* \neg p \vee \Box_{s'} p$.*

$$\dfrac{\dfrac{\dfrac{\dfrac{\dfrac{}{s' \preceq s \vdash \varphi, \Diamond_s \Diamond_* \neg p, \Box_{s'} p, (s')[\Diamond_* \neg p, \neg p, p]}(id)}{s' \preceq s \vdash \varphi, \Diamond_s \Diamond_* \neg p, \Box_{s'} p, (s')[\Diamond_* \neg p, p]}(\Diamond^2_*)}{s' \preceq s \vdash \varphi, \Diamond_s \Diamond_* \neg p, \Box_{s'} p, (s')[p]}(\Diamond^1_s)}{s' \preceq s \vdash \varphi, \Diamond_s \Diamond_* \neg p, \Box_{s'} p}(\Box_{s'})}{s' \preceq s \vdash \varphi}(\vee)$$

Observe that $(\Diamond^1_s)$ is applicable as $s' \preceq^*_\Gamma s$ holds due to the antecedent, and $(\Diamond^2_*)$ is applicable as $s' \preceq^*_\Gamma *$ holds by definition (see Def. 5).

We now prove that our calculi are sound (Thm. 1, building on Lem. 1), that is, that every nested sequent derivable in $\mathsf{NS}(\mathcal{V})$ is valid. We then state our completeness theorem, which is a consequence of the work in Sect. 4.

Lemma 1. *Let $\Gamma \vdash \Delta$ be a sequent, $\mathcal{M} = \langle \Pi, \sigma, \delta \rangle$ be a model with $\pi \in \Pi$, and $s, s' \in \mathcal{S}$. If $\mathcal{M}, \pi \models \bigwedge \Gamma$ and $s' \preceq^*_\Gamma s$, then $\mathcal{M}, \pi \models s' \preceq s$.*

Proof. Assume that $\mathcal{M}, \pi \models \bigwedge \Gamma$ and $s' \preceq^*_\Gamma s$ for some $s', s \in \mathcal{S}$. There are four cases to consider:

(1) $s = *$. The result is immediate as $\sigma(*) = \Pi$, and therefore, $\mathcal{M}, \pi \models s' \preceq *$ for every $s' \in \mathcal{S}$ by Def. 4.

(2) $s' \preceq s \in \Gamma$. From the assumption that $\mathcal{M}, \pi \models \bigwedge \Gamma$ it follows that $\mathcal{M}, \pi \models s' \preceq s$.

$$\frac{}{\Gamma \vdash \Delta\{p, \neg p\}_\pi} (id) \qquad \frac{\Gamma \vdash \Delta\{\varphi, \psi\}_\pi}{\Gamma \vdash \Delta\{\varphi \vee \psi\}_\pi} (\vee) \qquad \frac{\Gamma \vdash \Delta\{\varphi\}_\pi \qquad \Gamma \vdash \Delta\{\psi\}_\pi}{\Gamma \vdash \Delta\{\varphi \wedge \psi\}_\pi} (\wedge)$$

$$\frac{\Gamma \vdash \Delta\{\Box_s \varphi\}_\pi, (s)[\varphi]_{\pi'}}{\Gamma \vdash \Delta\{\Box_s \varphi\}_\pi} (\Box_s)^{\dagger_1} \qquad \frac{\Gamma \vdash \Delta, (s)[\emptyset]_{\pi'}}{\Gamma \vdash \Delta} (n_s)^{\dagger_1}$$

$$\frac{\Gamma \vdash \Delta\{\Diamond_s \varphi\}_\pi, (s')[\Sigma, \varphi]_{\pi'}}{\Gamma \vdash \Delta\{\Diamond_s \varphi\}_\pi, (s')[\Sigma]_{\pi'}} (\Diamond_s^1)^{\dagger_2} \qquad \frac{\Gamma \vdash \Delta, (s')[\Diamond_s \varphi, \varphi, \Sigma]_\pi}{\Gamma \vdash \Delta, (s')[\Diamond_s \varphi, \Sigma]_\pi} (\Diamond_s^2)^{\dagger_2} \qquad \frac{\Gamma \vdash \varphi, \Delta\{\Diamond_* \varphi\}_\pi}{\Gamma \vdash \Delta\{\Diamond_* \varphi\}_\pi} (\Diamond_*)$$

Figure 2: The nested calculus $\mathsf{NS}(\mathcal{V})$ with $\mathcal{V} = \langle \mathcal{P}, \mathcal{S} \rangle$ a vocabulary. We note that π is permitted to be any label from $\{\pi_i \mid i \in \mathbb{N} \setminus \{0\}\}$ and that $\mathsf{NS}(\mathcal{V})$ contains a copy of $(\Box_s)$, (n_s), $(\Diamond_s^1)$, and $(\Diamond_s^2)$ for each $s \in \mathcal{S}$. The side condition $\dagger_1$ stipulates that the rule is applicable only if the label π' is fresh and $\dagger_2$ stipulates that the rule is applicable only if $s' \preceq^*_\Gamma s$.

(3) $s = s'$. Then, it is trivially implied that $\mathcal{M}, \pi \models s' \preceq s$ since $\sigma(s') = \sigma(s) \subseteq \sigma(s)$ by Def. 4.

(4) There are some $s_1, \ldots, s_n \in \mathcal{S}$ such that $s' \preceq s_1, \in \Gamma$, $s_i \preceq s_{i+1} \in \Gamma$ for every $1 \leq i \leq n-1$, and $s_n \preceq s \in \Gamma$, that is, $s' \preceq^*_\Gamma s$ is obtained by transitivity on a path in $\mathcal{S}$. From this, together with the assumption that $\mathcal{M}, \pi \models \bigwedge \Gamma$, it directly follows that $\mathcal{M}, \pi \models s' \preceq s$ by Def. 4. □

Theorem 1 (Soundness)**.** *If* $\Gamma \vdash \Delta$ *is derivable in* $\mathsf{NS}(\mathcal{V})$, *then* $\Gamma \vdash \Delta$ *is valid.*

Proof. We prove the result by induction on the number of inferences in a given derivation, and assume that Δ is of the form $\Sigma_0, (s_1)[\Sigma_1], \ldots, (s_n)[\Sigma_n]$.

Base case. In the base case, our derivation consists of a single application of the (id) rule. Hence,

$$\iota(\Gamma \vdash \Delta\{p, \neg p\}_{\pi_i}) := \bigwedge \Gamma \rightarrow \bigvee \Sigma_0 \vee \bigvee_{1 \leq i \leq n} \Box_{s_i}(\bigvee \Sigma_i)$$

where $p, \neg p \in \Sigma_i$, for some $0 \leq i \leq n$. Regardless, the consequent of the implication above will be satisfied in any model $\mathcal{M}$, implying that the above implication is valid.

Inductive step. We make a case distinction based on the last rule applied, and show that if the conclusion of the rule is invalid, then at least one of the premises of the rule is invalid, that is to say, we show by contraposition that if the premise(s) is (are) valid, then the conclusion is valid. We only show the $(\Box_s)$ and $(\Diamond_s^1)$ cases as the remaining cases are simple or argued in a similar manner.

$(\Box_s)$. We assume that Σ_1 is of the form $\Box_s \varphi, \Sigma_1'$ with $\Box_s \varphi$ principal; all remaining cases are similar. Furthermore, let us suppose that $\iota(\Gamma \vdash \Delta\{\Box_s \varphi\}_{\pi_1}) :=$

$$\bigwedge \Gamma \rightarrow \bigvee \Sigma_0 \vee \Box_{s_1}(\Box_s \varphi \vee \bigvee \Sigma_1') \vee \bigvee_{2 \leq i \leq n} \Box_{s_i}(\bigvee \Sigma_i)$$

is invalid. Then, $\mathcal{M}, \pi \not\models \Box_{s_1}(\Box_s \varphi \vee \bigvee \Sigma_1')$ for some standpoint model $\mathcal{M} := \langle \Pi, \sigma, \delta \rangle$ with a precisification π. Hence, there exists a precisification $\pi' \in \sigma(s_1)$ such that $\mathcal{M}, \pi' \not\models \Box_s \varphi$, implying that there exists a precisification $\pi'' \in \sigma(s)$ such that $\mathcal{M}, \pi'' \not\models \varphi$. It thus follows that $\mathcal{M}, \pi \not\models \Box_s \varphi$, showing that the premise of $(\Box_s)$ is invalid.

$(\Diamond_s^1)$. Suppose that Σ_1 is of the form $\Diamond_s \varphi, \Sigma_1'$ with $\Diamond_s \varphi$ principal; all remaining cases are argued in a similar fashion. Assume that $s' \preceq^*_\Gamma s$ holds and that the following is invalid:

$$\iota(\Gamma \vdash \Delta\{\Diamond_s \varphi\}_\pi, (s')[\Sigma]_{\pi'}) := \bigwedge \Gamma \rightarrow \bigvee \Sigma_0 \vee$$

$$\Box_{s_1}(\Diamond_s \varphi \vee \bigvee \Sigma_1') \vee \Big(\bigvee_{2 \leq i \leq n} \Box_{s_i}(\bigvee \Sigma_i) \Big) \vee \Box_{s'}(\bigvee \Sigma)$$

Therefore, there is a standpoint model $\mathcal{M} := \langle \Pi, \sigma, \delta \rangle$ with $\pi \in \Pi$ such that $\mathcal{M}, \pi \not\models \Box_{s'}(\bigvee \Sigma)$ and $\mathcal{M}, \pi \not\models \Box_{s_1}(\Diamond_s \varphi \vee \bigvee \Sigma_1')$, and such that $\sigma(s') \subseteq \sigma(s)$, by $s' \preceq^*_\Gamma s$ and Lem. 1. This entails that there exists a precisification $\pi' \in \sigma(s')$ such that $\mathcal{M}, \pi' \not\models \bigvee \Sigma$, and that there exists a precisification $\pi_1 \in \sigma(s_1)$ such that $\mathcal{M}, \pi_1 \not\models \Diamond_s \varphi$. The latter further implies that for every precisification in $\sigma(s)$, and thus for π' (since $\pi' \in \sigma(s') \subseteq \sigma(s)$), that $\mathcal{M}, \pi' \not\models \varphi$. Thus, the premise has been shown invalid. □

Theorem 2 (Completeness)**.** *If* $\Gamma \vdash \Delta$ *is valid, then* $\Gamma \vdash \Delta$ *is provable in* $\mathsf{NS}(\mathcal{V})$.

Proof. The theorem follows from the correct (Thm. 3) and terminating (Thm. 4) proof-search procedure given in the subsequent section (Sect. 4). □

4 Automating Standpoint Logic via Proof-Search

We now employ our nested calculi in an algorithm that decides the validity of formulae for propositional standpoint logics. In particular, we design a proof-search algorithm (see Alg. 1 below) which takes a vocabulary $\mathcal{V}$ as a parameter and bottom-up applies rules from $\mathsf{NS}(\mathcal{V})$ in attempt to construct a proof of a given input sequent $\Gamma \vdash \varphi$. We may make the simplifying assumption that our proof-search algorithm only receives inputs of the form $\Gamma \vdash \varphi$ as any nested sequent $\Gamma \vdash \Delta$ with $\Delta = \Sigma_0, (s_1)[\Sigma_1], \ldots, (s_n)[\Sigma_n]$ is valid *iff* $\iota(\Gamma \vdash \Delta)$ is valid *iff* $\Gamma \vdash \varphi$ is valid, where $\varphi = \bigvee \Sigma_0 \vee \Box_{s_1}(\bigvee \Sigma_1) \vee \cdots \vee \Box_{s_n}(\bigvee \Sigma_n)$.

To decrease the complexity of proof-search and obtain (worst-case) complexity-optimality, we introduce a new technique in the context of nested sequents which we refer to as *coloring*. In essence, given the input $\Gamma \vdash \varphi$, the first step of proof-search guesses a *proper coloring* of the formula φ, that is, it labels the formula's subformulae with either an *active* label $\circ$ or an *inactive* label $\bullet$ in a particular manner. Recall that, due to the $(\wedge)$ rule, a proof in $\mathsf{NS}(\mathcal{V})$ has the structure of a binary tree, thus giving rise to the possibility

Algorithm 1: $\texttt{Prove}_{\mathcal{V}}$

Input: A Nested Sequent: $\Gamma \vdash \varphi$
Output: A Boolean: True, False
1 Choose a proper coloring $\widetilde{\varphi}$ of φ;
2 **return** $\texttt{ProofSearch}_{\mathcal{V}}(\Gamma \vdash \widetilde{\varphi})$;

that proof-search is exponential; therefore, our proof-search algorithm uses the aforementioned labels to only generate a single path in this binary tree relative to each coloring, which yields a worst-case complexity-optimal proof-search procedure in CoNP (for the validity problem of $\mathbb{S}(\mathcal{V})$).

Definition 7 (Coloring)**.** *We define a* colored formula *to be a formula generated via the following grammar in BNF:*

$$\widetilde{\varphi} ::= p^* \mid \neg p^* \mid (\widetilde{\varphi} \vee \widetilde{\varphi})^* \mid (\widetilde{\varphi} \wedge \widetilde{\varphi})^* \mid (\Diamond_s \widetilde{\varphi})^* \mid (\Box_s \widetilde{\varphi})^*$$

with $* \in \{\circ, \bullet\}$*. For any colored formula* $\widetilde{\varphi}$*, we let* φ *be the formula in* $\mathcal{L}_{\mathcal{V}}$ *obtained by removing all labels* $\circ$ *and* $\bullet$ *from* $\widetilde{\varphi}$*. A formula* $\widetilde{\varphi}$ *is* properly colored *iff* $\widetilde{\varphi} = f_{\circ}(\varphi)$*, where the non-deterministic* coloring function $f_{\circ}$ *and* $f_{\bullet}$ *are defined accordingly with* $* \in \{\circ, \bullet\}$*:*

- $f_*(p) = p^*$
- $f_*(\neg p) = \neg p^*$
- $f_*(\varphi \vee \psi) = (f_*(\varphi) \vee f_*(\psi))^*$
- $f_{\circ}(\varphi \wedge \psi) \in \{(f_{\circ}(\varphi) \wedge f_{\bullet}(\psi))^{\circ}, (f_{\bullet}(\varphi) \wedge f_{\circ}(\psi))^{\circ}\}$
- $f_{\bullet}(\varphi \wedge \psi) = (f_{\bullet}(\varphi) \wedge f_{\bullet}(\psi))^{\bullet}$
- $f_*(\Diamond_s \varphi) = (\Diamond_s f_*(\varphi))^*$
- $f_*(\Box_s \varphi) = (\Box_s f_*(\varphi))^*$

We define $\mathrm{pcs}(\varphi)$ *to be the set of all proper colorings of* φ*, and define a* colored nested sequent *to be a nested sequent that uses colored formulae as opposed to formulae from* $\mathcal{L}_{\mathcal{V}}$*.*

We now stipulate our *saturation conditions.* When such conditions are unsatisfied during proof-search it signals that certain inference rules still need to be applied bottom-up. Alternatively, once all such conditions are satisfied this signals that proof-search ought to terminate.

Definition 8 (Saturation Conditions)**.** *A colored nested sequent* $\Gamma \vdash \Sigma_0, (s_1)[\Sigma_1]_{\pi_1}, \dots, (s_n)[\Sigma_1]_{\pi_n}$ *is* saturated *iff for every* $i \in \{0, \dots, n\}$ *it satisfies the following conditions:*

id *If* $p^{\circ} \in \Sigma_i$*, then* $\neg p^{\circ} \notin \Sigma_i$*;*

$\vee$ *if* $(\widetilde{\varphi} \vee \widetilde{\psi})^{\circ} \in \Sigma_i$*, then* $\widetilde{\varphi}^{\circ}, \widetilde{\psi}^{\circ} \in \Sigma_i$*;*

$\wedge$ *if* $(\widetilde{\varphi} \wedge \widetilde{\psi})^{\circ} \in \Sigma_i$*, then either* $\widetilde{\varphi}^{\circ} \in \Sigma_i$ *or* $\widetilde{\psi}^{\circ} \in \Sigma_i$*;*

$\Diamond_s$ *if* $(\Diamond_s \widetilde{\varphi})^{\circ} \in \Sigma_i$ *and* $s' \preceq^*_{\Gamma} s$*, then for each* $j \in \{1, \dots, n\}$ *such that* $s_j = s'$*,* $\widetilde{\varphi}^{\circ} \in \Sigma_j$*;*

$\Diamond_*$ *if* $(\Diamond_* \widetilde{\varphi})^{\circ} \in \Sigma_i$*, then* $\widetilde{\varphi}^{\circ} \in \Sigma_0$*;*

$\Box_s$ *if* $(\Box_s \widetilde{\varphi})^{\circ} \in \Sigma_i$*, then for some* $j \in \{1, \dots, n\}$*,* $s_j = s$*, and* $\widetilde{\varphi}^{\circ} \in \Sigma_j$*;*

n_s *for each* $s \in \mathcal{S}$*, there exists a* $j \in \{1, \dots, n\}$ *such that* $s_j = s$*.*

Let us comment on the functionality of our (non-deterministic) proof-search algorithm $\texttt{Prove}_{\mathcal{V}}$ (Alg. 1), which takes $\texttt{ProofSearch}_{\mathcal{V}}$ (Alg. 2) as a subroutine. (NB. Alg. 2 is split between this page and the next due to its length.) As mentioned above, given an input $\Gamma \vdash \varphi$, the algorithm $\texttt{Prove}_{\mathcal{V}}$ guesses a proper coloring $\widetilde{\varphi}$ of φ, and then returns the value of $\texttt{ProofSearch}_{\mathcal{V}}(\Gamma \vdash \widetilde{\varphi})$. We note that $\texttt{ProofSearch}_{\mathcal{V}}$ applies the rules from $\mathsf{NS}(\mathcal{V})$ in a bottom-up manner (each corresponding to a recursive call of the algorithm with the exception of (id)). The application of each rule is as follows: (id) corresponds to lines 1–3, $(\vee)$ to lines 7–11, $(\wedge)$ to lines 12–16 and 17–21, that respectively yields the left and right premises of $(\wedge)$, $(\Diamond^1_s)$ and $(\Diamond^2_s)$ to lines 22–25, $(\Diamond_*)$ to lines 26–29, $(\Box_s)$ to lines 30–33, and (n_s) to lines 34–37.

Algorithm 2: $\texttt{ProofSearch}_{\mathcal{V}}$ (Part I)

Input: A Colored Nested Sequent:
$\Phi := \Gamma \vdash \Sigma_0, (s_1)[\Sigma_1]_{\pi_1}, \dots, (s_n)[\Sigma_n]_{\pi_n}$
Output: A Boolean: True, False
1 **if** *for some* $0 \leq i \leq n$, $p^{\circ}, \neg p^{\circ} \in \Sigma_i$ **then**
2 | **return** True;
3 **end**
4 **if** Σ *is saturated* **then**
5 | **return** False;
6 **end**
7 **if** *for some* $0 \leq i \leq n$, $(\widetilde{\varphi} \vee \widetilde{\psi})^{\circ} \in \Sigma_i$*, but* $\widetilde{\varphi}, \widetilde{\psi} \notin \Sigma_i$ **then**
8 | Let $\Sigma'_i := \Sigma_i, \widetilde{\varphi}, \widetilde{\psi}$;
9 | Let $\Phi' := \Gamma \vdash \Sigma_0, \dots, (s_i)[\Sigma'_i]_{\pi_i}, \dots, (s_n)[\Sigma_n]_{\pi_n}$;
| // Replace Σ_i by Σ'_i to obtain Φ'.
10 | **return** $\texttt{Prove}_{\mathcal{V}}(\Phi')$;
11 **end**
12 **if** *for some* $0 \leq i \leq n$, $(\widetilde{\varphi}^{\circ} \wedge \widetilde{\psi}^{\bullet})^{\circ} \in \Sigma_i$*, but* $\widetilde{\varphi}^{\circ} \notin \Sigma_i$ **then**
13 | Let $\Sigma'_i := \Sigma_i, \widetilde{\varphi}^{\circ}$;
14 | Let $\Phi' := \Gamma \vdash \Sigma_0, \dots, (s_i)[\Sigma'_i]_{\pi_i}, \dots, (s_n)[\Sigma_n]_{\pi_n}$;
| // Replace Σ_i by Σ'_i to obtain Φ'.
15 | **return** $\texttt{Prove}_{\mathcal{V}}(\Phi')$
16 **end**
17 **if** *for some* $0 \leq i \leq n$, $(\widetilde{\varphi}^{\bullet} \wedge \widetilde{\psi}^{\circ})^{\circ} \in \Sigma_i$*, but* $\widetilde{\psi}^{\circ} \notin \Sigma_i$ **then**
18 | Let $\Sigma'_i := \Sigma_i, \widetilde{\psi}^{\circ}$;
19 | Let $\Phi' := \Gamma \vdash \Sigma_0, \dots, (s_i)[\Sigma'_i]_{\pi_i}, \dots, (s_n)[\Sigma_n]_{\pi_n}$;
| // Replace Σ_i by Σ'_i to obtain Φ'.
20 | **return** $\texttt{Prove}_{\mathcal{V}}(\Phi')$
21 **end**

Moreover, $\texttt{ProofSearch}_{\mathcal{V}}$ contrasts with typical proof-search algorithms in that it utilizes the active and inactive labels $\circ$ and $\bullet$ in $\widetilde{\varphi}$ to guide its computation and only constructs *a single thread* of the proof.[2] In other words, if a nested sequent $\Gamma \vdash \varphi$ is derivable in $\mathsf{NS}(\mathcal{V})$, then the sequent has a proof in $\mathsf{NS}(\mathcal{V})$ such that $\texttt{ProofSearch}_{\mathcal{V}}$ generates each thread of the proof relative to each proper coloring of φ; as argued in the lemma below, all such threads may be 'zipped' together to reconstruct a full proof of $\Gamma \vdash \varphi$ in

[2] A *thread* in a proof is defined in the usual fashion as a path of sequents from the conclusion of the proof to an initial sequent (cf. (Takeuti 2013, p. 14)).

$\mathsf{NS}(\mathcal{V})$. In this way, our proof-search algorithm may be used to construct certificates witnessing the validity (by means of a proof in $\mathsf{NS}(\mathcal{V})$) or invalidity (by means of a counter-model) of any input $\Gamma \vdash \varphi$ (see Thm. 3 below for details).

Lemma 2. *Let $\Gamma \vdash \varphi$ be a sequent and $\mathrm{pcs}(\varphi)$ the (finite) set of proper colorings of φ. If $\mathtt{ProofSearch}_{\mathcal{V}}(\Gamma \vdash \widetilde{\varphi}) = \mathtt{True}$ for all $\widetilde{\varphi} \in \mathrm{pcs}(\varphi)$, then there is a proof of $\Gamma \vdash \varphi$ in $\mathsf{NS}(\mathcal{V})$.*

Proof. Assume that $\mathtt{ProofSearch}_{\mathcal{V}}(\Gamma \vdash \widetilde{\varphi}) = \mathtt{True}$ for every $\widetilde{\varphi} \in \mathrm{pcs}(\varphi)$, and the following thread of colored nested sequents is generated during its execution:

$$T(\widetilde{\varphi}) := \Gamma \vdash \Delta_0, \dots, \Gamma \vdash \Delta_h$$

such that $\Delta_0 = \widetilde{\varphi}$ and $\Gamma \vdash \Delta_h$ is an instance of (id) (by lines 1–3). Let $\mathcal{T}$ be the set of all such threads.

For a thread $\Gamma \vdash \Delta_0, \dots, \Gamma \vdash \Delta_h \in \mathcal{T}$ and $0 \leq k \leq h$, the colored nested sequent $\Gamma \vdash \Delta_k$ is:

- *left conjunctive iff* $\Gamma \vdash \Delta_{k+1}$ is obtained from $\Gamma \vdash \Delta_k$ by applying $(\wedge)$ yielding the left premise (lines 12–16), and
- *right conjunctive iff* $\Gamma \vdash \Delta_{k+1}$ is obtained from $\Gamma \vdash \Delta_k$ by applying $(\wedge)$ yielding the right premise (lines 17–21).

A colored nested sequent is *conjunctive iff* it is left or right conjunctive. We now explain how our threads may be transformed into a proof of $\Gamma \vdash \varphi$ in $\mathsf{NS}(\mathcal{V})$.

We assume w.l.o.g. that the initial segments of all threads up to and including the first conjunctive sequent $\Gamma \vdash \Delta_k$ are identical (i.e. we assume that the subroutine $\mathtt{ProofSearch}_{\mathcal{V}}$ executes in a deterministic fashion). Hence, we may form the 'pseudo-derivation' shown below left, by making use of the first k sequents of any given thread, where the rules $(r_1), \dots, (r_{k-1})$ are determined on the basis of which lines of $\mathtt{ProofSearch}_{\mathcal{V}}$ were executed.

$\dfrac{\dfrac{\Gamma \vdash \Delta_k}{\vdots}\,(r_{k-1})}{\Gamma \vdash \varphi}\,(r_1)$	$\dfrac{\dfrac{\dfrac{\Gamma \vdash \Delta^l_{k+1} \qquad \Gamma \vdash \Delta^r_{k+1}}{\Gamma \vdash \Delta_k}\,(\wedge)}{\vdots}\,(r_{k-1})}{\Gamma \vdash \varphi}\,(r_1)$

Let us define $T^k(\widetilde{\varphi}) := \Gamma \vdash \Delta_{k+1}, \dots, \Gamma \vdash \Delta_h$ to be the tail of a thread $T(\widetilde{\varphi})$ starting from $k+1$. Since the kth colored nested sequent of every thread is conjunctive, we may generate two sets of threads $\mathcal{T}_L$ and $\mathcal{T}_R$ from $\mathcal{T}$:

$$\mathcal{T}_L := \{T^k(\widetilde{\varphi}) \mid \Gamma \vdash \Delta_k \in T(\widetilde{\varphi}) \text{ is left conjunctive}\}$$

$$\mathcal{T}_R := \{T^k(\widetilde{\varphi}) \mid \Gamma \vdash \Delta_k \in T(\widetilde{\varphi}) \text{ is right conjunctive}\}$$

We now extend the 'pseudo-derivation' shown above left, with a bottom-up application of $(\wedge)$ to obtain the 'pseudo-derivation' shown above right, where $\Gamma \vdash \Delta^l_{k+1}$ and $\Gamma \vdash \Delta^r_{k+1}$ are the initial elements of each thread $\mathcal{T}_L$ and $\mathcal{T}_R$, respectively. By successively repeating the above described process over $\mathcal{T}_L$ and $\mathcal{T}_R$, a proof in $\mathsf{NS}(\mathcal{V})$ will eventually be built above $\Gamma \vdash \Delta^l_{k+1}$ and $\Gamma \vdash \Delta^r_{k+1}$, giving a proof of $\Gamma \vdash \varphi$ in $\mathsf{NS}(\mathcal{V})$. □

Example 3. *To illustrate the procedure in Lem. 2 above, we provide an example of the proof construction process of $\emptyset \vdash \varphi$ with $\varphi := \Box_s(p \vee (\neg p \wedge \neg p)) \wedge \Diamond_s(q \vee \neg q)$. First, observe that φ has three proper colorings, given below:*

Algorithm 2: $\mathtt{ProofSearch}_{\mathcal{V}}$ (Part II)

22 **if** *for some* $0 \leq i \leq n$, $(\Diamond_s \widetilde{\varphi})^\circ \in \Sigma_i$ *and* $s' \preceq^*_\Gamma s$, *and for some* $1 \leq j \leq n$, $s_j = s'$, *but* $\widetilde{\varphi} \notin \Sigma_j$ **then**
23   Let $\Phi' := \Gamma \vdash \Sigma_0, \dots, (s_j)[\Sigma_j, \widetilde{\varphi}]_{\pi_j}, \dots, (s_n)[\Sigma_n]_{\pi_n}$;
    // Add $\widetilde{\varphi}$ to the jth nesting to obtain Φ'.
24   **return** $\mathtt{Prove}_{\mathcal{V}}(\Phi')$;
25 **end**
26 **if** *for some* $0 \leq i \leq n$, $(\Diamond_* \widetilde{\varphi})^\circ \in \Sigma_i$, *but* $\widetilde{\varphi} \notin \Sigma_0$ **then**
27   Let $\Phi' := \Gamma \vdash \widetilde{\varphi}, \Sigma_0, (s_1)[\Sigma_1]_{\pi_1}, \dots, (s_n)[\Sigma_n]_{\pi_n}$;
    // Add $\widetilde{\varphi}$ to the 0th component to obtain Φ'.
28   **return** $\mathtt{Prove}_{\mathcal{V}}(\Phi')$;
29 **end**
30 **if** *for some* $0 \leq i \leq n$, $(\Box_s \widetilde{\varphi})^\circ \in \Sigma_i$, *but for each* $1 \leq j \leq n$ *such that* $s_j = s$, $\widetilde{\varphi} \notin \Sigma_j$ **then**
31   Let $\Sigma' := \Gamma \vdash \Sigma_0, \dots, (s_n)[\Sigma_n]_{\pi_n}, (s)[\widetilde{\varphi}]_{\pi_{n+1}}$;
    // Append $(s)[\widetilde{\varphi}]_{\pi_{n+1}}$ to obtain Φ' with π_{n+1} fresh.
32   **return** $\mathtt{Prove}_{\mathcal{V}}(\Phi')$;
33 **end**
34 **if** *for some* $s \in \mathcal{S}$ *there does not exist a* $1 \leq j \leq n$ *such that* $s_j = s$ **then**
35   Let $\Phi' := \Gamma \vdash \Sigma_0, \dots, (s_n)[\Sigma_n]_{\pi_n}, (s)[\emptyset]_{\pi_{n+1}}$;
    // Append $(s)[\emptyset]_{\pi_{n+1}}$ to obtain Φ' with π_{n+1} fresh.
36   **return** $\mathtt{Prove}_{\mathcal{V}}(\Phi')$;
37 **end**

$$\widetilde{\varphi}^1 := ((\Box_s(p^\circ \vee (\neg p^\circ \wedge \neg p^\bullet)^\circ)^\circ)^\circ \wedge (\Diamond_s(q^\bullet \vee \neg q^\bullet)^\bullet)^\bullet)^\circ$$
$$\widetilde{\varphi}^2 := ((\Box_s(p^\circ \vee (\neg p^\bullet \wedge \neg p^\circ)^\circ)^\circ)^\circ \wedge (\Diamond_s(q^\bullet \vee \neg q^\bullet)^\bullet)^\bullet)^\circ$$
$$\widetilde{\varphi}^3 := ((\Box_s(p^\bullet \vee (\neg p^\bullet \wedge \neg p^\bullet)^\bullet)^\bullet)^\bullet \wedge (\Diamond_s(q^\circ \vee \neg q^\circ)^\circ)^\circ)^\circ$$

Each proper coloring $\widetilde{\varphi}^i$ with $i \in \{1,2,3\}$ gives rise to a corresponding thread $T(i)$ (shown at the top of Fig. 3) when $\mathtt{ProofSearch}_{\mathcal{V}}(\emptyset \vdash \widetilde{\varphi}^i)$ is run. Note that in the figure we have omitted the active and inactive labels, as well as labels of the form π_i, from each thread $T(i)$ to improve readability, and each application of $(\wedge)$ is emphasized with a dashed inference line. By making use of the proof construction process described in Lem. 2, the three threads $T(1)$, $T(2)$, and $T(3)$ can be fused together to generate a proof of $\emptyset \vdash \varphi$ shown at the bottom of Fig. 3.

Theorem 3 (Correctness). *Let $\Gamma \vdash \varphi$ be a sequent.*

1. *If $\mathtt{ProofSearch}_{\mathcal{V}}(\Gamma \vdash \widetilde{\varphi}) = \mathtt{True}$ for all proper colorings of φ, then a proof in $\mathsf{NS}(\mathcal{V})$ may be constructed witnessing that $\Gamma \vdash \varphi$ is valid.*
2. *If $\mathtt{ProofSearch}_{\mathcal{V}}(\Gamma \vdash \widetilde{\varphi}) = \mathtt{False}$ for some proper coloring of φ, then a counter-model may be constructed witnessing that $\Gamma \vdash \varphi$ is invalid.*

Proof. The first claim follows by Lem. 2 and the soundness of each nested calculus (see Thm. 1); therefore, we focus on

$T(1) :=$

$$\begin{array}{c} \hline \emptyset \vdash \varphi, \psi_0, (s)[\psi_1, p, \neg p, \psi_2] \quad (id) \\ \hdashline \emptyset \vdash \varphi, \psi_0, (s)[\psi_1, p, \neg p \wedge \neg p] \quad (\wedge) \\ \hline \emptyset \vdash \varphi, \psi_0, (s)[p \vee (\neg p \wedge \neg p)] \quad (\vee) \\ \hline \emptyset \vdash \varphi, \Box_s(p \vee (\neg p \wedge \neg p)) \quad (\Box_s) \\ \hdashline \emptyset \vdash \varphi \quad (\wedge) \end{array}$$

$T(2) :=$

$$\begin{array}{c} \hline \emptyset \vdash \varphi, \psi_0, (s)[\psi_1, p, \neg p, \psi_2] \quad (id) \\ \hdashline \emptyset \vdash \varphi, \psi_0, (s)[\psi_1, p, \neg p \wedge \neg p] \quad (\wedge) \\ \hline \emptyset \vdash \varphi, \psi_0, (s)[p \vee (\neg p \wedge \neg p)] \quad (\vee) \\ \hline \emptyset \vdash \varphi, \Box_s(p \vee (\neg p \wedge \neg p)) \quad (\Box_s) \\ \hdashline \emptyset \vdash \varphi \quad (\wedge) \end{array}$$

$T(3) :=$

$$\begin{array}{c} \hline \emptyset \vdash \varphi, \Diamond_s(q \vee \neg q), (s)[\psi_3, q, \neg q] \quad (id) \\ \hline \emptyset \vdash \varphi, \Diamond_s(q \vee \neg q), (s)[q \vee \neg q] \quad (\vee) \\ \hline \emptyset \vdash \varphi, \Diamond_s(q \vee \neg q), (s)[\emptyset] \quad (\Diamond_s) \\ \hline \emptyset \vdash \varphi, \Diamond_s(q \vee \neg q) \quad (n_s) \\ \hdashline \emptyset \vdash \varphi \quad (\wedge) \end{array}$$

$$\dfrac{\dfrac{\dfrac{\dfrac{\dfrac{}{\emptyset \vdash \varphi, \psi_0, (s)[\psi_1, p, \neg p, \psi_2]}(id) \quad \dfrac{}{\emptyset \vdash \varphi, \psi_0, (s)[\psi_1, p, \neg p, \psi_2]}(id)}{\emptyset \vdash \varphi, \psi_0, (s)[\psi_1, p, \neg p \wedge \neg p]}(\wedge)}{\emptyset \vdash \varphi, \psi_0, (s)[p \vee (\neg p \wedge \neg p)]}(\vee)}{\emptyset \vdash \varphi, \Box_s(p \vee (\neg p \wedge \neg p))}(\Box_s) \quad \dfrac{\dfrac{\dfrac{\dfrac{}{\emptyset \vdash \varphi, \Diamond_s(q \vee \neg q), (s)[\psi_3, q, \neg q]}(id)}{\emptyset \vdash \varphi, \Diamond_s(q \vee \neg q), (s)[q \vee \neg q]}(\vee)}{\emptyset \vdash \varphi, \Diamond_s(q \vee \neg q), (s)[\emptyset]}(\Diamond_s)}{\emptyset \vdash \varphi, \Diamond_s(q \vee \neg q)}(n_s)}{\emptyset \vdash \varphi}(\wedge)$$

Figure 3: An example of how the threads $T(1)$, $T(2)$, and $T(3)$ may be 'zipped' together to construct the derivation shown above bottom. Note that $\varphi := \Box_s(p \vee (\neg p \wedge \neg p)) \wedge \Diamond_s(q \vee \neg q)$, $\psi_0 := \Box_s(p \vee (\neg p \wedge \neg p))$, $\psi_1 := p \vee (\neg p \wedge \neg p)$, $\psi_2 := \neg p \wedge \neg p$, and $\psi_3 := q \vee \neg q$.

the second claim. Suppose that $\texttt{ProofSearch}_{\mathcal{V}}(\Gamma \vdash \widetilde{\varphi}) = \texttt{False}$ for some chosen proper coloring of φ. Then, $\texttt{ProofSearch}_{\mathcal{V}}$ generates a saturated nested sequent $\Gamma \vdash \Delta$ with Δ of the form $\Sigma_0, (s_1)[\Sigma_1]_{\pi_1}, \ldots, (s_n)[\Sigma_n]_{\pi_n}$. We will use $\Gamma \vdash \Delta$ to construct a counter-model for $\Gamma \vdash \varphi$, thus proving the second claim. Let us define $\mathcal{M} := \langle \Pi, \sigma, \delta \rangle$ as:

- $\Pi := \{\pi_0, \pi_1, \ldots, \pi_n\}$;
- $\sigma(*) := \Pi$ and for each $s \in \mathcal{S} \setminus \{*\}$, we define $\sigma(s)$:
  (i) $\pi_i \in \sigma(s)$ for each $i \in \{1, \ldots, n\}$ such that $s_i = s$, and
  (ii) $\pi_j \in \sigma(s)$ for each $\pi_j \in \sigma(s')$ such that $s' \preceq^*_\Gamma s$;
- $\delta(p) := \{\pi_i \mid p^\circ \notin \Sigma_i\}$.

We know that the recursive definition of σ will eventually terminate since $\mathcal{S}$ is finite.

Let us now prove that $\mathcal{M}$ is indeed a standpoint model; afterward, we will show that $\mathcal{M}, \pi_0 \not\models \iota(\Gamma \vdash \Delta)$. First, observe that the inclusion of π_0 in Π ensures that the domain of precisifications is non-empty. Furthermore, δ is a function from $\mathcal{P}$ to 2^Π, for each $s \in \mathcal{S}$, we have that $\sigma(s) \neq \emptyset$ by the n_s saturation condition, and $\sigma(*) = \Pi$ by definition. We now show that (a) for each $s' \preceq s \in \Gamma$ and $i \in \{0, \ldots, n\}$, $\mathcal{M}, \pi_i \models s' \preceq s$, and (b) for each $i \in \{0, \ldots, n\}$ and $\widetilde{\psi} \in \Sigma_i$, $\mathcal{M}, \pi_i \not\models \psi$, from which $\mathcal{M}, \pi_0 \not\models \iota(\Gamma \vdash \varphi)$ follows as $\widetilde{\varphi} \in \Sigma_0$.

(a) Let $s' \preceq s \in \Gamma$ and assume that $\pi \in \sigma(s')$. Then, by the second clause in the definition of $\sigma(s)$ it follows that $\pi \in \sigma(s)$, thus showing that $\mathcal{M}, \pi \models s \preceq s'$ for all $\pi \in \Pi$.

(b) By induction on the complexity of ψ.

Base case. First, let us suppose that ψ is a propositional atom p where $p^\circ \in \Sigma_i$. Then, by the definition of δ, we have that $\pi_i \notin \delta(p)$, i.e. $\mathcal{M}, \pi_i \not\models p$. Similarly, if ψ is a negated atom $\neg p$ where $\neg p^\circ \in \Sigma_i$, then by the id saturation condition, we know that $p^\circ \notin \Sigma_i$, implying that $\pi_i \in \delta(p)$ by the definition of δ, thus showing that $\mathcal{M}, \pi_i \not\models \neg p$.

Inductive step. We suppose that $\widetilde{\psi}^\circ \in \Sigma_i$ and we show that $\mathcal{M}, \pi_i \not\models \psi$ making a case distinction based on the main connective of ψ.

$\psi = \chi \vee \xi$: By the $\vee$ saturation condition, $\widetilde{\chi}^\circ, \widetilde{\xi}^\circ \in \Sigma_i$. By IH, $\mathcal{M}, \pi_i \not\models \chi$ and $\mathcal{M}, \pi_i \not\models \xi$, showing $\mathcal{M}, \pi_i \not\models \psi$.

$\psi = \chi \wedge \xi$: By the $\wedge$ saturation condition, $\widetilde{\chi}^\circ \in \Sigma_i$ or $\widetilde{\xi}^\circ \in \Sigma_i$. By IH, $\mathcal{M}, \pi_i \not\models \chi$ or $\mathcal{M}, \pi_i \not\models \xi$, so $\mathcal{M}, \pi_i \not\models \psi$.

$\psi = \Diamond_s \chi$ with $s \in \mathcal{S} \setminus \{*\}$: Assume that $\pi_j \in \sigma(s)$. By the definition of $\sigma(s)$, π_j was added via the first (i) or second (ii) condition. If (i), then there is a nesting $(s)\{\Sigma_j\}_{\pi_j}$ in Δ, and by the $\Diamond_s$ saturation condition, $\widetilde{\chi}^\circ \in \Sigma_j$. By IH then, $\mathcal{M}, \pi_j \not\models \chi$. If (ii), then there is a chain of statements $s_0 \preceq s_1, \ldots, s_n \preceq s \in \Gamma$ such that a nesting of the form $(s_0)\{\Sigma_j\}_{\pi_j}$ exists in Δ. Again, by the $\Diamond_s$ saturation condition, it follows that $\widetilde{\chi}^\circ \in \Sigma_j$, which implies that $\mathcal{M}, \pi_j \not\models \chi$ by IH. Hence, $\mathcal{M}, \pi_i \not\models \Diamond_s \chi$.

$\psi = \Diamond_* \chi$: Since $*$ is maximal relative to the $\preceq^*_\Gamma$ relation, i.e. $s \preceq^*_\Gamma *$ for all $s \in \mathcal{S}$, we have $\widetilde{\chi}^\circ \in \Sigma_j$ for each $j \in \{0, \ldots, n\}$ by the $\Diamond_*$ and $\Diamond_s$ saturation conditions, hence for all $\pi_j \in \Pi$, $\mathcal{M}, \pi_j \not\models \chi$, i.e. $\mathcal{M}, \pi_i \not\models \Diamond_* \chi$.

$\psi = \Box_s \chi$: By the $\Box_s$ saturation condition, we know that there exists a $j \in \{1, \ldots, n\}$ such that $s_j = s$ and $\widetilde{\chi}^\circ \in \Sigma_j$. By IH, $\mathcal{M}, \pi_j \not\models \chi$, thus proving the case. □

Example 4. *Let us provide an example of the counter-model construction procedure given in Thm. 3. We assume that the (invalid) sequent $s \preceq s' \vdash \varphi$ with $\varphi := \Box_{s'} p \vee \Diamond_s \neg p$ is input into $\texttt{Prove}_{\mathcal{V}}$. Since φ has one proper coloring (with all subformulae active), only the following single thread is generated, yielding the saturated sequent shown at the top of the proof below. We omit the active labels for readability.*

$$\begin{array}{c} s \preceq s' \vdash \varphi, \Box_{s'} p, \Diamond_s \neg p, (s')[p]_{\pi_1}, (s)[\neg p]_{\pi_2}, (*)[\emptyset]_{\pi_3} \\ \hline s \preceq s' \vdash \varphi, \Box_{s'} p, \Diamond_s \neg p, (s')[p]_{\pi_1}, (s)[\neg p]_{\pi_2} \quad (n_*) \\ \hline s \preceq s' \vdash \varphi, \Box_{s'} p, \Diamond_s \neg p, (s')[p]_{\pi_1}, (s)[\emptyset]_{\pi_2} \quad (\Diamond^1_s) \\ \hline s \preceq s' \vdash \varphi, \Box_{s'} p, \Diamond_s \neg p, (s')[p]_{\pi_1} \quad (n_s) \\ \hline s \preceq s' \vdash \varphi, \Box_{s'} p, \Diamond_s \neg p \quad (\Box_{s'}) \\ \hline s \preceq s' \vdash \varphi \quad (\vee) \end{array}$$

Then, we may extract the following (counter-)model $\mathcal{M} = \langle \Pi, \sigma, \delta \rangle$ from the top, saturated sequent in the proof above.

- $\Pi := \{\pi_0, \pi_1, \pi_2, \pi_3\}$;
- $\sigma(*) := \Pi$, $\sigma(s) := \{\pi_2\}$, *and* $\sigma(s') := \{\pi_1\}$;
- $\delta(p) := \{\pi_0, \pi_2, \pi_3\}$.

It is readily verifiable that $\mathcal{M}, \pi_0 \not\models \Box_{s'} p \vee \Diamond_s \neg p$.

We now show that $\texttt{ProofSearch}_{\mathcal{V}}$ (and hence $\texttt{Prove}_{\mathcal{V}}$) terminates after at most polynomially many rule applications in the *size* of the input sequent. For an input $\Phi := \Gamma \vdash \varphi$, its size is defined to be $|\Phi| := |\mathcal{S}| + |\varphi|$. That is, the size of Φ is the sum of the cardinality of the set $\mathcal{S}$ of standpoints and the size of φ. The size of a sequent incorporates a measure on the set $\mathcal{S}$ from the associated vocabulary $\mathcal{V}$ as opposed to a measure on the set Γ of sharpening statements because Γ only plays a role in bottom-up applications of $(\Diamond_s^1)$ and $(\Diamond_s^2)$, which are bounded in part by the cardinality of $\mathcal{S}$ and in part by the number of $\Box_s$ modalities occurring in φ, as explained in the proof of Thm. 4 below.

Theorem 4 (Termination). *Let $\Phi := \Gamma \vdash \varphi$ be a sequent. Then, the number of recursive calls in $\texttt{ProofSearch}_{\mathcal{V}}(\Gamma \vdash \widetilde{\varphi})$, and thus $\texttt{Prove}_{\mathcal{V}}(\Gamma \vdash \varphi)$, is bounded by a polynomial*

$$p(|\Phi|) = \mathcal{O}(|\Phi|^2).$$

Proof. Let $\Phi := \Gamma \vdash \varphi$ be a nested sequent, and $N_\oplus$ be the number of occurrences of the connectives $\{\vee, \wedge\} \cup \{\Diamond_s \mid s \in \mathcal{S}\}$ in φ. By the saturation conditions (Def. 8), we know that for each $s \in \mathcal{S}$, the $(\Box_s)$ rule will be applied bottom-up at most one time for each occurrence of $\Box_s$ in φ, which are bounded by $|\varphi|$. Also, (n_s) will be applied at most once for each $s \in \mathcal{S}$. Since only $(\Box_s)$ and (n_s) introduce nestings, the number of components (i.e. the nestings plus the root) throughout the course of proof-search is bounded by:

$$K := 1 + |\mathcal{S}| + |\varphi|$$

For each occurrence of $\vee$, $\wedge$, and $\Diamond_s$ in φ (with $s \in \mathcal{S}$), we know by the saturation conditions that $(\vee)$, $(\wedge)$, $(\Diamond_s^1)$, $(\Diamond_s^2)$, and $(\Diamond_*)$ can be applied a maximum number of K times during proof search. Then, since $N_\vee + N_\wedge + \sum_{s \in \mathcal{S}} N_{\Diamond_s} \leq |\varphi|$, the number of recursive calls (i.e. bottom-up applications of rules) during proof-search is bounded by $N := |\varphi| \cdot K$. Finally, $|\mathcal{S}|, |\varphi| \leq |\Phi|$ holds trivially, implying:

$$N \leq |\Phi| \cdot (1 + |\Phi| + |\Phi|)$$

Therefore, it follows that a polynomial $p(|\Phi|) = \mathcal{O}(|\Phi|^2)$ bounds the number of recursive calls of $\texttt{Prove}_{\mathcal{V}}(\Phi)$. □

Corollary 1. *Let $\mathcal{V}$ be a vocabulary. Then,*

1. *$\mathbb{S}(\mathcal{V})$ is decidable;*
2. *$\mathbb{S}(\mathcal{V})$ has the finite model property;*
3. *$\texttt{Prove}_{\mathcal{V}}$ is worst-case complexity-optimal, deciding the validity problem for $\mathbb{S}(\mathcal{V})$ in* CoNP;
4. *The validity problem for $\mathbb{S}(\mathcal{V})$ is* CoNP*-complete.*

Proof. Statements 1 and 2 follow from the fact that $\texttt{Prove}_{\mathcal{V}}$ is a correct (Thm. 3) and terminating (Thm. 4) decision procedure for $\mathbb{S}(\mathcal{V})$ that, in particular, returns a finite counter-model when the input is invalid.

To show statement 3, observe that $\texttt{Prove}_{\mathcal{V}}$ is a non-deterministic algorithm that takes a sequent $\Phi := \Gamma \vdash \varphi$ as input, guesses a proper coloring of φ, and constructs a thread. Each such thread is polynomial in the size of its input, since the number of rule applications (i.e. the length of the thread) is bounded by a polynomial $p(|\Phi|) = \mathcal{O}(|\Phi|^2)$, by Thm. 4. Moreover, since any sequent generated during proof-search can have at most $K \leq 1 + |\mathcal{S}| + |\varphi|$ many components (as stated in the proof of Thm. 4), each of which can only be inhabited by at most $|\text{sufo}(\varphi)| = |\varphi|$ many formulae, it follows that the size of each nested sequent in the thread is bounded by $\mathcal{O}(|\Phi|^2)$ since $|\mathcal{S}|, |\varphi| \leq |\Phi|$. Taking the functionality of $\texttt{Prove}_{\mathcal{V}}$ into account, one can see that if $\texttt{Prove}_{\mathcal{V}}(\Phi) = \texttt{False}$, then the corresponding thread is generated in polynomial time and its size is bounded above by a polynomial $q(|\Phi|) = \mathcal{O}(|\Phi|^4)$. Additionally, note that $\texttt{Prove}_{\mathcal{V}}$ is worst-case complexity-optimal as the validity problem for classical propositional logic is CoNP-complete, and can be solved by $\texttt{Prove}_{\mathcal{V}}$ as (id), $(\vee)$, and $(\wedge)$ form a sound and complete proof system for propositional logic (cf. (Lyon 2021a, App. B)). Last, statement 4 is an immediate consequence of statement 3. □

5 Conclusion and Future Work

In this paper, we introduced and employed nested sequent systems to automate reasoning with propositional standpoint logics. To obtain worst-case complexity-optimal proof-search, we presented a novel proof-search technique, referred to as *coloring*, whereby the subformulae of an input formula are non-deterministically colored with (in)active labels, yielding partial proofs (i.e. *threads*) of the input. By means of our technique, we designed a non-deterministic proof-search algorithm deciding the validity of standpoint implications in CoNP, showing how certain threads could be transformed into a counter-model for an invalid input, and how all threads could be transformed into a proof for a valid input. The attainment of these "certificates" from proof-search serve as explanations for the (in)validity of standpoint formulae, thus motivating our proof-theoretic approach.

For future work, we aim to extend our nested systems and proof-search algorithm to cover (i) first-order standpoint logics that (ii) incorporate complex standpoints, which have interesting applications in knowledge integration scenarios. Regarding point (i), placing standpoint logic on a first-order base increases the applicability of the framework along with its expressivity to better match that of contemporary knowledge representation languages. Our focus in this area is to provide results that can then be extrapolated to widely used decidable fragments of FOL. Regarding point (ii), we note that the set-theoretic interpretation of standpoints permits the definition of complex standpoints built atop atomic ones; e.g. union $s_1 \cup s_2$ (integrating knowledge from multiple perspectives), intersection $s_1 \cap s_2$ (expressing the knowledge jointly shared between multiple perspectives), and difference $s_1 \setminus s_2$ (yielding the sharpening of s_1 by ignoring all precisifications of s_2). Beyond providing nested systems for more expressive formulations of standpoint logic, we also aim to write and evaluate theorem provers based on our nested calculi.

Acknowledgments

Lucía Gómez Álvarez was supported by the Bundesministerium fur Bildung und Forschung (BMBF, Federal Ministry of Education and Research) in the Center for Scalable Data Analytics and Artificial Intelligence (ScaDS.AI). Tim S. Lyon has received funding from the European Research Council (Grant Agreement no. 771779, DeciGUT).

References

Belnap, N. D. 1982. Display logic. *Journal of philosophical logic* 11(4):375–417.

Brünnler, K. 2009. Deep sequent systems for modal logic. *Arch. Math. Log.* 48(6):551–577.

Bull, R. A. 1992. Cut elimination for propositional dynamic logic without *. *Z. Math. Logik Grundlag. Math.* 38(2):85–100.

Buss, S. R. 1998. An introduction to proof theory. *Handbook of proof theory* 137:1–78.

Dyckhoff, R. 1992. Contraction-free sequent calculi for intuitionistic logic. *The Journal of Symbolic Logic* 57(3):795–807.

Fine, K. 1975. Vagueness, truth and logic. *Synthese* 30(3-4):265–300.

Fitting, M., and Kuznets, R. 2015. Modal interpolation via nested sequents. *Annals of pure and applied logic* 166(3):274–305.

Gentzen, G. 1935a. Untersuchungen über das logische Schließen. i. *Mathematische Zeitschrift* 39(1):176–210.

Gentzen, G. 1935b. Untersuchungen über das logische Schließen. ii. *Mathematische Zeitschrift* 39(1):405–431.

Gómez Álvarez, L., and Bennett, B. 2018. Dealing with conceptual indeterminacy: A framework based on supervaluation semantics. In *Joint Proceedings of MedRACER and WOMoCoE*, volume 2237, 38–50. CEUR.

Gómez Álvarez, L., and Rudolph, S. 2021. Standpoint logic: Multi-perspective knowledge representation. In Neuhaus, F., and Brodaric, B., eds., *Proceedings of the 12th International Conference on Formal Ontology in Information Systems*, volume 344 of *FAIA*, 3–17. IOS Press.

Gómez Álvarez, L.; Bennett, B.; and Richard-Bollans, A. 2017. Talking about forests: An example of sharing information expressed with vague terms. In *Proceedings of the Joint Ontology Workshops 2017*, volume 2050. CEUR.

Gómez Álvarez, L. 2020. *Standpoint logic: a logic for handling semantic variability, with applications to forestry information*. Ph.D. Dissertation, School of Computing, The University of Leeds.

Kashima, R. 1994. Cut-free sequent calculi for some tense logics. *Studia Logica* 53(1):119–135.

Keefe, R., and Smith, P. 1997. *Theories of vagueness*. The MIT press.

Lyon, T., and van Berkel, K. 2019. Automating agential reasoning: Proof-calculi and syntactic decidability for STIT logics. In Baldoni, M.; Dastani, M.; Liao, B.; Sakurai, Y.; and Zalila Wenkstern, R., eds., *Proceedings of the 22nd International Conference on Principles and Practice of Multi-Agent Systems*, volume 11873, 202–218. Springer.

Lyon, T.; Tiu, A.; Goré, R.; and Clouston, R. 2020. Syntactic interpolation for tense logics and bi-intuitionistic logic via nested sequents. In Fernández, M., and Muscholl, A., eds., *Proceedings of the 28th Annual Conference on Computer Science Logic*, volume 152 of *LIPIcs*, 28:1–28:16. Schloss Dagstuhl - Leibniz-Zentrum für Informatik.

Lyon, T. 2020. On the correspondence between nested calculi and semantic systems for intuitionistic logics. *Journal of Logic and Computation* 31(1):213–265.

Lyon, T. 2021a. *Refining Labelled Systems for Modal and Constructive Logics with Applications*. Ph.D. Dissertation, Technische Universität Wien.

Lyon, T. S. 2021b. Nested sequents for intuitionistic modal logics via structural refinement. In Das, A., and Negri, S., eds., *Automated Reasoning with Analytic Tableaux and Related Methods*, 409–427. Cham: Springer.

Pesquita, C.; Faria, D.; Santos, E.; and Couto, F. M. 2013. To repair or not to repair: Reconciling correctness and coherence in ontology reference alignments. In *Proceedings of the 8th International Conference on Ontology Matching*, volume 1111, 13–24. CEUR.

Poggiolesi, F. 2009. The method of tree-hypersequents for modal propositional logic. In Makinson, D.; Malinowski, J.; and Wansing, H., eds., *Towards Mathematical Philosophy*, volume 28 of *Trends in logic*. Springer. 31–51.

Simpson, A. K. 1994. *The proof theory and semantics of intuitionistic modal logic*. Ph.D. Dissertation, University of Edinburgh. College of Science and Engineering. School of Informatics.

Slaney, J. K. 1997. Minlog: A minimal logic theorem prover. In McCune, W., ed., *Proceedings of the 14th International Conference on Automated Deduction*, volume 1249 of *Lecture Notes in Computer Science*, 268–271. Springer.

Takeuti, G. 2013. *Proof theory*, volume 81. Courier Corporation.

Tiu, A.; Ianovski, E.; and Goré, R. 2012. Grammar logics in nested sequent calculus: Proof theory and decision procedures. In Bolander, T.; Braüner, T.; Ghilardi, S.; and Moss, L. S., eds., *Advances in Modal Logic 9, papers from the ninth conference on Advances in Modal Logic*, 516–537. College Publications.

Wansing, H. 2002. Sequent systems for modal logics. In Gabbay, D. M., and Guenthner, F., eds., *Handbook of Philosophical Logic: Volume 8*. Springer. 61–145.

Proceedings of the 19th International Conference on Principles of Knowledge Representation and Reasoning
Main Track

Towards an Enthymeme-Based Communication Framework in Multi-Agent Systems

Alison R. Panisson[1], **Peter McBurney**[2], **Rafael H. Bordini**[3]
[1]Department of Computing – UFSC, Brazil
[2]Department of Informatics – KCL, UK
[3]School of Technology – PUCRS, Brazil
alison.panisson@ufsc.br, peter.mcburney@kcl.ac.uk, rafael.bordini@pucrs.br

Abstract

Communication is one of the most important aspects of multi-agent systems. Among the different communication techniques applied to multi-agent systems, argumentation-based approaches have received special interest from the community, because allowing agents to exchange arguments provides a rich form of communication. In contrast to the benefits that argumentation-based techniques provide to multi-agent communication, extra weight on the communication infrastructure results from the additional information exchanged by agents, which could restrict the practical use of such techniques. In this work, we propose an argumentation framework whereby agents are able to exchange shorter messages when engaging in dialogues by omitting information that is common knowledge (e.g., information about a shared multi-agent organisation). In particular, we focus on using *enthymemes*, shared argumentation schemes (i.e., reasoning patterns from which arguments are instantiated), and common organisational knowledge to build an enthymeme-based communication framework. We show that our approach addresses some of Grice's maxims, in particular that agents can be brief in communication, without any loss in the content of the intended arguments.

1 Introduction

Enthymemes are arguments in which one or more statements (which are part of the argument) are not explicitly stated, i.e., they are arguments with "missing premises" or even "missing conclusions" (Walton, Reed, and Macagno 2008). They are more realistic arguments, in the sense that real-world arguments (i.e., arguments made by humans) usually do not have enough explicitly stated premises for the entailment of the claim. This is because there is common knowledge that can be assumed by the arguers which allows them to encode arguments into a shorter message by ignoring the common knowledge (Black and Hunter 2008). Further, when an arguer receives an enthymeme, it can deduce the intended argument, in a process of reconstruction of such argument, looking for the missing parts, assumptions, etc., in order to recover its intended meaning (Mailly 2016). However, attributing unstated information to an arguer is a dangerous kind of inference, given that this depends on interpreting what the arguer presumably meant to say (Walton, Reed, and Macagno 2008), and this needs to be treated carefully, in order not to change the intended meaning of exchanged arguments. Changing the meaning of arguments uttered by agents in Multi-Agent Systems (MAS) could be disastrous, considering the rigour expected in multi-agent communication methods.

Although using enthymemes could be dangerous in distorting the meaning of arguments in agent communication, if the involved process could ensure that arguments do not lose the intended meaning, enthymemes could be beneficial for agent communication, allowing agents to exchange only essential information needed for a particular purpose. In this work, in order to deal with this inherent problem in using enthymemes, we propose to use argumentation schemes (Walton, Reed, and Macagno 2008) as common organisational knowledge to guide the construction of enthymemes by the proponent of arguments, as well as to guide the reconstruction of the intended argument by the recipients of such enthymemes. Thus, agents are able to exchange only the content that is needed for them to understand each other in argumentation-based communication, and it can be ensured that the arguments will not lose content or the intended meaning.

The contributions of this work are: (i) we describe a complete framework for argumentation-based dialogues, where agents are able to communicate only the information that is required for mutual understanding using enthymemes, no more than that[1]; (ii) we guarantee that both the sender and the recipient will have the same understanding for the enthymemes exchanged; (iii) we empirically evaluate our implementation; (iv) we show that our approach has various advantages for argumentation-based communication in MAS, addressing some of Grice's maxims for cooperative communication.

2 Argumentation Schemes in MAS

Argumentation schemes could be available as common knowledge to all agents in a MAS, considering that they describe usual reasoning patterns. Furthermore, such reasoning patterns tend to be domain specific (Walton 2008). For example, there is work where agents use argumentation schemes that are specific for analysing the provenance of information (Toniolo et al. 2014), argumentation schemes

[1]Intuitively, this corresponds to Grice's maxim of quantity (Grice 1975).

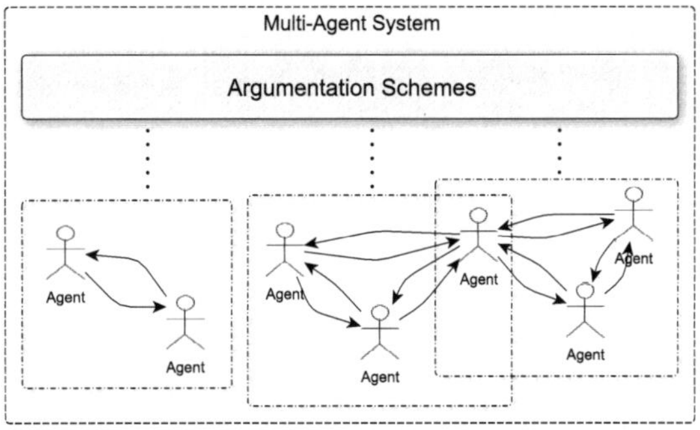

Figure 1: Argumentation schemes are shared by all agents.

for reasoning about trust (Parsons et al. 2012), argumentation schemes for arguing about human organ transplantation (Tolchinsky et al. 2007; Tolchinsky et al. 2012), argumentation schemes for reasoning about data access control (Panisson et al. 2018), argumentation schemes for reasoning about a proposed treatment (Kokciyan et al. 2018), and so forth.

Given the discussion in the relevant literature that argumentation schemes are normally both domain dependent and common knowledge, we propose an architecture for MAS where argumentation schemes are shared by all agents in the system. In particular, our approach is based on the specification of argumentation schemes as part of the organisational specifications (e.g., using the Moise organisational model (Hubner, Sichman, and Boissier 2007)), or as an interface to an external source of information such as the semantic web (Freitas et al. 2015; Freitas et al. 2017), etc. The only requirement is that all agents in the systems must have access to specifications of all such reasoning patterns at run time, so they are able to instantiate arguments from the available argumentation schemes, as well as to use such instantiated arguments to reason and to argue with other agents. An overview of our approach to argumentation schemes in MAS is shown in Figure 1, where all agents are able to instantiate arguments from the argumentation schemes at runtime.

2.1 Instantiating Arguments

To exemplify our approach, we use the argumentation schemes *Argument from Position to Know* from (Walton 1996), but here making reference to organisational concepts; for example, *roles* that agents play in the multi-agent organisation are referred to within the scheme:

> "Agent $\mathtt{Ag}$ is currently playing a role R (its position) that implies knowing things in a certain subject domain S containing proposition A (**Major Premise**). $\mathtt{Ag}$ asserts that A (in domain S) is true (or false) **(Minor Premise)**. A is true (or false) **(Conclusion)**".

The associated critical questions are: **CQ1**: Does playing role R imply knowing whether A holds? **CQ2**: Is $\mathtt{Ag}$ an honest (trustworthy, reliable) source? **CQ3**: Did $\mathtt{Ag}$ assert that A is true (or false)? **CQ4**: Is $\mathtt{Ag}$ playing role R?

Definition 1 (Argumentation Scheme). *An argumentation scheme is a tuple* $\langle \mathcal{SN}, \mathcal{C}, \mathcal{P}, \mathcal{CQ} \rangle$ *with* $\mathcal{SN}$ *the argumentation scheme name (which must be unique within the system),* $\mathcal{C}$ *the conclusion of the argumentation scheme,* $\mathcal{P}$ *the premises, and* $\mathcal{CQ}$ *the associated critical questions.*

The set of argumentation schemes available to agents is represented by $\Delta_{\mathtt{AS}}$. Such argumentation schemes can be represented in structured argumentation[2], using defeasible inferences, as described in (Prakken 2011; Panisson and Bordini 2017). Thus, in order to make explicit the representation of arguments, we introduce the language $\mathcal{L}$ used in this work. We use a first-order language as the basis for our representation, given that most agent-oriented programming languages are based on logic programming. In particular, we have a set of atomic formulæ $\{p_0, \ldots, p_n\} \in \mathcal{L}$, and a set of defeasible inference rules $\{(p_i, \ldots, p_j \Rightarrow p_k), \ldots, (p_l, \ldots, p_m \Rightarrow p_o)\} \in \mathcal{L}$. In order to refer to the unification process, we use a most general unifier θ (as usual in logic programming). We use uppercase letters to represent variables — e.g., `Ag` and `R` in `role(Ag,R)` — and lowercase letters to represent terms and ground literals — e.g., `john`, `doctor`, and `role(john,doctor)`. Using language $\mathcal{L}$, the argumentation scheme introduced above can be represented as the following defeasible inference:

$$\mathtt{role(Ag,R)}, \mathtt{knows(R,S)}, \mathtt{asserts(Ag,A)}, \mathtt{about(A,S)} \Rightarrow \mathtt{A}$$

with $\mathcal{P} = \{\mathtt{role(Ag,R)}, \mathtt{knows(R,S)}, \mathtt{asserts(Ag,A)}, \mathtt{about(A,S)}\}$, and $\mathcal{C} = \mathtt{A}$. In order to create an argument from this reasoning pattern, agents instantiate it using the knowledge available to them.

Definition 2 (Argument). *An argument is a tuple* $\langle S, c \rangle^{\theta}_{\mathtt{sn_i}}$*, where* $\mathtt{sn_i}$ *is the name of the argumentation scheme* $\langle \mathtt{sn_i}, \mathcal{C}, \mathcal{P}, \mathcal{CQ} \rangle \in \Delta_{\mathtt{AS}}$*,* θ *is a most general unifier for the premises in* $\mathcal{P}$ *and the agent's current belief base,* S *is the set of premises and the inference rule of the scheme used to draw* c *(the conclusion). That is,* S *includes all instantiated premises from* $\mathcal{P}$ *— i.e., for all* $p \in \mathcal{P}, p\theta \in S$ *— and the inference rule corresponding to the scheme* $(\mathcal{P} \Rightarrow \mathcal{C})$*; the conclusion* c *is the instantiation* $\mathcal{C}\theta$ *such that* $S \models c$*.*

Example 1. *Imagine that all agents know that* `john` *(an agent in the system) is playing the role of* `doctor` *—* `role(john,doctor)` *— within the organisational structure. Further, the agents know that doctors know about cancer —* `knows(doctor,cancer)`*. Therefore, if* `john` *asserts that "smoking causes cancer" —* `asserts(john,causes(smoking,cancer))`*, and causes of cancer are a subject matter related to cancer —* `about(causes(smoking,cancer),cancer)`*, all agents are able to conclude that smoking causes cancer:* `causes(smoking,cancer)`*.*

In this example, the organisational structure within the system ensures that all agents know that agent `john` plays the role of `doctor` within that organisational structure, and that doctors know about cancer, because it is one of the features of that role. Also, they could know that causes of cancer are a subject related to cancer, given the domain knowledge shared by them in the system. However, not all agents

[2]The best known frameworks for structured argumentation are (Modgil and Prakken 2014; García and Simari 2014; Besnard and Hunter 2014; Toni 2014).

will know that agent john has asserted that smoking causes cancer, only the ones john has communicated with. Therefore, not all agents are able to instantiate an argument from the reasoning pattern available, giving that not all premises are common knowledge.

2.2 Reasoning with Arguments

Instantiating arguments from argumentation schemes allows agents to use such arguments for both reasoning and communication processes. In both cases, agents will check conflicts among arguments they are able to instantiate, reaching acceptable conclusions, given the set of arguments available to them. There are many approaches to argumentation semantics in the literature, most of them based on Dung's well-known work (Dung 1995). In this work, for practical reasons, we use the *defeasible semantics* (Governatori et al. 2004), which has been chosen considering recent implementations of argumentation-based reasoning in the Jason platform (Bordini, Hübner, and Wooldridge 2007), as reported in (Panisson et al. 2014; Panisson and Bordini 2016; Berariu 2014). Other semantics could be used with minor changes in the framework.

Before we introduce the notion of conflicting arguments, we need to introduce the definition of conflicting information, which will point to conflicts between arguments later.

Definition 3 (Conflicting Information). *Two pieces of information φ and ψ are said to be in conflict if $\varphi \equiv \neg\psi$ (where "$\neg$" represents strong negation) or there is a semantic declaration that such pieces of information are conflicting, e.g., comp(φ, ψ), stating that φ and ψ are the complement of each other. Both cases are represented in our formalisation using a general operator for contradictory information, whereby $\overline{\varphi}$ is contradictory with φ, that is, $\overline{\varphi} \equiv \neg\varphi$ and $\overline{\neg\varphi} \equiv \varphi$.*

Two kinds of attacks between arguments are considered here, which are used to evaluate the acceptable arguments in the set of arguments available for each agent.

Definition 4 (Attack Between Arguments). *Let $\langle S_1, c_1\rangle^{\theta}_{\mathtt{sn_i}}$ and $\langle S_2, c_2\rangle^{\theta}_{\mathtt{sn_j}}$ be two arguments. Attacks between arguments can be generalised into two types:*

- $\langle S_1, c_1\rangle^{\theta}_{\mathtt{sn_i}}$ *rebuts* $\langle S_2, c_2\rangle^{\theta}_{\mathtt{sn_j}}$ *iff* $c_1 \equiv \overline{c_2}$.
- $\langle S_1, c_1\rangle^{\theta}_{\mathtt{sn_i}}$ *undercuts* $\langle S_2, c_2\rangle^{\theta}_{\mathtt{sn_j}}$ *iff* $c_1 \equiv \overline{\varphi}$ *for some* $\varphi \in S_2$.

Example 2. *Imagine that another agent playing also the role of doctor, called* pietro, *asserts that "smoking does not cause cancer", i.e.,* $\mathtt{asserts(pietro, \neg causes(smoking, cancer))}$. *Any agent aware of both assertions (i.e., John's and Pietro's assertions) is able to construct conflicting arguments for* $\mathtt{\neg causes(smoking, cancer)}$ *and* $\mathtt{causes(smoking, cancer)}$ *(both rebutting each other). However, the agents are able to check if* John *and* Pietro *are honest (trustworthy, reliable) sources, if they really play the role of* doctor, *and the other questionable points indicated by critical questions in the argumentation scheme used. For example, if an agent has an acceptable argument "Pietro does not have a degree, therefore he cannot be considered a doctor", i.e.,* $\mathtt{\neg has(pietro, degree)} \Rightarrow \mathtt{\neg role(pietro, doctor)}$, *such argument undercuts* $\mathtt{\neg causes(smoking, cancer)}$ *argument, and* $\mathtt{causes(smoking, cancer)}$ *becomes the acceptable conclusion for that agent.*

Definition 5 (Acceptable Arguments). *An argument $\langle S, c\rangle^{\theta}_{\mathtt{sn_i}}$ is acceptable to an agent* ag *(where $\Delta_{\mathtt{ag}}$ is its knowledge base) if it is not attacked by other arguments, or if every argument attacking $\langle S, c\rangle^{\theta}_{\mathtt{sn_i}}$ is defeated by some acceptable argument $\langle S_n, c_n\rangle^{\theta}_{\mathtt{sn_j}} \in \Delta_{\mathtt{ag}}$ (i.e., all arguments that attack $\langle S, c\rangle^{\theta}_{\mathtt{sn_i}}$ cannot be inferred from $\Delta_{\mathtt{ag}}$ because they are attacked by acceptable arguments in $\Delta_{\mathtt{ag}}$).*

In communication, the acceptability of arguments received from other agents is directly associated with the agent's rationality, i.e., when an agent ag receives an argument $\langle S, c\rangle^{\theta}_{\mathtt{sn_i}}$ from another agent, it is able to check if that information is or is not acceptable to itself, temporarily adding S to its knowledge base $\Delta_{\mathtt{ag}}$ (i.e., $\Delta_{\mathtt{ag}} = \Delta_{\mathtt{ag}} \cup S$) and checking the acceptability of c. We use $\Delta_{\mathtt{ag}} \models c$ to express that agent Ag is able to construct an acceptable argument $\langle S, c\rangle^{\theta}_{\mathtt{sn_i}}$, with $S \subset \Delta_{\mathtt{ag}}$. An agent will never have acceptable arguments for conflicting information, i.e., $\Delta_{\mathtt{ag}} \models c$ and $\Delta_{\mathtt{ag}} \models \overline{c}$ never both hold simultaneously. We use $\Delta_{\mathtt{ag}} \not\models c$ to denote that an agent is not able to construct an acceptable argument for c. $\Delta_{\mathtt{ag}} \not\models c$ does not imply $\Delta_{\mathtt{ag}} \models \overline{c}$; however, $\Delta_{\mathtt{ag}} \models c$ implies $\Delta_{\mathtt{ag}} \not\models \overline{c}$.

2.3 Referring to Organisational Components

Argumentation schemes as a specification on top of a MAS with an organisational model allows them to have several relations with other components in the organisational specifications of such systems, such as normative, structural, and functional specifications (although such specifications themselves are not the focus of this paper). Furthermore, there are some organisational components, such as roles, authority links, etc., that are commonly referred to from the premises and critical questions of argumentation schemes; they are also common knowledge (as ensured by existing organisation infrastructures) and, therefore, they play an important role in our approach. Of course, agents will have more common knowledge specific to the application domain; however, for simplicity, in this work we use only organisational information, which is guaranteed common knowledge in platforms for the development of MAS based on the organisational paradigm.

As described before, argument schemes could refer to organisational components, as it is the case in the argumentation schemes given as example above. In such organisational-based approaches, all agents/participants are aware of other agents' roles in the organisation and the associated features/abilities related to them. Therefore, it would be pointless to exchange such information in a communication process.

2.4 Agent Knowledge

We denote all knowledge coming from the organisational infrastructure available to agents as $\Delta_{\mathtt{Org}}$, and we emphasise that all agents are aware of the information in $\Delta_{\texttt{Org}}$ (and the organisation infrastructure ensures that this information is kept up to date with the state of open, dynamic organisations at runtime). Further, we denote all argumentation schemes, available for agents to instantiate arguments in the MAS as $\Delta_{\texttt{AS}}$; recall that, being one of the organisation specifications, argumentation schemes are also common knowledge in our approach. They represent defeasible inferences that entail a conclusion from the instantiated premises, and they point to possible doubts in such defeasible inferences by means of critical questions. Finally, we denote all knowledge available to an agent $\texttt{ag}_\texttt{i}$ as $\Delta_{\texttt{ag}_\texttt{i}}$, where $(\Delta_{\texttt{Org}} \cup \Delta_{\texttt{AS}}) \subset \Delta_{\texttt{ag}_\texttt{i}}$.

Normally, $(\Delta_{\texttt{ag}_\texttt{i}} \setminus (\Delta_{\texttt{Org}} \cup \Delta_{\texttt{AS}})) \neq \emptyset$ holds, given that agents are constantly perceiving the environment and exchanging knowledge, as well as agents have specialised knowledge depending on their position/role within the MAS. Thus, arguments are often constructed by agents using all knowledge available in $\Delta_{\texttt{ag}_\texttt{i}}$. In some cases, agents are able to construct arguments based on just $\Delta_{\texttt{Org}}$ and $\Delta_{\texttt{AS}}$, if the argument contains only organisational information. However, agents will never construct arguments using only $\Delta_{\texttt{AS}}$, given that it represents non-instantiated reasoning patterns. While we follow an approach in which agents have specialised knowledge, there are other approaches, like sharing a domain knowledge base, as presented in (Schmidt et al. 2016), that could be easily incorporated into our approach.

3 Enthymemes

Differently from logical arguments, where their supports have enough information to entail the conclusion, enthymemes only explicitly represent some of the premises needed for inferring a claim/conclusion (or even have a missing conclusion) (Walton, Reed, and Macagno 2008).

Using enthymemes in human activities has widely-known benefits, allowing for economy, efficiency, and efficacy, as claimed by Nettel in (Nettel 2011); in particular, Nettel claims that: (i) being shorter, enthymemes can be easier to follow by the audience; (ii) starting from what is known and already taken for granted is important, because the addressee will, in consequence, be well-disposed towards what is said; (iii) omitting premises is also justified by reasons of economy, where if something is well-known it is unnecessary to repeat it; (iv) omitting the conclusion has advantages in terms of economy, but might also be beneficial to efficiency because if the audience comes to the conclusion by itself, its acceptance is more easily acquired; and (v) allowing members of the audience to come to a conclusion by themselves might be more respectful towards them.

The use of enthymemes characterises more rational and "intelligent" agents; besides bringing them closer to human reasoning and communication, we also show that using enthymemes could bring some computational benefits for MAS.

When agents use enthymemes, the common knowledge is removed from the original argument by the proponent of the argument (such process is called *encoding* in (Black and Hunter 2008)), where it is assumed that all information removed from the original argument is known by the recipients and, therefore, they are able to reconstruct (or to *decode*)

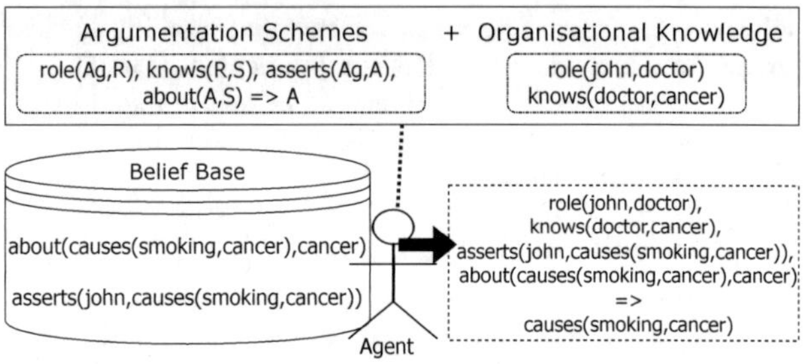

Figure 2: Constructing arguments using argumentation schemes and organisational information.

such an argument, understanding exactly what was meant to be communicated. If both the proponent and recipients in fact have the same common knowledge, then this process is straightforward (Hunter 2007). However, normally, this is not the case, and the recipients generate an approximation of such an argument in the reconstruction process, given the disparities between the different views on what constitutes common knowledge (Hunter 2007).

In our approach, however, we can guarantee that all agents, which are involved in an argumentation-based dialogue, will have the same understanding when using enthymemes, by means of guiding the reconstruction of arguments by the recipients using argumentation schemes and available organisational knowledge[3].

Definition 6 (Enthymeme). *Let* $\langle S, c\rangle^{\theta}_{\texttt{sn}}$ *be an acceptable argument to agent* $\texttt{ag}_\texttt{i}$. *An enthymeme for* $\langle S, c\rangle^{\theta}_{\texttt{sn}}$ *is a tuple* $\langle S', c\rangle^{\theta}_{\texttt{sn}}$, *where* $S' = (S \setminus (\Delta_{\texttt{Org}} \cup \Delta_{\texttt{AS}}))$.

Example 3. *An argument contains, in its support, all premises and inference rules needed to entail the conclusion, and it could be constructed as*[4]*:*
$\langle\{$`role(john,doctor),`
`asserts(john,causes(smoking,cancer)),`
`knows(doctor,cancer),`
`about(causes(smoking,cancer),cancer),`
`[role(Ag,R),knows(R,S),asserts(Ag,A),`
`about(A,S)` $\Rightarrow$ `A]`$\}$,
`causes(smoking,cancer)`$\rangle^{\theta}_{\texttt{position\_to\_know}}$
where $\theta = \{\texttt{Ag} \mapsto \texttt{john}, \texttt{R} \mapsto \texttt{doctor}, \texttt{S} \mapsto \texttt{cancer}, \texttt{A} \mapsto \texttt{causes}(\texttt{smoking}, \texttt{cancer})\}$. *The corresponding enthymeme has the following format (considering the common knowledge presented in Figure 2):*
$\langle\{$`asserts(john,causes(smoking,cancer)),`
`about(causes(smoking,cancer),cancer)`$\}$,
`causes(smoking,cancer)`$\rangle^{\theta}_{\texttt{position\_to\_know}}$

Based on the label `position_to_know` *and the most general unifier* θ, *an agent receiving the enthymeme is able to identify the missing premises and therefore conclude that* `causes(smoking,cancer)`, *given that all missing premises are organisational information and, therefore, common knowledge.*

[3]Also, recall that we have an infrastructure that ensures that all agents will have the same perception on what constitutes common knowledge.

[4]We use `[` and `]` in order to delimit the inference rules.

Further details about encoding arguments into enthymemes and decoding enthymemes into arguments will be discussed in the next section, where both processes are properly formalised.

4 Argumentation-Based Dialogues

In the multi-agent paradigm, communication is often based on the speech-act theory (Searle 1969). In such approaches, messages have the following format $\langle \texttt{Ags}, \texttt{performative}, \texttt{content} \rangle$, where `Ags` represents the agent (or set of agents) to which the message is addressed, `performative` denotes the illocutionary force of the speech act, and `content` is the (propositional) content of the message. The performatives we use in this work and their intended meaning are informally presented below:

- `assert`: the performative `assert` is used by agents to introduce a particular claim in the dialogue. The agents receiving such a message become aware of that claim.
- `question`: the performative `question` is used by agents to question a claim, part of arguments, or a critical question related to an argument, put forward by agents in the dialogue. The `content` will be a proposition φ that either: (i) refers to a claim put forward by some agent in the dialogue; or (ii) refers to part of an argument for which its corresponding enthymeme has been put forward by some agent in the dialogue, i.e., $\varphi \in S$ for some argument $\langle S, c \rangle^{\theta}_{\texttt{sn}}$ for which the enthymeme $\langle S', c \rangle^{\theta}_{\texttt{sn}}$ has been put forward by some agent in the dialogue; or (iii) a critical question associated to an argument for which its corresponding enthymeme has been put forward by some agent in the dialogue, i.e., $\varphi = q\theta_{\texttt{sn}}$, with $q \in \mathcal{CQ}$, for an argumentation scheme[5] $\langle \texttt{sn}, \mathcal{C}, \mathcal{P}, \mathcal{CQ} \rangle$, with $\langle S, c \rangle^{\theta}_{\texttt{sn}}$ the intended argument, and $\langle S', c \rangle^{\theta}_{\texttt{sn}}$ the previously received enthymeme.
- `justify`: the performative `justify` is used by agents to introduce an enthymeme in the dialogue. The content will be $\langle S', c \rangle^{\theta}_{\texttt{sn}}$, with $\langle S, c \rangle^{\theta}_{\texttt{sn}}$ the intended argument for c.
- `refuse`: the performative `refuse` is used by agents to refuse a previous proposition put forward by some agent in the dialogue.
- `accept`: the performative `accept` is used by agents to accept a previous proposition put forward by some agent in the dialogue.

In the course of argumentation-based dialogues, agents make commitments based on which speech act they use. These commitments are stored in the commitment store (CS) that consists of one or more structures, accessible to all agents in a dialogue[6]. The CS is simply a subset of the knowledge base, and the union of the CSs can be viewed as the global state of the dialogue at a given time (Parsons, Wooldridge, and Amgoud 2002). The rules that define how CSs are updated, depending on the speech act used by agents, are summarised as follows: (i) *assert*: the agent's CS is updated with the asserted content p, $CS \leftarrow CS \cup \{p\}$; (ii) *accept*: the agent's CS is updated with the accepted content p, $CS \leftarrow CS \cup \{p\}$; (iii) *question* and *refuse*: no effect over the CS; and (iv) *justify*: the agent's CS is updated with the justified content contained in the set of rules and facts S (the support of the intend argument for p), $CS \leftarrow CS \cup S$. Using these speech acts, various protocols can be specified.

It is important to mention that, when the agent receives a justify message, the content is an enthymeme. Thus, the enthymeme is decoded into the original sender's argument, guided by the argumentation scheme. The operational semantics for the performatives we use in this work, regarding decoding enthymemes into arguments and encoding arguments into enthymemes, is presented in the short paper presented in (Panisson and Bordini 2022). We define the encoding and decoding processes as follow:

Definition 7 (Encoding Arguments into Enthymemes)**.** *When an agent ag send a message $\langle sid, \texttt{justify}, \langle S, c \rangle^{\theta}_{sn} \rangle$, the argument $\langle S, c \rangle^{\theta}_{sn}$ is encoded into the enthymeme $\langle S', c \rangle^{\theta}_{sn}$ with $S' = (S \setminus (\Delta_{AS} \cup \Delta_{org}))$.*

Definition 8 (Decoding Enthymemes into Arguments)**.** *When an agent receives a message $\langle sid, \texttt{justify}, \langle S', c \rangle^{\theta}_{sn} \rangle$, the enthymeme $\langle S', c \rangle^{\theta}_{sn}$, instantiated from the argumentation scheme $\langle sn, \mathcal{C}, \mathcal{P}, \mathcal{CQ} \rangle$ is decoded to the argument $\langle S, c \rangle^{\theta}_{sn}$, i.e., for all $p \in \mathcal{P}$ with $p\theta \in S'$, then $p[s(sid)]\theta \in S$ (everything said by the agent sid), for all $p \in \mathcal{P}$ with $p\theta \notin S'$, then $p[s(sid), dec(\texttt{sn})]\theta \in S$, and $\mathcal{P} \Rightarrow \mathcal{C})[s(sid), dec(\texttt{sn})] \in S$ (everything decoded by the receiver agent).*

5 Example

Considering the example we introduced, we show a short real-world dialogue between a nurse and two patients in a hospital scenario using the argumentation scheme `position_to_know` and an additional argumentation scheme[7] called here *cc* — `[causes(A,I), evidences(P,A)` $\Rightarrow$ `is_consequence(I,A)]`$_{cc}$ — stating that *"if a long-term action A causes an illness I, and there is evidence that a patient P has been doing A, probably illness I is a consequence of A"*.

Imagine that the nurse is supposed to explain to two patients, *Alice* and *Bob*, who were diagnosed with cancer, how they probably got the illness[8]. Using the performatives introduced, the nurse starts a dialogue executing a `justify` move explaining that smoking causes cancer, in which the following enthymeme is built by the nurse (according to Definition 7):

$\langle$`{asserts(john,causes(smoking,cancer)),`
`about(causes(smoking,cancer),cancer)]},`
`causes(smoking,cancer)`$\rangle^{\theta}_{\texttt{position\_to\_know}}$

[5]Recall that S is different from $\mathcal{P}$, considering that $\mathcal{P}$ are non-instantiated premises, and S the entire support for c.

[6]Other names are used for CS, such as *dialogue obligation store* in (McBurney and Parsons 2004) and *dialogue store* in (Sadri, Toni, and Torroni 2001).

[7]We refer to this argumentation scheme as a domain-dependent version of the argumentation scheme *argument from cause to effect*, found in (Walton, Reed, and Macagno 2008, pg.328).

[8]It is important to mention that we assume the nurse was asked to explain the doctor's diagnosis; we do not assume that the nurse made the diagnosis themselves.

Based on the common knowledge that `john` is a doctor and doctors are experts in such domains (see Figure 2), both patients accept that "*smoking causes cancer*". After introducing this premise, following the nurse's strategy, another `justify` move is executed to explain that, probably, smoking is the cause of their illness. The enthymeme resulting (according to Definition 7) is:

$\langle\{\texttt{causes(smoking,cancer)}, \texttt{evidence(alice/bob,smoking)}\}, \texttt{is\_consequence(cancer,smoking)}\rangle^{\theta}_{\texttt{cc}}$

Considering that both *Bob* and *Alice* share the argumentation scheme *cc*, (i) *Bob* accepts the nurse's argument, given he has been smoking cigarettes for many years and he is able to make the same inference used by the nurse; and (ii) *Alice* questions the premise `evidence(alice,smoking)`, given she does not smoke. Thus, the nurse explains that she has been a second-hand smoker[9] because of her husband's smoking, thus she has been smoking for many years as well. Finally, she accepts the nurse's claim[10].

This example demonstrates that our enthymeme-based communication framework matches with real-world dialogues, which is a very important property, considering the AI community aims to achieve such rich dialogues when involving software agents too. Further, note that, when communicating the second enthymeme, the nurse uses the premise `causes(smoking,cancer)`, which is in the CS of both patients *Bob* and *Alice* (according to `accept` performative from Section 4). While for software agents it could be interesting to omit that information, given that all agents participating in that particular dialogue accepted that information and it became common knowledge for them, when involving human-agent interaction, it is wiser to repeat that information to make the link between the moves in a dialogue, which is important for example in fields such as storytelling (Bex and Bench-Capon 2010; Bex and Bench-Capon 2014; Bex and Bench-Capon 2017), and complex explanations (Sklar and Azhar 2018; Miller 2019). Also, it addresses some of Grice's maxims for cooperative communication as we discuss in the next section.

6 Properties

Grice (Grice 1975) claims that conversational statements are often linked together, forming a cooperative effort to achieve some goal of information exchange, or social goal. Thus, Grice proposes four categories of maxims that would help to achieve such cooperative principle, namely: *quality, quantity, relation* and *manner*. The category of *quality* includes two (sub)maxims: (1) *do not say things that are believed to be false*, and (2) *do not say things for which there is no sufficient evidence*. The category of *quantity* includes two (sub)maxims: (3) *make the contribution as informative as is required*, and (4) *do not make it more informative than is required*. The category of *relation* includes only the following maxim: (5) *be relevant*. The category of *manner* includes four (sub)maxims: (6) *avoid obscurity of expression*, (7) *avoid ambiguity*, (8) *be brief*, (9) *be orderly*.

These maxims are important aspects concerning communication in MAS, including those multi-agent applications that require human-agent interaction in the context of eXplainable AI (XAI) (Gunning 2017; Gunning et al. 2019) and Hybrid Intelligence (Akata et al. 2020). Clearly, in this work, our main contribution addressing Grice's maxims for cooperative communication is centred in the category of *quantity*, in which agents will exchange shorter arguments (enthymemes) and will understand each other as if they had communicated the full intended argument.

Proposition 1. *Agents always communicate shorter arguments (enthymemes) instead of the intended arguments.*

Proof. In our approach, agents only communicate arguments using the `justify` performative (see Section 4), which encode arguments into enthymemes according to Definition 7. That way, any information from $\Delta_{\texttt{Org}}$ and $\Delta_{\texttt{AS}}$ will be removed from the intended argument. Considering that agents are only able to instantiate arguments from the argumentation schemes in $\Delta_{\texttt{AS}}$ (Definition 2), if there exists an argument $\langle S, c\rangle^{\theta}_{\texttt{sn}_\texttt{i}}$, then there exists an argumentation scheme $\langle \texttt{sn}_\texttt{i}, \mathcal{C}, \mathcal{P}, \mathcal{CQ}\rangle \in \Delta_{\texttt{AS}}$. Even if such an argument does not refer to any information from $\Delta_{\texttt{Org}}$, the resulting enthymeme $\langle S', c\rangle^{\theta}_{\texttt{sn}_\texttt{i}}$ will be shorter than the intended argument $\langle S, c\rangle^{\theta}_{\texttt{sn}_\texttt{i}}$, given $S' = S \setminus (S \cap (\Delta_{\texttt{Org}} \cup \Delta_{\texttt{AS}}))$, i.e., at least $(\mathcal{P} \Rightarrow \mathcal{C}) \notin S'$. □

Proposition 2. *Agents understand each other as if they had communicated the intended arguments instead of enthymemes.*

Proof. In our approach, agents always communicate shorter arguments (enthymemes) instead of the intended arguments (Proposition 1). Enthymemes are represented as $\langle S', c\rangle^{\theta}_{\texttt{sn}_\texttt{i}}$, making reference to the argumentation scheme $\langle \texttt{sn}_\texttt{i}, \mathcal{C}, \mathcal{P}, \mathcal{CQ}\rangle \in \Delta_{\texttt{AS}}$ and the unifier θ used to instantiate the intended argument. When decoding an enthymeme $\langle S', c\rangle^{\theta}_{\texttt{sn}}$, according to Definition 8, agents recover all information $p \in S'$ plus the omitted content $p \in \mathcal{P}$ and $p\theta \notin S'$. All information is properly annotated with the source of that information $s(sid)$ and whether it has been decoded $dec(\texttt{sn})$ or not. The reference to the argumentation scheme sn and θ guarantees that, for all $p \notin S'$, $p \in S$, with S the support of the intended argument, with p properly annotated, i.e., $p[dec(\texttt{sn})]\}$. Thus, the agent receiving that enthymeme will have the same understanding as if it had received the intend argument — all $p \in S$ properly annotated $p[s(sid)]$ — also understanding which parts of the intended argument have been omitted in the enthymeme — for all $\forall p \in S$ and $p \notin S'$ properly annotated $p[dec(\texttt{sn}_\texttt{i})]$. □

Both properties are also supported by an empirical evaluation presented in the next section.

While Grice's maxims (3), (4), and (8) are directly addressed by our approach when using the concept of enthymemes, maxims (6) and (7) are addressed by agent communication languages through well defined semantics. In

[9] Someone who breaths other people's smoke.

[10] Note that when a patient has an argument against the causal generalisation or the evidences, the patient is able to use the critical questions listed in (Walton, Reed, and Macagno 2008, pg.328).

the context of an enthymeme-based communication framework, we also addressed those maxims through the operational semantics presented in (Panisson and Bordini 2022). Finally, Grice's maxims (1), (2), (5), and (9) can be addressed when specifying argumentation-based protocols, for example, addressing maxims (1) and (2) by constraining the justify move so that agents only introduce acceptable arguments in the dialogue. In the next section, we use two different argumentation-based protocols from the literature to evaluate the generality of our approach and support the properties described in this section, also presenting an empirical evaluation for our approach.

7 Empirical Evaluation

We have implemented our enthymeme-based communication framework using the JaCaMo Platform (Boissier et al. 2013), and its implementation is available open source[11]. Using that implementation, we have evaluated our framework using different scenarios of argumentation-based dialogues that use different argumentation schemes and different argumentation-based protocols from the literature.

The first scenario implemented is from (Panisson et al. 2018), in which the authors propose the following argumentation scheme for data-access control: (`as4dac` for short):

> Information I has security information-category C (**premise**). Agent A belongs to an access-category R which has (has no) access to information with security information-category C (**premise**). Agent A has (has no) access to information I (**conclusion**).

using this argumentation scheme and the *information-seeking* protocol specified below, the authors were able to implement data access control in MAS using an argumentation-based approach. The protocol from (Panisson et al. 2018) is specified as follow:

(1) a requester agent, named ag_i, sends a question message to an interface agent, named ag_j, asking access to a particular information φ; the protocol goes to (2);

(2) ag_j receives the request (or new information) from ag_i and checks whether it has an acceptable argument supporting $\mathtt{access}(\mathtt{ag_i}, \varphi)$. In case ag_j has an acceptable argument supporting that agent ag_i has access to the information φ, ag_j provides the information to ag_i, and the protocol goes to (4). Otherwise, when ag_j has an argument against ag_i having access to the information φ, ag_j justifies why ag_i has no access to the information φ, sending an argument supporting $\neg\mathtt{access}(\mathtt{ag_i}, \varphi)$ to `ra`; the protocol goes to (3);

(3) ag_i receives an argument supporting that it has no access to the requested information, then ag_i checks whether there is any information in support of the argument received from ag_j that it disagrees with, and in case there is some information with which ag_i disagrees, for example, ag_j was not able to identify the correct role of ag_i in the MAS, ag_i provides the correct information sending an assert message to ag_j, and the protocol goes to (2). Otherwise, when the ag_i is not able to identify any wrong information about itself, used to deny access to the requested information, the protocol goes to (4);

(4) the dialogue ends, either with ag_i receiving the information or realising it has no access to the information.

Using this protocol, the authors in (Panisson et al. 2018) describe a scenario that illustrates an emergency situation that requires sharing data between two different hospitals. The scenario involves a patient, named Bob, who is being monitored and receiving treatment in a hospital H1. The patient decides to travel to another country, receiving a bracelet that informs how to contact H1 in case of emergency. During the trip, Bob starts to feel strong pain in the chest, becomes unconscious, and goes to hospital H2. Then, a doctor, named Joe, from H2 calls the hospital H1 asking for Bob's records. However, the interface agent responsible for answering the request categorises Joe as an external hospital receptionist (considering that they are from different organisations so it has no access to H2's organisational structure). There is no access control rule that grants access to a patient's records to an external hospital receptionist, thus the interface agent denies access to that information with the following enthymeme[12]:

$$\langle\ \{\mathtt{info\_category(record,patient\_data)},\ \mathtt{ac\_category(joe,ext\text{-}hospital\text{-}receptionist)},\ \neg\mathtt{access\_rule(ext\text{-}hospital\text{-}receptionist,\ patient\_data)}\ \},\ \neg\mathtt{access(joe,record)}\ \rangle^{\theta}_{\mathrm{as4dac}}$$

in which `ac_category` stands for *access category*, and `inf_category` for *information category*, which are linked by access rules, specifying when an `ac_category` has access to an `inf_category`. Continuing this scenario, when Joe receives the argument above, he realises that his role has not been correctly identified, so he provides the information that he is a doctor. However, external doctors have no access to patient's records as well, and he receives the following argument:

$$\langle\ \{\mathtt{info\_category(record,patient\_data)},\ \mathtt{ac\_category(joe,external\text{-}doctor)},\ \neg\mathtt{access\_rule(external\text{-}doctor,patient\_data)}\ \},\ \neg\mathtt{access(joe,record)}\ \rangle^{\theta}_{\mathrm{as4dac}}$$

Finally, considering that Joe has been correctly categorised, Joe provides the information that the patient is unconscious, which means it is an emergency situation. That information enables the use of emergency rules, in which external doctors have access to patient's records in emergency situations, and Bob's records are granted to Joe.

Applying our approach to this protocol enables the interface agent to communicate enthymemes when justifying why the requester agent has no access to the re-

[11] https://github.com/AlisonPanisson/EBCF

[12] Note that, the interface agent knows the requester agents share the same argumentation schemes, but they do not share information about the organisational structure, considering they are from different organisations.

quested information, sending an enthymeme supporting $\neg\mathtt{access}(\mathtt{ag_i}, \varphi)$, with ag_i the requester agent. The implementation of this protocol, using our approach for enthymeme-based communication in MAS, including the scenarios from (Panisson et al. 2018), is available in our GitHub repository[13]. Also, the repository includes an empirical evaluation in which we measure the length of messages communicated by agents in this scenario. Our results show that our approach reduces from 45% to 46% the length of arguments (enthymemes) communicated by agents.

The second scenario implemented is from (Panisson, McBurney, and Bordini 2021; Panisson and Bordini 2017; Panisson 2017), in which the authors show different examples of argumentation-based dialogues about experts' assertions, based on the argumentation scheme from role to know described in this paper, using the protocol for *inquiry* dialogues described below:

(1) an agent ag_i starts a dialogue with another agent ag_j, asserting the information φ that becomes the subject of the dialogue; the protocol goes to (2).

(2) ag_j receives the assertion of φ and checks whether it has an argument against it. When it has no argument against φ, it accepts that information, and the protocol goes to (5). Otherwise, when ag_j is able to construct an argument against φ, ag_j questions the other agent for an argument supporting that assertion; the protocol goes to (3).

(3) ag_i receives a question and it responds with an argument that supports the questioned proposition; the protocol goes to (4).

(4) ag_j receives an argument and checks whether the information received from ag_i is enough to make it accept the subject of the dialogue, i.e., if it has no argument against the subject of the dialogue, considering the argument received from ag_i. In case ag_j has no argument against the subject of the dialogue, it accepts the subject of the dialogue; the protocol goes to (5). Otherwise, when ag_j is able to construct an argument against the subject of the dialogue, either (i) it asserts $\neg\varphi$, committing itself to provide support for $\neg\varphi$, and the protocol goes to (2); or (ii) it checks whether it is able to answer negatively any critical question related to the argumentation scheme sn that ag_i has used to instantiate its argument. In the case where it is able to answer negatively a critical question from sn, it asserts $\neg cq$, with cq the critical question; the protocol goes to (2).

(5) ag_j receives an accept message, and in the case where the accepted proposition is the subject of the dialogue, the dialogue ends with both agents believing that the subject of the dialogue holds. In the case where the accepted proposition is a critical question, the agent that accepts the critical question returns to step (4) of the protocol, accepting the subject of the dialogue, questioning another critical question, or committing itself to give support for the subject of the dialogue not being the case.

[13]https://github.com/AlisonPanisson/EBCF/blob/master/Scenario_DAC.md

Using this protocol, the authors (Panisson, McBurney, and Bordini 2021; Panisson and Bordini 2017; Panisson 2017) describe an example in which two agents argue about whether *smoking causes cancer* or not, the same scenario introduced in Sections 2. In that example, agents communicate arguments similar to those presented in Section 3. Below, we describe an enthymeme communicated by an agent from the implementation of this scenario:

$$\langle\{\mathtt{asserts(pietro,\neg causes(smoking,cancer))},\ \mathtt{about(causes(smoking,cancer),cancer)}\},\ \mathtt{causes(smoking,cancer)}\rangle^{\theta}_{\mathtt{position\_to\_know}}$$

in which it believes that *smoking does not cause cancer*, based on Pietro's assertion. Considering that Pietro is a doctor, it is a valid argument (enthymeme). However, in the course of the dialogue, another agent argues that Pietro is not a reliable source of information, and the dialogue ends with both agents reaching the conclusion that *smoking causes cancer*, based on John's assertion (the argument used as an example in Section 2).

Applying our approach to this protocol enables agents to communicate enthymemes when justifying their previous assertions. The implementation of this scenario and protocol is available in our GitHub repository [14]. Our empirical evaluation shows that our approach reduces the length of messages communicated by agents in this scenario from 45% to 51%. This second scenario achieves better results as agents are from the same organisation, i.e., they share the organisational structure of the MAS.

Implementing both protocols presented above, using the scenario introduced with each protocol by the authors, allowed us empirically validate our approach by executing a few experiments[15]. First, we were able to confirm that our approach reduces the length of arguments without losing the meaning of those communications, supporting both Propositions 1 and 2. Second, the experiments show the generality of our framework, which allows us to represent different argumentation schemes as well as specify different argumentation-based protocols using the performatives introduced in Section 4. More details, including the output for all experiments, are publicly available in our GitHub repository[16].

8 Related Work

In (Black and Hunter 2008), the authors investigate the use of enthymemes in inquiry dialogues, and show how enthymemes can be managed by the agents involved, and how common knowledge can evolve through dialogue. Also, the authors claim that when a recipient decodes an enthymeme, it does not know for certain what the intended argument is, and it is not guaranteed to find the same premises for it. But, if both have the same understanding of common knowledge,

[14]https://github.com/AlisonPanisson/EBCF/blob/master/Scenario_RK.md

[15]All experiments are available in https://github.com/AlisonPanisson/EBCF

[16]https://github.com/AlisonPanisson/EBCF

the intended argument (the original proponent's argument) is correctly interpreted by the recipient. Also, in that paper the authors say that enthymemes make the exchanges made by agents more sensible, since they avoid the use of common knowledge. But, in case of disparities in the so called cobases (the expected common knowledge) of the two agents, the enthymeme inquiry strategy in (Black and Hunter 2008) forces the agents to exchange quiz and posit moves (additional moves) when the recipient of an enthymeme cannot decode it. Our work differs from (Black and Hunter 2008) in that we guarantee that agents will only remove from the exchanged arguments information that all agents know, and the underlying platform ensures it is kept up to date to all agents, thus there are no disparities in the expected common knowledge. Thus, our approach avoids any extra moves such as the quiz and posit moves described in (Black and Hunter 2008). Also, we use argumentation schemes in order to guide the process agents use for encoding arguments into enthymemes and decoding enthymemes into arguments. Considering that practical MAS typically require accuracy in the communication process used by agents, our approach seems more applicable to MAS development.

In (Walton 2008), Walton proposes a new theory of enthymemes. That work describes three bases for the enthymeme in a formal dialogue system: (i) the participant's commitment sets; (ii) the set of argument schemes shared by both participants; and (iii) a set of propositions representing common knowledge shared by both participants. In (Walton 2008), Walton claims that "although there is much writing on the nature and importance of enthymemes, and their function in argumentation, very little appears to be known about how they actually work." Further, he says that the common-knowledge database is domain-dependent, because what is taken to be common knowledge varies widely depending on the context of the dialogue (Walton 2008). Our work takes inspiration from (Walton 2008); however we here consider structured argumentation in MAS, using concepts, features, and the infrastructure available in well-known multi-agent frameworks, such as JaCaMo (Boissier et al. 2013). While we already implemented (ii) and (iii) from Walton's theory, (i) can be easily implemented, and it is part of a planned extension of this work.

In (Black and Hunter 2009), extending their previous work in (Black and Hunter 2008), the authors argue that humans often engage in dialogues where enthymemes are used; however, proposals for logic-based formalisations of that process remain underdeveloped. In particular, in that work the authors use relevance-theoretic ideas of maximising cognitive effect and minimising cognitive effort. It aims to enable a proponent of an intended logical argument to construct an appropriate enthymeme for the intended recipient, and for the intended recipient to reconstruct the intended logical argument from the enthymeme. The authors argue that if a proponent wants to construct an appropriate enthymeme for a recipient, they need to know about the recipient's knowledge first. Similarly when the recipient deconstructs the enthymeme received from the proponent. Further, the authors have shown that if the recipient's view of the shared knowledge is the same as that of the proponent, then the deconstruction process is guaranteed to return an argument whose claim is the same as that of the intended argument (Black and Hunter 2009). Our work takes into consideration both those interesting points in (Black and Hunter 2009): the rationality of agents in constructing and deconstructing enthymemes, as well as considering the cognitive effects and efforts. As our approach guides such construction and deconstruction processes using argumentation schemes, the cognitive efforts can be reduced, while the cognitive effects are guaranteed, given that using the argumentation schemes for guidance, the recipient will have the same understanding of the proponent's argument.

9 Conclusion

In this work, we described an argumentation framework where agents exchange only the information needed to ensure that both sides, the proponent and recipient(s), will have the same understanding of the uttered arguments. Improving the efficiency of argumentation-based communication benefits all applications that use argumentation techniques, and decreasing the network usage benefits all applications that have restricted bandwidth, e.g., applications that use mobile networks such as (Schmidt et al. 2016; Koster, Bazzan, and de Souza 2016). Our approach is based on an organisation-centred paradigm, using organisational information and argumentation schemes as common knowledge; other approaches for describing common knowledge such as those in (Black and Hunter 2009; Black and Hunter 2008) could be considered without major changes. However, note that, considering organisational information and argumentation schemes as common knowledge, our approach allows agents to construct appropriate enthymemes not only for specific agents, but also to an entire "audience" belonging to the same organisation. Thus, when considering dialogues among more than two agents, our approach is more suitable than other approaches, given that agents will be able to use the same enthymemes for the entire audience, and all will have the same understanding of that communication.

Also, considering argumentation schemes in MAS from a practical point of view seems as yet an underdeveloped research topic. Here, we described how we used argumentation schemes integrated with multi-agent platforms, and how they are used by agents to instantiate arguments as well as to decode enthymemes into arguments instantiated from those argumentation schemes.

In future work, we intend to extend our approach to consider the public statements previously made by agents during dialogues (the *commitment stores*), covering all desiderata from (Walton 2008). However, as argued in this paper, it may depend on the context of different types of dialogues. While storytelling (Bex and Bench-Capon 2010; Bex and Bench-Capon 2014; Bex and Bench-Capon 2017) and complex explanations (Sklar and Azhar 2018; Miller 2019) require agents reinforcing previous conclusions (from their CS) in order to keep the link between arguments, other types of dialogues may not require such a link between moves, thus that information can be omitted.

References

Akata, Z.; Balliet, D.; de Rijke, M.; Dignum, F.; Dignum, V.; Eiben, G.; Fokkens, A.; Grossi, D.; Hindriks, K.; Hoos, H.; et al. 2020. A research agenda for hybrid intelligence: Augmenting human intellect with collaborative, adaptive, responsible, and explainable artificial intelligence. *Computer* 53(8):18–28.

Berariu, T. 2014. An argumentation framework for bdi agents. In Zavoral, F.; Jung, J. J.; and Badica, C., eds., *Intelligent Distributed Computing VII*, volume 511 of *Studies in Computational Intelligence*. Springer International Publishing. 343–354.

Besnard, P., and Hunter, A. 2014. Constructing argument graphs with deductive arguments: a tutorial. *Argument & Computation* 5(1):5–30.

Bex, F. J., and Bench-Capon, T. J. 2010. Persuasive stories for multi-agent argumentation. In *AAAI fall symposium: computational models of narrative*, volume 10, 04.

Bex, F., and Bench-Capon, T. J. 2014. Understanding narratives with argumentation. In *COMMA*, 11–18.

Bex, F., and Bench-Capon, T. 2017. Arguing with stories. In *Narration as Argument*. Springer. 31–45.

Black, E., and Hunter, A. 2008. Using enthymemes in an inquiry dialogue system. In *Proceedings of the 7th international joint conference on Autonomous agents and multiagent systems-Volume 1*, 437–444. International Foundation for Autonomous Agents and Multiagent Systems.

Black, E., and Hunter, A. 2009. A relevance-theoretic framework for constructing and deconstructing enthymemes. *Journal of Logic and Computation* 22(1):55–78.

Boissier, O.; Bordini, R. H.; Hübner, J. F.; Ricci, A.; and Santi, A. 2013. Multi-agent oriented programming with jacamo. *Science of Computer Programming* 78(6):747–761.

Bordini, R. H.; Hübner, J. F.; and Wooldridge, M. 2007. *Programming Multi-Agent Systems in AgentSpeak using Jason (Wiley Series in Agent Technology)*. John Wiley & Sons.

Dung, P. M. 1995. On the acceptability of arguments and its fundamental role in nonmonotonic reasoning, logic programming and n-person games. *Artificial Intelligence* 77:321–357.

Freitas, A.; Panisson, A. R.; Hilgert, L.; Meneguzzi, F.; Vieira, R.; and Bordini, R. H. 2015. Integrating ontologies with multi-agent systems through CArtAgO artifacts. In *2015 IEEE/WIC/ACM International Joint Conferences on Web Intelligence (WI) and Intelligent Agent Technologies (IAT)*, volume 2, 143–150.

Freitas, A.; Panisson, A. R.; Hilgert, L.; Meneguzzi, F.; Vieira, R.; and Bordini, R. H. 2017. Applying ontologies to the development and execution of multi-agent systems. In *Web Intelligence*, volume 15, 291–302. IOS Press.

García, A. J., and Simari, G. R. 2014. Defeasible logic programming: Delp-servers, contextual queries, and explanations for answers. *Argument & Computation* 5(1):63–88.

Governatori, G.; Maher, M. J.; Antoniou, G.; and Billington, D. 2004. Argumentation semantics for defeasible logic. *J. Log. Comput.* 14(5):675–702.

Grice, H. P. 1975. Logic and conversation. speech acts, ed. by peter cole and jerry morgan, 41-58.

Gunning, D.; Stefik, M.; Choi, J.; Miller, T.; Stumpf, S.; and Yang, G.-Z. 2019. Xai—explainable artificial intelligence. *Science Robotics* 4(37).

Gunning, D. 2017. Explainable artificial intelligence (xai). *Defense Advanced Research Projects Agency (DARPA), nd Web* 2:2.

Hubner, J. F.; Sichman, J. S.; and Boissier, O. 2007. Developing organised multiagent systems using the moise+ model: programming issues at the system and agent levels. *International Journal of Agent-Oriented Software Engineering* 1(3-4):370–395.

Hunter, A. 2007. Real arguments are approximate arguments. In *AAAI*, volume 7, 66–71.

Kokciyan, N.; Sassoon, I.; Young, A. P.; Chapman, M.; Porat, T.; Ashworth, C.; Modgil, S.; Parsons, S.; and Sklar, E. 2018. Towards an argumentation system for supporting patients in self-managing their chronic conditions. AAAI.

Koster, A.; Bazzan, A. L.; and de Souza, M. 2016. Liar liar, pants on fire; or how to use subjective logic and argumentation to evaluate information from untrustworthy sources. *Artificial Intelligence Review* 1–17.

Mailly, J.-G. 2016. Using enthymemes to fill the gap between logical argumentation and revision of abstract argumentation frameworks. *arXiv preprint arXiv:1603.08789*.

McBurney, P., and Parsons, S. 2004. Locutions for argumentation in agent interaction protocols. In van Eijk, R. M.; Huget, M.-P.; and Dignum, F., eds., *AC*, volume 3396 of *Lecture Notes in Computer Science*, 209–225. Springer.

Miller, T. 2019. Explanation in artificial intelligence: Insights from the social sciences. *Artificial Intelligence* 267:1–38.

Modgil, S., and Prakken, H. 2014. The aspic+ framework for structured argumentation: a tutorial. *Argument & Computation* 5(1):31–62.

Nettel, A. 2011. The enthymeme between persuasion and argumentation. In *Proceedings of the 7th conference on argumentation of the International Society for the Study of Argumentation*, 1359–1365.

Panisson, A. R., and Bordini, R. H. 2016. Knowledge representation for argumentation in agent-oriented programming languages. In *2016 Brazilian Conference on Intelligent Systems, BRACIS*.

Panisson, A. R., and Bordini, R. H. 2017. Argumentation schemes in multi-agent systems: A social perspective. In *International Workshop on Engineering Multi-Agent Systems*, 92–108. Springer.

Panisson, A. R., and Bordini, R. H. 2022. Towards an enthymeme-based communication framework. In *International Conference on Autonomous Agents and MultiAgent Systems*.

Panisson, A. R.; Meneguzzi, F.; Vieira, R.; and Bordini, R. H. 2014. An Approach for Argumentation-based Reasoning Using Defeasible Logic in Multi-Agent Programming

Languages. In *11th International Workshop on Argumentation in Multiagent Systems*.

Panisson, A. R.; Ali, A.; McBurney, P.; and Bordini, R. H. 2018. Argumentation schemes for data access control. In *COMMA*, 361–368.

Panisson, A. R.; McBurney, P.; and Bordini, R. H. 2021. A computational model of argumentation schemes for multi-agent systems. *Argument & Computation* (Preprint):1–39.

Panisson, A. R. 2017. Argumentation schemes and enthymemes in multi-agent systems. In *Proceedings of the 16th Conference on Autonomous Agents and MultiAgent Systems*, 1849–1850.

Parsons, S.; Atkinson, K.; Haigh, K.; Levitt, K.; Rowe, P. M. J.; Singh, M. P.; and Sklar, E. 2012. Argument schemes for reasoning about trust. *Computational Models of Argument: Proceedings of COMMA 2012* 245:430.

Parsons, S.; Wooldridge, M.; and Amgoud, L. 2002. An analysis of formal inter-agent dialogues. In *1st International Conference on Autonomous Agents and Multi-Agent Systems*, 394–401. ACM Press.

Prakken, H. 2011. An abstract framework for argumentation with structured arguments. *Argument and Computation* 1(2):93–124.

Sadri, F.; Toni, F.; and Torroni, P. 2001. Logic agents, dialogues and negotiation: An abductive approach. In *Proceedings AISB'01 Convention*. AISB.

Schmidt, D.; Panisson, A. R.; Freitas, A.; Bordini, R. H.; Meneguzzi, F.; and Vieira, R. 2016. An ontology-based mobile application for task managing in collaborative groups. In *Florida Artificial Intelligence Research Society Conference*.

Searle, J. R. 1969. *Speech Acts: An Essay in the Philosophy of Language*. Cambridge University Press.

Sklar, E. I., and Azhar, M. Q. 2018. Explanation through argumentation. In *Proceedings of the 6th International Conference on Human-Agent Interaction*, 277–285.

Tolchinsky, P.; Atkinson, K.; McBurney, P.; Modgil, S.; and Cortés, U. 2007. Agents deliberating over action proposals using the proclaim model. In *International Central and Eastern European Conference on Multi-Agent Systems*, 32–41. Springer.

Tolchinsky, P.; Modgil, S.; Atkinson, K.; McBurney, P.; and Cortés, U. 2012. Deliberation dialogues for reasoning about safety critical actions. *Autonomous Agents and Multi-Agent Systems* 25(2):209–259.

Toni, F. 2014. A tutorial on assumption-based argumentation. *Argument & Computation* 5(1):89–117.

Toniolo, A.; Cerutti, F.; Oren, N.; Norman, T. J.; and Sycara, K. 2014. Making informed decisions with provenance and argumentation schemes. In *Proceedings of the Eleventh International Workshop on Argumentation in Multi-Agent Systems, 2014*.

Walton, D.; Reed, C.; and Macagno, F. 2008. *Argumentation Schemes*. Cambridge University Press.

Walton, D. 1996. *Argumentation schemes for presumptive reasoning*. Routledge.

Walton, D. 2008. The three bases for the enthymeme: A dialogical theory. *Journal of Applied Logic* 6(3):361–379.

Proceedings of the 19th International Conference on Principles of Knowledge Representation and Reasoning
Main Track

Verification and Realizability in Finite-Horizon Multiagent Systems

Senthil Rajasekaran and Moshe Y. Vardi
Rice University
{sr79, vardi}@rice.edu

Abstract

The problems of *verification* and *realizability* are two central themes in the analysis of reactive systems. When multiagent systems are considered, these problems have natural analogues of existence (nonemptiness) of pure-strategy Nash equilibria and verification of pure-strategy Nash equilibria. Recently, this body of work has begun to include finite-horizon temporal goals. With finite-horizon temporal goals, there is a natural hierarchy of goal representation, ranging from deterministic finite automata (DFA), to nondeterministic finite automata (NFA), and to alternating finite automata (AFA), with a worst-case exponential gap between each successive representation. Previous works showed that the realizability problem with DFA goals was PSPACE-complete, while the realizability problem with temporal logic goals is in 2EXPTIME. In this work, we study both the realizability and the verification problems with respect to various goal representations. We first show that the realizability problem with NFA goals is EXPTIME-complete and with AFA goals is 2EXPTIME-complete, thus establishing strict complexity gaps between realizability with respect to DFA, NFA, and AFA goals. We then contrast these complexity gaps with the complexity of the verification problem, where we show that verification with respect to DFAs, NFA, and AFA goals is PSPACE-complete.

1 Introduction

Verification (Clarke, Emerson, and Sistla 1986) and *Realizability* (Pnueli and Rosner 1989) are two major decision problems in the study of reactive systems. When the goals of these systems are specified through linear temporal logics, game theory has provided a powerful modeling framework for both problems through a two-agent game in which one agent takes on the role of a system that tries to realize a property and the other takes on the role of the environment that tries to falsify the property. The verification problem corresponds to checking whether an input strategy is winning for the system agent in the relevant game (Kupferman and Vardi 1996), and the realizability (also called *nonemptiness*) problem corresponds to determining whether a winning strategy for the system agent exists (Pnueli and Rosner 1989).

When the number of autonomous agents increases, the games become *concurrent multiagent games*, suitable for analyzing concurrent multiagent systems (Shoham and Leyton-Brown 2009). In this setting, the notion of a winning strategy no longer corresponds to a meaningful solution concept, as there are no longer only two agents with a purely adversarial relationship. In these types of systems, the concept of a *pure-strategy Nash equilibria* (henceforth, Nash equilibria) has come to be a widely used solution concept (Bouyer et al. 2015). Informally, a Nash equilibria is a profile of strategies such that for each agent in the system deviating from the profile is never more profitable than not . In this sense, Nash equilibria represent a stable point that games naturally tend towards over repeated play (Nash 1950; Gutierrez, Harrenstein, and Wooldridge 2015a).

Concurrent multiagent games represent an extremely broad class of games. *Iterated Boolean Games* (Gutierrez, Harrenstein, and Wooldridge 2015b) are a restriction of concurrent multiagent games that naturally mirror the games that model the two-agent realizability and verification problems (Kupferman and Vardi 1996; Pnueli and Rosner 1989). In an iterated boolean game each agent has a temporal goal and at each time step assigns a setting to a unique collection of boolean variables under its control. Thus, when all agents' assignments are considered we are given a complete valuation of the boolean variables at each time step. This infinite sequence of valuations is then used to determine which temporal goals are satisfied and which are not. Finding Nash equilibria in such games corresponds to a useful method of analysis of the systems that these games model; as such, there is a very large of body finding Nash equilibria when agents' goals are given by an infinite-horizon logic such as *Linear Time Temporal Logic* (LTL) (Wooldridge 2009; Gutierrez et al. 2020; Mogavero et al. 2014; Grädel, Thomas, and Wilke 2002; Abate et al. 2021).

Some systems, however, are naturally modeled by agents with finite-horizon goals, such as when notions like 'completion' are considered. The concept of a finite-horizon temporal logic remains a relatively recent development in the study of temporal logics (Giacomo and Vardi 2013). While agents still create an infinite trace by setting their variables at every time step, satisfaction is considered over finite prefixes. The analogous problem of finding Nash equilibria in iterated boolean games in which each agent has been given a finite-horizon temporal goal has recently begun to receive attention (Rajasekaran and Vardi 2021; Gutierrez, Perelli, and Wooldridge 2017).

Our modelling of this problem is done from the viewpoint of a system designer. Specifically, when given a system in which multiple agents have finite-horizon temporal logic goals, we query a subset W of "good" agents to see if there is Nash equilibrium in which precisely the agents in W are able to satisfy their goals. By the definition of the Nash equilibrium, this means that agents not within W, which we consider as "bad" agents, are unable to unilaterally change their strategy and satisfy their own "bad" goal. In doing so we can naturally incorporate malicious agents with goals contrary to the designer's intent by specifying a set W that not contain such agents. This study of teams of cooperating agents has clear parallels in earlier work in rational synthesis (Fisman, Kupferman, and Lustig 2010; Kupferman, Perelli, and Vardi 2016).

Here we consider *Linear Time Temporal Logic on Finite Traces* (LTLf) (Giacomo and Vardi 2013) as our standard finite-horizon temporal logic, but by using an automata-based approach we are able to prove more general results that are independent of a specific logic by considering the size of the automata that represents the specification. Since finite-horizon temporal logics describe languages of finite words, they admit a variety of equivalent representations, ranging from deterministic finite automata (DFAs) to nondeterministic finite automata (NFAs) to alternating finite automata (DFAs) (Giacomo and Vardi 2013; Giacomo and Vardi 2015; Giacomo and Vardi 2016). While alternating finite automata are polynomial in the size with respect to their corresponding LTL_f formula, nondeterminstic automata are exponential and deterministic finite automata are doubly exponential (Giacomo and Vardi 2013). By reasoning about different types of input automata, we are able to reason broadly about finite-horizon temporal goals with different goal succinctness from a complexity-theoretic viewpoint. It is then natural to consider how the succinctness of the representation influences the complexities of the realizability and verification problems.

Our investigation sheds new light on the computational complexity of temporal Nash Equilibria. Note that, in prior work, the verification problem is usually proven to be easier than the realizability problem from a complexity-theoretic viewpoint. This corresponds to our intuition, since the verification problem checks a single input candidate strategy, while the realizability problem tries to find some solution strategy. Here, we observe the same phenomena of realizability being more difficult than verification. The succinctness of the representation does not, however, seem to effect the complexity of the verification problem in this setting. No matter which representation we use, we get a PSPACE-complete complexity result. In contrast, if we consider the realizability problem then we get a strict hierarchy. For DFA goals, the problem is PSPACE-complete (Rajasekaran and Vardi 2021) (the same as verification, an exception to the intuition that verification is easier than realizability). From NFAs goals, the problem is EXPTIME-complete. Finally, for AFA goals, the problem is 2EXPTIME-complete. This analysis extends the state of the art to include a complete set of results for both problems with varying representations.

Our approach follows the approach outlined in (Rajasekaran and Vardi 2021) in that we consider the Nash equilibria as two separate conditions - one that corresponds to correct behavior under deviation (the j-Deviant Trace Condition) and one that corresponds to correct behavior when no deviations are observed (the Primary-Trace condition). Using this characterization we are able to prove a suite of new results and prove novel variants of a few older results that appeared in previous works under this unified framework. Taken together, they represent a complete characterization of the complexity of both problems for the three main types of automata-theoretic representations common to the literature on finite-horizon temporal logic.

2 Background

The background presented here largely follows (Rajasekaran and Vardi 2021). We assume familiarity with automata theory, as in (Sipser 2006; Vardi 1996).

2.1 Games

In this section we provide some definitions related to two-agent games to provide a standard notation throughout this paper. The two agents are denoted agent 0 and agent 1.

Definition 2.1 (Arena). An *arena* is a four tuple $A = (V, V_0, V_1, E)$ where V is a finite set of vertices, V_0 and V_1 are disjoint subsets of V with $V_0 \cup V_1 = V$ that represent the vertices that belong to agent 0 and agent 1 respectively, and $E \subseteq V \times V$ is a set of directed edges, i.e. $(v, v') \mid \in E$ if there is an edge from v to v'.

Intuitively, the agent that owns a node decides which outgoing edge to follow. Since $V = V_0 \cup V_1$, we omit V and write $A = (V_0, V_1, E)$.

Definition 2.2 (Play). A *play* in an arena A is an infinite sequence $\rho = \rho_0\rho_1\rho_2 \ldots \in V^\omega$ such that $(\rho_n, \rho_{n+1}) \in E$ holds for all $n \in \mathbb{N}$. We say that ρ starts at ρ_0

Definition 2.3 (Game). A *game* $G = (A, Win)$ consists of an arena A with vertex set V and a set of winning plays $Win \subseteq V^\omega$. A play ρ is winning for agent 0 if $\rho \in Win$, otherwise it is winning for agent 1.

Note that in this formulation of a game, reaching a state $v \in V$ with no outgoing transitions is always losing for agent 0, as agent 0 is the one that must ensure that ρ is infinite (a member of V^ω).

A game is thus defined by its set of winning plays, often called the *winning condition*. One such widely used winning condition is the *safety condition*.

Definition 2.4 (Safety Games). Let $A = (V, V_0, V_1, E)$ be an arena and $S \subseteq V$ be a subset of A's vertices. Then, the *safety condition* $Safety(S)$ is defined as $Safety(S) = \{\rho \in V^\omega \mid Occ(\rho) \subseteq S\}$, where $Occ(\rho)$ denotes the subset of vertices that occur at least once in ρ. A game with the safety condition for a subset S is a *safety game* with the set S of *safe vertices*. Information about solving safety games, including notions of *winning strategies* and *winning sets* can be found here (McNaughton 1993).

2.2 Concurrent Games and iBGs

A *concurrent game structure* (CGS) is an 8-tuple

$$(Prop, \Omega, (ACT_i)_{i\in\Omega}, S, \lambda, \tau, s_0 \in S, (A^i)_{i\in\Omega})$$

where $Prop$ is a finite set of *propositions*, $\Omega = \{0, \dots k-1\}$ is a finite set of *agents*, ACT_i is a set of *actions*, where each ACT_i is associated with Agent i, the set of *decisions* is $D = ACT_0 \times ACT_1 \dots ACT_{k-1}$, S is a set of *states*, $\lambda : S \to 2^{Prop}$ is a *labeling function* that associates each state with a set of propositions that are interpreted as true in that state, $\tau : S \times D \to S$ is a deterministic *transition function* that takes a state and a decision as input and returns another state, $s_0 \in S$ is the *initial state*, and A^i is a *goal* specification for Agent i given in the form of an deterministic finite automaton (DFA), nondeterministic finite automaton (NFA), or alternating finite automaton (AFA). [1] We say that a finite word automaton accepts an infinite word ω if it accepts a finite prefix of ω. In a CGS, Agent i prefers plays in the game that satisfy A^i, that is, a play such that some finite prefix of the play is accepted by A^i. For a goal automaton we use the notation $A^i = \langle Q^i, q_0^i, \Sigma, \delta^i, F^i\rangle$, where Q^i is the state space, $q_0^i \in Q^i$ is the initial state, Σ is the alphabet, δ^i is the transition function, and F^i is the set of final states. In this paper we refer to arbitrary infinite sequences of states in a CGS as *traces*.

We now define *iterated boolean games* (iBG), a restriction on the CGS formalism (Gutierrez, Harrenstein, and Wooldridge 2015b). We follow the formulation of (Rajasekaran and Vardi 2021), as we take the set of actions to be a finite alphabet rather than a set of truth assignments. An iBG is defined by applying the following restrictions to the CGS formalism. Agent i 'owns" alphabet Σ_i. These Σ_i are disjoint and each Σ_i serves as the set of actions for Agent i-an action for agent i consists of choosing a letter in Σ_i. The set of decisions is then $\Sigma = \times_{i=0}^{k-1} \Sigma_i$. The set of states is also Σ, and the labeling function is the identity function, i.e., $\lambda(s) = s$. Our use of the iBG model is motivated by presentation, as iBGs offer a simple model in which agent actions influence global states - considering general CGS models would not influence the forthcoming complexity-theoretic results. Finally, the transition function τ is simply the right projection $\tau(s, d) = d$.

We now introduce the notion of a *strategy* for Agent i in the general CGS formalism.

Definition 2.5 (Strategy for Agent i). A strategy for Agent i is a function $\pi_i : S^* \to ACT_i$. Intuitively, this is a function that, given the observed history of the game (represented by an element of S^*), returns an action $act_i \in ACT_i$.

Recalling that $\Omega = \{0, 1 \dots k-1\}$ represents the set of agents, we now introduce the notion of a *strategy profile*.

Definition 2.6 (Strategy Profile). Let Π_i represent the set of strategies for agent i. We define the set of strategy profiles $\Pi = \times_{i\in\Omega} \Pi_i$ and denote a single strategy profile as π.

A strategy profile can be naturally thought of as a function of type $\Sigma^* \to \Sigma$, and we will call any function with such type a *global strategy*. Since a global strategy is deterministic, it yields a unique element of S^ω, which we call a *primary trace*.

Definition 2.7 (Primary Trace resulting from a Global Strategy). Given a global strategy $\pi : \Sigma^* \to \Sigma$, the primary trace of π is the unique trace t that satisfies

1. $t[0] = \pi(\epsilon)$
2. $t[i] = \pi(t[0], \dots t[i-1])$

We denote this trace as t_π.

Given a trace $t \in S^\omega$, define the *winning set* $W_t = \{i \in \Omega : t \models A^i\}$ to be the set of agents whose DFA goals are satisfied by a finite prefix of the trace t. The *losing set* is then defined as Ω / W_t.

A common solution concept in game theory is the *Nash equilibrium*, which we adapt to our iBG framework. In our framework, a Nash equilibrium is a strategy profile π such that for each Agent i, if A^i is not satisfied on t_π, then a unilateral strategy deviation for Agent i does not result in a trace that satisfies A^i.

Definition 2.8 (Nash Equilibrium). (Gutierrez, Harrenstein, and Wooldridge 2015b) Let G be an iBG and $\pi = \langle \pi_0, \pi_1 \dots \pi_{k-1}\rangle$ be a strategy profile. We denote $W_\pi = W_{t_\pi}$. The profile π is a *Nash equilibrium* if for every $i \in \Omega / W_t$ we have that for each strategy profile of the form $\pi' = \langle \pi_0, \pi_1 \dots \pi_i' \dots \pi_{k-1}\rangle$, with $\pi_i' \in \Pi_i$, it is the case that $i \in \Omega / W_{\pi'}$.

This definition provides an analogy for the Nash Equilibrium defined in (Nash 1950) by capturing the same property - no agent can unilaterally deviate to improve its own payoff (moving from an unsatisfied goal to a satisfied goal). Agents in the set W_π cannot have their payoff improved further, so we do not check their deviations. We say that π is a W-NE iff π is a Nash Equilibrium with $W_\pi = W$.

We have already defined the primary trace, which corresponds to the trace that results from no deviations to a profile π. Since we consider unilateral deviations from a single agent in our analysis, we define these traces as well.

Definition 2.9 (j-Deviant-Trace from a Strategy Profile). Given a strategy profile π, a j-Deviant-Trace (w.r.t π) is defined as follows. For $\alpha \in \Sigma$, we introduce the notation $\alpha[-j]$ to refer to $\alpha|_{\Sigma \setminus \Sigma_j}$ (that is, α with Σ_j projected out). A trace $t = y_0, y_1, \dots$ is j-deviant if

1. $y_0 = \varepsilon$
2. $y_{i+1} = y_0, \dots, y_i, \alpha$, where $\alpha \in \Sigma$ and $\alpha[-j] = \pi(y_i)[-j]$
3. t is not the primary trace

Our characterization of the Nash equilibria is based on (Rajasekaran and Vardi 2021), in which the Nash Equilibrium condition was decomposed into the *Primary-Trace* and *j-Deviant-Trace* Condition, which we reintroduce here. For a fixed strategy profile π we have:

1. Primary-Trace Condition: The primary infinite trace t_π defined by π satisfies the goals A^i for precisely $i \in W$.

[1] For automata-theoretic background, see (Vardi 1996)

2. j-Deviant-Trace Condition: Each j-*deviant* trace $t = y_0, y_1, \ldots$ (w.r.t π) for $j \notin W$, does not satisfy the goal A^j.

A strategy profile $\pi : \Sigma^* \to \Sigma$ is then a W-NE iff it satisfies both the Primary-Trace Condition and the j-Deviant Trace Condition w.r.t W. In this definition we work with a general notion of the goal A^j accepting a prefix, therefore this universally applies to DFA, NFA, and AFA goals.

The main insight of (Rajasekaran and Vardi 2021) was to show that these two conditions could be reasoned about through automata-theoretic means *separately* when considering DFA goals. In order to analyze the j-Deviant-Trace Condition for a single agent j with goal A^j, a safety game G_j with $V_0 = Q^j$ and $V_1 = \{Q^j \times \Sigma\}$ and edge relation E_j is defined as follows:

1. $(q, \langle q, \alpha \rangle)) \in E_j$ for $q \in Q^j \setminus F^j$ and all $\alpha \in \Sigma$.
2. $(\langle q, \alpha \rangle, q') \in E_j$ for $q \in Q^j$ and $q' \in Q^j$, where $q' = \delta^j(q, \beta)$ for some $\beta \in \Sigma$ such that $\alpha[-j] = \beta[-j]$.

The winning set of agent 0 in this game is denoted $Win_0(G_j)$; the winning set for agent 1 is $Win_1(G_j)$.

In order to reason about the Primary Trace, we construct the deterministic Büchi automaton (Vardi 1996) $A_W = \langle Q, q_0, \Sigma, \delta, F \rangle$ with

1. $Q = (\times_{j \in \Omega} Q^j) \times 2^\Omega$
2. $q_0 = \langle q_0^1, \ldots, q_0^n, W \rangle$
3. $F = (\times_{j \in \Omega} Q^j) \times \{\emptyset\}$
4. $\delta(\langle q_1, \ldots q_n, U \rangle, \alpha) = \langle q_1', \ldots q_n', V \rangle$ if $q_j' = \delta^i(q_j, \alpha)$, where $q_j' \notin F^j$ for $j \notin W$, and $V = U - \{i : q_i' \in F^i\}$.

The intuition is that a word in Σ^ω is accepted by A_W iff only the goals in W are satisfied on it.

The winning sets for agent 0 in the games G_j are now used to refine the state space and transition function of A_W to create the deterministic Büchi automaton $A'_W = (Q', q_0, \Sigma, \delta', F \cap Q')$, with $Q' = \times_{i \in W} Q^i \times \times_{j \in \Omega \setminus W} \{Win_0(G_j) \cap Q^j\} \times 2^\Omega$, and δ' defined as follows: $\delta'(q, \alpha) = \delta(q, \alpha)$ if, for all $j \notin W$, we have that $(q[j], \alpha) \in Win_0(G_j)$; otherwise, $\delta'(q, \alpha)$ is undefined. It was then shown that

Theorem 1. (Rajasekaran and Vardi 2021) *For a given iBG G, a W-NE strategy exists in G iff A'_W is nonempty.*

Since the goal automata being considered have an input alphabet that is the cross product of k other alphabets ($\Sigma = \Sigma_0 \times \Sigma_1 \ldots \Sigma_{k-1}$) , they can be seen as exponential constructions themselves. For this reason, we introduce *bounded-channel automata.*

Definition 2.10 (Bounded-Channel Automaton). Let $\Sigma = \Sigma_0 \times \Sigma_1 \ldots \Sigma_{k-1}$ and let $I \subset \{0 \ldots k-1\}$ be a strict subset of agents. A *bounded-channel automaton* is an automaton with a transition function ρ that satisfies the property that for all $\alpha, \beta \in \Sigma$ and states q in the automaton, if $\alpha_I = \beta_I$, i.e α and β agree on Σ_i for every $i \in I$, then $\rho(q, \alpha) = \rho(q, \beta)$, i.e. the transition function only considers Σ_i for $i \in I$ on a state q and a symbol $\alpha \in \Sigma$.

Intuitively, a bounded-channel automaton does not consider the actions of every agent through an element of Σ but has an input alphabet $\Sigma_B = \times_{i \in I} \Sigma_i$ where $I \subset \Omega$. Note that if $|I|$ is a constant w.r.t $|\Omega| = k$, then such automata have polynomial-sized alphabets. While the use of bounded-channel goal automata does not affect many of the complexity results in this paper, considering bounded channel automata allows us to reason about a more succinct input type that arguably better corresponds to realistic situations.

3 Realizability

In this section we study the *realizability problem* (referred to as the *nonemptiness problem* in (Gutierrez, Harrenstein, and Wooldridge 2015b; Rajasekaran and Vardi 2021)) in which we are are given an iBG G *and* a set $W \subseteq \Omega$ of agents and we wish to decide if a Nash equilibria strategy profile exists in which only the agents in W have their goals satisfied. In (Rajasekaran and Vardi 2021), this problem was proven to be PSPACE-complete for DFA goals, using the safety games G_j and Büchi automaton A'_W, as described in section 2.2. We now analyze the complexity for NFA and AFA goals.

3.1 NFA Goals

Assume the input goal automata are NFAs. By determinizing each goal automaton, we can readily apply the procedure from (Rajasekaran and Vardi 2021). Constructing the DFA goal automaton $A^j = \langle Q^j, q_0^j, \Sigma, \delta^j, F^j \rangle$ from the NFA goal input involves a worst-case exponential blowup in the number of states, with no blow-up in the size of the alphabet Σ. Therefore, the state space of each safety game G_j, given by $Q^j \cup \{Q^j \times \Sigma\}$ is overall exponential in the size of the goal NFAs. Safety games can be solved in time linear in the size of the game (McNaughton 1993), so each relevant G_j can be analyzed in EXPTIME.

The automaton A'_W from (Rajasekaran and Vardi 2021) has a state space Q' that is upper bounded by the size of the cross product of all DFA goals and 2^Ω. Each DFA goal has a state space that is exponential in the size of the NFA, so the product of all DFAs is still singly exponential with respect to the NFA goals. Furthermore, 2^Ω is also singly exponential, implying that A'_W is singly exponential in size with respect to the input. Testing a Büchi automaton for nonemptiness can be done in NLOGSPACE (Vardi and Wolper 1994), meaning that A'_W can be checked for nonemptiness in PSPACE. Since the safety games are in EXPTIME in the worst case, the overall complexity of this method is in EXPTIME. These results still hold when considering bounded-channel goals, as they are still polynomial in the size of the input.

The upper bound for the realizability problem with NFA goals is analyzed above. For lack of space, we do not include here the lower-bound proof, which holds even for two-agent iBGs (and therefore holds for the bounded-channel case as well). The proof is included in detail in our corresponding technical report (Rajasekaran and Vardi 2022) [2]

[2]https://arxiv.org/abs/2205.01029

Theorem 2. *The realizability problem with NFA goals is EXPTIME-complete.*

3.2 AFA Goals

We now analyze the case of the realizability problem when the agents' goals are specified by AFAs. Since AFAs are linear (in number of states) in the size of equivalent finite-trace temporal specifications such as LTL_f or LDL_f (Giacomo and Vardi 2013), we note that a similar problem of deciding whether any W-NE exists was given a 2EXPTIME upper bound, but no lower bound, in (Gutierrez, Perelli, and Wooldridge 2017). Here we focus on the a single agent set W and provide a tight 2EXPTIME bound.

Constructing the DFA goal automata A^j from the AFA goals involves a doubly exponential worst-case blowup in the number of states (Giacomo and Vardi 2013), with no blow-up in the size of the alphabet Σ - this holds for bounded-channel automata as well. The analysis now largely follows the NFA-goals case. The size of the safety game G_j is now doubly exponential in the size of the input due to the presence of Q^j, and so each G_j can be solved in 2EXPTIME. Meanwhile A'_W consists of the cross product of the doubly exponential Q^js and the singly exponential 2^Ω, so it is doubly exponential overall. Following the same logic as before yields a 2EXPTIME upper bound.

Theorem 3. *The realizability problem with AFA goals can be solved in 2EXPTIME.*

This result agrees with the result in (Gutierrez, Perelli, and Wooldridge 2017) (where W is not part of the input). We now extend the analysis by providing a matching lower bound, proving the problem to be 2EXPTIME-hard by reducing from the 2EXPTIME-complete problem of LTL_f realizability, noting that there is a linear-time conversion from LTL_f formulas to equivalent AFA for a fixed-size alphabet (Giacomo and Vardi 2013). We note that the 2EXPTIME lower bound for LTL_f realizability holds already for fixed alphabet goals, as in (Rosner 1992).

The *LTL_f realizability problem* (Giacomo and Vardi 2015) takes as input an LTL_f formula ϕ along with a partition of the variables V in ϕ into two sets X and Y. The problem asks whether an agent (Agent 0) that takes control of the variables in X can always ensure a trace satisfying ϕ with an antagonistic agent (Agent 1) setting the variables in Y. At each time step the agents set their variables, thus producing an infinite trace over $2^{X \cup Y}$. As before, ϕ is satisfied by an infinite trace if it is satisfied by some finite prefix of that infinite trace. The interaction is naturally modeled as a game between the two agents, which is called the *ϕ-realizability game*. There are several variations of these games, we consider the variation where Agent 0 and Agent 1 move concurrently, assigning values to the X and Y variables, respectively (Giacomo and Vardi 2015).

Given an instance of the LTL_f realizability problem with goal ϕ, we construct an iBG G_ϕ with two agents. Agent 0 is given the goal ϕ expressed as AFA and Agent 1 is given an empty goal, i.e., an AFA that accepts the empty language. Let $\Sigma_0 = 2^X$, $\Sigma_1 = 2^Y$, and the set W be the empty set. Since we assume that the temporal goal has a bounded alphabet, the translation to AFAs is linear in number of states.

Theorem 4. *Given an LTL_f formula ϕ, Agent 0 wins the ϕ-realizability game iff no $\emptyset$-NE exists in G_ϕ.*

Proof. ($\rightarrow$) Assume that Agent 0 wins the ϕ-realizability game. Then, there exists a strategy $\pi'_0 : (2^Y)^* \rightarrow 2^X$ that ensures that the formula ϕ is eventually satisfied given an arbitrary Agent 1 strategy $\pi_1 : (2^X)^* \rightarrow 2^Y$. Therefore, there can not be $\emptyset$-NE in G. Suppose to the contrary that the profile $\langle \pi_0, \pi_1 \rangle$ is an $\emptyset$-NE, which means that the primary trace does not satisfy ϕ. Agent 0 can now deviate from this profile and follow the strategy π'_0, so now Agent 0 and Agent 1 are following the profile $\langle \pi'_0, \pi_1 \rangle$. Since π'_0 is a winning strategy in the ϕ-realizability game, Agent 0 is able to force satisfaction of ϕ, so $\langle \pi_0, \pi_1 \rangle$ is not an $\emptyset$-NE.

($\leftarrow$) Assume to the contrary that there is an $\emptyset$-NE in G_ϕ. We show that it implies that Agent 1 wins the ϕ-realizability game. Let $\langle \pi_0, \pi_1 \rangle$ be the strategy profile for the $\emptyset$-NE in G_ϕ. This means that ϕ is not satisfied in the primary trace, and, furthermore, for every strategy profile $\langle \pi'_0, \pi_1 \rangle$ the primary trace does not satisfy ϕ. This means that π_1 is winning strategy for Agent 1 in the ϕ-realizability game. □

Since LTL_f-realizability is known to be 2EXPTIME-complete (Giacomo and Vardi 2015), we get:

Theorem 5. *The realizability problem with AFA goals is 2EXPTIME-complete.*

Since this lower bound was shown for two-agent games, it holds for the bounded-channel case as well.

4 Verification

We now address the verification problem in which we are given an iBG G, a set $W \subseteq \Omega$ of agents, and a strategy profile $\pi = \langle \pi_0 \dots \pi_{k-1} \rangle$, where $k = |\Omega|$. We are given the strategy profile in terms of the individual strategies: Each $\pi_i = \langle S^i, s^i_0, \Sigma, \Sigma_i, \rho^i, \gamma^i \rangle$ is a Moore machine (Sipser 2006) that represents a function of type $\Sigma^* \rightarrow \Sigma_i$, where S^i is the set of states, $s^i_0 \in S^i$ is the initial state, Σ_i is the alphabet controlled by agent i, $\rho^i : S^i \times \Sigma \rightarrow S^i$ is the transition function, and $\gamma^i : S^i \rightarrow \Sigma^i$ is the output function. $\Sigma = \times_{i \in \Omega} \Sigma_i$ is the common alphabet of the goals in G. The *verification problem* takes as inputs G, W, and π and outputs whether π is a W-NE in G.

We first construct a Moore machine for π from $\pi_0 \dots \pi_{k-1}$ using the standard product construction: $\pi = \langle S, s_0, \Sigma, \Sigma, \rho, \gamma \rangle$, where

1. $S = \times_{i \in \Omega} S^i$.
2. $s_0 = \langle s^0_0, \dots, s^{k-1}_0 \rangle$.
3. Σ is both the input and output alphabet in π.
4. The transition function ρ is defined component-wise. For $\bar{t} = \langle t_0, \dots, t_{k-1} \rangle \in S$ and $\alpha \in \Sigma$, we have $\rho(\bar{t}, \alpha) = \langle t'_0, \dots, t'_{k-1} \rangle$, where $t'_i = \rho^i(t_i, \alpha)$, for each $i \in \Omega$.
5. The output function γ is defined component-wise. For $\bar{t} = \langle t_0, \dots, t_{k_1} \rangle \in S$, we have $\gamma(\bar{t}) = \langle \sigma_0, \dots, \sigma_{k-1} \rangle$, where $\sigma_i = \gamma^i(t_i)$, for each $i \in \Omega$.

Note that the size of π is exponential in the sizes of $\pi_0 \dots \pi_{k-1}$.

We now define the state outcome of running π on input words in Σ^*, inductively:

- $\pi(\varepsilon) = s_0$, and
- $\pi(w\alpha) = \rho(\pi(w), \alpha)$, for $w \in \Sigma^*$ and $\alpha \in \Sigma$

The output of running π on a word $w \in \Sigma^*$ is then $\gamma(\pi(w))$. In this way, we get that π represents a function of type $\Sigma^* \to \Sigma$,i.e. a global strategy (see Definition 2.6), which yields a primary trace (Definition 2.7).

We can define bounded-channel Moore Machines for single-agent strategies in the same way we have defined bounded-channel goal automata. The construction is the same - instead of considering input alphabet Σ, we consider a restricted version that only considers some subset of agents. This allows us to consider single-agent strategies that have a succinct representation just as we considered goals with succinct representations. We now proceed to analyze the complexity of verification with respect to DFA, NFA, and AFA goals.

4.1 DFA Goals

As described in Section 2.2, the existence of a W-NE in an iBG G with DFA goals can be analyzed through solving safety games G_j and testing a Büchi word automaton A'_W for nonemptiness. Note, however, that A'_W had a state space that consisted of the cross product of all DFA goals. Since here we have a strategy profile specified explicitly by the Moore machine $\pi = \langle \pi_0 \dots \pi_{k-1} \rangle$, the Primary-Trace and j-Deviant-Trace Conditions can be checked separately for each agent, avoiding a cross-product construction. We begin our analysis by considering agents in W.

Checking Agents in W As mentioned before, we no longer need to create an automaton from the cross product of all DFA goals A^i to form $A_{W,\pi}$, which checks the primary trace for *all* agents at once. Since the primary trace of π is uniquely determined (Definition 2.7), we can check whether this trace satisfies the goal A^i for each agent $i \in W$.

For each agent $i \in W$, we construct a DFA $A^i \times \pi$ as the product of the goal $A^i = (Q^i, q_0^i, \Sigma, \delta^i, F^i)$ and π. In detail, $A^i \times \pi = (Q^i \times S, \langle q_0^i, s_0 \rangle, \emptyset, \tau^i, F^i \times S)$. Note that the alphabet of this automaton is empty, so transitions are defined between states. For $q \in Q^i$ and $s \in S$, We have $\tau^i(\langle q, s \rangle) = \langle q', s' \rangle$, where $q' = \delta^i(q, \gamma(s))$ and $s' = \rho(s, \gamma(s))$. Satisfaction of A^i on the primary trace now corresponds to nonemptiness of this product automaton (as the transition function τ^i simulates the run of A^i on the primary trace of π), which means that a state $\langle f, s \rangle$ with $f \in F^i$ is reachable from $\langle q_0^i, s_0 \rangle$. This implies that a prefix of the primary trace is accepted by A^i. Note that the state space of $A^i \times \pi$ is of exponential size, since the state space of π is of exponential size. Nonemptiness in a DFA with an exponential state space can be decided in NPSPACE=PSPACE.

If $A^i \times \pi$ is empty for some $i \in W$. then π is not a W-NE as the goal goal A^i for an agent i is not satisfied on the primary trace. We refer to these nonemptiness queries of $A^i \times \pi$ as the i-queries.

Safety Game for Deviating Agents We now move on to the analyzing the Primary Trace and Deviant Trace conditions for agents $j \notin W$. As before, we first construct a safety game to characterize the set of states from which successful deviations are possible. We adapt the safety game G_j to take in account the fact that we wish to check if π is a W-NE. Formally, we construct the safety game $G_{\pi,j} = (Q^j \times S, Q^j \times S \times \Sigma, E_{\pi,j})$. Agent 0 owns $Q^j \times S$ and agent 1 owns $Q^j \times S \times \Sigma$. The edge relation $E_{\pi,j}$ is defined as follows:

1. $(\langle q, s \rangle, \langle q, s, \alpha \rangle)) \in E_{\pi,j}$ for $q \in Q^j \setminus F^j$, $s \in S$, and $\alpha = \gamma(s)$.
2. $(\langle q, s, \alpha \rangle, \langle q', s' \rangle) \in E_{\pi,j}$ for $q, q' \in Q^j$ and $s, s' \in S$, where $q' = \delta^j(q, \beta)$ and $s' = \rho(s, \beta)$, for some $\beta \in \Sigma$ such that $\alpha[-j] = \beta[-j]$.

As in G_j, if $q \in F^j$, then $\langle q, s \rangle$ has no successor node, and agent 0 is stuck and loses the game. Since $G_{\pi,j}$ is a safety game, agent 0's goal is to avoid states in F^j and not get stuck. Unlike in G_j, however, agent 0 has no "discretion" in $G_{\pi,j}$; the move in state $(\langle q, s \rangle$ must be to $\langle q, s, \alpha \rangle)$, where $\alpha = \gamma(s)$. Intuitively, we check whether agent 0 can win this game while sticking to the strategy profile π. By keeping track of the state $s \in S$ of π, agent 0 must move in accordance with $\gamma(s)$. Therefore, solving the safety game $G_{\pi,j}$ amounts to a reachability query; agent 1 wins if she can reach a state $\langle q, s \rangle$, with $q \in F^j$. Because graph reachability is in NLOGSPACE and the size of the game $G_{\pi,j}$ is exponential in the input due to the exponential state space S, the game can be solved in NPSPACE=PSPACE. We denote the set of winning states for agent 0 as $Win_0(G_{\pi,j})$; $Win_1(G_{\pi,j})$ is the set of winning states for agent 1. Note that, in particular, $F^j \times S \subseteq Win_1(G_{\pi,j})$.

Checking the Agents in $\Omega \setminus W$

For an agent $j \notin W$, we construct a DFA that checks that the goal A^j is not satisfied on the primary trace or on a deviant trace. In detail, $A^j \times \pi = (Q^j \times S, \langle q_0^j, s_0 \rangle, \emptyset, \tau^j, Win_1(G_{\pi,j}))$ is defined in exactly the same way as the automaton $A^i \times \pi$ for $i \in W$ with the exception of the set of final states. We show below that if $A^j \times \pi$ is nonempty, then either the Primary Trace Condition or the Deviant Trace conditions is violated for Agent j.

So, we must make sure that no state in $Win_1(G_{\pi,j})$ is reachable in $A^j \times \pi$ from $\langle q_0^j, s_0 \rangle$. This is equivalent to the automaton being empty, so we have another nonemptiness query but now one that should fail. A path from $\langle q_0^j, s_0 \rangle$ to a state in $Win_1(G_{\pi,j})$ corresponds to either acceptance of A^j on the primary trace or a violation of the j-Deviant-Trace Condition , both of which contradicts π being a W-NE. We refer to these nonemptiness queries as the j-queries (a reference to $j \notin W$), and we note that they can be decided in NPSPACE=PSPACE by the exact same logic as i-queries. We now prove the correctness of checking the i-queries for the agents $i \in W$ and the j-queries for the agents $j \notin W$.

Theorem 6. *Given an iBG G with DFA goal inputs, a strategy profile π is a W-NE iff the i-queries succeed and the*

j-queries fail.

Proof. ($\rightarrow$). Assume that π is a W-NE. Therefore, it satisfies both the Primary-Trace Condition and the j-Deviant-Trace Condition. Since π satisfies the Primary-Trace Condition, there is a path from $\langle q_0^i, s_0\rangle$ to $F^i \times S$ in $A^i \times \pi$, so we have that the i-queries are successful.

Suppose now, for contradiction, that some j-query succeeds. This means that there is a run of A^j on the primary trace that enters a state $\langle q^j, s\rangle$ in $Win_1(G_{\pi,j})$. There are now two cases:

1. If $q^j \in F^j$, then A^j has just accepted on the primary trace, contradicting the assumption that π was a W-NE.
2. Otherwise, Agent j now has a winning strategy in $G_{\pi,j}$ from state $\langle q^j, s\rangle$. By following this strategy, the agent is able to reach a state in $F^j \times S$, which means that Agent j constructed a j-Deviant-Trace that satisfies A^j, violating the j-Deviant-Trace Condition of π and contradicting the assumption that π was a W-NE.

Therefore, we have that the i-queries must succeed and the j-queries must fail.

($\leftarrow$) Assume now that the i-queries succeed and the j-queries fail. We show that π satisfies the Primary-Trace Condition and the j-Deviant-Trace Condition.

For the Primary-Trace Condition, note that goals A^i, for $i \in W$, accept on the primary trace of π, since the i-queries succeeded. Furthermore, the goals A^j, for $j \notin W$, cannot accept on the primary trace of π, as this would correspond to a path in $A^j \times \pi$ from $\langle q_0^j, s_0\rangle$ to $F^j \times S \subseteq Win_1(G_{\pi,j})$ in $A^j \times \pi$. No such path exists since the j-queries failed.

For the j-Deviant-Trace Condition, we only need to study the j-queries, $j \notin W$. Note that $A^j \times \pi$ cannot enter a state in $Win_1(G_{\pi,j})$, since the j-queries failed. Thus, $A^j \times \pi$ stays in $Win_0(G_{\pi,j})$. A j-Deviant-Trace must separate from the primary trace at some time step $k \geq 0$, since deviant traces cannot be the primary trace, so at that point $A^j \times \pi$ is in some state $\langle q, s\rangle \in Win_0(G_{\pi,j})$. For A^j to accept on a deviant trace means that agent 1 can force reaching, in the games $G_{\pi,j}$, from $\langle q, s\rangle$ to some $\langle q', s'\rangle$ for $q \in F^j$ and $s \in S$. But that is not possible, since it would mean that $\langle q, s\rangle \in Win_1(G_{\pi,j})$. It follows that A^j cannot accept on a j-deviant trace. □

Complexity As noted before, each safety game and reachability query can be solved in PSPACE. Therefore, the entire algorithm has a PSPACE upper bound. The same holds for the bounded-channel case (for both goal automata and Moore machines), as the safety games and reachability queries would still be solved in PSPACE since S would still be exponential in the size of the input.

Theorem 7. *The verification problem with DFA goals can be solved in PSPACE.*

4.2 NFA and AFA Goals

NFA Goals The algorithm for NFA goals follows from the algorithm for DFA goals with some adaptation. Since we are dealing with nondeterministic automata now, we denote the transition function δ^i of the goal automaton A^i as a set of triples with $\langle q, \alpha, q'\rangle$ belonging to δ^i if it possible to transition from state q to state q' upon reading $\alpha \in \Sigma$. As before, we start by considering the agents in W.

Checking Agents in W Given a goal automaton $A^i = (Q^i, q_0^i, \Sigma, \delta^i, F^i)$ we use essentially the same construction of $A^i \times \pi = (Q^i \times S, \langle q_0^i, s_0\rangle, \emptyset, \tau^i, F^i \times S)$, which is now a nondeterministic finite automaton. The transition function τ^i is modified slightly to accommodate nondeterministic transitions. As before, the alphabet of this automaton is empty so transitions are defined between states; therefore τ^i is represented a set of pairs. For $q \in Q^i$ and $s \in S$, We have $\langle\langle q, s\rangle, \langle q', s'\rangle\rangle \in \tau^i$ if $\langle q, \gamma(s), q'\rangle \in \delta^i$ and $s' = \rho(s, \gamma(s))$. Once again we test these automata for nonemptiness, noting that a word accepted by $A^i \times \pi$ corresponds to A^i accepting a finite prefix of the primary trace of π. As before, we denote these nonemptiness queries as the i-queries. They can once again be tested for nonemptiness in NPSPACE=PSPACE, as they are once again equivalent to reachability testing in an exponentially large graph (caused by the exponential state space S).

As before, we proceed with the construction of safety games to analyze the set of states from which deviation is possible for an agent $j \notin W$.

Safety Game for Deviating Agents We construct the safety game $G_{\pi,j} = (Q^j \times S, Q^j \times S \times \Sigma, E_{\pi,j})$. agent 0 owns $Q^j \times S$, and agent 1 owns $Q^j \times S \times \Sigma$. The edge relation $E_{\pi,j}$ is defined as follows:

1. $(\langle q, s\rangle, \langle q, s, \alpha\rangle)) \in E_{\pi,j}$ for $q \in Q^j \setminus F^j$, $s \in S$, and $\alpha = \gamma(s)$.
2. $(\langle q, s, \alpha\rangle, \langle q', s'\rangle) \in E_{\pi,j}$ for $q, q' \in Q^j$ and $s, s' \in S$, if $\langle q, \beta, q'\rangle \in \delta^j$ and $s' = \rho(s, \beta)$, for some $\beta \in \Sigma$ such that $\alpha[-j] = \beta[-j]$.

This is a slight modification from the previous construction that takes into account that there are now multiple transitions possible for a state q and a letter $\beta \in \Sigma$ in A^j, so the fundamental structure of the game is unchanged. It still amounts to a reachability query, as agent 0 still has no choice in moves. As before, these safety games are exponential in the size of the input due to the presence of S, and therefore they can be solved in NPSPACE=PSPACE. We retain the notation that the set of winning states for agent 0 is given by $Win_0(G_{\pi,j})$ with $Win_1(G_{\pi,j})$ defined analogously.

Checking the Agents in $\Omega \setminus W$ Once again, the same argument from before applies. We create the NFA $A^j \times \pi = (Q^j \times S, \langle q_0^j, s_0\rangle, \emptyset, \tau^j, Win_1(G_{\pi,j}))$ from the goal NFA A^j, which differs from the previous construction of the NFA $A^i \times \pi$ in only the set of final states. As before, in the DFA case, we denote nonemptiness queries of $A^j \times \pi$ as the j-queries and they can once again be conducted in NPSPACE=PSPACE. It is once again integral to π being a W-NE that the j-queries fail. We state an equivalent theorem to Theorem 6 for NFA inputs.

Theorem 8. *Given an iBG G with NFA goal inputs, a strategy profile π is a W-NE iff the i-reachability queries succeed and the j-reachability queries fail.*

Proof. The proof of this theorem closely follows the proof of Theorem 6 and is therefore omitted. □

Complexity Each safety game and reachability query was conducted in PSPACE. Therefore, the entire algorithm has a PSPACE upper bound. Once again, S is exponential in the size of the input for even the bounded-channel case, so the result holds for the bounded-channel case as well.

Theorem 9. *The verification problem with NFA goals can be solved in PSPACE.*

We note that we can achieve the same upper bound by simply determinizing each goal automaton and then applying the DFA verification procedure. While both a DFA-based approach and the approach outlined in this section lie in PSPACE, the latter has better complexity in practice since it avoids a second exponential blowup. The approach in this section also prepares us to handle AFA goals.

AFA Goals A similar version of this problem in which a game G with LDL_f goal specifications was queried to see if some W-NE existed was presented in (Gutierrez, Perelli, and Wooldridge 2017) and was proven PSPACE-complete. In this section, we show that this upper bound also holds when W is specified and we are given AFA goals.

With AFA goals, we have a choice of converting to NFAs, incurring an exponential blowup, or DFAs, incurring a doubly exponential blowup. By converting to NFAs, we can avoid a second exponential blow up and show that this problem lies in PSPACE. Therefore given goal AFAs, we create equivalent NFAs A^i from the input and proceed as before.

The safety games constructed for NFA goals had a state space of $\{Q^j \times S\} \cup \{Q^j \times S \times \Sigma\}$. Since we converted from an AFA to NFA to obtain Q^j, Q^j is now exponential in the size of the input. Since S remains exponential and Σ was a part of the input, this game remains exponential in the size of the input. Therefore, these safety games can still be solved in PSPACE.

With respect to the automata constructed for the reachability queries, each vertex space $Q^i \times S$ still remains exponential in the size of the input even when Q^i is exponential in the size of the input. Therefore, these reachability queries can also be solved in PSPACE.

Theorem 10. *The verification problem with AFA goals can solved in PSPACE.*

Note that by employing an approach in which we check each agent individually, we have also avoided a situation in which we must take the cross product of exponentially large automata. If we are given k AFAs and wish to convert them in k NFAs, this represents an exponential blowup. At this point, we could take the cross product of all NFAs and still remain exponential in the size of the input. Note, however, that this would involve a quadratic blowup in the exponent - while 2^n and 2^{kn} are both exponential in n, there is an exponential (in k) gap between 2^n and 2^{kn}.

4.3 Lower Bound

We now prove PSPACE-hardness for the verification problem with DFA goals, which also serves as a lower bound for the verification problems with NFA and AFA goals.

We use the succinct representations of bounded-channel automata to show that the verification problem for DFA goals is PSPACE-hard through a polynomial time reduction from the following canonical PSPACE-complete problem : given a deterministic Turing machine M and a natural number n in unary, does M accept the empty tape using at most n space (Sipser 2006)? We further assume that M has a unique accepting configuration in which the tape consists solely of a special unused character $*$ with the head on the rightmost of the n cells. This standard assumption does not influence the complexity of the problem.

The Turing Machine M has a state set denoted by R and an alphabet denoted by Δ. Our reduction relies on the notion of an instantaneous description (ID) of a Turing Machine, which is a string that represents the content of the tape at a discrete time step in the run time of M. Such an ID includes

- The complete contents of the tape from left to right.
- The position and state of the head of M. As a matter of notation, if the head is on cell i then the character corresponding to the content of cell i is a pair consisting of the the element of Δ on the tape *and* an element of R representing the state of the machine.

As an example, an ID could be of the form $121\langle 0, q\rangle 31$. In this case, the content of the tape is 121031, while the pair $\langle 0, q\rangle$ denotes that the machine is currently reading the cell with symbol 0 while in state q. Since the machine is deterministic, a sequence of IDs corresponding to the computation run of M on the empty tape is uniquely given by the initial state and position of the head of M, which we will call ID_0. The machine then accepts if there is a sequence of IDs $ID_0 \dots ID_m$ such that ID_m is the unique accepting configuration of M and ID_{i+1} follows from ID_i according to the transition function of M. Our reduction strategy to the verification problem is to use a set of bounded-channel Moore Machines to simulate the transitions from one ID_i to ID_{i+1}, and a set bounded channel DFA goals of the agents to verify that the sequence is correct - that it starts at ID_0 and eventually reaches ID_m.

We now sketch a construction of a game $G_{M,n}$ and a strategy profile $\pi_{M,n} = \langle \pi_0 \dots \pi_{n-1}\rangle$ such that the Turing machine M accepts the empty tape in at most n steps iff π is an Ω-NE in G, i.e. a strategy profile that satisfies every agent's goal on its primary trace. The number of agents in this game is given by n, the same as the length of the unary input to the Turing Machine M.

We first consider the Σ_i assigned to each agent in G. This alphabet is $R \cup \{\Delta \times R\}$ for every agent. Intuitively, each Σ_i represents a single character of the ID, with Σ_i specifically corresponding to the i-th cell of the ID. Therefore taking all n alphabets together as Σ corresponds to an entire ID.

The strategy π_i of an agent i outputs the next configuration of cell i based on the previous configurations of the cell to the right, the cell to the left, and the cell itself. Thus, each strategy only needs to read at most three symbols, from

Σ_{i-1}, Σ_i, and Σ_{i+1}–since transitions in a Turing machine are determined locally–and output a symbol in Σ_i according to the transition function of M. (Agents 0 and $n-1$ need only consider two of the Σ_i since there are no cells to the left and right of these agents, respectively). If the computation moves out of bounds, then the Moore machine for the agent that moved it out of bounds (either 0 or $n-1$) immediately moves to a sink state that continuously outputs a special character that does not appear in the unique accepting configuration. Since each strategy only considers at most three Σ_i's as input and outputs a single Σ_i, these strategies can be represented by bounded-channel Moore machines. The state space of each machine has a size upper bound of $|R \cup \{\Delta \times R\}|^3$, meaning that each machine is polynomial in the size of the input.

We now consider the goals for the agents. The purpose of the goals is to check that the initial ID represent the empty tape, and the final ID is an accepting one. The goal for each agent except Agents 0 and $n-1$ is to see the symbol $*$ some time after reading the empty symbol $\perp$ as the first symbol corresponding to the empty tape input. The goal for Agent 0 is to eventually read the symbol $*$, after reading the first symbol $\langle \perp, q_0 \rangle$, where $q_0 \in R$ is the initial state of M. The goal for Agent $n-1$ is to read the pair $\langle *, q_F \rangle$ some time after seeing an empty cell as the first character, where $q_F \in R$ is the unique state corresponding to the accepting configuration ID_m since the head is moved all the way to the right in ID_m. The DFA representations of these goals are very simple, as they solely consist of eventually reading a single character after verifying an initial character. Therefore, all goal DFAs are bounded-channel automata and are therefore polynomial in the size of the input. Overall, we have a polynomial number of agents, each with a polynomial-sized Moore machine and a polynomial-sized goal DFA. Therefore, the game G can be constructed in polynomial time. We now prove the correctness of the reduction.

Theorem 11. *The strategy profile $\pi_{M,n} = \langle \pi_0 \dots \pi_{n-1} \rangle$ is an Ω-NE in $G_{M,n}$ iff M accepts the empty tape using at most space n.*

Proof. ($\rightarrow$) Assume that $\pi_{M,n}$ is an Ω-NE. By construction, the primary trace of $\pi_{M,n}$ simulates the sequence of IDs of M running on the empty tape with a built in check to ensure that the computation uses no more than n cells. Therefore, for the DFA goals to accept on this trace it means that in the final ID all cells except the last are filled with the special $*$ character and the last has the pair $\langle *, q_F \rangle$ and that each cell started empty. This means that there is a valid sequence of IDs generated by M upon reading the empty tape, meaning that M accepted the empty tape while staying in bounds.

($\leftarrow$)Assume that M accepts the empty tape using no more than n space. Then, it generates a unique valid sequence of IDs that eventually end at the unique accepting configuration. By construction, the primary trace of π consists of this same sequence of IDs, and ID_m must consist of the unique configuration consisting of $*$ on every cell but the rightmost with the pair $\langle *, q_F \rangle$. Therefore, all DFA goals will accept on the primary trace of $\pi_{M,n}$, so $\pi_{M,n}$ is an Ω-NE. □

We are able to construct the game $G_{M,n}$ and the profile $\pi_{M,n}$ in polynomial time due to the succinct representation of bounded-channel automata. Therefore, we have exhibited a polynomial time reduction from a known PSPACE-complete problem for the verification problem with DFA goal inputs. Therefore, we have:

Theorem 12. *The verification problems with DFA goals is PSPACE-complete.*

Since DFAs are a special case of both NFAs and AFAs, we get lower bounds for both corresponding verification problems as well.

Corollary 12.1. *The verification problems with NFA or AFA goals are PSPACE-complete.*

5 Concluding Remarks

In this work we provided complexity results for both the realizability and verification problems in the finite-horizon multiagent setting with different types of goal specifications, significantly extending previous works (Gutierrez, Perelli, and Wooldridge 2017; Rajasekaran and Vardi 2021). One of the key points of interest from this analysis is the complexity gap observed between the complexities of the realizability and verification problems. While realizability with DFA goals was proven to be PSPACE-complete in (Rajasekaran and Vardi 2021), here we have shown that realizability with NFA goals is EXPTIME-complete and realizability with AFA goals is 2EXPTIME-complete. Therefore, with respect to the realizability problem, we have shown that the succincness of goal specification greatly influences the complexity of the realizability problem. With respect to the verification problem, however, this distinction does not exist, as the verification problems with DFA,NFA, and AFA goals are all PSPACE-complete. Thus, the complexity for DFA goals is the same for both the realizability and the verification problems, but as the automata get more succinct the realizability problem grows in complexity while the verification problem remains PSPACE-complete. This complexity picture is similar to what is known in temporal reasoning in two-agent systems (system and environment), where the complexity of realizability rises from PTIME for DFA goals to 2EXPTIME for LTL_f goals, while verification, i.e., model checking, is PSPACE-complete for different types of goals, with the system *state-explosion problem* being the primary source of PSPACE-hardness, cf. (Vardi 1996)

Finally, by reasoning about the Primary-Trace Condition and the j-Deviant-Trace Conditions separately, as in (Rajasekaran and Vardi 2021), we were able to get algorithms that are easy to understand and optimal. This method of separation was made specifically to reason about Nash equilibria in qualitative games, by leveraging properties of both the Nash equilibria as a solution concept and qualitative goals themselves. By analyzing the j-Deviant-Trace Condition separately through the use of safety games we are able to get much better complexity bounds than if we dealt with the entire Nash equilibria at once. We believe that this principle of separation provides a powerful framework to reason about other qualitative multi-agent systems and perhaps even other solution concepts.

Acknowledgements

Work supported in part by NSF grants IIS-1527668, CCF-1704883, IIS-1830549, CNS-2016656, DoD MURI grant N00014-20-1-2787, and an award from the Maryland Procurement Office.

References

Abate, A.; Gutierrez, J.; Hammond, L.; Harrenstein, P.; Kwiatkowska, M.; Najib, M.; Perelli, G.; Steeples, T.; and Wooldridge, M. J. 2021. Rational verification: game-theoretic verification of multi-agent systems. *Appl. Intell.* 51(9):6569–6584.

Bouyer, P.; Brenguier, R.; Markey, N.; and Ummels, M. 2015. Pure Nash equilibria in concurrent deterministic games. *Log. Methods Comput. Sci.* 11(2).

Clarke, E.; Emerson, E.; and Sistla, A. 1986. Automatic verification of finite-state concurrent systems using temporal logic specifications. *ACM Transactions on Programming Languages and Systems* 8(2):244–263.

Fisman, D.; Kupferman, O.; and Lustig, Y. 2010. Rational synthesis. In *Proc. 16th Int'l Conf. on Tools and Algorithms for the Construction and Analysis of Systems*, volume 6015 of *Lecture Notes in Computer Science*, 190–204. Springer.

Giacomo, G. D., and Vardi, M. Y. 2013. Linear temporal logic and linear dynamic logic on finite traces. In *Proc. 23rd Int'l Joint Conf. on Artificial Intelligence*, 854–860. IJ-CAI/AAAI.

Giacomo, G. D., and Vardi, M. Y. 2015. Synthesis for LTL and LDL on finite traces. In Yang, Q., and Wooldridge, M. J., eds., *Proc. 24th Int'l Joint Conf. on Artificial Intelligence*, 1558–1564. AAAI Press.

Giacomo, G. D., and Vardi, M. Y. 2016. LTL_f and LDL_f synthesis under partial observability. In *Proc. 25th Int'l Joint Conf. on Artificial Intelligence*, 1044–1050. IJ-CAI/AAAI Press.

Grädel, E.; Thomas, W.; and Wilke, T. 2002. *Automata, Logics, and Infinite Games: A Guide to Current Research.* Lecture Notes in Computer Science 2500. Springer.

Gutierrez, J.; Najib, M.; Perelli, G.; and Wooldridge, M. J. 2020. Automated temporal equilibrium analysis: Verification and synthesis of multi-player games. *Artif. Intell.* 287:103353.

Gutierrez, J.; Harrenstein, P.; and Wooldridge, M. J. 2015a. Expresiveness and complexity results for strategic reasoning. In *Proc. 26th Int'l Conf. on Concurrency Theory*, volume 42 of *LIPIcs*, 268–282. Schloss Dagstuhl - Leibniz-Zentrum für Informatik.

Gutierrez, J.; Harrenstein, P.; and Wooldridge, M. J. 2015b. Iterated Boolean games. *Inf. Comput.* 242:53–79.

Gutierrez, J.; Perelli, G.; and Wooldridge, M. J. 2017. Iterated games with LDL goals over finite traces. In *Proc. 16th Conf. on Autonomous Agents and MultiAgent Systems*, 696–704. ACM.

Kupferman, O., and Vardi, M. 1996. Module checking. In *Proc. 8th Int. Conf. on Computer Aided Verification*, volume 1102 of *Lecture Notes in Computer Science*, 75–86. Springer.

Kupferman, O.; Perelli, G.; and Vardi, M. Y. 2016. Synthesis with rational environments. *Ann. Math. Artif. Intell.* 78(1):3–20.

McNaughton, R. 1993. Infinite games played on finite graphs. *Ann. Pure Appl. Logic* 65(2):149–184.

Mogavero, F.; Murano, A.; Perelli, G.; and Vardi, M. Y. 2014. Reasoning about strategies: On the model-checking problem. *ACM Trans. Comput. Log.* 15(4):34:1–34:47.

Nash, J. F. 1950. Equilibrium points in n-person games. *Proceedings of the National Academy of Sciences* 36(1):48–49.

Pnueli, A., and Rosner, R. 1989. On the synthesis of a reactive module. In *Proc. 16th ACM Symp. on Principles of Programming Languages*, 179–190.

Rajasekaran, S., and Vardi, M. Y. 2021. Nash equilibria in finite-horizon multiagent concurrent games. In *Proc. 20th Int'l Conf. on Autonomous Agents and MultiAgent Systems*, 1046–1054. Int'l Found. for Autonomous Agents and Multiagent Systems.

Rajasekaran, S., and Vardi, M. Y. 2022. Verification and realizability in finite-horizon multiagent systems.

Rosner, R. 1992. *Modular Synthesis of Reactive Systems.* Ph.D. Dissertation, Weizmann Institute of Science.

Shoham, Y., and Leyton-Brown, K. 2009. *Multiagent Systems - Algorithmic, Game-Theoretic, and Logical Foundations.* Cambridge University Press.

Sipser, M. 2006. *Introduction to the Theory of Computation.* Course Technology, second edition.

Vardi, M., and Wolper, P. 1994. Reasoning about infinite computations. *Information and Computation* 115(1):1–37.

Vardi, M. 1996. An automata-theoretic approach to linear temporal logic. In *Logics for Concurrency: Structure versus Automata*, volume 1043 of *Lecture Notes in Computer Science*, 238–266. Springer.

Wooldridge, M. J. 2009. *An Introduction to MultiAgent Systems, Second Edition.* Wiley.

Proceedings of the 19th International Conference on Principles of Knowledge Representation and Reasoning
Main Track

On Dynamics in Structured Argumentation Formalisms

Anna Rapberger[1] and **Markus Ulbricht**[2]
[1]TU Wien, Institute of Logic and Computation
[2]Leipzig University, Department of Computer Science
[1]arapberg@dbai.tuwien.ac.at [2]mulbricht@informatik.uni-leipzig.de

Abstract

In this paper we contribute to the investigation of dynamics in assumption-based argumentation (ABA) and investigate situations where a given knowledge base undergoes certain changes. We show that two frequently investigated problems, namely enforcement of a given target atom and deciding strong equivalence of two given ABA frameworks, are intractable in general. Interestingly, these problems are both tractable for abstract argumentation frameworks (AFs) which admit a close correspondence to ABA by constructing semantics-preserving instances. Inspired by this observation, we search for tractable fragments for ABA frameworks by means of the instantiated AFs. We argue that the usual instantiation procedure is not suitable for the investigation of dynamic scenarios since too much information is lost when constructing the AF. We thus consider an extension of AFs, called cvAFs, equipping arguments with conclusions and vulnerabilities in order to better anticipate their role after the underlying knowledge base is extended. We investigate enforcement and strong equivalence for cvAFs and present syntactic conditions to decide them. We show that the correspondence between cvAFs and ABA frameworks is close enough to capture ABA also in dynamic scenarios. This yields the desired tractable ABA fragment. We furthermore discuss consequences for the corresponding problems for logic programs.

1 Introduction

A currently highly relevant area of research in knowledge representation and reasoning is the investigation of dynamical environments, i.e., knowledge bases that change over time (Gabbay et al. 2021). Considering the inherently dynamic nature of argumentation it is not surprising that researchers in the field of formal argumentation have taken up this topic in various ways. In the area of abstract argumentation (Dung 1995) where argument acceptance is decided solely by looking at conflicts between arguments, several problems have been investigated.

Among the most prominent problems in this line of research is *strong equivalence*: Given a knowledge base $\mathcal{K}$, is it possible to replace a subset $\mathcal{H}$ of $\mathcal{K}$ by an equivalent one, say $\mathcal{H}'$, without changing the meaning of $\mathcal{K}$? Within the KR community it is folklore that this is usually not the case when considering non-monotonic formalisms. Driven by this observation, the notion of strong equivalence has been proposed, developed and investigated in various contexts (Lifschitz, Pearce, and Valverde 2001; Oikarinen and Woltran 2011). While strong equivalence is about comparing the behavior of different knowledge bases, the *enforcement problem* (Baumann 2012b; Wallner, Niskanen, and Järvisalo 2017; Doutre and Mailly 2018; Borg and Bex 2021) deals with manipulating a single one in order to ensure a certain outcome. Research concerned with this issue contributes to predict conceivable future scenarios and possible outcomes of a debate and can serve as a guidance when trying to defend a certain point of view. Both strong equivalence and enforcement have received increasing attention in the realm of abstract argumentation (Baumann et al. 2021). There are, however, only few studies on the aforementioned problems in structured argumentation; we refer the reader to Section 8 for pointers to related work.

In this paper, we study the enforcement and strong equivalence problem for structured argumentation with main focus on assumption-based argumentation (ABA) (Bondarenko, Toni, and Kowalski 1993). While for abstract argumentation, deciding strong equivalence as well as the basic argument enforcement (Baumann and Brewka 2010) is tractable, it is not clear whether, and if so, how these results survive the transition to structured argumentation formalisms. At first glance it seems that we can rely on well-established methods: viewing arguments as abstract entities, we can represent instances of structured argumentation formalisms as abstract Dung-style argumentation frameworks (AFs); cf. instantiations for ABA (Caminada et al. 2015a) or logic-based argumentation (Gorogiannis and Hunter 2011). A similar procedure also exists for logic programs (LPs) (Dung 1995; Caminada et al. 2015b). Such *instantiation procedures* provide a unifying framework to study properties that are common to a large class of non-monotonic formalisms; and one would expect that they can be utilized to prove tractability or identify tractable fragments of the respective problems in the original formalisms – it is for instance well-known that deciding strong equivalence in the closely related realm of LPs is intractable (Lifschitz, Pearce, and Valverde 2001); here, we would hope that transferring the results from abstract argumentation will be helpful to identify an LP fragment for which deciding strong equivalence is tractable.

A closer inspection of the aforementioned instantiation procedures however reveals a certain drawback that becomes apparent when moving from static to dynamic scenarios.

Example 1.1. *We consider an instantiation of an ABA framework* $D = (\mathcal{L}, \mathcal{R}, \mathcal{A}, ^-)$ *with assumptions* $\mathcal{A} = \{a, b\}$*, their contraries* $\overline{a}$ *and* $\overline{b}$*, resp., and rules* $r_1 = (p \leftarrow a.)$ *and* $r_2 = (\overline{a} \leftarrow b.)$*. We obtain the associated AF* F_D *as follows (cf. Section 2): each assumption* a, b *yields a corresponding argument and each rule* r_i *yields an argument* x_i*. Attacks depend on the conclusion of the attacking argument, e.g.,* x_2 *attacks* x_1 *because* $\overline{a}$ *is the contrary of* a*.*

F_D :

It turns out that we have abstracted away critical information: The rule r_2 *can be disabled by adding a rule with conclusion* $\overline{b}$*, e.g., the fact "*$\overline{b} \leftarrow .$*"; this is however not reflected in* F_D*. To illustrate this, let us consider an adjusted version* D' *of* D *by replacing* r_2 *with rule "*$r_2' : \overline{a} \leftarrow$*", i.e.,* $\overline{a}$ *can be considered as fact. The instantiation yields the same AF:*

$F_{D'}$:

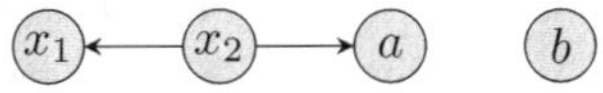

The instantiated AFs do not carry sufficient information to investigate dynamics. Consider the following questions:

- *Is it possible to accept assumption* a *by adding suitable rules? The answer is "yes" in* D*, but "no" in* D'*. This information cannot be extracted from* $F_D = F_{D'}$*.*
- *What are the stable models after adding the fact "*$\overline{b} \leftarrow .$*"? In* D*,* $\{a\}$ *is stable while in* D'*, we obtain* $\{b\}$*. We cannot judge the situation correctly by comparing* F_D *and* $F_{D'}$*.*
- *More generally, are* D *and* D' *strongly equivalent? The answer is clearly "no" when inspecting* D *and* D' *but again we cannot tell by comparing their associated AFs.*

In all of these questions, the missing peace of information is that x_2 *has a* hidden weakness $\overline{b}$ *in* F_D *but not in* $F_{D'}$*. It is thus impossible to attack* x_2 *in* $F_{D'}$ *whereas in* F_D*,* x_2 *can be attacked by an argument with conclusion* $\overline{b}$*.*

As this example shows, the minimal generalization to tailor AFs suitable for dynamic settings consists of two aspects: (i) the *conclusion* and (ii) the *vulnerabilities* of an argument. The latter describes all possibilities to attack an argument, i.e., it contains conclusions of all potential attackers. This means that for an argument $S \vdash_R p$ in the spirit of ABA, (i.e., atom p is derivable from assumptions S via rules R) the vulnerabilities are the contraries of the assumptions in S while p is the argument's conclusion. A potential weakness of the logic-based argument $(\{\alpha, \alpha \to \beta\}, \beta)$ is the sentence $\neg\alpha$; its conclusion is β. Considering ASPIC (Modgil and Prakken 2017), also a rule can be a vulnerability: an argument $B : q \Rightarrow p$ with defeasible rule $d_1 : q \Rightarrow p$ can be attacked by an argument with conclusion $\neg d_1$.

In this paper, we consider a generalization of AFs by augmenting arguments with *vulnerabilities* and a *conclusion*. This allows us to identify a fragment of ABA for which deciding enforcement and strong equivalence becomes tractable. Our main contributions are as follows:

- We study enforcement and strong equivalence for ABA. We show that, as anticipated, both problems lie on the first level of the polynomial hierarchy and are thus intractable, in contrast to their counterparts in abstract argumentation.
- We present our novel formalism: *conclusion and vulnerability augmented AFs (cvAFs)*. We show that they are a faithful generalization of standard instantiation procedures and discuss their relation to ABA.
- We present cvAF characterization results for argument and conclusion enforcement and show that strong equivalence can be characterized by so-called kernels. Our results show that both problems are tractable for cvAFs.
- We identify a tractable fragment for ABA by means of our cvAF enforcement and strong equivalence results.
- To demonstrate the flexibility of our approach, we also transfer our results to LPs and identify a fragment for which enforcement and strong equivalence is tractable.

2 Background

Abstract Argumentation. We fix a non-finite background set $\mathcal{U}$. An argumentation framework (AF) (Dung 1995) is a directed graph $F = (A, R)$ where $A \subseteq \mathcal{U}$ represents a set of arguments and $R \subseteq A \times A$ models *attacks* between them. For a set $E \subseteq A$, we let $E_F^+ = \{x \in A \mid \exists y \in E, (y, x) \in R\}$; also, E is *conflict-free* in F iff for no $x, y \in E$, $(x, y) \in R$. E *defends* an argument x if E attacks each attacker of x. A conflict-free set E is *admissible* in F ($E \in ad(F)$) iff it defends all its elements. A *semantics* is a function $\sigma : \mathcal{F} \to 2^{2^{\mathcal{U}}}$ with $F \mapsto \sigma(F) \subseteq 2^A$; each $E \in \sigma(F)$ is called a σ-*extensions*. Here we consider so-called *complete*, *grounded*, *preferred*, and *stable* semantics (abbr. co, gr, pr, stb).

Definition 2.1. *Let* $F = (A, R)$ *be an AF and* $E \in ad(F)$*.*

- $E \in co(F)$ *iff* E *contains all arguments it defends;*
- $E \in gr(F)$ *iff* E *is* $\subseteq$*-minimal in* $co(F)$*;*
- $E \in pr(F)$ *iff* E *is* $\subseteq$*-maximal in* $co(F)$*;*
- $E \in stb(F)$ *iff* $E^+ = A \setminus E$*.*

Assumption-based Argumentation. We assume a deductive system $(\mathcal{L}, \mathcal{R})$, where $\mathcal{L}$ is a formal language and $\mathcal{R}$ is a set of inference rules over $\mathcal{L}$. A rule $r \in \mathcal{R}$ has the form $a_0 \leftarrow a_1, \ldots, a_n$, $a_i \in \mathcal{L}$; $head(r) = a_0$ is the head and $body(r) = \{a_1, \ldots, a_n\}$ is the (possibly empty) body of r.

Definition 2.2. *An ABA framework is a tuple* $(\mathcal{L}, \mathcal{R}, \mathcal{A}, ^-)$*, where* $(\mathcal{L}, \mathcal{R})$ *is a deductive system,* $\mathcal{A} \subseteq \mathcal{L}$ *a non-empty set of assumptions, and a contrary function* $^- : \mathcal{A} \to \mathcal{L}$*.*

In this work, we focus on frameworks which are *flat*, i.e., $head(r) \notin \mathcal{A}$ for each rule $r \in \mathcal{R}$, and *finite*, i.e., $\mathcal{L}$, $\mathcal{R}$, $\mathcal{A}$ are finite; also, each rule is stated explicitly (given as input).

A sentence $p \in \mathcal{L}$ is tree-derivable from assumptions $S \subseteq \mathcal{A}$ and rules $R \subseteq \mathcal{R}$, denoted by $S \vdash_R p$, if there is a finite rooted labeled tree T such that the root is labeled with p, the set of labels for the leaves of T is equal to S or $S \cup \{\top\}$, and there is a surjective mapping from the set of internal nodes to R satisfying for each internal node v there is a rule $r \in R$ such that v labelled with $head(r)$ and the set of all successor nodes corresponds to $body(r)$ or $\top$ if $body(r) = \emptyset$.

A set of assumptions S *attacks* a set of assumptions T if there is $S' \subseteq S$, $R \subseteq \mathcal{R}$, such that $S \vdash_R \overline{a}$ for some $a \in T$. S is conflict-free if it does not attack itself; S is admissible if it defends itself. We next recall grounded, complete, preferred, and stable ABA semantics (abbr. gr, co, pr, stb).

Definition 2.3. *Let $D = (\mathcal{L}, \mathcal{R}, \mathcal{A}, \overline{\ })$ be an ABA framework. Further, let $S \subseteq \mathcal{A}$ be admissible in D.*

- *$S \in co(D)$ iff S contains every assumption set it defends;*
- *$S \in gr(D)$ iff S is $\subseteq$-minimal in $co(D)$;*
- *$S \in pr(D)$ iff S is $\subseteq$-maximal in $co(D)$;*
- *$S \in stb(D)$ iff S attacks each $\{x\} \subseteq \mathcal{A} \setminus S$.*

By $Th_D(S) = \{p \mid \exists S' \subseteq S : S' \vdash_R p\}$ we denote the set of all conclusions derivable from an assumption-set S in an ABA D. Observe that $S \subseteq Th_D(S)$ since per definition, each assumption $a \in \mathcal{A}$ is derivable from $\{a\} \vdash_\emptyset a$. We call $Th_D(S) \setminus S$ the set of *proper* conclusions of X. We say that an assumption $a \in \mathcal{A}$ (atom $p \in \mathcal{L}$) is *credulously accepted* wrt a semantics σ in an ABA D iff there is some $S \in \sigma(D)$ with $a \in S$ ($p \in Th_D(S)$, respectively).

Definition 2.4. *The associated AF $F_D = (A, R)$ of an ABA $D = (\mathcal{L}, \mathcal{R}, \mathcal{A}, \overline{\ })$ is given by $A = \{S \vdash p \mid \exists R \subseteq \mathcal{R} : S \vdash_R p\}$ and attack relation $(S \vdash p, S' \vdash p') \in R$ iff $p \in \overline{S'}$.*

For a set S of assumptions, we let $\overline{S} = \{\overline{a} \mid a \in S\}$; moreover, we write $asms(E) = \bigcup_{S \vdash p \in E} S$ to denote the set of assumptions of a given set of arguments $E \subseteq A$.

ABA and AFs are closely related (see (Čyras et al. 2018)).

Proposition 2.5. *Given an ABA $D = (\mathcal{L}, \mathcal{R}, \mathcal{A}, \overline{\ })$, its corresponding AF F and a semantics $\sigma \in \{gr, co, pr, stb\}$. If $E \in \sigma(F)$ then $asms(E) \in \sigma(D)$; if $S \in \sigma(D)$ then $\{S' \vdash p \mid \exists S' \subseteq S, R \subseteq \mathcal{R} : S' \vdash_R p\} \in \sigma(F)$.*

3 Dynamics in ABA

In this section, we discuss enforcement and strong equivalence notions for ABA. We show that, in contrast to analogous settings in abstract argumentation, deciding enforceability as well as strong equivalence is intractable.

We consider expansions of ABA frameworks that allow for the addition of rules and assumptions. We consider expansions componentwise, i.e., given $D = (\mathcal{L}, \mathcal{R}, \mathcal{A}, \overline{\ })$ and $H = (\mathcal{L}, \mathcal{R}', \mathcal{A}', \overline{\ })$ with $\mathcal{A} \cap \mathcal{A}' = \emptyset$, we denote the *expansion* of D by H as $D \cup H = (\mathcal{L}, \mathcal{R} \cup \mathcal{R}', \mathcal{A} \cup \mathcal{A}', \overline{\ })$.

3.1 Enforcement

Let us now introduce our version of the ABA enforcement problem. There are several variants of this problem proposed in the literature, based on credulous vs. skeptical reasoning and positive vs. negative enforcement. In order to keep our presentation concise we focus on one particular problem and demonstrate how our proposal can help tackling it. The following notion of enforcement is stated for a fixed class $\mathcal{C}$ of ABA frameworks. If not stated otherwise, we suppose $\mathcal{C}$ consists of all flat finite ABA frameworks.

Definition 3.1. *Given a class $\mathcal{C}$ of ABA frameworks. For $D = (\mathcal{L}, \mathcal{R}, \mathcal{A}, \overline{\ }) \in \mathcal{C}$ and a semantics σ, we say that an assumption $a \in \mathcal{A}$ (atom $p \in \mathcal{L}$) is* enforceable *wrt. σ if there is some expansion $H = (\mathcal{L}, \mathcal{R}', \mathcal{A}', \overline{\ })$ s.t. $D \cup H \in \mathcal{C}$ and a (p, resp.) is credulously accepted wrt σ (and p does not occur in any head of $\mathcal{R}'$) in $D \cup H$.*

We require that a conclusion p cannot be enforced by simply adding a fact with head p since this would trivialize the problem. Now, let us revisit our motivating example.

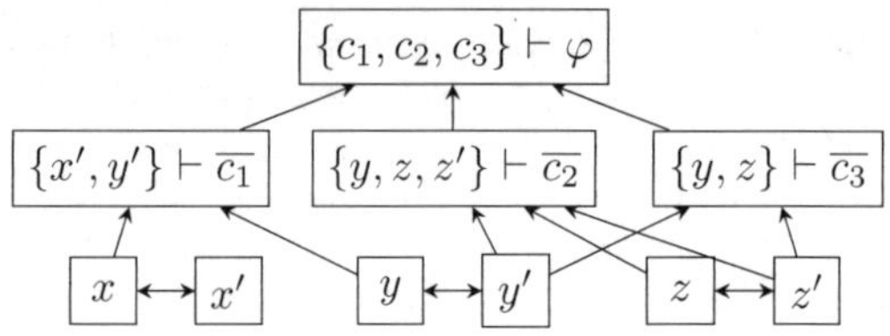

Figure 1: Example of the SAT reduction in Theorem 3.4 for the formula φ given by clauses $\{x, y\}, \{\neg y, z, \neg z\}\{\neg y, \neg z\}$.

Example 3.2. *In our running example ABA D (cf. Example 1.1), we observe that a is credulously enforceable since we can add e.g. the rule "$\overline{b} \leftarrow a$." in order to induce a counterattack from a to b.*

Enforcement is well-studied for abstract argumentation and we would hope that our investigation can benefit from this research. In terms of AFs, our enforcement problem amounts to deciding existence of a suitable expansion; corresponding (im-)possibility results can be found in (Baumann and Brewka 2010). Unfortunately, there are some obstacles which are best explained by our running example D'.

Example 3.3. *Consider the ABA framework D' (cf. Example 1.1). Judging from the associated AF $F_{D'}$, assumption a is easily enforceable by adding some argument attacking x_2. However, since this argument stems from a fact "$\overline{a} \leftarrow .$" it is not possible to add rules inducing a counterattack to x_2.*

As this example nicely illustrates, the structure of the ABA framework imposes constraints on the effect an additional argument may have. This observation, unfortunately, renders the corresponding research on enforcement for AFs inapplicable to our situation.

Hence, the next natural question would be whether this issue can be fixed by somehow making the classical enforcement results work for ABA as well. That is, can we perform some simple syntactical check and decide in polynomial time whether some atom is enforceable? As it turns out, under standard assumptions the answer is negative again.

Theorem 3.4. *Deciding whether an assumption a (conclusion p) is enforceable in a given ABA framework D w.r.t. a semantics $\sigma \in \{gr, co, pr, stb\}$ is* NP*-complete.*

Proof (conclusion enforcement, $\sigma = stb$). We reduce SAT: Given a CNF φ with clauses $\mathcal{C}$ over variables in X, we define a corresponding ABA framework $D = (\mathcal{L}, \mathcal{R}, \mathcal{A}, \overline{\ })$ with

- $\mathcal{A} = X \cup \{x' \mid x \in X\} \cup \mathcal{C}$ with $\overline{a} = a$ for all $a \in \mathcal{A}$;
- for each $c \in \mathcal{C}$, $\mathcal{R}$ contains a rule r with $head(r) = c'$ and $body(r) = \{x \mid \neg x \in c\} \cup \{x' \mid x \in c\}$, moreover, $\mathcal{R}$ contains a rule $\varphi \leftarrow \mathcal{C}$.

Instantiating this ABA as AF results in the well-known standard reduction (cf. (Dvorák and Dunne 2018, Reduction 3.6)); an example is given in Figure 1. It can be shown that φ is satisfiable iff φ is inferred by a stable extension of D.

Observe that it is not possible to defend the assumption set $\mathcal{C}$ by adding novel rules to D since this would require to introduce rules with head $\overline{x}$ or $\overline{x'}$. That is, in case φ is not satisfiable, it holds that φ cannot be enforced in D. □

3.2 Strong Equivalence

We consider the following natural notion of strong equivalence, where we assume that the background information and the assumptions are fixed and knowledge bases are characterized by their rules. If the class $\mathcal{C}$ is not specified, we suppose $\mathcal{C}$ contains all flat finite ABA frameworks.

Definition 3.5. *Let $\mathcal{C}$ be a class of ABA frameworks. Two ABA frameworks $D \in \mathcal{C}$ and $D' \in \mathcal{C}$ are* strongly equivalent w.r.t. σ *($D \equiv_s^\sigma D'$) if $\sigma(D \cup H) = \sigma(D' \cup H)$ for each expansion H satisfying $D \cup H \in \mathcal{C}$ as well as $D' \cup H \in \mathcal{C}$.*

We mention an alternative approach that considers equivalence on conclusion-level instead of assumption-level: Two ABAs $D, D' \in \mathcal{C}$ are *strongly conclusion-equivalent* to each other if they agree on their conclusion-extensions under all possible expansions ($D \equiv_s^{Th_\sigma} D'$ for short), formally, $\{Th(E) \mid E \in \sigma(D \cup H)\} = \{Th(E) \mid E \in \sigma(D' \cup H)\}$ for each expansion H s.t. $D \cup H \in \mathcal{C}$ and $D' \cup H \in \mathcal{C}$. It turns out that both notions are equivalent; also, it is equally possible to consider only proper conclusion-extensions.

Proposition 3.6. *For $\sigma \in \{gr, co, pr, stb\}$, for any two ABAs D and D', it holds that $D \equiv_s^{Th_\sigma} D'$ iff $D \equiv_s^\sigma D'$, even when considering only proper conclusion-extensions.*

Moreover, assumption-sets of strongly equivalent ABA frameworks agree on their conclusions.

Proposition 3.7. *For $\sigma \in \{gr, co, pr, stb\}$, for ABAs D, D', if $D \equiv_s^\sigma D'$ then $Th_D(E) = Th_{D'}(E)$ for all $E \in \sigma(D)$.*

As for the enforcement problem, strong equivalence is well-studied for abstract argumentation (Oikarinen and Woltran 2011). There is even another similarity: Deciding strong equivalence is also tractable for abstract argumentation, since one only needs to compute the so-called kernels of both AFs and check their syntactical coincidence.

However, we are facing the same issue regarding ABA.

Example 3.8. *Our running example ABAs D and D' both induce the same AF as we saw before. Hence, the abstract AFs F_D and $F_{D'}$ are clearly strongly equivalent. However, already from the fact that a is enforceable in D but not in D' we can infer that D and D' are not strongly equivalent.*

To complete the picture, we mention that for strong equivalence, we again do not expect the a polynomial-time syntactical check. Adapting the proof of Theorem 3.4 shows that deciding strong equivalence is coNP-complete.

Theorem 3.9. *Deciding whether two ABA frameworks are strongly equivalent w.r.t. a given semantics $\sigma \in \{gr, co, pr, stb\}$ is* coNP*-complete.*

4 An Instantiation For Dynamics

In this section, we present cvAFs ("conclusion and vulnerability augmented AFs") which extend Dung-style AFs with additional information concerning the occurring arguments. Our cvAFs incorporate the observation we made earlier in the introduction: arguments are typically characterized by their *conclusion* and their potential weaknesses (*vulnerabilites*) on which they can be attacked.

4.1 Instantiated Arguments

Recall our motivating Example 1.1. Given the ABA framework D from the introduction, our goal is to preserve conclusions and vulnerabilities during instantiation.

For this we observe that structured argumentation instantiation procedures make use of some meta-level information where each argument is augmented with the two aforementioned features, namely the conclusions as well as the vulnerabilities. However, when instantiating a Dung-style AF this information is lost. We therefore consider a slight generalization of AFs based on the following notion of instantiated arguments, which carry the information we require.

Definition 4.1. *Given a set $\mathcal{L}$ of sentences. An* instantiated argument *is a tuple $x = (vul(x), cl(x))$ where $vul(x) \subseteq \mathcal{L}$ are the* vulnerabilities *and $cl(x) \in \mathcal{L}$ is the* conclusion *of x.*

Instantiated arguments are a flexible tool and may stem from an arbitrary instantiation procedure which makes use of conclusions and vulnerabilities in a certain sense, e.g. ABA, ASPIC, or logic-based argumentation.

With our notion of instantiated arguments at hand we are ready to formally introduce cvAFs as generalization of AFs by replacing abstract arguments with instantiated arguments.

Definition 4.2. *A cvAF is a tuple $\mathcal{F} = (A, R)$ where A is a set of instantiated arguments and $R \subseteq A \times A$.*

An example of a cvAF is given by the representation of our running example as cvAF (cf. $\mathcal{F}_D$ below). Here, each argument contains its vulnerabilities (left) and its conclusion (right, in boldface), e.g., argument x_1 has a single vulnerability $\overline{a}$ and conclusion p.

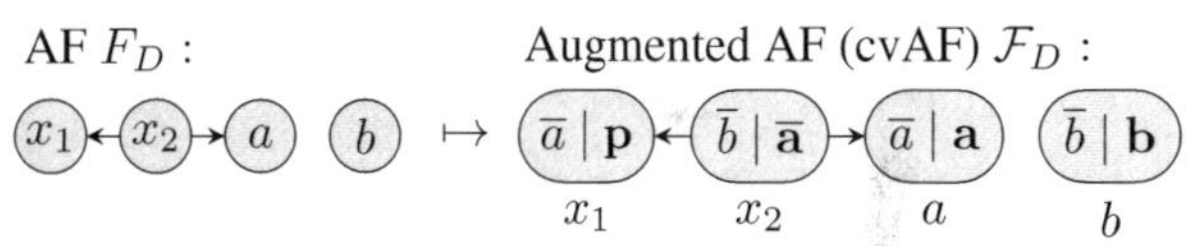

We consider a crucial property based on the following observation that appears in many structured argumentation formalisms: outgoing attacks usually depend on the conclusion of the attacking argument while incoming attacks are characterized by the vulnerabilities. This means that arguments with conclusion p attack all arguments with vulnerability p. A cvAFs adhering to this property is called well-formed.

Definition 4.3. *A cvAF is called $\mathcal{F} = (A, R)$* well-formed *if $(x, y) \in R$ iff $cl(x) \in vul(y)$ for each $x, y \in A$.*

Let us now turn our attention towards the semantics. By utilizing *instantiated* instead of *abstract* arguments when instantiating a knowledge base $\mathcal{K}$, we find a cvAF $\mathcal{F}_\mathcal{K}$ whose structure is isomorphic to the standard instantiation $F_\mathcal{K}$, but the arguments in $\mathcal{F}_\mathcal{K}$ carry more information. Since we do not intend to alter the meaning of the instantiation procedure, we stick to the classical AF semantics when evaluating $\mathcal{F}_\mathcal{K}$; we mention however that cvAFs are flexible in the sense that we can either focus on the arguments themselves or their conclusions.

Definition 4.4. *Given a cvAF $\mathcal{F}$ and an AF semantics σ. We call $\sigma(\mathcal{F})$ the σ-argument-extensions of $\mathcal{F}$ and $\sigma_{cl}(\mathcal{F}) := \{cl(E) \mid E \in \sigma(F)\}$ the σ-conclusion-extensions of $\mathcal{F}$.*

Note that for well-formed cvAFs, each σ-argument-extension corresponds to a unique σ-conclusion-extension.

Proposition 4.5. *For each well-formed cvAF $\mathcal{F}$, for each $\sigma \in \{gr, co, pr, stb\}$, it holds that $|\sigma(\mathcal{F})| = |\sigma_{cl}(\mathcal{F})|$.*

Let us now see or formalism at work when applied to ABA frameworks. We use the usual procedure, but consider instantiated arguments where the conclusions and underlying assumptions are made explicit. So suppose from our ABA framework we can construct an argument of the form $S \vdash p$. An argument of this form yields an instantiated argument $x = (vul(x), cl(x)) = (\overline{S}, p)$. Therefore, a natural instantiation with instantiated arguments is as follows.

Definition 4.6. *For an ABA framework D, $\mathcal{F}_D = (A, R)$ is the cvAF with instantiated arguments $A = \{(\overline{S}, p) \mid S \vdash p\}$ and $(x, y) \in R$ iff $cl(x) \in vul(y)$.*

Our cvAF instantiation is a faithful generalization of the usual one; moreover, each instantiated cvAF is well-formed.

Proposition 4.7. *For each ABA D, its associated cvAF $\mathcal{F}_D$ is well-formed. Moreover, for each $\sigma \in \{gr, co, pr, stb\}$,*

1. *if $S \in \sigma(D)$ then $\{(\overline{S'}, p) \in A \mid S' \subseteq S\} \in \sigma(\mathcal{F}_D)$;*
2. *if $E \in \sigma(\mathcal{F}_D)$ then $\bigcup_{(\overline{S}, p) \in E} S \in \sigma(D)$.*

Furthermore, $\{Th_D(S) \mid S \in \sigma(D)\} = \sigma_{cl}(\mathcal{F}_D)$.

Indeed, the ABA framework D from our running example yields the cvAF $\mathcal{F}_D$ depicted above. Moreover, $\sigma(\mathcal{F}_D) = \{\{x_2, b\}\}$ and hence $\sigma_{cl}(\mathcal{F}_D) = \{\{\overline{b},\}\}$ correctly reflects the semantics of D. We also mention that when instantiating D' from Example 1.1 we obtain a similar cvAF, but x_2 does not have any vulnerability. Hence we are indeed able to distinguish the two instantiations as desired.

Since our formalism of interest yields well-formed cvAFs, we restrict our studies to *well-formed cvAFs only*.

Assumption 4.8. *In the remaining part of the paper, we assume that each cvAF is well-formed.*

4.2 cvAFs and Dynamics

We are ready to investigate dynamics in structured argumentation by means of cvAFs. Suppose we are given a knowledge base $\mathcal{K}$ and the instantiated cvAF $\mathcal{F}_{\mathcal{K}}$. If we want to move to a superset $\mathcal{K} \cup \mathcal{H}$ we can construct $\mathcal{F}_{\mathcal{K} \cup \mathcal{H}}$ immediately by inspecting the relevant conclusions and vulnerabilities. This idea can be formalized as follows.

Definition 4.9. *Given a cvAF $\mathcal{F} = (A, R)$ and an instantiated argument x we define the expansion $f_e(\mathcal{F}, x)$ of $\mathcal{F}$ with x by letting $f_e(\mathcal{F}, x) = (A \cup \{x\}, R_x)$ be the cvAF where*

$$\begin{aligned} R_x = R &\cup \{(x, y) \mid y \in A, cl(x) \in vul(y)\} \\ &\cup \{(y, x) \mid y \in A, cl(y) \in vul(x)\}. \end{aligned}$$

We stipulate that $f_e(\mathcal{F}, X)$ is a shorthand for successively expanding $\mathcal{F}$ with each $x \in X$ in an arbitrary order.

Example 4.10. *Let D be our running example and $\mathcal{F}_D$ its instantiated cvAF as depicted above. Adding a fact "$\overline{b}$." yields an additional instantiated argument $x_3 = (\emptyset, \overline{b})$:*

4.3 cvAFs and Atomic ABA Frameworks

Our cvAFs are closely related to a certain fragment of ABA in dynamic scenarios which we will discuss next.

Definition 4.11. *Let $(\mathcal{L}, \mathcal{R}, \mathcal{A}, ^-)$ be an ABA framework. A rule r is* atomic *if $body(r) \subseteq \mathcal{A}$. The ABA framework is* atomic *if each rule $r \in \mathcal{R}$ is atomic.*

There are two decisive observations we make about atomic ABA frameworks. The first is concerning cvAFs.

Lemma 4.12. *Given an atomic ABA $D = (\mathcal{L}, \mathcal{R}, \mathcal{A}, ^-)$.*

- *If $a \in \mathcal{A}$, then $\mathcal{F}_{D \cup \{r\}} = f_e(\mathcal{F}_D, x)$ with $x = (\overline{a}, a)$.*
- *For each atomic (in D) rule $r = p \leftarrow S$, it holds that $\mathcal{F}_{D \cup \{r\}} = f_e(\mathcal{F}_D, x)$ with $x = (\overline{S}, p)$.*
- *If $x = (\overline{S}, p)$, then $\mathcal{F}_{D \cup H} = f_e(\mathcal{F}_D, x)$ with $H = (\mathcal{L}, \mathcal{R}', \mathcal{A}', ^-)$ with $\mathcal{R}' = \{(p \leftarrow S)\}$ and $\mathcal{A}' = \overline{S}$.*

Second, by moving from general to atomic ABA frameworks we do not lose expressive power; each framework can be transformed into an atomic one.

Proposition 4.13. *For each ABA D there is an atomic ABA D' such that $\sigma(D) = \sigma(D')$ for each considered semantics.*

We mention however that this transformation might result in an exponential blow-up in the number of rules. However, given an atomic ABA framework D we can be sure that the instantiated cvAF $\mathcal{F}_D$ is of linear size in D.

Proposition 4.14. *If $D = (\mathcal{L}, \mathcal{R}, \mathcal{A}, ^-)$ is atomic, then the cvAF $\mathcal{F}_D$ consists of $|\mathcal{R}| + |\mathcal{A}|$ arguments.*

5 The cvAF Enforcement Problem

In this section we develop a notion of the enforcement problem for cvAFs and establish criteria for deciding enforcability. At first glance, this yields results applicable to atomic ABAs due to Lemma 4.12; we will however discuss some subtle details of the notions which one needs to be aware of.

In line with our enforcement notion from Definition 3.1, we define conclusion enforcement for cvAFs by requiring that no new argument with the target conclusion is introduced. In addition, we introduce a natural notion of argument enforcement.

Definition 5.1. *Let $\mathcal{F} = (A, R)$ be a cvAF and σ a semantics. We say that a conclusion p is* σ-enforceable *if there is a set X of instantiated arguments s.t. $cl(x) \neq p$ for each $x \in X$ and p is credulously accepted in $f_e(\mathcal{F}, X)$. An argument $x \in A$ is* σ-enforceable *if there is a set X of instantiated arguments s.t. x is credulously accepted in $f_e(\mathcal{F}, X)$.*

Example 5.2. *Let $\mathcal{F}_D$ be our running example cvAF and consider the expansion $f_e(\mathcal{F}_D, x_3)$ with $x_3 = (\emptyset, \overline{b})$ (cf. Example 4.10). Since $co(f_e(\mathcal{F}_D, x)) = \{\{a, x_1, x_3\}\}$ with $cl(x_1) = p$ we obtain that conclusion p is co-enforceable.*

In the following we establish criteria to decide whether arguments and conclusions are enforceable in cvAFs. It turns out that it suffices to focus on argument enforcement:

Proposition 5.3. *Let $\mathcal{F} = (A, R)$ be a cvAF and σ a semantics. A conclusion $c \in cl(A)$ is enforceable iff there is some $x \in A$ with $cl(x) = c$ s.t. x is enforceable.*

The possible modifications of a cvAF are determined by the conclusions and vulnerabilities of its arguments. It is thus not possible to consider arbitrary expansions. We already saw this for our running example $\mathcal{F}_{D'}$ where a is not enforceable since it is attacked by some argument without any vulnerability (cf. Example 3.3).

In general, arguments of this kind will always be defeated in complete-based semantics. This is not only the case within the given cvAF, but also for any conceivable expansion. Motivated by this observation, we call such arguments *strongly defeated.*

Definition 5.4. *For a cvAF $\mathcal{F} = (A, R)$, $x \in A$ is* strongly defeated *if there is $y \in A$ with $(y, x) \in R$ and $vul(y) = \emptyset$.*

Example 5.5. *In our running example cvAF stemming from instantiating D', the argument x_1 is strongly defeated. In fact, it is verifiable with reasonable effort that x_2 is part of the grounded extension in any possible expansion $f_e(\mathcal{F}, X)$.*

The following proposition formalizes that the behavior we observed in the previous example generalizes to any cvAF and thus our intuition about strong defeat is indeed correct.

Proposition 5.6. *Let $\mathcal{F} = (A, R)$ be a cvAF. If $x \in A$ is strongly defeated, then for each set X of instantiated arguments, the grounded extension of $f_e(\mathcal{F}, X)$ attacks x.*

Consequently, we infer that strongly defeated arguments can never be enforced. It is therefore a reasonable conjecture that an argument is enforceable iff it is not strongly defeated. However, as the following example illustrates, the notion of strong defeat is not yet general enough.

Example 5.7. *Consider the cvAF $\mathcal{F}$ depicted below.*

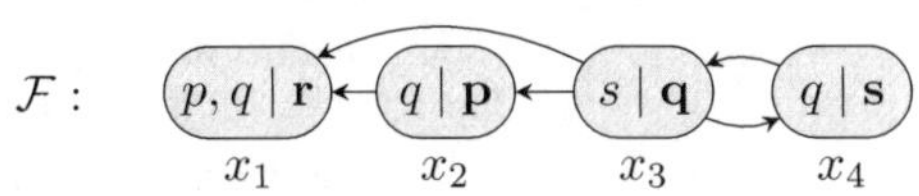

Suppose we want to enforce x_1. In order to achieve this goal we have to add an argument defeating x_2. However, the only vulnerability of x_2 is q and due to $q \in vul(x_1)$, such an argument would defeat x_1 as well.

In general, if there is some argument y with $(y, x) \in R$ and $vul(y) \subseteq vul(x)$, then x can never be defended by a conflict-free set. We call arguments of this kind *strongly unacceptable* since this holds also true for any expansion.

Definition 5.8. *For a cvAF $\mathcal{F} = (A, R)$, $x \in A$ is* strongly unacceptable *if there is $y \in A$ with $(y, x) \in R$ and $vul(y) \subseteq vul(x)$.*

By definition, each strongly defeated argument is strongly unacceptable. For $\sigma \in \{co, pr, stb\}$ we are now ready to state our enforcement results.

Theorem 5.9. *Let $\mathcal{F} = (A, R)$ be a cvAF and suppose $\sigma \in \{co, pr, stb\}$. An argument $x \in A$ is σ-enforceable if and only if it is not strongly unacceptable.*

For grounded semantics, however, we need to consider further unacceptability notions. The reason why Theorem 5.9 does not hold for grounded semantics is that an argument might be capable of defending itself, but is still not part of the iterative procedure which yields the grounded extension. To illustrate this we consider the following example.

Example 5.10. *Suppose we aim to gr-enforce x_1 in $\mathcal{F}$:*

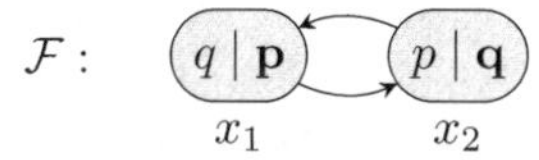

Since $gr(\mathcal{F}) = \emptyset$ we would have to introduce an argument defeating x_2 in order defend x_1 from the in-coming attack. However, an argument achieving this would possess p as conclusion which we want to avoid for this version of the enforcement notion. Indeed, x_1 is not gr-enforceable.

In general, for grounded semantics we require a notion which is similar to strong unacceptability, while taking the special case we just illustrated into account.

Definition 5.11. *For a cvAF $\mathcal{F} = (A, R)$, $x \in A$ is* strongly gr-unacceptable *if there is $y \in A$ with $(y, x) \in R$ and $vul(y) \setminus \{cl(x)\} \subseteq vul(x)$.*

The following condition characterizes gr-enforceability for cvAFs. Although it may appear technical at first glance, it simply ensures that an argument z can be defeated without attacking x, y, or introducing the target claim $cl(x) = cl(y)$.

Proposition 5.12. *Let $\mathcal{F} = (A, R)$ be a cvAF. An argument $x \in A$ is gr-enforceable if and only if one of the following two conditions hold:*

- *x is not strongly gr-unacceptable,*
- *there is some $y \in A$ with $cl(y) = cl(x) = q$ s.t.*
  - *if z attacks y, then $vul(z) \setminus (vul(x) \cup vul(y) \cup \{q\}) \neq \emptyset$,*
  - *if z attacks x, then $q \in vul(z)$ or $vul(z) \setminus (vul(x) \cup vul(y)) \neq \emptyset$.*

Let us now discuss corresponding results for conclusion enforcement. To enforce a conclusion $p \in cl(A)$ we need to enforce an argument $x \in A$ with $cl(x) = p$. Thus, as a corollary of Theorem 5.9 and Proposition 5.12 we obtain:

Corollary 5.13. *Let $\mathcal{F} = (A, R)$ be a cvAF and $\sigma \in \{ad, co, pr, stb\}$. An argument $a \in A$ is σ-enforceable if and only if it is not strongly unacceptable; it is gr-enforceable if and only if it is not strongly gr-unacceptable.*

Consequences for ABA. The introduced unacceptability notions yield syntactical conditions to decide the cvAF enforcement problem in polynomial time. In view of this, it might seem that Lemma 4.12 now implies tractability of the enforcement problem for atomic ABA frameworks. However, when inspecting the construction for the proof of Theorem 3.4 we see that the constructed ABA framework is atomic itself.

Corollary 5.14. *Deciding whether a (p) is enforceable wrt σ is* NP*-complete even for atomic ABA frameworks.*

The reason why this is no contradiction to tractability in cvAFs is rather subtle: When considering an arbitrary expansion $f_e(\mathcal{F}, X)$, it might happen that the resulting cvAF does not correspond to a flat ABA framework anymore due to $cl(X) \cap \mathcal{A} \neq \emptyset$. So even if we start with a cvAF corresponding to some flat ABA framework, we do not have a one to one correspondence between expansions of the cvAF and flat ABA framework extending the initial one.

To ensure that it is not necessary to introduce arguments with assumptions as conclusion when enforcing an argument $x \in A$, we consider a particular fragment of ABA where assumptions do not have out-going attacks.

Definition 5.15. *Let $D = (\mathcal{L}, \mathcal{R}, \mathcal{A}, \bar{\ })$ be an ABA framework. We say D has* separated contraries *if $\mathcal{A} \cap \overline{\mathcal{A}} = \emptyset$.*

Indeed, we are now ready to introduce a tractable fragment for the ABA enforcement problem.

Theorem 5.16. *Deciding whether an argument or conclusion is enforceable for atomic flat ABAs with separated contraries is tractable.*

We want to emphasize that moving from flat ABA to flat atomic ABA does not change the complexity class of the enforcement problem; but additional requiring separated contraries does, i.e., we found a rather minor condition pushing the enforcement problem over the edge to tractability.

6 The cvAF Strong Equivalence Problem

In this section, we establish methods to decide strong equivalence for cvAFs. We define further unacceptability notions, tailored for this setting. In accordance with the standard literature on strong equivalence we then can decide this problem for two cvAFs by comparing their so-called *kernels*, that is, we transform both cvAFs into a semantics-dependent normal form. Let us point out the following crucial difference: In contrast to strong equivalence characterizations in Dung AFs where kernels are constructed by removing redundant *attacks*, we identify redundant *arguments*. The kernels in cvAFs are constructed by *removing* as well as *manipulating* arguments that fall in certain redundancy categories.

We start by defining an appropriate strong equivalence notion for cvAFs.

Definition 6.1. *Two cvAFs $\mathcal{F}$, $\mathcal{G}$ are* strongly equivalent *wrt a semantics σ, for short $\mathcal{F} \equiv_s^\sigma \mathcal{G}$, if for each set X of instantiated arguments $\sigma_{cl}(f_e(\mathcal{F}, X)) = \sigma_{cl}(f_e(\mathcal{G}, X))$ holds.*

Example 6.2. *Consider again the cvAFs $\mathcal{F}_D$ and $\mathcal{F}_{D'}$ from Example 1.1. Judging from earlier results we anticipate that they are not strongly equivalent to each other. Indeed, adding the argument $x_3 = (\emptyset, \bar{b})$ yields the following cvAFs:*

$f_e(\mathcal{F}_D, x_3)$:

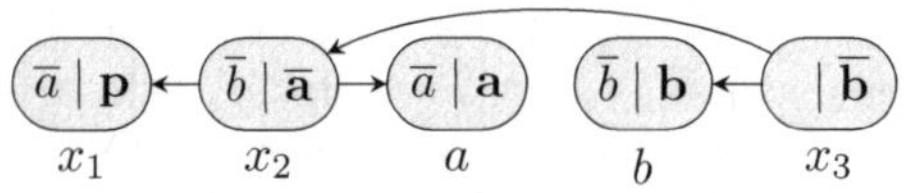

$f_e(\mathcal{F}_{D'}, x_3)$:

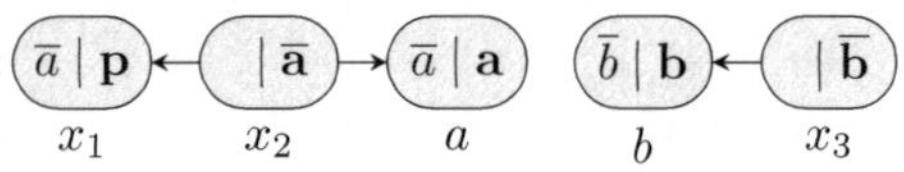

Now, $\{a, p, \bar{b}\}$ is stable in $f_e(\mathcal{F}_D, x_3)$ but not in $f_e(\mathcal{F}_{D'}, x_3)$. We obtain that $\mathcal{F}_D$ and $\mathcal{F}_{D'}$ are not strongly equivalent wrt stable semantics, i.e., $\mathcal{F}_D \not\equiv_s^{stb} \mathcal{F}_{D'}$.

In the above example, it was quite easy to come up with an appropriate counter example. Not only that finding a counter example might be more involved in other situations, it is usually not possible to verify strong equivalence by testing all possible expansions because there might be infinitely many of them. Instead, we identify, for each semantics, a specific kernel – checking strong equivalence then reduces to computing and comparing the respective kernels.

Let us first reconsider the unacceptability notions from Section 5. We have shown that strongly defeated arguments cannot be enforced; in fact, they can be removed without changing the σ_{cl}-extensions.

Proposition 6.3. *Given a cvAF $\mathcal{F} = (A, R)$, a semantics $\sigma \in \{gr, co, pr, stb\}$ and a strongly defeated argument $x \in A$. Then $\sigma_{cl}(\mathcal{F}) = \sigma_{cl}(\mathcal{F} \setminus \{x\})$.*

Likewise, for stable semantics, strongly unacceptable arguments can be deleted without affecting the outcome.

Proposition 6.4. *For a cvAF $\mathcal{F} = (A, R)$ and a strongly unacceptable argument $x \in A$, $stb_{cl}(\mathcal{F}) = stb_{cl}(\mathcal{F} \setminus \{x\})$.*

Considering grounded, complete, and preferred semantics, we observe that strongly unacceptable arguments are not necessarily defeated – removing them thus potentially results in a change of the σ_{cl}-extensions.

Example 6.5. *Consider the cvAF $\mathcal{F}$ from Example 5.7 together with a new argument $x_0 = (\{r\}, t)$:*

$f_e(\mathcal{F}, x_0)$:

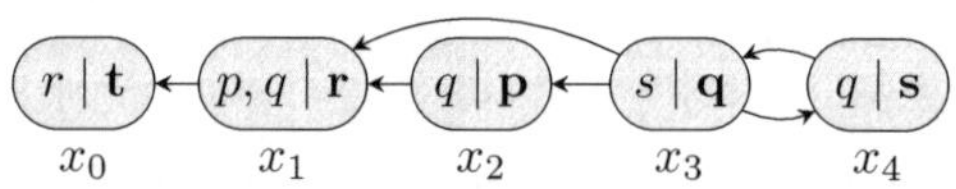

$f_e(\mathcal{F}, x_0)$ has three complete conclusion-extensions: $\emptyset$ (the grounded extension), $\{s, p, t\}$, and $\{q, t\}$. Recall that x_1 is strongly unacceptable w.r.t. x_2. Removing x_1 would make x_0 unattacked, changing the grounded extension to $\{t\}$.

Strongly unacceptable arguments can neither be enforced nor deleted in such situations. This means that on semantics level, it is not possible to distinguish if such arguments are self-attacking or not (analogous observations hold for *gr*-unacceptable arguments wrt grounded semantics).

Proposition 6.6. *Given a cvAF $\mathcal{F} = (A, R)$, a semantics $\sigma \in \{gr, co, pr, stb\}$ and a strongly unacceptable argument $x \in A$ and let $x' = (vul(x) \cup \{cl(x)\}, cl(x))$. Then $\sigma(\mathcal{F}) = \sigma(f_e(\mathcal{F} \setminus \{x\}, x'))$. If x is strongly gr-unacceptable, then $gr(\mathcal{F}) = gr((f_e(\mathcal{F} \setminus \{x\}, x'))$.*

Next we consider a redundancy notion that also appears in different contexts (Dvorák and Woltran 2020): We call an argument x *redundant* if there is some other argument y having the same conclusion but possesses less vulnerabilities.

Definition 6.7. *For a cvAF $\mathcal{F} = (A, R)$, $x \in A$ is* redundant *if there is $y \in A$ with $cl(y) = cl(x)$ and $vul(y) \subsetneq vul(x)$.*

Example 6.8. *The argument x_2 from the cvAF $\mathcal{F}_D$ from our running example is redundant wrt $x = (\emptyset, \bar{a})$ because $cl(x) = cl(x_2) = \bar{a}$ and $vul(x) = \emptyset \subsetneq \{\bar{b}\} = vul(x_2)$.*

Redundant arguments can be removed without changing the conclusion-based extensions of a given cvAF.

Proposition 6.9. *For a cvAF $\mathcal{F} = (A, R)$, a semantics $\sigma \in \{gr, co, pr, stb\}$ and a redundant argument $x \in A$, it holds that $\sigma_{cl}(\mathcal{F}) = \sigma_{cl}(\mathcal{F} \setminus \{x\})$.*

We are ready to define the complete and the grounded kernel for cvAFs. Following Proposition 6.6, the first adjustment we carry out is a modification on vulnerability level:

Each unacceptable argument x is turned into a self-attacker by adding $cl(x)$ to $vul(x)$; for grounded semantics, we modify each gr-unacceptable argument instead. In the next step, we remove all strongly defeated and redundant arguments.

Definition 6.10. *For a cvAF $\mathcal{F} = (A, R)$, let X denote the set of all strongly unacceptable arguments in A and let*

$$(A', R') = f_e(\mathcal{F} \setminus X, \{(vul(x) \cup \{cl(x)\}, cl(x)) \mid x \in X\}).$$

We define the complete kernel $\mathcal{F}^{ck} = (A^{ck}, R^{ck})$ *with*

$$A^{ck} = A' \setminus \{x \in A' \mid x \text{ is str. defeated or redundant}\},$$

and $R^{ck} = R' \cap (A^{ck} \times A^{ck})$. The grounded kernel $\mathcal{F}^{gk}$ *is defined analogously by replacing X with the set of all strongly gr-unacceptable arguments $x \in A$.*

Example 6.11. *The cvAF $\mathcal{F}_D$ from our running example coincides with its complete and grounded kernel since no arguments are strongly defeated, unacceptable or redundant. That is, we obtain $\mathcal{F}_D^{ck} = \mathcal{F}_D^{gk} = \mathcal{F}_D$. Recalling that x_2 is strongly unacceptable in $\mathcal{F}_{D'}$ we obtain the following picture (observe that $\mathcal{F}_{D'}^{ck} = \mathcal{F}_{D'}^{gk}$ also holds in this case):*

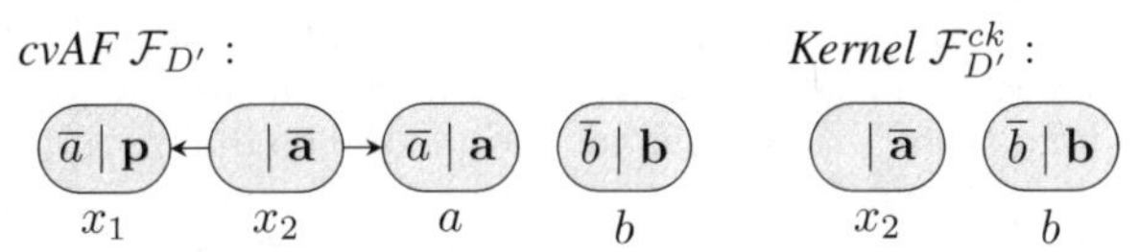

Next we consider a special case of strong unacceptability that affects only preferred semantics.

Definition 6.12. *For a cvAF $\mathcal{F} = (A, R)$, $x \in A$ is* strongly pr-unacceptable *if x is strongly unacceptable w.r.t. $y \in A$ and $vul(y) = \{cl(x)\}$.*

Observe that each strongly pr-unacceptable argument is self-attacking because $vul(y) = \{cl(x)\} \subseteq vul(x)$. It turns out that such arguments can be removed without changing the conclusion-based preferred extensions.

Proposition 6.13. *For a cvAF $\mathcal{F} = (A, R)$ and a strongly pr-unacceptable argument $x \in A$, $pr_{cl}(\mathcal{F}) = pr_{cl}(\mathcal{F} \setminus \{x\})$.*

The preferred kernel refines the complete kernel:

Definition 6.14. *For a cvAF $\mathcal{F} = (A, R)$, let $\mathcal{F}^{ck} = (A^{ck}, R^{ck})$ be as in Definition 6.10. We define the* preferred kernel $\mathcal{F}^{pk} = (A^{pk}, R^{pk})$ *with*

$$A^{pk} = A^{ck} \setminus \{x \in A^{ck} \mid x \text{ is str. } pr\text{-unacceptable}\},$$

and $R^{pk} = R^{ck} \cap (A^{pk} \times A^{pk})$.

Finally, we consider stable semantics. We start with the crucial observation that the particular conclusion of self-attacking arguments is not of importance.

Example 6.15. *Consider the following two cvAFs $\mathcal{F}$ and $\mathcal{G}$:*

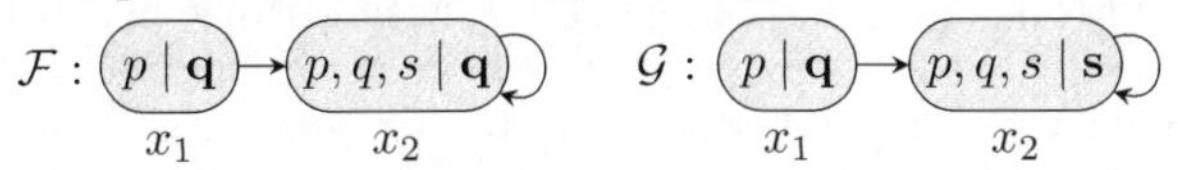

Essentially, $\mathcal{F}$ and $\mathcal{G}$ differ only in the conclusion of the self-attacking argument x_2. Observe that $\mathcal{F}$ and $\mathcal{G}$ both admit the same unique stable extension $\{q\}$. As we will see, this is not a coincidence: For stable semantics, self-attacking arguments are indistinguishable with respect to their conclusion.

Proposition 6.16. *Given a cvAF $\mathcal{F} = (A, R)$ and a self-attacking argument $x \in A$. For any $s \in vul(x)$, it holds that $stb_{cl}(\mathcal{F}) = stb_{cl}(f_e(\mathcal{F}, \{(vul(x), s)\}))$.*

We construct the stable kernel by (i) adding all such missing self-attackers before (ii) removing all redundant, strongly defeated, and strongly unacceptable arguments.

Definition 6.17. *For a cvAF $\mathcal{F} = (A, R)$, let X denote the set of all self-attacking arguments in A and let*

$$(A', R') = f_e(\mathcal{F}, \{(vul(x), s) \mid x \in X, s \in vul(x)\}).$$

We define the stable kernel $\mathcal{F}^{sk} = (A^{sk}, R^{sk})$ *with*

$$A^{sk} = A' \setminus \{x \in A' \mid x \text{ is str. defeated, str. unacceptable, or redundant}\},$$

and $R^{sk} = R' \cap (A^{sk} \times A^{sk})$.

Iterative application of the previously established propositions shows that the kernels are semantics-preserving. Below we write $\mathcal{F}^{k(\sigma)}$ to denote the σ-kernel of $\mathcal{F}$.

Lemma 6.18. *$\sigma(\mathcal{F}) = \sigma(\mathcal{F}^{k(\sigma)})$ for every cvAF $\mathcal{F}$ and semantics σ considered in this paper.*

The syntactical coherence is guaranteed by the following technical lemma which states that the order of adding additional arguments is not of importance.

Lemma 6.19. *For every cvAF $\mathcal{F}$, for every instantiated argument x, $(f_e(\mathcal{F}, \{x\}))^{k(\sigma)} = (f_e(\mathcal{F}^{k(\sigma)}, \{x\}))^{k(\sigma)}$.*

We are ready to present our characterization result for cvAF strong equivalence: strong equivalence can be decided by computing and comparing the respective kernels.

Theorem 6.20. *For any two cvAFs $\mathcal{F}$ and $\mathcal{G}$, for any $\sigma \in \{gr, co, pr, stb\}$, $\mathcal{F} \equiv_s^\sigma \mathcal{G}$ if and only if $\mathcal{F}^{k(\sigma)} = \mathcal{G}^{k(\sigma)}$.*

Recall that the cvAFs $\mathcal{F}_D$ and $\mathcal{F}_{D'}$ from our running example are not strongly equivalent to each other as already observed in Example 6.2. Theorem 6.20 now gives a criteria to check strong equivalence for any two cvAFs without searching for counter-examples. Considering for instance the cvAFs $\mathcal{F}$ and $\mathcal{G}$ from Example 6.15, we obtain

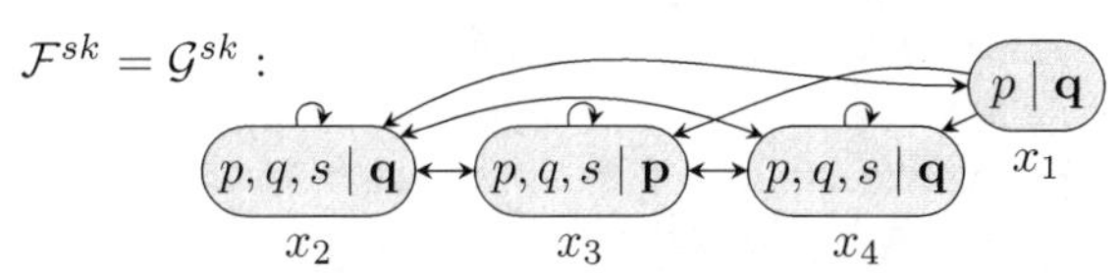

By Theorem 6.20 we thus can conclude that $\mathcal{F}$ and $\mathcal{G}$ are strongly equivalent w.r.t. stable semantics without testing each possible expansion.

Consequences for ABA By transferring the above results in the context of ABA we obtain that deciding strong equivalence for flat, atomic ABA frameworks with separated contraries is tractable.

Theorem 6.21. *For two atomic, flat ABA frameworks D, D' with separated contraries, deciding $D \equiv_s^\sigma D'$ is tractable.*

As in the case of enforcement, we want to emphasize that moving from flat ABA to flat atomic ABA does not change the complexity class of this problem. However, if we additionally require that the frameworks have separated assumptions we obtain the desired tractable fragment.

7 Consequences for Logic Programs

The attentive reader may have observed that we inferred our tractability results by changing the instantiation from AFs to cvAFs and then applying results for cvAFs instead of directly investigating ABA frameworks as deductive systems. While this technique seems cumbersome as a first glance, the established results for cvAFs turn out to be a convenient tool which we can now apply to logic programs almost immediately. This section demonstrates this approach.

We consider the logic programming semantics discussed in (Caminada et al. 2015b); for those, a close correspondence to AF semantics has been shown. We assume the reader to be familiar with these concepts; an introduction to LPs can be found in the supplementary material. We define credulous acceptance of an atom a occurring in P in the expected way. Given an LP P, the corresponding instantiated cvAF is denoted by $\mathcal{F}_P$. We proceed as for ABA frameworks by applying the cvAF results. Since they have been shown already, we only have left to give an LP version of Proposition 4.7 as well as Lemma 4.12.

Proposition 7.1. *For each LP P and its associated cvAF $\mathcal{F}_P$, for each $\sigma \in \{gr, co, pr, stb\}$, it holds that*

- *if $X \in \sigma(P)$ then $\{(X', s) \in A \mid X' \subseteq X\} \in \sigma(\mathcal{F}_P)$;*
- *if $E \in \sigma(\mathcal{F}_P)$ then $\bigcup_{(X,s)\in E} X \in \sigma(D)$.*

Lemma 7.2. *Given an atomic LP P and $B = \{b_1, \ldots, b_n\}$.*

- *For each atomic rule $r = c \leftarrow not\ b_1, \ldots, not\ b_n$, it holds that $\mathcal{F}_{P\cup\{r\}} = f_e(\mathcal{F}_P, x)$ with $x = (B, c)$.*
- *For each argument $x = (B, c)$, it holds that $\mathcal{F}_{P\cup\{r\}} = f_e(\mathcal{F}_P, x)$ with $r = c \leftarrow not\ b_1, \ldots, not\ b_n$.*

This suffices in order to efficiently investigate our two problems we considered before. The relation is even much closer since we do not need to handle additional assumptions. We define the LP enforcement problem as follows.

Definition 7.3. *Let P be a logic program and σ a semantics. An atom a is σ-*enforceable *if there is a set R of rules s.t. a is credulously accepted in $P \cup R$ w.r.t. σ.*

The NP-hardness proof we gave for ABA in Theorem 3.4 works analogously for LPs and thus, the enforcement problem is intractable for LPs in general. However, our cvAF results yield tractability for atomic LPs.

Theorem 7.4. *For atomic LPs, deciding whether some atom is enforceable is tractable.*

Analogously we discuss strong equivalence for LPs. As in the corresponding notion of ABA frameworks, we insist that the expansions are atomic as well.

Definition 7.5. *Two atomic LPs P, P' are* atomic strongly equivalent *w.r.t. a semantics σ, for short $P \equiv^{\sigma}_{ase} P'$, if for each atomic LP H $\sigma(P \cup H) = \sigma(P' \cup H)$ holds.*

Without the requirement of P, P', and H being atomic, intractability of strong equivalence is well-known from LP research (Lifschitz, Pearce, and Valverde 2001). Due to our cvAF results, we obtain a tractable fragment here as well.

Theorem 7.6. *Deciding whether two atomic LPs P and Q are atomic strongly equivalent is tractable.*

8 Discussion

We investigated strong equivalence and enforcement for ABA. We showed that in general, both tasks are intractable. Inspired by tractability of the corresponding problems for AFs, we proposed an adjusted instantiation procedure via cvAFs to obtain a closer relation between the knowledge base and the corresponding AF. Due to the close correspondence between atomic ABA frameworks and cvAFs, we demonstrated how our cvAF tractability results yield tractable fragments of ABA for these problems. Finally, we applied our techniques to LPs as well.

Our work extends research on dynamics in argumentation (Rotstein et al. 2010; Rotstein et al. 2008; Snaith and Reed 2017). In the context of AFs, both enforcement and strong equivalence are well-studied (Baumann and Brewka 2010; Oikarinen and Woltran 2011; Baumann 2012a; Wallner, Niskanen, and Järvisalo 2017). Similar to our setting, (Wallner 2020) considers situations where an AF undergoes certain changes, but the permitted modifications are constrained. Constraints on the possibly reachable expansions of a given cvAF are intrinsic to our approach. In a recent paper (Borg and Bex 2021) the authors study under which conditions in a structured argumentation formalism a given formula can be enforced; moreover, strong equivalence is similar in spirit to *stability* (Testerink, Odekerken, and Bex 2019). The authors in (Moguillansky et al. 2008) consider argumentative revision operators in the context of defeasible logic programming. In contrast to our enforcement approach, they allow for the deletion of rules (following some minimal change principle) to warrant a desired conclusion.

Our cvAFs are similar in spirit to CAFs (Dvorák and Woltran 2020) where arguments are equipped with claims. CAFs are well-studied (Dvorák, Rapberger, and Woltran 2020; Dvorák et al. 2021), including research on strong equivalence (Baumann, Rapberger, and Ulbricht 2021). However, since vulnerability awareness is crucial for dynamics in ABA, CAFs would not be suitable in this setting.

The redundancy notions we discussed are similar in spirit to the line of research on syntactic transformations for LPs, see., e.g., (Brass and Dix 1997; Eiter et al. 2004; Wang and Zhou 2005; Lin and Chen 2007), that gave rise to alternative characterizations of strong equivalence (Osorio, Pérez, and Arrazola 2001; Cabalar 2002) and set the ground for further complexity analysis of LP fragments (Eiter et al. 2007).

Future work directions include exploring further formalisms where cvAFs are applicable, i.e., investigating suitability for e.g. logic-based argumentation (Besnard and Hunter 2001). As demonstrated in our LP section, this technique may lead to quickly obtained results. Similarly, finding more reasoning tasks where cvAFs are applicable might contribute to this line of research. It would also be interesting to see under which conditions the requirement of atomic frameworks can be dropped. As a further future research direction we identify the design of efficient algorithms since our tractability results serve as a promising starting point for such an endeavor. We also want to mention that formalisms which incorporate preferences, e.g., ABA+ (Cyras and Toni 2016), do not always yield well-formed cvAFs, so research on this more general case is also worth the effort.

Acknowledgements

This work was supported by the German Federal Ministry of Education and Research (BMBF, 01/S18026A-F) by funding the competence center for Big Data and AI "ScaDS.AI" Dresden/Leipzig and by the Austrian Science Fund (FWF) through project W1255-N23 and by the Vienna Science and Technology Fund (WWTF) through project ICT19-065.

References

Baumann, R., and Brewka, G. 2010. Expanding argumentation frameworks: Enforcing and monotonicity results. In *Proc. COMMA'10*, volume 216 of *FAIA*, 75–86. IOS Press.

Baumann, R.; Doutre, S.; Mailly, J.-G.; and Wallner, J. P. 2021. Enforcement in formal argumentation. *J. Appl. Logic* 2:1623–1677.

Baumann, R.; Rapberger, A.; and Ulbricht, M. 2021. Equivalence in argumentation frameworks with a claim-centric view – classical results with novel ingredients. In *Proceedings of the 19th International Workshop on Non-Monotonic Reasoning (NMR'21)*, 71–80. To appear in Proc. AAAI'22.

Baumann, R. 2012a. Normal and strong expansion equivalence for argumentation frameworks. *Artificial Intelligence* 193:18–44.

Baumann, R. 2012b. What does it take to enforce an argument? minimal change in abstract argumentation. In *Proc. ECAI'12*, volume 242 of *FAIA*, 127–132. IOS Press.

Besnard, P., and Hunter, A. 2001. A logic-based theory of deductive arguments. *Artif. Intell.* 128(1-2):203–235.

Bondarenko, A.; Toni, F.; and Kowalski, R. A. 1993. An assumption-based framework for non-monotonic reasoning. In Pereira, L. M., and Nerode, A., eds., *Logic Programming and Non-monotonic Reasoning, Proceedings of the Second International Workshop, Lisbon, Portugal, June 1993*, 171–189. MIT Press.

Borg, A., and Bex, F. 2021. Enforcing sets of formulas in structured argumentation. In Bienvenu, M.; Lakemeyer, G.; and Erdem, E., eds., *Proceedings of the 18th International Conference on Principles of Knowledge Representation and Reasoning, KR 2021, Online event, November 3-12, 2021*, 130–140.

Brass, S., and Dix, J. 1997. Characterizations of the disjunctive stable semantics by partial evaluation. *J. Log. Program.* 32(3):207–228.

Cabalar, P. 2002. A three-valued characterization for strong equivalence of logic programs. In Dechter, R.; Kearns, M. J.; and Sutton, R. S., eds., *Proc. AAAI'02*, 106–111. AAAI Press / The MIT Press.

Caminada, M.; Sá, S.; Alcântara, J.; and Dvořák, W. 2015a. On the difference between assumption-based argumentation and abstract argumentation. *IfCoLog Journal of Logic and its Applications* 2(1):15–34.

Caminada, M.; Sá, S.; Alcântara, J. F. L.; and Dvorák, W. 2015b. On the equivalence between logic programming semantics and argumentation semantics. *Int. J. Approx. Reason.* 58:87–111.

Cyras, K., and Toni, F. 2016. ABA+: assumption-based argumentation with preferences. In Baral, C.; Delgrande, J. P.; and Wolter, F., eds., *Principles of Knowledge Representation and Reasoning: Proceedings of the Fifteenth International Conference, KR 2016, Cape Town, South Africa, April 25-29, 2016*, 553–556. AAAI Press.

Čyras, K.; Fan, X.; Schulz, C.; and Toni, F. 2018. Assumption-based argumentation: Disputes, explanations, preferences. In Baroni, P.; Gabbay, D.; Giacomin, M.; and van der Torre, L., eds., *Handbook of Formal Argumentation*. College Publications. chapter 7, 365–408.

Doutre, S., and Mailly, J. 2018. Constraints and changes: A survey of abstract argumentation dynamics. *Argument Comput.* 9(3):223–248.

Dung, P. M. 1995. On the acceptability of arguments and its fundamental role in nonmonotonic reasoning, logic programming and n-person games. *Artif. Intell.* 77(2):321–357.

Dvorák, W., and Dunne, P. E. 2018. Computational problems in formal argumentation and their complexity. In Baroni, P.; Gabbay, D.; Giacomin, M.; and van der Torre, L., eds., *Handbook of Formal Argumentation*. College Publications.

Dvorák, W., and Woltran, S. 2020. Complexity of abstract argumentation under a claim-centric view. *Artif. Intell.* 285:103290.

Dvorák, W.; Greßler, A.; Rapberger, A.; and Woltran, S. 2021. The complexity landscape of claim-augmented argumentation frameworks. In *Proc. AAAI'21*, 6296–6303. AAAI Press.

Dvorák, W.; Rapberger, A.; and Woltran, S. 2020. Argumentation semantics under a claim-centric view: Properties, expressiveness and relation to setafs. In *Proc. KR'20*, 341–350.

Eiter, T.; Fink, M.; Tompits, H.; and Woltran, S. 2004. Simplifying logic programs under uniform and strong equivalence. In Lifschitz, V., and Niemelä, I., eds., *Proc. LPNMR'04*, volume 2923 of *LNCS*, 87–99. Springer.

Eiter, T.; Fink, M.; Tompits, H.; and Woltran, S. 2007. Complexity results for checking equivalence of stratified logic programs. In *Proc. IJCAI'07*, 330–335.

Gabbay, D.; Giacomin, M.; Simari, G. R.; and Thimm, M., eds. 2021. *Handbook of Formal Argumentation*, volume 2. College Publications.

Gorogiannis, N., and Hunter, A. 2011. Instantiating abstract argumentation with classical logic arguments: Postulates and properties. *Artif. Intell.* 175(9-10):1479–1497.

Lifschitz, V.; Pearce, D.; and Valverde, A. 2001. Strongly equivalent logic programs. *ACM Transactions on Computational Logic (TOCL)* 2(4):526–541.

Lin, F., and Chen, Y. 2007. Discovering classes of strongly equivalent logic programs. *J. Artif. Intell. Res.* 28:431–451.

Modgil, S., and Prakken, H. 2017. Abstract rule-based argumentation. *FLAP* 4(8).

Moguillansky, M. O.; Rotstein, N. D.; Falappa, M. A.; García, A. J.; and Simari, G. R. 2008. Argument theory change applied to defeasible logic programming. In Fox, D., and Gomes, C. P., eds., *Proceedings of the Twenty-Third AAAI Conference on Artificial Intelligence, AAAI 2008, Chicago, Illinois, USA, July 13-17, 2008*, 132–137. AAAI Press.

Oikarinen, E., and Woltran, S. 2011. Characterizing strong equivalence for argumentation frameworks. *Artif. Intell.* 175(14-15):1985–2009.

Osorio, M.; Pérez, J. A. N.; and Arrazola, J. 2001. Equivalence in answer set programming. In Pettorossi, A., ed., *Proc. LOPSTR'01*, volume 2372 of *LNCS*, 57–75. Springer.

Rotstein, N. D.; Moguillansky, M. O.; Falappa, M. A.; García, A. J.; and Simari, G. R. 2008. Argument theory change: Revision upon warrant. In *Proc. COMMA'08*, volume 172 of *FAIA*, 336–347. IOS Press.

Rotstein, N. D.; Moguillansky, M. O.; García, A. J.; and Simari, G. R. 2010. A dynamic argumentation framework. In *Proc. COMMA'10*, volume 216 of *FAIA*, 427–438. IOS Press.

Snaith, M., and Reed, C. 2017. Argument revision. *J. Log. Comput.* 27(7):2089–2134.

Testerink, B.; Odekerken, D.; and Bex, F. 2019. A method for efficient argument-based inquiry. In *International Conference on Flexible Query Answering Systems*, 114–125. Springer.

Wallner, J. P.; Niskanen, A.; and Järvisalo, M. 2017. Complexity results and algorithms for extension enforcement in abstract argumentation. *J. Artif. Intell. Res.* 60:1–40.

Wallner, J. P. 2020. Structural constraints for dynamic operators in abstract argumentation. *Argument Comput.* 11(1-2):151–190.

Wang, K., and Zhou, L. 2005. Comparisons and computation of well-founded semantics for disjunctive logic programs. *ACM Trans. Comput. Log.* 6(2):295–327.

Kernel Contraction and the Order of Relevance

Jandson S. Ribeiro
University of Hagen, Germany
jandson.ribeiro@fernuni-hagen.de

Abstract

The postulate of *relevance* provides a suitable and general notion of minimal change for belief contraction. Relevance is tightly connected to smooth kernel contractions when an agent's epistemic state is represented as a logically closed set of formulae. This connection, however, breaks down when an agent's epistemic state is represented as a set of formulae not necessarily logically closed. We investigate the cause behind this schism, and we reconnect relevance with smooth kernel contractions by constraining the behaviour of their choice mechanisms and epistemic preference relations. Our first representation theorem connects smooth kernel contractions with a novel class of epistemic preference relations. For our second representation theorem, we introduce the principle of *symmetry of removal* that relates relevance to epistemic choices. For the last theorem, we devise a novel class of smooth kernel contractions, that satisfy relevance, which are based on epistemic preference relations that capture the principle of *symmetry of removal*.

1 Introduction

The field of *belief change* (Alchourrón, Gärdenfors, and Makinson, 1985; Hansson, 1999) studies how an agent should rationally maintain its body of beliefs as it evolves. The most interesting situations emerge when incoming information conflicts with the agent's current beliefs. In this case, for the sake of consistency, the agent must remove beliefs that conflict with the incoming information. This is known as *belief revision*, and a challenging task consists in deciding which information should be discarded. In essence, the agent should preserve most of its original beliefs, which is known as the principle of minimal change. Removal of information is by itself studied under the name of *belief contraction* and can be seen as a central problem in belief change, because it forms the cornerstone to properly define other kinds of changes. For instance, *belief revision* is in essence defined in terms of belief contraction: first remove any conflict with the incoming information by performing belief contraction, and thereafter accommodate the incoming information. When the underlying logic used to specify an agent's beliefs is closed under classical negation, this recipe for defining revision from contraction is formalised via the (external and internal) Levi Identity.

Belief contraction, and other forms of belief change, have been studied via two different, but equivalent, perspectives: (i) defining rationality postulates that conceptualise the principle of minimal change; and (ii) constructing classes of operations that explicitly capture such postulates. The first perspective provides a principled way for understanding what is a rational change, as well as identifying and forbidding counter-intuitive behaviours of belief change. The second perspective provides constructive apparatuses to understand how belief change behaves. The contrast between the two perspectives helps to understand how principles of minimal change (via rationality postulates) outline and constrain the epistemic choices an agent might make, and on which classes of epistemic preferences such choices can be based. Toward the first perspective, a major rationality postulate in belief contraction is *relevance* which intuitively states that a belief can only be removed for a good reason (see Section 2 for the formal definition). Hansson (1991) argues that *relevance* provides a general and suitable notion of minimal change, while Ribeiro et al. (2013) have shown that *relevance* is consistent with several non-classical logics.

As for the second perspective, the two dominating classes of belief contraction operations are: partial-meet functions (Alchourrón, Gärdenfors, and Makinson, 1985) which are based on a "what to keep" strategy; and (smooth) kernel contraction functions (Hansson, 1994) which are based on a "what to remove" strategy. These two classes of functions are dual, and are usually seen as two sides of the same coin (Falappa, Fermé, and Kern-Isberner, 2006). This duality permits to understand the rationality of relevance through two complementary constructive views. Indeed, in the most fundamental case, when an agent's epistemic state is represented as a logically closed set of formulae, called a theory, both *partial meet* and *smooth kernel contraction* satisfy relevance, and they collapse to the same class of functions (Hansson, 1999; Hansson and Wassermann, 2002).

Theories, however, are very restrictive, because they do not distinguish between implicit beliefs versus explicit beliefs. This distinction can be achieved by dropping the logical closure requirement, and simply representing an agent's epistemic state as a set of formulae, called a *belief base*. This alternative is more general and expressive than theories. However, for belief bases, the connection between relevance and *smooth kernel contraction* breaks down, though the connection between partial meet and relevance is not harmed. The reasons for this rupture are still unclear. Restoring the connection between relevance and smooth kernel contraction is extremely important to better support belief contraction for several reasons.

First, smooth kernel contraction and partial meet work as two complementary perspectives of belief contraction. At a first glance, it might not seem harmful to solely rely on partial meet as a canonical form for constructing belief contraction operations that satisfy relevance. It turns out that such a strategy severely limits the reach of belief contraction approaches in more expressive logics: in several non-classical logics, partial meet functions cannot even be defined (Ribeiro et al., 2013; Guerra and Wassermann, 2019), although belief contraction operations satisfying relevance do exist in such logics (Ribeiro, Nayak, and Wassermann, 2018). Kernel contraction operations could be studied in such logics as a natural alternative. Secondly, according to Hansson (2017) the way that partial meet functions conceptualise choices is counter-intuitive. Precisely, partial meet functions decide what to keep by forcing the agent to choose among the maximal conserving options, and intersecting the choices. This is counter-intuitive, because epistemically an agent's choice should not be based on maximising and maintaining the best of two or more scenarios. Therefore, partial-meet should not be taken as a canonical form to construct belief contraction operations. On the other hand, kernel contraction simply chooses beliefs to be removed, and therefore is not subject to this criticism. Moreover, kernel contraction appears as the dominating implementation strategy for handling inconsistencies in ontology repair (Horridge, 2011; Kalyanpur et al., 2007), whereas partial meet is almost unexplored (Cóbe and Wassermann, 2015).

Lastly, kernel contraction functions are closely related to other forms of belief dynamics, such as argumentation systems (Simari and Loui, 1992) and consistency maintenance approaches, such as culpability and inconsistency measures (Hunter and Konieczny, 2008, 2005).

Therefore, identifying the precise connection between kernel contractions and the postulate of relevance is of extreme importance to achieve a complete constructive overview of processes of rational belief contraction.

In this work, we restore the connection between smooth kernel contraction and relevance, by constraining the way that kernel contraction functions choose what to remove. We identify a principle relating relevance and epistemic choices, which we call *symmetry of removal*. We then examine how such a principle can be translated into epistemic preference relations. We start by defining a class of epistemic preference relations on the subsets of the agent's belief base, and we construct a novel class of kernel contraction functions based on such relations: the *spalled kernel contractions*. Thereafter, we devise a condition, *concordant-mirroring*, that embeds this principle in the epistemic preferences of an agent. This yields a new class of smooth kernel contraction functions which we call *mirrored kernel contraction*, and we show a representation theorem relating this novel class of kernel contraction functions and the relevance postulate.

Road map: In Section 2, we briefly review belief base contraction, its rationality postulates, including relevance, and smooth kernel contraction functions. In Section 3, we introduce the novel class of spalled kernel contraction functions. We show that spalled and smooth kernel contraction correspond to the same class of functions, with the difference that spalled kernel contraction explicitly realises the epistemic preference relations of an agent. In Section 4, we introduce the principle of *symmetry of removal* and the *concordant-mirroring* condition, and their respective representation theorems with relevance. In Section 5, we discuss some related works. Finally, in Section 6, we make some final considerations, and we discuss some future research lines worth to explore.

2 Belief Base Contraction

We assume that an agent's corpus of beliefs is represented as a belief base, which will be denoted by the letter $\mathcal{K}$. The term belief base has been used in the literature with two main purposes: (i) as a finite representation of an agent's beliefs (Nebel, 1990; Dixon, 1994; Dalal, 1988), and (ii) as a more general and expressive approach that distinguishes explicit from implicit beliefs (Fuhrmann, 1991; Hansson, 1999). We follow the latter approach, and therefore a belief base can be infinite. The power set of a set A is denoted by $\mathcal{P}(A)$. A belief base is specified in the language of an underlying logic. We treat a logic as a pair $\langle \mathcal{L}, Cn \rangle$, where $\mathcal{L}$ is a language, and $Cn : \mathcal{P}(\mathcal{L}) \to \mathcal{P}(\mathcal{L})$ is a logical consequence operator that indicates all the formulae that are entailed from a set of formulae in $\mathcal{L}$. We limit ourselves to logics whose consequence operator Cn satisfies:

monotonicity: if $A \subseteq B$ then $Cn(A) \subseteq Cn(B)$;

inclusion: $A \subseteq Cn(A)$;

idempotency: $Cn(Cn(A)) = Cn(A)$;

compactness: if $\varphi \in Cn(A)$ then there is some finite set $A' \subseteq A$ such that $\varphi \in Cn(A')$.

Consequence operators that satisfy the first three conditions above are called Tarskian. Some times we say that the logic itself is Tarskian. Throughout this work, unless otherwise stated, all the presented results regard logics whose consequence operators are both Tarskian and satisfy compactness. Let $\mathcal{K}$ be a belief base, a contraction function for $\mathcal{K}$ is a function $\dot{-} : \mathcal{L} \to \mathcal{P}(\mathcal{L})$ that given an unwanted piece of information α outputs a subset of $\mathcal{K}$ which does not entail α. A contraction function is subject to the following basic rationality postulates (Hansson, 1991, 1994):

(success): if $\alpha \notin Cn(\emptyset)$ then $\alpha \notin Cn(\mathcal{K} \dot{-} \alpha)$;
(inclusion): $\mathcal{K} \dot{-} \alpha \subseteq \mathcal{K}$;
(vacuity): if $\alpha \notin Cn(\mathcal{K})$ then $\mathcal{K} \dot{-} \alpha = \mathcal{K}$;
(uniformity): if for all $\mathcal{K}' \subseteq \mathcal{K}$ it holds that $\alpha \in Cn(\mathcal{K}')$ iff $\beta \in Cn(\mathcal{K}')$, then $\mathcal{K} \dot{-} \alpha = \mathcal{K} \dot{-} \beta$;
(core-retainment): if $\beta \in \mathcal{K} \setminus (\mathcal{K} \dot{-} \alpha)$ then there exists a $\mathcal{K}' \subseteq K$ s.t $\alpha \notin Cn(\mathcal{K}')$ but $\alpha \in Cn(\mathcal{K}' \cup \{\beta\})$;
(relative closure): if $\beta \in \mathcal{K} \cap Cn(\mathcal{K} \dot{-} \alpha)$ then $\beta \in \mathcal{K} \dot{-} \alpha$;

(relevance): if $\beta \in \mathcal{K} \setminus (\mathcal{K} \dot{-} \alpha)$ then there is some $\mathcal{K}'$ such that $\mathcal{K} \dot{-} \alpha \subseteq \mathcal{K}' \subseteq \mathcal{K}$, $\alpha \notin Cn(\mathcal{K}')$ but $\alpha \in Cn(\mathcal{K}' \cup \{\beta\})$

For a discussion on the rationale of this postulates, see (Hansson, 1999). It worth highlighting that relevance implies core-retainment. A contraction function that satisfies the six first rationality postulates above will be dubbed a *rational contraction function*. Additionally if a rational contraction function satisfies relevance, then we will say that it is *fully rational*. One of the most influential classes of rational contraction functions is the class of (smooth) kernel contraction functions (see Definition 5), which are defined on kernels and incision functions:

Definition 1. *An α-kernel of a belief base $\mathcal{K}$ is a set X such that (1) $X \subseteq \mathcal{K}$; (2) $\alpha \in Cn(X)$; and (3) if $X' \subset X$ then $\alpha \notin Cn(X')$.*

An α-kernel of a belief base $\mathcal{K}$ is a minimal subset of $\mathcal{K}$ that does entail α. Due to compactness, every kernel is finite. The set of all α-kernels of a belief base $\mathcal{K}$ is denoted by $\mathcal{K} \perp\!\!\!\perp \alpha$. Formulae that do not appear in any α-kernel are called α-free. As α-free formulae have no connection with the formula α to be contracted, they should be kept intact, while only not α-free formulae should be picked for removal. This choice of removal is realised by an incision function:

Definition 2. *Let $\mathcal{C}(\mathcal{K}) = \{\mathcal{K} \perp\!\!\!\perp \alpha \mid \alpha \in \mathcal{L}\}$ be the set of all kernel sets of $\mathcal{K}$. A standard incision function on a belief base $\mathcal{K}$ is a function $\sigma : \mathcal{C}(\mathcal{K}) \rightarrow \mathcal{P}(\mathcal{L})$ such that*

(1) $\sigma(\mathcal{K} \perp\!\!\!\perp \alpha) \subseteq \bigcup \mathcal{K} \perp\!\!\!\perp \alpha$;
(2) if $X \in \mathcal{K} \perp\!\!\!\perp \alpha$ and $X \neq \emptyset$, then $X \cap \sigma(\mathcal{K} \perp\!\!\!\perp \alpha) \neq \emptyset$.

Intuitively, in order to contract a formula α, an agent chooses at least one formula from each α-kernel, and only formulae from such kernels. An incision function works as an extra-logical device that realises an agent's epistemic preferences, and it chooses the least preferable formulae in each α-kernel to be removed. Incision functions, as per Definition 2, do not clearly reference such preferences, and the connection between epistemic preferences and choices is obscure. In Section 3, we devise a class of incision functions that are explicitly built on the agent's epistemic preferences. As such preferences depend on the formula α to be contracted, it will be convenient to explicitly reference the formula α to be contracted, rather than its α-kernels. Towards this end, to facilitate presentation, we slightly reformulate the signature of an incision function to receive as parameter a single formula instead of all α-kernels:

Definition 3. *A formula-based incision function, centred on a belief base $\mathcal{K}$, is a mapping $\sigma : \mathcal{L} \rightarrow \mathcal{P}(\mathcal{L})$ such that*

(1) $\sigma(\alpha) \subseteq \bigcup \mathcal{K} \perp\!\!\!\perp \alpha$;
(2) if $X \in \mathcal{K} \perp\!\!\!\perp \alpha$ and $X \neq \emptyset$, then $X \cap \sigma(\alpha) \neq \emptyset$;
(3) if $\mathcal{K} \perp\!\!\!\perp \alpha = \mathcal{K} \perp\!\!\!\perp \beta$ then $\sigma(\alpha) = \sigma(\beta)$.

In Definition 3, conditions (1) and (2) correspond respectively to the translation of conditions (1) and (2) of Definition 2. It is important to stress that standard incision functions are defined on kernel-sets with the only purpose of trivially capturing the behaviour imposed by the uniformity postulate: if two formulae, say α and β, are entailed exactly by the same subsets of $\mathcal{K}$ (we say α and β are $\mathcal{K}$-uniform), then α and β must present the same contraction result. This is equivalent to say that α and β present the same set of kernels. In this way, by working on kernel sets, the standard incision functions trivially captures *uniformity* behaviour. Condition (3) guarantees that this will also be the case for formula-based incision functions.

Proposition 4. *Formula-based incision functions and standard incision functions are interchangeable, that is,*

1. *for all standard incision function σ there is a formula-based incision function σ' such that $\sigma(\mathcal{K} \perp\!\!\!\perp \alpha) = \sigma'(\alpha)$, for all α;*
2. *for all formula-based incision function σ' there is a standard incision function σ such that $\sigma(\mathcal{K} \perp\!\!\!\perp \alpha) = \sigma'(\alpha)$, for all α;*

As shown in Proposition 4, standard and formula-based incision functions produce the same class of choices, and therefore we can use them interchangeably. From now on, we will employ solely the formula-based incision functions, and we will refer to them simply as incision functions.

A contraction operation can be constructed by removing the formulae picked by an incision function. Contraction functions that follow this recipe are called kernel contraction functions:

Definition 5. *(Hansson, 1994) Given a belief base $\mathcal{K}$ and an incision function σ for $\mathcal{K}$, the kernel contraction function $\dot{-}_\sigma$ is defined as: $\mathcal{K} \dot{-}_\sigma \varphi = \mathcal{K} \setminus \sigma(\varphi)$.*

Kernel contractions functions, however, are characterised only by the first five postulates:

Theorem 6. *(Hansson and Wassermann, 2002) A contraction function satisfies* success, inclusion, vacuity, uniformity, *and* core-retainment *iff it is a kernel contraction.*

To capture *relative-closure*, Hansson (1994) has proposed the *smoothness* property to be put upon incision functions:

smoothness if $\mathcal{K}' \subseteq \mathcal{K}$, and $\varphi \in Cn(\mathcal{K}')$ and $\varphi \in \sigma(\alpha)$ then $\mathcal{K}' \cap \sigma(\alpha) \neq \emptyset$.

Incision functions satisfying *smoothness* are called *smooth incision functions*, and kernel contraction functions built upon smooth incision functions are called *smooth kernel contraction functions*. Smoothness states that if a formula φ is picked for removal, then each subset of $\mathcal{K}$ that entails φ must also have some formula picked for removal. In propositional logics, smoothness captures relative-closure (Hansson, 1994). We extend this result for more expressive logics:

Theorem 7. *If Cn is Tarskian and satisfies compactness, then a contraction function satisfies* success, inclusion, vacuity, uniformity, core-retainment, *and* relative-closure *iff it is a smooth kernel contraction function.*

Though *smoothness* captures relative-closure, smoothness alone is not capable of connecting with *relevance* (Hansson, 1994). To fill this gap, at Section 4, we will first unveil in the next section the precise connection between smooth incision functions and epistemic preference relations.

3 Relational Incision Functions: Smoothness

Some beliefs might be deemed more reliable than others, and when performing a contraction, an agent should remove only the least reliable beliefs. Towards this end, an incision function realises such epistemic choices which are founded on the agent's epistemic preferences. However, incision functions, as presented in Section 2 do not make reference to the agent's epistemic preferences. Moreover, *smoothness* simply constrains what is rational to be chosen, but does not give any hint of how such choices relates to epistemic preferences. In this section, we devise a class of incision functions whose choices are explicitly founded on the epistemic preference relations of the agent, called *effacings*. We show that *effacings* and smooth incision functions coincide. This will serve as a basis to construct, in Section 4, smooth kernel contraction functions satisfying relevance.

An agent's epistemic preference relation could be specified via a single binary relation between its beliefs. Although this has been the dominating form of representing epistemic preferences on belief bases, such as *safe contraction* (Alchourrón and Makinson, 1985), and *ensconcements* (Williams, 1994), this strategy is very limiting because of the two main impossibility results for belief bases:

1. There are fully rational contractions that cannot be based on a single epistemic preference relation (Hansson, 1999);
2. There are natural epistemic preferences that can be specified between sets of beliefs, but are impossible to be translated in terms of formulae in the belief base (Hansson, 1999).

These impossibility results severely limit our alternatives for specifying epistemic preferences relations. In order to work around these issues, we will consider preference relations between the subsets of belief bases, and that an agent might present several epistemic preference relations. We move to give a brief overview of how our strategy will work, and thereafter we proceed to the formal definitions. Intuitively, when an agent wishes to relinquish a belief α from its current belief base $\mathcal{K}$, the agent shall consult an epistemic preference relation, say $\leqslant_\alpha \subseteq \mathcal{P}(\mathcal{K}) \times \mathcal{P}(\mathcal{K})$, that indicates the degree of reliability between its "blocks" of knowledge, or in other words, which clusters of information are deemed more reliable (or trustworthy) than others. A pair $A \leqslant_\alpha B$ means that A is at least as reliable as B, in the sense that the beliefs within A are jointly equally or more reliable than the joint beliefs within B. This means that the more reliable a set is, the more protected all the beliefs that it carries are. Towards this end, if a set is not among the least reliable ones, all the beliefs it carries are protected against contraction. We call such sets *resistant sets*.

Therefore, in order to contract α, the agent shall retain the beliefs within such resistant sets, whereas only the beliefs that do not fall within the resistant sets are *susceptible* for contraction. An incision function based on such epistemic preference relations picks the *susceptible* beliefs that appear in each α-kernel.

We move now to formalise this recipe. We assume that for each formula $\alpha \in \mathcal{L}$, an agent presents an epistemic preference relation $\leqslant_\alpha$ on the subsets of its current belief base $\mathcal{K}$. Such an assignment is given by a function τ, called a *spalling*. Clearly, not every binary relation can be regarded as suitable for specifying epistemic preferences, let alone yield rational contraction functions. Each of the relations assigned by τ shall then satisfy some minimal requirements,

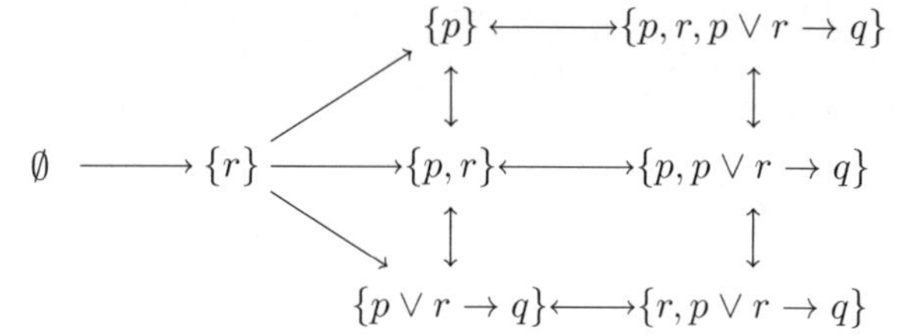

Figure 1: A q-shard on a belief base $\mathcal{K} = \{p, r, p \vee r \to q\}$. The relation is transitive, but to avoid visual pollution we omit edges obtained by transitivity.

which we present in Definition 8.

Definition 8. *Given a belief base $\mathcal{K}$, a spalling is a function $\tau : \mathcal{L} \to \mathcal{P}(\mathcal{P}(\mathcal{K}) \times \mathcal{P}(\mathcal{K}))$ that maps each formula $\alpha \in \mathcal{L}$ to a relation $\leqslant^\tau_\alpha$ on the subsets of $\mathcal{K}$ such that each $\leqslant^\tau_\alpha$ satisfies all the following conditions:*

transitivity: *if $A \leqslant^\tau_\alpha B$ and $B \leqslant^\tau_\alpha C$ then $A \leqslant^\tau_\alpha C$.*

isotonicity: *if $A \subseteq Cn(B)$ then $A \leqslant^\tau_\alpha B$.*

α-maximality: *if $\alpha \in Cn(A)$ then $B \leqslant^\tau_\alpha A$.*

α-discernment: *if $\{\psi\} \leqslant^\tau_\alpha \{\varphi\}$ and φ is α-free then ψ is α-free.*

relational uniformity: *if for all $\mathcal{K}' \subseteq \mathcal{K}$ it holds $\alpha \in Cn(\mathcal{K}')$ iff $\beta \in Cn(\mathcal{K}')$, then $\leqslant^\tau_\alpha = \leqslant^\tau_\beta$, where $\leqslant^\tau_\beta = \tau(\beta)$.*

conjunctiveness: *$A \cup B \leqslant^\tau_\alpha A$ or $A \cup B \leqslant^\tau_\alpha B$.*

Giving a spalling τ, we will write $\leqslant^\tau_\alpha$ as a shorthand for $\tau(\alpha)$. We call each $\leqslant^\tau_\alpha$, an α-shard. $A \leqslant^\tau_\alpha B$ means that A is at least as preferable as B. When it is clear from context, we will omit the superscript $^\tau$, and simply write $\leqslant_\alpha$. A spalling is similar in spirit to the concept of *faithful assignments* of Katsuno and Mendelzon (2003) used to specify preference relations for *belief update*. There are, however, many differences between our approach to the faithful assignments of Katsuno and Mendelzon. First, a spalling considers relations on the subsets of a belief base, while assignments are designed for relations between interpretations. Second, the properties put upon assignments and spallings are utterly different. Last, assignments are designed for belief update on theories finitely represented by a single formula, while spallings realise epistemic preferences for (possibly infinite) belief bases.

We proceed to explain each of the properties put upon the relations $\leqslant^\tau_\alpha$ assigned by spallings. To support the explanation of such properties, we will consider as an example the belief base $\mathcal{K} = \{p, r, p \vee r \to q\}$ and the q-shard depicted in Fig. 1. *Transitivity* is a widely explored property used to specify epistemic preferences: if one prefers A rather B and B rather C than one should also prefer A rather C. *Isotonicity* states that adding information does not make a set more reliable. For example, in Fig. 1, both $\{p\}$ and $\{r\}$ are at least as reliable as $\{p, r\}$: $\{p\}$ is as reliable as $\{p, r\}$, while $\{r\}$ is strictly more reliable than $\{p, r\}$. *Isotonicity* is the reverse of the *dominance* property used in both *Epistemic Entrenchment* and *Safe-contraction* (Hansson, 1999; Gärdenfors, 1988).

An agent should remove only the least reliable pieces of information. The property *α-maximality* imposes that a set A which entails the formula α to be contracted cannot be trusted, and therefore A must be among the least reliable ones. In our example, there are only three sets that entail the formula q, which are depicted at the rightmost column in Fig. 1: the belief base $\mathcal{K}$ itself and the two q-kernels. All of them are put among the least reliable sets. On the other hand, *α-discernment* states that α-free formulae are strictly more reliable than not α-free formulae. The property *α-discernment* jointly with *transitivity, isotonic,* and *conjunctiveness* states that finite α-free sets are strictly more reliable than not α-free sets. *Relational uniformity*, as the name suggests, is related to the *uniformity* postulate. It states that the epistemic preferences of an agent should not be syntax sensitive: if two formulae, even though not necessarily logically equivalent, are entailed exactly by the same subsets of the belief base $\mathcal{K}$, then they should present exactly the same epistemic preference relation.

For the rationale of *conjunctiveness*, consider a set $X = A \cup B$, and that a belief $\beta \in X$ is chosen to be removed during the contraction of a formula α. Intuitively, only information among the least reliable sets should be picked for removal, which means that X is among the least reliable sets. However, as β is in X, β appears either in A or in B. Therefore, it is plausible to assume that the subset in which β appears (either A or B), must also be among the least reliable sets, that is, either A or B must be as (un-)reliable as X (*conjunctiveness*). Consider, for instance, the q-shard in Fig. 1 and the set $\{p, r\}$ among the least preferable sets. According to *conjunctiveness*, at least one between $\{p\}$ or $\{r\}$ must be as (un-)reliable as $\{p, r\}$, which is the case of $\{p\}$ while $\{r\}$ is strictly more preferable than them.

We extend the notion of α-free from formulae to sets. We say that a set A is α-free, if and only if every formula in A is α-free. The maximal elements of a set A w.r.t a transitive relation $\leqslant$ is $\max_{\leqslant}(A) = \{a \in A \mid \text{for all } b \in A, \text{ if } a \leqslant b \text{ then } b \leqslant a\}$. An α-shard $\leqslant_\alpha \subseteq \mathcal{P}(\mathcal{K}) \times \mathcal{P}(\mathcal{K})$ realises the epistemic preference relation of an agent during the contraction of a formula α. Intuitively, $A \leqslant_\alpha B$ means that whole information in A is at least as reliable than the whole information in B. Additionally, if $A \leqslant_\alpha B$ and $B \not\leqslant_\alpha A$, then information within A as a whole is strictly more reliable than the whole information in B. This means that B is strictly more vulnerable to contraction than A. For instance, in the relation $\leqslant_q$ depicted in Fig. 1, the set $\{p \vee r \to q\}$ is strictly more vulnerable to contraction than $\{r\}$. Ideally, an agent should remove information only from the most vulnerable sets (the sets at the two rightmost columns at Fig. 1) while keeping all other sets, like $\{r\}$, intact. Sets whose information are not subject to removal are called resistant:

Definition 9. *A set $A \subseteq \mathcal{K}$ is a resistant set w.r.t an α-shard $\leqslant_\alpha$ iff A is α-free or there is some $B \subseteq \mathcal{K}$ such that $A \leqslant_\alpha B$ and $B \not\leqslant_\alpha A$. The resistant sets from $\mathcal{K}$ w.r.t $\leqslant_\alpha$ is given by*

$$\mathsf{resist}_{\leqslant_\alpha}(\mathcal{K}) = \mathcal{P}(\mathcal{K}) \setminus \mathsf{max}_{\leqslant_\alpha}(\{A \subseteq \mathcal{K} \mid A \textit{ is not } \alpha\textit{-free}\})$$

Intuitively, a resistant set carries information that shall be protected during contraction. As only not α-free formulae should be removed, every α-free set is by default resistant. *Resistant sets* are similar in spirit to the notion of safe-formulae used in safe-contraction. The main difference is that to be safe, a formula φ must be covered by some other formula in every α-kernel in which φ appears, whereas resistant sets only need to be covered by some other set. For instance, in Fig. 1, $\{r\}$ is resistant because it is strictly more preferable than $\{p\}$. As all the formulae within a resistant set shall be protected, the only information that can be removed are those that do not appear in any of the resistant sets modulo $\leqslant_\alpha$. We call such formulae α-susceptible.

Definition 10. *Within a belief base $\mathcal{K}$, a formula φ is α-susceptible w.r.t an α-shard $\leqslant_\alpha$ iff $\varphi \notin A$, for all $A \in \mathsf{resist}_{\leqslant_\alpha}(\mathcal{K})$.*

For conciseness, when the α-shard is clear from context, we will simply say that a formula is α-susceptible. For instance, in the q-shard illustrated at Fig. 1, we have only two resistant sets: $\emptyset$ and $\{r\}$. Therefore, the formulae p and $p \vee r \to q$ are q-susceptible, because they do not appear in any of the resistant sets. We highlight the following interesting properties regarding α-susceptible formulae, which will be useful for defining a new class of incision functions:

Proposition 11. *If $\leqslant_\alpha$ is an α-shard on a belief base $\mathcal{K}$,*

1. *every α-susceptible formula w.r.t $\leqslant_\alpha$ is not α-free;*
2. *α is not tautological and $\alpha \in Cn(\mathcal{K})$ iff there is an α-susceptible formula in $\mathcal{K}$.*

Proof sketch. For item 1, let φ be an α-susceptible formula w.r.t an α-shard $\leqslant_\alpha$. Thus, φ does not appear in any of the resistant sets. By definition, the set of all α-free formulae is resistant. Thus, φ does not appear in such a set, which means φ is not α-free. For item 2, the direction "$\Leftarrow$" follows from item 1, because an α-susceptible formula necessarily is not α-free which implies that $\mathcal{K}$ must entail α. For the direction "$\Rightarrow$", from $\alpha \in Cn(\mathcal{K})$ we get there is at least one α-kernel $X \in \mathcal{K} \perp\!\!\!\perp \alpha$, and from compactness we know that all of them are finite. Let us fix an α-kernel $X \in \mathcal{K} \perp\!\!\!\perp \alpha$. As α is not tautological, $X \neq \emptyset$. From α-maximality, we get that X is maximal, and from conjunctiviness, we can prove by induction on size of X that there is a $\varphi \in X$ such that $X \leqslant_\alpha \{\varphi\}$. Let us fix such a φ. Therefore, as X is maximal, we get that $\{\varphi\}$ is also maximal. This jointly with isotonicity, implies that every set in which φ appears is also maximal. Therefore, every set that φ appears is not resistant. This means that φ is α-susceptible. □

As every α-susceptible formula is not α-free, and their existence is guaranteed when the underlying belief base entails α, we can define an incision function that selects all α-susceptible formulae, called an *effacing*:

Definition 12. *Given a belief base $\mathcal{K}$, and a spalling τ on $\mathcal{K}$. An effacing is a function $\delta_\tau : \mathcal{L} \to \mathcal{P}(\mathcal{L})$ such that*

$$\delta_\tau(\alpha) = \{\varphi \in \mathcal{K} \mid \varphi \textit{ is } \alpha\textit{-susceptible w.r.t. } \leqslant^\tau_\alpha\}.$$

Although an effacing does not look inside each α-kernel to pick a formula for removal, an effacing does hit every α-kernel and it is therefore indeed an incision function:

Proposition 13. *Every effacing is an incision function.*

Proof sketch. *We have to show that every effacing δ_τ satisfies conditions (1), (2) and (3) from Definition 3. Condition (3) follows from relational uniformity. For condition (1), note that from Proposition 11, we have that every α-susceptible formula is not α-free. Thus, $\delta_\tau(\alpha) \subseteq \bigcup \mathcal{K} \perp\!\!\!\perp \alpha$. For condition (2), let $X \in \mathcal{K} \perp\!\!\!\perp \alpha$ such that $X \neq \emptyset$, we will show that there is some $\varphi \in X$ such that $\varphi \in \delta_\tau(\alpha)$. As X is an α-kernel, we get from compactness that X is finite. From α-maximality we get $X \in \max_{\leqslant_\alpha}(\mathcal{P}(\mathcal{K}))$, which means that X is not resistant. Thus, as $\leqslant_\alpha$ satisfies conjunctiveness, we can show by induction on the size of X that there is some $\varphi \in X$ such that $\{\varphi\}$ is also maximal. This jointly with isotonicity, implies that any set that contains φ will also be maximal, and therefore it is not resistant. Thus, φ is α-susceptible, which means that $\varphi \in \delta_\tau(\alpha)$.* □

As effacings are incision functions, we can use them to construct a new class of kernel contraction functions:

Definition 14. *Let τ be a spalling on a belief base $\mathcal{K}$. A kernel contraction founded on τ is defined as $\mathcal{K} \dot{-}_\tau \alpha = \mathcal{K} \setminus \delta_\tau(\alpha)$. We say that $\dot{-}_\tau$ is a spalled kernel contraction.*

Example I illustrates a spalled kernel contraction function, based on the α-shard depicted in Fig. 1.

Example I. *Let $\mathcal{K} = \{p, r, p \vee r \rightarrow q\}$, and τ be a spalling such that $\leqslant^\tau_\alpha$ q corresponds to the relation depicted at Fig. 1. The only q-susceptible formulae are p and $p \vee r \rightarrow q$. Thus, $\delta_\tau(q) = \{p, p \vee r \rightarrow q\}$, and $\mathcal{K} \dot{-}_\tau q = \mathcal{K} \setminus \delta_\tau(q) = \{r\}$. This contraction satisfies relative-closure, because $\{r\}$ does not imply either of the removed formulae.*

The class of kernel contractions based on effacings matches exactly the class of smooth kernel contractions. We present the first direction of this representation theorem:

Theorem 15. *Every spalled kernel contraction is smooth.*

Proof sketch. *Let $X \subseteq \mathcal{K}$ and $\varphi \in \delta_\tau(\alpha)$ such that $\varphi \in Cn(X)$. We will show that there is some $\psi \in X$ such that $\psi \in \delta_\tau(\alpha)$. From $\varphi \in Cn(X)$, we get that there is a $X' \in X \perp\!\!\!\perp \varphi$. Let us fix such a X'. Due to conjunctiveness, isotonicity and transitivity, we get that there is some $\psi \in X'$ such that $X' \leqslant_\alpha \{\psi\}$. From isotonicity, transitivity and α-discernment, we have that $\{\varphi\} \leqslant_\alpha \{\psi\}$, and ψ is not α-free. Moreover, as $\varphi \in \delta_\tau(\alpha)$, it follows that $\{\varphi\}$ is maximal among all not α-free sets. This implies from $\{\varphi\} \leqslant_\alpha \{\psi\}$ that $\{\psi\}$ is also maximal among all not α-free sets. This jointly with isotonicity implies that every set that has ψ is not resistant, and therefore ψ is α-susceptible.* □

To conclude the representation theorem between effacings and smooth kernel contractions, we will need to show that each smooth incision σ function is indeed an effacing, that is, that there is a spalling τ such that $\sigma(\alpha) = \delta_\tau(\alpha)$. The main strategy is to construct, for each formulae α, a relation $\leqslant^\sigma_\alpha$ such that the formulae in $\sigma(\alpha)$ corresponds exactly to the α-susceptible formulae modulo $\leqslant^\sigma_\alpha$. We call $\leqslant^\sigma_\alpha$ the α-projection of σ. The spalling can then be achieved by mapping each formula α to its α-projection. We call this mapping between formulae and projections the shadowing of σ. There are two essential conditions we need to capture in constructing such shadowing τ: (C1) $\delta_\tau(\alpha)$ matches $\sigma(\alpha)$, and (C2) that τ is indeed a spalling (all conditions at Definition 8 are satisfied). We start by presenting how α-projections are constructed:

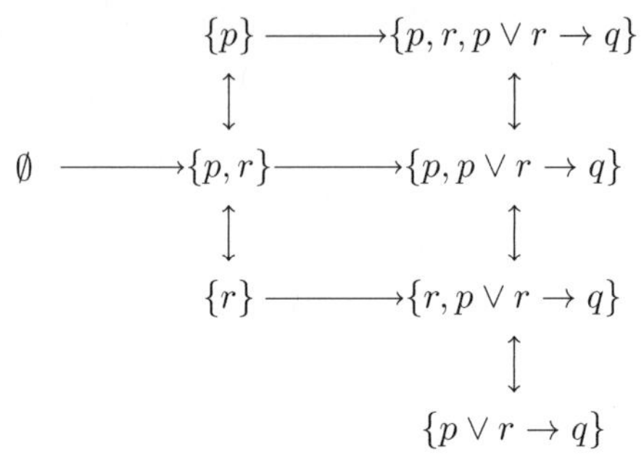

Figure 2: An α-projection of the incision function at Example II.

Definition 16. *Given an incision function σ for a belief base $\mathcal{K}$, and a formula α. The α-projection of σ is the smallest relation $\leqslant^\sigma_\alpha \subseteq \mathcal{P}(\mathcal{K}) \times \mathcal{P}(\mathcal{K})$ such that*

1. *if $A \cap \sigma(\alpha) \neq \emptyset$ then $B \leqslant^\sigma_\alpha A$.*
2. *if $A \subseteq Cn(B)$ then $A \leqslant^\sigma_\alpha B$*
3. *if A is α-free then $A \leqslant^\sigma_\alpha B$.*
4. *if both A and B are not α-free, and $(A \cup B) \cap \sigma(\alpha) = \emptyset$ then $A \leqslant^\sigma_\alpha B$*

If a formula φ is picked by $\sigma(\alpha)$, then every set A that has φ cannot be a resistant set. This can be done by putting such sets as the least preferable ones (Item 1). This not only captures α-maximality, but also guarantees that the α-susceptible formulae modulo $\leqslant^\sigma_\alpha$ match the formulae in $\sigma(\alpha)$, see Proposition 22 below. Item 2 is the *isotonicity* condition, while Item 3 captures α-discernment by putting each α-free set among the most preferable ones. Item 4 makes equally preferable any two sets that, though not α-free, have no formulae picked by $\sigma(\alpha)$. Item 4 jointly with Item 1 captures conjunctiveness. An α-projection also satisfies transitivity. Example II illustrates how an α-projection is constructed.

Example II. *Let $\mathcal{K} = \{p, r, p \vee r \rightarrow q\}$, and consider that we want to contract the formula q using the smooth incision function σ such that $\sigma(q) = \{p \vee r \rightarrow q\}$. The q-projection $\leqslant^\sigma_q$ of σ is depicted in Fig. 2. The relation $\leqslant^\sigma_q$, as we explain below, is transitive, and to avoid visual pollution, we have not drawn the transitive edges of $\leqslant^\sigma_q$ in Fig. 2. Let us explain how $\leqslant^\sigma_q$ is constructed according to Definition 16. First, every set that contains the formula $p \vee r \rightarrow q$ (sets at the rightmost side) is put as the most vulnerable ones, as imposed by condition 1. Condition 2 imposes the relation to satisfy isotonicity. For instance, $\{p\} \leqslant^\sigma_q \{p, r\}$. The empty set is the only α-free set, and therefore it is put as the most reliable one (condition 3). According to condition 4, each pair of non q-free sets that do not contain the formula $p \vee r \rightarrow q$ is put as equally preferable (sets in the middle column). To facilitate visualisation, we have split the relation into three columns. Sets in the same column are equally preferable (resp. equally vulnerable), while the sets towards* *the right are more vulnerable than all the sets towards the left end. From all this, we see that $\leqslant^\sigma_q$ is transitive.*

Lemma 17 below will be helpful in proving the properties of an α-projection. It states that any set that has no formulae in common with $\sigma(\alpha)$ is a resistant set.

Lemma 17. *For every smooth incision function and α-projection $\leqslant^\sigma_\alpha$, if $B \cap \sigma(\alpha) = \emptyset$ and $A \leqslant^\sigma_\alpha B$ then $A \cap \sigma(\alpha) = \emptyset$.*

Proposition 18. *If an incision function σ is smooth, then every α-projection of σ satisfies: isotonicity, α-maximality, α-discernment, conjunctiveness, and transitivity.*

According to Proposition 18 above, every α-projection from a smooth incision function satisfies almost all conditions put upon spallings. Another interesting property is related to *relational uniformity*: if two formulae are entailed exactly by the same subsets of a belief base $\mathcal{K}$, then their projections coincide.

Observation 19. *Let σ be an incision function on a belief base $\mathcal{K}$, and let α and β be two formulae. If for all $\mathcal{K}' \subseteq \mathcal{K}$, it holds that $\alpha \in Cn(\mathcal{K}')$ iff $\beta \in Cn(\mathcal{K}')$, then $\leqslant^\sigma_\alpha = \leqslant^\sigma_\beta$.*

We are ready to define the shadowing of an incision function σ, which basically maps each formula α to the respective α-projection of σ:

Definition 20. *Given an incision function σ, defined on a belief base $\mathcal{K}$. The shadowing of σ is the function $\mathcal{T}_\sigma : \mathcal{L} \to \mathcal{P}(\mathcal{P}(\mathcal{K}) \times \mathcal{P}(\mathcal{K}))$ such that $\mathcal{T}_\sigma(\alpha) = \leqslant^\sigma_\alpha$, where $\leqslant^\sigma_\alpha$ is the α-projection of σ.*

We can see, from Proposition 18 and Observation 19, that shadowings are spallings:

Corollary 21. *If an incision function is smooth, then its shadowing is a spalling.*

So far, we have shown how to construct a spalling from a smooth incision function σ. The only piece missing to complete the representation theorem is to show that the effacing based on the spalling $\mathcal{T}_\sigma$ actually matches σ. This follows directly from the construction of the α-projection:

Proposition 22. *If σ is a smooth incision function on a belief base $\mathcal{K}$, then for all formula α:*

$$\sigma(\alpha) = \{\varphi \in \mathcal{K} \mid \varphi \text{ is } \alpha\text{-susceptible modulo } \leqslant^\sigma_\alpha\}.$$

Proof sketch. We need to show that a formula $\varphi \in \mathcal{K}$ is α-susceptible modulo $\leqslant^\sigma_\alpha$ iff $\varphi \in \sigma(\alpha)$. The direction "$\Leftarrow$" follows directly from condition (1) at Definition 16. For direction "$\Rightarrow$", the proof is by its contrapositive. Let us suppose that $\varphi \notin \sigma(\alpha)$, and we will show that φ is not α-susceptible. The case that φ is α-free is trivial. Let suppose then that φ is not α-free. Thus, there is some $A \in \mathcal{K} \perp\!\!\!\perp \alpha$ such that $\varphi \in A$. Let $A' = A \setminus \sigma(\alpha)$. Note that $A' \cap \sigma(\alpha) \neq \emptyset$, as $\varphi \in A$ and $\varphi \notin \sigma(\alpha)$. As σ is an incision function, we have that $A \cap \sigma(\alpha) \neq \emptyset$. Thus, from condition (1) at Definition 16, we get that (i) $A' \leqslant^\sigma_\alpha A$; and from the contrapositive of Lemma 17 (on that lemma let B stand for A'), we get (ii) $A' \nleqslant^\sigma_\alpha A$. Therefore, A' is a resistant set, which implies that φ is not α susceptible. □

The representation theorem between smooth kernel contraction and spalled kernel contraction easily follows from Theorem 15 and Proposition 22:

Theorem 23. *A kernel contraction is smooth iff its a spalled kernel contraction.*

4 Concordance and Relevance

In this section, we present two representation theorems between kernel contraction functions and the postulate of relevance. In our first representation theorem, we identify a principle that relates incision functions and the postulate of relevance, which we call the *symmetry of removal*. This principle allows us to frame exactly the class of all incision functions that yield fully rational kernel contraction functions. The principle of *symmetry of removal*, similar to smoothness, states which properties an incision function must obey in order to capture relevance, but it does not tell us how to construct such incision functions nor how the epistemic preference relations of an agent should look. In our second representation theorem, we fill this gap by putting an extra constraint, called *concordant-mirroring*, upon the spalling of an effacing. The *concordant-mirroring* condition is inspired by the principle of *symmetry of removal*. Before we present this principle and *concordant-mirroring* we shall first introduce the notion of *completion* and *concordant sets*.

Definition 24. *Let $\mathcal{K}$ be a belief base, and α be a formula. An α-completion of a set $A \subseteq \mathcal{K}$ is a set X such that (a) $X \subseteq \mathcal{K}$, and (b) $\alpha \in Cn(A \cup X)$. The set of all α-completions of A is given by*

$$com_{\mathcal{K}}(A, \alpha) = \{X \subseteq \mathcal{K} \mid \alpha \in Cn(A \cup X)\}.$$

Intuitively, an α-completion of a set $A \subseteq \mathcal{K}$ is a set X that collaborates with A to entail α. Unlike kernels, which are required to entail α, an α-completion only carries information that "completes" the information of A towards entailing α. The following example illustrates the notion of α-completion.

Example III. *Let $\mathcal{K} = \{p, r, p \vee r \to q\}$. The set $X = \{p \vee r \to q\}$ is a q-completion of both $\{r\}$ and $\{p\}$, because $X \subseteq \mathcal{K}$, $q \in Cn(X \cup \{r\})$ and $q \in Cn(X \cup \{p\})$. The belief base $\mathcal{K}$ itself and the q-kernels $\{p, p \vee r \to q\}$ and $\{r, p \vee r \to q\}$ are trivially q-completions of both $\{p\}$ and $\{r\}$. There are no other q-completions for either $\{p\}$ or $\{r\}$. Thus, $com_{\mathcal{K}}(\{p\}, q) = com_{\mathcal{K}}(\{r\}, q)$.*

In Example III above, the sets $\{p\}$ and $\{r\}$, though not logically equivalent, present the same q-completions. Sets that agree upon the same collection of α-completions will be called α-concordant sets:

Definition 25. *Let α be a formula, and $\mathcal{K}$ a belief base $\mathcal{K}$. Two sets $A, B \subseteq \mathcal{K}$ are α-concordant within $\mathcal{K}$ iff $com_{\mathcal{K}}(A, \alpha) = com_{\mathcal{K}}(B, \alpha)$.*

Intuitively, α-concordant sets are indistinguishable w.r.t to their α-completions. When $\mathcal{K}$ is clear from context, we simply say that two sets are α-concordant. As we show in Proposition 26 below, α-concordant sets are tightly connected to the relevance postulate via the following principle:

symmetry of removal: if A and B are α-concordant within $\mathcal{K}$ then $A \cap \sigma(\alpha) \neq \emptyset$ iff $B \cap \sigma(\alpha) \neq \emptyset$.

The principle of *symmetry of removal* states that formulae are removed uniformly from α-concordant sets, that is, if two sets are α-concordant, then an incision function will either remove formulae from both of them or it will keep both of them intact. Back to Example III, the sets $\{r\}$ and $\{p\}$ are α-concordant. Thus, according to *symmetry of removal*, an incision function must remove both r and p, or remove neither. The contraction in Example I violates *relevance*, because the incision function removes p but does not remove r. On the other hand, the contraction illustrated in Example II does satisfy *relevance*, because the incision function removes neither p nor r.

Indeed, symmetry of removal is a necessary condition for incision functions to yield kernel contractions that satisfy relevance:

Proposition 26. *If a kernel contraction function $\dot{-}_\sigma$ satisfies relevance then σ satisfies symmetry of removal.*

Proposition 26 exhibits that relevance induces a symmetry of removal between α-concordant sets. Although symmetry of removal is a necessary condition for incision functions to yield kernel contraction functions that do satisfy relevance, it is important to stress that symmetry of removal alone is not strong enough to capture relevance:

Observation 27. *If an incision function satisfies symmetry of removal then its kernel contraction* ***does not necessarily*** *satisfy relevance.*

Proof. Consider the belief base $\mathcal{K} = \{p, p \vee q, p \to m, p \vee q \to m\}$, and the following incision function σ satisfying symmetry of removal: $\sigma(\alpha) = \{p \vee q, p \to m, p \vee q \to m\}$, if $\mathcal{K} \perp\!\!\!\perp \alpha = \mathcal{K} \perp\!\!\!\perp m$; and $\sigma(\alpha) = \bigcup \mathcal{K} \perp\!\!\!\perp \alpha$, otherwise. For violation of relevance, note that $\mathcal{K} \dot{-}_\sigma m = \{p\}$, while $p \vee q \in \sigma(m)$. □

We need both *symmetry of removal* and *smoothness* in order to capture relevance:

Proposition 28. *If an incision function σ satisfies smoothness and symmetry of removal then the smooth kernel contraction function $\dot{-}_\sigma$ satisfies relevance.*

Our first representation theorem relating relevance and kernel contraction functions follows from Proposition 26 and Proposition 28 :

Theorem 29. *A kernel contraction function satisfies relevance iff its incision function satisfies both smoothness and symmetry of removal.*

Theorem 29 states that the only way for kernel contractions to satisfy relevance is via incision functions satisfying both smoothness and symmetry of removal. Although this informs us which principles an incision function must satisfy, it does not relate such incision functions to the agent's epistemic preference relations. We already know from Section 3 that the choices made by smooth incision functions are based on epistemic preference relations founded on spallings. Thus, to capture relevance, we only need to constrain the behaviour of such spallings. The condition we will put upon the spallings must be sufficiently strong to capture *symmetry of removal*, and at the same time it must be general enough so it dispense with no spallings satisfying *symmetry of removal*. The condition we devise for this purpose is called *concordant-mirroring*, and spallings satisfying this condition will be called mirrored spallings:

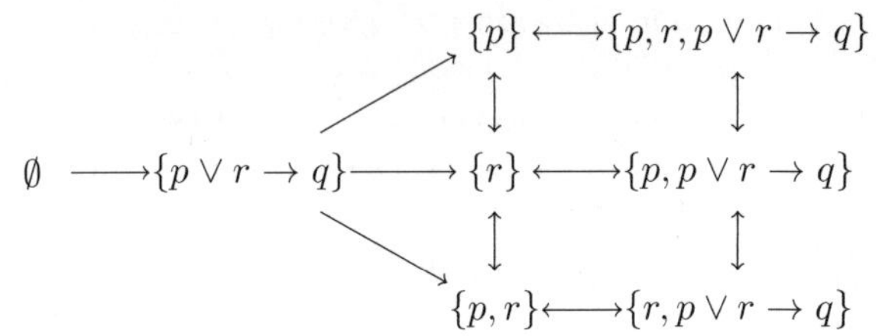

Figure 3: An α-shard satisfying *concordant-mirroring*. The relation is transitive, but to avoid visual pollution we omit edges obtained by transitivity.

Definition 30. *A spalling $\tau : \mathcal{K} \to \mathcal{P}(\mathcal{P}(\mathcal{K}) \times \mathcal{P}(\mathcal{K}))$ is mirrored iff for each formula α, the relation $\leqslant^\tau_\alpha$ satisfies*

> ***concordant-mirroring****: if A and B are α-concordant, and $X \leqslant^\tau_\alpha A$ then $X \leqslant^\tau_\alpha B$*

Intuitively, *concordant-mirroring* states that if two sets, say A and B, are α-concordant then they must be as resistant (resp. as vulnerable) as each other. Example IV below illustrates the notion of *concordant-mirroring*:

Example IV. *Let $\mathcal{K} = \{p, r, p \vee r \to q\}$, and τ be a spalling such that $\leqslant^\tau_\alpha$ is the q-shard depicted in Fig. 3. Except for $\{p \vee r \to q\}$ and the empty-set, all other sets are equally preferable, and are not resistant. To facilitate visualisation, q-concordant sets are put in the same column. It is easy to see in this way that $\leqslant_q$ satisfies concordant-mirroring. For instance, the sets $\{p\}, \{r\}$ and $\{p, r\}$ are all q-concordant. According to concordant-mirroring all of them must present the same preferences. Thus, as $\{p \vee r \to q\} \leqslant_q \{p\}$, the sets $\{r\}$ and $\{p, r\}$ must mimic such a preference, that is, $\{p \vee r \to q\} \leqslant_q \{r\}$ and $\{p \vee r \to q\} \leqslant_q \{p, r\}$.*

Note also that the only two resistant sets are $\{p \vee r \to q\}$ and $\emptyset$. Thus, $\delta_\tau(q) = \{p, r\}$, and $\mathcal{K} \dot{-}_\tau q = \{p \vee r \to q\}$. Note that this contraction satisfies relevance, as putting back either of the two removed formulae will restore q.

An effacing built upon a mirrored spalling will be called a mirrored effacing, and a kernel contraction built upon a mirrored effacing will be called a mirrored kernel contraction.

Definition 31. *A mirrored kernel contraction is a kernel contraction $\dot{-}_\tau$ such that δ_τ is a mirrored effacing.*

Example IV illustrates a mirrored kernel contraction satisfying relevance. Indeed, *concordant-mirroring* is all we need to capture symmetry of removal, and therefore relevance.

Theorem 32. *Mirrored effacings satisfy symmetry of removal, and every mirrored kernel contraction satisfies relevance.*

We have reached the first part of our second representation theorem between relevance and kernel contractions. To complete it, we need to show that *concordant-mirroring* preserves all fully rational kernel contractions. This corresponds to showing that the incision function of every fully rational kernel contraction is actually a mirrored effacing. We achieve this by employing the same strategy we used in Section 3 based on shadowing. Recall that the incision function σ of a fully rational kernel contraction function is smooth. Therefore, we already know from Proposition 22 and Corollary 21 that σ is indeed an effacing whose spalling is its shadowing $\mathcal{T}_\sigma$. The only thing missing is to show that the shadowing $\mathcal{T}_\sigma$ indeed satisfies *concordant-mirroring*:

Proposition 33. *If a smooth kernel contraction function* $\dot{-}_\sigma$ *satisfies relevance then the shadowing of* σ *is mirrored.*

We have already illustrated, in Example II, an α-projection from the shadowing of a smooth incision function whose kernel contraction satisfies relevance. Such an α-projection is shown in Fig. 2, and it does satisfy *concordant-mirroring*. We reach our second representation theorem:

Theorem 34. *A smooth kernel contraction satisfies relevance iff its a mirrored kernel contraction.*

5 Related Works

Few efforts have been made to investigate the connection between kernel contraction and relevance. Falappa, Fermé, and Kern-Isberner (2006) investigate the explicit connection between partial meet functions and kernel contraction functions in terms of their choice mechanisms: incision functions, for kernel contraction; and selection function for partial meet functions. The work focuses on translating selection functions and incision functions in terms of each other. For this inter-translation to work, it is assumed that the underlying smooth kernel contraction indeed satisfies relevance. However, it is not investigated which condition an incision function must satisfy in order to capture relevance. In our work, we fill this gap by showing precisely such a condition: *symmetry of removal*. Moreover, their correspondence between smooth incision functions and selection functions are confined to classical proposition logics, whereas our results are presented for more general logics, precisely for Tarskian compact logics. Booth et al. (2014) show that in Horn Logics (Horn, 1951), partial meet is too strong for contraction, and they introduce a more general operation, called infra-contraction, which coincides with kernel contraction. However, infra-contractions do not capture relevance.

For theories, several ways of specifying epistemic preferences are known, such as Epistemic Entrenchment (Gärdenfors, 1988), and Grove's system of spheres (Grove, 1988; Gärdenfors, 1988). However, few efforts have been made to construct epistemic preferences for belief bases. There are two main contraction operators that consider epistemic preferences for belief bases: *safe-contraction* (Alchourrón and Makinson, 1985) and *ensconscements* (Williams, 1994). Kernel contractions are generalisations of *safe-contractions*, in which epistemic preferences are represented as a single hierarchy: an acyclic strict total order on the formulae of a belief base. Safe-contractions, however, are too restrictive and, even for theories, there are fully rational contractions that cannot be defined as safe-contractions. This occurs not only because of the impossibility results listed in Section 3, but also because safe-contraction cannot handle cycles. Williams (1994) has introduced the ensconscements relations, which are in essence generalisations of epistemic entrenchment relations, originally defined for contraction on theories, to deal with belief bases. Fermé, Krevneris, and Reis (2008) have shown that ensconscements are so general that they not only violate *relevance*, but also they violate *core-retainment*.

Concordant-mirorring, introduced in Section 4, is inspired by the *mirroring* condition introduced by Ribeiro, Nayak, and Wassermann (2018). In that work, mirroring is introduced with the purpose to rationalise epistemic preference relations, over interpretations, on non-compact logics. While mirroring enforces that any two incomparable models must mimic each other's preferences, in our setting *concordant-mirroring* is a bit more relaxed and imposes the mimicking behaviour only on α-concordant sets. Mirroring is suitable for contraction on theories and was designed to capture the supplementary postulates of the AGM paradigm (Alchourrón, Gärdenfors, and Makinson, 1985).

6 Discussion and Future Works

In this work, we have restored the connection between kernel contraction and the postulate of relevance by constraining the behaviour of incision functions in two different, but equivalent, ways: (i) via the principle of *symmetry of removal*, and (ii) based on a suitable class of epistemic preference relations. For the former, we have shown that smooth incision functions can only satisfy relevance when they obey *symmetry of removal*. For the latter, we have started by proposing to represent an agent's epistemic preferences via binary relations on the subsets of its belief base. We have then defined the *mirrored-concordance* condition that translates symmetry of removal in terms of epistemic preferences, and shown a representation theorem connecting relevance and kernel contractions based on such preference relations. Our results are presented for logics that are Tarskian and compact. There are further interesting research questions worth to explore:

Smoothness and symmetry of removal: when an agent's epistemic state is represented as a theory, smooth kernel contractions are strong enough to capture relevance. Although this is not the case for belief bases, it is not hard to find belief bases where smoothness is still capable of capturing relevance. For instance, for the belief base $\mathcal{K} = \{p, r, p \vee r \rightarrow q, r \rightarrow q\}$, the contraction $\mathcal{K} \dot{-}_\sigma q$ satisfies relevance, as long as σ is smooth. Thus, another way of establishing the connection between kernel contraction and relevance is to frame precisely the class of belief bases in which smoothness implies *symmetry of removal*.

Inconsistency/Culpability measures: Recently, Ribeiro and Thimm (2021) have proposed to use inconsistency/culpability measures as a means to automatically disclose an agent's epistemic preference relation for contracting inconsistencies, known as *consolidation*. Their results are confined to smooth incision functions, and therefore are not strong enough to capture relevance. It will be worth to investigate how such inconsistency/culpability measures could be strengthened in order to capture relevance, and how such measures could be broadened to perform contraction beyond consolidation and classical propositional logics.

Acknowledgements

This research is supported by the German Research Association (DFG), project number 424710479. I would like to thank Dominik Klumpp for suggesting an intuitive reformulation of α-concordant sets.

References

Alchourrón, C. E., and Makinson, D. 1985. On the logic of theory change: Safe contraction. *Stud Logica* 44(4):405–422.

Alchourrón, C. E.; Gärdenfors, P.; and Makinson, D. 1985. On the logic of theory change: partial meet contraction and revision functions. *The Journal of Symbolic Logic* 50(2):510–530.

Booth, R.; Meyer, T.; Varzinczak, I. J.; and Wassermann, R. 2014. On the link between partial meet, kernel, and infra contraction and its application to horn logic. *CoRR* abs/1401.3902.

Cóbe, R., and Wassermann, R. 2015. Ontology repair through partial meet contraction. In *DARe@IJCAI*, volume 1423 of *CEUR Workshop Proceedings*. CEUR-WS.org.

Dalal, M. 1988. Investigations into a theory of knowledge base revision. In *Proceedings of the 7th National Conference on Artificial Intelligence*, 475–479. AAAI Press / The MIT Press.

Dixon, S. E. 1994. *Belief revision: A computational approach*. Ph.D. Dissertation, University of Sydney.

Falappa, M. A.; Fermé, E. L.; and Kern-Isberner, G. 2006. On the logic of theory change: Relations between incision and selection functions. In *ECAI 2006, 17th European Conference on Artificial Intelligence*, volume 141, 402–406. IOS Press.

Fermé, E.; Krevneris, M.; and Reis, M. D. L. 2008. An axiomatic characterization of ensconcement-based contraction. *J. Log. Comput.* 18(5):739–753.

Fuhrmann, A. 1991. Theory contraction through base contraction. *J. Philos. Log.* 20(2):175–203.

Gärdenfors, P. 1988. *Knowledge in flux: Modeling the dynamics of epistemic states*. The MIT press.

Grove, A. 1988. Two modellings for theory change. *J. Philos. Log.* 17(2):157–170.

Guerra, P. T., and Wassermann, R. 2019. Two AGM-style characterizations of model repair. *Annals of Mathematics and Artificial Intelligence* 87(3):233–257.

Hansson, S. O., and Wassermann, R. 2002. Local change. *Stud Logica* 70(1):49–76.

Hansson, S. O. 1991. Belief contraction without recovery. *Stud Logica* 50(2):251–260.

Hansson, S. O. 1994. Kernel contraction. *J. Symb. Log.* 59(3):845–859.

Hansson, S. O. 1999. *A textbook of belief dynamics - theory change and database updating*, volume 11 of *Applied logic series*. Kluwer.

Hansson, S. O. 2017. *Descriptor Revision: Belief Change Through Direct Choice*, volume 46. Springer.

Horn, A. 1951. On sentences which are true of direct unions of algebras. *J. Symb. Log.* 16(1):14–21.

Horridge, M. 2011. *Justification based explanation in ontologies*. Ph.D. Dissertation, University of Manchester, UK.

Hunter, A., and Konieczny, S. 2005. *Approaches to Measuring Inconsistent Information*. Berlin, Heidelberg: Springer Berlin Heidelberg. 191–236.

Hunter, A., and Konieczny, S. 2008. Measuring inconsistency through minimal inconsistent sets. In *Proceedings of the 11th International Conference on Knowledge Representation and Reasoning, KR 2008*, 358–366. AAAI Press.

Kalyanpur, A.; Parsia, B.; Horridge, M.; and Sirin, E. 2007. Finding all justifications of OWL DL entailments. In *ISWC/ASWC*, volume 4825 of *Lecture Notes in Computer Science*, 267–280. Springer.

Katsuno, H., and Mendelzon, A. O. 2003. On the difference between updating a knowledge base and revising it. In Gärdenfors, P., ed., *Belief revision*, 183–203. Cambridge University Press.

Nebel, B. 1990. *Reasoning and Revision in Hybrid Representation Systems*, volume 422 of *Lecture Notes in Computer Science*. Springer.

Ribeiro, J. S., and Thimm, M. 2021. Consolidation via tacit culpability measures: Between explicit and implicit degrees of culpability. In *Proceedings of the 18th International Conference on Principles of Knowledge Representation and Reasoning, KR 2021*, 529–538.

Ribeiro, M. M.; Wassermann, R.; Flouris, G.; and Antoniou, G. 2013. Minimal change: Relevance and recovery revisited. *Artif. Intell.* 201:59–80.

Ribeiro, J. S.; Nayak, A.; and Wassermann, R. 2018. Towards belief contraction without compactness. In *Principles of Knowledge Representation and Reasoning: Proceedings of the Sixteenth International Conference, KR 2018*, 287–296. AAAI Press.

Simari, G. R., and Loui, R. P. 1992. A mathematical treatment of defeasible reasoning and its implementation. *Artif. Intell.* 53(2-3):125–157.

Williams, M. 1994. On the logic of theory base change. In *Logics in Artificial Intelligence, European Workshop, JELIA '94, Proceedings*, volume 838 of *Lecture Notes in Computer Science*, 86–105. Springer.

Proceedings of the 19th International Conference on Principles of Knowledge Representation and Reasoning
Main Track

A Credal Least Undefined Stable Semantics for Probabilistic Logic Programs and Probabilistic Argumentation

Victor Hugo Nascimento Rocha , Fabio Gagliardi Cozman
Escola Politécnica, Universidade de São Paulo
{victor.hugo.rocha,fgcozman}@usp.br

Abstract

We present an approach to probabilistic logic programming and probabilistic argumentation that combines elements of the L-stable semantics and the credal semantics. We derive the complexity of inferences, propose an extended version of argumentation graphs with a semantics that maps to the L-stable semantics, and introduce a definition for the probability of an argument.

1 Introduction

In this paper we deal with probabilistic versions both of logic programs and of argumentation frameworks. On the one hand, we propose a semantics for probabilistic logic programs that is motivated by the needs of probabilistic argumentation. On the other hand, we obtain a novel approach to probabilistic argumentation that is derived from the features and semantics of logic programming.

In the remaining sections of the paper, we start with probabilistic logic programming and move to probabilistic argumentation, as this is the easiest way to chain the technical results. However, the work was developed in the reverse direction: we started with a few issues in probabilistic argumentation, then needed a novel approach to probabilistic logic programming. We follow this path in the next paragraph, as it better conveys the motivation for our proposals.

Our intended argumentation scenario is this. Consider an artificial agent that extracts arguments from various sources and organizes the arguments to help and support (not persuade) human agents, possibly dealing with assumptions and probabilities. Work on probabilistic argumentation typically assigns probability directly to abstract arguments, but it is often difficult to interpret the required probabilities. We assume our agent builds probabilistic arguments whose internal structure is based on rules and facts associated with probabilities; from those probabilities the agent can arrive at the probabilities of arguments. The whole pipeline is depicted in Figure 1: rules and probabilities are first extracted and then translated to arguments that support the human user. We do not deal with the extraction process in this paper, but we believe that rules and probabilistic facts offer a better target primary language for extraction than abstract arguments associated with probabilities.

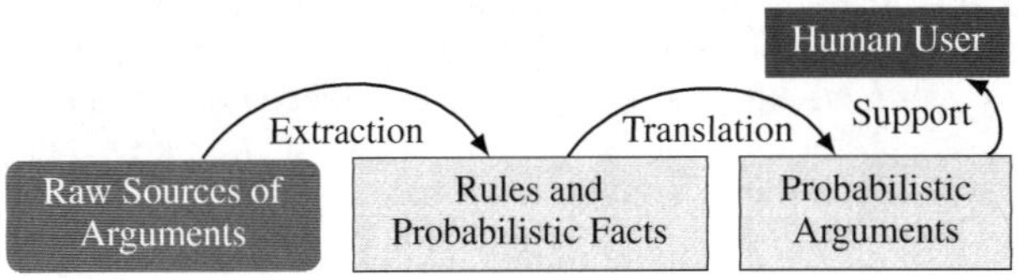

Figure 1: The conceptual pipeline.

In Section 2 we look at probabilistic logic programs that can serve the purpose outlined in the previous paragraph. To do so, we combine two ideas that have been investigated separately: the L-stable semantics for sets of rules and the credal semantics for probabilistic facts. We define the resulting *L-credal* semantics and its basic inference problem. We then derive the complexity of the inference problem. Even though our motivation arises from argumentation theory, we believe that our results are of general interest.

We then present, in Section 3, a new theory of probabilistic argumentation that is based on probabilistic logic programs under the L-credal semantics. We show how arguments can be constructed and how argumentation graphs can be enlarged so that their semantics meshes smoothly with the underlying L-stable semantics. We then propose a definition for the probability of an argument.

Conclusions and plans for future work appear in Section 4.

2 The L-Credal Semantics

Section 2.1 combines well-known concepts, and Section 2.2 introduces the L-credal semantics.

2.1 Rules and Probabilistic Facts

We start with a vocabulary with a finite set of names for *constants* and a finite set of names for *parameterized random variables* (Poole 2003). A parameterized random variable indexes, through its arguments, a set of random variables; for instance, if $\mathsf{brotherOf}$ is a parameterized random variable with two arguments, then $\mathsf{brotherOf}(\mathsf{Mary}, \mathsf{John})$ is a random variable. Each random variable has three values; logic programming typically resorts to labels true, false, and $\mathsf{undefined}$. The underlying sample space is the set of all configurations of random variables.

An *atom* consists of a parameterized random variable with arguments that may be constants or *logical variables*; for instance, $\mathsf{brotherOf}(\mathsf{Mary}, \mathsf{John})$, $\mathsf{brotherOf}(X, \mathsf{John})$, brotherOf$(X, Y)$. A *ground atom* is an atom without logical variables (hence, a random variable). An atom can be grounded into a ground atom by replacing its logical variables by constants. The Herbrand base is the (finite) set of all grounded atoms (random variables) that can be built with names in the vocabulary.

A rule is an expression of the form

$$H :- B_1, \ldots, B_m, \textbf{not } B_{m+1}, \ldots, \textbf{not } B_{m+n}.,$$

where H and each B_i is an atom. The atom H is the *head* of the rule; the righthand side is the *body* of the rule. A *fact* is a rule without body, written $H.$. A *logic program* is a set of rules (some of which may be facts).

We could use classic negation $\neg$ and also rules without heads (usually referred to as *constraints*), but, coupled with the semantics discussed later, these constructs can be compiled away (Eiter, Ianni, and Krennwalner 2009).

In the remainder of this paper we assume that all given rules have been grounded with all possible atoms. Thus we are dealing with logic programs without logical variables.

We take uncertainty to be coded by associating probabilities with selected facts as often done in probabilistic logic programming (Fierens et al. 2014; Sato 1995). Such a simple scheme cannot capture every subjective or objective kind of uncertainty in argumentation, but it seems to be an excellent compromise between expressivity and complexity — not just computational complexity, but also the complexity that a human user faces in dealing with the formalism.

We adopt ProbLog's syntax (Fierens et al. 2014) and specify a *probabilistic fact* using the syntax $\alpha :: F.$ to mean, intuitively, that with probability α the fact $F.$ is added to the program (and with probability $1-\alpha$ the fact $F.$ is discarded). A set of rules and probabilistic facts is a *probabilistic logic program*.

Before we move to a discussion of probabilistic semantics, we briefly review a few well-known semantics for logic programs (Caminada et al. 2015). A *three-valued interpretation* of a logic program $\mathbf{P}$ is a pair $(\mathcal{T}, \mathcal{F})$ such that $\mathcal{T} \cap \mathcal{F} = \emptyset$ and both $\mathcal{T}$ and $\mathcal{F}$ contain elements of the Herbrand base of $\mathbf{P}$. A *three-valued model* of $\mathbf{P}$ is an interpretation $(\mathcal{T}, \mathcal{F})$ such that: H is in $\mathcal{T}$ if there is a rule whose head is H and where each B not preceded by **not** is in $\mathcal{T}$; H is in $\mathcal{F}$ if every rule whose head is H is such that there is some B not preceded by **not** in $\mathcal{F}$. The *reduct* of $\mathbf{P}$ with respect to a three-valued interpretation $\mathcal{I}$, denoted $\mathbf{P}/\mathcal{I}$, is a logic program without **not**: first, remove from $\mathbf{P}$ every rule that contains **not** B in its body for some $B \in \mathcal{T}$; then, for each remaining rule, remove **not** B from the body of the rule if $B \in \mathcal{F}$; finally, replace any remaining occurrences of **not** B'' by some fresh symbol ♣ that represents "undefined". Then $\mathbf{P}/\mathcal{I}$ has a unique three-valued model with minimal $\mathcal{T}$ and maximal $\mathcal{F}$ (with respect to set inclusion); denote this model by $\Phi_{\mathbf{P}}(\mathcal{I})$. A *partial stable model* of $\mathbf{P}$ is an interpretation $\mathcal{I}$ such that $\Phi_{\mathbf{P}}(\mathcal{I}) = \mathcal{I}$. The *well-founded model* [*regular*] of $\mathbf{P}$ is the partial stable model with minimal [maximal] $\mathcal{T}$. A *stable model* of $\mathcal{P}$ is a partial stable model without undefined atoms.

2.2 The L-Credal Semantics

Our semantics for probabilistic facts is directly based on Sato's distribution semantics (Sato 1995; Fierens et al. 2014). A *choice* for probabilistic fact $\alpha :: F.$, where F is a ground atom, is a decision as to whether the probabilistic fact is replaced by the fact $F.$ or simply discarded (if F contains variables, we assume a probabilistic per grounding is generated before any semantics is applied). A *total choice* is a set of choices, one per probabilistic fact. All choices are assumed independent; for a set of probability facts $\{\alpha_i :: F_i.\}_{i=1}^N$, the probability of a total choice $\mathcal{O}$ is

$$\mathbb{P}(\mathcal{O}) = \prod_{\substack{(\alpha_i :: F_i.) \text{ not} \\ \text{discarded by } \mathcal{O}}} \alpha_i \prod_{\substack{(\alpha_i :: F_i.) \\ \text{discarded by } \mathcal{O}}} (1 - \alpha_i). \quad (1)$$

A total choice transforms a probabilistic logic program into a logic program. Thus, a probability distribution over total choices induces a probability distribution over logic programs. To have a complete semantics, we must decide which semantics to adopt for the induced logic programs.

Existing approaches to probabilistic logic programming adopt either the well-founded or the stable semantics for the logic programs induced by total choices. The well-founded semantics always exists and is unique; when it does not contain undefined values, it is equal to the stable semantics. It is thus not surprising that the well-founded semantics has been proposed in connection with probabilistic facts (Sato, Kameya, and Zhou 2005; Hadjichristodoulou and Warren 2012), for then the unique probability distribution over total choices induces a unique distribution over atoms. However, the well-founded semantics conflates two distinct situations into its undefined values. On the one hand, it may be the case that we *could* accept or reject an atom in more than one way, but the semantics simply refuses to make a decision. To use a well-known example, take the set of rules:

$$G_1 :- \textbf{not } G_2., \; G_2 :- \textbf{not } G_1., \; H :- G_1., \; H :- G_2..$$

The well-founded semantics leaves all atoms undefined. But we in fact can label G_1 as true and G_2 as false or the other way around while respecting all structural constraints of the logic program. In both cases H gets true, even though it is left undefined by the well-founded semantics. And then there is the entirely different situation, where we *cannot* take neither true nor false. An example is the logic program $\{H :- \textbf{not } H.\}$: atom H cannot be true nor false without breaking some structural assumption about logic programs. Even though the two logic programs in this paragraph are fundamentally different, the well-founded semantics handles both cases through the same undefined value.

The stable model semantics has no place for undefined values, at a cost: there may be, for a logic program, many stable models, or none. For instance, there are two stable models for the first example in the previous paragraph. One assigns false only to G_1 and true to the other atoms; the other assigns false only to G_2 and true to the other atoms. Intuitively, each stable model offers a solution to the constraints imposed by rules. For the second logic program in the previous paragraph, the stable model semantics does not exist, signifying that there is no way to satisfy the constraints.

If a total choice $\mathcal{O}$ leads to a logic program with more than one stable model, we have no information as to how to distribute the probability $\mathbb{P}(\mathcal{O})$. One solution is to distribute that probability mass uniformly over the stable models (Baral, Gelfond, and Rushton 2009; Totis, Kimmig, and Raedt 2021). In that approach, if we have two stable models, each one of them gets $\mathbb{P}(\mathcal{O})/2$. One may defend such a strategy through maximum entropy or some other kind of minimum commitment principle (Howson and Urbach 1993). However, it is *not* the case that such solution is neutral when it comes to beliefs and opinions (Walley 1991). A minimum commitment strategy can still be found, as originally proposed by Lukasiewicz (2005); take the set of *all* possible induced distribution over models prescribed by the adopted semantics. For instance, if we have two stable models for total choice $\mathcal{O}$, we can have a distribution that assigns $\mathbb{P}(\mathcal{O})$ to one of them and zero to the other, or $\mathbb{P}(\mathcal{O})/2$ to both, and so on. Because sets of probability distributions are often called *credal sets* (Augustin et al. 2014), the resulting semantics has been referred to as the *credal semantics* (Cozman and Mauá 2017).

For each distribution in the semantics, the probabilities of any value of an atom A are obtained by summing probabilities for all models in which A gets the value. Each distribution thus assigns a probability to each total choice $\mathcal{O}$, and of course that probability must agree with Expression 1.

To summarize: the credal semantics of a probabilistic logic program is the set of all probability distributions over stable models of logic programs induced by total choices, such that each probability distribution agrees with the probabilities of total choices. If every total choice induces a single stable model, the credal semantics induces a unique probability distribution over all atoms. In general, the credal semantics induces a closed convex set of probability distributions over atoms (Cozman and Mauá 2017).

Alas, the credal semantics breaks down when some total choices induce logic programs without stable models. In logic programming, where stable models are often the solution to a combinatorial problem (Eiter, Ianni, and Krennwallner 2009), absence of stable models can be useful information: it shows the constraints in the logic program cannot be satisfied. Instead, in probabilistic logic programming, the fact that a few scenarios cannot be satisfied should not break the semantics. This will be particularly important when we later move to probabilistic argumentation: it is not reasonable to stop the analysis of probabilistic arguments just because some scenarios leave a few atoms undefined. We must be able to proceed even when some total choices create scenarios that are partially, or even totally, unsatisfiable.

Our solution will be to adopt the *least undefined semantics*, often referred to as the *L-stable semantics*, for logic programs.

A *least undefined stable model*, or *L-stable model* for short, of a logic program $\mathbf{P}$ is a partial stable model with maximal $\mathcal{T} \cup \mathcal{F}$ (with respect to set inclusion). That is, a L-stable model is a partial stable model with a minimum number of undefined atoms. The set of L-stable models is the L-stable semantics of $\mathbf{P}$ (Sacca 1997). A nice feature of this semantics is that, if a logic program has one or more stable models, those are exactly the L-stable models. However, if a logic program has no stable models, then there will be partial stable models for it, but they will have undefined atoms (not necessarily all atoms will be undefined; just the minimum number of them).

	$v = \mathsf{true}$	$v = \mathsf{false}$	$v = \mathsf{undefined}$
$\mathbb{P}(A = v)$	0.5	0.5	0.0
$\mathbb{P}(B = v)$	0.5	0.5	0.0
$\mathbb{P}(C = v)$	$[0.5, 0.75]$	$[0.25, 0.5]$	0.0
$\mathbb{P}(D = v)$	$[0.5, 0.75]$	$[0.25, 0.5]$	0.0
$\mathbb{P}(E = v)$	0.0	0.5	0.5

	$v = \mathsf{true}$	$v = \mathsf{false}$	$v = \mathsf{inconsistent}$
$\mathbb{P}(A = v)$	0.0	0.5	0.5
$\mathbb{P}(B = v)$	0.25	0.25	0.5
$\mathbb{P}(C = v)$	0.125	0.375	0.5
$\mathbb{P}(D = v)$	0.375	0.125	0.5
$\mathbb{P}(E = v)$	0.0	0.5	0.5

Table 1: Top: tight probability intervals for Example 1; if an interval contains a single number, the interval is replaced by the number. Bottom: probabilities using the SMProbLog approach.

Definition 1. *Given a probabilistic logic program* $\mathbf{P}$*, its* credal least undefined stable *semantics, or* L-credal *semantics, is the set of all probability distributions over L-stable models of programs induced by total choices, such that each distribution agrees with the probabilities of total choices.*

An example should clarify the semantics.

Example 1. *Suppose we have the following rules:*
$\mathsf{worksInTown}(X) :- \mathsf{barber}(X).$,
$\mathsf{worksInRiver}(X) :- \mathsf{fisherman}(X).$,
$\mathsf{worksInTown}(X) :- \mathbf{not}\ \mathsf{worksInRiver}(X).$,
$\mathsf{worksInRiver}(X) :- \mathbf{not}\ \mathsf{worksInTown}(X).$,
$\mathsf{shaves}(X, Y) :- \mathsf{barber}(X), \mathbf{not}\ \mathsf{shaves}(Y, Y).$.
These rules state a few facts about professions in a village, and moreover state that a barber shaves everyone who does not shave himself (this is a combination of well-known examples in logic programming). Suppose additionally that we have two probabilistic facts:
$0.5 :: \mathsf{barber}(\mathsf{John}).$, $\quad 0.5 :: \mathsf{fisherman}(\mathsf{John}).$.
By grounding, we obtain a logic program of the form:
$C :- A.$, $D :- B.$, $C :- \mathbf{not}\ D.$, $D :- \mathbf{not}\ C.$, $E :- A, \mathbf{not}\ E.$, $0.5 :: A.$, $0.5 :: B.$. *There are four total choices ($\emptyset$, $\{A\}$, $\{B\}$, $\{A, B\}$), each with probability* 0.25. *For total choice $\emptyset$, the induced logic program has two L-stable models (both are also stable models): one where every atom is* false *except C that is* true, *and another where every atom is* false *except D that is* true. *For total choice $\{A\}$, there is a single L-stable model (that is also the well-founded model): E is* undefined, *while both A and C are* true *and both B and D are* false. *For total choice $\{B\}$, there is again a single L-stable model (that is the single stable model): A and C and E are* false *and both B and D are* true. *Finally, for total choice $\{A, B\}$ there is a single L-stable model (that is the well-founded model): all atoms are* true *except E that is* undefined. *By adding probabilities across models for all possible distributions in the semantics, we obtain the tight probability intervals in Table 1 (top).* □

Note that the L-credal semantics nicely differentiates between: (i) the uncertainty captured by the probabilities in probabilistic facts; (ii) the uncertainty regarding multiple stable models, captured by probability intervals; (iii) the uncertainty arising from inability to satisfy constraints, leading to non-zero probability for undefined values.

Previous literature has discussed situations where total choices induce logic programs without stable models. One proposal is to automatically repair logic programs whose rules cannot be satisfied (Ceylan, Lukasiewicz, and Peñaloza 2016). Another proposal in the literature is to set all atoms to a value inconsistent whenever a stable model does not exist (Totis, Kimmig, and Raedt 2021). As an interesting comparison, we collect in Table 1 (bottom) the probabilities obtained via the SMProbLog approach (Totis, Kimmig, and Raedt 2021), where uniform probabilities are distributed over multiple stable models and absence of stable models puts probability mass into inconsistent values. Note how large are the probabilities of inconsistent values, even for atoms that can always be assigned other values.

As a final point, we argue that words such as true, false and undefined are not really appropriate here. It seems better to use unsatisfiable or undecided rather than undefined, to avoid weird sentences such as "the probability that X is undefined" or, worse, "the conditional probability that X is undefined given that Y is undefined" (Cozman and Mauá 2017). And it seems also better to use accepted rather than true and rejected rather than false, to avoid controversies related to mixtures of probabilities and three-valued logic. From now on we use accepted, rejected, and undecided.

2.3 The Complexity of Inferences

The basic inference problem in probabilistic logic programming is to compute the marginal or conditional probability of a ground atom given a probabilistic logic program. For instance, one may be interested in the probability that John is not a barber given that he works in the river: in Example 1, this probability value can be anywhere within the probability interval $[1/3, 1/2]$. We refer to $\underline{\mathbb{P}}(H) \doteq \inf \mathbb{P}(H)$ as the *lower* probability of atom H; similarly, to $\overline{\mathbb{P}}(H) \doteq \inf \mathbb{P}(H)$ as the *upper* probability of atom H (Augustin et al. 2014; Walley 1991). And we refer to $\underline{\mathbb{P}}(H|G) \doteq \inf_{\mathbb{P}:\mathbb{P}(G)>0} \mathbb{P}(H|G)$ as the *lower conditional* probability of H given G; the latter is only defined if $\overline{\mathbb{P}}(G) > 0$ (likewise, $\overline{\mathbb{P}}(H|G) \doteq \sup_{\mathbb{P}:\mathbb{P}(G)>0} \mathbb{P}(H|G)$ is the upper conditional probability).

We must define a precise decision problem in order to study the complexity of inferences. Our *inference problem* receives: a grounded logic program $\mathbf{P}$ with probabilistic facts all defined by rational numbers, a nonempty set of *query atoms* that belong to the logic program, a set of selected ground atoms that belong to the logic program, referred to as the *evidence*, and a rational number γ. Denote by $\mathcal{Q}$ the event that the query atoms are all accepted, and by $\mathcal{E}$ the event that the evidence atoms are all accepted. If the evidence is empty, then the output is YES when $\underline{\mathbb{P}}(\mathcal{Q}) > \gamma$. If the evidence is nonempty and $\overline{\mathbb{P}}(\mathcal{E}) = 0$, then the output is NO (that is, "no probability measure satisfies $\mathbb{P}(\mathcal{Q}|\mathcal{E}) > \gamma$"). And if $\overline{\mathbb{P}}(\mathcal{E}) > 0$, then the output is YES if $\underline{\mathbb{P}}(\mathcal{Q}|\mathcal{E}) > \gamma$ and NO otherwise.

We will show that this inference problem is complete for a complexity class in Wagner's Polynomial Counting Hierarchy (Wagner 1986). We take as known concepts such as complexity classes, decision problems, many-one polynomial reductions, oracles; detailed definitions can be found elsewhere (Papadimitriou 1994). We use well-known complexity classes P, NP, coNP. We also use the complexity class PP: a language $\mathcal{L}$ is in PP when there is a nondeterministic Turing machine $\mathbb{M}$ such that $l \in \mathcal{L}$ iff more than half of computation paths of $\mathbb{M}$ accept l. The Polynomial Counting Hierarchy is the collection of complexity classes that includes P such that if $\mathcal{C}$ is in the hierarchy then so are the classes of decision problems computed by oracle machines $\mathsf{PP}^{\mathcal{C}}$, $\mathsf{NP}^{\mathcal{C}}$ and $\mathsf{coNP}^{\mathcal{C}}$. The Polynomial Counting Hierarchy therefore contains the Polynomial Hierarchy, which includes classes such as $\Sigma_k^p = \mathsf{NP}^{\Sigma_{k-1}^p}$ and $\Pi_k^p = \mathsf{coNP}^{\Sigma_{k-1}^p}$ for $k > 0$, with $\Sigma_0^p = \Pi_0^p = \mathsf{P}$, and also counting classes with oracles in the polynomial hierarchy, such as $\mathsf{PP}^{\Sigma_k^p}$.

We can now state our result:

Theorem 1. *The inference problem is* $\mathsf{PP}^{\Sigma_2^p}$*-complete.*

To prove Theorem 1 on the complexity of the inference problem, we need to adapt some previous results about the credal semantics. First recall that an infinitely monotone Choquet capacity is a set-function c from sets in an algebra over a set Ω to real numbers in $[0, 1]$ such that $c(\Omega) = 1 - c(\emptyset) = 1$ and $c(\cup_{i=1}^n E_i) \geq \sum_{J \subseteq \{1,\ldots,n\}} (-1)^{|J|-1} c(\cap_{j \in J} E_j)$ for any sets of events E_i in the algebra (Augustin et al. 2014). A set of functions dominates a Choquet capacity c if every function in the set is uniformly larger or equal to c. We then have:

Theorem 2. *The L-credal semantics of a logic program is a closed convex set of probability distributions that is the largest set dominating an infinitely monotone Choquet capacity.*

Proof. Identical to the proof of Theorem 1 of (Cozman and Mauá 2017). □

The proof of our complexity result will also need the following consequence of Theorem 2:

$$\underline{\mathbb{P}}(\mathcal{Q}|\mathcal{E}) = \frac{\underline{\mathbb{P}}(\mathcal{Q} \cap \mathcal{E})}{\underline{\mathbb{P}}(\mathcal{Q} \cap \mathcal{E}) + \overline{\mathbb{P}}(\mathcal{Q}^c \cap \mathcal{E})} \tag{2}$$

provided the denominator is larger than zero (Molchanov 2005). If the denominator of the latter expression is zero, then $\underline{\mathbb{P}}(\mathcal{Q}|\mathcal{E})$ is equal to one if there is *any* distribution such that $\mathbb{P}(\mathcal{Q} \cap \mathcal{E}) > 0$, and is undefined otherwise.

The proof of membership of Theorem 1 depends a few additional facts based on Theorem 2. To compute a lower probability $\underline{\mathbb{P}}(\mathcal{Q})$, we can go over all total choices and, for each total choice, examine whether all L-stable models are such that $\mathcal{Q}$ is obtained; if that happens, we add the probability of that total choice to some accumulator. At the end, the accumulator (that started from zero) contains the desired lower probability. That is, to obtain a lower probability we must go over the total choices running *cautious (logical) inference* for each logic program (sometimes referred to as *skeptical* inference) (Eiter, Leone, and Saccá 1998). Similarly, to obtain an upper probability we must run *brave (logical) inference* for each induced logic program – that is, we must check whether $\mathcal{Q}$ is obtained in some L-stable model (sometimes referred to as *credulous* inference).

We can now present the proof of Theorem 1:

Proof. To prove membership in $\mathsf{PP}^{\Sigma_2^p}$, we piece together some parts of previous proofs in the literature. First, we use the first part of the proof of Theorem 16 by Cozman and Mauá (2017) to build a nondeterministic Turing machine that generates a total choice (with probability given by Expression (1)). Then, for a total choice $\mathcal{T}$ selected through a polynomial sequence of non-deterministic moves, the machine builds the induced non-probabilistic logic program $\mathbf{P}_\mathcal{T}$. As in that proof, the Turing machine branches into different paths so as to decide whether $k_1\underline{\mathbb{P}}(\mathcal{Q} \cap \mathcal{E}) > k_2\overline{\mathbb{P}}(\mathcal{Q}^c \cap \mathcal{E})$ for suitable constants k_1 and k_2 (this inequality is derived from Expression (2)). Some of the paths require cautions inference, while others require brave inference; the specific branches are detailed in the proof of Theorem 25 by Cozman and Mauá (2017). Now, cautions inference can be solved by calling an oracle in Π_2^p. To see this, consider the decision as to whether an atom belongs to all L-stable models. It is enough to generate a L-stable model that does not contain the atom and negate the output. To do so, first generate, using a polynomial time nondeterministic machine, an interpretation $\mathcal{I}$; a polynomial time nondeterministic machine can be used as oracle to decide whether $\mathcal{I}$ is in fact a L-stable model. A similar reasoning shows that brave inference can be solved by calling an oracle in Σ_2^p.

To prove hardness, we start with the following $\mathsf{PP}^{\Sigma_2^p}$-complete problem (Wagner 1986): Decide whether

$$\#X_1, \dots, X_n : \forall Y_1, \dots, Y_m : \exists Z_1, \dots, Z_s : \phi > M,$$

where ϕ is a propositional formula in all propositional symbols bounded to quantifiers and in Conjunctive Normal Form (CNF) where each clause has at most three literals (propositional variables or propositional variables preceded by negation), and where M is an integer. The symbol $\#$ denotes a *counting* quantifier whose result is to count the number of configurations of bounded propositional variables that satisfy the enclosed formula.

Start with the Σ_2^p-complete decision problem (Papadimitriou 1994): decide whether Θ holds, where $\Theta \doteq \forall Y_1, \dots, Y_m : \exists Z_1, \dots, Z_s : \phi$. We treat ϕ as a set of clauses and each clause c as a set of literals. This decision problem can be reduced to the computation of the semi-stable semantics of an argumentation framework (Dvořák 2012, Theorem 12); an atom ϕ is introduced so that formula ϕ holds iff atom ϕ is accepted in all semi-stable argumentation labelings of the argumentation framework. Now we could translate this argumentation framework into a logic program using a well-known transformation (Caminada et al. 2015);[1] this translation has the important property that each labeling of the original argumentation framework corresponds to a L-stable model of the resulting program and vice-versa (Caminada et al. 2015, Theorem 29). Now consider including into this construction the counting quantifier and associated propositional variables X_i. First, we have a formula ϕ containing clauses where some literals may mention the X_i. Include arguments X_i and $\overline{X}_i$ in the argumentation framework above, and treat literals with X_i as all other propositional variables in Dvořák's reduction. The next step is to translate the argumentation framework into a logic program and replace, for each pair X_i and $\overline{X}_i$, the rules with them as heads by the probabilistic fact $0.5 :: X_i$. and the rule $\overline{X}_i :- X_i$.. The computation of the lower probability of the atom ϕ yields the probability of the total choices for which ϕ is in all L-stable models; using Dvořák's results, that is the probability ρ that formula Θ holds. By comparing $\rho > 1/2$, we decide whether $\#X_1, \dots, X_n : \Theta > 2^{n+m+s-1}$. □

[1] This translation is discussed in Section 3.3 (footnote 2).

Note that the corresponding result for the credal *stable* semantics yields $\mathsf{PP}^{\Sigma_1^p}$-completeness (Cozman and Mauá 2017); the L-stable semantics moves us one oracle up.

3 Probabilistic Argumentation: A Proposal

As we mentioned in Section 1, we began this work by looking for a formalism to represent arguments with uncertainty. In this section we offer an approach that, we feel, fixes a few difficulties found in existing approaches. In Section 3.1 we review terminology and existing literature on (probabilistic) argumentation frameworks. Section 3.2 describes our proposal, and Section 3.3 introduces a novel extension of argumentation graphs that is needed to connect logic programs and sets of arguments. And Section 3.4 introduces a new definition for the probability of an argument.

3.1 A Bit of Background on (Probabilistic) Argumentation Frameworks

Argumentation theory has been studied for centuries (van Eemeren et al. 2014); within artificial intelligence, two strong research agendas have been pursued: Abstract Argumentation Frameworks (AAF) and Assumption-based Argumentation Frameworks (ABAF). They have many variants; due to space constraints, we stick to basic definitions.

An AAF is a pair $(\mathcal{A}, \mathcal{R})$ where $\mathcal{A}$ is a finite set of arguments and $\mathcal{R} \subseteq \mathcal{A} \times \mathcal{A}$ is a relation between arguments (Dung 1995). If $(A, B) \in \mathcal{R}$, we say that A *attacks* B. An *argumentation labeling* associates each argument with a label, either accepted, rejected, or undecided. A *complete argumentation labeling* L is an argumentation labeling such that: (i) if argument A is rejected then there is argument B that is accepted and that attacks A; (ii) if argument A is accepted then for all arguments B that attack A we must have that B is rejected; (iii) if argument A is undecided then there is no argument B that is accepted and attacks A, and there is an argument C that attacks A and is not rejected. A *grounded argumentation labeling* is a complete argumentation labeling where the set of accepted arguments is minimal. A *preferred argumentation labeling* is a complete argumentation labeling where the set of accepted arguments is maximal. A *stable argumentation labeling* is a complete argumentation labeling with no undecided argument. A *semi-stable argumentation labeling* is a complete argumentation labeling where the set of undecided arguments is minimal. A semantics prescribes the labels for all arguments: the complete/grounded/preferred/stable/semi-stable semantics prescribe the corresponding argumentation labelings. An *argumentation graph* associated with an AAF is a graph where each node is an argument and each directed arrow corresponds to an attack.

An ABAF on the other hand emphasizes the structure of arguments (Bondarenko et al. 1997). Usually such a framework consists of a language, a set of rules, a set of *assumptions* in the language, and a *contrary* function that indicates a sentence that defeats an assumption (Toni 2014). An argument can be viewed as a finite tree with an element of the language in the root (the *conclusion*), nodes that represent rules, and assumptions in the leaves (Caminada and Schulz 2017). Logic programs and ABAFs can be directly translated to one another (Caminada and Schulz 2017). This sort of translation to/from logic programming applies also to many other structured argumentation and non-monotonic formalisms (Heyninck and Strasser 2016; Heyninck 2019). Given this, we stay with logic programs as the main structured representation for argumentation schemes, even though we certainly agree that many features such as supports, weights and preferences (Modgil and Prakken 2014), cannot be captured by logic programs.

Interest in probabilistic versions of argumentation frameworks has been growing for some time. Initial efforts focused on structured argumentation, some of them closer to probabilistic logic (Haenni 2001; Haenni 2009), while others concentrating on probabilistic ABAFs (Dung and Thang 2010; Riveret et al. 2007); however, their assumptions and probabilistic assessments are significantly different than ours. Recent work (Čyras, Heinrich, and Toni 2021; Hung 2017) operates closer to us by combining ABAFs with (what amounts to) probabilistic facts, but with semantics that are not related to our L-credal semantics. Relatively less work has appeared on probabilistic ABAFs than on probabilistic AAFs, and most (almost all) proposals for probabilistic argumentation assume that probabilities are assigned to arguments or to attacks, with differences on how these probabilities are to be interpreted. Fortunately a detailed recent survey can be consulted (Hunter et al. 2021), so here we only offer a very brief review of probabilistic argumentation and skip important topics that we do not need in this paper.

Probabilistic AAFs can basically be of two kinds. In the *constellation* approach, uncertainty lies in the graph topology: arguments and attacks may be present with given probabilities (Li, Oren, and Norman 2011; Mantadelis and Bistarelli 2020). In the *epistemic* approach the graph topology is fixed and there is uncertainty as to which degree arguments are believed — or justified, or acceptable; the interpretation varies in the literature (Baroni, Giacomin, and Vicig 2014; Hunter, Polberg, and Thimm 2020; Thimm 2012).

The constellation approach usually relies on the concepts of acceptance and rejection from (non-probabilistic) AAFs; for instance, one may be interested in the probability that some atom gets some argumentation labeling. The epistemic approach typically offers more notions of acceptance or conditions of rational behavior, often based on probabilistic ideas (for instance, an argument may be accepted only if its probability is larger than some threshold). In that sense, the epistemic approach moves away from AAFs in an attempt to model the human agents involved in argumentation.

As noted by Prakken (2018), in the constellation approach the probabilities are extrinsic to arguments, as they carry uncertainty about arguing agents, while in the epistemic approach probabilities are intrinsic to arguments. Clearly, one can contemplate mixtures of both approaches (Riveret et al. 2018). An interesting mixture appears in the work by Totis, Kimmig, and Raedt (2021): they employ probabilistic logic programming to build arguments but still assume that probabilities are assigned to arguments and attacks.

3.2 Building Probabilistic Arguments

A challenge in probabilistic argumentation is the lack of consensus over the meaning of probabilities (Prakken 2018). Existing proposals typically start from the probability that an argument is accepted, or that it is justified, or even that it is true; often it feels these approaches assume probabilities over events that should actually be the end result of argumentation. Another challenge is that almost all approaches are based on probabilities over supposedly independent abstract arguments; even approaches related to ABAFs often assign probabilities to arguments, not to their components. This strategy is not satisfactory when arguments must be extracted from human discourse (Figure 1), as in real life many arguments depend on common uncertain sources. The structure of arguments must matter.

Given this, we believe that probabilistic argumentation should be assumption-based, with probabilities attached to constituent atoms. Because logic programs capture most assumption-based argumentation schemes, we take that probabilistic logic programming is the right language from which to build arguments.

However, we also think there is significant value in argumentation graphs when it comes to interacting with human users. One advantage is that the user can focus on subsets of a logic program (the arguments) and look for explanations and justifications there. Another advantage is that the user can be informed about the probability of arguments and not just of atoms, thus enlarging the scope of the interaction.

Fortunately, there are well-known translations from logic programs to argumentation frameworks. We adopt the *WCG* (Wu, Caminada and Gabbay) translation algorithm (Caminada et al. 2015). We believe this algorithm is the best one at capturing the notion of an argument.

We summarize the WCG algorithm as follows. Starting with a set of rules, process one rule at a time. If we find a rule of the form H :− $\mathbf{not}\ B_1, \ldots, \mathbf{not}\ B_n$., then we generate an argument A written as $\langle H \leftarrow \mathbf{not}\ B_1, \ldots, \mathbf{not}\ B_n \rangle$. We say A has *conclusion* H, *rules* $\{H$:− $\mathbf{not}\ B_1, \ldots, \mathbf{not}\ B_n.\}$, *vulnerabilities* $\{B_1, \ldots, B_n\}$, and a singleton set of *subarguments* that contains A itself. Suppose instead we find a rule of the form H :− $B_1, \ldots, B_m, \mathbf{not}\ B_{m+1}, \ldots, \mathbf{not}\ B_{m+n}$.

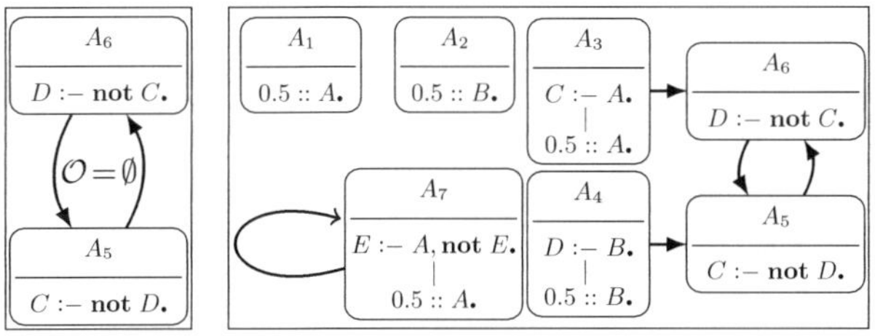

Figure 2: Arguments and graphs generated by running the WCG algorithm for a total choice (left) and with probabilistic facts (right).

Refer to this rule as r and suppose further that, for each $B_1, \ldots, B_m$ there is an argument A_i with conclusion B_i such that r is not in the set of rules of A_i. Then r generates an argument A written as $\langle H \leftarrow \langle A_1 \rangle, \ldots, \langle A_m \rangle, \mathbf{not}\ B_{m+1}, \ldots, \mathbf{not}\ B_{m+n} \rangle$. We say A has *conclusion* H, *rules* consisting of the union of the sets of rules for each A_i and the singleton with rule r, *vulnerabilities* consisting of the union of the sets of vulnerabilities for each A_i and the set $\{B_{m+1}, \ldots, B_{m+n}\}$, *subarguments* consisting of the union of the subarguments for each A_i and the singleton containing just A itself. Intuitively, an argument can be drawn as a tree-like structure, with the root containing a top rule whose head is the conclusion, and additional rules whose conclusions belong to the right hand side the top rule, and so on recursively. Say that A *attacks* A' iff the conclusion of A belongs to vulnerabilities of A'. Nicely, given a set of rules, this procedure generates an AAF.

Hence, a probabilistic logic program generates, for each total choice $\mathcal{O}$, an AAF through the WCG algorithm. The set of AAFs and their probabilities can be drawn in compact form if one is willing to depict the structure of arguments:

Example 2. *Consider again Example 1. Figure 2 (left) depicts the argumentation graph obtained by selecting total choice $\mathcal{O} = \emptyset$ and running the WCG algorithm. The argumentation graph show the structure of the arguments, even though this is not usually drawn in an argumentation graph. Figure 2 (right) is a bit different; there the arguments are built running the WCG algorithm* as if *the probabilistic facts were facts, and leaving them with their probabilities. On the one hand, if we erase the probabilities, we have the argumentation graph obtained by selecting total choice $\mathcal{O} = \{A, B\}$ and running the WCG algorithm. On the other hand, if we leave the probabilities, the right graph captures the whole gamut of total choices and their probabilities.* □

In Section 3.4 it will be important to use probabilistic logic programs "inside" arguments as generated in this example (we will refer to them as *attached probabilistic logic programs*).

At this point we have a complete pipeline corresponding to Figure 1. Alas, there is an unsatisfying snag. Existing results show that it is *impossible* to find a semantics for AAFs that maps back to the L-stable semantics (Caminada et al. 2015, Theorem 24). The last sentence must be made more precise. Suppose that we start with a logic program $\mathbf{P}$ and we generate an AAF by running the WCG algorithm. Suppose we find an argumentation labeling for arguments using a selected argumentation semantics. Suppose further that, for each atom C, we find the highest label amongst the labels of arguments whose conclusion is C, where accepted > undecided > rejected. We then assign respectively accepted/undecided/rejected to the atom C if the highest argument label is accepted/undecided/rejected. Can this *back mapping* procedure always generate L-stable models for the original program $\mathbf{P}$? Unfortunately, no, at least not with the tools we have so far.

Example 3. *Here is a short version of the key example by Caminada et al. (2015). Consider the following rules: E :– **not** E., A :– **not** B., B :– **not** A.. Now build a logic program $\mathbf{P}_1$ consisting of these rules and C :– **not** E. and C :– **not** A, **not** C.. And build another logic program $\mathbf{P}_2$ consisting of the three previous rules and D :– **not** E. and C :– **not** A, **not** C, **not** D.. The WCG algorithm generates the same argumentation graph for both logic programs:*

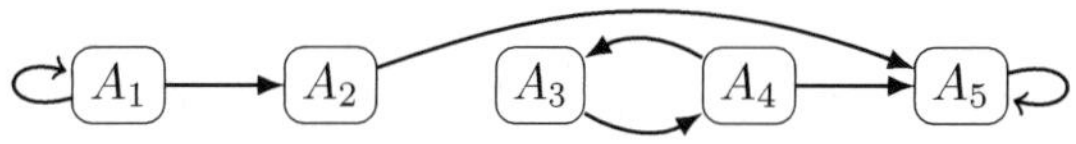

Programs $\mathbf{P}_1$ and $\mathbf{P}_2$ have respectively two and one L-stable models. Alas, it is not possible for a single graph, whatever the argumentation semantics, to map back to two distinct models. □

Somewhat surprisingly, the back mapping procedure *does* work for several pairs of program/argumentation semantics: We obtain respectively a partial stable/well-founded/regular/stable model of $\mathbf{P}$ if we use complete/grounded/preferred/stable argumentation labelings. But no argumentation semantics can always back map into the L-stable semantics.

Consequently, argumentation graphs are not really appropriate to convey the L-stable semantics, and hence the L-credal semantics, to a human user as envisioned in Figure 1. The next section solves this problem.

3.3 Conclusion-augmented Argumentation Frameworks (CAFs)

We wish to keep the L-stable semantics for logic programs but still be able to recover L-stable models from argumentation graphs. Our way out is straightforward: enlarge AAFs so that each argument is explicitly associated with a conclusion. As argumentation is about conclusions, it makes sense to give the latter a more prominent status. And the resulting framework is still rather abstract as no argument exhibits internal structure.

In fact, the same idea has been proposed in connection with *Claim-Augmented Argumentation Frameworks* (Dvorák and Woltran 2019; Dvořák, Rapberger, and Woltran 2020; Rapberger 2020). We prefer to use the term *conclusion* instead of *claim*, as the former seems to better fit the previous literature we work upon (Caminada et al. 2015). We also develop here what we hope is a more direct route to obtain correspondences to logic programming. Despite this, both frameworks are equivalent so the proposal itself is not a novel contribution of the present paper.

We define:

Definition 2. *A Conclusion-augmented Argumentation Framework (CAF) is a tuple $(\mathcal{A}, \mathcal{S}, f, \mathcal{R})$, where $\mathcal{A}$ is a finite set of arguments, $\mathcal{S}$ is a set of atoms referred to as conclusions, f is a function from arguments to conclusions, and $\mathcal{R} \subseteq \mathcal{A} \times \mathcal{A}$ is an attack relation as before.*

We write that for a conclusion c, the set of arguments associated with it is denoted by $f^{-1}(c)$. An *conclusion-augmented argumentation graph* is a directed graph where each node contains an argument and its conclusion, and each arrow goes from a node containing an attacking argument to a node containing an attacked argument.

Example 4. *The program in Example 2 with total choice $\mathcal{O} = \{A, B\}$ and program $\mathbf{P}_1$ in Example 3 respectively lead to the following conclusion-augmented argumentation graphs:*

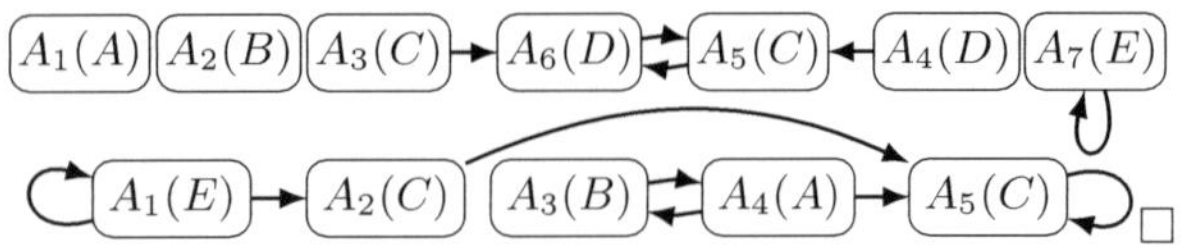

Given a CAF, we can label each conclusion as accepted, undecided, or rejected. Clearly such a *conclusion labeling* maps to an argumentation labeling through the function f. And the previous back-mapping procedure produces a conclusion labeling out of any given argumentation labeling.

Obviously, a CAF can be generated by any logic program by running the WCG algorithm with the small change that arguments are explicitly associated with their conclusions at the end. We refer to the resulting algorithms as the *extended* WCG algorithm.

Definitions related to argumentation labelings can be readily adapted to conclusion labelings. For instance, consider the definition of complete conclusion labeling:

Definition 3. *Let $(\mathcal{A}, \mathcal{S}, f, \mathcal{R})$ be a CAF and $\mathcal{L}$ a conclusion labeling of $\mathcal{S}$. Then $\mathcal{L}$ is a* complete conclusion labeling *iff (i) if a conclusion a is* rejected *then for every argument $A \in f^{-1}(a)$ there is an argument B that attacks A with* accepted *conclusion $f(B)$; (ii) if a conclusion a is* accepted *then for some argument $A \in f^{-1}(a)$, each argument B that attacks A must have a* rejected *conclusion $f(B)$. (iii) if a conclusion a is* undecided *then there is no argument $A \in f^{-1}(a)$ for which all arguments B that attack A have $f(B)$ as* rejected*; and for some argument $A \in f^{-1}(a)$, there is no argument B that attacks A with* accepted *conclusion $f(B)$, and there is an argument C that attacks that same A and whose conclusion $f(C)$ is not* rejected.

Using this definition, other semantics immediately follow:

Definition 4. *Let L be a conclusion labeling. L is grounded iff it is complete and the set of* accepted *conclusions is minimal. L is preferred iff it is complete and the set of* accepted *conclusions is maximal. L is stable iff it is complete and no conclusion is left* undecided. *L is semi-stable iff it is complete and the set of* undecided *conclusions is minimal.*

We then obtain the desired correspondence between logic program and argumentation semantics:

Theorem 3. *Let $\mathbf{P}$ be a logic program and $\mathbf{C} = (\mathcal{A}, \mathcal{S}, f, \mathcal{R})$ the CAF generated by the extended WCG algorithm. Then the complete, preferred, grounded, stable and semi-stable conclusion labelings of $\mathbf{C}$ are identical to the labels assigned respectively by the partial stable, regular, well-founded, stable and L-stable models of $\mathbf{P}$.*

Proof. As proved by Caminada et al. (2015), the complete semantics for $\mathbf{C}$ yields the same results as the partial stable semantics applied to $\mathbf{P}$. As the other semantics are computed by maximizing/minimizing specific labels at the conclusion level, they are equivalent to applying the desired semantics directly in the logic program. □

To conclude this section, we ask: Is it possible to translate *any* CAF to a logic program with equivalent semantics over conclusions? There is a well-known procedure that generates a logic program from an AAF such that all argumentation semantics discussed here are preserved, except the semi-stable semantics (Caminada et al. 2015).[2] Can a similar result be found for CAFs? In fact, we can do even better with CAFs. Consider the following procedure:

Definition 5. *Let $\mathbf{C} = (\mathcal{A}, \mathcal{S}, f, \mathcal{R})$ be a CAF. For each argument A, generate the rule $f(A)$:− **not** $f(B_1)$, ..., **not** $f(B_m)$. where the B_i are the arguments that attack A. Denote by $\mathbf{P_C}$ the logic program consisting of these rules.*

The next theorem proves the desired equivalence between the semantics before and after the translation.

Theorem 4. *Let $\mathbf{C} = (\mathcal{A}, \mathcal{S}, f, \mathcal{R})$ be a CAF and $\mathbf{P_C}$ be the corresponding logic program produced by Definition 5. Then the partial stable, regular, well-founded, stable, L-stable models of $\mathbf{P_C}$ assign the same labels to atoms as labels assigned respectively by the complete, preferred, grounded, stable, semi-stable conclusion labelings of $\mathbf{C}$.*

Proof. Denote by $\mathbf{C_{P_C}}$ the CAF produced by the extended WCG algorithm with $\mathbf{P_C}$ as input. Theorem 3 shows that labels are the same for $\mathbf{P_C}$ and $\mathbf{C_{P_C}}$ for all semantics in the theorem. Hence, if $\mathbf{C}$ and $\mathbf{C_{P_C}}$ produce the same conclusion labeling, we are done. Note that we allow $\mathbf{C}$ to have more than one argument with the same conclusion and that is attacked by the same arguments while $\mathbf{C_{P_C}}$ can have just one "copy" of that argument. Such repeated arguments in $\mathbf{C}$ do not affect the conclusion labelings. Now, if we assume that $\mathbf{C}$ and $\mathbf{C_{P_C}}$ have distinct conclusion labelings, the set of conclusions from their arguments is different and/or the set of vulnerabilities associated with them is different. In the translation shown in Definition 5, each rule of $\mathbf{P_C}$ contains in its head H the conclusion associated with an argument from $\mathbf{C}$ and, from extended the WCG algorithm, we know each rule becomes an argument in $\mathbf{C_P}$. Therefore the set of conclusions is the same. Similarly, the set of vulnerabilities must be the same in $\mathbf{C}$ and $\mathbf{C_{P_C}}$. Because of that, $\mathbf{C}$ and $\mathbf{C_{P_C}}$ produce the same conclusion labelings. □

[2]This is the translation also mentioned in the proof of Theorem 1: each argument maps to an atom (we use the same letters for both) and each atom H produced by an argument is associated with a rule H :− **not** $B_1, \ldots,$ **not** B_m., where $B_1, \ldots, B_m$ are the atoms corresponding to arguments that attack the argument H.

To summarize, we have proposed an argumentation framework that puts conclusions in center stage, the CAFs. We have proved that they do guarantee nice correspondences with logic programs, going beyond AAFs — as CAFs do even display a correspondence between L-stable models and semi-stable conclusion labelings.

3.4 Finally: The Probability of an Argument

Having put in place an infrastructure for probabilistic argumentation, we are ready to ask: What exactly is the probability of an argument? We do not believe that there is a unique probability value that captures all uncertainty around a given argument, and we can explore here a few ideas by examining the structure of arguments.

Note, first, that there is a difference between the probability of a conclusion and of an argument. A conclusion may be accepted due to many different arguments operating with respect to distinct total choices.

Instead, when computing the "probability of an argument", we should take into account only the information attached to the argument. We need some machinery for that. Suppose we have a probabilistic logic program $\mathbf{P}$ and some argument A in that program. Suppose also that we run the WCG algorithm with $\mathbf{P}$ as input, but we treat probabilistic facts as if they were facts (this is illustrated by the right graph in Figure 2 in connection with Example 2). The set *rules* generated by the WCG algorithm is a set that contains rules, some of which may be facts, and probabilistic facts. We refer to this suitably enlarged set *rules* as the *probabilistic logic program attached to* A. We then propose:

Definition 6. *Given a probabilistic conclusion-augmented argumentation graph* $\mathbf{C}$ *generated from a probabilistic logic program* $\mathbf{P}$*, and an argument* A *in* $\mathbf{C}$*, the* probability of argument A *is the probability that the conclusion of* A *is* accepted *in the probabilistic logic program attached to* A.

An example is important here, so as to clarify the idea:

Example 5. *In Example 2, the probability of arguments* A_1 *and* A_3*, as well as the probability of arguments* A_2 *and* A_4*, is* 0.5*. The probability of arguments* A_5 *and* A_6 *is one; this makes sense because, if we view* **not** *as introducing assumptions in the argument, these assumptions should be taken to hold when looking at the argument in isolation. In fact, the atoms preceded by* **not** *behave as Toulmin's warrants — that is, as statements that should be accepted when evaluating an argument (Besnard and Hunter 2008). Finally, the probability of argument* A_7 *is zero; regardless of atom* A*, atom* E *cannot be* accepted*. Note that if we had simply erased atoms preceded by* **not***, we would obtain the rule* E :− A*. and the probability of* E *would then be* 0.5*. Thus it makes sense to take the whole logic program inside an argument while evaluating the probability of the argument: the program may reveal internal connections between atoms.* □

Similar ideas have been proposed for variants of ABAFs, for instance by taking the probability of premises (Hunter 2013) or of premises and conclusion (Prakken 2018).

To conclude, we note that the conditional probability of the conclusion given the premises has been studied in the literature (Timmer et al. 2017). Such a notion deserves attention if we allow rules themselves to be probabilistically fired, for instance by resorting to ProbLog's *probabilistic rules* (Fierens et al. 2014). Such a rule is written $\alpha :: H :- \mathbf{B}.$, where $\mathbf{B}$ denotes the body; it is syntactic sugar for a rule $H :- \mathbf{B}.$ and a fresh probabilistic fact $\alpha :: F.$ whose atom F does not appear anywhere. For instance, suppose we have the following logic program associated with an argument:

$$H :- G_1, G_2, G_3, \mathbf{not}\ G_4., \quad 0.5 :: G_1., \quad 0.5 :: G_2., \quad 0.5 :: G_3 :- G_5, \mathbf{not}\ G_6. \quad 0.5 :: G_5..$$

Then the probability of the argument is $(0.5)^4$, but the conditional probability of H given G_1, G_2, G_3, G_5 all accepted is 0.5. We might even condition on $\mathbf{not}\ G_4$, $\mathbf{not}\ G_6$, and this may be an avenue to pursue in the future. Here we take the position that the atoms preceded by $\mathbf{not}$ carry the warrants of the argument and thus must not be conditioned upon.

4 Conclusion

In this paper we have dealt with two interrelated issues: how to handle non-singleton/empty sets of stable models in probabilistic logic programming, and how to put together a practical and meaningful theory of probabilistic argumentation. These challenges are connected by the fact that probabilistic facts and rules can be used to build probabilistic arguments, and probabilistic argumentation has specific needs concerning absence of stable extensions. Our solution is to combine the credal semantics (for probabilistic facts) with the L-stable semantics (for logic programs).

We have introduced the L-credal semantics for logic programs. We derived the complexity of the inference problem in the propositional case, proving $\mathsf{PP}^{\Sigma_2^p}$-completeness. We conjecture that similar proofs can be used to prove $\mathsf{PP}^{\Sigma_3^p}$-completeness for the inference problem when predicates have bounded arity. This is our next step. Another future step is the development of inference algorithms, possibly by combining techniques for probabilistic and credal inference (Cozman and Mauá 2020; Fierens et al. 2014; Totis, Kimmig, and Raedt 2021).

We also contributed with a different route to Conclusion(Claim)-augmented Argumentation Frameworks, an extended version of Dung's AAFs that smoothly connect the semantics of logic programming and the semantics of argumentation. We obtained a connection between probabilistic logic programs and probabilistic argumentation that is important within the pipeline suggested by Figure 1.

Finally, we have proposed a definition for the probability of an argument. While a single concept does not seem to capture all the uncertainty carried by an argument, our proposal is a step forward that can be extended in future work.

Overall, we have addressed the conceptual foundation behind the pipeline in Figure 1; we know how to represent rules and probabilistic facts, and how to build, present and evaluate probabilistic arguments. Of course, we have captured only a fraction of logic programming and argumentation theory; much more work is due to capture various semantics, disjunctive heads and aggregates, supports, weights and preferences. We will focus on that in future work.

Acknowledgements

This work was carried out at the Center for Artificial Intelligence (C4AI-USP), with support by the São Paulo Research Foundation (FAPESP grant 2019/07665-4) and by the IBM Corporation. The first author is partially supported by the Coordenação de Aperfeiçoamento de Pessoal de Nível Superior - Brasil (CAPES) grant 88887.616392/2021-00. The second author was partially supported by CNPq grant 312180/2018-7. We acknowledge support by CAPES - Finance Code 001.

References

Augustin, T.; Coolen, F. P. A.; de Cooman, G.; and Troffaes, M. C. M. 2014. *Introduction to Imprecise Probabilities*. Wiley.

Baral, C.; Gelfond, M.; and Rushton, N. 2009. Probabilistic reasoning with answer sets. *Theory and Practice of Logic Programming* 9(1):57–144.

Baroni, P.; Giacomin, M.; and Vicig, P. 2014. On rationality conditions for epistemic probabilities in abstract argumentation. In *Computational Models of Argument*, 121–132.

Besnard, P., and Hunter, A. 2008. *Elements of Argumentation*. MIT Press.

Bondarenko, A.; Dung, P.; Kowalski, R.; and Toni, F. 1997. An abstract, argumentation-theoretic approach to default reasoning. *Artificial Intellligence* 93:63–101.

Caminada, M., and Schulz, C. 2017. On the equivalence between assumption-based argumentation and logic programming. *Journal of Artificial Intelligence Research* 60:779–825.

Caminada, M.; Sá, S.; ao Alcântara, J.; and Dvorak, W. 2015. On the equivalence between logic programming semantics and argumentation semantics. *International Journal of Approximate Reasoning* 58:87–111.

Ceylan, Í. Í.; Lukasiewicz, T.; and Peñaloza, R. 2016. Complexity results for probabilistic Datalog$^{\pm}$. In *European Conference on Artificial Intelligence*, 1414–1422.

Cozman, F. G., and Mauá, D. D. 2017. On the semantics and complexity of probabilistic logic programs. *Journal of Artificial Intelligence Research* 60:221–262.

Cozman, F. G., and Mauá, D. D. 2020. The joy of Probabilistic Answer Set Programming: Semantics, complexity, expressivity, inference. *International Journal of Approximate Reasoning* 125:218–239.

Dung, P. M., and Thang, P. M. 2010. Towards (probabilistic) argumentation for jury-based dispute resolution. In *Frontiers in Artificial Intelligence and Applications*, volume 216, 171–182. IOS Press.

Dung, P. M. 1995. On the acceptability of arguments and its fundamental role in nonmonotonic reasoning, logic programming and n-person games. *Artificial Intelligence* 77(2):321–357.

Dvorák, W., and Woltran, S. 2019. Complexity of abstract argumentation under a claim-centric view. *33rd AAAI Conference on Artificial Intelligence, AAAI 2019, 31st Innovative Applications of Artificial Intelligence Conference, IAAI 2019 and the 9th AAAI Symposium on Educational Advances in Artificial Intelligence, EAAI 2019* 2801–2808.

Dvořǎk, W. 2012. *Computational Aspects of Abstract Argumentation*. Ph.D. Dissertation, Fakultät für Informatik der Technischen Universität Wien.

Dvořák, W.; Rapberger, A.; and Woltran, S. 2020. Argumentation semantics under a claim-centric view: Properties, expressiveness and relation to SETAFs. *17th International Conference on Principles of Knowledge Representation and Reasoning, KR 2020* 1:340–349.

Eiter, T.; Ianni, G.; and Krennwalner, T. 2009. Answer set programming: a primer. In *Reasoning Web: Semantic Technologies for Information Systems*.

Eiter, T.; Leone, N.; and Saccá, D. 1998. Expressive power and complexity of partial models for disjunctive deductive databases. *Theoretical Computer Science* 206:181–218.

Fierens, D.; Van den Broeck, G.; Renkens, J.; Shrerionov, D.; Gutmann, B.; Janssens, G.; and De Raedt, L. 2014. Inference and learning in probabilistic logic programs using weighted Boolean formulas. *Theory and Practice of Logic Programming* 15(3):358–401.

Hadjichristodoulou, S., and Warren, D. S. 2012. Probabilistic logic programming with well-founded negation. In *International Symposium on Multiple-Valued Logic*, 232–237.

Haenni, R. 2001. Cost-bounded argumentation. *International Journal of Approximate Reasoning* 26:101–127.

Haenni, R. 2009. Probabilistic argumentation. *Journal of Applied Logic* 7:155–176.

Heyninck, J., and Strasser, C. 2016. Relations between assumption-based approaches in nonmonotonic logic and formal argumentation. In *International Workshop on Non-Monotonic Reasoning*.

Heyninck, J. 2019. Relations between assumption-based approaches in nonmonotonic logic and formal argumentation: from structured argumentation to adaptive logics. *Journal of Applied Logics – IfCoLog Journal of Logics and their Applications* 6(2):317–357.

Howson, C., and Urbach, P. 1993. *Scientific Reasoning: the Bayesian Approach*. Chicago, Illinois: Open Court Publishing Company.

Hung, N. D. 2017. Inference procedures and engine for probabilistic argumentation. *International Journal of Approximate Reasoning* 90:163–191.

Hunter, A.; Polberg, S.; Potyka, N.; Rienstra, T.; and Thimm, M. 2021. Probabilistic argumentation: A survey. In *Handbook of Formal Argumentation*, volume 2. College Publications.

Hunter, A.; Polberg, S.; and Thimm, M. 2020. Epistemic graphs for representing and reasoning with positive and negative influences of arguments. *Artificial Intelligence* 281:103236.

Hunter, A. 2013. A probabilistic approach to modelling uncertain logical arguments. *International Journal of Approximate Reasoning* 54:47–81.

Li, H.; Oren, N.; and Norman, T. J. 2011. Probabilistic argumentation frameworks. In *International Workshop on Theories and Applications of Formal Argumentation*, 1–16.

Lukasiewicz, T. 2005. Probabilistic description logic programs. In *European Conference on Symbolic and Quantitative Approaches to Reasoning with Uncertainty (ECSQARU 2005)*, 737–749. Barcelona, Spain: Springer.

Mantadelis, T., and Bistarelli, S. 2020. Probabilistic abstract argumentation frameworks, a possible world view. *International Journal of Approximate Reasoning* 119:204–219.

Modgil, S., and Prakken, H. 2014. The *ASPIC*$^+$ framework for structured argumentation: a tutorial. *Argument and Computation* 5(1):31–62.

Molchanov, I. 2005. *Theory of Random Sets*. Springer.

Papadimitriou, C. H. 1994. *Computational Complexity*. Addison-Wesley Publishing.

Poole, D. 2003. First-order probabilistic inference. In *International Joint Conference on Artificial Intelligence (IJCAI)*, 985–991.

Prakken, H. 2018. Probabilistic Strength of Arguments with Structure. In *International Conference on Principles of Knowledge Representation and Learning*, 158–167.

Rapberger, A. 2020. Defining argumentation semantics under a claim-centric view. In *CEUR Workshop Proceedings*, volume 2655. CEUR-WS.

Riveret, R.; Rotolo, A.; Sartor, G.; Prakken, H.; and Roth, B. 2007. Success chances in argument games: a probabilistic approach to legal disputes. In *Conference on Legal Knowledge and Information Systems*, 99–108.

Riveret, R.; Baroni, P.; Gao, Y.; Governatori, G.; Rotolo, A.; and Sartor, G. 2018. A labelling framework for probabilistic argumentation. *Annals of Mathematics and Artificial Intelligence* 83(1):21–71.

Sacca, D. 1997. The expressive powers of stable models for bound and unbound DATALOG queries. *J. Comput. System Sci.* 54(3):444–464.

Sato, T.; Kameya, Y.; and Zhou, N.-F. 2005. Generative modeling with failure in PRISM. In *International Joint Conference on Artificial Intelligence*, 847–852.

Sato, T. 1995. A statistical learning method for logic programs with distribution semantics. In *Conference on Logic Programming*, 715–729.

Thimm, M. 2012. A probabilistic semantics for abstract argumentation. In *European Conference on Artificial Intelligence (ECAI)*, 750–755.

Timmer, S. T.; Meyer, J.-J.; Prakken, H.; Renooij, S.; and Verheij, B. 2017. A two-phase method for extracting explanatory arguments from bayesian networks. *International Journal of Approximate Reasoning* 80:475–494.

Toni, F. 2014. A tutorial on assumption-based argumentation. *Argument and Computation* 5(1):89–117.

Totis, P.; Kimmig, A.; and Raedt, L. D. 2021. SMProbLog: Stable model semantics in ProbLog and its applications in argumentation. Technical Report arXiv:2110.01990, arXiv.

van Eemeren, F. H.; Garssen, B.; Krabbe, E. C. W.; Henkemans, A. F. S.; Verheij, B.; and Wagemans, J. H. M. 2014. *Handbook of Argumentation Theory*. Springer.

Čyras, K.; Heinrich, Q.; and Toni, F. 2021. Computational complexity of flat and generic assumption-based argumentation, with and without probabilities. *Artificial Intelligence* 293.

Wagner, K. W. 1986. The complexity of combinatorial problems with succinct input representation. *Acta Informatica* 23:325–356.

Walley, P. 1991. *Statistical Reasoning with Imprecise Probabilities*. London: Chapman and Hall.

On the Representation of Darwiche and Pearl's Epistemic States for Iterated Belief Revision

Nicolas Schwind[1] , **Sébastien Konieczny**[2] , **Ramón Pino Pérez**[2]
[1]National Institute of Advanced Industrial Science and Technology, Tokyo, Japan
[2]CRIL - CNRS, Université d'Artois, Lens, France
nicolas-schwind@aist.go.jp, {konieczny,pinoperez}@cril.fr

Abstract

The seminal characterization of iterated belief revision was proposed by Darwiche and Pearl, which uses an abstract notion of epistemic states. In this work we look for a canonical representation of these epistemic states. Total preorders are not expressive enough to be used as such a canonical representation. Actually, we show that some operators can even not be represented on a countable epistemic space. Nonetheless, under a very reasonable assumption on the epistemic space, we show that OCFs (Ordinal Conditional Functions) can be considered as a canonical representation.

1 Introduction

Belief revision is an important issue in many domains. In particular, if one wants to conceive a truly autonomous agent, it has to be able to revise incorrect information on its model of its environment.

The standard model for belief revision as been proposed by Alchourron, Gärdenfors and Makinson (Alchourrón, Gärdenfors, and Makinson 1985; Gärdenfors 1988; Fermé and Hansson 2011), and is called the AGM theory. This theory perfectly gives account of a one step revision, as attested by several representation theorems (Alchourrón, Gärdenfors, and Makinson 1985; Alchourrón and Makinson 1985; Katsuno and Mendelzon 1991; Grove 1988; Hansson 1994; del Cerro and Herzig 1996), showing that the AGM rationality postulates correspond exactly to the most sensible way to build revision operators. The close formal links between belief revision and non-monotonic inference relations (Makinson and Gärdenfors 1989; Gärdenfors 1990) on one side and possibilistic logic (Dubois and Prade 1991) on the other side, also prove that this theory adequatly captures this fundamental process.

Nonetheless, one weakness of the AGM theory is that it provides no constraint on sequences of revision, allowing several inadequate behaviors. This may be seen as a real problem, since any autonomous agent is typically expected to perform a large number of revisions during its activity.

To fill the gap, many papers aimed to identify the correct model for *iterated* belief revision, which was a very active topic during the nineties (Nayak 1994; Nayak et al. 1994; Nayak et al. 1996; Rott 2009). What is considered now as the most convincing approach for iterated belief revision was proposed by Darwiche and Pearl (1997), who introduced four additional postulates about successive revisions. Some extensions of this work have also been investigated (Booth and Meyer 2006; Jin and Thielscher 2007; Konieczny and Pino Pérez 2008; Konieczny, Medina Grespan, and Pino Pérez 2010).

While the AGM framework uses simple logical theories to represent an agent's epistemic state, the Darwiche and Pearl's framework requires more complex objects (Darwiche and Pearl 1994; Freund and Lehmann 1994; Lehmann 1995; Friedman and Halpern 1999). Indeed, if one needs not only to represent the current beliefs of an agent but also some information on the relative plausibility of currently disbelieved information, then this additional information has to be represented somewhere to guide the iterated revision process. Yet epistemic states, in Darwiche and Pearl's framework, are very abstract objects: we know very little about them, besides the fact that each epistemic state is associated with a logical formula that represents the current beliefs of an agent. This can be seen both as a strength and a weakness of the approach. One can see it as a weakness, because as opposed to the standard AGM case, the Darwiche and Pearl's representation theorem is not definitional: one can characterize the revised beliefs of the agent (the formula associated with the epistemic state), but not the whole epistemic state. One can also see it as a strength, because it is general enough to encompass all possible ways to practically encode the epistemic states.

The Darwiche and Pearl's representation theorem is an extension of the Katsuno and Mendelzon's one for AGM belief revision (Katsuno and Mendelzon 1991). It states that each epistemic state can be associated with a total preorder on propositional worlds, such that the new beliefs after revision of this epistemic state is obtained by selecting the most plausible models of the new piece of information w.r.t. this total preorder. It may then be tempting to identify the epistemic states and these total preorders on worlds: not only the representation theorem itself seems to suggest total preorders on worlds as a canonical representation, but they are also a very intuitive way to represent the relative plausibility of each formula. In fact, some works explicitly choose this representation for epistemic states (Booth and Meyer 2011; Ramachandran, Nayak, and Orgun 2012; Booth and Chandler 2016; Booth and Chandler 2019), and this is enough for a lot of applications.

But one has to be aware not to make a step further, by considering these total preorders to be *the* canonical representation of Darwiche and Pearl's epistemic states, and to restrict them to this case, as it is done in some works[1]. For instance, Aravanis *et. al* (2019) showed an example of a revision operator that can not be represented as functional transitions between total preorders, would those total preorders be the ones given by the Darwiche and Pearl's representation theorem. In this paper, we show without any further assumption that total preorders are not the canonical representation of Darwiche and Pearl's epistemic states via an example using ordinal conditional functions (OCFs), a well-known representation of epistemic states for belief change. Then, we investigate the extent to which a canonical representation can be found for these epistemic states. To do so, based on the work initiated in (Aravanis, Peppas, and Williams 2019; Schwind and Konieczny 2020), we make precise the condition under which a revision operator defined on a given epistemic space can be "instantiated" into another epistemic space. Would such a target epistemic space exist for every Darwiche and Pearl's revision operator, that epistemic space could be considered as an appropriate canonical representation of Darwiche and Pearl's epistemic states.

We start from the important remark that whatever the chosen representation, every epistemic state can be viewed as a black box associating each *finite* sequence of formulae with a formula representing the beliefs of the agent after the successive revision of the epistemic state by each formula from the sequence. Based on that observation, two epistemic states are *strongly equivalent* according to a revision operator if they cannot be distinguished from each other by any such successive revision steps, which means that these epistemic states have the same behavior for that revision operator. So the question now is whether one can find a canonical representation of the whole *quotient set* of epistemic states under this strong equivalence relation. We show that in general this is not possible. The number of possible (quotient set of) epistemic states is just too large. Nevertheless, we show that under the very natural assumption that every epistemic state is reachable from an initial, "empty", epistemic state, through a finite succession of revisions, OCFs are a possible candidate of canonical representation of epistemic states. This suggests that to encode all such possible epistemic states, what is missing in the total preorder representation is the additional numerical information OCFs accordingly provide.

2 Preliminaries

We consider a propositional language $\mathcal{L}_P$ built up from a finite set of propositional variables P and the usual connectives. The set of consistent formulae is denoted by $\mathcal{L}^*_P$. $\bot$ (resp. $\top$) is the Boolean constant always false (resp. true). An interpretation (or world) is a mapping from P to $\{0, 1\}$. The set of all worlds on $\mathcal{L}_P$ is denoted by Ω. $\models$ denotes logical entailment, $\equiv$ logical equivalence, and $[\varphi]$ denotes the set of models of the formula φ.

[1]See (Meng, Kou, and Li 2015) for instance.

In iterated belief change, it is standard to assume that the current set of beliefs of an agent is represented by an *epistemic state*. An epistemic state allows one to represent the current beliefs of the agent and some conditional information guiding the revision process. In all generality, an epistemic state can be any object Ψ from which the set of beliefs of the agent can be extracted through a mapping Bel, so that $Bel(\Psi)$ is a propositional formula from $\mathcal{L}_P$. Formally:

Definition 1 (Epistemic Space). *An* epistemic space $\mathcal{E}$ *is a tuple* $\langle E, Bel\rangle$, *where* E *is a set and* Bel *is a mapping* $Bel : E \to \mathcal{L}^*_P$.

We illustrate this concept with some basic epistemic spaces:

Example 1. *Let us define the* TPO*-based epistemic space*[2] *The* TPO-based epistemic space *is the epistemic space* $\mathcal{E}_{tpo} = \langle U_{tpo}, B_{tpo}\rangle$ *where:*

- U_{tpo} *is the set of all total preorders over the set of all worlds from* Ω*;*
- B_{tpo} *is the mapping associating each total preorder* $\preceq$ *from* U_{tpo} *with a formula* $\psi \in \mathcal{L}^*_P$ *such that* $[\psi] = \min([\top], \preceq)$.

The second example of epistemic space is built with the ordinal conditional functions (OCFs) (Spohn 1988; Williams 1995). An OCF κ is a function associating each world with a non-negative integer[3] such that there is a world ω such that $\kappa(\omega) = 0$.

Example 2. *The* OCF-based epistemic space *is the epistemic space* $\mathcal{E}_{ocf} = \langle U_{ocf}, B_{ocf}\rangle$ *where:*

- U_{ocf} *is the set of all* OCFs *over* Ω*;*
- B_{ocf} *is the mapping associating each* OCF κ *from* U_{ocf} *with a formula* ψ *such that* $[\psi] = \{\omega \mid \kappa(\omega) = 0\}$.

Given an epistemic space $\mathcal{E} = \langle E, Bel\rangle$, a belief revision operator $\circ$ on $\mathcal{E}$ associates every epistemic state Ψ from E and every consistent formula μ with a new epistemic state from E, denoted by $\Psi \circ \mu$, i.e, $\circ$ is a mapping $\circ : E \times \mathcal{L}^*_P \to E$. In the rest of the paper, when a revision operator $\circ$ will be referred to without the epistemic space on which it is defined, we will implicitely assume that $\circ$ is defined on some epistemic space denoted by $\mathcal{E} = \langle E, Bel\rangle$.

Let us recall the set of postulates which are expected for such operators to have a good iterative behavior (Darwiche and Pearl 1997):

Definition 2 (DP operator (Darwiche and Pearl 1997)). *A revision operator* $\circ$ *is a* DP operator *if the following properties are satisfied, for each epistemic state* Ψ *and all formulae* μ, μ'*:*

(R*1) $Bel(\Psi \circ \mu) \models \mu$*;*
(R*2) *If* $Bel(\Psi) \wedge \mu \not\models \bot$, *then* $Bel(\Psi \circ \mu) \equiv Bel(\Psi) \wedge \mu$*;*
(R*3) *If* $\mu \not\models \bot$, *then* $Bel(\Psi \circ \mu) \not\models \bot$*;*

[2]TPO stands for total preorder.

[3]Note that in the original definition (Spohn 1988) OCFs are defined on ordinals. But here, as in mosts cases, the integer restriction is enough. Note however than using the full power of ordinals can prove useful in some cases (Konieczny 2009).

(R*4) *If* $\mu \equiv \mu'$, *then* $Bel(\Psi \circ \mu) \equiv Bel(\Psi \circ \mu')$;
(R*5) $Bel(\Psi \circ \mu) \wedge \mu' \models Bel(\Psi \circ (\mu \wedge \mu'))$;
(R*6) *If* $Bel(\Psi \circ \mu) \wedge \mu' \not\models \bot$,
then $Bel(\Psi \circ (\mu \wedge \mu')) \models Bel(\Psi \circ \mu) \wedge \mu'$.
(C1) *If* $\alpha \models \mu$, *then* $Bel((\Psi \circ \mu) \circ \alpha) \equiv Bel(\Psi \circ \alpha)$
(C2) *If* $\alpha \models \neg\mu$, *then* $Bel((\Psi \circ \mu) \circ \alpha) \equiv Bel(\Psi \circ \alpha)$
(C3) *If* $Bel(\Psi \circ \alpha) \models \mu$, *then* $Bel((\Psi \circ \mu) \circ \alpha) \models \mu$
(C4) *If* $Bel(\Psi \circ \alpha) \not\models \neg\mu$, *then* $Bel((\Psi \circ \mu) \circ \alpha) \not\models \neg\mu$

The postulates **(R*1-R*6)** are a direct adaptation of the standard KM postulates to epistemic states. The remaining four postulates, **(C1-C4)**, add constraints w.r.t. iteration.

Darwiche and Pearl also provided a characterization of DP operators in terms of total preorders over worlds:

Definition 3 (Faithful assignment). *Given an epistemic space* $\mathcal{E} = \langle E, Bel \rangle$, *a mapping* $\Psi \mapsto \preceq_\Psi$ *associating each epistemic state* $\Psi \in E$ *with a total preorder*[4] *over worlds* $\preceq_\Psi$ *is a* faithful assignment (on $\mathcal{E}$) *if and only if for all worlds* $\omega, \omega' \in \Omega$:

1. *If* $\omega \models Bel(\Psi)$ *and* $\omega' \models Bel(\Psi)$, *then* $\omega \simeq_\Psi \omega'$
2. *If* $\omega \models Bel(\Psi)$ *and* $\omega' \not\models Bel(\Psi)$, *then* $\omega \prec_\Psi \omega'$

Theorem 1 ((Darwiche and Pearl 1997)). *An operator* $\circ$ *is a DP operator if and only if there exists a faithful assignment* $\Psi \mapsto \preceq_\Psi$ *that satisfies the following properties:*

CR1. *If* $\omega \models \mu$ *and* $\omega' \models \mu$, *then* $\omega \preceq_\Psi \omega' \Leftrightarrow \omega \preceq_{\Psi\circ\mu} \omega'$
CR2. *If* $\omega \not\models \mu$ *and* $\omega' \not\models \mu$, *then* $\omega \preceq_\Psi \omega' \Leftrightarrow \omega \preceq_{\Psi\circ\mu} \omega'$
CR3. *If* $\omega \models \mu$ *and* $\omega' \not\models \mu$, *then* $\omega \prec_\Psi \omega' \Rightarrow \omega \prec_{\Psi\circ\mu} \omega'$
CR4. *If* $\omega \models \mu$ *and* $\omega' \not\models \mu$, *then* $\omega \preceq_\Psi \omega' \Rightarrow \omega \preceq_{\Psi\circ\mu} \omega'$,

and such that for each epistemic state Ψ *and each formula* μ, $[Bel(\Psi \circ \mu)] = \min([\mu], \preceq_\Psi)$.

When a faithful assignment exists for $\circ$, we will call such a faithful assignment a *DP assignment corresponding to* $\circ$. As a matter of fact, when such assignment exists it is unique[5].

Conditions (CR1-CR4) above correspond to the iteration postulates **(C1-C4)**. They impose constraints on the total preorder $\preceq_{\Psi\circ\mu}$: CR1 and CR2, the "rigidity" conditions, say that the order between models of μ is preserved and the order between models of $\neg\mu$ is also preserved. CR3 and CR4 say that there is no worsening between the models of μ and the models of $\neg\mu$.

Theorem 1 has important applications. One of them is that, for some epistemic spaces, it allows to define some DP operators in a constructive way, for which the verification that they satisfy indeed the DP postulates is done almost trivially. Let us illustrate this through the following examples.

Example 3. *We consider the Boutilier's natural revision operator* $\circ_B$ *defined over the epistemic space* $\mathcal{E}_{tpo}$. *This operator associates each total preorder* $\Psi \in U_{tpo}$ *and each formula* μ *with a total preorder* $\Psi \circ_B \mu$ *that satisfies* $\min(\Psi \circ \mu) = \min([\mu], \Psi)$ *and the following condition:*

[4] For each preorder $\preceq$, $\simeq$ denotes the corresponding indifference relation, and $\prec$ the corresponding strict ordering.

[5] That is due to the fact that if an assignment satisfies $[Bel(\Psi \circ \mu)] = \min([\mu], \preceq_\Psi)$, then $\omega \preceq_\Psi \omega'$ iff $\omega \in [\Psi \circ \alpha_{\omega,\omega'}]$ (where $[\alpha_{\omega,\omega'}] = \{\omega, \omega'\}$), from which the unicity follows.

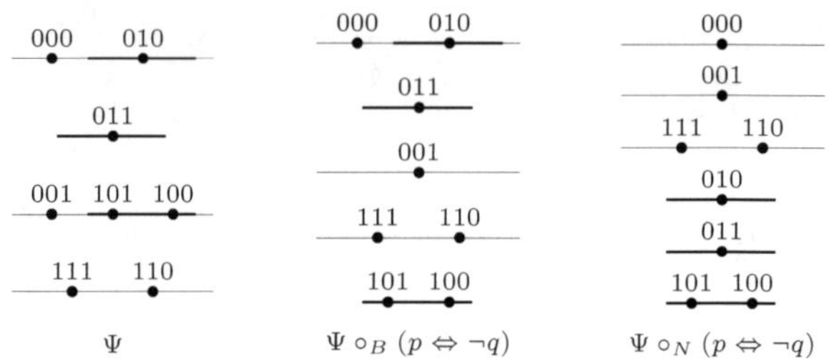

Figure 1: The Boutilier and Nayak operators.

B. *If* $\omega, \omega' \notin \min([\mu], \Psi)$, *then* $\omega \preceq_\Psi \omega' \Leftrightarrow \omega \preceq_{\Psi\circ_B\mu} \omega'$,

where $\preceq_\Psi$ *denotes* Ψ *and* $\preceq_{\Psi\circ_B\mu}$ *denotes* $\Psi \circ_B \mu$.

That is, Boutilier's revision operator on $\mathcal{E}_{tpo}$ consists in selecting the set of all models of μ that are minimal according to an input preorder, and defining this set as the first level of the revised preorder while leaving the rest of the preorder unchanged. This is a DP operator: one of the most easy ways to see that is to note that the assignment $\Psi \mapsto \Psi$ is a faithful assignment which satisfies the conditions (CR1-CR4), and that $\min(\Psi \circ \mu) = \min([\mu], \Psi)$. Then by Theorem 1, $\circ_B$ is a DP operator.

Example 4. *Another example is the Nayak's lexicographic operator* $\circ_N$ *defined also in the epistemic space* $\mathcal{E}_{tpo}$. *It is defined by* $\min(\Psi \circ \mu) = \min([\mu], \Psi)$, *conditions (CR1-CR4) and:*

N. *If* $\omega \models \mu$ *and* $\omega' \not\models \mu$, *then* $\omega \prec_{\Psi\circ_N\mu} \omega'$

Nayak's revision moves all models of μ below all models of $\neg\mu$, and keeps the relationships between worlds of μ (resp. of $\neg\mu$) unchanged. Using the same argument as in the previous example, one can see that this operator is also a DP operator.

Let us illustrate how the behaviors of Boutilier and Nayak revision operators depart from each other.

Example 5. *Let* $P = \{p, q, r\}$. *Figure 1 depicts a total preorder* Ψ *over worlds*[6] , *and the revised total preorders* $\Psi \circ_B (p \Leftrightarrow \neg q)$ *and* $\Psi \circ_N (p \Leftrightarrow \neg q)$. *We have that* $B_{tpo}(\Psi) \equiv p \wedge q$, *and* $B_{tpo}(\Psi \circ_B (p \Leftrightarrow \neg q) \equiv B_{tpo}(\Psi \circ_N (p \Leftrightarrow \neg q)) \equiv p \wedge \neg q$. *Then it is easy to see from the figure that:*

- $B_{tpo}(\Psi \circ_B (p \Leftrightarrow \neg q) \circ_B q \equiv p \wedge q$
- $B_{tpo}(\Psi \circ_N (p \Leftrightarrow \neg q) \circ_N q \equiv \neg p \wedge q \wedge r$,

i.e., $B_{tpo}(\Psi \circ_B (p \Leftrightarrow \neg q) \circ_B q \not\equiv B_{tpo}(\Psi \circ_N (p \Leftrightarrow \neg q) \circ_N q$.

The next example is an operator on the epistemic space of OCFs, that is, it is defined on $\mathcal{E}_{ocf}$.

Example 6. *Given an* OCF κ *and a formula* α, *we define* $\kappa(\alpha) = min\{n : \exists\omega \in [\alpha],\ \kappa(\omega) = n\}$.

Consider an OCF κ, *a formula* μ, *and an integer* x *such that* $x \geq 1$. *The* (μ, x)*-conditionalization (Spohn 1988) of* κ

[6] A world ω is at the same or at a lower level than a world ω' iff $\omega \leq_\Psi \omega'$. So minimal (i.e., most plausible) worlds are at the lowest levels.

is the OCF κ' *defined for each world* ω *by:*

$$\kappa'(\omega) = \begin{cases} \kappa(\omega) - \kappa(\mu) & \text{if } \omega \models \mu \\ \kappa(\omega) - \kappa(\neg\mu) + x & \text{if } \omega \not\models \mu \end{cases}$$

The operator $\circ_C$ *on* $\mathcal{E}_{ocf}$ *is defined for each* $\kappa \in U_{ocf}$ *and each* $\mu \in \mathcal{L}_P^*$ *by* $\kappa \circ_C \mu = \kappa'$*, where* κ' *is the* (μ, x)*-conditionalization of* κ*.*

Conditionalization was the first change operator proposed on OCFs (Spohn 1988) (see (Williams 1995) for a generalization and other operators on OCFs). The conditionalization of an OCF performs a (DP) revision under some conditions (if $x > 0$ and $\kappa(\mu) > 0$), but in the other cases we can obtain a contraction or a re-ordering. Please see Definition 7 in Section 4 for an example of a pure DP revision on OCFs.

The most commonly used epistemic spaces are $\mathcal{E}_{tpo}$ and $\mathcal{E}_{ocf}$. Their popularity can be explained by their simplicity and by the fact that the representation theorems for iterated change operators as (Darwiche and Pearl 1997; Booth and Meyer 2006; Konieczny and Pino Pérez 2008; Konieczny, Medina Grespan, and Pino Pérez 2010; Medina Grespan and Pino Pérez 2013) allow to define operators as transitions between states (cf. Example 3, 4 and 6. The choice of such epistemic spaces is for instance used in (Booth and Meyer 2011; Booth and Chandler 2019; Spohn 1988).

Before concluding this section, let us introduce a few notations that will be used in some subsequent proofs. Given a set E, $card(E)$ denotes the cardinality of E. Given any total preorder $\Psi \in U_{tpo}$ and any world ω, $rank(\Psi, \omega)$ denotes the rank of ω in Ψ. More precisely, $rank(\Psi, \omega) = k - 1$ when there is a chain $(\omega_1, \dots, \omega_k)$ of size k such that $\omega = \omega_k$ and for each i, j such that $i < j$, $\omega_i \prec \omega_j$ ($\prec$ denotes the strict ordering corresponding to Ψ), and such that no such chain of size k' with $k < k'$ exists. Then, given a non-negative integer i, $lvl(\Psi, i)$ denotes the set of models at the ith level in Ψ, i.e., $lvl(\Psi, i) = \{\omega \mid rank(\Psi, \omega) = i\}$, and $max(\Psi) = \max\{i \mid i \in \mathbb{N}, lvl(\Psi, i) \neq \emptyset\}$. Lastly, given an OCF $\kappa \in U_{ocf}$, $tpo(\kappa)$ denotes the total preorder associated with κ, i.e., $tpo(\kappa)$ is defined as the total preorder $\preceq$ where for all worlds ω, ω', $\omega \preceq \omega$ if and only if $\kappa(\omega) \leq \kappa(\omega')$.

3 Instantiability of Revision Operators

Each revision operator is defined on a given epistemic space, but can be equivalently defined on a different epistemic space. Intuitively, given two epistemic spaces $\mathcal{E} = \langle E, Bel\rangle$ and $\mathcal{I} = \langle U, B\rangle$, we say that a revision operator $\circ$ on $\mathcal{E}$ is "safely $\mathcal{I}$-instantiable" whenever one can find a revision operator $\circ_\mathcal{I}$ on $\mathcal{I}$ that has the same "behavior" as $\circ$, i.e., $\circ_\mathcal{I}$ models the same transitions between epistemic states from U as $\circ$ between those from $\mathcal{E}$, modulo the beliefs that can be observed from these epistemic states in the context of belief revision. The set of all epistemic states from E is mapped onto another set U, and B is used to associate with each mapped epistemic state from U its corresponding beliefs. Formally:

Definition 4 ((Safe) translation)**.** *Let* $\circ$ *be a revision operator on* $\mathcal{E} = \langle E, Bel\rangle$*, and let* $\mathcal{I} = \langle U, B\rangle$ *be an epistemic space. A* translation of $\circ$ into $\mathcal{I}$ *is a pair* $(f_\mathcal{E}, \circ_\mathcal{I})$*, where* $f_\mathcal{E}$ *is a mapping from* E *to* U *and* $\circ_\mathcal{I}$ *is a revision operator on* I *such that for each* $\Psi \in \mathcal{E}$*,* $Bel(\Psi) \equiv B(f_\mathcal{E}(\Psi))$*, and for each* $\Psi \in E$ *and each* $\mu \in \mathcal{L}_P^*$*,* $f_\mathcal{E}(\Psi \circ \mu) = f_\mathcal{E}(\Psi) \circ_\mathcal{I} \mu$*. Such a translation is said to be* safe *if there exists a mapping* $h_I : U \to E$ *such that* $(h_I, \circ)$ *is a translation of* $\circ_\mathcal{I}$ *into* $\mathcal{E}$*.*

When a such a (safe) translation exists we say that $\circ$ *is (safely)* $\mathcal{I}$*-instantiable.*

Note that the notion of translation is close to the notions of simulation in (Aravanis, Peppas, and Williams 2019) and of instantiation in (Schwind and Konieczny 2020). We intend now to explain why safe translations are of particular interest. Let $\mathcal{I} = (U, B)$, $\mathcal{I}' = (U', B')$ be two epistemic spaces, let $\circ_\mathcal{I}$ be a revision operator on $\mathcal{I}$ and $\circ_{\mathcal{I}'}$ be a revision operator on $\mathcal{I}'$. Given $\Psi \in U$ and $\Psi' \in U'$, we say that Ψ is *strongly equivalent*[7] to Ψ' w.r.t. $(\circ_\mathcal{I}, \circ_{\mathcal{I}'})$, denoted by $\Psi \equiv_{(\circ_\mathcal{I}, \circ_{\mathcal{I}'})} \Psi'$, if $B(\Psi) \equiv B'(\Psi')$ and for each finite sequence of formulae $\sigma = (\mu_1, \dots, \mu_k)$ with $k \geq 1$, $B(\Psi \circ_\mathcal{I} \sigma) \equiv B'(\Psi' \circ_{\mathcal{I}'} \sigma)$.

In the particular case where $\mathcal{I} = \mathcal{I}'$ and $\circ_\mathcal{I} = \circ_{\mathcal{I}'} = \circ$, we simply say that Ψ and Ψ' are strongly equivalent w.r.t. $\circ$ and simplify the notation $\Psi \equiv_{(\circ_\mathcal{I}, \circ_{\mathcal{I}'})} \Psi'$ into $\Psi \equiv_\circ \Psi'$. Then given a revision operator $\circ$ on $\mathcal{I} = (U, B)$, we denote by $U_{\equiv_\circ}$ the the quotient of U by the equivalence relation $\equiv_\circ$. That is, if $(\Psi)_{\equiv_\circ}$ denotes the equivalence class[8] of Ψ, then $U_{\equiv_\circ} = \{(\Psi)_{\equiv_\circ} \mid \Psi \in U\}$.

The notion of strong equivalence between epistemic states is very important. Indeed, each epistemic state, whatever the epistemic space to which it belongs, can actually be seen as a black box that associates each finite sequence of formulae with a formula representing the beliefs of the agent. And even if epistemic states may contain more complex information, this additional information does not have any further impact in the iterated revision process. That is, if two epistemic states have the same behavior for any Darwiche and Pearl's iterated revision, then they can not be distinguished from one another in this context, and in that case they belong to the same equivalence class.

Let us now use the notion of strong equivalence between epistemic states to define the notion of equivalence between two operators defined on two different epistemic spaces:

Definition 5. *Let* $\mathcal{I} = (U, B)$ *and* $\mathcal{I}' = (U', B')$ *be two epistemic spaces,* $\circ_\mathcal{I}$ *be a revision operator on* $\mathcal{I}$*, and* $\circ_{\mathcal{I}'}$ *be a revision operator on* $\mathcal{I}'$*. We say that* $\circ_\mathcal{I}$ *and* $\circ_{\mathcal{I}'}$ *are* equivalent *if there is a one-to-one and onto correspondence* g *from* $U_{\equiv_{\circ_\mathcal{I}}}$ *to* $U'_{\equiv_{\circ_{\mathcal{I}'}}}$ *such that for each* $V \in U_{\equiv_{\circ_\mathcal{I}}}$ *and for all* $\Psi \in V$*,* $\Psi' \in g(V)$*, we have that* $\Psi \equiv_{(\circ_\mathcal{I}, \circ_{\mathcal{I}'})} \Psi'$*.*

Let us state an important lemma:

Lemma 1. *Let* $\circ$ *be a revision operator,* $\mathcal{I} = (U, B)$ *be an epistemic space, and* $(f_\mathcal{E}, \circ_\mathcal{I})$ *be a translation of* $\circ$ *into* $\mathcal{I}$*. Then for each* $\Psi \in E$*, we have that* $\Psi \equiv_{(\circ, \circ_\mathcal{I})} f_\mathcal{E}(\Psi)$*.*

[7] In standard DP papers, two epistemic states are said to be equivalent iff $B(\Psi) \equiv B(\Psi')$. This is why we call this notion strong equivalence. Note that a similar distinction was made in (Konieczny and Pino Pérez 2000).

[8] $(\Psi)_{\equiv_\circ} = \{\Psi' \in U \mid \Psi' \equiv_\circ \Psi\}$

Proof. Let $\Psi \in E$. First, by definition of $f_{\mathcal{E}}$ we get that $Bel(\Psi) \equiv B(f_{\mathcal{E}}(\Psi))$. Second, for each sequence of formulae $\sigma = (\mu_1, \ldots, \mu_k)$, $k \geq 1$, we know that $Bel(\Psi \circ \sigma) \equiv B(f_{\mathcal{E}}(\Psi \circ \sigma))$. Since $f_{\mathcal{E}}(\Psi \circ \mu) = f_{\mathcal{E}}(\Psi) \circ_{\mathcal{I}} \mu$ for any formula μ, it is easy to see, by induction, that $f_{\mathcal{E}}(\Psi \circ \sigma) = f_{\mathcal{E}}(\Psi) \circ_{\mathcal{I}} \sigma$, thus $Bel(\Psi \circ \sigma) \equiv B(f_{\mathcal{E}}(\Psi) \circ_{\mathcal{I}} \sigma)$. This shows that $\Psi \equiv_{(\circ,\circ_{\mathcal{I}})} f_{\mathcal{E}}(\Psi)$. □

Taking advantage of Lemma 1, we are ready to make clear why the notion of safe translation is of particular interest:

Proposition 1. *Let $\circ$ be a revision operator and $\mathcal{I} = (U, B)$ be an epistemic space. If $(f_{\mathcal{E}}, \circ_{\mathcal{I}})$ is a safe translation of $\circ$ into $\mathcal{I}$, then $\circ$ and $\circ_{\mathcal{I}}$ are equivalent.*

Proof. Let $\circ$ be a revision operator on $\mathcal{E} = (E, Bel)$, $\mathcal{I} = (U, B)$ be an epistemic space, and $(f_{\mathcal{E}}, \circ_{\mathcal{I}})$ be a safe translation of $\circ$ into $\mathcal{I}$. For each $(\Psi)_{\equiv_\circ} \in E_{\equiv_\circ}$, let g be the mapping $(\Psi)_{\equiv_\circ} \mapsto (f_{\mathcal{E}}(\Psi))_{\equiv_{\circ_{\mathcal{I}}}}$. From Lemma 1, it is easy to see that g is well defined and defines an injective mapping from $E_{\equiv_\circ}$ to $U_{\equiv_{\circ_{\mathcal{I}}}}$, and we directly get for each $(\Psi)_{\equiv_\circ} \in E_{\equiv_\circ}$ and for all $\Psi_1 \in (\Psi)_{\equiv_\circ}$, $\Psi_2 \in (f_{\mathcal{E}}(\Psi))_{\equiv_{\circ_{\mathcal{I}}}}$, that $\Psi_1 \equiv_{(\circ,\circ_{\mathcal{I}})} \Psi_2$. Since $(f_{\mathcal{E}}, \circ_{\mathcal{I}})$ is safe, there is a mapping $h_{\mathcal{I}} : U \rightarrow E$ such that $(h_{\mathcal{I}}, \circ)$ is a translation of $\circ_{\mathcal{I}}$ into $\mathcal{E}$. Then, similar to g, let us define the function g', mapping each $(\Psi')_{\equiv_{\circ_{\mathcal{I}}}} \in U_{\equiv_{\circ_{\mathcal{I}}}}$ into $(h_{\mathcal{I}}(\Psi'))_{\equiv_\circ}$. From Lemma 1 again, g' defines an injective mapping from $U_{\equiv_{\circ_{\mathcal{I}}}}$ to $E_{\equiv_\circ}$, and it is easy to verify that for each $(\Psi)_{\equiv_\circ} \in E_{\equiv_\circ}$ and for each$(\Psi')_{\equiv_{\circ_{\mathcal{I}}}} \in U_{\equiv_{\circ_{\mathcal{I}}}}$ we have $g'(g((\Psi)_{\equiv_\circ})) = (\Psi)_{\equiv_\circ}$ and $g(g'((\Psi')_{\equiv_{\circ_{\mathcal{I}}}})) = (\Psi')_{\equiv_{\circ_{\mathcal{I}}}}$. Thus, g is a one-to-one and onto correspondence from $E_{\equiv_\circ}$ to $U_{\equiv_{\circ_{\mathcal{I}}}}$. Therefore, g satisfies the requirements of Definition 5, which means that $\circ$ and $\circ_{\mathcal{I}}$ are equivalent. □

We have also the following result:

Proposition 2. *If a revision operator $\circ$ is not $\mathcal{I}$-instantiable, then there is no revision operator on $\mathcal{I}$ equivalent to $\circ$.*

Proof. We prove the contrapositive of the statement. Let $\circ$ be a revision operator, $\mathcal{I} = (U, B)$ be an epistemic space, and let $\circ_{\mathcal{I}}$ be an operator on $\mathcal{I}$ that is equivalent to $\circ$. So there is a bijection $g : E_{\equiv_\circ} \rightarrow U_{\equiv_{\circ_{\mathcal{I}}}}$ such that for each $F \in E_{\equiv_\circ}$, each $\Psi \in F$ and each $\Psi' \in g(F)$, $\Psi \equiv_{(\circ,\circ_{\mathcal{I}})} \Psi'$. First, let $\delta_U : U_{\equiv_{\circ_{\mathcal{I}}}} \rightarrow U$ be a mapping associating every equivalence class $F \in U_{\equiv_{\circ_{\mathcal{I}}}}$ with an arbitrary chosen epistemic state from F, in particular, if $\delta_U(V) = \Psi$, then $V = (\Psi)_{\equiv_{\circ_{\mathcal{I}}}}$. Define now the revision operator $\circ'_{\mathcal{I}}$ on $\mathcal{I}$ for each $\Psi \in U$ and each $\mu \in \mathcal{L}^*_P$ by $\Psi \circ'_{\mathcal{I}} \mu = \delta_U((\Psi \circ_{\mathcal{I}} \mu)_{\equiv_{\circ_{\mathcal{I}}}})$. Obviously enough, $\circ'_{\mathcal{I}}$ is equivalent to $\circ_{\mathcal{I}}$, thus $\circ'_{\mathcal{I}}$ is equivalent to $\circ$. Now, define $f_{\mathcal{E}} : E \rightarrow U$ for each $\Psi \in E$ as $f_{\mathcal{E}}(\Psi) = \delta_U(g((\Psi)_{\equiv_\circ}))$. It is easy to see for each $\Psi \in E$ that $Bel(\Psi) \equiv B(f_{\mathcal{E}}(\Psi))$. And for each $\Psi \in \mathcal{E}$ and each $\mu \in \mathcal{L}^*_P$, $f_{\mathcal{E}}(\Psi) \circ'_{\mathcal{I}} \mu = \delta_U(g((\Psi)_{\equiv_\circ})) \circ'_{\mathcal{I}} \mu = \delta_U((\delta_U(g((\Psi)_{\equiv_\circ})) \circ_{\mathcal{I}} \mu)_{\equiv_{\circ_{\mathcal{I}}}}) = \delta_U(g((\Psi \circ \mu)_{\equiv_\circ})) = f_{\mathcal{E}}(\Psi \circ \mu)$. This shows that $(f_{\mathcal{E}}, \circ'_{\mathcal{I}})$ is a translation of $\circ$ into $\mathcal{I}$, i.e., $\circ$ is $\mathcal{I}$-instantiable. □

Propositions 1 and 2 show why the notion of (safe) instantiability is a key concept: (safe) $\mathcal{I}$-instantiability it is a (sufficient and) necessary condition for defining an operator equivalent to $\circ$ in the space $\mathcal{I}$.

Another important consequence of Lemma 1 is the following:

Proposition 3. *Let $\circ$ be a revision operator and $\mathcal{I} = (U, B)$ be an epistemic space. If $\circ$ is $\mathcal{I}$-instantiable, then $card(E_{\equiv_\circ}) \leq card(U)$.*

Proof. Let $\circ$ be a revision operator and $\mathcal{I} = (U, B)$ be an epistemic space. Assume that $\circ$ is $\mathcal{I}$-instantiable, and let $(f_{\mathcal{E}}, \circ_{\mathcal{I}})$ be a translation of $\circ$ into $\mathcal{I}$. So let $\Psi, \Psi' \in E$ and assume that $\Psi \not\equiv_\circ \Psi'$. From Lemma 1, we know that $f_{\mathcal{E}}(\Psi) \not\equiv f_{\mathcal{E}}(\Psi')$, thus $f_{\mathcal{E}}(\Psi) \neq f_{\mathcal{E}}(\Psi')$. This means that there is an injective mapping from $\mathcal{E}_{\equiv_\circ}$ to U. Hence, $card(E_{\equiv_\circ}) \leq card(U)$. □

This result is quite intuitive: in order to be used as an appropriate space for defining an operator equivalent to a given operator $\circ$, an epistemic space has to be "large enough" to encode all the equivalence classes (w.r.t. $\circ$) of epistemic states in the initial epistemic space. This point is important for our subsequent results.

4 TPO vs OCF

In this section, we investigate the links between the TPO and OCF epistemic spaces. We start by defining the notion of "structure preservation", in order to work with epistemic states that are closely related to the total preorders obtained by the representation theorem. Then we show how to find for every operator on the TPO epistemic space an equivalent operator on the OCF epistemic space. Lastly, we show that a converse translation is not possible.

A very interesting feature of operators defined in the spaces $\mathcal{E}_{tpo}$ and $\mathcal{E}_{ocf}$ is that they are typically built using the ordered structure of the epistemic states in a natural way. For instance, the DP assignment corresponding to the operators in Examples 3 and 4 is the identity, and the one corresponding to the operator on $\mathcal{E}_{ocf}$ introduced later in Definition 7 is "almost" the identity. An appealing property of an operator defined on $\mathcal{E}_{tpo}$ or $\mathcal{E}_{ocf}$ is thus to preserve the internal ordered structure of their epistemic states according to its corresponding assignment. Let us formalize this property:

Definition 6. *Let $\circ$ be a DP operator defined on $\mathcal{E}_{tpo}$ and $\Psi \mapsto \preceq_\Psi$ be the DP assignment corresponding to $\circ$. We say that $\circ$ is* structure preserving *if for each $\Psi \in U_{tpo}$, $\Psi = \preceq_\Psi$. Likewise, let $\circ$ be a DP operator defined on $\mathcal{E}_{ocf}$ and $\kappa \mapsto \preceq_\kappa$ be the DP assignment corresponding to $\circ$. We say that $\circ$ is* structure preserving *if for each $\kappa \in U_{ocf}$, $tpo(\kappa) = \preceq_\kappa$.*

One can wonder if there exist DP operators that are not structure preserving. The following example shows an operator defined on $\mathcal{E}_{tpo}$ which is not structuring preserving.

Example 7. *Consider a propositional language with two propositional variables. Thus, there are four interpretations ω_1, ω_2, ω_3 and ω_4. Let $\circ_N$ be the Nayak operator on $\mathcal{E}_{tpo}$. Consider the two following total preorders: Ψ_1 defined by $\omega_1 \sim \omega_2 \prec \omega_3 \prec \omega_4$ and Ψ_2 defined by $\omega_1 \sim \omega_2 \prec \omega_4 \prec$*

ω_3. Clearly $\Psi_1 \neq \Psi_2$ and $B_{tpo}(\Psi_1) \equiv B_{tpo}(\Psi_2)$. Now, define a new operator $\star$ as follows:

$$\Psi \star \mu = \begin{cases} \Psi_2 \circ_N \mu & \text{if } \Psi = \Psi_1 \\ \Psi_1 \circ_N \mu & \text{if } \Psi = \Psi_2 \\ \Psi \circ_N \mu, & \text{otherwise} \end{cases}$$

It is easy to see that $\star$ is a DP operator and, moreover, $\Psi_1 = \preceq^{\star}_{\Psi_2}$. Therefore $\star$ is not structure preserving.

However, we can show that:

Proposition 4. *An operator $\circ$ on $\mathcal{E}_{tpo}$ is a DP operator if and only if there is a structure preserving DP operator $\circ'$ on $\mathcal{E}_{tpo}$ that is equivalent to $\circ$.*

Proof. The (if) part of the proof is direct: since $\circ'$ is equivalent to $\circ$ and $\circ'$ is a DP operator, $\circ$ is a DP operator as well. Let us prove the (only if) part of the proof. Let $\circ$ be a DP operator. Let τ denote the faithful assignment corresponding to $\circ$ (recall that it is unique), and let us first show that τ is a one-to-one-correspondence on U_{tpo}. It is enough to prove that τ is surjective. In the following, $\tau(\Psi)$ will sometimes be denoted by $\preceq_\Psi$.

Let us start with a useful observation. Let $\Psi \in U_{tpo}$ and α be a formula such that $[\alpha] \subseteq lvl(\preceq_\Psi, max(\preceq_\Psi))$, i.e., α is a formula whose models lie at the last level of $\preceq_\Psi$. Then from the representation theorem (Theorem 1) and condition CR2, the total preorder $\preceq_{\Psi\circ\alpha}$ is uniquely defined by:

- if $\omega, \omega' \models \alpha$, then $\omega \preceq_{\Psi\circ\alpha} \omega'$
- if $\omega \models \alpha, \omega' \not\models \alpha$, then $\omega \prec_{\Psi\circ\alpha} \omega'$
- if $\omega, \omega' \not\models \alpha$, then $\omega \preceq_{\Psi\circ\alpha} \omega'$ iff $\omega \preceq_\Psi \omega'$

From this observation, we can show that every total preorder $\preceq$ corresponds to $\tau(\Psi)$ from some $\Psi \in U_{tpo}$. Indeed, let $\preceq$ be any total preorder from U_{tpo}, let $\Psi_\top \in U_{tpo}$ be such that $B_{tpo}(\Psi_\top) \equiv \top$ (note that $\preceq_{\Psi_\top}$ is always the "flat" total preorder defined for all worlds ω, ω' by $\omega \simeq_{\Psi_\top} \omega'$), and let $\sigma = (\alpha_1, \ldots, \alpha_{max(\preceq)})$ be a sequence of formulae such that for each α_i, $[\alpha_i] = lvl(\preceq, max(\preceq) - i)$. It is easy to see from the observation above that $\tau(\Psi_\top \circ \sigma) = \preceq$. This shows that τ is surjective, so it is a one-to-one correspondence.

Now, let us consider the operator $\circ'$ on $\mathcal{E}_{tpo}$ defined for each $\Psi \in U_{tpo}$ and each $\mu \in \mathcal{L}^*_P$ by $\Psi \circ' \mu = \tau(\tau^{-1}(\Psi) \circ \mu)$, and let us show that $(\tau, \circ')$ is a safe translation of $\circ$ into $\mathcal{E}_{tpo}$. Let $\Psi \in U_{tpo}$ and $\mu \in \mathcal{L}^*_P$. The fact that $B_{tpo}(\Psi) \equiv B_{tpo}(\tau(\Psi))$ is direct from the representation theorem (cf. Theorem 1) and conditions 1 and 2 of a faithful assignment. Yet we also have that $\tau(\Psi) \circ' \mu = \tau(\tau^{-1}(\tau(\Psi)) \circ \mu) = \tau(\Psi \circ \mu)$. This shows that $(\tau, \circ')$ is a translation of $\circ$ into $\mathcal{E}_{tpo}$. To show that $(\tau, \circ')$ is safe, it is enough to remark that $(\tau^{-1}, \circ)$ is a translation of $\circ'$ into $\mathcal{E}_{tpo}$, since $B_{tpo}(\Psi) \equiv B_{tpo}(\tau^{-1}(\Psi))$ and $\tau^{-1}(\Psi \circ' \mu) \equiv \tau^{-1}(\tau(\tau^{-1}(\Psi) \circ \mu)) = \tau^{-1}(\Psi) \circ \mu$.

Since $(\tau, \circ')$ is a safe translation of $\circ$ into $\mathcal{E}_{tpo}$, from Proposition 1 we get that $\circ$ and $\circ'$ are equivalent, which concludes the proof. □

This result is very important, since it means that we can always assume to work with structure preserving operators for any DP operator on $\mathcal{E}_{tpo}$.

Now, let us show that every revision operator on $\mathcal{E}_{tpo}$ is safely $\mathcal{E}_{ocf}$-instantiable. Let $\circ$ be any revision operator on $\mathcal{E}_{tpo}$. Let $f_{\mathcal{E}_{tpo}}$ be the mapping from U_{tpo} to U_{ocf} defined for each $\Psi \in U_{tpo}$ by $f_{\mathcal{E}_{tpo}}(\Psi) = \kappa_\Psi$, where κ_Ψ is the OCF defined for each world ω by $\kappa_\Psi(\omega) = rank(\Psi, \omega)$. Now, let us define a revision operator $\circ_{\mathcal{E}_{ocf}}$ on $\mathcal{E}_{ocf}$ for each $\kappa \in U_{ocf}$ and each $\mu \in \mathcal{L}^*_P$ as $\kappa \circ_{\mathcal{E}_{ocf}} \mu = f_{\mathcal{E}_{tpo}}(tpo(\kappa) \circ \mu)$. Then:

Proposition 5. *$(f_{\mathcal{E}_{tpo}}, \circ_{\mathcal{E}_{ocf}})$ is a safe translation of $\circ$ into $\mathcal{E}_{ocf}$.*

Proof. First, it is easy to see that for each $\Psi \in B_{tpo}$, we have that $B_{tpo}(\Psi) = B_{ocf}(\kappa_\Psi)$. Then, remark that for each $\Psi \in U_{tpo}$, by construction of κ_Ψ we get that $tpo(\kappa_\Psi) = \Psi$. Thus for each $\Psi \in U_{tpo}$ and each $\mu \in \mathcal{L}^*_P$ we get that $f_{\mathcal{E}_{tpo}}(\Psi) \circ_{\mathcal{E}_{ocf}} \mu = \kappa_\Psi \circ_{\mathcal{E}_{ocf}} \mu = f_{\mathcal{E}_{tpo}}(tpo(\kappa_\Psi) \circ \mu) = f_{\mathcal{E}_{tpo}}(\Psi \circ \mu)$. This shows that $(f_{\mathcal{E}_{tpo}}, \circ_{\mathcal{E}_{ocf}})$ is a translation of $\circ$ into $\mathcal{E}_{ocf}$.

To see that this is also a safe translation, simply consider the mapping $h_{\mathcal{E}_{ocf}} : U_{ocf} \to U_{tpo}$ defined for each $\kappa \in U_{ocf}$ as $h_{\mathcal{E}_{ocf}}(\kappa) = tpo(\kappa)$. On the one hand, it is easy to see that $B_{ocf}(\kappa) \equiv B_{tpo}(h_{\mathcal{E}_{ocf}}(\kappa))$. On the other hand, remark that for each $\Psi \in U_{tpo}$, $h_{\mathcal{E}_{ocf}}(f_{\mathcal{E}_{tpo}}(\Psi)) = tpo(\kappa_\Psi) = \Psi$. Hence, we get for each $\kappa \in U_{ocf}$ and each $\mu \in \mathcal{L}^*_P$ that $h_{\mathcal{E}_{ocf}}(\kappa \circ_{\mathcal{E}_{ocf}} \mu) = h_{\mathcal{E}_{ocf}}(f_{\mathcal{E}_{tpo}}(tpo(\kappa) \circ \mu)) = tpo(\kappa) \circ \mu = h_{\mathcal{E}_{ocf}}(\kappa) \circ \mu$. This shows that $(h_{\mathcal{E}_{ocf}}, \circ)$ is a translation of $\circ_{\mathcal{E}_{ocf}}$ into U_{tpo}, which proves that $(f_{\mathcal{E}_{tpo}}, \circ_{\mathcal{E}_{ocf}})$ is a safe translation of $\circ$ into $\mathcal{E}_{ocf}$. □

We call the pair $(f_{\mathcal{E}_{tpo}}, \circ_{\mathcal{E}_{ocf}})$ the *canonical* translation of $\circ$ into $\mathcal{E}_{ocf}$.

A particular consequence of Proposition 5 is that every revision operator $\circ$ on $\mathcal{E}_{tpo}$ is safely $\mathcal{E}_{ocf}$-instantiable. Moreover, it is easy to see by construction of $\circ_{\mathcal{E}_{ocf}}$ that if $\circ$ is a structure preserving DP operator, then $\circ_{\mathcal{E}_{ocf}}$ is also structure preserving. Hence, a direct consequence of Propositions 4 and 5 is that:

Corollary 1. *For every DP operator $\circ$ on $\mathcal{E}_{tpo}$, there is an operator on $\mathcal{E}_{ocf}$ equivalent to $\circ$ that is structure preserving.*

So we can encode any DP revision defined on TPOs into the OCF epistemic space by a structure preserving operator. Let us now show that the converse translation is not possible, by providing an example of operator that is defined on OCFs and that is not $\mathcal{E}_{tpo}$-instantiable.

Definition 7. *Let $\bullet_+$ be the revision operator on $\mathcal{E}_{ocf}$ defined for each $\kappa \in U_{ocf}$ and each $\mu \in \mathcal{L}^*_P$ by $\kappa' = \kappa \bullet_+ \mu$, where for each world $\omega \in \Omega$, $\kappa'(\omega)$ is defined by:*

$$\kappa'(\omega) = \begin{cases} 0 & \text{if } \omega \models \mu \text{ and } \kappa(\omega) = \kappa(\mu) \\ \kappa(\omega) & \text{if } \omega \models \mu \text{ and } \kappa(\omega) > \kappa(\mu) \\ \kappa(\omega) + 1 & \text{if } \omega \not\models \mu \end{cases}$$

This operator can be related with the $\bullet$ operator proposed by Darwiche and Pearl to illustrate their DP postulates (Darwiche and Pearl 1997), since $\bullet$ and $\bullet_+$ deal with the countermodels of μ in a similar way. However, $\bullet_+$ depart from $\bullet$ in its treatment of the models of μ that do not move (except in the case where they are the minimal ones).

First, please observe that :

Proposition 6. *$\bullet_+$ is a DP revision operator.*

Proof. Let τ be the mapping from U_{ocf} to U_{tpo} defined for each $\kappa \in U_{ocf}$ by $\tau(\kappa) = tpo(\kappa)$. The fact that $\bullet_+$ is a DP operator is shown as follows: one can easily observe by definition of $\bullet_+$ that τ satisfies conditions 1 and 2 of a faithful assignment and conditions (CR1-CR4) of Theorem 1, and for each $\kappa \in U_{ocf}$ and each $\mu \in \mathcal{L}_P^*$, $[B_{ocf}(\kappa \bullet_+ \mu)] = \min([\mu], tpo(\kappa))$. That is, τ defines a DP assignment corresponding to $\bullet_+$, which from Theorem 1 shows that $\bullet_+$ is a DP operator. □

Let us illustrate the behavior of this operator through the following example:

Example 8. *Let $P = \{p, q\}$, and consider the two* OCFs κ *and π defined by:*[9]
$\kappa(00) = 0$ $\kappa(01) = 1$ $\kappa(10) = 1$ $\kappa(11) = 2$
$\pi(00) = 0$ $\pi(01) = 1$ $\pi(10) = 1$ $\pi(11) = 4$
Then $\kappa \bullet_+ p = \kappa_1$, $\pi \bullet_+ p = \pi_1$, $\pi_1 \bullet_+ p = \pi_2$, $\pi_2 \bullet_+ p = \pi_3$, as illustrated in Figure 2.[10]

Note that $\bullet_+$ is structure preserving, so its corresponding faithful assignment associates κ and π with the same total preorder $\preceq$. Would $\bullet_+$ be safely $\mathcal{E}_{tpo}$-instantiable, Propositions 1 and 4 together show that there would be a structure preserving operator on $\mathcal{E}_{tpo}$ that is equivalent to $\bullet_+$, and so κ and π would be translated to the same total preorder. But this example shows that this can not be the case, since $B_{ocf}((\kappa \bullet_+ p) \bullet_+ q) \not\equiv B_{ocf}((\pi \bullet_+ p) \bullet_+ q)$, and so κ and π are not strongly equivalent. Similarly, one can remark that the TPO translated from π_1 and π_2 should be exactly the same, but $B_{ocf}((\pi_1 \bullet_+ p) \bullet_+ q) \not\equiv B_{ocf}((\pi_2 \bullet_+ p) \bullet_+ q)$.

This example is enough to conclude that $\bullet_+$ is not safely $\mathcal{E}_{tpo}$-instantiable, but let us give a more general result:

Proposition 7. *$U_{ocf,\equiv_{\bullet_+}}$ is countably infinite.*

Proof. Without loss of generality, assume that $\mathcal{L}_P$ is such that $|P| \geq 2$. Let $\omega_1, \omega_2, \omega_3$ be three distinct worlds from Ω. Since U_{ocf} is a countable set, $U_{ocf,\equiv_{\bullet_+}}$ is a countable set. Let $\mathbb{N}_*$ denotes the set of positive integers. To conclude the proof that $U_{ocf,\equiv_{\bullet_+}}$ is countably *infinite*, since $\mathbb{N}_*$ is infinite it is enough to build an injective mapping τ from $\mathbb{N}_*$ to $U_{ocf,\equiv_{\bullet_+}}$. So let us define $\tau : \mathbb{N}_* \to U_{ocf,\equiv_{\bullet_+}}$ for each $i \in \mathbb{N}_*$ as $\tau(i) = \kappa^i$, where κ^i is any arbitrary OCF that satisfies $\kappa^i(\omega_1) = 0$, $\kappa^i(\omega_2) = 1$, and $\kappa^i(\omega_3) = i + 2$. For each $k \in \mathbb{N}_*$, let σ^k be the sequence of formulae $(\alpha_{13}, \ldots, \alpha_{13})$ where $[\alpha_{13}] = \{\omega_1, \omega_3\}$ and α_{13} appears exactly k times in the sequence. Let us denote by κ^i_k the OCF $\kappa^i \bullet_+ \sigma^k$. By definition of $\bullet_+$, we get for all $i, k \in \mathbb{N}_*$ that $\kappa^i_k(\omega_1) = \kappa^i(\omega_1) = 0$, $\kappa^i_k(\omega_2) = \kappa^i(\omega_2) + k = k + 1$, and $\kappa^i_k(\omega_3) = \kappa^i(\omega_3) = i + 2$. Hence,

- $\kappa^i_{i+1}(\omega_2) = \kappa^i_{i+1}(\omega_3)$
- if $k < i + 1$, then $\kappa^i_k(\omega_2) < \kappa^i_k(\omega_3)$
- otherwise, i.e., if $k > i + 1$, then $\kappa^i_k(\omega_2) > \kappa^i_k(\omega_3)$

[9]A world is denoted by an ordered pair of two symbols from $\{0, 1\}$ according to the ordering $p < q$.

[10]$\kappa(\omega) = i$ iff ω appears at the level associated to the integer i.

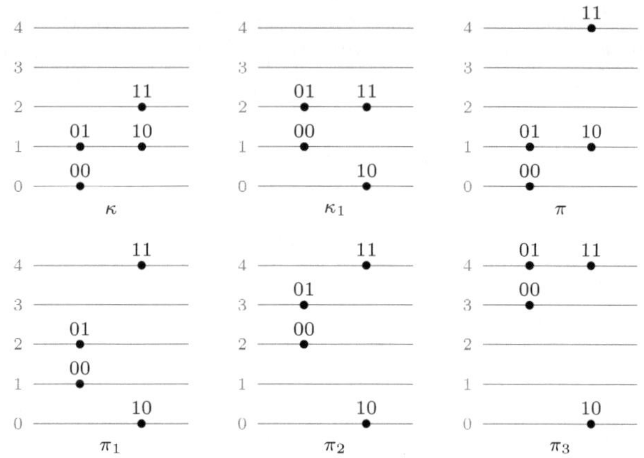

Figure 2: The DP operator $\bullet_+$

This shows that $B_{ocf}(\kappa^i_k \bullet_+ \alpha_{23}) \equiv \alpha_{23}$ if and only if $k = i + 1$, where $[\alpha_{23}] = \{\omega_2, \omega_3\}$. Stated otherwise, for all $i, j \in \mathbb{N}_*$, if $i \neq j$ then the sequence $\sigma = \sigma^{i+1} \cdot \alpha_{23}$ is such that $B_{ocf}(\kappa^i \bullet_+ \sigma) \not\equiv B_{ocf}(\kappa^j \bullet_+ \sigma)$. This means that if $i \neq j$ then $\kappa_i \not\equiv_{\bullet_+} \kappa_j$, which shows that τ is an injective mapping from $\mathbb{N}_*$ to $U_{ocf,\equiv_{\bullet_+}}$, and concludes the proof that $U_{ocf,\equiv_{\bullet_+}}$ is countably infinite. □

Then from Propositions 3 and 7 and from the fact that U_{tpo} is a finite set, we can conclude that:

Corollary 2. *$\bullet_+$ is not $\mathcal{E}_{tpo}$-instantiable.*

Proposition 7 is more interesting than the counterexample, since the fact that $U_{ocf,\equiv_{\bullet_+}}$ is countably infinite means not only that an operator on $\mathcal{E}_{tpo}$ that is equivalent to $\bullet_+$ can not be found on the same propositional language, but also that trying to use a larger language in order to gain in expressivity (i.e., artifically adding new atoms to have more TPOs) can not work either.

5 An Impossibility Result

Let us start this section by the definition of an epistemic space $\mathcal{I}$ being C-complete where C is a class of revision operators, meaning that $\mathcal{I}$ is rich enough to endorse any operator of a given class C (e.g., satisfying a set of postulates).

Definition 8. *Given a class C of revision operators, we say that an epistemic space $\mathcal{I} = (U, B)$ is C-complete if every operator from C is safely $\mathcal{I}$-instantiable.*

When C is the class of DP operators and $\mathcal{I}$ is C-complete, we simply say that $\mathcal{I}$ is DP-complete.

In this section, we intend to introduce an impossibility result, that is, no epistemic space $\mathcal{I} = (U, B)$ where U is countable is DP-complete. To this end, we intend to introduce a specific DP revision operator that is not $\mathcal{I}$-instantiable, for any $\mathcal{I} = (U, B)$ where U is a countable set.

Let us first define our revision operator, denoted by $\bullet^*$. Without loss of generality, we can assume that $\mathcal{L}_P$ is such that $|P| \geq 2$. Let $\omega_1, \omega_2, \omega_3$ be three distinct worlds from Ω. Let $\mathbb{B}^{\mathbb{N}}$ be the set of all (countably infinite) binary sequences of values from $\{0,1\}$. For each $\delta \in \mathbb{B}^{\mathbb{N}}$ and for each integer $i \geq 1$, $\delta(i)$ denotes the ith value of δ in the sequence, and $(\delta+1)$ denotes the sequence from $\mathbb{B}^{\mathbb{N}}$ defined for each integer $i \geq 1$ as $(\delta+1)(i) = \delta(i+1)$ (e.g., if $\delta = (00101\cdots)$, then $(\delta+1) = (0101\cdots)$). Moreover, let $\circ_B$ and $\circ_N$ be respectively the Boutilier revision operator and the Nayak lexicographic operator on $\mathcal{E}_{tpo}$ (recall that both operators are DP operators). Lastly, let Φ_{123} denote the subset of total preorders from U_{tpo} that satisfy $\omega_1 < \omega_2 < \omega_3$ and for each $\omega \notin \{\omega_1, \omega_2, \omega_3\}$, $\omega_3 < \omega$.

Let us now define an epistemic space $\mathcal{E}^* = \langle E^*, Bel^* \rangle$ as follows. Let $E^* = U_{tpo} \times \mathbb{B}^{\mathbb{N}}$, and let Bel^* be defined for each $(\Psi,\delta) \in E^*$ as $Bel^*((\Psi,\delta)) = B_{tpo}(\Psi)$. We now define the revision operator $\bullet^*$ on $\mathcal{E}^*$ as follows, for each $(\Psi,\delta) \in E^*$:

- $(\Psi,\delta) \bullet^* \mu = (\Psi \circ_N \mu, (\delta+1))$, if $\Psi \in \Phi_{123}, [\mu] = \{\omega_1, \omega_3\}$, and $\delta(1) = 1$,
- $(\Psi,\delta) \bullet^* \mu = (\Psi \circ_B \mu, (\delta+1))$, if $\Psi \in \Phi_{123}, [\mu] = \{\omega_1, \omega_3\}$, and $\delta(1) = 0$,
- $(\Psi,\delta) \bullet^* \mu = (\Psi \circ_B \mu, \delta)$, in the remaining cases.

Let us first show that:

Proposition 8. $\bullet^*$ *is a DP operator.*

Proof. Let τ be the mapping associating each epistemic state $(\Psi,\delta) \in E^*$ with the total preorder Ψ. On the one hand, since $Bel^*((\Psi,\delta)) = B_{tpo}(\Psi)$ for every $(\Psi,\delta) \in E^*$, by definition of $B_{tpo}(\Psi)$ we directly get that τ satisfies conditions 1 and 2 of a faithful assignment. On the other hand, by construction of $\bullet^*$, for every $(\Psi,\delta) \in E^*$, we have that $\tau((\Psi,\delta) \bullet^* \mu) \in \{\Psi \circ_N \mu, \Psi \circ_B \mu\}$. Yet $\circ_B$ and $\circ_N$ are both structure preserving, so the identity function on U_{tpo} defines a DP assignment corresponding to both $\circ_B$ and $\circ_N$. Then τ satisfies conditions (CR1-CR4) as well, and for each epistemic state (Ψ,δ) and each formula μ, $[Bel((\Psi,\delta) \bullet^* \mu)] = \min([\mu], \Psi)$. This means that τ is the DP assignment corresponding to $\bullet^*$. Then, by Theorem 1, $\bullet^*$ is a DP revision operator. $\square$

Our impossibility result is based on the following statement, which shows $E^*_{\equiv_{\bullet^*}}$ is uncountable:

Proposition 9. $card(\mathbb{B}^{\mathbb{N}}) \leq card(E^*_{\equiv_{\bullet^*}})$.

Proof. Let σ_{321} be the sequence of formulae $(\alpha_3, \alpha_2, \alpha_1)$ with $[\alpha_3] = \{\omega_3\}$, $[\alpha_2] = \{\omega_2\}$, and $[\alpha_1] = \{\omega_1\}$. Let Ψ be any total preorder from U_{tpo}, and let us note $\Psi' = \Psi \circ_B \sigma_{123}$. It is easy to verify by construction of $\circ_B$ that $\Psi' \in \Phi_{123}$. Yet by definition of $\circ_*$, we know that for each epistemic state $(\Psi,\delta) \in E^*$, $(\Psi,\delta) \bullet^* \sigma_{123} = (\Psi \circ_B \sigma_{123}, \delta)$. Hence, for each epistemic state $(\Psi,\delta) \in E^*$, $(\Psi,\delta) \bullet^* \sigma_{123}$ is an epistemic state (Ψ',δ) such that $\Psi' \in \Phi_{123}$.

Now, given any such epistemic state $(\Psi',\delta) \in \mathcal{E}^*$ such that $\Psi' \in \Phi_{123}$, when α_{13}, α_{23} are formulae such that $[\alpha_{13}] = \{\omega_1, \omega_3\}$ and $[\alpha_{23}] = \{\omega_2, \omega_3\}$, we have that:

- if $\delta(1) = 1$, then $(\Psi',\delta) \bullet^* \alpha_{13} \bullet^* \alpha_{23} = (\Psi' \circ_N \alpha_{13}, (\delta+1)) \bullet^* \alpha_{23} = (\Psi' \circ_N \alpha_{13} \circ_B \alpha_{23}, (\delta+1))$, which we denote by $(\Psi_1, (\delta+1))$; and
- if $\delta(1) = 0$, then $(\Psi',\delta) \bullet^* \alpha_{13} \bullet^* \alpha_{23} = (\Psi' \circ_B \alpha_{13}, (\delta+1)) \bullet^* \alpha_{23} = (\Psi' \circ_B \alpha_{13} \circ_B \alpha_{23}, (\delta+1))$, which we denote by $(\Psi_2, (\delta+1))$.

And it is easy to verify by construction of $\circ_B$ and $\circ_N$ that $B_{tpo}(\Psi_1) \equiv \alpha_3$ and $B_{tpo}(\Psi_2) \equiv \alpha_2$, thus $Bel((\Psi_1, (\delta+1)) \equiv \alpha_3$ and $Bel((\Psi_2, (\delta+1)) \equiv \alpha_2$.

Overall, we have shown that for each epistemic state $(\Psi,\delta) \in E^*$, when σ is the sequence of formulae $\sigma = \sigma_{123} \cdot \alpha_{13} \cdot \alpha_{23}$,

- if $\delta(1) = 1$, then $(\Psi,\delta) \bullet^* \sigma = (\Psi_1, (\delta+1))$ and $Bel((\Psi_1, (\delta+1))) \equiv \alpha_3$, and
- if $\delta(1) = 0$, then $(\Psi,\delta) \bullet^* \sigma = (\Psi_2, (\delta+1))$ and $Bel((\Psi_2, (\delta+1))) \equiv \alpha_2$.

That is, for all epistemic states $(\Psi,\delta), (\Psi,\delta') \in E^*$,

$$\delta(1) \neq \delta'(1) \Rightarrow Bel((\Psi,\delta) \bullet^* \sigma) \not\equiv Bel((\Psi,\delta') \bullet^* \sigma) \quad (1)$$

We intend now to show that if $(\Psi,\delta), (\Psi,\delta')$ are two epistemic states from E^* such that $\delta \neq \delta'$, then $(\Psi,\delta) \not\equiv_{\bullet^*} (\Psi,\delta')$. Given a vector $\delta \in \mathbb{B}^{\mathbb{N}}$ and an integer $k \geq 1$, δ can be rewritten as the concatenation of two vectors δ_{-k} and δ_{+k}, i.e., $\delta = \delta_{-k} \cdot \delta_{+k}$, where $\delta_{-k} = (\delta(1), \ldots, \delta(k-1))$ (δ_{-k} is possibly empty) and $\delta_{+k} = (\delta(k), \delta(k+1), \ldots)$. Now, let $\delta \neq \delta'$, then let i be the smallest integer such that $\delta(i) \neq \delta'(i)$, formally $i = \min(\{j \in \mathbb{N} \mid \delta(j) \neq \delta'(j)\})$. We have that $\delta_{-i} = \delta'_{-i}$ and $\delta_{+i}(1) \neq \delta'_{+i}(1)$. On the one hand, by definition of $\bullet^*$, we get that $(\Psi,\delta) \bullet^* \sigma^{(i)} = (\Psi_i, \delta_{+i})$ and $(\Psi,\delta') \bullet^* \sigma^{(i)} = (\Psi_i, \delta'_{+i})$ for some unique total preorder Ψ_i. On the other hand, we have shown in Equation 1 above that since $\delta_{+i}(1) \neq \delta'_{+i}(1)$, $Bel(\Psi_i, \delta_{+i}) \bullet^* \sigma \not\equiv Bel(\Psi_i, \delta'_{+i}) \bullet^* \sigma$. That is, the sequence of formulae $\sigma^{(i+1)}$ is such that $Bel((\Psi,\delta) \bullet^* \sigma^{(i+1)}) \not\equiv Bel((\Psi,\delta') \bullet^* \sigma^{(i+1)})$. This shows that $(\Psi,\delta) \not\equiv_{\bullet^*} (\Psi,\delta')$.

We have shown that each total preorder $\Psi \in U_{tpo}$ and for all $\delta, \delta' \in \mathbb{B}^{\mathbb{N}}$, if $\delta \neq \delta'$ then $(\Psi,\delta) \not\equiv_{\bullet^*} (\Psi,\delta')$. This shows that there is an injective mapping from $\mathbb{B}^{\mathbb{N}}$ to $E^*_{\equiv_{\bullet^*}}$, from which we can conclude that $card(\mathbb{B}^{\mathbb{N}}) \leq card(E^*_{\equiv_{\bullet^*}})$. $\square$

And so, as a consequence of Propositions 3 and 9 and from the fact that the set $\mathbb{B}^{\mathbb{N}}$ is uncountable, we get that:

Corollary 3. *Let $\mathcal{I} = (U, B)$ be an epistemic space such that U is a countable set. Then $\bullet^*$ is not $\mathcal{I}$-instantiable.*

We are ready to state our impossibility result. Since $\bullet^*$ is a DP operator (cf. Proposition 8), we get as a direct consequence of Corollary 3 that:

Corollary 4. *There is no DP-complete epistemic space $\mathcal{I} = (U, B)$ where U is a countable set.*

In particular, $\mathcal{E}_{ocf}$ and $\mathcal{E}_{tpo}$ are not DP-complete, and thus these epistemic spaces cannot be used to define *every* DP operator. This can be seen as a very negative result. But this is a simple consequence of the generality of Darwiche and Pearl's definition of epistemic states. Nevertheless, one can be more positive if one makes a very natural assumption on the operator and the epistemic space on which it is defined. This is the topic of the next section.

6 A Possibility Result

Let us now investigate a particular, yet very natural, case, where all epistemic states can be finitely generated from an initial empty epistemic state and a sequence of revisions.

Let $\mathcal{E} = \langle E, Bel \rangle$ be an epistemic space and $\circ$ be a revision operator on $\mathcal{E}$. We consider the following property:

(G) There exists a unique $\Psi_\top \in \mathcal{E}$ such that $Bel(\Psi_\top) \equiv \top$, and for each $\Psi \in \mathcal{E}$, there exists a finite sequence of formulae $\sigma = (\mu_1, \ldots, \mu_k)$ such that $\Psi = \Psi_\top \circ \sigma$

A DP operator satisfying **(G)** is said to be a DP+G operator. And when C is the class of DP operators satisfying **(G)** and $\mathcal{I}$ is C-complete, we simply say that $\mathcal{I}$ is DP+G-complete.

We intend to show that every DP+G operator is safely $\mathcal{E}_{ocf}$-instantiable. For this purpose, we intend to provide a canonical, safe translation of any DP+G operator $\circ$ into an equivalent operator on OCFs, denoted by $\circ_{\mathcal{E}_{ocf}}$. So let $\circ$ be any DP+G operator on $\mathcal{E} = (E, Bel)$. By condition **(G)**, every epistemic state from E can be identified by a finite sequence of formulae. Since the set of all finite sequence of formulae is a countable set, E is also countable. So one can denote by $(\Psi_1, \Psi_2, \ldots)$ the list of all epistemic states from E. For each $\Psi_i \in E$, let $\preceq_{\Psi_i}$ be the total preorder associated with Ψ_i by the DP assignment corresponding to $\circ$. Now, let $f_\mathcal{E}$ be the mapping from E to U_{ocf} defined for each $\Psi_i \in \mathcal{E}$ by $f_\mathcal{E}(\Psi_\top) = \kappa_\top$, where $\kappa_\top$ is the OCF defined for each world ω by $\kappa_\top(\omega) = 0$; and if $\Psi_i \neq \Psi_\top$, then $f_\mathcal{E}(\Psi_i) = \kappa_i$, where κ_i is the OCF defined for each world ω by $\kappa_i(\omega) = 0$ if ω is at the first level of $\preceq_{\Psi_i}$ otherwise $\kappa_i(\omega) = |\Omega| + i$ if $\omega \in lvl(\preceq_{\Psi_i}, max(\preceq_{\Psi_i}))$ (i.e., if ω lies at the last level of $\preceq_{\Psi_i}$), otherwise $\kappa_i(\omega) = rank(\preceq_{\Psi_i}, \omega)$. By construction, $f_\mathcal{E}$ is injective. Let $\mathsf{Im}(f_\mathcal{E})$ be the subset of OCFs from U_{ocf} that is the image of $f_\mathcal{E}$, i.e., $\mathsf{Im}(f_\mathcal{E}) = \{f_\mathcal{E}(\Psi_i) \mid \Psi_i \in \mathcal{E}\}$. The fact that $f_\mathcal{E}$ is injective allows one to define another mapping $h_{\mathcal{E}_{ocf}} : U_{ocf} \to E$ defined for each OCF $\kappa \in U_{ocf}$ by $h_{\mathcal{E}_{ocf}}(\kappa) = f_\mathcal{E}^{-1}(\kappa)$ if $\kappa \in \mathsf{Im}(f_\mathcal{E})$, otherwise $h_{\mathcal{E}_{ocf}}(\kappa) = \Psi_i$, where Ψ_i is any arbitrary chosen epistemic state from E such that $tpo(\kappa) = \preceq_{\Psi_i}$. (Note that such an epistemic state $\Psi_i \in E$ exists, since the DP assignment corresponding to $\circ$ is a surjective mapping from E to U_{tpo}: similar to the proof of Proposition 4 and by condition **(G)**, we can prove that for any total preorder $\preceq$, there exists a finite sequence σ such that $\Psi_i = \Psi_\top \circ \sigma$ and $\preceq = \preceq_{\Psi_i}$.) Then we define the revision operator $\circ_{\mathcal{E}_{ocf}}$ on $\mathcal{E}_{ocf}$ defined for each $\kappa \in U_{ocf}$ and each $\mu \in \mathcal{L}_P^*$ by $\kappa \circ_{\mathcal{E}_{ocf}} \mu = f_\mathcal{E}(h_{\mathcal{E}_{ocf}}(\kappa) \circ \mu)$.

Using this translation, we get that:

Proposition 10. *$(f_\mathcal{E}, \circ_{\mathcal{E}_{ocf}})$ is a safe translation of $\circ$ into $\mathcal{E}_{ocf}$.*

Proof. First, for each $\Psi_i \in E$, let $\preceq_{\Psi_i}$ be the total preorder associated with Ψ_i by the DP assignment corresponding to $\circ$. Then we know by conditions 1 and 2 of a faithful assignment that $[Bel(\Psi_i)] = \min(\Omega, \preceq_{\Psi_i})$. And by construction of $f_\mathcal{E}(\Psi_i) = \kappa_i$, we have that $\kappa_i(\omega) = 0$ if and only if $rank(\preceq_{\Psi_i}, \omega) = 0$ if and only if $\omega \in \min(\Omega, \preceq_{\Psi_i})$. Hence, for each $\Psi_i \in E$, we have that $Bel(\Psi_i) = B_{ocf}(f_\mathcal{E}(\Psi_i))$. Second, for each $\Psi_i \in E$ and each $\mu \in \mathcal{L}_P^*$ we get that $f_\mathcal{E}(\Psi_i) \circ_{\mathcal{E}_{ocf}} \mu = \kappa_i \circ_{\mathcal{E}_{ocf}} \mu = f_\mathcal{E}(h_{\mathcal{E}_{ocf}}(\kappa_i) \circ \mu) = f_\mathcal{E}(f_\mathcal{E}^- 1(\kappa_i) \circ \mu) = f_\mathcal{E}(\Psi_i \circ \mu)$. This shows that $(f_\mathcal{E}, \circ_{\mathcal{E}_{ocf}})$ is a translation of $\circ$ into $\mathcal{E}_{ocf}$.

Yet by definition of $h_{\mathcal{E}_{ocf}}$, on the one hand we get for each $\kappa \in U_{ocf}$ that $B_{ocf}(\kappa) \equiv Bel(h_{\mathcal{E}_{ocf}}(\kappa))$ (since by denoting $\Psi_i = h_{\mathcal{E}_{ocf}}(\kappa)$, we have that $tpo(\kappa) = \preceq_{\Psi_i}$). On the other hand, for each $\kappa \in U_{ocf}$ and each $\mu \in \mathcal{L}_P^*$ we get that $h_{\mathcal{E}_{ocf}}(\kappa \circ_{\mathcal{E}_{ocf}} \mu) = h_{\mathcal{E}_{ocf}}(f_\mathcal{E}(h_{\mathcal{E}_{ocf}}(\kappa) \circ \mu)) = f_\mathcal{E}^- 1(f_\mathcal{E}(\Psi_i \circ \mu)) = \Psi_i \circ \mu = h_{\mathcal{E}_{ocf}}(\kappa_i) \circ \mu$. This shows that $(h_{\mathcal{E}_{ocf}}, \circ)$ is a translation of $\circ_{\mathcal{E}_{ocf}}$ into $\mathcal{E}$. Hence, $(f_\mathcal{E}, \circ_{\mathcal{E}_{ocf}})$ is a safe translation of $\circ$ into $\mathcal{E}_{ocf}$. □

We know now that every DP+G operator $\circ$ is safely $\mathcal{E}_{ocf}$-instantiable. Moreover, by construction, $\circ_{\mathcal{E}_{ocf}}$ is structure preserving. Therefore:

Corollary 5. *For every DP+G operator $\circ$, the operator $\circ_{\mathcal{E}_{ocf}}$ is equivalent to $\circ$ and is structure preserving.*

And we can conclude that:

Corollary 6. *$\mathcal{E}_{ocf}$ is DP+G-complete.*

This means that every DP operator defined on any epistemic space and satisfying the property **(G)** (that simply states that there is an initial, empty, epistemic state and that each epistemic state is reachable from it through a finite sequence of revisions) can be safely translated to the OCF epistemic space. As a consequence, all these operators can be defined equivalently in the OCF epistemic space.

7 Conclusion

In this work, we focused on Darwiche and Pearl's epistemic states and iterated revision operators from the representational perspective. We defined epistemic spaces as the structures in which these epistemic states and revision operators are defined. We highlighted the fact that epistemic states can be distinguished from each other by revision operators only by their behavior under any finite sequence of successive revisions. This led us to focus on the notion of strong equivalence between epistemic states, and to define a notion of equivalence between revision operators defined on different epistemic spaces. Based on these notions, we made precise the condition under which an operator is "instantiable" into another epistemic space.

Then, we looked for a canonical representation for the whole quotient set of epistemic states under this strong equivalence relation. But we showed that in general, such a canonical representation can not exist. The number of possible (quotient set of) epistemic states is just too large.

But then, if we restrict ourselves to epistemic states finitely generated from an initial, "empty" epistemic state, that is a quite reasonable assumption, then we showed that we can find such a canonical representation in terms of OCFs (Ordinal Conditional Functions). OCFs are a well-known representation choice for belief change operators, and are really close to total preorders. But this paper shows that the numerical information they add compared to total preorders is what is missing in order to encode all possible finitely generated epistemic state spaces.

Acknowledgements

This work has benefited from the support of the AI Chair BE4musIA of the French National Research Agency (ANR-20-CHIA-0028) and of the JSPS KAKENHI Grant Number JP20K11947. The third author has also been partially funded by the program PAUSE of Collège de France.

References

Alchourrón, C. E., and Makinson, D. 1985. On the logic of theory change: Safe contraction. *Studia Logica* 44:405–422.

Alchourrón, C. E.; Gärdenfors, P.; and Makinson, D. 1985. On the logic of theory change: Partial meet contraction and revision functions. *Journal of Symbolic Logic* 50:510–530.

Aravanis, T. I.; Peppas, P.; and Williams, M. 2019. Observations on Darwiche and Pearl's approach for iterated belief revision. In *Proceedings of the 28th International Joint Conference on Artificial Intelligence (IJCAI'19)*, 1509–1515.

Booth, R., and Chandler, J. 2016. Extending the harper identity to iterated belief change. In *Proceedings of the 25th International Joint Conference on Artificial Intelligence (IJCAI'16)*, 987–993.

Booth, R., and Chandler, J. 2019. From iterated revision to iterated contraction: Extending the harper identity. *Artificial Intelligence* 277.

Booth, R., and Meyer, T. A. 2006. Admissible and restrained revision. *Journal of Artificial Intelligence Research* 26:127–151.

Booth, R., and Meyer, T. A. 2011. How to revise a total preorder. *Journal of Philosophical Logic* 40(2):193–238.

Darwiche, A., and Pearl, J. 1994. On the logic of iterated belief revision. In *Proceedings of the 5th Conference on Theoretical Aspects of Reasoning about Knowledge (TARK'94)*, 5–23.

Darwiche, A., and Pearl, J. 1997. On the logic of iterated belief revision. *Artificial Intelligence* 89(1-2):1–29.

del Cerro, L. F., and Herzig, A. 1996. Belief change and dependence. In *Proceedings of the 6th Conference of Theoretical Aspects of Rationality and Knowledge (TARK'96)*, 147–161.

Dubois, D., and Prade, H. 1991. Epistemic entrenchment and possibilistic logic. *Artificial Intelligence* 50:223–239.

Fermé, E., and Hansson, S. O. 2011. AGM 25 years: Twenty-five years of research in belief change. *Journal of Philosophical Logic* 40(2):295–331.

Freund, M., and Lehmann, D. 1994. Belief revision and rational inference. Technical Report TR-94-16, Institute of Computer Science, The Hebrew University of Jerusalem.

Friedman, N., and Halpern, J. Y. 1999. Belief revision: A critique. *Journal of Logic, Language and Information* 8(4):401–420.

Gärdenfors, P. 1988. *Knowledge in flux*. MIT Press.

Gärdenfors, P. 1990. Belief revision and nonmonotonic logic: Two sides of the same coin? In *Proceedings of the 9th European Conference on Artificial Intelligence (ECAI'90)*, 768–773.

Grove, A. 1988. Two modellings for theory change. *Journal of Philosophical Logic* 17(157-180).

Hansson, S. O. 1994. Kernel contraction. *The Journal of Symbolic Logic* 59(3):845–859.

Jin, Y., and Thielscher, M. 2007. Iterated belief revision, revised. *Artificial Intelligence* 171(1):1–18.

Katsuno, H., and Mendelzon, A. O. 1991. Propositional knowledge base revision and minimal change. *Artificial Intelligence* 52:263–294.

Konieczny, S., and Pino Pérez, R. 2008. Improvement operators. In *Proceedings of the 11th International Conference on Principles of Knowledge Representation and Reasoning (KR'08)*, 177–187.

Konieczny, S., and Pino Pérez, R. 2000. A framework for iterated revision. *Journal of Applied Non-Classical Logics* 10(3-4):339–367.

Konieczny, S.; Medina Grespan, M.; and Pino Pérez, R. 2010. Taxonomy of improvement operators and the problem of minimal change. In *Proceedings of the 12th International Conference on Principles of Knowledge Representation and Reasoning (KR'10)*, 161–170.

Konieczny, S. 2009. Using transfinite ordinal conditional functions. In *Proceedings of the 10th European Conference on Symbolic and Quantitative Approaches to Reasoning with Uncertainty (ECSQARU'09)*, 396–407.

Lehmann, D. 1995. Belief revision, revised. In *Proceedings of the 14th International Joint Conference on Artificial Intelligence (IJCAI'95)*, 1534–1540.

Makinson, D., and Gärdenfors, P. 1989. Relations between the logic of theory change and nonmonotonic logic. In *The Logic of Theory Change*, 185–205.

Medina Grespan, M., and Pino Pérez, R. 2013. Representation of basic improvement operators. In *Trends in Belief Revision and Argumentation Dynamics*. College Publications. 195–227.

Meng, H.; Kou, H.; and Li, S. 2015. Belief revision with general epistemic states. In *Proceedings of the 29th AAAI Conference on Artificial Intelligence (AAAI'15)*.

Nayak, A. C.; Foo, N. Y.; Pagnucco, M.; and Sattar, A. 1994. Entrenchment kinematics 101. In *Proceedings of the 7th Australian Joint Conference on Artificial Intelligence (AI'94)*, 157–164.

Nayak, A. C.; Foo, N. Y.; Pagnucco, M.; and Sattar, A. 1996. Changing conditional beliefs unconditionally. In *Proceedings of the 6th Conference of Theoretical Aspects of Rationality and Knowledge (TARK'96)*, 119–135.

Nayak, A. 1994. Iterated belief change based on epistemic entrenchment. *Erkenntnis* 41:353–390.

Ramachandran, R.; Nayak, A. C.; and Orgun, M. A. 2012. Three approaches to iterated belief contraction. *Journal of Philosophical Logic* 41(1):115–142.

Rott, H. 2009. Shifting priorities: Simple representations for twenty-seven iterated theory change operators. In Makinson, D.; Malinowski, J.; and Wansing, H., eds., *Towards Mathematical Philosophy*. Springer. 269–296.

Schwind, N., and Konieczny, S. 2020. Non-prioritized iterated revision: Improvement via incremental belief merging. In *Proceedings of the 17th International Conference on Principles of Knowledge Representation and Reasoning (KR'20)*, 738–747.

Spohn, W. 1988. *Ordinal Conditional Functions: A Dynamic Theory of Epistemic States*. Springer Netherlands. 105–134.

Williams, M.-A. 1995. Iterated theory base change: A computational model. In *Proceedings of the 14th International Joint Conference on Artificial Intelligence (IJCAI'95)*, 1541–1549.

Proceedings of the 19th International Conference on Principles of Knowledge Representation and Reasoning
Main Track

Who's the Expert? On Multi-source Belief Change

Joseph Singleton, **Richard Booth**
Cardiff University
{singletonj1,boothr2}@cardiff.ac.uk

Abstract

Consider the following belief change/merging scenario. A group of information sources gives a sequence of reports about the state of the world at various instances (e.g. different points in time). The true states at these instances are unknown to us. The sources have varying levels of expertise, also unknown to us, and may be knowledgeable on some topics but not others. This may cause sources to report false statements in areas they lack expertise. What should we believe on the basis of these reports? We provide a framework in which to explore this problem, based on an extension of propositional logic with expertise formulas. This extended language allows us to express beliefs about the state of the world at each instance, as well as beliefs about the expertise of each source. We propose several postulates, provide a couple of families of concrete operators, and analyse these operators with respect to the postulates.

1 Introduction

Consider the following belief change scenario in a hospital. We observe the results of a blood test of patient 1, confirming condition X. Assuming the test is reliable, the AGM paradigm (Alchourrón, Gärdenfors, and Makinson 1985) tells us how to revise our beliefs in light of the new information. Dr. A then claims that patient 2 suffers from the same condition, but Dr. B disagrees. Given that doctors specialise in different areas and may make mistakes, who should we trust? Since the *Success* postulate ($\alpha \in K * \alpha$) assumes information is reliable, we are outside the realm of AGM revision, and must instead apply some form of *non-prioritised* revision (Hansson 1999).

Suppose it now emerges that Dr. A had earlier claimed patient 1 did *not* suffer from condition X, contrary to the test results. We now have reason to suspect Dr. A may *lack expertise* on diagnosing X, and may subsequently revise beliefs about Dr. A's domain of expertise and the status of patient 2 (e.g. by opting to trust Dr. B instead).

While simple, this example illustrates the key features of the belief change problem we study: we consider multiple sources, whose expertise is *a priori* unknown, providing reports on various instances of a problem domain. On the basis of these reports we form beliefs both about the expertise of the sources and the state of the world in each instance.

By including a distinguished *completely reliable* source (the test results in the example) we extend AGM revision. In some respects we also extend approaches to non-prioritised revision (e.g. selective revision (Fermé and Hansson 1999), credibility-limited revision (Hansson et al. 2001), and trust-based revision (Booth and Hunter 2018)), which assume information about the reliability of sources is known up front. The problem is also related to *belief merging* (Konieczny and Pino Pérez 2002) which deals with combining belief bases from multiple sources; a detailed comparison will be given in Section 7.

Our work is also connected to trust and belief revision, if one interprets trust as *belief in expertise*. As Yasser and Ismail (2021) note in recent work, trust and belief are inexorably linked: we should accept reports from sources we believe are trustworthy, and we should trust sources whose reports turn out to be reliable. Trust and belief should also be revised in tandem, so that we may increase or decrease trust in a source as more reports are received, and revoke or reinstate previous reports from a source as its perceived trustworthiness changes.[1]

To unify the trust and belief aspects, we enrich a propositional language with *expertise statements* $E_i(\varphi)$, read as "source i has expertise on φ". The output of our belief change problem is then a collection of belief and knowledge sets in the extended language, describing what we *know* and *believe* about the expertise of the sources and the state of the world in each instance. For example, we should *know* reports from the reliable source are true, whereas reports from ordinary sources may only be believed.

Following recent work on logical approaches to expertise (Singleton 2021; Booth and Hunter 2018), we formally model expertise using a partition of propositional valuations for each source. Equivalently, each source has an *indistinguishibility equivalence relation* over valuations. A source is an expert on a proposition φ exactly when they can distinguish every φ valuation from every $\neg\varphi$ valuation.[2] As in Singleton (2021), we also use *soundness formulas* $S_i(\varphi)$, which intuitively say that φ is true *up the expertise of* i. For example, if i has expertise on p but not q, then the conjunction $p \wedge q$ is sound for i whenever p holds, since we can effectively ignore q. Formally, φ is sound for i if the "actual" state of the world is indistinguishable from a φ valu-

[1] This mutual dependence between trust and belief is also the core idea in *truth discovery* (Li et al. 2016).

ation. Note that expertise does not depend on the "actual" state, whereas soundness does. This provides a crucial link between expertise and truthfulness of information.

We then make the assumption that *sources only report sound propositions*. That is, reports are only false due to sources overstepping the bounds of their expertise. In particular, we assume sources are honest in their reports, and that experts are always right.

Note that in our introductory example, the fact that we had a report from Dr. A on patient 1 (together with reliable information on patient 1) was essential for determining the expertise of Dr. A, and subsequently the status of patient 2. While the patients are independent, reports on one can cause beliefs about the other to change, as we update our beliefs about the expertise of the sources.

In general we consider an arbitrary number of *cases*, which are seen as labels for instances of the domain. For example, a crowdsourcing worker may label multiple images, or a weather forecaster may give predictions for different locations. Each report in the input to the problem then refers to a specific case. Via these cases and the presence of the completely reliable source, we are able to model scenarios where some "ground truth" is available, listing how often sources have been correct/incorrect on a proposition (e.g. the *report histories* of Hunter (2021)). We can also generalise this scenario, e.g. by having only partial information about "previous" cases.

Throughout the paper we make the assumption that *expertise is fixed across cases*: the expertise of a source does not depend on the particular instance of the domain we look at. For instance, the expertise of Dr. A is the same for patient 1 as for patient 2. This is a simplifying assumption, and may rule out certain interpretations of the cases (e.g. if cases represent different points in time, it would be natural to let expertise evolve over time).

Contribution. Our contributions are threefold. First, we develop a logical framework for reasoning about the expertise of multiple sources and the state of the world in multiple cases. Second, we formulate a belief change problem within this framework, which allows us to explore how trust and belief should interact and evolve as reports are received from the various sources. Finally, we put forward several postulates and two concrete classes of operators – with a representation result for one class – and analyse these operators with respect to the postulates.

Paper Outline. In Section 2 we develop the formal framework. Section 3 introduces the problem and lists some core postulates. We give two constructions and specific example operators in Section 4. Section 5 introduces some further postulates concerning belief change on the basis of one new report. An analogue of selective revision (Fermé and Hansson 1999) is presented Section 6. Section 7 discusses related work, and we conclude in Section 8. Proofs are given in the appendix of the full version of the paper (Singleton and Booth 2022).

[2] The relationship between this notion of expertise and *S5 epistemic logic* is explored in a modal logic setting in Singleton (2021), and we revisit this connection in Section 7.

2 The Framework

Let $\mathcal{S}$ be a finite set of information sources. For convenience, we assume there is a *completely reliable* source in $\mathcal{S}$, which we denote by $*$. For example, we can treat our first-hand observations as if they are reported by $*$. Other sources besides $*$ will be termed *ordinary sources*. Let $\mathcal{C}$ be a finite set of *cases*, which we interpret as labels for different instances of the problem domain.

Syntax. There are two levels to our formal language. To describe properties of the world in each case $c \in \mathcal{C}$, we assume a fixed finite set $\mathcal{P}$ of propositional variables, and let $\mathcal{L}_0$ denote the set of propositional formulas generated from $\mathcal{P}$ using the usual propositional connectives. We use lower case Greek letters (φ, ψ etc) for formulas in $\mathcal{L}_0$. The classical logical consequence operator will be denoted by Cn_0, and $\equiv$ denotes equivalence of propositional formulas.

The extended *language of expertise* $\mathcal{L}$ additionally describes the expertise of the sources, and is defined by the following grammar:

$$\Phi ::= \varphi \mid \Phi \wedge \Phi \mid \neg\Phi \mid E_i(\varphi) \mid S_i(\varphi)$$

where $i \in \mathcal{S}$ and $\varphi \in \mathcal{L}_0$. We introduce Boolean connectives $\vee$, $\rightarrow$, $\leftrightarrow$ and $\bot$ as abbreviations. We use upper case Greek letters (Φ, Ψ etc) for formulas in $\mathcal{L}$. For $\Gamma \subseteq \mathcal{L}$, we write $[\Gamma] = \Gamma \cap \mathcal{L}_0$ for the propositional formulas in Γ.

The intuitive reading of $E_i(\varphi)$ is *source i has expertise on* φ, i.e., i is able to correctly identify the truth value of φ in any possible state. The intuitive reading of $S_i(\varphi)$ is that φ *sound* for i to report: that φ is true up to the expertise of i. That is, the parts of φ on which i has expertise are true. Note that both operators are restricted to propositional formulas, so we will not consider iterated formulas such as $E_i(S_j(\varphi))$.

Semantics. Let $\mathcal{V}$ denote the set of propositional valuations over $\mathcal{P}$. For each $\varphi \in \mathcal{L}_0$, the set of valuations making φ true is denoted by $\mathrm{mod}_0(\varphi)$. A *world* $W = \langle \{v_c\}_{c \in \mathcal{C}}, \{\Pi_i\}_{i \in \mathcal{S}} \rangle$ is a possible complete specification of the environment we find ourselves in:

- $v_c \in \mathcal{V}$ is the "true" valuation at case $c \in \mathcal{C}$;
- Π_i is a partition of $\mathcal{V}$ for each $i \in \mathcal{S}$, representing the "true" expertise of source i; and
- Π_* is the unit partition $\{\{v\} \mid v \in \mathcal{V}\}$.

Let $\mathcal{W}$ denote the set of all worlds. Note that the partition corresponding to the distinguished source $*$ is fixed in all worlds as the finest possible partition, reflecting the fact that $*$ is completely reliable.

For any partition Π and valuation v, write $\Pi[v]$ for the unique cell in Π containing v. For a set of valuations U, write $\Pi[U] = \bigcup_{v \in U} \Pi[v]$. For brevity, we write $\Pi[\varphi]$ for $\Pi[\mathrm{mod}_0(\varphi)]$. Then $\Pi[\varphi]$ is the set of valuations indistinguishable from a φ valuation.

For our belief change problem we will be interested in maintaining a collection of several belief sets, describing beliefs about each case $c \in \mathcal{C}$. Towards determining when a world W models such a collection, we define semantics for $\mathcal{L}$ formulas with respect to a world and a case:

$$\begin{array}{lll} W, c \models \varphi & \iff & v_c \in \mathrm{mod}_0(\varphi) \\ W, c \models E_i(\varphi) & \iff & \Pi_i[\varphi] = \mathrm{mod}_0(\varphi) \\ W, c \models S_i(\varphi) & \iff & v_c \in \Pi_i[\varphi] \end{array}$$

where $i \in \mathcal{S}$, $\varphi \in \mathcal{L}_0$, and the clauses for conjunction and negation are the expected ones. Since $\mathrm{mod}_0(\varphi) \subseteq \Pi_i[\varphi]$ always holds, we have that $E_i(\varphi)$ holds iff there is no $\neg\varphi$ valuation which is indistinguishable from a φ valuation (c.f. Booth and Hunter (2018)). Note that since each source i has only a single partition Π_i used to interpret the expertise formulas, the truth value of $E_i(\varphi)$ does not depend on the case c. On the other hand, $S_i(\varphi)$ holds in case c iff the c-valuation of W is indistinguishable from some model of φ. That is, it is consistent with i's expertise that φ is true.

Also note that if φ is a propositional tautology, $E_i(\varphi)$ holds for every source i. Thus, all sources are experts on *something*, even if just the tautologies.

Example 1. *Let us extend the hospital example from the introduction. Let $\mathcal{S} = \{*, a, b\}$ denote the reliable source, Dr. A and Dr. B, and let $\mathcal{C} = \{c_1, c_2\}$ denote patients 1 and 2. Consider propositional variables $\mathcal{P} = \{x, y\}$, standing for condition X and Y respectively. Suppose that Dr. A has expertise on diagnosing condition Y only, whereas Dr. B only has expertise on X. For the sake of the example, suppose that patient 1 suffers from both conditions, and patient 2 suffers only from condition Y. This situation is modelled by the following world $W = \langle \{v_c\}_{c \in \{c_1, c_2\}}, \{\Pi_i\}_{i \in \{*, a, b\}} \rangle$:*

$$\begin{array}{ll} v_{c_1} = xy; & v_{c_2} = \bar{x}y; \\ \Pi_a = xy, \bar{x}y \mid x\bar{y}, \bar{x}\bar{y}; & \Pi_b = xy, x\bar{y} \mid \bar{x}y, \bar{x}\bar{y}. \end{array}$$

We have $W, c \models E_a(y) \wedge E_b(x)$ for each $c \in \{c_1, c_2\}$. Also note that $W, c_1 \models x$ (patient 1 suffers from X), $W, c_1 \models S_a(\neg x)$ (it is sound for Dr. A to report otherwise; this holds since $\Pi_a[\neg x] = \{xy, \bar{x}y\} \cup \{x\bar{y}, \bar{x}\bar{y}\} \ni xy = v_{c_1}$), but $W, c_1 \models \neg S_b(\neg x)$ (the same formula is not *sound for Dr. B; we have $\Pi_b[\neg x] = \{\bar{x}y, \bar{x}\bar{y}\} = \mathrm{mod}_0(\neg x) \not\ni xy = v_{c_1}$).*

Say Φ is *valid* if $W, c \models \Phi$ for all $W \in \mathcal{W}$ and $c \in \mathcal{C}$. For future reference we collect a list of validities.

Proposition 1. *For any $i \in \mathcal{S}$, $c \in \mathcal{C}$ and $\varphi, \psi \in \mathcal{L}_0$, the following formulas are valid*

1. *$S_i(\varphi) \leftrightarrow S_i(\psi)$ and $E_i(\varphi) \leftrightarrow E_i(\psi)$, whenever $\varphi \equiv \psi$*
2. *$E_i(\varphi) \leftrightarrow E_i(\neg\varphi)$ and $E_i(\varphi) \wedge E_i(\psi) \rightarrow E_i(\varphi \wedge \psi)$*
3. *$E_i(p_1) \wedge \cdots \wedge E_i(p_k) \rightarrow E_i(\varphi)$, where $p_1, \ldots, p_k$ are the propositional variables appearing in φ*
4. *$E_i(\varphi) \wedge S_i(\varphi) \rightarrow \varphi$, and $S_i(\varphi) \wedge \neg\varphi \rightarrow \neg E_i(\varphi)$*
5. *$S_i(\varphi) \wedge S_i(\neg\varphi) \rightarrow \neg E_i(\varphi)$*
6. *$S_*(\varphi) \leftrightarrow \varphi$ and $E_*(\varphi)$*

(1) states syntax-irrelevance properties. (2) says that expertise is symmetric with respect to negation, and closed under conjunctions. Intuitively, symmetry means that i is an expert on φ if they know *whether or not* φ holds. (3) says that expertise on each propositional variable in φ is sufficient for expertise on φ itself. (4) says that, in the presence of expertise, soundness of φ is sufficient for φ to in fact be true. (5) says that if both φ and $\neg\varphi$ are true up to the expertise of i, then i cannot have expertise on φ. Finally, (6) says that the reliable source $*$ has expertise on *all* formulas, and thus φ is sound for $*$ iff it is true.

Case-Indexed Collections. In the remainder of the paper we will be interested in forming beliefs about each case $c \in \mathcal{C}$. To do so we use collections of belief sets $G = \{\Gamma_c\}_{c \in \mathcal{C}}$, with $\Gamma_c \subseteq \mathcal{L}$, indexed by cases. Say a world W is a *model* of G iff

$$W, c \models \Phi \text{ for all } c \in \mathcal{C} \text{ and } \Phi \in \Gamma_c,$$

i.e. iff W satisfies all formulas in G in the relevant case. Let $\mathrm{mod}(G)$ denote the models of G, and say that G is *consistent* if $\mathrm{mod}(G) \neq \emptyset$. For $c \in \mathcal{C}$, define the *c-consequences*

$$\mathrm{Cn}_c(G) = \{\Phi \in \mathcal{L} \mid \forall W \in \mathrm{mod}(G), W, c \models \Phi\}.$$

We write $\mathrm{Cn}(G)$ for the collection $\{\mathrm{Cn}_c(G)\}_{c \in \mathcal{C}}$.

Example 2. *Suppose $\mathcal{C} = \{c_1, c_2, c_3\}$, and define G by $\Gamma_{c_1} = \{S_i(p \wedge q)\}$, $\Gamma_{c_2} = \{E_i(p)\}$ and $\Gamma_{c_3} = \{E_i(q)\}$. Then, since expertise holds independently of case, any model W of G has $W, c_1 \models E_i(p) \wedge E_i(q)$. By Proposition 1 part (3), $W, c_1 \models E_i(p \wedge q)$. Since W satisfies Γ_{c_1} in case c_1, Proposition 1 part (4) gives $W, c_1 \models p \wedge q$. Since W was an arbitrary model of G, we have $p \wedge q \in \mathrm{Cn}_{c_1}(G)$, i.e. $p \wedge q$ is a c_1-consequence of G. This illustrates how information about distinct cases can be brought together to have consequences for other cases.*

For two collections $G = \{\Gamma_c\}_{c \in \mathcal{C}}$, $D = \{\Delta_c\}_{c \in \mathcal{C}}$, write $G \sqsubseteq D$ iff $\Gamma_c \subseteq \Delta_c$ for all c, and let $G \sqcup D$ denote the collection $\{\Gamma_c \cup \Delta_c\}_{c \in \mathcal{C}}$. With this notation, the case-indexed consequence operator satisfies analogues of the Tarskian consequence properties.[3]

Say a collection G is *closed* if $\mathrm{Cn}(G) = G$. Closed collections provide an idealised representation of beliefs, which will become useful later on. For instance, when G is closed we have $E_i(\varphi) \in \Gamma_c$ iff $E_i(\varphi) \in \Gamma_d$ for all $c, d \in \mathcal{C}$; i.e. expertise statements are either present for all cases or for none. We also have $\mathrm{Cn}_0\left[\Gamma_c\right] = \left[\Gamma_c\right]$, i.e. the propositional parts of G are (classically) closed.

In propositional logic, mod_0 is a 1-to-1 correspondence between closed sets of formulas and sets of valuations. This is not so in our setting, since some subsets of $\mathcal{W}$ do not arise as the models of any collection. Instead, we have a 1-to-1 correspondence into a restricted collection of sets of worlds. Borrowing the terminology of Delgrande, Peppas, and Woltran (2018), say a set of worlds $S \subseteq \mathcal{W}$ is *elementary* if $S = \mathrm{mod}(G)$ for some collection $G = \{\Gamma_c\}_{c \in \mathcal{C}}$.[4]

[3] That is, (i) $G \sqsubseteq \mathrm{Cn}(G)$, (ii) $G \sqsubseteq D$ implies $\mathrm{Cn}(G) \sqsubseteq \mathrm{Cn}(D)$, and (iii) $\mathrm{Cn}(\mathrm{Cn}(G)) = \mathrm{Cn}(G)$.

[4] Non-elementary sets can also exist for weaker logics (such as Horn logic (Delgrande, Peppas, and Woltran 2018)) which lack the syntactic expressivity to identify all sets of models. In our framework, $\mathcal{C}$-indexed collections are not expressive enough to specify *combinations of valuations*, since each Γ_c only says something about the valuation for c.

Elementariness is characterised by a certain closure condition. Say that two worlds W, W' are *partition-equivalent* if $\Pi_i^W = \Pi_i^{W'}$ for all sources i, and say W is a *valuation combination* from a set $S \subseteq \mathcal{W}$ if for all cases c there is $W_c \in S$ such that $v_c^W = v_c^{W_c}$. Then a set is elementary iff it is closed under valuation combinations of partition-equivalent worlds.

Proposition 2. *$S \subseteq \mathcal{W}$ is elementary if and only if the following condition holds: for all $W \in \mathcal{W}$ and $W_1, W_2 \in S$, if W is partition-equivalent to both W_1, W_2 and W is a valuation combination from $\{W_1, W_2\}$, then $W \in S$.*

3 The Problem

With the framework set out, we can formally define the problem. We seek an operator with the following behaviour:

- **Input:** A sequence of reports σ, where each report is a triple $\langle i, c, \varphi \rangle \in \mathcal{S} \times \mathcal{C} \times \mathcal{L}_0$ and $\varphi \not\equiv \bot$. Such a report represents that *source i reports φ to hold in case c*. Note that we only allow sources to make *propositional* reports.
- **Output:** A pair $\langle B^\sigma, K^\sigma \rangle$, where $B^\sigma = \{B_c^\sigma\}_{c \in \mathcal{C}}$ is a collection of *belief sets* $B_c^\sigma \subseteq \mathcal{L}$ and $K^\sigma = \{K_c^\sigma\}_{c \in \mathcal{C}}$ is a collection of *knowledge sets* $K_c^\sigma \subseteq \mathcal{L}$.

3.1 Basic Postulates

We immediately narrow the scope of operators under consideration by introducing some basic postulates which are expected to hold. In what follows, say a sequence σ is $*$-*consistent* if for each $c \in \mathcal{C}$ the set $\{\varphi \mid \langle *, c, \varphi \rangle \in \sigma\} \subseteq \mathcal{L}_0$ is classically consistent. Write G_{snd}^σ for the collection with $(G_{\mathsf{snd}}^\sigma)_c = \{S_i(\varphi) \mid \langle i, c, \varphi \rangle \in \sigma\}$, i.e. the collection of soundness statements corresponding to the reports in σ.

Closure $B^\sigma = \mathrm{Cn}(B^\sigma)$ and $K^\sigma = \mathrm{Cn}(K^\sigma)$

Containment $K^\sigma \sqsubseteq B^\sigma$

Consistency *If σ is $*$-consistent, B^σ and K^σ are consistent*

Soundness *If $\langle i, c, \varphi \rangle \in \sigma$, then $S_i(\varphi) \in K_c^\sigma$*

K-bound $K^\sigma \sqsubseteq \mathrm{Cn}(G_{\mathsf{snd}}^\sigma \sqcup K^\emptyset)$

Prior-Extension $K^\emptyset \sqsubseteq K^\sigma$

Rearrangement *If σ is a permutation of ρ, then $B^\sigma = B^\rho$ and $K^\sigma = K^\rho$*

Equivalence *If $\varphi \equiv \psi$ then $B^{\sigma \cdot \langle i, c, \varphi \rangle} = B^{\sigma \cdot \langle i, c, \psi \rangle}$ and $K^{\sigma \cdot \langle i, c, \varphi \rangle} = K^{\sigma \cdot \langle i, c, \psi \rangle}$*

Closure says that the belief and knowledge collections are closed under logical consequence. In light of earlier remarks, this implies that the propositional belief sets $[B_c^\sigma]$ are closed under (propositional) consequence, and that $E_i(\varphi) \in B_c^\sigma$ iff $E_i(\varphi) \in B_d^\sigma$. *Containment* says that everything which is known is also believed. *Consistency* ensures the output is always consistent, provided we are not in the degenerate case where $*$ gives inconsistent reports. *Soundness* says we *know* that all reports are sound in their respective cases. This formalises our assumption that sources are *honest*, i.e. that false reports only arise due to lack of expertise. By Proposition 1 part (4) it also implies *experts are always right*: if a source has expertise on their report then it must be true. While *Soundness* places a lower bound on knowledge, *K-bound* places an upper bound: knowledge cannot go beyond the soundness statements corresponding to the reports in σ together with the prior knowledge $K^\emptyset$. That is, from the point view of knowledge, a new report of $\langle i, c, \varphi \rangle$ only allows us to learn $S_i(\varphi)$ in case c (and to combine this with other reports and prior knowledge). Note that the analogous property for belief is *not* desirable: we want to be more liberal when it comes to beliefs, and allow for *defeasible inferences* going beyond the mere fact that reports are sound. *Prior-Extension* says that knowledge after a sequence σ extends the prior knowledge on the empty sequence $\emptyset$. *Rearrangement* says that the order in which reports are received is irrelevant. This can be justified on the basis that we are reasoning about *static worlds* for each case c, so that there is no reason to see more "recent" reports as any more or less important or truthful than earlier ones.[5] Consequently, we can essentially view the input as a *multi-set* of belief sets – one for each source – bringing us close to the setting of belief merging. This postulate also appears as the commutativity postulate **(Com)** in the work of Schwind and Konieczny (2020). Finally, *Equivalence* says that the syntactic form of reports is irrelevant.

Taking all the basic postulates together, the knowledge component K^σ is fully determined once $K^\emptyset$ is chosen.

Proposition 3. *Suppose an operator satisfies the basic postulates. Then*

1. $K^\sigma = \mathrm{Cn}(G_{\mathsf{snd}}^\sigma \sqcup K^\emptyset)$
2. $K^\emptyset = \mathrm{Cn}(\emptyset)$ *iff* $K^\sigma = \mathrm{Cn}(G_{\mathsf{snd}}^\sigma)$ *for all* σ.

The choice of $K^\emptyset$ depends on the scenario one wishes to model. While $\mathrm{Cn}(\emptyset)$ is a sensible choice if the sequence σ is all we have to go on, we allow $K^\emptyset \neq \mathrm{Cn}(\emptyset)$ in case *prior knowledge* is available (for example, the expertise of particular sources may be known ahead of time).

Another important property of knowledge, which follows from the basic postulates, says that *knowledge is monotonic*: knowledge after receiving σ and ρ together is just the case-wise union of K^σ and K^ρ.

K-conjunction $K^{\sigma \cdot \rho} = \mathrm{Cn}(K^\sigma \sqcup K^\rho)$

K-conjunction reflects the idea that one should be cautious when it comes to knowledge: a formula should only be accepted as known if it won't be given up in light of new information.

Proposition 4. *Any operator satisfying the basic postulates satisfies* K-conjunction.

The postulates also imply some useful properties linking *trust* (seen as belief in expertise) and *belief/knowledge*.

Proposition 5. *Suppose an operator satisfies the basic postulates. Then*

1. *If $\varphi \in K_c^\sigma$ and $\neg\psi \in \mathrm{Cn}_0(\varphi)$ then $\neg E_i(\psi) \in K_c^{\sigma \cdot \langle i, c, \psi \rangle}$.*
2. *If $\langle i, c, \varphi \rangle \in \sigma$ and $E_i(\varphi) \in B_c^\sigma$ then $\varphi \in B_c^\sigma$.*

[5] This argument is from (Delgrande, Dubois, and Lang 2006).

(1) expresses how knowledge can negatively affect trust: we should distrust sources who make reports we know to be false. (2) expresses how trust affects belief: we should believe reports from trusted sources. It can also be seen as a form of *success* for ordinary sources, and implies AGM success when $i = *$ (by Proposition 1 part (6) and *Closure*). We illustrate the basic postulates by formalising the introductory hospital example.

Example 3. *Set $\mathcal{S}, \mathcal{C}$ and $\mathcal{P}$ as in Example 1, and consider the sequence*

$$\sigma = (\langle *, c_1, x\rangle, \langle a, c_2, x\rangle, \langle b, c_2, \neg x\rangle, \langle a, c_1, \neg x\rangle).$$

What do we know on the basis of this sequence, assuming the basic postulates? First note that by Soundness, *Proposition 1 part (6) and* Closure, *the report from $*$ gives $x \in K^\sigma_{c_1}$, i.e. reliable reports are known.* Soundness *also gives $S_a(x) \wedge S_b(\neg x) \in K^\sigma_{c_2}$. Combined with Proposition 1 parts (2), (4) and* Closure, *this yields $\neg(E_a(x) \wedge E_b(x)) \in K^\sigma_c$ for all c, formalising the intuitive idea that Drs. A and B cannot both be experts on X, since they give conflicting reports. Considering the final report from a, we get $x \wedge S_a(\neg x) \in K^\sigma_{c_1}$, and thus $\neg E_a(x) \in K^\sigma_c$ by* Closure. *So in fact Dr. A is known to be a non-expert on X.*

What about beliefs? The basic postulates do not require beliefs to go beyond knowledge, so we cannot say much in general. An "optimistic" operator, however, may opt to believe that sources are experts unless we know otherwise, and thus maximise the information that can be (defeasibly) inferred from the sequence (in the next section we will introduce concrete operators obeying this principle). In this case we may believe that at least one source has expertise on x (i.e. $E_a(x) \vee E_b(x) \in B^\sigma_c$). Combined with $\neg E_a(x) \in K^\sigma_c$, Closure *and* Containment, *we get $E_b(x) \in B^\sigma_{c_2}$. Symmetry of expertise together with Proposition 5 part (2) then gives $\neg x \in B^\sigma_{c_2}$, i.e. we trust Dr. B in the example and believe patient 2 does not suffer from condition X.*

3.2 Model-Based Operators

While an operator is a purely syntactic object, it will be convenient to specify K^σ and B^σ in semantic terms by selecting a set of *possible* and *most plausible* worlds for each sequence σ. We call such operators *model-based.*

Definition 1. *An operator is* model-based *if for every σ there are sets $\mathcal{X}_\sigma, \mathcal{Y}_\sigma \subseteq \mathcal{W}$ such that (i) $\mathcal{X}_\sigma \supseteq \mathcal{Y}_\sigma$; (ii) $\Phi \in K^\sigma_c$ iff $W, c \models \Phi$ for all $W \in \mathcal{X}_\sigma$; and (iii) $\Phi \in B^\sigma_c$ iff $W, c \models \Phi$ for all $W \in \mathcal{Y}_\sigma$.*

In other words, K^σ_c (resp., B^σ_c) contains the formulas which hold at case c in *all worlds* in $\mathcal{X}_\sigma$ (resp., $\mathcal{Y}_\sigma$). It follows from the relevant definitions that $\mathcal{X}_\sigma \subseteq \mathrm{mod}(K^\sigma)$, and equality holds if and only if $\mathcal{X}_\sigma$ is elementary (similarly for $\mathcal{Y}^\sigma$ and B^σ). Model-based operators are characterised by our first two basic postulates.

Theorem 1. *An operator satisfies* Closure *and* Containment *if and only if it is model-based.*

Since we take *Closure* and *Containment* to be fundamental properties, all operators we consider from now on will be model-based. We introduce our first concrete operator.

Definition 2. *Define the model-based operator* weak-mb *by*

$$\mathcal{X}_\sigma = \mathcal{Y}_\sigma = \{W \mid W, c \models S_i(\varphi) \text{ for all } \langle i, c, \varphi\rangle \in \sigma\}.$$

That is, the possible worlds $\mathcal{X}_\sigma$ are exactly those satisfying the soundness constraint for each report in σ, i.e. false reports are only due to lack of expertise of the corresponding source. Syntactically, $K^\sigma = B^\sigma = \mathrm{Cn}(G^\sigma_{\mathsf{snd}})$.

Clearly weak-mb satisfies *Soundness*, and one can show that it satisfies all of the basic postulates of Section 3.1.[6] In fact, it is the *weakest* operator satisfying *Closure*, *Containment* and *Soundness*, in that for any other operator $\sigma \mapsto \langle \hat{B}^\sigma, \hat{K}^\sigma\rangle$ with these properties we have $B^\sigma \sqsubseteq \hat{B}^\sigma$ and $K^\sigma \sqsubseteq \hat{K}^\sigma$ for any σ.

Example 4. *Consider* weak-mb *applied to the sequence $\sigma = (\langle *, c, p\rangle, \langle i, c, \neg p \wedge q\rangle)$. By* Soundness, Closure *and the validities from Proposition 1, we have $p \in K^\sigma_c$ and $\neg E_i(p) \in K^\sigma_c$. In fact, by* Closure, *we have $\neg E_i(p) \in K^\sigma_d$ for all cases d. However, we cannot say much about q: neither q, $\neg q$, $E_i(q)$ nor $\neg E_i(q)$ are in $B^\sigma_c = K^\sigma_c$.*

4 Constructions

For model-based operators in Definition 1, the sets $\mathcal{X}_\sigma$ and $\mathcal{Y}_\sigma$ – which determine knowledge and belief – can depend on σ in a completely arbitrary manner. This lack of structure leads to very wide class of operators, and one cannot say much about them in general beyond the satisfaction of *Closure* and *Containment*. In this section we specialise model-based operators by providing two constructions.

4.1 Conditioning Operators

Intuitively, $\mathcal{Y}_\sigma$ is supposed to represent the *most plausible* worlds among the possible worlds in $\mathcal{X}_\sigma$. This suggests the presence of a *plausibility ordering* on $\mathcal{X}_\sigma$, which is used to select $\mathcal{Y}_\sigma$. For our first construction we take this approach: we condition a fixed plausibility total preorder[7] on the knowledge $\mathcal{X}_\sigma$, and obtain $\mathcal{Y}_\sigma$ by selecting the minimal (i.e. most plausible) worlds.

Definition 3. *An operator is a* conditioning operator *if there is a total preorder $\leq$ on $\mathcal{W}$ and a mapping $\sigma \mapsto \langle \mathcal{X}_\sigma, \mathcal{Y}_\sigma\rangle$ as in Definition 1 such that $\mathcal{Y}_\sigma = \min_\leq \mathcal{X}_\sigma$ for all σ.*

Note that $\leq$ is independent of σ: it is fixed before receiving any reports. All conditioning operators are model-based by definition. Clearly $\mathcal{Y}_\sigma$ is determined by $\mathcal{X}_\sigma$ and the plausibility order, so that to define a conditioning operator it is enough to specify $\leq$ and the mapping $\sigma \mapsto \mathcal{X}_\sigma$. Write $W \simeq W'$ iff both $W \leq W'$ and $W' \leq W$. We now present examples of how such an ordering can be defined.

Definition 4. *Define the conditioning operator* var-based-cond *by setting $\mathcal{X}_\sigma$ in the same way as* weak-mb *in Definition 2, and $W \leq W'$ iff $r(W) \leq r(W')$, where*

$$r(W) = -\sum_{i \in \mathcal{S}} \left|\{p \in \mathcal{P} \mid \Pi^W_i[p] = \mathrm{mod}_0(p)\}\right|.$$

[6] For *Consistency*, note that for any $*$-consistent sequence σ one can form a world W such that v_c is a model of all reports from $*$ at case c, and $\Pi_i = \{\mathcal{V}\}$ for all $i \neq *$. This satisfies all the soundness constraints, so $W \in \mathcal{X}_\sigma = \mathcal{Y}_\sigma$.

[7] A total preorder is a reflexive, transitive and total relation.

var-based-cond aims to trust each source on *as many propositional variables* as possible. One can check that var-based-cond satisfies the basic postulates.

Example 5. *Revisiting the sequence* $\sigma = (\langle *, c, p\rangle, \langle i, c, \neg p \wedge q\rangle)$ *from Example 4 with* var-based-cond, *the knowledge set* K^σ_c *is the same as before, but we now have* $q \wedge E_i(q) \in B^\sigma_c$. *This reflects the "credulous" behaviour of the ranking* $\leq$*: while it is not possible to believe* i *is an expert on* p*, we should believe they* are *an expert on* q *so long as this does not conflict with soundness. For the propositional beliefs generally, we have* $[B^\sigma_c] = \mathrm{Cn}_0(p \wedge q)$. *That is,* var-based-cond *takes the* q *part of the report from* i *(on which* i *is credulously trusted) while ignoring the* $\neg p$ *part (which is false due to report from* $*$*).*

Definition 5. *Define a conditioning operator* part-based-cond *with* $\mathcal{X}_\sigma$ *as for* var-based-cond, *and* $\leq$ *defined by the ranking function*

$$r(W) = -\sum_{i \in \mathcal{S}} |\Pi^W_i|.$$

part-based-cond aims to maximise the *number of cells* in the sources' partitions, and thereby maximise the number of propositions on which they have expertise. Unlike var-based-cond, the propositional variables play no special role. As expected, part-based-cond satisfies the basic postulates.

Example 6. *Applying* part-based-cond *to* σ *from Examples 4 and 5, we no longer extract* q *from the report of* i*:* $q \notin B^\sigma_c$ *and* $E_i(q) \notin B^\sigma_c$. *Instead, we have* $[B^\sigma_c] = \mathrm{Cn}_0(p)$*, and* $E_i(p \vee q) \in B^\sigma_c$.

Note that both var-based-cond and part-based-cond are based on the general principle of maximising the expertise of sources, subject to the constraint that all reports are sound. This intuition is formalised by the following postulate for conditioning operators. In what follows, write $W \preceq W'$ iff Π^W_i refines $\Pi^{W'}_i$ for all $i \in \mathcal{S}$, i.e. if all sources have broadly more expertise in W than in W'.[8]

Refinement *If* $W \preceq W'$ *then* $W \leq W'$

Since $\preceq$ is only a partial order on $\mathcal{W}$ there are many possible total extensions; var-based-cond and part-based-cond provide two specific examples.

We now turn to an axiomatic characterisation of conditioning operators. Taken with the basic postulates from Section 3.1, conditioning operators can be characterised using an approach similar to that of Delgrande, Peppas, and Woltran (2018) in their account of *generalised AGM belief revision*.[9] This involves a technical property Delgrande, Peppas, and Woltran call *Acyc*, which finds its roots in the *Loop* property of Kraus, Lehmann, and Magidor (1990).

Duplicate-removal *If* $\rho_1 = \sigma \cdot \langle i, c, \varphi\rangle$ and $\rho_2 = \rho_1 \cdot \langle i, c, \varphi\rangle$ then $B^{\rho_1} = B^{\rho_2}$ and $K^{\rho_1} = K^{\rho_2}$

Conditional-consistency *If* K^σ *is consistent then so is* B^σ

Inclusion-vacuity $B^{\sigma \cdot \rho} \sqsubseteq \mathrm{Cn}(B^\sigma \sqcup K^\rho)$*, with equality if* $B^\sigma \sqcup K^\rho$ *is consistent*

Acyc *If* $\sigma_0, \ldots, \sigma_n$ *are such that* $K^{\sigma_j} \sqcup B^{\sigma_{j+1}}$ *is consistent for all* $0 \leq j < n$ *and* $K^{\sigma_n} \sqcup B^{\sigma_0}$ *is consistent, then* $K^{\sigma_0} \sqcup B^{\sigma_n}$ *is consistent*

Inclusion-vacuity is so-named since it is analogous to the combination of *Inclusion* and *Vacuity* from AGM revision, if one informally views $B^{\sigma \cdot \rho}$ as the revision of B^σ by K^ρ. *Conditional-consistency* is another consistency postulate, which follows from *Consistency*, *Closure* and *Soundness*. *Acyc* is the analogue of the postulate of Delgrande, Peppas, and Woltran, which rules out cycles in the plausibility order constructed in the representation result.

As with the result of Delgrande, Peppas, and Woltran, a technical condition beyond Definition 3 is required to obtain the characterisation: say that a conditioning operator is *elementary* if for each σ the sets of worlds $\mathcal{X}_\sigma$ and $\mathcal{Y}_\sigma = \min_\leq \mathcal{X}_\sigma$ are elementary.[10]

Theorem 2. *Suppose an operator satisfies the basic postulates of Section 3.1.*[11] *Then it is an elementary conditioning operator if and only if it satisfies* Duplicate-removal, Conditional-consistency, Inclusion-vacuity *and* Acyc.

The proof roughly follows the lines of Theorem 4.9 in (Delgrande, Peppas, and Woltran 2018), although some differences arise due to the form of our input as finite sequences of reports. We note that while the requirement that $\mathcal{X}_\sigma$ and $\mathcal{Y}_\sigma$ are elementary is a technical condition,[12] the characterisation in Proposition 2 implies a simple sufficient condition for elementariness.

Proposition 6. *Suppose* $\leq$ *is such that* $W \simeq W'$ *whenever* W *and* W' *are partition-equivalent. Then* $\min_\leq S$ *is elementary for any elementary set* $S \subseteq \mathcal{W}$.

Proposition 6 implies that var-based-cond and part-based-cond are elementary. Indeed, for both operators $\mathcal{X}_\sigma = \mathrm{mod}(G^\sigma_{\mathsf{snd}})$ so is elementary by definition. Since the ranking $\leq$ for each operator only depends on the partitions of worlds, $\mathcal{Y}_\sigma = \min_\leq \mathcal{X}_\sigma$ is elementary also.

4.2 Score-Based Operators

The fact that the plausibility order $\leq$ of a conditioning operator is fixed may be too limiting. For example, consider

$$\sigma = (\langle i, c, p\rangle, \langle j, c, \neg p\rangle, \langle i, d, p\rangle).$$

If one sets $\mathcal{X}_\sigma$ to satisfy the soundness constraints (i.e. as in weak-mb), there is a possible world $W_1 \in \mathcal{X}_\sigma$ with $W_1, d \models \neg E_i(p) \wedge E_j(p) \wedge \neg p$ (i.e. W_1 sides with source j and p is false at d) and another world $W_2 \in \mathcal{X}_\sigma$ with $W_2, d \models E_i(p) \wedge \neg E_j(p) \wedge p$ (i.e. W_2 sides with source i). Appealing to symmetry, one may argue that neither world is *a priori* more plausible than the other, so any fixed plausibility order should have $W_1 \simeq W_2$. If these worlds are maximally plausible (e.g. if taking the "optimistic" view outlined

[8] Π refines Π' if $\forall A \in \Pi, \exists B \in \Pi'$ such that $A \subseteq B$.

[9] Note that while the result is similar, our framework is not an instance of theirs.

[10] Equivalently, there is a total preorder $\leq$ such that $\mathrm{mod}(B^\sigma) = \min_\leq \mathrm{mod}(K^\sigma)$ for all σ.

[11] Strictly speaking, we only need *Closure*, *Containment*, *K-conjunction*, *Equivalence* and *Rearrangement*.

[12] *Inclusion-vacuity* may fail for non-elementary conditioning.

in Example 3), conditioning gives $p \notin B^{\sigma}_{d}$ and $\neg p \notin B^{\sigma}_{d}$. However, there is an argument that W_2 should be considered more plausible than W_1 *given the sequence* σ, since W_2 validates the final report $\langle i, d, p\rangle$ whereas W_1 does not. Consequently, there is an argument that we should in fact have $p \in B^{\sigma}_{d}$.[13] This shows that we need the plausibility order to be responsive to the input sequence for adequate belief change.[14]

As a result of this discussion, we look for operators whose plausibility ordering can depend on σ. One approach to achieve this in a controlled way is to have a ranking for each *report* $\langle i, c, \varphi\rangle$, and combine these to construct a ranking for each sequence σ. We represent these rankings by *scoring functions*, and call the resulting operators *score-based.*

Definition 6. *An operator is* score-based *if there is a mapping* $\sigma \mapsto \langle \mathcal{X}_\sigma, \mathcal{Y}_\sigma\rangle$ *as in Definition 1 and functions* $r_0 : \mathcal{W} \to \mathbb{N}\cup\{\infty\}$, $d : \mathcal{W}\times(\mathcal{S}\times\mathcal{C}\times\mathcal{L}_0) \to \mathbb{N}\cup\{\infty\}$ *such that* $\mathcal{X}_\sigma = \{W \mid r_\sigma(W) < \infty\}$ *and* $\mathcal{Y}_\sigma = \operatorname{argmin}_{W\in\mathcal{X}_\sigma} r_\sigma(W)$, *where*

$$r_\sigma(W) = r_0(W) + \sum\nolimits_{\langle i,c,\varphi\rangle\in\sigma} d(W, \langle i, c, \varphi\rangle).$$

Here $r_0(W)$ is the *prior implausibility score* of W, and $d(W, \langle i, c, \varphi\rangle)$ is the *disagreement score* for world W and $\langle i, c, \varphi\rangle$. The set of most plausible worlds $\mathcal{Y}_\sigma$ consists of those W which minimise the sum of the prior implausibility and the total disagreement with σ. Note that by summing the scores of each report $\langle i, c, \varphi\rangle$ with equal weight, we treat each report independently. Score-based operators generalise elementary conditioning operators with *K-conjunction.*

Proposition 7. *Any elementary conditioning operator satisfying* K-conjunction *is score-based.*

We now give a concrete example.

Definition 7. *Define a score-based operator* excess-min *by setting* $r_0(W) = 0$ *and*

$$d(W, \langle i, c, \varphi\rangle) = \begin{cases} |\Pi^W_i[\varphi] \setminus \mathrm{mod}_0(\varphi)|, & W, c \models S_i(\varphi) \\ \infty, & \textit{otherwise.}\end{cases}$$

The set of possible worlds $\mathcal{X}_\sigma$ is the same as for the earlier operators. All worlds are *a priori* equiplausible according to r_0. The disagreement score d is defined as the number of propositional valuations in the "excess" of $\Pi^W_i[\varphi]$ which are not models of φ, i.e. the number of $\neg\varphi$ valuations which are indistinguishable from some φ valuation. The intuition here is that *sources tend to only report formulas on which they have expertise.* The minimum score 0 is attained exactly when i has expertise on φ; other worlds are ordered by how much they deviate from this ideal.

One can verify that excess-min satisfies the basic postulates of Section 3.1. It can also be seen that $\mathcal{X}_\sigma$ and $\mathcal{Y}_\sigma$ are elementary, and excess-min fails *Duplicate-removal* and *Inclusion-vacuity.* It follows from Theorem 2 that excess-min is *not* a conditioning operator.

[13] At the very least, the case $p \in B^{\sigma}_{d}$ should not be *excluded.*

[14] In Section 5 we make this argument more precise by providing an impossibility result which shows conditioning operators with some basic properties cannot accept p in sequences such as this.

Example 7. *To illustrate the differences between* excess-min *and conditioning, consider a more elaborate version of the example given at the start of this section:*

$$\sigma = (\langle i, c, p \to q\rangle, \langle j, c, p \to \neg q\rangle, \langle *, c, p\rangle, \langle i, d, p\rangle, \langle i, d, q\rangle).$$

Here the reports of i *and* j *in case* c *are consistent, but inconsistent when taken with the reliable information* p *from* $*$. *Should we believe* q *or* $\neg q$? *Both our conditioning operators* var-based-cond *and* part-based-cond *decline to decide, and have* $[B^{\sigma}_{c}] = \mathrm{Cn}_0(p)$. *However, since* excess-min *takes into account each report in the sequence, the fact that* i *reports both* p *and* q *in case* d *leads to* $E_i(p) \wedge E_i(q) \in B^{\sigma}_{c}$. *This gives* $E_i(p \to q) \in B^{\sigma}_{c}$ *by Proposition 1 part (3), so we can make use of the report from* i *in case* c: *we have* $[B^{\sigma}_{c}] = \mathrm{Cn}_0(p \wedge q)$. *This example shows that score-based operators can be* more credulous *than conditioning operators (e.g. we can believe* $E_i(p)$ *when* i *reports* p*), and can consequently hold stronger propositional beliefs.*

5 One-Step Revision

The postulates of Section 3.1 only set out very basic requirements for an operator. In this section we introduce some more demanding postulates which address how beliefs should change when a sequence σ is extended by a new report $\langle i, c, \varphi\rangle$. First, we address how propositional beliefs should be affected by reliable information.

AGM-$*$ *For any* σ *and* $c \in \mathcal{C}$ *there is an AGM operator* $\star$ *for* $[B^{\sigma}_{c}]$ *such that* $\left[B^{\sigma\cdot\langle *,c,\varphi\rangle}_{c}\right] = [B^{\sigma}_{c}] \star \varphi$ *whenever* $\neg\varphi \notin K^{\sigma}_{c}$

AGM-$*$ says that receiving information from the reliable source $*$ acts in accordance with the well-known AGM postulates (Alchourrón, Gärdenfors, and Makinson 1985) for propositional belief revision (provided we are not in the degenerate case where the new report φ was already *known* to be false). Since AGM revision operators are characterised by total preorders over valuations (Grove 1988; Katsuno and Mendelzon 1991), it is no surprise that our order-based constructions are consistent with *AGM-$*$*.

Proposition 8. var-based-cond, part-based-cond *and* excess-min *satisfy* AGM-$*$.

Thus, we do indeed extend AGM revision in the case of reliable information. What about non-reliable information? First note that the analogue of *AGM-$*$* for ordinary sources $i \neq *$ is *not* desirable. In particular, we should not have the *Success* postulate:

$$\varphi \in B^{\sigma\cdot\langle i,c,\varphi\rangle}_{c}.$$

Indeed, the sequence in Example 4 with $\varphi = \neg p \wedge q$ already shows that *Success* would conflict with the basic postulates. However, there are weaker modifications of *Success* which may be more appropriate. We consider two such postulates.

Cond-success *If* $E_i(\varphi) \in B^{\sigma}_{c}$ *and* $\neg\varphi \notin B^{\sigma}_{c}$, *then* $\varphi \in B^{\sigma\cdot\langle i,c,\varphi\rangle}_{c}$

Strong-cond-success *If* $\neg(E_i(\varphi) \wedge \varphi) \notin B^{\sigma}_{c}$, *then* $\varphi \in B^{\sigma\cdot\langle i,c,\varphi\rangle}_{c}$

Cond-success says that if i is deemed an expert on φ, which is consistent with current beliefs, then φ is accepted after i reports it. That is, the acceptance of φ is *conditional* on prior beliefs about the expertise of i (on φ). *Strong-cond-success* weakens the antecedent by only requiring that $E_i(\varphi)$ and φ are jointly consistent with current beliefs (i.e. i need not be considered an expert on φ). In other words, we should believe reports if there is no reason not to. It is easily shown that *Closure* and *Strong-cond-success* implies *Cond-success*. We once again revisit our examples.

Proposition 9. var-based-cond, part-based-cond *and* excess-min *satisfy* Cond-success, *and* excess-min *additionally satisfies* Strong-cond-success.

By omission, the reader may suppose that the conditioning operators fail *Strong-cond-success*. This is correct, and we can in fact say even more: *no* conditioning operator with a few basic properties – all of which are satisfied by var-based-cond and part-based-cond – can satisfy *Strong-cond-success*. In what follows, for a permutation $\pi : \mathcal{S} \to \mathcal{S}$ with $\pi(*) = *$, write $\pi(W)$ for the world with $v_c^{\pi(W)} = v_c^W$ and $\Pi_i^{\pi(W)} = \Pi_{\pi(i)}^W$. We have an impossibility result.

Proposition 10. *No elementary conditioning operator satisfying the basic postulates can simultaneously satisfy the following properties:*

1. $K^\emptyset = \mathrm{Cn}(\emptyset)$
2. *If* π *is a permutation of* $\mathcal{S}$ *with* $\pi(*) = *$, $W \simeq \pi(W)$
3. Refinement
4. Strong-cond-success

(1) says that before any reports are received, we only know tautologies. As remarked earlier, this is not an *essential* property, but is reasonable when no prior knowledge is available. (2) is an anonymity postulate: it says that permuting the "names" of sources does not affect the plausibility of a world, and is a desirable property in light of (1). *Refinement*, introduced in Section 4.1, says that worlds in which all sources have more expertise are preferred.

Proposition 10 highlights an important difference between conditioning and score-based operators, and hints that a fixed plausibility order may be too restrictive: we need to allow the order to be responsive to new reports in order to satisfy properties such as *Strong-cond-success*.

6 Selective Change

In the previous section we saw how a single formula φ may be accepted when it is received as an additional report. But what can we say about propositional beliefs when taking into account the *whole sequence* σ? To investigate this we introduce an analogue of *selective revision* (Fermé and Hansson 1999), in which propositional beliefs are formed by "selecting" part of each input report (intuitively, some part consistent with the source's expertise). In what follows, write $\sigma \upharpoonright c = \{\langle i, \varphi\rangle \mid \langle i, c, \varphi\rangle \in \sigma\}$ for the c-reports in σ.

Definition 8. *A* selection scheme *is a mapping* f *assigning to each* $*$*-consistent sequence* σ *a function* $f_\sigma : \mathcal{S} \times \mathcal{C} \times \mathcal{L}_0 \to \mathcal{L}_0$ *such that* $f_\sigma(i, c, \varphi) \in \mathrm{Cn}_0(\varphi)$. *An operator is* selective *if there is a selection scheme* f *such that for all* $*$*-consistent* σ *and* $c \in \mathcal{C}$,

$$[B_c^\sigma] = \mathrm{Cn}_0(\{f_\sigma(i, c, \varphi) \mid \langle i, \varphi\rangle \in \sigma \upharpoonright c\}).$$

Thus, an operator is selective if its propositional beliefs in case c are formed by weakening each c-report and taking their consequences. Note that for $\sigma = \emptyset$ we get $[B_c^\sigma] = \mathrm{Cn}_0(\emptyset)$, so selectivity already rules out non-tautological prior propositional beliefs. Also note that in the presence of *Closure*, *Containment* and *Soundness*, selectivity implies that $[B_c^\sigma] = [B_c^\rho]$, where ρ is obtained by replacing each report $\langle i, c, \varphi\rangle$ with $\langle *, c, f_\sigma(i, c, \varphi)\rangle$.

Selectivity can be characterised by a natural postulate placing an upper bound on the propositional part of B_c^σ. In what follows, let $\Gamma_c^\sigma = \{\varphi \in \mathcal{L}_0 \mid \exists i \in \mathcal{S} : \langle i, \varphi\rangle \in \sigma \upharpoonright c\}$.

Boundedness *If* σ *is* $*$*-consistent,* $[B_c^\sigma] \subseteq \mathrm{Cn}_0(\Gamma_c^\sigma)$

Boundedness says that the propositional beliefs in case c should not go beyond the consequences of the formulas reported in case c. In some sense this can be seen as an iterated version of *Inclusion* from AGM revision, in the case where $[B_c^\sigma] = \mathrm{Cn}_0(\emptyset)$. We have the following characterisation.

Theorem 3. *A model-based operator is selective if and only if it satisfies* Boundedness.

This result allows us to easily analyse when conditioning and score-based operators are selective; we show in the full paper (Singleton and Booth 2022) that var-based-cond, part-based-cond and excess-min are all selective.

6.1 Case Independence

In the definition of a selection scheme, we allow $f_\sigma(i, c, \varphi)$ to depend on the case c. If one views $f_\sigma(i, c, \varphi)$ as a weakening of φ which accounts for the lack of expertise of i, this is somewhat at odds with other aspects of the framework, where expertise is independent of case. For this reason it is natural to consider *case independent* selective schemes.

Definition 9. *A selection scheme* f *is* case independent *if* $f_\sigma(i, c, \varphi) \equiv f_\sigma(i, d, \varphi)$ *for all* $*$*-consistent* σ *and* $i \in \mathcal{S}$, $c, d \in \mathcal{C}$ *and* $\varphi \in \mathcal{L}_0$.

Say an operator is *case-independent-selective* if it is selective according to some case independent scheme. This stronger notion of selectivity can again be characterised by a postulate which bounds propositional beliefs. For any set of cases $H \subseteq \mathcal{C}$, sequence σ and $c \in \mathcal{C}$, write

$$\Gamma_c^{\sigma,H} = \{\varphi \in \mathcal{L}_0 \mid \exists i \in \mathcal{S} : \langle i, \varphi\rangle \in \sigma \upharpoonright c \text{ and } \forall d \in H : \langle i, \varphi\rangle \notin \sigma \upharpoonright d\}.$$

H-Boundedness For any $*$-consistent σ, $H \subseteq \mathcal{C}$ and $c \in \mathcal{C}$,

$$[B_c^\sigma] \subseteq \mathrm{Cn}_0\left(\Gamma_c^{\sigma,H} \cup \bigcup_{d \in H} [B_d^\sigma]\right)$$

Note that *Boundedness* is obtained as the special case where $H = \emptyset$. We illustrate with an example.

Example 8. *Consider case* c *in the following sequence:*

$$\sigma = (\langle i, c, p\rangle, \langle j, c, q\rangle, \langle j, d, q\rangle, \langle k, d, r\rangle)$$

Boundedness *requires that* $[B^\sigma_c] \subseteq \mathrm{Cn}_0(\{p, q\})$. *However, the instance of* H-Boundedness *with* $H = \{d\}$ *makes use of the fact that* j *reports* q *in both cases* c *and* d, *and requires* $[B^\sigma_c] \subseteq \mathrm{Cn}_0(\{p\} \cup [B^\sigma_d])$. *This also has an interesting implication for case* d: *if* $\varphi \in [B^\sigma_c]$, *then* $p \to \varphi \in [B^\sigma_d]$. *This follows since* $\beta \in \mathrm{Cn}_0(\{\alpha\} \cup \Gamma)$ *iff* $\alpha \to \beta \in \mathrm{Cn}_0(\Gamma)$ *for* $\alpha, \beta \in \mathcal{L}_0$. *Intuitively, this says that if* p *(from* i*) and* q *(from* j*) is enough to accept* φ *in case* c, *then* φ *is accepted in case* d if p is, *given that the report of* q *from* j *is repeated for* d.

Theorem 4. *A model-based operator is case-independent-selective if and only if it satisfies* H-Boundedness.

The question of whether our concrete operators satisfy *H-Boundedness* (equivalently, whether they are case-independent-selective) is still open.

7 Related Work

Belief Merging. In the framework of Konieczny and Pino Pérez (2002), a merging operator Δ maps a multiset of propositional formulas $\Phi = \{\varphi_1, \ldots, \varphi_n\}$ and an integrity constraint μ to a formula $\Delta_\mu(\Phi)$. This can be seen as the special case of our framework with a single case c: for Φ, μ we consider the sequence $\sigma_{\Phi,\mu}$ where $*$ reports μ and each source i reports φ_i. Any operator then gives rise to a merging operator $\Delta_\mu(\Phi) = \bigwedge [B^{\sigma_{\Phi,\mu}}_c]$.

We go beyond this setting by considering multiple cases and explicitly modelling expertise (and trust, via beliefs about expertise). While it may be possible to model expertise *implicitly* in belief merging (for example, say i is not trusted on ψ if $\Delta_\mu(\Phi) \not\vdash \psi$ when $\varphi_i \vdash \psi$), bringing expertise to the object level allows us to express more complex beliefs about expertise, such as $E_a(x) \vee E_b(x)$ in Example 3. It also facilitates postulates which refer directly to expertise, such as the weakenings of *Success* in Section 5.

However, our problem is more specialised than merging, since we focus specifically on conflicting information due to lack of expertise. Belief merging may be applied more broadly to other types of *information fusion*, e.g. subjective beliefs or goals (Grégoire and Konieczny 2006), where notions of objective expertise do not apply. While our framework *could* be applied in these settings, our postulates may no longer be desirable.

Epistemic Logic. Our notions of expertise and soundness are related to *S5 knowledge* from epistemic logic (van Ditmarsch et al. 2015). In such logics, an agent *knows* φ at a state x if φ holds at all states y "accessible" from x. Knowledge is thus determined by an *epistemic accessibility relation*, which describes the distinctions between states the agent can make. The logic of S5 arises when this relation is an equivalence relation (or equivalently, a partition).

Our previous work (Singleton 2021) – in which expertise and soundness were introduced in a modal logic framework – showed that "expertise models" are in 1-to-1 correspondence with S5 models, such that $E(\varphi)$ holds iff $A(\varphi \to K\varphi)$ holds in the S5 model, where A is the universal modality. By symmetry of expertise, we can also replace φ with its negation. Thus, expertise has a precise epistemic interpretation: it is the ability to *know whether* φ holds in *any possible state*. Similarly, $S(\varphi)$ translates to $\neg K \neg \varphi$. That is, φ is sound exactly when the source does not *know* φ is false.

In the present framework, if we set $W, c \models K_i(\varphi)$ iff $\Pi_i[v_c] \subseteq \mathrm{mod}_0(\varphi)$ and $W, c \models A\Phi$ iff $\forall v : W_{c=v}, c \models \Phi$, where $W_{c=v}$ is the world obtained from W by setting $v'_c = v$, then we have $E_i(\varphi) \equiv A(\varphi \to K_i(\varphi))$ and $S_i(\varphi) \equiv \neg K_i(\neg\varphi)$. While K_i is not quite an S5 modality (the **5** axiom requires iterating K_i, which is not possible in our framework), this shows the fundamental link between expertise, soundness and knowledge.

8 Conclusion

Summary. In this paper we studied a belief change problem – extending the classical AGM framework – in which beliefs about the state of the world in multiple cases, as well as expertise of multiple sources, must be inferred from a sequence of reports. This allowed us to take a fresh look at the interaction between trust (seen as *belief in expertise*) and belief. By inferring the expertise of the sources from the reports, we have generalised some earlier approaches to non-prioritised revision which assume expertise (or reliability, credibility, priority etc) is known up-front (e.g. (Fermé and Hansson 1999; Hansson et al. 2001; Booth and Hunter 2018; Delgrande, Dubois, and Lang 2006)). We went on to propose some concrete belief change operators, and explored their properties through examples and postulates.

We saw that conditioning operators satisfy some desirable properties, and our concrete instances make useful inferences that go beyond weak-mb. However, we have examples in which intuitively plausible inferences are blocked, and conditioning is largely incompatible with *Strong-cond-success*. Score-based operators, and in particular excess-min, offer a way around these limitations, but may come at the expense of some other seemingly reasonable postulates, such as *Duplicate-removal*.

Future Work. There are many possibilities for future work. Firstly, we have a representation result only for conditioning operators. A characterisation of score-based operators – either the class in general or the specific operator excess-min – remains to be found. This would help to further clarify the differences between conditioning and score-based operators. We have also not considered any computational issues. Determining the complexity of calculating the results of our example operators, and the complexity for conditioning and score-based operators more broadly, is left to future work. Secondly, there is scope for deeper postulate-based analysis. For example, there should be postulates governing how beliefs change in case c in response to reports in case d. We could also consider more postulates relating trust and belief, and compare these postulates with those of Yasser and Ismail (2021). Finally, our framework only deals with three levels of trust on a proposition: we can believe $E_i(\varphi)$, believe $\neg E_i(\varphi)$, or neither. Future work could investigate how to extend our semantics to talk about *graded expertise*, and thereby permit more fine-grained *degrees of trust* (Hunter 2021; Yasser and Ismail 2021; Delgrande, Dubois, and Lang 2006).

Acknowledgements

We thank the anonymous reviewers for their thoughtful comments and suggestions.

References

Alchourrón, C. E.; Gärdenfors, P.; and Makinson, D. 1985. On the logic of theory change: Partial meet contraction and revision functions. *Journal of symbolic logic* 510–530.

Booth, R., and Hunter, A. 2018. Trust as a Precursor to Belief Revision. *J. Artif. Intell. Res.* 61:699–722.

Delgrande, J. P.; Dubois, D.; and Lang, J. 2006. Iterated revision as prioritized merging. *KR* 6:210–220.

Delgrande, J. P.; Peppas, P.; and Woltran, S. 2018. General belief revision. *Journal of the ACM (JACM)* 65(5):1–34.

Fermé, E. L., and Hansson, S. O. 1999. Selective revision. *Studia Logica* 63(3):331–342.

Grove, A. 1988. Two modellings for theory change. *Journal of philosophical logic* 157–170.

Grégoire, E., and Konieczny, S. 2006. Logic-based approaches to information fusion. *Information Fusion* 7(1):4 – 18. Logic-based Approaches to Information Fusion.

Hansson, S. O.; Fermé, E. L.; Cantwell, J.; and Falappa, M. A. 2001. Credibility limited revision. *Journal of Symbolic Logic* 66(4):1581–1596.

Hansson, S. O. 1999. A survey of non-prioritized belief revision. *Erkenntnis* 50(2):413–427.

Hunter, A. 2021. Building trust for belief revision. In Pham, D. N.; Theeramunkong, T.; Governatori, G.; and Liu, F., eds., *PRICAI 2021: Trends in Artificial Intelligence*, 543–555. Cham: Springer International Publishing.

Katsuno, H., and Mendelzon, A. O. 1991. Propositional knowledge base revision and minimal change. *Artificial Intelligence* 52(3):263–294.

Konieczny, S., and Pino Pérez, R. 2002. Merging information under constraints: a logical framework. *Journal of Logic and Computation* 12(5):773–808.

Kraus, S.; Lehmann, D.; and Magidor, M. 1990. Nonmonotonic reasoning, preferential models and cumulative logics. *Artificial intelligence* 44(1-2):167–207.

Li, Y.; Gao, J.; Meng, C.; Li, Q.; Su, L.; Zhao, B.; Fan, W.; and Han, J. 2016. A Survey on Truth Discovery. *SIGKDD Explor. Newsl.* 17(2):1–16.

Schwind, N., and Konieczny, S. 2020. Non-Prioritized Iterated Revision: Improvement via Incremental Belief Merging. In *Proceedings of the 17th International Conference on Principles of Knowledge Representation and Reasoning*, 738–747.

Singleton, J., and Booth, R. 2022. Who's the expert? On multi-source belief change. https://arxiv.org/abs/2205.00077.

Singleton, J. 2021. A logic of expertise. *ESSLLI 2021 Student Session*. https://arxiv.org/abs/2107.10832.

van Ditmarsch, H.; van der Hoek, W.; Halpern, J.; and Kooi, B., eds. 2015. *Handbook of Epistemic Logic*. College Publications.

Yasser, A., and Ismail, H. O. 2021. Trust is all you need: From belief revision to information revision. In Faber, W.; Friedrich, G.; Gebser, M.; and Morak, M., eds., *Logics in Artificial Intelligence*, 50–65. Cham: Springer International Publishing.

Proceedings of the 19th International Conference on Principles of Knowledge Representation and Reasoning
Main Track

Hyperintensional Partial Meet Contractions

Marlo Souza[1,2] , **Renata Wassermann**[2]
[1]Federal University of Bahia, Salvador, Brazil
[2]University of São Paulo, São Paulo, Brazil
msouza1@ufba.br, renata@ime.usp.br

Abstract

Formal frameworks for Epistemology need to have enough logical structure to enable interesting conclusions regarding epistemic phenomena and to be expressive enough to model competing positions in the philosophical and logical literature. While beliefs are commonly accepted as hyperintensional attitudes, i.e., epistemic attitudes, which may differ even towards necessarily equivalent sentences, most work on standard epistemic logic has relied on idealised and intensional agents. This is particularly true in the area of AGM-inspired Belief Change. Although a few recent studies investigate hyperintensional models of belief change, few have been well connected to the AGM framework, the main paradigm in the area. This work investigates hyperintensional notions of belief base contraction and belief set contraction, as studied in the AGM framework, and its connections to partial meet contractions. We also provide suitable representation theorems, characterising the constructions by means of rationality postulates.

1 Introduction

Formal frameworks for Epistemology, i.e., frameworks to reason about beliefs and knowledge, face a double-edged requirement. They need at the same time to be sufficiently structured, in the sense that we can employ them to reason about a broad class of doxastic agents, but flexible and expressive enough to model different theoretical and philosophical positions in the field, as discussed by Berto and Hawke (2021).

Since the work of Hintikka (1962), the epistemic logic tradition has heavily relied on idealised agents, as discussed by Rantala (1982) and Halpern and Puccela (2011). For example, standard epistemic logic has received criticism on the nature of its idealised agents and the intentional nature of beliefs in its models, c. f. the work of Cresswell (1972). It has also been argued in the literature (Halpern and Pucella 2011; Wansing 1990; Jago 2009; Bjerring 2013) that resource-bounded agents are not required to believe all consequences of their currently held beliefs, as an agent can fail to reach the conclusion of a reasoning process due to a lack of cognitive resources.

Similarly, in Belief Change, the area that studies how doxastic agents change their minds after acquiring new information, one of the most influential approaches in the literature, namely the AGM framework (Alchourrón, Gärdenfors, and Makinson 1985), also relies on heavily idealised agents. AGM admits as a representation of an agent's belief state a consequentially-closed set of formulas, requiring thus that an agent believes in all consequences of their beliefs. In fact, Gärdenfors (1988, p. 9) acknowledges that AGM's notion of Belief is but merely an idealisation "judged in relation to the rationality criteria for the epistemological theory".

It is well recognised in the literature, however, as discussed by Özgün and Berto (2020), that beliefs and other mental attitudes are sensitive to hyperintensional distinctions and that these latter are connected to well-studied problems, such as logical omniscience. We call, after Cresswell (1975), *hyperintensional attitudes* those which depend on sentential contents finer-grained than intensions. In other words, these attitudes can draw distinctions between necessarily equivalent contents. For example, while the sentences "*3 is a prime number*" and "*3068 is divisible by 13*" have the same intension as mathematical necessities, they certainly cannot be transparently substituted for the other in the sentence "Alice believes that *3 is a prime number*."

Aiming to obtain a compromise between the logical power of standard epistemic logic, as well as its unrealistic computational demands and the lack of expressiveness to encode current positions in philosophical debate (Berto and Hawke 2021), Levesque (1984) proposes a logic in which we can distinguish the notions of explicit and implicit beliefs. Explicit beliefs represent the notions of Belief that need not be closed under logical consequence and purely intentional, while implicit beliefs represent those that an agent may achieve from their explicit beliefs. In Belief Change, a similar position was advocated by Hansson (1992), who proposes that the representation of an agent's belief state, and its dynamics, depends on the syntactic structure of agents' explicit beliefs.

Despite incorporating some form of hyperintensionality in the representation of beliefs (and belief change) in the area, Hansson's approach does not consider hyperintensional difference in the input, i.e. the received information. For example, let B be a set of logical formulas[1] representing the belief base of an agent, i.e. the representation of their belief state, φ and ψ be logical formulas, and $\star$ be a belief

[1]In this example, we do not require any specific logic. Later, in Section 3, we will define more clearly our notion of logic.

change operation. Hansson's postulate of *uniformity* implies that if $Cn(\varphi) = Cn(\psi)$, then $B \star \varphi = B \star \varphi$, thus belief base change still preserves dependence on intensionality in the dynamics of beliefs.

Recently, work on hyperintensional belief change has risen in the literature to deal with this limitation. Most prominent, Berto (2019) proposes a hyperintensional logic of conditional beliefs and investigates hyperintensional belief revision operations interpreted as conditional beliefs. Other work soon followed, such as Özgün and Berto (2020) who dynamify Berto's conditional logic, proposing a dynamic logic of hyperintensional belief revision. On the other hand, Souza (2020) and Souza and Wassermann (2021) investigate hyperintensional belief change operations using tools similar to that of the AGM framework, based on abstract logics. These authors propose connections between hyperintensional belief change and belief change in non-classical logics, showing that for several logics of interest to AI, we can obtain partial meet-like operations based on a classical logic.

The main drawback of the work of Souza and Wassermann (2021) is that hyperintensional belief change is defined through intensional operators. For example, let C be the consequence operator of Intuitionistic Propositional Calculus (IPC) (Van Dalen 1994), and let Cn be the consequence operator of Classical Propositional Calculus (CPC), Souza and Wassermann show how one can use Cn to compute Belief Change for the logic defined by operator C. However, let p be the proposition that "3068 is divisible by 13". A constructive agent, i.e. an agent with intuitionistic reasoning, with a belief state believing that $\neg p$ is not true, can be described by the set of beliefs $B = \{\neg\neg p\}$. As $\neg\neg p \rightarrow p$ is not valid in IPC, the agent cannot, over the risk of irrationality, state that p is true. However, if the agent comes to the conclusion that there is no support for p, there is no operation defined by Souza and Wassermann in which removing the belief in p from B does not result in a belief state in which the agent believes that $\neg\neg p$, even though the agent did not initially believe p.

In this work, we explore further the notion of hyperintensional belief change, as studied by Souza (2020) and Souza and Wassermann (2021), aiming to overcome their deficiencies. Further, by differentiating between the notions of hyperintensional belief base change and hyperintensional belief set change, we can study the connections between AGM contractions and partial meet contractions in a more general setting, establishing relations to earlier work on the definability of AGM contractions for non-classical logics, such as that of Flouris (2006) on AGM-compatibility and that of Ribeiro (2013) on partial meet contractions for non-classical logics.

Notice that, for Classical Propositional Logic, there is a strong connection between Belief Base Change and Belief Set Change, as demonstrated by Hansson (Hansson 1991; Hansson 1992). However, for non-classical logics this connections seems much more fragile. In fact, as seen in the literature, for some logics the notions of AGM Belief Set Change and Belief Base Change may differ (Ribeiro 2013). More yet, for non-monotonic and hyperintensional logics, the connection between syntactic representations of the agent's epistemic state, e.g. by sets of formulas, and their beliefs is much more complex. As such, for non-classic logics, the notions of Belief Base Change and Belief Set Change may not always coincide and must be investigated separately.

This work is structured as follows: in Section 2 we discuss some of the related literature focusing on hyperintensional phenomena in belief change; in Section 3, we present the basic concepts and notations employed in this work; in Section 4, we study partial meet belief base contractions and their hyperintensional variants; Section 5 discusses partial meet belief set contractions and varying hyperintensional belief set operations, connecting to previous work in the literature; in Section 6, we study the connection between hyperintensional partial meet contractions and AGM contractions, providing negative results regarding the definability of the latter by the former. Finally, in Section 7, we present our final considerations and future directions of our work.

2 Related Work

Work on hyperintensional phenomena in representations of beliefs and other mental attitudes has a long standing tradition on epistemic logic at least since the work of Cresswell (1972; 1975; 1982), c.f. also (Rantala 1982; Vardi 1986; Fagin and Halpern 1987; Wansing 1990).

Regarding hyperintensional phenomena in Belief Change, a smaller, but not insignificant, number of contributions in the literature investigated how belief change can be modelled based on syntactic representations of the agent's belief state. This is the case, for example, of the work of Hansson (1992), Williams (1995), Rott (1998), and Ågnotes and Walicki (2004).

Work on belief change for non-classical logics, such as that of Girard and Tanaka (2016), have investigated dynamic belief change operators, which in principle could be used to model some hyperintensional notions, as classical consequences need not be valid in such logics. Similarly, Santos et al. (2018) investigate pseudo-contractions, which can be used to study a particular kind of hyperintensional belief change, called by Souza and Wassermann (2021) C-dependent contractions. These strategies, however, deal with hyperintensionality in an implicit way, not providing theoretical and philosophical connections that allow us to understand their underlying commitments.

Work on genuinely hyperintensional models for belief change, i.e. that explicitly consider hyperintensional differences between formulas both in the agent's beliefs and in the input, is far more recent in the literature. To our knowledge, the first of such attempts was proposed by Berto (2019), who investigates a topic-sensitive hyperintensional logic of conditional beliefs, in which belief revision is interpreted as conditionalisation. This work was soon followed by that of Özgün and Berto (2020), who dynamify the previously proposed logic. Unlike their work, however, ours investigates how a general notion of hyperintensional belief change can be defined, based on the AGM approach, that can be connected to different semantic frameworks for hyperintensional reasoning.

Similarly, Bozdag (2021) proposes a hyperintensional doxastic logic, based on the HYPE framework (Leitgeb 2019), in which belief base revision can also be thought of as a form of conditionalisation. As before, it is not completely clear how we can compare her proposal with competing notions of belief change in the AGM-inspired literature since, as observed by Lindström and Rabinowicz (1999), Baltag and Smets (2008), or even Souza et al. (2020), modal-based semantic approaches to AGM Belief Change often surpass the expressive power of the original frameworks and, thus, postulates need to be generalised for these settings.

Our work follows directly the line delineated in (Souza 2020) and (Souza and Wassermann 2021), expanding their framework and establishing connections with belief change in non-classical logics and between different notions of hyperintensional belief change investigated in these previous works.

3 Preliminaries

In this work, we employ the tools from Abstract Logic to study classes of logics in which we can define partial meet-like hyperintensional belief change operations. Differently from work such as that of AGM (Alchourrón, Gärdenfors, and Makinson 1985), Flouris (2006), or Ribeiro (2013), we will not require logics to be Tarskian unless explicitly stated.

We will call a logic any pair $\mathcal{L} = \langle L, Cn\rangle$, where L is a non-empty set, called the logical language, and $Cn : 2^L \to 2^L$ is a function called a consequence operator.

A consequence relation may satisfy some important properties defined below. These are common properties of several logics of interest for Philosophy and Artificial Intelligence.

- **inclusion**: $\Gamma \subseteq Cn(\Gamma)$.
- **idempotence**: $Cn(\Gamma) = Cn(Cn(\Gamma))$.
- **monotonicity**: If $\Gamma \subseteq \Gamma'$ then $Cn(\Gamma) \subseteq Cn(\Gamma')$.
- **tarskianicity**: If Cn satisfies inclusion, idempotence and monotonicity.
- **compactness**: for any $\varphi \in Cn(\Gamma)$, there is some finite $\Gamma' \subseteq \Gamma$ s.t. $\varphi \in Cn(\Gamma')$.
- **distributivity**: for any $\Gamma \subseteq L$ and any finitely representable[2] $\Gamma', \Gamma'' \subseteq L$, it holds that $Cn(\Gamma \cup (Cn(\Gamma') \cap Cn(\Gamma''))) = Cn(\Gamma \cup \Gamma') \cap Cn(\Gamma \cup \Gamma'')$.
- **closure under negation**: for any $\Gamma \subseteq L$ finitely representable, there is $\Gamma' \subseteq L$ finitely representable s.t. $Cn(\Gamma \cup \Gamma') = L$ and $Cn(\Gamma \cap \Gamma') = Cn(\varnothing)$.
- **booleanicity**: Cn is tarskian, distributive and closed under negation.

We say a logic $\mathcal{L} = \langle L, Cn\rangle$ satisfies a certain property, say tarskianicity, if its consequence operator Cn does.

The term hyperintensionality describes phenomena in which it is possible to draw distinctions between necessarily equivalent formulas - or those having the same intension. As such, hyperintensionality is commonly explained through the relation between the contents of a sentence and its intension with respect to a standard semantics. In the remainder of this work, we will represent hyperintensional reasoning by means of the relationship between two consequence operators over a given language. Let us define this notion formally.

Definition 1. *Let $\mathcal{L} = \langle L, Cn\rangle$ be a logic, and $C : 2^L \to 2^L$ be a consequence operator. We say that:*

- *C is $\mathcal{L}$-sound, if for every $\Gamma \subseteq 2^L$, $C(\Gamma) \subseteq Cn(\Gamma)$;*
- *C is $\mathcal{L}$-complete, if for every $\Gamma \subseteq 2^L$, $Cn(\Gamma) \subseteq C(\Gamma)$.*

We will denote by $\mathcal{L}_C$ the logic defined by operator C, i.e. $\mathcal{L}_C = \langle L, C\rangle$.

Given a logic $\mathcal{L}$, the AGM authors investigate three basic belief change operators: expansion, contraction and revision. Belief expansion blindly integrates a new piece of information into the agent's beliefs. Belief contraction removes a currently believed sentence from the agent's set of beliefs with minimal alterations. Finally, belief revision is the operation of integrating new information into an agent's beliefs while maintaining consistency. Among these basic operations, only expansion can be univocally defined. The other two are defined by a set of rational constraints or postulates, usually referred to as the AGM postulates. These postulates define a class of suitable change operators representing different rational ways in which an agent can change their beliefs.

In this work, we will focus on hyperintensional contraction operations based on $\mathcal{L}$-sound consequences and characterise them through appropriate postulates, as commonly pursued by the AGM tradition. Contractions have a central role in the study of AGM Belief Change, based on AGM's result known as the Levi Identity (Alchourrón, Gärdenfors, and Makinson 1985), in which revisions may be defined using contraction operations. In the following, we investigate both notions of belief base contractions and belief set contractions, showing their connection.

4 Belief Base Contractions

The first kind of operation we study in this work is known as Belief Base Change, or more generally Belief Representation Change, in which the belief change operation acts on a representation of the agent's belief state to incorporate new information. These kinds of operations describe several belief change operations in the literature, related to ways of representing the agent's belief state, such as Hansson's belief base operations (Hansson 1992), Williams (1995) ensconcements, and Souza et al.'s (2019; 2021) graph transformations.

Hansson (1992) has advocated that belief dynamics should be dependent on explicit doxastic commitments of the agent, in the sense that some beliefs "have no independent standing, but arise only as inferences from our more basic beliefs" (Hansson 1992, p.240) and that "these consequences should be subject only to exactly those changes that follow from the changes of the primary beliefs"(Hansson 1992, p.240). As such, Belief Base Change aims to take

[2]We say a set $\Gamma \subseteq L$ is finitely representable if there is some finite $X \subseteq L$ s.t. $Cn(X) = Cn(\Gamma)$.

into consideration this relation between the agent's beliefs in its dynamics.

In this work, following Hansson (1992), we will focus on a representation of the agent's belief state as a set of formulas $B \subset L$, for a particular logic $\mathcal{L} = \langle L, Cn \rangle$. We call this set a belief base, representing the explicit beliefs held by the agent. As such, we can define the notion of a belief base change operator formally.

Definition 2. *Let $\mathcal{L} = \langle L, Cn \rangle$ be a logic, we call belief base change operator any function $\star : 2^L \times L \to 2^L$*

We begin our exposition with partial meet belief base contractions, as originally studied by Hansson (1992) and Hansson and Wassermann (2002), and introduce our generalisation of such notion taking into consideration hyperintensional reasoning.

4.1 Partial Meet Belief Base Contraction

A partial meet belief base contraction is an operation that preserves a maximal amount of "safe" information from the agent's explicit beliefs, i.e., information that cannot be used to derive what the agent has ceased to believe. To formalise this notion, Alchourrón and Makinson (1982) propose the notion of remainder set.

Definition 3. *(Hansson and Wassermann 2002) Let $B \subseteq L$ be a set of formulas and $\varphi \in L$ be a formula of L, the remainder set $B \bot_{\mathcal{L}} \varphi$ is the set of sets B' satisfying:*

- *$B' \subseteq B$*
- *$\varphi \notin Cn(B')$*
- *$B' \subset B'' \subseteq B$ implies $\varphi \in Cn(B'')$.*

When it is clear to which logic $\mathcal{L}$ we are referring, we will denote $B \bot_{\mathcal{L}} A$ by $B \bot A$.

A partial meet contraction $-$ is an operation for which there is a selection function γ, that characterises this operations. By selection function, we mean that the function γ satisfies (i) $\varnothing \neq \gamma(B \bot A) \subseteq B \bot A$ if $B \bot A \neq \varnothing$ and (ii) $\gamma(B \bot A) = \{B\}$ otherwise.

Definition 4. *(Hansson and Wassermann 2002) We say a belief base change operator $-$ is a belief base contraction on a set $B \subseteq L$ if there is a selection function γ, s.t. for any φ*

$$B - \varphi = \bigcap \gamma(B \bot \varphi).$$

Hansson and Wassermann (2002) show that for any monotonic and compact logic, an operation $-$ is a partial meet contraction on B if and only if it satisfies the following postulates:

(**success**) If $\varphi \notin Cn(\varnothing)$, then $\varphi \notin Cn(B - \varphi)$

(**inclusion**) $B - \varphi \subseteq B$

(**uniformity**) If for any $B' \subseteq B$ it holds that $\varphi \in Cn(B')$ iff $\psi \in Cn(B')$, then it holds that $B - \varphi = B - \psi$

(**relevance**) If $\psi \in B \backslash B - \varphi$, then there is some $B' \subseteq B$ s.t. $B - \varphi \subseteq B'$, $\varphi \notin Cn(B')$, and $\varphi \in Cn(B' \cup \{\psi\})$

Let us revisit the example discussed in the introduction of a constructive agent having a belief set based on the information that $\neg p$ is not true and apply this notion to investigate the example of trying to remove the information that p from their beliefs.

Example 5. *Let $\mathcal{L} = \langle L, Cn \rangle$ be the Classical Propositional Logic, C be the consequence operator of Intuitionistic Propositional Logic, and $p \in L$ a propositional symbol of L. Take $B = \{\neg\neg p\}$, then $B \bot p = \{\varnothing\}$ and thus $B - p = \varnothing$, for any belief base partial meet contraction $-$. However, $B \bot_{\mathcal{L}_C} p = \{B\}$.*

Notice in Example 5 that the partial meet belief base contractions defined in $\mathcal{L}$ and in $\mathcal{L}_C$ differ substantially, in the sense that there is no operation for which the result of $B - p$ coincides in both logics. In the next section, we will discuss how we can construct contraction operations for the logic $\mathcal{L}_C$ from partial meet contractions in the logic $\mathcal{L}$, thus removing the requirement for C to be compact in order to obtain such operations.

4.2 Hyperintensional Partial Meet Belief Base Contraction

To deal with the problem of providing an adequate answer to the example illustrated above, we will introduce the notion of a hyperintensional remainder set.

Definition 6. *Let $\mathcal{L} = \langle L, Cn \rangle$ be a monotonic and compact logic, C be a $\mathcal{L}$-sound consequence operator, $B \subseteq L$ be a set of formulas and $\varphi \in L$ a formula of $\mathcal{L}$. We define the hyperintensional remainder set of B by φ, relative to C, as the set:*

$$B \bot^C_{\mathcal{L}} \varphi = \{B' \subseteq B | \varphi \notin C(B') \text{ and } \exists B'' \in B \bot \varphi \text{ s.t. } B'' \subseteq B'\}$$

The hyperintensional remainder set of B by φ, relative to C, contains all the subsets of B that do not imply φ, according to the hyperintensional consequence operator C, while maintaining a maximal amount "safe" information in B, i.e. that does not imply φ according to Cn.

Lemma 7. *Let $\mathcal{L} = \langle L, Cn \rangle$ be a monotonic and compact logic, C be a $\mathcal{L}$-sound consequence operator. For any $B \subseteq L$ and $\varphi \in L$, $B \bot \varphi \subseteq B \bot^C_{\mathcal{L}} \varphi$.*

We can understand the hyperintensional remainder set of B by φ as a set of approximations of the 'optimal' sets that do not imply φ according to C. If C is monotonic and compact, the notion of 'optimal' commonly adopted in the literature is that of maximality and, indeed, all maximal subsets of B that do not imply φ, according to C, are in $B \bot^C_{\mathcal{L}} \varphi$.

Lemma 8. *Let $\mathcal{L} = \langle L, Cn \rangle$ be a monotonic and compact logic, C be a monotonic and compact $\mathcal{L}$-sound consequence operator. For any $B \subseteq L$ and $\varphi \in L$, $B \bot_{\mathcal{L}_C} \varphi \subseteq B \bot^C_{\mathcal{L}} \varphi$.*

With that, we can define the class of hyperintensional partial meet belief base contractions, as usual.

Definition 9. *Let $\mathcal{L} = \langle L, Cn \rangle$ be a monotonic and compact logic, C be a $\mathcal{L}$-sound consequence operator, and $B \subseteq L$ be a set of formulas. We say a belief base change operator $- : 2^L \times L \to 2^L$ is a hyperintensional belief base contraction* *on B, according to C, iff there is a selection function γ s.t. for any $\varphi \in L$:*

$$B - \varphi = \bigcap \gamma(B \perp_{\mathcal{L}}^{C} \varphi).$$

From Lemmas 7 and 8, it is easy to see that every partial meet belief base contraction (on Cn or on C) is a hyperintensional partial meet belief base contraction, in which the selection function always selects elements of $B \perp_{\mathcal{L}} \varphi$ ($B \perp_{\mathcal{L}_C} \varphi$). Thus, our notion is more general than that of Hansson, while maintaining the desideratum of preserving the maximal amount of 'safe' information from the agent's belief state.

Corollary 10. *Let $\mathcal{L} = \langle L, Cn \rangle$ be a monotonic and compact logic and C be any $\mathcal{L}$-sound consequence operator, every partial meet belief base contraction in $\mathcal{L}$ is a hyperintensional belief base contraction. Further, if C is a monotonic and compact $\mathcal{L}$-sound consequence operator, every partial meet belief base contraction in $\mathcal{L}_C$ is also a hyperintensional belief base contraction.*

Let us see that this notion can actually be used to give a proper response to our running example.

Example 11. *Let $\mathcal{L} = \langle L, Cn \rangle$ be the Classical Propositional Logic, C be the consequence operator of Intuitionistic Propositional Logic, and $p \in L$ a propositional symbol of L. Take the constructive agent with beliefs $B = \{\neg\neg p\}$, then $B \perp_{\mathcal{L}}^{C} p = \{\emptyset, \{\neg\neg p\}\}$. Clearly $B \in B \perp_{\mathcal{L}}^{C} p$ and, thus, there is some hyperintensional belief base partial meet contraction $-$ on B s.t. $B - p = B$.*

To characterise this operation, as commonly pursued by the AGM tradition, we will employ the following postulates - a modification of Hansson and Wassermann's (2002) postulates for belief base contraction.

(inclusion) $B - \varphi \subseteq B$

(C-success) If $\varphi \notin C(\emptyset)$, then $\varphi \notin C(B - \varphi)$

(hyperintensional uniformity) If for any $B', B'' \subseteq B$ it holds that

1. $\varphi \in Cn(B')$ iff $\psi \in Cn(B')$
2. $\varphi \notin Cn(B')$ and $\varphi \in C(B' \cup B'')$ implies that there is some $B''' \subseteq B$ s.t. $B' \subseteq B'''$, $\psi \notin Cn(B''')$ and $\psi \in C(B''' \cup B'')$
3. $\psi \notin Cn(B')$ and $\psi \in C(B' \cup B'')$ implies that there is some $B''' \subseteq B$ s.t. $B' \subseteq B'''$, $\varphi \notin Cn(B''')$ and $\varphi \in C(B''' \cup B'')$

then $B - \varphi = B - \psi$

(hyperintensional relevance) If $\psi \in B \backslash B - \varphi$, there is some $B' \subseteq B$ s.t. $B - \varphi \subseteq B'$, $\varphi \notin C(B')$ but $\psi \notin B'$ and $\varphi \in Cn(B' \cup \{\psi\})$. Furthermore, there is some $B'' \subseteq B'$ s.t. $\varphi \notin Cn(B'')$ but $\varphi \in Cn(B'' \cup \{\xi\})$ for any $\xi \in B \backslash B''$.

The postulate of *(inclusion)* states that no information not currently believed by the agent will be included in her belief state after performing a contraction. The postulate of *(C-success)* states that the agent will not believe the information being removed after contraction unless it is a C-validity. The postulate of *(hyperintensional uniformity)* reinforces Hansson's original *(uniformity)* requiring that the contraction operation coincides for any two formulas when they behave similarly with respect to the logic Cn, but also with respect to C in the subsets of a belief base B. Finally, the postulate of *(hyperintensional relevance)* states that if a formula ψ is removed in a contraction, there is a set containing a maximal set with respect to Cn, in which ψ can be used to prove the information to be removed.

With these postulates, we can prove the characterisation of hyperintensional partial meet belief contraction for a monotonic logic C.

Proposition 12. *Let $\mathcal{L} = \langle L, Cn \rangle$ be a monotonic and compact logic, C be a monotonic $\mathcal{L}$-sound consequence operator, and $B \subseteq L$ be a set of formulas. If $-$ is a hyperintensional belief base contraction on B, then $-$ satisfies (inclusion), (C-success), (hyperintensional uniformity) and (hyperintensional relevance).*

Proof. The proofs for *(inclusion)*, *(C-success)* and *(hyperintensional relevance)* are immediate by construction. Let's show that *(hyperintensional uniformity)* holds.

Take $\varphi, \psi \in L$ satisfying the hypothesis, we only need to show that $B \perp_{\mathcal{L}}^{C} \varphi = B \perp_{\mathcal{L}}^{C} \psi$. From $\varphi \in Cn(B')$ iff $\psi \in Cn(B')$ for every $B' \subseteq B$, we conclude that $B \perp \varphi = B \perp \psi$.

Take $B' \in B \perp_{\mathcal{L}}^{C} \varphi$, then $\varphi \notin C(B')$. As $B' \in B \perp_{\mathcal{L}}^{C} \varphi$, then there is some $B'' \in B \perp \varphi$ s.t. $B'' \subseteq B'$. As $B \perp \varphi = B \perp \psi$, we just need to show that $\psi \notin C(B')$. Suppose $\psi \in C(B')$, then $\psi \notin Cn(B'')$ and $\psi \in C(B'' \cup B' \backslash B'')$. By hypothesis, there is some $B''' \subseteq B$ s.t. $B'' \subseteq B'''$, $\varphi \notin B''$ and $\varphi \in C(B''' \cup B' \backslash B''')$. However, $B'' \in B \perp \varphi$, thus $B''' = B''$ and $\varphi \in C(B'' \cup B' \backslash B'') = C(B')$, which is a contradiction. Thus, $\psi \notin C(B')$ and $B' \in B \perp_{\mathcal{L}}^{C} \psi$.

□

More yet, any operation satisfying these postulates are hyperintensional partial meet belief base contractions.

Theorem 13. *Let $\mathcal{L} = \langle L, Cn \rangle$ be a monotonic and compact logic, C be a monotonic $\mathcal{L}$-sound consequence operator, and $B \subseteq L$ be a set of formulas. The operator $-$ is a hyperintensional belief base contraction on B iff $-$ satisfies (inclusion), (C-success), (hyperintensional uniformity) and (hyperintensional relevance).*

Proof. Proposition 12 already showed that hyperintensional belief base contractions satisfy the postulates when C is monotonic. Let us show that any belief base change operation satisfying these postulates is a hyperintensional belief base contraction.

Let $\star : 2^L \times L \to 2^L$ be a belief base change operation satisfying the four postulates for a given belief base B. Let us construct a selection function γ that coincides with the result of $B \star \varphi$ for any φ.

Define $\gamma : 2^{2^L} \to 2^{2^L}$ a function s.t. $\gamma(B \perp_{\mathcal{L}}^{C} \varphi) = \{B' \in B \perp_{\mathcal{L}}^{C} \varphi \mid B \star \varphi \subseteq B'\}$ if $B \perp_{\mathcal{L}}^{C} \varphi \neq \emptyset$ and $\gamma(B \perp_{\mathcal{L}}^{C} \varphi) = \{B\}$, otherwise.

We need to show that γ is a selection function and that $B \star \varphi = \bigcap \gamma(B \perp_{\mathcal{L}}^{C} \varphi)$. First, it suffices to see that if $B \perp_{\mathcal{L}}^{C} \varphi = B \perp_{\mathcal{L}}^{C} \psi$, then it holds that for any $B', B'' \subseteq B$: (i) $\varphi \in$

$Cn(B')$ iff $\psi \in Cn(B')$, (ii) if $\varphi \notin Cn(B')$ and $\varphi \in C(B' \cup B'')$, it holds that there is some $B''' \subseteq B$ s.t. $\psi \notin Cn(B''')$ and $\psi \in C(B''' \cup B'')$, and (iii) if $\psi \notin Cn(B')$ and $\psi \in C(B' \cup B'')$, then it holds that there is some $B''' \subseteq B$ s.t. $\varphi \notin Cn(B''')$ and $\varphi \in C(B''' \cup B'')$. By *(hyperintensional uniformity)* of $\star$, $B \star \varphi = B \star \psi$ and, thus, $\gamma(B\bot^C_{\mathcal{L}}\varphi) = \gamma(B\bot^C_{\mathcal{L}}\psi)$. Further, $\gamma(B\bot^C_{\mathcal{L}}\varphi) \neq \varnothing$ if $B\bot^C_{\mathcal{L}}\varphi \neq \varnothing$, as (i) if $\varphi \notin Cn(B \star \varphi)$, it holds that there is some $B' \in B\bot\varphi \subseteq B\bot^C_{\mathcal{L}}\varphi$ s.t. $B \star \varphi \subseteq B'$ and (ii) if $\varphi \in Cn(B \star \varphi)$, by *(hyperintensional relevance)* there is a $B' \in B\bot\varphi$ s.t. $\varphi \notin C(B' \cup B \star \varphi)$, thus $B' \cup B \star \varphi \in B\bot^C_{\mathcal{L}}\varphi$ and, by construction, $B' \cup B \star \varphi \in \gamma(B\bot^C_{\mathcal{L}}\varphi)$. Additionally, if $B\bot^C_{\mathcal{L}}\varphi = \varnothing$ then $\gamma(B\bot^C_{\mathcal{L}}\varphi) = \{B\}$, i.e. γ is a selection function.

Let us show that $B \star \varphi = \bigcap \gamma(B\bot^C_{\mathcal{L}}\varphi)$. Well, by construction, it is easy to see that $B \star \varphi \subseteq \bigcap \gamma(B\bot^C_{\mathcal{L}}\varphi)$, then we only need to show the opposite inclusion. Take $\psi \in \bigcap \gamma(B\bot^C_{\mathcal{L}}\varphi)$, then for any $B' \in B\bot^C_{\mathcal{L}}\varphi$ s.t. $B \star \varphi \subseteq B'$, $\psi \in B'$. Suppose $\psi \notin B \star \varphi$, then by *(hyperintensional relevance)* of $\star$, there is some $B' \subseteq B$ s.t. $B - \varphi \subseteq B'$, $\psi \notin B'$ and $\varphi \notin C(B')$, and there is $B'' \subseteq B'$ s.t. $\varphi \notin Cn(B'')$ but $\varphi \in Cn(B'' \cup \{\xi\})$ for any $\xi \in B \backslash B''$. Clearly, $B' \in \gamma(B\bot^C_{\mathcal{L}}\varphi)$, but $\psi \notin B'$, which is a contradiction to $\psi \in \bigcap \gamma(B\bot^C_{\mathcal{L}}\varphi)$. Thus, $\psi \in B \star \varphi$. □

5 Belief Set Contractions

In their seminal work, AGM defines a class of operations over the set of theories of a logic $\mathcal{L}$, i.e. sets of formulas satisfying $K = Cn(K)$. These sets of formulas represent the beliefs currently held by an agent. Belief Set Change operations, thus, represent how the currently held beliefs of an agent may be changed due to some new information. As discussed before, changes in belief sets and changes in belief bases may differ in nature for non-classical logics. In fact, the notion of belief set as a consequentially-closed set only applies to Tarskian logics, since for logics not satisfying **idempotence** (c.f. Section 3), there is no guarantee of the existence of such theories. As such, we need to generalise this notion to the context of non-classical logics.

Definition 14. *Let $\mathcal{L} = \langle L, Cn \rangle$ be a logic. The set of theories of $\mathcal{L}$, denoted by $Th(\mathcal{L})$, is the set of all conclusions of some set of hypotheses, i.e.*

$$Th(\mathcal{L}) = \{Cn(B) \mid B \subseteq \mathcal{L}\}.$$

We say a logic $\mathcal{L}$ is closed under intersection if its set of theories is closed under intersections, i.e. for any $T, T' \in Th(\mathcal{L})$, $T \cap T' \in Th(\mathcal{L})$. That is a common property of Tarskian logics, in fact of any monotonic and idempotent logic, but may not hold for all logics considered. Closure under intersection will be an important property of the logics to guarantee the existence of contractions that we investigate in the following.

We call, following AGM, a belief set any element of $Th(\mathcal{L})$, representing the beliefs of the agent obtained from the representation of their belief state as a set of formulas. Belief set contractions are, thus, functions that change the belief set of an agent. Notice that, since different belief bases can give rise to the same belief set and representing the explicit beliefs of an agent is an important feature for hyperintensional modellings of belief change, taking the original belief state of the agent into consideration when computing changes is of great importance. As such, we will employ pseudo-contractions (Santos et al. 2018) to construct belief set contractions in our work. Let us define this notion formally.

Definition 15. *Let $\mathcal{L} = \langle L, Cn \rangle$ be a logic. We say a function $\star : 2^L \times L \to 2^L$ is a belief set change operation if $B \star \varphi \in Th(\mathcal{L})$ for any B and φ.*

Finally, as our logics are not necessarily Tarskian, we need to establish a differentiation among the notions of a remainder set, as defined in Definition 3, used to define partial meet belief base changes, and a different notion, which we call residual beliefs, used to define partial meet belief set changes. The set of residuals describes the possible sets of beliefs after removing an information φ from an epistemic state described by a belief base B. Differently then remainder sets, residual sets do not preserve the structure of the epistemic state, i.e. the agent's explicit doxastic commitments.

Definition 16. *Let $\mathcal{L} = \langle L, Cn \rangle$ be a monotonic and compact logic, C be a $\mathcal{L}$-sound consequence operator, $B \subseteq L$ be a set of formulas and $\varphi \in L$ a formula of $\mathcal{L}$. The set of belief residuals from B by φ, according to $\mathcal{L}$, is the set*

$$B \triangle_{\mathcal{L}} \varphi = \{Cn(B') \mid B' \in B\bot\varphi\}.$$

Similarly,

$$B \triangle_{\mathcal{L}_C} \varphi = \{C(B') \mid B' \in B\bot\varphi\}.$$

Similarly to what we did for belief base change, in Definition 6, we will also define a hyperintensional notion of residuals, with which we define different notions of hyperintensional belief set contractions. Analogously to hyperintensional remainders, hyperintensional residuals describe the subsets of the agent's beliefs that do not support the information φ and contain some residual of the agent's beliefs after removing φ, representing the hyperintensional belief (sub)sets in which information φ does not hold, but maintain some maximal amount of "safe" information.

Definition 17. *Let $\mathcal{L} = \langle L, Cn \rangle$ be a monotonic and compact logic, C be a $\mathcal{L}$-sound consequence operator, $B \subseteq L$ be a set of formulas and $\varphi \in L$ a formula of $\mathcal{L}$. The set of hyperintensional belief residuals from B by φ, according to $\mathcal{L}$, is the set*

$$B \blacktriangle_{\mathcal{L}_C} \varphi = \{C(B') \mid B' \subseteq B, \varphi \notin C(B') \text{ and there is } K \in B \triangle_{\mathcal{L}_C} \varphi \text{ s.t. } K \subseteq C(B') \subseteq C(B)\}.$$

5.1 Partial Meet Belief Set Contraction

As for belief base contractions, let us define partial meet belief set contractions, as defined by AGM.

Definition 18. *Let $\mathcal{L} = \langle L, Cn \rangle$ be a monotonic and compact logic, and $B \subseteq L$ be a set of formulas. We say a belief set change operator $- : Th(\mathcal{L}) \times L \to Th(\mathcal{L})$ is partial meet belief set contraction on B iff there is a selection function γ s.t. for any $\varphi \in L$:*

$$B - \varphi = \bigcap \gamma(B \triangle_{\mathcal{L}} \varphi) \cap Cn(B).$$

Notice that, as is the case for AGM belief contraction and Hansson's belief base contractions, it is not always the case that partial meet belief set contractions coincide with the consequence of a partial meet base contraction. In fact, take $B = \{p, p \to q\}$, then $B \perp p = \{\{p \to q\}\}$, thus $B \triangle p = \{Cn(\{p \to q\})\}$, while $Cn(B) \perp p = \{Cn(\{p \to q\}), Cn(\{q\})\}$. This means that there is some partial meet belief base contraction $-$ s.t. for any partial meet belief set contraction $\ominus$, $B \ominus p \neq Cn(B) - p$. The reason for this is that $Cn(B) \perp p$ does not preserve the structure of the belief state B, as we intend to do.

Example 19. *Let $\mathcal{L} = \langle L, Cn \rangle$ be the Classical Propositional Logic, C be the consequence operator of Intuitionistic Propositional Logic, and $p \in L$ a propositional symbol of L. Take the constructive agent with beliefs $B = \{\neg\neg p\}$, then $B \triangle p = \{Cn(\varnothing)\}$ and thus $B - p = Cn(\varnothing)$, for any belief set partial meet contraction $-$.*

We will employ the following postulates to characterise partial meet belief set contraction for any monotonic and compact logic closed under intersection.

(logical closure) $B - \varphi = C(\Gamma)$, for some $\Gamma \subseteq L$

(logical inclusion) $B - \varphi \subseteq Cn(B)$

(success) If $\varphi \notin Cn(\varnothing)$, then $\varphi \notin B - \varphi$

(uniformity) If for any $B' \subseteq B$, $\varphi \in Cn(B')$ iff $\psi \in Cn(B')$, then $B - \varphi = B - \psi$

(logical relevance) If $\psi \notin Cn(B) \backslash B - \varphi$, then there is some $B' \subseteq B$ s.t. $B - \varphi \subseteq Cn(B')$, $\varphi \notin Cn(B')$, and $\varphi \in Cn(B' \cup \{\psi\})$

We will omit the proof of this characterisation since it is a simple modification of the one presented by Hansson and Wassermann (2002) to consider the set $B \triangle_{\mathcal{L}} \varphi$ instead of $B \perp \varphi$.

From the same structure of partial meet belief set contraction, we can define different notions hyperintensional belief set contraction, varying the elements used, i.e. substituting $B \triangle_{\mathcal{L}} \varphi$ for $B \triangle_{\mathcal{L}_C} \varphi$ or $B \blacktriangle_{\mathcal{L}_C} \varphi$, substituting $Cn(B)$ for $C(B)$, etc. These variations give rise to different operations previously investigated in the literature by Santos et al. (2018), Souza (2020) and Souza and Wassermann (2021), as well as some interesting new ones. In this work, we will focus on only two of them.

5.2 Belief Set C-base Contraction

Based on the definition of (a subclass of) belief base contractions using AGM contractions by Hansson, Souza and Wassermann (2021) proposed the notion of C-base contractions, a generalisation of the C-dependent contraction previously studied by Santos et al. (2018) and Souza (2020). C-base contractions are hyperintensional contractions in that they consider hyperintensional differences in the belief base to compute a contraction, generalising the reasoning behind Hansson's (1992) belief base contraction to any hyperintensional consequence C.

Definition 20. *Let $\mathcal{L} = \langle L, Cn \rangle$ be a monotonic and compact logic, C be a $\mathcal{L}$-sound consequence operator, and $B \subseteq L$ be a set of formulas. We say a belief base change operator $- : 2^L \times L \to 2^L$ is a C-base belief set contraction on B iff there is a selection function γ s.t. for any $\varphi \in L$:*

$$B - \varphi = \bigcap \gamma(B \triangle_{\mathcal{L}} \varphi) \cap C(B).$$

Let us apply this definition to investigate our running example.

Example 21. *Let $\mathcal{L} = \langle L, Cn \rangle$ be the Classical Propositional Logic and C be the consequence operator of Intuitionistic Propositional Logic and $p \in L$ a propositional symbol of L. Take the constructive agent with beliefs $B = \{\neg\neg p\}$, then $B \triangle p = \{Cn(\varnothing)\}$ and thus $B - p = C(\varnothing)$, for any belief set C-base contraction $-$.*

Notice that, in general, $\bigcap \gamma(B \triangle \varphi) \cap C(B)$ is not a C-theory, i.e. $\bigcap \gamma(B \triangle \varphi) \cap C(B) \notin Th(\mathcal{L}_C)$. Thus, to properly characterise this operation as a hyperintensional belief set contraction, we must require a further property of the logic C: upward closure under intersection.

Given a logic $\mathcal{L} = \langle L, Cn \rangle$ and a $\mathcal{L}$-sound consequence operator C. We say $\mathcal{L}_C$ is upwards closed under intersection if it is closed under intersection and for any $T \in Th(\mathcal{L})$ and $T' \in Th(\mathcal{L}_C)$, it holds that $T \cap T' \in Th(\mathcal{L}_C)$.

To characterise belief set C-base contractions, we employ the following postulates - a modified version of those presented previously (Souza and Wassermann 2021).

(logical closure) $B - \varphi = C(\Gamma)$, for some $\Gamma \subseteq L$

(C-logical inclusion) $B - \varphi \subseteq C(B)$.

(success) If $\varphi \notin Cn(\varnothing)$, then $\varphi \notin B - \varphi$

(uniformity) If for all $B' \subseteq Cn(B)$, it holds that $\varphi \in Cn(B')$ iff $\psi \in Cn(B')$, then $B - \varphi = B - \psi$

(C-local logical relevance) If $\psi \in C(B) \backslash B - \varphi$, then there is some $B' \subseteq B$, s.t. $B - \varphi \subseteq Cn(B')$, $\varphi \notin Cn(B')$ and $\varphi \in Cn(B' \cup \{\psi\})$.

Again, the proof of this characterisation, for any logic $\mathcal{L}_C$ upwards closed under intersection, can be obtained by a simple modification of the proof provided previously (Souza and Wassermann 2021) to account for the use of the residual set $B \triangle_{\mathcal{L}} \varphi$.

5.3 Hyperintensional Partial Meet Belief Set Contraction

Finally, analogously to how we defined hyperintensional partial meet belief base contractions, we can define a general notion of hyperintensional belief set contraction that allows us to approximate changes in the agent's beliefs to remove certain information. Differently than Definition 9, however, by using hyperintensional residuals, we are concerned not with the structure of the agent's resulting epistemic state but which beliefs are maintained by the agent after contraction. As a result, hyperintensional belief set contractions can select the hyperintensional subtheories of an agent's beliefs which do not imply the information to be removed.

Definition 22. *Let $\mathcal{L} = \langle L, Cn \rangle$ be a monotonic and compact logic, C be a $\mathcal{L}$-sound consequence operator, and $B \subseteq L$ be a set of formulas. We say a belief set change* *operator* $- : 2^L \times L \rightarrow Th(\mathcal{L}_C)$ *is a hyperintensional C-dependent belief set contraction on B, according to C, iff there is a selection function* γ *s.t. for any* $\varphi \in L$*:*

$$B - \varphi = \bigcap \gamma(B \blacktriangle_{\mathcal{L}_C} \varphi) \cap Cn(B).$$

As for hyperintensional partial meet belief base contractions, hyperintensional partial meet belief set contractions seek to obtain hyperintensional subtheories of the agent's belief set $Cn(B)$, i.e. elements $K \in Th(\mathcal{L}_C)$ s.t. $K \subseteq Cn(B)$, which do not prove the formula being removed. As for partial meet belief set contractions, it is not always the case that $\bigcap \gamma(B \blacktriangle_{\mathcal{L}_C} \varphi)) = C(\bigcap \gamma(B \bot^C_{\mathcal{L}} \varphi))$, so there is some hyperintensional partial meet belief base contraction $-$ for which there is no hyperintensional partial meet belief set contraction $\ominus$ satisfying $B - \varphi = B \ominus \varphi$.

Again, we can employ this operation to study our running example.

Example 23. *Let* $\mathcal{L} = \langle L, Cn \rangle$ *be the Classical Propositional Logic, C be the consequence operator of Intuitionistic Propositional Logic, and* $p \in L$ *a propositional symbol of L. Take the constructive agent with beliefs* $B = \{\neg\neg p\}$*, then* $B \blacktriangle_{\mathcal{L}_C} p = \{C(\varnothing), C(\{\neg\neg p\}\}$*. Clearly* $C(B) \in B \blacktriangle_{\mathcal{L}_C} p$ *and, thus, there is some hyperintensional belief set partial meet contraction* $-$ *s.t.* $B - p = C(B)$*.*

We can thus see that the hyperintensional residual set $B \blacktriangle_{\mathcal{L}_C} p$ contains subtheories of $C(B)$ that do not prove p. To characterise this operation, we will employ the following postulates:

(logical closure) $B - \varphi = C(\Gamma)$, for some $\Gamma \subseteq L$

(C-logical inclusion) $B - \varphi \subseteq C(B)$

(C-success) If $\varphi \notin C(\varnothing)$, then $\varphi \notin B - \varphi$

(hyperintensional uniformity) If for any $B', B'' \subseteq B$ it holds that

1. $\varphi \in Cn(B')$ iff $\psi \in Cn(B')$
2. $\varphi \notin Cn(B')$ and $\varphi \in C(B' \cup B'')$ implies that there is some $B''' \subseteq B$ s.t. $B' \subseteq B'''$, $\psi \notin Cn(B''')$ and $\psi \in C(B''' \cup B'')$
3. $\psi \notin Cn(B')$ and $\psi \in C(B' \cup B'')$ implies that there is some $B''' \subseteq B$ s.t. $B' \subseteq B'''$, $\varphi \notin Cn(B''')$ and $\varphi \in C(B''' \cup B'')$

then $B - \varphi = B - \psi$

(hyperintensional logical relevance) If $\psi \in Cn(B) \backslash B - \varphi$, there is some $B' \subseteq B$, s.t. $B - \varphi \subseteq C(B')$, $\varphi \notin C(B')$, and $\psi \notin C(B')$, but $\varphi \in Cn(B' \cup \{\psi\})$. Further, there is some $B'' \subseteq B$ s.t. $C(B'') \subseteq C(B')$, $\varphi \notin Cn(B'')$ but $\varphi \in Cn(B'' \cup \{\xi\})$ for any $\xi \in B \backslash B''$.

We can show that these postulates characterise hyperintensional partial meet belief set contraction for all monotonic and upwardly closed under intersection logics $\mathcal{L}_C$.

Theorem 24. *Let* $\mathcal{L} = \langle L, Cn \rangle$ *be a monotonic and compact logic, C be a monotonic* $\mathcal{L}$*-sound consequence operator with* $\mathcal{L}_C$ *an upwardly closed under intersection logic, and* $B \subseteq L$ *be a set of formulas. An operation* $- : 2^L \times L \rightarrow Th(\mathcal{L}_C)$ *is a hyperintensional belief set partial meet contraction iff it satisfies (C-logical inclusion), (C-success), (hyperintensional uniformity), and (hyperintensional logical relevance).*

Sketch of the proof. Satisfaction of the postulates is similar to that presented in Proposition 12, with *(logical closure)* following from upward closure by intersection of $\mathcal{L}_C$. To prove the characterisation, construct the selection function $\gamma(B \blacktriangle_{\mathcal{L}_C})\varphi = \{B' \in B \blacktriangle_{\mathcal{L}_C} \varphi \mid B - \varphi \subseteq B'\}$ if $B \blacktriangle_{\mathcal{L}_C} \varphi \neq \varnothing$ and $\gamma(B \blacktriangle_{\mathcal{L}_C} \varphi)\varphi = C(B)$, otherwise.

To prove that γ is selection function, similarly to the proof for hyperintensional partial meet base contraction, it suffices to see that *(hyperintensional logical relevance)* implies that if $B \blacktriangle_{\mathcal{L}_C} \varphi \neq \varnothing$ then $\gamma(B \blacktriangle_{\mathcal{L}_C} \varphi) \neq \varnothing$ and *(hyperintensional uniformity)* implies that if $B \blacktriangle_{\mathcal{L}_C} \varphi = B \blacktriangle_{\mathcal{L}_C} \psi$ then $\gamma(B \blacktriangle_{\mathcal{L}_C} \varphi) = \gamma(B \blacktriangle_{\mathcal{L}_C} \psi)$.

To show that $B - \varphi = \gamma(B \blacktriangle_{\mathcal{L}_C} \varphi) \cap Cn(B)$, it suffices to see that $B - \varphi \subseteq \gamma(B \blacktriangle_{\mathcal{L}_C} \varphi) \cap Cn(B)$ by construction and that for any $\psi \in \gamma(B \blacktriangle_{\mathcal{L}_C} \varphi) \cap Cn(B)$, $\psi \in B - \varphi$ by *(hyperintensional logical relevance)*. □

6 AGM Contractions and Hyperintensional Belief Set Contractions

In this section, we wish to explore whether AGM belief contraction can be understood as a form of partial meet hyperintensional belief contraction, as studied in this work. The motivation for such investigation lies in the fact that the notions of AGM contraction and partial meet contraction coincide in several logics of interest but diverge in some non-classical logics (Ribeiro 2013). Thus, we investigate whether these notions can be reconciled within a broader framework that explains these previous results.

Flouris (2006) studied the definability of AGM contraction operations, i.e. operations satisfying the original AGM postulates, in Tarskian logics, obtaining sufficient and necessary conditions for such definability. Let us introduce these notions in order to compare our hyperintensional belief change operations and AGM contractions.

Definition 25. *(Flouris 2006) A tarskian logic* $\mathcal{L} = \langle L, Cn \rangle$ *is said to be decomposable if for any* $B \subseteq L$ *and* $\varphi \in L$*, with* $\varphi \notin Cn(\varnothing)$*, the set*

$$K^{-\varphi} = \{B' \subseteq B \,|\, \varphi \notin Cn(B') \wedge Cn(B) = Cn(B' \cup \{\varphi\})\}$$

is not empty.

Flouris introduces the notion of decomposability as the possibility of constructing a contraction, i.e. that there is a set that is an admissible result for a contraction by a formula, for any set B and any formula φ. Further, the author shows that all Tarskian and boolean logics are decomposable.

Theorem 26. *(Flouris 2006) Any Tarskian logic* $\mathcal{L} = \langle L, Cn \rangle$ *that is also boolean is decomposable.*

Flouris (2006) show that decomposability is a necessary and sufficient condition for the definability of AGM-compliant contraction operations.

Proposition 27. *(Flouris 2006) Let* $\mathcal{L} = \langle L, Cn \rangle$ *be a decomposable logic and* $- : Th(\mathcal{L}) \times L \rightarrow Th(\mathcal{L})$ *be a belief change operation.* $-$ *is an AGM contraction, i.e. satisfies AGM's six original postulates, iff for any* $K = Cn(K)$ *and* $\varphi \notin Cn(\varnothing)$ *it holds that* $K - \varphi \in K^{-\varphi}$*.*

From AGM's original characterisation of AGM contractions as partial meet contractions, it is easy to obtain the following result.

Proposition 28. *Let $\mathcal{L} = \langle L, Cn\rangle$ be a monotonic and compact logic, and C be a tarskian, boolean and compact $\mathcal{L}$-sound consequence operator. For any set of formulas $K \subseteq L$ s.t. $K = C(K)$ and formula $\varphi \in L$, it holds that any set $K' \subseteq K$ s.t. $\varphi \notin K$ and $K = Cn(K' \cup \{\varphi\})$, $K' \in K\bot_{\mathcal{L}_C}\varphi$.*

From that, we can obtain the simple result that, if the logic $\mathcal{L}_C$ is compact and boolean, every AGM contraction on $\mathcal{L}$ can be obtained as a hyperintensional contraction on $\mathcal{L}$.

Corollary 29. *Let $\mathcal{L} = \langle L, Cn\rangle$ be a monotonic and compact logic, and C be a tarskian, boolean and compact $\mathcal{L}$-sound consequence operator. Let $- : Th(\mathcal{L}_C) \times L \to Th(\mathcal{L}_C)$ be an AGM contraction on C, then there is a hyperintensional C-base contraction $\ominus$ s.t. for any $K \subseteq L$ s.t. $K = C(K)$ and $\varphi \in L$, it holds that $K - \varphi = K \ominus \varphi$.*

This result is not particularly surprising since the connection between partial meet contractions and AGM contractions for boolean and compact logics has been known since the seminal work of AGM. It seems, however, that these connections cannot be extended further if the logic $\mathcal{L}_C$ does not satisfy one of such properties. Consider the following example.

Example 30. *Consider the tarskian logic $\mathcal{L} = \langle L, Cn\rangle$, with $L = \{a, b, p_0, p_1, \cdots, q_0, q_1, \cdots\}$ and Cn with:*

$Cn(L) = L$
$Cn(\varnothing) = \varnothing$
$Cn(a) = Cn(\{p_1\}) = Cn(\{p_2\}) = \cdots = \{a, p_0, p_1, \cdots\}$
$Cn(b) = Cn(\{q_1\}) = Cn(\{q_2\}) = \cdots = \{b, q_0, q_1, \cdots\}$
$Cn(\{p_0\}) = \{p_0\}$
$Cn(\{q_0\}) = \{q_0\}$
$Cn(\{p_i, q_j\}) = L$ *for* $i, j \in \mathbb{N}$

Take also the $\mathcal{L}$-sound consequence C with the following structure:

$C(L) = L$
$C(\varnothing) = \varnothing$
$C(a) = Cn(\{p_0, p_1, \cdots\} = \{a, p_0, p_1, \cdots\}$
$C(b) = Cn(\{q_0, q_1, \cdots\} = \{b, q_0, q_1, \cdots\}$
$C(\{p_i\}) = \{p_0, \cdots p_i\}$ *for* $i \in \mathbb{N}$
$C(\{q_i\}) = \{q_0, \cdots q_i\}$ *for* $i \in \mathbb{N}$
$C(\{p_i, q_j\}) = L$ *for* $i, i \in \mathbb{N}$

Clearly, Cn is boolean and compact and C is boolean. Consider the agent with a belief set $K = C(a)$, there is a set $K' = \varnothing \subseteq K$ s.t. $C(K' \cup \{a\}) = K$ and $K' \notin K\bot^C_{\mathcal{L}}a$. Thus, there is some AGM contraction $-$ with $K - a = \varnothing$ that is not a hyperintensional belief set contraction, for any of such notions investigated in this work.

More yet, Ribeiro (2013) shows a compact and non-distributive logic in which the notions of AGM contraction and partial meet contraction do not coincide. This indicates that these notions may be irreconcilable for non-boolean or non-compact logics.

7 Final Considerations

As Berto and Hawke (2021) point out, a useful framework for epistemic logic needs to be both robust enough, i.e. have enough logical structure, to allow one to draw interesting conclusions regarding epistemic phenomena, and flexible enough as to be able to encode disputing positions in the philosophical and logical literature. We believe our framework for hyperintensional belief change achieves this balance by allowing the construction of a broad class of belief change operations for a wide range of non-classical logics while still guaranteeing minimal criteria (or properties) for minimal change.

Besides the connections with belief change in non-classical logics, established in (Souza and Wassermann 2021), our approach also is similar, in some sense, to the idea of approximate belief change (Chopra, Parikh, and Wassermann 2001). In their work, Chopra et al. (2001) aim to approximate belief contraction operations on a logic $\mathcal{L}$ through belief change operations for a sequence $\mathcal{L}$-sound consequence operators C^i_S. Our approach, however, employs belief change operations in the "well-behaved" logic $\mathcal{L}$ to construct (or approximate) belief change operations in the logic defined by a $\mathcal{L}$-sound consequence operator C.

Notice that, by encoding hyperintensional reasoning using the relation among two different consequence operators C and Cn, our approach is general enough to be connected to different foundational theories of hyperintensionality - such as the structural perspective underlying the structured propositions tradition (Cresswell 1975) and the informational perspective of Berto's (2019) mereological treatment. This allows the investigation of dynamic phenomena in several modellings of hyperintensionality. In fact, the connection of these operations to one such framework, namely impossible-world semantics, is the object of future work developed by the authors.

Our framework also provides a richer setting to study the connection between different competing notions of rational belief change in the literature as partial meet belief change and AGM belief change. Our results indicate, for example, that these two notions may be irreconcilable in a wide variety of logics.

8 Acknowledgments

This study was financed in part by the Coordenação de Aperfeiçoamento de Pessoal de Nível Superior - Brasil (CAPES) - Finance Code 001 and in part by the Center for Artificial Intelligence (C4AI-USP), with support by the São Paulo Research Foundation (FAPESP grant #2019/07665-4) and by the IBM Corporation.

References

Ågotnes, T., and Walicki, M. 2004. Syntactic knowledge: A logic of reasoning, communication and cooperation. In *Proceedings of the Second European Workshop on Multi-Agent Systems (EUMAS), Barcelona, Spain*. Citeseer.

Alchourrón, C. E., and Makinson, D. 1982. On the logic of theory change: Contraction functions and their associated revision functions. *Theoria* 48(1):14–37.

Alchourrón, C. E.; Gärdenfors, P.; and Makinson, D. 1985. On the logic of theory change: Partial meet contraction and revision functions. *Journal of Symbolic Logic* 50(2):510–530.

Baltag, A., and Smets, S. 2008. A qualitative theory of dynamic interactive belief revision. *Texts in logic and games* 3:9–58.

Berto, F., and Hawke, P. 2021. Knowability relative to information. *Mind* 130(517):1–33.

Berto, F. 2019. Simple hyperintensional belief revision. *Erkenntnis* 84(3):559–575.

Bjerring, J. C. 2013. Impossible worlds and logical omniscience: an impossibility result. *Synthese* 190(13):2505–2524.

Bozdag, S. 2021. A semantics for hyperintensional belief revision based on information bases. *Studia Logica* 1–38.

Chopra, S.; Parikh, R.; and Wassermann, R. 2001. Approximate belief revision. *Logic Journal of the IGPL* 9(6):755–768.

Cresswell, M. J., and Von Stechow, A. 1982. "de re" belief generalized. *Linguistics and Philosophy* 503–535.

Cresswell, M. J. 1972. Intensional logics and logical truth. *Journal of Philosophical Logic* 1(1):2–15.

Cresswell, M. J. 1975. Hyperintensional logic. *Studia Logica: An International Journal for Symbolic Logic* 34(1):25–38.

Fagin, R., and Halpern, J. Y. 1987. Belief, awareness, and limited reasoning. *Artificial intelligence* 34(1):39–76.

Flouris, G. 2006. On belief change in ontology evolution. *AI Communications* 19(4):395–397.

Gärdenfors, P. 1988. *Knowledge in flux: Modeling the dynamics of epistemic states.* The MIT press.

Girard, P., and Tanaka, K. 2016. Paraconsistent dynamics. *Synthese* 193(1):1–14.

Halpern, J. Y., and Pucella, R. 2011. Dealing with logical omniscience: Expressiveness and pragmatics. *Artificial intelligence* 175(1):220–235.

Hansson, S. O., and Wassermann, R. 2002. Local change. *Studia Logica* 70(1):49–76.

Hansson, S. O. 1991. Belief contraction without recovery. *Studia logica* 50(2):251–260.

Hansson, S. O. 1992. In defense of base contraction. *Synthese* 91(3):239–245.

Hintikka, J. 1962. *Knowledge and Belief - An Introduction to the Logic of the Two Notions.* Ithaca: Cornell University Press.

Jago, M. 2009. Logical information and epistemic space. *Synthese* 167(2):327–341.

Leitgeb, H. 2019. HYPE: A system of hyperintensional logic (with an application to semantic paradoxes). *Journal of Philosophical Logic* 48(2):305–405.

Levesque, H. J. 1984. A logic of implicit and explicit belief. In *Proceedings of the Fourth National Conference on Artificial Intelligence*, 198–202. Austin, Texas: American Association for Artificial Intelligence.

Lindström, S., and Rabinowicz, W. 1999. DDL unlimited: Dynamic doxastic logic for introspective agents. *Erkenntnis* 50(2):353–385.

Rantala, V. 1982. Impossible worlds semantics and logical omniscience. *Acta Philosophica Fennica* 35:106–115.

Ribeiro, M. M. 2013. *Belief revision in non-classical logics.* Springer Science & Business Media.

Rott, H. 1998. 'just because': Taking belief bases seriously. In Samuel R. Buss, P. H. u. P. P., ed., *Lecture Notes in Logic*, volume 13, 387–408. Urbana, US: Association for Symbolic Logic.

Santos, Y. D.; Matos, V. B.; Ribeiro, M. M.; and Wassermann, R. 2018. Partial meet pseudo-contractions. *International Journal of Approximate Reasoning* 103:11–27.

Souza, M., and Moreira, Á. 2021. Belief base change as priority change: A study based on dynamic epistemic logic. *Journal of Logical and Algebraic Methods in Programming* 122:100689.

Souza, M., and Wassermann, R. 2021. Belief contraction in non-classical logics as hyperintensional belief change. In *Proceedings of the International Conference on Principles of Knowledge Representation and Reasoning*, volume 18, 588–598.

Souza, M.; Moreira, Á.; and Vieira, R. 2019. Iterated belief base revision: A dynamic epistemic logic approach. In *Proceedings of the Thirty-Third AAAI Conference on Artificial Intelligence*, 3076–3083. AAAI Press.

Souza, M.; Vieira, R.; and Moreira, Á. 2020. Dynamic preference logic meets iterated belief change: Representation results and postulates characterization. *Theoretical Computer Science* 872(8):15–40.

Souza, M. 2020. Towards a theory of hyperintensional belief change. In Cerri, R., and Prati, R. C., eds., *Intelligent Systems*, 272–287. Cham: Springer International Publishing.

Van Dalen, D. 1994. *Logic and structure*, volume 3. Springer.

Vardi, M. Y. 1986. On epistemic logic and logical omniscience. In *Theoretical aspects of reasoning about knowledge*, 293–305. Elsevier.

Wansing, H. 1990. A general possible worlds framework for reasoning about knowledge and belief. *Studia Logica* 49(4):523–539.

Williams, M.-A. 1995. Iterated theory base change: A computational model. In *Proceedings of the 14th International Joint Conference on Artificial intelligence*, 1541–1547.

Özgün, A., and Berto, F. 2020. Dynamic hyperintensional belief revision. *The Review of Symbolic Logic* 1–46.

Proceedings of the 19th International Conference on Principles of Knowledge Representation and Reasoning
Main Track

A Minimal Deductive System for RDFS with Negative Statements

Umberto Straccia[1], **Giovanni Casini**[1,2]
[1]ISTI-CNR, Pisa, Italy
[2]CAIR, University of Cape Town, Cape Town, South Africa
{umberto.straccia,giovanni.casini}@isti.cnr.it

Abstract

The triple language RDFS is designed to represent and reason with *positive* statements only (*e.g.*, "antipyretics are drugs"). In this paper, we extend RDFS to deal with various forms of negative statements under the Open World Assumption (OWA). To do so, we consider ρdf, a minimal, but significant RDFS fragment that covers all essential features of RDFS, and then extend it to $\rho df_\perp^\neg$, allowing express also statements such as "radio therapies are *non* drug treatments", "Ebola *has no* treatment", or "opioids and antipyretics are *disjoint* classes". The main features of our proposal are: (i) $\rho df_\perp^\neg$ remains syntactically a triple language by extending ρdf with new symbols with specific semantics and there is no need to revert to the reification method to represent negative triples; (ii) the logic is defined in such a way that any RDFS reasoner/store may handle the new predicates as ordinary terms if it does not want to take account of the extra capabilities; (iii) despite negated statements, every $\rho df_\perp^\neg$ knowledge base is satisfiable; (iv) the $\rho df_\perp^\neg$ entailment decision procedure is obtained from ρdf via additional inference rules favouring a potential implementation; and (v) deciding entailment in $\rho df_\perp^\neg$ ranges from P to NP.

1 Introduction

The *Resource Description Framework* (RDF)[1] and its extension *RDF Schema* (RDFS)[2] are both W3C standards, and nowadays quite popular knowledge representation languages. Essentially, a statement in RDF is a triple of the form (s, p, o), allowing to state that *subject* s is related to *object* o via the *property* p. For instance, (`fever`, `hasTreatment`, `paracetamol`) is such a triple whose intended meaning is "fever can be treated via paracetamol". RDFS is an extension of RDF providing mechanisms for describing groups of related terms and the relationships between these terms via a specific vocabulary of predicates. So, *e.g.*, the RDFS triple (`paracetamol`, type, `antipyretic`) express that "paracetamol *is an* antipyretic" (here type is the predicate for class membership specification), while (`antipyretic`, sc, `drug`) asserts that "antipyretic *is a subclass of* drug" (sc is the predicate for sub-class specification).

[1]http://www.w3.org/RDF/

[2]https://www.w3.org/TR/rdf-schema/

As both languages have been designed to represent and reason with *positive* statements only, they can not properly deal with *negative* statements such as

"opioids and antipyretics are *disjoint* classes"; (1)

"radio therapies are *non* drug treatments"; and (2)

"Ebola *has no* treatment". (3)

In particular, we may not infer that "paracetamol *is not* a treatment for Ebola". Such a statement could only be inferred with the major assumption that the Knowledge Base (KB) is complete — the so-called *Closed-World Assumption* (CWA) (Reiter 1978), which however is not realistic to be assumed in many cases. For instance, in medicine, it is important to distinguish between knowing about the absence of a biochemical reaction between substances, and not knowing about its existence at all, which rises then the need for explicitly stating salient *negative* statements (see, *e.g.*, (Arnaout et al. 2021b) for a recent work about it). This is particularly true in the case in which the information about the represented world is assumed to be incomplete, — the so-called *Open World Assumption* (OWA).

Contribution. In this paper we show how to extend RDFS to express and reason with various forms of negative statements under the OWA. To do so, we start from ρdf (Muñoz, Pérez, and Gutierrez 2009), a minimal, but significant RDFS fragment that covers all essential features of RDFS, and then extend it to $\rho df_\perp^\neg$, allowing express also negative statements via a specific expressions involving negated classes/properties, disjointness relationships, and no-value existence. So, for instance, the $\rho df_\perp^\neg$ triple (`opioid`, $\perp_{\mathsf{c}}$, `antipyretic`) expresses (1) ($\perp_{\mathsf{c}}$ is the vocabulary predicate for class disjointness specification), (`radiotherapy`, sc, ¬`drugTreatment`) expresses (2) (here, essentially we introduce class complements via the $\neg$ operator), while (`ebola`, ¬`hasTreatment`, $\star_{\texttt{treatment}}$) is meant to encode (3) (here, besides property complement, we also allow the $\star_c$ operator, which is the place holder for an universally quantified variable over domain c).[3]

The main and, to the best of our knowledge, unique features of our proposal are (*cf.*, related work below): (i)

[3]We refer the reader to Table 1 for an informal First-Order Logic (FOL) reading of some types of $\rho df_\perp^\neg$ triples.

$\rho df_{\perp}^{\neg}$ remains syntactically a triple language by extending ρdf with new symbols with specific semantics and there is no need to revert to the reification method to represent negative triples; (ii) the logic is defined in such a way that any RDFS reasoner/store may handle the new predicates as ordinary terms if it does not want to take account of the extra capabilities; (iii) despite negated statements, every $\rho df_{\perp}^{\neg}$ knowledge base is satisfiable, which is obtained via an intentional like four-valued semantics; (iv) the $\rho df_{\perp}^{\neg}$ entailment decision procedure is obtained from ρdf via additional inference rules favouring a potential implementation; and (v) deciding entailment in $\rho df_{\perp}^{\neg}$ ranges from P to NP.

Related Work. There have been various works in the past about extending RDFS with negative statements, or applications that would like or require to have such a feature, which we briefly summarise below and indeed inspired our work.

In (Arnaout et al. 2021b) and related works (Arnaout, Razniewski, and Weikum 2020; Arnaout et al. 2021a; Arnaout et al. 2021c), two types of negative statements are considered: (i) grounded negative statements of the form $\neg(s,p,o)$, with informal FOL reading $\neg p(s,o)$; and (ii) universally negative statements of the form $\neg\exists x.(s,p,x)$, meaning in FOL terms $\neg\exists x.p(s,x)$. The former type of triples have been proposed in (Analyti et al. 2004) (and subsequent works, see below), while the latter has been addressed in (Darari, Prasojo, and Nutt 2015). In (Arnaout et al. 2021b) essentially a statistical inference method is proposed to extract useful negative statements of this form, such as "Leonardo DiCaprio has never been married" and "United Kingdom is not the citizenship of Jimi Hendrix".[4] It also publishes datasets[5] that contain useful negative statements about entities in Wikidata.[6] Reasoning has not been addressed (and was not the focus of these works). Both types of negative statements are covered by $\rho df_{\perp}^{\neg}$ and, thus, our work is complementary to (Arnaout et al. 2021b) in the sense that we describe how then to reason with such information.

In (Darari, Prasojo, and Nutt 2015) the problem on how to express the non-existence of information is addressed, which has the form $No(\{(s_1,p_1,o_1),\ldots,(s_n,p_n,o_n)\})$, with informal FOL reading $\neg\exists\mathbf{x}.(p_1(s_1,o_1)\wedge\ldots\wedge p_n(s_n,o_n))$, or equivalently, $\forall\mathbf{x}.(\neg p_1(s_1,o_1)\vee\ldots\vee\neg p_n(s_n,o_n))$, where $\mathbf{x}$ are the variables occurring the triples. It shows how to represent it via the reification method and incorporate it into SPARQL[7] query answering. Reasoning is not addressed however. We consider here only the case $n=1$ via the expression $(s,\neg p,\star_c)$ as the general case $n\geq 2$ would introduce a disjunction, which we would like to avoid for computational reasons.

In (Analyti et al. 2008) and related works (Analyti, Damásio, and Antoniou 2015; Analyti, Antoniou, and Damásio 2008; Analyti, Antoniou, and Damásio 2009; Analyti, Antoniou, and Damásio 2011; Analyti et al. 2013; Analyti et al. 2005; Analyti et al. 2004; Damásio, Analyti, and Antoniou 2010) the authors deal with *Extended* RDF (ERDF), a non-monotonic logic, where an ERDF ontology consists of two parts: an ERDF graph and an ERDF logic program. An ERDF graph allows *negated* RDF triples of the form $\neg(s,p,o)$, informally in FOL terms $\neg p(s,o)$, while in the body of rules all the classical connectives $\neg,\supset,\wedge,\vee,\forall,\exists$, plus the weak negation (negation-as-failure) $\sim$ are allowed. Various "stable model" semantics have been proposed. From a computational complexity point view, decision problems in ERDF are non-polynomial (Analyti, Damásio, and Antoniou 2015). E.g., deciding model existence and, thus, model existence is not guaranteed, ranges from NP to PSPACE, while query answering goes from co-NP to PSPACE, depending on the setting.[8] In comparison, $\rho df_{\perp}^{\neg}$ does not use a rule layer, the triple language is more expressive, model existence is guaranteed and the computational complexity ranges between P and NP. Of course, all inference rules for $\rho df_{\perp}^{\neg}$ can be implemented in the rule layer of ERDF (and in Datalog in general).

Eventually, (Casini and Straccia 2020) considers $\rho df_{\perp}$ on top of which to develop a non-monotonic RDFS logic based on Rational Closure (Lehmann and Magidor 1992). $\rho df_{\perp}$ extends ρdf allowing to express disjointness among (positive) classes and relations.

In summary, our work aims at putting all together within RDFS to deal with expressions of the form *e.g.*, (1)–(3) in a generalised way.

We proceed as follows. As next we introduce the basic notions about ρdf we will rely on. Section 3 is the main part of this paper in which we extend ρdf to $\rho df_{\perp}^{\neg}$. The paper concludes with a summary of the contributions and addresses some topics for future work.

2 Preliminaries

For the sake of our purposes, we will rely on a minimal, but significant RDFS fragment, called ρdf (Muñoz, Pérez, and Gutierrez 2009; Muñoz, Pérez, and Gutiérrez 2007), that covers the essential features of RDFS. In fact, ρdf may be considered as the logic behind RDFS and suffices to illustrate the main concepts and algorithms we will consider. ρdf is defined as the following subset of the RDFS vocabulary:

$$\rho\text{df} = \{\mathsf{sp},\mathsf{sc},\mathsf{type},\mathsf{dom},\mathsf{range}\}\ . \quad (4)$$

Informally, (i) (p,sp,q) means that property p is a *sub property* of property q; (ii) (c,sc,d) means that class c is a *sub class* of class d; (iii) (a,type,b) means that a is of *type* b; (iv) (p,dom,c) means that the *domain* of property p is c; (v) (p,range,c) means that the *range* of property p is c.

Syntax. Assume pairwise disjoint alphabets $\mathbf{U}$ (*RDF URI references*), $\mathbf{B}$ (*Blank nodes*), and $\mathbf{L}$ (*Literals*). We assume $\mathbf{U},\mathbf{B}$, and $\mathbf{L}$ fixed, and for simplicity we will denote unions

[4] Optionally, triples may be annotated with a degree such as *e.g.*, "The Sultan Resort has no parking facility to degree 0.97". See *e.g.*, (Zimmermann et al. 2012) for a general framework to deal with annotated triples.

[5] https://github.com/HibaArnaout/usefulnegations

[6] https://www.wikidata.org

[7] http://www.w3.org/TR/sparql11-query/

[8] There are also many more works that use rule languages on top of RDFS, which however we are not going to discuss here (see, *e.g.*, (Casini and Straccia 2020).

of these sets simply concatenating their names. We call elements in $\mathbf{UBL}$ *terms* (denoted $a, b, \ldots, w$), and elements in $\mathbf{B}$ *variables* (denoted x, y, z).[9] A *vocabulary* is a subset of $\mathbf{UL}$ and we assume that $\mathbf{U}$ contains the ρdf vocabulary -see Eq. (4). A *triple* is of the form

$$(s, p, o) \in \mathbf{UBL} \times \mathbf{U} \times \mathbf{UBL} ,$$

where $s, o \notin \rho$df. We call s the *subject*, p the *predicate*, and o the *object*. A *graph* (or *RDF Knowledge Base*) G is a set of triples τ. A subgraph is a subset of a graph. The *universe* of G, denoted $\mathtt{uni}(G)$, is the set of terms in $\mathbf{UBL}$ that occur in the triples of G. The *vocabulary* of G, denoted by $\mathtt{voc}(G)$ is the set $\mathtt{uni}(G) \cap \mathbf{UL}$. A graph is *ground* if it has no blank nodes, *i.e.*, variables. A *map* (or *variable assignment*) is as a function $\mu : \mathbf{UBL} \to \mathbf{UBL}$ preserving URIs and literals, *i.e.*, $\mu(t) = t$, for all $t \in \mathbf{UL}$. Given a graph G, we define

$$\mu(G) = \{(\mu(s), \mu(p), \mu(o)) \mid (s, p, o) \in G\} .$$

We speak of a map μ from G_1 to G_2, and write $\mu : G_1 \to G_2$, if μ is such that $\mu(G_1) \subseteq G_2$.

Example 1 (Running example). *The following is a ρdf graph:*[10]

$$\begin{aligned} G = \{ & (\mathtt{paracetamol}, \mathsf{type}, \mathtt{antipyretic}), \\ & (\mathtt{antipyretic}, \mathsf{sc}, \mathtt{drugTreatment}), \\ & (\mathtt{morphine}, \mathsf{type}, \mathtt{opioid}), (\mathtt{opioid}, \mathsf{sc}, \mathtt{drugTreatment}), \\ & (\mathtt{drugTreatment}, \mathsf{sc}, \mathtt{treatment}), \\ & (\mathtt{brainTumour}, \mathsf{type}, \mathtt{tumour}), \\ & (\mathtt{hasDrugTreatment}, \mathsf{sp}, \mathtt{hasTreatment}), \\ & (\mathtt{hasTreatment}, \mathsf{dom}, \mathtt{illness}), \\ & (\mathtt{hasTreatment}, \mathsf{range}, \mathtt{treatment}), \\ & (\mathtt{hasDrugTreatment}, \mathsf{range}, \mathtt{drugTreatment}), \\ & (\mathtt{fever}, \mathtt{hasDrugTreatment}, \mathtt{paracetamol}) \\ & (\mathtt{brainTumour}, \mathtt{hasDrugTreatment}, \mathtt{morphine}) \} . \end{aligned}$$

Semantics. A ρdf *interpretation* $\mathcal{I}$ over a vocabulary V is a tuple

$$\mathcal{I} = \langle \Delta_{\mathsf{R}}, \Delta_{\mathsf{P}}, \Delta_{\mathsf{C}}, \Delta_{\mathsf{L}}, \mathsf{P}[\![\cdot]\!], \mathsf{C}[\![\cdot]\!], \cdot^{\mathcal{I}} \rangle ,$$

where the finite non-empty sets $\Delta_{\mathsf{R}}, \Delta_{\mathsf{P}}, \Delta_{\mathsf{C}}, \Delta_{\mathsf{L}}$ are the interpretation domains of $\mathcal{I}$ and $\mathsf{P}[\![\cdot]\!], \mathsf{C}[\![\cdot]\!], \cdot^{\mathcal{I}}$ are the interpretation functions of $\mathcal{I}$. They have to satisfy:

1. Δ_{R} are the resources;
2. Δ_{P} are property names;
3. $\Delta_{\mathsf{C}} \subseteq \Delta_{\mathsf{R}}$ are the classes;
4. $\Delta_{\mathsf{L}} \subseteq \Delta_{\mathsf{R}}$ are the literal values and contains all the literals in $\mathbf{L} \cap V$;
5. $\mathsf{P}[\![\cdot]\!]$ is a function $\mathsf{P}[\![\cdot]\!]\colon \Delta_{\mathsf{P}} \to 2^{\Delta_{\mathsf{R}} \times \Delta_{\mathsf{R}}}$;
6. $\mathsf{C}[\![\cdot]\!]$ is a function $\mathsf{C}[\![\cdot]\!]\colon \Delta_{\mathsf{C}} \to 2^{\Delta_{\mathsf{R}}}$;
7. $\cdot^{\mathcal{I}}$ maps each $t \in \mathbf{UL} \cap V$ into a value $t^{\mathcal{I}} \in \Delta_{\mathsf{R}} \cup \Delta_{\mathsf{P}}$, where $\cdot^{\mathcal{I}}$ is the identity for literals; and
8. $\cdot^{\mathcal{I}}$ maps each variable $x \in \mathbf{B}$ into a value $x^{\mathcal{I}} \in \Delta_{\mathsf{R}}$.

As next, for space reasons and without loosing the substantial ingredients, we illustrate the so-called *reflexive-relaxed* ρdf semantics (Muñoz, Pérez, and Gutierrez 2009, Definition 12), in which the predicates sc and sp are *not* assumed to be reflexive. Informally, the notion entailment is defined using the idea of *satisfaction* of a graph under certain interpretation. Intuitively a ground triple (s, p, o) in an RDF graph G will be true under the interpretation $\mathcal{I}$ if p is interpreted as a property name, s and o are interpreted as resources, and the interpretation of the pair (s, o) belongs to the extension of the property assigned to p. Moreover, blank nodes, *i.e.*, variables, work as existential variables. Intuitively the triple (x, p, o) with $x \in \mathbf{B}$ will be true under $\mathcal{I}$ if $\mathcal{I}$ maps x into a resource s such that the pair (s, o) belongs to the extension of the property assigned to p. Formally,

Definition 1 (Model/Satisfaction/Entailment $\models$). *A ρdf interpretation $\mathcal{I}$ is a* model *of a ρdf graph G, denoted $\mathcal{I} \models G$, if and only if $\mathcal{I}$ is an interpretation over the vocabulary ρdf $\cup$ $\mathtt{uni}(G)$ such that:*

Simple:

1. for each $(s, p, o) \in G$, $p^{\mathcal{I}} \in \Delta_{\mathsf{P}}$ and $(s^{\mathcal{I}}, o^{\mathcal{I}}) \in \mathsf{P}[\![p^{\mathcal{I}}]\!]$;

Subproperty:

1. $\mathsf{P}[\![\mathsf{sp}^{\mathcal{I}}]\!]$ is transitive over Δ_{P};

2. if $(p, q) \in \mathsf{P}[\![\mathsf{sp}^{\mathcal{I}}]\!]$ then $p, q \in \Delta_{\mathsf{P}}$ and $\mathsf{P}[\![p]\!] \subseteq \mathsf{P}[\![q]\!]$;

Subclass:

1. $\mathsf{P}[\![\mathsf{sc}^{\mathcal{I}}]\!]$ is transitive over Δ_{C};

2. if $(c, d) \in \mathsf{P}[\![\mathsf{sc}^{\mathcal{I}}]\!]$ then $c, d \in \Delta_{\mathsf{C}}$ and $\mathsf{C}[\![c]\!] \subseteq \mathsf{C}[\![d]\!]$;

Typing I:

1. $x \in \mathsf{C}[\![c]\!]$ if and only if $(x, c) \in \mathsf{P}[\![\mathsf{type}^{\mathcal{I}}]\!]$;

2. if $(p, c) \in \mathsf{P}[\![\mathsf{dom}^{\mathcal{I}}]\!]$ and $(x, y) \in \mathsf{P}[\![p]\!]$ then $x \in \mathsf{C}[\![c]\!]$;

3. if $(p, c) \in \mathsf{P}[\![\mathsf{range}^{\mathcal{I}}]\!]$ and $(x, y) \in \mathsf{P}[\![p]\!]$ then $y \in \mathsf{C}[\![c]\!]$;

Typing II:

1. for each $\mathsf{e} \in \rho df$, $\mathsf{e}^{\mathcal{I}} \in \Delta_{\mathsf{P}}$;

2. if $(p, c) \in \mathsf{P}[\![\mathsf{dom}^{\mathcal{I}}]\!]$ then $p \in \Delta_{\mathsf{P}}$ and $c \in \Delta_{\mathsf{C}}$;

3. if $(p, c) \in \mathsf{P}[\![\mathsf{range}^{\mathcal{I}}]\!]$ then $p \in \Delta_{\mathsf{P}}$ and $c \in \Delta_{\mathsf{C}}$;

4. if $(x, c) \in \mathsf{P}[\![\mathsf{type}^{\mathcal{I}}]\!]$ then $c \in \Delta_{\mathsf{C}}$.

A graph G is satisfiable *if it has a model $\mathcal{I}$. Moreover, given two graphs G and H, G* entails *H, denoted $G \models H$, if and only if every model of G is also a model of H.*

Example 2. *From G in Example 1, it can be shown that $G \models \{(\mathtt{fever}, \mathtt{hasTreatment}, x), (x, \mathsf{type}, \mathtt{drugTreatment})\}$.*

Deductive System for ρdf. We recap the sound and complete deductive system for ρdf (Muñoz, Pérez, and Gutierrez 2009). In every rule, A, B, C, D, E, X and Y stand for meta-variables to be replaced by actual terms. An *instantiation* of a rule is obtained by replacing all meta-variables with terms such that all triples after the replacement are ρdf triples.

[9] All symbols may have upper or lower script.

[10] For ease of presentation, we use the terms paracetomol, antipyretic, morphine and opioid to mean paracetomol-, antipyretic-, morphine- and opioid-treatement, respectively.

Definition 2 (Deductive rules for ρdf). *The* deductive rules for ρdf *are the following:*

1. *Simple:*
   (a) $\frac{G}{G'}$ *for a map* $\mu : G' \to G$ (b) $\frac{G}{G'}$ *for* $G' \subseteq G$
2. *Subproperty:*
   (a) $\frac{(A,\mathsf{sp},B),(B,\mathsf{sp},C)}{(A,\mathsf{sp},C)}$ (b) $\frac{(D,\mathsf{sp},E),(X,D,Y)}{(X,E,Y)}$
3. *Subclass:*
   (a) $\frac{(A,\mathsf{sc},B),(B,\mathsf{sc},C)}{(A,\mathsf{sc},C)}$ (b) $\frac{(A,\mathsf{sc},B),(X,\mathsf{type},A)}{(X,\mathsf{type},B)}$
4. *Typing:*
   (a) $\frac{(D,\mathsf{dom},B),(X,D,Y)}{(X,\mathsf{type},B)}$ (b) $\frac{(D,\mathsf{range},B),(X,D,Y)}{(Y,\mathsf{type},B)}$
5. *Implicit Typing:*
   (a) $\frac{(A,\mathsf{dom},B),(D,\mathsf{sp},A),(X,D,Y)}{(X,\mathsf{type},B)}$

   (b) $\frac{(A,\mathsf{range},B),(D,\mathsf{sp},A),(X,D,Y)}{(Y,\mathsf{type},B)}$

Definition 3 (Derivation $\vdash$). *Let G and H be ρdf-graphs. $G \vdash H$ if and only if there exists a sequence of graphs $P_1, P_2, \ldots, P_k$ with $P_1 = G$ and $P_k = H$ and for each j $(2 \leq j \leq k)$ one of the following cases hold:*

- *there is a map $\mu : P_j \to P_{j-1}$ (rule (1a));*
- *$P_j \subseteq P_{j-1}$ (rule (1b));*
- *there is an instantiation R/R' of one of the rules (2)-(5), such that $R \subseteq P_{j-1}$ and $P_j = P_{j-1} \cup R'$.*

Such a sequence of graphs is called a proof of $G \vdash H$. Whenever $G \vdash H$, we say that the graph H is derived from the graph G. Each pair (P_{j-1}, P_j), $1 \leq j \leq k$ is called a step of the proof which is labeled by the respective instantiation R/R' of the rule applied at the step.

Please note that if $G \vdash H$ then H is indeed a graph. Finally, the *closure* of a graph G, denoted $\mathsf{Cl}(G)$, is defined as

$$\mathsf{Cl}(G) = \{\tau \mid G \vdash^* \tau\},$$

where $\vdash^*$ is as $\vdash$ except that rule $(1a)$ is excluded.

Example 3. *Consider Example 1. Then it can be verified that* $\mathsf{Cl}(G) \supseteq \{(\texttt{morphine}, \mathsf{type}, \texttt{drugTreatment}), (\texttt{brainTumour}, \mathsf{type}, \texttt{illness})\}$.

The following proposition recaps salient results taken from (Gutiérrez et al. 2011; Muñoz, Pérez, and Gutierrez 2009; ter Horst 2005)

Proposition 1. *Every ρdf-graph is satisfiable. Moreover, let G and H be ρdf-graphs. Then*

1. *$G \vdash H$ if and only if $G \models H$;*
2. *if $G \models H$ then there is a proof of H from G where rule $(1a)$ is used at most once and at the end;*
3. *the closure of G is unique and $|\mathsf{Cl}(G)| \in \Theta(|G|^2)$;*
4. *deciding $G \models H$ is an NP-complete problem;*
5. *if G is ground then $\mathsf{Cl}(G)$ can be determined without using implicit typing rules (5);*
6. *if H is ground, then $G \models H$ if and only if $H \subseteq \mathsf{Cl}(G)$;*
7. *There is no triple τ such that $\emptyset \models \tau$.*

Remark 1. *Please note that: (i) a proof of NP-completeness of point 4. above can be found in (ter Horst 2005, Proposition 2.19) via a reduction of the k-clique problem encoding an undirected graph G into a ρdf graph G' (an edge $\langle v, w\rangle$ is encoded via two triples (v, e, w) and (w, e, v)) and H' consists of the triples (x, e, y), where x and y are distinct variables of new set of k blank nodes. Then, G has a clique of size $\geq k$ iff $G' \models H'$, i.e., there is a map μ: $H' \to G'$; and (ii) concerning the size of the closure, the lower bound is determined by triples $(p_1, \mathsf{sp}, p_2), \ldots, (p_n, \mathsf{sp}, p_{n+1})$, whose closure's size is $\Omega(n^2)$ via rule $(2a)$. The upper bound follows by an analysis of the rules, where the important point is the propagation of triples (s, p, o) via rule $(2b)$. This gives at most a quadratic upper bound (for triples with fixed predicate, the quadratic bound is trivial).*

Note that from Proposition 1 it follows that deciding if, for two ground ρdf-graphs G and H, $G \models H$ can be done in time $O(|H||G|^2)$ by computing first the closure of G and then check whether H is in that closure. An alternative method not requiring to compute the closure with a computational benefit is illustrated by the following proposition:

Proposition 2 ((Muñoz, Pérez, and Gutierrez 2009)). *Let G and H be two ground ρdf graphs. Then deciding if $G \models H$ can be done in time $O(|H||G| \log |G|)$. The result hods also in case each triple in H has at most one blank node.*

3 Extending ρdf with Negative Statements

In this section, we show how to extend ρdf allowing to represent negative statements.

3.1 Syntax

To start with, consider a new pair of predicates, $\bot_{\mathsf{c}}$ and $\bot_{\mathsf{p}}$, used to represent disjoint information: *e.g.*, (i) $(c, \bot_{\mathsf{c}}, d)$ indicates that the classes c and d are disjoint; analogously, (ii) $(p, \bot_{\mathsf{p}}, q)$ indicates that the properties p and q are disjoint.

We call $\rho df_\bot$ the vocabulary obtained from ρdf by adding $\bot_{\mathsf{c}}$ and $\bot_{\mathsf{p}}$, that is,

$$\rho df_\bot = \rho\text{df} \cup \{\bot_{\mathsf{c}}, \bot_{\mathsf{p}}\}\,. \quad (5)$$

Like for ρdf, we assume that $\mathbf{U}$ contains the $\rho df_\bot$ vocabulary. Now we extend the alphabet $\mathbf{U}$ in the following way:

1. for each (*atomic*) resource $r \in \mathbf{U} \setminus \rho df_\bot$, we add to $\mathbf{U}$ a new *negated resource* $\neg r$ of r. Let $\mathbf{U}'$ be the resulting alphabet. We will use the convention that $\neg\neg r$ is r. Informally, $\neg r$ is intended to represent the complement of r. So, for instance, $(\texttt{paracetamol}, \mathsf{type}, \neg\texttt{opioid})$ may encode "paracetamol is a non opioid treatment";

2. for each resource $c \in \mathbf{U}' \setminus \rho df_\bot$, we add to $\mathbf{U}'$ a new resource of the form $\star_c$. Let $\mathbf{U}''$ be the resulting alphabet. Informally, *e.g.*, a triple $(s, p, \star_c)$ represents an universal quantification on the third argument over instance of class c, *i.e.*, (s, p, t) is true for all $t \in$

$\rho df_\bot^\neg$	FOL
$(s, \neg p, o)$	$\neg p(s, o)$
$(s, \neg p, x)$	$\exists x. \neg p(s, x)$
$(a, \mathsf{type}, \neg c)$	$\neg c(a)$
$(c, \mathsf{sc}, \neg d)$	$\forall x.c(x) \to \neg d(x)$
$(p, \mathsf{dom}, \neg c)$	$\forall x \forall y.p(x, y) \to \neg c(x)$
$(\neg p, \mathsf{range}, d)$	$\forall x \forall y.\neg p(x, y) \to d(y)$
$(c, \bot_\mathsf{c}, \neg d)$	$\forall x.c(x) \wedge \neg d(x) \to \bot$
$(\neg p, \bot_\mathsf{p}, q)$	$\forall x \forall y.\neg p(x, y) \wedge q(x, y) \to \bot$
$(\star_c, p, o)$	$\forall x.c(x) \to p(x, o)$
$(s, \neg p, \star_c)$	$\forall y.c(y) \to \neg p(s, y)$ (*i.e.*, $\neg \exists y.c(y) \wedge p(s, y)$)

Table 1: Informal FOL reading of some types of $\rho df_\bot^\neg$-triples.

UL that are instances of the class c. For instance, $(\texttt{ebola}, \neg\texttt{hasTreatment}, \star_{\texttt{treatment}})$ may encode (3);[11]

3. finally, let **U** be **U**$''$.

Now, the definition of *$\rho df_\bot^\neg$-triples* extends the one for ρdf-triples in the following way:

Definition 4 ($\rho df_\bot^\neg$-triple). *A* $\rho df_\bot^\neg$-triple *is of the form* $(s, p, o) \in \mathbf{UBL} \times \mathbf{U} \times \mathbf{UBL}$, *where*

1. $s, o \notin \rho df_\bot$;
2. *p is not of the form $\star_c$;*
3. *s and o can not be both of the form $\star_c$;*
4. *if $p \in \rho df_\bot$ then neither s nor o are of the form $\star_c$.*

In Table 1, to ease the reading, we provide an informal FOL reading of various additional (non exhaustive) types of triples supported in $\rho df_\bot^\neg$.[12]

Example 4. *In the context of Example 1, let us extend the graph G with:*

$$\begin{aligned} G := G \cup \{ & (\texttt{opioid}, \bot_\mathsf{c}, \texttt{antipyretic}), \\ & (\neg\texttt{drugTreatment}, \mathsf{sc}, \texttt{treatment}), \\ & (\neg\texttt{hasDrugTreatment}, \mathsf{sp}, \texttt{hasTreatment}), \\ & (\neg\texttt{hasDrugTreatment}, \mathsf{range}, \neg\texttt{drugTreatment}), \\ & (\texttt{brainTumour}, \neg\texttt{hasDrugTreatment}, \texttt{radioTherapy}), \\ & (\neg\texttt{hasTreatment}, \mathsf{dom}, \texttt{illness}), \\ & (\neg\texttt{hasTreatment}, \mathsf{range}, \texttt{treatment}), \\ & (\texttt{ebola}, \neg\texttt{hasTreatment}, \star_{\texttt{treatment}}) \} . \end{aligned}$$

3.2 Semantics

The semantics of $\rho df_\bot^\neg$ has the following objectives:

1. we accommodate the new constructs in such a way that the resulting deductive system will be as for ρdf, plus some additional rules and, thus, any RDFS reasoner/store may handle the new triples as ordinary triples if it does not want to take account of the extra inference capabilities;
2. the semantics has to be such that, despite introducing negative statements, all $\rho df_\bot^\neg$ graphs have a canonical model (see Corollary 1 later on), and, thus, $\rho df_\bot^\neg$ remains a *paraconsistent* logic; and
3. deciding entailment in $\rho df_\bot^\neg$ still ranges from P to NP.

To do so, we will consider a *four-valued* logic semantics (Belnap 1977) variant of the semantics for ρdf. Specifically, we will have *positive extensions* of $\mathsf{P}[\![]\!]$ and $\mathsf{C}[\![]\!]$ (denoted $\mathsf{P}^+[\![]\!]$ and $\mathsf{C}^+[\![]\!]$, respectively) and *negative extensions* of $\mathsf{P}[\![]\!]$ and $\mathsf{C}[\![]\!]$ (denoted $\mathsf{P}^-[\![]\!]$ and $\mathsf{C}^-[\![]\!]$, respectively). Roughly, $\mathsf{C}^+[\![c]\!]$ will denote the set of resources *known to be* instances of class c, while $\mathsf{C}^-[\![c]\!]$ will denote the set of resources *known not to be* instances of class c (for properties the case is similar). Note that positive and negative extensions need not to be the complement of each other: *e.g.*, $r \notin \mathsf{C}^+[\![c]\!]$ does not imply necessarily that $r \in \mathsf{C}^-[\![c]\!]$ as $\mathsf{C}^-[\![c]\!]$ will not enforced to be *e.g.*, $\Delta_\mathsf{R} \setminus \mathsf{C}^+[\![c]\!]$.

The idea of having separate positive and negative extensions is not new at all and we may find already traces of it back in the mid 80s with the seminal work of Patel-Schneider (Patel-Schneider 1985; Patel-Schneider 1986; Patel-Schneider 1987; Patel-Schneider 1988; Patel-Schneider 1989) in which four-valued variants of *Terminological Logics* (TLs), *viz.*, the so-called *Description Logics* (DLs) (Baader et al. 2007) nowadays, have been proposed with the aim to obtain some gain from a computational complexity point of view. Later the works (Straccia 1997a; Straccia 1997b; Straccia 1999; Straccia 2000) have been inspired by the same idea, though also to model some sort of *relevance entailment*, besides being paraconsistent. More recently, a similar idea has been considered also in the context of RDFS (Analyti et al. 2004; Analyti et al. 2005; Analyti et al. 2013; Analyti, Damásio, and Antoniou 2015), which is also the semantics we start from and are going to adapt and extend to meet the before mentioned objectives.

A $\rho df_\bot^\neg$ *interpretation* $\mathcal{I}$ over a vocabulary V is a tuple

$$\mathcal{I} = \langle \Delta_\mathsf{R}, \Delta_\mathsf{P}, \Delta_\mathsf{C}, \Delta_\mathsf{L}, \mathsf{P}^+[\![\cdot]\!], \mathsf{P}^-[\![\cdot]\!], \mathsf{C}^+[\![\cdot]\!], \mathsf{C}^-[\![\cdot]\!], \cdot^\mathcal{I} \rangle ,$$

where the finite non-empty sets $\Delta_\mathsf{R}, \Delta_\mathsf{P}, \Delta_\mathsf{C}, \Delta_\mathsf{L}$ are the interpretation domains of $\mathcal{I}$ and $\mathsf{P}^+[\![\cdot]\!], \mathsf{P}^-[\![\cdot]\!], \mathsf{C}^+[\![\cdot]\!], \mathsf{C}^-[\![\cdot]\!], \cdot^\mathcal{I}$ are the interpretation functions of $\mathcal{I}$. They have to satisfy:

1. Δ_R are the resources;
2. Δ_P are property names;
3. $\Delta_\mathsf{C} \subseteq \Delta_\mathsf{R}$ are the classes;
4. for each domain $\Delta_\mathsf{R}, \Delta_\mathsf{P}$ and Δ_C, for each term t in it, there is an unique designated complement term of t, denoted $\neg t$, in it;[13]
5. $\Delta_\mathsf{L} \subseteq \Delta_\mathsf{R}$ are the literal values and contains all the literals in $\mathbf{L} \cap V$;
6. $\mathsf{P}^+[\![\cdot]\!]$ and $\mathsf{P}^-[\![\cdot]\!]$ are functions $\Delta_\mathsf{P} \to 2^{\Delta_\mathsf{R} \times \Delta_\mathsf{R}}$ such that $\mathsf{P}^+[\![\neg p]\!] = \mathsf{P}^-[\![p]\!]$, for each $p \in \Delta_\mathsf{P}$;
7. $\mathsf{C}^+[\![\cdot]\!]$ and $\mathsf{C}^-[\![\cdot]\!]$ are functions $\Delta_\mathsf{C} \to 2^{\Delta_\mathsf{R}}$ such that $\mathsf{C}^+[\![\neg c]\!] = \mathsf{C}^-[\![c]\!]$, for each $c \in \Delta_\mathsf{C}$;
8. $\cdot^\mathcal{I}$ maps each $t \in \mathbf{UL} \cap V$, that is not of the form $\star_c$, into a value $t^\mathcal{I} \in \Delta_\mathsf{R} \cup \Delta_\mathsf{P}$, such that $(\neg t)^\mathcal{I} = \neg\, t^\mathcal{I}$ and $\cdot^\mathcal{I}$ is the identity for literals; and
9. $\cdot^\mathcal{I}$ maps each variable $x \in \mathbf{B}$ into a value $x^\mathcal{I} \in \Delta_\mathsf{R}$.

[11] In the sense that "none of the treatments are treatments for ebola"

[12] The FOL reading is 'informal' as the translation isn't a bijection, *e.g.*,, we have a 4-valued intentional semantics and individuals may be classes, which may be negated.

[13] As for **U**, we will use the convention that $\neg\neg t$ is t.

In the following, we define

$$\begin{aligned}
\mathsf{P}^+[\![p]\!]\!\uparrow &= \{x \in \Delta_\mathsf{R} \mid (x,y) \in \mathsf{P}^+[\![p]\!]\} \\
\mathsf{P}^+[\![p]\!]\!\downarrow &= \{y \in \Delta_\mathsf{R} \mid (x,y) \in \mathsf{P}^+[\![p]\!]\} \\
\mathsf{P}^-[\![p]\!]\!\uparrow &= \{x \in \Delta_\mathsf{R} \mid (x,y) \in \mathsf{P}^-[\![p]\!]\} \\
\mathsf{P}^-[\![p]\!]\!\downarrow &= \{y \in \Delta_\mathsf{R} \mid (x,y) \in \mathsf{P}^-[\![p]\!]\}
\end{aligned}$$

as the projections of the property extension functions $\mathsf{P}^+[\![]\!]$ and $\mathsf{P}^-[\![]\!]$ on the first and second argument, respectively.

Now, the model/satisfaction/entailment definitions for ρdf are generalised to $\rho df_\bot^\neg$ as follows:

Definition 5 (Model/Satisfaction/Entailment $\models^\bot_\neg$)**.** *A $\rho df_\bot^\neg$ interpretation $\mathcal{I}$ is a $\rho df_\bot^\neg$-model of a $\rho df_\bot^\neg$ graph G, denoted $\mathcal{I} \models^\bot_\neg G$, if and only if $\mathcal{I}$ is a $\rho df_\bot^\neg$-interpretation over the vocabulary $\rho df_\bot^\neg \cup \mathtt{uni}(G)$ such that:*

Simple:

1. *if $(s,p,o) \in G$ and neither s nor o are of the form $\star_\mathsf{c}$, then $p^\mathcal{I} \in \Delta_\mathsf{P}$ and $(s^\mathcal{I}, o^\mathcal{I}) \in \mathsf{P}^+[\![p^\mathcal{I}]\!]$;*
2. *if $(s,p,\star_\mathsf{c}) \in G$, then $p^\mathcal{I} \in \Delta_\mathsf{P}, c^\mathcal{I} \in \Delta_\mathsf{C}$ and $(s^\mathcal{I}, y) \in \mathsf{P}^+[\![p^\mathcal{I}]\!]$, for all $y \in \mathsf{C}^+[\![c^\mathcal{I}]\!]$;*
3. *if $(\star_\mathsf{c},p,s) \in G$, then $p^\mathcal{I} \in \Delta_\mathsf{P}, c^\mathcal{I} \in \Delta_\mathsf{C}$ and $(x, s^\mathcal{I}) \in \mathsf{P}^+[\![p^\mathcal{I}]\!]$, for all $x \in \mathsf{C}^+[\![c^\mathcal{I}]\!]$;*
4. *if $(s,p,\star_\mathsf{c}) \in G$, then $p^\mathcal{I} \in \Delta_\mathsf{P}, c^\mathcal{I} \in \Delta_\mathsf{C}$ and $y \in \mathsf{C}^-[\![c^\mathcal{I}]\!]$, for all $(s^\mathcal{I}, y) \in \mathsf{P}^-[\![p^\mathcal{I}]\!]$;*
5. *if $(\star_\mathsf{c},p,s) \in G$, then $p^\mathcal{I} \in \Delta_\mathsf{P}, c^\mathcal{I} \in \Delta_\mathsf{C}$ and $x \in \mathsf{C}^-[\![c^\mathcal{I}]\!]$, for all $(x, s^\mathcal{I}) \in \mathsf{P}^-[\![p^\mathcal{I}]\!]$;*

Subproperty:

1. *$\mathsf{P}^+[\![\mathsf{sp}^\mathcal{I}]\!]$ is transitive over Δ_P;*
2. *if $(p,q) \in \mathsf{P}^+[\![\mathsf{sp}^\mathcal{I}]\!]$ then $p,q \in \Delta_\mathsf{P}$ and $\mathsf{P}^+[\![p]\!] \subseteq \mathsf{P}^+[\![q]\!]$;*
3. *$(p,q) \in \mathsf{P}^+[\![\mathsf{sp}^\mathcal{I}]\!]$ if and only if $(\neg q, \neg p) \in \mathsf{P}^+[\![\mathsf{sp}^\mathcal{I}]\!]$;*

Subclass:

1. *$\mathsf{P}^+[\![\mathsf{sc}^\mathcal{I}]\!]$ is transitive over Δ_C;*
2. *if $(c,d) \in \mathsf{P}^+[\![\mathsf{sc}^\mathcal{I}]\!]$ then $c,d \in \Delta_\mathsf{C}$ and $\mathsf{C}^+[\![c]\!] \subseteq \mathsf{C}^+[\![d]\!]$;*
3. *$(c,d) \in \mathsf{P}^+[\![\mathsf{sc}^\mathcal{I}]\!]$ if and only if $(\neg d, \neg c) \in \mathsf{P}^+[\![\mathsf{sc}^\mathcal{I}]\!]$;*

Typing I:

1. *$x \in \mathsf{C}^+[\![c]\!]$ if and only if $(x,c) \in \mathsf{P}^+[\![\mathsf{type}^\mathcal{I}]\!]$;*
2. *if $(p,c) \in \mathsf{P}^+[\![\mathsf{dom}^\mathcal{I}]\!]$ and $(x,y) \in \mathsf{P}^+[\![p]\!]$ then $x \in \mathsf{C}^+[\![c]\!]$;*
3. *if $(p,c) \in \mathsf{P}^+[\![\mathsf{range}^\mathcal{I}]\!]$ and $(x,y) \in \mathsf{P}^+[\![p]\!]$ then $y \in \mathsf{C}^+[\![c]\!]$;*
4. *if $(p,c) \in \mathsf{P}^+[\![\mathsf{dom}^\mathcal{I}]\!]$, $x \in \mathsf{C}^-[\![c]\!]$ and $y \in \mathsf{P}^+[\![p]\!]\!\downarrow$ then $(x,y) \in \mathsf{P}^-[\![p]\!]$;*
5. *if $(p,c) \in \mathsf{P}^+[\![\mathsf{range}^\mathcal{I}]\!]$, $y \in \mathsf{C}^-[\![c]\!]$ and $x \in \mathsf{P}^+[\![p]\!]\!\uparrow$ then $(x,y) \in \mathsf{P}^-[\![p]\!]$;*

Typing II:

1. *For each $\mathsf{e} \in \rho df_\bot^\neg$, $\mathsf{e}^\mathcal{I} \in \Delta_\mathsf{P}$;*
2. *if $(p,c) \in \mathsf{P}^+[\![\mathsf{dom}^\mathcal{I}]\!]$ then $p \in \Delta_\mathsf{P}$ and $c \in \Delta_\mathsf{C}$;*
3. *if $(p,c) \in \mathsf{P}^+[\![\mathsf{range}^\mathcal{I}]\!]$ then $p \in \Delta_\mathsf{P}$ and $c \in \Delta_\mathsf{C}$;*
4. *if $(x,c) \in \mathsf{P}^+[\![\mathsf{type}^\mathcal{I}]\!]$ then $c \in \Delta_\mathsf{C}$;*

Disjointness I:

1. *if $(c,d) \in \mathsf{P}^+[\![\bot_\mathsf{c}{}^\mathcal{I}]\!]$ then $c,d \in \Delta_\mathsf{C}$;*
2. *if $(p,q) \in \mathsf{P}^+[\![\bot_\mathsf{p}{}^\mathcal{I}]\!]$ then $p,q \in \Delta_\mathsf{P}$;*
3. *$\mathsf{P}^+[\![\bot_\mathsf{c}{}^\mathcal{I}]\!]$ is symmetric, sub-transitive and exhaustive over Δ_C;*
   Symmetry: *if $(c,d) \in \mathsf{P}^+[\![\bot_\mathsf{c}{}^\mathcal{I}]\!]$, then $(d,c) \in \mathsf{P}^+[\![\bot_\mathsf{c}{}^\mathcal{I}]\!]$;*
   Sub-Transitivity: *if $(c,d) \in \mathsf{P}^+[\![\bot_\mathsf{c}{}^\mathcal{I}]\!]$ and $(e,c) \in \mathsf{P}^+[\![\mathsf{sc}^\mathcal{I}]\!]$, then $(e,d) \in \mathsf{P}^+[\![\bot_\mathsf{c}{}^\mathcal{I}]\!]$;*
   Exhaustive: *if $(c,c) \in \mathsf{P}^+[\![\bot_\mathsf{c}{}^\mathcal{I}]\!]$ and $d \in \Delta_\mathsf{C}$ then $(c,d) \in \mathsf{P}^+[\![\bot_\mathsf{c}{}^\mathcal{I}]\!]$;*
4. *$\mathsf{P}^+[\![\bot_\mathsf{p}{}^\mathcal{I}]\!]$ is symmetric, sub-transitive and exhaustive over Δ_P;*
   Symmetry: *If $(p,q) \in \mathsf{P}^+[\![\bot_\mathsf{p}{}^\mathcal{I}]\!]$, then $(q,p) \in \mathsf{P}^+[\![\bot_\mathsf{p}{}^\mathcal{I}]\!]$;*
   Sub-Transitivity: *if $(p,q) \in \mathsf{P}^+[\![\bot_\mathsf{p}{}^\mathcal{I}]\!]$ and $(r,p) \in \mathsf{P}^+[\![\mathsf{sp}^\mathcal{I}]\!]$, then $(r,q) \in \mathsf{P}^+[\![\bot_\mathsf{p}{}^\mathcal{I}]\!]$;*
   Exhaustive: *if $(p,p) \in \mathsf{P}^+[\![\bot_\mathsf{p}{}^\mathcal{I}]\!]$ and $q \in \Delta_\mathsf{P}$ then $(p,q) \in \mathsf{P}^+[\![\bot_\mathsf{p}{}^\mathcal{I}]\!]$;*

Disjointness II:

1. *if $(p,c) \in \mathsf{P}^+[\![\mathsf{dom}^\mathcal{I}]\!]$, $(q,d) \in \mathsf{P}^+[\![\mathsf{dom}^\mathcal{I}]\!]$, and $(c,d) \in \mathsf{P}^+[\![\bot_\mathsf{c}{}^\mathcal{I}]\!]$, then $(p,q) \in \mathsf{P}^+[\![\bot_\mathsf{p}{}^\mathcal{I}]\!]$;*
2. *if $(p,c) \in \mathsf{P}^+[\![\mathsf{range}^\mathcal{I}]\!]$, $(q,d) \in \mathsf{P}^+[\![\mathsf{range}^\mathcal{I}]\!]$, and $(c,d) \in \mathsf{P}^+[\![\bot_\mathsf{c}{}^\mathcal{I}]\!]$, then $(p,q) \in \mathsf{P}^+[\![\bot_\mathsf{p}{}^\mathcal{I}]\!]$;*
3. *$(c,d) \in \mathsf{P}^+[\![\bot_\mathsf{c}{}^\mathcal{I}]\!]$ if and only if $(c, \neg d) \in \mathsf{P}^+[\![\mathsf{sc}^\mathcal{I}]\!]$;*
4. *$(p,q) \in \mathsf{P}^+[\![\bot_\mathsf{p}{}^\mathcal{I}]\!]$ if and only if $(p, \neg q) \in \mathsf{P}^+[\![\mathsf{sp}^\mathcal{I}]\!]$.*

A graph G is $\rho df_\bot^\neg$-satisfiable if it has a $\rho df_\bot^\neg$-model $\mathcal{I}$. Moreover, given two $\rho df_\bot^\neg$-graphs G and H, we say that G $\rho df_\bot^\neg$-entails H, denoted $G \models^\bot_\neg H$, if and only if every $\rho df_\bot^\neg$-model of G is also a $\rho df_\bot^\neg$-model of H.

In the following, if clear from the context, for ease of presentation, we will omit the prefix $\rho df_\bot^\neg$-.

Remark 2 (About Definition 5)**.** *Note that:*

1. *the positive extension of a negated class is the negative extension of that class;*
2. *by construction, we also have that for $(s, \neg p, o) \in G$, $(s^\mathcal{I}, o^\mathcal{I}) \in \mathsf{P}^+[\![(\neg p)^\mathcal{I}]\!] = \mathsf{P}^+[\![\neg\, p^\mathcal{I}]\!] = \mathsf{P}^-[\![p^\mathcal{I}]\!]$. That is, $(s, \neg p, o) \in G$ states that "(s,o) belongs to the negative extension of p, i.e., s has a non p that is an o";*
3. *by construction, e.g., if $(c,d) \in \mathsf{P}^+[\![\mathsf{sc}^\mathcal{I}]\!]$ then also $\mathsf{C}^-[\![d]\!] \subseteq \mathsf{C}^-[\![c]\!]$. Moreover, $x \in \mathsf{C}^-[\![c]\!]$ if and only if $(x, \neg c) \in \mathsf{P}^+[\![\mathsf{type}^\mathcal{I}]\!]$;*
4. *concerning e.g., point 5 in Typing I, the informal reading of (p, range, c) is $\forall x.\forall y.p(x,y) \to c(y)$ and $\forall x.\forall y \in p\!\downarrow .\neg c(y) \to \neg p(x,y)$. In the latter case, the aim is to limit the universal quantification in a reasonable way;*
5. *the presence of e.g., (a, type, b), (a, type, c) and $(b, \bot_\mathsf{c}, c)$ in a graph does not preclude its satisfiability. In fact, a $\rho df_\bot^\neg$ graph will always be satisfiable (see Corollary 1 later on) avoiding, thus, the* ex falso quodlibet *principle. This is in line with the ρdf semantics (Muñoz, Pérez, and Gutierrez 2009);*

6. *concerning the exhaustive property in Disjointness I: classically, c disjoint d means that the intersection of c and d is empty. So, c disjoint c tells us that c is empty, so disjoint from any other class. We preserved this property within our semantics.*

Example 5. *Consider Example 4. Then, it may be verified that*

$$G \models^{\perp}_{\neg} \{(\texttt{brainTumor}, \texttt{hasTreatment}, x), (x, \texttt{type}, \neg\texttt{antipyretic})\} \quad (6)$$

$$G \models^{\perp}_{\neg} (\texttt{ebola}, \neg\texttt{hasTreatment}, \texttt{paracetomol}) \quad (7)$$

$$G \not\models^{\perp}_{\neg} (\texttt{ebola}, \neg\texttt{hasTreatment}, \texttt{ebola})\,. \quad (8)$$

Note that the last entailment does not hold as "ebola is not a treatment", which instead would hold without the restriction on the domain of the universal quantification.

Remark 3. *As anticipated in the related work section, (Darari, Prasojo, and Nutt 2015) considers expressions of the form*

$$No(\{(s_1, p_1, o_1), \ldots, (s_n, p_n, o_n)\}) \quad (9)$$

in informal FOL terms $\neg\exists \mathbf{x}.(p_1(s_1, o_1) \land \ldots \land p_n(s_n, o_n))$, *or equivalently,* $\forall \mathbf{x}.(\neg p_1(s_1, o_1) \lor \ldots \lor \neg p_n(s_n, o_n))$, *where* $\mathbf{x}$ *are the variables occurring the triples. For instance,*

$$No(\{(\texttt{obama}, \texttt{child}, x), (x, \texttt{gender}, \texttt{male})\}) \quad (10)$$

expresses that "Obama has no son".

$\rho df_{\perp}^{\neg}$ *considers only the case* $n = 1$ *in* (9) *via the expression* $(s, \neg p, \star_c)$ *as the general case would introduce a disjunction, which we would like to avoid for computational reasons. Nevertheless, we may consider the option to use e.g.,* $(\texttt{obama}, \neg\texttt{child}, \star_{\texttt{malePerson}})$ *instead to express* (10).

3.3 Deductive System for $\rho df_{\perp}^{\neg}$

We now present a deductive system for $\rho df_{\perp}^{\neg}$.

Definition 6 (Deductive rules for $\rho df_{\perp}^{\neg}$). *The* deductive rules *for* $\rho df_{\perp}^{\neg}$ *are all rules for* ρdf *to which we add the following rules (Z is an additional meta-variable):*

2. *Subproperty:*
   - (c) $\frac{(A,\mathsf{sp},B)}{(\neg B,\mathsf{sp},\neg A)}$
   - (d) $\frac{(A,D,\star_C),(D,\mathsf{sp},E)}{(A,E,\star_C)}$ $\quad (e)$ $\frac{(\star_C,D,A),(D,\mathsf{sp},E)}{(\star_C,E,A)}$
3. *Subclass:*
   - (c) $\frac{(A,\mathsf{sc},B)}{(\neg B,\mathsf{sc},\neg A)}$
   - (d) $\frac{(A,D,\star_C),(B,\mathsf{sc},C)}{(A,D,\star_B)}$ $\quad (e)$ $\frac{(\star_C,D,A),(B,\mathsf{sc},C)}{(\star_B,D,A)}$
4. *Typing:*
   - (c) $\frac{(D,\mathsf{dom},B),(X,\mathsf{type},\neg B),(Z,D,Y)}{(X,\neg D,Y)}$
   - (d) $\frac{(D,\mathsf{range},B),(Y,\mathsf{type},\neg B),(X,D,Z)}{(X,\neg D,Y)}$
   - (e) $\frac{(A,D,\star_C),(Y,\mathsf{type},C)}{(A,D,Y)}$ $\quad (f)$ $\frac{(\star_C,D,B),(X,\mathsf{type},C)}{(X,D,B)}$
   - (g) $\frac{(A,D,\star_C),(A,\neg D,Y)}{(Y,\mathsf{type},\neg C)}$ $\quad (h)$ $\frac{(\star_C,D,B),(X,\neg D,B)}{(X,\mathsf{type},\neg C)}$
6. *Conceptual Disjointness:*
   - (a) $\frac{(A,\perp_c,B)}{(B,\perp_c,A)}$ $\quad (b)$ $\frac{(A,\perp_c,B),(C,\mathsf{sc},A)}{(C,\perp_c,B)}$
   - (c) $\frac{(A,\perp_c,A)}{(A,\perp_c,B)}$ $\quad (d)$ $\frac{(A,\perp_c,B)}{(A,\mathsf{sc},\neg B)}$
   - (e) $\frac{(A,\mathsf{sc},B)}{(A,\perp_c,\neg B)}$
7. *Predicate Disjointness:*
   - (a) $\frac{(A,\perp_p,B)}{(B,\perp_p,A)}$ $\quad (b)$ $\frac{(A,\perp_p,B),(C,\mathsf{sp},A)}{(C,\perp_p,B)}$
   - (c) $\frac{(A,\perp_p,A)}{(A,\perp_p,B)}$ $\quad (d)$ $\frac{(A,\perp_p,B)}{(A,\mathsf{sp},\neg B)}$
   - (e) $\frac{(A,\mathsf{sp},B)}{(A,\perp_p,\neg B)}$
8. *Crossed Disjointness:*
   - (a) $\frac{(A,\mathsf{dom},C),(B,\mathsf{dom},D),(C,\perp_c,D)}{(A,\perp_p,B)}$
   - (b) $\frac{(A,\mathsf{range},C),(B,\mathsf{range},D),(C,\perp_c,D)}{(A,\perp_p,B)}$

Now, the definition of derivation among $\rho df_{\perp}^{\neg}$-graphs G and H, denoted $G \vdash^{\perp}_{\neg} H$, is as for ρdf (see Definition 3), except that, of course, we now consider all rules of Definition 6 instead. Similarly, the *$\rho df_{\perp}^{\neg}$-closure* of a graph G, denoted $\mathsf{Cl}_{\perp}^{\neg}(G)$, is defined as

$$\mathsf{Cl}_{\perp}^{\neg}(G) = \{\tau \mid G \vdash^{\perp}_{\neg}{}^{*}\, \tau\}\,,$$

where $\vdash^{\perp}_{\neg}{}^{*}$ is as $\vdash^{\perp}_{\neg}$ except that rule $(1a)$ is excluded.

Example 6. *The following is a simple proof of Eq.* (6)*:*

(1)	$(\texttt{opioid}, \perp_c, \texttt{antipyretic})$	*Rule* $(1b)$
(2)	$(\texttt{opioid}, \mathsf{sc}, \neg\texttt{antipyretic})$	*Rule* $(6d)$: (1)
(3)	$(\texttt{morphine}, \texttt{type}, \texttt{opioid})$	*Rule* $(1b)$
(4)	$(\texttt{morphine}, \texttt{type}, \neg\texttt{antipyretic})$	*Rule* $(3b)$: (2), (3)
(5)	$(\texttt{brainTumour}, \texttt{hasDrugTreatment}, \texttt{morphine})$	*Rule* $(1b)$
(10)	$(\texttt{brainTumor}, \texttt{hasTreatment}, x)$	
	$(x, \texttt{type}, \neg\texttt{antipyretic})$	*Rule* $(1a)$: (4), (5)

In the following, we will also assume that the definition of entailment $\models$ is extended naturally to $\rho df_{\perp}^{\neg}$-graphs by considering $\perp_c$, $\perp_p$, $\neg p$ and $\star_c$ as resources without any specific semantic constraint. In a similar way, we assume $\vdash$ (and $\mathsf{Cl}(\cdot)$) to be extended to $\rho df_{\perp}^{\neg}$-graphs by assuming that triples involving $\perp_c$, $\perp_p$, $\neg p$ and $\star_c$ are considered as ρdf triples. Then, the following can easily be proven:

Proposition 3. *Let G and H be two $\rho df_{\perp}^{\neg}$-graphs. Then,*

1. *if* $G \models H$ *then* $G \models^{\perp}_{\neg} H$;
2. *if* $G \vdash H$ *then* $G \vdash^{\perp}_{\neg} H$;
3. $\mathsf{Cl}(G) \subseteq \mathsf{Cl}_{\perp}^{\neg}(G)$.

Of course, conditions 1.-3. above do not hold in general for the opposite direction. For instance, for $G = \{(a, \perp_c, b)\}$ we have $G \not\models (a, \mathsf{sc}, \neg b)$, $G \not\vdash (a, \mathsf{sc}, \neg b)$ and $(a, \mathsf{sc}, \neg b) \notin \mathsf{Cl}(G)$, but $G \vdash^{\perp}_{\neg} (a, \mathsf{sc}, \neg b)$ and $(a, \mathsf{sc}, \neg b) \in \mathsf{Cl}_{\perp}^{\neg}(G)$.

The next proposition shows the construction of the *canonical model* for $\rho df_{\perp}^{\neg}$ graphs and extends the result for ρdf (see Proposition 1), *i.e.*, all $\rho df_{\perp}^{\neg}$-graphs G are satisfiable.

Proposition 4 ($\rho df_{\bot}^{\neg}$ Canonical model). *Given a $\rho df_{\bot}^{\neg}$-graph G, define a $\rho df_{\bot}^{\neg}$ interpretation $\mathcal{I}_G$ as a tuple*

$$\mathcal{I}_G = \langle \Delta_\mathsf{R}, \Delta_\mathsf{P}, \Delta_\mathsf{C}, \Delta_\mathsf{L}, \mathsf{P}^+[\![\cdot]\!], \mathsf{P}^-[\![\cdot]\!], \mathsf{C}^+[\![\cdot]\!], \mathsf{C}^-[\![\cdot]\!], \cdot^{\mathcal{I}_G} \rangle$$

such that:

1. $\Delta_\mathsf{R} := \mathtt{uni}(G) \cup \{\neg r \mid r \in \mathtt{uni}(G)\} \cup \rho df$;
2. $\Delta'_\mathsf{P} := \{p \in \mathtt{uni}(G) \mid$ *either* (s,p,o), $(s,p,\star_c)$, $(\star_c,p,o)$, (p,sp,q), (q,sp,p), (p,dom,c), (p,range,d) *or* $(p,\bot_\mathsf{p},q)$ *is in* $\mathsf{Cl}_{\bot}^{\neg}(G)\} \cup \rho df_{\bot}^{\neg}$;
3. $\Delta_\mathsf{P} := \Delta'_\mathsf{P} \cup \{\neg p \mid p \in \Delta'_\mathsf{P}\}$;
4. $\Delta'_\mathsf{C} := \{c \in \mathtt{uni}(G) \mid$ *either* (x,type,c), (c,sc,d), (d,sc,c), (p,dom,c), (p,range,c), $(s,p,\star_c)$, $(\star_c,p,o)$ *or* $(c,\bot_\mathsf{c},d)$ *is in* $\mathsf{Cl}_{\bot}^{\neg}(G)\}$;
5. $\Delta_\mathsf{C} := \Delta'_\mathsf{C} \cup \{\neg c \mid c \in \Delta'_\mathsf{C}\}$;
6. $\Delta_\mathsf{L} := \mathtt{uni}(G) \cap \mathbf{L}$;
7. $\mathsf{P}^+[\![\cdot]\!]$ *and* $\mathsf{P}^-[\![\cdot]\!]$ *are extension functions* $\Delta_\mathsf{P} \to 2^{\Delta_\mathsf{R} \times \Delta_\mathsf{R}}$ *s.t.* $\mathsf{P}^+[\![p]\!] := \{(s,o) \mid (s,p,o) \in \mathsf{Cl}_{\bot}^{\neg}(G)\}$ *and* $\mathsf{P}^-[\![p]\!] := \mathsf{P}^+[\![\neg p]\!]$;
8. $\mathsf{C}^+[\![\cdot]\!]$ *and* $\mathsf{C}^-[\![\cdot]\!]$ *are extension functions* $\Delta_\mathsf{C} \to 2^{\Delta_\mathsf{R}}$ *s.t.* $\mathsf{C}^+[\![c]\!] := \{x \in \mathtt{uni}(G) \mid (x,\mathsf{type},c) \in \mathsf{Cl}_{\bot}^{\neg}(G)\}$ *and* $\mathsf{C}^-[\![c]\!] := \mathsf{C}^+[\![\neg c]\!]$;
9. $\cdot^{\mathcal{I}_G}$ *is the identity function over* Δ_R.

Then, $\mathcal{I}_G \models^{\bot}_{\neg} G$.

Proof. We prove that $\mathcal{I}_G$ satisfies the constraints in Definition 5. We illustrate here the proof of some of the conditions in Definition 5 only. The others can be worked out similarly.

Simple:

1. Suppose $(s,p,o) \in G$ and neither s nor o are of the form $\star_c$. Then by construction $p \in \Delta_\mathsf{P}$ and $(s,o) \in \mathsf{P}^+[\![p]\!]$, which concludes.
2. Suppose $(s,p,\star_c) \in G$. Then, by construction $p \in \Delta_\mathsf{P}$ and $c \in \Delta_\mathsf{C}$. Now, assume $y \in \mathsf{C}^+[\![c]\!]$ and, thus, by construction $(y,\mathsf{type},c) \in \mathsf{Cl}_{\bot}^{\neg}(G)$. Therefore, by rule $(4e)$ we have also $(s,p,y) \in \mathsf{Cl}_{\bot}^{\neg}(G)$ and, thus, $(s,y) \in \mathsf{P}^+[\![p]\!]$ by construction, which concludes.

Subclass:

2. Assume $(c,d) \in \mathsf{P}^+[\![\mathsf{sc}]\!]$. By construction, $(c,\mathsf{sc},d) \in \mathsf{Cl}_{\bot}^{\neg}(G)$ and $c,d \in \Delta_\mathsf{C}$. Now, assume $x \in \mathsf{C}^+[\![c]\!]$ and, thus, by construction $(x,\mathsf{type},c) \in \mathsf{Cl}_{\bot}^{\neg}(G)$. Therefore, by rule $(3b)$ we have also $(x,\mathsf{type},d) \in \mathsf{Cl}_{\bot}^{\neg}(G)$ and, thus, $x \in \mathsf{C}^+[\![d]\!]$ by construction. As a consequence, $\mathsf{C}^+[\![c]\!] \subseteq \mathsf{C}^+[\![d]\!]$. Eventually, assume $x \in \mathsf{C}^-[\![d]\!]$ and, thus, by construction both $x \in \mathsf{C}^+[\![\neg d]\!]$ and $(x,\mathsf{type},\neg d) \in \mathsf{Cl}_{\bot}^{\neg}(G)$ hold. But, $(c,\mathsf{sc},d) \in \mathsf{Cl}_{\bot}^{\neg}(G)$ implies, by rule $(3c)$, $(\neg d,\mathsf{sc},\neg c) \in \mathsf{Cl}_{\bot}^{\neg}(G)$ and, thus, by rule $(3b)$ we have $(x,\mathsf{type},\neg c) \in \mathsf{Cl}_{\bot}^{\neg}(G)$. Therefore, by construction $x \in \mathsf{C}^+[\![\neg c]\!] = \mathsf{C}^-[\![c]\!]$ and, thus, $\mathsf{C}^-[\![d]\!] \subseteq \mathsf{C}^-[\![c]\!]$, which concludes.

Typing I:

2. Assume $(p,c) \in \mathsf{P}^+[\![\mathsf{dom}^{\mathcal{I}}]\!]$ and $(x,y) \in \mathsf{P}^+[\![p]\!]$. By construction, both (p,dom,c) and (x,p,y) are in $\mathsf{Cl}_{\bot}^{\neg}(G)$. Therefore, by rule $(4a)$, $(x,\mathsf{type},c) \in \mathsf{Cl}_{\bot}^{\neg}(G)$ and, thus, by construction $x \in \mathsf{C}^+[\![c]\!]$, which concludes.
4. Assume $(p,c) \in \mathsf{P}^+[\![\mathsf{dom}^{\mathcal{I}}]\!]$, $x \in \mathsf{C}^-[\![c]\!]$ and $y \in \mathsf{P}^+[\![p]\!] \downarrow$. By construction, we have that $\{(p,\mathsf{dom},c),(x,\mathsf{type},\neg c),(z,p,y)\} \subseteq \mathsf{Cl}_{\bot}^{\neg}(G)$. Therefore, by rule $(4c)$, $(x,\neg p,y) \in \mathsf{Cl}_{\bot}^{\neg}(G)$ and, thus, by construction, $(x,y) \in \mathsf{P}^+[\![\neg p]\!] = \mathsf{P}^-[\![p]\!]$, which concludes.

Typing II:

2. Assume $(p,c) \in \mathsf{P}^+[\![\mathsf{dom}^{\mathcal{I}}]\!]$. Then, by construction $(p,\mathsf{dom},c) \in \mathsf{Cl}_{\bot}^{\neg}(G)$ and, thus, $p \in \Delta'_\mathsf{P} \subseteq \Delta_\mathsf{P}$ and $c \in \Delta'_\mathsf{C} \subseteq \Delta_\mathsf{C}$, which concludes.

Disjointness I:

3. **Symmetry:** Assume $(c,d) \in \mathsf{P}^+[\![\bot_\mathsf{c}{}^{\mathcal{I}}]\!]$. By construction, $(c,\bot_\mathsf{c},d) \in \mathsf{Cl}_{\bot}^{\neg}(G)$ and, thus, by rule $(4a)$ $(d,\bot_\mathsf{c},c) \in \mathsf{Cl}_{\bot}^{\neg}(G)$. Therefore, by construction, $(d,c) \in \mathsf{P}^+[\![\bot_\mathsf{c}{}^{\mathcal{I}}]\!]$, which concludes.

Disjointness II:

1. Assume $(p,c) \in \mathsf{P}^+[\![\mathsf{dom}^{\mathcal{I}}]\!]$, $(q,d) \in \mathsf{P}^+[\![\mathsf{dom}^{\mathcal{I}}]\!]$, and $(c,d) \in \mathsf{P}^+[\![\bot_\mathsf{c}{}^{\mathcal{I}}]\!]$. Then, by construction, we have that $\{(p,\mathsf{dom},c),(q,\mathsf{dom},d),(c,\bot_\mathsf{c},d)\} \subseteq \mathsf{Cl}_{\bot}^{\neg}(G)$ and, thus, by rule $(8a)$ $(p,\bot_\mathsf{p},q) \in \mathsf{Cl}_{\bot}^{\neg}(G)$. Therefore, by construction, $(p,q) \in \mathsf{P}^+[\![\bot_\mathsf{p}{}^{\mathcal{I}}]\!]$, which concludes.
3. If $(c,d) \in \mathsf{P}^+[\![\bot_\mathsf{c}{}^{\mathcal{I}}]\!]$ then, by construction, $(c,\bot_\mathsf{c},d) \in \mathsf{Cl}_{\bot}^{\neg}(G)$ and, thus, by rule $(6d)$ $(c,\mathsf{sc},\neg d) \in \mathsf{Cl}_{\bot}^{\neg}(G)$. Therefore, by construction, $(c,\neg d) \in \mathsf{P}^+[\![\mathsf{sc}^{\mathcal{I}}]\!]$. Vice-versa, if $(c,\neg d) \in \mathsf{P}^+[\![\mathsf{sc}^{\mathcal{I}}]\!]$ then by construction, $(c,\mathsf{sc},\neg d) \in \mathsf{Cl}_{\bot}^{\neg}(G)$ and, thus, by rule $(6e)$ $(c,\bot_\mathsf{c},d) \in \mathsf{Cl}_{\bot}^{\neg}(G)$. Therefore, by construction, $(c,d) \in \mathsf{P}^+[\![\bot_\mathsf{c}{}^{\mathcal{I}}]\!]$, which concludes.

□

By Proposition 4, it follows that

Corollary 1. *Every $\rho df_{\bot}^{\neg}$-graph is satisfiable.*

We prove now soundness and completeness of our deduction system for $\rho df_{\bot}^{\neg}$. The proofs are inspired by the analogous ones in (Muñoz, Pérez, and Gutierrez 2009) for ρdf.

The following proposition is needed for soundness.

Proposition 5 (Soundness). *Let G and H be $\rho df_{\bot}^{\neg}$-graphs and let one of the following statements hold:*

1. *there is a map* $\mu : H \to G$;
2. $H \subseteq G$;
3. *there is an instantiation R/R' of one of the rules in Definition 6, such that $R \subseteq G$ and $H = G \cup R'$.*

Then, $G \models^{\bot}_{\neg} H$.

Proof. By Corollary 1 we know that G is satisfiable. So, let

$$\mathcal{I} = \langle \Delta_\mathsf{R}, \Delta_\mathsf{P}, \Delta_\mathsf{C}, \Delta_\mathsf{L}, \mathsf{P}^+[\![\cdot]\!], \mathsf{P}^-[\![\cdot]\!], \mathsf{C}^+[\![\cdot]\!], \mathsf{C}^-[\![\cdot]\!], \cdot^{\mathcal{I}} \rangle$$

be a model of G, *i.e.*, $\mathcal{I} \models^{\bot}_{\neg} G$. Therefore, $\mathcal{I}$ satisfies the constraints in Definition 5. We have to prove that $\mathcal{I} \models^{\bot}_{\neg} H$. The proof is split in cases depending on rule applications of which we address here only some of them. The other cases can be shown similarly.

Rule $(4e)$**.** Let $\{(s,p,\star_c),(o,\mathsf{type},c)\} \subseteq R$ for some $R \subseteq G$, $R' = \{(s,p,o)\}$, obtained via the application of rule $(4e)$, and $H = G \cup R'$. As $\mathcal{I} \models^{\bot}_{\neg} G$ and $R \subseteq G$, $\mathcal{I} \models^{\bot}_{\neg} R$ follows. Therefore, $\mathcal{I} \models^{\bot}_{\neg} (o,\mathsf{type},c)$ and, thus, $o^{\mathcal{I}} \in \mathsf{C}^{+}[\![c^{\mathcal{I}}]\!]$ follows. But, also $\mathcal{I} \models^{\bot}_{\neg} (s,p,\star_c)$ and, thus, by condition Simple, case 2. in Definition 5, we have that $(s^{\mathcal{I}},o^{\mathcal{I}}) \in \mathsf{P}^{+}[\![p^{\mathcal{I}}]\!]$. That is, $\mathcal{I} \models^{\bot}_{\neg} (s,p,o)$. Hence, from $\mathcal{I} \models^{\bot}_{\neg} R'$, $\mathcal{I} \models^{\bot}_{\neg} G$ and $H = G \cup R'$, $\mathcal{I} \models^{\bot}_{\neg} H$ follows.

Rule $(6d)$**.** Let $(c,\bot_{\mathsf{c}},d) \in R$ for some $R \subseteq G$, $R' = \{(c,\mathsf{sc},\neg d)\}$, obtained via the application of rule $(6d)$, and $H = G \cup R'$. As $\mathcal{I} \models^{\bot}_{\neg} G$ and $R \subseteq G$, $\mathcal{I} \models^{\bot}_{\neg} R$ follows. Therefore, $\mathcal{I} \models^{\bot}_{\neg} (c,\bot_{\mathsf{c}},d)$ and, thus, $(c^{\mathcal{I}},d^{\mathcal{I}}) \in \mathsf{P}^{+}[\![\bot_{\mathsf{c}}{}^{\mathcal{I}}]\!]$. But, by condition Disjointness II, case 3. in Definition 5 we have that $(c^{\mathcal{I}},\neg d^{\mathcal{I}}) \in \mathsf{P}^{+}[\![\mathsf{sc}^{\mathcal{I}}]\!]$ and, thus, $(c^{\mathcal{I}},(\neg d)^{\mathcal{I}}) \in \mathsf{P}^{+}[\![\mathsf{sc}^{\mathcal{I}}]\!]$. Therefore, $\mathcal{I} \models^{\bot}_{\neg} (c,\mathsf{sc},\neg d)$. Hence, from $\mathcal{I} \models^{\bot}_{\neg} R'$, $\mathcal{I} \models^{\bot}_{\neg} G$ and $H = G \cup R'$, $\mathcal{I} \models^{\bot}_{\neg} H$ follows.

□

Proposition 6. *Let G and H be $\rho df_{\bot}^{\neg}$-graphs. If $G \models^{\bot}_{\neg} H$ then there is a map $\mu : H \to \mathsf{Cl}_{\bot}^{\neg}(G)$.*

Proof. Consider the canonical model

$$\mathcal{I}_G = \langle \Delta_{\mathsf{R}}, \Delta_{\mathsf{P}}, \Delta_{\mathsf{C}}, \Delta_{\mathsf{L}}, \mathsf{P}^{+}[\![\cdot]\!], \mathsf{P}^{-}[\![\cdot]\!], \mathsf{C}^{+}[\![\cdot]\!], \mathsf{C}^{-}[\![\cdot]\!], \cdot^{\mathcal{I}_G} \rangle$$

of G, as defined in Proposition 4. As $G \models^{\bot}_{\neg} H$, $\mathcal{I}_G \models^{\bot}_{\neg} H$ follows. Therefore, for each $(s,p,o) \in H$, $p^{\mathcal{I}_G} \in \Delta_{\mathsf{P}}$ and $(s^{\mathcal{I}_G},o^{\mathcal{I}_G}) \in \mathsf{P}^{+}[\![p^{\mathcal{I}_G}]\!]$. By construction, $p^{\mathcal{I}_G} = p$, and $\mathsf{P}^{+}[\![p^{\mathcal{I}_G}]\!] = \mathsf{P}^{+}[\![p]\!] = \{(t,t') \mid (t,p,t') \in \mathsf{Cl}_{\bot}^{\neg}(G)\}$. Finally, since $(s^{\mathcal{I}_G},o^{\mathcal{I}_G}) \in \mathsf{P}^{+}[\![p]\!]$, we have that $(s^{\mathcal{I}_G},p,o^{\mathcal{I}_G}) \in \mathsf{Cl}_{\bot}^{\neg}(G)$, *i.e.*, $(s^{\mathcal{I}_G},p^{\mathcal{I}_G},o^{\mathcal{I}_G}) \in \mathsf{Cl}_{\bot}^{\neg}(G)$. Therefore, $\cdot^{\mathcal{I}_G}$ is a map such that $H^{\mathcal{I}_G} \subseteq \mathsf{Cl}_{\bot}^{\neg}(G)$, *i.e.*, a map $\cdot^{\mathcal{I}_G} : H \to \mathsf{Cl}_{\bot}^{\neg}(G)$, which concludes. □

From Proposition 6 we get the following corollary:

Corollary 2. *Let G and H be $\rho df_{\bot}^{\neg}$-graphs. If $G \models^{\bot}_{\neg} H$ then there is a proof of H from G where rule $(1a)$ is used at most once and at the end.*

Eventually, combining previous Propositions 5 and 6, we get soundness and completeness of our deductive system.

Theorem 1 (Soundness & Completeness)**.** *Let G and H be $\rho df_{\bot}^{\neg}$-graphs. Then $G \vdash^{\bot}_{\neg} H$ iff $G \models^{\bot}_{\neg} H$.*

Proof. Concerning soundness, if $G \vdash^{\bot}_{\neg} H$ then, by Proposition 5, $G \models^{\bot}_{\neg} H$. Concerning completeness, if $G \models^{\bot}_{\neg} H$ then, by Proposition 6, H can be obtained from $\mathsf{Cl}_{\bot}^{\neg}(G)$ using rule (1a). Therefore, as $G \vdash^{\bot}_{\neg} \mathsf{Cl}_{\bot}^{\neg}(G)$, $G \vdash^{\bot}_{\neg} H$ follows, which concludes. □

Finally, unlike ρdf (see Proposition 1), the size of the closure of a $\rho df_{\bot}^{\neg}$ graph G is $\Theta(|G|^3)$. The upper bound comes from the fact that in a triple (s,p,o), for each s,p and o we may have at most $|G|$ terms, while the lower bound is given by the following example.

Example 7. *It can easily be verified that for $1 \le i < j \le n$ and $1 \le l,k,h \le n$*

$$\{(a_i,\mathsf{type},c),(a_i,p_1,\star_c),(p_i,\mathsf{sp},p_j)\} \models^{\bot}_{\neg} (a_l,p_k,a_h)\,,$$

and, thus, the number of triples in the closure is $\Omega(|G|^3)$.

Furthermore, it is not difficult to see that if $\star_c$ terms do not occur in a $\rho df_{\bot}^{\neg}$ graph G, then the closure of G remains quadratically upper bounded. As case (i) in Remark 1 also applies to $\rho df_{\bot}^{\neg}$, it can be shown that

Proposition 7. *Let G and H be $\rho df_{\bot}^{\neg}$-graphs. Then*

1. *the closure of G is unique and $|\mathsf{Cl}_{\bot}^{\neg}(G)| \in \Theta(|G|^3)$;*
2. *if $\star_c$ terms do not occur in G then $|\mathsf{Cl}_{\bot}^{\neg}(G)| \in \Theta(|G|^2)$;*
3. *deciding $G \models^{\bot}_{\neg} H$ is an NP-complete problem;*
4. *if G is ground then $\mathsf{Cl}_{\bot}^{\neg}(G)$ can be determined without using implicit typing rules (5);*
5. *if H is ground, then $G \models^{\bot}_{\neg} H$ if and only if $H \subseteq \mathsf{Cl}_{\bot}^{\neg}(G)$;*
6. *There is no triple τ such that $\emptyset \models \tau$.*

Eventually, by Proposition 7 it follows immediately that

Corollary 3. *Let G and H be two ground $\rho df_{\bot}^{\neg}$ graphs. Then deciding if $G \models^{\bot}_{\neg} H$ can be done in time $O(|H||G|^3)$ and in time $O(|H||G|^2)$ if $\star_c$ terms do not occur in G.*

4 Conclusions

We have addressed the problem to add negative statements of various form considered as relevant for RDFS by the literature. We have presented a sound and complete deductive system that consists of RDFS rules plus some additional rules to deal with the extra type of triples we allow. The design of the semantics has been such that to preserve features such as the canonical model property and computational attractiveness.

As future work, Corollary 3 tells us that there is still some computational complexity gap w.r.t. ρdf (see Proposition 2), which we would like to reduce as much as possible. In particular, we want to investigate whether the principles of the method proposed in (Muñoz, Pérez, and Gutierrez 2009) for ρdf can be adapted to $\rho df_{\bot}^{\neg}$ as well. Additionally, we would like to address query answering, in particular to extend our framework to SPARQL and to verify whether and how it impacts w.r.t. $\rho df_{\bot}^{\neg}$ graphs. Eventually, we would like to develop a FOL encoding of our semantics in the spirit of (Franconi et al. 2013), which encodes, *e.g.*, subclass transitivity via $\forall x,y,z.\mathsf{sc}(x,y) \land \mathsf{sc}(y,z) \to \mathsf{sc}(x,z)$, and determine whether our semantics can be reformulated in terms of a well-know paraconsistent semantics, such as *e.g.*, Quasi-classical logic (Marquis and Porquet 2001).

Acknowledgments

This research was partially supported by TAILOR (Foundations of Trustworthy AI – Integrating Reasoning, Learning and Optimization), a project funded by EU Horizon 2020 research and innovation programme under GA No 952215.

References

Analyti, A.; Antoniou, G.; and Damásio, C. V. 2008. A principled framework for modular web rule bases and its semantics. In Brewka, G., and Lang, J., eds., *Principles of Knowledge Representation and Reasoning: Proceedings of the Eleventh International Conference, KR 2008, Sydney, Australia, September 16-19, 2008*, 390–400. AAAI Press.

Analyti, A.; Antoniou, G.; and Damásio, C. V. 2009. A formal theory for modular ERDF ontologies. In Polleres, A., and Swift, T., eds., *Web Reasoning and Rule Systems, Third International Conference, RR 2009, Chantilly, VA, USA, October 25-26, 2009, Proceedings*, volume 5837 of *Lecture Notes in Computer Science*, 212–226. Springer.

Analyti, A.; Antoniou, G.; and Damásio, C. V. 2011. Mweb: A principled framework for modular web rule bases and its semantics. *ACM Trans. Comput. Log.* 12(2):17:1–17:46.

Analyti, A.; Antoniou, G.; Damásio, C. V.; and Wagner, G. R. 2004. Negation and negative information in the w3c resource description framework. *Annals of Mathematics, Computing & Teleinformatics* 1(2):25–34.

Analyti, A.; Antoniou, G.; Damásio, C. V.; and Wagner, G. 2005. Stable model theory for extended RDF ontologies. In Gil, Y.; Motta, E.; Benjamins, V. R.; and Musen, M. A., eds., *The Semantic Web - ISWC 2005, 4th International Semantic Web Conference, ISWC 2005, Galway, Ireland, November 6-10, 2005, Proceedings*, volume 3729 of *Lecture Notes in Computer Science*, 21–36. Springer.

Analyti, A.; Antoniou, G.; Damásio, C. V.; and Wagner, G. 2008. Extended RDF as a semantic foundation of rule markup languages. *J. Artif. Intell. Res.* 32:37–94.

Analyti, A.; Antoniou, G.; Damásio, C. V.; and Pachoulakis, I. 2013. A framework for modular ERDF ontologies. *Annals of Mathematics and Artificial Intelligence* 67(3-4):189–249.

Analyti, A.; Damásio, C. V.; and Antoniou, G. 2015. Extended RDF: computability and complexity issues. *Annals of Mathematics and Artificial Intelligence* 75(3-4):267–334.

Arnaout, H.; Razniewski, S.; Weikum, G.; and Pan, J. Z. 2021a. Negative knowledge for open-world wikidata. In Leskovec, J.; Grobelnik, M.; Najork, M.; Tang, J.; and Zia, L., eds., *Companion of The Web Conference 2021*, 544–551. ACM / IW3C2.

Arnaout, H.; Razniewski, S.; Weikum, G.; and Pan, J. Z. 2021b. Negative statements considered useful. *Journal of Web Semantics* 71(100661).

Arnaout, H.; Razniewski, S.; Weikum, G.; and Pan, J. Z. 2021c. Wikinegata: a knowledge base with interesting negative statements. *Proceedings of VLDB Endowment* 14(12):2807–2810.

Arnaout, H.; Razniewski, S.; and Weikum, G. 2020. Enriching knowledge bases with interesting negative statements. In Das, D.; Hajishirzi, H.; McCallum, A.; and Singh, S., eds., *Conference on Automated Knowledge Base Construction, AKBC 2020, Virtual, June 22-24, 2020*.

Baader, F.; Calvanese, D.; McGuinness, D.; Nardi, D.; and Patel-Schneider, P., eds. 2007. *The Description Logic Handbook: Theory, Implementation and Applications*. Cambridge University Press, 2 edition.

Belnap, N. D. 1977. A useful four-valued logic. In Epstein, G., and Dunn, J. M., eds., *Modern uses of multiple-valued logic*. Dordrecht, NL: Reidel. 5–37.

Casini, G., and Straccia, U. 2020. Defeasible RDFS via rational closure. Technical report, Computing Research Repository. Available as CoRR technical report at http://arxiv.org/abs/2007.07573.

Damásio, C. V.; Analyti, A.; and Antoniou, G. 2010. Implementing simple modular ERDF ontologies. In Coelho, H.; Studer, R.; and Wooldridge, M. J., eds., *ECAI 2010 - 19th European Conference on Artificial Intelligence, Lisbon, Portugal, August 16-20, 2010, Proceedings*, volume 215 of *Frontiers in Artificial Intelligence and Applications*, 1083–1084. IOS Press.

Darari, F.; Prasojo, R. E.; and Nutt, W. 2015. Expressing no-value information in RDF. In Villata, S.; Pan, J. Z.; and Dragoni, M., eds., *Proceedings of the ISWC 2015 Posters & Demonstrations Track co-located with the 14th International Semantic Web Conference (ISWC-2015), Bethlehem, PA, USA, October 11, 2015*, volume 1486 of *CEUR Workshop Proceedings*. CEUR-WS.org.

Franconi, E.; Gutiérrez, C.; Mosca, A.; Pirrò, G.; and Rosati, R. 2013. The logic of extensional RDFS. In Alani, H.; Kagal, L.; Fokoue, A.; Groth, P.; Biemann, C.; Parreira, J. X.; Aroyo, L.; Noy, N. F.; Welty, C.; and Janowicz, K., eds., *The Semantic Web - ISWC 2013 - 12th International Semantic Web Conference, Sydney, NSW, Australia, October 21-25, 2013, Proceedings, Part I*, volume 8218 of *Lecture Notes in Computer Science*, 101–116. Springer.

Gutiérrez, C.; Hurtado, C. A.; Mendelzon, A. O.; and Pérez, J. 2011. Foundations of semantic web databases. *J. Comput. Syst. Sci.* 77(3):520–541.

Lehmann, D., and Magidor, M. 1992. What does a conditional knowledge base entail? *Artificial Intelligence Journal* 55(1):1–60.

Marquis, P., and Porquet, N. 2001. Computational aspects of quasi-classical entailment. *J. Appl. Non Class. Logics* 11(3-4):295–312.

Muñoz, S.; Pérez, J.; and Gutierrez, C. 2009. Simple and Efficient Minimal RDFS. *Web Semantics: Science, Services and Agents on the World Wide Web* 7(3):220–234.

Muñoz, S.; Pérez, J.; and Gutiérrez, C. 2007. Minimal deductive systems for RDF. In *4th European Semantic Web Conference (ESWC-07)*, volume 4519 of *Lecture Notes in Computer Science*, 53–67. Springer Verlag.

Patel-Schneider, P. F. 1985. A decidable first-order logic for knowledge representation. In *Proceedings of IJCAI-85, 9th International Joint Conference on Artificial Intelligence*, 455–458.

Patel-Schneider, P. F. 1986. A four-valued semantics for frame-based description languages. In *Proceedings of AAAI-86, 5th Conference of the American Association for Artificial Intelligence*, 344–348.

Patel-Schneider, P. F. 1987. A hybrid, decidable, logic-based knowledge representation system. *Computational Intelligence* 3:64–77.

Patel-Schneider, P. F. 1988. Adding number restrictions to a four-valued terminological logic. In *Proc. of the 7th Nat. Conf. on Artificial Intelligence (AAAI-88)*, 485–490.

Patel-Schneider, P. F. 1989. A four-valued semantics for terminological logics. *Artificial Intelligence* 38:319–351.

Reiter, R. 1978. On closed world data bases. In Gallaire, H., and Minker, J., eds., *Logic and data bases*. New York, NY: Plenum Press. 55–76.

Straccia, U. 1997a. A four-valued fuzzy propositional logic. In *Proceedings of the 15th International Joint Conference on Artificial Intelligence (IJCAI-97)*, 128–133.

Straccia, U. 1997b. A sequent calculus for reasoning in four-valued description logics. In *Proc. of the Int. Conf. on Analytic Tableaux and Related Methods (TABLEAUX-97)*, volume 1227 of *Lecture Notes in Artificial Intelligence*, 343–357.

Straccia, U. 1999. *Foundations of a Logic Based Approach to Multimedia Document Retrieval*. Ph.D. Dissertation, Department of Computer Science, University of Dortmund, Dortmund, Germany.

Straccia, U. 2000. A framework for the retrieval of multimedia objects based on four-valued fuzzy description logics. In Crestani, F., and Pasi, G., eds., *Soft Computing in Information Retrieval: Techniques and Applications*. Heidelberg, Germany: Physica Verlag (Springer Verlag). 332–357.

ter Horst, H. J. 2005. Completeness, decidability and complexity of entailment for rdf schema and a semantic extension involving the owl vocabulary. *Journal of Web Semantics* 3(2-3):79–115.

Zimmermann, A.; Lopes, N.; Polleres, A.; and Straccia, U. 2012. A general framework for representing, reasoning and querying with annotated semantic web data. *Journal of Web Semantics* 11:72–95.

Proceedings of the 19th International Conference on Principles of Knowledge Representation and Reasoning
Main Track

Discovering User-Interpretable Capabilities of Black-Box Planning Agents

Pulkit Verma, Shashank Rao Marpally, and **Siddharth Srivastava**
Autonomous Agents and Intelligent Robots Lab,
School of Computing and Augmented Intelligence, Arizona State University, USA
{verma.pulkit, smarpall, siddharths}@asu.edu

Abstract

Several approaches have been developed for answering users' specific questions about AI behavior and for assessing their core functionality in terms of primitive executable actions. However, the problem of summarizing an AI agent's broad capabilities for a user is comparatively new. This paper presents an algorithm for discovering from scratch the suite of high-level "capabilities" that an AI system with arbitrary internal planning algorithms/policies can perform. It computes conditions describing the applicability and effects of these capabilities in user-interpretable terms. Starting from a set of user-interpretable state properties, an AI agent, and a simulator that the agent can interact with, our algorithm returns a set of high-level capabilities with their parameterized descriptions. Empirical evaluation on several game-based scenarios shows that this approach efficiently learns descriptions of various types of AI agents in deterministic, fully observable settings. User studies show that such descriptions are easier to understand and reason with than the agent's primitive actions.

1 Introduction

AI systems are rapidly developing to an extent where their users may not understand what they can and cannot do safely. In fact, the limits and capabilities of many AI systems are not always immediately clear even to the experts, as they may use black box policies, e.g., ATARI game-playing agents (Greydanus et al. 2018), text summarization tools (Paulus, Xiong, and Socher 2018), mobile manipulators (Popov et al. 2017), etc.

Ongoing research on the topic focuses on the significant problem of how to answer users' questions about the system's behavior while assuming that the user and AI share a common action vocabulary (Chakraborti et al. 2017; Dhurandhar et al. 2018; Anjomshoae et al. 2019; Barredo Arrieta et al. 2020). Furthermore, most non-experts hesitate to ask questions about new AI tools (Mou and Xu 2017) and often do not know which questions to ask for assessing the safe limits and capabilities of an AI system. This problem is aggravated in situations where an AI system can carry out planning or sequential decision making. Lack of understanding about the limits of an imperfect system can result in unproductive usage or, in the worst-case, serious accidents (Randazzo 2018). This, in turn, limits the adoption and productivity of AI systems.

This work presents a new approach for *discovering* capabilities of a black-box AI system. The AI system may use arbitrary internal models, representations, and processes for computing solutions to user-assigned tasks. Prior work on the topic addresses complementary problems of deriving symbolic descriptions for pre-defined skills (Konidaris, Kaelbling, and Lozano-Perez 2018) and of learning users' conceptual vocabularies (Kim et al. 2018; Sreedharan et al. 2022). However, they do not address the problem of *discovering* high-level user-interpretable capabilities that an agent can perform using arbitrary, internal behavior synthesis algorithms (see Sec. 5 for a greater discussion).

As a starting point, in this paper, we assume determinism and full observability on part of the AI system. Since there are no solution approaches for solving the problem even in this foundational setting, our framework can serve as a foundation for solutions to the more general setting in the future.

Running example Consider a game based on "The Legend of Zelda" (Fig. 1) featuring a protagonist player *Link* who must defeat the antagonist monster *Ganon*, and escape through the door using a key. (Fig. 1)(a) shows the game state as the agent sees it; its primitive actions are keystrokes as shown in (b). These keystrokes do not help convey the agent's capabilities because (i) they are too fine-grained, and (ii) they show the set of actions available to the AI system, although its true capabilities depend on its AI planning and learning algorithms. Fig. 1(c) shows common English terms that a user might understand (called the *user's vocabulary*), and the types of capabilities that they may want to know about. Fig. 1(d) shows a parameterized capability discovered by our method. Intuitively, Fig. 1(d) captures the "defeat Ganon" capability.

This paper shows how we can discover and describe an agent's capabilities in the form of Fig. 1(d). This capability description can be readily transcribed as "If the *player1* is at *cell1*; the *monster1* is at *cell2*; the *monster1* is *alive* (not defeated); and the *monster1* is next to the *player1*; then the *player1* can act to reach a state where *cell2* is empty; the *monster1* is *not alive* (defeated); the *monster1* is *not at cell2*; and the *player1* is not next to the *monster1*." Our empirical evaluation shows that our system effectively discovers such high-level capabilities; our user study shows that the discovered capabilities help users effectively estimate black-box

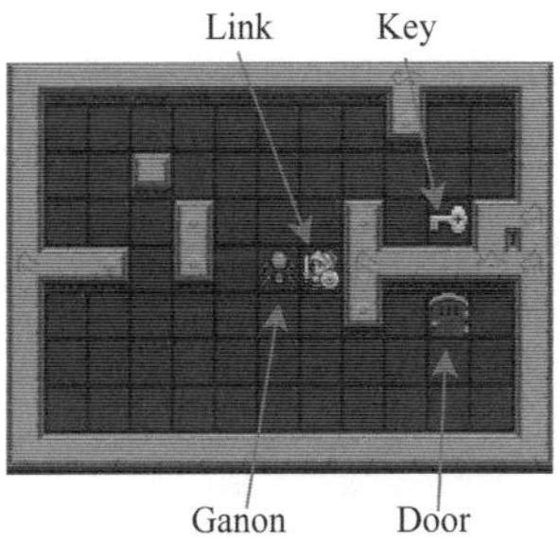

(a)

State as available to the agent:

```
(pixel 1-1 #FD2310)
(pixel 1-1 #B24319)
.
.
```

Agent actions (keystrokes):

```
W,A,S,D,E
```

(b)

State in User's Vocabulary:

```
(at ganon 5-3)
(at key 9-4)
(alive ganon)
.
.
```

Desired:
Capabilities such as:

```
(Go next to Key),(Pick Key),(Go next to Door),
(Go next to Ganon),(Open Door),(Defeat Ganon)
```

(c)

```
(:capability c4
 :parameters (?player1 ?cell1
   ?monster1 ?cell2)
 :precondition
  (and (alive ?monster1)
    (at ?player1 ?cell1)
    (at ?monster1 ?cell2)
    (next_to ?monster1))
 :effect
  (and (clear ?cell2)
   (not(alive ?monster1))
   (not(at ?monster1 ?cell2))
   (not(next_to ?monster1))))
```

(d)

Figure 1: From pixels to interpretable capabilities. (a) A Zelda-like game; (b) States available to the agent and its actions; (c) States represented in user vocabulary, and possible set of desired capabilities; (d) A parameterized capability description learned by our method.

agent capabilities.

The rest of this paper is organized as follows. The next section presents a formal framework for capabilities as well as notions of correctness for discovered agent capabilities. Sec. 3 describes our main algorithms and their formal properties and Sec. 4 presents empirical results and results from user studies. Sec. 5 discusses the relationship of the presented methods with prior work. Finally, Sec. 6 presents our conclusion and future directions.

2 Formal Framework

We model an AI system ("agent" henceforth) as a 3-tuple $\langle S, A, T\rangle$, where S is the state space, A is the set of actions that the agent can execute, $T : S \times A \to S$ is a deterministic black-box transition function determining the effects of the agent's primitive actions on the environment. For brevity of notation, we use $a(s)$ to represent $T(s, a)$, where $a \in A$, and $s \in S$. Given a goal set $G \subseteq S$, a black-box *deterministic policy* $\Pi : S \to A$ maps each state to the action that the agent should execute in that state to reach a $g \in G$.

In this paper, we use "actions" to refer to the core *functionality* of the agent, denoting the agent's decision choices, or primitive actions that the agent could execute (e.g., keystrokes in our running example). In contrast, we use the term "capabilities" to refer to the *high-level behaviors* that the agent can perform using its AI algorithms for behavior synthesis, including planning and learning (e.g., defeating Ganon or picking up the key). Thus, actions refer to the set of choices that a tabular-rasa agent may possess, while capabilities are a result of its agent function (Russell 1997) and can change as a result of algorithmic updates even as the agent uses the same actions.

2.1 Abstraction

We now define the notion of abstraction used in this work. Several approaches have explored the use of abstraction in planning (Sacerdoti 1974; Giunchiglia and Walsh 1992; Helmert et al. 2007; Bäckström and Jonsson 2013; Srivastava, Russell, and Pinto 2016). We refer to $\tilde{S}$ as the set of *high-level* or *abstract* states, and S as the set of *low-level* or *concrete* states. We define abstraction as in (Srivastava, Russell, and Pinto 2016):

Definition 1. Let S and $\tilde{S}$ be sets such that $|\tilde{S}| \leq |S|$. An *abstraction* from S to $\tilde{S}$ is defined by a surjective function $f : S \to \tilde{S}$. For any $\tilde{s} \in \tilde{S}$, the concretization function $f^{-1}(\tilde{s}) = \{s \in S : f(s) = \tilde{s}\}$ denotes the set of states represented by the abstract state $\tilde{s}$.

Following this, we use $\tilde{}$ whenever we refer to a state, a predicate, or an action pertaining to the abstract state space.

2.2 Capability Descriptions

We express capability descriptions using a STRIPS-like representation (Fikes and Nilsson 1971; McDermott et al. 1998). This is because, when used with a user's vocabulary, such a representation can be readily transcribed into statements such as "in situations where X holds, if the agent executes actions $a_1, \ldots, a_k$ it would result in Y", where X and Y are in the user's vocabulary (Camacho and McIlraith 2019; Verma, Marpally, and Srivastava 2021). Such representations have been shown to be intuitive for humans in understanding deliberative behaviors of other agents (Malle 2004; Miller 2019). In our running example, such a description could indicate that if Link is next to Ganon then Link can defeat it. We now formally define a capability.

Definition 2. Given a set of objects $\tilde{O}$; and a finite set of predicates $\tilde{P} = \{\tilde{p}_1^{k_1}, \ldots, \tilde{p}_n^{k_n}\}$ with arities k_i; a *grounded capability* $\tilde{c}^*$ is defined as a tuple $\langle pre(\tilde{c}^*), eff(\tilde{c}^*)\rangle$ where precondition $pre(\tilde{c}^*)$ and effect $eff(\tilde{c}^*)$ are conjunctions of literals over $\tilde{P}$ and $\tilde{O}$.

We also refer to the tuple $\langle \tilde{c}^*, pre(\tilde{c}^*), eff(\tilde{c}^*)\rangle$ as the *capability description* for a capability $\tilde{c}^*$. Here each atom could be absent, positive, or negative (henceforth referred to as the *mode*) in the precondition and the effect of an action. However, we disallow atoms to be positive (or negative) in both the preconditions and the effects of an action simultaneously to avoid redundancy. Semantics of capabilities are close to those of STRIPS actions, but they address vocabulary disparity: an agent can execute a capability $\tilde{c}^*$ in any concrete state s where $\tilde{s} \models pre(\tilde{c}^*)$; as a result, the system reaches a concrete state s' (a member of an abstract state $\tilde{s}'$). Atoms that don't appear in $eff(\tilde{c}^*)$ retain their truth values from $\tilde{s}$ in $\tilde{s}'$ while others are set to their modes (positive, negative, or absent) in $\mathit{eff}(\tilde{c}^*)$, i.e., $\forall \ell \in \mathit{eff}(\tilde{c}^*), \tilde{s}' \models \ell$. For brevity, we represent this as $\tilde{s}' = \tilde{c}^*(\tilde{s})$.

We refer to the capabilities defined in Def. 2 as grounded capabilities as they are instantiated with a specific set of objects in $\tilde{O}$. We use * whenever we refer to a grounded capability. We define a lifted form of capabilities as parameterized capabilities.

Definition 3. Given a set of objects $\tilde{O}$; a finite set of predicates $\tilde{P} = \{\tilde{p}_1^{k_1}, \ldots, \tilde{p}_n^{k_n}\}$ with arities k_i; a *parameterized capability* $\tilde{c}$ is defined a 3-tuple $\langle \mathit{args}(\tilde{c}), \mathit{pre}(\tilde{c}), \mathit{eff}(\tilde{c})\rangle$ where $\mathit{args}(\tilde{c})$ is the set of arguments that can be initialized with a set of objects $\tilde{o} \subseteq \tilde{O}$; and $\mathit{pre}(\tilde{c})$ and $\mathit{eff}(\tilde{c})$ are sets of literals over $\tilde{P}$ and $\mathit{args}(\tilde{c})$.

A set of parameterized capabilities constitutes a parameterized capability model. Formally, a *parameterized capability model* is a tuple $\tilde{M} = \langle \tilde{P}, \tilde{C}\rangle$, where $\tilde{P}$ is a finite set of predicates, and $\tilde{C}$ is a finite set of parameterized capabilities.

Our objective is to develop a capability discovery algorithm that learns a parameterized capability model of a black-box AI agent using as input (i) the agent, (ii) a compatible simulator using which the agent can simulate its primitive action sequences, and (iii) the user's concept vocabulary, which may be insufficient to express the simulator's state representation. Such assumptions on the agent are common. In fact, the use of third-party simulators for development and testing is the bedrock of most of the research on taskable AI systems today (including game-playing AI, autonomous cars, and factory robots). Providing simulator access for assessment is reasonable as it would allow AI developers to retain freedom and proprietary controls on internal software while supporting calls for assessment and regulation using approaches such as ours.

Our user studies show the efficacy of this approach using spoken English terms for concepts without an explicit process for vocabulary synchronization. Several threads of ongoing research address the problem of identifying user-specific concept vocabularies (e.g., Kim et al. (2018), Sreedharan et al. (2022)), and the field of intelligent tutoring systems develops methods for helping users understand a fixed concept vocabulary. These methods can be used to either elicit or impart a vocabulary for a given user and such systems can be used to complement the methods developed in this paper.

However, since the problem of capability discovery is not well understood even in settings where user-concept definitions are readily available, we focus on capability discovery with a given vocabulary with known definitions and formalize our approach using them. Furthermore, our empirical evaluation and user studies don't place requirements on user concept vocabularies and show the efficacy of this representation. We formalize these concept definitions as follows:

Definition 4. Given a concrete state $s \in S$, a set of objects $\tilde{O}$ and their tuples $\tilde{O}^{\leq d}$ (of dimension at most d, where d is a positive integer), a set of *concepts/predicates* $\tilde{P} = \tilde{p}_1^{k_1}, \ldots, \tilde{p}_n^{k_n}$ with their arities k_i and an associated Boolean evaluation function $\psi_{\tilde{p}_i} : S \times \tilde{P} \times \tilde{O}^{\leq \mathit{max}(k_i)} \rightarrow \{T, F\}$, $j \leq \mathit{max}(k_i)$, we define $s \models_{\psi_{\tilde{p}_i}} \tilde{p}_i(\tilde{o}_1, \ldots, \tilde{o}_j)$ iff $\psi_{\tilde{p}_i}(s, \tilde{p}_i, \tilde{o}_1, \ldots, \tilde{o}_j) = T$. We define *the abstraction* $\tilde{s}_{\tilde{P},\tilde{O}}$ *of a state* $s \in S$ as the set of all literals over $\tilde{P}$ and $\tilde{O}$ that are true in s. $\tilde{S}_{\tilde{P},\tilde{O}}$ denotes the abstract state space $\{\tilde{s}_{\tilde{P},\tilde{O}} : s \in S\}$.

Algorithm 1: Interactive Capability Model Learning

```
Input  : predicates P̃, agent 𝒜
Output : M̃
E ← generate_execution_traces(𝒜)
C̃* ← generate_partial_capability_descriptions(E)
C̃′ ← parameterize_partial_capabilities(C̃*)
M̃ ← generate_parameterized_capability_model(C̃′)
Set L̃ ← {pre, eff}
for each ⟨L̃, C̃, P̃⟩ in M̃ do
    Generate M̃₊, M̃₋, M̃_∅ by setting P̃ in C̃ at L̃ to
      +, −, ∅ in M̃
    for each pair M̃_x, M̃_y in {M̃₊, M̃₋, M̃_∅} do
        q̃ ← generate_query(M̃₁, M̃₂)
        ϱ̃ ← generate_waypoints(q̃)
        ϱ ← refine_waypoints(ϱ̃, P̃)
        for i in range[0, k − 1] do
            θ ← ask_agent(𝒜, ⟨s_i, s_{i+1}⟩)
            break if θ = ⊥
        M̃ ← consistent_description(i, s̃_i, M̃_x, M̃_y)
return M̃
```

We omit subscripts $\tilde{P}$ and $\tilde{O}$ unless needed for clarity. As mentioned, we assume availability of an evaluation function $\psi_{\tilde{p}}$ associated with each predicate $\tilde{p} \in \tilde{P}$. E.g., for a 3-D Blocksworld simulator with objects a and b, and coordinates x, y, and z, "$\mathit{on}(a, b)$ is true exactly for states where $z(a) > z(b)$, $x(a) = x(b)$, and $y(a) = y(b)$." As this example illustrates, such vocabularies can be inaccurate. The abstraction function f (Def. 4) can be modeled as a conjunction of these evaluation functions $\psi_{\tilde{p}}$. We now discuss how we discover capabilities and learn their descriptions.

3 Active Capability Discovery

Our overall approach consists of two main phases: (1) discovering candidate capabilities and their partial descriptions from a set of execution traces of the agent's behavior (Sec. 3.1); and (2) completing the descriptions of the candidate capabilities discovered in step (1) by asking the agent queries designed to assess under which conditions it can execute those capabilities and what their effects are (Sec. 3.2). The interactive Capability Model Learning (iCaML) algorithm (Alg. 1) performs both these steps using user interpretable predicates $\tilde{P}$ and the agent $\mathcal{A}$ as inputs. We now explain these two phases in detail.

3.1 Discovering Candidate Partial Capabilities

Generating execution traces As a first step, Alg. 1 collects a set of execution traces E from the agent (line 1). An *execution trace* e is a sequence of states of the form $\langle s_0, s_1, \ldots, s_{n-1}, s_n \rangle$, such that $\forall j \in [1, n] \ \ \exists a_i \in A \ \ a_j(s_{j-1}) = s_j$. To obtain the traces $e \in E$, a set of random tasks of the form $\langle s_I, s_G \rangle$, where $s_I, s_G \in S$, are given to the agent $\mathcal{A}$, and the agent is asked to reach s_G from s_I. Intermediate states that the agent goes through form the set of execution traces E.

Discovering candidate capabilities To discover candidate capabilities, we abstract the low-level execution traces E in terms of the user's vocabulary (line 2). This abstraction of a low-level execution trace $\langle s_0, s_1, \ldots, s_{n-1}, s_n \rangle$ gives a high-level execution trace $\langle \tilde{s}_0, \tilde{s}_1, \ldots, \tilde{s}_{n-1}, \tilde{s}_n \rangle$. Since we do not assume that the user's vocabulary is precise enough to discern all the states available to the agent, more than one low-level state in an execution trace may be abstracted to a single high-level abstract state in $\tilde{S}$. Hence for some $j \in [0, n-1]$, it is possible that $\tilde{s}_j = \tilde{s}_{j+1}$. E.g., in Fig. 1(a), the state available to the agent in the simulator expresses pixel-level details of the game (Fig. 1(b)), whereas the user's vocabulary can express it only as an abstract state that represents multiple similar low-level states (Fig. 1(c)). Formally, an *abstract execution trace* is the longest subsequence of $\tilde{s}_1, \ldots, \tilde{s}_n$ such that no two subsequent elements are identical. We remove the repetitions from the high-level execution trace to get the abstract execution trace $\tilde{e} = \langle \tilde{s}_0, \ldots, \tilde{s}_m \rangle$, where $m \leq n$.

We store each transition $\tilde{s}_i, \tilde{s}_{i+1}$ in $\tilde{e}$ as a new grounded candidate capability $\tilde{c}^*_{\tilde{s}_i, \tilde{s}_{i+1}}$.

Generating partial capability descriptions For each candidate capability $\tilde{c}^*_{\tilde{s}_i, \tilde{s}_{i+1}}$, the set of predicates $\tilde{s}_{i+1} \setminus \tilde{s}_i$ is added to the effects of $\tilde{c}^*_{\tilde{s}_i, \tilde{s}_{i+1}}$ in positive form (add effects); whereas the set $\tilde{s}_i \setminus \tilde{s}_{i+1}$ is added to the same candidate capability's effects in negative form (delete effects). As an optimization, in a manner similar to Stern and Juba (2017), we also store that the predicates true in $\tilde{s}_i$ cannot be negative preconditions for this capability, whereas the predicates false in $\tilde{s}_i$ cannot be positive preconditions.

Lifting the partial capability descriptions After line 2 of Alg. 1, we get a set of candidate capabilities with their partial descriptions that are in terms of predicates $\tilde{P}$ instantiated with objects in $\tilde{O}$. For each such grounded partial capability description, the predicates in the preconditions and effects are sorted in some lexicographic order. The choice of ordering is not important as long as it stays consistent throughout Alg. 1. The objects used in predicate arguments are assigned unique IDs corresponding to this capability in the order of their appearance in ordered predicates. These IDs are then used as variables representing capability parameters. E.g., suppose we have a grounded partial capability description with a precondition: *(alive ganon), (at link cell6), (at ganon cell5),(next_to ganon)*. Traversing the predicates in this order, the objects used in these predicates are given IDs as follows: $\{$*ganon: 1, link: 2, cell6: 3, cell5: 4*$\}$. Note that there is only one assignment per object, hence *ganon* in *(at ganon cell5)* was not given a separate ID. This procedure is extended to effects while assigning new IDs for any unseen objects in the partial capability description. Finally, the parameterized partial capability description is constructed by replacing all occurrences of objects in the partial capability description with variables corresponding to their unique IDs.

Combining candidate capabilities Multiple candidate partial capabilities can be combined if their precondition and effect conjunctions are unifiable. E.g., for any capability to match the capability discussed above, it's precondition should be in the form: *(alive ?1), (at ?2 ?3), (at ?1 ?4), (next_to ?1)*. Its effects should also be unifiable in terms of these parameters. The algorithm also keeps track of which grounded partial candidate capabilities map to each parameterized partial capability description. These descriptions are partial as they are generated using limited execution traces and may not capture all the preconditions or effects of a capability. E.g., suppose a capability adds a literal on its execution. If that literal is already present in the state where the capability was executed, it will not be captured in the effect of the capability's partial description. Hence, we next try to complete the partial capability descriptions. Note that all parameterized partial capability descriptions are collectively used as the parameterized capability model $\tilde{M}$ (line 4).

3.2 Completing Partial Capability Descriptions

To complete the partial capability descriptions $\tilde{M}$, Alg. 1 generates queries aimed to gain more information about the conditions under which the capability can be executed and the state properties that become true or false upon its execution. These queries give the agent a sequence of states, called waypoints, to traverse. Based on the agent's ability to traverse them, we derive the precondition and effect of each capability. Alg. 1 iterates through the combinations of predicates and capabilities generated earlier to determine how each predicate will appear in each capability's precondition and effect (line 6). For each combination, it generates a query as follows.

Active query generation For each combination of predicate, capability, and precondition (or effect), three possible capability descriptions $M_+, M_-, M_\emptyset$ are possible, one each for the predicate appearing in the precondition (or effect) of the capability in positive, negative, or absent mode, respectively (line 7). As noted when generating partial capability descriptions in Sec. 3.1, some of the models will not be considered if we know that a form is not possible for a particular predicate. The algorithm iteratively picks two such models M_x, M_y from $M_+, M_-, M_\emptyset$ (line 8) and generates a query $\tilde{q}$ in the form of a state $\tilde{s}_0$ and a capability sequence $\tilde{\pi}$ such that the result of executing the sequence $\tilde{\pi}$ on $\tilde{s}_0$ is different in M_x and M_y (line 9). We use the agent interrogation algorithm (AIA), from our prior work Verma, Marpally, and Srivastava (2021) (henceforth referred to as VMS21). For their process, AIA reduces query generation to a planning problem. The resulting query $\tilde{q}$ is of the form $\langle \tilde{s}_0, \tilde{\pi}\rangle$, asking the model (or an agent) about the length of the plan $\tilde{\pi}$ that it can successfully execute when starting from state $\tilde{s}_0$. Here plan $\tilde{\pi}$ is a sequence of capabilities $\langle \tilde{c}_1^*, \dots, \tilde{c}_n^*\rangle$ grounded with objects in $\tilde{O}$.

Generating waypoints from queries The queries described above cannot be directly posed to an agent, as the plan $\tilde{\pi}$ is in terms of high-level capabilities $\tilde{c}_i^* \in \tilde{C}^*$, which the agent will not be able to comprehend. Additionally, these high-level capabilities cannot be converted directly to low-level actions, as each capability may correspond to a different sequence of low-level actions depending on the state in which it is executed. Hence, we pose the queries to the agent in the form of high-level state transitions induced by the capabilities in the query's capability sequence.

To accomplish this, Alg. 1 converts the query $\tilde{q}$ to a sequence of waypoints $\tilde{\varrho} = \langle \tilde{s}_0, \dots, \tilde{s}_n\rangle$. Starting from the initial state $\tilde{s}_0$, these are generated by applying the capability $\tilde{c}_i^*$, for $i \in [1, n]$, in the state $\tilde{s}_{i-1}$ according to the partial capability description of $\tilde{c}_i^*$. Note that the waypoints $\tilde{\varrho}$ cannot be presented to the agent as the agent may not know the high-level vocabulary. Hence these high-level waypoints must be refined into the low-level waypoints $\varrho = \langle s_0, \dots, s_n\rangle$ (with each s_i similar to state shown in Fig. 1(b)) that agent understands.

Alg. 1 first converts the high-level waypoints $\tilde{\varrho}$ to a sequence of low-level waypoints $\varrho = \langle s_0, \dots, s_n\rangle$ using the predicate definitions (line 11). Then each consecutive pair of states $\langle s_i, s_{i+1}\rangle$ is given sequentially to the agent as a *state reachability query* asking if it can reach from state s_i to s_{i+1} using its internal black-box policy (line 13).

Updating partial models based on agent responses Using its internal planning mechanism and the simulator, the agent attempts to reach from state s_i to s_{i+1}. If it succeeds, the response to the query is recorded as true; if it fails, the response is recorded as false. The algorithm keeps track of the waypoints that were successfully traversed. Based on the waypoint pairs that the agent was able to traverse, we discard the capability descriptions among M_x and M_y that are not consistent with the agent's response (line 15).

E.g., suppose the algorithm is trying to determine how the predicate *(alive ?monster1)* should appear in the precondition of capability *c4* shown in Fig. 1(d). Now the two possible capability descriptions M_1 and M_2 that Alg. 1 is considering in line 6 are M_+ and M_-, corresponding to *(alive ?monster1)* being in *c4*'s precondition in positive and negative form, respectively. The algorithm will generate query with its corresponding waypoints $\tilde{\varrho} = \langle \tilde{s}_0, \tilde{s}_1\rangle$, where $\tilde{s}_0$ will correspond to the state shown in Fig 1(a), and $\tilde{s}_1$ will be $\tilde{s}_0$ without Ganon. Now the agent uses its own internal mechanism to try to reach $\tilde{s}_1$ from $\tilde{s}_0$ and succeeds. Since this is not possible according to M_-, M_- will be discarded.

We now define and prove the theoretical properties of iCaML algorithm. To do this, we use two key properties of VMS21 relevant to this work: (1) if there exists a distinguishing query for two models then it will be generated (Thm. 1 in VMS21); and (2) the algorithm will not discard any model that is consistent with the agent (Thm. 2 in VMS21). Interested readers can refer to VMS21 for further details.

3.3 Formal Analysis

Alg. 1 has two main desirable properties: (1) the partial capability model (that is maintained as $\tilde{M}$) is always maximally consistent, i.e, adding any more literals into it would be unsupported by the execution traces that we obtain; and (2) the final parameterized capability is complete in the limit of infinite execution traces given to Alg. 1. We first define these concepts and then formalize the results under Thm. 1 and Thm. 2.

Definition 5. Let $e = \langle s_0, \dots, s_n\rangle$ be an execution trace with a corresponding abstract execution trace $\tilde{e} = \langle \tilde{s}_0, \dots, \tilde{s}_m\rangle$, where $m \leq n$. A *parameterized capability model* $\tilde{M} = \langle \tilde{P}, \tilde{C}, \tilde{O}\rangle$ is consistent with E iff $\forall i \in [0, m-1]\ \exists \tilde{c}^* \in \tilde{C}^*\ \tilde{s}_{i+1} = \tilde{c}^*(\tilde{s}_i)$, where $\tilde{C}^*$ is a set of grounded capabilities that can be generated by instantiating the parameters of capabilities $\tilde{c} \in \tilde{C}$ with objects in $\tilde{O}$.

We extend this terminology to say that a capability model is consistent with a set of execution traces E iff it is consistent with every trace in E. This notion of consistency captures completeness as a parameterized capability model $\tilde{M}$ that is consistent with a set of execution traces E, is also complete w.r.t. E. We next define a stronger notion of completeness that our algorithm provides in the form of maximal consistency. This helps to assess the succinctness of a capability model with a set of execution traces E.

Definition 6. Let E be a set of execution traces, and Λ be the set of possible agents that can generate all execution traces in E. A *parameterized capability model* $\tilde{M} = \langle \tilde{P}, \tilde{C}, \tilde{O}\rangle$ *is maximally consistent with a set of execution traces* E iff (i) $\tilde{M}$ is consistent with E, and (ii) adding any predicate as positive or negative precondition or effect of a capability in $\tilde{M}$ makes it inconsistent with at least one execution trace that can be generated by at least one agent $\mathcal{A}^\# \in \Lambda$.

An abstraction satisfies *local connectivity* iff $\forall \tilde{s}\ \forall s_i, s_j \in f^{-1}(\tilde{s})$ there exists a sequence of primitive actions $\langle a_i, \dots, a_n\rangle$ such that $a_n(a_{n-1} \cdots (a_1(s_i)) \dots) = s_j$. We use this to show that the parameterized capability model learned by Alg. 1 is maximally consistent.

Theorem 1. *Let $\mathcal{A} = \langle S, A, T\rangle$ be an agent operating in a deterministic, fully observable, and stationary environment with a state space S using a set of primitive actions A. Given an input vocabulary $\tilde{P}$, and the set of execution traces E generated by $\mathcal{A}$, if local connectivity holds, then the capability model $\tilde{M}$ maintained by Alg. 1 is* consistent *with the set of execution traces E.*

Proof. We show that given the set of all execution traces E, the parameterized capability model $\tilde{M}$ maintained by Alg. 1 is consistent with E, i.e., for every high-level transition $\tilde{s}, \tilde{s}'$ corresponding to a transition in E, there exists a capability $\tilde{c}$ which has a grounding $\tilde{c}^*$ such that $\tilde{c}^*(s) = \tilde{s}'$. We prove this by contradiction. The partial capability model

$\tilde{M}$ is initially generated using observed transitions $\tilde{s}, \tilde{s}'$ corresponding to the transitions in E as grounded capabilities $\tilde{c}^*_{\tilde{s},\tilde{s}'}$ (lines 2 to 4 in Alg. 1). So the model $\tilde{M}$ is consistent with the set of traces to start with. At each step, Alg. 1 adds a new literal l to a capability $\tilde{c}$ in $\tilde{M}$ such that adding l keeps $\tilde{M}$ consistent with the agent $\mathcal{A}$ (Thm. 2 from VMS21). Now consider that adding l to $\tilde{M}$ makes it inconsistent with an execution trace in E, i.e., there must exist a transition $\tilde{s}_1, \tilde{s}_2$ such that no capability $\tilde{c}^* \in \tilde{C}^*$ corresponds to it.

Consider the version of $\tilde{c}_1$ corresponding to $c^*_{\tilde{s}_1,\tilde{s}_2}$ that was modified by Alg. 1. We show that modifications inconsistent with this transition are not possible under the assumption that the agent's capabilities can be expressed using the input vocabulary.

Case 1: Suppose Alg. 1 added a literal l in the precondition of $\tilde{c}_1$ that was not true in $\tilde{s}_1$. Thm. 2 in VMS21 implies that absent and negated forms of l were inconsistent with executions of $\tilde{c}_1$ using the same agent that generated E. In other words, the agent sometimes requires l as a precondition to execute $\tilde{c}_1$, even though l was not a part of $\tilde{s}_1$. This contradicts the assumption that $\tilde{c}_1$ is expressible using the input vocabulary in the form of Def. 3.

Case 2: Suppose Alg. 1 added a literal l in the effect of $\tilde{c}_1$ that was not present in $\tilde{s}_2$. This implies that the negation and absence of l in the result of $\tilde{c}_1$ were inconsistent with the agent's execution of $\tilde{c}_1$ in query-responses generated by Alg. 1. A similar contradiction about the assumption of expressiveness follows.

Hence, the capability model $\tilde{M}$ maintained by Alg. 1 is *consistent* with the set of execution traces E. □

Theorem 2. *Let $\mathcal{A} = \langle S, A, T\rangle$ be an agent operating in a deterministic, fully observable, and stationary environment with a state-space S using a set of primitive actions A. Given an input vocabulary $\tilde{P}$, and the set of execution traces E generated by $\mathcal{A}$, if local connectivity holds, then the capability model $\tilde{M}$ returned by Alg. 1 is* maximally consistent *with the set of execution traces E.*

Proof. We will prove the two conditions for maximal consistency separately. The first condition is that the model $\tilde{M}$ returned by Alg. 1 is consistent with E follows directly from Thm. 1. Since the model maintained by Alg. 1 at each step is consistent with E, hence the same model returned after the last iteration is also consistent with E.

Next, we show that adding any predicate as a positive or negative precondition or effect of a capability in $\tilde{M}$ returned by Alg. 1 makes it inconsistent with at least one execution trace that can be generated by at least one agent $\mathcal{A}^{\#} \in \Lambda$, where Λ is the set of possible agents that can generate all execution traces in E. We prove this by contradiction. Note that a literal is not added by Alg. 1 to an action's precondition (or effect) only if (1) in the observed traces, it was not present in the state where (immediately after) that action was executed; or (2) adding it in the precondition (or effect) of an action resulted in a response to a query that was inconsistent with that of the agent. Also, note that a predicate corresponding to a literal is always added to the model in some form in each precondition (or effect). Suppose a literal l that was not added by Alg. 1 is added to $\tilde{M}$ in precondition (or effect) of a capability $\tilde{c}$ without making it inconsistent with the agent. Since a predicate p corresponding to this literal l is already present in $\tilde{c}$, this implies that the form of the predicate p added by Alg. 1 is incorrect. But this is not possible as shown by Thm. 1 and Thm. 2 of VMS21. Hence this is not possible and adding an additional literal in any form to an action's precondition or effect would make it inconsistent with the agent. This means that it also makes the model inconsistent with at least one agent $\mathcal{A}^{\#} \in \Lambda$. □

Next, we formalize the notion of downward refinability, that the discovered capabilities are indeed within the agent's scope. In this work, refinability is similar to the notion of forall-exists abstractions (Srivastava, Russell, and Pinto 2016) for deterministic systems. Recall the notion of abstraction functions (Def. 4).

Definition 7. Let $\tilde{M} = \langle \tilde{P}, \tilde{C}, \tilde{O}\rangle$ be a capability model with $\tilde{S}$, the induced state space over $\tilde{P}, \tilde{O}$ using an abstraction function f, for an agent $\mathcal{A} = \langle S, A, T\rangle$; and $\tilde{C}^*$ be a set of grounded capabilities that can be generated by instantiating the arguments of capabilities $\tilde{c} \in \tilde{C}$ with objects in $\tilde{O}$. A capability $\tilde{c}^* \in \tilde{C}^*$ is *realizable w.r.t.* $\mathcal{A}$ iff $\forall \tilde{s} \in \tilde{S}$, if $\tilde{s} \models pre(\tilde{c}^*)$ then $\forall s \in f^{-1}(\tilde{s})\ \exists a_1, \ldots, a_n \in A : a_n(a_{n-1} \ldots (a_1(s)) \ldots) \in \tilde{c}^*(\tilde{s})$. The model M is *realizable w.r.t.* $\mathcal{A}$ iff all capabilities $\tilde{c}^* \in \tilde{C}^*$ are realizable.

In these terms, discovered capabilities are more likely to be useful if they are accurate in the sense that they are consistent with execution traces and realizable, i.e., true representations of what the agent can do. Realizability captures the soundness of the model wrt the execution of the capabilities. We now show that the parameterized capability model that we learn is realizable.

Theorem 3. *Let $\tilde{P}$ be a set of predicates $\tilde{P}$, $\mathcal{A} = \langle S, A, T\rangle$ be an agent with a deterministic transition system T. If a high-level model is expressible deterministically using the predicates $\tilde{P}$, and local connectivity is ensured, then the parameterized capability model $\tilde{M}$ learned by Alg. 1 is* realizable.

Proof. We will prove that for all capabilities in $\tilde{C}$ learned as part of the parameterized capability model $\tilde{M}$, for all groundings $\tilde{C}^*$, if the capability is executed in an abstract state $\tilde{s}$ such that $\tilde{s} \models pre(\tilde{c}^*)$ then there exists a sequence of low-level states that the agent can traverse to reach a state $\tilde{s}' \in \tilde{c}^*(\tilde{s})$.

We prove this by cases. Consider a capability $\tilde{c} \in \tilde{C}$ whose description is learned using Alg. 1. Using Thm. 1, the precondition and effect of $\tilde{c}$ will be consistent with E generated by the agent. Now consider a grounded capability $\tilde{c}^*$ corresponding to the capability $\tilde{c}$. There are only two cases possible: (1) either $\tilde{c}^*$ appeared in the observed traces or was executed successfully by the agent in response to one of the queries posed to the agent; or (2) it was not present in either. We prove each case separately.

Case 1: There exists a set of low-level states s and s' such that $\tilde{c}^*(\tilde{s}) = \tilde{s}'$, where $\tilde{s} = f(s)$ and $\tilde{s}' = f(s')$. Now due to local connectivity, all states in $f^{-1}(s)$ are connected with each other and same is true for all states in $f^{-1}(s')$. Hence the agent can traverse from any state in $f^{-1}(s)$ to any state in $f^{-1}(s')$ on executing the capability $\tilde{c}^*$. This makes the capability $\tilde{c}^*$ realizable.

Case 2: Since $\tilde{c}^*$ was not observed directly and the only way capabilities are added to $\tilde{M}$ is if they are lifted forms of capabilities identified from observation traces E, $\tilde{c}^*$ must be a grounding of the lifted form $\tilde{c}_1$ of a capability $\tilde{c}_1^*$ that is of the type considered in case 1. Alg. 1 constructs precondition and effect of $\tilde{c}_1$ while ensuring consistency with query responses and observations under the assumption that the capability model is expressible as in Def. 3. When this assumption holds, the effect or precondition of a capability can only depend on the vocabulary of available predicates, which are considered exhaustively (hierarchically) by Alg. 1. This implies that there must be a path from a concrete state s in the grounding corresponding to $\tilde{c}_1$'s precondition to a concrete state s' that satisfies the effects of grounding of $\tilde{c}_1$'s effects. By local connectivity, this extends to all concrete states in the same abstract state as $\tilde{s}$ corresponding to s.

Hence if a high-level model is expressible deterministically using the predicates $\tilde{P}$, and local connectivity is ensured, then the parameterized capability model $\tilde{M}$ learned by Alg. 1 is *realizable*. □

Note that here expressibility of a high-level model refers to the class of models of the form defined in Def. 3. Together, the notions of maximal consistency and realizability establish the completeness and soundness of our approach wrt a set of execution traces E. Note that this approach will also work when we have access to a stream of execution traces E being collected at random, independent of our active querying mechanism. We next show that in the limit of infinite randomly generated execution traces, our approach will capture all possible agent capabilities with probability 1. Here, capturing all possible agent capabilities in a learned model $\tilde{M} = \langle \tilde{P}, \tilde{C}, \tilde{O} \rangle$ means that if the agent can go from $\tilde{s}_i$ to $\tilde{s}_j$, then one of the capabilities in $\tilde{C}$ will be instantiable to result in $\tilde{s}_j$ when executed from $\tilde{s}_i$.

Theorem 4. *Let $\tilde{P}$ be a set of predicates, $\mathcal{A} = \langle S, A, T \rangle$ be an agent with a deterministic transition system T. Suppose random samples of agent behavior in the form of execution traces E are coming from a distribution that assigns non-zero probability to at least one transition corresponding to each ground capability ($\tilde{c}^*_{\tilde{s}_i,\tilde{s}_j}$, $\tilde{s}_i, \tilde{s}_j \subseteq \tilde{P}$). If a high-level model is expressible deterministically using the predicates $\tilde{P}$ and local connectivity holds, then in the limit of infinite execution traces E, the probability of discovering all capabilities $\tilde{c} \in \tilde{C}$ expressible using the predicates $\tilde{P}$ is 1.*

Proof. Consider every possible abstract transition that the agent can make. There are finite (let's consider L) such transitions possible given the predicate vocabulary $\tilde{P}$ and a fixed set of objects $\tilde{O}$. Now we are getting random execution traces E from a distribution that assigns non-zero probability to at least one transition corresponding to each ground capability ($\tilde{c}^*_{\tilde{s}_i,\tilde{s}_j}$). This means that the probability of not observing this finite set of cardinality L will reduce with each successive collection of L execution traces. Hence we will eventually observe at least one transition corresponding to each ground capability ($\tilde{c}^*_{\tilde{s}_i,\tilde{s}_j}$). Then as shown in Thm. 1, we will discover the capability $\tilde{c}$ corresponding to the ground transition $\tilde{c}^*_{\tilde{s}_i,\tilde{s}_j}$ with probability 1. □

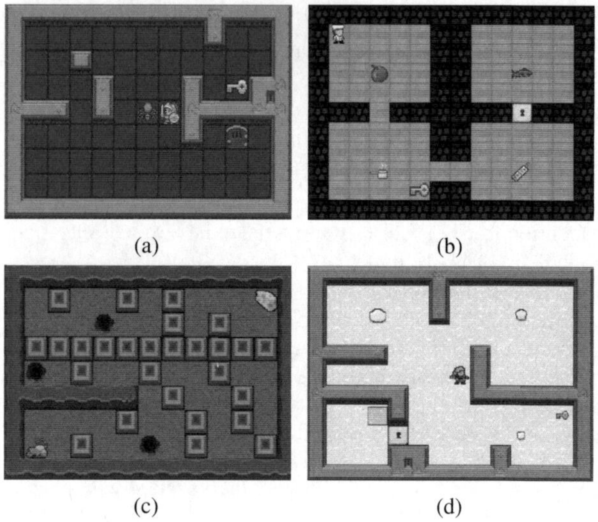

(a) (b) (c) (d)

Figure 2: GVGAI's domains; (a) Zelda, (b) Cook-Me-Pasta, (c) Escape, and (d) Snowman.

4 Empirical Evaluation

We implemented Alg. 1 in Python to empirically verify its effectiveness.[1] To show that our approach can work with different internal agent implementations, we evaluated Alg. 1 with two broad categories of input test agents: *Policy agents* can use (possibly learned) black-box policies to plan and to respond to state reachability queries. We used policy agents with hand-coded policies for this evaluation. *Search agents* respond to the state reachability queries using arbitrary search algorithms. We used search agents that use A* search (Hart, Nilsson, and Raphael 1968). We now describe the setup of our experiments used for evaluation.

4.1 Experimental Setup

Our test agents use the General Video Game Artificial Intelligence framework (Perez-Liebana et al. 2016; Perez-Liebana et al. 2019). Domains in GVGAI are two-dimensional ATARI-like games defined using the Video Game Description Language PyVGDL (Schaul 2013). We performed experiments on four such game domains – Zelda, Cook-Me-Pasta, Escape, and Snowman (Fig. 2). All these domains require the agent to navigate in a grid-based environment and complete a set of tasks (in some partial order) to complete the game. More details about these domains and the input user vocabularies are available in the extended version of the paper (Verma, Marpally, and Srivastava 2022).

[1]Code: https://github.com/AAIR-lab/iCaML

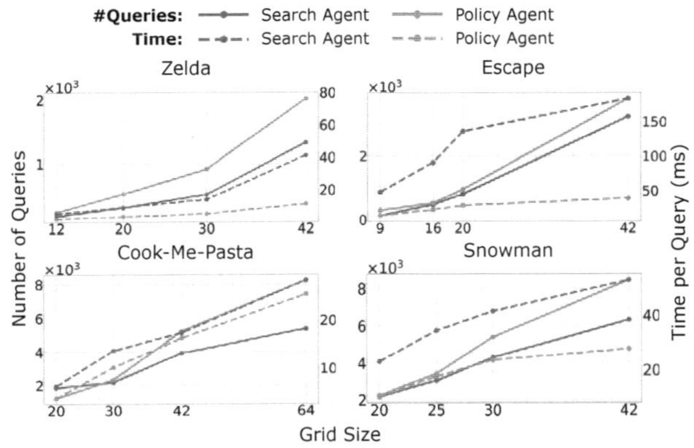

Figure 3: Performance comparison of search-based agents and policy-based agents in terms of the number of queries asked and time taken per query when increasing the grid size (number of cells in the grid) in the four GVGAI domains.

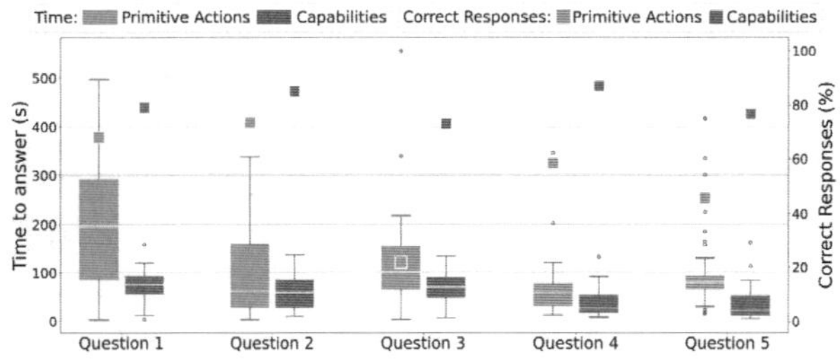

Figure 4: Data from behavior analysis shows that using computed capability descriptions took lesser time and yielded more accurate results. See Sec.4.3 for details.

Since the complete list of an agent's capabilities may be irrelevant to a user's current needs, w.l.o.g, our implementation supports an input including sets of formulas representing the properties that may be of interest to the user. This set can be the set of all grounded predicates in the user's concept vocabulary. We also consider object types to be a subset of the unary predicates in the vocabulary and assume that each object has exactly one type. These types are used and discovered in capability like any other predicate. In addition, they are used in creating parameterized capability parameters as shown in Fig. 1(d).

For each domain, and for each grid size in that domain, we create a random game instance with the goal of achieving one of the user's specified properties of interest. To generate these instances, the number of obstacles in all domains, except Escape, is set to 20% of the total cells in the grid, whereas all other objects are generated randomly. We use the solution to that instance to generate the execution trace that is used in lines 1-2 of Alg. 1. These solutions are not always optimal. All experiments are run on 5.0 GHz Intel i9 CPUs with 64 GB RAM running Ubuntu 18.04.

As shown in Sec.3.3, Alg. 1 is guaranteed to compute capability descriptions that are correct in the sense that they are consistent with the execution traces, and refinable and executable with respect to the true capabilities of the agent. We now present the main conclusions of our empirical analysis.

We evaluated our algorithm's performance along two aspects; (i) how the performance of our approach changes with respect to the size of the problem; and (ii) how its performance differs for search-based vs policy-based agents.

4.2 Empirical Results

Scalability analysis We increase the size of each domain to analyze its effect on the performance of the search and policy agents. Fig. 3 shows the graphs for the experimental runs on the four domains. In all four domains, for both kinds of agents, *the number of queries increases as we increase the grid size*. The increasing number of queries is an expected behavior and this is also clear in approaches that use passive observations of agent behavior (Yang, Wu, and Jiang 2007; Aineto, Celorrio, and Onaindia 2019).

Agent type analysis The *number of queries required by the policy agent is higher than that of the search agent* in almost all cases. This is because a large number of state reachability queries fail on the policy agent as the sequence of waypoints in these queries does not always align with the policy of the agent. However, *the time per query is lesser for the policy agents* as they can answer the state reachability queries by following their policy, whereas the search agents perform an exhaustive search of the state space for every such query.

4.3 User Study

We conducted a user study to evaluate the utility of the capability descriptions discovered and computed by Alg. 1. Intuitively, our notion of interpretability matches that of common English and its use in AI literature, e.g., as enunciated by Doshi-Velez and Kim (2018): *"the ability to explain or to present in understandable terms to a human."* We evaluate this through the following operational hypothesis:

H1. The discovered capabilities make it easier for users to analyze and predict the outcome of the agent's possible behaviors.

We designed the following study to evaluate H1.

Behavior analysis study This study compares the predictability and analyzability of agent behavior in terms of the agent's low-level actions and high-level capabilities. Each user is explained the rules of a Zelda-like game. One group of users – called the *primitive action group* – are presented with text descriptions of the agent's primitive actions, while the users in the other group – called the *capability group* – are presented with a text description of the six learned capabilities. The capability group users are asked to choose a short summarization for each capability description, out of the eight possible summarizations that we provide, whereas the primitive action group users are asked to choose a short summarization for each primitive action description, out of the five possible summarizations that we provide. Then each user is given the same 5 questions in order. Each question contains two game-state images; start and end state. The user is asked what sequence of actions or capabilities that the agent should execute to reach the end state from the start state. Each question has 5 possible options for the user to choose from, and these options differ depending on their group. We then collect the data about the accuracy of the answers, and the time taken to answer each question.

Study design 108 participants were recruited from Amazon Mechanical Turk and randomly divided into two groups of 54 each. Each user was provided with a survey on Qualtrics (Qualtrics 2005) that explained the rules of GVGAI's Zelda game. We used screeners (Kennedy et al. 2020; Arndt et al. 2021) to ensure quality of the data collected, and discarded 23 responses. The results are based on the responses of 41 and 43 users in the primitive action and capability group, respectively.

Results The results of the behavior analysis study are shown in (Fig. 4) To evaluate the statistical significance (p-value) of the difference in the mean of the time taken by the two groups, we used Student's t-test (Student 1908). The results indicate that the test results were statistically significant with p-values less than 0.05 for all five questions. Also, the users took less time to answer questions and they got more responses correct when using the capabilities as compared to using primitive actions. This validates H1 that the discovered capabilities made it easier for the users to analyze and predict the agent's behavior correctly. Detailed information about the user study is available in the extended version of the paper (Verma, Marpally, and Srivastava 2022).

5 Related Work

High-level skills from input options Given a set of options encoding skills as input, Konidaris, Kaelbling, and Lozano-Perez (2018) and James, Rosman, and Konidaris (2020) propose methods for learning high-level propositional models of options representing various "skills." They assume access to predefined options and learn the high-level symbols that describe those options at the high-level. While they use options or skills as inputs to learn models defining when those skills will be useful in terms of auto-generated symbols (for which explanatory semantics could be derived in a post-hoc fashion), our approach uses user-provided interpretable concepts as apriori inputs to learn agent capabilities: high-level actions as well as their interpretable descriptions in terms of the input vocabulary.

Learning symbolic models using physics simulators Multiple approaches learn different kinds of symbolic models of the functionality of ATARI or physics-based simulators using methods like conjunctions of binary input features (Kansky et al. 2017), graph neural networks (Battaglia et al. 2016; Cranmer et al. 2020), CNNs (Agrawal et al. 2016; Fragkiadaki et al. 2016), etc. Some methods create interpretable descriptions of reinforcement learning policies using trees (Liu et al. 2018) or specialized programming languages (Verma et al. 2018). These approaches solve the orthogonal problem of learning the functionality of an agent that could help a user understand how an agent would solve a problem, whereas we focus on learning capabilities of the agent that could help a user understand and answer what type of problems it could solve.

Action model learning The planning community has also worked on learning STRIPS-like action models of agent functionality from observations of its behavior (Gil 1994; Yang, Wu, and Jiang 2007; Cresswell, McCluskey, and West 2009; Zhuo and Kambhampati 2013; Stern and Juba 2017; Aineto, Celorrio, and Onaindia 2019; Bonet and Geffner 2020). Jiménez et al. (2012) and Arora et al. (2018) present a comprehensive review of such approaches. These methods work with broad assumptions that the agent model is internally expressed in the same vocabulary as the user's (Gil 1994; Weber, Morwood, and Bryce 2011; Juba, Le, and Stern 2021), or at a similar level of abstraction (Mehta, Tadepalli, and Fern 2011; Verma, Marpally, and Srivastava 2021; Nayyar, Verma, and Srivastava 2022). Additionally, such methods have as input a given set of predicates in terms of which they learn the functionality descriptions of the agent.

High-level actions Works like Madumal et al. (2020) explain an agent's policy in terms of high-level actions but they assume that high-level actions are a part of the input whereas our approach discovers these actions. There is an orthogonal thread of research on using high-level actions in AI planning as tasks, and learning low-level policies for each of those tasks (Yang et al. 2018; Lyu et al. 2019; Illanes et al. 2020; Kokel et al. 2021). These works assume the high-level actions as input and learn the corresponding low-level policies.

As compared to the above two classes of methods, our work focuses on solving the harder problem of discovering the capabilities of the agent behavior resulting from its planning/learning algorithms and learning the descriptions of these capabilities.

6 Conclusion

We presented a novel approach for learning the capability description of an AI system in terms of user-interpretable concepts by combining information from passive execution traces and active query answering. Our approach works for settings where the user's conceptual vocabulary is imprecise and cannot directly express the agent's capabilities. Our empirical analysis showed that for the agents that internally use black-box deterministic policies, or search techniques, we can successfully discover the capabilities and their descriptions. Extending this approach for partially observable settings and relaxing the various assumptions we made are some of the promising future directions for this work.

Acknowledgements

We thank Nancy Cooke, Akkamahadevi Hanni, and Sydney Wallace for their help with the user study. We also thank anonymous reviewers for their helpful feedback on the paper. This work was supported in part by the NSF under grants IIS 1942856, IIS 1909370, and the ONR grant N00014-21-1-2045.

References

Agrawal, P.; Nair, A. V.; Abbeel, P.; Malik, J.; and Levine, S. 2016. Learning to Poke by Poking: Experiential Learning of Intuitive Physics. In *Proc. NIPS*.

Aineto, D.; Celorrio, S. J.; and Onaindia, E. 2019. Learning Action Models With Minimal Observability. *Artificial Intelligence* 275:104–137.

Anjomshoae, S.; Najjar, A.; Calvaresi, D.; and Främling, K. 2019. Explainable Agents and Robots: Results from a Systematic Literature Review. In *Proc. AAMAS*.

Arndt, A. D.; Ford, J. B.; Babin, B. J.; and Luong, V. 2021. Collecting Samples from Online Services: How to Use Screeners to Improve Data Quality. *International Journal of Research in Marketing*.

Arora, A.; Fiorino, H.; Pellier, D.; Métivier, M.; and Pesty, S. 2018. A Review of Learning Planning Action Models. *The Knowledge Engineering Review* 33:E20.

Bäckström, C., and Jonsson, P. 2013. Bridging the Gap Between Refinement and Heuristics in Abstraction. In *Proc. IJCAI*.

Barredo Arrieta, A.; Díaz-Rodríguez, N.; Del Ser, J.; Bennetot, A.; Tabik, S.; Barbado, A.; Garcia, S.; Gil-Lopez, S.; Molina, D.; Benjamins, R.; Chatila, R.; and Herrera, F. 2020. Explainable Artificial Intelligence (XAI): Concepts, Taxonomies, Opportunities and Challenges toward Responsible AI. *Information Fusion* 58:82–115.

Battaglia, P.; Pascanu, R.; Lai, M.; Jimenez Rezende, D.; and Kavukcuoglu, K. 2016. Interaction Networks for Learning about Objects, Relations and Physics. In *Proc. NIPS*.

Bonet, B., and Geffner, H. 2020. Learning First-Order Symbolic Representations for Planning from the Structure of the State Space. In *Proc. ECAI*.

Camacho, A., and McIlraith, S. A. 2019. Learning interpretable models expressed in linear temporal logic. In *Proc. ICAPS*.

Chakraborti, T.; Sreedharan, S.; Zhang, Y.; and Kambhampati, S. 2017. Plan Explanations as Model Reconciliation: Moving Beyond Explanation as Soliloquy. In *Proc. IJCAI*.

Cranmer, M.; Sanchez Gonzalez, A.; Battaglia, P.; Xu, R.; Cranmer, K.; Spergel, D.; and Ho, S. 2020. Discovering Symbolic Models from Deep Learning with Inductive Biases. In *Proc. NeurIPS*.

Cresswell, S.; McCluskey, T.; and West, M. 2009. Acquisition of Object-Centred Domain Models from Planning Examples. In *Proc. ICAPS*.

Dhurandhar, A.; Chen, P.-Y.; Luss, R.; Tu, C.-C.; Ting, P.; Shanmugam, K.; and Das, P. 2018. Explanations based on the Missing: Towards Contrastive Explanations with Pertinent Negatives. In *Proc. NeurIPS*.

Doshi-Velez, F., and Kim, B. 2018. *Considerations for Evaluation and Generalization in Interpretable Machine Learning*. Springer International Publishing. 3–17.

Fikes, R. E., and Nilsson, N. J. 1971. STRIPS: A New Approach to the Application of Theorem Proving to Problem Solving. *Artificial Intelligence* 2(3-4):189–208.

Fragkiadaki, K.; Agrawal, P.; Levine, S.; and Malik, J. 2016. Learning Visual Predictive Models of Physics for Playing Billiards. In *Proc. ICLR*.

Gil, Y. 1994. Learning by Experimentation: Incremental Refinement of Incomplete Planning Domains. In *Proc. ICML*.

Giunchiglia, F., and Walsh, T. 1992. A Theory of Abstraction. *Artificial Intelligence* 57(2-3):323–389.

Greydanus, S.; Koul, A.; Dodge, J.; and Fern, A. 2018. Visualizing and Understanding Atari Agents. In *Proc. ICML*.

Hart, P. E.; Nilsson, N. J.; and Raphael, B. 1968. A Formal Basis for the Heuristic Determination of Minimum Cost Paths. *IEEE Transactions on Systems Science and Cybernetics* 4(2):100–107.

Helmert, M.; Haslum, P.; Hoffmann, J.; et al. 2007. Flexible Abstraction Heuristics for Optimal Sequential Planning. In *Proc. ICAPS*.

Illanes, L.; Yan, X.; Icarte, R. T.; and McIlraith, S. A. 2020. Symbolic Plans as High-Level Instructions for Reinforcement Learning. In *Proc. ICAPS*.

James, S.; Rosman, B.; and Konidaris, G. 2020. Learning Portable Representations for High-Level Planning. In *Proc. ICML*.

Jiménez, S.; De La Rosa, T.; Fernández, S.; Fernández, F.; and Borrajo, D. 2012. A Review of Machine Learning for Automated Planning. *The Knowledge Engineering Review* 27(4):433–467.

Juba, B.; Le, H. S.; and Stern, R. 2021. Safe Learning of Lifted Action Models. In *Proc. KR*.

Kansky, K.; Silver, T.; Mély, D. A.; Eldawy, M.; Lázaro-Gredilla, M.; Lou, X.; Dorfman, N.; Sidor, S.; Phoenix, S.; and George, D. 2017. Schema Networks: Zero-shot Transfer with a Generative Causal Model of Intuitive Physics. In *Proc. ICML*.

Kennedy, R.; Clifford, S.; Burleigh, T.; Waggoner, P. D.; Jewell, R.; and Winter, N. J. G. 2020. The Shape of and Solutions to the MTurk Quality Crisis. *Political Science Research and Methods* 8(4):614–629.

Kim, B.; Wattenberg, M.; Gilmer, J.; Cai, C.; Wexler, J.; Viegas, F.; and Sayres, R. 2018. Interpretability Beyond Feature Attribution: Quantitative Testing with Concept Activation Vectors (TCAV). In *Proc. ICML*.

Kokel, H.; Manoharan, A.; Natarajan, S.; Ravindran, B.; and Tadepalli, P. 2021. RePReL: Integrating Relational Planning and Reinforcement Learning for Effective Abstraction. In *Proc. ICAPS*.

Konidaris, G.; Kaelbling, L. P.; and Lozano-Perez, T. 2018. From Skills to Symbols: Learning Symbolic Representations for Abstract High-Level Planning. *Journal of Artificial Intelligence Research* 61(1):215–289.

Liu, G.; Schulte, O.; Zhu, W.; and Li, Q. 2018. Toward Interpretable Deep Reinforcement Learning with Linear Model U-Trees. In *Proc. ECML PKDD*.

Lyu, D.; Yang, F.; Liu, B.; and Gustafson, S. 2019. SDRL: Interpretable and Data-Efficient Deep Reinforcement Learning Leveraging Symbolic Planning. In *Proc. AAAI*.

Madumal, P.; Miller, T.; Sonenberg, L.; and Vetere, F. 2020. Explainable Reinforcement Learning Through a Causal Lens. In *Proc. AAAI*.

Malle, B. F. 2004. *How the Mind Explains Behavior: Folk Explanations, Meaning, and Social Interaction*. The MIT Press.

McDermott, D.; Ghallab, M.; Howe, A.; Knoblock, C.; Ram, A.; Veloso, M.; Weld, D. S.; and Wilkins, D. 1998. PDDL – The Planning Domain Definition Language. Technical Report CVC TR-98-003/DCS TR-1165, Yale Center for Comp. Vision and Control.

Mehta, N.; Tadepalli, P.; and Fern, A. 2011. Autonomous Learning of Action Models for Planning. In *Proc. NIPS*.

Miller, T. 2019. Explanation in Artificial Intelligence: Insights from the Social Sciences. *Artificial Intelligence* 267:1–38.

Mou, Y., and Xu, K. 2017. The Media Inequality: Comparing the Initial Human-Human and Human-AI Social Interactions. *Computers in Human Behavior* 72:432–440.

Nayyar, R. K.; Verma, P.; and Srivastava, S. 2022. Differential Assessment of Black-Box AI Agents. In *Proc. AAAI*.

Paulus, R.; Xiong, C.; and Socher, R. 2018. A Deep Reinforced Model for Abstractive Summarization. In *Proc. ICML*.

Perez-Liebana, D.; Samothrakis, S.; Togelius, J.; Schaul, T.; and Lucas, S. 2016. General Video Game AI: Competition, Challenges and Opportunities. In *Proc. AAAI*.

Perez-Liebana, D.; Liu, J.; Khalifa, A.; Gaina, R. D.; Togelius, J.; and Lucas, S. M. 2019. General Video Game AI: A Multitrack Framework for Evaluating Agents, Games, and Content Generation Algorithms. *IEEE Transactions on Games* 11(3):195–214.

Popov, I.; Heess, N.; Lillicrap, T.; Hafner, R.; Barth-Maron, G.; Vecerik, M.; Lampe, T.; Tassa, Y.; Erez, T.; and Riedmiller, M. 2017. Data-efficient Deep Reinforcement Learning for Dexterous Manipulation. *arXiv preprint arXiv:1704.03073*.

Qualtrics. 2005. Qualtrics XM. https://www.qualtrics.com/. Accessed: 2022-05-10.

Randazzo, R. 2018. What went wrong with Uber's Volvo in fatal crash? Experts shocked by technology failure. *The AZ Republic*.

Russell, S. J. 1997. Rationality and Intelligence. *Artificial Intelligence* 94(1-2):57–77.

Sacerdoti, E. D. 1974. Planning in a Hierarchy of Abstraction Spaces. *Artificial Intelligence* 5(2):115–135.

Schaul, T. 2013. A Video Game Description Language for Model-based or Interactive Learning. In *2013 IEEE Conference on Computational Intelligence in Games (CIG)*.

Sreedharan, S.; Soni, U.; Verma, M.; Srivastava, S.; and Kambhampati, S. 2022. Bridging the Gap: Providing Post-Hoc Symbolic Explanations for Sequential Decision-Making Problems with Inscrutable Representations. In *Proc. ICLR*.

Srivastava, S.; Russell, S.; and Pinto, A. 2016. Metaphysics of Planning Domain Descriptions. In *Proc. AAAI*.

Stern, R., and Juba, B. 2017. Efficient, Safe, and Probably Approximately Complete Learning of Action Models. In *Proc. IJCAI*.

Student. 1908. The Probable Error of a Mean. *Biometrika* 6(1):1–25.

Verma, A.; Murali, V.; Singh, R.; Kohli, P.; and Chaudhuri, S. 2018. Programmatically Interpretable Reinforcement Learning. In *Proc. ICML*.

Verma, P.; Marpally, S. R.; and Srivastava, S. 2021. Asking the Right Questions: Learning Interpretable Action Models Through Query Answering. In *Proc. AAAI*.

Verma, P.; Marpally, S. R.; and Srivastava, S. 2022. Discovering User-Interpretable Capabilities of Black-Box Planning Agents. *CoRR* abs/2107.13668.

Weber, C.; Morwood, D.; and Bryce, D. 2011. Goal-Directed Knowledge Acquisition. In *ICML 2011 Workshop on Planning and Acting with Uncertain Models*.

Yang, F.; Lyu, D.; Liu, B.; and Gustafson, S. 2018. Peorl: Integrating Symbolic Planning and Hierarchical Reinforcement Learning for Robust Decision-Making. In *Proc. IJCAI*.

Yang, Q.; Wu, K.; and Jiang, Y. 2007. Learning Action Models from Plan Examples Using Weighted MAX-SAT. *Artificial Intelligence* 171(2-3):107–143.

Zhuo, H. H., and Kambhampati, S. 2013. Action-Model Acquisition from Noisy Plan Traces. In *Proc. IJCAI*.

Open Relation Extraction with Non-existent and Multi-span Relationships

Huifan Yang[1], Da-Wei Li[2], Zekun Li[1], Donglin Yang[1], Bin Wu[1]

[1]Beijing Key Laboratory of Intelligence Telecommunication Software and Multimedia,
Beijing University of Posts and Telecommunications
[2]Microsoft Software Technology Center Asia
{huifunny, lizekun, iceberg, wubin}@bupt.edu.cn, daweilee@microsoft.com

Abstract

Open relation extraction (ORE) aims to assign semantic relationships among arguments, essential to the automatic construction of knowledge graphs (KG). The previous ORE methods and some benchmark datasets consider a relation between two arguments as definitely existing and in a simple single-span form, neglecting possible non-existent relationships and flexible, expressive multi-span relations. However, detecting non-existent relations is necessary for a pipelined information extraction system (first performing named entity recognition then relation extraction), and multi-span relationships contribute to the diversity of connections in KGs. To fulfill the practical demands of ORE, we design a novel **Q**uery-based **Mu**lti-head **O**pen **R**elation **E**xtractor (**QuORE**) to extract single/multi-span relations and detect non-existent relationships effectively. Moreover, we re-construct some public datasets covering English and Chinese to derive augmented and multi-span relation tuples. Extensive experiment results show that our method outperforms the state-of-the-art ORE model LOREM in the extraction of existing single/multi-span relations and the overall performances on four datasets with non-existent relationships.

Context (*English*): *Donna Karan was born in Long Island, New York. She has a special comprehension of New York, known by the world as a cosmopolitan city.*

Given Argument Tuple	Open Relation
(*Donna Karan, Long Island*)	(*born in*) Single-span
(*a special comprehension, the world*)	Non-existent
(*Donna Karan, a special comprehension, New York*)	(*has, of*) Multi-span
(*New York, the world, a cosmopolitan city*)	(*known by, as*) Multi-span

Context (*Chinese*): *唐娜・凯伦出生于纽约长岛，对纽约这个闻名世界的大都会有着一份特殊的感悟* 。

Given Argument Tuple	Open Relation
(*唐娜・凯伦, 长岛*)	(*出生于*) Single-span
(*世界, 一份特殊的感悟*)	Non-existent
(*唐娜・凯伦, 纽约, 一份特殊的感悟*)	(*对, 有着*) Multi-span

Figure 1: An illustration of our task: open relation extraction with single-span, multi-span, and non-existent relationships. (We present cases in English and Chinese due to the datasets of the two languages used in this paper.)

1 Introduction

Relation extraction (RE) from unstructured text is fundamental to a variety of downstream tasks, such as constructing knowledge graphs and computing sentence similarity. Conventional closed relation extraction considers only a predefined set of relation types on small and homogeneous corpora, which is far less effective when shifting to general-domain text mining that has no limits in relation types or languages. To alleviate the constraints of closed RE, Banko et al. introduce a new paradigm: open relation extraction (ORE), predicting a text span as the semantic connection between arguments from within a context, where a span is a contiguous subsequence. However, the previous works and some widely-used datasets regard an arbitrary argument pair as having a definitely existing relation by default and constrain their task to extract a simple single-span relation between two arguments, ignoring possible non-existent relationships and flexible multi-span relations. To extend ORE for practical demands of general-domain text mining, this paper describes the further tasks of ORE with non-existent and multi-span relationships, and proposes a novel query-based multi-head open relation extractor (QuORE) developed from our re-constructed datasets.

We illustrate the ORE task of this paper in Figure 1. Provided a context and an argument tuple, open relation extraction identifies a single span or multiple spans to specify a semantic connection among the arguments, or detects a non-existent relationship if the arguments do not entail an open relation. (An argument is a text span representing an adverbial, adjectival, nominal phrase, and so on, which is not limited to an entity.)

Conventional ORE systems are largely based on syntactic patterns and heuristic rules that depend on external tools of natural language processing (e.g., PoS-taggers) and language-specific relation formations. For example, ReVerb (Fader, Soderland, and Etzioni 2011), ClausIE (Corro and Gemulla 2013), OpenIE4 (Mausam 2016) for English and CORE (Tseng et al. 2014), ZORE (Qiu and Zhang 2014) for Chinese, leverage external tools to obtain part-of-speech tags or dependency features and generate syntactic patterns to extract relational facts. These pattern-based approaches cannot handle the complexity and diversity of languages well, and the extraction is usually far from satisfactory. To alleviate the burden of designing manual features, some neural ORE models have been proposed, typically adopting the methods of either sequence labeling or span selection. But their tasks still do not consider non-existent or multi-span relations. MGD-GNN (Lyu et al. 2021) for Chinese ORE constructs a multi-grained dependency graph and utilizes a span selection model to predict based on character features. Compared with our method, MGD-GNN heavily relies on dependency information and cannot deal with multiple languages. Jia, Xiang, and Chen transform English ORE into a sequence labeling process and present a hybrid neural network NST, whereas a dependency on PoS-taggers may introduce error propagation to NST. Improving NST, the current state-of-the-art ORE model LOREM (Harting, Mesbah, and Lofi 2020) works as a multilingual-embedded sequence-labeling method based on CNN/BiLSTM. Identical to our model, LOREM does not rely on language-specific knowledge or external tools. However, LOREM is restricted to binary-argument relation extraction and tends to output single spans rather than multi-span relations. Furthermore, based on our comparison of architectures in Section 4.1, LOREM suffers from inherent problems in learning long-range sequence dependencies (Vaswani et al. 2017), basic to computing token relevances to gold relations.

The benchmark ORE datasets in English (*En*) and Chinese (*Zh*) include OpenIE4^{En} (Mausam 2016), LSOIE-wiki^{En}, LSOIE-sci^{En} (Solawetz and Larson 2021), COER^{Zh} (Tseng et al. 2014), and SAOKE^{Zh} (Sun et al. 2018), whose contexts are complex or multiple sentences. Nevertheless, the five datasets do not contain tuples with non-existent relations. Moreover, tuples in the datasets except SAOKE^{Zh} are in a fixed triple form of (Arg_1, *Single-span Rel.*, Arg_2) without tuples of multi-span relations and possible polyadic arguments. To our best knowledge, SAOKE^{Zh} is the only multi-span Chinese ORE dataset, and there are no English datasets with multi-span relations so far. We need to clarify that the triple-form data take the majority of tuples in common KGs and their extraction accuracy is the most influential part of the overall performance. But it is also significant to measure the multi-span extraction ability of an extractor since the multi-span form can express rich semantics and constitute diverse relationships in existing languages.

The motivations of our work are as follows. **(1) Non-existent relations**: Most knowledge graphs are constructed using a pipeline of named entity recognition (NER), relation extraction (with open relation normalization), and entity linking (Martínez-Rodríguez, López-Arévalo, and Ríos-Alvarado 2018). However, an arbitrary argument tuple identified from NER does not necessarily entail a semantic relationship, especially when the arguments are separated distantly from each other in a long context (typically in complex-sentence-level or document-level relation extraction). Thus, it is significant to facilitate ORE methods with the twofold ability to extract existing relation spans and detect non-existent relationships. **(2) Multi-span relations**: Some languages, such as Chinese, express the connections among the arguments in a flexible way of single and multiple spans, as illustrated in Figure 1. Multi-span relations are often linked to polyadic arguments from our observation of SAOKE^{Zh}. The multi-span form of relations generally represents richer and more precise meanings, thus playing an essential role in the diverse relationships in KGs. The above two further tasks of ORE are practical and vital demands of KG construction and general-domain information extraction, but neglected by the previous works. **(3) Data augmentation**: Since there are no datasets with non-existent relationships, we re-construct four public ORE datasets covering English and Chinese to derive the corresponding augmented datasets with non-existent relations for training models. **(4) Proposed QuORE framework**: We design a query-based multi-head framework QuORE to extract single/multi-span relations and detect non-existent relationships effectively. Given an argument tuple and its context, we first create a query template containing the argument information and derive a contextual representation of query and context via a pre-trained language model BERT (Devlin et al. 2019), which provides a deep understanding of query and context, and models the information interaction between them. The two sub-modules of multi-head framework are SSE (Single-span Extraction) and QASL (Query-based Sequence Labeling), which have different specialties in extraction. The sub-module SSE is used for effective single-span relation extraction, while QASL is designed for labeling non-existent relation sequences and multi-span relationships. Finally, our multi-head framework dynamically decides which sub-module (i.e., head) to predict a relation depending on the input.

To summarize, the main contributions of this work[1] are:

- We define two further tasks of open relation extraction with non-existent and multi-span relationships considering the practical demands of ORE.
- By re-constructing some existing ORE datasets, we derive and publicize four augmented datasets with non-existent relationships and a multi-span relation dataset.
- We propose a query-based multi-head framework QuORE to extract single/multi-span relations and detect non-existent relationships effectively. We conduct extensive experiments, showing that our models outperform the state-of-the-art ORE method LOREM in the extraction of existing single/multi-span relations and the overall performances of non-existent relationships. We also give an in-depth analysis of the functions of QuORE sub-modules.

2 QuORE Framework

An overview of our QuORE framework is visualized in Figure 2. Given a context and an argument tuple, we first create a query from the arguments based on a template and encode the combination of query and context using the pre-trained BERT. The multi-head selection process dynamically determines a sub-module (SSE or QASL) to output a predicted open relation depending on the input.

[1] https://github.com/farahhuifanyang/QuORE

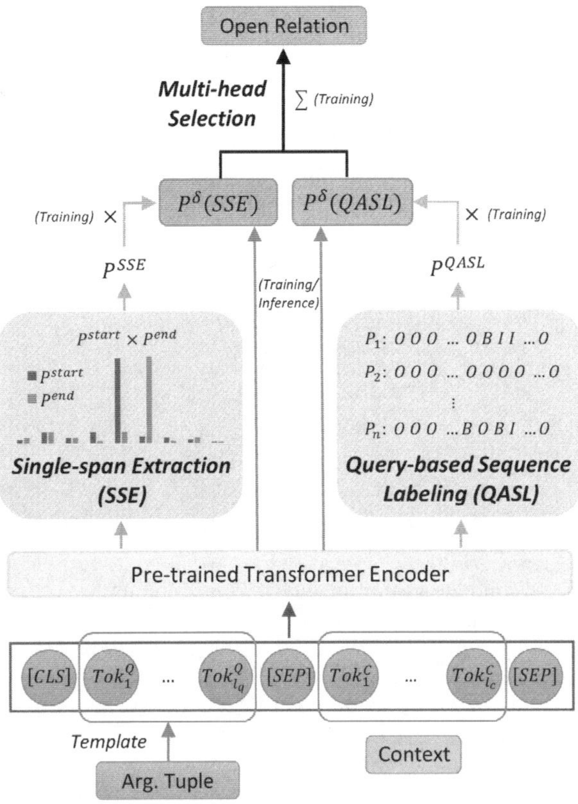

Figure 2: An overview of QuORE framework

2.1 Task Description

Given a context C and an argument tuple $\boldsymbol{A} = (A_1, A_2, ..., A_n)$ in C, an ORE model needs to find the semantic relationship within the tuple $\boldsymbol{A}$ and detect non-existent relation cases, where n is the number of arguments. We denote the context as a word token sequence $\boldsymbol{C} = \{x_i^c\}_{i=1}^{l_c}$ and an argument as a text span $A_k = \{x_i^{a_k}\}_{i=1}^{l_{a_k}}$, where l_c is the context length and l_{a_k} is the k-th argument length. Our goal is to predict a relation $\boldsymbol{R} = (R_1, R_2, ..., R_u)$, a tuple of spans in the context, or return an empty string if there is no open relation, where u is the span number of $\boldsymbol{R}$, a relation span $R_j = \{x_i^{r_j}\}_{i=1}^{l_{r_j}}$ and l_{r_j} is the j-th relation span length.

2.2 Query Template Creation

Provided an argument tuple $(A_1, A_2, ..., A_n)$, we adopt a rule-based method to create the query template

$$\boldsymbol{T} = \langle s_1 \rangle \, A_1 \, \langle s_2 \rangle \, A_2 ... \langle s_n \rangle \, A_n \, \langle s_{n+1} \rangle \tag{1}$$

having $n+1$ slots for a possible relation $(R_1, R_2, ..., R_{n+1})$ with the span number up to $n+1$, where $\langle s_i \rangle$ indicates the i-th slot. The tokens filling a slot are separators of the adjacent arguments (e.g., double-quotes, a comma, or words of natural languages) or a placeholder for a relation span (e.g., a question mark or words of natural languages). In this paper, we adopt the question-mark (QM) style template $\boldsymbol{T}_{QM}$, taking the form of a structured argument-relationship tuple.

$$\boldsymbol{T}_{QM} = \text{“}A_1\text{”?“}A_2\text{”?...?“}A_n\text{”} \tag{2}$$

We also construct other templates, such as the w/o QM style, comma style, and language-specific natural-language (NL) style, but obtain marginal performance differences, where the experiments and analysis can be found in Appendix A.

2.3 Encoder

Given a context $\boldsymbol{C} = \{x_i^c\}_{i=1}^{l_c}$ with l_c tokens and a query $\boldsymbol{Q} = \{x_j^q\}_{j=1}^{l_q}$ with l_q tokens, we employ a pre-trained language model BERT (Devlin et al. 2019) as the encoder to learn the contextual representation for each token. First, we concatenate the query $\boldsymbol{Q}$ and the context $\boldsymbol{C}$ to derive the input $\boldsymbol{I}$ of encoder:

$$\boldsymbol{I} = \{[CLS], x_1^q, ..., x_{l_q}^q, [SEP], x_1^c, ..., x_{l_c}^c, [SEP]\} \tag{3}$$

where $[CLS]$ and $[SEP]$ denote the beginning token and the segment token, respectively.

Next, we generate the initial embedding $\boldsymbol{e}_i$ for each token by summing its word embedding $\boldsymbol{e}_i^w$, position embedding $\boldsymbol{e}_i^p$, and segment embedding $\boldsymbol{e}_i^s$. The sequence embedding $\boldsymbol{E} = \{\boldsymbol{e}_1, \boldsymbol{e}_2, ..., \boldsymbol{e}_m\}$ is then fed into the deep Transformer layers to learn contextual representations with **long-range sequence dependencies via the self-attention mechanism** (Vaswani et al. 2017). Finally, we obtain the last-layer hidden states $\boldsymbol{H} = \{\boldsymbol{h}_1, \boldsymbol{h}_2, ..., \boldsymbol{h}_m\}$ as the contextual representation for the input sequence $\boldsymbol{I}$, where $\boldsymbol{h}_i \in \mathbb{R}^{d_h}$ and d_h indicates the dimension of the last hidden layer of BERT. The length of the sequences $\boldsymbol{I}, \boldsymbol{E}, \boldsymbol{H}$ is denoted as m where $m = l_q + l_c + 3$.

2.4 Single-span Extraction (SSE) Head

Span Prediction The SSE head aims to find a single span in a context as open relation. We utilize two learnable parameter matrices (feed-forward networks) $f_{start} \in \mathbb{R}^{d_h}$ and $f_{end} \in \mathbb{R}^{d_h}$ followed by the softmax normalization, then take each contextual token representation $\boldsymbol{h}_i$ in $\boldsymbol{H}$ as the input to produce the probability of each token i being selected as the start/end of relation span:

$$p_i^{start} = softmax(f_{start}(\boldsymbol{h}_1), ..., f_{start}(\boldsymbol{h}_m))_i \tag{4}$$

$$p_i^{end} = softmax(f_{end}(\boldsymbol{h}_1), ..., f_{end}(\boldsymbol{h}_m))_i \tag{5}$$

We denote $\boldsymbol{p}^{start} = \{p_i^{start}\}_{i=1}^m$ and $\boldsymbol{p}^{end} = \{p_i^{end}\}_{i=1}^m$.

Training The training objective of span prediction is defined as minimizing the cross entropy loss for the start and end selections,

$$p_k^{SSE} = p_{y_k^s}^{start} \times p_{y_k^e}^{end} \tag{6}$$

$$\mathbb{L}^{SSE} = -\frac{1}{N}\sum_k^N \log p_k^{SSE} \tag{7}$$

where y_k^s and y_k^e are respectively ground-truth start and end positions of example k. N is the number of examples.

Inference In the inference process, the relation span is extracted by finding the indices (s, e):

$$(s, e) = \arg\max_{s \leq e}(p_s^{start} \times p_e^{end}) \tag{8}$$

2.5 Query-based Sequence Labeling (QASL) Head

We tackle multi-span and non-existent ORE with query-based sequence labeling. The QASL head utilizes the same contextual representation $\boldsymbol{H}$ from the encoder as the SSE head, but instead of predicting the start and end probabilities, it outputs a probability distribution over a set of labels for each token. We use $\mathbb{V}$ to denote a label set. Formally, given $\boldsymbol{H}$, for each of the m tokens, the QASL head computes the probability of a label assigned to the i-th token as

$$\boldsymbol{p}_i^{label} = softmax(\boldsymbol{h}_i \boldsymbol{W}_{\mathbb{V}} + \boldsymbol{b}_{\mathbb{V}}) \tag{9}$$

where d_h is the hidden dimension of the encoder, $\boldsymbol{W}_{\mathbb{V}} \in \mathbb{R}^{d_h \times |\mathbb{V}|}$ and $\boldsymbol{b}_{\mathbb{V}} \in \mathbb{R}^{|\mathbb{V}|}$ are trainable parameters.

In this paper, we experiment with the `BIO` labeling scheme (Sang 2000; Huang, Xu, and Yu 2015), including three label types: `B` (beginning of a relation span), `I` (internal word in a relation span), and `O` (not part of a relation span). The labeling for a sequence of a non-existent relationship is all `O`. We illustrate the labeling for a sequence consisting of a multi-span relation with an instance from Figure 1: "*Donna*$_{\texttt{O}}$ *Karan*$_{\texttt{O}}$ *was*$_{\texttt{O}}$ *born*$_{\texttt{O}}$ *in*$_{\texttt{O}}$ *Long*$_{\texttt{O}}$ *Island*$_{\texttt{O}}$,$_{\texttt{O}}$ *New*$_{\texttt{O}}$ *York*$_{\texttt{O}}$.$_{\texttt{O}}$ *She*$_{\texttt{O}}$ *has*$_{\texttt{O}}$ *a*$_{\texttt{O}}$ *special*$_{\texttt{O}}$ *comprehension*$_{\texttt{O}}$ *of*$_{\texttt{O}}$ *New*$_{\texttt{O}}$ *York*$_{\texttt{O}}$,$_{\texttt{O}}$ *known*$_{\texttt{B}}$ *by*$_{\texttt{I}}$ *the*$_{\texttt{O}}$ *world*$_{\texttt{O}}$ *as*$_{\texttt{B}}$ *a*$_{\texttt{O}}$ *cosmopolitan*$_{\texttt{O}}$ *city*$_{\texttt{O}}$.$_{\texttt{O}}$"

Training We train the QASL head for predicting the correct sequence labeling $\boldsymbol{L} = (y_1, y_2, ..., y_m)$ corresponding to a ground-truth relation by minimizing the loss $\mathbb{L}^{QASL}$:

$$p_k^{QASL} = p(\boldsymbol{L}|\boldsymbol{H}_k) = \prod_{i=1}^{m} p(y_i|y_1, ..., y_{i-1}, \boldsymbol{H}_k) \tag{10}$$

$$\mathbb{L}^{QASL} = -\frac{1}{N}\sum_{k}^{N} \log p_k^{QASL} \tag{11}$$

where m denotes the length of $\boldsymbol{L}$, and $\boldsymbol{H}_k$ is the encoding output of example k. N is the number of examples.

Inference At test time, we would like to find and decode the most likely labeling $\hat{\boldsymbol{L}}$ from all the valid labelings. For the `BIO` scheme, the set of all valid labelings $\mathbb{S}$ includes all labelings that do not have an `I` after an `O`. Given $\boldsymbol{H}$, we hope to find:

$$\hat{\boldsymbol{L}} = \arg\max_{\boldsymbol{L}_s \in \mathbb{S}} p(\boldsymbol{L}_s|\boldsymbol{H}) \tag{12}$$

where the used maximization method is the Viterbi algorithm (Viterbi 1967) that performs in linear time.

2.6 Multi-head Framework

We employ a multi-head framework to handle diverse open relations in single/multi-span or non-existent forms. A head $\boldsymbol{\theta}$ is a module that inputs the contextual representation $\boldsymbol{H}$ and calculates a probability distribution over predictions. To derive a relation $\boldsymbol{R}_k$ for the example k having a context $\boldsymbol{C}_k$ and an argument tuple $\boldsymbol{A}_k$, a head $\boldsymbol{\theta}$ computes

$$p_k^{\boldsymbol{\theta}} = p^{\boldsymbol{\theta}}(\boldsymbol{R}_k|\boldsymbol{A}_k, \boldsymbol{C}_k) = p^{\boldsymbol{\theta}}(\boldsymbol{R}_k|\boldsymbol{H}_k) \tag{13}$$

In addition, we train an extra module $\boldsymbol{\delta}$ to decide which head to use for each example:

$$p_k^{\boldsymbol{\delta}} = p^{\boldsymbol{\delta}}(\boldsymbol{\theta}|\boldsymbol{A}_k, \boldsymbol{C}_k) = p^{\boldsymbol{\delta}}(\boldsymbol{\theta}|\boldsymbol{H}_k) \tag{14}$$

Training The training object of multi-head framework is to minimize the loss $\mathbb{L}^{MH}$ corresponding to the cumulative probability of each head's prediction:

$$p(\boldsymbol{R}_k|\boldsymbol{A}_k, \boldsymbol{C}_k) = \sum_{\boldsymbol{\theta}} p^{\boldsymbol{\delta}}(\boldsymbol{\theta}|\boldsymbol{A}_k, \boldsymbol{C}_k) \times p^{\boldsymbol{\theta}}(\boldsymbol{R}_k|\boldsymbol{A}_k, \boldsymbol{C}_k) \tag{15}$$

$$\mathbb{L}^{MH} = -\frac{1}{N}\sum_{k}^{N} \log p(\boldsymbol{R}_k|\boldsymbol{A}_k, \boldsymbol{C}_k) \tag{16}$$

Inference In the inference process, we first predict which head to function using Equation 14, then output the prediction from the chosen head.

With this framework, we integrate both SSE and QASL heads, dynamically deciding which head to utilize based on the input and achieving different forms of open relations.

3 Experimental Setup

We propose the following hypotheses and design a set of experiments to examine the performances of QuORE multi-head framework and its sub-modules. We choose LOREM as the comparison baseline because it is the state-of-the-art ORE method and the only multi-lingual neural model capable of processing English and Chinese texts. We arrange the hypotheses based on the following considerations: $\mathbf{H_1}$: As stated in Introduction, the extraction of (*Arg₁, Single-span Rel., Arg₂*) is the most influential part of the overall performance since the triple form takes the majority of tuples in KGs. Thus, we first evaluate on the original single-span OpenIE4^{En}, LSOIE-wiki^{En}, LSOIE-sci^{En}, COER^{Zh} datasets. $\mathbf{H_2}$: As a follow-up to $\mathbf{H_1}$, we augment the above four datasets and investigate the twofold abilities of existing and non-existent relation extraction. $\mathbf{H_3}$ explores the multi-span relation extraction capabilities on the existing multi-span-style SAOKE^{Zh}.

- $\mathbf{H_1}$: For extracting existent single-span open relations, QuORE can outperform the SOTA model LOREM with notable performances of the multi-head framework and the SSE model.
- $\mathbf{H_2}$: For open relation extraction with non-existent relationships, our multi-head framework can process an input using a suitable sub-module, flexibly determining whether to extract or not and exceeding LOREM in overall performances.
- $\mathbf{H_3}$: For a challenging Chinese ORE dataset SAOKE^{Zh} with multi-span relations and polyadic arguments, QuORE shows effectiveness in extracting relations with a diverse number of spans.

	OpenIE4^{En}			LSOIE-wiki^{En}			LSOIE-sci^{En}			COER^{Zh}			SAOKE^{Zh}	
	#Con	#Tup$_{ori}$	#Tup$_{aug}$	#Con	#Tup$_{ori}$	#Tup$_{aug}$	#Con	#Tup$_{ori}$	#Tup$_{aug}$	#Con	#Tup$_{ori}$	#Tup$_{aug}$	#Con	#Tup$_{ori}$
Train	11998	21295	30143	11872	11872	19145	11983	11983	18931	12000	13914	20463	11680	24451
Dev	1500	2660	3749	3142	3142	5045	1498	1498	2376	1500	1746	2572	1480	3059
Test	1499	2567	3647	3202	3202	5065	1499	1499	2380	1500	1771	2633	1461	3126

Table 1: Statistics of five datasets and corresponding augmentations. *(Con: Contexts; Tup: Tuples; ori: original; aug: augmented.)*

3.1 Datasets and Augmentation

We evaluate the performances of our proposed QuORE framework on five public datasets covering English (*En*) and Chinese (*Zh*). Table 1 lists the statistics of the used training, development and test sets.

- **OpenIE4^{En}**[2] was bootstrapped from extractions of OpenIE4 (Mausam 2016) from Wikipedia and annotated with POS and dependency information by Zhan and Zhao.
- **LSOIE-wiki^{En}** and **LSOIE-sci^{En}**[3] (Solawetz and Larson 2021) were algorithmically re-purposed from the QA-SRL BANK 2.0 dataset (FitzGerald et al. 2018), covering the domains of Wikipedia and science, respectively.
- **COER^{Zh}**[4] is a high-quality Chinese knowledge base, created by an unsupervised open extractor (Tseng et al. 2014) from heterogeneous web text.
- **SAOKE^{Zh}**[5] (Sun et al. 2018) is a human-annotated large-scale dataset for Chinese open information extraction, containing a single/multi-span relation and binary/polyadic arguments in a tuple.

In the data cleaning process, we only retain argument-relation tuples whose components are spans of a context. From our statistics, a tuple from OpenIE4^{En}, LSOIE-wiki^{En}, LSOIE-sci^{En}, and COER^{Zh} is made up of a single-span relation and binary arguments. After preprocessing, we reconstruct SAOKE^{Zh} into a dataset with single/multi-span relations and binary/polyadic arguments.

To adapt the data to our setting of ORE with non-existent relations, we augment the datasets that only contain binary-argument tuples. We implement a rule-based augmentation method, as shown in Algorithm 1. In this way, we add 0 or 1 non-existent relation to each context and consider the arguments having an order to specify the direction of a relation. The number of tuples before and after augmentation are recorded in Table 1 as #Tup$_{ori}$ and #Tup$_{aug}$, respectively. By randomly dividing a dataset, we obtain close ratios $R_{o/a} = \frac{\#Tup_{\text{ori}}}{\#Tup_{\text{aug}}}$ among the training, development, and test sets. The percents $R_{o/a}$ (%) of test sets in OpenIE4^{En}, LSOIE-wiki^{En}, LSOIE-sci^{En}, and COER^{Zh} are respectively 70.48, 63.22, 62.98, and 67.26. We omit to augment SAOKE^{Zh} for the complexity of permutations of multiple arguments and the ambiguity of Chinese that an argument tuple can entail a certain relation when containing some unnecessary argument or not.

[2]https://github.com/zhanjunlang/Span_OIE

[3]https://github.com/Jacobsolawetz/large-scale-oie

[4]https://github.com/TJUNLP/COER

[5]https://ai.baidu.com/broad/introduction?dataset=saoke

Algorithm 1 Augmentation for Non-existent Open Relations

Input: All tuples $Tps = [tps_1, tps_2, ..., tps_k]$ of existent relations in the corresponding k contexts, where $tps_i = [(A_{i,j,1}, R_{i,j}, A_{i,j,2})_{j=1}^{l_i}]$, $i \in [1, k]$ and l_i is the number of tuples in tps_i

Output: Augmented tuples $Tps^{aug} = [tps_1^{aug}, tps_2^{aug}, ..., tps_k^{aug}]$ with non-existent relations

Let Tps^{aug} be an empty list
for tuples tps in Tps **do**
  Let S_{arg} be an empty set and tps^{aug} be a deep copy of tps
  for tuple tp in tps **do**
    Find the arguments A_1, A_2 in tp
    S_{arg}.*ADD*(A_1) and S_{arg}.*ADD*(A_2)
  end for
  Construct the argument-pair permutations P_{arg} of length 2 from S_{arg}
  for tuple tp in tps **do**
    Remove the pair (A_1, A_2) of tp from P_{arg}
  end for
  Add a special empty pair (A_0, A_0) to P_{arg}
  Randomly select a pair $p_{non} = (A_x, A_y)$ from P_{arg}
  if $p_{non} \neq (A_0, A_0)$ **then**
    Create a non-existent relation tuple $tp_{non} = (A_x, empty\_str, A_y)$
    tps^{aug}.*ADD*(tp_{non}) then Tps^{aug}.*ADD*(tps^{aug})
  else
    Tps^{aug}.*ADD*(tps^{aug})
  end if
end for
return Tps^{aug}

3.2 Implementations

Encoder We utilize the *bert-base-cased* language model as the encoder on English datasets and *bert-base-chinese* on Chinese datasets.

Model Training BertAdam optimizer is used with default parameters and a learning rate of 3e-5. We train on a single NVIDIA Tesla P100 GPU with a batch size of 12 for 15 epochs with an early-stopping patience of 5. Evaluation is performed with our token-level evaluation script.

Sub-modules In some experiments, we implement the multi-head QuORE model along with its individual sub-modules (i.e., SSE and QASL models) which work solely controlled by our *not-to-integrate* option.

	OpenIE4^{En}				LSOIE-wiki^{En}			
	P	R	F1	EM	P	R	F1	EM
SSE	**.9911**	**.9934**	**.9910**	**.9817**	.9639	**.9703**	**.9650**	.9572
QASL	.9820	.9861	.9821	.9677	.9587	.9671	.9611	.9472
Multi-H	.9897	.9913	.9891	.9790	**.9653**	.9666	**.9650**	**.9600**
LOREM	.9287	.9441	.9216	.8098	.7199	.7108	.7138	.7017
	LSOIE-sci^{En}				COER^{Zh}			
	P	R	F1	EM	P	R	F1	EM
SSE	.9678	.9746	.9690	.9566	.9435	**.9585**	**.9377**	**.8837**
QASL	.9640	.9730	.9664	.9500	.9396	.9504	.9318	.8758
Multi-H	**.9730**	**.9793**	**.9740**	**.9620**	**.9475**	.9529	.9356	.8826
LOREM	.7812	.7698	.7736	.7585	.4537	.4535	.4228	.2693

Table 2: Evaluation on four datasets with all existing open relations. *(Multi-H: Multi-head.)*

3.3 Evaluation Metrics

We keep track of the metrics of F1 score, precision, recall, and Exact Match (EM). (1) For existing relations, the metrics are token-level. The F1 score measures the average overlap between a model's prediction and the ground-truth relation. Formally, F1 denotes the harmonic mean of precision and recall, where precision is defined as the ratio of correctly predicted tokens to the total number of predicted relation tokens. Recall, meanwhile, is the ratio of correctly predicted tokens to the total number of tokens in the ground-truth relation. Exact Match considers if a prediction exactly matches the correct relation, which means every token is the same. (2) For non-existent relations, we regard the values of F1, precision, and recall as the same as Exact Match, indicating if the prediction suggests non-existent, then the four metrics are all 1; if existing, then 0.

4 Experimental Results

4.1 $\mathbf{H_1}$: QuORE for Existing Single-span Relations

In $\mathbf{H_1}$, we train three individual models of SSE, QASL and multi-head to compare with the SOTA method LOREM. From Table 2, we observe that all the models of QuORE outperform LOREM on four existing single-span relation datasets of English and Chinese, with notable performances from the multi-head and SSE models. We next explain the advantages of QuORE over LOREM by comparing the two architectures.

LOREM encodes an input sequence using pre-trained word embeddings and adds argument tag vectors to the word embeddings. The argument tag vectors are simple one-hot encoded vectors indicating if a word is part of an argument. Then LOREM utilizes CNN and BiLSTM layers to form a representation of each word. The CNN is used to capture the local feature information, as LOREM considers that certain parts of the context might have higher chances of containing relation words than others. Meanwhile, the BiLSTM captures the forward and backward context of each word. Next, a CRF layer tags each word using the NST tagging scheme (Jia, Xiang, and Chen 2018): `S` (Single-word relation), `B` (Beginning of a relation), `I` (Inside a relation), `E` (Ending of a relation), `O` (Outside a relation).

Our QuORE framework generates the initial representations with word embeddings and position embeddings from BERT (Devlin et al. 2019). Unlike the simple one-hot argument vectors of LOREM, QuORE derives the argument information by creating a query template of arguments. We combine the query with the context to form the input of encoder, and the encoder outputs a contextual representation that we utilize to compute the relevance of each token to a gold relation (Equation 4, 5 for SSE and Equation 9 for QASL). Moreover, by employing the self-attention mechanism of the Transformers-based encoder, QuORE has the benefit of learning long-range dependencies easier and deriving a better representation for computing relevances, which we interpret in the following. Learning long-range dependencies is a key challenge in encoding sequences and solving related tasks (Vaswani et al. 2017). One key factor affecting the ability to learn such dependencies is the length of the paths forward and backward signals have to traverse between any two input and output positions in the network. The shorter these paths between any combination of positions in the input and output sequences, the easier it is to learn long-range dependencies. Vaswani et al. also provide the maximum path length between any two input and output positions in self-attention, recurrent, and convolutional layers, which are $O(1)$, $O(n)$, and $O(\log_k(n))$, respectively. (k is the kernel width of a convolutional layer.) The constant path length of self-attention makes it easier to learn long-range dependencies than CNN and BiLSTM layers. Despite the gating in LSTMs and gradient clipping (Graves 2013), recurrent layers are difficult to optimize for such long dependencies due to gradient vanishing and explosion problems. As for CNNs, the way they derive dependencies is by applying different kernels to a sequence. For example, a kernel of size 2 learns connections between pairs of words, a kernel of size 3 captures connections between triplets of words. The evident problem here is that the number of kernels required to capture dependencies among all combina-

	$\text{OpenIE4}^{\text{En}}_{\text{Aug}}$				$\text{LSOIE-wiki}^{\text{En}}_{\text{Aug}}$			
	P	R	F1	EM	P	R	F1	EM
Multi-H [All]	.9602	.9624	**.9605**	.9544	.9165	.9170	**.9159**	.9102
[Exg.]	.9744	.9774	**.9748**	.9661	.9582	.9589	**.9572**	.9482
[Non.]	.9265	.9265	**.9265**	.9265	.8449	.8449	.8449	.8449
LOREM [All]	.8971	.8855	.8816	.8108	.7811	.7751	.7771	.7692
[Exg.]	.9024	.8859	.8803	.7798	.7205	.7111	.7142	.7017
[Non.]	.8847	.8847	.8847	.8847	.8857	.8857	**.8857**	.8857

	$\text{LSOIE-sci}^{\text{En}}_{\text{Aug}}$				$\text{COER}^{\text{Zh}}_{\text{Aug}}$			
	P	R	F1	EM	P	R	F1	EM
Multi-H [All]	.9402	.9450	**.9411**	.9345	.9415	.9397	**.9307**	.8959
[Exg.]	.9605	.9680	**.9619**	.9513	.9396	.9369	**.9235**	.8718
[Non.]	.9058	.9058	.9058	.9058	.9455	.9455	**.9455**	.9455
LOREM [All]	.7983	.7912	.7935	.7840	.6053	.5888	.5784	.4839
[Exg.]	.7225	.7111	.7149	.6998	.4420	.4175	.4020	.2614
[Non.]	.9281	.9281	**.9281**	.9281	.9408	.9408	.9408	.9408

Table 3: Evaluation on four augmented datasets with non-existent open relations. *(Multi-H: Multi-head; Exg.: Existing; Non.: Non-existent; Aug: Augmented.)* The measures of [All], [Exg.], and [Non.] are the performances on a whole dataset and the subsets of existing and non-existent relationships, respectively.

tions of words would be enormous and unpractical, because of the exponentially growing combinations when increasing the maximum length of sequences. Overall, QuORE achieves substantial improvements over LOREM in extracting existing relations due to the better sequence representations with long-term dependencies, a basis of computing token relevances to gold relations.

If we focus on the performances of SSE, QASL and multi-head models, we find that the results from multi-head and SSE are relatively more significant than QASL. The SSE model exceeds QASL with marginal improvements in F1 scores on the four datasets of single-span relations, which is in line with the advantage of SSE on the single-span extraction task. The results also suggest that the single/multi-span QASL may be used by itself as a more general extraction method on these single-span relation datasets. Meanwhile, we observe that the multi-head models maintain high precisions due to integration.

4.2 H_2: QuORE with Non-existent Relations

For open relation extraction with non-existent relationships, we compare our multi-head QuORE model and LOREM on four augmented datasets, as shown in Table 3. We also provide an in-depth analysis of the functions of each submodule (i.e., head) in our multi-head framework via the visualization in Figure 3.

Table 3 presents the evaluation results of multi-head QuORE and LOREM on the augmented datasets and their subsets of existing and non-existent relationships. Our multi-head model achieves more precise outcomes on the overall performances and the parts of existing relations than LOREM on all four datasets. LOREM, meanwhile, outperforms on the non-existent relation subsets of $\text{LSOIE-wiki}^{\text{En}}_{\text{Aug}}$ and $\text{LSOIE-sci}^{\text{En}}_{\text{Aug}}$. If we focus on contrasting the partial measures between the [Exg.] and [Non.] parts of multi-head QuORE itself, we observe that the performances in [Non.] part are not compatible with the ones in [Exg.] on the datasets except $\text{COER}^{\text{Zh}}_{\text{Aug}}$, implying there exists improvement space for the task of verifying non-existent relations.

We further probe into the functions of SSE and QASL heads in our multi-head framework by studying the data percents processed by each head and the corresponding F1 scores in Figure 3. By observation, the Subfigures 3a, 3c, and 3d present a similar trend in the data distribution while the Subfigure 3b is different. In the following, we first analyze the performances on the three datasets of $\text{OpenIE4}^{\text{En}}_{\text{Aug}}$, $\text{LSOIE-sci}^{\text{En}}_{\text{Aug}}$, and $\text{COER}^{\text{Zh}}_{\text{Aug}}$.

In the Subfigures 3a, 3c, and 3d, the vast majority of examples with existing relations are distributed to the SSE head due to the observed high precision of SSE in extracting single spans from Table 2. Meanwhile, the QASL head is responsible for most non-existent relationships, obtaining notable results with F1 scores (%) of 97.27, 94.10, and 95.88 on its processed [Non.] parts of $\text{OpenIE4}^{\text{En}}_{\text{Aug}}$, $\text{LSOIE-sci}^{\text{En}}_{\text{Aug}}$, and $\text{COER}^{\text{Zh}}_{\text{Aug}}$, respectively. We also observe that SSE is not available to detect non-existent relations from 3a and 3c, and QASL cannot extract effectively if given only a small portion of existing relation examples.

The data distribution in $\text{LSOIE-wiki}^{\text{En}}_{\text{Aug}}$ (Subfigure 3b) is different from the other three datasets, suggesting that our multi-head framework can dynamically decide which head to use if the overall data feature of a dataset changes. In Subfigure 3b, the non-existent relations are allocated to the QASL head similarly to the other three charts, but QASL also processes the large part of existing relations, illustrating that QASL has the general ability to extract existing relations and detect non-existent relationships.

On the whole, the overall performances from Table 3 and

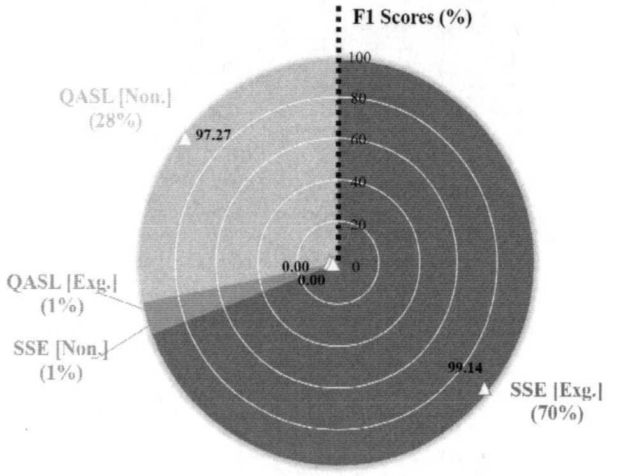

(a) OpenIE4$^{\text{En}}_{\text{Aug}}$

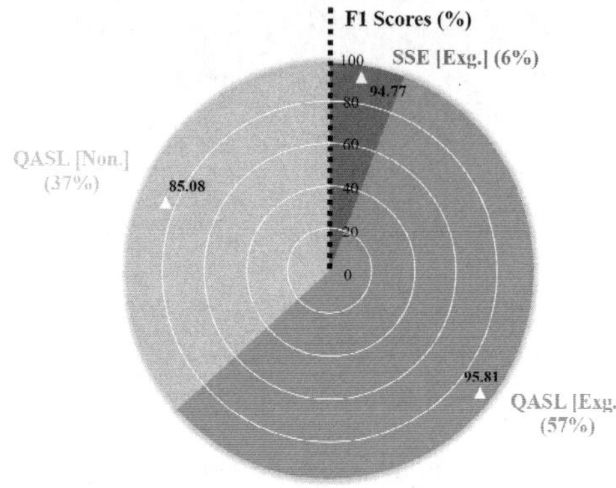

(b) LSOIE-wiki$^{\text{En}}_{\text{Aug}}$

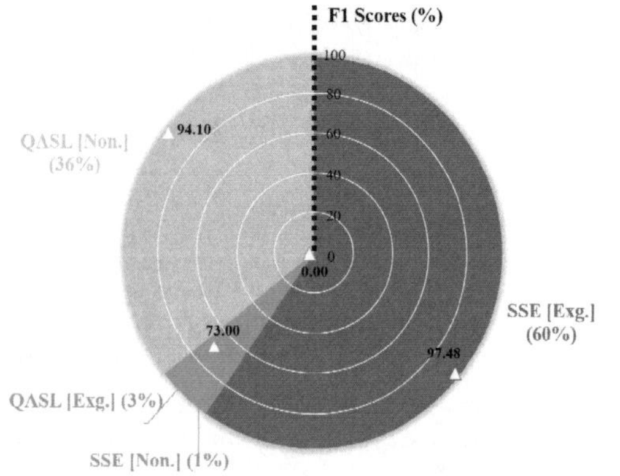

(c) LSOIE-sci$^{\text{En}}_{\text{Aug}}$

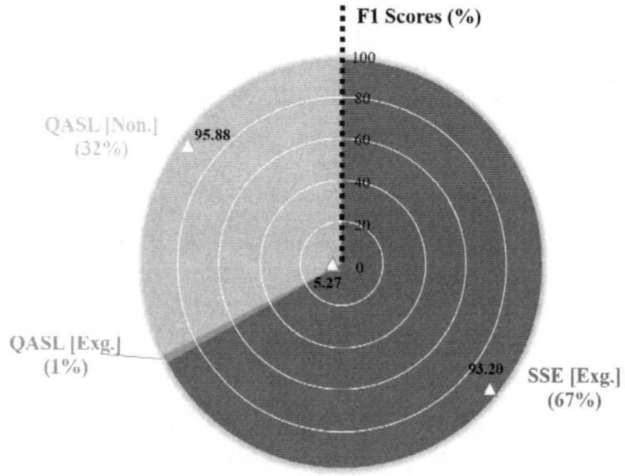

(d) COER$^{\text{Zh}}_{\text{Aug}}$

Figure 3: Performances of the SSE and QASL sub-modules in multi-head QuORE on existing and non-existent relations from the four augmented datasets. *(Exg.: Existing; Non.: Non-existent.)* The percents in the parentheses are the data percentage processed by a sub-module, and [Exg.] or [Non.] denotes the relation type. The F1 scores are beside the triangles of each part in a pie chart.

the detailed measures of each head in Figure 3 show that our multi-head model can determine a suitable sub-module to work dynamically based on the input data mixed with both existing and non-existent relationships.

4.3 H_3: QuORE with Multi-span Relations

In the challenging Chinese dataset SAOKE^{Zh}, the relation tuples are not necessarily in the form of single-span relations and binary arguments; some have multi-span relations along with polyadic arguments, as shown in Figure 1. We evaluate the multi-span extraction abilities of QuORE and LOREM on SAOKE^{Zh} and present the results in Table 4 and Figure 4.

Table 4 shows that our individual SSE, QASL and multi-head models all outperform LOREM. We also investigate from the results on SAOKE^{Zh} and COER^{Zh} from Tables 2 and 4 that the performances of LOREM on the Chinese datasets are dissatisfactory. If we focus on the extracted number of spans by the multi-head QuORE and LOREM in Figure 4, we discover that LOREM tends to output single-span relations while QuORE is able to generate a various number of spans dynamically depending on the input and achieve relatively high precisions. The sub-module SSE accounts for the effective single-span extraction, and QASL contributes to the diverse outputs of multi-span relationships. Thus, the overall performance of multi-head model is influenced by the above specialties of its two sub-modules.

4.4 Case Study

We conduct case studies of the above three hypotheses to compare the predictions of the multi-head QuORE and LOREM. We present context words in double-quotes.

- Cases in $\mathbf{H_1}$: (1) We notice that QuORE is better at handling cases where arguments separately locate in main and subordinate clauses than LOREM. For instance, given a sentence "*Different enzymes that catalyze the same chemical reaction are called isozymes.*" and the arguments ("*Different enzymes*", "*the same chemical reaction*"), QuORE gives out the gold relation "*catalyze*" whereas LOREM predicts "*called*" incorrectly. (2) We summarize that the major errors of QuORE occur in cases where the relation concerns modal verbs or auxiliary verbs, such as "*can*" and "*have been*". QuORE may

	SAOKE^{Zh}			
	P	R	F1	EM
SSE	**.9123**	.8015	.8114	.6045
QASL	.8937	.9162	.8867	**.7389**
Multi-H	.8918	**.9220**	**.8887**	.7347
LOREM	.6904	.5349	.5657	.3544

Table 4: Evaluation on SAOKE^{Zh} with multi-span relations

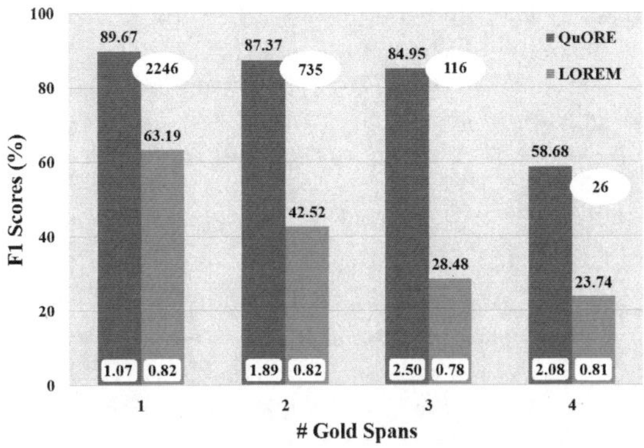

Figure 4: Comparison of QuORE (multi-head) and LOREM on the test set of SAOKE^{Zh} by the number of spans in gold relations. Labels at the bottom indicate the average number of predicted spans. Ovals at the top denote the number of examples.

extract either fewer or more words than a gold relation, e.g., provided a sentence "*Algae had covered moist land areas for millions of years.*" and the arguments ("*Algae*", "*moist land areas*"), QuORE predicts "*covered*" as the relation, fewer than the ground truth "*had covered*". Meanwhile, we observe that LOREM also outputs "*covered*".

- Case in $\mathbf{H_2}$: QuORE can take the argument order into account and detect a non-existent relation. Given a context "*The bus was out-of-control and going downhill when it struck a truck from behind.*" and the arguments ("*downhill*", "*The bus*"), our model correctly predicts a non-existent relationship considering the reverse order of arguments.
- Case in $\mathbf{H_3}$: Provided a multi-span case of a context "“远望5号”测量船给“嫦娥一号”下达指令，指示“嫦娥”不断变轨，使其按照固定轨道顺利运行。" and the arguments ("“远望5号”", "“嫦娥”"), QuORE outputs the gold multi-span relation ("指示", "不断变轨").

5 Related Work

We have reviewed the previous open relation extraction systems and datasets in the Introduction. In this section, we focus on the related works of our model framework.

Multi-span Extraction Some recent studies on machine reading comprehension have designed different models to extract multi-span answers. Segal et al. cast the multi-span question answering task as a sequence tagging problem, predicting for each token whether it is part of the answer. Yang, Zhang, and Zhao modify the single-span extraction method by adding a special virtual span to generate multi-span answers. Hu et al. propose to predict the number of output spans for each question and use a non-differentiable inference procedure to find them in the text.

Multi-head Models There has been substantial interest in training a multi-head model for multiple tasks, including the fields of languages (Collobert and Weston 2008; Liu et al. 2019; McCann et al. 2018; Dua et al. 2019; Hu et al. 2019; Segal et al. 2020), computer vision (Lu et al. 2020), and robotics (Teh et al. 2017).

6 Conclusion

Our work targets the practical demands of open relation extraction with non-existent and multi-span relationships using a novel query-based multi-head framework QuORE. The experiments and analyses present the effective performances in the multiple tasks and corresponding explanations. In the future, we will enhance the model architecture, transfer our model to other languages, and explore the few/zero-shot learning abilities in low-resource languages and domains.

A Different Query Templates

We analyze the effects of different query templates by experimenting with the question-mark (QM) style $\boldsymbol{T}_{QM}$, w/o QM style $\boldsymbol{T}_{w/oQM}$, comma style $\boldsymbol{T}_{comma}$, and language-specific natural-language (NL) style $\boldsymbol{T}_{NL}$ in English (*En*) or Chinese (*Zh*), as listed below. However, the evaluation results of these templates have marginal differences, which is observed on all datasets used in this paper. We present the evaluation of different queries on LSOIE-wiki^{En} in Table 5. The possible reason for the marginal results is that all the templates consist of the necessary argument information, and the representations learned via a pre-trained Transformers encoder are similar due to the robust expression ability of the encoder.

- $\boldsymbol{T}_{w/oQM}$ = "A_1" "A_2" ... "A_n"
- $\boldsymbol{T}_{comma}$ = "A_1", "A_2", ..., "A_n"
- $\boldsymbol{T}_{NL^{En}}$ = What is the relation among "A_1", ..., and "A_n"?
- $\boldsymbol{T}_{NL^{Zh}}$ = "A_1", "A_2", ..., "A_n"之间的关系是?

		QM	w/o QM	Comma	NL^{En}
SSE	F1	0.9650	0.9654	0.9660	**0.9663**
	EM	0.9572	0.9594	0.9588	**0.9597**
QASL	F1	**0.9611**	0.9548	0.9537	0.9585
	EM	**0.9472**	0.9422	0.9419	0.9403
Multi-H	F1	0.9650	0.9664	**0.9674**	0.9640
	EM	**0.9600**	0.9582	**0.9600**	0.9572

Table 5: Evaluation of different queries on LSOIE-wiki^{En}

Acknowledgments

This work is supported by the NSFC-General Technology Basic Research Joint Funds under Grant (U1936220), the National Natural Science Foundation of China under Grant (61972047) and the National Key Research and Development Program of China (2018YFC0831500).

References

Banko, M.; Cafarella, M. J.; Soderland, S.; Broadhead, M.; and Etzioni, O. 2007. Open information extraction from the web. In Veloso, M. M., ed., *IJCAI 2007, Proceedings of the 20th International Joint Conference on Artificial Intelligence, Hyderabad, India, January 6-12, 2007*, 2670–2676.

Collobert, R., and Weston, J. 2008. A unified architecture for natural language processing: deep neural networks with multitask learning. In Cohen, W. W.; McCallum, A.; and Roweis, S. T., eds., *Machine Learning, Proceedings of the Twenty-Fifth International Conference (ICML 2008), Helsinki, Finland, June 5-9, 2008*, volume 307 of *ACM International Conference Proceeding Series*, 160–167. ACM.

Corro, L. D., and Gemulla, R. 2013. Clausie: clause-based open information extraction. In Schwabe, D.; Almeida, V. A. F.; Glaser, H.; Baeza-Yates, R.; and Moon, S. B., eds., *22nd International World Wide Web Conference, WWW '13, Rio de Janeiro, Brazil, May 13-17, 2013*, 355–366. International World Wide Web Conferences Steering Committee / ACM.

Devlin, J.; Chang, M.; Lee, K.; and Toutanova, K. 2019. BERT: pre-training of deep bidirectional transformers for language understanding. In Burstein, J.; Doran, C.; and Solorio, T., eds., *Proceedings of the 2019 Conference of the North American Chapter of the Association for Computational Linguistics: Human Language Technologies, NAACL-HLT 2019, Minneapolis, MN, USA, June 2-7, 2019, Volume 1 (Long and Short Papers)*, 4171–4186. Association for Computational Linguistics.

Dua, D.; Wang, Y.; Dasigi, P.; Stanovsky, G.; Singh, S.; and Gardner, M. 2019. DROP: A reading comprehension benchmark requiring discrete reasoning over paragraphs. In Burstein, J.; Doran, C.; and Solorio, T., eds., *Proceedings of the 2019 Conference of the North American Chapter of the Association for Computational Linguistics: Human Language Technologies, NAACL-HLT 2019, Minneapolis, MN, USA, June 2-7, 2019, Volume 1 (Long and Short Papers)*, 2368–2378. Association for Computational Linguistics.

Fader, A.; Soderland, S.; and Etzioni, O. 2011. Identifying relations for open information extraction. In *Proceedings of the 2011 Conference on Empirical Methods in Natural Language Processing, EMNLP 2011, 27-31 July 2011, John McIntyre Conference Centre, Edinburgh, UK, A meeting of SIGDAT, a Special Interest Group of the ACL*, 1535–1545. ACL.

FitzGerald, N.; Michael, J.; He, L.; and Zettlemoyer, L. 2018. Large-scale QA-SRL parsing. In Gurevych, I., and Miyao, Y., eds., *Proceedings of the 56th Annual Meeting of the Association for Computational Linguistics, ACL 2018, Melbourne, Australia, July 15-20, 2018, Volume 1: Long Papers*, 2051–2060. Association for Computational Linguistics.

Graves, A. 2013. Generating sequences with recurrent neural networks. *CoRR* abs/1308.0850.

Harting, T.; Mesbah, S.; and Lofi, C. 2020. LOREM: language-consistent open relation extraction from unstructured text. In Huang, Y.; King, I.; Liu, T.; and van Steen, M., eds., *WWW '20: The Web Conference 2020, Taipei, Taiwan, April 20-24, 2020*, 1830–1838. ACM / IW3C2.

Hu, M.; Peng, Y.; Huang, Z.; and Li, D. 2019. A multi-type multi-span network for reading comprehension that requires discrete reasoning. In Inui, K.; Jiang, J.; Ng, V.; and Wan, X., eds., *Proceedings of the 2019 Conference on Empirical Methods in Natural Language Processing and the 9th International Joint Conference on Natural Language Processing, EMNLP-IJCNLP 2019, Hong Kong, China, November 3-7, 2019*, 1596–1606. Association for Computational Linguistics.

Huang, Z.; Xu, W.; and Yu, K. 2015. Bidirectional LSTM-CRF models for sequence tagging. *CoRR* abs/1508.01991.

Jia, S.; Xiang, Y.; and Chen, X. 2018. Supervised neural models revitalize the open relation extraction. *CoRR* abs/1809.09408.

Liu, X.; He, P.; Chen, W.; and Gao, J. 2019. Multi-task deep neural networks for natural language understanding. In Korhonen, A.; Traum, D. R.; and Màrquez, L., eds., *Proceedings of the 57th Conference of the Association for Computational Linguistics, ACL 2019, Florence, Italy, July 28-August 2, 2019, Volume 1: Long Papers*, 4487–4496. Association for Computational Linguistics.

Lu, J.; Goswami, V.; Rohrbach, M.; Parikh, D.; and Lee, S. 2020. 12-in-1: Multi-task vision and language representation learning. In *2020 IEEE/CVF Conference on Computer Vision and Pattern Recognition, CVPR 2020, Seattle, WA, USA, June 13-19, 2020*, 10434–10443. Computer Vision Foundation / IEEE.

Lyu, Z.; Shi, K.; Li, X.; Hou, L.; Li, J.; and Song, B. 2021. Multi-grained dependency graph neural network for chinese open information extraction. In Karlapalem, K.; Cheng, H.; Ramakrishnan, N.; Agrawal, R. K.; Reddy, P. K.; Srivastava, J.; and Chakraborty, T., eds., *Advances in Knowledge Discovery and Data Mining - 25th Pacific-Asia Conference, PAKDD 2021, Virtual Event, May 11-14, 2021, Proceedings, Part III*, volume 12714 of *Lecture Notes in Computer Science*, 155–167. Springer.

Martínez-Rodríguez, J.; López-Arévalo, I.; and Ríos-Alvarado, A. B. 2018. Openie-based approach for knowledge graph construction from text. *Expert Syst. Appl.* 113:339–355.

Mausam. 2016. Open information extraction systems and downstream applications. In Kambhampati, S., ed., *Proceedings of the Twenty-Fifth International Joint Conference on Artificial Intelligence, IJCAI 2016, New York, NY, USA, 9-15 July 2016*, 4074–4077. IJCAI/AAAI Press.

McCann, B.; Keskar, N. S.; Xiong, C.; and Socher, R. 2018.

The natural language decathlon: Multitask learning as question answering. *CoRR* abs/1806.08730.

Qiu, L., and Zhang, Y. 2014. ZORE: A syntax-based system for chinese open relation extraction. In Moschitti, A.; Pang, B.; and Daelemans, W., eds., *Proceedings of the 2014 Conference on Empirical Methods in Natural Language Processing, EMNLP 2014, October 25-29, 2014, Doha, Qatar, A meeting of SIGDAT, a Special Interest Group of the ACL*, 1870–1880. ACL.

Sang, E. F. T. K. 2000. Transforming a chunker to a parser. In Daelemans, W.; Sima'an, K.; Veenstra, J.; and Zavrel, J., eds., *Computational Linguistics in the Netherlands 2000, Selected Papers from the Eleventh CLIN Meeting, Tilburg, November 3, 2000*, volume 37 of *Language and Computers - Studies in Practical Linguistics*, 177–188. Rodopi.

Segal, E.; Efrat, A.; Shoham, M.; Globerson, A.; and Berant, J. 2020. A simple and effective model for answering multi-span questions. In Webber, B.; Cohn, T.; He, Y.; and Liu, Y., eds., *Proceedings of the 2020 Conference on Empirical Methods in Natural Language Processing, EMNLP 2020, Online, November 16-20, 2020*, 3074–3080. Association for Computational Linguistics.

Solawetz, J., and Larson, S. 2021. LSOIE: A large-scale dataset for supervised open information extraction. In Merlo, P.; Tiedemann, J.; and Tsarfaty, R., eds., *Proceedings of the 16th Conference of the European Chapter of the Association for Computational Linguistics: Main Volume, EACL 2021, Online, April 19 - 23, 2021*, 2595–2600. Association for Computational Linguistics.

Sun, M.; Li, X.; Wang, X.; Fan, M.; Feng, Y.; and Li, P. 2018. Logician: A unified end-to-end neural approach for open-domain information extraction. In Chang, Y.; Zhai, C.; Liu, Y.; and Maarek, Y., eds., *Proceedings of the Eleventh ACM International Conference on Web Search and Data Mining, WSDM 2018, Marina Del Rey, CA, USA, February 5-9, 2018*, 556–564. ACM.

Teh, Y. W.; Bapst, V.; Czarnecki, W. M.; Quan, J.; Kirkpatrick, J.; Hadsell, R.; Heess, N.; and Pascanu, R. 2017. Distral: Robust multitask reinforcement learning. In Guyon, I.; von Luxburg, U.; Bengio, S.; Wallach, H. M.; Fergus, R.; Vishwanathan, S. V. N.; and Garnett, R., eds., *Advances in Neural Information Processing Systems 30: Annual Conference on Neural Information Processing Systems 2017, December 4-9, 2017, Long Beach, CA, USA*, 4496–4506.

Tseng, Y.; Lee, L.; Lin, S.; Liao, B.; Liu, M.; Chen, H.; Etzioni, O.; and Fader, A. 2014. Chinese open relation extraction for knowledge acquisition. In Bouma, G., and Parmentier, Y., eds., *Proceedings of the 14th Conference of the European Chapter of the Association for Computational Linguistics, EACL 2014, April 26-30, 2014, Gothenburg, Sweden*, 12–16. The Association for Computer Linguistics.

Vaswani, A.; Shazeer, N.; Parmar, N.; Uszkoreit, J.; Jones, L.; Gomez, A. N.; Kaiser, L.; and Polosukhin, I. 2017. Attention is all you need. In Guyon, I.; von Luxburg, U.; Bengio, S.; Wallach, H. M.; Fergus, R.; Vishwanathan, S. V. N.; and Garnett, R., eds., *Advances in Neural Information Processing Systems 30: Annual Conference on Neural Information Processing Systems 2017, December 4-9, 2017, Long Beach, CA, USA*, 5998–6008.

Viterbi, A. J. 1967. Error bounds for convolutional codes and an asymptotically optimum decoding algorithm. *IEEE Trans. Inf. Theory* 13(2):260–269.

Yang, J.; Zhang, Z.; and Zhao, H. 2021. Multi-span style extraction for generative reading comprehension. In Veyseh, A. P. B.; Dernoncourt, F.; Nguyen, T. H.; Chang, W.; and Celi, L. A., eds., *Proceedings of the Workshop on Scientific Document Understanding co-located with 35th AAAI Conference on Artificial Inteligence, SDU@AAAI 2021, Virtual Event, February 9, 2021*, volume 2831 of *CEUR Workshop Proceedings*. CEUR-WS.org.

Zhan, J., and Zhao, H. 2020. Span model for open information extraction on accurate corpus. In *The Thirty-Fourth AAAI Conference on Artificial Intelligence, AAAI 2020, The Thirty-Second Innovative Applications of Artificial Intelligence Conference, IAAI 2020, The Tenth AAAI Symposium on Educational Advances in Artificial Intelligence, EAAI 2020, New York, NY, USA, February 7-12, 2020*, 9523–9530. AAAI Press.

Proceedings of the 19th International Conference on Principles of Knowledge Representation and Reasoning
Main Track

Act for Your Duties but Maintain Your Rights

Shufang Zhu*, **Giuseppe De Giacomo**
Sapienza University of Rome, Rome, Italy
{zhu,degiacomo}@diag.uniroma1.it

Abstract

Most of the synthesis literature has focused on studying how to synthesize a strategy to fulfill a task. This task is a duty for the agent. In this paper, we argue that intelligent agents should also be equipped with rights, that is, tasks that the agent itself can choose to fulfill (e.g., the right of recharging the battery). The agent should be able to maintain these rights while acting for its duties. We study this issue in the context of LTL_f synthesis: we give duties and rights in terms of LTL_f specifications, and synthesize a suitable strategy to achieve the duties that can be modified on-the-fly to achieve also the rights, if the agent chooses to do so. We show that handling rights does not make synthesis substantially more difficult, although it requires a more sophisticated solution concept than standard LTL_f synthesis. We also extend our results to the case in which further duties and rights are given to the agent while already executing.

1 Introduction

Consider the following example: we give to a robot the task of cleaning one by one series of rooms. The robot has a model of the world describing the effects of its actions, and, given the task specification, it synthesizes a strategy to accomplish its cleaning task. However, in going after its task, the robot would like to be sure to be able to recharge its battery, if it thinks the battery level is getting too low. Both cleaning and recharging batteries are (temporally extended) tasks. Once the cleaning task is accepted, the agent must fulfill it, i.e., the cleaning task is a *duty*. Instead, recharging the battery, is what we may call a *right* of the robot, i.e., a task that the agent must be given the ability to fulfil, such that the agent itself can decide to actually fulfill or not. Handling both *duties* and *rights* is the issue studied in this paper.

The literature on strategy synthesis (Pnueli and Rosner 1989; Finkbeiner 2016), as well as the literature on planning (Ghallab, Nau, and Traverso 2016; Haslum et al. 2019), focus only on fulfilling duties, without considering rights. Instead, our notion of rights is implicitly related to the notion of *ability* studied in autonomous agents and reasoning about actions, see e.g., (Lespérance et al. 2000). Indeed, the ability of performing some task requires the existence of strategies for fulfilling the task, but not necessarily the decision to follow such strategy to actually fulfill it. In our case the agent has the *ability* of satisfying also its *rights* while executing the strategy for satisfying the duties, but actually satisfies the rights only if it wants to do so. Also, talking about duties and rights calls for connections with *obligations* and *permissions* in Deontic Logic (Gabbay et al. 2013). However, here we focus mainly on synthesis and leave the exact connection with Deontic Logic for future studies.

Specifically, in this paper, we study how to handle duties and rights in the context of Linear Temporal Logic on finite traces (LTL_f), see (De Giacomo and Vardi 2013) for a survey. LTL_f, on the one hand, allows for specifying a rich set of temporally extended specifications (Bacchus and Kabanza 2000; de Silva, Meneguzzi, and Logan 2020), and on the other hand, focuses on finite traces, which makes it particularly suitable for specifying tasks of intelligent agents. Note that intelligent agents will not get stuck accomplishing a task for all their lifetime, but only for a finite (but unbounded) number of steps.

Technically, our starting point is LTL_f synthesis under environment specifications (De Giacomo and Vardi 2015; Aminof et al. 2019; De Giacomo et al. 2021a). We assume the agent is acting in an environment that is specified through safety specifications, which can be thought of as an extension, possibly with non-Markovian features (Gabaldon 2011), of nondeterministic fully observable planning domains (Cimatti et al. 2003; Ghallab, Nau, and Traverso 2016), as discussed, e.g., in (Camacho, Bienvenu, and McIlraith 2018; Aminof et al. 2018). Wlog, we are going to use LTL_f, also for these environment safety specifications as in (De Giacomo et al. 2021b). Over this environment, we give duties and rights to the agent, expressing both of them as arbitrary LTL_f specifications. The problem that we want to solve is to synthesize a suitable strategy to achieve the duties that can be modified while in execution to achieve also the rights, if the agent chooses to do so.

We show that handling duties and rights is 2EXPTIME-complete, as standard LTL_f synthesis (De Giacomo and Vardi 2015), though it requires a more sophisticated solution concept. Essentially, we do not only compute the winning strategy as a transducer, but we guarantee that during its execution such a strategy never leaves the *winning region* (which technically captures the ability to fulfil) of both the duties and the rights. Moreover, by storing such winning region, we can readily build a further transducer represent-

*Corresponding Author

ing a strategy to fulfil also the rights at the moment the agent decides to do so while executing the first strategy.

We then study the case in which further duties and rights are given to the agent while the agent is already executing the strategy for the original duties and rights. Handling further duties that are given while already executing a strategy is related to *live synthesis*, which has been recently introduced in Formal Methods (Finkbeiner, Klein, and Metzger 2021). So as a by-product of our work, we devise a technique for live synthesis in LTL_f. We however extend this form of synthesis to handle also rights. We show that, even in this case, synthesis remains 2EXPTIME-complete, and we present techniques to effectively compute such kind of strategies with only a small overhead.

2 Preliminaries

2.1 LTL_f Basics

Linear Temporal Logic on finite traces (LTL_f) is a specification language to express temporal properties on finite traces (De Giacomo and Vardi 2013). In particular, LTL_f has the same syntax as LTL, one of the popular specification languages in Formal Methods, which is interpreted over infinite traces (Pnueli 1977). Given a set of propositions $Prop$, the formulas of LTL_f are generated as follows:

$$\varphi ::= a \mid (\neg\varphi) \mid (\varphi \wedge \varphi) \mid (\circ\varphi) \mid (\varphi\,\mathcal{U}\,\varphi),$$

where $a \in Prop$ is an atom, $\circ$ for *Next*, and $\mathcal{U}$ for *Until* are temporal operators. We make use of standard Boolean abbreviations, such as $\vee$ (or) and $\rightarrow$ (implies), $true$ and $false$. Moreover, we have the following abbreviations for temporal operators, *Eventually* as $\Diamond\varphi \equiv true\,\mathcal{U}\,\varphi$ and *Always* as $\Box\varphi \equiv \neg\Diamond\neg\varphi$. In addition, we have the *Weak Next* operator $\bullet$ as abbreviation of $\bullet\varphi \equiv \neg\circ\neg\varphi$.

A *trace* $\pi = \pi_0\pi_1\ldots$ is a sequence of propositional interpretations (sets), where for every $i \geq 0$, $\pi_i \in 2^{Prop}$ is the i-th interpretation of π. Intuitively, π_i is interpreted as the set of propositions that are $true$ at instant i. A trace π is an *infinite* trace if $last(\pi) = \infty$, which is formally denoted as $\pi \in (2^{Prop})^\omega$; otherwise π is a *finite* trace, denoted as $\pi \in (2^{Prop})^*$. Moreover, by $\pi^k = \pi_0 \ldots \pi_k$ we denote the *prefix* of π up to the k-th instant. Sometimes we call a prefix of a trace *history*. We denote by ϵ the empty prefix, i.e., the history of length 0. LTL_f formulas are interpreted over finite and nonempty traces. Given $\pi \in (2^{Prop})^+$, we define when an LTL_f formula φ *holds* at instant i ($0 \leq i \leq last(\pi)$), written as $\pi, i \models \varphi$, inductively on the structure of φ, as:

- $\pi, i \models a$ iff $a \in \pi_i$ (for $a \in Prop$);
- $\pi, i \models \neg\varphi$ iff $\pi, i \not\models \varphi$;
- $\pi, i \models \varphi_1 \wedge \varphi_2$ iff $\pi, i \models \varphi_1$ and $\pi, i \models \varphi_2$;
- $\pi, i \models \circ\varphi$ iff $i < last(\pi)$ and $\pi, i+1 \models \varphi$;
- $\pi, i \models \varphi_1\,\mathcal{U}\,\varphi_2$ iff $\exists j$ such that $i \leq j \leq last(\pi)$ and $\pi, j \models \varphi_2$, and $\forall k, i \leq k < j$, we have that $\pi, k \models \varphi_1$.

We say π *satisfies* φ, written as $\pi \models \varphi$, if $\pi, 0 \models \varphi$.

2.2 LTL_f for Safety Properties

Safety properties assert that *undesired things never happen*, i.e., a trace always behaves within some allowed boundaries. Thereby, safety properties exclude traces that can be violated by a "bad" finite prefix. Typically, safety properties are captured as LTL formulas (Kupferman and Vardi 2001), interpreted over infinite traces. Alternatively, it has been shown in (De Giacomo et al. 2021b) that, one can use LTL_f formulas to capture safety properties over both of finite and infinite traces, by applying an alternative notion of satisfaction that interprets an LTL_f formula over *all* prefixes of a trace.

Definition 1. *A (finite or infinite) trace π satisfies an LTL_f formula φ on* all prefixes, *denoted $\pi \models_\forall \varphi$, if every nonempty finite prefix of π satisfies φ. That is, $\pi^k = \pi_0\pi_1\ldots\pi_k \models \varphi$, for every $0 \leq k \leq last(\pi)$.*

Moreover, all safety properties expressible in LTL, i.e., all first-order (logic) safety properties (Lichtenstein, Pnueli, and Zuck 1985), can be specified using LTL_f on all prefixes.

Theorem 1. *(De Giacomo et al. 2021b) Every first-order safety property can be expressed as an LTL_f formula on all prefixes.*

2.3 LTL_f Synthesis with Safety Env Specs

Reactive synthesis can be viewed as a game between the *environment* and the *agent*, contrasting each other by controlling two disjoint sets of variables $\mathcal{X}$ and $\mathcal{Y}$, respectively. The goal of reactive synthesis is to synthesize an agent strategy such that no matter how the environment behaves, the combined trace from two players satisfy desired properties (Pnueli and Rosner 1989). In standard synthesis, the agent assumes the environment to be free to choose an arbitrary move at each step, but in AI typically the agent has some knowledge of how the environment works. The environment knowledge that the agent knows apriori is called *environment specification* (De Giacomo and Vardi 2015; Aminof et al. 2019; De Giacomo et al. 2021a).

In particular, we focus on the environment specifications that are formed by safety properties. In this way our environment specifications can be thought as an extension of fully observable nondeterministic domains (Cimatti et al. 2003; Ghallab, Nau, and Traverso 2016), see also (Rintanen 2004). Formally, an environment specification is an LTL_f safety formula env, while the agent task is expressed as a standard LTL_f formula φ_{task}. We describe the synthesis problem as a tuple $\mathcal{P} = (env, \varphi_{task})$. Note that for simplicity, we do not explicitly list $\mathcal{X}$ and $\mathcal{Y}$ here, since they are given as inputs by default and thus are clear from the context.

An environment strategy is a function $\gamma : (2^{\mathcal{Y}})^* \rightarrow 2^{\mathcal{X}}$, and an agent strategy is a function $\sigma : (2^{\mathcal{X}})^+ \rightarrow 2^{\mathcal{Y}}$. A trace $\pi = (X_0 \cup Y_0)(X_1 \cup Y_1)\cdots \in (2^{\mathcal{X}\cup\mathcal{Y}})^\omega$, is *compatible* with an environment strategy γ if $\gamma(\epsilon) = X_0$ and $\gamma(Y_0Y_1\ldots Y_i) = X_{i+1}$ for every i. A trace π being compatible with an agent strategy σ is defined analogously. Sometimes, we write $\sigma(\pi^k)$ instead of $\sigma(X_0X_1\cdots X_k)$ for simplicity. We denote the unique infinite sequence that is compatible with γ and σ as $\mathsf{Trace}(\gamma, \sigma)$. We also generalize these definitions to finite traces in the obvious way.

Turning to agent strategies, wlog, we require them to be *stopping*, i.e., we require the agent to perform a mandatory stop action. More specifically, every action of the agent is considered as an assignment over $\mathcal{Y}$, and $\mathbf{stop}$ is one of them. For convenience, wlog, $\mathbf{stop}$ is encoded as an assignment where all variables in $\mathcal{Y}$ are set to $false$, i.e., $\mathbf{stop} = \bigwedge_{y \in \mathcal{Y}} \neg y$.

Definition 2. *(De Giacomo et al. 2021a) A* stopping *agent strategy is a function $\sigma : (2^{\mathcal{X}})^+ \to 2^{\mathcal{Y}}$, such that for every trace $\pi \in (2^{\mathcal{X}\cup\mathcal{Y}})^\omega$ that is compatible with σ, there exists $i \in \mathbb{N}$ such that $\sigma(\pi^j) = \mathbf{stop}$ for every $j \geq i$ and $\sigma(\pi^h) \neq \mathbf{stop}$ for every $h < i$.*

Having *stopping* agent strategies, we define the *play* induced by given γ and σ as the finite prefix of $\mathsf{Trace}(\gamma, \sigma)$ that ends right before the first $\mathbf{stop}$, denoted by $\mathsf{Play}(\gamma, \sigma)$. Formally, $\mathsf{Play}(\gamma, \sigma) = (X_0 \cup Y_0)(X_1 \cup Y_1) \dots (X_i \cup Y_i)$ where $Y_{i+1} = \mathbf{stop}$, and $Y_j \neq \mathbf{stop}$ for every $0 \leq j \leq i$.

Given an environment safety specification env, which is an LTL_f formula, an environment strategy γ *enforces* env, written $\gamma \rhd env$, if for every agent strategy σ, it holds that $\mathsf{Trace}(\gamma, \sigma) \models_\forall env$. We denote the set of environment strategies enforcing env by $[\![env]\!]$.

Definition 3. *(De Giacomo et al. 2021a) The problem of synthesis is described as a tuple $\mathcal{P} = (env, \varphi_{task})$. Realizability of $\mathcal{P}$ checks whether there exists an agent strategy σ such that $\forall \gamma \in [\![env]\!]$, $\mathsf{Play}(\gamma, \sigma) \models \varphi_{task}$. Synthesis of $\mathcal{P}$ computes such a strategy if exists.*

As usual, we require that env must be *environment realizable*, i.e., $[\![env]\!]$ is nonempty. As shown in (De Giacomo et al. 2021a; De Giacomo et al. 2021b), this kind of synthesis can be solved through a reduction to a suitable two-player game constructed from LTL_f formulas env and φ_{task}, which takes 2EXPTIME. The problem itself is 2EXPTIME-complete.

2.4 Two-player Games

A *two-player game* is a game between the *environment* and the *agent*, controlling two disjoint sets of variables $\mathcal{X}$ and $\mathcal{Y}$, respectively. The game is described by a *deterministic automaton* (DA), which is a tuple $\mathcal{A} = (2^{\mathcal{X}\cup\mathcal{Y}}, Q, I, \delta, \alpha)$, where $2^{\mathcal{X}\cup\mathcal{Y}}$ is the alphabet, Q is a finite set of states, $I \in Q$ is the initial state, $\delta : Q \times 2^{\mathcal{X}\cup\mathcal{Y}} \to Q$ is the transition function, and $\alpha \subseteq Q^\omega$ is an acceptance condition. Given an infinite word $\pi = \pi_0\pi_1\pi_2 \ldots \in (2^{\mathcal{X}\cup\mathcal{Y}})^\omega$, the *run* $\rho = \mathsf{Run}(\mathcal{A}, \pi)$ of $\mathcal{A}$ on π is an infinite sequence $\rho = q_0q_1q_2 \ldots \in Q^\omega$, where $q_0 = I$ and $q_{i+1} \in \delta(q_i, \pi_i)$ for every $i \geq 0$. The run of $\mathcal{A}$ on a finite prefix π^k is defined analogously, and so $\mathsf{Run}(\mathcal{A}, \pi^k) = q_0q_1q_2 \ldots q_{k+1}$. A run ρ is *accepting* if $\rho \in \alpha$. The *language* of $\mathcal{A}$, denoted by $\mathcal{L}(\mathcal{A})$, is the set of words accepted by $\mathcal{A}$. In this work, we specifically consider the following acceptance conditions:

- *Reachability.* Given a set $R \subseteq Q$, $\text{Reach}(R) = \{q_0q_1q_2 \ldots \in Q^\omega \mid \exists k \geq 0 : q_k \in R\}$, i.e., a state in R is visited at least once.
- *Safety.* Given a set $S \subseteq Q$, $\text{Safe}(S) = \{q_0q_1q_2 \ldots \in Q^\omega \mid \forall k \geq 0 : q_k \in S\}$, i.e., only states in S are visited.
- *Reachability-Safety.* Given two sets $R, S \subseteq Q$, $\text{Reach–Safe}(R, S) = \{q_0q_1q_2 \ldots \in Q^\omega \mid \exists k \geq 0 : q_k \in R$ and $\forall j, 0 \leq j \leq k : q_j \in S\}$, i.e., a state in R is visited at least once, and until then only states in S are visited.

Notably, a DA with reachability acceptance condition defines a deterministic finite automaton (DFA). Depending on the actual acceptance condition α, we get reachability, safety, or reachability-safety games.

Theorem 2. *(De Giacomo et al. 2021b) Reachability-safety game can be solved by a linear-time reduction to a reachability game.*

Given a game $\mathcal{A} = (2^{\mathcal{X}\cup\mathcal{Y}}, Q, I, \delta, \alpha)$ defined above, an agent strategy σ is *winning* if $\forall \gamma. \mathsf{Trace}(\gamma, \sigma) \in \mathcal{L}(\mathcal{A})$. A state $q \in Q$ is an agent (resp. environment) *winning* state if the agent (resp. environment) has a winning strategy in $\mathcal{A}' = (2^{\mathcal{X}\cup\mathcal{Y}}, Q, q, \delta, \alpha)$, i.e., same structure but a new initial state q. By Agn (resp. Env) we denote the set of all agent (resp. environment) winning states, also called the agent (environment) *winning region*. All the games defined above are *determined*, i.e., $q \in Q$ is an agent winning state ($q \in \mathsf{Agn}$) iff q is not an environment winning state ($q \notin \mathsf{Env}$) (Martin 1975).

3 Synthesis with Duties and Rights

In a common synthesis setting, the agent typically follows a strategy blindly. In other words, any action that the agent performs is expected to serve the task. In this paper, we would like to assign more freedom to the agent, and thus look into the scenario where the agent has its own rights of doing some work in its own favor. For example, along the way in cleaning a series of rooms, the robot should remain able to recharge the battery, if it thinks the battery level is getting too low. Note that the robot must make sure that the rooms are cleaned when it stops, no matter whether it chooses or not to recharge the battery while cleaning.

In this synthesis setting, we divide agent tasks into two types: *duties*, expressed as an LTL_f formula φ_{d}, specifying the mandatory tasks that the agent has to accomplish; *rights*, expressed as an LTL_f formula φ_{r}, specifying the optional tasks that the agent has the right to decide whether to accomplish. To make sure that the agent can purse φ_{r} whenever it chooses to do so, the agent should be equipped with the ability of accomplishing also φ_{r} while achieving φ_{d}.

We start with defining a strategy that enforces a specification φ with respect to a history h, indicating the moment that the agent chooses to pursue φ.

Definition 4. *Let φ be an LTL_f formula and $h \in (2^{\mathcal{X}\cup\mathcal{Y}})^*$ be a history. An agent strategy σ* enforces *φ, with respect to history h, denoted by $\sigma \rhd_h \varphi$, if $\forall \gamma \in [\![env]\!]$ such that $\mathsf{Play}(\gamma, \sigma)$ has h as a prefix, we have that $\mathsf{Play}(\gamma, \sigma) \models \varphi$.*

It should be noted that, in Definition 4, we only consider the cases where both the environment strategy γ and the agent strategy σ are compatible with h. That is, $h = (X_0 \cup Y_0)(X_1 \cup Y_1) \ldots (X_i \cup Y_i) \in (2^{\mathcal{X}\cup\mathcal{Y}})^*$ is such that for every $0 \leq j \leq i$: $\sigma(X_0X_1 \cdots X_j) = Y_j$ and $Y_j \neq \mathbf{stop}$; $\gamma(\epsilon) = X_0$ and $\gamma(Y_0Y_1 \cdots Y_j) = X_{j+1}$.

Computing such a strategy is analogous to computing a strategy that enforces φ. We start with computing $[\![env]\!]$ by taking the following steps:

1. Build $\mathcal{A}_{\text{e}} = (2^{\mathcal{X}\cup\mathcal{Y}}, Q_{\text{e}}, I_{\text{e}}, \delta_{\text{e}}, \text{Safe}(S))$ that accepts a trace π iff $\pi \models_\forall env$.
2. Solve the safety game on $\mathcal{A}_{\text{e}}$ for the environment, thus obtaining the *environment winning region* Env.

3. Restrict $\mathcal{A}_e$ with Env into $\mathcal{A}'_e = (2^{\mathcal{X}\cup\mathcal{Y}}, \mathsf{Env}, I_e, \delta'_e, \mathrm{Safe}(\mathsf{Env}))$, $\delta'_e(q, X \cup Y) = $ undefined, if $\exists Y' \in 2^{\mathcal{Y}}.\delta_e(q, X \cup Y') \notin \mathsf{Env}$; $\delta'_e(q, X \cup Y) = \delta_e(q, X \cup Y)$ otherwise.

It should be noted that for safety games, there exists a unique "nondeterministic" strategy that can capture the set of all winning strategies. This strategy can be intuitively interpreted as a "staying in the winning region" strategy (Bernet, Janin, and Walukiewicz 2002). Therefore, $\mathcal{A}'_e$ precisely captures $[\![env]\!]$.

Now we translate LTL$_f$ formula φ into DA $\mathcal{A}_\varphi = (2^{\mathcal{X}\cup\mathcal{Y}}, Q_\varphi, I_\varphi, \delta_\varphi, \mathrm{Reach}(R_\varphi))$ that accepts a trace π iff $\pi^k \models \varphi$ for some $k \geq 0$, and take the product of $\mathcal{A}'_e$ and $\mathcal{A}_\varphi$ into $\mathcal{A} = (2^{\mathcal{X}\cup\mathcal{Y}}, Q, I, \delta, \mathrm{Reach}(R))$, where $Q = \mathsf{Env} \times Q_\varphi$, $I = (I_e, I_\varphi)$, $\delta((q_1, q_2), X \cup Y) = (\delta_e(q_1, X \cup Y), \delta_\varphi(q_2, X \cup Y))$, and $R = R_\varphi$ (for simplicity, we omit the projection of states in R to R_φ here, we do the same later for similar usage). Indeed, $\delta((q_1, q_2), X \cup Y) = $ undefined, if $\delta_e(q_1, X \cup Y) = $ undefined. At the end, solve a reachability game on $\mathcal{A}$ for the agent via a least fixpoint computation and obtain the *agent winning region* $\mathsf{Agn}_\varphi = \bigcup_{0 \leq l \leq u} \mathsf{Agn}^l_\varphi$, where Agn^l_φ are the "approximates" of the fixpoint computation. Clearly, if $\mathcal{A}$ does not have an agent winning strategy, i.e., $I \notin \mathsf{Agn}_\varphi$, or $\mathsf{Run}(\mathcal{A}, h)$ does not always visit states in Agn_φ, then there does not exist an agent strategy enforcing φ with respect to h. Otherwise, we abstract σ enforcing φ with respect to h, by first restricting σ to be compatible with h, considering only the environment strategies that are compatible with h, then following the least fixpoint computation to get closer to R_φ at every step until reaching R_φ. At the end, σ keeps playing **stop** right after reaching R_φ. The correctness of the construction is justified by the following lemma, which is easy to prove by construction.

Lemma 1. *Let φ be an LTL$_f$ formula, $h \in (2^{\mathcal{X}\cup\mathcal{Y}})^*$ be a finite history, and σ be constructed as above. Then σ enforces φ with respect to h.*

The following theorem shows that computing a strategy that enforces φ with respect to a history h is not more difficult than computing a strategy that just enforces φ.

Theorem 3. *Let φ be an LTL$_f$ formula and $h \in (2^{\mathcal{X}\cup\mathcal{Y}})^*$ be a history. Computing an agent strategy that enforces φ with respect to history h is 2EXPTIME-complete in φ.*

For the synthesis setting that allows agent rights φ_r while pursuing φ_d, we expect an agent strategy being able to enforce φ_d, and along the execution until then, the agent is always able to enforce also φ_r, i.e., to enforce $\varphi_d \wedge \varphi_r$.

Definition 5. *Agent strategy σ enforcing φ_d is right-aware for φ_r if $\forall \gamma \in [\![env]\!]$:*

- $\mathsf{Play}(\gamma, \sigma) \models \varphi_d$*;*
- *for every prefix h of $\mathsf{Play}(\gamma, \sigma)$, there exists an agent strategy σ_h that enforces $\varphi_d \wedge \varphi_r$ with respect to history h, i.e., $\sigma_h \rhd_h \varphi_d \wedge \varphi_r$.*

The problem of LTL$_f$ synthesis with duties and rights is defined as follows.

Definition 6 (LTL$_f$ synthesis with duties and rights)**.** *The problem is described as a tuple $\mathcal{P} = (env, \varphi_d, \varphi_r)$, where env is an LTL$_f$ formula specifying the environment safety specification, φ_d and φ_r are LTL$_f$ formulas specifying the duties and rights, respectively. Realizability of $\mathcal{P}$ checks whether there exists an agent strategy σ enforcing φ_d that is right-aware for φ_r. Synthesis of $\mathcal{P}$ computes a strategy σ if exists.*

This class of synthesis problem is able to naturally reflect the problem structure of many autonomous agent applications. We illustrate this with a relatively simple example.

Example 1. *Consider a cleaning robot working in a circular hallway, where the charging station is located close to the entrance. Suppose the robot gets assigned a duty of "cleaning room A" $\varphi_d = \Diamond(\neg Dust\_A \wedge RobotOut\_A)$, together with the rights of "fully charging battery" $\varphi_r = \Diamond(BatteryFull)$. In this hallway, the robot has two strategies to enforce φ_d:*

1. *Take the direction that passes the charging station to room A and clean it. The remaining battery after enforcing φ_d still allows the robot to reach the charging station;*
2. *Take the other direction to reach room A and clean it. The remaining battery after enforcing φ_d is not enough for the robot to reach the charging station.*

Although both strategies allow the robot to enforce φ_d, only strategy (1) allows the robot to enforce φ_d and be right-aware of φ_r "fully charging battery".

3.1 Synthesis Technique

Following the construction explained above, we can compute $[\![env]\!]$ and represent it as $\mathcal{A}'_e = (2^{\mathcal{X}\cup\mathcal{Y}}, \mathsf{Env}, I_e, \delta'_e, \mathrm{Safe}(\mathsf{Env}))$. Moreover, we know that both duties φ_d and rights φ_r can be represented by DAs $\mathcal{A}_d$ and $\mathcal{A}_r$ with reachability conditions, respectively. The crucial difference is that, apart from achieving φ_d through a reachability game on $\mathcal{A}_d$, agent rights allow the agent to decide whether to achieve φ_r. To do so, the agent should have the ability to make such decision, which can be naturally captured by the agent winning region of the reachability game on $\mathcal{A}_r$.

Given the synthesis problem $\mathcal{P} = (env, \varphi_d, \varphi_r)$, we have the following: regardless of which strategy the environment chooses to enforce env, thus staying in $\mathcal{A}'_e$, the desired agent strategy must make sure that the generated trace satisfies the reachability condition of $\mathcal{A}_d$, and that if the agent decides to pursue also φ_r, there exists a strategy that the agent can take to satisfy the reachability conditions of $\mathcal{A}_d$ and $\mathcal{A}_r$.

To synthesize such a strategy, we do the following: (*i*) compute the agent winning region Agn_r, from where the agent is able to lead the trace to satisfy the reachability conditions of $\mathcal{A}_d$, also $\mathcal{A}_r$; (*ii*) compute an agent winning strategy σ s.t. for every $\gamma \in [\![env]\!]$, $\mathsf{Trace}(\gamma, \sigma)$ satisfies the reachability condition of $\mathcal{A}_d$ by visiting *only* states in Agn_r. In this way, the agent maintains the ability of also satisfying the reachability conditions of $\mathcal{A}_r$. We now elaborate on every step.

Step 1. Compute Agn_r. Build $\mathcal{A}_d = (2^{\mathcal{X}\cup\mathcal{Y}}, Q_d, I_d, \delta_d, \mathrm{Reach}(R_d))$ that accepts a trace π iff $\pi^k \models \varphi_d$ for some $k \geq 0$, and $\mathcal{A}_r = (2^{\mathcal{X}\cup\mathcal{Y}}, Q_r, I_r, \delta_r, \mathrm{Reach}(R_r))$ that accepts a trace π iff $\pi^k \models \varphi_r$ for some $k \geq 0$. Take the product of $\mathcal{A}'_e$, $\mathcal{A}_d$, and $\mathcal{A}_r$ into $\mathcal{A} =$

$(2^{\mathcal{X}\cup\mathcal{Y}}, Q, I, \delta, \text{Reach}(R))$, where $Q = \mathsf{Env} \times Q_d \times Q_r$, $I = (I_e, I_r, I_d)$, $\delta((q_1, q_2, q_3), X \cup Y) = (\delta_e(q_1, X \cup Y), \delta_d(q_2, X \cup Y), \delta_r(q_3, X \cup Y))$, and $R = R_d \cap R_r$. Indeed, $\delta((q_1, q_2, q_3), X \cup Y) = \text{undefined}$, if $\delta_e(q_1, X \cup Y) = \text{undefined}$. At the end, solve a reachability game on $\mathcal{A}$ for the agent via a least fixpoint computation, thus obtaining $\mathsf{Agn}_r = \bigcup_{0 \leq i \leq m} \mathsf{Agn}_r^i$. If $I \notin \mathsf{Agn}_r$, return "unrealizable".

Lemma 2. *Let $\mathcal{P}$ be a problem of* LTL$_f$ *synthesis with duties and rights, and Agn_r the agent winning region of the reachability game on $\mathcal{A} = (2^{\mathcal{X}\cup\mathcal{Y}}, Q, I, \delta, \text{Reach}(R_d \cap R_r))$ computed as above. Then $\mathcal{P}$ is realizable iff $I \in \mathsf{Agn}_r$.*

Proof. We prove the lemma in both directions.

($\Leftarrow$) We need to show that if $I \in \mathsf{Agn}_r$, then $\mathcal{P}$ is realizable. By construction, $I \in \mathsf{Agn}_r$ shows that there exists an agent strategy σ such that, for every $\gamma \in [\![env]\!]$, $\pi = \mathsf{Trace}(\gamma, \sigma)$ is such that $\pi \in \mathcal{L}(\mathcal{A})$. That is to say, $\pi^k \models \varphi_d \wedge \varphi_r$ for some $k \geq 0$, thus it also holds that $\pi^k \models \varphi_d$. In this case, σ starts playing **stop** after π^k, and so we have $\mathsf{Play}(\gamma, \sigma) = \pi^k$. Moreover, for every prefix h of $\mathsf{Play}(\gamma, \sigma)$, we can construct an agent strategy σ_h that works exactly the same as σ, which indeed enforces $\varphi_d \wedge \varphi_r$ with respect to history h.

($\Rightarrow$) We prove by contradiction. If $I \notin \mathsf{Agn}_r$, then there does not exist an agent winning strategy of the reachability game on $\mathcal{A}$. Suppose the agent decides to pursue also φ_r at the very beginning, then the agent does not have a strategy that enforces $\varphi_d \wedge \varphi_r$ with respect to history $h = \epsilon$, i.e., empty trace. Hence, $\mathcal{P}$ is unrealizable. □

Step 2. Compute strategy σ. Note that σ needs to lead the play to reach R_d by visiting states in Agn_r only. First, we define a new DA with reachability-safety condition $\mathcal{A}_1 = (2^{\mathcal{X}\cup\mathcal{Y}}, Q, I, \delta, \text{Reach–Safe}(R_d, \mathsf{Agn}_r))$ from $\mathcal{A} = (2^{\mathcal{X}\cup\mathcal{Y}}, Q, I, \delta, \text{Reach}(R_d \cap R_r))$. It has been shown in (De Giacomo et al. 2021b) that $\mathcal{A}_1$ can be reduced to a new DA $\mathcal{A}'_1 = (2^{\mathcal{X}\cup\mathcal{Y}}, Q, I, \delta', \text{Reach}(R'))$ with δ' and R' as follows:

- $\delta'(q, X \cup Y) = \begin{cases} \delta(q, X \cup Y) & \text{if } q \in \mathsf{Agn}_r \\ q & \text{if } q \notin \mathsf{Agn}_r \end{cases}$
- $R' = R_d \cap \mathsf{Agn}_r$

Intuitively, the only change in δ' is to turn all non-safe states (states not in Agn_r) into sink states, while R' requires reaching a goal state (a state in R_d) that is also safe (i.e., it is in Agn_r). Then we solve a reachability game on $\mathcal{A}'_1$ via a least fixpoint computation and obtain $\mathsf{Agn} = \bigcup_{0 \leq j \leq n} \mathsf{Agn}^j$. Note that $I \in \mathsf{Agn}$ indeed holds, which is guaranteed by the reachability game for computing Agn_r in the previous step. Finally, we define a strategy generator based on $\mathsf{Agn} = \bigcup_{0 \leq j \leq n} \mathsf{Agn}^j$, represented as a transducer $\mathcal{T} = (2^{\mathcal{X}\cup\mathcal{Y}}, Q, I, \varrho, \tau)$, where

- $2^{\mathcal{X}\cup\mathcal{Y}}$, Q and I are the same as in $\mathcal{A}$;
- $\varrho : Q \times 2^{\mathcal{X}} \to 2^Q$ is the transition function such that $\varrho(q, X) = \{q' \mid q' = \delta(q, X \cup Y) \text{ and } Y \in \tau(q)\}$;
- $\tau : Q \times 2^{\mathcal{X}} \to 2^{2^{\mathcal{Y}}}$ is the output function s.t. $\forall X \in 2^{\mathcal{X}}$, $\tau(q, X) = \{Y \mid \delta(q, X \cup Y) \in \mathsf{Agn}^j\}$ if $q \in (\mathsf{Agn}^{j+1} \backslash \mathsf{Agn}^j)$, otherwise $\tau(q, X) = 2^{\mathcal{Y}}$.

This transducer generates an agent strategy $\sigma : (2^{\mathcal{X}})^+ \to 2^{\mathcal{Y}}$ in the following way: for every $\xi^k \in (2^{\mathcal{X}})^+$ $(k \geq 0)$

$$\sigma(\xi^k) = \begin{cases} \textbf{stop} & \text{if } \mathsf{Run}(\mathcal{A}, \pi^{k-1}) \text{ visited } R_d, \\ Y \in \tau(q_k, X_k) & \text{otherwise.} \end{cases}$$

where $\mathsf{Run}(\mathcal{A}, \pi^{k-1}) = q_0 q_1 q_2 \ldots q_k$ s.t. $q_0 = I$, and $\pi^{k-1} = (X_0 \cup Y_0)(X_1 \cup Y_1) \ldots (X_{k-1} \cup Y_{k-1})$. Note that $\mathcal{T}$ generates a strategy in the way of restricting τ to return only one of its values (chosen arbitrarily).

Lemma 3. *Let $\mathcal{P}$ be a problem of* LTL$_f$ *synthesis with duties and rights, and $\mathcal{T}$ constructed as above. Any strategy returned by $\mathcal{T}$ is a strategy that solves the synthesis of $\mathcal{P}$.*

Proof. Let σ be an arbitrary strategy generated by $\mathcal{T}$, i.e., $I \in \mathsf{Agn}$, and $\gamma \in [\![env]\!]$ be an arbitrary environment strategy that enforces env. First, $\mathcal{T}$ already restricts the environment to be able to only choose strategies from $[\![env]\!]$. Then, by construction, $\mathsf{Play}(\gamma, \sigma)$ satisfies the following:

- $\mathsf{Play}(\gamma, \sigma) \models \varphi_d$, since σ forces $\mathsf{Play}(\gamma, \sigma)$ to get closer to R_d at every step until reaching R_d. Moreover, σ starts playing **stop** only after then.
- there exists $\sigma_h \rhd_h \varphi_d \wedge \varphi_r$ for every prefix h of $\mathsf{Play}(\gamma, \sigma)$. This holds since σ restricts $\mathsf{Play}(\gamma, \sigma)$ to visit states in Agn_r only. Therefore, for every prefix h of $\mathsf{Play}(\gamma, \sigma)$, there exists an agent strategy $\hat{\sigma}$ of the reachability game on $\mathcal{A}_h = (2^{\mathcal{X}\cup\mathcal{Y}}, Q, \delta(I, h), \delta, \text{Reach}(R_d \cap R_r))$. Hence, we can construct an agent strategy σ_h that first copies h until reaching $\delta(I, h)$ and works as $\hat{\sigma}$ until reaching $R_d \cap R_r$, then plays **stop** forever. Therefore, σ_h holds that $\sigma_h \rhd_h \varphi_d \wedge \varphi_r$. □

Notice that by the construction described above, if the reachability game on $\mathcal{A}$ (in Step 1) does not have an agent winning strategy, then $\mathcal{T}$ trivially returns *no strategy* and indeed, by Lemma 2, $\mathcal{P}$ is unrealizable. As an immediate consequence of Lemmas 2&3, we have:

Theorem 4. *Let $\mathcal{P}$ be a problem of* LTL$_f$ *synthesis with duties and rights. Realizability of $\mathcal{P}$ can be solved by reducing to a suitable reachability game. Synthesis of $\mathcal{P}$ can be solved by generating a strategy from $\mathcal{T}$ constructed as above.*

Theorem 5. *Let $\mathcal{P}$ be a problem of* LTL$_f$ *synthesis with duties and rights. Realizability of $\mathcal{P}$ is 2EXPTIME-complete.*

Theorem 6. *Let $\mathcal{P}$ be a problem of* LTL$_f$ *synthesis with duties and rights. Then computing a strategy solving $\mathcal{P}$ can take, in the worst case, double-exponential time in the size of $|\varphi_d| + |\varphi_r| + |env|$.*

We observe that if env is specified, for example, using, e.g., PDDL (Haslum et al. 2019) instead of LTL$_f$, then the complexity with respect to the environment specification env only becomes EXPTIME-complete (membership from a construction, hardness from planning of Fully Observable Nondeterministic Domains (FOND) (Rintanen 2004)).

Enforcing also rights while executing. Given problem $\mathcal{P} = (env, \varphi_d, \varphi_r)$, suppose we have synthesized a strategy σ for $\mathcal{P}$, which enforces φ_d and is right-aware for φ_r, and while executing σ, the agent wants to satisfy also its rights φ_r. Then we can consider the history h generated with the environment so far, and synthesize a strategy σ_h, that enforces $\varphi_d \wedge \varphi_r$ with respect to history h. This can take 2EXPTIME, as shown by Theorem 3.

Nevertheless, if we consider the construction above, we actually do not need to compute the new strategy σ_h from scratch. This is because we can, base on the immediate results obtained from computing the original strategy σ, to construct a transducer $\mathcal{T}_r$ for generating σ_h of a given history h. In particular, this transducer is independent of h. Therefore, we can construct $\mathcal{T}_r$ apriori, and use it to obtain σ_h when the agent chooses to satisfy φ_r after history h. The essential ingredients for constructing $\mathcal{T}_r$ is the DA $\mathcal{A} = (2^{\mathcal{X}\cup\mathcal{Y}}, Q, I, \delta, \mathrm{Reach}(R_d \cap R_r))$ and the agent winning region $\mathsf{Agn}_r = \bigcup_{0\leq i\leq m} \mathsf{Agn}_r^i$. We construct $\mathcal{T}_r = (2^{\mathcal{X}\cup\mathcal{Y}}, Q, I, \varrho_r, \tau_r)$ as follows:

- $2^{\mathcal{X}\cup\mathcal{Y}}$, Q and I are the same as in $\mathcal{A}$;
- $\varrho_r : Q \times 2^{\mathcal{X}} \to 2^Q$ is the transition function such that $\varrho_r(q, X) = \{q' \mid q' = \delta(q, X \cup Y) \text{ and } Y \in \tau_r(q)\}$;
- $\tau_r : Q \times 2^{\mathcal{X}} \to 2^{2^{\mathcal{Y}}}$ is the output function such that $\forall X \in 2^{\mathcal{X}}$, $\tau_r(q, X) = \{Y \mid \delta(q, X \cup Y) \in \mathsf{Agn}_r^i\}$ if $q \in \mathsf{Agn}_r^{i+1} \backslash \mathsf{Agn}_r^i$, otherwise $\tau_r(q, X) = 2^{\mathcal{Y}}$.

Suppose while executing σ, which enforces φ_d and is right-aware for φ_r, the agent chooses to satisfy φ_r after history h, the transducer $\mathcal{T}_r$ generates an agent strategy $\sigma_h : (2^{\mathcal{X}})^+ \to 2^{\mathcal{Y}}$ in the following way: for every $\xi^k \in (2^{\mathcal{X}})^+$ that is compatible with history $h = (X_0 \cup Y_0)(X_1 \cup Y_1) \dots (X_i \cup Y_i)$

$$\sigma_h(\xi^k) = \begin{cases} Y_k & \text{if } 0 \leq k \leq i \\ \textbf{stop} & \text{if } \mathsf{Run}(\mathcal{A}, \pi^{k-1}) \text{ visited } R_d \cap R_r \\ Y \in \tau(q_k, X_k) & \text{otherwise.} \end{cases}$$

where $\mathsf{Run}(\mathcal{A}, \pi^{k-1}) = q_0 q_1 q_2 \dots q_k$ such that $q_0 = I$, and $\pi^{k-1} = (X_0 \cup Y_0)(X_1 \cup Y_1) \dots (X_{k-1} \cup Y_{k-1})$. Intuitively, given history h, $\mathcal{T}_r$ generates a strategy σ_h by first following h, and after h, choosing suitable agent action to enforce the play to get closer to $R_d \cap R_r$. At the end, σ_h keeps playing **stop** right after visiting $R_d \cap R_r$.

Theorem 7. *Let $\mathcal{P}$ be a problem of* LTL$_f$ *synthesis with duties and rights, σ be an agent strategy computed by $\mathcal{T}$ that solves the synthesis of $\mathcal{P}$, and σ_h be an agent strategy that is generated by $\mathcal{T}_r$ for a history $h \in (2^{\mathcal{X}\cup\mathcal{Y}})^*$. Then σ_h* enforces *$\varphi_d \wedge \varphi_r$, with respect to history h, i.e., $\sigma_h \rhd_h \varphi_d \wedge \varphi_r$.*

Proof. Let σ_h be an arbitrary strategy generated by $\mathcal{T}_r$ for history h, and $\gamma \in [\![env]\!]$ be an arbitrary environment strategy that enforces env. By Lemma 3, we have that $\mathsf{Run}(\mathcal{A}, h)$ only visits states in Agn_r. By construction of σ_h, $\mathsf{Play}(\gamma, \sigma)$ has h as a prefix, and $\mathsf{Play}(\gamma, \sigma) \models \varphi_d \wedge \varphi_r$. Therefore, $\sigma_h \rhd_h \varphi_d \wedge \varphi_r$ holds. □

The advantage of building transducer $\mathcal{T}_r$ is that this transducer works for any history h generated by σ that enforces φ_d and is right-aware for φ_r. Moreover, when building the transducer $\mathcal{T}$ for σ, we already have all the ingredients to build also $\mathcal{T}_r$, with only a constant overhead (i.e., since we are computing two transducers, sharing essentially the same cost, instead of one).

We now extend Example 1 to show how to utilize the transducer $\mathcal{T}_r$ in the presence of robot also achieving rights.

Example 2. *Suppose the robot decides to also achieve its rights $\varphi_r = \Diamond(BatteryFull)$ while cleaning room A. Let us assume that the by now the running history is h. The robot will look into $\mathcal{T}_r$ and choose a strategy σ_h out of $\mathcal{T}_r$ that allows it to enforce $\varphi_d \wedge \varphi_r$.*

4 Handling Further Duties and Rights While Executing

Let us focus on duty only first. Commonly in synthesis the agent only gets one task (duty) to accomplish, after which, the agent can terminate. However, in practice, further tasks might arrive while executing the current task, e.g., a new room to clean while the robot is cleaning the rooms it got assigned at the beginning. Intuitively, the new task can be considered as an update of the previous task.

Synthesizing updated specifications has been recently studied in Formal Methods, under the name of *live synthesis* (Finkbeiner, Klein, and Metzger 2021), where the desired properties are specified in LTL and can get updated while executing a strategy of the original LTL specification. The goal of live synthesis is to synthesize a new strategy to replace an already running strategy. In particular, the correct handover from the already running strategy to the new strategy is specified by an extension of LTL, called LiveLTL. For specifications in LiveLTL, the synthesis problem shares the same complexity bound as standard LTL synthesis.

Despite that synthesis problems of LTL$_f$ can be solved by a reduction to suitable problems of LTL, since LTL$_f$ can be encoded in LTL, such reductions do not seem promising, as shown in (Zhu et al. 2017) for LTL$_f$ synthesis, and (Zhu et al. 2020; De Giacomo et al. 2020) for LTL$_f$ synthesis under environment specifications. So while we want to consider an LTL$_f$ variant of live synthesis, we avoid a detour to LiveLTL synthesis and devise a direct synthesis technique for LTL$_f$.

We start by observing that the crucial difference between new duties and the ongoing duties is that, the agent should enforce ongoing duties from the very beginning, but enforce new duties after a history, i.e., starting from the moment that the new duties are assigned to the agent.

Definition 7. *Let φ be an* LTL$_f$ *formula and $h \in (2^{\mathcal{X}\cup\mathcal{Y}})^*$ be a history. An agent strategy σ* enforces *φ after history h, denoted by $\sigma \rhd_{\mathrm{af(h)}} \varphi$, if $\forall\gamma \in [\![env]\!]$ such that* $\mathsf{Play}(\gamma, \sigma)$ *has h as a prefix, we have that* $\mathsf{Play}(\gamma, \sigma), |h| \models \varphi$.

Recall that Definition 4 describes how an *agent strategy enforces φ with respect to a history h*, and Definition 7 above describes how an *agent strategy enforces φ after a history h*. There is a significant difference between these two notions, since we use them to differentiate how agent strategies enforce ongoing duties and new duties. In particular, an agent strategy enforces ongoing duties with respect to a history h, but enforces new duties after a history h.

Note that the environment strategy enforcing env in any case starts from the very beginning. Moreover, we only consider the cases where both the environment strategy γ and the agent strategy σ are compatible with h. In other words, we need to consider environment strategies that are in the set $[\![env]\!]^h = \{\gamma \mid \forall\sigma$ that is compatible with h we have $\mathsf{Trace}(\gamma,\sigma)$ has h as a prefix and $\mathsf{Trace}(\gamma,\sigma) \models_\forall env\}$.

In order to compute a strategy σ that enforces φ after h, we split the trace $\mathsf{Trace}(\gamma,\sigma)$ into two phases. In phase I, both strategies γ and σ are compatible with h. In phase II, the agent focuses on the environment strategies that enforce env with respect to h. We show how to compute a strategy σ enforcing φ after h by addressing two phases in reverse order. Specifically, we first compute the set of environment strategies that start executing after h, but enforce env when the compatible traces are concatenated to h. We denote this set of environment strategies by

$$[\![env, \mathrm{af(h)}]\!] = \{\gamma \mid \forall\sigma.\ h \cdot \mathsf{Trace}(\gamma,\sigma) \models_\forall env\}.$$

The fact that we can focus on this set of environment strategies is justified by the following lemma, which is easy to prove considering the two definitions of $[\![env]\!]^h$ and $[\![env, \mathrm{af(h)}]\!]$.

Lemma 4. *For every $\gamma \in [\![env]\!]^h$ there exists $\gamma' \in [\![env, \mathrm{af(h)}]\!]$ s.t. for every $\lambda = h|_\mathcal{Y} \cdot \lambda'$ we have $\gamma(\lambda) = \gamma'(\lambda')$.*

Viceversa, for every $\gamma' \in [\![env, \mathrm{af(h)}]\!]$ there exists $\gamma \in [\![env]\!]^h$ s.t. for every $\lambda = h|_\mathcal{Y} \cdot \lambda'$ we have $\gamma(\lambda) = \gamma'(\lambda')$.

To compute $[\![env, \mathrm{af(h)}]\!]$, we first compute $[\![env]\!]$, represented as $\mathcal{A}'_\mathrm{e} = (2^{\mathcal{X}\cup\mathcal{Y}}, \mathsf{Env}, I_\mathrm{e}, \delta'_\mathrm{e}, \mathsf{Safe}(\mathsf{Env}))$, as described in Section 3. In order to synchronize the starting point of the environment to be aligned with the instant after history h, we run $\mathcal{A}'_\mathrm{e}$ on h to obtain a new DA $\mathcal{A}'_{\mathrm{e,af(h)}} = (2^{\mathcal{X}\cup\mathcal{Y}}, \mathsf{Env}, I_{\mathrm{e,af(h)}}, \delta'_\mathrm{e}, \mathsf{Safe}(\mathsf{Env}))$ that differs from $\mathcal{A}'_\mathrm{e}$ only on the initial state, and $I_{\mathrm{e,af(h)}} = \delta'_\mathrm{e}(I_\mathrm{e}, h)$. The following lemma shows that $\mathcal{A}'_{\mathrm{e,af(h)}}$ precisely captures $[\![env, \mathrm{af(h)}]\!]$, which is easy to prove by construction.

Lemma 5. *Let env be an LTL_f formula specifying a safety property, $h \in (2^{\mathcal{X}\cup\mathcal{Y}})^*$ be a finite history, and $\mathcal{A}'_\mathrm{e}$ be constructed as above. Then $\mathcal{A}'_{\mathrm{e,af(h)}}$ represents the set $[\![env, \mathrm{af(h)}]\!]$.*

Having $[\![env, \mathrm{af(h)}]\!]$ represented as DA $\mathcal{A}'_{\mathrm{e,af(h)}}$, we can first construct the DA $\mathcal{A}_\varphi$ and then solve a reachability game on the product $\mathcal{A}'_{\mathrm{e,af(h)}} \times \mathcal{A}_\varphi$ to abstract an agent strategy $\hat{\sigma}$ that guides the play to satisfy the reachability condition of $\mathcal{A}_\varphi$, hence enforcing φ. The final agent strategy enforcing φ after h can be obtained by first copying h, and then switching to $\hat{\sigma}$ after h. Formally, for every $\xi^k \in (2^\mathcal{X})^+$ that is compatible with $h = (X_0 \cup Y_0)(X_1 \cup Y_1)\ldots(X_i \cup Y_i) \in (2^{\mathcal{X}\cup\mathcal{Y}})^*$

$$\sigma(\xi^k) = \begin{cases} Y_k & \text{if } 0 \le k \le i, \\ \hat{\sigma}(\iota) & \text{if } \xi^k = h \cdot \iota. \end{cases}$$

Lemma 6. *Let φ be an LTL_f formula, $h \in (2^{\mathcal{X}\cup\mathcal{Y}})^*$ be a history, and σ be constructed as above. Then σ enforces φ after h.*

Proof. Note that σ is constructed from h and a strategy $\hat{\sigma}$, which holds that for every $\hat{\gamma} \in [\![env, \mathrm{af(h)}]\!]$, $\mathsf{Play}(\hat{\gamma},\hat{\sigma}) \models \varphi$. Hence, together with Lemma 4, it holds that for every $\gamma' \in [\![env]\!]^h$, $\mathsf{Play}(\gamma',\sigma), |h| \models \varphi$. Clearly, σ holds that for every $\gamma \in [\![env]\!]$ such that $\mathsf{Play}(\gamma',\sigma)$ has h as a prefix, then $\mathsf{Play}(\gamma,\sigma), |h| \models \varphi$. Therefore, σ enforces φ after h. □

The following theorem shows that computing an agent strategy enforcing φ after a history h is not more difficult than computing a strategy that just enforces φ.

Theorem 8. *Let φ be an LTL_f formula and $h \in (2^{\mathcal{X}\cup\mathcal{Y}})^*$ be a history. Computing an agent strategy that enforces φ after history h is 2EXPTIME-complete in φ.*

Building on the above results and the results in Section 3, we now enrich our synthesis setting by allowing both further duties and further rights, specified as LTL_f formulas φ_fd and φ_fr, respectively.

Definition 8. *Let h be the formed history when further duties φ_fd and rights φ_fr arrive. Agent strategy σ enforcing φ_fd is right-aware for φ_fr after h, if $\forall\gamma \in [\![env]\!]$:*

- *$\mathsf{Play}(\gamma,\sigma)$ has h as a prefix and $\mathsf{Play}(\gamma,\sigma), |h| \models \varphi_\mathrm{fd}$;*
- *for every prefix l of $\mathsf{Play}(\gamma,\sigma)$ that has h as a prefix, there exists an agent strategy σ_l that enforces $\varphi_\mathrm{fd} \wedge \varphi_\mathrm{fr}$ after history h, i.e., $\sigma_l \rhd_{\mathrm{af(h)}} \varphi_\mathrm{fd} \wedge \varphi_\mathrm{fr}$.*

The enriched synthesis problem that allows further duties and rights is defined as follows.

Definition 9 (LTL_f synthesis for further duties and rights)**.** *The problem is described as a tuple $\hat{\mathcal{P}} = (env, \varphi_\mathrm{d}, \varphi_\mathrm{r}, \varphi_\mathrm{fd}, \varphi_\mathrm{fr}, h)$, where env is an LTL_f formula specifying the environment safety specification, φ_d and φ_r are LTL_f formulas specifying duties and rights, respectively, φ_fd and φ_fr are LTL_f formulas specifying further duties and rights that arrive after history h, respectively. Realizability of $\hat{\mathcal{P}}$ checks whether there exists an agent strategy σ s.t.:*

- *it enforces φ_d and is right-aware for φ_r wrt h;*
- *it enforces φ_fd and is right-aware for φ_fr after h.*

Synthesis of $\hat{\mathcal{P}}$ computes a strategy σ if exists.

Notice that, in Definition 9, we also only consider the cases where both the environment strategies and the agent strategies are compatible with h.

We extend Example 1 to address the intuition of this class of synthesis problem.

Example 3. *Suppose the robot is on its way to room A, while receiving a new duty of "cleaning room B" $\varphi_\mathrm{fd} = \Diamond(\neg Dust\_B \wedge RobotOut\_B)$. The robot has generated a history h when receiving φ_fd. Now, the robot has one strategy to enforce φ_d with respect to h and enforce φ_fd after h:*

- *Take the direction that passes the charging station to reach room A and clean it. Then go to room B and clean it. The remaining battery after cleaning is not enough for the robot to reach the charging station.*

In this case, the robot would refuse the new duty φ_fd, since completing it would be conflicted with maintaining the robot rights φ_r.

On the other hand, let us consider the situation where the cleaning robot is able to handle original duties and rights, together with further duties and rights.

Example 4. *Suppose the cleaning robot is cleaning room A, while receiving a new duty of "cleaning room C" $\varphi_\mathrm{fd} = \Diamond(\neg Dust\_C \wedge RobotOut\_C)$, and a new right of "emptying the garbage collector" $\varphi_\mathrm{fr} = \Diamond(Collector\_Empty)$. The* *robot has generated a history h when receiving φ_{fd} and φ_{fr}. Since this is a circular hallway, the robot again has two directions to reach room C. Nevertheless, the robot only takes the strategy that allows it to reach the charging station, and the garbage station whenever it wants.*

4.1 Synthesis Technique

Given problem $\hat{\mathcal{P}} = (env, \varphi_{\mathrm{d}}, \varphi_{\mathrm{r}}, \varphi_{\mathrm{fd}}, \varphi_{\mathrm{fr}}, h)$, the main complication comes from further duties and rights that arrive after history h. This is because apart from enforcing φ_{fd} while maintaining φ_{fr}, the agent should also enforce unfinished φ_{d} and be right-aware for φ_{r}. To synthesize an agent strategy that is able to do so, we do the following: (*i*) compute the agent winning region $\mathsf{Agn}_{\mathrm{r}}$ from where the agent is able to lead the trace to satisfy φ_{d} and φ_{r}; (*ii*) compute the agent winning region $\mathsf{Agn}_{\mathrm{r}\wedge\mathrm{fr}}$ from where the agent is able to lead the trace to also satisfy both φ_{fd} and φ_{fr}, but after h; (*iii*) synthesize an agent strategy σ enforcing φ_{d} and is right-aware for φ_{r} wrt h, also enforcing φ_{fd} being right-aware for φ_{fr}, but after h. We now elaborate on every step.

Step 1. Compute $\mathsf{Agn}_{\mathrm{r}}$. As described in Section 3.1, we can construct the corresponding DAs $\mathcal{A}_{\mathrm{d}} = (2^{\mathcal{X}\cup\mathcal{Y}}, Q_{\mathrm{d}}, I_{\mathrm{d}}, \delta_{\mathrm{d}}, \mathrm{Reach}(R_{\mathrm{d}}))$ and $\mathcal{A}_{\mathrm{r}} = (2^{\mathcal{X}\cup\mathcal{Y}}, Q_{\mathrm{r}}, I_{\mathrm{r}}, \delta_{\mathrm{r}}, \mathrm{Reach}(R_{\mathrm{r}}))$ of φ_{d} and φ_{r}, respectively. The agent winning region $\mathsf{Agn}_{\mathrm{r}}$ can be computed via a least fixpoint computation on the product DA $\mathcal{A}_{\mathrm{d}\wedge\mathrm{r}} = (2^{\mathcal{X}\cup\mathcal{Y}}, Q_{\mathrm{d}\wedge\mathrm{r}}, I_{\mathrm{d}\wedge\mathrm{r}}, \delta_{\mathrm{d}\wedge\mathrm{r}}, \mathrm{Reach}(R)_{\mathrm{d}\wedge\mathrm{r}})$ constructed out of $\mathcal{A}'_{\mathrm{e}}$, $\mathcal{A}_{\mathrm{d}}$, and $\mathcal{A}_{\mathrm{r}}$, where $\mathcal{A}'_{\mathrm{e}}$ captures $[\![env]\!]$.

Step 2. Compute $\mathsf{Agn}_{\mathrm{r}\wedge\mathrm{fr}}$. Build DA $\mathcal{A}_{\mathrm{fd}} = (2^{\mathcal{X}\cup\mathcal{Y}}, Q_{\mathrm{fd}}, I_{\mathrm{fd}}, \delta_{\mathrm{fd}}, \mathrm{Reach}(R_{\mathrm{fd}}))$ of φ_{fd}, and DA $\mathcal{A}_{\mathrm{fr}} = (2^{\mathcal{X}\cup\mathcal{Y}}, Q_{\mathrm{fr}}, I_{\mathrm{fr}}, \delta_{\mathrm{fr}}, \mathrm{Reach}(R_{\mathrm{fr}}))$ of φ_{fr}. In order to synthesize an agent strategy that enforces φ_{fd} and is right-aware φ_{fr} after h, we need to run $\mathcal{A}_{\mathrm{d}\wedge\mathrm{r}}$ on h to obtain a new DA $\mathcal{A}'_{\mathrm{d}\wedge\mathrm{r}}$ that differs from $\mathcal{A}_{\mathrm{d}\wedge\mathrm{r}}$ only on the initial state, and $\mathcal{A}_{\mathrm{d}\wedge\mathrm{r,af(h)}} = (2^{\mathcal{X}\cup\mathcal{Y}}, Q_{\mathrm{d}\wedge\mathrm{r}}, I_{\mathrm{d}\wedge\mathrm{r,af(h)}}, \delta_{\mathrm{d}\wedge\mathrm{r}}, \mathrm{Reach}(R))$, where $I_{\mathrm{d}\wedge\mathrm{r,af(h)}} = \delta(I_{\mathrm{d}\wedge\mathrm{r}}, h)$. Clearly, if $\mathsf{Run}(\mathcal{A}_{\mathrm{d}\wedge\mathrm{r}}, h)$ does not visit states in $\mathsf{Agn}_{\mathrm{r}}$ only, return "unrealizable", since every agent strategy that is compatible with h cannot enforce φ_{d} and be right-aware for φ_{r}, thus $\hat{\mathcal{P}}$ is simply unrealizable, and so $\mathsf{Agn}_{\mathrm{r}\wedge\mathrm{fr}} = \emptyset$.

Otherwise, we continue as follows. Since the final agent strategy should be able to guide the play to reach R_{d} and R_{fd}, and always able to reach also R_{r} and R_{fr}, we take the product of $\mathcal{A}_{\mathrm{d}\wedge\mathrm{r,af(h)}}$, $\mathcal{A}_{\mathrm{fd}}$ and $\mathcal{A}_{\mathrm{fr}}$ into $\mathcal{A} = (2^{\mathcal{X}\cup\mathcal{Y}}, Q, I, \delta, \mathrm{Reach}(R))$, where $Q = Q_{\mathrm{d}\wedge\mathrm{r}} \times Q_{\mathrm{fd}} \times Q_{\mathrm{fr}}$, $I = (I_{\mathrm{d}\wedge\mathrm{r,af(h)}}, I_{\mathrm{fd}}, I_{\mathrm{fr}})$, $\delta((q_1, q_2, q_3), X \cup Y) = (\delta_{\mathrm{d}\wedge\mathrm{r}}(q_1, X\cup Y), \delta_{\mathrm{fd}}(q_2, X\cup Y), \delta_{\mathrm{fr}}(q_3, X\cup Y))$. Furthermore, $\delta((q_1, q_2, q_3), X\cup Y) =$ undefined, if $\delta_{\mathrm{d}\wedge\mathrm{r}}(q_1, X\cup Y) =$ undefined. Finally, $R = R_{\mathrm{d}} \cap R_{\mathrm{r}} \cap R_{\mathrm{fd}} \cap R_{\mathrm{fr}}$. We now solve a reachability game on $\mathcal{A}$ for the agent via a least fixpoint computation, to obtain $\mathsf{Agn}_{\mathrm{r}\wedge\mathrm{fr}} = \bigcup_{0\leq i\leq m} \mathsf{Agn}^i_{\mathrm{r}\wedge\mathrm{fr}}$. If $I \notin \mathsf{Agn}_{\mathrm{r}\wedge\mathrm{fr}}$, i.e., $\mathcal{A}$ does not have an agent winning strategy, return "unrealizable".

Lemma 7. *Let $\hat{\mathcal{P}}$ be a problem of* LTL_f *synthesis for further duties and rights, and $\mathsf{Agn}_{\mathrm{r}\wedge\mathrm{fr}}$ the agent winning region of the reachability game on $\mathcal{A} = (2^{\mathcal{X}\cup\mathcal{Y}}, Q, I, \delta, \mathrm{Reach}(R))$ computed as above. $\hat{\mathcal{P}}$ is realizable iff $I \in \mathsf{Agn}_{\mathrm{r}\wedge\mathrm{fr}}$.*

Proof. We prove the lemma in both directions.

($\Leftarrow$) We need to show that if $I \in \mathsf{Agn}_{\mathrm{r}\wedge\mathrm{fr}}$, then $\hat{\mathcal{P}}$ is realizable. By construction, $I \in \mathsf{Agn}_{\mathrm{r}\wedge\mathrm{fr}}$ shows that there exists an agent strategy σ such that, for every $\gamma \in [\![env, \mathrm{af(h)}]\!]$, $\pi = \mathsf{Trace}(\gamma, \sigma)$ is such that $\pi \in \mathcal{L}(\mathcal{A})$. That is to say, $\pi^k \models \varphi_{\mathrm{fd}} \wedge \varphi_{\mathrm{fr}}$ for some $k \geq 0$, thus it also holds that $\pi^k \models \varphi_{\mathrm{fd}}$. Moreover, since $I = (I_{\mathrm{d}\wedge\mathrm{r,af(h)}}, I_{\mathrm{fd}}, I_{\mathrm{fr}})$, where $I_{\mathrm{d}\wedge\mathrm{r,af(h)}} = \delta_{\mathrm{d}\wedge\mathrm{r}}(I, h)$, it also holds that $h \cdot \pi^k \models \varphi_{\mathrm{d}} \wedge \varphi_{\mathrm{r}}$, and thus $h \cdot \pi^k \models \varphi_{\mathrm{d}}$. Moreover, for every prefix l of $\mathsf{Play}(\gamma, \sigma)$ that has h as a prefix, we can construct an agent strategy σ_l that works exactly the same as σ, which indeed enforces φ_{r} with respect to h, and enforces φ_{fr} after h.

($\Rightarrow$) We prove by contradiction. If $I \notin \mathsf{Agn}_{\mathrm{r}\wedge\mathrm{fr}}$, then either $\mathsf{Agn}_{\mathrm{r}\wedge\mathrm{fr}} = \emptyset$, i.e., $\mathsf{Run}(\mathcal{A}_{\mathrm{d}\wedge\mathrm{r}}, h)$ does not visit states in $\mathsf{Agn}_{\mathrm{r}}$ only, then $\hat{\mathcal{P}}$ is simply unrealizable; or there does not exist an agent winning strategy of reachability game on $\mathcal{A}$. Therefore, suppose the agent decides to achieve both rights φ_{r} and φ_{fr} immediately after history h, then the agent does not have a strategy that enforces $\varphi_{\mathrm{d}} \wedge \varphi_{\mathrm{r}}$ with respect to history h, and $\varphi_{\mathrm{fd}} \wedge \varphi_{\mathrm{fr}}$ after h. Hence, $\hat{\mathcal{P}}$ is unrealizable. □

Step 3. Compute strategy σ. Note that strategy σ needs to lead the play to reach R_{d} and R_{fd} by visiting states in $\mathsf{Agn}_{\mathrm{r}\wedge\mathrm{fr}}$ only. Moreover, if the agent already decides to achieve φ_{r} along h, here the strategy σ should lead the play to reach, instead, $R_{\mathrm{d}} \cap R_{\mathrm{fd}} \cap R_{\mathrm{r}}$, by visiting states in $\mathsf{Agn}_{\mathrm{r}\wedge\mathrm{fr}}$ only. The following computation focuses on the former case (computing a strategy for the latter case is similar). Therefore, we can build a new DA with reachability-safety condition $\mathcal{A}_1 = (2^{\mathcal{X}\cup\mathcal{Y}}, Q, I, \delta, \mathrm{Reach\text{–}Safe}(R_{\mathrm{d}} \cap R_{\mathrm{fd}}, \mathsf{Agn}_{\mathrm{r}\wedge\mathrm{fr}}))$ out of $\mathcal{A} = (2^{\mathcal{X}\cup\mathcal{Y}}, Q, I, \delta, \mathrm{Reach}(R))$, and solve it by reducing to a reachability game, which is analogous to the construction presented in Section 3.1.

Then we solve the reduced reachability game via a least fixpoint computation and obtain $\mathsf{Agn} = \bigcup_{0\leq j\leq n} \mathsf{Agn}^j$. Note that $I \in \mathsf{Agn}$ indeed holds, which is guaranteed by the reachability game for computing $\mathsf{Agn}_{\mathrm{r}\wedge\mathrm{fr}}$ in the previous step. We now define a strategy generator that starts serving after h, based on $\mathsf{Agn} = \bigcup_{0\leq j\leq n} \mathsf{Agn}^j$, represented as a transducer $\hat{\mathcal{T}} = (2^{\mathcal{X}\cup\mathcal{Y}}, Q, I, \varrho, \tau)$, where

- $2^{\mathcal{X}\cup\mathcal{Y}}$, Q and I are the same as in $\mathcal{A}$;
- $\varrho : Q \times 2^{\mathcal{X}} \to 2^Q$ is the transition function s.t. $\varrho(q, X) = \{q' \mid q' = \delta(q, X\cup Y) \text{ and } Y \in \tau(q)\}$;
- $\tau : Q \times 2^{\mathcal{X}} \to 2^{2^{\mathcal{Y}}}$ is the output function s.t. $\forall X \in 2^{\mathcal{X}}$, $\tau(q, X) = \{Y \mid \delta(q, X\cup Y) \in \mathsf{Agn}^j\}$ if $q \in (\mathsf{Agn}^{j+1} \backslash \mathsf{Agn}^j)$, otherwise $\tau(q, X) = 2^{\mathcal{Y}}$.

The transducer $\hat{\mathcal{T}}$, together with history h, generates an agent strategy $\sigma : (2^{\mathcal{X}})^+ \to 2^{\mathcal{Y}}$ as follows: $\forall \xi^k \in (2^{\mathcal{X}})^+$ that is compatible with $h = (X_0 \cup Y_0)(X_1 \cup Y_1)\ldots(X_i \cup Y_i) \in (2^{\mathcal{X}\cup\mathcal{Y}})^*$,

$$\sigma(\xi^k) = \begin{cases} Y_k & \text{if } 0 \leq k \leq i, \\ \textbf{stop} & \text{if } \mathsf{Run}(\mathcal{A}, \pi^{k-1}) \text{ visited } R_{\mathrm{d}} \cap R_{\mathrm{fd}}, \\ \tau(q_k, X_k) & \text{otherwise.} \end{cases}$$

where $\mathsf{Run}(\mathcal{A}, \pi^{k-1}) = q_0 q_1 q_2 \ldots q_k$ such that $q_0 = I$, and $\pi^{k-1} = (X_0 \cup Y_0)(X_1 \cup Y_1)\ldots(X_{k-1} \cup Y_{k-1})$.

Intuitively, given a history $h \in (2^{\mathcal{X} \cup \mathcal{Y}})^*$, the final strategy σ is generated by first following h, and starts taking $\hat{\mathcal{T}}$ by choosing suitable agent action to enforce the play to get closer to $R_{\mathrm{d}} \cap R_{\mathrm{fd}}$, then keeps playing **stop** right after visiting $R_{\mathrm{d}} \cap R_{\mathrm{fd}}$.

Lemma 8. *Let $\hat{\mathcal{P}}$ be a problem of* LTL$_f$ *synthesis for further duties and rights, and $\hat{\mathcal{T}}$ be constructed as above. Any strategy returned by $\hat{\mathcal{T}}$ solves the synthesis of $\hat{\mathcal{P}}$.*

Proof. Let σ be an arbitrary strategy generated by $\hat{\mathcal{T}}$, i.e., $I \in \mathsf{Agn}_{\mathrm{r} \wedge \mathrm{fr}}$, and $\gamma \in [\![env]\!]$ be an arbitrary environment strategy that enforces env such that $\mathsf{Play}(\gamma, \sigma)$ has h as a prefix. By construction, $\mathsf{Play}(\gamma, \sigma)$ satisfies the following:

- $\mathsf{Play}(\gamma, \sigma) \models \varphi_{\mathrm{d}}$ and $\mathsf{Play}(\gamma, \sigma), |h| \models \varphi_{\mathrm{fd}}$, since after h, σ forces $\mathsf{Play}(\gamma, \sigma)$ to get closer to $R_{\mathrm{d}} \cap R_{\mathrm{fd}}$ at every step until reaching $R_{\mathrm{d}} \cap R_{\mathrm{fd}}$. Moreover, only after reaching $R_{\mathrm{d}} \cap R_{\mathrm{fd}}$, σ starts playing **stop**.
- for every prefix l of $\mathsf{Play}(\gamma, \sigma)$, if l is a prefix of h, then by definition, there exists an agent strategy σ_l that enforces $\varphi_{\mathrm{d}} \wedge \varphi_{\mathrm{r}}$ with respect to history l, i.e., $\sigma_l \rhd_l \varphi_{\mathrm{d}} \wedge \varphi_{\mathrm{r}}$. Otherwise, l has h as a prefix, then by construction, after h, $\mathsf{Play}(\gamma, \sigma)$ only visits states in $\mathsf{Agn}_{\mathrm{r} \wedge \mathrm{fr}}$. Therefore, for any of the following cases, there exists an expected agent strategy that satisfies the conditions:
  - enforcing $\varphi_{\mathrm{d}} \wedge \varphi_{\mathrm{r}}$ with respect to h, and φ_{fd} after h, if the agent chooses to achieve φ_{r} only;
  - enforcing φ_{d} with respect to h, and $\varphi_{\mathrm{fd}} \wedge \varphi_{\mathrm{fr}}$ after h, if the agent chooses to achieve φ_{fr} only;
  - enforcing $\varphi_{\mathrm{d}} \wedge \varphi_{\mathrm{r}}$ with respect to h, and $\varphi_{\mathrm{fd}} \wedge \varphi_{\mathrm{fr}}$ after h, if the agent chooses to achieve both φ_{r} and φ_{fr}. □

By the construction described above, if the reachability game on $\mathcal{A}$ does not have an agent winning strategy, then $\hat{\mathcal{T}}$ trivially returns *no strategy*, and indeed by Lemma 7, $\hat{\mathcal{P}}$ is unrealizable. As an immediate consequence of Lemmas 7&8, we have:

Theorem 9. *Let $\hat{\mathcal{P}}$ be a problem of* LTL$_f$ *synthesis for further duties and rights. Realizability of $\hat{\mathcal{P}}$ can be solved by a reduction to a suitable reachability game. Synthesis of $\hat{\mathcal{P}}$ can be solved by generating a strategy from $\hat{\mathcal{T}}$, as constructed above.*

Theorem 10. *Let $\hat{\mathcal{P}}$ be a problem of* LTL$_f$ *synthesis for further duties and rights. Realizability of $\hat{\mathcal{P}}$ is 2EXPTIME-complete.*

Theorem 11. *Let $\hat{\mathcal{P}}$ be a problem of* LTL$_f$ *synthesis for further duties and rights. Then computing a strategy solving $\hat{\mathcal{P}}$ can take, in the worst case, double-exponential time in $|env| + |\varphi_{\mathrm{d}}| + |\varphi_{\mathrm{r}}| + |\varphi_{\mathrm{fd}}| + |\varphi_{\mathrm{fr}}|$.*

Analogously to Section 3.1, given problem $\hat{\mathcal{P}} = (env, \varphi_{\mathrm{d}}, \varphi_{\mathrm{r}}, \varphi_{\mathrm{fd}}, \varphi_{\mathrm{fr}}, h)$, suppose we have a strategy σ for $\hat{\mathcal{P}}$, and while executing σ, the agent wants to satisfy also its rights φ_{r} or φ_{fr} (maybe both). Then we can again, base on the immediate results obtained from the construction above, to construct three transducers $\hat{\mathcal{T}}_{\mathrm{r}}$, $\hat{\mathcal{T}}_{\mathrm{fr}}$ and $\hat{\mathcal{T}}_{\mathrm{r} \wedge \mathrm{fr}}$, corresponding to agent options of achieving also φ_{r} only, φ_{fr} only, and φ_{r} together with φ_{fr}, following the construction described in Section 3.1. Indeed, if the agent already decides to satisfy φ_{r} along h, i.e., before further duties and rights arrive, then the agent needs to stay with its choice of satisfying φ_{r}. In this case, when further duties and rights arrive, the agent can only choose whether to satisfy also further rights φ_{fr}.

We extend the cleaning robot example and demonstrate how the robot deal with further duties and rights.

Example 5. *Suppose the cleaning robot decides to achieve also its new rights "emptying the garbage collector" $\varphi_{\mathrm{fr}} = \Diamond(Collector\_Empty)$ when being on its way to the charging station after cleaning rooms A and C. In other words, the robot already made the decision of achieving its rights "fully charging battery", so the current strategy indeed comes from $\hat{\mathcal{T}}_{\mathrm{r}}$. Let us assume that $\hat{\mathcal{T}}_{\mathrm{r} \wedge \mathrm{fr}}$ is not prepared in advance and by now the running history is h'. Note that h' is different from the running history h generated when the robot receives further duties and rights. The robot will now compute $\hat{\mathcal{T}}_{\mathrm{r} \wedge \mathrm{fr}}$, and choose a strategy $\sigma_{h'}$ out of $\hat{\mathcal{T}}_{\mathrm{r} \wedge \mathrm{fr}}$ that allows it to enforce $\varphi_{\mathrm{d}} \wedge \varphi_{\mathrm{r}}$ with respect to h, and $\varphi_{\mathrm{fd}} \wedge \varphi_{\mathrm{fr}}$ after h.*

It should be noted that, one can generalize the problem of LTL$_f$ synthesis with further duties and rights to allow multiple further duties and rights. In this case, computing such transducers in advance might lead to a tradeoff, since there can be an exponential number of agent options of choosing which rights to achieve. Therefore, it might be better to just keep the winning regions and compute the strategy for achieving the chosen rights only if and when the agent demands it.

5 Conclusion

We have studied synthesis for duties respecting rights. We have shown that we can actually compute such strategies with a small overhead wrt to the state-of-the-art LTL$_f$ synthesis techniques (Zhu et al. 2017; Bansal et al. 2020; De Giacomo and Favorito 2021). We can do so by enriching the arena to contain also the information needed to handle the rights. For simplicity, we have considered a single duties specification and a single rights specification at the time. Considering multiple duties specifications simultaneously actually is like considering as duties the conjunction of the duties specifications. However, considering multiple rights specifications would require to consider satisfying arbitrary subsets of rights, as chosen by the agent. This can still be done with our techniques, though precomputing solutions as in Section 3 can lead to a combinatorial explosion. In fact, our solution to handle further duties and rights in Section 4 can be already applied to handle multiple duties and rights as well, by considering as history the empty history. Note that the technique presented there also handle contradicting rights, i.e., rights that cannot actually be satisfied simultaneously (but see the discussion at the end of Section 4). These extensions tighten up even more the connection with Deontic Logic, in particular in combination with actions (Gabbay et al. 2013). We leave though exploring this connection to future work.

Acknowledgements

This work is partially supported by the ERC Advanced Grant WhiteMech (No. 834228), the EU ICT-48 2020 project TAILOR (No. 952215), the PRIN project RIPER (No. 20203FFYLK), the JPMorgan AI Faculty Research Award "Resilience-based Generalized Planning and Strategic Reasoning"

References

Aminof, B.; De Giacomo, G.; Murano, A.; and Rubin, S. 2018. Planning and synthesis under assumptions. *CoRR* abs/1807.06777.

Aminof, B.; De Giacomo, G.; Murano, A.; and Rubin, S. 2019. Planning under LTL environment specifications. In *ICAPS*.

Bacchus, F., and Kabanza, F. 2000. Using temporal logics to express search control knowledge for planning. *Artif. Intell.* 116(1-2):123–191.

Bansal, S.; Li, Y.; Tabajara, L. M.; and Vardi, M. Y. 2020. Hybrid Compositional Reasoning for Reactive Synthesis from Finite-Horizon Specifications. In *AAAI*, 9766–9774.

Bernet, J.; Janin, D.; and Walukiewicz, I. 2002. Permissive strategies: from parity games to safety games. *RAIRO Theor. Informatics Appl.* 36(3):261–275.

Camacho, A.; Bienvenu, M.; and McIlraith, S. A. 2018. Finite LTL synthesis with environment assumptions and quality measures. In *KR*, 454–463. AAAI Press.

Cimatti, A.; Pistore, M.; Roveri, M.; and Traverso, P. 2003. Weak, strong, and strong cyclic planning via symbolic model checking. 1–2(147).

De Giacomo, G., and Favorito, M. 2021. Compositional approach to translate $\mathrm{LTL}_f/\mathrm{LDL}_f$ into deterministic finite automata. In *ICAPS*, 122–130.

De Giacomo, G., and Vardi, M. Y. 2013. Linear Temporal Logic and Linear Dynamic Logic on Finite Traces. In *IJCAI*, 854–860.

De Giacomo, G., and Vardi, M. Y. 2015. Synthesis for LTL and LDL on Finite Traces. In *IJCAI*, 1558–1564.

De Giacomo, G.; Di Stasio, A.; Vardi, M. Y.; and Zhu, S. 2020. Two-stage technique for ltlf synthesis under LTL assumptions. In *KR*, 304–314.

De Giacomo, G.; Di Stasio, A.; Perelli, G.; and Zhu, S. 2021a. Synthesis with Mandatory Stop Actions. In *KR*.

De Giacomo, G.; Di Stasio, A.; Tabajara, L. M.; Vardi, M. Y.; and Zhu, S. 2021b. Finite-trace and generalized-reactivity specifications in temporal synthesis. In *IJCAI*, 1852–1858.

de Silva, L.; Meneguzzi, F.; and Logan, B. 2020. BDI agent architectures: A survey. In *IJCAI*, 4914–4921. ijcai.org.

Finkbeiner, B.; Klein, F.; and Metzger, N. 2021. Live synthesis. *CoRR* abs/2107.01136.

Finkbeiner, B. 2016. Synthesis of reactive systems. In *Dependable Software Systems Engineering*, volume 45 of *NATO Science for Peace and Security Series - D: Information and Communication Security*. 72–98.

Gabaldon, A. 2011. Non-markovian control in the situation calculus. *Artif. Intell.* 175(1):25–48.

Gabbay, D.; Horty, J.; Parent, X.; van der Meyden, R.; and van der Torre, L. 2013. *Handbook of Deontic Logic and Normative System, Volume 2*. College Publications.

Ghallab, M.; Nau, D. S.; and Traverso, P. 2016. *Automated planning and acting*. Cambridge.

Haslum, P.; Lipovetzky, N.; Magazzeni, D.; and Muise, C. 2019. *An Introduction to the Planning Domain Definition Language*.

Kupferman, O., and Vardi, M. Y. 2001. Model Checking of Safety Properties. *Formal Methods in System Design* 19(3):291–314.

Lespérance, Y.; Levesque, H. J.; Lin, F.; and Scherl, R. B. 2000. Ability and knowing how in the situation calculus. *Stud Logica* 66(1):165–186.

Lichtenstein, O.; Pnueli, A.; and Zuck, L. D. 1985. The Glory of the Past. In *Logics of Programs*, 196–218.

Martin, D. 1975. Borel Determinacy. *Annals of Mathematics* 65:363–371.

Pnueli, A., and Rosner, R. 1989. On the Synthesis of a Reactive Module. In *POPL*, 179–190.

Pnueli, A. 1977. The temporal logic of programs. In *FOCS*, 46–57.

Rintanen, J. 2004. Complexity of planning with partial observability. In *ICAPS*, 345–354. AAAI.

Zhu, S.; Tabajara, L. M.; Li, J.; Pu, G.; and Vardi, M. Y. 2017. Symbolic LTL_f Synthesis. In *IJCAI*, 1362–1369.

Zhu, S.; De Giacomo, G.; Pu, G.; and Vardi, M. Y. 2020. LTL_f synthesis with fairness and stability assumptions. In *AAAI*, 3088–3095.

Proceedings of the 19th International Conference on Principles of Knowledge Representation and Reasoning
Main Track

On the Relationship between Shy and Warded Datalog+/-

Teodoro Baldazzi[1] , **Luigi Bellomarini**[2] , **Marco Favorito**[2,3] , **Emanuel Sallinger**[4,5]
[1]Università Roma Tre, Italy
[2]Bank of Italy
[3]Università Sapienza, Italy
[4]TU Wien, Austria
[5]University of Oxford, UK
teodoro.baldazzi@uniroma3.it, {luigi.bellomarini,marco.favorito}@bancaditalia.it, sallinger@dbai.tuwien.ac.at

Abstract

Datalog$^\exists$ is the extension of Datalog with existential quantification. While its high expressive power, underpinned by a simple syntax and the support for full recursion, renders it particularly suitable for modern applications on knowledge graphs, query answering (QA) over such language is known to be undecidable in general. For this reason, different fragments have emerged, introducing syntactic limitations to Datalog$^\exists$ that strike a balance between its expressive power and the computational complexity of QA, to achieve decidability. In this short paper, we focus on two promising tractable candidates, namely Shy and Warded Datalog$^\pm$. Reacting to an explicit interest from the community, we shed light on the relationship between these fragments. Moreover, we carry out an experimental analysis of the systems implementing Shy and Warded, respectively DLV$^\exists$ and Vadalog.

1 Introduction

The last decade has witnessed a rising interest, both in academia and industry, towards querying and exploiting data in the form of *knowledge graphs* (KGs), modeled by combining extensional knowledge with ontological theories to infer intensional information. This led to the adoption of novel intelligent systems that perform *ontological reasoning* and *ontology-based query answering* (QA) tasks over KGs, employing powerful logic languages for knowledge representation (Krötzsch and Thost 2016).

Among the main requirements such languages must exhibit, a high expressive power is essential in modern applications on KGs, so as to model and reason on complex domains with full recursion and existential quantification (Bellomarini et al. 2017). At the same time, decidability and tractability of QA must be sustained, limiting the data complexity to a polynomial degree (Gottlob and Pieris 2015).

In this context, Datalog$^\exists$, the natural extension of Datalog with existential quantification in rule heads, became particularly relevant. Its semantics is specified in an operational way via the CHASE (Maier, Mendelzon, and Sagiv 1979), an algorithmic tool that takes as input a database D and a set Σ of rules, and modifies D by adding new tuples until Σ is satisfied. While this language encompasses both a high expressiveness and a simple syntax that enable powerful knowledge-modeling, QA over it is known to be undecidable in general (Calì, Gottlob, and Kifer 2013). For this reason, recent years have witnessed a rise of proposals for decidable classes of Datalog$^\exists$ in the literature (Calì, Gottlob, and Lukasiewicz 2012; Calì, Gottlob, and Pieris 2012; Baget, Leclère, and Mugnier 2010; Baget et al. 2011), defined by imposing proper syntactic limitations to strike a good balance between the expressive power of the language and the computational complexity of QA.

In this paper, we focus on two particularly promising languages, namely, *Shy Datalog*$^\exists$ (Leone et al. 2019) and *Warded Datalog*$^\pm$ (Gottlob and Pieris 2015), which have been independently introduced. Indeed, they both cover the requirements for knowledge representation, restricting Datalog$^\exists$, though with notably different constraints, and featuring PTIME data complexity for Boolean conjunctive QA (BCQA). Shy and Warded are employed in state-of-the-art reasoning systems. Specifically, Shy was introduced as part of the *parsimonious* class (Leone et al. 2012) and is adopted in the system *DLV*$^\exists$ (Leone et al. 2017). Likewise, Warded was recently introduced as fragment of the Datalog$^\pm$ family (Calì et al. 2010) and is implemented as logic core of the reasoner *Vadalog system* (Bellomarini et al. 2020). Both find many industrial applications in the financial, media intelligence, security, logistics, pricing domains, and more (Berger et al. 2019; Adrian et al. 2018).

Previous works have thoroughly discussed how these two languages individually compare to the other main decidable classes (Leone et al. 2019; Gottlob, Lukasiewicz, and Pieris 2014). However, to our surprise, determining the relationship between Shy and Warded is still an unexplored research topic, despite known to be recurring in the Datalog$^\exists$ academic and practitioner communities.

This paper aims at providing an answer to such question, by contributing the results summarized below. After a brief overview of Shy and Warded, we present a novel **theoretical analysis** of the relationship between the languages. From a syntactical point of view, we conclude that they intersect in a newly defined fragment, named **Protected Datalog**$^\pm$. Regarding semantics, we show that the CHASE procedures adopted by Shy and Warded are equivalent over Protected settings with respect to BCQA. To enrich the analysis with a more empirical perspective, we then illustrate an **experimental comparison** between DLV$^\exists$ and the Vadalog system on QA tasks over Protected settings.

Overview. This paper is organized as follows. In Section 2, we provide an overview of Shy and Warded. In Section 3, we discuss the relationship between them. In Section 4, we provide the experimental evaluation of DLV$^{\exists}$ and the Vadalog system. We draw our conclusions in Section 5.

2 Shy Datalog$^{\exists}$ and Warded Datalog$^{\pm}$

To guide our discussion, we briefly recall some relevant notions and provide an overview of the two fragments at issue. Let C, N, and V be disjoint countably infinite sets of *constants*, *(labelled) nulls* and *(regular) variables*, respectively. A *(relational) schema* $\mathbf{S}$ is a finite set of relation symbols (or *predicates*) with associated arity. A *term* is either a constant or variable. An *atom* over $\mathbf{S}$ is an expression of the form $R(\bar{v})$, where $R \in \mathbf{S}$ is of arity $n > 0$ and $\bar{v}$ is an n-tuple of terms. A *database (instance)* over $\mathbf{S}$ associates to each relation symbol in $\mathbf{S}$ a relation of the respective arity over the domain of constants and nulls. The members of the relations are called *tuples* or *facts*. Given two conjunctions of atoms ς_1 and ς_2, we define a *homomorphism* from ς_1 to ς_2 as a mapping $h : C \cup N \cup V \to C \cup N \cup V$ such that $h(t) = t$ if $t \in C$, $h(t) \in C \cup N$ if $t \in N$ and if $a(t_1, \ldots, t_n)$ is an atom $\in \varsigma_1$, then $a(h(t_1), \ldots, h(t_n)) \in \varsigma_2$: ς_1 and ς_2 are *isomorphic* if h^{-1} is a homomorphism from ς_2 to ς_1.

A Datalog$^{\exists}$ program consists of a set of facts and *existential rules* $\forall\bar{x}\forall\bar{y}(\varphi(\bar{x}, \bar{y}) \to \exists\bar{z}\ \psi(\bar{x}, \bar{z}))$, where φ (the *body*) and ψ (the *head*) are conjunctions of atoms. We omit $\forall$ and denote conjunction by comma. Let Σ be a set of Datalog$^{\exists}$ rules and $p[i]$ a position (i.e., the i-th term of a predicate p with arity k, where $i = 1, \ldots, k$). We define $p[i]$ as *affected* if (i) p appears in a rule in Σ with an existentially quantified variable ($\exists$-*variable*) in i-th term or, (ii) there is a rule in Σ such that a universally quantified variable ($\forall$-*variable*) is only in affected body positions and in $p[i]$ in the head.

Shy Datalog$^{\exists}$. Let y be an $\exists$-variable in Σ. We define the position $p[i]$ as *invaded* by y if there is a rule $\rho \in \Sigma$ such that *head*(ρ) = $p(t_1, \ldots, t_k)$ and either (i) $t_i = y$ or, (ii) t_i is a $\forall$-variable that occurs in *body*(ρ) only in positions that are invaded by y. By such definition, if $p[i]$ is invaded, then it is affected, but not vice versa. Let $x \in \mathbf{X}$ be a variable in a conjunction of atoms $\varsigma_{[\mathbf{X}]}$. We say that x is *attacked* in $\varsigma_{[\mathbf{X}]}$ by y if x occurs in $\varsigma_{[\mathbf{X}]}$ only in positions invaded by y. If x is not attacked by any variable, x is *protected* in $\varsigma_{[\mathbf{X}]}$.

We define a set Σ as *Shy Datalog*$^{\exists}$ (or shy) if, for each rule $\sigma \in \Sigma$: (S1) if a variable x occurs in more than one body atom, then x is protected in *body*(σ); and, (S2) if two distinct $\forall$-variables are not protected in *body*(σ) but occur both in *head*(σ) and in two different body atoms, then they are not attacked by the same variable (Leone et al. 2019).

Warded Datalog$^{\pm}$. A $\forall$-variable x is *harmful*, wrt a rule ρ in Σ, if x appears only in affected positions in ρ, otherwise it is *harmless*. A (join) rule that contains a harmful (join) variable is a *harmful (join) rule*. If the harmful variable is in *head*(ρ), it is *dangerous* (Gottlob and Pieris 2015).

We define a set Σ as *Warded Datalog*$^{\pm}$ (or warded) if, for each rule $\sigma \in \Sigma$: (W1) all the dangerous variables appear in a single body atom, called *ward*; and, (W2) the ward only shares harmless variables with other atoms in the body.

Chase and Semantics. Chase-based procedures enforce the satisfaction of Σ over a database D ($\langle D,\Sigma\rangle$), incrementally expanding D into new instances I with facts derived from the application of the rules in $\langle D,\Sigma\rangle$, until Σ is satisfied ($chase(D, \Sigma)$). Such facts may contain labelled nulls as placeholders for the $\exists$-variables (Calì et al. 2010). We refer to its *oblivious* variant with $ochase$. Consider an instance $I' \supseteq I$. Given a rule $\sigma : \varphi(\bar{x}, \bar{y}) \to \exists\bar{z}\ \psi(\bar{x}, \bar{z})) \in \Sigma$, a *chase step* $\langle\sigma,h\rangle$ is *applicable* to I' if there exists a homomorphism h that maps the atoms of $\varphi(\bar{x}, \bar{y})$ to facts of I (i.e., $h(\varphi(\bar{x}, \bar{y})) \subseteq I$). When the chase step is applicable, the atom $h'(\psi(\bar{x}, \bar{z}))$ is added to I', where h' is obtained by extending h so that $h'(z_i) \in N$ is a fresh labelled null, $\forall\ z_i \in \bar{z}$.

However, in the presence of recursion, especially jointly with existential quantification, infinite labelled nulls could be generated in $ochase$, causing the procedure not to terminate and inhibiting the decidability of the QA task (Calì, Gottlob, and Lukasiewicz 2009). To practically achieve termination and decidability, shy and warded both employ variants of the $ochase$, based on *firing conditions* that limit the applicability of the chase steps. Specifically, shy adopts the so-called *parsimonious* chase ($pchase$): the chase step $\langle\sigma,h\rangle$ is applicable wrt $I' \supseteq I$ if, additionally, there is no homomorphism from *h(head(σ))* to I'. To cover decidability of CQ cases and preserve correctness of the evaluation, $pchase$ is extended into its variant *with resumption* ($pchase_r$) (Leone et al. 2019), which iteratively "resumes" the chase in the same state it was after termination but considering previous nulls as constants. Similarly, warded employs an *isomorphism-based* chase ($ichase$): the chase step $\langle\sigma,h\rangle$ is applicable wrt $I' \supseteq I$ if, additionally, there is no isomorphic embedding of *h(head(σ))* to I'. Here, decidability of CQA derives from (Bellomarini, Sallinger, and Gottlob 2018, Theorem 1, Theorem 2), as we shall see.

A *Boolean Conjunctive Query* (BCQ) is a first-order expression $q : \exists\mathbf{Y}\ \varsigma_{[\mathbf{X}\cup\mathbf{Y}]}$, where $\mathbf{X} \in C$. The answer of q over an instance I (namely, BCQA) is *true*, denoted by $I \models q$, if and only if there is a homomorphism h: $\mathbf{Y} \to C \cup N$ s.t. $h(\varsigma_{[\mathbf{X}\cup\mathbf{Y}]}) \subseteq I$. It holds that q is true over $chase(D, \Sigma)$, denoted by $chase(D, \Sigma) \models q$, if and only if $\langle D,\Sigma\rangle \models q$. We recall that the query output tuple problem (decision version of CQ evaluation) and BCQ evaluation are AC_0-reducible to each other (Calì, Gottlob, and Lukasiewicz 2012). Therefore, we only consider BCQ evaluation.

3 Relationship between Shy and Warded

We now have the means to discuss the relationship between shy and warded. Let us start by showing that the two fragments are not characterized by any form of syntactical containment (represented with the symbol $\not\subseteq$).

Proposition 1. shy $\not\subseteq$ warded

Proof. We prove the claim by showing that there exists a program that is shy but not warded. Let Σ be the following:

$$E_1(x) \to \exists y\, I_1(x, y) \qquad (\alpha)$$
$$E_2(x) \to \exists z\, I_2(z, x) \qquad (\beta)$$
$$I_1(x, y), I_2(z, x) \to I_3(x, y, z) \qquad (\rho)$$

Here, rules α and β are existential rules, both shy and warded, and introduce affectedness in positions $I_1[2]$ and $I_2[1]$, respectively. Rule ρ has a harmless join on x and propagates the harmful variables y and z to the head. Indeed, ρ is not warded, as y and z are dangerous and there is no ward (condition (W1) is not satisfied). However, it is shy, as the join variable x is protected (condition (S1)), whereas y and z are attacked by distinct variables, respectively y_α and z_β (condition (S2)). Therefore Σ is shy but it is not warded. □

Proposition 2. warded $\not\subseteq$ shy

Proof. We prove the claim by showing that there exists a program that is warded but not shy. Let Σ be the following:

$$E_1(\mathrm{x}) \rightarrow \exists \mathrm{y}\, I_1(\mathrm{x},\mathrm{y}) \qquad (\alpha)$$

$$I_1(\mathrm{x},\mathrm{y}), I_1(\mathrm{z},\mathrm{y}) \rightarrow I_2(\mathrm{x},\mathrm{z}) \qquad (\rho)$$

Here, rule α is an existential rule, both warded and shy, and introduces affectedness in position $I_1[2]$. Rule ρ contains a harmful join on y and propagates the harmless variables x and z to the head. Indeed, ρ is warded, as no dangerous variables occur in the rule. However, it is not shy, as the join variable y is attacked by y_α (condition (S1) is not satisfied). Therefore Σ is warded but it is not shy. □

Protected Datalog$^\pm$. To further explore the relationship between shy and warded, we first introduce the notion of *protected harmful* variable. Given a Datalog$^\exists$ set Σ, a $\forall$-variable x is protected harmful, with respect to a rule $\rho \in \Sigma$, if it appears in affected positions in ρ that are not invaded by the same $\exists$-variable: if the invading variable is the same, x is an *attacked harmful* variable. Without loss of generality (as more complex joins can be broken into steps (Bellomarini et al. 2020)), we define *protected harmful join rule* as a rule:

$$A(x_1, y_1, h), B(x_2, y_2, h) \rightarrow \exists z\, C(\overline{x}, z) \qquad (\tau)$$

where A, B and C are atoms, $A[3]$ and $B[3]$ are positions invaded (and thus affected) by distinct $\exists$-variables, $x_1, x_2 \subseteq \overline{x}$, $y_1, y_2 \subseteq \overline{y}$ are disjoint tuples of harmless variables or constants and h is a protected harmful variable. By definition of protected variables and labelled nulls, the join on h only activates on constant values in the CHASE. If h is attacked, τ is an *attacked harmful join rule*.

We define a set Σ as *Protected Datalog$^\pm$* (or protected) if, for each rule $\sigma \in \Sigma$: (P1) σ does not contain attacked harmful joins; and, (P2) σ is warded (it satisfies (W1) and (W2)). With reference to the relationship between shy and warded, we first show that protected corresponds to the syntactical intersection of the two fragments (represented with $\cap$).

Theorem 1. warded $\cap$ shy $=$ protected.

Proof. We prove the equivalence by showing the containment in both directions of implication.

warded $\cap$ shy $\subseteq$ protected. Let Σ be a generic set of rules $\in$ warded $\cap$ shy. Then, Σ satisfies condition (P2) by definition. Regarding condition (P1), we proceed by contrapositive and show that $\neg(P1) \implies \neg(S1)$. Indeed, if Σ does not satisfy condition (P1), then there exists a rule $\sigma \in \Sigma$ with an attacked harmful join. However, this means that σ contains a variable that occurs in more than one body atom and it is not protected in *body*(σ) (condition $(S1)$ is not satisfied). Therefore, by contrapositive, $\Sigma \in$ protected.

protected $\subseteq$ warded $\cap$ shy. Let Σ be a generic set of rules $\in$ protected. By condition (P2), $\Sigma \in$ warded. Also, by condition (P1), Σ may only contain harmless joins and protected harmful joins, thus an attacked variable cannot occur in both body atoms by definition. Therefore, condition (S1) is satisfied. Finally, we proceed by contrapositive and show that $\neg(S2) \implies \neg(P2)$. Indeed, if Σ does not satisfy condition (S2), then there exists a rule $\sigma \in \Sigma$ with two dangerous attacked variables in distinct body atoms. However, this means that σ does not contain a ward, thus it is not warded (condition $(P2)$ is not satisfied). Therefore, by contrapositive, $\Sigma \in$ warded $\cap$ shy. This concludes the proof. □

Figure 1 illustrates the syntactic containment of these fragments, as well as their data complexity.

With reference to the semantic perspective of this analysis, let us first develop the following consideration.

Observation 1. *$pchase(D,\Sigma) \subseteq ichase(D,\Sigma)$, $\forall\Sigma \in$ Datalog$^\exists$, $\forall D$. This derives from the definition of pchase and ichase, as the applicability of their chase steps depends on fact homomorphism and fact isomorphism, respectively. In particular, whenever a pchase step $\langle\sigma, h\rangle$ is applicable with respect to $I' \supseteq I$, the absence of homomorphisms from $h(head(\sigma))$ to I' implies the absence of isomorphic embeddings of $h(head(\sigma))$ to I' (and not vice versa). The ichase step is therefore applicable as well.*

Since, by Theorem 1, protected is a syntactical subset of warded, its data complexity is also PTIME, as shown in Figure 1. Moreover, we observe that reasoning with protected can adopt both $pchase_r$ and $ichase$. Based on these notions, we make an additional step in the comparative analysis of the fragments, stating that $pchase_r$ and $ichase$ are equivalent over protected settings, with respect to BCQA (i.e., a generic BCQ has the same answer).

Lemma 1. *Let $\Sigma \in$ shy, D a database and q a BCQ. Then, $ochase(D,\Sigma) \models q$ if and only if $pchase_r(D,\Sigma) \models q$.*

Proof. The result directly follows from (Leone et al. 2019, Theorem 4.9) for BCQA decidability over shy. □

Lemma 2. *Let $\Sigma \in$ warded, D a database and q a BCQ. Then, $ochase(D,\Sigma) \models q$ if and only if $ichase(D,\Sigma) \models q$.*

Proof. Completeness, namely $ochase(D,\Sigma) \models q$ implies $ichase(D,\Sigma) \models q$, directly follows from (Bellomarini, Sallinger, and Gottlob 2018, Theorem 1, Theorem 2), as chase subgraphs derived from isomorphic facts are isomorphic, thus irrelevant for BCQA. Soundness, namely $ichase(D,\Sigma) \models q$ implies $ochase(D,\Sigma) \models q$, holds because $ichase(\Sigma) \subseteq ochase(\Sigma)$ by definition. □

Theorem 2. *Let $\Sigma \in$ protected, D a database and q a BCQ. Then, $pchase_r(D,\Sigma) \models q$ if and only if $ichase(D,\Sigma) \models q$.*

Proof. By Theorem 1 and by definition of protected fragment, we know that $\Sigma \in$ shy and $\Sigma \in$ warded. Therefore, the result directly follows from Lemma 1 and Lemma 2. □

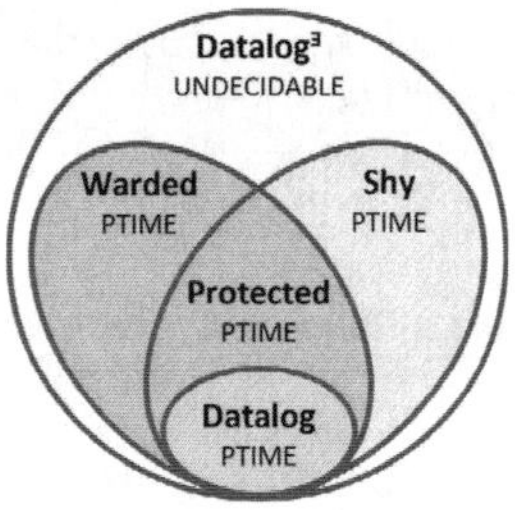

Figure 1: Syntactic containment of fragments and data complexity.

4 DLV$^\exists$ and Vadalog System

We integrate the analysis of shy and warded with an experimental comparison between their main state-of-the-art implementations, namely DLV$^\exists$ and the Vadalog system (VADALOG). Indeed, it follows from Section 3 that the two systems are comparable over protected settings.

Systems Overview. DLV$^\exists$ is an extension of the answer set programming system DLV (Leone et al. 2006), enriched with $pchase_r$ for CQA over shy programs. To answer CQs, it employs a *materialization* approach, producing and storing all the facts for each predicate via the so-called *semi-naive* evaluation (Abiteboul, Hull, and Vianu 1995), where rules are evaluated according to a bottom-up strategy from the initial database. It is available online (Leone et al. 2017). VADALOG is a well-known system for KG management, implementing warded and $ichase$ for reasoning and CQA (Bellomarini, Sallinger, and Gottlob 2018). To answer CQs, it employs a *streaming* approach, building a *reasoning query graph* as a processing pipeline, where nodes correspond to algebra operators that perform transformations over the data pulled from their predecessors, and edges are dependency connections between the rules. It is available upon request. While DLV$^\exists$ integrates powerful optimization techniques that VADALOG has yet to incorporate, the latter is also extended with multiple features of practical utility, such as aggregations and equality-generating dependencies.

Experiments and Results. We compared DLV$^\exists$ and VADALOG over distinct reasoning scenarios and QA tasks. The experiments were run on a local installation of the two systems, using a machine equipped with an Intel Core i7-8665U CPU running at 1.90 GHz and 16 GB of RAM. The results of the experiments, as well as the steps to reproduce them on DLV$^\exists$, were made public (Baldazzi et al. 2022).

The first set of experiments is based on a financial recursive scenario about persons and companies (Bellomarini, Sallinger, and Gottlob 2018) and real datasets extracted from DBPedia (DBpedia 2018). A *person of significant control* (PSC) for a company is a person that directly or indirectly has some control over the company. The goal of this task is finding all the PSCs for the companies in DBPedia. We ran it for all the 67K available companies and for 1K, 10K, 100K, 500K and 1M of the available persons. Figure 2 illustrates similar execution times for the two systems, all under 5 seconds. Specifically, DLV$^\exists$ has better times in the first cases, partially due to VADALOG's longer pre-processing phase for the creation of the query graph. With larger datasets, VADALOG's performance progressively improves, thanks to its efficient recursion control to avoid the exploration of redundant areas of the reasoning space, and its *routing strategies* to traverse the query graph (Bellomarini et al. 2020).

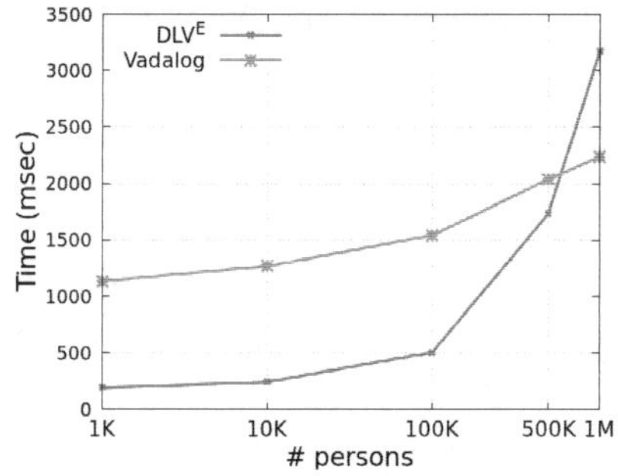

Figure 2: QA times for DBPedia PSC scenarios.

The second set of experiments is based on *Doctors*, a data integration task from the schema mapping literature (Mecca, Papotti, and Santoro 2014), included in the CHASEBENCH benchmark (Benedikt et al. 2017). It represents a plausible real-world case related to the healthcare domain and it features existential quantification. We ran it for 10K, 100K, 500K and 1M of all the datasets and over 7 distinct queries, of which we report the average times. Figure 3 illustrates that, while both systems show very good behaviour even in the most demanding cases, DLV$^\exists$ outperforms VADALOG. This is motivated by the powerful optimization techniques integrated in DLV$^\exists$ that limit the loading of redundant data for the query and reduce the space needed for materializing the output of $pchase_r$ (Leone et al. 2019).

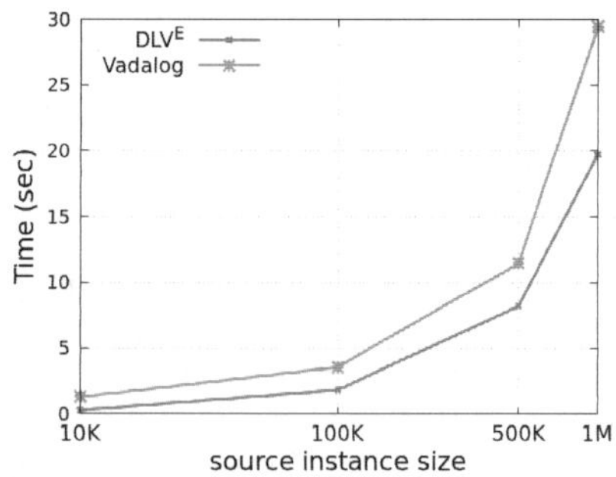

Figure 3: QA times for CHASEBENCH Doctors scenarios.

5 Conclusion

Shy Datalog$^\exists$ and Warded Datalog$^\pm$ are two relevant languages that extend Datalog with existential quantification while sustaining decidability of BCQA. Reacting to an explicit interest of the community, we provided an analysis of the fragments in terms of syntactical relationship and query evaluation, as well as an experimental comparison of their main implementations. Future work includes investigating their mutual reduction into the intersection fragment we defined and its impact in terms of their semantic relationship.

Acknowledgements

The work on this paper was supported by the Vienna Science and Technology Fund (WWTF) grant VRG18-013

References

Abiteboul, S.; Hull, R.; and Vianu, V. 1995. *Foundations of databases*, volume 8. Addison-Wesley Reading.

Adrian, W. T.; Alviano, M.; Calimeri, F.; Cuteri, B.; Dodaro, C.; Faber, W.; Fuscà, D.; Leone, N.; Manna, M.; Perri, S.; Ricca, F.; Veltri, P.; and Zangari, J. 2018. The ASP system DLV: advancements and applications. *Künstliche Intell.* 32(2-3):177–179.

Baget, J.-F.; Mugnier, M.-L.; Rudolph, S.; and Thomazo, M. 2011. Walking the complexity lines for generalized guarded existential rules. In *Twenty-Second International Joint Conference on Artificial Intelligence*.

Baget, J.-F.; Leclère, M.; and Mugnier, M.-L. 2010. Walking the decidability line for rules with existential variables. *KR* 10:466–476.

Baldazzi, T.; Bellomarini, L.; Favorito, M.; and Sallinger, E. 2022. Experimental evaluation. https://github.com/TeodoroBaldazzi/Shy-Warded-Datalog-KR2022. Accessed: 2022-02-01.

Bellomarini, L.; Gottlob, G.; Pieris, A.; and Sallinger, E. 2017. Swift logic for big data and knowledge graphs. In *IJCAI*, 2–10. Springer.

Bellomarini, L.; Benedetto, D.; Gottlob, G.; and Sallinger, E. 2020. Vadalog: A modern architecture for automated reasoning with large knowledge graphs. *IS*.

Bellomarini, L.; Sallinger, E.; and Gottlob, G. 2018. The Vadalog System: Datalog-based reasoning for knowledge graphs. *VLDB* 11(9).

Benedikt, M.; Konstantinidis, G.; Mecca, G.; Motik, B.; Papotti, P.; Santoro, D.; and Tsamoura, E. 2017. Benchmarking the chase. In *Proceedings of the 36th ACM SIGMOD-SIGACT-SIGAI Symposium on Principles of Database Systems*, 37–52.

Berger, G.; Gottlob, G.; Pieris, A.; and Sallinger, E. 2019. The space-efficient core of vadalog. In *PODS*, 270–284. ACM.

Calì, A.; Gottlob, G.; Lukasiewicz, T.; Marnette, B.; and Pieris, A. 2010. Datalog+/-: A family of logical knowledge representation and query languages for new applications. In *2010 25th Annual IEEE LICS*, 228–242. IEEE.

Calì, A.; Gottlob, G.; and Kifer, M. 2013. Taming the infinite chase: Query answering under expressive relational constraints. *Journal of Artificial Intelligence Research* 48:115–174.

Calì, A.; Gottlob, G.; and Lukasiewicz, T. 2009. A general datalog-based framework for tractable query answering over ontologies. In *PODS*, 77–86.

Calì, A.; Gottlob, G.; and Lukasiewicz, T. 2012. A general datalog-based framework for tractable query answering over ontologies. *Journal of Web Semantics* 14:57–83.

Calì, A.; Gottlob, G.; and Pieris, A. 2012. Towards more expressive ontology languages: The query answering problem. *Artificial Intelligence* 193:87–128.

DBpedia. 2018. Global and unified access to knowledge graphs. http://wiki.dbpedia.org/services-resources/downloads/dbpedia-tables. Accessed: 2022-02-01.

Gottlob, G., and Pieris, A. 2015. Beyond sparql under owl 2 ql entailment regime: Rules to the rescue. In *Twenty-Fourth International Joint Conference on Artificial Intelligence*.

Gottlob, G.; Lukasiewicz, T.; and Pieris, A. 2014. Datalog+/-: Questions and answers. In *Fourteenth International Conference on the Principles of Knowledge Representation and Reasoning*.

Krötzsch, M., and Thost, V. 2016. Ontologies for knowledge graphs: Breaking the rules. In *International Semantic Web Conference (1)*, volume 9981 of *LNCS*, 376–392.

Leone, N.; Pfeifer, G.; Faber, W.; Eiter, T.; Gottlob, G.; Perri, S.; and Scarcello, F. 2006. The dlv system for knowledge representation and reasoning. *ACM Transactions on Computational Logic (TOCL)* 7(3):499–562.

Leone, N.; Manna, M.; Terracina, G.; and Veltri, P. 2012. Efficiently computable datalog^E programs. In *Thirteenth international conference on the principles of knowledge representation and reasoning*.

Leone, N.; Manna, M.; Terracina, G.; and Veltri, P. 2017. Dlv^E system. https://www.mat.unical.it/dlve/. Accessed: 2022-02-01.

Leone, N.; Manna, M.; Terracina, G.; and Veltri, P. 2019. Fast query answering over existential rules. *ACM Transactions on Computational Logic (ToCL)* 20(2):1–48.

Maier, D.; Mendelzon, A. O.; and Sagiv, Y. 1979. Testing implications of data dependencies. *ACM Transactions on Database Systems* 4(4):455–468.

Mecca, G.; Papotti, P.; and Santoro, D. 2014. Iq-meter-an evaluation tool for data-transformation systems. In *2014 IEEE 30th International Conference on Data Engineering*, 1218–1221. IEEE.

Proceedings of the 19th International Conference on Principles of Knowledge Representation and Reasoning
Main Track

Projection of Belief in the Presence of Nondeterministic Actions and Fallible Sensing

Jens Claßen[1] **, James P. Delgrande**[2]
[1]Department of People and Technology, Roskilde University, Denmark
[2]School of Computing Science, Simon Fraser University, Burnaby, BC, Canada
classen@ruc.dk, jim@cs.sfu.ca

Abstract

We recently presented a Situation Calculus-based framework for modelling an agent who has incomplete or inaccurate knowledge about its environments, whose actions are nondeterministic, and whose sensors might give incorrect results. Generalizing earlier proposals, the approach represented the agent's epistemic state by a set of situations ranked by their respective plausibility, and which would then be updated by modifying the plausibility ranks accordingly. Here we extend our earlier work by considering *projection* in this framework, i.e. the question whether a certain (epistemic) formula will hold after a given sequence of actions. We present results on both *regression*, where the query is transformed into an equivalent one about the initial situation, as well as *progression*, where the knowledge base is updated to reflect the situation after executing the action sequence in question.

1 Introduction

In a recent paper (Claßen and Delgrande 2021), we presented a framework based on the Situation Calculus (McCarthy and Hayes 1969; Reiter 2001) for representing an agent that has incomplete or inaccurate knowledge about its environment, whose actions are non-deterministic, and whose sensors might be fallible. The approach generalizes earlier proposals (Shapiro et al. 2011; Delgrande and Levesque 2012; Delgrande and Levesque 2019) where the agent's epistemic state is presented by a set of situations ranked by their respective plausibility, and which would then be updated according to the executed action and its sensing outcome. Two notions of belief were distinguished, an extensional "bird's eye" view, and an intensional one from the agent's perspective. Here we extend this work by considering the *projection problem*, which means deciding whether a formula will hold after a given sequence of actions, which is in particular needed for the purpose of planning. We present results on both *regression*, where the query is transformed into an equivalent one about the initial situation, as well as *progression*, where the knowledge base is updated to reflect the situation after executing the action sequence in question. For brevity, we only discuss the extensional case, but it is straightforward to adapt our results to the intensional one.

As a motivating example, we adapt the extended litmus paper problem from (Hunter and Delgrande 2011). The original example is due to Moore (1985): There is a liquid in a beaker that is either an acid or a base, and the agent has a piece of litmus paper. After dipping the paper into the liquid and observing its colour, the agent will learn that the liquid is an acid, if the paper turned red, and a base, if the paper turned blue. In the extended version, the agent most plausibly *believes* that the paper is litmus, however also allows for the possibility that it is just a plain piece of white paper. After dipping it and observing that it remained white, the agent will revise its beliefs so that it now most plausibly believes that the paper is (and initially was) in fact not litmus paper.

We present preliminaries in Section 2, discuss regression in Section 3, progression in Section 4, and then conclude.

2 Preliminaries

2.1 The Situation Calculus

The Situation Calculus is a dialect of first-order logic, with some second-order features, for reasoning about action and change. There is a sort for *actions*, one for *situations*, and one for *objects* (everything else, including numbers). Situations describe possible sequences of actions, where a term $do(\alpha, \sigma)$ denotes the situation resulting from applying action α in situation σ, and S_0 is a constant representing the initial situation. We will use σ (possibly with decorations) to denote *terms* of sort situation, and s (possibly with decorations) as situation *variables*. Similarly, α and β will refer to action *terms*, whereas a is used as action variable. For convenience, we may use sequence notation for do where $do(\beta, do(\alpha, S_0))$ can be written as $do(\langle\alpha;\beta\rangle, S_0)$. Changing properties are represented by *fluents*, which are predicates that take a situation as their last argument, e.g. $Re(s)$ to express that the litmus paper is red in situation s. A formula is called *uniform in* σ if the only situation term it mentions is σ (ruling out quantification and equalities over situations).

2.2 Nondeterminism, Fallible Sensing, Belief

Here we only give a brief summary of our framework for nondeterministic actions, fallible sensing, and extensional belief, and refer to (Claßen and Delgrande 2021) for details. Nondeterminism is handled by distinguishing two types of action parameters: the ones under the control of the agent, and those under "nature's" control (we henceforth omit the scare quotes). For example, $flip(x, y)$ might denote the action of flipping a coin x, for which nature then determines outcome y (e.g., heads, tails, or some form of failure).

We use three special predicates: $Ieq(a, a')$ expresses that actions a and a' are *intensionally equivalent*, meaning they are identical except maybe for arguments set by nature. $Apl(a, p, s)$ says that action a has *argument plausibility* p in situation s, where $p = 0$ corresponds to the most plausible outcome(s), and higher values to less plausible ones. The *sensing fluent* $SF(a, s)$ holds iff action a reports sensing result "true" in situation s. Fallible sensing is again handled by a special argument set by nature, e.g. indicating that a light sensor works correctly ($sL(ok)$), or has a fault where it transiently reports the light being on ($sL(on)$) or off ($sL(off)$).

For beliefs, we allow for multiple initial situations s, denoted by $Init(s)$, in addition to S_0. We use an accessibility predicate $B(s', p, s)$ to express that in situation s, the agent considers situation s' possible with plausibility p. A formula ϕ is believed in situation s, written $Bel(\phi, s)$, iff it is true in all most plausible (MP) situations s' accessible from s:

$$MP(s', s) \doteq \exists p. B(s', p, s) \land \forall s'', p' (B(s'', p', s) \supset p \leq p')$$
$$Bel(\phi, s) \doteq \forall s'. MP(s', s) \supset \phi[s'].$$

(As convention, free variables are assumed to be universally quantified from the outside.) A successor state axiom for B then determines what is believed after executing an action a:

$$\begin{aligned} B(s', n, do(a, s)) \equiv\ & \exists p', s^*, n^*, a^*, p^*. B(s^*, n^*, s) \land \\ & Apl(a, p', s) \land Ieq(a, a^*) \land Apl(a^*, p^*, s^*) \land s' = do(a^*, s^*) \\ & \land (SF(a^*, s^*) \equiv SF(a, s)) \land n = n^* + p' + p^* \end{aligned} \quad (1)$$

We call formulas that don't mention SF, Apl, Ieq, or B *objective* formulas. A formula is *situation-independent* if it does not mention any fluents (including special ones such as B), but perhaps includes equalities over situation terms. Finally, we say that a (non-objective) formula is *about a ground situation term* $\sigma = do(\vec{\alpha}, S_i)$ if: (a) only σ occurs as right-hand side argument of B; (b) every other situation term in it is either a variable or a ground situation $do(\vec{\beta}, S_j)$ with $|\vec{\beta}| = |\vec{\alpha}|$; (c) if a fluent atom $F(\vec{t}, s)$ has a variable s as its situation argument, s is restricted to range only over situations such that $B(s, p, \sigma)$ for some p or $Init(s)$ holds. In particular any $Bel(\psi, \sigma)$ formula then is about σ.

2.3 Basic Action Theories

In order to describe a dynamic domain, we use action theories very similar to the ones proposed by Reiter (2001), but with additional axioms for the new special predicates:

Definition 1 (Basic Action Theory). *A basic action theory (BAT) consists of the union of the following sets of formulas:*

- Σ_0 *is an initial theory that is given by a finite set of sentences about* S_0*, satisfying that initial situations are only* B*-related to other initial situations, and that plausibility values are a function of the pair of situations:*
$$Init(s) \land B(s', n, s) \supset Init(s')$$
$$Init(s) \land B(s', n_1, s) \land B(s', n_2, s) \supset n_1 = n_2$$
- Σ_{post} *is a finite set of successor state axioms, one for each fluent predicate* $F(\vec{x}, s)$*, of the form*
$$F(\vec{x}, do(a, s)) \equiv \gamma_F(\vec{x}, a, s),$$
where γ_F *is an objective formula uniform in* s *whose free variables are among* $\vec{x}$*,* a*, and* s*;*
- Σ_{sense} *is a singleton sentence of the form*
$$SF(a, s) \equiv \varphi_{SF}(a, s),$$
where φ_{SF} *is an objective formula uniform in* s *whose free variables are among* a *and* s*;*
- Σ_{Ieq} *is a singleton sentence of the form*
$$Ieq(a_1, a_2) \equiv \varphi_{Ieq}(a_1, a_2),$$
where $\varphi_{Ieq}(a_1, a_2)$ *is a situation-independent objective formula whose free variables are among* a_1 *and* a_2*;*
- Σ_{Apl} *is a singleton sentence of the form*
$$Apl(a, p, s) \equiv \varphi_{Apl}(a, p, s),$$
where φ_{Apl} *is an objective formula uniform in* s *whose free variables are among* a*,* p*, and* s*;*
- Σ_{una} *is a set of unique names axioms for actions;*
- Σ_{fnd} *is the set of foundational axioms that defines the set of situations to form a forest of isomorphic trees rooted at initial situations, where* $Init(s) \doteq \neg\exists a, s'. s = do(a, s')$.

We ignore preconditions here for brevity, but they would be straightforward to include. Compared to (Claßen and Delgrande 2021), we also make the simplifying assumption that axioms for *Ieq*, *Apl*, and *SF* are given as a single equivalence each, instead of multiple guarded axioms. It is conceivable, though significantly more involved, to extend our projection results to include guarded axioms along the lines of what is described in (De Giacomo and Levesque 1999).

Example 1. *We formalize the extended litmus scenario as follows. Fluents* $Ac(s)$*,* $Li(s)$*,* $Re(s)$*, and* $Bl(s)$ *denote that in situation* s*, the liquid is an acid, the paper is litmus paper, the paper is red, and the paper is blue, respectively. The action of dipping the paper in the liquid is denoted by* dip*, and the action of sensing whether the paper is white by* $sW(y)$*.*

- Σ_0*: Initially, the agent considers four situations possible: It does not know whether the liquid is acid, but believes (*$p = 0$*) that the paper is litmus, while allowing for the possibility (*$p = 1$*) that the paper is not litmus. It is certain though that the paper is white (neither red nor blue).*
$$\begin{aligned} & Init(s) \equiv s = S_0 \lor s = S_1 \lor s = S_2 \lor s = S_3, \\ & B(s, p, S_0) \equiv (s = S_1 \land p = 0) \lor (s = S_2 \land p = 0) \lor \\ & \quad (s = S_0 \land p = 1) \lor (s = S_3 \land p = 1), \\ & \neg Ac(S_0) \land \neg Li(S_0) \land \neg Re(S_0) \land \neg Bl(S_0), \\ & \quad Ac(S_1) \land Li(S_1) \land \neg Re(S_1) \land \neg Bl(S_1), \\ & \neg Ac(S_2) \land Li(S_2) \land \neg Re(S_2) \land \neg Bl(S_2), \\ & \quad Ac(S_3) \land \neg Li(S_3) \land \neg Re(S_3) \land \neg Bl(S_3). \end{aligned}$$
- Σ_{post}*: In this example,* $Ac(s)$ *and* $Li(s)$ *are rigid predicates, and don't change their value due to any action.* $Re(do(a, s))$ *will be true iff* a *is a dip action, the liquid is acid, and the paper is litmus. Similar for* Bl*.*
$$\begin{aligned} & Ac(do(a, s)) \equiv Ac(s), \quad Li(do(a, s)) \equiv Li(s), \\ & Re(do(a, s)) \equiv a = dip \land Ac(s) \land Li(s) \lor Re(s), \\ & Bl(do(a, s)) \equiv a = dip \land \neg Ac(s) \land Li(s) \lor Bl(s). \end{aligned}$$

- Σ_{sense}: *When working correctly (outcome ok), sW senses whether the paper is neither red nor blue. In addition, we allow for transitory on and off failures. Thus:*

$$SF(a,s) \equiv (a = sW(ok) \wedge \neg(Re(s) \vee Bl(s))) \vee (a = sW(on))$$

- Σ_{Ieq}: *The dip action is deterministic, and so only intensionally equivalent to itself. The sensing action has a nature's argument to allow for transitory errors.*

$$Ieq(a_1,a_2) \equiv (a_1 = a_2 = dip) \vee \bigvee_{\substack{c_1,c_2 \in \\ \{ok,on,off\}}} (a_1 = sW(c_1) \wedge a_2 = sW(c_2))$$

- Σ_{Apl}: *Due to being deterministic, the dip action always has plausibility 0. The sensing action most plausibly returns the correct result, less plausibly has a transitory off failure, and even less plausibly a transitory on failure.*

$$\begin{aligned} &Apl(a,p,s) \equiv \\ &\quad (a = dip \wedge p = 0) \vee (a = sW(ok) \wedge p = 0) \vee \\ &\quad (a = sW(off) \wedge p = 1) \vee (a = sW(on) \wedge p = 2) \end{aligned}$$

3 Regression

The idea behind regression is to turn a query formula about a future situation into an equivalent one about the initial situation, and then test it against the initial theory of the BAT:

Definition 2 (Regression). *Let Σ be a BAT, $\vec{\alpha}$ a sequence of ground action terms, and ψ a formula about $do(\vec{\alpha}, S_0)$. Then a formula ϕ is a* regression of ψ wrt Σ *if it is about S_0 and $\Sigma \models \psi$ iff $\Sigma_0 \cup \Sigma_{una} \models \phi$.*

Reiter (2001) presented a regression operator $\mathfrak{R}$ that achieves this for objective formulas by iteratively replacing subexpressions deemed equivalent by the BAT. It is straightforward to extend it to the new SF, Ieq, and Apl predicates:

- $\mathfrak{R}[F(\vec{t}, do(\alpha,\sigma))] = \mathfrak{R}[\gamma_F(\vec{t},\alpha,\sigma)]$, if F is a fluent;
- $\mathfrak{R}[P(\vec{t})] = \mathfrak{R}[\varphi_P(\vec{t})]$ for $P \in \{SF, Ieq, Apl\}$;
- $\mathfrak{R}[\phi] = \phi$ for every other atomic formula ϕ;
- $\mathfrak{R}$ distributes over $\neg, \wedge, \forall$, e.g. $\mathfrak{R}[\phi \wedge \psi] = \mathfrak{R}[\phi] \wedge \mathfrak{R}[\psi]$.

In principle, formulas involving B and Bel could be handled similarly, given that (1) is a successor state axiom for B. A technical problem is that the axiom as well as Bel formulas use quantification over situations, and due to nesting, we may end up with a formula such as $\exists s'.\, s' = do(a,s) \wedge P(s')$ that cannot immediately be regressed further, unless we rewrite it to $P(do(a,s))$. The solution below makes use of this idea, together with the fact that if situations σ and σ' are B-related, then they are the result of applying action sequences *of the same length* to B-related initial situations.

We here restrict ourselves to regressing belief atoms of the form $Bel(\phi, do(\vec{\alpha}, S_0))$, where $\vec{\alpha} = \langle \alpha_0, \ldots, \alpha_{k-1}\rangle$ is a sequence of ground actions of length k. Let $\vec{a}'$,$\vec{a}''$ denote sequences of action variables of the same length, and $\vec{\alpha}_i$ the prefix $\langle \alpha_0, \ldots, \alpha_i \rangle$, with $\vec{\alpha}_{-1} \doteq \langle\rangle$. We add the rules

- $\mathfrak{R}[Bel(\phi, do(\vec{\alpha}, S_0))] = \mathfrak{R}[\forall \vec{a}', s_0'.\, MP(do(\vec{a}', s_0'), do(\vec{\alpha}, S_0)) \supset \phi[do(\vec{a}', s_0')]]$;
- $\mathfrak{R}[MP(do(\vec{a}', s_0'), do(\vec{\alpha}, S_0))] = \mathfrak{R}[\exists p'.\, B(do(\vec{a}', s_0'), p', do(\vec{\alpha}, S_0)) \wedge \forall \vec{a}'', s_0'', p''\,(B(do(\vec{a}'', s_0''), p'', do(\vec{\alpha}, S_0)) \supset p' \leq p'')]$;
- $\mathfrak{R}[B(do(\vec{a}', s_0'), n, do(\vec{\alpha}, S_0))] = \mathfrak{R}[\exists n_0, \ldots, n_k.\, B(s_0', n_0, S_0) \wedge (n = n_k) \wedge \bigwedge_{i=0}^{k-1} \Psi_i]$,

where the Ψ_i formulas in the last line are given by

$$\begin{aligned} \Psi_i \doteq\ & \exists p_i, p_i'.\, n_{i+1} = n_i + p_i + p_i' \wedge Ieq(\alpha_i, a_i') \wedge \\ & Apl(\alpha_i, p_i, do(\vec{\alpha}_{i-1}, S_0)) \wedge Apl(a_i', p_i', do(\vec{a}_{i-1}', s_0')) \wedge \\ & (SF(a_i', do(\vec{a}_{i-1}', s_0')) \equiv SF(\alpha_i, do(\vec{\alpha}_{i-1}, S_0))). \end{aligned}$$

Theorem 1. *For any belief atom $\psi = Bel(\phi, do(\vec{\alpha}, S_0))$, $\mathfrak{R}[\psi]$ is a regression of ψ wrt Σ.*

Proof. (Sketch) $\mathfrak{R}[\psi]$ clearly has the right form, and hence only depends on $\Sigma_0 \cup \Sigma_{una}$. Correctness follows from the fact that subformulas are only substituted by equivalent ones, except for the $\forall$-quantified s' and s'' in Bel and MP being replaced by $do(\vec{a}', s_0')$ and $do(\vec{a}'', s_0'')$, respectively. The latter is shown to be "safe" by an induction over $\vec{\alpha}$. □

Example 2. *To decide if $Bel(\neg Li, do(\langle dip; sW(ok)\rangle, S_0))$ is entailed by the BAT from Ex. 1, we need to determine $\mathfrak{R}[B(do(\langle a_0'; a_1'\rangle, s_0'), n, do(\langle dip; sW(ok)\rangle, S_0))]$, i.e.*

$$\begin{aligned} \mathfrak{R}[\ & \exists n_0, n_1, n_2.\, B(s_0', n_0, S_0) \wedge n = n_2 \wedge \\ & \exists p_0, p_0'.\, n_1 = n_0 + p_0 + p_0' \wedge Ieq(dip, a_0') \wedge \\ & \quad Apl(dip, p_0, S_0) \wedge Apl(a_0', p_0', s_0') \wedge \\ & \quad (SF(a_0', s_0') \equiv SF(dip, S_0)) \wedge \\ & \exists p_1, p_1'.\, n_2 = n_1 + p_1 + p_1' \wedge Ieq(sW(ok), a_1') \wedge \\ & \quad Apl(sW(ok), p_1, do(dip, S_0)) \wedge \\ & \quad Apl(a_1', p_1', do(a_0', s_0')) \wedge \\ & \quad (SF(a_1', do(a_0', s_0')) \equiv SF(sW(ok), do(dip, S_0)))\ ]. \end{aligned}$$

During further evaluation, many subexpressions can be simplified. For example, $SF(sW(ok), do(dip, S_0))$ reduces to TRUE, *and $Ieq(dip, a_0')$ to $(a_0' = dip)$. We thus obtain*

$$\begin{aligned} \exists n_0.\, & B(s_0', n_0, S_0) \wedge a_0' = dip \wedge \\ & (a_1' = sW(ok) \wedge n = n_0 \wedge \neg Li(s_0') \vee \\ & \ a_1' = sW(on) \wedge n = n_0 + 2). \end{aligned}$$

$MP(...)$ now describes those $do(\langle a_0'; a_1'\rangle, s_0')$ situations with minimal n, and $Bel(...)$ requires Li to be false there. Both $do(\langle dip; sW(ok)\rangle, S_0)$ and $do(\langle dip; sW(ok)\rangle, S_3)$ satisfy this with $n = 1$. The agent hence believes the paper is not litmus after dipping and sensing that it is white.

4 Progression

We follow (Vassos and Levesque 2013) and define:

Definition 3 (Progression). *Let Σ be a BAT, α a ground action term, and Σ_α a set of sentences about $do(\alpha, S_0)$. Then Σ_α is a* progression *of Σ_0 wrt α, Σ iff for every sentence ϕ about $do(\alpha, S_0)$, $\Sigma \models \phi$ iff $(\Sigma - \Sigma_0) \cup \Sigma_\alpha \models \phi$.*

Lin and Reiter (1997) showed that even in the objective case, the progression of a theory may require second-order logic. However, they also presented special cases for which progression is first-order definable, one of them being the *relatively complete databases*. Here, we generalize this class to the case of extensional belief. Let us call a BAT relatively complete if Σ_0 comprises exactly the following formulas:

1. The formula
$$Init(s) \;\equiv\; s = S_0 \vee \cdots \vee s = S_k,$$
where $S_0, \ldots, S_k$ denote all and only initial situations;
2. one formula of the form
$$B(s, p, S_0) \;\equiv\; \Pi_B^{S_0}(s, p),$$
where $\Pi_B^{S_0}$ is a situation-independent objective formula whose free variables are among s, p;
3. for each fluent F and each S_i, one formula of the form
$$F(\vec{x}, S_i) \;\equiv\; \Pi_F^{S_i}(\vec{x}),$$
where $\Pi_F^{S_i}(\vec{x})$ is a situation-independent objective formula whose free variables are among $\vec{x}$.

Also assume that a ground action α has only finitely many β with $\Sigma_{una} \models Ieq(\alpha, \beta)$. Let $\mathfrak{P}$ now be an operator replacing B and F subformulas by corresponding Π expressions:

- $\mathfrak{P}[B(\sigma, t, S_0)] = \Pi_B^{S_0}(\sigma, t)$;
- $\mathfrak{P}[F(\vec{t}, \sigma)] = \bigvee_{0 \leq i \leq k}(\sigma = S_i) \wedge \Pi_F^{S_i}(\vec{t})$;
- $\mathfrak{P}[P(\vec{t})] = \mathfrak{P}[\varphi_P(\vec{t})]$ for $P \in \{SF, Ieq, Apl\}$;
- $\mathfrak{P}[\phi] = \phi$ for every other atomic formula ϕ;
- $\mathfrak{P}$ distributes over $\neg, \wedge, \forall$, e.g. $\mathfrak{P}[\phi \wedge \psi] = \mathfrak{P}[\phi] \wedge \mathfrak{P}[\psi]$.

Theorem 2. *Let Σ be a relatively complete BAT, α a ground action, and $\gamma_B(s', p, a, s)$ the right-hand side of axiom (1). We construct a set Σ_α consisting of the following formulas:*

1. The formula
$$B(s, p, do(\alpha, S_0)) \;\equiv\; \mathfrak{P}[\gamma_B(s, p, \alpha, S_0)].$$
2. For each fluent F, each S_i, and each ground action β such that $\Sigma_{una} \models Ieq(\alpha, \beta)$, the formula
$$F(\vec{x}, do(\beta, S_i)) \;\equiv\; \mathfrak{P}[\gamma_F(\vec{x}, \beta, S_i)].$$

Then Σ_α is a progression of Σ_0 through α wrt Σ.

Proof. (Sketch) Σ_α obviously has the right form. Soundness follows from the fact that we only replace equivalent subformulas, completeness from the fact that the set gives a complete description for all fluents and situations. □

Notice that Σ_α has the right form to apply progression repeatedly, if we treat the finitely many $do(\beta, S_i)$ as new initial situations (e.g. by replacing each by a new constant S_β^i).

Example 3. *Suppose we want to progress the BAT from Example 1 through $\langle dip; sW(ok)\rangle$, i.e. determine what the agent believes after dipping the paper and then performing a sense-white action. Notice that the BAT has the right form if we understand expressions like $\neg Ac(S_2)$ as shorthand for $Ac(S_2) \equiv$ FALSE. After the dip action, each initial situation is updated by the results of the dip (let $S_i' \doteq do(dip, S_i)$):*

$$\begin{array}{l}
\neg Ac(S_0') \wedge \neg Li(S_0') \wedge \neg Re(S_0') \wedge \neg Bl(S_0') \\
Ac(S_1') \wedge Li(S_1') \wedge Re(S_1') \wedge \neg Bl(S_1') \\
\neg Ac(S_2') \wedge Li(S_2') \wedge \neg Re(S_2') \wedge Bl(S_2') \\
Ac(S_3') \wedge \neg Li(S_3') \wedge \neg Re(S_3') \wedge \neg Bl(S_3')
\end{array}$$

The situations' plausibilities remain unchanged, but for those situations where Li is true, the agent will believe the paper is red if the liquid is acid, and blue if base. Consequently the agent believes the paper is either red or blue.

$$\begin{array}{rl}
B(s, p, S_0') \equiv & (s = S_1' \wedge p = 0) \vee (s = S_2' \wedge p = 0) \vee \\
& (s = S_0' \wedge p = 1) \vee (s = S_3' \wedge p = 1)
\end{array}$$

After the sense-white action, the physical fluents retain their previous value, but the belief state changes as follows:

$$\begin{array}{l}
B(s, p, do(\langle dip; sW(ok)\rangle, S_0)) \;\equiv \\
\quad (s = do(\langle dip; sW(ok)\rangle, S_0) \wedge p = 1) \vee \\
\quad (s = do(\langle dip; sW(ok)\rangle, S_3) \wedge p = 1) \vee \\
\quad (s = do(\langle dip; sW(on)\rangle, S_1) \wedge p = 2) \vee \\
\quad (s = do(\langle dip; sW(on)\rangle, S_2) \wedge p = 2) \vee \\
\quad (s = do(\langle dip; sW(on)\rangle, S_0) \wedge p = 3) \vee \\
\quad (s = do(\langle dip; sW(on)\rangle, S_3) \wedge p = 3)
\end{array}$$

The two situations with minimum ($p = 1$) implausibility are those where sensing worked correctly. In both, the paper is not litmus, but Ac only holds in one. Other situations ($p > 1$) record less plausible circumstances where the sensing action failed. Hence the agent believes the paper is not litmus and does not know whether the liquid is acid or base.

5 Conclusion

We presented results on both regression and progression in a Situation Calculus-based framework for reasoning about the beliefs of an agent who is dealing with conflicting information, nondeterministic actions, and fallible sensing. As the two main solutions to the projection problem, they are paramount ingredients for any practical application of the formalism. A prototype implementation of our methods in SWI-Prolog with the examples from this paper is available on GitHub (Claßen 2022). For future work, we want to investigate their use as basis for an epistemic planner, possibly in combination with first-order knowledge compilation techniques (Claßen 2018). Without going into detail, we believe that our approach lends itself very well for this purpose when compared to similar work (Fang, Liu, and Wen 2015; Schwering and Lakemeyer 2015; Arenas et al. 2016). While (Shapiro et al. 2011) do not even consider projection, (Hunter and Delgrande 2011) only keep track of the most plausible set of situations, albeit in an action language (Gelfond and Lifschitz 1998) framework. In case of a contradiction, they regress to the initial situation, carry out belief revision, and progress through the action sequence again. We avoid this by keeping track of all possible outcomes, and in case of a sensing conflict, only need to look at the most plausible situations compatible with the sensing outcome.

Acknowledgements

We thank the reviewers for their helpful and pertinent comments. Financial support was gratefully received from the Natural Sciences and Engineering Research Council of Canada.

References

Arenas, M.; Baier, J. A.; Navarro, J. S.; and Sardiña, S. 2016. Incomplete causal laws in the situation calculus using free fluents. In Kambhampati, S., ed., *Proceedings of the Twenty-Fifht International Joint Conference on Artificial Intelligence (IJCAI 2016)*, 907–914. AAAI Press.

Claßen, J., and Delgrande, J. 2021. An account of intensional and extensional actions, and its application to belief, nondeterministic actions, and fallible sensors. In Bienvenue, M.; Erdem, E.; and Lakemeyer, G., eds., *Proceedings of the Eighteenth International Conference on the Principles of Knowledge Representation and Reasoning (KR 2021)*, 194–204. ijcai.org.

Claßen, J. 2018. Symbolic verification of Golog programs with first-order BDDs. In Thielscher, M.; Toni, F.; and Wolter, F., eds., *Proceedings of the Sixteenth International Conference on the Principles of Knowledge Representation and Reasoning (KR 2018)*, 524–529. AAAI Press.

Claßen, J. 2022. Belief Projection Prototype in SWI-Prolog. https://github.com/jens-classen/belief_projection.

De Giacomo, G., and Levesque, H. J. 1999. Projection using regression and sensors. In Dean, T., ed., *Proceedings of the Sixteenth International Joint Conference on Artificial Intelligence (IJCAI 1999)*, 160–165. Morgan Kaufmann Publishers Inc.

Delgrande, J. P., and Levesque, H. J. 2012. Belief revision with sensing and fallible actions. In Brewka, G.; Eiter, T.; and McIlraith, S. A., eds., *Proceedings of the Thirteenth International Conference on the Principles of Knowledge Representation and Reasoning (KR 2012)*. AAAI Press.

Delgrande, J. P., and Levesque, H. J. 2019. An epistemic approach to nondeterminism: Believing in the simplest course of events. *Studia Logica* 107(5):859–886.

Fang, L.; Liu, Y.; and Wen, X. 2015. On the progression of knowledge and belief for nondeterministic actions in the situation calculus. In Yang, Q., and Wooldridge, M., eds., *Proceedings of the Twenty-Fourth International Joint Conference on Artificial Intelligence (IJCAI 2015)*, 2955–2963. AAAI Press.

Gelfond, M., and Lifschitz, V. 1998. Action languages. *Electronic Transactions on AI* 3.

Hunter, A., and Delgrande, J. P. 2011. Iterated belief change due to actions and observations. *Journal of Artificial Intelligence Research* 40:269–304.

Lin, F., and Reiter, R. 1997. How to progress a database. *Artificial Intelligence* 92(1–2):131–167.

McCarthy, J., and Hayes, P. 1969. Some philosophical problems from the standpoint of artificial intelligence. In *Machine Intelligence 4*. New York: American Elsevier. 463–502.

Moore, R. C. 1985. A formal theory of knowledge and action. In Hobbs, J. R., and Moore, R. C., eds., *Formal Theories of the Commonsense World*. Norwoord, NJ, USA: Ablex Publishing. 319–358.

Reiter, R. 2001. *Knowledge in Action: Logical Foundations for Specifying and Implementing Dynamical Systems*. MIT Press.

Schwering, C., and Lakemeyer, G. 2015. Projection in the epistemic situation calculus with belief conditionals. In Bonet, B., and Koenig, S., eds., *Proceedings of the Twenty-Ninth AAAI Conference on Artificial Intelligence (AAAI 2015)*, 1583–1589. AAAI Press.

Shapiro, S.; Pagnucco, M.; Lespérance, Y.; and Levesque, H. J. 2011. Iterated belief change in the situation calculus. *Artificial Intelligence* 175(1):165–192.

Vassos, S., and Levesque, H. J. 2013. How to progress a database III. *Artificial Intelligence* 195:203–221.

Proceedings of the 19th International Conference on Principles of Knowledge Representation and Reasoning
Main Track

Inference with System W Satisfies Syntax Splitting

Jonas Haldimann , Christoph Beierle
FernUniversität in Hagen, 58084 Hagen, Germany
{jonas.haldimann, christoph.beierle}@fernuni-hagen.de

Abstract

In this paper, we investigate inductive inference with system W from conditional belief bases with respect to syntax splitting. The concept of syntax splitting for inductive inference states that inferences about independent parts of the signature should not affect each other. This was captured in work by Kern-Isberner, Beierle, and Brewka in the form of postulates for inductive inference operators expressing syntax splitting as a combination of relevance and independence; it was also shown that c-inference fulfils syntax splitting, while system P inference and system Z both fail to satisfy it. System W is a recently introduced inference system for nonmonotonic reasoning that captures and properly extends system Z as well as c-inference. We show that system W fulfils the syntax splitting postulates for inductive inference operators by showing that it satisfies the required properties of relevance and independence. This makes system W another inference operator besides c-inference that fully complies with syntax splitting, while in contrast to c-inference, also extending rational closure.

1 Introduction

An important subject in the field of knowledge representation and reasoning is the reasoning with conditional knowledge (Lehmann and Magidor 1992). A conditional formalizes a defeasible rule "If A then usually B" for logical formulas A, B, denoted here as $(B|A)$. Two well known inference methods for conditional belief bases consisting of such conditionals are p-entailment that is characterized by the axioms of System P (Adams 1965; Kraus, Lehmann, and Magidor 1990) and system Z (Pearl 1990; Goldszmidt and Pearl 1996). Newer approaches include inference with c-representations (Kern-Isberner 2001; Kern-Isberner 2004), skeptical c-inference taking all c-representations into account (Beierle et al. 2018; Beierle et al. 2021), and the recently introduced system W (Komo and Beierle 2020; Komo and Beierle 2022).

While all reasoning approaches cited above satisfy the axioms of system P, called the "industry standard" for qualitative nonmonotonic inference (Hawthorne and Makinson 2007), there are differences among them with respect to other properties. This also applies to the highly desirable property of syntax splitting for nonmonotonic reasoning. The concept of syntax splitting was originally developed by Parikh (Parikh 1999) for belief sets in order to formulate a postulate for belief revision stating that the revision with a formula that contains only variables from one part of the signature should only affect the information about that part of the signature. The notion of syntax splitting was later extended, e.g. (Peppas et al. 2015; Kern-Isberner and Brewka 2017). In (Kern-Isberner, Beierle, and Brewka 2020), syntax splitting is introduced for nonmonotic resoning as a combination of *relevance* and *independence*, stating that only conditionals from a considered part of the syntax splitting of a belief base are relevant for corresponding inferences, and that inferences using only atoms from one part of the syntax splitting should be independent of the other parts. It is shown that c-inference fulfils syntax splitting, while system P and system Z both fail to satisfy it (Kern-Isberner, Beierle, and Brewka 2020).

System W has been shown (Komo and Beierle 2022) to exhibit high-quality properties like capturing and properly extending p-entailment, system Z, and c-inference, or avoiding the drowning problem (Pearl 1990; Benferhat et al. 1993). In this paper, we show that system W also satisfies the required properties of relevance and independence, making it another inference operator, besides c-inference, to fully comply with the highly desirable property of syntax splitting. Furthermore, system W also extends, in contrast to c-inference, rational closure and thus inheriting its desirable properties (Lehmann and Magidor 1992).

After briefly recalling the needed basics of conditional logic in Sec. 2, the syntax splitting postulates are given in Sec. 3. In Sec. 4, we present a syntax splitting example and illustrate how system W handles it, and Sec. 5 shows that system W satisfies syntax splitting. Sec. 6 concludes and points out further work.

2 Reasoning with Conditional Logic

A *(propositional) signature* is a finite set Σ of identifiers. For a signature Σ, we denote the propositional language over Σ by $\mathcal{L}_\Sigma$. Usually, we denote elements of the signatures with lowercase letters $a, b, c, \dots$ and formulas with uppercase letters $A, B, C, \dots$. We may denote a conjunction $A \wedge B$ by AB and a negation $\neg A$ by $\overline{A}$ for brevity of notation. The set of interpretations over a signature Σ is denoted as Ω_Σ. Interpretations are also called *worlds*. An interpretation $\omega \in \Omega_\Sigma$ is a *model* of a formula $A \in \mathcal{L}_\Sigma$ if A holds in ω. This is denoted as $\omega \models A$. The set of models of a formula (over a signature Σ) is denoted as $Mod_\Sigma(A) = \{\omega \in \Omega_\Sigma \mid \omega \models A\}$. A formula A *entails* a formula B if $Mod_\Sigma(A) \subseteq Mod_\Sigma(B)$.

Worlds over (sub-)signatures can be merged or marginalized. Let Σ be a signature with disjunct sub-signatures Σ_1, Σ_2 such that $\Sigma = \Sigma_1 \cup \Sigma_2$. Let $\omega_1 \in \Omega_{\Sigma_1}$ and $\omega_2 \in \Omega_{\Sigma_2}$. Then $(\omega_1 \cdot \omega_2)$ denotes the world from Ω_Σ that assigns the truth values for variables in Σ_1 as ω_1 and truth values for variables in Σ_2 as ω_2. For $\omega \in \Omega_\Sigma$, the world from Ω_{Σ_1} that assigns the truth values for variables in Σ_1 as ω is denoted as $\omega_{|\Sigma_1}$.

A *conditional* $(B|A)$ connects two formulas A, B and represents the rule "If A then usually B". The conditional language over a signature Σ is denoted as $(\mathcal{L}|\mathcal{L})_\Sigma = \{(B|A) \mid A, B \in \mathcal{L}_\Sigma\}$. A finite set of conditionals is called a *(conditional) belief base* Δ. A belief base Δ is called *consistent* if there is a ranking model for Δ (Goldszmidt and Pearl 1996).

We use a three-valued semantics of conditionals in this paper (de Finetti 1937). For a world ω a conditional $(B|A)$ is either *verified* by ω if $\omega \models AB$, *falsified* by ω if $\omega \models A\overline{B}$, or *not applicable* to ω if $\omega \models \overline{A}$.

Reasoning with conditionals is often modelled by inference relations. An *inference relation* is a binary relation $\mid\!\sim$ on formulas over an underlying signature Σ with the intuition that $A \mid\!\sim B$ means that A (plausibly) entails B. (Nonmonotonic) inference is closely related to conditionals: an inference relation $\mid\!\sim$ can also be seen as a set of conditionals $\{(B|A) \mid A, B \in \mathcal{L}_\Sigma, A \mid\!\sim B\}$.

Definition 1 (inductive inference operator (Kern-Isberner, Beierle, and Brewka 2020)). *An* inductive inference operator *is a mapping* $C : \Delta \mapsto \mid\!\sim_\Delta$ *that maps each belief base to an inference relation such that direct inference (DI) and trivial vacuity (TV) are fulfilled, i.e.,*

(DI) *if* $(B|A) \in \Delta$ *then* $A \mid\!\sim_\Delta B$ *and*

(TV) *if* $\Delta = \emptyset$ *and* $A \mid\!\sim_\Delta B$ *then* $A \models B$.

Examples for inductive inference operators are p-entailment (Adams 1965) and system Z (Pearl 1990).

3 Syntax Splitting for Inductive Inference

First, we recall the notion of syntax splitting for belief bases.

Definition 2 (syntax splitting for belief bases (adapted from (Kern-Isberner, Beierle, and Brewka 2020))). *Let* Δ *be a belief base over a signature* Σ. *A partitioning* $\{\Sigma_1, \dots, \Sigma_n\}$ *of* Σ *is a* syntax splitting *for* Δ *if there is a partitioning* $\{\Delta_1, \dots, \Delta_n\}$ *of* Δ *such that* $\Delta_i \subseteq (\mathcal{L}|\mathcal{L})_{\Sigma_i}$ *for every* $i = 1, \dots, n$. *A syntax splitting* $\{\Sigma_1, \Sigma_2\}$ *of* Δ *with two parts and corresponding partition* $\{\Delta_1, \Delta_2\}$ *of* Δ *is denoted as*

$$\Delta = \Delta_1 \bigcup_{\Sigma_1, \Sigma_2} \Delta_2.$$

Here, we will focus on syntax splittings in two sub-signatures. Results for belief bases with syntax splittings in more than two parts can be obtained by iteratively applying the postulates presented here.

For belief bases with syntax splitting, the postulate *Relevance* (Rel) describes that conditionals corresponding to one part of the syntax splitting do not have any influence on inferences that only use the other part of the syntax splitting, i.e., that only conditionals from the considered part of the syntax splitting are relevant.

(Rel) An inductive inference operator $C : \Delta \mapsto \mid\!\sim_\Delta$ satisfies **(Rel)** (Kern-Isberner, Beierle, and Brewka 2020) if for any $\Delta = \Delta_1 \bigcup_{\Sigma_1, \Sigma_2} \Delta_2$, and for any $A, B \in \mathcal{L}_{\Sigma_i}$ for $i = 1, 2$ we have that

$$A \mid\!\sim_\Delta B \quad \text{iff} \quad A \mid\!\sim_{\Delta_i} B. \tag{1}$$

The postulate *Independence* (Ind) describes that inferences should not be affected by beliefs in formulas over other subsignatures in the splitting, i.e., inferences using only atoms from one part of the syntax splitting should be drawn independently of beliefs about other parts of the splitting.

(Ind) An inference operator $C : \Delta \mapsto \mid\!\sim_\Delta$ satisfies **(Ind)** (Kern-Isberner, Beierle, and Brewka 2020) if for any $\Delta = \Delta_1 \bigcup_{\Sigma_1, \Sigma_2} \Delta_2$, and for any $A, B \in \mathcal{L}_{\Sigma_i}, D \in \mathcal{L}_{\Sigma_j}$ for $i, j \in \{1, 2\}, i \neq j$ such that D is consistent, we have

$$A \mid\!\sim_\Delta B \quad \text{iff} \quad AD \mid\!\sim_\Delta B. \tag{2}$$

Syntax splitting is the combination of (Rel) and (Ind):

(SynSplit) An inductive inference operator satisfies **(SynSplit)** (Kern-Isberner, Beierle, and Brewka 2020) if it satisfies (Rel) and (Ind).

Among the inductive inference operators investigated in (Kern-Isberner, Beierle, and Brewka 2020), only reasoning with c-representations satisfies (SynSplit).

4 System W

Recently, system W has been introduced as a new inductive inference operator (Komo and Beierle 2020; Komo and Beierle 2022). System W takes into account both the tolerance information expressed by the ordered partition of Δ and the structural information about which conditionals are falsified.

Definition 3 (inclusion maximal tolerance partition (Pearl 1990)). *A conditional* $(B|A)$ *is* tolerated *by* Δ *if there exists a world* $\omega \in \Omega_\Sigma$ *such that* ω *verifies* $(B|A)$ *and* ω *does not falsify any conditional in* Δ. *The* inclusion maximal tolerance partition $OP(\Delta) = (\Delta^0, \dots, \Delta^k)$ *of a consistent belief base* Δ *is defined as follows. The first set* Δ^0 *in the tolerance partitioning contains all conditionals from* Δ *that are tolerated by* Δ. *Analogously,* Δ^i *contains all conditionals from* $\Delta \backslash (\bigcup_{j<i} \Delta^j)$ *which are tolerated by* $\Delta \backslash (\bigcup_{j<i} \Delta^j)$, *until* $\Delta \backslash (\bigcup_{j<k+1} \Delta^j) = \emptyset$.

It is well-known that $OP(\Delta)$ exists iff Δ is consistent; moreover, because the Δ^i are chosen inclusion-maximal, the tolerance partitioning is unique (Pearl 1990).

Definition 4 (ξ^j, ξ, preferred structure $<^{\mathsf{w}}_\Delta$ on worlds (Komo and Beierle 2022)). *Consider a consistent belief base* $\Delta = \{r_i = (B_i|A_i) \mid i \in \{1, \dots, n\}\}$ *with the tolerance partition* $OP(\Delta) = (\Delta^1, \dots, \Delta^k)$. *For* $j = 0, \dots, k$, *the functions* ξ^j *and* ξ *are the* functions mapping worlds to the set of falsified conditionals *from the set* Δ^j *in the tolerance partition and from* Δ, *respectively, given by*

$$\xi^j(\omega) := \{r_i \in \Delta^j \mid \omega \models A_i\overline{B_i}\}, \tag{3}$$

$$\xi(\omega) := \{r_i \in \Delta \mid \omega \models A_i\overline{B_i}\}. \tag{4}$$

The preferred structure on worlds *is given by the binary relation* $<^{\mathsf{w}}_{\Delta} \subseteq \Omega \times \Omega$ *defined by, for any* $\omega, \omega' \in \Omega$,

$$\omega <^{\mathsf{w}}_{\Delta} \omega' \text{ iff there exists } m \in \{0, \dots, k\} \text{ such that}$$
$$\xi^i(\omega) = \xi^i(\omega') \quad \forall i \in \{m+1, \dots, k\}, \text{ and}$$
$$\xi^m(\omega) \subsetneqq \xi^m(\omega'). \tag{5}$$

Thus, $\omega <^{\mathsf{w}}_{\Delta} \omega'$ if and only if ω falsifies strictly less conditionals than ω' in the partition with the biggest index m where the conditionals falsified by ω and ω' differ. Note, that $<^{\mathsf{w}}_{\Delta}$ is a strict partial order. The inductive inference operator system W based on $<^{\mathsf{w}}_{\Delta}$ is defined as follows.

Definition 5 (system W, $\mid\!\sim^{\mathsf{w}}_{\Delta}$(Komo and Beierle 2022))**.** *Let* Δ *be a belief base and* A, B *be formulas. Then* B *is a* system W inference from A (in the context of Δ), *denoted* $A \mid\!\sim^{\mathsf{w}}_{\Delta} B$ *if for every* $\omega' \in \Omega_{A\overline{B}}$ *there is an* $\omega \in \Omega_{AB}$ *such that* $\omega <^{\mathsf{w}}_{\Delta} \omega'$.

System W extends system Z and c-inference and enjoys further desirable properties for nonmonotonic reasoning like avoiding the drowning problem. For more information on system W we refer to (Komo and Beierle 2022). We illustrate system W with an example.

Example 1. *Consider the belief base* $\Delta = \{(f|b), (\overline{v}|d), (b|p), (\overline{f}|p)\}$ *over the signature* $\Sigma = \{b, p, f, v, d\}$ *from (Kern-Isberner, Beierle, and Brewka 2020, Example 2) with the intended meanings birds (b), penguins (p), being able to fly (f), being visible in the night (v), dark objects (d). The preferred structure* $<^{\mathsf{w}}_{\Delta}$ *on worlds is given in in Figure 1.*

We have $\Delta = \Delta_1 \bigcup_{\Sigma_1,\Sigma_2} \Delta_2$ *with* $\Sigma_1 = \{b, p, f\}$, $\Sigma_2 = \{v, d\}$ *and* $\Delta_1 = \{(f|b), (b|p), (\overline{f}|p)\}$, $\Delta_2 = \{(\overline{v}|d)\}$.

The conditional $(\overline{v}|d)$ *can be deduced from* Δ *with every inductive inference operator because of (DI). But the conditional* $(\overline{v}|dp)$ *cannot be deduced from* Δ *with either p-entailment and System Z; in both cases, the additional information* p *from an independent part of the signature prevents the deduction of* $\neg v$. *Therefore, p-entailment and system Z do not fulfil (SynSplit). Using the preferred structure* $<^{\mathsf{w}}_{\Delta}$ *given in in Figure 1, it is straightforward to verify that for each world* ω' *with* $\omega' \models dpv$ *there is a world* ω *with* $\omega \models dp\overline{v}$ *such that* $\omega <^{\mathsf{w}}_{\Delta} \omega'$. *Thus, system W licences the inference* $dp \mid\!\sim^{\mathsf{w}}_{\Delta} \overline{v}$, *complying with (SynSplit).*

Example 1 is an example of system W complying with (Ind), which is the part of (SynSplit) that system Z and p-entailment fail to fulfil.

5 System W fulfils Syntax Splitting

For proving that system W fulfils syntax splitting, we first present four lemmas on the properties of $<^{\mathsf{w}}_{\Delta}$ in the presence of a syntax splitting $\Delta = \Delta_1 \bigcup_{\Sigma_1,\Sigma_2} \Delta_2$. Note, that we consider the belief bases Δ_1, Δ_2 as belief bases over the signature $\Sigma = \Sigma_1 \cup \Sigma_2$ in this section. Thus, in particular $<^{\mathsf{w}}_{\Delta_1}$ and $<^{\mathsf{w}}_{\Delta_2}$ are relations on Ω_Σ and the inference relations induced by Δ_1, Δ_2 are calculated with respect to Σ.

The following Lemma 1 shows how a syntax splitting on a belief base carries over to the corresponding inclusion maximal tolerance partitioning.

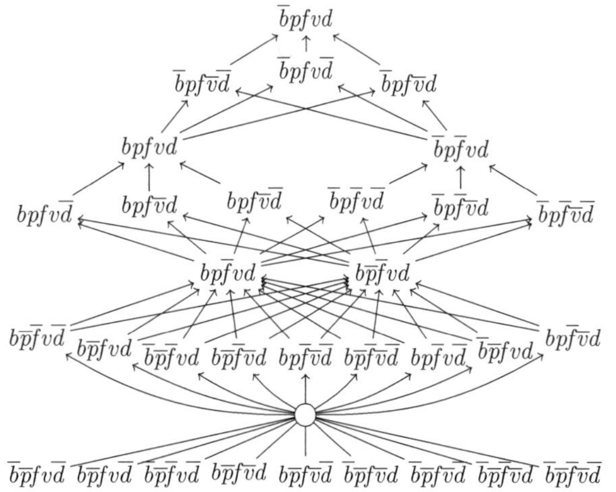

Figure 1: The preferred structure on worlds induced by the belief base Δ from Example 1. Edges that can be obtained from transitivity are omitted for lucidity.

Lemma 1. *Let* $\Delta = \Delta_1 \bigcup_{\Sigma_1,\Sigma_2} \Delta_2$ *be a consistent belief base with syntax splitting. Let* $OP(\Delta) = (\Delta^0, \dots, \Delta^k)$ *be the inclusion maximal tolerance partitioning of* Δ. *Let* $OP(\Delta_i) = (\Delta_i^0, \dots, \Delta_i^{l_i})$ *be the inclusion maximal tolerance partition of* Δ_i *for* $i = 1, 2$.

1. *For* $i = 1, 2$ *and* $j = 0, \dots, l_i$ *we have* $\Delta_i^j = \Delta^j \cap \Delta_i$ *and thus especially* $\Delta_i^j \subseteq \Delta^j$.
2. $\max\{l_1, l_2\} = k$
3. *If* $l_1 \leqslant l_2$, *then* $\Delta^j = \begin{cases} \Delta_1^j \cup \Delta_2^j & \text{for } j = 1, \dots, l_1 \\ \Delta_2^j & \text{for } j = l_1 + 1, \dots, k. \end{cases}$

If we have $\omega <^{\mathsf{w}}_{\Delta} \omega'$, then there is some conditional r that falsifies ω' but not ω and thus causes the $\subsetneqq$ relation in (5) in Definition 4. If $\Delta = \Delta_1 \bigcup_{\Sigma_1,\Sigma_2} \Delta_2$, this r is either in Δ_1 or in Δ_2. Lemma 2 states that the relation $\omega <^{\mathsf{w}}_{\Delta} \omega'$ can also be obtained using only Δ_1 or only Δ_2.

Lemma 2. *Let* $\Delta = \Delta_1 \bigcup_{\Sigma_1,\Sigma_2} \Delta_2$ *and let* $\omega, \omega' \in \Omega$. *If* $\omega <^{\mathsf{w}}_{\Delta} \omega'$, *then* $\omega <^{\mathsf{w}}_{\Delta_1} \omega'$ *or* $\omega <^{\mathsf{w}}_{\Delta_2} \omega'$.

Note, that both $\omega <^{\mathsf{w}}_{\Delta_1} \omega'$ and $\omega <^{\mathsf{w}}_{\Delta_2} \omega'$ might be true.

The next Lemma 3 considers the reverse direction of Lemma 2 and shows a situation where we can infer $\omega <^{\mathsf{w}}_{\Delta} \omega'$ from $\omega <^{\mathsf{w}}_{\Delta_1} \omega'$ for a belief base with syntax splitting.

Lemma 3. *Let* $\Delta = \Delta_1 \bigcup_{\Sigma_1,\Sigma_2} \Delta_2$ *and let* $\omega, \omega' \in \Omega$. *If* $\omega <^{\mathsf{w}}_{\Delta_1} \omega'$ *and* $\omega_{|\Sigma_2} = \omega'_{|\Sigma_2}$, *then* $\omega <^{\mathsf{w}}_{\Delta} \omega'$.

The next Lemma 4 captures that in a world the variable assignment for variables that do not occur in the belief set has no influence on the position of this world in the resulting preferential structure on worlds.

Lemma 4. *Let* $\Delta = \Delta_1 \bigcup_{\Sigma_1,\Sigma_2} \Delta_2$ *and* $\omega^a, \omega^b, \omega' \in \Omega_\Sigma$ *with* $\omega^a{}_{|\Sigma_1} = \omega^b{}_{|\Sigma_1}$. *Then we have* $\omega^a <^{\mathsf{w}}_{\Delta_1} \omega'$ *iff* $\omega^b <^{\mathsf{w}}_{\Delta_1} \omega'$.

Proofs for Lemmas 1 to 4 are given in (Haldimann and Beierle 2022). We now show that system W fulfils (Rel) and (Ind).

Proposition 1. *System W fulfils (Rel).*

Proof. Let $\Delta = \Delta_1 \bigcup_{\Sigma_1,\Sigma_2} \Delta_2$ and let $A, B \in \mathcal{L}_{\Sigma_1}$ be propositional formulas. W.l.o.g. we need to show that

$$A \mid\!\sim^{\mathsf{w}}_{\Delta} B \text{ if and only if } A \mid\!\sim^{\mathsf{w}}_{\Delta_1} B. \tag{6}$$

Direction ⇒ of (6): Assume that $A \mid\!\sim^{\mathsf{w}}_{\Delta} B$. Let ω' be any world in $\Omega_{A\overline{B}}$. Now choose $\omega'_{min} \in \Omega$ such that

1. $\omega'_{min} \leqslant^{\mathsf{w}}_{\Delta} \omega'$,
2. $\omega'_{|\Sigma_1} = \omega'_{min|\Sigma_1}$, and
3. there is no world ω'_{min2} with $\omega'_{min2} <^{\mathsf{w}}_{\Delta} \omega'_{min}$ that fulfils (1.) and (2.).

Such an ω'_{min} exists because ω' fulfils properties (1.) and (2.), $<^{\mathsf{w}}_{\Delta}$ is irreflexive and transitive, and there are only finitely many worlds in Ω. Because of (2.) and because $\omega' \models A\overline{B}$ we have that $\omega'_{min} \models A\overline{B}$. Because $A \mid\!\sim^{\mathsf{w}}_{\Delta} B$, there is a world ω such that $\omega \models AB$ and $\omega <^{\mathsf{w}}_{\Delta} \omega'_{min}$. Lemma 2 yields that $\omega <^{\mathsf{w}}_{\Delta_1} \omega'_{min}$ or $\omega <^{\mathsf{w}}_{\Delta_2} \omega'_{min}$.

The case $\omega <^{\mathsf{w}}_{\Delta_2} \omega'_{min}$ is not possible: Assuming $\omega <^{\mathsf{w}}_{\Delta_2} \omega'_{min}$, it follows that $\omega'_{min2} = (\omega'_{min|\Sigma_1} \cdot \omega_{|\Sigma_2}) <^{\mathsf{w}}_{\Delta_2} \omega'_{min}$ with Lemma 4. With Lemma 3 it follows that $\omega'_{min2} <^{\mathsf{w}}_{\Delta} \omega'_{min}$. This contradicts (3.). Hence, $\omega <^{\mathsf{w}}_{\Delta_1} \omega'_{min}$. Because of (2.) and Lemma 4 it follows that $\omega <^{\mathsf{w}}_{\Delta_1} \omega'$.

As we can find an ω such that $\omega <^{\mathsf{w}}_{\Delta_1} \omega'$ and $\omega \models AB$ for every $\omega' \models A\overline{B}$ we have that $A \mid\!\sim^{\mathsf{w}}_{\Delta_1} B$ as required.

Direction ⇐ of (6): Assume that $A \mid\!\sim^{\mathsf{w}}_{\Delta_1} B$. Let ω' be any world in $\Omega_{A\overline{B}}$. Because $A \mid\!\sim^{\mathsf{w}}_{\Delta_1} B$, there is a world ω^* such that $\omega^* \models AB$ and $\omega^* <^{\mathsf{w}}_{\Delta_1} \omega'$. Let $\omega = (\omega^*_{|\Sigma_1} \cdot \omega'_{|\Sigma_2})$. Because $\omega^* \models AB$ we have that $\omega \models AB$. With Lemma 4 it follows that $\omega <^{\mathsf{w}}_{\Delta_1} \omega'$ and thus $\omega <^{\mathsf{w}}_{\Delta} \omega'$ due to Lemma 3.

As we can construct ω such that $\omega <^{\mathsf{w}}_{\Delta} \omega'$ and $\omega \models AB$ for every $\omega' \models A\overline{B}$ we have that $A <^{\mathsf{w}}_{\Delta} B$ as required. □

Proposition 2. *System W fulfils (Ind).*

Proof. Let $\Delta = \Delta_1 \bigcup_{\Sigma_1,\Sigma_2} \Delta_2$. W.l.o.g. let $A, B \in \mathcal{L}_{\Sigma_1}$ and $C \in \mathcal{L}_{\Sigma_2}$ such that C is consistent. We need to show that

$$A \mid\!\sim^{\mathsf{w}}_{\Delta} B \text{ if and only if } AC \mid\!\sim^{\mathsf{w}}_{\Delta} B. \tag{7}$$

Direction ⇒ of (7): Assume that $A \mid\!\sim^{\mathsf{w}}_{\Delta} B$. Let ω' be any world in $\Omega_{A\overline{B}C}$. Now choose $\omega'_{min} \in \Omega$ such that

1. $\omega'_{min} \leqslant^{\mathsf{w}}_{\Delta} \omega'$,
2. $\omega'_{|\Sigma_1} = \omega'_{min|\Sigma_1}$, and
3. there is no world ω'_{min2} with $\omega'_{min2} <^{\mathsf{w}}_{\Delta} \omega'_{min}$ that fulfils (1.) and (2.).

Such an ω'_{min} exists because ω' fulfils properties (1.) and (2.), $<^{\mathsf{w}}_{\Delta}$ is irreflexive and transitive, and there are only finitely many worlds in Ω. Because of (2.) and because $\omega' \models A\overline{B}C$ we have that $\omega'_{min} \models A\overline{B}$. Because $A \mid\!\sim^{\mathsf{w}}_{\Delta} B$, there is a world ω^* such that $\omega^* \models AB$ and $\omega^* <^{\mathsf{w}}_{\Delta} \omega'_{min}$. Lemma 2 yields that either $\omega^* <^{\mathsf{w}}_{\Delta_1} \omega'_{min}$ or $\omega^* <^{\mathsf{w}}_{\Delta_2} \omega'_{min}$.

The case $\omega^* <^{\mathsf{w}}_{\Delta_2} \omega'_{min}$ is not possible: Assuming $\omega^* <^{\mathsf{w}}_{\Delta_2} \omega'_{min}$, it follows that $\omega'_{min2} = (\omega'_{min|\Sigma_1} \cdot \omega^*_{|\Sigma_2}) <^{\mathsf{w}}_{\Delta_2} \omega'_{min}$ with Lemma 4. With Lemma 3 it follows that $\omega'_{min2} <^{\mathsf{w}}_{\Delta} \omega'_{min}$. This contradicts (3.). Hence, $\omega^* <^{\mathsf{w}}_{\Delta_1} \omega'_{min}$. Let $\omega = (\omega^*_{|\Sigma_1} \cdot \omega'_{|\Sigma_2})$. Because $\omega^* \models AB$ we have that $\omega \models AB$. Because $\omega' \models C$ we have that $\omega \models C$. Because of (2.) and Lemma 4 it follows that $\omega <^{\mathsf{w}}_{\Delta_1} \omega'$ and thus with Lemma 3 $\omega <^{\mathsf{w}}_{\Delta} \omega'$.

As we can construct an ω such that $\omega <^{\mathsf{w}}_{\Delta} \omega'$ and $\omega \models ABC$ for every $\omega' \models A\overline{B}C$ we have $AC \mid\!\sim^{\mathsf{w}}_{\Delta} B$ as required.

Direction ⇐ of (7): Assume that $AC \mid\!\sim^{\mathsf{w}}_{\Delta} B$. Let ω' be any world in $\Omega_{A\overline{B}}$. Now choose $\omega'_{min} \in \Omega$ such that

1. $\omega'_{min} \models C$
2. $\omega'_{|\Sigma_1} = \omega'_{min|\Sigma_1}$, and
3. there is no world ω'_{min2} with $\omega'_{min2} <^{\mathsf{w}}_{\Delta} \omega'_{min}$ that fulfils (1.) and (2.).

Such an ω'_{min} exists because C is consistent, $C \in \mathcal{L}_{\Sigma_2}$, $<^{\mathsf{w}}_{\Delta}$ is irreflexive and transitive, and there are only finitely many worlds in Ω. Because of (2.) and because $\omega' \models A\overline{B}$ we have that $\omega'_{min} \models A\overline{B}$. Because of (1.) we have that $\omega'_{min} \models C$. Because $AC \mid\!\sim^{\mathsf{w}}_{\Delta} B$, there is a world ω^* such that $\omega^* \models ABC$ and $\omega^* <^{\mathsf{w}}_{\Delta} \omega'_{min}$. Lemma 2 yields that either $\omega^* <^{\mathsf{w}}_{\Delta_1} \omega'_{min}$ or $\omega^* <^{\mathsf{w}}_{\Delta_2} \omega'_{min}$.

The case $\omega^* <^{\mathsf{w}}_{\Delta_2} \omega'_{min}$ is not possible: Assuming $\omega^* <^{\mathsf{w}}_{\Delta_2} \omega'_{min}$, it follows that $\omega'_{min2} = (\omega'_{min|\Sigma_1} \cdot \omega^*_{|\Sigma_2}) <^{\mathsf{w}}_{\Delta_2} \omega'_{min}$ with Lemma 4. With Lemma 3 it follows that $\omega'_{min2} <^{\mathsf{w}}_{\Delta} \omega'_{min}$. This contradicts (3.). Hence, $\omega^* <^{\mathsf{w}}_{\Delta_1} \omega'_{min}$. Let $\omega = (\omega^*_{|\Sigma_1} \cdot \omega'_{|\Sigma_2})$. Because $\omega^* \models AB$ we have that $\omega \models AB$. Because of (2.) and Lemma 4 it follows that $\omega <^{\mathsf{w}}_{\Delta_1} \omega'$ and thus with Lemma 3 $\omega <^{\mathsf{w}}_{\Delta} \omega'$.

As we can construct an ω such that $\omega <^{\mathsf{w}}_{\Delta} \omega'$ and $\omega \models AB$ for every $\omega' \models A\overline{B}$ we have $A \mid\!\sim^{\mathsf{w}}_{\Delta} B$ as required. □

Combining Propositions 1 and 2 yields that system W fulfils (SynSplit).

Proposition 3. *System W fulfils (SynSplit).*

6 Conclusions and Further Work

In this short paper, we showed that the recently introduced System W that extends rational closure and c-inference, also fully complies with syntax splitting. In a new publication parallel to this one, lexicographic inference (Lehmann 1995) is shown to fulfill syntax splitting as well (Heyninck, Kern-Isberner, and Meyer 2022). In our current work, we are studying the effect of syntax splitting on the preferred structure on worlds and further properties of system W; first results of these further studies are given in (Haldimann and Beierle 2022), along with the observation that lexicographic inference extends system W and thus also c-inference. Furthermore, we investigate normal forms of conditional belief bases respecting system W inferences (Beierle and Haldimann 2022), and we will extend the online reasoning platform InfOCF-Web (Kutsch and Beierle 2021) by a system W implementation.

Acknowledgements

This work was supported by the Deutsche Forschungsgemeinschaft (DFG, German Research Foundation), grant BE 1700/10-1 awarded to Christoph Beierle as part of the priority program "Intentional Forgetting in Organizations" (SPP 1921). Jonas Haldimann is supported by this grant.

References

Adams, E. 1965. The Logic of Conditionals. *Inquiry* 8(1-4):166–197.

Beierle, C., and Haldimann, J. 2022. Normal forms of conditional belief bases respecting inductive inference. In *Proceedings of the Thirty-Fifth International Florida Artificial Intelligence Research Society Conference (FLAIRS)*. (to appear).

Beierle, C.; Eichhorn, C.; Kern-Isberner, G.; and Kutsch, S. 2018. Properties of skeptical c-inference for conditional knowledge bases and its realization as a constraint satisfaction problem. *Ann. Math. Artif. Intell.* 83(3-4):247–275.

Beierle, C.; Eichhorn, C.; Kern-Isberner, G.; and Kutsch, S. 2021. Properties and interrelationships of skeptical, weakly skeptical, and credulous inference induced by classes of minimal models. *Artificial Intelligence* 297.

Benferhat, S.; Cayrol, C.; Dubois, D.; Lang, J.; and Prade, H. 1993. Inconsistency Management and Prioritized Syntax-Based Entailment. In *Proceedings of the Thirteenth International Joint Conference on Artificial Intelligence (IJCAI'93)*, volume 1, 640–647. San Francisco, CA, USA: Morgan Kaufmann Publishers.

de Finetti, B. 1937. La prévision, ses lois logiques et ses sources subjectives. *Ann. Inst. H. Poincaré* 7(1):1–68. Engl. transl. *Theory of Probability*, J. Wiley & Sons, 1974.

Goldszmidt, M., and Pearl, J. 1996. Qualitative probabilities for default reasoning, belief revision, and causal modeling. *Artificial Intelligence* 84(1-2):57–112.

Haldimann, J., and Beierle, C. 2022. Properties of system W and its relationships to other inductive inference operators. In *FoIKS 2022, Helsinki, Finland, June 20-23, 2022, Proceedings*, Lecture Notes in Computer Science. Springer. (to appear).

Hawthorne, J., and Makinson, D. 2007. The quantitative/qualitative watershed for rules of uncertain inference. *Studia Logica* 86(2):247–297.

Heyninck, J.; Kern-Isberner, G.; and Meyer, T. 2022. Lexicographic entailment, syntax splitting and the drowning problem. In *31st International Joint Conference on Artificial Intelligence, IJCAI 2022*. ijcai.org. (to appear).

Kern-Isberner, G., and Brewka, G. 2017. Strong syntax splitting for iterated belief revision. In *Proceedings of the Twenty-Sixth International Joint Conference on Artificial Intelligence, IJCAI 2017, Melbourne, Australia, August 19-25, 2017*, 1131–1137.

Kern-Isberner, G.; Beierle, C.; and Brewka, G. 2020. Syntax splitting = relevance + independence: New postulates for nonmonotonic reasoning from conditional belief bases. In *KR-2020*, 560–571.

Kern-Isberner, G. 2001. *Conditionals in Nonmonotonic Reasoning and Belief Revision – Considering Conditionals as Agents*. Number 2087 in Lecture Notes in Computer Science. Berlin, DE: Springer Science+Business Media.

Kern-Isberner, G. 2004. A thorough axiomatization of a principle of conditional preservation in belief revision. *Ann. Math. Artif. Intell.* 40(1-2):127–164.

Komo, C., and Beierle, C. 2020. Nonmonotonic inferences with qualitative conditionals based on preferred structures on worlds. In Schmid, U.; Klügl, F.; and Wolter, D., eds., *KI 2020: Advances in Artificial Intelligence - 43rd German Conference on AI, Bamberg, Germany, September 21-25, 2020, Proceedings*, volume 12325 of *LNCS*, 102–115. Springer.

Komo, C., and Beierle, C. 2022. Nonmonotonic reasoning from conditional knowledge bases with system W. *Ann. Math. Artif. Intell.* 90(1):107–144.

Kraus, S.; Lehmann, D. J.; and Magidor, M. 1990. Nonmonotonic Reasoning, Preferential Models and Cumulative Logics. *Artificial Intelligence* 44(1-2):167–207.

Kutsch, S., and Beierle, C. 2021. InfOCF-Web: An online tool for nonmonotonic reasoning with conditionals and ranking functions. In Zhou, Z., ed., *Proceedings of the Thirtieth International Joint Conference on Artificial Intelligence, IJCAI 2021, Virtual Event / Montreal, Canada, 19-27 August 2021*, 4996–4999. ijcai.org.

Lehmann, D., and Magidor, M. 1992. What does a conditional knowledge base entail? *Artif. Intell.* 55:1–60.

Lehmann, D. 1995. Another perspective on default reasoning. *Ann. Math. Artif. Intell.* 15(1):61–82.

Parikh, R. 1999. Beliefs, belief revision, and splitting languages. *Logic, Language, and Computation* 2:266–278.

Pearl, J. 1990. System Z: A natural ordering of defaults with tractable applications to nonmonotonic reasoning. In *Proc. of the 3rd Conf. on Theoretical Aspects of Reasoning About Knowledge (TARK'1990)*, 121–135. San Francisco, CA, USA: Morgan Kaufmann Publ. Inc.

Peppas, P.; Williams, M.-A.; Chopra, S.; and Foo, N. Y. 2015. Relevance in belief revision. *Artificial Intelligence* 229((1-2)):126–138.

Iterated Belief Change, Computationally

Kai Sauerwald , Christoph Beierle
FernUniversität in Hagen, Knowledge-Based Systems, 58084 Hagen, Germany
{kai.sauerwald, christoph.beierle}@fernuni-hagen.de

Abstract

This paper considers belief change in the Darwiche-Pearl framework. We demonstrate that iterative belief revision is Turing complete by showing how revision operators over ranking functions can simulate every Turing machine. Our result holds even under the condition that the broadly accepted Darwiche-Pearl postulates for iterated revision hold.

1 Introduction

The question of how an agent should change her belief according to new information is a central task for agents and AI systems. The belief change community developed a very fruitful unique research approach to this subject. The approach is top-down, by considering postulates, while being at the same time agent-centric, by taking a subjective perspective on the phenomenon of belief change.

Iterated belief change considers relations between a change and changes that happen priorly or posteriorly. In this area, changes of epistemic states are considered, which may contain "meta-information" in addition to the plain beliefs. The framework by Darwiche and Pearl (1997) deals with the aspect of meta-information elegantly by considering belief change over abstract sets of epistemic states. The computation complexity in specific sets of epistemic states was investigated for iterated belief revision (Liberatore 1997; Schwind et al. 2020), however, investigations on the general computability are missing.

In this paper, we focus on the computational aspect of iterated belief change. We quantify its computational power by providing corresponding notions and a construction that demonstrate that iterated belief change is Turing complete, even when the prominent iteration principles of Darwiche and Pearl (1997) are satisfied. We will therefore consider iterated revision in the Darwiche-Pearl framework and instantiate the set of epistemic states by ranking functions.

2 Formal Background

Let $\Sigma = \{a, b, c, \dots\}$ be a propositional signature (non empty finite set of propositional variables) and $\mathcal{L}$ a propositional language over Σ. The set of propositional interpretations is denoted by Ω. Propositional entailment is denoted by $\models$, the set of models of α with $[\![\alpha]\!]$, and $L \subseteq \mathcal{L}$ is deductively closed if $L = \{\beta \mid L \models \beta\}$. For a set of worlds $\Omega' \subseteq \Omega$ and a total preorder $\preceq \subseteq \Omega \times \Omega$ (total, reflexive and transitive relation), we denote with $\min(\Omega', \preceq) = \{\omega \in \Omega' \mid \omega \preceq \omega' \text{ for all } \omega' \in \Omega'\}$ the set of all minimal worlds of Ω' with respect to $\preceq$. For a total preorder $\preceq$, we say $x \prec y$ if $x \preceq y$ and $y \not\preceq x$. With $\leq$ we denote the usual ordering on the integers and with $<$ we denote the strict part of $\leq$.

3 Iterated Belief Revision in the Darwiche-Pearl Framework

AGM theory, by Alchourrón, Gärdenfors and Makinson (1985), deals with the dynamics of beliefs in the context of belief sets, i.e., deductively closed sets of propositions.

The area of iterated belief change abstracts from belief sets to *epistemic states*, in which the agent maintains necessary information for all used belief change operators. The most prominent approach for iterated belief change is the framework by Darwiche and Pearl (1997), which does leave open what an epistemic state is, but assumes that for every epistemic state Ψ we can obtain the set of plausible sentences $\mathrm{Bel}(\Psi) \subseteq \mathcal{L}$ of Ψ, which is deductively closed.

While the Darwiche-Pearl framework is very successful, an ontological problem of belief change itself appears in their framework: when describing change operators over epistemic states, we have to specify on which epistemic states the changes happen, an aspect which was not explicitly treated by Darwiche and Pearl and rediscovered several times (Friedman and Halpern 1996; Aravanis, Peppas, and Williams 2019; Schwind and Konieczny 2020).

We solve this problem by considering an abstract set of epistemic states $\mathcal{E}$, and assume in this paper that $\mathcal{E}$ is a countable infinite set and that for every belief set $L \subseteq \mathcal{L}$ there exists infinite many epistemic states $\Psi \in \mathcal{E}$ with $\mathrm{Bel}(\Psi) = L$. We write $\Psi \models \alpha$ if $\alpha \in \mathrm{Bel}(\Psi)$ and we define $[\![\Psi]\!] = [\![\mathrm{Bel}(\Psi)]\!]$.

Definition 1. *A* belief change operator *(for $\mathcal{E}$ and $\mathcal{L}$) is a function $\circ : \mathcal{E} \times \mathcal{L} \to \mathcal{E}$.*

As we do not specify in detail what an epistemic states in $\mathcal{E}$ is, one has to identify the additional information for the elements of Ψ for realizing certain operators. Formally, we do this by assigning additional information (similar as Katsuno and Mendelzon, 1992) to epistemic states.

Definition 2. *A function $\Psi \mapsto \preceq_\Psi$ which assigns to each epistemic states $\Psi \in \mathcal{E}$ a preorder $\preceq_\Psi$ over Ω is called a* faithful assignment *if $[\![\Psi]\!] \neq \emptyset$ implies $[\![\Psi]\!] = \min(\Omega, \preceq_\Psi)$.*

AGM revision is characterized by selecting minimal models in the respective assigned total preorders.

Proposition 3 (AGM Revision for Epistemic States (Darwiche and Pearl 1997))**.** *A belief change operator $\star$ is an* AGM revision operator for epistemic states *if there is a faithful assignment $\Psi \mapsto \preceq_\Psi$, which assigns to Ψ a total preorder $\preceq_\Psi$ such that:*

$$[\![\Psi \star \alpha]\!] = \min([\![\alpha]\!], \preceq_\Psi) \quad (1)$$

Darwiche and Pearl (1997) proposed the following postulates:

(DP1) if $\beta \models \alpha$, then $\mathrm{Bel}(\Psi \star \alpha \star \beta) = \mathrm{Bel}(\Psi \star \beta)$

(DP2) if $\beta \models \neg\alpha$, then $\mathrm{Bel}(\Psi \star \alpha \star \beta) = \mathrm{Bel}(\Psi \star \beta)$

(DP3) if $\Psi \star \beta \models \alpha$, then $(\Psi \star \alpha) \star \beta \models \alpha$

(DP4) if $\Psi \star \beta \not\models \neg\alpha$, then $(\Psi \star \alpha) \star \beta \not\models \neg\alpha$

It is well-known that these operators can be characterised in the semantic framework of total preorders.

Proposition 4 (Darwiche and Pearl (1997))**.** *Let $\star$ be an AGM revision operator for epistemic states. Then $\star$ satisfies* (DP1)–(DP4) *if and only there exists a faithful assignment $\Psi \mapsto \preceq_\Psi$ such that $\preceq_\Psi$ is a total preorder, Equation* (1) *holds, and the following postulates are satisfied:*

(CR1) *if* $\omega_1, \omega_2 \in [\![\alpha]\!]$, *then* $\omega_1 \preceq_\Psi \omega_2 \Leftrightarrow \omega_1 \preceq_{\Psi\star\alpha} \omega_2$

(CR2) *if* $\omega_1, \omega_2 \in [\![\neg\alpha]\!]$, *then* $\omega_1 \preceq_\Psi \omega_2 \Leftrightarrow \omega_1 \preceq_{\Psi\star\alpha} \omega_2$

(CR3) *if* $\omega_1 \in [\![\alpha]\!]$, $\omega_2 \in [\![\neg\alpha]\!]$, *then* $\omega_1 \prec_\Psi \omega_2 \Rightarrow \omega_1 \prec_{\Psi\star\alpha} \omega_2$

(CR4) *if* $\omega_1 \in [\![\alpha]\!]$, $\omega_2 \in [\![\neg\alpha]\!]$, *then* $\omega_1 \preceq_\Psi \omega_2 \Rightarrow \omega_1 \preceq_{\Psi\star\alpha} \omega_2$

The postulates (DP1)–(DP4) are accepted today as very importation iteration principles for revision.

4 Turing Completeness

In this section, we will show that iterated belief revision is inherently computationally powerful, in particular, we will see that belief change operators can simulate Turing machines.

4.1 Computability Theory

At first, we recall basic concepts of computability theory and formal language theory. In the following, $\Gamma = \{\sigma, \ldots\}$ will denote a finite (non-empty) alphabet and $\Gamma^* = \{\varepsilon, \sigma, \sigma\sigma, \ldots\}$ denotes the set of all finite words over Γ, where $\cdot^*$ is the Kleene star operator and ε denotes the empty word.

A (deterministic) *Turing machine* is a tuple $T = \langle Q, \Gamma, \delta, q_s\rangle$ where $Q = \{q_1, \ldots, q_n\}$ is a finite set of *states* where $q_s \in Q$ is the *starting state*, the set Γ is the finite alphabet of tape symbols, and $\delta : Q \times \Gamma \to Q \times \{\leftarrow, \downarrow, \rightarrow\}$ is the *transition function* of T. The state $q_{\mathtt{halt}} := q_n$ is used a special state, indicating that the machine T has stopped. We describe the *position* on the tape of T as triple $\langle t_l, t_c, t_r\rangle \in \Gamma^* \times \Gamma \cup \{\varepsilon\} \times \Gamma^*$. A *configuration* of T is a tuple $\langle q, \langle t_l, t_c, t_r\rangle\rangle \in Q \times \Gamma^* \times \Gamma \cup \{\varepsilon\} \times \Gamma^*$. The start configuration for T by input $\gamma = \sigma_1\sigma_2 \ldots \sigma_n \in \Gamma^*$ is $(q_s, \langle \varepsilon, \sigma_1, \sigma_2 \ldots \sigma_n\rangle)$. The run r of T by input $\gamma \in \Gamma^*$ is defined in the usual way as a (possible infinite) sequence of configurations, starting in the corresponding start configuration by input $\gamma \in \Gamma^*$, and all subsequent configurations are determined by δ in the usual way. A configuration $\langle q, \langle t_l, t_c, t_r\rangle\rangle$ with $q = q_{\mathtt{halt}}$ is a *halting configuration*, and we require that after a halting configuration there are no subsequent configurations in a run. If the run r starting in γ ends in a halting configuration $\langle q, \langle t_l, t_c, t_r\rangle\rangle$ we say the word $t_l t_c t_r$ is the output of γ by T, if r does not halt, then ∞ is the output of γ by T.

Definition 5. *A partial function*[1] $f : \Gamma^* \to \Gamma^*$ *is called* Turing computable *if there is a Turing machine $T = \langle Q, \Gamma, \delta, q_s\rangle$ such that $f(\gamma)$ is the output of γ by T for every $\gamma \in \Gamma^*$. If this is the case, we say that T* computes *f.*

4.2 Ranking Function-Based Change Operators

A function $\kappa : \Omega \to \mathbb{N}_0$ is a *ranking function*, introduced (in a more general form) by Spohn (1988; 2012), if there exists some $\omega \in \Omega$ such that $\kappa(\omega) = 0$. Let $[\![\kappa]\!] = \{\omega \in \Omega \mid \kappa(\omega) = 0\}$ and $\mathrm{Bel}(\kappa) = \{\alpha \in \mathcal{L} \mid [\![\kappa]\!] \subseteq [\![\alpha]\!]\}$. Every κ gives rise to a total preorder $\preceq_\kappa$, given by $\omega_1 \preceq_\kappa \omega_2$ if $\kappa(\omega_1) \leq \kappa(\omega_2)$. For our main theorem we make use of special change operators, which can be characterized by information in form of a ranking function.

Definition 6. *A belief change operator $\circ$ is called* ranking function-based *if there is an assignment $\Psi \mapsto (\kappa_\Psi, b_\Psi)$ such that the following is satisfied:*

(RFA0) *if* $[\![\Psi]\!] = \emptyset$, *then* $b_\Psi = \bot$; *otherwise* $b_\Psi = \top$

(RFA1) *if* $b_\Psi = \top$, *then* $[\![\kappa]\!] = [\![\Psi]\!]$

(RFA2) *if* $\kappa_\Psi = \kappa_\Phi$ *and* $b_\Psi = b_\Phi$, *then* $\Psi \circ \alpha = \Phi \circ \alpha$

Note that Definition 6 makes again no assumption about the real form of epistemic states, but guarantees that the behaviour of a belief change operator is representable by an assigned ranking function κ_Ψ. The following proposition relies heavily on our assumptions about $\mathcal{E}$.

Proposition 7. *A belief change operator $\star$ is an AGM revision operator for epistemic states if and only if $\star$ is ranking function-based with $\Psi \mapsto (\kappa_\Psi, b_\Psi)$ such that:*

$$[\![\Psi \star \alpha]\!] = \min([\![\alpha]\!], \preceq_{\kappa_\Psi}) \quad (2)$$

Proof. We consider both directions of the proof independently, but due to space reasons we focus only on Ψ with $[\![\Psi]\!] \neq \emptyset$, and do not consider the b_Ψ-part. *The "if" direction.* Let $\Psi \mapsto \preceq_\Psi$ be a faithful assignment which satisfies Equation (1), guaranteed by Proposition 3. With $\mathrm{Behv}(\Psi) = \{\Phi \in \mathcal{E} \mid \preceq_\Psi = \preceq_\Phi \text{ and } \Psi \star \alpha = \Phi \star \alpha \text{ for all } \alpha \in \mathcal{L}\}$ we denote all *behavioural* equivalent states to Ψ. Clearly, $\Phi \in \mathrm{Behv}(\Psi)$ if and only if $\mathrm{Behv}(\Psi) = \mathrm{Behv}(\Phi)$. Note that $\mathrm{Behv}(\Psi)$ is countable and that for each $\preceq_\Psi$ there exist countably infinite many ranking functions κ with $\preceq_\Psi = \preceq_\kappa$. Because of these properties, we can construct $\Psi \mapsto \kappa_\Psi$ by choosing for each different set $\mathrm{Behv}(\Psi)$ a unique ranking function κ_Ψ with $\preceq_\Psi = \preceq_{\kappa_\Psi}$. By construction (RFA1), (RFA2) and Equation (2) are satisfied by $\Psi \mapsto \kappa_\Psi$.

The "only if" direction. Every assignment $\Psi \mapsto \kappa_\Psi$ as given in Definition 6 which satisfies Equation (2) yields a faithful assignment $\Psi \mapsto \preceq_{\kappa_\Psi}$ which satisfies Equation (1). Thus, by Proposition 3, existence of $\Psi \mapsto \kappa_\Psi$ as above implies that $\star$ is an AGM revision operator for epistemic states. $\square$

[1] $f(\gamma) = \infty$ denotes undefined

Rank	ω	Intended Meaning
$\vdots$		
$n+3$	$\omega_{\mathtt{pos}}$	$\langle \varepsilon; a; baba \rangle$
$n+2$		-
$n+1$		$\langle aab; b; baba \rangle$
n	$\omega_{\mathtt{halt}}$	$q = q_{\mathtt{halt}}$
$\vdots$		$\vdots$
2	$\omega_{\mathtt{q}}$	$q = q_2$
1		$q = q_1$
0	ω_0	-

Figure 1: Sketch of a ranking function represent a configuration.

Because of Proposition 7, we will focus on ranking function-based change operators and identify epistemic states with ranking functions, and use κ as a synonym for Ψ with $[\![\Psi]\!] \neq \emptyset$.

4.3 Simulation Machinery

We will simulate one step of a Turing machine by multiple changes. The simulation uses four types of ranking functions with special meaning in the simulation of T:

CONF Intended to represent a configuration of T.

PEEK Intended to check where T is in a halting state.

TRANS Describing the change of the state in a transition (before modifying the tape).

POST An intermediate state after updating state and tape.

In particular, simulation of a transition to a new configuration will take three steps. As first step we will compute a **TRANS** ranking function where we update the state of T (while saving the old state). Then we update the tape, obtaining a **POST** ranking function. Adjusting some ranks yields a **CONF** ranking function representing the new configuration (see Algorithm 1 for an overview).

The ranking functions of these types are given over a signature Σ with $|\Sigma| = 2$. Consequently, Ω has four elements, which we denote by $\omega_0, \omega_{\mathtt{halt}}, \omega_q, \omega_{\mathtt{pos}}$. Each interpretation from Ω will serve a special purpose (see Figure 1). We use the rank of ω_q as indicator for the current state of T. The interpretation $\omega_{\mathtt{pos}}$ will encode the tape position of T using the rank of $\omega_{\mathtt{pos}}$. Therefore, remember, that it is well-known that (by a variation of a Gödel numbering) for a fixed Γ we can encode positions $\langle t_l, t_c, t_r \rangle$ into natural numbers. Let $\mathtt{enc} : \Gamma^* \times \Gamma \times \Gamma^* \to \mathbb{N}$ be such an injective encoding function. We use $\omega_{\mathtt{halt}}$ to check if the halting state is reached (**PEEK**) and for saving the prior state of T (**TRANS**). The interpretation ω_0 has rank 0 in most situations; the purpose is to ensure that we always have a ranking function.

In the following we will describe the four types of ranking functions in more detail:

CONF. A **CONF** ranking function κ is given if

$$\kappa(\omega_0) = 0 \qquad 1 \leq \kappa(\omega_q) \leq n$$
$$\kappa(\omega_{\mathtt{halt}}) = n \qquad n < \kappa(\omega_{\mathtt{pos}})$$

Algorithm 1: Simulate-TM$(T, \circ, \gamma)$

Input: A word $\gamma \in \Gamma^*$
Output: A word over Γ or ∞ if it runs infinit

(**CONF**) $\kappa \leftarrow \kappa_\gamma^T$ `// inital conf.`
(**PEEK**) $\kappa \leftarrow \kappa \circ \varphi_{q,\mathtt{halt}}$ `// prepare peek`
while $\omega_{\mathtt{halt}} \notin [\![\kappa]\!]$ `// check if` $q \neq q_{\mathtt{halt}}$
do
  (**CONF**) $\kappa \leftarrow \kappa \circ \varphi_{\mathbf{0},\mathtt{pos}}$ `// obtain conf.`
  (**TRANS**) $\kappa \leftarrow \kappa \circ \varphi_{\mathbf{0}}$ `// update state`
  (**POST**) $\kappa \leftarrow \kappa \circ \varphi_{\mathbf{0},q,\mathtt{halt}}$ `// update tape`
  (**CONF**) $\kappa \leftarrow \kappa \circ \varphi_{\mathbf{0},q,\mathtt{pos}}$ `// restore` $\omega_{\mathtt{halt}}$
  (**PEEK**) $\kappa \leftarrow \kappa \circ \varphi_{q,\mathtt{halt}}$ `// prepare peek`
end
$\langle q, \langle t_l, t_c, t_r \rangle \rangle \leftarrow \mathtt{conf}(\kappa \circ \varphi_{\mathbf{0},\mathtt{pos}})$
return $t_l t_c t_r$

and $\mathtt{enc}^{-1}(\kappa(\omega_{\mathtt{pos}}) - (n+1)) \neq \emptyset$ holds. For such a ranking function let $\mathtt{conf}(\kappa) = \langle q_{\kappa(\omega_q)}, \mathtt{enc}^{-1}(\kappa(\omega_{\mathtt{pos}}) - (n+1)) \rangle$ denote the represented configuration of T. Note that we can provide for each possible configuration a ranking function that represents the configuration. In particular, for a given Turing machine T we denote with κ_γ^T a ranking function representing the start configuration for T by input $\gamma \in \Gamma^*$.

PEEK. When performing a revision on a **CONF** ranking function by a formula having $\omega_{\mathtt{halt}}$ and ω_q as models, rank 0 of $\omega_{\mathtt{halt}}$ in the posterior ranking function implies that T has reached a halting state. Ranking functions κ which are the result of such a revision are called **PEEK** and obey the following characteristics

$$\kappa(\omega_q) = 0 \qquad 0 \leq \kappa(\omega_{\mathtt{halt}}) \leq n-1$$
$$\kappa(\omega_0) = 1 \qquad n+1 < \kappa(\omega_{\mathtt{pos}})$$

and $\mathtt{enc}^{-1}(\kappa(\omega_{\mathtt{pos}}) - (n+2)) \neq \emptyset$. For such a ranking function let $\mathtt{conf}(\kappa) = \langle q_{n-\kappa(\mathtt{halt})}, \mathtt{enc}^{-1}(\kappa(\omega_{\mathtt{pos}}) - (n+2)) \rangle$ denote the represented configuration.

TRANS. A **TRANS** ranking function κ is given if:

$$\kappa(\omega_0) = 0 \qquad 1 \leq \kappa(\omega_q) \leq n$$
$$\kappa(\omega_{\mathtt{pos}}) > n \qquad 2 \leq \kappa(\omega_{\mathtt{halt}}) \leq n$$

For such a ranking function κ we define $\mathtt{post\text{-}state}(\kappa) = q_{\kappa(\omega_q)}$. Moreover, let $\mathtt{conf}(\kappa) = \langle q_{\kappa(\omega_q)-n+\kappa(\omega_{\mathtt{halt}})}, \mathtt{enc}^{-1}(\kappa(\omega_{\mathtt{pos}})-(n+1)) \rangle$ denote the represented configuration (before the transition). Note that $\kappa(\omega_q)$ encodes the posterior state, but the current (prior) state is reconstructible from $\kappa(\omega_q)$ and the difference between n and $\kappa(\omega_{\mathtt{halt}})$.

POST. Any ranking function κ with

$$\kappa(\omega_0) = 0 \qquad 1 \leq \kappa(\omega_q) \leq n$$
$$\kappa(\omega_{\mathtt{halt}}) = n \qquad n < \kappa(\omega_{\mathtt{pos}})$$

and with $\mathtt{enc}^{-1}(\kappa(\omega_{\mathtt{pos}}) - (n+1)) \neq \emptyset$. Such a ranking function represents the configuration $\mathtt{conf}(\kappa) = \langle q_{\kappa(\omega_q)}, \mathtt{enc}^{-1}(\kappa(\omega_{\mathtt{pos}}) - (n+1)) \rangle$.

Simulation is performed by continuously revising by specific formulas (Algorithm 1). With $\varphi_{\mathbf{0},\mathtt{pos}}$ we denote a formula with $[\![\varphi_{\mathbf{0},\mathtt{pos}}]\!] = \{\omega_0, \omega_{\mathtt{pos}}\}$. This extends analogously to $\varphi_{q,\mathtt{halt}}$, $\varphi_{\mathbf{0}}$, $\varphi_{\mathbf{0},q,\mathtt{halt}}$ and $\varphi_{\mathbf{0},q,\mathtt{pos}}$.

Definition 8. *Let $f : \Gamma^* \to \Gamma^*$ be a partial function computed by a Turing machine T. A ranking function-based belief change operator $\circ$ is said to* simulate T *if Simulate-TM$(T, \circ, \gamma)$ (Algorithm 1) yields the output of γ by T for all $\gamma \in \Gamma^*$. If $\circ$ simulates T, then we say $\circ$* computes f.

4.4 Main Theorem

We will now provide a construction for an AGM revision operator $\star$ which simulates a given Turing machine and show correctness of the construction.

Theorem 9. *Every Turing computable function f is computable by a ranking function-based AGM revision operator that satisfies the postulates* (DP1)–(DP4).

Proof. Let $T = \langle Q, \Gamma, \delta, q_s \rangle$ be a (deterministic) Turing machine computing f. We construct a ranking function-based AGM revision operator $\star$ and an assignment $\Psi \mapsto (\kappa_\Psi, b_\Psi)$. We start by letting $\Psi \mapsto (\kappa_\Psi, b)$ be a bijective function such that for each ranking function κ there exist exactly two epistemic states $\Psi^\kappa, \Psi^\kappa_\perp \in \mathcal{E}$ with $[\![\Psi^\kappa]\!] = [\![\kappa]\!]$, $\kappa_{\Psi^\kappa} = \kappa$ and $b_{\Psi^\kappa} = \top$; and with $[\![\Psi^\kappa_\perp]\!] = \emptyset$, $\kappa_{\Psi^\kappa_\perp} = \kappa$ and $b_{\Psi^\kappa_\perp} = \perp$. Such a mapping exists by the properties of $\mathcal{E}$. In the following we ease notation and just write κ for Ψ^κ and $\kappa_\perp$ for $\Psi^\kappa_\perp$.

Next, we provide how $\star$ behaves in all cases appearing in runs of Simulate-TM$(T, \star, \gamma)$ (Algorithm 1), depending on the ranking function type of κ:

CONF. We consider two different cases. *These case of* $\alpha = \varphi_{q,\mathtt{halt}}$. For this case let $\star$ yield the following ranking function $\kappa \star \alpha$:

$$\kappa \star \alpha(\omega_{\mathbf{0}}) = 1 \qquad \kappa \star \alpha(\omega_{\mathtt{halt}}) = \kappa(\omega_{\mathtt{halt}}) - \kappa(\omega_q)$$
$$\kappa \star \alpha(\omega_q) = 0 \qquad \kappa \star \alpha(\omega_{\mathtt{pos}}) = \kappa(\omega_{\mathtt{pos}}) + 1$$

Note that $\kappa \star \alpha$ is a **PEEK** ranking function and $\mathtt{conf}(\kappa) = \mathtt{conf}(\kappa \star \alpha)$. *The case of* $\alpha = \varphi_{\mathbf{0}}$. Let κ_Ψ be a ranking function representing a configuration $C = \langle q_i, \langle t_l, t_c, t_r \rangle \rangle$ of T. Let $\langle q_j, \langle t'_l, t'_c, t'_r \rangle \rangle$ be the successor configuration provided by δ. Then $\star$ yields the following ranking function $\kappa \star \alpha$:

$$\kappa \star \alpha(\omega_{\mathbf{0}}) = 0 \qquad \kappa \star \alpha(\omega_{\mathtt{halt}}) = \kappa(\omega_{\mathtt{halt}}) - (i - j)$$
$$\kappa \star \alpha(\omega_q) = j \qquad \kappa \star \alpha(\omega_{\mathtt{pos}}) = \kappa(\omega_{\mathtt{pos}}) - (i - j)$$

Note that $\kappa \star \alpha$ is a **TRANS** ranking function with $\mathtt{post\text{-}state}(\kappa \star \alpha) = q_j$ and $\mathtt{conf}(\kappa) = \mathtt{conf}(\kappa \star \alpha)$.

PEEK. Based on Algorithm 1 we consider $\alpha = \varphi_{\mathbf{0},\mathtt{pos}}$. Then $\star$ is constructed such that it yields $\kappa \star \alpha$ by input κ and α with:

$$\kappa \star \alpha(\omega_{\mathbf{0}}) = 0 \qquad \kappa \star \alpha(\omega_q) = n - \kappa(\omega_{\mathtt{halt}})$$
$$\kappa \star \alpha(\omega_{\mathtt{halt}}) = n \qquad \kappa \star \alpha(\omega_{\mathtt{pos}}) = \kappa(\omega_{\mathtt{pos}}) - 1$$

The ranking function $\kappa \star \alpha$ is of **CONF** and $\mathtt{conf}(\kappa) = \mathtt{conf}(\kappa \star \alpha)$.

TRANS. Let $\mathtt{post\text{-}state}(\kappa \star \alpha) = q_j$ and conf$(\kappa) = \langle q_i, \langle t_l, t_c, t_r \rangle \rangle$ and successor configuration $C = \langle q_j, \langle t'_l, t'_c, t'_r \rangle \rangle$. For $\alpha = \varphi_{\mathbf{0},q,\mathtt{halt}}$ let $\star$ yield the ranking function $\kappa \star \alpha$ given by:

$$\kappa \star \alpha(\omega_{\mathbf{0}}) = 0 \qquad \kappa \star \alpha(\omega_{\mathtt{halt}}) = \kappa(\omega_{\mathtt{halt}})$$
$$\kappa \star \alpha(\omega_q) = \kappa(\omega_q) \qquad \kappa \star \alpha(\omega_{\mathtt{pos}}) = n + \mathtt{enc}(C) + 1$$

Note that $\kappa \star \alpha$ is a **POST** ranking function which represents the posterior configuration C, i.e. $C = \mathtt{conf}(\kappa \star \alpha)$.

POST. As last case consider $\alpha = \varphi_{\mathbf{0},q,\mathtt{pos}}$. We define $\star$ as follows:

$$\kappa \star \alpha(\omega_{\mathbf{0}}) = 0 \qquad \kappa \star \alpha(\omega_{\mathtt{halt}}) = n$$
$$\kappa \star \alpha(\omega_q) = \kappa(\omega_q) \qquad \kappa \star \alpha(\omega_{\mathtt{pos}}) = \kappa(\omega_{\mathtt{pos}})$$

The resulting $\kappa \star \alpha$ is a **CONF** ranking function.

Consideration of Algorithm 1 yields that all operations $\star$ performed in Algorithm 1 are covered by the cases described here. In every step of Algorithm 1 every ranking function constructed is of one of the four types and only parameters treated above are applied. In particular, observe that in Lines 6 to 8 a complete transition to a new configuration is performed. Clearly, if $\omega_{\mathtt{halt}} \in [\![\kappa]\!]$, where κ is of type **PEEK**, then T has also reached the halting state and κ represents the content of the tape of T in that configuration. Thus, Line 11 of Algorithm 1 yields the output of T.

Next, we complete $\star$ to a ranking function-based belief change operator, by setting $\kappa \star \alpha = \kappa^\kappa_\alpha$ for all remaining unspecified cases of $\star$, where κ^κ_α is given as follows: If α is consistent, let κ^κ_α denote the ranking function with:

$$\kappa^\star_\alpha(\omega) = \begin{cases} \kappa(\omega) - \min_{\omega' \in [\![\alpha]\!]}(\kappa(\omega')) & \text{if } \omega \in [\![\alpha]\!] \\ \kappa(\omega) + 1 & \text{if } \omega \notin [\![\alpha]\!] \end{cases}$$

If α is inconsistent, let $\kappa^\kappa_\alpha = \kappa_\perp$. A careful examination shows that $\star$ satisfies the quantitative postulates:

(Q1) if $\omega, \omega' \in [\![\alpha]\!]$, then $\kappa(\omega) - \kappa(\omega') = \kappa \star \alpha(\omega) - \kappa \star \alpha(\omega')$

(Q2) if $\omega, \omega' \in [\![\neg\alpha]\!]$, then $\kappa(\omega) - \kappa(\omega') = \kappa \star \alpha(\omega) - \kappa \star \alpha(\omega')$

(Q3) if $\omega \in [\![\alpha]\!]$ and $\omega' \in [\![\neg\alpha]\!]$,
then $\kappa(\omega) < \kappa(\omega') \Rightarrow \kappa \star \alpha(\omega) < \kappa \star \alpha(\omega')$

(Q4) if $\omega \in [\![\alpha]\!]$ and $\omega' \in [\![\neg\alpha]\!]$,
then $\kappa(\omega) \leq \kappa(\omega') \Rightarrow \kappa \star \alpha(\omega) \leq \kappa \star \alpha(\omega')$

Consequently, by Proposition 7 and Proposition 4, $\star$ is an AGM revision operator that satisfies (DP1)–(DP4). □

Theorem 9 gives rise to the central observation.

Observation. *Iterated belief change is Turing complete.*

5 Conclusions and Future Work

In this paper we showed that iterated belief change is Turing complete; this includes iterated AGM revision. In particular, we showed how Turing machines can be encoded in a belief revision operator over ranking functions. The results of Turing-completeness still hold when assuming the Darwiche-Pearl iteration principles for belief revision.

It is reasonable that (in certain situations) iterated belief change should be limited in its computational power, e.g., when modeling human reasoning (Ragni et al. 2020). In future work, we will identify such situations formally and investigate computational properties and restrictions by means of iteration postulates.

Acknowledgements

We thank the anonymous reviewers for their valuable hints and comments that helped us to improve the paper. This work was supported by the Deutsche Forschungsgemeinschaft (DFG, German Research Foundation), grants BE 1700/9-1 and BE 1700/10-1 awarded to Christoph Beierle as part of the priority program "Intentional Forgetting in Organizations" (SPP 1921). Kai Sauerwald is supported by the grants BE 1700/9-1 and BE 1700/10-1.

References

Alchourrón, C. E.; Gärdenfors, P.; and Makinson, D. 1985. On the logic of theory change: Partial meet contraction and revision functions. *J. Symb. Log.* 50(2):510–530.

Aravanis, T.; Peppas, P.; and Williams, M. 2019. Observations on Darwiche and Pearl's approach for iterated belief revision. In Kraus, S., ed., *Proceedings of the Twenty-Eighth International Joint Conference on Artificial Intelligence, IJCAI 2019, Macao, China, August 10-16, 2019*, 1509–1515. ijcai.org.

Darwiche, A., and Pearl, J. 1997. On the logic of iterated belief revision. *Artificial Intelligence* 89:1–29.

Friedman, N., and Halpern, J. Y. 1996. Belief revision: A critique. In Aiello, L. C.; Doyle, J.; and Shapiro, S. C., eds., *Proceedings of the Fifth International Conference on Principles of Knowledge Representation and Reasoning (KR'96), Cambridge, Massachusetts, USA, November 5-8, 1996*, 421–431. Morgan Kaufmann.

Katsuno, H., and Mendelzon, A. O. 1992. Propositional knowledge base revision and minimal change. *Artif. Intell.* 52(3):263–294.

Liberatore, P. 1997. The complexity of iterated belief revision. In Afrati, F. N., and Kolaitis, P. G., eds., *Database Theory - ICDT '97, 6th International Conference, Delphi, Greece, January 8-10, 1997, Proceedings*, volume 1186 of *Lecture Notes in Computer Science*, 276–290. Springer.

Ragni, M.; Kern-Isberner, G.; Beierle, C.; and Sauerwald, K. 2020. Cognitive logics - features, formalisms, and challenges. In Giacomo, G. D.; Catalá, A.; Dilkina, B.; Milano, M.; Barro, S.; Bugarín, A.; and Lang, J., eds., *Proceedings of the 24nd European Conference on Artificial Intelligence (ECAI 2020)*, volume 325 of *Frontiers in Artificial Intelligence and Applications*, 2931–2932. IOS Press.

Schwind, N., and Konieczny, S. 2020. Non-Prioritized Iterated Revision: Improvement via Incremental Belief Merging. In *Proceedings of the 17th International Conference on Principles of Knowledge Representation and Reasoning*, 738–747.

Schwind, N.; Konieczny, S.; Lagniez, J.; and Marquis, P. 2020. On computational aspects of iterated belief change. In Bessiere, C., ed., *Proceedings of the Twenty-Ninth International Joint Conference on Artificial Intelligence, IJCAI 2020*, 1770–1776.

Spohn, W. 1988. Ordinal conditional functions: a dynamic theory of epistemic states. In Harper, W., and Skyrms, B., eds., *Causation in Decision, Belief Change, and Statistics, II.* Kluwer Academic Publishers. 105–134.

Spohn, W. 2012. *The Laws of Belief: Ranking Theory and Its Philosophical Applications.* Oxford University Press.

Chasing Streams with Existential Rules

Jacopo Urbani[1], **Markus Krötzsch**[2], **Thomas Eiter**[3]
[1]Department of Computer Science, Vrije Universiteit Amsterdam, The Netherlands
[2]Knowledge-Based Systems Group, TU Dresden, Germany
[3]Institute of Logic and Computation, Technische Universität Wien, Austria
jacopo@cs.vu.nl,markus.kroetzsch@tu-dresden.de,eiter@kr.tuwien.ac.at

Abstract

We study reasoning with existential rules to perform query answering over streams of data. On static databases, this problem has been widely studied, but its extension to rapidly changing data has not yet been considered. To bridge this gap, we extend LARS, a well-known framework for rule-based stream reasoning, to support existential rules. For that, we show how to translate LARS with existentials into a semantics-preserving set of existential rules. As query answering with such rules is undecidable in general, we describe how to leverage the temporal nature of streams and present suitable notions of acyclicity that ensure decidability.

1 Introduction

Streaming data arises in many applications, fostered by the need of deriving timely insights from emerging information and the inherent impossibility of storing all available data (Margara et al. 2014). Stream reasoning has become a productive area of KR with many formalisms (Anicic et al. 2011; Le-Phuoc et al. 2011; Barbieri et al. 2010; Tiger and Heintz 2016; Dell'Aglio et al. 2017; Kharlamov et al. 2019; Wałega, Kaminski, and Cuenca Grau 2019). This multiplicity is justified by the breadth of scenarios where stream processing is useful. Many of the approaches are distinguished from classical temporal reasoning, e.g., since data snapshots (*windows*) play an important role to reduce data volumes.

A well-known formalism in this space is LARS (Beck, Dao-Tran, and Eiter 2018), which is a rule-based language for stream reasoning that combines concepts from logic programming with dedicated stream operators to express windows and temporal quantifiers. For example, the LARS rule r_1: $\boxplus^3 \Box \mathsf{beltTmp}(X,Y) \wedge \mathsf{high}(Y) \rightarrow \mathsf{warn}(X)$ issues a warning if the temperature on a conveyor belt has been high for all ($\Box$) last three time points ($\boxplus^3$).

Another prominent field in KR are *existential rules*, which are also used as a basis for ontological models, especially in applications with large amounts of data (Baget et al. 2011; Cuenca Grau et al. 2013; Gottlob, Lukasiewicz, and Pieris 2014). Other common names for these rules include *tuple-generating dependencies* (Abiteboul, Hull, and Vianu 1994) and *Datalog*$^{\pm}$ (Calì et al. 2010). As a simple example, the rule r_2: $\mathsf{belt}(X) \rightarrow \exists Y.\mathsf{beltOperator}(X,Y)$ expresses that every belt has an operator (even if unknown). Existential quantification is central for ontologies and provides high expressivity beyond plain Datalog (Krötzsch, Marx, and Rudolph 2019). While reasoning with existential rules is known to be undecidable in general (Beeri and Vardi 1981), many well-behaved language fragments and practical implementations exist (Benedikt et al. 2017; Urbani et al. 2018; Bellomarini, Sallinger, and Gottlob 2018).

Until now, however, these areas have not been combined, and stream reasoning approaches do not support existential rules. Even for logic-based ontology languages in general, solutions only seem to exist for specific cases where queries are rewritable (Kharlamov et al. 2019; Kalaycı et al. 2019). As a consequence, it is often unclear how existing ontological background knowledge can be used in stream reasoning.

Additionally, the lack of existential quantification prevents useful modelling techniques for stream analysis. In particular, existential quantification can be used to represent temporal events, possibly spanning multiple time points, or to track unknown individuals. For instance, it can be used to create a new incident ID if the temperature on a belt is high for too long, or to track a not-yet-recognized object within a bounding box in a video stream. Notice that while in principle events could be modeled without value invention, i.e., using ad-hoc relations, doing so would put an upper bound to the number of possible events which might be undesirable as the future stream is typically unknown. A similar argument applies to the example above about objects within bounding boxes: it is arguably more natural to introduce new values and treat them as first-class individuals.

With this motivation in mind, we developed an extension of existential rules with LARS-based temporal quantifiers called LARS$^+$. Due to the undecidability of query answering with existential rules, our objective are decidable fragments, with the following contributions:

- We introduce LARS$^+$ as an existential stream reasoning language with a model-theoretic semantics.
- We give a semantics-preserving transformation from LARS$^+$ to existential rules to allow query answering. Doing so allows us to exploit existing decidability results, but these are limited in their use of time. We thus present *time-aware extensions of acyclicity notions* for LARS$^+$ programs.
- Initial experiments suggest that our method is promising.[1]

[1]Source code is at https://github.com/karmaresearch/elars; for a longer version of this paper see (Urbani, Krötzsch, and Eiter 2022).

2 LARS$^+$

Currently, LARS and DatalogMTL (Brandt et al. 2017; Wałega, Kaminski, and Cuenca Grau 2019) are popular for rule-based reasoning on data streams. While we focus on LARS, some of our work may be adapted to DatalogMTL.

To cope with big data volumes, LARS allows one to restrict streams to data snapshots (i.e., substreams) taken by generic window operators $\boxplus$. Typically, windows are used to consider only the knowledge in the most recent past, but this is not enough to avoid a complexity explosion or even undecidability that could arise from reasoning over an indefinite future. To overcome this problem, it is common in this domain to restrict future predictions up to a horizon of interest h, which is moved forward indefinitely.

Our language LARS$^+$ can be viewed as an extension of existential rules with temporal features of LARS. In the choice of data-snapshot operators, we take inspiration from *plain LARS*, which is a LARS fragment that is apt for efficient implementation (Bazoobandi, Beck, and Urbani 2017).

Syntax We consider a two-sorted logic with abstract elements and the natural numbers $\mathbb{N}$ as time points. We assume infinite sets $\mathcal{V}_A$ of *abstract variables*, $\mathcal{V}_T$ of *time variables*, $\mathcal{N}$ of *labelled nulls*, and $\mathcal{C}$ of *constants* that are mutually disjoint and disjoint from $\mathbb{N}$. *Abstract terms* (resp. *time terms*) are elements of $\mathcal{V}_A \cup \mathcal{N} \cup \mathcal{C}$ (resp., $\mathcal{V}_T \cup \mathbb{N}$).

Predicates p are from a set $\mathcal{P}$ of predicates and have arity $\mathsf{ar}(p) \geq 0$, with each position typed (abstract or time sort). A *normal atom* is an expression $p(\mathbf{t})$, $\mathbf{t} = t_1, \ldots, t_{\mathsf{ar}}(p)$, where t_i is a term of proper sort. An *arithmetic atom* has the form $t_1 \leq t_2$ or $t_1 = t_2 + t_3$ for time terms t_1, t_2, t_3. The set of all *atoms* (normal and arithmetic) is denoted $\mathcal{A}$. For an atom α (or any other logical expression introduced below), the *domain* $\mathsf{dom}(\alpha)$ of α is the set of all terms in α; we write $\alpha[\mathbf{x}]$ to state that $\mathbf{x} = \mathsf{dom}(\alpha) \cap (\mathcal{V}_A \cup \mathcal{V}_T)$; and we say that α is *ground* if it contains no variables.

A predicate $p \in \mathcal{P}$ is *simple* if it has no position of time sort, while an atom is *simple* if it normal and has a simple predicate. A *LARS$^+$ atom* α has the form

$$\alpha := a \mid b \mid @_T b \mid \boxplus^n @_T b \mid \boxplus^n \Diamond b \mid \boxplus^n \Box b \qquad (1)$$

where a is an arithmetic atom, b is either a null-free simple atom or $\top$ (which holds true at all times), T is a time term, and $n \in \mathbb{N}$. *Window operators* $\boxplus^n$ restrict attention back to n time points in the past, and $@_T$ (resp. $\Box$, $\Diamond$) indicates that a formula holds at time T (resp., *every*, *some* time point).

Arithmetic atoms do not depend on time, whereas atoms $@_T b$ refer to a specific time T. All other LARS$^+$ atoms are interpreted relative to some current time point. Simple atoms b can equivalently be written as $\boxplus^0 \Diamond b$ or as $\boxplus^0 \Box b$.

Definition 1. A *LARS$^+$ rule* is an expression of the form

$$r = \Box \forall \mathbf{x}, \mathbf{y}.(B[\mathbf{x}, \mathbf{y}] \rightarrow \exists \mathbf{v}.H[\mathbf{y}, \mathbf{v}]) \qquad (2)$$

where $\mathbf{x}$, $\mathbf{y}$, and $\mathbf{v}$ are mutually disjoint sets of variables, and $\mathbf{v}$ contains only abstract variables; the body $B[\mathbf{x}, \mathbf{y}]$ is a conjunction of LARS$^+$ atoms; and the head $H[\mathbf{y}, \mathbf{v}]$ is a conjunction of atoms of the form b or $@_T b$ in (1). We set $\mathsf{b}(r) := B$ and $\mathsf{h}(r) := H$, and we usually omit the leading $\Box$ and universal quantifiers when writing rules.

A *LARS$^+$ program* is a finite set of *LARS$^+$ rules*; we denote the set of all such programs by $\mathbf{L}^+$.

Semantics Like for LARS, the semantics of LARS$^+$ is based on streams. Formally, a *stream* $S = (\mathbf{T}, v)$ consists of a timeline $\mathbf{T} = [0, h] \subset \mathbb{N}$ and an *evaluation function* $v : \mathbb{N} \rightarrow 2^{\mathcal{A}}$ such that, for all $t \in \mathbb{N}$, $v(t)$ is a set of ground normal atoms and $v(t) = \emptyset$ if $t \notin \mathbf{T}$. We call S a *data stream* if only extensional atoms occur in S, i.e., atoms with designated predicates not occurring in rule heads. Given $n \in \mathbb{N}$ and $t \in \mathbf{T}$, we write $w_n(S, t)$ for the stream $([0, t], v')$ where for any $t' \in \mathbb{N}$, $v'(t') = v(t')$ if $t - n \leq t' \leq t$, and $v'(t) = \emptyset$ otherwise; we call $w_n(S, t)$ a *window* of size n on S at t.

Models of LARS$^+$ are special streams. For a stream $S = (\mathbf{T}, v)$, a simple ground atom b, and $t, t', n \in \mathbb{N}$, we write:

$$\begin{array}{ll} S, t \models b \quad \text{if } b \in v(t), & S, t \models @_{t'} b \quad \text{if } S, t' \models b, \\ S, t \models \Diamond b \,/\, \Box b & \text{if } S, t'' \models b \text{ for some / all } t'' \in \mathbf{T}, \\ S, t \models \boxplus^n \beta & \text{if } w_n(S, t), t \models \beta. \end{array}$$

Further, $S, t \models \top$ holds for all $t \in \mathbf{T}$ and $S, t \models a$ for all ground arithmetic atoms a that express a true relation on $\mathbb{N}$. To define satisfaction of rules on a stream S at time point t, we introduce the auxiliary notion of $\mathbf{T}$-*match* σ for a set C of atoms on S and t as a sort-preserving mapping from the variables of C to terms, s.t. (i) each time variable X is mapped to $\mathbf{T}$ ($X\sigma \in \mathbf{T}$) and (ii) $S, t \models \alpha\sigma$ for each $\alpha \in C$.

Definition 2. A LARS$^+$ rule r as in (2) is *satisfied* by a stream $S = (\mathbf{T}, v)$, written $S \models r$, if either (i) $\mathsf{h}(r)$ contains some time point $t \notin \mathbf{T}$ (i.e., ignore inference out of scope), or (ii) for all $t \in \mathbf{T}$, every $\mathbf{T}$-match σ of $\mathsf{b}(r)$ on S and t is extendible to a $\mathbf{T}$-match $\sigma' \supseteq \sigma$ of $\mathsf{b}(r) \cup \mathsf{h}(r)$ on S and t.

A program $P \in \mathbf{L}^+$ is satisfied by S, written $S \models P$, if $S \models r$ for all $r \in P$. A data stream $D = (\mathbf{T}', v')$ is satisfied by S, written $S \models D$, if $\mathbf{T}' \subseteq \mathbf{T}$ and $v'(t) \subseteq v(t)$ for all $t \in \mathbf{T}'$. We then call S a *model* of P resp. D.

Example 1. Consider the data stream $D = ([0, 9], v)$, where $v(t) = \{\mathsf{belt}(b_1), \mathsf{high}(90), \mathsf{beltTmp}(b_1, tmp(t))\}$ for each $t \in [0, 9]$, where $tmp(t) = 90$ if $t \leq 4$ and $tmp(t) = 70$ otherwise. Then any model S of the rules r_1, r_2 in Section 1 and D fulfills $S, 4 \models \mathsf{warn}(b_1) \wedge \mathsf{beltOperator}(b_1, v)$ for some constant or null v. Similarly $S, 5 \models \mathsf{beltOperator}(b_1, v')$ for some constant or null v' while $S, 5 \models \mathsf{warn}(b_1)$ may fail.

3 Query Answering with LARS$^+$

The query answering problem in LARS$^+$ is as follows.

Definition 3. A *LARS$^+$ Boolean Conjunctive Query (BCQ)* q has the form $\exists \mathbf{x}.Q[\mathbf{x}]$, where Q is a conjunction of LARS$^+$ atoms. A stream $S = (\mathbf{T}, v)$ satisfies q at time t, written $S, t \models q$, if some $\mathbf{T}$-match σ of Q on S and t exists. A program $P \in \mathbf{L}^+$ and data stream D *entail* q at time t, written $P, D, t \models q$, if $S, t \models q$ for every model S of P and D.

For instance, a BCQ could be $\exists X.\, \boxplus^5 \Box \mathsf{warn}(X)$, which asks if there has been a warning over the same belt in the last 5 time points. To solve BCQ answering with LARS$^+$, we propose a consequence-preserving rewriting $\mathsf{rew}(\cdot)$ to existential rules with a time sort. This rewriting is useful because it will allow us to exploit known results for existential rules, e.g., acyclicity notions (Cuenca Grau et al. 2013).

Our proposed rewriting of P into $\mathsf{rew}(P)$ has 5 steps:
(1) Each atom $\boxplus^n \Diamond p(\mathbf{t})$ is replaced by $\boxplus^n @_T\, p(\mathbf{t})$, where T is a fresh variable used only in one atom.
(2) For any simple predicate p, we add auxiliary predicates $[\![\boxplus\Box\, p]\!]$ and $[\![\boxplus @\, p]\!]$ of arity $\mathsf{ar}(p){+}2$ resp. $\mathsf{ar}(p){+}3$. Intuitively, $[\![\boxplus\Box\, p]\!](\mathbf{t}, n, C)$ and $[\![\boxplus @\, p]\!](\mathbf{t}, n, T, C)$ mean that $\boxplus^n \Box p(\mathbf{t})$ and $\boxplus^n @_T\, p(\mathbf{t})$ hold at time C, respectively.
(3) Using a fresh variable C to represent the current time, we rewrite non-arithmetic atoms α in P (where $\top$ is $\top()$) to

$$\mathsf{rew}(\alpha) = \begin{cases} [\![\boxplus\Box\, p]\!](\mathbf{t}, 0, C) & \text{if } \alpha = p(\mathbf{t}), \\ [\![\boxplus\Box\, p]\!](\mathbf{t}, 0, T) & \text{if } \alpha = @_T\, p(\mathbf{t}), \\ [\![\boxplus\Box\, p]\!](\mathbf{t}, n, C) & \text{if } \alpha = \boxplus^n \Box p(\mathbf{t}), \\ [\![\boxplus @\, p]\!](\mathbf{t}, n, T, C) & \text{if } \alpha = \boxplus^n @_T\, p(\mathbf{t}) \end{cases}$$

(4) We add $[\![\boxplus\Box\, \top]\!](0, C)$ in rule bodies not containing C.
(5) For every predicate p (including $\top$), we add the following rules to P, where $\mathbf{X}$ is a list of variables of length $\mathsf{ar}(p)$ and $m = \max(0, n \mid \boxplus^n$ occurs in $P)$:

$$0 \le C \rightarrow [\![\boxplus\Box\, \top]\!](0, C) \qquad (3)$$

$$[\![\boxplus\Box\, p]\!](\mathbf{X}, 0, 0) \rightarrow [\![\boxplus\Box\, p]\!](\mathbf{X}, m, 0) \qquad (4)$$

$$[\![\boxplus\Box\, p]\!](\mathbf{X}, N', C) \wedge N'{=}N{+}1 \rightarrow [\![\boxplus\Box\, p]\!](\mathbf{X}, N, C) \qquad (5)$$

$$\begin{aligned} &[\![\boxplus\Box\, p]\!](\mathbf{X}, N, C) \wedge N'{=}N{+}1 \wedge N'{\le}m \wedge C'{=}C{+}1 \\ &\quad \wedge [\![\boxplus\Box\, p]\!](\mathbf{X}, 0, C') \rightarrow [\![\boxplus\Box\, p]\!](\mathbf{X}, N', C') \end{aligned} \qquad (6)$$

$$[\![\boxplus\Box\, p]\!](\mathbf{X}, 0, C) \rightarrow [\![\boxplus @\, p]\!](\mathbf{X}, 0, C, C) \qquad (7)$$

$$\begin{aligned} &[\![\boxplus @\, p]\!](\mathbf{X}, N, T, C) \wedge N'{\le}m \wedge N'{=}N{+}1 \\ &\quad \wedge I \le 1 \wedge C'{=}C{+}I \rightarrow [\![\boxplus @\, p]\!](\mathbf{X}, N', T, C') \end{aligned} \qquad (8)$$

We rewrite a LARS$^+$ BCQ $\exists \mathbf{x}.Q$ and time point t similarly to $\mathsf{rew}(\exists \mathbf{x}.Q, t) = \exists \mathbf{x}. \bigwedge_{\alpha \in Q} \mathsf{rew}(\alpha) \wedge C{\le}t \wedge t{\le}C$ (treating atoms $\boxplus^n \Diamond p(\mathbf{t})$ as before), and a stream $S = (\mathbf{T}, v)$ to facts $\mathsf{rew}(S) = \{[\![\boxplus\Box\, p]\!](\mathbf{t}, 0, s) \mid p(\mathbf{t}) \in v(t), t \in \mathbf{T}\}$.

Example 2. We illustrate the rewriting on r_1. Step (2) creates predicates $[\![\boxplus\Box\mathsf{beltTmp}]\!]$, $[\![\boxplus\Box\mathsf{high}]\!]$, and $[\![\boxplus\Box\mathsf{warn}]\!]$ and Step (3) the rule $[\![\boxplus\Box\mathsf{high}]\!](X, Y, 3, C) \wedge [\![\boxplus\Box\mathsf{high}]\!](Y, 0, C) \rightarrow [\![\boxplus\Box\mathsf{warn}]\!](X, 0, C)$. Step (5) adds auxiliary rules to implement the semantics; e.g., rule (6) ensures that "$\boxplus\Box$"-facts survive across time points, say if $[\![\boxplus\Box\mathsf{beltTmp}]\!](a, b, 0, 6)$ and $[\![\boxplus\Box\mathsf{beltTmp}]\!](a, b, 2, 5)$ hold, then $[\![\boxplus\Box\mathsf{beltTmp}]\!](a, b, 3, 6)$ should hold as well.

Let us denote by $P' \models_{\mathbf{T}} q'$ entailment of a BCQ q' from existential rules P' with timeline $\mathbf{T}$, which is defined using $\mathbf{T}$-matches as $P, D, t \models q$ but disregarding D and t. Then:

Theorem 1. *For any $P \in \mathbf{L}^+$, BCQ q, data stream D on $\mathbf{T}$, and $t \in \mathbf{T}$ holds $P, D, t \models q$ iff $\mathsf{rew}(P) \cup \mathsf{rew}(D) \models_{\mathbf{T}} \mathsf{rew}(q, t)$.*

Theorem 1 is important as it allows us to implement BCQ answering in LARS$^+$ using existential rule engines, e.g., GLog (Tsamoura et al. 2021); arithmetic atoms over $\mathbf{T}$ can be simulated with regular atoms: simply add the set $\mathsf{rew}(\mathbf{T})$ of all true instances of arithmetic atoms in P over $\mathbf{T}$ and view $\mathsf{rew}(P) \cup \mathsf{rew}(D) \cup \mathsf{rew}(\mathbf{T})$ as a single-sorted theory.

4 Decidability

As BCQ entailment over existential rules is undecidable, we desire that the rewriting $\mathsf{rew}(\cdot)$ falls into a known decidable fragment. Such may be defined by *acyclicity conditions* (Cuenca Grau et al. 2013), which ensure that a suitable *chase*, which is a versatile class of reasoning algorithms for existential rules (Benedikt et al. 2017) based on "applying" rules iteratively, will terminate over a given input. We use a variant of the *skolem chase* (Marnette 2009), using nulls instead of skolem terms (aka *semi-oblivious chase*), extended to the time sort (see (Urbani, Krötzsch, and Eiter 2022)).

Conditions like the canonical *weak acyclicity (WA)* (Fagin et al. 2005) ensure in fact *universal termination*, i.e., chase termination for a given rule set over all sets of input facts. We can thus apply such criteria to $\mathsf{rew}(P)$ (viewed as single-sorted theory) while ignoring $\mathsf{rew}(D)$ and $\mathsf{rew}(\mathbf{T})$. Universal termination may here be seen as an analysis that disregards time. To formalise this, let $\mathsf{strip}(P)$ result from P by deleting all arithmetic atoms, window operators, and temporal quantifiers, and let $\mathbf{CT}$ and $\mathbf{WA}$ be the classes of all rule sets on which the skolem chase universally terminates and of all weakly acyclic rule sets, respectively. Then:

Theorem 2. *For any $P \in \mathbf{L}^+$, we have (i) $\mathsf{strip}(P) \in \mathbf{CT}$ iff $\mathsf{rew}(P) \in \mathbf{CT}$ and (ii) $\mathsf{strip}(P) \in \mathbf{WA}$ iff $\mathsf{rew}(P) \in \mathbf{WA}$.*

Analogous results hold for elaborated acyclicity notions (Cuenca Grau et al. 2013). Notably, we can check acyclicity on the simpler rule set $\mathsf{strip}(P)$. With WA as a representative notion, we let $\mathbf{L}^+_{\mathsf{LWA}} = \{P \in \mathbf{L}^+ \mid \mathsf{strip}(P) \in \mathbf{WA}\}$.

While easy to check, universal termination also considers situations that are impossible on properly encoded streams.

Example 3. Consider $P = \{@_T\, p(X, Y) \wedge T'{=}T{+}1 \rightarrow \exists V. @_{T'}\, p(Y, V)\}$. The skolem chase on $\mathsf{rew}(P) \cup \mathsf{rew}(D) \cup \mathsf{rew}(\mathbf{T})$ terminates on all $\mathbf{T}$ and D, but not universally for non-standard timelines where e.g., $0 = 0 + 1$ holds. That is, reasoning with P always terminates despite $P \notin \mathbf{L}^+_{\mathsf{LWA}}$.

We thus introduce *time-aware acyclicity*, which retains relevant temporal information instead of working with $\mathsf{strip}(P)$ only. First, to simplify P, we fix a fresh time variable N and replace all LARS$^+$ atoms in all rules as follows:

$$p(\mathbf{t}) \mapsto @_N\, p(\mathbf{t}) \quad (9) \qquad \boxplus^n @_T\, p(\mathbf{t}) \mapsto @_T\, p(\mathbf{t}) \quad (11)$$

$$\boxplus^n \Box p(\mathbf{t}) \mapsto @_N\, p(\mathbf{t}) \quad (10) \qquad \boxplus^n \Diamond p(\mathbf{t}) \mapsto @_U\, p(\mathbf{t}) \quad (12)$$

where (9) refers to atoms with no surrounding LARS$^+$ operators and U in (12) is a fresh time variable unique for each replacement; arithmetic atoms are kept unchanged. The resulting program is denoted by $\mathsf{wfree}(P)$ ("*window-free*").

Example 4. Let P consist of the following rules:

$$\boxplus^3 \Box p(X) \rightarrow \exists Y. q(X, Y) \qquad (13)$$

$$@_T\, q(X, Y) \wedge U = T + 1 \rightarrow @_U\, p(Y) \qquad (14)$$

As in Example 3, the skolem chase on $\mathsf{rew}(P)$ terminates if the given input data encodes a valid timeline, else it may not (indeed, $P \notin \mathbf{L}^+_{\mathsf{LWA}}$). In $\mathsf{wfree}(P)$, (13) is changed to

$$@_N\, p(X) \rightarrow \exists Y. @_N\, q(X, Y) \qquad (15)$$

Intuitively, in $\mathsf{wfree}(P)$, N is the time at which rules are evaluated and localises all simple atoms to it; windows are removed and their restrictions relaxed: $\boxplus^n \Box$ ("at all times in window up to now") becomes $@_N$ ("now"); $\boxplus^n @_T$ ("at T if in window") becomes $@_T$; and $\boxplus^n \Diamond$ ("at some time in window") becomes $@_U$ ("at some time"). As this logically weakens rule bodies, $\mathsf{wfree}(P)$ has more logical consequences than P. We obtain the following useful insight:

Theorem 3. *For every $P \in \mathbf{L}^+$ and data stream D, if the skolem chase terminates on* $\mathsf{rew}(\mathsf{wfree}(P))$ *and* $\mathsf{rew}(D)$, *then it also terminates on* $\mathsf{rew}(P)$ *and* $\mathsf{rew}(D)$.

To exploit Theorem 3, we study the chase termination over $\mathsf{rew}(\mathsf{wfree}(P))$ while restricting to actual timelines, which are incorporated by partial grounding.

Definition 4. The *partial grounding* $\mathsf{grnd}_A(P)$ of a program P for a set A of null-free facts over a set $\mathcal{P}_A$ of predicates not occurring in rule heads of P, is the set of all rules $(B\backslash B_A \rightarrow \exists\mathbf{z}.H)\sigma$, where B_A are the atoms in B with predicate in $\mathcal{P}_A$, s.t. a rule $B \rightarrow \exists\mathbf{z}.H \in P$ and a homomorphism σ between B_A and A exist, i.e., a sort- and constant- preserving mapping $\sigma : \mathsf{dom}(B_A) \rightarrow \mathsf{dom}(A)$ s.t. $B_A\sigma \subseteq A$.

As long as A comprises all facts over $\mathcal{P}_A$, $\mathsf{grnd}_A(P)$ has the same models as P and the chase is also preserved. We use this to ground the time sort in LARS$^+$:

Definition 5. Given a program P, the *temporal grounding* of $\mathsf{wfree}(P)$ for a timeline $\mathbf{T}$, denoted $\mathsf{tgrnd}_\mathbf{T}(P)$, is the partial grounding $\mathsf{grnd}_{a(\mathbf{T},P)}(P')$ where

- P' results from $\mathsf{rew}(\mathsf{wfree}(P))$ by adding, for each $T \in \mathcal{V}_T$ in each rule body B, an atom $T \leq T$ to B and
- $a(\mathbf{T}, P)$ is the set of all ground instances of arithmetic atoms in P with values from $\mathbf{T}$ that are true over $\mathbb{N}$.

Example 5. For $\mathsf{wfree}(P)$ from Example 4 and timeline $\mathbf{T} = [0, 1]$, the temporal grounding is as follows (the deleted ground instances of B_A are shown in parentheses):

$$[\![\boxplus\Box\, p]\!](X,0,0) \rightarrow \exists Y.[\![\boxplus\Box\, q]\!](X,Y,0,0) \qquad (0\leq 0)$$
$$[\![\boxplus\Box\, p]\!](X,0,1) \rightarrow \exists Y.[\![\boxplus\Box\, q]\!](X,Y,0,1) \qquad (1\leq 1)$$
$$[\![\boxplus\Box\, q]\!](X,Y,0,0) \rightarrow [\![\boxplus\Box\, p]\!](Y,0,1) \qquad (1=0+1)$$

While universal termination on $\mathsf{tgrnd}_\mathbf{T}(P)$, which can be recognized in Example 5 using e.g. MFA (Cuenca Grau et al. 2013), ensures chase termination on $\mathsf{rew}(P)$ and $\mathsf{rew}(D)$ for all data streams D on $\mathbf{T}$, simpler, position-based notions like WA still fail. We thus encode time into predicate names:

Definition 6. Let P be an existential rules program with atoms of form $[\![\boxplus\Box\, p]\!](\mathbf{s},0,t)$ only, where t is a time point. Then $\mathsf{tfree}(P)$ is obtained by replacing each $[\![\boxplus\Box\, p]\!](\mathbf{s},0,t)$ with $[\![p]\!]_t(\mathbf{s})$ for a fresh predicate $[\![p]\!]_t$ of proper signature.

Let $\mathsf{tfgrnd}_\mathbf{T}(P) := \mathsf{tfree}(\mathsf{tgrnd}_\mathbf{T}(P))$. The following result shows that this is a good basis to check for acyclicity.

Theorem 4. *If* $\mathsf{tfgrnd}_\mathbf{T}(P)$ *is weakly acyclic for* $P \in \mathbf{L}^+$ *and timeline* $\mathbf{T}$, *then the skolem chase terminates on* $\mathsf{rew}(P)$ *and* $\mathsf{rew}(D)$ *for all data streams D on* $\mathbf{T}$.

Example 6 (cont'd)**.** As $\mathsf{tfgrnd}_\mathbf{T}(P)$ is WA, by Theorem 4 the skolem chase on $\mathsf{rew}(P)$ and $\mathsf{rew}(D)$ always terminates.

In view of Theorem 4, we call $P \in \mathbf{L}^+$ *temporally weakly acyclic* (TLWA) over $\mathbf{T}$ if $\mathsf{tfgrnd}_\mathbf{T}(P)$ is WA, and denote by $\mathbf{L}^+_{\mathsf{TLWA}}(\mathbf{T})$ the class of all such programs P. We then have:

Theorem 5. $\mathbf{L}^+_{\mathsf{LWA}} \subset \mathbf{L}^+_{\mathsf{TLWA}}(\mathbf{T})$ *holds for all* $\mathbf{T}$ *s.t.* $|\mathbf{T}| \geq 2$.

Regarding complexity, as $\mathsf{rew}(\mathbf{T})$ is polynomial *in the length of* $\mathbf{T}$, it is exponential if $\mathbf{T}$ is encoded in binary. However, a polynomial axiomatisation of time is feasible, following the idea to encode numbers 0,1,...,m using sequences of $\lceil \log_2 m \rceil$ bits and to define predicates on them, cf. (Dantsin et al. 2001), such that for the resulting rewriting $\mathsf{rew}_\mathbf{T}(\cdot)$ instead of $\mathsf{rew}(\cdot)$, Theorems 1 and 2 hold analogously.

BCQ answering for $\mathbf{L}^+_{\mathsf{TLWA}}(\mathbf{T})$ is as for WA rules 2EXPTIME-complete in general (on extensional streams, i.e, all $v(t)$, $t \in \mathbf{T}$, are listed). The P-complete data complexity for WA rules carries over to $\mathbf{L}^+_{\mathsf{LWA}}$ but gets 2EXPTIME-hard for $\mathbf{L}^+_{\mathsf{TLWA}}(\mathbf{T})$, as hardest WA programs with bounded predicate arities (Calì, Gottlob, and Pieris 2010) can be emulated.

S_A: $p_1/p_2/p_3$	*Run*	*Mem*	*Out*	S_B: n	*Run*	*Mem*	*Out*
0.0/0.0/0.0	13.12ms	21.9	10.5k	0	0.6s	45.0	36k
0.3/0.3/0.5	13.34ms	22.7	10.7k	2	1.3s	81.8	64k
0.7/0.7/1.0	13.67ms	22.9	10.7k	4	2.6s	114.4	82k

Table 1: Preliminary experiments for scenario S_A and S_B

5 Preliminary Evaluation and Conclusion

We implemented an experimental prototype in Python, which is fed with the stream pointwise. At each time point, it computes the LARS$^+$ model with the stream collected up to the last ℓ time points, using the rewriting in Section 3 and the chase implementation of GLog (Tsamoura et al. 2021).

We considered two scenarios S_A and S_B. The first, S_A, is a toy example with conveyor belts and sensors that measure speed and temperature. The program contains 5 simple rules and the stream is parametrized by probability values p_1, p_2, and p_3 that regulate the number of rule executions (higher values lead to more reasoning). Scenario S_B is much more complex than S_A. We considered the dataset *Deep100* from the *ChaseBench* suite (Benedikt et al. 2017), which is a stress test of chase engines. We created a stream by copying all facts on each time point and rewrote the original rules using LARS$^+$ operators and different window sizes n. More details are available at (Urbani, Krötzsch, and Eiter 2022).

Table 1 reports multiple metrics obtained using a laptop, viz. avg. runtime (*Run*), avg. peak use of RAM (in MB, *Mem*), and avg. model size (# facts, *Out*). Notably, a LARS$^+$ model can be computed rather quickly, viz. in $\approx$13ms with an hypothetical input like S_A. This suggests that our approach can be used in scenarios that need fast response times. For "heavier" scenarios like S_B, the runtime increases but still stays within few seconds. Moreover, reasoning used at most 114MB of RAM; thus it may be done on limited hardware, e.g., sensors or edge devices.

Conclusion. Our work shows that combining existential rules with LARS can give rise to a versatile stream reasoning formalism with expressive features which is still decidable. A worthwhile future objective is to develop more efficient algorithms to compute the models. Our translation to existential rules is a good basis, but many optimisations are conceivable. On the theoretical side, a study of further decidability paradigms, especially related to guarded logics, is suggestive. Finally, further extensions towards nonmonotonic reasoning or other issues, like window validity (Ronca et al. 2018), are challenging for existential rules, but would be very useful for stream reasoning.

Acknowledgments

The authors would like to thank Mike Spadaru for his work on earlier versions of the prototype used in this work.

This work was partly supported by *Deutsche Forschungsgemeinschaft* (DFG) in project 389792660 (TRR 248, Center for Perspicuous Systems), by the *Bundesministerium für Bildung und Forschung* (BMBF) in project ScaDS.AI (Center for Scalable Data Analytics and Artificial Intelligence), and by the Center for Advancing Electronics Dresden (cfaed).

References

Abiteboul, S.; Hull, R.; and Vianu, V. 1994. *Foundations of Databases*. Addison Wesley.

Anicic, D.; Fodor, P.; Rudolph, S.; and Stojanovic, N. 2011. EP-SPARQL: A Unified Language for Event Processing and Stream Reasoning. In *WWW*, 635–644.

Baget, J.-F.; Leclère, M.; Mugnier, M.-L.; and Salvat, E. 2011. On rules with existential variables: Walking the decidability line. *Artificial Intelligence* 175(9–10):1620–1654.

Barbieri, D. F.; Braga, D.; Ceri, S.; Valle, E. D.; and Grossniklaus, M. 2010. C-SPARQL: a continuous query language for rdf data streams. *International Journal of Semantic Computing* 04(01):3–25.

Bazoobandi, H. R.; Beck, H.; and Urbani, J. 2017. Expressive Stream Reasoning with Laser. In *ISWC*, 87–103.

Beck, H.; Dao-Tran, M.; and Eiter, T. 2018. LARS: A Logic-based framework for Analytic Reasoning over Streams. *Artificial Intelligence* 261:16–70.

Beeri, C., and Vardi, M. Y. 1981. The Implication Problem for Data Dependencies. In *ICALP*, 73–85.

Bellomarini, L.; Sallinger, E.; and Gottlob, G. 2018. The Vadalog System: Datalog-based Reasoning for Knowledge Graphs. *PVLDB* 11(9):975–987.

Benedikt, M.; Konstantinidis, G.; Mecca, G.; Motik, B.; Papotti, P.; Santoro, D.; and Tsamoura, E. 2017. Benchmarking the Chase. In *PODS*, 37–52.

Brandt, S.; Kalaycı, E. G.; Kontchakov, R.; Ryzhikov, V.; Xiao, G.; and Zakharyaschev, M. 2017. Ontology-Based Data Access with a Horn Fragment of Metric Temporal Logic. In *AAAI*, 1070–1076.

Calì, A.; Gottlob, G.; Lukasiewicz, T.; Marnette, B.; and Pieris, A. 2010. Datalog+/-: A Family of Logical Knowledge Representation and Query Languages for New Applications. In *LICS*, 228–242.

Calì, A.; Gottlob, G.; and Pieris, A. 2010. Query Answering under Non-guarded Rules in Datalog+/-. In *RR*, 1–17.

Cuenca Grau, B.; Horrocks, I.; Krötzsch, M.; Kupke, C.; Magka, D.; Motik, B.; and Wang, Z. 2013. Acyclicity notions for existential rules and their application to query answering in ontologies. *J. Artif. Intell. Res.* 47:741–808.

Dantsin, E.; Eiter, T.; Gottlob, G.; and Voronkov, A. 2001. Complexity and expressive power of logic programming. *ACM Computing Surveys* 33(3):374–425.

Dell'Aglio, D.; Della Valle, E.; van Harmelen, F.; and Bernstein, A. 2017. Stream reasoning: A survey and outlook. *Data Science* 1(1-2):59–83.

Fagin, R.; Kolaitis, P. G.; Miller, R. J.; and Popa, L. 2005. Data exchange: semantics and query answering. *Theoretical Computer Science* 336(1):89 – 124.

Gottlob, G.; Lukasiewicz, T.; and Pieris, A. 2014. Datalog+/-: Questions and Answers. In *KR*, 682–685.

Kalaycı, E. G.; Brandt, S.; Calvanese, D.; Ryzhikov, V.; Xiao, G.; and Zakharyaschev, M. 2019. Ontology-based access to temporal data with ontop: A framework proposal. *Applied Mathematics and Computer Science* 29(1):17–30.

Kharlamov, E.; Kotidis, Y.; Mailis, T.; Neuenstadt, C.; Nikolaou, C.; Özçep, Ö. L.; Svingos, C.; Zheleznyakov, D.; Ioannidis, Y. E.; Lamparter, S.; Möller, R.; and Waaler, A. 2019. An ontology-mediated analytics-aware approach to support monitoring and diagnostics of static and streaming data. *Journal of Web Semantics* 56:30–55.

Krötzsch, M.; Marx, M.; and Rudolph, S. 2019. The Power of the Terminating Chase. In *ICDT*, 3:1–3:17.

Le-Phuoc, D.; Dao-Tran, M.; Xavier Parreira, J.; and Hauswirth, M. 2011. A Native and Adaptive Approach for Unified Processing of Linked Streams and Linked Data. In *ISWC*, 370–388.

Margara, A.; Urbani, J.; Van Harmelen, F.; and Bal, H. 2014. Streaming the web: Reasoning over dynamic data. *Journal of Web Semantics* 25:24–44.

Marnette, B. 2009. Generalized Schema-Mappings: from Termination to Tractability. In *PODS*, 13–22.

Ronca, A.; Kaminski, M.; Cuenca Grau, B.; and Horrocks, I. 2018. The Window Validity Problem in Rule-Based Stream Reasoning. In *KR*, 571–581.

Tiger, M., and Heintz, F. 2016. Stream Reasoning Using Temporal Logic and Predictive Probabilistic State Models. In *TIME*, 196–205.

Tsamoura, E.; Carral, D.; Malizia, E.; and Urbani, J. 2021. Materializing knowledge bases via trigger graphs. *PVLDB* 14(6):943–956.

Urbani, J.; Krötzsch, M.; Jacobs, C. J. H.; Dragoste, I.; and Carral, D. 2018. Efficient Model Construction for Horn Logic with VLog - System Description. In *IJCAR*, 680–688.

Urbani, J.; Krötzsch, M.; and Eiter, T. 2022. Chasing Streams with Existential Rules. *arXiv:2205.02220 [cs]*. http://arxiv.org/abs/2205.02220.

Wałega, P. A.; Kaminski, M.; and Cuenca Grau, B. 2019. Reasoning over Streaming Data in Metric Temporal Datalog. In *AAAI*, 3092–3099.

Proceedings of the 19th International Conference on Principles of Knowledge Representation and Reasoning
Special Session on KR and Machine Learning

Embed2Sym - Scalable Neuro-Symbolic Reasoning via Clustered Embeddings

Yaniv Aspis[1] , **Krysia Broda**[1] , **Jorge Lobo**[2,3] , **Alessandra Russo**[1]
[1]Imperial College London
[2]ICREA
[3]Universitat Pompeu Fabra
{yaniv.aspis17, k.broda, a.russo}@imperial.ac.uk, jorge.lobo@upf.edu

Abstract

Neuro-symbolic reasoning approaches proposed in recent years combine a neural perception component with a symbolic reasoning component to solve a downstream task. By doing so, these approaches can provide neural networks with symbolic reasoning capabilities, improve their interpretability and enable generalization beyond the training task. However, this often comes at the cost of poor training time, with potential scalability issues. In this paper, we propose a scalable neuro-symbolic approach, called Embed2Sym. We complement a two-stage (perception and reasoning) neural network architecture designed to solve a downstream task end-to-end with a symbolic optimisation method for extracting learned latent concepts. Specifically, the trained perception network generates clusters in embedding space that are identified and labelled using symbolic knowledge and a symbolic solver. With the latent concepts identified, a neuro-symbolic model is constructed by combining the perception network with the symbolic knowledge of the downstream task, resulting in a model that is interpretable and transferable. Our evaluation shows that Embed2Sym outperforms state-of-the-art neuro-symbolic systems on benchmark tasks in terms of training time by several orders of magnitude while providing similar if not better accuracy.

1 Introduction

Research into methods of combining neural and symbolic approaches to AI has accelerated in recent years (Sarker et al. 2021). Neural networks have achieved high success over a large range of tasks involving perception, such as object recognition (Zhao et al. 2019) or acoustic event detection (Xia et al. 2019). However, tasks involving reasoning are generally considered challenging for a neural network. While an architecture can be devised to solve specific tasks (Palm, Paquet, and Winther 2018; Lample and Charton 2020), a trained network lacks the true generalization capabilities that a reasoning system should possess, while also not being interpretable. Neuro-symbolic methods are seen as a method of enhancing a neural network by providing it with some of the reasoning capabilities and interpretability that a symbolic system traditionally has.

Broadly speaking, many systems are built around differentiable neural architectures that learn to approximate symbolic computation from data (Minervini et al. 2018; Riegel et al. 2020). A different approach that has recently gained attention involves extending the capabilities of symbolic solvers by (1) allowing the system to depend on the output of a neural component, and (2) using inconsistent results arising from the neural output, reasoning process and data to guide the training of the network. These systems see neuro-symbolic reasoning on raw data as a combination of two tasks: a perception task, handled by a neural component, and a reasoning downstream task, handled by the symbolic solver. In this paper we refer to these systems as "neuro-symbolic reasoning systems". Prominent examples include DeepProbLog (Manhaeve et al. 2021) and NeurASP (Yang, Ishay, and Lee 2020).

In neuro-symbolic reasoning, the output of the neural component is associated with a symbolic concept (typically a predicate of a logic program). We refer to these concepts as "latent" as one does not typically provide labels for them. In fact, the ability of neuro-symbolic reasoning systems to train a neural network by only using the labels of the downstream task ("target labels") is one of their great advantages. Additional advantages include increased interpretability, and the ability to generalize to downstream tasks other than the one the system was trained on (by keeping the perception component fixed and applying different rules). However, experiments have shown that the training time for these systems can be significantly long even when the perception task is simple (Tsamoura, Hospedales, and Michael 2021; Yang, Ishay, and Lee 2020). The difficulty in training is inherent in current approaches: in order to train, the symbolic component must "work backwards" from a given target label to a set of possible latent labels, which can be exponential in size. This fact has so far hindered most neuro-symbolic reasoning systems from being applied to tasks involving a larger number of inputs and more complex perception tasks are usually not considered, with a few exceptions, e.g. (Huang et al. 2021).

In contrast, approaches such as Concept Bottleneck models (Koh et al. 2020) have demonstrated that performing the reasoning step with a second neural network can achieve competitive accuracy when latent concepts are effectively integrated into the neural architecture, without loss of scalability. But they require latent bottleneck concepts to be labelled to preserve interpretability and generalization. They are also not typically applied in a neuro-symbolic setting where multiple raw inputs must be considered together.

In this paper, we introduce Embed2Sym, a novel approach to neuro-symbolic reasoning that is scalable, able to produce neuro-symbolic models that are interpretable and generalize beyond the training task, and does not require latent concepts to be labelled. Embed2Sym works in three steps. First, a neural network composed of a perception component and a reasoning component is trained on the downstream task end-to-end. The architecture for this network has previously been shown to be effective in solving diagrammatic reasoning tasks (Wang, Jamnik, and Liò 2018). Here we consider its use within the context of a general neuro-symbolic approach. By training the perception component in this manner, rather than through evaluation of a logical formula, we avoid the combinatorial difficulty that other neuro-symbolic reasoning systems confront. Second, we search for latent concepts that have been learned by the perception component by analysing the clustered structure of datapoints in embedding space. Third, we identify the discovered latent concepts and assign them their symbolic meaning by means of an optimisation task solved using a symbolic system (Clingo) and background knowledge of the task. In this way, we are able to lift a purely neural model into a neuro-symbolic one that is interpretable and can generalize to tasks the neural network alone could not perform.

We evaluate Embed2Sym on several tasks previously introduced to benchmark neuro-symbolic systems. Results confirm Embed2Sym achieves similar or better accuracy to competing systems while training faster by orders of magnitude. The scalability of Embed2Sym allows it to train on tasks involving at least dozens of raw inputs, such as adding two 15-digit numbers given as MNIST images, which other systems find infeasible. We also confirm Embed2Sym can scale to tasks involving more challenging perception domains such as the CIFAR-10 dataset.

The paper is structured as follows: Section 2 discusses related work. Section 3 covers the various aspects of the Embed2Sym algorithm for neuro-symbolic training and inference. Section 4 presents the results of an evaluation of the system confirming its performance and scalability. Section 5 discusses the results and Section 6 concludes the paper.

2 Related Work

Research on combining neural networks and symbolic reasoning has a long history, and approaches vary greatly, see survey in (Besold et al. 2017). For example, Neural Theorem Prover (Minervini et al. 2018) uses soft unification to learn symbol embeddings to correctly satisfy queries. Logic Tensor Networks (Badreddine et al. 2022) represent First-Order Logic constructs as vectors and differentiable functions, and uses fuzzy logical operations. Logical Neural Networks (Riegel et al. 2020) implement conjunction and disjunction using a perceptron whose weights and bias are learned with a tailored activation function designed to preserve two-valued semantics as much as possible.

We consider our work to be most closely related to neuro-symbolic reasoning systems that extend a symbolic solver with neural capabilities. DeepProbLog (Manhaeve et al. 2021) is an extension of the ProbLog system (De Raedt, Kimmig, and Toivonen 2007). A new construct in the form of a neural Annotated Disjunction allows for the output of a network to be interpreted as the probabilities of atoms. A formula computing the probability of a query is compiled and transformed into an arithmetic circuit which can be evaluated and used to produce gradient information for the network. DeepStochLog (Winters et al. 2021) is an analogous framework that uses Stochastic Definite Clause Grammars rather than probabilistic logic programs.

NeurASP (Yang, Ishay, and Lee 2020) extends Answer Set Programming with neural predicates. The predicate is linked to a neural network and translated by NeurASP into a choice rule representing the various output of the network. The answer sets of the program are assigned probabilities based on the network predictions, and the network is then trained to optimise a semantic loss function (Xu et al. 2018).

Abductive Learning (Dai et al. 2019) considers the output of a neural network in the absence of latent labels as incomplete knowledge and therefore uses abductive reasoning to generate these labels. Neurolog (Tsamoura, Hospedales, and Michael 2021) generalizes this concept by producing all abductive solutions for a given goal, and then applying a semantic loss. More recently, abductive learning has been extended into ABL-sim that uses vector embedding of latent concepts to guide the training of the neural network (Huang et al. 2021), which is trained using an additional loss term.

Similarly to the neuro-symbolic reasoning systems mentioned above, we divide a task into perception and reasoning sub-tasks. We also enhance a symbolic paradigm, in our case Answer Set Programming, by providing it with a means to reason over unstructured data. Unlike these approaches, we do not use the symbolic component to guide the training of the network. Instead, we use it to extract and label the latent concepts discovered by the network through end-to-end training. Like ABL-Sim, we consider the representation of latent concepts in embedding space. However, in our approach, these embeddings are not used as tools for guiding the training of the perception component, and hence we do not require any additional loss terms. Instead, these embeddings arise naturally when training the neural network, and are used to extract symbolic concepts out of the trained network for downstream symbolic computations.

3 Method

We wish to learn functions of the form $f = h \circ g : \mathcal{X} \rightarrow \mathcal{Z} \rightarrow \mathcal{Y}$, where f can be decomposed into a perception function $g : \mathcal{X} \rightarrow \mathcal{Z}$ and a reasoning function $h : \mathcal{Z} \rightarrow \mathcal{Y}$. $\mathcal{X}$ is the space of inputs, $\mathcal{Y}$ the space of target labels and $\mathcal{Z}$ a space of latent concept values relevant for the task.

A latent concept is a tuple $C = (n_C, S_C)$ where n_C is the name of the latent concept and S_C is an associated set of values, which we assume to be finite. The task input X to the function f itself is composed of multiple inputs $X = x_1 \times x_2 \times ... \times x_m$ where each x_i is either a raw input (e.g. image, text) or a symbolic input. While there could be many latent concepts, we assume w.l.o.g. that each x_i is associated with a single one. To deal with multiple latent concepts per input, we can construct a composite latent concept. For example, if x_i should be associated with

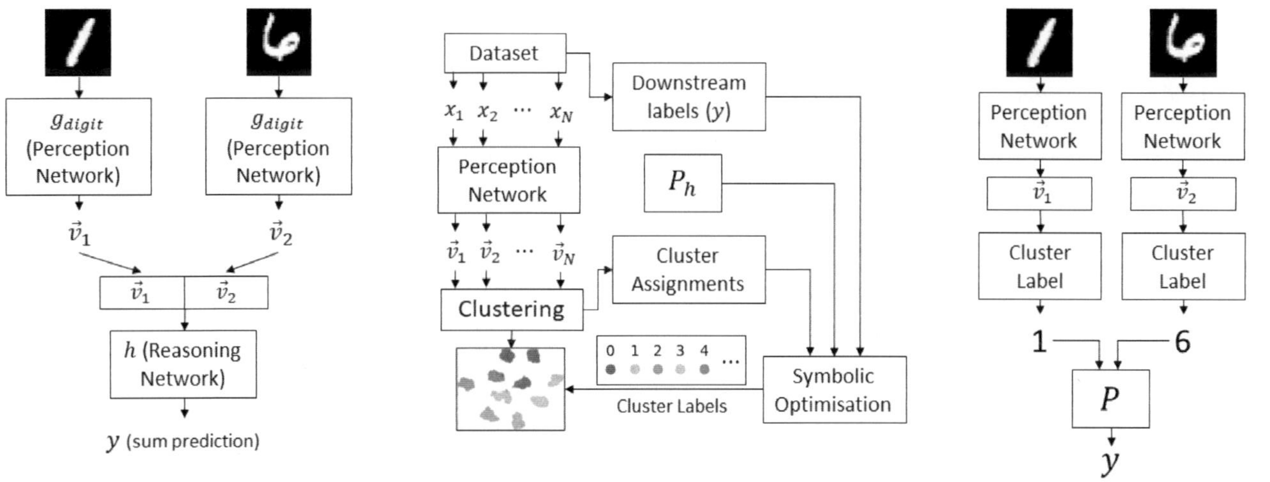

Figure 1: Embed2Sym architecture. Left: An example of a fully neural architecture for the MNIST Addition task. Middle: After training the fully neural network, clustering is applied on embedding vectors computed by the perception network. Symbolic optimisation is used to label the clusters together with the rules P_h. Right: An example inference on MNIST digits. The cluster labels are used as symbolic inputs to the program P (which may differ from P_h).

both $C_1 = (n_{C_1}, S_{C_1})$ and $C_2 = (n_{C_2}, S_{C_2})$ then we construct $C_{1,2} = (n_{C_{1,2}}, S_{C_1} \times S_{C_2})$. $\mathcal{Y}$ is a set of target labels that represent the output of the full neuro-symbolic reasoning task. $\mathcal{C}$ is the set of latent concepts of the task.

To train our model, we are given a dataset of samples $\mathcal{D} = \{X, y\} \subset \mathcal{X} \times \mathcal{Y}$. Crucially $\mathcal{D}$ does not contain any information about the correct latent labels in $\mathcal{Z}$. To perform well at the task, the model would have to learn how to correctly map a raw input x_i to its latent concept value, which is the responsibility of the g function. g in general is in fact several functions, one for each latent concept. We denote the perception function associated with latent concept C as g_C. Each g_C is effectively a classifier for the latent concept C trained via a weakly supervised learning task using $\mathcal{D}$.

Example 1. *Consider the MNIST Addition task (Manhaeve et al. 2021). In this task, we are given two images of MNIST digits (LeCun, Cortes, and Burges 2010) and must output their sum. The task input X is a composition of the two 28x28 pixel images x_1 and x_2. Each image is associated with the latent concept ("digit", $\{0, 1, ..., 9\}$). The target labels are the 19 possible sums $\mathcal{Y} = \{0, 1, ..., 18\}$. Samples in $\mathcal{D}$ are of the form (, , 7). g is just a single function g_{digit} that maps an MNIST image to its corresponding digit. g_{digit} must be trained when the only given label is the sum.*

As is common in neuro-symbolic reasoning settings, we assume the reasoning component h can be represented by a given set of rules P_h that is known in advance and can be considered background knowledge for the task. It may have been provided by a human, online knowledge bases such as WordNet (Fellbaum 1998) and ConceptNet (Speer, Chin, and Havasi 2017), or an inductive rule learning system (Law, Russo, and Broda 2020). In settings where such knowledge is not known in advance, the rules would have to be learned in conjunction with the perception module g. We leave such cases for future work and for now assume we have been given this knowledge.

3.1 Fully Neural Model

Since h can be implemented correctly using the known rules P_h, training the perception component g remains the primary goal. However, since the rules are not differentiable, this can present some challenges. Some authors have taken the approach of replacing hard logical rules with probabilistic or continuous approximations (Manhaeve et al. 2021; Xu et al. 2018). We choose a different path. We begin by training a fully neural model. In this model, h is modeled as a neural network that is trained from the data as an approximate reasoner. Although this may look at first to be counter-intuitive, as we are interested in a neuro-symbolic model, this neural model is useful in three ways. First, it allows us to train the perception function g in a setting where neural networks excel: continuous space with dense representations. Second, we will see that even though g is not trained using domain knowledge, it still discovers structure in the data that is relevant to the domain and can be used to lift our differentiable model into a neuro-symbolic one. Third, it allows us to scale very well with the number of raw inputs the model receives.

For each latent concept C, we have a function $g_C : \mathcal{X}_C \rightarrow \mathbb{R}^k$ as a neural network. $\mathcal{X}_C$ is the space of raw inputs that can be mapped to values of C. In the MNIST Addition task, this will be 28x28 grayscale images. g_C maps these inputs to a vector space of *embeddings* of size k. k is a hyperparameter that can be set to different values for each C. The embeddings should form a dense representation of the latent concept values and a good g_C function would map raw inputs having the same concept values close together. The function h is also a neural network that operates on the set of embedding vectors produced from each input, and outputs the predicted label $y \in \mathcal{Y}$.

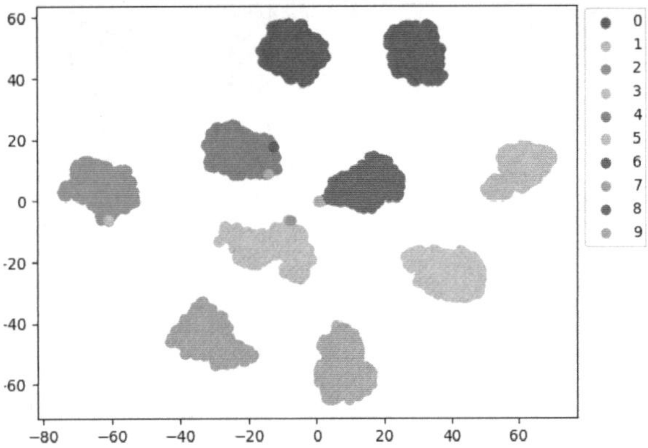

Figure 2: t-SNE visualization of g_{digit} embedding space post-training, clearly showing clusters representing 10 different digits.

More formally, for each input x_i in X let $C(i)$ be its associated latent concept. The fully neural model is composed as follows:

$$\forall i = 1...m \quad \vec{v}_i = g_{C(i)}(x_i) \qquad (1)$$

$$y = h(\vec{v}_1, \vec{v}_2, ..., \vec{v}_m) \qquad (2)$$

Figure 1 (left) illustrates this architecture for the MNIST Addition example when $m = 2$. g_{digit} in this case could be a CNN such as a LeNet, but modified to output an embedding vector ($\vec{v}_1/\vec{v}_2$) instead of a probability simplex vector, as commonly done by using a softmax operation. This change is important, as softmax outputs of the perception module do not make much sense in a purely neural setting. In addition, its use of exponents tends to cause one argument to dominate the others, sending a sparser signal to the reasoning component. For this task, h can simply be an MLP with an output layer of size 19, corresponding to the 19 possible sums, activated using softmax. The outputs of g_{digit} are concatenated before being fed into the h component.

3.2 Identifying Latent Concepts

The fully neural model described above can be trained to solve the task using $\mathcal{D}$. As the various g_C functions are trained, they tend to cluster datapoints corresponding to the same latent value together. So if $C = (n_C, \{v_1, v_2, v_3\})$, g_C will converge to a function that maps datapoints to three distinct clusters in embedding space. An example of this is shown in Figure 2. The plot depicts a t-SNE visualization of the embedding space of MNIST images after training the fully neural model depicted in Figure 1 (left) on the MNIST Addition task. Even though this model was not given any knowledge about relevant latent concepts for the task, 10 clear clusters emerged, each associated with a specific digit.

This observation is key to lifting the fully neural model into a neuro-symbolic one. To achieve neuro-symbolic reasoning, we need to transform each g_C function into a classifier for C. We can exploit the clustering behaviour to do so. After training g_C, we identify the various clusters in embedding space. Then, we label each cluster with the best latent concept value. The process for cluster discovery and labelling is depicted in Figure 1 (middle). When we wish to predict the latent concept value associated with a raw input x_i, we compute $g_C(x_i)$, check which cluster it belongs to and predict the label of that cluster.

```
latent_concept(n_c, s_i, i).

cluster_assignment(sample_id, n_c, x_i, j).

{cluster_mapping(n_c, X, Y) : Y=0..|S_C|} = 1 :-
    X=0..|S_C|.
:- cluster_mapping(n_c, X, Z),
    cluster_mapping(n_c, Y, Z), X != Y.

holds(Id, C, RawInput, Value) :-
    cluster_assignment(Id, C, RawInput, ClusterIdx),
    cluster_mapping(C, ClusterIdx, ValueIdx).
    latent_concept(C, Value, ValueIdx).

% Task-specific rules defining the label
% in terms of the ''holds'' predicate

:~ holds(sample_id, target, y). [-1, 0]
```

Listing 1: ASP encoding for the cluster labelling task.

Cluster Discovery To perform the clustering in embedding space, we employ the K-Means Clustering algorithm. K-Means has the advantages of being simple and fast, although it assumes clusters are isotropic in Euclidean distance. However, we believe this is sufficient to demonstrate our approach and have observed good results over the range of experiments we performed. Future work may be directed at investigating other clustering algorithms, such as DBScan (Ester et al. 1996) or Deep Clustering methods (Caron et al. 2018; Moradi Fard, Thonet, and Gaussier 2020).

Cluster Labelling So far we have identified the clusters in g_C's embedding space, but we have yet to discover which symbolic latent value of C is associated with each cluster. In other words, the clusters are unlabelled. For the labelling, we take advantage of the fact that the reasoning component h can be given an alternative representation using P_h.

An assignment of clusters to labels of C is simply a one-to-one mapping. We can evaluate such an assignment using the dataset $\mathcal{D}$. For each $(X, y) \in \mathcal{D}$, apply g to X to receive a sequence of embeddings. Each embedding is mapped to a cluster by K-Means, and then a latent concept value by the chosen assignment. We can then apply h in its symbolic rule form (P_h) to compute a prediction y'. The amount of datapoints misclassified is a measure of the assignment score. The smaller this value is, the better the assignment.

We can therefore define the task of labelling clusters as an optimisation problem, which we encode using an Answer Set Program. The syntax of Answer Set Programs supports an extensive range of programs allowing the expression of a large variety of neuro-symbolic problems. To solve the task, we use Clingo 5.5.1 (Gebser et al. 2017).

A summary of the ASP encoding of the optimisation task appears in Listing 1. For each latent concept $C = (n_C, \{s_0, s_2, ..., s_l\})$ we assign its various latent values indices. These are encoded as facts as can be seen in line 1. Next, we encode the various assignments of samples to clusters as provided by K-Means. For a sample with ID "sample_id", raw input x_i and its associated latent concept C, and the assigned cluster index j, we add a fact as in line 3.

For each latent concept C, we add a choice rule requiring each cluster to be mapped to a latent concept value (lines 5-6). We add an additional restriction that two clusters cannot be mapped to the same value (lines 7-9). For example, for MNIST Addition, we would have the following lines:

```
{cluster_mapping(digit, X, Y) : Y=0..9} = 1 :- X=0..9.
:- cluster_mapping(digit, X, Z),
     cluster_mapping(digit, Y, Z), X != Y.
```

These rules require that each cluster is mapped to exactly one of the digits 0-9 in an answer set. The next rule, seen in lines 10-13, defines the "holds" predicate that states that a raw input of a sample has been assigned a particular latent concept value in the answer set. A raw input x_i associated with latent concept C has been assigned a latent concept value $Value$ if the following three conditions hold. First, it has been assigned by K-Means to a cluster with index $ClusterIdx$ (indicated by the "cluster_assignment" predicate). Second, $ClusterIdx$ has been mapped to a latent concept value with index $ValueIdx$ (indicated by the "cluster_mapping" predicate). Third, the latent concept value with index $ValueIdx$ has value $Value$ (indicated by the "latent_concept" predicate).

With these rules in place, we can add the background knowledge related to the task (line 15). These are the rules that are given by P_h. The rules should be specified in terms of the "holds" predicate to establish a connection to the cluster assignment for each sample. For example, adding two MNIST digits together, we can add the following rule:

```
holds(Id, sum, Z) :- holds(Id, digit, x1, X),
        holds(Id, digit, x2, Y), Z = X+Y.
```

The "holds" atoms in the body will become true if their respective raw inputs have been mapped to a cluster that has been labelled by the variable X (for the first raw input x_1) or Y (for the second raw input x_2). The task's target output, in this case the sum, will also be indicated by a "holds" predicate, defined by the rule. The sample "Id" will have a target output "sum" whose value Z equals $X + Y$, as required.

Once the rules of h have been added, the optimisation process can produce predictions for every sample, once a cluster mapping has been chosen. To compute a score for each mapping, for each sample (X, y) with ID "sample_id", we add the weak constraint appearing in line 18, indicating its prediction for output "target" should be y. Each constraint has a penalty of -1, indicating that its body should be true. An optimal answer set has a minimal score, indicating the best coverage over the dataset. Using weak constraints in this way also allows us to deal with the fact that our data is noisy - the cluster assignments are not perfect. Once the task is solved, we extract the optimal cluster mapping out of the answer set, thus successfully labelling the clusters.

Algorithm 1 Embed2Sym Training

Input: $\mathcal{D}, \mathcal{C}, P_h$
Output: g, K, π

Train fully neural model $f = h \circ g$ on $\mathcal{D}$
Select $\mathcal{D}_2 \subseteq \mathcal{D}$
$K \leftarrow \emptyset$
for $c \in \mathcal{C}$ **do**
  $V \leftarrow \emptyset$
  for $(X, y) \in \mathcal{D}_2$ **do**
    for $x_i \in X$ s.t. c latent concept of x_i **do**
      Add $g_c(x_i)$ to V
    end for
  end for
  Train K_C on V using K-Means Clustering.
  Add K_C to K
end for
Encode task O as in listing 1 using $\mathcal{D}_2, \mathcal{C}, K, P_H$
Solve O and select optimal answer set A
$\pi \leftarrow \emptyset$
for $c \in \mathcal{C}$ **do**
  $\pi_c \leftarrow \emptyset$
  for $cluster\_mapping(n_C, i, j) \in A$ **do**
    Assign $\pi_c(i) = j$
  end for
  Add π_c to π
end for
return g, K, π

3.3 Neuro-Symbolic Model

With the various components laid out, we can now present the full Embed2Sym training and inference algorithms. These are listed in Algorithm 1 and 2, respectively. An example inference process is also depicted in Figure 1 (right). In the algorithms we use some notations that we define here.

The perception component, g, is a cartesian product of perception networks applied to each raw input individually. If C_i is the latent concept corresponding to input x_i, then:

$$g(X) = g(x_1 \times x_2 \times \cdots \times x_m) = \\ = g_{C_1}(x_1) \times g_{C_2}(x_2) \times \cdots \times g_{C_m}(x_m) = \\ = \vec{v}_1 \times \vec{v}_2 \times \cdots \times \vec{v}_m = \vec{v} \tag{3}$$

K_C is a clustering function associated with latent concept C. It maps vectors from the embedding space associated with C to their cluster index. Formally, $K_C : \mathbb{R}^{k_C} \rightarrow \{1, ..., |S_C|\}$ where k_C is the dimensionality of the embeddings space $C = (n_C, S_C)$. Generally, K_C will be applied to the embeddings of several raw inputs. K denotes the cartesian product of the K_C's analogously to g above. We have:

$$K(\vec{v}) = K_{C_1}(\vec{v}_1) \times K_{C_2}(\vec{v}_2) \times \cdots \times K_{C_m}(\vec{v}_m) = \\ = (i_1, i_2, ..., i_m) = I \tag{4}$$

π_C is the mapping of cluster indices to value indices for the latent concept C. π_C is always a permutation of $\{1, ..., |S_C|\}$. π is defined analogously to g and K:

$$\pi(I) = \pi_{C_1}(i_1) \times \pi_{C_2}(i_2) \times \cdots \times \pi_{C_m}(i_m) = \\ = (j_1, j_2, ..., j_m) = J \tag{5}$$

Algorithm 2 Embed2Sym Inference

Input: X, g, K, π, P, $target$
Output: y

$\vec{v} \leftarrow g(X)$
$I \leftarrow K(\vec{v})$
$J \leftarrow \pi(I)$
$Facts \leftarrow \emptyset$
for $j \in J$ **do**
  Let s be the latent concept value of C corresponding to j
  Let x_i be the raw input name corresponding to j
  Add $holds(0, n_C, x_i, s)$ to $Facts$
end for
Let A be an answer set of $P \cup Facts$
return y s.t. $holds(0, target, y) \in A$

In line 2 of Algorithm 1 we make a selection of a subset of the dataset $\mathcal{D}$. This is motivated by the fact that both K-Means clustering and cluster labelling using Clingo are quite data efficient. These steps can therefore be sped up by selecting a much smaller subset of $\mathcal{D}$ than was required for training the perception module. Selection would typically be done by uniformly sampling from $\mathcal{D}$ without replacement.

An important aspect of Embed2Sym is that P_h of Algorithm 1 and P of Algorithm 2 need not be the same. This allows the rules of the reasoning component to be changed, as long as they are still concerned with the same latent concepts. For example, if the model was trained on the addition of MNIST images, it can perform multiplication as well at inference time. Hence, despite starting with a non-generalizing neural model, we achieved the same level of generalization other neuro-symbolic systems have, and the same level of interpretability.

4 Experiments

In this section, we present results following an evaluation of our Embed2Sym implementation in benchmark tasks involving both perception and reasoning. In designing these experiments, we aimed to answer the following questions:

1. Is Embed2Sym capable of solving tasks involving both perception and reasoning?
2. Is Embed2Sym able to scale to more challenging tasks involving a larger number of raw inputs?
3. Can Embed2Sym cope with challenging perception tasks?
4. How does Embed2Sym compare to other neuro-symbolic systems in terms of accuracy and training time?

To answer questions 1 & 2, we tested Embed2Sym on three benchmark tasks introduced before to evaluate neuro-symbolic systems, namely MNIST Addition, Member (Tsamoura, Hospedales, and Michael 2021) and Forth Sort (Bošnjak et al. 2017). We chose these tasks in particular as a means of testing the scalability of Embed2Sym when confronted with a large number of raw inputs, and increasing this number is straightforward for both. To answer question 3, we took the same approach previously introduced to benchmark the ABL-Sim algorithm (Huang et al. 2021) and created a CIFAR-10 Addition task as a more challenging version of the MNIST Addition task. To answer question 4, we also compare our models to two state-of-the-art neuro-symbolic systems, DeepProbLog and NeurASP, as they are both well known and have code available that allows for easy adaptation to the tasks we chose. When reporting results, we use the shorthand notations "E2S - FN", "E2S - NS", "DPLog" to refer to the fully neural, neuro-symbolic models and DeepProbLog, respectively. Our implementation of Embed2Sym was developed in Python3.8 using the TensorFlow framework, and can be found at the following link: https://github.com/YanivAspis/Embed2Sym.

Experiments were performed on a system running Ubuntu 18.04.6 with the following specifications: Intel i7-6700 CPU @ 3.40 GHz, 8 GB RAM and a single GeForce GTX 970 GPU. Hyperparameters for the experiments were determined by performance on a separate validation set separate from the test set. The K-Means and logical optimisation steps were performed using a subset of the dataset of 100 samples ($\mathcal{D}_{\in}$ of algorithm 1). We ran each experiment 5 times and report the average test accuracy and training time to account for the effects of random initialisation of the weights. If a system takes longer than 4 hours to train for any run, we stop training and declare a timeout.

N	1	2	3	4	15
E2S - FN	97.40	82.10	22.50	00.73	00.00
E2S - NS	97.73	94.31	93.90	91.61	66.40
DPLog	96.02	T/O	T/O	T/O	T/O
NeurASP	96.07	95.00	T/O	T/O	T/O

Table 1: Average test sum accuracy (%) on the MNIST Addition task for varying number of digits. T/O stands for "timeout".

4.1 MNIST Addition

We have used the MNIST Addition task as a running example throughout the paper to illustrate our approach. Here we consider the generalized task that allows for the addition of numbers with multiple digits. Specifically, each summand has N digits and so the number of raw inputs the model receives is $2N$. For the fully neural model, we can follow the architecture depicted in Figure 1 for small values of N. However, as N grows, the number of target labels (possible sums) grows exponentially, resulting in an output layer of exponential size. To resolve this, the reasoning component outputs each digit of the sum separately, so the number of output neurons grows linearly. Otherwise, the architecture is unchanged, where the g_{digit} component is applied to each of the $2N$ MNIST images, and their embeddings are concatenated before the reasoning component is applied. We generated for every N a training set of 30,000 samples, 500 validation samples and 5000 test samples. Results are summarised in Tables 1, 2 and 3. The results reported in each column are for training and testing on the number of digits appearing at the top.

Table 1 shows that Embed2Sym is able to produce models that solve this task with close or better accuracy than that

N	1	2	3	4	15
E2S - NS	98.86	98.54	98.96	98.92	98.64
DPLog	98.04	T/O	T/O	T/O	T/O
NeurASP	98.02	98.72	T/O	T/O	T/O

Table 2: Average test digit accuracy (%) on the MNIST Addition task for varying number of digits. T/O stands for "timeout".

N	1	2	3	4	15
E2S - FN	38.2	65.0	93.7	115.7	412.3
E2S - NS	40.9	69.0	99.6	122.6	434.1
DPLog	1033.4	T/O	T/O	T/O	T/O
NeurASP	919.7	3414.6	T/O	T/O	T/O

Table 3: Average training time (sec) on the MNIST Addition task for varying number of digits. Training time of "E2S - FN" includes the training time of "E2S - NS". T/O stands for "timeout". Results reported here for DeepProbLog are after only 1 epoch of training.

of competing systems. For $N = 1$ the fully neural model performs quite well, despite not having the advantage of being given any knowledge on the task. Note that in order to get the answer correct, the fully neural model must get each digit of the sum correct. Table 2 confirms that even though the fully neural scores poorly on larger values of N, digit accuracy remains high, meaning the perception network is still well trained. As N grows, the reasoning task becomes very difficult, as statistically speaking the network is likely to get at least one digit in the sum wrong. Therefore the fully neural model by itself is incapable of solving the task for large N in a satisfying manner.

However, all of this is solved once the model is lifted into a neuro-symbolic form. Despite not succeeding in the downstream task, clusters still form in the perception network's embedding space, and this can be exploited by Embed2Sym to create a neuro-symbolic model fully capable of adding MNIST numbers of large lengths. Note that for $N = 15$, a downstream average task accuracy of 66.40% is due to the statistical independence of predicting each individual input digit. An average accuracy of 98.64% in predicting each of 30 individual inputs correctly corresponds to a theoretical overall accuracy of 66.31% in predicting them all at once. Hence a result of 66.40% is in fact as high as one would expect for such a length.

The results suggest two important conclusions. First, even though the reasoning component did not achieve good accuracy, Embed2Sym is still able to extract the latent concepts from the perception component's embedding space. In this sense, the neuro-symbolic model can be used to improve upon the fully neural one in tasks where the reasoning steps may be more complex, by exploiting background knowledge. Second, this improvement can be achieved using only a limited portion of the dataset.

While other neuro-symbolic systems also provide a neural network with generalization capabilities, we see the advantage of Embed2Sym in its scalability in terms of training time. For small N, training is still feasible for NeurASP and DeepProbLog. NeurASP trains faster than DeepProbLog as it relies on the fast Clingo engine, being able to train on 2 digit addition within the time limit. However, as we move to 3 digits or more, training becomes infeasible to both NeurASP and DeepProbLog, while Embed2Sym can train up to $N = 15$ within minutes, and theoretically could go higher. Analysing the results deeper, we see that Embed2Sym spends most of its training time at the fully neural stage, with the process of lifting to a neuro-symbolic one only taking a few more seconds. In fact, our analysis shows that those few seconds are mostly spent computing the embeddings using the perception component (lines 6-10 of Algorithm 1), while K-Means clustering and Clingo each take less than a second on their part. This suggests training time can be further reduced by decreasing the number of epochs spent training the fully neural model, although at the possible cost of reduced accuracy.

	Task (%)	Image (%)	Training Time
E2S - FN	84.68	—	5883.6
E2S - NS	84.45	91.74	5908.6
DPLog	55.29	73.75	(T/O) 14400.0
NeurASP	6.52	12.75	(T/O) 14400.0

Table 4: Results for the CIFAR-10 Single Digit Addition experiment. Task % = Test accuracy in predicting the sum correctly. Image % = Test accuracy in predicting the digit (object) correctly. The fully neural model produces embeddings for the latent concepts and therefore cannot be assessed on Image Accuracy. Training time is in seconds.

4.2 CIFAR-10 Addition

CIFAR-10 (Krizhevsky and Hinton 2009) is a dataset of images depicting 10 classes of objects including animals and vehicles. In this task we consider each class to be a digit instead. We created a dataset for CIFAR-10 Addition where the MNIST images have been replaced with images from CIFAR-10 and the sum label is computed based on the digit each image label has been mapped to. Hence, the task involves the same level of reasoning as MNIST Addition but with a far more complex perception task. For the perception component, we use a ResNet56 architecture (He et al. 2016). If a system does not converge within 4 hours, we declare a timeout and report the accuracy achieved at that point.

Results are summarised in Table 4. The experiment confirms Embed2Sym is capable of learning even in this more difficult setting, completing training in less than 2 hours. DeepProbLog did not achieve satisfying accuracy within the time limit, although results could be higher if more time is given. NeurASP was unable to learn as it could only train for 1 epoch. We suspect that the limitation to a batch size of 1 is also affecting the training process negatively.

4.3 Member

In the Member task (Tsamoura, Hospedales, and Michael 2021), we are given a set of MNIST images, and a digit in symbolic form. We must determine if the digit appears in

N	3	4	5	20
E2S - FN	98.67	98.22	98.57	99.49
E2S - NS	96.82	96.51	97.53	93.46
DPLog	97.71	97.23	88.52	86.75
NeurASP	97.41	T/O	T/O	T/O

Table 5: Average test membership accuracy (%) on the Member task for a varying size of the set. T/O stands for "timeout".

N	3	4	5	20
E2S - NS	94.52	94.23	94.33	90.54
DPLog	96.94	95.94	78.85	79.46
NeurASP	95.36	T/O	T/O	T/O

Table 6: Average test digit accuracy (%) on the Member task for varying number of digits. T/O stands for "timeout".

one of the images in the set (In other words, if it is a member of the set). For sets of N elements, the task has the following specification:

- **Latent Concept:** ("$digit$", $\{0, 1, ..., 9\}$)
- **Raw inputs:** x_1, x_2, ..., x_N, each a 28x28 image.
- **Symbolic input:** t, one of the values '0' to '9'.
- **Target labels:** "True" and "False" (membership).

From a time complexity point of view, this task is interesting as the number of ways one can interpret the set of raw inputs increases exponentially with N. However, the label gives minimal information: If it is true, we know one of the images is labelled t, but we do not know which. If it is false, all images must not be labelled t, but we have no further information about their label. Therefore the label does not eliminate the exponential number of sets that can be interpreted. We generated for every N 10,000 training samples, 1000 validation samples and 2000 test samples.

For the fully neural model, we keep the perception component unchanged. The symbolic input t is fed directly into the reasoning component, using one-hot encoding to represent the 10 possible values of t. This one-hot vector is transformed using fully connected layers to an embedding vector, which is joined to the other embedding vectors being fed into the h component. For h, we use an attention-like mechanism where the embedding of t is compared to the embedding of each x_i, and the results are then passed through multiple layers before the true/false prediction is made. For all N, we train the fully neural model for 30 epochs.

Results of this experiment are listed in Tables 5, 6 and 7. In terms of accuracy, we see that Embed2Sym again achieves comparable or better accuracy to competing systems. In this case, the fully neural model is slightly better than the neuro-symbolic one, especially for $N = 20$. This is most likely due to its more relaxed representation. The fully neural model can retrieve the correct answer to the question of membership, without having to commit to the exact identities of the images. For example, if it is asked if the digit 4 is in the set, it can answer "yes" as long as it believes

N	3	4	5	20
E2S - FN	33.2	40.0	51.6	169.2
E2S - NS	35.6	42.6	54.9	177.2
DPLog	190.4	239.8	304.2	998.9
NeurASP	2044.4	T/O	T/O	T/O

Table 7: Average training time (sec) on the Member task for varying number of digits. Training time of "E2S - FN" includes the training time of "E2S - NS". T/O stands for "timeout".

there are several images that could be a 4. It need not decide between them. In contrast, the neuro-symbolic model must assign a digit to each image. While this does mean that the switch from the neural model to the neuro-symbolic one comes with some cost of accuracy, there is a gain in the form of sound reasoning and interpretability. The ability to correctly predict membership without correctly predicting all set members also explains why all systems demonstrate lower digit accuracy than one would expect based on their accuracy on the downstream task.

Once again, Embed2Sym is much faster to train than competing systems. NeurASP is unable to scale beyond small values, timing out already at $N = 4$. This is due to the time spent by NeurASP computing all answer sets that satisfy a label, as this number grows exponentially with N. DeepProbLog, on the other hand, relies only on the various proof paths to its query, which grows linearly with N. This allows DeepProbLog to scale well on the Member task, while other tasks such as MNIST Addition remain infeasible due to the exponential number of proofs. This is in contrast to the MNIST Addition task, where NeurASP performed better, showing that the scalability on tasks can vary significantly between systems. However, Embed2Sym is able of scaling well on both tasks, and is about 5-6 times faster than DeepProbLog. We also noticed that DeepProbLog had more difficulty training for higher values of N, at times failing to converge, which explains the lower average accuracy.

4.4 Forth Sort

The experiments so far have all been concerned with classification of images to latent labels. However Embed2Sym can be applied in a broader range of settings. To demonstrate this, we performed the Forth Sort experiment (Bošnjak et al. 2017) that is concerned with the induction of an operation, namely the decision to swap two elements in a list during sorting. The input to this task is a list of symbolic digits. Note the assumption that we do not know how to compare two digits, and therefore cannot use this as background knowledge. Instead, a "perception" network is employed to learn if two digits should be swapped or not. The latent concept "swap" therefore has two values: true and false. The perception network receives every pair of digits in the list and outputs an embedding. The reasoning network takes these embeddings and outputs an approximate permutation matrix to apply to the original list, and the sorted list is used as a label. The background knowledge for the task involves sorting based on the decision of swap/not swap for every

N	4	5	6	7	8
E2S - NS	13.6	31.4	50.2	74.6	277.4
DPLog (B)	70.2	271.4	2277.3	T/O	T/O
DPLog (Q)	27.7	213.5	791.3	1602.8	T/O

Table 8: Average training time (sec) for the Forth Sort task on various list lengths. Time to reach 100% accuracy on the test set is reported. T/O stands for "timeout". B/Q = Bubble/Quick Sort.

possible pair of digits.

Results are reported in Table 8. Following the DeepProbLog paper, we report the time it takes to reach 100% accuracy on a test set. In the DeepProbLog paper results for Bubble Sort alone are reported. As we are concerned with training time, we also report results for DeepProbLog using Quick Sort. The results not only confirm that Embed2Sym can be used to solve the Forth Sort task, but can do so much faster than DeepProbLog.

5 Discussion

With regards to the four questions raised at the beginning of section 4, we can now provide the following answers: 1) Embed2Sym successfully solves tasks involving perception and reasoning, as confirmed by the Addition, Member and Forth Sort experiments. 2) Embed2Sym is capable of scaling to tasks involving dozens of raw inputs and potentially more. In particular, we have shown Embed2Sym is capable of solving 15-digit MNIST addition and 20-digit Member. 3) Embed2Sym can learn even when the perception task is more complex, as confirmed by the CIFAR-10 Addition experiment. 4) Embed2Sym achieves similar or better test accuracy to competing systems on all the tested tasks, while training faster by several orders of magnitude and scaling to tasks infeasible to other systems.

Embed2Sym offers a more scalable approach to neuro-symbolic reasoning by embracing a different philosophy than other systems. While most approaches attempt to turn logical formulas into differentiable operations, Embed2Sym uses the neural and symbolic components as a means to complement each other. The difficulty in creating a scalable version of differentiable logic is highlighted by the combinatorial issues existing systems encounter. Backpropagation through a differentiable logic gate requires answering the question "Which input values would result in the correct output". Systems such as NeurASP and ABL link this question to logical abduction. In the case of ABL this is done only in the context of definite programs, whereas NeurASP uses the full expressivity of Answer Set Programming. The difficulty in using abduction is that these systems need to find the full set of solutions which in general can be exponential in size. DeepProbLog takes a proof-theoretical view to this question, constructing a (weighted) boolean formula that satisfies a given query. The time complexity of this construction can be $\#P$-complete (Fierens et al. 2015). We see these difficulties manifest in practice particularly in the MNIST Addition experiment, where even for small values of N, training becomes infeasible for both NeurASP and DeepProbLog.

Embed2Sym solves this issue by embracing the approximate nature of neural network inference. The training of the fully neural model creates a structure in embedding space that a symbolic system can later identify and exploit. This gives a symbolic reasoning system access to inference on raw data while circumventing the difficulties arising from differentiable logic operations. The logical optimisation step, which is the critical step in creating the neuro-symbolic model, scales well with an increased number of raw inputs because it builds upon the advances in solving an optimisation problem in Answer Set Programming. We see from experiment that the logical optimisation step is very fast (less than 1 second), and it is in fact the training of the neural network that has a significant effect on training time.

It should be noted that while Embed2Sym works by identifying latent concepts discovered by a neural network, it should not be understood as an explainability method. Embed2Sym makes no attempt at explaining why the perception network associates a given raw input with a latent concept value. It merely states that it did. Specifically, it is not designed to discover if this relationship is due to a statistical correlation rather than a causal relation. Note that other neuro-symbolic systems do not address this issue either.

Future work will be directed at further development of the Embed2Sym method and testing on more challenging domains. Embed2Sym may benefit from more sophisticated methods of discovering cluster information in embedding space (Guo, Lin, and Ye 2021). In the experiments in this paper, we used a simple MLP for the reasoning component during the neural training stage. But in general more sophisticated models could be required, as reasoning gets more complex. For example, reasoning involving differentiating and integrating mathematical functions has been shown to be possible using tree generating Seq2Seq models (Lample and Charton 2020). We also wish to explore the possibility of learning the logic program from data, rather than being provided with the rules.

6 Summary

We introduced Embed2Sym, a novel approach to neuro-symbolic reasoning that is capable of solving tasks involving both perception and reasoning, interpretable and can generalize to other downstream tasks. Most importantly, our system scales far better than competing systems, being capable of solving tasks involving a far larger amount of raw inputs and to more complex perception tasks. Experiments confirm Embed2Sym is much faster to train than competing systems and can scale to many raw inputs, being able to train on the addition of 15 digits numbers (at least), far larger than any competing system has so far achieved. Results on CIFAR-10 Addition confirm the system is capable of training on more complex perception tasks, while other systems time out. Future work will be directed toward experimentation in more challenging domains, experimenting with more sophisticated clustering and reasoning networks, and exploring the possibility of learning rules from data.

References

Badreddine, S.; d'Avila Garcez, A.; Serafini, L.; and Spranger, M. 2022. Logic tensor networks. *Artificial Intelligence* 303:103649.

Besold, T. R.; d'Avila Garcez, A.; Bader, S.; Bowman, H.; Domingos, P.; Hitzler, P.; Kuehnberger, K.-U.; Lamb, L. C.; Lowd, D.; Lima, P. M. V.; de Penning, L.; Pinkas, G.; Poon, H.; and Zaverucha, G. 2017. Neural-symbolic learning and reasoning: A survey and interpretation.

Bošnjak, M.; Rocktäschel, T.; Naradowsky, J.; and Riedel, S. 2017. Programming with a differentiable forth interpreter. In Precup, D., and Teh, Y. W., eds., *Proceedings of the 34th International Conference on Machine Learning*, volume 70 of *Proceedings of Machine Learning Research*, 547–556. PMLR.

Caron, M.; Bojanowski, P.; Joulin, A.; and Douze, M. 2018. Deep clustering for unsupervised learning of visual features. In *Proceedings of the European Conference on Computer Vision (ECCV)*, 132–149.

Dai, W.-Z.; Xu, Q.; Yu, Y.; and Zhou, Z.-H. 2019. Bridging machine learning and logical reasoning by abductive learning. *Advances in Neural Information Processing Systems* 32.

De Raedt, L.; Kimmig, A.; and Toivonen, H. 2007. Problog: A probabilistic prolog and its application in link discovery. In *IJCAI*, volume 7, 2462–2467. Hyderabad.

Ester, M.; Kriegel, H.-P.; Sander, J.; Xu, X.; et al. 1996. A density-based algorithm for discovering clusters in large spatial databases with noise. In *KDD*, volume 96, 226–231.

Fellbaum, C., ed. 1998. *WordNet: An Electronic Lexical Database*. Language, Speech, and Communication. Cambridge, MA: MIT Press.

Fierens, D.; Van den Broeck, G.; Renkens, J.; Shterionov, D.; Gutmann, B.; Thon, I.; Janssens, G.; and De Raedt, L. 2015. Inference and learning in probabilistic logic programs using weighted boolean formulas. *Theory and Practice of Logic Programming* 15(3):358–401.

Gebser, M.; Kaminski, R.; Kaufmann, B.; and Schaub, T. 2017. Multi-shot ASP solving with clingo. *CoRR* abs/1705.09811.

Guo, W.; Lin, K.; and Ye, W. 2021. Deep embedded k-means clustering. In *2021 International Conference on Data Mining Workshops (ICDMW)*, 686–694. Los Alamitos, CA, USA: IEEE Computer Society.

He, K.; Zhang, X.; Ren, S.; and Sun, J. 2016. Deep residual learning for image recognition. In *Proceedings of the IEEE conference on computer vision and pattern recognition*, 770–778.

Huang, Y.-X.; Dai, W.-Z.; Cai, L.-W.; Muggleton, S.; and Jiang, Y. 2021. Fast abductive learning by similarity-based consistency optimization. *Advances in Neural Information Processing Systems* 34.

Koh, P. W.; Nguyen, T.; Tang, Y. S.; Mussmann, S.; Pierson, E.; Kim, B.; and Liang, P. 2020. Concept bottleneck models. In *International Conference on Machine Learning*, 5338–5348. PMLR.

Krizhevsky, A., and Hinton, G. 2009. Learning multiple layers of features from tiny images. Technical report, University of Toronto, Toronto, Ontario.

Lample, G., and Charton, F. 2020. Deep learning for symbolic mathematics. In *8th International Conference on Learning Representations, ICLR 2020, Addis Ababa, Ethiopia, April 26-30, 2020*. OpenReview.net.

Law, M.; Russo, A.; and Broda, K. 2020. The ilasp system for inductive learning of answer set programs. *arXiv preprint arXiv:2005.00904*.

LeCun, Y.; Cortes, C.; and Burges, C. 2010. Mnist handwritten digit database. *ATT Labs [Online]. Available: http://yann.lecun.com/exdb/mnist* 2.

Manhaeve, R.; Dumančić, S.; Kimmig, A.; Demeester, T.; and De Raedt, L. 2021. Neural probabilistic logic programming in deepproblog. *Artificial Intelligence* 298:103504.

Minervini, P.; Bosnjak, M.; Rocktäschel, T.; and Riedel, S. 2018. Towards neural theorem proving at scale. *arXiv preprint arXiv:1807.08204*.

Moradi Fard, M.; Thonet, T.; and Gaussier, E. 2020. Deep k-means: Jointly clustering with k-means and learning representations. *Pattern Recognition Letters* 138:185–192.

Palm, R.; Paquet, U.; and Winther, O. 2018. Recurrent relational networks. *Advances in Neural Information Processing Systems* 31.

Riegel, R.; Gray, A.; Luus, F.; Khan, N.; Makondo, N.; Akhalwaya, I. Y.; Qian, H.; Fagin, R.; Barahona, F.; Sharma, U.; et al. 2020. Logical neural networks. *arXiv preprint arXiv:2006.13155*.

Sarker, M. K.; Zhou, L.; Eberhart, A.; and Hitzler, P. 2021. Neuro-symbolic artificial intelligence: Current trends. *arXiv preprint arXiv:2105.05330*.

Speer, R.; Chin, J.; and Havasi, C. 2017. Conceptnet 5.5: An open multilingual graph of general knowledge. In *Proceedings of the Thirty-First AAAI Conference on Artificial Intelligence*, AAAI'17, 4444–4451. AAAI Press.

Tsamoura, E.; Hospedales, T.; and Michael, L. 2021. Neural-symbolic integration: A compositional perspective. *Proceedings of the AAAI Conference on Artificial Intelligence* 35(6):5051–5060.

Wang, D.; Jamnik, M.; and Liò, P. 2018. Investigating diagrammatic reasoning with deep neural networks. In *Diagrams*.

Winters, T.; Marra, G.; Manhaeve, R.; and De Raedt, L. 2021. Deepstochlog: Neural stochastic logic programming. *arXiv preprint arXiv:2106.12574*.

Xia, X.; Togneri, R.; Sohel, F.; Zhao, Y.; and Huang, D. 2019. A survey: neural network-based deep learning for acoustic event detection. *Circuits, Systems, and Signal Processing* 38(8):3433–3453.

Xu, J.; Zhang, Z.; Friedman, T.; Liang, Y.; and Van den Broeck, G. 2018. A semantic loss function for deep learning with symbolic knowledge. In Dy, J., and Krause, A., eds., *Proceedings of the 35th International Conference on Machine Learning*, volume 80 of *Proceedings of Machine Learning Research*, 5502–5511. PMLR.

Yang, Z.; Ishay, A.; and Lee, J. 2020. Neurasp: Embracing neural networks into answer set programming. In Bessiere, C., ed., *Proceedings of the Twenty-Ninth International Joint Conference on Artificial Intelligence, IJCAI-20*, 1755–1762. International Joint Conferences on Artificial Intelligence Organization. Main track.

Zhao, Z.-Q.; Zheng, P.; Xu, S.-T.; and Wu, X. 2019. Object detection with deep learning: A review. *IEEE Transactions on Neural Networks and Learning Systems* 30(11):3212–3232.

Proceedings of the 19th International Conference on Principles of Knowledge Representation and Reasoning
Special Session on KR and Machine Learning

Looking Inside the Black-Box: Logic-based Explanations for Neural Networks

João Ferreira , Manuel de Sousa Ribeiro , Ricardo Gonçalves , João Leite
NOVA LINCS, NOVA University Lisbon, Portugal
{jmdi.ferreira, mad.ribeiro}@campus.fct.unl.pt, {rjrg, jleite}@fct.unl.pt

Abstract

Deep neural network-based methods have recently enjoyed great popularity due to their effectiveness in solving difficult tasks. Requiring minimal human effort, they have turned into an almost ubiquitous solution in multiple domains. However, due to the size and complexity of typical neural network models' architectures, as well as the sub-symbolical nature of the representations generated by their neuronal activations, neural networks are essentially opaque, making it nearly impossible to explain to humans the reasoning behind their decisions. We address this issue by developing a procedure to induce human-understandable logic-based theories that attempt to represent the classification process of a given neural network model, based on the idea of establishing mappings from the values of the activations produced by the neurons of that model to human-defined concepts to be used in the induced logic-based theory. Exploring the setting of a synthetic image classification task, we provide empirical results to assess the quality of the developed theories for different neural network models, compare them to existing theories on that task, and give evidence that the theories developed through our method are faithful to the representations learned by the neural networks that they are built to describe.

1 Introduction

In this paper, we investigate how to induce logic-based theories that reflect a given neural network's classification process. Our results suggest that this is achievable by using an inductive reasoning framework and relating the activations of a neural network with human-defined concepts, without the need to retrain or modify the neural network, while requiring few labeled data.

Artificial neural networks have allowed for multiple breakthroughs in different challenging areas in the last few years, being capable of matching or surpassing state-of-the-art approaches in real-time object detection (Ren et al. 2017), video classification (Karpathy et al. 2014) and segmentation (Fu et al. 2021), translation (Bahdanau, Cho, and Bengio 2015), even outperforming humans at facial recognition (Wang and Deng 2021), playing strategic games (Silver et al. 2017), just to name a few. For this reason, they have gained popularity, and are now being applied to solve the most varied tasks in multiple different domains, e.g., in medical diagnosis, (Sun, Zheng, and Qian 2016), self-driving vehicles (Kanagaraj et al. 2021), crime prevention (Lin, Chen, and Yu 2017) and fraud detection (Benchaji et al. 2021).

Despite all the successes and popularity achieved by artificial neural network-based methods, neural network models are typically viewed as black boxes (Guidotti et al. 2019), i.e., their input-output behavior is typically considered of highest importance, while the inner representations learned by these models are largely disregarded.

On the one hand, the opaqueness of neural network models might be attributed to their typical size and complexity, having potentially many billions of parameters spread across several dozens of layers performing non-linear transformations (Brown et al. 2020). On the other hand, these models are subsymbolic in nature, meaning that their internal representations are generally based on a high-dimensional Euclidean space, i.e., real-valued tensors, which do not possess an associated declarative meaning (Hitzler et al. 2020). In practice, when a neural network is used to make a prediction, there is no human-interpretable indication regarding why a particular output was produced.

This shortfall led to the search for methods for explaining how to these models are achieving their results, ultimately contributing to the rise of the field of explainable AI (Ignatiev 2020), which we briefly review in Section 6.

There are many different ways one can look at explanations (Miller 2019), but they are usually taken to be answers to (often interactive sequences of) "why" questions, whose selection and evaluation requires a) a language containing human-understandable concepts and meaningful relations between those concepts, b) some knowledge about the domain, and c) one or more forms of reasoning e.g., deductive, abductive, counterfactual, etc.

One recent proposal (de Sousa Ribeiro and Leite 2021), takes a step towards providing *richer* explanations for the outputs of neural network models by exploring the idea of establishing mappings from the values of the activations produced by the neurons of a neural network model, to human-defined concepts from a selected existing logic-based theory. These mappings are established by what is referred in (de Sousa Ribeiro and Leite 2021) as mapping networks – small neural networks built to predict a single human-defined concept from the activations of a given neural network model. When input is fed to a particular *main network* – the neural network model whose outputs we want to justify – it is possible to use these mapping networks and observe whether the concepts they were trained to predict were identified in the main network's activations, thus acquiring additional knowledge about how the main network has processed its input. The justifications are then obtained using logic-based reasoning methods over the selected logic-based theory, together with the observations made for a given input regarding each mapped concept. They are minimal sets of axioms from the selected logic-based theory that, together with the mapping networks' observations, entail the output of the main network. They are symbolic, human-understandable, since they are expressed in the language of the chosen logic-based theory, and we can reason about them. While the selected logic-based theory provides the necessary language and background knowledge to adequately convey justifications for the main networks' output, the established mappings provide additional knowledge about how the main network has processed its input, allowing for an interpretation of its internal representations.

However, the fact that the justifications discussed in (de Sousa Ribeiro and Leite 2021) depend not only on the mapping networks' observations of the input but also on the selected existing logic-based theory, raise two important questions. First, because of the dependency on the selected logic-based theory, one cannot really take them to be exact representations of how a neural network reaches its output, but rather plausible and understandable rationalisations of how it might have arrived at its results, based on the selected logic-based theory. The axioms of the theory that are included in the justification might not be warranted by how the neural network is achieving its results. Second, a logic-based theory might not be available, either because our main network solves a task in a domain where there is little background knowledge available, or no one has yet encoded it as a logic-based theory.

What if we do not have a logic-based theory, or we do not want to rely on existing ones because we suspect that they are in some way incorrect or do not properly reflect how our main network might be achieving its results?

To address this issue, in this paper, instead of using the output of the mapping networks as knowledge about how the main network has processed its input to be used together with an existing logic-based theory, we explore its use to *generate* a logic-based theory. We use the mapping networks to provide additional labels to a data set which we then use to induce a logic-based theory. By choosing an appropriate set of human-defined concepts to build the mapping networks, the generated logic-based theory will provide explanations in a language with the required level of abstraction. By relying on the mapping networks, hence on the internal representations of the main neural network, the generated logic-based theory will better reflect the classification process of that neural network model. Hence, following the method described in (de Sousa Ribeiro and Leite 2021), it can be used for the generation of justifications that are more than just rationalisations – they are closer to providing a global description of how a given neural network is achieving its classifications, based on human-defined concepts.

In this paper, after presenting a formal account of neural networks in Section 2, we proceed, in Section 3, with a formalization of the process of extracting concepts from a neural network using mapping networks, only informally described in (de Sousa Ribeiro and Leite 2021). In Section 4, we describe our method to generate the logic-based theories. Then, in Section 5, we describe a series of experiments conducted to empirically test the proposed method, including evaluating the quality of the generated theories; how the generated theories depend on the concepts used to construct the mapping networks, regarding both their level of abstraction and their adequacy; the cost of the method; and whether the generated theories are indeed a good reflection of the classification process of the neural network model. In Section 6 we discuss related work, and conclude in Section 7.

2 Neural Networks

In this section, we formally introduce the necessary notions and notation on neural networks.

We start by defining the mathematical objects that neural networks manipulate, *tensors*. Formally, a *tensor space* is a subset $\mathbb{A}$ of $\mathbb{R}^{n_1 \times \cdots \times n_s}$, with $s \geq 1$, and each $\mathbf{T} \in \mathbb{A}$ is called a tensor. Vectors and matrices are particular cases of tensors, namely elements of $\mathbb{R}^n$ and $\mathbb{R}^{n \times m}$, respectively. We denote by $size(\mathbb{A}) = \Pi_{i \in \{1,...,s\}} n_i$ the size of $\mathbb{A}$, that is, the number of components of $\mathbb{A}$. Given a tensor $\mathbf{T} \in \mathbb{A}$ and an index $j \in \{1, \ldots, n_1\} \times \cdots \times \{1, \ldots, n_s\}$, by $\mathbf{T}_j$ we denote the j-component of $\mathbf{T}$.

A useful operation on tensors is the vectorization of a sequence of tensors, also known as flattening, which corresponds to the representation of such sequence using a vector that preserves the components of the tensors. We abstract the details of possible vectorizations, and assume that for each sequence $(\mathbb{A}_1, \ldots, \mathbb{A}_k)$ of tensors spaces, there is a function $vec : \mathbb{A}_1 \times \ldots \times \mathbb{A}_k \to \mathbb{R}^n$, with $n = \sum_{i \in \{1,...,k\}} size(\mathbb{A}_i)$, that gives the vectorization of each sequence of tensors.

The basic elements of neural networks are called *units* or *neurons*, and are defined as functions $u \colon \mathbb{I}_u \times \mathbb{S}_u \to \mathbb{R}$, where $\mathbb{I}_u$ and $\mathbb{S}_u$ are tensor spaces, representing the input and the parameters space of u, respectively. Units that share input and parameters spaces can be combined to form *layers*. Formally, a layer is a function $L \colon \mathbb{I}_L \times \mathbb{S}_L \to \mathbb{O}_L$, where $\mathbb{I}_L$, $\mathbb{S}_L$, and $\mathbb{O}_L$ are tensor spaces, where $\mathbb{O}_L$ is called the output tensor space. The units of a given layer L, one for each component j of the output tensor space $\mathbb{O}_L$, are given by the functions $L_i \colon \mathbb{I}_L \times \mathbb{S}_L \to \mathbb{R}$, where $L_i(\mathbf{X}; \boldsymbol{\theta}) = L(\mathbf{X}; \boldsymbol{\theta})_i$.

As an example, a fully connected sigmoid layer with two units can be defined as $L \colon \mathbb{R}^k \times \mathbb{R}^{2(k+1)} \to [0, 1]^2$ such that $L(\boldsymbol{x}; (\boldsymbol{\theta}_1, \boldsymbol{\theta}_2)) = (\phi(\boldsymbol{x}\boldsymbol{w}_1 + b_1), \phi(\boldsymbol{x}\boldsymbol{w}_2 + b_2))$, where ϕ is the sigmoid activation function, k the size of the input $\boldsymbol{x}$, $\boldsymbol{\theta}_i = (\boldsymbol{w}_i, b_i)$, where $\boldsymbol{w}_i$ and b_i are the weights and biases of the corresponding unit i. The output of each unit is the projection of the output of the layer into the respective component, i.e., $L_i(\boldsymbol{x}; (\boldsymbol{\theta}_1, \boldsymbol{\theta}_2)) = L(\boldsymbol{x}; (\boldsymbol{\theta}_1, \boldsymbol{\theta}_2))_i = \phi(\boldsymbol{x}\boldsymbol{w}_i + b_i)$.

A *neural network* N is a sequence $(L^1, \ldots, L^d)$ of layers such that the input of one layer is the same as the output of the previous layer, that is, $\mathbb{I}_{L^j} = \mathbb{O}_{L^{j-1}}$, for all $j \in \{2, \ldots d\}$. The outputs of all layers of N are also usually called the activations of N.

Given a neural network $N = (L^1, \ldots, L^d)$, its input

space is equal to the input space of the first layer, that is, $\mathbb{I}_N = \mathbb{I}_{L^1}$, its output space is equal to the output space of the last layer, that is, $\mathbb{O}_N = \mathbb{O}_{L^d}$, its parameter space is the product of the parameter spaces of each layer, that is, $S_N = \mathbb{S}_{L^1} \times \cdots \times \mathbb{S}_{L^d}$, and its size is the number of units it has, that is, $size(N) = \sum_{i \in \{1,\ldots,d\}} size(\mathbb{O}_{L^i})$.

A neural network N is said to be for *classification* if there exists a set of concepts $\mathcal{C}_N$ and a function $concept_N : \mathbb{O}_N \times \mathcal{C}_N \to \{0,1\}$, such that $concept_N(\mathbf{Y}, \mathsf{C}) = 1$ indicates that concept C can be identified in output $\mathbf{Y}$.

As a simple example of a classification neural network, take N with a single output, that is, $\mathbb{O}_N = [0,1]$, and a single concept $\mathcal{C}_N = \{\mathsf{C}\}$. Then, $concept_N$ can be defined as $concept_N(y, \mathsf{C}) = 1$ iff $y > 0.5$, that is, concept C is only identified when the output value is larger than 0.5.

A *neural network model* is pair $\mathcal{M} = (N, \overline{\boldsymbol{\theta}})$, where N is a neural network and $\overline{\boldsymbol{\theta}}$ is a choice of parameters for each layer of N, that is, $\overline{\boldsymbol{\theta}} \in S_N$. Given a model $\mathcal{M} = (N, \overline{\boldsymbol{\theta}})$, with $N = (L^1, \ldots, L^d)$ and $\overline{\boldsymbol{\theta}} = (\boldsymbol{\theta}_1, \ldots, \boldsymbol{\theta}_d)$, the output of a layer j can be obtained using a function $F^j_{\mathcal{M}} : \mathbb{I}_N \to \mathbb{O}_{L^j}$ defined as the composition of the layers up to layer j, that is, $F^j_{\mathcal{M}}(\mathbf{X}) = L^j(L^{j-1}(\ldots L^1(\mathbf{X}; \boldsymbol{\theta}_1)\ldots; \boldsymbol{\theta}_{j-1}); \boldsymbol{\theta}_j)$. The function associated with the entire model $F_{\mathcal{M}} : \mathbb{I}_N \to \mathbb{O}_N$ is exactly the function of the last layer, that is, $F_{\mathcal{M}} = F^d_{\mathcal{M}}$.

A *training set* for a neural network N is a set of labeled examples, that is, a set of pairs $\{(\mathbf{X}^1, \mathbf{Y}^1), \ldots, (\mathbf{X}^k, \mathbf{Y}^k)\}$, with $\{\mathbf{X}^1, \ldots, \mathbf{X}^k\} \subseteq \mathbb{I}_N$ and $\{\mathbf{Y}^1, \ldots, \mathbf{Y}^k\} \subseteq \mathbb{O}_N$.

Given a neural network model $(N, \overline{\boldsymbol{\theta}})$, the *training process* consists in finding a new model $(N, \overline{\boldsymbol{\theta}}')$, by optimizing some objective function with respect to the parameters space S_N over a training set for N. The *accuracy* of a classification model $\mathcal{M}$ over a set of samples $\mathbb{X}$, denoted by $acc_{\mathbb{X}}(\mathcal{M})$, is the proportion of well-classified examples from the sample set. We may omit $\mathbb{X}$ when it is implicit.

3 Extracting Concepts from Neural Networks

In this section we formalize the method proposed in (de Sousa Ribeiro and Leite 2021) to extract human-understandable concepts from the activation patterns of a trained neural network, usually called main network.

We assume the main network model $\mathcal{M} = (N, \overline{\boldsymbol{\theta}})$ to be fixed, where $N = (L^1, \ldots, L^d)$ is a classification network for a set $\mathcal{C}_N$ of concepts. We also assume a vectorization $vec : \mathbb{O}_{L^1} \times \ldots \times \mathbb{O}_{L^d} \to \mathbb{R}^k$, with $k = size(N)$, that transforms the activations of N into a vector form.

The fundamental elements of the method are the *mapping networks*, each being a classification network M that has as input the activations of the main network and is associated with a single concept C_M. Formally, a mapping network over $\mathcal{M}$ is a classification network M, with $\mathbb{I}_M = \mathbb{R}^k$, where $k = size(N)$, $\mathbb{O}_M = [0,1]$, and $\mathcal{C}_M = \{\mathsf{C}_M\}$.

To allow mapping networks to consider only a subset of the set of all units of the main network N, we associate to each a sequence of selection tensors, $sel_M = (\mathbf{S}^1, \ldots, \mathbf{S}^d)$, one for each layer of N, such that each $\mathbf{S}^i$ has the same dimension as $\mathbb{O}_{L^i}$ but is restricted to $0's$ and $1's$[1]. The positions of $\mathbf{S}^i$ with a 1 correspond to the units of the main network that are to be considered as input for the mapping network M. Given a possible output of the main network, $(\mathbf{O}^1, \ldots, \mathbf{O}^d) \in \mathbb{O}_{L^1} \times \ldots \times \mathbb{O}_{L^d}$, the corresponding input for a mapping network M is $vec(\mathbf{O}^1 \cdot \mathbf{S}^1, \ldots, \mathbf{O}^d \cdot \mathbf{S}^d)$, where $\cdot$ is the point-wise multiplication of tensors.

As an example, let $\mathcal{M} = (N, \overline{\boldsymbol{\theta}})$ be a main network model where N has two layers, one with 3×2 units and the other with 4 units. The vectorization transforms the output of the two layers in a vector of size 10, the size of the input vector of every mapping network for $\mathcal{M}$. The selection sequence of each mapping network M is a pair $sel_M = (\mathbf{S}^1, \mathbf{S}^2)$, where $\mathbf{S}^1$ is a 3×2 binary matrix and $\mathbf{S}^2$ is a size 4 binary vector.

A mapping network is trained to identify its associated concept C_M, given the activations of the main network. Therefore, the training set of a mapping network is a set of pairs, each composed by the activations of the main network together with a label that indicates whether C_M was identified on the input to the main network that generated such activations. To build such training sets, we first need to label samples of the main network with the concepts associated with the mapping networks. Given a concept C and a set of samples $\mathbb{X} \subseteq \mathbb{I}_N$, a *labeling function* for C is of the form $label_{\mathsf{C}} : \mathbb{X} \to \{0,1\}$, such that $label_{\mathsf{C}}(\mathbf{X}) = 1$ indicates whether concept C is present in a given sample $\mathbf{X} \in \mathbb{X}$. A training set for a mapping network M can then be obtained by labeling the output of the units of the main network model generated by an input sample $\mathbf{X}$ with the corresponding label $label_{\mathsf{C}_M}(\mathbf{X})$. Formally, given a set of samples $\mathbb{X} \subseteq \mathbb{I}_N$, the training set for M generated by $\mathbb{X}$ is the set of pairs $(vec(F^1_{\mathcal{M}}(\mathbf{X}) \cdot \mathbf{S}^1, \ldots, F^d_{\mathcal{M}}(\mathbf{X}) \cdot \mathbf{S}^d), label_{\mathsf{C}_M}(\mathbf{X}))$, $\mathbf{X} \in \mathbb{X}$. The cost of training a mapping network is labeling the samples, which usually needs domain expert knowledge.

After training a mapping network M, the resulting model $\mathcal{M}_M = (M, \overline{\boldsymbol{\theta}}_M)$ can be used to predict its associated concept C_M from the activations of the main network. Therefore, we can associate to each $\mathcal{M}_M$ a labeling function $label_{\mathcal{M}_M} : \mathbb{I}_N \to \{0,1\}$ where $label_M(\mathbf{X})$ is given by $concept_M(F_{\mathcal{M}_M}(vec(F^1_{\mathcal{M}}(\mathbf{X}) \cdot \mathbf{S}^1, \ldots, F^d_{\mathcal{M}}(\mathbf{X}) \cdot \mathbf{S}^d)))$, for each $\mathbf{X} \in \mathbb{I}_N$. Intuitively, this labeling function is the application of the function associated with $\mathcal{M}$ to the activations of N generated by $\mathbf{X}$. Then, $concept_M$ indicates whether the concept C_M was identified in the activations of N. It is important to note that, once a mapping network is trained, its labeling function has almost negligible cost (one forward pass of both the main and the mapping network), specially when compared with the cost of manually labeling data.

4 Inducing Logical Theories from Neural Networks

In this section we describe our method to induce human-understandable logic-based theories that aim to represent the

[1]For the sake of presentation, we assumed that the size of the input vector of each mapping network is equal to the number of units of N. In practice, the size of the input vector of each mapping network is the size of the considered subset of units of N.

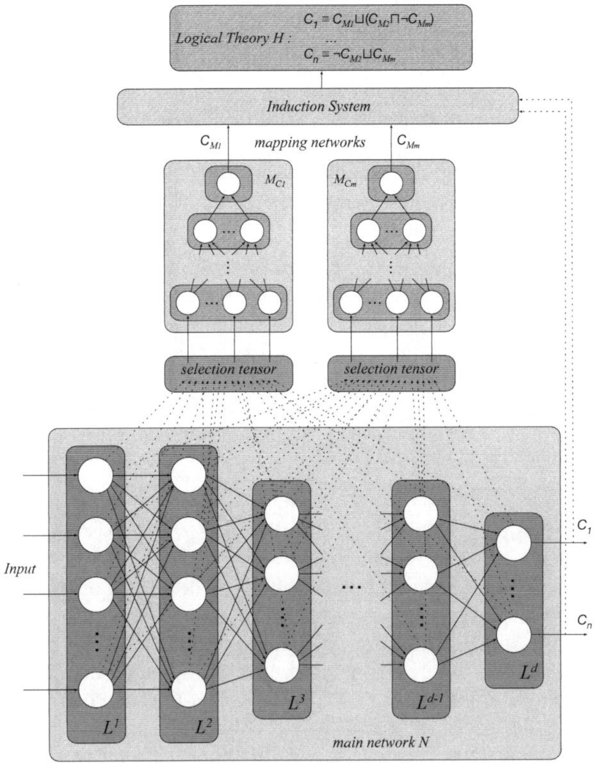

Figure 1: Architecture.

classification process of a neural network model, based on the output of mapping networks, illustrated in Figure 1. We assume a fixed trained main network model $\mathcal{M} = (N, \overline{\boldsymbol{\theta}})$. To represent the classification process of $\mathcal{M}$ and the domain of interest, we need a logical language $\mathcal{L}$ that is rich enough to allow for the representation of concepts, relations between them, and knowledge specific to the individuals of the domain of discourse. Our method is general in the sense that it is parametric on the choice of a logical language (e.g. Description Logics (Baader et al. 2003), Answer-Set Programming (Brewka, Eiter, and Truszczynski 2011), etc.) and an induction framework defined over that language. We just assume that $\mathcal{L}$ is defined over a given set of concepts that includes the concepts in $\mathcal{C}_N$ and a set of concepts of interest $\mathcal{C}$, which are concepts relevant to the domain of the main network N that would normally be obtained from domain experts, and be dependent on the end-users' preferences or level of expertise (e.g., a health practitioner would probably require a set of concepts different than those required by a patient). For example, for a neural network trained on the CIFAR-10 dataset (Krizhevsky and Hinton 2009) we could use concepts such as 'wheels', 'horns', or 'water', while for one trained on the HAM10000 dataset (Tschandl, Rosendahl, and Kittler 2018), we could use concepts such as 'asymmetric', or 'patchy'. We also assume a fixed set of constants $c_N = \{c_{\mathbf{X}} : \mathbf{X} \in \mathbb{I}_N\}$, representing the individuals of the domain of interest, corresponding to the possible input elements of the main network, i.e., its input space.

The elements of $\mathcal{L}$ are called formulas, and should include as basic elements the atoms of the form $\mathsf{C}(c)$, for $\mathsf{C} \in \mathcal{C} \cup \mathcal{C}_N$ and $c \in c_N$. We assume given a consequence relation $\models \subseteq 2^{\mathcal{L}} \times \mathcal{L}$ over $\mathcal{L}$. Then, an inductive framework over $(\mathcal{L}, \models)$ has three ingredients: the so called background knowledge, denoted by BK, which is a subset of $\mathcal{L}$ and represents the known knowledge; a set Pos of atoms, usually called the positive examples; and a set Neg of atoms, called the negative examples. The goal of the inductive framework is to induce an *hypothesis*, which is a set of formulas that together with the background knowledge entails all the positive examples and none of the negative examples. Formally, a set $H \subseteq \mathcal{L}$ is called an inductive hypothesis if $BK \cup H \models \mathsf{C}(c)$ for every $\mathsf{C}(c) \in Pos$, and $BK \cup H \not\models \mathsf{C}(c)$ for every $\mathsf{C}(c) \in Neg$.

In our method, the positive and negative examples will refer to the concepts in $\mathcal{C}_N$, while the background knowledge will contain knowledge about the concepts of interest in $\mathcal{C}$. This way, we can obtain a logical theory representing the classification process of N by characterizing the concepts in $\mathcal{C}_N$ in terms of those in $\mathcal{C}$. To construct the sets BK, Pos and Neg, we fix a set of samples $\mathbb{X} \subseteq \mathbb{I}_N$. For each sample $\mathbf{X} \in \mathbb{X}$, we check using the main network model, if the concepts of $\mathcal{C}_N$ are identified or not in $\mathbf{X}$, adding this information to the positive or negative examples, accordingly. Formally, for each $\mathsf{C} \in \mathcal{C}_N$, we define: $Pos^{\mathsf{C}} = \{\mathsf{C}(c_{\mathbf{X}}) : \mathbf{X} \in \mathbb{X} \text{ and } concept_N(F_{\mathcal{M}}(\mathbf{X}), \mathsf{C}) = 1\}$; $Neg^{\mathsf{C}} = \{\mathsf{C}(c_{\mathbf{X}}) : \mathbf{X} \in \mathbb{X} \text{ and } concept_N(F_{\mathcal{M}}(\mathbf{X}), \mathsf{C}) = 0\}$. The sets of positive and negative examples are defined as $Pos = \cup_{\mathsf{C} \in \mathcal{C}_N} Pos^{\mathsf{C}}$ and $Neg = \cup_{\mathsf{C} \in \mathcal{C}_N} Neg^{\mathsf{C}}$, respectively.

The distinctive characteristic of our method is the use of mapping networks to obtain such background knowledge. The fact that mapping networks learn to classify using the activations of the main network is fundamental to assure that this classification is intrinsic to the main network. For each concept $\mathsf{C} \in \mathcal{C}$ we train a mapping network M_{C} as described in Sect. 2, resulting in a mapping network model $\mathcal{M}_{\mathsf{C}}$. Since some of these mapping networks may not learn to correctly identify its associated concept, we assume some threshold α for the accuracy of the mapping networks, below which we do not use them to build the background knowledge. Then, only the concepts in $\mathcal{C}_\alpha = \{\mathsf{C} \in \mathcal{C} : acc(\mathcal{M}_{\mathsf{C}}) > \alpha\}$ will be used to build the background knowledge. Formally, we have $BK = \{\mathsf{C}(c_{\mathbf{X}}) : \mathbf{X} \in \mathbb{X} \text{ and } \mathsf{C} \in \mathcal{C}_\alpha \text{ and } label_{\mathcal{M}_{\mathsf{C}}}(\mathbf{X}) = 1\}$. Note that the set BK could also include additional background knowledge over $\mathcal{C}$, e.g. provided by a domain expert, but we do not further explore that possibility in this paper.

Given the sets Pos, Neg and BK defined above, the logic-based theory given by the induction framework can be seen as a representation over $\mathcal{L}$ of the classification process of the main network, describing in a human-understandable logical language the characterization of the concepts of the main network in terms of the concepts of interest.

5 Empirical Evaluation

In this section, we empirically evaluate our proposed method using the XTRAINS Dataset (de Sousa Ribeiro, Krippahl, and Leite 2020). After introducing the dataset in Section 5.1 and the experimental setting in Section 5.2, we discuss the

Figure 2: Sample images from the XTRAINS dataset.

direct application of our method to this dataset in Section 5.3, followed by a set of experiments to highlight different aspects of our proposal: –Section 5.4 discusses how the induced theories are affected when using concepts with different levels of abstraction; –Section 5.5 analyzes how our method behaves when provided with insufficient concepts to induce a theory for a neural network; –Section 5.6 evaluates the cost of applying our method, and how it performs with different amounts of available data; and –Section 5.7 examines the importance of using mapping networks when inducing a theory for the classification process of a neural network model.

5.1 Dataset and Main Networks

The XTRAINS is an image dataset containing representations of trains, such as those in Figure 2. The images are labeled according to their visual features, which correspond to human-understandable concepts. Having an accompanying ontology, this dataset provides a controlled environment for the experiments. The use of images is challenging since human-understandable concepts cannot be directly extracted from pixel representations.

The dataset images can be seen as $152 \times 152 \times 3$ tensors, and are highly diverse. The trains vary in the number, size, and shape of their wagons and wheels, and in the quantity, size and relative position of the geometric shapes inside each wagon, but also in the distance between each wagon, the thickness of the wagons' walls or the height of the trains' couplers. Also, noise is present in the form of missing pixels from the trains' representations.

The ontology accompanying the dataset is represented using Description Logics, which are a family of logic based knowledge representation languages, consisting of decidable fragments of First-Order Logic.[2] Figure 3 presents a subset of this ontology, which agrees with the labels of the XTRAINS dataset. The ontology represents how different concepts are related, e.g., a train has a wagon or locomotive, and how trains are classified in this domain, e.g., a type A train is either a war train or an empty train.

In our experiments, we consider three different main network models – referred to as $\mathcal{M}_{\mathsf{A}}$, $\mathcal{M}_{\mathsf{B}}$, $\mathcal{M}_{\mathsf{C}}$. Each of these models was trained to identify, respectively, trains with the following descriptions, each illustrated in Figure 2, and described in the accompanying ontology, cf. Figure 3:

- TypeA – trains having either, a wagon with at least a circle inside and a wagon with two walls in each side, or no wagons with geometric figures inside them;
- TypeB – trains having a long wagon, or two wagons, with at least a circle inside, or trains having at least two long wagons, or three wagons, with at least two of which with a geometric figure inside that is not a circle;
- TypeC – trains having a wagon with no geometric figure inside and either, a wagon with a circle inside and a wagon with a geometric figure inside that is not a circle, or no long wagons and a wagon with a figure inside.

Each of the three main networks[3] was trained using a set of 25 000 images and achieved an accuracy of about 99% on a test set of 10 000 images. The three main networks possess different architectures, but all start with a set of convolutional, batch normalization, pooling, and dropout layers, followed by a varying number of fully connected and batch normalization layers, with a single output unit at the end.

5.2 Experimental Setting

The mapping networks used in the following experiments all have the same architecture, being composed solely by an input layer, receiving the main network's activations, and an output layer with a single neuron using the sigmoid activation function. Similarly to the main networks, the mapping networks were trained using the optimization algorithm Adam (Kingma and Ba 2015), with a learning rate of 0.001, the binary cross entropy as loss function, and early stopping with a patience value of 20 (30 for main networks). Each mapping network was trained using a balanced set of 800 samples and tested using 1 000 samples, with the exception of those in Section 5.6, where we discuss the effects of varying the amount of available training samples.

The accuracy threshold α, used to select which mapping networks should be considered when building the background knowledge, is set to be $\alpha = 90\%$.

We choose ontologies over Description Logics as our logical language, a standard choice for taxonomic classification, which also allow us to compare our induced theories with the accompanying ontology of the dataset. As for the induction system, we use DL-Learner framework (Lehmann 2009), which supports supervised ontology induction. Other alternatives for learning logic-based theories could have been used, such as ILASP (Law, Russo, and Broda 2014) or even differentiable logic machines (Zimmer et al. 2021). We use the CELOE algorithm (Lehmann et al. 2011), which is biased to minimize the induced theory, and consider a positive-negative learning problem using closed world reasoning with a maximum execution time of 60 seconds. In all experiments, the theories are induced using a set of 3 000 samples, and tested with a set of 1 000 samples.

The main metric to quantitatively evaluate the quality of our induced theories is the fidelity measure (F_{Main}), which computes how well a given theory *imitates* the classifications of the main network model it was induced from. This metric is computed as the ratio of samples where the classifications of the main network coincide with those obtained from the induced theory together with the knowledge obtained from the outputs of the mapping networks.

[2]We assume basic familiarity with Description Logics (see (Baader et al. 2003)).

[3]The networks are available at https://bit.ly/XTrainsModels

$$\begin{aligned}
&\mathsf{Train} \equiv \exists\mathsf{has}.(\mathsf{Wagon} \sqcup \mathsf{Locomotive})\\
&\mathsf{TypeA} \equiv \mathsf{WarTrain} \sqcup \mathsf{EmptyTrain}\\
&\mathsf{TypeB} \equiv \mathsf{PassengerTrain} \sqcup \mathsf{LongFreightTrain}\\
&\mathsf{TypeC} \equiv \mathsf{RuralTrain} \sqcup \mathsf{MixedTrain}\\
&\mathsf{LongFreightTrain} \equiv \mathsf{LongTrain} \sqcap \mathsf{FreightTrain}\\
&\mathsf{EmptyTrain} \equiv \forall\mathsf{has}.(\mathsf{EmptyWagon} \sqcup \mathsf{Locomotive}) \sqcap \exists\mathsf{has}.\mathsf{EmptyWagon}\\
&\exists\mathsf{has}.\mathsf{EmptyWagon} \sqcap \exists\mathsf{has}.(\mathsf{PassengerCar} \sqcup \mathsf{FreightWagon}) \sqcap \neg\exists\mathsf{has}.\mathsf{LongWagon} \sqsubseteq \mathsf{RuralTrain}\\
&\exists\mathsf{has}.\mathsf{FreightWagon} \sqcap \exists\mathsf{has}.\mathsf{PassengerCar} \sqcap \exists\mathsf{has}.\mathsf{EmptyWagon} \sqsubseteq \mathsf{MixedTrain}\\
&\exists\mathsf{has}.(\mathsf{PassengerCar} \sqcap \mathsf{LongWagon}) \sqcup (\geq 2\ \mathsf{has}.\mathsf{PassengerCar}) \sqsubseteq \mathsf{PassengerTrain}\\
&\exists\mathsf{has}.\mathsf{ReinforcedCar} \sqcap \exists\mathsf{has}.\mathsf{PassengerCar} \sqsubseteq \mathsf{WarTrain}\\
&(\geq 2\ \mathsf{has}.\mathsf{LongWagon}) \sqcup (\geq 3\ \mathsf{has}.\mathsf{Wagon}) \sqsubseteq \mathsf{LongTrain}\\
&(\geq 2\ \mathsf{has}.\mathsf{FreightWagon}) \sqsubseteq \mathsf{FreightTrain}
\end{aligned}$$

Figure 3: A subset of the XTRAINS dataset's ontology.

Given the high accuracy of the three main networks being studied, we consider another fidelity metric ($F_{XTrains}$), which measures the concordance of the induced theories with respect to the XTRAINS dataset labeling. This metric is computed as the ratio of samples where the classifications of the XTRAINS labels (for the main network's output concepts $\mathcal{C}_N$) coincide with those obtained from the induced theory together with the knowledge obtained from the labels of the mapped concepts ($\mathcal{C}_\alpha$). This metric allows us to compare whether the induced theories are better suited to the classifications of our main and mapping networks, or to the labeling of the dataset. Even when obtaining high F_{Main} scores, it is relevant to also examine $F_{XTrains}$, since if it is significantly greater than F_{Main}, it could mean that our method was overfitting to the dataset labels.

Additionally, we also inspect how the induced theories logically compare with the existing XTRAINS' ontology. However, whereas an existing logical relation between both could serve as confirmation of the quality of the induced theory, it is worth noting that the absence of such a relation should not be seen as evidence of an induced theory with poor quality since the main networks may have learned to perform the same classifications through a different internal process.

Each experiment was run 20 times, using different balanced sets of samples for training and testing purposes. Throughout the paper, the induced theories that we present and logically analyze are the mode of the 20 runs, while the discussed fidelity scores correspond to the runs' averages.

5.3 Inducing a Main Network's Theory

In this section, we test our main hypothesis, namely that we can leverage on the classifications provided by mapping networks, trained to identify concepts of interest, and use them as basis to induce a human-understandable theory describing how a neural network processes its inputs.

To that end, for each main network, we trained mapping networks to identify the following 11 concepts[4] from the ontology in Figure 3: EmptyTrain, FreightTrain, LongTrain, MixedTrain, PassengerTrain, RuralTrain, WarTrain, ∃has.FreightWagon, ∃has.LongWagon, ∃has.OpenRoof, ∃has.ReinforcedCar. In this process, we treat each complex concept, e.g., ∃has.FreightWagon, as an atomic concept.

Using our method, we induced the following theories for each of the three main networks:

$$\mathsf{TypeA} \equiv \mathsf{WarTrain} \sqcup \mathsf{EmptyTrain}$$
$$\mathsf{TypeB} \equiv (\mathsf{FreightTrain} \sqcap \mathsf{LongTrain}) \sqcup (\mathsf{PassengerTrain} \sqcap \neg\mathsf{EmptyTrain})$$
$$\mathsf{TypeC} \equiv \mathsf{MixedTrain} \sqcup \mathsf{RuralTrain}$$

For example, the theory induced for $\mathcal{M}_\mathsf{A}$ states that a sample is classified as being a TypeA train if and only if it is either a war train or an empty train, whereas the theory induced for $\mathcal{M}_\mathsf{B}$ states that a sample is classified as being a TypeB train if and only if it is either a freight train and a long train, or a passenger train and not an empty train.

It is worth noting that, despite the usage of 11 concepts when inducing each theory, only 3 of those concepts were used on average. This suggests that the proposed method was able to properly select the concepts better suited to describe each neural network's classification process.

A logical comparison of the induced theories with the ontology that accompanies the XTRAINS dataset allows us to observe that both the definitions of concepts TypeA and TypeC in the induced theories for $\mathcal{M}_\mathsf{A}$ and $\mathcal{M}_\mathsf{C}$, respectively, are equivalent to the respective definitions of TypeA and TypeC in the datasets' ontology. The concept of TypeB in the induced theory for $\mathcal{M}_\mathsf{B}$ is a subclass of TypeB as defined in the XTRAINS ontology, meaning that any individual of TypeB in the induced theory is also considered to be of TypeB according to the XTRAINS ontology.

	F_{Main}	$F_{XTrains}$
$\mathcal{M}_\mathsf{A}$	$99.72 \pm 0.18\%$	$99.92 \pm 0.35\%$
$\mathcal{M}_\mathsf{B}$	$98.71 \pm 0.31\%$	$99.83 \pm 0.76\%$
$\mathcal{M}_\mathsf{C}$	$99.33 \pm 0.32\%$	$99.52 \pm 1.52\%$

Table 1: Fidelity scores for the theories of each main network.

Table 1 shows the fidelity scores of the induced theories. The resulting high F_{Main} scores provide evidence that the resulting theories are properly reflecting the main network's internal classification process, strongly supporting our main hypothesis. Furthermore, one can observe that the induced theories are also faithful to the dataset's labels, achieving similar $F_{XTrains}$ and F_{Main} scores. This is an interesting indication that the main networks have learned to classify their samples in similar fashion to how they are classified by the ontology accompanying the XTRAINS dataset.

5.4 Levels of Abstraction

It is often the case that different scenarios require different levels of abstraction and detail to interpret a neural networks' classification process. For example, we may want to

[4]We selected the same 11 concepts that were explored in (de Sousa Ribeiro and Leite 2021)

understand how a neural network is classifying some type of train based on other known types of trains, or otherwise wish to be more specific and understand how particular kinds of wagons are influencing the output of the neural network.

To investigate how our method performs when faced with concepts at different levels of abstraction, we crafted the following sets of concepts:

Train-level:

$$\{\mathsf{EmptyTrain}, \mathsf{LongFreightTrain}, \mathsf{MixedTrain}, \mathsf{PassengerTrain}, \mathsf{RuralTrain}, \mathsf{WarTrain}\}$$

Wagon-Level:

$$\{\exists \mathsf{has.EmptyWagon}, \exists \mathsf{has.FreightWagon}, \exists \mathsf{has.LongWagon}, \exists \mathsf{has.}(\mathsf{LongWagon} \sqcap \mathsf{PassengerCar}) \exists \mathsf{has.PassengerCar}, \exists \mathsf{has.ReinforcedCar}, \geq 2\mathsf{has.FreightWagon}, \geq 2\mathsf{has.LongWagon}, \geq 2\mathsf{has.PassengerCar}, \geq 3\mathsf{has.Wagon}\}$$

The application of our method to the three main networks, using the train-level concepts, resulted in the theories:

$$\mathsf{TypeA} \equiv \mathsf{EmptyTrain} \sqcup \mathsf{WarTrain}$$
$$\mathsf{TypeB} \equiv \mathsf{LongFreightTrain} \sqcup \mathsf{PassengerTrain}$$
$$\mathsf{TypeC} \equiv \mathsf{MixedTrain} \sqcup \mathsf{RuralTrain}$$

While with the wagon-level concepts we obtained:

$$\mathsf{TypeA} \equiv (\exists \mathsf{has.PassengerCar} \sqcup \neg\exists \mathsf{has.FreightWagon}) \sqcap (\exists \mathsf{has.ReinforcedCar} \sqcup \neg\exists \mathsf{has.PassengerCar})$$
$$\mathsf{TypeB} \equiv \exists \mathsf{has.}(\mathsf{LongWagon} \sqcap \mathsf{PassengerCar}) \sqcup (\geq 3\mathsf{has.Wagon} \sqcap \geq 2\mathsf{has.FreightWagon})$$
$$\mathsf{TypeC} \equiv \exists \mathsf{has.EmptyWagon} \sqcap (\neg\exists \mathsf{has.LongWagon} \sqcup (\geq 3\mathsf{has.Wagon} \sqcap \exists \mathsf{has.PassengerCar}))$$

Comparing the induced theories with the dataset's ontology, the induced definitions for the train-level theories of TypeA, TypeB, and TypeC are all logically equivalent to the ones in the dataset's ontology. Turning to the wagon-level induced theories, we can observe that the induced definition of TypeB is a subclass of the corresponding definition in the dataset's ontology, while neither the induced definitions of TypeA and TypeC are subclasses or superclasses of their corresponding definitions in the dataset's ontology.

However, when we turn to the fidelity scores for both groups of induced theories, shown in Table 2, we can observe that the train-level theories achieve, on average, a slightly higher value (99.35%) than the wagon-level ones (96.74%), but they are all high, showing that our method is able to generate high-quality theories using concepts at different levels of abstraction. The slight difference in fidelity between the results achieved by the train-level and wagon-level induced theories can be attributed to the difference in accuracy of the mapping networks – 97.43% on average for the train-level concepts and 96.07% for the wagon-level ones – amplified by the fact that the wagon-level induced theories use more concepts.

5.5 Insufficient Concepts

Having shown that the proposed method is able to induce theories that represent a neural network's classification process, even when using concepts with different levels of abstraction, we now turn our attention to the case where the chosen concepts of interest are somehow insufficient to describe the neural networks' classification process. This is relevant since, in real-life, it may occur that we are unable to determine a set of concepts that is adequate, or sufficient, to describe a neural networks' classification process.

		F_{Main}	$F_{XTrains}$
Train-level	$\mathcal{M}_\mathsf{A}$	$99.76 \pm 0.19\%$	$100.00 \pm 0.0\%$
	$\mathcal{M}_\mathsf{B}$	$98.82 \pm 0.39\%$	$100.00 \pm 0.0\%$
	$\mathcal{M}_\mathsf{C}$	$99.46 \pm 0.20\%$	$100.00 \pm 0.0\%$
Wagon-level	$\mathcal{M}_\mathsf{A}$	$94.55 \pm 10.14\%$	$94.44 \pm 11.12\%$
	$\mathcal{M}_\mathsf{B}$	$97.50 \pm 0.52\%$	$96.73 \pm 1.18\%$
	$\mathcal{M}_\mathsf{C}$	$98.16 \pm 0.36\%$	$99.02 \pm 0.56\%$

Table 2: Fidelity scores of the train- and wagon-level theories.

We expect the fidelity of the resulting theories to reflect the adequacy of the concepts C being mapped. If the chosen concepts are insufficient to properly describe a main network's $\mathcal{M}$ classification process, then the induced theory would have a diminished F_{Main} fidelity. Otherwise, it would mean that our method could be picking up on spurious correlations to describe $\mathcal{M}$'s classification process.

To test this, we sampled 20 random sets of 5 concepts among all concepts defined in the XTRAINS ontology, and induced theories for each of the three main networks. The average fidelity scores F_{Main} and $F_{XTrains}$ of the resulting theories were, respectively, 72.6% and 71.9%, which are considerably lower than the ones obtained in Sections 5.3 and 5.4. These results back our hypothesis that the inadequacy of the selected concepts negatively reflects in the quality of the resulting theories.

As an example, using the set $\{\mathsf{LongFreightTrain}, \exists \mathsf{has.LongWagon}, \exists \mathsf{has.PassengerCar}, \geq 3\mathsf{has.Wagon}, \geq 2\mathsf{has.PassengerCar}\}$, resulted in the following theories:

$$\mathsf{TypeA} \equiv \top$$
$$\mathsf{TypeB} \equiv\ \geq 3\mathsf{has.Wagon} \sqcup \mathsf{LongFreightTrain}$$
$$\mathsf{TypeC} \equiv (\geq 3\mathsf{has.Wagon} \sqcap \exists \mathsf{has.PassengerCar}) \sqcup (\neg(\geq 2\mathsf{has.PassengerCar}) \sqcap \neg\exists \mathsf{has.LongWagon})$$

A logical comparison of these theories with the dataset's ontology shows that the definition of TypeA in the dataset's ontology is a subclass of the induced definition of TypeA, although this is hardly interesting since that would be the case for any concept. The definitions of TypeB and TypeC are not directly comparable with their respective definitions in the dataset's ontology, given that they are neither their subclasses or superclasses. The poor quality of these theories is reflected in their fidelity scores, shown in Table 3. The high fidelity of the theory obtained for $\mathcal{M}_\mathsf{B}$ can be explained by the use of concepts $\geq 3\mathsf{has.Wagon}$ and $\mathsf{LongFreightTrain}$, which, based on the experiments of Sections 5.3 and 5.4, are adequate to describe the classification process of $\mathcal{M}_\mathsf{B}$.

5.6 Theory Induction's Cost

The experiments presented so far provide evidence that our method is able to perform properly in multiple scenarios, as long as the mapped concepts are sufficient to describe a neural network's classification process. However, in order to verify the method's feasibility, its cost needs to be assessed.

	F_{Main}	$F_{XTrains}$
$\mathcal{M}_\mathsf{A}$	$50.16 \pm 0.26\%$	$50.00 \pm 0.00\%$
$\mathcal{M}_\mathsf{B}$	$92.53 \pm 2.75\%$	$92.70 \pm 1.43\%$
$\mathcal{M}_\mathsf{C}$	$76.78 \pm 1.99\%$	$76.99 \pm 0.94\%$

Table 3: Fidelity scores of the theories with randomly selected concepts.

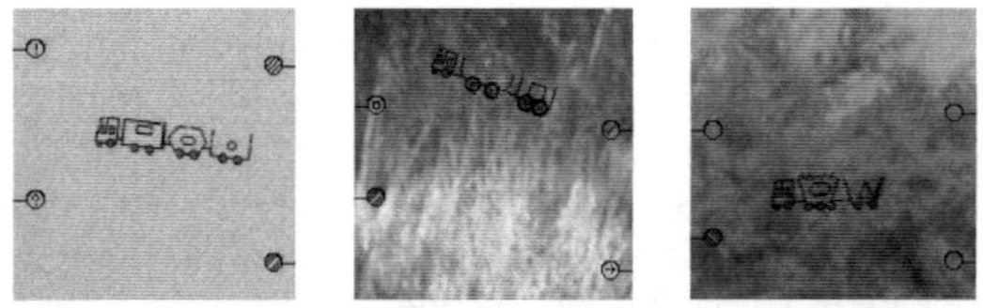

Figure 4: Sample images of the designed classification problem.

The method requires the training of multiple mapping networks, and a set of samples to induce the theory. The mapping networks' development adds little computational overhead, given their simple architectures, but requires data labeled with respect to the concepts $\mathcal{C}$ to be mapped. However, this data can be repurposed to induce the theory, by relabeling it according to the mapping networks' classifications.

Hence, if the quality of our resulting theories would mostly depend on the accuracy of the mapping networks, and assuming the availability of enough unlabeled data, then the main cost of applying our method would be in labeleling the data required to train the mapping networks. Consequently, since mapping networks are known to require few labeled data to train, as shown in (de Sousa Ribeiro and Leite 2021), the cost of our method would be relatively low, depending mostly on the amount of concepts $\mathcal{C}$ to be mapped.

To test whether the quality of the resulting theories mostly depends on the accuracy of the mapping networks, for each of the three main networks used throughout this paper, we induced theories using the 11 concepts selected in Section 5.3, while varying the amount of data used for their training between 50 and 1200 samples. The amount of data used to induce the theories remained constant at 3000 samples. A Pearson's correlation test on fidelity F_{Main} and the average accuracy of the mapping networks for $\mathcal{C}_\alpha$, with $\alpha = 90\%$, shows a significant strong correlation ($r = 0.8161$, $p < 0.0001$), thus indicating that when the mapping networks' accuracy increases, the quality of the induced theories increases as well. Since mapping networks are able to achieve high accuracies even with few training data, and that this data is typically the limiting factor, the cost of our method can be considered to be quite moderate. Even when considering only 50 samples to both train the mapping networks and induce the theories, the resulting theories were typically quite accurate, with an average fidelity F_{Main} of about 96%.

5.7 Importance of the Mappings

The goal of our proposed method is to develop a human-understandable theory representing the classification process of a given neural network model. Given that our theories are induced based on the results of mapping networks, which in turn were trained based on labeled data, one might wonder why they should bother with using mapping networks, instead of inducing the theories directly from the labels used to train the mapping networks. We hypothesize that theories induced directly from labeled data, even if faithful to the data classification, can misrepresent the classification process of the neural network model they were built to represent. Conversely, we hypothesize that the theories induced through our method, being reliant on the internal representations of the model obtained through the mapping networks, will more faithfully represent its internal process.

To test our hypotheses, we designed a classification problem where four traffic signals are added to each image of the XTRAINS dataset, as shown in Figure 4. A traffic signal is said to be *on* if it contains any symbol inside it, and *off* if it does not contain any symbol inside or if it only contains diagonal stripes inside. The images were then labeled regarding 5 different concepts: $\mathsf{TopLeftOn}$, $\mathsf{TopRightOn}$, $\mathsf{BottomLeftOn}$, $\mathsf{BottomRightOn}$, with obvious meaning, and On whenever some traffic signal is on. The dataset was designed such that whenever one of the top traffic signals is on, at least one of the bottom traffic signals is on as well, and vice versa. A neural network is then tasked with identifying whether some traffic signal is on in a given image. Notice that, due to the way the dataset was designed, it is enough to look at either the top, or bottom signals to be able to identify if any traffic signal is on. Thus, one would expect that neural networks trained to perform this task would sometimes learn to identify the top signals, sometimes learn to identify the bottom ones, and sometimes learn to identify them all.

In this setting, we trained 50 different main networks with a test accuracy higher than 90%. When inducing a theory for each of the developed main networks, using their outputs and the dataset labels (instead of the mapping network outputs), the same theory was always obtained: $\{\mathsf{On} \equiv \mathsf{BottomLeftOn} \sqcup \mathsf{BottomRightOn}\}$.[5] This observation strongly supports our first hypothesis, suggesting that due to the high accuracy of the main networks' outputs, when using the dataset labels, the induced theories are instead describing how the dataset was labeled. Hence, having no relation to the main networks classification process.

However, if we apply our proposed method to the same 50 main networks, which considers the outputs of the mapping networks, we observe diverse induced theories. Our results reveal that 22% of the main networks learned to classify their outputs just by considering whether the two top signals were on, resulting in the induced theory $\{\mathsf{On} \equiv \mathsf{TopLeftOn} \sqcup \mathsf{TopRightOn}\}$, while 42% *looked at* the two bottom signals, resulting in the induced theory $\{\mathsf{On} \equiv \mathsf{BottomLeftOn} \sqcup \mathsf{BottomRightOn}\}$. This indicates that different main networks learned to classify their inputs differently, which was captured by the induced theories using the outputs of the mapping networks, but not when only the

[5]Despite the existence of two minimal theories that describe the dataset's labels, $\{\mathsf{On} \equiv \mathsf{BottomLeftOn} \sqcup \mathsf{BottomRightOn}\}$ and $\{\mathsf{On} \equiv \mathsf{TopLeftOn} \sqcup \mathsf{TopRightOn}\}$, DL-Learner always presents the same one because it is not non-deterministic – the induced theory depends on the order in which the concepts were presented.

dataset labels were used. The remaining main networks learned to classify their inputs based on some other combination of signals, e.g., by observing all signals. Interestingly, our results hint that some of these networks did not seem to have learned the concepts that we considered, but instead had learned to classify their inputs based on some other spurious correlations present in the dataset.

6 Related Work

The success of artificial neural network-based methods, along with their characteristic opaqueness, led to the development of many methods with the goal of increasing the interpretability of artificial neural network models. One of the most popular approaches being saliency and attribution methods (Li et al. 2021; Sundararajan, Taly, and Yan 2017; Wang et al. 2020), where the explanation for a neural network's behavior is given in terms of the contribution of each input feature for a given prediction. This is the case of gradient-based methods (Ancona et al. 2018), which compute the gradient of the output with respect to the input to approximate the input features' contributions, and backpropagation-based methods (Montavon et al. 2019; Rebuffi et al. 2020), where a set of propagation rules is used to propagate the output backwards, in order to compute the relevancy of each input feature. There also exist saliency and attribution methods based on perturbation (Zeiler and Fergus 2014; Ivanovs, Kadikis, and Ozols 2021), where the input features' contributions are estimated by measuring how the output changes when masking different parts of the input, or based on abduction (Ignatiev, Narodytska, and Marques-Silva 2019), where inputs are selected based on an encoding of the model as a set of constrains.

Other methods, known as proxy-based methods (Gilpin et al. 2018), attempt to substitute the model being interpreted for another one that has a similar behavior and is inherently interpretable. One popular proxy-based method is LIME (Ribeiro, Singh, and Guestrin 2016), where local linear models are used as a simplified proxy for the full model. Automatic rule extraction algorithms (Guidotti et al. 2019) are a large subgroup of proxy-based methods, where different approaches can be found. Pedagogical rule extraction algorithms (Augasta and Kathirvalavakumar 2012; Schmitz, Aldrich, and Gouws 1999) treat the neural network as a black-box and attempt to produce rules based only on its input-output behavior, decompositional rule extraction algorithms (Zilke, Mencía, and Janssen 2016) consider the inner structure of a neural network model to generate its rules, and eclectic rule extraction algorithms (Towell and Shavlik 1993) apply both elements of pedagogical and decompositional rule extraction algorithms. Recently, multilayer perceptrons were mapped into quantitative bipolar argumentation frameworks (Potyka 2021), although the meaning of the resulting arguments, and the added-value, is yet unclear.

While the above mentioned methods increase the interpretability of neural network models in some way, most only do so in terms of the inputs of the model being interpreted, with explanations consisting only of sets of input features and their corresponding contribution values. However, user studies (Adebayo et al. 2020; Chu, Roy, and Andreas 2020; Shen and Huang 2020) have shown that such explanations typically end up being ignored or unhelpful to end users. We attribute this to the fact that this kind of explanations do not explicitly present any kind of clarification regarding the underlying phenomena that lead to the production of a particular output from a given input to the model, leaving to the user the burden of understanding why the explanation, e.g., a particular set of input features and contribution values, justifies the output of a neural network. Works such has TCAV (Kim et al. 2018) use a notion of "human-interpretable concepts", but no account is given regarding how these concepts relate to the output of the neural network.

The field of neuro-symbolic AI (Besold et al. 2017) and inductive logic-based explainable AI (Schmid 2018) have also contributed to the increase of the interpretability of subsymbolic models. Works such as LIME-FOLD (Shakerin and Gupta 2019) and SHAP-FOIL (Shakerin and Gupta 2020) induce a theory for explaining a model's input-output behavior, by leveraging local explanation methods to determine input feature importance, while (Sarker et al. 2017) attempts to induce such a theory based on labels describing a model's inputs and outputs. (D'Asaro et al. 2020) employs a similar approach, but addresses preference learning tasks, using ILASP (Law, Russo, and Broda 2014) and its ability to learn weak constraints to explain a model. However, given that these methods are pedagogical rule-extraction methods, they are limited to only describing a model's input-output behavior, and thus might fail to be truthful to a neural networks' internal representations.

7 Conclusions

In this paper, we proposed a method for inducing logic-based theories that represent the classification process of a neural network model, providing a human-understandable description of how a neural network is achieving its results based on human-defined concepts.

We provide a formalization of our method along with an experimental evaluation. We were able to show that the method is capable of inducing theories that are faithful to a neural network's classifications. The method has shown to be able to deal with unnecessary concepts, and select the ones that are adequate, depending on the neural network model to which it is being applied. Moreover, it was able to induce theories at different levels of abstraction, and shown to be applicable even when few labeled data is available. Our results indicate that it is indeed possible to obtain logic-based theories that reflect the internal classification process of a given neural network, by leveraging the knowledge hidden in its internal representations to extract symbolic human-defined concepts. This allows us to better understand how a neural network model is performing its classifications, at an adequate level of abstraction, and thus better interpret that model.

Regarding future work, an interesting avenue of research is to explore how to induce probabilistic theories based on the accuracy of the mapping networks, in order to obtain theories that better represent the internal classification process of neural network models.

Acknowledgments

The authors would like to thank the anonymous reviewers for their helpful comments, and acknowledge the support provided by Calouste Gulbenkian Foundation through its "New Talents in AI" program, and by FCT through PhD grant (UI/BD/151266/2021), project FORGET (PTDC/CCI-INF/32219/2017), project RIVER (PTDC/CCI-COM/30952/2017) and strategic project NOVA LINCS (UIDB/04516/2020).

References

Adebayo, J.; Muelly, M.; Liccardi, I.; and Kim, B. 2020. Debugging tests for model explanations. In *Procs. of NeurIPS'20*.

Ancona, M.; Ceolini, E.; Öztireli, C.; and Gross, M. 2018. Towards better understanding of gradient-based attribution methods for deep neural networks. In *Procs. of ICLR'18*. OpenReview.net.

Augasta, M. G., and Kathirvalavakumar, T. 2012. Reverse engineering the neural networks for rule extraction in classification problems. *Neural Process. Lett.* 35(2):131–150.

Baader, F.; Calvanese, D.; McGuinness, D. L.; Nardi, D.; and Patel-Schneider, P. F., eds. 2003. *The Description Logic Handbook: Theory, Implementation, and Applications*. Cambridge University Press.

Bahdanau, D.; Cho, K.; and Bengio, Y. 2015. Neural machine translation by jointly learning to align and translate. In *Procs. of ICLR'15*.

Benchaji, I.; Douzi, S.; Ouahidi, B. E.; and Jaafari, J. 2021. Enhanced credit card fraud detection based on attention mechanism and LSTM deep model. *J. Big Data* 8(1):151.

Besold, T. R.; d'Avila Garcez, A. S.; Bader, S.; Bowman, H.; Domingos, P. M.; Hitzler, P.; Kühnberger, K.; Lamb, L. C.; Lowd, D.; Lima, P. M. V.; de Penning, L.; Pinkas, G.; Poon, H.; and Zaverucha, G. 2017. Neural-symbolic learning and reasoning: A survey and interpretation. *CoRR* abs/1711.03902.

Brewka, G.; Eiter, T.; and Truszczynski, M. 2011. Answer set programming at a glance. *Commun. ACM* 54(12):92–103.

Brown, T. B.; Mann, B.; Ryder, N.; Subbiah, M.; Kaplan, J.; Dhariwal, P.; Neelakantan, A.; Shyam, P.; Sastry, G.; Askell, A.; Agarwal, S.; Herbert-Voss, A.; Krueger, G.; Henighan, T.; Child, R.; Ramesh, A.; Ziegler, D. M.; Wu, J.; Winter, C.; Hesse, C.; Chen, M.; Sigler, E.; Litwin, M.; Gray, S.; Chess, B.; Clark, J.; Berner, C.; McCandlish, S.; Radford, A.; Sutskever, I.; and Amodei, D. 2020. Language models are few-shot learners. In *Procs. of NeurIPS'20*.

Chu, E.; Roy, D.; and Andreas, J. 2020. Are visual explanations useful? A case study in model-in-the-loop prediction. *CoRR* abs/2007.12248.

D'Asaro, F. A.; Spezialetti, M.; Raggioli, L.; and Rossi, S. 2020. Towards an inductive logic programming approach for explaining black-box preference learning systems. In *Procs. of KR'20*, 855–859.

de Sousa Ribeiro, M., and Leite, J. 2021. Aligning artificial neural networks and ontologies towards explainable AI. In *Procs. of AAAI'21*, 4932–4940. AAAI Press.

de Sousa Ribeiro, M.; Krippahl, L.; and Leite, J. 2020. Explainable abstract trains dataset. *CoRR* abs/2012.12115.

Fu, Y.; Yang, L.; Liu, D.; Huang, T. S.; and Shi, H. 2021. Compfeat: Comprehensive feature aggregation for video instance segmentation. In *Procs. of AAAI'21*, 1361–1369. AAAI Press.

Gilpin, L. H.; Bau, D.; Yuan, B. Z.; Bajwa, A.; Specter, M. A.; and Kagal, L. 2018. Explaining explanations: An overview of interpretability of machine learning. In *Procs. of DSAA'18*, 80–89. IEEE.

Guidotti, R.; Monreale, A.; Ruggieri, S.; Turini, F.; Giannotti, F.; and Pedreschi, D. 2019. A survey of methods for explaining black box models. *ACM Comput. Surv.* 51(5):93:1–93:42.

Hitzler, P.; Bianchi, F.; Ebrahimi, M.; and Sarker, M. K. 2020. Neural-symbolic integration and the semantic web. *Semantic Web* 11(1):3–11.

Ignatiev, A.; Narodytska, N.; and Marques-Silva, J. 2019. Abduction-based explanations for machine learning models. In *Procs. of AAAI'19*, 1511–1519. AAAI Press.

Ignatiev, A. 2020. Towards trustable explainable AI. In *Procs. of IJCAI'20*, 5154–5158. ijcai.org.

Ivanovs, M.; Kadikis, R.; and Ozols, K. 2021. Perturbation-based methods for explaining deep neural networks: A survey. *Pattern Recognit. Lett.* 150:228–234.

Kanagaraj, N.; Hicks, D.; Goyal, A.; Tiwari, S. M.; and Singh, G. 2021. Deep learning using computer vision in self driving cars for lane and traffic sign detection. *Int. J. Syst. Assur. Eng. Manag.* 12(6):1011–1025.

Karpathy, A.; Toderici, G.; Shetty, S.; Leung, T.; Sukthankar, R.; and Fei-Fei, L. 2014. Large-scale video classification with convolutional neural networks. In *Procs. of CVPR'14*, 1725–1732. IEEE Computer Society.

Kim, B.; Wattenberg, M.; Gilmer, J.; Cai, C. J.; Wexler, J.; Viégas, F. B.; and Sayres, R. 2018. Interpretability beyond feature attribution: Quantitative testing with concept activation vectors (TCAV). In *Procs. of ICML'18*, volume 80 of *Proceedings of Machine Learning Research*, 2673–2682. PMLR.

Kingma, D. P., and Ba, J. 2015. Adam: A method for stochastic optimization. In *Procs. of ICLR'15*.

Krizhevsky, A., and Hinton, G. 2009. Learning multiple layers of features from tiny images. Technical report, University of Toronto.

Law, M.; Russo, A.; and Broda, K. 2014. Inductive learning of answer set programs. In *Procs. of JELIA'14*, volume 8761 of *Lecture Notes in Computer Science*, 311–325. Springer.

Lehmann, J.; Auer, S.; Bühmann, L.; and Tramp, S. 2011. Class expression learning for ontology engineering. *J. Web Semant.* 9(1):71–81.

Lehmann, J. 2009. Dl-learner: Learning concepts in description logics. *J. Mach. Learn. Res.* 10:2639–2642.

Li, X.; Shi, Y.; Li, H.; Bai, W.; Cao, C. C.; and Chen, L. 2021. An experimental study of quantitative evaluations on saliency methods. In *Procs. of KDD'21*, 3200–3208. ACM.

Lin, Y.; Chen, T.; and Yu, L. 2017. Using machine learning to assist crime prevention. In *Procs. of IIAI-AAI'17*, 1029–1030. IEEE Computer Society.

Miller, T. 2019. Explanation in artificial intelligence: Insights from the social sciences. *Artif. Intell.* 267:1–38.

Montavon, G.; Binder, A.; Lapuschkin, S.; Samek, W.; and Müller, K. 2019. Layer-wise relevance propagation: An overview. In *Explainable AI: Interpreting, Explaining and Visualizing Deep Learning*, volume 11700 of *Lecture Notes in Computer Science*. Springer. 193–209.

Potyka, N. 2021. Interpreting neural networks as quantitative argumentation frameworks. In *Procs. of AAAI'21*, 6463–6470. AAAI Press.

Rebuffi, S.; Fong, R.; Ji, X.; and Vedaldi, A. 2020. There and back again: Revisiting backpropagation saliency methods. In *Procs. of CVPR'20*, 8836–8845. Computer Vision Foundation / IEEE.

Ren, S.; He, K.; Girshick, R. B.; and Sun, J. 2017. Faster R-CNN: towards real-time object detection with region proposal networks. *IEEE Trans. Pattern Anal. Mach. Intell.* 39(6):1137–1149.

Ribeiro, M. T.; Singh, S.; and Guestrin, C. 2016. "why should I trust you?": Explaining the predictions of any classifier. In *Procs. of KDD'16*, 1135–1144. ACM.

Sarker, M. K.; Xie, N.; Doran, D.; Raymer, M. L.; and Hitzler, P. 2017. Explaining trained neural networks with semantic web technologies: First steps. In *Procs. of NeSy'17*, volume 2003 of *CEUR Workshop Proceedings*. CEUR-WS.org.

Schmid, U. 2018. Inductive programming as approach to comprehensible machine learning. In *Procs. of DKB'18 and KIK'18*, volume 2194 of *CEUR Workshop Proceedings*, 4–12. CEUR-WS.org.

Schmitz, G. P. J.; Aldrich, C.; and Gouws, F. S. 1999. ANN-DT: an algorithm for extraction of decision trees from artificial neural networks. *IEEE Trans. Neural Networks* 10(6):1392–1401.

Shakerin, F., and Gupta, G. 2019. Induction of non-monotonic logic programs to explain boosted tree models using LIME. In *Procs. of AAAI'19*, 3052–3059. AAAI Press.

Shakerin, F., and Gupta, G. 2020. White-box induction from SVM models: Explainable AI with logic programming. *Theory Pract. Log. Program.* 20(5):656–670.

Shen, H., and Huang, T. K. 2020. How useful are the machine-generated interpretations to general users? A human evaluation on guessing the incorrectly predicted labels. *CoRR* abs/2008.11721.

Silver, D.; Schrittwieser, J.; Simonyan, K.; Antonoglou, I.; Huang, A.; Guez, A.; Hubert, T.; Baker, L.; Lai, M.; Bolton, A.; Chen, Y.; Lillicrap, T. P.; Hui, F.; Sifre, L.; van den Driessche, G.; Graepel, T.; and Hassabis, D. 2017. Mastering the game of go without human knowledge. *Nat.* 550(7676):354–359.

Sun, W.; Zheng, B.; and Qian, W. 2016. Computer aided lung cancer diagnosis with deep learning algorithms. In *Procs. of MICAD'16*, volume 9785 of *SPIE Proceedings*, 97850Z. SPIE.

Sundararajan, M.; Taly, A.; and Yan, Q. 2017. Axiomatic attribution for deep networks. In *Procs. of ICML'17*, volume 70 of *Proceedings of Machine Learning Research*, 3319–3328. PMLR.

Towell, G. G., and Shavlik, J. W. 1993. Extracting refined rules from knowledge-based neural networks. *Mach. Learn.* 13:71–101.

Tschandl, P.; Rosendahl, C.; and Kittler, H. 2018. The HAM10000 dataset: A large collection of multi-source dermatoscopic images of common pigmented skin lesions. *CoRR* abs/1803.10417.

Wang, M., and Deng, W. 2021. Deep face recognition: A survey. *Neurocomputing* 429:215–244.

Wang, Z.; Mardziel, P.; Datta, A.; and Fredrikson, M. 2020. Interpreting interpretations: Organizing attribution methods by criteria. In *Procs. of CVPR'20 Workshops*, 48–55. Computer Vision Foundation / IEEE.

Zeiler, M. D., and Fergus, R. 2014. Visualizing and understanding convolutional networks. In *Procs. of ECCV'14*, volume 8689 of *Lecture Notes in Computer Science*, 818–833. Springer.

Zilke, J. R.; Mencía, E. L.; and Janssen, F. 2016. Deepred - rule extraction from deep neural networks. In *Procs. of DS'16*, volume 9956 of *Lecture Notes in Computer Science*, 457–473.

Zimmer, M.; Feng, X.; Glanois, C.; Jiang, Z.; Zhang, J.; Weng, P.; Hao, J.; Li, D.; and Liu, W. 2021. Differentiable logic machines. *CoRR* abs/2102.11529.

Proceedings of the 19th International Conference on Principles of Knowledge Representation and Reasoning
Special Session on KR and Machine Learning

A Graph Neural Network Reasoner for Game Description Language

Alvaro Gunawan[1] , **Ji Ruan**[1] , **Xiaowei Huang**[2]
[1]Auckland University of Technology,
[2]University of Liverpool
{alvaro.gunawan, ji.ruan}@aut.ac.nz, xiaowei.huang@liverpool.ac.uk

Abstract

General Game Playing (GGP) aims to develop agents that are able to play any game with only rules given. The game rules are encoded in the Game Description Language (GDL). A GGP player processes the game rules to obtain game states and expand the game tree search for an optimal move. The recent accomplishments of AlphaGo and AlphaZero have triggered new work in extending the neural network approach to GGP. In these works, the neural networks are used only for optimal move selection, while the components dealing with GDL still use the logic-based methods. This motivates us to explore if a neural network based method would be able to approximate the logical inference in GDL with a high accuracy. The structured nature of logic tends to be a difficulty for neural networks, which rely heavily on statistical features. Inspired by the recent work on neural network learning for logical entailments, we propose a neural network based reasoner that is able to learn logical inferences for GDL. We present three key contributions: (i) a general, game-agnostic graph-based representation for game states described in GDL, (ii) methods for generating samples and datasets to frame the GDL inference task as a neural network based machine learning problem and (iii) a GNN based *neural reasoner* that is able to learn and infer various game states with high accuracy and has some capability of transfer learning across games.

1 Introduction

General Game Playing (GGP) (Love et al. 2008) aims to develop agents that are able to play any game with only the rules given. The game rules are encoded in Game Description Language (GDL), a logical language that is a variant of Datalog with function symbols and a few known keywords. In order to play games, the players in GGP parse the game rules using logic-based inferences to obtain game states and expand the game tree to search for an optimal move. These inferences are typically done through Prolog or PropNet (propositional networks) (Schkufza, Love, and Genesereth 2008) implementations. The recent accomplishments of AlphaGo (Silver et al. 2016) and AlphaGo Zero (Silver et al. 2017b) use Monte-Carlo Tree Search (MCTS), deep neural networks and learning through self-play to achieve super-human performance in Go. The generality of this method is extended in AlphaZero(Silver et al. 2017a) to also allow the agent to play Chess and Shogi effectively. However, AlphaZero is limited in that it does not automatically extend to play other games without additional human information and the game types are always assumed to be two-player, turn-taking and zero-sum. In the domain of GGP, an agent must be able to account for games with any number of players, simultaneous action and non-zero-sum, without the aid of human information. GDL serves the purpose of representing such games in a flexible way.

In this paper, we propose methods for a neural network based reasoner that is able to learn logical inferences for GDL. As GDL allows flexible representation of various games, the reasoner has to handle game states with various sizes and features; e.g., a state in Tic-Tac-Toe is quite different to a state in Connect Four. Typical neural network architectures such as multilayer perceptrons and convolutional networks would not be able to capture the general nature of the different state features of various games without introducing unintended biases.

To overcome this, we propose graph-based representations of GDL rules and game states, using a Graph Neural Network (GNN) based architecture for inference. This combination provides an avenue for the development and implementation of GNN based reasoners that are able to learn to infer the rules of general games. We present three key contributions: (i) a general, game-agnostic graph-based representation for game states described in GDL, (ii) methods for generating samples and datasets to frame the GDL inference task as a neural network based machine learning problem and (iii) a GNN based *neural reasoner* that is able to learn and infer various game states with high accuracy and has some capability of transfer learning across games.

The rest of the paper is organised as follows: Section 2 gives an overview of the different components of our neural reasoner. Section 3 describes a general representation for game states in GGP, and in particular we propose *instantiated rule graphs*. Section 4 introduces our proposed GNN architecture that is able to handle the instantiated rule graphs and outputs the predicted legal actions and next fluents. Section 5 presents and discusses the results of our neural reasoner across a variety of games as well as a mixture of games. The neural reasoner is evaluated across a set of games to investigate its generalisation capability. In particular, we find that our reasoner can achieve 100% accuracy in several games and over 80% for the majority. The design of the GNN architecture also allows us to transfer learned

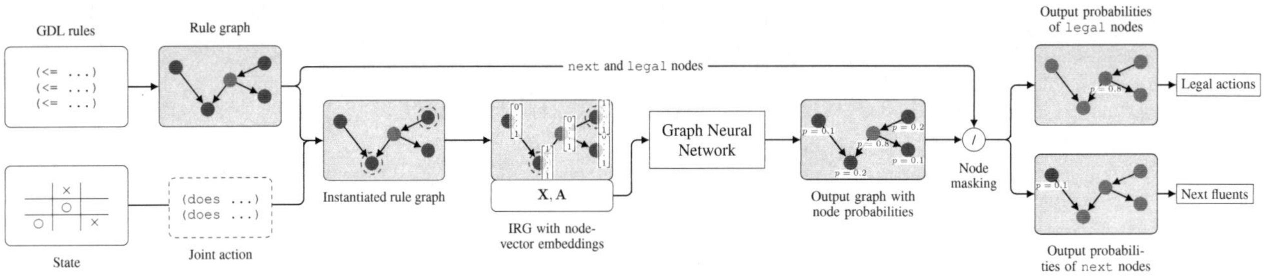

Figure 1: Overview of the Neural Reasoner

knowledge from one game to a different game which we demonstrate with experimental results showing the neural reasoner's transfer learning capability. We discuss in Section 6 related work in graph neural networks and GGP. Finally, we discuss the limitations of the approaches we have presented and conclude with possible future directions for research.

2 Overview of the Neural Reasoner

We first show the inference tasks in GGP that our neural reasoner learns to approximate and then present an overview of the different components in the neural reasoner. Games in the GGP setting are described using Game Description Language (GDL), a logical programming language based on Datalog that can describe game states and mechanics with logical rules. Figure 2 shows an example fragment of the description for game Tic-Tac-Toe. The left rule states that in the next state, `(cell 1 1 o)` is true if `oplayer` does action `(mark 1 1)` and `(cell 1 1 b)` is true in the current state. The right rule states that it is legal for `oplayer` to take the action `(mark 1 1)` if `(cell 1 1 b)` and `(control oplayer)` are true in the current state. A full GDL description of a game will consist of many other rules to define the full dynamics of the game.

```
(<= (next (cell 1 1 o))              (<= (legal oplayer (mark 1 1))
    (does oplayer (mark 1 1))            (true (cell 1 1 b))
    (true (cell 1 1 b)))                 (true (control oplayer)))
```

Figure 2: Fragment of GDL description of Tic-Tac-Toe.

A game state described with GDL consists of a set of dynamic predicates called *fluents*, such as `(cell 1 1 o)`, `(cell 1 1 b)` `(control oplayer)`. A subsequent state (next-state) can be logically derived by the combination of rules, fluents present in the current state and the actions made by the players. Suppose we have a game G, defined as a set of rules in GDL, two key inference tasks are to find out *(1) what are the legal actions for the players at the current state and (2) what is the next state if the agents make a joint move*. Task (1) can be formalized as the following: to find out for each player i, its legal move m at the current state s, as in a logical representation $G \wedge s \models legal(i, m)$. There can be multiple legal actions in a state. Task (2) can be formalized as the following: to find out all the fluent f that holds in the next state, given each player $i \in [1, k]$ doing a move m_i at the current state s, as in a logical representation $G \wedge s \wedge does(1, m_1) \wedge ... \wedge does(k, m_k) \models next(f)$.

Figure 1 gives an overview of the different components in our neural reasoner for GGP. We start with a game described as a set of rules in GDL. It is converted into a rule graph, which is built upon the dependency of the fluents or other predicates in such rules. The rule graph is then combined with a game state into an instantiated rule graph (IRG). We apply a node-vector embedding to the nodes of the IRG to prepare it as input of the Graph Neural Network component. The output of the GNN component is a rule graph with node probabilities. Node masking is then applied based on node type to extract the probabilities of the `legal` and `next` nodes, using information from the input rule graph. During training, the output probabilities are compared to the ground truth training targets to calculate the error for backpropagation. Finally, the nodes with output probabilities greater than a threshold are selected as the legal actions and next fluents.

The training samples, generated by a logical reasoner, are in the form of the pairs $((G, s), S_{\text{legal}})$ for Task (1) and $((G, s, Does), S_{\text{next}})$ for Task (2), where G is a game, s the current state, S_{legal} the set of legal actions, $Does$ the joint action set, and S_{next} the set of fluents true in the next state. Once the graph neural network is trained, we then use it to predict the legal actions and next fluents. In the next two sections, we will provide more details on these components.

3 Game State Representations

A key element of applying neural networks to games is finding a state representation that allows for effective feature extraction, while also being computationally efficient. Typically, these representations consists of a vector, matrix or tensor based structure, depending on the type of neural network architecture used. For example, in Chess or Go, the game board can be directly translated into a matrix, with elements representing the presence of different pieces on the board. These matrices can then be used directly as input to a convolutional neural network, as the grid-structure of the matrix retains the positional information of the various pieces. Although they are effective and efficient, these vector or matrix based representations are "fixed" in size for each game and are not compatible across different games.

As different games described in GDL may have varying sets of possible fluents, a simple vector or matrix is not capable of representing the general features of various game states. Consider the games Tic-Tac-Toe and Connect-Four: one could represent various GDL states by constructing a one-hot vector representing all possible fluents that could be present in a state, such as `cell(1, 1, o)`, `cell(1, 2, x)` and so on. However, as Tic-Tac-Toe and Connect-Four have different numbers of fluents (28 and 127 respectively), these vectors would have different sizes. Likewise, if we were to instead represent a state by mapping its board positions to a matrix, these matrices would also have different sizes. A multilayer perceptron or convolutional neural network would have a fixed size for its input layer and would not be able to take both Tic-Tac-Toe and Connect-Four states as input without additional preprocessing or padding, which may introduce unintended biases. This means a different neural network needs to be trained for each game separately.

In this section, we propose a more general "game-agnostic" representation that suits the domain of GGP better. This representation will be able to fully capture the features present in states, while still allowing for states of various games to be valid inputs for the same neural network. The basis of this representation is a *rule graph*, a graph-based representation of game rules first introduced in (Kuhlmann and Stone 2007), initially used to identify similarity in game descriptions. The rule graph captures the relational inductive biases present in the game rules. We first give the details of rule graphs in section 3.1 and then propose to extend the rule graphs to be a general state representation in section 3.2.

3.1 Rule Graphs

Rule graphs are coloured, directed graphs consisting of four types of nodes: keyword nodes, predicate nodes, label nodes and label argument nodes. *Keyword nodes* represent logical and relational sentences consisting of a predefined GDL keyword such as `legal`, `next`, `does`, etc. *Predicate nodes* represent sentences consisting of non-keyword nodes, i.e., custom defined predicates declared specifically for the game. In the fragment in Figure 1, the predicates `mark` and `cell` are examples of non-keyword predicates. *Label nodes* are used to identify which predicates are the same throughout the description without keeping explicit or specific lexical labels. This is done by drawing an edge from label nodes to each predicate which is an instance of said label. Finally, *label argument nodes* are used to identify the position of arguments in a predicate, encoding the positional information of predicates into the rule graph. Similarly to label nodes, an edge is drawn between the label argument node to each instance of an argument given its position. Additionally, variable nodes can also be included, however for our purposes the game descriptions are initially grounded which instantiates all variables. Edges are drawn between predicates and their arguments, constructing a syntax tree.

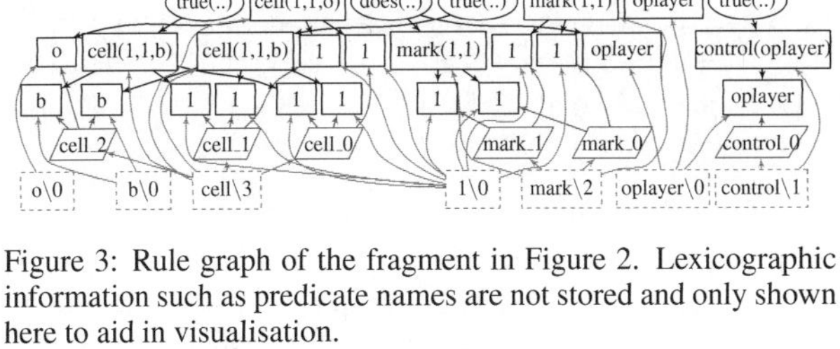

Figure 3: Rule graph of the fragment in Figure 2. Lexicographic information such as predicate names are not stored and only shown here to aid in visualisation.

Figure 3 shows the rule graph generated from the rule fragment presented in Figure 2. Oval nodes are keyword nodes. Rectangular nodes are predicate nodes. Red nodes are label nodes. Blue nodes are label argument nodes. Lexical labels are only for visualisation and are not retained in the actual rule graph. To generate a rule graph from a game description G, we follow the method in (Schiffel 2010):

- Ground all rules to eliminate all variables in G.
- For each logical sentence, relational sentence and predicate in G, create a node in the graph. E.g.,
  - The rule graph in Figure 3 consists of nodes for each keyword and predicate present in the fragment in Figure 2: the keyword `legal` is represented by an oval keyword node and the predicate `(control oplayer)` is represented by a rectangular predicate node.
- Add an edge between each term's node to all the term's argument nodes. For the backwards implication node, add edges from the head node to the body nodes. E.g.,
  - The node `legal(oplayer,mark(1,1))` has edges to its arguments, nodes `oplayer` and `mark(1,1)`. Aditionally, as it is the head argument of a backwards implication node, it has edges to the body nodes `true(control(oplayer))` and `true(cell(1,1,b))`.
- For each unique non-keyword predicate in the game description, create a label node and an edge to each node that represents an instance of that predicate being used. E.g.,
  - As the predicate `mark` is used in both rules, the red `mark\2` label node has edges to each instance of the predicate.
- For each label node's predicate with arity i, create i label argument nodes, representing each possible argument's position. Add an edge from the label node to each corresponding label argument node. Add an edge to each node that represents an argument with the corresponding label argument node according to its position. E.g.,
  - The blue `mark\2` node has two label argument nodes: `mark_0` and `mark_1`.

As the rule graphs only retain the relations and positions of the various predicates without storing actual predicate names, the representation is isomorphic to predicate scrambling. Two different descriptions of the same game that have their predicate names changed would have the same rule graph representation. Additionally, similar features defined in different games would have similar subgraphs within their rule graph representations.

3.2 Instantiated Rule Graphs

Although GDL provides a representation for rules that are general across different games, it does not provide a general *state* representation. Likewise, the rule graphs discussed in the previous section are still only a representation of game rules and are not a general representation of game states. To overcome this limitation, we present *instantiated rule graphs*, a general state representation generated by instantiating the rule graph of a game, localising it to a specific state by providing a unique node labelling for each state.

Definition 3.1. Instantiated Rule Graph. Given a rule graph $R = (V, E)$ and a state $S = \{f_1, f_2, \ldots, f_n\}$ consisting of fluents f_i, an instantiated rule graph is a graph $I = (V, E, L)$ where V, E are the same as in rule graph R and $L_S : V \rightarrow \{false, true\}$ is a labelling function based on state S and the following requirements:

For node n in rule graph R and current state S:

- If node n is a predicate node that corresponds to a fluent in state S and parent node n_p is a `true` node with edge $(n_p, n) \in E$, then nodes $L_S(n) = true$, $L_S(n_p) = true$ and $L_S(n_c) = true$ for all children nodes given $(n, n_c) \in E$.
- For all other nodes, $L_S(n_o) = false$.

Figure 4 shows the rule graph from Figure 3 instantiated to a state S where fluent `cell(1,1,b)` $\in S$. Nodes labelled $true$ are shaded in blue. All other nodes are labelled $false$. A benefit of the instantiated rule graphs is that any modifications or improvements can be made to the labelling function without loss of generality across all games.

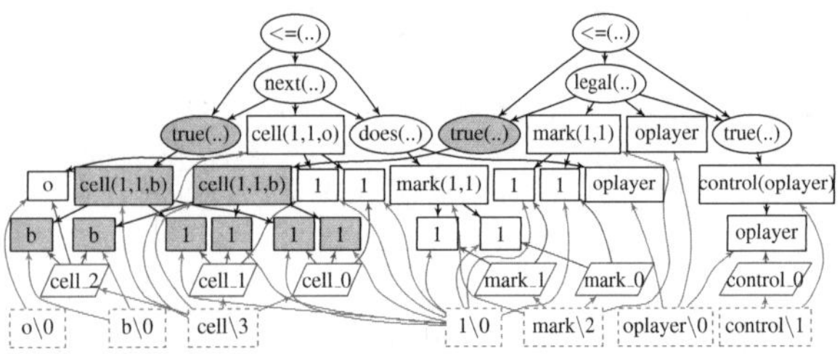

Figure 4: An example of an instantiated rule graph

4 Neural Network Architecture

This section outlines the neural network architecture used with instantiated rule graphs. Firstly we introduce our strategy of embedding the node features into a vector. Secondly, we provide details of the graph neural network based architecture. Thirdly, we present a general method of generating datasets for different games. Finally, we provide details on the training of the neural network itself.

4.1 Node-Vector Embeddings

To prepare the instantiated rule graph as input for a neural network, we convert the labelling and the node types into a vector embedding. For node $n \in V$ in instantiated rule graph $I = (V, E, L)$, we construct a vector embedding $\vec{v}^n \in \{0, 1\}^{19}$. This embedding provides a general fixed length vector that can represent without ambiguity the various types of nodes and labelling present in an instantiated rule graph. The first value of the vector directly corresponds to the labelling function, with $true$ and $false$ represented by values 1 and 0 directly. The rest of the vector acts as a one-hot encoding representing the type of node, with the first four corresponding to the non-keyword node types and the rest corresponding to the keywords present in GDL. Table 1 shows the node feature that each value $\vec{V}_{1\ldots19}$ corresponds to.

Index	Node Embedding
1	True in state (label)
2	Constant symbol
3	Variable symbol
4	Predicate
5	Variable

(a) Label and non-keywords

Index	Node Embedding
6	`<=`
7	`not`
8	`or`
9	`distinct`
10	`does`
11	`goal`
12	`init`
13	`legal`
14	`next`
15	`role`
16	`terminal`
17	`true`
18	`input`
19	`base`

(b) Keywords

Table 1: Vector embedding values

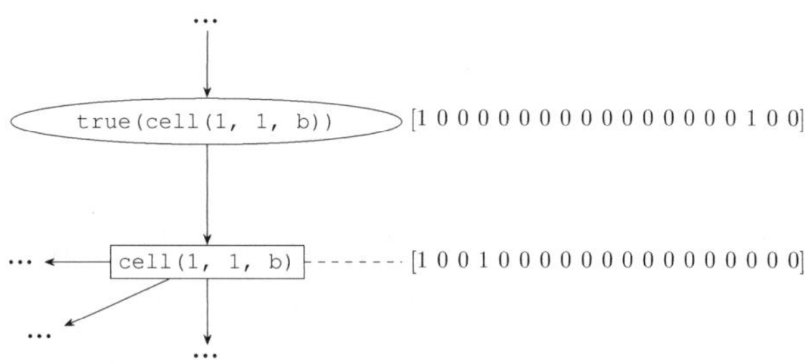

Figure 5: Example vector embedding of two nodes of the instantiated rule graph from Figure 4.

Figure 5 shows an example of a vector embedding of the `cell(1, 1, b)` nodes in the instantiated rule graph from Figure 4. Note that as the node is a predicate node, the value of $\vec{v}_4^n = 1$. The node `true(cell(1, 1, b))` is a `true` keyword node, resulting in the value of $\vec{v}_{17}^n = 1$. Both nodes are labelled $true$ by the labelling function, so both vectors will have the value $\vec{v}_1^n = 1$.

The vector embeddings of all nodes in the graph are then stacked to create node feature matrix $\mathbf{X} \in \{0, 1\}^{|V| \times 19}$. Alongside the adjacency matrix of the graph $\mathbf{A}$, the node feature matrix $\mathbf{X}$ is used as the input for the graph neural network described in the next section.

4.2 Graph Neural Network Architecture

As the game state representation we have discussed in the previous section is defined as a graph, we use a graph neural network. The overall architecture of our GNN, shown

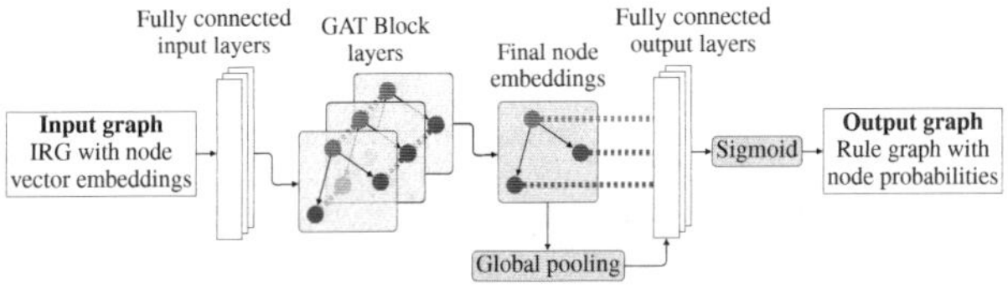

Figure 6: Architecture of Our Graph Neural Network

in Figure 6, consists of three distinct layers: an initial set of fully connected input embedding layers, a set of 3 GAT Block layers and finally a set of fully connected output layers. The GAT Blocks consist of two pairs of Graph Attention Networks (GAT) (Veličković et al. 2018) acting as bidirectional edge layers, a skip connection and ReLU nonlinearity.

An input IRG with node vector embeddings is first passed through a set of fully connected input layers, attending only to individual node embeddings. Then, the graph is passed through a set of GAT Blocks, propogating messages to update the node embeddings. After the last GAT Block, final node embeddings are generated. Global soft attention (Li et al. 2016) is applied across the final node embeddings to pool into a graph-level embedding. This graph-level embedding is combined with each individual final node embedding and passed through the fully connected output layers. Lastly a sigmoid activation is used to provide the final output node probabilities.

We chose the Graph Attention Network architecture for the graph neural network layers as they provided the best balance between performance and memory usage. Experiments with other architectures such as Graph Convolutional Networks (Kipf and Welling 2017) exhibited worse performance, while more complex architectures such as Directed Acyclic Graph Neural Networks (Thost and Chen 2021) restricted the size of games that were usable while providing minimal improvement in performance.

4.3 Dataset Generation

To train the neural network, we require a dataset of training samples containing game states and the inferred legal actions and next fluents. Using the definition of IRGs and node-vector embeddings, we propose a general method of generating training datasets for a game described in GDL.

To generate a dataset, the GDL description of the selected game G is used to play out random games. As new states are visited throughout the game plays, we store the states as instantiated rule graphs and use a Prolog based reasoner to generate ground truth logical inferences for the states as the training target. While inferring the legal actions only requires the fluents of a state, inferring the fluents present in the next state additionally requires the actions selected. To account for this, we additionally store a randomly selected legal joint action in a given state. The training targets for each example is the truth valuations of the `legal` and `next` rules for a given state or state and joint action pair respectively. These correspond directly to the `legal` and `next` nodes present in the IRG. The task of the neural network is then to learn to approximate a function that converts each initial node-vector embedding into an output probability. As such, the dataset can be seen as a partial node classification task across multiple graphs.

Game	IRG size		Outdegree		Mean path
	Nodes	Edges	Max	Mean	length
blocker	5087	12201	559	2.40	4.23
connectfour (C4)	19672	47221	2249	2.40	4.33
connectfour3p ($C4_{3p}$)	17076	42623	1731	2.50	4.25
hamilton	14963	31516	1601	2.11	5.27
hanoi6disks	28055	70237	4098	2.50	4.98
knightstour	12291	30154	1393	2.45	4.45
parallelbuttonsandlights	1602	3245	182	2.03	4.93
tictactoe (TTT)	4810	11031	591	2.29	4.19
doubletictactoe (TTT_D)	7379	16338	803	2.21	4.61
tictactoelarge (TTT_L)	3553	8185	323	2.30	4.69
connectfour-flat	21450	51477	2543	2.40	4.29
doubletictactoe-flat	27280	64342	2583	2.36	4.52
tictactoelarge-flat	4203	9735	423	2.32	4.60

Table 2: Graph metrics of game datasets

In our implementation, a game description G is used to generate dataset $\mathcal{D}_G$ consisting of training examples of the form $((\mathbf{X}, \mathbf{A}), \vec{l})$ for legal actions and $((\mathbf{X}_a, \mathbf{A}), \vec{n})$ for next fluents. For a given state S and joint action $a = does(1, m_1) \wedge \ldots \wedge does(k, m_k)$, $\mathbf{X}$ is the node feature matrix of IRG $I = (V, E, L)$ of S and $\mathbf{X}_a$ is the the node feature matrix of the IRG $I_a = (V, E, L_a)$ of S with `does` nodes labelled $true$ according to actions a in addition to the standard fluent labelling. $\mathbf{A}$ is the adjacency matrix of IRGs I and I_a. The training targets $\vec{l} = \{0,1\}^{|V|}$ and $\vec{n} = \{0,1\}^{|V|}$ are the target output probabilities of the nodes V that the network must predict. As $\mathbf{X}_i$ corresponds to node i, if node i is a `legal` node, $\vec{l_i} = 1$ if the valuation of the legal rule represented by node i is $true$ and $\vec{l_i} = 0$ otherwise. Likewise, for `next` node j, $\vec{n}_j = 1$ if the valuation of the next rule represented by node j is $true$ and $\vec{n}_j = 0$ otherwise.

The above method is general and can be applied to any game described using GDL. For the experiments in Section 5, we generate 12000 training examples for each game. Although the datasets are generated on a per-game basis for simplicity, multiple datasets can be combined for multi-game mixed training or sequential training.

Table 2 shows some metrics of the IRGs present in the game datasets generated. Although the IRGs are directed graphs, we calculate the average path length by treating them as undirected graphs as the graph neural network architecture is able to propagate messages along both directions separately. While the size of the IRG gives a sense of the complexity of the game description, it is distinct from the state complexity of the game itself. These metrics highlight the discrepancy between game state complexity and game description complexity. For example, while TTT_L has a larger number of game states compared to standard TTT due to its larger board size, the IRG for TTT_L is smaller in both the number of nodes and edges. These metrics correspond roughly to the complexity of the game description, as the IRG size corresponds directly to the number and length of rules present in the description, while the average path length corresponds to the average distance of logical dependencies present in the rules. In the end of the table, G-flat refers to an equivalent game of G, which we examine later in Section 5.4.

We have only generated the datasets for 10 different games which are typically used in GGP tournaments, but there are many other game descriptions that exist in various repositories such as the Stanford [1] and Dresden[2] GGP repositories. Explanations of game rules and example game plays can also be found on these repositories. Descriptions for more complex games like Chess and Go are also available, but due to hardware limitations we avoid using these games for our experiments. Additional game descriptions can be written for games that do not have a description already available. This presents an opportunity to provide an extensive benchmark for the inference tasks in GDL, which we encourage others to use in further graph neural network research.

4.4 Training Details

We train the neural network using the cross-entropy loss criterion for both legal action and next fluent prediction. Only `legal` and `next` node output probabilities are used in the calculations for the cross-entropy loss, with other nodes masked out. These other nodes contribute to the loss values implicitly through the message propagation mechanism in the GAT layers and the global pooling operator. The Adam optimiser (Kingma and Ba 2015) is used with a base learning rate of 0.0001 and dropout is applied to the fully connected layers during training. Additionally, we use Pairnorm (Zhao and Akoglu 2020) normalisation throughout the graph neural network layers.

The neural reasoner is trained on datasets generated from various games with 10% of each dataset reserved as a validation split. A batch size of 32 examples are used for most games, however for larger game descriptions a smaller batch size is used due to hardware limitations. Once the network training is complete, threshold values for `next` and `legal` node probabilities are selected. For each task, threshold values $0.1, 0.15, 0.2, \ldots, 0.9$ are used to discretise the output probabilities, selecting the threshold value that provides the lowest mean squared error between the discretised output probabilities and the examples from the validation set. These selected threshold values are used for each game during evaluation.

5 Results and Discussion

We conduct a series of experiments to evaluate the performance of the neural reasoner on a collection of games and to investigate training behaviour in a variety of settings and learning modalities. Section 5.1 presents the performance of the neural reasoner trained on individual games. Section 5.2 investigates the neural reasoner's ability to transfer its learned knowledge across to different games as well as a mixed training scheme with multiple games being learned simultaneously. Section 5.3 compares the mixed training scheme with a sequential training scheme. Finally, Section 5.4 present a solution to the issues faced with unflattened rules that causes poorer performance in certain games.

All experiments are conducted on an Intel Xeon Silver 4210 CPU with 96 GB of memory running Ubuntu 20.04.2 LTS and 4 NVIDIA GeForce RTX2080 Ti. The implementation is written in Python using the PyTorch Geometric library (Fey and Lenssen 2019) and PySwip (Tekol and contributors 2020).

5.1 Individual Game Experiments

As the networks are trained to predict `legal` actions and `next` fluents, we measure the accuracy of the neural reasoner over 100 randomly played games. For a given input state, the predicted legal actions and next fluents are given by the neural reasoner's output node probabilities that are greater than the selected threshold. This is then compared to the ground truth which is inferred with a Prolog based reasoner.

Game	Next fluents (%)	Legal actions (%)
parallelbuttonsandlights	84.35%	100.00%
tictactoe (TTT)	100.00%	100.00%
tictactoelarge (TTT_L)	100.00%	63.69%
doubletictactoe (TTT_D)	100.00%	91.96%
connectfour (C4)	93.58%	100.00%
connectfour3p ($C4_{3p}$)	95.50%	91.75%
blocker	88.94%	100.00%
knightstour	100.00%	100.00%
hamilton	94.94%	100.00%
hanoi6disks	87.55%	72.66%

Table 3: Neural reasoner accuracy over 100 games.

Table 3 shows the accuracy of the neural reasoner on 10 different games, over 100 game plays on each. Across all games, the neural reasoner shows fairly high accuracy, achieving 100% at several games and at least 80% accuracy in most games. Notable exceptions are TTT_L and hanoi6disks at legal prediction, which we investigate further in Section 5.4.

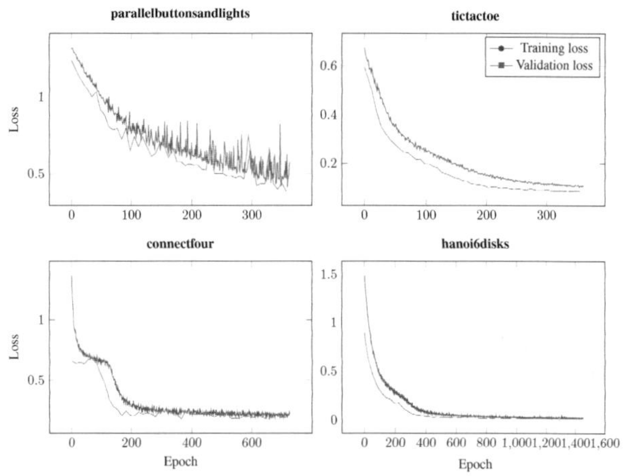

Figure 7: Training loss for parallelbuttonsandlights, tictactoe, connectfour and hanoi6disks.

[1]http://ggp.stanford.edu

[2]http://general-game-playing.de

Figure 7 shows that the training behaviour across four different games. The differences exhibited here also contribute to the varying levels of accuracy that the neural reasoner achieves for different games. Dropout is not applied when calculating the validation loss, leading to the the lower values. The differences in epochs correspond to smaller batch sizes due to hardware limitations as mentioned earlier in Section 4.4.

5.2 Transfer and Mixed Learning

To evaluate the neural reasoner's transfer learning capabilities, we run evaluations across the following games: Tic-Tac-Toe (TTT), Connect-Four (C4), Double Tic-Tac-Toe (TTT_D) and Tic-Tac-Toe Large (TTT_L). We evaluate the neural reasoner on games it has not learned. Additionally, we conduct mixed training, where the reasoner is trained on all four games simultaneously with a uniform random mixture of game states. All networks are initialised with random weights. Table 4 shows the results of the training conducted. Interestingly, the results have shown the potential to achieve "zero-step generalisation" as the network is able to achieve 100% accuracy on several games that it was not trained for, which ideally shows that the network is learning to reason GDL more generally. However we can see that in several cases this transfer does not occur, such as the network trained on TTT_L which shows poor performance across all other games.

The network trained on all games jointly shows balanced performance across the board - notably it outperforms the C4 trained network on C4 itself on `next` prediction and achieves equal or comparable performance in other games. This shows that mixed training can be used to train a neural reasoner that can reason multiple games simultaneously with high accuracy.

5.3 Sequential vs Mixed Training

While the mixed-game training shows that the neural reasoner can achieve similar accuracy to its solely trained counterpart, the method in which the examples are mixed might not be practical or well-suited for all game-playing scenarios. In particular, we would like to see if a *sequential training* scheme is possible. Rather than mixing the examples from various games into a single dataset, the network is trained on the different game datasets sequentially. There are two questions this raises: Firstly, does the sequential training cause the network to "forget" the earlier trained games? Secondly, can the prior training on other games assist the later training, leading to faster convergence? To answer this, we train a neural reasoner on the game sequence $TTT \rightarrow TTT_D \rightarrow TTT_L \rightarrow$ C4 and compare its accuracy to mixed training.

Table 5 shows the accuracy of the sequentially trained neural reasoner compared to the mixed training reasoner. The sequentially trained neural reasoner shows similar performance to the mixed trained neural reasoner. This shows that the network does not "forget" its learned reasoning on earlier games after training on the other games. Like with the mixed neural reasoner, the network shows balanced performance across the games it is trained on when compared to the individually trained networks as in Section 5.2.

However, as Figure 8 shows, the sequentially trained neural reasoner exhibits much more instability during training as can be seen in the fluctuating validation loss. The sequentially trained network is still able to achieve final loss values equivalent to the mixed training counterpart despite the instability. The random mixing of various game states likely acts as a type of regularisation, whereas the sequential training can potentially lead to overfitting on each individual game before moving on to the next. Regardless, sequential training presents an alternative training scheme when mixing is not possible or impractical.

5.4 Rule Flattening

Of note in Section 5.1 was the relatively poor performance of the variants of TTT, namely TTT_D and TTT_L, when compared to default TTT. We discovered that a potential cause

Training method		TTT	TTT_D	TTT_L	C4
Mixed	Next	100.00%	100.00%	100.00%	98.00%
	Legal	100.00%	82.62%	55.80%	100.00%
Sequential	Next	100.00%	100.00%	92.52%	93.63%
	Legal	100.00%	82.35%	64.45%	100.00%

Table 5: Neural reasoner accuracy in mixed and sequential trainings.

Train dataset	TTT	TTT_D	TTT_L	C4
TTT	100.00%	100.00%	100.00%	93.45%
TTT_D	100.00%	100.00%	94.77%	93.53%
TTT_L	40.66%	41.06%	100.0%	40.92%
C4	100.00%	94.68%	92.49%	93.58%
Mixed	100.00%	100.00%	100.00%	98.00%

(a)

Train dataset	TTT	TTT_D	TTT_L	C4
TTT	100.00%	1.35%	56.02%	100.00%
TTT_D	91.36%	91.96%	64.66%	89.71%
TTT_L	59.02%	14.18%	63.69%	12.85%
C4	100.00%	1.39%	56.47%	100.00%
Mixed	100.00%	82.62%	55.80%	100.00%

(b)

Table 4: Neural reasoner accuracy over 100 games for (a) `next` and (b) `legal` prediction.

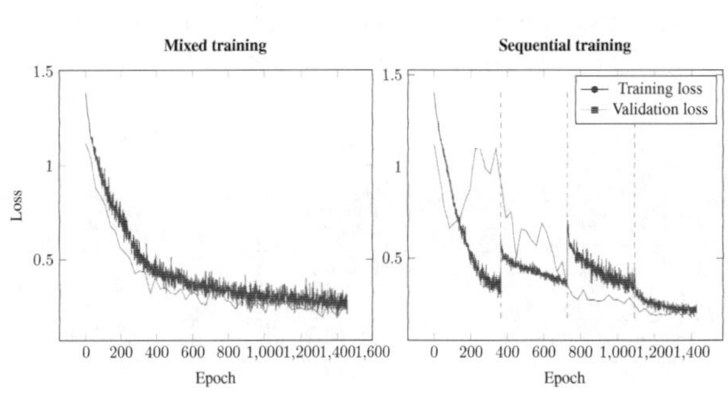

Figure 8: Comparison of mixed training and sequential training. Dashed lines show dataset transitions.

for this disparity is in the way some rules are defined. In TTT, all of the legal and next rules are defined in a *flat* manner, with the heads (legal or next predicates) directly depending on fluents that represent the basic features of the states. However, in other games such as TTT_D and TTT_L, several of the legal and next predicates have a longer dependency on fluents via other intermediate predicates.

For example, in the rule fragments shown in Figure 9, the left two rules are from the standard description of TTT_L. The legal predicate `legal(.)` in the first rule depends on the predicate `emptycell(.)`, which is not a fluent and further depends on the fluent `cell(.)` in the second rule. While in the rule on the right, the legal predicate `legal(.)` directly depends on the fluent `cell(.)`. We give simple flattening as a process analogous to substitution, inserting the body of the second rule into the first rule. In particular, `emptycell(.)` is replaced with its corresponding body. This process shall retain the equivalence of the games.

```
(<= (legal xplayer (mark 1 1 x))
    (true (control xplayer))
    (emptycell 1 1))

(<= (emptycell 1 1)
    (index 1)
    (index 1)
    (not (true (cell 1 1 x)))
    (not (true (cell 1 1 o))))
```

```
(<= (legal xplayer (mark 1 1 x))
    (true (control xplayer))
    (index 1)
    (index 1)
    (not (true (cell 1 1 x)))
    (not (true (cell 1 1 o))))
```

Figure 9: Left: Standard definition of rules in TTT_L. Right: Flattened version of the same rules

Figure 10 shows the rule graphs of the unflattened and flattened rules, highlighting the effect of this process: the dependency path from the `legal(..)` node to the fluent `cell(1,1,x)` node reduces from 6 in unflattened version to 3 in the flattened version. This shortened dependency between nodes can be seen when comparing the average path lengths of the unflattened and flattened versions of the same game in Table 2 (last three rows), with all the flattened versions showing shorter average paths lengths than their unflattened counterparts.

To test whether the poor performance seen in some games is caused by the behaviour seen in unflattened rules, we train and evaluate the neural reasoner on the flattened versions and compare the performance to the standard, unflattened versions. Table 6 shows the improved accuracy of the neural reasoner trained on flattened rules compared to the standard unflattened rules, on the three games.

These results suggest that the distance of the dependency of legal and next predicates to the fluents is an important factor in our representation and flattening the rules could reduce the distance and potentially increase overall performance of the neural reasoner. Some limitation of this approach is that a systematic automated flattening process can be difficult, e.g., with recursively defined rules and exponential growth of the number of the rules. Note that game hanoi6disks also exhibited a large number of unflattened legal rules, which could not be easily flattened.

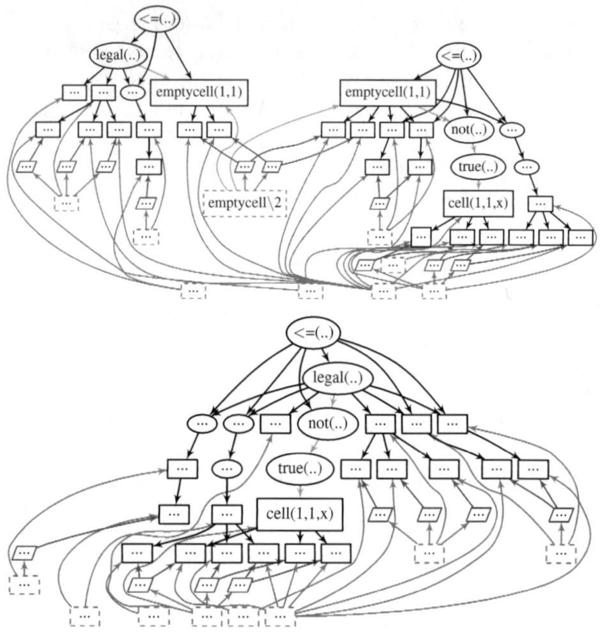

Figure 10: Rule graphs of unflattened (top) and flattened (bottom) fragment from Figure 9. Labels have been removed for clarity.

Game	Next fluents accuracy	Legal actions
TTT-L (standard)	100.00%	63.69%
TTT-L (flat)	100.00%	100.00%
TTT-D (standard)	100.00%	91.96%
TTT-D (flat)	100.00%	100.00%
C4 (standard)	93.58%	100.00%
C4 (flat)	100.00%	100.00%

Table 6: Terminal prediction for 100 games of standard and flattened games

6 Related Work

Work in the 90s and early 2000s on the modelling of logic programming using neural networks (Garcez and Zaverucha 1999; Abdullah 1992; Garcez et al. 2002) laid the foundations of neuro-symbolic computing - the synthesis of logic and neural networks. Early work in the field rely on directly translating the logical statements to the neural network structure itself.

Recently, there has been a resurgence in applying neural network based methods to logical domains, following their successes in computer vision and natural language processing. This more recent work focuses on using the logical statements themselves as input to the neural networks, allowing for more general neural network architectures. However, the structured nature of logic tends to be a difficulty for neural networks, which rely heavily on statistical features. Evans et al. introduced a dataset of logical entailment examples to train and evaluate neural network architectures on (Evans et al. 2018), as well as their model PossibleWorldNet which was able to outperform several benchmarks. Rawson and Reger (Rawson and Reger 2020) were able to further extend this by taking advantage of the relational inductive bias present in the logical dataset. Their work presented a

GNN-based architecture and a graph based encoding for the logical statements, which combined was able to outperform PossibleWorldNet in several of the categories of the dataset.

Beyond the two mentioned earlier, many other researchers have applied graph neural networks to the logical domain (Thost and Chen 2021; Abdelaziz et al. 2021; Glorot et al. 2019; Paliwal et al. 2020; Crouse et al. 2019; Olšák, Kaliszyk, and Urban 2019). Most work in the logical domain focus on tasks such as entailment and automated theorem proving, which typically uses much smaller graphs as the logical formulae consist of fewer clauses than an entire GDL game description. Additionally, these tasks are typically formulated as a graph classification problem, which differs from our approach, which is more akin to a node classification problem across multiple graphs.

Some recent work such as (Silver et al. 2020; Lin et al. 2022) has applied graph neural networks to planning problems. However, most work in this field typically use graphical representations of the objects in the environment and their relationships instead of directly modelling a logical description. As such, the GNNs are tasked to learn the importance and probabilities of the objects themselves, rather than learning to infer legal actions or transition dynamics.

Some of the most notable recent work applying neural network based approaches to games is that of AlphaGo, AlphaGo Zero and AlphaZero (Silver et al. 2016; Silver et al. 2017b; Silver et al. 2017a), which were able to achieve super-human performance on Go, Chess and Shogi. The networks were used for policy and value estimation and trained through self-play. Although the architecture presented in AlphaZero was general across the three games, the networks had were specific for each game and had to be trained separately due to the varying state representations. Several recent work (Goldwaser and Thielscher 2020; Gunawan et al. 2020) have extended the methods in AlphaZero to the domain of GGP and shown their effectiveness. The neural networks are used similarly as in AlphaZero for optimal move selection and are specific for individual games too. There are two main differences in our work. Firstly our graph neural networks are able to handle the game states more generally. Secondly, we use neural networks in approximating the logical reasoning, instead of the move selection.

Alongside the initial introduction of rule graphs by Kuhlmann and Stone (Kuhlmann and Stone 2007), they have also investigated other applications of transfer learning in GGP. In their work rule graphs are used to identify similar games, to which they transfer known value mappings for Q-learning. Schiffel (Schiffel 2010) further extends this work and uses rule graphs for symmetry detection within games. As these make use of standard rule graphs, they do not apply their methods to individual game states. Additionally, they do not make use of graph neural networks, instead using more traditional approaches such as graph isomorphism algorithms.

7 Limitations

The current implementation of instantiating the rule graph as described can be improved both in expressiveness and efficiency. Firstly, the most effective labelling function for instantiating the rule graph is still not known and the current implementation can be improved for a more expressive representation. Secondly, the current instantiation method requires the game description to be grounded, which is a computationally expensive process that can lead to extremely large graphs. It is possible that only targeted rules need to be grounded instead, as the rule graph representation is capable of representing ungrounded variables.

A key limitation we have discovered is the poor performance of the neural reasoner on games that are described using unflattened rules. We found that by flattening these rules, the neural reasoner was able to improve its accuracy. However, as mentioned before, this flattening process is resource intensive. Furthermore, there are several games where this flattening is not possible without completely rewriting the rules. More generally, this issue is likely due to the graph neural network architecture being unable to make inferences across long-range dependencies. This also includes other relational structures such as negation, which can be seen as a two-hop dependency.

Currently, we have only trained the neural reasoner to predict legal actions and next fluents. To implement a complete GDL reasoner, we also need to infer whether a state is terminal and the goal values of each player when the state is terminal. We leave this as an open problem as there are issues that arise from the unbalanced nature of the dataset (there are more non-terminal states than terminal states) as well as the limitations faced due to unflattened rules (most terminal and goal rules are unflattened).

8 Conclusion and Further Work

In this paper we have presented a method to approach GDL reasoning with neural networks in a general manner. The translation of the GDL rules and game states to a graph-based representation allows for the application of graph neural networks that are able take as input various games without resorting to game-specific networks. We have implemented a neural reasoner that is able to learn to infer the legal actions and next fluents in various games, with high accuracy in most of them. Furthermore, we show that with the general instantiated rule graph representation and graph neural network architecture, we are able to train the neural reasoner on multiple games simultaneously as well as transfer across unlearned games. Sequential training is also possible: the neural reasoner is able to be trained on a sequence of various games without forgetting the earlier trained games. This is likely the most practical method of training a neural reasoner for use in a game player, as this allows the neural reasoner to learn new games as they are introduced to it. However, we have highlighted several limitations.

While the instantiated rule graph representation and the graph neural network architectures have been used to learn the reasoning task in this paper, further work could extend these methods to apply them to the task of game playing. Using a modified network architecture based on these approaches in an AlphaZero style self-learning agent would allow for the agent to learn and play multiple game simultaneously, in a truly general manner.

References

Abdelaziz, I.; Crouse, M.; Makni, B.; Austil, V.; Cornelio, C.; Ikbal, S.; Kapanipathi, P.; Makondo, N.; Srinivas, K.; Witbrock, M.; et al. 2021. Learning to guide a saturation-based theorem prover. *arXiv preprint arXiv:2106.03906*.

Abdullah, W. A. T. W. 1992. Logic programming on a neural network. *International journal of intelligent systems* 7(6):513–519.

Crouse, M.; Abdelaziz, I.; Cornelio, C.; Thost, V.; Wu, L.; Forbus, K.; and Fokoue, A. 2019. Improving graph neural network representations of logical formulae with subgraph pooling. *arXiv preprint arXiv:1911.06904*.

Evans, R.; Saxton, D.; Amos, D.; Kohli, P.; and Grefenstette, E. 2018. Can neural networks understand logical entailment? *arXiv preprint arXiv:1802.08535*.

Fey, M., and Lenssen, J. E. 2019. Fast graph representation learning with pytorch geometric. *CoRR* abs/1903.02428.

Garcez, Artur S d'Avila, A. S., and Zaverucha, G. 1999. The connectionist inductive learning and logic programming system. *Applied Intelligence* 11(1):59–77.

Garcez, A. S. d.; Broda, K.; Gabbay, D. M.; et al. 2002. *Neural-symbolic learning systems: foundations and applications*. Springer Science & Business Media.

Glorot, X.; Anand, A.; Aygun, E.; Mourad, S.; Kohli, P.; and Precup, D. 2019. Learning representations of logical formulae using graph neural networks. In *Neural Information Processing Systems, Workshop on Graph Representation Learning*.

Goldwaser, A., and Thielscher, M. 2020. Deep reinforcement learning for general game playing. In *AAAI*, 1701–1708.

Gunawan, A.; Ruan, J.; Thielscher, M.; and Narayanan, A. 2020. Exploring a learning architecture for general game playing. In *AI 2020: Advances in Artificial Intelligence - 33rd Australasian Joint Conference, AI 2020, Proceedings*, 294–306. Springer.

Kingma, D. P., and Ba, J. 2015. Adam: A method for stochastic optimization. In Bengio, Y., and LeCun, Y., eds., *3rd International Conference on Learning Representations, ICLR 2015, San Diego, CA, USA, May 7-9, 2015, Conference Track Proceedings*.

Kipf, T. N., and Welling, M. 2017. Semi-supervised classification with graph convolutional networks. In *International Conference on Learning Representations (ICLR)*.

Kuhlmann, G., and Stone, P. 2007. Graph-based domain mapping for transfer learning in general games. In *European Conference on Machine Learning*, 188–200. Springer.

Li, Y.; Tarlow, D.; Brockschmidt, M.; and Zemel, R. S. 2016. Gated graph sequence neural networks. In Bengio, Y., and LeCun, Y., eds., *4th International Conference on Learning Representations, ICLR 2016, San Juan, Puerto Rico, May 2-4, 2016, Conference Track Proceedings*.

Lin, Y.; Wang, A. S.; Undersander, E.; and Rai, A. 2022. Efficient and interpretable robot manipulation with graph neural networks. *IEEE Robotics and Automation Letters*.

Love, N.; Hinrichs, T.; Haley, D.; Schkufza, E.; and Genesereth, M. 2008. General game playing: Game description language specification.

Olšák, M.; Kaliszyk, C.; and Urban, J. 2019. Property invariant embedding for automated reasoning. *arXiv preprint arXiv:1911.12073*.

Paliwal, A.; Loos, S.; Rabe, M.; Bansal, K.; and Szegedy, C. 2020. Graph representations for higher-order logic and theorem proving. In *Proceedings of the AAAI Conference on Artificial Intelligence*, volume 34(03), 2967–2974.

Rawson, M., and Reger, G. 2020. Directed graph networks for logical entailment. Technical report, EasyChair.

Schiffel, S. 2010. Symmetry detection in general game playing. In *Twenty-Fourth AAAI Conference on Artificial Intelligence*.

Schkufza, E.; Love, N.; and Genesereth, M. 2008. Propositional automata and cell automata: Representational frameworks for discrete dynamic systems. In *Australasian Joint Conference on Artificial Intelligence*, 56–66. Springer.

Silver, D.; Huang, A.; Maddison, C. J.; Guez, A.; Sifre, L.; Van Den Driessche, G.; Schrittwieser, J.; Antonoglou, I.; Panneershelvam, V.; Lanctot, M.; et al. 2016. Mastering the game of go with deep neural networks and tree search. *nature* 529(7587):484.

Silver, D.; Hubert, T.; Schrittwieser, J.; Antonoglou, I.; Lai, M.; Guez, A.; Lanctot, M.; Sifre, L.; Kumaran, D.; Graepel, T.; et al. 2017a. Mastering chess and shogi by self-play with a general reinforcement learning algorithm. *arXiv preprint arXiv:1712.01815*.

Silver, D.; Schrittwieser, J.; Simonyan, K.; Antonoglou, I.; Huang, A.; Guez, A.; Hubert, T.; Baker, L.; Lai, M.; Bolton, A.; et al. 2017b. Mastering the game of go without human knowledge. *nature* 550(7676):354–359.

Silver, T.; Chitnis, R.; Curtis, A.; Tenenbaum, J.; Lozano-Perez, T.; and Kaelbling, L. P. 2020. Planning with learned object importance in large problem instances using graph neural networks. *arXiv preprint arXiv:2009.05613*.

Tekol, Y., and contributors. 2020. PySwip v0.2.10.

Thost, V., and Chen, J. 2021. Directed acyclic graph neural networks. In *International Conference on Learning Representations*.

Veličković, P.; Cucurull, G.; Casanova, A.; Romero, A.; Liò, P.; and Bengio, Y. 2018. Graph Attention Networks. *International Conference on Learning Representations*.

Zhao, L., and Akoglu, L. 2020. Pairnorm: Tackling oversmoothing in gnns. In *International Conference on Learning Representations*.

Proceedings of the 19th International Conference on Principles of Knowledge Representation and Reasoning
Special Session on KR and Machine Learning

Sum-Product Loop Programming: From Probabilistic Circuits to Loop Programming

Viktor Pfanschilling[1], **Hikaru Shindo**[1], **Devendra Singh Dhami**[1,3], **Kristian Kersting**[1,2,3]
[1]Computer Science Department, Technical University of Darmstadt, Germany
[2]Center for Cognitive Science, Technical University of Darmstadt, Germany
[3]Hessian Center for AI, Darmstadt, Germany
{viktor.pfanschilling, hikaru.shindo, devendra.dhami, kersting}@cs.tu-darmstadt.de

Abstract

Recently, Probabilistic Circuits such as Sum-Product Networks have received growing attention, as they can represent complex features but still provide tractable inference. Although quite successful, unfortunately, they lack the capability of handling control structures, such as for and while loops. In this work, we introduce Sum-Product Loop Language (SPLL), a novel programming language that is capable of tractable inference on complex probabilistic code that includes loops. SPLL has dual semantics: every program has generative semantics familiar to most programmers and probabilistic semantics that assign a probability to each possible result. This way, the programmer can describe how to generate samples almost like in any standard programming language. The language takes care of computing the probability values of all results for free at run time. We demonstrate that SPLL inherits the beneficial properties of PCs, namely tractability and differentiability, while generalizing to other distributions and programs, and retains substantial computational similarities.

1 Introduction

Sum-Product Networks (SPNs) can be viewed as a deep learning architecture as well as a graphical model with tractable inference (Poon and Domingos 2011). SPNs are based on the concept of modeling network polynomials and are closely related to arithmetic circuits (Darwiche 2003). They exploit the efficiency of deep learning while abstracting the representation of the underlying model by implementing compositions of functions. As a result of such compositions, SPNs can model different distributions efficiently when compared to pure deep learning models and can compute any marginalization and conditioning query in time linear to the size of the network. That is, we can answer questions such as "what is the probability of X being 0.3 and Y being any value" or "what is the probability of X being greater than 0.3 and Y being greater than 0.5" efficiently. The inherent probabilistic formulation of SPNs enables effective reasoning about the uncertainty in the underlying domain.

Deep probabilistic programming languages (DPPLs) such as DeepProblog (Manhaeve et al. 2018), Pyro (Bingham et al. 2019) and Edward (Tran et al. 2017), to name a few, leverage the expressive power of deep neural networks within probabilistic programming systems, especially at inference

```
A = coinflip(theta1)
if(A) {
  B = coinflip(theta2)
} else {
  B = A
}
```

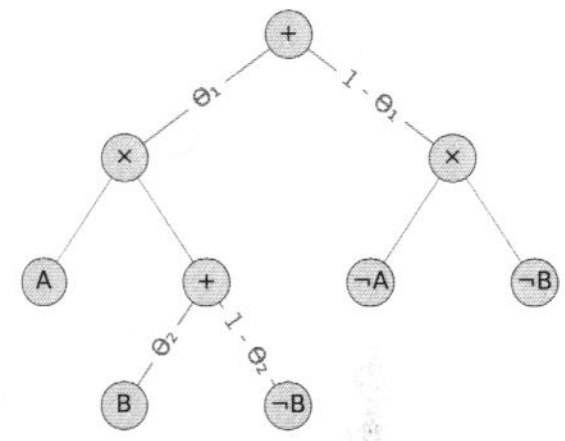

Figure 1: A simple program with randomness (left) and an SPN encoding the same distribution(right).

time. These deep neural architectures allow sampling in the DPPLs but the computation of marginal probabilities remains an issue. Such a computation can quickly become intractable, especially for continuous variables, thus limiting the types of queries that can be handled efficiently by DPPLs.

Looking at programs with random outcomes as ways to encode distributions, for some programs we can find SPNs or other probabilistic representations that encode the same distribution as that program (Holtzen, Millstein, and Broeck 2019). For example, consider figure 1 that shows an SPN representation for a simple program. This probabilistic representation is useful because it enables us to learn, as the distribution is differentiable in its parameters. It also encodes the joint distribution in a way that enables more complicated queries like maximum a posteriori (MAP) or most probable explanations (MPE).

Hand-crafting the equivalent SPN structure for a given program is tedious, and quite complicated once we introduce recursion or other complex control flow, such as for and while loops, into the program. In order for an SPN to be a valid distribution, one of the constraints is that of *completeness* which states that each child of a sum node must cover the same set of variables, that is, have the same scope. If a loop that generates more samples is introduced, then the children of the sum node that decides on whether to keep iterating or to stop will have different scopes, thereby violating the completeness constraint and rendering the SPN invalid.

Consider for example the following program where crafting the SPN structure is impossible, due to the number of involved variables:

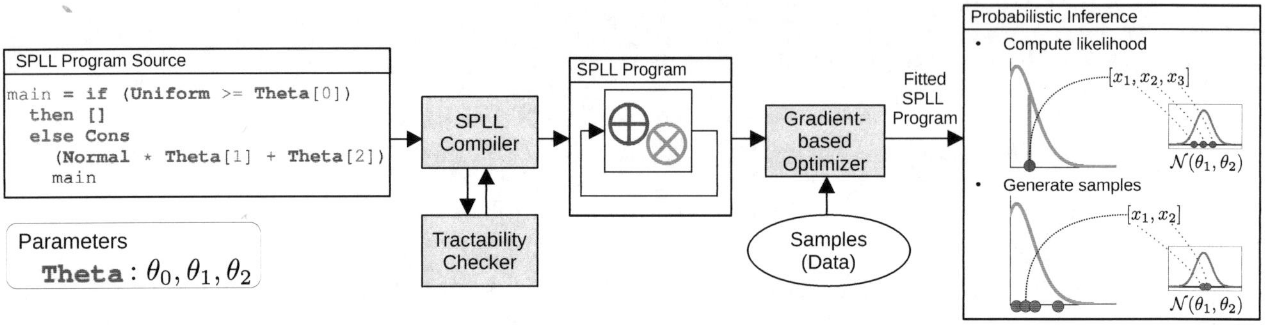

Figure 2: An overview of SPLL, for the task of parameter estimation. The source program of SPLL is compiled into executable SPLL programs by the compiler. During the compilation, SPLL checks the tractability of the program. The parameters in the program can be trained by gradient descent using samples. Using the fitted SPLL program, users can perform different types of probabilistic inference, e.g. compute the likelihood given samples or generate samples. We note that each data point in SPLL can be structured, e.g. as a list of values. In the example code, each data point is a list of values, and each value is following a Gaussian distribution which is parameterized by θ_1 and θ_2.

```
main = if coinflip(theta1) {
  (coinflip(theta2) : main)
} else {
  []
}
```

To handle these control structures, we introduce Sum-Product Loop Language (SPLL), a novel programming language capable of tractable inference on complex code that includes loops and produces a probabilistic representation from the program code. By allowing recursive programs, we can e.g. model distributions that describe a heterogeneous number of variables. In SPLL, every program has generative semantics that most programmers are familiar with and probabilistic semantics that assign a probability to each possible result. Thus, SPLL enables programmers to describe a generative process similarly to any standard programming language. The language produces code for computing the probability of values for free. At the core of SPLL lie two interpreters: one generates a sample from a program and its parameterization while the other differentiably computes the probability of a sample given a program and its parameterization. Overall, we make the following contributions:

1. We propose sum-product loop language (SPLL), a novel probabilistic programming language capable of handling loops in complex probabilistic code.
2. We describe the syntax as well as the generative and probabilistic semantics of SPLL (Section 2).
3. We demonstrate that SPLL is at least as capable as Sum Product Networks and inherits the beneficial properties of PCs, namely tractability and differentiability(Section 5).
4. We illustrate that SPLL can neatly solve some problems that are fundamentally unsolvable using Sum Product Networks (Section 6).

We proceed as follows. We start off by introducing SPLL, including its corresponding semantics. Then we introduce the notion of tractable programs within SPLL and then show the training procedure. Before concluding we show SPLL is at least as powerful as sum-product networks and also how SPLL extends beyond them.

2 Sum-Product Loop Language (SPLL)

Figure 2 shows the overall architecture of SPLL as presented for the task of parameter estimation. The SPLL source code, written in the manner of a standard programming language, is compiled to an SPLL program after going through a tractability checker. The tractability checker determines if the source SPLL program is efficiently solvable. The SPLL program parameters are then trained using gradient descent. The fitted program can then be used for inference and sample generation.

2.1 SPLL by Example

For an intuitive introduction, we construct a few compact SPLL programs and give a brief explanation from the view of generative semantics. We will cover the path to probabilistic semantics in section 2.3. Our first program will simply draw from a $\mathcal{N}(0, 1)$ distribution.

```
main = Normal
```

Our next program will linearly transform the $\mathcal{N}(0, 1)$ samples using parameters *Theta* to produce a $\mathcal{N}(\mu, \sigma)$-distribution.

```
main = Normal * Theta[0] + Theta[1]
```

We can also produce boolean variables, for example by comparing a uniform random sample against a parameter. This results in a Bernoulli distribution.

```
main = Uniform >= Theta[0]
```

Our final example will introduce list construction and conditional statements. It returns either [True] or [].

```
main = if Uniform >= Theta[0]
  then Cons True Null
  else Null
```

2.2 SPLL Syntax

We now introduce the core syntax of SPLL. An SPLL program can consist of multiple functions, each assigning an expression to a name. These functions can call each other, also recursively, thereby extending existing first-order functional

$$\mathcal{E} \rightarrow \textit{if } \mathcal{E} \textit{ then } \mathcal{E} \textit{ else } \mathcal{E}$$
$$\mathcal{E} \rightarrow \mathcal{E} >= \mathcal{E}$$
$$\mathcal{E} \rightarrow \textit{theta}[\mathbb{Z}]$$
$$\mathcal{E} \rightarrow \textit{uniform}$$
$$\mathcal{E} \rightarrow \textit{normal}$$
$$\mathcal{E} \rightarrow \textit{constant } \mathcal{V}$$
$$\mathcal{E} \rightarrow \mathcal{E} * \mathcal{E}$$
$$\mathcal{E} \rightarrow \mathcal{E} + \mathcal{E}$$
$$\mathcal{E} \rightarrow \textit{null}$$
$$\mathcal{E} \rightarrow \textit{cons } \mathcal{E}\ \mathcal{E}$$
$$\mathcal{E} \rightarrow \textit{call } \mathcal{F}$$

Figure 3: The syntax for SPLL.

languages such as DICE (Holtzen, Millstein, and Broeck 2019). SPLL programs can be queried by an interpreter.

Formally, the syntax for SPLL expressions is defined as in Fig. 3. $\mathcal{E}$ refers to the expressions in SPLL and $\mathbb{Z}$ refers to the set of whole numbers and is used to index the θ vector. The $\mathcal{V}$ nonterminal refers to the set of all values supported by the language and $\mathcal{F}$ refers to any function in the SPLL program. Overall, SPLL's syntax follows the syntax of standard functional programming languages, e.g. Haskell, closely.

2.3 SPLL Semantics

Now that we have covered the syntax, let us turn to the semantics. We first show how to draw samples and then derive the probability distribution of the generative semantics.

(1) Generative Semantics The generative semantics of SPLL are accessed by calling the *generate* function on an SPLL program. The semantics again draw from functional languages such as Haskell, albeit with randomness as a first-class part of the language. The generative semantics of the syntax elements are aligned with the syntax, i.e. the programs can be read as a generative description of its distribution. We use *cons* and *null* for list construction. Types in the generative semantics are restricted to *Bool*, *Float*, and *Lists*. SPLL prevents certain ill-typed expressions at compile time such as using a non-boolean for the condition of an if-expression.

Loops are implemented in SPLL using recursion. This as well as the functional language simplify control flow and thus simplify reasoning about the resulting distribution. θ denotes the parameters; each index refers to a real-valued variable marked as subject to parameter optimization. We adopt the definition of most syntax elements from Haskell.

Theorem 1 (Generative Semantics). *Any properly typed SPLL program with a complete parameterization θ that is not recursing indefinitely can be used to draw samples from its distribution.*

Proof. The syntax of SPLL programs encompasses a set of simple functional programs with well-known semantics. We can execute these programs to generate samples. The only syntax not usually found in functional languages is our θ-parameteriziation, which will yield a result as long as the provided θ-vector is long enough with respect to the indices used. □

(2) Probabilistic Semantics The probabilistic semantics of SPLL, given a sample, follow a similar recursive formulation. The resulting probabilities will add to 1 if integrated or summed over all possible outcomes of the program. They express the chance of that sample being emitted by the *generate* function. Some expressions introduce requirements and assumptions beyond what is readily apparent from their generative semantics. For example, *cons*-statements assume statistical independence of the head and tail elements, which is trivially true, since SPLL does not allow variable bindings, thus preventing information flow between the subexpressions.

We will next prove that the generative and probabilistic semantics describe the same distribution:

Theorem 2. *For any properly typed SPLL program with a complete parameterization θ, the analytical probability function accurately represents the empirical sample probability resulting from the associated generative process.*

Proof. In order to demonstrate that the *probability* function is aligned with the sample probability, we look at how it computes probabilities for each sample. In Table 1, we provide the probability $p(x|\texttt{expr})$ of a sample x arising from a program `expr`. We use these probabilities directly in interpreting the *probability* function. Intuitively, conditionals weigh the outcomes of each branch by the probability of the condition selecting that branch. Meanwhile, comparisons (which have one integrable and one deterministic argument), such as $p(\top|\texttt{a >= b})$, integrate the probability of the random variable up to the deterministic boundary. Please mind the distinction of which side is deterministic and which side of c is integrated. As for arithmetic expressions, here we compute the deterministic operand and use it to invert the operation to deduce the value of the random subexpression. For multiplication, we additionally need to apply a correction factor: The inversion widens the graph of the distribution. To ensure it integrates to 1, we divide the probability by y. Finally, keep in mind that we can safely assume independence of the subexpressions of *cons*. These probabilities were derived from the generative semantics. □

These semantics preserve and expect data type consistency. For example, queries such as $p(\top|\texttt{Normal})$ will not arise and the condition in if-statements must return a boolean. This, as well as the typing rules of the generative process, guarantee type safety. The type system of the probabilistic semantics ensures that (sub-)expressions that are integrated or deterministically evaluated in the above computations are indeed integrable or deterministic. Please refer back to the semantics in Table 1 for when these conditions apply and see Section 3 for how these conditions are enforced.

$$p(x|\texttt{if c then a else b}) = p(\top|\texttt{c})p(x|\texttt{a}) + p(\bot|\texttt{c})p(x|\texttt{b})$$

$$p(x|\texttt{uniform}) = \varphi_{\mathcal{U}(0,1)}(x)$$

$$p(x|\texttt{normal}) = \varphi_{\mathcal{N}(0,1)}(x)$$

$$p(x|\texttt{constant y}) = \begin{cases} 1, \textit{if } x = y \\ 0, \textit{if } x \neq y \end{cases}$$

$$p(x|\texttt{theta[y]}) = \begin{cases} 1, \textit{if } x = \theta_y \\ 0, \textit{if } x \neq \theta_y \end{cases}$$

$$p(x|\texttt{a} * \texttt{b}) = \begin{cases} p(x/y|\texttt{a})y \textit{ if det(b)} \to y \\ p(x/y|\texttt{b})y \textit{ if det(a)} \to y \end{cases}$$

$$p(x|\texttt{a} + \texttt{b}) = \begin{cases} p(x-y|\texttt{a}) \textit{ if det(b)} \to y \\ p(x-y|\texttt{b}) \textit{ if det(a)} \to y \end{cases}$$

$$p(x|\texttt{null}) = \begin{cases} 1 \textit{ if } x = [] \\ 0 \textit{ otherwise} \end{cases}$$

$$p(x|\texttt{cons a b}) = \begin{cases} 0 \textit{ if } x = [] \\ p(y|\texttt{a})p(ys|\texttt{b}) \\ \qquad \textit{if } x = (y{:}ys) \end{cases}$$

$$p(x|\texttt{call "f"}) = p(x|\texttt{f})$$

$$p(\top|\texttt{a} >= \texttt{b}) = \int_c^{\infty} p(x|\texttt{a})\, dx \quad \textit{where det(b)} \to c$$

$$p(\bot|\texttt{a} >= \texttt{b}) = 1 - \int_c^{\infty} p(x|\texttt{a})\, dx \quad \textit{where det(b)} \to c$$

$$p(\top|\texttt{a} >= \texttt{b}) = \int_{-\infty}^{c} p(x|\texttt{b})\, dx \quad \textit{where det(a)} \to c$$

$$p(\bot|\texttt{a} >= \texttt{b}) = 1 - \int_{-\infty}^{c} p(x|\texttt{b})\, dx \quad \textit{where det(a)} \to c$$

Table 1: Semantics for SPLL expressions. We denote 'expression a is deterministic with result x' with $det(a) \to x$; the density function of a distribution d with φ_d, and the name of a function and its implementation with "`f`" and `f`. The difference of probability densities and probabilities is left implicit.

3 Tractable Programs via Typing

In order to help the user avoid intractable programs, we provide rudimentary type inference that returns a compile-time error if no efficient implementation of the probability function is available. These probability types describe the operations we can efficiently do on a given expression. Generally, the type of an expression depends on the types of its subexpressions, but can have unique requirements such as the need to integrate over values of one subexpression or the need for a subexpression to be deterministic. Therefore, the type system keeps track of whether an expression is deterministic or allows efficient integration. If SPLL does not have a tractable solution to the probability function of a program, SPLL will raise a type error.

We developed rules that derive the type of an expression. For example, uniform and normal distributions can be integrated. Parameters θ and constants behave deterministically.

Conditional statements can be integrated over if both branches can be integrated over. The condition, being of generative type *bool*, is either tractably solvable or not; playing no further role in typing beyond failing if it is intractable.

The $a >= b$ operator requires that one argument be deterministic and the other be integrable, as the semantics integrate the random variable up to the deterministic boundary. Arithmetics are considered tractable if either argument is deterministic.

Different algorithms and along with them different typing rules can coexist within the SPLL compiler. For example, the solution of addition has two symmetrical variants. It is possible to add more variants that cover additional cases, thus expanding the set of valid programs. We will elaborate on such future expansions in section 8.

Tractable Programs as SPNs Now that we have a way to guarantee that the program is tractable, we can try to find a way back towards more familiar tractable structures. First, let us constrain the set of considered programs further, in order to characterize programs with useful gradients:

Definition 1. *An SPLL program is consistent if it has the following properties: (A) For any sample, every execution path resulting in this sample must have finite length. (B) The probability functions of* `constant` *and* `theta` *are not called or integrated.*

Note that (A) is true in particular for programs that recursively construct lists, as this way the recursion depth is connected to the number of list elements. Meanwhile (B) implies that deterministic expressions are only used where the probability rules expect them.

Theorem 3. *For any sample and consistent program, the computation of the probability function is equivalent to a finite SPN. That is, a program induces a set of SPNs, potentially one per sample.*

Proof. Looking at the previous formulas for the probability of a sample in Table 1, large parts collapse at compile-time into structures familiar from SPNs: leaf nodes containing primitive distributions, weighted sums, and products. The indicator functions associated with deterministic behavior in `constant` and `theta` are not actually called upon in the probability computation of consistent programs. Some expressions result in behaviors that are not trivially mapped to an SPN. We now illustrate how these map to SPNs:

(A) Arithmetics query its subexpressions normally, analogous to an SPN. Since y is deterministic, the transformations upon x it imparts do not change the distribution fundamentally. In order to construct an equivalent SPN, these transformations can be represented as changes to the leaf nodes.

(B) Function calls attach another function's computational graph in place, potentially recursively. Due to consistency of the SPLL program, the resulting graph has a finite depth.

(C) The indicator functions in the probabilities of *cons* and *null* develop interesting behavior though: They can be seen as rejecting samples that are ill-structured. In particular, *cons* rejects empty lists or shortens a list for further evaluation, thus guaranteeing termination for finite lists when applied recursively. We can also view this behavior as pruning an infinite, recursive SPN down to a finite SPN, subject to information from the sample.

This way, we can represent the computation of the probability function as an SPN, where the structure and parameters of that SPN depend on compile-time information and runtime information from the sample. □

Tractability Inference in general is known to be an intractable problem (Darwiche 2009). We have demonstrated that consistent SPLL programs are computationally equivalent to a set of SPNs. With SPNs known to be tractable, this makes SPLLs tractable, at least with respect to the size of the equivalent SPN model. The size of this model is dependent on recursion behavior and the SPLL code length. For any program that can be constrained in its recursion behavior, for example by recursively constructing lists, we can thus show tractability. We discuss the impact of tractability on the design decisions of SPLL and on future expansions in Section 8.

4 Training SPLL Programs

Now that we have formalized the syntax and semantics, we will look at the task of parameter estimation, using the following learning setup:

> **Given** a set of samples X and a consistent SPLL program, **find** the parameterization θ of the program that best maximizes log-likelihood $\mathcal{L}$ of all samples given a program and parameters: $\mathcal{L} = \sum_{x \in X} -log(p(x|\theta))$.

For this learning setting, it is natural to follow a standard gradient approach for maximizing log-likelihood, and we will describe that next. However, we have to be a bit more careful and we will explain that afterward.

4.1 Gradients via Automatic Differentiation

The gradient of the likelihood function with respect to a program's `theta[i]` can be computed using automatic differentiation. This works well for most expressions except for the following: Uniform, deterministic expressions and list construction.

Specifically, *Uniform* distributions do not exhibit useful gradients. However, when integrated they are very useful. We thus use them in the argument of comparisons, so as to produce more understandable code. Furthermore, the indicator functions for *deterministic expressions* provide no usable gradients, but for consistent SPLL programs, this is no problem, as their probability function will not be evaluated. *List construction* has, in spite of appearances, proper gradients, as the discrete jump between empty and full list does not happen via variation of `theta` but only by deconstructing x.

While it may seem like we can not train thetas, as the derivative of $p(x|\texttt{theta[y]})$ is 0 everywhere, this is not true. Note how other probabilities, namely arithmetics and comparisons, depend on the result of deterministic expressions. The derivatives of their probabilities will contain the derivatives of said result, as opposed to the derivative of the probability of the result. The derivative of the result of a `theta[i]`-expression is a vector with 1 at index i, thus providing a non-zero base case for SPLL gradients.

Given the gradients and a learning rate λ, we can train the parameters θ of an SPLL program in the following way: We initialize θ randomly and iteratively update it using $\theta := \theta + \lambda \cdot \partial\mathcal{L}/\partial\theta$. Assuming that the given program is adequate for the dataset, we can reconstruct the exact distribution of the data.

Although the above approach seems natural, consider the following SPLL program:

```
main = if 0.5 >= Theta[0]
  then True
  else False
```

This program is interesting as it has gradients that do not allow the training of θ at all, even though θ affects the distribution. While it would be easy to brush this program aside as inconsistent, let us instead investigate remedial actions for it and programs like it.

4.2 Gradients via Continuous Relaxations

We can use continuous relaxations to produce a gradient that resembles that of the original distribution, while also being much better behaved. The consequence of this is giving up exactness as the relaxations will result in approximate solutions.

In the case where both $det(l) \to l_d$ and $det(r) \to r_d$, by smoothing the discrete comparison result with a sigmoid, the probabilities of comparisons can be written as

$$p(\top|\texttt{l} >= \texttt{r}) = \sigma(l_d - r_d)$$
$$p(\bot|\texttt{l} >= \texttt{r}) = 1 - \sigma(l_d - r_d)$$

and their corresponding gradients can be computed as:

$$\nabla p(\top|\texttt{l} >= \texttt{r}) = \sigma'(l_d - r_d)\nabla l_d - \sigma'(l_d - r_d)\nabla r_d$$
$$\nabla p(\bot|\texttt{l} >= \texttt{r}) = \sigma'(l_d - r_d)\nabla r_d - \sigma'(l_d - r_d)\nabla l_d \,.$$

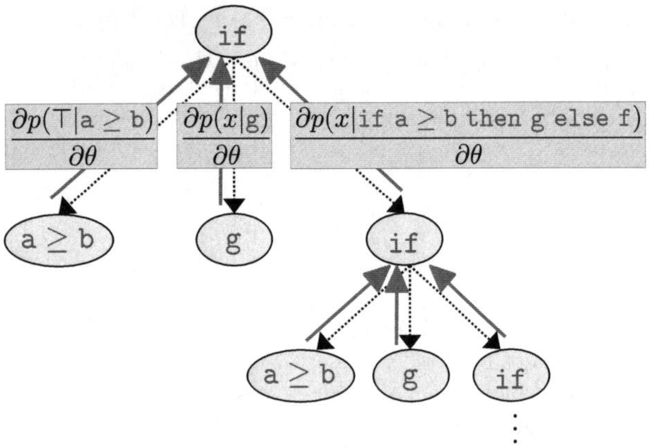

Figure 4: Gradient flow in the SPLL program. Each node represents a component of the program. Dotted arrows represent the forward path, and colored arrows represent the backward path, respectively. The gradient of an entire SPLL program can be computed by automatic differentiation even if the program contains complex control flow such as recursions and conditionals.

The changes affect conditional statements and thus propagate even to recursive calls. Consider how this affects conditionals: With the probability of the condition returned to smoothness using the above relaxations, we can again compute reasonable gradients for conditional statements.

Let us now return to the above code example. We will assume a sample of $x = \texttt{True}$. We will omit a few terms due to redundancy arising from symmetry. To disambiguate the factor 0.5 from the program constant 0.5, we will write out the usually implicit `constant` expression. The gradient of the program, ignoring the symmetrical $\perp$ case would be the following:

$$
\begin{aligned}
&\frac{\partial}{\partial\theta} p(\mathtt{T}|\texttt{if c then a else b}) \\
&= p(\mathtt{T}|\mathtt{a}) \cdot \frac{\partial}{\partial\theta} p(\mathtt{T}|\mathtt{c}) + p(\mathtt{T}|\mathtt{c}) \cdot \frac{\partial}{\partial\theta} p(\mathtt{T}|\mathtt{a}) + \ldots \\
&= 1 \cdot \frac{\partial}{\partial\theta} p(\mathtt{T}|\texttt{constant 0.5} >= \texttt{theta[0]}) + p(\mathtt{T}|\mathtt{c}) \cdot 0 \\
&= \sigma'(0.5 - \theta_0) \frac{\partial}{\partial\theta} (\texttt{constant 0.5}) - \\
&\quad \sigma'(0.5 - \theta_0) \frac{\partial}{\partial\theta} (\texttt{theta[0]}) \\
&= \; -\sigma'(0.5 - \theta_0) \;,
\end{aligned}
$$

where the last step is because θ consists of `theta[0]` only.

As we can see, we restored the gradient of θ. We can convince ourselves that the gradient is viable by observing that the gradient is always negative, most strongly so around $\theta = 0.5$. From the source code, we can learn that a lower theta will tend to produce more `True` samples, as it will move the program towards the respective side of the decision boundary of the condition. That is exactly the property we want to maximize.

We can restore gradients even if a branch of the conditional recurses: Note the original semantics for recursion are

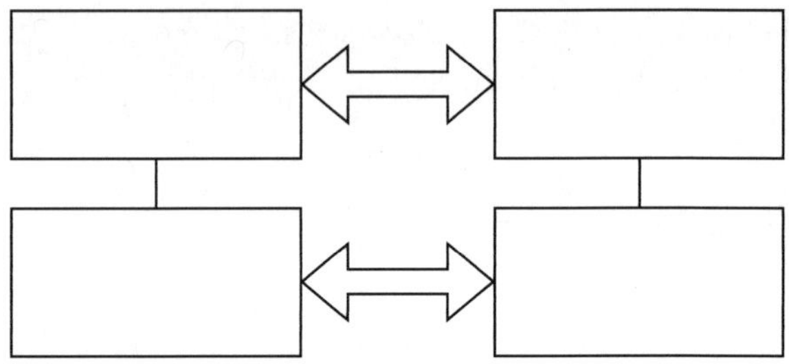

Figure 5: Mapping between SPN and SPLL functions for simple SPLL programs.

quite benign; the heavy lifting of computing likelihoods and gradients happens in the conditional and comparison expressions. The question of whether to recurse or not is decided by the plausibility of the desired outcome under the recursive and the non-recursive branch, and that decision is made in the conditional. Thus, restoring gradients to conditionals is sufficient to restore gradients even to more complex, recursive programs.

By using Automatic Differentiation, the gradient for an entire SPLL program, including any recursions can be computed by computing the gradient of each component and applying the chain rule. Consider the following SPLL program:

```
f = if a >= b
  then g
  else f
```

where `f` is a recursive function that calls itself or the function `g`. Figure 4 shows the gradient flow of the program. The gradient of each component can be computed as presented above. SPLL allows computing the gradients even if the program contains complex control flows such as if-then-else and recursions.

5 SPLL Covers Sum-Product Networks

Because SPNs offer good guarantees of e.g. tractability, it is desirable to demonstrate that SPLL can fall back on those guarantees if the problem at hand is sufficiently simple. These guarantees are also valuable if the SPLL program can divide the problem into SPN-solvable sub-problems. Therefore, we will now show how any SPN can be expressed in SPLL, and which subset of SPLL maps cleanly to SPNs.

Firstly: we can express any SPN in our language simply by writing out its sampling procedure. That is to say, we need an SPLL code's generative process to match an SPN's generative process, i.e. its sampling procedure. Under that condition, their distributions also align (See Figure 5).

To implement this sampling procedure in SPLL, we need to concatenate two disjointed sets of variables and perform weighted random sampling from two branches. These operations are exactly equivalent to if-then-else and list concatenation, with the respective probabilities being weighted sums and products respectively. More explicitly, `if Bernoulli(p) then A else B` is equivalent to a sum node that associates node A with weight p and node B with weight $(1-p)$. Similarly, `concat A B` is equivalent to a product node over A and B, in that the probability of the concatenation is the product of the probabilities of the sublists. Consequently, we express a trivariate distribution using the list [x1, x2, x3]. We should add that proper SPN-equivalence requires the use of "chaotic" concatenation, where we can e.g. concatenate [x1, x4] and [x2, x3] into [x1, x2, x3, x4]. This is necessary because product nodes in SPNs can split the domain of variables arbitrarily. This can be implemented in our language as an operation that rearranges a single list.

Thus, a minimal grammar for SPLL programs that cover SPNs would be:

Expr → *if* (*bernoulli p*) *then Expr else Expr*

Expr → *normal* μ σ

Expr → *null*

Expr → *cons Expr Expr*

Every other element of the grammar of SPLL, like function calls or arithmetic, is there to support more complex programs or to aid in flexibility of the language.

Experimentally, we confirm the above theoretical considerations by modelling a simple mixture of Gaussians using an SPN and using our language. To this end, we used two Gaussians centered at (0.3, 0.3) and (0.7, 0.7), with $\sigma = 0.1$ and a mixture ratio of 0.4 to 0.6. We modeled this distribution using the SPLL code shown in Listing 1. We will compare this to an SPN using SPFlow (Molina et al. 2019).

We find that in both cases, the parameters of the respective structures match those found in the distribution: SPN and SPLL both get the mixture ratios and the underlying parameters of the normal distribution right to within a small approximation error. Please refer also to Figure 7, where we display the probability density of $[X, Y]$ for both models. Both models exhibit a stronger peak at (0.7, 0.7) and a weaker peak at (0.3, 0.3), which reflects the method of data synthesis, including the mixture ratio. The resulting figures line up to the point of being indistinguishable.

6 SPLL Moves Beyond SPNs

To illustrate why recursive programs can generate more varied distributions than SPNs, consider for example a process that generates one sample from a Gaussian mixture

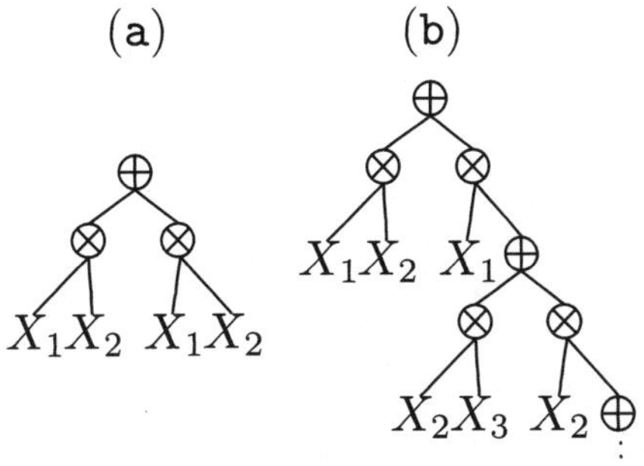

Figure 6: SPNs are SPLL programs. (a) A valid SPN. (b) An invalid SPN caused by recursions. Note that the topmost sum node in (b) covers different sets of variables in its left and right branch.

Listing 1 Multivariate mixture of Gaussians

```
main = if Uniform >= Theta[0]
  then [Normal * Theta[1] + Theta[2],
        Normal * Theta[3] + Theta[4]]
  else [Normal * Theta[5] + Theta[6],
        Normal * Theta[7] + Theta[8]]
```

Listing 2 Recursive lists of mixture of Gaussians

```
main = if Uniform >= Theta[0]
  then Null
  else Cons
    if Uniform >= Theta[1]
      then Normal * Theta[2] + Theta[3]
      else Normal * Theta[4] + Theta[5]
    main
```

distribution per iteration, with some probability of stopping each time. The resulting distribution contains lists of variable length with no upper limit, where longer lists are exponentially less likely. Distributions such as this can not be modelled by SPNs. Since the resulting number of variables varies, an SPN would need to cover a heterogeneous number of variables, which would violate completeness. For example, consider the SPN in Fig. 6(a) which is defined over two random variables X_1 and X_2. Note that the scope of the childern of the only sum node is $\{X_1, X_2\}$ as both the random variables are present on both the left and right child product nodes. Now consider the SPN in Fig. 6(b) obtained after recursion on the underlying SPN in Fig. 6(a) where one of the leaf node is replaced by the underlying SPN but can contain a new random variable X_3. The children of the topmost sum node then have the scope $\{X_1, X_2\}$ for the left child product node and $\{X_1, X_2, X_3\}$ for the right child product node thus specifying different scopes and violating the completeness property of the SPN.

With SPLL, we can solve this by modelling the generative process (see Listing 2). The likelihood function correctly determines the amount of times the recursion condition fired before failing and consequently provides a gradient for optimizing θ_0. The gradient is also passed through to the parameters of the Gaussian distributions. While estimating θ_0 is of course possible from just the list lengths, SPLL can do this without much modelling work and for more complex programs where connections are not as readily apparent. For such a recursive mixture model as well as a recursive simple gaussian model, we conducted experiments by sampling from the ground truth parameterization 1000 times and training a random parameterization via maximum likelihood.

The convergence behavior of these programs can be seen in Figure 8. We trace the path parameters take while the program is training, in relation to the ground truth configuration. Note that in the mixture model, most of the parameters except θ_0 go through a phase of non-monotonic behavior while the program can not provide a clear assignment of samples to mixture components. Note that due to model

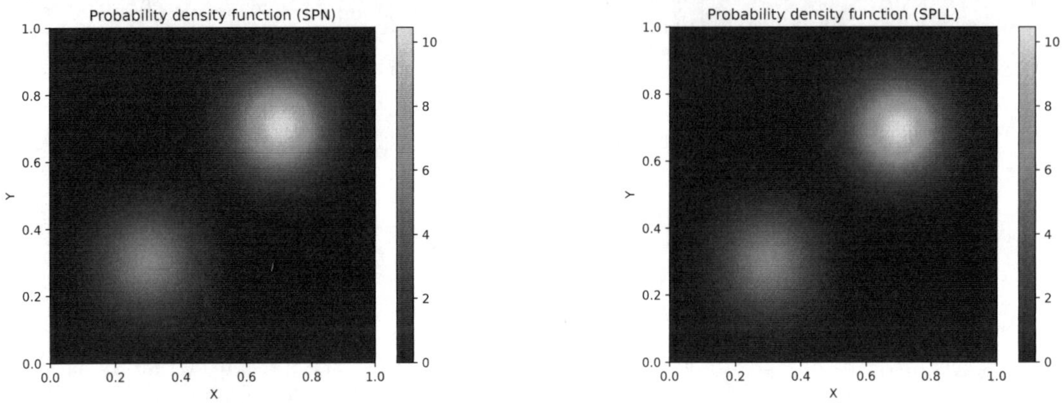

Figure 7: Comparison of the learned density functions of an SPN (left) and SPLL (right). We can see that the density functions learned by both are identical thus showing empirically that SPLLs are at least as powerful as SPNs.

symmetry it is possible for θ to converge on an inverted but equivalent parameterization. This would not affect sample quality or log-likelihood.

7 Related Work

Deep probabilistic programming languages (DPPLs) such as DeepProblog (Manhaeve et al. 2018), Pyro (Bingham et al. 2019) and Edward (Tran et al. 2017) have been developed to enable users to write probabilistic programs as SPLL. However, they do not ensure tractable inference. DICE (Holtzen, Van den Broeck, and Millstein 2020) is a probabilistic programming language that can perform exact discrete probabilistic program inference. DICE supports tractable inference but unlike SPLL only on discrete, non-recursive programs. Church (Goodman et al. 2008) is a functional language for generative models. It has a similar motivation as SPLL to introduce a language to describe stochastic processes in a functional programming style. However, church has less of a focus on tractability and thus can not provide the guarantees we do around tractable programs. For both languages, continuous relaxations for training have not been proposed yet.

Another important line of research is that of logic-based probabilistic programming (Raedt, Kimmig, and Toivonen 2007; Riguzzi and Swift 2011; Fierens et al. 2014; Vlasselaer et al. 2015). In contrast to these frameworks, SPLL defines its own syntax and semantics supporting traditional programming language constructs.

Probabilistic models to perform tractable inference have been proposed such as Sum Product Network (SPNs) (Poon and Domingos 2011) and Probabilistic Sentential Decision Diagrams (PSDDs) (Kisa et al. 2014). These models are called *Probabilistic Circuits (PCs)* (Choi, Vergari, and Van den Broeck 2020). However, these models are not capable of handling structured programs that contain loops or recursion. SPLL offers the capability of tractable inference and the handling of structured programs. Sum-Product Probabilistic Language (SPPL) has been proposed as a generalization of SPNs to a programming language with an extension of symbolic expressions (Saad, Rinard, and Mansinghka 2021). SPPL achieves tractable exact inference. However, it does so by restricting the user to bounded loops.

Since we pass a gradient through a program, we can also compare our work to Continuous Relaxations (Berthet et al. 2020; Petersen et al. 2021), which smoothes over discrete control flow decisions by interpolating the outcomes. In contrast, SPLL offers exact computations, where the distribution of the generator is guaranteed to align with that of the likelihood function. Meanwhile Continuous Relaxations can lead to unintended program behavior, where the act of relaxing control flow conditions can lead to e.g. impossible paths in the program being possible. The cost of this exactness is that some programs can not be expressed in SPLL and some others scale badly in their computational cost. (Petersen et al. 2021) has proposed to use continuous relaxations to produce a gradient that resembles the original distribution, while also being much better behaved. SPLL adopts the approach to compute the gradients for parameters in places where it not otherwise possible.

Previous work has addressed the integration of symbolic programs and neural networks (Manhaeve et al. 2018; Yang, Ishay, and Lee 2020; Evans and Grefenstette 2018; Rocktäschel and Riedel 2017; Mao et al. 2019). SPLL can be placed here as a new approach to use a differentiable probabilistic programming language for neuro-symbolic learning, where the available set of computations on the symbolic representation receives a new degree of freedom.

8 Conclusions

Triggered by the success of probabilistic circuits such as sum-product networks, we have moved beyond circuits and introduced Sum-Product Loop Language, a novel programming language that is capable of tractable inference on complex probabilistic code that includes recursion. SPLL has dual semantics: every program has generative semantics fa-

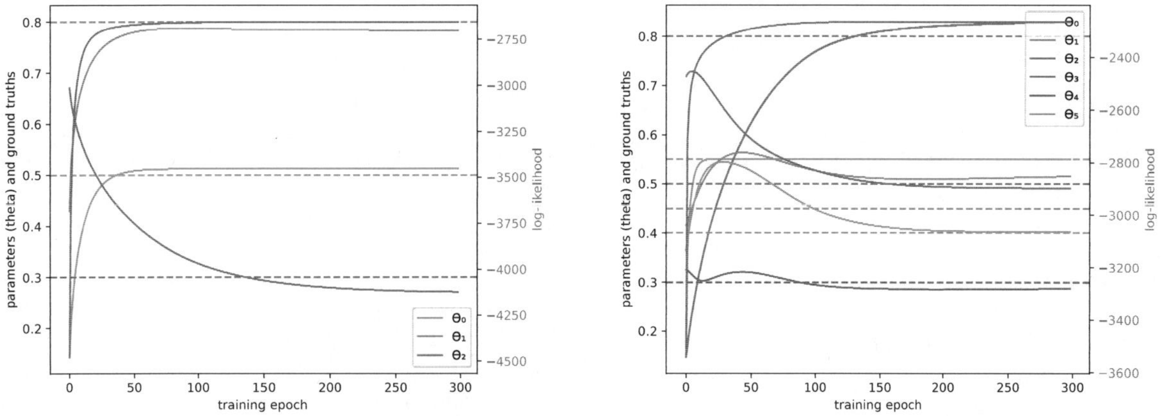

Figure 8: Training SPLL programs: Parameter convergence and likelihood fit(blue) for variable-length Gaussian sequences (left) as well as for variable length mixture-of-Gaussian sequences(right). Dashed lines indicate the ground truth of the respective parameter. Slightly off convergence points can arise from the sampling error of the training set.

miliar to most programmers and probabilistic semantics that assign a probability to each possible result. This way, the programmer can describe how to generate samples almost like in any standard programming language. The language takes care of computing the probability values of all results for free at run time. Overall, we showed that SPLL inherits tractability and differentiability from PCs, while generalizing to other distributions and programs.

Our work provides several interesting avenues for future work on tractability for more complicated programs, the introduction of memory, more supported queries, and incorporating deep learning by means of neural function calls.

Tractability. Limitations of the language arise from the tractability of the probabilistic semantics: It is quite simple to produce code for which the analytical computation of the probability is impossible. For example, we might encounter problems in a program that adds two random variables: Computing the probability of the result generally involves integrating over all possible values of one variable, making even a relatively simple program intractable. Consider, however, the case of the sum of two Gaussian variables. The sum of two Gaussian-distributed variables is again Gaussian. Such an algorithm and many like it could be added to SPLL. Thus, it is possible to expand tractability beyond what our language currently offers. In such cases, identifying and pushing the boundary of intractability will be important future work.

Queries. SPNs support many more queries than SPLL. Implementing these queries for the SPN-equivalent subset of the language should straightforwardly follow their SPN implementation, while for the wider language, this might offer interesting insights into degrees of tractability while making the language more usable. Instead of implementing these as different interpretation methods of the same program, a promising approach could be to implement them within the language. For example, if we refer back to the recursive lists of Gaussians in Listing 2, we might query the length of the resulting list like this:

```
query = length main >= 2
```

to find the probability that a list is at least 2 elements long. Using this approach, enabling more queries would entail expanding the expressiveness of the language fundamentally.

Memory. Another interesting avenue is the introduction of memory: If we could tractably compute $p(x|\texttt{let y} = \texttt{e1 in e2})$, we would introduce many different interesting programs into the language. These programs could for example be made efficient if the result "witnesses" *y* as would be the case in $[\texttt{y}, \texttt{f(y)}]$, if we restrict the permitted subexpressions, or if the type of *y* is small enough to allow enumeration. However, care must be taken to not accidentally allow intractable programs. For example, a program like

```
main = let x1 = expr
  in let x2 = expr2 x1
  in expr3 x2
```

might result in evaluating a number of execution paths exponential in the number of variables x_i.

Neural Function Calls. In order to integrate SPLL with Neural Networks, which offer high performance in many fields of machine learning, we could introduce a new syntax element. First, we impose that compatible neural networks must output their predictions "distribution-like", e.g. using a softmax layer. The *probability* function is the output of the neural network, while the *generate* function draws a sample from this distribution. Implementing it this way also guarantees that we can train the neural network end to end, as the gradients can be propagated to the softmax layer. We could then solve tasks such as MNIST-Addition (Manhaeve et al. 2018) as simply as:

```
main img1 img2 =
  (read_NN img1) + (read_NN img2)
```

With these additions to SPLL, it becomes feasible to tackle problems that integrate neural and symbolic representations and move into the domain of neuro-symbolic AI.

Acknowledgements

This work was supported by the Federal Ministry for Economic Affairs and Climate Action (BMWK) AI lighthouse project "SPAICER" (01MK20015E), the EU ICT-48 Network of AI Research Excellence Center "TAILOR" (EU Horizon 2020, GA No 952215), and the Collaboration Lab "AI in Construction" (AICO) with Nexplore/HochTief. The work has also benefited from the Hessian Ministry of Higher Education, Research, Science and the Arts (HMWK) cluster projects "The Third Wave of AI" and "The Adaptive Mind".

References

Berthet, Q.; Blondel, M.; Teboul, O.; Cuturi, M.; Vert, J.-P.; and Bach, F. 2020. Learning with differentiable pertubed optimizers. In *NeurIPS*.

Bingham, E.; Chen, J. P.; Jankowiak, M.; Obermeyer, F.; Pradhan, N.; Karaletsos, T.; Singh, R.; Szerlip, P.; Horsfall, P.; and Goodman, N. D. 2019. Pyro: Deep universal probabilistic programming. *The Journal of Machine Learning Research* 20(1):973–978.

Choi, Y.; Vergari, A.; and Van den Broeck, G. 2020. Probabilistic circuits: A unifying framework for tractable probabilistic models. UCLA. URL: http://starai.cs.ucla.edu/papers/ProbCirc20.pdf.

Darwiche, A. 2003. A differential approach to inference in Bayesian networks. *JACM*.

Darwiche, A. 2009. *Modeling and reasoning with Bayesian networks*. Cambridge university press.

Evans, R., and Grefenstette, E. 2018. Learning explanatory rules from noisy data. *JAIR*.

Fierens, D.; den Broeck, G. V.; Renkens, J.; Shterionov, D.; Gutmann, B.; Thon, I.; Janssens, G.; and Raedt, L. D. 2014. Inference and learning in probabilistic logic programs using weighted boolean formulas. *Theory and Practice of Logic Programming* 15(3).

Goodman, N. D.; Mansinghka, V. K.; Roy, D. M.; Bonawitz, K. A.; and Tenenbaum, J. B. 2008. Church: a language for generative models. In *UAI*.

Holtzen, S.; Millstein, T.; and Broeck, G. V. d. 2019. Symbolic exact inference for discrete probabilistic programs. *arXiv preprint arXiv:1904.02079*.

Holtzen, S.; Van den Broeck, G.; and Millstein, T. 2020. Scaling exact inference for discrete probabilistic programs. *Proc. ACM Program. Lang.*

Kisa, D.; Van den Broeck, G.; Choi, A.; and Darwiche, A. 2014. Probabilistic sentential decision diagrams. In *KR*.

Manhaeve, R.; Dumancic, S.; Kimmig, A.; Demeester, T.; and De Raedt, L. 2018. Deepproblog: Neural probabilistic logic programming. *Advances in Neural Information Processing Systems* 31.

Mao, J.; Gan, C.; Kohli, P.; Tenenbaum, J. B.; and Wu, J. 2019. The Neuro-Symbolic Concept Learner: Interpreting Scenes, Words, and Sentences From Natural Supervision. In *ICLR*.

Molina, A.; Vergari, A.; Stelzner, K.; Peharz, R.; Subramani, P.; Mauro, N. D.; Poupart, P.; and Kersting, K. 2019. Spflow: An easy and extensible library for deep probabilistic learning using sum-product networks.

Petersen, F.; Borgelt, C.; Kuehne, H.; and Deussen, O. 2021. Learning with algorithmic supervision via continuous relaxations. In *NeurIPS*.

Poon, H., and Domingos, P. 2011. Sum-product networks: A new deep architecture. In *UAI*.

Raedt, L. D.; Kimmig, A.; and Toivonen, H. 2007. Problog: A probabilistic prolog and its application in link discovery. In Veloso, M. M., ed., *IJCAI*.

Riguzzi, F., and Swift, T. 2011. The pita system: Tabling and answer subsumption for reasoning under uncertainty. *Theory and Practice of Logic Programming* 11(4-5):433–449.

Rocktäschel, T., and Riedel, S. 2017. End-to-end Differentiable Proving. In *NeurIPS*.

Saad, F. A.; Rinard, M. C.; and Mansinghka, V. K. 2021. Sppl: Probabilistic programming with fast exact symbolic inference. In *ICPLI*.

Tran, D.; Hoffman, M. D.; Saurous, R. A.; Brevdo, E.; Murphy, K.; and Blei, D. M. 2017. Deep probabilistic programming.

Vlasselaer, J.; Van den Broeck, G.; Kimmig, A.; Meert, W.; and De Raedt, L. 2015. Anytime inference in probabilistic logic programs with Tp-compilation. In *IJCAI*.

Yang, Z.; Ishay, A.; and Lee, J. 2020. Neurasp: Embracing neural networks into answer set programming. In *IJCAI*.

Neural-Probabilistic Answer Set Programming

Arseny Skryagin[1] , **Wolfgang Stammer**[1,3] , **Daniel Ochs**[1] ,
Devendra Singh Dhami[1,3] , **Kristian Kersting**[1,2,3]
[1]Computer Science Department, Technical University Darmstadt, Germany
[2]Centre for Cognitive Science, TU Darmstadt
[3]Hessian Center for AI (hessian.AI)
{arseny.skryagin, wolfgang.stammer, daniel.ochs, devendra.dhami, kersting}@cs.tu-darmstadt.de

Abstract

The goal of combining the robustness of neural networks and the expressivity of symbolic methods has rekindled the interest in Neuro-Symbolic AI. One specifically interesting branch of research is deep probabilistic programming languages (DPPLs) which carry out probabilistic logical programming via the probability estimations of deep neural networks. However, recent SOTA DPPL approaches allow only for limited conditional probabilistic queries and do not offer the power of true joint probability estimation. In our work, we propose an easy integration of tractable probabilistic inference within a DPPL. To this end we introduce SLASH, a novel DPPL that consists of Neural-Probabilistic Predicates (NPPs) and a logical program, united via answer set programming. NPPs are a novel design principle allowing for the unification of all deep model types and combinations thereof to be represented as a single probabilistic predicate. In this context, we introduce a novel +/- notation for answering various types of probabilistic queries by adjusting the atom notations of a predicate. We evaluate SLASH on the benchmark task of MNIST addition as well as novel tasks for DPPLs such as missing data prediction, generative learning and set prediction with state-of-the-art performance, thereby showing the effectiveness and generality of our method.

1 Introduction

In recent years, Neuro-Symbolic AI approaches to learning (Hudson and Manning 2019; d'Avila Garcez et al. 2019; Jiang and Ahn 2020; d'Avila Garcez and Lamb 2020) have gained traction. In general, these integrate low-level perception with high-level reasoning by combining data-driven neural modules with logic-based symbolic modules. This combination of sub-symbolic and symbolic systems has been shown to have several advantages for various tasks such as visual question answering and reasoning (Yi et al. 2018), concept learning (Mao et al. 2019) and improved properties for explainable and revisable models (Ciravegna et al. 2020; Stammer, Schramowski, and Kersting 2021).

Rather than designing specifically tailored neuro-symbolic architectures, where often the neural and symbolic modules are disjoint and trained independently (Yi et al. 2018; Mao et al. 2019; Stammer, Schramowski, and Kersting 2021), deep probabilistic programming languages (DPPLs) provide an exciting alternative (Bingham et al. 2019; Tran et al. 2017; Manhaeve et al. 2018; Yang, Ishay, and Lee 2020). Specifically, DPPLs integrate neural and symbolic modules via a unifying programming framework with probability estimates acting as the *"glue"* between separate modules, thus allowing for reasoning over noisy, uncertain data and, importantly, joint training of the modules. Additionally, prior knowledge and biases in the form of logical rules can easily and explicitly be added into the learning process with DPPLs. This stands in contrast to specifically tailored, implicit architectural biases of, e.g., purely subsymbolic deep learning approaches. Ultimately, DPPLs thereby allow to integrate neural networks easily into downstream logical reasoning tasks.

Recent state of the art DPPLs, such as DeepProbLog (Manhaeve et al. 2018) and NeurASP (Yang, Ishay, and Lee 2020) allow for conditional class probability estimates as both works base their probability estimates on neural predicates. Although certain tasks may only require conditional class probabilities, we argue that for the overall expressive and utilization power of a DPPL, it is necessary to also be able to integrate and process joint probability estimates. The world is uncertain, and often it becomes necessary to reason in settings, e.g., in which variables of an observation might be missing or even manipulated.

In this work, we therefore make two main contributions. First, we propose a novel form of predicates for DPPLs, termed Neural Probabilistic Predicates (NPPs) that allow for task-specific probability queries. NPPs consist of neural and/or probabilistic circuit (PC) modules and act as a unifying term, encompassing the neural predicates of DeepProbLog and NeurASP, as well as purely probabilistic predicates. Further, we introduce a much more powerful *"flavor"* of NPPs that consist jointly of neural and PC modules, taking advantage of the power of neural computations together with true density estimation of PCs via tractable probabilistic inference.

Second, having introduced NPPs, we next construct a novel DPPL, SLASH, to efficiently combine NPPs with logic programming. Similar to the punctuation symbol, this can be used to efficiently combine several paradigms into one. Specifically, SLASH represents for the first time an efficient and scalable programming language that seamlessly integrates probabilistic logical programming with neural representations and tractable probabilistic estimations. This allows for the integration of all forms of probability estima-

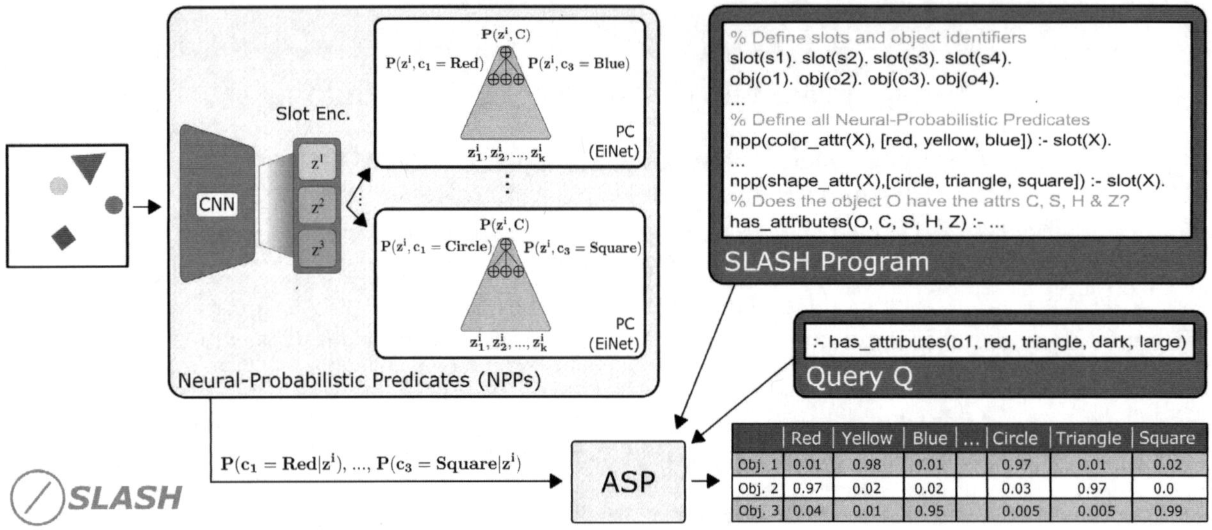

Figure 1: NPPs consist of neural and/or probabilistic circuit modules and can produce task-specific probability estimates. In our novel DPPL, SLASH, NPPs are integrated with a logic program via an ASP module to answer logical queries about data samples. In the depicted instantiation of SLASH (*SLASH Attention*) the Neural-Probabilistic Predicates consist of a slot attention encoder and Probabilistic Circuits (PCs) realized via EiNets. The slot encoder is shared over all NPPs, where each EiNet computes a joint distribution at the root node, thereby, learning the joint distribution over slot encodings, z^i, and object attributes, C, of a specific category, e.g., color attributes. Via targeted queries to the NPPs, one can obtain task-related probabilities, e.g., conditional probabilities for a visual reasoning task.

tions, not just class conditionals, thus extending the works of (Manhaeve et al. 2018) and (Yang, Ishay, and Lee 2020).

Apart from NPPs, SLASH[1] additionally consists of a logical program, containing a set of facts and logical statements that define the state of the world of an underlying task. Lastly, an ASP module is used to combine the NPP(s) with the logic program. Given a logical query about the input data, the logical program and the probability estimates obtained from the NPP(s), the ASP module produces a probability estimate about the truth value of the query. Finally, training in SLASH is performed efficiently in a batch-wise and end-to-end fashion, by integrating the parameters of all modules (neural and probabilistic) into a single loss term.

Fig. 1 exemplifies the building blocks of SLASH and NPPs for a specific instantiation of SLASH, termed SLASH Attention. This is designed for the task of set prediction from images. In this example, the NPPs consist of a slot attention encoder (Locatello et al. 2020) and several EinSum PCs (Peharz et al. 2020). The slot encoder is shared across all NPPs, whereas the PC of each NPP models a separate category of attributes. This way, each NPP models the joint distribution over slot encodings and object attribute values, such as color of an object. By querying the NPP, one can obtain task-related probability estimations, such as the conditional attribute probability. Finally, via the logic program, the user can predefine a set of statements and rules, e.g., of when an object possesses a specific set of attributes, and query if an observed image contains a large, dark red triangle.

To show the effectiveness and advantages of SLASH and thus NPPs, we provide extensive experimental evaluations on various data sets and tasks. Specifically, we investigate the advantages of SLASH in comparison to SOTA DPPLs on the benchmark task of MNIST-Addition (Manhaeve et al. 2018). We further expand on this benchmark for a missing data setup as well as generative MNIST Addition task. Our results indicate the advantage of true probabilistic density estimation via appropriate NPPs. Finally, we show that SLASH Attention provides superior results for set prediction in terms of accuracy and generalization abilities compared to a baseline slot attention encoder. Both image generation and set prediction are novel benchmark tasks that no previous DPPL has tackled. With our results, we show that SLASH is a realization of "one system – two approaches" (Bengio 2019), that can successfully be used for performing various tasks and on a variety of data types.

In summary, we make the following contributions:

- introduce neural-probabilistic predicates,
- efficiently integrate answer set programming with probabilistic inference via NPPs within our novel DPPL, SLASH.
- successfully train neural, probabilistic and logic modules within SLASH for complex data structures end-to-end via a simple, single loss term.
- show that the integration of NPPs in SLASH provides various advantages across a variety of tasks and data sets compared to state-of-the-art DPPLs and neural models.

We proceed as follows. We start off by introducing NPPs, including its contribution to the loss function when learning. Then we introduce SLASH programs with the corresponding semantics and loss function. Before concluding, we touch upon our experimental evaluation.

[1]Code and supplements at: https://github.com/askrix/SLASH

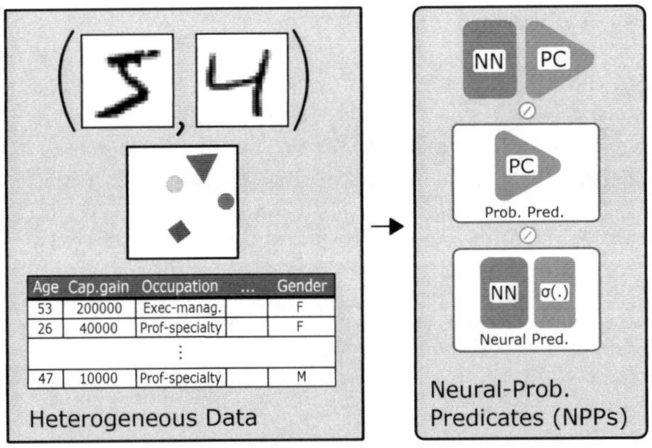

SLASH Program for set prediction:

```
# Define slots and identifiers for the objects in the image
slot(s1). slot(s2). slot(s3). slot(s4).
obj(o1). obj(o2). obj(o3). obj(o4).
# Assign each slot to an object identifier (matching)
{assign_one_slot_to_one_object(X, O): slot(X)}=1 :- obj(O).
...
# Define all Neural-Probabilistic Predicates
npp(color_attr(X), [red, blue, green, grey, brown,
                    magenta, cyan, yellow, bg]) :- slot(X).
...
# Object O has the attributes C and S and H and Z if ...
has_attributes(O, C, S, H, Z) :- slot(X), obj(O),
                    assign_one_slot_to_one_object(X, O),
                    color(+X, -C), shape(+X, -S),
                    shade(+X, -H), size(+X, -Z).
```

Query for set prediction:

```
# Does object o1 have the attributes red, circle, bright, small?
:- has_attributes(o1, red, circle, bright, small)
```

Figure 2: Basic SLASH building blocks and how to use them: (left) NPPs come in various flavors depending on the data and underlying task. Depending on the data set and underlying task, SLASH requires a suitable Neural-Probabilistic Predicate (NPP) that computes query-dependent probability estimates. A NPP can be composed of neural and probabilistic modules, or (depicted via slash symbol) only one of these two. (right) A minimal SLASH program and query for the set prediction task, here only showing the NPP that models the color category per object. For the full program, we refer to the supplements.

2 SLASH by Means of NPPs and Vice Versa

We begin our work by first introducing the novel framework of probabilistic predicates, neural probabilistic predicates (NPPs). After this, we introduce the novel DPPL, SLASH, which easily integrates NPPs via answer set programming with logical programming. We finally end this section with the learning procedure in SLASH, allowing to train all modules via a joint loss term.

2.1 Neural-Probabilistic Predicates

Previous DPPLs, DeepProbLog (Manhaeve et al. 2018) and NeurASP (Yang, Ishay, and Lee 2020), introduced the *Neural Predicate* as an annotated-disjunction or as a propositional atom, respectively, to acquire conditional class probabilities, $P(C|X)$, via the softmax function at the output of an arbitrary DNN. As mentioned in the introduction, this approach has certain limitations concerning inference capabilities. To resolve this issue, we introduce *Neural-Probabilisitic Predicates* (NPPs).

Formally, we denote with

$$npp\,(h(x), [v_1, \dots, v_n]) \tag{1}$$

a Neural-Probabilistic Predicate h. Thereby, (i) *npp* is a reserved word to label a NPP, (ii) *h* a symbolic name of either a PC, NN or a joint of a PC and NN (*cf.* Fig. 2)(left), e.g., *color_attr* is the name of a NPP of Fig. 2(right). Additionally, (iii) x denotes a "term" and (iv) $v_1, \dots, v_n$ are the n possible outcomes of h. For example, the placeholders for *color_attr* are the color attributes of an object (*Red, Blue, Green, etc.*).

A NPP abbreviates a rule of the form $c = v$ with $c \in \{h(x)\}$ and $v \in \{v_1, \dots, v_m\}$. Furthermore, we denote with Π^{npp} a set of NPPs of the form stated in (Eq. 1) and r^{npp} the set of all rules $c = v$ of one NPP, which denotes the possible outcomes, obtained from a NPP in Π^{npp}, e.g. $r^{color\_attr} = \{c = Red, c = Blue, c = Green, ...\}$ for the example depicted in Fig. 2(right).

Rules of the form $npp\,(h(x), [v_1, \dots, v_n]) \leftarrow Body$ are used as an abbreviation for application to multiple entities, e.g., multiple slots for the task of set prediction (*cf.* Fig. 2(right)). Hereby, the *Body* of the rule is identified by $\top$ (tautology, true) or $\bot$ (contradiction, false) during grounding. Rules of the form *Head* $\leftarrow$ *Body* with r^{npp} appearing in *Head* are prohibited for Π^{npp}.

In this work, we largely make use of NPPs that contain probabilistic circuits, which allow for tractable density estimation and modelling of joint probabilities. The term probabilistic circuit (PC) (Choi, Vergari, and Van den Broeck 2020) represents a unifying framework that encompasses all computational graphs which encode probability distributions and guarantee tractable probabilistic modelling. These include Sum-Product Networks (SPNs) (Poon and Domingos 2011) which are deep mixture models represented via a rooted directed acyclic graph with a recursively defined structure. In this way, with PCs it is possible to answer a much richer set of probabilistic queries, i.e. $P(X, C)$, $P(X|C)$, $P(C|X)$ and $P(C)$.

In addition to NPPs based purely on PCs, we introduce the arguably more interesting type of NPP that combines a neural module with a PC. Hereby, the neural module learns to map the raw input data into an optimal latent representation, e.g., object-based slot representations. The PC, in turn, learns to model the joint distribution of these latent variables and produces the final probability estimates. This type of NPP nicely combines the representational power of neural networks with the advantages of PCs in probability estimation and query flexibility.

For making the different probabilistic queries distinguishable in a SLASH program, we introduce the following notation. We denote a given variable with $+$ and the query variable with $-$. E.g., within the running example of set prediction (*cf.* Fig. 1 and 2(right)), with the query $color\_attr(+X, -C)$ one is asking for $P(C|X)$. Similarly, with $color\_attr(-X, +C)$ one is asking for $P(X|C)$ and, finally, with $color\_attr(+X,+C)$ for $P(X,C)$. And, in the case when no data is available, i.e, $color\_attr(-X,-C)$, we are querying for the prior $P(C)$.

To summarize, a NPP can consist of neural and/or probabilistic modules and produces query-dependent probability estimates. Due to the flexibility of its definition, the term NPP contains the predicates of previous works (Manhaeve et al. 2018; Yang, Ishay, and Lee 2020), but also more interesting predicates discussed above. The specific "flavor" of a NPP should be chosen depending on what type of probability estimation is required (*cf.* Fig 2(left)).

Lastly, for parameter learning NPPs possess a unified loss function of the negative log-likelihood,

$$L_{NPP} := -\log LH(x,\hat{x}) = \sum_{i=1}^{n} LH(x_i,\hat{x}_i) = \\ -\sum_{i=1}^{n} x_i \cdot \log(P_\xi^{(X,C)}(x_i)) \geq -\sum_{i=1}^{n} \log(P_\xi^{(X,C)}(x_i)) \tag{2}$$

whereby LH is an abbreviation for likelihood. Further, we assume data to be i.i.d., ground truth x_i to be the all-ones vector, ξ to be the parameters of the NPP and $P_\xi^{(X,C)}(x_i)$ are the predictions $\hat{x}_i$ obtained from the PC encoded in the NPP.

2.2 SLASH: a Novel DPPL for Integrating NPPs

Let us now introduce SLASH, a novel DPPL that efficiently integrates NPPs with logic programming.

SLASH Language and Semantics We continue in the pipeline on how to use the probability estimates of NPPs for answering logical queries, and begin by formally defining a SLASH program.

Definition 1. *A SLASH program* Π *is the union of* Π^{asp}, Π^{npp}. *Therewith,* Π^{asp} *is the set of propositional rules (standard rules from ASP-Core-2 (Calimeri et al. 2020)), and* Π^{npp} *is a set of Neural-Probabilistic Predicates of the form stated in Eq. 1.*

Similar to NeurASP, SLASH requires ASP and as such adopts its **syntax** to most part. Compared to ProbLog, ASP rarely goes into an infinite loop (*c.f.* chapter 2.9 of (Lifschitz 2019) for a simple code example leading to infinite loops with ProbLog) and is therefore preferable as a backbone. Fig. 2(right) presents a minimal SLASH program for the task of set prediction, exemplifying a set of propositional rules and neural predicates.

We now address how to integrate NPPs into an ASP compatible form to obtain the success probability for the logical query given all potential solutions. Thus, we define **SLASH's semantics**. For SLASH to translate the program Π to the ASP-solver's compatible form, the rules (Eq. 1) will be rewritten to the set of rules:

$$1\{h(x) = v_1; \ldots; h(x) = v_m\}1 \tag{3}$$

The ASP-solver should understand this as "Pick exactly one rule from the set". After the translation is done, we can ask an ASP-solver for the solutions for Π. We denote a set of ASP constraints in the form $\leftarrow$ *Body*, as *queries* Q and each of the solutions regarding Q as a *potential solution*, I, (referred to as *stable model* in ASP).

With $I|_{r^{npp}}$ we denote the projection of the I onto r^{npp}, $Num(I|_{r^{npp}},\Pi)$ – the number of the potential solutions of the program Π agreeing with $I|_{r^{npp}}$ on r^{npp}. Because we aim to calculate the success probability of a query Q, we formalize the probability of potential solution I beforehand.

Definition 2. *We specify the probability of the potential solution, I, for the program Π as the product of the probabilities of all atoms $c = v$ in $I|_{r^{npp}}$ divided by the number of potential solutions of Π agreeing with $I|_{r^{npp}}$ on r^{npp}:*

$$P_\Pi(I) = \begin{cases} \frac{\prod_{c=v \in I|_{r^{npp}}} P_\Pi(c=v)}{Num(I|_{r^{npp}},\Pi)}, & \text{if } I \text{ is pot. sol. of } \Pi, \\ 0, & \text{otherwise.} \end{cases} \tag{4}$$

Thus, we can now define the probability of a query.

Definition 3. *The probability of the query Q given the set of potential solutions I is defined as*

$$P_\Pi(Q) := \sum_{I \models Q} P_\Pi(I). \tag{5}$$

Thereby, $I \models Q$ reads as "I satisfies Q". The probability of the set of queries $\mathbf{Q} = \{Q_1,\ldots,Q_n\}$ is defined as the product of the probability of each. I.e.

$$P_\Pi(\mathbf{Q}) := \prod_{Q_i \in \mathbf{Q}} P_\Pi(Q_i) = \prod_{Q_i \in \mathbf{Q}} \sum_{I \models Q} P_\Pi(I). \tag{6}$$

Parameter Learning in SLASH We denote with $\Pi(\boldsymbol{\theta})$ the SLASH program under consideration, where $\boldsymbol{\theta}$ is the set of the parameters associated with Π. Further, making the i.i.d. assumption of the query set $\mathbf{Q}$, we follow (Manhaeve et al. 2018) and (Skryagin et al. 2020), and use the *learning from entailment* setting. That is, the training examples are logical queries that are known to be true in the SLASH program $\Pi(\boldsymbol{\theta})$. The goal is to learn the parameters $\boldsymbol{\theta}$ of the program $\Pi(\boldsymbol{\theta})$ so that the observed queries are most likely.

To this end, we employ the negative log-likelihood and the cross-entropy of the observed queries $P_{\Pi(\theta)}(Q_i)$ and their predicted probability value $P^{(X_\mathbf{Q},C)}(x_{Q_i})$, assuming the NPPs are fixed:

$$L_{ENT} := \\ -\log LH\left(\log(P_{\Pi(\theta)}(\mathbf{Q})), P^{(X_\mathbf{Q},C)}(x_\mathbf{Q})\right) = \\ -\sum_{j=1}^{m} \log(P_{\Pi(\theta)}(Q_{ij})) \cdot \log\left(P^{(X_\mathbf{Q},C)}(x_{Q_{ij}})\right). \tag{7}$$

This loss function aims at maximizing the estimated success probability. We remark that the defined loss function is true regardless of the NPP's form (NN with Softmax, PC or PC jointly with NN). The only difference will be the second term, e.g., $P^{(C|X_\mathbf{Q})}(x_\mathbf{Q})$ or $P^{(X_\mathbf{Q}|C)}(x_\mathbf{Q})$) depending on the NPP and task. Furthermore, we assume that for the set of queries $\mathbf{Q}$ it holds that,

$$P_{\Pi(\boldsymbol{\theta})}(Q) > 0 \quad \forall\, Q \in \mathbf{Q}.$$

In accordance with the semantics, we seek to reward the right solutions $v = c$ and penalize the wrong ones $v \neq c$. Referring to the probabilities in r^{npp} (i.e., the set of logical rules denoting NPPs; see Def. 2) as $\mathbf{p}$, one can compute their gradients w.r.t. $\boldsymbol{\theta}$ via backpropagation as

$$\sum_{Q\in\mathbf{Q}} \frac{\partial \log\left(P_{\Pi(\boldsymbol{\theta})}(Q)\right)}{\partial \boldsymbol{\theta}} = \sum_{Q\in\mathbf{Q}} \frac{\partial \log\left(P_{\Pi(\boldsymbol{\theta})}(Q)\right)}{\partial \mathbf{p}} \times \frac{\partial \mathbf{p}}{\partial \boldsymbol{\theta}}. \tag{8}$$

The term $\frac{\partial \mathbf{p}}{\partial \boldsymbol{\theta}}$ can now be computed as usual via backward propagation through the NPPs (see Eq.11 in the supplementary materials (Suppl.) A for details). By letting p to be the label of the probability of an atom $c = v$ in r^{npp} and denoting $P_{\Pi(\boldsymbol{\theta})}(c = v)$, the term $\frac{\partial \log\left(P_{\Pi(\boldsymbol{\theta})}(Q)\right)}{\partial \mathbf{p}}$ follows from NeurASP (Yang, Ishay, and Lee 2020) as

$$\frac{\partial \log\left(P_{\Pi(\boldsymbol{\theta})}(Q)\right)}{\partial \mathbf{p}} = \frac{\displaystyle\sum_{\substack{I:I\models Q\\ I\models c=v}} \frac{P_{\Pi(\boldsymbol{\theta})}(I)}{P_{\Pi(\boldsymbol{\theta})}(c=v)} - \sum_{\substack{I:I,v'\models Q\\ I\models c=v', v\neq v'}} \frac{P_{\Pi(\boldsymbol{\theta})}(I)}{P_{\Pi(\boldsymbol{\theta})}(c=v')}}{\displaystyle\sum_{I:I\models Q} P_{\Pi(\boldsymbol{\theta})}(I)}. \tag{9}$$

Doing this is a sensible idea. For instance, if a query to be true is not likely to be entailed, the gradient is positive. Putting everything together, the final loss function is

$$L_{SLASH} = L_{NPP} + L_{ENT} \tag{10}$$

and we perform training using coordinate descent, i.e., we train the NPPs, then train the program with fixed NPPs, train the NPPs with the program fixed, and so on.

Complementary, we formulate the proposition in the following, showing exactly the way the parameter learning is performed via the logical entailment loss function L_{ENT}, i.e., we derive its gradients.

Proposition 1. *The average derivative of the logical entailment loss function L_{ENT} defined in Eq. 7 can be estimated as follows*

$$\frac{1}{n}\frac{\partial}{\partial \mathbf{p}} L_{ENT} \geq -\frac{1}{n}\sum_{i=1}^{n} \frac{\partial \log(P_{\Pi(\theta)}(Q_i))}{\partial \mathbf{p}} \cdot \log(P^{(X_{\mathbf{Q}},C)}(x_{Q_i}))$$

Proof. Applying the i.i.d assumption over the likelihood and the definition of the cross-entropy for two vectors y_i and $\hat{y}_i$ we obtain

$$L_{ENT} = -\log LH(y,\hat{y}) = \sum_{i=1}^{n} H(y_i,\hat{y}_i)$$
$$= -\sum_{i=1}^{n}\sum_{j=1}^{m} \log(P_{\Pi(\theta)}(Q_{ij})) \cdot \log\left(P^{(X_{\mathbf{Q}},C)}(x_{Q_{ij}})\right).$$

With m being the number of classes defined in the domain of a NPP. Recognizing that the second term of the derivative

$$\frac{\partial}{\partial \mathbf{p}} H(y_i,\hat{y}_i) = -\sum_{j=1}^{m}\left[\frac{\partial \log(P_{\Pi(\theta)}(Q_{ij}))}{\partial \mathbf{p}} \cdot \log\left(P^{(X_{\mathbf{Q}},C)}(x_{Q_{ij}})\right) + \log(P_{\Pi(\theta)}(Q_{ij})) \cdot \frac{\partial \log\left(P^{(X_{\mathbf{Q}},C)}(x_{Q_{ij}})\right)}{\partial \mathbf{p}}\right],$$

is a constant and assembling all intermediate steps, we obtain the desired inequality. □

Similarly one can derive the derivative of the NPP loss function (Eq. 2) as:

$$\frac{\partial}{\partial \xi} L_{NPP} = \frac{\partial x_{Q_i}}{\partial \xi}\left(-\sum_{i=1}^{n} \frac{1}{\left(P_{\xi}^{(X_{\mathbf{Q}},C)}(x_{Q_i})\right)} \frac{\partial}{\partial x_{Q_i}}\left(P_{\xi}^{(X_{\mathbf{Q}},C)}(x_{Q_i})\right)\right)$$

For more details of the proof and derivations, we refer to the Suppl. A. It also includes the details on parameter learning for such NPPs, as depicted for SLASH Attention.

Importantly, with the learning schema described above, rather than requiring a novel loss function for each individual task and data set, with SLASH, it is now possible to simply incorporate specific task and data requirements into the logic program. The training loss, however, remains the same.

3 Empirical Evaluations

Let us now turn to experimental evaluations. In particular, a main advantage of SLASH lies in the efficient integration of neural, probabilistic and symbolic computations. To emphasize this, but also the particular advantages of integrating true probabilistic density estimation into logic programming via NPPs, we conduct a variety of experimental evaluations showing the advantages and usability of SLASH on novel tasks for DPPLs.

3.1 Experimental Details

We use two benchmark data sets, namely MNIST (LeCun, Cortes, and J.C. Burges 1998) for the task of MNIST-Addition and a variant of the ShapeWorld data set (Kuhnle and Copestake 2017) for object-centric set prediction. For all experiments, we present the average and the standard deviation over five runs with different random seeds for parameter initialization.

For ShapeWorld experiments, we generate a data set we refer to as ShapeWorld4. Images of ShapeWorld4 contain between one and four objects, with each object consisting of four attributes: a color (red, blue, green, gray, brown, magenta, cyan or yellow), a shade (bright, or dark), a shape (circle, triangle, or square) and a size (small or big). Thus, each object can be created from 84 different combinations of attributes. Fig. 1 depicts an example image.

	Test Acc. (%)
DeepProbLog	98.49 ± 0.18
NeurASP	98.21 ± 0.30
SLASH (PC)	95.52 ± 0.32
SLASH (DNN)	$\mathbf{98.99} \pm \mathbf{0.04}$

	DeepProbLog	NeurASP	**SLASH** (DNN)	**SLASH** (PC)
50%	$\mathbf{97.73} \pm \mathbf{0.12}$	25.75 ± 31.32	96.0 ± 0.02	97.59 ± 0.01
80%	76.07 ± 18.38	10.29 ± 0.83	95.4 ± 0.01	$\mathbf{96.8} \pm \mathbf{0.00}$
90%	69.15 ± 29.15	13.28 ± 4.94	75.6 ± 0.18	$\mathbf{95.00} \pm \mathbf{0.00}$
97%	32.46 ± 22.48	11.94 ± 0.95	67.4 ± 0.09	$\mathbf{84.2} \pm \mathbf{0.03}$

Table 1: MNIST Addition and missing data MNIST Addition Results. Test accuracy corresponds to the percentage of correctly classified test images. (left) Baseline MNIST Addition task with various DPPLs, including SLASH with a NPP that models the joint probabilities (SLASH (PC)) and one that models only conditional probabilities (SLASH (DNN)). (right) MNIST Addition task with missing pixels. The amount of missing pixels was varied between 50% and 97% of the pixels per image.

We measure performance via classification accuracies in the MNIST-Addition task. In our ShapeWorld4 experiments, we present the average precision. We refer to Suppl. B for the SLASH programs and queries of each experiment, and Suppl. C for a detailed description of hyperparameters and further details. Lastly, we remark to have trained all experiments but Generative MNIST-Addition by discriminative fashion only.

3.2 Experimental Results

Let us now present our experimental findings.

Evaluation 1: SLASH outperforms SOTA DPPLs in MNIST-Addition. The task of MNIST-Addition (Manhaeve et al. 2018) is to predict the sum of two MNIST digits, presented only as raw images. During test time, however, a model should classify the images directly. Thus, although a model does not receive explicit information about the depicted digits, it must learn to identify digits via indirect feedback on the sum prediction.

We compare the test accuracy after convergence between the three DPPLs: DeepProbLog (Manhaeve et al. 2018), NeurASP (Yang, Ishay, and Lee 2020) and SLASH, using a probabilistic circuit (PC) or a deep neural network (DNN) as NPP. Notably, the DNN used in SLASH (DNN) is the LeNet5 model (LeCun et al. 1998) of DeepProbLog and NeurASP. When using the PC as NPP, we have also extracted conditional class probabilities $P(C|X)$, by marginalizing the class variables C to acquire the normalization constant $P(X)$ from the joint $P(X, C)$, and calculating $P(X|C)$.

The results can be seen in Tab. 1(left). We observe that training SLASH with a DNN NPP produces SOTA accuracies compared to DeepProbLog and NeurASP, confirming that SLASH's loss computation leads to improved performances. Apart from improved mean accuracies, it is important to note that the training of SLASH (DNN) also led to the massively reduced standard deviation in the test accuracy, suggesting that SLASH allows for much more stable results than the other DPPLs.

We further observe that the test accuracy of SLASH with a PC NPP is slightly below the other DPPLs. However, we argue that this may be since a PC, in comparison to a DNN, is learning a true mixture density rather than just conditional probabilities. The advantages of doing so will be investigated in the next experiments. Note that, optimal architecture search for PCs, e.g., for computer vision, is an open research question. We also refer to the Suppl. E, indicating substantial improvements in terms of inference time (even with a PC-based NPP, thus performing tractable probabilistic inference) due to our efficient implementation of SLASH with the batchwise learning and parallel calls to the ASP solver of SLASH.

These evaluations, in summary, show SLASH's advantages on the benchmark MNIST-Addition task. Additional benefits will be made clear in the following experiments.

Evaluation 2: Handling Missing Data with SLASH. SLASH offers the advantage of flexibility to use various kinds of NPPs. Thus, in comparison to previous DPPLs, one can easily integrate NPPs into SLASH that perform joint probability estimation. For this evaluation, we again consider the task of MNIST-Addition with missing data. Specifically, in this evaluation, all three DPPLs were trained with the MNIST-Addition task with images in which a percentage of pixels per image has been removed. Importantly, whereas DeepProbLog, NeurASP and SLASH (DNN) handle the missing data simply as background pixels, SLASH (PC) specifically models the missing data as uncertain data by marginalizing the denoted pixels at inference time.

As can be seen in Tab. 1(right), regardless of the NPP's form and the rate of the missing pixels per image, SLASH outperforms other DPPLs, both in terms of higher mean test accuracy and lower standard deviation. We observe that at 50%, DeepProbLog and SLASH produce almost equal accuracies. With 80% percent missing pixels, there is a substantial difference in the ability of the two DPPLs to correctly classify images, with SLASH having quite stable results, and delivering only slightly decreased performance. By further increasing the percentage of missing pixels, this difference becomes even more substantial with SLASH (PC) still reaching a 84% test accuracy even when 97% of the pixels per image are missing, whereas DeepProbLog degrades to an average of 32% test accuracy.

We further note that SLASH, in comparison to DeepProbLog, produces largely reduced standard deviations over runs. Notably, over all seeds and settings, the test accuracy measured by NeurASP diverged after several epochs and did not recover. We presume this to be an effect of exploding gradients. We also refer to Suppl. D, containing results of training on the full MNIST data set, but testing on a set with missing pixels, further indicating benefits of SLASH for out-of-distribution data.

In summary, using the power of true density estimation, SLASH can produce robust results in comparison to other DPPLs in a task with missing data.

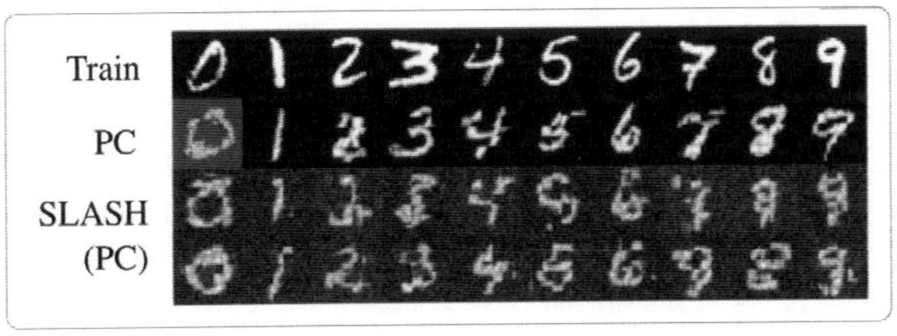

Figure 3: Qualitative comparison of Generative MNIST-Addition: each row is entailing images per class. The first one are ground truths obtained from the dataset, the second one represents the sampled images from a PC trained solely in a generative way. The last two rows are sampled from the NPP trained within SLASH. The third row depicts images after an epoch of the discriminative learning step, and the last row after a one epoch of generative step.

Evaluation 3: True density estimation allows for generative learning. As previously mentioned, thanks to the NPP's design, SLASH allows us to embrace true density estimation in logic programming. Having such a model for joint probability estimation allows for posing a much broader range of questions, e.g., based on generative learning.

In this evaluation, we investigate the situation where only a part of the overall dataset is available and the task is to discover the missing part through high-level reasoning and generative learning. This evaluation differs from evaluation 2 in that a model receives as input the result of the addition and one of the two images that contributes to the sum. Thus, an entire image is missing, and we wish not only to find the value of the missing digit, but also generate the corresponding image as well. Using the $\pm$ notation, we are thus querying for the class prior of the missing image, a type of query that no previous DPPLs can handle.

To train SLASH for this challenging task, we require not only discriminative, but also generative learning. For this purpose, we applied coordinate descent with an Adam optimizer (Kingma and Ba 2015) to minimize the SLASH loss (discriminative learning) and expectation maximization (EM) to maximize the log-likelihood (generative learning). In other words, the data set consisted of available and sampled images during the generative phase of the training.

As neither of the previous DPPLs have generative capabilities, we here revert to comparing the generative abilities of SLASH with an PC-based NPP and trained via coordinate descent to a stand-alone PC trained solely via EM. Both PCs were constructed using the same set of settings and entail the same number of learnable parameters. We further revert here to a qualitative analysis of generated samples. Thus, the point of the results is to indicate the quality of generated samples via SLASH in comparison to the current SOTA image generation results via PCs.

As with other tasks, we present the corresponding program in the Suppl. B. Fig. 3 presents the qualitative comparison per class between the ground truths (data), images sampled from a PC trained in the generative fashion and images sampled from the NPP after training. We observe that SLASH generated digits, though not as qualitative as the stand-alone PC digits, still clearly depict characteristic features of the classes. This is a surprising result given that both objectives are perpendicular in their nature towards each other, and thus it is far more challenging for the sampled images to be as distinct and without artifacts as after pure generative training of stand-alone PCs.

Thus, utilizing the generative property of NPPs with the ability of joint probability estimation, we show that via the $\pm$-notation one can easily perform generative learning out-of-the-box via SLASH. Overall, the results are a first step of generative learning via a DPPL. We note that the quality of the generated samples is improvable, and hypothesize that employing two different optimizers for each step of coordinate descent surely does not have an optimal effect on the PC NPP. A promising approach for future work is to investigate the hybrid generative-discriminative loss proposed in RAT-SPN (eq. 5) (Peharz et al. 2019) that unifies the training and mitigates the need for coordinate descent.

Evaluation 4: Improved Concept Learning via SLASH. Let us now turn to a very different setting of object-centric set prediction, a fascinating, yet challenging task that no DPPL has tackled up to now. Recent advances in object-centric deep learning (OCDL) have shown great architectural improvements for the performances of neural networks in complex visual tasks, such as object set prediction from images (Greff et al. 2019; Lin et al. 2020; Locatello et al. 2020). We propose that these advancements can be improved even further by integrating such neural components into DPPLs, and adding logical constrains about objects and their properties. For the fourth set of evaluations, we thus revert to the ShapeWorld4 dataset.

For set prediction, a model is trained to predict the discrete attributes of a set of objects in an image (*cf.* Fig. 1 for an example ShapeWorld4 image). The difficulty lies therein that the model must match an unordered set of corresponding attributes of a varying number of objects, with its internal representations of the image.

The slot attention module introduced by (Locatello et al. 2020) allows for an attractive object-centric approach to this task. Specifically, this module represents a pluggable, differentiable module that can be easily added to any architecture and, through a competitive softmax-based attention mechanism, can enforce the binding of specific parts of a latent representation into permutation-invariant, task-specific vectors, called slots. In our experiments, we wish to show that by adding logical constraints in the training setting, one can improve the overall performances and generalization properties of such a model. For this, we train SLASH with NPPs as depicted in Fig. 1 consisting of a shared slot encoder and separate PCs, each modelling the mixture of latent slot variables and the attributes of one category, e.g., color. For ShapeWorld4, we thereby have altogether four NPPs. Finally, SLASH is trained via queries of the kind exemplified in Fig.10 in the supplements. We refer to this configuration as *SLASH Attention*.

We compare SLASH Attention to a baseline slot attention

	Slot Att.	**SLASH Att.**
	ShapeWorld4	
Test Set	90.24 ± 0.93	$\mathbf{95.58 \pm 0.61}$
	CoGenT	
Test Cond. A	90.37 ± 2.19	$\mathbf{96.85 \pm 0.43}$
Test Cond. B	27.15 ± 2.36	$\mathbf{40.58 \pm 1.99}$

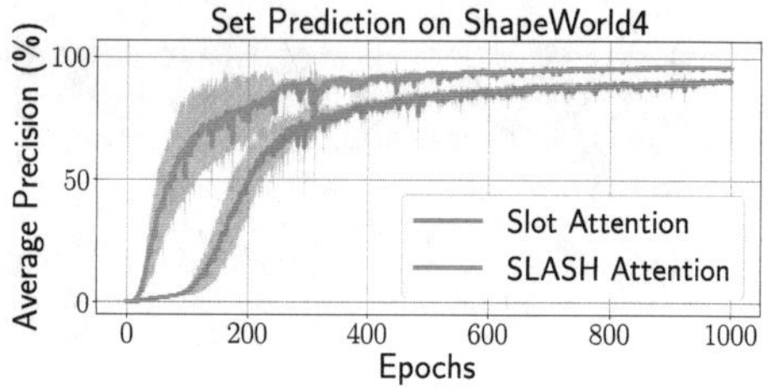

Figure 4: ShapeWorld4 Experiments. (Left) Converged test average precision scores for the set prediction task with ShapeWorld4 (top) and ShapeWorld4 CoGenT (bottom). (Right) Test average precision scores for set prediction with ShapeWorld4 over the training epochs. In these experiments, we compared a baseline slot encoder versus SLASH Attention with slot attention and PC-based NPPs. For the CoGenT experiments, a model is trained on one training set and tested on two separate test conditions. Condition A test set contains attribute compositions which were also seen during training. Condition B test set contains attribute compositions which were not seen during training, e.g., yellow circles were not present in the training set, but present in Condition B test set.

encoder using an MLP and Hungarian loss for predicting the object properties from the slot encodings as in (Locatello et al. 2020). The key difference between these two models lies in the logical constraint we are employing in SLASH Attention. In their original work, the authors of (Locatello et al. 2020) utilize a single MLP trained via Hungarian loss, i.e., they assume shared parameters for all attributes. In comparison, in SLASH attention, we make an independence assumption about the parameters for the object attributes and encode this via logical constraints. We refer to Fig. 2 (right) for a minimal version of the program, and Suppl. C for the full version.

The results of these experiments can be found in Fig. 4 (left). We observe that the average precision after convergence on the held-out test set with SLASH Attention is greatly improved to that of the baseline model. Additionally, in Fig. 4 (right), we observe that SLASH Attention reaches the average precision value of the baseline model in much fewer number of epochs.

The goal of this evaluation was to test if we can observe any overall advantage of SLASH and NPPs for such a challenging visual reasoning task for which we had introduced the specific instantiation of SLASH, SLASH Attention. We can summarize that indeed by adding logical knowledge to the training procedure via SLASH one can greatly improve the capabilities of a neural module exemplified here for set prediction. These results suggest that the question of the independence of object attributes (e.g., an object has one color, one form, etc.) can be solved effectively by logic constraints. Consequentially, the monolithic multicategorical MLP with shared parameters used by (Locatello et al. 2020) is sufficient but not necessary.

Evaluation 5: Improved Compositional Generalization with SLASH. Lastly, to test the hypothesis that SLASH Attention possesses improved generalization properties in comparison to a baseline neural model, we ran experiments on a variant of ShapeWorld4 similar to the CLEVR Compositional Generalization Test (CoGenT) (Johnson et al. 2017). The goal of CoGenT is to investigate a model's ability to handle novel combinations of attributes that were not seen during training.

For this purpose, we established two conditions within a ShapeWorld4 CoGenT data set: **Condition (A)** – the training and test data set contains squares with the colors *gray*, *blue*, *brown*, or *yellow*, triangles with the colors *red*, *green*, *magenta*, or *cyan* and circles of *all* colors. **Condition (B)** – the training set is as in Condition (A). However, the test set contains squares with the colors *red*, *green*, *magenta*, or *cyan*, triangles with the colors *gray*, *blue*, *brown*, or *yellow* and circles of *all* colors. The goal is to investigate how well a model can generalize that, e.g., also squares can have the color red, although never having seen evidence for this during training.

The resulting average precision test scores are presented in Fig. 4a (left). We observe that, even though SLASH Attention with its corresponding program was not explicitly designed to handle composition generalization, it shows greatly improved generalization capabilities. This can be seen in the approx. 13% higher average precision scores on the Condition (B) test set in comparison to the baseline model. Importantly, this trend still holds even when taking the overall higher performance of SLASH Attention observed in Condition (A) into account.

To summarize our findings from the experiments on set prediction: we observe that adding prior knowledge in the form of logical constraints via SLASH can greatly improve a neural module in terms of performance and generalizability. On a side note: training neural networks for novel tasks, often involves defining explicit loss functions, e.g., Hungarian loss for set prediction. This stands in contrast to SLASH: no matter the choice of NPP and underlying task, the training loss remains the same. Task-related requirements simply need to be added as lines of code to the SLASH program. Thus, it highlights SLASH's versatility and flexibility even further.

Summary of Empirical Results. All empirical results together demonstrate that the expressiveness and flexibility of SLASH is highly beneficial and can easily outperform state-of-the-art: one can freely combine what is required to solve the underlying task — (deep) neural networks, PCs, and logic. Importantly, the results indicate the potential of NPPs in general and PC-based NPPs, in particular, via SLASH.

4 Related Work

Neuro-Symbolic AI can be divided into two lines of research, depending on the starting point, though both have the same final goal: to combine low-level perception with logical constraints and reasoning.

A key motivation of Neuro-Symbolic AI (d'Avila Garcez, Lamb, and Gabbay 2009; Mao et al. 2019; Hudson and Manning 2019; d'Avila Garcez et al. 2019; Jiang and Ahn 2020; d'Avila Garcez and Lamb 2020) is to combine the advantages of symbolic and neural representations into a joint system. This is often done in a hybrid approach where a neural network acts as a perception module that interfaces with a symbolic reasoning system, e.g., (Mao et al. 2019; Yi et al. 2018). The goal of such an approach is to mitigate the issues of one type of representation by the other, e.g., using the power of symbolic reasoning systems to handle the generalizability issues of neural networks and on the other hand handle the difficulty of noisy data for symbolic systems via neural networks. Recent work has also shown the advantage of approaches for explaining and revising incorrect decisions (Ciravegna et al. 2020; Stammer, Schramowski, and Kersting 2021). Many of these previous works, however, train the sub-symbolic and symbolic modules separately.

Deep Probabilistic Programming Languages (DPPLs) are programming languages that combine deep neural networks with probabilistic models and allow a user to express a probabilistic model via a logical program. Similar to neuro-symbolic architectures, DPPLs thereby unite the advantages of different paradigms. DPPLs are related to earlier works such as Markov Logic Networks (MLNs) (Richardson and Domingos 2006). Thereby, the binding link is the Weighted Model Counting (WMC) introduced in LP^{MLN} (Lee and Wang 2016). Several DPPLs have been proposed by now, among which are Pyro (Bingham et al. 2019), Edward (Tran et al. 2017), DeepProbLog (Manhaeve et al. 2018), and NeurASP (Yang, Ishay, and Lee 2020).

To resolve the scalability issues of DeepProbLog, which use Sentential Decision Diagrams (SDDs) (Darwiche 2011) as the underlying data structure to evaluate queries, NeurASP (Yang, Ishay, and Lee 2020), offers a solution by utilizing Answer Set Programming (ASP) (Dimopoulos, Nebel, and Koehler 1997; Soininen and Niemelä 1999; Marek and Truszczynski 1999; Calimeri et al. 2020). In contrast to query evaluation in Prolog (Colmerauer and Roussel 1993; Clocksin and Mellish 1981) which may lead to an infinite loop, many modern answer set solvers use Conflict-Driven-Clause-Learning (CDPL) which, theoretically, always terminates. In this way, NeurASP changes the paradigm from query evaluation to model generation, i.e., instead of constructing an SDD or similar knowledge representation system, NeurASP generates a set of all potential solutions (one model per solution) and estimates the probability for the truth value of each of these solutions. Of those DPPLs that handle learning in a relational, probabilistic setting and in an end-to-end fashion, all of these are limited to estimating only conditional class probabilities.

Object-centric deep learning has recently brought forth several exciting avenues of research by introducing inductive biases to neural networks to extract objects from visual scenes in an unsupervised manner (Zhang, Hare, and Prügel-Bennett 2019; Burgess et al. 2019; Engelcke et al. 2020; Greff et al. 2019; Lin et al. 2020; Locatello et al. 2020; Jiang and Ahn 2020). We refer to (Greff, van Steenkiste, and Schmidhuber 2020) for a detailed overview. A motivation for this specific line of investigation, which notably has been around for a longer period of time (Fodor and Pylyshyn 1988; Marcus 2019), is that objects occurring as natural building blocks in human perception and possess advantageous properties for many cognitive tasks, such as scene understanding and reasoning. These works have shown great success in extracting object-based representations via their implicit architectural biases. However, an interesting avenue is to also add explicit logical biases, e.g., via constraints about objects and their properties in the form of logical statements such as color singularity.

5 Conclusion and Future Work

We introduce SLASH, a novel DPPL that integrates neural computations with tractable probability estimates and logical statements. The key ingredient of SLASH to achieve this are Neural-Probabilistic Predicates (NPPs) that can be flexibly constructed out of neural and/or probabilistic circuit modules based on the data and underlying task. With these NPPs, one can produce task-specific probability estimates. The details and additional prior knowledge of a task are neatly encompassed within a SLASH program with only few lines of code. Finally, via Answer Set Programming and Weighted Model Counting, the logical SLASH program and probability estimates from the NPPs are combined to estimate the truth value of a task-specific query. Our experiments show the power and efficiency of SLASH, improving upon previous DPPLs in the benchmark MNIST-Addition task in terms of performance, efficiency, and robustness. Furthermore, the generative MNIST-Addition task demonstrates that via the generation of images which encapsulate logical knowledge bases, we are moving from data-rich to knowledge-rich AI. Importantly, by integrating a SOTA slot attention encoder into NPPs and adding few logical constraints, SLASH demonstrates improved performances and generalizability in comparison to the pure slot encoder for the task of object-centric set prediction; a setting no DPPL has tackled yet. Our results show the effectiveness and improved utility of SLASH over previous DPPLs, as well as the great potential overall of DPPLs to elegantly combine logical reasoning with neural computations and uncertainty estimates.

Interesting avenues for future work include benchmarking SLASH on additional data types and tasks. One should explore unsupervised and weakly supervised learning using logic with SLASH and investigate how far logical constraints can help unsupervised object discovery. An interesting and important avenue for a broader usability of NPPs, in particular, is to investigate the construction of multicategorical NPPs. Furthermore, the ideas of the generative MNIST-Addition task should be investigated further. As mentioned, one interesting approach to this end is the hybrid generative-discriminative loss of (Peharz et al. 2019).

Acknowledgements

This work was partly supported by the Federal Minister of Education and Research (BMBF) and the Hessian Ministry of Science and the Arts (HMWK) within the National Research Center for Applied Cybersecurity ATHENE, the ICT-48 Network of AI Research Excellence Center "TAILOR" (EU Horizon 2020, GA No 952215, and the Collaboration Lab with Nexplore "AI in Construction" (AICO). It also benefited from the BMBF AI lighthouse project "SPAICER" (01MK20015E), the Hessian research priority programme LOEWE within the project WhiteBox, as well as the HMWK cluster projects "The Third Wave of AI" and "The Adaptive Mind".

References

Bengio, Y. 2019. From System 1 Deep Learning to System 2 Deep Learning. Invited talk NeurIPS.

Bingham, E.; Chen, J. P.; Jankowiak, M.; Obermeyer, F.; Pradhan, N.; Karaletsos, T.; Singh, R.; Szerlip, P. A.; Horsfall, P.; and Goodman, N. D. 2019. Pyro: Deep universal probabilistic programming. *Journal of Machine Learning Research* 28:1–28:6.

Burgess, C. P.; Matthey, L.; Watters, N.; Kabra, R.; Higgins, I.; Botvinick, M.; and Lerchner, A. 2019. Monet: Unsupervised scene decomposition and representation. *CoRR*.

Calimeri, F.; Faber, W.; Gebser, M.; Ianni, G.; Kaminski, R.; Krennwallner, T.; Leone, N.; Maratea, M.; Ricca, F.; and Schaub, T. 2020. Asp-core-2 input language format. *Theory and Practice of Logic Programming* 294–309.

Choi, Y.; Vergari, A.; and Van den Broeck, G. 2020. Probabilistic circuits: A unifying framework for tractable probabilistic models. Technical report, UCLA.

Ciravegna, G.; Giannini, F.; Gori, M.; Maggini, M.; and Melacci, S. 2020. Human-driven FOL explanations of deep learning. In *IJCAI*, 2234–2240.

Clocksin, W. F., and Mellish, C. 1981. *Programming in Prolog*.

Colmerauer, A., and Roussel, P. 1993. The birth of prolog. In *HOPL-II*, 37–52.

Darwiche, A. 2011. SDD: A new canonical representation of propositional knowledge bases. In *IJCAI*, 819–826.

d'Avila Garcez, A., and Lamb, L. C. 2020. Neurosymbolic AI: the 3rd wave. *CoRR*.

d'Avila Garcez, A. S.; Gori, M.; Lamb, L. C.; Serafini, L.; Spranger, M.; and Tran, S. N. 2019. Neural-symbolic computing: An effective methodology for principled integration of machine learning and reasoning. *FLAP* 611–632.

d'Avila Garcez, A. S.; Lamb, L. C.; and Gabbay, D. M. 2009. *Neural-Symbolic Cognitive Reasoning*. Cognitive Technologies.

Dimopoulos, Y.; Nebel, B.; and Koehler, J. 1997. Encoding planning problems in nonmonotonic logic programs. In *ECP*, Lecture Notes in Computer Science, 169–181.

Engelcke, M.; Kosiorek, A. R.; Jones, O. P.; and Posner, I. 2020. GENESIS: generative scene inference and sampling with object-centric latent representations. In *ICLR*.

Fodor, J. A., and Pylyshyn, Z. W. 1988. Connectionism and cognitive architecture: A critical analysis. *Cognition* 3–71.

Greff, K.; Kaufman, R. L.; Kabra, R.; Watters, N.; Burgess, C.; Zoran, D.; Matthey, L.; Botvinick, M.; and Lerchner, A. 2019. Multi-object representation learning with iterative variational inference. In *ICML*, 2424–2433.

Greff, K.; van Steenkiste, S.; and Schmidhuber, J. 2020. On the binding problem in artificial neural networks. *CoRR*.

Hudson, D. A., and Manning, C. D. 2019. Learning by abstraction: The neural state machine. In *NeurIPS*, 5901–5914.

Jiang, J., and Ahn, S. 2020. Generative neurosymbolic machines. In *NeurIPS*.

Johnson, J.; Hariharan, B.; van der Maaten, L.; Fei-Fei, L.; Zitnick, C. L.; and Girshick, R. B. 2017. CLEVR: A diagnostic dataset for compositional language and elementary visual reasoning. In *CVPR*, 1988–1997.

Kingma, D. P., and Ba, J. 2015. Adam: A method for stochastic optimization. In *ICLR 2015*.

Kuhnle, A., and Copestake, A. A. 2017. Shapeworld - A new test methodology for multimodal language understanding. *CoRR*.

LeCun, Y.; Bottou, L.; Bengio, Y.; and Haffner, P. 1998. Gradient-based learning applied to document recognition. 2278–2324.

LeCun, Y.; Cortes, C.; and J.C. Burges, C. 1998. THE MNIST DATABASE of handwritten digits.

Lee, J., and Wang, Y. 2016. Weighted rules under the stable model semantics. In *KR*, 145–154.

Lifschitz, V. 2019. *Answer Set Programming*. Springer International Publishing.

Lin, Z.; Wu, Y.; Peri, S. V.; Sun, W.; Singh, G.; Deng, F.; Jiang, J.; and Ahn, S. 2020. SPACE: unsupervised object-oriented scene representation via spatial attention and decomposition. In *ICLR*.

Locatello, F.; Weissenborn, D.; Unterthiner, T.; Mahendran, A.; Heigold, G.; Uszkoreit, J.; Dosovitskiy, A.; and Kipf, T. 2020. Object-centric learning with slot attention. In *NeurIPS*.

Manhaeve, R.; Dumancic, S.; Kimmig, A.; Demeester, T.; and Raedt, L. D. 2018. Deepproblog: Neural probabilistic logic programming. 3753–3763.

Mao, J.; Gan, C.; Kohli, P.; Tenenbaum, J. B.; and Wu, J. 2019. The neuro-symbolic concept learner: Interpreting scenes, words, and sentences from natural supervision. In *ICLR*.

Marcus, G. F. 2019. *The algebraic mind: Integrating connectionism and cognitive science*. MIT press.

Marek, V. W., and Truszczynski, M. 1999. Stable models and an alternative logic programming paradigm. In *The Logic Programming Paradigm - A 25-Year Perspective*, Artificial Intelligence. 375–398.

Peharz, R.; Vergari, A.; Stelzner, K.; Molina, A.; Trapp, M.; Shao, X.; Kersting, K.; and Ghahramani, Z. 2019. Random sum-product networks: A simple and effective approach to probabilistic deep learning. In *UAI*, 334–344.

Peharz, R.; Lang, S.; Vergari, A.; Stelzner, K.; Molina, A.; Trapp, M.; den Broeck, G. V.; Kersting, K.; and Ghahramani, Z. 2020. Einsum networks: Fast and scalable learning of tractable probabilistic circuits. In *ICML*, 7563–7574.

Poon, H., and Domingos, P. M. 2011. Sum-product networks: A new deep architecture. In *UAI*, 337–346.

Richardson, M., and Domingos, P. M. 2006. Markov logic networks. *Machine Learning* 107–136.

Skryagin, A.; Stelzner, K.; Molina, A.; Ventola, F.; and Kersting, K. 2020. Splog: Sum-product logic. In *ProbProg*.

Soininen, T., and Niemelä, I. 1999. Developing a declarative rule language for applications in product configuration. In *PADL*, Lecture Notes in Computer Science, 305–319.

Stammer, W.; Schramowski, P.; and Kersting, K. 2021. Right for the right concept: Revising neuro-symbolic concepts by interacting with their explanations. In *CVPR*, 3619–3629.

Tran, D.; Hoffman, M. D.; Saurous, R. A.; Brevdo, E.; Murphy, K.; and Blei, D. M. 2017. Deep probabilistic programming. In *ICLR*.

Yang, Z.; Ishay, A.; and Lee, J. 2020. NeurASP: Embracing neural networks into answer set programming. In *IJCAI*, 1755–1762.

Yi, K.; Wu, J.; Gan, C.; Torralba, A.; Kohli, P.; and Tenenbaum, J. 2018. Neural-symbolic VQA: disentangling reasoning from vision and language understanding. In *NeurIPS*, 1039–1050.

Zhang, Y.; Hare, J. S.; and Prügel-Bennett, A. 2019. Deep set prediction networks. In *NeurIPS*, 3207–3217.

Proceedings of the 19th International Conference on Principles of Knowledge Representation and Reasoning
Special Session on KR and Machine Learning

Learning Generalized Policies without Supervision Using GNNs

Simon Ståhlberg[1] , **Blai Bonet**[2] , **Hector Geffner**[3,2,1]
[1]Linköping University, Sweden
[2]Universitat Pompeu Fabra, Spain
[3]Institució Catalana de Recerca i Estudis Avançats (ICREA), Barcelona, Spain
simon.stahlberg@liu.se, bonetblai@gmail.com, hector.geffner@upf.edu

Abstract

We consider the problem of learning generalized policies for classical planning domains using graph neural networks from small instances represented in lifted STRIPS. The problem has been considered before but the proposed neural architectures are complex and the results are often mixed. In this work, we use a simple and general GNN architecture and aim at obtaining crisp experimental results and a deeper understanding: either the policy greedy in the learned value function achieves close to 100% generalization over instances larger than those used in training, or the failure must be understood, and possibly fixed, logically. For this, we exploit the relation established between the expressive power of GNNs and the C_2 fragment of first-order logic (namely, FOL with 2 variables and counting quantifiers). We find for example that domains with general policies that require more expressive features can be solved with GNNs once the states are extended with suitable "derived atoms" encoding role compositions and transitive closures that do not fit into C_2. The work follows an existing approach based on GNNs for learning optimal general policies in a supervised fashion, but the learned policies are no longer required to be optimal (which expands the scope, as many planning domains do not have general optimal policies) and are learned without supervision. Interestingly, value-based reinforcement learning methods that aim to produce optimal policies, do not always yield policies that generalize, as the goals of optimality and generality are in conflict in domains where optimal planning is NP-hard.

1 Introduction

Generalized planning is concerned with the computation of general policies for families of planning instances over the same domain that span different state spaces. For example, a general policy for solving Blocks problems can place all blocks on the table and stack then the desired towers, bottom up, one at at time. The formulation and the computation of general policies is particularly interesting at it involves ideas from planning, knowledge representation, and learning. Indeed, the language for representing the general policies is key, in particular in domains where the set of ground actions change from instance to instance (Bonet and Geffner 2018). Also learning policies from examples has been found to be simpler than synthesizing them from specifications (Khardon 1999; Srivastava, Immerman, and Zilberstein 2008; Bonet, Palacios, and Geffner 2009; Hu and De Giacomo 2011; Belle and Levesque 2016; Segovia, Jiménez, and Jonsson 2016). In planning, it is common to approach the problem assuming that domain predicates are known, while some deep learning and deep reinforcement learning approaches address the problem with no domain knowledge, representing the states, for example, as 2D images (Chevalier-Boisvert et al. 2019; Campero et al. 2021; Cobbe et al. 2020).

In this paper, we consider the problem of learning generalized policies for classical planning domains using *graph neural networks* (Scarselli et al. 2008; Hamilton 2020) from small instances represented in lifted STRIPS. The problem has been considered before but using neural architectures that are more complex and with results that are often less crisp, involving in certain cases heuristic information or search (Toyer et al. 2020; Garg, Bajpai, and Mausam 2020; Rivlin, Hazan, and Karpas 2020; Karia and Srivastava 2021; Shen, Trevizan, and Thiébaux 2020). We use a simple and general GNN architecture and aim at obtaining crisp experimental results and a deeper understanding: either the policy greedy in the learned value function achieves close to 100% generalization over instances larger than those used in training, or the failure must be understood and, possibly fixed, using logical methods. For this, we exploit the relation between the expressive power of GNNs and the two-variable fragment of first-order logic with counting, C_2, that includes the standard description logics (Barceló et al. 2020; Grohe 2020). Description logic features have been used indeed for expressing general policies and general value functions (Martín and Geffner 2004; Fern, Yoon, and Givan 2006; Bonet, Francès, and Geffner 2019; Francès et al. 2019; Francès, Bonet, and Geffner 2021). We find for example that domains with general policies that require more expressive features can be solved with GNNs once the states are extended with suitable "derived atoms" for encoding role compositions and transitive closures that do not fit into C_2.

The work follows the GNN approach for learning optimal general policies in a supervised fashion (Ståhlberg, Bonet, and Geffner 2022) but the learned policies are no longer required to be optimal, which expands the scope of the approach, as many planning domains do not admit general optimal policies, and are learned without supervision. The learning problem becomes the problem of learning a value function V that can be applied to the states s of any domain instance, such that the greedy policy in V

solves the training instances. Versions of this idea have been used in combinatorial settings (Francès et al. 2019; Francès, Bonet, and Geffner 2021). Interestingly, value-based reinforcement learning methods that aim to produce optimal value functions $V = V^*$ are shown not to generalize as well in domains that admit (non-optimal) general policies but where optimal planning is NP-hard.

The rest of the paper is organized as follows. First we discuss related research, then cover the background (classical planning, general policies and value functions, and GNNs) and the actual GNN architecture and loss functions used for learning. This is followed by the experimental section, analyses, and a summary.

2 Related Work

Some related research threads are the following.

Generalized planning (GP). Formulations of generalized planning differ in the way in which general policies are represented; most often, as logic programs, finite-state controllers, or programs with loops (Khardon 1999; Srivastava, Immerman, and Zilberstein 2008; Bonet, Palacios, and Geffner 2009; Hu and De Giacomo 2011; Belle and Levesque 2016; Segovia, Jiménez, and Jonsson 2016). In all cases, the most compact policies that manage to solve a family of examples are sought, and the key question is how the space of possible programs or controllers is defined.

GP with logical features. An alternative approach is to define the general policies as collection of rules over a set of logical features (Bonet and Geffner 2018), often derived from the domain predicates using a description logic grammar (Martín and Geffner 2004; Fern, Yoon, and Givan 2006). Recent methods learn such policies from pools of such features (Bonet, Francès, and Geffner 2019; Francès, Bonet, and Geffner 2021); in some cases, by learning value functions (Francès et al. 2019). The Boolean and numerical features are closely related to the variables used in qualitative numerical planning models (Srivastava et al. 2011; Bonet and Geffner 2020b).

Generalized policies using deep learning. Deep learning and deep reinforcement learning methods have been used to compute general policies from sampled problems without having to predefine the space of possible features. In some cases, the planning representation of the domains is used (Toyer et al. 2020; Garg, Bajpai, and Mausam 2020; Rivlin, Hazan, and Karpas 2020); in other cases, it is not (Groshev et al. 2018; Chevalier-Boisvert et al. 2019; Campero et al. 2021; Cobbe et al. 2020). Also in some cases, the learning is supervised; in others, it is based on reinforcement learning (Bertsekas 1995; Sutton and Barto 2018; François-Lavet et al. 2018). The neural networks learn to map states into a feature representation that is mapped into the value or policy associated to the state.

GNNs and logic. A graph neural network learns to map vertices of a graph into feature representations that can be aggregated and fed into a feedforward neural network for classifying graphs, and more generally, for computing functions over graphs independently of their size (Scarselli et al. 2008; Hamilton 2020). Since the computational model is based on message passing, GNNs cannot distinguish all pairs of graphs that are not isomorphic but can distinguish those that are distinguished by the WL coloring procedure (Morris et al. 2019; Xu et al. 2019). These correspond in turn to those that can be distinguished by formulas in the two-variable fragment of first-order logic with counting quantifiers, C_2, which includes the standard description logics (Barceló et al. 2020; Grohe 2020).

GNNs and optimal general policies. Ståhlberg, Bonet, and Geffner (2022) use GNNs to learn optimal general policies in a supervised fashion from targets $V^*(s)$ and sampled states s, taking advantange of a GNN architecture introduced for learning to solve Max-CSPs (Toenshoff et al. 2021), extended to the more general relational structures underlying planning states where objects define the universe, predicates define the relations, and atoms define their denotations. In this work, we build on these results to learn general policies that are not necessarily optimal (and which hence cover more domains) without supervision and without having to predefine a pool of features (Francès et al. 2019).

3 Classical Planning

A classical planning problem is a pair $P = \langle D, I \rangle$ where D is a first-order *domain* and I contains information about the instance (Geffner and Bonet 2013; Ghallab, Nau, and Traverso 2016; Haslum et al. 2019a). The domain D contains a set of predicate symbols p and a set of action schemas with preconditions and effects given by atoms $p(x_1, \ldots, x_k)$ where each x_i is an argument of the schema. An instance is a tuple $I = \langle O, Init, Goal \rangle$ where O is a set of object names c_i, and *Init* and *Goal* are sets of *ground atoms* $p(c_1, \ldots, c_k)$.

A classical problem $P = \langle D, I \rangle$ encodes a state model $S(P) = \langle S, s_0, S_G, Act, A, f \rangle$ in compact form where the states $s \in S$ are sets of ground atoms from P, s_0 is the initial state I, S_G is the set of goal states s such that $S_G \subseteq s$, *Act* is the set of ground actions in P, $A(s)$ is the set of ground actions whose preconditions are (true) in s, and f is the transition function so that $f(a, s)$ for $a \in A(s)$ represents the state s' that follows action a in the state s. An action sequence $a_0, \ldots, a_n$ is applicable in P if $a_i \in A(s_i)$ and $s_{i+1} = f(a_i, s_i)$, for $i = 1, \ldots, n$, and it is a plan if $s_{n+1} \in S_G$. The *cost* of a plan is assumed to be given by its length and a plan is *optimal* if there is no shorter plan.

The representation of planning problems P in two parts D and I, one that is general, and the other that is specific, is essential for defining and computing general policies, as the instances are assumed to come all from the same domain. Recent work has addressed the problem of learning the action schemas and predicates (Cresswell, McCluskey, and West 2013; Asai 2019; Bonet and Geffner 2020a; Rodriguez et al. 2021).

4 General Policies and Value Functions

One approach for expressing general policies is as rules $C \mapsto E$ where the condition C and the effect E are defined in terms of state features (Bonet and Geffner 2018). State features or simply, features, refer to functions ϕ over the state, and Boolean and numerical features refer to state functions that return Boolean and numerical values. For example, a general policy for clearing a block x can be expressed in terms of the two features $\Phi = \{H, n\}$, where H is a true in a state if a block is being held, and n represents the number of blocks above x. The policy rules are

$$\neg H, n > 0 \mapsto H, n\downarrow \quad , \quad H \mapsto \neg H \tag{1}$$

that say that, when the gripper is empty and there are blocks above x, any action that decreases n and makes H true should be selected, and that when the gripper is not empty, any action that makes H false and does not affect n should be selected. General policies of this form can be learned without supervision by solving a combinatorial optimization problem $T(\mathcal{S}, \mathcal{F})$ where $\mathcal{S}$ is a set of sampled state transitions and $\mathcal{F}$ is a large but finite pool of description logic features obtained from the domain predicates (Bonet, Francès, and Geffner 2019; Francès, Bonet, and Geffner 2021).

Another way to represent (general) policies is by means of (general) value functions. In dynamic programming and RL (Bellman 1957; Sutton and Barto 2018; Bertsekas 1995), a value function V defines a (non-deterministic) *greedy policy* π_V that selects in a state s any possible successor state s' with minimum $V(s')$ value under the assumption that actions are deterministic and have the same cost. A policy π solves an instance P if the state transitions compatible with π, starting with the initial state, eventually end up in a goal state. If V is optimal, i.e., $V = V^*$, the greedy policy π_V is optimal too, selecting state transitions along optimal paths.

General value functions for a class of problems are defined in terms of features ϕ_i that have well-defined values over all states of such problems as:

$$V(s) \;=\; F(\phi_1(s), \ldots, \phi_k(s))\,. \tag{2}$$

Linear value functions have the form

$$V(s) \;=\; \sum\nolimits_{1 \le i \le k} w_i \phi_i(s) \tag{3}$$

where the coefficients w_i are constants that do not depend on the states. For example, a general, linear value function for clearing block x while having an empty gripper is $V = 2n + H$, where the states are left implicit, and the Boolean feature H is assumed to have value 1 when true, and 0 otherwise.

Linear value functions using description logic features (Bonet, Francès, and Geffner 2019), called generalized potential heuristics, can be learned from small instances via a mixed integer programming formulation, leading to an alternative representation of general policies that solve many standard planning domains (Francès et al. 2019).

5 Features

Logical features derived from the domain predicates using a description logic grammar have been used to define and learn *policies* of the form (1) and *value functions* of the form (3).[1] The complexity of such features is defined in terms of the number of grammar rules required to derive them, and the pool of features used is obtained by placing a bound on the complexity of the features. An important limitation of these methods is that the pool of features grows exponentially with the complexity bound, and that some domains require complex features. For example, Francès et al. (2019) cannot learn general value functions for Logistics and Blocks because they appear to require features of complexity 22 and 49, respectively. Interestingly, the features required to express the policy rules for some of these domains is much smaller (Francès, Bonet, and Geffner 2021).

For learning general policies without using a precomputed pool of features, it turns out to be simpler and more direct to learn general value functions, and then define greedy policies from them. A first step in this direction was taken by Ståhlberg, Bonet, and Geffner (2022) where the value function V was learned in a supervised fashion using graph neural networks from optimal targets V^*. Graph neural networks have also been used in other approaches to generalized planning using deep nets (Toyer et al. 2020; Garg, Bajpai, and Mausam 2020; Rivlin, Hazan, and Karpas 2020), but in combination with other techniques and without drawing on the relation between the features that can be learned by GNNs and those that are actually needed.

6 Graph Neural Networks

The GNN architecture for learning value functions follows the one used by Ståhlberg, Bonet, and Geffner (2022): it accepts states s over arbitrary instances of a given planning domain, and outputs the scalar value $V(s)$. For this, the form of the general value function $V(s)$ in (2) is reformulated as:

$$V(s) \;=\; F(\phi(o_1), \ldots, \phi(o_n)) \tag{4}$$

where $o_1, \ldots, o_n$ represent the objects in the instance where the state s is drawn from, $\phi(o)$ is a vector of feature values associated with object o in state s (dependence on s omitted), represented as a vector of real numbers, and F is a function that aggregates these feature vectors and produces the scalar output $V(s)$. The vectors $\phi(o)$ are usually called *object embeddings* and the function F, the readout. Before revising the details of the architecture, it is worth discussing the meaning and the implication of the transition from the fully general value function form expressed in (2) to the specific form expressed in (4).

6.1 From State Features to Object Embeddings

We are moving from state features to object features $\phi(o)$ that depend not just on the state s but on the objects o. In addition, the same feature function ϕ is applied to all the objects, and the same aggregation function F is applied to the states s of any of the domain instances so that the number of feature vectors $\phi(o)$ expands or contracts according to the number of objects in the instance. This is key for having a well-defined value function over the whole collection of domain instances that involve a different numbers of objects, not necessarily bounded.

The reasons for why the restricted value function form (4) is rich enough for capturing the value functions needed

[1] These logical features have also been used to encode "sketches", a generalization of policies that split problems into (polynomial) subproblems of bounded width (Drexler, Seipp, and Geffner 2021). Policies are a special type of sketches where the subproblems can be solved in one step (Bonet and Geffner 2021).

for generalized planning can be understood by comparing (4) with the linear value functions (3) used by Francès et al. (2019) in combination with description logic features. These Boolean and numerical features $b_q(s)$ and $n_q(s)$ are defined in terms of derived unary predicates q, where $b_q(s) = 1$ (true) if there is an object o such that $q(o)$ is true in s, otherwise 0; and $n_q(s) = m$ is the number of objects o for which $q(o)$ is true in s. Clearly, if the feature vectors $\phi(o_i)$ in (4) contain a bit encoding whether $q(o)$ is true in s, then the readout function F would just need to take the *max* and the *sum* of the bits $q(o)$ as

$$b_q(s) = \max_o q(o)\,, \tag{5}$$

$$n_q(s) = \sum_o q(o)\,, \tag{6}$$

in order to capture such features, where the objects o range over all the objects o in the instance. In other words, the object-embedding form (4) is no less expressive than the linear form that uses description logic features, provided that the feature vectors $\phi(o)$ are expressive enough to represent the bits $q_i(o)$ for unary predicates q_i derived from the domain predicates using the description logic grammar. This in turn is known to be within the capabilities of standard, message passing GNNs, that can capture the properties that can be expressed in the guarded fragment of the variable logic with counting C_2, which includes the standard description logics (Barceló et al. 2020).

Below we follow the terminology of graph neural networks and refer to graphs and not states, and to vertex embeddings $f(v)$ and not object embeddings $\phi(o)$. After considering standard GNNs for undirected graphs, we introduce the generalization needed for dealing with the relational structures represented by planning states.

6.2 GNNs on Graphs

GNNs represent trainable, parametric, and generalizable functions over graphs (Scarselli et al. 2008; Hamilton 2020) specified by means of aggregate and combination functions agg_i and $comb_i$, and a readout function F. For each vertex v of the input graph G, the GNN maintains a state (vector) $f_i(v) \in \mathbb{R}^k$, the vertex embedding, $i = 0, \ldots, L$, where L is the number of iterations or layers. The vertex embeddings $f_0(v)$ are fixed and the embeddings f_{i+1} for all v are computed from the f_i embeddings as:

$$f_{i+1}(v) := comb_i\big(f_i(v), agg_i(\{\!\{f_i(w) | w \in N_G(v)\}\!\})\big) \tag{7}$$

where $N_G(v)$ is the set of neighbors for vertex v in G, and $\{\!\{\ldots\}\!\}$ denotes a multiset. In words, the embeddings $f_{i+1}(v)$ at iteration $i + 1$ are obtained by combining the aggregation of neighbors' embeddings $f_i(w)$ at iteration i with v's own embeddings $f_i(v)$. This process is usually seen as an exchange of messages among neighbor nodes in the graph. The aggregation functions agg_i map arbitrary collections of real vectors of dimension k into a single $\mathbb{R}^k$ vector. Common aggregation functions are *sum*, *max*, and *smooth-max* (a smooth approximation of the max function). The combination functions $comb_i$ map pairs of $\mathbb{R}^k$ vectors into a single

Algorithm 1: GNN maps state s into scalar $V(s)$

Input: State s: set of atoms true in s, set of objects
Output: V(s)

$f_0(o) \sim \mathbf{0}^{k/2}\mathcal{N}(0,1)^{k/2}$ for each object $o \in s$;
for $i \in \{0, \ldots, L-1\}$ **do**
    for *each atom* $q := p(o_1, \ldots, o_m)$ *true in* s **do**
        `// Msgs` $q \rightarrow o$ `for each` $o = o_j$ `in` q
        $m_{q,o} := [\mathbf{MLP}_p(f_i(o_1), \ldots, f_i(o_m))]_j$;
    for *each* o *in* s **do**
        `// Aggregate, update embeddings`
        $f_{i+1}(o) := \mathbf{MLP}_U\big(f_i(o), agg(\{\!\{m_{q,o} | o \in q\}\!\})\big)$;
`// Final Readout`
$V := \mathbf{MLP}_2\big(\sum_{o \in s} \mathbf{MLP}_1(f_L(o))\big)$

$\mathbb{R}^k$ vector. The embeddings $f_L(v)$ in the last layer are aggregated and mapped into the output of the GNN by means of a readout function F. In our setting, the output will be a scalar V, and the aggregation and combination functions agg_i and $comb_i$ will be homogeneous and not depend on the layer index i. All the functions are parametrized with weights that are adjusted by minimizing a suitable loss function. By design, the function computed by a GNN is *invariant* with respect to graph isomorphisms, and once a GNN is trained, its output is well defined for any graph G regardless size.

6.3 GNNs for Planning States

States s in planning do not represent graphs but more general relational structures that are defined by the set objects, the set of domain predicates, and the atoms $p(o_1, \ldots, o_m)$ that are true in the state: the objects define the universe, the domain predicates, the relations, and the atoms, their denotations. The set of predicate symbols p and their arities are fixed by the domain, but the sets of objects o_i may change from instance to instance. The adaptation of the basic GNN architecture for dealing with planning states s follows (Ståhlberg, Bonet, and Geffner 2022), which is an elaboration of the architecture for learning to solve Max-CSP problems over a fixed class of binary relations introduced by Toenshoff et al. (2021). The new GNN still maintains just the object embeddings $f_i(o)$ for each of the objects o in the input state s, $i = 0, \ldots, L$, but now rather than messages flowing from "neighbor" objects to objects as in (7), the messages flow from objects o_i to the true atoms q in s that include o_i, $q = p(o_1, \ldots, o_m)$, $1 \leq i \leq m$, and from such atoms q to all the objects o_j involved in q as:

$$f_{i+1}(o) := comb_U\big(f_i(o), agg(\{\!\{m_{q,o} | o \in q, q \in s\}\!\})\big) \tag{8}$$

where $m_{q,o}$ for $q = p(o_1, \ldots, o_m)$ and $o = o_j$ is:

$$m_{q,o} := [comb_p(f_i(o_1), \ldots, f_i(o_m))]_j\,. \tag{9}$$

In these updates, the combination function $comb_U$ takes the concatenation of two real vectors of size k and outputs a vector of size k, while the combination function $comb_p$, that depends on the predicate symbol p, takes the concatenation of m vectors of size k, where m is the arity of p, and outputs m vectors of size k as well, one for each object involved in the p-atom. The expression $[\ldots]_j$ in (9) selects the j-th such vector in the output.

The resulting trainable function that maps states s into their values $V(s)$ is shown in Algorithm 1 with all the combination functions replaced by the multilayer perceptrons (MLPs) that implement them. During the iterations $i = 0, \ldots, L$, a single $\mathbf{MLP}_U$ is used for updating the object embeddings following (7), and a single $\mathbf{MLP}_p$ per predicate is used to collect the messages from atoms to objects as in (9). The readout function, the last line in Algorithm 1, uses two MLPs and a sum aggregator. Finally, for the aggregator in line 6, we use the differentiable smooth max function $smax(x_1, \ldots, x_n)$ defined as

$$x^* + \alpha^{-1} \log \left(\sum_{1 \leq j \leq n} \exp(\alpha(x_j - x^*)) \right) \qquad (10)$$

where $x^* = \max\{x_1, \ldots, x_n\}$ and $\alpha = 8$.

All MLPs consists of a dense layer with a ReLU activation function, followed by a dense layer with a linear activation function. The hyperparameter in the networks are the embedding dimension k and the number of layers L. The initial embeddings $f_0(o)$ are obtained by concatenating a zero vector with a random vector, each of dimension $k/2$, to break symmetries. Random initialization increase expressive power for instances of fixed size (Abboud et al. 2021), however, we aim to learn policies for arbitrary sizes. Key for the GNN to apply to any state over the domain is the use of a single MLP_p for each predicate symbol p in the domain.

7 Learning the GNN Parameters

The parameters of the network displayed in Algorithm 1 are learned by stochastic gradient descent by minimizing a loss function. In the work of Ståhlberg, Bonet, and Geffner (2022), the training data $\mathcal{D}$ is a collection of pairs $\langle s, V^*(s) \rangle$ for sampled states s from selected instances, and $V^*(s)$ is the optimal cost for reaching the goal from s (min. number of steps). The loss is the average sum of the differences

$$L(s) \;=\; |V(s) - V^*(s)| \qquad (11)$$

over the states s in the training set. The computation of the optimal targets $V^*(s)$ is not a problem because we are computing them over small instances. The real problem is that by forcing the value function to be optimal over the training instances, domains such as Blocks or Miconic, where optimal planning is NP-hard (Gupta and Nau 1992; Helmert 2001), are excluded (except when the goals are restricted to be single atoms).

Interestingly, as discussed in the next section, this limitation pops up also in unsupervised, reinforcement learning approaches where the optimal target values $V^*(s)$ are not given but are sought by minimizing the Bellman error:

$$L_0'(s) \;=\; |V(s) - (1 + \min_{s' \in N(s)} V(s'))| \qquad (12)$$

for non-goal states s, where $N(s)$ are the states reachable from s in one step (possible successor states). For goal states, $L_0'(s)$ is $|V(s)|$. The optimal function V^* is the unique value function that minimizes the resulting loss, provided that actions costs are all 1 and the goal is reachable from all states. In this work, rather than penalizing departures from the Bellman optimality equation

$$V(s) \;=\; 1 + \min_{s' \in N(s)} V(s') \,, \qquad (13)$$

departures from the inequality $V(s) \geq 1 + \min_{s' \in N(s)} V(s')$ are penalized with a loss for non-goal states s defined as

$$L_1'(s) \;=\; \max\{0, (1 + \min_{s' \in N(s)} V(s')) - V(s)\} \,. \quad (14)$$

Furthermore, this loss is extended with two regularization terms that penalize large departures from V^*; namely, as done by Francès, Bonet, and Geffner (2021), we want a value function V that also satisfies $V^* \leq V \leq \delta V^*$, and thus settle for the minimization of the loss:

$$\begin{aligned} L_1(s) \;=\; & L_1'(s) + \max\{0, V^*(s) - V(s)\} + \\ & \max\{0, V(s) - \delta V^*(s)\} \,, \end{aligned} \qquad (15)$$

where $\delta = 2$. The loss over a set $\mathcal{S}$ of states is the sum of the average of $L_1(s)$ for non-goal states $s \in \mathcal{S}$ and the average of $|V(s)|$ for goal states $s \in \mathcal{S}$. For comparison purposes, the L_0' loss is extend into the regularized L_0 loss as well as:

$$\begin{aligned} L_0(s) \;=\; & L_0'(s) + \max\{0, V^*(s) - V(s)\} + \\ & \max\{0, V(s) - \delta V^*(s)\} \,, \end{aligned} \qquad (16)$$

If all the states in a small instance are in $\mathcal{S}$ and the overall loss is close to zero, the loss function L_1 results in value functions that lead greedily to the goal (by picking the min-V successors), while the loss L_0 results in value functions that lead greedily and *optimally* to the goal. For simplicity, it is assumed that the domains considered do not have *dead-ends*, i.e. states from which the goal is not reachable and where $V^*(s)$ is not well-defined. Learning to plan in such domains requires an slight extension, with extra inputs, for labeling states as dead-ends in the training data, and extra outputs, for predicting if a state is a dead-end (Ståhlberg, Francès, and Seipp 2021). This extension is implemented and tested, but it will be skipped over in the presentation.

8 Experiments

The experiments are aimed to test the generalization, coverage, and quality of the plans obtained by the policy π_V greedy in the learned value function V, using the unsupervised losses L_0 and L_1. We describe the training and testing data used, and the results. A key difference with prior work (Ståhlberg, Bonet, and Geffner 2022) is that the test instances are standard IPC planning problems from standard planning domains, several of which are intractable for optimal planning. We seek crisp experimental results, which means close to 100% generalization, or alternatively, crisp explanations of why this is not possible, with logical fixes that restore generalization in certain cases.

Data. The states in the training and validation sets are obtaining by fully expanding selected instances from the initial state through a breadth-first search. For each reachable state, the length of the shortest path to a goal state is computed. For instances with large state spaces we keep up to $40,000$ sampled reachable states to avoid large instances from dominating the training set. The actual size of the instances used

Domain	Train	Validation	Test
Blocks	[4, 7]	[8, 8]	[9, 17]
Delivery	[12, 20]	[28, 28]	[29, 85]
Gripper	[8, 12]	[14, 14]	[16, 46]
Logistics	[5, 18]	[13, 16]	[15, 37]
Miconic	[3, 18]	[18, 18]	[21, 90]
Reward	[9, 100]	[100, 100]	[225, 625]
Spanner*	[6, 33]	[27, 30]	[22, 320]
Visitall	[4, 16]	[16, 16]	[25, 121]

Table 1: Instance sizes used training, validation, and testing datasets, as measured by the number of objects involved. E.g., the training set for Blocks consists of IPC instances with a number of blocks between 4 and 7. There is no instance that is in more than 1 set (same number of objects, initial state and goal description).

in training, validation, and testing are shown in Table 1, measured by the number of objects involved. In almost all cases, the testing instances are IPC (International Planning Competition) instances. The exception is the domain Spanner*, which is a slight variant of the Spanner domain that does not give rise to dead-end states by allowing the agent to move not just forward but also backward.

Domains. The domains are those used by Francès, Bonet, and Geffner (2021) with the addition of Logistics, and the above modification of Spanner. Briefly, Blocks is the standard blocks world. Delivery is the problem of picking up objects in an empty grid and delivering them one by one to a target cell. Gripper is about moving balls from one room to another with a moving robot that can have more than one gripper. Logistics involves trucks and airplanes that move within city locations and across cities, where packages have to be moved from one location to another location, possibly in a different city. Miconic is about controlling an elevator to pick up passengers in different floors to their destination floors. Rewards is about reaching certain cells in a grid while avoiding others. Spanner is about collecting spanners spread in a one dimensional grid, each one to be used to tighten up a single nut at the other end. Visitall is about visiting all or some cells in an empty grid.

Setup. The hyperparameters k and L in Algorithm 1 are set to 64 and 30, respectively: k is the number of "features" per object; i.e., the size of the real object embedding vectors; and L the number of layers in the GNN (fixed for training and testing). Both hyperparameters affect training speed, memory, and generalization. Hyperparameter L affects how far messages can propagate in the graph, and indeed, the GNN cannot capture shortest paths between two objects if longer than L, even if the existence of paths up to length $2L$ can be determined. The architecture is implemented in PyTorch (Paszke and et. al. 2019) and the optimizer Adam (Kingma and Ba 2015) is used with a learning rate of 0.0002.[2] The networks are trained with NVIDIA A100 GPUs for up to 12 hours. Five models for each domain are trained to ensure that the optimizer did not get stuck in "bad" local minima, and the final model used is the one with the best validation loss (i.e., loss measured on the validation set). The quality of the plans obtained by following the greedy policy π_V for the learned value function V are evaluated in comparison with optimal plans that are computed with the Fast Downward (FD) planner (Helmert 2006) using the *seq-opt-merge-and-shrink* configuration with time and memory outs set to 10 minutes and 64 GB, respectively, on a Ryzen 9 5900X CPU.

[2]Code and data: https://doi.org/10.5281/zenodo.6511809

8.1 Testing the Greedy Policy π_V: Two Modes

The greedy policy π_V selects the action applicable in a non-goal state s that leads to the child state s' with minimum $V(s')$ value (action costs are all assumed to be 1). It is common to add "noise" in this selection process by either breaking ties randomly or by choosing the action leading to the best child probabilistically, by soft-mapping the children values $V(s')$ into probabilities that add up to 1. The addition of "noise" in action selection has the benefit that it helps to avoid cycles in the execution, but at the same time, it blurs the results. Instead, Table 2 shows (on the right) the results of the executions that follow the deterministic greedy policy π_V, which always chooses the action leading to the child s' with lowest $V(s')$ value, breaking ties for the first such action encountered. Since the learned value function is not perfect, we show on the left the execution of the greedy policy but with *cycle avoidance*; namely, executions keep track of the visited states and deterministically select the first action leading to the best *unvisited* child (min-V value). When there are no such children, the execution fails. Executions are also terminated when the goal is not reached within $1,000$ steps.

8.2 Results: L_1 Loss

Table 2 shows the results for various experiments: learning using the L_1 loss (top), learning using the L_0 loss (middle), and learning using states augmented with derived atoms in domains that benefit from C_3 features (explained below). Furthermore, the three subtables are divided horizontally in two, according to the way in which the greedy policy π_V for the learned value function V is used: with cycle avoidance, on the left, and without cycle avoidance, on the right. We focus now on the top part of the table.

Coverage. The first thing to notice is that in 4 out of the 8 domains considered, Blocks, Delivery, Gripper, and Miconic, the deterministic greedy policy π_V for the learned value function V solves all the test instances. This is pretty remarkable as the resulting plans are often long. In Blocks, the average plan length is $790/20 = 39.5$ steps, while in Miconic, it is $7,331/120 = 61.09$. As we will see, while the plans are not optimal, they are very good, and moreover, in none of these cases, the deterministic greedy policy generates an execution where a state is revisited. Indeed, if revisits are explicitly excluded by executing the greedy policy while avoiding cycles (left), a fifth domain is solved in full: Visitall. The other three domains are not solved in full in either mode: Logistics, Reward, and Spanner. In the case of Logistics, the reason, as we will see, is purely logical:

	Deterministic policy π_V with cycle avoidance			Deterministic policy π_V alone		
Domain (#)	Coverage (%)	L	PQ = PL / OL (#)	Coverage (%)	L	PQ = PL / OL (#)
			L_1 **Loss**			
Blocks (20)	20 (100%)	790	1.0427 = 440 / 422 (13)	20 (100%)	790	1.0427 = 440 / 422 (13)
Delivery (15)	15 (100%)	400	1.0000 = 400 / 400 (15)	15 (100%)	404	1.0100 = 404 / 400 (15)
Gripper (16)	16 (100%)	1,286	1.0000 = 176 / 176 (4)	16 (100%)	1,286	1.0000 = 176 / 176 (4)
Logistics (28)	17 (60%)	4,635	9.7215 = 3,665 / 377 (15)	0 (0%)	0	—
Miconic (120)	120 (100%)	7,331	1.0052 = 1,170 / 1,164 (35)	120 (100%)	7,331	1.0052 = 1,170 / 1,164 (35)
Reward (15)	11 (73%)	1,243	1.2306 = 1,062 / 863 (10)	3 (20%)	237	1.1232 = 237 / 211 (3)
Spanner*-30 (41)	30 (73%)	1,545	1.0000 = 1,545 / 1,545 (30)	24 (58%)	940	1.0000 = 940 / 940 (24)
Visitall (14)	14 (100%)	904	1.0183 = 556 / 546 (10)	11 (78%)	631	1.0107 = 471 / 466 (9)
Total (269)	243 (90%)	18,134	1.6410 = 9,014 / 5,493 (132)	209 (77%)	11,619	1.0156 = 3,838 / 3,779 (103)
			L_0 **Loss**			
Blocks (20)	0 (0%)	0	—	0 (0%)	0	—
Delivery (15)	12 (80%)	278	1.0000 = 278 / 278 (12)	12 (80%)	278	1.0000 = 278 / 278 (12)
Gripper (16)	16 (100%)	1,288	1.0000 = 176 / 176 (4)	12 (75%)	816	1.0000 = 176 / 176 (4)
Logistics (28)	1 (3%)	134	16.7500 = 134 / 8 (1)	0 (0%)	0	—
Miconic (120)	120 (100%)	7,758	1.0241 = 1,192 / 1,164 (35)	108 (90%)	6,438	1.0000 = 1,084 / 1,084 (33)
Reward (15)	12 (80%)	1,362	1.1226 = 861 / 767 (9)	7 (46%)	661	1.0285 = 505 / 491 (6)
Spanner*-30 (41)	24 (58%)	1,221	1.0374 = 1,221 / 1,177 (24)	14 (34%)	475	1.0000 = 475 / 475 (14)
Visitall (14)	14 (100%)	838	1.0073 = 550 / 546 (10)	12 (85%)	664	1.0073 = 550 / 546 (10)
Total (269)	199 (73%)	12,879	1.0719 = 4,412 / 4,116 (95)	165 (61%)	9,332	1.0059 = 3,068 / 3,050 (79)
			Derived Atoms (L_1 **Loss)**			
Logistics-atoms (28)	28 (100%)	8,147	5.5711 = 2,546 / 457 (17)	4 (14%)	88	1.0353 = 88 / 85 (4)
Spanner*-10 (36)	12 (33%)	557	1.0000 = 557 / 557 (12)	8 (22%)	373	1.0000 = 373 / 373 (8)
Spanner*-atoms-5 (36)	31 (86%)	1,370	1.0000 = 1,112 / 1,112 (27)	28 (77%)	1,190	1.0000 = 996 / 996 (25)
Spanner*-atoms-2 (36)	36 (100%)	1,606	1.0000 = 1,348 / 1,348 (32)	36 (100%)	1,606	1.0000 = 1,348 / 1,348 (32)
Total (136)	107 (78%)	11,680	1.6013 = 5,563 / 3,474 (88)	76 (55%)	3,257	1.0011 = 2,805 / 2,802 (69)

Table 2: Performance of the deterministic greedy policy π_V for the learned value function V when executed with cycle avoidance (left) and without (right). Three subtables shown: results when using the L_1 loss (top), results when using the L_0 loss (middle), and results using L_1 loss when states are extended with derived atoms (encoding role compositions and transitive closures). The domains are shown on the left with the number of instances tested in each. Coverage is the number of solved problems. L is the sum of the solution lengths over the test instances solved by the learned policy. PQ is a measure of overall plan quality given by the ratio of the sum of the plan lengths found by the policy (PL) and the optimal plan lengths (OL) found by FD, over the instances solved by both within the time and memory limits (number of problems solved by FD shown after OL in parenthesis).

given the domain representation of Logistics, the feature expressing that a package is in a location or in a city, while possibly within a vehicle, involves the composition of two or three binary relations, requiring three variables, which is not possible in C_2. We address this expressive limitation of GNNs below by adding suitable "derived" atoms to the state that bypass the need for such compositions. The limitations observed in Reward and Spanner are not logical: these two domains, as others in the list, require the computation of distances to determine in which direction to move (e.g., to the nearest reward or right exit). Yet GNNs cannot compute distances that exceed their number of layers L. Actually, there are other domains solved in full that require the computation of distances, but the magnitude of the distances needed in the test set does not defy these bounds. Indeed, even a simple problem such a clearing a block x may be found to be unsolvable by the learned policy if the number of blocks above x is much larger than L. Interestingly, this limitation has an easy logical "fix" in some of the domains, where derived atoms capturing the *transitive closure* of some binary predicates manage to decouple the computation of distances from the number of layers in the GNN. In the domains where these expressive limitations arise, the greedy policy with cycle avoidance does better than the pure greedy policy, as the latter is more likely to be trapped in cycles.

Quality. Somewhat surprisingly, the quality of the executions delivered by the models trained with the L_1 loss is very close to optimal, as measured with respect to the optimal plans computed by FD. The only exception is the Logistics domain where plans are up to 10 times longer than optimal, on average. These results are surprising not just because the L_1 loss does not force the value function V to be optimal, but because optimal planning in several of these domains, certainly Blocks, Miconic, and Logistics, and possibly in Reward and Visitall as well, is NP-hard (Gupta and Nau 1992; Helmert 2001). For example, FD with the given time and memory bounds computes optimal solutions for 35 instances in Miconic comprising a total of 1,164 actions, while the sum of execution lengths for the learned, greedy policy π_V with or without cycle avoidance on the same 35 instances is 1,170. Indeed, the execution lengths that follow from the learned value function do not exceed the optimal plan lengths in more than 12% with the exception of Logistics.

8.3 L_0 Loss: General Policies and RL

The differences between the L_1 loss (15) and the L_0 loss (16) are small but significant. Zero loss for L_0 arises just when the learned V function has zero Bellman error over the training set; i.e. when $V(s) = 1 + \min_{s' \in N(s)} V(s')$ for the possible children s' of s, and thus when V is the optimal cost function V^*. Zero loss for L_1, on the other hand, arises just when the learned V function is such that $V(s) \geq 1 + \min_{s' \in N(s)} V(s')$. Thus, zero L_0 loss implies zero L_1 loss, but not the other way around, as the L_1 loss captures just one half of Bellman's optimality equation. Provided that only the goal states have zero value and that non-goal states have positive values, one can use a value function V with zero L_1 loss to solve problems *greedily* by always moving to the best child (min V). On the other hand, a value function V with zero L_0 loss can be used in the same manner to solve problems greedily and *optimally*. The difference between solving a class of problems optimally or suboptimally is crucial in domains where optimal planning is NP-hard. Such domains, like Blocks, often admit general policies but no general policies that are optimal.

So the question arises as to whether the minimization of the L_0 loss leads to greedy policies π_V that are as good as, or better than those obtained by minimization of the L_1 loss. The question is particularly relevant because the standard methods for learning policies without supervision are usually based on reinforcement learning, which in their value-based variant (as opposed to the policy gradient version) are based on the minimization of Bellman error (Sutton and Barto 2018). The expectation is that the minimization of L_0 loss will not be as good. Indeed, the value functions V that yield greedy policies π_V that generalize correctly over domains that are intractable for optimal planning are unlikely to yield zero L_0 loss.

The middle part of Table 2 shows the results of the greedy policies π_V for value functions V learned by minimizing L_0 loss instead of L_1. The L_0-based policies are observed to perform worse than the L_1-based policies. The extreme case is precisely in Blocks where coverage drops from 100% to 0% when using the greedy policy with cycle avoidance and also without. A big difference also surfaces in Logistics where coverage drops from 60% to 3% with cycle avoidance (otherwise no instances are solved). For the other domains, the drops are not as drastic, yet the greedy policy with no cycle avoidance based on L_1 solves four domains fully (100% coverage) while the same policy based on L_0 does not solve fully any single domain. The L_0-policies, however, do slightly better in two of the domains where the L_1-policy is not good: Reward and Visitall where coverage increases from 20% and 78% to 46% and 86%. As expected, the lower coverage of L_0-policies goes along with executions whose lengths are better overall. With cycle avoidance, the performance resulting from the two loss functions is closer, with the aforementioned exceptions. In general, the ability of the learned value functions V to yield greedy policies that generalize can be predicted from the corresponding loss on the validation set. In both Blocks and Logistics, the validation loss after L_1 training is close to zero, but significantly higher than zero after L_0 training.

8.4 Derived Atoms: Beyond C_2

The failure of the learned policies to generalize fully when using the L_1 loss function in domains such as Logistics, Reward, and Spanner* can be traced to two limitations. Logistics requires features that cannot be expressed in C_2 and which therefore are not captured by GNNs (Barceló et al. 2020; Grohe 2020). Spanner*, like Reward and other domains, involves the computation of distances in the test instances that exceed the number of layers used in the GNN. The bottom part of Table 2 shows the results that are obtained in Logistics and Spanner* when these limitations are addressed logically by extending the states (in training, validation, and testing) with suitable derived atoms and predicates, a facility provided by PDDL (Thiébaux, Hoffmann, and Nebel 2005; Haslum et al. 2019b). For example, one can extend the states in Blocks with the derived predicate $above$ that corresponds to the transitive closure of the domain predicate on, so that every state s contains additional atoms $above(x, y)$ when block x is above block y in s.

In Logistics, four derived predicates are added, following the four role compositions used by Francès et al. (2019) to obtain a general value function. These role compositions go beyond the expressive capabilities of C_2 and GNNs. In Logistics, there are binary predicates (roles) to express that a package or truck is at some location ('at'), to express that a package is inside a truck or airplane ('in'), and to express that a location is in a city ('in-city'). Additionally, as done in previous works, "goal versions" of these predicates (indeed, of all predicates) denoted by 'at@', 'in@' and 'in-city@' whose denotation is provided by the goal descriptions are added to the domain. The Logistics domain is extended with the following role compositions from Francès et al. (2019):

- 'at∘in-city' and 'at@∘in-city' that tells the city where a package is located, either in the current or goal state,
- 'in∘at' that tells the location of a package that is inside a truck, and
- 'in∘at∘in-city' that tells the city where a package that is inside a truck is located.

In Spanner*, a single derived predicate is added which is the transitive closure of the 'link' predicate. Provided with the new link$^+$ predicate, the required distances in Spanner* are not restricted by the number of layers L in the GNN and can be computed in a single layer, as the distance to the exit location equals the number of locations to the right of the current location c; i.e., dist2exit $= |\{x \mid \text{link}^+(c, x)\}|$.

The results obtained by learning from states with these derived predicates in Logistics and Spanner* are shown at the bottom of Table 2. In Logistics, the simple addition of the atoms makes the coverage jump from from 0% to 14% for the greedy policy alone, and from 60% to 100% for the greedy policy with cycle avoidance. For Spanner*, three rows are shown: the first is for the domain without derived atoms but with two modifications that preclude comparison with the Spanner* results reported previously in the same table. The first is that the test instances involving more than 100 locations have been replaced by smaller instances with up to 45 and 50 locations. The second is that the number of layers L in the GNN are reduced from 30 to 10. These modifications provide a more convenient baseline for evaluating the impact of derived atoms: with 100 locations, there are $10,000 = 100^2$ extra derived atoms in the states, that make training and testing much slower (this is a weakness of adding derived atoms). It is because of these modifications, and in particular from the reduction in the value of L from 30 to 10, that the coverage of the learned policies in the modified Spanner* setting is reduced to 33% and 22% percent (first of the last three rows in the table). This number however increases to 86% and 77% when the derived atoms are included, even if the number of GNN layers is reduced from 10 to 5 (second of the last three rows in table). Moreover, coverage increases further to 100% when the derived atoms are included and the number of GNN layers is reduced further to just 2 (last row in the table). This additional increase in coverage is likely due by reduced overfitting as the number of layers L is reduced from 5 to 2.

9 Conclusions

We have considered the problem of learning generalized policies for classical planning domains from small instances represented in lifted STRIPS. Unlike previous work that makes uses of a predefined pool of features based on description logic and combinatorial solvers, we have followed the GNN approach for learning general policies advanced by Ståhlberg, Bonet, and Geffner (2022) that exploits the relation between C_2 features and those that can be computed by GNNs. However, instead of learning optimal value functions in a supervised manner, we learn non-optimal value functions without supervision. For this, the change is technically small, as it affects the loss function and not the GNN architecture, but the consequences are interesting as the new method can be applied to domains that have general policies but no general policies that are optimal. We have shown that 100% generalization is achieved in many such domains, and have discussed and addressed two important additional issues: the limitations of value-based RL methods for computing general policies over domains where optimal planning is intractable, and the limitations of GNNs for capturing general value functions that require non-C_2 features. We have addressed the first limitation by using a novel loss function (L_1) different than the more natural loss function L_0 associated with value-based RL methods, and the second limitation, by extending planning states with derived atoms. In the future, we would like to make the point about the limitations of RL methods for learning generalized plans, sharper, and to consider the use of recent GNN architectures that compute features beyond C_2 (Bevilacqua et al. 2021). At the same time, we are interested in "domesticating" the use of deep learning engines in the context of planning and representation learning for planning, so that they can be used as alternatives to ASP and Weighted Max-SAT solvers, for avoiding scalability issues and for opening up new possibilities. This requires understanding what can be computed with them in a clean way and how. This work is also a step in that direction.

Acknowledgments

The code framework Tarski (Francés, Ramirez, and Collaborators 2018) was very useful during this research. This research was partially supported by the European Research Council (ERC), Grant No. 885107, and by project TAILOR, Grant No. 952215, both funded by the EU Horizon research and innovation programme. This work was partially supported by the Wallenberg AI, Autonomous Systems and Software Program (WASP) funded by the Knut and Alice Wallenberg Foundation. The computations were enabled by the supercomputing resource Berzelius provided by National Supercomputer Centre at Linköping University and the Knut and Alice Wallenberg foundation.

References

Abboud, R.; Ceylan, I. I.; Grohe, M.; and Lukasiewicz, T. 2021. The surprising power of graph neural networks with random node initialization. In *Proc. IJCAI*.

Asai, M. 2019. Unsupervised grounding of plannable first-order logic representation from images. In *Proc. ICAPS*.

Barceló, P.; Kostylev, E. V.; Monet, M.; Pérez, J.; Reutter, J.; and Silva, J. P. 2020. The logical expressiveness of graph neural networks. In *ICLR*.

Belle, V., and Levesque, H. J. 2016. Foundations for generalized planning in unbounded stochastic domains. In *Proc. KR*, 380–389.

Bellman, R. 1957. *Dynamic Programming*. Princeton University Press.

Bertsekas, D. 1995. *Dynamic Programming and Optimal Control, Vols 1 and 2*. Athena Scientific.

Bevilacqua, B.; Frasca, F.; Lim, D.; Srinivasan, B.; Cai, C.; Balamurugan, G.; Bronstein, M. M.; and Maron, H. 2021. Equivariant subgraph aggregation networks. *arXiv preprint arXiv:2110.02910*.

Bonet, B., and Geffner, H. 2018. Features, projections, and representation change for generalized planning. In *Proc. IJCAI*, 4667–4673.

Bonet, B., and Geffner, H. 2020a. Learning first-order symbolic representations for planning from the structure of the state space. In *Proc. ECAI*.

Bonet, B., and Geffner, H. 2020b. Qualitative numeric planning: Reductions and complexity. *JAIR* 69:923–961.

Bonet, B., and Geffner, H. 2021. General policies, representations, and planning width. In *Proc. AAAI*, 11764–11773.

Bonet, B.; Francès, G.; and Geffner, H. 2019. Learning features and abstract actions for computing generalized plans. In *Proc. AAAI*, 2703–2710.

Bonet, B.; Palacios, H.; and Geffner, H. 2009. Automatic derivation of memoryless policies and finite-state controllers using classical planners. In *Proc. ICAPS-09*, 34–41.

Campero, A.; Raileanu, R.; Kuttler, H.; Tenenbaum, J. B.; Rocktäschel, T.; and Grefenstette, E. 2021. Learning with AMIGo: Adversarially motivated intrinsic goals. In *ICLR*.

Chevalier-Boisvert, M.; Bahdanau, D.; Lahlou, S.; Willems, L.; Saharia, C.; Nguyen, T. H.; and Bengio, Y. 2019. Babyai: A platform to study the sample efficiency of grounded language learning. In *ICLR*.

Cobbe, K.; Hesse, C.; Hilton, J.; and Schulman, J. 2020. Leveraging procedural generation to benchmark reinforcement learning. In *Proc. ICML*, 2048–2056.

Cresswell, S. N.; McCluskey, T. L.; and West, M. M. 2013. Acquiring planning domain models using LOCM. *The Knowledge Engineering Review* 28(2):195–213.

Drexler, D.; Seipp, J.; and Geffner, H. 2021. Expressing and exploiting the common subgoal structure of classical planning domains using sketches. In *Proc. KR*, 258–268.

Fern, A.; Yoon, S.; and Givan, R. 2006. Approximate policy iteration with a policy language bias: Solving relational markov decision processes. *JAIR* 25:75–118.

Francès, G.; Corrêa, A. B.; Geissmann, C.; and Pommerening, F. 2019. Generalized potential heuristics for classical planning. In *Proc. IJCAI*.

Francès, G.; Bonet, B.; and Geffner, H. 2021. Learning general planning policies from small examples without supervision. In *Proc. AAAI*, 11801–11808.

Francés, G.; Ramirez, M.; and Collaborators. 2018. Tarski: An AI planning modeling framework. https://github.com/aig-upf/tarski. Accessed: 2022-05-16.

François-Lavet, V.; Henderson, P.; Islam, R.; Bellemare, M. G.; and Pineau, J. 2018. An introduction to deep reinforcement learning. *Found. Trends. Mach. Learn.*

Garg, S.; Bajpai, A.; and Mausam. 2020. Symbolic network: generalized neural policies for relational mdps. In *Proc. ICML*.

Geffner, H., and Bonet, B. 2013. *A Concise Introduction to Models and Methods for Automated Planning*. Morgan & Claypool Publishers.

Ghallab, M.; Nau, D.; and Traverso, P. 2016. *Automated planning and acting*. Cambridge U.P.

Grohe, M. 2020. The logic of graph neural networks. In *Proc. of the 35th ACM-IEEE Symp. on Logic in Computer Science*.

Groshev, E.; Goldstein, M.; Tamar, A.; Srivastava, S.; and Abbeel, P. 2018. Learning generalized reactive policies using deep neural networks. In *Proc. ICAPS*.

Gupta, N., and Nau, D. S. 1992. On the complexity of blocks-world planning. *AIJ* 56(2-3):223–254.

Hamilton, W. L. 2020. Graph representation learning. *Synth. Lect. on Artif. Intell. Mach. Learn.* 14(3):1–159.

Haslum, P.; Lipovetzky, N.; Magazzeni, D.; and Muise, C. 2019a. *An Introduction to the Planning Domain Definition Language*. Morgan & Claypool.

Haslum, P.; Lipovetzky, N.; Magazzeni, D.; and Muise, C. 2019b. An introduction to the planning domain definition language. *Synth. Lect. on Artif. Intell. Mach. Learn.* 13(2):1–187.

Helmert, M. 2001. On the complexity of planning in transportation domains. In *Proc. ECP*.

Helmert, M. 2006. The Fast Downward planning system. *JAIR* 26:191–246.

Hu, Y., and De Giacomo, G. 2011. Generalized planning: Synthesizing plans that work for multiple environments. In *Proc. IJCAI*, 918–923.

Karia, R., and Srivastava, S. 2021. Learning generalized relational heuristic networks for model-agnostic planning. In *AAAI*.

Khardon, R. 1999. Learning action strategies for planning domains. *AIJ* 113:125–148.

Kingma, D. P., and Ba, J. 2015. Adam: A method for stochastic optimization. In Bengio, Y., and LeCun, Y., eds., *Proc. ICLR*.

Martín, M., and Geffner, H. 2004. Learning generalized policies from planning examples using concept languages. *Appl. Intell.* 20(1):9–19.

Morris, C.; Ritzert, M.; Fey, M.; Hamilton, W. L.; Lenssen, J. E.; Rattan, G.; and Grohe, M. 2019. Weisfeiler and leman go neural: Higher-order graph neural networks. In *Proc. AAAI*, 4602–4609.

Paszke, A., and et. al. 2019. Pytorch: An imperative style, high-performance deep learning library. In Wallach, H.; Larochelle, H.; Beygelzimer, A.; d'Alché Buc, F.; Fox, E.; and Garnett, R., eds., *Adv. Neural Inf. Process. Syst. 32*. Curran Associates, Inc. 8024–8035.

Rivlin, O.; Hazan, T.; and Karpas, E. 2020. Generalized planning with deep reinforcement learning. *arXiv preprint arXiv:2005.02305*.

Rodriguez, I. D.; Bonet, B.; Romero, J.; and Geffner, H. 2021. Learning first-order representations for planning from black-box states: New results. In *KR*. arXiv preprint arXiv:2105.10830.

Scarselli, F.; Gori, M.; Tsoi, A. C.; Hagenbuchner, M.; and Monfardini, G. 2008. The graph neural network model. *IEEE transactions on neural networks* 20(1):61–80.

Segovia, J.; Jiménez, S.; and Jonsson, A. 2016. Generalized planning with procedural domain control knowledge. In *Proc. ICAPS*, 285–293.

Shen, W.; Trevizan, F.; and Thiébaux, S. 2020. Learning domain-independent planning heuristics with hypergraph networks. In *Proc. ICAPS*, volume 30, 574–584.

Srivastava, S.; Zilberstein, S.; Immerman, N.; and Geffner, H. 2011. Qualitative numeric planning. In *AAAI*.

Srivastava, S.; Immerman, N.; and Zilberstein, S. 2008. Learning generalized plans using abstract counting. In *Proc. AAAI*, 991–997.

Ståhlberg, S.; Bonet, B.; and Geffner, H. 2022. Learning general optimal policies with graph neural networks: Expressive power, transparency, and limits. In *Proc. ICAPS*.

Ståhlberg, S.; Francès, G.; and Seipp, J. 2021. Learning generalized unsolvability heuristics for classical planning. In *Proc. IJCAI*, volume 4, 4175–4181.

Sutton, R. S., and Barto, A. G. 2018. *Reinforcement learning: An introduction*. MIT Press.

Thiébaux, S.; Hoffmann, J.; and Nebel, B. 2005. In defense of pddl axioms. *AIJ* 168(1-2):38–69.

Toenshoff, J.; Ritzert, M.; Wolf, H.; and Grohe, M. 2021. Graph neural networks for maximum constraint satisfaction. *Front. Artif. Intell. Appl.* 3:98.

Toyer, S.; Thiébaux, S.; Trevizan, F.; and Xie, L. 2020. Asnets: Deep learning for generalised planning. *JAIR* 68:1–68.

Xu, K.; Hu, W.; Leskovec, J.; and Jegelka, S. 2019. How powerful are graph neural networks? In *ICLR*.

Proceedings of the 19th International Conference on Principles of Knowledge Representation and Reasoning
Special Session on KR and Machine Learning

Faithful Approaches to Rule Learning

David J. Tena Cucala , Bernardo Cuenca Grau , Boris Motik
University of Oxford
{ david.tenacucala, bernardo.grau, boris.motik }@cs.ox.ac.uk

Abstract

Rule learning involves developing machine learning models that can be applied to a set of logical facts to predict additional facts, as well as providing methods for extracting from the learned model a set of logical rules that explain symbolically the model's predictions. Existing such approaches, however, do not describe formally the relationship between the model's predictions and the derivations of the extracted rules; rather, it is often claimed without justification that the extracted rules 'approximate' or 'explain' the model, and rule quality is evaluated by manual inspection. In this paper, we study the formal properties of Neural-LP—a prominent rule learning approach. We show that the rules extracted from Neural-LP models can be both unsound and incomplete: on the same input dataset, the extracted rules can derive facts not predicted by the model, and the model can make predictions not derived by the extracted rules. We also propose a modification to the Neural-LP model that ensures that the extracted rules are always sound and complete. Finally, we show that, on several prominent benchmarks, the classification performance of our modified model is comparable to that of the standard Neural-LP model. Thus, *faithful* learning of rules is feasible from both a theoretical and practical point of view.

1 Introduction

Datalog (Abiteboul, Hull, and Vianu 1995) is a widely-used formalism that can represent 'if-then' *rules*. Datalog rules are iteratively applied to a set of facts to derive fresh facts until a fixpoint is reached, allowing Datalog to express important second-order properties such as transitive closure. Due to its expressive power, Datalog is often used as a knowledge representation formalism in the AI community (Eisner and Filardo 2010), and it is seen as the quintessential recursive query language in the database community (Arni et al. 2003; Green et al. 2013).

As with most logic-based KR languages, a key hindrance in practice is that Datalog rules typically need to be constructed manually by experts familiar with both the application domain and the principles of logical deduction. Such expertise is often scarce, and the rule construction process is laborious and costly. Thus, numerous approaches have been proposed with the aim of automating rule construction.

Rule mining approaches analyse a set of facts to identify patterns (e.g., paths of connected facts) and generalise them to rules (Galárraga et al. 2015; Meilicke et al. 2019; Ahmadi et al. 2020). They are typically based on heuristics and do not provide any formal guarantees about their output.

Inductive Logic Programming (ILP) techniques take as input positive and negative examples of inferences, and output a set of rules that can reproduce all such inferences (Muggleton 1991; Cropper et al. 2021). Standard ILP techniques, however, satisfy all examples *exactly* and, as a result, are intolerant to noise: small inconsistencies in the input examples can significantly affect the quality of the produced rules (Evans and Grefenstette 2018).

The approaches in the next group define a transformation $T_{\mathcal{M}}$ of datasets by introducing an ML model $\mathcal{M}$, showing how to encode a set of facts so that $\mathcal{M}$ can be applied, and describing how the model's output is decoded back into a set of facts. The objective is to learn $\mathcal{M}$ so that transformation $T_{\mathcal{M}}$ satisfies the training examples *optimally* (rather than exactly) and thus increase resilience to noise in the training data. Model $\mathcal{M}$ is usually designed to simulate aspects of logical reasoning. For example, the immediate consequence operator of certain classes of logic programs can be approximated by recurrent (Hölldobler, Kalinke, and Störr 1999), fibring (Bader, d'Avila Garcez, and Hitzler 2005), and feed-forward networks (Bader et al. 2007). Also, certain neural-symbolic architectures can simulate the intuition of forward (Dong et al. 2019; Campero et al. 2018) and backwards chaining (Rocktäschel and Riedel 2017) of Horn clauses. Although these techniques are sometimes described as *rule learning* approaches, they do not provide a way to extract rules from the model $\mathcal{M}$. Thus, operator $T_{\mathcal{M}}$ is a 'black box' that aims to mimic Datalog reasoning, but whose inferences cannot be explained symbolically.

Finally, *rule learning* approaches follow the principles outlined in the previous paragraph, but they also specify how to extract a set of Datalog rules $\mathcal{R}_{\mathcal{M}}$ from $\mathcal{M}$. Neural-LP (Yang, Yang, and Cohen 2017) is a prominent example that has been very influential in the field, and it has spurred the development of several refinements (Sadeghian et al. 2019) and extensions to more complex rules (Wang et al. 2020). The ∂ILP (Evans and Grefenstette 2018) and RNNLogic (Qu et al. 2021) frameworks follow the same principle, but use a different kind of ML model.

The rule learning approaches mentioned in the previous paragraph promise to deliver the best of both symbolic reasoning and machine learning. To the best of our knowledge, however, these approaches do not provide any formal guarantees on the relationship between $\mathcal{R}_{\mathcal{M}}$ and $T_{\mathcal{M}}$. In particular, $\mathcal{R}_{\mathcal{M}}$ should at least be a *sound* approximation of $T_{\mathcal{M}}$, in the sense that, for an arbitrary set of facts D, all the facts obtained by applying $\mathcal{R}_{\mathcal{M}}$ to D should be contained in the result of applying $T_{\mathcal{M}}$ to D. Without this property, the extent to which the extracted rules explain the model's predictions is inherently unclear. Ideally, though, $\mathcal{R}_{\mathcal{M}}$ should represent $\mathcal{M}$ *faithfully*: applying either $T_{\mathcal{M}}$ or $\mathcal{R}_{\mathcal{M}}$ to an arbitrary set of facts should produce *exactly* the same results. Surprisingly, this issue has been overlooked in the literature: it is often claimed without justification that the extracted rules 'approximate' or 'explain' the model, and rule quality is usually evaluated just by manual inspection.

In this paper, we make the first steps towards studying formally the rule extraction procedures proposed in the literature. We focus on Neural-LP since, on the one hand, Yang, Yang, and Cohen (2017) present explicitly the rule extraction algorithm for their approach, and, on the other hand, Neural-LP has been successfully trained on large inputs and has inspired many other approaches (Sadeghian et al. 2019; Wang et al. 2020). While our results (naturally) depend on the specifics of the Neural-LP model, we believe they can be adapted to other rule learning approaches.

After recapitulating the definitions of Neural-LP in Section 2, we analyse the formal properties of Neural-LP models and the rule extraction algorithm in Section 3. To this end, we first reformulate the definitions of Neural-LP and discuss the underlying intuitions. The extraction procedure takes as input a threshold parameter. We then show that, for arbitrary thresholds, the extracted rules can be unsound (i.e., on some datasets, the rules can derive facts not predicted by the model); however, we can always ensure soundness by selecting the threshold in a specific way. In contrast, we prove that it is *impossible* to devise a procedure that takes an arbitrary Neural-LP model and produces rules that faithfully represent the model's predictions. Intuitively, predictions of Neural-LP models can depend on *how many times* a rule body matches the data, whereas inferences in standard Datalog can only depend on whether there is at least one way to match a rule body to the data.

As a possible remedy, in Section 4 we propose a new family of *max-Neural-LP models* for which the rule extraction procedure by Yang, Yang, and Cohen (2017) always produces faithful rules. Intuitively, our proposal prevents models from making predictions based on the number of matches of a rule body, which in turn reduces the expressive power of models to fit within that of standard Datalog and thus makes the extraction of faithful rules theoretically feasible.

Rule learning approaches have commonly been evaluated on knowledge graph completion tasks in the literature (Rossi et al. 2021; Bordes et al. 2013; Teru, Denis, and Hamilton 2020). Following this practice, we evaluated our techniques using several benchmarks in this area, and we present our results in Section 5. We first show that the rules extracted from Neural-LP models do not accurately approximate the models in practice: on our benchmarks, the extracted rules derive only a fraction of the facts predicted by the trained models. Thus, the extracted rules are insufficient to explain or characterise the transformation induced by the models. We then compare the classification performance of Neural-LP and our max-Neural-LP models. Our results show that the proposed modifications do not impact the model's practical ability to make useful predictions: on all benchmarks, max-Neural-LP models can be effectively trained in practice to achieve performance similar to that of standard Neural-LP. We thus show that effective rule learning can be realised in practice without sacrificing faithfulness of rule extraction.

2 Background

We now recapitulate the definitions of Datalog, introduce the Neural-LP model, and discuss its rule extraction algorithm.

Datalog assumes a *signature* consisting of *constants* and *predicates*, where each predicate is associated with a non-negative integer *arity*. A *term* is a *variable* or a constant; an *atom* is an expression of the form $R(t_1, \dots, t_n)$ where R is an n-ary predicate and each t_i, $1 \leq i \leq n$, is a term; a *fact* is a variable-free atom; and a *dataset* is a finite set of facts. A (Datalog) *rule* is an expression of form (1), where $n \geq 0$, H is a *head* atom, and each B_i with $1 \leq i \leq n$ is a *body* atom.

$$H \leftarrow B_1 \wedge \dots \wedge B_n \tag{1}$$

A (Datalog) *program* is a finite set of rules. We use (possibly indexed) letters $a, b, c \dots$ for constants, letters $x, y, z \dots$ for variables, and letters $R, S, T, \dots$ for predicates.

A *substitution* σ is a partial mapping of variables to constants with a finite domain. For α a term, atom, rule, or a set of rules, $\alpha\sigma$ is the result of replacing each occurrence of a variable x in α with $\sigma(x)$, provided that σ is defined on x.

Each rule r of the form (1) gives rise to the *immediate consequence* operator T_r, whose application to a dataset D is defined as the smallest dataset $T_r(D)$ containing $H\sigma$ for each substitution σ of the variables of r to constants of D that satisfies $\{B_1\sigma, \dots, B_n\sigma\} \subseteq D$. For $\mathcal{R}$ a program, let $T_{\mathcal{R}}(D) = \bigcup_{r \in \mathcal{R}} T_r(D)$. Operator $T_{\mathcal{R}}$ is *monotonic*: for all datasets D_1 and D_2, if $D_1 \subseteq D_2$, then $T_{\mathcal{R}}(D_1) \subseteq T_{\mathcal{R}}(D_2)$. Thus, for each dataset D, operator $T_{\mathcal{R}}$ has a unique least fixpoint $T_{\mathcal{R}}^{\infty}(D)$; this set, as well as the process of computing it, are often called the *materialisation* of $\mathcal{R}$ on D.

In our work, we allow rules to be *unsafe* (i.e., variables may occur in the rule head without also occurring in the rule body), and we allow rule bodies to be empty. These assumptions allow us to present the definitions of Neural-LP more seamlessly, but they do not affect the fundamental nature of Datalog. In particular, operator T_r remains well defined; for example, if r is $R(x, y) \leftarrow$ and $D = \{S_1(a), S_2(b)\}$, then $T_r(D) = \{R(a, a), R(a, b), R(b, a), R(b, b)\}$.

For μ a mapping of constants to constants and D a dataset, $\mu(D)$ is the dataset obtained from D by replacing each occurrence of a constant c in D with $\mu(c)$ (and eliminating any duplicate facts so that $\mu(D)$ is a set). It is well known that each Datalog program $\mathcal{R}$ is *invariant* under any μ that maps each constant occurring in $\mathcal{R}$ to itself—that is, for any such μ, we have $\mu(T_{\mathcal{R}}(D)) \subseteq T_{\mathcal{R}}(\mu(D))$ for each dataset D.

Vectors, Matrices, and Tensors. We use tensors over the set $\mathbb{R}$ of real numbers. For $\mathbf{A}$ a tensor with n dimensions, $a_{i_1, i_2, \dots, i_n}$ is its element in position i_1 of the first dimension, position i_2 of the second dimension, etc. We consider vectors and matrices as tensors with one and two dimensions, respectively. Finally, $\mathbf{v}^\intercal$ is the transpose of a vector $\mathbf{v}$.

Neural-LP assumes a signature consisting of a finite number δ of *binary* predicates arranged in an arbitrary (but fixed) sequence $R_1, \ldots, R_\delta$. Each dataset or rule can mention only the predicates given in the signature, so fixing an enumeration of the predicates allows us to represent an arbitrary dataset as an adjacency tensor.

The objective of Neural-LP is to learn an operator $T_\mathcal{M}$ that mimics the immediate consequence operator of a set of *chain rules* of the form (2), where $n \geq 0$.

$$R_h(x_n, x_0) \leftarrow R_{k_n}(x_n, x_{n-1}) \wedge \cdots \wedge R_{k_1}(x_1, x_0) \quad (2)$$

For $n = 0$, rule (2) reduces to $R_h(x_0, x_0) \leftarrow$; when applied to a dataset D, this rule derives $R_h(a, a)$ for each constant a in D. Instead of listing the rules explicitly, $T_\mathcal{M}$ is defined by a machine learning model $\mathcal{M}$. We next define $\mathcal{M}$ and $T_\mathcal{M}$, and we leave the analysis of the model's properties and the discussion of the intuitions behind it to Section 3.

A Neural-LP model $\mathcal{M}$ is a triple $(\mathbf{A}, \mathbf{B}, \beta)$ where, for a positive integer L called the *depth* of the model, $\mathbf{A}$ is a tensor of dimension $\delta \times \delta \times L$, $\mathbf{B}$ is a tensor of dimension $\delta \times (L+1) \times (L+1)$, and $\beta \in \mathbb{R}$. The elements of tensors $\mathbf{A}$ and $\mathbf{B}$ are learnable, whereas β is a classification threshold that is typically given explicitly. The formal description of Neural-LP does not impose any restriction on the range of the components of $\mathbf{A}$ and $\mathbf{B}$; however, the Neural-LP implementation computes $\mathbf{A}$ and $\mathbf{B}$ using the softmax function, so their elements have values between zero and one.

We next discuss how to compute $T_\mathcal{M}(D)$ for a dataset D. First, we identify the number ϵ of distinct constants in D, we order all constants into an arbitrary sequence $c_1, \ldots, c_\epsilon$, and we construct an adjacency tensor $\mathbf{M}$ of dimension $\delta \times \epsilon \times \epsilon$ such that $m_{k,i,j}$ is set to 1 if $R_k(c_i, c_j) \in D$ and to 0 otherwise. For k with $1 \leq k \leq \delta$, we let $\mathbf{M}_k$ be the matrix of dimension $\epsilon \times \epsilon$ where $(m_k)_{i,j} = m_{k,i,j}$. Second, for each fact of the form $R_h(c_i, c_j)$ with $1 \leq h \leq \delta$ and $1 \leq i, j \leq \epsilon$, we determine whether $R_h(c_i, c_j)$ should be added to $T_\mathcal{M}(D)$ as follows.

- We define a vector $\mathbf{u}^0$ of dimension ϵ such that $u_j^0 = 1$ and all other components are zero.
- For each $\ell \in \{1, \ldots, L\}$, we inductively compute vectors $\mathbf{u}^\ell$ using the following formula:

$$\mathbf{u}^\ell = \sum_{k=1}^{\delta} a_{h,k,\ell} \cdot \mathbf{M}_k \times \left(\sum_{\ell'=0}^{\ell-1} b_{h,\ell,\ell'+1} \cdot (\mathbf{u}^{\ell'})^\intercal \right). \quad (3)$$

- We compute vector $\mathbf{u}^{L+1}$ as follows:

$$\mathbf{u}^{L+1} = \sum_{\ell=0}^{L} b_{h,L+1,\ell+1} \cdot \mathbf{u}^\ell. \quad (4)$$

- We add $R_h(c_i, c_j)$ to $T_\mathcal{M}(D)$ if and only if $u_i^{L+1} > \beta$.

Neural-LP also provides a procedure for extracting a set of rules from a model $\mathcal{M}$, which we show in Algorithm 1. The procedure is parameterised by a threshold γ (which can be different from the model's classification threshold β). Since the aim is to learn only chain rules, the body of each such rule is represented in the extraction algorithm as a possibly empty sequence of predicates $[R_{k_\ell}, \ldots, R_{k_1}]$; we use $[]$ as the empty sequence and $[\rho|R]$ as the concatenation of sequence ρ with predicate R. The algorithm considers each predicate R_h in the signature and produces in lines 2–15 all chain rules of depth up to L with R_h in the head. To this end, the algorithm computes a sequence $\mathcal{R}_0, \ldots, \mathcal{R}_{L+1}$ of pairs of the form $\langle s, \rho \rangle$, where ρ is a sequence corresponding to a subset of the rule body and s is a real-valued confidence factor; we explain the intuition behind this step in more detail in Section 3. Finally, the algorithm selects each rule body whose confidence exceeds the threshold γ in line 14, and it converts it into a rule with R_h in the head in line 15.

Algorithm 1 Neural-LP's Rule Extraction Algorithm

Inputs: a Neural-LP model $\mathcal{M} = (\mathbf{A}, \mathbf{B}, \beta)$ of depth L, a threshold $\gamma \in \mathbb{R}$
Output: a Datalog program

1: $\mathcal{R} := \emptyset$
2: **for** $h \in \{1, \ldots, \delta\}$ **do**
3: $\quad \mathcal{R}_0 := \{\langle 1, [] \rangle\}$
4: $\quad$ **for** $\ell \in \{1, \ldots, L+1\}$ **do**
5: $\quad\quad \hat{\mathcal{R}}_\ell := \emptyset$
6: $\quad\quad$ **for** $\ell' \in \{1, \ldots, \ell\}$ and $\langle s, \rho \rangle \in \mathcal{R}_{\ell'-1}$ **do**
7: $\quad\quad\quad$ add $\langle s \cdot b_{h,\ell,\ell'}\ ,\ \rho \rangle$ to $\hat{\mathcal{R}}_\ell$
8: $\quad\quad$ **if** $\ell \leq L$ **then**
9: $\quad\quad\quad \mathcal{R}_\ell := \emptyset$
10: $\quad\quad\quad$ **for** $\langle s, \rho \rangle \in \hat{\mathcal{R}}_\ell$ and $k \in \{1, \ldots, \delta\}$ **do**
11: $\quad\quad\quad\quad$ add $\langle s \cdot a_{h,k,\ell}\ ,\ [\rho | R_k] \rangle$ to $\mathcal{R}_\ell$
12: $\quad\quad$ **else**
13: $\quad\quad\quad \mathcal{R}_\ell := \hat{\mathcal{R}}_\ell$
14: $\quad$ **for** $\langle s, [R_{k_n}, \ldots, R_{k_1}] \rangle \in \mathcal{R}_{L+1}$ such that $s > \gamma$ **do**
15: $\quad\quad$ add rule (2) to $\mathcal{R}$
16: **return** $\mathcal{R}$

3 Analysing the Neural-LP Model

In this section we investigate the formal properties of the Neural-LP approach. In particular, in Section 3.1 we describe intuitively the inferences that a Neural-LP model can make, and we reformulate equations (3) and (4) in a way that allows us to draw additional insights and prove our technical results more easily. In Section 3.2, we present a succinct characterisation of the Datalog programs produced by Algorithm 1. Finally, in Section 3.3 we discuss how the predictions of a Neural-LP model and the derivations of the rules extracted from the model relate on arbitrary datasets.

3.1 Analysing the Neural-LP Model

Yang, Yang, and Cohen (2017) motivate their formulation of Neural-LP by the desire to obtain a trainable model that mimics the application of chain rules of varying length. The definitions of Neural-LP can perhaps be better understood if we observe that the model does not simulate chain rules directly; rather, it simulates a nonstandard application of rules of the form (5)–(7) instantiated for all h, k, ℓ, and ℓ' satisfying $1 \leq h, k \leq \delta$ and $0 \leq \ell' < \ell \leq L$.

$$U_{h,0}(x, x) \leftarrow \tag{5}$$

$$U_{h,\ell}(x, z) \leftarrow R_k(x, y) \wedge U_{h,\ell'}(y, z) \tag{6}$$

$$U_{h,L+1}(x, y) \leftarrow U_{h,\ell}(x, y). \tag{7}$$

Here, $U_{h,\ell}$ are auxiliary binary predicates distinct from the signature predicates $R_1, \ldots, R_\delta$; we assume that $U_{h,\ell}$ do not occur in any input dataset, so we consider them to be 'internal' to the model. A model $\mathcal{M} = (\mathbf{A}, \mathbf{B}, \beta)$ assigns a weight to each body atom in the aforementioned rules:

- in each rule (6), element $a_{h,k,\ell}$ of $\mathbf{A}$ determines the weight of atom $R_k(x, y)$, and element $b_{h,\ell,\ell'+1}$ of $\mathbf{B}$ determines the weight of atom $U_{h,\ell'}(x, z)$; and
- in each rule (7), element $b_{h,L+1,\ell+1}$ of $\mathbf{B}$ determines the weight of atom $U_{h,\ell}(x, y)$.

Note that elements $b_{h,\ell,\ell'+1}$ of $\mathbf{B}$ with $\ell' \geq \ell$ are not used in the predictions made by $\mathcal{M}$.

The application of model $\mathcal{M}$ to a dataset can then be seen as applying rules (5)–(7) in the following nonstandard way. Assume that each fact in the dataset is annotated with a confidence value; for uniformity, we define the confidence value of all facts not contained in the dataset as zero. An application of a rule *increases* the confidence value of the derived fact by the product of the weights of all body atoms and the confidence values of the matched facts; for rules with empty bodies, we define this product to be one.

We can now reinterpret equations (3) and (4) as applying rules (5)–(7) with weighted atoms. In particular, let D be an arbitrary dataset and let D' be obtained by applying rules (5)–(7) as outlined in the previous paragraph, but where atoms $R_k(x, y)$ are only matched to facts in D with confidence value of one. Finally, assume that, to check whether $R_h(c_i, c_j)$ should be added to $T_\mathcal{M}(D)$, we compute vectors $\mathbf{u}^\ell$ as specified in Section 2. Then, for each $0 \leq \ell \leq L + 1$ and $1 \leq p \leq \epsilon$, the confidence of fact $U_{h,\ell}(c_p, c_j)$ in D' is equal to u_p^ℓ; moreover, $R_h(c_i, c_j) \in T_\mathcal{M}(D)$ if and only if the confidence of $U_{h,L+1}(c_i, c_j)$ is larger than β. Indeed, for $\ell = 0$, facts of the form $U_{h,0}(c_p, c_j)$ are derived only by (5), so the confidence of each fact is $u_p^0 = 1$ if $p = j$ and $u_p^0 = 0$ if $p \neq j$. For $1 \leq \ell \leq L$, equation (3) can be rewritten as

$$\mathbf{u}^\ell = \sum_{k=1}^{\delta} \sum_{\ell'=0}^{\ell-1} a_{h,k,\ell} \cdot b_{h,\ell,\ell'+1} \cdot \mathbf{M}_k \times (\mathbf{u}^{\ell'})^\intercal, \tag{8}$$

which clearly corresponds to the computations of rules (6). Finally, equation (4) corresponds to applying rules (7).

Chain rules of varying length can be obtained by *unfolding* the auxiliary predicates. For example, we can eliminate predicate $U_{h,1}$ in rules $U_{h,2}(x, z) \leftarrow R_2(x, y) \wedge U_{h,1}(y, z)$ and $U_{h,1}(x, z) \leftarrow R_3(x, y) \wedge U_{h,0}(y, z)$ by unifying and then resolving away the atoms containing $U_{h,1}$; we thus obtain $U_{h,2}(x, z) \leftarrow R_2(x, y) \wedge R_3(y, w) \wedge U_{h,0}(w, z)$ where w is a fresh variable. It is straightforward to see that, if we extend rules (5)–(7) with rules

$$R_h(x, y) \leftarrow U_{h,L+1}(x, y) \text{ for } h \in \{1, \ldots, \delta\} \tag{9}$$

and then unfold all auxiliary predicates, we obtain all chain rules of the form (2) with $0 \leq n \leq L$.

We next formalise the intuitions of such unfolding in a way that will facilitate the proofs of our main results. Our reformulation uses (possibly empty) sequences of integers that we will use as indexes into the model's tensors.

- For each $s \in \{0, \ldots, L\}$, let $\mathcal{L}_s$ be the set of all nonempty integer sequences $[\ell_0, \ldots, \ell_n]$ such that $0 \leq n \leq s$ and $0 = \ell_0 < \ell_1 < \cdots < \ell_n = s$. Note that $\mathcal{L}_0 = \{[0]\}$.
- Let $\mathcal{L} = \bigcup_{0 \leq s \leq L} \mathcal{L}_s$.
- For $\lambda = [\ell_0, \ldots, \ell_n] \in \mathcal{L}$, let $\mathcal{K}_\lambda$ be the set of all sequences $[k_1, \ldots, k_n]$ where each k_p satisfies $1 \leq k_p \leq \delta$.
- For $\lambda = [\ell_0, \ldots, \ell_n] \in \mathcal{L}$ and $i, j \in \{1, \ldots, \epsilon\}$, let $\mathcal{T}_{\lambda,i,j}$ be the set of all sequences $[t_0, \ldots, t_n]$ where $t_0 = j$, $t_n = i$, and each t_p satisfies $1 \leq t_p \leq \epsilon$.

Note that all sequences are nonempty apart from the only sequence in $\mathcal{K}_{[0]} = \{[]\}$. Furthermore, for $h \in \{1, \ldots, \delta\}$ and $\lambda = [\ell_0, \ldots, \ell_n]$, $\kappa = [k_1, \ldots, k_n]$, and $\tau = [t_0, \ldots, t_n]$, let

$$\varphi(h, \kappa, \lambda) = \prod_{i=1}^{n} a_{h,k_i,\ell_i} \cdot b_{h,\ell_i,\ell_{i-1}+1},$$

$$\psi(\kappa, \tau) = \prod_{i=1}^{n} m_{k_i,t_i,t_{i-1}}, \quad \text{and}$$

$$\theta(h, \kappa, \lambda) = b_{h,L+1,\ell_n+1} \cdot \varphi(h, \kappa, \lambda).$$

With these definitions in place, we can now show that equations (3) and (4) are equivalent to (10) and (11), respectively.

Proposition 1. *Let $\mathcal{M} = (\mathbf{A}, \mathbf{B}, \beta)$ be a Neural-LP model, let D be a dataset, and let $\mathbf{u}^0, \ldots, \mathbf{u}^{L+1}$ be the vectors computed by equations* (3) *and* (4) *when checking whether fact $R_h(c_i, c_j)$ should be added to $T_\mathcal{M}(D)$. Then,* (10) *and* (11) *hold for each $0 \leq \ell \leq L$ and each $1 \leq p \leq \epsilon$.*

$$u_p^\ell = \sum_{\lambda \in \mathcal{L}_\ell} \sum_{\kappa \in \mathcal{K}_\lambda} \varphi(h, \kappa, \lambda) \sum_{\tau \in \mathcal{T}_{\lambda,p,j}} \psi(\kappa, \tau) \tag{10}$$

$$u_p^{L+1} = \sum_{\lambda \in \mathcal{L}} \sum_{\kappa \in \mathcal{K}_\lambda} \theta(h, \kappa, \lambda) \sum_{\tau \in \mathcal{T}_{\lambda,p,j}} \psi(\kappa, \tau) \tag{11}$$

Proof. We prove (10) by induction on ℓ. Consider $\ell = 0$. Then, we have $\mathcal{L}_0 = \{\lambda\}$ for $\lambda = [0]$, and $\mathcal{K}_\lambda = \{\kappa\}$ where $\kappa = []$; in addition, $\varphi(h, \kappa, \lambda) = 1$. Furthermore, if $p \neq j$, then $\mathcal{T}_{\lambda,p,j} = \emptyset$ and so $u_p^\ell = 0$. Otherwise, $\mathcal{T}_{\lambda,j,j} = \{[j]\}$, so $\sum_{\tau \in \mathcal{T}_{\lambda,j,j}} \psi(\kappa, \tau) = 1$ and we have $u_j^\ell = 1$.

Now assume that (10) holds for $\ell - 1$ and consider some u_p^ℓ computed by (8). The formula for u_p^ℓ can be rewritten as in Figure 1 using the distributive properties of multiplication and summation. In the last step, note that $\lambda \in \mathcal{L}_{\ell'}$ extended with ℓ produces a sequence $\lambda' \in \mathcal{L}_\ell$, extending κ with k produces κ', and extending τ with t produces τ'. The proof of formula (11) is analogous and is omitted for brevity. □

Intuitively, these formulas correspond to the 'unfolding' of rules (5)–(7). Each sequence $\lambda \in \mathcal{L}$ determines a path through the auxiliary body predicates, and each sequence

$$
\begin{aligned}
u_p^\ell &= \sum_{k=1}^{\delta} \sum_{\ell'=0}^{\ell-1} a_{h,k,\ell} \cdot b_{h,\ell,\ell'+1} \left(\sum_{t=1}^{\epsilon} m_{k,p,t} \cdot u_t^{\ell'} \right) = \\
&= \sum_{\ell'=0}^{\ell-1} \sum_{k=1}^{\delta} a_{h,k,\ell} \cdot b_{h,\ell,\ell'+1} \left(\sum_{t=1}^{\epsilon} m_{k,p,t} \sum_{\lambda \in \mathcal{L}_{\ell'}} \sum_{\kappa \in \mathcal{K}_\lambda} \varphi(\kappa, \lambda) \sum_{\tau \in \mathcal{T}_{\lambda,p,j}} \psi(\kappa, \tau) \right) = \\
&= \sum_{\ell'=0}^{\ell-1} \sum_{k=1}^{\delta} a_{h,k,\ell} \cdot b_{h,\ell,\ell'+1} \left(\sum_{\lambda \in \mathcal{L}_{\ell'}} \sum_{\kappa \in \mathcal{K}_\lambda} \varphi(\kappa, \lambda) \sum_{b=1}^{\epsilon} \sum_{\tau \in \mathcal{T}_{\lambda,p,j}} m_{k,p,t} \cdot \psi(\kappa, \tau) \right) = \\
&= \sum_{\ell'=0}^{\ell-1} \sum_{\lambda \in \mathcal{L}_{\ell'}} \sum_{k=1}^{\delta} \sum_{\kappa \in \mathcal{K}_\lambda} a_{h,k,\ell} \cdot b_{h,\ell,\ell'+1} \cdot \varphi(\kappa, \lambda) \sum_{t=1}^{\epsilon} \sum_{\tau \in \mathcal{T}_{\lambda,p,j}} m_{k,p,t} \cdot \psi(\kappa, \tau) = \sum_{\lambda' \in \mathcal{L}_\ell} \sum_{\kappa' \in \mathcal{K}_{\lambda'}} \varphi(\kappa', \lambda') \sum_{\tau' \in \mathcal{T}_{\lambda',p,j}} \psi(\kappa', \tau')
\end{aligned}
$$

Figure 1: Equivalences in the Proof of Proposition 1

$\kappa \in \mathcal{K}_\lambda$ identifies the body predicates associated to this path. In particular, each ℓ_i in λ and k_i in κ together identify a rule of the form (6) for which $\ell = \ell_i$, $\ell' = \ell_{i-1}$, and $k = k_i$. Finally, each sequence $\tau \in \mathcal{T}_{\lambda,p,j}$ identifies a possible set of facts $R_{k_i}(c_{t_i}, c_{t_{i-1}})$ that can potentially be matched to the body atoms of the unfolded rule, and elements $m_{k_i,t_i,t_{i-1}}$ determine whether these facts are contained in D. Thus, equations (10) and (11) can indeed be understood as applications of the unfolding of rules (5)–(7) to D.

3.2 Characterisation of Rule Extraction

This idea of unfolding is also reflected in the rule extraction procedure shown in Algorithm 1. In particular, when the loop in lines 2–15 completes for some h, all unfoldings having predicate $U_{h,\ell}$, $0 \leq \ell \leq L$, in the head are described by $\mathcal{R}_\ell$, and all unfoldings having predicate R_h in the head are described by $\mathcal{R}_{L+1}$. Specifically, for each $\langle s, \rho \rangle$ in one of these sets, s corresponds to the product of the weights of all body atoms in the unfolding, and ρ describes the body of the unfolding. This claim can be easily proved by induction on ℓ. For $\ell = 0$, the only unfolding with $U_{h,0}$ in the head is $U_{h,0}(x, x) \leftarrow$ and the product of all body weights is 1, which matches the definition of $\mathcal{R}_0$ in line 3. For $1 \leq \ell \leq L$, the induction hypothesis and lines 5–7 ensure that, for each $\langle s, \rho \rangle \in \hat{\mathcal{R}}_\ell$, sequence ρ describes the body of an unfolding with some $U_{h,\ell'}$ in the head, where $0 \leq \ell' < \ell$, and s is the product of the body weights of that unfolding and the weight of atom $U_{h,\ell'}(y, z)$ in a rule of form (6); but then, lines 9–11 clearly extend each such $\langle s, \rho \rangle$ to the relevant unfoldings with $U_{h,\ell}$ in the head. Finally, line 13 ensures that $\mathcal{R}_{L+1}$ captures the unfoldings generated from rules of form (7).

Rules (5)–(7) can often be unfolded in different ways to the same rule. For example, rule $R_5(x, y) \leftarrow R_7(x, y)$ can be obtained by unfolding (7) for $\ell = 3$, (6) for $k = 7$, $\ell = 3$, and $\ell' = 1$, and (5), as well as by unfolding (7) for $\ell = 2$, (6) for $k = 7$, $\ell = 2$, and $\ell' = 1$, and (5). Each such unfolding can derive facts with different confidence factors.

Before proceeding, we present a more direct characterisation of the output of Algorithm 1, which will allow us to formalise other statements about Neural-LP more easily.

Definition 1. *For $\mathcal{M} = (\mathbf{A}, \mathbf{B}, \beta)$ a Neural-LP model and $\gamma \in \mathbb{R}$, program $\mathcal{R}_\mathcal{M}^\gamma$ contains a rule of the form (2) for each index $h \in \{1, \ldots, \delta\}$, each sequence $\lambda \in \mathcal{L}$, and each sequence $\kappa = [k_1, \ldots, k_n] \in \mathcal{K}_\lambda$ such that $\theta(h, \kappa, \lambda) > \gamma$.*

Proposition 2. *For each Neural-LP model $\mathcal{M}$ and each $\gamma \in \mathbb{R}$, Algorithm 1 outputs $\mathcal{R}_\mathcal{M}^\gamma$.*

Proof. Consider an arbitrary index $h \in \{1, \ldots, \delta\}$ and let $\mathcal{R}_0, \ldots, \mathcal{R}_{L+1}$ be the sets computed by Algorithm 1 when the iteration of the loop in lines 2–15 finishes for h. We show that, for each $\ell \in \{0, \ldots, L\}$, each sequence of predicates $\rho = [R_{k_n}, \ldots, R_{k_1}]$ with $0 \leq n \leq \ell$, and each $s \in \mathbb{R}$, we have $\langle s, \rho \rangle \in \mathcal{R}_\ell$ if and only if there exists a sequence $\lambda \in \mathcal{L}_\ell$ such that $\varphi(h, \kappa, \lambda) = s$ where $\kappa = [k_1, \ldots, k_n]$. The proof is by an easy induction on ℓ and is omitted. Then, lines 6–7 and line 13 for $L{+}1$, and the way in which the rules are produced in lines 14–15 ensures the claim for h. □

3.3 Relating Model to Extracted Rules

The rule extraction algorithm of Neural-LP is intuitive, but Yang, Yang, and Cohen (2017) never discussed the extent to which the extracted rules characterise the model's inferences. We study this question in the rest of this section. As we mentioned in Section 2, the Neural-LP implementation uses the softmax function to compute $\mathbf{A}$ and $\mathbf{B}$ so the elements of these tensors are nonnegative; but then, it is also reasonable to require the classification threshold to be nonnegative too. Consequently, we shall restrict our attention to models that are *regular* as per the following definition.

Definition 2. *A Neural-LP model $\mathcal{M} = (\mathbf{A}, \mathbf{B}, \beta)$ is* regular *if $\beta \geq 0$ and no element of tensor $\mathbf{A}$ or $\mathbf{B}$ is negative.*

Before proceeding with our analysis, we introduce several notions that capture possible relationships between a model and the extracted rules.

Definition 3. *Let $\mathcal{M}$ be a Neural-LP model, and let $\mathcal{R}$ be a Datalog program. Then, program $\mathcal{R}$ is* sound *(resp.* complete*) for $\mathcal{M}$ if, for each dataset D, $T_\mathcal{R}(D) \subseteq T_\mathcal{M}(D)$ (resp. $T_\mathcal{R}(D) \supseteq T_\mathcal{M}(D)$). Moreover, $\mathcal{R}$ is* faithful *to $\mathcal{M}$ if $\mathcal{R}$ is both sound and complete for $\mathcal{M}$.*

In other words, a sound program $\mathcal{R}$ can derive only consequences also derived by $\mathcal{M}$, but it may not necessarily derive all consequences of $\mathcal{M}$; in contrast, a complete program derives all consequences of $\mathcal{M}$, but it may also derive consequences that are 'incorrect' according to $\mathcal{M}$. Ideally, we would like $\mathcal{R}$ to be faithful to $\mathcal{M}$ since program $\mathcal{R}$ then provides an exact symbolic account of all inferences that $\mathcal{M}$ can make on an arbitrary dataset.

We are now ready to present two results that relate a regular Neural-LP model $\mathcal{M}$ and the corresponding program $\mathcal{R}^{\gamma}_{\mathcal{M}}$. We show that $\mathcal{R}^{\gamma}_{\mathcal{M}}$ is sound for $\mathcal{M}$ if we choose $\gamma \geq \beta$, but otherwise $\mathcal{R}^{\gamma}_{\mathcal{M}}$ can be unsound for $\mathcal{M}$.

Theorem 1.

1. *For each regular Neural-LP model $\mathcal{M} = (\mathbf{A}, \mathbf{B}, \beta)$ and each $\gamma \geq \beta$, program $\mathcal{R}^{\gamma}_{\mathcal{M}}$ is sound for $T_{\mathcal{M}}$.*
2. *There exists a regular Neural-LP model $\mathcal{M} = (\mathbf{A}, \mathbf{B}, \beta)$ such that, for $\gamma < \beta$, program $\mathcal{R}^{\gamma}_{\mathcal{M}}$ is unsound for $\mathcal{M}$.*

Proof of Claim 1. Fix an arbitrary regular Neural-LP model $\mathcal{M} = (\mathbf{A}, \mathbf{B}, \beta)$, real number $\gamma \geq \beta$, dataset D, and fact $R_h(c_i, c_j) \in T_{\mathcal{R}^{\gamma}_{\mathcal{M}}}(D)$. Then, there exists a rule $r \in \mathcal{R}^{\gamma}_{\mathcal{M}}$ of the form (2) and facts

$$\{R_{k_n}(c_{t_n}, c_{t_{n-1}}), \dots, R_{k_1}(c_{t_1}, c_{t_0})\} \subseteq D$$

such that applying r to these facts derives $R_h(c_i, c_j)$. Now let $\kappa = [k_1, \dots, k_n]$ and $\tau = [t_0, \dots, t_n]$. By Definition 1, there exists a sequence $\lambda \in \mathcal{L}$ such that $\theta(h, \kappa, \lambda) > \gamma$. Note that $\kappa \in \mathcal{K}_{\lambda}$ and $\tau \in \mathcal{T}_{\lambda,i,j}$; moreover, $m_{j,t_i,t_{i-1}} = 1$ for each $1 \leq i \leq n$, so $\psi(\kappa, \tau) = 1$. Now let $\mathbf{u}^0, \dots, \mathbf{u}^{L+1}$ be the vectors computed as specified in equations (3) and (4) for checking whether $R_h(c_i, c_j)$ should be added to $T_{\mathcal{M}}(D)$. By Proposition 1, the value of u_i^{L+1} is given by equation (11); all numbers in this equation are nonnegative because model $\mathcal{M}$ is regular, so $\psi(\kappa, \tau) = 1$ and $\theta(h, \kappa, \lambda) > \gamma \geq \beta$ clearly imply $u_i^{L+1} > \beta$. Therefore, $R_h(c_i, c_j)$ is added to $T_{\mathcal{M}}(D)$, and our claim holds. □

Proof of Claim 2. Let $\delta = 2$, but note that we can handle larger signatures by padding tensors $\mathbf{A}$ and $\mathbf{B}$ with zeros if needed. Now let $\mathcal{M} = (\mathbf{A}, \mathbf{B}, \beta)$ be the regular Neural-LP model of depth $L = 1$ where $\beta = 0.5$ and tensors $\mathbf{A}$ and $\mathbf{B}$ contain zeros everywhere apart from $a_{1,2,1} = 0.5$ and $b_{1,1,1} = b_{1,2,2} = 1$. Moreover, let $D = \{R_2(a, a)\}$; one can easily check that $T_{\mathcal{M}}(D) = \emptyset$. However, for each $\gamma < \beta$, by Definition 1 program $\mathcal{R}^{\gamma}_{\mathcal{M}}$ contains rule (12).

$$R_1(x, y) \leftarrow R_2(x, y) \tag{12}$$

One can easily check that $T_{\mathcal{R}^{\gamma}_{\mathcal{M}}}(D) = \{R_1(a, a)\}$; hence, program $\mathcal{R}^{\gamma}_{\mathcal{M}}$ is unsound for $\mathcal{M}$. □

Theorem 1 is quite intuitive. In particular, note that each rule extracted from $\mathcal{M}$ corresponds to an element of the sum in equation (11). Thus, by selecting γ such that $\gamma \geq \beta$, we make sure that the consequences of each extracted rule are also consequences of $\mathcal{M}$. In contrast, if we select γ such that $\gamma < \beta$, then the confidence factors of the facts derived by (5)–(7) may not exceed the threshold β and we run the risk of extracting unsound rules.

Along these lines, one might hope that we can ensure completeness by selecting $\gamma = \beta$; however, we next show that this is not the case. In fact, our result is much stronger: we show that there exists a Neural-LP model whose inferences do not correspond to inferences of any Datalog program. As a result, no algorithm can extract a sound and complete program given an arbitrary regular Neural-LP model.

Theorem 2. *There exists a regular Neural-LP model $\mathcal{M}$ such that no Datalog program $\mathcal{R}$ is faithful to $\mathcal{M}$.*

Proof. Let $\delta = 2$, but note that we can handle larger signatures by padding tensors $\mathbf{A}$ and $\mathbf{B}$ with zeros. Now let $\mathcal{M} = (\mathbf{A}, \mathbf{B}, \beta)$ be the regular Neural-LP model of depth $L = 2$ where $\beta = 0.75$ and tensors $\mathbf{A}$ and $\mathbf{B}$ contain zeros everywhere apart from

$$a_{1,2,1} = 0.5 \quad \text{and}$$
$$a_{1,2,2} = b_{1,1,1} = b_{1,2,2} = b_{1,3,3} = 1.$$

Now assume that there exists a Datalog program $\mathcal{R}$ that is faithful to $\mathcal{M}$, and let D_1 and D_2 be the following datasets, where constant c does not appear in $\mathcal{R}$.

$$D_1 = \{R_2(a, b), R_2(b, d)\} \tag{13}$$
$$D_2 = D_1 \cup \{R_2(a, c), R_2(c, d)\} \tag{14}$$

It is straightforward to check using the definitions of Neural-LP that $T_{\mathcal{M}}(D_1) = \emptyset$ and $T_{\mathcal{M}}(D_2) = \{R_1(a, d)\}$. Since $\mathcal{R}$ is complete for $\mathcal{M}$, we have $T_{\mathcal{R}}(D_2) = \{R_1(a, d)\}$. Now let μ be the mapping of constants to constants that is the identity everywhere apart from $\mu(c) = b$. Note that $\mu(D_2) = D_1$ and $\mu(T_{\mathcal{R}}(D_2)) = \{R_1(a, d)\}$. Now constant c does not occur in $\mathcal{R}$ and μ is the identity on all other constants, so program $\mathcal{R}$ is invariant under μ and

$$\{R_1(a, d)\} = \mu(T_{\mathcal{R}}(D_2)) \subseteq T_{\mathcal{R}}(\mu(D_2)) = T_{\mathcal{R}}(D_1)$$

holds. But then, $R_1(a, d) \in T_{\mathcal{R}}(D_1)$ implies that $\mathcal{R}$ is unsound for $\mathcal{M}$, which is a contradiction. □

Theorem 2 can be understood as follows. Model $\mathcal{M}$ used in the proof describes rules whose unfolding corresponds to

$$R_1(x, z) \leftarrow R_2(x, y) \wedge R_2(y, z) \tag{15}$$

where the weights of atoms $R_2(x, y)$ and $R_2(y, z)$ are 1 and 0.5, respectively. Now the body of rule (15) can be matched just once in dataset D_1, so $R_1(a, d)$ is derived with confidence factor 0.5, which does not exceed the classification threshold $\beta = 0.75$. In contrast, the body of (15) matches twice in dataset D_2, so $R_1(a, d)$ is derived with confidence factor 1. In other words, the derivations of Neural-LP can count how many times a rule body matches to a dataset. Indeed, this is shown in equation (11): each κ corresponds to a chain rule of the form (2), and $\psi(\kappa, \tau) = 1$ if the rule matches to the facts identified by the sequence τ; thus, $\sum_{\tau \in \mathcal{T}_{\lambda,p,j}} \psi(\kappa, \tau)$ gives us the number of body matches. Counting the matches of a rule body is not possible in standard Datalog: each Datalog rule can only determine whether the rule body matches or not. Such inferences can be captured only using nonstandard extensions of Datalog such as arithmetic and aggregate functions, but these drastically change the computational properties of Datalog.

4 Ensuring Faithfulness of Rule Extraction

Theorems 1 and 2 suggest that any rule extraction procedure for Neural-LP faces fundamental limitations: the best we can hope for is soundness. One may also wonder whether program $\mathcal{R}^{\beta}_{\mathcal{M}}$ is 'sufficiently complete' in practice in the sense that it derives *most* consequences of a model $\mathcal{M}$. We show empirically in Section 5 that this is not the case: the number of facts derived by $\mathcal{R}^{\beta}_{\mathcal{M}}$ and $T_{\mathcal{M}}$ can be different by several orders of magnitude on commonly used benchmarks. These observations motivate the question of whether the Neural-LP model can be modified in a way that makes extracting faithful Datalog programs possible.

We answer this question positively: we propose a new family of *max-Neural-LP models* for which Algorithm 1 always produces faithful Datalog programs. Intuitively, our modification allows us to replace the sums in equations (10) and (11) with maximum operators. This prevents the model from making predictions based on how many times a rule body matches to the data, which in turn reduces the expressive power of the model to fit that of standard Datalog.

Towards this goal, we note that the sum over sequences τ in equations (10) and (11) actually originates from the matrix product in equation (3). To replace this sum with a maximum, we define a *max-product* $\otimes$ of matrices as follows.

Definition 4. *Let* $\mathbf{M}$ *and* $\mathbf{N}$ *be matrices of dimension* $m \times n$ *and* $n \times p$*, respectively. The* max-product *of* $\mathbf{M}$ *and* $\mathbf{N}$*, written* $\mathbf{M} \otimes \mathbf{N}$*, is a matrix of dimension* $m \times p$ *whose element at position* i *and* j *is equal to*

$$\max_{1 \leq k \leq n} a_{i,k} \cdot b_{k,j}.$$

It is straightforward to see that the max-product has the same properties as the standard matrix product, such as associativity and distributivity with respect to the sum. However, sum and maximum do not commute, so we cannot just replace $\times$ with $\otimes$ in equation (3) and hope to reformulate the model's equations analogously to Proposition 1. To facilitate such a reformulation, we also replace alls sums in equations (3) and (4) with maximums too. Thus, for matrices $\mathbf{M}$ and $\mathbf{N}$ of equal dimensions, we let $\max\{\mathbf{M}, \mathbf{N}\}$ be the matrix obtained by taking the element-wise maximum—that is, its element at position i and j is equal to $\max\{m_{i,j}, n_{i,j}\}$. We are now ready to define our max-Neural-LP model.

Definition 5. *A* max-Neural-LP *model is defined as the standard Neural-LP model, but equations* (3) *and* (4) *are replaced with equations* (16) *and* (17)*, respectively.*

$$\mathbf{u}^{\ell} = \max_{1 \leq k \leq \delta} \max_{0 \leq \ell' < \ell} a_{h,k,\ell} \cdot b_{h,\ell,\ell'+1} \cdot \mathbf{M}_k \otimes (\mathbf{u}^{\ell'})^{\intercal} \quad (16)$$

$$\mathbf{u}^{L+1} = \max_{0 \leq \ell \leq L} b_{h,L+1,\ell+1} \cdot \mathbf{u}^{\ell} \quad (17)$$

Just like a standard Neural-LP model, each max-Neural-LP model $\mathcal{M}$ defines an operator $T_{\mathcal{M}}$ on datasets, so we can straightforwardly apply the notions of soundness, completeness, and faithfulness to max-Neural-LP models. Moreover, a max-Neural-LP model is regular if all of its components are nonnegative. We are now ready to show that Algorithm 1 produces programs that are both sound and complete for each max-Neural-LP model provided we use the same threshold for fact classification and rule extraction. Towards this goal, we first adapt Proposition 1 to max-Neural-LP.

Proposition 3. *Let* $\mathcal{M} = (\mathbf{A}, \mathbf{B}, \beta)$ *be a regular max-Neural-LP model, let* D *be a dataset, and let* $\mathbf{u}^0, \ldots, \mathbf{u}^{L+1}$ *be the vectors computed by* (16) *and* (17) *when checking whether* $R_h(c_i, c_j)$ *should be added to* $T_{\mathcal{M}}(D)$*. Then,* (18) *and* (19) *hold for each* $0 \leq \ell \leq L$ *and each* $1 \leq p \leq \epsilon$.

$$u^{\ell}_p = \max_{\lambda \in \mathcal{L}_{\ell}} \max_{\kappa \in \mathcal{K}_{\lambda}} \varphi(h, \kappa, \lambda) \max_{\tau \in \mathcal{T}_{\lambda,p,j}} \psi(\kappa, \tau) \quad (18)$$

$$u^{L+1}_p = \max_{\lambda \in \mathcal{L}} \max_{\kappa \in \mathcal{K}_{\lambda}} \theta(h, \kappa, \lambda) \max_{\tau \in \mathcal{T}_{\lambda,p,j}} \psi(\kappa, \tau) \quad (19)$$

Proof. The following identities clearly hold for each set of numbers b_i, each set of numbers $c_{i,j}$, and each $\alpha \geq 0$:

$$\alpha \max{}_i \, b_i = \max{}_i \, \alpha \cdot b_i,$$
$$\max{}_i \max{}_j \, c_{i,j} = \max{}_j \max{}_i \, c_{i,j}.$$

Thus, since $\mathcal{M}$ is regular, equations (16) and (17) can be rewritten to (18) and (19) in the same way as in Figure 1, but while using $\max$ instead of $\sum$. □

Intuitively, Proposition 3 suggests that each rule corresponding to the unfolding of rules (5)–(7) is applied in a max-Neural-LP model in isolation, and the confidence of the resulting fact is the maximum derived by one unfolding. The rule application now matches the rule extraction procedure, so we can show that, for $\gamma = \beta$, Algorithm 1 produces a program that is faithful to the model.

Theorem 3. *For* $\mathcal{M} = (\mathbf{A}, \mathbf{B}, \beta)$ *a regular max-Neural-LP model, program* $\mathcal{R}^{\beta}_{\mathcal{M}}$ *is faithful to* $\mathcal{M}$.

Proof. The poof that $\mathcal{R}^{\beta}_{\mathcal{M}}$ is sound is analogous to the proof of the first claim of Theorem 1 so we omit it for the sake of brevity. To show that $\mathcal{R}^{\beta}_{\mathcal{M}}$ is complete for $\mathcal{M}$, consider an arbitrary dataset D and fact $R_h(c_i, c_j) \in T_{\mathcal{M}}(D)$, and let $\mathbf{u}^0, \ldots, \mathbf{u}^{L+1}$ be the vectors computed by (16) and (17) when checking whether $R_h(c_i, c_j)$ should be added to $T_{\mathcal{M}}(D)$. Also, choose arbitrary sequences $\lambda \in \mathcal{L}$, $\kappa \in \mathcal{K}_{\lambda}$, and $\tau \in \mathcal{T}_{\lambda,i,j}$ that maximise $\theta(h, \kappa, \lambda) \cdot \psi(\kappa, \tau)$. Then, we have $u^{L+1}_i = \theta(h, \kappa, \lambda) \cdot \psi(\kappa, \tau) > \beta$, where the equality holds by Proposition 3, and the inequality holds because $R_h(c_i, c_j) \in T_{\mathcal{M}}(D)$. Now $\beta \geq 0$ ensures $\psi(\kappa, \tau) = 1$; but then, for $\kappa = [k_1, \ldots, k_n]$ and $\tau = [t_0, \ldots, t_n]$, we have

$$\{R_{k_n}(c_{t_n}, c_{t_{n-1}}), \ldots, R_{k_1}(c_{t_1}, c_{t_0})\} \subseteq D. \quad (20)$$

Finally, we have $\theta(h, \kappa, \lambda) > \beta$, so Definition 1 ensures that $\mathcal{R}^{\beta}_{\mathcal{M}}$ contains the chain rule (2). This rule clearly derives $R_h(c_i, c_j)$ on the facts from equation (20), as required. □

5 Evaluation

To evaluate our approach, we ported the code of Neural-LP to TensorFlow 2.7.0 and extended it with the ability to learn max-Neural-LP models. To reduce memory consumption, Neural-LP uses a sparse representation of adjacency tensors, and and it relies on TensorFlow's highly optimised implementation of multiplication of a sparse matrix by a dense one. To use the same approach in max-Neural-LP, we extended TensorFlow with a custom implementation of the max-product of a sparse matrix by a dense one. We ran our experiments on a laptop running macOS 12.2 and Python 3.8.5 with 8 GB of RAM and an Intel Core i5 2.30 GHz CPU. We evaluated the two versions of Neural-LP on several well-known benchmarks. All systems, scripts, and datasets used in the experiments are available online.[1]

5.1 Benchmarks and Training

We evaluate our models on knowledge graph (KG) completion tasks, where the aim is to extend an incomplete KG represented as a dataset D to its complete version D' by adding missing facts. When seen as a classification problem, the objective of KG completion is to learn a Boolean function that takes as input a dataset D and a fact α over a fixed set of binary predicates and returns true if and only if $\alpha \in D'$.

We used the 12 benchmark datasets by Teru, Denis, and Hamilton (2020) based on FB15K-237 by Bordes et al. (2013), NELL-995 by Xiong, Hoang, and Wang (2017), and WN18RR by Dettmers et al. (2018). Each benchmark provides disjoint datasets $\mathcal{T}$, $\mathcal{V}$, and $\mathcal{S}$ for training, validation, and testing, respectively; relevant statistics are shown in Table 1. The benchmarks also provide means for splitting the test dataset $\mathcal{S}$ into disjoint subsets $\mathcal{S}_I$ and $\mathcal{S}_M$, where the former plays the role of the incomplete test KG and the latter contains the missing facts.

We trained both versions of Neural-LP as denoising autoencoders (Vincent et al. 2010). We split the training dataset $\mathcal{T}$ with a 3:1 ratio into an incomplete training KG $\mathcal{T}_I$ and a set $\mathcal{T}_M$ of missing facts, and we used $(\mathcal{T}_I, \alpha)$ for each fact $\alpha \in \mathcal{T}_M$ as a positive example. We trained models of depth $L = 3$ using Adam optimisation with the standard learning rate 0.001, a batch size of 64, and a maximum of 10 epochs. Following Yang, Yang, and Cohen (2017) in their evaluation of Neural-LP, we used log-likelihood loss with sum reduction, minimum probability threshold of 10^{-20}, and target value 1. We trained both versions of Neural-LP using an RNN neural controller system by Yang, Yang, and Cohen (2017). For each system and benchmark, the training process yields a pair of tensors $\mathbf{A}$ and $\mathbf{B}$ whose elements are computed using the softmax function and are thus between zero and one. We then combine these tensors with different nonnegative classification thresholds β to obtain models $\mathcal{M} = (\mathbf{A}, \mathbf{B}, \beta)$ that are regular according to Definition 2.

5.2 Rule Extraction Completeness for Neural-LP

As discussed in Section 3.3, Algorithm 1 produces sound programs for Neural-LP models if the rule extraction threshold γ is greater or equal to the model's classification threshold β. Using $\gamma = \beta$ clearly produces the largest such program, and one may wonder whether this program is 'sufficiently complete' in practice.

To answer this question, for each benchmark, we trained tensors $\mathbf{A}$ and $\mathbf{B}$ as described. Then, for each value of β shown in Table 2, we used Neural-LP's implementation of Algorithm 1 to extract the program $\mathcal{R}^{\beta}_{\mathcal{M}}$ from the model $\mathcal{M} = (\mathbf{A}, \mathbf{B}, \beta)$; we computed the sets of facts $T_{\mathcal{R}^{\beta}_{\mathcal{M}}}(\mathcal{S}_I)$ and $T_{\mathcal{M}}(\mathcal{S}_I)$ that the program and the model produce on the incomplete test dataset $\mathcal{S}_I$; and we calculated the percentage ratio of the sizes of these two sets. This provided us with a 'measure of completeness' of the extracted programs on the test datasets. Our results are shown in Table 2.

For benchmarks based on FB15K and NELL-995, the extracted rules often derive less than 3% of the facts predicted by the model; for benchmarks based on WN18RR, the rules typically derive 5%–30% of the predicted facts. We take this as empirical evidence that the extracted rules do not sufficiently explain the predictions of Neural-LP models. We observe also that the extracted rules provide a better approximation for smaller thresholds. This is because the number of extracted rules decreases quickly when γ rises to 0.01 and above: for models of depth 3, the values $\theta(h, \kappa, \lambda)$ are a product of 7 elements of $\mathbf{A}$ and $\mathbf{B}$; now these elements are typically smaller than 0.5, and $0.5^7 \approx 0.008$.

5.3 Knowledge Graph Completion Performance

We next compared the performance of Neural-LP and max-Neural-LP models on KG completion. For each benchmark, we proceeded as follows. For each fact $\alpha \in \mathcal{S}_M$, we took $(\mathcal{S}_I, \alpha)$ as a positive testing example. We generated negative testing examples by uniformly sampling at random $|\mathcal{S}_M|$ facts from the set of all facts $R(a, b) \notin \mathcal{S}$ where predicate R is used in the benchmark, and constants a and b are at distance at most 3 in $\mathcal{S}_I$—that is, either $a = b$, or there exist facts $\{R_1(a, c_1), \dots, R_n(c_{n-1}, b)\} \subseteq \mathcal{S}_I$ for $n \in \{1, 2, 3\}$. We used this negative sampling strategy because a model's depth fundamentally limits the type of inferences the model can make: a fact of the form $R(a, b)$ can be derived on a dataset D only if the distance of constants a and b in D is at most the model's depth. For each system and benchmark, we computed the F1 score on the validation dataset for a range of classification thresholds β between 0 and 1, and we selected the threshold that maximised this score. For Neural-LP models, this threshold was between 0.001 and 1 for most benchmarks, whereas for max-Neural-LP models, the threshold was typically around 10^{-5}. For the selected threshold, we classified the positive and negative testing examples, and we computed precision, recall, accuracy, and F1 score as usual. Finally, we computed the area under the precision-recall curve (AUC) using the thresholds considered during validation. Our results are shown in Table 3.

The performance of max-Neural-LP models is on a par with that of Neural-LP models. Recall values of both systems are generally low in all benchmarks; this can be explained by the fact that many positive examples involve constants separated by more than three steps in $\mathcal{S}_I$, so they cannot be predicted by either approach. The benchmarks based on WN18RR were difficult for both systems: the systems produced many false positives, which led to lower precision scores. Finally, the training times of Neural-LP and max-Neural-LP models were comparable.

Our results confirm that max-Neural-LP models can be effectively trained in practice to achieve performance comparable to Neural-LP models. Yang, Yang, and Cohen (2017)

[1] http://krr-nas.cs.ox.ac.uk/2022/max-Neural-LP/

	FB15K-237				NELL-995				WN18RR			
	v1	v2	v3	v4	v1	v2	v3	v4	v1	v2	v3	v4
# Facts for Training	4,245	9,739	17,986	27,203	4,687	8,219	16,393	7,546	5,410	15,262	25,901	7,940
# Facts for Validation	489	1,166	2,194	3,352	414	922	1,851	876	630	1,838	3,097	934
# Facts for Testing	2,198	4,623	8,271	13,138	933	5,062	8,857	7,804	1,806	4,452	6,932	13,763
# Predicates	180	200	215	219	14	88	142	76	9	10	11	9

Table 1: Numbers of Predicates and Facts in Training, Validation, and Testing Datasets Per Benchmark

	GraIL-BM/FB15K-237				GraIL-BM/NELL-995				GraIL-BM/WN18RR			
Threshold β	v1	v2	v3	v4	v1	v2	v3	v4	v1	v2	v3	v4
0.001	4.2	2.4	1.1	0.97	29	3.2	1.3	1.6	43	37	9.9	54
0.002	1.5	1.1	0.62	0.55	25	2.0	0.63	1.7	35	27	6.0	39
0.005	0.29	0.28	0.31	0.24	3.9	0.76	0.33	0.52	26	17	11	25
0.01	0.089	0.13	0.21	0.20	4.9	0.50	0.28	0.23	20	11.5	8.2	20
0.02	0.056	0.15	0.14	0.19	3.1	0.43	0.17	0.14	17	7.9	6.6	12
0.05	0.054	0.10	0.14	0.21	1.1	0.35	0.13	0.22	7.9	5.6	3.2	7.9
0.1	0.051	0.089	0.086	0.14	0.58	0.18	0.051	0.24	6.1	3.3	3.2	5.6
0.2	0.044	0.0	0.0	0.0075	0.18	0.098	0.0	0.51	0.98	4.4	3.9	5.1
0.5	0.0	0.0	0.0	0.0	0.0	0.0	0.0	0.0	0.0	0.0	0.0	0.0

Table 2: Percentage of Facts Derived by Neural-LP Model $\mathcal{M}$ for Threshold β Also Derived by $\mathcal{R}^{\beta}_{\mathcal{M}}$

		GraIL-BM/FB15K-237				GraIL-BM/NELL-995				GraIL-BM/WN18RR			
	Model	v1	v2	v3	v4	v1	v2	v3	v4	v1	v2	v3	v4
Precision	Neural-LP	**37.8**	45.4	67.1	64.6	38.5	69.8	76.8	59.5	19.7	**18.2**	3.8	16.1
	Max-Neural-LP	30.7	**75.1**	**74.7**	**85.4**	**39.5**	**80.1**	**77.1**	**70.4**	**20.5**	12.5	**5.8**	**16.9**
Recall	Neural-LP	16.6	**34.1**	**25.7**	**33.7**	60.0	26.7	30.3	6.8	**13.8**	0.9	0.3	**11.1**
	Max-Neural-LP	**19.0**	31.0	25.5	30.4	**62.0**	**35.9**	**40.8**	**53.4**	13.3	**7.7**	**4.3**	11.0
Accuracy	Neural-LP	**44.6**	46.5	56.5	57.6	32.0	57.6	60.6	51.1	28.7	**48.4**	**46.0**	26.7
	Max-Neural-LP	38.0	**60.4**	**58.4**	**62.6**	**33.5**	**63.7**	**64.3**	**65.5**	**30.9**	26.8	17.0	**28.5**
F1 Score	Neural-LP	23.1	38.9	37.1	44.3	46.9	38.6	43.4	12.3	**16.3**	1.7	0.6	13.1
	Max-Neural-LP	**23.5**	**43.9**	**38.1**	**44.8**	**47.3**	**49.7**	**64.3**	**60.7**	16.1	**9.5**	**4.9**	**13.3**
AUC	Neural-LP	23.3	39.3	40.7	48.5	20.6	45.4	50.1	48.9	**14.0**	**9.6**	**3.1**	**9.7**
	Max-Neural-LP	**25.4**	**44.8**	**44.1**	**50.4**	**56.7**	**55.1**	**53.4**	**56.7**	11.5	8.1	2.8	8.3
Training Time	Neural-LP	3.8	**7.5**	46.2	90.7	0.4	5.7	35.8	**2.4**	0.4	2.8	**4.8**	1.6
	Max-Neural-LP	**3.3**	14.3	**39.4**	**85.9**	0.4	**5.2**	**32.3**	4.5	**0.3**	**2.7**	9.5	1.6

Table 3: Classification Metrics (%) and Training Times (minutes) for Both Systems

compare Neural-LP with other rule learning and rule mining approaches, and their results transfer to max-Neural-LP as well. The crucial benefit of max-Neural-LP models is that we can extract from each model a program that faithfully captures the model's predictions on any dataset.

6 Conclusion and Future Work

In this paper, we studied the formal properties of the Neural-LP approach to rule learning. We showed that there is a fundamental mismatch between the predictions made by Neural-LP models and the inferences of the rules extracted from such models. We proposed a novel family of max-Neural-LP models for which the extracted Datalog rules completely characterise the models' predictions. Our max-Neural-LP models achieve comparable performance to that of Neural-LP on knowledge graph completion benchmarks. Thus, we show that it is possible to devise practical rule learning approaches with a formally well-understood relationship between the model and the extracted rules.

For our future work, we shall extend our results to approaches that build on top of Neural-LP such as those by Sadeghian et al. (2019) and Wang et al. (2020), as well as approaches based on different types of models, such as those by Evans and Grefenstette (2018) and Qu et al. (2021).

Acknowledgments

This work was supported by the AIDA project (Alan Turing Institute, EP/N510129/1), the SIRIUS Centre for Scalable Data Access (Research Council of Norway, project number 237889), Samsung Research UK, Siemens AG, and the EPSRC projects ConCur (EP/V050869/1), OASIS (EP/S032347/1) and UK FIRES (EP/S019111/1).

References

Abiteboul, S.; Hull, R.; and Vianu, V. 1995. *Foundations of Databases*. Addison Wesley.

Ahmadi, N.; Huynh, V.-P.; Meduri, V. V.; Ortona, S.; and Papotti, P. 2020. Mining Expressive Rules in Knowledge Graphs. *Journal of Data and Information Quality* 12(2):8:1–8:27.

Arni, F.; Ong, K.; Tsur, S.; Wang, H.; and Zaniolo, C. 2003. The deductive database system LDL++. *TPLP* 3(1):61–94.

Bader, S.; Hitzler, P.; Hölldobler, S.; and Witzel, A. 2007. A Fully Connectionist Model Generator for Covered First-Order Logic Programs. In Veloso, M. M., ed., *Proc. of the 20th Int. Joint Conf. on Artificial Intelligence (IJCAI 2007)*, 666–671.

Bader, S.; d'Avila Garcez, A. S.; and Hitzler, P. 2005. Computing First-Order Logic Programs by Fibring Artificial Neural Networks. In Russell, I., and Markov, Z., eds., *Proc. of the 18th Int. Florida Artificial Intelligence Research Society Conference (FLAIRS 2005)*, 314–319. AAAI Press.

Bordes, A.; Usunier, N.; García-Durán, A.; Weston, J.; and Yakhnenko, O. 2013. Translating embeddings for modeling multi-relational data. In Burges, C. J. C.; Bottou, L.; Ghahramani, Z.; and Weinberger, K. Q., eds., *NeurIPS*, 2787–2795.

Campero, A.; Pareja, A.; Klinger, T.; Tenenbaum, J.; and Riedel, S. 2018. Logical rule induction and theory learning using neural theorem proving. *CoRR* abs/1809.02193.

Cropper, A.; Dumancic, S.; Evans, R.; and Muggleton, S. H. 2021. Inductive logic programming at 30. *CoRR* abs/2102.10556.

Dettmers, T.; Minervini, P.; Stenetorp, P.; and Riedel, S. 2018. Convolutional 2D knowledge graph embeddings. In McIlraith, S. A., and Weinberger, K. Q., eds., *AAAI*, 1811–1818. AAAI Press.

Dong, H.; Mao, J.; Lin, T.; Wang, C.; Li, L.; and Zhou, D. 2019. Neural Logic Machines (Poster). In *Proc. of the 7th Int. Conf. on Learning Representations (ICLR 2019)*.

Eisner, J., and Filardo, N. W. 2010. Dyna: Extending Datalog for Modern AI. In *Datalog Reloaded—First International Workshop, Datalog 2010. Revised Selected Papers*, 181–220. Oxford, UK: Springer.

Evans, R., and Grefenstette, E. 2018. Learning Explanatory Rules from Noisy Data. *Journal of Artificial Intelligence Research* 61:1–64.

Galárraga, L.; Teflioudi, C.; Hose, K.; and Suchanek, F. M. 2015. Fast Rule Mining in Ontological Knowledge Bases with AMIE+. *VLDB J.* 24(6):707–730.

Green, T. J.; Huang, S. S.; Loo, B. T.; and Zhou, W. 2013. Datalog and Recursive Query Processing. *Foundations and Trends in Databases* 5(2):105–195.

Hölldobler, S.; Kalinke, Y.; and Störr, H.-P. 1999. Approximating the Semantics of Logic Programs by Recurrent Neural Networks. *Applied Intelligence* 11(1):45–58.

Meilicke, C.; Chekol, M. W.; Ruffinelli, D.; and Stuckenschmidt, H. 2019. Anytime Bottom-Up Rule Learning for Knowledge Graph Completion. In Kraus, S., ed., *Proc. of the 28th Int. Joint Conf. on Artificial Intelligence (IJCAI 2019*, 3137–3143.

Muggleton, S. 1991. Inductive Logic Programming. *New Generation Computing* 8(4):295–318.

Qu, M.; Chen, J.; Xhonneux, L.-P. A. C.; Bengio, Y.; and Tang, J. 2021. RNNLogic: Learning Logic Rules for Reasoning on Knowledge Graphs. In *Proc. of the 9th Int. Conf. on Learning Representations (ICLR 2021)*.

Rocktäschel, T., and Riedel, S. 2017. End-to-end Differentiable Proving. In Guyon, I.; von Luxburg, U.; Bengio, S.; Wallach, H. M.; Fergus, R.; Vishwanathan, S. V. N.; and Garnett, R., eds., *Proc. of the 31st Conf. on Neural Information Processing Systems (NeurIPS 2017)*, 3788–3800.

Rossi, A.; Barbosa, D.; Firmani, D.; Matinata, A.; and Merialdo, P. 2021. Knowledge graph embedding for link prediction: A comparative analysis. *ACM Trans. Knowl. Discov. Data* 15(2):14:1–14:49.

Sadeghian, A.; Armandpour, M.; Ding, P.; and Wang, D. Z. 2019. DRUM: End-To-End Differentiable Rule Mining On Knowledge Graphs. In Wallach, H. M.; Larochelle, H.; Beygelzimer, A.; d'Alché-Buc, F.; Fox, E. B.; and Garnett, R., eds., *Proc. of the 33rd Conf. on Neural Information Processing Systems (NeurIPS 2017)*, 15321–15331.

Teru, K. K.; Denis, E.; and Hamilton, W. 2020. Inductive relation prediction by subgraph reasoning. In *ICML*, volume 119 of *Proceedings of Machine Learning Research*, 9448–9457. PMLR.

Vincent, P.; Larochelle, H.; Lajoie, I.; Bengio, Y.; Manzagol, P.-A.; and Bottou, L. 2010. Stacked denoising autoencoders: Learning useful representations in a deep network with a local denoising criterion. *J. of Machine Learning Res.* 11(12).

Wang, P.-W.; Stepanova, D.; Domokos, C.; and Kolter, J. Z. 2020. Differentiable learning of numerical rules in knowledge graphs. In *Proc. of the 8th Int. Conf. on Learning Representations (ICLR 2020)*.

Xiong, W.; Hoang, T.; and Wang, W. Y. 2017. Deeppath: A reinforcement learning method for knowledge graph reasoning. In *EMNLP*, 564–573. Association for Computational Linguistics.

Yang, F.; Yang, Z.; and Cohen, W. W. 2017. Differentiable Learning of Logical Rules for Knowledge Base Reasoning. In Guyon, I.; von Luxburg, U.; Bengio, S.; Wallach, H. M.; Fergus, R.; Vishwanathan, S. V. N.; and Garnett, R., eds., *Proc. of the 31st Conf. on Neural Information Processing Systems (NeurIPS 2017)*, 2319–2328.

Proceedings of the 19th International Conference on Principles of Knowledge Representation and Reasoning
Special Session on KR and Machine Learning

Learning Typed Rules over Knowledge Graphs

Hong Wu[1], Zhe Wang[1], Kewen Wang[1], Yi-Dong Shen[2]
[1]School of Information and Communication Technology, Griffith University, Australia
[2]State Key Laboratory of Computer Science, Institute of Software, Chinese Academy of Sciences, China
hong.wu2@griffithuni.edu.au, {zhe.wang, k.wang}@griffith.edu.au, ydshen@ios.ac.cn

Abstract

Rule learning from large datasets has regained extensive interest as rules are useful for developing explainable approaches to many applications in knowledge graphs. However, existing methods for rule learning are still limited in terms of rule expressivity and rule quality. This paper presents a new method for learning typed rules by employing type information. Our experimental evaluation shows the superiority of our system compared to state-of-the-art rule learners. In particular, we demonstrate the usefulness of typed rules in reasoning for link prediction.

1 Introduction

Knowledge graphs (KGs) are a special kind of knowledge bases that highlight interconnection among entities and represent such knowledge as graphs. They have found wide applications in information retrieval, recommender systems, question answering, and semantic data integration (Ji et al. 2020). A number of large-scale and general-purpose knowledge graphs have been developed, such as WordNet (Miller 1995), YAGO (Suchanek, Kasneci, and Weikum 2007), and Freebase (Bollacker et al. 2008). Although significant progress has been made, some important research challenges remain open. One challenge is to extract high-level schema information from large KGs, and another is KG completion or link prediction, as most KGs are still highly incomplete.

Hence, the problem of learning first-order rules over KGs has recently regained extensive interest, as rules provide a promising tool for KG reasoning in various KG applications. Compared to methods purely based on deep neural networks, logic rules are human-comprehensible knowledge and naturally offer explainability of reasoning. Several scalable rule learners have been proposed, including (Galárraga et al. 2015; Chen, Wang, and Goldberg 2016b; Yang, Yang, and Cohen 2017; Omran, Wang, and Wang 2018; Meilicke et al. 2019; Ahmadi et al. 2020; Pirrò 2020), and the learned rules have been successfully applied to link prediction and demonstrated competitive performance (Meilicke et al. 2019; Pirrò 2020).

Several recent rule learners can only extract so-called *closed path rules* (or *CP-rules*) (Yang et al. 2014; Chen, Wang, and Goldberg 2016b; Omran, Wang, and Wang 2018; Pirrò 2020). A major shortcoming of such rules is their limited expressivity. Consider an example, $B(x, y) \wedge C(y, z) \rightarrow N(x, z)$ is a CP-rule for the head predicate $N(x, z)$, which means that if person x was born in city y of country z, then x has the nationality z. So this CP-rule is essentially intended to express the typed rule $B(x : \mathit{person}, y : \mathit{city}) \wedge C(y : \mathit{city}, z : \mathit{country}) \rightarrow N(x : \mathit{person}, z : \mathit{country})$. In fact, this typed rule can be expressed as a first order Horn rule $B(x, y) \wedge C(y, z) \wedge \mathit{person}(x) \wedge \mathit{city}(y) \wedge \mathit{country}(z) \rightarrow N(x, z)$. But such Horn rules cannot be expressed by the syntax of CP-rules. Thus, typed rules provide a natural and useful extension of CP-rules.

More importantly, a KG usually contains rich type information on entities (Hao et al. 2019; Zhang et al. 2020), which is useful for optimising the search of rules. However, this has not received sufficient attention in the literature on rule learning over KGs, except for ScaLeKB (Chen, Wang, and Goldberg 2016b) and RARL (Pirrò 2020), which are based on ontological pathfinding (OP) (Chen et al. 2016a). While these approaches utilise type information in both rule search and rule evaluation, they do not learn typed rules. Also, ontological pathfinding approaches typically use type information as hard constraints on the candidate rules, i.e., each of them must represent a path going through entities belonging to some types. Yet in practice, type information in KGs is often highly incomplete, which would make such hard constraints too restrictive. Besides path-based rule learning, embedding-based rule learning has recently been proposed and shows promising performance (Omran, Wang, and Wang 2018), which employs latent representations from Statistical Relational Learning.

In this paper, we propose a new rule learning approach that is able to learn typed rules and better utilises type information to guide the rule search. We adopt a combined approach of both path-based and embedding-based strategies for our rule search. In the path-based strategy, candidate rules are obtained from both ABox paths and TBox paths. Moreover, type information is employed to confine the path exploration. In the embedding-based strategy, a novel scoring function is defined and used for rule evaluation, in which type information is encoded as latent representations to refine the embedding model.

We have implemented a prototype system TyRuLe and evaluated its performance on both standard benchmarks and a real-life KG AirGraph. The experiments show that our system can learn high-quality and informative rules, and the advantages of using type information are demonstrated through both quantitative and qualitative analysis. As a commonly used rule quality indicator, link prediction results show that TyRuLe outperforms existing rule learners and is competitive compared to embedding-based link prediction systems.

The rest of this paper is organised as follows. Section 2 provides a brief review on models for rule learning and link prediction for knowledge graphs. Section 3 introduces some basics of knowledge graphs and rule technologies. Section 4 describes technical details of our proposed TyRuLe, including KG sampling, a path-based strategy and an embedding-based strategy for rule extraction. Our experimental results are presented in Section 5. Finally, we conclude the paper in Section 6.

2 Related Work

In what follows, we discuss existing works on rule learning and link prediction that are closely related to this paper.

2.1 Rule Learning

First-order rule learning has been extensively studied in Inductive Logic Programming (ILP) literature (Muggleton 1990; Muggleton 1991; Cropper et al. 2022) by exploring the rule space through refinement operators. Classical ILP systems like QuickFOIL (Zeng, Patel, and Page 2014) cannot be used directly to handle KGs due to the lack of negative examples and the large data sizes. Recently, rule learners such as AMIE and its extensions (Galárraga et al. 2015) have been developed with the aim to handle large datasets like KGs, which use plausibility metrics adapted from association rule mining to address the lack of negative examples. Some work has been proposed to propose new completeness-aware confidence metrics to better assess the quality of rules (Pellissier Tanon et al. 2017). Also, learning non-monotonic rules have been studied (Gad-Elrab et al. 2016; Lisi and Weikum 2017).

Another group of approaches generates candidate rules by exploring paths in KGs. AnyBURL (Meilicke et al. 2019) is a bottom-up approach that substitutes entities from sampled paths with variables, to generalise path instances to patterns for rule generation. This allows AnyBURL to learn a large number of rules, which together provide more accurate link prediction than many of the embedding-based approaches. Ontological pathfinding approaches ScaLeKB (Chen, Wang, and Goldberg 2016b) and RARL (Pirrò 2020) adopt a top-down approach by exploring the schema-level knowledge in KGs, i.e., entity types and their relations. They construct path patterns directly from schema-level graphs.

Recently, there is an emerging interest of applying deep neural networks (DNNs) in rule learning. Differentiable rule learners NeuralLP (Yang, Yang, and Cohen 2017) and DRUM (Sadeghian et al. 2019) have been proposed to learn rules directly using DNNs, by optimising objective functions that roughly correspond to plausible path patterns. In (Yang et al. 2014), the authors first suggest to use KG embeddings extracted from neural networks for rule learning, and RLvLR (Omran, Wang, and Wang 2018) is, and as far as know, the only rule learner that can handle large-scale KGs like DBpedia or Wikidata, by using a sampling strategy and matrix computation techniques.

Path-based and DNN-based rule learners can only learn rules that resemble path patterns, with only binary predicates. While ontological pathfinding approaches use type information, the rules learned by them do not contain unary predicates either; that is, type information is only used to confine path search and the learned rules do not contain types. While ILP-based methods do not necessarily have such restrictions, scalable systems like AMIE$^+$ adopt a language bias that only slightly extends path patterns and do not contain unary predicates either.

2.2 Link Prediction

Link prediction is a major inference task for KG completion. Intensive research has been conducted to embed entities and relations in KGs into low-dimensional latent representations, known as *embeddings*. Approaches to link prediction train various scoring functions based on embeddings to estimate the plausibility of triples. Existing approaches along this line can be roughly divided into three categories: tensor decomposition models (Yang et al. 2014; Trouillon et al. 2016), geometric translational models (Bordes et al. 2013; Sun et al. 2019) and deep neural models (Dettmers et al. 2018; Nguyen et al. 2018).

Some recent approaches also explore the type information in KGs and propose embeddings for types. TKRL (Xie et al. 2016) is based on translation model and embeds hierarchical types as projection matrices for entities. JOIE (Hao et al. 2019) adopts a more flexible approach that allows various embedding models as base embeddings and uses nonlinear transformations to capture class membership and hierarchies. HAKE (Zhang et al. 2020) uses a more complex embedding model based on polar coordinate systems to capture hierarchical types.

Compared to black-box neural models, rules are explicit knowledge and are also used for KG reasoning with human-understandable explanations for the results. And link prediction is also considered an important indicator for the quality of rules learned over KGs. With the recent advance of rule learning, rule learners are increasingly used for link prediction and demonstrate competitive accuracy and sometimes significantly better scalability over embedding-based approaches (Omran, Wang, and Wang 2018; Meilicke et al. 2019; Pirrò 2020).

3 Preliminaries

In this section, we briefly introduce some basics of knowledge graphs and rules as well as fixing some notations to be used later.

3.1 Knowledge Graphs

A *knowledge graph* (*KG*) is a directed multi-relational graph, often expressed as a set of *triples* of the form (s, p, o), i.e., $(\textit{subject}, \textit{relation}, \textit{object})$, where subjects and objects are the vertices of the graph and they are connected via relations. Triples in a KG $\mathcal{K}$ can be separated into two

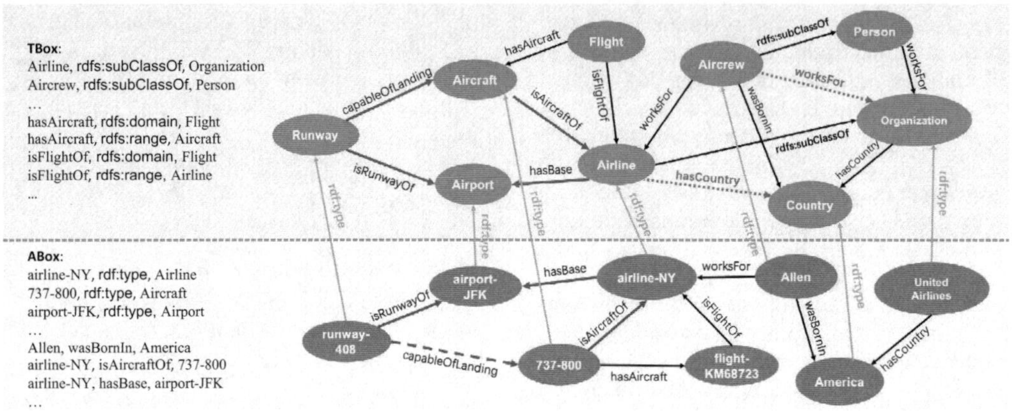

Figure 1: An example knowledge graph.

categories, i.e., $\mathcal{K} = \mathcal{T} \cup \mathcal{A}$, where $\mathcal{T}$ is the *TBox* and $\mathcal{A}$ is the *ABox*. ABox $\mathcal{A}$ describes instance level (or assertional) knowledge about *entities* and their *properties*; for instance, a triple (airline-NY, hasBase, airport-JFK) describes that the two entities airline-NY and airport-JFK are associated by the property hasBase. A property is a binary predicate. $\mathcal{A}$ also describes the *classes* of entities, such as a triple (airline-NY, rdf:type, Airline) expressing that airline-NY is a member of the class Airline. A class is a unary predicate. TBox $\mathcal{T}$, on the other hand, describes schema level (or terminological) knowledge about the relations between classes and between classes and properties. For example, triple (Airline, rdfs:subClassOf, Organization) says that class Airline is a subclass of Organization, and the two triples (hasBase, rdfs:domain, Airline) and (hasBase, rdfs:range, Airport) state that property hasBase has a domain Airline and a range Airport.

Formally, let sets of entities, classes, and properties in the KG $\mathcal{K}$ be respectively $\mathcal{E}$, $\mathcal{C}$, and $\mathcal{P}$. Triples in $\mathcal{A}$ are of the forms

- (e_1, p, e_2) with $e_1, e_2 \in \mathcal{E}$ and $p \in \mathcal{P}$, and
- $(e, \text{rdf:type}, c)$ with $e \in \mathcal{E}$, $p \in \mathcal{P}$, and $c \in \mathcal{C}$.

Following the tradition in knowledge bases, we denote the two types of ABox triples as *facts* of the forms $p(e_1, e_2)$ and $c(e)$, respectively. We write $c(e) \in \mathcal{A}$ or $p(e_1, e_2) \in \mathcal{A}$ meaning the triple occurs in the ABox. Triples in $\mathcal{T}$ are of forms

- $(c_1, \text{rdfs:subClassOf}, c_2)$ with $c_1, c_2 \in \mathcal{C}$,
- $(p, \text{rdfs:domain}, c)$ with $p \in \mathcal{P}$ and $c \in \mathcal{C}$, and
- $(p, \text{rdfs:range}, c)$ with $p \in \mathcal{P}$ and $c \in \mathcal{C}$.

For simplicity, the first type of triple is denoted $c_1 \sqsubseteq c_2$. We use $\sqsubseteq^*$ to denote the transitive closure of the relation $\sqsubseteq$. Following (Hao et al. 2019; Pirrò 2020), we denote each pair of triples $(p, \text{rdfs:domain}, c_1)$ and $(p, \text{rdfs:range}, c_2)$ as a single triple (c_1, p, c_2), and they should not be confused with ABox triples.

Triples of the form $c_1 \sqsubseteq c_2$ are sometimes referred to as class (or type) hierarchy, (c_1, p, c_2) as domain and range constraints, and $c(e)$ as class (or type) membership. They together are called *type information* in the KG. In this paper, we will use the terms "class" and "type" interchangeably. For a relation p, p^- denotes its *inverse*, i.e., triple (o, p^-, s) is equivalent to (s, p, o). Let $\mathcal{P}^* = \mathcal{P} \cup \{p^- \mid p \in \mathcal{P}\}$.

3.2 Rules

Existing rule learners mostly focus on *closed-path (CP)* rules (Yang et al. 2014; Chen, Wang, and Goldberg 2016b; Omran, Wang, and Wang 2018; Pirrò 2020) of the form

$$p_1(x_0, x_1) \wedge p_2(x_1, x_2) \wedge \cdots \wedge p_n(x_{n-1}, x_n) \rightarrow p(x_0, x_n),$$

where $p \in \mathcal{P}$, $p_i \in \mathcal{P}^*$ $(1 \leq i \leq n)$ and x_j's $(0 \leq j \leq n)$ are variables.

For instance, a Horn rule

$$\mathsf{hasAircraft}(x, y) \wedge \mathsf{isFlightOf}(x, z) \rightarrow \mathsf{isAircraftOf}(y, z)$$

says if a flight x has an aircraft y and x is a flight of an airline z then y is an aircraft of z. It corresponds to a CP rule

$$\mathsf{hasAircraft}^-(x_0, x_1) \wedge \mathsf{isFlightOf}(x_1, x_2) \\ \rightarrow \mathsf{isAircraftOf}(x_0, x_2).$$

As discussed in the introduction, it is useful to include types of variables in the rules.

$$\mathsf{hasAircraft}^-(x_0 : \mathsf{Aircraft}, x_1 : \mathsf{Flight}) \\ \wedge \mathsf{isFlightOf}(x_1 : \mathsf{Flight}, x_2 : \mathsf{Airline}) \\ \rightarrow \mathsf{isAircraftOf}(x_0 : \mathsf{Aircraft}, x_2 : \mathsf{Airline}).$$

Such types can be naturally expressed as unary predicates, and hence we want to learn first-order Horn rules with unary predicates in the rule body.

A *typed rule* (or simply a *rule*) r is of the form

$$c_0(x_0) \wedge p_1(x_0, x_1) \wedge c_1(x_1) \wedge p_2(x_1, x_2) \wedge \\ \cdots \wedge p_n(x_{n-1}, x_n) \wedge c_n(x_n) \rightarrow p(x_0, x_n). \quad (1)$$

Each c_i $(1 \leq i \leq n-1)$ is either a class from $\mathcal{C}$ or $\top$, where $\top$ is the class of all entities and $\top(e)$ is always valid for any entity e. A variable in the rule body does not have to be attached a type, and multiple occurrences of the same variable may have multiple types. If no specific type is attached, it has the $\top$ type. Clearly, CP-rules are a special case of typed rules where all the c_i's are $\top$. The atom $p(x_0, x_n)$ is the *head* of r and the set of atoms $\{c_0(x_0), p_1(x_0, x_1), c_1(x_1), p_2(x_1, x_2), \cdots, p_n(x_{n-1}, x_n), c_n(x_n)\}$ is the body of r. The *length* of the rule body is n. Note that the rule heads only contain binary predicates as we learn such rules mainly for link prediction.

A key step in rule learning is to assess the plausibility of candidate rules, and most rule learners for KGs use *support*, *standard confidence*, and *head coverage* (Chen, Wang, and Goldberg 2016b; Omran, Wang, and Wang 2018), or their variants (Galárraga et al. 2015), as metrics for rule plausibility. For a rule r of the form (1), $ins_H(r)$ consists of all the pairs of entities $e_0, e_n \in \mathcal{E}$ such that when x_0 and x_n are replaced with e_0 and e_n, the fact obtained from the head of r occurs in $\mathcal{A}$. Similarly, $ins_B(r)$ consists of all the pairs of entities $e_0, e_n \in \mathcal{E}$ such that there exist $e_1, \ldots, e_{n-1} \in \mathcal{E}$, when each x_i is replaced with e_i ($0 \leq i \leq n$), all the facts obtained from the body of r occur in $\mathcal{A}$. Then, the *support* of r is defined as $|ins_H(r) \cap ins_B(r)|$. That is, the support of r is defined as the number of entity pairs that satisfy both the head and the body of r. The *standard confidence* (*SC*) and *head coverage* (*HC*) of r are defined as follows

$$sc(r) = \frac{|ins_H(r) \cap ins_B(r)|}{|ins_B(r)|} \quad \text{and}$$

$$hc(r) = \frac{|ins_H(r) \cap ins_B(r)|}{|ins_H(r)|}$$

Hence, SC is the normalisation of support through the number of entity pairs that satisfy the body, while HC is the normalisation of support through the number of entity pairs that satisfy the head. The higher the values are for these metrics, the more plausible the rule is.

3.3 Rule-based Link Prediction

Link prediction is the task that given an entity $e \in \mathcal{E}$ and a property $p \in \mathcal{P}^*$, to predict entities e' such that $p(e, e')$ is plausible. Unlike embedding-based approaches that rank the possible entities e' via scoring functions, a rule-based approach tries to derive plausible facts $p(e, e')$ by applying the learned rules to the existing facts in the KG. For a rule r of the form (1), the derived facts are $p(e_0, e_n)$ for $e_0, e_n \in \mathcal{E}$ such that there exist $e_1, \ldots, e_{n-1} \in \mathcal{E}$, when each x_i is replaced with e_i ($0 \leq i \leq n$), all the facts obtained from the body of r occur in $\mathcal{A}$.

The ranking of the derived fact is obtained from the confidences of the rules deriving it. Note that each fact α can be derived by multiple rules $r_1, \ldots, r_m$. We adopt the ranking method called Max-Aggregation (Meilicke et al. 2019), which ranks a fact based on the maximum SC of all rules deriving it. More specifically, let $\mathbf{d}_\alpha$ be a vector of the SC values of all the rules deriving α in descending order, i.e., $\mathbf{d}_\alpha = (sc(r_{k_1}), \ldots, sc(r_{k_m}))$ with $1 \leq k_1, \ldots, k_m \leq m$ and $sc(r_{k_i}) \geq sc(r_{k_{i+1}})$ for $1 \leq i < m$. Then, $\mathbf{d} < \mathbf{d}'$ if there exists some $i \geq 0$ such that $d_i < d'_i$ and $d_j = d'_j$ for all $0 \leq j < i$, where d_i (resp., d'_i) is the i-th element of $\mathbf{d}$ (resp., $\mathbf{d}'$).

4 Rule Learning

In this section, we introduce our approach for rule learning. The proposed approach combines path-based and embedding-based methods for candidate rule generation. To obtain such an effective combination, major challenges include how to use type information to narrow down the path search, and how to embed type information and utilize the embedding.

To learn the following rule for a property isAircraftOf

$$\mathsf{Aircraft}(x_0) \wedge \mathsf{hasAircraft}^-(x_0, x_1) \wedge \mathsf{Flight}(x_1) \wedge \mathsf{isFlightOf}(x_1, x_2) \wedge \mathsf{Airline}(x_2) \rightarrow \mathsf{isAircraftOf}(x_0, x_2),$$

we essentially want to extract a sequence of types and properties like (Aircraft, hasAircraft$^-$, Flight, isFlightOf, Airline). For simplicity, we refer such a sequence as a *path pattern*. In a knowledge graph, there are at least two ways for obtaining a path pattern for the target property isAircraftOf. It can be achieved by exploring a path in the TBox in Figure 1 formed by the two triples (Aircraft, hasAircraft$^-$, Flight) and (Flight, isFlightOf, Airline). Alternatively, the rule can be obtained by exploring many paths in the ABox in Figure 1 such as (737-800, hasAircraft$^-$, flight-KM68732) and (flight-KM68732, isFlightOf, airline-NY).

Given a knowledge graph $\mathcal{K}$, a *path* is a sequence of triples $(s_1, p_1, o_1), (s_2, p_2, o_2), \ldots, (s_n, p_n, o_n)$ in $\mathcal{K}$ where $o_i = s_{i+1}$ ($1 \leq i < n$), denoted $(s_1, p_1, s_2, p_2, \ldots, p_n, o_n)$, and its *length* is n. A *TBox path* (resp., *ABox path*) is a path where $s_i, o_i \in \mathcal{C}$ ($s_i, o_i \in \mathcal{E}$) and $p_i \in \mathcal{P}^*$ ($1 \leq i \leq n$).

Thus, we formally define *path patterns* in KGs as follows.

Definition 1. *A* path pattern *of a KG $\mathcal{K}$ is of the form $\theta = (c_0, p_1, c_1, p_2, \cdots, p_n, c_n)$, where $c_i \in \mathcal{C}$ ($0 \leq i \leq n$) and $p_j \in \mathcal{P}^*$ ($1 \leq j \leq n$).*

A path $\beta = (s_0, p_1, s_1, p_2, \ldots, p_n, s_n)$ in $\mathcal{K}$ is an instance *of θ if for each $0 \leq i \leq n$,*

- *if $s_i \in \mathcal{C}$, $s_i \sqsubseteq^* c_i$, and*
- *if $s_i \in \mathcal{E}$, $c(s_i) \in \mathcal{A}$ for some $c \sqsubseteq^* c_i$.*

Conversely, θ is a pattern *of β.*

Clearly, each TBox path is a path pattern, but not necessarily vice versa, as a path pattern does not necessarily consist of triples in the KG. Learning rules of the form (1) is essentially learning path patterns with significant numbers of ABox paths as instances of the form $(e_0, p_1, e_1, p_2, \ldots, p_n, e_n)$ such that $p(e_0, e_n) \in \mathcal{A}$.

In our approach, we first extract a subgraph of $\mathcal{K}$ for each p, which contains the relevant paths and type information (Section 4.1). Then, we search path patterns on both the TBox graph and ABox graph levels, while the type information is used to reduce the search space (Section 4.2). Meanwhile, we embed the entities, relations, and classes in a latent space, and use the embeddings to complement the search (Section 4.3). Finally, the generated candidate rules, which are in a much more manageable number, are assessed using the SC and HC metrics.

4.1 KG Modules

Sampling of large-scale KGs has been shown to be effective in significantly reducing the data sizes (Omran, Wang, and Wang 2018). For each predicate p that can occur in the head of rules and a maximum rule body length n, we extract a subgraph of $\mathcal{K}$ that is sufficient to generate path patterns.

Definition 2. *For a property $p \in \mathcal{P}$ and an integer $n \geq 1$, a (p, n)*-module *of $\mathcal{K}$ is a subgraph of $\mathcal{K}$ that contains all the ABox paths $\beta = (e_0, p_1, e_1, p_2, \ldots, p_n, e_n)$ with $p(e_0, e_n) \in \mathcal{A}$, and all the triples containing some classes in the patterns of β.*

To extract a (p, n)-module, our method deploys a breath-first tree search. Let $l = \lfloor \frac{n+1}{2} \rfloor$.

- Take $\mathcal{A}_0$ as the set of triples in $\mathcal{A}$ that contain p, and $\mathcal{E}_0$ is the set of entities in $\mathcal{A}_0$;
- For each $1 \leq i \leq l$, let $\mathcal{A}_i$ be the set of triples in $\mathcal{A}$ that contain some entity in $\mathcal{E}_{i-1}$, $\mathcal{E}_i$ and $\mathcal{C}_i$ be the set of respectively entities and classes in $\mathcal{A}_i$, and $\mathcal{T}_i$ be the set of triples in $\mathcal{T}$ that contain some class in $\mathcal{C}_i$.

Observation 1. *$\mathcal{T}_l \cup \mathcal{A}_l$ is a (p, n)-module of $\mathcal{K}$.*

For example, consider an ABox path of length 3, $(e_0, p_1, e_1, p_2, e_2, p_3, e_3)$, such that $p(e_0, e_3) \in \mathcal{A}$, then $e_0, e_3 \in \mathcal{E}_0$, $p_1(e_0, e_1), p_3(e_2, e_3) \in \mathcal{A}_1$, $e_1, e_2 \in \mathcal{E}_1$, and $p_2(e_1, e_2) \in \mathcal{A}_2$.

Compared with the sampling in RLvLR (Omran, Wang, and Wang 2018), our method has superior time efficiency, taking only about half the time RLvLR uses. Also, our method preserves all relevant path patterns, whereas RLvLR is not necessary the case, as its method has to limit the entities or relations in each iteration due the large sizes of sampling. In (Pirrò 2020), the author extracts a reduced ABox for each candidate rule body that can be used to assess the plausibility. We extract a module for each head property, which can be used to generate all candidate bodies.

After we obtain a (p, n)-module, we use two strategies to search for path patterns on the module to form candidate rules. One strategy is to explore paths in both the TBox and ABox in the module, and the other strategy is through embeddings over the module. We present the two strategies in the following two subsections. When the context is clear, for annotation simplicity, we will consider the module as our KG and use $\mathcal{K}$ to represent the module.

4.2 Path-based Strategy

TBox Paths For a KG $\mathcal{K}$, we define its *TBox coverage* (TC) as the ratio t/s, where t (resp., s) is the number of TBox paths (resp., all path patterns) in $\mathcal{K}$ that have some ABox paths as their instances. A KG is *fully TBox covered* if its TBox coverage is 1. When the TBox coverage is relatively high, exploring TBox paths is an effective way to generate candidate rules, as shown in (Chen, Wang, and Goldberg 2016b; Pirrò 2020).

Yet generating candidate rules directly from TBox patterns may cause important information in the class hierarchies being neglected. For example, suppose there are two triples (Aircrew, worksFor, Airline) and (Organization, hasCountry, Country) in the TBox, they do not form a TBox path from Aircrew to Country. Yet we know airlines are organizations and have their associated countries. With the class hierarchy Airline $\sqsubseteq$ Organization in the TBox, the two path patterns are both reasonable, (Aircrew, worksFor, Airline, hasCountry, Country) and (Aircrew, worksFor, Organization, hasCountry, Country).

Based on this observation, we first relax the condition of a TBox path to consider class hierarchies.

Definition 3. *For a path formed by triples $(s_1, p_1, o_1), \ldots, (s_n, p_n, o_n)$, suppose p_i is $\sqsubseteq$ or its inverse with some $1 \leq i \leq n$, then a result of* bridging *is obtained by replacing s_i with o_i, or vice versa, and removing the i-th triple.*

An extended TBox path *is obtained by recursively bridging a path formed by triples from $\mathcal{T}$ till all the remaining relations are from $\mathcal{P}^*$.*

In (Chen, Wang, and Goldberg 2016b), the authors replace classes in each TBox path with their subclasses. This is different from our bridging operation. For instance, suppose there is a class hierarchy EuropeAirline $\sqsubseteq$ Airline, their approach would add a triple (Aircrew, worksFor, EuropeAirline), which may not be expected.

The notions TBox coverage and being fully TBox covered can be extended by considering extended TBox paths instead of TBox paths.

We explore the extended TBox paths for path patterns that can be used for candidate rules. In particular, to learn rules of the form (1), for each pair of classes $c, c' \in \mathcal{C}$ that is directly connected by p in the TBox, we check all the extended TBox paths from c to c'. Our exploration method is combined with the KG module extraction process, as all extended TBox paths of length k that have ABox path instances can be constructed from $\mathcal{T}_l$ with $l = \lfloor \frac{k+1}{2} \rfloor$.

ABox Paths Generating candidate rules directly from extended TBox paths may have the following issues. First, many extended TBox paths may have few or no instances in the ABox, which means the support of such rules will be low. Second, for KGs with low TBox coverage, their extended TBox paths may fail to capture many plausible path patterns. We address these two issues by exploring ABox paths.

To address the first issue, we use ABox paths to filter the extended TBox paths. This can be done on KG modules, by evaluating whether the extended TBox paths have significant numbers of ABox path instances. This can efficiently eliminate irrelevant path patterns before the plausibility assessment via the SC and HC metrics. For the second issue, we use lift ABox paths to complement the path patterns extracted from the TBox. Unlike the bottom-up approach in (Meilicke et al. 2019), where individual ABox paths are lifted by substituting entities with variables, we use vector computations to efficiently evaluate large numbers of ABox paths together.

Our goal is to explore path patterns, from extended TBox paths or lifted ABox paths, that have significant ABox path instances. The ABox instances of a path pattern can be retrieved using a SPARQL query, which is rather inefficient as one query is needed for each path pattern. We use a lightweight check for rapid evaluation as below. For each $p \in \mathcal{P}^*$, let $dom(p) = \{e \in \mathcal{E} \mid p(e, e') \in \mathcal{A}\}$ and $ran(p) = \{e \in \mathcal{E} \mid p(e', e) \in \mathcal{A}\}$. Intuitively, for a path pattern that forms the body of rule (1), there should be a significant number of ABox path instances of the form $(e_0, p_1, e_1, p_2, \dots, p_n, e_n)$ such that $p(e_0, e_n) \in \mathcal{A}$; that is, a significant number of entities exist in the following sets

- $dom(p) \cap dom(p_1)$ (i.e., as e_0),
- $ran(p) \cap ran(p_n)$ (i.e., as e_n), and
- $ran(p_i) \cap dom(p_{i+1})$ (i.e., as e_i for $1 \leq i < n$).

This is similar to the co-occurrence measure proposed in (Omran, Wang, and Wang 2018), where embeddings of $dom(p)$ and $ran(p)$ are defined as the averages of the embeddings of the entities occurring in the corresponding positions. Yet the meaning of such averages is less clear. Unlike (Omran, Wang, and Wang 2018), we use one-hot encodings for $dom(p)$ and $ran(p)$. Suppose all the entities in $\mathcal{E}$ are indexed from 1 to $|\mathcal{E}|$. Let $\mathbf{p}^{\text{dom}}$ (resp., $\mathbf{p}^{\text{ran}}$) be a vector of length $|\mathcal{E}|$, such that the scalar at position i is $\frac{1}{|dom(p)|}$ (resp., $\frac{1}{|ran(p)|}$) if $e_i \in dom(p)$ (resp., $e_i \in ran(p)$), and 0 otherwise, for $1 \leq i \leq |\mathcal{E}|$.

The *path scoring function* is defined as follows.

$$f_{path}(r) = sim(\mathbf{p}_1^{\text{dom}}, \mathbf{p}^{\text{dom}}) + sim(\mathbf{p}_n^{\text{ran}}, \mathbf{p}^{\text{ran}}) + sim(\mathbf{p}_1^{\text{ran}}, \mathbf{p}_2^{\text{dom}}) + \dots + sim(\mathbf{p}_{n-1}^{\text{ran}}, \mathbf{p}_n^{\text{dom}}),$$

where $sim(\cdot,\cdot)$ is defined by the Frobenius norm, i.e. $sim(\mathbf{v}_1, \mathbf{v}_2) = \exp(-\|\mathbf{v}_1 - \mathbf{v}_2\|)_F$.

Our one-hot encoding is a computational method to obtain statistics on entity distributions over predicates, which is simple and effective in calculating ABox support. Hence, we use the path scoring function to filter extended TBox paths and to generate other path patterns from the ABox. While the path scoring function does not include classes, classes of entities on the ABox paths can be added and validated through the SC and HC metrics.

4.3 Embedding-based Strategy

Our path exploration method can effectively generate potentials rules that are well supported by ABox facts, yet some useful rules can be overlooked in such a search, especially when the TBox coverage is not high, i.e., when many ABox paths cannot be captured by extended TBox paths. In this subsection, we present our embedding-based method that further complements the path-based methods.

Embedding models capture the graph structure of KGs through latent representations, which provide better granularity in modelling and can be efficiently manipulated. We embed each entity $e \in \mathcal{E}$ and each property or its inverse $p \in \mathcal{P}^*$ as d_A-dimensional vectors respectively $\mathbf{e}, \mathbf{p} \in \mathbb{R}^{d_A}$, where d_A is an integer, as in TransE (Bordes et al. 2013). In TransE, the embeddings are generated such that for each triple (e_1, p, e_2) in the ABox, their embeddings satisfy $\mathbf{e}_1 + \mathbf{p} \approx \mathbf{e}_2$. Intuitively, the embedding $\mathbf{p}$ of a property p is a translation from $\mathbf{e}_1$ to $\mathbf{e}_2$ for each pair of entities e_1, e_2 such that $p(e_1, e_2) \in \mathcal{A}$. For ABox paths of the form $(e_0, p_1, e_1, p_2, \dots, p_n, e_n)$, it should satisfy $\mathbf{e}_0 + \mathbf{p}_1 + \mathbf{p}_2 + \dots + \mathbf{p}_n \approx \mathbf{e}_n$; that is $\mathbf{p}_1 + \mathbf{p}_2 + \dots + \mathbf{p}_n$ is a translation from $\mathbf{e}_0$ to $\mathbf{e}_n$ for each pair of entities e_0, e_n connected via an ABox paths as above.

Hence, for a CP rule of the form $p_1(x_0, x_1) \wedge p_2(x_1, x_2) \wedge \dots \wedge p_n(x_{n-1}, x_n) \to p(x_0, x_n)$, it is expected that $\mathbf{p_1} + \mathbf{p}_2 + \dots + \mathbf{p}_n \approx \mathbf{p}$. We can use such an intuition to search for potential rules as in (Omran, Wang, and Wang 2018). Unlike the matrix embeddings adopted in (Omran, Wang, and Wang 2018), TransE embeddings can significantly improve learning efficiency. Yet, this approach do not take classes into consideration. In what follows, we will extend it with class embeddings that can describe class membership and class hierarchy.

We embed each class $c \in \mathcal{C}$ as a d_T-dimensional vector $\mathbf{c} \in \mathbb{R}^{d_T}$, where d_T is an integer that can be different from d_A; that is, class embeddings can be in a different latent space from that of the entity embeddings. The class embeddings should capture the following three kinds of knowledge: (i) membership of entities $c(e) \in \mathcal{A}$; (ii) class hierarchy $c_1 \sqsubseteq c_2 \in \mathcal{T}$; and (iii) domain and range constraints of the form $(c_1, p, c_2) \in \mathcal{T}$.

Our embedding approach for (i) and (ii) are inspired by (Hao et al. 2019), and we map embeddings of entities (resp., subclasses) to those of their classes (resp., superclasses) through transformations. In particular, let $f_M(\mathbf{e}) = \sigma(\mathbf{W}_M \cdot \mathbf{e} + \mathbf{b}_M)$ be a non-linear affine transformation that maps an entity embedding $\mathbf{e}$ to that of its class, where $\mathbf{W}_M \in \mathbb{R}^{d_T \times d_A}$ is a weight matrix, $\mathbf{b}_M \in \mathbb{R}^{d_T}$ is a bias vector, and $\sigma(\cdot)$ is a non-linear activation function such as tanh. Similarly, $f_H(\mathbf{c}) = \sigma(\mathbf{W}_H \cdot \mathbf{c} + \mathbf{b}_H)$ is another non-linear transformation that maps a class embedding $\mathbf{c}$ to that of its superclass, with $\mathbf{W}_H \in \mathbb{R}^{d_T \times d_T}$ and $\mathbf{b}_H \in \mathbb{R}^{d_T}$. Then, our class embeddings should satisfy

- for each $c(e) \in \mathcal{A}$, $f_M(\mathbf{e}) \approx \mathbf{c}$; and
- for each $c_1 \sqsubseteq c_2 \in \mathcal{T}$, $f_H(\mathbf{c}_1) \approx \mathbf{c}_2$.

For (iii), the embedding method in (Hao et al. 2019) treats $(c_1, p, c_2) \in \mathcal{T}$ in the same way as a triple $(e_1, p, e_2) \in \mathcal{A}$, which is not intuitive for domain and range constraints. Also, the approach in (Hao et al. 2019) assumes the properties in the TBox do not overlap with those in the ABox, which would result in the TBox coverage of the KG being 0. Indeed, what (c_1, p, c_2) conveys is the membership of entities in $dom(p)$ and $ran(p)$. Hence, our class embeddings should satisfy for each $(c_1, p, c_2) \in \mathcal{T}$:

- for each $e \in dom(p)$, $f_M(\mathbf{e}) \approx \mathbf{c_1}$; and
- for each $e \in ran(p)$, $f_M(\mathbf{e}) \approx \mathbf{c_2}$.

With the class embeddings trained together with the entity and property embeddings, the property embeddings would satisfy the domain and range constraints, and each entity occurring on an ABox path is always confined by its class membership. The *embedding scoring function* is defined as follows.

$$f_{embd}(r) = sim(\mathbf{p}_1 + \dots + \mathbf{p}_n, \mathbf{p}),$$

where $sim(\cdot,\cdot)$ is the L2 norm of vector distance as in TransE, i.e. $sim(\mathbf{v}_1, \mathbf{v}_2) = -\|\mathbf{v}_1 - \mathbf{v}_2\|_2$.

We use the embedding scoring function to generate path patterns to complement those generated from the path-based strategy. Again, although the embedding scoring function does not include classes, type information is utilized through embeddings to search for path patterns and classes can be added to the candidate rules and validated through the SC and HC metrics.

5 Experiments

We have implemented a prototype system TyRuLe (Typed Rule Learning) and conducted experiments on rule learning and link prediction over both standard benchmarks and a real-life dataset. Our experiments are designed to validate the following claims:

1. TyRuLe can learn quality and informative typed rules, and the benefit of such typed rules over CP rules is also shown in enhancing the accuracy of link prediction.
2. TyRuLe outperforms major rule learners and several embedding models on link prediction.
3. Both our path-based and embedding-based components contribute to the typed rule learning.

For Claim 1, we first show the intuitiveness of typed rules TyRuLe learns on a real-life dataset in the aviation domain, which is extracted from Web sources and contains very specific domain knowledge. We also compare the rules learned by TyRuLe with and without type information, and demonstrate the benefit of typed rules in enhancing the accuracy of link prediction. For Claim 2, we compare TyRuLe with existing rule learners and embedding models on link prediction over two commonly used benchmarks FB15K-237 and WN18RR, and show the advantages of TyRuLe. Finally, for Claim 3, we conduct an ablation study to analyse the respective benefits of our path-based and embedding-based measures.

All the experiments are conducted on a PC with Intel Xeon Gold 5215 CPU at 2.50GHz and with 16G of RAM, running on Ubuntu 18.04.3. Our system and benchmarks can be found at https://github.com/Rainbow0625/TyRuLe.

5.1 Datasets

Our experiments use three commonly used benchmarks and one real-life KG. Statistics of the four datasets are shown in Table 1.

KG	#Entity	#Relation	#Class	#Triple
FB15K237	14541	237	79	310116
WN18RR	40943	11	-	89969
YAGO26K906	26078	34	106	390738
AirGraph	64782	40	24	360650

Table 1: Statistics of datasets.

FB15K237 (Toutanova and Chen 2015) and WN18RR (Dettmers et al. 2018) are widely used benchmarking datasets obtained from respectively Freebase and WordNet. They are considered challenging benchmarks for link prediction, and were developed to address the test leakage issues in FB15K and WN18 (Toutanova and Chen 2015). We included explicit type information in FB15K237, which is extracted from FB15K following (Xie et al. 2016). Note that the type information is extracted from the original FB15K dataset and should not be considered as external knowledge. As most of the classes contain a very small number of entities, we only kept the classes that contain at least 1000 entities and those asserted as domains and ranges of relations, which leads to a total number of 79 classes. The version of WN18RR is the same as in (Dettmers et al. 2018) and we did not add explicit type information.

Another dataset is YAGO26K906 from (Hao et al. 2019), which is obtained from YAGO with explicit type information. The TBox and ABox in YAGO26K906 have disjoint sets of properties, which means ontological pathfinding approaches cannot be applied, and we adopted it mainly for comparison with embedding model JOIE (Hao et al. 2019) for which the dataset was initially used.

Finally, since existing benchmarks are obtained from established general-purpose KGs, we add a dataset we developed about a specific domain called AirGraph. AirGraph is a KG about airlines, airports, and aircraft, obtained by extracting and integrating data from four major sources: Federal Aviation Administration (FAA)[1], ourairports.com[2], openflights.org[3], and DBpedia. The AirGraph is unavoidably more noisy and incomplete compared to the established KGs, which poses challenges to rule learners and link prediction systems. On the other hand, it has very focused domain knowledge so it is easier to compare rules learned from different systems.

5.2 Rule Learning

In the first set of experiments, we evaluate the performance of TyRuLe in rule learning. We evaluate the benefits of learning typed rules from both quantitative and qualitative aspects. In particular, we compare the number of rules learned by TyRuLe with the rule learners AMIE+ (Galárraga et al. 2015) and AnyBURL (Meilicke et al. 2019) on AirGraph. RARL (Pirrò 2020) was not compared since we could not access the system at the time of the experiment. The maximum rule body length is 3 and the minimum SC is 0.001 for all the rule learners. A time limit of 3 hours per head property is set for each rule learner, as AnyBURL is an anytime rule learner and did not stop in 3 hours.

As AnyBURL learns partial-grounded rules, i.e., CP rules with some variables substituted by entities, several such rules can be obtained from a single CP rule. For a fair comparison on rule numbers, we also record the CP rules learned by AnyBURL. On AirGraph, TyRuLe learned 941 typed rules, including 815 CP rules. In the given time, AnyBURL could learn 173396 rules (mostly partial-grounded) including 357 CP rules, and AMIE+ could learn 76 rules.

In Table 2, we list the top 3 rules learned by each system on the head property capableOfLanding with their standard

[1] https://www.faa.gov/data_research/

[2] https://ourairports.com/

[3] https://openflights.org/data.html

AMIE+	r_1:0.114	capableOfLanding(x, z_1) ∧ hasPhysicalClass(z_1, z_2) ∧ hasGearConfig(z_2, y) → capableOfLanding(x, y),
AnyBURL	r_2:0.044	capableOfLanding(x, z_1) ∧ isAircraftOf(z_1, z_2) ∧ isAircraftOf(y, z_2) → capableOfLanding(x, y),
	r_3:0.042	hasSurface(x, z_1) ∧ hasSurface(z_2, z_1) ∧ capableOfLanding(z_2, y) → capableOfLanding(x, y),
	r_4:0.038	capableOfLanding(x, z_1) ∧ hasWakeCategory(z_1, z_2) ∧ hasGearConfig(y, z_2) → capableOfLanding(x, y),
TyRuLe	r_5:0.851	Runway(x) ∧ capableOfLanding(x, z_1) ∧ Aircraft(z_1) ∧ isAircraftEventOf(z_2, z_1) ∧ Event(z_2) ∧isAircraftEventOf(z_2, y) ∧ Aircraft(y) → capableOfLanding(x, y),
	r_6:0.507	capableOfLanding(x, z_1) ∧ hasGearConfig(z_1, z_2) ∧ hasWingtip(y, z_2) → capableOfLanding(x, y),
	r_7:0.098	Runway(x) ∧ isRunwayOf(x, z_1) ∧ Airport(z_1) ∧ hasBase(z_2, z_1) ∧ Airline(z_2) ∧isAircraftOf(y, z_2) ∧ Aircraft(y) → capableOfLanding(x, y)

Table 2: Rules learned by different systems.

confidence degrees. This property is interesting as it associates data from various original sources, such as aircraft information from FAA, airline data from openflights.org, and airport and runway information from ourairports.com. For this property, AMIE+ could only learn one rule with an SC of 0.114, AnyBURL learned 17 CP rules with the maximum SC of 0.044, and TyRuLe learned 25 typed rules with some SC as high as 0.851. For the convenience of reading, inverse properties are flipped around.

Both rules r_5 and r_7 are typed rules, and we observe that specifying types of variables can (while not always) lead to higher SC. Intuitively, with variable types, it can constrain the grounding of the rules to those potentially well supported by the ABox (i.e., with significant numbers of instances). The typed rules are intuitive, for example, rule r_7 says if an aircraft y belongs to an airline z_2 that has a base airport z_1 with a runway x, then y can land on the runway x. Rule r_5 says if an aircraft is involved in an event on a specific runway then the aircraft can land on the runway. Rules r_2 and r_3 explore some commonalities between aircrafts (i.e., same airline) and between runways (i.e., same surface). Finally, rules r_1, r_4 and r_6 discover some physical features of the aircraft and runway that are related to landing capability.

5.3 Link Prediction

A major quantitative indicator on the quality of learned rules is their performance in link prediction. Hence, in the second set of experiments, we evaluate the performance of TyRuLe in link prediction on various datasets. The way to apply the learned rules for link prediction is described in Section 3.3.

First, we evaluated TyRuLe on FB15K-237 and WN18RR, in comparison with rule learners AMIE+ (Galárraga et al. 2015), NeuralLP (Yang, Yang, and Cohen 2017), RLvLR (Omran, Wang, and Wang 2018), AnyBURL (Meilicke et al. 2019) and RARL (Pirrò 2020), as well as with major embedding-based models RESCAL (Nickel, Tresp, and Kriegel 2011), TransE (Bordes et al. 2013), DistMult (Yang et al. 2014), ComplEx (Trouillon et al. 2016), ConvE (Dettmers et al. 2018), RotatE (Sun et al. 2019) and HAKE (Zhang et al. 2020). We adopt the standard metrics for link prediction, namely Mean Reciprocal Rank (MRR) and the proportion of top n hits (Hits@1 and Hits@10), to represent the accuracy of prediction. And we follow the literature to filter the predictions before ranking (Bordes et al. 2013).

Table 3 shows the results. Besides the results of HAKE is from (Zhang et al. 2020), all the other embedding-based models for FB15K237 and WN18RR are obtained from (Broscheit et al. 2020). The results of AMIE+, AnyBURL and RARL are from (Pirrò 2020). And NeuralLP and RLvLR are from (Omran, Wang, and Wang 2018). The best results are highlighted in bold, and the second best ones are underlined.

From Table 3, we can see that TyRuLe outperforms all the rule learners in link prediction, especially on Hits@1, where an improvement of up to 6.8% is achieved. This shows the quality of the rules learned by TyRuLe and the benefit of type information in link prediction. The performance of TyRuLe is even comparable to the embedding methods, and outperforms all the models on two metrics for FB15K237. For WN18RR, as type information is implicit, HAKE, which employs a more complex embedding for implicit hierarchical structures, shows better performance. And our performance is still close to HAKE.

Following the comparison in Section 5.2 on AirGraph, we compared the quality of learned rule through link prediction. Table 4 shows the results. The rules learned by TyRuLe again show better accuracy for link prediction, which confirms the quality of the learned rules.

Finally, as our embedding method is inspired from JOIE (Hao et al. 2019), we compare with JOIE on YAGO26K-906. The results are shown in Table 5, where JOIE-X is the version of JOIE that uses a base embedding method X with a configuration closest to ours (regarding the embedding of class membership and hierarchies), and the results on JOIE are from (Hao et al. 2019).

From Table 5, we can see that with the combination of path-based and embedding-based strategies, our approach can effectively utilize the type information and outperforms JOIE, sometimes by a significant margin.

5.4 Ablation Study

In this set of experiments, we analyse the contributing factors of TyRuLe's outstanding performance. First, we evaluate the usefulness of type information in rule learning. More specifically, we compare the quantities and quality of the learned rules with and without types. In particular, we separate the rules learned by TyRuLe into two groups, the CP rules (with no types) and the other rules (with types, called T-rules). We also group the rules by their body lengths $n = 1, 2, 3$. Table 6 shows the numbers of learned rules per head property (#Rule) and the overall link prediction results (LP) of different groups of rules learned by TyRuLe on FB15K237.

	Model	FB15K237			WN18RR		
		MRR	Hits@1	Hits@10	MRR	Hits@1	Hits@10
Link Predictor	RESCAL	35.6	26.3	54.1	46.7	43.9	51.7
	TransE	31.3	22.1	49.7	22.8	5.3	52.0
	DistMult	34.3	25.0	53.1	45.2	41.3	53.0
	ComplEx	34.8	25.3	53.6	47.5	43.8	54.7
	ConvE	33.9	24.8	52.1	44.2	41.1	50.4
	RotatE	33.3	24.0	52.2	47.8	43.9	55.3
	HAKE	34.6	25.0	**54.2**	**49.7**	**45.2**	**58.1**
Rule Learner	AMIE+		17.4	40.9		35.8	38.8
	NeuralLP	24		36.1			
	RLvLR	24		39.3			
	AnyBURL	31	23.3	48.6	47	44.1	55.2
	RARL	32	25.1	49.1	36.13	35.1	40.9
	TyRuLe	**39.5**	**33.5**	52.0	48.3	44.8	54.1

Table 3: Link prediction on FB15K237 and WN18RR: TyRuLe outperforms all rule learner and competitive to other models for link prediction.

Model	MRR	Hits@1	Hits@3	Hits@10
AMIE+	12.3	11.9	12.7	12.9
AnyBURL	31.3	26.2	34.3	43.1
TyRuLe	**35.3**	**30.6**	**37.5**	**45.1**

Table 4: Link prediction on AirGraph.

Model	MRR	Hits@1	Hits@10
JOIE-TransE	30.6	18.6	51.7
JOIE-DistMult	29.6	19.4	45.5
JOIE-HolE	32.7	22.4	**52.4**
TyRuLe	**42.8**	**37.7**	**52.4**

Table 5: Link prediction on YAGO26K-906.

#Rule	$n = 1$	$n = 2$	$n = 3$	Total
CP rules	2.9	29.0	127.3	159.2
T-rules	1.7	23.5	116.5	141.7
Together	4.6	52.5	243.8	300.9
LP	MRR	Hits@1	Hits@3	Hits@10
CP rules	33.7	26.7	35.5	47.9
T-rules	38.7	32.8	40.1	50.8
Together	39.5	33.5	40.9	52.0

Table 6: Link prediction with and without types.

	Path		Emb.		Overlap	
Property	CP	TR	CP	TR	CP	TR
modeTransportation	201	101	168	73	143	65
disciplineOrSubject	21	6	18	2	16	2
parentGenre	45	36	80	43	27	21
eventLocation	122	113	141	130	115	109
directorFilm	157	153	237	208	144	130

Table 7: Path-based vs embedding-based strategies.

We can see that while the numbers of T-rules are smaller than those of CP rules, which may be due to the limited type information, the T-rules achieve higher accuracy in link prediction. And the link prediction accuracy is further enhanced when the two groups rules are combined. This shows the benefits of type information in both enriching and enhancing the quality of learned rules.

Then, we analyse the contributions of our path-based and embedding-based strategies in rule learning. We separate the rules respectively learned through the two strategies on FB15K237. Table 7 shows the numbers of rules learned for some head properties by the two different strategies, where we separately record the numbers of CP rules (CP) and T-rules (TR).

6 Conclusion

In this paper, we have developed a novel approach to learn typed rules over KGs, by exploiting the rich type information in KGs. Instead of using such type information as hard constraints for rule search, we adopted a combined approach using both path-based and embedding-based strategies for the search of candidate rules. Type information from the KG is used both in the path exploration and embedding generation, and the selected paths and generated embeddings in turn are used to generate typed rules. We have evaluated our prototype system in both rule learning and link prediction tasks, through quantitative and qualitative analysis. TyRuLe showed superior performance over existing rule learners in link prediction, and is competitive compared to embedding models, which shows the quality of our learned rules.

In our typed rules, type atoms can only appear in the body part of the rule. Next, we plan to extend our approach to learn more expressive rules with type in the rule heads. Furthermore, we will also explore the application of learned rules in reasoning tasks over KGs, such as question answering, to provide explainability of predictions.

Acknowledgments

The authors would like to thank three anonymous referees for their helpful comments. This work was partially supported by National Natural Science Foundation of China (NSFC) (61976153).

References

Ahmadi, N.; Huynh, V.-P.; Meduri, V.; Ortona, S.; and Papotti, P. 2020. Mining expressive rules in knowledge graphs. *Journal of Data and Information Quality* 12(2):1–27.

Bollacker, K.; Evans, C.; Paritosh, P.; Sturge, T.; and Taylor, J. 2008. Freebase: a collaboratively created graph database for structuring human knowledge. In *Proc. of SIGMOD-08*, 1247–1250.

Bordes, A.; Usunier, N.; Garcia-Duran, A.; Weston, J.; and Yakhnenko, O. 2013. Translating embeddings for modeling multi-relational data. *Proc. of NIPS-13* 26:2787–2795.

Broscheit, S.; Ruffinelli, D.; Kochsiek, A.; Betz, P.; and Gemulla, R. 2020. LibKGE - A knowledge graph embedding library for reproducible research. In *Proc. of EMNLP-20 (Demos)*, 165–174.

Chen, Y.; Goldberg, S.; Wang, D. Z.; and Johri, S. S. 2016a. Ontological pathfinding. In *Proc. of COMAD-16*, 835–846.

Chen, Y.; Wang, D. Z.; and Goldberg, S. 2016b. Scalekb: scalable learning and inference over large knowledge bases. *The VLDB Journal* 25(6):893–918.

Cropper, A.; Dumančić, S.; Evans, R.; and Muggleton, S. H. 2022. Inductive logic programming at 30. *Mach. Learn.* 111(1):147–172.

Dettmers, T.; Minervini, P.; Stenetorp, P.; and Riedel, S. 2018. Convolutional 2d knowledge graph embeddings. In *Proc. of AAAI-18*, 1811–1818.

Gad-Elrab, M. H.; Stepanova, D.; Urbani, J.; and Weikum, G. 2016. Exception-enriched rule learning from knowledge graphs. In *Proc. of ISWC-16*, 234–251.

Galárraga, L.; Teflioudi, C.; Hose, K.; and Suchanek, F. M. 2015. Fast rule mining in ontological knowledge bases with amie+. *The VLDB Journal* 24(6):707–730.

Hao, J.; Chen, M.; Yu, W.; Sun, Y.; and Wang, W. 2019. Universal representation learning of knowledge bases by jointly embedding instances and ontological concepts. In *Proc. of KDD-19*, 1709–1719.

Ji, S.; Pan, S.; Cambria, E.; Marttinen, P.; and Yu, P. S. 2020. A survey on knowledge graphs: Representation, acquisition and applications. *CoRR* abs/2002.00388.

Lisi, F. A., and Weikum, G. 2017. Towards nonmonotonic relational learning from knowledge graphs. In *Proc. of ILP-17*, 94.

Meilicke, C.; Chekol, M. W.; Ruffinelli, D.; and Stuckenschmidt, H. 2019. Anytime bottom-up rule learning for knowledge graph completion. In *Proc. of IJCAI-19*, 3137–3143.

Miller, G. A. 1995. Wordnet: a lexical database for english. *Communications of the ACM* 38(11):39–41.

Muggleton, S. 1990. Inductive logic programming. In Arikawa, S.; Goto, S.; Ohsuga, S.; and Yokomori, T., eds., *Proc.of ALT-90*, 42–62.

Muggleton, S. 1991. Inductive logic programming. *New Gener. Comput.* 8(4):295–318.

Nguyen, T. D.; Nguyen, D. Q.; Phung, D. Q.; et al. 2018. A novel embedding model for knowledge base completion based on convolutional neural network. In *Proc. of NAACL-HLT-18*, 327–333.

Nickel, M.; Tresp, V.; and Kriegel, H.-P. 2011. A three-way model for collective learning on multi-relational data. In *Proc. of ICML-28*, 809–816.

Omran, P. G.; Wang, K.; and Wang, Z. 2018. Scalable rule learning via learning representation. In *Proc. of IJCAI-18*, 2149–2155.

Pellissier Tanon, T.; Stepanova, D.; Razniewski, S.; Mirza, P.; and Weikum, G. 2017. Completeness-aware rule learning from knowledge graphs. In *Proc. of ISWC-17*, 507–525.

Pirrò, G. 2020. Relatedness and tbox-driven rule learning in large knowledge bases. In *Proc. of AAAI-20*, 2975–2982.

Sadeghian, A.; Armandpour, M.; Ding, P.; and Wang, D. Z. 2019. Drum: End-to-end differentiable rule mining on knowledge graphs. *Proc. of NIPS-19* 32:15321–15331.

Suchanek, F. M.; Kasneci, G.; and Weikum, G. 2007. Yago: a core of semantic knowledge. In *Proc. of WWW-07*, 697–706.

Sun, Z.; Deng, Z.; Nie, J.; and Tang, J. 2019. Rotate: Knowledge graph embedding by relational rotation in complex space. In *Proc. of ICLR-19(Poster)*.

Toutanova, K., and Chen, D. 2015. Observed versus latent features for knowledge base and text inference. In *Proc. of CVSC-15*, 57–66.

Trouillon, T.; Welbl, J.; Riedel, S.; Gaussier, É.; and Bouchard, G. 2016. Complex embeddings for simple link prediction. In *Proc. of ICML-16*, 2071–2080.

Xie, R.; Liu, Z.; Sun, M.; et al. 2016. Representation learning of knowledge graphs with hierarchical types. In *Proc. of IJCAI-16*, 2965–2971.

Yang, B.; Yih, W.-t.; He, X.; Gao, J.; and Deng, L. 2014. Embedding entities and relations for learning and inference in knowledge bases. In *Proc. of ICLR-14*.

Yang, F.; Yang, Z.; and Cohen, W. W. 2017. Differentiable learning of logical rules for knowledge base reasoning. *Proc. of NIPS-2017* 30:2319–2328.

Zeng, Q.; Patel, J. M.; and Page, D. 2014. Quickfoil: Scalable inductive logic programming. *Proc. of the VLDB Endowment-14* 8(3):197–208.

Zhang, Z.; Cai, J.; Zhang, Y.; and Wang, J. 2020. Learning hierarchy-aware knowledge graph embeddings for link prediction. In *Proc. of AAAI-20*, 3065–3072.

Proceedings of the 19th International Conference on Principles of Knowledge Representation and Reasoning
Special Session on KR and Machine Learning

Explaining Causal Models with Argumentation: the Case of Bi-variate Reinforcement

Antonio Rago[1] , **Pietro Baroni**[2] and **Francesca Toni**[1]
[1]Department of Computing, Imperial College London, UK
[2]Dipartimento di Ingegneria dell'Informazione, Università degli Studi di Brescia, Italy
{a.rago, ft}@imperial.ac.uk, pietro.baroni@unibs.it

Abstract

Causal models are playing an increasingly important role in machine learning, particularly in the realm of explainable AI. We introduce a conceptualisation for generating argumentation frameworks (AFs) from causal models for the purpose of forging explanations for the models' outputs. The conceptualisation is based on reinterpreting desirable properties of semantics of AFs as *explanation moulds*, which are means for characterising the relations in the causal model argumentatively. We demonstrate our methodology by reinterpreting the property of *bi-variate reinforcement* as an explanation mould to forge *bipolar AFs* as explanations for the outputs of causal models. We perform a theoretical evaluation of these argumentative explanations, examining whether they satisfy a range of desirable explanatory and argumentative properties.

1 Introduction

The field of explainable AI (XAI) has in recent years become a major focal point of the efforts of researchers, with a wide variety of models for explanation being proposed (see e.g. (Guidotti et al. 2019) for an overview). More recently, incorporating a causal perspective into explanations has been explored by some, e.g. (Schwab and Karlen 2019; Madumal et al. 2020). The link between causes and explanations has long been studied (Halpern and Pearl 2001); indeed, the two have even been equated (under a broad sense of the concept of "cause") (Woodward 1997). Causal reasoning is, in fact, how humans explain to one another (de Graaf and Malle 2017), and so mimicking such a trend lends credence to the hypothesis that machines should do likewise when their explanations target humans. Further, research from the social sciences (Miller 2019) has indicated the value of causal links, particularly in the form of counterfactual reasoning, within explanations, and that the importance of such information surpasses that of probabilities or statistical relationships for users. In this paper we outline a methodology for obtaining explanations from *causal models* (Pearl 1999), based on *(computational) argumentation* (see (Atkinson et al. 2017; Baroni et al. 2018) for recent overviews).

Argumentation has received increasing attention in recent years as a means for providing explanations of the outputs of a number of AI models (see (Vassiliades, Bassiliades, and Patkos 2021; Cyras et al. 2021) for recent overviews on argumentative XAI), e.g. for recommender systems (Teze, Godo, and Simari 2018), neural classifiers (Dejl et al. 2021), Bayesian networks (Timmer et al. 2015) and PageRank (Albini et al. 2020a). *Argumentative explanations* have also been advocated in the social sciences (Antaki and Leudar 1992; Miller 2019), and several works focus on the power of argumentation to provide a bridge between explained models and users, validated by user studies (Madumal et al. 2019; Rago et al. 2020). While argumentative explanations are wide-ranging in their application, their links with causal models have remained largely unexplored to date.

In this paper, we introduce a conceptualisation for generating *argumentation frameworks* (AFs) from causal models for the purpose of forging explanations for the models' outputs. Like (Albini et al. 2020b; Albini et al. 2021), we focus on explaining by *relations* – rather than by features, as is more conventional (e.g. for feature attribution methods such as (Lundberg and Lee 2017)). Our method is based on a reinterpretation of properties of argumentation semantics from the literature as *explanation moulds*, i.e. means for characterising argumentative relations (§3). Here, we focus on reinterpreting the property of *bi-variate reinforcement* (Amgoud and Ben-Naim 2018) as a basis for extracting bipolar AFs (Cayrol and Lagasquie-Schiex 2005) which may be used as explanations for the outputs of causal models. We provide a theoretical assessment of these explanations (§4), demonstrating how they satisfy desirable properties from both explanatory and argumentative viewpoints.

2 Background

Here, we provide the core background on causal models and computational argumentation, on which our method relies.

Causal models. A *causal model* (Pearl 1999) is a triple $\langle U, V, E\rangle$, where: U is a (finite) set of *exogenous variables*, i.e. variables whose values are determined by external factors (outside the causal model); V is a (finite) set of *endogenous variables*, i.e. variables whose values are determined by internal factors, namely by (the values of some of the) variables in $U \cup V$; each variable may take any value in its associated *domain*; we refer to the domain of $W_i \in U \cup V$ as $\mathcal{D}(W_i)$; E is a (finite) set of *structural equations* that, for each endogenous variable $V_i \in V$, define V_i's values as a function f_{V_i} of the values of V_i's *parents* $PA(V_i) \subseteq U \cup V \setminus \{V_i\}$. We use the term *binary* *causal model* to refer to any causal model $\langle U, V, E\rangle$ such that $\forall W_i \in U \cup V$, $\mathcal{D}(W_i) = \{0, 1\}$ (where 0 stands for "false" and 1 stands for "true", where suitable), and the term *gradual causal model* to refer to any causal model $\langle U, V, E\rangle$ such that $\forall W_i \in U \cup V$, $\mathcal{D}(W_i)$ is equipped with a partial order (we refer to this partial order as $\leq$; as usual, $a < b$ stands for $a \leq b$ and $b \not\leq a$). Note that a binary causal model is a gradual causal model (with $0 < 1$).

Given a causal model $\langle U, V, E\rangle$ where $U = \{U_1, \ldots, U_i\}$, we denote with $\mathcal{U} = \mathcal{D}(U_1) \times \ldots \times \mathcal{D}(U_i)$ the set of all possible combinations of values of the exogenous variables (called *inputs*). Abusing notation, we refer to the value of any $W_i \in U \cup V$ given $\mathbf{u} \in \mathcal{U}$ as $f_{W_i}[\mathbf{u}]$: if W_i is an exogenous variable, $f_{W_i}[\mathbf{u}]$ is its assigned value in $\mathbf{u}$; if W_i is an endogenous variable, it is the value dictated by the structural equations in the causal model. We use the *do* operator (Pearl 2012) to indicate *interventions*, i.e., for any variable $V_i \in V$ and value thereof $v_i \in \mathcal{D}(V_i)$, $do(V_i = v_i)$ implies that f_{V_i} is replaced by the constant function v_i. We use the notation $set(W_i = w_i)$, for $w_i \in \mathcal{D}(W_i)$, to indicate that $do(W_i = w_i)$ if $W_i \in V$ or that W_i is assigned w_i if $W_i \in U$.

Argumentation. An *argumentation framework* (AF) is any tuple $\langle \mathcal{A}, \mathcal{R}_1, \ldots, \mathcal{R}_l\rangle$ with $\mathcal{A}$ a set (of *arguments*), and $\mathcal{R}_i \subseteq \mathcal{A} \times \mathcal{A}$, for $i \in \{1, \ldots, l\}$, (binary and directed) *dialectical relations* between arguments (Gabbay 2016; Baroni et al. 2017). In the abstract argumentation (Dung 1995) tradition, arguments in these AFs are unspecified *abstract* entities that can correspond to different concrete instances in different settings. Several specific choices of dialectical relations can be made, giving rise to specific AFs, including *bipolar AFs* (BFs, our focus in this paper) (Cayrol and Lagasquie-Schiex 2005), with $l = 2$ and $\mathcal{R}_1$ and $\mathcal{R}_2$ dialectical relations of *attack* and *support*, respectively, referred to later as $\mathcal{R}_-$ and $\mathcal{R}_+$. Given a BF $\langle \mathcal{A}, \mathcal{R}_-, \mathcal{R}_+\rangle$, for $\alpha_1 \in \mathcal{A}$, we will use the notation $\mathcal{R}_-(\alpha_1) = \{\alpha_2 | (\alpha_2, \alpha_1) \in \mathcal{R}_-\}$ and $\mathcal{R}_+(\alpha_1) = \{\alpha_2 | (\alpha_2, \alpha_1) \in \mathcal{R}_+\}$. The meaning of BFs (including the intended dialectical role of the relations) may be given in terms of *gradual semantics* (e.g. see (Baroni et al. 2017; Baroni, Rago, and Toni 2018)), defined by means of mappings $\sigma : \mathcal{A} \rightarrow \mathbb{V}$, with $\mathbb{V}$ a given set of *values* of interest for evaluating arguments. The choice of gradual semantics for BFs may be guided by *properties* that σ should satisfy (e.g. as in (Baroni, Rago, and Toni 2018)). We will utilise, in §3, a variant of the property of *bi-variate reinforcement* for BFs from (Amgoud and Ben-Naim 2018). We will also use, in §4, the following notions of coherence from (Cayrol and Lagasquie-Schiex 2005). Let a *path* from $\alpha_x \in \mathcal{A}$ to $\alpha_y \in \mathcal{A}$ via a relation $\mathcal{R} \subseteq \mathcal{R}_- \cup \mathcal{R}_+$ be a sequence of arguments $\alpha_1, \ldots, \alpha_n$, $n \geq 1$, such that $\alpha_1 = \alpha_x$, $\alpha_n = \alpha_y$, and for each i, $1 \leq i < n$, $(\alpha_n, \alpha_{n+1}) \in \mathcal{R}$. Then, a set of arguments $S \subseteq \mathcal{A}$ is *internally coherent* iff $\forall \alpha_x, \alpha_y \in S$, $\nexists$ a path $\alpha_1, \ldots, \alpha_n$ from α_x to α_y via $\mathcal{R}_- \cup \mathcal{R}_+$ such that $(\alpha_{n-1}, \alpha_n) \in \mathcal{R}_-$ and for $1 \leq i < n-1$, $(\alpha_i, \alpha_{i+1}) \in \mathcal{R}_+$, nor such that $(\alpha_1, \alpha_2) \in \mathcal{R}_-$ and for $2 \leq i < n$, $(\alpha_i, \alpha_{i+1}) \in \mathcal{R}_+$. S is said to be *externally coherent* iff $\forall \alpha_x, \alpha_y \in S$, $\nexists \alpha_z \in \mathcal{A}$ such that $\exists$ a path from α_x to α_z via $\mathcal{R}_+$ and $\exists$ a path $\alpha_1, \ldots, \alpha_n$ from α_y to α_z via $\mathcal{R}_- \cup \mathcal{R}_+$ such that $(\alpha_{n-1}, \alpha_n) \in \mathcal{R}_-$ and for $1 \leq i < n-1$, $(\alpha_i, \alpha_{i+1}) \in \mathcal{R}_+$, or such that $(\alpha_1, \alpha_2) \in \mathcal{R}_-$ and for $2 \leq i < n$, $(\alpha_i, \alpha_{i+1}) \in \mathcal{R}_+$.

i.

U_1	U_2	V_1	V_2
1 margherita	1 pineapple	0 ~Italian	0 ~enter
1 margherita	0 ~pineapple	1 Italian	1 enter
0 margarita	1 pineapple	0 ~Italian	0 ~enter
0 margarita	0 ~pineapple	0 ~Italian	0 ~enter

ii. **iii.**

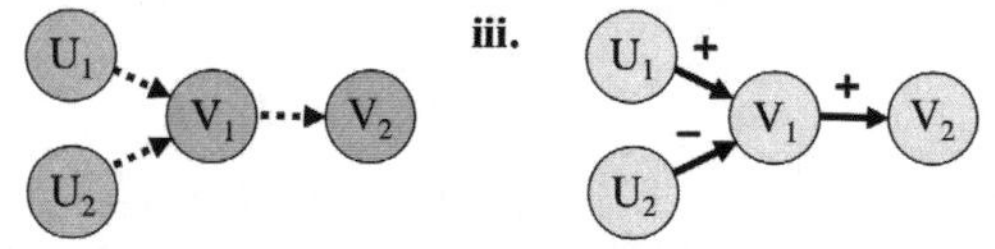

Figure 1: Toy example. (i) Combinations of values (1 or 0) resulting from the structural equations (the assignment of 1 to U_1 may be read as *"margherita" is spelt correctly on the menu* – simply given as 'margherita' in the table, the assignment of U_2 to 0 may be read as *there is no pineapple on the pizzas* – simply given as '~pineapple' in the table, etc.). (ii) Graphical representation of the influence graph, with (exogenous/endogenous) variables in the causal model indicated by (blue/red respectively) nodes and influences represented by dashed arrows. (iii) RX for $\mathbf{u} \in \mathcal{U}$ such that $f_{U_1}[\mathbf{u}] = 1$ and $f_{U_2}[\mathbf{u}] = 0$.

3 From Causal Models to Explanation Moulds and Argumentative Explanations

We see the task of obtaining *explanations* for causal models' assignments of values to variables as a two-step process: first we define *moulds* characterising the core ingredients of explanations; then we use these moulds to obtain, automatically, (instances of) AFs as argumentative explanations. Moulds and explanations are defined in terms of *influences* between variables in the causal model, in turn defined in terms of the parent relation underpinning the model.

Definition 1. *The* influence graph *corresponding to a causal model* $\langle U, V, E\rangle$ *is the pair* $\langle \mathcal{V}, \mathcal{I}\rangle$, *where* $\mathcal{V} = U \cup V$ *and* $\mathcal{I} \subseteq \mathcal{V} \times \mathcal{V}$ *such that* $\mathcal{I} = \{(W_1, W_2) | W_1 \in PA(W_2)\}$ *(referred to as the set of* influences*)*.

Note that influence graphs are closely related to the notion of *causal diagrams* (Pearl 1995). While straightforward, they are useful as they underpin much of what follows.

Throughout, for illustration we will use a toy example with a simple (binary) causal model $\langle U, V, E\rangle$ comprising $U = \{U_1, U_2\}$, $V = \{V_1, V_2\}$ and $\forall W_i \in U \cup V$, $\mathcal{D}(W_i) = \{0, 1\}$. Figure 1i gives the combinations of values for the variables resulting from the structural equations E (amounting to $V_1 = U_1 \wedge \neg U_2$ and $V_2 = V_1$) and Figure 1ii visualises the influence graph $\langle \{U_1, U_2, V_1, V_2\}, \{(U_1, V_1), (U_2, V_1), (V_1, V_2)\}\rangle$ (we ignore Figure 1iii for the moment: this will be discussed later). This causal model may represent a group's decision on whether to enter a restaurant, with variables U_1: *"margherita" is spelt correctly on the menu, not like the drink*; U_2: *there is pineapple on the pizzas*; V_1: *the pizzeria seems to be legitimately Italian*; and V_2: *the group chooses to enter the pizzeria.*

Influence graphs synthetically express which variables affect which others but do not give an account of how the influences actually occur in the context the user may be interested in, as expressed by the given values to the exogenous variables. For example, the influence graph in Figure 1ii alone shows which variables affect other variables but provides little intuition on *how* they do so. Thus, our standpoint is that each influence can be assigned an explanatory role, indicating how that influence is actually working in that context. We assume that each explanatory role is specified by a *relation characterisation*, i.e. a Boolean logical requirement, that is used as a *mould to forge explanations* to be presented to users by indicating which relations play a role therein.

Definition 2. *Given a causal model* $\langle U, V, E\rangle$ *with corresponding influence graph* $\langle \mathcal{V}, \mathcal{I}\rangle$, *an* explanation mould *is a non-empty set* $\{c_1,\dots,c_m\}$ *where,* $\forall i \in \{1,\dots,m\}$, $c_i : \mathcal{U}\times\mathcal{I} \rightarrow \{true, false\}$ *is a* relation characterisation, *in the form of a Boolean condition in some formal language.*

Here, we do not prescribe any formal language for specifying relation characterisations: several may be suitable. The use of this definition requires an up-front choice of the number of relations and their characterisations. This choice then applies to all inputs in need of explaining.

Given an input $\mathbf{u}$, based on an explanation mould we can obtain an AF including, as dialectical relations, the influences satisfying the (different) relation characterisations for the given $\mathbf{u}$. Thus, the choice of relation characterisations is to a large extent dictated by the specific form of *argumentative explanation* the intended users expect. In general, argumentative explanations can be generated as follows.

Definition 3. *Given a causal model* $\langle U, V, E\rangle$, *its corresponding influence graph* $\langle \mathcal{V}, \mathcal{I}\rangle$ *and an explanation mould* $\{c_1,\dots,c_m\}$, *an* argumentative explanation for $\langle U, V, E\rangle$ and $\mathbf{u} \in \mathcal{U}$ *is an AF* $\langle \mathcal{A}, \mathcal{R}_1,\dots\mathcal{R}_m\rangle$, *where* $\mathcal{A} \subseteq \mathcal{V}$, *and* $\mathcal{R}_1,\dots,\mathcal{R}_m \subseteq \mathcal{I}\cap(\mathcal{A}\times\mathcal{A})$ *such that, for any* $i = 1\dots m$, $\mathcal{R}_i = \{(W_1, W_2) \in \mathcal{I}\cap(\mathcal{A}\times\mathcal{A}) | c_i(\mathbf{u}, (W_1, W_2)) = true\}$.

Note that these argumentative explanations are *local*, namely they focus on the causal model's behaviour for (any) input $\mathbf{u}$. Thus, different argumentative explanations may be obtained for different inputs. Note also that we have left open the choice of $\mathcal{A}$ (as a generic, possibly non-strict subset of $\mathcal{V}$). In practice, $\mathcal{A}$ may be the full $\mathcal{V}$, but we envisage that users may prefer to restrict attention to some variables of interest (for example, excluding variables not "involved" in any influence satisfying the relation characterisations). For example, an argumentative explanation of a counterfactual nature for the causal model in Figure 1i and the input in the first row may choose to neglect U_1 since changing its value in this case does not affect the other variables' values.

The choice of (number and form of) relation characterisations in explanation moulds is crucial for the generation of argumentative explanations. Here we demonstrate a novel concept for utilising properties of gradual semantics for AFs for this choice, based on "property inversion". The idea is to interpret the variable values in the causal model as generated by a "hypothetical" gradual semantics embedded in the model itself. This is similar, in spirit, to recent work to extract (weighted) BFs from multi-layer perceptrons (MLPs) (Potyka 2021), using the underlying computation of the MLPs as a gradual semantics, and to proposals to explain recommender systems via tripolar AFs (Rago, Cocarascu, and Toni 2018) or BFs (Rago et al. 2020), using the underlying predicted ratings as a gradual semantics. A natural semantic choice for causal models, given that we are trying to explain why endogenous variables are assigned specific values, given assignments to the exogenous variables, is to use the assignments as a gradual semantics.

Then, the idea of inverting properties of semantics to obtain dialectical relations in AFs can be recast to obtain relation characterisations in explanation moulds as follows: *given an influence graph and a selected value assignment to exogenous variables, if an influence satisfies a given, desirable semantics property, then the influence can be cast as part of a dialectical relation with explanatory purposes in the resulting AF.* We will illustrate this concept with the property of *bi-variate reinforcement* for BFs (Amgoud and Ben-Naim 2018), which we posit is intuitive in the realm of explanations. In our formulation of this property, we require that increasing the value of variables which are attackers (supporters) can only decrease (increase, respectively) the values of variables they attack (support, respectively).

Definition 4. *Given a gradual causal model* $\langle U, V, E\rangle$ *and influence graph* $\langle \mathcal{V}, \mathcal{I}\rangle$, *a* reinforcement explanation mould *is an explanation mould* $\{c^r_-, c^r_+\}$ *such that, given some* $\mathbf{u} \in \mathcal{U}$ *and* $(W_1, W_2) \in \mathcal{I}$:

- $c^r_-(\mathbf{u}, (W_1, W_2)) = true$ *iff:*
  1. $\forall w_+ \in \mathcal{D}(W_1)$ *such that* $w_+ > f_{W_1}[\mathbf{u}]$, *it holds that* $f_{W_2}[\mathbf{u}, set(W_1 = w_+)] <_* f_{W_2}[\mathbf{u}]$ *with* $<_* = \leq$;
  2. $\forall w_- \in \mathcal{D}(W_1)$ *such that* $w_- < f_{W_1}[\mathbf{u}]$, *it holds that* $f_{W_2}[\mathbf{u}, set(W_1 = w_-)] >_* f_{W_2}[\mathbf{u}]$ *with* $>_* = \geq$;
  3. $\exists_{\geq 1} w_+ \in \mathcal{D}(W_1)$ *or* $\exists_{\geq 1} w_- \in \mathcal{D}(W_1)$ *satisfying the conditions at points 1 and 2 with* $<_* = <$ *and* $>_* = >$.
- $c^r_+(\mathbf{u}, (W_1, W_2)) = true$ *iff:*
  1. $\forall w_+ \in \mathcal{D}(W_1)$ *such that* $w_+ > f_{W_1}[\mathbf{u}]$, *it holds that* $f_{W_2}[\mathbf{u}, set(W_1 = w_+)] >_* f_{W_2}[\mathbf{u}]$ *with* $>_* = \geq$;
  2. $\forall w_- \in \mathcal{D}(W_1)$ *such that* $w_- < f_{W_1}[\mathbf{u}]$, *it holds that* $f_{W_2}[\mathbf{u}, set(W_1 = w_-)] <_* f_{W_2}[\mathbf{u}]$ *with* $<_* = \leq$;
  3. $\exists_{\geq 1} w_+ \in \mathcal{D}(W_1)$ *or* $\exists_{\geq 1} w_- \in \mathcal{D}(W_1)$ *satisfying the conditions at points 1 and 2 with* $<_* = <$ *and* $>_* = >$.

We call any argumentative explanation for $\langle U,V,E\rangle$ *and* $\mathbf{u}$, *given a reinforcement explanation mould* $\{c^r_-, c^r_+\}$, *a* reinforcement explanation *(RX) (for* $\langle U, V, E\rangle$ *and* $\mathbf{u}$*).*

For illustration, Figure 1iii shows the RX for the causal model in Figure 1i and $\mathbf{u}$ as in the caption. Note that the causal model can only be understood by inspection of the structural equations; instead, the argumentative explanations provide a qualitative characterisation of influences, without requiring an understanding of the structural equations. Note also that conditions 1 and 2 for the attack and support relations in RXs correspond to a weak form of local monotonicity of the model. For instance, since U_2 attacks V_1, the user knows that, all else remaining the same, any increase in the value of U_2 cannot give rise to an increase of the value of V_1, while a decrease of U_2 will not decrease the value of V_1. Condition 3 adds a guarantee of effectiveness: there is at least one variation of U_2, which, all else remaining the same, enforces a variation of V_1. Thus RXs have a counterfactual nature, as they suggest to the user the kind of local changes with respect to the current situation that could give rise to a desired change of outcome. In this respect, note that the role assigned to variables refers to the selected value assignment to exogenous variables. For example, in the RX for the input in the first line of the table in Figure 1i, the fact that "margherita" is spelt correctly on the menu does not play a role in determining that the pizzeria is not legitimately Italian (indeed this is determined solely by pineapple being on the pizza), thus the support (U_1, V_1) is not present in the RX for this input. Such differences reflect the fact that only some (or possibly none) of the individual changes of variables U_1 and U_2 are guaranteed to produce a change in V_1's value, depending on the initial context. The local nature of RXs, corresponding to the local nature of bi-variate reinforcement, ensures simplicity and a rather intuitive interpretation but at the same time clearly limits expressiveness, in particular RXs are not meant to cover cases where multiple variable changes are needed to produce an effect. Other, explanation moulds may be needed to satisfy differing users' explanatory requirements. Note that some explanation moulds may be unsuitable to some causal models, e.g. our reinforcement explanation mould is not directly applicable to causal models with variables whose domains lack a partial order.

4 Properties

We perform a theoretical evaluation of RXs with regards to their satisfaction of various properties (besides a variant of bi-variate reinforcement, satisfied by design and easy to see from Definition 4). Unless specified otherwise, we assume some RX $\langle \mathcal{A}, \mathcal{R}_-, \mathcal{R}_+ \rangle$ for gradual causal model $\langle U, V, E \rangle$ and $\mathbf{u} \in \mathcal{U}$ with influence graph $\langle \mathcal{V}, \mathcal{I} \rangle$.

The first result shows the deterministic nature of RXs.

Proposition 1 (Uniqueness). *There is no $\langle \mathcal{A}, \mathcal{R}'_-, \mathcal{R}'_+ \rangle$ for $\langle U, V, E \rangle$ and $\mathbf{u}$, such that $\langle \mathcal{A}, \mathcal{R}'_-, \mathcal{R}'_+ \rangle$ is different from $\langle \mathcal{A}, \mathcal{R}_-, \mathcal{R}_+ \rangle$ (i.e. such that $\mathcal{R}'_- \neq \mathcal{R}_-$ or $\mathcal{R}'_+ \neq \mathcal{R}_+$).*

This guarantees *stability* (e.g. as discussed in (Sokol and Flach 2020)), i.e. a user would never be shown two different explanations for the same causal model and input given the choice of $\mathcal{A}$. We posit that this is important to avoid possible user uncertainty and confusion.

Further, RXs are acyclic when seen as graphs.

Proposition 2 (Acylicity). *Let (n, e) be the graph with $n = \mathcal{A}$ and $e = \mathcal{R}_- \cup \mathcal{R}_+$. Then, (n, e) is acyclic.*

This follows directly from acyclicity of causal models. It prevents potentially undesirable behaviour such as a self-attacking or self-supporting variable assignments in RXs.

An argument in RXs may not both attack and support another argument therein:

Proposition 3 (Unambiguity). *$\forall W_1 \in \mathcal{A}$, $\mathcal{R}_-(W_1) \cap \mathcal{R}_+(W_1) = \emptyset$, or, equivalently, $\mathcal{R}_- \cap \mathcal{R}_+ = \emptyset$.*

Violation of this property would clearly provide contradictory indications to the user.

The following proposition states that argumentative relations in RXs are derived from causal relationships.

Proposition 4 (Relevance). *$\mathcal{R}_- \cup \mathcal{R}_+ \subseteq \mathcal{I}$.*

Note that, while straightforward for RXs, this property may be violated by (model-agnostic) explanation methods which do not leverage upon the underlying causal model. This property is in the same spirit as other properties in the XAI literature, e.g. *Dummy* (Sundararajan and Najmi 2020), which states that a feature which does not affect a classification is given a zero attribution value. This may be particularly important in some cases, e.g. in the running example, it may not be enough to use the absence of pineapple on pizza ($U_2 = 0$) as a reason for entering a restaurant ($V_2 = 1$), and $V_1 = 1$ provides a useful intermediate justification that the restaurant seems to be legitimately Italian.

The following requires that changing attackers or supporters in binary causal models necessitates a change in the value of the argument they attack or support, respectively.

Proposition 5 (Bipolar Counterfactuality). *If $\langle U, V, E \rangle$ is binary, then $\forall (W_1, W_2) \in \mathcal{I}$ where $(W_1, W_2) \in \mathcal{R}_- \cup \mathcal{R}_+$, for every $w \neq f_{W_1}[\mathbf{u}]$: $f_{W_2}[\mathbf{u}, set(W_1 = w)] \neq f_{W_2}[\mathbf{u}]$.*

This is a powerful explanatory characteristic of RXs since attacks and supports indicate counterfactuals (in the binary case). For example, given the RX in Figure 1iii, a user can immediately see that changing the value of V_2 can be achieved by changing the value of V_1, which itself can be achieved by changing the value of U_1 or U_2.

The next property shows that behaviour similar to attacks and supports with discrete semantics (see (Cayrol and Lagasquie-Schiex 2005)) arises in RXs for binary models.

Proposition 6 ((Dis)agreement). *If $\langle U, V, E \rangle$ is binary, then, $\forall W_1 \in \mathcal{A}$: if $\exists W_2 \in \mathcal{R}_-(W_1)$ then $f_{W_2}[\mathbf{u}] \neq f_{W_1}[\mathbf{u}]$; if $\exists W_3 \in \mathcal{R}_+(W_1)$ then $f_{W_3}[\mathbf{u}] = f_{W_1}[\mathbf{u}]$.*

We thus observe that attacks indicate a contradiction between two arguments while supports indicate harmony between them. Clearly this is the case in Figure 1, where assigning U_2 value 1 will reduce the value of V_1 to 0: a contradiction. Meanwhile, any input which changes V_1's value to 0 will necessitate the same result in V_2: a harmony.

The set of arguments assigned value 1 in an RX for a binary causal model satisfies coherence (see §2).

Proposition 7 ((Internal and External) Coherence). *If $\langle U, V, E \rangle$ is binary, then the set of* accepted arguments *$\mathcal{A}_a = \{W_1 \in \mathcal{A} | f_{W_1}[\mathbf{u}] = 1\}$ is internally and externally coherent.*

This result indicates that the basic principles of argumentation are upheld in RXs, which hence can support some genuine forms of argumentative reasoning on the model by the user. For example, if the RX in Figure 1iii were given for an input $\mathbf{u}'$ with $f_{U_2}[\mathbf{u}'] = 1$ and $f_{V_1}[\mathbf{u}'] = 1$, the set of accepted arguments would contain a contradiction, which is not intuitive since the accepted attacker has no effect.

5 Future Work

We believe that our approach provides the groundwork for many future directions. The computational complexity of RXs deserves attention. Moulds inspired by other properties, and resulting in other forms of AFs, could be devised. A full empirical analysis of RXs, including user studies, also seems worthwhile. Links between our work and existing XAI methods, particularly those utilising argumentation, could be instructive, while counterfactuals and causality also warrant investigation in our approach.

Acknowledgements

Toni was partially funded by the European Research Council (ERC) under the European Union's Horizon 2020 research and innovation programme (grant agreement No. 101020934). Rago and Toni were partially funded by J.P. Morgan and by the Royal Academy of Engineering under the Research Chairs and Senior Research Fellowships scheme. Any views or opinions expressed herein are solely those of the authors listed. The authors would like to thank Fabrizio Russo and Emanuele Albini for their helpful contributions to discussions in the build up to this work.

References

Albini, E.; Baroni, P.; Rago, A.; and Toni, F. 2020a. PageRank as an argumentation semantics. In *COMMA*, 55–66.

Albini, E.; Rago, A.; Baroni, P.; and Toni, F. 2020b. Relation-based counterfactual explanations for Bayesian network classifiers. In *IJCAI*, 451–457.

Albini, E.; Rago, A.; Baroni, P.; and Toni, F. 2021. Influence-driven explanations for Bayesian network classifiers. In *PRICAI*, 88–100.

Amgoud, L., and Ben-Naim, J. 2018. Weighted bipolar argumentation graphs: Axioms and semantics. In *IJCAI*, 5194–5198.

Antaki, C., and Leudar, I. 1992. Explaining in conversation: Towards an argument model. *European Journal of Social Psychology* 22:181–194.

Atkinson, K.; Baroni, P.; Giacomin, M.; Hunter, A.; Prakken, H.; Reed, C.; Simari, G. R.; Thimm, M.; and Villata, S. 2017. Towards artificial argumentation. *AI Magazine* 38(3):25–36.

Baroni, P.; Comini, G.; Rago, A.; and Toni, F. 2017. Abstract games of argumentation strategy and game-theoretical argument strength. In *PRIMA*, 403–419.

Baroni, P.; Gabbay, D.; Giacomin, M.; and van der Torre, L., eds. 2018. *Handbook of Formal Argumentation*. College Publications.

Baroni, P.; Rago, A.; and Toni, F. 2018. How many properties do we need for gradual argumentation? In *AAAI*, 1736–1743.

Cayrol, C., and Lagasquie-Schiex, M. 2005. On the acceptability of arguments in bipolar argumentation frameworks. In *ECSQARU*, 378–389.

Cyras, K.; Rago, A.; Albini, E.; Baroni, P.; and Toni, F. 2021. Argumentative XAI: A survey. In *IJCAI*, 4392–4399.

de Graaf, M. M. A., and Malle, B. F. 2017. How people explain action (and autonomous intelligent systems should too). In *AAAI Fall Symposia*, 19–26.

Dejl, A.; He, P.; Mangal, P.; Mohsin, H.; Surdu, B.; Voinea, E.; Albini, E.; Lertvittayakumjorn, P.; Rago, A.; and Toni, F. 2021. Argflow: A toolkit for deep argumentative explanations for neural networks. In *AAMAS*, 1761–1763.

Dung, P. M. 1995. On the Acceptability of Arguments and its Fundamental Role in Nonmonotonic Reasoning, Logic Programming and n-Person Games. *Artificial Intelligence* 77(2):321–358.

Gabbay, D. M. 2016. Logical foundations for bipolar and tripolar argumentation networks: preliminary results. *Journal of Logic and Computation* 26(1):247–292.

Guidotti, R.; Monreale, A.; Ruggieri, S.; Turini, F.; Giannotti, F.; and Pedreschi, D. 2019. A survey of methods for explaining black box models. *ACM Computing Surveys* 51(5):93:1–93:42.

Halpern, J. Y., and Pearl, J. 2001. Causes and explanations: A structural-model approach: Part 1: Causes. In *UAI*, 194–202.

Lundberg, S. M., and Lee, S. 2017. A unified approach to interpreting model predictions. In *NeurIPS*, 4765–4774.

Madumal, P.; Miller, T.; Sonenberg, L.; and Vetere, F. 2019. A grounded interaction protocol for explainable artificial intelligence. In *AAMAS*, 1033–1041.

Madumal, P.; Miller, T.; Sonenberg, L.; and Vetere, F. 2020. Explainable reinforcement learning through a causal lens. In *AAAI*, 2493–2500.

Miller, T. 2019. Explanation in artificial intelligence: Insights from the social sciences. *Artificial Intelligence* 267:1–38.

Pearl, J. 1995. Causal diagrams for empirical research. *Biometrika* 82(4):669–710.

Pearl, J. 1999. Reasoning with cause and effect. In *IJCAI*, 1437–1449.

Pearl, J. 2012. The do-calculus revisited. In *UAI*, 3–11.

Potyka, N. 2021. Interpreting neural networks as quantitative argumentation frameworks. In *AAAI*, 6463–6470.

Rago, A.; Cocarascu, O.; Bechlivanidis, C.; and Toni, F. 2020. Argumentation as a framework for interactive explanations for recommendations. In *KR*, 805–815.

Rago, A.; Cocarascu, O.; and Toni, F. 2018. Argumentation-based recommendations: Fantastic explanations and how to find them. In *IJCAI*, 1949–1955.

Schwab, P., and Karlen, W. 2019. CXPlain: Causal explanations for model interpretation under uncertainty. In *NeurIPS*, 10220–10230.

Sokol, K., and Flach, P. A. 2020. Explainability fact sheets: a framework for systematic assessment of explainable approaches. In *FAT**, 56–67.

Sundararajan, M., and Najmi, A. 2020. The many shapley values for model explanation. In *ICML*, 9269–9278.

Teze, J. C.; Godo, L.; and Simari, G. R. 2018. An argumentative recommendation approach based on contextual aspects. In *SUM*, 405–412.

Timmer, S. T.; Meyer, J. C.; Prakken, H.; Renooij, S.; and Verheij, B. 2015. Explaining bayesian networks using argumentation. In *ECSQARU*, 83–92.

Vassiliades, A.; Bassiliades, N.; and Patkos, T. 2021. Argumentation and Explainable Artificial Intelligence: A Survey. *The Knowledge Engineering Review* 36(2).

Woodward, J. 1997. Explanation, invariance, and intervention. *Philosophy of Science* 64:S26–S41.

Special Session on KR and Robotics

Proceedings of the 19th International Conference on Principles of Knowledge Representation and Reasoning
Special Session on KR and Robotics

Online Grounding of Symbolic Planning Domains in Unknown Environments

Leonardo Lamanna[1,2] , **Luciano Serafini**[1] , **Alessandro Saetti**[2] , **Alfonso Gerevini**[2] , **Paolo Traverso**[1]

[1]Fondazione Bruno Kessler, Trento, Italy
[2]University of Brescia, Italy
{llamanna,serafini,traverso}@fbk.eu {l.lamanna,
alessandro.saetti,alfonso.gerevini}@unibs.it

Abstract

If a robotic agent wants to exploit symbolic planning techniques to achieve some goal, it must be able to properly ground an abstract planning domain in the environment in which it operates. However, if the environment is initially unknown by the agent, the agent needs to explore it and discover the salient aspects of the environment necessary to reach its goals. Namely, the agent has to discover: (i) the objects present in the environment, (ii) the properties of these objects and their relations, and finally (iii) how abstract actions can be successfully executed. The paper proposes a framework that aims to accomplish the aforementioned perspective for an agent that perceives the environment partially and subjectively, through real value sensors (e.g., GPS, and on-board camera) and can operate in the environment through low level actuators (e.g., move forward of 20 cm). We evaluate the proposed architecture in photo-realistic simulated environments, where the sensors are RGB-D on-board camera, GPS and compass, and low level actions include movements, grasping/releasing objects, and manipulating objects. The agent is placed in an unknown environment and asked to find objects of a certain type, place an object on top of another, close or open an object of a certain type. We compare our approach with a state of the art method on object goal navigation based on reinforcement learning, showing better performances.

1 Introduction

Symbolic planners are powerful and flexible tools (Ghallab, Nau, and Traverso 2016) that, given a general symbolic description of an available set of actions (i.e., a planning domain) and a detailed description of an environment, are capable of generating plans for achieving ideally any goal about (known) objects in the environment. In several applications, the information about the environment required to instantiate a planning domain is not available from the beginning. In particular, when an agent is placed in a new environment, it does not know the objects that populate the environment, and therefore it does not know their specific properties and relations. Consider, for instance, a robot that has to move around and manipulate objects in a kitchen (tables, chairs, apples, etc.) without knowing which and how many objects are really in the room. In this setting, the exploitation of a planning domain is a compelling challenge for three main reasons. First, in realistic environments, it is unfeasible for the robot to acquire a complete/correct and sufficiently detailed description of the environment before starting to plan and execute actions towards the achievement of its goals. Second, a robotic agent usually has a first-person perspective and partial view of the environment (e.g., by an on-board camera), so that the only way to acquire symbolic knowledge suitable for planning is by executing actions, observing their effects through its sensors, and mapping the sensory data (e.g., raw images) in a symbolic state. Third, high level actions of the planning domain are not directly executable by the robot, and therefore they need to be compiled to low level actions executable in the environment by the agent actuators. For instance, given an object instance identified by a constant c_0, the action $\mathsf{goCloseTo}(c_0)$ is compiled into a sequence of robot movements and rotations, which follow the path provided by a path-planner, and moves the robot to the (nearest) location close to object c_0.

This paper proposes a framework for agents that incrementally instantiate a planning domain, specified in PDDL, by planning, acting, and sensing, in an unknown environment. At each time-point, the belief of the agent about the current state of the environment is represented by three components, namely: (i) the set of objects currently known by the agent and their properties expressed with the predicates of the PDDL domain, e.g., $\mathsf{table}(c_0)$, $\mathsf{apple}(c_1)$, and $\mathsf{on}(c_1, c_0)$; (ii) for each known object, a set of low-level features as perceived by the agent, e.g., visual features and positions of c_0 and c_1; (iii) a set of global features associated to the current environment state, e.g., an occupancy map of the environment, and the current pose of the robot.

For this framework, we propose an online iterative algorithm, called OGAMUS (Online Grounding of Action Models in Unknown Situations), that allows an agent, equipped with a lifted PDDL planning domain, and placed in an unknown environment, to achieve a set of goals expressed in the language of its PDDL action model. The agent is initialized without prior knowledge about the environment where it has to operate, i.e., with the empty set of objects, the empty set of their properties, and all the points of the occupancy map set as traversable. OGAMUS attempts to achieve the goal by combining four main activities, namely: (i) *exploring the environment* to acquire the knowledge needed to achieve the goals; (ii) *abstracting the sensor information* obtained at every step into a symbolic state; (iii) performing *symbolic planning* in the abstract model grounded with the current beliefs and current abstract state; (iv) *executing* the planned abstract actions by compiling them into low-level operations suitable for the current state of the environment.

The main features of OGAMUS are the following. *Generality:* OGAMUS is able to deal with any goal that can be expressed by a (first-order) formula using the predicates of the PDDL domain. For instance the goal of putting "two apples on a table" can be specified by the formula $\exists x\, y\, z.\mathsf{on}(x, z) \wedge \mathsf{on}(y, z) \wedge \mathsf{apple}(x) \wedge \mathsf{apple}(y) \wedge \mathsf{table}(z) \wedge x \neq y$. Notice that goals are expressed with existentially quantified variables; this is because, initially, the agent is not aware of any objects in the domain. An important step, necessary to achieve a goal containing existential variables, concerns discovering the object instances of the proper types (apple and table in the previous example) for instantiating all the existential variables. *Explainability*: The behaviour of the agent, its plans, and the effects of actions are represented at a symbolic level in which the states of the PDDL domain are derived at every step by abstracting the sensory data. *Robustness:* The action model, the obtained symbolic state representation, and the action compilation are not required to be fault free. As experimentally shown in this paper, OGAMUS achieves high success rate even with low precision object detectors and classifiers.

We have implemented and experimentally evaluated OGAMUS in the ITHOR (Kolve et al. 2017) and ROBOTHOR (Deitke et al. 2020) simulated photo-realistic environments for embodied AI. We evaluate OGAMUS on different tasks including "go close to an object of a certain type" (e.g., "go close to a fridge"). In the area of Embodied AI, this class of tasks is called "object goal navigation", and it is still considered a challenging and open problem. Our framework and evaluation go beyond such a challenge, considering more complex tasks, such as "open/close an object of a certain type" (e.g., "open a laptop"), and "put an object of a type on top of an object of another type" (e.g., "put an apple on a table"). We compared our results with the state-of-the-art approaches on the object goal navigation task. In particular, we show that, in the benchmarks of the last ROBOTHOR object goal navigation challenge, our approach outperforms the state of the art methods based on Reinforcement Learning (RL).[1] The evaluation on the other tasks leads to very positive performance, but we cannot compare them with any state-of-the-art approach since, to the best of our knowledge, we are the first solving such types of tasks in the ITHOR and ROBOTHOR environment.

The paper is structured as follows: firstly we analyze the related literature, then we describe the framework and the algorithm adopted by the agent to reach a specific goal in an unknown environment; finally, we present the experimental evaluation and a comparison with RL-based approaches.

2 Related Work

The problem of integrating symbolic action models with low level sensory data and actions has been addressed by different approaches. Most of them are based on RL techniques. Lyu et al. (2019) propose a framework, called SDRL, which combines symbolic planning and Deep RL to learn policies that compile high level actions into low level operations. SDRL assumes that a grounded domain model is provided in input and never updated. A fundamental difference w.r.t. our approach is that OGAMUS, instead, learns how to ground the domain model with new objects discovered online. Moreover, SDRL assumes a perfect oracle that maps low level perceptions into symbolic states, while OGAMUS deals with faulty mappings without assuming to have an oracle.

NSRL (Ma et al. 2021) represents abstract domains in first-order logic and uses RL to learn high level policies. NSRL generates a compact representation of the learned policies as a set of rules via Inductive Logic Programming. Similarly to SDRL, NSRL assumes a given and fixed abstract domain instantiation and a perfect mapping from sensory data to symbolic states, while OGAMUS overcomes these assumptions.

DPDL (Kase et al. 2020) represents abstract domains in PDDL. It learns online both mappings from sensory data to symbolic states and low level policies for high level actions. In OGAMUS, instead, the mapping from perceptions to symbolic states is obtained by combining a set of neural networks trained off-line. Moreover some of the high level actions are pre-compiled in low level operations (e.g., pick-up an object at a given position), while policies for moving actions are computed online via path planning. As the other methods mentioned above, DPDL assumes a given and fixed grounded PDDL domain, while this is not the case for OGAMUS. Moreover, it focuses on performing manipulation tasks in a single scene type (i.e., a kitchen). OGAMUS, instead, can work on different scenes (we evaluate it on 35 different scenes grouped by kitchens, living-rooms, bedrooms, and bathrooms). Finally, DPDL works with an external fixed camera, while OGAMUS uses egocentric and dynamic views. This makes the tasks more difficult for OGAMUS, since the agent needs to navigate, explore the environment, and find new objects outside of its current view.

Differently from the above mentioned works, in the approach proposed by Garnelo, Arulkumaran, and Shanahan (2016), like in OGAMUS, the agent instantiate the abstract domain online by augmenting the set of objects every time it discovers new ones. The states of the instantiated abstract model is represented with a set of propositional atoms on the current set of constants. However, this approach is evaluated only with an extremely simple environment, while OGAMUS is tested in accurate and photo-realistic simulated environments with complex objects and egocentric views. Furthermore, the approach in (Garnelo, Arulkumaran, and Shanahan 2016) does not take advantage of the power of symbolic planning techniques on PDDL domain descriptions, and it does not generalize over different tasks. On the contrary, OGAMUS exploits symbolic planning which allows to accomplish variegated tasks that can be specified using PDDL.

(Lamanna et al. 2021a) proposes a method for learning an extensional representation of a discrete planning domain from continuous observations. However, it focuses on discovering states as atoms, while in OGAMUS states are structured entities composed of object instances, with properties and relationships between them. In (Lamanna et al. 2021b),

[1]https://ai2thor.allenai.org/

the same authors propose an approach that deals with action schema learning, a different but related problem w.r.t. action schema instantiation. In OGAMUS, the action schema is known in advance, and we focus on mapping continuous perceptions into symbolic states, while (Lamanna et al. 2021b) does not address the problem of inferring high-level states from perceptions, i.e., it assumes to directly observe the truth value of the current state atoms.

We experimentally evaluate OGAMUS on the Object Goal Navigation task that has recently received much attention in the embodied AI community (Mirowski et al. 2017; Savva et al. 2017; Fang et al. 2019; Mousavian et al. 2019; Campari et al. 2020; Wortsman et al. 2019; Chaplot et al. 2019; Chaplot et al. 2020; Ye et al. 2021). We experimentally show that, in the benchmark of the last ROBOTHOR object goal navigation challenge, OGAMUS performs better than a method based on DD-PPO (Wijmans et al. 2019), which won the challenge using pure RL based on low-level features, without exploiting a symbolic domain.

3 The Framework

In this section, we start by introducing the basic definitions of our reference framework. We then introduce the OGAMUS algorithm. The section closes with the description of what are the basic components that need to be specified in order to cope with new abstract predicates or actions of the PDDL domain.

3.1 Preliminary Definitions

Let $\mathcal{P}$ be a set of first order predicates, $\mathcal{V}$ a set of variables (also called parameters), and $\mathcal{C}$ a set of constants. We use $\mathcal{P}(\mathcal{V})$ to denote the set of atoms $P(x_1, \ldots, x_m)$, where $x_i \in \mathcal{V}$ and $P \in \mathcal{P}$, and $\mathcal{P}(\mathcal{C})$ to denote the set of atoms obtained by grounding $\mathcal{P}(\mathcal{V})$ with the constants in $\mathcal{C}$.

Definition 1 (Action model). *Given a set of operators* $\mathcal{O}$, *an* action model $\mathcal{M}$ *associates to each* $op \in \mathcal{O}$ *an* action schema, *which is a tuple* $\langle \mathsf{par}(op), \mathsf{pre}(op), \mathsf{eff}^+(op), \mathsf{eff}^-(op) \rangle$, *where* $\mathsf{par}(op) \subseteq \mathcal{V}$, $\mathsf{pre}(op)$, $\mathsf{eff}^+(op)$, *and* $\mathsf{eff}^-(op)$ *are subsets of* $\mathcal{P}(\mathsf{par}(op))$.

Definition 2 (Ground action). *The* ground action $op(\mathbf{c})$ *of an operator* $op \in \mathcal{O}$ *with* $\mathbf{c} = \langle c_1, \ldots, c_n \rangle$ *constants in* $\mathcal{C}$ *is the tuple* $\langle \mathsf{pre}(op(\mathbf{c})), \mathsf{eff}^+(op(\mathbf{c})), \mathsf{eff}^-(op(\mathbf{c})) \rangle$, *obtained by instantiating the atoms of* $\mathsf{pre}(op)$, $\mathsf{eff}^+(op)$, *and* $\mathsf{eff}^-(op)$ *with* $\mathbf{c}$.

Definition 3 (Planning problem). *A* planning problem *is a tuple* $\langle \mathcal{M}, \mathcal{C}, s_0, \mathcal{G} \rangle$ *where* $\mathcal{M}$ *is an action model,* $\mathcal{C}$ *is a (possibly empty) set of constants,* $s_0 \subseteq \mathcal{P}(\mathcal{C})$ *is the initial state, and* $\mathcal{G}$ *is a first order formula over* $\mathcal{P}$, $\mathcal{V}$ *and* $\mathcal{C}$.

Definition 4 (Plan). *A* plan *for a planning problem* $\langle \mathcal{M}, \mathcal{C}, s_0, \mathcal{G} \rangle$ *is a sequence* $\langle op_1(\mathbf{c}_1), \ldots, op_n(\mathbf{c}_n) \rangle$ *such that there is a sequence* $\langle s_1, \ldots, s_n \rangle$ *of subsets of* $\mathcal{P}(\mathcal{C})$ *(aka states), such that for every* $0 \leq i < n$, $\mathsf{pre}(op_i(\mathbf{c}_i)) \subseteq s_i$, $s_i = s_{i-1} \cup \mathsf{eff}^+(op_i(\mathbf{c}_i)) \setminus \mathsf{eff}^-(op_i(\mathbf{c}_i))$, *and* $s_n \models \mathcal{G}$.

Notice that our definition of planning problem allows to express first-order goal formula $\mathcal{G}$. We say that a state $s \models \mathcal{G}$ iff $\bigwedge_{P(\mathbf{c}) \in s} P(\mathbf{c}) \wedge \bigwedge_{P(\mathbf{c}) \in \mathcal{P}(\mathcal{C}) \setminus s} \neg P(\mathbf{c}) \models \mathcal{G}$, under the assumption that all the elements of the problem are in $\mathcal{C}$.

In order to use an abstract model, an agent needs to *anchor* the symbols occurring in the states of the planning domain with the real-world perceptions, and to map abstract actions into actions executable in the real world (Coradeschi and Saffiotti 2003). We suppose that the agent can *partially* observe the current state of the environment through a set of sensors, for instance images provided by an RGB-D camera, which do not directly correspond to the states of the abstract model. Furthermore, the set of sensors provide only a partial and subjective view of the environment. For instance, the RGB-D camera provides only an egocentric view of a portion of the room visible by the agent. We also suppose that the agent interacts with the environment by executing low-level operations (e.g., move 25 cm forward, rotate 30° left, pick up or put down an object at the GPS-coordinates (x, y, z)), which are different from the actions in the abstract action model. We need therefore to link the abstract state to real perceptions, and the abstract actions to operations executable by the actuators of the agent. Let us first consider the relationship between abstract states and perceptions.

Object and state anchoring. Every object that the agent is aware of at a given instant is represented by a constant $c \in \mathcal{C}$ that is the internal identifier for such an object. Following the approaches to symbol anchoring proposed in the literature (Coradeschi and Saffiotti 2003; Persson et al. 2019), every constant $c \in \mathcal{C}$ is associated with a tuple of numeric features denoted by $\boldsymbol{z}_c$. For instance, $\boldsymbol{z}_c$ might include the estimated position of c and a set of visual features of the different views of c. In addition, for each state s determined by the agent, we have a vector of state features $\boldsymbol{z}_s$, consisting of the 3D position of the agent in the environment, the orientation of the agent relative to its initial pose, the information about the success of the last low-level operation made by the agent, and an occupancy map of the environment. The occupancy map is a 2D map of the environment storing the areas that are believed to be traversable by the robot. The occupancy map is initialized so that every point is traversable.

Predicate predictors. In order to map the perceptions about objects into atoms of the symbolic state, the agent associates to every predicate a probabilistic model, e.g., a neural network, that computes the probability of a certain atom $P(\mathbf{c})$ to be true given the features associated to $\mathbf{c}$ and the current state ones, i.e., $Pr(Y_{P(\mathbf{c})} = \text{True} \mid \boldsymbol{z}_\mathbf{c}, \boldsymbol{z}_s)$, where $Y_{P(\mathbf{c})}$ is a boolean random variable associated to the atom $P(\mathbf{c})$. These probabilistic models can be updated during execution on the basis of new observations. In this paper, however, we suppose that these probabilistic models are given (e.g., a pre-trained neural network), and they are not modified during execution.

We call *belief state* the agent's knowledge about object/state anchoring and predicate predictors.

Definition 5. *An agent belief state is a 5-tuple* $\langle \mathcal{C}, \boldsymbol{z}_\mathcal{C}, s, \boldsymbol{z}_s, \mathbf{Pr} \rangle$ *where:*

– $\mathcal{C}$ *is a set of constants;*

Algorithm 1 OGAMUS algorithm

Input: $\mathcal{M}$, $\mathcal{G}$, $\mathbf{Pr}$ and MAXITER $\in \mathbb{N}$.
Output: SUCCESS/FAIL

1: $\langle \mathcal{C}, \boldsymbol{z}_{\mathcal{C}}, s, \boldsymbol{z}_s \rangle \leftarrow \langle \emptyset, \emptyset, \emptyset, (\mathbf{0}, nil, \emptyset) \rangle$
2: **for** $1 = 0$ **to** MAXITER **do**
3:   **if** $s \models \mathcal{G}$ **then**
4:     **return** SUCCESS
5:   **end if**
6:   $\pi \leftarrow$ PLAN$(\mathcal{M}, \mathcal{C}, s, \mathcal{G})$
7:   **if** $\pi =$ NONE **then**
8:     $\boldsymbol{e} \leftarrow$ EXPLORE$(\boldsymbol{z}_s)$
9:   **else**
10:     $op(\mathbf{c}) \leftarrow$ POP(π)
11:     $\boldsymbol{e} \leftarrow$ COMPILE$(op(\mathbf{c}), \boldsymbol{z}_{\mathbf{c}}, \boldsymbol{z}_s)$
12:   **end if**
13:   $e_1 \leftarrow Pop(\boldsymbol{e})$
14:   $\boldsymbol{x} \leftarrow$ EXEC(e_1)
15:   $\boldsymbol{z}_s \leftarrow$ GETSTATEFEATURES$(\boldsymbol{x})$
16:   $\mathcal{C}_{\boldsymbol{x}}, \boldsymbol{z}_{\mathcal{C}_{\boldsymbol{x}}} \leftarrow$ GETOBJS$(\boldsymbol{x})$
17:   $\mathcal{C}, \boldsymbol{z}_{\mathcal{C}} \leftarrow$ UPDATEOBJS$(\mathcal{C}, \boldsymbol{z}_{\mathcal{C}}, \mathcal{C}_{\boldsymbol{x}}, \boldsymbol{z}_{\mathcal{C}_{\boldsymbol{x}}})$
18:   $Pr(\boldsymbol{Y}_{\mathcal{P}(\mathcal{C})}) \leftarrow$ PREDICTSTATE$(\boldsymbol{z}_{\mathcal{C}}, s, \boldsymbol{z}_s)$
19:   $s \leftarrow \{p(\mathbf{c}) \in \mathcal{P}(\mathcal{C}) \mid Pr(Y_{p(\mathbf{c})} = True \mid \boldsymbol{z}_{\mathbf{c}}) > 1 - \epsilon\}$
20:   **if** $\pi \neq$ NONE and SUCCEED$(op(\mathbf{c}))$ **then**
21:     $s \leftarrow s \cup \mathsf{eff}^{+}(op(\mathbf{c})) \setminus \mathsf{eff}^{-}(op(\mathbf{c})))$
22:   **end if**
23: **end for**
24: **return** FAIL

- $\boldsymbol{z}_{\mathcal{C}} = \{\boldsymbol{z}_c\}_{c \in \mathcal{C}}$ *is a set of object feature vectors* $\boldsymbol{z}_c$*;*
- $s \subseteq \mathcal{P}(\mathcal{C})$ *is the set of atoms that are believed to be true;*
- $\boldsymbol{z}_s$ *is a vector of state features;*
- $\mathbf{Pr} = \{Pr(Y_{P(\mathbf{c})} \mid \boldsymbol{z}_{\mathbf{c}}, \boldsymbol{z}_s)\}_{P \in \mathcal{P}}$ *is the set of probabilistic models used to predict the truth value of* $P(\mathbf{c})$ *given the features* $\boldsymbol{z}_s$ *and* $\boldsymbol{z}_{\mathbf{c}}$ *associated with the constants in* $\mathbf{c}$*.*

3.2 The OGAMUS Algorithm

So far, we have not considered how the set $\mathcal{C}$ of constants identifying objects is obtained by the agent. We do not assume that they are given a priori to the agent; instead, we are interested in providing the agent with the capability to discover objects by adding new constants to the representation of the environment, updating the anchor to an object, merging two constants anchored to the same object, and deleting a constant from the representation that was erroneously identifying a non existing object in the environment.

Let $\boldsymbol{x}$ be the vector that contains the data returned by the sensors (i.e., the observations) at a given time; the agent extracts from $\boldsymbol{x}$ a set of objects $\mathcal{C}_{\boldsymbol{x}}$, and for each object $c \in \mathcal{C}_{\boldsymbol{x}}$ a feature vector $\boldsymbol{z}_c$. Since the agent can also recognize objects that it has already seen, it is possible that $\mathcal{C}_{\boldsymbol{x}} \cap \mathcal{C} \neq \emptyset$.

In the following, we shortly describe the OGAMUS algorithm (Algorithm 1).

- The algorithm takes as input an action model $\mathcal{M}$, a set $\mathbf{Pr}$ of probabilistic models for predicting the predicates in $\mathcal{P}$, a goal formula $\mathcal{G}$, and a maximum number of iterations. Notice that the goal $\mathcal{G}$ cannot contain constants, since we suppose that at the beginning the agent is not aware of any object. For instance, the goal requiring that an apple is inside a box can be encoded by the PDDL expression representing formula $\exists x, y\ \mathsf{apple}(x) \wedge \mathsf{box}(y) \wedge \mathsf{in}(x, y)$.
- The agent starts by initializing all the components of its state to the emptyset (line 1). We assume indeed that the agent is not aware of any object in the environment, therefore $\mathcal{C} = \emptyset$. Since $\mathcal{C}$ is empty, $\boldsymbol{z}_{\mathcal{C}}$, $\mathcal{P}(\mathcal{C})$ and s are also empty. The information in $\boldsymbol{z}_s$ representing the position and orientation of the agent is initialized with a vector of 0's; the information in $\boldsymbol{z}_s$ about the success of the last operation is set to *nil*; finally, the occupancy map of the environment in $\boldsymbol{z}_s$ is set to an empty map so that all the points are traversable.
- Then the agent iterates for a maximum number of steps, checking if the current state s satisfies the goal (line 4); when this is the case, it returns SUCCESS.
- Otherwise, the agent invokes a planner (line 6) to solve the planning problem defined on the input action model, the current set of objects, the current state, and the input goal formula $\mathcal{G}$.
- If the planner does not find a plan that satisfies the goal, then the agent explores the environment in order to discover new objects that are needed to satisfy the goal. For instance, if the goal is to put an apple into a box, then the planner can find a plan only if in the current state s there is at least one object of type apple and one of type box. For the exploration phase (line 8), the agent randomly selects a target position on the occupancy map (stored in $\boldsymbol{z}_s$) that it believes to be free from other obstacles. As shown in Figure 1, EXPLORE$(\boldsymbol{z}_s)$ calls a path planner that checks if such a position is reachable (if it is not reachable a new position is selected) and returns a sequence $\boldsymbol{e}$ of low-level navigation and rotation operations, which, according to the current knowledge of the agent, moves the agent from its current position to the selected target. For efficiency reasons, this path is computed in an approximated occupancy map obtained by discretizing the occupancy map through a grid. The execution of such a sequence of operations might fail due to the partial or incorrect knowledge

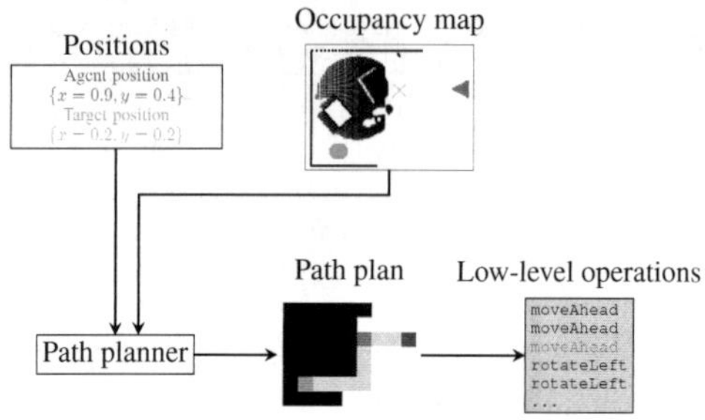

Figure 1: Example of EXPLORE$(\boldsymbol{z}_s)$. The occupancy map, agent position (in blue) and target position (in green) are given as input to a path planner which discretizes the occupancy map, computes a path plan, and compile the path plan into a sequence of low-level operations.

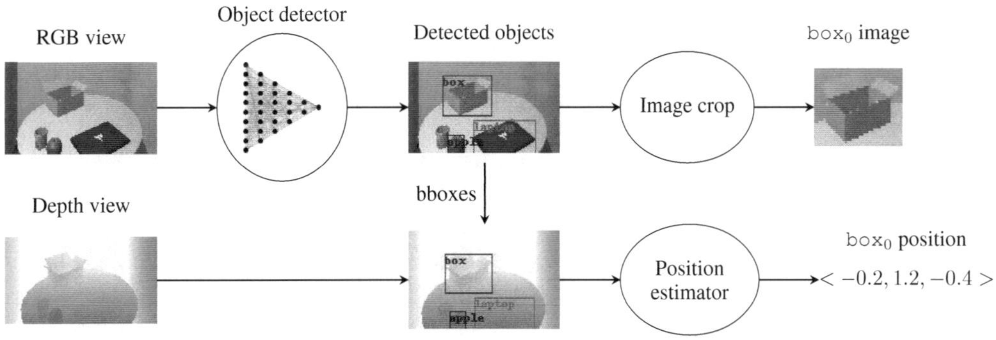

Figure 2: Example of object features extraction. The object detector takes as input the perception composed by the agent view RGB image, and returns a set of bounding boxes together with the detected object types. The object bounding boxes are used with the agent view depth image to estimate their positions (in meters w.r.t. the initial agent position). The lighter the pixels in the box, the farther the associated object.

of the agent, i.e., when the agent wrongly believes that a certain area on the path returned by the path-planner is traversable while there is an obstacle. In Figure 1, the agent fails to reach the red cell. Indeed, the execution of the third moveAhead action fails because the robot bumps into a table, whose size was only partially determined at the beginning of the exploration phase. The exploration terminates whenever the goal is reachable according to the learned problem. For example, consider the goal requiring that an apple is in a box and assume that an apple has already been discovered in the environment. The execution of the computed sequence of operations terminates in advance, when the agent detects the presence of a box on the table in Figure 1, as it approaches the table by executing the first operations in the sequence.

- If instead the planner succeeds and returns a valid plan π, then the first action of π is compiled into a sequence of low-level operations $\boldsymbol{e}$ (line 11). The compilation of the action is based on the object and state features available in the agent's state. For instance, the high level action $\mathsf{pickup}(c)$ is compiled into the low-level operation $\mathsf{pickup}(x, y, z)$ where (x, y, z) is the current (believed) position of object c, memorized in $\boldsymbol{z}_c$. The simulator executes such an operation by picking up what is present at these coordinates. To compile the action $\mathsf{goCloseTo}(c)$ instead, the agent calls a path-planner that provides a path from the current position of the agent (memorized in $\boldsymbol{z}_s$) to a position close to c.
- Successively, the first operation of sequence $\boldsymbol{e}$ is executed (line 14), and a new observation $\boldsymbol{x}$ is obtained. The execution of the first operation may fail or not. In both cases, the agent can acquire new knowledge (e.g., discover new objects or an obstacle), which can be used to produce a better compilation of an high-level action, and/or produce a better plan. Then, the new state features $\boldsymbol{z}_s$ are extracted from the sensory data $\boldsymbol{x}$ (line 15). The information about the occupancy map is updated using the information of success/failure of the action and the depth image.
- Then the agent runs an object detector (line 16) on the RGB image contained in observation $\boldsymbol{x}$ which returns a set of objects $\mathcal{C}_{\boldsymbol{x}}$, each associated with a vector of numeric features $\boldsymbol{z}_c$. These features include the bounding box, an estimation of the object position, and a vector of visual features extracted from the cropping of the image with the bounding box. Figure 2 gives an example of extraction of a number of objects, including a box, from the egocentric view of an agent robot, together with the bounding-box image of such a box and the estimate of its position.
- Next, at line 17, the agent merges the objects $\mathcal{C}_{\boldsymbol{x}}$ recognized in the current perception with the ones already known, i.e., $\mathcal{C}$. For every object $c' \in \mathcal{C}_{\boldsymbol{x}}$ there are two possible situations: (i) c' does not match with any object $c \in \mathcal{C}$, and therefore it is added to $\mathcal{C}$ with the corresponding features $\boldsymbol{z}_{c'}$; (ii) c' matches with a $c \in \mathcal{C}$; in this case the features $\boldsymbol{z}_c$ of c are extended/updated with the features $\boldsymbol{z}_{c'}$. In the implementation, we use a very simple matching criteria which considers only the estimated position of the objects. Two objects are matched when their distance is less then a given threshold (set to 20cm). More sophisticated criteria can be adopted by defining a suitable distance measure between the entire set of object features. However, this simple criteria turned out to be sufficiently effective in our experiments.
- In line 18, the agent predicts the truth values of each atom in $\mathcal{P}(\mathcal{C})$ for the updated set of constants $\mathcal{C}$ by applying the predictors $\mathbf{Pr}$ on the features $\boldsymbol{z}_{\mathcal{C}}$. For predicate closeToAgent, the prediction takes also as input the agent position in $\boldsymbol{z}_s$. All the atoms involving new or merged objects must be evaluated; the remaining atoms are evaluated only if the corresponding predictor takes as input some feature that has been updated after the execution of the last action. For instance, if the agent executes a move action, then all the atoms $\mathsf{closeToAgent}(c)$ for all $c \in \mathcal{C}$ must be evaluated. Each atom $\mathsf{closeToAgent}(c)$ is predicted true if the euclidean distance between the position of the object represented by c in z_c and the agent position in z_s is lower than a given threshold (set to 140 cm). When the action $\mathsf{open}(\mathsf{box}_0)$ is executed, the visual features of box_0 probably change, and the truth value of predicate $\mathsf{isOpen}(\mathsf{box}_0)$ is predicted as depicted in Figure 3. Notice that, after executing an open operation it is

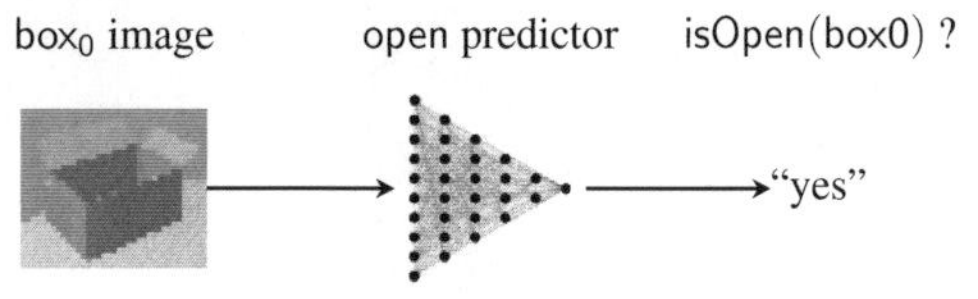

Figure 3: Example of predictor for the open predicate. The predictor takes as input the RGB images associated to box_0, and returns the predicted truth value of $\mathsf{isOpen}(\mathsf{box}_0)$.

not guaranteed that the object will be open, as the action might fail.

- At line 19, the new state s is created with all predicates $P(\boldsymbol{c})$ such that $Pr(Y_{P(\boldsymbol{c})} = True \mid \boldsymbol{z_c}, \boldsymbol{z}_s)$ is higher than a given threshold $1 - \epsilon$ with $\epsilon \in [0, 1]$. Our approach does not assume to have access to the correct abstract state. Indeed, the agent can produce inconsistent states (e.g., a box is both on the table and on another box), or states that do not comply with action effects. Inconsistent states do not prevent OGAMUS to further plan and, whether a failure occurs, revise the agent's knowledge making them consistent. In the second case, the agent monitors the execution of high-level actions by comparing the state predicted by the PDDL model with the perceived state, and it solves inconsistencies in favour of the action effects in the model.
- At line 21, when SUCCEED$(op(\boldsymbol{c}))$ is true, i.e., the entire sequence $\boldsymbol{e}$ of operations compiling the first action $op(\boldsymbol{c})$ of π is successfully executed, the state s is updated according to the effects of $op(\boldsymbol{c})$.
- If the agent does not reach a state s that satisfies the goal $\mathcal{G}$ after MAXITER steps, then the algorithm returns FAIL (line 24).

3.3 Knowledge Revision for New Tasks

To show the generality and the modularity of the proposed framework, we describe how it can be easily extended to cope with new tasks that can possibly involve a set of new (PDDL) actions, predicates, and object types. To allow the agent to accomplish a new task t_{new}, we firstly need to encode t_{new} in a PDDL goal formula. If the encoding of t_{new} does not require the introduction of new predicates, actions, or object types, then to solve the task it is sufficient to invoke OGAMUS with the goal formula encoding t_{new}. If, instead, the encoding of t_{new} requires some new predicates, actions, or object types, then we have to provide the agent with the capability of (1) recognizing objects of the new types, (2) predicting the truth value of the new predicates, and (3) compiling the new actions in low-level operations executable by the agent's actuators. Consider, for instance, the case where t_{new} is the task turning a lamp on: t_{new} can be specified by the goal formula $\exists x.\mathsf{lamp}(x) \wedge \mathsf{turned\_on}(x)$, where lamp is a new object type and turned_on a new unary predicate.

To detect objects with the newly introduced type e.g., lamp, the object detector need to be extended and retrained with the new object type. This implies that the upper part of the detector (which is responsible of classifying the objects in their types) need to be extended with the new type and re-trained on a dataset containing also examples for this new type. The introduction of a new predicate, in our example turned_on, requires the deployment of a new classifier that predicts if the predicate holds for the objects detected from the sensory data. In case the predictor is based on a supervised learning model, then a training dataset with object labelled with positive and negative examples of the predicate need to be provided. Finally, if the new task requires adding new actions to the PDDL model, (e.g., to make the predicate $\mathsf{turned\_on}(x)$ true/false we need to introduce two new action turn_on and turn_off) we need to specify how the new action can be compiled into a sequence of low-level operations executable by the agent. For example, action $\mathsf{turn\_on}(c)$ will be compiled into a low-level operation $\mathsf{turn\_on}(x, y, z)$ where (x, y, z) is the believed position of object c.

4 Experiments

We perform two sets of experiments. First, we experimentally evaluate OGAMUS with a simulated environment on four tasks that involves going close and move objects present in a number of rooms. Then, we compare OGAMUS with a state-of-the-art approach on the specific task of object goal navigation in different apartments.

4.1 Evaluating OGAMUS

The tasks and the corresponding goals on which we evaluate OGAMUS are the following:

1. Object goal navigation (OBJNAV t_1): given an object type t_1, the agent has to find, go close to, and look at an object of type t_1. For instance, the agent has to go close to an apple and look at it. The corresponding goal is $\exists x(\mathsf{Apple}(x) \wedge \mathsf{CloseToAgent}(x) \wedge \mathsf{Visible}(x))$. The agent is close to an object when the distance from the object is less than 1.5 meter.
2. Open/close an object (OPEN/CLOSE t_1): the agent is required to go close to an object of type t_1, look at it, and open/close it. For instance the agent has to open a drawer; the corresponding goal is $\exists x(\mathsf{Drawer}(x) \wedge \mathsf{Open}(x))$. In order to manipulate an object the agent need to be at a distance less than 1.5 meter.
3. Stack an object of type t_1 on an object of type t_2 (ON t_1 t_2): the agent has to find two objects of types t_1 and t_2 and put the one of type t_1 on top of the other of type t_2. For instance the agent has to put an apple on a table. The corresponding goal is: $\exists xy(\mathsf{Apple}(x) \wedge \mathsf{Table}(y) \wedge \mathsf{On}(x, y))$.

Since these tasks do not involve numerical resources or temporal constraints, we adopted propositional PDDL planning.

Simulator. We used the ITHOR (Kolve et al. 2017) simulator, an open source interactive environment for Embodied AI. ITHOR provides 120 different scenes, such as kitchens, living-rooms, bathrooms, and bedrooms, and allows a realistic simulation of the environment, including the physics of the objects. The scenes contain objects of 118 different types. The agent perceives the current state of the environment through an RGB-D on-board camera that provides a photo-realistic rendering of its egocentric view. The agent also perceives its position and orientation via a GPS and a compass (relative to the initial pose, which is unknown). The agent can navigate the environment by moving ahead of a given distance (set to 25cm), turn left or right, and look up or down of a given angle (set to 30°).[2] The agent can pick up objects, move them around, and change their state (e.g., a fridge can be opened or a laptop switched on).

For the object goal navigation task, we also considered a second simulator, ROBOTHOR (Deitke et al. 2020). ROBOTHOR is another simulation environment designed to develop embodied AI agents. Recently, ROBOTHOR hosted a competition that tackles an object goal navigation challenge; in our experiments, we also compared OGAMUS with the approaches that took part in the competition.

Object detector. As an object detector we used the Faster-RCNN model available in PyTorch 1.9 (Paszke et al. 2019), pre-trained on the COCO dataset (Lin et al. 2014) and fine-tuned on a self-generated dataset. In addition to the bounding box of the detected object, the object detector returns also the classification in one of the 118 classes. The object detector has been trained on a dataset composed by 69,095 training and validation images. The labeling of the dataset has been done by using the ground-truth provided by ITHOR. We tested it on 12,892 images obtaining a precision and recall of 50.99% and 65.18%, respectively.

Predicate predictors. For predicting predicate ON, we trained a feed-forward neural network (Svozil, Kvasnicka, and Pospichal 1997) with 244 input features composed by the bounding boxes coordinates of the two objects involved in the predicate relation and the 1-hot encoding of the two predicted classes returned by the object detector. For such a predicate, the training (and validation) sets is composed of 36,344 labelled pairs of objects. We evaluate the prediction of predicate ON on a test set composed of 8678 object pairs, obtaining 98.32% of both precision and recall. For predicting the unary predicate OPEN, we used a ResNet50 neural network (He et al. 2016) to extract features from the cropped object image, followed by a linear layer with input size 2048.[3] We trained it on 48,476 labelled examples, and test it on 9685 examples, obtaining 92.84% precision and 92.54% recall. The unary predicate CLOSETOAGENT, meaning that the agent is near to the object mentioned by the predicate, is computed directly from the features of the object. Specifically, we check if the distance between the agent position memorized in $\boldsymbol{z}_s$ and the object position memorized in the object feature vector is less than the manipulation distance, which is set to 1.5 meter in ITHOR and 1 meter in ROBOTHOR. Finally, we have to predict the equality predicate, i.e., when two objects c and d with features $\boldsymbol{z}_c$ and $\boldsymbol{z}_d$ represent the same object. To this purpose, we compute the distance between the two estimated object positions, and assign the object features to the same object instance whether such a distance is lower than a given threshold (set to 20 cm in our experiments). All the training, validation, and testing data have been extracted from a set of images collected by navigating in the ITHOR simulator.

	Success ↑		*DTS* ↓		$P_\mathcal{C}$ ↑		$R_\mathcal{C}$ ↑		$P_\mathcal{P}$ ↑		$R_\mathcal{P}$ ↑	
	$\mathcal{C}$	$\mathcal{C}_{GT}$	$\mathcal{C}$	$\mathcal{C}_{GT}$	$\mathcal{C}$	$\mathcal{C}_{GT}$	$\mathcal{C}$	$\mathcal{C}_{GT}$	$\mathcal{C}$	$\mathcal{C}_{GT}$	$\mathcal{C}$	$\mathcal{C}_{GT}$
ON	0.5	0.8	1	0.37	0.28	1	0.86	1	0.83	0.82	0.8	0.87
OPEN	0.75	0.87	0.45	0.25	0.35	1	0.78	1	0.82	0.81	0.72	0.82
CLOSE	0.78	0.89	0.39	0.16	0.32	1	0.8	1	0.8	0.79	0.73	0.82
OBJNAV	0.78	0.83	0.27	0.19	0.42	1	0.8	1	0.82	0.8	0.75	0.84

Table 1: Performance of OGAMUS with/out the ground-truth object detection, evaluated on the considered tasks in the ITHOR simulator. ↑/↓ means the higher/lower the better.

Evaluation metrics. The evaluation is provided by calculating a number of standard metrics over a set of episodes. For each task, an episode is obtained by randomly placing the agent in a random unseen scene and providing it a randomly generated goal for the given task. The generated goals are feasible since the object types used in their definitions are randomly chosen from a proper set of types; e.g., the goal to open a box is defined by randomly choosing the type "box" from a the set of object types that can be opened. For all the tasks we adopt the following standard evaluation metrics:

- **Success rate (Success):** is equal to the fraction of successful episodes on the total number of episodes.
- **Distance To Success (DTS):** For tasks (OBJNAV t_1), (OPEN t_1), and (CLOSE t_1), it is the average distance between the agent and the closest object of type t_1; for the task (ON t_1 t_2), it is the average distance between the closest pair of objects of types t_1 and t_2. If the episode succeeds such a distance is set to 0.

In order to measure the impact of errors in object detecting, for each task we consider two versions of OGAMUS. In a version the set of objects $\mathcal{C}$ are those returned by our object detector; in the second version the set of objects $\mathcal{C}_{GT}$ are those returned by the ITHOR simulator, which corresponds to a ground-truth object detector. Moreover, for all tasks, we evaluate the precision $P_\mathcal{C}$ and recall $R_\mathcal{C}$ of the detected objects, and the precision $P_\mathcal{P}$ and recall $R_\mathcal{P}$ of their predicate relations. $P_\mathcal{P}$ and $R_\mathcal{P}$ take into account only the objects that match with ground-truth ones. The matching is performed by computing the Intersection over Union (IoU) among the 2D bounding box detected during the episode and the ground-truth ones: if the IoU is higher than 50% for a ground-truth object of the same class, then the detected object matches with it.

Experimental results. In our experiments, a run of OGAMUS consists of 200 steps, where at each step a low-level operation is performed; we call each of these runs an episode. For all tasks, the episode dataset uses the *test* scenes of ITHOR, i.e., all environments that does not appear in the

[2]These settings are those indicated by the simulator developers for their proposed challenges.

[3]Further technical details about the hyper-parameters and datasets are available in the supplementary material.

datasets generated for training the predicate classifiers and object detector.

In Table 1, we report the average results of all tasks with and without ground-truth object detection over the considered episodes. For task ON, we randomly generated 400 different goals, defining 400 episodes; for tasks OPEN and CLOSE, we randomly generated 100 goals, defining 100 episodes for each task; for the object goal navigation task, we used the test set of goals proposed in (Wortsman et al. 2019), defining 2133 episodes. It is worth noting that, for the object goal navigation task, two different episodes often have the same goal but a different initial pose of the agent.

The impact of errors in object detecting for tasks OBJNAV, OPEN and CLOSE is pretty low and, as expected, it is the half of the impact for task ON, since this latter task requires to detect two objects, while all other tasks requires to detect a single object. Without ground-truth object detection, OGAMUS achieves the best success rate on the object goal navigation task; same or similar results are also provided in tasks OPEN and CLOSE, since they can be seen as an extension of the object goal navigation task where, after finding and going near to an object, the agent has only to open or close the object. In the ON task, the success rate decreases significantly, because it requires moving towards two objects, instead of only one, and has two additional complexities given by the facts that one object must be placed on the other one in a clear place, i.e., a place not obstructed by other objects, and that the total encumbrance of the agent increases when it carries an object, which causes more collisions during the navigation.

Metric $P_{\mathcal{C}}$ measures the amount of false positive object detections. Although the value of $P_{\mathcal{C}}$ is quite low for almost all the tasks, the success rate is relatively high because: (i) many false positive objects are not involved in the goals definition; (ii) the agent acts by using the objects with the highest confidence, which usually correspond to ground truth objects. $P_{\mathcal{C}}$ is higher for the object goal navigation task, because in this task the agent achieves the goal in fewer steps than for other tasks, and this reduces the number of predictions and the chance of detecting false positive objects.

Metric $R_{\mathcal{C}}$ measures the amount of true positive detected objects. The values for $R_{\mathcal{C}}$ are quite high, and hence the real existing objects are often detected, although in our experiments the agent sometimes fails to recognize objects when they are far from the agent. Moreover, the values of $P_{\mathcal{P}}$ and $R_{\mathcal{P}}$ are relatively high, and hence the agent can construct a symbolic state that is quite correct and complete, enabling an effective planning.

As expected, when OGAMUS is provided with ground-truth object detection, all metrics are better than or similar to using our object detection. Only $P_{\mathcal{P}}$ is slightly lower when ground-truth object detection is used; we think this is due to the fact that sometimes the ground-truth object detection identifies objects which are only partially seen by the agent camera and predicting their properties more likely fails (e.g., the agent fails in predicting whether a fridge is open when it sees only a corner of the fridge).

	Success ↑	*SPL* ↑
Random	1.72%	1.33%
DD-PPO	35.11%	17.37%
DD-PPO$_{boost}$	36.61%	17.49%
OGAMUS	**56.78%**	**24.87%**

Table 2: Performance of OGAMUS w.r.t. the random baseline, DD-PPO, and DD-PPO$_{boost}$, evaluated on the object goal navigation task in the ROBOTHOR simulator.

4.2 Comparison on Object Goal Navigation

We did not find other approaches using simulator ITHOR that solve the tasks considered in our experiments. Therefore, in our experimental analysis we considered a second simulator, ROBOTHOR (Deitke et al. 2020), for which the last challenge concerning the object goal navigation was launched in 2021.

For the object goal navigation task, we compared OGAMUS with a random baseline, an RL baseline provided in the challenge, called DD-PPO, and the winner of the challenge, called DD-PPO$_{boost}$. Both the RL baseline and the winner exploit the DD-PPO algorithm (Wijmans et al. 2019) where the hidden state is computed by providing, as input to a GRU (Cho et al. 2014), the visual features of the RGB-D images computed by a ResNet-18 (He et al. 2016). The baseline and the winner approach have been trained on 108,000 episodes for 300 and about 10 million steps, respectively.

For this experiment, we adopt an additional metric, called Success weighted by Path Length (SPL) and introduced by Anderson et al. (2018). This metric measures the efficiency of the agent in reaching the goals and is defined as:

$$SPL = \frac{1}{N} \cdot \sum_{i=1}^{N} \left(s_i \cdot \frac{p_i^\star}{max(p_i, p_i^\star)} \right)$$

where N is the number of episodes, $p_i^\star$ is the shortest-path distance from the initial position of the agent to the closest goal in the i-th episode, p_i is the length of the agent path in the i-th episode, and s_i is a boolean variable equal to 1 when the i-th episode succeeds, and equal to 0 otherwise. If the path of the agent is the shortest one, the term in parenthesis is 1. The longer the path, the lower the term in parenthesis and the worse the metric.

For the experiment, we considered the validation episode dataset provided in the challenge, which is composed by 1800 episodes set in the 15 validation scenes of ROBOTHOR. We did not consider the test episode dataset of the challenge, because for such a dataset the evaluation can be done only by the organizers of the challenge who require that the evaluated approach plays by the challenge rule. This is not the case for OGAMUS because it allows the agent to perceive its pose, which is not available in the challenge. While the usage of this additional information can in principle favors OGAMUS w.r.t. the approaches that took part in the challenge, it is worth noting that the agent position can be approximately derived from the RGB-D egocentric views by means of visual simultaneous localization and mapping methods (Taketomi, Uchiyama, and Ikeda 2017). Most importantly, the usage of the validation dataset of ROBOTHOR

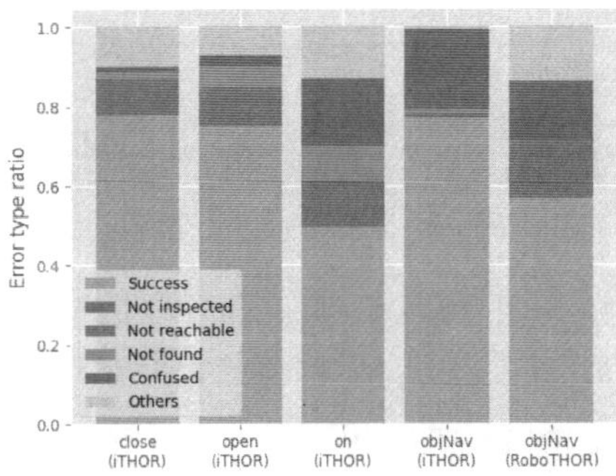

Figure 4: Ratio of the occurrences of different error types made by OGAMUS.

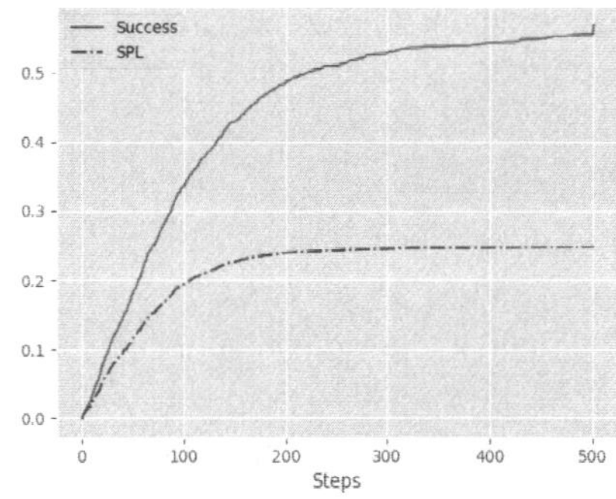

Figure 5: Average performance of OGAMUS for the goal object navigation task in the ROBOTHORsimulator, using a number of steps ranging from 0 to 500.

disfavors OGAMUS w.r.t. the other compared approaches because the object detector and predicate classifiers of OGAMUS are trained using the training and validation scenes of a different simulation environment, ITHOR, while the other compared approaches are trained and validated on the training and validation scenes of ROBOTHOR.

Each episode of the dataset consists of 500 steps, and regards finding and moving toward objects of 12 types. We trained an object detector similarly to the one for ITHOR simulator, but focused on the 12 goal object types of ROBOTHOR, which provides a performance slightly higher than the object detector trained using all the 118 object types of ITHOR, obtaining 59.02% precision and 69.06% recall.

Table 2 shows the results of the comparison. The random baseline provides poor performances. This indicates that, for the ROBOTHOR simulator, the object goal navigation task is quite challenging. The complexity of the task is confirmed by the performance of the RL baseline which is higher than the random baseline but still quite low. DD-PPO$_{boost}$ provides results slightly higher than the RL baseline. Remarkably, OGAMUS outperforms DD-PPO$_{boost}$ in terms of success rate and *SPL*. This confirms that the integration of symbolic planning with state recognition from sensory data can provide competitive results w.r.t. RL approaches.

4.3 Error Analysis

In Figure 4, we analyze the errors made by OGAMUS on all tasks. For few episodes, denoted as "Not inspected", the agent detects a far object of the same type as the type used for the goal definition, and subsequently approaches the object but is no more able to recognize it. This is due to the fact that either the object does not really exists, or the agent does not recognize an existing object, despite being close to and looking at it. For some episodes, namely "Not reachable", the agent finds a goal object but cannot reach a position close enough to the object. This can be due to the fact that either the agent collides or the goal object estimated position is farther than the real one. Collisions more often happen for the task ON, when the agent holds an object as the agent encumbrance increases. An error in the estimation of the object position is more likely for large objects, such as tables or televisions, since the agent considers the center of the object as its position. There are few episodes, labelled as "Not found", where the agent does not find the object, due to either an ineffective exploration of the environment or false negatives of the object detector. We observed that the latter case is more likely than the former, because the agent almost always explores the entire environment within the given number of steps. The errors labelled by "Confused" denote episodes for which the agent believes it succeeded while the task has not been completed. This is due to false positives of the object detector. Finally, "Others" denote all other task-dependent failures. E.g., for the ON, OPEN and CLOSE tasks, the agent sometimes fails to identify the object position when it has to manipulate an object. This more likely happens for small objects, such as spoons or saltshakers. Moreover, for the ON predicate an agent can fail to put an object on a table due to the fact that the target position is already occupied, or there is not enough space on the table.

Figure 5 shows the success rate and *SPL* for a number of steps ranging from 0 to 500. For almost all episodes the agent achieves the goal in 300 steps. For few episodes, the agent achieves the goal only after 500 steps. This happens because the agent is actually close to and looks at a goal object, but it fails to recognize the object.

5 Conclusions and Future Work

We have proposed a framework, called OGAMUS, for the online grounding of planning domains in unknown environments. Our approach enables an agent to map the sensory data into a symbolic state, allowing to perform and exploit efficient planning in a wide variety of different environments. We have tested the proposed method on different tasks obtaining better results than recent RL-based approaches. Future work will focus on learning a policy to compile the high-level actions into low-level executable operations, and on learning, online, the mapping of the sensory representations to symbolic ones.

Acknowledgments

This work is partially supported by the EU ICT-48 2020 project TAILOR (No. 952215) and the EU H2020 project AIPlan4EU (No. 101016442).

References

Anderson, P.; Chang, A.; Chaplot, D. S.; Dosovitskiy, A.; Gupta, S.; Koltun, V.; Kosecka, J.; Malik, J.; Mottaghi, R.; Savva, M.; et al. 2018. On evaluation of embodied navigation agents. *arXiv preprint arXiv:1807.06757.*

Campari, T.; Eccher, P.; Serafini, L.; and Ballan, L. 2020. Exploiting scene-specific features for object goal navigation. In *European Conference on Computer Vision*, 406–421. Springer.

Chaplot, D. S.; Gandhi, D.; Gupta, S.; Gupta, A.; and Salakhutdinov, R. 2019. Learning to explore using active neural slam. In *International Conference on Learning Representations.*

Chaplot, D. S.; Gandhi, D. P.; Gupta, A.; and Salakhutdinov, R. R. 2020. Object goal navigation using goal-oriented semantic exploration. In Larochelle, H.; Ranzato, M.; Hadsell, R.; Balcan, M. F.; and Lin, H., eds., *Advances in Neural Information Processing Systems*, volume 33, 4247–4258. Curran Associates, Inc.

Cho, K.; van Merriënboer, B.; Bahdanau, D.; and Bengio, Y. 2014. On the properties of neural machine translation: Encoder–decoder approaches. In *Proceedings of SSST-8, Eighth Workshop on Syntax, Semantics and Structure in Statistical Translation*, 103–111.

Coradeschi, S., and Saffiotti, A. 2003. An introduction to the anchoring problem. *Robotics and autonomous systems* 43(2-3):85–96.

Deitke, M.; Han, W.; Herrasti, A.; Kembhavi, A.; Kolve, E.; Mottaghi, R.; Salvador, J.; Schwenk, D.; VanderBilt, E.; Wallingford, M.; Weihs, L.; Yatskar, M.; and Farhadi, A. 2020. RoboTHOR: An Open Simulation-to-Real Embodied AI Platform. In *CVPR.*

Fang, K.; Toshev, A.; Fei-Fei, L.; and Savarese, S. 2019. Scene memory transformer for embodied agents in long-horizon tasks. In *Proceedings of the IEEE Conference on Computer Vision and Pattern Recognition*, 538–547.

Garnelo, M.; Arulkumaran, K.; and Shanahan, M. 2016. Towards deep symbolic reinforcement learning. *arXiv preprint arXiv:1609.05518.*

Ghallab, M.; Nau, D. S.; and Traverso, P. 2016. *Automated Planning and Acting.* Cambridge University Press.

He, K.; Zhang, X.; Ren, S.; and Sun, J. 2016. Deep residual learning for image recognition. In *Proceedings of the IEEE conference on computer vision and pattern recognition*, 770–778.

Kase, K.; Paxton, C.; Mazhar, H.; Ogata, T.; and Fox, D. 2020. Transferable task execution from pixels through deep planning domain learning. In *2020 IEEE International Conference on Robotics and Automation (ICRA)*, 10459–10465. IEEE.

Kolve, E.; Mottaghi, R.; Han, W.; VanderBilt, E.; Weihs, L.; Herrasti, A.; Gordon, D.; Zhu, Y.; Gupta, A.; and Farhadi, A. 2017. AI2-THOR: An Interactive 3D Environment for Visual AI. *arXiv.*

Lamanna, L.; Gerevini, A. E.; Saetti, A.; Serafini, L.; and Traverso, P. 2021a. On-line learning of planning domains from sensor data in pal: Scaling up to large state spaces. In *Proceedings of the AAAI Conference on Artificial Intelligence*, volume 35, 11862–11869.

Lamanna, L.; Saetti, A.; Serafini, L.; Gerevini, A.; and Traverso, P. 2021b. Online learning of action models for pddl planning. In *IJCAI-2021.*

Lin, T.-Y.; Maire, M.; Belongie, S.; Hays, J.; Perona, P.; Ramanan, D.; Dollár, P.; and Zitnick, C. L. 2014. Microsoft coco: Common objects in context. In *European conference on computer vision*, 740–755. Springer.

Lyu, D.; Yang, F.; Liu, B.; and Gustafson, S. 2019. Sdrl: interpretable and data-efficient deep reinforcement learning leveraging symbolic planning. In *Proceedings of the AAAI Conference on Artificial Intelligence*, volume 33, 2970–2977.

Ma, Z.; Zhuang, Y.; Weng, P.; Zhuo, H. H.; Li, D.; Liu, W.; and Hao, J. 2021. Learning symbolic rules for interpretable deep reinforcement learning. *arXiv preprint arXiv:2103.08228.*

Mirowski, P.; Pascanu, R.; Viola, F.; Soyer, H.; Ballard, A. J.; Banino, A.; Denil, M.; Goroshin, R.; Sifre, L.; Kavukcuoglu, K.; et al. 2017. Learning to navigate in complex environments. *ICLR.*

Mousavian, A.; Toshev, A.; Fišer, M.; Košecká, J.; Wahid, A.; and Davidson, J. 2019. Visual representations for semantic target driven navigation. In *2019 International Conference on Robotics and Automation (ICRA)*, 8846–8852. IEEE.

Paszke, A.; Gross, S.; Massa, F.; Lerer, A.; Bradbury, J.; Chanan, G.; Killeen, T.; Lin, Z.; Gimelshein, N.; Antiga, L.; et al. 2019. Pytorch: An imperative style, high-performance deep learning library. *Advances in neural information processing systems* 32:8026–8037.

Persson, A.; Dos Martires, P. Z.; De Raedt, L.; and Loutfi, A. 2019. Semantic relational object tracking. *IEEE Transactions on Cognitive and Developmental Systems* 12(1):84–97.

Savva, M.; Chang, A. X.; Dosovitskiy, A.; Funkhouser, T.; and Koltun, V. 2017. Minos: Multimodal indoor simulator for navigation in complex environments. *arXiv preprint arXiv:1712.03931.*

Svozil, D.; Kvasnicka, V.; and Pospichal, J. 1997. Introduction to multi-layer feed-forward neural networks. *Chemometrics and intelligent laboratory systems* 39(1):43–62.

Taketomi, T.; Uchiyama, H.; and Ikeda, S. 2017. Visual slam algorithms: a survey from 2010 to 2016. *IPSJ Transactions on Computer Vision and Applications* 9(1):1–11.

Wijmans, E.; Kadian, A.; Morcos, A.; Lee, S.; Essa, I.; Parikh, D.; Savva, M.; and Batra, D. 2019. Dd-ppo: Learning near-perfect pointgoal navigators from 2.5 billion frames. In *International Conference on Learning Representations*.

Wortsman, M.; Ehsani, K.; Rastegari, M.; Farhadi, A.; and Mottaghi, R. 2019. Learning to learn how to learn: Self-adaptive visual navigation using meta-learning. In *Proceedings of the IEEE/CVF Conference on Computer Vision and Pattern Recognition*, 6750–6759.

Ye, J.; Batra, D.; Das, A.; and Wijmans, E. 2021. Auxiliary tasks and exploration enable objectnav. *arXiv preprint arXiv:2104.04112*.

Applications and Systems

Proceedings of the 19th International Conference on Principles of Knowledge Representation and Reasoning
Applications and Systems

Querying Inconsistent Prioritized Data with ORBITS: Algorithms, Implementation, and Experiments

Meghyn Bienvenu[1] , **Camille Bourgaux**[2]
[1] CNRS, University of Bordeaux, Bordeaux INP, LaBRI, Talence, France
[2] DI ENS, ENS, CNRS, PSL University & Inria, Paris, France
meghyn.bienvenu@labri.fr, camille.bourgaux@ens.fr

Abstract

We investigate practical algorithms for inconsistency-tolerant query answering over prioritized knowledge bases, which consist of a logical theory, a set of facts, and a priority relation between conflicting facts. We consider three well-known semantics (AR, IAR and brave) based upon two notions of optimal repairs (Pareto and completion). Deciding whether a query answer holds under these semantics is (co)NP-complete in data complexity for a large class of logical theories, and SAT-based procedures have been devised for repair-based semantics when there is no priority relation, or the relation has a special structure. The present paper introduces the first SAT encodings for Pareto- and completion-optimal repairs w.r.t. general priority relations and proposes several ways of employing existing and new encodings to compute answers under (optimal) repair-based semantics, by exploiting different reasoning modes of SAT solvers. The comprehensive experimental evaluation of our implementation compares both (i) the impact of adopting semantics based on different kinds of repairs, and (ii) the relative performances of alternative procedures for the same semantics.

1 Introduction

The question of how to handle data that is inconsistent w.r.t. expressed constraints, be they given by database dependencies or ontologies, has great practical relevance. Data cleaning addresses this problem by modifying datasets so that they satisfy the constraints, often using heuristics to decide how to resolve contradictions, which may result in wrong facts being kept, or true facts removed (as discussed e.g. in (Fan 2015)). An alternative, more principled, approach is to adopt inconsistency-tolerant semantics in order to extract meaningful information from the contradictory data.

In the database setting, such an approach goes by the name of *consistent query answering* (CQA) and has been extensively studied since the seminal work of Arenas, Bertossi, and Chomicki (1999), see e.g. the recent survey by Wijsen (2019). A central notion is that of a *(subset) repair*, defined as a maximal subset of the dataset that satisfies the constraints. Intuitively, repairs represent all different ways of minimally modifying the data to satisfy the constraints. As we do not know which repair corresponds to the true part of the data, the CQA semantics stipulates that a tuple is a query answer if it is an answer w.r.t. every repair (in line with how skeptical inference is defined in many KR settings).

Inconsistency-tolerant semantics have also drawn considerable interest in the setting of ontology-mediated query answering (OMQA) (Poggi et al. 2008; Bienvenu and Ortiz 2015; Xiao et al. 2018), where the ontology not only specifies constraints on the data but also captures other forms of domain knowledge, which can be exploited at query time. In addition to the *AR semantics* (the OMQA analog of the CQA semantics), several other inconsistency-tolerant semantics have been proposed (see (Bienvenu and Bourgaux 2016; Bienvenu 2020) for surveys and references), among which: the *brave semantics* (Bienvenu and Rosati 2013), which only requires a tuple to be an answer w.r.t. some repair, provides a natural notion of possible answer, and the *IAR semantics* (Lembo et al. 2010), which answers queries over the intersection of the repairs, identifies the most reliable answers.

The basic notion of repair can be refined by exploiting preference information. A prominent approach, introduced by Staworko, Chomicki, and Marcinkowski (2012) in the database setting and recently explored in the OMQA setting (Bienvenu and Bourgaux 2020), assumes that preferences are given by a binary *priority relation* between conflicting facts. Three notions of 'best' repairs w.r.t. a priority relation were proposed, namely, Pareto-optimal, globally-optimal, and completion-optimal repairs, and can be used in place of subset repairs in any repair-based semantics.

The complexity of answering queries under (optimal) repair-based semantics has been extensively studied in the database and OMQA settings, refer to (Wijsen 2019; Bienvenu and Bourgaux 2016) for an overview and references. We can briefly summarize these (many!) complexity results as follows: query answering under the AR (or CQA) semantics is coNP-hard in data complexity even in the simplest of settings (e.g. key constraints, class disjointness), and adopting optimal repairs in place of subset repairs leads to (co)NP-hardness for the brave and IAR semantics as well. Membership in (co)NP holds for AR, brave, and IAR semantics w.r.t. subset, Pareto-optimal, and completion-optimal repairs in the most commonly considered settings i.e. for database constraints given by primary keys or more generally, functional dependencies (FDs), and for ontologies formulated in data-tractable description logics such as those of the DL-Lite family (Calvanese et al. 2007).

The preceding (co)NP complexity results naturally suggest the interest of employing SAT solvers. Two recent systems, CQAPri and CAvSAT, have begun to explore such an approach. CQAPri (Bienvenu, Bourgaux, and Goasdoué 2014; 2019) uses tractable approximations together with calls to SAT solvers to answer queries over inconsistent DL-Lite knowledge bases, under the AR, brave, and IAR semantics, w.r.t. subset repairs as well as optimal repairs for the restricted class of score-structured priority relations. CAvSAT (Dixit and Kolaitis 2019) targets relational databases equipped with denial constraints (which include FDs as a special case) and computes query answers under the AR semantics w.r.t. subset repairs. While geared to different forms of constraints, the two systems solve essentially the same problem, yet they employ SAT solvers in different ways. CQAPri makes a single SAT call for each candidate query answer, whereas CAvSAT treats all candidate answers at the same time via calls to a weighted MaxSAT solver.

This paper presents a comprehensive study of the use of SAT-based approaches for inconsistency-tolerant query answering, which abstracts from the particular setting and provides a solid foundation for the future development of such systems. Our contributions can be summarized as follows. In Section 3, we provide propositional encodings of the AR, brave, and IAR semantics, including the first encodings for Pareto- and completion-optimal repairs. Our encodings are generic and are built in a modular manner from a core set of basic formulas. Based upon these encodings, we develop in Section 4 several SAT-based algorithms, which utilize different functionalities of modern SAT solvers: weighted MaxSAT, MUS enumeration, iterative SAT calls with assumptions. In Section 5, we present our implemented system, ORBITS, which computes query answers under the chosen semantics using the selected encoding and algorithm. Section 6 presents the result of our extensive experimental evaluation, using existing OMQA and database benchmarks, aimed at comparing the different semantics, and understanding the relative performances of different encodings and/or algorithms for the same semantics. Proofs, pseudo-code for algorithms, and details on the experimental evaluation are provided in the appendix of (Bienvenu and Bourgaux 2022).

2 Querying Inconsistent Knowledge Bases

We introduce notation and terminology for talking about knowledge bases and then recall different inconsistency-tolerant semantics. We shall assume throughout the paper that readers are familiar with propositional and first-order logic. Key notions are illustrated in Example 1.

Knowledge bases By *knowledge base (KB)*, we mean a pair $\mathcal{K} = (\mathcal{D}, \mathcal{T})$ consisting of a *dataset* $\mathcal{D}$ and a *logical theory* $\mathcal{T}$. The dataset $\mathcal{D}$ is a finite set of ground *facts*, i.e. atoms $P(c_1, \ldots, c_n)$ where P is an n-ary predicate and each c_i is a constant. The theory $\mathcal{T}$ is a finite set of first-order logic (FOL) sentences. An $\mathcal{L}$ *KB* is a KB whose theory is formulated in the $\mathcal{L}$ fragment of FOL. Typically, $\mathcal{T}$ will be either an *ontology* (with $\mathcal{L}$ a description logic or decidable class of existential rules) or a set of *database constraints*, for instance, letting $\mathcal{L}$ be the class of *denial constraints*, which take the form $\forall \vec{x} \neg(\alpha_1 \wedge \ldots \wedge \alpha_n)$, where each α_i is a relational or inequality atom whose variables are among $\vec{x}$. Denial constraints generalize the more well-known functional dependencies (FDs) and (primary) key constraints.

A KB $\mathcal{K} = (\mathcal{D}, \mathcal{T})$ is *consistent*, and its dataset $\mathcal{D}$ is called $\mathcal{T}$*-consistent*, if $\mathcal{D} \cup \mathcal{T}$ has at least one model. Otherwise, $\mathcal{K}$ is *inconsistent*, denoted $\mathcal{K} \models \bot$. To identify the reasons for a KB $\mathcal{K} = (\mathcal{D}, \mathcal{T})$ being inconsistent, we use the notion of a *conflict* of $\mathcal{K}$, defined as an inclusion-minimal subset $\mathcal{D}' \subseteq \mathcal{D}$ such that $(\mathcal{D}', \mathcal{T}) \models \bot$. We use $Conf(\mathcal{K})$, or $Conf(\mathcal{D}, \mathcal{T})$, to refer to the set of all conflicts of $\mathcal{K} = (\mathcal{D}, \mathcal{T})$. Note that $Conf(\mathcal{D}, \mathcal{T}) \subseteq Conf(\mathcal{D}', \mathcal{T})$ whenever $\mathcal{D} \subseteq \mathcal{D}'$. In particular, this means that adding more facts cannot render an inconsistent KB consistent.

We will be interested in answering queries over KBs. In this paper, when we speak of queries, we mean *conjunctive queries*, which take the form of conjunctions of relational atoms $P(t_1, \ldots, t_n)$ (with each t_i a constant or variable), where some variables may be existentially quantified. Given a query $q(\vec{x})$, with free variables $\vec{x} = (x_1, \ldots, x_k)$, and a tuple of constants $\vec{a} = (a_1, \ldots, a_k)$, we denote by $q(\vec{a})$ the first-order sentence obtained by replacing each variable in $\vec{x}$ by the corresponding constant in $\vec{a}$. A *(certain) answer* to $q(\vec{x})$ over $\mathcal{K} = (\mathcal{D}, \mathcal{T})$ is a tuple of constants $\vec{a}$ from $\mathcal{D}$ such that $q(\vec{a})$ holds in every model of $\mathcal{K}$. We use $\mathcal{K} \models q(\vec{a})$ to indicate that $\vec{a}$ is a certain answer to $q(\vec{x})$ over $\mathcal{K}$.

Certain answers are preserved under the addition of facts: if $(\mathcal{D}, \mathcal{T}) \models q(\vec{a})$ and $\mathcal{D} \subseteq \mathcal{D}'$, then $(\mathcal{D}', \mathcal{T}) \models q(\vec{a})$. It thus makes sense to consider the minimal subsets of the data responsible for an answer. We call a $\mathcal{T}$-consistent subset $\mathcal{C} \subseteq \mathcal{D}$ a *cause* for $q(\vec{a})$ w.r.t. $\mathcal{K} = (\mathcal{D}, \mathcal{T})$ if $(\mathcal{C}, \mathcal{T}) \models q(\vec{a})$ and $(\mathcal{C}', \mathcal{T}) \not\models q(\vec{a})$ for every $\mathcal{C}' \subsetneq \mathcal{C}$; the set of causes for $q(\vec{a})$ w.r.t. $\mathcal{K}$ is denoted by $Causes(q(\vec{a}), \mathcal{K})$.

Observe that if $\mathcal{K}$ is inconsistent, then $\mathcal{K} \models q(\vec{a})$ for *every* candidate answer $\vec{a}$, which is uninformative and motivates the need for alternative inconsistency-tolerant semantics.

Repairs In order to extract meaningful information from an inconsistent KB, it is useful to consider the parts of the data that are consistent with the theory. This can be formalized using the notion of repair:

Definition 1. A *(subset) repair* of a KB $\mathcal{K} = (\mathcal{D}, \mathcal{T})$ is an inclusion-maximal subset $\mathcal{R} \subseteq \mathcal{D}$ such that $(\mathcal{R}, \mathcal{T}) \not\models \bot$. We use $SRep(\mathcal{K})$ to denote the set of repairs of KB $\mathcal{K}$.

Subset repairs treats all facts equally. However, preferences between conflicting facts should be taken into account when they are available. Following (Staworko, Chomicki, and Marcinkowski 2012; Bienvenu and Bourgaux 2020), we assume such preferences are given as a priority relation:

Definition 2. A *priority relation* $\succ$ for a KB $\mathcal{K} = (\mathcal{D}, \mathcal{T})$ is an acyclic binary relation over the facts of $\mathcal{D}$ such that if $\alpha \succ \beta$, then there exists $\mathcal{C} \in Conf(\mathcal{K})$ such that $\{\alpha, \beta\} \subseteq \mathcal{C}$. We say that $\succ$ is *total* if for every pair $\alpha \neq \beta$ such that $\{\alpha, \beta\} \subseteq \mathcal{C}$ for some $\mathcal{C} \in Conf(\mathcal{K})$, either $\alpha \succ \beta$ or $\beta \succ \alpha$. A *completion* of $\succ$ is a total priority relation $\succ' \supseteq \succ$.

Definition 3. A *prioritized KB* $\mathcal{K}_\succ$ consists of a KB $\mathcal{K} = (\mathcal{D}, \mathcal{T})$ and a priority relation $\succ$ for $\mathcal{K}$.

We recall two[1] natural ways of refining the notion of re-

[1] Staworko et al. (2012) defined a third notion, *globally-optimal repairs*, which we do not consider due to their higher complexity.

pair to exploit priority relations (Staworko, Chomicki, and Marcinkowski 2012; Bienvenu and Bourgaux 2020):

Definition 4. Consider a prioritized KB $\mathcal{K}_{\succ}$ with $\mathcal{K} = (\mathcal{D}, \mathcal{T})$, and let $\mathcal{R} \in SRep(\mathcal{K})$.

- A *Pareto improvement* of $\mathcal{R}$ is a $\mathcal{T}$-consistent $\mathcal{B} \subseteq \mathcal{D}$ such that there is $\beta \in \mathcal{B} \setminus \mathcal{R}$ with $\beta \succ \alpha$ for every $\alpha \in \mathcal{R} \setminus \mathcal{B}$.

The repair $\mathcal{R}$ is a:

- *Pareto-optimal repair* of $\mathcal{K}_{\succ}$ if there is no Pareto improvement of $\mathcal{R}$.
- *completion-optimal repair* of $\mathcal{K}_{\succ}$ if $\mathcal{R}$ is a Pareto-optimal repair of $\mathcal{K}_{\succ'}$, for some completion $\succ'$ of $\succ$.

We denote by $PRep(\mathcal{K}_{\succ})$ and $CRep(\mathcal{K}_{\succ})$ the sets of Pareto- and completion-optimal repairs.

It is known that $CRep(\mathcal{K}_{\succ}) \subseteq PRep(\mathcal{K}_{\succ}) \subseteq SRep(\mathcal{K})$, with each of the inclusions potentially strict. Interestingly, however, if $\succ$ is induced by assigning scores to facts, then Pareto- and completion-optimal repairs coincide:

Definition 5. A priority relation $\succ$ for $\mathcal{K} = (\mathcal{D}, \mathcal{T})$ is *score-structured* if there exists a scoring function $s : \mathcal{D} \to \mathbb{N}$ such that for every pair of facts α and β that appear together in a conflict of $\mathcal{K}$, we have $\alpha \succ \beta$ iff $s(\alpha) > s(\beta)$.

Theorem 1. *(Livshits and Kimelfeld 2017; Bourgaux 2016) Let $\mathcal{K}_{\succ}$ be a prioritized KB such that $\succ$ is score-structured. Then $CRep(\mathcal{K}_{\succ}) = PRep(\mathcal{K}_{\succ})$.*

Bourgaux (2016) further shows that for score-structured priorities, Pareto- and completion-optimal repairs also coincide with the $\subseteq_P$-repairs from (Bienvenu, Bourgaux, and Goasdoué 2014) based upon lexicographic set inclusion.

Repair-based semantics We next recall three prominent inconsistency-tolerant semantics (brave, AR, and IAR), which we parameterize by the considered type of repair:

Definition 6. Fix X $\in \{S, P, C\}$ and consider a prioritized KB $\mathcal{K}_{\succ}$ with $\mathcal{K} = (\mathcal{D}, \mathcal{T})$, query $q(\vec{x})$, and tuple of constants $\vec{a}$ from $\mathcal{D}$ with $|\vec{x}| = |\vec{a}|$. Then $\vec{a}$ is an answer to q over $\mathcal{K}_{\succ}$

- under *X-brave semantics*, denoted $\mathcal{K}_{\succ} \models^X_{\text{brave}} q(\vec{a})$, if $(\mathcal{R}, \mathcal{T}) \models q(\vec{a})$ for some $\mathcal{R} \in XRep(\mathcal{K}_{\succ})$
- under *X-AR semantics*, denoted $\mathcal{K}_{\succ} \models^X_{\text{AR}} q(\vec{a})$, if $(\mathcal{R}, \mathcal{T}) \models q(\vec{a})$ for every $\mathcal{R} \in XRep(\mathcal{K}_{\succ})$
- under *X-IAR semantics*, denoted $\mathcal{K}_{\succ} \models^X_{\text{IAR}} q(\vec{a})$, if $(\mathcal{B}, \mathcal{T}) \models q(\vec{a})$ where $\mathcal{B} = \bigcap_{\mathcal{R} \in XRep(\mathcal{K}_{\succ})} \mathcal{R}$

The AR semantics is arguably the most natural way of defining *plausible* query answers, and it is the semantics used for consistent query answering in databases (Bertossi 2011). The brave semantics captures the notion of *possible* answers, while the IAR semantics identifies the answers that can be obtained using only the *most reliable* facts. Observe that $\mathcal{K}_{\succ} \models^X_{\text{IAR}} q \Rightarrow \mathcal{K}_{\succ} \models^X_{\text{AR}} q \Rightarrow \mathcal{K}_{\succ} \models^X_{\text{brave}} q$.

Example 1. Let $\mathcal{K} = (\mathcal{D}, \mathcal{T})$ where $\mathcal{D}$ contains four facts $\alpha = R(a, b)$, $\beta = R(a, c)$, $\gamma = S(d, c)$, and $\delta = S(d, b)$, and $\mathcal{T}$ contains FDs $\forall x, y, z \neg(R(x, y) \wedge R(x, z) \wedge y \neq z)$, $\forall x, y, z \neg(S(x, y) \wedge S(x, z) \wedge y \neq z)$ and the denial constraint $\forall x, y, z \neg(R(y, x) \wedge S(z, x))$.

The conflicts of $\mathcal{K}$ are $\{\alpha, \beta\}$, $\{\gamma, \delta\}$, $\{\alpha, \delta\}$ and $\{\beta, \gamma\}$, hence $SRep(\mathcal{K}) = \{\{\alpha, \gamma\}, \{\beta, \delta\}\}$. If we define $\succ$ by $\alpha \succ \beta$ and $\gamma \succ \delta$, we obtain $PRep(\mathcal{K}_{\succ}) = SRep(\mathcal{K})$ but $CRep(\mathcal{K}_{\succ}) = \{\{\alpha, \gamma\}\}$. Indeed, any completion $\succ'$ of $\succ$ is such that $\alpha \succ' \delta$ or $\gamma \succ' \beta$ by acyclicity.

If $q(x) = \exists y R(x, y)$, $Causes(q(a), \mathcal{K}) = \{\{\alpha\}, \{\beta\}\}$. Hence, $\mathcal{K}_{\succ} \models^C_{\text{IAR}} q(a)$, $\mathcal{K}_{\succ} \models^P_{\text{AR}} q(a)$ but $\mathcal{K}_{\succ} \not\models^P_{\text{IAR}} q(a)$.

We briefly recall what is known about the complexity of query answering under (optimal) repair-based semantics. Note that *when we speak of complexity, we mean data complexity*, measured solely in terms of the size of the dataset.

Theorems 2 and 3 summarize upper and lower bounds from the database and ontology settings. All of them are known (Staworko, Chomicki, and Marcinkowski 2012; Bienvenu and Bourgaux 2020; Rosati 2011), except the lower bounds for X-brave and X-IAR semantics in the case of FDs, proven in (Bienvenu and Bourgaux 2022). We say that a logic $\mathcal{L}$ *enjoys* PTIME *consistency checking (resp. query entailment)* if the problem of deciding whether $\mathcal{K} \models \bot$ (resp. $\mathcal{K} \models q(\vec{a})$) for an input $\mathcal{L}$ KB is in PTIME.

Theorem 2. *Let $\mathcal{L}$ be any FOL fragment that enjoys* PTIME *consistency checking and query entailment, and let $X \in \{S, P, C\}$. Then query entailment for $\mathcal{L}$ KBs is*

- *in* NP *under X-brave semantics, and*
- *in* coNP *under X-AR and X-IAR semantics.*

Theorem 3. *Query entailment for $\mathcal{L}$ KBs is*

- NP*-hard under X-brave semantics ($X \in \{P, C\}$)*
- coNP*-hard under X-AR semantics ($X \in \{S, P, C\}$)*
- coNP*-hard under X-IAR semantics ($X \in \{P, C\}$)*

for any $\mathcal{L}$ that extends DL-Lite$_{\text{core}}$, $\mathcal{EL}_\bot$, or FDs.

Remark 1. Query entailment under S-brave and S-IAR is tractable both for DL-Lite ontologies and denial constraints (Bienvenu and Rosati 2013).

3 SAT Encodings

The (co)NP complexity results from the previous section suggest a SAT-based approach to query entailment under (optimal) repair-based semantics. While our work is not the first to explore SAT encodings for inconsistency-tolerant semantics, our contribution is a uniform approach that covers a wide range of semantics and settings, and provides the first encodings for Pareto- and completion-optimal repairs.

3.1 Overview

Our propositional encodings are built from:

- the set $Conf(\mathcal{K})$ of conflicts of the considered KB $\mathcal{K}$,
- a set $PotAns$ of *potential answers*, and for each $\vec{a} \in PotAns$, the (non-empty[2]) set $Causes(q(\vec{a}), \mathcal{K})$,
- the priority relation $\succ$ of $\mathcal{K}$,

and are of polynomial size w.r.t. to these inputs. Note that for DL-Lite ontologies and denial constraints, the sets of conflicts, candidate answers, and their causes, can be computed in PTIME via database query evaluation, so our encodings will yield procedures of the expected co(NP) complexity.

[2]If $Causes(q(\vec{a}), \mathcal{K}) = \emptyset$, $q(\vec{a})$ holds for none of our semantics.

To simplify the treatment, *we shall assume that every conflict contains at most two facts*, a property that is satisfied by the most common DL-Lite dialects and for FDs. (The extension to non-binary conflicts is discussed later in the section.) By restricting our attention to binary conflicts, we can *use a convenient notation $\alpha \bot \beta$ in place of $\{\alpha, \beta\} \in Conf(\mathcal{K})$*, and define a graph representation of conflicts and priorities. The *directed conflict graph $\mathcal{G}_{\mathcal{K}_\succ}$* has facts from $Conf(\mathcal{K})$ as nodes and an edge from α to β iff $\alpha \bot \beta$ and $\alpha \not\succ \beta$.

Our encodings will use variables of the form x_α to indicate whether fact α appears in a (partial) repair. Including one such variable for each fact in $\mathcal{D}$ would yield prohibitively large encodings, which is why we use $\mathcal{G}_{\mathcal{K}_\succ}$ to focus on relevant facts: given any $F \subseteq \mathcal{D}$, we let $\mathsf{R}(F)$ be the set of all *facts that are reachable in $\mathcal{G}_{\mathcal{K}_\succ}$* from some $\alpha \in F$.

Before proceeding to the details, let us give a high-level overview of our encodings. All of the encodings try to construct a set of facts that is consistent with the theory (i.e. does not contain any conflicts) and that can be extended to an optimal repair. For the X-AR semantics, we are trying to build an optimal repair that does *not* entail the considered query answer(s), which can be done by including facts that contradict each of the answer(s) causes. For the X-brave semantics, we must ensure that the repair entails the considered query answer(s), achieved by requiring the presence of some cause in the chosen subset. Finally, for the X-IAR semantics, we ensure the existence of optimal repairs that omit a given cause or fact appearing in a cause by including facts that contradict the considered cause or fact.

In the next section, we will present SAT-based algorithms that consider each potential answer in turn, as well as algorithms that treat all potential answers conjointly. For that reason, in what follows, we will present encodings both for a single answer and for several answers at a time.

3.2 Basic Building Blocks

Our various encodings rely upon some common ingredients, which are presented next.

Absence or presence of causes To contradict a specific cause C, we use $\varphi_{\neg C}$, with two alternative definitions inspired respectively by the CQAPri and CAvSAT encodings:

$$\varphi_{\neg C} = \bigvee_{\alpha \in C} \bigvee_{\alpha \bot \beta, \alpha \not\succ \beta} x_\beta \qquad (\mathsf{neg}_1)$$

$$\varphi_{\neg C} = \bigvee_{\alpha \in C} \neg x_\alpha \wedge \bigwedge_{\alpha \in C} (x_\alpha \vee \bigvee_{\alpha \bot \beta, \alpha \not\succ \beta} x_\beta) \qquad (\mathsf{neg}_2)$$

For encodings with multiple answers, we use a variant $\varphi'_{\neg C}(y)$ obtained by adding $\neg y$ as a disjunct of the (first) clause of $\varphi_{\neg C}$, so it is only 'active' when the given variable y is true. To block all causes of the BCQ $q(\vec{a})$, we can use

$$\varphi_{\neg q(\vec{a})} = \bigwedge_{C \in Causes(q(\vec{a}), \mathcal{K})} \varphi_{\neg C}$$

or, in the case of encodings for several answers, a variant $\varphi'_{\neg q(\vec{a})}$ obtained by replacing $\varphi_{\neg C}$ by $\varphi'_{\neg C}(x_{\vec{a}})$.

If instead we want to force that cause C holds, we use:

$$\varphi_C = \bigwedge_{\alpha \in C} x_\alpha$$

and to ensure *some* cause for BCQ $q(\vec{a})$ is present, we use:

$$\varphi_{q(\vec{a})} = (\bigvee_{C \in Causes(q(\vec{a}), \mathcal{K})} x_C) \wedge \bigwedge_{C \in Causes(q(\vec{a}), \mathcal{K})} \bigwedge_{\alpha \in C} \neg x_C \vee x_\alpha$$

or, for multi-answer encodings, a variant $\varphi'_{q(\vec{a})}$ obtained from $\varphi_{q(\vec{a})}$ by adding $\neg x_{\vec{a}}$ as a disjunct of the first clause.

Consistency We use $\varphi_{\mathsf{cons}}(F)$ to ensure that the valuation of $\{x_\alpha \mid \alpha \in F\}$ corresponds to a $\mathcal{T}$-consistent set of facts:

$$\varphi_{\mathsf{cons}}(F) = \bigwedge_{\alpha, \beta \in F, \alpha \bot \beta} \left(\neg x_\alpha \vee \neg x_\beta\right).$$

Extension to optimal repair The most intricate part of the encoding is ensuring that the selected set of facts can be extended to a repair of the desired type. To this end, we introduce formulas of the form $\varphi_{\mathsf{X\text{-}max}}(F)$, where F provides the facts that may appear, and X is the type of repair.

- Subset repairs: we can simply set $\varphi_{\mathsf{S\text{-}max}}(F) = \top$, as every consistent set of facts extends to some S-repair.
- Pareto-optimal repairs: we prove that the following encoding of maximality for $\subseteq_P$-repairs (w.r.t. score-structured $\succ$) from Bienvenu et al. (2014) in fact also works for Pareto-optimal repairs and arbitrary $\succ$:

$$\varphi_{\mathsf{P_1\text{-}max}}(F) = \bigwedge_{\alpha \in \mathsf{R}(F)} (x_\alpha \vee \bigvee_{\alpha \bot \beta, \alpha \not\succ \beta} x_\beta)$$

  Essentially, it states that a relevant fact can only be omitted if we include a non-dominated contradicting fact. We also propose an alternative encoding with fewer variables:

$$\varphi_{\mathsf{P_2\text{-}max}}(F) = \bigwedge_{\alpha \in \mathsf{R}^-(F)} \bigwedge_{\beta \succ \alpha} (\neg x_\alpha \vee \bigvee_{\beta \bot \gamma, \beta \not\succ \gamma} x_\gamma)$$

  where $\mathsf{R}^-(F) = \bigcup_{i=1}^{\infty} \mathsf{R}_i$ with $\mathsf{R}_0 = F$ and

$$\mathsf{R}_{i+1} = \mathsf{R}_i \cup \{\gamma \mid \exists \alpha \in \mathsf{R}_i, \beta \succ \alpha, \beta \bot \gamma, \beta \not\succ \gamma\}.$$

  Intuitively, to include $\alpha \in F$, we must contradict every more preferred fact that conflicts with α, then do the same for selected contradicting facts.
- Completion-optimal repairs (w.r.t. arbitrary $\succ$): we use

$$\varphi_{\mathsf{C\text{-}max}}(F) = \varphi_{\mathsf{pref}} \wedge \varphi_{\mathsf{compl}} \wedge \varphi_{\mathsf{acyc}}$$

  where the subformulas φ_{pref}, φ_{compl}, and φ_{acyc} are defined in Figure 1. The formula φ_{pref} states that if x_α is omitted, then we must include a contradicting fact β that is preferred to α according to $\succ'$. We use φ_{compl} to ensure that $\succ'$ compares all contradicting facts and extends $\succ$, while the acyclicity of $\succ'$ is ensured by φ_{acyc}, which uses variables $t_{\alpha,\beta}$ to compute the transitive closure of $\succ'$.

Non-binary conflicts We briefly discuss how to modify the preceding formulas to handle non-binary conflicts. The most essential difference is that instead of choosing a single contradicting fact, we may need to choose a conjunction of facts, and use additional variables to refer to them. We must also redefine $\mathcal{G}_{\mathcal{K}_\succ}$ as a directed hypergraph, and use hypergraph reachability to define $\mathsf{R}(F)$. Details of the required modifications are provided in (Bienvenu and Bourgaux 2022).

$$\varphi_{\mathsf{pref}} = \bigwedge_{\alpha \in \mathsf{R}(F)} \Big(x_\alpha \vee \bigvee_{\beta \in \mathsf{R}(F), \alpha \perp \beta} x_{\beta \to \alpha}\Big) \wedge \bigwedge_{\alpha,\beta \in \mathsf{R}(F), \alpha \perp \beta} \Big((\neg x_{\beta \to \alpha} \vee x_\beta) \wedge (\neg x_{\beta \to \alpha} \vee x_{\beta \succ' \alpha})\Big)$$

$$\varphi_{\mathsf{compl}} = \bigwedge_{\alpha,\beta \in \mathsf{R}(F), \alpha \perp \beta} \Big(x_{\alpha \succ' \beta} \vee x_{\beta \succ' \alpha}\Big) \wedge \bigwedge_{\alpha,\beta \in \mathsf{R}(F), \alpha \perp \beta} \Big(\neg x_{\alpha \succ' \beta} \vee \neg x_{\beta \succ' \alpha}\Big) \wedge \bigwedge_{\alpha,\beta \in \mathsf{R}(F), \alpha \succ \beta} x_{\alpha \succ' \beta}$$

$$\varphi_{\mathsf{acyc}} = \bigwedge_{\alpha,\beta \in \mathsf{R}(F), \alpha \perp \beta} \Big(\neg x_{\alpha \succ' \beta} \vee t_{\alpha,\beta}\Big) \wedge \bigwedge_{\alpha,\beta \in \mathsf{R}(F), \alpha \perp \beta} \Big(\neg x_{\alpha \succ' \beta} \vee \neg t_{\beta,\alpha}\Big) \wedge \bigwedge_{\alpha,\beta,\gamma \in \mathsf{R}(F), \beta \perp \gamma} \Big(\neg t_{\alpha,\beta} \vee \neg x_{\beta \succ' \gamma} \vee t_{\alpha,\gamma}\Big)$$

Figure 1: Subformulas of $\varphi_{\mathsf{C\text{-}max}}(F)$, which is used to ensure it is possible to extend the selected subset of F to a completion-optimal repair.

3.3 Propositional Encodings

We now present our encodings, built from the preceding components following the intuitions given in Section 3.1.

Note that the following results hold no matter which variant of $\varphi_{\neg\mathcal{C}}$ we use and with $\varphi_{\mathsf{P\text{-}max}}$ instantiated as either $\varphi_{\mathsf{P_1\text{-}max}}$ or $\varphi_{\mathsf{P_2\text{-}max}}$. The notation $\mathsf{facts}(\varphi)$ will be used for the set of facts α such that the variable x_α occurs in φ.

X-AR semantics Formula $\Phi_{X\text{-}AR}(q(\vec{a}))$ in Figure 2 is used to test whether a particular tuple $\vec{a}$ holds. Roughly speaking, it selects a way to contradict every clause, checking that the resulting set of facts is contained in a X-optimal repair. The second formula $\Psi_{X\text{-}AR}(PotAns)$ simultaneously handles all tuples in $PotAns$. Clauses of the form $x_{\vec{a}}$ can be added to activate $\varphi'_{\neg q(\vec{a})}$.

The correctness of our encodings is given in the next result, which applies to all $X \in \{S, P, C\}$ and $\vec{a} \in PotAns$:

Theorem 4. *The following are equivalent : (i)* $\mathcal{K}_\succ \models^X_{AR} q(\vec{a})$, *(ii)* $\Phi_{X\text{-}AR}(q(\vec{a}))$ *is unsatisfiable, and (iii)* $x_{\vec{a}}$ *is false in every satisfying assignment of* $\Psi_{X\text{-}AR}(PotAns)$.

X-brave semantics Figure 2 presents our encodings for the X-brave semantics. Formula $\Phi_{X\text{-}brave}(q(\vec{a}))$ checks a particular tuple $\vec{a}$ and is essentially the same as $\Phi_{X\text{-}AR}(q(\vec{a}))$, but with $\varphi_{q(\vec{a})}$ in place of $\varphi_{\neg q(\vec{a})}$. A variant $\Phi_{X\text{-}brave}(\mathcal{C})$ can be used to check whether a particular cause $\mathcal{C}$ holds in some X-optimal repair. For a multi-answer encodings, we use the formula $\Psi_{X\text{-}brave}(PotAns)$, again adding clauses of the form $x_{\vec{a}}$ to activate $\varphi'_{q(\vec{a})}$. We obtain an analogous correctness result:

Theorem 5. *The following are equivalent: (i)* $\mathcal{K}_\succ \models^X_{brave} q(\vec{a})$, *(ii)* $\Phi_{X\text{-}brave}(q(\vec{a}))$ *is satisfiable, (iii)* $\Phi_{X\text{-}brave}(\mathcal{C})$ *is satisfiable for some* $\mathcal{C} \in Causes(q(\vec{a}), \mathcal{K})$, *and (iv)* $x_{\vec{a}}$ *is true in some satisfying assignment of* $\Psi_{X\text{-}brave}(PotAns)$.

X-IAR semantics Formula $\Phi_{X\text{-}IAR}(\mathcal{C})$ from Figure 2 can be used to test whether there exists a X-optimal repair that excludes cause $\mathcal{C}$. To check a potential answer $\vec{a}$, we use $\Phi_{X\text{-}IAR}(q(\vec{a}))$, which is essentially the conjunction of $\Phi_{X\text{-}IAR}(\mathcal{C})$ for every cause $\mathcal{C}$ of $q(\vec{a})$, but where the *conjuncts for different causes use distinct variables* ($x^{\mathcal{C}}_\alpha$ in place of x_α). A multi-answer encoding $\Psi_{X\text{-}IAR}(PotAns)$ can be obtained by taking the conjunction of $\Phi_{X\text{-}IAR}(q(\vec{a}))$ for all $\vec{a} \in PotAns$, but with $\varphi^{\mathcal{C}}_{\neg\mathcal{C}}$ replaced by $\varphi'^{\mathcal{C}}_{\neg\mathcal{C}}(x_{\vec{a}})$ (see the appendix of (Bienvenu and Bourgaux 2022) for details). We obtain the following:

Theorem 6. *The following are equivalent: (i)* $\mathcal{K}_\succ \models^X_{IAR} q(\vec{a})$, *(ii)* $\Phi_{X\text{-}IAR}(q(\vec{a}))$ *is unsatisfiable, (iii)* $\Phi_{X\text{-}IAR}(\mathcal{C})$ *is unsatisfiable for some* $\mathcal{C} \in Causes(q(\vec{a}), \mathcal{K})$, *and (iv)* $x_{\vec{a}}$ *is false in every satisfying assignment of* $\Psi_{X\text{-}IAR}(PotAns)$.

We shall also require encodings for individual facts, using

$$\Phi_{X\text{-}IAR}(\alpha) = \Phi_{X\text{-}IAR}(\{\alpha\})$$

to test if α holds in all X-optimal repairs. We also consider a multi-fact version $\Psi_{X\text{-}IAR}(Rel)$, parameterized by a set of facts Rel, and to which we add clause y_α to activate $\varphi'_{\neg\{\alpha\}}(y_\alpha)$.

Theorem 7. *For every* $\alpha \in \mathcal{D}$, *the following are equivalent: (i)* $\mathcal{K}_\succ \models^X_{IAR} \alpha$, *(ii)* $\Phi_{X\text{-}IAR}(\alpha)$ *is unsatisfiable, and (iii) if* $\alpha \in Rel$ *then* y_α *is false in every satisfying assignment of* $\Psi_{X\text{-}IAR}(Rel)$.

4 Algorithms

Inspired by the different use of SAT solvers made by CQAPri and CAvSAT, we propose several algorithms based on the encodings of Section 3. The pseudo code of all algorithms is available in (Bienvenu and Bourgaux 2022).

Before describing the algorithms, note that we can show that the encodings of Section 3 are still valid if $Causes(q(\vec{a}), \mathcal{K})$ is actually *a superset of the causes* such that every superfluous $\mathcal{B}$ in it either (1) includes a real cause of $q(\vec{a})$ or (2) contains two distinct facts that form a conflict. Since checking consistency and minimality to obtain the real causes can be costly in practice, our algorithms accept such 'sets of causes'. They actually even accept the presence of self-inconsistent facts in the 'causes' (which would make the encodings for X-AR and X-IAR not applicable) and handle them in a preprocessing step.

Our high-level algorithm takes as input a semantics Sem $\in$ {brave, AR, IAR}, a repair notion $X \in \{S, P, C\}$, a directed conflict graph $\mathcal{G}_{\mathcal{K}_\succ}$, and a set of potential answers $PotAns$ with their causes, and outputs the set of tuples from $PotAns$ that are answers under the X-Sem semantics.

An initial preprocessing step serves to (1) check whether $\mathcal{G}_{\mathcal{K}_\succ}$ contains some self-inconsistent facts, remove them from $\mathcal{G}_{\mathcal{K}_\succ}$, discard all causes that contain such facts, then all answers that do not have any cause left, and (2) find some answers that trivially hold under X-Sem. To do so, it removes from the causes all facts that do not have any outgoing edge in the directed conflict graph, and thus trivially belong to all

$$\Phi_{X\text{-}AR}(q(\vec{a})) = \varphi_{\neg q(\vec{a})} \wedge \varphi_{\text{X-max}}(F_1) \wedge \varphi_{\text{cons}}(F_2) \qquad F_1 = \text{facts}(\varphi_{\neg q(\vec{a})}), F_2 = F_1 \cup \text{facts}(\varphi_{\text{X-max}}(F_1))$$

$$\Psi_{X\text{-}AR}(PotAns) = \bigwedge_{\vec{a} \in PotAns} \varphi'_{\neg q(\vec{a})} \wedge \varphi_{\text{X-max}}(F'_1) \wedge \varphi_{\text{cons}}(F'_2) \qquad F'_1 = \text{facts}(\bigwedge_{\vec{a} \in PotAns} \varphi'_{\neg q(\vec{a})}), F'_2 = F'_1 \cup \text{facts}(\varphi_{\text{X-max}}(F'_1))$$

$$\Phi_{X\text{-}brave}(q(\vec{a})) = \varphi_{q(\vec{a})} \wedge \varphi_{\text{X-max}}(G_1) \wedge \varphi_{\text{cons}}(G_2) \qquad G_1 = \text{facts}(\varphi_{q(\vec{a})}), G_2 = G_1 \cup \text{facts}(\varphi_{\text{X-max}}(G_1))$$

$$\Phi_{X\text{-}brave}(\mathcal{C}) = \varphi_{\mathcal{C}} \wedge \varphi_{\text{X-max}}(G_1^*) \wedge \varphi_{\text{cons}}(G_2^*) \qquad G_1^* = \text{facts}(\varphi_{\mathcal{C}}), G_2^* = G_1^* \cup \text{facts}(\varphi_{\text{X-max}}(G_1^*))$$

$$\Psi_{X\text{-}brave}(PotAns) = \bigwedge_{\vec{a} \in PotAns} \varphi'_{q(\vec{a})} \wedge \varphi_{\text{X-max}}(G'_1) \wedge \varphi_{\text{cons}}(G'_2) \qquad G'_1 = \text{facts}(\bigwedge_{\vec{a} \in PotAns} \varphi'_{q(\vec{a})}), G'_2 = G'_1 \cup \text{facts}(\varphi_{\text{X-max}}(G'_1))$$

$$\Phi_{X\text{-}IAR}(\mathcal{C}) = \varphi_{\neg\mathcal{C}} \wedge \varphi_{\text{X-max}}(H_1) \wedge \varphi_{\text{cons}}(H_2) \qquad H_1 = \text{facts}(\varphi_{\neg\mathcal{C}}), H_2 = H_1 \cup \text{facts}(\varphi_{\text{X-max}}(H_1))$$

$$\Phi_{X\text{-}IAR}(q(\vec{a})) = \bigwedge_{\mathcal{C} \in Causes(q(\vec{a}),\mathcal{K})} \left(\varphi^{\mathcal{C}}_{\neg\mathcal{C}} \wedge \varphi^{\mathcal{C}}_{\text{X-max}}(H_1^{\mathcal{C}}) \wedge \varphi^{\mathcal{C}}_{\text{cons}}(H_2^{\mathcal{C}})\right) \qquad H_1^{\mathcal{C}} = \text{facts}(\varphi^{\mathcal{C}}_{\neg\mathcal{C}}), H_2^{\mathcal{C}} = H_1^{\mathcal{C}} \cup \text{facts}(\varphi^{\mathcal{C}}_{\text{X-max}}(H_1^{\mathcal{C}}))$$

Figure 2: Single- and multi-answer encodings for X-AR (top) and X-brave (middle) semantics, single-answer encodings for X-IAR (bottom).

optimal repairs. The *trivial answers* that have some cause that contains only such facts hold under X-Sem semantics and are filtered during this step.

It then remains to filter the remaining potential answers. The four first algorithms we propose to do so are generic in the sense that they can be used for all semantics.

- Simple is similar to the algorithm used by CQAPri. For each answer to filter $\vec{a}$, it checks whether $\Phi_{X\text{-Sem}}(q(\vec{a}))$ is satisfiable, which decides whether $\mathcal{K}_{\succ} \models^{X}_{\text{Sem}} q(\vec{a})$.
- All-MaxSAT is similar to the CAvSAT algorithm. It constructs a weighted MaxSAT instance $\Psi_{X\text{-Sem}}(PotAns) \wedge \bigwedge_{\vec{a} \in PotAns} x_{\vec{a}}$, where the $x_{\vec{a}}$ are soft clauses, and all other clauses are hard. It then relies on the solver to maximize the number of soft clauses satisfied, which filters the corresponding answers. After each iteration, the $\neg x_{\vec{a}}$ corresponding to the satisfied soft clauses are added to the set of assumed literals for the next iteration.
- All-MUSes is based on the observation that if $x_{\vec{a}}$ is false in every satisfying assignment of $\Psi_{X\text{-Sem}}(PotAns)$, then $\{x_{\vec{a}}\}$ is a minimal unsatisfiable subset (MUS) of $\bigwedge_{\vec{a} \in PotAns} x_{\vec{a}}$ w.r.t. $\Psi_{X\text{-Sem}}(PotAns)$. All-MUSes relies on the solver to compute all MUSes, and decides whether $\mathcal{K}_{\succ} \models^{X}_{\text{Sem}} q(\vec{a})$ by looking at those of size one.
- Assumptions iteratively evaluates $\Psi_{X\text{-Sem}}(PotAns)$, treating the variables $x_{\vec{a}}$, with $\vec{a} \in PotAns$ as assumptions. If $\Psi_{X\text{-Sem}}(PotAns)[x_{\vec{a}}]$ is satisfiable, there exists a satisfying assignment of $\Psi_{X\text{-Sem}}(PotAns)$ in which $x_{\vec{a}}$ is true, which decides whether $\mathcal{K}_{\succ} \models^{X}_{\text{Sem}} q(\vec{a})$.

While we may need to consider all causes to decide whether an answer holds under X-AR semantics, in the X-brave or X-IAR case it is sufficient to find a single cause that belongs to some or all optimal repairs. Moreover, the encoding $\Phi_{X\text{-}IAR}(q(\vec{a}))$ is a conjunction of independent subproblems built on distinct variables for each cause, which does not seem very fit for a SAT solver. We hence propose algorithms specific to these cases.

- Cause-by-cause can be used for X-brave and X-IAR. For each answer to filter $\vec{a}$, it checks whether there is a cause $\mathcal{C}$ of $q(\vec{a})$ such that $\Phi_{X\text{-Sem}}(\mathcal{C})$ is (un)satisfiable: if Sem = brave and $\Phi_{X\text{-Sem}}(\mathcal{C})$ is satisfiable, or Sem = IAR and $\Phi_{X\text{-Sem}}(\mathcal{C})$ is unsatisfiable, then $\mathcal{K}_{\succ} \models^{X}_{\text{Sem}} q(\vec{a})$; if no cause witnesses $\mathcal{K}_{\succ} \models^{X}_{\text{Sem}} q(\vec{a})$, then $\mathcal{K}_{\succ} \not\models^{X}_{\text{Sem}} q(\vec{a})$.
- IAR-causes is specific to X-IAR. It considers the answers in turn while maintaining two sets of facts: the X-IAR facts that belong to the intersection of the optimal repairs and the non-X-IAR facts. For each cause $\mathcal{C}$ of $q(\vec{a})$ that does not contain any known non X-IAR fact, it removes the known X-IAR facts from $\mathcal{C}$. If $\mathcal{C}$ becomes empty, then $\mathcal{K}_{\succ} \models^{X}_{\text{IAR}} q(\vec{a})$. Otherwise, for each remaining $\alpha \in \mathcal{C}$, it checks whether $\mathcal{K}_{\succ} \models^{X}_{\text{IAR}} \alpha$ using $\Phi_{X\text{-}IAR}(\alpha)$ and adds α to the corresponding set of facts. If every $\alpha \in \mathcal{C}$ is such that $\mathcal{K}_{\succ} \models^{X}_{\text{IAR}} \alpha$, then $\mathcal{K}_{\succ} \models^{X}_{\text{IAR}} q(\vec{a})$.
- IAR-facts is also specific to X-IAR and considers the answers in turn while maintaining the two sets of X-IAR and non X-IAR facts. The difference is that for each answer, it uses $\Psi_{X\text{-}IAR}(Rel) \wedge \bigwedge_{\alpha \in Rel} y_{\alpha}$ and a weighted MaxSAT solver to decide which facts hold under X-IAR among the set Rel of facts that belong to some cause and have not already been assigned to one of the two sets. Then it checks whether there is a cause that only contains X-IAR facts.

5 Implementation & Experimental Setting

We implemented the algorithms presented in Section 4 in java 11. Our system ORBITS (Optimal Repair-Based Inconsistency-Tolerant Semantics) takes as input two JSON files containing the directed conflict graph $\mathcal{G}_{\mathcal{K}_{\succ}}$, and the potential answers $PotAns$ of the query associated with their causes. The user specifies a semantics (AR, IAR, or brave), a value X (among S, P_1, P_2, or C) to use in $\varphi_{\text{X-max}}(F)$, the desired encoding for $\varphi_{\neg\mathcal{C}}$ (neg_1 or neg_2), and the algorithm to use to compute the answers w.r.t. the chosen semantics. The set of answers is output as a JSON file.

ORBITS relies on the Sat4j java library (version 2.3.4) to solve the SAT, weighted MaxSAT, and MUS enumeration problems (Berre and Parrain 2010). In principle, a standalone solver could be used, but we found that the time needed to print out the encoding to pass it to an external solver tends to be prohibitive compared to using Sat4j.

The source code of ORBITS is available at https://github.com/bourgaux/orbits, the inputs files we used in the experiments at https://zenodo.org/record/5946827, and details on the experimental setting in (Bienvenu and Bourgaux 2022).

Experimental Environment All experiments were run with 16GB of RAM in a cluster node running CentOS 7.9 with linux kernel 3.10.0, with processor 2x Cascade Lake Intel Xeon 5218 16 cores, 2.4GHz. Reported times are averaged over 5 runs, with a 30 minutes time-out. Since we aim at comparing our different algorithms and encodings, in what follows, we focus on the time needed to filter the candidate answers, excluding the time needed to load the inputs from the JSON files or serialize the output. This input loading time is generally below 1 second and never exceeds a few seconds. However, in real-world applications, we would not use ORBITS as a standalone tool, but rather make it a library to be integrated in a full query answering system.

Test KBs We evaluate ORBITS on three (sets of) KBs. The first is the CQAPri benchmark (Bourgaux 2016), a synthetic benchmark crafted to evaluate inconsistency-tolerant query answering over DL-Lite KBs, adapted from the $\text{LUBM}^{\exists}_{20}$ benchmark (Lutz et al. 2013). The two others, called Food Inspection and Physicians, are real-world datasets built from public open data, which have already been used to evaluate data cleaning and consistent query answering systems (Rekatsinas et al. 2017; Dixit and Kolaitis 2019). They consist of relational databases built from the original csv files, on which typical integrity constraints have been added. We briefly summarize their main characteristics below.

We use the DL-Lite ontology (which includes 875 disjointness axioms) and 20 queries of the CQAPri benchmark, together with the 18 datasets named uXcY with $X \in \{1, 5, 20\}$ and $Y \in \{1, 5, 10, 20, 30, 50\}$. Parameters X and Y are related to the size and the proportion of facts involved in some conflicts respectively (the higher the bigger), and the datasets are such that uXcY $\subseteq$ uXcY$'$ for $Y \leq Y'$ and uXcY $\subseteq$ uX$'$cY for $X \leq X'$. Their sizes range from 75K to 2M facts and their proportions of facts involved in some conflict from 3% to 46%. The induced conflict graphs contain from 2K to 946K facts and from 2K to 3M conflicts.

The Food Inspection dataset contains data about inspection of restaurants in New York and Chicago (Dat c; Dat a). We use the database schema and six queries proposed by Dixit and Kolaitis (2019): there are four relations, each having a key constraint and one having a further FD. The dataset contains 523K facts, 37% of them belong to some conflict. The conflict graph contains 192K facts and 219K conflicts.

We build the Physicians dataset from the National Downloadable File provided by the Centers for Medicare & Medicaid Services (Dat b). It contains information on medical professionals and their affiliations. We decompose it into seven relations, add four reasonable key constraints and two FDs, and design six queries. In total, the dataset contains more than 8M facts and 2% of them are in some conflict. The conflict graph contains 183K facts and 2.7M conflicts.

Priority Relations We build score-structured priority relations by randomly assigning each fact a score between 1 and n. To construct a non-score-structured priority relation, we consider each conflict and assign a random direction to the corresponding edge in the conflict graph with a probability p, except if doing so creates a cycle, and verify that the resulting priority is indeed not score-structured. On the Food Inspection and Physicians datasets, we build four priority relations: two score-structured with $n = 2$ and $n = 5$, and two non-score-structured with $p = 0.5$ and $p = 0.8$. For the CQAPri benchmark, we build two priority relations, one score-structured with $n = 5$ and one non-score-structured with $p = 0.8$, on our largest dataset (u20c50), then propagate them to the other datasets.

	Triv.	IAR\Triv.	AR\IAR	brave\AR	not brave
S	1,655		7	77	0
{P,C}-2	1,668	0	7	48	16
{P,C}-5	1,679	1	7	29	23
P-0.5	1,671	1	7	45	15
C-0.5	1,671	23	0	30	15
P-0.8	1,680	5	7	25	22
C-0.8	1,680	24	0	13	22

Table 1: Number of answers of q1 over the Physicians dataset depending on the priority relation (none, score-structured with $n = 2$ or $n = 5$, and not score-structured with $p = 0.5$ or $p = 0.8$) and type of repairs (standard, Pareto- or completion-optimal).

6 Experimental Evaluation

Our experimental evaluation aims at assessing (i) the impact of adopting different kinds of repairs, and (ii) the relative performances of alternative procedures for the same semantics. More precisely, we consider the following questions.

- What is the impact in terms of number of answers of adopting optimal repairs rather than standard repairs, or completion-optimal repairs instead of Pareto-optimal repairs when the priority relation is not score-structured?
- What is the impact of using one kind of repairs rather than another on the computation time?
- Given a semantics and type of repair, what is the impact in terms of computation times of the choice of:
  - how to encode optimality (P_1 or P_2 for Pareto-optimal repairs, P_1, P_2 or C when $\succ$ is score-structured)?
  - how to encode contradictions ($\varphi_{\neg\mathcal{C}}$ with neg_1 or neg_2)?
  - the algorithm used to filter the non-trivial answers?

In what follows, we summarize our main observations. Detailed results are given in (Bienvenu and Bourgaux 2022).

Comparing Semantics w.r.t. Number of Answers Table 1 shows the impact on the number of answers of the type of priority relation and chosen notion of optimal repairs for an example query. For each priority relation and repair type X, it gives the number of answers that: are trivially X-IAR (i.e. some cause contains only facts without outgoing edges in the directed conflict graph), hold under X-IAR but not trivially, hold under X-AR but not under X-IAR, hold under X-brave but not X-AR, and do not hold under X-brave semantics.

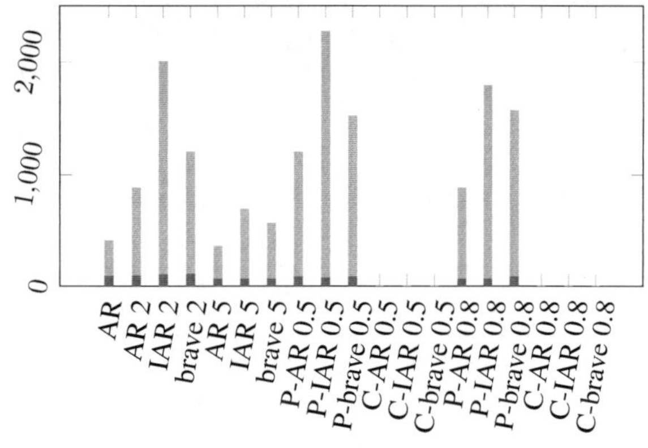

Figure 3: Best running times (in milliseconds) for each semantics and priority relation (none, score-structured with $n = 2$ or $n = 5$, not score-structured with $p = 0.5$ or $p = 0.8$) for query q2 over the Food Inspection dataset. An empty bar means that the query ran out of time / memory for all possible algorithms and encodings. The lower part of bars is the time to identify self-inconsistent facts and trivial answers, the upper part the time to filter non-trivial answers.

Priority relations leads to fewer edges in the directed conflict graph, which in turn makes more answers hold trivially. The more the priority relation sets preferences between facts (higher parameter n or p of the priority relation), the more trivially X-IAR answers we obtain. Adopting optimal repairs also significantly increases the number of potential answers that do not hold under X-brave semantics, which are very rare when using classical subset repairs.

An interesting observation is that while, in the absence of a priority relation, many queries of the CQAPri benchmark do not have any AR answers that are not trivial, which makes trivial answers a good approximation of AR, this is no longer the case for optimal repairs. It hence seems even more important to actually compute the answers that hold under the desired semantics rather simply computing the polynomial lower bound given by the trivial answers.

Regarding the impact of the choice between Pareto- and completion-optimal repairs, in many cases ORBITS did not manage to compute the answers for completion-optimal repairs in our given time and memory limits. When it does manage to compute them (for 5 queries on the Physicians dataset; none on the Food Inspection dataset; and from between 7 and 13 on uXc1 to less than 3 on uXc50), we observe a difference with Pareto-answers in only two cases.

Comparing Semantics w.r.t. Computation Time Figure 3 shows the best running times (across all algorithms and encoding variants) for each semantics and an example query. We did this comparison for all queries on Physicians and Food Inspection datasets and two CQAPri datasets.

Given a kind of repair X, the relative difficulty of the X-AR, X-IAR and X-brave semantics depends on the query, dataset and sometimes the nature of the priority relation.

Comparing S-AR, P-AR, and C-AR semantics, we observe that using optimal repairs may either increase or decrease the answer filtering time, intuitively because there are more trivial answers, but the encodings are more complex.

		q1	q2	q3	q4	q5	q6
Alg. 1	P_1	417	141	350	12,799	224	4,009
	P_2	804	142	379	326,594	213	8,684
	C	252,694	179	550	oom	284	t.o
Alg. 2	P_1	268	166	326	1,730	214	11,263
	P_2	502	163	333	2,961	221	10,833
	C	oom	632	t.o	t.o	551	oom
Alg. 3	P_1	272	154	313	t.o	211	245,804
	P_2	466	146	281	t.o	201	241,030
	C	oom	624	t.o	t.o	550	oom
Alg. 4	P_1	362	166	997	42,544	281	559,923
	P_2	566	193	972	36,923	304	546,199
	C	oom	764	t.o	t.o	846	oom
Alg. 5	P_1	383	135	335	8,192	211	3,419
	P_2	565	157	309	225,170	207	5,963
	C	192,429	164	544	oom	238	t.o

Table 2: Query answer filtering time (in milliseconds, t.o:time out, oom:out of memory) under X-brave semantics (X $\in$ {P,C}), for each algorithm and encoding $\varphi_{\text{X-max}}$, on Physicians dataset with score-structured priority ($n = 2$). Alg. 1: Simple, Alg. 2: All-MaxSAT, Alg. 3: All-MUSes, Alg. 4: Assumptions, Alg. 5: Cause-by-cause. Best time in bold red and 'close to best times' (i.e., not exceeding the best by more than 50ms or 10%) on grey.

Given a dataset, query and semantics, if we compare two priority relations of the same kind (score-structured or not), the one that sets preferences between more facts leads to lower running times. This can be explained by the increase of the number of trivial answers and maybe by the fact that the encodings involve less facts and encode more 'forced choices' between facts so that there are less possibilities to explore. When we compare the 'easiest' non score-structured priority relations ($p = 0.8$) and the hardest score-structured ones ($n = 2$), which lead to comparable sizes of directed conflict graphs, score-structured priority relations seem to be easier than non-score-structured ones.

Finally, we conclude that our procedures do not perform well for completion-optimal repair-based semantics, which form most of the cases that fail due to lack of time or memory, and very often have higher running times than Pareto-optimal-based semantics with the same priority relation.

Choice of Algorithm & Encoding for Given Semantics Table 2 presents the time needed to filter the candidate answers that hold under brave semantics based on optimal-repairs (score-structured case) for some example queries. It illustrates the huge impact that the choice of an algorithm and encoding can have. For example, q6 answers are filtered in 3.5s with algorithm Cause-by-cause and $\varphi_{\text{P}_1\text{-max}}$, but need at least 546s with the Assumptions algorithm, at least 5.9s with $\varphi_{\text{P}_2\text{-max}}$, and cannot be filtered in our time and memory limits with encoding $\varphi_{\text{C-max}}$. For X-AR and X-IAR semantics, we also observe sometimes huge variations when using the neg_1 or neg_2 version of $\varphi_{\neg\mathcal{C}}$. For example, for X-AR semantics on u20c50 with a score-structured priority relation, the best times for queries q2 and q18 are both obtained

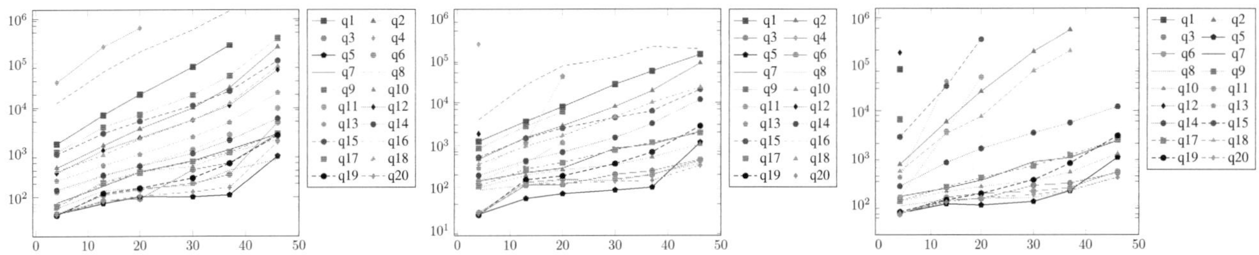

(a) Simple (b) All-MaxSAT (c) All-MUSes

Figure 4: Time (in milliseconds, log. scale) to filter query answers under X-AR semantics (X $\in$ {P,C}) w.r.t. percentage of facts involved in some conflict for u20cY with score-structured priority relation ($\varphi_{\mathsf{P_1\text{-}max}}$ and neg_1 encoding). Missing queries ran out of time or memory.

with algorithm All-MaxSAT and $\varphi_{\mathsf{P_1\text{-}max}}$, but with the neg_2 variant for q2 (50 seconds versus 85 with neg_1) and neg_1 for q18 (23 seconds versus 47 with neg_2). The comparison of the possible procedures for each semantics on the different datasets and queries shows that there is not a 'best' method in general. However, we still gain some relevant insights.

The first one concerns the choice of $\varphi_{\mathsf{X\text{-}max}}$. The encoding $\varphi_{\mathsf{P_1\text{-}max}}$ is generally the best one for Pareto-optimal repairs, in the sense that it achieves 'close to best times' (cf. Table 2) much more often than the others. However, there are a few cases where $\varphi_{\mathsf{P_2\text{-}max}}$ performs significantly better, especially on the CQAPri datasets with fewer conflicts (e.g., on u20c1 with a score-structured priority relation, the best time for filtering q9 answers under P-AR semantics is 480ms with $\varphi_{\mathsf{P_2\text{-}max}}$, while the best time with another encoding is 825ms). When the priority relation is score-structured, $\varphi_{\mathsf{C\text{-}max}}$ never significantly outperforms $\varphi_{\mathsf{P_1\text{-}max}}$ and $\varphi_{\mathsf{P_2\text{-}max}}$ and leads to much more time or memory failures.

The second concerns the choice of algorithm for X-IAR semantics. For all kinds of repairs, algorithm IAR-causes is generally better than the others in terms of frequency of 'close to best times'. It is sometimes outperformed by algorithms Cause-by-cause or IAR-facts. The 'generic' algorithms (Simple, All-MaxSAT, All-MUSes, Assumptions) perform quite poorly, except on the simplest cases.

For the AR and brave semantics, it is more difficult to find an algorithm that is superior to the others. For non-score-structured priority relations and completion-optimal repairs, algorithm Simple seems to be the best choice for both C-AR and C-brave semantics, but all algorithms fail in most cases. A related observation is that algorithms that consider answers individually and use smaller encodings seems to be often more robust in terms of time-out and out-of-memory, with a notable exception for P-AR and P-brave semantics on u20c50 with non-score-structured priority, where algorithms All-MaxSAT and All-MUSes are more robust. For S-AR, P-AR and P-brave, we observe different behaviours depending on the benchmark: All-MaxSAT and All-MUSes tend to perform better for the CQAPri benchmark, while Simple tends to perform better for the Food Inspection dataset.

Finally, comparing neg_1 and neg_2 versions of $\varphi_{\neg\mathcal{C}}$, we observe that the relative performance depends on the dataset, query, algorithm, and choice of $\varphi_{\mathsf{X\text{-}max}}$. However, we note that $\varphi_{\mathsf{P_2\text{-}max}}$ usually works better with neg_1. Even if there is not a direct relationship between the encoding sizes and the running times, this is probably due to the fact that neg_2 enforces that both the facts that occur in the causes and their conflicts are part of the encoding, which significantly increases the size of $\varphi_{\mathsf{P_2\text{-}max}}$, but has little impact on $\varphi_{\mathsf{P_1\text{-}max}}$.

Figure 4 shows the evolution of the running times of three algorithms using the same encoding variants as the proportion of facts involved in some conflicts grows, on the u20cY datasets with a score-structured priority for X-AR semantics (X $\in$ {P,C}). It illustrates the fact that the relative performance of the algorithms depends on the query and dataset (here, the proportion of facts involved in some conflict): For example, All-MaxSAT is the best for q9 over the three first datasets, but runs out of time on the three last (more that 20% of facts in conflict), while Simple can handle them.

7 Conclusion

We have presented a comprehensive exploration of SAT-based approaches to querying inconsistent data using (optimal) repair-based inconsistency tolerant semantics, including the proposal of novel encodings and algorithms. Our generic framework places existing approaches into a broader context and makes our results and system directly applicable to both the (pure) database and OMQA settings.

Our experimental comparison of different SAT-based algorithms and encoding variants shows that the choice of algorithm and encoding may have huge impact on the computation time. While in some cases our results can be used to single out some approaches as more effective, more often there are no clear winner(s). This suggests that to minimize runtimes, it may make sense to launch multiple algorithms in parallel, and/or devise methods that can help predict which algorithm and encoding will perform best on a given dataset and query, e.g. using machine learning techniques.

Our work lays important foundations for the future development of mature systems for querying inconsistent data. We plan to investigate different ways of improving the performance for optimal repair-based semantics. For example, it would be interesting to explore alternative approaches for completion-optimal repairs based upon SAT modulo graph techniques (Gebser, Janhunen, and Rintanen 2014). Another promising direction is to employ more refined polynomial lower approximations than the trivial answers, such as the grounded semantics (Bienvenu and Bourgaux 2020).

Acknowledgements

This work was supported by the ANR AI Chair INTENDED (ANR-19-CHIA-0014).

References

Arenas, M.; Bertossi, L. E.; and Chomicki, J. 1999. Consistent query answers in inconsistent databases. In *Proceedings of the 18th ACM SIGMOD-SIGACT-SIGAI Symposium on Principles of Database Systems (PODS)*, 68–79.

Berre, D. L., and Parrain, A. 2010. The sat4j library, release 2.2. *JSAT* 7(2-3):59–64.

Bertossi, L. E. 2011. *Database Repairing and Consistent Query Answering*. Synthesis Lectures on Data Management. Morgan & Claypool Publishers.

Bienvenu, M., and Bourgaux, C. 2016. Inconsistency-tolerant querying of description logic knowledge bases. In *Tutorial Lectures of the 12th International Reasoning Web Summer School*, 156–202.

Bienvenu, M., and Bourgaux, C. 2020. Querying and repairing inconsistent prioritized knowledge bases: Complexity analysis and links with abstract argumentation. In *Proceedings of the 17th International Conference on Principles of Knowledge Representation and Reasoning (KR)*, 141–151.

Bienvenu, M., and Bourgaux, C. 2022. Querying inconsistent prioritized data with ORBITS: Algorithms, implementation, and experiments. arxiv.org/abs/2202.07980 [cs.LO].

Bienvenu, M., and Ortiz, M. 2015. Ontology-mediated query answering with data-tractable description logics. In *Tutorial Lectures of the 11th Reasoning Web International Summer School*, 218–307.

Bienvenu, M., and Rosati, R. 2013. Tractable approximations of consistent query answering for robust ontology-based data access. In *Proceedings of the 23rd International Joint Conference on Artificial Intelligence (IJCAI)*.

Bienvenu, M.; Bourgaux, C.; and Goasdoué, F. 2014. Querying inconsistent description logic knowledge bases under preferred repair semantics. In *Proceedings of the 28th AAAI Conference on Artificial Intelligence (AAAI)*, 996–1002.

Bienvenu, M.; Bourgaux, C.; and Goasdoué, F. 2019. Computing and explaining query answers over inconsistent DL-Lite knowledge bases. *Journal of Artificial Intelligence Research (JAIR)* 64:563–644.

Bienvenu, M. 2020. A short survey on inconsistency handling in ontology-mediated query answering. *Künstliche Intelligenz* 34(4):443–451.

Bourgaux, C. 2016. *Inconsistency Handling in Ontology-Mediated Query Answering. (Gestion des incohérences pour l'accès aux données en présence d'ontologies)*. Ph.D. Dissertation, University of Paris-Saclay, France.

Calvanese, D.; De Giacomo, G.; Lembo, D.; Lenzerini, M.; and Rosati, R. 2007. Tractable reasoning and efficient query answering in description logics: The DL-Lite family. *Journal of Automated Reasoning (JAR)* 39(3):385–429.

Dataset: Food Inspections, Chicago Data Portal. https://data.cityofchicago.org/Health-Human-Services/Food-Inspections/4ijn-s7e5. Accessed December 7, 2020.

Dataset: National Downloadable File, Centers for Medicare & Medicaid Services. https://data.cms.gov/provider-data/dataset/mj5m-pzi6. Accessed December 10, 2020.

Dataset: New York City Restaurant Inspection Results, Department of Health and Mental Hygiene (DOHMH), NYC Open Data. https://data.cityofnewyork.us/Health/DOHMH-New-York-City-Restaurant-Inspection-Results/43nn-pn8j. Accessed December 7, 2020.

Dixit, A. A., and Kolaitis, P. G. 2019. A SAT-based system for consistent query answering. In *Proceedings of the 22nd International Conference on Theory and Applications of Satisfiability Testing (SAT)*, 117–135.

Fan, W. 2015. Data quality: From theory to practice. *SIGMOD Rec.* 44(3):7–18.

Gebser, M.; Janhunen, T.; and Rintanen, J. 2014. SAT modulo graphs: Acyclicity. In *Proceedings of the 14th European Conference on Logics in Artificial Intelligence (JELIA)*, 137–151.

Lembo, D.; Lenzerini, M.; Rosati, R.; Ruzzi, M.; and Savo, D. F. 2010. Inconsistency-tolerant semantics for description logics. In *Proceedings of the 4th International Conference on Web Reasoning and Rule Systems (RR)*, 103–117.

Livshits, E., and Kimelfeld, B. 2017. Counting and enumerating (preferred) database repairs. In *Proceedings of the 36th ACM SIGMOD-SIGACT-SIGAI Symposium on Principles of Database Systems (PODS)*, 289–301.

Lutz, C.; Seylan, I.; Toman, D.; and Wolter, F. 2013. The combined approach to OBDA: Taming role hierarchies using filters. In *Proceedings of the 12th International Semantic Web Conference (ISWC)*, 314–330.

Poggi, A.; Lembo, D.; Calvanese, D.; De Giacomo, G.; Lenzerini, M.; and Rosati, R. 2008. Linking data to ontologies. *Journal of Data Semantics* 10:133–173.

Rekatsinas, T.; Chu, X.; Ilyas, I. F.; and Ré, C. 2017. Holoclean: Holistic data repairs with probabilistic inference. *Proceedings of the VLDB Endowment (PVLDB)* 10(11):1190–1201.

Rosati, R. 2011. On the complexity of dealing with inconsistency in description logic ontologies. In *Proceedings of the 22nd International Joint Conference on Artificial Intelligence (IJCAI)*, 1057–1062.

Staworko, S.; Chomicki, J.; and Marcinkowski, J. 2012. Prioritized repairing and consistent query answering in relational databases. *Annals of Mathematics and Artifcial Intelligence (AMAI)* 64(2-3):209–246.

Wijsen, J. 2019. Foundations of query answering on inconsistent databases. *SIGMOD Record* 48(3):6–16.

Xiao, G.; Calvanese, D.; Kontchakov, R.; Lembo, D.; Poggi, A.; Rosati, R.; and Zakharyaschev, M. 2018. Ontology-based data access: A survey. In *Proceedings of the 27th International Joint Conference on Artificial Intelligence (IJCAI)*, 5511–5519.

Proceedings of the 19th International Conference on Principles of Knowledge Representation and Reasoning
Applications and Systems

Forecasting Argumentation Frameworks

Benjamin Irwin, **Antonio Rago** and **Francesca Toni**
Imperial College London
{benjamin.irwin19, a.rago, ft}@imperial.ac.uk

Abstract

We introduce *Forecasting Argumentation Frameworks (FAFs)*, a novel argumentation-based methodology for forecasting informed by recent judgmental forecasting research. FAFs comprise update frameworks which empower (human or artificial) agents to argue over time about the probability of outcomes, e.g. the winner of a political election or a fluctuation in inflation rates, whilst flagging perceived *irrationality* in the agents' behaviour with a view to improving their forecasting accuracy. FAFs include five argument types, amounting to standard *pro/con* arguments, as in bipolar argumentation, as well as novel *proposal* arguments and *increase/decrease amendment* arguments. We adapt an existing gradual semantics for bipolar argumentation to determine the aggregated dialectical strength of proposal arguments and define irrational behaviour. We then give a simple aggregation function which produces a final group forecast from rational agents' individual forecasts. We identify and study properties of FAFs and conduct an empirical evaluation which signals FAFs' potential to increase the forecasting accuracy of participants.

1 Introduction

Historically, humans have performed inconsistently in judgemental forecasting (Makridakis, Hogarth, and Gaba 2010; Tetlock 2017), which incorporates subjective opinion and probability estimates to predictions (Lawrence et al. 2006). Yet, human judgement remains essential in cases where pure statistical methods are not applicable, e.g. where historical data alone is insufficient or for one-off, more 'unknowable' events (Petropoulos, Fildes, and Goodwin 2016; Arvan et al. 2019; Baets and Harvey 2020). Judgemental forecasting is widely relied upon for decision-making (Nikolopoulos 2021), in myriad fields from epidemiology to national security (Nikolopoulos et al. 2015; Litsiou et al. 2019). Effective tools to help humans improve their predictive capabilities thus have enormous potential for impact. Two recent global events – the COVID-19 pandemic and the US withdrawal from Afghanistan – underscore this by highlighting the human and financial cost of predictive deficiency. A multi-purpose system which could improve our ability to predict the incidence and impact of events by as little as 5%, could save millions of lives and be worth trillions of dollars per year (Tetlock and Gardner 2016).

Research on judgemental forecasting (see (Lawrence et al. 2006; Zellner et al. 2021) for overviews), including the recent, groundbreaking 'Superforecasting Experiment' (Tetlock and Gardner 2016), is instructive in establishing the desired properties for systems for supporting forecasting. In addition to reaffirming the importance of fine-grained probabilistic reasoning (Mellers et al. 2015b), this literature points to the benefits of some group techniques versus solo forecasting (Landeta, Barrutia, and Lertxundi 2011; Tetlock et al. 2014), of synthesising qualitative and quantitative information (Lawrence et al. 2006), of combating agents' irrationality (Chang et al. 2016) and of high agent engagement with the forecasting challenge, e.g. robust debating (Landeta, Barrutia, and Lertxundi 2011) and frequent prediction updates (Mellers et al. 2015b).

Meanwhile, *computational argumentation* (see (Atkinson et al. 2017; Baroni et al. 2018) for recent overviews) is a field of AI which involves reasoning with uncertainty and resolving conflicting information, e.g. in natural language debates. As such, it is an ideal candidate for aggregating the broad, polymorphous set of information involved in judgemental group forecasting. An extensive and growing literature is based on various argumentation frameworks – rule-based systems for aggregating, representing and evaluating sets of arguments, such as those applied in the contexts of *scheduling* (Cyras et al. 2019), *fact checking* (Kotonya and Toni 2020) or in various instances of *explainable AI* (Cyras et al. 2021). Subsets of the requirements for forecasting systems are addressed by individual formalisms, e.g. *probabilistic argumentation* (Dung and Thang 2010; Thimm 2012; Hunter 2013; Fazzinga, Flesca, and Furfaro 2018) may effectively represent and analyse uncertain arguments about the future. However, we posit that a purpose-built argumentation framework for forecasting is essential to effectively utilise argumentation's reasoning capabilities in this context.

In this paper, we attempt to cross-fertilise these two as of yet unconnected academic areas. We draw from forecasting literature to inform the design of a new computational argumentation approach: *Forecasting Argumentation Frameworks* (FAFs). FAFs empower (human and artificial) agents to structure debates in real time and to deliver argumentation-based forecasting. They offer an approach in the spirit of *deliberative democracy* (Bessette 1980) to respond to a forecasting problem over time. The steps which

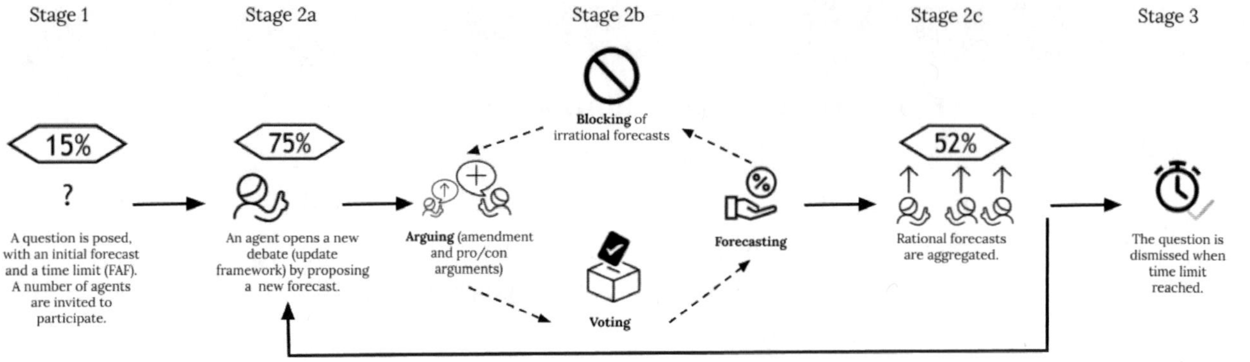

Figure 1: The step-by-step process of a FAF over its lifetime.

underpin FAFs are depicted in Figure 1 (referenced throughout) and can be described in simple terms as follows: a FAF is initialised with a time limit (for the overall forecasting process and for each iteration therein) and a pre-agreed 'base-rate' forecast $\mathcal{F}$ (Stage 1), e.g. based on historical data. Then, the forecast is revised by one or more (non-concurrent) debates, in the form of 'update frameworks' (Stage 2), opened and resolved by participating agents (until the specified time limit is reached). Each update framework begins with a proposed revision to the current forecast (Stage 2a), and proceeds with a cycle of argumentation (Stage 2b) about the proposed forecast, voting on said argumentation and forecasting. Forecasts deemed 'irrational' with a view to agents' argumentation and voting are blocked. Finally, the rational forecasts are aggregated and the result replaces the current group forecast (Stage 2c). This process may be repeated over time in an indefinite number of update frameworks (thus continually revising the group forecast) until the (overall) time limit is reached. The composite nature of this process enables the appraisal of new information relevant to the forecasting question as and when it arrives. Rather than confronting an unbounded forecasting question with a diffuse set of possible debates open at once, all agents concentrate their argumentation on a single topic (a proposal) at any given time.

After giving the necessary background on forecasting and argumentation (§2), we formalise our update frameworks for Step 2a (§3). We then give our notion of rationality (Step 2b), along with our new method for aggregating rational forecasts (Step 2c) from a group of agents (§4) and FAFs overall. We explore the underlying properties of FAFs (§5), before describing an experiment with a prototype implementing our approach (§6). Finally, we conclude and suggest potentially fruitful avenues for future work (§7).

2 Background

2.1 Forecasting

Studies on the efficacy of judgemental forecasting have shown mixed results (Makridakis, Hogarth, and Gaba 2010; Tetlock 2017; Goodwin, Gönül, and Önkal-Atay 2019). Limitations of the judgemental approach are a result of well-documented cognitive biases (Kahneman 2012), irrationalities in human probabilistic reasoning which lead to distortion of forecasts. Manifold methodologies have been explored to improve judgemental forecasting accuracy to varying success (Lawrence et al. 2006). These methodologies include, but are not limited to, prediction intervals (Lawrence and Makridakis 1989), decomposition (MacGregor and Armstrong 1994), structured analogies (Green and Armstrong 2007; Nikolopoulos et al. 2015) and unaided judgement (Litsiou et al. 2019). Various group forecasting techniques have also been explored (Linstone and Turoff 1975; Delbecq, Van den Ven, and Gustafson 1975; Landeta, Barrutia, and Lertxundi 2011), although the risks of groupthink (McNees 1987) and the importance of maintaining the independence of each group member's individual forecast are well established (Armstrong 2001). Recent advances in the field have been led by Tetlock and Mellers' superforecasting experiment (Tetlock and Gardner 2016), which leveraged geopolitical forecasting tournaments and a base of 5000 volunteer forecasters to identify individuals with consistently exceptional accuracy (top 2%). The experiment's findings underline the effectiveness of group forecasting orientated around debating (Tetlock et al. 2014), and demonstrate a specific cognitive-intellectual approach conducive for forecasting (Mellers et al. 2015a; Mellers et al. 2015b), but stop short of suggesting a concrete universal methodology for higher accuracy. Instead, Tetlock draws on his own work and previous literature to crystallise a broad set of methodological principles by which superforecasters abide (Tetlock and Gardner 2016, pg.144):

- *Pragmatic*: not wedded to any idea or agenda;
- *Analytical:* capable of stepping back from the tip-of-your-nose perspective and considering other views;
- *Dragonfly-eyed:* value diverse views and synthesise them into their own;
- *Probabilistic:* judge using many grades of maybe;
- *Thoughtful updaters:* when facts change, they change their minds;
- *Good intuitive psychologists:* aware of the value of checking thinking for cognitive and emotional biases.

Subsequent research after the superforecasting experiment has included exploring further optimal forecasting tournament preparation (Horowtiz et al. 2021; Katsagounos et al. 2021) and extending Tetlock and Mellers' approach to answer broader, more time-distant questions (Page, Aiken, and Murdick 2020). It should be noted that there have been no recent advances on computational toolkits for the field similar to that proposed in this paper.

2.2 Computational Argumentation

We posit that existing argumentation formalisms are not well suited for the aforementioned future-based arguments, which are necessarily semantically and structurally different from arguments about present or past concerns. Specifically, forecasting arguments are inherently probabilistic and must deal with the passage of time and its implications for the outcomes at hand. Further, several other important characteristics can be drawn from the forecasting literature which render current argumentation formalisms unsuitable, e.g. the paramountcy of dealing with bias (in data and cognitive), forming granular conclusions, fostering group debate and the co-occurrence of qualitative and quantitative arguing.

Nonetheless, several of these characteristics have been previously explored in argumentation and our formalisation draws from several existing approaches. First and foremost, it draws in spirit from abstract argumentation frameworks (AAFs) (Dung 1995), in that the arguments' inner contents are ignored and the focus is on the relationships between arguments. However, we consider arguments of different types and an additional relation of support (pro), rather than attack (con) alone as in (Dung 1995). Past work has also introduced probabilistic constraints into argumentation frameworks. Probabilistic AAFs (prAAFs) propose two divergent ways for modelling uncertainty in abstract argumentation using probabilities - the constellation approach (Dung and Thang 2010; Li, Oren, and Norman 2011) and the epistemic approach (Hunter 2013; Hunter and Thimm 2014; Hunter, Polberg, and Thimm 2020). These formalisations use probability as a means to assess uncertainty over the validity of arguments (epistemic) or graph topology (constellation), but do not enable reasoning *with* or *about* probability, which is fundamental in forecasting. In exploring temporality, (Cobo, Martínez, and Simari 2010) augment AAFs by providing each argument with a limited lifetime. Temporal constraints have been extended in (Cobo, Martínez, and Simari 2011) and (Baron et al. 2014). Elsewhere, (Rago and Toni 2017) have used argumentation to model irrationality or bias in agents. Finally, a wide range of gradual evaluation methods have gone beyond traditional qualitative semantics by measuring arguments' acceptability on a scale (normally [0,1]) (Leite and Martins 2011; Evripidou and Toni 2012; Amgoud et al. 2017; Amgoud and Ben-Naim 2018; Amgoud and Ben-Naim 2016). Many of these approaches have been unified as Quantitative Bipolar Argumentation Frameworks (QBAFs) in (Baroni, Rago, and Toni 2018).

Amongst existing approaches, of special relevance in this paper are Quantitative Argumentation Debate (QuAD) frameworks (Baroni et al. 2015), i.e. 5-tuples $\langle \mathcal{X}^a, \mathcal{X}^c, \mathcal{X}^p, \mathcal{R}, \tau \rangle$ where $\mathcal{X}^a$ is a finite set of *answer* arguments (to implicit *issues*); $\mathcal{X}^c$ is a finite set of *con* arguments; $\mathcal{X}^p$ is a finite set of *pro* arguments; $\mathcal{X}^a$, $\mathcal{X}^c$ and $\mathcal{X}^p$ are pairwise disjoint; $\mathcal{R} \subseteq (\mathcal{X}^c \cup \mathcal{X}^p) \times (\mathcal{X}^a \cup \mathcal{X}^c \cup \mathcal{X}^p)$ is an acyclic binary relation; $\tau : (\mathcal{X}^a \cup \mathcal{X}^c \cup \mathcal{X}^p) \rightarrow [0, 1]$ is a total function: $\tau(a)$ is the *base score* of a. Here, attackers and supporters of arguments are determined by the pro and con arguments they are in relation with. Formally, for any $a \in \mathcal{X}^a \cup \mathcal{X}^c \cup \mathcal{X}^p$, the set of *con (pro) arguments* of a is $\mathcal{R}^-(a) = \{b \in \mathcal{X}^c | (b, a) \in \mathcal{R}\}$ ($\mathcal{R}^+(a) = \{b \in \mathcal{X}^p | (b, a) \in \mathcal{R}\}$, resp.). Arguments in QuAD frameworks are scored by the *Discontinuity-Free QuAD* (DF-QuAD) algorithm (Rago et al. 2016), using the argument's intrinsic base score and the *strengths* of its pro/con arguments. Given that DF-QuAD is used to define our method (see Def. 4), for completeness we define it formally here. DF-QuAD's *strength aggregation function* is defined as $\Sigma : [0, 1]^* \rightarrow [0, 1]$, where for $S = (v_1, \ldots, v_n) \in [0, 1]^*$: if $n = 0$, $\Sigma(S) = 0$; if $n = 1$, $\Sigma(S) = v_1$; if $n = 2$, $\Sigma(S) = f(v_1, v_2)$; if $n > 2$, $\Sigma(S) = f(\Sigma(v_1, \ldots, v_{n-1}), v_n)$; with the *base function* $f : [0, 1] \times [0, 1] \rightarrow [0, 1]$ defined, for $v_1, v_2 \in [0, 1]$, as: $f(v_1, v_2) = v_1 + (1 - v_1) \cdot v_2 = v_1 + v_2 - v_1 \cdot v_2$. After separate aggregation of the argument's pro/con descendants, the combination function $c : [0, 1] \times [0, 1] \times [0, 1] \rightarrow [0, 1]$ combines v^- and v^+ with the argument's base score (v^0): $c(v^0, v^-, v^+) = v^0 - v^0 \cdot \mid v^+ - v^- \mid \ if\ v^- \geq v^+$ and $c(v^0, v^-, v^+) = v^0 + (1 - v^0) \cdot \mid v^+ - v^- \mid if v^- < v^+$, resp. The inputs for the combination function are provided by the *score function*, $\sigma : \mathcal{X}^a \cup \mathcal{X}^c \cup \mathcal{X}^p \rightarrow [0, 1]$, which gives the argument's strength, as follows: for any $x \in \mathcal{X}^a \cup \mathcal{X}^c \cup \mathcal{X}^p$: $\sigma(x) = c(\tau(x), \Sigma(\sigma(\mathcal{R}^-(x))), \Sigma(\sigma(\mathcal{R}^+(x))))$ where if $(x_1, \ldots, x_n)$ is an arbitrary permutation of the ($n \geq 0$) con arguments in $\mathcal{R}^-(x)$, $\sigma(\mathcal{R}^-(x)) = (\sigma(x_1), \ldots, \sigma(x_n))$ (similarly for pro arguments). Note that the DF-QuAD notion of σ can be applied to any argumentation framework where arguments are equipped with base scores and pro/con arguments. We will do so later, for our novel formalism.

3 Update Frameworks

We begin by defining the individual components of our frameworks, starting with the fundamental notion of a *forecast*. This is a probability estimate for the positive outcome of a given (binary) question.

Definition 1. *A* forecast $\mathcal{F}$ *is the probability* $P(\mathcal{Q} = true) \in [0, 1]$ *for a given* forecasting question $\mathcal{Q}$.

Example 1. *Consider the forecasting question* $\mathcal{Q}$: 'Will the Tokyo 2020 Summer Olympics be cancelled/postponed to another year?'. *Here, the* $true$ *outcome amounts to the Olympics being cancelled/postponed (and* $false$ *to it taking place in 2020 as planned). Then, a forecast* $\mathcal{F}$ *may be* $P(\mathcal{Q} = true) = 0.15$ *which amounts to a 15% probability of the Olympics being cancelled/postponed. Note that* $\mathcal{F}$ *may have been introduced as part of an update framework (herein described), or as an initial base rate at the outset of a FAF (Stage 1 in Figure 1).*

In the remainder, we will often drop $\mathcal{Q}$, implicitly assuming it is given, and use $P(true)$ to stand for $P(\mathcal{Q} = true)$.

In order to empower agents to reason about probabilities and thus support forecasting, we need, in addition to *pro/con* arguments as in QuAD frameworks, two new argument types:

- *proposal* arguments, each about some forecast (and its underlying forecasting question); each proposal argument $\mathcal{P}$ has a *forecast* and, optionally, some supporting *evidence*; and
- *amendment* arguments, which suggest a modification to some forecast's probability by increasing or decreasing it, and are accordingly separated into disjoint classes of *increase* and *decrease* (amendment) arguments.[1]

Note that amendment arguments are introduced specifically for arguing about a proposal argument, given that traditional QuAD pro/con arguments are of limited use when the goal is to judge the acceptability of a probability, and that in forecasting agents must not only decide *if* they agree/disagree but also *how* they agree/disagree (i.e. whether they believe the forecast is too low or too high considering, if available, the evidence). Amendment arguments, with their increase and decrease classes, provide for this.

Example 2. *A proposal argument $\mathcal{P}$ in the Tokyo Olympics setting may comprise forecast:* 'There is a 75% chance that the Olympics will be cancelled/postponed to another year'. *It may also include evidence:* 'A new poll today shows that 80% of the Japanese public want the Olympics to be cancelled. The Japanese government is likely to buckle under this pressure.' *This argument may aim to prompt updating the earlier forecast in Example 1.* A decrease *amendment argument may be $x_1^{\downarrow}$:* 'The International Olympic Committee and the Japanese government will ignore the views of the Japanese public'. *An* increase *amendment argument may be $x_1^{\uparrow}$:* 'Japan's increasingly popular opposition parties will leverage this to make an even stronger case for cancellation'.

Intuitively, a proposal argument is the focal point of the argumentation. It typically suggests a new forecast to replace prior forecasts, argued on the basis of some new evidence (as in the earlier example). We will see that proposal arguments remain immutable through each debate (update framework), which takes place via amendment arguments and standard pro/con arguments. Note that, wrt QuAD argument types, proposal arguments replace issues and amendment arguments replace answers, in that the former are driving the debates and the latter are the options up for debate. Note also that amendment arguments merely state a direction wrt $\mathcal{F}^{\mathcal{P}}$ and do not contain any more information, such as *how much* to alter $\mathcal{F}^{\mathcal{P}}$ by. We will see that alteration can be determined by *scoring* amendment arguments.

[1]Note that we decline to include a third type of amendment argument for arguing that $\mathcal{F}^{\mathcal{P}}$ is just right. This choice rests on the assumption that additional information always necessitates a change to $\mathcal{F}^{\mathcal{P}}$, however granular that change may be. This does not restrict individual agents arguing about $\mathcal{F}^{\mathcal{P}}$ from casting $\mathcal{F}^{\mathcal{P}}$ as their own final forecast. However, rather than cohering their argumentation around $\mathcal{F}^{\mathcal{P}}$, which we hypothesise would lead to high risk of groupthink (McNees 1987), agents are compelled to consider the impact of their amendment arguments on this more granular level.

Proposal and amendment arguments, alongside pro/con arguments, form part of our novel update frameworks (Stage 2 of Figure 1), defined as follows:

Definition 2. *An* update framework *is a nonad $\langle \mathcal{P}, \mathcal{X}, \mathcal{X}^-, \mathcal{X}^+, \mathcal{R}^p, \mathcal{R}, \mathcal{A}, \mathcal{V}, \mathcal{F}^{\mathcal{A}} \rangle$ such that:*

- *$\mathcal{P}$ is a single proposal argument with* forecast $\mathcal{F}^{\mathcal{P}}$ *and, optionally,* evidence $\mathcal{E}^{\mathcal{P}}$ *for this forecast;*
- *$\mathcal{X} = \mathcal{X}^{\uparrow} \cup \mathcal{X}^{\downarrow}$ is a finite set of* amendment arguments *composed of subsets $\mathcal{X}^{\uparrow}$ of* increase *arguments and $\mathcal{X}^{\downarrow}$ of* decrease *arguments;*
- *$\mathcal{X}^-$ is a finite set of* con *arguments;*
- *$\mathcal{X}^+$ is a finite set of* pro *arguments;*
- *the sets $\{\mathcal{P}\}$, $\mathcal{X}^{\uparrow}$, $\mathcal{X}^{\downarrow}$, $\mathcal{X}^-$ and $\mathcal{X}^+$ are pairwise disjoint;*
- *$\mathcal{R}^p \subseteq \mathcal{X} \times \{\mathcal{P}\}$ is a directed acyclic binary relation between amendment arguments and the proposal argument (we may refer to this relation informally as 'probabilistic');*
- *$\mathcal{R} \subseteq (\mathcal{X}^- \cup \mathcal{X}^+) \times (\mathcal{X} \cup \mathcal{X}^- \cup \mathcal{X}^+)$ is a directed acyclic, binary relation from pro/con arguments to amendment/pro/con arguments (we may refer to this relation informally as 'argumentative');*
- *$\mathcal{A} = \{a_1, \ldots, a_n\}$ is a finite set of* agents *$(n > 1)$;*
- *$\mathcal{V} : \mathcal{A} \times (\mathcal{X}^- \cup \mathcal{X}^+) \rightarrow [0, 1]$ is a total function such that $\mathcal{V}(a, x)$ is the* vote *of agent $a \in \mathcal{A}$ on argument $x \in \mathcal{X}^- \cup \mathcal{X}^+$; with an abuse of notation, we let $\mathcal{V}_a : (\mathcal{X}^- \cup \mathcal{X}^+) \rightarrow [0, 1]$ represent the votes of a* single *agent $a \in \mathcal{A}$, e.g. $\mathcal{V}_a(x) = \mathcal{V}(a, x)$;*
- *$\mathcal{F}^{\mathcal{A}} = \{\mathcal{F}^{\mathcal{A}}_{a_1}, \ldots, \mathcal{F}^{\mathcal{A}}_{a_n}\}$ is such that $\mathcal{F}^{\mathcal{A}}_{a_i}$, where $i \in \{1, \ldots n\}$, is the* forecast *of agent $a_i \in \mathcal{A}$.*

Note that pro (con) arguments can be seen as supporting (attacking, resp.) other arguments via $\mathcal{R}$, as in the case of conventional QuAD frameworks (Baroni et al. 2015).

Example 3. *A possible update framework in our running setting may include $\mathcal{P}$ as in Example 2 as well as (see Table 1) $\mathcal{X} = \{x_1^{\downarrow}, x_2^{\downarrow}, x_1^{\uparrow}\}$, $\mathcal{X}^- = \{x_1^-, x_2^-, x_3^-\}$, $\mathcal{X}^+ = \{x_1^+, x_2^+\}$, $\mathcal{R}^p = \{(x_1^{\downarrow}, \mathcal{P}), (x_2^{\downarrow}, \mathcal{P}), (x_3^{\uparrow}, \mathcal{P})\}$, and $\mathcal{R} = \{(x_1^-, x_1^{\downarrow}), (x_2^-, x_1^{\downarrow}), (x_3^-, x_1^{\uparrow}), (x_1^+, x_2^{\downarrow}), (x_2^+, x_1^{\uparrow})\}$. Figure 2 gives a graphical representation of these arguments and relations. Assuming $\mathcal{A} = \{alice, bob, charlie\}$, $\mathcal{V}$ may be such that $\mathcal{V}_{alice}(x_1^-) = 1$, $\mathcal{V}_{bob}(x_1^+) = 0$, and so on.*

Several considerations about update frameworks are in order. Firstly, they represent 'stratified' debates: graphically, they can be represented as trees with the proposal argument as root, amendment arguments as children of the root, and pro/con arguments forming the lower layers, as shown in Figure 2. This tree structure serves to focus argumentation towards the proposal (i.e. the probability and, if available, evidence) it puts forward. Second, we have chosen to impose a 'structure' on proposal arguments, whereby their forecast is distinct from their (optional) evidence. Here the forecast has special primacy over the evidence, because forecasts are the vital reference point and the drivers of debates in FAFs. They are, accordingly, both mandatory and required to 'stand out' to participating agents. In the spirit of abstract argumentation (Dung 1995), we nonetheless treat all arguments, including proposal arguments, as

	Content
$\mathcal{P}$	'A new poll today shows that 80% of the Japanese public want the Olympics to be cancelled owing to COVID-19, and the Japanese government is likely to buckle under this pressure ($\mathcal{E}^{\mathcal{P}}$). Thus, there is a 75% chance that the Olympics will be cancelled/postponed to another year' ($\mathcal{F}^{\mathcal{P}}$).
$x_1^{\downarrow}$	'The International Olympic Committee and the Japanese government will ignore the views of the Japanese public'.
$x_2^{\downarrow}$	'This poll comes from an unreliable source.'
$x_1^{\uparrow}$	'Japan's increasingly popular opposition parties will leverage this to make an even stronger case for cancellation.'
x_1^{-}	'The IOC is bluffing - people are dying, Japan is experiencing a strike. They will not go ahead with the games if there is a risk of mass death.'
x_2^{-}	'The Japanese government may renege on its commitment to the IOC, and use legislative or immigration levers to block the event.'
x_3^{-}	'Japan's government has sustained a high-approval rating in the last year and is strong enough to ward off opposition attacks.'
x_1^{+}	'This pollster has a track record of failure on Japanese domestic issues.'
x_2^{+}	'Rising anti-government sentiment on Japanese Twitter indicates that voters may be receptive to such arguments.'

Table 1: Arguments in the update framework in Example 3.

'abstract', and focus on relations between them rather between their components. In practice, therefore, amendment arguments may relate to a proposal argument's forecast but also, if present, to its evidence. We opt for this abstract view on the assumption that the flexibility of this approach better suits judgmental forecasting, which has a diversity of use cases (e.g. including politics, economics and sport) where different argumentative approaches may be deployed (i.e. quantitative, qualitative, directly attacking amendment nodes or raising alternative POVs) and wherein forecasters may lack even a basic knowledge of argumentation. We leave the study of structured variants of our framework (e.g. see overview in (Besnard et al. 2014)) to future work: these may consider finer-grained representations of all arguments in terms of different components, and finer-grained notions of relations between components, rather than full arguments. Third, in update frameworks, voting is restricted to pro/con arguments. Preventing agents from voting directly on amendment arguments mitigates against the risk of arbitrary judgements: agents cannot make off-the-cuff estimations but can only express their beliefs via (pro/con) argumentation, thus ensuring a more rigorous process of appraisal for the proposal and amendment arguments. Note that rather than facilitating voting on arguments using a two-valued perspective (i.e. positive/negative) or a three-valued

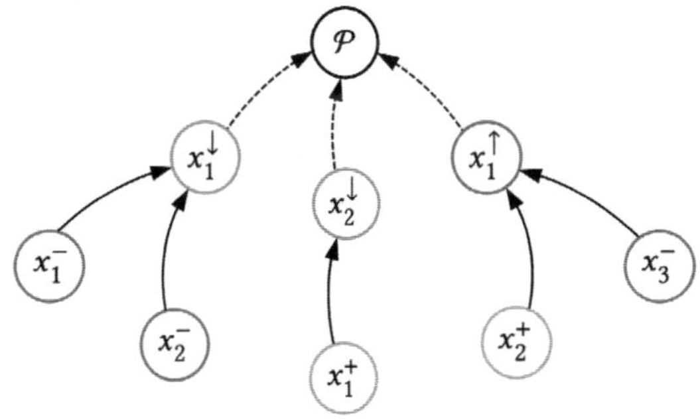

Figure 2: A graphical representation of arguments and relations in the update framework from Example 3. Nodes represent proposal ($\mathcal{P}$), increase ($\uparrow$), decrease ($\downarrow$), pro ($+$) and con ($-$) arguments, while dashed/solid edges indicate, resp., the $\mathcal{R}^p/\mathcal{R}$ relations.

perspective (i.e. positive/negative/neutral), $\mathcal{V}$ allows agents to cast more granular judgements of (pro/con) argument acceptability, the need for which has been highlighted in the literature (Mellers et al. 2015b). Finally, although we envisage that arguments of all types are put forward by agents during debates, we do not capture this mapping in update frameworks. Thus, we do not capture who put forward which arguments, but instead only use votes to encode and understand agents' views. This enables more nuanced reasoning and full engagement on the part of agents with alternative viewpoints (i.e. an agent may freely argue both for and against a point before taking an explicit view with their voting). Such conditions are essential in a healthy forecasting debate (Landeta, Barrutia, and Lertxundi 2011; Mellers et al. 2015b).

In the remainder of this paper, with an abuse of notation, we often use $\mathcal{F}^{\mathcal{P}}$ to denote, specifically, the probability advocated in $\mathcal{F}^{\mathcal{P}}$ (e.g. 0.75 in Example 2).

4 Aggregating Rational Forecasts

In this section we formally introduce (in §4.1) our notion of rationality and discuss how it may be used to identify, and subsequently 'block', undesirable behaviour in forecasters. We then define (in §4.2) a method for calculating a revised forecast (Stage 2c of Figure 1), which aggregates the views of all agents in the update framework, whilst optimising their overall forecasting accuracy.

4.1 Rationality

Characterising an agent's view as irrational offers opportunities to refine the accuracy of their forecast (and thus the overall aggregated group forecast). Our definition of rationality is inspired by, but goes beyond, that of QuAD-V (Rago and Toni 2017), which was introduced for the e-polling context. Whilst update frameworks eventually produce a single aggregated forecast on the basis of group deliberation, each agent is first evaluated for their rationality on an individual basis. Thus, as in QuAD-V, in order to define rationality for individual agents, we first reduce frameworks to *delegate frameworks* for each agent, which are the restriction of update frameworks to a single agent.

Definition 3. *A* delegate framework *for an agent a is $u_a = \langle \mathcal{P}, \mathcal{X}, \mathcal{X}^-, \mathcal{X}^+, \mathcal{R}^p, \mathcal{R}, a, \mathcal{V}_a, \mathcal{F}_a^{\mathcal{A}} \rangle$.*

Note that all arguments in an update framework are included in each agent's delegate framework, but only the agent's votes and forecast are carried over.

Recognising the irrationality of an agent requires comparing the agent's forecast against (an aggregation of) their opinions on the amendment arguments and, by extension, on the proposal argument. To this end, we evaluate the different parts of the update framework as follows. We use the DF-QuAD algorithm (Rago et al. 2016) to score each amendment argument for the agent, in the context of the pro/con arguments 'linked' to the amendment argument, using $\mathcal{R}$, in the context of the agent's delegate framework. We refer to the DF-QuAD score function as σ. This requires a choice of base scores for amendment arguments as well as pro/con arguments. We assume the same base score $\tau(x) = 0.5$ for all $x \in \mathcal{X}$; in contrast, the base score of pro/con arguments is a result of the votes they received from the agent, in the spirit of QuAD-V (Rago and Toni 2017). The intuition behind assigning a neutral (0.5) base score for amendment arguments is that an agent's estimation of their strength from the outset would be susceptible to bias and inaccuracy. Once each amendment argument has been scored (using σ) for the agent, we aggregate the scores of all amendment arguments (for the same agent) to to calculate the agent's *confidence score* in the proposal argument (which underpins our rationality constraints), by weighting the mean average strength of this argument's increase amendment relations against that of the set of decrease amendment relations:

Definition 4. *Given a delegate framework $u_a = \langle \mathcal{P}, \mathcal{X}, \mathcal{X}^-, \mathcal{X}^+, \mathcal{R}^p, \mathcal{R}, a, \mathcal{V}_a, \mathcal{F}_a^{\mathcal{A}} \rangle$, let $\mathcal{X}^\uparrow = \{x_1^\uparrow, x_2^\uparrow, \ldots, x_i^\uparrow\}$ and $\mathcal{X}^\downarrow = \{x_1^\downarrow, x_2^\downarrow, \ldots, x_j^\downarrow\}$. Then, a's* confidence score *is as follows:*

$$\text{if } i \neq 0, j \neq 0: \quad \mathcal{C}_a(\mathcal{P}) = \frac{1}{i}\sum_{k=1}^{i} \sigma(x_k^\uparrow) - \frac{1}{j}\sum_{l=1}^{j} \sigma(x_l^\downarrow);$$

$$\text{if } i \neq 0, j = 0: \quad \mathcal{C}_a(\mathcal{P}) = \frac{1}{i}\sum_{k=1}^{i} \sigma(x_k^\uparrow);$$

$$\text{if } i = 0, j \neq 0: \quad \mathcal{C}_a(\mathcal{P}) = -\frac{1}{j}\sum_{l=1}^{i} \sigma(x_l^\downarrow);$$

$$\text{if } i = 0, j = 0: \quad \mathcal{C}_a(\mathcal{P}) = 0.$$

Note that $\mathcal{C}_a(\mathcal{P}) \in [-1, 1]$, which denotes the overall views of the agent on the forecast $\mathcal{F}^\mathcal{P}$ (i.e. as to whether it should be *increased* or *decreased*, and how far). A negative (positive) $\mathcal{C}_a(\mathcal{P})$ indicates that an agent believes that $\mathcal{F}^\mathcal{P}$ should be amended down (up, resp.). The size of $\mathcal{C}_a(\mathcal{P})$ reflects the degree of the agent's certainty in either direction. In turn, we can constrain an agent's forecast $\mathcal{F}_a^{\mathcal{A}}$ if it contradicts this belief as follows.

Definition 5. *Given a delegate framework $u_a = \langle \mathcal{P}, \mathcal{X}, \mathcal{X}^-, \mathcal{X}^+, \mathcal{R}^p, \mathcal{R}, a, \mathcal{V}_a, \mathcal{F}_a^{\mathcal{A}} \rangle$, a's forecast $\mathcal{F}_a^{\mathcal{A}}$ is* strictly rational *(wrt u_a) iff:*

$$if\ \mathcal{C}_a(\mathcal{P}) < 0\ then\ \mathcal{F}_a^{\mathcal{A}} < \mathcal{F}^\mathcal{P}$$

$$if\ \mathcal{C}_a(\mathcal{P}) > 0\ then\ \mathcal{F}_a^{\mathcal{A}} > \mathcal{F}^\mathcal{P}$$

$$\mid \mathcal{C}_a(\mathcal{P}) \mid \geq \frac{\mid \mathcal{F}^\mathcal{P} - \mathcal{F}_a^{\mathcal{A}} \mid}{\mathcal{F}^\mathcal{P}}$$

Hereafter, we refer to forecasts which violate the first two constraints as, resp., *irrational increase* and *irrational decrease* forecasts, and to forecasts which violate the final constraint as *irrational scale* forecasts.

This definition of rationality preserves the integrity of group forecast in two ways. First, it prevents agents from forecasting against their beliefs: an agent cannot increase $\mathcal{F}^\mathcal{P}$ if $\mathcal{C}_a(\mathcal{P}) < 0$ and an agent cannot decrease $\mathcal{F}^\mathcal{P}$ if $\mathcal{C}_a(\mathcal{P}) > 0$; further, it ensures that agents cannot make forecasts disproportionate to their confidence score – *how far* an agent a deviates from the proposed change $\mathcal{F}^\mathcal{P}$ is restricted by $\mathcal{C}_a(\mathcal{P})$; finally, an agent must have $\mathcal{C}_a(\mathcal{P})$ greater than or equal to the relative change to $\mathcal{F}^\mathcal{P}$ denoted in their forecast $\mathcal{F}_a^{\mathcal{A}}$. Note that the *irrational scale* constraint deals with just one direction of proportionality (i.e. providing only a maximum threshold for $\mathcal{F}_a^{\mathcal{A}}$'s deviation from $\mathcal{F}^\mathcal{P}$, but no minimum threshold). Here, we avoid bidirectional proportionality on the grounds that such a constraint would impose an arbitrary notion of arguments' 'impact' on agents. An agent may have a very high $\mathcal{C}_a(\mathcal{P})$, indicating their belief that $\mathcal{F}^\mathcal{P}$ is too low, but may, we suggest, rationally choose to increase $\mathcal{F}^\mathcal{P}$ by only a small amount (e.g. if, despite their general agreement with the arguments, they believe the overall issue at stake in $\mathcal{P}$ to be minor or low impact to the overall forecasting question). Our definition of rationality, which relies on notions of argument strength derived from DF-QuAD, thus informs but does not wholly dictate agents' forecasting, affording them considerable freedom. We leave alternative, stricter definitions of rationality, which may derive from probabilistic conceptions of argument strength, to future work.

Example 4. *Consider our running Tokyo Olympics example, with the same arguments and relations from Example 3 and an agent alice with a confidence score $\mathcal{C}_{alice}(\mathcal{P}) = -0.5$. From this we know that alice believes that the suggested $\mathcal{F}^\mathcal{P}$ in the proposal argument $\mathcal{P}$ should be decreased. Then, under our definition of rationality, alice's forecast $\mathcal{F}_{alice}^{\mathcal{A}}$ is 'rational' if it decreases $\mathcal{F}^\mathcal{P}$ by up to 50%.*

If an agent's forecast $\mathcal{F}_a^{\mathcal{A}}$ violates these rationality constraints then it is 'blocked' and the agent is prompted to return to the argumentation graph. From here, they may carry out one or more of the following actions to render their forecast rational:

a. Revise their forecast;

b. Revise their votes on arguments;

c. Add new arguments (and vote on them).

Whilst a) and b) occur on an agent-by-agent basis, confined to each delegate framework, c) affects the shared update framework and requires special consideration. Each time new arguments are added to the shared graph, every agent must vote on them, even if they have already made a rational forecast. In certain cases, after an agent has voted on a new argument, it is possible that their rational forecast is made irrational. In this instance, the agent must resolve their irrationality via the steps above. In this way, the update framework can be refined on an iterative basis until the graph is no longer being modified and all agents' forecasts are rational. At this stage, the update framework has reached a stable state and the agents $\mathcal{A}$ are collectively rational:

Definition 6. *Given an update framework* $u = \langle \mathcal{P}, \mathcal{X}, \mathcal{X}^-, \mathcal{X}^+, \mathcal{R}^p, \mathcal{R}, \mathcal{A}, \mathcal{V}, \mathcal{F}^\mathcal{A} \rangle$, *$\mathcal{A}$ is* collectively rational *(wrt* u*) iff* $\forall a \in \mathcal{A}$, *$a$ is individually rational (wrt the delegate framework* $u_a = \langle \mathcal{P}, \mathcal{X}, \mathcal{X}^-, \mathcal{X}^+, \mathcal{R}^p, \mathcal{R}, a, \mathcal{V}_a, \mathcal{F}^\mathcal{A}_a \rangle$*).*

When $\mathcal{A}$ is collectively rational, the update framework u becomes immutable and the aggregation (defined next) produces a group forecast $\mathcal{F}^g$, which becomes the new $\mathcal{F}$.

4.2 Aggregating Forecasts

After all the agents have made a rational forecast, an aggregation function is applied to produce one collective forecast. One advantage of forecasting debates vis-a-vis the many other forms of debate, is that a ground truth always exists – an event either happens or does not. This means that, over time and after enough FAF instantiations, data on the forecasting success of different agents can be amassed. In turn, the relative historical performance of forecasting agents can inform the aggregation of group forecasts. In update frameworks, a weighted aggregation function based on Brier Scoring (Brier 1950) is used, such that more accurate forecasting agents have greater influence over the final forecast. Brier Scores are a widely used criterion to measure the accuracy of probabilistic predictions, effectively gauging the distance between a forecaster's predictions and an outcome after it has(n't) happened, as follows.

Definition 7. *Given an agent a, a non-empty series of forecasts* $\mathcal{F}^\mathcal{A}_a(1), \ldots, \mathcal{F}^\mathcal{A}_a(\mathcal{N}_a)$ *with corresponding actual outcomes* $\mathcal{O}_1, \ldots, \mathcal{O}_{\mathcal{N}_a} \in \{true, false\}$ *(where $\mathcal{N}_a > 0$ is the number of forecasts a has made in a non-empty sequence of as many update frameworks), a's Brier Score* $b_a \in [0,1]$ *is as follows:*

$$b_a = \frac{1}{\mathcal{N}_a} \sum_{t=1}^{\mathcal{N}_a} (\mathcal{F}^\mathcal{A}_a(t) - val(\mathcal{O}_t))^2$$

where $val(\mathcal{O}_t) = 1$ *if* $\mathcal{O}_t = true$*, and 0 otherwise.*

A Brier Score b is effectively the mean squared error used to gauge forecasting accuracy, where a low b indicates high accuracy and high b indicates low accuracy. This can be used in the update framework's aggregation function via the weighted arithmetic mean as follows. Each Brier Score is inverted to ensure that more (less, resp.) accurate forecasters have higher (lower, resp.) weighted influences on $\mathcal{F}^g$:

Definition 8. *Given a set of agents* $\mathcal{A} = \{a_1, \ldots, a_n\}$, *their corresponding set of Brier Scores* $b = \{b_{a_1}, \ldots, b_{a_n}\}$ *and their forecasts* $\mathcal{F}^\mathcal{A} = \{\mathcal{F}^\mathcal{A}_{a_1}, \ldots, \mathcal{F}^\mathcal{A}_{a_n}\}$, *and letting, for* $i \in \{1, \ldots, n\}$, $w_i = 1 - b_{a_i}$, *the* group forecast $\mathcal{F}^g$ *is as follows:*

$$\text{if } \sum_{i=1}^{n} w_i \neq 0: \qquad \mathcal{F}^g = \frac{\sum_{i=1}^{n} w_i \mathcal{F}^\mathcal{A}_{a_i}}{\sum_{i=1}^{n} w_i};$$

$$\text{otherwise}: \qquad \mathcal{F}^g = 0.$$

This group forecast could be 'activated' after a fixed number of debates (with the mean average used prior), when sufficient data has been collected on the accuracy of participating agents, or after a single debate, in the context of our general *Forecasting Argumentation Frameworks*:

Definition 9. *A* Forecasting Argumentation Framework *(FAF) is a triple* $\langle \mathcal{F}, \mathcal{U}, \mathcal{T} \rangle$ *such that:*

- $\mathcal{F}$ *is a* forecast*;*
- $\mathcal{U}$ *is a finite, non-empty sequence of update frameworks with $\mathcal{F}$ the forecast of the proposal argument in the first update framework in the sequence; the forecast of each subsequent update framework is the group forecast of the previous update framework's agents' forecasts;*
- $\mathcal{T}$ *is a preset time limit representing the lifetime of the FAF;*
- *each agent's forecast wrt the agent's delegate framework drawn from each update framework is strictly rational.*

Example 5. *Consider our running Tokyo Olympics example: the overall FAF may be composed of* $\mathcal{F} = 0.15$, *update frameworks* $\mathcal{U} = \{u_1, u_2, u_3\}$ *and time limit* $\mathcal{T} = 14\ days$, *where u_3 is the latest (and therefore the only open) update framework after, for example, four days.*

The superforecasting literature explores a range of forecast aggregation algorithms: extremizing algorithms (Baron et al. 2014), variations on logistic and Fourier L_2E regression (Cross et al. 2018), with considerable success. These approaches aim at ensuring that less certain or less accurate forecasts have a lesser influence over the final aggregated forecast. We believe that FAFs apply a more intuitive algorithm since much of the 'work' needed to bypass inaccurate and erroneous forecasting is expedited via argumentation.

5 Properties

We now undertake a theoretical analysis of FAFs by considering mathematical properties they satisfy. Note that the properties of the DF-QuAD algorithm (see (Rago et al. 2016)) hold (for the amendment and pro/con arguments) here. For brevity, we focus on novel properties unique to FAFs which relate to our new argument types. These properties focus on aggregated group forecasts wrt a debate (update framework). They imply the two broad, and we posit, desirable, principles of *balance* and *unequal representation*. We assume for this section a generic update framework $u = \langle \mathcal{P}, \mathcal{X}, \mathcal{X}^-, \mathcal{X}^\uparrow, \mathcal{R}^p, \mathcal{R}, \mathcal{A}, \mathcal{V}, \mathcal{F}^\mathcal{A} \rangle$ with group forecast $\mathcal{F}^g$.

Balance. The intuition for these properties is that differences between $\mathcal{F}^g$ and $\mathcal{F}^\mathcal{P}$ correspond to imbalances between the *increase* and *decrease* amendment arguments.

The first result states that $\mathcal{F}^g$ only differs from $\mathcal{F}^\mathcal{P}$ if $\mathcal{F}^\mathcal{P}$ is the dialectical target of amendment arguments.

Proposition 1. *If* $\mathcal{X}=\emptyset$ *(*$\mathcal{X}^\downarrow=\emptyset$ *and* $\mathcal{X}^\uparrow=\emptyset$*), then* $\mathcal{F}^g=\mathcal{F}^\mathcal{P}$.

Proof. If $\mathcal{X}^{\downarrow}=\emptyset$ and $\mathcal{X}^{\uparrow}=\emptyset$ then $\forall a \in \mathcal{A}$, $\mathcal{C}_a(\mathcal{P})=0$ by Def. 4 and $\mathcal{F}_a^{\mathcal{A}} = \mathcal{F}^{\mathcal{P}}$ by Def. 5. Then, $\mathcal{F}^g = \mathcal{F}^{\mathcal{P}}$ by Def. 8. □

This simple proposition conveys an important property for forecasting:for an agent to put forward a different forecast, amendment arguments must have been introduced.

Example 6. *In the Olympics setting, the group of agents could only forecast higher or lower than the proposed forecast $\mathcal{F}^{\mathcal{P}}$ after the addition of at least one of the amendment arguments $x_1^{\downarrow}$, $x_2^{\downarrow}$ or $x_1^{\uparrow}$.*

In the absence of increase (decrease) amendment arguments, if there are decrease (increase, resp.) amendment arguments, then $\mathcal{F}^g$ is not higher (lower, resp.) than $\mathcal{F}^{\mathcal{P}}$.

Proposition 2. *If $\mathcal{X}^{\downarrow} \neq \emptyset$ and $\mathcal{X}^{\uparrow} = \emptyset$, then $\mathcal{F}^g \leq \mathcal{F}^{\mathcal{P}}$. If $\mathcal{X}^{\downarrow} = \emptyset$ and $\mathcal{X}^{\uparrow} \neq \emptyset$, then $\mathcal{F}^g \geq \mathcal{F}^{\mathcal{P}}$.*

Proof. If $\mathcal{X}^{\downarrow}\neq\emptyset$ and $\mathcal{X}^{\uparrow}=\emptyset$ then $\forall a \in \mathcal{A}$, $\mathcal{C}_a(\mathcal{P})\leq 0$ by Def. 4 and then $\mathcal{F}_a^{\mathcal{A}} \leq \mathcal{F}^{\mathcal{P}}$ by Def. 5. Then, by Def. 8, $\mathcal{F}^g \leq \mathcal{F}^{\mathcal{P}}$. If $\mathcal{X}^{\downarrow}=\emptyset$ and $\mathcal{X}^{\uparrow}\neq\emptyset$ then $\forall a \in \mathcal{A}$, $\mathcal{C}_a(\mathcal{P}) \geq 0$ by Def. 4 and then $\mathcal{F}_a^{\mathcal{A}} \geq \mathcal{F}^{\mathcal{P}}$ by Def. 5. Then, by Def. 8, $\mathcal{F}^g \geq \mathcal{F}^{\mathcal{P}}$. □

This proposition demonstrates that, if a decrease (increase) amendment argument has an effect on proposal arguments, it can only be as its name implies.

Example 7. *In the Olympics setting, the agents could not forecast higher than the proposed forecast $\mathcal{F}^{\mathcal{P}}$ if either of the decrease amendment arguments $x_1^{\downarrow}$ or $x_2^{\downarrow}$ had been added, but the increase argument $x_1^{\uparrow}$ had not. Likewise, the agents could not forecast lower than $\mathcal{F}^{\mathcal{P}}$ if $x_1^{\uparrow}$ had been added, but neither of $x_1^{\downarrow}$ or $x_2^{\downarrow}$ had.*

If $\mathcal{F}^g$ is lower (higher) than $\mathcal{F}^{\mathcal{P}}$, there is at least one decrease (increase, resp.) argument.

Proposition 3. *If $\mathcal{F}^g < \mathcal{F}^{\mathcal{P}}$, then $\mathcal{X}^{\downarrow} \neq \emptyset$. If $\mathcal{F}^g > \mathcal{F}^{\mathcal{P}}$, then $\mathcal{X}^{\uparrow} \neq \emptyset$.*

Proof. If $\mathcal{F}^g < \mathcal{F}^{\mathcal{P}}$ then, by Def. 8, $\exists a \in \mathcal{A}$ where $\mathcal{F}_a^{\mathcal{A}} < \mathcal{F}^{\mathcal{P}}$, for which it holds from Def. 5 that $\mathcal{C}_a(\mathcal{P}) < 0$. Then, irrespective of $\mathcal{X}^{\uparrow}$, $\mathcal{X}^{\downarrow} \neq \emptyset$. If $\mathcal{F}^g > \mathcal{F}^{\mathcal{P}}$ then, by Def. 8, $\exists a \in \mathcal{A}$ where $\mathcal{F}_a^{\mathcal{A}} > \mathcal{F}^{\mathcal{P}}$, for which it holds from Def. 5 that $\mathcal{C}_a(\mathcal{P}) > 0$. Then, irrespective of $\mathcal{X}^{\downarrow}$, $\mathcal{X}^{\uparrow} \neq \emptyset$. □

We can see here that the only way an agent can decrease (increase) the forecast is by adding decrease (increase, resp.) arguments, ensuring the debate is structured as intended.

Example 8. *In the Olympics setting, the group of agents could only produce a group forecast $\mathcal{F}^g$ lower than $\mathcal{F}^{\mathcal{P}}$ due to the presence of* decrease *amendment arguments $x_1^{\downarrow}$ or $x_2^{\downarrow}$. Likewise, the group of agents could only produce a $\mathcal{F}^g$ higher than $\mathcal{F}^{\mathcal{P}}$ due to the presence of $x_1^{\uparrow}$.*

Unequal representation. AFs exhibit instances of unequal representation in the final voting process. In formulating the following properties, we distinguish between two forms of unequal representation. First, *dictatorship*, where a single agent dictates $\mathcal{F}^g$ with no input from other agents. Second, *pure oligarchy*, where a group of agents dictates $\mathcal{F}^g$ with no input from other agents outside the group. In the forecasting setting, these properties are desirable as they guarantee higher accuracy from the group forecast $\mathcal{F}^g$.

An agent with a forecasting record of *some* accuracy exercises *dictatorship* over the group forecast $\mathcal{F}^g$, if the rest of the participating agents have a record of total inaccuracy.

Proposition 4. *If $a_d \in \mathcal{A}$ has a Brier score $b_{a_d} < 1$ and $\forall a_z \in \mathcal{A} \setminus \{a_d\}$, $b_{a_z} = 1$, then $\mathcal{F}^g = \mathcal{F}_{a_d}^{\mathcal{A}}$.*

Proof. By Def. 8: if $b_{a_z}=1$ $\forall a_z \in \mathcal{A}\setminus\{a_d\}$, then $w_{a_z}=0$; and if $b_{a_d}<1$, then $w_{a_d}>0$. Then, again by Def. 8, $\mathcal{F}_{a_d}^{\mathcal{A}}$ is weighted at 100% and $\mathcal{F}_{a_z}^{\mathcal{A}}$ is weighted at 0% so $\mathcal{F}^g=\mathcal{F}_{a_d}^{\mathcal{A}}$. □

This proposition demonstrates how we will disregard agents with total inaccuracy, even in the extreme case where we allow one (more accurate) agent to dictate the forecast.

Example 9. *In the running example, if alice, bob and charlie have Brier scores of 0.5, 1 and 1, resp., bob's and charlie's forecasts have no impact on $\mathcal{F}^g$, whilst alice's forecast becomes the group forecast $\mathcal{F}^g$.*

A group of agents with a forecasting record of *some* accuracy exercises *pure oligarchy* over $\mathcal{F}^g$ if the rest of the agents all have a record of total inaccuracy.

Proposition 5. *Let $\mathcal{A} = \mathcal{A}_o \cup \mathcal{A}_z$ where $\mathcal{A}_o \cap \mathcal{A}_z = \emptyset$, $b_{a_o} < 1$ $\forall a_o \in \mathcal{A}_o$ and $b_{a_z} = 1$ $\forall a_z \in \mathcal{A}_z$. Then, $\mathcal{F}_{a_o}^{\mathcal{A}}$ is weighted at $> 0\%$ and $\mathcal{F}_{a_z}^{\mathcal{A}}$ is weighted at 0%.*

Proof. By Def. 8: if $b_{a_z} = 1$ $\forall a_z \in \mathcal{A}_z$, then $w_{a_z} = 0$; and if $b_{a_o} < 1$ $\forall a_o \in \mathcal{A}_o$, then $w_{a_o} > 0$. Then, again by Def. 8, $\mathcal{F}_{a_o}^{\mathcal{A}}$ is weighted at $> 0\%$ and $\mathcal{F}_{a_z}^{\mathcal{A}}$ is weighted at 0%. □

This proposition extends the behaviour from Proposition 4 to the (more desirable) case where fewer agents have a record of total inaccuracy.

Example 10. *In the running example, if alice, bob and charlie have Brier scores of 1, 0.2 and 0.6, resp., alice's forecast has no impact on $\mathcal{F}^g$, whilst bob and charlie's aggregated forecast becomes the group forecast $\mathcal{F}^g$.*

6 Evaluation

We conducted an experiment using a dataset obtained from the 'Superforecasting' project, Good Judgment Inc (Good Judgment Inc 2014), to simulate four past forecasting debates in FAFs. This dataset contained 1770 datapoints (698 'forecasts' and 1072 'comments') posted by 242 anonymised users with a range of expertise. The original debates had occurred on the publicly available group forecasting platform, the Good Judgment Open (GJO)[2], providing a suitable baseline against which to compare FAFs' accuracy.

For the experiment, we used a prototype implementation of FAFs in the form of the publicly available web platform called *Arg&Forecast* (see (Irwin, Rago, and Toni 2022) for an introduction to the platform and an additional human experiment with FAFs). Python's Gensim topic modelling library (Řehůřek and Sojka 2010) was used to separate the datapoints for each debate into contextual-temporal groups

[2]https://www.gjopen.com/

Q	Group b	$min(b)$	$max(b)$
Q1	0.1013 (0.1187)	0.0214 (0)	0.4054 (1)
Q2	0.216 (0.1741)	0 (0)	0.3853 (1)
Q3	0.01206 (0.0227)	0.0003 (0)	0.0942 (0.8281)
Q4	0.5263 (0.5518)	0 (0)	0.71 (1)
All	**0.2039 (0.217)**	**0 (0)**	**1 (1)**

Table 2: The accuracy of the platform group versus control, where 'Group b' is the aggregated (mean) Brier score, '$min(b)$' is the lowest individual Brier score and '$max(b)$' is the highest individual Brier score. Q1-Q4 indicate the four simulated debates.

Q	$\overline{C}$	Forecasts	Irrational Forecasts		
			Increase	*Decrease*	*Scale*
Q1	-0.0418	366	63	101	170
Q2	0.1827	84	11	15	34
Q3	-0.4393	164	53	0	86
Q4	0.3664	84	4	19	15
All	-0.0891	698	131	135	305

Table 3: Auxiliary results from the experiment, where $\overline{C}$ is the average confidence score, 'Forecasts' is number of forecasts made in each question and 'Irrational Forecasts' the number in each question which violated each constraint in §4.1.

that could form update frameworks. In each update framework the proposal forecast was set to the mean average of forecasts made in the update framework window and each argument appeared only once. Gensim was further used to simulate voting, matching users to specific arguments they (dis)approved of. Some 4,700 votes were then generated with a three-valued system (where votes were taken from $\{0,0.5,1\}$) to ensure consistency: if a user voiced approval for an argument in the debate time window, their vote for the corresponding argument(s) was set to 1; disapproval for an argument led to a vote of 0, and (in the most common case) if a user did not mention an argument at all, their vote for the corresponding argument(s) defaulted to 0.5.

With the views of all participating users wrt the proposal argument encoded in each update framework's votes, forecasts could then be simulated. If a forecast was irrational, violating any of the three constraints in Def. 5 (referred to in the following as *increase*, *decrease* and *scale*, resp.), it was blocked and, to mimic real life use, an automatic 'follow up' forecast was made. The 'follow up' forecast would be the closest possible prediction (to their original choice) a user could make whilst remaining 'rational'.

Note that evaluation of the aggregation function described in §4.2 was outside this experiment, since the past forecasting accuracy of the dataset's 242 anonymised users was unavailable. Instead, we used the mean average whilst adopting the GJO's method for scoring the accuracy of a user and/or group over the lifetime of the question (Roesch 2015). This meant calculating a daily forecast and daily Brier score for each user, for every day of the question. After users made their first rational forecast, that forecast became their 'daily forecast' until it was updated with a new forecast. Average and range of daily Brier scores allowed reliable comparison between (individual and aggregated) performance of the GJO versus the FAF implementation.

Results. As Table 2 demonstrates, simulating forecasting debates from GJO in *Arg&Forecast* led to predictive accuracy improvements in three of the four debates. This is reflected in these debates by a substantial reduction in Brier scores versus control. The greatest accuracy improvement in absolute terms was in Q4, which saw a Brier score decrease of 0.0255. In relative terms, Brier score decreases ranged from 5% (Q4) to 47% (Q3). The average Brier score decrease was 33%, representing a significant improvement in forecasting accuracy across the board. Table 3 demonstrates how our rationality constraints drove forward this improvement. 82% of forecasts made across the four debates were classified as irrational and subsequently moderated with a rational 'follow up' forecast. Notably, there were more *irrational scale* forecasts than *irrational increase* and *irrational decrease* forecasts combined. These results demonstrate how argumentation-based rationality constraints can play an active role in facilitating higher forecasting accuracy, signalling the early promise of FAFs.

7 Conclusions

We have introduced the Forecasting Argumentation Framework (FAF), a multi-agent argumentation framework which supports forecasting debates and probability estimates. FAFs are composite argumentation frameworks, comprised of multiple non-concurrent update frameworks which themselves depend on three new argument types and a novel definition of rationality for the forecasting context. Our theoretical and empirical evaluation demonstrates the potential of FAFs, namely in increasing forecasting accuracy, holding intuitive properties, identifying irrational behaviour and driving higher engagement with the forecasting question (more arguments and responses, and more forecasts in the user study). These strengths align with requirements set out by previous research in the field of judgmental forecasting.

There is a multitude of possible directions for future work. First, FAFs are equipped to deal only with two-valued outcomes but, given the prevalence of forecasting issues with multi-valued outcomes (e.g. 'Who will win the next UK election?'), expanding their capability would add value. Second, further work may focus on the rationality constraints, e.g. by introducing additional parameters to adjust their strictness, or by implementing alternative interpretations of rationality. Third, future work could explore constraining agents' argumentation. This could involve using past Brier scores to limit the quantity or strength of agents' arguments and also to give them greater leeway wrt the rationality constraints. Fourth, our method relies upon acyclic graphs: we believe that they are intuitive for users and note that all Good Judgment Open debates were acyclic; nonetheless, the inclusion of cyclic relations (e.g. to allow con arguments that attack each other) could expand the scope of the argumentative reasoning in in FAFs. Finally, there is an immediate need for larger scale human experiments.

Acknowledgements

The authors would like to thank Prof. Anthony Hunter for his helpful contributions to discussions in the build up to this work. Special thanks, in addition, go to Prof. Philip E. Tetlock and the Good Judgment Project team for their warm cooperation and for providing datasets for the experiments. Finally, the authors would like to thank the anonymous reviewers and meta-reviewer for their suggestions, which led to a significantly improved paper.

References

Amgoud, L., and Ben-Naim, J. 2016. Evaluation of arguments from support relations: Axioms and semantics. In *IJCAI*, 900–906.

Amgoud, L., and Ben-Naim, J. 2018. Weighted bipolar argumentation graphs: Axioms and semantics. In *IJCAI*, 5194–5198.

Amgoud, L.; Ben-Naim, J.; Doder, D.; and Vesic, S. 2017. Acceptability semantics for weighted argumentation frameworks. In *IJCAI*, 56–62.

Armstrong, J. S. 2001. *Evaluating Forecasting Methods*. Boston, MA: Springer US. 443–472.

Arvan, M.; Fahimnia, B.; Reisi, M.; and Siemsen, E. 2019. Integrating human judgement into quantitative forecasting methods: A review. *Omega (United Kingdom)* 86.

Atkinson, K.; Baroni, P.; Giacomin, M.; Hunter, A.; Prakken, H.; Reed, C.; Simari, G. R.; Thimm, M.; and Villata, S. 2017. Towards artificial argumentation. *AI Magazine* 38(3):25–36.

Baets, S. D., and Harvey, N. 2020. Using judgment to select and adjust forecasts from statistical models. *European Journal of Operational Research* 284(3):882–895.

Baron, J.; Mellers, B. A.; Tetlock, P. E.; Stone, E.; and Ungar, L. H. 2014. Two reasons to make aggregated probability forecasts more extreme. *Decision Analysis* 11.

Baroni, P.; Romano, M.; Toni, F.; Aurisicchio, M.; and Bertanza, G. 2015. Automatic evaluation of design alternatives with quantitative argumentation. *Argument and Computation* 6.

Baroni, P.; Gabbay, D.; Giacomin, M.; and van der Torre, L., eds. 2018. *Handbook of Formal Argumentation*. College Publications.

Baroni, P.; Rago, A.; and Toni, F. 2018. How many properties do we need for gradual argumentation? In *AAAI*, 1736–1743.

Besnard, P.; García, A. J.; Hunter, A.; Modgil, S.; Prakken, H.; Simari, G. R.; and Toni, F. 2014. Introduction to structured argumentation. *Argument and Computation* 5(1):1–4.

Bessette, J. M. 1980. Deliberative democracy: The majority principle in republican government. In *How Democractic is the Constitution?* Washington: American Enterprise Institute for Public Policy Research. 102–116.

Brier, G. W. 1950. Verification of forecasts expressed in terms of probability. *Monthly Weather Review* 78.

Chang, W.; Chen, E.; Mellers, B.; and Tetlock, P. E. 2016. Developing expert political judgment: The impact of training and practice on judgmental accuracy in geopolitical forecasting tournaments. *Judgment and Decision Making* 11.

Cobo, M. L.; Martínez, D. C.; and Simari, G. R. 2010. On admissibility in timed abstract argumentation frameworks. In *ECAI*, 1007–1008.

Cobo, M. L.; Martínez, D. C.; and Simari, G. R. 2011. Stable extensions in timed argumentation frameworks. In *TAFA*, 181–196.

Cross, D.; Ramos, J.; Mellers, B.; Tetlock, P. E.; and Scott, D. W. 2018. Robust forecast aggregation: Fourier l2e regression. *Journal of Forecasting* 37.

Cyras, K.; Letsios, D.; Misener, R.; and Toni, F. 2019. Argumentation for explainable scheduling. In *AAAI*, 2752–2759.

Cyras, K.; Rago, A.; Albini, E.; Baroni, P.; and Toni, F. 2021. Argumentative XAI: A survey. In *IJCAI*, 4392–4399.

Delbecq, A.; Van den Ven, A.; and Gustafson, D. 1975. *Group Techniques for Program Planning: A Guide to Nominal Group and Delphi Processes*. Scott Foresman.

Dung, P. M., and Thang, P. M. 2010. Towards (probabilistic) argumentation for jury-based dispute resolution. In *COMMA*, 171–182.

Dung, P. M. 1995. On the acceptability of arguments and its fundamental role in nonmonotonic reasoning, logic programming and n-person games. *Artificial Intelligence* 77.

Evripidou, V., and Toni, F. 2012. Argumentation and voting for an intelligent user empowering business directory on the web. In *RR*, 209–212.

Fazzinga, B.; Flesca, S.; and Furfaro, F. 2018. Probabilistic bipolar abstract argumentation frameworks: complexity results. In *IJCAI*, 1803–1809.

Good Judgment Inc. 2014. https://goodjudgment.com/. [Online; accessed 09-October-2021].

Goodwin, P.; Gönül, M. S.; and Önkal-Atay, D. 2019. When providing optimistic and pessimistic scenarios can be detrimental to judgmental demand forecasts and production decisions. *European Journal of Operational Research* 273(3):992–1004.

Green, K. C., and Armstrong, J. S. 2007. Structured analogies for forecasting. *International Journal of Forecasting* 23.

Horowtiz, M. C.; Ciocca, J.; Kahn, L.; and Ruhl, C. 2021. Keeping score: A new approach to geopolitical forecasting. *Penn Global*.

Hunter, A., and Thimm, M. 2014. Probabilistic argumentation with incomplete information. In *ECAI*, 1033–1034.

Hunter, A.; Polberg, S.; and Thimm, M. 2020. Epistemic graphs for representing and reasoning with positive and negative influences of arguments. *Artificial Intelligence* 281.

Hunter, A. 2013. A probabilistic approach to modelling uncertain logical arguments. *International Journal of Approximate Reasoning* 54.

Irwin, B.; Rago, A.; and Toni, F. 2022. Argumentative forecasting – extended abstract. In *AAMAS*. (To appear).

Kahneman, D. 2012. *Thinking, fast and slow*. Farrar, Straus and Giroux.

Katsagounos, I.; Thomakos, D. D.; Litsiou, K.; and Nikolopoulos, K. 2021. Superforecasting reality check: Evidence from a small pool of experts and expedited identification. *European Journal of Operational Research* 289(1):107–117.

Kotonya, N., and Toni, F. 2020. Explainable automated fact-checking for public health claims. In *EMNLP*, 7740–7754.

Landeta, J.; Barrutia, J.; and Lertxundi, A. 2011. Hybrid delphi: A methodology to facilitate contribution from experts in professional contexts. *Technological Forecasting and Social Change* 78.

Lawrence, M., and Makridakis, S. 1989. Factors affecting judgmental forecasts and confidence intervals. *Organizational Behavior and Human Decision Processes* 43.

Lawrence, M.; Goodwin, P.; O'Connor, M.; and Önkal, D. 2006. Judgmental forecasting: A review of progress over the last 25 years. *International Journal of Forecasting* 22.

Leite, J., and Martins, J. G. 2011. Social abstract argumentation. In *IJCAI*, 2287–2292.

Li, H.; Oren, N.; and Norman, T. J. 2011. Probabilistic argumentation frameworks. In *TAFA*, 1–16.

Linstone, H., and Turoff, M. 1975. *The Delphi Method: Techniques and Applications*. Addison-Wesley Publishing Company.

Litsiou, K.; Polychronakis, Y.; Karami, A.; and Nikolopoulos, K. 2019. Relative performance of judgmental methods for forecasting the success of megaprojects. *International Journal of Forecasting*.

MacGregor, D. G., and Armstrong, J. 1994. Judgmental decomposition: when does it work? *International Journal of Forecasting* 10(4):495–506.

Makridakis, S.; Hogarth, R. M.; and Gaba, A. 2010. Why forecasts fail. what to do instead. *MIT Sloan Management Review* 51.

McNees, S. K. 1987. Consensus forecasts: tyranny of the majority? *New England Economic Review* 15-21.

Mellers, B.; Stone, E.; Atanasov, P.; Rohrbaugh, N.; Metz, S. E.; Ungar, L.; Bishop, M. M.; Horowitz, M.; Merkle, E.; and Tetlock, P. E. 2015a. The psychology of intelligence analysis: Drivers of prediction accuracy in world politics. *Journal of Experimental Psychology: Applied* 21.

Mellers, B.; Stone, E.; Murray, T.; Minster, A.; Rohrbaugh, N.; Bishop, M.; Chen, E.; Baker, J.; Hou, Y.; Horowitz, M.; Ungar, L.; and Tetlock, P. E. 2015b. Identifying and cultivating superforecasters as a method of improving probabilistic predictions. *Perspectives on Psychological Science* 10.

Nikolopoulos, K.; Litsa, A.; Petropoulos, F.; Bougioukos, V.; and Khammash, M. 2015. Relative performance of methods for forecasting special events. *Journal of Business Research* 68.

Nikolopoulos, K. 2021. We need to talk about intermittent demand forecasting. *European Journal of Operational Research* 291(2):549–559.

Page, M.; Aiken, C.; and Murdick, D. 2020. How crowd forecasting can inform the big picture. *Georgetown CSET*.

Petropoulos, F.; Fildes, R.; and Goodwin, P. 2016. Do 'big losses' in judgmental adjustments to statistical forecasts affect experts' behaviour? *European Journal of Operational Research* 249(3):842–852.

Rago, A., and Toni, F. 2017. Quantitative argumentation debates with votes for opinion polling. In *PRIMA*, 369–385.

Rago, A.; Toni, F.; Aurisicchio, M.; and Baroni, P. 2016. Discontinuity-free decision support with quantitative argumentation debates. In *KR*, 63–73.

Řehůřek, R., and Sojka, P. 2010. Software Framework for Topic Modelling with Large Corpora. In *LREC*, 45–50.

Roesch, B. 2015. Measuring accuracy in prediction markets and opinion. https://www.cultivatelabs.com/posts/measuring-accuracy-in-prediction-markets-and-opinion-poll-pools. [Online; accessed 05-February-2022].

Tetlock, P. E., and Gardner, D. 2016. *Superforecasting: the art and science of prediction*. Crown Publishers.

Tetlock, P. E.; Mellers, B. A.; Rohrbaugh, N.; and Chen, E. 2014. Forecasting tournaments: Tools for increasing transparency and improving the quality of debate. *Current Directions in Psychological Science* 23.

Tetlock, P. E. 2017. *Expert political judgment: How good is it? How can we know?* Princeton University Press.

Thimm, M. 2012. A probabilistic semantics for abstract argumentation. In *ECAI*, 750–755.

Zellner, M.; Abbas, A. E.; Budescu, D. V.; and Galstyan, A. 2021. A survey of human judgement and quantitative forecasting methods. *Royal Society open science* 8(2):201187.

Proceedings of the 19th International Conference on Principles of Knowledge Representation and Reasoning
Applications and Systems

Stream Reasoning with Cycles

Periklis Mantenoglou[2,1] , **Manolis Pitsikalis**[3] , **Alexander Artikis**[4,1]
[1]NCSR Demokritos, Athens, Greece
[2]National and Kapodistrian University of Athens, Greece
[3]University of Liverpool, UK
[4]University of Piraeus, Greece
periklismant@di.uoa.gr, E.Pitsikalis@liverpool.ac.uk, a.artikis@iit.demokritos.gr

Abstract

Temporal specifications, such as those of multi-agent systems, often include cyclic dependencies. Moreover, there is an increasing need to evaluate such specifications in an online manner, upon streaming data. Consider, e.g., the online computation of the normative positions of the agents engaging in an e-commerce protocol. We present a formal computational framework that deals with cyclic dependencies in an efficient way. Moreover, we demonstrate the effectiveness of our framework on large synthetic and real data streams, from multi-agent systems and composite event recognition.

1 Introduction

The temporal specifications of many contemporary applications include cyclic dependencies. In multi-agent e-commerce protocols, e.g., a contract may be awarded to an agent that has not been suspended, while an agent may be suspended when not fulfilling the terms of a(nother) contract. As another example, consider the recognition of the different stages of a fishing trip, which is important for managing fishing activity and port traffic. For instance, a fishing vessel is said to be: (a) *approaching* a fishing area if it has ended another trip and goes in motion, i.e., 'under way'; (b) *trawling* when it stops the approach, i.e., it has reached the fishing area, and starts making consecutive turns; (c) *returning* when it stops trawling and goes under way; moreover, a vessel is said to have (d) *ended* its trip when it completes its return by becoming anchored or moored.

Contemporary applications also require the processing of large, evolving streams of data. Stream reasoning systems process such data streams by continuously applying temporal queries/patterns on incoming data and reporting instances of pattern satisfaction. Examples of stream reasoning systems may be found in various fields (Dell'Aglio et al. 2019). Consider, e.g., the recognition of (illegal) fishing on streams of vessel position signals. Furthermore, consider the online computation of the normative positions (Sergot 2001) of agents negotiating about a contract, given the messages exchanged between them. In all these cases, complex temporal specifications need to be evaluated with minimal latency in order to support real-time decision-making.

To deal efficiently with cyclic dependencies in temporal specifications, we present an extension of the 'Event Calculus for Run-Time reasoning' (RTEC), i.e., a logic programming implementation of the Event Calculus (Kowalski and Sergot 1986), designed to handle high-velocity data streams (Artikis, Sergot, and Paliouras 2015). The specifications in our proposed extension, $RTEC_{\circ}$, are locally stratified logic programs. Furthermore, $RTEC_{\circ}$ includes an algorithm for incremental caching, designed to avoid unnecessary re-computations when evaluating cyclic dependencies.

The contributions of the paper may be summarised as follows. First, we present $RTEC_{\circ}$, an open-source formal computational framework[1] for reasoning over real-world data streams and temporal specifications with cyclic dependencies. Second, we evaluate $RTEC_{\circ}$ by means of a complexity analysis and identify the benefits of incremental caching. Third, we present an extensive, *reproducible* empirical evaluation on large synthetic and real data streams. Moreover, we present an empirical comparison of $RTEC_{\circ}$ with a related computational framework and demonstrate the benefits of our approach.

We employ a voting procedure from multi-agent systems to illustrate $RTEC_{\circ}$. We follow the formalisation of Pitt et al. (2006), which may be summarised as follows: a committee sits and the chair opens the meeting; a member proposes a motion; another member seconds the motion; the members debate the motion; the chair calls for those in favour/against to cast their vote; finally, the motion is carried, or not, according to the standing rules of the committee.

2 Event Calculus for Run-Time Reasoning

The Event Calculus for Run-Time reasoning (RTEC) (Artikis, Sergot, and Paliouras 2015) is a logic programming implementation of the Event Calculus (Kowalski and Sergot 1986), designed for reasoning over data streams. We summarise the language of RTEC and its reasoning algorithms.

Representation. The time model is linear and includes integer time-points. Variables start with an upper-case letter, while predicates and constants start with a lower-case letter. A *fluent* is a property that is allowed to have different values at different points in time. The term $F\!=\!V$ denotes that fluent F has value V. Boolean fluents are a special case in which the possible values are true and false. The application-

[1]$RTEC_{\circ}$ is written in Prolog and the code is available at: https://github.com/aartikis/RTEC

specific part of a formalisation in RTEC is called *event description*.

Definition 1 (Event Description). An *event description* is a set of:

1. Ground happensAt facts, expressing a stream of event instances. happensAt$(E,\ T)$ denotes that event E occurs at time-point T.
2. Rules with head initiatedAt or terminatedAt, expressing the effects of events on fluents. initiatedAt$(F = V,\ T',\ T,\ T'')$ (respectively terminatedAt$(F = V,\ T',\ T,\ T'')$) denotes that a time period during which a fluent F has value V is initiated (resp. terminated) at a time-point T, such that $T' \leq T < T''$. ■

Definition 2 (Syntax). The rules defining initiatedAt predicates in RTEC have the following syntax:

$$\begin{aligned}
&\text{initiatedAt}(F = V,\ T',\ T,\ T'') \leftarrow \\
&\quad \text{happensAt}(E_1,\ T),\ T' \leq T < T'', \\
&\quad [[\ [\text{not}]\ \text{happensAt}(E_2,\ T),\ \ldots, \\
&\quad\ [\text{not}]\ \text{happensAt}(E_i,\ T), \\
&\quad\ [\text{not}]\ \text{holdsAt}(F_1 = V_1,\ T),\ \ldots, \\
&\quad\ [\text{not}]\ \text{holdsAt}(F_k = V_k,\ T).\ ]]
\end{aligned} \tag{1}$$

The first body literal of an initiatedAt rule is a positive happensAt predicate; this is followed by a possibly empty set of positive/negative happensAt and holdsAt predicates denoted by '[[ ]]'. holdsAt$(F = V,\ T)$ expresses that fluent F has value V at a given time-point T. The evaluation of holdsAt predicates will be discussed shortly. 'not' expresses negation-by-failure (Clark 1978), while '[not]' denotes that 'not' is optional. All (head and body) predicates are evaluated on the same time-point T. T' and T'', which are added at compile-time in a process transparent to the user, specify the temporal range of T. T' and T'' are always ground in queries, allowing search optimisations through indexing. terminatedAt rules have the same form. ■

According to the common-sense law of inertia, $F = V$ holds at a particular time-point T, i.e., holdsAt$(F = V,\ T)$, if $F = V$ has been *initiated* by an event at some earlier time-point, and not *terminated* by another event in the meantime.

Example 1. Consider the following rule from voting:

$$\begin{aligned}
&\text{initiatedAt}(voted(Ag, M) = Vote,\ T',\ T,\ T'') \leftarrow \\
&\quad \text{happensAt}(vote(Ag, M, Vote),\ T),\ T' \leq T < T'', \\
&\quad \text{holdsAt}(status(M) = voting,\ T).
\end{aligned}$$

$voted(Ag, M) = Vote$ is a fluent-value pair (FVP) recording the $Vote$, i.e., *aye*/*nay*, of agent Ag on motion M. $vote(Ag, M, Vote)$ expresses the act of voting, while $status(M)$ is a fluent recording the status of motion M, i.e., *proposed*, *voting*, *voted* or *null*. The above rule expresses the effects of casting a 'valid' vote, i.e., the vote for a motion M is recorded if the status of M is *voting*. ♦

Semantics. An event description in RTEC defines a *dependency graph* expressing the relationships between the FVPs of the event description.

Definition 3 (Dependency Graph). The dependency graph of an event description is a directed graph such that:

1. Each vertex denotes a FVP $F = V$;
2. There exists an edge $(F_j = V_j, F_i = V_i)$ iff there is an initiatedAt or terminatedAt rule for $F_i = V_i$ having holdsAt$(F_j = V_j,\ T)$ as one of its conditions. ■

RTEC restricts attention to event descriptions defining *acyclic* dependency graphs whereby it is possible to define a function *level* that maps all FVPs $F = V$ to the non-negative integers according to the following definition.

Definition 4 (FVP Level in RTEC). Given a dependency graph in RTEC, the *level* of a FVP $F = V$ is:

1. 1, if the vertex of $F = V$ has no incoming edges. In other words, $F = V$ is defined only in terms of events.
2. $n > 1$, if the vertex of $F = V$ has at least one incoming edge from a vertex of a FVP of level $n-1$, and zero or more incoming edges from vertices of FVPs of levels lower than $n-1$. ■

Proposition 1 (Semantics of RTEC). An event description in RTEC is a locally stratified logic program (Przymusinski 1987). ◇

A stratification of an event description may be constructed as follows. The first stratum contains all groundings of happensAt. The remaining strata are formed by following, in a bottom-up fashion, the FVP levels of the dependency graph.

Reasoning. The key reasoning task of RTEC is the computation of the maximal intervals during which a fluent-value pair (FVP) of an event description holds continuously. To achieve this, RTEC computes the initiation points of $F = V$ by evaluating the initiatedAt rules for $F = V$. If there is at least one initiation point, then RTEC computes all time-points T at which $F = V$ is 'broken'. $F = V$ is said to be 'broken' at time-point T if $F = V$ is terminated or F is initiated with a value $V' \neq V$ at T. These are the termination points of $F = V$. Subsequently, RTEC constructs the list of maximal intervals of $F = V$ by matching each initiation point T_i of $F = V$ with the first termination point T_b after T_i, ignoring every intermediate initiation point between T_i and T_b. holdsFor$(F = V,\ I)$ denotes that $F = V$ holds continuously in the maximal intervals of the list I. holdsAt$(F = V,\ T)$ is then evaluated by checking whether T belongs to one of the maximal intervals of list I for which holdsFor$(F = V,\ I)$.

RTEC employs a simple caching mechanism to avoid unnecessary re-computations, according to which the FVPs of an event description are processed in an order specified by its dependency graph. RTEC processes FVPs in a bottom-up manner, computing and caching their intervals level-by-level. This way, the intervals of the FVPs that are required for the processing of a FVP of level n are fetched from the cache without the need for re-computation.

RTEC performs continuous query processing to compute the maximal intervals of FVPs. At each query time q_i, the events that fall within a specified sliding window ω are taken into consideration. All events that took place before or at $q_i - \omega$ are discarded/'forgotten'. This way, the cost of reasoning depends on the size of ω and not on the complete stream. The size of ω and the temporal distance between two consecutive query times, i.e., the 'step' $q_i - q_{i-1}$, are parameters that may be manually chosen or optimised to meet the requirements of a given application. In the case that events arrive at RTEC with delays, e.g., due to network delays, it is preferable to make ω longer than the step. This way, we may compute, at q_i, the effects of events that took place in $(q_i - \omega,\ q_{i-1}]$, but arrived after q_{i-1}.

3 Cyclic Dependencies

Temporal specifications, such as those found in composite event recognition (Giatrakos et al. 2020) and multi-agent systems, often include cyclic dependencies.

Example 2. Consider, e.g., the specification of the status of a motion in voting:

$$\begin{aligned}&\mathsf{initiatedAt}(\mathit{status}(M) = \mathit{proposed},\ T',\ T,\ T'') \leftarrow\\&\quad \mathsf{happensAt}(\mathit{propose}(P, M),\ T),\ T' \leq T < T'',\\&\quad \mathsf{holdsAt}(\mathit{status}(M) = \mathit{null},\ T).\end{aligned} \tag{2}$$

$$\begin{aligned}&\mathsf{initiatedAt}(\mathit{status}(M) = \mathit{voting},\ T',\ T,\ T'') \leftarrow\\&\quad \mathsf{happensAt}(\mathit{second}(S, M),\ T),\ T' \leq T < T'',\\&\quad \mathsf{holdsAt}(\mathit{status}(M) = \mathit{proposed},\ T).\end{aligned} \tag{3}$$

$$\begin{aligned}&\mathsf{initiatedAt}(\mathit{status}(M) = \mathit{voted},\ T',\ T,\ T'') \leftarrow\\&\quad \mathsf{happensAt}(\mathit{close\_ballot}(C, M),\ T),\ T' \leq T < T'',\\&\quad \mathsf{holdsAt}(\mathit{status}(M) = \mathit{voting},\ T).\end{aligned} \tag{4}$$

$$\begin{aligned}&\mathsf{initiatedAt}(\mathit{status}(M) = \mathit{null},\ T',\ T,\ T'') \leftarrow\\&\quad \mathsf{happensAt}(\mathit{declare}(C, M, R),\ T),\ T' \leq T < T'',\\&\quad \mathsf{holdsAt}(\mathit{status}(M) = \mathit{voted},\ T).\end{aligned} \tag{5}$$

The first condition of each rule expresses an agent action; $\mathit{declare}(C, M, R)$, e.g., expresses that agent C declared the outcome R of voting on motion M. In all actions, the first argument denotes the agent that performed the action, while the second argument denotes the motion. The formalisation above expresses the various stages of a motion M: $\mathit{proposed}$ (the motion needs to be seconded before voting may start), voting (voters may cast their votes), voted (voting has ended and the chair may declare the outcome) and null. The effects of an agent message on $\mathit{status}(M)$ depend on the value of this fluent at the time of issuing the message. A message $\mathit{propose}(P, M)$, e.g., from a proposer P results in $\mathit{status}(M) = \mathit{proposed}$ provided that $\mathit{status}(M) = \mathit{null}$ at the time of sending $\mathit{propose}(P, M)$. Performing this action when $\mathit{status}(M) \neq \mathit{null}$ has no effect on $\mathit{status}(M)$. The effects of the remaining actions are formalised similarly. The specification of status includes an initial value for this fluent — this is omitted to simplify the presentation. ♦

The top part of Figure 1 displays the dependency graph defined by the event description of a voting protocol. This graph contains a cycle which is formed by rules (2)–(5). As another example, the bottom part of Figure 1 displays a dependency graph of NetBill, a protocol for exchanging encrypted digital goods (Sirbu 1997; Artikis and Sergot 2010), also including a cycle. In this specification, a contract concerning digital goods may be awarded to an agent that has not been suspended, while an agent may be (temporarily) suspended when not fulfilling the obligations of some other contract. The complete formalisations of voting and NetBill are publicly available[1].

RTEC cannot handle cyclic dependencies. When computing the initiation points of, e.g., $\mathit{status}(M) = \mathit{proposed}$ we

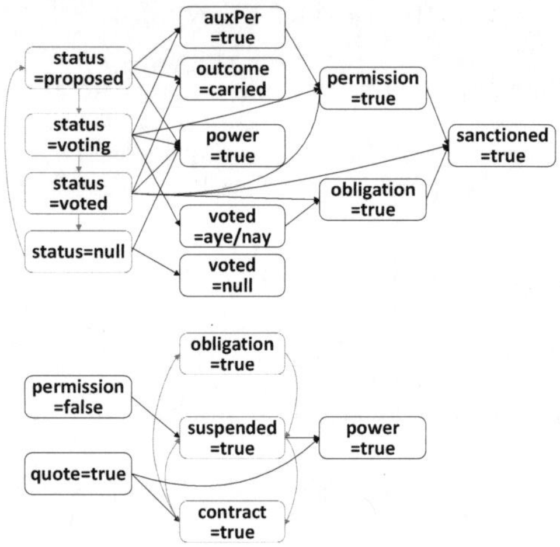

Figure 1: Dependency Graphs: Voting (top) and NetBill (bottom). We omit the arguments of fluents, and group FVPs with the same conditions into a single node, to simplify the presentation. Cycles are coloured red. Apart from the basic features of these protocols, e.g., motions in voting and quotes for digital goods in NetBill, the specifications express the normative positions of the agents, such as institutionalised power, permission and obligation, as well as sanctions/suspensions for handling non-conformance with obligations and the performance of forbidden actions.

cannot assume, as RTEC does, that the FVPs appearing in the body of rule (2) have been processed and thus their intervals can be fetched from the cache. $\mathit{status}(M) = \mathit{proposed}$ depends on $\mathit{status}(M) = \mathit{null}$ which in turn depends on $\mathit{status}(M) = \mathit{proposed}$.

This is not an issue, however, for other Event Calculus dialects, which can process FVPs with cyclic dependencies. Consider, e.g., the formalisation below:

$$\begin{aligned}&\mathsf{holdsAt}(F = V,\ T) \leftarrow\\&\quad \mathsf{initiatedAt}(F = V,\ q_i - \omega,\ T_i,\ T),\\&\quad \mathsf{not\ brokenBetween}(F = V,\ T_i,\ T).\end{aligned} \tag{6}$$

$$\begin{aligned}&\mathsf{brokenBetween}(F = V,\ T_i,\ T) \leftarrow\\&\quad \mathsf{terminatedAt}(F = V,\ T_i,\ T_b,\ T).\end{aligned} \tag{7}$$

$$\begin{aligned}&\mathsf{brokenBetween}(F = V,\ T_i,\ T) \leftarrow\\&\quad \mathsf{initiatedAt}(F = V',\ T_i,\ T_b,\ T),\ V \neq V'.\end{aligned} \tag{8}$$

Rule (6) specifies that $F = V$ holds at time-point T if it was initiated at some time-point T_i between the beginning of the current window $q_i - \omega$ and T, and has not been 'broken' between T_i and T. $F = V$ is broken between T_i and T if it is terminated in that interval (see rule (7)). A fluent cannot have more than one value at any time. Rule (8) captures this feature: if $F = V'$ is initiated at time $T_b \in [T_i, T)$ then $F = V$ is said to be broken in $[T_i, T)$, for all possible values V, other than V', of F.

Example 3. Assume that the current window $(q_i - \omega, q_i]$

	Predicate	Rule
1	initiatedAt$(s(m) = proposed,\ q_i{-}\omega,\ T,\ q_i)$?	(2)
2	happensAt$(propose(ag_p, m),\ t_4)$ ✓	(2), (9)
3	holdsAt$(s(m) = null,\ t_4)$?	(2), (6)
4	initiatedAt$(s(m) = null,\ q_i{-}\omega,\ T_i,\ t_4)$?	(6), (5)
5	happensAt$(declare(ag_c, m, not_carried),\ t_3)$ ✓	(5), (9)
6	holdsAt$(s(m) = voted,\ t_3)$?	(5), (6)
7	initiatedAt$(s(m) = voted,\ q_i{-}\omega,\ T_i',\ t_3)$?	(6), (4)
8	happensAt$(close_ballot(ag_c, m),\ t_2)$ ✓	(4), (9)
9	holdsAt$(s(m) = voting,\ t_2)$?	(4), (6)
10	initiatedAt$(s(m) = voting,\ q_i{-}\omega,\ T_i'',\ t_2)$?	(6), (3)
11	happensAt$(second(ag_s, m),\ t_1)$ ✓	(3), (9)
12	holdsAt$(s(m) = proposed,\ t_1)$?	(3), (6)
13	initiatedAt$(s(m) = proposed, q_i{-}\omega, T_i''', t_1)$?	(6)
14	initiatedAt$(s(m) = proposed, q_i{-}\omega, q_i{-}\omega, t_1)$ ✓	(10)
15	brokenBetween$(s(m) = proposed,\ q_i{-}\omega,\ t_1)$?	(6), (8)
16	initiatedAt$(s(m) = voting,\ q_i{-}\omega,\ T_b,\ t_1)$ ×	(8), (3)
17	initiatedAt$(s(m) = voted,\ q_i{-}\omega,\ T_b,\ t_1)$ ×	(8), (4)
18	initiatedAt$(s(m) = null,\ q_i{-}\omega,\ T_b,\ t_1)$ ×	(8), (5)
19	brokenBetween$(s(m) = proposed, q_i{-}\omega, t_1)$ ×	(8), (6)
20	holdsAt$(s(m) = proposed,\ t_1)$ ✓	(6), (3)
21	initiatedAt$(s(m) = voting,\ q_i{-}\omega,\ t_1,\ t_2)$ ✓	(3), (6)
22	brokenBetween$(s(m) = voting,\ t_1,\ t_2)$ ×	(6), (8)
23	holdsAt$(s(m) = voting,\ t_2)$ ✓	(6), (4)
24	initiatedAt$(s(m) = voted,\ q_i{-}\omega,\ t_2,\ t_3)$ ✓	(4), (6)
25	brokenBetween$(s(m) = voted,\ t_2,\ t_3)$ ×	(6), (8)
26	holdsAt$(s(m) = voted,\ t_3)$ ✓	(6), (5)
27	initiatedAt$(s(m) = null,\ q_i{-}\omega,\ t_3,\ t_4)$ ✓	(5), (6)
28	brokenBetween$(s(m) = null,\ t_3,\ t_4)$ ×	(6), (8)
29	holdsAt$(s(m) = null,\ t_4)$ ✓	(6), (2)
30	initiatedAt$(s(m) = proposed,\ q_i{-}\omega,\ t_4,\ q_i)$ ✓	(2)

Table 1: Narrative assimilation in the Event Calculus. '$status(m)$' is abbreviated as '$s(m)$' to fit the column margins. The second column shows the evaluated predicates and the third column refers to the rules used in their evaluation. We use '?' to indicate that we will illustrate predicate evaluation, '✓' to express a successful evaluation, and '×' to denote an unsuccessful evaluation. The predicates in the second column are indented to distinguish between the head and body atoms of a rule.

consists of the following event narrative/stream:

$$\begin{aligned}&\mathsf{happensAt}(second(ag_s, m),\ t_1).\\&\mathsf{happensAt}(close\_ballot(ag_c, m),\ t_2).\\&\mathsf{happensAt}(declare(ag_c, m, not\_carried),\ t_3).\\&\mathsf{happensAt}(propose(ag_p, m),\ t_4).\\&\text{where } q_i{-}\omega < t_1 < t_2 < t_3 < t_4 < q_i\end{aligned} \tag{9}$$

Moreover, the initial value of $status(M)$, in the current window, is set to *proposed*:

$$\mathsf{initiatedAt}(status(M) = proposed,\ q_i{-}\omega,\ q_i{-}\omega,\ T) \leftarrow \\ T > q_i{-}\omega. \tag{10}$$

To compute the maximal intervals for which $status(m) = proposed$ holds continuously, we first need to compute the initiation points of this FVP. Table 1 illustrates this process. To save space, we omit from this table the evaluation of the second condition (double inequality) of the initiatedAt and terminatedAt rules (see e.g. rule (2)); moreover, in the middle part of the table (see lines 14–19) we omit the presentation of the happensAt calls, while in the lower part of the table (see lines 20–30) we do not show the proof of brokenBetween. A solution to the initiatedAt call of line 1, i.e., a initiation point of $status(m) = proposed$ in $[q_i{-}\omega, q_i)$, is shown in line 30 (initiation point: t_4). ♦

Rule-set (6)–(8) constitutes a very inefficient implementation, leading to numerous unnecessary re-computations. Assume, e.g., that the event stream (9) includes an additional event:

$$\begin{aligned}&\mathsf{happensAt}(propose(ag_p, m),\ t_5).\\&\text{where } t_4 < t_5 < q_i\end{aligned} \tag{11}$$

In this case, most predicate calls presented in Table 1 would have to be repeated, in order to determine whether the above event creates new initiation points for $status(m) = proposed$. More precisely, the predicate calls presented in lines 1–27 of Table 1 would be repeated, with the exception that time-point t_4 is replaced by t_5, i.e., the time-point of the *propose* event of expression (11). Subsequently, the call to brokenBetween$(status(m) = null, t_3, t_5)$ would succeed, since $status(m) = null$ is broken at t_4, thus leading to no new initiation points for $status(m) = proposed$. Similarly, additional messages in the event stream, such as several agents proposing or seconding a motion, would increase significantly the number of unnecessary re-computations.

Furthermore, consider, e.g., the computation of the maximal intervals for which $status(M) = voting$ holds continuously, that could follow the computation of the maximal intervals for which $status(M) = proposed$. First, we would have to compute the initiation points of $status(M) = voting$, i.e.:

$$\mathsf{initiatedAt}(status(M) = voting,\ q_i{-}\omega,\ T,\ q_i).$$

To calculate these initiation points, we would have to repeat the computations presented in lines 10–21 of Table 1, i.e., we would have to prove again that holdsAt$(status(M) = proposed, t_1)$. Similarly, to calculate the maximal intervals for which $status(M) = voted$, we would have to repeat the computations presented in lines 7–24 of Table 1, for computing the initiation points of this FVP, while to calculate the maximal intervals for which $status(M) = null$, we would have to repeat the computations presented in lines 4–27 of Table 1.

4 Efficient Treatment of Cyclic Dependencies

To address these issues, we propose RTEC$_\circ$, an extension of RTEC that computes, in an efficient way, the maximal intervals during which a FVP with cyclic dependencies holds continuously. To achieve this, RTEC$_\circ$ performs incremental caching when processing FVPs in a cycle. Below we present the semantics, reasoning algorithms and complexity of RTEC$_\circ$. The syntax of the rules in RTEC$_\circ$ is the same as that of RTEC.

Semantics. In RTEC$_\circ$, the dependency graph of an event description may include cycles. Thus, we need to modify Definition 4 of FVP level to cater for cyclic dependency graphs. The strongly connected components (SCCs) of a cyclic dependency graph include either a single vertex of a FVP with no cyclic dependencies or a set of vertices of FVPs among which there are cyclic dependencies. A dependency graph becomes acyclic by contracting its SCCs into single vertices.

Definition 5 (SCC Contracted Graph)**.** Given a directed graph G, its set of vertices V, its set of edges E and its SCCs $S_1, S_2, \dots, S_n$, the *SCC contracted graph* $G' = (V',\ E')$ of G is defined as follows:

1. $V' = \bigcup_{1 \leq i \leq n} \{v_{S_i}\}$.
2. $e = (v_{S_i},\ v_{S_j}) \in E'$ iff $\exists v_i, v_j \in V$, such that $v_i \in S_i$, $v_j \in S_j$ and $e = (v_i,\ v_j) \in E$. ■

By construction, G' is acyclic. To construct the SCC contracted graph of voting (resp. NetBill), for example, we must merge the red nodes of the top (bottom) dependency graph shown in Figure 1 into a single node.

Definition 6 (FVP Level in RTEC$_\circ$)**.** Given a dependency graph G in RTEC$_\circ$ and the SCC contracted graph G' of G, the *level* of a FVP $F{=}V$ included in the SCC S_i of G is equal to the level of the vertex v_{S_i} of G', which is derived by following Definition 4. ■

According to Definition 6, all FVPs whose vertices are in the same cycle, and thus in the same SCC of the dependency graph, have the same level.

Proposition 2 (Semantics of RTEC$_\circ$)**.** An event description in RTEC$_\circ$ is a locally stratified logic program. ◊

Unlike RTEC, a local stratification of an event description in RTEC$_\circ$ cannot be derived solely by partitioning the groundings of its predicates in terms of the level of the FVP they concern. The ground predicates for FVPs with cyclic dependencies have to be stratified further in terms of their time-stamp. At each FVP level (with cyclic dependencies), additional strata may be introduced for each time-point of the window ω.

Reasoning. Similar to RTEC, RTEC$_\circ$ computes and caches the maximal intervals of FVPs in a bottom-up manner, following their level in the dependency graph, while the intervals of FVPs in the same level may be computed and cached in any order. In contrast to RTEC, RTEC$_\circ$ supports cyclic dependencies, and employs Algorithms 1 and 2 to evaluate the holdsAt predicates found in the bodies of initiatedAt and terminatedAt rules defining FVPs in a cycle. Algorithms 1 and 2 are an efficient implementation of rules (6)–(8), i.e., they incorporate an incremental caching technique to avoid unnecessary re-computations, such as those mentioned in Section 3.

To compute holdsAt($F = V,\ T$), RTEC$_\circ$ first checks whether $F{=}V$ has been processed at the current query-time q_i (see line 1 of Algorithm 1), i.e., whether the maximal intervals for which $F{=}V$ holds continuously have been computed. If they have been computed, then RTEC$_\circ$ fetches them from the cache (line 2) and checks whether T belongs in these intervals (line 3). If the intervals have not been computed yet, then RTEC$_\circ$ checks whether some time-points, before or at T, for which $F{=}V$ holds or not have already been cached (see cachedLEQ in line 4). If that is the

Algorithm 1 holdsAt($F = V,\ T$)

1: **if** processed($F = V$) **then**
2:     holdsFor($F = V,\ I$)
3:     **if** $T \in I$ **then return** true
4: **else if** cachedLEQ($T,\ F = V$) $\neq []$ **then**
5:     *last*(cachedLEQ($T,\ F = V$), ($T_{lCP},\ Tval_{lCP}$))
6:     **if** $T == T_{lCP}$ **then**
7:         **if** $Tval_{lCP} == +$ **then return** true
8:     **else if** holdsAtEC($F = V,\ T_{lCP},\ T,\ Tval_{lCP}$) **then**
9:         updateCache($F = V,\ T,\ +$)
10:         **return** true
11:     **else** updateCache($F = V,\ T,\ -$)
12: **else**
13:     **if** holdsAtEC($F = V,\ q_i{-}\omega,\ T,\ -$) **then**
14:         updateCache($F = V,\ T,\ +$)
15:         **return** true
16:     **else** updateCache($F = V,\ T,\ -$)
17: **return** false

Algorithm 2 holdsAtEC($F = V,\ T_{lCP},\ T,\ Tval_{lCP}$)

1: **if** $T_{lCP} < T$ **then**
2:     **if** $Tval_{lCP} == +$ **then**
3:         **if** brokenAt($F = V,\ T_{lCP},\ T_b,\ T$) **then**
4:             **if** holdsAtEC($F = V,\ T_b{+}1,\ T,\ -$) **then**
5:                 **return** true
6:         **else return** true
7:     **else**
8:         **if** initiatedAt($F = V,\ T_{lCP},\ T_i,\ T$) **then**
9:             **if** holdsAtEC($F = V,\ T_i{+}1,\ T,\ +$) **then**
10:                 **return** true
11: **return** false

case (lines 4–11), then RTEC$_\circ$ retrieves the cached time-point T_{lCP} closer to T along with the truth value $Tval_{lCP}$ of $F{=}V$ at T_{lCP} (line 5). If T_{lCP} coincides with T (line 6), then its truth value is returned; '$+$' denotes that $F{=}V$ holds and '$-$' that it does not. Otherwise, i.e., if T_{lCP} does not coincide with T (lines 8–11), RTEC$_\circ$ computes whether $F{=}V$ holds at T restricting the evaluation in $[T_{lCP},\ T)$; the evaluation is performed by means of holdsAtEC, which is presented in Algorithm 2. Moreover, the outcome of the evaluation is cached (lines 9 and 11). Finally, if no time-points for $F{=}V$ have been cached (lines 12–16), then RTEC$_\circ$ computes whether $F{=}V$ holds at T performing the evaluation in $[q_i{-}\omega,\ T)$ (line 13) and caching the outcome.

Algorithm 2 presents the steps for evaluating holdsAtEC($F = V,\ T_{lCP},\ T,\ Tval_{lCP}$), i.e., calculating whether $F{=}V$ holds at T restricting the search in $[T_{lCP},\ T)$ and taking into consideration $Tval_{lCP}$, i.e., the truth value of $F{=}V$ at T_{lCP}. All arguments of holdsAtEC are ground. First, if $F{=}V$ holds at T_{lCP} (see lines 2–6 of Algorithm 2), then we check whether $F{=}V$ is broken at some time $T_b \in [T_{lCP},\ T)$. brokenAt is a simple variation of brokenBetween (see rules (7) and (8)) returning the time-point at which a FVP is broken. If $F{=}V$ is not broken in $[T_{lCP},\ T)$, then RTEC$_\circ$ returns that $F{=}V$ holds at T. Otherwise, i.e., if $F{=}V$ is broken at some $T_b \in [T_{lCP},\ T)$, RTEC$_\circ$ calls recursively holdsAtEC, this time restricting the

Predicate	Rule/Alg.
1 initiatedAt($s(m)=proposed,\ q_i-\omega,\ T,\ q_i$) ?	(2)
2 happensAt($propose(ag_p, m),\ t_5$) ✓	(2), (11)
3 holdsAt($s(m)=null,\ t_5$) ?	(2), a1
4 processed($s(m)=null$) ×	a1
5 $last$(cachedLEQ($t_5,\ s(m)=null$), $(t_4, +)$) ✓	a1, (12)
6 holdsAtEC($s(m)=null,\ t_4,\ t_5,\ +$) ?	a1, a2
7 brokenAt($s(m)=null,\ t_4,\ t_4,\ t_5$) ✓	a2
8 holdsAtEC($s(m)=null,\ t_4+1,\ t_5,\ -$) ×	a2
9 holdsAtEC($s(m)=null,\ t_4,\ t_5,\ +$) ×	a2, a1
10 updateCache($s(m)=null,\ t_5,\ -$) ✓	a1
11 holdsAt($s(m)=null,\ t_5$) ×	a1, (2)
12 initiatedAt($s(m)=proposed,\ q_i-\omega,\ T,\ q_i$) ×	(2)
13 initiatedAt($s(m)=voting,\ q_i-\omega,\ T,\ q_i$) ?	(3)
14 happensAt($second(ag_s, m),\ t_1$) ✓	(3), (9)
15 holdsAt($s(m)=proposed,\ t_1$) ?	(3), a1
16 processed($s(m)=proposed$) ✓	a1
17 holdsFor($s(m)=proposed,\ I$), $t_1 \in I$ ✓	a1
18 holdsAt($s(m)=proposed,\ t_1$) ✓	a1, (3)
19 initiatedAt($s(m)=voting,\ q_i-\omega,\ t_1,\ q_i$) ✓	(3)
20 initiatedAt($s(m)=null,\ q_i-\omega,\ T,\ q_i$) ?	(5)
21 happensAt($declare(ag_c, m),\ t_3$) ✓	(5), (9)
22 holdsAt($s(m)=voted,\ t_3$) ?	(5), a1
23 processed($s(m)=voted$) ×	a1
24 $last$(cachedLEQ($t_3,\ s(m)=voted$), $(t_3, +)$) ✓	a1, (12)
25 holdsAt($s(m)=proposed,\ t_3$) ✓	a1, (5′)
26 initiatedAt($s(m)=null,\ q_i-\omega,\ t_3,\ q_i$) ✓	(5)

Table 2: Stream reasoning with RTEC$_\circ$. '$status(m)$' is abbreviated as '$s(m)$'. a1–a2 refer to Algorithms 1–2.

evaluation interval to $[T_b+1,\ T)$, where T_b+1 denotes the next time-point of T_b, and starting from the negative truth value of $F=V$ at T_b. Second, if $F=V$ does not hold at T_{ICP} (see lines 7–10), then RTEC$_\circ$ determines whether $F=V$ is initiated at some $T_i \in [T_{ICP},\ T)$. If $F=V$ is initiated in this interval, RTEC$_\circ$ calls holdsAtEC with the evaluation interval $[T_i+1,\ T)$ and the initial truth value of $F=V$ being positive. The example below illustrates the incremental caching of RTEC$_\circ$.

Example 4. Consider the stream consisting of events (9) and (11), while the initial value of $status(m)$ in the current window is *proposed* (see formula (10)). The computation of the initiation points of $status(m)=proposed$ commences with the evaluation presented in Table 1, with some additional calls, e.g., to processed (see Algorithm 1), to check for cached intervals and time-points. Furthermore, RTEC$_\circ$ caches all computed time-points for which a FVP holds. In this example, RTEC$_\circ$ caches the following:

$$\begin{aligned} &\text{holdsAt}(status(m)=proposed,\ t_1).\\ &\text{holdsAt}(status(m)=voting,\ t_2).\\ &\text{holdsAt}(status(m)=voted,\ t_3).\\ &\text{holdsAt}(status(m)=null,\ t_4).\end{aligned} \qquad (12)$$

The top part of Table 2 (lines 1–12) shows the remaining evaluation concerning the initiation points of $status(m)=proposed$, and, in particular, the processing of the event $propose(ag_p, m)$ at t_5. As in Table 1, we show a subset of the predicate calls to simplify the presentation. To prove whether $status(m)=null$ holds at t_5, as required by rule (2), RTEC$_\circ$ follows Algorithm 1 and consults the cache, first by determining if the intervals of this FVP have already been computed—at this stage they have not—and then by looking for cached time-points. The closest cached time-point to t_5 is t_4, while $status(m)=null$ holds at t_4 (see cache (12)). Subsequently, RTEC$_\circ$ follows Algorithm 2 to prove whether $status(m)=null$ still holds at t_5. This is not the case, since $status(m)=null$ is broken at t_4 (by the occurrence of a *propose* event at that time) and not re-initiated in the meantime. Consequently, no new initiation points are computed for $status(m)=proposed$.

With the use of caching, RTEC$_\circ$ can restrict attention to the events that have not been processed so far, avoiding unnecessary re-computations. In this example, without the cached time-points of *status* we would have to repeat most of the steps presented in Example 3, only to compute again the values of *status* before t_5.

The middle part of Table 2 (lines 13–19) shows the computation of the initiation points of $status(m)=voting$. At this stage, the intervals I for which $status(m)=proposed$ holds continuously have been computed and cached, and are $(q_i-\omega,\ t_1]$ and $(t_4,\ \infty)$. In other words, m is said to be 'proposed' from the beginning of the current window until t_1, and since t_4. As can be seen from Table 2, the computation of the initiation points of $status(m)=voting$ is very efficient. RTEC$_\circ$ quickly computes that $status(m)=proposed$ holds at t_1, as required by rule (3), since the intervals of this FVP may be fetched from the cache. This way, the unnecessary re-computations discussed after Example 3 are avoided.

The bottom part of Table 2 (lines 20–26) presents another illustration of the effects of incremental caching, by showing the computation of the initiation points of $status(m)=null$. Again, reasoning is very efficient: we fetch from the cache (12) time-point t_3 for which $status(m)=voted$ holds, and directly prove rule (5) expressing the conditions in which $status(m)=null$ is initiated. ♦

Complexity. We present the worst-case complexity of Algorithms 1 and 2, and compare it against the complexity of reasoning with cycles in the absence of incremental caching. According to Algorithms 1 and 2, RTEC$_\circ$ consults its cache to evaluate holdsAt($F=V,\ T$), and when reasoning is necessary, it is restricted to intervals that have not been explored so far. Moreover, after the end of the evaluation of holdsAt($F=V,\ T$) the cache is updated. Therefore, in the worst-case, RTEC$_\circ$ will have to evaluate each initiatedAt/terminatedAt rule for $F=V$ at every-time point of ω, but no more than that. In other words, the worst-case complexity is

$$\mathcal{O}(\omega k), \qquad (13)$$

where ω denotes the window size and k is the cost of computing whether a FVP is initiated or terminated at a given time-point (see (Artikis, Sergot, and Paliouras 2015) for an estimation of k).

In the absence of incremental caching, we do not mark the intervals that have been explored so far, and thus we may repeat evaluations that have already been performed. In the worst-case, the evaluation of all earlier initiation and termination points of FVPs in a cycle has to repeated ω times.

Thus, the worst-case complexity is

$$\mathcal{O}(\omega^2 rk), \tag{14}$$

where r is the number of FVPs in a cycle.

In real-world applications, ω, i.e., the window size, can be large. Therefore, the use of the caching mechanism of RTEC$_\circ$ leads to significant performance gains (compare expressions (13) and (14)). This is key difference of our proposed computational framework from related work.

5 Experimental Analysis

5.1 Experimental Setup

We evaluated RTEC$_\circ$ on two multi-agent systems (MAS) protocols, formalising a voting procedure and NetBill, an e-commerce procedure, as well as on composite event recognition for maritime situational awareness. The complete event descriptions of all applications, including the corresponding datasets, are available with the code of RTEC$_\circ$[1], allowing the *reproducibility* of our empirical analysis.

Voting & NetBill. The voting protocol is our running example (Pitt et al. 2006). Agents occupy the roles of proposer, seconder, voter and/or chair, and deliberate over various motions over time. NetBill includes consumers and merchants negotiating over digital goods (Sirbu 1997). Consumers request quotes for goods and the interested merchants reply with the quotes, or even proactively advertise their goods. A timely acceptance of a quote leads to a contract, which defines the processes of sending the digital goods and payment (Artikis and Sergot 2010). In both protocols, a set of normative positions, such as institutionalised power, permission and obligation, guide the behaviour of the agents (Sergot 2001). Moreover, sanctions deal with the performance of forbidden actions and non-compliance with obligations. Figure 1 displays the dependency graphs of these protocols.

Synthetic data generators produced the event streams of the two protocols. In the case of voting, multiple agents and motions were generated, and the agents were assigned roles. Then, agents proposed motions, some of which were subsequently seconded and voted for. In the case of NetBill, quotes were progressively requested, presented, accepted and sometimes fulfilled. To simulate realistic MAS, the data generators produced events which do not comply with the rules, e.g. closing the ballot before all votes are cast, and not complying with the terms of a contract in NetBill. RTEC$_\circ$ was instructed to compute, in an online fashion, the maximal intervals of the FVPs presented in Figure 1, e.g., compute the maximal intervals in which an agent is permitted to perform an action.

Maritime Situational Awareness. In this application, the input events are Automatic Identification System (AIS) position signals emitted by vessels, including information about their heading, speed and navigational status. FVPs express various types of dangerous, suspicious and illegal vessel activity, such as ship-to-ship transfer of goods in the open sea, that must be detected in real-time. We extended the event description of Pitsikalis et al. (2019) with cyclic dependencies among FVPs, as required by domain experts, in order to capture more accurately the maritime behaviours of interest, such as fishing. We evaluated RTEC$_\circ$ on a publicly available dataset[2] of 18M AIS position signals, emitted from 5K vessels sailing in the Atlantic Ocean around the port of Brest, France, between October 2015–March 2016. Moreover, we employed a much larger dataset, made available to us by IMIS Global[3], containing 55M position signals from 34K vessels sailing in the European seas between January 1-30, 2016. A description of both datasets may be found in (Pitsikalis et al. 2019).

RTEC$_\circ$ is written in Prolog[1]. Our experiments were conducted using YAP-6.3 Prolog, on a single node of a desktop PC running Ubuntu 20.04, with Intel Core i7-4770 CPU @ 3.40GHz and 16GB RAM.

5.2 Experimental Results

We begin with a set of experiments which demonstrate the benefits of our caching mechanism for processing FVPs with cyclic dependencies. For this purpose, we employed a downgraded version of RTEC$_\circ$, named RTEC$_\circ$-naive, which processes FVPs with cyclic dependencies without a caching mechanism. Figure 2a shows the experimental results in voting and NetBill. The presented reasoning times are an average of 100 windows, while RTEC$_\circ$ and RTEC$_\circ$-naive always produced the same FVP intervals. We used a maximum response time of 10 seconds per window, i.e., when the reasoning time exceeded this threshold, then we stopped the execution. The reasoning times of RTEC$_\circ$-naive, using windows of 80 time-points, exceeded this threshold for both MAS protocols and, therefore, are not presented in Figure 2a. Our experimental results show that, as we increase the window size, the reasoning times of RTEC$_\circ$-naive increase exponentially, while RTEC$_\circ$ scales much better. These results are consistent with our complexity analysis, which indicated that the absence of the caching mechanism of RTEC$_\circ$ results in unnecessary re-computations, that increase with the window size.

In the next set of experiments, we compared RTEC$_\circ$ against jREC, a Java-Prolog implementation of the 'Reactive Event Calculus' (Chesani et al. 2010; Montali et al. 2013). jREC has been evaluated in several application domains (Bragaglia et al. 2012; Chesani et al. 2013; Loreti et al. 2019). Moreover, it is an open-source implementation[4], which facilitates the comparison against RTEC$_\circ$. Figure 2b shows the results of the comparison. Both systems were evaluated on a fragment of the event description of the voting protocol. We restricted attention to the $status$ fluent, the specification of which creates a cycle in the dependency graph (see Figure 1). The task, therefore, was to compute the maximal intervals for which $status$ has some value ($proposed$, $voting$, $voted$, $null$) continuously. We used a window size of 10 time-points for RTEC$_\circ$ and instructed jREC to evaluate the trace of input events every 10 time-points. We performed experiments for windows with 800–6,400 events, and made sure that both systems computed the same FVP intervals. Figure 2b shows that the use of RTEC$_\circ$ leads to significant performance gain. Moving

[2]https://zenodo.org/record/1167595

[3]https://imisglobal.com/

[4]https://www.inf.unibz.it/~montali/tools.html

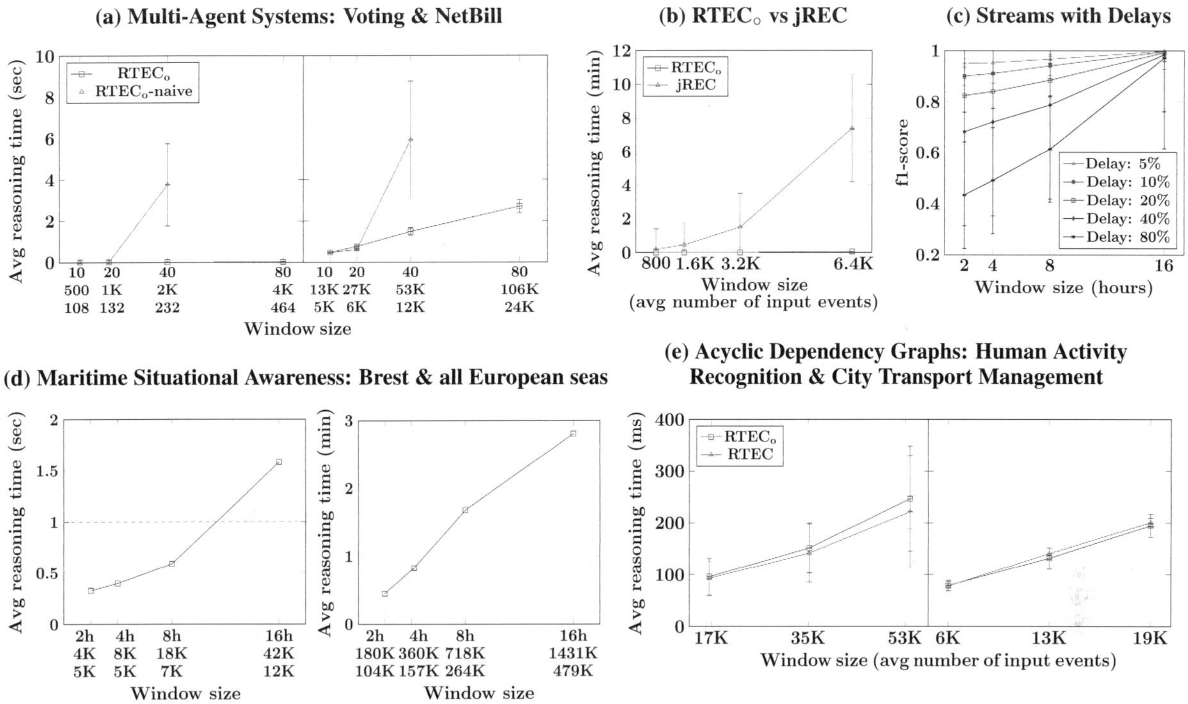

Figure 2: (a) The reasoning times of RTEC$_\circ$ and RTEC$_\circ$-naive in voting (left) and NetBill (right). The horizontal axis denotes window size in terms of time-points (top), average number of input entities (middle) and average number of computed FVP intervals (bottom) per window. (b) RTEC$_\circ$ and jREC computing the maximal intervals of the *status* fluent of the voting protocol. (c) The predictive accuracy of RTEC$_\circ$ in the presence of delayed events on the dataset of Brest. (d) RTEC$_\circ$ for maritime situational awareness on the datasets of Brest (left) and Europe (right). The window size is presented as in figure (a). (e) The reasoning times of RTEC$_\circ$ and RTEC in temporal specifications without cyclic dependencies: human activity recognition (left) and city transport management (right).

from 800 events to 6,400 events barely affects the performance of RTEC$_\circ$. In contrast, jREC requires considerably more time to process the increasing number of input events.

In addition to MAS, we evaluated RTEC$_\circ$ on composite event recognition for maritime situational awareness. We relied on real data, i.e., position signals from thousands of vessels, producing millions of input events. Real data streams often include delayed events. In the maritime domain, vessel position signals may arrive with a delay that exceeds 6 hours, especially when such signals are relayed through satellites. This issue may be addressed by longer, overlapping windows (see Section 2). To simulate realistic scenarios, we introduced delays into the maritime datasets. The temporal extent of the delay was set using a Gamma distribution. The percentage of delayed events, which were chosen uniformly, ranges from 5% to 80%. Figure 2c shows the predictive accuracy of RTEC$_\circ$ when processing data streams with delayed events. The step, i.e., the temporal distance between two consecutive query times, was set to 2 hours. We varied the size of the windows from 2 hours to 16 hours. The f1-scores were derived by comparing the intervals computed by RTEC$_\circ$ on data streams with delayed events to the intervals computed by RTEC$_\circ$ on the respective data streams without delayed events. Figure 2c demonstrates the necessity of longer windows in the maritime domain.

Figure 2d displays the average reasoning times of RTEC$_\circ$ per window size when processing real maritime data. In the dataset of Brest, the 2-hour window includes on average 4K events/vessel position signals, while the 16-hour window includes approximately 42K events. The computed FVP intervals range from 5K, in the 2-hour window, to 12K in the 16-hour window. In the significantly larger dataset concerning all European seas, the windows include 180K–1,431K events, while the computed FVP intervals range between 104K and 479K. We introduced delays to 40% of the inputs events in the data streams. Figure 2d shows that RTEC$_\circ$ is capable of real-time stream reasoning in real-world applications. In the dataset of Brest, e.g., RTEC$_\circ$ reasons about the events of a 16-hour window in just over 1.5 seconds, in order to recognise a wide range of maritime activities of interest, such as fishing, tugging, etc., while in the dataset of all European seas, RTEC$_\circ$ requires just below 3 minutes to reason about a 16-hour window.

For completeness, we compared RTEC$_\circ$ and RTEC in temporal specifications without cyclic dependencies, i.e., the specifications used for human activity recognition and city transport management in (Artikis, Sergot, and Paliouras 2015). Figure 2e displays the average reasoning times. In both applications, the reasoning times of $RTEC_{\circ}$ are comparable to those of RTEC. In other words, the mechanism of $RTEC_{\circ}$ for handling FVPs with cyclic dependencies does not impose a computational overhead in applications without such dependencies.

6 Related Work

Numerous computational frameworks based on the Event Calculus have been proposed in the literature. The 'Macro-Event Calculus' (Cervesato and Montanari 2000), e.g., leverages the concept of 'macro-event' to support composite/macro event operators such as sequence, disjunction, parallelism and iteration. The 'Interval-based Event Calculus' (Paschke and Bichler 2008) supports the representation of durative events and includes various event operators, such as sequence, concurrency and negation. The F2LP system translates a reformulation of the Event Calculus into answer set programs, so that the efficient answer set programming solvers may be used for reasoning (Lee and Palla 2012). The 'Reactive Event Calculus' (REC) (Chesani et al. 2010; Montali et al. 2013) adopts a lightweight version of the *update-time* reasoning of the 'Cached Event Calculus' (Chittaro and Montanari 1996), which retrieves and revises the necessary fluent intervals upon the arrival of (delayed) events.

None of these frameworks handles effectively cyclic dependencies. $RTEC_{\circ}$ includes an incremental caching technique for dealing with such dependencies efficiently, and consequently may scale to high-velocity data streams. Our complexity analysis showed the performance gains of $RTEC_{\circ}$. Furthermore, our extensive empirical analysis, and comparison with jREC, i.e., the Java-Prolog implementation of REC, demonstrated the effectiveness of our approach.

Various frameworks for reasoning over streams have been proposed in the literature (Dell'Aglio et al. 2017; Dell'Aglio et al. 2019). Ronca (2020), e.g., provides tight complexity bounds for a temporal extension of negation-free Datalog. LARS is a well-known stream reasoning language featuring built-in window constructs (Beck, Dao-Tran, and Eiter 2018). Laser (Bazoobandi, Beck, and Urbani 2017) is a reasoner that employs a fixed-point materialisation of restricted LARS formulas to handle data streams. The empirical analysis of Beck et al. (2018) showed that Laser outperforms other related reasoners (Beck, Eiter, and Folie 2017; Le-Phuoc et al. 2011; Barbieri et al. 2010). Laser, however, cannot express the event descriptions of $RTEC_{\circ}$ since it is restricted to stratified negation.

Eiter et al. (2019) presented a distributed architecture using 'stream stratification' (Beck, Dao-Tran, and Eiter 2018) in order to decompose LARS programs into sub-programs that may be evaluated in parallel, while Dodaro et al. (2020) presented an approach handling constraint satisfaction problems in a streaming setting by means of reinforcement learning. These issues are orthogonal to our work; e.g., we aim to develop distributed reasoning techniques (Giatrakos et al. 2020) for $RTEC_{\circ}$ as part of our future work.

In the field of composite event recognition, one of the best known logic-based stream reasoning systems is the Chronicle Recognition System (Dousson and Maigat 2007). TESLA (Cugola and Margara 2010) is an event pattern language that supports content and temporal filters, negation, timers, aggregates and customisable selection and consumption policies. Neither of these frameworks supports cyclic dependencies. ETALIS (Anicic et al. 2012) is a logic programming framework that aims to support event recognition by combining reasoning over streams and background knowledge. ETALIS does not allow for the explicit representation of time, complicating the specification of fluent value changes, including the formalisation of the commonsense law of inertia. Moreover, it is unclear how one may model cyclic dependencies, such as those of the applications presented in this paper, in the language of ETALIS.

A key difference between our work and the aforementioned stream reasoning frameworks lies in the use of the Event Calculus, which allows us to develop expressive temporal specifications for a wide range of applications, such as MAS and composite event recognition. At the same time, the built-in representation of inertia allows us to develop succinct specifications, supporting code maintenance and reasoning efficiency. With the use of the Event Calculus, one may develop intuitive specifications, facilitating the interaction between data scientist and domain (e.g. maritime) expert, and pave the way for explainability. Furthermore, we may develop custom optimisation techniques, such as those presented in this paper, to meet the requirements of contemporary applications concerning latency.

Wan (2009) presented a framework for belief logic programming that eliminates cyclic dependencies by introducing auxiliary rules and atoms representing intermediate results. The number of these auxiliary clauses increases with the length of the cycle. On the contrary, $RTEC_{\circ}$ handles cycles by utilising the Event Calculus, e.g., the formalisation of the law of inertia, and does not require auxiliary clauses. Moura and Damásio (2015) presented an approach for modular logic programming that supports positive cycles, i.e., cycles without negation. In contrast, $RTEC_{\circ}$ is not restricted to positive cycles. Moreover, we presented reasoning algorithms for handling cycles in an efficient manner.

7 Summary & Further Work

We presented $RTEC_{\circ}$, a formal computational framework for reasoning over real-world streams and temporal specifications including cyclic dependencies. The event descriptions in $RTEC_{\circ}$ are locally stratified logic programs. $RTEC_{\circ}$ includes a novel incremental caching mechanism, which avoids unnecessary re-computations and thus optimises stream reasoning. We evaluated $RTEC_{\circ}$ by means of a complexity analysis and showed its benefits. Furthermore, we presented an extensive, reproducible empirical evaluation, on both synthetic and real data streams, including millions of events. For further work, we will investigate the use of distributed reasoning techniques in $RTEC_{\circ}$ (Eiter, Ogris, and Schekotihin 2019; Giatrakos et al. 2020).

Acknowledgements

This work was supported by the INFORE project, which has received funding from the European Union's Horizon 2020 research and innovation programme, under grant agreement No 825070.

References

Anicic, D.; Rudolph, S.; Fodor, P.; and Stojanovic, N. 2012. Real-time complex event recognition and reasoning-a logic programming approach. *Applied Artificial Intelligence* 26(1-2):6–57.

Artikis, A., and Sergot, M. 2010. Executable specification of open multi-agent systems. *Logic Journal of the IGPL* 18(1):31–65.

Artikis, A.; Sergot, M.; and Paliouras, G. 2015. An event calculus for event recognition. *IEEE TKDE* 27(4):895–908.

Barbieri, D. F.; Braga, D.; Ceri, S.; Valle, E. D.; and Grossniklaus, M. 2010. C-SPARQL: a continuous query language for RDF data streams. *Int. J. Semantic Comput.* 4(1):3–25.

Bazoobandi, H. R.; Beck, H.; and Urbani, J. 2017. Expressive stream reasoning with laser. In *ISWC*, volume 10587, 87–103.

Beck, H.; Dao-Tran, M.; and Eiter, T. 2018. LARS: A logic-based framework for analytic reasoning over streams. *Artif. Intell.* 261:16–70.

Beck, H.; Eiter, T.; and Folie, C. 2017. Ticker: A system for incremental asp-based stream reasoning. *Theory Pract. Log. Program.* 17(5-6):744–763.

Bragaglia, S.; Chesani, F.; Mello, P.; Montali, M.; and Torroni, P. 2012. Reactive event calculus for monitoring global computing applications. In *Logic Programs, Norms and Action*, volume 7360, 123–146.

Cervesato, I., and Montanari, A. 2000. A calculus of macro-events: Progress report. In *TIME*, 47–58.

Chesani, F.; Mello, P.; Montali, M.; and Torroni, P. 2010. A logic-based, reactive calculus of events. *Fundam. Informaticae* 105(1-2):135–161.

Chesani, F.; Mello, P.; Montali, M.; and Torroni, P. 2013. Representing and monitoring social commitments using the event calculus. *Auton. Agents Multi Agent Syst.* 27(1):85–130.

Chittaro, L., and Montanari, A. 1996. Efficient temporal reasoning in the cached event calculus. *Computational Intelligence* 12(3):359–382.

Clark, K. 1978. Negation as failure. In Gallaire, H., and Minker, J., eds., *Logic and Databases*. 293–322.

Cugola, G., and Margara, A. 2010. Tesla: a formally defined event specification language. In *DEBS*, 50.

Dell'Aglio, D.; Valle, E. D.; van Harmelen, F.; and Bernstein, A. 2017. Stream reasoning: A survey and outlook. *Data Sci.* 1(1-2):59–83.

Dell'Aglio, D.; Eiter, T.; Heintz, F.; and Phuoc, D. L. 2019. Special issue on stream reasoning. *Semantic Web* 10(3):453–455.

Dodaro, C.; Eiter, T.; Ogris, P.; and Schekotihin, K. 2020. Managing caching strategies for stream reasoning with reinforcement learning. *TPLP* 20(5):625–640.

Dousson, C., and Maigat, P. L. 2007. Chronicle recognition improvement using temporal focusing and hierarchisation. In *IJCAI*, 324–329.

Eiter, T.; Ogris, P.; and Schekotihin, K. 2019. A distributed approach to LARS stream reasoning (system paper). *TPLP* 19(5-6):974–989.

Giatrakos, N.; Alevizos, E.; Artikis, A.; Deligiannakis, A.; and Garofalakis, M. N. 2020. Complex event recognition in the big data era: a survey. *VLDB J.* 29(1):313–352.

Kowalski, R., and Sergot, M. 1986. A logic-based calculus of events. *New Generation Computing* 4(1):67–96.

Le-Phuoc, D.; Dao-Tran, M.; Xavier Parreira, J.; and Hauswirth, M. 2011. A native and adaptive approach for unified processing of linked streams and linked data. In *The Semantic Web – ISWC*, 370–388.

Lee, J., and Palla, R. 2012. Reformulating the situation calculus and the event calculus in the general theory of stable models and in answer set programming. *J. Artif. Intell. Res.* 43:571–620.

Loreti, D.; Chesani, F.; Mello, P.; Roffia, L.; Antoniazzi, F.; Cinotti, T. S.; Paolini, G.; Masotti, D.; and Costanzo, A. 2019. Complex reactive event processing for assisted living: The habitat project case study. *Expert Systems with Applications* 126:200–217.

Montali, M.; Maggi, F. M.; Chesani, F.; Mello, P.; and van der Aalst, W. M. P. 2013. Monitoring business constraints with the event calculus. *ACM Trans. Intell. Syst. Technol.* 5(1):17:1–17:30.

Moura, J., and Damásio, C. V. 2015. Allowing cyclic dependencies in modular logic programming. In *Progress in Artificial Intelligence*, 363–375.

Paschke, A., and Bichler, M. 2008. Knowledge representation concepts for automated SLA management. *Decis. Support Syst.* 46(1):187–205.

Pitsikalis, M.; Artikis, A.; Dreo, R.; Ray, C.; Camossi, E.; and Jousselme, A. 2019. Composite event recognition for maritime monitoring. In *DEBS*, 163–174.

Pitt, J.; Kamara, L.; Sergot, M.; and Artikis, A. 2006. Voting in multi-agent systems. *Computer Journal* 49(2):156–170.

Przymusinski, T. 1987. On the declarate semantics of stratified deductive databases and logic programs. In *Foundations of Deductive Databases and Logic Programming*.

Ronca, A. 2020. *Rule-based stream reasoning*. Ph.D. Dissertation, University of Oxford, UK.

Sergot, M. 2001. A computational theory of normative positions. *ACM Transactions on Computational Logic* 2(4):522–581.

Sirbu, M. 1997. Credits and debits on the Internet. *IEEE Spectrum* 34(2):23–29.

Wan, H. 2009. Belief logic programming with cyclic dependencies. In *Web Reasoning and Rule Systems*, volume 5837, 150–165.

Proceedings of the 19th International Conference on Principles of Knowledge Representation and Reasoning
Applications and Systems

Symbolic Knowledge Extraction from Opaque Machine Learning Predictors: GridREx & PEDRO

Federico Sabbatini[1] , **Roberta Calegari**[2]
[1]Dipartimento di Scienze Pure e Applicate (DiSPeA),
Università degli Studi di Urbino "Carlo Bo", Italy
[2]Alma AI—Alma Mater Research Institute for Human-Centered Artificial Intelligence,
ALMA MATER STUDIORUM–Università di Bologna, Italy
f.sabbatini1@campus.uniurb.it, roberta.calegari@unibo.it

Abstract

Procedures aimed at explaining outcomes and behaviour of opaque predictors are becoming more and more essential as machine learning (ML) black-box (BB) models pervade a wide variety of fields and, in particular, critical ones – e.g., medical or financial –, where it is not possible to make decisions on the basis of a blind automatic prediction. A growing number of methods designed to overcome this BB limitation is present in the literature, however some ML tasks are nearly or completely neglected—e.g., regression and clustering. Furthermore, existing techniques may be not applicable in complex real-world scenarios or they can affect the output predictions with undesired artefacts.

In this paper we present the design and the implementation of GridREx, a pedagogical algorithm to extract knowledge from black-box regressors, along with PEDRO, an optimisation procedure to automate the GridREx hyper-parameter tuning phase with better results than manual tuning. We also report the results of our experiments involving the application of GridREx and PEDRO in real case scenarios, including GridREx performance assessment by using as benchmarks other similar state-of-the-art techniques. GridREx proved to be able to give more concise explanations with higher fidelity and predictive capabilities.

1 Introduction & Motivation

Nowadays machine learning (ML) techniques – e.g., artificial neural networks (ANNs) – are among the most widespread tools to face almost any kind of task (Rocha, Papa, and Meira 2012). The learning process consists of the model internal parameter tuning in order to maximise its predictive capability w.r.t. the domain data. Despite the impressive predictive power of ML algorithms even in complex scenarios, the major drawback in the application of these techniques is their *opacity*, intended as their inability to provide any intelligible representation of the acquired knowledge. Opaque models are commonly named *black boxes* (BBs), because they can only represent knowledge in a *sub-symbolic* way. Since there exist critical fields where it is not possible to accept BB predictions or recommendations – for instance, healthcare, finance and law domains as well as areas where decision making may affect human lives in terms of health, wealth and freedom – it is of paramount importance to rely on *explainable* predictions to let humans retain accountability and liability over the decisions they make.

According to Guidotti et al. (2018), different strategies can be exploited to pursue the purpose of explainability. For instance, it is possible to obtain explainable data-driven solutions *only* by using *interpretable* algorithms (Rudin 2019)—such as generalised linear models, decision trees, etc. However, in general this can have repercussions on the predictive performance, as the most effective algorithms are excluded—e.g., ANNs. Another strategy consists of deriving *post-hoc* explanations (Kenny et al. 2021), aimed at reverse-engineering the BB inner operation to make it explicit. In this way data scientists are allowed to adopt prediction-effective (but opaque) algorithms without sacrificing human readability. The extraction algorithm presented in this paper belongs to the latter strategy.

Symbolic knowledge extraction (SKE) is among the most promising means to derive *post-hoc* explanations from sub-symbolic BBs. Its main idea is to build a *symbolic* – and thus interpretable – model that mimics the behaviour (a.k.a., output predictions) of the original BB. Symbols may consist of intelligible knowledge—e.g., lists or trees of *rules* that can be exploited to either derive predictions or to better understand the BB behaviour. SKE has been applied, for instance, to credit-risk evaluation (Baesens et al. 2003; Baesens et al. 2001; Steiner et al. 2006), healthcare (Bologna and Pellegrini 1997; Hayashi, Setiono, and Yoshida 2000), credit card screening (Setiono, Baesens, and Mues 2011), intrusion detection systems (Hofmann, Schmitz, and Sick 2003), and keyword extraction (Azcarraga, Liu, and Setiono 2012).

Despite the large amount of SKE techniques existing in the literature, only few of them are explicitly designed for regression—for instance ITER (Huysmans, Baesens, and Vanthienen 2006), REFANN (Setiono, Leow, and Zurada 2002) and GridEx (Sabbatini, Ciatto, and Omicini 2021). Furthermore, they present several limitations in their applications. REFANN is a *decompositional* (Andrews, Diederich, and Tickle 1995) extraction procedure only applicable to 3-layer ANNs and it requires a prior minimisation (not always feasible without loss of predictive performance) of the number of hidden neurons to simplify the extraction process. It is then poorly suited for modern *deep* neural networks. Conversely, ITER and GridEx are *pedagogical* (Andrews, Diederich, and Tickle 1995) approaches which can be applied to any kind of BB regressor since they do not make assumptions on the type and structure of the underlying model. However, ITER predictive performance degrades when applied to *high-dimensional* data sets. GridEx extends ITER in order to overcome its major drawbacks, but both algorithms produce rule lists where each rule is associated to a constant value, so they introduce an undesired discretisation in the output predictions.

In this work we propose GridREx, a new pedagogical knowledge-extraction procedure extending GridEx to overcome the output discretisation issue. While doing so, GridREx is able to produce more concise rule lists with better predictive performances and fidelity w.r.t. the data and the underlying model predictions, respectively. We demonstrate the effectiveness of GridREx by reporting our experiments on real-world scenarios and comparing its performance with the the most exploited state-of-the-art techniques – namely, ITER, GridEx and CART (Breiman et al. 1984) – trained on the same data. Furthermore, since GridREx – as many other SKE algorithms – has several hyper-parameters to be configured to obtain the best output and since the manual tuning of these parameters can be often tedious and unsatisfactory, we also discuss PEDRO, an optimiser explicitly designed to automate the selection of the best GridREx hyper-parameter values. PEDRO is designed according to the hyper-parameters optimisation methodology widely discussed in the literature (Yang and Shami 2020; Feurer and Hutter 2019; Hutter, Kotthoff, and Vanschoren 2019) targeting progressive automation of ML, based on principles from optimization and machine learning itself.

It is worth mentioning that the experiments reported in Section 5 – aimed at producing logic rules as for output – are grouped into two sections. In the first group we report the results of GridREx trained by using as target values the BB predictor outputs instead of the data set original variable. The performance of GridREx is then compared with that of analogous techniques. In the second group we demonstrate how, under some particular circumstances, GridREx can be applied *directly* to the initial training set as well, to obtain an equivalent model performing *rule induction* (Grzymala-Busse 2005). Although this hypothesis requires further investigation, from our first experiments it appears that it is convenient to exploit the predictor when dealing with scattered training sets. More precisely, a sparse data set can be increased by creating a certain number of new random samples and by using the BB predictor as an oracle to obtain corresponding output values. In this way it is possible to augment the data set and thus produce fewer and more precise rules.

2 Related Works

To ease the reader, in the following we provide a brief description of the knowledge-extraction techniques adopted in the experiments presented in Section 5.

ITER ITER is a pedagogical technique based on the iterative creation and expansion of hypercubes in the input feature space. The algorithm terminates if one of the following conditions holds: *(i)* the input space is entirely covered; *(ii)* it is not possible to expand/add further cubes; *(iii)* the maximum number of iterations is reached. Output rules are produced by creating a certain amount of random samples into each cube, then by using the underlying BB to predict the corresponding output values and finally by averaging the predictions to obtain the mean cube output. Thus, each cube corresponds to a human-comprehensible rule and each rule is associated with a constant output.

GridEx GridEx extends the core concepts of ITER to avoid issues concerning computational time, exhaustivity and fidelity. As a consequence, GridEx can be applied under the same circumstances as ITER, but it returns better results in terms of output rule amount and predictive accuracy. GridEx follows a completely different strategy to create the hypercubes associated with the output rules. It iteratively partitions the input space according to given strategies and a sensitivity threshold parameter. As ITER, it outputs rules associated with constant values.

CART CART is a pedagogical algorithm able to induce a regression tree on a data set or a trained BB. The extraction of human-readable rules is based on the conversion of each possible path from the root to leaves into an *if-then* rule. Also in this case the output value is a constant.

3 GridREx

GridREx – Grid Regressive Extractor – is a pedagogical knowledge-extraction method designed for regression tasks. Consequently, it can be applied to any kind of machine learning predictor if the output variable is numeric. GridREx also requires the input attributes to be numeric, so it cannot be applied if the problem domain is described by relevant categorical variables. The algorithm is designed only for univariate regression, but it is possible to split a multivariate regression task into several univariate tasks and then apply the extractor to each one.

The basic idea behind GridREx is to partition the input feature space into hypercubes, by observing the input instances of the data set and the output predictions of the underlying BB. The algorithm leverages on the assumption according to which close input samples should exhibit similar outputs, or at least output values following a similar regression law w.r.t. the input variables. After having identified these hypercubic clusters of similar data points, GridREx creates a human-readable rule for each one. Output rules are *first-order logic* rules, where the premise is a conjunction of conditions on the input variables – i.e., each variable should belong to a specific interval of values – and the action is a regression rule describing the output variable in terms of a linear combination of the input attributes.

3.1 Hyper-Parameters

The behaviour of the GridREx algorithm can be controlled through several user-defined hyper-parameters. These parameters define how to perform the input space partitioning and thus the amount and quality of the output rules. More precisely, the algorithm hyper-parameters are:

1. $n \in \mathbb{N}_{>0}$, i.e., the number of iterations to perform;
2. $m \in \mathbb{N}_{>0}$, i.e., the minimum number of samples to consider in each hypercube;
3. $\theta \in \mathbb{R}_{>0}$, i.e., the hypercube predictive error threshold;
4. $S_1, \ldots, S_n$, i.e., the splitting strategy to adopt at each algorithm iteration $i, i = 1, \ldots, n$.

The notion of *hypercube predictive error* refers to the mean absolute error between the output value provided by GridREx and that of the underlying BB for all the training samples belonging to a hypercube. The threshold parameter can be exploited by users to set the preferred trade-off between *quality* and *readability* of the output rules—intended as average predictive capability of the hypercubes and number of rules, respectively. Please notice that the more the quality increases, the more the readability decreases.

As for the splitting strategies, GridREx allows users to select a different criterion for each iteration by choosing one of the following:

1. a fixed strategy, parametrised with an integer value k, performing k slices along each input dimension, and
2. an adaptive strategy, parametrised with an increasingly-monotone function of the form $f : [0, 1] \to \mathbb{N}_{>0}$, performing $f(r)$ slices along each input dimension with *relevance* equal to r.

For feature relevance, we intend numeric information about how an input feature is important to determine the output variable. GridREx assumes that this measure is normalised in the $[0, 1]$ interval, with the most relevant feature having a relevance equal to 1. Importance values can be estimated in several ways—e.g., (Zien et al. 2009; Zhuang et al. 2019; Altmann et al. 2010). Since we have implemented our algorithm in Python, we exploited a simple feature selection method available within the SciKit-Learn Python library: `feature_selection.f_regression`[1].

Experimental results showed that fixed strategies are a good choice when dealing with data sets described by input attributes having comparable relevance. When this condition does not hold, it is possible to reduce the number of partitions along the less relevant dimensions in order to have fewer output rules without noticeable degradation of their quality. It is worthwhile to notice that the number of partitions greatly impacts on the GridREx performances, in terms of efficiency as well as predictive capabilities and output rules readability. In other words, a large number of partitions implies the same amount of rules, so – despite being more accurate – these rules cover smaller input space regions w.r.t. those produced with fewer partitions. As concerns human readability, the output rule set readability decreases as its dimension grows. Accordingly – considering also that the output variable can depend more on some variables and almost not depend at all on others – we develop adaptive strategies allowing GridREx to create more slices on relevant dimensions and fewer partitions on the others, without losses in the extracted rules' quality. In the following, we refer to the term *grid* to identify an object incapsulating both the maximum number of GridREx iterations and the strategy to adopt at each iteration.

[1]cf. https://scikit-learn.org/stable/modules/generated/sklearn.feature_selection.f_regression.html

3.2 Algorithm

The GridREx algorithm, reported in Algorithm 1, requires a data set of training samples – e.g., the one adopted to train the underlying model – and a BB regressor to be used as an *oracle*. This basic version of GridREx can be modified to perform rule induction from data instead of BB explanation. It is sufficient to use the original output of the data set instances as target during the training phase. Conversely, when adopted as knowledge extractor, GridREx firstly substitutes the output values of the training data set with the corresponding underlying BB model predictions.

The main idea behind GridREx is to partition the *surrounding hypercube* – i.e., the minimal region including all the input instances – in a number of (hyper)cubic regions such that the output values of all the samples in each partition can be described with the same linear combination of the input variables. At the end of the partitioning, each hypercube is converted into an *if-then* logical rule.

GridREx adopts a top-down recursive partitioning, starting from a single region equal to the surrounding hypercube. At each iteration, all the eligible regions are split as specified in the user-defined list of strategies. A region is *eligible* if it contains input samples and its error is above the user-defined threshold. Otherwise, regions can be *negligible* if they contain no input samples or *permanent* if their error is smaller than the threshold. The former are discarded, so there will be no rules associated with them, whereas the latter will be no further partitioned. If a partition contains not enough training instances to provide accurate predictions, GridREx generates random samples, using the underlying BB as an oracle to predict the corresponding output values. The minimum number of samples to be present in each hypercube is one of the hyper-parameters described in the previous section. Obviously, this augmentation phase cannot be performed when GridREx is applied for rule induction.

After every splitting iteration a merging phase is performed to reduce the number of eligible regions. GridREx attempts to pair-wise merge adjacent hypercubes containing samples having similar behaviours, on the basis of the threshold parameter. Specifically, two adjacent hypercubes are joined only if the merged cube predictive error does not exceed the threshold, in order not to hinder the resulting rule quality.

GridREx stopping criteria are the absence of eligible regions to split and the reaching of the user-defined maximum number of iterations. If at least one of these two conditions holds, the algorithm terminates.

To calculate the predictive error corresponding to the identified regions as well as to associate a rule to each one of

Algorithm 1 GridREx pseudocode

Require: grid G, predictive error threshold θ, minimum number of samples per hypercube m to be provided

```
function GRIDREX(R, D)
    H_0 ← SURROUNDINGCUBE(D)
    return SPLIT(1, H_0, R, D)

function SURROUNDINGCUBE(D)
    return the minimal hypercube including all the samples of D

function SPLIT(i, H, R, D)
    d ← depth of G,   Π ← ∅,   Π' ← ∅
    if i > d then
        return {H}
    for all H' ∈ PARTITIONS(H, i) s.t. H' ∩ D ≠ ∅ do
        D ← D ∪ GENERATESAMPLESIN(H', D)
        if PREDICTIVEERROR(H', R, D) ≤ θ then
            Π ← Π ∪ {H'}
        else
            Π' ← Π' ∪ {H'}
    Π'' ← MERGE(Π, R, D)
    for all H' ∈ Π' do
        Π'' ← Π'' ∪ SPLIT(i + 1, H', R, D)                ▷ Recursive step
    return Π''

function PARTITIONS(H, i)
    return { all the partitions of H according to the i-th level of the grid G }

function GENERATESAMPLESIN(H, D)
    c ← |H ∩ D|
    if c < m then
        return { (m − c) random points in H }
    else
        return ∅

function PREDICTIVEERROR(H, R, D)
    return the predictive error of R w.r.t. the samples of D included in H

function MERGE(Π, R, D)
    C ← ADJACENTCUBES(Π)
    while (|C| > 0) do
        (H*_1, H*_2) ← argmin_{(H_1,H_2)∈C} { PREDICTIVEERROR(H_1 ∪ H_2, R, D) }
        H ← H*_1 ∪ H*_2
        if PREDICTIVEERROR(H, R, D) ≤ θ then
            Π ← Π \ {H*_1, H*_2} ∪ {H}
            C ← ADJACENTCUBES(Π)
        else
            return Π
    return Π

function ADJACENTCUBES(Π)
    return { (H_1, H_2) | H_1, H_2 ∈ Π ∧ H_1 ≠ H_2 ∧ (H_1 and H_2 are adjacent) }
```

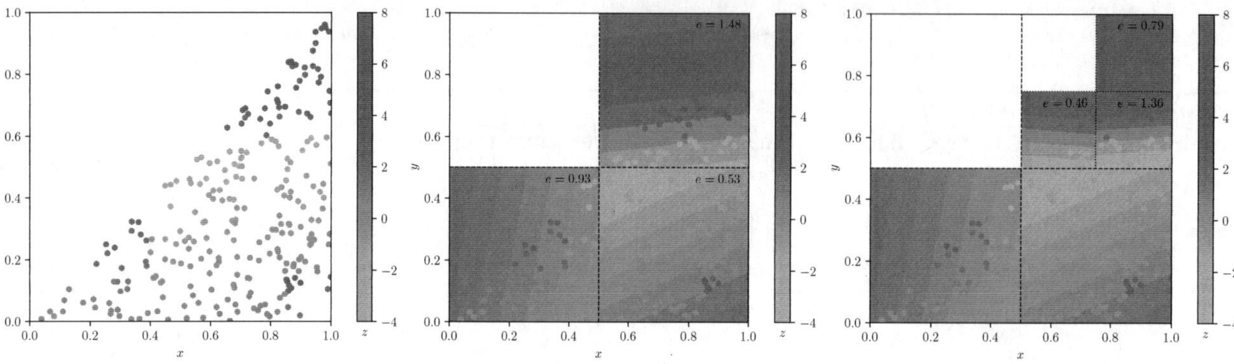

(a) Surrounding cube.

(b) Iteration 1.

(c) Iteration 2.

Figure 1: Example of GridREx partitioning (without merging step) performed with fixed strategies ($k = 2$) and threshold equal to 1.

them, a different linear model is trained for each hypercube. As for the evaluation of the feature importance, we relied on a simple model available within the SciKit-Learn Python library: `linear_model.LinearRegression`[2]. The predictions of these linear models are compared with the training target values (the underlying BB predictions or the data set output values) to calculate the error of each region, while output rules are created by reading the estimated coefficients of the linear models. To make predictions, GridREx accepts input data belonging to the surrounding hypercube and outputs the response of the linear models corresponding to the hypercubes including the provided data.

In Figure 1 is reported an example of partitioning performed by GridREx on a 2-dimensional data set by using for each iteration a fixed strategy with $k = 2$. The Figure shows the first 2 iterations and the threshold parameter value is set to 1. Figure 1a represents the surrounding hypercube with the data set samples. The first iteration (see Figure 1b) produces 4 hypercubes. One is negligible (white background) since it contains no training samples. Inside the other three regions different linear models are trained and the corresponding predictive errors are calculated on the training samples and reported on the top right corner of each hyper-cube. By comparing these errors with the threshold it can be noticed that the bottom cubes are permanent, so they will not be further partitioned during successive iterations. Conversely, the top right region error exceeds the threshold, so it is partitioned into 4 smaller cubes (see Figure 1c) in a recursive fashion.

4 PEDRO

The tuning of GridREx hyper-parameters may be quite challenging if performed manually. For such a reason we developed PEDRO, a Proficient and Easy Direct Reliable Optimiser that helps users to find the best values for the critical hyper-parameters.

Among all the GridREx parameters, the minimum number of examples to consider in each hypercube is the only one with negligible impact on the algorithm performance, so PEDRO does not focus on this one. The main idea behind the optimiser is to compare GridREx executions differing only for one hyper-parameter, according to some *ad hoc defined* metrics evaluating both the rule quality enhancements and the readability losses. A (small) worsening in the final rule set readability is acceptable only when it is balanced by a (large enough) enhancement in the average predictive performance (details in the next subsection). This is achieved by iteratively exploring the hyper-parameter space in several directions until the trade-off between the two metrics is no more favourable. Then, after having selected a set of candidate optimal solutions, different scoring metrics are adopted to select the best values for the GridREx parameters in terms of best readability, best predictive performance and best trade-off between the two requirements.

PEDRO is based on the following general assumptions about the behaviour of GridREx:

1. a small (large) threshold produces a large (small) number of small (large) partitions with small (large) predictive error, thus hindering readability in favour of rule quality;
2. analogously, an extra iteration produces (a possibly very high number of) smaller regions with smaller average error;
3. the optimisation *desideratum* is the minimisation of both the number of rules and the corresponding predictive error, so an adequate scoring function should be multiplicative w.r.t. both quantities conveniently weighted.

These assumptions are encoded in the following equations—please notice that it is desirable to have large values for the improvement indices. The improvement between two GridREx executions (G_1, G_2) having growing thresholds ($\theta_1 < \theta_2$; Item 1) is calculated as:

$$thresholdImprovement = 1 - \frac{r_2}{r_1} + \frac{E_1}{E_2}, \quad (1)$$

being r_i and E_i the number of extracted rules and the predictive error, respectively, associated to the i-th GridREx execution G_i. Differently, the improvement between two

[2]cf. https://scikit-learn.org/stable/modules/generated/sklearn.linear_model.LinearRegression.html

GridREx executions (G_1, G_2) having growing maximum iteration values ($n_1 < n_2$; Item 2) is calculated as:

$$depthImprovement = \frac{1}{\left(1 - \frac{E_2}{E_1}\right)^{0.1} \cdot \frac{\lceil r_2 \cdot RTO \rceil}{\lceil r_1 \cdot RTO \rceil}}, \quad (2)$$

where r_i and E_i have the same meaning as before and RTO is the readability trade-off parameter. Finally, the scoring function of each GridREx execution (Item 3) is calculated as:

$$score = E \cdot \lceil 2 \cdot r \cdot RTO \rceil . \quad (3)$$

A good execution has a small score.

4.1 Hyper-Parameters

To exploit PEDRO the following parameters have to be provided to the algorithm:

1. a threshold to stop the iterative research when the predictive error worsens too much;
2. analogously, a threshold to identify when the gain in the model readability is not large enough;
3. a patience parameter to relax the threshold-based stopping criteria, in order to avoid optimal solutions that are only local for a limited parameter space region;
4. a trade-off parameter to define the importance of readability w.r.t. the predictive performance;
5. the maximum number of GridREx iterations to perform for each hyper-parameter combination;
6. the focus of the optimisation—i.e., maximise the fidelity of GridREx w.r.t. the underlying BB predictions or the predictive accuracy w.r.t. the data.

Tuning these parameters is not a hard task, since the maximum number of GridREx iterations is cut off by the thresholding mechanism in the majority of cases and the default threshold values are usually adequate. The patience and trade-off parameters affect the parameter space research and thus the total computational time of the optimisation process. Small (large) patience values imply the premature (delayed) algorithm termination. Small (large) trade-off values tend to disadvantage (privilege) the role of the readability w.r.t. that of the predictive performance when calculating the score of GridREx outputs. The optimisation focus should concern the BB if the goal of the extraction process is to explain the model behaviour or on the data if the goal is to obtain an interpretable and accurate predictor to be used in substitution of the underlying BB. However, with well-performing BBs there is not an appreciable difference between the two choices.

4.2 Algorithm

PEDRO finds the optimal hyper-parameters through iterative research inside the parameter space as reported in Algorithm 2. It finds the optimal GridREx error threshold, the number of iterations it should perform and the splitting strategy to adopt in each iteration. The current implementation of PEDRO assumes that every GridREx iteration adopts the same strategy, that can be fixed or adaptive.

The parameter space exploration starts from 25 different points, corresponding to 25 different splitting strategies (2 fixed and 23 adaptive). This choice is an optimal trade-off between combinatorial exhaustivity and search efficiency. Indeed, fixed strategies performing more than 3 slices per dimension result in an explosion of the number of output rules, hindering readability, so as for fixed strategies testing 2 of them (performing 2 and 3 slices, respectively) is sufficient. On the other hand, 23 adaptive strategies were always more than sufficient in our experiments to cover all the interesting splitting combinations: as a matter of fact, they generally result in duplicate strategies. Since they are chosen by default, it is common to have more than one strategy equivalent to others, depending on the input feature importance of the data set to analyse. When this is the case, equivalent strategies are collapsed. For instance, by taking as an example a regression task with 2 input dimensions, if we define 3 adaptive strategies by imposing a certain number of partitions for features having relevance above 0.3, 0.5 and 0.8, respectively, and the actual feature relevancies are 0.1 and 1, all the strategies will perform the same partitioning, leading to the same output. It is worth noting that strategies, especially when dealing with high-dimensional data sets, can lead to an explosion of the number of rules. For this reason, PEDRO automatically excludes all those strategies performing a number of partitions greater than a given value. Such value is equal to 3 times the number of partitions obtained with a fixed strategy performing 2 slices along each dimension. Additionally, after collapsing duplicated strategies, the average amount of partitions is calculated. This enables more strict patience policies to be adopted for strategies having more partitions than the average since they are supposed to be more time-consuming (due to better readability, this detail is not included in the pseudo-code).

For each strategy and for each possible number of GridREx iterations between 1 and the maximum user-defined value, the best threshold of the extraction procedure parametrised with the particular strategy is selected. An early stopping is performed if the loss in readability is no more balanced with the gain in quality (see Equation (2)).

To find the best threshold for a strategy, given a number of iterations, the following steps are executed. Firstly, an initial threshold t_0 and update step s are set to $0.9e$ and $0.5e$, respectively, being e the mean absolute error of the underlying BB. This choice derives from the consideration according to which it is generally not possible to achieve a significantly better performance than the underlying BB by using an extraction procedure that exploits the outputs of such BB as target values. Then GridREx is performed with growing threshold values, starting from t_0 and incrementing it at each iteration by an amount equal to s. If an iteration results in no improvement, the step value s is augmented. It is worth noticing that a rule amount reduction smaller than the user defined value is not considered an improvement. The search terminates if GridREx produces only one output rule, if the worsening w.r.t. the error obtained with the initial threshold t_0 is beyond the user-defined value, or if there are no improvements even by considering the patience parameter (see Equation (1)).

Algorithm 2 PEDRO pseudocode

Require: parameters $maxDepth$, $maxErrorIncrease$, $minRuleDecrease$, $readTradeoff$, $patience_0$ to be provided

function PEDRO(R, D)
  $maxPartitions \leftarrow$ MAXPARTITIONNUMBER(D)
  $S \leftarrow$ INITIALIZESTRATEGIES($D, maxPartitions$)
  return SEARCH(S, R, D, $maxPartitions$)

function MAXPARTITIONNUMBER(D)
  return an upperbound for the number of partitions calculated w.r.t. the number of input features describing D

function INITIALIZESTRATEGIES(D, $maxPartitions$)
  $S \leftarrow$ a set of default strategies
  return $\{ s \mid s \in S \wedge$ NPARTITIONS$(D, s) < maxPartitions \}$

function NPARTITIONS(D, $strategy$)
  return the number of partitions produced by $strategy$ applied to D

function SEARCH(S, R, D, $maxPartitions$)
  return $\bigcup_{s \in S}$ DEPTHSEARCH($s, R, D, maxPartitions$)

function DEPTHSEARCH(s, R, D, $maxPartitions$)
  $\Pi \leftarrow \varnothing, \quad i \leftarrow 1, \quad best' \leftarrow$ **undefined**
  while $i < maxDepth$ **do**
    $grid \leftarrow$ GRID(i, s)
    $\Pi' \leftarrow$ THRESHOLDSEARCH($grid, R, D, maxPartitions$)
    $best \leftarrow$ SELECTBEST(Π')
    $\Pi \leftarrow \Pi \cup \Pi'$
    if $(|\Pi| > 1) \wedge$ (IMPROVEMENT($best, best'$, "depth") < 1.2) **then return** Π
    $i \leftarrow i + 1$
    $best' = best$
  return Π

function SELECTBEST(Π)
  return the best output in Π w.r.t. both predictive performance and readability according to $readTradeoff$

function IMPROVEMENT($output_1$, $output_2$, $criterion$) ▷ $criterion$ is either "depth" or "threshold"
  return a numeric evaluation of $output_1$ w.r.t. $output_2$ according to $criterion$

function THRESHOLDSEARCH($grid$, R, D, $maxPartitions$)
  $\theta_0 \leftarrow$ PREDICTIVEERROR(D, R)
  $\Pi \leftarrow \varnothing, \quad \theta \leftarrow 0.9\,\theta_0, \quad patience \leftarrow patience_0, \quad step = 0.5\,\theta_0$
  while $patience > 0$ **do**
    $E \leftarrow$ GRIDREX(R, D)
    $p \leftarrow$ parameters of E
    $n \leftarrow$ number of rules extracted by E
    $e \leftarrow$ PREDICTIVEERROR(D, E)
    if $\Pi = \varnothing$ **then** $e_0 \leftarrow e$
    else if $n = 1$ **then return** $\Pi \cup \{(p, n, e)\}$
    else if $n > maxPartitions$ **then return** Π
    else if $e > e_0 \cdot maxErrorIncrease$ **then return** Π
    else if (IMPROVEMENT($(n, e), (n', e')$, "threshold") $\leq 1) \bigvee (n > \lceil n' \cdot minRuleDecrease \rceil)$ **then**
      $patience \leftarrow patience - 1$
      $step \leftarrow \max\{step,\ |e - \theta|\} \,/\, \max\{patience,\ 1\}$
    $\Pi \leftarrow \Pi \cup \{(p, n, e)\}$
    $n' \leftarrow n$
    $e' \leftarrow e$
    $\theta \leftarrow \theta + step$
  return Π

function PREDICTIVEERROR(D, P) ▷ Predictor P may be a BB or an extractor
  return the predictive error of P applied to the samples of D

At the end of the parameter space search PEDRO ranks each solution according to 3 different dimensions: *(i)* the number of extracted rules, a.k.a., the readability; *(ii)* the predictive error, a.k.a., the quality; *(iii)* the *ad hoc* scoring function explicitly designed to select the best trade-off between readability and quality, involving the user-defined specific parameter (see Equation (3)).

5 Comparison in PSyKE

5.1 Knowledge Extraction

In order to assess the performance of GridREx and PEDRO[3] we applied our algorithms to 6 different real-world data sets from the StairwAI[4] EU project. These data sets are composed uniquely of continuous input and output features. 2 data sets have 5 input attributes, whereas the others have 1 input variable. All data sets count 12 100 instances and we adopted an 80%-20% train-test split. The test set was never used to train the BBs or the extractors.

Our results are summarised in Table 1. We used PEDRO to estimate the best GridREx hyper-parameters for each data set. Other state-of-the-art extraction procedures – namely, ITER, GridEx, and CART – applied on the same data sets are used as benchmarks to compare with GridREx.

We performed a complete comparison by collecting the same indicators for each extractor. For regression tasks, the most used indicators are the mean absolute/squared error (MAE/MSE) and the R^2 score. Due to space limitations, we report in Table 1 only the MAE (aligned to the results of other indicators).For each data set, the number of input variables, the MAE of the BB model applied to it and the results of the 4 extraction procedures applied to the data sets and the corresponding BBs are reported in Table 1. For each extractor, the number of extracted rules (R) and the MAE w.r.t. both the data (D) and the underlying BB are reported as well. Since ITER can be a non-exhaustive procedure, for this algorithm we included also the percentage of missed test predictions (MTP), i.e., how many test samples ITER is not able to predict w.r.t. the size of the test set.

GridREx proved to be the best extractor for all the case studies, being able to provide the fewest number of rules and, at the same time, achieving the highest predictive performance of all the tested extractors w.r.t. both the data and the underlying BB predictions. This is not surprising, since all the other techniques are not able to produce actual regression rules, but only constant values assigned to defined input space regions. This undesired output discretisation hinders their predictive performance as well as their readability, since they may fragment regions dominated by the same linear relationship into a number of smaller regions having constant outputs.

[3]Experiments have been run exploiting the Python implementations provided by PSyKE (Sabbatini et al. 2021), cf. https://apice.unibo.it/xwiki/bin/view/PSyKE/ and https://github.com/psykei/psyke-python/

[4]https://cordis.europa.eu/project/id/101017142; data sets will be publicly available accordingly to the timeline of the StairwAI EU project

Obviously, the results reported in Table 1 are not the unique possible. The number of rules and the MAE of each procedure may greatly vary with different algorithm parameters. While we used PEDRO to choose the best GridREx and GridEx hyper-parameters, different considerations are mandatory for the other algorithms. We selected for CART a maximum depth equal to 2, in order to have not more than 4 output rules. This choice derives from the fact that GridREx produces 3-5 output rules for all the data sets; in such a way it is possible to compare the predictive performance of CART and GridEx in terms of MAE to parity of human readability. It is worth noticing that CART can achieve a predictive performance almost as good as that of GridREx at the expense of readability—i.e., with larger depths and, therefore, larger rule sets. For instance, by using a maximum depth equal to 3, resulting in 8 output rules, it is possible to have better predictive performance. However, since CART outputs are constant values while those of GridREx are not, the latter is able to outperform the former in the general case.

On the other hand, ITER shows quite good results in terms of MAE when applied to data sets with only one input feature, but it tends to have smaller readability than GridREx and furthermore its rules are always non-exhaustive. For ITER we report here the best results obtained after a manual hyper-parameter tuning phase. As *best* we intend the predictive performance w.r.t. the output model readability.

5.2 Rule Induction

In the following we describe the results of GridREx applied to the same aforementioned data sets without the intermediate "interference" of the BB predictor. These results are summarised in Table 2 as a comparison between the extraction performed by GridREx on the BB regressor and the rule induction directly performed by GridREx on the data sets. We describe the GridREx executions in terms of MAE and R^2 score as predictive error/performance measurement and the number of output rules as readability index.

Our goal is to demonstrate that this procedure can be exploited instead of ML techniques to learn relationships from data without loss of predictive performance. Extraction techniques from BB predictors imply prior training and tuning phases regarding the BB itself, often a time-consuming task that offers no certainty about the optimality of the selected final hyper-parameters. On the other hand, rule induction is not able to rely on an ML oracle to augment the data set under study, nor can learn complex relationships as other widespread ML algorithms do—for instance, ANNs. For these reasons, GridREx should be exploited for this purpose only when a dense data set is available, so as to have the possibility to obtain rules corresponding to hypercubes naturally including a proper amount of samples—used to construct robust and accurate output rules.

From the results reported in Table 2 it is clear how GridREx can be applied to perform rule induction obtaining approximatively the same results as the rule extraction from an ML BB—and, in some cases, even slightly better results. For this reason, we suggest directly applying GridREx to the data set when possible, in order to avoid the training and tuning phases of the underlying regressor. PEDRO can be ex-

Data set	Input var.	BB MAE	GridREx R	GridREx MAE D	GridREx MAE BB	ITER R	ITER MAE D	ITER MAE BB	ITER MTP (%)	GridEx R	GridEx MAE D	GridEx MAE BB	CART R	CART MAE D	CART MAE BB
#1	5	0.4	3	1.4	1.5	76	9.5	7.2	6.3	5	14.5	14.6	4	14.6	14.6
#2	1	4.3	5	5.0	3.3	20	6.3	4.3	1.7	5	15.3	14.7	4	17.8	17.5
#3	1	8.3	5	11.3	6.7	14	12.2	7.5	1.8	5	17.6	14.9	4	17.1	12.9
#4	5	1.5	4	22.1	21.9	83	23.2	21.4	9.6	5	28.4	28.3	4	26.2	26.1
#5	1	3.8	5	4.7	1.8	4	4.6	2.0	1.7	3	4.8	2.2	4	4.7	1.9
#6	1	0.8	5	1.0	0.7	15	1.6	1.3	1.9	5	3.2	3.1	4	3.9	3.8

Table 1: Results of GridREx applied to the 6 described data sets in terms of number of extracted rules (R) and MAE w.r.t. the data (D) and the underlying BB model. Results are compared with those of ITER, GridEx and CART applied to the same data sets. For each data set the number of input variables and the BB MAE are reported, as well as the percentage of missed test predictions (MTP) for ITER.

Data set	Input variables	BB MAE (data)	BB R^2 (data)	GridREx (extraction) # Rules	GridREx (extraction) MAE (data)	GridREx (extraction) R^2 (data)	GridREx (extraction) MAE (BB)	GridREx (extraction) R^2 (BB)	GridREx (induction) # Rules	GridREx (induction) MAE (data)	GridREx (induction) R^2 (data)
#1	5	0.4	1.00	3	1.4	1.00	1.5	1.00	3	1.5	1.00
#2	1	4.3	0.99	5	5.0	0.99	3.3	1.00	5	4.6	0.99
#3	1	8.3	0.97	5	11.3	0.92	6.7	0.97	5	11.4	0.91
#4	5	1.5	0.99	4	22.1	0.67	21.9	0.67	5	21.8	0.70
#5	1	3.8	0.28	5	4.7	0.05	1.8	0.19	5	3.91	-0.1
#6	1	0.8	1.00	5	1.0	0.99	0.7	1.00	5	1.9	0.99

Table 2: Comparison in terms of readability, predictive error and R^2 score of GridREx applied to the 6 described data sets by exploiting the underlying BB (knowledge extraction) as well as without any intermediate ML predictor (rule induction).

ploited to detect the best GridREx hyper-parameters also for the case of rule induction. We adopted it to tune GridREx during our rule induction experiments to obtain the results reported in the Table 2.

5.3 Discussion on the Execution Time

Except for CART, the execution time of the compared algorithms strictly depends on the number of extracted rules. In all our experiments, CART always produces its output within a second. The same holds for GridEx and GridREx when less than 10 hyper-cubes are created. These two techniques may require up to one minute when dealing with huge amounts of hyper-cubes—e.g., above 500. ITER results to be slower than the others, due to the creation and discard of many data structures during its execution, as well as for the repetition of the same operations several times. These considerations can be drawn by analysing the algorithm description given by the authors of ITER. In our experiments, ITER terminates within a second only when less than 6 rules are extracted. The execution in the other cases may take up to some minutes, depending on its hyper-parameters.

6 Conclusions

In this paper we present the design and application of GridREx and PEDRO, a pedagogical knowledge-extraction algorithm for BB regressors of any kind and an optimisation procedure applicable to it to help human users during the hyper-parameter tuning phase of GridREx. GridREx is able to overcome at the same time the major limitations of similar algorithms described in the literature—i.e., the inability to output regression rules and the application restricted to specific BBs. PEDRO can provide the best hyper-parameter values for GridREx, taking into account the readability of the output rule set, the corresponding predictive performance, or both of the two criteria, combining them according to a user-provided trade-off threshold. PEDRO outperforms manual tuning executed by human experts even when launched with default parameters.

Even though GridREx proved to outperform several state-of-the-art analogous techniques, some considerations can be taken into account for future improvements. Two examples are *(i)* the possibility to customise the relationship between input and output inside single hypercubes – such as polynomial functions instead of linear ones – and *(ii)* the introduction of a splitting technique disentangled from the equal-size partitioning criterion, possibly critical when dealing with strongly asymmetrical data sets.

In the future we also plan to enrich PEDRO, making it more configurable by users. For example, we find it useful to let users choose among more than one criterion to measure the predictive error – or, more generally, performance – of a given regressor/extractor—for instance, MSE and R^2 score, as well as user-defined loss functions. We also plan to modify the search of the input parameter space to include grids having not only one single strategy for every iteration, but also different strategies automatically selected by PEDRO.

Acknowledgements

This work has been partially supported by the EU ICT-48 2020 project TAILOR (No. 952215) and by the European Union's Horizon 2020 research and innovation programme under G.A. no. 101017142 (StairwAI project).

References

Altmann, A.; Toloşi, L.; Sander, O.; and Lengauer, T. 2010. Permutation importance: a corrected feature importance measure. *Bioinformatics* 26(10):1340–1347.

Andrews, R.; Diederich, J.; and Tickle, A. B. 1995. Survey and critique of techniques for extracting rules from trained artificial neural networks. *Knowledge-Based Systems* 8(6):373–389.

Azcarraga, A.; Liu, M. D.; and Setiono, R. 2012. Keyword extraction using backpropagation neural networks and rule extraction. In *The 2012 International Joint Conference on Neural Networks (IJCNN 2012)*, 1–7. IEEE.

Baesens, B.; Setiono, R.; De Lille, V.; Viaene, S.; and Vanthienen, J. 2001. Building credit-risk evaluation expert systems using neural network rule extraction and decision tables. In Storey, V. C.; Sarkar, S.; and DeGross, J. I., eds., *ICIS 2001 Proceedings*, 159–168. Association for Information Systems.

Baesens, B.; Setiono, R.; Mues, C.; and Vanthienen, J. 2003. Using neural network rule extraction and decision tables for credit-risk evaluation. *Management Science* 49(3):312–329.

Bologna, G., and Pellegrini, C. 1997. Three medical examples in neural network rule extraction. *Physica Medica* 13:183–187.

Breiman, L.; Friedman, J.; Stone, C. J.; and Olshen, R. A. 1984. *Classification and Regression Trees*. CRC Press.

Feurer, M., and Hutter, F. 2019. Hyperparameter optimization. In *Automated machine learning*. Springer, Cham. 3–33.

Grzymala-Busse, J. W. 2005. Rule induction. In Maimon, O., and Rokach, L., eds., *The Data Mining and Knowledge Discovery Handbook*. Springer. 277–294.

Guidotti, R.; Monreale, A.; Ruggieri, S.; Turini, F.; Giannotti, F.; and Pedreschi, D. 2018. A survey of methods for explaining black box models. *ACM Computing Surveys* 51(5):1–42.

Hayashi, Y.; Setiono, R.; and Yoshida, K. 2000. A comparison between two neural network rule extraction techniques for the diagnosis of hepatobiliary disorders. *Artificial intelligence in Medicine* 20(3):205–216.

Hofmann, A.; Schmitz, C.; and Sick, B. 2003. Rule extraction from neural networks for intrusion detection in computer networks. In *2003 IEEE International Conference on Systems, Man and Cybernetics*, volume 2, 1259–1265. IEEE.

Hutter, F.; Kotthoff, L.; and Vanschoren, J. 2019. *Automated machine learning: methods, systems, challenges*. Springer Nature.

Huysmans, J.; Baesens, B.; and Vanthienen, J. 2006. ITER: An algorithm for predictive regression rule extraction. In *Data Warehousing and Knowledge Discovery (DaWaK 2006)*, 270–279. Springer.

Kenny, E. M.; Ford, C.; Quinn, M.; and Keane, M. T. 2021. Explaining black-box classifiers using post-hoc explanations-by-example: The effect of explanations and error-rates in XAI user studies. *Artificial Intelligence* 294:103459.

Rocha, A.; Papa, J. P.; and Meira, L. A. A. 2012. How far do we get using machine learning black-boxes? *International Journal of Pattern Recognition and Artificial Intelligence* 26(02):1261001–(1–23).

Rudin, C. 2019. Stop explaining black box machine learning models for high stakes decisions and use interpretable models instead. *Nature Machine Intelligence* 1(5):206–215.

Sabbatini, F.; Ciatto, G.; Calegari, R.; and Omicini, A. 2021. On the design of PSyKE: A platform for symbolic knowledge extraction. In Calegari, R.; Ciatto, G.; Denti, E.; Omicini, A.; and Sartor, G., eds., *WOA 2021 – 22nd Workshop "From Objects to Agents"*, volume 2963 of *CEUR Workshop Proceedings*, 29–48. Sun SITE Central Europe, RWTH Aachen University. 22nd Workshop "From Objects to Agents" (WOA 2021), Bologna, Italy, 1–3 September 2021. Proceedings.

Sabbatini, F.; Ciatto, G.; and Omicini, A. 2021. GridEx: An algorithm for knowledge extraction from black-box regressors. In Calvaresi, D.; Najjar, A.; Winikoff, M.; and Främling, K., eds., *Explainable and Transparent AI and Multi-Agent Systems. Third International Workshop, EXTRAAMAS 2021, Virtual Event, May 3–7, 2021, Revised Selected Papers*, volume 12688 of *LNCS*. Basel, Switzerland: Springer Nature. 18–38.

Setiono, R.; Baesens, B.; and Mues, C. 2011. Rule extraction from minimal neural networks for credit card screening. *International Journal of Neural Systems* 21(04):265–276.

Setiono, R.; Leow, W. K.; and Zurada, J. M. 2002. Extraction of rules from artificial neural networks for nonlinear regression. *IEEE Transactions on Neural Networks* 13(3):564–577.

Steiner, M. T. A.; Steiner Neto, P. J.; Soma, N. Y.; Shimizu, T.; and Nievola, J. C. 2006. Using neural network rule extraction for credit-risk evaluation. *International Journal of Computer Science and Network Security* 6(5A):6–16.

Yang, L., and Shami, A. 2020. On hyperparameter optimization of machine learning algorithms: Theory and practice. *Neurocomputing* 415:295–316.

Zhuang, J.; Dvornek, N. C.; Li, X.; Yang, J.; and Duncan, J. 2019. Decision explanation and feature importance for invertible networks. In *2019 IEEE/CVF International Conference on Computer Vision Workshop (ICCVW)*, 4235–4239. IEEE.

Zien, A.; Krämer, N.; Sonnenburg, S.; and Rätsch, G. 2009. The feature importance ranking measure. In *Joint European Conference on Machine Learning and Knowledge Discovery in Databases (ECML PKDD 2009)*, 694–709. Springer.

Proceedings of the 19th International Conference on Principles of Knowledge Representation and Reasoning
Applications and Systems

ALASPO: An Adaptive Large-Neighbourhood ASP Optimiser

Thomas Eiter[1], **Tobias Geibinger**[1], **Nelson Higuera**[1],
Nysret Musliu[1,2], **Johannes Oetsch**[1], **Daria Stepanova**[3]
[1]Institute for Logic and Computation, TU Wien, Favoritenstraße 9-11, 1040 Vienna, Austria,
[2]CD-Lab Artis, TU Wien,
[3]Bosch Center for AI, Robert Bosch Campus 1, 71272 Renningen, Germany
{eiter, oetsch, nhiguera}@kr.tuwien.ac.at, {tgeibing, musliu}@dbai.tuwien.ac.at,
daria.stepanova@de.bosch.com

Abstract

We present the system ALASPO which implements Adaptive Large-neighbourhood search for Answer Set Programming (ASP) Optimisation. Large-neighbourhood search (LNS) is a meta-heuristic where parts of a solution are destroyed and reconstructed in an attempt to improve an overall objective. ALASPO currently supports the ASP solver clingo, as well as its extensions clingo-dl and clingcon for difference and full integer constraints, and multi-shot solving for an efficient implementation of the LNS loop. Neighbourhoods can be defined in code or declaratively as part of the ASP encoding. While the method underlying ALASPO has been described in previous work, ALASPO also incorporates portfolios for the LNS operators along with self-adaptive selection strategies as a technical novelty. This improves usability considerably at no loss of solution quality, but on the contrary often yields benefits. To demonstrate this, we evaluate ALASPO on different optimisation benchmarks.

1 Introduction

Answer-set programming (ASP) (Brewka, Eiter, and Truszczyński 2011; Lifschitz 2019; Gebser et al. 2012) is a declarative KR paradigm that is increasingly used to solve challenging optimisation problems. We present the system ALASPO (Adaptive Large-neighbourhood search for ASP Optimisation) that leverages ASP optimisation with *large-neighbourhood search* (LNS) (Shaw 1998; Pisinger and Ropke 2010), a powerful meta-heuristic where parts of a solution are destroyed and reconstructed in an attempt to improve an overall objective.

LNS is commonly used for MIP (Danna, Rothberg, and Pape 2005; Rothberg 2007) and CP (Shaw 1998; Perron, Shaw, and Furnon 2004; Berthold et al. 2011; Björdal et al. 2020), but for ASP it has only recently been exploited (Eiter et al. 2022; Geibinger, Mischek, and Musliu 2021). The method starts by obtaining a first solution for an optimisation problem encoded in ASP (either with a construction heuristic or from an ASP solver). Then, a *neighbourhood*, i.e., a part of the solution, is *relaxed*, i.e., deleted from the answer set. Next, an ASP solver is used to reconstruct a solution with a better overall objective value. Relaxation and reconstruction steps proceed until a global time limit is reached.

The system currently supports the ASP solver clingo (Gebser et al. 2019; Gebser et al. 2016), as well as its extensions clingo-dl (Janhunen et al. 2017) and clingcon (Banbara et al. 2017) for difference and full integer constraints, respectively. For an efficient implementation of the LNS loop, it exploits multi-shot solving to preserve the solver state and avoid unnecessary grounding between solver calls. The system features pre-defined neighbourhood definitions that can be used out-of-the-box, but also supports custom neighbourhoods provided by the user. They can be given either in code or, more conveniently, declaratively as part of the ASP encoding.

The method underlying ALASPO is described and evaluated in recent work (Eiter et al. 2022). As a major technical novelty, ALASPO allows to bundle neighbourhoods and search configurations into portfolios. Switching between operators can be done on the fly during search, but the system also provides full self-adaptive modes where no user intervention is required. In previous work (Eiter et al. 2022), one could only use a single neighbourhood operator. With ALASPO, the user can select a set of operators, and the tool self-adapts to use effective ones through selection strategies. Therefore, the solver requires less tuning which improves usability We evaluate the adaptive modes introduced in this paper on different optimisation benchmarks.

The system is publicly available under the MIT licence: https://gitlab.tuwien.ac.at/kbs/BAI/alaspo.

2 Architecture & Functionality

ALASPO is a system for ASP optimisation with support for different ASP solvers, search configurations, and neighbourhood definitions. Figure 1 gives on overview of how its components play together to realise the system's functionality.

The LNS loop. At the heart of ALASPO lies an LNS loop, where an incumbent solution is repeatedly relaxed and reconstructed by an ASP solver to continuously obtain better objective values for the optimisation problem at hand.

An *initial solution* is generated by the ASP solver as either the first solution without optimisation or after letting the solver pre-optimise the problem for a specified amount of time. Alternatively, it can be obtained by a custom procedure using a construction heuristic, which however is problem specific and must be provided by the user as an implementation of an abstract class in Python 3.

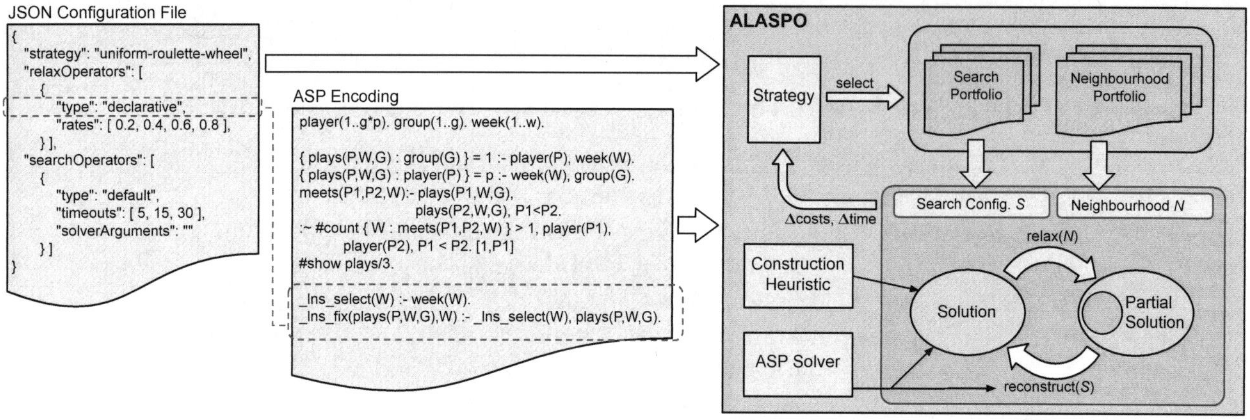

Figure 1: Adaptive LNS for ASP in the system ALASPO.

In each iteration of the LNS loop, the currently best solution I is relaxed using a *neighbourhood operator* N, which is a procedure to select a subset of the atoms in I. For instance, N could pick 20% of the visible atoms at random. Then, the resulting partial solution is reconstructed using the ASP solver with a constraint to obtain a better objective value than I. This reconstruction step depends on a search configuration S which defines solver options and a time limit. If a better solution is found within the time limit, it becomes the new incumbent solution, otherwise (i.e., the solver runs into a timeout or yields unsatisfiability), the old solution I remains the best known one.

The optimisation problem is formulated in ASP and stored in one or multiple input files. The currently supported ASP solvers are clingo, clingo-dl, and clingcon from the Potassco family.[1] All solvers feature multi-shot solving and solving under assumptions (Gebser et al. 2019). The former is used to keep learned heuristics and constraints between solver calls and to avoid unnecessary grounding, the latter is used to technically realise the relaxation step by fixing the parts of the solution that are not relaxed with assumptions prior to the next solver call.

Search and neighbourhood portfolios. The effectiveness of LNS is predicated upon suitable choices for search and neighbourhood operators. Different such operators can be bundled together into portfolios to choose from. A search configuration typically involves different time limits used in the reconstruction step. Likewise, a neighbourhood operator specifies the type of the neighbourhood, which corresponds to the structure and selection strategy of atoms, as well as different rates to control the size of the selection. The portfolios contain some pre-defined neighbourhoods, but custom ones can be added.

The tool provides two problem independent pre-defined neighbourhood types: random-atoms and random-constants. *Random-atoms* relaxes a random sample of the visible atoms of an answer set. Although quite simple, this method is often surprisingly effective (Eiter et al. 2022). *Random-constants* selects a random sample from all constant symbols from the visible atoms, and relaxes all atoms that contain any constants from that selection. The idea is that often atoms are not independent and shared constants help to relax groups of related atoms together. Relaxation rates refer to the size of the random sample for both types.

Neighbourhood types can also be defined declaratively as part of the ASP encoding using dedicated predicates `_lns_select/1` and `_lns_fix/2`. An example appears in Fig. 1 for the Social Golfer problem; details are discussed in (Eiter et al. 2022). Roughly, `_lns_select` defines a set of terms from which a sample is selected. The size of that sample, as for the pre-defined types, is controlled using a respective relaxation rate. Predicate `_lns_fix` defines a mapping from terms of the sample to atoms that should not be relaxed between solver calls.

Neighbourhood operators can also be defined in code which can be useful for highly customised applications. An advanced example for a parallel machine scheduling problem is discussed by Eiter et al. (2022).

Strategies for adaptive LNS. While the system performs well with the right choice of search and neighbourhood operators, it is often better to make changes when the search gets stuck. ALASPO can be run in *interactive mode*, where the user can interrupt search when intervention seems necessary. Before search is resumed, a better fitting configuration from the portfolios can be selected. We also provide several *selection strategies* that do not require any user intervention. After each iteration of the LNS loop, they take information like change in objective value, elapsed time, and whether a new solution was found, and then select from the portfolio potentially more suitable LNS operators for the next iteration. A JSON file can be used to select a strategy and to specify neighbourhood operators with types and relaxation rates and search configurations with different time limits. This is then internally used to set up respective portfolios in ALASPO.

The first strategy implemented in ALASPO is a *self-adaptive roulette-wheel strategy* from the literature (Laborie

[1]https://potassco.org/.

and Godard 2007; Pisinger and Ropke 2007): each pair (S, N) of search and neighbourhood operators gets an initial weight. After each iteration of the LNS loop, the weight of the currently used pair (S, N) is updated according to the reinforcement learning formula $weight_{new} = (1 - \alpha) \cdot weight_{old} + \alpha \cdot r$ where r is the *effectiveness score* of the operator defined as the ratio of cost improvement over time needed, and α is the *learning rate*. Then, a new pair of operators is selected with probability proportional to the weights.

The system implements also a simple non-adaptive version of the first strategy, *uniform roulette-wheel strategy*, where all pairs of operators have equal weight, and are thus selected with equal probability in each iteration.

The third strategy, which we call *dynamic strategy*, attempts to escape a stuck search by varying relaxation rates and time limits. Operators as well as neighborhoods are not changed as long as they give some improvement. If the solver reports unsatisfiability three times in a row, we increase the relaxation rate of the currently used neighbourhood to the next largest rate; after the largest one is reached, new operators are randomly selected and search is resumed with the smallest relaxation rate for the new neighbourhood. If the solver times out however, it decides by coin flip to either decrease the relaxation rate to its lowest setting or to increase the time limit of the search operator; if this is not possible, new operators are randomly chosen.

3 Usage

ALASPO can be used out-of-the-box with little or no configuration. If needed, it can also be customised through either the command-line or an additional JSON configuration file.

Invocation. The tool is called in standard configuration for a problem stored in `program.lp`:

```
> python alaspo -i program.lp
```

where it runs the system with its *default portfolio* which uses neighborhood relax-atoms with relaxation rates 0.1, 0.2, 0.4, 0.6, and 0.8, neighbourhood relax-constants with rates 0.1, 0.2, 0.3, 0.4, 0.5, time limits of 5, 15, 30, and 60 seconds for the search configurations, and the dynamic selection strategy. During execution, the solver will continuously report when new solutions are found.

Further command-line arguments and neighbourhoods. Additional command-line arguments can be used to change the global time limit, and to select an ASP solver other than clingo (clingo-dl and clingcon are currently supported as well). Sometimes, it is beneficial to let the ASP solver optimise the problem for some time before the LNS loop starts; to this end, a time limit for pre-optimisation can be specified.

Instead of the default portfolio, the user can select a single neighbourhood type from the pre-defined ones (random-atoms or random constants), or specify that declaratively defined one from the ASP program should be used instead. A relaxation rate, an argument list that is passed to the ASP solver, and a time limit for reconstruction steps can be set in the command-line as well. In the mode where single search and neighbourhood operators are used, a new neighbourhood in the LNS loop is only selected if the current one stops to yield improvements and is fully exploited. Option `--help` gives a complete description of the command-line.

Portfolios and search strategies. The features described so far allow one to run the tool with a simple default portfolio or with single LNS operators. With a good relaxation rate and time limit for LNS steps, better solutions can indeed be found starting from the relaxed solution while the search space is small enough for the solver to actually succeed within the time limit. Such calibration needs in general some trials; alternatively user-defined portfolios with different selection strategies can be employed.

A novel feature is that several declarative neighbourhoods can be specified for use in the operator portfolio of the system. Alternative definitions are disambiguated in the encoding by giving them a name as additional first argument of `lns_select` and `lns_fix`. Examples of how to define neighbourhoods in ASP can be found in previous work (Eiter et al. 2022), one of which is shown in Fig. 1.

Portfolios can be specified in an additional JSON file as depicted in Fig. 1. There, the user lists all LNS operators that should be used. For each neighbourhood, a type (random-atoms, random-constants, or declarative), an optional name in case there are several declarative neighbourhoods in the encoding, and a list of relaxation rates for instances of the operator are given. Search configurations can be defined with a list of time limits on LNS iterations.

The selection strategy for the portfolio (roulette-wheel or dynamic) can be specified in the JSON file. Alternatively, the user can select the interactive mode from the command line and interrupt the solver during search to switch to other operators when search gets stuck.

Custom applications. We mention in passing that the system can be extended for custom applications by defining new neighbourhood types in code. Furthermore, if an ASP solver cannot produce a good first solution, construction heuristics, e.g., a simple greedy procedure, can be specified by instantiating a respective abstract class. An example developed for a challenging parallel machine scheduling problem can be found in previous work (Eiter et al. 2022).

4 Experiments

An evaluation of ASP with LNS was given in the companion paper (Eiter et al. 2022). We revisit some of the benchmarks from there to evaluate how the new self-adaptive modes perform in comparison with hand-selected search and neighbourhood operators used previously.

All experiments were run on a cluster of 13 nodes with 2 Intel Xeon CPUs E5-2650 v4 (max. 2.90GHz, 12 physical cores, no hyperthreading) per node and a memory limit of 20GB for each process. Encodings, instances, logs, and random seeds are available at www.kr.tuwien.ac.at/research/projects/bai/kr22.zip.

	single LNS operators (Eiter et al. 2022)	portfolio with selection strategy uniform	self-adaptive $\alpha = 0.2$	$\alpha = 0.4$	$\alpha = 0.6$	$\alpha = 0.8$	dynamic
SG	15.91 ± 2.05	17.14 ± 2.45	18.36 ± 3.20	$\mathbf{20.00} \pm 2.79$	17.14 ± 1.73	18.36 ± 2.79	19.18 ± 2.19
TSP	$\mathbf{35.85} \pm 0.60$	19.65 ± 3.61	20.75 ± 3.13	20.54 ± 2.46	20.74 ± 2.72	21.17 ± 2.55	29.03 ± 2.32
SPG	$\mathbf{3.33} \pm 0.00$	0.47 ± 0.52	0.00 ± 0.00	2.38 ± 0.52	1.90 ± 0.80	-0.95 ± 0.80	$\mathbf{3.33} \pm 0.43$
WSC	39.70 ± 0.77	39.83 ± 0.52	40.01 ± 0.41	40.17 ± 1.25	39.96 ± 0.79	$\mathbf{40.25} \pm 1.27$	39.44 ± 1.71
SD	7.29 ± 2.22	$\mathbf{12.14} \pm 1.66$	11.47 ± 0.56	11.22 ± 1.24	10.95 ± 2.12	10.61 ± 1.69	6.61 ± 2.02

Table 1: Average percentual improvement and standard deviation over plain clingo for ASP with (adaptive) LNS.

Benchmark problems and setup. In our previous experiments, LNS was used with a single search configuration and single hand-selected neighbourhood for each benchmark. We used clingo (v. 5.5.1) with the same search configuration (the default configuration if not stated otherwise) as the LNS approach to establish a baseline. The benchmark problems and settings are as follows:

Social Golfer (SG) is an NP-hard scheduling problem where golfers must be grouped in a weekly schedule such that individuals meet again as little as possible. The global time limit is $1800s$ per instance, and we use a declaratively specified neighbourhood (shown in Fig. 1 with the problem encoding) to relax entire weeks per iteration, a relaxation rate of 20%, and a time limit of $20s$ for the LNS reconstruction step.

Travelling Salesman Problem (TSP) is the problem of finding a round trip with minimal costs in a graph. The global time limit is $300s$, and we use random-atoms with a time limit of $5s$ and a relaxation rate of 30% for LNS.

Sudoku Puzzle Generation (SPG) requests to generate a Sudoku puzzle with a minimal number of hints such that the solution is unique. The global time limit is $600s$, and we use "`--many -t4`" for clingo (the default portfolio for multi-treading with 4 threads). For LNS, we use random-atoms with a rate of 20% and time limit of $20s$.

Weighted Strategic Companies (WSC) is a version of the Σ_2^P-hard Strategic Companies Problem (Cadoli, Eiter, and Gottlob 1997) with additional weights for companies and the objective to find strategic sets with minimal total weight. Here, the global time limit is $1800s$, and we use random-atoms with a rate of 20% and a time limit of $30s$ for LNS.

Shift Design (SD) requires to align shifts such that over- and understaffing is avoided (Abseher et al. 2016). The global time limit is $3600s$ and the search configuration is "`--opt-strategy=usc,3 --configuration=handy`" which selects unsat-core based optimisation and defaults for large problems. For LNS, we use random-atoms with a rate of 70% and a time limit of $30s$. Also, pre-optimisation for 50 minutes is used to initialise search.

For our comparisons with the adaptive modes of ALASPO with portfolios, we used the solver settings described above and time limits from the default portfolio (cf. Section 3). For the neighbourhood operators, we included both random-atoms and random-constants with relaxation rates from the default portfolio. For Social Golfer, we used all the declarative neighbourhoods for that problem from previous work together in a portfolio.

Results. The results of our experiments are summarised in Table 1. For all problems, we report the relative improvement in objective value for ASP with LNS in comparison with plain clingo averaged over 5 runs. The first column gives the results for LNS with single hand-selected LNS operators that fit the problem best as described above. The remaining columns show results obtained with the portfolio described above for different selection strategies.

Overall, clingo with LNS is able to produce better results than plain clingo on all benchmarks. The only case where the baseline is not reached is Sudoku Puzzle Generation with roulette-wheel selection and a high learning rate where suboptimal operators become preferred ones. The setting with single hand-selected LNS operators is the sole winner in performance gain for the Travelling Salesperson Problem only, while it is outperformed by the portfolio approaches in three out of the four remaining problems. Notably, putting LNS operators into a portfolio is less effort for a user than determining manually which ones work best. The self-adaptive roulette-wheel strategy performs better than the uniform one in most of the cases, at least with the right learning rate, except for Shift Design, where uniform roulette works best overall. The dynamic strategy gives most consistently excellent improvements though not in all cases the best ones.

5 Discussion

The experiments show that our method of combining ASP with LNS is quite effective even with a single neighbourhood operator and a fixed relaxation rate. Often better results are achieved however with more customised configurations. Portfolios, as implemented in ALASPO in contrast to previous work where only single LNS operators were supported (Eiter et al. 2022), ease the burden on the user to find such configurations. Our experiments confirm that the investigated adaptive strategies with reasonable portfolios achieve very good results most of the time. Adaptive LNS has thus indeed the potential to enhance ASP optimisation in many applications; for some, this has already been demonstrated, others are planned.

For future work, we want to extend ALASPO to support further ASP systems like WASP (Alviano et al. 2015), add more pre-defined neighbourhoods, and to continue research on new self-adaptive strategies.

Acknowledgements

This work was supported by funding from the Bosch Center for AI at Renningen, Germany.

References

Abseher, M.; Gebser, M.; Musliu, N.; Schaub, T.; and Woltran, S. 2016. Shift design with answer set programming. *Fundamenta Informaticae* 147(1):1–25.

Alviano, M.; Dodaro, C.; Leone, N.; and Ricca, F. 2015. Advances in WASP. In *Proceeding of the 13th International Conference on Logic Programming and Nonmonotonic Reasoning (ICLP 2015)*, volume 9345 of *LNCS*, 40–54. Springer.

Banbara, M.; Kaufmann, B.; Ostrowski, M.; and Schaub, T. 2017. Clingcon: The next generation. *Theory and Practice of Logic Programming* 17(4):408–461.

Berthold, T.; Heinz, S.; Pfetsch, M. E.; and Vigerske, S. 2011. Large neighborhood search beyond mip. In *Proceedings of the 9th Metaheuristics International Conference (MIC 2011)*, 51–60.

Björdal, G.; Flener, P.; Pearson, J.; Stuckey, P. J.; and Tack, G. 2020. Solving satisfaction problems using large-neighbourhood search. In *Proceedings of the 26th International Conference on Principles and Practice of Constraint Programming (CP 2020)*, volume 12333 of *LNCS*, 55–71. Springer.

Brewka, G.; Eiter, T.; and Truszczyński, M. 2011. Answer Set Programming at a Glance. *Communications of the ACM* 54(12):92–103.

Cadoli, M.; Eiter, T.; and Gottlob, G. 1997. Default logic as a query language. *IEEE Transactions on Knowledge and Data Engineering* 9(3):448–463.

Danna, E.; Rothberg, E.; and Pape, C. L. 2005. Exploring relaxation induced neighborhoods to improve MIP solutions. *Mathematical Programming* 102(1):71–90.

Eiter, T.; Geibinger, T.; Ruiz, N. H.; Musliu, N.; Oetsch, J.; and Stepanova, D. 2022. Large-neighbourhood search for optimisation in answer-set solving. In *36th AAAI Conference on Artificial Intelligence (AAAI-22)*. http://www.kr.tuwien.ac.at/research/projects/bai/aaai22.pdf.

Gebser, M.; Kaminski, R.; Kaufmann, B.; and Schaub, T. 2012. Answer Set Solving in Practice. *Synthesis Lectures on Artificial Intelligence and Machine Learning* 6(3):1–238.

Gebser, M.; Kaminski, R.; Kaufmann, B.; Ostrowski, M.; Schaub, T.; and Wanko, P. 2016. Theory Solving Made Easy with Clingo 5. In *Technical Communications of the 32nd International Conference on Logic Programming (ICLP 2016)*, volume 52 of *OASIcs*, 2:1–2:15. Schloss Dagstuhl-Leibniz-Zentrum für Informatik.

Gebser, M.; Kaminski, R.; Kaufmann, B.; and Schaub, T. 2019. Multi-shot ASP Solving with clingo. *Theory and Practice of Logic Programming* 19(1):27–82.

Geibinger, T.; Mischek, F.; and Musliu, N. 2021. Constraint logic programming for real-world test laboratory scheduling. In *Proceedings of the 35th AAAI Conference on Artificial Intelligence (AAAI 21)*, 6358–6366. AAAI Press.

Janhunen, T.; Kaminski, R.; Ostrowski, M.; Schellhorn, S.; Wanko, P.; and Schaub, T. 2017. clingo goes Linear Constraints over Reals and Integers. *Theory and Practice of Logic Programming* 17(5-6):872–888.

Laborie, P., and Godard, D. 2007. Self-adapting large neighborhood search: Application to single-mode scheduling problems. *In Proceedings of the 3rd Multidisciplinary International Conference on Scheduling: Theory and Applications (MISTA 2007)*.

Lifschitz, V. 2019. *Answer Set Programming*. Springer.

Perron, L.; Shaw, P.; and Furnon, V. 2004. Propagation guided large neighborhood search. In *Proceedings of the 10th International Conference on Principles and Practice of Constraint Programming (CP 2004)*, volume 3258 of *LNCS*, 468–481. Springer.

Pisinger, D., and Ropke, S. 2007. A general heuristic for vehicle routing problems. *Computers & Operations Research* 34(8):2403–2435.

Pisinger, D., and Ropke, S. 2010. Large neighborhood search. In *Handbook of Metaheuristics*. Springer. 399–419.

Rothberg, E. 2007. An evolutionary algorithm for polishing mixed integer programming solutions. *INFORMS Journal on Computing* 19(4):534–541.

Shaw, P. 1998. Using constraint programming and local search methods to solve vehicle routing problems. In *Proceedings of the 4th International Conference on Principles and Practice of Constraint Programming (CP 1998)*, volume 1520 of *LNCS*, 417–431. Springer.

AUTHOR INDEX